Financial reporting

THIRD EDITION

Janice Loftus

Ken Leo

Sorin Daniliuc

Noel Boys

Belinda Luke

Hong Ang

Karyn Byrnes

WILEY

Third edition published 2020 by
John Wiley & Sons Australia, Ltd
42 McDougall Street, Milton Qld 4064

Typeset in 10/12pt Times LT Std

Wiley
Terry Burkitt (Director, Publishing and Course Development), Mark Levings (Executive Publisher), Kylie Challenor (Senior Manager, Knowledge & Learning Content Management), Rebecca Campbell (Production Editor), Emily Echlin (Publishing Coordinator), Emily Brain (Production Assistant), Renee Bryon (Copyright & Image Research), Delia Sala (Cover Design)

Cover: © the_burtons / Getty Images; shuoshu / Getty Images Australia

Typeset in India by diacriTech

Printed in Singapore by
Markono Print Media Pte Ltd

10 9 8 7 6 5 4 3 2 1

BRIEF CONTENTS

CONTENTS

CHAPTER 13

Share capital and reserves 473

CHAPTER 14

Share-based payment 524

CHAPTER 15

Revenue 558

CHAPTER 16

Presentation of financial statements 587

CHAPTER 17

Statement of cash flows 634

CHAPTER 24

Translation of foreign currency financial statements 837

CHAPTER 25

Business combinations 875

CHAPTER 26

Consolidation: controlled entities 909

CHAPTER 33

Insolvency and liquidation 1231

CHAPTER 34

Accounting for mineral resources 1281

CHAPTER 35

Agriculture   1299

CHAPTER 1

Accounting regulation and the *Conceptual Framework*

CHAPTER AIM

This chapter introduces the regulatory framework that governs financial reporting in Australia, including the *Conceptual Framework for Financial Reporting* (*Conceptual Framework*) and accounting standards issued by the Australian Accounting Standards Board (AASB) and the International Accounting Standards Board (IASB), the *Corporations Act 2001* and the Australian Securities Exchange Listing Rules.

LEARNING OBJECTIVES

After studying this chapter, you should be able to:

1.1 understand the major sources of regulation of financial reporting in Australia

1.2 identify the roles of the key bodies involved in financial reporting regulation in Australia

1.3 explain the structure, role and processes of the IASB and the IFRS Interpretations Committee

1.4 explain the key components of the *Conceptual Framework*

1.5 explain the qualitative characteristics that make information in financial statements useful

1.6 describe the objective and scope of financial statements prepared by a reporting entity

1.7 define the basic elements in financial statements — assets, liabilities, equity, income and expenses

1.8 explain the criteria for recognising and derecognising the elements of financial statements

1.9 compare alternative measurement bases for measuring the elements of financial statements

1.10 explain the concepts that underpin how information should be presented and disclosed

1.11 outline concepts of capital

1.12 explain how inconsistencies may arise between the *Conceptual Framework* and accounting standards.

CONCEPTS FOR REVIEW

Before studying this chapter, you should understand and, if necessary, revise:
- the basic accounting system used to record and classify transactions
- the rules of double-entry accounting and how to apply these rules in analysing transactions
- the purpose and basic format of accounting journals, ledger accounts and financial statements.

1.1 Key sources of regulation of financial reporting in Australia

LEARNING OBJECTIVE 1.1 Understand the major sources of regulation of financial reporting in Australia.

The major sources of regulation of financial reporting in Australia are:
- the *Corporations Act 2001*
- Australian accounting standards
- the *Conceptual Framework for Financial Reporting* (*Conceptual Framework*)
- the Australian Securities Exchange Listing Rules.

1.1.1 The Corporations Act

Australian companies must comply with the requirements of the *Corporations Act 2001* (the **Corporations Act**). The Corporations Act covers many aspects of the management of companies and the relationships between the company — as a legal person — and directors, shareholders and others. Our discussion of the Corporations Act will focus on its implications for the preparation of financial statements, which arise from Part 2M.3 of Chapter 2M of the Act.

Section 292(1) of the Corporations Act requires the preparation of a financial report and directors' report each financial year by:

    (a) all disclosing entities; and
    (b) all public companies; and
    (c) all large proprietary companies; and
    (d) all registered schemes.

In limited circumstances, some small proprietary companies may be required to prepare a financial report and directors' report if directed to do so by shareholders, members or the Australian Securities and Investments Commission (ASIC).

We will briefly describe each type of entity that may be required to prepare a financial report and directors' report.
- Whether an entity is a *disclosing entity* (Corporations Act s. 111AC) generally depends on the type of securities it has on issue. With few exceptions, entities whose securities are listed on a securities exchange are disclosing entities.
- A *public company* means any company other than a proprietary company (defined next).
- To qualify for registration as a *proprietary company* under s. 45A of the Corporations Act a company must:
  - be limited by shares or be an unlimited company with a share capital
  - have no more than 50 non-employee shareholders
  - not do anything that would require disclosure to investors under Chapter 6D (except in limited circumstances).

  Section 45A of the Act further classifies proprietary companies as small or large, as follows.
  - A *small proprietary company* is a proprietary company that satisfies at least two of the following criteria, specified in s. 45A(2).
    - The consolidated revenue for the financial year of the company and the entities it controls is less than $50 million.
    - The value of the consolidated gross assets at the end of the financial year of the company and the entities it controls is less than $25 million.
    - The company and the entities it controls have fewer than 100 employees at the end of the financial year.
  - A *large proprietary company* is any proprietary company that does not satisfy the definition of a small proprietary company.
- A *registered scheme* refers to a managed investment scheme that is registered under s. 601EB of the Corporations Act.

Figure 1.1 can assist in determining whether an entity is required to prepare an annual report under Part 2M.3 of the Corporations Act.

FIGURE 1.1 Determining whether an entity is required to prepare an annual report under Part 2M.3 of the Corporations Act

Source: Deloitte (2018, p. 12).

Preparation of a financial report according to the Corporations Act

Nature Walk Resort Pty Ltd is a proprietary company that operates a resort in the Australian outback. It has 10 shareholders and 88 employees. According to internal accounting records, Nature Walk Resort Pty Ltd has total assets of $28 million and total liabilities of $10 million. Its revenue for the current year was $54 million. Neither ASIC nor shareholders have made a direction for the preparation of a financial report.

Required

Is Nature Walk Resort Pty Ltd required to prepare a financial report?

Solution

Nature Walk Resort Pty Ltd is required to prepare a financial report in accordance with s. 292 of the Corporations Act because it is a *large proprietary company*. Nature Walk Resort Pty Ltd fails to satisfy the definition of a small proprietary company because it does not meet the minimum of two of the three criteria specified in s. 45A(2) of the Corporations Act. The company has less than 100 employees, but its total revenue is more than $50 million and total assets are more than $25 million.

In addition to specifying which entities must prepare financial reports, the Corporations Act imposes requirements in relation to those reports.

- Part 2M.2 of the Act requires the entity to retain all financial records that record and explain the transactions of the entity and enable true and fair financial statements to be prepared and audited. The entity shall keep the records for 7 years after the transactions covered by the records are completed.
- Section 297 of the Act requires that an entity's financial statements, including the notes, for a financial year must provide a true and fair view of the financial position and performance of the entity.
- Section 296 of the Corporations Act requires that if an entity is required to produce a financial report for a financial year then that report must comply with accounting standards, which are discussed in section 1.1.2.

1.1.2 Australian accounting standards

The Financial Reporting Council (FRC) is a statutory body with responsibility for overseeing the effectiveness of financial reporting in Australia. Under its direction, the AASB adopted **International Financial Reporting Standards (IFRSs)**, effective for reporting periods commencing on or after 1 January 2005. To implement this, the AASB issues Australian accounting standards with requirements that are the same as those of IFRSs for application by for-profit entities.

International Financial Reporting Standards comprise the authoritative pronouncements issued by the International Accounting Standards Board (IASB). They include two series of accounting standards and two series of interpretations:

- standards that are labelled IFRS (e.g. IFRS 8 *Operating Segments*)
- standards that originated as part of the older series of International Accounting Standards, originally issued by the International Accounting Standards Committee and reissued or revised and reissued by the IASB (e.g. IAS 16 *Property, Plant and Equipment*)
- interpretations that are issued by the IFRS Interpretations Committee (e.g. IFRIC 10 *Interim Financial Reporting and Impairment*)
- interpretations that were issued by the former Standing Interpretations Committee (e.g. SIC 32 *Intangible Assets — Website Costs*).

The Australian equivalents of the IASB's 'IFRS' series are numbered from AASB 1. For example, the Australian equivalent of IFRS 8 *Operating Segments* is AASB 8 *Operating Segments*. The Australian equivalents of the IASB's 'IAS' series are numbered from AASB 101. For example, the Australian equivalent of IAS 16 *Property, Plant and Equipment* is AASB 116 *Property, Plant and Equipment*.

The AASB also issues Australian accounting standards that are not an equivalent of a corresponding standard issued by the IASB. These standards typically cover specific local requirements, such as additional disclosure requirements, and requirements for not-for-profit and public-sector entities; for example, AASB 1051 *Land Under Roads*, which applies to the financial statements of various public-sector entities.

Note that IFRSs include both standards and interpretations issued by the IASB. Interpretations do not have the same status as accounting standards under the Corporations Act. The AASB has addressed this problem by bringing the content of interpretations into the ambit of accounting standards. This is achieved through AASB 1048 *Interpretation of Standards*.

AASB 1053 *Application of Tiers of Australian Accounting Standards* was issued in 2010 to apply a two-tier **differential reporting** system for companies preparing general purpose financial statements (GPFS). GPFS are defined in AASB 101 *Presentation of Financial Statements*, paragraph 7, as financial statements:

> intended to meet the needs of users who are not in a position to require an entity to prepare reports tailored to their particular information needs.

Tier 1 and Tier 2 share reporting requirements in relation to recognition, measurement and presentation, but Tier 2 has significantly reduced disclosure requirements compared with Tier 1. Each Australian accounting standard sets out the disclosure requirements from which Tier 2 entities are exempted.

AASB 1053 originally differentiated between entities required to comply with Tier 1 and entities required to comply with Tier 2 using a particular definition of the **reporting entity**. However, the adoption of a revised *Conceptual Framework* for annual reporting periods commencing on or after 1 January 2020 introduced a different reporting entity concept, necessitating a change in how the two tiers are differentiated, which has been accomplished by amending various standards, including AASB 1053.

In terms of Tier 1 reporting requirements, paragraph 11 of AASB 1053 states:

> The following types of entities shall prepare general purpose financial statements that comply with Tier 1 reporting requirements:
> (a) for-profit private sector entities that have public accountability and are required by legislation to comply with Australian Accounting Standards; and
> (b) the Australian Government and State, Territory and Local Governments.

Appendix A of AASB 1053 specifies that an entity has public accountability if:

> (a) its debt or equity instruments are traded in a public market or it is in the process of issuing such instruments for trading in a public market (a domestic or foreign stock exchange or an over-the-counter market, including local and regional markets); or
> (b) it holds assets in a fiduciary capacity for a broad group of outsiders as one of its primary businesses.

Entities that hold assets in a fiduciary capacity on behalf of others as a primary business include banks, insurance companies, and securities brokers.

Tier 1 reporting requirements in AASB 1053 require the application of the revised *Conceptual Framework*, effective for annual reporting periods commencing on or after 1 January 2020. Companies complying with Tier 1 requirements will comply with all relevant accounting standards.

In terms of Tier 2 reporting requirements, paragraph 13 of AASB 1053 states:

> Tier 2 reporting requirements shall, as a minimum, apply to the general purpose financial statements of the following types of entities:
> (a) for-profit private sector entities that do not have public accountability;
> (b) not-for-profit private sector entities; and
> (c) public sector entities, whether for-profit or not-for-profit, other than the Australian Government and State, Territory and Local Governments.

A large proprietary company must at least prepare Tier 2 financial statements.

As an interim measure, entities to which Tier 2 reporting requirements apply will continue to apply the *Framework for the Preparation and Presentation of Financial Statements* (*Framework*) rather than move to the revised *Conceptual Framework* that applies to Tier 1 for annual reporting periods commencing on or after 1 January 2020. Entities applying the *Framework* are referred to as AusCF entities.

Companies complying merely with Tier 2 requirements cannot state compliance with all relevant accounting standards. The entities listed in paragraph 13 may, however, elect to also apply Tier 1 reporting requirements.

The AASB is considering adopting a new approach to the identification and presentation of Tier 2 disclosures. In 2017, it issued exposure draft ED 277 *Reduced Disclosure Requirements for Tier 2 Entities* as part of a joint project with the New Zealand Accounting Standards Board (NZASB). ED 277 proposes a new set of principles to be used in determining required disclosures for Tier 2 entities and a new approach to presenting the Tier 2 disclosures in the Australian accounting standards. It recommends adding an appendix to each accounting standard and interpretation to outline the Tier 2 disclosure requirements. This would replace the current approach of shading those disclosures that are not applicable to Tier 2 reporting entities.

Accounting standards issued by the AASB have legislative backing under s. 334 of the Corporations Act and s. 296 requires compliance with accounting standards issued by the AASB. However, an exception is provided for small proprietary companies that prepare financial reports under the direction of shareholders or members where the direction specifies that the report does not have to comply with accounting standards.

Small proprietary companies preparing financial statements in accordance with an ASIC direction or a shareholder direction that did *not* specify an exemption from compliance with accounting standards may still receive relief from complying with the full range of Australian accounting standards. This occurs because many Australian accounting standards are limited to reporting entities. For AusCF entities (i.e. those applying the *Framework* rather than the *Conceptual Framework*), AASB 1057 *Application of Australian Accounting Standards* and Statement of Accounting Concepts 1 *Definition of the Reporting Entity* define a reporting entity as follows.

> An entity in respect of which it is reasonable to expect the existence of users who rely on the entity's general purpose financial statements for information that will be useful to them for making and evaluating decisions about the allocation of resources.

Thus, small proprietary companies are not reporting entities as defined by AASB 1057 and SAC 1 for AusCF entities and therefore are typically not required to comply with most Australian accounting standards. This does not mean, however, that their financial statements are unregulated. ASIC's Regulatory Guide 85: *Reporting requirements for non-reporting entities* specifies that the recognition and measurement requirements of Australian accounting standards should also be applied by entities that are not required to prepare GPFS. Figure 1.2 provides extracts from Regulatory Guide 85 that explain why non-reporting entities should apply the recognition and measurement requirements of Australian accounting standards when preparing financial reports in accordance with the Corporations Act.

FIGURE 1.2 Application of recognition and measurement requirements to non-reporting entities

Section 2. Accounting provisions applicable to non-reporting entities

2.1 The accounting standards provide a framework for determining a consistent meaning of 'financial position' and 'profit or loss' in financial reporting across entities.

2.2 In the absence of any such framework, the figures disclosed in financial statements would lose their meaning and could be determined completely at the whim of the directors of individual entities. The profit or loss reported by an individual entity would vary greatly depending upon which individuals were responsible for the preparation of its financial statements.

2.4 The following requirements of accounting standards that apply to all entities reporting under Chapter 2M are also relevant:

(a) Paragraph 13 of accounting standard AASB 101 *Presentation of Financial Statements* requires the financial report to present fairly the financial position, financial performance and cash flows. Fair presentation requires 'the faithful representation of the effects of transactions, other events and conditions' in accordance with the definitions and recognition criteria for 'assets', 'liabilities', 'income' and 'expenses' set out in the [conceptual framework].

(b) Paragraph 25 of AASB 101 requires all entities reporting under Chapter 2M to apply the accrual basis of accounting.

(c) Paragraphs 10 and 11 of AASB 108 *Accounting Policies, Changes in Accounting Estimates and Errors* provides that, in the absence of an Australian accounting standard that specifically applies to a transaction, other event or condition, management should refer to, and consider the applicability of, the following sources in descending order:

(i) the requirements and guidance in Australian Accounting Standards dealing with similar and related issues; and

(ii) the definitions, recognition criteria and measurement concepts for assets, liabilities, income and expenses in the [conceptual framework]

> 2.5 Hence, the recognition and measurement requirements of accounting standards must also be applied in order to determine the financial position and profit or loss of any entity preparing financial reports in accordance with the Act.
>
> 2.6 As noted earlier, the recognition and measurement requirements of the accounting standards include requirements relating to depreciation of non-current assets, tax effect accounting, lease accounting, measurement of inventories, and recognition and measurement of liabilities for employee entitlements.
>
> 2.7 The provisions of accounting standards dealing with the classification of items as assets, liabilities, equity, income and expenses also apply. This would include the provisions of AASB 132 [*Financial Instruments: Presentation*] concerning the classification of financial instruments issued as debt or equity.
>
> **Source:** ASIC (2005, pp. 5–6).

Paragraph 3.5 of ASIC's Regulatory Guide 85 requires all entities preparing a financial report in accordance with Chapter 2M of the Corporations Act (including those eligible for the Tier 2 reporting reduced disclosure requirements and whether they are reporting entities or not) to apply in full the following Australian accounting standards:

- AASB 101 *Presentation of Financial Statements* (see chapter 16)
- AASB 107 *Statement of Cash Flows* (see chapter 17)
- AASB 108 *Accounting Policies, Changes in Accounting Estimates and Errors* (see chapter 18)
- AASB 1048 *Interpretation of Standards*.

ILLUSTRATIVE EXAMPLE 1.2

Application of Australian accounting standards

Seaside Resorts Pty Ltd is a proprietary company that operates a holiday resort in the Whitsundays. It has 10 shareholders, all of whom are involved in the management of the company. Seaside Resorts Pty Ltd has 66 employees. According to internal accounting records, Seaside Resorts Pty Ltd has total assets of $56 million and total liabilities of $20 million, most of which represents a secured bank loan. Seaside Resorts Pty Ltd must provide the bank with financial information each year as specified in the loan agreement. Seaside Resorts Pty Ltd's revenue for the current year was $48 million. Neither ASIC nor shareholders have made a direction for the preparation of a financial report.

Required

Does Seaside Resorts Pty Ltd need to prepare a financial report and apply Australian accounting standards?

Solution

To address this question, it is necessary to first consider whether the Corporations Act requires Seaside Resorts Pty Ltd to prepare a financial report. If so, then we must consider which tier of reporting applies to Seaside Resorts Pty Ltd. If Tier 2 applies, we would also need to consider whether Seaside Resorts Pty Ltd is a reporting entity as defined for AusCF entities.

Seaside Resorts Pty Ltd is not required to prepare a financial report in accordance with s. 292 of the Corporations Act because it is a small proprietary company. Seaside Resorts Pty Ltd satisfies the definition of a small proprietary company because it meets two of the three criteria specified in s. 45A(2) of the Corporations Act, by having fewer than 100 employees and revenue less than $50 million even though the company's total assets exceed $25 million.

As described in section 1.1.1, the Corporations Act requires that financial statements present a true and fair view. The Act also requires compliance with the accounting standards. So what should the directors of a company do if they believe that compliance with accounting standards would not produce a true and fair view? In these circumstances the Corporations Act requires compliance with accounting standards and the inclusion of additional information in the notes to the financial statements so as to give a true and fair view.

The expression 'true and fair' is not defined in the Corporations Act. However, paragraph 25 of auditing standard ASA 700 *Forming an Opinion and Reporting on a Financial Report* indicates that 'gives a true and fair view' and 'presents fairly in all material respects' are equivalent.

According to paragraph 15 of AASB 101, fair presentation requires the:

> faithful representation of the effects of transactions, other events and conditions in accordance with the definitions and recognition criteria for assets, liabilities, income and expenses set out in the *Conceptual Framework for Financial Reporting*.

The requirements for additional disclosure in the notes when necessary to present a true and fair view are considered further in chapter 16.

1.1.3 A conceptual framework

A conceptual framework is not a standard. It does not override any accounting standard or any requirement in a standard. The purpose of a conceptual framework is to provide a coherent set of principles:
- to assist standard setters to develop accounting standards for the preparation of financial statements that are based on consistent concepts
- to assist preparers of financial statements in the application of accounting standards and in dealing with topics that are not the subject of an existing applicable accounting standard
- to assist users in the interpretation of information in financial statements.

AASB 108/IAS 8 *Accounting Policies, Changes in Accounting Estimates and Errors* requires financial statement preparers to consider the definitions, recognition criteria and measurement concepts in the conceptual framework when developing accounting policies for transactions, events or conditions in the absence of an Australian accounting standard that specifically applies or that applies to similar circumstances. AASB 108/IAS 8 is considered in more detail in chapter 18.

Prior to 2020, the conceptual framework applied in Australia included the conceptual framework issued by the IASB and Statement of Accounting Concepts SAC 1 *Definition of the Reporting Entity*. The IASB issued a revised conceptual framework — the *Conceptual Framework for Financial Reporting* (*Conceptual Framework*) — in March 2018 and this has been adopted by the AASB, effective for annual reporting periods beginning on or after 1 January 2020. In order to apply the revised *Conceptual Framework* in Australia, the AASB has to address the following two problems:
- a clash in the way 'reporting entity' is defined
- whether to phase out the ability for entities to prepare special purpose financial statements (SPFS) rather than GPFS if management determines that the entity is not a 'reporting entity' as defined in SAC 1.

For AusCF entities, the definition of a reporting entity is used to determine whether the entity's financial statements need to comply with Australian accounting standards. The term 'special purpose financial reports' is used to refer to the financial reports prepared by entities that are not identified as reporting entities as defined by SAC 1.

Research by the AASB (Carey, Potter & Tanewski 2014) indicates that approximately 55% to 60% of entities publicly lodge SPFS in Australia, suggesting a strong need to find a solution to improve the consistency, comparability, usefulness and credibility of financial reporting in Australia.

Following consultation, the AASB decided to adopt a two-phased approach to applying the IASB's revised conceptual framework:
- maintain IFRS compliance for publicly accountable entities and entities voluntarily claiming IFRS compliance in the short term (phase 1)
- maintain IFRS as a base by removing the Australian reporting entity concept, removing SPFS from Australian accounting standards and providing an alternative Tier 2 GPFS framework in the medium term (phase 2).

The two-phased approach maintains IFRS compliance for publicly accountable entities while retaining the status quo for all other entities in the short-to-medium term, allowing time for the AASB to consult and determine an alternative Tier 2 GPFS framework to replace SPFS in Australian accounting standards. Figure 1.3 summarises the two-phased approach to applying the IASB's revised *Conceptual Framework*.

FIGURE 1.3   A summary of the AASB's two-phased approach to applying the revised *Conceptual Framework*

Phase 1: Short-term approach — operate with two conceptual frameworks to maintain IFRS compliance for publicly accountable entities. This involves:
(a) the [revised conceptual framework] being applied to publicly accountable for-profit entities and other entities voluntarily reporting compliance with IFRS to enable them to maintain IFRS compliance;

(b) all other entities continuing to apply the existing *Framework*, enabling them to continue using the 'Australian reporting entity concept'; and

(c) amendments being made to the definition of 'public accountability' in AASB 1053 *Application of Tiers of Australian Accounting Standards* to align with the revised IASB definition in IFRS for Small and Medium-sized Entities (SMEs).

Phase 2: Medium-term approach — maintain IFRS compliance for publicly accountable entities and entities voluntarily claiming IFRS compliance, maintain IFRS as a base for all other entities, by having one conceptual framework, remove SPFS and provide a new GPFS Tier 2 alternative. This involves:

(a) the [revised conceptual framework] being applied to all entities required by legislation or otherwise to comply with [Australian accounting standards];

(b) the Tier 2 framework in AASB 1053 being revised to be **one** of the following:

   (i) Alternative 1: GFPS — Reduced Disclosure Requirements (RDR) — Existing Tier 2 (full recognition and measurement with **reduced disclosures** from each Accounting Standard, includes consolidation and equity accounting where applicable); **OR**

   (ii) Alternative 2: GFPS — Specified Disclosure Requirements (SDR) — New Tier 2 (full recognition and measurement with **specified disclosures** from some Accounting Standards, includes consolidation and equity accounting where applicable); and

(c) consequential amendments being made to [Australian accounting standards] and transitional relief for entities moving from SPFS to GPFS or to another tier of reporting.

Source: AASB (2018).

1.1.4 Australian Securities Exchange Listing Rules

The **Australian Securities Exchange (ASX) Group** requires companies that list on its exchange to comply with the **ASX Listing Rules**, which deal with listing and quotation, market information, trading and settlement, and general supervisory matters. The principles underlying the Listing Rules embrace the interests of listed entities and investors and seek to maintain the reputation of the market. Figure 1.4 shows some of the principles that underpin the ASX Listing Rules, selected on the basis of their relevance to financial reporting.

FIGURE 1.4   Selected principles that underpin the ASX Listing Rules

- An entity should satisfy appropriate minimum standards of quality, size and operations and disclose sufficient information about itself before it is admitted to the official list.
- Timely disclosure should be made of information which may have a material effect on the price or value of an entity's securities.
- Information should be produced to high standards and, where appropriate, enable ready comparison with similar information.
- Information should be disclosed to enable investors to assess an entity's corporate governance practices.

Source: ASX (2016).

The Listing Rules include requirements for continuous disclosure and periodic reporting. In accordance with ASX General Rule 3.1, if an entity 'is or becomes aware of any information concerning it that a reasonable person would expect to have a material effect on the price or value of the entity's securities, the entity must immediately tell ASX that information'. Listing Rule 3.1A provides for exceptions to General Rule 3.1 where all of the following conditions are satisfied.

- A reasonable person would not expect the information to be disclosed.
- The information is confidential and ASX has not formed the view that the information ceased to be confidential.
- At least one of the following applies.
  - It would be a breach of a law to disclose the information.
  - The information concerns an incomplete proposal of negotiation.
  - The information comprises matters of supposition or is insufficiently definite to warrant disclosure.
  - The information is generated for the internal management purposes of the entity.
  - The information is a trade secret.

The Listing Rules are primarily concerned with disclosure rather than with the accounting policies applied in determining classifications and amounts reported in financial statements.

1.2 The roles of key players in financial reporting regulation

LEARNING OBJECTIVE 1.2 Identify the roles of the key bodies involved in financial reporting regulation in Australia.

The key players in standard setting in Australia are the FRC and the AASB. A diagrammatic representation of the Australian accounting standard-setting institutional arrangements is shown in figure 1.5.

FIGURE 1.5   Australian accounting standard-setting institutional arrangements

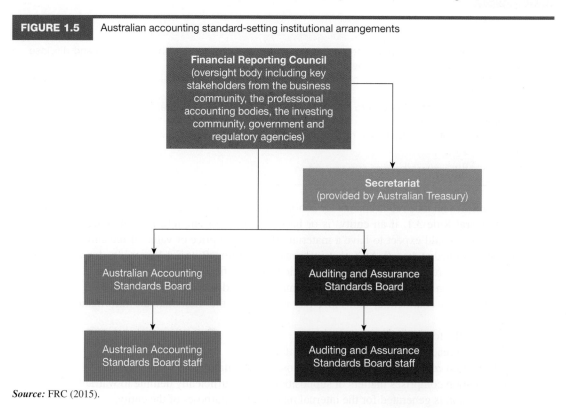

Source: FRC (2015).

Other key players in financial reporting regulation include the Australian Securities and Investments Commission (ASIC), the Australian Prudential Regulation Authority (APRA) and the ASX. The role of each body is discussed, in turn, below.

Professional accounting bodies, such as CPA Australia, Chartered Accountants Australia and New Zealand (created by the combination of the former Institute of Chartered Accountants Australia and the New Zealand Institute of Chartered Accountants) and the Institute of Public Accountants, also play a part in accounting regulation. They contribute to the standard-setting process by responding to exposure drafts and other invitations to comment, as well as communicating information to their members about developments in accounting standards and other accounting regulations, and providing professional development resources. Another important role of the professional bodies is in the regulation of accountants through professional codes of conduct. The focus of this chapter is on the regulation of financial reporting, rather than the regulation of accountants. As such, we do not elaborate on the role of the professional bodies. More information about the professional accounting bodies can be obtained from their websites:

- CPA Australia: www.cpaaustralia.com.au
- Chartered Accountants Australia and New Zealand: www.charteredaccountantsanz.com
- the Institute of Public Accountants: www.publicaccountants.org.au.

1.2.1 Financial Reporting Council (FRC)

The **Financial Reporting Council (FRC)** is a statutory body under the *Australian Securities and Investments Commission Act 2001* (the ASIC Act 2001), as amended by the *Corporate Law Economic Reform Program* (*Audit Reform and Corporate Disclosure*) *Act 2004*. The FRC has responsibility for overseeing the effectiveness of the financial reporting system in Australia and is thereby the key external adviser to the Australian government on the financial reporting system. It provides broad oversight of the processes for setting accounting and auditing standards. It also provides strategic advice on the quality of audits conducted by Australian auditors and advises the Minister on these and related matters to the extent that they affect the financial reporting system in Australia. The general functions of the FRC established by s. 225(1) of the ASIC Act 2001 are:

(a) to provide broad oversight of the processes for setting accounting standards in Australia; and
(b) to provide broad oversight of the processes for setting auditing standards in Australia; and
(d) to give the Minister reports and advice about the matters referred to in paragraphs (a) and (b); and
(e) the functions specified in subsections (2) (specific accounting standards functions), (2A) (specific auditing standards functions) and (2B) (specific auditor quality functions); and
(f) to establish appropriate consultative mechanisms; and
(g) to advance and promote the main objects of this Part; and
(h) any other functions that the Minister confers on the FRC by written notice to the FRC Chair.

Section 225(2) details the specific accounting standards functions of the FRC, these being:

(a) appointing the members of the AASB (other than the Chair); and
(b) giving the AASB advice or feedback on the AASB's:
    (i) priorities; and
    (ii) business plans; and
    (iii) procedures; and
(ba) giving the Office of the AASB advice or feedback on the Office's:
    (i) budgets; and
    (ii) staffing arrangements (including level, structure and composition of staffing); and
(c) determining the AASB's broad strategic direction; and
(e) monitoring the development of international accounting standards and the accounting standards that apply in major international financial centres; and
(f) furthering the development of a single set of accounting standards for world-wide use with appropriate regard to international developments; and
(g) promoting the continued adoption of international best practice accounting standards in the Australian accounting standard setting processes if doing so would be in the best interests of both the private and public sectors in the Australian economy; and
(h) monitoring:
    (i) the operation of accounting standards to assess their continued relevance and their effectiveness in achieving their objectives in respect of both the private and public sectors of the Australian economy; and
    (ii) the effectiveness of the consultative arrangements used by the AASB.

In 2002, the FRC exercised its power to determine the AASB's broad strategic direction with a directive to adopt IFRSs. As a result, Australia adopted IFRSs effective for reporting periods commencing on or after 1 January 2005. Notwithstanding this strategic direction, the key determinant in selecting Australian accounting standards is that they be in the best interests of both the private and public sectors in the Australian economy. Sections 225(5) and 225(6) impose explicit limits on the power of the FRC:

(5) The FRC does not have power to direct the AASB in relation to the development, or making, of a particular standard.

(6) The FRC does not have power to veto a standard made, formulated or recommended by the AASB.

Although the FRC may provide strategic direction to the AASB, it cannot direct the board to make a specific standard or to provide specific solutions to accounting issues. This ensures the independence of the standard-setting boards. Details about the rules of operation of the FRC, including meeting procedures, charter of functions and framework for appointment of members, are available on the FRC website, www.frc.gov.au.

1.2.2 Australian Accounting Standards Board (AASB)

The AASB is an Australian government agency under the ASIC Act 2001. The FRC appoints the members of the AASB, except the chair, who is appointed by the treasurer of the Australian government. The AASB has the authority delegated by the Federal Parliament to issue Australian accounting standards. The functions of the AASB are specified in s. 227(1) of the ASIC Act 2001 as follows:

(a) to develop a conceptual framework, not having the force of an accounting standard, for the purpose of evaluating proposed accounting standards and international standards; and

(b) to make accounting standards under Section 334 of the Corporations Act for the purposes of the corporations legislation (other than the excluded provisions); and

(c) to formulate accounting standards for other purposes; and

(d) to participate in and contribute to the development of a single set of accounting standards for world-wide use; and

(e) to advance and promote the main objects of this Part.

The ASIC Act also sets out key objectives for accounting standards in Australia. These are as follows.

• Accounting standards should support the Australian economy by reducing the cost of capital and enabling Australian entities to compete effectively overseas, and should maintain investor confidence in the Australian economy, including its capital markets.

• Accounting standards should support the Australian economy by being clearly stated and easy to understand.

The AASB must have regard to the interests of Australian corporations that raise or propose to raise capital in major international financial centres. This requirement can be a source of tension because Australian accounting standards must also be applied by many entities that do not raise finance in international capital markets. The provision of certain disclosures has expected benefits in terms of lower cost of capital. Such benefits are more likely to be realised by entities that compete for funds in global capital markets.

The AASB may formulate an accounting standard by issuing the text of an international accounting standard (s. 227(4) of the ASIC Act 2001). The text of the international accounting standard may be 'modified to the extent necessary to take account of the Australian legal or institutional environment and, in particular, to ensure that any disclosure and transparency provisions in the standard are appropriate to the Australian legal or institutional environment'. While the ASIC Act 2001 limits the modifications that the AASB may make, it does not limit the capacity of the AASB to formulate new accounting standards (i.e. standards that are not equivalent to or modifications of international accounting standards). For example, AASB 1054 *Australian Additional Disclosures*, which was issued by the AASB, is not based on a standard issued by the IASB. The Australian Federal Parliament has a power to disallow standards issued by the AASB.

The AASB has power under s. 227(3) of the ASIC Act 2001 to establish committees, advisory panels and consultative groups. Figure 1.6 shows the relationships between the AASB and other bodies.

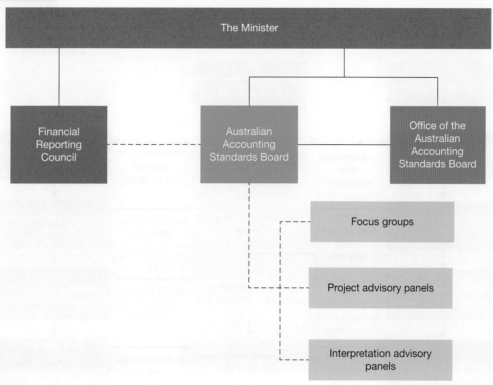

FIGURE 1.6 Relationship between AASB and other bodies

The Minister

Financial Reporting Council

Australian Accounting Standards Board

Office of the Australian Accounting Standards Board

Focus groups

Project advisory panels

Interpretation advisory panels

Source: AASB (n.d.).

At the time of writing, the AASB has two focus groups.

- The User Focus Group was established to help the AASB better understand the information needs of investors and investment professionals, equity and credit analysts, credit grantors and rating agencies, and how those stakeholders use financial reports. It thus increases the contribution of analysts to AASB processes, including standard setting.
- The Not-for-Profit (Private Sector) Focus Group was established to help the AASB better understand the information needs of preparers, donors, credit grantors and community agencies, and the financial reporting issues affecting them. It increases participation of those involved in not-for-profit private-sector entities in the accounting standard-setting process and other AASB processes.

Project advisory panels comprise a group of people appointed for their expertise on a particular topic.

The AASB may appoint an interpretation advisory panel, constituted as a committee of the AASB, to prepare alternative views on an issue and make recommendations for consideration by the AASB.

Figure 1.7 outlines the process for setting Australian accounting standards. Technical issues may be identified by:

- the IASB
- the IFRS Interpretations Committee (IFRIC)
- the International Public Sector Accounting Standards Board (IPSASB)
- members or staff of the AASB
- other individual or organisational Australian stakeholders.

Issues on the IASB and IFRIC work programs are included on the AASB work program, although the AASB's involvement varies depending on the issue. The AASB undertakes work on issues on the IPSASB work program when they are significant to public-sector financial reporting in Australia. Technical issues identified by the AASB in relation to for-profit entities are usually referred to the IASB or IFRIC, whereas issues affecting not-for-profit entities are addressed domestically or referred to IPSASB. The AASB also considers issues raised by Australian stakeholders.

Following identification of a technical issue, the AASB develops a project proposal that examines costs, benefits, resources and timing. The AASB reviews this proposal to decide whether the project should be added to its work program.

FIGURE 1.7 AASB standard-setting process

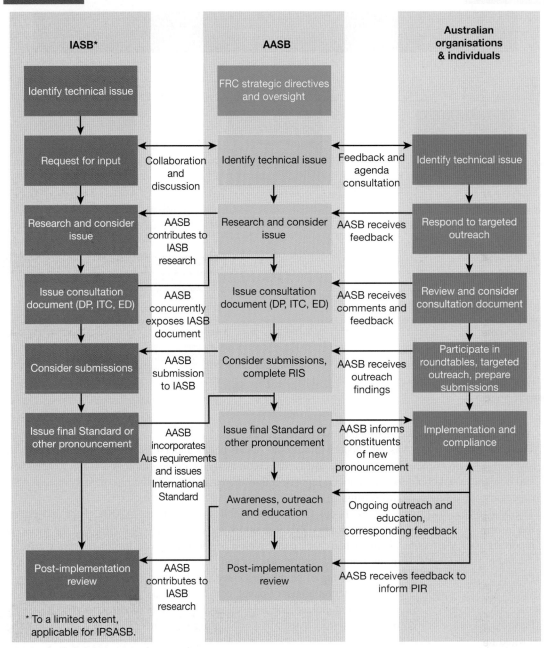

Source: AASB (2019).

If the AASB decides to proceed with the project, AASB staff develop and present agenda papers that will be discussed by the AASB. Once research is complete, the AASB releases one of the following types of documents for public comment.

• Discussion Paper or Consultation Paper — usually outlines a wide range of possible accounting policies on a particular topic
• Draft Interpretation — a draft of a proposed interpretation of a standard
• Invitation to Comment — seeking feedback on broad proposals; it may include a discussion or consultation paper
• Exposure Draft — a draft of a proposed pronouncement such as a new standard or an amendment to a standard

In addition to documents issued for public comment, the AASB may undertake stakeholder consultation through roundtable discussions, focus groups, project advisory panels and interpretation advisory panels.

After the AASB has fully considered an issue on its work program, it may issue a pronouncement (e.g. a standard, interpretation or conceptual framework document) or give its view via a Board decision or the minutes of a Board meeting.

The AASB monitors how entities implement accounting standards and interpretations. Compliance is also monitored by ASIC, APRA, CPA Australia, Chartered Accountants Australia and New Zealand (CAANZ) and the Institute of Public Accountants (IPA). AASB standards may be revised or submissions may be made to the IASB or IPSASB to propose amendments if monitoring suggests they are required.

1.2.3 Australian Securities and Investments Commission (ASIC)

The **Australian Securities and Investments Commission (ASIC)** administers the Corporations Act and the ASIC Act 2001. ASIC is an independent federal government body established under the ASIC Act 2001. It acts as Australia's corporate, markets, financial services and consumer credit regulator and aims to develop and maintain a fair, strong and efficient financial system for all Australians.

Figure 1.8 outlines the functions of ASIC under the ASIC Act 2001 and figure 1.9 lists its powers under the ASIC Act 2001 and the Corporations Act.

FIGURE 1.8	Functions of ASIC

The *Australian Securities and Investments Commission Act 2001* requires ASIC to:
- maintain, facilitate and improve the performance of the financial system and entities in it
- promote confident and informed participation by investors and consumers in the financial system
- administer the law effectively and with minimal procedural requirements
- enforce and give effect to the law
- receive, process and store, efficiently and quickly, information that [it receives]
- make information about companies and other bodies available to the public as soon as practicable
- take whatever action [it] can, and which is necessary, to enforce and give effect to the law.

Source: ASIC (2019).

FIGURE 1.9	Powers of ASIC

The *Australian Securities and Investments Commission Act 2001* and *Corporations Act 2001* give ASIC the facilitative, regulatory and enforcements powers to:
- register companies and managed investment schemes
- grant Australian financial services licenses and Australian credit licences
- register auditors and liquidators
- grant relief from various provisions of the legislation [that it] administer[s]
- maintain publicly accessible registers of information about companies, financial services licensees and credit licensees
- make rules aimed at ensuring the integrity of financial markets
- stop the issue of financial products under defective disclosure documents
- investigate suspected breaches of the law and in so doing require people to produce books or answer questions at an examination
- issue infringement notices in relation to alleged breaches of some laws
- ban people from engaging in credit activities or providing financial services
- seek civil penalties from the courts
- commence prosecutions — these are generally conducted by the Commonwealth Director of Public Prosecutions, although there are some categories of matters which [ASIC prosecutes itself].

Source: ASIC (2019).

ASIC undertakes financial reporting surveillance with the purpose of improving the quality of financial reporting. Entities' financial statements are selected for review. The selection is based on several criteria including the current issues, or 'hot topics', in financial reporting and public complaints. The financial statements are reviewed for compliance with the Corporations Act and Australian accounting standards. ASIC informs the entity if it has any concerns about its financial statements and invites the issuer to explain the accounting treatment used. ASIC publishes the findings of its surveillance program on its website, www.asic.gov.au. Figure 1.10 provides an overview of the accounting issues examined by ASIC in its review of 30 June 2018 financial reports.

FIGURE 1.10	Issues examined in ASIC's review of 30 June 2018 financial reports

1. Asset values and impairment testing
   - Reasonableness of cash flows and assumptions
   - Determining the carrying amount of cash generating units
   - Use of fair value
   - Impairment indicators
   - Disclosures
2. Revenue recognition
3. Tax accounting
4. Consolidation accounting
5. Business combinations
6. Expense deferral
7. Estimates and accounting policy judgements

Source: ASIC (2019).

1.2.4 Australian Prudential Regulation Authority (APRA)

The **Australian Prudential Regulation Authority (APRA)** is the prudential regulator of the Australian financial services industry. It oversees:

- banks
- credit unions
- building societies
- general insurance and reinsurance companies
- life insurance
- friendly societies
- most members of the superannuation industry.

APRA identifies the key risks taken by an entity, ensures the risks are adequately measured, managed and monitored, and assesses the adequacy of the entity's financial resources to accommodate potential losses. The aim of APRA's supervision is to promote financial stability by requiring these institutions to manage risk prudently so as to minimise the likelihood of financial losses to depositors, policy holders and superannuation fund members.

Regulated entities provide financial and other information to APRA. Summary statistics, such as monthly banking statistics, are reported by APRA. More information about the activities of APRA and its publications are provided on its website, www.apra.gov.au.

1.2.5 Australian Securities Exchange Group (ASX)

The Australian Securities Exchange Group (ASX) operates the largest securities market in Australia. Several of its functions have implications for financial reporting practice. As discussed in section 1.1.4, the ASX establishes Listing Rules for entities that offer securities on its exchange. The ASX oversees compliance with its operating rules, promotes standards of corporate governance among Australia's listed companies and helps to educate retail investors. The ASX relies on a range of subsidiary brands to monitor and enforce compliance with its operating rules. These subsidiaries are as follows.

- Australian Securities Exchange — which handles ASX's primary, secondary and derivative market services. It encompasses ASX (formerly Australian Stock Exchange) and ASX 24 (formerly Sydney Futures Exchange).
- ASX Clearing Corporation — the brand under which ASX's clearing services are promoted. It encompasses ASX Clear (formerly the Australian Clearing House) and ASX Clear (Futures) (formerly SFE Clearing Corporation).
- ASX Settlement Corporation — the brand under which ASX Group's settlement services are promoted. It encompasses ASX Settlement (formerly ASX Settlement and Transfer Corporation) and Austraclear.

- ASX Compliance — the brand under which services are provided to the ASX Group for the ongoing monitoring and enforcement of compliance with the ASX operating rules. This entity replaces ASX Markets Supervision.

More information about the ASX can be obtained from its website, www.asx.com.au.

LEARNING CHECK

- ☐ The key players in standard setting in Australia are the Financial Reporting Council (FRC) and the AASB. Other key players in financial reporting regulation include the Australian Securities and Investments Commission (ASIC), the Australian Prudential Regulation Authority (APRA) and the Australian Securities Exchange Group (ASX).
- ☐ The FRC provides broad oversight of the accounting standard-setting process in Australia.
- ☐ The AASB formulates and issues accounting standards in Australia.
- ☐ ASIC is the regulator of corporations, markets and financial services. It administers the Corporations Act and the ASIC Act.
- ☐ APRA regulates the financial services industry and aims to promote financial stability so as to minimise the likelihood of financial losses to investors.
- ☐ The ASX operates the largest securities market in Australia. It establishes Listing Rules, oversees compliance with its operating rules, and promotes standards of corporate governance for entities that list on its exchange.

1.3 The International Accounting Standards Board (IASB)

LEARNING OBJECTIVE 1.3 Explain the structure, role and processes of the IASB and the IFRS Interpretations Committee.

As noted in section 1.1.2, Australia adopts accounting standards issued by the **International Accounting Standards Board (IASB)**. The IASB is an independent standard-setting board that develops and approves International Financial Reporting Standards (IFRSs). As at 2018, approximately 87% of jurisdictions require the use of IFRS standards for most domestically accountable companies (IFRS 2018). The IFRS Interpretations Committee (formerly known as International Financial Reporting Interpretations Committee) issues interpretations (IFRICs) and guidance for accounting standards and for specific transactions or events. Compliance with IFRSs includes compliance with IFRICs. The IASB and IFRS Interpretations Committee are appointed and overseen by a geographically and professionally diverse group of trustees (IFRS Foundation Trustees) who are publicly accountable to a monitoring board comprising public capital market authorities. The IFRS Foundation Trustees appoint an IFRS Advisory Council, which provides strategic advice to the IASB and informs the IFRS Foundation Trustees. The Trustees are accountable to the Monitoring Board, which comprises public authorities including the International Organization of Securities Commissions.

Further information about the IASB and international standard-setting arrangements is available on the IASB website, www.ifrs.org.

LEARNING CHECK

- ☐ The IASB is responsible for the development and publication of IFRSs, which are adopted in Australia as AASBs.

1.4 The components of the *Conceptual Framework*

LEARNING OBJECTIVE 1.4 Explain the key components of the *Conceptual Framework*.

The role of a conceptual framework of accounting is to provide guidance to standard setters in developing accounting standards and to guide preparers on accounting issues that are not addressed by accounting standards. In 1989, the International Accounting Standards Committee (IASC), the predecessor to the IASB, adopted the *Framework for the Preparation and Presentation of Financial Statements*.

This document was superseded by the *Conceptual Framework for Financial Reporting* in 2010 and revised in 2018. The revised *Conceptual Framework* takes effect for annual periods beginning on or after 1 January 2020. The IASB's *Conceptual Framework* comprises the following eight chapters.
- Chapter 1. The objective of general purpose financial reporting
- Chapter 2. Qualitative characteristics of useful financial information
- Chapter 3. Financial statements and the reporting entity
- Chapter 4. The elements of financial statements
- Chapter 5. Recognition and derecognition
- Chapter 6. Measurement
- Chapter 7. Presentation and disclosure
- Chapter 8. Concepts of capital and capital maintenance

As discussed in section 1.1.2, under the direction of the FRC, the AASB adopted accounting standards issued by the IASB as well as the conceptual framework. Further, as discussed in section 1.1.3, the AASB has adopted a two-phased approach to adopting the revised *Conceptual Framework* issued by the IASB, thus limiting the requirement to apply the new framework to publicly accountable entities for annual reporting periods commencing on or after 1 January 2020. As the focus of this text is the application of Australian accounting standards, the discussion in this section will focus on the revised *Conceptual Framework*.

1.4.1 The objective of financial reporting

Paragraph 1.2 of the *Conceptual Framework* states the objective of general purpose financial reporting is:

> to provide financial information about the reporting entity that is useful to existing and potential investors, lenders and other creditors in making decisions relating to providing resources to the entity.

This objective forms the foundation of the *Conceptual Framework*. The *Conceptual Framework* is designed to aid the development of accounting standards; assist financial statement preparers to develop consistent accounting policies; and assist all parties to understand and interpret the standards.

Without a defined group of primary users of financial statements, the *Conceptual Framework* would risk becoming unduly abstract or vague. Capital providers are the primary user group to which GPFS are directed (paragraph 1.5). Other parties (e.g. regulators) may find GPFS useful, but GPFS are not primarily directed to these groups.

As described in paragraph 1.2 of the *Conceptual Framework*, users of financial statements make decisions about buying, selling or holding equity and debt instruments, providing or settling loans, and voting on management actions related to the use of the entity's economic resources. As noted in paragraph 1.23 of the *Conceptual Framework*, capital providers need to assess the returns on their investments through:
- the prospects for future net cash inflows to the entity
- the assessment of management's stewardship of the entity's economic resources entrusted to their care.

Because individual primary users have varying needs, accounting standards aim to have financial statements provide information that meets the needs of the maximum number of primary users (*Conceptual Framework* paragraph 1.8). Entities can also include additional information that may be more useful to a particular subset of users. Information that meets the needs of the specified primary users is likely to meet many of the needs of other users.

GPFS cannot provide all of the information that capital providers need; they need to consider relevant information from other sources as well. GPFS provide information that helps users estimate the value of the entity, but they are not themselves intended to show the value of the entity.

The *Conceptual Framework* emphasises that investors need information on both:
- financial performance — income and expenses
- financial position — assets, liabilities and equity.

Paragraph 1.12 of the *Conceptual Framework* states:

> General purpose financial reports provide information about the financial position of a reporting entity, which is information about the entity's economic resources and the claims against the reporting entity. Financial reports also provide information about the effects of transactions and other events that change a reporting entity's economic resources and claims. Both types of information provide useful input for decisions relating to providing resources to an entity.

Before the objective of general purpose financial reporting can be implemented in practice, the basic qualitative characteristics of financial reporting information need to be specified. Further, it is necessary to define the basic elements — assets, liabilities, equity, income and expenses — used in financial statements. This is done in the following sections.

LEARNING CHECK

☐ The *Conceptual Framework* is designed to assist standard setters to develop accounting standards, assist preparers to develop consistent accounting policies, and assist all parties to understand and interpret the standards.
☐ Users of financial reports are an entity's existing and potential investors, lenders and other creditors. They must rely on GPFS for much of the financial information they need.

1.5 Qualitative characteristics of useful information

LEARNING OBJECTIVE 1.5 Explain the qualitative characteristics that make information in financial statements useful.

What characteristics should financial information have in order to be included in general purpose external financial statements? The following discusses both the qualitative characteristics of useful information and the constraint on providing useful information. The qualitative characteristics are divided into fundamental qualitative characteristics and enhancing qualitative characteristics.

1.5.1 Fundamental qualitative characteristics

For financial information to be decision useful, it must possess two fundamental qualitative characteristics:
• relevance
• faithful representation.

Relevance

Paragraphs 2.6 to 2.10 of the *Conceptual Framework* elaborate on the qualitative characteristic of **relevance**. Information is relevant if:
• it is capable of making a difference in the decisions made by the users of that financial information. This applies regardless of whether or not the information has actually made a difference in the past, will make a difference in the future, users choose to take advantage of it or users are already aware of it from other sources.
• it has predictive value, confirmatory value or both. Predictive value occurs where the information is useful as an input into the users' decision models to predict future outcomes. Confirmatory value arises where the information provides feedback that confirms or changes previous evaluations.

Information about the financial position and past performance is often used as the basis for predicting future financial position and performance and other matters in which users are directly interested, such as future dividends and wage payments, future share prices and the ability of the reporting entity to pay its debts when they fall due. The predictive ability of information may be improved if unusual or infrequent transactions and events are reported separately in the statement of profit or loss and other comprehensive income.

Materiality is an entity-specific aspect of the relevance of information. Information is **material** if its omission, misstatement or obscuration could be expected to influence the decisions that users make about a specific reporting entity (paragraph 2.11). Therefore, no uniform quantitative threshold can be specified for materiality for an entity or in a particular situation.

For example, small expenditures for non-current assets (e.g. tools) are often expensed immediately rather than depreciated over their useful lives to save the clerical costs of recording depreciation and because the effects on performance and financial position measures over their useful lives are not large enough to affect decisions. Another example of the application of materiality is the common practice by large companies of rounding amounts to the nearest thousand dollars in their financial statements.

Materiality is a relative matter — what is material for one entity may be immaterial for another. A $10 000 error may not be important in the financial statements of a multimillion-dollar company, but it may be critical to a small business. The materiality of an item may depend not only on its relative size but also on its nature. For example, the discovery of a $10 000 bribe is a material event even for a large company. Judgements as to the materiality of an item or event are often difficult. Accountants make judgements based on their knowledge of the company and on past experience, and users of financial statements must generally rely on the accountants' judgements.

Faithful representation

Paragraphs 2.12 to 2.19 of the *Conceptual Framework* elaborate on the concept of **faithful representation**. Financial reports are designed to represent economic phenomena of an entity in words and numbers. To be useful, the financial information presented must faithfully represent the substance of the phenomena that it purports to represent. To be a perfectly faithful representation it must have three characteristics — it must be complete, neutral and free from error.

- A depiction is complete if it includes all information, descriptions and explanations required for a user to understand the phenomenon (paragraph 2.14).
- Neutrality is the absence of bias in the selection or presentation of financial information. Neutral information avoids any manipulations that may influence how users perceive it. Neutrality is supported by prudence, which is an exercise of caution when making judgements under conditions of uncertainty (paragraph 2.15).
- Free from error does not require the report to be perfectly accurate, but rather that the descriptions of economic phenomena are free of errors or omissions, and that there are no errors in the selection and application of the process used to produce the information. For example, an estimate of an unobservable value cannot be stated to be accurate, but can be faithfully represented if it is described as an estimate, explains the estimating process, and no errors were made in selecting and applying the estimation process (paragraph 2.18).

Paragraph 2.19 describes measurement uncertainty as a factor affecting faithful representation. Measurement uncertainty arises when amounts cannot be observed directly and so must be estimated. Reasonable estimates that are clearly and accurately described and explained do not undermine the usefulness of financial reports and even estimates with a high level of measurement uncertainty can provide useful information.

To be useful, information must be both relevant and a faithful representation. However, sometimes a trade-off between relevance and faithful representation may be necessary to meet the objective of financial reporting to provide useful information. For example, the measurement base that provides the most relevant information about an asset will not always provide the most faithful representation.

The *Conceptual Framework* (paragraph 2.21) stipulates the following process for applying the fundamental qualitative characteristics.

1. Identify the economic phenomenon to be communicated to users of the entity's financial information.
2. Identify the most relevant type of information about that phenomenon.
3. Determine whether that information is available and can provide a faithful representation.

If the conditions in point 3 are met, the process of satisfying the fundamental qualitative characteristics ends at that point. If not, the process is repeated using the next most relevant type of information.

1.5.2 Enhancing qualitative characteristics

The *Conceptual Framework* (paragraph 2.23) identifies four enhancing qualitative characteristics:
- comparability
- verifiability
- timeliness
- understandability.

These characteristics are *complementary* to the fundamental characteristics. They cannot make information useful if the information lacks relevance or is not a faithful representation. They can, however, be used to help choose between alternative ways to depict a phenomenon if the alternatives provide equally relevant information and an equally faithful representation. In relation to these enhancing qualities, note the following.

- **Comparability** is the quality of information that enables users to identify and understand similarities in and differences between two or more economic phenomena. Making decisions about one entity may be enhanced if comparable information is available about similar entities; for example, profit for the period per share.

- **Verifiability** is a quality of information that helps assure users that information faithfully represents the economic phenomena that it purports to represent. Verifiability is achieved if different knowledgeable and independent observers could reach the same general conclusions that the information represents the economic phenomena or that a particular recognition or measurement model has been appropriately applied. Direct verification involves direct observation (e.g. counting cash). Indirect verification involves checking the data used in a model or formula and using the same methodology to determine whether the same outputs are achieved.
- **Timeliness** means having information available to decision makers in time to be capable of influencing their decisions. If such capacity is lost, then the information loses its relevance. Information may continue to be timely after it has been initially provided; for example, in trend analysis.
- **Understandability** is the quality of information that enables users to comprehend its meaning. Information may be more understandable if it is classified, characterised and presented clearly and concisely. Users of financial statements are assumed to have a reasonable knowledge of business and economic activities and to be able to read a financial report. Entities shall not exclude complex information simply because they are trying to make the financial reports easier to understand as to do so could make the report incomplete and therefore possibly misleading.

Alternative accounting policies exist in the treatment of many items, such as inventories and cost of sales, non-current assets and depreciation, and intangible assets (e.g. patents, copyrights and goodwill). The standard setters have expressed their position regarding the consistency of accounting methods in accounting standard AASB 108/IAS 8, which states that an entity must select and apply its accounting policies in a consistent manner from one period to another. Consistency of practices between entities is also desired. Any change made in an accounting policy by an entity must be disclosed by stating the nature of the change, the reasons the change provides reliable and more relevant information, and the effect of the change in monetary terms on each financial statement item affected. For example, the reason for a change in accounting policy may be disclosed in a note such as this:

> During the year, the company changed from the first-in first-out to the weighted average cost method of accounting for inventories because the weighted average cost method provides a more relevant measure of the entity's financial performance. The effect of this change was to increase cost of sales by $460 000 for the current financial year.

Note that the need for consistency does not require a given accounting method to be applied throughout the entity. An entity may very well use different methods for different types of inventories and different depreciation methods for different kinds of non-current assets. (Different inventories costing and depreciation methods are discussed in chapters 4 and 5.) Furthermore, the need for consistency should not be allowed to hinder the introduction of better accounting methods. Consistency from year to year or entity to entity is not an end in itself, but a means for achieving greater comparability in the presentation of information in GPFS. The need for comparability should not be confused with mere uniformity or consistency. It is not appropriate for an entity to continue to apply an accounting policy if the policy is not in keeping with the qualitative characteristics of relevance and faithful representation.

1.5.3 Cost constraint on useful financial reporting

Paragraphs 2.39 to 2.43 of the *Conceptual Framework* note that cost is the constraint that limits the information provided by financial reporting. The provision of information incurs costs. The costs of supplying information should not exceed the benefits. Costs include costs of collecting and processing information, costs of verifying information and costs of disseminating information. Users ultimately bear those costs in the form of reduced returns. The non-provision of information also imposes costs on the users of financial information as they seek alternative sources of information. As described in paragraph 2.41 of the *Conceptual Framework:*

> Reporting financial information that is relevant and faithfully represents what it purports to represent helps users to make decisions with more confidence. This results in more efficient functioning of capital markets and a lower cost of capital for the economy as a whole.

However, given the cost constraint, it is not possible to provide all the information that every user finds relevant.

☐ To be useful for decision making, financial information must be relevant and faithfully represent the economic phenomena.

☐ Accounting information is more useful when it possesses comparability, verifiability, timeliness and understandability.

☐ The provision of accounting information is constrained by the cost of providing that information. It is not possible to provide all the information that every user finds relevant.

1.6 Financial statements and the reporting entity

LEARNING OBJECTIVE 1.6 Describe the objective and scope of financial statements prepared by a reporting entity.

Chapters 1 and 2 of the *Conceptual Framework* discuss information provided in general purpose financial reports and Chapters 3 to 8 discuss information provided in GPFS, which are a particular form of general purpose financial report. Paragraph 3.2 of the *Conceptual Framework* states the following.

> The objective of financial statements is to provide financial information about the reporting entity's assets, liabilities, equity, income and expenses that is useful to users of financial statements in assessing the prospects for future net cash inflows to the reporting entity and in assessing management's stewardship of the entity's economic resources.

Financial statements provide information about transactions and other events viewed from the perspective of the reporting entity as a whole, rather than from the perspective of any particular group of the entity's existing or potential investors, lenders or other creditors. Paragraph 3.4 specifies that financial statements are prepared for a reporting period and provide information about:

(a) assets and liabilities — including unrecognised assets and liabilities — and equity that existed at the end of the reporting period, or during the reporting period; and
(b) income and expenses for the reporting period.

A reporting entity shall provide comparative information for at least one preceding reporting period to help users of financial statements to identify and assess changes and trends. It shall also provide information about possible future transactions and events in financial statements if it relates to the entity's assets, liabilities, equity, income or expenses for the reporting period and is useful to users of financial statements. Information about transactions and other events that have occurred after the end of the reporting period also shall be included in the financial statements when necessary to meet the objective of financial statements.

1.6.1 Going concern assumption

Paragraph 3.9 of the *Conceptual Framework* states that financial statements are prepared under the assumption that the entity is a going concern and will continue to operate for the foreseeable future. Hence, it is assumed that the entity has neither the intention nor the need to enter liquidation or to cease trading. This assumption is called the **going concern assumption** or sometimes the *continuity assumption*. Past experience indicates that the continuation of operations in the future is highly probable for most entities. Thus, it is usually assumed that an entity will continue to operate at least long enough to carry out its existing commitments.

Adoption of the going concern assumption has important implications in accounting. For example, it is an assumption used by some to justify the use of historical costs in accounting for non-current assets and for the systematic allocation of their costs to depreciation expense over their useful lives. Because it is assumed that the assets will not be sold in the near future but will continue to be used in operating activities, current market values of the assets are sometimes assumed to be of little importance. If the entity continues to use the assets, fluctuations in their market values cause no gain or loss, nor do they increase or decrease the usefulness of the assets. The going concern assumption also supports the inclusion of some assets, such as prepaid expenses and acquired goodwill, in the statement of financial position even though they may have little, if any, sales value.

If management intends to liquidate the entity's operations, the going concern assumption is set aside and financial statements are prepared on the basis of expected liquidation (forced sale) values. Thus, assets are reported at their expected sales values and liabilities at the amount needed to settle them immediately. Paragraph 25 of AASB 101/IAS 1 details disclosures required when an entity does not prepare financial statements on a going concern basis (see chapter 16).

1.6.2 The reporting entity

The IASB and AASB do not consider that they have the authority to determine who should or could prepare GPFS. Hence, the revised *Conceptual Framework* provides a general description of a reporting entity, rather than stating who should or could prepare GPFS. Paragraph 3.10 of the *Conceptual Framework* describes a reporting entity as:

> an entity that is required, or chooses, to prepare financial statements. A reporting entity can be a single entity or a portion of an entity or can comprise more than one entity. A reporting entity is not necessarily a legal entity.

An entity that is required by legislation to prepare financial statements, or chooses to do so, is a reporting entity. Financial statements of reporting entities could differ based on the *boundary* of a reporting entity. A reporting entity's financial statements could be:
- consolidated financial statements — if one entity (parent) has control over another entity (subsidiary) and the reporting entity comprises both the parent and its subsidiaries
- unconsolidated financial statements — if a reporting entity is the parent alone
- combined financial statements — if a reporting entity comprises two or more entities that are not all linked by a parent–subsidiary relationship.

The boundary of the reporting entity is driven by the information needs of the primary users of the reporting entity's financial statements and the financial reporting regulation of the relevant jurisdiction.

LEARNING CHECK

☐ The objective of financial statements is to provide financial information about the reporting entity's assets, liabilities, equity, income and expenses that is useful to users of financial statements in assessing the prospect for future net cash inflows to the reporting entity and in assessing management's stewardship of the entity's economic resources.
☐ Financial statements are prepared under the going concern assumption; that is, the assumption that an entity will continue to operate for the foreseeable future.
☐ A reporting entity is an entity that is required, or chooses, to prepare financial statements.

1.7 Definition of the elements of financial statements

LEARNING OBJECTIVE 1.7 Define the basic elements in financial statements — assets, liabilities, equity, income and expenses.

The *Conceptual Framework* identifies and defines the elements of financial statements: assets, liabilities, equity, income and expenses.

1.7.1 Assets

An **asset** is defined in paragraph 4.3 of the *Conceptual Framework* as:

> a present economic resource controlled by the entity as a result of past events.

Paragraph 4.4 defines an economic resource as 'a right that has the potential to produce economic benefits'. The definition of an asset refers to the economic resource, not to the resulting economic benefits. Although an asset derives its value from its potential to produce future economic benefits, what the entity controls is the present right that contains that potential. The entity does not control the future economic benefits.

The definitions of an asset and economic resources involve three aspects: rights, potential to produce economic benefits and control.

Rights

Paragraph 4.9 of the *Conceptual Framework* specifies that the rights, in order to be an asset of the entity, must:

> both have the potential to produce for the entity economic benefits beyond the economic benefits available to all other parties . . . and be controlled by the entity.

Hence, not all of an entity's rights are assets of that entity. For example, rights to access public goods are available to all parties and hence are typically not assets for the entities that hold them.

In principle, each of an entity's rights is a separate asset (paragraph 4.11). For example, a right that is established by a contract that gives a lessee a right or use of a leased object is an asset of the entity. However, for accounting purposes, related rights are often treated as a single asset. For example, legal ownership of a physical object gives rise to several rights, including, but not limited to, the right to:

- use the object
- transfer rights over the object
- pledge rights over the object.

In this instance, the economic resource is not the physical object but the set of rights over the object. In many cases, the set of rights arising from legal ownership of a physical object is accounted for as a single asset. Describing the set of rights as the physical object will often provide a faithful representation of those rights in the most concise and understandable way (paragraph 4.12).

An entity cannot have a right to obtain economic benefits from itself (paragraph 4.10). For example, if an entity repurchases and holds debt instruments or equity instruments issued previously by the entity, the repurchased instruments are not an economic resource of the entity.

Potential to produce economic benefits

Paragraph 4.14 of the *Conceptual Framework* states the following.

> An economic resource is a right that has the potential to produce economic benefits. For that potential to exist, it does not need to be certain, or even likely, that the right will produce economic benefits. It is only necessary that the right already exists and that, in at least one circumstance, it would produce for the entity economic benefits beyond those available to all other parties.

There are numerous ways that an entity could use an economic resource to produce economic benefits. Examples include (paragraph 4.16):

- receiving contractual cash flows
- exchanging economic resources with another party on favourable terms
- producing cash inflows or avoiding cash outflows by using the economic resource to produce goods or provide services, or to enhance the value of other economic resources, or lease the economic resource to another party
- extinguishing liabilities by transferring the economic resource.

Paragraph 4.17 states:

> Although an economic resource derives its value from its present potential to produce future economic benefits, the economic resource is the present right that contains that potential, not the future economic benefits that the right may produce. For example, a purchased option derives its value from its potential to produce economic benefits through exercise of the option at a future date. However, the economic resource is the present right — the right to exercise the option at a future date. The economic resource is not the future economic benefits that the holder will receive if the option is exercised.

Control

Paragraph 4.20 of the *Conceptual Framework* defines control in the following terms.

> An entity controls an economic resource if it has the present ability to direct the use of the economic resource and obtain the economic benefits that may flow from it. Control includes the present ability to prevent other parties from directing the use of the economic resource and from obtaining the economic benefits that may flow from it.

Paragraph 4.19 states:

> Control links an economic resource to an entity. Assessing whether control exists helps to identify the economic resource for which the entity accounts. For example, an entity may control a proportionate share

in a property without controlling the rights arising from ownership of the entire property. In such cases, the entity's asset is the share in the property, which it controls, not the rights arising from ownership of the entire property, which it does not control.

Paragraph 4.22 notes that control of an economic resource usually arises from the ability to enforce legal rights, but it can also exist if an entity has some other means of ensuring that it has the exclusive present ability to 'direct the use of the economic resource and obtain the benefits that may flow from it'. This may be the case when, for example, an entity can control a right to use know-how that is not in the public domain if it has access to the know-how and can keep it secret even if it is not protected by a registered patent (and thus there is no ability to enforce a legal right). For example, an entity engaged in processing and selling foods may maintain control over its recipes by keeping them in a secure location and entering into confidentiality agreements with suppliers and employees.

1.7.2 Liabilities

A **liability** is defined in paragraph 4.26 of the *Conceptual Framework* as:

> a present obligation of the entity to transfer an economic resource as a result of past events.

Thus, a liability only exists when:
- the entity has an obligation
- the obligation is to transfer an economic resource
- the obligation is a present obligation that exists as a result of past events.

Obligation

Paragraph 4.29 describes an obligation as follows.

> An obligation is a duty or responsibility that an entity has no practical ability to avoid. An obligation is always owed to another party (or parties). The other party (parties) could be a person or another entity, a group of people or other entities, or society at large. It is not necessary to know the identity of the party (or parties) to whom the obligation is owed.

A legal debt constitutes a liability, but a liability is not restricted to being a legal debt. An obligation may also be imposed by notions of equity or fairness (referred to as an 'equitable' obligation), and by customary practices, published policies or particular statements (referred to as a 'constructive' obligation) if the entity has no practical ability to avoid complying. For example, an entity may publish a policy that it will rectify faults in its products beyond the expiry of the legal warranty period. Hence, the entity has a constructive obligation in respect of goods already sold. The action must be unavoidable. It is not sufficient for an entity merely to have an intention to sacrifice economic benefits in the future.

Paragraph 4.32 notes that:

> In some situations, an entity's duty or responsibility to transfer an economic resource is conditional on a particular future action that the entity itself may take [such as] operating a particular business or operating in a particular market on a specified future date ... In such situations, the entity has an obligation if it has no practical ability to avoid taking that action.

Transfer of an economic resource

The obligation must have the potential to require the entity to transfer an economic resource to another party. It does not need to be certain, or even likely, that the entity will be required to transfer an economic resource. For example, the transfer may be required only if a specified uncertain future event occurs such as a customer making a warranty claim. It is only necessary that the obligation already exists and it would require the entity to transfer an economic resource in at least one circumstance.

Present obligation as a result of past events

An important characteristic of a liability is present obligation as a result of past events. Paragraph 4.43 states a present obligation arises as a result of past events only if:

(a) the entity has already obtained economic benefits or taken an action; and
(b) as a consequence, the entity will or may have to transfer an economic resource that it would not otherwise have had to transfer.

A present obligation needs to be distinguished from a future commitment. A decision by management to buy an asset in the future does not give rise to a present obligation. An obligation normally arises when the asset is delivered, or the entity has entered into an irrevocable agreement to buy the asset, with a substantial penalty if the agreement is revoked. A liability must have resulted from a *past event* (sometimes referred to as the *obligating event*). For example, the acquisition of goods and the work done by staff give rise to accounts payable and wages payable respectively. Wages to be paid to staff for work they will do in the future is not a liability as there is no past transaction or event and no present obligation.

1.7.3 Equity

Paragraph 4.63 of the *Conceptual Framework* defines **equity** as:

> the residual interest in the assets of the entity after deducting all its liabilities.

Defining equity in this manner shows clearly that it cannot be defined independently of the other elements in the statement of financial position. The characteristics of equity are as follows.
- Equity is a residual; that is, something left over. In other words:

$$\text{Equity} = \text{Assets} - \text{Liabilities}$$

- Equity increases as a result of profitable operations (i.e. the excesses of income over expenses) and by contributions by owners. Similarly, equity is diminished by unprofitable operations and by distributions to owners (drawings and dividends).
- Equity is influenced by the measurement system adopted for assets and liabilities and by the concepts of capital and capital maintenance adopted in the preparation of general purpose external financial statements. (These aspects are discussed later in the chapter.)
- Equity may be subclassified in the statement of financial position; for example, into contributed funds from owners, retained earnings, other reserves representing appropriations of retained earnings and reserves representing capital maintenance adjustments.

1.7.4 Income

The *Conceptual Framework* defines **income** in paragraph 4.68 as:

> increases in assets, or decreases in liabilities, that result in increases in equity, other than those relating to contributions from holders of equity claims.

Note that this definition of income is linked to the definitions of assets and liabilities. The definition of income is wide in its scope, in that income in the form of increases in assets or decreases in liabilities can arise from providing goods or services, investing in or lending to another entity, holding and disposing of assets, and receiving contributions such as grants and donations. To qualify as income, the increase in assets or decrease in liabilities must have the effect of increasing equity, excluding capital contributions by owners. Also excluded are certain increases in equity under various inflation accounting models that require the recognition of capital maintenance adjustments.

Another important aspect of the definition is that, if income arises as a result of an increase in assets or a decrease in liabilities, it is necessary for the entity to *control* that increase in economic benefits. If control does not exist, then no asset exists. Income arises once control over the increase in economic benefits has been achieved and an asset exists, provided there is no equivalent increase in liabilities. For example, in the case of magazine subscriptions received in advance, no income exists on receipt of the cash because an equivalent obligation also has arisen for services to be performed through supply of magazines to clients in the future.

Income can also exist through a reduction in liabilities that increase the entity's equity. An example of a liability reduction is if a liability of the entity is 'forgiven'. Income arises as a result of that forgiveness, unless the forgiveness of the debt constitutes a contribution by owners.

Under the *Conceptual Framework*, income encompasses both revenue and gains. A definition of **revenue** is contained in Appendix A of AASB 15/IFRS 15 *Revenue from Contracts with Customers*:

> Income arising in the course of an entity's ordinary activities.

Thus, revenue represents income which has arisen from the ordinary activities of an entity. On the other hand, *gains* represent income that does not necessarily arise from the ordinary activities of the entity; for example, gains on the disposal of non-current assets or on the revaluation of marketable securities. Gains are usually disclosed in the statement of profit or loss and other comprehensive income net of any related expenses, whereas revenues are reported at a gross amount. As revenues and gains are both income, there is no need to regard them as separate elements under the *Conceptual Framework*.

1.7.5 Expenses

Paragraph 4.69 of the *Conceptual Framework* contains the following definition of **expenses**.

> Expenses are decreases in assets, or increases in liabilities, that result in decreases in equity, other than those relating to distributions to holders of equity claims.

To qualify as an expense, a reduction in an asset or an increase in a liability must have the effect of decreasing the entity's equity. For example, paying rent for the current month is an expense because it reduces assets (cash) and reduces equity. However, the purchase of an item of plant is not an expense. Although the transaction reduces one asset (cash) there is a corresponding increase in another asset (plant). An expense arises whenever the economic benefits in the asset are consumed, expire or are lost. Like income, the definition of expenses is expressed in terms of changes in assets, liabilities and equity. This concept of expense is broad enough to encompass items that have typically been reported in financial statements as 'losses'; for example, losses on foreign currency transactions, losses from fire or flood, or losses on the sale of an asset.

LEARNING CHECK

- [ ] The *Conceptual Framework* identifies and defines the elements of financial statements: assets, liabilities, equity, income and expenses.
- [ ] An asset is a present economic resource controlled by the entity as a result of past events. An economic resource is a right that has the potential to produce economic benefits.
- [ ] A liability is a present obligation of the entity to transfer an economic resource as a result of past event.
- [ ] Equity is the residual interest in the assets of the entity after deducting all its liabilities.
- [ ] Income is defined as increases in assets, or decreases in liabilities, that result in increases in equity, other than those relating to contributions from holders of equity claims.
- [ ] Expenses are decreases in assets, or increases in liabilities, that result in decreases in equity, other than those relating to distributions to holders of equity claims.

1.8 Recognition and derecognition of the elements of financial statements

LEARNING OBJECTIVE 1.8 Explain the criteria for recognising and derecognising the elements of financial statements.

There are recognition criteria to be followed in the preparation and presentation of financial statements. These criteria have been set down as part of the *Conceptual Framework*. **Recognition** means the process of incorporating into the statement of financial position or the statement of profit or loss and other comprehensive income an item that meets the definition of one of the elements of financial statements — an asset, a liability, equity, income or expense. In other words, it involves the inclusion of dollar amounts in the entity's accounting system known as *carrying amounts*. Note that an item must satisfy the definition of an element before it is 'recognised'. However, not all items that meet the definition of the elements are recognised.

1.8.1 Recognition criteria

The *Conceptual Framework* states in paragraph 5.7 that an asset or liability is recognised only if recognition of that asset or liability and of any resulting income, expenses or changes in equity provides users of financial statements with useful information. Recognition must provide:

- *relevant* information about the asset or liability and about any resulting income, expenses or changes in equity
- a *faithful representation* of the asset or liability and of any resulting income, expenses or changes in equity.

Paragraph 5.8 further provides that an asset or liability is recognised if the benefits of recognising and providing the information to users of financial statements are likely to justify the costs of providing and using that information. The recognition criteria serve to avoid cluttering financial statements with lots of assets and liabilities for which the probability of an inflow or outflow is so low that recognising them would not provide relevant information about the entity's financial position to users of financial statements.

Relevance

The recognition of items that satisfy the definition of elements of financial statements, such as assets and liabilities, would not always result in relevant information. This may be the case if:
- it is uncertain whether an asset or liability exists, or
- an asset or liability exists, but the probability of an inflow or outflow of economic benefits is low.

The presence of one or both of these factors does not automatically lead to a conclusion that the information provided by recognition lacks relevance. It may be a combination of factors that determines whether recognition provides relevant information. Whether or not the asset or liability is recognised, an entity may need to provide explanatory information in the financial statements about the uncertainties associated with it.

Faithful representation

An entity will need to measure the item or event before it can be recognised. In many cases, such measures need to be estimated and are subject to *measurement uncertainty*. As noted in section 1.5.1, the use of reasonable estimates is an essential part of the preparation of financial information and does not undermine the usefulness of financial information if the estimates are clearly and accurately described and explained.

In some cases, measurement of an asset or liability may involve such a high level of measurement uncertainty that it becomes questionable whether the estimate would provide a sufficient faithful representation of that asset or liability and of any resulting income, expenses or changes in equity; for example, a measure that is exceptionally sensitive to small changes in the input estimates or a measure for which the range of possible outcomes is exceptionally wide and the probability of each outcome is exceptionally difficult to estimate.

In limited circumstances, if all relevant measures of an asset or liability are subject to such high measurement uncertainty that recognition would not provide useful information about the asset or liability — even if accompanied by a description of the estimates made and an explanation of the uncertainties that affect those estimates — the asset or liability would not be recognised.

ILLUSTRATIVE EXAMPLE 1.3

Asset recognition

Sustainable Ltd purchased solar panels, which were installed on the roof of a building owned by the company. The cost of the solar panels was $20 000. The solar panels create electricity from solar energy and feed it into the grid, resulting in savings in electricity costs for the company. Sustainable Ltd also purchased a ticket in a lottery operated by a charity. The lottery ticket cost $200 and gives Sustainable Ltd one chance in 10 000 (0.01 per cent probability) of winning the prize, which is a house in Sydney.

Required
Should Sustainable Ltd recognise the following as assets in accordance with the *Conceptual Framework*: (a) the solar panels, (b) the sun and (c) the lottery ticket?

Solution
The first step is to consider whether the item is an asset in accordance with the definition of an asset in the *Conceptual Framework*. If so, we proceed to the second step, which is to consider whether it satisfies the criteria for recognition in financial statements.

An asset is defined as an economic resource controlled by the entity as a result of past events. For the item to be an economic resource, it must be a right with the potential to produce economic benefits.

(a) Sustainable Ltd has the right to use the solar panels, which was established by the past events of purchasing them and having them installed on the roof of a building that the company owns. The solar panels have the potential to produce economic benefits because they can draw solar energy and feed it into the grid. This is an economic benefit because it reduces electricity costs. Thus the solar panels satisfy the definition of an asset.

It is reasonable to expect that recognition of the solar panels as assets would provide useful information about them, by indicating that the investment in solar panels may provide economic benefits beyond the current reporting period. The solar panels can be faithfully represented by the cost of obtaining that resource, $20 000. Therefore, Sustainable Ltd should recognise the solar panels as an asset.

(b) Although the sun has the potential to produce economic benefits, it is a public good. Control links the economic resource to the entity. Sustainable Ltd does not control the rights to the sun because it is a right shared by everyone. Thus the sun is not an asset of Sustainable Ltd and therefore should not be recognised as an asset.

(c) The lottery ticket is a right to the chance of winning a prize. It has the potential to produce economic benefits in the form of a house in Sydney because the ticket might win. Sustainable Ltd controls the lottery ticket as a result of the past event, which was to purchase it. Thus the lottery ticket is an asset as defined by the *Conceptual Framework*.

Although the lottery ticket can be faithfully represented at its cost of $200, it is highly unlikely that the recognition of this asset would provide relevant information, because the probability of it providing benefits is so low. Therefore, the expenditure on lottery tickets should not be recognised as an asset. Instead, it should be recognised as an expense.

1.8.2 Derecognition

An entity must remove all or part of a recognised asset or liability from an entity's statement of financial position when the item no longer meets the definition of an asset or a liability. This is known as derecognition. For an asset, derecognition normally occurs when the entity loses *control* of all or part of the recognised asset or the potential benefits are fully used or expire. For example, prepaid rent is derecognised when the rental period expires. For a liability, derecognition normally occurs when the entity no longer has a *present obligation* for all or part of the recognised liability. For example, if an entity settles a bank loan, it would derecognise the bank loan because it no longer has an obligation to the bank. Paragraphs 5.27 and 5.28 of the *Conceptual Framework* stipulate that derecognition aims to *faithfully represent* both:

- any assets and liabilities retained after the transaction or other event that led to the derecognition (the control approach)
- the change in the entity's assets and liabilities as a result of that transaction or other event (the risks-and-rewards approach).

This aim can be achieved by:

- derecognising any assets or liabilities that have expired or have been consumed, collected, fulfilled or transferred, and recognising any resulting income and expenses (referred to as the *transferred component*)
- continuing to recognise the assets or liabilities retained (referred to as the *retained component*), if any
- including in the financial statement:
  - presentation of any retained component separately in the statement of financial position
  - presentation separately in the statement of financial performance any income and expenses recognised as a result of the derecognition of the transferred component
  - explanatory information.

In some cases, an entity may appear to transfer an asset or liability, but in fact it remains an asset or liability of the entity; for example, if an entity has transferred an asset to another party that holds the asset as an agent of the entity (e.g. sales on consignment), the transferor still controls the asset. In this case, an entity shall not derecognise the asset or liability because it would not achieve the aims of faithfully representing both any assets and liabilities retained and the resulting income or expenses.

LEARNING CHECK

☐ An item or transaction must meet the definition of an element of financial statements to be recognised in financial statements.

☐ Recognition is appropriate if it results in both relevant information about assets, liabilities, equity, income and expenses and a faithful representation of those items so that the financial statement provides information that is useful to the users of financial statements.

▶

☐ An entity shall derecognise an asset or liability from an entity's statement of financial position when the item no longer meets the definition of an asset or a liability. This occurs when the entity loses control of all or part of the recognised asset or the entity no longer has a present obligation for all or part of the liability.

1.9 Measurement of the elements of financial statements

LEARNING OBJECTIVE 1.9 Compare alternative measurement bases for measuring the elements of financial statements.

Chapter 6 of the *Conceptual Framework* describes various measurement bases, the information provided by each measurement base and factors to consider when selecting a basis for **measurement**. It describes two categories of measurement bases: historical cost and current value. Both bases can provide useful information; hence, the *Conceptual Framework* does not favour one over the other.

- Historical cost — the initial value of the costs incurred in acquiring or creating the asset. It comprises the value of the consideration paid to acquire or create the asset plus transaction costs.
- Current value — reflects conditions at the measurement date. It includes:
  - fair value
  - value in use for assets and fulfilment value for liabilities
  - current cost.

Table 1.1 summarises the definition and information provided by each measurement basis.

Table 6.1 of the *Conceptual Framework* also provides a summary of information provided by particular measurement bases for each asset, liability, income and expense.

In some circumstances, it may not be possible to identify a cost (e.g. an exchange of an asset without incurring a cost) or the cost may not provide relevant information about the asset or liability. In such case, a current value of the asset or liability is used as a deemed cost on initial recognition.

TABLE 1.1	A summary of the definition and information provided by each measurement basis	
Measurement basis	**Definition of the measurement basis**	**Entry or exit value**
Historical cost	• *Asset:* The value of the costs incurred in acquiring or creating the asset, comprising the consideration paid to acquire or create the asset plus transaction cost (paragraph 6.5) • *Liability:* The value of the consideration received to incurred or take on the liability minus transaction costs (paragraph 6.5)	Entry
Fair value	The price that would be received to sell an asset, or paid to transfer a liability, in an orderly transaction between market participants at the measurement date (paragraph 6.12)	Exit
Value in use (for assets) and fulfilment value (for liabilities)	• *Asset:* The present value of the cash flows, or other economic benefits, that an entity expects to derive from the use of an asset and from its ultimate disposal (paragraph 6.17) • *Liability:* The present value of the cash, or other economic resources, that an entity expects to be obliged to transfer as it fulfils a liability (paragraph 6.17) Value in use and fulfilment value include the present value of any transaction costs an entity expects to incur on the ultimate disposal of the asset or on fulfilling the liability (paragraph 6.18).	Exit
Current cost	• *Asset:* The cost of an equivalent asset at the measurement date. It comprises the consideration that would be paid at the measurement date plus the transaction costs that would be incurred at that date (paragraph 6.21). • *Liability:* The consideration that would be received for an equivalent liability at the measurement date minus the transaction costs that would be incurred at that date (paragraph 6.21)	Entry

1.9.1 Factors to consider when selecting a measurement basis

When selecting a measurement basis, an entity shall consider the nature of the information that the measurement basis will produce in both the statement of financial position and the statement of financial performance. The information provided by a measurement basis must be useful to users of financial statements; that is, to provide relevant information that faithfully represents the underlying substance of a transaction.

Relevance

The *Conceptual Framework* acknowledges that the relevance of information provided by a measurement basis for an asset, a liability and for related income and expenses is affected by:

- *the characteristics of the asset or liability* — for example, if the value of an asset or liability is sensitive to market factors, its historical cost might differ significantly from its current value. In such cases, historical cost may not provide relevant information if information about changes in value is important to users of financial statements.
- *how the asset or liability contributes to future cash flows* — for example, for assets and liabilities that produce cash flows directly, such as assets that can be sold independently without a significant economic penalty (e.g. without significant business disruption), the measurement basis that provides the most relevant information is likely to be a current value that incorporates current estimates of the amount, timing and uncertainty of the future cash flows. However, a current value may be less relevant for assets that the entity holds in order to collect contractual cash flows such as loans receivable, because changes in current value do not affect the amount of benefits that the entity expects to obtain from them.

Faithful representation

The *Conceptual Framework* describes that *measurement inconsistency* and *measurement uncertainty* may lead to financial statements not faithfully representing some aspects of the entity's financial position and financial performance.

Measurement inconsistency may arise when assets and liabilities that are related in some way are measured using different measurement bases (accounting mismatch). Therefore, using the same measurement basis for related assets and liabilities may provide users of financial statements with information that is more useful than the information that would result from using different measurement bases.

Measurement uncertainty arises when prices cannot be directly observed in an active market and estimation must be used. The level of measurement uncertainty may affect whether information provided by a particular measurement basis provides a faithful representation of an entity's financial position and financial performance. Nevertheless, if a particular measurement basis will provide relevant information, then a high level of measurement uncertainty does not necessarily prevent its use. In the event that measurement uncertainty results in information that does not faithfully represent the underlying information an entity should consider selecting a different measurement base.

Enhancing qualitative characteristics and the cost of constraint

Comparability, understandability and verifiability influence the selection of a measurement basis as follows.

- Comparability — using the same measurement bases for the same items from period to period within a reporting entity or in a single period across entities can increase the comparability of financial statements.
- Understandability — a change in measurement basis can reduce the understandability of financial statements, but may be justified if other factors outweigh the effect on understandability. If an entity makes a change in measurement basis, explanatory information may be needed to help users understand the effects of the change.
- Verifiability — independent corroboration enhances the verifiability of measures used in financial statements. If a measure cannot be verified, either directly by observing prices or indirectly by checking observable inputs to a model, users of financial statements may need additional explanatory information, such as key estimates used, to understand how the item has been measured.

No single enhanced qualitative characteristic is determinative in choosing a measurement basis. The relative importance of each factor will depend on facts and circumstances, and cost constraints may play a role. An entity will likely consider whether the benefits of the information provided to users of financial statements by a measurement basis justify the costs of providing that information.

1.10 Presentation and disclosure

LEARNING OBJECTIVE 1.10 Explain the concepts that underpin how information should be presented and disclosed.

Chapter 7 of the *Conceptual Framework* notes that the financial statements of an entity provide a means to effectively communicate financial information. Paragraph 7.2 states that effective communication of information in financial statements requires:

(a) focusing on presentation and disclosure objectives and principles rather than focusing on rules;
(b) classifying information in a manner that groups similar items and separates dissimilar items; and
(c) aggregating information in such a way that it is not obscured either by unnecessary detail or by excessive aggregation.

Paragraph 7.5 of the *Conceptual Framework* states that including presentation and disclosure requirements in accounting standards supports effective communication. Paragraph 7.4 establishes two principles for accounting standard setters when developing presentation and disclosure requirements: a reporting entity should have flexibility to provide relevant information that faithfully represents its assets, liabilities, equity, income and expenses; and information should be comparable over time and between entities. In specifying or encouraging certain methods of presentation, including classification, and disclosures, standard setters need to achieve a balance between these potentially competing principles.

Effective communication of financial information is assisted by providing entity-specific information rather than standardised descriptions. Duplication of information in different parts of the financial statements is usually unnecessary and can reduce understandability.

1.10.1 Classification

Entities commonly classify assets, liabilities, equity, income and expenses based on shared characteristics (e.g. the nature of the item, its function and how it is measured). Dissimilar items should not be classified together as this undermines usefulness.

Classification of assets and liabilities

An entity classifies assets and liabilities by applying the unit of account it has selected for the asset or liability. For example, an entity may recognise its obligations to pay wages to each of its employees as a single liability for wages payable. Sometimes, it may improve usefulness to separate an asset or liability into components that have different characteristics and classify those components separately (e.g. separating an asset or liability into current and non-current components) (paragraph 7.9).

Assets and liabilities that have been recognised and measured separately, such as cash at bank and bank loan payable, should not be offset (paragraph 7.10). This means that such assets and liabilities should not be combined and presented as a net asset or net liability.

Classification of equity

An entity may need to classify equity claims separately if (paragraphs 7.12–7.13):
- the equity claims have different characteristics
- some of the components of equity are subject to particular legal, regulatory or other requirements (e.g. where dividends can only be distributed to equity holders from specified distributable reserves, it is useful to present those reserves separately).

Classification of income and expenses

Income and expenses are classified and included in either the statement of profit or loss or in other comprehensive income.

The statement of profit or loss serves as the primary source of information about financial performance for the reporting period. As a default, income and expenses are classified and included in the statement of profit or loss. However, in paragraph 7.17 of the *Conceptual Framework*, it is noted that the AASB/IASB may decide that income or expenses arising from changes in the current value of an asset or liability should be reported in other comprehensive income if that would result in more relevant information presented in profit or loss or provide a more faithful representation of the entity's financial performance.

Generally, income or expenses included in other comprehensive income in one period should be reclassified to the statement of profit or loss in a future period, when doing so results in the statement of profit or loss providing more relevant information or providing a more faithful representation of the entity's financial performance for that period. However, an accounting standard may allow that income or expenses included in other comprehensive income are not to be subsequently recycled if there is no clear basis for identifying the period in which classification would improve the information in the statement of profit or loss (paragraph 7.19).

1.10.2 Aggregation

Aggregation summarises a large volume of information by adding together assets, liabilities, equity, income or expenses that have shared characteristics and are included in the same classification, but it conceals some detail. An entity needs to find a balance between summarising and providing sufficient detail.

LEARNING CHECK

☐ Entity-specific information is more useful than standardised description.
☐ An entity should avoid duplicating information in different parts of the financial statements.
☐ Assets and liabilities should not be offset.
☐ As a default, all income and expenses should be included in the statement of profit or loss, but in exceptional circumstances accounting standards may require that some income or expense shall instead be included in other comprehensive income.
☐ Income or expenses included in other comprehensive income in one period may need to be reclassified to the statement of profit or loss in a future period.

1.11 Concepts of capital

LEARNING OBJECTIVE 1.11 Outline concepts of capital.

Scant attention has been given to the concept of capital in accounting in the last few decades, but it was a topic that received considerable focus during the current value debates of the 1960s to the early 1980s. It was argued then, and now, that before an entity can determine its income for any period, it must adopt not only a measurement basis for assets and liabilities but also a concept of capital. An entity's choice of concept of capital should be based on the needs of the users of financial statements. Two concepts of capital discussed in paragraphs 8.1 and 8.2 of the *Conceptual Framework* are:
- *a financial concept of capital* — capital is synonymous with the net assets or equity of the entity. A financial concept of capital should be adopted if users are mainly concerned with the maintenance of invested capital or the purchasing power of invested capital.
- *a physical concept of capital* — capital is seen as the productive capability of the entity's assets, such as units of output per day. A physical concept of capital should be adopted if users are mainly concerned with the operating capability of the entity.

The *Conceptual Framework* does not prescribe a particular model. Most entities adopt a financial concept of capital. The recognition and measurement principles underlying Australian accounting standards applicable to the for-profit sector, and the determination of profit in accordance with Australian accounting standards are consistent with a financial concept of capital.

The two concepts of capital give rise to two concepts of capital maintenance. Capital maintenance links the concepts of profit and capital: only inflows of assets in excess of amounts needed to maintain capital may be regarded as profit and thus a return on capital.

- *Financial capital maintenance* can be measured in the following ways.
  - Nominal monetary units — profit is the increase in nominal money capital over the period and includes increases in the prices of assets held over the period
  - Constant purchasing power units — profit is the increase in purchasing power of invested capital over the period and thus only asset price increases in excess of the increase in the general level of prices is regarded as profit. The balance of the increase is treated as a capital maintenance adjustment (i.e. as part of equity).
- *Physical capital maintenance* measures profit as the increase in the physical productive capacity of the entity during the year. If a physical concept of capital is used, it would be necessary to apply a current cost measurement basis for assets and liabilities. Changes in the cost of replacing assets (i.e. the cost of maintaining operating capacity) are treated as capital maintenance adjustments, which are part of equity rather than profit.

The revaluation or restatement of assets and liabilities results in increases or decreases in equity. Although they satisfy the definition of income or expense according to the *Conceptual Framework*, they would be accounted for as a capital maintenance adjustment or revaluation reserves under some concepts of capital maintenance (paragraph 8.10).

LEARNING CHECK

☐ Two main concepts of capital are discussed in the *Conceptual Framework*: a financial concept of capital and a physical concept of capital.

☐ Under the financial concept of capital, capital is synonymous with the net assets or equity of the entity. Profit is measured either in terms of increases in the prices of assets held over the period or after considering the general level of prices and thus purchasing power.

☐ Under the physical concept of capital, capital is seen as the operating capability of the entity's assets. Profit is measured as the increase in the net assets after adjusting for the amount needed to maintain the operating capacity of the entity's assets, applying a current cost measurement basis.

1.12 Inconsistencies between the *Conceptual Framework* and accounting standards

LEARNING OBJECTIVE 1.12 Explain how inconsistencies may arise between the *Conceptual Framework* and accounting standards.

Although a purpose of the *Conceptual Framework* is to assist standard setters to develop accounting standards, inconsistencies sometimes arise between accounting standards and the *Conceptual Framework*. There are several reasons why this occurs.

First, many of the current accounting standards were developed under an earlier conceptual framework for accounting, which adopted different definitions and recognition criteria. For example, under the previous framework an asset or liability could not be recognised unless the flow of future economic benefits to or from the entity was probable. Thus some accounting standards still apply this principle (e.g. paragraph 14(b) of AASB 137/IAS 37 *Provisions, Contingent Liabilities and Contingent Assets* states that for a provision to be recognised it must be probable that an outflow of resources embodying economic benefits will be required to settle the obligation). It may take quite some time for the IASB and, hence, the AASB to revise all accounting standards for the implications of the revised *Conceptual Framework*.

Second, standard setters may impose more restrictive recognition criteria or restrict the choice of measurement base in order to avoid creative application of principles and accounting policies. For example, paragraph 54 of AASB 138/IAS 38 *Intangible Assets* prohibits the recognition of costs of internally generated intangible assets where those costs are incurred during the research phase of the project. There is a presumption that the entity cannot demonstrate that the resource will generate probable future economic benefits during the research phase.

Last, standard setting is, in part, a political process. There are instances where compromises are made in the interest of achieving the overall objective of developing a single set of high-quality global accounting standards.

The requirements of accounting standards override the *Conceptual Framework*. Thus in preparing GPFS, the entity must apply the requirements of accounting standards even if they differ from the principles established in the *Conceptual Framework*.

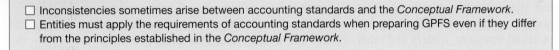

LEARNING CHECK

☐ Inconsistencies sometimes arise between accounting standards and the *Conceptual Framework*.
☐ Entities must apply the requirements of accounting standards when preparing GPFS even if they differ from the principles established in the *Conceptual Framework*.

SUMMARY

This chapter has provided an overview of key sources of regulation of financial reporting. While the Corporations Act is an overriding authority, Australian accounting standards are a very important source of regulation of financial reporting. The requirements of specific Australian accounting standards are covered throughout this text. The adoption of IFRSs has increased the importance of developments in international standards setting for financial reporting in Australia.

The *Conceptual Framework* describes the basic concepts that underlie financial statements prepared in conformity with accounting standards. It serves as a guide to the standard setters in developing accounting standards and in resolving accounting issues that are not addressed directly in an accounting standard. The *Conceptual Framework* identifies the principal classes of users of an entity's GPFS and states that the objective of financial statements is to provide information — about the financial position, performance and changes in financial position of an entity — that is useful to existing and potential investors, lenders and other creditors, in making decisions about providing resources to the entity. It specifies the fundamental qualities that make financial information useful, namely relevance and faithful representation. The usefulness of financial information is enhanced by comparability, verifiability, timeliness and understandability, and constrained by cost. The *Conceptual Framework* also defines the elements of financial statements (assets, liabilities, equity, income and expenses) and provides principles for the recognition and derecognition, measurement and presentation and disclosure for items reported in financial statements.

The *Conceptual Framework* also discusses alternative concepts of capital maintenance.

KEY TERMS

asset A present economic resource controlled by the entity as a result of past events. An economic resource is a right that has the potential to produce economic benefits.

ASX Listing Rules The set of rules that the Australian Securities Exchange Group imposes on companies that list on the ASX.

Australian Prudential Regulation Authority (APRA) The Australian financial services industry regulator.

Australian Securities and Investments Commission (ASIC) The Australian corporate, markets and financial services regulator, responsible for administering the Corporations Act.

Australian Securities Exchange (ASX) Group Australia's principal securities exchange (and the company that operates it).

comparability The quality of information that enables users to identify similarities in and differences between two sets of economic phenomena.

Corporations Act The *Corporations Act 2001* is Australian Commonwealth legislation that covers many aspects of the operations of Australian companies, including requiring certain types of entities to prepare financial statements.

differential reporting Provision within accounting standards or a regulatory framework that facilitates different reporting requirements for different categories of entities.

equity The residual interest in the assets of the entity after deducting all its liabilities.

expenses Decreases in assets or increases in liabilities, that result in decreases in equity, other than those relating to distributions to holders of equity claims.

faithful representation When an economic phenomenon is depicted completely, neutrally and free from material error.

Financial Reporting Council (FRC) The statutory body that oversees the accounting standard-setting process in Australia.

going concern assumption The assumption that the entity will continue to operate for the foreseeable future.

income Increases in assets, or decreases in liabilities, that result in increases in equity, other than those relating to contributions from holders of equity claims.

International Accounting Standards Board (IASB) An independent international body that sets International Financial Reporting Standards (IFRSs).

International Financial Reporting Standards (IFRSs) Accounting standards issued by the International Accounting Standards Board (IASB).

liability A present obligation of the entity to transfer an economic resource as a result of past events.

material The quality of information that exists when the omission or misstatement of the information could influence the decision that users make.

measurement The process of determining the monetary amounts at which the elements of the financial statements are to be recognised and carried in the statement of financial position or recognised in the statement of profit or loss and other comprehensive income.

recognition The process of capturing for inclusion in the statement of financial position or statement of profit or loss and other comprehensive income an item that meets the definition of one of the elements of financial statements — an asset, a liability, equity, income or expenses.

relevance The quality of information that is capable of making a difference in the decisions made by the users of financial information.

reporting entity An entity that is required, or chooses, to prepare financial statements.

revenue Income arising in the course of an entity's ordinary activities.

timeliness The quality of information being available to decision makers in time to be capable of influencing their decisions.

understandability The quality of information that arises from classifying, characterising and presenting information clearly and concisely.

verifiability The quality of information that different observers could broadly agree the information is a faithful representation, thus helping assure users that information faithfully represents the economic phenomena it purports to represent.

COMPREHENSION QUESTIONS

1 What are the key sources of regulation in Australia for a listed company?

2 Describe the standard-setting process of the AASB.

3 Distinguish between the roles of the FRC and the AASB.

4 How does the IASB influence financial reporting in Australia?

5 Explain the potential benefits and problems that can result from the adoption of IFRSs in Australia.

6 What is the difference between Australian accounting standards and IFRSs?

7 Specify the objectives of general purpose financial reporting, the nature of users and the information to be provided to users to achieve the objectives as provided in the *Conceptual Framework*.

8 One of the functions of the FRC is to ensure that the Australian accounting standards are 'in the best interests of both the private and public sectors in the Australian economy'. How might the FRC assess this?

9 Outline the fundamental qualitative characteristics of information that is useful to users of financial statements.

10 Discuss the importance of the going concern assumption to the practice of accounting.

11 Discuss the essential characteristics of an asset as described in the *Conceptual Framework*.

12 Discuss the essential characteristics of a liability as described in the *Conceptual Framework*.

13 A government gives a parcel of land to a company at no charge. The company builds a factory on the land and employs people at the factory to produce jam that is sold in local and interstate markets. Considering the definition of income in the *Conceptual Framework*, do you think the receipt of the land is income to the company? Would your answer depend on how the land is measured?

14 Discuss the difference, if any, between income, revenue and gains.

15 Describe the qualitative characteristics of financial information according to the *Conceptual Framework*, distinguishing between fundamental and enhancing characteristics.

16 Define 'equity'. Explain why the *Conceptual Framework* does not prescribe any recognition criteria for equity.

17 In relation to the following multiple-choice questions, discuss your choice of correct answer.

(a) Which of the following statements about the *Conceptual Framework* is incorrect?

(i) The *Conceptual Framework* overrides any accounting standard that is in conflict with the International Financial Reporting Standards (IFRS).

(ii) The *Conceptual Framework* states that the elements directly related to the measurement of financial position are assets, liabilities and equity.

(iii) The *Conceptual Framework* determines capital providers as the primary user group of general purpose financial statements.

(iv) In accordance with the *Conceptual Framework*, income is recognised if it provides users of the financial statements with information that is relevant and faithfully represented.

(b) The *Conceptual Framework*'s enhancing qualitative characteristics include:
  (i) understandability, timeliness, verifiability and comparability
  (ii) faithful representation, relevance, understandability and verifiability
  (iii) comparability and reliability
  (iv) substance over form and relevance.

(c) Which of the following statements about the *Conceptual Framework*'s definition of expenses is correct?
  (i) Expenses include distributions to owners.
  (ii) Expenses are always in the form of outflows or depletions of assets.
  (iii) Expenses exclude losses.
  (iv) Expenses are always decreases in economic benefits.

(d) In accordance with the *Conceptual Framework*, from the perspective of the lender the forgiveness of its $20 000 interest-free loan results in:
  (i) an increase in income and a decrease in a liability
  (ii) an increase in an expense and a decrease in an asset
  (iii) an increase in an asset and an increase in income
  (iv) an increase in an expense and a decrease in a liability.

CASE STUDY 1.1

The AASB

Visit the AASB website (www.aasb.gov.au) and answer the following.
1. Who is the Chair of the AASB?
2. Who are the members?
3. Which accounting standards have been issued in the past year?
4. Why are there differences in the numbering systems for current accounting standards (e.g. AASB x, AASB xxx and AASB xxxx)?
5. What current projects (if any) is the AASB working on in collaboration with the IASB?

CASE STUDY 1.2

The IASB

Visit the website of the International Accounting Standards Board (www.ifrs.org). Report on:
1. the resources that are provided by the IASB for the accounting profession
2. the membership of the IASB and which countries the members come from
3. the goals of the IASB
4. a current project being undertaken by the IASB.

CASE STUDY 1.3

ASIC

Visit the website of the Australian Securities and Investments Commission (www.asic.gov.au). Report on:
1. what ASIC is and its role
2. the types of investigations and enforcement performed by ASIC
3. the policy statements and practice notes issued by ASIC.

CASE STUDY 1.4

The FRC

Visit the website of the Financial Reporting Council (www.frc.gov.au). Locate its strategic plan and report on:
1. the strategic priorities of the FRC's current strategic plan
2. the key environmental factors that impact the FRC.

APPLICATION AND ANALYSIS EXERCISES

★ BASIC | ★ ★ MODERATE | ★ ★ ★ DIFFICULT

1.1 Requirements to prepare a financial report ★   LO1

Apple Isle Transport Pty Ltd operates tours and transport services throughout Tasmania. The company has 50 employees. Its accounting records show that it has total assets of $30 million, equity of $25 million and revenue of $50 million. The directors of Apple Isle Transport Pty Ltd have not received a request for a financial report from the shareholders or ASIC. Is Apple Isle Transport Pty Ltd required to prepare a financial report? If so, explain whether Apple Isle Transport Ltd needs to apply Tier 1 or Tier 2 reporting requirements.

1.2 Relevant information ★   LO5, 8

A year ago you bought shares in an investment company. The investment company in turn buys, holds and sells shares of business enterprises. You want to use the financial statements of the investment company to assess its performance over the past year.

Required

1. What financial information about the investment company's holdings would be most relevant to you?
2. The investment company earns profits from appreciation of its investment securities and from dividends received. How would the concepts of recognition in the *Conceptual Framework* apply here?

1.3 Measuring inventories ★   LO8

AASB 102/IAS 2 *Inventories* allows producers of gold and silver to measure inventories of these commodities at selling price even before they have sold them, which means income is recognised at production. In nearly all other industries, however, income from the sale of goods is recognised only when the inventories are sold to outside customers. What concepts in the *Conceptual Framework* are reflected in accounting for gold and silver production?

1.4 Recognising a loss ★   LO8

The law in your community requires store owners to shovel snow and ice from the footpath in front of their shops. You failed to do that and a pedestrian slipped and fell, resulting in serious and costly injury. The pedestrian has sued you. Your lawyers say that while they will vigorously defend you in the lawsuit, you should expect to lose $30 000 to cover the injured party's costs. A court decision, however, is not expected for at least a year. What aspects of the *Conceptual Framework* might help you in deciding the appropriate accounting for this situation?

1.5 Financial statements ★   LO5, 9

An entity purchases a rental property for $5 000 000 as an investment. The building is fully rented and is in a good area. At the end of the current year, the entity hires an appraiser who reports that the fair value of the building is $7 500 000 plus or minus 15%. Depreciating the building over 40 years would reduce the carrying amount to $4 875 000.

Required

1. What are the relevance and faithful representation accounting considerations in deciding how to measure the building in the entity's financial statements?
2. Does the *Conceptual Framework* lead to measuring the building at $7 500 000? Or at $4 875 000? Or at some other amount?

1.6 The *Conceptual Framework* versus interpretations ★   LO3, 4, 8, 9

Applying the *Conceptual Framework* is subjective and requires judgement. Would the IASB be better off to abandon the *Conceptual Framework* entirely and instead rely on a very active interpretations committee that develops detailed guidance in response to requests from constituents?

1.7 Meaning of 'decision useful' ★   LO5

What is meant by saying that accounting information should be 'decision useful'? Provide examples.

1.8 Performance of a business entity ★   LO5

A financial analyst said:

> I advise my clients to invest for the long term. Buy good shares and hang onto them. Therefore, I am interested in a company's long-term earning power. Accounting standards that result in earnings volatility obscure long-term earning power. Accounting should report earning power by deferring and amortising costs and revenues.

Is this analyst's view consistent with the fundamental characteristics of financial information established in the *Conceptual Framework*?

1.9 Going concern ★ **LO6, 9**

What measurement principles might be most appropriate for a company that has ceased to be a going concern (e.g. creditors have appointed a receiver who is seeking buyers for the company's assets)?

1.10 Assessing probabilities in accounting recognition ★ **LO7, 8**

The *Conceptual Framework* defines an asset as a present economic resource controlled by the entity as a result of past events. At the same time the *Conceptual Framework* establishes that an asset is to be recognised only if it provides information to the users of the financial statements that is relevant and has faithful representation. Discuss the recognition criteria of 'relevance' and 'faithful representation' and provide examples, if any, when an asset may not be recognised in the financial statements.

1.11 Definitions of elements ★ **LO7, 8**

Explain how Beachside Ltd should account for the following items/situations, justifying your answers by reference to the *Conceptual Framework*'s definitions and recognition criteria.
1. Receipt of artwork of sentimental value only.
2. Beachside Ltd is the guarantor for an employee's bank loan:
   (a) You have no reason to believe the employee will default on the loan.
   (b) As the employee is in serious financial difficulties, you think it likely that he will default on the loan.
3. Beachside Ltd receives 5000 shares in Monty Ltd, trading at $6 each, as a gift from a grateful client.
4. The panoramic view of the coast from Beachside Ltd's café windows, which you are convinced attracts customers to the café.
5. The court has ordered Beachside Ltd to repair the environmental damage it caused to the local river system. You have no idea how much this repair work will cost.

1.12 Definitions and recognition criteria ★ **LO7, 8**

Explain how Simpkins Ltd should account for the following items, justifying your answers by reference to the definitions and recognition criteria in the *Conceptual Framework*. Also state, where appropriate, which ledger accounts should be debited and credited.
1. Photographs of the company's founders, which are of great sentimental and historical value.
2. (a) Simpkins Ltd has been sued for negligence — likely it will lose the case.
   (b) Simpkins Ltd has been sued for negligence — likely it will win the case.
3. Obsolete machinery now retired from use.
4. Simpkins Ltd receives a donation of $5000.

1.13 Definitions and recognition criteria ★ **LO7, 8**

Gunnedah Accounting Services has just invoiced one of its clients $4800 for accounting services provided to the client. Explain how Gunnedah Accounting Services should recognise this event, justifying your answer by reference to relevant *Conceptual Framework* definitions and recognition criteria. Would your answer be different if the services had not yet been provided; that is, the payment is in advance?

1.14 Recognition and derecognition ★ ★ **LO8**

The following events occurred in relation to assets and liabilities recognised by Watson Ltd.

(a) Watson Ltd settled (paid) an account payable.
(b) Watson Ltd sold an item of inventory to a customer.
(c) Watson Ltd had been using the fair value measurement base for its plant but estimates of fair value have become unreliable due to changes in market conditions.
(d) A debtor, Holmes Pty Ltd, is facing financial difficulties and has advised that it might be unable to pay the amount owing to Watson Ltd.

Required

For each event, state whether it would be likely to result in derecognition of an asset or liability in accordance with the *Conceptual Framework*. Give reasons for your answer.

1.15 Asset definition and recognition ★ **LO7, 8**

Recently, $16 000 cash was stolen from Fisher Ltd's night safe. Explain how Fisher should account for this event, justifying your answer by reference to relevant *Conceptual Framework* definitions and recognition criteria.

REFERENCES

Australian Accounting Standards Board (AASB) 2018, *ITC 39 Consultation Paper: applying the IASB's revised conceptual framework and solving the reporting entity and special purpose financial statement problems*, www.aasb.gov.au.
—— 2019, *The standard-setting process*, www.aasb.gov.au.
—— n.d., *Organisational structure*, www.aasb.gov.au.
Australian Securities and Investments Commission (ASIC) 2005, *Regulatory Guide 85: reporting requirements for non-reporting entities,* July, www.asic.gov.au.
—— 2019, *19-014MR Findings from 30 June 2018 financial reports*, 25 January, www.asic.gov.au.
——2019, 'Our role', www.asic.gov.au.
Australian Securities Exchange Group (ASX) 2016, 'ASX admission framework', *Listed@ASX compliance update*, 21 April, www.asic.gov.au.
Carey, P, Potter, B & Tanewski, G 2014, *AASB Research Report No 1: application of the reporting entity concept and lodgement of special purpose financial statements*, Australian Accounting Standards Board Research Centre, www.aasb.gov.au.
Deloitte 2018, *Australian financial reporting guide: financial reporting periods ending on or after 30 June 2018*, p. 12, www2.deloitte.com.
Financial Reporting Council (FRC) 2015, *Financial Reporting Council annual report 2014–15*, www.frc.gov.au.

ACKNOWLEDGEMENTS

Photo: © Inc / Shutterstock.com
Figure 1.1: © Deloitte 2018
Figure 1.2: © ASIC 2015
Figures 1.3, 1.6, 1.7 and text: © 2019 Australian Accounting Standards Board (AASB). The text, graphics and layout of this publication are protected by Australian copyright law and the comparable law of other countries. No part of the publication may be reproduced, stored or transmitted in any form or by any means without the prior written permission of the AASB except as permitted by law. For reproduction or publication, permission should be sought in writing from the AASB. Requests in the first instance should be addressed to the National Director, Australian Accounting Standards Board, PO Box 204, Collins Street West, Victoria 8007.
Figure 1.4: © ASX Limited, ABN 98 008 624 691, ASX 2016. All rights reserved. This material is reproduced with the permission of ASX. This material should not be reproduced, stored in a retrieval system or transmitted in any form whether in whole or in part without the prior written permission of ASX.
Figure 1.5: © FRC 2015
Figures 1.8, 1.9, 1.10: © ASIC 2019
Text: © IFRS. This publication contains copyright material of the IFRS Foundation in respect of which all rights are reserved. Reproduced by John Wiley & Sons Australia, Ltd with the permission of the IFRS Foundation. No permission granted to third parties to reproduce or distribute. For full access to IFRS Standards and the work of the IFRS Foundation please visit http://eifrs.ifrs.org. The International Accounting Standards Board, the IFRS Foundation, the authors and the publishers do not accept responsibility for any loss caused by acting or refraining from acting in reliance on the material in this publication, whether such loss is caused by negligence or otherwise.
Text: *Corporations Act 2001.* Sourced from the Federal Register of Legislation at 8 November 2018. For the latest information on Australian Government law, please go to https://www.legislation.gov.au.
Text: *Australian Securities and Investments Commission Act 2001.* Sourced from the Federal Register of Legislation at 8 November 2018. For the latest information on Australian Government law, please go to https://www.legislation.gov.au.

CHAPTER 2

Application of accounting theory

CHAPTER AIM

This chapter examines the notion of an accounting policy, including its four components: definition, recognition, measurement and disclosure. It considers the meaning of accounting theory, different types of theories and their role in professional judgement in accounting.

LEARNING OBJECTIVES

After studying this chapter, you should be able to:

2.1 describe the role of professional judgement in the preparation of financial reports

2.2 identify the major decision areas in considering policies to account for transactions and other events

2.3 explain how normative and positive theories are used in accounting

2.4 explain the implications of positive accounting theory for accounting policy choice

2.5 compare the implications of the mechanistic hypothesis and the efficient market hypothesis for financial reporting.

CONCEPTS FOR REVIEW

Before studying this chapter, you should understand and, if necessary, revise:

- the *Conceptual Framework*, particularly the definition of elements of financial statements
- the statement of financial position.

2.1 Professional judgement in accounting

LEARNING OBJECTIVE 2.1 Describe the role of professional judgement in the preparation of financial reports.

Accounting is not merely following a set of accounting rules or procedures — accountants are often called upon to exercise **professional judgement**. While there are various decision contexts in which accountants might exercise professional judgement, we will focus on judgements about accounting policies made in the preparation of financial statements. For example, the accountant may need to exercise professional judgement in deciding how to account for a transaction that is not covered by a specific accounting standard.

Accounting standards do not remove the need for accountants to exercise professional judgement. Even when a particular transaction or event is covered by a specific accounting standard, accountants often still need to exercise professional judgement in applying the standard. Accountants may need to exercise professional judgement in deciding how to measure an asset or a liability where the relevant accounting standard permits choice, or in the estimation of expected inflows or outflows used in the measurement of assets and liabilities. For example, in measuring a provision for warranty, the accountant must estimate the cost of settling the obligation at the end of the reporting period.

The accounting standards issued by the International Accounting Standards Board (IASB) and the Australian Accounting Standards Board (AASB) are considered to be predominantly principles-based, rather than rules-based.

A rules-based standard attempts to prescribe the accounting treatment for every possibility, leaving little room for judgement or discretion in its application. Rules-based accounting standards use objective criteria in determining which accounting treatment should be applied to a transaction, such as whether an item of expenditure should be accounted for as an asset or an expense. For example, a rules-based standard might state that all expenditure on advertising, internally generated brand names and internally generated mastheads must be accounted for as an expense. This leaves little scope for professional judgement. If the entity spends money on an advertising campaign, in applying the standard the accountant must classify the expenditure as an expense because it was for advertising. The accountant would not need to consider whether the entity controlled the advertising campaign or whether future economic benefits were expected to flow to the entity as a result of the advertising campaign.

In contrast, a principles-based standard prescribes principles that can be applied to a range of different situations. The application of the standard involves subjective assessment in applying the principles to various circumstances. For example, let us assume that a principles-based standard specifies that a purchased intangible asset should be recognised if it meets all of the following conditions.
- The entity has control over the intangible asset as a result of a past transaction or event.
- The intangible asset is expected to generate future economic benefits for the entity.
- It is probable that the future economic benefits will flow to the entity.
- The intangible asset has a cost that can be measured reliably.

In applying this principles-based standard to the acquisition of a patent, the accountant would need to exercise judgement, particularly in assessing the probability that the patent will generate future economic benefits.

Theories can help us to predict accounting policy choice and to understand the implications of alternative accounting policies, as well as providing a source of guidance for our accounting policy decisions.

LEARNING CHECK

- ☐ The application of accounting standards to the preparation of financial statements requires accountants to exercise professional judgement.
- ☐ Professional judgement may involve making estimates in the measurement process, assessing probability, choosing an accounting policy from alternatives permitted by accounting standards, and making decisions about how to account for transactions and events that are not specifically addressed by accounting standards.

2.2 What is an accounting policy?

LEARNING OBJECTIVE 2.2 Identify the major decision areas in considering policies to account for transactions and other events.

Accounting for routine transactions is typically straightforward. For example, you are probably quite familiar with accounting for cash sales by recording an increase in cash and an increase in income. Entities develop policies for transactions that are routine for their operations. For example, the entity may adopt a policy of recognising property, plant and equipment as an asset when acquired and measuring it at cost, with subsequent depreciation on a straight-line basis over the remaining useful life of the item. Accounting policy decisions may also need to be made for one-off transactions or events, such as accounting for major renovations to the entity's head office building.

Whether we are accounting for a one-off transaction or developing a policy for routine transactions, the **accounting policy** decision involves four components, as follows.

- *Definition*. Did a past event give rise to an item that meets the definition of a financial statement element?
- *Recognition*. When does the item satisfy the recognition criteria?
- *Measurement*. How should it be measured initially and, in the case of an asset or a liability, how should it be measured subsequent to initial measurement?
- *Disclosure*. How should the information be presented and disclosed?

ILLUSTRATIVE EXAMPLE 2.1

Accounting policy for an asset

Sun Power Ltd spent $30 000 installing solar panels on the roof of its office building.

Required

What must Sun Power Ltd's accountant consider in deciding how to account for the expenditure?

Solution

Sun Power Ltd's accountant must consider the definition, recognition, measurement and disclosure components of the accounting policy.

First, the accountant must consider whether the modifications to the roof meet the definition of an asset. Recall from chapter 1 that an asset is defined in paragraph 4.3 of the *Conceptual Framework* as follows.

A present economic resource controlled by the entity as a result of past events.

Paragraph 4.4 states:

An economic resource is a right that has the potential to produce economic benefits.

The accountant needs to make a judgement about whether the solar panels are controlled by Sun Power Ltd and whether they have the potential to provide economic benefits, either in the form of cash inflows or a reduction in cash outflows, for Sun Power Ltd.

Does Sun Power Ltd control the solar panels? Perhaps Sun Power Ltd owns the building on which they have been installed. Alternatively, Sun Power Ltd might have control over the building, and therefore the solar panels, under a long-term lease. The relevant past events here would be the acquisition or lease of the building and the installation of the solar panels on the roof of the building.

In forming a judgement about whether the solar panels are an asset, it is also necessary to consider whether they have the potential to produce economic benefits for Sun Power Ltd. In this case, the solar panels could provide benefits in the form of reduced electricity costs.

If the solar panels meet the definition of an asset, the accountant will need to form a judgement about whether they satisfy the recognition criteria of an asset. According to the *Conceptual Framework*, an entity should recognise an item that meets the definition of an asset if recognition would provide relevant information about the asset and a faithful representation of the asset.

The application of the recognition criteria requires the accountant to exercise judgement. The recognition of the solar panels as an asset is likely to provide relevant information to users of Sun Power Ltd's financial statements because the potential savings in electricity costs may affect their estimates of the entity's future cash flows and profitability. The solar panels could be represented faithfully at cost.

If the accountant decides that the solar panels should be recognised as an asset, it will be necessary to consider how to measure them. Initial recognition is usually at cost. A related measurement consideration is how the asset would be measured subsequent to initial recognition. This may involve a choice of depreciation method and the estimation of useful life. Subsequent measurement of property, plant and equipment also involves a choice between the cost model and revaluation based on **fair value**, which is the price that would be received to sell an asset, or paid to transfer a liability, in an orderly transaction between market participants.

Last, there is the disclosure component of accounting for the acquisition of solar panels. The accountant must consider how the information should be presented in the financial statements and what disclosures should be made. For example, Sun Power Ltd might disclose in the notes to the financial statements the depreciation method used for the solar panels and other items of property, plant and equipment.

LEARNING CHECK

☐ In developing or selecting accounting policies, decisions must be made about the definition, recognition, measurement and disclosure of items.

☐ Decisions about accounting policies require professional judgement, particularly in the context of principles-based accounting standards.

2.3 What is accounting theory?

LEARNING OBJECTIVE 2.3 Explain how normative and positive theories are used in accounting.

Theories are constantly used in the world around us. Builders, engineers and architects rely on structural engineering and mathematical theories in building design and development. Structural theories are based on physical laws and research that explain the structural performance of materials. Governments use economic theories to formulate policies and strategies, such as whether to increase or decrease taxes, or whether to introduce a new tax. These theories relate to the effect of expenditure or taxes on inflation and the national debt, as well as social justice considerations, such as unemployment.

You may have come across various theories in finance, economics or other discipline areas that you have studied, but what do we mean by *theory*? Hendriksen (1970, p. 1) defines **theory** as the 'coherent set of hypothetical, conceptual and pragmatic principles forming a general framework of reference for a field of inquiry'. This is a broadly applicable definition that applies to different types of theories, which are discussed in section 2.3.1.

Despite popular opinion, accounting involves much more than recording financial transactions according to a set of rules or standards. Accountants need to make decisions about what information to provide, how accounting methods are to be applied and the extent of information to disclose to users. Accounting is a human activity, and while we can never fully know what motivates people to make the decisions they do, theories can be useful in helping us to understand and to explain what might have influenced the decision-making process. Theories in accounting can help us to understand decisions of financial information preparers, as well as those of users of the output of the accounting system, including investors, lenders and other creditors.

Theories that examine the operation of capital markets explain how share prices change when accounting information is provided to the market. Other theories explain and predict managerial choice of accounting methods and how they relate to remuneration contracts and lending agreements.

Rather than explaining actions, some accounting theories can assist in determining what methods should be used, or how accounting information should be measured and reported. Such theories are designed to provide solutions or improvements.

2.3.1 Types of theories

There are two main types of theories used in accounting:
- normative theories
- positive theories.

Normative theories

A **normative theory** provides recommendations about what *should* happen. It *prescribes* what ought to be the case based on a specific goal or objective. The outcome of a normative theory is derived from logical development based upon a stated objective. The conceptual framework is one example of a normative theory. Based upon the objective of financial reporting stated in the conceptual framework, a range of principles are established about who should report; what qualities financial information should have; how elements, such as assets and liabilities, should be defined; how the recognition of items in the financial statements should be determined; and how information should be presented to be meaningful. Normative theories are also referred to as prescriptive theories.

A normative theory is not necessarily based upon what is happening in the world, but on what *should* be done given the objective upon which the theory is based. That does not mean that the development of normative theories is completely divorced from reality. Often normative theories evolve from observations and research into practice, undertaken using positive theories. For example, research might provide evidence of the relevance or understandability of various types of financial information.

Positive theories

The purpose of a **positive theory** is to describe, explain or predict activities or outcomes. For example, a positive theory might be *descriptive* of accounting practice. Another theory might *explain* why managers choose particular accounting methods in situations where accounting standards allow such choice, and could be used to *predict* what other entities might do when faced with similar circumstances. Positive theories can help us to understand what is happening in the world, and why entities act the way they do. As such they rely on real-world observations. Positive theories can assist us to understand the decisions that users make with regards to accounting information, which can facilitate more informed decisions about how to present information.

2.3.2 Development of theories

Theories may be derived from inductive reasoning or from deductive reasoning. Both the inductive and deductive approaches to the development of theory share common basic elements of objectives, assumptions, principles and definitions or actions. However, the logic linking the elements flows in opposite directions for inductive and deductive reasoning.

Inductive reasoning

The process of **inductive reasoning** is illustrated in figure 2.1.

| FIGURE 2.1 | Inductive approach to theory development |

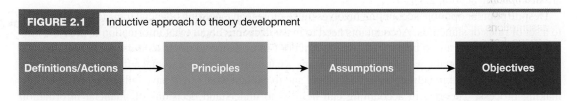

A person developing a theory using inductive reasoning would begin by observing definable activities and actions. Based on the definable activities and actions, the theorist would then infer the principles that conform to the observations. Having inferred certain principles on the basis of detailed observations, the theorist would then attempt to infer higher level assumptions and objectives. Illustrative example 2.2 illustrates the inductive approach to developing a theory.

Inductive approach to theory development

Theo intends to develop a theory to explain why some gains and losses are recognised in profit or loss, while others are recognised in other comprehensive income. Gains and losses that are recognised in other comprehensive income are reported below profit in the statement of profit or loss and other comprehensive income. (Chapter 16 considers the statement of profit or loss and other comprehensive income in detail.) Theo intends to develop a theory that goes beyond a simple explanation of compliance with accounting standards. He will attempt to infer the underlying principles and objectives reflected in the accounting treatment prescribed or permitted by accounting standards, and identify assumptions that have been made.

Required

Describe an inductive approach to the development of Theo's theory.

Solution

Actions

Theo begins with observations of gains/losses that are recognised in profit and gains/losses that are recognised in other comprehensive income (OCI). For simplicity, we will just consider a few observations of accounting treatment (actions).

Gains/losses recognised in profit	Gains/losses recognised in OCI
Downward revaluation of property, plant and equipment (AASB 116/IAS 16 *Property, Plant and Equipment*)	Upward revaluation of property, plant and equipment (AASB 116/IAS 16 *Property, Plant and Equipment*)
Change in fair value of animals classified as biological assets and used in agricultural activity (AASB 141/IAS 41 *Agriculture*)	

Principles

Theo's next step is to identify principles that are consistent with the observed actions. For example, a principle that gains should be recognised in OCI while losses should be recognised in profit or loss is not consistent with all of the observations. It holds for property, plant and equipment, but is inconsistent for biological assets under AASB 141/IAS 41 where all changes in fair value are recognised in profit or loss.

Theo infers the following principles from the observations.

1. Fair value adjustments should be recognised in profit if they capture biological transformations that reflect the performance of the entity during the period.
2. Where the fair value is not easily determined, use of fair value should be discouraged by requiring downward revaluations to be charged against profit while not allowing upward revaluations to be included in profit.

(Please note, these principles are merely made up for the purpose of illustrating inductive reasoning and are not intended to suggest that these were the basis for conclusions of the standard setters.)

Assumptions

Next, Theo would identify assumptions that have been made in identifying the principles, such as assumptions about performance measurement, what is meant by profit and the rationale for the observed actions. For example, the first principle assumes that changes in the fair value of biological assets result from biological transformation that reflects the performance of the entity. (In fact, changes in the fair value may also result from changes in market conditions.) The second principle assumes that the measurement of the fair value of property, plant and equipment is not easily determined. (This may be a valid assumption for some items, such as plant and equipment, but is unlikely to hold for most real estate assets.)

Objectives

Last, Theo makes broad generalisations from the principles and assumptions reached. For example, Theo might make a broad generalisation about the objectives for the reporting of profit and comprehensive income. This would provide general rules that could then be applied to new observations or emerging issues, such as how to account for changes in the fair value of assets arising under emissions trading schemes.

Inductive reasoning is useful for developing a positive theory. A limitation of the inductive approach is that it tends to maintain *the status quo*. It does not attempt to improve on how things are done. The inductive approach does not question the appropriateness of the observed actions. Under the inductive approach, observations of practice lead the development of principles. Accordingly, if we used only an inductive approach to develop accounting theories, undesirable accounting practices may emerge. However, if accounting principles had already been developed, the undesirable accounting practices might have been avoided.

Deductive reasoning

The process of **deductive reasoning** is illustrated in figure 2.2.

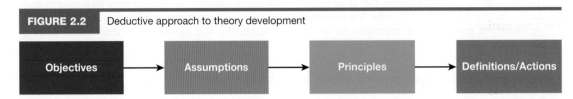

FIGURE 2.2 — Deductive approach to theory development

A person developing a theory using deductive reasoning would begin by setting objectives. The theorist uses his or her own normative values to set the objectives. Having set the objectives, the theorist would then identify the assumptions that underlie those objectives and how they can be achieved. Then, the theorist derives the principles that flow logically from both the objectives and the assumptions. The principles, in turn, enable the theorist to derive the definitions and observable actions that should result.

Deductive logic can be used to develop a prescriptive (or normative) theory, which sets out the way things should be done. The conceptual framework is an example of a normative theory that has been developed through a deductive approach. The conceptual framework commences with the objective of financial statements, to provide information about the reporting entity that is useful to existing and potential investors, lenders and other creditors for making decisions about providing resources to the entity. The conceptual framework then presents assumptions about the information needs of the target users. For example, the conceptual framework assumes that users of financial statements need information to assess the prospects for future cash flows. Based on these assumptions, the developers of the conceptual framework established principles that serve the objective of providing information that is useful for decision making. For example, one of the principles established in the conceptual framework is that information provided in financial statements should be relevant and should represent faithfully that which it purports to represent. Lastly, definitions and actions, such as the definition and recognition criteria for assets and liabilities, are derived from the principles.

We will now examine a few theories commonly used in accounting and disclosure research. While most of these theories are positive theories, some also have normative underpinnings.

LEARNING CHECK

- ☐ An accounting theory is a coherent set of principles that provides a framework for understanding, predicting and guiding the process, preparation and use of accounting information.
- ☐ A normative accounting theory prescribes how accounting information should be prepared, based on a specified objective.
- ☐ A positive accounting theory describes or explains observed behaviour or predicts actions pertaining to the preparation or use of accounting information.

2.4 Positive accounting theory

LEARNING OBJECTIVE 2.4 Explain the implications of positive accounting theory for accounting policy choice.

As the name suggests, positive accounting theory is a *positive* theory used to explain and predict accounting practice. It is 'designed to explain and predict which firms will and which firms will not use a particular method' (Watts & Zimmerman 1986, p. 7). The term, positive accounting theory, can be a source of confusion because it is used in two different ways. *Positive accounting theory* can be used to refer to a type of theory, one which is positive rather than normative. *Positive accounting theory* is also used more narrowly to refer to a specific theory about accounting policy choice. In this section positive accounting theory is used in this narrower sense.

Positive accounting theory attempts to explain accounting policy decisions by examining a range of relationships, or contracts, between the entity and suppliers of equity capital (owners), managerial labour (management) and debt capital (lenders or debtholders). It is based on the 'rational economic person' assumption that all individuals act in their own self-interest and are rational wealth maximisers. Positive accounting theory is underpinned by the nexus of contracts view of the firm and agency theory. We will consider each of these in turn.

2.4.1 Nexus of contracts

The organisation is characterised as a 'nexus of contracts' or as the centre of contractual relationships, with the contracting parties having rights and responsibilities under the contracts (Smith & Watts 1982). It is argued that an organisation is an efficient way of organising economic activity (Coase 1937). The contracting parties include shareholders, lenders, managers, employees, suppliers and customers (Smith & Watts 1982). While an entity can facilitate a wide array of contracts, positive accounting theory focuses on three relationships: managerial contracts and debt contracts, both of which are agency contracts used to manage relationships where there is a separation between management and capital providers; and political 'contracts', which refer to relationships between the entity and other parties such as governments, trade unions and community groups.

2.4.2 Agency theory

Agency theory is used to understand relationships whereby a person or group of persons (the principal) employs the services of another (the agent) to perform some activity on their behalf. In doing so the principal delegates the decision-making authority to the agent. An *agency relationship* exists where one party (the principal) employs another (the agent) to perform some activity on their behalf. For example, the shareholders of a company (the principal) may employ a manager (the agent) to conduct the business of the company, including the negotiation of contracts with other parties.

While the agent has a legal and fiduciary duty to act in the best interests of the principal, the assumption that both parties are utility maximisers means that the agent will not always act in the interests of the principal (Jensen & Meckling 1976). Jensen and Meckling identify three types of **agency costs**:
- monitoring costs
- bonding costs
- residual loss.

Monitoring costs

Monitoring costs are costs incurred by the principal to observe, evaluate and control the agent's behaviour. Monitoring activities include having the financial statements audited, corporate governance arrangements, other operating policies and procedures, and implementing a management remuneration plan (also referred to as a management compensation plan). Monitoring costs are initially incurred by the principal who will pass them on to the agent. For example, owners, as principals, will incur costs to monitor management and pass the costs on to the manager through reduced remuneration. In the case of debt contracts, lenders are concerned about the financial performance of entities they lend to, and how this might affect the risk involved in lending. Lenders, as principals, will monitor managers (who act as agents for both lenders and shareholders). For example, lenders might obtain valuations on properties used as collateral for loans. Lenders are likely to increase interest rates charged on loans or lend for a shorter period if they are required to undertake more monitoring of the entity.

Bonding costs

Bonding costs are costs incurred by the agent when implementing mechanisms to provide assurance that they are acting in the principal's best interests. Agents have an incentive to do this because, as explained above, the agents will actually bear the costs of monitoring through lower remuneration or higher interest rates. Because of this, managers (the agents in both of the managerial and debt contracts) are likely to provide some assurance that they are making decisions in the best interests of the principals. One example might be incurring the time and effort involved in producing and providing quarterly accounting reports to lenders; or by agreeing to link part of their remuneration payment to entity performance. Linking remuneration to entity performance gives management an incentive to enhance entity performance, which is also in the interests of owners.

Residual loss

Monitoring and bonding activities can never completely remove all situations where the agent does not act in the best interests of the principal, as it is too costly to do so. For instance, it might be too costly to monitor the use of a manager's travel expenses to ensure they are only for business purposes, or to monitor his or her use of business stationery for personal use. Residual loss is the amount by which the net value of the agent's output is less than it would be if the agent always acted in the principal's best interest. In other words, it is the loss in value of the entity that results from the separation of ownership and control, when the marginal cost exceeds the expected benefit of additional monitoring and bonding. The majority of monitoring and bonding costs are borne by agents through reduced remuneration (in a managerial contract) or higher interest rates (in a debt contract). Accordingly, managers have incentives to minimise these costs. However, principals can never estimate perfectly the full impact of the agent's behaviour. Agents know this and perceive that they will not be fully penalised for all behaviour that is not in the interests of principals. Consequently, residual loss is borne by both the principal and the agent.

Accounting plays a large role in monitoring and bonding mechanisms. Accounting information is used to design the contracts to bond agents' behaviour, as well as to monitor performance against those contracts. As such, agency theory relies heavily on the accounting function. We will now discuss how accounting plays a role in owner–manager relationships and manager–lender relationships, as well as in managing political costs.

2.4.3 Owner–manager agency relationships

As previously mentioned, the separation of ownership and control means that managers, as agents, are likely to act in their own interests, and these actions might not necessarily align with those of the principal, or owners. The theory suggests that when there is separation of ownership and control, managers will act in their own interests through excessive consumption of perquisites and avoidance of effort. Perquisites are non-cash benefits of the job. An extreme example is a manager using entity resources, including internet access, office facilities and time during business hours to operate their own business 'on the side'.

Although the theory is often applied to explain accounting and management practice in large modern corporations with many shareholders, illustrative example 2.3 uses a simple, small-entity setting to illustrate the principles and concepts underlying the theory.

ILLUSTRATIVE EXAMPLE 2.3

Agency relationships

For the purpose of this simplified example, we will ignore the effects of taxation. Mary is both the owner and manager of Poppins Ltd. There is no separation of ownership and control because she is the owner of the business and has control over its operations. Mary has an incentive to work hard in the business because she will reap the rewards of any effort that she exerts in the business. Mary has no incentive to overspend on perquisites because any extra expenditure incurred by the business reduces profit, and thus reduces the benefits she receives as the only shareholder of Poppins Ltd. If Mary spends $4000 of Poppins Ltd's money on unnecessary travel, profit will be reduced by $4000. Mary's share of profit is 100%. Therefore, her share of profit will be reduced by $4000 if she spends an extra $4000 on unnecessary travel. Thus, there is no benefit to Mary, the manager, of overspending on perquisites when she is the only shareholder.

Now assume that Mary decides to raise additional capital for Poppins Ltd and issues more shares to new shareholders. Mary is still the manager but she now owns only 75% of the shares and the new external shareholders own the remaining 25% of the shares. The new shareholders are not managers and they do not have the opportunity, nor would it be efficient for them, to observe Mary's efforts in managing Poppins Ltd.

Required
Explain why Mary now has less incentive to work hard and more incentive to overspend on perquisites.

Solution
Mary has less incentive to work hard because the rewards of her extra effort must be shared with the other shareholders.

Mary has an incentive to overspend on perquisites because the cost of the perquisites will be shared with the external shareholders. For example, if Mary spends $4000 of Poppins Ltd's money on unnecessary travel, profit will be reduced by $4000. Mary's share of profit is 75% because she owns 75% of the shares.

Therefore, her share of profit will be reduced by $3000 if she spends an extra $4000 on unnecessary travel. However, she will obtain all of the benefit of the additional expenditure on travel, resulting in a net benefit of $1000, being the benefit of $4000 less Mary's $3000 share of reduced profit. Thus Mary, as manager, has an incentive to overspend on perquisites when she does not own all of the shares.

Smith and Watts (1982) identify three major problems that can arise in owner–manager agency relationships:
- the horizon problem
- risk aversion
- dividend retention.

Horizon problem

The horizon problem stems from the differing time horizons that are important to shareholders and managers. Many shareholders have an interest in the long-term growth and value of the entity, as the current market value of the entity's shares reflects the market's estimates of the present value of the expected future cash flows over the long term. Even shareholders who do not intend to hold their shares in the long term are interested in long-term growth to the extent that it is reflected in the price of their shares when they choose to sell them. Consequently, management's decisions that affect the long-term future cash flows of the entity are important to shareholders. However, management's interest in the cash flow potential may be limited to the period over which they expect to be employed by the entity. This problem is potentially greater when managers are approaching retirement. Managers who are seeking to move to another entity within the short term are more likely to wish to demonstrate the short-term profitability of the entity as evidence of effective management. Doing so is likely to enhance their capacity to find alternative employment as well as the remuneration they can command in the new position.

Managers can demonstrate short-term profitability in a number of ways. For example, they could delay undertaking maintenance or reduce research and development expenditure. While increasing short-term profitability, these activities can have adverse long-term consequences for the future productivity of the entity. For example, if an airline reduced maintenance expenditure, it would have lower maintenance expense, and thus higher reported profit. However, if aircraft are not adequately maintained, the airline may be grounded by aviation authorities, resulting in a loss of income and reputation.

The horizon problem can be reduced by linking management rewards to the entity's performance over a longer period. This occurs through the managerial remuneration contract. Management interests can be aligned, to some extent, with the long-term interests of shareholders through share-based remuneration, such as shares or executive share options. Paying a portion of managerial remuneration as shares or share options encourages managers to focus on long-term performance because it is likely to affect their own wealth. Linking a greater proportion of managerial pay to share price movements as the manager approaches retirement is also likely to encourage managers to maximise long-term performance.

Risk aversion

The problem of risk aversion is that managers generally prefer less risk than do shareholders. Shareholders are not likely to hold all their resources as shares in only one entity. They are able to diversify their risk through investing across multiple entities or other forms of investment, such as real estate. Shareholders may also receive regular income from other sources, such as a personal salary. In addition, shareholders' liability is limited to the amount they are required to pay for their shares. Managers, on the other hand, have more capital invested in the entity than shareholders through their 'human capital' or managerial expertise. It is likely that their remuneration is their primary source of income. As such, losing their job or being paid less can have a substantial impact on their personal wealth.

Economic theory proposes that higher risk potentially leads to higher returns. Shareholders, therefore, prefer that managers invest in more risky projects, which are likely to increase the value of the entity. Managers meanwhile wish to take less risk when deciding on projects for the entity because they have more to lose.

Managerial remuneration contracts can include incentives to encourage managers to invest in more risky projects. For instance, linking a bonus to profits can encourage managers to consider more risky projects that have the potential to increase profits. Share-based remuneration such as executive shares and share option schemes can be less effective in encouraging managers to invest in more risky projects because the cost to the manager of diversifying risk increases with managerial share ownership. For example, the manager of XYZ Ltd may hold other shares in order to diversify the risk associated with the holding of XYZ executive shares. If the number of executive shares increased, the manager may need to purchase more shares in other entities to maintain a balanced portfolio.

Dividend retention

The dividend retention problem refers to managers' preference to maintain a greater level of funds within the entity, and to distribute less of the entity's earnings to shareholders as dividends. Managers wish to retain money within the business to expand the size of the business they control (empire building) and to pay their own salaries and benefits. Shareholders, on the other hand, may have a preference for increased dividends.

Paying a bonus that is linked to a dividend payout ratio may encourage managers to maintain high dividend payouts to shareholders. Similarly, linking a bonus to profits will also encourage managers to seek additional profit which, in turn, increases funds available for dividends.

Many entities use executive remuneration schemes that reward management with combinations of salaries, bonuses, shares and stock options. The performance criteria used in executive contracts use a range of accounting measures. Figure 2.3 illustrates how CSR Limited uses its remuneration scheme to help align the interests of key management personnel (KMP) with those of shareholders through performance-based short-term incentive (STI) and long-term incentive (LTI) plans.

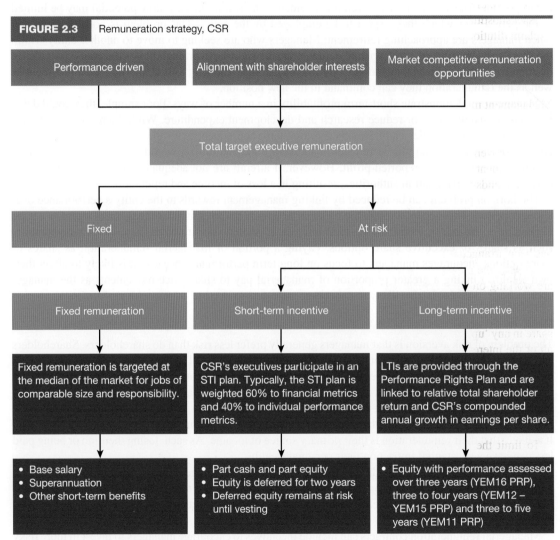

FIGURE 2.3 Remuneration strategy, CSR

Note: CSR Limited's financial year ends on 31 March. YEM = year ended March.

Source: CSR Limited (2016, p. 28).

2.4.4 Manager–lender agency relationships

Agency theory has also been used to understand the relationship between lenders and management. The lender is the principal, and the manager is the agent, with a duty to comply with the debt contract, but the manager also acts on behalf of shareholders when entering into contracts with lenders.

When a lender agrees to provide funds to an entity, there is the risk that the borrower may not honour its obligation to repay all of the borrowed funds with interest. This is referred to as credit risk. Lenders, such as banks and other financial institutions, seek to be compensated for credit risk through the returns earned in the form of interest. Accordingly, if the lender assesses the loan to be of higher risk, a higher rate of interest is charged. This is referred to as price protection. Conversely, if the loan is assessed to be of low risk, a lower interest rate will be charged.

Debt contracts can contain restrictions, known as debt covenants, which are designed to protect the interest of lenders. According to agency theory, managers will agree to debt covenants in the debt contract that restrict them from acting in a way that is detrimental to lenders because it will reduce the risk to the lender, resulting in lower interest costs being imposed on the borrower. For example, a debt covenant may restrict leverage to 60% of total assets. As a result of agreeing to debt covenants, managers are able to borrow funds at lower rates of interest, borrow larger amounts, or borrow for longer periods. Accounting numbers such as total liabilities and total tangible assets are used in debt covenants. Financial statements are then used to monitor compliance with debt covenants.

Smith and Warner (1979) identify four major problems that can increase the lender's risk:
- excessive dividend payments to owners
- asset substitution
- claim dilution
- underinvestment.

Excessive dividend payments

Management may make excessive dividend payments to shareholders. When lending funds, lenders price the debt to take into account an assumed level of dividend payout. If managers pay more dividends, the entity may have insufficient funds to service the debt. To reduce this problem, managers and lenders agree to covenants that restrain dividend policy and restrict dividend payouts as a function of profits. A requirement to maintain a minimum working capital ratio can also discourage payment of excessive cash dividends that reduce working capital.

Asset substitution

The agency problem of asset substitution refers to management investing in riskier assets after the loan has been arranged. For example, the entity may borrow money to expand mining production facilities but then spend the money on mining exploration which carries the risk of non-discovery. Because managers are working on behalf of owners and are often also owners themselves, they have incentives to use the debt finance to invest in alternative, higher risk assets in the expectation that it will lead to higher returns to shareholders. Lenders bear the risk of this strategy as they are subject to the 'downside' risk, but do not share in any 'upside' effects of the investment decision. If the project fails, the entity may be unable to pay all of the interest and principal of the loan. However, no matter how successful the project becomes, the lender will not earn any more than the agreed interest.

Lenders are aware of the agency problem that management might use borrowed funds for more risky assets or projects than those to which they have agreed and, accordingly, factor this risk into determining the interest rate and terms of the loan. Therefore, managers are willing to agree to debt covenants that restrict their actions in order to reduce creditors' risk, and thus reduce the cost of borrowing.

To limit the agency problem of asset substitution, debt contracts will often impose restrictions on investment opportunities of the entity, including mergers and takeovers. The lender might also secure the debt against specific assets. Establishing a minimum ratio of debt to tangible assets can also mitigate asset substitution by restricting investment in intangible assets.

Claim dilution

Claim dilution arises when entities take on debt of an equal or higher priority. For example, after obtaining an unsecured loan, management might offer a secured charge over the entity's real estate assets to obtain additional funding from another lender. This reduces the assets available to the original, unsecured creditor in the event of default. The most common method of avoiding claim dilution is to restrict the borrowing of higher priority debt, or debt with an earlier maturity date.

Underinvestment

The remaining agency problem of debt, underinvestment, can arise when the entity faces financial difficulty. If the entity is struggling to repay the principal and interest components of debt, the extra cash flows that might be generated by additional projects would go to repaying the debt rather than increasing shareholder wealth. Creditors rank above owners in order of payments in the event that an entity is liquidated; thus any funds from these projects would go towards debt rather than equity if the entity were liquidated. Managers, acting on behalf of owners, may have little or no incentive to undertake positive net present value (NPV) projects if the projects would only lead to increased funds being available to lenders.

2.4.5 Political relationships

From an economic perspective, political processes can be viewed as a competition for wealth transfers. Based on an assumption of self-interest, individuals face incentives to join forces to compete for wealth transfers. For example, workers may join forces, such as a union, to seek wealth transfers from other providers of factors of production, such as shareholders.

Political costs refer to wealth transfers imposed on an entity. For example, the government might impose a new tax, which would be a political cost to firms operating in industries that are subject to the tax. Economic sanctions are another example of political costs. A retailer obtaining inventory from suppliers that use child labour may attract political costs from powerful non-governmental organisations, such as a campaign to discourage consumers from purchasing goods from that retailer.

Figure 2.4 provides an example of political processes in response to a decision by Adelaide Zoo to discontinue purchases of ice-cream from a local supplier.

| **FIGURE 2.4** | Political processes at Adelaide Zoo |

Pressure on Adelaide Zoo over Golden North ice-cream

Adelaide Zoo actively promoted a campaign against the commercial production of palm oil because the associated unsustainable clearing of tropical forests threatens the natural habitat of endangered species. In conjunction with that campaign, Golden North, a local supplier of ice-cream to Adelaide Zoo, undertook substantial modifications to its production processes to eliminate palm oil from its product. However, in mid 2014, Adelaide Zoo terminated its contract with Golden North in favour of Unilever, a large multinational corporation, whose products contained the contentious palm oil.

There was mounting public outcry in response to the zoo's decision. Senator Nick Xenophon protested outside the zoo by distributing non–palm oil ice-cream and collecting signatures from Zoos SA members on a petition for a special meeting of the Royal Zoological Society. He aimed to place pressure on the zoo's management and board to reverse their decision, explaining, 'What they've done by dumping Golden North actually goes against their aims of conservation'. Some commentators raised concerns about the impact the negative publicity could have on the capacity of the zoo to attract sponsorship and other forms of financial support.

In response to an enormous amount of pressure, particularly through social media, the zoo partly backed down on its previous position. The zoo announced that it would continue to sell Golden North's non-palm oil ice-cream, albeit alongside Unilever products. Unilever aims to source all of its palm oil from certified sustainable sources by 2020.

Sources: Adapted from ABC News (2014) and News.com.au (2014).

Lobbying and other forms of political action are costly to those who conduct them. One of the costs of political action is obtaining information about the entity, the effects of its operations and its capacity to change operations or redistribute wealth.

Due to the costs of political action and limited resources, lobby groups are more likely to take action against larger, more profitable entities, which control more resources and have power to affect more people. For example, if an environmental interest group intends to lobby against the use of plastic drinking cups, the effect of those actions may be greater if targeted against a large chain of restaurants that uses tens of thousands of cups daily, than against a small retailer that uses less than 100 cups each week. Accordingly, politicians, organisations and other groups within society may draw on financial statement information to identify larger and more profitable firms in deciding how to employ scarce resources in political processes.

2.4.6 Role of accounting information in reducing agency problems

As we saw previously, accounting information forms one of the major components of both manager remuneration and lending contracts. Terms are written into managerial remuneration contracts to link managers' performance to shareholder interests. Bonuses can be tied to accounting measures of entity financial performance, such as earnings per share, or market-based measures, such as growth in share price.

Accounting information plays several related roles in the contracting process. First, it is used in writing terms of the remuneration contract, including the specification of performance hurdles and targets, as well as formulas for determining the amount of remuneration. For example, a CEO's remuneration contract might specify that she will receive a cash bonus of 0.5% of profit before tax, subject to meeting a performance hurdle of a return on equity of 10%. Second, accounting information presented in financial statements is used to measure performance against the terms of the contracts to determine whether the manager is eligible for a bonus. Finally, the accounting information may be used to determine the amount of bonus and other components of remuneration that managers will receive.

Debt contracts may include covenants that reflect different measures of entity performance, such as leverage, dividend payout or interest coverage ratios. For example, a debt contract might include a covenant that the ratio of total liabilities to total assets does not exceed 60%. The interest cover restriction might be in the form of an ongoing requirement, such as maintaining a minimum *times interest earned* (profit before interest and taxes/interest) of 3.0. Alternatively, some lenders require minimum average *times interest earned* to have been maintained over several years for a potential borrower to be eligible for a loan. Lenders rely on audited financial statements to determine whether entities are maintaining accounting-based debt covenants.

Accounting is a source of information about the entity in political processes. For example, lobby groups may use an entity's financial statements to assess its capacity to meet their demands. However, various parties with an interest in the entity may differ in terms of their demands and information needs and it is often not cost effective for individuals, or smaller interest groups, to incur costs to analyse financial information. Thus, the extent to which information is generated for political purposes depends on factors including the effects of government policy and the costs and effectiveness of lobbying by interest groups.

As explained above, accounting numbers may be used in management remuneration contracts, debt contracts and political processes. Financial statements are also used to monitor performance against the terms or expectations specified in the contract. The use of accounting information to monitor performance can give rise to incentives for accounting policy choice in the preparation of financial statements.

2.4.7 Implications of agency theory for accounting policy choice

The choice of one accounting policy over another can have economic consequences for contracting parties. Agency theory is used to derive hypotheses about accounting policy choice. These hypotheses are described in general terms below.

- *Bonus plan/management compensation hypothesis: managers of entities with bonus plans prefer accounting policies that increase profit.* Management compensation contracts do not usually specify which accounting policies should be used in the preparation of financial statements. First, it would be very costly, if not impossible, because it would require prediction and specification of all the different types of transactions that might arise and accounting judgements that might be made. Second, it may be in the interests of shareholders to allow managers some discretion so they can strategically select accounting policies that yield more favourable outcomes for shareholders in terms of the entity's contracts with other parties, such as debtholders and governments.

  Managers, acting in their own interest, prefer more remuneration. If their remuneration is based on a bonus, managers may be able to increase their bonus by choosing accounting policies that increase profit. This may involve accounting policies that accelerate the recognition of income or defer the recognition of expenses. For example, management may prefer straight-line depreciation over the diminishing balance method because the straight-line method recognises lower depreciation expenses in the first few years of the useful life of the asset. The amount of profit recognised in the long term will be the same because the total depreciation expense over the useful life of the asset is the same, irrespective of which depreciation method is used. Managers are expected to prefer to report more profit sooner so that they will receive their bonus sooner rather than later. This preference reflects both the time value of the money and the shorter horizon of the manager.

Some more complicated variations of the general management compensation hypothesis allow for minimum profit hurdles that must be met. The manager is expected to prefer accounting policies that reduce profit in periods when the profit hurdle cannot be achieved. The rationale is that if the entity's profit is so low that the manager will not be eligible for a bonus in the current period, the manager would prefer to recognise more expenses in the current period, so as to increase the prospects of exceeding the profit hurdle and getting a bonus in the next period.

- *Debt hypothesis: managers of entities with high leverage prefer accounting policies that increase profit and equity.* Entities with high leverage are more likely to be close to leverage constraints in debt contracts. Managers are expected to act in the interests of shareholders in the entity's relationships with providers of debt finance because management's interests are more aligned with those of shareholders than with those of debtholders. Debt contracts usually allow for some discretion in accounting policy choice because it would be too costly, if not impossible, to specify in advance how to account for every transaction that might arise.

  Agency theory implies that, when faced with restrictive debt covenants, managers will prefer accounting policies that increase profit and equity so as to reduce the risk of breaching a debt contract and to lower the cost of raising further finance. For example, managers may prefer to capitalise expenditure (i.e. recognise expenditure as an asset) rather than recognising it as an expense. Capitalising expenditure would result in more reported assets and equity than would occur if the expenditure were recognised as an expense. The higher reported assets and equity reduce the proximity to restrictive debt covenants that are expressed in terms of the ratio of debt to total assets.

- *Political cost (size) hypothesis: managers of larger entities are more likely to prefer accounting policies that reduce profit.* Managers of firms that are more politically visible are expected to prefer lower reported profit so as to reduce political visibility, thus reducing potential political costs. Large entities are assumed to be more politically visible. Accordingly, managers of large entities are expected to prefer accounting policies that reduce profit to deflect political costs. For example, management of a large financial institution may prefer to recognise more bad and doubtful debts expense, so as to reduce pressure from governments and society to pass on interest rate cuts to borrowers.

While agency theory suggests some factors that may influence accounting policy choice, other factors may also be relevant. For example, some accounting policies may be common within certain industries. In some jurisdictions and for some accounting issues, entities need to select the same accounting policy for financial reporting purposes that they intend to use for purposes of determining income tax obligations.

LEARNING CHECK

☐ Positive accounting theory is based on the view of the firm as a nexus of contracts and on the assumption that individuals are rational wealth maximisers.

☐ Positive accounting theory attempts to explain accounting policy decisions by examining agency relationships between managers and both shareholders and debtholders, as well as political processes.

☐ Accounting numbers are used in management remuneration contracts to establish performance targets and to specify how the amount of remuneration will be determined.

☐ Debt contracts use accounting numbers in setting restrictions such as a maximum leverage ratio.

☐ Accounting numbers reported in financial statements are used to monitor compliance with the terms of debt contracts.

☐ Accounting numbers reported in financial statements are used to measure performance against the terms of management remuneration contracts to determine the eligibility for, and amount of, rewards, such as the amount of a manager's bonus.

☐ While contracts serve to align the interests of agents with those of the principals, they also provide incentives for managers to choose particular accounting policies. Agency theory and economic theory about political processes are used to derive hypotheses about accounting policy choice.

2.5 The role of accounting in capital markets

LEARNING OBJECTIVE 2.5 Compare the implications of the mechanistic hypothesis and the efficient market hypothesis for financial reporting.

Investors and potential investors are considered to be important groups of users of general purpose financial statements. In this section we will consider two competing theories about the role of accounting information in capital markets: the mechanistic hypothesis and the efficient market hypothesis. Both of these hypotheses are based on theories about how the market and, therefore, share prices respond to information.

2.5.1 The mechanistic hypothesis

The **mechanistic hypothesis** predicts that the market reacts mechanistically to changes in accounting numbers. This means that investors are assumed to ignore differences in accounting policies when analysing financial statements. The mechanistic hypothesis suggests that investors respond to an increase in profit in the same way, regardless of whether it has cash flow implications, such as an increase in profit that results from additional sales revenue, or whether it has no cash flow implications, such as an increase in profit resulting from a change of depreciation method. This hypothesis is based on the assumption that investors are functionally fixated on reported numbers.

An implication of the mechanistic hypothesis is that investors could be easily fooled by cosmetic changes in accounting policies, that is, changes that have no cash flow implications. For example, if management changes the straight-line depreciation rate from 20% to 10%, the depreciation expense will decrease and reported profit will be higher than under the former depreciation rate. Of course, this does not mean the entity is generating more cash flows. It simply means that depreciation is being spread over a longer estimated useful life. According to the mechanistic hypothesis, share prices would be overstated because investors would be tricked into believing the shares are worth more because profit is increased. The mechanistic hypothesis implies that accounting standard setters and regulators should be concerned about accounting policy choice because the use of different accounting methods can be used to mislead investors.

2.5.2 The efficient market hypothesis

The **efficient market hypothesis** is a proposition that markets are efficient. A market is efficient if security prices in that market rapidly adjust to new information so that prices fully reflect the available information (Fama 1970). If good news about an entity's future prospects were released, investors would interpret this as indicating that the entity's shares were more valuable and the increased demand for the shares would rapidly drive up the share price. An implication of market efficiency is that, on average, it is not possible to earn economic profits by trading on information. That is, investors are unable to earn returns beyond those commensurate with the level of risk, by using information in an efficient market because the share price reflects the information available about the shares.

Fama (1970) identifies the following three forms of market efficiency which differ in terms of the information set reflected in share prices.

- The *weak form of market efficiency* implies that a security's price at a particular time fully reflects the information contained in its sequence of past prices. If the market is efficient in the weak form, investors would not be able to earn abnormal returns from trading strategies that are based on charting and analysing past prices to identify cycles or patterns.
- The *semi-strong form of market efficiency* implies a security's price at a particular time fully reflects all publicly available information, including the information contained in past prices. If the market is efficient in the semi-strong form, investors would not be able to earn abnormal returns from trading strategies that involve analysing publicly available economic, legal, political or financial information, such as financial statements.
- The *strong form of market efficiency* implies a security's price at a particular time fully reflects all information, including information that is not publicly available. If the market is efficient in the strong form, investors would not be able to earn abnormal returns by trading on private information, which is referred to as 'insider trading'. Insider trading is prohibited by securities regulations and laws because capital markets are not considered to be efficient in the strong form.

Figure 2.5 presents a diagram of the three forms of market efficiency. Each circle depicts an information set. The inner circle is the weak form, in which the market is efficient with respect to information in past security prices only. The next circle reflects the semi-strong form in which the information set to which the market is efficient includes all publicly available information. The information set of the weak form of market efficiency is entirely within the information set of the semi-strong form of market efficiency because past share prices are a component of all publicly available information. Lastly, the outer circle reflects the strong form of market efficiency in which the market is efficient with respect to all public and private information.

FIGURE 2.5   Weak, semi-strong and strong forms of market efficiency

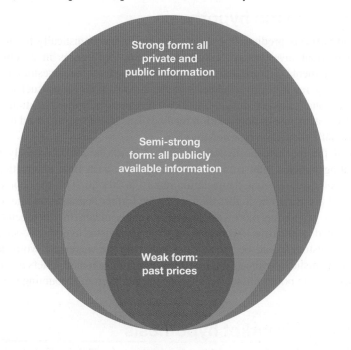

The semi-strong form of market efficiency is of greatest relevance to financial reporting because general purpose financial statements form part of the publicly available set of information about entities. Much of the empirical research undertaken on the effects of accounting policy choice and disclosures on share prices assumes the semi-strong form of capital market efficiency. This is a reasonable assumption although the market is unlikely to be fully efficient in the semi-strong form because market efficiency assumes (Fama 1970):

- there are no transaction costs in trading securities
- all information is available free of cost to all market participants
- market participants agree on the implications of current information for the current price and distribution of future prices of each security.

Clearly these assumptions are not met in modern capital markets. The presence of transaction costs, such as stamp duty and brokerage fees, limit the efficiency of capital markets. While information may be available at low cost, many investors incur information costs to obtain sophisticated analyses and interpretation of financial information. Lastly, there are often differences in the assessment of the implications of new information for the valuation of shares, even among sophisticated analysts.

If the capital market is efficient, the share price will rapidly respond to the release of information, irrespective of whether an item is recognised in the financial statements, or merely disclosed in the notes to the financial statements. For example, according to the efficient market hypothesis, the share price would react to information about an obligation to make future cash payments, regardless of whether it is reported as a liability in the statement of financial position or disclosed as a commitment in the notes to the financial statements.

The semi-strong form of market efficiency implies that what is disclosed is more important than how the information is presented. It does not matter where the information is reported because the share price incorporates all publicly available information. Disclosure is important because if the market is efficient in the semi-strong form, but not in the strong form, information must be made publicly available to be incorporated in share prices.

2.5.3 What does accounting theory tell us about accounting policies?

The capital markets theories considered in sections 2.5.1 and 2.5.2 attempt to explain the effects of accounting policy choice on share prices. The mechanistic hypothesis predicts that investors ignore differences in accounting policy choice and fixate on reported numbers. In contrast, the efficient market hypothesis predicts that in a market that is characterised by the semi-strong form of efficiency, the share price will rapidly incorporate all publicly available information. This implies that the share price would reflect the information about the effect of the choice of accounting policy on profit.

Let us consider an example in which management changes the depreciation policy from the diminishing balance method to the straight-line method, resulting in an increase in reported profit. Information about the change of accounting policy is disclosed in the notes to the financial statements. We will also assume that the change of accounting policy does not affect the entity's tax obligations. The mechanistic hypothesis predicts that the share price will respond to the increase in profit, ignoring that it is the result of a cosmetic change of accounting policy. The efficient market hypothesis predicts that if the increase in profit results from a change of accounting policy that has no cash flow effects, the share price would not be affected. If the share price actually increased in response to this cosmetic accounting policy change, how would we interpret this in light of the competing theories about the behaviour of share prices? One interpretation is that if the share price responds to a cosmetic accounting policy change, it is evidence in support of the mechanistic hypothesis. That is, investors respond to the increase in profit and ignore the additional information in the notes to the financial statements that the increased profit is merely the result of a change of accounting policy. An alternative interpretation is that the change of accounting policy has implications for the entity's contracts with other parties. For example, the increase in profit resulting from the change of depreciation policy may increase the entity's interest coverage and reduce the risk of a breach of its debt contract. The increase in the share price would be consistent with the efficient market hypothesis if it reflects a more sophisticated response that incorporates the economic consequences of the change of accounting policy in terms of the entity's contracts with other parties.

LEARNING CHECK

☐ The mechanistic hypothesis assumes that investors ignore differences in accounting policy choice when analysing financial statements.

☐ The semi-strong form of market efficiency implies a market in which the share price rapidly adjusts to reflect all publicly available information, including disclosures about accounting policies.

SUMMARY

At the beginning of this chapter we considered the need for professional judgement in deciding on a policy to account for transactions and other events in the context of applying accounting standards. The major decision areas include determining:

- whether the transaction or event results in an item that meets the definition of an element of financial statements
- whether the item should be recognised (i.e. have the recognition criteria been satisfied)
- how the item will be measured both initially and, with respect to assets and liabilities, subsequent to initial recognition
- the nature and scope of detail that is disclosed about a transaction, event or item reported in financial statements.

Accounting theory refers to a set of hypothetical, conceptual and pragmatic principles that form a general framework of accounting. Accounting theory can provide guidance, explanations and predictions about accounting policies that are, or could be, used in practice. Normative accounting theories, such as the conceptual framework, prescribe how we should account for transactions and events. In contrast, positive accounting theories seek to explain or predict phenomena pertaining to accounting practice. Some positive theories try to explain differences in accounting policies between entities, while other theories are more concerned with the effects of different accounting policies or disclosures on users' decisions.

We considered selected positive accounting theories, including agency theory which is used to explain and predict accounting policy choice. Separation of ownership and control gives rise to incentives to overspend on perquisites and can provide disincentives for managerial effort. Specific major agency problems in the owner–manager relationship include the horizon problem, risk aversion and dividend retention. The agency problems relating to the contractual relationship between lenders and managers are:

- excessive dividend payments, which could lead to insufficient funds available to service the debt
- asset substitution — the risk to lenders of managers using the debt finance to invest in riskier assets
- claim dilution, when management takes on debt of an equal or higher priority than that on issue
- underinvestment, which arises when managers have incentives not to undertake positive NPV projects that would lead to increased funds being available to lenders.

Contracts are designed to reduce monitoring and bonding costs and the resulting residual loss in the relationship between agents and principals. Accounting information is used to specify performance targets and covenants in contracts. It is also used to monitor actual performance against the contractual terms and determine the amount of rewards.

Accounting policies, such as whether an item is accounted for as an asset or as an expense, or whether a financial instrument is classified as a liability or equity, also have significant effects on the financial statements. The timing and amount of recognition of items can have significant effects on financial statements which are used to monitor performance in relation to contracts and to determine outcomes, such as the amount of a manager's bonus. Thus, accounting policy choice can have economic consequences for the entity and other parties with which it enters into contracts.

Agency theory posits that managers who are remunerated with bonuses linked to the entity's profit prefer accounting policies that increase reported profit. Similarly, if the entity has a lending agreement with a leverage covenant, management will prefer accounting policies that increase reported assets and equity.

Last, we considered selected theories that try to explain the effect of accounting policies and disclosures on share prices. The mechanistic hypothesis assumes investors fixate on accounting numbers, without regard to differences in accounting policies, and thus respond mechanistically to changes in reported profit. In contrast, the efficient market hypothesis predicts that the share price responds rapidly to new information. The semi-strong form of market efficiency implies that the share price rapidly incorporates all publicly available information. Thus, if the market is efficient in the semi-strong form, the share price would also reflect the information about the accounting policy applied in the preparation of financial statements.

KEY TERMS

accounting policy The specific principles, bases, conventions, rules and practices applied by an entity in preparing and presenting financial statements.

agency costs The monitoring and bonding costs borne by the principal and agent, respectively, and residual loss in value of the firm, arising from agency relationships.

agency theory The theory that deals with problems caused by separating ownership from control in the modern corporation.

deductive reasoning An approach to theory development that begins with a description of desired outcomes and leads to principles and, in turn, specific actions that should result in those desired outcomes.

efficient market hypothesis The proposition that a market is 'efficient' if security prices fully reflect the available information about the securities.

fair value The price that would be received to sell an asset or paid to transfer a liability in an orderly transaction between market participants at the measurement date.

inductive reasoning An approach to theory development that begins with observations of practice and leads to inferences about principles, assumptions and objectives.

mechanistic hypothesis The hypothesis that share prices respond mechanistically to changes in accounting numbers, ignoring the effects of accounting policies.

normative theory A theory that prescribes what should be done based on a specific goal or objective.

political costs Wealth transfers imposed on the entity, resulting from political processes.

positive theory A theory that describes, explains or predicts activities or outcomes.

professional judgement The use of professional knowledge and skills to make decisions and solve problems.

theory A coherent set of hypothetical, conceptual and pragmatic principles forming a general framework of reference for a field of inquiry.

COMPREHENSION QUESTIONS

1 Describe the four components of an accounting policy. Illustrate your answer with examples.

2 Differentiate normative accounting theory from positive accounting theory. Provide an example of each.

3 What is the difference between the deductive and inductive processes of developing a theory?

4 What is an agency relationship? Explain how monitoring costs, bonding costs and residual loss arise in agency relationships.

5 Why would managers' interests differ from those of shareholders?

6 Explain the following agency problems that can arise in the relationship between owners and managers.
   (a) The horizon problem
   (b) Risk aversion
   (c) Dividend retention

7 Outline the four agency problems that can arise in the relationship between lenders and managers.

8 What is a debt covenant and why is it used in a lending agreement?

9 Why would managers agree to enter into lending agreements that incorporate covenants?

10 How does accounting information reduce agency problems in relationships between management and shareholders?

11 How does accounting information reduce agency problems in relationships between management and debtholders?

12 What are the factors a manager might consider in making various expensing–capitalising choices?

13 Linking managerial remuneration to entity performance motivates managers to act in the interests of shareholders. However, it also burdens managers with greater risks than they may like. How do entities balance these two considerations in management remuneration plans?

14 Bonus plans are used to reduce agency problems between managers and shareholders. Discuss two of these problems specific to the relationship between shareholders and managers and identify how bonus plans can be used to reduce the agency problems you have identified. In your answer you should provide examples of specific components that may be included in a bonus plan to address the issues identified.

15 What are political costs? How might political visibility influence accounting policy choice?

16 Distinguish between the three forms of market efficiency. Which form is more relevant for financial reporting? Justify your answer.

CASE STUDY 2.1

ACCOUNTING POLICY DECISION

Mandy Ltd made the following disclosure in the notes to its financial statements about how it accounts for insurance premiums.

Other current assets

Insurance premiums are paid in advance and recognised as 'Prepaid insurance' asset at the time of settlement. 'Other current assets' includes an amount of $10 000, which represents the unexpired portion of the insurance contract. The expired portion of the insurance contract is recognised as an expense.

Required

1. List the four components of an accounting policy decision.
2. Analyse Mandy Ltd's policy for accounting for the insurance premium in terms of each component.

CASE STUDY 2.2

AGENCY THEORY

At the beginning of the current reporting period City Retail Ltd launched a new logo and spent $500 000 on new signage for all its premises. The expenditure on signage was originally accounted for as part of property, plant and equipment. It was recognised as a depreciable asset with a useful life of 10 years.

Tony has been engaged as the new accountant for City Retail Ltd. Tony believes that the expenditure for signage should be recognised as an expense because it is in the nature of advertising and the signage has no resale value. Eager to impress the senior managers, Tony gave a presentation on how he would 'improve' the forthcoming annual financial statements, by expensing signage costs. An extract from his presentation is provided below.

	Before change $'000	% of total assets
Total assets (includes signage with carrying amount of $450 000)	4 200	100
Total liabilities (includes a long-term debt agreement)	2 500	60
Shareholders' equity	1 700	40
Profit (includes depreciation expense of $50 000)	600	14

Tony was puzzled by the senior managers' response: 'You don't understand our business. What might look like an improvement for your financial statements, looks like devastating economic consequences for us.'

Additional information

• Managers receive a bonus, subject to profit exceeding 10% of total assets.
• The long-term debt agreement restricts borrowing to a maximum of 65% of total assets.

Required

For simplicity, assume that the change in accounting treatment has no implications on tax or tax expense.

1. Describe and quantify the effects of recognising the signage costs as an expense in City Retail Ltd's financial statements for the year ended 30 June.
2. How would agency theory explain why the managers of City Retail Ltd did not welcome Tony's accounting treatment for the expenditure on signage?

CASE STUDY 2.3

ACCOUNTING THEORIES

Rocky Retail Ltd had experienced a difficult year with declining sales as a result of increased competition from online retailers. The accountant for Rocky Retail Ltd presented a set of draft financial statements to management to review before the final set of financial statements were published. Management was very worried because the draft financial statements showed a profit of only $460 000 for 2022, compared with $600 000 in 2021. They were concerned that a reduction in profit would result in a fall in the company's share price.

The statement of profit or loss and other comprehensive income included an expense of $160 000 for stamp duty on long-term rental properties. One of the managers announced a 'clever plan' to increase profit, suggesting the company 'classify the stamp duty as an asset and expense it over the term of the lease'.

The accountant did some calculations and advised that if Rocky Retail Ltd accounted for the stamp duty costs of $160 000 as 'Prepayments', and then progressively allocated it to expenses over the term of each lease, only $10 000 would be recognised as an expense in 2022. Everyone seemed happy with that plan and the accountant got to work writing the note disclosure about the accounting policy. She explained, 'We must disclose this to comply with accounting standards, but don't worry . . . I think the shareholders and investors will be too busy looking at the profit to read what is says in the notes'.

Required

1. Ignoring taxes, calculate Rocky Retail Ltd's profit for 2022 after the decision to account for stamp duty as an asset.
2. Explain which of the theories discussed in this chapter best describes the managers' expectations about how shareholders and investors will react to the reported profit for 2022.
3. Define the semi-strong form of market efficiency and discuss its implications for how the investors and, therefore, the share price might respond to the release of the financial statements. Assume that the market is efficient in the semi-strong form.

APPLICATION AND ANALYSIS EXERCISES

★ BASIC | ★ ★ MODERATE | ★ ★ ★ DIFFICULT

2.1 Debt covenants and accounting information ★   LO4

You have recently been appointed as a lending officer in the commercial division of a major bank. The bank is concerned about lending in the current economic environment, where there has been an economic downturn.

Required

Prepare a report outlining what agency problems the bank should be concerned with, how covenants in debt agreements can be used to reduce those problems, and how accounting information can be used to assist in this process.

2.2 Management remuneration plans and performance ★ ★   LO4

XYZ is a global financial institution with an executive remuneration scheme that includes both cash-based and share-based remuneration and a mix of shorter term and longer term awards. At least 80% of the performance-based award is deferred. At least 50% of the total performance award (or bonus) is awarded through a share ownership plan, in which the executive receives XYZ shares that vest in three instalments over 3 to 5 years. The senior executives do not become legally entitled to the shares until they vest. In addition, 30% of the total performance award is awarded under a deferred contingent capital plan. This award does not vest for 5 years and is conditional upon further performance targets being satisfied. The award is reduced if XYZ makes a loss during the 5 years until it vests.

Required

1. Explain how the use of a bonus plan linked to performance and the deferral of part of the bonus can reduce the agency problems of the owner–manager relationship.
2. How does the senior executive equity ownership plan reduce agency problems beyond that which is achieved by the bonus plan?

2.3 Agency theory and management remuneration ★ ★   LO4

Publicly listed companies provide a remuneration report as a component of the annual report, which is often available on the company's website.

Required

Obtain the remuneration report for a publicly listed company. Examine the remuneration arrangement for the chief executive officer (CEO). Prepare a report which summarises your findings for each of the following.

1. What amount of the CEO's remuneration is in the nature of salary and cash bonus for the current year, and for the previous year?
2. What forms of remuneration other than salaries and cash bonuses does the CEO receive?
3. What proportion of the CEO's pay for the current reporting period is fixed and what proportion is performance based?
4. What measures of accounting performance, if any, are used to determine the CEO's bonus?
5. Explain the incentives for accounting policy choice that arise from the CEO's remuneration contract according to agency theory. Use specific accounting policies to illustrate your answer.
6. Can agency theory provide an explanation for the various remuneration components? Justify your answer.

2.4 Debt covenants and agency relationships ★ ★   LO4

On 1 July 2019, Medical Supplies Ltd borrowed $15 million to finance an investment in a laboratory for developing and testing surgical supplies. The loan is due 30 June 2029. The lender insisted on a debt covenant in the loan agreement, specifying that the ratio of total liabilities to total tangible assets not exceed 65%. Medical Supplies Ltd complied with the requirement in 2020 when the ratio of total liabilities to total tangible assets was 64%.

Medical Supplies Ltd also invested in plant and equipment used exclusively to manufacture latex gloves. However, due to a decline in demand for latex gloves, analysts are predicting that the company may need to write down some of its plant and equipment.

Required

1. Debt covenants or restrictions are commonly used in Australian lending agreements. Discuss how they are used to reduce agency problems that exist in the relationship between management and lenders.
2. Why would management choose to enter into a lending agreement that contains a covenant that restricts the company's leverage?
3. How might a write-down of plant and equipment increase the risk of breaching debt contracts?
4. If a company is close to breaching its leverage covenant what actions might it take?

2.5 Accounting policies ★ ★ ★   LO1, 2, 3, 4

In small teams, obtain the financial statements of three publicly listed companies. Refer to the notes to the financial statements pertaining to accounting policies and the note pertaining to property, plant and equipment reported in the statement of financial position.

Required

1. Describe the measurement and disclosure components of each company's policy for accounting for each class of property, plant and equipment.
2. Prepare a report on the comparability of the accounting policies used by the three companies. Drawing on theories explored in this chapter, do you think all companies should be required to use identical accounting policies?

2.6 Leases and efficient market hypothesis ★ ★ ★   LO5

Accounting standard setters introduced changes to the requirements for accounting for leases from 1 January 2019. Prior to then, if a lease was classified as a finance lease, the leased asset and a corresponding lease liability were recognised in the statement of financial position of the lessee. However, if a lease was classified as an operating lease, a lease asset and a lease liability were not recognised by the lessee. Instead, lease payments were recognised as expenses as incurred and lease commitments were disclosed in the notes to the financial statements. The following statement has been made in relation to the 2019 changes to accounting for leases.

> If the efficient market hypothesis is correct, management would be indifferent between classifying the lease as a finance lease or as an operating lease.

Required

Critically evaluate this statement.

2.7 Mechanistic hypothesis and efficient market hypothesis ★ ★ LO5

Hudson Ltd had always classified interest paid as an operating cash flow. In 2022 Hudson Ltd changed its accounting policy and classified interest paid of $50 000 as a financing cash flow in its statement of cash flows. The reported amounts are summarised below.

	2021 $'000	2022 $'000
Net cash inflows from operating activities	400	450
Net cash outflows for investing activities	(300)	(300)
Net cash outflows from financing activities	(50)	(100)
Net movement in cash	50	50

Required

1. Describe the mechanistic hypothesis. What does the mechanistic hypothesis predict about how investors and, therefore, share prices will respond to the increase in operating cash flows reported in Hudson Ltd's 2022 financial statements?
2. Describe the semi-strong form of market efficiency. What does the efficient market hypothesis predict about how investors and, therefore, share prices will respond to the increase in operating cash flows reported in Hudson Ltd's 2022 financial statements?

2.8 Mechanistic hypothesis and efficient market hypothesis ★ ★ LO5

Due to a change of accounting standards Lily Ltd reclassified some of its financial instruments in preparing its financial statements for the year ended 30 June 2022. The fair value of the financial instruments actually declined by $2 000 000. The effect of the reclassification was that changes in the fair value of the financial instruments were no longer recognised in the financial statements and this enabled Lily Ltd to report a profit of $6 000 000, which was an increase of 5% over the previous year's profit. The amount of the decline in the fair value of the financial instruments was disclosed in the notes to the financial statements.

Required

1. What does the mechanistic hypothesis predict about how investors and, therefore, share prices will respond to information about the profit reported in Lily Ltd's 2022 financial statements?
2. Distinguish between the mechanistic hypothesis and the semi-strong form of market efficiency. What does the efficient market hypothesis predict about how investors and, therefore, share prices will respond to information about the profit reported in Lily Ltd's 2022 financial statements?

REFERENCES

ABC News 2014, 'Independent Senator Nick Xenophon increases pressure on Adelaide Zoo over palm oil ice creams', 9 August, www.abc.net.au.

Coase, R 1937, 'The nature of the firm', *Econometrica,* vol. 4, pp. 386–405.

CSR Limited 2016, *Annual report 2016,* www.csr.com.au.

Fama, EF 1970, 'Efficient capital markets: a review of theory and empirical work', *Journal of Finance,* vol. 25, pp. 383–417.

Hendriksen, E 1970, *Accounting theory,* Richard D Irwin, Illinois.

Jensen, M & Meckling, W 1976, 'Theory of the firm: managerial behaviour, agency costs and ownership structure', *Journal of Financial Economics,* vol. 3, October, pp. 305–60.

News.com.au 2014, 'Adelaide Zoo backflips over Golden North ice cream', 15 August, www.news.com.au.

Smith, CW & Warner, JB 1979, 'On financial contracting: an analysis of bond covenants', *Journal of Financial Economics,* June, pp. 117–61.

Smith, CW & Watts, RL 1982, 'Incentive and tax effects of executive compensation plans', *Australian Journal of Management,* vol. 7, pp. 139–57.

Watts, RL & Zimmerman, JL 1986, *Positive accounting theory,* Prentice Hall, Englewood Cliffs, NJ.

ACKNOWLEDGEMENTS

Photo: © zstock / Shutterstock.com

Figure 2.3: © CSR Limited 'CSR's remuneration strategy'. Figure 2 from p. 28 of CSR Limited *Annual report 2016* (copy of report supplied and downloadable from: http://www.csr.com.au/investor-relations-and-news/annual-meetings-and-reports).

Text: © 2019 Australian Accounting Standards Board (AASB). The text, graphics and layout of this publication are protected by Australian copyright law and the comparable law of other countries. No part of the publication may be reproduced, stored or transmitted in any form or by any means without the prior written permission of the AASB except as permitted by law. For reproduction or publication permission should be sought in writing from the Australian Accounting Standards Board. Requests in the first instance should be addressed to the National Director, Australian Accounting Standards Board, PO Box 204, Collins Street West, Victoria, 8007.

CHAPTER 3

Fair value measurement

CHAPTER AIM

This chapter discusses the application of AASB 13/IFRS 13 *Fair Value Measurement*. The objectives of this standard are: to define fair value, set out a framework for measuring fair value, and establish disclosures about fair value measurement.

LEARNING OBJECTIVES

After studying this chapter, you should be able to:

3.1 identify the need for an accounting standard on fair value measurement

3.2 explain the definition of fair value

3.3 measure the fair value of non-financial assets

3.4 apply the fair value measurement principles to liabilities

3.5 discuss the measurement of the fair values of an entity's own equity instruments

3.6 explain some of the issues relating to financial instruments

3.7 appreciate the disclosures required where assets, liabilities or equity is measured at fair value.

CONCEPTS FOR REVIEW

Before studying this chapter, you should understand and, if necessary, revise:

* the nature of a liability under the *Conceptual Framework*
* the nature of an asset under the *Conceptual Framework*.

3.1 Introduction and scope

LEARNING OBJECTIVE 3.1 Identify the need for an accounting standard on fair value measurement.

This chapter explains the meaning and measurement of fair value as set out in AASB 13/IFRS 13 *Fair Value Measurement*. Fair value is used extensively in Australian accounting standards as a measurement basis for assets, liabilities, equity instruments, revenues and expenses. Topics that require an understanding of fair value include:

- applying the revaluation method to property, plant and equipment under AASB 116/IAS 16 *Property, Plant and Equipment* (see chapter 5)
- applying the revaluation method to intangibles under AASB 138/IAS 38 *Intangible Assets* (see chapter 6)
- measuring recoverable amounts when applying impairment tests under AASB 136/IAS 36 *Impairment of Assets* (see chapter 7)
- measuring defined benefit plan assets under AASB 119/IAS 19 *Employee Benefits* (see chapter 9)
- classification of leases by the lessor under AASB 16/IFRS 16 *Leases* (see chapter 10)
- applying the revaluation model to exploration and evaluation assets under AASB 6/IFRS 6 *Exploration for and Evaluation of Mineral Resources* (see chapter 34)
- measuring investment property using the fair value model under AASB 140/IAS 40 *Investment Property*
- measuring biological assets and agricultural assets under AASB 141/IAS 41 *Agriculture* (see chapter 35)
- measuring fair values of financial instruments under AASB 9/IFRS 9 *Financial Instruments* (see chapter 11)
- measuring equity-settled share-based payment transactions under AASB 2/IFRS 2 *Share-based Payment* (see chapter 14)
- measuring non-cash consideration under AASB 15/ IFRS 15 *Revenue from Contracts with Customers* (see chapter 15)
- measuring non-current assets or disposal groups classified as held for sale under AASB 5/IFRS 5 *Non-current Assets Held for Sale and Discontinued Operations* (see chapter 16)
- measuring fair values in accounting for foreign currency transactions and hedges under AASB 9/ IFRS 9 *Financial Instruments* (see chapter 23)
- measuring the identifiable assets acquired and the liabilities assumed at their acquisition-date fair values in a business combination under AASB 3/IFRS 3 *Business Combinations* (see chapter 25)
- measuring the non-controlling interest using the full goodwill method under AASB 3/IFRS 3 *Business Combinations* (see chapter 29)
- measuring the consideration received and any investment retained in the subsidiary at fair value under AASB 127/IAS 27 *Consolidated and Separate Financial Statements* (see chapter 30)
- measuring non-monetary government grants under AASB 120/IAS 20 *Accounting for Government Grants and Disclosure of Government Assistance*
- measuring contributions (e.g. the donations) of not-for-profit entities under AASB 1004 *Contributions*
- measuring the assets and liabilities of superannuation entities under AASB 1056 *Superannuation Entities*.

In Australia, companies have been allowed to use fair values for measurement of certain non-current assets for many years. This has not been the case in the United States. As far back as the 1940s, the Securities and Exchange Commission (SEC) in the United States had effectively removed the option of upward revaluation of property, plant and equipment for financial statements filed with SEC registration documents. However, fair values were still applied in relation to acquisitions and contracts entered into by companies. Following various accounting scandals and corporate collapses, some involving irregularities in fair value numbers, the accounting standard-setters moved to issue an accounting standard on the measurement of fair value. In May 2011, the International Accounting Standards Board (IASB) issued IFRS 13 *Fair Value Measurement*. The Australian Accounting Standards Board (AASB) issued the equivalent standard AASB 13 in September of the same year. According to paragraph 1 of AASB 13/ IFRS 13, the standard's three objectives are to:

1. define fair value
2. set out a framework for measuring fair value
3. require disclosures about fair value measurements.

The standard does not introduce new requirements for the use of fair value as a required measurement method or eliminate current practicability exceptions to the measurement of fair value, such as in accounting for agriculture (see chapter 35). Furthermore, the requirements of the standard do not extend to the use of fair values in share-based payment transactions within the scope of AASB 2/IFRS 2 *Share-based Payment* (see chapter 14) and accounting for leases by lessors within the scope of AASB 16/IFRS 16 *Leases* (see chapter 10). In some accounting standards, terms other than fair value are used, including net realisable value (used in AASB 102/IAS 2 *Inventories* — see chapter 4) or value in use (used in AASB 136/IAS 36 *Impairment of Assets* — see chapter 7). It is important in applying AASBs/IFRSs and interpreting financial information to also understand the meaning of these terms and how they differ from fair value.

LEARNING CHECK

☐ In 2011, the AASB/IASB issued AASB 13/IFRS 13 *Fair Value Measurement*.
☐ AASB 13/IFRS 13 has three main objectives:
  – to define fair value
  – to establish a framework for measuring fair value
  – to require disclosures about fair value measurements.
☐ Measurement at fair value based on AASB 13/IFRS 13 is permitted or required in a number of current accounting standards.

3.2 The definition of fair value

LEARNING OBJECTIVE 3.2 Explain the definition of fair value.

Appendix A of AASB 13/IFRS 13 defines **fair value** as follows.

> The price that would be received to sell an asset or paid to transfer a liability in an orderly transaction between market participants at the measurement date.

The measurement of fair value is based on a *hypothetical* transaction. The three key elements of fair value are as follows.
1. It is a current exit price.
2. The asset is sold or the liability is transferred in an orderly transaction.
3. The transaction is between market participants.

3.2.1 Current exit price

Appendix A of AASB 13/IFRS 13 defines **exit price** as follows.

> The price that would be received to sell an asset or paid to transfer a liability.

An important feature of the definition of fair value is that it is an exit price based on the perspective of the entity that holds the asset or owes the liability. The exit price is based on expectations about the future cash flows that would be generated by the asset subsequent to its sale or that would be needed to transfer a liability to an acquiring entity. These cash flows may be generated from the use of the asset or from the sale of the asset by the acquiring entity. Even where the entity holding the asset intends to use it rather than sell it, the fair value is measured as an exit price by reference to the sale of the asset to a market participant who will use the asset or sell it. Similarly, with a liability, an entity may continue to hold a liability until settlement, or transfer the liability to another entity. The fair value in both cases is based on the price to transfer the liability to a market participant, which can be determined by reference to the expected cash outflows for the settlement of the liability.

In contrast to an exit price, an entry price is one that would be paid to buy an asset or received to incur a liability. According to paragraph BC44 of the Basis for Conclusions on AASB 13/IFRS 13, the IASB concluded that a current entry price and a current exit price will be equal when they relate to the same asset or liability on the same date in the same form in the same market. When an entity acquires an asset or assumes a liability in an exchange transaction, the transaction price is the amount paid by the entity — this is an *entry* price. In contrast, the fair value of the acquired asset or assumed liability is the price that would be received by the entity when it sold the asset or paid to transfer the liability to another entity — this is an *exit* price.

3.2.2 Orderly transactions

Appendix A of AASB 13/IFRS 13 defines an **orderly transaction** as follows.

> A transaction that assumes exposure to the market for a period before the measurement date to allow for marketing activities that are usual and customary for transactions involving such assets or liabilities; it is not a forced transaction (e.g. a forced liquidation or distress sale).

Fair value is determined by considering a hypothetical transaction in a market. To measure that fair value, the entity will make observations in current markets. The markets to be observed must be those containing orderly transactions. It is not appropriate to base fair value measurements on prices of goods sold at 'sale price' or in a liquidation or fire sale or in a transaction in which the entities are not at arm's length. Factors that would indicate a transaction is not orderly include the following.

- The seller is in or near bankruptcy.
- The seller was forced to sell to meet regulatory or legal requirements.

Hence, if an entity acquired an asset as a result of a transaction that was not orderly, the amount paid — the actual price (an entry price) — is not necessarily equal to the fair value of the asset.

3.2.3 Market participants

Appendix A of AASB 13/IFRS 13 defines **market participants** as follows.

> Buyers and sellers in the principal (or most advantageous) market for the asset or liability that have all of the following characteristics:
> (a) They are independent of each other, i.e. they are not related parties as defined in AASB 124 [*Related Party Disclosures*], although the price in a related party transaction may be used as an input to a fair value measurement if the entity has evidence that the transaction was entered into at market terms.
> (b) They are knowledgeable, having a reasonable understanding about the asset or liability and the transaction using all available information, including information that might be obtained through due diligence efforts that are usual and customary.
> (c) They are able to enter into a transaction for the asset or liability.
> (d) They are willing to enter into a transaction for the asset or liability, i.e. they are motivated but not forced or otherwise compelled to do so.

This is the same in concept as 'knowledgeable, willing parties in an arm's length transaction', a phrase that was used to describe fair value before the issue of AASB 13/IFRS 13.

As the fair value is determined by reference to a hypothetical transaction, an entity must measure fair value using the assumptions that relevant market participants would use when pricing the asset or liability. The assumptions are those of the market participants, *not* those of the entity using the valuation. It is presumed that market participants act in their economic best interest. Neither party to an exchange transaction is perfectly informed, but it is assumed that both will undertake sufficient efforts to obtain the relevant information about an asset or a liability prior to committing to the transaction.

An entity does not have to identify specific market participants; rather the entity has to identify characteristics that distinguish market participants generally. For example, the entity does not need to identify, say, BHP Group Ltd as a potential market participant, but rather the characteristics of an entity that is a large manufacturer of iron and steel and uses certain assets in that process.

According to paragraph 23 of AASB 13/IFRS 13, the entity needs to consider factors specific to the transaction such as the:

- actual asset or liability being measured
- principal (or most advantageous) market for the asset or liability
- market participants with whom the entity would enter into a transaction in that market.

3.2.4 Transaction and transport costs

Two types of costs need to be considered when measuring fair value: transaction costs and transport costs.

Transaction costs are defined in Appendix A of AASB 13/IFRS 13 as follows.

> The costs to sell an asset or transfer a liability in the principal (or most advantageous) market for the asset or liability that are directly attributable to the disposal of the asset or the transfer of the liability and meet both of the following criteria:
> (a) They result directly from and are essential to that transaction.
> (b) They would not have been incurred by the entity had the decision to sell the asset or transfer the liability not been made (similar to costs to sell, as defined in AASB 5 [IFRS 5]).

Transaction costs include selling costs and handling costs because these are incremental and directly attributable to a transaction. The level of transaction costs affects the determination of the principal (or most advantageous) market in which an asset may be sold, and hence the market in which the fair value is measured. However, the price used to measure the fair value of an asset or liability is *not* adjusted for transaction costs. The reason for this is that these costs are specific to a transaction with a particular entity and would change from transaction to transaction. They are not considered to be a characteristic of the asset or liability itself. For example, the registration costs of a bus are not included in the fair value measurement of the bus.

Transport costs are defined in Appendix A of AASB 13/IFRS 13 as follows.

> The costs that would be incurred to transport an asset from its current location to its principal (or most advantageous) market.

An asset may have to be transported from its present location to the market in which it is to be sold. As the location of an asset or a liability is a characteristic of the asset or liability, associated transport costs *do* affect the fair value. The measurement of the fair value of an asset is therefore net of any transport costs.

For example, the fair value of a bus in an isolated country town is lower than the fair value of one located in the city because of the transport costs associated with getting the bus to the market.

Illustrative example 3.1 shows how transport costs and transaction costs affect the measurement of fair value.

ILLUSTRATIVE EXAMPLE 3.1

Transaction costs and transport costs

Pilbara Ltd, a mining company in Western Australia, owns a number of heavy-duty machines used in the extraction of ore. A downturn in demand from Chinese companies has prompted Pilbara Ltd to consider selling one of its machines. Pilbara Ltd therefore wishes to determine the fair value of a heavy-duty machine. Similar machines are sold in the market for $100 000. In order to sell the machine, Pilbara Ltd would need to incur advertising costs of $250, legal costs of $300 and possibly informational costs (to investigate the market for these machines) of $120. The cost of transporting the machine from the mine site to the nearest town with railway and shipping facilities is $300.

Required
Determine the transaction costs, transport costs and fair value of the heavy-duty machine.

Solution

$$\text{Transaction costs} = \$250 + \$300 + \$120$$
$$= \$670$$
$$\text{Transport costs} = \$300$$

In calculating the fair value of the machine, only transport costs are taken into account.

$$\text{Fair value} = \$100\,000 - \$300$$
$$= \$99\,700$$

LEARNING CHECK

☐ AASB 13/IFRS 13 introduced a new definition of fair value, different from that used previously in accounting standards.

☐ Fair value is defined as an exit price rather than an entry price.

▶

3.3 Application to non-financial assets

LEARNING OBJECTIVE 3.3 Measure the fair value of non-financial assets.

In this chapter, the measurement of fair value is considered in relation to non-financial assets and liabilities, and equity. This section considers non-financial assets. Sections 3.4 and 3.5 consider liabilities and equity instruments, respectively. Whereas financial assets include cash, shares in other entities and rights to receive cash from other entities, non-financial assets include property, plant and equipment, and intangibles.

According to paragraph B2 of Appendix B *Application guidance* of AASB 13/IFRS 13, an entity needs to undertake the following four steps to make a fair value measurement for a non-financial asset.

Step 1. Determine 'the particular asset that is the subject of the measurement (consistent with its unit of account)'.

Step 2. Determine 'the valuation premise that is appropriate for the measurement (consistent with its highest and best use)'.

Step 3. Determine 'the principal (or most advantageous) market for the asset'.

Step 4. Determine 'the valuation technique(s) appropriate for the measurement, considering the availability of data with which to develop inputs that represent the assumptions that market participants would use when pricing the asset and the level of the fair value hierarchy within which the inputs are categorised'.

These four steps are now discussed in more detail.

3.3.1 Step 1. What is the particular asset being measured?

According to paragraph 11 of AASB 13/IFRS 13, a fair value measurement is for a particular asset. When measuring the fair value of an asset, it is necessary to consider the particular characteristics of the asset that market participants would take into account when pricing the asset.

Some of the key questions that need to be asked when considering the characteristics of the asset to be measured are as follows.

- *What is the location of the asset?* If the asset is located away from the market, it will need to be transported to the market and transport costs will be incurred. Time constraints or difficulties in transporting the asset may affect its fair value.
- *What is the condition of the asset?* Many of the factors that are considered in depreciating an asset are relevant to assessing the condition of an asset, such as remaining useful life, physical condition, expected usage, and technical or commercial obsolescence. Assets may be new or second-hand, and may be well or poorly maintained.
- *Are there any restrictions on sale or use of the asset?* There may be legal limits on the use of the asset; for example, patents, licences or expiry dates of related lease contracts. It may be illegal to sell certain assets in some countries.
- *Is the asset a stand-alone asset or is it a group of assets?* Where a fair value is being calculated for impairment purposes, the assets being valued may be a cash generating unit as defined in AASB 136/IAS 36 *Impairment of Assets* (see chapter 7). Similarly, if the fair value relates to a business, the definition of a business in AASB 3/IFRS 3 *Business Combinations* would need to be considered (see chapter 25).

The premise for considering these factors is that the market participants will be taking these factors into consideration when determining how they would price the asset or liability.

According to paragraph 69 of AASB 13/IFRS 13, blockage factors should *not* be considered when measuring fair value. Blockage factors relate to the volume of assets being sold. In general, price per unit can be expected to fall if a large volume of units is sold as a package; for example, the price per vehicle in the sale of a fleet of vehicles would be less than the price in the sale of a single vehicle. Blockage is hence an entity-specific factor. According to paragraph BC42 of the Basis for Conclusions on AASB 13/IFRS 13, the transaction being considered between the market participants is a hypothetical transaction, and as such, the determination of fair value does not consider any entity-specific factors that might influence the transaction. Hence, assets should be measured on a per unit basis.

3.3.2 Step 2. What is the appropriate measurement valuation premise?

The fair value of an asset is determined by considering the price a market participant would pay to buy the asset from a seller. The market participant would determine this price by considering the potential cash flows from the asset, whether from its sale or use. The market participant may have a number of alternative ways in which it can sell or use the asset. Fair value is measured by considering the highest and best use of the asset. **Highest and best use** is defined in Appendix A of AASB 13/IFRS 13 as follows.

> The use of a non-financial asset by market participants that would maximise the value of the asset or the group of assets and liabilities (e.g. a business) within which the asset would be used.

According to paragraph 28 of AASB 13/IFRS 13, the highest and best use must be:
(a) physically possible, taking into account the physical characteristics of the asset
(b) legally permissible, considering any legal restrictions (e.g. zoning regulations on the use of land)
(c) financially feasible, in that the use of the asset must generate adequate income or cash flows to produce an investment return that market participants would require from the asset.

The highest and best use is not based on how the entity is currently using the asset. Note the following.

- The highest and best use is based on how the market participants will use the asset; for example, a competing use for land on which a factory currently stands may be use of the land for a housing development.
- The entity does not have to make an intensive search for other potential uses if there is no evidence to suggest that the current use is not its highest and best use (AASB 13/IFRS 13 paragraph 29). On 2 November 2009 at an IASB roundtable, one participant argued that it is rare that the highest and best use of a commodity would be something other than its actual current use in its current form, citing that an entity with crude oil should not have to look to all the different potential uses of that oil such as refined oil, gasoline and electricity generation through oil-burning plants.
- For competitive reasons, the entity may have decided not to use an acquired asset; for example, an entity may have acquired a competing trademark and then not used it. However, the fair value of the acquired trademark is based on its highest and best use by market participants, not on the current use by the entity holding the asset. Disclosure is also required where an asset is not being used in its highest and best use.

The highest and best use of an asset establishes the valuation premise to be used to measure the fair value of the asset (AASB 13/IFRS 13 paragraph 31). There are two valuation premises: the in-combination valuation premise and the stand-alone valuation premise.

In-combination valuation premise

When a fair value is determined under the in-combination valuation premise, the highest and best use of the asset is where the market participants obtain maximum value through using the asset *in combination with other assets as a group*.

Paragraph 31(a) of AASB 13/IFRS 13 states that if the fair value of an asset is measured under this premise, it is based on the price that would be received in a current transaction to sell the asset assuming that the asset would be used with other assets and liabilities as a group and that those assets and liabilities would be available to market participants. For example, if the asset is work-in-progress which would be converted into finished goods, in determining the fair value of the work-in-progress it is assumed that the market participants have or would be able to acquire any necessary machinery for that conversion process.

The fair value is based on the asset being sold to other market participants to be used by them. The asset is sold as an individual asset, not as part of a group of assets. However, the asset will then be used by the market participants in conjunction with other assets. The fair value of an asset used in conjunction with other assets is not determined by an allocation of the fair value of the group of assets. The fair value is the exit price for the asset. The unit of account of the asset depends on what is specified in other accounting standards and can be an individual asset (AASB 13/IFRS 13 paragraph 32). For example, the measurement requirements of AASB 116 /IAS 16 *Property, Plant and Equipment* apply on an item by item basis.

Sometimes the asset being sold is a specialised asset; that is, it has been made specifically for use by the entity. An item of specialised equipment would generally be used in conjunction with other assets; hence the valuation premise would be in-use rather than in-exchange. The exit price is then based on the sale of the specialised equipment to market participants who will use the specialised equipment in conjunction with other assets to obtain a return. The in-use valuation premise assumes there are market participants who will use the asset in combination with other assets and that those assets are available to them.

Stand-alone valuation premise

When fair value is determined under the stand-alone valuation premise, the highest and best use of the asset is where market participants obtain maximum value from using the asset on a stand-alone basis. Paragraph 31(b) of AASB 13/IFRS 13 states the fair value of the asset is the price that would be received in a current transaction to sell the asset to market participants who would use the asset *on a stand-alone basis*; that is, not in combination with other assets or liabilities.

Decisions concerning the highest and best use of an asset and the relevant valuation premise are considered in illustrative examples 3.2 and 3.3.

ILLUSTRATIVE EXAMPLE 3.2

Determining highest and best use and valuation premise

Atlantic Brands Ltd is an Australian company whose business interests include the acquisition of other Australian companies. It recently acquired the assets and liabilities of Craft Ltd, makers of jam and related products. One of the assets of Craft Ltd was the brand *Crunchy Peanut Butter*. Craft Ltd had not yet produced a saleable product related to this brand but was working on a manufacturing process to generate a suitable product.

Under AASB 3/IFRS 3 *Business Combinations*, the acquiring entity must measure all assets acquired in a business combination at fair value. Atlantic Brands Ltd must then determine a fair value for the acquired brand *Crunchy Peanut Butter*. To do this it needs to determine the highest and best use of the asset by the market participants and the valuation premise.

One of the assets already held by Atlantic Brands Ltd is the brand *Smoothy Peanut Butter*, which relates to one of the company's top-selling products. Atlantic Brands Ltd does not want to put another peanut paste product on the market to compete with its *Smoothy Peanut Butter* so it plans to discontinue the use of the *Crunchy Peanut Butter* brand and concentrate on the sole production of the smooth peanut paste alongside other jams and related products previously owned by Craft Ltd.

Required
How is the fair value of the *Crunchy Peanut Butter* brand determined?

Solution
The fair value of the *Crunchy Peanut Butter* brand is not based on what Atlantic Brands Ltd plans to do with the brand as this would be an entity-specific valuation. The determination of the fair value of the brand is based on the potential uses of the brand by market participants. Some possible situations are as follows.
- The highest and best use may be where market participants want to use the brand in conjunction with their own manufacturing processes and develop a market-acceptable crunchy peanut paste to compete with smooth peanut paste. The brand is then used in-combination with other assets held by market participants to produce a viable product for sale. The calculation of the fair value of the brand would be based on the price that would be received from market participants who are planning to use the brand in conjunction with their own manufacturing assets.
- The highest and best use may be where market participants do not want the brand to reach the market as it would compete with the products they presently produce. To ensure the brand does not reach the market other market participants may be willing to buy the brand as a stand-alone asset. The fair value is then based on the price that market participants would pay to gain control of the asset so that it would be discontinued in use. The fair value is then unrelated to any future cash flows from the sales of crunchy peanut paste, but rather an analysis of sales potentially lost if the crunchy peanut paste were manufactured.

ILLUSTRATIVE EXAMPLE 3.3

Determining highest and best use and valuation premise

The main business of Greens Development Company is the development of real estate for sale of residential land in Western Australia. It is currently in the process of acquiring properties in Madora Bay for the purpose of developing the properties into beachside residential land. Greens is in negotiation with many local companies that have businesses in Madora Bay. One of these is Bazza's Olive Oil Company. Bazza has land on which he cultivates olive trees from which he produces high-quality olive oil products for local and export markets. Although Greens Development Company has made many offers to Bazza's Olive Oil Company for the acquisition of the olive groves, Bazza has refused to sell off the family business.

Required
How would Bazza determine the fair value of the land held by Bazza's Olive Oil Company?

Solution
To measure the fair value of the land held by Bazza's Olive Oil Company the highest and best use of the land would need to be determined. Two possible uses of the land are as follows.
- The land could continue to be used by Bazza's Olive Oil Company for the production of olive oil products. The valuation premise in this case is the in-combination valuation premise. Determining the value of the land would be based on selling the land and the olive oil factory to market participants who would use these assets to make olive oil products for sale. The value of the land relates to its suitability to the growing of olive trees, such as the composition of the soil, drainage and fertility. The fair value of the factory would be based on the continued use of the land to support the olive oil production process.
- An alternative use of the land is its sale to developers such as Greens Development Company. The valuation premise used in the determination of fair value of the land is the stand-alone valuation premise as the land is sold as a stand-alone asset, separate from the factory. It would be expected that development companies would demolish the factory and then develop the land into residential blocks. The factory has value only as scrap. The fair value of the land is based on the amount that would be received on sale of the land to the development companies.

It may be that Bazza's Olive Oil Company determines that the highest and best use of the land is sale for residential purposes as this generates the higher value. However, Bazza may still continue to use the land for the production of olive oil. This decision may be based on family tradition and a perceived need to continue to pass the business on to the next generation of the family. Note that where an asset is used in a way that differs from its highest and best use, and is measured at fair value, according to paragraph 93(i) of AASB 13/IFRS 13, the entity must disclose this fact and why the entity is using the asset in a manner that differs from its highest and best use.

3.3.3 Step 3. What is the principal (or most advantageous market) for the asset?

According to paragraph 16 of AASB 13/IFRS 13, a fair value measurement assumes that the transaction to sell the asset takes place either in the:
(a) principal market for the asset; or
(b) absence of a principal market, in the most advantageous market for the asset.

Appendix A of AASB 13/IFRS 13 defines the **principal market** as follows.

> The market with the greatest volume and level of activity for the asset or liability.

The principal market is then the largest market for the non-financial asset. An entity does not have to make an exhaustive search of all markets in order to determine which market is the principal market. In fact, unless evidence to the contrary exists, the market the entity usually enters to sell this type of asset is presumed to be the principal market.

On the measurement date, the price in the principal market may be less than in another market. According to paragraph 18 of AASB 13/IFRS 13, when measuring fair value the price in the principal market takes precedence. Paragraph BC52 of the Basis for Conclusions on AASB 13/IFRS 13 considers the principal market to be the most liquid market and to provide the most representative input for a fair value measurement if the entity can access the market at the measurement date.

Where there is no principal market, the entity needs to determine the most advantageous market. Appendix A of AASB 13/IFRS 13 defines the **most advantageous market** as follows.

> The market that maximises the amount that would be received to sell the asset or minimises the amount that would be paid to transfer the liability, after taking into account transaction costs and transport costs.

The determination of the most advantageous market is then based on a comparison of the amounts receivable from entering a number of markets. The most advantageous market is the one that offers the highest return. Illustrative example 3.4 provides an example of determining the most advantageous market, with a consideration of transport and transaction costs.

Most advantageous market

An asset held by Butcher Bird Ltd is sold in two different active markets at different prices. Butcher Bird Ltd conducts transactions in both markets and at all times is able to access the prices in both markets for the asset. Relevant information about both markets is as follows.

	Market A	Market B
Price that would be received	$54 000	$52 000
Transaction costs	(4 000)	(4 000)
Costs to transport to market	(6 000)	(2 000)
Net amount receivable	$44 000	$46 000

Required

What is the fair value of the asset?

Solution

The fair value of an asset is the amount receivable in the most advantageous market. The most advantageous market is the one that maximises the amount that would be received to sell the asset — this being an amount net of both transaction and transport costs.

Using the figures above, the most advantageous market to Butcher Bird Ltd is Market B as it has the highest net amount receivable. The fair value of the asset is $50 000, being the amount receivable in Market B less any transport costs in Market B. Transaction costs are used to determine the most advantageous market, but are not used in the measurement of fair value.

An entity may be in a situation where it may be able to access different markets at different points of time; that is, not all markets are always accessible to the entity. According to paragraph 19 of AASB 13/IFRS 13, the principal (or most advantageous) market must be one that the entity can access at the measurement date.

Most entities make operational decisions based upon an objective of maximisation of profits; therefore entities would choose the most advantageous market in which to conduct operations. The most advantageous market would then often be the market that the entity usually enters, or expects to enter.

In some situations there may be no observable market for a specific asset; for example, a patent or a trademark. According to paragraph 21 of AASB 13/IFRS 13, the entity must assume that a transaction takes place at the measurement date, consider the characteristics of market participants who might be involved in a transaction to acquire the asset under consideration, and consider how that asset would be dealt with by those participants.

3.3.4 Step 4. What is the appropriate valuation technique for the measurement of the asset?

Having determined the nature of the asset being valued, the valuation premise applicable (consistent with its highest and best use) and the principal (or most advantageous) market in which the asset can be sold, the next step is to estimate the price in an orderly transaction between market participants.

Valuation techniques

According to paragraph 61 of AASB 13/IFRS 13, an entity must use valuation techniques to measure fair value that:
- are appropriate to the circumstances
- have sufficient data available
- maximise the use of relevant observable inputs and minimise the use of unobservable inputs.

The objective of using a valuation technique is to estimate the price at which an orderly transaction would take place between market participants at the measurement date under current market conditions. Paragraph 62 of AASB 13/IFRS 13 notes three widely used valuation techniques:
1. market approach
2. cost approach
3. income approach.

The **market approach** is defined in Appendix A of AASB 13/IFRS 13 as follows.

A valuation technique that uses prices and other relevant information generated by market transactions involving identical or comparable (i.e. similar) assets, liabilities or a group of assets and liabilities, such as a business.

The market approach involves direct observation of what is occurring in a market. Prices are obtained directly from information gathered from the activities in markets. For example, applying the market approach to measure the fair value of used vehicles would involve obtaining prices based on market transactions at auctions and second-hand car yards. Assets such as cars do not have to be *identical* (e.g. in terms of the colour or extent of rust spots); prices may be based on *comparable* assets in the market. Sometimes an asset may have features that make it different from the asset whose fair value is being measured (e.g. a vehicle may have a sunroof or a satellite navigation device). The fair value would then be based on the price for the vehicle in the market adjusted for the differences between the two vehicles. Similarly, the market approach might be applied to a power station by relying on the price of quoted securities for a comparable power company.

The **cost approach** is defined in Appendix A of AASB 13/IFRS 13 as follows.

A valuation technique that reflects the amount that would be required currently to replace the service capacity of an asset (often referred to as current replacement cost).

The cost approach is based on the amount a market participant would pay to acquire or construct an asset that has the same qualities as the asset being valued. The cost may be that for the construction of an identical asset by the entity itself or by paying another entity to physically make the asset. Where the asset being valued is a used asset, the cost of a new version of the asset is adjusted for physical deterioration and technological changes; for example, the cost of a new Boeing 787 Dreamliner adjusted for wear and tear based on flight hours.

The **income approach** is defined in Appendix A of AASB 13/IFRS 13 as follows.

Valuation techniques that convert future amounts (e.g. cash flows or income and expenses) to a single current (i.e. discounted) amount. The fair value measurement is determined on the basis of the value indicated by current market expectations about those future amounts.

The fair value determined under the income approach is based upon market expectations about future cash flows, or income and expenses associated with the asset. Present value techniques are an example of techniques used in applying the income approach. The fair value of an asset is generated by discounting the expected net cash flows from the use of the asset by a market participant. In determining a present value measurement, a number of components need to be present. These are detailed in paragraph B13 of AASB 13/IFRS 13:

(a) an estimate of future cash flows for the asset or liability being measured.
(b) expectations about possible variations in the amount and timing of the cash flows representing the uncertainty inherent in the cash flows.
(c) the time value of money, represented by the rate on risk-free monetary assets that have maturity dates or durations that coincide with the period covered by the cash flows and pose neither uncertainty in timing nor risk of default to the holder (i.e. the risk-free interest rate).
(d) the price for bearing the uncertainty inherent in the cash flows (i.e. a *risk premium*).
(e) other factors that market participants would take into account in the circumstances.
(f) for a liability, the non-performance risk relating to that liability, including the entity's (i.e. the obligor's) own credit risk.

In using a present value technique, it is necessary to make assumptions about cash flows and discount rates. According to paragraph B14 of AASB 13/IFRS 13:

(a) Cash flows and discount rates should reflect assumptions that market participants would use when pricing the asset or liability.
(b) Cash flows and discount rates should take into account only the factors attributable to the asset or liability being measured.
(c) To avoid double-counting or omitting the effects of risk factors, discount rates should reflect assumptions that are consistent with those inherent in the cash flows. For example, a discount rate that reflects the uncertainty in expectations about future defaults is appropriate if using contractual cash flows of a loan (i.e. a discount rate adjustment technique). That same rate should not be used if using expected

(i.e. probability-weighted) cash flows (i.e. an expected present value technique) because the expected cash flows already reflect assumptions about the uncertainty in future defaults; instead a discount rate that is commensurate with the risk inherent in the expected cash flows should be used.

(d) Assumptions about cash flows and discount rates should be internally consistent. For example, nominal cash flows, which include the effect of inflation, should be discounted at a rate that includes the effect of inflation. The nominal risk-free rate includes the effect of inflation. Real cash flows, which exclude the effect of inflation, should be discounted at a rate that excludes the effect of inflation. Similarly, after-tax cash flows should be discounted using an after-tax discount rate. Pre-tax cash flows should be discounted at a rate consistent with those cash flows.

(e) Discount rates should be consistent with the underlying economic factors of the currency in which the cash flows are denominated.

Choice of technique

The choice of technique will ultimately depend on the circumstances, the data available and the extent of observable and non-observable inputs. Some techniques are likely to be better than others in some circumstances. For example, the appropriate technique to determine the fair value of one share in Telstra Corporation Limited at a measurement date is invariably the market approach. In contrast, the appropriate technique to determine the fair value of a highly specialised and unique item of plant may be the income approach. Judgement is required in selecting an appropriate technique for the situation. In some cases, different techniques might be considered, but the eventual choice must be weighed and evaluated against the three criteria in paragraph 61 of AASB 13/IFRS 13. In this regard, the standard includes a fair value hierarchy based on the inputs to the valuation techniques to assist the judgement process.

Valuation techniques used to measure fair value must be consistently applied. A change in technique may, however, be appropriate in some circumstances, such as when market conditions change, new markets develop, new information becomes available or new valuation techniques emerge. Illustrative example 3.5 shows how different valuation techniques may be used for an asset.

ILLUSTRATIVE EXAMPLE 3.5

Valuation techniques for an asset

As a by-product of its own manufacturing, the Australian company Magpie Ltd has developed a tool that enables certain machines to run more productively. There are a number of other non-competing Australian companies that can use this tool in their manufacturing processes. Rather than manufacture and sell this tool, Magpie Ltd decided to allow these other companies to manufacture and use the tool under a licensing program.

Required
How would Magpie Ltd measure the fair value of the licence?

Solution
In measuring the fair value of the licence, Magpie Ltd has to determine the highest and best use of the licence. The company has determined that the highest and best use of the licence is in conjunction with other assets in the manufacturing process. The valuation premise is then 'in-combination'.

The licence for the tool is unique as there are no comparable items of machinery in the market to determine fair value. Two possible valuation techniques could be used to measure the fair value of the licence for the tool.

1. *The income approach.* The present value of the fees obtainable from selling licences to other entities over the economic life of the licence is determined.
2. *The cost approach.* The cost of a licence from developing a comparable tool using current manufacturing techniques and at current costs is determined.

Inputs to valuation techniques

Appendix A of AASB 13/IFRS 13 defines **inputs** as follows.

The assumptions that market participants would use when pricing the asset or liability, including assumptions about risk, such as the following:
(a) the risk inherent in a particular valuation technique used to measure fair value (such as a pricing model); and
(b) the risk inherent in the inputs to the valuation technique.

Assumptions will be made in the application of a valuation technique, regardless of which technique is used. A key aspect of the inputs is their classification into *observable* or *unobservable* inputs. **Observable inputs** are defined in Appendix A of AASB 13/IFRS 13 as follows.

> Inputs that are developed using market data, such as publicly available information about actual events or transactions, and that reflect the assumptions that market participants would use when pricing the asset or liability.

Unobservable inputs are defined in Appendix A of AASB 13/IFRS 13 as follows.

> Inputs for which market data are not available and that are developed using the best information available about the assumptions that market participants would use when pricing the asset or liability.

The valuation technique applied in the measurement of fair value of an asset must maximise the use of observable inputs and minimise the use of unobservable inputs. Hence, an income approach valuation technique that maximises the use of observable inputs and minimises the use of unobservable inputs may provide a better measure of fair value than a market valuation technique that requires significant adjustment using unobservable inputs.

Fair value hierarchy — prioritising inputs

To achieve consistency and comparability in the measurement of fair values, there is a hierarchy that shows which inputs are given higher priority in determining a fair value measurement. Four points critical to understanding the uses of inputs are as follows.

1. The inputs are *prioritised* into three levels: Level 1 (highest), Level 2 and Level 3 (lowest) (AASB 13/IFRS 13 paragraph 72).
2. The fair value hierarchy gives the *highest priority* to quoted market prices in active markets for identical assets and liabilities and the *lowest priority* to unobservable inputs (AASB 13/IFRS 13 paragraph 72).
3. Where observable inputs are used, they must be *relevant* observable inputs (AASB 13/IFRS 13 paragraph 67). As noted in paragraph BC151 of the Basis for Conclusions on AASB 13/IFRS 13, some respondents to the IASB expressed concerns about being required to use observable inputs during the global financial crisis of 2007–08 when the available observable inputs were not representative of the asset or liability being measured at fair value. Observability is not the only criteria applied when selecting inputs; the inputs must be relevant as well as observable. Market conditions may require adjustments to be made to current observable inputs in measuring fair value.
4. The availability of inputs and their relative subjectivity potentially affect the selection of the valuation technique; however, the fair value hierarchy prioritises the *inputs* to the valuation techniques, not the techniques themselves (AASB 13/IFRS 13 paragraph 74).

Having selected the inputs and applied a valuation technique(s), a fair value measurement is made. According to paragraph 73 of AASB 13/IFRS 13, the fair value measure must then be categorised *in its entirety* at the same level as the *lowest* level input that is significant to the entire measurement. Hence, a valuation technique that relies solely on Level 1 inputs produces a Level 1 valuation measurement. A measurement that uses some Level 2 and some Level 3 inputs that are significant to the fair value measure would be classified as a Level 3 valuation measurement. Paragraph 93(b) of AASB 13/IFRS 13 requires, for each class of assets and liabilities measured at fair value, the disclosure of the level of the fair value hierarchy within which the fair value measurements are categorised in their entirety (Level 1, 2 or 3).

Level 1 inputs

Level 1 inputs are defined in Appendix A of AASB 13/IFRS 13 as follows.

> Quoted prices (unadjusted) in active markets for identical assets or liabilities that the entity can access at the measurement date.

The term **active market** is also defined, as follows.

> A market in which transactions for the asset or liability take place with sufficient frequency and volume to provide pricing information on an ongoing basis.

Markets such as those for vehicles, property, taxi licences and equity instruments on a securities exchange would generally be regarded as active markets. In contrast, active markets do not generally exist for intangible assets such as patents and trademarks. According to paragraph 77 of AASB 13/IFRS 13, a quoted price in an active market provides the most reliable evidence of fair value and shall be used without adjustment whenever available.

A market would not be considered to be active if:

- there has been a significant decrease in the volume and level of activity for the asset when compared with normal market activity
- there are few recent transactions
- price quotations are not based on current information
- price quotations vary substantially over time or among market-makers.

Shares and other financial instruments — both financial assets — are examples of assets that are identical and traded in active markets. Level 1 inputs must also be prices for *identical* assets. Buildings, for example, may be similar, but they are not identical. New vehicles may be identical, but it is unlikely that used vehicles would be identical — because of different usage and history.

According to paragraph 79 of AASB 13/IFRS 13 an adjustment to a Level 1 input can only be made in limited circumstances; for example, quoted prices where a significant event (new information) has emerged after the close of business for the market. When such an adjustment is made the fair value measurement is categorised at a lower level in the hierarchy.

Level 2 inputs

Level 2 inputs are defined in Appendix A of AASB 13/IFRS 13 as follows.

> Inputs other than quoted prices included within Level 1 that are observable for the asset or liability, either directly or indirectly.

Similar to Level 1 inputs, Level 2 inputs are observable. In contrast to Level 1 inputs, Level 2 inputs do not have to be for identical assets or liabilities. According to paragraph 82 of AASB 13/IFRS 13, Level 2 inputs include:

- quoted prices for similar assets or liabilities in active markets
- quoted prices for identical or similar assets or liabilities in markets that are not active
- inputs other than quoted prices that are observable for the asset or liability, such as interest rates and yield curves at commonly quoted intervals, implied volatilities, and credit spreads
- inputs that are derived from or corroborated by observable market data by correlation or other means.

It may be necessary to make adjustments to Level 2 inputs. For example, in relation to quoted prices for similar assets, adjustments may be needed for the condition or location of the asset or the volume/level of activity of the market in which the inputs are observed. Depending where the information for the adjustments is found, making adjustments may lead to the fair value measure being categorised at Level 3 rather than Level 2.

Paragraph B35 of AASB 13/IFRS 13 contains some examples of Level 2 inputs, as follows.

- *Finished goods inventory at a retail outlet.* Level 2 inputs include either a price to customers in a retail market or a wholesale price to retailers in a wholesale market adjusted for differences between the condition and location of the inventory item and a comparable (i.e. similar) inventory item.
- *Building held and used.* A Level 2 input would be the price per square metre for the building derived from observable market data, or derived from prices in observed transactions involving comparable buildings in similar locations.
- *Cash-generating unit.* A Level 2 input could be obtained by observing transactions of similar businesses (e.g. obtaining a multiple of earnings or revenue from observable market data).

In all cases, reference is made to market data, and the prices are observable either directly (i.e. the price is available) or indirectly (i.e. information is derived from prices).

Level 3 inputs

Level 3 inputs are defined in Appendix A of AASB 13/IFRS 13 as follows.

> Unobservable inputs for the asset or liability.

Whereas Level 1 and Level 2 inputs are based on observable market data, Level 3 inputs are unobservable. The data used may be that of the entity itself, and may be adjusted to reflect factors that market participants may build into the valuation or to eliminate the effects of variables that are specific to this entity but not relevant to other market participants.

Paragraph B36 of AASB 13/IFRS 13 contains some examples of Level 3 inputs as follows.

- *Cash-generating unit*. A Level 3 input would include a financial forecast of cash flow or earnings based on the entity's own data.
- *Trademark*. A Level 3 input would be to measure the expected royalty rate that could be obtained by allowing other entities to use the trademark to produce the products covered by the trademark.
- *Accounts receivable*. A Level 3 input would be to measure the asset based upon the amount expected to be recovered given the entity's historical record of recoverability of accounts receivable.

In all cases the fair value measure is based upon inputs that are not observable in a market.

Illustrative example 3.6 discusses different valuation techniques that could be used to measure the fair value of an asset, with a consideration of the level of inputs that might be used.

ILLUSTRATIVE EXAMPLE 3.6

Valuation techniques and inputs used

Kookaburra Ltd is a building supplies company servicing large construction businesses as well as the do-it-yourself home improvements market. Its products are sold out of warehouses that display the goods for sale in racks separated by aisles. Kookaburra Ltd recently acquired the business of a competitor, Kingfisher Ltd, which also uses the warehouse type structure for sale of hardware products. However, the warehouses operated by Kingfisher Ltd have aisles that are smaller than normal. Hence, the trolleys used by Kingfisher Ltd to move products between the shelves had to be adapted for use in smaller aisles.

In measuring the fair value of the trolleys used in Kingfisher Ltd's warehouses, it has been determined that the highest and best use of the trolleys is in combination with other assets. The trolleys by themselves do not generate income. Income is generated by the warehouses, which are generally regarded as the appropriate cash generating units.

Required
Which valuation techniques could be used to measure the fair value of the trolleys? What inputs would be required for each? How would the final choice of technique be made?

Solution
In choosing valuation techniques to measure fair value, both the market approach and the cost approach are appropriate. The income approach is not appropriate as there is no income stream associated with the trolleys themselves.

- *Market approach*. Using the market approach, it is necessary to obtain quoted prices of comparable used trolleys available in the market. These quoted market prices would need to be adjusted for such factors as current condition (wear and tear, and age), location and transport costs as well as any costs associated with converting these trolleys for use in the narrow aisles of the Kingfisher Ltd warehouses. The inputs used under the market approach are classified as Level 2 inputs as they are observable market prices but are not for identical assets.
- *Cost approach*. Using the cost approach, it is necessary to determine the cost of constructing a trolley of the same size, quality and usefulness as those held by Kingfisher Ltd. Because the cost would be the cost of a new machine, adjustments would need to be made for the effects of wear and tear as experienced by the currently held trolleys. The inputs used in this calculation are also Level 2 inputs as they are based on market prices of raw materials and labour costs used in the construction process.

In choosing between the two methods, it's important to consider:
- the level of estimation used in the calculations, as this affects the objectivity of the fair value
- if there are alternative markets for trolleys, the effects of availability and the range of prices given
- the effects on the calculations of the need to adjust the trolleys for use by Kingfisher Ltd. As adjusted trolleys are not available in the market, this tends to suggest it is better to use the cost method. Under the latter the cost of adjusting the machines is directly considered
- under the market approach, if there are no readily found second-hand markets for used trolleys then the determination of the market value of used trolleys is more difficult.

In both the market approach and cost approach, the final fair value measure is likely to be classified as a Level 2 valuation as the significant inputs are classified as Level 2.

3.4 Application to liabilities

LEARNING OBJECTIVE 3.4 Apply the fair value measurement principles to liabilities.

The measurement of a liability at cost is based on the amount required to *settle* the present obligation. As per its definition in AASB 13/IFRS 13 however, fair value is the amount paid to *transfer* a liability. The fair value measurement thus assumes that the liability is transferred to another market participant at the measurement date. According to paragraph 34(a) of AASB 13/IFRS 13, the transfer assumes the:

- liability would remain outstanding
- market participant transferee would be required to fulfil the obligation
- liability would not be settled with the counterparty or otherwise extinguished on the measurement date.

Paragraph BC82 of the Basis for Conclusions on AASB 13/IFRS 13 notes that the fair value of a liability from the perspective of a market participant who owes the liability is the same regardless of whether it is settled or transferred. This is because both settlement and transfer of a liability reflect all costs incurred, whether direct or indirect. Therefore, the entity faces the same risks as a market participant transferee. Similar thought processes are needed to estimate both the amount to settle a liability and the amount to transfer that liability.

Many of the principles dealing with the measurement of fair value of non-financial assets also apply to the measurement of the fair value of liabilities. There are four steps in measuring the fair value of an asset. In contrast, no valuation premise is required for liabilities. Hence, there are only *three* steps in the measurement process for liabilities — the entity must determine the:

1. particular liability that is the subject of the measurement (consistent with its unit of account)
2. principal (or most advantageous) market for the liability
3. valuation technique(s) appropriate for the measurement.

The question of the highest and best use applies only when determining the fair value of an asset. Paragraph BC65 of the Basis for Conclusions of AASB 13/IFRS 13 states the highest and best use concept does not apply to liabilities. The ability of an entity to discharge a liability in a number of ways, such as immediate settlement or fulfilment of the contract, is not seen as a liability having alternative uses. Also entity-specific factors are not considered to affect fair value.

For some liabilities, such as financial liabilities, an observable market may exist and a quoted price may be obtained to measure the fair value of the liability. Where this is not available, valuation techniques must be used. The objective of a fair value measurement of a liability, when using a valuation technique, is to estimate the price that would be paid to transfer the liability between market participants at the measurement date under current market conditions. In all cases, an entity must maximise the use of relevant observable inputs and minimise the use of unobservable inputs.

3.4.1 Corresponding asset approach

In most circumstances, a liability will be *held as an asset* by another entity. For example, a loan is recognised as a payable by one entity (the recipient of the loan) and a receivable by another entity (the lender). Paragraph 37 of AASB 13/IFRS 13 recognises this symmetry. If a quoted price for the transfer of an identical or similar liability is unavailable, then the measurement of the fair value of the liability must be calculated from the perspective of a market participant that holds the identical item as an asset at measurement date. In this case, the fair value of the liability equals the fair value of a properly defined corresponding asset.

Paragraph 38 of AASB 13/IFRS 13 states that the measurement of the corresponding asset should be made, in descending order of preference, by:
- using the quoted price of the asset in an active market
- using the quoted price for the asset in a market that is not active
- applying a valuation technique, such as:
  - an income approach — present value techniques could be employed using the future cash flows a market participant would expect to receive from holding the liability as an asset
  - a market approach — the measure would be based on quoted prices for similar liabilities held by other parties as assets.

Illustrative example 3.7 provides an example of a liability measured by reference to the asset held by another entity.

ILLUSTRATIVE EXAMPLE 3.7

Liability held as an asset by another entity

On 1 July 2021, Parrot Ltd issued 100 000 5% debentures. These were bought by a wide variety of investors and the debentures were traded in the local securities market. At the end of the financial year these securities were trading at $990 per $1000 of debentures.

Required
How would Parrot Ltd measure the liability relating to the debentures at fair value?

Solution
As the local securities market is an active market, Parrot Ltd would measure the fair value of the debentures based upon the quoted market price at year-end. Hence, Parrot Ltd would measure the fair value of the debentures at $990 000 at 30 June 2022.

If the market was not considered active because the trade in the securities was not of sufficient volume or frequency to provide pricing information, then potentially a valuation method such as present value or a measure based on quoted prices for similar liabilities would need to be used.

In some circumstances, a *corresponding asset is not held* by another entity, such as in the case of an entity that must decommission an oil platform when drilling ceases. Here, the entity measuring the fair value of the liability must use a valuation technique from the perspective of a market participant that owes the liability (AASB 13/IFRS 13 paragraph 40). In such cases a present value technique could be applied.

Paragraph B13 of AASB 13/IFRS 13 notes that the following elements will be captured by using a present value technique:
- an estimate of future cash flows
- expectations about variations in the amount and timing of the cash flows representing the uncertainty inherent in the cash flows
- the time value of money, represented by a risk-free interest rate
- a risk premium, being the price for bearing the uncertainty inherent in the cash flows
- other factors that market participants would take into account
- non-performance risk.

An example of the use of the present value technique for a simple debt obligation is given in illustrative example 3.8. The present value technique may also be used for non-financial liabilities, such as when a mining company is required to restore the land subsequent to the completion of mining activities. In such cases all future outlays necessary for restoration of the land, such as future labour costs and raw materials, would need to be discounted to the date of measuring the fair value of the liability. The discount rate used would reflect the time value of money adjusted by the non-performance risk associated with the company not being able to meet its obligation, including its own credit risk.

ILLUSTRATIVE EXAMPLE 3.8

Present value technique: debt obligation

Using the same information as in illustrative example 3.7 assume the market was not considered to be active and a present value method was used to measure fair value. The present value is calculated at 30 June 2022. The expected cash flows are the payment of interest of $5000 at the end of each of the next 4 years (i.e. an annuity of $5000 for 4 years) and the return of the $100 000 face value of the debentures at the end of the fourth year. The interest rate is based on the market rate for similar liabilities at 30 June 2022. Assume at 30 June 2022 this is 6%.

Required
How would the fair value be measured?

Solution
The fair value should reflect the price that would be paid by Parrot Ltd to transfer the liability to market participants at the measurement date under current market conditions. The present value (PV) is calculated as follows.

$5000 × 3.4651 (PV of an annuity for 4 years at 6%)	$17 326
$100 000 × 0.792094 (PV of a single sum at the end of 4 years at 6%)	79 209
	$96 535

The fair value of the debentures at 30 June 2022 is $96 535.

3.4.2 Non-performance risk and credit enhancements

According to paragraph 43 of AASB 13/IFRS 13, when measuring the fair value of a liability, it is necessary to consider the effect of an entity's credit risk and any other risk factors that may influence the likelihood that the obligation will not be fulfilled. The effect may differ depending on:

(a) whether the liability is an obligation to deliver cash (a financial liability) or an obligation to deliver goods or services (a non-financial liability).
(b) the terms of credit enhancements related to the liability, if any.

The fair value of a liability will reflect the effect of credit risk or **non-performance risk**, which is defined in Appendix A of AASB 13/IFRS 13 as follows.

> The risk that an entity will not fulfil an obligation. Non-performance risk includes, but may not be limited to, the entity's own credit risk [or credit standing].

Non-performance risk includes an entity's own credit risk. The fair value will also include the effect of any credit enhancement such as a third-party guarantee of debt.

Illustrative example 3.9 demonstrates the valuation of liabilities with a consideration of non-performance risk.

ILLUSTRATIVE EXAMPLE 3.9

Valuation of liabilities and non-performance risk

At 1 July 2022 Blue Ltd lent $10 000 each to two other entities, Red Ltd and Green Ltd.

Red Ltd agreed to pay the $10 000 back in 3 years' time. At 30 June 2023, based upon its own credit rating, Red Ltd can borrow money at 5.5%.

At 30 June 2023, because of an improvement in its credit rating, Green Ltd can borrow money at 4.9%.

Required
What is the fair value of the liability of Red Ltd and Green Ltd at 30 June 2023?

Solution
Red Ltd would calculate its liability using an interest rate that reflects its own ability to pay, this being affected by its own credit risk. The fair value of the liability at 30 June 2023 by Red Ltd is then the present value of the payment of $1000 at the end of 2 years using the 5.5% interest rate applicable to Red Ltd.

$10 000 × 0.8985 (PV of a single sum at the end of 2 years at 5.5%)	$8985

In contrast, at 30 June 2023 Green Ltd can borrow money at 4.9%. The fair value of the liability of Green Ltd at 30 June 2023 is then calculated in the same way as for Red Ltd but instead a 4.9% interest rate would be applied.

| $10 000 × 0.9088 (PV of a single sum at the end of 2 years at 4.9%) | $9088 |

In the initial recognition of the liability by Red Ltd and Green Ltd, as well as at the measurement of the fair value at each subsequent year-end, the credit standing of the entities is taken into account in determining the interest rate to be applied in the measurement of fair value using the present value method. Hence, as a company's credit rating declines and cost of borrowing increases, the fair value of a liability based on present value measurement may decrease. If accounting standards permitted restatement of the liability, the decrease in fair value arising from the decline in credit rating would result in a gain, which is somewhat counterintuitive.

3.5 Application to an entity's own equity instruments

LEARNING OBJECTIVE 3.5 Discuss the measurement of the fair values of an entity's own equity instruments.

Measurement of equity instruments may be needed in circumstances where an entity undertakes a business combination and issues its own equity instruments in exchange for a business. The principles relating to the fair value measurement of liabilities generally apply to equity instruments also.

The fair value measure assumes that an entity's own equity instruments are transferred to a market participant at measurement date. According to paragraph 34(b) of AASB 13/IFRS 13, the transfer assumes that an entity's own equity instrument would remain outstanding and the market participant transferee would take on the rights and responsibilities associated with the instrument. The instrument would not be cancelled or otherwise extinguished on the measurement date.

In measuring an equity instrument at fair value, as with assets and liabilities, the objective is to estimate an exit price at measurement date from the perspective of a market participant who holds the instrument as an asset. If a company is the issuer of an equity instrument such as an ordinary share, then in order to exit from that instrument, the company must either cancel the share or repurchase the share. The company must then measure the fair value of the equity instrument from the perspective of a market participant who holds the instrument as an asset; for example, the company would have to consider what it would need to pay a shareholder to repurchase the share.

3.6 Issues relating to application to financial instruments

LEARNING OBJECTIVE 3.6 Explain some of the issues relating to financial instruments.

Financial instruments consist of both financial assets and financial liabilities. AASB 132/IAS 32 *Financial Instruments: Presentation* contains definitions of these terms. This section covers two issues relating to the fair value measurement of financial instruments.

3.6.1 Inputs based on bid and ask prices

Some input measures are based on market prices where there are both bid prices (the price a dealer is willing to pay) and ask prices (the price a dealer is willing to sell). An example is a foreign exchange dealer who is willing to exchange one currency for another, such as exchanging Australian dollars for Japanese yen. In such cases, paragraph 70 of AASB 13/IFRS 13 states that the price within a bid–ask spread that is most representative of fair value should be used to measure fair value. Paragraph 71 of AASB 13/ IFRS 13 notes that a mid-market price may be used as a practical expedient for fair value measurements within a bid–ask spread.

3.6.2 Offsetting positions

An entity may hold both financial assets and financial liabilities, and as such is exposed to both market risk and credit risk. An entity may hold both assets and liabilities in a particular market and manage these as a group, having a net exposure to risk.

In such a situation, an entity may apply an exception in the measurement of fair value. Paragraph 48 of AASB 13/IFRS 13 states that in such circumstances the measurement of the net financial asset may be based on the price that would be received to sell a net long position, while for a net financial liability the measurement would be based on the price to transfer a net short position for a particular risk exposure in an orderly market.

Paragraph 49 of AASB 13/IFRS 13 provides conditions under which this exception may be applied, including that an entity must manage the group of financial assets and liabilities on a net exposure basis as a part of its documented risk management strategy.

LEARNING CHECK

☐ Measuring the fair value of financial assets and liabilities requires the application of the general principles applicable to measuring the fair value of non-financial assets and liabilities.
☐ Where a market has both a bid and an ask process, the most representative price is used in measuring fair value.

3.7 Disclosure requirements

LEARNING OBJECTIVE 3.7 Appreciate the disclosures required where assets, liabilities or equity is measured at fair value.

Paragraphs 91–99 of AASB 13/IFRS 13 set out the disclosures required for fair value measurements. The key principle is stated in paragraph 91:

> An entity shall disclose information that helps users of its financial statements assess both of the following:
> (a) for assets and liabilities that are measured at fair value on a recurring or non-recurring basis in the statement of financial position after initial recognition, the valuation techniques and inputs used to develop those measurements.
> (b) for recurring fair value measurements using significant unobservable inputs (Level 3), the effect of the measurements on profit or loss or other comprehensive income for the period.

'Recurring' fair value measures are those that other accounting standards require or permit in the statement of financial position at the end of the reporting period; for example, the fair value of property under AASB 116/IAS 16 *Property, Plant and Equipment*. 'Non-recurring' fair value measurements are those that other accounting standards require or permit in particular circumstances; for example, the fair value less costs to sell of a non-current asset held for sale under AASB 5/IFRS 5 *Non-current Assets Held for Sale and Discontinued Operations*.

In order for users of the financial statements to be able to assess the relevance of the fair value information provided, the disclosure of both the valuation techniques used to measure fair value as well as the inputs used to measure fair value is required. All fair value methods are potentially able to provide reliable measures of fair value; however, users need disclosures about the methods used and the inputs in order to be able to assess the extent of subjectivity of the techniques used.

Paragraph 93 of AASB 13/IFRS 13 requires the following be disclosed for each class of assets and liabilities measured at fair value:

(a) ... the fair value measurement at the end of the reporting period and, for non-recurring measurements, the reasons for the measurement

(b) ... the level of the fair value hierarchy within which the fair value measurements are categorised in their entirety (Level 1, 2 or 3)

(c) ... the amounts of any transfers between Level 1 and Level 2 of the fair value hierarchy, the reasons for those transfers and the entity's policy for determining when transfers between levels are deemed to have occurred

(d) ... the valuation techniques used and the inputs [relating to] fair value measurements [categorised within Level 2 and Level 3 of the fair value hierarchy]. If there has been a change in [the] valuation technique [used, this fact must be disclosed as well as the reasons for change. Where the inputs are categorised as Level 3], an entity [must disclose] quantitative information about the significant unobservable inputs used in the fair value measurement

(e) ... a reconciliation from the opening balances to the closing balances, disclosing separately changes ... [for recurring fair value measurements categorised within Level 3 of the fair value hierarchy]

(f) ... the amount of [unrealised] gains and losses for the period ... and the line item(s) in profit or loss [where those gains and losses are recognised for recurring fair value measurements categorised within Level 3 of the fair value hierarchy]

(g) ... the valuation processes used ... including how an entity decides its valuation policies and procedures and analyses changes in [fair value for] fair value measurements [categorised within Level 3 of the fair value hierarchy]

(h) ... the sensitivity of the fair value measurement to changes in unobservable inputs, [including] reasonably possible alternative assumptions [for recurring fair value measurements categorised within Level 3 of the fair value hierarchy]

(i) ... [the fact that the *current use* of an asset differs from] its *highest and best use* [as well as the reasons the] asset is being used in a manner that differs from its highest and best use.

According to paragraph 94 of AASB 13/IFRS 13, the classes of assets and liabilities for the disclosure requirements must be determined on the basis of: the nature, characteristics and risks of the asset or liability; and the level of the fair value hierarchy within which the fair value measurement is categorised. It is expected that the number of classes for Level 3 will be greater than Levels 1 and 2 because of the relatively greater degree of uncertainty and subjectivity at Level 3. Paragraph 99 of AASB 13/ IFRS 13 requires that any quantitative disclosures be presented in a tabular format unless another format is more appropriate.

Paragraph 97 of AASB 13/IFRS 13 also requires the disclosures set out at paragraphs 93 (b), (d) and (i) — except the quantitative information for significant unobservable inputs at Level 3 — for each class of assets and liabilities that is not measured at fair value but for which fair value is disclosed in the notes to the financial statements.

Figure 3.1 demonstrates the disclosures required to comply with paragraphs 93(a) and (b) of AASB 13/IFRS 13.

FIGURE 3.1 Disclosure requirements complying with paragraphs 93(a) and (b) of AASB 13/IFRS 13

| (CU in millions) | Fair value measurements at the end of the reporting period using | | | | |
Description	31/12/X9	Quoted prices in active markets for identical assets (Level 1)	Significant other observable inputs (Level 2)	Significant unobservable inputs (Level 3)	Total gains (losses)
Recurring fair value measurements					
Trading equity securities[a]:					
Real estate industry	93	70	23		
Oil and gas industry	45	45			
Other	15	15			
Total trading equity securities	153	130	23		

(CU in millions)		Fair value measurements at the end of the reporting period using			
Description	31/12/X9	Quoted prices in active markets for identical assets (Level 1)	Significant other observable inputs (Level 2)	Significant unobservable inputs (Level 3)	Total gains (losses)
Other equity securities[a]:					
Financial services industry	150	150			
Healthcare industry	163	110		53	
Energy industry	32			32	
Private equity fund investments[b]	25			25	
Other	15	15			
Total other equity securities	385	275		110	
Debt securities:					
Residential mortgage-backed securities	149		24	125	
Commercial mortgage-backed securities	50			50	
Collateralised debt obligations	35			35	
Risk-free government securities	85	85			
Corporate bonds	93	9	84		
Total debt securities	412	94	108	210	
Hedge fund investments:					
Equity long/short	55		55		
Global opportunities	35		35		
High-yield debt securities	90			90	
Total hedge fund investments	180		90	90	
Derivatives:					
Interest rate contracts	57		57		
Foreign exchange contracts	43		43		
Credit contracts	38			38	
Commodity futures contracts	78	78			
Commodity forward contracts	20		20		
Total derivatives	236	78	120	38	
Investment properties:					
Commercial — Asia	31			31	
Commercial — Europe	27			27	
Total investment properties	58			58	
Total recurring fair value measurements	1 424	577	341	506	
Non-recurring fair value measurements					
Assets held for sale[c]	26		26		(15)
Total non-recurring fair value measurements	26		26		(15)

[a]On the basis of its analysis of the nature, characteristics and risks of the securities, the entity has determined that presenting them by industry is appropriate.

[b]On the basis of its analysis of the nature, characteristics and risks of the investments, the entity has determined that presenting them as a single class is appropriate.

[c]In accordance with IFRS 5, assets held for sale with a carrying amount of CU35 million were written down to their fair value of CU26 million, less costs to sell of CU6 million (or CU20 million), resulting in a loss of CU15 million, which was included in profit or loss for the period.

(*Note:* A similar table would be presented for liabilities unless another format is deemed more appropriate by the entity.)

Source: IFRS 13, Example 15 — Assets measured at fair value, pp. 26–7.

LEARNING CHECK

☐ Disclosures are required for assets and liabilities measured at fair value.

☐ Users should be able to assess the methods and inputs used to develop the measures of fair value.

☐ Disclosures are required where a class of assets and liabilities is not measured at fair value but where the fair value is disclosed by way of note disclosure.

☐ Disclosures are required where the current use of an asset differs from its highest and best use.

SUMMARY

This chapter has covered the principles of measurement of fair values as contained in AASB 13/IFRS 13 *Fair Value Measurement*. Some of the key principles are as follows.

- Fair value is defined as an exit price, not an entry price.
- The concepts of orderly transactions and market participants assist in determining the market in which the fair value is measured.
- There are four steps in the measurement of the fair values of non-financial assets.
- The highest and best use of an asset establishes the valuation premise — stand-alone or in-combination — to be used in measuring the fair value.
- The measurement of fair value requires the determination of the principal (or most advantageous) market for the asset.
- Three valuation techniques are the market approach, the cost approach and the income approach.
- There is a hierarchy of information inputs into the valuation techniques which is prioritised into three levels: Level 1 (highest), Level 2 and Level 3 (lowest).
- Observable inputs have a higher priority than unobservable inputs.
- A fair value measure is categorised in its entirety at the same level as the lowest level input that is significant to the entire measurement.

KEY TERMS

active market A market in which transactions for the asset or liability take place with sufficient frequency and volume to provide pricing information on an ongoing basis.

cost approach A valuation technique that reflects the amount that would be required currently to replace the service capacity of an asset (often referred to as current replacement cost).

exit price The price that would be received to sell an asset or paid to transfer a liability.

fair value The price that would be received to sell an asset or paid to transfer a liability in an orderly transaction between market participants at the measurement date.

highest and best use The use of a non-financial asset by market participants that would maximise the value of the asset or the group of assets and liabilities (e.g. a business) within which the asset would be used.

income approach Valuation techniques that convert future amounts (e.g. cash flows or income and expenses) to a single current (i.e. discounted) amount. The fair value measurement is determined on the basis of the value indicated by current market expectations about those future amounts.

inputs The assumptions that market participants would use when pricing the asset or liability, including assumptions about risk.

Level 1 inputs Quoted prices (unadjusted) in active markets for identical assets or liabilities that the entity can access at the measurement date.

Level 2 inputs Inputs other than quoted prices included within Level 1 that are observable for the asset or liability, either directly or indirectly.

Level 3 inputs Unobservable inputs for the asset or liability.

market approach A valuation technique that uses prices and other relevant information generated by market transactions involving identical or comparable (i.e. similar) assets, liabilities or a group of assets and liabilities, such as a business.

market participants Buyers and sellers in the principal market that are independent of each other, knowledgeable, and willing and able to enter into a transaction.

most advantageous market The market that maximises the amount that would be received to sell the asset or minimises the amount that would be paid to transfer the liability, after taking into account transaction costs and transport costs.

non-performance risk The risk that an entity will not fulfil an obligation. Non-performance risk includes, but may not be limited to, the entity's own credit risk.

observable inputs Inputs that are developed using market data, such as publicly available information about actual events or transactions, and reflect the assumptions that market participants would use when pricing the asset or liability.

orderly transaction A transaction that assumes exposure to the market for a period before the measurement date to allow for marketing activities that are usual and customary for transactions involving such assets or liabilities; it is not a forced transaction (e.g. a forced liquidation or distress sale).

principal market The market with the greatest volume and level of activity for the asset.

transaction costs Incremental costs that are directly attributable to the acquisition, issue or disposal of a financial asset or financial liability.

transport costs The costs that would be incurred to transport an asset from its current location to its principal (or most advantageous) market.

unobservable inputs Inputs for which market data are not available and that are developed using the best information available about the assumptions that market participants would use when pricing the asset or liability.

COMPREHENSION QUESTIONS

1 Name three current accounting standards that permit or require the use of fair values for the measurement of assets or liabilities.

2 What are the main objectives of AASB 13/IFRS 13? Discuss why such a standard was considered necessary.

3 What are the key elements of the definition of 'fair value'? Explain the effects of the inclusion of each element in the definition.

4 Compare entry price to exit price for specialised plant. How does AASB 13/IFRS 13 resolve the debate on which price to use?

5 What are market participants? Is the entity applying AASB 13/IRFS 13 a market participant?

6 Does the measurement of fair value take into account transport costs and transaction costs? Explain.

7 How does the measurement of the fair value of a liability differ from that of an asset? What are the key steps in determining a fair value measure?

8 Explain the difference between the current use of an asset and the highest and best use of that asset.

9 Explain the difference between the in-combination valuation premise and the stand-alone valuation premise.

10 What is the difference between an entity's principal market and its most advantageous market?

11 What are the issues associated with fair value measurement of assets without an active market?

12 What valuation techniques are available to measure fair value?

13 Discuss the differences between the various levels in the fair value hierarchy. Do you agree that the outcomes at all three levels should be described as 'fair values'?

14 Discuss the use of entity-specific information in the generation of fair value measurements under AASB 13/IFRS 13.

CASE STUDY 3.1

FAIR VALUES CAUSING TENSION IN THE ACCOUNTING PROFESSION

Find and read the following article: Cain, A 2013, 'Fair value continues to captivate', *Charter*, vol. 84, no. 6, 2 July, pp. 31–2.

ABSTRACT

A new accounting standard attempted to clear up the uncertainty, but the whole process of placing a value on something still requires attention.

Required

What difficulties have been identified by accounting practitioners in relation to the application of fair value measurement?

CASE STUDY 3.2

FAIR VALUES AND ENRON

Find and read the following article: Benston, G 2006, 'Fair value accounting: a cautionary tale from Enron', *Journal of Accounting and Public Policy*, vol. 25, no. 4, pp. 465–84.

ABSTRACT

The FASB's 2004 Exposure Draft, Fair-Value Measurements, would have companies determine fair values by reference to market prices on the same assets (level 1), similar assets (level 2) and, where these prices are not available or appropriate, present value and other internally generated estimated values (level 3). Enron extensively used level three estimates and, in some instances, level 2 estimates, for its external and internal reporting. A description of its use and misuse of fair-value accounting should provide some insights into the problems that auditors and financial statement users might face when companies use level 2 and, more importantly, level 3 fair valuations. Enron first used level 3 fair-value accounting for energy contracts, then for trading activities generally and undertakings designated as 'merchant' investments. Simultaneously, these fair values were used to evaluate and compensate senior employees. Enron's accountants (with Andersen's approval) used accounting devices to report cash flow from operations rather than financing and to otherwise cover up fair-value overstatements and losses on projects undertaken by managers whose compensation was based on fair values. Based on a chronologically ordered analysis of its activities and investments, I believe that Enron's use of fair-value accounting is substantially responsible for its demise.

Required

Describe the fair value accounting practices that emerged from the Enron scandal. In your view, are there sufficient safeguards to prevent a similar scandal in future?

CASE STUDY 3.3

FAIR VALUES

Find and read the following article: Whittington, G 2008 'Fair value and the IASB/FASB Conceptual Framework project: an alternative view', *Abacus*, vol. 44, no. 2, pp. 139–68.

ABSTRACT

This paper analyses various controversial issues arising from the ... project of the IASB and FASB to develop a joint conceptual framework for financial reporting standards. It discusses their possible implications for measurement and, in particular, for the use of fair value as the preferred measurement basis. Two competing world views are identified as underlying the debate: a Fair Value View, implicit in the IASB's public pronouncements, and an Alternative View implicit in publicly expressed criticisms of the IASB's pronouncements. The Fair Value View assumes that markets are relatively perfect and complete and that, in such a setting, financial reports should meet the needs of passive investors and creditors by reporting fair values derived from current market prices. The Alternative View assumes that markets are relatively imperfect and incomplete and that, in such a market setting, financial reports should also meet the monitoring requirements of current shareholders (stewardship) by reporting past transactions and events using entity-specific measurements that reflect the opportunities actually available to the reporting entity. The different implications of the two views are illustrated by reference to specific issues in recent accounting standards. Finally, the theoretical support for the two views is discussed. It is concluded that, in a realistic market setting, the search for a universal measurement method may be fruitless and a more appropriate approach to the measurement problem might be to define a clear measurement objective and to select the measurement method that best meets that objective in the particular circumstances that exist in relation to each item in the accounts. An example of such an approach is deprival value, which is not, at present, under consideration by the IASB.

Required

Whittington argues there are two broad schools of thought in relation to measurement: the fair value view and the alternative view. What are the main conceptual features of these two views? Explain which view you prefer.

CASE STUDY 3.4

FAIR VALUES OF PROPERTY, PLANT AND EQUIPMENT IN THE UNITED STATES

Find and read the following article: Hermann, D, Saudagaran, S & Thomas, W 2006, 'The quality of fair value measures for property, plant and equipment', *Accounting Forum*, vol. 30, no. 1, July, pp. 43–59.

ABSTRACT

Based on Statement of Financial Accounting Concepts (SFAC) No. 2, this paper argues for fair value measures of property, plant, and equipment and challenges the primary arguments in support of maintaining the current status quo in the United States — strict historical costs for all property, plant, and equipment unless the asset is impaired. We first provide a summary of the valuation of property, plant, and equipment internationally noting that revaluations to fair value are an acceptable practice under international and many national accounting standards. We also provide a brief historical perspective of accounting in the United States where prior to 1940 the upward valuation of property, plant, and equipment was an acceptable accounting alternative. We then evaluate fair value versus historical cost measures for property, plant, and equipment based on the qualitative characteristics of accounting information in SFAC No. 2. We argue that fair value measures for property, plant, and equipment are superior to historical cost based on the characteristics of predictive value, feedback value, timeliness, neutrality, representational faithfulness, comparability, and consistency. Verifiability appears to be the sole qualitative characteristic favoring historical cost over fair value. Finally, we address key measurement concepts for property, plant, and equipment. The United States could learn from the practices already established in other countries and in international financial reporting standards by reconsidering fair value measures for property, plant, and equipment.

Required

Summarise the history of revaluations of property, plant and equipment in the United States. What concerns led the United States to prevent property, plant and equipment being carried at an amount above cost to the entity?

CASE STUDY 3.5

FAIR VALUE ACCOUNTING: THE SHORTCOMINGS

Find and read the following article: Benston, G 2008, 'The shortcomings of fair value accounting described in SFAS 157', *Journal of Accounting and Public Policy*, vol. 27, no. 2, March–April, pp. 101–14.

ABSTRACT

Analysis of the examples given by the FASB to show how fair values, defined as exit prices, should be determined in specified circumstances is revealing. Such prices require determining what hypothetical companies might pay for assets, a costly procedure at best. Even though SFAS 157 specifies exit values, several examples employ values in use and entrance values. Although transaction costs must be excluded, they often are not. Fair valuation of non-financial assets, required in certain circumstances (e.g. business combinations), is particularly difficult to apply. Furthermore, exit values of such assets as work-in-process inventories and special-purpose machines, as defined by SFAS 157, often are zero or negative. Importantly, assets and liabilities restated at exit prices yield balance sheets and income statements that are of little, if any, value to investors in ongoing firms. Further, the examples presented show that fair values could be readily manipulated. Implementation of SFAS 157, therefore, is likely to be costly to investors and independent public accountants.

Required

Summarise Benston's main criticisms of fair value accounting in the United States and discuss if they are also applicable to AASB 13/IFRS 13.

CASE STUDY 3.6

FAIR VALUE MEASUREMENT DISCLOSURES

Find a recent annual report of a top 50 company listed on the Australian Securities Exchange (www.asx.com.au) that includes some assets and/or liabilities measured at fair value at the reporting date.

Required

Consistent with the requirements of AASB 13/IFRS 13, what disclosures have been made in the notes to the financial statements regarding the fair value measurement of assets and liabilities? Describe why the disclosures provide useful information to the users of the financial statements.

APPLICATION AND ANALYSIS EXERCISES

★ BASIC | ★ ★ MODERATE | ★ ★ ★ DIFFICULT

3.1 Valuation premise for measurement of fair value ★   LO3

Maple Ltd conducts a business that makes women's handbags. It operates a factory in an inner suburb of Perth. The factory contains a large amount of equipment that is used in the manufacture of handbags. Maple Ltd owns both the factory and the land on which the factory stands. The land was acquired in 2013 for $400 000 and the factory was built in that year at a cost of $1 040 000. Both assets are recorded at cost, with the factory having a carrying amount at 30 June 2023 of $520 000.

In recent years a property boom in Perth has seen residential house prices double. The average price of a house is now approximately $1 000 000. A property valuation group used data about recent sales of land in the area to value the land on which the factory stands at $2 000 000. The land is now considered prime residential property given its closeness to the coast and, with its superb ocean views, its suitability for building executive apartments. It would cost $200 000 to demolish the factory to make way for these apartments to be built. It is estimated that to build a new factory on the current site would cost around $1 560 000.

Required

The directors of Maple Ltd want to measure both the factory and the land at fair value as at 30 June 2023. Discuss how you would measure these fair values.

3.2 Valuation techniques and inputs used ★   LO3

An entity acquired a machine in a business combination that is held and used in its operations. The machine was initially acquired from a supplier and was then customised by the entity for use in its own operations. The highest and best use of the machine is its use in combination with other assets as a group. The valuation premise is then 'in-combination'.

Required

1. What two valuation techniques could be used to determine the fair value of the machine?
2. What would be the level of the inputs to the two valuation techniques?

3.3 Highest and best use ★   LO3

A response to the IASB's *Exposure Draft 2009/5 Fair Value Measurements*, stated:

> In practical terms we doubt that an asset measured on any other basis than its intended use will provide more useful information to readers.
>
> The fact that, say, a site used for production would have a higher market value if it were redeveloped for retail purposes, is not relevant if the entity is not engaged in retail or, more obviously, needs the site in order to carry out its production operations.
>
> The risk here is that the fair value measure, as redefined, results in irrelevant information.

Required

Discuss the issues associated with measuring the fair value of a site currently used for production, but which could be redeveloped for retail purposes.

3.4 Highest and best use ★   LO3

Cellar Ltd is in the business of bottling wine, particularly for small wineries that cannot afford sophisticated technical equipment and prefer to concentrate on the growing of the grapes. The white wine and champagne bottles used by Cellar Ltd have a built-in insulation device that keeps the contents of the bottle cold even when held in the hand.

In January 2023, Solar-Blue, a company experimenting with energy sources useful in combating climate change, produced a device which, when attached to the outside of a container, could display the temperature of the liquid inside. The temperature was displayed by the highlighting of certain colours on the device. How this device could be used with wine bottles had yet to be determined. However, Cellar Ltd believed that its employees had the skills that would enable the company to determine the feasibility of such a project. Whether the costs of incorporating the device into wine bottles would be prohibitive was unknown.

Cellar Ltd was concerned that competing wine-bottling companies might acquire the device from Solar-Blue, so it paid $100 000 for the exclusive rights to use the device in conjunction with bottles.

Required

The accountant wants to measure the fair value of the asset acquired. Discuss the process of determining this fair value.

3.5 'In-combination' valuation premise ★   LO3

Palm Ltd acquired a business that used a large number of assets that worked in combination to produce a product saleable in offshore markets. The assets of the business include a computer program that transfers the inputs to the manufacturing process around the assets that work together to produce the output.

In measuring the fair value of the computer program, management of Palm Ltd determined that the valuation premise was 'in-combination' as the program worked together with other assets in the business.

Required

Discuss how the various valuation approaches may be applied in the determination of the fair value of the computer program.

3.6 Most advantageous market ★   LO3

Asset PYJ is sold in three different active markets.

- In Market I, the price that would be received is $54; transaction costs are $4 and the transport costs are $6.
- In Market II, the price that would be received is $52; transaction costs are $4 and the transport costs are $2.
- In Market III, the price that would be received is $58; transaction costs are $8 and the transport costs are $2.

Required

1. What is the most advantageous market for Asset PYJ and what is its fair value?
2. If the principal market for Asset PYJ were Market I, then what would be the fair value of Asset PYJ?

3.7 Characteristics of an asset ★   LO3

Dr Mosby owned a large house on a sizeable piece of land in Darwin. His ancestors had been some of the first settlers in the area and the property had been in the family since around 1889. Dr Mosby was 92 years old and had become incapable of taking care of the large property. He wanted to move into a retirement village and so sold his property to the RuralMed Group, which was an association of doctors. The doctors wanted to use the house for their medical practice as it was centrally situated, had many rooms and had an 'old-world' atmosphere that would make patients feel comfortable.

The house was surrounded by a large group of trees that had been planted by the Anderson family over the years. The trees covered a large portion of the land. RuralMed did not want to make substantial alterations to the house as it was already suitable for a doctors' surgery. Only minor alterations to the inside of the house and some maintenance to the exterior were required. However, RuralMed wanted to divide the land and sell the portion adjacent to the house. This portion was currently covered in trees. The property sold would be very suitable for up-market apartment blocks.

It was a condition of the sale of the property to RuralMed that while Dr Mosby remained alive the trees on the property could not be cut down, as it would have caused him great distress. This clause in the contract would restrict the building of the apartment blocks. However, this restriction would not be enforceable on subsequent buyers of the property if RuralMed wanted to sell the property in the future. A further issue affecting the building of the apartment blocks was that across one corner of the block there was a gas pipeline that was a part of the city infrastructure for the supply of gas to Darwin residents.

Required

Outline any provisions in AASB 13/IFRS 13 that relate to consideration of restrictions on the measurement of fair values of assets. Describe how the restrictions would affect the measurement of the fair value of the property by RuralMed.

3.8 Market participants ★   **LO3**

Brumby Ltd recognises that the concept of 'market participants' is an important part of the measurement of fair value. It has determined that market participants are buyers and sellers in the principal (or most advantageous) market for the asset or liability that have the following characteristics.

- They are independent of each other.
- They are knowledgeable, having a reasonable understanding about the asset or liability and the transaction.
- They are able to enter into a transaction for the asset or liability.
- They are willing to enter into a transaction for the asset or liability.

Required

The group accountant for Brumby Ltd has asked for your advice on the following matters. Provide a response to the group accountant, referring to relevant paragraphs of AASB 13/IFRS 13.
1. Does an entity have to specifically identify market participants?
2. How should an entity determine what assumptions a market participant would make in measuring fair value?
3. If an entity is unwilling to transact at a price provided by a market participant, can that price be disregarded?

3.9 Determination of fair value ★   **LO3**

Pine Ltd holds an asset that is traded in three different markets: Market A, Market B and Market C. Pine Ltd normally trades in Market C. Some information gathered in relation to these three markets is as follows.

	Market A	Market B	Market C
Annual volume	30 000	12 000	6 000
Price (per unit)	$100	$96	$106
Transport costs (per unit)	$6	$6	$8
Transaction costs (per unit)	$2	$4	$4

Required

Using the above information, explain how Pine Ltd should measure the fair value of the asset it holds.

3.10 Liability held as an asset ★   **LO3, 4**

On 1 January 2022, Kangaroo Ltd issues at par $2 million A-rated 5-year fixed rate debt securities with an annual coupon interest rate of 8%. On 31 December 2022, investments in the debt securities are trading as an asset in an active market at $1900 per $2000 of par value after payment of accrued interest. Kangaroo Ltd uses the quoted price of the asset in an active market as its initial input into the fair value measurement of the debt securities liability.

Required

Determine the fair value of the debt securities at 31 December 2022. What other factors may need to be included when determining the fair value of the liability?

3.11 Present value technique: decommissioning liability ★ ★   **LO4**

On 1 July 2022, Panda Ltd assumed a decommissioning liability in a business combination. The entity is legally required to dismantle and remove an offshore oil platform at the end of its useful life, which is estimated to be 10 years. If Panda Ltd were contractually allowed to transfer its decommissioning liability to a market participant, Panda Ltd considers that the market participant would need to take into account the following inputs.

- Expected labour costs: $152 500
- Allocation of overhead costs: $115 000
- Contractor's profit margin: 20% of total labour and overhead costs
- Inflation factor: 4% p.a. for 10 years
- Market risk premium paid for undertaking risks involved: 5%
- Time value of money, represented by the risk-free rate: 5%
- Non-performance risk including Panda Ltd's own credit risk: 3.5%

Required

Determine the fair value of the decommissioning liability at 1 July 2022 using the present value technique.

3.12 Valuation of liabilities and non-performance risk ★★ LO4

Wallaby Ltd and Dingo Ltd enter into a contractual obligation to pay cash of $50 000 to Bandicoot Ltd in 5 years' time. Wallaby Ltd has a AA credit rating and can borrow at 4%. Dingo Ltd has a BBB credit rating and can borrow at 10%. At initial recognition, the fair value of the liability of each entity must reflect the credit standing of that entity.

Required

1. Determine the fair values of the contractual obligations of Wallaby Ltd and Dingo Ltd to Bandicoot Ltd on initial recognition.
2. Assume Wallaby Ltd's credit rating decreases to AA− by the end of the first year and its borrowing rate changes to 6%, while Dingo Ltd's credit rating improves to BB and its borrowing rate changes to 8%. Determine the fair value measurements of the contractual obligations after based on the new credit ratings. If the change in fair value of the liability were recognised, would a decline in the credit rating give rise to a gain or loss?

3.13 Present value technique: debt obligation ★★ LO5

On 1 January 2022, Koala Ltd issued at par in a private placement 42 million BBB-rated 5-year fixed rate debt securities with an annual coupon interest rate of 10%. At 31 December 2022, Koala Ltd still carried a BBB credit rating. Market conditions, including interest rates and credit spreads for a BBB-quality credit rating and liquidity, remain unchanged from the date of issue. However, Koala Ltd's credit spread had deteriorated by 50 basis points because of a change in its risk of non-performance. If the debt securities were issued at 31 December 2022, they would be priced at an interest rate of 10.5%.

Required

Determine the fair value of the debt securities at 31 December 2022 using the present value technique.

REFERENCE

IASB 2011, IFRS 13 *Fair Value Measurement, Illustrative Examples*, Example 15 — Assets measured at fair value, pp. 26–7.

ACKNOWLEDGEMENTS

Photo: © bukinnet / Shutterstock.com

Figure 3.1: © 2019 Australian Accounting Standards Board (AASB) and IFRS. The text, graphics and layout of this publication are protected by Australian copyright law and the comparable law of other countries. No part of the publication may be reproduced, stored or transmitted in any form or by any means without the prior written permission of the AASB except as permitted by law. For reproduction or publication permission should be sought in writing from the Australian Accounting Standards Board. Requests in the first instance should be addressed to the National Director, Australian Accounting Standards Board, PO Box 204, Collins Street West, Victoria 8007.

Case study 3.2: © Benston, G 2006, 'Fair value accounting: a cautionary tale from Enron', *Journal of Accounting and Public Policy*, vol. 25, no. 4, pp. 465–84.

Case study 3.3: © Whittington, G 2008 'Fair value and the IASB/FASB Conceptual Framework project: an alternative view', *Abacus*, vol. 44, no. 2, pp. 139–68.

Case study 3.4: © Hermann, D, Saudagaran, S & Thomas, W 2006, 'The quality of fair value measures for property, plant and equipment', *Accounting Forum*, vol. 30, no. 1, July, pp. 43–59.

Case study 3.5: © Benston, G 2008, 'The shortcomings of fair value accounting described in SFAS 157', *Journal of Accounting and Public Policy*, vol. 27, no. 2, March–April, pp. 101–14.

Application and analysis exercise 3.3: © IASB

Text: © 2019 Australian Accounting Standards Board (AASB). The text, graphics and layout of this publication are protected by Australian copyright law and the comparable law of other countries. No part of the publication may be reproduced, stored or transmitted in any form or by any means without the prior written permission of the AASB except as permitted by law. For reproduction or publication permission should be sought in writing from the Australian Accounting Standards Board. Requests

---

in the first instance should be addressed to the National Director, Australian Accounting Standards Board, PO Box 204, Collins Street West, Victoria, 8007.

CHAPTER 4

Inventories

CHAPTER AIM

This chapter discusses the application of AASB 102/IAS 2 *Inventories*. The objectives of this standard are to prescribe the accounting treatment for inventories, including the provision of guidance on: the determination of cost; the recognition of inventories as an expense, including any write-down to net realisable value; and the cost formulas that are used to assign costs to inventories.

LEARNING OBJECTIVES

After studying this chapter, you should be able to:

4.1 explain the definition of inventories

4.2 explain how to initially recognise and measure inventories

4.3 explain what costs are included in the cost of inventories

4.4 account for inventories transactions using both the periodic and the perpetual methods

4.5 explain and apply end-of-period procedures for inventories under both the periodic and the perpetual methods

4.6 explain why cost flow assumptions are required and apply both the FIFO and weighted average cost formulas

4.7 explain the net realisable value basis of measurement and account for adjustments to net realisable value

4.8 account for inventories expense

4.9 identify the disclosure requirements of AASB 102/IAS 2.

CONCEPTS FOR REVIEW

Before studying this chapter, you should understand and, if necessary, revise:
- the definitions of asset and expense in the *Conceptual Framework*
- the recognition criteria for an asset in the *Conceptual Framework*.

4.1 The nature of inventories

LEARNING OBJECTIVE 4.1 Explain the definition of inventories.

AASB 102/IAS 2 *Inventories* is the accounting standard that deals with accounting for inventories. Paragraph 6 of AASB 102/IAS 2 defines **inventories** as follows.

> Inventories are assets:
> (a) held for sale in the ordinary course of business;
> (b) in the process of production for such sale; or
> (c) in the form of materials or supplies to be consumed in the production process or in the rendering of services.

This definition classifies inventories into three categories based on retailing and the production cycle. To illustrate, the inventories of an entity that manufactures wooden furniture for sale include:

(a) finished goods — the finished wooden furniture available for sale from the warehouse or in retail outlets
(b) work in progress — the furniture that is in the factory in the process of being made ready for sale
(c) raw materials — the timber, screws and varnishes that are stored and available for use in the manufacturing process.

In its 2018 annual report, Wesfarmers Limited reported these three categories of inventories as shown in figure 4.1. Wesfarmers is a diversified company. Its businesses include Bunnings, Officeworks, Target, Kmart and many others. Consider Wesfarmers' Bunnings division, which consists of the Bunnings, Bunnings Warehouse and Bunnings Trade stores in Australia and New Zealand. Bunnings is a leading retailer of hardware, home improvement and outdoor products and a major supplier to tradespeople and the housing industry. At 30 June 2018, Bunnings operated out of 369 trading locations including 259 warehouse-style stores. A typical Bunnings warehouse store stocks more than 45 000 different items. Similarly, Wesfarmers' Officeworks division sells tens of thousands of different products, including office supplies, ink cartridges, computers, furniture, catering products, cleaning supplies and copy services. Wesfarmers' Industrials division includes the manufacture and supply of chemicals and fertilisers to the Western Australian mining and agricultural sectors respectively (Wesfarmers Limited 2018).

FIGURE 4.1   Disclosure of types of inventories, Wesfarmers

6: Inventories

	CONSOLIDATED	
	2018 $m	2017 $m
Raw materials	37	91
Work in progress	2	15
Finished goods	5 972	6 424
	6 011	**6 530**

Inventories recognised as an expense for the year ended 30 June 2018 totalled $50 122 million (2017: $49 083 million).

Source: Wesfarmers Limited (2018, p. 112).

For retailers, such as Bunnings and Officeworks, and for manufacturing companies, inventories are the most active asset and may make up a significant proportion of current assets. For such companies, accounting for inventories is an important part of operations. Information about inventories is provided in two key areas of the financial statements of a company as follows.

- In the statement of profit or loss and other comprehensive income, the company reports **cost of sales**, being the cost of the inventories sold.
- In the statement of financial position, in the current assets section, the company lists the balance of inventories on hand at the end of the reporting period.

Obviously the two numbers are linked. A company commences its reporting period with a balance of inventories on hand. During the period, inventories are sold and new inventories are manufactured or purchased. At the end of the period, as a result of these activities, the company has a new balance of inventories on hand. See figure 4.1 for the opening and closing balances of each type of inventory for Wesfarmers Limited.

Note the following points in relation to the nature of inventories.

1. The assets are held for sale in the ordinary course of business. The accounting standards do not define 'ordinary', but AASB 5/IFRS 5 *Non-current Assets Held for Sale and Discontinued Operations* requires that non-current assets held for sale be distinguished from inventories. This indicates that the term 'inventories' should be applied only to those assets that are always intended for sale or for consumption in producing saleable goods or services. Hence, a company whose primary business is selling food products would not regard as inventory a delivery van that it is selling because it needs a larger van.

2. Accounting for assets held for use by the entity is covered by other accounting standards according to the nature of the assets. For example, AASB 116/IAS 16 *Property, Plant and Equipment* covers tangible assets such as production equipment (see chapter 5), while AASB 138/IAS 38 *Intangible Assets* covers intangible assets such as patents (see chapter 6).

3. Supplies or materials such as stationery would not be treated as inventories unless they are held for sale or are used in producing goods for sale.

4. Spare parts and servicing equipment are usually carried as inventories unless those spare parts are expected to be used during more than one period, or can be used only in conjunction with an item of property, plant and equipment (AASB 116/IAS 16 paragraph 8). Spare parts are categorised as inventories where those items are consumed regularly during the production process, such as bobbin winders on commercial sewing machines.

Paragraph 66 of AASB 101/IAS 1 *Presentation of Financial Statements* provides criteria for classifying assets as current. The following apply or may apply to inventories.

- They are expected to be realised in, or are intended for sale or consumption in, the entity's normal operating cycle. The operating cycle of an entity is the time between the acquisition of assets for processing and their realisation in cash or cash equivalents (paragraph 68). In some industries (e.g. retailing) the operating cycle may be very short, but for others (e.g. winemaking) the operating cycle could cover a number of years. When the entity's operating cycle is not clearly identifiable, its duration is assumed to be 12 months.
- They are held primarily for the purpose of being traded.
- They are expected to be realised within 12 months after the reporting period.

While AASB 102/IAS 2 is the accounting standard that deals with the recognition, measurement and disclosure of inventories, paragraphs 2 and 3 of AASB 102/IAS 2 specifically exclude the following from the standard:

- financial instruments dealt with under AASB 132/IAS 32 *Financial Instruments: Presentation* and AASB 9/IFRS 9 *Financial Instruments*
- biological assets relating to agricultural activity and agricultural produce at the point of harvest dealt with under AASB 141/IAS 41 *Agriculture*
- the measurement of inventories held by producers of agricultural and forest products, agricultural produce after harvest, and minerals and mineral products to the extent they are measured at net realisable value in accordance with established industry practice
- the measurement of inventories held by commodity broker-traders who measure their inventories at fair value less costs to sell.

LEARNING CHECK

☐ The accounting standard that deals with inventories is AASB 102/IAS 2 *Inventories*.
☐ There are three categories of inventories:
  – assets held for sale in the ordinary course of business
  – assets in the process of production for such sale
  – assets in the form of materials or supplies to be consumed in the production process or in the rendering of services.

4.2 Recognition and measurement of inventories

LEARNING OBJECTIVE 4.2 Explain how to initially recognise and measure inventories.

Generally, accounting standards for assets specify recognition criteria (e.g. AASB 116/IAS 16 *Property, Plant and Equipment*) and these are couched in the same or similar terms to those in the *Conceptual Framework*. However, AASB 102/IAS 2 does not specify recognition criteria for inventories. When an accounting standard does not deal specifically with recognition issues paragraph 11 of AASB 108/ IAS 8 *Accounting Policies, Changes in Accounting Estimates and Errors* requires reference to the *Conceptual Framework*. Paragraph 5.7 of the *Conceptual Framework* states that assets and liabilities are recognised only if recognition provides users of financial statements with information that is useful (i.e. information that is relevant and is a faithful representation).

The measurement of inventories subsequent to initial recognition is governed by paragraph 9 of AASB 102/IAS 2 as follows.

> Inventories shall be measured at the lower of cost and net realisable value.

Normally, inventories are initially measured at cost, and then, if the net realisable value becomes lower than cost, an adjustment is made to reduce the carrying amount in subsequent measurement.

Paragraph 6 of AASB 102/IAS 2 defines net realisable value but cost is undefined. Therefore, the traditional meaning of cost in generally accepted accounting practice applies. The measurement of inventories at cost is specifically addressed in AASB 102/IAS 2, as discussed in section 4.3.

LEARNING CHECK

☐ AASB 102/IAS 2 includes no recognition criteria for inventories — initial recognition occurs when recognition would provide users of financial statements with useful information.
☐ Inventories are subsequently measured at the lower of cost and net realisable value.

4.3 Measurement at cost

LEARNING OBJECTIVE 4.3 Explain what costs are included in the cost of inventories.

Inventories are measured initially at cost. As a rule of thumb, the cost of inventories includes all costs necessarily incurred in getting the inventories ready for sale or use. Paragraph 10 of AASB 102/IAS 2 requires that the costs of inventories comprise:
 (a) costs of purchase
 (b) costs of conversion
 (c) other costs incurred in bringing the inventories to their present location and condition.

Costs of purchase are applicable to retailing, wholesaling and manufacturing entities. Bunnings as a retailer has costs of purchase for outdoor table settings whereas Wesfarmers' Industrials as a manufacturer has costs of purchase for raw materials to make fertilisers. Costs of conversion apply only to manufacturers where raw materials and other supplies are purchased and then converted into finished goods through a production process.

4.3.1 Costs of purchase

According to paragraph 11 of AASB 102/IAS 2, the costs of purchase comprise the purchase price, import duties and other taxes (other than those recoverable by the entity from the tax authorities), transport, handling and other costs directly attributable to the acquisition of finished goods, materials and services. Trade discounts, rebates and other similar items are deducted in determining the costs of purchase.

Purchase price

Purchase price means the supplier's invoice price before any trade discounts or rebates. In the case of Bunnings there is an invoice price from the supplier of its outdoor table settings. In the case of Wesfarmers' Industrials division there is an invoice price for natural gas that is used in the production process.

Import duties and other taxes

Many countries levy import duties or taxes on transactions involving the exchange of goods and services, and require entities engaging in such activities to collect and remit the import duties and tax to the government. These duties and taxes are included in the costs of purchase unless recoverable by the purchasing entity from the tax authorities.

In the case of Bunnings, if the outdoor table setting is imported from a supplier overseas and import duties are levied but not recoverable, then the duties are included in the costs of purchase. In contrast, if the outdoor table setting is acquired from a local manufacturer and the purchase invoice includes goods and services tax (GST), then the GST is not included in the costs of purchase because Bunnings can recover it from the Australian Taxation Office when lodging its business activity statement.

Transport and handling costs

Transport and handling costs to get inventories ready for sale or use are included in the costs of purchase. Inwards transport costs from suppliers may be included in the costs of purchase; however, outwards transport costs to customers are not. The costs of packing goods into a warehouse are likewise included in the costs of purchase.

In identifying the costs of purchase, consideration must be given to the terms of sale relating to inventories because such terms determine the treatment of transport costs associated with purchase. If goods are sold *FOB (free on board) shipping point*, freight costs incurred from the point of shipment are paid by the buyer, and are *included* in the costs of purchase. If goods are sold *FOB destination*, the seller pays all freight costs, and these costs are *not directly included* in the costs of purchase because they are not incurred by the purchaser.

Trade discounts

Trade discounts are reductions in selling prices granted to customers. Such discounts may be granted as an incentive to buy, as a means for a supplier to quit ageing inventories or as a reward for placing large orders for goods. As the discount effectively reduces the purchase cost, it is deducted when determining the cost of inventories. Similarly, if a cash discount is offered for immediate payment for the inventories the cost of inventories is the amount actually paid after the cash discount.

Supplier rebates

Supplier rebates granted to entities purchasing inventories can arise in a variety of scenarios. 'Scan rebates' arise where the purchaser is entitled to credit or cash from a supplier as it sells the inventories on to a customer; that is, as they are scanned at a store checkout. 'Over and above rebates' arise where the purchaser is entitled to credit or cash from a supplier once it meets some agreed target. Examples of targets include an agreed buying volume, an agreed period of custom or an agreed program of qualifying advertising costs to sell goods onto customers.

The standard setters (the AASB and IASB) considered the accounting treatment of supplier rebates during 2004–05. In light of this, the AASB made the following statements.
- Supplier rebates subject to a binding agreement based on purchasing volume or period of custom should be recognised as a reduction of the costs of purchase, provided they are probable and reliably measurable. This may be based on the progress towards meeting the specified requirements for the rebate.
- Supplier rebates that are discretionary should be recognised only when credited or paid by the supplier or when the supplier becomes obligated to credit or pay them.

- Supplier rebates that relate to the purchase of inventories (e.g. scan rebates and over and above rebates based on volume of purchasing activity) should be taken into consideration in the measurement of the cost of inventories.
- Supplier rebates that genuinely refund selling expenses such as advertising costs should not be deducted from the cost of inventories.
- If supplier rebates exceed the selling costs being reimbursed, then the excess should be deducted from the cost of inventories.

Recently, various media outlets have published allegations that some Australian and UK retailers may have recognised supplier rebates incorrectly — before there is an entitlement to the rebate or before inventories are sold — in order to manipulate profits.

Settlement discounts

Settlement discounts arise when inventories are purchased on credit terms. Purchase invoices or contracts often take the form '2/10, n/30', which means that the buyer will receive a 2% discount if the invoice is paid within ten days of the invoice date or has 30 days to pay without discount. Settlement discounts are allowed by suppliers as an incentive for the purchaser to pay the invoice prior to the end of the credit period.

The standard setters (the AASB and IASB) considered the accounting treatment of settlement discounts during 2004–05. They decided that settlement discounts should be deducted from the costs of inventories. The basis of this decision is that a purchaser who declines to take advantage of settlement discounts available from a supplier is, in substance, financing the acquisition of inventories using the credit terms offered by the supplier. Hence, the cost of inventories is the net amount after taking into account any settlement discounts that are offered by the supplier. Illustrative example 4.1 compares the accounting if the purchaser takes advantage of settlement discounts and if they do not.

ILLUSTRATIVE EXAMPLE 4.1

Accounting with and without settlement discount

Sydney Ltd purchases garden furniture settings from Melbourne Pty Ltd to sell in its retail outlets. Melbourne Pty Ltd, the supplier, offers credit terms to Sydney Ltd, the purchaser, of 2/10, n/30.

On 1 August 2021, Sydney Ltd purchased 30 settings from Melbourne Pty Ltd at $670 each on credit terms of 2/10, n/30.

Required

Prepare the journal entries necessary to record the purchase and settlement of the account assuming:
1. the account is settled within 10 days on 8 August 2021 and settlement discount applies
2. the account is settled on 31 August 2021 and settlement discount does not apply.

Solution

1. The first step is to record the purchase of the 30 settings.

Inventories	Dr	19 698	
Accounts payable	Cr		19 698
(Purchase of 30 settings — 30 × $670 × (1 − 0.02))			

The second step is to record the settlement with the discount applied.

Accounts payable	Dr	19 698	
Cash	Cr		19 698

2. The first step is to record the purchase of the 30 settings.

Inventories	Dr	19 698	
Accounts payable	Cr		19 698
(Purchase of 30 settings — 30 × $670 × (1 − 0.02))			

The second step is to record the settlement without a discount.

Accounts payable	Dr	19 698	
Finance expense	Dr	402	
Cash	Cr		20 100

In both cases, the cost of inventories is net of the discount offered ($19 698). The settlement of account is $19 698 with the discount or $20 100 without a discount (with a finance expense of $402 recorded).

4.3.2 Costs of conversion

Costs of conversion arise when a manufacturing process converts raw materials into units of production or finished goods. Paragraph 12 of AASB 102/IAS 2 describes the costs of conversion as the costs directly related to the units of production, such as direct labour. They also include a systematic allocation of fixed and variable production overheads that are incurred in the production process. Fixed production overhead are indirect costs that are constant regardless of the volume of production and are allocated to the cost of inventories on the basis of normal production capacity, such as depreciation of a factory or plant. Variable production overhead is the indirect costs that vary directly with the volume of production and are allocated to each unit of production on the basis of actual use of production facilities, such as the indirect labour of a supervisor in a factory.

According to paragraph 14 of AASB 102/IAS 2, where a production process simultaneously produces one or more products, the costs of conversion are allocated between products on a systematic and rational basis. Costing methodologies are a managerial accounting issue and outside the scope of this text.

4.3.3 Other costs

Paragraph 15 of AASB 102/IAS 2 requires other costs be included in the cost of inventories only if they are incurred in bringing the inventories to their *present location and condition*. Other costs could include design costs incurred in producing tailor-made goods for individual customers.

The phrase 'to their present location and condition' is critical as it sets a limit to the outlays that can be capitalised into the cost of the inventories. Outlays on inventories subsequent to the point of their present location and condition are expensed. For example, refrigeration costs in a supermarket would be recognised as an expense rather than as part of the cost of the inventories.

Paragraph 16 of AASB 102/IAS 2 lists examples of costs excluded from the cost of inventories. These costs are not directly attributable to getting the inventories into their present location and condition, and include:

(a) abnormal amounts of wasted materials, labour or other production costs;
(b) storage costs, unless those costs are necessary in the production process before a further production stage;
(c) administrative overheads [e.g. the costs of head office functions such as employee relations and accounting] that do not contribute to bringing inventories to their present location and condition; and
(d) selling costs [e.g. the salaries of sales staff].

Illustrative example 4.2 shows how the cost of inventories is determined for a retailer purchasing goods for sale from an overseas supplier.

ILLUSTRATIVE EXAMPLE 4.2

Determination of cost for a retailer

Swan Ltd, an Australian company, received the following invoice from Expresso Garments Ltd, an Italian garment manufacturer.

	Expresso Garments		Invoice: 37962
	112a Industrial Estate GENOA ITALY		Date: 18/04/23

Swan Ltd 2 Baskerville Street PERTH WA 6108 Australia	Shipping details Tiamaru -ex Genoa Port 17/4/23 to Fremantle Australia

Customer no.	Order no.	Order date	Dispatch date	Dispatch no.	Delivered by	Terms of sale
17632-A	726BI	16/3/23	17/4/23	19635-6	TNT Freight	FOB shipping

Code	Qty ordered	Qty sent	Description	Unit price excl. VAT	VAT/Tax amount	Value of goods
				€	€	€
GTF-16	100	60	Basic T-shirt size 16	8.25		495.00
GTA-14	1200	1200	Glamour Tee size 14	11.22		13464.00
SZ6-10	600	560	Superseded T-shirt size 10*	5.90		3304.00
			*15% discount on list price applies			

VAT %	VAT incl.		
15%	€ 00.00	Value of goods dispatched	17263
		Freight costs	695
		Total payable	17958

Credit terms net 60 days

The goods arrived at Fremantle port on 29 May 2023 and were held in a bond store pending payment of import duties and taxes. After the payment of storage costs of A$145, import duty at 1.5% of the total value of goods in Australian dollars, GST of 10% and local freight charges of A$316, the goods were received at Swan Ltd's warehouse on 6 June 2023.

The invoice was received on 8 June and a liability of A$23 628.95 recorded using the exchange rate of A$1 = €0.76 at that date. The invoice was paid in full on 8 July by the remittance of A$23 322.08 (at an exchange rate of A$1 = €0.77). Swan Ltd paid A$167 to acquire the euros. Upon receipt of the goods, Swan Ltd attaches its own logo to the T-shirts and repackages them for sale. The cost of this further processing is A$2.54 per T-shirt.

Required
Calculate the cost of inventories.

Solution
The cost of inventories would include the following amounts.

Purchase price	€17 263.00
Shipping costs	695.00
	€17 958.00
Conversion to Australian dollars:	
€17 958 ÷ 0.76	A$23 628.95
Storage costs — bond store	145.00
Import duty (€17 263.00 ÷ 0.76) × 1.5%	340.72
Freight costs	316.00
Foreign exchange commission	167.00
Logo and repackaging (1820 items × $2.54)	4 622.80
Total cost	A$29 220.47

Where a cost per unit for each type of T-shirt is required, some method of allocating the 'generic' costs of shipping, storage, freight and foreign exchange commission would need to be employed. In this case, such costs could be allocated on a per garment basis. For example, the cost per unit for the Basic T-shirts is calculated as follows.

	A$
Purchase price (€8.25 ÷ $0.76)	10.86
Import duty (1.5% × $10.86)	0.16
Shipping and other costs*	0.85
Logo and repackaging	2.54
Cost per unit	14.41

*(A$145 + 316 + 167 + [€695 ÷ 0.76] = A$1542.47/1820 garments = A$0.85 per garment)

Note that the exchange gain of $306.87 arising from the change in euro–dollar exchange rates between the recognition of the liability and its payment is not incorporated in the calculation of cost as it is not associated with the acquisition transaction. Additionally, the GST of 10% is not included in inventories as it is a transaction tax receivable by Swan Ltd against GST collected on sale of inventories.

4.3.4 Estimating cost

Paragraph 21 of AASB 102/IAS 2 notes that techniques for estimating cost, such as the standard cost method or the retail method, may be used for convenience so long as the resulting values approximate cost.

The standard cost method is a practical expedient for determining the cost of inventories if there is large-scale production activity. Under the standard cost method, a manufacturer determines a 'standard' value of materials, direct and indirect labour and overheads for each product based on normal levels of efficiency and capacity utilisation. Adjustments are made at the end of the reporting period to account for variances between standard and actual costs. Standard costs must be regularly reviewed and amended as required.

The retail method is used to measure inventories of large numbers of rapidly changing items with similar margins for which it is impracticable to use other costing methods. Supermarket chains and department store chains generally employ this method of approximating cost. Cost is determined by reducing the sales value of the inventories by an appropriate percentage gross margin or an average percentage margin. In applying this method, care must be taken to ensure that gross margins are adjusted for goods that have been discounted below their original selling price. Illustrative example 4.3 shows how to apply the retail method in a simple case where it is assumed that all products have the same gross margin.

ILLUSTRATIVE EXAMPLE 4.3

Simple retail method

Mandurah Foods determined the following information in relation to its inventories.

	Cost	Retail
Beginning inventories	$30 000	$45 000
Purchases	40 000	55 000
Sales	—	80 000

Required
Estimate the ending inventories.

Solution
The ending inventories are estimated as follows.

	Cost	Retail
Beginning inventories	$30 000	$45 000
Purchases	40 000	55 000
Inventories available for sale	$70 000	100 000

Cost to retail: $70 000/$100 000 = 70%

Gross margin: 100% − 70% = 30%

Less: Sales	80 000
Ending inventories	20 000
Estimate of ending inventories: $20 000 × (1 − 0.3)	$14 000

The cost of inventories sold can be determined as $56 000, being $70 000 inventories available for sale less the estimate of ending inventories of $14 000.

4.3.5 Cost of inventories of a service provider

Previously, AASB 102/IAS 2 also applied to the inventories of service providers such as companies offering cleaning, catering, facilities management, legal or accounting services. Because a service is being provided, the costs would have consisted primarily of the labour of those employees directly engaged in providing the service. The concept of inventories of service providers meant that the costs billed against client work-in-process (WIP) at year-end (e.g. the charge-out rates of employees providing the service) could not factor in profit margins because this would have resulted in measuring inventories at a value greater than cost.

In July 2015, AASB 102/IAS 2 was amended to remove the concept of inventories of service providers. Accordingly, the WIP of service providers in no longer considered inventories. The WIP of service providers is now governed by the requirements for the recognition and measurement of revenues in AASB 15/IFRS 15 *Revenue from Contracts with Customers*. The application of AASB 15/IFRS 15 is discussed in chapter 15 of this text.

4.3.6 Inventories of not-for-profit entities

The AASB has inserted Australian paragraphs into AASB 102 to deal with issues in the accounting of inventories by not-for-profit entities. Paragraphs Aus9.1 and Aus9.2 of AASB 102 explain how under certain circumstances, not-for-profit entities use current replacement cost rather than net realisable value to measure a loss in the service potential of inventories held for distribution.

Paragraph Aus10.1 of AASB 102 states that where inventories are acquired by not-for-profit entities at no cost, or for nominal consideration, the cost shall be the current replacement cost at the date of acquisition. For example, if used clothing is donated to a charitable organisation, the charity records the used clothing at cost, measured as the current replacement cost of the used clothing at the date the charity became the owner.

LEARNING CHECK

- ☐ Inventories are measured initially at cost.
- ☐ Cost comprises costs of purchase, costs of conversion and other costs incurred in bringing the inventories to their present location and condition.
- ☐ Costs of purchase comprise the purchase price, import duties and other non-recoverable taxes, transport, handling and other costs directly attributable to the acquisition of finished goods, materials and services less trade discounts, rebates and other similar items.
- ☐ Costs of conversion are the costs directly related to the units of production, such as direct labour, plus a systematic allocation of fixed and variable production overheads that are incurred in converting materials into finished goods.
- ☐ Other costs can be included only if they are incurred in bringing the inventories to their present location and condition.

4.4 Methods of record keeping for inventory control

LEARNING OBJECTIVE 4.4 Account for inventories transactions using both the periodic and the perpetual methods.

Inventory controls include safeguards for physical protection and keeping accurate records that can be used for internal management and external financial reports. There are two main methods of record keeping for inventory control: the periodic method and the perpetual method. These two methods potentially result in different amounts for cost of sales and the cost of inventories on hand at the end of the period.

4.4.1 Periodic method

Under the **periodic method**:
- *inventories on hand* is determined periodically (e.g. annually). This is done by conducting a physical count — a stocktake — and multiplying the number of units of each item by the cost per unit of the item. A current asset, inventories, is then recognised and measured at the amount consistent with the stocktake. The inventories balance remains unchanged until the next stocktake.
- *purchases* of inventories and *inwards freight costs* for the period are posted directly to expense accounts
- *purchase returns* for the period may be recognised separately as a contra account to purchases so that the accounting system records any problem stock issues with suppliers
- *cost of sales* for the period is determined as follows. For a merchandiser, cost of sales for the period is opening inventories plus the costs of purchase less closing inventories. For a manufacturer, cost of sales for the period is opening finished goods plus the costs of manufacture of finished goods less closing finished goods.

Accounting for inventories using the periodic method is cost effective because it is relatively easy to apply and does not require timely inventory records. Its major disadvantage is that the exact quantity and cost of inventories cannot be determined on a day-to-day or regular basis, making it more difficult to manage inventories for sales opportunities and customer demand. It is not possible to identify stock losses from theft and spoilage (sometimes referred to as inventory shrinkage) or posting errors. In the periodic method, the details regarding theft, spoilage and accounting errors are subsumed into the cost of sales for the period. The periodic method is best suited to inventories that are homogeneous and for which quantities are more readily observable; for example, mineral products such as iron ore.

Illustrative example 4.4 shows how to determine the cost of sales of a retailer using the periodic method.

ILLUSTRATIVE EXAMPLE 4.4

Cost of sales — periodic method

Hobart Ltd sells kitchen appliances. On 30 June 2021, a stocktake determined that inventories amounted to $250 000. An extract of Hobart Ltd's trial balance for 30 June 2021 is as follows.

	Debit	Credit
Inventories at 1 July 2020	$130 000	
Purchases expense	840 000	
Purchase returns		$15 000
Freight inwards expense	10 000	
Finance expense	20 000	

Required

Calculate the cost of sales using the periodic method.

Solution

The calculation of cost of sales under the periodic method is as follows.

Opening inventories		$ 130 000
+ Purchases	$840 000	
+ Freight inwards	10 000	
− Purchase returns	(15 000)	835 000
− Closing inventories		(250 000)
Cost of sales		$ 715 000

> Recall from section 4.3.1 that if the entity does not take advantage of a settlement discount, the additional cost is a financing expense and therefore not part of cost of sales.

4.4.2 Perpetual method

Under the **perpetual method** there is a running record for inventories. The records are updated each time there is a transaction involving inventories. Hence:

- *inventories on hand* can be determined at any point of time from the accounting records
- *purchases* of inventories and *purchase returns* are recognised using the inventories account
- *cost of sales* is recorded at point of sale such that each sale is associated with a revenue and an expense.

Up-to-date information about the quantity and cost of inventories on hand will always be available, enabling the entity to provide better customer service and maintain better control over its inventories. The perpetual method also makes it possible to identify stock losses from theft or spoilage when stocktakes occur.

The perpetual method is a more complicated and expensive system to operate than the periodic method but, with the advent of user-friendly computerised accounting packages and point-of-sale machines linked directly to accounting records, most businesses today can afford to and do use the perpetual method.

The perpetual method requires a subsidiary ledger to be maintained, either manually or electronically, with a separate record for each inventory item detailing all movements in both quantity and cost. This subsidiary record is linked to the general ledger account for inventories, and regular reconciliations are carried out to ensure the accuracy and completeness of the accounting records. Illustrative example 4.5 demonstrates the perpetual method and compares it with the periodic method.

ILLUSTRATIVE EXAMPLE 4.5

Comparing the periodic and the perpetual inventories methods

Sydney Ltd sells garden furniture settings. This example illustrates the journal entries necessary for Sydney Ltd to record the normal inventories transactions that would occur during an accounting period, and the reporting of gross profit from the sale of inventories under both accounting systems.

The inventories account in the general ledger of Sydney Ltd at the beginning of the year under both methods is shown below.

Inventories		
1/7/23	Balance b/d	6 700
	(10 units @ $670)	

The following transactions took place during the year.
(a) Purchased 354 settings (FOB shipping) at $670 each on credit terms of n/30 from Melbourne Pty Ltd.
(b) Sold, on credit, 352 settings for $975 each.
(c) Returned four settings to the supplier.
(d) Seven settings were returned by customers.

Required

1. Prepare the journal entries to record these transactions under the perpetual inventories method and the periodic inventories method.
2. Prepare the general ledger account for each inventories method after posting the journal entries.
3. Determine the gross profit earned under each inventories method assuming that the physical count at the end of the reporting period found 15 settings on hand at a cost of $670 each.

Solution

1. The journal entries necessary to record each transaction are shown below for each inventories accounting method.

(a) Purchased 354 settings (FOB shipping) at $670 each on credit terms of n/30 from Melbourne Pty Ltd.

Perpetual inventories method				Periodic inventories method			
Inventories	Dr	237 180		Purchases	Dr	237 180	
A/cs payable	Cr		237 180	A/cs payable	Cr		237 180

(b) Sold, on credit, 352 settings for $975 each.

Perpetual inventories method				Periodic inventories method			
A/cs receivable	Dr	343 200		A/cs receivable	Dr	343 200	
Sales revenue	Cr		343 200	Sales revenue	Cr		343 200
Cost of sales	Dr	235 840					
Inventories	Cr		235 840				

(c) Returned four settings to the supplier.

Perpetual inventories method				Periodic inventories method			
A/cs payable	Dr	2 680		A/cs payable	Dr	2 680	
Inventories	Cr		2 680	Purchase returns	Cr		2 680

(d) Seven settings were returned by customers.

Perpetual inventories method				Periodic inventories method			
Sales returns	Dr	6 825		Sales returns	Dr	6 825	
A/cs receivable	Cr		6 825	A/cs receivable	Cr		6 825
Inventories	Dr	4 690					
Cost of sales	Cr		4 690				

Important differences to note between the two methods of accounting for inventories are as follows.

• Purchases are posted directly to the asset account under the perpetual method, and are posted to expense accounts under the periodic method.
• When goods are sold, a second entry is necessary under the perpetual method to transfer the cost of those goods from the inventories account to the expense account, cost of sales.
• When goods are returned to suppliers, the return is adjusted directly to inventories under the perpetual method, and is posted to a purchase returns account under the periodic method.
• When goods are returned from customers, a second journal entry is necessary under the perpetual method to transfer the cost of these goods out of the cost of sales account and back into the inventories account.
• Under the periodic method, freight is normally posted to a separate account. Under the perpetual method, freight is included in the cost of inventories unless the amounts are immaterial, in which case freight costs are accumulated in a separate expense account.
• If inventories being returned to the supplier have been paid for, an accounts receivable account is opened pending a cash refund from the supplier.
• If sales returns have been paid for, an accounts payable entry is raised to recognise the need to refund cash to the customer.

2. After posting the journal entries, the general ledger account appears as follows.

Perpetual inventories method

Inventories				
1/7/23	Balance b/d	6 700	Cost of sales	235 840
	Accounts payable	237 180	Accounts payable	2 680
	Cost of sales	4 690	Balance c/d	10 050
		248 570		248 570
	Balance b/d	10 050		

Periodic inventories method

Inventories		
1/7/23	Balance	6 700

3. Assuming that the physical count at the end of the reporting period found 15 settings on hand at a cost of $670 each, the gross profit earned on sales of the garden furniture settings is determined as follows.

Perpetual inventories method	
Sales revenue	$ 343 200
Sales returns and allowances	(6 825)
Net sales revenue	336 375
Cost of sales	(231 150)
Gross profit	$ 105 225

Periodic inventories method		
Sales revenue		$ 343 200
Sales returns		(6 825)
Net sales revenue		336 375
Cost of sales		
Opening inventories	$ 6 700	
Purchases	237 180	
	243 880	
Purchase returns	(2 680)	
Goods available for sale	241 200	
Closing inventories	(10 050)	(231 150)
Gross profit		$ 105 225

Note that in this example the same gross profit is reported irrespective of the inventories recording method adopted. However, gross profit will differ if there are damaged or lost inventories, because they are recorded separately under the perpetual method but absorbed in cost of sales under the periodic method.

LEARNING CHECK

☐ The periodic method of accounting for inventories involves physically counting inventories on hand (usually annually) and multiplying the number of units by a cost per unit to value the inventories on hand. This amount is then recognised as a current asset and remains unchanged until the next count. Purchases are posted directly to an expense account. Cost of sales during the year is determined from opening inventories, purchases, freight inwards, returns and closing inventories. The periodic method provides no way to know precise inventories levels at any point during the year.

☐ The perpetual method of accounting for inventories involves updating inventories records each time a transaction involving inventories takes place. Using this method, the balance of the inventories account indicates inventories on hand at any point in time, purchases and returns are adjusted against the inventories account and cost of sales is recorded at point of sale.

4.5 End-of-period accounting

LEARNING OBJECTIVE 4.5 Explain and apply end-of-period procedures for inventories under both the periodic and the perpetual methods.

Certain procedures are carried out at the end of each accounting period to ensure that reported figures for inventories, cost of sales and other expenses are accurate and complete. Good internal controls are required to protect inventories from fraud and loss, and ensure that inventories figures are complete and accurate.

This section examines the physical count, end-of-year cut-off and reconciliation procedures.

4.5.1 Physical count

Physical counts are done under both the periodic and perpetual methods, but for different reasons.
- Under the *periodic method*, inventories are counted at the end of each accounting period to determine the balance of closing inventories.
- Under the *perpetual method*, physical counts are made to verify the accuracy of recorded quantities for each inventory item, although not necessarily at the end of the reporting period if inventories differences are historically found to be immaterial.

The way in which the physical count is conducted depends on the types of inventories and the accounting system of the entity. Electronic goods would be counted on their shelves. Stockpiled inventories such as mineral sands may require the use of surveyors to measure quantities on hand and assay tests to determine mineral content.

Some steps that are generally taken to ensure the accuracy of a physical count are as follows.
- The warehouse, retail store or storage facility is arranged so as to facilitate counting with a clear segregation of non-inventory items.
- Cut-off procedures are put in place and final numbers of important documents such as dispatch notes and invoices are recorded.
- Pre-numbered count sheets, tags or cards are produced, detailing inventories codes and descriptions. A supervisor should record all numbers used and account for spoiled documents to ensure that the count details are complete. Alternatively, where inventory items have bar codes, electronic scanners can be used to record the count.
- Counting is done in teams of at least two people: one counter and one checker. All team members should sign the count records.
- Any damaged or incomplete items located during the count are clearly listed on the count records.
- The supervisor should ensure that all goods have been counted before the count sheets are collected.

Periodic method

Once the count is completed, under the periodic method the count quantities are then costed and the balance of inventories at period-end is brought to account. This adjustment can be done in a number of ways, but the simplest is to post the following two journal entries, which are based on illustrative example 4.5.

Opening inventories (cost of sales)	Dr	6 700	
Inventories	Cr		6 700
(Transfer of opening balance to cost of sales expense)			
Inventories	Dr	10 050	
Closing inventories (cost of sales)	Cr		10 050
(Recognition of final inventories balance)			

Under the periodic method, inventory losses and fraud cannot be identified and recorded as a separate expense. The movement in inventories balances plus the cost of purchases is presumed to represent the cost of sales during the reporting period.

Accordingly, the general ledger account for cost of sales consistent with illustrative example 4.5 is as follows.

Cost of sales			
Inventories (op.)	6 700	Purchase returns	2 680
Purchases	237 180	Inventories (cl.)	10 050
		Income summary	231 150
	243 880		243 880

Perpetual method

Once the physical count is completed, under the perpetual method the quantities on hand are then compared to recorded quantities and discrepancies investigated. Recording errors cause discrepancies; for example, the wrong code number or quantity might have been entered, or a transaction might not have been processed in the correct period. Alternatively, discrepancies may reveal losses of goods caused by damage or fraud. Recording errors can be corrected but the value of goods that have been lost must be written off.

Continuing with the data in illustrative example 4.5, if a stocktake found that only $8710 of inventories was on hand at year-end, but the accounting records showed $10 050, then the following entry would be necessary to adjust the accounting records to the physical count.

Inventories losses expense	Dr	1 340	
Inventories	Cr		1 340
(Recognition of inventories losses during the period)			

Note that it is only in the perpetual method where this entry applies. In contrast to the perpetual method, the periodic method does not have a control account for inventories that would enable comparison with the physical count.

Inventory losses must also be disclosed separately in the notes to the financial statements if material.

4.5.2 Cut-off procedures

Both the periodic and the perpetual methods require cut-off procedures that ensure the accounting records properly reflect the results of the physical count and include all transactions relevant to the accounting period, while excluding those that belong to other periods. For all inventories transactions (sales, purchases and returns) it is possible for inventories records to be updated before transaction details are posted to the general ledger accounts. For example, goods are normally entered into inventories records when the goods are received, but accounts payable records will not record the liability until the invoice arrives because shipping documents may not record price details.

The periodic method requires a proper cut-off between the general ledger recording of goods received, shipped and returned, and the inventories counted. The perpetual method requires that all inventories movements are properly recorded in the perpetual records so that a valid comparison is made between inventories counted and the perpetual record quantities. Further, if the perpetual method is not integrated with the general ledger, there is a need to ensure a proper cut-off between the general ledger and the perpetual records. Thus, at the end of the reporting period it is essential that proper cut-off procedures be implemented.

The following situations could give rise to errors unless cut-off procedures are put into place.
- Goods have been received into inventories, but the purchase invoice has not been processed.
- Goods have been returned to a supplier, and deleted from inventories, but the credit note has not been processed.
- Goods have been sold and dispatched to a customer, but the invoice has not been raised.
- Goods have been returned by a customer, but the credit note has not been issued.

If inventories movements have been processed before invoices and credit notes, adjusting entries are needed to bring both sides of the transaction into the same accounting period.

4.5.3 Goods in transit

Accounting for goods in transit at the end of the reporting period depends upon the terms of trade. Where goods are purchased on an FOB shipping basis, the goods belong to the purchaser from the time they are shipped, and are included in inventories/accounts payable at the end of the reporting period. All such purchases in transit need to be identified and the following adjusting journal entry posted.

Goods in transit (inventories)	Dr	1 500	
Accounts payable	Cr		1 500
(Recognition of inventories in transit at the end of the reporting period)			

If goods are purchased on FOB destination terms, no adjustment is required because the goods still legally belong to the supplier.

If goods are sold on FOB destination terms, they belong to the entity until they arrive at the customer's premises. Because the sale will have been recorded in the current year, the following adjusting entries are required to remove that sale and reinstate the inventories.

Inventories	Dr	3 000	
Cost of sales	Cr		3 000
(Reversal of sale for goods in transit at the end of the reporting period)			
Sales revenue	Dr	4 500	
Accounts receivable	Cr		4 500
(Reversal of sale for goods in transit at the end of the reporting period)			

4.5.4 Consignment inventories

Care must be taken in the treatment of consignment inventories. Under a consignment arrangement, an agent (the consignee) agrees to sell goods on behalf of the consignor on a commission basis. The transfer of goods to the consignee is not a legal sale/purchase transaction. Legal ownership remains with the consignor until the agent sells the goods to a third party. Steps must be taken to ensure that goods held on consignment are not included in the physical count. Equally, goods owned by the entity that are held by consignees must be added to the physical count.

4.5.5 Control account/subsidiary ledger reconciliation

The perpetual method requires that the general ledger account balance be reconciled with the total of the subsidiary ledger (manual or computerised) at the end of the period. This reconciliation process is not required under the periodic method.

Recording errors and omissions may cause differences between the general ledger control and the subsidiary inventory ledgers accounts. Any material discrepancies should be investigated and corrected. This process will identify only amounts that have not been posted to both records; it cannot identify errors within the subsidiary records, such as posting a purchase to the wrong inventories item code. However, the physical count/recorded figure reconciliation will isolate these errors.

Illustrative example 4.6 demonstrates various end-of-period adjustments.

ILLUSTRATIVE EXAMPLE 4.6

End-of-period adjustments

John Smith, trading as Adelaide Pty Ltd, completed his first year of trading as a toy wholesaler on 30 June 2024. He is worried about his end-of-year physical and cut-off procedures.

The inventories ledger account balance at 30 June 2024, under the perpetual inventories method, was $78 700. His physical count, however, revealed the cost of inventories on hand at 30 June 2024 to be only $73 400. While John expected a small inventories shortfall due to breakage and petty theft, he considered this shortfall to be excessive.

Upon investigating reasons for the inventories 'shortfall', John discovered the following.

- Goods costing $800 were sold on credit to R Jones for $1300 on 26 June 2024 on FOB destination terms. The goods were still in transit at 30 June 2024. Adelaide Pty Ltd recorded the sale on 26 June 2024 but did not include these goods in the physical count.
- Included in the physical count were $2200 of goods held on consignment.
- Goods costing $910 were purchased on credit from Tugun Ltd on 25 June 2024 and received on 28 June 2024. The purchase was unrecorded at 30 June 2024 but the goods were included in the physical count.
- Goods costing $400 were purchased on credit from Mandurah Supplies on 23 June 2024 on FOB shipping terms. The goods were delivered to the transport company on 27 June 2024. The purchase was recorded on 27 June 2024 but, as the goods had not yet arrived, Adelaide Pty Ltd did not include these goods in the physical count.

- At 30 June 2024 Adelaide Pty Ltd had unsold goods costing $3700 out on consignment. These goods were not included in the physical count.
- Goods costing $2100 were sold on credit to Toowoomba Ltd for $3200 on 24 June 2024 on FOB shipping terms. The goods were shipped on 28 June 2024. The sale was unrecorded at 30 June 2024 and Adelaide Pty Ltd did not include these goods in the physical count.
- Goods costing $1500 had been returned to Newcastle Garments on 30 June 2024. A credit note was received from the supplier on 5 July 2024. No payment had been made for the goods prior to their return.

These transactions and events must be analysed to determine if adjustments are required to the ledger accounts (general and subsidiary) and/or the physical count records as follows.

Workings	Recorded balance $	Physical count $
Balance prior to adjustment	$78 700	$73 400
Add: Goods sold, FOB destination and in transit at 30 June	800	800
Less: Goods held on consignment	—	(2 200)
Add: Unrecorded purchase	910	—
Add: Goods purchased, FOB shipping and in transit at 30 June	—	400
Add: Goods out on consignment	—	3 700
Less: Unrecorded sale	(2 100)	—
Less: Unrecorded purchase returns	(1 500)	—
	$76 810	$76 100

If, after all adjustments are made, the recorded balance cannot be reconciled to the physical count, the remaining discrepancy is presumed to represent inventories losses and a final adjustment is made as follows.

Adjusted balances	$76 810	$76 100
Inventories shortfall	(710)	—
	$76 100	$76 100

Required

Prepare the journal entries necessary on 30 June 2024 to correct the errors and adjust the inventories ledger accounts.

Solution

The required journal entries are as follows.

ADELAIDE PTY LTD General journal			
2024 30 June			
Sales revenue Accounts receivable (R Jones) (Correction of sale recorded in error)	Dr Cr	1 300	1 300
Inventories (Item X) Cost of sales (Correction of sale recorded in error)	Dr Cr	800	800
Inventories (Item Y) Accounts payable (Tugun Ltd) (Correction of unrecorded purchase)	Dr Cr	910	910
Accounts receivable (Toowoomba Ltd) Sales revenue (Correction of unrecorded sale)	Dr Cr	3 200	3 200
Cost of sales Inventories (Item Z) (Correction of unrecorded sale)	Dr Cr	2 100	2 100

ADELAIDE PTY LTD General journal			
Accounts payable (Newcastle Garments) Inventories (Item W) (Correction of unrecorded purchase return)	Dr Cr	1 500	1 500
Inventories losses and write-downs Inventories (Unexplained variance (physical/records) written off)	Dr Cr	710	710

LEARNING CHECK

☐ Physical count, end-of-year cut-off and reconciliation procedures are undertaken to ensure that reported figures for inventories, cost of sales and other expenses are accurate and complete.

☐ Inventories are counted under the *periodic method* at the end of each accounting period to determine the balance of closing inventories. The movement in inventories balances plus the cost of purchases is presumed to represent the cost of sales during the reporting period.

☐ Inventories are counted under the *perpetual method* to compare actual quantities on hand with recorded quantities. Discrepancies are investigated.

☐ Cut-off procedures are used to ensure that the accounting and the physical count include all transactions relevant to the accounting period, while excluding those that belong to other periods.

☐ Goods in transit at the end of the reporting period are identified and accounted for according to the terms of trade.

☐ Goods held by the entity on consignment are excluded from the physical count. Goods owned by the entity that are held by consignees are added to the physical count.

☐ Under the perpetual method, the general ledger account balance must be reconciled with the total of the subsidiary ledger. Any material discrepancies should be investigated and corrected.

4.6 Assigning costs to inventories on sale

LEARNING OBJECTIVE 4.6 Explain why cost flow assumptions are required and apply both the FIFO and weighted average cost formulas.

The method of recording inventories held by an entity does not affect initial recognition at cost but has a significant impact when those inventories are sold. As shown in illustrative example 4.5, under the perpetual system the cost of inventories is transferred to a 'cost of sales' expense account on sale, and under the periodic system a 'cost of sales' figure is calculated at the end of the reporting period. This is an easy task if the nature of inventories is such that it is possible to clearly identify the exact inventory item that has been sold and its cost, but what if it is not possible to identify exactly the cost of the item sold? How can you measure the cost of a tonne of wheat when it is extracted from a stockpile consisting of millions of tonnes acquired at different prices over the accounting period?

There are two rules for determining the cost of inventories sold.

1. *Specific identification* (AASB 102/IAS 2 paragraph 23). The inventories are specifically identified and assigned an individual specific cost — this is applicable to inventories that are not interchangeable, and goods and services produced under specific projects, such as works of art. On sale of the item the exact cost is recorded as cost of sales.

2. *Assigned cost* (AASB 102/IAS 2 paragraph 25). Where a specific cost cannot be determined, the cost of inventories is assigned by using the first-in, first-out (FIFO) or weighted average cost formula. This means that, where a specific cost cannot be identified because of the nature of the item sold, then some method has to be adopted to estimate that cost. This process is known as 'assigning' cost. Most inventories fall into this category; for example, identical items of food and clothing and bulk items like oil and minerals. Note that only two methods — FIFO and weighted average — are permitted in Australia.

4.6.1 First-in, first-out (FIFO) cost formula

As described in paragraph 27 of AASB 102/IAS 2, the **first-in, first-out (FIFO) cost formula** assumes that items of inventory that were purchased or produced first are sold first, and the items remaining in inventories at the end of the period are those most recently purchased or produced. Thus, more recent purchase costs are assigned to the inventories asset account, and older costs are assigned to the cost of sales expense account.

To illustrate, assume an entity has 515 Blu-ray players on hand at 30 June 2024, and recent purchase invoices showed the following costs.

28 June	180 players at $49.00
15 June	325 players at $48.50
31 May	200 players at $47.00

The value of ending inventories is found by starting with the most recent purchase and working backwards until all items on hand have been priced (on the assumption that it is not known when any particular Blu-ray player was sold). The value of ending inventories is $25 052.50, determined as follows.

180 players at $49.00	$ 8 820.00
325 players at $48.50	15 762.50
10 players at $47.00	470.00
515 players	$25 052.50

Proponents of the FIFO method argue that this method best reflects the physical movement of inventories, particularly perishable goods or those subject to changes in fashion or rapid obsolescence (as in the case of Blu-ray players). If the oldest goods are normally sold first, then the oldest costs should be assigned to expense. In accounting for sales returns it is assumed that the inventories returned were the most recently sold, that is, the cost of the inventories returned is based on a last-out, first-returned basis. This is consistent with the principle of the oldest goods being sold first.

4.6.2 Weighted average cost formula

Under the **weighted average cost formula**, the cost of each item sold is determined from the cost of similar items purchased or produced during the period. The average may be calculated on a periodic basis (periodic weighted average method), or as each additional shipment is received (moving weighted average method).

Using a *periodic weighted average method*, the cost of inventories on hand at the beginning of the period plus all inventories purchased during the year is divided by the total number of items available for sale during the period (opening quantity plus purchased quantity). This produces the cost per unit. For example, consider inventories held and acquired over the 2022–23 year.

Inventories on hand at 1 July 2022	134 units at $25.67 (average)	$ 3 439.78
Purchases during the year:		
	200 units at $27.50	5 500.00
	175 units at $28.35	4 961.25
	300 units at $29.10	8 730.00
	120 units at $29.00	3 480.00
Inventories on hand at 30 June 2023	929 units	$26 111.03
Periodic weighted average cost	= $26 111.03/929 units	
	= $28.11 per unit	

Using the *moving weighted average method*, the average unit cost is recalculated each time there is an inventories purchase or purchase return. This is demonstrated in illustrative example 4.7.

ILLUSTRATIVE EXAMPLE 4.7

Application of cost formulas

The following information has been extracted from the records of Armidale Parts about one of its products. Armidale Parts uses the perpetual inventories method and its reporting period ends on 31 December.

▶

Date	Details	No. of units	Unit cost $	Total cost $
2024				
01/01	Beginning balance	800	7.00	5 600
06/01	Purchased	300	7.05	2 115
05/02	Sold @ $12.00 per unit	1 000		
19/03	Purchased	1 100	7.35	8 085
24/03	Purchase returns	80	7.35	588
10/04	Sold @ $12.10 per unit	700		
22/06	Purchased	8 400	7.50	63 000
31/07	Sold @ $13.25 per unit	1 800		
04/08	Sales returns @ $13.25 per unit	20		
04/09	Sold @ $13.50 per unit	3 500		
06/10	Purchased	500	8.00	4 000
27/11	Sold @ $15.00 per unit	3 100		

Required

1. Calculate the cost of inventories on hand at 31 December 2024 and the cost of sales for the year ended 31 December 2024, assuming:
   (a) the FIFO method
   (b) the moving weighted average method (round the average unit costs to the nearest cent, and round the total cost amounts to the nearest dollar).
2. Prepare the trading section of the statement of profit or loss and other comprehensive income for the year ended 31 December 2024 for the FIFO method and the moving weighted average method.

Solution

1. (a) FIFO method

Date	Details	Purchases No. units	Purchases Unit cost	Purchases Total cost	Cost of sales No. units	Cost of sales Unit cost	Cost of sales Total cost	Balance[1] No. units	Balance[1] Unit cost	Balance[1] Total cost
01/01	Inventories balance							800	7.00	5 600
06/01	Purchases	300	7.05	2 115				800	7.00	5 600
								300	7.05	2 115
05/02	Sales				800	7.00	5 600			
					200	7.05	1 410	100	7.05	705
19/03	Purchases	1 100	7.35	8 085				100	7.05	705
								1 100	7.35	8 085
24/03	Purchase returns	(80)	7.35	(588)				100	7.05	705
								1 020	7.35	7 497
10/04	Sales				100	7.05	705			
					600	7.35	4 410	420	7.35	3 087
22/06	Purchases	8 400	7.50	63 000				420	7.35	3 087
								8 400	7.50	63 000
31/07	Sales				420	7.35	3 087			
					1 380	7.50	10 350	7 020	7.50	52 650
04/08	Sales returns[2]				(20)	7.50	(150)	7 040	7.50	52 800
04/09	Sales				3 500	7.50	26 250	3 540	7.50	26 550
06/10	Purchases	500	8.00	4 000				3 540	7.50	26 550
								500	8.00	4 000
22/11	Sales				3 100	7.50	23 250	440	7.50	3 300
								500	8.00	4 000
				76 612			74 912			

Notes: 1. As it is assumed the earliest purchases are sold first, a separate balance of each purchase at a different price must be maintained.

2. The principle of 'last-out, first-in' is applied to sales returns.

(b) Moving weighted average method

Date	Details	Purchases			Cost of sales[1]			Balance		
		No. units	Unit cost	Total cost	No. units	Unit cost	Total cost	No. units	Unit cost	Total cost
01/01	Inventories balance							800	7.00	5 600
06/01	Purchases	300	7.05	2 115				1 100	7.01	7 715
05/02	Sales				1 000	7.01	7 010	100	7.01	705
19/03	Purchases	1 100	7.35	8 085				1 200	7.33	8 790
24/03	Purchase returns	(80)	7.35	(588)				1 120	7.32	8 202
10/04	Sales				700	7.32	5 124	420	7.32	3 078
22/06	Purchases	8 400	7.50	63 000				8 820	7.49	66 078
31/07	Sales				1 800	7.49	13 482	7 020	7.49	52 596
04/08	Sales returns				(20)	7.49	(150)	7 040	7.49	52 746
04/09	Sales				3 500	7.49	26 215	3 540	7.49	26 531
06/10	Purchases	500	8.00	4 000				4 040	7.56	30 531
22/11	Sales				3 100	7.56	23 436	940	7.55	7 095
				76 612			75 117			

Notes: 1. The 'average' cost on the date of sale is applied to calculate the 'cost of sales'.
2. The average cost per unit is recalculated each time there is a purchase or a purchase return at a different cost.
3. The unit cost for cost of sales and the unit cost of inventories held differ on 22/11 as a result of rounding.

2. The trading section of the statement of profit or loss and other comprehensive income for the year ended 31 December 2024 is as follows.

ARMIDALE PARTS Statement of profit or loss and other comprehensive income (extract) for the year ended 31 December 2024	FIFO	Moving weighted average
Sales revenue	$138 070	$138 070
Less: Sales returns	(265)	(265)
Net sales	137 805	137 805
Less: Cost of sales	(74 912)	(75 117)
Gross profit	$ 62 893	$ 62 688

Because the purchase price has been rising throughout the year, using the FIFO method produces a lower cost of sales (higher gross profit) and a higher inventories balance than the moving weighted average method.

4.6.3 Which costing method to use?

The choice of method is a matter for management judgement and depends on the nature of the inventories, the information needs of management and financial statement users, and the cost of applying the formulas. For example, the weighted average method is easy to apply and is particularly suited to inventories where homogeneous products are mixed together, such as iron ore or spring water. On the other hand, first-in, first-out may be a better reflection of the actual physical movement of goods, such as those with use-by dates where the first produced must be sold first to avoid loss due to obsolescence, spoilage or legislative restrictions.

Entities with diversified operations may use both methods because they carry different types of inventories. According to paragraph 26 of AASB 102/IAS 2, using diverse methods is acceptable but reasons such as 'a difference in geographical location of inventories' are not sufficient to justify the use of different cost formulas. The nature of the inventories themselves should determine the choice of formula.

4.6.4 Consistent application of costing methods

In accordance with paragraphs 13 and 14 of AASB 108/IAS 8 *Accounting Policies, Changes in Accounting Estimates and Errors*, once a cost formula has been selected, management cannot randomly switch from one formula to another. Because the choice of method can have a significant impact on an entity's reported profit and asset figures, particularly in times of volatile prices, indiscriminate changes in formulas could result in the reporting of financial information that is neither comparable nor reliable. Accounting policies must be consistently applied to ensure comparability of financial information. Changes in accounting policies are allowed only when required by an accounting standard or where the change results in reporting more relevant and reliable financial information. Therefore, unless the nature of inventories changes, it is unlikely that the cost formula will change.

A switch from the FIFO to the weighted average method must be disclosed. According to paragraph 19 of AASB 108/IAS 8, the change must be applied retrospectively, and the information disclosed as if the new accounting policy had always been applied. Hence, a change from the FIFO method to the weighted average method requires adjustments to the financial statements to show the information as if the weighted average method had always been applied. The accounting treatment and disclosures required for a change of accounting policy are considered in chapter 18 of this text.

LEARNING CHECK

☐ Where a specific cost cannot be determined, the cost of inventories is assigned by using the first-in, first-out (FIFO) cost formula or the weighted average cost formula.

☐ The FIFO formula assumes that items of inventory that were purchased or produced first are sold first, and the items remaining in inventories at the end of the period are those most recently purchased or produced. Thus, more recent purchase costs are assigned to the inventories asset account, and older costs are assigned to the cost of sales expense account.

☐ Under the weighted average cost formula, the cost of each item sold is determined from the cost of similar items purchased or produced during the period. The average may be calculated on a periodic basis (periodic weighted average method) or as each additional shipment is received (moving weighted average method).

☐ Using a *periodic weighted average method*, the cost per unit of inventory is determined by dividing the inventories on hand at the beginning of the period plus all inventories purchased during the year by the total number of items available for sale during the period (opening quantity plus purchased quantity).

☐ Using the *moving weighted average method*, the average unit cost is recalculated each time there is an inventories purchase or purchase return.

☐ Under AASB 108/IAS 8, once a cost formula has been selected, it must be consistently applied to ensure comparability of financial information, with changes being allowed only in specified circumstances.

4.7 Net realisable value

LEARNING OBJECTIVE 4.7 Explain the net realisable value basis of measurement and account for adjustments to net realisable value.

Recall that in AASB 102/IAS 2, the measurement rule for inventories is the lower of cost and net realisable value, so an estimate of net realisable value must be made to determine whether inventories must be written down. Normally, this estimate is done before preparing the financial reports. However, where management become aware during the reporting period that goods or services can no longer be sold at a price above cost, inventories values should be written down to net realisable value. As noted in paragraph 28 of AASB 102/IAS 2, the rationale for this measurement rule is that assets should not be carried in excess of amounts expected to be realised from their sale or use.

Net realisable value is the net amount that an entity expects to realise from the sale of inventories in the ordinary course of business. Paragraph 6 of AASB 102/IAS 2 defines it as:

> the estimated selling price in the ordinary course of business less the estimated costs of completion and the estimated costs necessary to make the sale.

Net realisable value may fall below cost for a number of reasons including:
- a fall in selling price (e.g. fashion garments)
- physical deterioration of inventories (e.g. fruit and vegetables)

- product obsolescence (e.g. computers and electrical equipment)
- a decision, as part of an entity's marketing strategy, to manufacture and sell products for the time being at a loss (e.g. new products)
- miscalculations or other errors in purchasing or production (e.g. overstocking)
- an increase in the estimated costs of completion or the estimated costs of making the sale (e.g. labour force problems during the manufacturing stage).

Net realisable value is specific to an individual entity and is not necessarily equal to fair value less selling costs because the latter is based on the hypothetical exit price from the perspective of a market participant.

4.7.1 Estimating net realisable value

Estimates of net realisable value must be based on the most reliable evidence available at the time the estimate is made. Thus, estimates must be made of:
- expected selling price
- estimated costs of completion (if any)
- estimated selling costs.

These estimates take into consideration fluctuations of price or cost occurring after the end of the reporting period to the extent that such events confirm conditions existing at the end of the reporting period. The purpose for which inventories are held should be taken into account when reviewing net realisable values. For example, the net realisable value of inventories held to satisfy firm sales or service contracts is based on the contract price. If the sales contracts are for less than the inventories quantities held, the net realisable value of the excess is based on general selling prices. Estimated selling costs include all incremental costs likely to be incurred in securing and filling customer orders such as advertising costs, sales personnel salaries and operating costs, and the costs of storing and shipping finished goods.

It is possible to use formulas based on predetermined criteria to initially estimate net realisable value. These formulas normally take into account, as appropriate, the age, past movements, expected future movements and estimated scrap values of the inventories. However, the results must be reviewed in the light of any special circumstances not anticipated in the formulas, such as changes in the current demand for inventories or unexpected obsolescence. As a rule of thumb, there may be a net realisable value problem if the inventory item has a last sales price that is lower than its cost.

4.7.2 Materials and other supplies

According to paragraph 32 of AASB 102/IAS 2, materials and other supplies held for use in the production of inventories are not written down below cost if the finished goods in which they will be incorporated are expected to be sold at or above cost. When the sale of finished goods is not expected to recover the costs, then materials are to be written down to net realisable value. In some situations, replacement cost of the materials or other supplies may be the best measure of their net realisable value.

4.7.3 Write-down to net realisable value

Inventories are usually written down to net realisable value on an item-by-item basis (AASB 102/IAS 2 paragraph 29). It is not appropriate to write inventories down on the basis of a classification of inventories (e.g. finished goods) or all the inventories in a particular industry or geographical segment. Where it is not practicable to separately evaluate the net realisable value of each item within a product line, the write-down may be applied on a group basis provided that the products have similar purposes or end uses, and are produced and marketed in the same geographical area.

The journal entry to process a write-down of $800 is as follows.

Inventories write-down expense	Dr	800
Inventories	Cr	800
(Write-down to net realisable value)		

In its 2017 annual report, Energy Resources of Australia reported a write-down of inventories to net realisable value, as shown in figure 4.2.

FIGURE 4.2　Write-down to net realisable value

9 Inventories — current

	2017 $'000	2016 $'000
Stores and spares	17 182	16 128
Ore stockpiles at cost	8 863	37 340
Work in progress at cost	3 737	2 424
Finished product U_3O_8 at cost	86 144	71 382
Total current inventory	**115 926**	**127 274**

Inventory expense

Obsolescence of inventory provided for and recognised as an expense during the year ended 31 December 2017 amounted to nil (2016: $840 635).

Write-downs of inventories to net realisable value recognised as an expense during the year ended 31 December 2017 amounted to $7 102 511 (2016: $24 780 087). The expense has been included in 'Changes in Inventories' in statement of comprehensive income.

11 Inventories — non-current

	2017 $'000	2016 $'000
Ore stockpiles at cost	0	9 791

Source: Energy Resources of Australia (2017, p. 78).

4.7.4 Reversal of prior write-down to net realisable value

If the circumstances that previously caused inventories to be written down below cost change, or if a new assessment confirms that net realisable value has increased, the amount of a previous write-down can be reversed (subject to an upper limit of the original write-down). This could occur if an item of inventory that has been written down to net realisable value because of falling sales prices is still on hand at the end of a subsequent period and its selling price has recovered.

The journal entry to process the reversal is as follows.

Inventories	Dr	800	
Inventories write-down expense	Cr		800
(Write-up to revised net realisable value)			

Illustrative example 4.8 demonstrates the application of the lower of cost and net realisable value measurement rule where there are multiple items of inventories.

ILLUSTRATIVE EXAMPLE 4.8

Application of measurement rule

Albany Pty Ltd retails gardening equipment and has four main product lines: mowers, vacuum blowers, edgers and garden tools.

At 30 June 2022, cost and net realisable values for each line were as shown below.

Application of lower of cost and net realisable value measurement rule

Inventories item	Quantity	Cost per unit $	NRV per unit $	Lower of cost and NRV $
Mowers	16	215.80	256.00	3 452.80
Vacuum blowers	113	62.35	60.00	6 780.00
Edgers	78	27.40	36.00	2 137.20
Garden tools	129	12.89	11.00	1 419.00
Inventories at the lower of cost and net realisable value				13 789.00

As the inventories have been recorded at cost, the following journal entry would be required at 30 June 2022 to adjust inventories values to net realisable value.

Inventories write-down expense	Dr	509.36	
Inventories	Cr		509.36
(Write-down to net realisable value — vacuum blowers $265.55 (113 × $2.35) and garden tools $243.81 (129 × $1.89))			

LEARNING CHECK

☐ Because the measurement rule for inventories is the lower of cost and net realisable value, an estimate of net realisable value must be made to determine whether inventories should be written down.

☐ Estimates of net realisable value must be based on the most reliable evidence available at the time and consider expected selling price, estimated costs of completion and estimated selling costs.

☐ Inventories are usually written down to net realisable value on an item-by-item basis. However, where it is not practicable to separately evaluate the net realisable value of each item within a product line, then under specified conditions the write-down may be applied on a group basis.

☐ The amount of a previous write-down can be reversed (subject to an upper limit of the original write-down).

4.8 Recognition as an expense

LEARNING OBJECTIVE 4.8 Account for inventories expense.

According to paragraph 34 of AASB 102/IAS 2, the following items must be recognised as expenses:
- carrying amount of inventories in the period in which the related revenue is recognised; in other words, cost of sales
- write-down of inventories to net realisable value
- all losses of inventories.

The only exception to this rule relates to inventories used by an entity as components in self-constructed property, plant or equipment. The cost of these items is capitalised and recognised as an expense via depreciation.

Where inventories have been written down to net realisable value and this has been reversed in the current period, the amount of any reversal is recognised as a reduction in the amount of inventories recognised as an expense in the period in which the reversal occurs.

LEARNING CHECK

☐ The following items must be recognised as expenses: cost of sales, write-down of inventories to net realisable value and all losses of inventories.

☐ The amount of any reversal of write-downs to net realisable value is recognised as a reduction in the amount of inventories recognised as an expense.

4.9 Disclosure

LEARNING OBJECTIVE 4.9 Identify the disclosure requirements of AASB 102/IAS 2.

According to paragraph 36 of AASB 102/IAS 2, the financial statements of an entity must disclose:

(a) the accounting policies adopted in measuring inventories, including the cost formula used;
(b) the total carrying amount of inventories and the carrying amount in classifications appropriate to the entity;
(c) the carrying amount of inventories carried at fair value less costs to sell;
(d) the amount of inventories recognised as an expense during the period;
(e) the amount of any write-down of inventories recognised as an expense in the period in accordance with paragraph 34;
(f) the amount of any reversal of any write-down that is recognised as a reduction in the amount of inventories recognised as expense in the period in accordance with paragraph 34;
(g) the circumstances or events that led to the reversal of a write-down of inventories in accordance with paragraph 34; and
(h) the carrying amount of inventories pledged as security for liabilities.

In relation to the disclosures required by paragraph 36(a) of AASB 102/IAS 2, Wesfarmers Limited provided the information shown in figure 4.3.

FIGURE 4.3 Accounting policy on inventories, Wesfarmers

Recognition and measurement

Inventories are valued at the lower of cost and net realisable value. The net realisable value of inventories is the estimated selling price in the ordinary course of business less estimated costs to sell.

Key estimate: net realisable value

The key assumptions, which require the use of management judgement, are the variables affecting costs recognised in bringing the inventory to their location and condition for sale, estimated costs to sell and the expected selling price. These key assumptions are reviewed at least annually. The total expense relating to inventory writedowns during the year was $78 million (2017: $11 million), which is inclusive of the $66 million writedown of stock made during the financial year for BUKI [Bunnings United Kingdom and Ireland, disposed of during the year]. Any reasonably possible change in the estimate is unlikely to have a material impact.

Costs incurred in bringing each product to its present location and condition are accounted for as follows.

- *Raw materials:* purchase cost on a weighted average basis.
- *Manufactured finished goods and work in progress:* cost of direct materials and labour and a proportion of manufacturing overheads based on normal operating capacity, but excluding borrowing costs. Work in progress also includes run-of-mine coal stocks for Resources, consisting of production costs of drilling, blasting and overburden removal.
- *Retail and wholesale merchandise finished goods:* purchase cost on a weighted average basis, after deducting any settlement discounts, supplier rebates and including logistics expenses incurred in bringing the inventories to their present location and condition.

Volume-related supplier rebates, and supplier promotional rebates where they exceed spend on promotional activities, are accounted for as a reduction in the cost of inventory and recognised in the income statement when the inventory is sold.

Key estimate: supplier rebates

The recognition of certain supplier rebates in the income statement requires management to estimate both the volume of purchases that will be made during a period of time and the related product that was sold and remains in inventory at reporting date. Management's estimates are based on existing and forecast inventory turnover levels and sales. Reasonably possible changes in these estimates are unlikely to have a material impact.

Source: Wesfarmers Limited (2018, p. 112).

Paragraph 37 of AASB 102/IAS 2 notes that information about the carrying amounts held in different classifications of inventories is useful to financial statement users. Such disclosure was provided by Energy Resources of Australia as shown in figure 4.2.

SUMMARY

This chapter has covered the principles of measurement of inventories as contained in AASB 102/IAS 2 *Inventories*. Some of the key principles are as follows.

- Inventories consist of raw materials, work-in-progress and finished goods.
- Inventories are measured at the lower of cost and net realisable value.
- Cost consists of costs of purchase, costs of conversion and other costs incurred in bringing the inventories to their present location and condition.
- There are two main record-keeping methods for inventories, namely the periodic method and the perpetual method.
- At the end of a period, a physical count is undertaken under both the inventories methods, but for different purposes.
- To measure the cost of inventories, if possible, specific cost is used.
- Where specific cost cannot be measured, costs are assigned to inventories using either the FIFO or weighted average cost formulas.
- When the net realisable value falls below cost, inventories must be written down with an expense recognised in the period of write-down.
- Previous write-downs to net realisable value may be reversed.

KEY TERMS

cost of sales The cost of inventories sold.

first-in, first-out (FIFO) cost formula A method of assigning the cost of inventories which assumes that items of inventory that were purchased or produced first are sold first, and the items remaining in inventories at the end of the period are those most recently purchased or produced.

inventories Assets held for sale in the ordinary course of business, in the process of production for such sale, or in the form of materials or supplies to be consumed in the production process or in the rendering of services.

net realisable value The estimated selling price in the ordinary course of business less the estimated costs of completion and the estimated costs necessary to make the sale.

periodic method A method of accounting for inventories in which the amount of inventories on hand is determined periodically by conducting a physical count and multiplying the number of units by a cost per unit to measure the inventories on hand.

perpetual method A method of accounting for inventories in which the inventories account is updated each time a transaction involving inventories takes place.

weighted average cost formula A method of assigning the cost of inventories in which the cost of each item sold is determined from the cost of similar items purchased or produced during the period.

DEMONSTRATION PROBLEMS

4.1 Reconciling the inventories control ledger and the physical account

Brisbane Outfitters sells outdoor adventure equipment. The entity uses the perpetual method to account for inventories transactions and assigns costs using the moving weighted average formula. All purchases and sales are made on FOB destination, 30-day credit terms.

At 30 June 2022, the balance of the inventories control account in the general ledger was $248 265. A physical count showed goods worth $256 100 to be on hand. Investigations of the discrepancy between the general ledger account balance and the count total revealed the following.

- Damaged ropes worth $1200 were returned to the supplier on 29 June, but this transaction has not yet been recorded.
- During the stocktake, staff found that a box of leather gloves worth $595 had suffered water damage during a recent storm. The gloves were damaged beyond repair and so were not included in the count, but they are still recorded in the inventories records.
- Equipment worth $1500, which was sold for $2500 on 29 June, was still in transit to the customer on 30 June. The sale was recorded on 29 June and the equipment was not included in the physical count. The equipment was sold on FOB destination terms.

- An error occurred when posting the purchase journal totals for May 2022. The correct total of $25 100 was erroneously posted as $21 500.
- The physical count included goods worth $7600 that were being held on consignment for All Weather Gear Pty Ltd.
- An all-terrain kit worth $1570 was returned by a customer on 28 June. The sales return transaction was correctly journalised and posted to the ledgers, but the kit was not returned to the warehouse and therefore was not included in the physical count.

Required

Adjust and reconcile the inventories control ledger account balance to the physical account (adjusted as necessary).

SOLUTION

The balance of the inventories control account is as follows:

Unadjusted balance	$248 265
(a) Purchase return not recorded	(1 200)
(b) Damaged goods written off	(595)
(c) Goods in transit	1 500
(d) Error in posting May purchases	3 600
Adjusted balance (cost)	$251 570

The reasoning for each of the adjustments to the unadjusted balance of inventories is as follows.
(a) The inventories have been returned to the supplier. They should no longer be included in the entity's inventories as they are no longer assets of the entity. However, as no recording has yet taken place they are still included in the entity's inventories account. The inventories account needs to be reduced by $1200.
(b) The damaged goods are not included in the physical count. As they are damaged beyond repair they need to be removed from the inventories account. The inventories account needs to be reduced by $595.
(c) Accounting for goods in transit depends on the terms of trade. If goods are sold on FOB destination terms, they belong to the entity until they arrive at the customer's premises. An adjustment entry is necessary to remove the recorded sale and reinstate the inventories. $1500 needs to be added back to the unadjusted balance of inventories.
(d) The error involved increasing inventories by $21 500 instead of by $25 100. The inventories account needs to be increased by $3600.

The reconciliation of the inventories control account to the physical count is as follows.

Physical count	$256 100
(e) Goods in transit	1 500
(f) Consignment stock	(7 600)
(g) Returned goods not included	1 570
Adjusted count	251 570
Control account balance	$251 570

The adjustments to the physical count are explained as follows.
(e) As the goods were sold on FOB destination terms they still belong to the inventories of the entity, and so have to be added back.
(f) As the inventories were only held on consignment they are not the assets of the entity. Hence, the physical stock must be reduced to calculate only the inventories that belong to the entity.
(g) The sales return of the all-terrain kit has been correctly journalised. However, it should also have been included in the count of the inventories on hand. Hence, $1570 is added onto the physical count.

The adjusted physical count is now the same amount as the adjusted balance of the inventories control account.

4.2 Inventories, cost of sales and reporting

The following information has been extracted from the records of Townsville Trading about one of its products for the year ended 30 September 2023. Townsville Trading uses the perpetual system.

		No. of units	Unit cost $	Total cost $
01/10	Beginning balance	1 600	14.00	22 400
06/10	Purchased	600	14.10	8 460
05/11	Sold @ $24.00 per unit	2 000		
19/12	Purchased	2 200	14.70	32 340
24/12	Purchase returns	160	14.70	2 352
10/01	Sold @ $24.20 per unit	1 400		
22/03	Purchased	16 800	15.00	252 000
30/04	Sold @ $26.50 per unit	3 600		
04/05	Sales returns @ $26.50 per unit	40		
04/06	Sold @ $27.00 per unit	7 000		
06/08	Purchased	1 000	16.00	16 000
27/09	Sold @ $30.00 per unit	6 200		

Required

1. Calculate the cost of inventories on hand at 30 September 2023 and the cost of sales for the year ended 30 September 2023, using the:
   (a) FIFO method
   (b) moving weighted average method (round the average unit costs to the nearest cent, and round the total cost amounts to the nearest dollar).
2. Prepare the trading section of the statement of profit or loss and other comprehensive income for the year ended 30 September 2023, using the FIFO method and the moving weighted average method.

SOLUTION

1. (a) FIFO method

   The cost of the inventories on hand and the cost of sales under the FIFO method is calculated as follows.

Date	Details	Purchases No. units	Purchases Unit cost	Purchases Total cost	Cost of sales No. units	Cost of sales Unit cost	Cost of sales Total cost	Balance No. units	Balance Unit cost	Balance Total cost
01/10	Inventories balance							1 600	14.00	22 400
06/10	Purchases	600	14.10	8 460				1 600	14.00	22 400
								600	14.10	8 460
05/11	Sales				1 600	14.00	22 400			
					400	14.10	5 640	200	14.10	2 820
19/12	Purchases	2 200	14.70	32 340				200	14.10	2 820
								2 200	14.70	32 340
24/12	Purchase returns	(160)	14.70	(2 352)				200	14.10	2 820
								2 040	14.70	29 988
10/01	Sales				200	14.10	2 820			
					1 200	14.70	17 640	840	14.70	12 348
22/03	Purchases	16 800	15.00	252 000				840	14.70	12 348
								16 800	15.00	252 000
30/04	Sales				840	14.70	12 348			
					2 760	15.00	41 400	14 040	15.00	210 600
04/05	Sales returns				(40)	15.00	(600)	14 080	15.00	211 200
04/06	Sales				7 000	15.00	105 000	7 080	15.00	106 200
06/08	Purchases	1 000	16.00	16 000				7 080	15.00	106 200
								1 000	16.00	16 000
27/09	Sales				6 200	15.00	93 000	880	15.00	13 200
								1 000	16.00	16 000
				306 448			299 648			

(b) Moving weighted average method

The cost of the inventories on hand and the cost of sales under the moving weighted average method is calculated as follows.

Date	Details	Purchases No. units	Purchases Unit cost	Purchases Total cost	Cost of sales No. units	Cost of sales Unit cost	Cost of sales Total cost	Balance No. units	Balance Unit cost	Balance Total cost
01/10	Inventories balance							1 600	14.00	22 400
06/10	Purchases	600	14.10	8 460				2 200	14.03	30 860
05/11	Sales				2 000	14.03	28 060	200	14.00	2 800
19/12	Purchases	2 200	14.70	32 340				2 400	14.64	35 140
24/12	Purchase returns	(160)	14.70	(2 352)				2 240	14.64	32 788
10/01	Sales				1 400	14.64	20 496	840	14.63	12 292
22/03	Purchases	16 800	15.00	252 000				17 640	14.98	264 292
30/04	Sales				3 600	14.98	53 928	14 040	14.98	210 364
04/05	Sales returns				(40)	14.98	(599)	14 080	14.98	210 963
04/06	Sales				7 000	14.98	104 860	7 080	14.99	106 103
06/08	Purchases	1 000	16.00	16 000				8 080	15.11	122 103
27/09	Sales				6 200	15.11	93 682	1 880	15.12	28 421
				306 448			300 427			

2. Statement of profit or loss and other comprehensive income

The trading sections of the statement of profit or loss and other comprehensive income for the year ended 30 September 2023 under the two methods are as follows.

TOWNSVILLE TRADING Statement of profit or loss and other comprehensive income (extract) for the year ended 30 September 2023		
	FIFO	Moving weighted average
Sales revenue	$551 220	$551 220
Less: Sales returns	1 060	1 060
Net sales	550 160	550 160
Less: Cost of sales	299 648	300 427
Gross profit	**$250 512**	**$249 733**

COMPREHENSION QUESTIONS

1 Define 'cost' as applied to the valuation of inventories.

2 What is meant by the term 'net realisable value'? Is this the same as fair value? If not, why not?

3 Explain the concept of lower of cost and net realisable value for inventories.

4 Which is more expensive to maintain: a perpetual method or a periodic method? Why?

5 In what circumstances must assumptions be made in order to assign a cost to inventories when they are sold?

6 'Estimating the value of inventories is not sufficiently accurate to justify using such an approach. Only a full physical count can give full accuracy.' Discuss.

7 What is the difference between the first-in, first-out formula and the weighted average formula of assigning cost?

8 Compare and contrast the impact on the reported profit and asset value for an accounting period of the first-in, first-out formula and the weighted average formula.

9 Why is the lower of cost and net realisable value rule used in the accounting standard? Is it permissible to revalue inventories upwards? If so, when?

10 What effect do the terms of trade have on the determination of the quantity and value of inventories on hand where goods are in transit at the end of the reporting period?

CASE STUDY 4.1

CALCULATION OF INVENTORIES

As a part of the auditing team assigned in relation to Mandurah Ltd, you have been asked to verify the inventories at the Halls Head branch at 30 June 2023. The company uses a perpetual method to account for inventories. In undertaking the task you note that there is a shipping container beside the main warehouse containing goods that Mandurah Ltd wants to sell. You ask the accountant at the Halls Head branch whether he plans to include the goods in the truck in the calculation of the inventories on hand at 30 June 2023. The accountant says that the goods will not be included.

You then obtain a copy of the invoice in relation to the container of goods. The container was shipped on 24 June from Sydney, marked FOB Sydney, and the total invoice price was $200 000. The freight bill amounted to $12 000, with terms requiring payment within 30 days. The accountant says he will not pay the invoice until mid-July, and so the inventories will not be included in determining the inventories on hand at 30 June 2023.

Required

Write a report to your supervisor advising on the following issues.

1. Does Mandurah Ltd have a liability that should be recorded at 30 June 2023?
2. Should the container of goods be included in the determination of the inventories balance at 30 June 2023? If so, what journal entry would be required?

CASE STUDY 4.2

INVENTORIES COSTS

You have been assigned a new graduate as part of your audit team and they have asked you a number of questions in relation to accounting for inventories at the Lake Clifton Ltd plant.

Required

Provide an answer and reasoning to the new graduate's questions, as follows.

1. Should Lake Clifton Ltd include in its inventories normal brand-name goods purchased from its suppliers but not yet received if the terms of purchase are FOB shipping point?
2. Should Lake Clifton Ltd include freight-in expenditures as an inventories cost?
3. If Lake Clifton Ltd acquires its goods on terms 5/10, n/30, should the purchases be recorded gross or net?
4. What are products on consignment, and should they be included in the inventories balance in the statement of financial position?

CASE STUDY 4.3

PURCHASE DISCOUNTS

Bunker Bay Ltd is considering alternative methods of accounting for the cash discounts it takes when paying for its supplies promptly.

Required

From a theoretical standpoint, discuss the acceptability of each of the following methods.

1. Financial income when payments are made
2. Reduction of cost of sales for the period when payments are made
3. Direct reduction of purchase cost

CASE STUDY 4.4

INVENTORIES COSTS

As a new graduate you have been assigned to the accounting team led by Andy Steel. Andy wants to determine your expertise in relation to accounting for inventories.

Required

Andy has given you the following list of questions and asked you to provide a detailed response.

1. A company is involved in the wholesaling and retailing of tyres for foreign-made cars. Most of the inventories are imported, and are valued on the company's records at the actual inventories cost plus freight-in. At year-end, the warehousing costs are pro-rated over costs of goods sold and ending inventories. Are warehousing costs a product cost or a period cost?
2. A certain portion of the company's inventories consists of obsolete items. Should obsolete items be classified as part of inventories?
3. A company purchases aeroplanes for sale to other entities. However, until they are sold, the company charters and services the planes. What is the proper way to report these aeroplanes in the company's financial statements?

APPLICATION AND ANALYSIS EXERCISES

★ BASIC | ★ ★ MODERATE | ★ ★ ★ DIFFICULT

4.1 Statement of financial position classification ★
LO1

Where, if at all, should the following items be classified on a statement of financial position?
1. Goods held by customers pending their approval of a sales contract
2. Goods in transit that were recently purchased FOB destination
3. Land held by a real estate firm for sale
4. Raw materials
5. Goods received on consignment
6. Stationery supplies

4.2 Disclosures relating to inventories ★
LO9

Ballina Pty Ltd reported inventories in its statement of financial position as follows.

Inventories	$12 094 300

Required

What additional disclosures might be necessary to present the inventories fairly?

4.3 Recording inventories transactions ★
LO3, 4

William Ltd began business on 1 March 2024. William Ltd balances the books at month-end and uses the periodic method. William Ltd's transactions for March 2024 are detailed below.

March	1	William Ltd invested $32 000 cash and $20 000 office equipment into the business.
	2	Purchased merchandise from B Broome on account for $4800 on terms of 2/15, n/30.
	5	Sold merchandise to S Moree on account for $2400 on terms of n/30.
	8	Purchased merchandise for cash, $860 on cheque no. 003.
	12	Purchased merchandise from N Narrabri on account for $4000 on terms of 2/10, n/30.
	14	Paid B Broome for 2 March purchase on cheque no. 004.
	15	Received $2400 from S Moree in payment of the account.
	21	Sold merchandise to Forbes Ltd on account for $3200 on terms of n/30.
	21	Paid N Narrabri for 12 March purchase on cheque no. 005.
	22	Purchased merchandise from B Geelong on account for $2400 on terms of 2/15, n/30.
	23	Sold merchandise for $2600 cash.
	25	Returned defective merchandise that cost $600 to B Geelong.
	28	Paid salaries of $1800 on cheque no. 006.

Required

Prepare journal entries for March 2024, using the pro-forma journals provided.

Cash receipts journal						
Date	Account	Ref.	Cash	Sales	A/c rec.	Other

Cash payments journal

Date	Account	Ch.	Ref.	Other	A/c pay.	Purch.	Interest exp.	Cash

Purchases journal

Date	Account	Terms	Ref.	Amount

Sales journal

Date	Account	Terms	Ref.	Amount

General journal

Date	Account	Ref.	Dr	Cr

4.4 Determining inventories cost and cost of sales (periodic method) ⋆ 　　　　　　　　　**LO3, 4**

Select the correct answer. Show any workings required and provide reasons to justify your choice.

1. The cost of inventories on hand at 1 January 2023 was $25 000 and at 31 December 2023 was $35 000. Inventories purchases for the year amounted to $160 000, freight outwards expense was $500, and purchase returns were $1400. What was the cost of sales for the year ended 31 December 2023?
   - (a) $148 100
   - (b) $148 600
   - (c) $149 100
   - (d) $150 000

2. The following inventories information relates to K Cooroy, who uses a periodic method and rounds the average unit cost to the nearest dollar.

Beginning inventories	10 units @ average cost of $25 each = $250
January purchase	10 units @ $24 each
July purchase	39 units @ $26 each
October purchase	20 units @ $24 each
Ending inventories	25 units

   What is the cost of ending inventories using the weighted average costing formula?
   - (a) $625
   - (b) $620
   - (c) $618.75
   - (d) $610

4.5 Assigning cost (perpetual method) ⋆ 　　　　　　　　　　　　　　　　　　　　**LO4**

Select the correct answer. Show any workings required and provide reasons to justify your choice.

Cairns Ltd uses the perpetual method. Cairns Ltd's inventories transactions for August 2024 were as follows.

		No.	Unit cost	Total cost
Aug. 1	Beginning inventories	20	$4.00	$80.00
7	Purchases	10	$4.20	$42.00
10	Purchases	20	$4.30	$86.00
12	Sales	15	?	?
16	Purchases	20	$4.60	$92.00
20	Sales	40	?	?
28	Sales returns	3	?	?

1. Using this information, assume that Cairns Ltd uses the FIFO cost formula and that the sales returns relate to the 20 August sales. The sales return should be costed back into inventories at what unit cost?
   (a) $4.00
   (b) $4.20
   (c) $4.30
   (d) $4.60

2. Assuming that Cairns Ltd uses the moving weighted average cost formula, the 12 August sales should be costed at what unit cost?
   (a) $4.16
   (b) $4.07
   (c) $4.06
   (d) $4.00

4.6 End-of-period adjustments ★ **LO5**

An extract from Geebung Ltd's unadjusted trial balance as at 30 June 2023 appears below. Geebung Ltd's reporting period ends on 30 June and it uses the perpetual method to record inventories transactions.

	$	$
Inventories	97 200	
Sales		315 885
Sales returns	3 205	
Cost of sales	234 320	
Inventories losses	6 339	

Additional information

- On 24 June 2023, Geebung Ltd recorded a $660 credit sale of goods costing $600. These goods, which were sold on FOB destination terms and were in transit at 30 June 2023, were included in the physical count.
- Inventories on hand at 30 June 2023 (determined via physical count) had a cost of $97 800 and a net realisable value of $97 370.

Required

1. Prepare any adjusting journal entries required on 30 June 2023.
2. Prepare the trading section of the statement of profit or loss and other comprehensive income for the year ended 30 June 2023.

4.7 End-of-period adjustments ★ ★ **LO5**

A physical count of inventories at 31 December 2023 revealed that Karalee Pty Ltd had inventories on hand at that date with a cost of $441 000. Karalee Pty Ltd uses the periodic method to record inventories transactions. Inventories at 1 January 2023 were $397 000. The annual audit identified that the following items were excluded from this amount.

- Merchandise of $61 000 is held by Karalee Pty Ltd on consignment. The consignor is Romsey Ltd.
- Merchandise costing $38 000 was shipped by Karalee Pty Ltd FOB destination to a customer on 31 December 2023. The customer was expected to receive the goods on 6 January 2024.
- Merchandise costing $46 000 was shipped by Karalee Pty Ltd FOB shipping to a customer on 29 December 2023. The customer was scheduled to receive the goods on 2 January 2024.
- Merchandise costing $83 000 shipped by a vendor FOB destination on 31 December 2023 was received by Karalee Pty Ltd on 4 January 2024.
- Merchandise costing $51 000 purchased FOB shipping was shipped by the supplier on 31 December 2023 and received by Karalee Pty Ltd on 5 January 2024.

Required

1. Based on the above information, calculate the amount that should appear for inventories on Karalee Pty Ltd's statement of financial position at 31 December 2023.
2. Prepare any journal entries necessary to adjust the inventories general ledger account to the amount calculated in requirement 1.

4.8 Consignment of inventories ★ **LO5**

Weijing Ltd reported in a recent financial statement that approximately $12 million of merchandise was received on consignment. Should the company recognise this amount on its statement of financial position? Explain.

4.9 Selection of formulas for assigning costs ★ **LO6**

Under what circumstances would each of the following formulas for assigning costs to inventories be appropriate?

1. Specific identification
2. Last-in, first-out
3. Average cost
4. First-in, first-out
5. Retail method

4.10 Applying the lower of cost and NRV rule ★ ★ **LO7**

The following information relates to the inventories on hand at 30 June 2023 held by Canberra Ltd.

Item no.	Quantity	Cost per unit $	Cost to replace $	Estimated selling price $	Cost of completion and disposal $
A1458	1 200	4.30	4.41	5.75	2.49
A1965	1 630	5.40	5.26	5.50	2.55
B6730	1 498	9.34	9.35	12.00	2.95
D0943	196	3.23	3.14	3.00	2.12
G8123	312	5.56	5.56	7.70	2.67
W2167	2 984	8.12	8.15	9.66	2.36

Required

Calculate the value of inventories on hand at 30 June 2023.

4.11 Assignment of cost (periodic and perpetual methods) ★ ★ **LO4, 5, 6**

Darwin Ltd's inventories transactions for April 2024 are shown below.

	Purchases			Cost of sales			Balance		
Date	No. units	Unit cost	Total cost	No. units	Unit cost	Total cost	No. units	Unit cost	Total cost
April 1							20	$8.00	$160.00
4	90	$8.40	$756.00						
7	100	$8.60	$860.00						
10				50					
13	(20)	$8.60	($172.00)						
18				70					
21				(5)					
29				40					

Required

For each question, select the correct answer. Show any workings required and provide reasons to justify your choice.

1. If Darwin Ltd uses the perpetual method with the moving weighted average cost formula, the 18 April sale would be costed at what unit cost?
   (a) $8.60
   (b) $8.46
   (c) $8.44
   (d) $8.42
2. If Darwin Ltd uses the periodic method with the FIFO cost formula, what would be the cost of sales for April?
   (a) $1303.00
   (b) $1508.60
   (c) $1310.00
   (d) $1324.00

3. If Darwin Ltd uses the perpetual method with the FIFO cost formula, the 21 April sales return (relating to the 18 April sale) would be costed at what unit cost?
   (a) $8.00
   (b) $8.60
   (c) $8.40
   (d) $8.50

4. If Darwin Ltd uses the periodic method with the weighted average cost formula, what would be the value of closing inventories at 30 April 2024? (Round average cost to the nearest cent.)
   (a) $295.40
   (b) $301.00
   (c) $253.20
   (d) $297.50

Note: Exercises 4.12, 4.13 and 4.14 concern the same entity, Pacific Emporium. Completing the three exercises will help you to integrate different aspects of accounting for inventories.

4.12 Assignment of cost ★ ★   **LO4, 5, 6**

Pacific Emporium is a gift shop situated in a small fishing village. The business carries a range of merchandise that it accounts for under the perpetual method. Cost is assigned using the FIFO cost formula. All purchases are on FOB shipping terms, with 30 days credit. The end of the reporting period is 30 June.

The following information lists the transactions during October 2022 for one item of inventories (wind chimes).

Date	Detail	Number	Unit cost
Oct. 1	Opening balance	35	8.40
4	Purchase	40	8.50
8	Sale	50	
11	Purchase	60	8.60
14	Purchase returns	10	8.60
19	Sale	60	
24	Sale returns (on 19 Oct. sale)	5	
28	Purchase	30	8.70

Required

For the inventories item (wind chimes), calculate October's cost of sales expense and the cost of inventories on hand at 31 October 2022. Round all figures to the nearest cent.

4.13 End-of-reporting-period reconciliation and NRV ★ ★ ★   **LO5, 7**

Pacific Emporium is a gift shop situated in a small fishing village. The business carries a range of merchandise that it accounts for under the perpetual method. Cost is assigned using the FIFO cost formula. All purchases are on FOB shipping terms, with 30 days credit. The end of the reporting period is 30 June.

A physical count of inventories at 30 June 2023 found inventories worth $284 475. The inventories control ledger account at that date had a balance of $290 550. Investigations of the discrepancy between these two figures revealed the following.

• An unopened carton containing posters worth $630 had not been included in the count.
• Seven large conch shells were found to be damaged beyond repair and were not recorded in the count. The shells, worth $330, are still recorded in the inventories records.
• Goods costing $885 were ordered on 27 June 2023 and delivered to the transport company by the supplier on 29 June. As the goods were in transit on 30 June, they were not included in the count. The purchase was recorded when the goods arrived at the shop on 2 July 2023.
• Pacific Emporium has a number of paintings on display in local restaurants on a consignment basis. The paintings are worth $6300 and were not included in the count.
• A telescope had been sold for $1800 on 30 June. As the telescope was still in the shop awaiting collection by the owner, it was included in the count. The telescope cost $1425.
• Five missing dolphin statues worth $240 could not be located and are presumed to have been stolen from the shop.

Required

1. Reconcile the inventories control ledger account balance with the physical count figure (adjust both figures as necessary).
2. Prepare any journal entries necessary to achieve the reconciliation.

4.14 End-of-reporting-period reconciliation and NRV ★ ★ **LO5, 7**

Pacific Emporium is a gift shop situated in a small fishing village. The business carries a range of merchandise that it accounts for under the perpetual method. Cost is assigned using the FIFO cost formula. All purchases are on FOB shipping terms, with 30 days credit. The end of the reporting period is 30 June.

Inventories must be recorded at the lower of cost and net realisable value. C Bligh, the owner of Pacific Emporium, assessed the net realisable value of her inventories at 30 June 2023 and concluded that the net realisable value of all items (except barometers) exceeded cost. The six barometers on hand cost $120 each, but C Bligh is of the opinion that they will need to be discounted to $70 in order to sell them.

Required

Explain what is meant by the term 'net realisable value' and detail the action C Bligh must take in respect to the wall barometers.

4.15 Allocating cost (weighted average formula), reporting gross profit and applying the NRV rule ★ ★
LO4, 5, 6, 7

Nanning Ltd wholesales bicycles. It uses the perpetual method and allocates cost to inventories using the moving weighted average formula. The company's reporting date is 31 March. At 1 March 2024, inventories on hand consisted of 400 bicycles at $92 each and 54 bicycles at $96 each. During the month ended 31 March 2024, the following inventories transactions took place (all purchase and sales transactions are on credit).

March 1	Sold 200 bicycles for $150 each.
3	Five bicycles were returned by a customer. They had originally cost $92 each and were sold for $150 each.
9	Purchased 60 bicycles at $94 each.
10	Purchased 80 bicycles at $98 each.
15	Sold 62 bicycles for $165 each.
17	Returned one damaged bicycle to the supplier. This bicycle had been purchased on 9 March.
22	Sold 74 bicycles for $155 each.
26	Purchased 82 bicycles at $104 each.
29	Two bicycles, sold on 22 March, were returned by a customer. The bicycles were badly damaged so it was decided to write them off. They had originally cost $94 each.

Required

1. Calculate the cost of inventories on hand at 31 March 2024 and the cost of sales for the month of March. (Round the average unit cost to the nearest cent, and round the total cost amounts to the nearest dollar.)
2. Prepare the inventories general ledger control account (in T-format) as it would appear at 31 March 2024.
3. Calculate the gross profit on sales for the month of March 2024.

4.16 End-of-year adjustments ★ ★ **LO5**

The inventories control account balance of St George Fashions at 30 June 2023 was $10 510 using the perpetual method. A physical count conducted on that day found inventories on hand worth $110 100. Net realisable value for each inventories item held for sale exceeded cost. An investigation of the discrepancy revealed the following.

- Goods worth $3300 held on consignment for Rockhampton Accessories had been included in the physical count.
- Goods costing $600 were purchased on credit from Yun Ltd on 27 June 2023 on FOB shipping terms. The goods were shipped on 28 June 2023 but, as they had not arrived by 30 June 2023, were not included in the physical count. The purchase invoice was received and processed on 30 June 2023.
- Goods costing $1200 were sold on credit to Noosa Pty Ltd for $1950 on 28 June 2023 on FOB destination terms. The goods were still in transit on 30 June 2023. The sales invoice was raised and processed on 29 June 2023.

- Goods costing $1365 were purchased on credit (FOB destination) from Launceston Handbags on 28 June 2023. The goods were received on 29 June 2023 and included in the physical count. The purchase invoice was received on 2 July 2023.
- On 30 June 2023, St George Fashions sold goods costing $3150 on credit (FOB shipping) terms to Kurnell's Boutique for $4800. The goods were dispatched from the warehouse on 30 June 2023 but the sales invoice had not been raised at that date.
- Damaged inventories valued at $1325 were discovered during the physical count. These items were still recorded on 30 June 2023 but were omitted from the physical count records pending their write-off.

Required

Prepare any journal entries necessary on 30 June 2023 to correct any errors and to adjust inventories.

4.17 Allocating cost (FIFO), reporting gross profit and applying the NRV rule ★ ★ ★   **LO3, 4, 5, 6, 7**

Zixingche Ltd wholesales bicycles. It uses the perpetual method and allocates cost to inventories using the first-in, first-out formula. The company's reporting period ends on 31 March. At 1 March 2023, inventories on hand consisted of 175 bicycles at $164 each and 22 bicycles at $170 each. During the month ended 31 March 2023, the following inventories transactions took place (all purchase and sales transactions are on credit).

March 1	Sold 100 bicycles for $240 each.
3	Five bicycles were returned by a customer. They had originally cost $164 each and were sold for $240 each.
9	Purchased 85 bicycles at $182 each.
10	Purchased 52 bicycles at $192 each.
15	Sold 75 bicycles for $270 each.
17	Returned one damaged bicycle to the supplier. This bicycle had been purchased on 9 March.
22	Sold 450 bicycles for $250 each.
26	Purchased 68 bicycles at $196 each.
29	Two bicycles, sold on 22 March, were returned by a customer. The bicycles were badly damaged so it was decided to write them off. They had originally cost $182 each.

Required

1. Calculate the cost of inventories on hand at 31 March 2023 and the cost of sales for the month of March.
2. Show the inventories general ledger control account (in T-format) as it would appear at 31 March 2023.
3. Calculate the gross profit on sales for the month of March 2023.
4. AASB 102/IAS 2 requires inventories to be measured at the lower of cost and net realisable value. Identify three reasons why the net realisable value of the bicycles on hand at 31 March 2023 may be below their cost.
5. If the net realisable value is below cost, what action shouldZixingche Ltd take?

4.18 Assigning costs and end-of-period adjustments ★ ★ ★   **LO3, 4, 5, 6, 7**

Kempsey Ltd is a food wholesaler that supplies independent grocery stores. The company operates a perpetual method, with the first-in, first-out formula used to assign costs to inventories. Freight costs are not included in the calculation of unit costs. Transactions and other related information regarding two of the items (baked beans and plain flour) carried by Kempsey Ltd are given below for June 2023, the last month of the company's reporting period.

	Baked beans	**Plain flour**
Unit of packaging	Case containing 25 × 410 g cans	Box containing 12 × 4 kg bags
Inventories @		
1 June 2023	350 cases @ $29.60	625 boxes @ $48.40
Purchases	1. 10 June: 200 cases @ $29.50 plus freight of $140	1. 3 June: 150 boxes @ $48.45
	2. 19 June: 470 cases @ $29.70 per case plus freight of $215	2. 15 June: 200 boxes @ $48.45
		3. 29 June: 240 boxes @ $49.00
Purchase terms	n/30, FOB shipping	n/30, FOB destination
June sales	730 cases @ $38.50	950 boxes @ 50.00

	Baked beans	Plain flour
Returns and allowances	A customer returned 50 cases that had been shipped in error. The customer's account was credited for $1925.	As the 15 June purchase was unloaded, 10 boxes were discovered damaged. A credit of $484.50 was received by Kempsey Ltd.
Physical count at 30 June 2023	326 cases on hand	15 boxes on hand
Explanation of variance	No explanation found — assumed stolen	Boxes purchased on 29 June still in transit on 30 June
Net realisable value at 30 June 2023	$39.00 per case	$48.50 per box

Required

1. Calculate the number of units in inventories and the FIFO unit cost for baked beans and plain flour as at 30 June 2023 (show all workings).
2. Calculate the total dollar amount of the inventories for baked beans and plain flour, applying the lower of cost and net realisable rule on an item-by-item basis. Prepare any necessary journal entries (show all workings).

4.19 Allocating cost (moving weighted average), end-of-period adjustments and write-downs to NRV ★ ★ ★   **LO4, 5, 7**

Part A

Swims Ltd uses the perpetual method and special journals, balances the books at month-end, and uses control accounts and subsidiary ledgers for all accounts receivable and accounts payable. All sales and purchases are made on n/30, FOB destination terms. The moving weighted average formula is used to assign cost to inventories.

The following information has been extracted from Swims Ltd's books and records for May and June 2024.

	$
Inventories control ledger account balance at 31 May	21 007.30
Accounts payable control ledger account balance at 31 May	8 015.40
Inventories purchases on credit during June	11 618.90
Cash paid to trade creditors during June	10 445.90
Inventories sales on credit during June	16 250.00

Inventories ledger card balances at 1 June:

		$
Pool filters	43 @ $242.50	10 427.50
Pool pumps	21 @ $503.80	10 579.80
		21 007.30

The inventories purchased during June comprised the following.

		$
June 4	5 pool pumps @ $486.10 each	2 430.50
17	3 pool pumps @ $501.30 each	1 503.90
18	12 pool filters @ $246.70 each	2 960.40
24	2 pool pumps @ $501.30 each	1 002.60
29	15 pool filters @ $248.10 each	3 721.50
		11 618.90

The inventories sold during June comprised the following.

		$
June 1	1 pool pump @ $540 and 1 pool filter @ $320	860
5	18 pool filters @ $320 each	5 760
18	4 pool pumps @ $570 each	2 280
23	15 pool filters @ $350 each	5 250
28	5 pool filters @ $350 each	2 100
		16 250

Other movements in inventories during June were:

June 9	2 pool filters, sold 5 June (not paid for) were returned by the customer
20	3 pool filters purchased 18 June (not paid for) were returned to the supplier
26	1 pool pump, purchased 4 June (paid for) was returned to the supplier

Required

1. Prepare the perpetual inventories records for June 2024.
2. Prepare the inventories control and accounts payable control general ledger accounts (in T-format) for the month of June 2024.

Part B

At 30 June 2024, Swims Ltd conducted a physical stocktake that found 14 pool filters and 26 pool pumps on hand. An investigation of discrepancies between the inventories card balances and the physical count showed that the 15 pool filters purchased on 29 June 2024 were still in transit from the supplier's factory on 30 June 2024, and one pool pump, sold on 18 June, had been returned by a customer on 30 June. No adjustment has been made in the books for the sales return. The customer had not paid for the returned pump.

Required

Prepare any general journal entries necessary to correct the inventories control general ledger account balance as at 30 June 2024. (Narrations are not required, but show all workings.) Do not adjust the perpetual inventories records prepared in Part A.

Part C

On 30 June 2024, Swims Ltd determined that its inventories have the following net realisable values.

Pool filters	$252 each
Pool pumps	$566 each

Required

1. What does the term 'net realisable value' mean?
2. What sources of evidence could Swims Ltd examine to determine net realisable value?
3. What action should Swims Ltd take as at 30 June 2024 with respect to these net realisable values? Why?

REFERENCES

Energy Resources of Australia Ltd 2017, *Annual report 2017*, Energy Resources of Australia Ltd, www.energyres.com.au.
Wesfarmers Limited 2018, *Annual report 2018*, Wesfarmers Limited, www.wesfarmers.com.au.

ACKNOWLEDGEMENTS

Photo: © v.gi / Shutterstock.com
Photo: © Katarzyna Mikolajczyk / Shutterstock.com
Photo: © kurhan / Shutterstock.com
Figures 4.1, 4.3: © Wesfarmers Limited 2018
Figure 4.2: © Energy Resources of Australia 2017
Text: © 2019 Australian Accounting Standards Board (AASB). The text, graphics and layout of this publication are protected by Australian copyright law and the comparable law of other countries. No part of the publication may be reproduced, stored or transmitted in any form or by any means without the prior written permission of the AASB except as permitted by law. For reproduction or publication, permission should be sought in writing from the AASB. Requests in the first instance should be addressed to the National Director, Australian Accounting Standards Board, PO Box 204, Collins Street West, Victoria 8007.

CHAPTER 5

Property, plant and equipment

CHAPTER AIM

This chapter discusses accounting for property, plant and equipment (PPE) in accordance with AASB 116/IAS 16 *Property, Plant and Equipment*. AASB 116/IAS 16 establishes when PPE should be recognised as assets, prescribes how the carrying amounts of PPE should be determined and establishes how depreciation charges should be determined.

LEARNING OBJECTIVES

After studying this chapter, you should be able to:

5.1 discuss the nature of property, plant and equipment

5.2 outline the recognition criteria for initial recognition of property, plant and equipment

5.3 explain how to measure property, plant and equipment on initial recognition

5.4 explain the alternative ways in which property, plant and equipment can be measured subsequent to initial recognition

5.5 explain the cost model of measurement and understand the nature and calculation of depreciation

5.6 explain the revaluation model of measurement

5.7 account for derecognition

5.8 outline the disclosure requirements of AASB 116/IAS 16.

CONCEPTS FOR REVIEW

Before studying this chapter, you should understand and, if necessary, revise:
- the concept of an asset in the *Conceptual Framework*.
- the concept of an expense in the *Conceptual Framework*.

5.1 The nature of property, plant and equipment

LEARNING OBJECTIVE 5.1 Discuss the nature of property, plant and equipment.

This chapter is concerned with accounting for the property, plant and equipment (PPE) in which companies invest. The relevant accounting standard is AASB 116/IAS 16 *Property, Plant and Equipment*.

Paragraph 6 of AASB 116/IAS 16 defines **property, plant and equipment** as:

> tangible items that:
> (a) are held for use in the production or supply of goods or services, for rental to others, or for administrative purposes; and
> (b) are expected to be used during more than one period.

Note the following points in relation to the nature of PPE.

- *The assets are 'tangible' assets.* The distinction between tangible and intangible assets is discussed in depth in chapter 6. However, a key feature of tangible assets is that they are physical assets, such as land, rather than non-physical, such as patents and trademarks.
- *The assets have specific uses within an entity.* Specific uses are in production/supply, rental or administration. Assets that are held for sale, including land, or held for investment are not included under property, plant and equipment.
- *The assets are non-current.* PPE assets are expected to be used for more than one accounting period. PPE may be divided into classes for disclosure purposes, a class of assets being a grouping of assets of a similar nature and use in an entity's operations. Examples of classes of PPE are land, machinery, motor vehicles and office equipment.

Note that AASB 116/IAS 16 does not apply to PPE held for sale, biological assets related to agricultural activity other than bearer plants (living plants used in the supply or production of agricultural produce), or mineral rights and mineral reserves such as oil and gas, each of which is governed by different accounting standards.

In this chapter, accounting for PPE is considered in terms of:

- recognition of the asset — the point at which the asset is brought into the accounting records
- initial measurement of the asset — determining the initial amount at which the asset is recorded in the accounts
- measurement subsequent to initial recognition — determining the amount at which the asset is reported subsequent to acquisition, including the recording of any depreciation of the asset
- derecognition of the asset — accounting for the asset when it is removed from the records, either as a result of sale or the asset has been fully used up
- disclosure requirements.

LEARNING CHECK

- ☐ 'Property, plant and equipment' is specifically defined in paragraph 6 of AASB 116/IAS 16 to include tangible items held for use in the production or supply of goods or services, for rental to others, or for administrative purposes, and which are expected to be used during more than one period.
- ☐ AASB 116/IAS 16 does not apply to intangible assets.
- ☐ AASB 116/IAS 16 does not apply when PPE assets are classified as held for sale.

5.2 Initial recognition of PPE

LEARNING OBJECTIVE 5.2 Outline the recognition criteria for initial recognition of property, plant and equipment.

PPE is initially recognised at cost. Paragraph 7 of AASB 116/IAS 16 contains the two criteria that must be met before the cost of PPE can be recognised as an asset.

> The cost of an item of property, plant and equipment shall be recognised as an asset if, and only if:
> (a) it is probable that future economic benefits associated with the item will flow to the entity; and
> (b) the cost of the item can be measured reliably.

Note that these recognition criteria are applied to the initial recognition of an asset, replacement parts of the asset, and costs incurred in relation to the asset during its life. To recognise a cost outlay as an asset, the outlay must give rise to the expectation of *future* economic benefits. One of the key problems for the entity is determining whether the outlay should be recorded as an expense or capitalised and recorded as an asset. That decision is based on whether the entity expects there to be future economic benefits, whether the receipt of those benefits is probable, and whether the benefits will flow specifically to the entity.

As PPE consists of physical assets such as land and machinery, such assets are normally traded in a market. One test of the existence of future benefits is then to determine whether a market exists for the item in question. A problem with some assets is that once items have been acquired and installed, there is no active market for them. However, in many cases, the expected economic benefits arise because of the use of that asset in conjunction with other assets held by the entity. At a minimum, the future benefits would be the scrap value of the item.

Paragraph 11 of AASB 116/IAS 16 notes that certain assets may not of themselves generate future benefits, but instead the assets may be necessary for the entity as a whole to generate future benefits. For example, some items of PPE may be acquired for safety or environmental reasons, such as equipment associated with the safe storage of dangerous chemicals. Benefits from using the chemicals can occur only if the safety equipment exists. Hence, even if the safety equipment does not of itself generate cash flows, its existence is necessary for the entity to be able to use chemicals within the business.

The term 'measured reliably' refers to recognition of PPE only where the measurement purports to faithfully represent the economic substance of the item and is free from material error or bias. As a result of reliable measurement, users can depend on this information to make economic decisions.

5.2.1 The significant parts approach

The total PPE of an entity may be broken down into separate assets. This is sometimes referred to as a 'significant parts' approach to asset recognition. An entity allocates the amount initially recognised in respect of an asset to its significant parts and accounts for each part separately.

Paragraph 9 of AASB 116/IAS 16 notes that the identification of what constitutes a separate item or part of plant and equipment requires the exercise of judgement, because there is no rule regarding the unit of measure for recognition. The key element in determining whether an asset should be further subdivided into its significant parts is an analysis of what is going to happen to that asset in the future. Having identified an asset, the entity needs to recognise both the value of the asset and the expected benefits consumed by the entity during the period in which the benefits are received. Hence, if an asset has a number of significant parts that have different useful lives then parts with different useful lives need to be identified and accounted for separately.

For example, consider an aircraft as an item of PPE. Is it sufficient to recognise the aircraft as a single asset? An analysis of the aircraft may reveal that there are various significant parts of the aircraft that have different useful lives including:
- the engines
- cockpit equipment, including computers, navigation equipment and so on
- the frame of the aircraft
- kitchen facilities
- the fittings (seats, floor coverings etc.).

Each of these may have different lives and residual values. It may be necessary to refit major parts of the aircraft such as passenger seating every 5 years, whereas the engines may last twice as long.

Similarly, seats in a lecture theatre would be recognised separately to the lecture building. An entity that deals with the refining of metals may have a blast furnace, the lining of which needs to be changed periodically. The lining of the blast furnace therefore needs to be separated from the external structure in terms of asset recognition and subsequent accounting for the asset.

Further, as noted in paragraph 9 of AASB 116/IAS 16, it may be appropriate to aggregate individually insignificant items (such as moulds, tools and dies) and apply the criteria to the aggregate value.

LEARNING CHECK

☐ Recognition of PPE depends on two criteria being met:
  1. the existence of probable future economic benefits, *and*
  2. the ability to measure an asset's cost reliably.
☐ The specific assets recognised are affected by an analysis of the significant parts of the assets acquired.

5.3 Initial measurement of PPE

LEARNING OBJECTIVE 5.3 Explain how to measure property, plant and equipment on initial recognition.

Having established that an asset can be recognised, the entity must assign a monetary amount to it. As noted in paragraph 15 of AASB 116/IAS 16, the initial measurement is the *cost* of the asset.

> An item of property, plant and equipment that qualifies for recognition as an asset shall be measured at its cost.

Paragraph 16 of AASB 116/IAS 16 specifies three components of cost:
* purchase price
* directly attributable costs
* the initial estimate of the costs of dismantling and removing the item or restoring the site on which it is located.

5.3.1 Purchase price

The purchase price is the basic **cost** of the asset — the amount given up by the acquirer to acquire the asset at the acquisition date.

ILLUSTRATIVE EXAMPLE 5.1

Acquisition of asset for cash

Big Ltd acquired a vehicle from Wave Ltd for $100 000. Big Ltd paid $20 000 cash and borrowed $80 000 from the bank. The total cost is $100 000.

Required
How would Big Ltd record the acquisition?

Solution

Vehicle	Dr	100 000	
Cash	Cr		20 000
Loan payable	Cr		80 000
(Acquisition of vehicle)			

Acquisition could involve an outflow of cash or cash equivalent, or other consideration including other non-current assets, such as in a trade-in situation or a swap of assets. Where the entity acquires another asset and gives in exchange one or more of its own non-current assets, the entity should remeasure the transferred assets to their **fair values** as at the acquisition date, and recognise any resultant gains or losses in profit or loss. For example, where land is exchanged for machinery, it is necessary to measure the fair value of the land given up. This would be done in accordance with AASB 13/IFRS 13 *Fair Value Measurement* (see chapter 3).

The purchase price of the asset acquired then consists of the fair value of all assets given up by the acquiring entity.

ILLUSTRATIVE EXAMPLE 5.2

Trade-in of other asset

Big Ltd acquires a BMW vehicle from Wave Ltd for $100 000. In exchange, Big Ltd gives $70 000 cash and trades in a Ford motor vehicle, currently recorded at $28 000. The fair value of the Ford at the time of the exchange is then calculated to be $30 000 (i.e. $100 000 – $70 000 cash).

Required
How would Big Ltd account for this transaction?

According to paragraph 34 of AASB 101/IAS 1 *Presentation of Financial Statements*, the gains and losses on disposal of several items of PPE during the period may be offset and disclosed as a net amount in the statement of profit or loss and other comprehensive income. (See section 5.7 for further details regarding disposal and derecognition of PPE.)

Paragraph 16(a) of AASB 116/IAS 16 notes that the purchase price also includes import duties and non-refundable purchase taxes, and is calculated after deducting any trade discounts and rebates.

Acquisition date

The cost of the asset acquired is measured at acquisition date. Some likely dates that may be considered in determining the acquisition date are:
- the date the contract to exchange the assets is signed
- the date the consideration is paid
- the date on which the assets acquired are received by the acquirer
- the date on which an offer becomes unconditional.

The advantage of these dates is that they relate to a specific point of time and can be determined objectively. A problem is that there may be a number of dates involved if, for example, an item of equipment arrives in stages or payment for the equipment is to be made in instalments over time.

The date on which the fair values should be measured is the date on which the acquirer *obtains control of the asset or assets acquired* — hereafter referred to as the 'acquisition date'. There is no specific date defined in AASB 116/IAS 16. However, in AASB 3/IFRS 3 *Business Combinations*, acquisition date is defined as 'the date on which the acquirer obtains control of the acquiree'. This same principle is applied in the acquisition of non-current assets.

Acquisition of multiple assets

The above principles of determining purchase price apply to the acquisition of an individual item of PPE as well as when an entity acquires more than one asset, such as a block of land and a number of items of machinery. The acquirer may acquire the assets as a group, paying one total amount for the bundle of assets.

The cost of acquiring the bundle of assets is measured at the fair value of what is given up by the acquirer to determine the purchase price, to which is added any directly attributable costs. However, even if the total cost of the bundle of assets can be determined, for accounting purposes it is necessary to measure the cost of each of the separate assets as they may be in different classes, or some may be depreciable and others not.

The basic principle of recording assets acquired is to record at cost. According to paragraph 2(b) of AASB 3/IFRS 3, where a bundle of assets is acquired, the cost of the separate assets must be estimated, and the fair values of the assets acquired can be used in this process. The cost of each asset (to be recorded separately) is calculated by allocating the cost of the bundle of assets over the individual assets acquired in proportion to their fair values.

Acquisition of multiple assets

Blue Ltd acquired land, buildings and furniture at a total cost of $300 000 cash. In order to separately record each asset acquired at cost, Blue Ltd measures the fair value of each asset as follows.

Land	$ 40 000
Buildings	200 000
Furniture	80 000
	$320 000

Required

Allocate the cost of the bundle of assets over the individual assets acquired in proportion to their fair values.

Solution

The total cost of $300 000 is allocated to each asset on the basis of the fair values as follows.

Land	$40 000/$320 000 × $300 000 =	$ 37 500
Buildings	$200 000/$320 000 × $300 000 =	187 500
Furniture	$80 000/$320 000 × $300 000 =	75 000
		$300 000

The acquisition of the three assets is recorded by Blue Ltd as follows.

Land	Dr	37 500	
Buildings	Dr	187 500	
Furniture	Dr	75 000	
Cash	Cr		300 000
(Acquisition of multiple assets for cash)			

5.3.2 Directly attributable costs

To determine which costs can be capitalised into the cost of the asset, the following question is asked.

Are the costs directly attributable to bringing the asset to the location and condition necessary for it to be capable of operating in the manner intended by management?

According to paragraph 16 of AASB 116/IAS 16, if the answer is 'yes', then the costs are capitalised into the cost of the asset; if the answer is 'no', then the costs are expensed and recognised in profit or loss.

Costs to be included

Paragraph 17 of AASB 116/IAS 16 notes various costs which meet the criterion in the question above, including:
- *costs of employee benefits* arising directly from the construction or acquisition of the item of PPE
- *costs of site preparation*
- *initial delivery and handling costs*
- *installation and assembly costs* — where buildings are acquired, associated costs could be the costs of renovation
- *costs of testing whether the asset is functioning properly*
- *professional fees*.

It can be seen that all these costs are incurred before the asset is used, and are necessary in order for the asset to be usable by the entity. Note the use of the word 'necessary' in this criterion. There may be costs incurred that were not necessary; for example, the entity may have incurred fines, or a concrete platform may have been placed in the wrong position, then had to be destroyed and a new one put in the right place. These costs should be written off as an expense rather than capitalised as part of the cost of the acquired asset.

Costs not to be included

Paragraphs 19 and 20 of AASB 116/IAS 16 include the following examples of costs that should not be included in directly attributable costs.

- *'Costs of opening a new facility'*. These costs are incurred after the item of PPE is capable of being used; the opening ceremony, for example, does not enhance the operating ability of the asset.
- *'Costs of introducing a new product or service (including costs of advertising and promotional activities)'*. These costs do not change the location or working condition of the asset.
- *'Costs of conducting business in a new location or with a new class of customer (including costs of staff training)'*. Unless the asset is relocated, there is no change in the asset's ability to operate.
- *'Administration and other general overhead costs'*. These costs are not directly attributable to the asset, but are associated generally with the operations of the entity.
- *'Costs incurred while an item capable of operating in the manner intended by management has yet to be brought into use or is operated at less than full capacity'*. These costs are incurred because of management's decisions regarding the timing of operations rather than being attributable to getting the asset in a position for operation.
- *'Initial operating losses, such as those incurred while demand for the item's output builds up'*. These are not incurred before the asset is ready for use.
- *'Costs of relocating or reorganising part or all of the entity's operations'*. If a number of currently operating assets are relocated to another site, then the costs of relocation are general expenses, and not directly attributable to the item of PPE.

Income earned

According to paragraph 17(e) of AASB 116/IAS 16, the cost of the asset should be measured after deducting the net proceeds from selling any items produced when bringing the asset to the location and condition ready for operation, such as proceeds from the sale of samples produced during the testing process.

The principle here is that any revenue flows, whether in or out, that occur before the asset is in a position to operate as management intends must be taken into account in measuring the cost of the asset. The testing process is often a necessary part of readying the asset for its ultimate use.

ILLUSTRATIVE EXAMPLE 5.4

Directly attributable costs

Small Ltd has acquired a warehouse for $400 000 and incurred the following costs.
(a) Stamp duty
(b) The real estate agent's fees
(c) The architect's fees for drawings of internal adjustments to the warehouse required to be made before use
(d) Interest on the bank loan to acquire the warehouse
(e) Application fee to the bank for the loan, which is secured over the warehouse
(f) Cost of refurbishing the warehouse to enhance the storage space available
(g) Cost of landscaping around the building
(h) Cost of providing a car parking area

Required
Assess which of the costs should be included in the cost of the warehouse.

Solution
The costs that would be included in the cost of the asset are: (a) stamp duty, (b) real estate agent's fees, (c) architect's fees, (d) interest on the bank loan, (e) application fee to the bank for the loan and (f) the cost of refurbishing the warehouse. (*Note:* Interest on the bank loan may be expensed or capitalised. According to AASB 123/IAS 23 *Borrowing Costs*, borrowing costs that are directly attributable to the acquisition, construction or production of a *qualifying asset* should be capitalised as part of that asset. A qualifying asset is one that requires a substantial period of time to get ready for its intended use.)

The cost that would not be included in the cost of the warehouse (but instead would be treated as separate assets) are: (g) the cost of landscaping around the building and (h) the cost of providing a car parking area (assuming that the car park is not an integral part of the building).

5.3.3 Acquisition for zero or nominal cost

An entity may acquire an asset for zero cost, or be required to pay an amount substantially different from the fair value of the asset. For example, an entity may be given a computer for no charge, or be required to pay only half price for a block of land or a building. Where there is zero cost, the entity receiving the asset would not record the asset. In the case of a heavily discounted asset, for example, where a mining company was required to pay a nominal amount (e.g. $50 000) for land, the asset would be recorded at the cost, namely the purchase price paid plus the directly attributable costs.

Land	Dr	50 000	
Cash	Cr		50 000
(Recognition of asset acquired at nominal cost)			

However, different accounting is applied in not-for-profit entities. According to paragraph Aus15.1 of AASB 116, where a not-for-profit entity acquires an asset at no cost or for a nominal amount, the 'cost' is deemed to be its fair value at acquisition date. An example is the contribution (donation) of land by a developer to enable the local government to develop a park. Charities such as the Red Cross may also receive items of PPE such as equipment at zero or nominal cost. The appropriate journal entry in this situation to record the receipt of such assets is as follows.

Equipment	Dr	Fair value	
Gain	Cr		Fair value
(Recognition of asset acquired at zero cost)			

5.3.4 Costs of dismantling, removal or restoration

At the date the asset is initially recognised, an entity is required to estimate any costs necessary to eventually dismantle and remove an asset and restore the site. For example, when an asset such as an offshore oil platform is constructed, an entity knows that in the future it is required by law to dismantle and remove the platform in such a manner that the environment is cared for.

The construction of the platform gives rise to a liability for restoration under AASB 137/IAS 37 *Provisions, Contingent Liabilities and Contingent Assets*. The expected costs, measured on a present value basis, are capitalised into the cost of the platform as the construction of the platform brings with it the responsibility of dismantling and removing the platform and restoring the site. Acceptance of the liability for dismantling, removal and restoration is an essential condition of having the asset available for use. Thus, the dismantling, removal and restoration costs are included in the value of the asset and depreciated over its useful life.

Note that in order for such costs to be capitalised, a liability to dismantle, remove or restore must exist at acquisition date. No costs would be capitalised purely because management had an intention, but not a liability, to dismantle, remove or restore at a later date.

ILLUSTRATIVE EXAMPLE 5.5

Costs of dismantling and removal

Shore Ltd constructs an offshore oil platform, which involves the following costs.

Construction	$6 000 000
Insurance	$ 300 000 p.a.
Dismantling	$1 500 000

The platform has a projected useful life of 20 years after which the time it must be dismantled.

Required

How would Shore Ltd account for the cost of the asset in the year of construction, assuming construction costs have been paid in full?

Solution

The cost of the asset would be recorded as $7 500 000, as follows.

Oil platform	Dr	7 500 000	
Cash	Cr		6 000 000
Dismantling fees liability	Cr		1 500 000

Note: Insurance would be recorded as an expense in the relevant period.

LEARNING CHECK

☐ Property, plant and equipment are initially measured at the cost of acquisition.

☐ The cost of acquisition is measured at the acquisition date.

☐ The cost consists of the fair value of the consideration paid plus any directly attributable costs, including estimated costs of dismantling, removal and restoration.

☐ Where multiple assets are acquired as a package, the cost of each asset is measured by allocating the cost of the package to each asset in proportion to the fair value of each asset acquired.

5.4 Measurement subsequent to initial recognition

LEARNING OBJECTIVE 5.4 Explain the alternative ways in which property, plant and equipment can be measured subsequent to initial recognition.

At the point of initial recognition of an item of PPE, the asset is measured at cost, which is the purchase price plus directly attributable costs and dismantling, removal and/or restoration costs. After this initial recognition, an entity has a choice regarding the measurement basis to be adopted. Paragraph 29 of AASB 116/IAS 16 details two possible measurement models:

- the cost model
- the revaluation model.

The choice of model is an accounting policy decision. That policy is not applied to individual assets but to an entire *class* of PPE. Hence, for each class of assets (e.g. land, motor vehicles, office equipment), an entity must decide the measurement model to be used. The cost model is discussed in section 5.5 and the revaluation model in section 5.6.

Having chosen a particular measurement model for a specific class of assets, the entity may later change to the alternative basis. For example, an entity that initially chose the revaluation model may at a later date change to the cost model. In order to change from one basis to another, the principles of AASB 108/IAS 8 *Accounting Policies, Changes in Accounting Estimates and Errors* must be applied. The key is whether the change in measurement basis will make the financial statements more useful to users; in particular, will the information be more relevant and/or more reliable — a requirement under AASB 108/IAS 8 paragraph 14.

In general, a change from the cost model to the revaluation model would be expected to increase the relevance of information provided because more current information is being made available. However, the change may make the information less reliable, as the determination of fair value may require estimation to occur. Accordingly, an entity would need to assess the overall benefit of the change in order to justify the change. Such a change is accounted for by applying AASB 116/IAS 16.

In contrast, changing from the revaluation model to the cost model would generally lead to a decrease in the relevance of the information. However, it may be that the measurement of fair value has become so unreliable that the fair values have little meaning. Again, a judgement of the relative trade-offs between relevance and reliability needs to be made. Such a change is accounted for by applying AASB 108/IAS 8, which would require retrospective application of the cost model (see chapter 18).

5.5 The cost model

LEARNING OBJECTIVE 5.5 Explain the cost model of measurement and understand the nature and calculation of depreciation.

Subsequent to initial recognition, management may outlay funds in relation to the asset. In particular, management may have to undertake certain outlays to keep the asset running efficiently. In relation to a vehicle that is needed to take a driver from point A to point B, the vehicle needs to run efficiently and at a required safety level without breakdowns. This means that the vehicle needs regular servicing, tune-ups and other routine checks. Costs associated with keeping PPE in the required working condition are expensed as incurred, and not added to the depreciable cost of the asset. These expenses are generally referred to as *repairs and maintenance*.

In other cases, management may outlay funds to refine the ability of the asset to operate. These outlays may increase the capacity of the asset, improve the quality of the output or adjust the operating costs of the asset. In order to capitalise (include) these outlays into the cost of the asset the general recognition criteria are applied. There needs to be an increase in probable future economic benefits embodied in the asset; that is, in excess of its standard of performance at the time the expenditure is made. The comparison is not with the original capacity of the asset but rather with the capacity of the asset at the time the expenditure is made. Further, the costs incurred at the time the capacity is changed must be able to be measured reliably.

ILLUSTRATIVE EXAMPLE 5.6

Cost model: repairs and maintenance vs improvements

Swift Ltd purchases a delivery vehicle which is serviced annually at a cost of approximately $1000 p.a. After 5 years, the following amounts were paid as part of the service cost.

Annual service costs	$1200
Fix rear bumper (due to accident)	$ 700
Replace existing engine with new one of increased capacity	$2700

Required
Advise Swift Ltd which amounts should be expensed and which amounts should be capitalised.

Solution
An amount of $1900 would be expensed as repairs and maintenance, comprising annual service costs and fixing the rear bumper. An amount of $2700 would be capitalised as an asset, comprising the new engine.

5.5.1 Depreciation

Under the cost model, after initial recognition, an asset continues to be recorded at historical cost (original cost). The subsequent carrying amount is determined after adjustments are made for depreciation and impairment losses (impairment losses are discussed in chapter 7). In this section, the emphasis is on the measurement (calculation) of depreciation.

In order to understand accounting for depreciation, the terms **depreciation**, **depreciable amount**, **useful life** and **residual value** need to be understood. Paragraph 6 of AASB 116/IAS 16 defines these terms as follows.

Depreciation is the systematic allocation of the depreciable amount of an asset over its useful life.

Depreciable amount is the cost of an asset, or other amount substituted for cost, less its residual value.

The *residual value* of an asset is the estimated amount that an entity would currently obtain from disposal of the asset, after deducting the estimated costs of disposal, if the asset were already of the age and in the condition expected at the end of its useful life.

Useful life is:
(a) the period over which an asset is expected to be available for use by an entity; or
(b) the number of production or similar units expected to be obtained from the asset by an entity.

A systematic allocation

Depreciation is a process of allocation. On acquiring an asset, an entity estimates the expected future economic benefits to be received from the asset. The entity estimates not only the value of the benefits but also the period over which the benefits are expected to be received and the pattern of these benefits; for example, to be received evenly over the asset's life, or to be received more in the early part of the asset's life.

The purpose of determining the depreciation expense per period is to measure the consumption of benefits in each period so that each period is allocated a share of the cost of the asset. Paragraphs 50 and 60 of AASB 116/IAS 16 note that:

> 50 The depreciable amount of an asset shall be allocated on a systematic basis over its useful life.
> 60 The depreciation method used shall reflect the pattern in which the asset's future economic benefits are expected to be consumed by the entity.

The accounting standards do not specify what is meant by 'systematic'. To be systematic a method, such as an equal amount over the useful life (e.g. 10% per period), must be applied, rather than just a random allocation of numbers.

Depreciation is *not* a measure of change in value. It is an allocation of the cost of the asset over its useful life. A common example relates to what occurs when a new car is acquired. It is generally recognised that the new car declines in value immediately once it is driven out of the showroom. The decline in value of the car is probably higher in the first year of its life than in the second year. However, if the entity acquired the car with an expectation of using the car in a similar fashion over a 3-year period, then the consumption of benefits is equal in each of those 3 years.

Similarly, an asset may increase in value because of market demand, but still be depreciated. An example relates to the acquisition of a building. It is generally recognised that the building increases in value over time. However, for accounting purposes the building will be depreciated over its useful life.

Similarly, as noted in paragraph 55 of AASB 116/IAS 16, depreciation continues to be charged even if an asset becomes temporarily idle, dependent on movements in residual value and expected useful life.

Methods of depreciation

The method of depreciation chosen by an entity is the one that systematically allocates the cost of an asset over its useful life in a manner that reflects the pattern of benefits expected to be received.

Paragraph 62 of AASB 116/IAS 16 describes three common depreciation methods used in practice.
- *Straight-line method.* This is used where the benefits are expected to be received evenly over the useful life of the asset. The depreciation charge for the period is calculated as:
$$\frac{\text{Cost} - \text{Residual value}}{\text{Useful life}}$$

If an item of plant had an original cost of $100 000, a residual value of $10 000 and a useful life of 4 years, the depreciation charge each year is:
$$\text{Depreciation expense p.a.} = \frac{\text{Cost} - \text{Residual value}}{\text{Useful life}}$$
$$= \frac{\$100\,000 - \$10\,000}{4}$$
$$= \$22\,500$$

The depreciation expense for the first 4 years following acquisition is shown below.

Year	Cost of asset	Carrying amount opening balance	Depreciation expense	Accumulated depreciation	Carrying amount closing balance
1	100 000	100 000	22 500	22 500	77 500
2	100 000	77 500	22 500	45 000	55 000
3	100 000	55 000	22 500	67 500	32 500
4	100 000	32 500	22 500	90 000	10 000

Note: Carrying amount opening balance − Depreciation expense = Carrying amount closing balance
Accumulated depreciation = Total depreciation to date

The journal entry for each of years 1 to 4 is:

Depreciation expense — plant	Dr	22 500	
Accumulated depreciation — plant	Cr		22 500
(Annual depreciation on plant)			

Note that both the residual value and the useful life may change during the life of the asset as expectations change.

- *Diminishing balance method.* This method is used where the pattern of benefits is such that more benefits are received in the earlier years of the asset's life, resulting in a higher depreciation expense. As the asset increases in age, the benefits each year are expected to reduce, resulting in a lower depreciation expense. The depreciation charge *each* year is calculated by multiplying the rate of depreciation by the carrying amount at the beginning of the year.

It is possible to calculate a rate of depreciation that would result in the depreciable amount being written off over the useful life. The formula is:

$$\text{Depreciation rate} = 1 - \sqrt[n]{\frac{r}{c}}$$

where n = useful life
r = residual value
c = cost or other revalued amount

Using the same information as in the example for the straight-line method, the depreciation rate under the diminishing balance method is:

$$\text{Depreciation rate} = 1 - \sqrt[n]{\frac{r}{c}}$$

$$= 1 - \sqrt[4]{\frac{10\,000}{100\,000}}$$

$$= 44\% \text{ (rounded)}$$

The depreciation expense for the first 4 years following acquisition is shown below.

Year	Cost of asset	Carrying amount opening balance	Depreciation expense	Accumulated depreciation	Carrying amount closing balance
1	100 000	100 000	44 000[(a)]	44 000	56 000
2	100 000	56 000	24 640[(b)]	68 640	31 360
3	100 000	31 360	13 798[(c)]	82 438	17 562
4	100 000	17 562	7 562[(d)]	90 000	10 000

Note: For years 1 to 3, depreciation expense = carrying amount opening balance × 44%
(a) 44% × $100 000 = $44 000
(b) 44% × $56 000 = $24 640
(c) 44% × $31 360 = $13 798
For year 4, depreciation expense = carrying amount opening balance − residual value (or carrying amount closing balance)
(d) $17 562 − $10 000 = $7562

The journal entries for years 1 to 4 are:

Depreciation expense — plant		Dr	44 000	
Accumulated depreciation — plant		Cr		44 000
(Annual depreciation — year 1)				
Depreciation expense — plant		Dr	24 640	
Accumulated depreciation — plant		Cr		24 640
(Annual depreciation — year 2)				
Depreciation expense — plant		Dr	13 798	
Accumulated depreciation — plant		Cr		13 798
(Annual depreciation — year 3)				
Depreciation expense — plant		Dr	7 562	
Accumulated depreciation — plant		Cr		7 562
(Annual depreciation — year 4)				

The depreciation charge then reflects a decreasing pattern of benefits over the asset's useful life.

- *Units-of-production method.* This method is based on the expected use or output of the asset. Variables used could be production hours or production output.

Using the above example again, assume that over the asset's 4-year life the expected output of the asset is as follows.

Year 1	17 000 units
Year 2	15 000 units
Year 3	12 000 units
Year 4	6 000 units
	50 000 units

The depreciation expense in each of the 4 years is based on the number of units produced in a year divided by the total units to be produced over the life of the asset, multiplied by the depreciable amount. Recall the depreciable amount is the cost minus the residual value (i.e. $100 000 – $10 000 = $90 000).

Year	Cost of asset	Carrying amount opening balance	Depreciation expense	Accumulated depreciation	Carrying amount closing balance
1	100 000	100 000	30 600[(a)]	30 600	69 400
2	100 000	69 400	27 000[(b)]	57 600	42 400
3	100 000	42 200	21 600[(c)]	79 200	20 800
4	100 000	20 800	10 800[(d)]	90 000	10 000

(a) $17/50 \times \$90\,000 = \$30\,600$
(b) $15/50 \times \$90\,000 = \$27\,000$
(c) $12/50 \times \$90\,000 = \$21\,600$
(d) $6/50 \times \$90\,000 = \$10\,800$

The journal entries for years 1 to 4 are:

Depreciation expense — plant		Dr	30 600	
Accumulated depreciation — plant		Cr		30 600
(Annual depreciation — year 1)				
Depreciation expense — plant		Dr	27 000	
Accumulated depreciation — plant		Cr		27 000
(Annual depreciation — year 2)				
Depreciation expense — plant		Dr	21 600	
Accumulated depreciation — plant		Cr		21 600
(Annual depreciation — year 3)				
Depreciation expense — plant		Dr	10 800	
Accumulated depreciation — plant		Cr		10 800
(Annual depreciation — year 4)				

An entity is not required to use any particular method of depreciation. The method chosen should be that which most closely reflects the expected pattern of consumption of the future economic benefits embodied in the asset.

An entity has to periodically review the depreciation method it is using. This should occur at least at the end of each annual reporting period. If the pattern of benefits has changed, then a more appropriate method should be chosen to reflect the changed pattern of benefits.

Useful life

Determination of useful life requires estimation of the asset's useful life to the entity. This is done by management, because the way in which an item of PPE is used (and the potential for changes in the market for that item) affects estimates of useful life.

The following list of factors, described in paragraph 56 of AASB 116/IAS 16, should be considered when determining an asset's useful life:

- the *expected usage* of the asset by the entity, which is assessed by reference to the asset's expected capacity or physical output
- the *expected physical wear and tear*, which depends on operational factors such as the number of work shifts for which the asset will be used and the repair and maintenance program of the entity, and the care and the maintenance of the asset while it is idle
- the *technical or commercial obsolescence* arising from changes or improvements in production, or from a change in the market demand for the product or service output of the asset. For example, computers may be regarded as having a relatively short useful life. The actual period over which they may be expected to work is probably considerably longer than the period over which they may be considered to be technologically efficient. The useful life for depreciation purposes is related to the period over which the entity intends to use the asset, which is probably closer to its technological life than the period over which it would be capable of being used
- the *legal or similar limits* on the use of the asset, such as expiry dates of related leases.

There is no necessary relationship between the asset's useful life to the entity and the economic life of the asset. Management may want to hold only relatively new assets, and a policy of replacement after specified periods of time may mean that assets are held for only a proportion of their economic lives. In other words, useful life for the purpose of calculating depreciation is defined in terms of the asset's expected usefulness to the entity. The useful life of an asset covers the entire time the asset is available for use, including the time the asset is idle but available for use.

Paragraph 58 of AASB 116/IAS 16 notes that land is a special type of PPE. Unless the land is being used for a purpose where there is a limited life imposed on the land, such as a quarry, it is assumed to have an unlimited life. Land with an unlimited life is not subject to depreciation. Hence, when accounting for land and buildings, these assets are dealt with separately so that buildings are subject to depreciation. If, however, the cost of land includes the expected costs of dismantling, removal or restoration, then these costs are depreciated over the period in which the benefits from use of the land are received.

Just as the depreciation method requires a periodic review, so does the useful life of an asset need reviewing. According to paragraph 51 of AASB 116/IAS 16, the review should occur at least at the end of each annual reporting period. A change in the assessment of the useful life will result in a change in the depreciation rate used.

ILLUSTRATIVE EXAMPLE 5.7

Assessment of useful life

An entity is in the business of making camera lenses. The machine used in this process is expected to make lenses for another 20 years. As the machine is computer-driven, the efficiency of making lenses is affected by the sophistication of the related computer program.

Technological advances are being made all the time, and it is thought that a new machine with advanced technology will be available within the next 5 years. The type of lens required is also a function of what cameras are considered to be in demand by consumers. Even if there is a change in technology, it is thought that cameras with the old style lens could still be marketable for another 7 years.

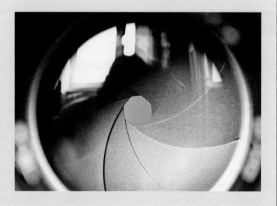

▶

Required

What useful life should management use in calculating depreciation on the machine?

Solution

Three specific time periods are mentioned:

- physical life: 20 years
- technical life: 5 years
- commercial life: 7 years.

A key element in determining the appropriate life is assessing the strategy used by management in marketing its products. If management believes that to retain market share and reputation it needs to be at the cutting edge of technology, 5 years will be appropriate. If, however, the marketing strategy is aimed at the general consumer, 7 years will be appropriate. In essence, management needs to consider at what point it expects to replace the machine.

Residual value

Residual value is an estimate based on what the entity would currently obtain on the asset's disposal; that is, what could be obtained at the time of the estimate — not at the expected date of disposal (at the end of the useful life). The estimate is based on what could be obtained from disposal of similar assets that are currently (at the date of the estimate) at the end of their useful lives, and which have been used in a similar fashion to the asset being investigated.

For assets that are unique, this estimation process is much more difficult than for assets that are constantly being replaced. An asset such as a vehicle may have a useful life of 2 years as the company replaces all its vehicles every 2 years. In such a case, the residual value of a new vehicle is the net amount that could be obtained now for a 2-year-old vehicle of the same type as the one being depreciated.

This form of assessment means that the residual value is not adjusted for expected changes in prices. It is also debatable whether the residual value should take into account possible technological developments. In relation to computers it may reasonably be expected that there will be such changes within a relatively short period of time, whereas with other assets (e.g. motor vehicles), predicting input changes is more difficult. Management is not required to be a predictor of future inventions. Expectations of technological change are already built into current second-hand asset prices. Management should then take into account reasonable changes in technological development and the effect on prices. Where an asset is expected to be used for the whole or the majority of its useful life, the residual value is zero or immaterial.

Where residual values are material, paragraph 51 of AASB 116/IAS 16 requires an entity to review the residual value at the end of each annual reporting period. If a change is required, the change is presented as a change in estimate and is accounted for prospectively as an adjustment to future depreciation (see chapter 18).

The accounting policy adopted by mining company BHP Group Ltd in relation to its PPE is disclosed in Note 10 to its financial statements. Figure 5.1 shows the information disclosed in BHP Group's 2018 annual report. Note in particular the use of the straight-line and units of production depreciation methods, as well as estimates of useful lives for the straight-line method.

FIGURE 5.1 Disclosure of policy on PPE, BHP Group

Recognition and measurement

Property, plant and equipment

Property, plant and equipment is recorded at cost less accumulated depreciation and impairment charges. Cost is the fair value of consideration given to acquire the asset at the time of its acquisition or construction and includes the direct costs of bringing the asset to the location and the condition necessary for operation and the estimated future costs of closure and rehabilitation of the facility.

Depreciation

Depreciation of assets, other than land, assets under construction and capitalised exploration and evaluation that are not depreciated, is calculated using either the straight-line (SL) method or units of production (UoP) method, net of residual values, over the estimated useful lives of specific assets. The depreciation method and rates applied to specific assets reflect the pattern in which the asset's benefits are expected to be used by the Group.

The Group's reported reserves are used to determine UoP depreciation unless doing so results in depreciation charges that do not reflect the asset's useful life. Where this occurs, alternative approaches to determining reserves are applied, such as using management's expectations of future oil and gas prices rather than yearly average prices, to provide a phasing of periodic depreciation charges that better reflects the asset's expected useful life.

Where assets are dedicated to a mine or petroleum lease, the below useful lives are subject to the lesser of the asset category's useful life and the life of the mine or petroleum lease, unless those assets are readily transferable to another productive mine or lease.

The estimation of useful lives, residual values and depreciation methods require significant management judgement and are reviewed annually. Any changes to useful lives may affect prospective depreciation rates and asset carrying values.

. . .

The table below summarises the principal depreciation methods and rates applied to major asset categories by the Group.

Category	Typical depreciation methodology	Depreciation rate
Buildings	SL	25–50 years
Plant and equipment	SL	3–30 years
Mineral rights and petroleum interests	UoP	Based on the rate of depletion of reserves
Capitalised exploration, evaluation and development expenditure	UoP	Based on the rate of depletion of reserves

Source: BHP Group Ltd (2018, pp. 177, 179).

Significant parts depreciation

It was mentioned earlier in this chapter that a significant parts approach requires an entity to allocate the cost of an asset to its significant parts and account for each part separately; for example, the cost of an aeroplane is allocated to parts, such as the frame, the engines and the fittings. According to paragraph 43 of AASB 116/IAS 16:

> Each part of an item of property, plant and equipment with a cost that is significant in relation to the total cost of the item shall be depreciated separately.

Thus, each part is depreciated separately. Any remainder is also depreciated *separately*.

Once an asset is separated into the relevant significant parts, if one of those parts needs regular replacing or renewing, the part is generally accounted for as a separate asset. The replaced asset (part) is depreciated over its useful life and derecognised (removed from the accounting records) on replacement.

To illustrate the accounting for significant parts, consider the case of a building with an elevator that periodically needs replacing. If the elevator is accounted for as a separate part (a separate asset), it is depreciated separately. On replacement, the carrying amount (if any) of the old elevator is written off. In order for this derecognition to occur, it is necessary to know the original cost of the elevator and the depreciation charged to date. The new elevator is accounted for as the acquisition of a new asset, assessed using the recognition criteria and, if capitalised as an asset, subsequently depreciated. If, however, the elevator is not treated as a separate component from the acquisition date of the building, then on replacement of the elevator, an entity cannot carry both the replacement and the replaced portion as assets. Calculation of the amount to be derecognised is more difficult where no separate part is recognised because the depreciation of the building has not been separated from the depreciation of the elevator.

Another example of dealing with a part of an asset arises where assets are subject to regular major inspections to ensure that they meet safety and quality requirements. According to paragraph 14 of AASB 116/IAS 16, such major inspections may be capitalised as a replacement component provided certain recognition criteria are satisfied. In particular, it must be probable that future economic benefits associated with the outlay will flow to the entity. For example, if there is a 5-year inspection of an aeroplane by a specific party, and this is required every 5 years in order for the plane not to be grounded, then the cost of the inspection provides benefits to the aeroplane owner by effectively providing a licence to continue flying. The capitalised amount is then depreciated over the relevant useful life (e.g. the time until the next inspection).

ILLUSTRATIVE EXAMPLE 5.8

The cost model

Mandurah Manufacturing Ltd's post-closing trial balance at 30 June 2021 included the following amounts.

Machinery control (at cost)	$ 244 480
Accumulated depreciation — machinery control	113 800

The machinery control and accumulated depreciation — machinery control accounts are supported by subsidiary ledgers. Details of Machine 2 owned at 30 June 2021 are as follows.

Machine	Acquisition date	Cost	Estimated useful life	Estimated residual value
2	1 February 2019	82 400	5 years	4 400

Additional information
- Mandurah Manufacturing Ltd uses the general journal for all journal entries, and records amounts to the nearest dollar.
- The company uses straight-line depreciation for machinery.

Required
Prepare journal entries to record the following transactions and events that occurred during the year ended 30 June 2022.

2021	
Oct. 1	Traded in Machine 2 for a new machine (Machine 5) that cost $90 740. A trade-in allowance of $40 200 was received and the balance was paid in cash. Freight charges of $280 and installation costs of $1600 were also paid in cash. Mandurah Manufacturing Ltd estimated Machine 5's useful life and residual value to be 6 years and $5500 respectively.

Solution
Step 1
It is necessary to calculate the depreciation on the depreciable asset so that when events such as a sale occur, depreciation up to the date of sale can be calculated. Depreciation is calculated as:

$$\frac{\text{Cost} - \text{Residual value}}{\text{Useful life}}$$

For Machine 2, the depreciation per month is calculated as follows.

$$\text{Machine 2 depreciation} = \frac{\text{Cost} - \text{Residual value}}{\text{Useful life}}$$

$$= \frac{\$82\,400 - \$4400}{60\,\text{months}}$$

$$= \$1300\,\text{per month}$$

Step 2
On 1 October, Machine 2 is traded in for Machine 5. Depreciation up to point of sale on Machine 2 is determined, being $1300 per month for the 3 months from July to September.

Oct. 1	Depreciation — machinery (M2) [$1300 × 3 months]	Dr	3 900	
	Accumulated depreciation — machinery (M2)	Cr		3 900

Step 3

Next, the machine is remeasured to fair value. This involves:

- related accumulated depreciation being written out of the records (Dr accumulated depreciation)
- the machine being reduced from original cost to its fair value (Cr adjustment for the difference between the original cost and the amount of the trade-in allowance)
- a gain/loss on sale being recognised for the difference.

Accumulated depreciation — machinery (M2) [$1300 × 32 months]	Dr	41 600	
Loss on sale of machinery (M2)	Dr	600	
Machinery (M2) [$82 400 – $40 200]	Cr		42 200

Step 4

Machine 5 is recorded at cost. Cost is determined as the sum of the purchase price and directly attributable costs. Purchase price is the fair value of consideration given up by the acquirer. In the absence of a fair value for Machine 2, the consideration is based on the fair value of Machine 5, namely $90 740. The directly attributable costs are the freight charges of $280 and installation costs of $1600, both being necessarily incurred to get the asset into the condition for management's intended use. Therefore, Machinery (M5) is debited for $92 620.

The trade-in allowance is used as the measure of the fair value of the asset. The cash outlay is then the sum of the balance paid to the seller of Machine 5 and the directly attributable costs (freight and installation). Given the cost of machinery and other directly attributable costs is $92 620 and the trade-in allowance is $40 200, the cash payment required is the difference between the two amounts ($52 420).

Machinery (M5) [$90 740 + $280 + $1600]	Dr	92 620	
Machinery (M2) [trade-in value]	Cr		40 200
Cash [$90 740 – $40 200 + $280 + $1600]	Cr		52 420

Step 5

The depreciation per month for Machine 5 is then calculated:

$$\text{Machine 5 depreciation} = (\$92\,620 - \$5500)\,/72\text{ months}$$
$$= \$1210\text{ per month}$$

LEARNING CHECK

- ☐ Under the cost model, measurement subsequent to initial recognition is affected by depreciation charges and impairment losses.
- ☐ Depreciation is the systematic allocation of the cost of the asset over its useful life.
- ☐ The allocation process reflects the consumption of benefits rather than changes in value.
- ☐ The depreciation method used should reflect the consumption of benefits.
- ☐ Residual value is determined by reference to current disposal prices and not future disposal prices.

5.6 The revaluation model

LEARNING OBJECTIVE 5.6 Explain the revaluation model of measurement.

Subsequent to initial recognition of the asset at cost, an entity may choose to apply the revaluation model. Under this model, the asset is measured at fair value. Fair value is measured in accordance with AASB 13/IFRS 13 *Fair Value Measurement* (see chapter 3) and must be able to be measured reliably.

Paragraph 31 of AASB 116/IAS 16 describes the use of the revaluation model. There is no specific time period (e.g. annually) as to how often an entity has to revalue an asset. The principle for revaluation of the asset is that revaluations must be made with sufficient regularity so that at any point of time the carrying amount of the asset does not differ materially from that which would be determined using fair value at the end of the reporting period. An entity adopting this model would need internal processes in place to keep track of movements in fair values of specific types of assets to know when material changes had occurred. For example, assume an entity has an office building in the centre of Perth and applies the revaluation model to this asset. The entity then tracks movements in prices of inner city office buildings.

In other words, it does not have to keep employing a valuer to obtain the fair value of the actual building owned, but instead obtains statistics on movements in prices in relation to this type of asset.

According to paragraph 36 of AASB 116/IAS 16, an entity cannot apply the revaluation model to a single asset. The revaluation measurement policy must be applied to classes of assets. Paragraph 37 of AASB 116/IAS 16 notes examples of separate asset classes:

(a) land;
(b) land and buildings;
(c) machinery;
(d) ships;
(e) aircraft;
(f) motor vehicles;
(g) furniture and fixtures;
(h) office equipment; and
(i) bearer plants.

There are two purposes for requiring revaluation to be done on a class of assets rather than on an individual asset basis. First, this limits the ability of management to 'cherry-pick' or selectively choose which assets to revalue. Second, the requirement to have all assets within the class measured on a fair value basis means that there is consistent measurement for the same type of assets in the entity.

5.6.1 Revaluation increases and decreases

Paragraphs 39 and 40 of AASB 116/IAS 16 contain the principles for applying the fair value method to revaluation. While the revaluation model requires a *class* of assets to be revalued, the revaluations in that class are done on an *asset-by-asset* basis. Where there is an increase in the fair value of an asset, the increase is not recognised in profit or loss but in other comprehensive income (OCI). The increase is accumulated in equity under the heading of asset revaluation surplus, which is reported in the reserves section of the statement of financial position.

ILLUSTRATIVE EXAMPLE 5.9

Revaluation increases

On 1 January, an entity carries an item of land at a cost of $100 000. The land is revalued to $120 000.

The new carrying amount is $120 000, giving rise to an increase in the value of the asset and a corresponding increase in the value of the asset revaluation surplus account.

Required
What are the appropriate accounting entries on revaluation of the asset?

Solution
1. The $20 000 increase in value of the asset is recorded with the gain being recognised as a part of other comprehensive income, not in profit or loss.

Land	Dr	20 000	
Gain on revaluation of land (OCI)	Cr		20 000
(Recognition of revaluation increase)			

2. The gain on revaluation of the asset previously recognised in other comprehensive income is accumulated in, or transferred to, equity (similar to closing entries to transfer revenue and expense amounts to the profit or loss account), the specific equity account being asset revaluation surplus.

Gain on revaluation of land (OCI)	Dr	20 000	
Asset revaluation surplus	Cr		20 000
(Accumulation of net revaluation gain in equity)			

Where there is a revaluation adjustment (increase or decrease) to a depreciable asset, the accumulated depreciation must first be written off. In the case of a revaluation decrease for example, the accumulated depreciation is written off and the decrease is then recognised as an expense in profit or loss in the period it occurs. The journal entries are shown in illustrative example 5.10.

Revaluation decrease

An item of plant has a carrying amount of $50 000, being original cost of $60 000 less accumulated depreciation of $10 000. The asset is revalued downwards to $24 000.

Required

What are the appropriate journal entries to record this revaluation decrease?

Solution

1. The first step is to write-off the accumulated depreciation of the plant, which reduces the recorded amount of the asset to $50 000.

Accumulated depreciation	Dr	10 000	
Plant	Cr		10 000
(Write-down asset to $50 000)			

2. The second step is to write the asset down to its fair value with the decrease being recognised as a loss in profit or loss.

Loss — downward revaluation of plant (P/L)	Dr	26 000	
Plant	Cr		26 000
(Revaluation of asset from recorded amount of $50 000 to fair value			
of $24 000)			

5.6.2 Revaluation increases and decreases involving reversals

According to paragraph 40 of AASB 116/IAS 16, where there is a revaluation decrease (due to a change in the fair value of an asset) and there *has previously been a revaluation increase to that asset*, the decrease must firstly be recognised in other comprehensive income to the extent of any credit balance remaining in the revaluation surplus in respect of that asset. The decrease also reduces the amount accumulated in equity under the heading of asset revaluation surplus. The reduction in other comprehensive income and asset revaluation surplus eliminates the effects of the previous increase. Any balance of decrease remaining is then recognised as an expense in profit or loss. The journal entries are shown in illustrative example 5.11.

Where an asset revaluation surplus has been raised via a previous revaluation increase, in accounting for a subsequent revaluation decrease for the same asset, the surplus must be eliminated before any loss on revaluation is recognised.

Similarly, where there is a revaluation increase to an asset that had previously recorded a revaluation decrease in the profit or loss, the increase must first be recognised in the profit or loss to the extent of the previous decrease, and any balance of increase remaining is then recognised in other comprehensive income.

Revaluation decrease following previous revaluation increase

An entity has a block of land with a carrying amount of $200 000, previously revalued upwards from $100 000. The following entries were recorded when the asset was revalued upwards.

Land	Dr	100 000	
Gain on revaluation of land (OCI)	Cr		100 000
(Revaluation of land)			
Gain on revaluation of land (OCI)	Dr	100 000	
Asset revaluation surplus	Cr		100 000
(Accumulation of net revaluation gain in equity)			

Required

What are the appropriate entries if:
(a) the asset is subsequently revalued downwards to $160 000
(b) revalued downwards from $200 000 to $80 000?

Solution

(a) *The asset is subsequently revalued downwards to $160 000.*
In this case the $40 000 write-down is a partial reversal of the previous revaluation increase of $100 000. The accounting entries for the decrease must reflect the decrease in other comprehensive income as well as the decrease in accumulated equity; that is, the asset revaluation surplus. The appropriate entries are as follows.
1. The first step is to recognise the decrease in other comprehensive income to the extent of the previous increase.

Loss on revaluation of land (OCI)	Dr	40 000	
Land	Cr		40 000
(Revaluation downwards of land)			

2. The next step is to reduce the amount accumulated in asset revaluation surplus by the decrease recognised in other comprehensive income.

Asset revaluation surplus	Dr	40 000	
Loss on revaluation of land (OCI)	Cr		40 000
(Reduction in accumulated equity due to devaluation of land)			

(b) *The asset is revalued downwards from $200 000 to $80 000.*
In this case, as there is a decrease of $120 000, the asset is written down to an amount $20 000 less than the previous increase of $100 000. The downward revaluation requires a loss to be recognised in profit or loss, as well as a decrease in other comprehensive income. Further, there has to be an elimination of the asset revaluation surplus previously raised when the revaluation increase was recognised. The appropriate entries are as follows.
1. The first step is to recognise the whole reduction in the value of the land ($120 000) and apportion the decrease to the reduction in other comprehensive income previously recognised ($100 000), and profit or loss for the amount that the asset is further written down ($20 000).

Loss on revaluation of land (P/L)	Dr	20 000	
Loss on revaluation of land (OCI)	Dr	100 000	
Land	Cr		120 000
(Downward revaluation of land)			

2. The next step is to reduce the amount accumulated in asset revaluation surplus by the decrease recognised in other comprehensive income.

Asset revaluation surplus	Dr	100 000	
Loss on revaluation of land (OCI)	Cr		100 000
(Reduction in accumulated equity due to revaluation decrease on land)			

Figure 5.2 shows the treatment of these revaluation adjustments, based on whether they represent increases (and related reversals) to the original cost of the asset (and are therefore shown as an adjustment to OCI), or decreases to the original cost of the asset (and are therefore shown as an adjustment in the profit or loss).

FIGURE 5.2	Treatment of revaluation adjustments

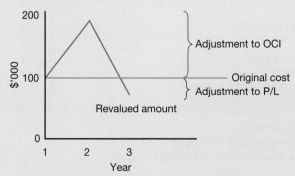

5.6.3 Depreciation of revalued assets

Section 5.6.1 discussed the accounting for revaluation of assets. Depreciation was described earlier in this chapter as a process of allocation. This applies for both the cost model and the revaluation model. Hence, even though an asset is measured at fair value, depreciation is not determined simply as the change in fair value of the asset over a period. As with the cost method, depreciation for a period is calculated after considering the pattern of economic benefits relating to the asset and the residual value of the asset.

ILLUSTRATIVE EXAMPLE 5.12

Depreciation of revalued assets

An entity has an item of plant that was revalued to $1000 at 30 June 2021. The asset is expected to have a remaining useful life of 5 years, with benefits being received evenly over that period. The residual value is calculated to be $100.

Required

What are the appropriate journal entries for 2021–22 for each of the following situations?

(a) *Situation 1:* At 30 June 2022, no formal revaluation occurs and the management of the entity assess that the carrying amount of the plant is not materially different from fair value.

(b) *Situation 2:* At 30 June 2022, a formal revaluation occurs and the external valuers assess the fair value of the plant to be $890.

Solution

(a) *Situation 1*

At 30 June 2022, no formal revaluation occurs and the management of the entity assess that the carrying amount of the plant is not materially different from fair value.

The appropriate journal entry for the 2021–22 period is as follows.

2022				
June 30	Depreciation expense	Dr	180	
	Accumulated depreciation	Cr		180
	(Depreciation on plant 1/5[$1000 – $100])			

The asset is reported in the statement of financial position at a carrying amount of $820, equal to a gross amount of $1000 less accumulated depreciation of $180, the carrying amount being equal to fair value.

(b) *Situation 2*

At 30 June 2022, a formal revaluation occurs and the external valuers assess the fair value of the plant to be $890.

The appropriate journal entries for the 2021–22 period are as follows.

2022				
June 30	Depreciation expense	Dr	180	
	Accumulated depreciation	Cr		180
	(Depreciation on plant 1/5[$1000 – $100])			
	Accumulated depreciation	Dr	180	
	Plant	Cr		180
	(Write down asset to its carrying amount of $820)			
	Plant	Dr	70	
	Gain on revaluation of plant (OCI)	Cr		70
	(Revaluation of plant from $820 to $890)			
	Gain on revaluation of plant (OCI)	Dr	70	
	Asset revaluation surplus	Cr		70
	(Accumulation of revaluation gain in equity)			

Hence, there is a two-step process. Depreciation is allocated in accordance with normal depreciation principles. Then, as a formal revaluation occurs, the accumulated depreciation is written off and the asset revalued to fair value. The asset is reported in the statement of financial position at fair value of $890 with no associated accumulated depreciation. Subsequent depreciation calculations are based on the fair value of the asset.

In summary, the basic steps in the process of revaluation of depreciable assets are as follows.
1. Check that depreciation is recorded up to the date of revaluation.
2. Write off accumulated depreciation (which adjusts the asset to its carrying amount).
3. Revalue the asset (reversing any previous valuation adjustments, where applicable).
4. Recalculate depreciation based on the revalued amount.

LEARNING CHECK

☐ Under the revaluation model, an asset is reported at fair value.
☐ The revaluation model is applied to classes of assets and not to individual assets.
☐ Revaluation increases are recognised in other comprehensive income and accumulated in an asset revaluation surplus, an equity account.
☐ Revaluation decreases affect current profit or loss for the period.
☐ The accounting for both revaluation decreases and increases is affected by the existence of previous revaluation decreases and increases.

5.7 Derecognition

LEARNING OBJECTIVE 5.7 Account for derecognition.

AASB 116/IAS 16 deals with the disposal of PPE that have not been previously classified as held for sale. The standard does not apply to non-current assets classified as held for sale and accounted for under AASB 5/IFRS 5 *Non-current Assets Held for Sale and Discontinued Operations*.

Paragraph 67 of AASB 116/IAS 16 identifies two circumstances in which derecognition of an item of PPE should occur:
1. on disposal, such as the sale of an asset
2. when the asset is fully consumed (i.e. no future economic benefits are expected).
   On sale of an item of PPE, the entity must:
1. account for any depreciation from the beginning of the period up to the point of sale
2. account for the sale, including the recognition of a gain or loss, equal to the difference between the proceeds from sale and the carrying amount of the asset at point of sale.

The gain or loss on sale is included in the current period profit or loss. Gains and losses on the sale of PPE can be netted off, as such activities are not considered to be the main revenue producing activities of an entity.

ILLUSTRATIVE EXAMPLE 5.13

Derecognition of an asset on sale

An entity acquired an item of plant on 1 July 2020 for $100 000. The asset had an expected useful life of 10 years and a residual value of $20 000.
On 1 January 2023, the entity sold the asset for $81 000.

Required
Prepare the entity's journal entries relating to this asset in the year of sale.

Solution
Depreciation per annum is calculated as:

$$(\$100\,000 - \$20\,000)/10 = \$8000 \text{ p.a.}$$

At the point of sale, the depreciation on the asset must be calculated for that part of the year for which the asset was held before the sale. Hence, for the half-year before the sale, under the straight-line method, depreciation of $4000 (i.e. ½ × $8000) must be charged as an expense.
The entry is as follows.

Depreciation expense	Dr	4 000	
Accumulated depreciation	Cr		4 000
(Depreciation expense for the year ended 30 June 2020 up to point of sale)			

The gain or loss on sale is the difference between the proceeds on sale of $81 000 and the carrying amount at time of sale of $80 000 (i.e. $100 000 − $20 000 [2.5 yrs × $8000]). Thus, the gain is $1000. The required journal entry is as follows.

Cash	Dr	81 000	
Accumulated depreciation	Dr	20 000	
Plant	Cr		100 000
Gain on sale of plant	Cr		1 000
(Sale of plant and recognition of gain)			

Required

In the above scenario, the asset was sold for $81 000. Assume that the asset, now referred to as Plant A, was instead traded in for another asset, Plant B, with Plant B having a fair value of $280 000. The entity makes a cash payment of $202 000 as well as giving up Plant A. The trade-in amount is then $78 000, considered to be the fair value of Plant A as part of the consideration.

Solution

The journal entries to record this transaction are as follows.

Accumulated depreciation — Plant A	Dr	20 000	
Loss on sale of Plant A	Dr	2 000	
Plant A	Cr		22 000
(Remeasurement of Plant A to fair value on sale)			
Plant B	Dr	280 000	
Plant A	Cr		78 000
Cash	Cr		202 000
(Acquisition of Plant B)			

LEARNING CHECK

☐ Derecognition occurs when assets are disposed of, or when no future benefits remain.

☐ When assets are derecognised during an accounting period, depreciation is determined up to the point of derecognition.

☐ Gains or losses on sale are included in current period profit or loss and are normally disclosed on a net basis.

5.8 Disclosure

LEARNING OBJECTIVE 5.8 Outline the disclosure requirements of AASB 116/IAS 16.

According to paragraph 73 of AASB 116/IAS 16, entities are required to disclose:

- the measurement bases used
- the depreciation methods used
- the useful lives or the depreciation rates used.

The accounting policy disclosures made by BHP Group Ltd were shown in figure 5.1. According to paragraph 73 of AASB 116/IAS 16, entities must also disclose the gross carrying amounts of the assets at the beginning and end of the period, the accumulated depreciation, and a reconciliation between the beginning and end of period carrying amounts. Figure 5.3 shows how BHP Group made these disclosures in the notes to the financial statements in its 2018 annual report.

If the revaluation model is used, then according to paragraph 77 of AASB 116/IAS 16, entities must disclose:

- the effective date of the revaluation
- whether an independent valuer was involved
- for each revalued class of PPE, the carrying amount that would have been recognised if the cost model had been applied
- any revaluation surplus, indicating the change for the period and any restrictions on the distribution of the balance to shareholders.

FIGURE 5.3   Disclosure of PPE, BHP Group Ltd

10 Property, plant and equipment

	Land and buildings US$m	Plant and equipment US$m	Other mineral assets US$m	Assets under construction US$m	Exploration and evaluation US$m	Total US$m
Net book value — 30 June 2018						
At the beginning of the financial year	8 547	49 427	15 557	5 536	1 430	80 497
Additions[(1)(2)]	(20)	110	873	5 423	258	6 644
Depreciation for the year	(548)	(6 467)	(730)	—	—	(7 745)
Impairments, net of reversals[(3)]	(9)	(507)	(260)	—	(62)	(838)
Disposals	(7)	(26)	(36)	(1)	(9)	(79)
Transferred to assets held for sale	(21)	(4 426)	(5 563)	(662)	—	(10 672)
Exchange variations taken to reserve	—	1	—	—	—	1
Transfers and other movements	210	2 773	(867)	(2 742)	—	(626)
At the end of the financial year	**8 152**	**40 885**	**8 974**	**7 554**	**1 617**	**67 182**
— Cost	12 525	91 037	13 212	7 554	2 400	126 728
— Accumulated depreciated and impairments	(4 373)	(50 152)	(4 238)	—	(783)	(59 546)
Net book value — 30 June 2017						
At the beginning of the financial year	9 005	47 766	15 942	9 561	1 701	83 975
Additions[(1)(2)]	—	809	416	3 773	314	5 312
Depreciation for the year	(552)	(6 419)	(765)	—	—	(7 736)
Impairments, net of reversals	(8)	(83)	—	—	(69)	(160)
Disposals	(27)	(56)	(25)	(1)	(152)	(261)
Divestment and demerger of subsidiaries and operations	(47)	(105)	—	(42)	—	(194)
Exchange variations taken to reserve	—	—	(1)	—	—	(1)
Transfers and other movements	176	7 515	(10)	(7 755)	(364)	(438)
At the end of the financial year	**8 547**	**49 427**	**15 557**	**5 536**	**1 430**	**80 497**
— Cost	12 387	106 332	31 196	5 538	2 213	157 666
— Accumulated depreciation and impairments	(3 840)	(56 905)	(15 639)	(2)	(783)	(77 169)

(1) Includes net foreign exchange gains/(losses) related to the closure and rehabilitation provisions. Refer to note 13 'Closure and rehabilitation provisions'.

(2) Property, plant and equipment of US$3 million (2017: US$593 million; 2016: US$ nil) was acquired under finance lease. This is a non-cash investing transaction that has been excluded from the Consolidated Cash Flow Statement.

(3) Includes impairment charges related to Onshore US assets of US$520 million (2017: US$ nil). Refer to note 26 'Discontinued operations'.

Source: BHP Group Ltd (2018, p. 177).

- ☐ The accounting policy choice relating to the asset measurement model must be disclosed.
- ☐ The movements in property, plant and equipment from the beginning of the period to the end of the period must be disclosed, including additions, disposals, depreciation and impairment losses.
- ☐ Movements in revaluation surplus must be disclosed.
- ☐ Information on the depreciation of assets, including depreciation methods and useful lives, must also be disclosed.

SUMMARY

The key principles for accounting for property, plant and equipment as described in AASB 116/IAS 16 *Property, Plant and Equipment* include the following.

- A PPE asset can only be recognised if it meets the recognition criteria of probable future benefits and reliable measurement of cost.
- PPE assets are initially measured at cost.
- Subsequent to initial recognition, PPE assets can be measured under either the cost model or the revaluation model.
- Depreciation is a process of allocation, both under the cost model and the revaluation model.
- Measurement of depreciation requires judgement, particularly in relation to useful lives, residual values and patterns of benefits.
- The revaluation model is applied to a class of assets but accounted for on an asset-by-asset basis.
- Unless they follow prior revaluation decreases, revaluation increases result in recognition of other comprehensive income and are accumulated in equity via the asset revaluation surplus.
- Unless they follow prior revaluation increases, revaluation decreases are recognised in profit or loss in the period in which they occur.

KEY TERMS

cost The amount of cash or cash equivalents paid or the fair value of other consideration given to acquire an asset at the time of its acquisition or construction.

depreciable amount The cost of an asset, or other amount substituted for cost, less its residual value.

depreciation The systematic allocation of the depreciable amount of an asset over its useful life.

fair value The price that would be received to sell an asset or paid to transfer a liability in an orderly transaction between market participants at the measurement date.

property, plant and equipment Tangible items that: (a) are held for use in the production or supply of goods or services, for rental to others, or for administrative purposes; and (b) are expected to be used during more than one period.

residual value The estimated amount that an entity would currently obtain from disposal of the asset, after deducting the estimated costs of disposal, if the asset were already of the age and in the condition expected at the end of its useful life.

useful life The period over which an asset is expected to be available for use by an entity; or the number of production or similar units expected to be obtained from the asset by an entity.

DEMONSTRATION PROBLEM

5.1 Recording property, plant and equipment transactions

Mandurah Manufacturing Ltd's post-closing trial balance at 30 June 2023 included the following balances.

Machinery control (at cost)	$244 480
Accumulated depreciation — machinery control	113 800
Fixtures (at cost; purchased 2 December 2020)	308 600
Accumulated depreciation — fixtures	134 138

The machinery control and accumulated depreciation — machinery control accounts are supported by subsidiary ledgers. Details of machines owned at 30 June 2023 are as follows.

Machine	Acquisition date	Cost	Estimated useful life	Estimated residual value
1	1 May 2019	$74 600	5 years	$3800
2	1 February 2021	82 400	5 years	4400
3	1 April 2022	87 480	6 years	5400

Additional information
- Mandurah Manufacturing Ltd uses the general journal for all journal entries, balances its books every 6 months, and records amounts to the nearest dollar.
- The company uses straight-line depreciation for machinery and diminishing balance depreciation at 20% p.a. for fixtures.

Required

Prepare journal entries to record the following transactions and events that occurred from 1 July 2023 onwards.

	2023	
(a)	July 1	Exchanged items of fixtures (having a cost of $100 600; a carrying amount at exchange date of $56 872; and a fair value at exchange date of $57 140) for a used machine (Machine 4). Machine 4's fair value at exchange date was $58 000. Machine 4 originally cost $92 660 and had been depreciated by $31 790 to exchange date in the previous owner's accounts. Mandurah Manufacturing Ltd estimated Machine 4's useful life and residual value to be 3 years and $4580 respectively.
(b)	Oct. 1	Traded in Machine 2 for a new machine (Machine 5) that cost $90 740. A trade-in allowance of $40 200 was received and the balance was paid in cash. Freight charges of $280 and installation costs of $1600 were also paid in cash. Mandurah Manufacturing Ltd estimated Machine 5's useful life and residual value to be 6 years and $5500 respectively.
	2024	
(c)	May 1	Overhauled Machine 3 at a cash cost of $16 910, after which Mandurah Manufacturing Ltd revised its residual value to $5600 and extended its useful life by 2 years.
(d)	June 1	Paid for scheduled repairs and maintenance on the machines of $2370.
(e)	June 30	Recorded depreciation and scrapped Machine 1.

SOLUTION

It is necessary to calculate the depreciation on each of the depreciable assets so that when events such as a sale occur, depreciation up to the date of the transaction can be calculated. Depreciation is calculated as:

$$\text{(Cost – Residual value)/Expected useful life}$$

For the three items of machinery, the depreciation per month is calculated:

$$\text{Machine 1 depreciation} = (\$74\,600 - \$3800)/60 \text{ months} = \$1180 \text{ per month}$$
$$\text{Machine 2 depreciation} = (\$82\,400 - \$4400)/60 \text{ months} = \$1300 \text{ per month}$$
$$\text{Machine 3 depreciation} = (\$87\,480 - \$5400)/72 \text{ months} = \$1140 \text{ per month}$$

(a) On 1 July, the company exchanges items of fixtures for a machine. The first journal entry derecognises the accumulated depreciation on the fixtures and remeasures the asset to fair value.

2023				
July 1	Accumulated depreciation — fixtures	Dr	43 728[(a)]	
	Fixtures [$100 600 – $57 140]	Cr		43 460[(b)]
	Gain on sale of fixtures	Cr		268[(c)]

(a) $100 600 − $56 872; reversal of accumulated depreciation
(b) Cost − FV of fixtures
(c) (a) − (b); alternatively FV $57 140 − carrying amount $56 872

The second journal entry recognises the acquired machine (Machine 4) at cost. Cost is measured using the fair value of the consideration given by the acquirer, namely the fair value of the fixtures. As cost is the measurement used, the fair value of the machine is not relevant. Similarly, the carrying amount of the asset in the seller's records is also not relevant.

	Machinery (M4)	Dr	57 140	
	Fixtures	Cr		57 140

The depreciation per month for M4 is then calculated:

$$\text{Machine 4 depreciation} = (\$57\,140 - \$4580)/36 \text{ months} = \$1460 \text{ per month}$$

(b) On 1 October, Machine 2 is traded in for Machine 5. Depreciation up to point of sale on Machine 2 is determined, being $1300 per month for the 3 months from July to September.

| Oct. 1 | Depreciation — machinery (M2) [$1300 × 3 months] | Dr | 3 900 | |
| | Accumulated depreciation — machinery (M2) | Cr | | 3 900 |

Machine 2 is remeasured to fair value and related accumulated depreciation is written out of the records and a gain/loss on sale is recognised.

	Accumulated depreciation — machinery (M2) [$1300 × 32 months]	Dr	41 600	
	Loss on sale of machinery (M2) [$42 200 – $41 600]	Dr	600	
	Machinery (M2) [$82 400 – $40 200]	Cr		42 200

Machine 5 is recorded at cost. Cost is determined as the sum of the purchase price and directly attributable costs. Purchase price is the fair value of consideration given up by the acquirer. In the absence of a fair value for Machine 2, the consideration is based on the fair value of Machine 5, namely $90 740. The directly attributable costs are the freight charges of $280 and installation costs of $1600, both necessary to prepare the asset for its intended use. Therefore Machinery (M5) is debited for $92 620.

The trade-in allowance is used as the measure of the fair value of the asset. The cash outlay is then the sum of the balance paid to the seller of Machine 5 and the directly attributable costs. Given the cost of machinery with the inclusion of the directly attributable costs is $92 620 and the trade in allowance $40 200, the cash balance is $52 420.

	Machinery (M5) [$90 740 + $280 + $1600]	Dr	92 620	
	Machinery (M2)	Cr		40 200
	Cash	Cr		52 420

The depreciation per month for Machine 5 is then calculated:

Machine 5 depreciation = ($92 620 – $5500)/72 months = $1210 per month

(c) On 1 May 2024, Machine 3 received an overhaul. This resulted in a change in the capacity of the machine, which increased the residual value and extended its useful life. Because this results in a change in the depreciation per month, depreciation based on the rate before the overhaul for the period up to the date of the overhaul is recorded.

2024				
May 1	Depreciation — machinery (M3) [$1140 × 10 months]	Dr	11 400	
	Accumulated depreciation — machinery (M3)	Cr		11 400

Because the overhaul increases the expected benefits from the asset; that is, the outlay for the overhaul results in probable future benefits, the cost of the overhaul is capitalised, increasing the overall cost of the asset.

| | Machinery (M3) | Dr | 16 910 | |
| | Cash | Cr | | 16 910 |

The overhaul results in a change in expectations, so it is necessary to calculate a revised depreciation per month.

M3: New depreciable amount = $87 480 + $16 910 – $5600 = $98 790
Accumulated depreciation balance = $1140 × 25 months = $28 500
Carrying amount to be depreciated = $98 790 – $28 500 = $70 290
New useful life = 72 months – 25 months + 24 months = 71 months
Revised depreciation = $70 290/71 months = $990 per month

(d) Because outlays on repairs and maintenance do not lead to increased future benefits, these outlays are expensed.

| June 1 | Repairs and maintenance expense | Dr | 2 370 | |
| | Cash | Cr | | 2 370 |

At the end of the reporting period, depreciation is accrued on all depreciable assets.

Machinery:	M1	$1180 × 10 months	$ 11 800
	M3	$990 × 2 months	1 980
	M4	$1460 × 12 months	17 520
	M5	$1210 × 9 months	10 890
			$ 42 190*
Fixtures:		$308 600 – $100 600	$208 000
		Less: $134 138 – $43 728	90 410
			$117 590
		20% × $117 590	$ 23 518**

(e) Journal entries to record the depreciation are as follows.

June 30	Depreciation — machinery*	Dr	42 190	
	Depreciation — fixtures**	Dr	23 518	
	Accumulated depreciation — machinery	Cr		42 190
	Accumulated depreciation — fixtures	Cr		23 518

Machine 1 is scrapped, so the asset is derecognised by writing off the asset and related accumulated depreciation. A residual value of $3800 was expected but not received, so the company incurs a loss of $3800.

Accumulated depreciation — machinery (M1) [$1180 × 60 months]	Dr	70 800	
Loss on derecognition — machinery (M1) [$74 600 – $70 800]	Dr	3 800	
Machinery (M1)	Cr		74 600

COMPREHENSION QUESTIONS

1 What assets constitute property, plant and equipment?

2 What are the recognition criteria for property, plant and equipment?

3 How should items of property, plant and equipment be measured at initial recognition?

4 How is cost determined?

5 What choices of measurement model exist subsequent to assets being initially recognised?

6 What factors should entities consider in choosing alternative measurement models?

7 What is meant by 'depreciation expense'?

8 How is useful life determined?

9 What is meant by 'residual value' of an asset?

10 How does an entity choose between depreciation methods; for example, straight-line versus diminishing balance models?

11 What is meant by 'significant parts depreciation'?

12 Under the revaluation model, how is a revaluation increase accounted for?

13 Under the revaluation model, how is a revaluation decrease accounted for?

14 Should accounting for revaluation increases and decreases be done on an asset-by-asset basis or on a class-of-assets basis?

15 When should property, plant and equipment be derecognised?

CASE STUDY 5.1

FAIR VALUE BASIS FOR MEASUREMENT

The management of Rocky Ltd has decided to use the fair value basis for the measurement of its equipment. Some of this equipment is difficult to obtain and has in fact increased in value over the current period. Management is arguing that, as there has been no decline in fair value, no depreciation should be charged on these pieces of equipment.

Required

Discuss management's position.

CASE STUDY 5.2

STRAIGHT-LINE VS DIMINISHING BALANCE DEPRECIATION

Ag Ltd uses tractors as part of its operating equipment, and it applies the straight-line depreciation method to these assets. Ag Ltd has just taken over Spector Ltd, which uses similar tractors in its operations. However, Spector Ltd has been using a diminishing balance method of depreciation for these tractors. The accountant in Ag Ltd is arguing that for both entities the same depreciation method should be used for tractors.

Required

Provide arguments for and against this proposal.

CASE STUDY 5.3

ANNUAL DEPRECIATION CHARGE

A company is in the movie rental business. Movies are generally rented out over a period of 2 years and then either sold or destroyed. However, management wants to show increased profits, and believes that the annual depreciation charge can be lowered by keeping the movies for 3 years.

Required

Discuss management's position.

CASE STUDY 5.4

DEPRECIATION CHARGES

A new accountant has been appointed to Outlander Ltd and has implemented major changes in the calculation of depreciation. As a result, some parts of the factory have much larger depreciation charges. This has angered some operations managers who believe that, as they take particular care with the maintenance of their machines, their machines should not attract large depreciation charges that reduce the profitability of their operations and reflect badly on their management skills. The operations managers plan to meet the accountant and ask for change.

Required

Explain how the new accountant should respond.

CASE STUDY 5.5

DEPRECIATION CHARGES

The management of Predator Ltd has been analysing the financial reports provided by the accountant, who has been with the firm for a number of years. Management has expressed its concern over depreciation charges being made in relation to the company's equipment. In particular, management believes that the depreciation charges are not high enough in relation to the factory machines because new technology applied in that area is rapidly making the machines obsolete. Management's concern is that the machines will have to be replaced in the near future and, with the low depreciation charges, the funds will not be sufficient to pay for the replacement machines.

Required

Discuss management's position.

APPLICATION AND ANALYSIS EXERCISES

★ BASIC | ★ ★ MODERATE | ★ ★ ★ DIFFICULT

5.1 Revaluation adjustments and reversals ★ LO6

On 1 January 2022, Lima Ltd revalued land from $200 000 to $400 000. On 1 January 2023, the company subsequently revalued the land to $320 000. And on 1 January 2024, the company again revalued the asset downwards to $160 000.

Required

Prepare the journal entries required to record the revaluation adjustment for the year ended:
1. 30 June 2022
2. 30 June 2023
3. 30 June 2024.

5.2 Revaluation adjustments and reversals ★ LO6

The following data from Lyre Ltd's accounts relates to two assets at 30 June 2021.

Asset	Value	Accumulated depreciation	Carrying amount
Land	$2 400 000	0	$2 400 000
Plant and equipment	$ 300 000	$60 000	$ 240 000

At 30 June 2021 Lyre Ltd decides to adopt the revaluation model for both these assets. On this date land has a fair value of $2 250 000 and plant and equipment has a fair value of $330 000. On 30 June 2022 Lyre Ltd reviews the value of its assets. The fair value of land is reassessed as $2 325 000. Plant and equipment has no change in value on that date.

Required

Prepare the journal entries required to revalue the assets for the year ended 30 June 2021 and the year ended 30 June 2022.

5.3 Revaluation model ★ LO6

One of the board of directors of Crane Ltd has proposed that the company adopt the revaluation model for fixed assets. Some of these assets are difficult to obtain and certain items have increased in value in the current period; however, it is difficult to know what their fair value is. The director is arguing that fair value will improve the 'look' of the company's statement of financial position, and may eliminate the need for depreciation.

Required

Prepare a report to the board on whether it should adopt the director's proposal.

5.4 Purpose of depreciation ★ LO5

Recently Sea Eagle Ltd experienced a workers' strike that affected a number of its operating plants. The group accountant of Sea Eagle Ltd indicated that it was not appropriate to report depreciation expense during this period as the equipment was not used during the strike. She stated that during the strike the equipment did not depreciate and an inappropriate matching of costs and revenues would result if depreciation were charged. She based her position on the following points.
1. It is inappropriate to charge the period with costs for which there are no related revenues arising from production.
2. The basic factor of depreciation in this instance is wear and tear, and because the equipment was idle, no wear and tear occurred.

Required

You are part of the auditing team that analyses the accounts of Sea Eagle Ltd. Write a report to your supervisor in relation to the views of the group accountant of Sea Eagle Ltd.

5.5 Determination of cost ★ LO2

Seagull Ltd purchased land for use as its corporate headquarters. A small factory that was on the land when it was purchased was torn down before construction of the office building began. A substantial amount of rock blasting and removal of soil then had to be done to the site before construction of the foundations of the building. Because the office building was set back from the public road, Seagull Ltd had the construction company build a paved road that led from the public highway to the entrance of the office building.

Required

Write a report to the group accountant of Seagull Ltd detailing which of the above expenditures should be capitalised.

5.6 Costs of acquisition ★ LO3

Rainbow Ltd has recently acquired a machine for an invoice price of $75 000. Various other costs relating to the acquisition and installation of the machine include transportation, electrical wiring and preparing a platform for installation. These amounted to $11 250. The machine has an estimated useful life of 10 years, with no residual value at the end of that period.

One of the accounting team has suggested that the incidental costs of $11 250 be charged to expense immediately for the following reasons.

1. If the machine is sold, these costs cannot be recovered in the sales price.
2. The inclusion of the $11 250 in the machinery account on the records will not necessarily result in a closer approximation of the market price of the asset over the years because of the possibility of changing demand and supply levels.
3. Charging the $11 250 to expense immediately will lower the depreciation expense in future years.

Required

Prepare a response to these arguments to be presented at the next meeting of the Rainbow Ltd accounting team.

5.7 Purpose of depreciation ★   **LO5**

A new accountant has been appointed to Flamingo Ltd and has implemented major changes in the calculation of depreciation. As a result, some parts of the factory are now subject to higher depreciation charges. This has incensed some operations managers who argue that they take particular care in the maintenance of their machines and, as a result, should not attract such large depreciation charges. They are concerned that these extra charges will reduce the profitability of their sections and may therefore lead to lower bonuses and maybe even the firing of some employees. These operations managers have complained to the group accountant.

Required

Write a report to these operations managers explaining the reasons for the depreciation policies adopted by Flamingo Ltd.

5.8 Determination of cost ★   **LO3**

Grantham Ltd has acquired a new building. Assess which of the following items should be included in the cost of the building. Provide a reason for your conclusions.

1. Stamp duty
2. Real estate agent's fees
3. Architect's fees for drawings for internal adjustments to the building needed to be made before use
4. Interest on the bank loan to acquire the building, and an application fee to the bank to get the loan, which is secured on the building
5. Cost of changing the name on the building
6. Cost of changing the parking bays
7. Cost of refurbishing the lobby to the building to attract customers and make it more user-friendly

5.9 Determination of cost ★   **LO3**

Corella Ltd has acquired new equipment, which it has now installed in its factory. Assess which of the following items should be capitalised into the cost of the building. Provide a reason for your conclusions.

1. Labour and travel costs for managers to inspect possible new items of equipment and for negotiating for the new equipment
2. Freight costs and insurance to get the new equipment to the factory
3. Costs for renovating a section of the factory, in anticipation of the new equipment's arrival, to ensure that all the other parts of the factory will have easy access to the new equipment
4. Cost of a cooling machine to assist in the efficient operation of the new equipment
5. Costs of repairing the factory door, which was damaged by the installation of the new equipment
6. Training costs of workers who will use the equipment

5.10 Determination of cost ★   **LO3**

Kingfisher Ltd has acquired a new building for $1 500 000. It has incurred incidental costs of $30 000 in the acquisition process for legal fees, the real estate agent's fees and stamp duties. Management believes that these costs should be expensed because they have not increased the value of the building and, if the building was immediately resold, these amounts would not be recouped. In other words, the fair value of the building is considered to still be $1 500 000.

Required

Discuss how these costs should be accounted for.

5.11 Depreciation and revaluation of assets ★ **LO5, 6**

In the 30 June 2022 annual report of Wombat Ltd, the equipment was reported as follows.

Equipment (at cost)	$250 000
Accumulated depreciation	75 000
	175 000

The equipment consisted of two machines, Machine A and Machine B. Machine A had cost $150 000 and had a carrying amount of $90 000 at 30 June 2022. Machine B had cost $100 000 and had a carrying amount of $85 000. Both machines are measured using the cost model and depreciated on a straight-line basis over a 10-year period.

On 31 December 2022, the directors of Wombat Ltd decided to change the basis of measuring the equipment from the cost model to the revaluation model. Machine A was revalued to $90 000 with an expected useful life of 6 years, and Machine B was revalued to $77 500 with an expected useful life of 5 years.

At 1 July 2023, Machine A was assessed to have a fair value of $81 500 with an expected useful life of 5 years, and Machine B's fair value was $68 250 with an expected useful life of 4 years.

Required

1. Prepare journal entries to record depreciation during the year ended 30 June 2023, assuming there was no revaluation.
2. Prepare the journal entries for Machine A for the period 1 July 2022 to 30 June 2023 on the basis that it was revalued on 31 December 2022.
3. Prepare the journal entries for Machine B for the period 1 July 2022 to 30 June 2023 on the basis that it was revalued on 31 December 2022.
4. Prepare the revaluation journal entries required for 1 July 2023.
5. According to accounting standards, on what basis may management change the method of asset measurement, for example, from cost to fair value?

5.12 Revaluation of assets ★ **LO5, 6**

On 30 June 2022, the statement of financial position of Kookaburra Ltd showed the following non-current assets after charging depreciation.

Building	$600 000	
Accumulated depreciation	(200 000)	$400 000
Motor vehicle	240 000	
Accumulated depreciation	(80 000)	160 000

The company has adopted fair value for the valuation of non-current assets. This has resulted in the recognition in previous periods of an asset revaluation surplus for the building of $28 000. On 30 June 2022, an independent valuer assessed the fair value of the building to be $320 000 and the vehicle to be $180 000.

Required

1. Prepare any necessary entries to revalue the building and the vehicle as at 30 June 2022.
2. Assume that the building and vehicle had remaining useful lives of 25 years and 4 years respectively, with zero residual value. Prepare entries to record depreciation expense for the year ended 30 June 2023 using the straight-line method.

5.13 Depreciation ★ **LO5, 6**

Willow Ltd was formed on 1 July 2020 to courier packages between the city and the airport. On this date, the company acquired a delivery truck from Lyons Trucks. The company paid cash of $50 000 to Lyons Trucks, which included government charges of $600 and registration of $400. Insurance costs for the first year amounted to $1200. The truck is expected to have a useful life of 5 years. At the end of the useful life, the asset is expected to be sold for $24 000, with costs relating to the sale amounting to $400.

The company prospered in its first year, and management decided at 1 July 2021 to add another vehicle, a flat-top, to the fleet. This vehicle was acquired from a liquidation auction at a cash price of $30 000. The vehicle needed some repairs for the elimination of rust (cost $2300), major servicing to the engine (cost $480) and the replacement of all tyres (cost $620). The company believed it would use the flat-top for another 2 years and then sell it. Expected selling price was $15 000, with selling costs estimated to be $400. On 1 July 2021, both vehicles were fitted with a radio communication system at a cost per vehicle of $300. This was not expected to have any material effect on the future selling price of either vehicle. Insurance costs for the 2021–22 period were $1200 for the first vehicle and $900 for the newly acquired vehicle.

All went well for the company except that, on 1 August 2022, the flat-top that had been acquired at auction broke down. Willow Ltd thought about acquiring a new vehicle to replace it but, after considering the costs, decided to repair the flat-top instead. The vehicle was given a major overhaul at a cost of $6500. Although this was a major expense, management believed that the company would keep the vehicle for another 2 years. The estimated selling price in 3 years' time is $12 000, with selling costs estimated at $300. Insurance costs for the 2022–23 period were the same as for the previous year.

Required

Prepare the journal entries for the recording of the vehicles and the depreciation of the vehicles for each of the 3 years. The end of the reporting period is 30 June.

5.14 Depreciation ★ **LO5, 6**

Sejenis Ltd constructed a building for use by its freight department. The completion date was 1 July 2015, and the construction cost was $840 000. The company expected to remain in the building for the next 20 years, at which time the building would probably have no real salvage value.

In December 2021, following some severe weather in the city, the roof of the freight building was considered to be in poor shape so the company decided to replace it. On 1 July 2022, a new roof was installed at a cost of $220 000. The new roof was of a different material to the old roof, which was estimated to have cost only $140 000 in the original construction, although at the time of construction it was thought that the roof would last for the 20 years that the company expected to use the building. Because the company had spent the money replacing the roof, it thought that it would delay construction of a new building, thereby extending the original life of the building from 20 years to 25 years.

Required

Discuss how you would account for the depreciation of the building and how the replacement of the roof would affect the depreciation calculations.

5.15 Calculation of depreciation ★ ★ **LO5**

On 1 July 2022, Eagle Airlines acquired a new aeroplane for a total cost of $20 million. A breakdown of the costs to build the aeroplane was given by the manufacturers.

Aircraft body	$6 000 000
Engines (2)	8 000 000
Fitting out of aircraft:	
Seats	2 000 000
Carpets	100 000
Electrical equipment:	
Passenger seats	400 000
Cockpit	3 000 000
Food preparation equipment	500 000

All costs include installation and labour costs associated with the relevant part.

It is expected that the aeroplane will be kept for 10 years and then sold. The main value of the plane at that stage is the body and the engines. The expected selling price is $4.2 million, with the body and engines retaining proportionate value.

Costs in relation to the aircraft over the next 10 years are expected to be as follows.

(a) *Aircraft body*. This requires an inspection every 2 years for cracks and wear and tear, at a cost of $20 000.

(b) *Engines*. Each engine has an expected life of 4 years before being sold for scrap. It is expected that the engines will be replaced in 2026 for $9 million and again in 2030 for $12 million. These engines are expected to incur annual maintenance costs of $600 000. The manufacturer has informed Eagle Airlines that a new prototype engine with an extra 10% capacity should be on the market in 2028, and that existing engines could be upgraded at a cost of $2 million.

(c) *Fittings*. Seats are replaced every 3 years. Expected replacement costs are $2.4 million in 2025 and $3 million in 2031. The repair of torn seats and faulty mechanisms is expected to cost

$200 000 p.a. Carpets are replaced every 5 years. They will be replaced in 2028 at an expected cost of $130 000, but will not be replaced again before the aircraft is sold in 2032. Cleaning costs amount to $20 000 p.a. The electrical equipment (such as the TV) for each seat has an annual repair cost of $30 000. It is expected that, with the improvements in technology, the equipment will be totally replaced in 2028 by substantially better equipment at a cost of $700 000. The electrical equipment in the cockpit is tested frequently at an expected annual cost of $500 000. Major upgrades to the equipment are expected every 2 years at expected costs of $500 000 (in 2021), $600 000 (in 2023), $690 000 (in 2025) and $820 000 (in 2030). The upgrades will take into effect the expected changes in technology.

(d) *Food preparation equipment.* This incurs annual costs for repair and maintenance of $40 000. The equipment is expected to be totally replaced in 2028.

Required

1. Discuss how the costs relating to the aircraft should be accounted for with respect to the following.
   (a) Aircraft body
   (b) Engines
   (c) Fittings
   (d) Food preparation equipment
2. Determine the expenses recognised for the 2022–23 financial year.

5.16 Acquisition and sale of assets, depreciation ★ ★　　　　　　　　　　　　　　　**LO2, 3, 5, 6**

Simon's Turf Farm owned the following items of property, plant and equipment as at 30 June 2022.

Land (at cost)		$120 000
Office building (at cost)	$150 000	
Accumulated depreciation	(23 375)	126 625
Turf cutter (at cost)	65 000	
Accumulated depreciation	(42 230)	22 770
Water desalinator (at fair value)		189 000

Additional information (at 30 June 2022)

- The straight-line method of depreciation is used for all depreciable items of PPE. Depreciation is charged to the nearest month and all figures are rounded to the nearest dollar.
- The office building was constructed on 1 April 2018. Its estimated useful life is 20 years and it has an estimated residual value of $40 000.
- The turf cutter was purchased on 21 January 2019, at which date it had an estimated useful life of 5 years and an estimated residual value of $3200.
- The water desalinator was purchased and installed on 2 July 2021 at a cost of $200 000. On 30 June 2022, the plant was revalued upwards by $7000 to its fair value on that day. Additionally, its useful life and residual value were re-estimated to 9 years and $18 000 respectively.

The following transactions occurred during the year ended 30 June 2023. (*Note:* All payments are made in cash.)

(i) On 10 August 2022, new irrigation equipment was purchased from Pond Supplies for $37 000. On 16 August 2022, the business paid $500 to have the equipment delivered to the turf farm. William Wagtail was contracted to install and test the new system. In the course of installation, pipes worth $800 were damaged and subsequently replaced on 3 September. The irrigation system was fully operational by 19 September and William Wagtail was paid $9600 for his services. The system has an estimated useful life of 4 years and a residual value of $0.

(ii) On 1 December 2022, the turf cutter was traded in on a new model worth $80 000. A trade-in allowance of $19 000 was received and the balance paid in cash. The new machine's useful life and residual value were estimated at 6 years and $5000 respectively.

(iii) On 1 January 2023, the turf farm's owner decided to extend the office building by adding three new offices and a meeting room. The extension work started on 2 February and was completed by 28 March at a cost of $49 000. The extension is expected to increase the useful life of the building by 4 years and increase its residual value by $5000.

(iv) On 30 June 2023, depreciation expense for the year was recorded. The fair value of the water desalination plant was $165 000.

Required

Prepare general journal entries to record the transactions and events for the reporting period ended 30 June 2023 in relation to the following assets.

(a) Office building
(b) Turf cutters
(c) Water desalinator
(d) Irrigation equipment

5.17 Acquisitions, disposals, depreciation ★ ★ LO5, 6, 7

Swan Ltd purchased machinery on 1 July 2021 for $119 400 cash. Transport and installation costs of $12 600 were paid on 5 July 2021. Useful life and residual value were estimated to be 10 years and $5400 respectively. Swan Ltd depreciates machinery using the straight-line method to the nearest month, and reports annually on 30 June. The company tax rate is 30%.

In June 2023, changes in technology caused the company to revise the estimated useful life from 10 years to 5 years, and the residual value from $5400 to $3600. This revised estimate was made before recording the depreciation for the reporting period ended 30 June 2023.

(a) On 30 June 2023, the company adopted the revaluation model to account for machinery. An expert valuation was obtained showing that the machinery had a fair value of $90 000 at that date.

(b) On 30 June 2024, depreciation for the year was charged and the machinery's carrying amount was remeasured to its fair value of $48 000.

(c) On 30 September 2024, the machinery was sold for $25 200 cash.

Required

1. Prepare general journal entries to record depreciation of the machinery for the years ended 30 June 2022 and 2023.

2. Prepare general journal entries to record the transactions and events for the period 1 July 2022 to 30 September 2024 for items (a) to (c). (Narrations are not required.) (Show all workings and round amounts to the nearest dollar.)

5.18 Revaluation model ★ ★ LO2, 3, 5, 6, 7

On 1 July 2022, Resonante Ltd acquired two assets within the same class of plant and equipment. Information on these assets is as follows.

	Cost	Expected useful life
Machine A	$200 000	5 years
Machine B	120 000	3 years

The machines are expected to generate benefits evenly over their useful lives. The class of plant and equipment is measured using fair value.

At 30 June 2023, information about the assets is as follows.

	Fair value	Expected useful life
Machine A	$168 000	4 years
Machine B	76 000	2 years

On 1 January 2024, Machine B was sold for $58 000 cash. On the same day, Resonante Ltd acquired Machine C for $160 000 cash. Machine C has an expected useful life of 4 years. Resonante Ltd also made a bonus issue of 20 000 shares at $1 per share, using $16 000 from the general reserve and $4000 from the asset revaluation surplus created as a result of measuring Machine A at fair value.

At 30 June 2024, information on the machines is as follows.

	Fair value	Expected useful life
Machine A	$122 000	3 years
Machine C	137 000	3.5 years

Required

1. Prepare the journal entries in the records of Resonante Ltd to record the events for the year ended 30 June 2023.
2. Prepare journal entries to record the events for the year ended 30 June 2024.

5.19 Determining the cost of assets ★ ★ LO3

Magpie Ltd uses many kinds of machines in its operations. It constructs some of these machines itself and acquires others from the manufacturers. The following information relates to two machines that it has recorded in the 2023–24 period. Machine A was acquired, and Machine B was constructed by Magpie Ltd itself.

Machine A	
Cash paid for equipment, including GST of $4000	$44 000
Costs of transporting machine — insurance and transport	1 500
Labour costs of installation by expert fitter	2 500
Labour costs of testing equipment	2 000
Insurance costs for 2023–24	750
Costs of training for personnel who will use the machine	1 250
Costs of safety rails and platforms surrounding machine	3 000
Costs of water devices to keep machine cool	4 000
Costs of adjustments to machine during 2023–24 to make it operate more efficiently	3 750

Machine B	
Cost of material to construct machine, including GST of $3500	$38 500
Labour costs to construct machine	21 500
Allocated overhead costs — electricity, factory space etc.	11 000
Allocated interest costs of financing machine	5 000
Costs of installation	6 000
Insurance for 2023–24	1 000
Profit saved by self-construction	7 500
Safety inspection costs prior to use	2 000

Required

Determine the amount at which each of these machines should be recorded in the records of Magpie Ltd. For items not included in the cost of the machines, note how they should be accounted for.

5.20 Classification of acquisition costs ★ ★ LO2, 3

Harrier Ltd began operations on 1 July 2022. During the following year, the company acquired a tract of land, demolished the building on the land and built a new factory. Equipment was acquired for the factory and, in March 2023, the factory was ready. A gala opening was held on 18 March, with the local parliamentarian opening the factory. The first items were ready for sale on 25 March. During this period, the following inflows and outflows occurred.

(a)	While searching for a suitable block of land, Harrier Ltd placed an option to buy with three real estate agents at a cost of $200 each. One of these blocks of land was later acquired.	
(b)	Payment of option fees	$ 600
(c)	Receipt of loan from bank	800 000
(d)	Payment to settlement agent for title search, stamp duties and settlement fees	20 000
(e)	Payment of arrears in rates on building on land	10 000
(f)	Payment for land	200 000
(g)	Payment for demolition of current building on land	24 000
(h)	Proceeds from sale of material from old building	11 000
(i)	Payment to architect	46 000
(j)	Payment to council for approval of building construction	24 000
(k)	Payment for safety fence around construction site	6 800
(l)	Payment to construction contractor for factory building	480 000
(m)	Payment for external driveways, parking bays and safety lighting	108 000
(n)	Payment of interest on loan	80 000
(o)	Payment for safety inspection on building	6 000
(p)	Payment for equipment	128 000
(q)	Payment of freight and insurance costs on delivery of equipment	11 200
(r)	Payment of installation costs on equipment	24 000
(s)	Payment for safety fence surrounding equipment	22 000
(t)	Payment for removal of safety fence	4 000

(u)	Payment for new fence surrounding the factory	16 000
(v)	Payment for advertisements in the local paper about the forthcoming factory and its benefits to the local community	1 000
(w)	Payment for opening ceremony	12 000
(x)	Payments to adjust equipment to more efficient operating levels subsequent to initial operation	6 600

Required

Using the information provided, determine what assets Harrier Ltd should recognise and the amounts at which they would be recorded.

5.21 Acquisitions, disposals, trade-ins, overhauls, depreciation ★ ★   **LO2, 3, 4, 5, 6, 7**

Li Na is the owner of Kestrel Fishing Charters. The business's final trial balance on 30 June 2022 (end of the reporting period) included the following balances.

Processing plant (at cost, purchased 4 April 2020)	$ 148 650
Accumulated depreciation — processing plant	(81 274)
Charter boats	291 200
Accumulated depreciation — boats	(188 330)

The following boats were owned at 30 June 2022.

Boat	Purchase date	Cost	Estimated useful life	Estimated residual value
1	23 February 2018	$62 000	5 years	$3000
2	9 September 2018	$66 400	5 years	$3400
3	6 February 2019	$78 600	4 years	$3600
4	20 April 2020	$84 200	6 years	$3800

Kestrel Fishing Charters calculates depreciation to the nearest month using straight-line depreciation for all assets except the processing plant, which is depreciated at 30% using the diminishing balance method. Amounts are recorded to the nearest dollar.

Required

1. Prepare general journal entries (with narrations) to record the transactions and events for the year ended 30 June 2023.
2. Assume the transactions and events listed in (a) to (d) below occurred during the year ended 30 June 2023. Prepare general journal entries (with narrations) to record the transactions and events for the year ended 30 June 2023, incorporating the information detailed in (a) to (d).

	2022	
(a)	July 26	Traded in Boat 1 for a new boat (Boat 5) which cost $84 100. A trade-in allowance of $8900 was received and the balance was paid in cash. Registration and stamp duty costs of $1500 were also paid in cash. Li Na estimated Boat 5's useful life and residual value at 6 years and $4120 respectively.
(b)	Dec. 4	Overhauled the processing plant at a cash cost of $62 660. As the modernisation significantly expanded the plant's operating capacity and efficiency, Li Na decided to revise the depreciation rate to 25%.
	2023	
(c)	Feb. 26	Boat 3 reached the end of its useful life but no buyer could be found, so the boat was scrapped.
(d)	June 30	Recorded depreciation.

3. On 26 March, Li Na was offered fish-finding equipment with a fair value of $9500 in exchange for Boat 2. The fish-finder originally cost its owner $26 600 and had a carrying value of $9350 at the date of offer. The fair value of Boat 2 was $9100. If River Song accepts the exchange offer, what amount would the business use to record the acquisition of the fish-finding equipment? Why? Justify your answer by reference to the requirements of AASB 116/IAS 16 relating to the initial recognition of a PPE item.

5.22 Acquisitions, revaluations, replacements, depreciation ★ ★ **LO2, 3, 5, 6, 7**

Robin Trading operates in a very competitive field. To maintain its market position, it purchased two new machines for cash on 1 January 2021. It had previously rented its machines. Machine A cost $40 000. Machine B cost $100 000. Each machine was expected to have a useful life of 10 years, and residual values were estimated at $2000 for Machine A and $5000 for Machine B.

On 30 June 2022, Robin Trading adopted the revaluation model to account for the class of machinery. The fair values of Machine A and Machine B were determined to be $32 000 and $90 000 respectively on that date. The useful life and residual value of Machine A were reassessed to 8 years and $1500. The useful life and residual value of Machine B were reassessed to 8 years and $4000.

On 2 January 2023, extensive repairs were carried out on Machine B for $66 000 cash. Robin Trading expected these repairs to extend Machine B's useful life by 3.5 years, and it revised Machine B's estimated residual value to $9450.

Owing to technological advances, Robin Trading decided to replace Machine A. It traded in Machine A on 31 March 2023 for new Machine C, which cost $64 000. A $28 000 trade-in was allowed for Machine A, and the balance of Machine C's cost was paid in cash. Transport and installation costs of $950 were incurred in respect to Machine C. Machine C was expected to have a useful life of 8 years and a residual value of $8000.

Robin Trading uses the straight-line depreciation method, recording depreciation to the nearest month and the nearest dollar. The end of its reporting period is 30 June.

On 30 June 2023, fair values were determined to be $140 000 and $65 000 for Machines B and C respectively.

Required

Prepare general journal entries to record the above transactions and the depreciation journal entries required at the end of each reporting period up to 30 June 2023.

5.23 Depreciation calculation ★ ★ ★ **LO5**

Dove Ltd operates a factory that contains a large number of machines designed to produce knitted garments. These machines are generally depreciated at 10% p.a. on a straight-line basis. In general, machines are estimated to have a residual value on disposal of 10% of cost. At 1 July 2023, Dove Ltd had a total of 50 machines, and the statement of financial position showed a total cost of $630 000 and accumulated depreciation of $195 000. During 2023–24, the following transactions occurred.

(a) On 1 September 2023, a new machine was acquired for $22 500. This machine replaced two other machines. One of the two replaced machines was acquired on 1 July 2020 for $12 300. It was traded in on the new machine, with Dove Ltd making a cash payment of $13 200 on the new machine. The second replaced machine had cost $13 500 on 1 April 2021 and was sold for $10 950.

(b) On 1 January 2024, a machine that had cost $6000 on 1 July 2014 was retired from use and sold for scrap for $750.

(c) On 1 January 2024, a machine that had been acquired on 1 January 2021 for $10 500 was repaired because its motor had been damaged from overheating. The motor was replaced at a cost of $7200. It was expected that this would increase the life of the machine by an extra 2 years.

(d) On 1 April 2024, Dove Ltd fitted a new form of arm to a machine used for putting special designs onto garments. The arm cost $1800. The machine had been acquired on 1 April 2021 for $15 000. The arm can be used on a number of other machines when required and has a 15-year life. It will not be sold when any particular machine is retired, but retained for use on other machines.

Required

1. Record each of the transactions. The end of the reporting period is 30 June.
2. Determine the depreciation expense for Dove Ltd for 2023–24.

5.24 Depreciation ★ ★ ★ **LO5**

Hawk Ltd started operations on 1 September 2017. Hawk Ltd's accounts at 31 December 2020 included the following balances.

Equipment (at cost)				$182 000
Accumulated depreciation — equipment				96 400
Vehicles (at cost; purchased 21 November 2019)				93 600
Accumulated depreciation — vehicles				39 312
Land (at cost; purchased 25 October 2017)				162 000
Building (at cost; purchased 25 October 2017)				371 440
Accumulated depreciation — building				57 228

Details of equipment owned at 31 December 2020 are as follows.

Machine	Purchase date	Cost	Useful life	Residual value
1	7 October 2017	$86 000	5 years	$5000
2	4 February 2018	$96 000	6 years	$6000

Additional information
- Hawk Ltd calculates depreciation to the nearest month and balances the records at month-end. Recorded amounts are rounded to the nearest dollar, and the end of the reporting period is 31 December.
- Hawk Ltd uses straight-line depreciation for all depreciable assets except vehicles, which are depreciated on the diminishing balance at 40% p.a.
- The vehicles account balance reflects the total paid for two identical delivery vehicles, each of which cost $46 800.
- On acquiring the land and building, Hawk Ltd estimated the building's useful life and residual value at 20 years and $10 000 respectively.

Required
Prepare general journal entries to record the following transactions that occurred from 1 January 2021.

2021	
Jan. 3	Bought new equipment (Equipment 3) for a cash price of $114 000. Freight charges of $884 and installation costs of $3516 were paid in cash. The useful life and residual value were estimated at 5 years and $8000 respectively.
June 22	Bought a second-hand vehicle for $30 400 cash. Repainting costs of $1310 and four new tyres costing $690 were paid for in cash.
Aug. 28	Exchanged Equipment 1 for office furniture that had a fair value of $25 000 at the date of exchange. The fair value of Equipment 1 at the date of exchange was $23 000. The office furniture originally cost $72 000 and, to the date of exchange, had been depreciated by $48 200 in the previous owner's books. Hawk Ltd estimated the office furniture's useful life and residual value at 8 years and $1080 respectively.
Dec. 31	Recorded depreciation.
2022	
April 30	Paid for repairs and maintenance on the equipment at a cash cost of $1856.
May 25	Sold one of the vehicles bought on 21 November 2019 for $13 200 cash.
June 26	Installed a fence around the property at a cash cost of $11 000. The fence has an estimated useful life of 10 years and zero residual value. (Debit the cost to a land improvements asset account.)
Dec. 31	Recorded depreciation.
2023	
Jan. 5	Overhauled Equipment 2 at a cash cost of $24 000, after which Hawk Ltd estimated its remaining useful life at 1 additional year and revised its residual value to $10 000.
June 20	Traded in the remaining vehicle bought on 21 November 2019 for a new vehicle. A trade-in allowance of $7400 was received and $44 000 was paid in cash. Stamp duty of $1000 and registration and third-party insurance of $1600 were also paid for in cash.
Oct. 4	Scrapped the vehicle bought on 22 June 2021, as it had been so badly damaged in a traffic accident that it was not worthwhile repairing it.
Dec. 31	Recorded depreciation.

5.25 Applying accounting theory to property, plant and equipment ★ ★ **LO5, 6**

Beatrix was recently appointed as the accountant for Lorikeet Ltd. She was surprised to learn that the company uses the cost model for its buildings. Her previous employer, Raven Ltd, had used the revaluation model for its buildings.

Eager to make a good impression with management, Beatrix proposed to adopt the fair value model for buildings, effective from 1 July 2021, in preparing the financial statements of Lorikeet Ltd for the year ended 30 June 2022. She presented the following analysis to senior management to show the effect of adopting the revaluation model.

LORIKEET LTD Summarised statement of financial position as at 1 July 2021	Cost model $m	Revaluation $m
Other assets	80	80
Buildings (net)	70	120
Total assets	**150**	**200**
Liabilities	50	50
Equity	100	150
Total liabilities and equity	**150**	**200**

Additional information
- Profit before interest and taxes is usually about $20 million each year.
- The remaining useful life of the buildings is 10 years.
- Lorikeet Ltd's senior management are paid a fixed salary plus a share-based bonus if return on investment (ROI) exceeds 10%, where ROI is calculated as profit before interest and taxes/total assets at the beginning of the year.

Required
1. Calculate the effect of the revaluation of buildings on depreciation expense for the year ended 30 June 2022. Assume the straight-line depreciation method is used.
2. Using the positive accounting theory perspective discussed in chapter 2 of this text, explain why senior management of Lorikeet Ltd might not be in favour of adopting the revaluation model for buildings.

REFERENCE

BHP Group Ltd 2018, *2018 annual report*, www.bhp.com.

ACKNOWLEDGEMENTS

Photo: © Manuel Gutjahr / iStockphoto
Photo: © Vladimir Arndt / Shutterstock.com
Figures 5.1, 5.3: © BHP Group Ltd 2018

CHAPTER 6

Intangible assets

CHAPTER AIM

This chapter discusses the accounting treatment for intangible assets, the criteria for the recognition of intangible assets by entities, how intangible assets are measured and the disclosures required in relation to intangible assets.

LEARNING OBJECTIVES

After studying this chapter, you should be able to:

6.1 explain the need for an accounting standard on intangible assets

6.2 explain the key characteristics of an intangible asset

6.3 discuss the recognition criteria applied to intangible assets

6.4 discuss the measurement at initial recognition of intangible assets

6.5 describe how to amortise intangible assets

6.6 explain the accounting for intangible assets subsequent to initial recognition

6.7 discuss the disclosures required for intangible assets.

CONCEPTS FOR REVIEW

Before studying this chapter, you should understand and, if necessary, revise:
- the definition of an asset in the *Conceptual Framework*
- the recognition criteria for an asset under the *Conceptual Framework*
- the accounting for property, plant and equipment, particularly criteria for recognition, concepts of depreciation, application of the cost model, and application of the revaluation model
- the concept of fair value measurement.

6.1 Introduction and scope

LEARNING OBJECTIVE 6.1 Explain the need for an accounting standard on intangible assets.

For many companies, there is a substantial difference between their financial position as measured by the net assets (book value) shown in their annual report and their market capitalisation as measured by their worth on the stock market on which they are listed. For example, at April 2019, the Commonwealth Bank of Australia had a price/book (P/B) ratio (being current market price/book value per share) of 1.96, Alphabet (Google) had a P/B ratio of 4.979 and Facebook had a P/B ratio of 6.318. In each case, the stock market valued the company at an amount greater than the net assets reported in their financial statements. In some cases, the P/B ratio can be extremely high, based on expectations of the future prospects of the company. For example, the health sciences company PuriCore plc at one point in time had a P/B ratio as high as 84.75, based on speculation about the potential value of the intellectual property arising from its research and development activities.

Market capitalisation may be greater than book value for many reasons. One reason is that accountants in general apply the historical cost method, as opposed to fair value, when measuring assets. Another reason is that accounting standards do not allow the recognition of some items that the market considers to be valuable. Consider the following items that may affect a company's value.

- *Human resources.* Accounting standards specifically exclude the recognition of skilled staff, training and technical talent from recognition as intangible assets. In some cases it can be argued that some personnel are extremely valuable to an entity. One example is Jony Ive and his value to Apple as its chief design officer (having been with the company since 1992 and having been a confidant of Steve Jobs). When it was announced that Ive would be leaving to start his own company, Apple's shares fell 1.5 per cent, losing nearly AU$13 billion in value (Nellis 2019).
- *Brand names.* All those who consider the brand of an item when making a purchase are aware of the importance of brands to the value of an entity. Table 6.1 provides information on the most valuable brands in Australia. These brand values, calculated by Brand Finance, are based on the value a company would need to pay to license its brand if it did not own it. However, not all brands appear on the financial statements of the companies that own the brand. For example, in the Qantas Airways Ltd (Qantas) annual report, the brand 'Jetstar' is recognised as an asset, but the brand 'Qantas' (which Brand Finance ranks as Australia's thirteenth-most valuable brand) does not appear. As discussed further in this chapter, accounting for brands under accounting standards provides different methods of measurement, dependent on how the brand was generated.
- *Customer satisfaction.* Companies investigate customer satisfaction as an indicator of their performance. Figure 6.1 provides information on the customer satisfaction levels perceived within the Australian domestic airlines industry. Customer satisfaction is considered to be valuable. The market capitalisation of an entity most likely includes some value for customer satisfaction as the market perceives that the value of an entity is affected by its customer satisfaction ratings. However, accountants do not recognise such resources as assets on the statement of financial position.

TABLE 6.1 Australia's 10 most valuable brands, 2018

Rank	Brand	Value
1	Telstra Corporation	$12.436 billion
2	Commonwealth Bank	$ 8.283 billion
3	ANZ	$ 8.248 billion
4	Woolworths Group Limited	$ 7.145 billion
5	Coles	$ 6.574 billion
6	National Australia Bank	$ 6.507 billion
7	Westpac	$ 5.833 billion
8	BHP Group	$ 5.104 billion
9	Optus	$ 3.946 billion
10	Rio Tinto	$ 3.103 billion

Source: Brand Finance (2018).

FIGURE 6.1 Customer satisfaction in Australian domestic airlines

Rated brands	Overall satisfaction*	Service	Value for money	Flight schedule /availability	In-flight offerings	Flight punctuality
Qantas	★★★★★	★★★★★	★★★★	★★★★★	★★★★★	★★★★★
Jetstar	★★★★	★★★★	★★★★	★★★★	★★	★★★★
Tiger Airways	★★★★	★★★	★★★★★	★★★★	★★	★★★
Virgin Australia	★★★★	★★★★★	★★★★	★★★★★	★★★★	★★★★★
Rex	★★★	★★★★	★★★	★★★	★★	★★★★

Overall satisfaction is an individual rating and not a combined total of all ratings.

Source: Canstar Blue (2018).

Even though accountants are reluctant to recognise human assets, customer satisfaction and some brands, they do recognise assets other than financial assets and tangible assets such as property, plant and equipment. These assets are referred to as 'intangible assets'.

The relevant accounting standard is AASB 138/IAS 38 *Intangible Assets*. This standard contains the definition of an intangible asset as well as the limitations on the recognition and measurement of these assets. The standard covers all intangible assets except where these are covered by other accounting standards, such as financial assets, mineral exploration rights, leases, deferred tax assets and goodwill acquired in a business combination. The focus of this chapter is on the accounting for intangible assets as set out in AASB 138/IAS 38.

LEARNING CHECK

☐ Accounting standards do not allow the recognition of some items that the market considers to be valuable, leading to potential differences between the book value and the market capitalisation of a company.

☐ AASB 138/IAS 38 *Intangible Assets* covers the definition, recognition and measurement of intangible assets.

6.2 The nature of intangible assets

LEARNING OBJECTIVE 6.2 Explain the key characteristics of an intangible asset.

Myer Holdings Ltd discloses brand names, trademarks, lease rights, software and goodwill as its intangible assets, while the Qantas Group lists airport landing slots, software, brand names and trademarks as well as customer contracts amongst its intangible assets. Paladin Energy Ltd, an Australian mining company with major interests in uranium mines and development projects in Australia and Africa, listed a number of interesting intangible assets in Note 23 of its 2018 annual report, as shown in figure 6.2.

FIGURE 6.2 Types of intangible assets, Paladin Energy

Description of the group's intangible assets

1. Right to supply of power
   LHUPL has entered into a contract with NamPower in Namibia for the right to access power at LHM. In order to obtain this right, the power line connection to the mine was funded by LHM. However, ownership of the power line rests with NamPower. The amount funded is being amortised on a unit of production basis.
2. Right to supply of water
   LHUPL has entered into a contract with NamWater in Namibia for the right to access water at LHM. In order to obtain this right, the water pipeline connection to the mine was funded by LHM. However, ownership of the pipeline rests with NamWater. The amount funded is being amortised on a unit of production basis.

Source: Paladin Energy Ltd (2018, p. 118).

Some other forms of intangible assets include the following.
- Plays, operas, ballets
- Computer software
- Internet domain names
- Musical works, song lyrics
- Formulas, recipes
- Broadcast rights
- Films and TV programs
- Trademarks
- Construction permits
- Royalties on books
- Newspaper mastheads
- Carbon trading rights
- Franchise agreements
- Customer lists
- Data bases
- Patents
- Pictures and photographs
- Package design, shape

Paragraph 8 of AASB 138/IAS 38 defines an **intangible asset** as:

> an identifiable non-monetary asset without physical substance.

For there to be an intangible asset, there must firstly be an asset — a resource controlled by an entity as a result of a past event and from which future economic benefits are expected to flow to the entity. For an asset to be classified as an intangible asset it must have three characteristics. An intangible asset must be:
- identifiable
- non-monetary in nature
- without physical substance.

Items that do not meet all three characteristics cannot be recognised as intangible assets in financial statements. Hence, the definition itself leads to the exclusion of some items from the statement of financial position.

6.2.1 Identifiable

The term 'identifiable' is not defined in AASB 138/IAS 38. However, paragraph 12 of AASB 138/IAS 38 states that an asset is identifiable if it is separable or arises from contractual or other legal rights.

The asset is separable

To be separable an asset must be capable of being separated from the entity. The asset could be separated if the entity could sell, license, rent, exchange or transfer the asset.

Assets such as brands and trademarks are separable, as an entity could sell them to other entities. Goodwill, however, is not separable as this asset cannot be transferred between entities. Goodwill is therefore not an intangible asset, even though many Australian companies include it in the intangibles section of their statements of financial position. Although AASB 138/IAS 38 does deal with internally generated goodwill (see section 6.4.4), it is AASB 3/IFRS 3 *Business Combinations* that establishes the accounting for goodwill (see chapter 25). In a discussion paper on intangible assets, the Australian Accounting Standards Board (AASB) (2008, paragraph 15) identified some other assets that are not separable:

> For example, the identifiability criterion scopes out customer service capability, presence in geographic markets or locations, strong labour relations, ongoing training or recruiting programs, knowledge, eco-logical attitudes, outstanding credit ratings and access to capital markets, and favourable government relations...

Figure 6.1 noted that customer satisfaction is valuable to companies. However, customer satisfaction is not separable from an entity. For example, Virgin Australia cannot transfer some of its customer satisfaction to another airline. Because customer satisfaction is not an identifiable asset (and does not arise from contractual or other legal rights), it is excluded from recognition as an intangible asset.

The inclusion of separability in the definition of an intangible asset relates to reliability of measurement. If an asset can be transferred from one entity to another then it is probable that a market exists for the asset. If there is a market, there is a market price. To include assets such as customer satisfaction on the statement of financial position, an entity would have to use some form of non-market valuation method to measure the asset. The standard setters were concerned about the reliability of such measures. Investors can include their own valuations in assessing the market price of the shares, but an entity cannot include unreliable measures on a statement of financial position. The existence of separability as a test of an intangible asset places a limit on the assets that can appear on a statement of financial position.

Some intangible aspects of assets are included in the measures of assets. For example, the measurement of the value of a block of land with a view over the ocean will include the intangible component of the view. Similarly the trademark 'Coca-Cola' has no value unless it is combined with the formula to manufacture the drink. Such assets are linked to each other and not separated into tangible and intangible components for accounting purposes.

The asset arises from contractual or other legal rights

As noted earlier, an alternative criterion to separability is whether the asset arises from contractual or other legal rights. Examples of assets that are not separable but arise from contractual or other legal rights generally relate to situations where a government gives or sells a right to an entity, such as:
- an entity has a right to use 2 million litres of water per annum in its production process
- an entity has broadcasting rights used in operating a television station.

A condition of receiving these rights is that they cannot be transferred between entities. If an entity uses, for example, only 1 million litres of water, it cannot sell/transfer the remaining right to water use to another entity. As such, the right is not separable. However, these rights are assets that can be distinguished from other assets of an entity and as such are recognisable as intangible assets.

6.2.2 Non-monetary in nature

According to paragraph 8 of AASB 138/IAS 38, **monetary assets** are:

> money held and assets to be received in fixed or determinable amounts of money.

'Non-monetary' is included as a required characteristic of an intangible asset in order to exclude financial assets, such as loans receivable, from being classified as intangible assets. These assets are accounted for under other accounting standards such as AASB 9/IFRS 9 *Financial Instruments*.

6.2.3 Lack of physical substance

Physical substance relates to the ability to be able to see and touch an asset, such as a building or machinery. This characteristic is included in the definition to exclude items of property, plant and equipment from being classified as intangible assets. In essence, identifiable, non-monetary tangible assets are accounted for under other accounting standards such as AASB 116/IAS 16 *Property, Plant and Equipment*.

Some intangible assets may be associated with a physical item, such as software contained on a computer disk. However, the asset is the software rather than the computer disk.

In 2016–17 in Australia a number of car manufacturing companies, including Toyota, Holden and Ford, closed manufacturing plants. It is interesting to note that the fragile assets in relation to car manufacturing are the plant and equipment used to make the cars — the tangible assets — while the strong assets are the brands of the car manufacturers — the intangible assets. The brands endure regardless of where the companies decide to manufacture the vehicles.

LEARNING CHECK

☐ The three key characteristics of intangible assets are identifiability, non-monetary nature and lack of physical substance.
☐ For an asset to be identifiable it must be separable or arise from contractual or other legal rights.
☐ Goodwill is not an intangible asset, as it is not separable.

6.3 Recognition of intangible assets

LEARNING OBJECTIVE 6.3 Discuss the recognition criteria applied to intangible assets.

An asset that has met the three criteria noted in section 6.2 is classified as an intangible asset. Before the asset can be included in the accounting records it must meet the recognition criteria described in paragraph 21 of AASB 138/IAS 38:

> (a) it is probable that the expected future economic benefits that are attributable to the asset will flow to the entity; and
> (b) the cost of the asset can be measured reliably.

These are the same as the criteria for recognition of property, plant and equipment. Note that it is the *cost* of the asset that must be measured reliably. As discussed later in this chapter, this has particular consequences for intangible assets. Unlike tangible assets, companies develop many of their intangible assets internally; for example, a brand name or a patent for a product. These intangible assets may be developed internally over many years. Even though a value may be able to be placed on these assets, unless the cost can be reliably measured, the assets cannot be recognised.

Even though these two recognition criteria are generally required, as discussed in section 6.4, under certain circumstances they are assumed to be met. In such circumstances there is no need to apply the recognition tests.

There are other intangible assets that can *never* be recognised, regardless of whether they meet the recognition tests.

- *Specific internally generated intangible assets.* These assets arise as a result of the entity internally generating them (as opposed to acquiring them). According to paragraph 63 of AASB 138/IAS 38, 'internally generated brands, mastheads, publishing titles, customer lists and items similar in substance shall not be recognised as intangible assets'. The reason for non-recognition relates to the perceived inability to be able to measure the cost of these assets as they are internally generated. The cost of developing these assets is seen to be indistinguishable from the cost of developing the business as a whole (AASB 138/IAS 38 paragraph 64). For example, the cost of generating the brand 'Vegemite' is seen to be the same as the cost of developing the business, in that the brand is useless without the product itself. The brand 'Vegemite' could not be sold by itself as a separate asset as it cannot be applied to any other product in any useful way. Internally generated intangible assets are discussed further in section 6.4.3.
- *Research costs.* Outlays classified as being on research can never be recognised as assets by the entity incurring those costs. These costs must always be expensed. This non-recognition applies only to internally generated research and not to in-process research acquired from other entities. The nature of research outlays is discussed further in section 6.4.3.

LEARNING CHECK

- ☐ The criteria for recognition of intangible assets are the same as those for recognition of property, plant and equipment.
- ☐ The recognition criteria require that it is probable that the future economic benefits will flow to the entity and that the cost can be measured reliably.
- ☐ Some intangible assets can never be recognised, regardless of whether they meet the recognition criteria, including internally generated intangible assets and research costs.

6.4 Measurement

LEARNING OBJECTIVE 6.4 Discuss the measurement at initial recognition of intangible assets.

According to paragraph 24 of AASB 138/IAS 38, an intangible asset must be measured initially at cost. This is the same as the measurement rule for property, plant and equipment. **Cost** is defined in paragraph 8 of AASB 138/IAS 38 as:

> the amount of cash or cash equivalents paid or the fair value of other consideration given to acquire an asset at the time of its acquisition or construction.

As with the recognition criteria, this measurement principle is applied differently depending on the circumstances.

- Not-for-profit entities sometimes receive assets as gifts or contributions. For example, a donor may give the Red Cross the right to use land or a building in its charity work. In such cases, the cost is zero. In Australia, when a not-for-profit entity receives an intangible asset at zero or nominal cost, paragraph Aus24.1 of AASB 138 specifies that the asset must be measured at its fair value at the date of acquisition.
- The measurement of the cost of intangible assets is based on how the assets were obtained by an entity. The various modes are:
  - separate acquisition
  - acquisition as part of a business combination
  - internally generated intangible assets.

6.4.1 Separate acquisition

Separate acquisition means that an entity acquires an individual intangible asset, not a group of assets; for example, an entity may acquire a brand or a patent from another entity.

According to paragraph 25 of AASB 138/IAS 38, in applying the *recognition criteria* for separately acquired assets, it is always assumed that the probability recognition criterion is met. The rationale for this is the belief that a buyer of an asset will determine the price to be paid by taking into account the probability of the future benefits to be received.

Further, as described in paragraph 26 of AASB 138/IAS 38, it is usual in a separate acquisition that the cost of the asset can be reliably measured, particularly if the consideration consists of cash or other monetary assets. As a result, usually both recognition criteria are met for separately acquired intangible assets.

Assets obtained by separate acquisition are measured at cost. According to paragraph 27 of AASB 138/IAS 38, the cost is determined as the sum of the purchase price and the directly attributable costs (i.e. in the same way as for property, plant and equipment under AASB 116/IAS 16). The purchase price is measured as the fair value of what is given up by the acquirer plus the directly attributable costs necessarily incurred to get the asset into the condition where it is capable of operating in the manner intended by management.

6.4.2 Acquisition as part of a business combination

The nature of a business combination is discussed in detail in chapter 25. In this section, a reference to a business combination indicates that the acquiring entity has acquired a group of assets rather than a single asset and one of the assets in the group is an intangible asset. The group of assets could be an operating division or a segment of another entity.

According to paragraph 33 of AASB 138/IAS 38, where an intangible asset is acquired as part of a business combination, *no recognition criteria* need be applied as it is considered that the recognition criteria are always satisfied. Provided the assets meet the definition of an intangible asset, they must be recognised as separate assets. As with separately acquired assets, the effect of probability of future benefits is reflected in the measurement of the asset. The acquirer expects future benefits even if they are uncertain. The reliable measurement criterion is also considered to be always satisfied.

An intangible asset acquired as part of a business combination will initially be measured at fair value. According to AASB 3/IFRS 3 the cost of such an intangible asset is its fair value at the acquisition date. Fair value is measured in accordance with AASB 13/IFRS 13 *Fair Value Measurement*, discussed in chapter 3. **Fair value** is defined in paragraph 8 of AASB 138/IAS 38 as:

> the price that would be received to sell an asset or paid to transfer a liability in an orderly transaction between market participants at the measurement date.

This may mean that the acquirer in a business combination may recognise assets that were not recognised in the records of the seller. The seller may not be able to recognise an intangible asset because it could not reliably measure the cost, or because it was one of the internally generated assets never to be recognised (see section 6.3) such as brands, mastheads and publishing titles. However, the acquirer in a business combination will recognise these assets. The acquirer will recognise the assets at fair value and the fair value is always considered measurable. To the acquirer, if the assets are brands, mastheads or publishing titles, these are acquired intangible assets, not internally generated assets.

6.4.3 Internally generated intangible assets

An internally generated asset may be created over a period of time, in contrast to separate acquisition and business combinations where there is a single acquisition date. For example, an entity may outlay funds to design a machine suitable for use by astronauts landing on the moon. There is no guarantee of success at the commencement of the project; the project may take an extended period of time; and the end result may be success or failure.

According to paragraph 52 of AASB 138/IAS 38, to determine whether an internally generated intangible asset should be recognised, an entity has to classify the generation of the asset into:

- a research phase
- a development phase.

Research

Research is defined in paragraph 8 of AASB 138/IAS 38 as:

> original and planned investigation undertaken with the prospect of gaining new scientific or technical knowledge and understanding.

In any project, research would be undertaken in the early stages of the project. Research activities include activities aimed at obtaining new knowledge as opposed to refining existing knowledge.

If outlays are incurred during the research phase, then according to paragraph 54 of AASB 138/IAS 38 no intangible asset can be recognised. The outlays are expensed as they are incurred.

Development

Development is defined in paragraph 8 of AASB 138/IAS 38 as:

> the application of research findings or other knowledge to a plan or design for the production of new or substantially improved materials, devices, products, processes, systems or services before the start of commercial production or use.

When a project proceeds beyond the research phase, it enters the development phase. If an entity cannot distinguish the research phase from the development phase, the expenditure on the project must be treated as if it occurred in the research phase.

An intangible asset can arise from development outlays. The *recognition criteria* are such that an intangible asset can only be recognised from development outlays if *all* the criteria from paragraph 57 of AASB 138/IAS 38 are met:

(a) the technical feasibility of completing the intangible asset so that it will be available for use or sale.
(b) its intention to complete the intangible asset and use or sell it.
(c) its ability to use or sell the intangible asset.
(d) how the intangible asset will generate probable future economic benefits. Among other things, the entity can demonstrate the existence of a market for the output of the intangible asset or the intangible asset itself or, if it is to be used internally, the usefulness of the intangible asset.
(e) the availability of adequate technical, financial and other resources to complete the development and to use or sell the intangible asset.
(f) its ability to measure reliably the expenditure attributable to the intangible asset during its development.

Note that these six criteria relate to determining the probability of future benefits from the project and the reliable measurement of the cost or expenditure — in other words, they are an expansion of the criteria in paragraphs 21 and 22 of AASB 138/IAS 38. If all these recognition criteria are met, the asset is *measured* at *cost*, being the sum of expenditure incurred from the point of time the recognition criteria are met. Any expenditure on development while the recognition criteria are not met must be expensed. Thus, costs incurred to internally generate an intangible asset are capitalised only if they are incurred in the development phase and all the criteria in paragraph 57 have been met.

As noted earlier with internally generated brands, mastheads, publishing titles, customer lists and similar items, regardless of whether they are in the research or development phase, the outlays on these items must be expensed (AASB 138/IAS 38 paragraph 63).

According to paragraph 71 of AASB 138/IAS 38, if amounts are expensed during either the research or development phases, and subsequently an intangible asset is raised, the amounts expensed cannot subsequently be capitalised into the asset with an adjustment to equity.

Note that although an entity must follow these principles for internally generated intangible assets, if an entity *acquires* in-process research and development from another entity it is accounted for either as acquisition of a separate asset or as part of a business combination. With the latter, in-process research and development *must* be recognised as an asset and measured at fair value.

ILLUSTRATIVE EXAMPLE 6.1

Research and development outlays

Two Rocks Ltd is a highly successful engineering company that manufactures filters for air-conditioning systems. Due to its dissatisfaction with the quality of the filters currently available, on 1 January 2023 it commenced a project to design a more efficient filter. The following notes record the events relating to that project.

2023

January	Paid $145 000 in salaries of company engineers and consultants who conducted basic tests on available filters with varying modifications.
February	Spent $165 000 on developing a new filter system, including the production of a basic model. It became obvious that the model in its current form was not successful because the material in the filter was not as effective as required.
March	Acquired the fibres division of Sand Hill Ltd for $330 000. The fair values of the tangible assets of this division were: property, plant and equipment, $180 000; inventories, $60 000.
	This business was acquired because one of the products it produced was a fibrous compound sold under the brand name Foamy, which Two Rocks Ltd considered would be excellent for including in the filtration process.
	By buying the fibres division, Two Rocks Ltd acquired the patent for this fibrous compound. Two Rocks Ltd valued the patent at $50 000 and the brand name at $40 000, using a number of valuation techniques. The patent had a further 10-year life but was renewable on application. Further costs of $54 000 were incurred on the new filter system during March.
April	Spent a further $135 000 on revising the filtration process to incorporate the fibrous compound. By the end of April, Two Rocks Ltd was convinced that it now had a viable product because preliminary tests showed that the filtration process was significantly better than any other available on the market.
May	Developed a prototype of the filtration component and proceeded to test it within a variety of models of air-conditioners. The company preferred to sell the filtration process to current manufacturers of air-conditioners if the process worked with currently available models. If this proved not possible, the company would then consider developing its own brand of air-conditioners using the new filtration system. By the end of May, the filtration system had proved successful on all but one of the currently available commercial models. Costs incurred were $65 000.
June	Various air-conditioner manufacturers were invited to demonstrations of the filtration system. Costs incurred were $25 000, including $12 000 for food and beverages for the prospective clients. The feedback from a number of the companies was that they were prepared to enter negotiations for acquiring the filters from Two Rocks Ltd. The company now believed it had a successful model and commenced planning the production of the filters. Ongoing costs of $45 000 to refine the filtration system, particularly in the light of comments by the manufacturers, were incurred in the latter part of June.

Required

Explain the accounting for the various outlays incurred by Two Rocks Ltd.

Solution

The main problem in accounting for the costs is determining at what point of time costs can be capitalised. This is resolved by applying all of the six criteria that must be met before capitalisation of outlays can occur.

- *Technical feasibility.* At the end of April, the company believed that the filtration process was technically feasible.
- *Intention to complete and sell.* At the end of April, the company was not yet sure that the system was adaptable to currently available models of air-conditioners. If it was not adaptable, the company would have to test whether development of its own brand of air-conditioners would be a commercial proposition. Hence, it was not until the end of May that the company was convinced it could complete the project and had a product that it could sell.

- *Ability to use or sell.* By the end of May, the company believed it had a product it had the ability to sell. Being a filter manufacturer, it knew the current costs of competing products and so could make an informed decision about the potential for the commercial sale of its own filter.
- *Existence of a market.* The market comprised the air-conditioning manufacturers. By selling to the manufacturers, the company had the potential to generate probable future cash flows. This criterion was met by the end of May.
- *Availability of resources.* From the beginning of the project, the company was not short of resources, being a highly successful company in its own right.
- *Ability to measure costs reliably.* Costs are readily attributable to the project throughout its development.

On the basis of the above analysis, the six recognition criteria were all met for the first time at the end of May. Therefore, costs incurred before this point are expensed, and those incurred after this point are capitalised.

Hence, the following costs would be written off as incurred.

January	$145 000
February	165 000
March	54 000
April	135 000
May	65 000

In acquiring the fibres division from Sand Hill Ltd, Two Rocks Ltd would pass the following entry.

Property, plant and equipment	Dr	180 000	
Inventories	Dr	60 000	
Brand	Dr	40 000	
Patent	Dr	50 000	
Cash	Cr		330 000
(Acquisition of assets)			

The patent would initially be depreciated over a 10-year useful life. However, this would need to be reassessed upon application of the fibrous compound to the air-conditioning filtration system. This alternative use may extend the expected useful life of the product, and hence of the patent. The brand name would be depreciated over the same useful life of the patent, because it is expected that the brand has no real value unless backed by the patent. See section 6.5 for a detailed discussion of amortisation of intangible assets.

The company would then capitalise development costs of $45 000 in June.

The marketing costs incurred in June of $25 000 would be expensed because they are not part of the development process.

Table 6.2 contains a summary of the recognition criteria and measurement principles for intangible assets.

TABLE 6.2   Recognition criteria and measurement principles

			Internally generated	
	Separate acquisition	Acquired as part of business combination	Research	Development
Recognition criteria				
1. Benefits to the entity are probable	Always met	Always met	Never recognise	1. Recognise if all 6 criteria in paragraph 57 are met.
2. Cost can be reliably measured	Usually met	Always met		2. Never recognise assets in paragraph 63.
Measurement	Cost	Fair value		Cost — limited to those incurred after the paragraph 57 criteria are met.

6.4.4 Internally generated goodwill

AASB 138/IAS 38 deals with intangible assets. As noted previously, goodwill is not an intangible asset as it is not a separable asset, and an entity does not have legal or contractual rights to the asset. Accounting for acquired goodwill is determined in accordance with the principles in AASB 3/IFRS 3. However, accounting for internally generated goodwill is covered in AASB 138/IAS 38, which states in paragraph 48 that:

> Internally generated goodwill shall not be recognised as an asset.

The main reason for non-recognition of internally generated goodwill is that the cost of the asset cannot be reliably measured. Potentially, the fair value of the current goodwill of an entity can be measured by comparing the fair value of the whole entity and the net fair value of the identifiable assets and liabilities of the entity. However, recognition of an asset requires a reliable measurement of cost, not fair value.

6.4.5 Examples of recognition and measurement of intangible assets

Qantas carries a number of intangible assets in its statement of financial position. Figure 6.3 shows how Qantas recognised and measured these intangible assets in the company's 2018 annual report.

FIGURE 6.3	Accounting policies on intangible assets, Qantas

(K) INTANGIBLE ASSETS

i. Recognition and measurement

Goodwill	Goodwill is stated at cost less any accumulated impairment losses. With respect to investments accounted for under the equity method, the carrying amount of goodwill is included in the carrying amount of the investment.
Airport landing slots	Airport landing slots are stated at cost less any accumulated impairment losses.
Software	Software is stated at cost less accumulated amortisation and impairment losses. Software development expenditure, including the cost of materials, direct labour and other direct costs, is only recognised as an asset when the Qantas Group controls future economic benefits as a result of the cost incurred and it is probable that those future economic benefits will eventuate and the costs can be measured reliably.
Brand names and trademarks	Brand names and trademarks are carried at cost less any accumulated impairment losses.
Customer contracts/ relationships	Customer contracts/relationships are carried at their fair value at the date of acquisition less accumulated amortisation and impairment losses.
Contract intangible assets	Contract intangible assets are stated at cost less accumulated amortisation. Amortisation commences when the asset is ready for use.

Source: Qantas Airways Ltd (2018, p. 91).

Australian Pharmaceutical Industries (API) Ltd reported its policies on accounting for research and development in Note 11b to its 2018 financial statements, as shown in figure 6.4.

FIGURE 6.4	Research and development accounting policies, API

Research and development

Expenditure on research activities, undertaken with the prospect of gaining new technical knowledge and understanding, is recognised in the income statement as an expense as incurred.

Expenditure on development activities, where research findings are applied to a plan or design for the production of new or substantially improved products and processes, is capitalised if the product or process is technically and commercially feasible and the Group has sufficient resources to complete development. The expenditure capitalised includes the cost of materials, direct labour and appropriate proportion of overheads. Other development expenditure is recognised against profit as an expense as incurred.

Source: Australian Pharmaceutical Industries Ltd (2018, p. 55).

API reported capitalised development costs in Note 11 of the 2018 annual report along with the company's other intangible assets, as shown in figure 6.5.

11. INTANGIBLE ASSETS

			As at 31 August		
	Goodwill $'000	Brand names $'000	Software $'000	Development costs $'000	Total $'000
Financial year 2018					
Cost	178 355	99 000	123 728	1 996	403 079
Accumulated amortisation	(56 360)	(2 640)	(77 240)	(1 121)	(137 361)
Net book value	**121 995**	**96 360**	**46 488**	**875**	**265 718**
Balance 1 September 2017	50 019	96 360	46 929	351	193 659
Transfer from property, plant and equipment	—	—	10 711	758	11 469
Additions from business acquisitions	70 849	—	—	—	70 849
Additions from stores acquired	1 017	—	—	—	1 017
Disposals	—	—	(2)	—	(2)
Amortisation expense for the year	—	—	(11 171)	(239)	(11 410)
Foreign currency exchange differences	110	—	21	5	136
Balance at 31 August 2018	**121 995**	**96 360**	**46 488**	**875**	**265 718**
Financial year 2017					
Cost	106 379	99 000	112 759	1 225	319 363
Accumulated depreciation and impairment	(56 360)	(2 640)	(65 830)	(874)	(125 704)
Net book value	**50 019**	**96 360**	**46 929**	**351**	**193 659**
Balance 1 September 2016	46 973	96 360	46 266	376	189 975
Transfer from property, plant and equipment	—	—	12 202	42	12 244
Additions from stores acquired	3 917	—	—	—	3 917
Disposals	—	—	(3)	—	(3)
Amortisation expense for the year	—	—	(11 464)	(119)	(11 583)
Foreign currency exchange differences	(871)	—	(72)	52	(891)
Balance at 31 August 2017	**50 019**	**96 360**	**46 929**	**351**	**193 659**

Source: Australian Pharmaceutical Industries Ltd (2018, p. 54).

LEARNING CHECK

☐ Initial measurement of intangible assets is at cost, but this is measured differently depending on how the intangible asset arose.

☐ Where an intangible assets is acquired in a business combination, it is initially measured at fair value, and this fair value may be determined in a variety of ways.

☐ Recognition of internally generated intangible assets is more difficult, with outlays being classified into research and development.
 – Research outlays are always expensed.
 – Development outlays are capitalised only if strict criteria are met.

☐ Certain intangible assets are allowed to be recognised if acquired in a business combination, but cannot be recognised if internally generated.

6.5 Amortisation of intangible assets

LEARNING OBJECTIVE 6.5 Describe how to amortise intangible assets.

Having recognised the intangible assets, the question of **amortisation** of these assets arises. Amortisation has the same meaning as depreciation and is defined in paragraph 8 of AASB 138/IAS 38 as:

> the systematic allocation of the depreciable amount of an intangible asset over its useful life.

The **depreciable amount** is defined as:

> the cost of an asset, or other amount substituted for cost, less its residual value.

In determining any amortisation charge, an assessment of useful life must be undertaken. With intangible assets, it is necessary to consider whether the assets have a finite life or an indefinite life. Indefinite life does not mean that an asset is going to last forever (i.e. have an infinite life); rather that, with proper maintenance, there is no foreseeable end to the life of the asset.

According to paragraph 90 of AASB 138/IAS 38, to determine the **useful life** of an intangible asset, the following factors should be considered:

(a) the expected usage of the asset by the entity and whether the asset could be managed efficiently by another management team;

(b) typical product life cycles for the asset and public information on estimates of useful lives of similar assets that are used in a similar way;

(c) technical, technological, commercial or other types of obsolescence;

(d) the stability of the industry in which the asset operates and changes in the market demand for the products or services output from the asset;

(e) expected actions by competitors or potential competitors;

(f) the level of maintenance expenditure required to obtain the expected future economic benefits from the asset and the entity's ability and intention to reach such a level;

(g) the period of control over the asset and legal or similar limits on the use of the asset, such as the expiry dates of related leases; and

(h) whether the useful life of the asset is dependent on the useful life of other assets of the entity.

To maintain the expected useful life it may be necessary for companies to incur further expenditure, such as advertising in relation to brand names. Also, continuous monitoring and adaptation to the changes in markets may be necessary to maintain the expected useful lives of intangible assets.

6.5.1 Finite useful lives

In general, as described in paragraph 98 of AASB 138/IAS 38, the principles of amortisation are the same as those for depreciating property, plantand equipment under AASB 116/IAS 16. In both cases, the process involves the allocation of the depreciable amount on a systematic basis over the useful life, with the method chosen reflecting the pattern in which the economic benefits are expected to be consumed by the entity. It is rare that any amortisation method applied by an entity would produce an amortisation expense that is initially lower than that determined under a straight-line method.

According to paragraph 104 of AASB 138/IAS 38, the amortisation period and amortisation method should be reviewed at least at the end of each annual reporting period, which is the same principle applied to property, plant and equipment. However, with intangible assets the following specific rules are to be applied in respect to amortisation.

• Where the pattern of benefits cannot be determined reliably, the straight-line method is to be used (AASB 138/IAS 38 paragraph 97). This is, presumably, to bring some consistency and comparability into the calculations.

• Because of the unique nature of many intangible assets and the uncertainty associated with their expected useful lives, the residual value of an intangible asset with a finite useful life is assumed to be zero (AASB 138/IAS 38 paragraph 100). Paragraph 8 of AASB 138/IAS 38 defines **residual value** as:

> the estimated amount that an entity would currently obtain from disposal of the asset, after deducting the estimated costs of disposal, if the asset were already of the age and in the condition expected at the end of its useful life.

A residual value other than zero is allowed where:

(a) there is a commitment by a third party to purchase the asset at the end of its useful life; *or*

(b) there is an active market for the asset; *and*

   (i) the residual value can be determined by reference to that market; *and*

   (ii) it is probable that such a market will exist at the end of the asset's useful life.

6.5.2 Indefinite useful lives

Where it is assessed that an intangible asset has an indefinite useful life, there is no amortisation expense for that asset. According to paragraph 109 of AASB 138/IAS 38, the useful life should, however, be reviewed each year. Further, in accordance with paragraph 10 of AASB 136/IAS 36 *Impairment of Assets*, irrespective of whether there is any indication of impairment, an entity must test an intangible asset with an indefinite useful life by comparing its carrying amount with its recoverable amount. (See chapter 7 for more detail on impairment testing of assets.)

If an entity changes the useful life from an indefinite life to a finite life, this is accounted for as a change in estimates, and affects the amortisation charge both in the current period and in future periods.

For example, intangible assets recognised by Qantas (see figure 6.3) are amortised as follows.

- *Airport landing slots* — no amortisation, as these assets are assumed to have indefinite lives
- *Software* — amortised on a straight-line basis over a 3- to 10-year period
- *Brand names and trademarks* — no amortisation, as these assets are assumed to have indefinite useful lives
- *Customer contracts/relationships* — amortisation based on estimated timing of benefits over a 5- to 10-year period

As shown in figure 6.6, Qantas reported the amortisation of its intangible assets as well as movements in the assets over the year in its 2018 annual report.

| **FIGURE 6.6** | Reporting amortisation of intangible assets, Qantas |

11. INTANGIBLE ASSETS

	2018 $m			2017 $m		
	At cost	Accumulated amortisation and impairment	Net book value	At cost	Accumulated amortisation and impairment	Net book value
Goodwill	207	—	207	207	—	207
Airport landing slots	35	—	35	35	—	35
Software	1 681	(924)	757	1 523	(824)	699
Brand names and trademarks	26	—	26	25	—	25
Customer contracts/ relationships	4	(3)	1	5	(4)	1
Contract intangible assets	87	—	87	58	—	58
Total intangible assets	**2 040**	**(927)**	**1 113**	**1 853**	**(828)**	**1 025**

2018 $m	Opening net book value	Additions[1]	Disposals of controlled entity	Transfers[2]	Transferred (to)/from assets classified as hold for sale	Amortisation	Other[3]	Closing net book value
Goodwill	207	—	(1)	—	—	—	1	207
Airport landing slots	35	—	—	—	—	—	—	35
Software	699	200	(7)	1	(9)	(127)	—	757
Brand names and trademarks	25	—	—	—	—	—	1	26
Customer contracts/ relationships	1	—	—	—	—	—	—	1
Contract intangible assets	58	29	—	—	—	—	—	87
Total intangible assets	**1 025**	**229**	**(8)**	**1**	**(9)**	**(127)**	**2**	**1 113**

2018 $m	Opening net book value	Additions[1]	Disposals of controlled entity	Transfers[2]	Transferred (to)/from assets classified as hold for sale	Amortisation	Other[3]	Closing net book value
Goodwill	208	—	—	—	—	—	(1)	207
Airport landing slots	35	—	—	—	—	—	—	35
Software	602	197	—	2	—	(105)	3	699
Brand names and trademarks	26	—	—	—	—	—	(1)	25
Customer contracts/ relationships	2	—	—	—	—	(1)	—	1
Contract intangible assets	36	22	—	—	—	—	—	58
Total intangible assets	**909**	**219**	**—**	**2**	**—**	**(106)**	**1**	**1025**

1. Additions include capitalised interest of $5 million (2017: $3 million)
2. Transfers include transfers between categories of intangible assets and transfers from/(to) other balance sheet sheer accounts.
3. Other includes foreign exchange movements, non-cash additions, impairments of intangible assets.

Source: Qantas Airways (2018, pp. 66–7).

ILLUSTRATIVE EXAMPLE 6.2

Amortisation of intangible assets

On 1 January 2022 Kendall Ltd acquired the following assets for cash.

- A customer list of a large newspaper for $600 000. This customer database includes name, contact information, subscription history and demographic information. Kendall Ltd expects to benefit from this information evenly over the next 5 years.
- The brand name 'Lawson Lines' for $500 000. Lawson Lines is a well-established brand and Kendall Ltd believes that it is expected to be popular indefinitely.

Required

Prepare the journal entries for the year ended 30 June 2022 in relation to these acquisitions.

Solution

Both the customer list and the brand qualify as intangible assets under AASB 138/IAS 38. Both will be recognised as assets and measured at the cost of acquisition on 1 January 2022. The customer list is a limited-life intangible asset and will be amortised on a straight-line basis over a 5-year period. The brand name is considered to have an indefinite useful life and is then not subject to amortisation. It is subject to annual impairment testing.

The journal entries required are as follows.

2022				
Jan. 1	Customer list	Dr	600 000	
	Cash	Cr		600 000
	(Acquisition of customer list)			
	Brand name	Dr	500 000	
	Cash	Cr		500 000
	(Acquisition of brand 'Lawson Lines')			
June 30	Amortisation expense — customer list	Dr	60 000	
	Accumulated amortisation — customer list	Cr		60 000
	(Amortisation of asset: $\frac{1}{2} \times \frac{1}{5} \times $600\,000$)			

6.6 Measurement subsequent to initial recognition

LEARNING OBJECTIVE 6.6 Explain the accounting for intangible assets subsequent to initial recognition.

Consistent with AASB 116/IAS 16, paragraph 72 of AASB 138/IAS 38 notes that after the initial recognition of an intangible asset at cost, an entity must choose for each class of intangible asset whether to measure the assets using the cost model or the revaluation model.

According to paragraph 74 of AASB 138/IAS 38, under the *cost model*, the asset is recorded at the initial cost and then subject to amortisation, as detailed in section 6.5, and impairment, as detailed in chapter 7 of this text.

According to paragraph 75 of AASB 138/IAS 38, under the *revaluation model*, the asset is carried at fair value and is subject to amortisation and impairment charges. As with property, plant and equipment, if the revaluation model is chosen, revaluations are made with sufficient regularity so that the carrying amount of the asset does not materially differ from the current fair value at the end of the reporting period.

One specification that applies to intangible assets but not to property, plant and equipment is how the fair value is to be measured. With intangible assets, the revaluation model can only be used if the fair value can be measured by reference to an active market. An **active market** is defined in Appendix A of AASB 13/IFRS 13 as:

> [a] market in which transactions for the asset or liability take place with sufficient frequency and volume to provide pricing information on an ongoing basis.

As noted in paragraph 78 of AASB 138/IAS 38, it is uncommon for an active market to exist for an intangible asset. This then limits the use of the revaluation model in measuring intangible assets. However, for some assets, such as taxi or fishing licences, an active market may exist.

One effect of this is in relation to intangible assets acquired as part of a business combination. These assets may be measured initially at fair value using valuation methods. However, adoption of the revaluation model would not allow those valuation models to be used in the continuing measurement of fair value, as only fair values arising from active markets can be used.

Not all intangible assets can be measured using the revaluation model. The assets described in paragraph 63 of AASB 138/IAS 38 as not being able to be recognised when internally generated could be recognised if separately acquired or acquired as part of a business combination. These assets (e.g. brands, newspaper mastheads, patents and trademarks) are prohibited from being measured using the revaluation model. This is because there is no active market for these assets, as they are considered unique.

Accounting for intangible assets measured using the revaluation model is exactly the same as for property, plant and equipment (see chapter 5). According to paragraph 85 of AASB 138/IAS 38, where there is a revaluation increase, the asset is increased, and the increase is recognised in other comprehensive income and accumulated in an asset revaluation surplus. However, if the revaluation increase reverses a previous revaluation decrease relating to the same asset, the revaluation increase is recognised in profit or loss. Any accumulated amortisation is eliminated at the time of revaluation.

According to paragraph 86 of AASB 138/IAS 38, where there is a revaluation decrease, the decrease is recognised as an expense unless there has been a previous revaluation increase. In the latter case, the adjustment must first be made against any existing revaluation surplus before recognising an expense. Any accumulated amortisation is eliminated at the time of the revaluation.

According to paragraph 87 of AASB 138/IAS 38, as with a revaluation surplus on property, plant and equipment, the revaluation surplus may be transferred to retained earnings when the surplus is realised on the retirement or disposal of the asset. Alternatively, the revaluation surplus may progressively be taken to retained earnings in proportion to the amortisation of the asset.

6.6.1 Subsequent expenditure

Once an intangible asset has been recognised, an entity may expend more funds on that asset. In general, such expenditures are not additions to the asset, but rather are used to maintain the expected economic benefits embodied in the existing asset. Hence, as described in paragraph 20 of AASB 138/IAS 38, the expectation is that subsequent expenditure is expensed.

With assets such as brands, mastheads, publishing titles and customer lists, subsequent expenditure on these assets is always expensed.

In relation to subsequent expenditure on in-process research or development projects, the same principles as noted in section 6.4.2 apply (paragraphs 42 and 43 of AASB 138/IAS 38):

- expense any research expenditure
- expense any development expenditure if it does not meet all the six recognition criteria
- capitalise development expenditure that meets the recognition criteria.

LEARNING CHECK

- ☐ As with property, plant and equipment, subsequent to initial recognition intangible assets may be measured using the cost model or the revaluation model.
- ☐ The revaluation model can only be applied where the fair value can be determined by reference to an active market.
- ☐ Subsequent expenditure on an intangible asset is generally expensed.
- ☐ Subsequent development expenditure may be capitalised if the recognition criteria are met.

6.7 Disclosure

LEARNING OBJECTIVE 6.7 Discuss the disclosures required for intangible assets.

Disclosures for intangible assets are based on classes of assets. Paragraph 119 of AASB 138/IAS 38 provides examples of classes of intangible assets:

    (a) brand names;
    (b) mastheads and publishing titles;
    (c) computer software;
    (d) licences and franchises;
    (e) copyrights, patents and other industrial property rights, service and operating rights;
    (f) recipes, formulas, models, designs and prototypes; and
    (g) intangible assets under development.

According to paragraph 118 of AASB 138/IAS 38, general information to be disclosed includes:

- whether the useful lives are finite or indefinite and, if finite, either the useful life or amortisation rate used
- the amortisation methods used for assets with finite lives
- the gross carrying amount and any accumulated amortisation, aggregated with accumulated impairment losses, at the beginning and end of the period
- the line item in the statement of profit or loss and other comprehensive income that includes the amortisation expense
- a reconciliation of the beginning and end of period carrying amounts, showing the movements during the period, such as additions separately acquired, additions from internal development, additions arising from business combinations, disposals, revaluations, reclassifications, amortisation and impairment.

According to paragraph 122(a) of AASB 138/IAS 38, for an intangible asset having an indefinite useful life, an entity must disclose the carrying amount of the asset and the reasons why the entity assessed it to have an indefinite useful life. These reasons must include a description of the factor(s) that played a significant role in determining the existence of an indefinite useful life.

Figure 6.7 shows the disclosures made by Rio Tinto Ltd in its 2018 annual report in relation to assessment of useful lives of its intangible assets.

FIGURE 6.7 Assessment of lives of intangible assets, Rio Tinto

Purchased intangible assets are initially recorded at cost. Finite-life intangible assets are amortised over their useful economic lives on a straight line or units of production basis, as appropriate. Intangible assets that are deemed to have indefinite lives and intangible assets that are not yet ready for use are not amortised; they are reviewed annually for impairment or more frequently if events or changes in circumstances indicate a potential impairment in accordance with accounting policy note 1(i).

The Group considers that intangible assets have indefinite lives when, based on an analysis of all of the relevant factors, there is no foreseeable limit to the period over which the asset is expected to generate cash flows for the Group. The factors considered in making this judgment include the existence of contractual rights for unlimited terms or evidence that renewal of the contractual rights without significant incremental cost can be expected for indefinite future periods in view of the Group's investment intentions. The life cycles of the products and processes that depend on the asset are also considered.

Source: Rio Tinto Ltd (2018, pp. 155–6).

If the entity has chosen to use the revaluation model subsequent to initial recognition of an intangible asset, paragraph 124 of AASB 138/IAS 38 requires the entity to disclose the:
- effective date of revaluation
- carrying amount of the revalued assets
- carrying amount that would have been recognised if the cost model had been used instead of the revaluation model
- amount of any asset revaluation surplus that relates to intangible assets at the beginning and at the end of the reporting period.

According to paragraph 126 of AASB 138/IAS 38, in the statement of profit or loss and other comprehensive income, an entity must disclose the aggregate amount of research and development recognised as an expense in the current period.

Figure 6.8 contains the disclosures made by Rio Tinto Ltd in its 2018 annual report in relation to its intangible assets.

FIGURE 6.8 Disclosure of intangible assets, Rio Tinto

13. INTANGIBLE ASSETS

Year ended 31 December 2018	Exploration and evaluation[a] US$m	Trademarks, patented and non-patented technology US$m	Contract-based intangible assets[b] US$m	Other intangible assets US$m	Total US$m
Net book value					
At 1 January 2018	393	75	2 188	463	3 119
Adjustment on currency translation	(25)	(3)	(171)	(46)	(245)
Expenditure during the year	90	1	—	83	174
Amortisation for the year[c]	—	(14)	(23)	(96)	(133)
Impairment charges[d]	—	—	—	(2)	(2)
Disposals, transfers and other movements[e]	(225)	—	(12)	103	(134)
At 31 December 2018	**233**	**59**	**1 982**	**505**	**2 779**
– Cost	2 346	217	3 114	1 538	7 215
– Accumulated amortisation and impairment	(2 113)	(158)	(1 132)	(1 033)	(4 436)

Year ended 31 December 2017	Exploration and evaluation[a] US$m	Trademarks, patented and non-patented technology US$m	Contract-based intangible assets[b] US$m	Other intangible assets US$m	Total US$m
Net book value					
At 1 January 2017	711	78	2 103	387	3 279
Adjustment on currency translation	27	10	150	29	216
Expenditure during the year	57	—	—	65	122
Amortisation for the year[c]	—	(13)	(67)	(97)	(177)
Impairment charges[d]	(357)	—	—	—	(357)
Disposals, transfers and other movements[e]	(45)	—	2	79	36
At 31 December 2017	**393**	**75**	**2 188**	**463**	**3 119**
– Cost	2 658	224	3 438	1 537	7 857
– Accumulated amortisation and impairment	(2 265)	(149)	(1 250)	(1 074)	(4 738)

(a) Exploration and evaluation assets' useful lives are not determined until transferred to property, plant and equipment.

(b) The Group benefits from certain intangible assets acquired with Alcan, including power supply contracts, customer contracts and water rights. The water rights are expected to contribute to the efficiency and cost-effectiveness of operations for the foreseeable future: accordingly, these rights are considered to have indefinite lives and are not subject to amortisation but are tested annually for impairment. These water rights constitute the majority of the amounts in 'Contract-based intangible assets'.

The remaining carrying value of the water rights (US$1 684 million) as at 31 December 2018 relates wholly to the Quebec smelters CGU. The Quebec smelters CGU was tested for impairment by reference to FVLCD using discounted cash flows, which is in line with the policy set out in note 1(i). The recoverable amount of the Quebec smelters is classified as level 3 under the fair value hierarchy. In arriving at FVLCD, post-tax cash flows expressed in real terms have been estimated over the expected useful economic lives of the underlying smelting assets and discounted using a real post-tax discount rate of 6.8% (2017: 6.7%).

The recoverable amounts were determined to be significantly in excess of carrying value, and there are no reasonably possible changes in key assumptions that would cause the remaining water rights to be impaired.

(c) Finite life intangible assets are amortised over their useful economic lives on a straight line or units of production basis, as appropriate. Where amortisation is calculated on a straight line basis, the following useful lives have been determined:

Trademarks, patented and non-patented technology
Trademarks: 14 to 20 years
Patented and non-patented technology: ten to 20 years

Contract-based intangible assets
Power contracts/water rights: two to 45 years
Other purchase and customer contracts: five to 15 years

Other intangible assets
Internally generated intangible assets and computer software: two to five years
Other intangible assets: two to 20 years

(d) Impairment charges in 2018 relate to the ISAL Smelter (see note 6). Impairment charges in 2017 relate to the full write-off of the Roughrider deposit in Canada (see note 6).

(e) Disposals, transfers and other movements includes transfers to assets held for sale relating to Rossing Uranium and ISAL assets, transfers to Mining properties and leases in relation to the Koodaideri mine from Exploration and evaluation, offset by transfers into other intangibles as part of the Autohaul project. Disposals, transfers and other movements for Exploration and evaluation in 2017 included US$34 million transferred to Mining Property in relation to the Kemano tunnel following approval of the project.

Source: Rio Tinto Ltd (2018, p. 177).

LEARNING CHECK

☐ AASB 138/IAS 38 requires extensive disclosures about an entity's intangible assets, with disclosures being made by class of intangible asset.

☐ Separate disclosures are required for internally generated intangible assets.

☐ Disclosures about the useful lives of intangible assets are required, with explanations required where assets are assessed to have indefinite useful lives.

☐ Where the revaluation model is used, specific disclosures are required, including that the carrying amount would have been under the cost model.

SUMMARY

The key principles of accounting for intangible assets as described in AASB 138/IAS 38 *Intangible Assets* are as follows.

- Intangible assets have three characteristics: they are identifiable, non-monetary in nature and lack physical substance.
- The recognition and measurement of intangible assets differs depending on how the asset is generated.
- For intangible assets acquired as separate assets, the probability recognition criterion is always met and the reliable measurement criterion is usually met. These assets are measured at cost.
- For intangible assets acquired as part of a business combination, both the probability and reliable measurement recognition criteria are always met. The assets are measured at fair value at acquisition date.
- For internally generated intangible assets, expenditure is classified as research or development. Research outlays are expensed, and development outlays may be capitalised if all six specified recognition criteria are met.
- Internally generated goodwill is never recognised.
- Amortisation of intangible assets requires an assessment of whether assets have finite or indefinite useful lives.
- Subsequent to initial recognition, the cost model or the revaluation model may be used; however, there are restrictions on when the revaluation model can be used.

KEY TERMS

active market A market in which transactions for the asset or liability take place with sufficient frequency and volume to provide pricing information on an ongoing basis.

amortisation The systematic allocation of the depreciable amount of an intangible asset over its useful life.

cost The amount of cash or cash equivalents paid or the fair value of other consideration given to acquire an asset at the time of its acquisition or construction.

depreciable amount The cost of an asset, or other amount substituted for cost, less its residual value.

development The application of research findings or other knowledge to a plan or design for the production of new or substantially improved materials, devices, products, processes, systems or services before the start of commercial production or use.

fair value The price that would be received to sell an asset or paid to transfer a liability in an orderly transaction between market participants at the measurement date.

intangible asset An identifiable non-monetary asset without physical substance.

monetary assets Money held and assets to be received in fixed or determinable amounts of money.

research Original and planned investigation undertaken with the prospect of gaining new scientific or technical knowledge and understanding.

residual value The estimated amount that an entity would currently obtain from disposal of the asset, after deducting the estimated costs of disposal, if the asset were already of the age and in the condition expected at the end of its useful life.

useful life The period over which an asset is expected to be available for use by an entity; or the number of production or similar units expected to be obtained from the asset by an entity.

DEMONSTRATION PROBLEM

6.1 Accounting for patents

During the 2021–22 period, Stitches Ltd acquired two patents, as well as incurring expenses in relation to the development of a new process that it expects to patent for subsequent use.

(a) Patent XC456 was acquired from a leather manufacturing firm on 1 October 2021 for $425 000. Given the continued demand for men's leather shoes it is expected that the life of this patent is indefinite.

(b) Patent CU254 was obtained as part of the business acquired from the conglomerate U-Beaut Fashions. The business was acquired on 1 January 2022 for $5 200 000. Patent CU254 was considered to have a fair value of $400 000 at the acquisition date. The patent was considered to have a 10-year life with benefits to be received evenly over this period.

(c) Stitches Ltd continued to incur expenses in relation to the development of a new process for softening leather, which it expects to patent for subsequent use. Expenses incurred were:

1 September 2021	$50 000
10 November 2021	$35 000
2 May 2022	$52 000

Following the work done up to 31 December 2021, Stitches Ltd believed that the project had progressed from the research stage to the development stage as it was now technically feasible to soften the leather as required. Stitches Ltd expected to continue with the project, as it considered that the company would be able to use the project results in its manufacturing process when the project was completed.

Required

Prepare a detailed report on which accounting standard would apply and the principles of how to account for patents. Explain the appropriate accounting procedures for the examples above.

SOLUTION

Issue 1. Which accounting standard should be applied in accounting for these patents?

The patents are *assets* as they are under the control of Stitches Ltd subsequent to their acquisition and are expected to generate future benefits for the company.

The patents can be classified as *intangible assets* as they meet the following characteristics of an intangible asset.

- *Non-monetary in nature.* Patents are not money held or assets to be received in fixed or determinable amounts of money.
- *Lack physical substance.* Patents exist on paper only. Unlike machinery to manufacture leather goods, patents cannot be seen or touched.
- *Identifiable.* Patents are separable in that they can be sold or transferred to other entities.

Hence, the appropriate accounting standard to apply in accounting for these patents is AASB 138/ IAS 38 *Intangible Assets.*

Issue 2. How should the various patents be accounted for at initial recognition?

- *Patent XC456.* This is an intangible asset acquired in a single acquisition. In relation to recognition of the asset, the probable flow recognition criterion is always met. The recognition criterion that needs to be examined is that of reliable measurement. Given the asset was acquired in a single transaction this recognition criterion should easily be met. The asset is measured at cost, being purchase price plus any directly attributable costs. In the case of Patent XC456 the cost is $425 000.

The appropriate journal entry at 1 October 2021 is as follows.

Patent XC456	Dr	425 000	
Cash	Cr		425 000
(Acquisition of Patent XC456)			

- *Patent CU254.* This asset was acquired as part of the acquisition of a business and is accounted for under AASB 3/IFRS 3 *Business Combinations.* There are no recognition criteria to be applied as they are assumed to be met where a business combination occurs. The asset is initially measured at fair value, which is considered to be the cost of the asset. In this case there is not sufficient information to provide the journal entry in relation to the business combination. However, as part of the entries prepared at acquisition date, the patent is recognised at its fair value of $400 000.
- *Patent in process.* Amounts spent on the internal generation of a patent must be classified into research and development outlays. If classified as research, then the outlays are expensed as incurred. If classified as development, then paragraph 57 of AASB 138/IAS 38 is applied. When all the six criteria in that paragraph are met, subsequent outlays are capitalised as an asset. Paragraph 63 of AASB 138/IAS 38 does exclude some assets from being recognised, but patents are not in this list of assets. In this case, it would appear that the criteria noted in paragraph 57 are met at 31 December 2021 — it is now technically feasible to complete the asset; the entity intends

to complete the asset; and the entity sees how it can use the asset in its manufacturing process. Note that all six criteria in paragraph 57 must be met before recognition occurs. Hence, all outlays prior to 31 December 2021 are research outlays and should be expensed, while outlays subsequent to that date are development outlays, meet the paragraph 57 criteria, and should be capitalised.

The appropriate journal entries are as follows.

2021				
Sept. 1	Research expense Cash (Research outlays on patent expensed)	Dr Cr	50 000	50 000
Nov. 10	Research expense Cash (Research outlays on patent expensed)	Dr Cr	35 000	35 000
2022				
May 2	Patent-in-process Cash (Capitalisation of development outlays on patent)	Dr Cr	52 000	52 000

Issue 3. How should patents be accounted for subsequent to initial measurement?
Under AASB 138/IAS 38, subsequent to initial recognition, an entity may choose to use the revaluation model or the cost model. Use of the revaluation model requires the existence of an active market in order to measure the fair value. Stitches Ltd is not able to use the revaluation model because the existence of an active market for identical patents is not feasible.

The amortisation of the patents should also be considered. The first determination here is that of the useful lives of the patents. With Patent XC456, the useful life is considered to be indefinite so no amortisation needs to be charged for this asset. However, annual impairment tests will need to be undertaken.

With Patent CU254 there is an expected useful life of 10 years so amortisation will need to be charged. Where an expected useful life is finite the determination of the useful life will require an analysis of the factors detailed in paragraph 90 of AASB 138/IAS 38 such as expected actions by competitors, the stability of the industry and changes in market demand. The depreciable amount of the asset is then written off over the useful life on a systematic basis, with the method chosen reflecting the pattern in which the expected benefits are expected to be consumed by the entity. If the pattern of benefits cannot be reliably determined then a straight-line method is used. Further, the residual value is assumed to be zero unless there is a commitment by a third party to acquire the asset in the future or there exists an active market. In the case of Patent CU254 the straight-line method should be used with an annual depreciation charge of $40 000 (being 10% × $400 000). The journal entry at 30 June 2022 is as follows.

2022				
June 30	Amortisation expense — Patent CU254 Accumulated amortisation — Patent CU254 (Amortisation for half a year on Patent CU254)	Dr Cr	20 000	20 000

With the patent in process, no amortisation is necessary unless the project becomes impaired.

COMPREHENSION QUESTIONS

1 What are the key characteristics of an intangible asset?
2 Explain what is meant by 'identifiability'.
3 How do the principles for amortisation of intangible assets differ from those for depreciation of property, plant and equipment?
4 How is the useful life of an intangible asset determined?
5 What intangible assets can never be recognised if internally generated? Why?
6 Explain the difference between 'research' and 'development'.
7 Explain when development outlays can be capitalised.

8 Explain how intangible assets are initially measured, and whether the measurement differs depending on whether the assets are acquired in a business combination or internally generated by an entity.

9 What are the recognition criteria for intangible assets?

10 Explain the application of the revaluation model for intangible assets.

11 Explain the use of fair values in the accounting for intangible assets.

CASE STUDY 6.1

ACCOUNTING FOR BRANDS

West Ltd is a leading company in the sale of frozen and canned fish produce. These products are sold under two brand names.

- Fish caught in southern Australian waters are sold under the brand 'Antarctic Fresh', which is the brand the company developed when it commenced operations and which is still used today.
- Fish caught in the northern oceans are sold under the brand name 'Tropical Taste', a brand developed by Fishy Tales Ltd. West Ltd acquired all the assets and liabilities of Fishy Tales Ltd a number of years ago when it took over that company's operations.

West Ltd has always marketed itself as operating in an environmentally responsible manner, and is an advocate of sustainable fishing. The public regards it as a dolphin-friendly company as a result of its previous campaigns to ensure dolphins are not affected by tuna fishing. The marketing manager of West Ltd has noted the efforts of the ship, the *Steve Irwin*, to disrupt and hopefully stop the efforts of whalers in the southern oceans and the publicity that this has received. He has recommended to the board of directors that West Ltd strengthen its environmentally responsible image by guaranteeing to repair any damage caused to the *Steve Irwin* as a result of attempts to disrupt the whalers. He believes that this action will increase West Ltd's environmental reputation, adding to the company's goodwill. He has told the board that such a guarantee will have no effect on West Ltd's reported profitability. He has explained that, if any damage to the *Steve Irwin* occurs, West Ltd can capitalise the resulting repair costs to the carrying amounts of its brands, as such costs will have been incurred basically for marketing purposes. Accordingly, as the company's net asset position will increase, and there will be no effect on the statement of profit or loss and other comprehensive income, this will be a win–win situation for everyone.

Required

The chairman of the board is well aware that the marketing manager is very effective at selling ideas but knows little about accounting. The chairman has, therefore, asked you to provide him with a report advising the board on how the proposal should be accounted for under accounting standards and how such a proposal would affect West Ltd's financial statements.

CASE STUDY 6.2

ACCOUNTING FOR INTANGIBLE ASSETS

Mags Ltd is an Australian mail-order company. Although the sector in Australia is growing slowly, Mags Ltd has reported significant increases in sales and net income in recent years. Sales increased from $50 million in 2015 to $120 million in 2021. Profit increased from $3 million to $12 million over the same period. The stock market and analysts believe that the company's future is very promising. In early 2022, the company was valued at $350 million, which was three times 2021 sales and 26 times estimated 2022 profit.

Company management and many investors attribute the company's success to its marketing flair and expertise. Instead of competing on price, Mags Ltd prefers to focus on service and innovation, including:

- free delivery
- a free gift with orders over $200.

As a result of such innovations, customers accept prices that are 60% above those of competitors, and Mags maintains a gross profit margin of around 40%.

Nevertheless, some investors have doubts about the company as they are uneasy about certain accounting policies the company has adopted. For example, Mags Ltd capitalises the costs of its direct mailings to prospective customers ($4.2 million at 30 June 2021) and amortises them on a straight-line basis over 3 years. This practice is considered to be questionable as there is no guarantee that customers will be obtained and retained from direct mailings.

In addition to the mailing lists developed by in-house marketing staff, Mags Ltd purchased a customer list from a competitor for $800 000 on 4 July 2022. This list is also recognised as a non-current asset. Mags Ltd estimates that this list will generate sales for at least another 2 years, more likely another 3 years. The company also plans to add names, obtained from a phone survey conducted in August 2022, to the list. These extra names are expected to extend the list's useful life by another year.

Mags Ltd's 2021 statement of financial position also reported $7.5 million of marketing costs as non-current assets. If the company had expensed marketing costs as incurred, 2021 net income would have been $10 million instead of the reported $12 million. The concerned investors are uneasy about this capitalisation of marketing costs, as they believe that Mags Ltd's marketing practices are relatively easy to replicate. However, Mags Ltd argues that its accounting is appropriate. Marketing costs are amortised at an accelerated rate (55% in year 1, 29% in year 2 and 16% in year 3), based on 25 years' knowledge and experience of customer purchasing behaviour.

Required

Explain how Mags Ltd's costs should be accounted for under AASB 138/IAS 38 *Intangible Assets*, giving reasons for your answer.

APPLICATION AND ANALYSIS EXERCISES

★ BASIC | ★ ★ MODERATE | ★ ★ ★ DIFFICULT

6.1 Financial statements and intangible assets ★   LO1

Upton (2001, p. 50) notes:

> There is a popular view of financial statements that underlies and motivates many discussions of intangible assets. That popular view often sounds something like this:
>> If accountants got all the assets and liabilities into financial statements, and they measured all those assets and liabilities at the right amounts, stockholders' equity would equal market capitalization. Right?

Required

Comment on the truth of this 'popular view'.

6.2 Useful life of trademark ★   LO2, 4, 6

Snapper Ltd holds a trademark that is well known within consumer circles and has enabled the company to be a market leader in its area. The trademark has been held by the company for 9 years. The legal life of the trademark is 5 years, but is renewable by the company at little cost to it.

Required

Discuss how the company should determine the useful life of the trademark, noting in particular what form of evidence it should collect to justify its selection of useful life.

6.3 Research and development ★   LO4

Sandy Beach Ltd's research and development section has an idea for a project on using cane toad poison for medicinal purposes. The board of directors believes the project has promise and could lead to future profits. The project is, however, very expensive and needs approval from the board.

The company's chief financial officer, Mr Stone, has expressed concern that the profits of the firm have not been strong in recent years and he does not want to see research and development costs charged as expenses to the profit or loss. Mr Stone has proposed that Sandy Beach Ltd should hire an outside firm, Shell Ltd, to undertake the work and obtain the patent. Sandy Beach Ltd could then acquire the patent from Shell Ltd, with no effect on the profit or loss of Sandy Beach Ltd.

Required

Discuss whether Mr Stone's proposal is a sound idea, particularly in relation to the effect on the profit or loss of Sandy Beach Ltd.

6.4 Recognition of intangible assets ★   LO3

Arrow Ltd has the following.

1. An investment in a subsidiary company
2. Training costs associated with a new product
3. The cost of testing in search for product alternatives
4. Legal costs incurred in securing a patent
5. Long-term receivables

Required

Which of these should be included as an intangible asset in the accounts of Arrow Ltd? Give reasons for your answer.

6.5 Recognition of intangible assets ★   **LO3**

Nemo Ltd has the following.

1. The cost of purchasing a trademark
2. Unrecovered costs of a successful lawsuit to protect a patent
3. Goodwill acquired in the purchase of a business
4. Costs of developing a patent
5. The cost of engineering activity to advance the design of a product to the manufacturing stage
6. Payments to an advertising agency for advertisements to increase the goodwill of the company

Required

Which of these should be included as an intangible asset in the accounts of Nemo Ltd? Give reasons for your answer.

6.6 Brands and formulas ★   **LO3, 4**

Wayne Upton (2001, p. 71) in his discussion of the lives of intangible assets noted that the formula for Coca-Cola has grown more valuable over time, not less, and that Sir David Tweedie, former chairman of the IASB, jokes that the brand name of his favourite Scotch whisky is older than the United States of America — and, in Sir David's view, the formula for Scotch whisky has contributed more to the sum of human happiness.

Required

Outline the accounting for brands under AASB 138/IAS 38, and discuss the difficulties for standard setters in allowing the recognition of all brands and formulas on statements of financial position.

6.7 Internally generated intangible assets ★ ★   **LO4**

In their article entitled 'U.S. firms challenged to get "intangibles" on the books', Byrnes and Aubin (2011) noted that in the United States some companies were accounting for intangibles such as brands, patents and information technology differently when they were developed internally rather than being acquired. This could mean major differences in accounting numbers where internally generated intangibles developed at low costs by one company were sold for large amounts to another company. They noted:

> The accounting difference could result in distorted behaviour, warns Abraham Briloff, a professor emeritus of accountancy at Baruch College, tempting companies to buy intellectual property rather than doing research themselves...

Required

1. Explain the accounting for internally generated intangible assets in AASB 138/IAS 38.
2. Discuss any differences between accounting for internally generated intangible assets and acquired intangible assets in AASB 138/IAS 38.
3. Discuss why companies may be reluctant to press for changes in AASB 138/IAS 38 to require more recognition of internally generated intangible assets.

6.8 Intangible assets acquired in a business combination ★ ★   **LO4**

Blue Sky, an internet services provider, acquired ConnectUs, a social networking company, for $2.4 billion. At the date of acquisition, it recognised three amortisable intangible assets, namely:

	$'000
Developed technology	1 256 800
Customer contracts and related relationships	473 500
Trade name	244 000

These intangible assets were acquired as part of a business combination.

Required

Discuss the accounting for intangible assets acquired in a business combination and how it differs from the recognition and measurement of other intangible assets.

6.9 Recognition of intangible assets ★ ★ LO3, 6, 7

The Global Alliance (2013) provided the following statement in a press release on its website.

> During an event organised by the Spanish Association of Communication Directors, Dircom, in the framework of the 8th World Public Relations Forum, due to be held in Madrid from 21 to 23 September 2014, [Anne] Gregory [chair of the Global Alliance for Public Relations and Communication Management] has made it clear that CEOs have a key role to play in this new business environment, which should be governed by authenticity and the heart. 'Nowadays over 80% of company assets are intangible, which means we need to communicate what makes us unique through our business values.'
>
> She believes this shift has changed the roles within organisations: 'Intangible assets are increasingly important with regard to other areas of the organisation, such as the finance department. Reputation, brand and the meaning our job conveys to society, the company and our stakeholders are taking precedence over figures and transactions.'

Required

Discuss the limitations placed on the recognition of intangible assets in the financial statements of by AASB 138/IAS 38 *Intangible Assets*.

6.10 Recognition of intangible assets ★ ★ LO3, 4

The latest annual report of Local Media Ltd states that the principal activities of the group are 'the production and broadcasting of television programs, local and national radio production and broadcasting, the sale of advertising airtime and space in these media'.

In the statement of financial position of Local Media Ltd, although goodwill is recognised, no intangible assets are identified.

Required

1. List intangible assets that Local Media Ltd is likely to own and state the arguments for and against capitalising each in the statement of financial position.
2. Explain why the statement of financial position excludes some assets that could have been separately identified.

6.11 Research and development ★ ★ LO4

General Labs Ltd manufactures and distributes a wide range of general pharmaceutical products. Selected preliminary figures for the reporting period ended 31 December 2022 are as follows.

Gross profit	$ 26 400 000
Profit before income tax	2 550 000
Income tax expense	750 000
Profit for the period	1 800 000
Total assets:	
Current	10 950 000
Non-current	171 250 000

The company uses a standard mark-up on cost.

Total research and development expenditure for the year amounted to $7 050 000. This amount is substantially higher than in previous years and has eroded the profitability of the company. Mr Birkdale, the company's finance director, has asked for your firm's advice on whether it is acceptable accounting practice for the company to carry forward any of this expenditure to a future accounting period.

Your analysis reveals that the main reason for the significant increase in research and development costs was the introduction of a planned 5-year laboratory program to attempt to find an antidote for the common cold. Salaries and identifiable equipment costs associated with this program amounted to $3 525 000 for the year ended 31 December 2022.

The following additional items were included in research and development costs for the year.

(a) Costs to test a new tamper-proof dispenser pack for the company's major selling line (20% of sales) of antibiotic capsules — $1 140 000. The new packs are to be introduced in the 2023 financial year.

(b) Experimental costs to convert a line of headache powders to liquid form — $885 000. The company hopes to phase out the powder form if the tests to convert to the stronger and better handling liquid form prove successful.

(c) Quality control required by stringent company policy and by law on all items of production for the year — $1 125 000.

(d) Costs of a time and motion study aimed at improving production efficiency by redesigning plant layout of existing equipment — $75 000.

(e) Construction and testing of a new prototype machine for producing hypodermic needles — $300 000. Testing has been successful to date and is nearing completion. Hypodermic needles accounted for 1% of the company's sales in the current year, but it is expected that the company's market share will increase following introduction of this new machine.

Required

Respond to Mr Birkdale's question for each item above.

6.12 Recognition of copyright ★ LO4, 7

Marlene Ltd acquired two copyrights during 2022. One copyright related to a textbook that was developed internally at a cost of $12 500. This book is estimated to have a useful life of 5 years from 1 September 2022, the date it was published. The second copyright was purchased from the King George University Press on 1 December 2022 for $24 000. This book, which analyses Aboriginal history in Western Australia prior to 2000, is considered to have an indefinite useful life.

Required

Discuss how these two copyrights should be reported in the statement of financial position of Marlene Ltd at 30 June 2023.

6.13 Recognition of intangible assets ★ ★ ★ LO4

JK Ltd is unsure of how to obtain computer software. Four possibilities are:

1. employ its own programmers to write software that the company will use
2. buy computer software to incorporate into a product that the company will develop
3. purchase computer software externally, including packages for payroll and general ledger
4. contract to independent programmers to develop specific software for the company's own use.

Required

Discuss whether the accounting will differ depending on which method is chosen.

6.14 Research and development outlays ★ ★ ★ LO4

A small manufacturing company, Ousmane Ltd, has significantly increased it expenditure on research and development over the past year.

Required

Advise Ousmane Ltd on how research and development expenditure should be accounted for under AASB 138/IAS 38 (disregard any discussion on amortisation of intangible assets).

6.15 Research and development outlays ★ ★ ★ LO4

Rosalie Ltd has been involved in a project to develop an engine that runs on fuel extracted from sugar cane. It started the project in February 2023. Between then and 30 June 2023, the end of the company's reporting period, Rosalie Ltd spent $508 000 on the project. At 30 June 2023, there was no indication that the project would be commercially feasible, although the company had made significant progress and was sufficiently confident of future success that it was prepared to outlay more funds on the project.

After spending a further $240 000 during July and August, the company had built a prototype that appeared to be successful. The prototype was demonstrated to a number of engineering companies during September, and several of these companies expressed interest in the further development of the engine. Convinced that it now had a product that it would be able to sell, Rosalie Ltd spent a further $130 000 during October adjusting for the problems that the engineering firms had pointed out. On 1 November, Rosalie Ltd applied for a patent on the engine, incurring legal and administrative costs of $70 000. The patent had an expected useful life of 7 years, but was renewable for a further 7 years upon application.

Between November and December 2023, Rosalie Ltd spent an additional amount of $164 000 on engineering and consulting costs to develop the project such that the engine was at manufacturing stage. This resulted in changes in the overall design of the engine, and costs of $10 000 were incurred to add minor changes to the patent authority.

On 1 January 2024, Rosalie Ltd invited tenders for the manufacture of the engine for commercial sale.

Required

Discuss how Rosalie Ltd should account for these costs. Provide journal entries with an explanation of why these are the appropriate entries.

Future Enterprises Ltd, a listed company, commenced a research and development (R&D) project in July 2022 to modify the method of recharging batteries used in its products. The project was successfully completed in June 2023 and the company applied for a patent for the design.

Future Enterprises Ltd plans to modify all products in its consumer range over the next 3 years and has incorporated these plans into its financial budget. The entity expects to derive economic benefits from the new battery recharging technology over the next 10 years.

The accountant was unsure how to account for the project so they used the New Project R&D account to accumulate the salaries of all engineers involved in the project during the year ended 30 June 2023. The following analysis of the salaries expenditure is based on the engineers' time sheets.

	$
Cost of time spent searching for and evaluating alternative materials	150 000
Cost of time designing models, and constructing and testing prototypes	1 050 000
Cost of time spent on training maintenance workers for the new design	300 000

The value in use of the design, estimated using present value techniques, is $6 000 000. However, the fair value of the design is estimated to be only $4 500 000 because the only potential buyer would need to modify the design to adapt it to its own products.

The following conversation took place between the chief executive officer (CEO) and the accountant (ACC).

CEO: That 'R&D asset' should make our financial statements look great this year. We can show it is worth $6 000 000 in the balance sheet and add an extra $4 500 000 to profit because it cost only $1 500 000.

ACC: I haven't finalised accounting for it yet but I am quite sure the accounting standard requires us to measure it at historical cost, and some of it will probably have to be recognised as an expense.

CEO: It isn't fair. These conservative accounting rules make it impossible to show investors that our project was successful — and expensing any of it will cause our share price to go down because the investors will think it didn't work.

Required

1. How should the project be accounted for in the financial statements for the year ended 30 June 2023? Justify your answer with reference to relevant paragraphs of AASB 138/IAS 38.
2. To what extent might the rules or restrictions in AASB 138/IAS 38 reduce the comparability of financial statements?
3. Write a response to the CEO, drawing on your understanding of AASB 138/IAS 38 and the efficient market hypothesis (refer to chapter 2 of this text). Include a recommendation as to how the company might mitigate concerns about investors' interpretation of the information reported in the financial statements.

REFERENCES

Australian Accounting Standards Board 2008, *Initial accounting for internally generated intangible assets*, discussion paper, Australian Accounting Standards Board.

Australian Pharmaceutical Industries Ltd 2018, *Annual report 2018*, Australian Pharmaceutical Industries Ltd, www.api.net.au.

Brand Finance 2018, *Australia 100 2018*, February, http://brandfinance.com/images/upload/brand_finance_australia_100_2018_locked.pdf.

Byrnes, N & Aubin, D 2011, 'U.S. firms challenged to bet "intangibles" on the books', *Reuters*, 2 September, www.reuters.com.

Canstar Blue 2018, *Domestic airlines*, April, www.canstarblue.com.au/domestic-airlines.

Nellis, S 2019, 'Apple shares lose $13b in value as designer behind the iPhone announces he is leaving to start his own company', *The Sydney Morning Herald*, 28 June, www.smh.com.au.

Paladin Energy Ltd 2018, *Annual report 2018*, Paladin Energy Ltd, www.paladinenergy.com.au.

Global Alliance 2013, 'Intangible assets are taking control at organisations', www.globalalliancepr.usi.ch/website/sites/default/files/nolie/Communication/Member%20Events/20131217-Desayuno-Anne%20Gregory.pdf.

Qantas Airways Ltd 2018, *Qantas annual report 2018*, www.qantas.com.au.

Rio Tinto Ltd 2018, *2018 annual report*, www.riotinto.com.

Upton, WS 2001, 'Business and financial reporting, challenges from the new economy', *Financial Accounting Series*, no. 219-A, Financial Accounting Standards Board, Norwalk, Connecticut, USA.

ACKNOWLEDGEMENTS

Photo: © iStockphoto / Getty Images

Figure 6.1: © Canstar Blue 2018

Figure 6.2: © Paladin Energy Ltd 2018

Figures 6.3, 6.6: © Qantas Airways Ltd 2018

Figures 6.4, 6.5: © Australian Pharmaceutical Industries Ltd 2018

Figures 6.7, 6.8: © Rio Tinto Ltd 2018

Table 6.1: © Brand Finance 2018

Text: © 2019 Australian Accounting Standards Board (AASB). The text, graphics and layout of this publication are protected by Australian copyright law and the comparable law of other countries. No part of the publication may be reproduced, stored or transmitted in any form or by any means without the prior written permission of the AASB except as permitted by law. For reproduction or publication, permission should be sought in writing from the AASB. Requests in the first instance should be addressed to the National Director, Australian Accounting Standards Board, PO Box 204, Collins Street West, Victoria 8007.

Text: © IFRS. This publication contains copyright material of the IFRS Foundation in respect of which all rights are reserved. Reproduced by John Wiley & Sons Australia, Ltd with the permission of the IFRS Foundation. No permission granted to third parties to reproduce or distribute. For full access to IFRS Standards and the work of the IFRS Foundation please visit http://eifrs.ifrs.org. The International Accounting Standards Board, the IFRS Foundation, the authors and the publishers do not accept responsibility for any loss caused by acting or refraining from acting in reliance on the material in this publication, whether such loss is caused by negligence or otherwise.

Text: © Global Alliance for Public Relations and Communication Management 2013

CHAPTER 7

Impairment of assets

CHAPTER AIM

This chapter discusses the application of AASB 136/IAS 36 *Impairment of Assets*. The objectives of the standard are to prescribe accounting procedures to ensure that assets are carried at amounts not greater than their recoverable amounts, that impairment losses are recognised if an asset's carrying amount is greater than its recoverable amount, that impairment losses are reversed when appropriate, and that appropriate disclosures are made.

LEARNING OBJECTIVES

After studying this chapter, you should be able to:

7.1 explain the nature and purpose of an impairment test

7.2 explain when an impairment test should be undertaken

7.3 outline the components of the impairment test

7.4 describe how to account for an impairment loss for a single asset

7.5 describe how to account for an impairment loss for a cash-generating unit

7.6 explain when an impairment loss can be reversed and how to account for it

7.7 identify the disclosures required in relation to impairment of assets.

CONCEPTS FOR REVIEW

Before studying this chapter, you should understand and, if necessary, revise:
- the *Conceptual Framework*
- the concepts of depreciation and the revaluation model adopted in AASB 116/IAS 16 *Property, Plant and Equipment*
- the nature of acquired goodwill and its accounting treatment under AASB 3/IFRS 3 *Business Combinations*.

7.1 Introduction and scope

LEARNING OBJECTIVE 7.1 Explain the nature and purpose of an impairment test.

Every entity hopes that it will have a profitable future. However, an entity's profitability may be affected by any number of external factors besides the ability of management.

For an entity in any year there may be declines in expected benefits from single assets as well as groups of assets. A major question when preparing the statement of financial position is whether the carrying amounts of the assets on that statement represent amounts that are recoverable by the entity.

The accounting profession has introduced an impairment test that entities apply to test the recoverability of their assets, which is aimed at providing reassurance to users of financial statements about the relevance and faithful representation of the accounting numbers disclosed.

Chapters 5 and 6 discuss the measurement and recognition criteria for property, plant and equipment and intangible assets respectively. These assets can be measured at either cost or a revalued amount and this is subsequently allocated over the **useful life** as **depreciation** or **amortisation**. The exception is where the asset (such as land or certain intangible assets) is assessed to have an indefinite useful life, in which case no allocation is made.

The degree of judgement involved in the depreciation/amortisation process — estimates of useful life, residual values and the expected pattern of benefits — leads to the question at the end of the reporting period: does the **carrying amount** of the asset reported in the statement of financial position overstate the value of the asset? In other words, can an entity expect to recover, in future periods, the carrying amounts of the assets reported? This recovery could come from continued use or sale of the assets.

Besides the judgements made in measuring carrying amounts, assets may have lost value for other reasons, such as a global economic downturn or a natural disaster. In recent years, mining companies have announced significant impairment losses due to declines in world commodity prices. In other cases, impairment write-downs may arise due to management identifying the need to restructure operations. The article in figure 7.1 discusses how Woolworths' decision to exit from the home improvement market had an adverse effect on its financial results.

FIGURE 7.1	Effects on expected profits

Woolworths reports almost $1 billion loss in half-year results

Woolworths has posted an after-tax loss of $972.7 million in its half-year results, after the retailer's failed venture into the home improvement market dragged on its bottom line.

The financial result represents the grocery giant's first loss since it was listed on the Australian stock exchange 23 years ago.

In the six months to January 3, Woolworths said first-half results slumped 176 per cent from the $1.28 billion profit the supermarket giant posted in the previous corresponding period.

Woolworths said impairment charges and costs to exit its Masters Home Improvement arm would total $1.89 billion.

Losses at Masters increased by 22.9 per cent to $137.9 million, on the back of costly store openings and mixed gross margins.

'We are rebuilding the Woolworths business,' said chairman Gordon Cairns in a statement released to the Australian Securities Exchange.

'While we have made progress, it will be a three to five year journey and there is much to do.'

'The decision to exit home improvement will allow Woolworths to focus its energy and resources on strengthening and executing its plans in its core businesses.'

Last month, Woolworths announced it would exit the loss-making Masters business, by selling or winding up the stores, after buying out its US partner, Lowe's.

'It appears it's been poorly executed,' said Roger Montgomery, chief investment officer at Montgomery Investment Management.

'It didn't appeal to the trade market, it was designed to appeal to a different market, that market didn't make the purchasing decisions [of] the sorts of products hardware stores are expected to sell.'

'So arguably, there was a mismatch between the design of the store and the most profitable audience.'

Source: Hyam and Ong (2016).

Paragraph 6 of AASB 136/IAS 36 *Impairment of Assets* defines an **impairment loss** as:

> the amount by which the carrying amount of an asset or a cash-generating unit exceeds its recoverable amount.

So, if an entity expects to recover less than the carrying amount of an asset, the entity has suffered an impairment loss in relation to that asset.

This chapter examines the impairment test for assets. Under AASB 136/IAS 36, an entity is required to conduct impairment tests for its assets to see whether it has incurred any impairment loss. The purpose of the impairment test is to ensure that assets are not carried at amounts that exceed their recoverable amounts or, more simply, that assets are not overstated.

Some key questions answered in this chapter are as follows.
- How does the test work?
- What is recoverable amount?
- Is the test the same for all assets?
- Should the test apply to individual assets or to groups of assets? If applied to groups, which groups?
- Is the accounting treatment the same for assets measured at cost and for those measured at revalued amount?
- When should the test be carried out? Should it be done annually; every 3 years; or over some other period?
- Can the results of the impairment test be reversed; that is, if an asset is written down because it is impaired, can later events lead to the reversal of that write-down?

The impairment test is not applied to all assets. Assets to which AASB 136/IAS 36 is not applied are:
- inventories
- assets arising from construction contracts
- deferred tax assets (see chapter 12)
- assets arising from employee benefits
- financial assets that are within the scope of AASB 9/IFRS 9 *Financial Instruments*
- investment property that is measured at fair value
- biological assets related to agricultural activity that are measured at fair value less costs of disposal
- deferred acquisition costs and intangible assets, arising from an insurer's contractual rights under insurance contracts
- non-current assets (or disposal groups) classified as held for sale.

The accounting standards dealing with the above assets require the assets to be measured at fair value or fair value less costs of disposal. Where assets are recorded at fair value, there is no need for an impairment test as the fair values reflect recoverability of benefits.

Note particularly the accounting for inventories. Under paragraph 9 of AASB 102/IAS 2 *Inventories*, inventories shall be measured at the lower of cost and net realisable value. As net realisable value is defined in terms of estimated price, the measurement of inventories has a 'built-in' impairment test requiring inventories to be written down when the cost is effectively greater than the recoverable amount.

LEARNING CHECK

- ☐ The carrying amounts of assets in an entity's statement of financial position are the result of judgements and estimations.
- ☐ The purpose of the impairment test is to ensure that assets are not overstated in the statement of financial position.
- ☐ Not all assets are written down as a result of an impairment test under AASB 136/IAS 36, but the standard that governs the accounting for those assets may be considered to have a 'built-in' impairment test.

7.2 When to undertake an impairment test

LEARNING OBJECTIVE 7.2 Explain when an impairment test should be undertaken.

Paragraph 9 of AASB 136/IAS 36 states:

> An entity shall assess at the end of each reporting period whether there is any indication that an asset may be impaired. If any such indication exists, the entity shall estimate the recoverable amount of the asset.

An impairment test is not necessarily undertaken at the end of each reporting period or at the end of any set period of time. The impairment test is undertaken when there is an *indication* that an asset may be impaired. An entity, therefore, has to determine — after analysing certain sources of information — whether there is sufficient evidence to suspect that an asset may be impaired.

If there is insufficient evidence, then an entity can assume no impairment has occurred, and no impairment test is conducted.

For most assets, the need for an impairment test can be assessed by analysing sources of evidence. However, paragraph 10 of AASB 136/IAS 36 specifies some assets for which an impairment test *must* be undertaken every year. These assets are:

- intangible assets with indefinite useful lives
- intangible assets not yet available for use (e.g. capitalised development outlays)
- goodwill acquired in a business combination.

The reason for singling these assets out for annual impairment tests is that the carrying amounts of these assets are considered to be more uncertain than those of other assets. Other assets tend to be reduced each year as a result of annual depreciation/amortisation charges. The above assets, however, are not subject to depreciation/amortisation reductions.

7.2.1 Evidence of impairment

The purpose of the impairment test is to determine whether the carrying amount of an asset exceeds its recoverable amount. The evidence of impairment relates to variables that may support the belief that the book value of the asset under investigation overstates the future cash flows expected to be generated from its use or sale. Management should take into account the nature and use of a specific asset and determine the factors that may indicate impairment.

Indicators of impairment can be described in two groups: external sources of information (looking at what is occurring outside the entity) and internal sources of information (looking at events occurring within the entity itself).

External sources of information

Paragraph 12 of AASB 136/IAS 36 identifies four possible sources of information relating to the external environment in which the entity operates, as follows.

1. '[T]here are observable indications that the asset's value has declined during the period significantly more than would be expected as a result of the passage of time or normal use.' This may occur for many reasons relating to changes in expectations concerning the operation of the entity. For example, there may have been a significant reduction in the entity's sales when new products or technologies that the entity planned to introduce within a certain timeframe were not introduced within that timeframe. Further, there may have been movements in key personnel that affected the productivity of the entity itself and brought increased pressure from competitors who employed those people.
2. '[S]ignificant changes with an adverse effect on the entity have taken place during the period, or will take place in the near future, in the technological, market, economic or legal environment in which the entity operates or in the market to which an asset is dedicated.' A significant drop in commodity prices, for example, would have an adverse impact on the estimation of future cash flows when determining the value in use of a mining company's property, plant and equipment.
3. '[M]arket interest rates or other market rates of return on investments have increased during the period, and those increases are likely to affect the discount rate used in calculating an asset's value in use and decrease the asset's recoverable amount materially.' Such increases have the potential to increase the discount rate used in assessing an entity's present value of future cash flows.
4. '[T]he carrying amount of the net assets of the entity is more than its market capitalisation.' This would indicate that, in the market's view at least, the assets of the entity are overstated.

Internal sources of information

Paragraph 12 of AASB 136/IAS 36 goes on to identify three possible sources of information based on events occurring within the entity itself, as follows.

1. '[E]vidence is available of obsolescence or physical damage of an asset.' Examples include an item of machinery that has been superseded by technology or major flood damage to an uninsured building.
2. '[S]ignificant changes with an adverse effect on the entity have taken place during the period, or are expected to take place in the near future, in the extent to which, or manner in which, an asset is used or expected to be used. These changes include the asset becoming idle, plans to discontinue or restructure the operation to which an asset belongs, plans to dispose of an asset before the previously expected date, and reassessing the useful life of an asset as finite rather than indefinite.' For example, when Ford Australia announced it would close its Australian plants, it would clearly result in an adverse effect on any local car parts supplier for whom Ford was a major customer. A car parts supplier would have needed to reassess its estimation of future cash flows from its own assets.
3. '[E]vidence is available from internal reporting that indicates that the economic performance of an asset is, or will be, worse than expected.' Evidence of this consists of:
   (a) actual cash flows for maintenance or operation of the asset may be significantly higher than expected
   (b) actual cash inflows or profits may be lower than expected
   (c) expected cash flows for maintenance or operations may have increased, or expected profits may be lower.

In analysing the information from the above sources, paragraph 15 of AASB 136/IAS 36 requires that materiality be taken into account. If, in previous analyses, the carrying amount of an asset was significantly lower than the asset's recoverable amount, minor movements in the factors listed above may cause the recoverable amount to be closer to the carrying amount but not large enough to expect the carrying amount to be greater than the recoverable amount.

Woolworths' 2018 annual report provided the disclosure note shown in figure 7.2.

FIGURE 7.2	Impairment disclosure note extract, Woolworths

3.5 Impairment of non-financial assets

Significant accounting policies

Impairment of non-financial assets
The carrying amounts of the Group's property, plant and equipment (refer to Note 3.3), goodwill and intangible assets (refer to Note 3.4) are reviewed for impairment as follows:

Property, plant and equipment and finite life intangibles	When there is an indication that the asset may be impaired (assessed at least each reporting date) or when there is an indication that a previously recognised impairment may have changed
Goodwill and indefinite life intangibles	At least annually and when there is an indication that the asset may be impaired

Source: Woolworths Group Limited (2018, p. 80).

Impairment tests are conducted both on individual assets and groups of assets, the latter being referred to as cash-generating units (CGUs).

LEARNING CHECK

☐ With the exception of the mandatory tests for goodwill (addressed later in this chapter) and intangible assets with an indefinite useful life, an impairment test is conducted only when there is evidence that assets have been impaired.
☐ Evidence of impairment may be obtained from external and/or internal sources.
☐ External sources relate to factors outside the entity such as changes in market prices, whereas internal sources relate to factors within the entity such as idle time of machinery held by the entity.

7.3 The impairment test

LEARNING OBJECTIVE 7.3 Outline the components of the impairment test.

The impairment test is shown diagrammatically in figure 7.3 as a two-step process.

FIGURE 7.3	The impairment test

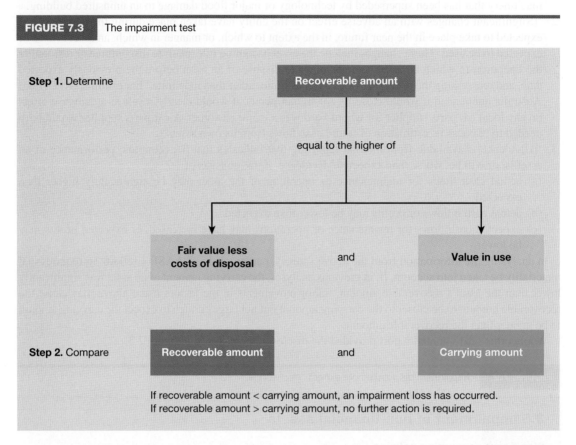

The *first step* is to determine the recoverable amount of an asset, which is done by considering the following three components defined in paragraph 6 of AASB 136/IAS 36.

- **Fair value** — 'the price that would be received to sell an asset or paid to transfer a liability in an orderly transaction between market participants at the measurement date.' See chapter 3 for more information on the measurement of fair value.
- **Costs of disposal** — 'incremental costs directly attributable to the disposal of an asset or cash-generating unit, excluding finance costs and income tax expense'. Examples of such costs are legal costs, stamp duty and similar transaction taxes, costs of removing the asset and direct incremental costs to bring the asset into condition for its sale.
- **Value in use** — 'the present value of the future cash flows expected to be derived from an asset or cash-generating unit'. See later in this section for more details on its measurement.

Considering these three components, the **recoverable amount** of an asset or a CGU is the higher of:
- its fair value less costs of disposal
- its value in use.

Thus, recoverable amount is the benefits or cash flows expected from the asset. Note that, for any asset, there are two possible sources of benefits: (i) benefits from holding on to the asset and using it, and (ii) benefits from selling the asset. For example, if a person owns a car, they can either use the car or sell the car. If they decide to use the car, it is because they have reasoned that the benefits from use are greater than the benefits from selling the car. This rationale can be applied to all assets held by an entity.

For non-current assets, the benefits from using the assets are presumed to be greater than the benefits from selling them. This is why an entity will hold property, plant and equipment, intangible assets and financial assets. These assets are held and used to produce cash flows rather than cash flows being obtained from selling these assets.

The *second step* is then to compare the recoverable amount with the *carrying amount* of the asset as recorded by the entity. An impairment loss is the amount by which the carrying amount of an asset or CGU exceeds its recoverable amount.

- If the recoverable amount is greater than the carrying amount, there is no impairment loss.
- If the recoverable amount is less than the carrying amount, an impairment loss has occurred.

It is not always necessary to calculate both fair value less costs of disposal and value in use for an asset when testing for impairment. If one of the amounts is greater than carrying amount, the asset is not impaired. In general, it is often easier to calculate fair value less costs of disposal rather than value in use.

7.3.1 Fair value less costs of disposal

Fair value is measured in accordance with AASB 13/IFRS 13 *Fair Value Measurement* and discussed in detail in chapter 3. Fair value is defined as an exit price and can be measured applying a number of valuation techniques using various observable or unobservable inputs.

7.3.2 Value in use

Value in use is the present value of future cash flows relating to the asset being measured. Paragraph 30 of AASB 136/IAS 36 notes that:

> The following elements shall be reflected in the calculation of an asset's value in use:
> (a) an estimate of the future cash flows the entity expects to derive from the asset;
> (b) expectations about possible variations in the amount or timing of those future cash flows;
> (c) the time value of money, represented by the current market risk-free rate of interest;
> (d) the price for bearing the uncertainty inherent in the asset; and
> (e) other factors, such as illiquidity, that market participants would reflect in pricing the future cash flows the entity expects to derive from the asset.

The objective is to measure the present value of the cash flows relating to the asset; in other words, to determine the cash flows and apply a discount rate. Some of the elements noted above — particularly (b), (d) and (e) — may affect either the measurement of the cash flows or the discount rate. Figure 7.4 shows a calculation of value in use.

FIGURE 7.4	Calculation of value in use			
Year	Long-term growth rates	Future cash flows	Present value factor at 15% discount rate	Discounted future cash flows
2009		$230*	0.869 57	$ 200
2010		253*	0.756 14	191
2011		273*	0.657 52	180
2012		290*	0.571 75	166
2013		304*	0.497 18	151
2014	3%	313**	0.432 33	135
2015	2%	307**	0.375 94	115
2016	6%	289**	0.326 90	94
2017	15%	245**	0.284 26	70
2018	25%	184**	0.247 19	45
2019	67%	61**	0.214 94	13
Value in use				$1360

* Based on management's best estimate of net cash flow projections.
** Based on an extrapolation from preceding year cash flow using declining growth rates.

Source: Based on Example 2 in the illustrative examples accompanying AASB 136/IAS 36.

As can be seen from figure 7.4, the calculation of value in use requires the estimation of future cash flows and a discount rate applied to these future cash flows.

LEARNING CHECK

☐ The impairment test for a single asset requires a comparison between the carrying amount of the asset and its recoverable amount, the latter being the higher of fair value less costs of disposal, and value in use.

▶

- [ ] For any non-current asset, future cash flows are generated from either continued use or sale, and recoverable amount is the greater of these two estimates.
- [ ] Value in use is calculated by estimating the future cash flows relating to the asset being tested, then discounting these cash flows to a present value. Such a calculation requires assumptions and estimates to be made about future events.

7.4 Impairment loss: individual assets

LEARNING OBJECTIVE 7.4 Describe how to account for an impairment loss for a single asset.

If the recoverable amount of an asset is less than its carrying amount, an impairment loss occurs. The asset must then be written down to the recoverable amount. The accounting involved depends on whether the asset is measured under the cost model or the revaluation model. According to paragraph 59 of AASB 136/IAS 36:

> If, and only if, the recoverable amount of an asset is less than its carrying amount, the carrying amount of the asset shall be reduced to its recoverable amount. That reduction is an impairment loss.

Under the *cost model*, an impairment loss is recognised immediately in profit or loss by debiting an expense account and crediting the contra-asset account Accumulated depreciation and impairment losses. This is demonstrated in illustrative example 7.1.

ILLUSTRATIVE EXAMPLE 7.1

Recognition of an impairment loss under the cost model

A motor vehicle with a carrying amount of $100 after accumulated depreciation of $60 has a recoverable amount of $90.

Required
What is the appropriate journal entry to recognise the impairment loss of $10? How would the asset be carried and disclosed in the financial statements?

Solution
The journal entry is as follows.

Impairment loss	Dr	10	
Accumulated depreciation and impairment losses	Cr		10
(Recognition of impairment loss)			

The asset would then be carried and disclosed in the financial statements as follows.

Motor vehicle	160
Less: Accumulated depreciation and impairment losses	70
	90

According to paragraph 60 of AASB 136/IAS 36:

> An impairment loss shall be recognised immediately in profit or loss, unless the asset is carried at revalued amount in accordance with another Standard (for example, in accordance with the revaluation model in AASB 116 [IAS 16]). Any impairment loss of a revalued asset shall be treated as a revaluation decrease in accordance with that other Standard.

Under the *revaluation model*, where the asset is measured at fair value, an impairment loss is treated as a downward revaluation and accounted for as in AASB 116/IAS 16 *Property, Plant and Equipment*. Hence, the downward revaluation is treated as an expense unless there has been a previous revaluation increase for that particular asset, in which case the downward revaluation reduces the existing revaluation surplus and is recognised in other comprehensive income. This is demonstrated in illustrative examples 7.2 and 7.3.

Recognition of an impairment loss under the revaluation model

Assume the motor vehicle from illustrative example 7.1 is carried under the revaluation model, has a carrying amount of $100 after accumulated depreciation of $60, and the recoverable amount of the asset is determined to be $90.

Required
What is the accounting entry, assuming the net method?

Solution

Accumulated depreciation	Dr	60	
Motor vehicle	Cr		60
(Writing back the accumulated depreciation)			
Loss on revaluation	Dr	10	
Motor vehicle	Cr		10
(Recognition of loss on revaluation)			

Recognition of an impairment loss subsequent to a prior revaluation increase

As before, a motor vehicle is carried under the revaluation model, has a carrying amount of $100 after accumulated depreciation of $60, and the recoverable amount of the asset is determined to be $90. Assume the vehicle had been subject to a revaluation increase of $20 in a prior period.

Required
How would the impairment loss be recognised?

Solution

Accumulated depreciation	Dr	60	
Motor vehicle	Cr		60
(Writing back the accumulated depreciation)			
Revaluation surplus (OCI)	Dr	10	
Motor vehicle	Cr		10
(Recognition of loss on revaluation)			

LEARNING CHECK

- ☐ Where an impairment loss is identified, the asset is written down immediately.
- ☐ The accounting treatment depends on whether the cost or revaluation model is being used for the asset.
- ☐ Under the cost model an impairment expense is recognised in profit or loss.
- ☐ Under the revaluation model the impairment is treated as a revaluation decrease in accordance with AASB 116/IAS 16.

7.5 Impairment loss: cash-generating units

LEARNING OBJECTIVE 7.5 Describe how to account for an impairment loss for a cash-generating unit.

In order to calculate an impairment loss it is necessary to determine the value in use. This requires the calculation of the cash flows that are expected to be generated from using the asset. However, many assets do not individually generate cash flows. The cash flows arise as a result of a combination of several assets working together. For example, the motor vehicle used by a sales manager does not by itself generate cash flows. The cash flows are generated by the sales of inventories produced by combining many assets, including machinery, raw materials, buildings and vehicles.

According to paragraph 66 of AASB 136/IAS 36:

> If there is any indication that an asset may be impaired, recoverable amount shall be estimated for the individual asset. If it is not possible to estimate the recoverable amount of the individual asset, an entity shall determine the recoverable amount of the cash-generating unit to which the asset belongs (the asset's cash-generating unit).

Paragraph 6 of AASB 136/IAS 36 defines a **cash-generating unit** (CGU) as:

> the smallest identifiable group of assets that generates cash inflows that are largely independent of the cash inflows from other assets or groups of assets.

7.5.1 Identifying a cash-generating unit

Identification of a CGU requires judgement. The key is to determine the smallest identifiable group of assets that creates independent cash flows from continuing use. Paragraphs 67 to 73 of AASB 136/IAS 36 provide some guidelines to assist in this judgement, as follows.

- Consider how management monitors the entity's operations (such as by product lines, businesses, individual locations, districts or regional areas).
- Consider how management makes decisions about continuing, or disposing of, the entity's assets and operations.
- If an active market exists for the output of a group of assets, this group constitutes a CGU.
- Even if some of the output of a group is used internally, if the output could be sold externally, then these prices can be used to measure the value in use of the group of assets.
- CGUs should be identified consistently from period to period for the same group of assets.

To assist in understanding the nature of a CGU, consider your local McDonald's restaurant. This restaurant has a number of assets including the building, shop fittings and furniture as well as the equipment that is used to produce the food both for take-away and in-house dining.

None of these assets by itself generates independent cash flows. The cash flows come from the sale of products such as hamburgers. The cash flows are produced by the combination of assets working together leading to the sale of the products.

The key question is: how many CGUs are there in your local McDonald's restaurant — in particular, where the McDonald's restaurant is also a McCafé? A McCafé not only sells the usual range of hamburgers and fries, but a customer can choose to sit in a more comfortable area and consume a cappuccino and a muffin or pastry.

To determine how many CGUs there are in a McCafé restaurant, it is necessary to determine the number of groups of assets that independently generate cash flows. It can be argued that there are two CGUs in a McCafé restaurant. The *first* CGU relates to the assets that combine to sell hamburgers and fries. The *second* CGU relates to the assets that combine to sell the coffee and cakes. Looking at the guidelines raised at the beginning of this section:

- *how does management monitor the entity's operations?* The profitability of the McCafé section would be determined separately from the profitability of the hamburgers and fries section. These two product lines are different.
- *how would management make decisions about continuing or disposing of the entity's assets?* Consider the situation where a Coffee Club was built across the road from the McDonald's, and that local consumers preferred the Coffee Club coffee to the McCafé coffee. This would lead to a decline in the profitability of the McCafé section of the McDonald's restaurant. The management of McDonald's could continue to operate the hamburger and fries section of McDonald's even if they closed down the McCafé section. The two operations are independent.

Application of the guidelines would support the existence of two CGUs in the McDonald's restaurant.

Note that there are assets that are common to both CGUs — in particular, the building which houses both CGUs. Such common or corporate assets are dealt with in section 7.5.4 later in this chapter.

The identification of a CGU within an entity is arbitrary. It requires judgement on the part of management, and comparability between entities is generally not available. It may be possible to view the segments of an entity as determined under application of AASB 8/IFRS 8 *Operating Segments* (see chapter 20) to assist in identifying CGUs within an entity.

7.5.2 Goodwill and CGUs

According to paragraph 80 of AASB 136/IAS 36:

> For the purpose of impairment testing, goodwill acquired in a business combination shall, from the acquisition date, be allocated to each of the acquirer's cash-generating units, or groups of cash-generating units, that is expected to benefit from the synergies of the combination . . .

Goodwill is recognised only when it is acquired in a business combination. When a business combination occurs, the goodwill acquired is allocated to one or more CGUs based upon the expected benefits from the synergies of the business combination.

When deciding how to allocate the goodwill, consideration should be given to how management monitors or manages the goodwill. The goodwill should be allocated to the *lowest level* within the entity at which management monitors the goodwill. When the business combination occurred, the acquirer would have analysed the earning capacity of the entity it proposed to acquire, and would have equated aspects of goodwill to various CGUs. It is possible that the allocation of goodwill would be made to each of the segments identified by management under AASB 8/IFRS 8 *Operating Segments*. The units to which goodwill is allocated should not be larger than an operating segment.

In its 2018 annual report, Woolworths Group Limited identified six reportable segments. Figure 7.5 shows Woolworths' accounting policies relating to goodwill impairment and how Woolworths allocated goodwill across its segments. Note from figure 7.2 how goodwill and other intangible assets with indefinite lives are reviewed annually for impairment.

| FIGURE 7.5 | Accounting policies relating to impairment and allocation of goodwill to segments, Woolworths |

3.4 Intangible assets

3.4.2 Allocation of indefinite life intangible assets to groups of cash-generating units

	GOODWILL		BRAND NAMES		LIQUOUR, GAMING LICENCES AND OTHER	
	2018 $m	2017 $m	2018 $m	2017 $m	2018 $m	2017 $m
Australian Food	360	360	—	—	—	—
New Zealand Food	2 109	2 181	243	249	—	—
Endeavour Drinks[1]	516	510	7	7	274	272
ALH Group	1 170	1 165	—	—	1 711	1 697
	4 155	4 216	250	256	1 985	1 969

1. Excludes ALH owned retail sites, which are included in ALH Group.

3.5 Impairment of non-financial assets

Calculation of recoverable amount

In assessing impairment, the recoverable amount of the asset is estimated in order to determine the extent of the impairment loss (if any).

The recoverable amount of an asset is the greater of its VIU and its fair value less costs to dispose (FVLCTD). For an asset that does not generate largely independent cash inflows, recoverable amount is assessed at the cash generating unit (CGU) level, which is the smallest group of assets generating cash inflows independent of other CGUs that benefit from the use of the respective asset. Goodwill is allocated to those CGUs or groups of CGUs that are expected to benefit from the business combination in which the goodwill arose, identified according to operating segments and grouped at the lowest levels for which goodwill is monitored for internal management purposes.

An impairment loss is recognised whenever the carrying amount of an asset or its CGU exceeds its recoverable amount. Impairment losses are recognised in the Consolidated Statement of Profit or Loss.

Impairment losses recognised in respect of a CGU will be allocated first to reduce the carrying amount of any goodwill allocated to the CGU and then to reduce the carrying amount of other assets in the CGU on a pro-rata basis to their carrying amounts.

Source: Woolworths Group Limited (2018, pp. 79, 80).

7.5.3 Impairment loss for a CGU

Having identified the CGU, at the end of a reporting period, management assess the sources of information determining whether there is an indication of impairment. If it is probable that the assets of the CGU are impaired, management then:

- calculate the recoverable amount of the CGU
- compare it with the total carrying amount of the assets of the CGU
- determine whether an impairment loss exists.

In determining the recoverable amounts for the CGUs, an entity makes many assumptions. Entities are required to disclose those assumptions so that users of financial reports can make assessments about the relative risks involved in their investments. Figure 7.6 shows the assumptions made by Woolworths in the calculation of both value in use and fair value less costs of disposal.

FIGURE 7.6   Critical accounting estimates in determining recoverable amount, Woolworths

Critical accounting estimates

Key assumptions used in determining the recoverable amount of assets include expected future cash flows, long-term growth rates (terminal value assumptions) and discount rates.

In assessing VIU, estimated future cash flows are based on the Group's most recent board approved business plan covering a period not exceeding five years. Cash flows beyond the approved business plan period are extrapolated using estimated long-term growth rates.

Long-term growth rates are based on past experience, expectations of external market operating conditions, and other assumptions which take account of the specific features of each business unit.

The recoverable amount has been determined using a VIU discounted cash flow model. In assessing VIU, the estimated future pre-tax cash flows are discounted to their present value using a pre-tax discount rate that reflects the current market assessments of the time value of money and risks specific to the asset. Pre-tax discount rates used vary depending on the nature of the business and the country of operation.

The ranges of rates used in determining recoverable amounts are set out below:

	2018 %	2017 %
Long-term growth rate	2.5	2.5
Pre-tax discount rate	12–17	13–17

The Group believes that any reasonably possible change in the key assumptions applied would not cause the carrying value of assets to exceed their recoverable amount and result in a material impairment based on current economic conditions and CGU performance.

Source: Woolworths Group Limited (2018, p. 81).

Once the recoverable amount of a CGU is determined, it is compared with the sum of the carrying amounts of the assets in the CGU. If an impairment loss is identified, the loss must be written off against the assets of the CGU. The allocation process has two steps:

1. reduce the carrying amount of any goodwill allocated to the CGU
2. allocate any balance of impairment loss to the other assets of the CGU pro rata on the basis of the carrying amount of each asset in the CGU.

Specifically, paragraph 104 of AASB 136/IAS 36 states:

> The impairment loss shall be allocated to reduce the carrying amount of the assets of the unit (group of units) in the following order:
> (a) first, to reduce the carrying amount of any goodwill allocated to the cash-generating unit (group of units); and
> (b) then, to the other assets of the unit (group of units) pro rata on the basis of the carrying amount of each asset in the unit (group of units).
> These reductions in carrying amounts shall be treated as impairment losses on individual assets and recognised in accordance with paragraph 60.

Step 1. Reduce the carrying amount of any goodwill allocated to the CGU

Because goodwill has been calculated as a residual rather than independently determined as in the case of the identifiable assets, both its carrying amount and its existence are considered less reliable than that of the identifiable assets. Hence, it is written off before any write-down of the identifiable assets.

ILLUSTRATIVE EXAMPLE 7.4

Write-down of goodwill as a result of an impairment loss

Gift Ltd has two CGUs, Blue and Box. A comparison of the assets of these CGUs and their recoverable amounts is shown below.

	CGU — Blue	CGU — Box
Property, plant and equipment	$1 000 000	$ 900 000
Goodwill	300 000	200 000
Accumulated impairment — goodwill	(100 000)	(50 000)
Carrying amount	1 200 000	1 050 000
Recoverable amount	1 100 000	880 000
Impairment loss	$ 100 000	$ 170 000

Required

Prepare the journal entries to write down the goodwill.

Solution

In accounting for the impairment losses, the first step requires the write-down of goodwill. With the Blue CGU, only some of the goodwill is written off, while with the Box CGU all the goodwill is written off. With the Box CGU further journal entries (see step 2 below) are needed to recognise the balance of the impairment loss.

The journal entries are:

Impairment loss	Dr	100 000	
Accumulated impairment losses — goodwill	Cr		100 000
(Recognition of impairment loss for Blue CGU)			
Impairment loss	Dr	150 000	
Accumulated impairment losses — goodwill	Dr	50 000	
Goodwill	Cr		200 000
(Write-off of goodwill for Box CGU)			

Step 2. Allocate any balance of impairment loss to the other assets

The assets of the CGU are then listed and the impairment loss allocated on a proportional basis to each asset. The reduction in the carrying amount of each asset is accounted for in the same way as for single assets in section 7.4. The losses are recognised immediately in profit or loss.

ILLUSTRATIVE EXAMPLE 7.5

Impairment of a CGU

The Box CGU in illustrative example 7.4 was assessed for impairment and it was determined that the unit had incurred an impairment loss of $170 000 with the first $150 000 written off against goodwill. The carrying amounts of the CGU's other assets and the allocation of the remaining $20 000 impairment loss on a proportional basis are as shown below.

	Carrying amount	Proportion	Allocation of impairment loss	Net carrying amount
Buildings	$360 000	360/900	$ 8 000	$352 000
Equipment	225 000	225/900	5 000	220 000
Land	180 000	180/900	4 000	176 000
Fittings	135 000	135/900	3 000	132 000
	$900 000		$20 000	$880 000

Required

Prepare the journal entry to reflect the recognition of the impairment loss.

Solution

Impairment loss	Dr	20 000	
Accumulated depreciation and impairment losses — buildings	Cr		8 000
Accumulated depreciation and impairment losses — equipment	Cr		5 000
Accumulated impairment losses — land	Cr		4 000
Accumulated depreciation and impairment losses — fittings	Cr		3 000

However, there are restrictions on an entity's ability to write down assets as a result of the allocation of the impairment loss across the carrying amounts of the CGU's assets. According to paragraph 105 of AASB 136/IAS 36:

> In allocating an impairment loss in accordance with paragraph 104, an entity shall not reduce the carrying amount of an asset below the highest of:
> (a) its fair value less costs of disposal (if measurable);
> (b) its value in use (if determinable); and
> (c) zero.
> The amount of impairment loss that would otherwise have been allocated to the asset shall be allocated pro rata to the other assets of the unit (group of units).

In general, the value in use for individual assets would not be known — the CGU is the smallest group of assets independently generating cash flows. Hence, the test is generally in relation to the net fair value.

If there is an amount of impairment loss allocated to an asset, but a part of it would reduce the asset below, say, its fair value less costs of disposal, then that part is allocated across the other assets in the CGU on a pro rata basis.

ILLUSTRATIVE EXAMPLE 7.6

Impairment of a CGU

The Box CGU in illustrative example 7.4 was assessed for impairment and it was determined that the unit had incurred an impairment loss of $170 000 with the first $150 000 written off against goodwill. The carrying amounts of the CGU's other assets and the allocation of the remaining $20 000 impairment loss on a proportional basis are as follows.

	Carrying amount	Proportion	Allocation of impairment loss	Net carrying amount
Buildings	$360 000	360/900	$ 8 000	$352 000
Equipment	225 000	225/900	5 000	220 000
Land	180 000	180/900	4 000	176 000
Fittings	135 000	135/900	3 000	132 000
	$900 000		$20 000	$880 000

Required

Assume the fair value less costs of disposal of the buildings was $355 000. Applying paragraph 105, this is the maximum to which this asset could be reduced. Hence, the balance of the allocated impairment loss to buildings of $3000 (i.e. $8000 [$360 000 $355 000]) has to be allocated across the other assets. Allocate the impairment loss on a proportional basis to the other assets. Prepare the journal entry to reflect the recognition of the impairment loss.

	Carrying amount	Proportion	Allocation of impairment loss	Net carrying amount
Buildings				$355 000
Equipment	$220 000	220/528	$1 250	218 750
Land	176 000	176/528	1 000	175 000
Fittings	132 000	132/528	750	131 250
	$528 000		$3 000	$880 000

The journal entry to reflect the recognition of the impairment loss is:

Impairment loss	Dr	20 000	
Accumulated depreciation and impairment losses — buildings	Cr		5 000
Accumulated depreciation and impairment losses — equipment			
[$5000 + $1250]	Cr		6 250
Accumulated impairment losses — land [$4000 + $1000]	Cr		5 000
Accumulated depreciation and impairment losses — fittings			
[$3000 + $750]	Cr		3 750

7.5.4 Corporate assets

One problem that arises when dividing an entity into separate CGUs is dealing with **corporate assets**. Corporate assets, such as the headquarters building or the information technology support centre, are integral to all CGUs generating cash flows but do not independently generate cash flows. In section 7.5.1, the example of the McCafé McDonald's restaurant was used. If such a restaurant has two CGUs, namely the coffee and pastries CGU and the hamburgers and fries CGU, then the McDonald's building is a corporate asset — it is used by both CGUs.

Paragraph 102 of AASB 136/IAS 36 describes the two steps in accounting for impairment losses where corporate assets exist. To illustrate these two steps, assume the CGU being tested for impairment is the coffee and pastries CGU within the McCafé entity.

Step 1

If any corporate assets *can* be allocated on a reasonable and consistent basis to CGUs, then this should be done. Each CGU is then, where appropriate, tested for an impairment loss. Where a loss occurs in a CGU, the loss is allocated pro rata across the assets, including the portion of the corporate asset allocated to the CGU. In the McCafé example, this procedure would occur if the carrying amount of the building could be allocated across the two CGUs.

Step 2

If any corporate assets *cannot* be allocated across the CGUs, the entity should do the following.
• Compare the carrying amount of each CGU being tested (excluding the unallocated corporate asset) with its recoverable amount and recognise any impairment loss by allocating the loss across the assets of the CGU. Using the McCafé example, this would mean testing the carrying amounts of the assets of the coffee and pastries CGU, excluding any amount for buildings, with the recoverable amount of the CGU.
• Identify the smallest CGU that includes the unit under review and to which a portion of the unallocated corporate asset can be allocated on a reasonable and consistent basis. Using the McCafé example, the smallest group of CGUs containing the unallocated building asset is the entity as a whole.
• Compare the carrying amount of the smallest group of CGUs containing the corporate asset with its recoverable amount. Any impairment loss is then allocated across the assets of this group of CGUs, including the corporate asset. Using the McCafé example, the recoverable amount of the entity as a whole is compared with the sum of the carrying amount of the building and the carrying amounts of each of the two CGUs (after any adjustment for impairment).

Illustrative example 7.7 contains an example of accounting for corporate assets. One of the corporate assets is allocated across the two CGUs, while the other corporate asset cannot be allocated across the CGUs.

Allocation of corporate assets

Elements Ltd has two CGUs, Bronze and Empire. The assets of the two units are as follows.

	Bronze CGU	Empire CGU
Plant	$500	$400
Land	300	220

The entity has two corporate assets: the headquarters building and a research centre. The headquarters is assumed to be used equally by both units. The carrying amount of the research centre cannot be allocated on a reasonable basis to the two units. The headquarters building has a carrying amount of $160. The research centre's assets consist of furniture of $40 and equipment of $30. Neither of the corporate assets produces cash flows for the entity.

The recoverable amounts of the two CGUs are as follows.

Bronze CGU	$900
Empire CGU	$665

Required

Account for the corporate assets.

Solution

The *first* step is to calculate the impairment losses for each of the CGUs. To do this, the carrying amount of the headquarters building is allocated equally between the two units as it is used equally by the CGUs. Impairment losses are then as follows.

	Bronze	Empire
Plant	$500	$400
Land	300	220
Headquarters building	80	80
Carrying amount	880	700
Recoverable amount	900	665
Impairment loss	$ 0	$ 35

The impairment loss of $35 for Empire is then allocated across all non-excluded assets in that CGU.

	Carrying amount	Proportion of loss	Loss	Adjusted carrying amount
Plant	$400	400/700	$20	$380
Land	220	220/700	11	209
Headquarters building	80	80/700	4	76
	$700		$35	$665

The *second* step is to deal with the research centre. This requires the determination of any impairment loss for the smallest CGU that includes the research centre. In this case, the smallest CGU is the entity as a whole. The impairment loss is calculated as follows.

Bronze CGU	
Plant	$ 500
Land	300
Empire CGU	
Plant	380
Land	209
Headquarters building [$80 + $76]	156
Research centre	
Furniture	40
Equipment	30
	1 615
Recoverable amount [$900 + $665]	1 565
Impairment loss	$ 50

This impairment loss is then allocated across these assets on a pro rata basis.

	Carrying amount	Proportion of loss	Loss	Adjusted carrying amount
Bronze CGU				
Plant	$ 500	500/1615	$15	$ 485
Land	300	300/1615	9	291
Empire CGU				
Plant	380	380/1615	12	368
Land	209	209/1615	7	202
Headquarters building	156	156/1615	5	151
Research centre				
Furniture	40	40/1615	1	39
Equipment	30	30/1615	1	29
	$1 615		$50	$1 565

LEARNING CHECK

☐ A CGU is the smallest identifiable group of assets that generates cash inflows that are largely independent of the cash inflows from other assets or groups of assets.
☐ AASB 136/IAS 36 provides indicators or guidelines to help determine the CGUs in an entity.
☐ For the purposes of impairment testing, goodwill is allocated to the various CGUs or groups of CGUs of an entity.
☐ In allocating impairment losses in a CGU the loss is first allocated to any goodwill.
☐ Where an impairment loss occurs in a CGU and either no goodwill exists or the goodwill has been previously written-off, the impairment loss is allocated across the carrying amounts of the remaining assets in the unit.
☐ There are restrictions on how much an individual asset in a CGU can be written down in the allocation process.
☐ Corporate assets should be allocated to CGUs if possible; otherwise they are tested within the smallest unit that contains the corporate asset.

7.6 Reversal of an impairment loss

LEARNING OBJECTIVE 7.6 Explain when an impairment loss can be reversed and how to account for it.

If an entity has written down some assets as a result of incurring an impairment loss, can the entity, in a subsequent period, reverse that loss? A reversal would allow the entity to write the assets up, and recognise the increase as income. According to paragraph 110 of AASB 136/IAS 36:

> An entity shall assess at the end of each reporting period whether there is any indication that an impairment loss recognised in prior periods for an asset other than goodwill may no longer exist or may have been decreased. If any such indication exists, the entity shall estimate the recoverable amount of that asset.

In assessing whether there is any indication of an impairment reversal, paragraph 111 of AASB 136/IAS 36 states that an entity shall consider, as a minimum, the following indications.

External sources of information
(a) there are observable indications that the asset's value has increased significantly during the period.
(b) significant changes with a favourable effect on the entity have taken place during the period, or will take place in the near future, in the technological, market, economic or legal environment in which the entity operates or in the market to which the asset is dedicated.
(c) market interest rates or other market rates of return on investments have *decreased* during the period, and those decreases are likely to affect the discount rate used in calculating the asset's value in use and increase the asset's recoverable amount materially.

Internal sources of information
(d) significant changes with a favourable effect on the entity have taken place during the period, or are expected to take place in the near future, in the extent to which, or manner in which, the asset is used or

is expected to be used. These changes include costs incurred during the period to improve or enhance the asset's performance or restructure the operation to which the asset belongs.

(e) evidence is available from internal reporting that indicates that the economic performance of the asset is, or will be, better than expected.

The procedure with a reversal is the same as for determining an impairment loss. An entity must determine by an assessment of external and internal sources of information that there is evidence to indicate the reversal of an impairment loss. The sources of information are the same as those for assessing the indication of an impairment loss except that whereas with an impairment loss the evidence suggested bad news, with a reversal the evidence shows good news.

7.6.1 Individual assets

According to paragraph 117 of AASB 136/IAS 36:

> The increased carrying amount of an asset other than goodwill attributable to a reversal of an impairment loss shall not exceed the carrying amount that would have been determined (net of amortisation or depreciation) had no impairment loss been recognised for the asset in prior years.

The reason for this restriction is the application of the historical cost model. To increase an asset above the carrying amount calculated using the historical model would effectively involve a revaluation of the asset.

According to paragraph 119 of AASB 136/IAS 36:

> A reversal of an impairment loss for an asset other than goodwill shall be recognised immediately in profit or loss, unless the asset is carried at revalued amount in accordance with another Standard (for example, the revaluation model in AASB 116 IAS 16). Any reversal of an impairment loss of a revalued asset shall be treated as a revaluation increase in accordance with that other Standard.

So, under the cost model an increase in the carrying amount of an asset is recognised immediately in profit or loss. The basic form of the journal entry, using a depreciable asset, is as follows.

Accumulated depreciation and impairment loss	Dr	xxx
Income — impairment loss reversal	Cr	xxx
(Reversal of impairment loss)		

This procedure is demonstrated in illustrative example 7.8.

Under the revaluation model, the increase is treated as a revaluation increase in accordance with AASB 116/IAS 16. In general this means the recognition of an asset revaluation surplus. If the increase reversed a previous decrease recognised in profit or loss then it would be recognised as income.

Subsequent to the recognition of a reversal, management needs to reassess the depreciation/amortisation of the asset. This involves assessment of such variables as expected future life, residual value and pattern of benefit to be received.

7.6.2 Cash-generating units

According to paragraph 122 of AASB 136/IAS 36:

> A reversal of an impairment loss for a cash-generating unit shall be allocated to the assets of the unit, except for goodwill, pro rata with the carrying amounts of those assets. These increases in carrying amounts shall be treated as reversals of impairment losses for individual assets and recognised in accordance with paragraph 119.

The accounting for the reversals for each asset is done as discussed earlier for reversals of individual assets.

According to paragraph 123 of AASB 136/IAS 36:

> In allocating a reversal of an impairment loss for a cash-generating unit in accordance with paragraph 122, the carrying amount of an asset shall not be increased above the lower of:
> (a) its recoverable amount (if determinable); and
> (b) the carrying amount that would have been determined (net of amortisation or depreciation) had no impairment loss been recognised for the asset in prior periods.

The amount of the reversal of the impairment loss that would otherwise have been allocated to the asset shall be allocated pro rata to the other assets of the unit, except for goodwill.

Paragraph 124 imposes a further restriction on reversing a previous impairment loss with a definitive statement in relation to goodwill:

An impairment loss recognised for goodwill shall not be reversed in a subsequent period.

The rationale for this is that increasing the carrying amount of goodwill would be seen as recognising internally generated goodwill, which is not allowed under AASB 138/IAS 38 *Intangible Assets*.

The procedure for reversing impairment losses in a CGU is demonstrated in illustrative example 7.8.

ILLUSTRATIVE EXAMPLE 7.8

Reversal of an impairment loss

At 30 June 2023, Owl Ltd incurred an impairment loss of $5000, of which $3000 was used to write off the goodwill and $2000 to write down the other assets. The allocation of the impairment loss to these other assets was as follows.

	Carrying amount	Proportion of loss	Impairment loss	Adjusted carrying amount
Land	$10 000	1/5	$ 400	$ 9 600
Plant	40 000	4/5	1 600	38 400
	$50 000		$2 000	

The plant had previously cost $100 000 and was being depreciated at 10% p.a. prior to 30 June 2023, requiring a depreciation charge of $10 000 p.a. Subsequent to the impairment, the asset was depreciated on a straight-line basis over 3 years, being $12 800 p.a.

At 30 June 2024 the business situation had improved and the entity believed that it should reverse past impairment losses. A comparison of the carrying amounts of the assets at 30 June 2024 and their recoverable amount revealed the following.

Land	$ 9 600
Plant [$38 400 − $12 800]	25 600
Furniture (acquired during the current period)	800
Carrying amount	36 000
Recoverable amount	38 800
Excess of recoverable amount over carrying amount	$ 2 800

Required

Reverse the impairment loss.

Solution

The excess cannot be allocated to goodwill as impairment losses on goodwill can never be reversed.

If the excess is allocated to the assets it can only be allocated to the assets *existing at the previous impairment write-down* as assets cannot be written up above their original cost. The excess of recoverable amount is then allocated to the relevant assets on a pro rata basis.

	Carrying amount	Share of reversal	Adjusted carrying amount
Land	$ 9 600	$ 764	$10 364
Plant	25 600	2 036	27 636
	$35 200	$2 800	$38 000

These assets cannot be written up above the amounts that they would have been recorded at if there had been no previous impairment. These amounts would be as follows.

Land	$10 000	
Plant	$30 000	[$40 000 less $10 000 depreciation for the 2023–24 year]

Writing plant up to $27 636 does not exceed the maximum write-up amount of $30 000. However, the land cannot be written up above $10 000. This means that $364 of the $764 that was allocated to the land must be reallocated to the plant. This increases the carrying amount of the plant to $28 000 (being $27 636 + $364). This is still less than the maximum of $30 000.

The journal entry to record the reversal of the impairment loss is as follows.

Accumulated impairment losses — land	Dr	400	
Accumulated depreciation and impairment loss — plant	Dr	2 400	
Income — impairment loss reversal	Cr		2 800
(Reversal of impairment loss)			

If the allocation of the excess of recoverable amount over carrying amount exceeded the maximum write-up amounts, then not all the excess would be recognised as income.

LEARNING CHECK

- ☐ Impairment losses from prior periods may be reversed.
- ☐ The assessment of possible reversal is based on an analysis of external and internal indicators.
- ☐ For an individual asset, a reversal of an impairment loss will result in an entity recognising income, depending on the measurement model being used.
- ☐ Impairment losses for goodwill cannot be reversed.
- ☐ AASB 136/IAS 36 restricts the amount by which impairment losses for other assets can be reversed, in particular requiring that the new carrying amount after the reversal cannot exceed the recoverable amount or the carrying amount that would have been determined had no impairment loss been recognised for the asset in previous periods.

7.7 Disclosure

LEARNING OBJECTIVE 7.7 Identify the disclosures required in relation to impairment of assets.

Paragraph 126 of AASB 136/IAS 36 requires that:

An entity shall disclose the following for each class of assets:
(a) the amount of impairment losses recognised in profit or loss during the period and the line item(s) of the statement of comprehensive income in which those impairment losses are included.
(b) the amount of reversals of impairment losses recognised in profit or loss during the period and the line item(s) of the statement of comprehensive income in which those impairment losses are reversed.
(c) the amount of impairment losses on revalued assets recognised in other comprehensive income during the period.
(d) the amount of reversals of impairment losses on revalued assets recognised in other comprehensive income during the period.

Paragraph 130 of AASB 136/IAS 36 requires that for each material impairment loss recognised or reversed during the period for an individual asset, including goodwill, or a CGU, an entity must also disclose:
- the events and circumstances that led to the recognition or reversal of the impairment loss
- the amount of any impairment loss recognised or reversed
- for an individual asset: the nature of the asset
- for a CGU:
  - a description of the CGU (e.g. a business operation or geographical area)
  - the amount of the impairment loss recognised or reversed by class of assets
- whether the recoverable amount of asset or CGU is its fair value less costs of disposal or its value in use

- if recoverable amount is fair value less costs of disposal, the basis of the measurement
- if recoverable amount is value in use, the discount rates used.

Paragraphs 134 and 135 of AASB 136/IAS 36 specify detailed disclosure requirements in relation to the estimates used to measure recoverable amounts of CGUs containing goodwill and other intangible assets with indefinite lives. These details include:

- carrying amounts of such assets
- the basis for determining recoverable amount (i.e. value in use or fair value less costs of disposal)
- a description of key assumptions and approaches used in estimating value in use and fair value less costs of disposal (e.g. projected growth rates, discount rates and time periods used).

Figure 7.7 is an extract from Santos Limited's 2017 annual report, disclosing details of its $703 million impairment charge during the reporting period.

| **FIGURE 7.7** | Disclosures relating to impairment charges, Santos Limited |

Notes to the consolidated financial statements

Section 3: Capital expenditure, operating assets and restoration obligations

3.3 IMPAIRMENT OF NON-CURRENT ASSETS

The carrying amounts of the Group's oil and gas assets are reviewed at each reporting date to determine whether there is any indication of impairment. Where an indicator of impairment exists, a formal estimate of the recoverable amount is made.

Indicators of impairment — exploration and evaluation assets

The carrying amounts of the Group's exploration and evaluation assets are reviewed at each reporting date, to determine whether any of the following indicators of impairment exists:

- tenure over the licence area has expired during the period or will expire in the near future, and is not expected to be renewed; or
- substantive expenditure on further exploration for, and evaluation of, mineral resources in the specific area is not budgeted or planned; or
- exploration for, and evaluation of, resources in the specific area have not led to the discovery of commercially viable quantities of resources, and the Group has decided to discontinue activities in the specific area; or
- sufficient data exists to indicate that although a development is likely to proceed, the carrying amount of the exploration and evaluation asset is unlikely to be recovered in full from successful development or from sale.

Cash generating units — oil and gas assets

Oil and gas assets, land, buildings, plant and equipment are assessed for impairment on a cash-generating unit ('CGU') basis. A CGU is the smallest grouping of assets that generates independent cash inflows, and generally represents an individual oil or gas field, or oil and gas fields, that are being produced through a common facility. Impairment losses recognised in respect of CGUs are allocated to reduce the carrying amount of the assets in the CGU on a pro-rata basis.

Individual assets within a CGU may become impaired if their ongoing use changes or if the benefits to be obtained from ongoing use are likely to be less than the carrying value of the individual asset. An impairment loss is recognised in the income statement whenever the carrying amount of an asset or its CGU exceeds its recoverable amount.

Recoverable amount

The recoverable amount of an asset is the greater of its fair value less costs of disposal ('FVLCD') (based on level 3 fair value hierarchy) and its value-in-use ('VIU'), using an asset's estimated future cash flows (as described below) discounted to their present value using a pre-tax discount rate that reflects current market assessments of the time value of money and the risks specific to the asset.

Significant judgement — Impairment of oil and gas assets

For oil and gas assets, the expected future cash flow estimation is based on a number of factors, variables and assumptions, the most important of which are estimates of reserves, future production profiles, commodity prices, costs and foreign exchange rates. In most cases, the present value of future cash flows is most sensitive to estimates of future oil price and discount rates.

The estimated future cash flows for the VIU calculation are based on estimates, the most significant of which are hydrocarbon reserves, future production profiles, commodity prices, operating costs including third-party gas purchases and any future development costs necessary to produce the reserves. Under a FVLCD calculation, future cash flows are based on estimates of hydrocarbon reserves in addition to other

▸

relevant factors such as value attributable to additional resource and exploration opportunities beyond reserves based on production plans.

Estimates of future commodity prices are based on the Group's best estimate of future market prices with reference to external market analysts' forecasts, current spot prices and forward curves. Future commodity prices are reviewed at least annually. Where volumes are contracted, future prices are based on the contracted price.

Future prices (US$/bbl) used were:

2018	2019	2020	2021	2022[1]	2023[1]
55.00	60.00	65.00	70.00	77.29	78.83

1. Based on US$70/bbl (2017 real) from 2022 escalated at 2.0% p.a.

Forecasts of the foreign exchange rate for foreign currencies, where relevant, are estimated with reference to observable external market data and forward values, including analysis of broker and consensus estimates. The future estimated rate applied is A$1/US$0.75.

The discount rates applied to the future forecast cash flows are based on the weighted average cost of capital, adjusted for risks where appropriate, including functional currency of the asset, and risk profile of the countries in which the asset operates. The range of pre-tax discount rates that have been applied to non-current assets is between 11% and 14%.

In the event that future circumstances vary from these assumptions, the recoverable amount of the Group's oil and gas assets could change materially and result in impairment losses or the reversal of previous impairment losses.

Due to the interrelated nature of the assumptions, movements in any one variable can have an indirect impact on others and individual variables rarely change in isolation. Additionally, management can be expected to respond to some movements, to mitigate downsides and take advantage of upsides, as circumstances allow. Consequently, it is impracticable to estimate the indirect impact that a change in one assumption has on other variables and hence, on the likelihood, or extent, of impairments, or reversals of impairments under different sets of assumptions in subsequent reporting periods.

Impairment expense	2017 US$m	2016 US$m
Current assets		
Assets held for sale	–	4
Other receivables	5	–
Total impairment of current assets	5	4
Non-current assets		
Exploration and evaluation assets	163	59
Oil and gas assets	765	1 489
Land and buildings	5	9
Total impairment of non-current assets	933	1 557
Total impairment	**938**	**1 561**

Recoverable amounts and resulting impairment write-downs/(reversals) recognised in the year ended 31 December 2017 are:

2017	Segment	Subsurface assets $m	Plant and equipment $m	Total $m	Recoverable amount[1] $m
Exploration and evaluation assets:					
Ande Ande Lumut – Indonesia	Other	149	–	149	Nil[2]
Gunnedah Basin	Other	10	–	10	Nil[2]
Papua New Guinea – PPL 287	Exploration	4	–	4	Nil[2]
Total impairment of exploration and evaluation assets		163	–	163	
Oil and gas assets – producing:					
GLNG	Queensland	–	1 238	1 238	4 099
Barrow	Other	–	6	6	Nil
Cooper – unconventional resources[3]	Cooper Basin	1	–	1	Nil

Cooper Basin	Cooper Basin	(256)	(224)	(480)	1 388
Total impairment of oil and gas assets		(255)	1 020	765	
Total impairment of exploration and evaluation and oil and gas assets		**(92)**	**1 020**	**928**	

1. Recoverable amounts represent the carrying values of assets before deducting the carrying value of restoration liabilities. All producing oil and gas asset amounts are calculated using the VIU method, whilst all exploration and evaluation asset amounts use the FVLCD method.
2. Impairment of exploration and evaluation assets relates to certain individual licences/areas of interest that have been impaired to nil.
3. Cooper — unconventional resources comprises exploration and evaluation expenditure pending commercialisation within oil and gas assets, producing assets. The impairment in the current year relates to Paragoona-ATP 820P.

Exploration and evaluation assets
The impairment of Ande Ande Lumut has arisen mainly from the impact of lower oil prices.

Oil and gas assets

GLNG
The impairment of GLNG has arisen mainly due to a reduction in the US$ oil price assumption, combined with a higher discount rate and lower assumed volumes of third-party gas, partially offset by higher assumed equity gas volumes resulting from positive upstream performance and lower costs.

Cooper Basin
Whilst the Cooper Basin has been impacted by lower US$ oil price assumptions, this has been more than offset by lower forecast development and operating costs, combined with increased drilling activity and production, resulting in a reversal of impairment.

Sensitivity analysis
To the extent the CGUs have been written down to their respective recoverable amounts in the current and prior years, any change in key assumptions on which the valuations are based would further impact asset carrying values. When modelled in isolation, it is estimated that changes in the key assumptions would result in the following additional impairments/lower impairment reversals in 2017 for the GLNG and Cooper Basin CGUs, respectively:

Sensitivity	Production decrease 5% US$m	Discount rate increase 0.50% US$m	Oil price decrease US$5/bbl all years US$m
GLNG	271	219	566
Cooper Basin	222	85	262

As identified above, the impact of changes in key assumptions such as reserves, production levels, commodity prices and discount rates are significant on the determination of recoverable amount. Due to the number of factors that could impact any of these assumptions, as well as any actions taken to respond to adverse changes, actual future determinations of recoverable amount may vary from those stated above.

Source: Santos Limited (2017, pp. 78–81).

LEARNING CHECK

☐ AASB 136/IAS 36 requires extensive disclosures regarding impairment of assets.
☐ Impairment losses and reversals of impairment losses must be separately disclosed for each class of asset.
☐ Any material impairment losses and reversals of impairment losses must be disclosed for any individual asset, including goodwill, or a CGU as well as details of the events and circumstances leading to these.
☐ Because of the judgements required in measuring variables such as value in use, AASB 136/IAS 36 requires disclosures about estimates and judgements made in the impairment testing process.

SUMMARY

The key principles of accounting for impairment of assets contained in AASB 136/IAS 36 *Impairment of Assets* are as follows.

- The purpose of the impairment test is to ensure that the carrying amounts of assets are recoverable; that is, assets are not overstated.
- For an entity to conduct an impairment test there must be indications of impairment determined by analysing various internal and external sources of information.
- The impairment test involves comparing the carrying amounts of assets with their recoverable amounts, the latter determined as the higher of fair value less costs of disposal and value in use.
- Impairment tests may be conducted on separate assets with impairment losses being recognised immediately in profit or loss.
- As many assets do not independently produce cash flows, the impairment test may be conducted on a group of assets, known as a CGU.
- Where a CGU incurs an impairment loss, the loss is written off against any recorded goodwill, and any balance then allocated on a pro rata basis across the assets of the CGU.
- Where improvements occur in the recoverable amounts of assets, impairment losses may be reversed, except in the case of goodwill.

KEY TERMS

amortisation The systematic allocation of the depreciable amount of an intangible asset over its useful life.

carrying amount The amount at which an asset or liability is recognised after deducting any accumulated depreciation (amortisation), accumulated impairment losses and allowances thereon.

cash-generating unit The smallest identifiable group of assets that generates cash inflows that are largely independent of the cash inflows from other assets or groups of assets.

corporate assets Assets other than goodwill that contribute to the future cash flows of both the CGU under review and other CGUs.

costs of disposal Incremental costs directly attributable to the disposal of an asset or cash-generating unit, excluding finance costs and income tax expense.

depreciation The systematic allocation of the depreciable amount of an asset over its useful life.

fair value The price that would be received to sell an asset or paid to transfer a liability in an orderly transaction between market participants at the measurement date.

impairment loss The amount by which the carrying amount of an asset or a cash-generating unit exceeds its recoverable amount.

recoverable amount The higher of an asset's fair value less costs of disposal and its value in use.

useful life The period over which an asset is expected to be available for use by an entity; or the number of production or similar units expected to be obtained from the asset by an entity.

value in use The present value of the future cash flows expected to be derived from an asset or cash-generating unit.

DEMONSTRATION PROBLEMS

7.1 Impairment losses, no corporate assets

Sarah Ltd has two divisions, Arena and Gibbs, each of which is a separate CGU. Sarah Ltd adopts a decentralised management approach and unit managers are expected to operate their units. However, one corporate asset — the information technology network — is centrally controlled and provides a computer network to the company as a whole. The information technology network is not a depreciable asset.

At 30 June 2023 the net assets of each division, including its allocated share of the information technology network, were as follows.

	Arena	Gibbs
Information technology (IT) network	$ 284 000	$ 116 000
Land	450 000	290 000
Plant (20% p.a. straight-line depreciation)	1 310 000	960 000
Accumulated depreciation (plant)	(917 000)	(384 000)
Goodwill	46 000	32 000
Patent (10% straight-line amortisation)	210 000	255 000
Accumulated amortisation (patent)	(21 000)	(102 000)
Cash	20 000	12 000
Inventories	120 000	80 000
Receivables	34 000	40 000
	1 536 000	1 299 000
Liabilities	(276 000)	(189 000)
Net assets	$1 260 000	$1 110 000

Additional information as at 30 June 2023
- Arena's land had a fair value less costs of disposal of $437 000.
- Gibbs' patent had a carrying amount below fair value less costs of disposal.
- Gibbs' plant had a fair value less costs of disposal of $540 000.
- Receivables were considered to be collectable.

Required

Sarah Ltd's management undertook impairment testing at 30 June 2023 and determined the recoverable amount of each CGU to be: $1 430 000 for Arena and $1 215 000 for Gibbs. Prepare any journal entries necessary to record the results of the impairment testing for each of the CGUs.

SOLUTION

Step 1

Determine whether either CGU has an impairment loss. This is done by comparing the carrying amount of the assets of each CGU with the recoverable amount of these assets. Note that it is the carrying amount of the assets, not the net assets, that is used — the test is for the impairment of assets, not net assets.

	Arena	Gibbs
Carrying amount of assets	$1 536 000	$1 299 000
Recoverable amount	1 430 000	1 215 000
Impairment loss	$ (106 000)	$ (84 000)

As a result of the comparison, both CGUs have suffered impairment losses.

Step 2

For each CGU, the impairment loss is used to write off any goodwill and then to allocate any balance across the other assets in proportion to their carrying amounts.

Arena CGU

Arena has goodwill of $46 000. Therefore, the first step is to write off goodwill of $46 000. The second step is to allocate the remaining impairment loss of $60 000 (i.e. $106 000 – $46 000).

Note that although all the assets are included in the calculation to determine whether the CGU has incurred an impairment loss, the allocation of that loss is only to those assets that will be written down as a result of the allocation process. Cash and receivables are not written down as they are recorded at amounts equal to fair value. The inventories are recorded under AASB 102/IAS 2 at the lower of cost and net realisable value and, as such, are excluded from the impairment test write-down under AASB 136/IAS 36. The allocation of the balance of the impairment loss is done on a pro rata basis, in proportion to the assets' carrying amounts.

	Carrying amount	Proportion	Allocation of loss	Adjusted carrying amount
IT network	$ 284 000	284/1 316	$12 948	$271 052
Land	450 000	450/1 316	20 517	429 483
Plant	393 000	393/1 316	17 918	375 082
Patent	189 000	189/1 316	8 617	180 383
	$1 316 000		$60 000	

After the initial allocation across the assets, a check has to be made on the amount of each write-down, as AASB 136/IAS 36 (paragraph 105) places limitations on the amount to which assets can be written down. For each asset the carrying amount should not be reduced below the highest of:

- its fair value less costs of disposal
- its value in use
- zero.

In this example, the land has a fair value less costs of disposal of $437 000. Hence, it cannot be written down to $429 483 as per the above allocation table. Only $13 000 (to write the asset down from $450 000 to $437 000) of the impairment loss can be allocated to it. Therefore, the remaining $7517 allocated loss (i.e. $20 517 – $13 000) must be allocated to the other assets. This allocation is based on the adjusted carrying amounts, which are shown in the right-hand column of the previous table.

	Carrying amount	Proportion	Allocation of loss	Adjusted carrying amount
IT network	$271 052	271 052/826 517	$2 465	$268 587
Plant	375 082	375 082/826 517	3 411	371 671
Patent	180 383	180 383/826 517	1 641	178 742
	$826 517		$7 517	

The impairment loss for each asset is then based, where relevant, on the accumulation of both allocations. The subsequent write-downs are accounted for by increasing the respective contra-asset amounts of each asset.

The journal entry for Arena is as follows.

Impairment loss	Dr	106 000	
Accumulated impairment losses — goodwill	Cr		46 000
Accumulated impairment losses — land	Cr		13 000
Accumulated depreciation and impairment losses — IT network [$12 948 + $2465]	Cr		15 413
Accumulated depreciation and impairment losses — plant [$17 918 + $3411]	Cr		21 329
Accumulated amortisation and impairment losses — patent [$8617 + $1641]	Cr		10 258

Gibbs CGU

As with the Arena CGU, the impairment loss is used to write off the goodwill balance, $32 000, and then the balance of the impairment loss, $52 000 (i.e. $84 000 – $32 000), is allocated across the remaining assets, except for cash, receivables and inventories. Further, no impairment loss can be allocated to the patent, as its carrying amount is below fair value less costs of disposal.

	Carrying amount	Proportion	Allocation of loss	Adjusted carrying amount
IT network	$116 000	116/982	$ 6 143	$109 857
Land	290 000	290/982	15 356	274 644
Plant	576 000	576/982	30 501	545 499
	$982 000		$ 52 000	

Because the plant has a fair value less costs of disposal of $540 000 and this is below the adjusted carrying amount of $545 499, the full impairment loss of $30 501 can be allocated to it.

The journal entry for Gibbs is as follows.

Impairment loss	Dr	84 000	
Accumulated impairment losses — goodwill	Cr		32 000
Accumulated depreciation and impairment losses — IT network	Cr		6 143
Accumulated impairment losses — land	Cr		15 356
Accumulated depreciation and impairment losses — plant	Cr		30 501

7.2 Impairment losses, corporate asset

Skaro Ltd has three CGUs, a head office and a research facility. The carrying amounts of the assets and their recoverable amounts are as follows.

	Unit A	Unit B	Unit C	Head office	Research facility	Skaro Ltd
Carrying amount	$100	$150	$200	$150	$50	$650
Recoverable amount	129	164	271			584

The assets of the head office are allocable to the three units as follows.
- Unit A: $19
- Unit B: $56
- Unit C: $75

The assets of the research facility cannot be reasonably allocated to the CGUs.

Required

Assuming all assets can be adjusted for impairment, prepare the journal entry relating to any impairment of the assets of Skaro Ltd.

SOLUTION

For each CGU, a comparison is required between the carrying amounts and recoverable amounts of the assets of the CGU to determine which, if any, of the CGUs is impaired. As the asset of the head office can be allocated to each of the units, the carrying amounts of each of the CGUs must then include the allocated part of the head office.

Calculation of impairment losses for CGUs

	Unit A	Unit B	Unit C
Carrying amount	$119	$206	$275
Recoverable amount	129	164	271
Impairment loss	$ 0	$ 42	$ 4

Because the assets of Unit A are not impaired, no write-down is necessary. For Units B and C, the impairment losses must be allocated to the assets of the units. The allocation is in proportion to the carrying amounts of the assets.

Allocation of impairment loss

	Unit B		Unit C	
To head office	$11	[42 × 56/206]	$1	[4 × 75/275]
To other assets	31	[42 × 150/206]	3	[4 × 200/275]
	$42		$4	

In relation to the research centre, the assets of the centre cannot be allocated to the units, so the impairment test is based on the smallest CGU that contains the research centre, which in this case is the entity as a whole, Skaro Ltd. For this calculation, the carrying amounts of the assets of the units as well as the head office are reduced by the impairment losses already allocated. The total assets of Skaro Ltd consist of all the assets of the entity.

Impairment testing for Skaro Ltd as a whole

	Unit A	Unit B	Unit C	Head office	Research centre	Skaro Ltd
Carrying amount	$100	$150	$200	$150	$50	$650
Impairment loss	—	31	3	12	—	46
Net	$100	$119	$197	$138	$50	604
Recoverable amount						584
Impairment loss						$ 20

Because the recoverable amount of the entity is less than the carrying amount of the assets of Skaro Ltd, the entity has incurred an impairment loss. This loss is allocated across all the assets of the entity in proportion to their carrying amounts.

Allocation of impairment loss

	Carrying amount	Proportion	Allocation of loss	Adjusted carrying amount
Unit A	$100	100/604 × 20	$ 3	$ 97
Unit B	119	119/604 × 20	4	115
Unit C	197	197/604 × 20	6	191
Head office	138	138/604 × 20	5	133
Research centre	50	50/604 × 20	2	48
	$604		$20	$584

Journal entry for impairment loss

The journal entry for the impairment loss recognises the reduction in each of the assets. As the composition of the assets is not detailed in this question, the credit adjustments are made against the aggregated asset accounts. They could also have been made against an accumulated depreciation and impairment losses account. If the composition of each of the assets of each unit had been given, the impairment loss would have been allocated to specific assets rather than assets as a total category as in the solution here.

Impairment loss	Dr	66	
Assets — Unit A	Cr		3
Assets — Unit B ($31 + $4)	Cr		35
Assets — Unit C ($3 + $6)	Cr		9
Assets — Head office ($12 + $5)	Cr		17
Assets — Research facility	Cr		2

COMPREHENSION QUESTIONS

1 What is an impairment test?

2 Why is an impairment test considered necessary?

3 When should an entity conduct an impairment test?

4 What are some external indicators of impairment?

5 What are some internal indicators of impairment?

6 What is meant by recoverable amount?

7 How is an impairment loss calculated in relation to a single asset accounted for?

8 What are the limits to which an asset can be written down in relation to impairment losses?

9 What is a cash-generating unit (CGU)?

10 How are impairment losses accounted for in relation to cash-generating units?

11 Are there limits in adjusting assets within a cash-generating unit when impairment losses occur?

12 How is goodwill tested for impairment?

13 What is a corporate asset?

14 How are corporate assets tested for impairment?

15 When can an entity reverse past impairment losses?

16 What are the steps involved in reversing an impairment loss?

CASE STUDY 7.1

INDICATIONS AND DETERMINATION OF IMPAIRMENT LOSSES

BHP Billiton (now known as BHP Group) released the following announcement to investors and media on 15 January 2016.

Onshore US asset review

BHP Billiton expects to recognise an impairment charge of approximately US$4.9 billion post-tax (or approximately US$7.2 billion pre-tax) against the carrying value of its Onshore US assets. This charge will be recognised as an exceptional item in the financial results for the half year ended 31 December 2015.

The impairment follows the bi-annual review of the Company's asset values and reflects changes to price assumptions, discount rates and development plans which have more than offset substantial productivity improvements. The impairment will reduce Onshore US net operating assets to approximately US$16 billion.[1]

The oil and gas industry has recently experienced significant volatility and much weaker prices.

The US gas price remains low as industry-wide productivity improvements have resulted in higher than expected supply at lower cost. BHP Billiton has previously suspended development of its dry gas acreage. The Company has now also reduced its medium and long-term gas price assumptions.

In addition, the oil price has fallen by more than 30 per cent over the last three months following the disruption of OPEC and stronger than anticipated non-OPEC production. Although we expect prices to improve from their current lows, we have reduced our oil price assumptions for the short to medium term. Our long-term price assumptions continue to reflect the market's attractive supply and demand fundamentals.

The increased volatility in prices has also increased the discount rates applied by BHP Billiton, which has a significant flow through impact on the Company's assessment of its Onshore US asset value.

The Group will reduce the number of operated rigs in its Onshore US business from seven to five in the March 2016 quarter. This will comprise three rigs in the Black Hawk and two rigs in the Permian. Beyond this, investment and development plans for the remainder of the 2016 financial year are under review, with a focus on preserving cash flow.

BHP Billiton Chief Executive Officer, Andrew Mackenzie, said 'Oil and gas markets have been significantly weaker than the industry expected. We responded quickly by dramatically cutting our operating and capital costs, and reducing the number of operated rigs in the Onshore US business from 26 a year ago to five by the end of the current quarter.

'While we have made significant progress, the dramatic fall in prices has led to the disappointing write down announced today. However, we remain confident in the long-term outlook and the quality of our acreage. We are well positioned to respond to a recovery.'

The broader carrying value assessment of the Group's assets will be finalised in conjunction with the interim financial results to be released on 23 February 2016.

1. This excludes a deferred tax liability of approximately US$4 billion.

Source: BHP Group (2016).

Required

1. Describe the process undertaken by BHP Group in determining:
   (a) its assets may have been impaired
   (b) the value of the impairment losses.
2. In percentage terms, what was the extent of BHP Group's impairment charge against its Onshore US assets?
3. Explain the impact of an impairment loss on a company's gearing ratio.

CASE STUDY 7.2

DETERMINATION OF CGUs

The Scenic City Council contracts out the bus routes in and around Scenic City to various subcontractors based on a tender arrangement. Some routes, such as the Express to City routes, are quite profitable, while others, such as those transporting schoolchildren to and from school in the more remote areas, are unprofitable or only barely profitable. As a result, to ensure the unprofitable and less profitable routes are serviced, the council requires tenderers to take a package of routes, some profitable, some less so.

The Saferide Bus Company has won a contract to provide bus services to the Scenic City Council. The contract to operate its buses involves a package of five separate routes, one of which operates at a significant loss. Specific buses are allocated by the Saferide Bus Company to each route, and cash flows can be isolated to each route because drivers and takings are specific to each route.

Required

Based on the information given above, write a report to the accountant of Saferide Bus Company which includes the following information.

1. An explanation of why impairment testing may require the use of CGUs, rather than being based on a single asset.
2. An explanation of the factors that should be considered in determining a CGU for Saferide Bus Company.
3. Your determination as to the identification of CGUs for the Saferide Bus Company.

CASE STUDY 7.3

GOODWILL WRITE-OFFS

Gu and Lev (2011) argue that the root cause of many goodwill write-offs is that the shares of the *buyer* are overpriced at the acquisition date.

Figure 7.8 presents eBay's cumulative stock return against the S&P 500 index from 2003. In mid-September 2005, eBay acquired the internet phone company Skype for $2.6 billion. On 1 October 2007, it announced a massive goodwill write-off of $1.43 billion (55% of the acquisition price) related to the Skype acquisition.

Gu and Lev argue that the root cause of this behaviour is the incentives of managers of overvalued firms to acquire businesses, whether to exploit the overpricing for shareholders' benefit or to justify and prolong the overpricing to maintain a facade of growth. Goodwill write-offs are accordingly an important business event signalling a flawed investment strategy.

| **FIGURE 7.8** | eBay vs S&P 500: The Skype acquisition — cumulative stock returns |

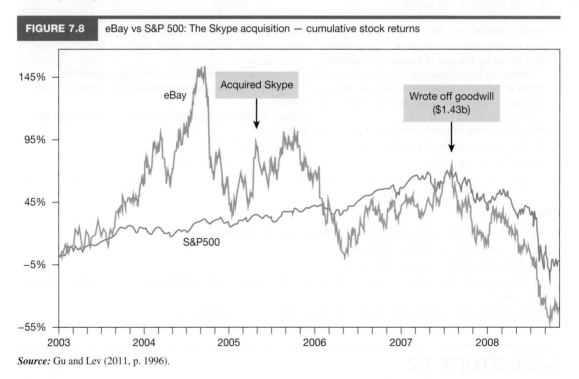

Source: Gu and Lev (2011, p. 1996).

Required

1. Explain the circumstances under which goodwill is recognised and how any subsequent write-off occurs.
2. Explain why a significant goodwill write-off may signal a 'flawed investment strategy'.

CASE STUDY 7.4

IMPAIRMENT UNDER THE REVALUATION MODEL

'Impairment is only relevant to assets carried under the cost model. For assets carried under the revaluation model, such as our land and buildings, increases and decreases in fair value dictate whether carrying amounts are adjusted up or down. We don't bother testing land and buildings for impairment.'

Required

Critically evaluate the above statement.

CASE STUDY 7.5

IMPACT OF IMPAIRMENT LOSSES

On 28 August 2014, Qantas announced an annual statutory loss after tax of $2.8 billion for the 12 months ended 30 June. This result included a massive $2.6 billion write-down of its international aircraft fleet. These losses were the largest in the airline's history and were seen to represent 'one of the biggest clearing of the decks in corporate history' (Bartholomeusz 2014).

In the media release announcing the loss, Qantas CEO Alan Joyce was quoted: 'There is no doubt today's numbers are confronting', yet he remained remarkably optimistic about the future, going on to say 'We expect a rapid improvement in the Group's financial performance — and a return to Underlying PBT profit in the first half of FY15' (Qantas Group 2014).

Required

1. Explain how such a massive impairment loss could be linked to any improved future performance.
2. Review the 2015 and 2016 annual reports of Qantas to determine if Alan Joyce's optimism was justified.

APPLICATION AND ANALYSIS EXERCISES

★ BASIC | ★ ★ MODERATE | ★ ★ ★ DIFFICULT

7.1 Determining recoverable amount and impairment adjustments ★   **LO3, 4**

Consider the following information relating to five different items of plant and equipment at the reporting date.

Asset	Carrying amount $	Fair value $	Costs of disposal $	Value in use $
A	200 000	210 000	6 000	220 000
B	100 000	90 000	2 000	96 000
C	160 000	170 000	4 000	164 000
D	400 000	380 000	10 000	440 000
E	240 000	240 000	6 000	230 000

Required

1. Calculate the recoverable amount for each of the five items of plant and equipment.
2. Assuming plant and equipment is carried under the cost model, determine the amount of any impairment adjustment necessary.
3. Assuming plant and equipment is carried under the revaluation model, determine the amount of any revaluation adjustment necessary.

7.2 Impairment of an individual asset ★   **LO3, 4**

On 1 April 2021 the construction of a fixed oil platform is completed and ready for use at a total cost of $500 million. The useful life of the rig is linked to the 25-year exploration rights granted to the company. Due to the specific nature of the platform it is deemed to have no realisable value (other than minimal scrap value) at any stage throughout its life. All impairment tests are therefore based on value-in-use estimations.

On 30 June 2023 a rapid and significant decline in world oil prices has provided an indication that the asset may be impaired. On this date, the rig's value in use is estimated to be $414 million.

On 30 June 2024 a major contract was cancelled after one of the company's customers was declared bankrupt. This led directors to believe the value in use of the rig was now $374 million.

Required

Prepare the necessary journal entries to record adjustments for impairment on 30 June 2023 and 30 June 2024.

7.3 Impairment of an individual asset, calculating value-in-use ★   **LO3, 4**

Flash Ltd acquired a machine for $125 000 on 1 July 2022. It depreciated the asset at 10% p.a. on a straight-line basis. On 30 June 2024, Flash Ltd conducted an impairment test on the asset. It determined that the asset could be sold to other entities for $77 000 with costs of disposal of $1000. Management expect to use the machine for the next 4 years with expected cash flows from use of the machine being as follows.

2024	$84 000
2025	30 000
2026	25 000
2027	20 000

The rate of return expected by the market on this machine is 8%.

Required

Assess whether the machine is impaired. If necessary, provide the appropriate journal entry to recognise any impairment loss.

7.4 Impairment of an individual asset ★   **LO3, 4**

On 1 July 2023 an item of equipment is acquired at a cost of $3 million. The asset is to be depreciated using the straight-line method on the basis of an estimated useful life of 15 years and a negligible residual value.

On 30 June 2026 it is determined that the asset has a value in use of $2 million and a fair value of $1.8 million before costs of disposal of $50 000. The remaining useful life of the asset is reassessed to be 8 years.

On 30 June 2028 it is determined that the asset has a value in use of $1.2 million and a fair value of $1.1 million before costs of disposal of $50 000. The remaining useful life of the asset is reassessed to be 5 years.

Required

Prepare the journal entries for any depreciation and impairment adjustments on the following dates.
1. 30 June 2026
2. 30 June 2028
3. 30 June 2029

7.5 Impairment loss of an individual asset incorporating revaluation model ★   **LO3, 4**

At 30 June 2023, Harrod Ltd holds a block of land from which it generates revenue through leasing to agricultural enterprises. The land has a carrying amount of $2.5 million. An independent market appraisal has valued the land at $2.36 million but costs to dispose of the land are estimated at $100 000. The value in use of land is determined to be $2.33 million.

Required

1. Determine the recoverable amount of the land.
2. Prepare the appropriate journal entry to record any impairment loss that should be recognised.

Suppose now that this same block of land was carried under the revaluation model.

3. Prepare the journal entry to record any necessary adjustment assuming there had been no prior revaluations.
4. Prepare the journal entry to record any necessary adjustment assuming there had been a prior revaluation increase of $200 000.
5. Prepare the journal entry to record any necessary adjustment assuming there had been a prior revaluation increase of $120 000.

7.6 Impairment of a CGU ★ ★ LO5

Robin Ltd reported the following information in its statement of financial position at 30 June 2022.

Plant	$325 000
Accumulated depreciation — plant	(75 000)
Intangible assets	150 000
Accumulated amortisation	(50 000)
Land	150 000
Total non-current assets	500 000
Cash	25 000
Inventories	90 000
Total current assets	115 000
Total assets	615 000
Liabilities	74 000
Net assets	**$540 000**

At 30 June 2022, Robin Ltd analysed the internal and external sources of information that would indicate deterioration in the worth of its assets. It determined that there were indications of impairment.

Robin Ltd calculated the recoverable amount of the assets to be $490 000.

Required

Provide the journal entry for any impairment loss at 30 June 2022.

7.7 Impairment of a CGU ★ ★ LO5

Rainier Ltd reported the following assets in its statement of financial position at 30 June 2022.

Plant	$ 800 000
Accumulated depreciation	(240 000)
Land	300 000
Patent	240 000
Office equipment	620 000
Accumulated depreciation	(340 000)
Inventories	220 000
Cash and cash equivalents	180 000
	$1 780 000

The recoverable amount of the entity was calculated to be $1 660 000. The fair value less costs of disposal of the land was $280 913.

Required

Prepare the journal entry for any impairment loss at 30 June 2022.

7.8 Impairment of a CGU, goodwill ★ ★ LO5

Crossbow Ltd manufactures leather footwear for women. It has undertaken a strategy of buying out companies that had competing products. These companies were liquidated and the assets and liabilities brought into Crossbow Ltd.

At 30 June 2022, Crossbow Ltd reported the following assets in its statement of financial position.

Cash	$ 40 000
Leather and other inventories	360 000
Brand 'Crossbow Shoes'	320 000
Shoe factory at cost	1 640 000
Accumulated depreciation — factory	(240 000)
Machinery for manufacturing shoes	1 280 000
Accumulated depreciation — machinery	(480 000)
Goodwill on acquisition of competing companies	80 000
	$3 000 000

In response to competition from overseas, as customers increasingly buy online rather than visit Crossbow Ltd's stores, Crossbow Ltd assessed its impairment position at 30 June 2022. The indicators suggested that an impairment loss was probable. Crossbow Ltd calculated a recoverable amount of its company of $2 840 000.

Required

Prepare the journal entry(ies) for any impairment loss occurring at 30 June 2022.

7.9 Reversal of impairment losses ★ ★ ★

LO5

At 30 June 2022, Boxes Ltd reported the following assets.

Land	$ 50 000
Plant	250 000
Accumulated depreciation	(50 000)
Goodwill	8 000
Inventories	40 000
Cash	2 000

All assets are measured using the cost model.

At 30 June 2022, the recoverable amount of the entity, considered to be a single CGU, was $272 000.

For the period ending 30 June 2023, the depreciation charge on plant was $18 400. If the plant had not been impaired the charge would have been $25 000.

At 30 June 2023, the recoverable amount of the entity was calculated to be $13 000 greater than the carrying amount of the assets of the entity. As a result, Boxes Ltd recognised a reversal of the previous year's impairment loss.

Required

Prepare the journal entries relating to impairment at 30 June 2022 and 2023.

7.10 Impairment of a CGU ★ ★

LO5

Mitch Ltd has determined that its fine china division is a CGU. The carrying amounts of the assets at 30 June 2022 are as follows.

Factory	$210 000
Land	150 000
Equipment	120 000
Inventories	60 000

Mitch Ltd calculated the recoverable amount of the division to be $510 000.

Required

Provide the necessary journal entries for the impairment loss.

7.11 Impairment loss, goodwill ★ ★

LO5

On 1 January 2021, Ted Ltd acquired all the assets and liabilities of Mosby Ltd. Mosby Ltd has a number of operating divisions, including one whose major industry is the manufacture of toy trains, particularly models of trains of historical significance. The toy trains division is regarded as a CGU. In paying $2 million for the net assets of Mosby Ltd, Ted Ltd calculated that it had acquired goodwill of $360 000. The goodwill was allocated to each of the divisions, and the assets and liabilities acquired measured at fair value at acquisition date.

At 31 December 2023, the carrying amounts of the assets of the toy train division were as follows.

Factory	$375 000
Inventories	225 000
Brand — 'Froggy'	75 000
Goodwill	75 000

There is a declining interest in toy trains because of the aggressive marketing of computer-based toys, so the management of Ted Ltd measured the value in use of the toy train division at 31 December 2023, determining it to be $712 500.

Required

1. Prepare the journal entries to account for the impairment loss at 31 December 2023.
2. Prepare the journal entries as above but now assuming the value in use of the train division at 31 December 2023 was determined to be $634 500.

7.12 Impairment loss and reversal of an individual asset ★ ★ **LO4, 6**

On 30 June 2023, an item of machinery had a carrying amount of $525 000. The machinery's cost at acquisition was $750 000 at which time its estimated useful life was 10 years with no residual value.

On 30 June 2023, the same item of machinery was assessed as having a recoverable amount of $455 000 and a remaining useful life of 7 years.

On 30 June 2026, the machinery was assessed as having a recoverable amount of $315 000 and a remaining useful life of 3 years.

All machinery is carried under the cost model.

Required

Show the journal entries for depreciation and any adjustments relating to impairment on each of the following dates.

1. 30 June 2023
2. 30 June 2026
3. 30 June 2027

7.13 Impairment loss for a CGU, reversal of impairment loss ★ ★ ★ **LO5, 6**

One of the CGUs of Canal Ltd is associated with the manufacture of wine barrels. At 30 June 2022, Canal Ltd believed, based on an analysis of economic indicators, that the assets of the unit were impaired.

The carrying amounts of the assets and liabilities of the unit at 30 June 2022 were as follows.

Buildings	$ 420 000
Accumulated depreciation — buildings*	(180 000)
Factory machinery	220 000
Accumulated depreciation — machinery**	(40 000)
Goodwill	15 000
Inventories	80 000
Receivables	40 000
Allowance for doubtful debts	(5 000)
Cash	20 000
Accounts payable	30 000
Loans	20 000

*Depreciated at $60 000 p.a.
**Depreciated at $45 000 p.a.

Canal Ltd determined the recoverable amount of the unit to be $535 000. The receivables were considered to be collectable, except those considered doubtful. The company allocated the impairment loss in accordance with AASB 136/IAS 36.

During the 2022–23 period, Canal Ltd increased the depreciation charge on buildings to $65 000 p.a. and to $50 000 p.a. for factory machinery. The inventories on hand at 1 July 2022 were sold by the end of the year. At 30 June 2023, Canal Ltd, because of a return in the market to the use of traditional barrels for wines and an increase in wine production, assessed the recoverable amount of the CGU to be $30 000 greater than the carrying amount of the unit. As a result, Canal Ltd recognised a reversal of the impairment loss.

Required

1. Prepare the journal entries for Canal Ltd at 30 June 2022 and 2023.
2. What differences would arise in relation to the answer in requirement 1 if the recoverable amount at 30 June 2023 was $20 000 greater than the carrying amount of the unit?
3. If the recoverable amount of the buildings at 30 June 2023 was $175 000, how would this change the answer to requirement 2?

Honey Ltd has two divisions, Time and Leisure. Each of these is regarded as a separate CGU.

At 31 December 2022, the carrying amounts of the assets of the two divisions were as follows.

	Time	Leisure
Plant	$3 000	$2 400
Accumulated depreciation	(1 300)	(750)
Patent	480	—
Inventories	108	150
Receivables	150	164
Goodwill	50	40

The receivables were regarded as collectable, and the inventories' fair value less costs of disposal was equal to its carrying amount. The patent had a fair value less costs of disposal of $440. The plant at Time was depreciated at $600 p.a. The plant at Leisure was depreciated at $500 p.a.

Honey Ltd undertook impairment testing at 31 December 2022, and determined the recoverable amounts of the two divisions to be as follows.

Time	$2 088
Leisure	1 980

As a result, management increased the depreciation of the Time plant from $600 to $700 p.a. for the year 2022.

By 31 December 2023, the performance in both divisions had improved, and the carrying amounts of the assets of both divisions and their recoverable amounts were as follows.

	Time	Leisure
Carrying amount	$2 644	$2 866
Recoverable amount	3 004	3 040

Required

Determine how Honey Ltd should account for the results of the impairment tests at both 31 December 2022 and 31 December 2023.

7.15 Corporate assets ★ ★   **LO5**

Barney Ltd has two divisions, each regarded as a separate CGU. The carrying amounts of the net assets within each division at the most recent reporting date were as follows.

	Division One	Division Two
Cash	$ 5 000	$ 8 000
Inventories	30 000	40 000
Receivables	20 000	8 000
Plant	320 000	300 000
Accumulated depreciation	(120 000)	(120 000)
Land	80 000	50 000
Buildings	110 000	100 000
Accumulated depreciation	(40 000)	(60 000)
Furniture and fittings	40 000	30 000
Accumulated depreciation	(15 000)	(10 000)
Total assets	430 000	346 000
Provisions	20 000	40 000
Borrowings	30 000	66 000
Total liabilities	50 000	106 000
Net assets	**$380 000**	**$240 000**

Barney Ltd also recorded goodwill of $14 000 (net of accumulated impairment losses of $12 000) and had corporate assets consisting of a head office building carried at $150 000 (net of depreciation of $50 000) and furniture and fittings of $80 000 (net of depreciation of $20 000).

Barney Ltd determined that the recoverable amount of the entity's assets was $950 000.

The management of Barney Ltd then completed the accounting for impairment losses. The receivables in both divisions were considered to be collectable.

Required
1. Prepare the journal entry to record the impairment loss at the reporting date.
2. Prepare a table of the assets and liabilities of Barney Ltd, using the headings 'Division One', 'Division Two' and 'Corporate', after the completion of accounting for impairment losses.

7.16 Allocation of corporate assets and goodwill ★ ★   **LO5**

Lily Ltd acquired all the assets and liabilities of Marshall Ltd on 1 January 2023. Marshall Ltd's activities were run through three separate businesses, namely the Alpha Unit, the Beta Unit and the Gamma Unit. These units are separate CGUs. Lily Ltd allowed unit managers to effectively operate each of the units, but certain central activities were run through the corporate office. Each unit was allocated a share of the goodwill acquired, as well as a share of the corporate office.

At 31 December 2023, the assets allocated to each unit were as follows.

	Alpha	Beta	Gamma
Factory	$ 205	$190	$115
Accumulated depreciation	(105)	(95)	(85)
Land	50	75	40
Equipment	75	105	140
Accumulated depreciation	(15)	(80)	(80)
Inventories	30	20	25
Goodwill	10	15	10
Corporate property	50	40	30

Lily Ltd determined the recoverable amounts of each of the business units at 31 December 2023.

Alpha	$290
Beta	225
Gamma	205

Required
Determine how Lily Ltd should allocate any impairment loss at 31 December 2023.

7.17 Reversal of impairment losses ★ ★ ★   **LO5, 6**

Saxon Ltd conducted an impairment test at 30 June 2021. As a part of that exercise, it measured the recoverable amount of the entity, considered to be a single CGU, to be $217 600. The carrying amounts of the assets of the entity at 30 June 2021 were as follows.

Equipment	$200 000
Accumulated depreciation	(40 000)
Patent	40 000
Goodwill	6 400
Inventories	32 000
Receivables	1 600

The receivables held by Saxon Ltd were all considered to be collectable. The inventories were measured in accordance with AASB 102/IAS 2 *Inventories*.

For the period ending 30 June 2022, the depreciation charge on equipment was $14 720. If the plant had not been impaired the charge would have been $20 000.

At 30 June 2022, the recoverable amount of the entity was calculated to be $10 400 greater than the carrying amount of the assets of the entity. As a result, Saxon Ltd recognised a reversal of the previous year's impairment loss.

Required

Prepare the journal entry(ies) accounting for the impairment loss at 30 June 2021 and the reversal of the impairment loss at 30 June 2022.

7.18 CGUs, reversal of impairment losses ★ ★ ★   **LO5, 6**

The two CGUs of Dark Forest Ltd are referred to as the Lady CGU and the Lake CGU. At 31 July 2021, the carrying amounts of the assets of the two divisions were as follows.

	Lady CGU	Lake CGU
Equipment	$18 000	$14 400
Accumulated depreciation	(7 800)	(4 500)
Brand	2 880	—
Inventories	648	900
Receivables	900	984
Goodwill	300	240

The receivables were regarded as collectable, and the inventories were measured according to AASB 102/IAS 2 *Inventories*. The brand had a fair value less costs of disposal of $2640. The equipment held by the Lady CGU was depreciated at $3600 p.a. and the equipment of Lake CGU was depreciated at $3000 p.a.

Dark Forest Ltd undertook impairment testing in July 2021, and determined the recoverable amounts of the two CGUs at 31 July 2021 to be as follows.

Lady CGU	$12 528
Lake CGU	11 880

The relevant assets were written down as a result of the impairment testing affecting the financial statements of Dark Forest Ltd at 31 July 2021. As a result of the impairment testing, management reassessed the factors affecting the depreciation of its non-current asset. The depreciation of the equipment held by the Lady CGU was increased from $3600 p.a. to $4200 p.a. for the year 2021–22.

By 31 July 2022, the performance in both divisions had improved, and the carrying amounts of the assets of both divisions and their recoverable amounts were as follows.

	Lady CGU	Lake CGU
Carrying amounts of assets	$15 864	$17 196
Recoverable amount of CGU	18 024	18 240

Required

Determine how Dark Forest Ltd should account for the results of the impairment tests at both 31 July 2021 and 31 July 2022.

7.19 CGUs, corporate assets, goodwill ★ ★ ★   **LO5**

Charleston Ltd manufactures children's toys. Its operations are carried out through three operating divisions, namely the Merlin Division, the Hollow Division and the Hills Division. These divisions are separate CGUs. In accounting for any impairment losses, all central management assets are allocated to each of these divisions.

At 31 July 2022, the assets allocated to each division were as follows.

	Merlin CGU	Hollow CGU	Hills CGU
Buildings	$ 656	$ 600	$ 368
Accumulated depreciation	(336)	(304)	(272)
Land	160	240	120
Machinery	240	328	448
Accumulated depreciation	(48)	(256)	(248)
Inventories	96	64	80
Goodwill	32	40	24
Head Office assets	160	120	96

In relation to land values, the land relating to the Merlin and Hills Divisions have carrying amounts less than their fair values as standalone assets. The land held by the Hollow Division has a fair value less costs of disposal of $234.

Charleston Ltd determined the recoverable amount of each of the CGUs at 31 July 2022 as follows.

Merlin	$936
Hollow	720
Hills	640

Required

Prepare the journal entry(ies) for Charleston Ltd to record any impairment loss at 31 July 2022.

7.20 Goodwill, corporate assets ★ ★ ★   **LO5**

A large manufacturing company, Dalby Ltd, has its operations in Newcastle. It has two CGUs, Red Unit and Dragon Unit. At 30 June 2022, the management of the company decided to conduct impairment testing. It calculated that the recoverable amounts of the two divisions were $1 245 000 (Red Unit) and $930 000 (Dragon Unit). In considering the assets of the CGUs the company allocated the assets of the corporate area equally to the units.

The carrying amounts of the assets and liabilities of the two CGUs and the corporate assets at 30 June 2022 were as follows.

	Red Unit	Dragon Unit	Corporate
Equipment	$ 960 000	—	
Accumulated depreciation — equipment	(360 000)	—	
Land	270 000	$450 000	
Buildings	330 000	420 000	$630 000
Accumulated depreciation — buildings	(120 000)	(180 000)	(150 000)
Furniture and fittings	—	90 000	
Accumulated depreciation — furniture and fittings	—	(30 000)	
Goodwill	—	—	42 000
Cash	36 000	24 000	
Inventories	90 000	120 000	
Receivables	60 000	24 000	
Total assets	1 266 000	918 000	$522 000
Provisions	60 000	120 000	
Debentures	90 000	198 000	
Total liabilities	150 000	318 000	
Net assets	**$1 016 000**	**$600 000**	

In relation to these assets:
- the receivables of both units were considered to be collectable
- the land held by the Dragon Unit had a fair value less costs of disposal of $405 000.

Required

Prepare the journal entry(ies) required at 30 June 2022 to account for any impairment losses.

7.21 Impairment loss ★ ★ ★   **LO5**

Excalibur Ltd operates in the Swan Valley in Western Australia where it is involved in the growing of grapes and the production of wine. In June 2022, it anticipated that its assets may be impaired due to a glut on the market for grapes and an impending tax from the Australian government seeking to reduce binge drinking of alcohol by teenage Australians.

Land is measured by Excalibur Ltd at fair value. At 30 June 2022, the entity revalued the land to its fair value of $120 000. The land had previously been revalued upwards by $20 000.

As a result of its impairment testing, Excalibur Ltd calculated that the recoverable amount of the entity's assets was $1 456 000.

The carrying amounts of the assets of Excalibur Ltd prior to adjusting for the impairment test and the revaluation of the land were as follows.

Non-current assets	
Buildings	$3 400 000
Accumulated depreciation	(776 000)
Land (at fair value 1/7/21)	512 000
Plant and equipment	5 816 000
Accumulated depreciation	(3 000 000)
Goodwill	240 000
Accumulated impairment losses	(176 000)
Trademarks — wine labels	320 000
Current assets	
Cash	28 000
Receivables	36 000

Required

1. Prepare the journal entries required on 30 June 2022 in relation to the measurement of the assets of Excalibur Ltd.
2. Assume that, as the result of the allocation of the impairment loss, the plant and equipment was written down to $2 560 000. If the fair value less costs of disposal of the plant and equipment was determined to be $2 400 000, outline the adjustments, if any, that would need to be made to the journal entries you prepared in part 1 of this question, and explain why adjustments are or are not required.

7.22 Accounting theory and impairment losses ★ ★   **LO1, 2, 7**

In an article published in the March 2015 issue of *Company Director*, Commissioner John Price of the Australian Securities & Investments Commission (ASIC) noted that some 'entities have made significant impairment write-downs in response to ASIC inquiries. Some companies continue to use unrealistic cash flows and assumptions in estimating the recoverable amount. There have also been some instances of material mismatches between cash flows used and assets tested' (Price 2015).

Required

1. Explain how the use of subjective estimates and assumptions can affect whether an impairment loss is recognised, and the magnitude and timing of the recognition of impairment losses.
2. How can positive accounting theory be used to explain management's preference or reluctance to recognise an impairment loss? (*Hint:* Positive accounting theory is discussed in chapter 2 of this text.) Your response should address:
   (a) management compensation incentives
   (b) debt contracting incentives
   (c) political costs.

REFERENCES

Bartholomeusz, S 2014, 'Mammoth loss just could be the turning point for Qantas', *The Australian*, 29 August, www.theaustralian.com.au.

BHP Group Ltd 2016, 'Onshore US asset review', media release, 15 January, www.bhp.com.

Gu, F & Lev, B 2011, 'Overpriced shares, ill-advised acquisitions, and goodwill impairment', *The Accounting Review*, vol. 86, no. 6, pp. 1995–2022.

Hyam, R & Ong, T 2016, 'Woolworths reports almost $1 billion loss in half-year results', *ABC News*, 26 February, www.abc.net.au.

Price, J 2015, 'The regulator: Improving financial reporting' [online], *Company Director*, vol. 31, no. 2, March, p. 14.

Qantas Group 2014, 'Qantas Group financial results', media release', 28 August, www.qantas.com.au.

Santos Ltd 2017, *Annual report 2017*, www.santos.com.

Woolworths Group Ltd 2018, *Annual report 2018*, www.woolworthslimited.com.au.

ACKNOWLEDGEMENTS

Photo: © Mila Supinskaya / Shutterstock.com

Figure 7.1: © *ABC News* 26 February 2016, www.abc.net.au/news/2016-02-26/woolworths-reports-almost-$1-billion-loss/7202004

Figures 7.2, 7.5, 7.6: © Woolworths Group Ltd 2018

Figure 7.7: © Santos Ltd 2017

Figure 7.8: © American Accounting Association. Figure 1 from Gu, F & Lev, B 2011, 'Overpriced shares, ill-advised acquisitions, and goodwill impairment', *The Accounting Review*, vol. 86, no. 6, p. 1996.

Case study 7.1: © BHP Group Ltd 2016

Text: © 2019 Australian Accounting Standards Board (AASB). The text, graphics and layout of this publication are protected by Australian copyright law and the comparable law of other countries. No part of the publication may be reproduced, stored or transmitted in any form or by any means without the prior written permission of the AASB except as permitted by law. For reproduction or publication, permission should be sought in writing from the AASB. Requests in the first instance should be addressed to the National Director, Australian Accounting Standards Board, PO Box 204, Collins Street West, Victoria 8007.

CHAPTER 8

Provisions, contingent liabilities and contingent assets

CHAPTER AIM

This chapter explains the recognition, measurement and presentation of provisions, contingent liabilities and contingent assets in accordance with AASB 137/IAS 37 *Provisions, Contingent Liabilities and Contingent Assets*.

LEARNING OBJECTIVES

After studying this chapter, you should be able to:

8.1 describe the purpose of AASB 137/IAS 37

8.2 outline the concept of a provision and how it is distinguished from other liabilities

8.3 outline the concept of a contingent liability and how it is distinguished from other liabilities

8.4 explain when a provision should be recognised

8.5 explain how a provision, once recognised, should be measured

8.6 apply the definitions, recognition and measurement criteria for provisions and contingent liabilities to practical situations

8.7 outline the concept of a contingent asset

8.8 describe the disclosure requirements for provisions, contingent liabilities and contingent assets

8.9 compare the requirements of AASB 3/IFRS 3 regarding contingent liabilities with those of AASB 137/IAS 37.

CONCEPTS FOR REVIEW

Before studying this chapter, you should understand and, if necessary, revise:

• the definition of assets and liabilities in the *Conceptual Framework*
• the recognition criteria as stipulated in the *Conceptual Framework*
• journal entries to record assets and liabilities.

8.1 Introduction and scope

LEARNING OBJECTIVE 8.1 Describe the purpose of AASB 137/IAS 37.

AASB 137/IAS 37 *Provisions, Contingent Liabilities and Contingent Assets* deals with the recognition, measurement and presentation of provisions, contingent liabilities and contingent assets. The standard:

- defines provisions
- specifies recognition criteria and measurement requirements for the recognition of provisions in financial statements
- defines contingent liabilities and contingent assets
- prohibits the recognition of contingent liabilities and contingent assets in the financial statements, but requires their disclosure when certain conditions are met
- requires the provisions be measured at present value where the effect of the time value of money is material
- requires that where provisions are discounted to their present value at the reporting date, an entity shall specify the discount rate to be used for this purpose
- prohibits providing for future operating losses
- defines onerous contracts
- requires provisions for the estimated net losses under onerous contracts
- specifies recognition criteria for restructuring provisions
- identifies the types of costs that may be included in restructuring provisions
- requires extensive disclosures relating to provisions, contingent liabilities and contingent assets.

AASB 137/IAS 37 prescribes the accounting and disclosure for all provisions, contingent liabilities and contingent assets except:

(a) those resulting from financial instruments (see AASB 9/IFRS 9 *Financial Instruments*, covered in chapter 11)

(b) those resulting from executory contracts, except where the contract is onerous (Executory contracts are contracts under which neither party has performed any of its obligations or both parties have partially performed their obligations to an equal extent.)

(c) those specifically covered by another standard. For example, certain types of provisions are also addressed in standards on:
   - income taxes (see AASB 112/IAS 12 *Income Taxes*, covered in chapter 12)
   - leases (see AASB 16/IFRS 16 *Leases*, covered in chapter 10)
   - employee benefits (see AASB 119/IAS 19 *Employee Benefits*, covered in chapter 9)
   - insurance contracts (see AASB 4/IFRS 4 *Insurance Contracts*, AASB 1023 *General Insurance Contracts*, and AASB 1038 *Life Insurance Contracts*)
   - contingent consideration of an acquirer in a business combination (see AASB 3/IFRS 3 *Business Combinations*, covered in chapter 25)
   - revenue from contracts with customers (see AASB 15/IFRS 15 *Revenue from Contracts with Customers*, covered in chapter 15) except where the contract is onerous.

Sometimes the term 'provision' is used in the context of items such as depreciation, impairment of assets and doubtful debts. These are adjustments to the carrying amounts of assets and are not addressed in AASB 137/IAS 37. Refer to AASB 136/IAS 36 *Impairment of Assets*, which is covered in chapter 7.

Other standards specify whether expenditures are treated as assets or as expenses. These issues are not addressed in AASB 137/IAS 37. Accordingly, AASB 137/IAS 37 neither prohibits nor requires capitalisation of the costs recognised when a provision is made. Refer to AASB 138/IAS 38 *Intangible Assets*, which deals partly with this issue, and is covered in chapter 6.

AASB 137/IAS 37 applies to provisions for restructuring (including discontinued operations). Where a restructure meets the definition of a discontinued operation, additional disclosures may be required by AASB 5/IFRS 5 *Non-current Assets Held for Sale and Discontinued Operations*. AASB 3/IFRS 3 deals with accounting for restructuring provisions arising in business combinations. This chapter covers the relevant requirements of AASB 3/IFRS 3.

In June 2019, the IASB reactivated a research project into IAS 37. The project had been put on hold in 2016, awaiting the revised *Conceptual Framework for Financial Reporting (Conceptual Framework)*. The project is intended to identify whether aspects of IAS 37 should be amended, in which case it would be added to the IASB's work program (see chapter 1).

8.2 Definition of a provision

LEARNING OBJECTIVE 8.2 Outline the concept of a provision and how it is distinguished from other liabilities.

As explained in chapter 1, paragraph 4.26 of the *Conceptual Framework* defines a liability as:

> a present obligation of the entity to transfer an economic resource as a result of past events.

Paragraph 10 of AASB 137/IAS 37, however, retains a variation on the definition of a **liability**:

> A liability is a present obligation of the entity arising from past events, the settlement of which is expected to result in an outflow from the entity of resources embodying economic benefits.

A **provision** is a subset of liabilities (i.e. it is a type of liability). Paragraph 10 of AASB 137/IAS 37 defines a provision as:

> a liability of uncertain timing or amount.

It is this *uncertainty* that distinguishes provisions from other liabilities.

An essential characteristic of a liability is that the entity has a **present obligation**. An obligation is a duty or responsibility to act or perform in a certain way. Obligations may be legally enforceable as a consequence of a binding contract, for example. This is normally the case with amounts payable for goods or services received, which are described as 'payables' or 'trade creditors'. However, legal enforceability is not a necessary requirement to demonstrate the existence of a liability. An entity may have an equitable or constructive obligation, arising from normal business practice or custom, to act in an equitable manner. Alternatively, the obligation is construed from the circumstances. Determining whether an equitable or constructive obligation exists is often more difficult than identifying a legal obligation. AASB 137/IAS 37 does not specifically acknowledge the concept of an equitable obligation; however, it does define a **constructive obligation**, in paragraph 10, as:

> an obligation that derives from an entity's actions where:
> (a) by an established pattern of past practice, published policies or a sufficiently specific current statement, the entity has indicated to other parties that it will accept certain responsibilities; and
> (b) as a result, the entity has created a valid expectation on the part of those other parties that it will discharge those responsibilities.

A present obligation exists only where the entity has no realistic alternative but to make the sacrifice of economic benefits to settle the obligation (*Conceptual Framework* paragraphs 4.29–4.31). For example, assume that an entity makes a public announcement that it will match the financial assistance provided by other entities to victims of a natural disaster and, because of custom and moral considerations, has no realistic alternative but to provide the assistance. (In this case the events have already taken place — the natural disaster — and the public announcement is the obligating event.)

Importantly, a decision by the entity's management or governing body does not, by itself, create a constructive obligation. This is because the management or governing body would retain the ability to reverse that decision. A present obligation would come into existence when the decision was communicated publicly to those affected by it. This would result in the valid expectation that the entity would fulfil the obligation, thus leaving the entity with little or no discretion to avoid the sacrifice of economic benefits.

8.2.1 Distinguishing provisions from other liabilities

A provision may arise from either a legal or constructive obligation. As stated previously, the key distinguishing feature of a provision is the uncertainty relating to either the timing of settlement or the amount to be settled. This contrasts with liabilities such as trade payables and accruals, as described in paragraph 11 of AASB 137/IAS 37:

(a) trade payables are liabilities to pay for goods or services that have been received or supplied and have been invoiced or formally agreed with the supplier; and
(b) accruals are liabilities to pay for goods or services that have been received or supplied but have not been paid, invoiced or formally agreed with the supplier, including amounts due to employees (for example, amounts relating to accrued vacation pay). Although it is sometimes necessary to estimate the amount or timing of accruals, the uncertainty is generally much less than for provisions.

Accruals are often reported as part of trade and other payables, whereas provisions are reported separately.

Note, however, that employee benefits are addressed specifically by AASB 119/IAS 19 *Employee Benefits* and are not included in the scope of AASB 137/IAS 37.

Some examples of typical provisions include provisions for warranty, restructuring provisions and provisions for onerous contracts. These are discussed in more detail later in this chapter.

> **LEARNING CHECK**
>
> ☐ A liability is defined in AASB 137/IAS 37 as a present obligation arising from past events, the settlement of which is expected to result in an outflow of resources embodying economic benefits.
> ☐ A present obligation exists where the entity has no realistic alternative but to settle the obligation.
> ☐ A provision is a liability of *uncertain* timing or amount.
> ☐ The key distinction between a provision and other liabilities is that a provision involves uncertainty relating to the timing of settlement or the amount to be settled.
> ☐ Typical provisions include provisions for warranties, restructuring and onerous contracts.

8.3 Definition of a contingent liability

LEARNING OBJECTIVE 8.3 Outline the concept of a contingent liability and how it is distinguished from other liabilities.

Paragraph 10 of AASB 137/IAS 37 defines a **contingent liability** as:

(a) a possible obligation that arises from past events and whose existence will be confirmed only by the occurrence or non-occurrence of one or more uncertain future events not wholly within the control of the entity; or
(b) a present obligation that arises from past events but is not recognised because:
  (i) it is not probable that an outflow of resources embodying economic benefits will be required to settle the obligation; or
  (ii) the amount of the obligation cannot be measured with sufficient reliability.

The definition of a contingent liability is interesting because it encompasses two distinctly different concepts. The first, part (a) of the definition, is the concept of a *possible* obligation. This fails one of the essential characteristics of a liability — the requirement for the existence of a present obligation. If there is no present obligation, only a possible one, there is no liability. Hence, part (a) of the definition does not meet the definition of a liability and one could argue that the term 'contingent *liability*' is misleading, because items falling into category (a) are not liabilities by definition.

Part (b) of the definition, on the other hand, deals with liabilities that fail the recognition criteria. They are present obligations, so they meet the essential requirements of the definition of liabilities, but they do not meet the recognition criteria (probability of outflow of economic benefits and reliability of measurement).

8.3.1 Distinguishing a contingent liability from a provision

Unlike provisions, contingent liabilities do not meet the recognition criteria stated in the *Conceptual Framework* and therefore are not recognised in the financial statements. It must be disclosed in the notes to the financial statements unless the possibility of an outflow in settlement is remote.

Paragraph 12 of AASB 137/IAS 37 states that:

> In a general sense, all provisions are contingent because they are uncertain in timing or amount. However, within this Standard the term 'contingent' is used for liabilities and assets that are not recognised because their existence will be confirmed only by the occurrence or non-occurrence of one or more uncertain future events not wholly within the control of the entity. In addition, the term 'contingent liability' is used for liabilities that do not meet the recognition criteria.

Figure 8.1 illustrates the difference between a contingent liability and a provision. Note, however, that financial guarantees are specifically covered by AASB 9/IFRS 9 and must be accounted for in accordance with that standard or AASB 4/IFRS 4 (see chapter 11).

FIGURE 8.1	Example of the difference between a provision and a contingent liability

When Company A provides a guarantee to a bank in relation to a bank loan provided to Company B, a contingent liability exists and Company A shall provide a disclosure in the notes to the financial statements in relation to the guarantee provided if Company B is solvent and able to repay the loan without breaching any debt covenants. However, if Company B has breached the debt covenants and it is probable that Company A will be called upon as guarantor of the loan by the bank, a provision should be recognised by Company A for the amount likely to be paid to the bank. This assumes that there is still uncertain timing or amount; otherwise the amount would be a liability.

LEARNING CHECK

- ☐ A contingent liability refers to:
  - – a possible obligation that will be confirmed (or not) by future events not entirely within the control of the entity
  - – a present obligation where it is not probable that an outflow of resources will be required for settlement or the amount of the obligation cannot be reliably measured.
- ☐ Contingent liabilities are not recognised in the financial statements because contingent liabilities either do not meet the definition of a liability or do not meet the recognition criteria.
- ☐ Contingent liabilities must be disclosed in the notes to the financial statements unless the possibility of an outflow in settlement is remote.

8.4 The recognition criteria for provisions

LEARNING OBJECTIVE 8.4 Explain when a provision should be recognised.

Paragraph 14 of AASB 137/IAS 37 states that a provision should be recognised when:

- (a) an entity has a present obligation (legal or constructive) as a result of a past event;
- (b) it is probable that an outflow of resources embodying economic benefits will be required to settle the obligation; and
- (c) a reliable estimate can be made of the amount of the obligation.

If these conditions are not met, no provision shall be recognised.

The concept of probability stated in paragraph 14(b) refers to the likelihood of something eventuating. If it is more likely rather than less likely, AASB 137/IAS 37 regards the outflow as *probable*. Probability is assessed for each obligation separately, unless the obligations form a group of similar obligations (such as product warranties) in which case the probability that an outflow will be required in settlement is determined by assessing the class of obligations as a whole.

Paragraphs 15 and 16 of AASB 137/IAS 37 discuss the concepts of a present obligation and probability, giving some useful examples:

15. In rare cases it is not clear whether there is a present obligation. In these cases, a past event is deemed to give rise to a present obligation if, taking account of all available evidence, it is more likely than not that a present obligation exists at the end of the reporting period.

16. In almost all cases it will be clear whether a past event has given rise to a present obligation. In rare cases, for example in a lawsuit, it may be disputed either whether certain events have occurred or whether those events result in a present obligation. In such a case, an entity determines whether a present obligation exists at the end of the reporting period by taking account of all available evidence, including, for example, the opinion of experts. The evidence considered includes any additional evidence provided by events after the end of the reporting period. On the basis of such evidence:

    (a) where it is more likely than not that a present obligation exists at the end of the reporting period, the entity recognises a provision (if the recognition criteria are met); and

    (b) where it is more likely that no present obligation exists at the end of the reporting period, the entity discloses a contingent liability, unless the possibility of an outflow of resources embodying economic benefits is remote [in which case no disclosure is made].

A past event that leads to a present obligation is called an obligating event. As discussed in the section on constructive obligations, for an event to be an obligating event the entity must have no realistic alternative to settling the obligation created by the event.

- In the case of a *legal obligation* this is because the settlement of the obligation can be enforced by law.
- In the case of a *constructive obligation* the event needs to create a valid expectation in other parties that the entity will discharge the obligation.

Reliable estimation is the final criterion for recognition of a provision. Although the use of estimates is a necessary part of the preparation of financial statements, in the case of provisions the uncertainty associated with reliable measurement is greater than for other liabilities. Accordingly, AASB 137/IAS 37 goes on to give more detailed guidance on measurement of provisions, which we will discuss later in the chapter. However, it is expected that, except in very rare cases, an entity will be able to determine a reliable estimate of the obligation.

Note the concept of 'probability' in the recognition criteria for liabilities, including provisions, contrasted with the concept of 'possibility' in determining whether or not a contingent liability should be disclosed. Paragraph 86 of AASB 137/IAS 37 requires contingent liabilities to be disclosed in the financial statements '[u]nless the possibility of any outflow in settlement is remote'. AASB 137/IAS 37 interprets 'probable' as meaning more likely than not to occur (paragraph 23). AASB 137/IAS 37 does not, however, provide any further guidance on what it means by 'possibility'. In plain English terms 'probability' addresses the likelihood of whether or not something will happen, whereas 'possibility' has a broader meaning — virtually anything is possible, but how probable is it? Given this distinction, we should assume that the intention of AASB 137/IAS 37 is that most contingent liabilities should be disclosed and that only in very rare circumstances is no disclosure appropriate.

Contingent liabilities need to be continually assessed to determine whether or not they have become actual liabilities. This is done by considering whether the recognition criteria for liabilities have been met. If it becomes probable that an outflow of economic benefits will be required for an item previously dealt with as a contingent liability and the amount can be reliably determined, a provision is recognised in the financial statements in the period in which the change in probability occurs (AASB 137/IAS 37 paragraph 30).

8.4.1 Putting it all together — a useful decision tree

In sections 8.2 through 8.4 we discussed the definitions of provisions and contingent liabilities, the recognition criteria for provisions and when a contingent liability must be disclosed. The decision tree (figure 8.2), reproduced from Guidance on Implementing AASB 137 part B, summarises this discussion.

FIGURE 8.2 Decision tree

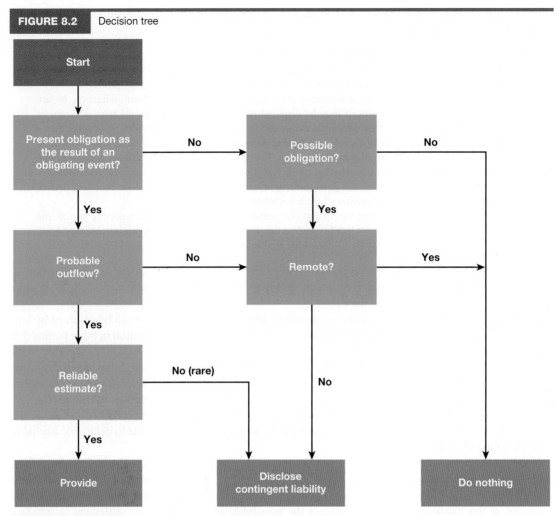

Source: AASB 137, Guidance on Implementing AASB 137 part B.

8.5 Measurement of provisions

LEARNING OBJECTIVE 8.5 Explain how a provision, once recognised, should be measured.

8.5.1 Best estimate

When measuring a provision, the amount recognised should be the **best estimate** of the consideration required to settle the present obligation at the end of the reporting period (AASB 137/IAS 37 paragraph 36). This amount is often expressed as the amount which represents, as closely as possible, what the entity would rationally pay to settle the present obligation at the end of the reporting period or to provide consideration to a third party to assume it. The fact that it is difficult to measure the provision and that estimates have to be used does not mean that the provision is not reliably measurable.

Paragraphs 39 and 40 of AASB 137/IAS 37 address the issue of how to deal with the uncertainties surrounding the amount to be recognised as a provision:

39. Uncertainties surrounding the amount to be recognised as a provision are dealt with by various means according to the circumstances. Where the provision being measured involves a large population of items, the obligation is estimated by weighting all possible outcomes by their associated probabilities. The name for this statistical method of estimation is 'expected value'. The provision will therefore be different depending on whether the probability of a loss of a given amount is, for example, 60 per cent or 90 per cent. Where there is a continuous range of possible outcomes, and each point in that range is as likely as any other, the mid-point of the range is used.

Example

An entity sells goods with a warranty under which customers are covered for the cost of repairs of any manufacturing defects that become apparent within the first six months after purchase. If minor defects were detected in all products sold, repair costs of $1 million would result. If major defects were detected in all products sold, repair costs of $4 million would result. The entity's past experience and future expectations indicate that, for the coming year, 75 per cent of the goods sold will have no defects, 20 per cent of the goods sold will have minor defects and 5 per cent of the goods sold will have major defects. In accordance with paragraph 24, an entity assesses the probability of an outflow for the warranty obligations as a whole.

The expected value of the cost of repairs is:

$$(75\% \text{ of nil}) + (20\% \text{ of } \$1m) + (5\% \text{ of } \$4m) = \$400\,000$$

---

40. Where a single obligation is being measured, the individual most likely outcome may be the best estimate of the liability. However, even in such a case, the entity considers other possible outcomes. Where other possible outcomes are either mostly higher or mostly lower than the most likely outcome, the best estimate will be a higher or lower amount. For example, if an entity has to rectify a serious fault in a major plant that it has constructed for a customer, the individual most likely outcome may be for the repair to succeed at the first attempt at a cost of 1000, but a provision for a larger amount is made if there is a significant chance that further attempts will be necessary.

The provision is measured before tax. Any tax consequences are accounted for in accordance with AASB 112/IAS 12 *Income Taxes*.

The need to use judgement in determining the best estimate is clearly evident. Judgement is used in assessing, amongst other things:

- what the likely consideration required to settle the obligation will be
- when the consideration is likely to be settled
- whether there are various scenarios that are likely to arise
- what the probability of those various scenarios arising will be.

The distinguishing characteristic of provisions — the uncertainty relating to either the timing of settlement or the amount to be settled — is illustrated in the above discussion. Because of the extent of judgement required in measuring provisions, auditors focus more on auditing provisions than on other normal liabilities such as trade creditors and accruals. This is particularly the case if a change in one of the assumptions, such as the probability of a particular scenario eventuating or the likely consideration required to settle the obligation, would have a material impact on the amount recognised as a provision and thus on the financial statements.

8.5.2 Risks and uncertainties

Paragraph 42 of AASB 137/IAS 37 requires that the risks and uncertainties surrounding the events and circumstances should be taken into account in reaching the best estimate of a provision. Paragraph 43 states that:

Risk describes variability of outcome. A risk adjustment may increase the amount at which a liability is measured. Caution is needed in making judgements under conditions of uncertainty, so that income or assets are not overstated and expenses or liabilities are not understated. However, uncertainty does not justify the creation of excessive provisions or a deliberate overstatement of liabilities. For example, if the projected costs of a particularly adverse outcome are estimated on a prudent basis, that outcome is not then deliberately treated as more probable than is realistically the case. Care is needed to avoid duplicating adjustments for risk and uncertainty with consequent overstatement of a provision.

Disclosure of the uncertainties surrounding the amount or timing of expected outflows is required by paragraph 85(b) of AASB 137/IAS 37.

8.5.3 Present value

Provisions are required to be *discounted to present value* where the effect of discounting is material (AASB 137/IAS 37 paragraph 45). AASB 137/IAS 37 (paragraph 47) requires that the discount rate used must be a pre-tax rate that reflects current market assessments of the time value of money and the *risks specific to the liability*. Where future cash flow estimates have been adjusted for risk, the discount rate should not reflect this risk — otherwise the risk would be duplicated.

In practical terms it is often difficult to determine reliably a liability-specific discount rate. Usually entities use a rate available for a liability with similar terms and conditions or, if a similar liability is not available, a risk-free rate for a liability with the same term (e.g. a government bond — assumed to be risk-free, although this is not always true — with a 5-year term may be used as the basis for a company's specific liability with a 5-year term) and this rate is then adjusted for the risks pertaining to the liability in question.

The higher the discount rate, the lower the amount that will be recognised as a liability. This seems counter-intuitive — seemingly the higher the risk attached to the liability, the lower the amount at which it is recognised. However, a risk-adjusted rate for a liability would be a *lower* rate than the risk-free rate. This is demonstrated in illustrative example 8.1.

ILLUSTRATIVE EXAMPLE 8.1

Calculation of a risk-adjusted rate

HEF Pty Ltd has a liability to clean up a site in 4 years' time. The potential cost of the clean-up lies in a range between $5000 and $8000. It is estimated that there is a 30% chance that HEF will need to pay $8000 and a 70% chance that it will need to pay $5000 in due course. At the risk-free rate of 4%, the provision for the expected value of the cash outflow in 4 years' time is $5900 (i.e. 30% × $8000 + 70% × $5000).

HEF Pty Ltd can settle the liability with a payment of $6500, payable in 4 years' time, rather than be exposed to the risk of paying potentially as much as $8000. The risk-adjusted cash flow of $6500 can be discounted at the risk-free (unadjusted) rate of 4%, giving a present value of $5560.

Viewed in another way, the expected payment of $5900 (unadjusted) in 4 years' time discounted to the present value of $5560 requires a risk-adjusted rate of 1.5%. The lower discount rate (1.5% versus 4%) for the provision (i.e. liability) reflects the fact HEF Pty Ltd is prepared to pay more to remove the risk that the actual cost could be higher.

This situation is in contrast to an asset such as a loan, where the lender requires a risk-adjusted rate that is higher than the risk-free rate in order to compensate for the risk that the loan may not be repaid in full.

Perhaps an easier way to factor in risk is to use it in assessing the probability of outcomes (as discussed in section 8.5.1) and then use a risk-free rate in discounting the cash flows. Paragraph 83 of AASB 119/IAS 19 *Employee Benefits* states that the discount rate for long-term employee benefit obligations should be determined by reference to market yields at the end of the reporting period on high-quality corporate bonds or, where there is no deep market in such bonds, the market yield on government bonds. The currency and term of the corporate bonds or government bonds should be consistent with the currency and estimated term of the employee benefit obligations. Although there may be some debate about how to determine the risk-free rate, market yields on high-quality corporate bonds or government bonds are reasonable approximations.

Illustrative example 8.2 shows the way a provision should be measured, taking into account risks and the time value of money.

Measuring a provision

An entity estimates that the expected cash outflows to settle its warranty obligations at the end of the reporting period are as follows. (Note that the probability of cash outflows has already been adjusted for risk similar to the example in section 8.5.1 and, accordingly, no further adjustment for risk is made to the discount rate.) The entity has used a discount rate based on government bonds with the same term and currency as the expected cash outflows.

Expected cash outflow	Timing	Discount rate	Present value of cash outflow
$400 000	In 1 year	6.0%	$377 358
100 000	In 2 years	6.5%	88 166
20 000	In 3 years	6.9%	16 372
Present value			$481 896

8.5.4 Future events

Anticipated future events expected to affect the amount required to settle the entity's present obligation must be reflected in the amount provided, when there is reliable evidence that they will occur. As an example, paragraph 49 of AASB 137/IAS 37 states:

Expected future events may be particularly important in measuring provisions. For example, an entity may believe that the cost of cleaning up a site at the end of its life will be reduced by future changes in technology. The amount recognised reflects a reasonable expectation of technically qualified, objective observers, taking account of all available evidence as to the technology that will be available at the time of the clean-up. Thus it is appropriate to include, for example, expected cost reductions associated with increased experience in applying existing technology or the expected cost of applying existing technology to a larger or more complex clean-up operation than has previously been carried out. However, an entity does not anticipate the development of a completely new technology for cleaning up unless it is supported by sufficient objective evidence.

8.5.5 Expected disposal of assets

Gains from the expected disposal of assets must not be taken into account when measuring the amount of a provision (AASB 137/IAS 37 paragraph 51), even if the expected disposal is closely linked to the event giving rise to the provision. Rather, when the gain on disposal is made it should be recognised at that time in accordance with the relevant international accounting standard. Therefore, it is clear that only expected cash *outflows* must be taken into account in measuring the provision. Any cash inflows are treated separately from the measurement of the provision.

8.5.6 Reimbursements

When some of the amount required to settle a provision is expected to be recovered from a third party, AASB 137/IAS 37 requires that the recovery be recognised as an asset, but only when it is *virtually certain* that the reimbursement will be received if the entity settles the obligation (paragraph 53). This differs from the normal asset recognition criteria, which require that the inflow of future economic benefits be *probable*. Presumably, the standard setters were concerned about an uncertain asset related to an uncertain liability, and therefore decided to make the recognition criteria stricter for these types of assets. When such an asset is recognised the amount should not exceed the amount of the provision. AASB 137/IAS 37 allows the income from the asset to be set off against the expense relating to the provision in the statement of profit or loss and other comprehensive income. However, it does not mention set off in the statement of financial position of the asset and the provision. One of the disclosures required, in paragraph 85(c), is the amount of any asset that has been recognised for expected reimbursements; therefore, it is reasonable to assume that AASB 137/IAS 37 did not intend for the provision and asset to be set off in the statement of financial position. This is alluded to in paragraph 56:

In most cases the entity will remain liable for the whole of the amount in question so that the entity would have to settle the full amount if the third party failed to pay for any reason. In this situation, a provision is recognised for the full amount of the liability, and a separate asset for the expected reimbursement is recognised when it is virtually certain that reimbursement will be received if the entity settles the liability.

8.5.7 Changes in provisions and use of provisions

AASB 137/IAS 37 requires provisions to be reviewed at the end of each reporting period and adjusted to reflect the current best estimate. If it is no longer probable that an outflow of resources embodying economic benefits will be required to settle the obligation, the provision should be reversed (paragraph 59).

Where discounting is used, the carrying amount of a provision increases in each period to reflect the passage of time. This increase is recognised as borrowing cost. This is similar to the way finance lease liabilities are accounted for under AASB 16/IFRS 16 *Leases*, as shown in chapter 10.

A provision should be used only for expenditures for which the provision was originally recognised. Illustrative example 8.3 shows how a provision is accounted for where discounting is applied and where the provision is adjusted to reflect the current best estimate.

ILLUSTRATIVE EXAMPLE 8.3

Accounting for a provision

Ant Ltd estimates that it will be required to pay $100 000 in 3 years' time to settle a warranty obligation. The risk-free discount rate applied is 5.5%. The probability of cash outflows has been assessed (i.e. adjusted for risk) in determining the $100 000.

Required

How is the provision accounted for over the 3 years? Prepare the journal entries.

Solution

The following table shows how the provision is accounted for over the 3 years.

A. Year	B. Present value at the beginning of the year	C. Interest expense at 5.5% (B × 5.5%)	D. Cash flows	E. Present value at the end of the year (B + C − D)
1	85 161	4 684	—	89 845
2	89 845	4 942	—	94 787
3	94 787	5 213	(100 000)	—

The journal entries are as follows.

On initial recognition in year 1:			
Warranty expense	Dr	85 161	
Warranty provision	Cr		85 161
On recognition of interest in year 1:			
Interest expense	Dr	4 684	
Warranty provision	Cr		4 684
On recognition of interest in year 2:			
Interest expense	Dr	4 942	
Warranty provision	Cr		4 942
On recognition of interest in year 3:			
Interest expense	Dr	5 213	
Warranty provision	Cr		5 213
On settlement of provision, end of year 3:			
Warranty provision	Dr	100 000	
Cash	Cr		100 000

Required

At the end of year 2, Ant Ltd re-estimates the amount to be paid to settle the obligation at the end of year 3 to be $90 000. The appropriate discount rate remains at 5.5%. How is the re-estimation accounted for? Prepare the journal entries.

Solution

The present value of $90 000 at the end of year 2 is $85 308. Ant Ltd thus adjusts the provision by $9479 ($94 787 − $85 308) to reflect the revised estimated cash flows.

The journal entries are as follows.

Revision of estimate at end of year 2:			
Warranty provision	Dr	9 479	
Warranty expense (statement of comprehensive income)	Cr		9 479
On recognition of interest in year 3:			
Interest expense ($85 308 × 5.5% rounded)	Dr	4 692	
Warranty provision	Cr		4 692
On settlement of provision, end of year 3:			
Warranty provision	Dr	90 000	
Cash	Cr		90 000

The re-estimated cash flows are adjusted against the warranty expense recorded in the statement of comprehensive income, while the unwinding of the discount continues to be recorded as interest expense (AASB 137/IAS 37 paragraph 60). Any change in the discount rate used would also be adjusted against interest expense.

LEARNING CHECK

☐ The amount recognised as a provision shall be the best estimate of the consideration required to settle the present obligation at the end of the reporting period.

☐ The fact that it is difficult to measure the provision and that estimates have to be used does not mean that the provision is not reliably measurable. The 'expected value' of a provision can be estimated by weighting all possible outcomes by their associated probabilities.

☐ The measurement of a provision should take into account risks and uncertainties surrounding the events and circumstances, time value of money and anticipated future events expected to affect the amount required to settle the entity's present obligation, but shall exclude gains from the expected disposal of assets.

☐ Provisions recognised shall be reviewed at the end of each reporting period and adjusted to reflect the current best estimate. It shall be reversed if it is no longer probable that an outflow of resources embodying economic benefits will be required to settle the obligation.

8.6 Application of the definitions, recognition and measurement rules

LEARNING OBJECTIVE 8.6 Apply the definitions, recognition and measurement criteria for provisions and contingent liabilities to practical situations.

8.6.1 Future operating losses

Paragraph 63 of AASB 137/IAS 37 states that provisions must not be recognised for future operating losses. Even if a sacrifice of future economic benefits is expected, a provision for future operating losses is not recognised because a past event creating a present obligation has not occurred. This is because the entity's management will generally have the ability to avoid incurring future operating losses by either disposing of or restructuring the operation in question. An expectation of future operating losses may, however, be an indicator that an asset is impaired and the requirements of AASB 136/IAS 36 *Impairment of Assets* should be applied.

8.6.2 Onerous contracts

An **onerous contract** is defined in paragraph 10 of AASB 137/IAS 37 as:

> a contract in which the unavoidable costs of meeting the obligations under the contract exceed the economic benefits expected to be received under it.

If an entity is a party to an onerous contract, a provision for the present obligation under the contract must be recognised (AASB 137/IAS 37 paragraph 66). The reason these losses should be provided for is that the entity is contracted to fulfil the contract. Therefore, entry into an onerous contract gives rise to a present obligation.

Examples of onerous contracts include:

- where an electricity retailer has entered into a contract to supply electricity at a price lower than the price that it is contracted to pay to the electricity generator
- where a manufacturer has entered into a supply contract at a price below the costs of production.

AASB 137/IAS 37 does not go into a lot of detail regarding onerous contracts and the requirements of the standard are quite vague in this area. Therefore, judgement has to be applied on a case-by-case basis to assess whether or not individual contracts qualify as onerous contracts under the standard.

For the purpose of raising a provision in respect of an onerous contract, paragraph 68 of AASB 137/IAS 37 states that the amount to be recognised is the least net cost of exiting the contract; that is, the lesser of:

- the cost of fulfilling the contract, and
- any compensation or penalties arising from failure to fulfil the contract.

AASB 137/IAS 37 also requires that before a separate provision is made for an onerous contract, an entity must first recognise any impairment loss that has occurred on assets dedicated to that contract. This is demonstrated in illustrative example 8.4.

ILLUSTRATIVE EXAMPLE 8.4

Accounting for an onerous contract

Pastels Ltd enters into a supply agreement with Buyers Ltd on 1 January 2023. The agreement states that:

- Pastels Ltd must supply Buyers Ltd with 100 chairs at a price of $150 per chair
- if Pastels Ltd cannot deliver the chairs on time and under the terms of the contract it must pay Buyers Ltd a penalty of $12 000
- the delivery date is 31 March 2023.

Pastels Ltd begins manufacturing the chairs on 1 March, but experiences a series of production problems that result in the production cost of each chair totalling $200 as at 31 March 2023.

Required

How should Pastels Ltd account for the contract?

Solution

The costs of fulfilling the contract (100 × $200 = $20 000) exceed the agreed amount to be received (100 × $150 = $15 000). As at 31 March, Pastels Ltd identifies an onerous contract in accordance with AASB 137/IAS 37. The cost of the chairs is recognised as inventories as at 31 March 2023. Assuming the end of Pastels Ltd's reporting period is 31 March, it must first recognise an impairment loss on the inventories. This would be calculated and recorded as $5000 (lower of cost and net realisable value (ignoring costs of disposal) under AASB 102/IAS 2 *Inventories* — see chapter 4). Once this impairment loss has been recognised, there is no amount to be recorded as a provision under the onerous contract. However, if Pastels Ltd had not yet recorded any costs as inventories it would need to determine what amount to recognise as a provision for the onerous contract. This would be the lesser of the penalty required to be paid to Buyers Ltd ($12 000) and the cost of fulfilling the contract (assume $20 000 if the costs have not yet been recognised). Thus, Pastels Ltd would record a provision of $12 000.

8.6.3 Restructuring provisions

Perhaps the most controversial aspect of AASB 137/IAS 37 is the recognition criteria for restructuring provisions. AASB 3/IFRS 3 *Business Combinations* addresses restructuring provisions arising as part of a business combination, whereas AASB 137/IAS 37 addresses restructuring provisions arising other than as part of a business combination. Although the fundamental criteria are consistent, AASB 3/IFRS 3 has more prescriptive requirements than AASB 137/IAS 37. For ease of discussion, both types of restructuring provision are discussed here.

During the 1990s, standard setters in various jurisdictions set tougher rules on when a restructuring provision could be recognised, particularly when the provision related to the acquisition of a business. The reason for the crackdown was the tendency for companies to create restructuring provisions deliberately to avoid the recognition of an expense in future periods. Illustrative example 8.5 demonstrates this point.

Restructuring provisions

Tuesday Ltd acquired Skopps Ltd on 1 February 1994. The identifiable net assets and liabilities of Skopps Ltd were $400 million. Tuesday Ltd paid $500 million cash as purchase consideration. The goodwill arising on acquisition was thus $100 million. Tuesday Ltd then decided to create a restructuring provision of $60 million for future possible restructuring activities related to Skopps Ltd. Tuesday Ltd recorded the following additional entry as part of its acquisition accounting entries.

Goodwill	Dr	60m	
Restructuring provision	Cr		60m

Required

Why did Tuesday Ltd have an incentive to record this entry?

Solution

The entry increased the amount recorded as goodwill, and in the 1990s goodwill was required to be amortised in most jurisdictions. Why would Tuesday Ltd have wanted to expose itself to future goodwill amortisation? Because the restructuring provision was recorded directly against goodwill, an expense for the restructuring will *never* be recorded. When Tuesday Ltd incurred the expenditure in the future, the outflows could then be recorded against the provision. Tuesday Ltd would likely have been able to highlight goodwill amortisation as a separate item either in its statement of comprehensive income or the attached notes, and thus would have been satisfied that the amortisation expense was effectively quarantined from the rest of its reported profit. The benefit for Tuesday Ltd was that the restructuring expense never affected its profit, and thus the creation of the restructuring provision as part of the acquisition entries protected Tuesday Ltd's future profits.

Paragraph 70 of AASB 137/IAS 37 provides the following examples of events that may be considered to be restructurings:

(a) sale or termination of a line of business;
(b) the closure of business locations in a country or region or the relocation of business activities from one country or region to another;
(c) changes in management structure, for example, eliminating a layer of management; and
(d) fundamental reorganisations that have a material effect on the nature and focus of the entity's operations.

In broad terms, to be able to raise a restructuring provision, three conditions need to be met.
1. The entity must have a *present obligation (either legal or constructive)* to restructure such that it cannot realistically avoid going ahead with the restructuring and thus incurring the costs involved.
2. Only costs that are *directly and necessarily* caused by the restructuring and *not associated with the ongoing activities* of the entity may be included in a restructuring provision.
3. If the restructuring involves the sale of an operation, no obligation is deemed to arise for the sale of an operation until the entity is committed to the sale by a *binding sale agreement*.
Each of these requirements is considered in more detail below.

Present obligation

Usually management initiates a restructuring and thus it is rare that a legal obligation will exist for a restructuring. AASB 137/IAS 37 therefore focuses on the conditions that need to be met for a constructive obligation to exist. As we saw earlier, a constructive obligation is defined in paragraph 10 as:

an obligation that derives from an entity's actions where:
(a) by an established pattern of past practice, published policies or a sufficiently specific current statement, the entity has indicated to other parties that it will accept certain responsibilities; and
(b) as a result, the entity has created a valid expectation on the part of those other parties that it will discharge those responsibilities.

In respect of restructuring provisions, paragraph 72 of AASB 137/IAS 37 states that a constructive obligation to restructure arises only when an entity:

(a) has a detailed formal plan for the restructuring identifying at least:
 (i) the business or part of a business concerned;
 (ii) the principal locations affected;
 (iii) the location, function, and approximate number of employees who will be compensated for terminating their services;
 (iv) the expenditures that will be undertaken; and
 (v) when the plan will be implemented; and
(b) has raised a valid expectation in those affected that it will carry out the restructuring by starting to implement that plan or announcing its main features to those affected by it.

Therefore, we see that the entity needs to have a *detailed formal plan* and must have raised a *valid expectation* in those affected. Paragraphs 73–75 of AASB 137/IAS 37 state that an entity can only recognise a restructuring provision in a reporting period if:

- the entity has started implementing a restructuring plan prior to the end of the reporting period (e.g. by dismantling plant or selling assets or by the public announcement of the main features of the plan); or
- the entity has announced the main features of the restructuring plan to those affected by it in a sufficient manner to raise a valid expectation in them that the entity will carry out the restructuring.

For a plan to be sufficient to give rise to a constructive obligation when communicated to those affected by it, its implementation needs to be scheduled to begin as soon as possible and to be completed in a timeframe that makes significant changes to the plan unlikely. If it is expected that there will be a long delay before the restructuring begins or that the restructuring will take an unreasonably long time, it is unlikely that the plan will raise a valid expectation on the part of others that the entity is at present committed to restructuring, because the timeframe allows opportunities for the entity to change its plans.

Recording restructuring provisions

Where a provision for restructuring costs arises on the acquisition of an entity, it must be recognised as a liability in the statement of financial position of the acquiree and not in the books of the acquirer or as a consolidation entry. The provision for the restructuring costs must be taken into account by the acquirer when measuring the fair value of the net assets acquired. Illustrative example 8.6 demonstrates this principle further.

ILLUSTRATIVE EXAMPLE 8.6

Recording restructuring provisions in the books of the acquiree

Clavinet Ltd acquires Wong Ltd, which has a head office in the city centre and a manufacturing plant in an industrial area. As part of the acquisition, Clavinet Ltd decides to close Wong Ltd's head office premises and move Wong Ltd's staff to Clavinet Ltd's own city premises. Wong Ltd will be paying the $120 000 cost of closing the office.

Required
How will the restructuring provisions be recorded by Wong Ltd?

Solution
Wong Ltd will record the following journal entry at or before the date of acquisition.

Restructuring costs	Dr	120 000	
Restructuring provision	Cr		120 000

In determining the fair value of the net assets acquired in Wong Ltd (in accordance with AASB3/IFRS 3), Clavinet Ltd will include the restructuring provision recorded by Wong Ltd. On the other hand, if Wong Ltd did not have an obligation to pay the restructuring costs, Wong Ltd would not have recorded them. Clavinet Ltd would then *not* be permitted to create a provision for restructuring costs as part of its acquisition entries in accordance with AASB 3/IFRS 3.

We saw above that in order to satisfy the 'valid expectation' test in AASB 137/IAS 37, the entity needs to have started to implement the detailed formal plan or announced the main features to those affected by it.

An entity can do this by:

- having already entered into firm contracts to carry out parts of the restructuring. These contracts would be of such a nature that they effectively force the entity to carry out the restructuring. This would be the case if they contained severe penalty provisions or the costs of not fulfilling the contract were so high that it would effectively leave the entity with no alternative but to proceed.
- starting to implement the detailed restructuring. This could include, for example, selling assets, notifying customers that supplies will be discontinued, notifying suppliers that orders will be ceasing, dismantling plant and equipment, and terminating employees' service.
- announcing the main features of the plan to those affected by it (or their representatives). There may be a number of ways in which such an announcement could be made. It could be through written communication, meetings or discussions with the affected parties.

It is important that the communication is made in such a way that it raises a valid expectation in the affected parties such that they can be expected to act as a result of the communication, and by them doing so the entity would be left with no realistic alternative but to go ahead with the restructuring. For example, affected employees would start looking for other employment and customers would seek alternative sources of supply.

Figure 8.3 provides examples of where a present obligation does and does not arise on a restructuring as a result of an acquisition.

| FIGURE 8.3 | Examples of the existence of a present obligation under AASB 3/IFRS 3 and AASB 137/IAS 37 |

Example 1

The acquired entity has developed a detailed plan for the restructuring. Details of the plan have not been made public but, as at the date of acquisition, agreement about key features of the plan has been reached with, or information about the plan has been disclosed to, relevant third parties. These parties include employee representatives, lessors and regulatory bodies. As at the acquisition date, no elements of the plan had begun to be implemented.

A present obligation exists because the key features of the plan have been communicated to those affected and a detailed plan has been developed. The fact that parts of the plan have not begun to be implemented at the acquisition date does not negate the constructive obligation. Importantly, the *acquired entity* has the obligation.

Example 2

The acquiring entity has developed a detailed plan for the restructuring as at the date of acquisition. That plan involves the closure of a number of operating sites and the retrenchment of all employees at those sites. As at the date of acquisition, key features of the plan have not been made public; however, employee representatives have been informed. Lessors of premises that will no longer be required have been informed of the entity's intentions, and negotiations on potential lease-termination penalty costs have commenced. Expressions of interest have been sought regarding the sale of plant and equipment that will be surplus should the acquisition proceed. Preliminary commitments have been made, and, conditional on the acquisition proceeding, agreements have been reached with third parties regarding the relocation or alternative supply of certain goods and services currently provided from the sites to be closed. The planned restructuring is such that on closure of the sites the continued employment of affected employees is not possible.

A present obligation does not exist for the *acquired entity*, so no provision is permitted under AASB 3/IFRS 3.

Qualifying restructuring costs

The second requirement for recognition of a restructuring provision is that the provision can include only costs that are directly and necessarily caused by the restructuring and not associated with the ongoing activities of the entity (AASB 137/IAS 37 paragraph 80).

Examples of the types of costs that would be included in a restructuring provision include the costs of:

- terminating leases and other contracts as a direct result of the restructuring
- operations conducted in effecting the restructuring, such as employee remuneration while they are engaged in such tasks as dismantling plant, disposing of surplus stocks and fulfilling contractual obligations
- making employees redundant.

Paragraph 81 of AASB 137/IAS 37 specifically indicates that the types of costs excluded from provisions for restructuring would be the costs of retraining or relocating the continuing staff, marketing costs and costs related to investment in new systems and distribution networks. These types of costs relate to the future conduct of the entity and do not relate to present obligations.

These requirements relating to the types of costs that qualify as restructuring costs apply equally to internal restructurings as well as to restructurings occurring as part of an acquisition. Figure 8.4 provides examples of costs that qualify as restructuring costs and figure 8.5 provides examples of costs that *do not* qualify as restructuring costs.

FIGURE 8.4	Examples of costs that qualify as restructuring costs

Example 1
A restructuring plan includes discontinuing operations currently performed in a facility that is leased under an operating lease. A lease-cancellation penalty fee payable on terminating the lease is a restructuring cost.

Example 2
A restructuring plan includes relocating operations currently performed in a facility leased by the acquired entity to a site that is owned by the acquirer. The lessor will not release the acquired entity from the lease agreement and will not permit the acquirer or acquiree to sublease the facility. The acquirer does not intend to re-open the facility prior to the lease's expiration. The leased space provides no future benefit to the enterprise. The lease payments by the acquiree for the remaining non-cancellable term of the operating lease after operations cease are a restructuring cost.

FIGURE 8.5	Examples of costs that do not qualify as restructuring costs

Example 1
The acquired entity used to share computer resources with its previous parent company. Therefore, the restructuring plan includes activities to separate the acquired entity from its previous parent and establish independent computer resources. The costs include costs of installing a LAN, moving head office PCs, moving a call centre, moving dedicated systems and acquisitions of new software. Such costs are associated with the ongoing activities of the entity and so are not restructuring costs.

Example 2
The restructuring plan includes costs to hire outside consultants to identify future corporate goals and strategies for organisational structure. The consultants' costs are associated with the ongoing activities of the entity and so are not restructuring costs.

It is important to note that, although certain costs have occurred only because of restructuring, this fact alone does not qualify them for recognition as restructuring costs. They also have to be costs that are not associated with the ongoing activities of the entity.

Binding sale agreement

The final requirement for recognition of a restructuring provision is that if the restructuring involves the sale of an operation, no obligation is deemed to arise for the sale until the entity is committed to the sale by a binding sale agreement (AASB 137/IAS 37 paragraph 78). Paragraph 79 explains:

> Even when an entity has taken a decision to sell an operation and announced that decision publicly, it cannot be committed to the sale until a purchaser has been identified and there is a binding sale agreement. Until there is a binding sale agreement, the entity will be able to change its mind and indeed will have to take another course of action if a purchaser cannot be found on acceptable terms. When the sale of an operation is envisaged as part of a restructuring, the assets of the operation are reviewed for impairment, under AASB 136 [IAS 36]. When a sale is only part of a restructuring, a constructive obligation can arise for the other parts of the restructuring before a binding sale agreement exists.

8.6.4 Other applications

The examples in figures 8.6 to 8.14, sourced from AASB 137/IAS 37 and modified to aid understanding, illustrate other applications of the recognition requirements of AASB 137/IAS 37.

FIGURE 8.6	Warranties

A manufacturer gives warranties at the time of sale to purchasers of its product. Under the terms of the contract for sale the manufacturer undertakes to make good, by repair or replacement, manufacturing defects that become apparent within three years from the date of sale. On past experience, it is probable (i.e. more likely than not) that there will be some claims under the warranties.

Present obligation as a result of a past obligating event — The obligating event is the sale of the product with a warranty, which gives rise to a legal obligation.

An outflow of resources embodying economic benefits in settlement — Probable for the warranties as a whole.

Conclusion — A provision is recognised for the best estimate of the costs of making good under the warranty products sold before the end of the reporting period.

Source: AASB 137, Guidance on Implementing AASB 137 part C, Example 1.

FIGURE 8.7	Contaminated land — legislation virtually certain to be enacted

An entity in the oil industry causes contamination but cleans up only when required to do so under the laws of the particular country in which it operates. One country in which it operates has had no legislation requiring cleaning up, and the entity has been contaminating land in that country for several years. At 31 December 2021, it is virtually certain that a draft law requiring a clean up of land already contaminated will be enacted shortly after the year end.

Present obligation as a result of a past obligating event — The obligating event is the contamination of the land (past event) which gives rise to a present obligation because of the virtual certainty of legislation requiring cleaning up.

An outflow of resources embodying economic benefits in settlement — Probable.

Conclusion — A provision is recognised for the best estimate of the costs of the clean-up.

Source: AASB 137, Guidance on Implementing AASB 137 part C, Example 2A.

FIGURE 8.8	Contaminated land and constructive obligation

An entity in the oil industry causes contamination and operates in a country where there is no environmental legislation. However, the entity has a widely published environmental policy in which it undertakes to clean up all contamination that it causes. The entity has a record of honouring this published policy.

Present obligation as a result of a past obligating event — The obligating event is the contamination of the land, which gives rise to a constructive obligation because the conduct of the entity has created a valid expectation on the part of those affected by it that the entity will clean up contamination.

An outflow of resources embodying economic benefits in settlement — Probable.

Conclusion — A provision is recognised for the best estimate of the costs of clean-up [the entity has a constructive obligation].

Source: AASB 137, Guidance on Implementing AASB 137 part C, Example 2B.

FIGURE 8.9	Offshore oilfield

An entity in the oil industry causes contamination and operates in a country where there is no environmental legislation. However, the entity has a widely published environmental policy in which it undertakes to clean up all contamination that it causes. The entity has a record of honouring this published policy.

Present obligation as a result of a past obligating event — The obligating event is the contamination of the land, which gives rise to a constructive obligation because the conduct of the entity has created a valid expectation on the part of those affected by it that the entity will clean up contamination.

An outflow of resources embodying economic benefits in settlement — Probable.

Conclusion — A provision is recognised for the best estimate of the costs of clean-up [the entity has a constructive obligation].

Source: AASB 137, Guidance on Implementing AASB 137 part C, Example 2B.

FIGURE 8.10   Refunds policy

A retail store has a policy of refunding purchases by dissatisfied customers, even though it is under no legal obligation to do so. Its policy of making refunds is generally known.

Present obligation as a result of a past obligating event — The obligating event is the sale of the product, which gives rise to a constructive obligation because the conduct of the store has created a valid expectation on the part of its customers that it will refund purchases.

An outflow of resources embodying economic benefits in settlement — Probable, a proportion of goods are returned for refund.

Conclusion — A provision is recognised for the best estimate of the costs of refunds.

Source: AASB 137, Guidance on Implementing AASB 137 part C, Example 4.

FIGURE 8.11   Legal requirement to fit smoke filters

Under new legislation, an entity is required to fit smoke filters to its factories by 30 June 2022. The entity has not fitted the smoke filters.

(a) At the end of the reporting period, 31 December 2021:

Present obligation as a result of a past obligating event — There is no obligation because there is no obligating event either for the costs of fitting smoke filters or for fines under the legislation.

Conclusion — No provision is recognised for the cost of fitting the smoke filters.

(b) At the end of the reporting period, 31 December 2022:

Present obligation as a result of a past obligating event — There is still no obligation for the costs of fitting smoke filters because no obligating event has occurred (the fitting of the filters). However, an obligation might arise to pay fines or penalties under the legislation because the obligating event has occurred (the non-compliant operation of the factory).

An outflow of resources embodying economic benefits in settlement — Assessment of the probability of incurring fines and penalties by non-compliant operation depends on the details of the legislation and the stringency of the enforcement regime.

Conclusion — No provision is recognised for the costs of fitting smoke filters. However, a provision is recognised for the best estimate of any fines and penalties that are more likely than not to be imposed.

Source: AASB 137, Guidance on Implementing AASB 137 part C, Example 6.

FIGURE 8.12   An onerous contract

An entity operates profitably from a factory that it has leased under an operating lease. During December 2022 the entity relocates its operations to a new factory. The lease on the old factory continues for the next four years. It cannot be cancelled and the factory cannot be re-let to another user.

Present obligation as a result of a past obligating event — The obligating event is the signing of the lease contract, which gives rise to a legal obligation.

An outflow of resources embodying economic benefits in settlement — When the lease becomes onerous, an outflow of resources embodying economic benefits is probable. (Until the lease becomes onerous, the entity accounts for the lease under [AASB 16/IFRS 16 *Leases*].)

Conclusion — A provision is recognised for the best estimate of the unavoidable lease payments.

Source: AASB 137, Guidance on Implementing AASB 137 part C, Example 8.

FIGURE 8.13   Repairs and maintenance: refurbishment costs — no legislative requirement

Some assets require, in addition to routine maintenance, substantial expenditure every few years for major refits or refurbishment and the replacement of major components. AASB 116 [IAS 16] *Property, Plant and Equipment* gives guidance on allocating expenditure on an asset to its component parts where these components have different useful lives or provide benefits in a different pattern.

A furnace has a lining that needs to be replaced every five years for technical reasons. At the end of the reporting period, the lining has been in use for three years.

Present obligation as a result of a past obligating event — There is no present obligation.

Conclusion — No provision is recognised.

The cost of replacing the lining is not recognised because, at the end of the reporting period, no obligation to replace the lining exists independently of the company's future actions — even the intention to incur the expenditure depends on the company deciding to continue operating the furnace or replace the lining. Instead of a provision being recognised, the depreciation of the lining takes account of its consumption (i.e. it is depreciated over five years). The re-lining costs then incurred are capitalised with the consumption of each new lining shown by depreciation over the subsequent five years.

Source: AASB 137, Guidance on Implementing AASB 137 part C, Examples 11 and 11A.

FIGURE 8.14   Repairs and maintenance: refurbishment costs — legislative requirement

An airline is required by law to overhaul its aircraft once every three years.

Present obligation as a result of a past obligating event — There is no present obligation.

Conclusion — No provision is recognised.

The costs of overhauling aircraft are not recognised as a provision for the same reasons the cost of replacing the lining is not recognised as a provision in [figure 8.13]. Even a legal requirement to overhaul does not make the costs of overhaul a liability, because no obligation exists to overhaul the aircraft independently of the entity's future actions — the entity could avoid the future expenditure by its future actions, for example, by selling the aircraft. Instead of a provision being recognised, the depreciation of the aircraft takes account of the future incidence of maintenance costs (i.e. an amount equivalent to the expected maintenance costs is depreciated over three years).

Source: AASB 137, Guidance on Implementing AASB 137 part C, Example 11B.

It is interesting to contrast figures 8.13 and 8.14 with figures 8.7 and 8.8. In figures 8.7 and 8.8, the entity had a present obligation for the costs of clean-up or removal, which were independent of the cost and useful life of the asset in question. In addition, in those examples the entity was unable to avoid the clean-up or removal, although it could be argued that it could avoid those actions and incur any resultant fines (as in figure 8.11). In that case, provision would be made for the best estimate of the costs of non-compliance with the relevant legislation.

LEARNING CHECK

☐ Provisions must not be recognised for future operating losses.
☐ If an entity has an onerous contract, it must recognise it as a provision at an amount that reflects the least net cost of exiting from the contract, which is the lower of the cost of fulfilling it and any compensation or penalties arising from failure to fulfil it.

▶

□ A restructuring provision shall be recorded in the statement of financial position of the acquiree if the entity has a present obligation to restructure; costs that are directly and necessarily caused by the restructuring (excluding costs associated with ongoing activities of the entity) can be measured reliably; and the entity is committed to the sale of an operation, if applicable, by a binding sale agreement.

8.7 Contingent assets

LEARNING OBJECTIVE 8.7 Outline the concept of a contingent asset.

Paragraph 10 of AASB 137/IAS 37 defines a **contingent asset** as:

> a possible asset that arises from past events and whose existence will be confirmed only by the occurrence or non-occurrence of one or more uncertain future events not wholly within the control of the entity.

Paragraph 31 of AASB 137/IAS 37 states that an entity should *not recognise* a contingent asset. Paragraph 89 requires that a contingent asset be *disclosed* where an inflow of benefits is probable.

Note the lack of symmetry between the definition of a contingent asset and a contingent liability. The definition of a contingent liability includes both possible liabilities and liabilities that fail the recognition criteria. A contingent asset includes only possible assets. The standard setters were presumably concerned with overstatement of assets and therefore wanted to apply a more stringent test to the definition, although arguably an asset that fails the recognition criteria is more of an asset than a possible asset! Further, paragraph 35 of AASB 137/IAS 37 permits a contingent asset to be reclassified and recognised as an actual asset only when it has become virtually certain that an inflow of economic benefits will arise. Contrast this with the test of probability, which is applied to asset recognition generally. It could be argued that AASB 137/IAS 37 is biased towards ensuring that contingent liabilities are disclosed in almost all circumstances and reclassified and recognised as actual liabilities as soon as they meet the liability recognition criteria. Contingent assets, however, can be disclosed only in rare circumstances and reclassified to actual assets only when they meet strict recognition criteria.

An example of a contingent asset would be the possible receipt of damages arising from a court case, which has been decided in favour of the entity as at the end of the reporting period. The hearing to determine damages, however, will be held after the end of the reporting period. The outcome of the hearing is outside the control of the entity, but the receipt of damages is probable because the case has been decided in the entity's favour. The asset meets the definition of a contingent asset because it is possible that the entity will receive the damages and the hearing is outside its control. In addition, the contingent asset is disclosed because it is probable that the damages (the inflow of economic benefits) will flow to the entity.

LEARNING CHECK

□ AASB 137/IAS 37 defines a contingent asset as a possible asset that arises from past events and whose existence will be confirmed only by the occurrence or non-occurrence of one or more uncertain future events not wholly within the control of the entity.
□ An entity should not recognise a contingent asset.
□ A contingent asset must be disclosed where an inflow of benefits is probable.

8.8 Disclosure

LEARNING OBJECTIVE 8.8 Describe the disclosure requirements for provisions, contingent liabilities and contingent assets.

The disclosure requirements of AASB 137/IAS 37 are self-explanatory and are reproduced below.

> 84. For each class of provision, an entity shall disclose:
>   (a) the carrying amount at the beginning and end of the period;
>   (b) additional provisions made in the period, including increases to existing provisions;
>   (c) amounts used (i.e. incurred and charged against the provision) during the period;
>   (d) unused amounts reversed during the period; and
>   (e) the increase during the period in the discounted amount arising from the passage of time and the effect of any change in the discount rate.
>   Comparative information is not required.

85. An entity shall disclose the following for each class of provision:
   (a) a brief description of the nature of the obligation and the expected timing of any resulting outflows of economic benefits;
   (b) an indication of the uncertainties about the amount or timing of those outflows. Where necessary to provide adequate information, an entity shall disclose the major assumptions made concerning future events, as addressed in paragraph 48; and
   (c) the amount of any expected reimbursement, stating the amount of any asset that has been recognised for that expected reimbursement.
86. Unless the possibility of any outflow in settlement is remote, an entity shall disclose for each class of contingent liability at the end of the reporting period a brief description of the nature of the contingent liability and, where practicable:
   (a) an estimate of its financial effect, measured under paragraphs 36–52;
   (b) an indication of the uncertainties relating to the amount or timing of any outflow; and
   (c) the possibility of any reimbursement.
89. Where an inflow of economic benefits is probable, an entity shall disclose a brief description of the nature of the contingent assets at the end of the reporting period, and, where practicable, an estimate of their financial effect, measured using the principles set out for provisions in paragraphs 36–52.
91. Where any of the information required by paragraphs 86 and 89 is not disclosed because it is not practicable to do so, that fact shall be stated.
92. In extremely rare cases, disclosure of some or all of the information required by paragraphs 84–89 can be expected to prejudice seriously the position of the entity in a dispute with other parties on the subject matter of the provision, contingent liability or contingent asset. In such cases, an entity need not disclose the information, but shall disclose the general nature of the dispute, together with the fact that, and reason why, the information has not been disclosed.

The disclosures required for contingent liabilities and assets necessarily involve judgement and estimation. Many analysts consider the contingent liabilities note to be one of the most important notes provided by a company because it helps the analyst to make his or her own decision about the likely consequences for the company and is useful in providing an overall view of the company's exposures. Thus, the use of the exemption permitted in paragraph 92 of AASB 137/IAS 37 should be treated with caution because it could be interpreted as deliberate concealment of the company's exposures.

An example of the disclosures required by paragraph 85 is included in Guidance on Implementing AASB 137 part D, shown in figure 8.15.

FIGURE 8.15	Warranties

A manufacturer gives warranties at the time of sale to purchasers of its three product lines. Under the terms of the warranty, the manufacturer undertakes to repair or replace items that fail to perform satisfactorily for two years from the date of sale. At the end of the reporting period, a provision of $60 000 has been recognised. The provision has not been discounted as the effect of discounting is not material. The following information is disclosed:

A provision of $60 000 has been recognised for expected warranty claims on products sold during the last three [annual reporting periods]. It is expected that the majority of this expenditure will be incurred in the next [annual reporting period], and all will be incurred within two years [of the end of the reporting period].

Source: AASB 137, Guidance on Implementing AASB 137 part D, Example 1.

A good example of extensive disclosures of provisions, related assumptions and contingent liabilities is included in the annual report of Bayer AG, a global enterprise based in Germany, reporting under IFRS. Figure 8.16 is an extract from the contingencies note (Note 31) and the first part of the note on legal risks (Note 32). Refer to the annual report at www.bayer.com for the full Note 32.

FIGURE 8.16	Example of disclosures of contingencies, Bayer

31. Contingent liabilities and other financial commitments

Contingent liabilities
The following warranty contracts, guarantees and other contingent liabilities existed at the end of the reporting period:

▶

Contingent liabilities

	Dec. 31, 2016 € million	Dec. 31, 2017 € million
Warranties	100	88
Guarantees	264	148
Other contingent liabilities	444	614
Total	**808**	**850**

The guarantees mainly comprise a declaration issued by Bayer AG to the trustees of the U.K. pension plans guaranteeing the pension obligations of Bayer Public Limited Company and Bayer CropScience Limited. Under the declaration, Bayer AG — in addition to the two companies — undertakes to make further payments into the plans upon receipt of a payment request from the trustees. The net liability with respect to these defined benefit plans as of December 31, 2017, declined to €148 million (2016: €264 million).

Other financial commitments

The other financial commitments were as follows:

Other financial commitments		B 31/2
€ million	Dec. 31, 2016	Dec. 31, 2017
Operating leases	1 101	801
Commitments under purchase agreements for property, plant and equipment	479	493
Contractual obligation to acquire intangible assets	243	83
Capital contribution commitments	182	149
Binding acquisition agreement with Monsanto Company, St. Louis, Missouri, U.S.A.[1]	53 000	47 000
Unpaid portion of the effective initial fund	1 213	1 005
Potential payment obligations under R&D collaboration agreements	2 444	2 349
Revenue-based milestone payment commitments	1 839	1 903
Total	**60 501**	**53 508**

1. The contingent financial commitment of approximately US$56 billion was translated at the closing rate and rounded.

On September 14, 2016, Bayer signed a definitive merger agreement with Monsanto Company, St. Louis, Missouri, United States, which provides for Bayer's acquisition of all outstanding shares in Monsanto Company against a cash payment of US$128 per share. Bayer thus has a contingent financial commitment in the amount of approximately US$56 billion to acquire Monsanto's entire outstanding capital stock. Further details of this planned acquisition are given in Note [6.2].

Financial commitments resulting from orders already placed under purchase agreements related to planned or ongoing capital expenditure projects totaled €493 million (2016: €479 million) while contractual obligations to acquire intangible assets totaled €83 million (2016: €243 million).

The nondiscounted future minimum lease payments relating to operating leases totaled €801 million (2016: €1 101 million). The decline is largely due to the deconsolidation of Covestro. The maturities of the respective payment obligations were as follows:

Operating leases			B 31/3
Maturing in	Dec. 31, 2016 € million	Maturing in	Dec. 31, 2017 € million
2017	237	2018	166
2018	192	2019	143
2019	161	2020	124
2020	138	2021	93
2021	102	2022	73
2022 or later	271	2023 or later	201
Total	**1 101**	**Total**	**801**

The Bayer Group has entered into cooperation agreements with third parties under which it has agreed to fund various research and development projects or has assumed other payment obligations based on the achievement of certain milestones or other specific conditions. If all of these payments have to be made, their maturity distribution as of December 31, 2017, was expected to be as set forth in the following table. The amounts shown represent the maximum payments to be made, and it is unlikely that they will all fall due. Since the achievement of the conditions for payment is highly uncertain, both the amounts and the dates of the actual payments may vary considerably from those stated in the table.

Potential payment obligations under R&D collaboration agreements

Maturing in	Dec. 31, 2016 € million	Maturing in	Dec. 31, 2017 € million
2017	233	2018	157
2018	151	2019	510
2019	333	2020	143
2020	66	2021	143
2021	28	2022	54
2022 or later	1 633	2023 or later	1 342
Total	**2 444**	**Total**	**2 349**

In addition to the above commitments, there were also revenue-based milestone payment commitments totaling €1923 million (2016: €1839 million), of which €1764 million (2016: €1834 million) was not expected to fall due until 2023 (2016: 2022) or later. These commitments are also highly uncertain.

32. Legal risks

As a global company with a diverse business portfolio, the Bayer Group is exposed to numerous legal risks, particularly in the areas of product liability, competition and antitrust law, anticorruption, patent disputes, tax assessments and environmental matters. The outcome of any current or future proceedings cannot normally be predicted. It is therefore possible that legal or regulatory judgments or future settlements could give rise to expenses that are not covered, or not fully covered, by insurers' compensation payments and could significantly affect our revenues and earnings.

Source: Bayer AG (2017, pp. 295–6).

LEARNING CHECK

☐ AASB 137/IAS 37 lists disclosure requirements for each class of provision. This includes a reconciliation of increases and decreases during the financial period (comparative information is not required), a brief description of the nature of the obligation and the expected timing of any resulting outflows of economic benefits and the relevant uncertainties involved, and the amount of any expected reimbursement.

☐ The disclosures required for contingent liabilities and assets involve judgement and estimation.

☐ Many analysts consider the contingent liabilities note to be one of the most important notes provided by a company. The use of the exemption permitted in paragraph 92 should be treated with caution because it could be interpreted as deliberate concealment of the company's exposures.

8.9 Comparison between AASB 3/IFRS 3 and AASB 137/IAS 37 in respect of contingent liabilities

LEARNING OBJECTIVE 8.9 Compare the requirements of AASB 3/IFRS 3 regarding contingent liabilities with those of AASB 137/IAS 37.

AASB 3/IFRS 3 *Business Combinations* contains a number of requirements that are inconsistent with AASB 137/IAS 37. However, as discussed in section 8.6.3, the requirements in respect of restructuring provisions are consistent with AASB 137/IAS 37. The two areas of difference are in respect of contingent liabilities acquired in a business combination and contingent consideration.

8.9.1 Contingent liabilities acquired in a business combination

As discussed in section 8.3.1, AASB 137/IAS 37 states that contingent liabilities must *not* be recognised in the statement of financial position. Instead, they are disclosed if certain conditions are met. However, AASB 3/IFRS 3 (paragraph 23) states that the requirements of AASB 137/IAS 37 *do not apply* in determining which contingent liabilities to recognise at the acquisition date. Instead, the acquirer *must* recognise contingent liabilities assumed in a business combination — just as it must recognise all

---

other liabilities assumed in a business combination. The only conditions for recognising the contingent liability are:

(a) it must be a present obligation arising from past events
(b) its fair value can be measured reliably.

Condition (a) means that contingent liabilities falling within part (a) of the contingent liability definition (i.e. a possible obligation — see section 8.3) are not recognised in a business combination — only those that fall within part (b) of the definition are eligible for recognition (i.e. there is a present obligation) provided their value can be reliably measured. This means that an acquirer must identify which contingent liabilities of the acquiree are present obligations that failed the recognition criteria from the perspective of the acquiree but which can be assigned a fair value by the acquirer. This is shown in illustrative example 8.7.

ILLUSTRATIVE EXAMPLE 8.7

Contingent liabilities in a business combination

Guitar Ltd is being acquired by Piano Ltd. Guitar Ltd had identified damages payable in a lawsuit as a present obligation because it had lost the case, but it did not record the contingent liability as a liability because it could not reliably measure the amount payable.

Required
How should Piano Ltd account for the obligation?

Solution
The acquirer, Piano Ltd, would need to estimate the fair value of the amount payable and recognise it as one of the liabilities assumed in the business combination.

8.9.2 Contingent consideration in a business combination

Sometimes an acquirer may enter into an agreement with the vendor of the acquiree that entitles the vendor to additional consideration if certain conditions are met in the future. This is referred to as contingent consideration. AASB 3/IFRS 3 paragraph 39 requires the acquirer to include the fair value of that contingent consideration as part of the consideration transferred in exchange for the acquiree. This means that the acquirer must make an estimate, if necessary, to determine the fair value and would record a liability for the amount of the contingency. This applies unless the contingent consideration is in the form of equity instruments, in which case the amount would be recorded as an equity instrument. This is illustrated in illustrative example 8.8.

ILLUSTRATIVE EXAMPLE 8.8

Accounting for contingent consideration in a business combination

Atlas Ltd acquires 100% of Maps Ltd from Carto Ltd. The purchase consideration comprises cash of $1 500 000 plus an agreement to pay a further $200 000 in cash to Carto Ltd if Maps Ltd achieves certain profit targets within 3 years of the acquisition date. The fair value of the net assets of Maps Ltd acquired is $1 200 000. Atlas Ltd estimates the acquisition date fair value of the contingent consideration to be $140 000 based on its expectations of Maps Ltd's future performance and the time value of money.

Required
How would Atlas Ltd record the transaction at the date of acquisition?

Solution
Atlas Ltd records the following journal entry at the date of acquisition. (See chapter 25 for more details on how to account for a business combination.)

Net assets of Maps Ltd	Dr	1 200 000	
Goodwill	Dr	440 000	
Cash	Cr		1 500 000
Liability to Pay Carto Ltd	Cr		140 000

Note that if the contingent consideration was not recorded (i.e. if the requirements of AASB 137/IAS 37 were followed) goodwill would be lower. Companies wishing to minimise the amount of goodwill arising on acquisition would thus want to record a lower amount for contingent consideration.

Table 8.1 summarises the similarities and differences between AASB 3/IFRS 3 and AASB 137/IAS 37.

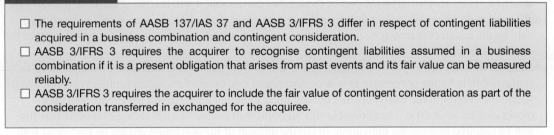

TABLE 8.1   **Similarities and differences between AASB 3/IFRS 3 and AASB 137/IAS 37**

	AASB 137/IAS 37	AASB 3/IFRS 3	Same/different
Contingent liabilities — part (a) of the definition of a contingent liability	Possible liabilities are not recognised by the entity.	Possible liabilities are not recognised by the acquirer.	Same
Contingent liabilities — part (b) of the definition of a contingent liability	A present obligation that fails either of the recognition criteria must not be recognised by the entity.	A present obligation whose fair value can be reliably measured must be recognised by the acquirer.	Different
Contingent consideration	Contingent consideration is not specifically addressed, but applying the definition of a contingent liability would likely result in no amount being recognised by the entity.	Contingent consideration must be recognised by the acquirer at its acquisition date fair value.	Different
Restructuring provisions	A restructuring provision is recognised by the entity only if the criteria in AASB 137/IAS 37 are met.	A restructuring provision is recognised by the *acquiree* only if the criteria in AASB 137/IAS 37 are met.	Same

LEARNING CHECK

☐ The requirements of AASB 137/IAS 37 and AASB 3/IFRS 3 differ in respect of contingent liabilities acquired in a business combination and contingent consideration.

☐ AASB 3/IFRS 3 requires the acquirer to recognise contingent liabilities assumed in a business combination if it is a present obligation that arises from past events and its fair value can be measured reliably.

☐ AASB 3/IFRS 3 requires the acquirer to include the fair value of contingent consideration as part of the consideration transferred in exchanged for the acquiree.

SUMMARY

AASB 137/IAS 37 deals with the recognition, measurement and presentation of provisions and contingent assets and contingent liabilities. The standard contains specific requirements regarding the recognition of restructuring provisions and onerous contracts.

The standard:

- defines provisions and specifies recognition criteria and measurement requirements for the recognition of provisions in financial statements
- defines contingent liabilities and contingent assets and prohibits their recognition in the financial statements but requires their disclosure when certain conditions are met
- requires that where provisions are measured using estimated cash flows, that the cash flows be discounted to their present value at the reporting date and specifies the discount rate to be used for this purpose
- prohibits providing for future operating losses
- defines onerous contracts and requires the estimated net loss under onerous contracts to be provided for
- specifies recognition criteria for restructuring provisions and identifies the types of costs that may be included in restructuring provisions
- requires extensive disclosures relating to provisions, recoveries, contingent liabilities and contingent assets.

The standard differs from AASB 3/IFRS 3 *Business Combinations* in respect of the recognition of contingent liabilities and contingent consideration. However, it is consistent with AASB 3/IFRS 3 in respect of restructuring provisions.

KEY TERMS

best estimate The amount which represents, as closely as possible, what the entity would rationally pay to settle the present obligation at the end of the reporting period or to provide consideration to a third party to assume it.

constructive obligation An obligation that derives from an entity's actions where: (a) by an established pattern of past practice, published policies or a sufficiently specific current statement, the entity has indicated to other parties that it will accept certain responsibilities; and (b) as a result, the entity has created a valid expectation on the part of those other parties that it will discharge those responsibilities.

contingent asset A possible asset that arises from past events and whose existence will be confirmed only by the occurrence or non-occurrence of one or more uncertain future events not wholly within the control of the entity.

contingent liability (a) A possible obligation that arises from past events and whose existence will be confirmed only by the occurrence or non-occurrence of one or more uncertain future events not wholly within the control of the entity; or (b) a present obligation that arises from past events but is not recognised because: (i) it is not probable that an outflow of resources embodying economic benefits will be required to settle the obligation; or (ii) the amount of the obligation cannot be measured with sufficient reliability.

liability A present obligation of the entity to transfer an economic resource as a result of past events.

onerous contract A contract in which the unavoidable costs of meeting the obligations under the contract exceed the economic benefits expected to be received under it.

present obligation A duty or responsibility to act or perform in a certain way.

provision A liability of uncertain timing or amount.

DEMONSTRATION PROBLEM

8.1 Reporting provisions, contingent liabilities and contingent assets

LMI Ltd is a lawnmower manufacturer. Its reporting period ends 30 June. Following is an extract from its financial statements at 30 June 2023.

Current liabilities	
Provisions	
Provision for warranties	$525 000
Non-current liabilities	
Provisions	
Provision for warranties	131 004
Non-current assets	
Plant and equipment	
At cost	$4 000 000
Accumulated depreciation	1 000 000
Carrying amount	3 000 000

Plant and equipment has a useful life of 8 years and is depreciated on a straight-line basis.

Note 37 — contingent liabilities

LMI signed an agreement with BankSouth on 3 April 2023 to the effect that LMI guarantees a loan made by BankSouth to LMI's subsidiary, LSS Ltd. LSS's loan with BankSouth was $56 million as at 30 June 2023. LSS was in a strong financial position at 30 June 2023 and accordingly LMI believes that it is not probable that the guarantee will be called (AASB 137/IAS 37 paragraph 86).

The provision for warranties at 30 June 2023 was calculated using the following assumptions (there was no balance carried forward from the prior year).

Estimated cost of repairs — products with minor defects	$2 000 000
Estimated cost of repairs — products with major defects	$5 500 000
Expected % of products sold during FY 2023 having no defects in FY 2024	75%
Expected % of products sold during FY 2023 having minor defects in FY 2024	20%
Expected % of products sold during FY 2023 having major defects in FY 2024	5%
Expected timing of settlement of warranty payments — those with minor defects	90% in FY 2024, 10% in FY 2025
Expected timing of settlement of warranty payments — those with major defects	60% in FY 2024, 40% in FY 2025
Discount rate	7%. The effect of discounting for FY 2024 is considered to be immaterial.

During the year ended 30 June 2024, the following occurred.
- In relation to the warranty provision of $656 004 at 30 June 2023, $420 000 was paid out of the provision. Of the amount paid, $360 000 was for products with minor defects and $60 000 was for products with major defects, all of which related to amounts that had been expected to be paid in the 2024 financial year.
- In calculating its warranty provision for 30 June 2024, LMI made the following adjustments to the assumptions used for the prior year.

Estimated cost of repairs — products with minor defects	$2 500 000
Estimated cost of repairs — products with major defects	$6 000 000
Expected % of products sold during FY 2024 having no defects in FY 2025	80%
Expected % of products sold during FY 2024 having minor defects in FY 2025	17%
Expected % of products sold during FY 2024 having major defects in FY 2025	3%
Expected timing of settlement of warranty payments — those with minor defects	All in FY 2025
Expected timing of settlement of warranty payments — those with major defects	50% in FY 2025, 50% in FY 2026
Discount rate	No change. The effect of discounting for FY 2025 is considered to be immaterial.

- LMI determined that part of its machinery needed an overhaul — the plasma cutter on one of its machines would need to be replaced in about June 2025 at an estimated cost of $550 000. The carrying amount of the plasma cutter at 30 June 2023 was $300 000. Its original cost was $400 000.
- The subsidiary of LMI, LSS Ltd, was in a strong financial position at 30 June 2024. However, LSS was sued by one of its competitors for patent infringement in April 2024. The compensation claimed in relation to the patent infringement is $87 million. The hearing for the dispute had not been scheduled as at the date the financial statements for 2024 were authorised for issue. The legal adviser of LSS was of opinion that there was a 30% chance that LSS would be found guilty. If found guilty, there was a 60% chance that LSS would need to pay $50 million as compensation to the plaintiff, and a 40% chance it would have to pay $30 million compensation.

Required

Prepare the relevant extracts from the financial statements (including the notes) of LMI Ltd as at 30 June 2024, in compliance with AASB 137/IAS 37 and related accounting standards. Include comparative figures where required. Show all workings separately. Perform your workings in the following order.

(a) Calculate the warranty provision as at 30 June 2023. This should agree with the financial statements provided in the question.
(b) Calculate the warranty provision as at 30 June 2024.
(c) Calculate the movement in the warranty provision for the year ended 30 June 2024.
(d) Calculate the prospective change in depreciation required as a result of the shortened useful life of the plasma cutter.
(e) Determine whether the bank guarantee meets the definition of a provision or a contingent liability for the year ended 30 June 2024 given the patent infringement action against LSS.
(f) Prepare the financial statement disclosures.

SOLUTION

(a) *Warranty provision at 30 June 2023*

	$
No defect + (75% × 0) =	0
Minor defects + (20% × $2 000 000) =	400 000
Major defects + (5% × $5 500 000) =	275 000
	$675 000
Timing:	
FY 2024	
Minor defects + (90% × $400 000) =	$360 000
Major defects + (60% × $275 000) =	165 000
	525 000 (current portion)
FY 2025	
Minor defects + (10% × $400 000 discount at 7% [for 2 years]) = $40 000/1.145	34 934
Major defects + (40% × $275 000 discounted at 7% [for 2 years]) = $110 000/1.145	96 070
	131 004 (non-current portion)
Therefore total provision = $525 000 + $131 004 =	$656 004

(b) *Warranty provision at 30 June 2024*

	$
No defect + (80% × 0)	0
Minor defects + (17% × $2 500 000)	425 000
Major defects + (3% × $6 000 000)	180 000
	$605 000
Timing:	
FY 2025	
Minor defects + $425 000	$425 000
Major defects + (50% × $180 000)	90 000
	515 000 (current portion)
FY 2026	
Major defects + (50% × $180 000 discounted at 7% [for 2 years]) = $90 000/1.145	78 603 (non-current portion)
Therefore total new provision for FY 2024 = $515 000 + $78 603 =	$593 603

(c) *Movement in the warranty provision*

Opening balance	$656 004	
Plus: Increase in the provision	593 603	
Less: Amounts used during the year	(420 000)	
Less: Unused amounts reversed during the year	(105 000)	[$525 000 expected to be paid in FY 2024, $420 000 was actually paid]
Plus: Increase in discounted amount arising from the passage of time	18 996	[$150 000* − $131 004]
Closing balance	743 603	
Balance of provision from FY 2023 payable in FY 2025	150 000	(current portion)
Therefore total provision = $665 000 + $78 603 =	$743 603	

*$150 000 = 10% of $400 000 (minor defects) + 40% of $275 000 (major defects) = $40 000 + $110 000

(d) *Prospective change in depreciation*

The expected overhaul is not a provision as LMI has no present obligation to conduct the overhaul. Rather, it is evidence that the plasma cutter's useful life has been shortened. The change in the depreciation rate must be accounted for prospectively in accordance with paragraph 61 of AASB 116/IAS 16 as follows.

Plasma cutter	As at 30 June 2023	As at 30 June 2024
Original cost	$400 000	$400 000
Accumulated depreciation	100 000	250 000
Carrying amount	300 000	150 000

The following adjustment should be made.

Original expected life	8 years
Expired life at 30 June 2023	2 years
New expected life	4 years (2 years old at 30 June 2023, approximately 2 years left)
Therefore, remaining life at 30 June 2023	2 years
Therefore, new depreciation amount should be	$150 000 per annum (i.e. $300 000/2 years)
Therefore, accumulated depreciation as at 30 June 2024	$250 000 ($100 000 + $150 000)

Calculations for disclosure of machinery:

	Excluding cutter (8-year life)	Cutter (4-year life)	Total
Cost	$3 600 000	$400 000	$4 000 000
Accumulated depreciation to 30 June 2024	1 350 000	250 000	1 600 000
Carrying amount	2 250 000	150 000	2 400 000

(e) *Bank guarantee*

LMI's guarantee of the loan made by BankSouth to LSS Ltd would be disclosed as a contingent liability rather than recorded as a provision because LSS was in a good financial position at 30 June 2024. There is a low possibility that LSS would be found guilty on the lawsuit. Therefore, while LMI has a present obligation under the guarantee, it is not probable that an outflow of economic benefits will be required to settle the obligation.

(f) *Extracts from financial statements of LMI Limited as at 30 June 2024*

	30 June 2024 $	30 June 2023 $	Reference
Current liabilities			AASB 101/IAS 1 paragraph 60
Provisions			AASB 101/IAS 1 paragraph 54
— Provision for warranties (Note X)	665 000	525 000	
Non-current liabilities			AASB 101/IAS 1 paragraph 60
— Provision for warranties (Note X)	78 603	131 004	AASB 101/IAS 1 paragraph 54
Non-current assets			AASB 101/IAS 1 paragraph 60
Plant and equipment (Note Y)	2 400 000	3 000 000	AASB 101/IAS 1 paragraph 54

Note X: Provision for warranties

LMI provides for expected amounts payable under warranties for products sold during the financial year. The portion of the warranty provision that is expected to be settled more than 1 year after the end of the reporting period is classified as a non-current provision. Assumptions used in calculating the warranty are based on past history and experience and include the percentage of products having minor defects versus those having major defects, the expected costs of rectifying those defects and the expected timing of settlement.			AASB 137/IAS 37 paragraph 85

Reconciliation of warranty provision:			AASB 137/IAS 37 paragraph 84
Opening balance		656 004	
Plus: Additional provision made in the current year		593 603	
Less: Amounts used during the year		(420 000)	
Less: Unused amounts reversed during the year		(105 000)	
Plus: Increase in discounted amount arising from the passage of time		18 996	
Closing balance		743 603	

Note 1: Summary of significant accounting policies
(y) Plant and equipment

Plant and equipment is measured at cost less depreciation. Cost includes expenditure that is directly attributable to the acquisition of the items. Depreciation is calculated on a straight-line basis. Useful lives of the assets vary from 4 years to 8 years.			AASB 116/IAS 16 paragraph 73

Note Y			AASB 116/IAS 16 paragraph 73
— At cost	4 000 000	4 000 000	
— Accumulated depreciation	1 600 000	1 000 000	
— Carrying amount	2 400 000	3 000 000	

Note 37: Contingent liabilities

LMI has an agreement with BankSouth to the effect that LMI guarantees a loan made by BankSouth to LMI's subsidiary, LSS Ltd. LSS's loan with BankSouth was $49 million as at 30 June 2024 (2023: $56 million). LSS was in a strong financial position at 30 June 2024 and accordingly LMI believes that it is not probable that the guarantee will be called (AASB 137/IAS 37 paragraph 86).			AASB 137/IAS 37 paragraph 86

COMPREHENSION QUESTIONS

1 How is present value related to the concept of a liability?
2 Define (a) a contingency and (b) a contingent liability.
3 What are the characteristics of a provision?
4 Define a constructive obligation.
5 What is the key characteristic of a present obligation?
6 What are the recognition criteria for provisions?
7 At what point would a contingent liability become a provision?
8 Compare and contrast the requirements of AASB 3/IFRS 3 and AASB 137/IAS 37 in respect of restructuring provisions and contingent liabilities.

CASE STUDY 8.1

DISTINGUISH BETWEEN PROVISIONS AND CONTINGENT LIABILITIES

Provisions are recognised as a liability in the statement of financial position whereas contingent liabilities are not recognised in the financial statements but disclosed in the notes to financial statements. Paragraph 12 of AASB 137/IAS 37 *Provisions, Contingent Liabilities and Contingent Assets* states that 'in a general sense, all provisions are contingent because they are uncertain in timing or amount'.

Required

What are some of the possible reasons that provisions are recognised in the financial statements but contingent liabilities are not?

CASE STUDY 8.2

MANAGEMENT JUDGEMENTS

Moolie Ltd is a manufacturer and retailer of surfboards. It gives purchasers a warranty at the time of sale for manufacturing defects that become apparent within 2 years from the date of sale. Based on past experience, Moolie expects to have 5% of its sales returned for manufacturing defects.

Required

Figure 8.2 provides a useful decision tree to help management make judgements on classifying a liability. Using this decision tree, determine how the case should be recorded.

CASE STUDY 8.3

LACK OF SYMMETRY BETWEEN A CONTINGENT ASSET AND A CONTINGENT LIABILITY

Jackshire Ltd filed a lawsuit against Bormire Ltd for compensation of $23 million after Bormire failed to deliver goods on time. At the end of the financial year the outcome of the hearing is unknown. The lawyer is of the opinion that there is a 40% chance that Bormire Ltd will be found liable for the damages.

Required

Discuss how this court case should be recorded by Bormire Ltd and Jackshire Ltd.

APPLICATION AND ANALYSIS EXERCISES

★ BASIC | ★ ★ MODERATE | ★ ★ ★ DIFFICULT

8.1 Distinguishing between liabilities, provisions and contingent liabilities ★ ★   **LO2, 3, 4, 6**

Kasey Ltd's financial statements are authorised for issue on 24 August 2022.

Required

Identify whether each of the following would be a liability, a provision or a contingent liability, or none of the above, in the financial statements of Kasey Ltd as at the end of its reporting period of 30 June 2022.

1. An amount of $42 000 owing to Petal Ltd for services rendered during May 2022.
2. Long service leave, estimated to be $350 000, owing to employees in respect of past services.
3. Costs of $12 000 estimated to be incurred for relocating an employee from Kasey Ltd's head office location to another city. The staff member will physically relocate during July 2022.
4. Provision of $40 000 for the overhaul of a machine. The overhaul is needed every 5 years and the machine was 5 years old as at 30 June 2022.
5. Damages awarded against Kasey Ltd resulting from a court case decided on 26 June 2022. The judge has announced that the amount of damages will be set at a future date, expected to be in September 2022. Kasey Ltd has received advice from its lawyers that the amount of the damages could be anything between $50 000 and $2 million.

8.2 Recognising a provision ★   **LO4**

When should liabilities for each of the following items be recorded in the accounts of the business entity?

1. Acquisition of goods by purchase on credit
2. Salaries

3. Annual bonus paid to management

4. Dividends

8.3 Recognising a provision ★   LO4

The government introduces a number of changes to the goods and services (value-added) tax system. As a result of these changes, Welles Ltd, a manufacturing company, will need to retrain a large proportion of its administrative and sales workforce to ensure compliance with the new tax regulations. At the end of the reporting period, no retraining of staff has taken place.

Required

Should Welles Ltd provide for the costs of the staff training at the end of the reporting period?

8.4 Recognising a provision ★ ★   LO4

Tray Ltd is a listed company that provides food to function centres that host events such as weddings and engagement parties. After an engagement party held by one of Tray Ltd's customers in June 2023, 80 people became seriously ill, possibly as a result of food poisoning from products sold by Tray Ltd.

Legal proceedings were commenced seeking damages from Tray Ltd. Tray Ltd disputed liability by claiming that the function centre was at fault for handling the food incorrectly. Up to the date of authorisation for issue of the financial statements for the year to 30 June 2023, Tray Ltd's lawyers advised that it was probable that Tray Ltd would not be found liable. However, 2 weeks after the financial statements were published, Tray Ltd's lawyers advised that, owing to developments in the case, it was probable that Tray Ltd would be found liable and the estimated damages would be material to the company's reported profits.

Required

Should Tray Ltd recognise a liability for damages in its financial statements at 30 June 2023? How should it deal with the information it receives 2 weeks after the financial statements are published?

8.5 Recognising a provision ★ ★   LO4

In each of the following scenarios, explain whether or not Margot Ltd would be required to recognise a provision.

1. As a result of its plastics operations, Margot Ltd has contaminated the land on which it operates. There is no legal requirement to clean up the land, and Margot Ltd has no record of cleaning up land that it has contaminated.

2. As a result of its plastics operations, Margot Ltd has contaminated the land on which it operates. There is a legal requirement to clean up the land.

3. As a result of its plastics operations, Margot Ltd has contaminated the land on which it operates. There is no legal requirement to clean up the land, but Margot Ltd has a long record of cleaning up land that it has contaminated.

8.6 Risk and present value of cash flows ★ ★   LO5

Using examples, explain how a liability-specific discount rate could cause the amount calculated for a provision to be lower when the risk associated with that provision is high. How could this problem be averted in practice?

8.7 Restructuring costs ★ ★   LO6

A division of an acquired entity will be closed and activities discontinued. The division will operate for 6 months after the date of acquisition. At the end of the 6 months, a few divisional employees will be retained to finalise closure of the division, but the rest will be retrenched.

Required

Which of the following costs, if any, are restructuring costs?

1. The costs of employees (salaries and benefits) to be incurred after operations cease and that are associated with the closing of the division

2. The costs of leasing the factory space occupied by the division for the period after the date of acquisition

3. The costs of modifying the division's purchasing system to make it consistent with that of the acquirer's

8.8 Restructuring costs ★ ★   LO6

Groucho Ltd acquires Harpo Ltd. The restructuring plan, which satisfies the criteria for the existence of a present obligation under AASB 137/IAS 37 and AASB 3/IFRS 3, includes an advertising program to promote the new company image. The restructuring plan also includes costs to retrain and relocate existing employees of the acquired entity.

Required

Are these costs restructuring costs?

8.9 Recognising a provision — measurement ★ **LO5, 6**

Explain how a borrowing cost could arise as part of the measurement of a provision. Illustrate your explanation with a simple example.

8.10 Contingent liabilities — disclosure ★★ **LO3, 6, 8**

A customer filed a lawsuit against Beta Ltd in December 2023 for costs and damages allegedly incurred as a result of the failure of one of Beta Ltd's electrical products. The amount claimed was $2 million. Beta Ltd's lawyers have advised that the amount claimed is extortionate and that Beta Ltd has a good chance of winning the case. However, the lawyers have also advised that if Beta Ltd loses the case its expected costs and damages would be about $400 000.

Required

How should Beta Ltd disclose this event in its financial statements as at 31 December 2023?

8.11 Calculation of a provision ★★ **LO5, 6**

In May 2022, Savoir Ltd relocated an employee from head office to an office in another city. As at 30 June 2022, the end of Savoir Ltd's reporting period, the costs were estimated to be $44 000. Analysis of the costs is as follows.

Costs for shipping goods	$ 4 000
Airfare	8 000
Temporary accommodation costs (May and June)	6 000
Temporary accommodation costs (July and August)	8 000
Reimbursement for lease break costs (paid in July; lease was terminated in May)	3 000
Reimbursement for cost-of-living increases (for the period 15 May 2022 – 15 May 2023)	15 000

Required

Calculate the provision for relocation costs for Savoir Ltd's financial statements as at 30 June 2022. Assume that AASB 137/IAS 37 applies to this provision and that the effect of discounting is immaterial.

8.12 Restructuring provisions on acquisition ★★★ **LO4, 6**

Steel Ltd acquires Nail Ltd, effective 1 March 2023. At the date of acquisition, Steel Ltd intends to close a division of Nail Ltd. As at the date of acquisition, management has developed and the board has approved the main features of the restructuring plan and, based on available information, best estimates of the costs have been made. As at the date of acquisition, a public announcement of Steel Ltd's intentions has been made and relevant parties have been informed of the planned closure. Within a week of the acquisition being effected, management commences the process of informing unions, lessors, institutional investors and other key shareholders of the broad characteristics of its restructuring program. A detailed plan for the restructuring is developed within 3 months and implemented soon thereafter.

Required

Should Steel Ltd create a provision for restructuring as part of its acquisition accounting entries? Explain your answer. How would your answer change if all the circumstances are the same as those above except that Steel Ltd decided that, instead of closing a division of Nail Ltd, it would close down one of its own facilities?

8.13 Measuring a restructuring provision ★★ **LO6**

Technic Ltd's directors decided on 3 May 2023 to restructure the company's operations as follows.
- Factory Z would be closed down and put on the market for sale.
- 200 employees working in Factory Z would be retrenched on 31 May 2023, and would be paid their accumulated entitlements plus 3 months wages.
- The remaining 40 employees working in Factory Z would be transferred to Factory X, which would continue operating.
- Six head-office staff would be retrenched on 30 June 2023, and would be paid their accumulated entitlements plus 3 months wages.

As at the end of Technic Ltd's reporting period, 30 June 2023, the following transactions and events had occurred.
- Factory Z was shut down on 31 May 2023. An offer of $6 million had been received for Factory Z but there was no binding sales agreement.
- The 200 retrenched employees had left and their accumulated entitlements had been paid. However, an amount of $34 000, representing a portion of the 3 months wages for the retrenched employees, had still not been paid.

- Costs of $35 000 were expected to be incurred in transferring the 40 employees to their new work in Factory X. The transfer is planned for 14 July 2023.
- Five of the six head-office staff who have been retrenched have had their accumulated entitlements paid, including the 3 months wages. However, one employee, Jerry Perry, remains in order to complete administrative tasks relating to the closure of Factory Z and the transfer of staff to Factory X. Jerry is expected to stay until 31 July 2023. His salary for July will be $6000 and his retrenchment package will be $15 000, all of which will be paid on the day he leaves. He estimates that he would spend 60% of his time administering the closure of Factory Z, 30% on administering the transfer of staff to Factory X, and the remaining 10% on general administration.

Required

Calculate the amount of the restructuring provision recognised in Technic Ltd's financial statements as at 30 June 2023, in accordance with AASB 137/IAS 37.

8.14 Comprehensive problem ★ ★ ★   **LO2, 3, 5, 6, 7, 8**

Wizards Ltd, a listed company, is a manufacturer of confectionery and biscuits. The end of its reporting period is 30 June. Relevant extracts from its financial statements at 30 June 2023 are as follows.

Current liabilities		
Provisions		
Provision for warranties		$540 000
Non-current liabilities		
Provisions		
Provision for warranties		320 000
Non-current assets		
Plant and equipment		
At cost	$2 000 000	
Accumulated depreciation	600 000	
Carrying amount	1 400 000	

Plant and equipment has a useful life of 10 years and is depreciated on a straight-line basis.

Note 36 — contingent liabilities

Wizards is engaged in litigation with various parties in relation to allergic reactions to traces of peanuts alleged to have been found in packets of fruit gums. Wizards strenuously denies the allegations and, as at the date of authorising the financial statements for issue, is unable to estimate the financial effect, if any, of any costs or damages that may be payable to the plaintiffs.

The provision for warranties at 30 June 2023 was calculated using the following assumptions (no balance carried forward from the prior year).

Estimated cost of repairs — products with minor defects	$3 000 000
Estimated cost of repairs — products with major defects	$9 000 000
Expected % of products sold during FY 2023 having no defects in FY 2024	80%
Expected % of products sold during FY 2023 having minor defects in FY 2024	15%
Expected % of products sold during FY 2023 having major defects in FY 2024	5%
Expected timing of settlement of warranty payments — those with minor defects	All in FY 2024
Expected timing of settlement of warranty payments — those with major defects	40% in FY 2024, 60% in FY 2025
Discount rate	6%. The effect of discounting for FY 2024 is considered to be immaterial.

During the year ended 30 June 2024, the following occurred.
(a) In relation to the warranty provision of $860 000 at 30 June 2023, $350 000 was paid out of the provision. Of the amount paid, $250 000 was for products with minor defects and $100 000 was

for products with major defects, all of which related to amounts that had been expected to be paid in the 2024 financial year.

(b) In calculating its warranty provision for 30 June 2024, Wizards made the following adjustments to the assumptions used for the prior year.

Estimated cost of repairs — products with minor defects	No change
Estimated cost of repairs — products with major defects	$6 000 000
Expected % of products sold during FY 2024 having no defects in FY 2025	80%
Expected % of products sold during FY 2024 having minor defects in FY 2025	15%
Expected % of products sold during FY 2024 having major defects in FY 2025	5%
Expected timing of settlement of warranty payments — those with minor defects	All in FY 2025
Expected timing of settlement of warranty payments — those with major defects	25% in FY 2025, 75% in FY 2026
Discount rate	No change. The effect of discounting for FY 2024 is considered to be immaterial.

(c) Wizards determined that part of its plant and equipment needed an overhaul — the conveyor belt on one of its machines would need to be replaced in about May 2025 at an estimated cost of $250 000. The carrying amount of the conveyor belt at 30 June 2023 was $140 000. Its original cost was $200 000.

(d) Wizards was unsuccessful in its defence of the peanut allergy case and was ordered to pay $1 500 000 to the plaintiffs. As at 30 June 2024, Wizards had paid $800 000.

(e) Wizards commenced litigation against one of its advisers for negligent advice given on the original installation of the conveyor belt referred to in (c) above. In April 2024 the court found in favour of Wizards. The hearing for damages had not been scheduled as at the date the financial statements for 2024 were authorised for issue. Wizards estimated that it would receive about $425 000.

(f) Wizards signed an agreement with BankSweet to the effect that Wizards would guarantee a loan made by BankSweet to Wizards' subsidiary, CCC Ltd. CCC's loan with BankSweet was $1 500 000 as at 30 June 2024. CCC was in a strong financial position at 30 June 2024.

Required
Prepare the relevant extracts from the financial statements (including the notes) of Wizards Ltd as at 30 June 2024, in compliance with AASB 137/IAS 37 and related accounting standards. Include comparative figures where required. Show all workings separately. Perform your workings in the following order.

1. Calculate the warranty provision as at 30 June 2023. This should agree with the financial statements provided in the question.
2. Calculate the warranty provision as at 30 June 2024.
3. Calculate the movement in the warranty provision for the year.
4. Calculate the prospective change in depreciation required as a result of the shortened useful life of the conveyor belt.
5. Determine whether the unpaid amount owing as a result of the peanut allergy case is a liability or a provision.
6. Determine whether the receipt of damages for the negligent advice meets the definition of an asset or a contingent asset.
7. Determine whether the bank guarantee meets the definition of a provision or a contingent liability.
8. Prepare the financial statement disclosures.

8.15 Applying accounting theory ★ ★ ★   **LO1, 4, 5, 6**
In June 2021 Great Southern Ltd built a submarine under a contract with the Australian Navy. The contract required Great Southern Ltd to provide a 1-year warranty. The accountant was unsure how to measure the warranty because the design of the submarine differed from those previously built by Great Southern Ltd. The trainee accountant was asked to obtain more information, so she asked some engineers for their advice on the expected cost of servicing the warranty. The trainee's report is summarised below.

Engineers' estimates and accompanying explanations	
Worst-case scenario	$1 000 000
Best-case scenario	200 000
Most probable scenario	500 000
Quote from a Japanese company to take on the warranty	700 000
Recommendation: The provision for warranty should not be recognised because it is too difficult to measure.	

The accountant needs to decide whether to recognise a provision for warranty and, if so, how to measure it.

Required

1. Describe two principles from AASB 137/IAS 37 that are relevant to the accountant's decision.
2. Use the principles identified in requirement 1 to evaluate the trainee accountant's recommendation.
3. Describe an accounting policy to account for the provision for warranty.
4. Explain how the policy that you proposed in requirement 3 is consistent with AASB 137/IAS 37.
5. Identify assumptions made in the exercise of judgement in proposing an accounting policy for the warranty.

REFERENCE

Bayer AG 2017, *Annual report 2017*, Bayer AG, Germany, www.bayer.com.

ACKNOWLEDGEMENTS

Photo: © PhotoAlto / Getty Images

Figures 8.2, 8.6–8.15 and text: © 2019 Australian Accounting Standards Board (AASB). The text, graphics and layout of this publication are protected by Australian copyright law and the comparable law of other countries. No part of the publication may be reproduced, stored or transmitted in any form or by any means without the prior written permission of the AASB except as permitted by law. For reproduction or publication, permission should be sought in writing from the AASB. Requests in the first instance should be addressed to the National Director, Australian Accounting Standards Board, PO Box 204, Collins Street West, Victoria 8007.

Figure 8.16: © Bayer AG 2017

CHAPTER 9

Employee benefits

CHAPTER AIM

This chapter discusses accounting for short-term, long-term and post-employment employee benefits in accordance with AASB 119/IAS 19 *Employee Benefits*.

LEARNING OBJECTIVES

After studying this chapter, you should be able to:

9.1 outline the scope, purpose and principles of accounting for employee benefits under AASB 119/IAS 19

9.2 prepare journal entries to account for short-term liabilities for employee benefits, such as wages and salaries, sick leave and annual leave

9.3 compare defined benefit and defined contribution post-employment benefit plans

9.4 prepare entries to account for expenses, assets and liabilities arising from defined contribution post-employment plans

9.5 prepare entries to record expenses, assets and liabilities arising from defined benefit post-employment plans

9.6 explain how to measure and record other long-term liabilities for employment benefits, such as long service leave

9.7 explain when a liability should be recognised for termination benefits and how it should be measured.

CONCEPTS FOR REVIEW

Before studying this chapter, you should understand and, if necessary, revise:

- the concept of a liability in the *Conceptual Framework*
- the concept of an asset in the *Conceptual Framework*
- the concept of a provision under AASB 137/IAS 37.

9.1 Introduction to accounting for employee benefits

LEARNING OBJECTIVE 9.1 Outline the scope, purpose and principles of accounting for employee benefits under AASB 119/IAS 19.

Employee benefits typically represent a significant component of an entity's expenses. Employees are remunerated for the service they provide in the form of salary or wages (which may be paid weekly, fortnightly or monthly) and entitlements such as sick leave, annual leave, long service leave and post-employment benefits (i.e. superannuation or pension plan contributions).

Employee benefits arise from formal agreements, which are often referred to as 'workplace agreements', between an entity and its individual employees. Alternatively, employee benefits may arise from agreements between an entity and groups of employees or their representatives. These agreements are often referred to as enterprise bargaining agreements. Employee benefits also include requirements specified by legislation or industry arrangements (e.g. for employers to contribute to an industry, state or national superannuation plan). Internal organisational practices that generate a constructive obligation, such as payment of annual bonuses, also fall within the scope of employee benefits.

AASB 119/IAS 19 *Employee Benefits* applies to all employee benefits except those relating to share-based payments (which are covered under AASB 2/IFRS 2 *Share-based Payment*). Chapter 14 considers share-based payments, including share-based employee remuneration. The purpose of AASB 119/IAS 19 is to prescribe the measurement and recognition of expenses, assets and liabilities arising from service provided by employees.

Paragraph 8 of AASB 119/IAS 19 defines **employee benefits** as:

> all forms of consideration given by an entity in exchange for service rendered by employees or for the termination of employment.

Employee benefits are usually paid to employees, but the term also includes amounts paid to their dependants or to other parties.

Liabilities arise when employees provide employment service in exchange for benefits payable by the employer. The measurement of short-term liabilities for employee benefits, such as wages payable, sick leave and annual leave, is relatively straightforward. Accounting for some employee benefits including post-employment benefits (e.g. superannuation), however, is complicated because they may be provided many years after the related employment service. Further, some employee benefits for past service (e.g. long service leave, which accumulates over time but is only payable after 10 years of continuous service) may be conditional upon the continuation of employment.

LEARNING CHECK

- ☐ Employee remuneration includes salary and wages as well as entitlements such as sick leave, annual leave, long service leave and post-employment benefits (e.g. superannuation).
- ☐ Employee benefits arise from agreements between employees and employers and include benefits specified by legislation, negotiated benefits and informal practices.
- ☐ AASB 119/IAS 19 *Employee Benefits* applies to all employee benefits (except those to which AASB 2/IFRS 2 *Share-based Payment* applies) and prescribes the measurement and recognition of expenses, assets and liabilities arising from employment service provided by employees.
- ☐ Paragraph 8 of AASB 119/IAS 19 defines employee benefits as all forms of consideration given by an entity in exchange for service rendered by employees or for the termination of employment.
- ☐ Liabilities arise when employees provide service in exchange for benefits payable by the employer.
- ☐ Accounting for employee benefits is complicated because some benefits may be provided many years after employees have provided service, and some employee benefits for past service may be conditional upon an employee's continued employment.

9.2 Short-term employee benefits

LEARNING OBJECTIVE 9.2 Prepare journal entries to account for short-term liabilities for employee benefits, such as wages and salaries, sick leave and annual leave.

Paragraph 8 of AASB 119/IAS 19 defines **short-term employee benefits** as:

> employee benefits (other than termination benefits) that are expected to be settled wholly before twelve months after the end of the annual reporting period in which the employees render the related service.

Short-term employee benefits include payment for employment service (e.g. wages, salaries, bonuses and profit-sharing arrangements) as well as paid leave entitlements (e.g. sick leave and annual leave) for which employees may be eligible. AASB 119/IAS 19 refers to various forms of leave entitlements as 'paid absences'.

Short-term employee benefits also include non-monetary benefits, which are often referred to as 'fringe benefits'. Non-monetary benefits include the provision of health insurance, housing and motor vehicles, provided at the employer's discretion. An entity may offer non-monetary benefits to attract staff (e.g. a mining company may provide housing to employees where there are no major towns located near its mining sites). Non-monetary benefits may also arise from salary sacrifice arrangements, also referred to as 'salary packaging' (e.g. an employee may elect to forgo a portion of salary or wages in return for other benefits, such as a motor vehicle, provided by the employer).

9.2.1 Payroll

The subsystem for regular recording and payment of employee benefits is referred to as the **payroll**. The payroll involves:
- recording the amount of wages or salaries for the pay period
- updating personnel records for the appointment of new employees
- updating personnel records for the termination of employment contracts
- calculating the amount to be paid to each employee, net of deductions
- remitting payment of net wages or salaries to employees
- remitting payment of deductions to various external parties
- complying with regulatory requirements, such as reporting to taxation authorities.

Businesses may process several payrolls. For example, a business may process a payroll each fortnight for general employees and process a separate monthly payroll for management.

Employers are typically required to deduct and withhold income tax from employees' wages and salaries. Thus, the employee receives a payment that is net of tax and the employer subsequently pays the amount of income tax deducted to the taxation authority.

Employers may offer a service of deducting other amounts from employees' wages and salaries and paying other parties on their behalf. For example, the employer may deduct union membership fees from employees' wages and make payments to the various unions on the employees' behalf. Similarly, the employer may deduct health insurance premiums from the employees' wages and remit payments to the various health insurance funds that its employees have joined.

Payments made on behalf of an employee from wages or salaries deductions (e.g. income tax or union membership fees) form part of the entity's wages and salaries expense. As these amounts are typically paid in the month following the payment of wages and salaries, they represent a short-term employee benefits liability for the entity at the end of each month.

Paragraph 11(a) of AASB 119/IAS 19 requires short-term employee benefits for service rendered during the period to be recognised as a liability after deducting any amounts already paid. Short-term liabilities for employee benefits must be measured at the nominal (undiscounted) amount that the entity expects to pay.

9.2.2 Accounting for the payroll

Illustrative example 9.1 demonstrates accounting for the payroll, including deductions from employees' remuneration, the remittance of payroll deductions and the measurement of resulting liabilities at the end of the period.

ILLUSTRATIVE EXAMPLE 9.1

Accounting for the payroll

Curtin Ltd pays its managers on a monthly basis. All of Curtin Ltd's salaries are recognised as expenses. Curtin Ltd's employees can elect to have their monthly health insurance premiums deducted from their salaries and paid to their health insurance fund on their behalf. The company provides a similar service for the payment of union membership fees. Curtin Ltd also operates a giving scheme under which employees can elect to have donations to nominated charities deducted from their salaries and wages and remitted on their behalf to the selected charities. Figure 9.1 summarises the managerial payrolls for May and June 2022.

▶

FIGURE 9.1   Summary of Curtin Ltd's payroll

	May 2022		June 2022	
	$	$	$	$
Gross payroll for the month		2 400 000		2 500 000
Deductions payable to:				
Taxation authority	530 000		600 000	
Total Care Health Fund	40 000		40 000	
National Health Fund	20 000		20 000	
UNICEF donation	3 000		3 000	
National Heart Research Fund donation	4 000		4 000	
Union fees	12 000		12 500	
Total deductions for the month		609 000		679 500
Net salaries paid		1 791 000		1 820 500

Each time the monthly payroll is processed, the cost of the salaries is charged to expense accounts and a liability is accrued for the gross wages payable. Payments of net wages and salaries and remittance of payroll deductions to taxation authorities and other parties reduce the payroll liability account.

The managerial payroll is processed on the second Monday of the month and net salaries are paid to employees on the following Tuesday. During May, managers earned salaries of $2.4 million. After deducting amounts for income tax, union membership fees, contributions to health funds and donations, Curtin Ltd paid its managers a net amount of $1 791 000 during May. All of the deductions are paid to the various external bodies in the following month. Health insurance deductions and union subscriptions are remitted on the first Friday of the following month. Thus, the deductions for health insurance and union subscriptions for the May payroll are remitted on Friday 3 June. Income tax withheld is remitted on the 20th of the following month. Deductions for donations are paid on the 21st of the following month.

The balance of Curtin Ltd's accrued managerial payroll account at 1 June 2022 is $609 000, being the deductions from managers' salaries for income tax, health insurance premiums, union fees and donations for May 2022. These amounts are paid during June 2022.

During June 2022, Curtin Ltd's managers earned gross salaries of $2.5 million. The managers actually received $1 820 500, being the net wages and salaries after deductions for income tax, health insurance premiums, union fees and donations to charities. In total, $679 500 was deducted from managers' salaries for June 2022. This amount is a liability at the end of June 2022. The amounts deducted from employees' salaries during June 2022 are remitted during July 2022.

Required

Prepare the journal entries to record Curtin Ltd's payroll and remittances for June 2022.

Solution

The journal entries are as follows.

June 3	Accrued payroll	Dr	40 000	
	Cash	Cr		40 000
	(Payment of May payroll deductions for Total Health Care Fund)			
	Accrued payroll	Dr	20 000	
	Cash	Cr		20 000
	(Payment of May payroll deductions for National Health Fund)			
	Accrued payroll	Dr	12 000	
	Cash	Cr		12 000
	(Payment of May payroll deductions for union fees)			
13	Salaries expense	Dr	2 500 000	
	Accrued payroll	Cr		2 500 000
	(Managerial payroll for June)			
14	Accrued payroll	Dr	1 820 500	
	Cash	Cr		1 820 500
	(Payment of net salaries for June)			
20	Accrued payroll	Dr	530 000	
	Cash	Cr		530 000
	(Payment of May payroll deductions for withheld income tax)			

21	Accrued payroll	Dr	3 000	
	Cash	Cr		3 000
	(Payment of May payroll deductions for UNICEF)			
	Accrued payroll	Dr	4 000	
	Cash	Cr		4 000
	(Payment of May payroll deductions for National Heart Research Fund)			

9.2.3 Accrual of wages and salaries

The end of the payroll period often differs from the end of the reporting period because payrolls are usually determined on a weekly or fortnightly basis. Accordingly, it is usually necessary to recognise an expense and a liability for employee benefits for the business days between the last payroll period and the end of the reporting period. This is demonstrated in illustrative example 9.2.

ILLUSTRATIVE EXAMPLE 9.2

Accrual of wages and salaries

Canterbury Ltd pays its employees on a fortnightly basis. The last payroll in the year ended 31 October 2022 was for the fortnight (10 working days) ended Friday 28 October 2022. There was one business day between the end of the final payroll period and the end of the reporting period. The cost of employee benefits for the remaining day was $120 000.

Required
How would Canterbury Ltd record the accrual of wages and salaries?

Solution
Canterbury Ltd would record the following accrual.

Wages and salaries expense	Dr	120 000	
Accrued wages and salaries	Cr		120 000
(Accrual of wages and salaries)			

The accrued wages and salaries is a liability for short-term employee benefits. Paragraph 16 of AASB 119/IAS 19 requires accrued short-term employee benefits to be measured at nominal value (i.e. the amount expected to be paid to settle the obligation).

9.2.4 Short-term paid absences

As noted in section 9.2, employees may be entitled to be paid during certain absences, such as annual recreational leave or short periods of illness. Some entities also offer other forms of paid leave, including maternity leave, parental leave, carers' leave and bereavement leave. Entitlements to **short-term paid absences** are those entitlements that are expected to be settled within 12 months after the end of the reporting period.

Short-term paid absences may be either accumulating or non-accumulating (AASB 119/IAS 19 paragraph 14). **Non-accumulating paid absences** are leave entitlements that the employee may not carry forward to a future period. For example, an employment agreement may provide for 5 days of paid, non-cumulative sick leave. If the employee does not take sick leave during the year, the unused leave lapses (i.e. it does not carry forward to an increased entitlement in the following year).

Paragraph 15 of AASB 119/IAS 19 describes **accumulating paid absences** as leave entitlements that the employee may carry forward to a future period if unused in the current period. For example, an employment agreement may provide for 20 days of paid annual leave. If the employee only takes 15 days of annual leave during the year, the remaining 5 days may be carried forward and taken in the following year.

Accumulating paid absences may be vesting or non-vesting. If accumulating paid absences are vesting, the employee is entitled, upon termination of employment, to cash settlement for any unused leave. If accumulating paid absences are non-vesting, the employee has no entitlement to cash settlement of their unused leave. For example, an employment contract may provide for cumulative annual leave of 20 days per annum, vesting to a maximum of 30 days, and non-vesting cumulative sick leave of 10 days per annum. After 2 years of service, the employee would have been entitled to take 40 days of annual leave and 20 days of sick leave, but if the employee resigned after 2 years of employment, during which no annual leave or sick leave had been taken, the termination settlement would include payment for 30 days' unused annual leave (the maximum allowed by the employment agreement). There would be no cash settlement of the unused sick leave because it was non-vesting.

Paragraph 13 of AASB 119/IAS 19 requires expected short-term accumulating paid absences to be recognised when the employee renders service that increases the entitlement. For example, if an entity's employees are entitled to 2 weeks of cumulative sick leave for every year of service, the entity is required to accrue the sick leave throughout the year. The employee benefit (i.e. the accumulated leave) is measured as the amount that the entity expects to pay to settle the obligation at the end of the reporting period. If the leave is cumulative but non-vesting, it is possible that there will not be a future settlement (i.e. if the sick leave remains unused when the employment contract is terminated). However, the sick leave must still be accrued throughout the period of employment, because the employee remains entitled to the leave while they remain employed, and as such there is an obligation. If the leave is non-vesting, it is necessary to estimate the amount of accumulated paid absence that the entity expects to pay.

For non-accumulating short-term paid absences, paragraph 13 of AASB 119/IAS 19 requires the entity to recognise the employee benefit when the paid absence occurs. A liability is not recognised for unused non-accumulating leave entitlements because the employee is not entitled to carry them forward to a future period.

The alternative forms of short-term paid absences and the corresponding recognition and measurement requirements are detailed in figure 9.2.

FIGURE 9.2	Short-term paid absences		
Accumulation	**Vesting/non-vesting**	**Recognition**	**Liability measurement**
Accumulating — employee may carry forward unused entitlement	Vesting — employee is entitled to cash settlement for unused leave	Recognised as employee provides service giving rise to entitlement	Nominal, amount expected to be paid (i.e. total vested accumulated leave)
	Non-vesting — no cash settlement for unused leave	Recognised as employee provides service giving rise to entitlement	Nominal, amount expected to be paid, requires estimation of amount that will be used
Non-accumulating — unused entitlement lapses each period		Recognised when paid absences occur	No liability is recognised

Illustrative example 9.3 demonstrates accounting for annual leave. Illustrative example 9.4 demonstrates accounting for short-term paid absences.

Accounting for annual leave

Southern Cross Ltd has four employees in its Queensland branch. Each employee is entitled to 20 days of paid recreational leave per annum, referred to as annual leave (AL). A loading of 17.5% is paid when annual leave is taken. At 1 July 2021, the balance of the provision for annual leave was $5123. During the year employees took a total of 70 days of annual leave, which cost Southern Cross Ltd $10 763. After annual leave taken during the year had been recorded, the provision for annual leave had a credit balance of $5640 in the trial balance at 30 June 2022 before end-of-period adjustments. All annual leave accumulated

at 30 June 2022 is expected to be paid by 30 June 2023. The following information is obtained from the payroll records for the year ended 30 June 2022.

Employee	Wage per day ($)	AL 1 July 2021 (days)	Increase in entitlement (days)	Amount of AL taken (days)	AL balance 30 June 2022 (days)	AL liability 30 June 2022 ($)
East	120	9	20	16	13	1 833
North	160	7	20	16	11	2 068
South	180	8	20	14	14	2 961
West	90	8	20	24	4	423
						7 285

Required

How would Southern Cross Ltd account for accumulated annual leave?

Solution

A liability must be recognised for accumulated annual leave at 30 June 2022. This is measured as the amount that is expected to be paid. As annual leave is vesting, all accumulated leave is expected to be paid. The first step in measuring the liability is to calculate the number of days of accumulated annual leave for each employee at 30 June 2022. Although this calculation would normally be performed by payroll software, we will manually calculate the number of days to demonstrate this process. The next step is to multiply the number of days of accumulated annual leave by each employee's daily wage, increased by 17.5% for the annual leave loading.

The calculations of accumulated annual leave in days and the resultant liability are as follows.

East: 9 + 20 − 16 = 13 days × $120 per day × 117.5% = $1833
North: 7 + 20 − 16 = 11 days × $160 per day × 117.5% = $2068
South: 8 + 20 − 14 = 14 days × $180 per day × 117.5% = $2961
West: 8 + 20 − 24 = 4 days × $90 per day × 117.5% = $423

The above calculations show that a liability of $7285 should be recognised for annual leave at 30 June 2022. After recording annual leave taken during the year, the unadjusted trial balance shows a credit balance of $5640 for the provision for annual leave. Thus, a journal entry is required to record an increase of $1645.

Wages and salaries expense	Dr	1 645	
Provision for annual leave	Cr		1 645
(Accrual of liability for annual leave)			

In illustrative example 9.3, an annual adjustment was made to the provision for annual leave. Some entities make accruals for annual leave more frequently to facilitate more comprehensive internal reporting to management. This is easily achieved with electronic accounting systems or payroll software.

Accounting for accumulating sick leave is demonstrated in illustrative example 9.4. In this illustration, the accumulating sick leave is non-vesting.

ILLUSTRATIVE EXAMPLE 9.4

Accounting for accumulating sick leave

Massey Ltd has 10 employees who are each paid $500 per week for a 5-day working week (i.e. $100 per day). Employees are entitled to 5 days of accumulating non-vesting sick leave each year. At 1 July 2021, the accumulated sick leave brought forward from the previous year was 10 days in total. During the year ended 30 June 2022, employees took 35 days of paid sick leave and 10 days of unpaid sick leave. One employee resigned at the beginning of the year. At the time of her resignation she had accumulated 5 days of sick leave. It is estimated that 60% of the unused sick leave will be taken during the following year and that the remaining 40% will not be taken at all.

After recording sick leave taken during the year, the unadjusted trial balance shows that the balance of the provision for sick leave at 30 June 2022 is $700 Cr.

The 9 employees who were employed for all of the year ended 30 June 2022 became entitled to 5 days of sick leave during the year. Thus, the total increase in entitlement during the year is 45 days. During the year, 35 days of paid sick leave were taken and 5 days of sick leave entitlement lapsed because an employee with 5 days accumulated sick leave resigned without having used her entitlement. Thus, the aggregate sick leave entitlement reduced by 40 days during the year.

Required

How would Massey Ltd account for its liability for sick leave?

Solution

The amount of the liability at 30 June 2022 is measured by first calculating the number of days of accumulated sick leave entitlement at 30 June 2022.

	Days
Brought forward July 2021	10
Increase in entitlement for service provided in the current year	45
Sick leave entitlement taken or lapsed during the year	(40)
Sick leave carried forward 30 June 2022	15

The number of days of accumulated sick leave at the end of the reporting period is multiplied by the proportion of days expected to be taken, in this case, 60%. This amount, 9 days, is then multiplied by the current rate of pay per day.

$$15 \text{ days} \times 60\% \times \$100 \text{ per day} = \$900$$

Thus, a provision for sick leave of $900 Cr should be recognised at 30 June 2022. The unadjusted balance of the provision for sick leave is $700 Cr. Accordingly, the provision must be increased by $200 as follows.

Wages and salaries expense	Dr	200	
Provision for sick leave	Cr		200
(Accrual of liability for sick leave)			

For simplicity, the accrual adjustment to recognise sick leave is made at the end of the year in this example. Many companies make such adjustments throughout the year to provide more complete internal reporting to management. This is facilitated by payroll software that automates the calculation of accumulated entitlements.

9.2.5 Profit-sharing and bonus plans

Employers may offer profit-sharing arrangements and bonuses to their employees. Bonuses may be determined as a lump-sum amount or based on accounting or market-based measures of performance. Many large companies use bonuses in management incentive schemes. The bonus forms part of a management remuneration package designed to align the interests of the manager with the interests of the entity or its owners. Figure 9.3 shows an extract from BHP Group Ltd's 2018 annual report, detailing the short-term and long-term incentives in the company's executive remuneration policy.

Paragraph 19 of AASB 119/IAS 19 requires an entity to recognise the expected cost of profit-sharing and bonus payments if:

(a) the entity has a present legal or constructive obligation to make such payments as a result of past events; and

(b) a reliable estimate of the obligation can be made.

A present obligation exists when, and only when, the entity has no realistic alternative but to make the payments.

Although the entity may have no legal obligation to pay the bonus, a constructive obligation arises if the entity has a well-established practice of paying the bonus and it has no realistic alternative but to pay the bonus (e.g. non-payment may be harmful to the entity's relations with its employees). (See chapter 8 for further details on provisions and contingent liabilities.)

3.3.8 Components of remuneration

The components of remuneration for other Executive KMP are . . . described below.

STI

STI performance measures for other Executive KMP are similar to those of the CEO which are outlined at section 3.3.2; however, the weighting of each performance measure will vary to reflect the focus required from each Executive KMP role.

Individual performance measures are determined at the start of the financial year. These include the other Executive KMP's contribution to the delivery of projects and initiatives within the scope of their role and the overall performance of the Group. Individual performance of other Executive KMP was reviewed against these measures by the Committee and, on average, was considered slightly above target.

LTI

LTI awards granted to other Executive KMP have a maximum face value of 350 per cent of base salary, which is a fair value of 143.5 per cent of base salary under the current plan design (with a fair value of 41 per cent, taking into account the performance condition: 350 per cent × 41 per cent = 143.5 per cent).

Source: BHP Group Ltd (2018, pp. 140–1).
Note: STI: short-term incentive, LTI: long-term incentive.

Liabilities for short-term profit-sharing arrangements and bonuses are measured at the nominal (i.e. undiscounted) amount that the entity expects to pay. Thus, if the payment under a profit-sharing arrangement is subject to the employee still being employed when the payment is due, the amount recognised as a liability is reduced by the amount that is expected to go unpaid due to staff turnover. For example, assume an entity has a profit-sharing arrangement in which it is obligated to pay 1% of profit for the period to employees and the amount becomes payable 3 months after the end of the reporting period. Based on staff turnover in prior years, the entity estimates that only 95% of employees will be eligible to receive a share of profit 3 months after the end of the reporting period. Accordingly, the amount of the liability that should be recognised for the profit-sharing scheme is equal to 0.95% of the entity's profit for the period. In this simple example it is assumed the bonus is distributed equally among employees.

LEARNING CHECK

☐ Paragraph 8 of AASB 119/IAS 19 describes short-term employee benefits as those that are expected to be settled wholly within 12 months after the end of the annual reporting period in which the employee renders the service.

☐ Short-term employee benefits include wages, salaries, bonuses, profit-sharing arrangements, and paid absences (e.g. sick leave and annual leave), as well as non-monetary benefits or 'fringe benefits' (e.g. health insurance, housing and motor vehicles).

☐ Short-term paid absences may be accumulating or non-accumulating (i.e. not able to be carried forward).

☐ Accumulating paid leave absences can be vesting or non-vesting (i.e. the employee has no entitlement to cash settlement where the leave is unused).

☐ Paragraph 19 of AASB 119/IAS 19 requires an entity to recognise the expected cost of profit-sharing and bonus payments if:
  (a) the entity has a present legal or constructive obligation to make such payments as a result of past events; and
  (b) a reliable estimate of the obligation can be made.

9.3 Post-employment benefits

LEARNING OBJECTIVE 9.3 Compare defined benefit and defined contribution post-employment benefit plans.

Post-employment benefits are benefits, other than termination benefits (which are considered in section 9.5), that are payable after completion of employment, typically after the employee retires. Where post-employment benefits involve significant obligations, it is common (and in some countries compulsory) for employers to contribute to a post-employment benefit plan for employees. For example, in Australia, it is compulsory for most private sector employers to contribute to a superannuation plan for employees.

Post-employment benefit plans are defined in paragraph 8 of AASB 119/IAS 19 as:

> formal or informal arrangements under which an entity provides post-employment benefits for one or more employees.

Post-employment benefit plans are also referred to as superannuation plans, employee retirement plans and pension plans. The employer makes payments (contributions) to the employee's nominated fund, and this money is available for the employee to access at a later date (e.g. upon reaching retirement age). The fund, which is a separate entity (typically a trust) invests the contributions and provides post-employment benefits to the employee, who is a member of the fund. Figure 9.4 shows the relations between the employer, the superannuation fund (plan) and the employee (member of the fund).

FIGURE 9.4 Relationships between the employer, the superannuation fund (plan) and the employee

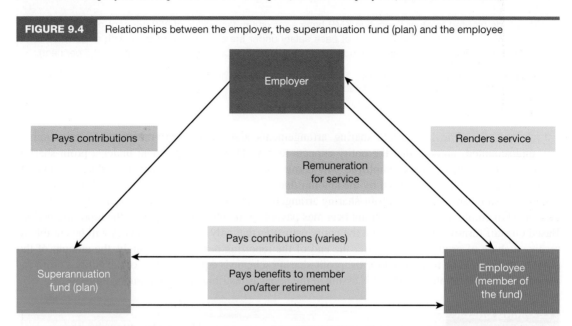

The two types of post-employment benefit plans are defined benefit plans and defined contribution plans, including multi-employer plans (where more than one employer contributes to the plan).

Paragraph 8 of AASB 119/IAS 19 refers to **defined contribution plans** as post-employment plans for which an entity (employer) pays fixed contributions to a separate entity (e.g. superannuation fund) on behalf of the employee. The contributions are normally based on a percentage of the wages and salaries paid to employees. Under a defined contribution plan, the contributing entity (employer) has no legal or constructive obligation to pay further contributions if the fund does not hold sufficient assets to pay all employee benefits relating to the employee's service in the current and prior periods. The amount received by an employee on retirement is dependent upon the level of contributions made and the return earned by the fund on its investments.

In paragraph 8 of AASB 119/IAS 19, **defined benefit plans** are defined as post-employment plans other than defined contribution plans; that is, if a post-employment plan is not classified as a defined contribution plan, then it is a defined benefit plan. Critical to the definition of a defined contribution post-employment benefit plan is the absence of an obligation for the employer to make further payments if the fund is unable to pay all the benefits accruing to members for their past service. Thus, defined benefit post-employment plans are those in which the employer has some obligation to pay further contributions such that the fund can pay members' benefits. In a defined benefit post-employment plan, the benefit received by members on retirement is determined by a formula reflecting their years of service and level of remuneration. It is not dependent upon the performance of the fund. If the performance of the fund is insufficient to pay members' post-employment benefits, the trustee of the fund will require the employer, who is the sponsor of the fund, to make additional payments to the fund. Similarly, if the fund achieves higher returns than are required to pay members' post-employment benefits, the employer may be able to take a 'contribution holiday' (i.e. cease making contributions until there are insufficient funds to pay members' post-employment benefits).

Most private sector (and many public sector) post-employment benefit plans are defined contribution plans. Employers often prefer defined contribution plans because there is no risk of liability for further contributions if the fund fails to earn an adequate return.

AASB 119/IAS 19 prescribes accounting treatment for contributions to post-employment benefit funds and assets and liabilities arising from post-employment benefit plans from the perspective of the employer. It does not prescribe accounting requirements for the post-employment benefit fund. The preparation and presentation of financial statements by post-employment benefit funds is prescribed by AASB 1056 *Superannuation Entities*.

LEARNING CHECK

- ☐ Post-employment benefits are benefits, other than termination benefits, that are payable after completion of employment (typically after the employee retires).
- ☐ In Australia it is compulsory for most private sector employers to contribute to a superannuation plan for employees.
- ☐ The two types of post-employment benefit plans are defined benefit plans and defined contribution plans, including multi-employer plans.
- ☐ In a defined contribution plan, an entity (employer) pays fixed contributions into a separate entity (fund). The amount received by an employee on retirement is dependent upon the level of contributions and the return earned by the fund on its investments.
- ☐ In a defined benefit plan, the employer has an obligation to pay contributions to enable the fund to pay members' benefits. The benefit received by members on retirement is determined by a formula reflecting their years of service and level of remuneration.
- ☐ AASB 119/IAS 19 prescribes accounting treatment for contributions to post-employment benefit funds and assets and liabilities arising from post-employment benefit plans from the perspective of the employer.

9.4 Accounting for defined contribution post-employment plans

LEARNING OBJECTIVE 9.4 Prepare entries to account for expenses, assets and liabilities arising from defined contribution post-employment plans.

As described above, entities that participate in defined contribution post-employment plans make payments to a post-employment benefit fund, such as a superannuation fund. The amount is determined as a percentage of remuneration paid to employees who are members of the fund. Contributions payable to defined contribution funds are recognised in the period the employee renders employment service. The contributions payable during the period are recognised as expenses unless another standard permits the cost of employment benefits to be allocated to the carrying amount of an asset, such as internally constructed plant in accordance with AASB 116/IAS 16 *Property, Plant and Equipment* (see chapter 5, section 5.3).

If the amount paid to the defined contribution fund by the entity (employer) during the year is less than the amount of contributions payable, a liability for unpaid contributions must be recognised at the end of the period. The liability is measured at the undiscounted amount payable for contributions due within 12 months after the reporting period. Paragraph 52 of AASB 119/IAS 19 requires discounting of liabilities for contributions to defined contribution plans that are due more than 12 months after the reporting period in which the employee provides the related employment service. The rate used to discount a post-employment benefit obligation is determined by reference to market yields on high-quality corporate bonds in accordance with paragraph 83 of AASB 119/IAS 19. If the obligation is to be settled in a country that does not have a deep market in high-quality corporate bonds, the market yield on government bonds must be used. Under AASB 119, Australian entities must use the corporate rather than government bond rate to discount post-employment benefits and other long-term employee liabilities.

If the amount paid to the defined contribution fund by the entity (employer) during the year is greater than the amount of contributions payable, the entity recognises an asset to the extent that it is entitled to a refund or reduction in future contributions. In this situation, the asset would be a prepayment, or prepaid expenses.

Accounting for defined contribution post-employment plans

Monash Ltd provides a defined contribution superannuation plan for its employees. Under the plan, Monash Ltd is required to contribute 9% of gross wages, salaries and commissions payable for service rendered by employees. Monash Ltd makes quarterly payments of $80 000 to the superannuation plan. Monash Ltd's annual reporting period ends on 30 June. If the amount paid to the superannuation fund during the financial year is less than 9% of gross wages, salaries and commissions for that year, Monash Ltd must pay the outstanding contributions by 30 September of the following financial year. If the amount paid during the financial year is more than 9% of the gross wages, salaries and bonuses for the year, the excess contributions are deducted from amounts payable in the following year.

Monash Ltd's employee benefits for the year ended 30 June 2022 comprise the following.

Gross wages and salaries	$3 900 000
Gross commissions	100 000
	$4 000 000

Required

Determine the deficiency in Monash Ltd's superannuation contributions for the year ended 30 June 2022. How would the company record the liability for the unpaid superannuation contributions?

Solution

The deficit in Monash Ltd's superannuation contributions is determined as follows.

Contributions payable:	
9% gross wages, salaries and bonuses	$360 000
Contributions paid during 2022: $80 000 × 4	320 000
Superannuation contribution payable	$ 40 000

Monash Ltd must recognise a liability for the unpaid superannuation contributions. The liability is not discounted because it is a short-term liability for employee benefits. Monash Ltd would record the following entry for 30 June 2022.

Wages and salaries expense	Dr	40 000	
Superannuation payable	Cr		40 000
(Accrual of liability for unpaid superannuation contributions)			

- ☐ Contributions payable to defined contribution funds are recognised in the period the employee renders service.
- ☐ The contributions payable during the period are recognised as expenses unless another standard permits the cost of employment benefits to be allocated to the carrying amount of an asset.
- ☐ If the amount paid to the defined contribution fund by the entity during the year is less than the amount payable, a liability for unpaid contributions must be recognised at the end of the period. The liability is measured at the undiscounted amount payable to the extent that contributions are due within 12 months after the reporting period. Paragraph 52 of AASB 119/IAS 19 requires discounting of liabilities for contributions due more than 12 months after the reporting period in which the employee provides the related service.
- ☐ If the amount paid to the defined contribution fund by the entity during the year is greater than the amount of contributions payable, the entity recognises an asset to the extent that it is entitled to a refund or reduction in future contributions. In this situation, the asset would be a prepayment, or prepaid expenses.

9.5 Accounting for defined benefit post-employment plans

LEARNING OBJECTIVE 9.5 Prepare entries to record expenses, assets and liabilities arising from defined benefit post-employment plans.

As described in section 9.3, the employer pays contributions to a fund, which is a separate entity from the employer. The fund accumulates assets through contributions and returns on investments. The accumulated assets are used to pay post-employment benefits to members (retired employees). The return on investments held by the superannuation fund comprises dividend and interest income and changes in the fair value of investments. The benefits paid to members are a function of their remuneration levels while employed and the number of years of service. If there is a shortfall in the fund's capacity to pay benefits to members, the trustee of the fund may require the employer to make additional contributions. Thus, the employer effectively underwrites the actuarial and investment risks of the plan. In other words, the entity (employer) bears the risk of the fund being unable to pay benefits.

The assets of the superannuation plan, which are mostly investments, do not always equal its obligation to pay post-employment benefits to members. If the present value of the defined benefit obligation (i.e. post-employment benefits that are expected to be paid to employees for their service up to the end of the reporting period) exceeds the fair value of the plan assets, the superannuation plan has a deficit. Conversely, when the fair value of the plan assets exceeds the present value of the defined benefit obligation, a surplus arises.

Whether the deficit (or surplus) of the defined benefit superannuation plan is a liability (or asset) of the sponsoring employer is debatable. Some argue that the surplus in the superannuation plan does not satisfy all of the characteristics of an asset. Arguably, the assets of the plan are not controlled by the employer because they cannot be used for its benefit. For example, the employer may not use the surplus of the defined benefit superannuation plan to pay its debts; the assets of the plan are only used to generate cash flows to pay post-employment benefits to the members of the plan. Although the surplus is expected to result in future cash savings (i.e. lower future contributions for the employer), it could be argued that the employer has not obtained control over those benefits. Further, any reduction in superannuation contributions is at the discretion of the superannuation fund trustee.

Similarly, it has been argued that a deficit in the defined benefit superannuation fund is not a liability of the sponsoring employer because it does not have a present obligation to make good the shortfall. For instance, the employer may modify the post-employment benefits payable so as to avoid some of the obligation.

The perspective adopted in AASB 119/IAS 19 is that the surplus (or deficit) of the defined benefit superannuation plan is an asset (or liability) of the sponsoring employer. In some cases, the entity might not have a legal obligation to address any shortfall in the fund's assets. For example, the terms of the trust deed may allow the employer to change or terminate its obligation under the plan. Although the employer might not have a legal obligation to compensate for any shortfall, it typically has a constructive obligation because terminating its obligations under the plan may make it difficult to retain and recruit staff. Accordingly, the accounting treatment prescribed by AASB 119/IAS 19 for an entity's obligations arising from sponsorship of a defined benefit plan assumes that the entity will continue to meet the post-employment benefits it committed to, over the remaining working lives of its employees. Similarly, AASB 119/IAS 19 reflects the view that any surplus of the fund represents expected future inflows (resulting in reduced employer contributions in the future), due to contributing more than required previously.

If adopting the view that a deficit (or surplus) of the defined benefit superannuation plan is a liability (or asset) of the sponsoring employer, recognition and measurement issues need to be addressed. The possible approaches are shown in figure 9.5. At one extreme, the deficit or surplus is not recognised in the financial statements of the entity (employer) that sponsors the defined benefit superannuation plan. In other words, the superannuation deficit or surplus is 'off-balance sheet'. At the other extreme, referred to as 'net capitalisation', the deficit (or surplus) of the fund is recognised as a liability (or asset) on the statement of financial position of the entity (employer) that sponsors the defined benefit superannuation plan. Under net capitalisation, the net superannuation liability (or asset) is usually measured as the difference between the present value of post-employment benefits earned by employees for service in the current and prior periods, and the fair value of plan assets. Between these two extremes are various partial capitalisation methods in which some amount of the surplus (or deficit) of the fund remains off-balance sheet.

For example, the previous version of AASB 119 permitted increments in the defined benefit obligation resulting from prior periods to be recognised progressively over the average remaining period until they become vested.

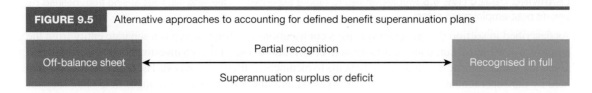

| FIGURE 9.5 | Alternative approaches to accounting for defined benefit superannuation plans |

In the absence of accounting regulation, preparers were able to select different approaches to accounting for defined benefit post-employment benefits, ranging from off-balance sheet to net capitalisation. However, the use of different methods of accounting for post-employment benefits reduced the comparability of financial statements. Concerns were also raised about delays in recognition of liabilities, which were perpetuated by partial capitalisation methods. The IASB and the FASB jointly undertook a project to enhance the comparability and transparency of accounting for post-employment benefits (IASB 2008). The outcome of that project was a revised version of IAS 19 *Employee Benefits*, requiring the net capitalisation approach, the equivalent of which is adopted in Australia as AASB 119.

Under the net capitalisation approach, the sponsoring employer recognises a net defined benefit liability (or asset), representing its exposure to the defined benefit superannuation fund at the end of the reporting period. Contributions paid into the fund by the employer increase the assets of the fund, and thus increase a surplus (or reduce any deficit) of the fund. The employer accounts for its contributions to the fund as a decrease in the net defined benefit liability (or an increase in the net defined benefit asset). The employer recognises expenses in relation to its sponsorship of the defined benefit superannuation fund when service costs and interest costs are incurred by the fund, rather than when contributions are paid.

The key steps involved in accounting by the employer for a defined benefit post-employment fund in accordance with AASB 119/IAS 19 (paragraph 57) are:
1. determine the deficit or surplus of the fund
2. determine the amount of the net defined benefit liability (or asset), which is the amount of the deficit or the surplus, adjusted for any effect of limiting a net defined benefit asset to the asset ceiling (explained below)
3. determine the amounts to be recognised in profit or loss for current service cost, any past service cost and net interest expense (or income) on the net defined benefit liability (or asset)
4. determine the remeasurement of the net defined benefit liability (or asset) to be recognised in other comprehensive income, which comprises actuarial gains and losses, return on plan assets (other than amounts included in net interest), and any change in the effect of the asset ceiling (other than amounts included in net interest).

We will now take a closer look at each step.

9.5.1 Step 1. Determine the deficit or surplus of the fund

There are two elements to determining the deficit (or surplus) of the fund:
1. the obligation to pay benefits
2. any fund/plan assets.

Paragraph 67 of AASB 119/IAS 19 requires an entity to use the projected unit credit method to determine the present value of post-employment benefits accumulated by employees for service in the current and prior periods. Other names for the projected unit credit method include the *accrued benefit method pro-rated on service* and the *benefits/years of service method*. The projected unit credit method, which attributes a proportionate amount of additional benefit to each period of employees' service, is shown in illustrative example 9.6.

Determining the present value of the defined benefit obligation using the projected unit credit method

Darwin Ltd provides a defined benefit superannuation plan in which employees receive post-employment benefits determined as 1% of their final year salary for every year of service. Salaries are expected to increase by 5% (compound) each year. The accountant has determined that the appropriate discount rate is 10% p.a. Charles commenced working for Darwin Ltd on 1 July 2022 with an annual salary of $40 000 and is expected to retire on 30 June 2025.

Required

Determine the present value of the defined benefit obligation using the projected unit credit method.

Solution

The first step is to determine the fair value of the plan assets at the end of 2023, 2024 and 2025.

At 30 June 2025 Charles will be entitled to 1% of his final year salary for each of his 3 years of service. If his salary increases by 5% p.a., his salary for the year ended 30 June 2025 will be $44 100. At 3% of final year salary, Charles' post-employment benefit will be $1323 ($44 100 × 3%). Note that this is the amount in the schedule below in the 'Total current and prior years' row of the column labelled 'Year ended 30/6/25'.

The benefit attributed to each year is $1/n$ of the total benefit payable after n years. The amount attributed to each year is therefore 1/3 of $1323, or $441. In the schedule below, the amount of $441 is the amount in the row labelled 'Current year' in the column for each year. The total current and prior year amount for each year is carried forward in the table as the prior year amount in the next year.

Schedule of changes in the defined benefit obligation			
Benefit attributed to:	Year ended 30/6/23 $	Year ended 30/6/24 $	Year ended 30/6/25 $
Prior year	0	441	882
Current year	441	441	441
Total current and prior years	441	882	1323

The second step is to determine the obligation at the end of each period. The obligation is measured as the present value of the accumulated post-employment benefit at the end of each period. Each period the present value increases partly as a result of another year's benefits being added, and partly because of the reduced discounting period (i.e. the time to settlement decreases). The difference in the present value attributable to discounting over a shorter period is accounted for as an interest expense. The interest component is calculated for each period by multiplying the opening balance of the liability by the interest rate.

The following table illustrates the increase in the defined benefit obligation over the three-year period, separating the service cost and interest. The opening obligation is the present value of the benefit attributed to Charles' prior years' service (i.e. employment). The interest cost for the year ended 30 June 2023 is nil because the opening balance of the obligation is nil. The interest cost for the year ended 30 June 2024 is $36, being $365 × the discount rate of 10%. The current service cost is the present value of the defined benefit attributed to the current year, where present value (PV) is calculated as follows.

$$PV = FV/(1 + i)^n$$

where:

FV = future value
i = discount rate
n = number of years

For example, for the year ended 30 June 2023 the benefit attributed to current service is $441, as per the schedule above. This is the increase in Charles' defined benefit entitlements attributable to his service during the year ended 30 June 2023. This amount is expected to be settled on 30 June 2025 (i.e. 2 years later). Accordingly, the current service cost for the year ended 30 June 2023 (i.e. the present value of the benefit attributed to the year ended 30 June 2023), is calculated as $441/(1 + 0.1)^2$. The closing balance of the obligation is the present value of the benefit attributed to current and prior years.

Schedule of current service cost, interest and present value of the defined benefit obligation

Defined benefit obligation	Year ended 30/6/23 $	Year ended 30/6/24 $	Year ended 30/6/25 $
Opening obligation	0	365	802
Interest at 10%	0	36	80
Current service cost	365	401	441
Closing obligation	365	802	1323

Illustrative example 9.6 was based on an individual to simplify the calculations of accrued benefits. However, the fund would typically include multiple members and the plan assets would generate cash inflows to be used to settle obligations to all members.

The deficit or surplus of the fund is equal to the difference between the fair value of plan assets and the present value of the defined benefit obligation.

- If the defined benefit obligation exceeds the fair value of the plan assets, then that excess is the deficit of the fund.
- If the fair value of plan assets exceeds the present value of the defined benefit obligation, then that excess is the surplus of the defined benefit superannuation fund.

Illustrative example 9.7 illustrates how to determine this deficit or surplus.

ILLUSTRATIVE EXAMPLE 9.7

Determining the deficit or surplus of the defined benefit superannuation fund

The following table provides information about the assets and obligations for post-employment benefits of Darwin Employees Superannuation Fund.

	30/6/23 $	30/6/24 $	30/6/25 $
Closing obligation	4900	5700	6550
Fair value of plan assets	4500	5400	6600

Required
Determine the deficit or surplus of the defined benefit superannuation fund at the end of each reporting period.

Solution
The deficit or surplus of the fund is calculated simply as the difference between the fair value of plan assets and the present value of the defined benefit obligation. The closing obligation in the table above is the present value of the defined benefit obligation at the end of each reporting period.

At 30 June 2023, the present value of the defined benefit obligation exceeded the fair value of plan assets by $400 ($4900 − $4500). Thus, the fund has a deficit of $400 at 30 June 2023.

At 30 June 2024, the present value of the defined benefit obligation exceeded the fair value of plan assets by $300 ($5700 − $5400). Thus, the fund has a deficit of $300 at 30 June 2024.

At 30 June 2025, the fair value of plan assets exceeded the defined benefit obligation by $50 ($6550 − 6600). Accordingly, the defined benefit superannuation fund has a surplus of $50 at 30 June 2025.

	30/6/23 $	30/6/24 $	30/6/25 $
Closing obligation	4 900	5 700	6 550
Fair value of plan assets	4 500	5 400	6 600
Deficit (surplus) of the fund	400	300	(50)

Obligations to pay pensions during employees' lives (or lives of their eligible dependants) can further complicate the measurement of accrued benefits because the total payment is dependent upon the mortality rate of the employees and their eligible beneficiaries. Companies often rely on actuarial assessments to estimate the defined benefit obligation and the level of investment required to enable the fund to pay accumulated benefits when they fall due. Actuaries apply mathematical, statistical, economic and financial analysis to assess risks associated with contracts, such as insurance contracts and superannuation funds. Actuarial estimates rely on assumptions, such as the employee retention rates and the rate at which salaries are expected to increase. Some companies employ their own actuaries, while many others engage actuaries as professional consultants.

9.5.2 Step 2. Determine the amount of the net defined benefit liability (asset)

A net defined benefit liability arises when the defined benefit superannuation fund has a deficit (i.e. the amount payable is more than the amount available). The net defined benefit liability is calculated following the procedure described in step 1. For example, in illustrative example 9.7 the amount of the net defined benefit liability for the year ended 30 June 2024 is $300.

A net defined benefit asset arises when the defined benefit superannuation fund has a surplus. The net defined benefit asset is measured as the lower of the surplus of the defined benefit superannuation fund and the asset ceiling. The **asset ceiling** is defined in paragraph 8 of AASB 119/IAS 19 as:

> the present value of any economic benefits available in the form of refunds from the plan or reductions in future contributions to the plan.

For example, if we assume that the present value of reductions in Darwin Ltd's future contributions to the plan at 30 June 2025 were $60, the net defined benefit asset of Darwin Ltd would be measured as $50, being the lower of the surplus of the defined benefit fund and the asset ceiling. However, if the present value of reductions in Darwin Ltd's future contributions to the plan at 30 June 2025 was only $40, its net defined benefit asset would be measured as $40.

9.5.3 Step 3. Determine the amounts to be recognised in profit or loss

The amount of the net defined benefit liability (or asset) is affected by the present value of the defined benefit obligation and the fair value of plan assets. The present value of the defined benefit obligation is affected by the service cost, which comprises current service cost, past service cost and any gain or loss on settlement of the defined benefit.

Current service cost is defined in paragraph 8 of AASB 119/IAS 19 as:

> the increase in the present value of the defined benefit obligation resulting from employee service in the current period.

The service cost for each year in illustrative example 9.6 is a current service cost to Darwin Ltd because it is the increase in the present value of the defined benefit obligation attributed to employment service rendered by Charles during each year.

Past service cost is defined in paragraph 8 of AASB 119/IAS 19 as:

> the change in the present value of the defined benefit obligation for employee service in prior periods, resulting from a plan amendment (the introduction or withdrawal of, or changes to, a defined benefit plan) or a curtailment (a significant reduction by the entity in the number of employees covered by a plan).

Illustrative example 9.8 draws on the information used in illustrative example 9.6, with the addition of an amendment to the terms of the superannuation plan on 1 July 2024.

Modifications to a defined benefit superannuation plan

On 1 July 2024, Darwin Ltd modified the terms of the defined benefit superannuation plan from 1% of final year salary per year of service to 0.9% of final year salary per year of service. The modification applies retrospectively to service rendered before 1 July 2024. Accordingly, after the modification the defined benefit payable at 30 June 2025 is expected to be 2.7% of final year salary instead of 3% of final salary (which had been used in the measurement of the defined benefit obligation at 30 June 2024). The discount rate remains 10% as in illustrative example 9.6.

Required

Determine the closing obligation for the years ended 30 June 2023, 30 June 2024 and 30 June 2025 on the basis of the revised terms.

Solution

The first step is to prepare a schedule of changes in the defined benefit obligation using the same method as in illustrative example 9.6.

The revised defined benefit payable to Charles after 3 years (i.e. at 30 June 2025) is 2.7% of Charles' final year salary (2.7% × $44 100), or $1191. Applying the projected credit method, the annual service cost is $397 (1/3 × $1191).

Schedule of changes in the defined benefit obligation			
Benefit attributed to:	Year ended 30/6/23 $	Year ended 30/6/24 $	Year ended 30/6/25 $
Prior year	0	397	794
Current year	397	397	397
Total current and prior years	397	794	1191

The second step is to determine the present value of the increase in the defined benefit obligation attributed to current service cost for the years ended 30 June 2023 and 30 June 2024, using the 10% discount rate:
- 30/6/2023: Current service cost = $397/(1 + 0.1)^2 = $328
- 30/6/2024: Current service cost = $397/(1 + 0.1)^1 = $361.

The third step is to determine the interest cost for the years ended 30 June 2024 and 30 June 2025 based on the closing obligation of the previous year:
- 30/6/2024: Interest cost = $328 × 10% = $33
- 30/6/2025: Interest cost = $722 × 10% = $72

The following schedule shows the current service cost, interest cost and present value of the defined benefit obligation on the basis of the revised terms of the plan, under which the benefit payable is 0.9% of salary for each year of service.

Schedule of current service cost, interest and present value of the defined benefit obligation			
Defined benefit obligation	Year ended 30/6/23 $	Year ended 30/6/24 $	Year ended 30/6/25 $
Opening obligation	0	328	722
Interest at 10%	0	33	72
Current service cost	328	361	397
Closing obligation	328	722	1191

Recall that the terms of the defined benefit superannuation plan were modified on 1 July 2024. Until 30 June 2024, the measurement of the present value of the defined benefit obligation had been based on a benefit of 1% of final salary for each year of service. This yielded a present value of $802 at 30 June 2024 as shown in illustrative example 9.6. From 1 July 2024, the amount of the present value of the defined benefit obligation should be remeasured based on a benefit of only 0.9% of final year salary for each year of service. This yields a present value of $722 as shown in the immediately preceding schedule. Step 4, then, is to adjust the opening obligation for the year ended 30 June 2025 for a past service cost (of $80) as follows.

	Year ended 30/6/24 $	Year ended 30/6/25 $
Opening obligation	365	802
Past service costs arising from modifications to the plan	—	(80)
Adjusted obligation		722
Interest at 10%	36	72
Current service cost	401	397
Closing obligation	802	1191

Current and past service cost, interest income or expense and settlement gains or losses are recognised in profit or loss.

Paragraph 8 of AASB 119/IAS 19 defines the **net interest on the net defined benefit liability (asset)** as the change in the net defined benefit liability (asset) that arises over time. The net interest on net defined benefit liability (asset) is measured by multiplying the discount rate that is used to measure the defined benefit obligation at the beginning of the period by the net defined benefit liability (asset) (AASB 119/IAS 19 paragraph 123).

Paragraph 83 requires the discount rate to be determined with reference to market yields on high-quality corporate bonds. In jurisdictions in which there is no deep market in such bonds, the market yield on government bonds should be used instead. The standard requires contributions received by the fund and benefits paid to be taken into account when calculating interest. This would involve recalculating interest for part of the year each time the plan assets were increased by a contribution or where payment of benefits resulted in settlement gains or losses, giving rise to change in the net defined benefit liability or asset. Throughout this text, this process is simplified by applying the discount rate to the opening balance of the net defined benefit liability (or asset), effectively assuming contributions and benefits are paid at the end of each year.

When the superannuation fund pays benefits to a member, both the plan assets and the defined benefit obligation are reduced. If, at the time of settlement, the carrying amount of the obligation to the member is equal to the amount actually payable, the settlement will have no effect on the surplus or deficit of the fund. However, the carrying amount of the defined benefit obligation is based on numerous actuarial estimates, resulting in potential inaccuracy in measurement. Differences between the carrying amount of the defined benefit obligation of the fund and the amount actually paid to a member give rise to a gain or loss on settlement, which is a service cost recognised in profit or loss.

9.5.4 Step 4. Determine the remeasurements of the net defined benefit liability (asset) to be recognised in other comprehensive income

The effects of remeasurements of the net defined benefit liability (or asset) are recognised in other comprehensive income. Changes in the net defined benefit liability (or asset) that result from remeasurements comprise actuarial gains and losses, return on plan assets (other than amounts included in net interest) and any change in the effect of the asset ceiling (excluding amounts included in net interest).

Actuarial gains and losses occur when changes in actuarial assumptions or 'experience adjustments' (discussed below) affect the present value of the defined benefit obligation. The measurement of the defined benefit obligation is sensitive to assumptions such as employee turnover and the rate of increase in salaries. For example, a higher rate of salary would increase the expected future settlement (due to a higher final year salary) and hence the present value of the defined benefit obligation, resulting in an actuarial loss. Another example of a change in an actuarial assumption is a change in the discount rate used to determine the present value of the obligation. An increase in the discount rate results in an actuarial gain because it reduces the present value of the defined benefit obligation. Similarly, a decrease in the discount rate results in an actuarial loss.

Experience adjustments refer to differences between the actual results and previous actuarial estimates used to measure the defined benefit obligation. An example is the difference between the estimated employee turnover for the year and the actual employee turnover during the year. Experience adjustments may also relate to early retirement, mortality rates and the rate of increase in salaries.

The return on plan assets is determined after deducting the costs of managing the plan assets and tax payable by the superannuation fund on its income derived from plan assets. Other administration costs are not deducted from the return on plan assets (AASB 119/IAS 19 paragraph 130).

The net capitalisation method can result in large gains and losses being recognised in profit or loss, or other comprehensive income, due to changes in the surplus or deficit of the fair value of plan assets over the present value of accrued benefits. For instance, the present value of the defined benefit obligation increases if employee retention is greater than the amount assumed in the previous actuarial estimate, resulting in a deficit in the superannuation fund. Similarly, an unexpected decline in the return on investment of plan assets may cause the plan assets to grow at a slower rate than the present value of the defined benefit obligation, giving rise to an increase in the superannuation liability recognised by the employer. The net capitalisation method is unpopular with some preparers of financial statements who would prefer less volatility of earnings. However, classification of actuarial gains and losses as items of other comprehensive income shields reported profit from the volatility that would arise from the recognition of actuarial gains and losses.

ILLUSTRATIVE EXAMPLE 9.9

Accounting for a defined benefit plan

Flinders Ltd has a defined benefit superannuation plan for its senior managers. Members of the plan had been entitled to 10% of their average salary for every year of service.

The following information is available about the Flinders DB (Defined Benefit) Superannuation Fund.

		$'000
30 June 2022		
Present value of defined benefit obligation at 30 June 2022		26 000
Fair value of plan assets at 30 June 2022		30 000
Asset ceiling at 30 June 2022		4 200
Interest rate used to measure the defined benefit obligation at 30 June 2022	7%	
1 July 2022		
Past service costs		5 000
Year ended 30 June 2023		
Current service cost		4 000
Contributions received by the fund		4 500
Benefits paid by the fund		Nil
Return on plan assets		800
Actuarial gain resulting from change in the discount rate, 30 June 2023		1 470
Present value of defined benefit obligation at 30 June 2023		35 700
Fair value of plan assets at 30 June 2023		37 400
Asset ceiling at 30 June 2023		2 500
Interest rate used to measure the defined benefit obligation at 30 June 2023	8%	

Additional information
- The current service cost is given as $4 million. This estimation is based on actuarial advice and provided by the manager of the superannuation fund.
- Actuarial advice has been obtained for the present value of the defined benefit obligation at 30 June 2022 and 30 June 2023.
- On 1 July 2022 Flinders Ltd revised its defined benefits and increased the entitlement to 11% of average salary. The revision to the defined benefit plan resulted in an increase in the defined benefit obligation of $5 million on 1 July 2022.
- During the year ended 30 June 2023, Flinders Ltd contributed $4 800 000 to the fund. All of the contributions to the Flinders DB Superannuation Fund are paid by Flinders Ltd. The senior managers of Flinders Ltd, who are the members of the fund, do not pay any superannuation contributions.
- The discount rate used to measure the defined benefit obligation was increased from 7% to 8% on 30 June 2023, resulting in a decrease of $1 470 000 in the present value of the defined benefit obligation.
- The fair value of plan assets is derived from valuations performed by Hope & Moore Valuers as at 30 June 2023.

Required

Prepare a defined benefit worksheet to provide working papers for the journal entries to account for the defined benefit superannuation plan in the books of Flinders Ltd in accordance with AASB 119/IAS 19.

Solution

First, we will read the amount of the net defined benefit liability (asset) at 30 June 2022 from the schedule above. We can see that Flinders DB Superannuation Fund had a surplus of $4 000 000, being the excess of the fair value of plan assets over the present value of the defined benefit obligation ($30 000 000 − $26 000 000), at 30 June 2022. Given this surplus was less than the asset ceiling at 30 June 2022 of $4 200 000, Flinders Ltd simply recognised a net defined benefit asset of $4 000 000.

Next we will consider the four steps involved in accounting by the employer for a defined benefit post-employment fund identified by paragraph 57 of AASB 119/IAS 19. The defined benefit worksheet (shown below for the Flinders DB Superannuation Fund), incorporates the four steps. It provides workings for the summary journal entries to account for the defined benefit post-employment fund in the books of the employer and provides a basis for the disclosure requirements required by AASB 119/IAS 19.

FLINDERS DB SUPERANNUATION FUND
Defined benefit worksheet
for the year ended 30 June 2023

	Flinders Ltd				Flinders DB Superannuation Fund	
	Profit/ loss $'000	OCI $'000	Bank $'000	Net DBL(A) $'000	DBO $'000	Plan assets $'000
Balance 30/6/22				4 000 Dr	26 000 Cr	30 000 Dr
Past service cost	5 000 Dr				5 000 Cr	
Revised balance 1/7/22				1 000 Cr	31 000 Cr	30 000 Dr
Net interest at 7%	70 Dr				2 170 Cr	2 100 Dr
Current service cost	4 000 Dr				4 000 Cr	
Contributions to the fund			4 500 Cr			4 500 Dr
Benefits paid by the fund					0	0
Return on plan assets		800 Cr				800 Dr
Actuarial gain: DBO		1 470 Cr			1 470 Dr	
Journal entry	**9 070 Dr**	**2 270 Cr**	**4 500 Cr**	**2 300 Cr**		
Balance 30/6/23				1 700 Dr	35 700 Cr	37 400 Dr
Adjustment for asset ceiling if < deficit				Not applicable		
Balance 30/6/23				**1 700 Dr**	**35 700 Cr**	**37 400 Dr**

Step 1. Determine the deficit or surplus of the fund

At 30 June 2023, the deficit or surplus of the Flinders DB Superannuation Fund is calculated as the difference between the fair value of plan assets ($37 400 000) and the present value of the defined benefit obligation (DBO) ($35 700 000). This indicates a surplus of $1 700 000. This is shown in the last row of the defined benefit worksheet.

Step 2. Determine the amount of the net defined benefit liability (asset)

The net defined benefit asset is $1 700 000, being the lesser of the surplus of $1 700 000 and the asset ceiling of $2 500 000 at 30 June 2023.

Step 3. Determine the amounts to be recognised in profit or loss

The increase in the DBO of $5 000 000 resulting from the past service cost is recognised as an expense in profit or loss. The revised balance of the net defined benefit liability is calculated as the deficit of the fund, being the excess of the DBO over the fair value of plan assets after accounting for the past service cost ($31 000 000 − $30 000 000), or $1 000 000. The revised balance of the defined benefit liability (asset) is shown in order to facilitate the calculation of the interest cost.

The net interest is $70 000, determined as 7% of the revised net defined benefit liability, and is recognised in profit or loss. The interest component of the increase in the DBO and the fair value of plan assets is $2 170 000 and $2 100 000 respectively.

The current service cost of $4 000 000 increases the DBO and is recognised in profit or loss. These three items correspond to step 3 and are recognised in profit or loss. The past service cost, the net interest and the current service cost amount to $9 070 000, as shown in the following journal entry (consistent with the defined benefit worksheet).

Summary entry	Superannuation expense (P/L)	Dr	9 070 000	
	Superannuation gain (OCI)	Cr		2 270 000
	Cash	Cr		4 500 000
	Net superannuation asset	Cr		2 300 000
	(Payment of superannuation contributions and recognition of changes in net superannuation asset)			

Step 4. Determine the amount of remeasurements to be recognised in other comprehensive income

There are two remeasurements of the net defined benefit asset during the year ended 30 June 2023. One of the remeasurements results from the return on plan assets exceeding the interest income included in net interest recognised in profit or loss. The return on plan assets ($800) affects the fair value of plan assets as shown in the defined benefit worksheet. The other remeasurement results from the increase in the discount rate used to measure the present value of the DBO, and is recognised in other comprehensive income (OCI).

Contributions during the year ended 30 June 2023 increase the net defined benefit asset and the plan assets of the fund.

Any benefits paid by the fund to members during the period would reduce both the plan assets and the DBO. (*Note:* It is a transaction of the fund, not a transaction of the sponsoring employer.)

The defined benefit worksheet provides working papers for the journal entries to account for the defined benefit superannuation plan in the books of Flinders Ltd.

The worksheet also provides a basis for preparation of notes to the financial statements for some of the disclosures required by AASB 119/IAS 19 in respect of defined benefit post-employment plans. Paragraph 140 includes a requirement for a reconciliation of the opening balance to the closing balance of the net defined benefit liability (asset), showing separate reconciliations for plan assets, the present value of the defined benefit obligation and the effect of the asset ceiling. Each reconciliation is required to show the effect, if applicable, of past service cost and gains and losses arising on settlement, current service cost, interest income or expense, and remeasurement of the net defined liability (asset), showing separately return on plan assets (excluding amounts included in interest), actuarial gains arising from changes in demographic assumptions, actuarial gains and losses arising from changes in financial assumptions and changes in the effect, if any, of the asset ceiling (AASB 119/IAS 19 paragraph 141). Paragraph 141 also requires disclosure of contributions, distinguishing between those paid by the employer and those paid by the members of the plan, and benefits paid. Other reconciliation items include the effects of changes in foreign exchange rates and the effects of business combinations and disposals, where applicable.

LEARNING CHECK

☐ A defined benefit fund accumulates assets through contributions from the employer and returns on investments (dividends, interest and changes in the fair value of investments).

☐ Accumulated assets are used to pay post-employment benefits to members (retired employees). The benefits paid to members are a function of their remuneration levels while employed and the number of years of service.

☐ A deficit occurs when the present value of the defined benefit obligation (i.e. post-employment benefits that are expected to be paid to employees for their employment service up to the end of the reporting period) exceeds the fair value of the plan assets.

☐ A surplus arises when the fair value of the plan assets exceeds the present value of the defined benefit obligation.

☐ Under AASB 119/IAS 19, a surplus (or deficit) of the defined benefit superannuation plan is an asset (or liability) of the sponsoring employer.

☐ The key steps involved in accounting by the employer for a defined benefit post-employment fund in accordance with AASB 119/IAS 19 are:
  – determine the deficit or surplus of the fund
  – determine the amount of the net defined benefit liability (or asset), which is the amount of the deficit or the surplus, adjusted for any effect of limiting a net defined benefit asset to the asset ceiling
  – determine the amounts to be recognised in profit or loss for current service cost, any past service cost and net interest expense (or income) on the net defined benefit liability (or asset)
  – determine the remeasurement of the net defined benefit liability (or asset) to be recognised in other comprehensive income, which comprises actuarial gains and losses, return on plan assets (other

9.6 Other long-term employment benefits

LEARNING OBJECTIVE 9.6 Explain how to measure and record other long-term liabilities for employment benefits, such as long service leave.

Long-term employee benefits are benefits for service provided in the current period that will not be paid until more than 12 months after the end of the period. Post-employment benefits were considered in section 9.5. This section considers long-term employee benefits that are provided to employees during the period of their employment. A common form of long-term employee benefits is **long service leave**, which is a paid absence after the employee has provided a long period of service, such as 3 months of paid leave after 10 years of continuous employment.

Long service leave accrues to employees as they provide service to the entity. The principle adopted by AASB 119/IAS 19 is that an obligation arises for long service leave when the employees provide employment service to the employer, even though the employees may have no legal entitlement to the leave. Thus, a liability is recognised for long service leave as it accrues. Long service leave payments reduce an entity's long service leave liability.

Accounting for other long-term employee benefits is similar to accounting for defined benefit post-employment plans, except that the effects of remeasurements are not recognised in other comprehensive income (AASB 119/IAS 19 paragraphs 154–55). Thus, the net liability (asset) for long-term employee benefits is measured as the net of the present value of the defined benefit obligation at the end of the reporting period minus the fair value at the reporting date of plan assets (if any) out of which the obligations are to be settled directly. Similar to defined benefit plans, the fair value of the plan assets may be limited by the effects of an asset ceiling (if applicable).

In Australia, it is extremely unusual to establish plan assets to provide for the payment of long service leave benefits to employees. Thus, the accounting treatment for long service leave benefits is usually confined to the recognition of the present value of the obligation measured in accordance with the projected unit credit method.

The projected unit credit method measures the obligation for long-term employee benefits by calculating the present value of the expected future payments that will result from employee service provided to date. The measurement of the present value of the long service leave payment obligation is complicated by the need to make several estimates. These include estimation of when the leave will be taken, projected salary levels, and the proportion of employees who will continue in the entity's employment long enough to become entitled to long service leave. Actuarial advice is often used in the measurement of long service leave obligations.

The steps involved in the measurement of a liability for long service leave are as follows.

1. *Estimate the number of employees who are expected to become eligible for long service leave.* The probability that employees will become eligible for long service leave generally increases with employees' period of employment. For example, if an entity provides long service leave after 10 years of employment, the probability that employees who have already been working for the entity for 7 years will continue in employment for another 3 years is very high, as the closer proximity to long service leave entitlement provides an incentive for employees to stay with their current employer. Thus, the proportion of employees who are expected to become eligible for long service leave is usually calculated separately for employees with different levels (years) of prior service.

2. *Estimate the projected wages and salaries at the time that long service leave is expected to be paid.* This step involves the application of expected inflation rates (or other cost adjustment rates) over the remaining period before long service leave is paid. Applying an estimated inflation rate:

$$\text{Projected salaries} = \text{Current salaries} \times (1 + \text{Inflation rate})^n$$

where n = number of years until long service leave is expected to be paid

For example, for employees who have 3 years remaining before long service leave is expected to be paid, current salaries are projected over a period of 3 years.

3. *Determine the accumulated benefit.* The projected unit credit is determined as the proportion of projected long service leave attributable to service that has already been provided by the employee. The accumulated benefit is calculated as follows.

$$\frac{\text{Years of employment}}{\text{Years required for long service leave}} \times \frac{\text{Weeks of paid leave}}{52} \times \text{Projected salaries}$$

4. *Measure the present value of the accumulated benefit.* The accumulated benefit is discounted at a rate determined by reference to market yields on high-quality corporate bonds, in accordance with paragraph 83 of AASB 119/IAS 19. If the country in which the long service leave entitlement will be paid does not have a deep market in high-quality corporate bonds, the government bond rate is used.

$$\text{Present value} = \frac{\text{Accumulated benefit}}{(1 + i)^n}$$

where i = the interest rate on high-quality corporate bonds maturing n years later

The liability for long service leave is a provision. After determining the amount of the obligation for long service leave at the end of the period, following steps 1 to 4 above, the provision is increased or decreased as required.

Illustrative example 9.10 demonstrates the measurement of the obligation for long service leave, applying the projected unit credit method in accordance with AASB 119/IAS 19, and the entries to account for changes in the provision for long service leave.

ILLUSTRATIVE EXAMPLE 9.10

Accounting for long service leave

Griffith Ltd commenced operations on 1 July 2021 and had 150 employees. Average salaries were $60 000 per annum for the year. Griffith Ltd accounts for all recognised employee costs as expenses. Employees are entitled to 13 weeks of long service leave after 10 years of employment.

Part 1
The following information is based on advice received from actuarial consultants at 30 June 2022.

Number of years unit credit	1 year
Number of years until long service leave is expected to be paid	9 years
Probability that long service leave will be taken (proportion of employees expected to stay long enough to become entitled to long service leave)	50%
Expected increase in salaries (based on inflation)	2% p.a.
Yield on 9-year high-quality corporate bonds at 30/6/2022	10%

Required
Determine the obligation for long service leave at 30 June 2022, applying the projected unit credit method in accordance with AASB 119/IAS 19, and prepare the journal entry to account for changes in the provision for long service leave.

Solution
The discount rate is determined using 9-year bonds because the long service leave is expected to be paid 9 years after the end of the reporting period.

Step 1. Estimate the number of employees who are expected to become eligible for long service leave

$$55\% \times 150 \text{ employees} = 75 \text{ employees}$$

Step 2. Estimate the projected salaries

$$= \text{Salary} \times (1 + \text{Inflation rate})^n$$
$$= \$60\,000 \times 75 \text{ employees} \times (1 + 0.02)^9$$
$$= \$5\,377\,917$$

The current salary is inflated over 9 years because employees are expected to take long service leave 9 years after the end of the reporting period.

Step 3. Determine the accumulated benefit

$$= \frac{\text{Years of employment}}{\text{Years required for long service leave}} \times \frac{\text{Weeks of paid leave}}{52} \times \text{Projected salaries}$$

$$= \frac{1}{10} \times \frac{13}{52} \times \$5\,377\,917$$

$$= \$134\,448$$

Step 4. Measure the present value of the accumulated benefit

$$= \frac{\text{Accumulated benefit}}{(1 + i)^n}$$

$$= \$134\,448/(1 + 0.1)^9 \text{ [or } \$134\,448 \times 0.4241]$$

$$= \$57\,019$$

The change in the provision for long service leave is recorded by the following journal entry.

2022				
30 June	Long service leave expense	Dr	57 019	
	Provision for long service leave	Cr		57 019
	(Increase in provision for long service leave)			

Note there was no beginning of period provision for long service leave as this is the entity's first year of operations.

Part 2

During the following year, Griffith Ltd's 150 employees continued to work for the company. Average salaries increased to $68 000 per annum for the year. The following information is based on advice received from actuarial consultants at 30 June 2023.

Number of years unit credit	2 years
Number of years until long service leave is expected to be paid	8 years
Probability that long service leave will be taken (proportion of employees expected to stay long enough to be entitled)	55%
Expected increase in salaries (based on inflation)	2% p.a.
Yield on 8-year high-quality corporate bonds 30/6/2023	9%

Required

Determine the obligation for long service leave at 30 June 2023, applying the projected unit credit method in accordance with AASB 119/IAS 19, and prepare the journal entry to account for changes in the provision for long service leave.

Solution

The discount rate is determined using 8-year bonds because the long service leave is expected to be paid 8 years after the end of the reporting period.

Step 1. Estimate the number of employees who are expected to become eligible for long service leave

$$55\% \times 150 \text{ employees} = 82.5 \text{ employees}$$

Step 2. Estimate the projected salaries

$$= \text{Salary} \times (1 + \text{Inflation rate})^n$$

$$= \$68\,000 \times 82.5 \text{ employees} \times (1 + 0.02)^8$$

$$= \$6\,573\,009$$

The current salary is inflated over 8 years because employees are expected to take long service leave 8 years after the end of the reporting period.

Step 3. Determine the accumulated benefit

$$= \frac{\text{Years of employment}}{\text{Years required for long service leave}} \times \frac{\text{Weeks of paid leave}}{52} \times \text{Projected salaries}$$

$$= \frac{2}{10} \times \frac{13}{52} \times \$6\,573\,009$$

$$= \$328\,650$$

Step 4. Measure the present value of the accumulated benefit

$$= \frac{\text{Accumulated benefit}}{(1 + i)^n}$$

$$= \$328\,650/(1 + 0.09)^8 \; [\text{or } \$328\,650 \times 0.50187]$$

$$= \$164\,939$$

The increase in the long service leave can be calculated as $164 939 less $57 019. Note that there have been no long service leave payments during the year to reduce the provision from the amount recognised at the end of the previous year. The change in the provision for long service leave is recorded by the following journal entry.

2023				
30 June	Long service leave expense	Dr	107 920	
	Provision for long service leave	Cr		107 920
	(Increase in provision for long service leave)			

The increase in the provision for long service leave during 2023 can be attributed to several factors:
- an increase in unit credit accumulated by employees. In the first year, the employees' accumulation was 10% of the leave, but, by the end of the second year, 20% had been accumulated because the employees had completed 2 of the 10 years of service required to become eligible for long service leave.
- the interest cost, being the increase in the present value arising from discounting the future cash flows over a shorter period
- an increase in projected salaries resulting from an increase in remuneration; that is, salaries increased beyond the projected 2% during 2023
- a reduction in the interest rate used from 10% at 30 June 2022 to 9% at 30 June 2023.

LEARNING CHECK

☐ Long service leave is a paid absence after the employee has provided a long period of service. Under AASB 119/IAS 19 a liability is recognised for long service leave as it accrues. Long service leave payments reduce the long service leave liability.

☐ In Australia, the accounting treatment for long service leave benefits is usually calculated based on the present value of the obligation measured in accordance with the projected unit credit method (i.e. the present value of the expected future payments that will result from employee service provided to date).

☐ Measurement of the present value of the obligation for long service leave payments is complicated by the need to estimate when the leave will be taken, what the salary will be and how many employees will continue in the entity's employment long enough to become entitled to long service leave.

☐ Accounting for other long-term employee benefits is similar to accounting for defined benefit post-employment plans except that the effects of remeasurements are not recognised in other comprehensive income. Thus, the net liability (or asset) for long-term employee benefits is measured as the difference between the present value of the defined benefit obligation at the end of the reporting period and the fair value at reporting date of plan assets (if any) from which the obligation will be settled (subject to the effects of an asset ceiling, if applicable).

9.7 Termination benefits

LEARNING OBJECTIVE 9.7 Explain when a liability should be recognised for termination benefits and how it should be measured.

When an employee is retrenched or made redundant, the employer may be obliged to pay termination benefits. For example, a downturn in the economy may cause a manufacturer to reduce the scale of its operations, resulting in some portion of the entity's workforce being made redundant. Termination benefits are typically lump sum payments. Paragraph 8 of AASB 119/IAS 19 refers to **termination benefits** as employee benefits that are payable as a result of either:

(a) an entity's decision to terminate an employee's employment before the normal retirement date; or
(b) an employee's decision to accept an offer of benefits in exchange for the termination of employment.

Thus, termination benefits can be distinguished from other forms of employee benefits because the obligation to pay termination benefits arises from the termination of an employment contract, rather than from past service provided by the employee. Although the obligation arises from a decision to terminate employment, the extent of past service provided by each employee is usually a factor in determining the amount of the payment.

The decision by an entity to undertake a redundancy program is not sufficient for the recognition of a liability for termination benefits (i.e. it does not create an obligation to a third party).

Paragraph 165 of AASB 119/IAS 19 requires an entity to recognise an expense and a liability for termination benefits at the earlier of the following dates:

(a) when the entity can no longer withdraw the offer of those benefits; and
(b) when the entity recognises costs for a restructuring that is within the scope of AASB 137 [IAS 37] and that involves the payment of termination benefits.

Paragraphs 166 and 167 of AASB 119/IAS 19 elaborate on when an entity can no longer withdraw from an offer. Paragraph 166 refers to termination benefits that become payable as a result of the employee accepting an offer of benefits in exchange for the termination of employment, such as a voluntary redundancy arrangement. Once the employee accepts, the entity can no longer withdraw the offer. Further, the entity may be prevented from withdrawing an offer by restrictions such as existing regulations, contracts or laws.

Paragraph 167 of AASB 119/IAS 19 is concerned with termination benefits that become payable as a result of the entity's decision to terminate employment. This situation differs from the circumstances in the preceding paragraph because the termination decision is made by the employer — the employee does not have a choice. When the termination benefits result from the entity's decision to terminate an employee's employment, the offer can no longer be withdrawn when the entity has communicated to affected employees a plan of termination that meets all the following criteria (AASB 119/IAS 19 paragraph 167).

(a) Actions required to complete the plan indicate that it is unlikely that significant changes to the plan will be made.
(b) The plan identifies the number of employees whose employment is to be terminated, their job classifications or functions and their locations (but the plan need not identify each individual employee) and the expected completion date.
(c) The plan establishes the termination benefits that employees will receive in sufficient detail that employees can determine the type and amount of benefits they will receive when their employment is terminated.

If at the time of initial recognition termination benefits are expected to be settled wholly within 12 months after the end of the annual reporting period, they are measured using the same principles as other short-term employee benefits (i.e. at the nominal [undiscounted] amount that the entity expects to pay). However, if the termination benefits are not expected to be settled wholly within 12 months after the end of the reporting period, they must be measured at present value. The expected payments required to settle the obligation are discounted at a rate determined by reference to market yields on high-quality corporate bonds, in accordance with paragraph 83 of AASB 119/IAS 19. This is consistent with the measurement of other long-term employee benefits.

Termination benefits

During June 2021, the board of directors of Universal Ltd approved a plan to outsource the company's data processing operations. The closure of the data processing operations is expected to result in the retrenchment of 180 employees throughout Australia and New Zealand. The chief financial officer provided an estimate of redundancy costs of A\$1.2 million. The board expected that it would take at least 6 months to select a contractor for outsourcing the data processing and that it would take a further 3 months for training before internal data processing operations could be discontinued.

During May 2022, redundancy packages were negotiated with trade union representatives and communicated to employees. Data processing operations were to be transferred to an external service provider in India on 1 October 2022.

Required

When should Universal Ltd recognise an expense and liability for the redundancy payments?

Solution

2021

The termination benefits become payable as a result of Universal Ltd's decision to terminate employment, rather than as a result of an offer being accepted by employees. Accordingly, Universal Ltd must recognise a liability for termination benefits when it can no longer withdraw from a plan of termination communicated to affected employees, and that plan meets the criteria specified in paragraph 167 of AASB 119/IAS 19.

At 30 June 2021, the termination plan meets some of the criteria. Management had specified the location (Australia and New Zealand) and function (data processing) of the employees becoming redundant, and estimated their number at 180. The termination benefit payable for each job specification is likely to have formed the basis of the estimated redundancy costs of A\$1.2 million. However, until Universal Ltd has identified an alternative source of data processing, it will not be able to decide on a time at which the redundancy plan should be implemented. Further, although the decision to discontinue the internal data processing operations has been made by Universal Ltd's board of directors, it has not been communicated to the employees. Therefore, Universal Ltd should not recognise an expense and liability for termination benefits in association with the planned closure of its data processing operations at 30 June 2021 in accordance with AASB 119/IAS 19.

2022

By June 2022, the company had completed the formal detailed termination plan by specifying when it is to be implemented. The negotiations with unions over the amount of redundancy payments and entering into a contract with an external provider demonstrate that it is unlikely that significant changes will be made to the amount or timing of the redundancy plan. The termination plan has been communicated to affected employees. Accordingly, Universal Ltd should recognise an expense and a liability for termination benefits in association with the planned closure of its data processing operations in its financial statements for the period ended 30 June 2022 in accordance with AASB 119/IAS 19.

☐ Termination benefits are employee benefits payable as a result of an entity's decision to terminate an employee's employment before the normal retirement date or an employee's decision to accept an offer of benefits in exchange for the termination of employment.

☐ AASB 119/IAS 19 requires an entity to recognise an expense and a liability for termination benefits at the earlier of: when the entity can no longer withdraw the offer of the benefits; or when the entity recognises costs for a restructuring that is within the scope of AASB 137/AASB 37 and that involves the payment of termination benefits.

☐ If at the time of initial recognition, termination benefits are expected to be settled wholly within 12 months after the end of the annual reporting period, they are measured using the same principles as other short-term employee benefits.

☐ If the termination benefits are not expected to be settled wholly within 12 months after the end of the reporting period, they must be measured at present value.

SUMMARY

Employee benefit costs are a significant expense for most reporting entities. Accounting for employee benefits is complicated by the diversity of arrangements for employee remuneration and the different methods prescribed by AASB 119/IAS 19 *Employee Benefits* to account for various forms and categories of employee benefits.

- Liabilities for short-term employee benefits, such as salaries, wages, sick leave, annual leave and bonuses payable within 12 months after the reporting period, are measured at the undiscounted amount that the entity expects to pay.
- Long-term liabilities for defined benefits, such as long service leave, are measured at the present value of the defined benefit obligations (less the fair value of plan assets, if any, out of which the obligation is to be settled). The obligation for long service leave is measured using the projected unit credit method.
- AASB 119/IAS 19 prescribes the accounting treatment for post-employment benefit plans. Accounting for defined contribution post-employment plans is relatively straightforward: a liability is recognised by the entity for contributions payable for the period in excess of contributions paid. Conversely, an asset is recognised if contributions paid exceed the contributions payable, to the extent that the entity expects the excess contributions to be refunded or deducted from future contribution obligations. An entity's net exposure to a defined benefit post-employment plan is measured at the present value of the defined benefit obligations less the fair value of plan assets. If the defined benefit fund has a surplus, the net defined benefit asset recognised by the entity is subject to an asset ceiling.
- The measurement of a liability for termination benefits depends on whether they are expected to be settled wholly within 12 months of the annual reporting period in which they were first recognised. The principles for the measurement of the termination benefits liability are consistent with those for short-term employee benefits and other long-term employee benefits.

KEY TERMS

accumulating paid absences Leave entitlements that the employee may carry forward to a future period if unused in the current period.

asset ceiling The present value of any economic benefits available in the form of refunds from the plan or reductions in future contributions to the plan.

current service cost The increase in the present value of defined benefit obligation resulting from employee service in the current period.

defined benefit plans Post-employment plans other than defined contribution plans.

defined contribution plans Post-employment plans for which an employer pays fixed contributions into a separate entity (e.g. superannuation fund) on behalf of the employee.

employee benefits All forms of consideration given by an entity in exchange for service rendered by employees or for the termination of employment.

long service leave A paid absence after the employee has provided a long period of continuous employment.

net interest on the net defined benefit liability (or asset) The change in the net defined benefit liability (or asset) that arises over time.

non-accumulating paid absences Leave entitlements that the employee may not carry forward to a future period.

past service cost The change in the present value of the defined benefit obligation for employee service in prior periods, resulting from a plan amendment or a curtailment.

payroll The subsystem for regular recording and payment of employee benefits.

post-employment benefits Benefits, other than termination benefits, that are payable after completion of employment, typically after the employee retires; includes pensions, other retirement benefits, post-employment life insurance and post-employment medical care.

short-term employee benefits Employee benefits (other than termination benefits) that are expected to be settled wholly within 12 months after the end of the annual reporting period in which the employees render the related service.

short-term paid absences Leave entitlements to absences that are expected to be settled within 12 months after the end of the reporting period.

termination benefits Employee benefits that are payable as a result of either: (a) an entity's decision to terminate an employee's employment before the normal retirement date; or (b) an employee's decision to accept an offer of benefits in exchange for the termination of employment.

DEMONSTRATION PROBLEM

9.1 Accounting for bonuses and defined contribution superannuation plans

Orchid Ltd contributes to a defined contribution superannuation plan for its employees. Contributions have been established as 10% of wages and salaries, including bonuses, actually paid during the year. Contributions based on budgeted payroll costs were set at $100 000 per month. There is annual net settlement of superannuation contributions payable or refundable based on actual audited payroll information. The net settlement occurs on 30 September for the preceding year ended 30 June.

Managers are entitled to a bonus calculated at 5% of their base salary if Orchid Ltd's profit before tax (excluding the bonus) is more than 20% of market capitalisation of the company at the beginning of the year. The profit target was achieved in 2021 and 2022. The bonus is payable 6 months after the end of the reporting period, provided the manager has remained in the company's employment.

	2022 $	2021 $
Managerial salaries expense	4 500 000	4 000 000
Other salaries and wages	8 000 000	7 800 000
	12 500 000	11 800 000
Accrued wages and salaries	300 000	250 000
Accrued managerial bonuses	?	400 000

At 30 June 2021, Orchid Ltd correctly anticipated that all managers would be eligible for the bonus because staff turnover among managers had been very low. However, by 30 June 2022, the company had moved to new premises and one manager, with a salary of $800 000, indicated that the additional travel was causing him to reconsider his position. The directors estimated that there was a 50% probability that the manager would resign by 31 December 2022 and an 80% probability that he would resign by 30 June 2023.

Required

1. Prepare the journal entry to record the contribution to the superannuation plan for June 2022.
2. Prepare a journal entry to record the liability, if any, arising from the bonus plan at 30 June 2022.
3. Prepare a journal entry to account for the superannuation asset or liability, if any, at 30 June 2022.

SOLUTION

1. *Record the contribution*

   Based on the information provided, monthly contributions are $100 000. As such, the journal entry for the month of June is as follows.

June 30	Contribution expenses	Dr	100 000	
	Bank	Cr		100 000
	(Payment of contribution to superannuation plan)			

2. *Record the liability*

   Using the information provided, bonuses are calculated at 5% of salary and wages expense. However, it is uncertain whether one manager will continue to be employed. Hence, the amount of his bonus (5%) is multiplied by the probability of him staying with the company (50%).

Workings:

	Salary $	Bonus payable $	Probability applied %	Expected payment $
Manager considering leaving	800 000	40 000	50	20 000
Other managers	3 700 000	185 000	100%	185 000
	4 500 000	225 000		205 000

Accordingly, the journal entry to record the liability relating to the bonus plan at 30 June 2022 is as follows.

June 30	Wages and salaries expense	Dr	205 000	
	Accrued managerial bonuses	Cr		205 000
	(Accrual of managerial bonuses)			

3. Account for the asset or liability

The amount of the superannuation asset or liability is determined by comparing:
(a) the amount of contributions payable, in accordance with the terms of the defined contribution plan
(b) the amount of contributions paid during the period.
The amount of contributions paid is: $100 000 per month $\times$ 12 months = $1 200 000
The amount of contributions payable is calculated as follows.

Total wages and salaries expense for 2022 excluding bonuses	$12 500 000
Less: Accrual 30 June 2022	(300 000)
Add: Accrual 30 June 2021	250 000
Wages and salaries paid during 2022	12 450 000
Managerial bonuses for 2021 paid during 2022	400 000
Total wages, salaries and bonuses paid during 2022	12 850 000
Superannuation contribution — 10% $\times$ $12 850 000	1 285 000
(a) Superannuation contributions payable for the year	1 285 000
(b) Contributions paid	(1 200 000)
Contributions payable at year end	85 000

As such, the journal entry to record the superannuation liability (amount payable) at 30 June 2022 is as follows.

June 30	Superannuation expense	Dr	85 000	
	Superannuation liability	Cr		85 000
	(Accrual of superannuation expense)			

COMPREHENSION QUESTIONS

1 What is a paid absence? Provide an example.
2 What is the difference between accumulating and non-accumulating sick leave? How does the recognition of accumulating sick leave differ from the recognition of non-accumulating sick leave?
3 What is the difference between vesting and non-vesting sick leave? How does the recognition of vesting sick leave differ from the recognition of non-vesting sick leave?
4 Explain how a defined contribution superannuation plan differs from a defined benefit superannuation plan.
5 During October 2008, there was a sudden global decline in the price of equity securities and credit securities. Many superannuation funds made negative returns on investments during this period. How would this event affect the wealth of employees and employers? Consider both defined benefit and defined contribution superannuation funds in your answer to this question.

6 Explain how an entity should account for its contribution to a defined contribution superannuation plan in accordance with AASB 119/IAS 19.

7 Compare the off-balance sheet approach to accounting for a defined benefit post-employment plan with the net capitalisation approach adopted by AASB 119/IAS 19. Can these approaches be explained by different underlying views as to whether a deficit or surplus in the fund meets the definition of a liability or asset of the sponsoring employer?

8 In relation to defined benefit post-employment plans, paragraph 56 of AASB 119/IAS 19 states, 'the entity is, in substance, underwriting the actuarial and investment risks associated with the plan'. Evaluate whether the requirements for the recognition and measurement of the net defined benefit liability reflect the underlying assumptions about the entity's risks.

9 Identify and discuss the assumptions involved in the measurement of a provision for long service leave. Assess the consistency of these requirements with the fundamental qualitative characteristics of financial information prescribed by the *Conceptual Framework*.

10 Explain the projected unit credit method of measuring and recognising an obligation for long-term employee benefits. Illustrate your answer with an example.

CASE STUDY 9.1

TERMINATION BENEFITS

The board of directors of Launceston Ltd met in June 2022 and decided to close down a branch of the company's operations when the lease expired in the following February. The chief financial officer advised that termination benefits of $2 million are likely to be paid.

Required

Advise the company's accountant whether the company should recognise a liability for termination benefits in its financial statements for the year ended June 2022. Explain your advice with reference to the requirements of AASB 119/IAS 19.

CASE STUDY 9.2

VESTING ENTITLEMENTS

Monash Ltd is a newly formed company and is formulating its policies in terms of employee benefits. The company would like to offer employees payment for any accumulated unused sick leave if they resign from the company.

Required

Explain to the CEO the effect on the financial statements if sick leave entitlements are vesting versus non-vesting.

CASE STUDY 9.3

LONG SERVICE LEAVE

The accountant of Oxford Ltd believes that long service leave should not be considered as a liability in the accounts until employees have commenced their tenth year of service, given this leave entitlement only applies to Oxford Ltd employees after 10 years of continuous service.

Required

Advise the accountant on whether this approach is acceptable, and what requirements exist under AASB 119/IAS 19.

CASE STUDY 9.4

BONUSES

Bond Ltd pays bonuses to its staff 3 months after year-end, provided profit targets are met and staff remain employed with the company at the time the bonuses are paid. At 30 June 2022 the company determines it has exceeded its profit target for the year, but prefers not to record a liability for bonuses payable until it confirms how many staff continue to be employed with the company in September, given there has been significant variation in turnover rates in recent years.

Required

Advise whether the proposed approach is acceptable.

APPLICATION AND ANALYSIS EXERCISES

★ BASIC | ★ ★ MODERATE | ★ ★ ★ DIFFICULT

9.1 Accounting for the payroll ★   LO2

Kingfisher Ltd pays its employees on a monthly basis. The payroll is processed on the 5th day of the month and payable on the 7th day of the month. Gross salaries for July were $600 000, from which $150 000 was deducted in tax. All of Kingfisher Ltd's salaries are accounted for as expenses. Deductions for health insurance were $12 000. Payments for health insurance and employee income taxes withheld are due on the 20th day of the following month.

Required

1. Prepare all journal entries to record the July payroll, the payment of July salaries and the remittance of deductions.
2. Calculate the balance of the accrued payroll account at the end of July.

9.2 Accrual of wages and salaries ★   LO2

Zhang Ltd has a weekly payroll of $140 000. The last payroll processed before the end of the annual reporting period was for the week ended Friday 24 June. Employees do not work during weekends.

Required

Prepare a journal entry to accrue the weekly payroll as at 30 June.

9.3 Accounting for the payroll ★   LO2

Malee Ltd pays management on a monthly basis and staff on a fortnightly basis. Payroll is processed and paid on the 1st of each month for management, and the 1st and 15th of each month for staff. Gross management salaries per month are $360 000 (less $162 000 tax). Gross staff wages per month are $540 000 (less $175 500 tax), and paid in equal instalments on the 1st and 15th of each month. Tax is remitted on the 15th of the following month.

Required

Prepare journal entries for January payroll.

9.4 Accounting for sick leave ★   LO2

Magpie Ltd has 80 employees who each earn a gross wage of $120 per day. In an attempt to reduce absenteeism, Magpie Ltd introduced a new workplace agreement providing all employees with entitlement to 5 days of non-vesting, accumulating sick leave per annum, effective from 1 July 2021. Under the previous workplace agreement, all sick leave was non-cumulative. During the year ended 30 June 2022, 240 days of paid sick leave were taken by employees. It is estimated that 70% of unused sick leave will be taken during the year ended 30 June 2023 and that 30% will not be taken at all.

Required

Prepare a journal entry to recognised Magpie Ltd's liability, if any, for sick leave at 30 June 2022.

9.5 Accounting for sick leave ★   LO2

Omu Ltd has 220 employees who each earn a gross wage of $145 per day. Omu Ltd provides 5 days of paid non-accumulating sick leave for each employee per annum. During the year, 160 days of paid sick leave and 20 days of unpaid sick leave were taken. Staff turnover is negligible.

Required

Calculate the employee benefits expense for sick leave during the year and the amount that should be recognised as a liability, if any, for sick leave at the end of the year.

9.6 Accounting for annual leave ★   LO2

Burung Ltd provides employees with 4 weeks (20 days) of annual leave for each year of service. The annual leave is accumulating and vesting up to a maximum of 6 weeks. Thus, all employees take their annual leave within 6 months after the end of each reporting period so that it does not lapse. Burung Ltd pays a loading of 17.5% on annual leave; that is, employees are paid an additional 17.5% of their regular wage while taking annual leave. Refer to the following extract from Burung Ltd's payroll records for the year ended 30 June 2022.

Employee	Wage/days $	AL 1 July 2021 (days)	Increase in entitlement (days)	AL taken (days)
Chand	150	8	20	15
Kettle	115	5	20	12
Sander	140	4	20	10
Zhou	100	6	20	15

Required

Calculate the amount of annual leave that should be accrued for each employee.

9.7 Accounting for profit-sharing arrangements ★ **LO2**

Ren Ltd has a profit-sharing arrangement in which 1% of profit for the period is payable to employees, paid 3 months after the end of the reporting period. Employees' entitlements under the profit-sharing arrangement are subject to their continued employment at the time the payment is made. Based on past staff turnover levels, it is expected that 95% of the share of profit will be paid. Ren Ltd's profit for the period was $70 million.

Required

Prepare a journal entry to record Ren Ltd's liability for employee benefits arising from the profit-sharing arrangement at the end of the reporting period.

9.8 Accounting for the payroll and accrual of wages and salaries ★ ★ **LO2**

Lyrebird Ltd pays its employees on a fortnightly basis. All employee benefits are recognised as expenses. The following information is provided for its July and August payrolls.

	July $	July $	August $	August $
Fortnightly payroll		680 000		800 000
		820 000		700 000
Gross payroll for the month		1 500 000		1 500 000
Deductions payable to:				
Taxation authority	260 000		255 000	
Health fund	20 000		20 000	
Community charity	4 000		4 000	
Union fees	6 500		6 500	
Total deductions for the month		290 500		285 500
Net wages and salaries paid				
14 July, 11 August	553 775		648 230	
28 July, 25 August	655 725	1 209 500	566 270	1 214 500
		1 500 000		1 500 000

The two fortnightly payrolls in August were for the fortnight ended Friday 7 August and Friday 21 August. The payrolls were processed and paid on the following Monday and Tuesday respectively. Payroll deductions are remitted as follows.

Health fund deductions	7th day of the following month
Union fees	7th day of the following month
Taxation authority	14th day of the following month
Community charity	21st day of the following month

Required

1. Prepare all journal entries to account for the August payroll and all payments relating to employee benefits during August.
2. Prepare a journal entry to accrue wages for the remaining days in August not included in the final August payroll. Use the same level of remuneration as per the final payroll for August.

9.9 Accounting for annual leave ★ ★ **LO2**

Niao Ltd provides 4 weeks (20 days) of accumulating vested annual leave for each year of service. The company policy is that annual leave must be taken within 6 months of the end of the period in which it accrues. Annual leave is paid at the base salary rate (which excludes commissions, bonuses and overtime). A 17.5% loading is applied to annual leave payments.

The following summary data is derived from Niao Ltd's payroll records for the year ended 30 June 2022. Base pay rates have increased during the year. The amounts shown are applicable at 30 June 2022.

Employee category	Base pay/day $	Annual leave Balance b/d 1 July 2021 (days)	Annual leave Accumulated during year (days)	Annual leave Taken during year (days)
Managers	440	100	200	260
Sales staff	220	150	600	630
Office workers	110	120	400	387
Other	100	60	200	240

Additional information

After leave taken during the year had been recorded, Niao Ltd's trial balance revealed that the provision for annual leave had a debit balance of $262 460 at 30 June 2022.

Required

Prepare journal entries to account for the liability for annual leave at 30 June 2022.

9.10 Accounting for annual leave ★ ★ LO2

Assume the same details as in exercise 9.9, except that Niao Ltd's trial balance showed the provision for annual leave had a credit balance of $62 640.

Required

1. Prepare journal entries to account for the annual leave liability at 30 June 2022.
2. Prepare journal entries to account for the annual leave liability at 30 June 2022 if the provision for annual leave had a credit balance of $62 640, but there was no loading applied to annual leave payments.

9.11 Accounting for sick leave ★ ★ LO2

Drake Ltd opened a call centre on 1 July 2021. The company provides 1 week (5 days) of sick leave entitlement for the employees working at the call centre. The following information has been obtained from Drake Ltd's payroll records and actuarial assessments for the year ended 30 June 2022. The column headed 'Term. in 2022' indicates the leave entitlement pertaining to service of employees whose employment was terminated during the year. The actuary has estimated the percentage of unused leave that would be taken within 12 months if Drake Ltd allowed leave to accumulate. Due to high staff turnover, the remaining leave would lapse (or be settled in cash, if vesting) within 1 year after the end of the reporting period.

Employee category	Base pay/day $	Current service (days)	Leave taken in 2022 (days)	Term. in 2022 (days)	Estimated leave used 2022 %	Estimated termination 2022 %
Supervisors	150	30	20	3	90	10
Operators	90	500	400	60	70	30

Required

Calculate the employee benefits expense for sick leave for the year and the amount that should be recognised as a liability for sick leave at 30 June 2022, assuming that sick leave entitlements are:

1. non-accumulating
2. accumulating and non-vesting
3. accumulating and vesting.

9.12 Accounting for defined contribution superannuation plans ★ LO4

Bachstelze Ltd provides a defined contribution superannuation fund for its employees. The company pays contributions equivalent to 10% of annual wages and salaries. Contributions of $60 000 per month were paid for the year ended 30 June 2022. Actual wages and salaries were $8 million. Three months after the reporting period, there is a settlement of the difference between the amount paid and the annual amount payable determined with reference to Bachstelze Ltd's audited payroll information. The settlement at 30 September involves either an additional contribution payment by Bachstelze Ltd or a refund of excess contributions paid.

Required

Prepare all journal entries required during June 2022 for Bachstelze Ltd's payment of, and liability for, superannuation contributions.

9.13 Accounting for defined benefit superannuation plans ★ ★ ★   **LO5**

Lily Ltd provides a defined benefit superannuation plan for its managers. The following information is available in relation to the plan.

	2022 $
Present value of the defined benefit obligation 1 July 2021	5 000 000
Fair value of plan assets 1 July 2021	4 750 000
Current service cost	575 000
Contributions paid by Lily Ltd to the fund during the year	500 000
Benefits paid by the fund during the year	600 000
Present value of the defined benefit obligation 30 June 2022	5 375 000
Fair value of plan assets at 30 June 2022	5 023 750

Additional information

- No past service costs were incurred during the year ended 30 June 2022.
- The interest rate used to measure the present value of defined benefits at 30 June 2021 was 9%.
- The interest rate used to measure the present value of defined benefits at 30 June 2022 was 10%.
- There was an actuarial gain pertaining to the present value of the defined benefit obligation as a result of an increase in the interest rate.
- The only remeasurement affecting the fair value of plan assets is the return on plan assets.
- The asset ceiling was nil at 30 June 2021 and 30 June 2022.
- All contributions received by the funds were paid by Lily Ltd. Employees make no contributions.

Required

1. Determine the surplus or deficit of Lily Ltd's defined benefit plan at 30 June 2022.
2. Determine the net defined benefit asset or liability that should be recognised by Lily Ltd at 30 June 2022.
3. Calculate the net interest for the year ended 30 June 2022.
4. Calculate the actuarial gain or loss for the defined benefit obligation for the year ended 30 June 2022.
5. Calculate the return on plan assets, excluding any amount recognised in net interest, for the year ended 30 June 2022.
6. Present a reconciliation of the opening balance to the closing balance of the net defined benefit liability (asset), showing separate reconciliations for plan assets and the present value of the defined benefit obligation.
7. Prepare a summary journal entry to account for the defined benefit superannuation plan in the books of Lily Ltd for the year ended 30 June 2022.

9.14 Accounting for defined benefit superannuation plans ★ ★ ★   **LO5**

Some years ago, Bidulgi Ltd established a defined benefit superannuation plan for its employees. The company has since introduced a defined contribution plan, which all new staff join when commencing employment with Bidulgi Ltd. Although the defined benefit plan is now closed to new recruits, the fund continues to provide for employees who have been with the company for a long time. The following actuarial report has been received for the defined benefit plan.

	2022 $
Present value of the defined benefit obligation 1 January	20 000 000
Past service cost	2 000 000
Net interest	?
Current service cost	800 000
Benefits paid	2 100 000
Actuarial loss on DBO	100 000
Present value of the defined benefit obligation 31 December	23 000 000
Fair value of plan assets at 1 January	19 000 000
Return on plan assets	?

Contributions paid to the fund during the year				1 000 000
Benefits paid by the fund during the year				2 100 000
Fair value of plan assets at 30 June 2022				20 130 000

Additional information

- All contributions received by the funds were paid by Bidulgi Ltd. Employees make no contributions.
- The interest rate used to measure the present value of the defined benefit obligation was 10% at 31 December 2021 and 31 December 2022.
- The asset ceiling was nil at 31 December 2021 and 31 December 2022.

Required

1. Determine the surplus or deficit of Bidulgi Ltd's defined benefit plan at 31 December 2022.
2. Determine the net defined benefit asset or liability that should be recognised by Bidulgi Ltd at 31 December 2022.
3. Calculate the net interest and the return on plan assets for the year ended 31 December 2022.
4. Present a reconciliation of the opening balance to the closing balance of the net defined benefit liability (asset), showing separate reconciliations for plan assets and the present value of the defined benefit obligation.
5. Prepare a summary journal entry to account for the defined benefit superannuation plan in the books of Bidulgi Ltd for the year ended 31 December 2022.

9.15 Accounting for defined benefit superannuation plans ★ ★ **LO5**

Pigeon Ltd provides a defined benefit superannuation plan for its managers. The assistant accountant has completed some sections of the defined benefit worksheet based on information provided in an actuary's report on the Pigeon DB Superannuation Fund for the year ended 30 June 2023.

PIGEON DB SUPERANNUATION FUND Defined benefit worksheet for the year ended 30 June 2023						
	Pigeon Ltd				Pigeon DB Superannuation Fund	
	Profit/ loss $'000	OCI $'000	Bank $'000	Net DBL(A) $'000	DBO $'000	Plan assets $'000
Balance 30/6/22				1 500 Cr	9 000 Cr	7 500 Dr
Net interest at 10%						
Current service cost					600 Cr	
Contributions to the fund			900 Cr			900 Dr
Benefits paid by the fund					150 Dr	150 Cr
Actuarial loss: DBO					450 Cr	
Journal entry						
Balance 30/6/23					10 800 Cr	9 000 Dr
Adjustment for asset ceiling if < deficit						
Balance 30/6/23						

Additional information

The asset ceiling was $900 000 at 30 June 2023.

Required

1. Determine the surplus or deficit of the fund at 30 June 2023.
2. Determine the net defined benefit asset or liability at 30 June 2023.
3. Calculate the net interest and distinguish between the interest expense component of the defined benefit obligation and the interest income component of the change in the fair value of plan assets for the year ended 30 June 2023.
4. Determine the amount to be recognised in profit or loss in relation to the defined benefit superannuation plan for the year ended 30 June 2023.
5. Determine the amount to be recognised in other comprehensive income in relation to the defined benefit superannuation plan for the year ended 30 June 2023.

9.16 Accounting for defined benefit superannuation plans ★ ★   **LO5**

Which of the following items in relation to a defined benefit fund are recognised in (i) profit or loss and (ii) other comprehensive income in accordance with AASB 119/IAS 19?

1. Current service cost
2. Past service cost incurred during the period
3. Net interest
4. Return on plan assets excluding amounts recognised in net interest
5. Benefits paid to members
6. Current period actuarial gains in relation to the defined benefit obligation
7. Current period actuarial losses in relation to the defined benefit obligation
8. Current period actuarial gains in relation to the assets of the plan
9. Current period actuarial losses in relation to the assets of the plan
10. Contributions paid

9.17 Accounting for defined benefit superannuation plans ★ ★   **LO5**

For each of the following scenarios, determine (i) the surplus or deficit in the defined benefit superannuation fund and (ii) the net defined benefit liability or asset that should be recognised by the sponsoring employer in accordance with AASB 119/IAS 19.

	Present value of DBO	Fair value of plan assets	Asset ceiling
1.	$2 600 000	$2 000 000	$nil
2.	$3 100 000	$2 400 000	$nil
3.	$4 000 000	$4 400 000	$200 000
4.	$4 800 000	$5 000 000	$500 000

9.18 Accounting for long service leave ★   **LO6**

Victoria Ltd provides long service leave entitlement of 13 weeks of paid leave after 10 years of continuous employment. The provision for long service leave had a credit balance of $180 000 at 30 June 2022. During the year ended 30 June 2023, long service leave of $45 000 was paid. At the end of the year, the present value of the defined benefit obligation for long service leave was $160 000.

Required

Prepare all journal entries in relation to long service leave for the year ended 30 June 2023.

9.19 Accounting for sick leave ★ ★   **LO2, 6**

Finch Ltd provides 1 week (5 days) of accumulating non-vesting sick leave for each year of service. Sick leave is paid at the base pay rate, which does not include commissions, bonuses and overtime. The proportion of accumulated sick leave that will be taken is estimated for each category of employee due to differences in staff turnover rates. The following summary data is derived from Finch Ltd's payroll records for the year ended 30 June 2022.

			Sick leave		% of unused leave expected to be taken		
Employee category	Base pay/day $	Balance b/d 1 July 2021 (days)	Increase in leave for current service (days)	Leave taken or lapsed (days)	Within 12 months	1 year later	2 years later
Managers	450	120	50	10	20	10	5
Consultants	300	110	100	90	75	10	0
Clerical staff	100	80	100	70	65	9	0

Additional information

The yield on high-quality corporate bonds at 30 June 2022 is 7% for one-year bonds and 8% for two-year bonds. After leave taken during the year had been recorded Finch Ltd's trial balance at 30 June 2022 revealed the provision for sick leave had a credit balance of $13 000.

Required

1. Prepare journal entries to account for the liability for sick leave at 30 June 2022.
2. State how much of the provision should be classified as a non-current liability.

9.20 Accounting for long service leave ★ ★   **LO6**

Oca Ltd provides long service leave for its retail staff. Long service leave entitlement is determined as 13 weeks of paid leave for 10 years of continued service. The following information is obtained from Oca Ltd's payroll records and actuarial reports for its retail staff at 30 June 2022.

Unit credit (years)	No. of employees	% expected to become entitled	Annual salary per employee	No. of years until vesting	Yield on HQ corporate bonds
1	80	20	$45 000	9	10%
2	70	30	$45 000	8	9%
3	50	50	$45 000	7	9%
4	30	60	$45 000	6	9%

Additional information

- The estimated annual increase in retail wages is 1% p.a. for the next 10 years, reflecting expected inflation.
- The provision for long service leave for retail staff at 30 June 2021 was $22 000.
- No employees were eligible to take long service leave during the year ended 30 June 2022.

Required

Prepare the journal entry to account for Oca Ltd's provision for long service leave at 30 June 2022.

9.21 Accounting for long service leave ★ ★ ★   **LO6**

Bluebird Ltd provides credit services. Bluebird Ltd provides its employees with long service leave entitlements of 13 weeks of paid leave for every 10 years of continuous service. As the company has been operating for only 5 years, no employees have become entitled to long service leave. However, the company recognises a provision for long service leave using the projected unit credit approach required by AASB 119/IAS 19. The following information is obtained from Bluebird Ltd's payroll records and actuarial reports for the non-managerial staff of its debt collection business at 30 June 2022.

Unit credit (years)	No. of employees	% expected to become entitled	Average annual salary	No. of years until vesting	Yield on govt corporate bonds
1	100	20	$46 000	9	6%
2	85	26	$48 000	8	6%
3	40	35	$50 000	7	5%
4	32	50	$52 500	6	5%
5	25	65	$55 600	5	5%

Additional information

- The estimated annual increase in retail wages is 5% p.a. for the next 10 years, reflecting Bluebird Ltd's policy of increasing salaries of its debt collection staff for each year of additional experience.
- At 30 June 2021, the provision for long service leave for non-managerial debt collection staff was $132 000.

Required

Prepare the journal entry to account for Bluebird Ltd's provision for long service leave at 30 June 2022 in relation to the non-managerial employees of the company's debt collection business.

REFERENCE

BHP Group Ltd 2018, *Annual report 2018*, www.bhp.com.

ACKNOWLEDGEMENTS

Photo: © Mila Supinskaya / Shutterstock.com

Photo: © Goodluz / Shutterstock.com

Figure 9.3: © BHP Group Ltd 2018

Text: © 2019 Australian Accounting Standards Board (AASB). The text, graphics and layout of this publication are protected by Australian copyright law and the comparable law of other countries. No part of the publication may be reproduced, stored or transmitted in any form or by any means without the prior written permission of the AASB except as permitted by law. For reproduction or publication, permission should be sought in writing from the AASB. Requests in the first instance should be addressed to the National Director, Australian Accounting Standards Board, PO Box 204, Collins Street West, Victoria 8007.

CHAPTER 10

Leases

CHAPTER AIM

This chapter explains the accounting requirements for leases from the perspective of both the lessee and the lessor in accordance with AASB 16/IFRS 16 *Leases*.

LEARNING OBJECTIVES

After studying this chapter, you should be able to:

10.1 explain the purpose of AASB 16/IFRS 16

10.2 account for leases from the perspective of a lessee

10.3 classify lease arrangements from the perspective of the lessor

10.4 account for finance leases from the perspective of a financier lessor

10.5 account for finance leases from the perspective of a manufacturer/dealer lessor

10.6 account for operating leases from the perspective of a lessor

10.7 summarise the disclosure requirements regarding leases.

CONCEPTS FOR REVIEW

Before studying this chapter, you should understand and, if necessary, revise:

- the definition of an asset in the *Conceptual Framework*
- the definition of a liability in the *Conceptual Framework*.

10.1 Introduction and scope

LEARNING OBJECTIVE 10.1 Explain the purpose of AASB 16/IFRS 16.

Leasing is a means of gaining access to the benefits of an asset without owning the asset. In a lease arrangement, payments are made by the lessee to the lessor for the right to use the asset for a specified period of time. AASB 16/IFRS 16 *Leases* requires the lessee to recognise all their leases on the statement of financial position.

Paragraph 1 of AASB 16/IFRS 16 states the objective of the standard:

> This Standard sets out the principles for the recognition, measurement, presentation and disclosure of *leases*. The objective is to ensure that *lessees* and *lessors* provide relevant information in a manner that faithfully represents those transactions. This information gives a basis for users of financial statements to assess the effect that leases have on the financial position, financial performance and cash flows of an entity.

10.1.1 What is a lease?

Appendix A of AASB 16/IFRS 16 defines a **lease** as follows.

> A contract, or part of a contract, that conveys the right to use an asset (the underlying asset) for a period of time in exchange for consideration.

Paragraphs B9–B31 provide detailed guidance to help in assessing whether a contract is, or contains, a lease. The transfer of the **right to use** is essential in the definition and therefore the guidance focuses on clarifying the concept of the right to use. According to paragraph B9, that includes:

(a) the right to obtain substantially all of the economic benefits from use of the identified asset (as described in paragraphs B21–B23); and

(b) the right to direct the use of the identified asset (as described in paragraphs B24–B30).

The concept of *underlying asset* and *identified asset* are used interchangeably. Nevertheless, paragraph B13 provides the following explanation about what constitutes an identified asset.

> An asset is typically identified by being explicitly specified in a contract. However, an asset can also be identified by being implicitly specified at the time that the asset is made available for use by the customer.

ILLUSTRATIVE EXAMPLE 10.1

Identified asset

OCO Ltd is the owner of a fibre-optic cable that connects Sydney to Jakarta. The cable has 20 fibres. Telco Ltd enters into a contract with OCO Ltd for access to the fibre-optic cable. The contract allows Telco Ltd to use any of the 20 fibres during the contract term to transmit data.

Required
Does the contract qualify as a lease?

Solution
Although the amount of fibres that Telco Ltd uses is specified in the contract, there is no identified asset and therefore there is no lease. The contract is for access to the capacity of an asset rather than an explicitly or implicitly specified asset.

If OCO Ltd dedicated specific fibres in the cable to the exclusive use of Telco Ltd, then the contract would be for an identified asset and could qualify as a lease.

The customer's ability to derive benefits from use of the underlying asset refers to substantially the whole of the potential economic benefits throughout the lease term. The customer can obtain the benefits either directly (e.g. by holding and using the asset itself) or indirectly (e.g. by subleasing the asset to another entity). A customer does not have the ability to derive benefits from the underlying asset if the benefits can only be derived by using the asset in conjunction with other goods and services provided by the supplier (and not available for separate purchase from the supplier or alternative suppliers).

The customer's ability to direct the use of an asset is determined by its ability to make the decisions that are most significant to the derivation of the economic benefits from the underlying asset during the lease term. The customer's ability to direct the use of the underlying asset would normally be evident in whether it can determine:
- how and for what purpose the asset is employed
- how the asset is operated
- the operator of the asset.

ILLUSTRATIVE EXAMPLE 10.2

Bundle of goods and services

Neighbours Ltd is a healthcare provider that enters into a 4-year contract with a supplier for specialised diagnostic radiography equipment. Neighbours Ltd will hold and use the equipment at one of its private hospitals to provide healthcare services to patients. The equipment can only be operated in conjunction with consumable products. The purchase of the consumable products is included in the contract with the supplier. The consumables are available for purchase separately from the supplier or other suppliers.

Required
Does the contract qualify as a lease?

Solution
There is a lease in this case because the right to use the specialised equipment is a separate component to the contract. Neighbours Ltd can derive benefits from the underlying asset with or without the purchase of consumables from this specific supplier.

Note that if the lessor has the right to substitute an alternative asset for the specified asset (referred to in paragraph B14 of AASB 16/IFRS 16 as a **substantive right to substitute the asset**), the contract cannot be recognised as a lease as the right to use the asset cannot be considered to have been transferred. A 'substantive right to substitute the asset' would exist if the lessor has the practical ability to substitute an alternative for the asset at any time without needing the lessee's approval and can benefit from doing so. Note that a substantive right does not exist if the supplier can only substitute an alternative for the underlying asset when the asset is not operating properly or when a technical upgrade is available — therefore, in those cases, the contract can be recognised as a lease.

ILLUSTRATIVE EXAMPLE 10.3

Substitution rights

MBOP Ltd supplies electronic data storage. Telco Ltd enters into a contract with MBOP Ltd for the use of a dedicated server to store data. The contract allows MBOP Ltd to substitute another identical server for the dedicated server at any time without Telco Ltd's consent. MBOP Ltd can give effect to the substitution at a nominal cost to it.

Required
Does the contract qualify as a lease?

Solution
There is no lease because there is no identified asset. The supplier has a 'substantive right to substitute the asset' at any time at nominal cost.

If the substitution required MBOP Ltd to incur significant costs in the transfer or back up of the data, then the supplier would not have substantive right of substitution. In this case, the contract would be for an identified asset and could qualify as a lease.

There are two parties to the lease contract: the lessor and the lessee. The **lessor** is the owner of the asset and retains ownership under the lease arrangement. The **lessee** obtains the right to use the asset, not the ownership of the asset itself, in return for making a payment or series of payments to the lessor. Consider the situation where Mary Smith goes to her local Radio Rentals store and rents a Blu-ray player for 2 years at $15 a month. In essence, Mary enters into a lease agreement with Radio Rentals for the Blu-ray player. Note:

- the lessor, Radio Rentals, retains ownership of the Blu-ray player
- the lessee, Mary Smith, obtains the right to use the Blu-ray player
- the lessee, Mary Smith, agrees to make a payment of $15 each month for the right to use the Blu-ray player.

In signing a lease agreement, a lessee may agree to make payments for additional services provided by the lessor. For example, an individual (the lessee) may lease a motor vehicle through a leasing company (the lessor) for $500 per month. Under the lease agreement the lessor will give the lessee the right to use the vehicle but the lessor will also pay for the regular servicing of the vehicle as well as for the fuel consumed (by providing fuel cards). The $500 payment by the lessee is covering the right to use of the vehicle, as well as the costs incurred for the other services provided by the lessor, referred to in this chapter as **executory costs**. These additional services are not considered part of the lease according to the definition from AASB 16/IFRS 16 — they are non-lease components of the lease agreement. Even though they ensure that the asset can be used, they do not involve the right to use the asset; that is, the lessee would still have the right to use the asset even if the lease agreement does not specify that the lessor will provide those extra services. In accounting for leases it is essential that the payment for the right to use the asset (the lease component) is distinguished from the payments for executory costs (the non-lease components). Nevertheless, if the service component is relatively small, the accounting standard does not require for it to be separately accounted; instead, it allows it be treated as a lease component.

All leases are covered under AASB 16/IFRS 16 except for those specifically excluded by paragraph 3:

    (a) leases to explore for or use minerals, oil, natural gas and similar non-regenerative resources;
    (b) leases of biological assets within the scope of AASB 141 [IAS 41] *Agriculture* held by a lessee;
    (c) service concession arrangements within the scope of [AASB] Interpretation 12 [IFRIC 12] *Service Concession Arrangements*;
    (d) licences of intellectual property granted by a lessor within the scope of AASB 15 [IFRS 15] *Revenue from Contracts with Customers*; and
    (e) rights held by a lessee under licensing agreements within the scope of AASB 138 [IAS 38] *Intangible Assets* for such items as motion picture films, video recordings, plays, manuscripts, patents and copyrights.

For leases involving intangible assets other than those described above, the lessee is allowed to ignore AASB 16/IFRS 16 if it so chooses. Also, a lessee is granted exemptions from applying the requirements of this standard for leases with a duration of 12 months or less and leases for low-value assets. For those leases, the lessee can recognise the payments as expenses and the only assets and liabilities that may be recognised are for the payments due, but not yet made at the end of the period (a liability) and the payments made in advance (an asset). These exemptions were introduced in response to the feedback received from various parties complaining about the complexities in applying the new requirements.

LEARNING CHECK

☐ The accounting standard on leases is AASB 16/IFRS 16 *Leases*.
☐ A lease gives a lessee the right to use a lessor's identified asset for an agreed period of time in return for a series of payments.
☐ Additional services provided by the lessor are considered as non-lease components of the lease agreement as they do not involve the right to use an asset.
☐ AASB 16/IFRS 16 does not apply to most leases relating to non-regenerative or biological resources or to licensing agreements for motion picture films, video recordings, plays, manuscripts, patents and copyrights.
☐ AASB 16/IFRS 16 gives some lessees the option to ignore the requirements of this standard, especially for leases with a duration of 12 months or less or leases for low-value assets.

10.2 Accounting for leases by lessees

LEARNING OBJECTIVE 10.2 Account for leases from the perspective of a lessee.

AASB 16/IFRS 16 requires the lessee to recognise an asset and a related liability for all their leases with a term of more than 12 months, unless the underlying asset is of low value. In this section, a detailed description is provided of the rules from AASB 16/IFRS 16 related to the initial recognition, measurement and disclosure of this asset and liability.

10.2.1 Initial recognition

Paragraph 22 of AASB 16/IFRS 16 requires the lessee, at the **commencement date of the lease**, to recognise a right-of-use asset and a lease liability. According to the Preface of AASB 16:

> A lessee is required to recognise a right-of-use asset representing its right to use the underlying leased asset and a lease liability representing its obligations to make lease payments.

The commencement of the lease is the date from which the lessee is entitled to exercise its right to use the underlying asset.

Lease liability

The liability is to be measured at the present value of the lease payments that are not paid at the commencement date of the lease (AASB 16/IFRS 16 paragraph 26). The present value is calculated based on the interest rate implicit in the lease, or, if the implicit rate is not readily determined, the lessee's incremental borrowing rate.

Lease payments are defined in Appendix A of AASB 16/IFRS 16 as payments for the right to use the underlying asset made during the lease term and include:

(a) fixed payments (including in-substance fixed payments), less any lease incentives;
(b) variable lease payments that depend on an index or a rate;
(c) the exercise price of a purchase option if the lessee is reasonably certain to exercise that option; and
(d) payments of penalties for terminating the lease, if the lease term reflects the lessee exercising an option
  to terminate the lease.

For the lessee, lease payments also include amounts expected to be payable by the lessee under residual value guarantees.

If any of the payments are made at commencement date, they are still considered lease payments, but they are not included in the initial amount recognised for the lease liability (as the obligation to pay the amount was already settled). If any of the payments above include a payment for executory costs (i.e. insurance, maintenance, consumable supplies, replacement parts and rates) reimbursed by the lessee after being paid by the lessor on behalf of the lessee, those costs should be deducted before calculating the lease payments. That is because, as discussed in section 10.1, those costs are related to additional services provided by the lessor that are not related to the right to use the underlying asset and therefore are not considered lease components.

Fixed payments include payments by the lessee for the right to use the asset that do not change throughout the lease term and are adjusted for payments made or reimbursements by the lessor to the lessee (i.e. **lease incentives**). **Variable lease payments** may be increased or decreased during the lease term because of changes in facts and circumstances occurring after the asset is made available to the lessee to use, other than the passage of time. To be included in the lease payments, the **purchase option** should allow the lessee to purchase the asset at the end of the lease for a pre-set amount, significantly less than the expected residual value at the end of the lease term (as such, it is normally referred to as a *bargain purchase option*). The **residual value guarantee**, in general, is that part of the residual value of the underlying asset guaranteed by the lessee, a party related to the lessee or a third party unrelated to the lessor. The lessor will estimate the residual value of the underlying asset at the end of the lease term based on market conditions at the inception of the lease, and the lessee, a party related to the lessee or a third party unrelated to the lessor will guarantee that, when the asset is returned to the lessor, it will realise at least that amount. The guarantee may range from 1% to 100% of the residual value and is a matter for negotiation between lessor and lessee or a third party unrelated to the lessor. Where a lessee guarantees some or all of the residual value of the asset, the lessor has transferred risks associated with movements in the residual value to the lessee. The lessee will recognise as part of the lease payments only the residual value guarantees expected to be payable by them. The part of the residual value that the lessor is not assured that will be realised or that is guaranteed solely by a party related to the lessor is identified as the **unguaranteed residual value**.

The **interest rate implicit in the lease** that is normally used to calculate the present value of the lease payments is defined by Appendix A of AASB 16/IFRS 16 as follows.

> The rate of interest that causes the present value of (a) the lease payments and (b) the unguaranteed residual value to equal the sum of (i) the fair value of the underlying asset and (ii) any initial direct costs of the lessor.

The **fair value** of the underlying asset is calculated from the lessor's perspective and is defined in Appendix A of AASB 16/IFRS 16 as follows.

> For the purpose of applying the lessor accounting requirements in this Standard, the amount for which an asset could be exchanged, or a liability settled, between knowledgeable, willing parties in an arm's length transaction.

Note that this is not the same as the definition used in AASB 13/IFRS 13 *Fair Value Measurement*. The fair value is normally a market price. The fair value is regarded as representing the future benefits available to the user of the asset, discounted by the market to allow for the risk that those benefits will not eventuate and for changes in the purchasing power of money over time.

Initial direct costs of the lessor are incremental costs that are directly attributable to negotiating and arranging a lease, except for such costs incurred by manufacturer/dealer lessors in connection with a finance lease. According to paragraph 74 of AASB 16/IFRS 16, initial direct costs incurred by a manufacturer/dealer lessor are excluded from the definition of initial direct costs because the costs of negotiating and arranging a finance lease are 'mainly related to earning the manufacturer or dealer's selling profit'. Thus, for the purposes of determining the interest rate implicit in the lease, any initial direct costs incurred by a lessee or a manufacturer/dealer lessor are ignored.

Note that the interest rate implicit in the lease can be seen as the rate of return for the lessor on their investment in the lease. That is because the fair value of the underlying asset plus the initial direct costs of the lessor constitute the investment by the lessor in the lease, while the lease payments plus the unguaranteed residual value make up the returns on that investment.

The interest rate implicit in the lease will be determined normally by trial and error using the above definition. However, this rate is not always easy to determine due to the difficulties in measuring the fair value of some underlying assets or the residual value (and by extension, the unguaranteed part). For example, if the underlying asset is unique (e.g. an intangible asset), the lessee may be unable to reliably estimate its fair value or the unguaranteed residual value. In those situations, the accounting standard prescribes the use of the lessee's incremental borrowing rate in the calculation of the present value of the lease payments. Appendix A of AASB 16/IFRS 16 defines the **lessee's incremental borrowing rate** as follows.

> The rate of interest that a lessee would have to pay to borrow over a similar term, and with a similar security, the funds necessary to obtain an asset of a similar value to the right-of-use asset in a similar economic environment.

Right-of-use asset

According to the Preface to AASB 16/IFRS 16, the lessee 'measures right-of-use assets similarly to other non-financial assets (such as property, plant and equipment)'. Therefore, the initial measurement of the right-of-use asset is very similar to the initial measurement of an item of property, plant and equipment prescribed by AASB 116/IAS 16 *Property, Plant and Equipment*. According to AASB 116/IAS 16, items of property, plant and equipment are initially measured at cost which includes the purchase price (after deducting trade discounts and rebates), directly attributable costs and the initial estimate of the costs of dismantling and removing the item. Similarly, the right-to-use asset should be measured as cost and that will include:

- the amount recognised as the lease liability (i.e. the present value of the lease payments that are not paid at that date)
- any lease payments made before or at the commencement date, less any lease incentives received
- any initial direct costs incurred by the lessee
- an estimate of the costs to dismantle and remove the underlying asset, to restore the site on which it is located and to restore the asset to the conditions required by the lease contract.

The first two items included in the cost of the right-of-use asset can be seen as the 'purchase price', while the third item identifies the directly attributable costs. Note that the initial direct costs incurred by the lessee are conceptually similar to the initial direct costs of the lessor referred above in the discussion of the implicit rate in the lease — they are incremental costs that are directly attributable to negotiating and arranging a lease, but they are incurred by the lessee.

10.2.2 Subsequent measurement

The Preface to AASB 16/IFRS 16 states that the right-of-use asset needs to be measured similarly to other non-financial assets, while the related liability should be measured similarly to other financial liabilities. Therefore, after initial recognition, the right-of-use asset is subject to depreciation and the lessee should recognise interest on the lease liability and classify cash repayments of the lease liability into a principal portion and an interest portion. This section provides a detailed description of those aspects.

Lease liability

Because lease payments are made over the lease term, paragraph 36 of AASB 16/IFRS 16 requires the payments to be divided into components consisting of:
- interest expense incurred
- reduction of the lease liability.

The lease liability recognised at the commencement of the lease term represents the present value of future lease payments relating to the use of the asset. This present value is determined by applying the interest rate implicit in the lease (or the lessee's incremental borrowing rate). Thus, the interest expense for a period can be obtained by applying this rate to the outstanding lease liability at the beginning of the payment period. A payments schedule can be used to determine the interest expense and the reduction in the liability over the lease period.

Right-of-use asset

After initial recognition, the right-of-use assets are depreciated. According to paragraph 31 of AASB 16/IFRS 16, the depreciation policy for depreciable right-of-use assets is consistent with that for depreciable assets that are owned, and the depreciation recognised is calculated in accordance with AASB 116/IAS 16.

Depreciable assets are those whose future benefits are expected to expire over time or by use. The asset is depreciated over its useful life in a pattern reflecting the consumption or loss of the rewards embodied in the asset. The length of a right-of-use asset's useful life from the lessee's perspective depends on whether or not ownership of the asset will transfer at the end of the lease term. If the asset is to be returned to the lessor, then its useful life for the lessee is the lease term. If ownership is reasonably certain to transfer to the lessee, then its useful life is its economic life or remainder thereof.

10.2.3 Accounting for executory costs

The accounting standard does not provide details about the treatment of the payments for the non-lease components of leases; that is, for the additional services provided by the lessor. However, as the cost of such items is effectively borne by the lessee, the payment should be recognised as an expense (if it is made after the service is received) or prepayment (if it is made in advance).

ILLUSTRATIVE EXAMPLE 10.4

Accounting for leases by lessees

On 30 June 2022, Face Ltd leased a vehicle to Book Ltd. Face Ltd had purchased the vehicle on that day for its fair value of $89 721. The lease agreement, which cost Face Ltd $1457 to have drawn up, contained the following.

▶

Lease term	4 years
Annual payment, payable in advance on 30 June each year	$23 900
Economic life of vehicle	6 years
Estimated residual value at end of lease term	$15 000
Residual value guarantee	$7 500

Included in the annual payment is an amount of $1900 to cover reimbursement for the costs of insurance and maintenance paid by the lessor.

Required

What will be the journal entries recorded by Book Ltd to recognise the lease and the related payments throughout the lease?

Solution

At the start of the lease, the lessee should recognise the lease liability based on the present value of the lease payments not made on or before the start of the lease. The discount rate to calculate the present value of lease payments is *interest rate implicit in the lease*; that is, the rate that discounts the lease payments and the unguaranteed residual value to the aggregate of the asset's fair value and any initial direct costs to the lessor.

As the lease payments in this example consist of fixed lease payments and the residual value guarantee, the discount rate is the rate that discounts the annual fixed lease payments net of executory costs of $22 000 (i.e. $23 900 − $1900), the residual value guarantee of $7500 and the unguaranteed residual of $7500 to $91 178, which is the sum of the asset's fair value at 30 June 2022 of $89 721 and the initial direct costs of $1457 incurred by the lessor. This rate is found by trial and error using present value (PV) tables (see the appendix of this text) or a financial calculator.

The implicit interest rate in this example seems to be 7% as shown below.

$$\text{PV of LP} = \$22\,000 + (\$22\,000 \times 2.6243\,[T_2, 7\%, 3\text{ years}])$$
$$+ \$7500 \times 0.7629\,[T_1, 7\%, 4\text{ years}]$$
$$= \$85\,457$$
$$\text{PV of unguaranteed residual} = \$7500 \times 0.7629\,[T_1, 7\%, 4\text{ years}]$$
$$= \$5722$$
$$\text{PV} = \$85\,457 + \$5722$$
$$= \$91\,178$$
$$\text{FV} + \text{IDC} = \$89\,721 + \$1457$$
$$= \$91\,178$$

where T_1 = table for the present value of $1

T_2 = table for the present value of an annuity of $1

Note the following.

- As the first payment is made at the inception of the lease, it does not need to be discounted.
- The first discount factor used is an annuity factor based on three fixed lease payments of $22 000 for the next 3 years at 7%.
- The second discount factor used in the calculation of the present value of lease payments (PV of LP) is based on a single payment of $7500 (the residual value guarantee) at the end of the lease term in 4 years' time at a rate of 7%. The same discount factor is used in the calculation of the present value of the unguaranteed residual value.
- As the discount rate of 7% makes the present value of the lease payments, the residual value guarantee and the unguaranteed residual equal to the sum of the fair value plus the initial direct costs by the lessor, the implicit rate in the lease is 7%.

Before preparing the journal entries, a lease payments schedule needs to be prepared to identify the interest expense incurred and the reduction in liability for each period. The lease payments schedule starts with the balance of the lease liability at the start of the lease that should capture the present value of lease payments not made on or before the start of the lease; that is, $85 475 − $22 000 = $63 457.

Therefore, the lease payments schedule prepared by Book Ltd, based on the remaining three annual lease payments of $22 000 for the vehicle due after the start of the lease (with a present value of $63 457), the residual value guarantee of $7500 and the implicit rate in the lease of 7%, would be as follows.

BOOK LTD			
Lease payments schedule			
	Lease payments[a]	Interest expense[b]	Reduction in liability[c]	Balance of liability
30 June 2022[e]				$63 457[f]
30 June 2023	$22 000	$ 4 442	$17 558	45 899
30 June 2024	22 000	3 213	18 787	27 112
30 June 2025	22 000	1 898	20 102	7 010
30 June 2026	7 500	490	7 010	—
	$73 500	$10 043	$63 457	

(a) The lease payments consist of three annual payments of $22 000 payable in advance on 30 June of each year (excluding the lease payment made at 30 June 2022), plus a residual value guarantee of $7500 transferred on the last day of the lease. The guarantee part of the payment is in the form of the underlying asset being returned to the lessor and potentially cash being paid by the lessee to cover any deficiency in the actual residual value.

(b) Interest expense is the balance of liability at the beginning of each year multiplied by 7%. No interest expense is incurred in the first year because payment is made at the commencement of the lease.

(c) Reduction in liability is calculated as lease payments less interest expense. The total of this column must equal the initial liability; due to rounding errors in the calculation of the initial liability, the final interest expense figure may require rounding.

(d) The balance of liability is reduced each year by the amount in the 'Reduction in liability' column.

(e) 30 June 2022 is the lease inception date, which in this example is the same as the commencement date. For simplicity, this chapter always assumes that the inception date (i.e. the date of the lease agreement or commitment to the lease terms and conditions, whichever is earlier) is the same as the commencement date (i.e. the date on which the underlying asset is available to use by the lessee).

(f) Initial liability is equal to the present value of lease payments and includes the three annual payments made after the commencement of the lease and the residual value guarantee.

The payment schedule is used to prepare lease journal entries for the lessee and disclosure notes each year. The journal entries recorded by Book Ltd for the 4 years of the lease are as follows.

Year ended 30 June 2022

30 June 2022:			
Right-of-use vehicle	Dr	85 457	
Lease liability	Cr		63 457
Prepaid executory costs*	Dr	1 900	
Cash	Cr		23 900
(Initial recording of lease asset/liability)			

*Executory costs were recognised as prepayments because the insurance and maintenance benefits will not be received until the next reporting period.

Year ended 30 June 2023

1 July 2022:			
Executory costs	Dr	1 900	
Prepaid executory costs	Cr		1 900
(Reversal of prepayment)			
30 June 2023:			
Lease liability	Dr	17 558	
Interest expense	Dr	4 442	
Prepaid executory costs	Dr	1 900	
Cash	Cr		23 900
(Second lease payment)			
Depreciation expense	Dr	19 489	
Accumulated depreciation	Cr		19 489
(Depreciation charge for the period [$85 457 − $7500]/4)*			

*Because the asset will be returned at the end of the lease term, the useful life for the lessee is the lease term of 4 years and the depreciable amount is the cost less the guaranteed residual value.

Year ended 30 June 2024			
1 July 2023:			
Executory costs	Dr	1 900	
Prepaid executory costs	Cr		1 900
(Reversal of prepayment)			
30 June 2024:			
Lease liability	Dr	18 787	
Interest expense	Dr	3 213	
Prepaid executory costs	Dr	1 900	
Cash	Cr		23 900
(Third lease payment)			
Depreciation expense	Dr	19 489	
Accumulated depreciation	Cr		19 489
(Depreciation charge for the period [$85 457 − $7500]/4)			
Year ended 30 June 2025			
1 July 2024:			
Executory costs	Dr	1 900	
Prepaid executory costs	Cr		1 900
(Reversal of prepayment)			
30 June 2025:			
Lease liability	Dr	20 102	
Interest expense	Dr	1 898	
Prepaid executory costs	Dr	1 900	
Cash	Cr		23 900
(Fourth lease payment)			
Depreciation expense	Dr	19 489	
Accumulated depreciation	Cr		19 489
(Depreciation charge for the period [$85 457 − $7500]/4)			
Year ended 30 June 2026			
1 July 2025:			
Executory costs	Dr	1 900	
Prepaid executory costs	Cr		1 900
(Reversal of prepayment)			
30 June 2026:			
Lease liability	Dr	7 010	
Interest expense	Dr	490	
Right-of-use vehicle*	Cr		7 500
(Return of leased vehicle)			
Depreciation expense	Dr	19 490	
Accumulated depreciation	Cr		19 490
(Depreciation charge for the period [$85 457 − $7500]/4)			
Accumulated depreciation	Dr	77 957	
Right-of-use vehicle	Cr		77 957
(Fully depreciated asset written off)			

*The final 'payment' is the return of the asset at its guaranteed residual value. If the asset is being purchased, this entry will record a cash payment. Another entry will then be required to reclassify the undepreciated balance of the asset from a 'right-of-use' asset to an 'owned' asset.

☐ A lessee must recognise, for each lease, a liability at the commencement of the lease term equal to the present value of the lease payments.

☐ Lease payments in respect of the use of the underlying asset must be allocated between reduction of the lease liability and interest expense using the interest rate implicit in the lease.

☐ Payments for executory costs are recognised as an expense as incurred, with consideration being given to normal accrual accounting principles.

10.3 Classifying leases by lessor

LEARNING OBJECTIVE 10.3 Classify lease arrangements from the perspective of the lessor.

Paragraph 61 of AASB 16/IFRS 16 requires lessors to classify each lease as either *a finance lease* or *an operating lease*. This classification process is vitally important because the accounting treatment and disclosures prescribed for the lessors for each type of lease differ significantly.

A **finance lease** is defined in Appendix A of AASB 16/IFRS 16 as follows.

A lease that transfers substantially all the risks and rewards incidental to ownership of an underlying asset.

Appendix A defines an **operating lease** as follows.

A lease that does not transfer substantially all the risks and rewards incidental to ownership of an underlying asset.

The key criterion of a finance lease is the transfer of substantially all the risks and rewards, making it almost equivalent to a sale, but without an immediate transfer of ownership. The classification process therefore consists of three steps, as follows.

1. Identify the potential risks and rewards associated with the ownership of the asset.
2. Analyse the lease to determine what risks and rewards are transferred from the lessor to the lessee.
3. Assess whether the risks and rewards associated with the ownership of the asset have been substantially passed to the lessee.

According to paragraph B53 of AASB 16/IFRS 16, the *risks* of ownership include the possibilities of *losses* from:

- idle capacity
- technological obsolescence
- variations in return because of changing economic conditions.

For example, if Helen Zhang leases a computer with a 3-year useful life from a Harvey Norman store under a 3-year lease agreement that cannot be cancelled unless a substantial penalty is paid, the risks associated with technological obsolescence are transferred to Helen. If a new innovation in computers occurs within the 3-year period, Helen may not be able to obtain the new model unless she breaks the lease, incurring a substantial loss due to the penalty payable; if she doesn't obtain the new model, she will bear the costs of productivity loss. On the other hand, if the lease agreement can be cancelled by Helen without incurring penalties, the risks associated with technological obsolescence stay with Harvey Norman; Helen would be able to return the asset to Harvey Norman if a new model appears on the market and Harvey Norman will have to bear the losses associated with a technologically obsolete, and potentially unsaleable, computer.

The *rewards* of ownership according to B53 of AASB 16/IFRS 16 include the possibilities of *gains* related to:

- any benefits obtained from profitable operation over the underlying asset's economic life
- appreciation in value
- realisation of a residual value.

For example, consider the case of Mary Smith renting a small building that has a 20-year useful life to operate a restaurant under a 10-year lease agreement. If the agreement allows Mary to buy the building at the end of the lease term for a fixed price set at the beginning of the lease, the rewards in the form of increases in value of that building may transfer to Mary. If a property developer builds a residential complex in the neighbourhood of the building leased by Mary, the value of the building may increase over the price set at the beginning of the lease and Mary will benefit from that increase.

There is no definition of the term 'substantially'. This determination is left to professional judgement. The classification decision is then in the hands of accountants and managers who must decide what is 'substantial' for their entity and under their particular circumstances. While this provides flexibility, the disadvantage of this approach is that similar or even identical lease agreements may be classified differently because of varying interpretations of what the term 'substantially' means.

10.3.1 Classification guidance

To help the lessor in the classification process, paragraph 63 of AASB 16/IFRS 16 sets out the following examples or indicators of situations that, either individually or in combination, *would normally* lead to a lease being classified as a finance lease:

    (a) the lease transfers ownership of the underlying asset to the lessee by the end of the lease term [transfer of ownership test];

    (b) the lessee has the option to purchase the underlying asset at a price that is expected to be sufficiently lower than the *fair value* at the date the option becomes exercisable for it to be reasonably certain, at the *inception date*, that the option will be exercised [purchase option test];

    (c) the lease term is for the major part of the *economic life* of the underlying asset even if title is not transferred [lease term test];

    (d) at the inception date, the present value of the lease payments amounts to at least substantially all of the fair value of the underlying asset [present value test]; and.

    (e) the underlying asset is of such a specialised nature that only the lessee can use it without major modifications [specialised nature test].

Paragraph 64 notes the following situations that *could* lead to a lease being classified as a finance lease:

    (a) if the lessee can cancel the lease, the lessor's losses associated with the cancellation are borne by the lessee [cancellability test];

    (b) gains or losses from the fluctuation in the fair value of the residual accrue to the lessee (for example, in the form of a rent rebate equaling most of the sales proceeds at the end of the lease) [residual value test]; and

    (c) the lessee has the ability to continue the lease for a secondary period at a rent that is substantially lower than market rent [continuity test].

These can serve as guidelines for assessing whether substantially all the risks and rewards of ownership are transferred. As the risks and rewards of ownership are normally transferred when the ownership title is transferred through a sale transaction, the indicators in paragraph 63 seem to describe situations that predict, or are very similar to, an actual sale. The indicators in paragraph 64 seem to focus on situations that indicate that the lessee will bear the losses for the decreases in the underlying asset's expected future economic benefits (i.e. risks of ownership), while being able to gain from increases in those economic benefits (i.e. rewards of ownership).

The above guidelines are not exhaustive, nor always conclusive. If other features of the lease agreement clearly point out that the lease does not transfer substantially all the risks and rewards of ownership, the lease should be classified as an operating lease. Moreover, if the lessee can cancel the lease without incurring significant penalties (that would otherwise act as a disincentive to cancel), the lessee will most likely cancel it if they will incur losses by keeping the lease agreement alive — the other features of the lease agreement will not matter as they will not be enforceable and therefore in this situation the risks of ownership are not transferred to the lessee, making the lease an operating lease (even though the rewards of ownership are arguably transferred).

Of the above guidelines, at least two require some clarification. This is provided in the following.

Asset's economic life versus lease term (lease term test)

This classification guidance requires measurement of the lease term against the asset's economic life. Appendix A of AASB 16/IFRS 16 defines both these terms. The **lease term** is the non-cancellable period for which the lessee has contracted (or is reasonably expected) to lease the asset. The **economic life** is the period of time over which the underlying asset is expected to be economically usable, or the number of production units expected to be obtained from the asset.

If ownership title to the asset is transferred to the lessee at the end of the lease, or if there is a reasonable expectation at lease inception date that the lessee will purchase the asset (via a favourable purchase option clause) at the end of the lease term, then the lessee effectively holds the asset for all (or the balance remaining) of the asset's economic life — this implies that all the risks and rewards of ownership of the underlying asset in the lease are transferred to the lessee. Where the asset is to be returned to the lessor at the end of the lease term, then judgement must be applied to assess whether there is a transfer of risks and rewards of ownership. Arguably, it is assumed that if the lessee is going to keep the asset for the major part of the economic life of that asset, the lease would transfer substantially all the risks and rewards of ownership to the lessee.

What percentage of the asset's economic life represents a 'major' part? 60%? 70%? 80%? The lack of clear guidance in the accounting standard could result in differing classifications of similar lease arrangements. For example, a 6-year lease of an asset with an economic life of 8 years could be classified as a finance lease by Entity A on the grounds that the lease term is greater than 70% of the asset's economic life, but treated as an operating lease by Entity B, which applies an 80% 'cut off'. Normally, a cut-off of 75% is considered appropriate to capture the major part of the asset's economic life.

This classification guidance assumes that the consumption pattern of economic benefits across the economic life of the asset will be straight-line (equal in each year). However, some assets, such as vehicles, may provide more of their benefits in the early years of their economic lives, so this time-based classification criterion may not be appropriate.

Asset's fair value versus present value of lease payments (present value test)

At lease inception date, the fair value of the asset measures the present value of the total benefits associated with the asset. The lease payments represent payments for benefits transferred to the lessee. This test therefore indicates the proportion of benefits being paid for by the lessee. If that proportion is close to 100% (i.e. substantially all), the lease contract is arguably very similar to a sale contract where the customer pays the fair value to acquire the asset; as such, it is assumed that the lease would transfer substantially all risks and rewards of ownership to the lessee.

To apply this guidance, the information that must be gathered or determined at the inception of the lease is:

1. the fair value of the underlying asset
2. lease payments
3. the discount rate (i.e. the rate implicit in the lease).

These items were discussed in section 10.2. The present value of the lease payments will be compared to the fair value of the underlying asset and a judgement needs to be made as to whether this represents 'substantially' all of the fair value of the asset from the lessor to the lessee. A lack of quantitative guidelines may result in the inconsistent classification of similar lease arrangements. Normally, the ratio between the present value of the lease payments and the fair value of the underlying asset can be expressed as a percentage and a cut-off of 90% may be considered appropriate to capture substantially all the fair value of the underlying asset.

ILLUSTRATIVE EXAMPLE 10.5

Classification of a lease agreement

Using the facts from illustrative example 10.4, assume now that the lease is cancellable, but cancellation will incur a monetary penalty equivalent to 2 years' rental payments. The directors of Book Ltd have indicated that they intend to return the asset to Face Ltd at the end of the lease term.

Required
How will the lessor classify this lease?

Solution
The lease must be classified as either a finance lease or an operating lease, based on the extent to which the risks and rewards associated with the vehicle have been transferred from Face Ltd to Book Ltd. To help with this, the tests described above to determine whether the lease can be classified as a finance lease can be used here as follows.

- There is no purchase option (purchase option test: failed). Moreover, the expectation is that the asset will be returned to the lessor; therefore, the ownership title over the asset will not be transferred to the lessee (transfer of ownership test: failed). The asset is also not of a specialised nature that would make it useful only for the lessee (specialised nature test: failed). There is no information that can be used to employ the residual value test and the continuity test.

▶

- The lease agreement is *cancellable*, but a significant monetary penalty equal to 2 years' rental payments will apply to the lessee. Arguably, that penalty is included in the lease to make sure that the lessor's losses associated with the cancellation are borne by the lessee. This feature indicates a transfer of risks to the lessee and is one of the indicators of finance leases according to paragraph 64 of AASB 16/IFRS 16 (cancellability test: passed).
- The lease term is 4 years, which is 66.67% of the asset's economic life of 6 years. If expected benefits were receivable evenly over the asset's useful life, it may be argued that the lease arrangement is for the major part of the asset's life; that is, a major part of the rewards associated with the asset have been transferred to the lessee (lease term test: passed).
- The present value of lease payments, calculated in illustrative example 10.4, is compared to the fair value of the asset to determine whether it represents substantially all of the fair value as follows.

$$PV \text{ of } LP = \$85\,457$$
$$FV = \$89\,721$$
$$PV \text{ of } LP/FV = (\$85\,457/\$89\,721) \times 100\%$$
$$= 95.25\%$$

At a 95.25% level, the present value of the lease payments is considered to be substantially all of the fair value of the underlying asset; that is, a major part of the benefits associated with the asset has been transferred to the lessee (present value test: passed).

Classification of the lease
Application of the guidelines provides mixed signals. The key criterion in classifying leases is whether substantially all the risks and rewards incident to ownership have been transferred. This requires an overall analysis of the situation, but insufficient information is given in the example to do this. The different signals coming from the lease term test and the present value test may be due to the fact that the majority of the rewards will be transferred in the early stages of the life of the asset, as with motor vehicles. This is reflected in the relatively low residual value at the end of the lease term. These mixed signals demonstrate that the guidelines must be used for guidance only and not treated as specific criteria that must be met.

Given no extra information, it is concluded that the lease agreement may be classified as a finance lease because arguably substantially all the risks and rewards incident to ownership have been passed to the lessee.

10.3.2 Further classification of finance leases by lessor

It is important to note that finance leases need to further be classified into (a) finance leases involving a financier lessor and (b) leases involving manufacturers or dealers, as the accounting standard prescribes different accounting requirements for those two types of finance leases. With financier lessors, the lessor acquires the asset at fair value and then enters into a lease arrangement with the lessee and will only recognise income periodically throughout the lease term. With manufacturer/dealer lessors, the assets are normally being carried in the records of the lessor at an amount (cost) different from fair value. At the beginning of the lease, manufacturer/dealer lessors will recognise a selling profit. Further discussion of the accounting requirements for these two different types of finance leases will be provided in section 10.4 and 10.5 respectively.

However, there is another difference in the treatment of leases involving financier lessors and leases involving manufacturers or dealers with regards to the recognition of the initial direct costs. The definition of the initial direct costs to the lessor provided in Appendix A of AASB 16/IFRS 16 specifically excludes the initial direct costs incurred by the manufacturer or dealer lessor. According to paragraph 74 of AASB 16/IFRS 16, the initial direct costs incurred by the manufacturer/dealer in negotiating and arranging the lease are recognised as an expense when the profit is recognised. Such costs are regarded as part of earning the profit on sale rather than a cost of leasing. As the initial direct costs to the lessor are used in determining the implicit rate in the lease, this differential treatment of initial direct costs incurred by the manufacturer or dealer lessor implies that the implicit rate in such leases is considered as being the discount rate that makes those present values equal to the fair value of the underlying asset only. As the present values calculated are used in the present value test to classify a lease as a finance or operating lease, the classification of lessors into financiers and manufacturers or dealers should precede the classification of leases into finance or operating leases.

10.4 Accounting for finance leases by financier lessors

LEARNING OBJECTIVE 10.4 Account for finance leases from the perspective of a financier lessor.

On signing a lease a lessor continues to own the underlying asset, but transfers the right to use the asset to the lessee. When a lease is classified as a finance lease, the lessor transfers substantially all the risks and rewards incidental to ownership of the underlying asset to the lessee, making the transaction similar to a sale. As a consequence, the lessor will need to 'derecognise' the underlying asset. In its place, the lessor will record a lease receivable to reflect the payments they will receive as a result of the lease. The lease receivable represents the lessor's return on the investment in the lease. This consists of the expected lease payments receivable from the lessee as well as the estimated unguaranteed residual value of the asset once the lease term has expired.

10.4.1 Initial recognition

Paragraph 67 of AASB 16/IFRS 16 requires the lessor to recognise assets held under a finance lease in its statement of financial position and present them as a receivable at an amount equal to the net investment in the lease. Appendix A of AASB 16/IFRS 16 defines the **net investment in the lease** as follows.

> The gross investment in the lease discounted at the interest rate implicit in the lease.

It defines the **gross investment in the lease** as:

> The sum of:
> (a) the lease payments receivable by the lessor under a finance lease; and
> (b) any unguaranteed residual value accruing to the lessor.

The net investment in the lease would normally equate to the fair value of the asset at the inception of the lease plus any initial direct costs incurred by the lessor. Therefore, the initial direct costs of the lessor are included in the net investment. The definition of interest rate implicit in the lease automatically includes initial direct costs in the finance lease receivable, so there is no need to add them separately.

10.4.2 Subsequent measurement

As the lease payments are received from the lessee over the lease term, the receipts need to be analysed into these components:
- interest revenue earned
- reduction of the lease receivable reimbursement of costs paid on behalf of the lessee.

The latter may be easily determined by reference to the lease agreement, but the first two need to be calculated in a similar fashion to that used by the lessee. The lease receivable recognised at the commencement of the lease term represents the present value of future lease payments relating to the use of the underlying asset. This present value is determined by applying the interest rate implicit in the lease. Thus, the interest revenue can be obtained by applying the same rate to the outstanding lease receivable at the beginning of the payment period. A receipts schedule can be used to determine the interest revenue and the reduction in the receivable over the lease period.

AASB 16/IFRS 16 does not provide details on the treatment of the reimbursements for the services provided/paid for on behalf of the lessee. However, as these receipts meet the definition of income in the *Conceptual Framework*, and reimbursements should be recorded as revenue in the same period in which the related expenses are incurred, then if these receipts are received in advance, they are going to be recognised as revenue received in advance.

ILLUSTRATIVE EXAMPLE 10.6

Accounting for finance leases by lessors

Use the facts from illustrative examples 10.4 and 10.5.

Required

What are the journal entries recorded by Face Ltd to recognise the lease and the related receipts throughout the lease?

Solution

As demonstrated in the answer to illustrative example 10.5, Face Ltd would apply AASB 16/IFRS 16 guidelines and classify the lease as a finance lease. The lease receipts schedule starts with the balance of the lease receivable at the start of the lease that should capture the present value of lease payments and the present value of unguaranteed residual, calculated as follows.

$$\text{PV of LP} = \$22\,000 \times (\$22\,000 \times 2.6243\,[T_2, 7\%, 3\text{ years}])$$
$$+ \$7500 \times 0.7629\,[T_1, 7\%, 4\text{ years}]$$
$$= \$85\,457$$
$$\text{PV of unguaranteed residual} = \$7500 \times 0.7629\,[T_1, 7\%, 4\text{ years}]$$
$$= \$5722$$
$$\text{PV} = \$85\,457 + \$5722$$
$$= \$91\,178$$

Therefore, the lease receipts schedule based on annual payments of $22 000 for the vehicle, the residual value guarantee of $7500, the unguaranteed residual value of $7500 and an interest rate implicit in the lease of 7% shows would be as follows.

FACE LTD
Lease receipts schedule

	Lease receipts[a]	Interest revenue[b]	Reduction in receivable[c]	Balance of receivable[d]
30 June 2022				$91 178[e]
30 June 2022	$ 22 000	$ —	$22 000	69 178
30 June 2023	22 000	4 842	17 158	52 020
30 June 2024	22 000	3 641	18 359	33 661
30 June 2025	22 000	2 356	19 644	14 017
30 June 2026	15 000	983	14 017	—
	$103 000	$11 822	$91 178	

(a) The lease receipts are made out of four annual receipts of $22 000 payable in advance on 30 June of each year, plus a residual value of $15 000 (of which $7500 is guaranteed by the lessee and the other $7500 is unguaranteed residual) on the last day of the lease.
(b) Interest revenue is calculated as the balance of receivable each year multiplied by 7%.
(c) The reduction in receivable is the excess of the receipts in a year over the interest revenue earned during that year; that is, lease receipts less interest revenue. The total of this column must equal the initial amount recognised for lease receivable — to ensure this, the final interest revenue figure may require rounding.
(d) The balance is reduced each year by the amount in the 'Reduction in receivable' column.
(e) Initial receivable is calculated as the fair value of $89 721 plus initial direct costs of $1457. This figure equals the present value of lease payments receivable and the present value of the unguaranteed residual value.

The lease receipts schedule is used to prepare lease journal entries and disclosure notes each year, as follows.

30 June 2022:			
Vehicle	Dr	89 721	
Cash	Cr		89 721
(Purchase of motor vehicle)			
Lease receivable	Dr	89 721	
Vehicle	Cr		89 721
(Lease of vehicle to Book Ltd)			
Lease receivable	Dr	1 457	
Cash	Cr		1 457
(Payment of initial direct costs)			
Cash	Dr	23 900	
Lease receivable	Cr		22 000
Reimbursement in advance*	Cr		1 900
(Receipt of first lease payment)			

*The reimbursement of executory cost has been carried forward to the 2022–23 period, when Face Ltd will pay the costs.

1 July 2022:			
Reimbursement in advance	Dr	1 900	
Reimbursement revenue	Cr		1 900
(Reversal of accrual)			
30 June 2023:			
Insurance and maintenance	Dr	1 900	
Cash	Cr		1 900
(Payment of costs on behalf of lessee)			
Cash	Dr	23 900	
Lease receivable	Cr		17 158
Interest revenue	Cr		4 842
Reimbursement in advance	Cr		1 900
(Receipt of second lease payment)			

1 July 2023:			
Reimbursement in advance	Dr	1 900	
Reimbursement revenue	Cr		1 900
(Reversal of accrual)			
30 June 2024:			
Insurance and maintenance	Dr	1 900	
Cash	Cr		1 900
(Payment of costs on behalf of lessee)			
Cash	Dr	23 900	
Lease receivable	Cr		18 359
Interest revenue	Cr		3 641
Reimbursement in advance	Cr		1 900
(Receipt of third lease payment)			

1 July 2024:			
Reimbursement in advance	Dr	1 900	
Reimbursement revenue	Cr		1 900
(Reversal of accrual)			
30 June 2025:			
Insurance and maintenance	Dr	1 900	
Cash	Cr		1 900
(Payment of costs on behalf of lessee)			
Cash	Dr	23 900	
Lease receivable	Cr		19 644
Interest revenue	Cr		2 356
Reimbursement in advance	Cr		1 900
(Receipt of fourth lease payment)			

Year ended 30 June 2026			
1 July 2025:			
Reimbursement in advance	Dr	1 900	
Reimbursement revenue	Cr		1 900
(Reversal of accrual)			
30 June 2026:			
Insurance and maintenance	Dr	1 900	
Cash	Cr		1 900
(Payment of costs on behalf of lessee)			
Vehicle	Dr	15 000	
Interest revenue	Cr		983
Lease receivable	Cr		14 017
(Return of vehicle at end of lease)			

LEARNING CHECK

☐ At the inception of a finance lease, a lessor recognises a receivable asset equal to the net investment in the lease being the sum of the present values of the lease payments and the unguaranteed residual value.

☐ The definition of the interest rate implicit in the lease ensures that the net investment in the lease equates with the fair value of the underlying asset plus initial direct costs for a non-manufacturer/non-dealer lessor.

☐ Lease receipts must be allocated between a reduction of the lease receivable and interest revenue using the interest rate implicit in the lease.

10.5 Accounting for finance leases by manufacturer or dealer lessors

LEARNING OBJECTIVE 10.5 Account for finance leases from the perspective of a manufacturer/dealer lessor.

When manufacturers/dealers offer customers the choice of either buying or leasing an asset, a lease arrangement gives rise to two types of income:
- profit or loss equivalent to the outright sale of the underlying asset being leased
- finance income over the lease term.

Accounting for the lease is identical to that required by financier lessors except for an initial entry to recognise profit or loss and the fact that initial direct costs are *not* included in the lease receivable amount (and not used in the calculation of the implicit rate in the lease).

10.5.1 Initial recognition

Paragraph 71 of AASB 16/IFRS 16 requires manufacturer/dealer lessors to recognise selling profit or loss at the commencement of the lease, in accordance with the policy followed by the entity for outright sales. Where artificially low interest rates have been offered to entice the customer to enter the lease, the selling profit recorded must be restricted to that which would apply if a market rate of interest had been charged.

Hence, as well as recognising the lease receivable, the manufacturer/dealer records the profit or loss on sale (at market interest rates) at the commencement of the lease by recognising:
- *sales revenue* as the fair value of the underlying asset or, if lower, the present value of lease payments discounted at a market rate of interest
- *cost of sale expense* as the cost or carrying amount of the underlying asset less the present value of any unguaranteed residual value.

The sales revenue recognises the amount that is going to be received in the form of lease payments, while the cost of sales is adjusted for the unguaranteed residual value to recognise the true cost of the asset transferred, after taking into consideration the amount that may be received from parties unrelated to the customer (i.e. the lessee). Additionally, as previously discussed, according to paragraph 74 of AASB 16/IFRS 16, the initial direct costs incurred by the manufacturer/dealer in negotiating and arranging the lease are recognised as an expense when the profit is recognised. Such costs are regarded as part of earning the profit on sale rather than a cost of leasing.

10.5.2 Subsequent measurement

Accounting for the lease after the initial entry is identical to that required by financier lessors.

ILLUSTRATIVE EXAMPLE 10.7

Calculating and recognising profit on sale with initial direct costs

Skye Ltd manufactures specialised moulding machinery for both sale and lease. On 1 July 2023, Skye leased a machine to Witter Ltd, incurring $1500 in costs to negotiate, prepare and execute the lease document. The machine cost Skye Ltd $195 000 to manufacture, and its fair value at the inception of the lease was $212 514. The interest rate implicit in the lease is 10%, which is in line with current market rates. Under the terms of the lease, Witter Ltd has guaranteed $25 000 of the asset's expected residual value of $37 000 at the end of the 5-year lease term. Witter Ltd agreed to pay an annual lease payment of $50 000 starting on 30 June 2024. Skye Ltd does not provide any additional services as part of the lease agreement.

Required
What will be the journal entries recorded by Skye Ltd to recognise the lease at the beginning of the lease?

Solution
Before the journal entries can be prepared, the lease must be classified as either a finance lease or an operating lease based on the extent to which the risks and rewards associated with the specialised moulding machinery have been effectively transferred between Skye Ltd and Witter Ltd. There is no sufficient information to assess all terms and conditions of the lease contract, but we can still perform the present value test to see whether the present value of the lease payments is substantially all the fair value of the underlying asset. The lease payments consist of five payments, in arrears, of $50 000 and the residual guarantee of $25 000. There are no variable lease payments or executory costs. The present value of those lease payments is calculated as follows.

$$\text{PV of LP} = \$50\,000 \times 3.7908 \, [T_2, 10\%, 5 \text{ years}]$$
$$+ \$25\,000 \times 0.6209 \, [T_1, 10\%, 5 \text{ years}]$$
$$= \$205\,063$$
$$\text{PV of LP/FV} = \$205\,063/\$215\,514 \times 100\%$$
$$= 95.15\%$$

On the basis of the evidence available, it can be argued that there has been an effective transfer of substantially all the risks and rewards associated with the specialised moulding machinery to the lessee. Hence, considering also that the lessor is the manufacturer of the underlying asset, the lease should be classified and accounted for as a *finance lease involving a manufacturer lessor*.

The following journal entries would be passed in the books of the lessor on 1 July 2023.

Lease receivable[(a)]	Dr	212 514	
Sales revenue[(b)]	Cr		205 063
Cost of sales[(c)]	Dr	187 549	
Inventories[(d)]	Cr		195 000
(Initial recognition of lease receivable and recording sale of machine)			
Lease costs	Dr	1 500	
Cash	Cr		1 500
(Payment of initial direct costs)			

Notes:
(a) The lease receivable represents the net investment in the lease and is equal to the fair value of the leased machine (the initial direct costs are ignored here as the lessor is a manufacturer).
(b) Sales revenue represents the present value of the lease payments, which in this situation is less than the fair value of the asset due to the existence of an unguaranteed residual value.
(c) Cost of sales represents the cost of the leased machine ($195 000) less the present value of the unguaranteed residual value ($12 000 × 0.6209 = $7451).
(d) Inventories is reduced by the cost of the leased machine.

10.6 Accounting for operating leases by lessors

LEARNING OBJECTIVE 10.6 Account for operating leases from the perspective of a lessor.

Operating leases are those where substantially all the risks and rewards incident to ownership remain with the lessor. Such arrangements are treated as rental agreements, with all payments treated as income by the lessor. Note that the lessee treats the operating leases the same as finance leases.

10.6.1 Lease receipts

Paragraph 81 of AASB 16/IFRS 16 requires lessors to account for receipts from operating leases as income on a straight-line basis over the lease term unless another systematic basis is more representative of the time pattern in which the benefit derived from the underlying asset is diminished.

10.6.2 Initial direct costs

According to paragraph 83 of AASB 16/IFRS 16, any initial direct costs incurred by lessors in negotiating operating leases are to be added to the carrying amount of the underlying asset and recognised as an expense over the lease term on the same basis as the lease income. Given that the underlying asset is to be depreciated over the useful life (which in operating leases is normally longer than the lease term), while the initial direct costs are to be recognised as an expense over the lease term, the initial direct costs are capitalised into a separate deferred costs account; however, the balance of that account is nevertheless included in the calculation of the carrying amount of the underlying asset, just like the balance of the accumulated depreciation is taken into consideration when calculating that carrying amount. Therefore, the carrying amount of the underlying asset will be calculated as follows.

Underlying asset	$ xxx
Less: Accumulated depreciation	(xxx)
Plus: Initial direct costs recognised as deferred costs at the start of the lease	xxx
Less: Costs recognised as expenses up to the end of period out of the initial direct costs	(xxx)
Carrying amount of underlying asset	$ xxx

10.6.3 Depreciation of underlying assets

According to paragraph 84 of AASB 16/IFRS 16, depreciation of underlying assets provided under operating leases should be consistent with the lessor's normal depreciation policy for similar assets, and should be calculated in accordance with AASB 116/IAS 16 and AASB 138/IAS 38 *Intangible Assets.*

ILLUSTRATIVE EXAMPLE 10.8

Accounting for operating leases

On 1 July 2023, Big Ltd leased a network server from Pond Ltd. The server cost Pond Ltd $35 966 on that same day. The finance lease agreement, which cost Pond Ltd $381 to have drawn up, contained the following.

Lease term		3 years
Estimated economic life of the network server		10 years
The lease is cancellable		
Annual rental payment, in arrears (commencing 30/6/24)		$3 900
Residual value at end of the lease term		$24 500
Residual guaranteed by Big Ltd		$0
Interest rate implicit in lease		6%

Required

What will be the journal entries recorded by Pond Ltd to recognise the lease and the related receipts for the year ended 30 June 2024?

Solution

Before the journal entries can be prepared, the lease must be classified as either a finance lease or an operating lease based on the extent to which the risks and rewards associated with the vehicle have been effectively transferred between Big Ltd and Pond Ltd.

The lease agreement is cancellable; either party can walk away from the arrangement without penalty. Therefore, the lease is considered an operating lease — the other terms and conditions of the lease contract do not matter. However, they also seem to indicate that the risks and rewards are not transferred to the lessee as:

- Big Ltd expects to return the network server to Pond Ltd; that is, the title of ownership is not transferred in the lease
- the lease term is 3 years, which is only 30% of the network server's economic life of 10 years; therefore, it would appear that the lease arrangement is not for the major part of the asset's life
- a present value test can also be performed.

The lease payments consist of three payments, in arrears, of $3900. There are no variable lease payments, executory costs or guaranteed residual value. The present value of those lease payments is calculated as follows.

$$PV \text{ of } LP = \$3900 \times 2.6730 \, [T_2, 6\%, 3 \text{ years}]$$
$$= \$10\,425$$
$$PV \text{ of } LP/FV = \$10\,425/\$35\,966 \times 100\%$$
$$= 29\%$$

On the basis of the evidence available, there has not been an effective transfer of substantially all the risks and rewards associated with the network server to the lessee. Hence, the lease should be classified and accounted for as an *operating lease*.

The following journal entries would be passed in the books of the lessor for the year ended 30 June 2024.

POND LTD			
General journal			
1 July 2023:			
Plant and equipment	Dr	35 966	
Cash	Cr		35 966
(Purchase of network server)			
Deferred initial direct costs — plant and equipment	Dr	381	
Cash	Cr		381
(Initial direct costs incurred for lease)			
30 June 2024:			
Cash	Dr	3 900	
Lease income	Cr		3 900
(Receipt of first year's rental)			
Lease expense	Dr	127	
Deferred initial direct costs — plant and equipment	Cr		127
(Recognition of initial direct cost: $381/3 years)			
Depreciation expense	Dr	3 597	
Accumulated depreciation	Cr		3 597
(Depreciation charge for the period: $35 966/10 years)			

10.7 Disclosure requirements

LEARNING OBJECTIVE 10.7 Summarise the disclosure requirements regarding leases.

AASB 16/IFRS 16 contains extensive disclosure requirements for both the lessee and the lessor. The information required to be disclosed is expected to help users of financial statements to assess the effect of leases on the financial position, financial performance and cash flows of the lessee and the lessor.

10.7.1 Disclosures required by lessees

The disclosure requirements related to lessees are based on the general principle stated in paragraph 51 of AASB 16/IFRS 16 that the lessee should provide information that helps the users of financial statements assess the effect of leases on the financial position, financial performance and cash flows of the lessee. More specifically, paragraph 53 of AASB 16/IFRS 16 requires lessees to disclose the following information for the reporting period:

(a) depreciation charge for right-of-use assets by class of underlying asset;
(b) interest expense on lease liabilities;
(c) the expense relating to short-term leases accounted for applying paragraph 6. This expense need not include the expense relating to leases with a lease term of one month or less;
(d) the expense relating to leases of low-value assets accounted for applying paragraph 6. This expense shall not include the expense relating to short-term leases of low-value assets included in paragraph 53(c);
(e) the expense relating to variable lease payments not included in the measurement of lease liabilities;
(f) income from subleasing right-of-use assets;
(g) total cash outflow for leases;
(h) additions to right-of-use assets;
(i) gains or losses arising from sale and leaseback transactions; and
(j) the carrying amount of right-of-use assets at the end of the reporting period by class of underlying asset.

Additional information should be provided according to paragraph 59 if that helps fulfil the general principle stated in paragraph 51. Paragraph 59 notes that this additional information may include, but is not limited to, information that helps users of financial statements to assess:

(a) the nature of the lessee's leasing activities;
(b) future cash outflows to which the lessee is potentially exposed that are not reflected in the measurement of lease liabilities. This includes exposure arising from:
   (i) variable lease payments (as described in paragraph B49);
   (ii) extension options and termination options (as described in paragraph B50);
   (iii) residual value guarantees (as described in paragraph B51); and
   (iv) leases not yet commenced to which the lessee is committed.
(c) restrictions or covenants imposed by leases; and
(d) sale and leaseback transactions (as described in paragraph B52).

10.7.2 Disclosures required by lessors

Paragraph 90 of AASB 16/IFRS 16 requires lessors to disclose the following information separately in the financial statements in respect to leases:

(a) for finance leases:
   (i) selling profit or loss;
   (ii) finance income on the net investment in the lease; and
   (iii) income relating to variable lease payments not included in the measurement of the net investment in the lease.

(b) for operating leases, lease income, separately disclosing income relating to variable lease payments that do not depend on an index or a rate.

The lessor is also required to provide additional qualitative and quantitative information necessary to ensure that the users of financial statements can assess the effect of leases on the financial position, financial performance and cash flows of the lessor. According to paragraph 92 of AASB 16/IFRS 16, that additional information may include, but is not limited to, information that helps the users assess:

(a) the nature of the lessor's leasing activities; and
(b) how the lessor manages the risk associated with any rights it retains in underlying assets.

Paragraphs 93–94 and 95–97 of AASB 16/IFRS 16 describe in detail specific disclosure requirements for the lessor for finance and operating leases respectively. For finance leases, the lessor should:
- provide an explanation of the significant changes in the carrying amount of the net investment in the finance leases
- disclose the undiscounted lease payments to be received on an annual basis for a minimum of each of the first 5 years and a total of the amounts for the remaining years, and
- reconcile the undiscounted lease payments to the net investment in the lease, identifying the unearned finance income relating to the lease payments receivable and any discounted unguaranteed residual value.

For the operating leases, the lessor should:
- provide the disclosures required by AASB 116/IAS 16 for property, plant and equipment assets subject to an operating lease (by class of underlying asset) separately from owned assets held and used by the lessor
- apply the disclosure requirements, where relevant, from AASB 136/IAS 36 *Impairment of Assets*, AASB 138/IAS 38 *Intangible Assets*, AASB 140/IAS 40 *Investment Property* and AASB 141/IAS 41 *Agriculture* for assets subject to the operating leases
- disclose the undiscounted lease payments to be received on an annual basis for a minimum of each of the first five years and a total of the amounts for the remaining years.

LEARNING CHECK

☐ Lessees are required to make certain disclosures in respect of leases as set out in AASB 16/IFRS 16 to help users of financial information assess the effect of leases on the financial position, financial performance and cash flows of the lessee.
☐ A lessor is required to make extensive disclosures of future lease payments and their present values in relation to finance leases.
☐ The total and timing of the lease payments must be disclosed by lessors for operating leases.

SUMMARY

Some of the key principles of accounting for leases contained in AASB 16/IFRS 16 *Leases* are as follows.

* A lease agreement consists of a transfer of the right to use of an underlying asset for an agreed period of time in exchange for a consideration.
* The lessee (i.e. the entity that receives the right to use the underlying asset) must recognise for all leases a right-of-use asset and a related liability.
* Lessees initially recognise a liability equal in amount to the present value of the lease payments not made on, or before, the start of the lease. The right-of-use asset is recognised based on the cost that includes the value of the liability plus all other payments made in advance or that are expected to be made for the right to use the underlying asset. Subsequent to initial recognition, as lease payments are made and the asset is used, the lease liability is reduced by the balance of the payment that does not represent interest expense determined via the use of an effective interest method, while the right-of-use asset is depreciated.
* The lessor (i.e. the entity that transfers the right to use) needs to classify the lease as either a finance lease or an operating lease.
* The key criterion for the classification of leases into finance or operating leases by the lessor is the transfer of substantially all the risks and rewards of ownership.
* Finance lessors must be classified into financiers and manufacturer/dealer lessors based on whether the lessor carries the asset to be leased at fair value or cost.
* For a financier lessor, a lease receivable is recognised at an amount equal to the fair value of the underlying asset plus any initial direct costs incurred by the lessor. With manufacturer/dealer lessors there are no initial direct costs involved. Any costs associated with negotiating the lease are expensed and therefore the initial amount recognised as lease receivable is equal to the fair value of the underlying asset only.
* With manufacturer/dealer lessors, a profit or loss is recognised at the commencement of the lease. More specifically, the lessor recognises sales revenue based on the fair value of the underlying asset or the present value of lease payments if lower, and cost of sales at the carrying amount of the underlying asset less the present value of any unguaranteed residual value of the underlying asset.
* Subsequent to initial measurement of the lease receivable, a lessor will, on receipt of lease payments from the lessee, reduce the lease receivable and recognise interest revenue earned.
* With operating leases, all payments are treated as income by the lessor. The lessee will still recognise a right-of-use asset and a related lease liability.

KEY TERMS

commencement date of the lease The date on which a lessor makes an underlying asset available for use by a lessee.

economic life The period of time over which the underlying asset is expected to be economically usable.

executory costs Costs incurred by the lessor on behalf of the lessee for the additional services provided as part of the lease agreement.

fair value The price that would be received to sell an asset or paid to transfer a liability in an orderly transaction between market participants at the measurement date.

finance lease A lease that transfers substantially all the risks and rewards incidental to ownership of an underlying asset.

fixed payments Payments made by a lessee to a lessor for the right to use an underlying asset during the lease term, excluding variable lease payments.

gross investment in the lease The sum of the lease payments receivable by the lessor under a finance lease, and any unguaranteed residual value accruing to the lessor.

initial direct costs Incremental costs that are directly attributable to negotiating and arranging a lease, except for such costs incurred by manufacturer/dealer lessors.

interest rate implicit in the lease The discount rate that, at the inception of the lease, causes the aggregate present value of (a) the lease payments; and (b) the unguaranteed residual value, to be equal to the sum of: (i) the fair value of the underlying asset, and (ii) any initial direct costs of the lessor.

lease An agreement whereby the lessor conveys to the lessee in return for a payment or series of payments the right to use an asset for an agreed period of time.

lease incentives Payments made by a lessor to a lessee associated with a lease, or the reimbursement or assumption by a lessor of costs of a lessee.

lease payments The total amounts payable by the lessee to the lessor under the lease agreement for the right to use the underlying asset (not including any executory costs and lease incentives).

lease term The non-cancellable period for which the lessee has contracted to lease the asset.

lessee The party that obtains the right to use the asset, not the asset itself, in return for making a series of payments to the lessor under the lease arrangement.

lessee's incremental borrowing rate The rate of interest that a lessee would have to pay to borrow over a similar term, and with a similar security, the funds necessary to obtain an asset of a similar value to the right-of-use asset in a similar economic environment.

lessor The party that owns the asset and retains ownership under the lease arrangement.

net investment in the lease The gross investment in the lease discounted at the interest rate implicit in the lease.

operating lease A lease other than a finance lease.

purchase option A clause in the lease agreement allowing the lessee to purchase the asset at the end of the lease for a pre-set amount, significantly less than the expected residual value at the end of the lease term.

residual value guarantee That part of the residual value of the underlying asset guaranteed by a party not related to the lessor.

right to use The right to direct the use of and obtain substantially all the economic benefits from the use of an asset.

substantive right to substitute the asset When the lessor has the practical ability to substitute the asset at any time without needing the lessee's approval and can benefit from substituting the asset.

unguaranteed residual value That part of the residual value of the underlying asset, the realisation of which by a lessor is not assured or is guaranteed solely by a party related to the lessor.

variable lease payments The portion of payments made by a lessee to a lessor for the right to use an underlying asset during the lease term that varies because of changes in facts or circumstances occurring after the commencement date, other than the passage of time.

DEMONSTRATION PROBLEMS

10.1 Manufacturer lessor

On 1 July 2023, Hot Ltd leased a photocopier from Mail Ltd, a company that manufactures, retails and leases copiers. The photocopier had cost Mail Ltd $30 000 to make but had a fair value on 1 July 2023 of $35 080. The lease agreement contained the following provisions.

Lease term	3 years
Annual payment, payable in advance on 1 July each year	$14 500
Economic life of the copier	4 years
Estimated residual value at the end of the lease term when the copier is returned to Mail Ltd	$3 000
Residual value guarantee by Hot Ltd	$1 500
Interest rate implicit in the lease	10%
The lease is cancellable, provided another lease is immediately entered into.	

The annual payment included an amount of $2500 p.a. to reimburse Mail Ltd for the cost of paper and toner supplied to Hot Ltd. Mail Ltd's solicitor prepared the lease agreement for a fee of $1365. On 30 June 2026, at the end of the lease term, Hot Ltd returned the copier to Mail Ltd, which sold the copier for $3000.

Required

Part A

1. Prepare the lease payments schedule and the journal entries for the lessee for the year ended 30 June 2026 only.
2. Classify the lease from the perspective of the lessor. Justify your answer.
3. Prepare the lease receipts schedule and the journal entries for the lessor for the year ended 30 June 2024 only.

Part B

Assume that the lease term is for 2 years, payments are $14 500 immediately and a further $14 500 in 12 months' time (both payments include an amount of $2500 p.a. to reimburse the cost of paper and toner supplied to Hot Ltd). The estimated residual value at the end of the lease term is $14 728 and no part of this residual value has been guaranteed by Hot Ltd, but by a party related to Mail Ltd.

1. Prepare the journal entries for the lessee for the year ended 30 June 2024 only.
2. Classify the lease from the perspective of the lessor. Justify your answer.
3. Prepare the lease receipts schedule and the journal entries for the lessor for the year ended 30 June 2024 only.

SOLUTION

Part A

1. *Prepare the lease payments schedule and the journal entries for the lessee for the year ended 30 June 2026 only.*

The lessee is required to make annual payments of $14 500 in advance, but included in these is an amount of $2500 p.a. to cover operational costs paid by the lessor (i.e. executory costs). Also, the lessee guarantees $1500 out of the estimated residual value. Thus, the lease payments recognised for the copier are one payment of $12 000 immediately, two future payments of $12 000 and a residual value guarantee of $1500. Applying the provided implicit rate in the lease to the lease payments, the present value of those payments is as follows.

$$\text{PV of LP} = \$12\,000 + (\$12\,000 \times 1.7355) \, [T_2, 10\%, 2 \text{ years}])$$
$$+ \$1500 \times 0.7513 \, [T_1, 10\%, 3 \text{ years}])$$
$$= \$33\,953$$

The lease payments schedule starts with the balance of the lease liability at the start of the lease that should capture the present value of lease payments not made on or before the start of the lease; that is, $33 953 − $12 000 = $21 953. The lease payments schedule is presented below.

HOT LTD (lessee) Lease payments schedule			
	Lease payments[a]	Interest expense[b]	Reduction in liability[c]	Balance of liability[d]
1 July 2023				$21 953[e]
1 July 2024	$12 000	$2 195	$ 9 805	12 148
1 July 2025	12 000	1 215	10 785	1 363
30 June 2026	1 500	137	1 363	—
	$25 500	$3 547	$21 953	

(a) The lease payments consist of two annual payments of $12 000 payable in advance on 1 July of each year (excluding the lease payment made at 1 July 2023), plus a residual value guarantee of $1500 transferred on the last day of the lease. The guarantee part of the payment is in the form of the underlying asset being returned to the lessor and potentially cash being paid by the lessee to cover any deficiency in the actual residual value.

(b) Interest expense is the balance of liability at the beginning of each year multiplied by 10%. No interest expense is incurred in the first year because payment is made at the commencement of the lease.

(c) Reduction in liability is calculated as lease payments less interest expense. The total of this column must equal the initial liability; due to rounding errors in the calculation of the initial liability, the final interest expense figure may require rounding.

(d) The balance of liability is reduced each year by the amount in the 'Reduction in liability' column.

(e) Initial liability is equal to the present value of lease payments and includes the two annual payments made after the commencement of the lease and the residual value guarantee.

Based on the lease payments schedule, the journal entries posted by Hot Ltd for the year ended 30 June 2026 are as follows.

HOT LTD (lessee) Journal entries for year ended 30 June 2026			
1 July 2025:			
Lease liability	Dr	10 785	
Interest payable	Dr	1 215	
Prepaid executory costs	Dr	2 500	
Cash	Cr		14 500
(Recording the third and final lease payment; the part of this payment related to interest covers the interest expense incurred in the previous year, i.e. from the last payment on 1 July 2024 to 30 June 2025)			
30 June 2026:			
Depreciation expense	Dr	10 817	
Accumulated depreciation	Cr		10 817
(Recognition of the depreciation of the leased asset for the year [($33 953 – $1500)/3])			
Lease liability	Dr	1 363	
Interest expense	Dr	137	
Accumulated depreciation	Dr	32 453	
Right-of-use asset	Cr		33 953
(Return of the copier at the end of the lease term)			
Executory costs	Dr	2 500	
Prepaid executory costs	Cr		2 500
(Recognition of the expired prepayment of executory costs)			

2. *Classify the lease from the perspective of the lessor.*
   (a) Determine whether the lessor is a financier or a manufacturer/dealer. This is essential as it changes the accounting treatment for initial direct costs paid by the lessor and the impacts on the determination of the interest rate implicit in the lease.
      (i) Mail Ltd is a manufacturer lessor. Accordingly, the initial direct costs are treated as part of expenses and are not included in calculating the interest rate implicit in the lease (they are not considered as part of the lessor's investment in the lease).
   (b) Determine whether substantially all of the risks and rewards associated with ownership of the copier have been transferred to the lessee; that is, whether the lease is a finance lease or an operating lease.
      (i) *Cancellability test.* The lease is cancellable, but on cancellation the lessee would have to immediately enter another lease. Arguably, this condition implies that the lease transferred some risks and rewards to the lessee.
      (ii) *Transfer of ownership test.* The copier will be returned to the lessor at the end of the lease term. However, the lessee guarantees a part of the residual value at the end of the lease, which may imply that the lease transferred some risks and rewards to the lessee.
      (iii) *Lease term test.* The lease term at 3 years is 75% of the copier's economic life. Arguably, this represents a major part of that economic life, which may imply that the lease transferred some risks and rewards to the lessee.
      (iv) *Present value test.* Applying the provided implicit rate in the lease to the lease payments, we find the present value of those payments to be 96.8% of the fair value of the copier (i.e. substantially all of that fair value).

$$\text{PV of LP} = \$12\,000 + (\$12\,000 \times 1.7355\ [T_2, 10\%, 2\ \text{years}])$$
$$+ \$1500 \times 0.7513\ [T_1, 10\%, 3\ \text{years}])$$
$$= \$33\,953$$
$$\text{PV of LP/FV} = \$33\,953/\$35\,080$$
$$= 96.8\%$$

Given the above evidence, the lessor will classify the transaction as a finance lease.

3. *Prepare a lease receipts schedule and journal entries for the lessor for the year ended 30 June 2024 only.*

The lease receipts schedule reflects annual payments in advance of $12 000 for the copier, the residual value guarantee of $1500, the unguaranteed residual value of $1500 and an interest rate implicit in the lease of 10%.

MAIL LTD (lessor) Lease receipts schedule			
	Lease receipts[a]	Interest revenue[b]	Reduction in receivable[c]	Balance of receivable[d]
1 July 2023				$35 080[e]
1 July 2023	$12 000	$ —	$12 000	23 080
1 July 2024	12 000	2 308	9 692	13 388
1 July 2025	12 000	1 339	10 661	2 727
30 June 2026	3 000	273	2 727	—
	$39 500	$3 920	$35 080	

(a) The lease receipts are made out of three annual lease receipts of $12 000 payable in advance on 1 July of each year, plus a residual value of $3000 (of which $1500 is guaranteed by the lessee and the other $1500 is unguaranteed residual) on the last day of the lease.
(b) Interest revenue is calculated as the balance of receivable each year multiplied by 10%.
(c) The reduction in receivable is the excess of the receipts in a year over the interest revenue earned during that year; that is, lease receipts less interest revenue. The total of this column must equal the initial amount recognised for lease receivable — to ensure this, the final interest revenue figure may require rounding.
(d) The balance is reduced each year by the amount in the 'Reduction in receivable' column.
(e) Initial receivable is calculated as the fair value of $35 080. This figure equals the present value of lease payments receivable and the present value of the unguaranteed residual value.

Based on the lease schedule prepared above, the journal entries are posted as follows. Note that because Mail Ltd is a manufacturer lessor, the first journal entry must record the profit or loss on sale of the asset as required by AASB 16/IFRS 16.

MAIL LTD (lessor) Journal entries for year ended 30 June 2024			
1 July 2023:			
Lease receivable	Dr	35 080	
Sales revenue*	Cr		33 953
Cost of sales**	Dr	28 873	
Inventories	Cr		30 000
(Recognition of lease receivable and recording the 'sale' of copier)			
*PV of LP			
**Cost less PV of unguaranteed residual ($1500 × 0.7513)			
Lease costs	Dr	1 365	
Cash	Cr		1 365
(Payment of initial direct costs)			
Cash	Dr	14 500	
Lease receivable	Cr		12 000
Reimbursement of executory costs in advance	Cr		2 500
(Receipt of first payment)			
30 June 2024:			
Paper and toner expense	Dr	2 500	
Cash	Cr		2 500
(Payment of executory costs)			
Interest receivable	Dr	2 308	
Interest revenue	Cr		2 308
(Interest expense accrual)			
Reimbursement of executory costs in advance	Dr	2 500	
Executory costs reimbursement	Cr		2 500
(Recognition of revenue related to the reimbursement of executory costs by the lessee)			

Part B

1. *Prepare the journal entries for the lessee for the year ended 30 June 2024 only.*

The lessee is required to make two annual payments of $14 500 in advance, but included in these is an amount of $2500 p.a. to cover operational costs paid by the lessor (i.e. executory costs); there is no residual value guarantee. Thus, the lease payments recognised for the copier are one payment of $12 000 immediately and one future payment of $12 000. Applying the provided implicit rate in the lease to the lease payments, the present value of those payments is as follows.

$$\text{PV of LP} = \$12\,000 + (\$12\,000 \times 0.9091\ [T_2, 10\%, 1\ \text{year}])$$
$$= \$22\,909$$

The lease payments schedule starts with the balance of the lease liability at the start of the lease that should capture the present value of lease payments not made on or before the start of the lease; that is, $22 909 − $12 000 = $10 909. The lease payments schedule is as follows.

HOT LTD (lessee) Lease payments schedule				
	Lease payments	Interest expense	Reduction in liability	Balance of liability
1 July 2023				$10 909
1 July 2024	$12 000	$1 091	$10 909	—

Based on the lease payments schedule, the journal entries posted by Hot Ltd for the year ended 30 June 2024 are as follows.

HOT LTD (lessee) Journal entries for year ended 30 June 2024			
1 July 2023:			
Right-of-use asset	Dr	22 909	
Prepaid executory costs	Dr	2 500	
Cash	Cr		14 500
Lease liability	Cr		10 909
(Recording at the start of the lease the right-of-use asset, the lease liability and the payment in advance of the first lease payment and the executory costs)			
30 June 2024:			
Depreciation expense	Dr	11 455	
Accumulated depreciation	Cr		11 455
(Recognition of the depreciation of the leased asset for the year: $22 909/2)			
Interest expense	Dr	1 091	
Interest payable	Cr		1 091
(Recognition of the interest expense incurred during the year which will be paid on 1 July 2024)			

2. *Classify the lease from the perspective of the lessor.*

(a) Determine whether the lessor is a financier or a manufacturer/dealer. This is essential as it changes the accounting treatment for initial direct costs paid by the lessor and also the definition of the interest rate implicit in the lease.

Mail Ltd is a manufacturer lessor. Accordingly, the initial direct costs are treated as part of cost of sales and are not included in calculating the interest rate implicit in the lease.

(b) Determine whether substantially all of the risks and rewards associated with ownership of the copier have been transferred to the lessee; that is, whether the lease is a finance lease or an operating lease.

(i) *Cancellability test.* The lease is cancellable, but on cancellation the lessee would have to immediately enter another lease. Arguably, this condition implies that the lease transferred some risks and rewards to the lessee.

(ii) *Transfer of ownership test.* The copier will be returned to the lessor at the end of the lease term. Moreover, the lessee does not guarantee any part of the residual value at the end of the lease, which may imply that the lease has not transferred risks and rewards to the lessee.

(iii) *Lease term test.* The lease term at 2 years is 50% of the copier's economic life. Arguably, this does not represent a major part of that economic life, which may imply that the lease has not transferred some risks and rewards to the lessee.

(iv) *Present value test.* Applying the provided implicit rate in the lease to the lease payments, we find the present value of those payments to be 65.3% of the fair value of the copier and not substantially all of the fair value of the copier.

$$\text{PV of LP} = \$12\,000 + (\$12\,000 \times 0.9091\,[T_2, 10\%, 1\text{ year}])$$
$$= \$22\,909$$
$$\text{PV of LP/FV} = \$22\,909/\$35\,080$$
$$= 65.3\%$$

Given the above evidence, the lessor may classify the transaction as an operating lease.

3. *Prepare the journal entries for the lessor for the year ended 30 June 2024 only.*

MAIL LTD (lessor) Journal entries for year ended 30 June 2024			
1 July 2023:			
Cash	Dr	12 000	
Rental income	Cr		12 000
(Recording the first lease receipt)			
Deferred initial direct costs	Dr	1 365	
Cash	Cr		1 365
(Initial direct costs incurred for lease)			
30 June 2024:			
Depreciation expense	Dr	7 500	
Accumulated depreciation	Cr		7 500
(Depreciation on copier for the year: $30 000/4)			
Lease expense	Dr	683	
Deferred initial direct costs	Cr		683
(Recognition of initial direct cost: $1365/2)			

10.2 Financier lessor

On 30 June 2023, Adobe Ltd leased a vehicle to Acrobat Ltd. Adobe Ltd had purchased the vehicle on that day for its fair value of $90 720. The lease agreement, which cost Adobe Ltd $457 and Acrobat Ltd $567 to have drawn up, contained the following provisions.

Lease term	4 years
Annual payment, payable in advance on 30 June each year	$23 900
Economic life of vehicle	6 years
Estimated residual value at end of economic life	$3 000
Estimated residual value at end of lease term	$15 000
Residual value guarantee by lessee	$13 500
Interest rate implicit in the lease	7%

The lease is cancellable, but cancellation will incur a monetary penalty equivalent to 2 years' rental payments. Included in the annual payment is an amount of $1900 to cover reimbursement for the costs of insurance and maintenance paid by the lessor. The directors of Acrobat Ltd have indicated that they are interested in acquiring the asset at the end of the lease.

Required

1. Prepare for the lessee, Acrobat Ltd:
   (a) the lease payments schedule (show all workings)
   (b) the journal entries for the years ended 30 June 2023 and 30 June 2024.
2. Explain why Adobe Ltd classify the above transaction as a finance lease.
3. Prepare for the lessor, Adobe Ltd:
   (a) the lease receipts schedule (show all workings)
   (b) the journal entries for the years ended 30 June 2023 and 30 June 2024.

SOLUTION

1. (a) *Prepare the lease payments schedule for the lessee, Acrobat Ltd.*

The lessee is required to make annual payments of $23 900 in advance over the lease term of 4 years, but included in these is an amount of $1900 p.a. to cover operational costs paid by the lessor (i.e. executory costs). The lessee guarantees $13 500 out of the estimated residual value at the end of the lease. Thus, the lease payments recognised for the vehicle are one payment of $22 000 immediately, three future payments of $22 000 and a residual value guarantee of $13 500. Applying the provided implicit rate in the lease to the lease payments of 7%, the present value of those payments is as follows.

$$\text{PV of LP} = \$22\,000 + (\$22\,000 \times 2.6243) \ [T_2, 7\%, 3 \text{ years}])$$
$$+ \$13\,500 \times 0.7629 \ [T_1, 7\%, 4 \text{ years}])$$
$$= \$90\,033$$

The lease payments schedule starts with the balance of the lease liability at the start of the lease that should capture the present value of lease payments not made on or before the start of the lease; that is, $90 033 − $22 000 = $68 033. The lease payments schedule is as follows.

		ACROBAT LTD (lessee) Lease payments schedule		
	Lease payments	Interest expense	Reduction in liability	Balance of liability
30 June 2023				$68 033
30 June 2024	$22 000	$ 4 762	$17 238	50 795
30 June 2025	22 000	3 556	18 444	32 351
30 June 2026	22 000	2 265	19 735	12 616
30 June 2027	13 500	884	12 616	—
	$79 500	$11 467	$68 033	

(b) *Prepare the journal entries for Acrobat Ltd for the years ended 30 June 2023 and 2024.*

ACROBAT LTD (lessee) Journal entries for years ended 30 June 2023 and 2024			
Year ended 30 June 2023:			
Right-of-use vehicle	Dr	90 600	
Prepaid executory costs	Dr	1 900	
Lease liability	Cr		68 033
Cash	Cr		24 467
(Recognition of lease and the first payment in advance, together with the payment of the initial direct costs incurred by Acrobat Ltd — those costs are included in the capitalised amount for the right-of-use asset as they are directly attributable costs)			
Year ended 30 June 2024:			
Executory costs	Dr	1 900	
Prepaid executory costs	Cr		1 900
(Executory costs prepayment expired during the year)			
Depreciation expense	Dr	14 600	
Accumulated depreciation	Cr		14 600
(Depreciation of right-of-use asset for the year ($90 600 − $3000)/6 (use economic life as ownership may be transferred))			
Lease liability	Dr	17 238	
Interest expense	Dr	4 762	
Prepaid executory costs	Dr	1 900	
Cash	Cr		23 900
(Second lease payment)			

2. *Classify the lease from the perspective of the lessor.*
   (a) Determine whether the lessor is a financier or a manufacturer/dealer. This is essential as it changes the accounting treatment for initial direct costs paid by the lessor and the definition of the interest rate implicit in the lease.

   Adobe Ltd is a financier lessor. Accordingly, the initial direct costs are treated as part of the lease receivable and are included in calculating the interest rate implicit in the lease.
   (b) Determine whether substantially all of the risks and rewards associated with ownership of the vehicle have been transferred to the lessee; that is, whether the lease is a finance lease or an operating lease.
       (i) *Cancellability test.* The lease is cancellable, but on cancellation the lessee would incur a monetary penalty equivalent to 2 years' rental payments. Arguably, this condition implies that the lease transferred some risks and rewards to the lessee.
       (ii) *Transfer of ownership test.* The directors of Acrobat Ltd have indicated that they are interested in acquiring the asset at the end of the lease term. Additionally, they have guaranteed most of its residual value at that date, which may imply that the lease transferred some risks and rewards to the lessee.
       (iii) *Lease term test.* The lease term at 4 years is 66.67% of the vehicle's economic life. Arguably, this represents a major part of that economic life, which may imply that the lease transferred some risks and rewards to the lessee.
       (iv) *Present value test.* Applying the provided implicit rate in the lease to the lease payments, we find the present value of those payments to be 99.24% of the fair value of the vehicle (i.e. substantially all of that fair value).

$$\text{PV of LP} = \$22\,000 + (\$22\,000 \times 2.6243\ [T_2, 7\%, 3 \text{ years}])$$
$$+ \$13\,500 \times 0.7629\ [T_1, 7\%, 4 \text{ years}])$$
$$= \$90\,033$$
$$\text{PV of LP/FV} = \$90\,033/\$90\,720$$
$$= 99.24\%$$

Given the above evidence, the lessor will classify the transaction as a finance lease.
3. (a) *Prepare the lease receipts schedule for the lessor, Adobe Ltd.*

   The lease receipts schedule based on the four annual payments in advance of $22\,000 for the vehicle, the residual value guarantee of $13\,500, the unguaranteed residual value of $1500 and an interest rate implicit in the lease of 7% is presented below. The initial amount recognised for the lease receivable is calculated as the fair value of $90\,720 plus the initial direct costs of the lessor of $457. This figure is also equal to the present value of lease payments receivable ($90\,033) plus the present value of the unguaranteed residual value ($1144).

	Lease receipts	Interest revenue	Reduction in receivable	Balance of receivable
ADOBE LTD (lessor)				
Lease receipts schedule				
30 June 2023				$91 177
30 June 2023	$ 22 000	$ —	$22 000	69 177
30 June 2024	22 000	4 842	17 158	52 019
30 June 2025	22 000	3 641	18 359	33 660
30 June 2026	22 000	2 356	19 644	14 016
30 June 2027	15 000	984	14 016	—
	$103 000	$11 823	$91 177	

   (b) *Prepare the journal entries for Adobe Ltd for years ended 30 June 2023 and 30 June 2024.*
       Since Adobe Ltd is a financier lessor, the initial direct costs are included in the lease receivable.

ADOBE LTD (lessor) Journal entries for years ended 30 June 2023 and 2024			
Year ended 30 June 2023:			
Vehicle	Dr	90 720	
Cash	Cr		90 720
(Purchase of vehicle to be leased)			
Lease receivable	Dr	91 177	
Vehicle	Cr		90 720
Cash	Cr		457
(Lease of vehicle and payment of initial direct costs)			
Cash	Dr	23 900	
Lease receivable	Cr		22 000
Reimbursement of executory costs in advance	Cr		1 900
(Receipt of first payment)			
Year ended 30 June 2024:			
Insurance and maintenance	Dr	1 900	
Cash	Cr		1 900
(Costs paid on behalf of lessee)			
Reimbursement of executory costs in advance	Dr	1 900	
Reimbursement of executory costs revenue	Cr		1 900
(Transfer of reimbursement revenue)			
Cash	Dr	23 900	
Interest revenue	Cr		4 842
Lease receivable	Cr		17 158
Reimbursement of executory costs in advance	Cr		1 900
(Receipt of second payment)			

COMPREHENSION QUESTIONS

1 What characteristics should a contract have to be considered a lease?

2 Explain the 'right to use' of an identified asset.

3 What are 'lease payments'?

4 If a lease agreement states that 'the lessee guarantees a residual value, at the end of the lease term, of $20 000', what does this mean?

5 What is meant by 'the interest rate implicit in a lease' and 'the lessee's incremental borrowing rate'?

6 Where a lessor incurs initial direct costs in establishing a lease agreement, how are these costs to be accounted for?

7 Where a lessee incurs initial direct costs in establishing a lease agreement, how are these costs to be accounted for?

8 How are leases to be accounted for by lessees according to AASB 16/IFRS 16?

9 What are operating and finance leases?

10 How are finance leases to be accounted for by lessors?

11 How does the accounting treatment for a finance lease change if the lessor is a manufacturer/dealer lessor?

12 How are operating leases to be accounted for by lessors?

13 Identify three possible adverse effects on an entity's financial statements arising from recognition of a lease arrangement on the statement of financial position.

CASE STUDY 10.1

ACCOUNTING FOR LEASES BY LESSEE

Farm Ltd leases some parcels of land from their owner for a period of 10 years at a time. The lease agreement can be cancelled, but a significant penalty will be incurred by Farm Ltd. The lease payments required include a payment up-front of $300 000, followed by another 9 payments of equal value at the end of every year up to the end of the ninth year. The implicit rate in the lease is 10%.

Required

Prepare the journal entries for Farm Ltd to recognise the lease under AASB 16/IFRS 16.

CASE STUDY 10.2

IDENTIFICATION OF LEASES

For the following arrangements, discuss whether they are lease transactions, and thus fall under the ambit of AASB 16/IFRS 16.

1. Entity A enters into a contract with Entity B, whereby Entity B will provide 5 SUV vehicles for Entity A to use over the next 3 years. The vehicles have been selected by Entity A from a large pool of similar vehicles and are explicitly identified in the contract. Entity B is only allowed to substitute the vehicles if, and only for the period when, the vehicles are being repaired.
2. Entity C enters into a contract with Entity D, whereby Entity D will provide 2 aeroplanes for Entity C to use over the next 5 years. The aeroplanes have been selected by Entity C from a large pool of similar aircraft, but remain in the airport hangar owned by Entity D when not in use and can be substituted at any time by Entity C.
3. Entity E enters into a contract with Entity F, a shopping centre operator, whereby Entity E will be offered a space for a pop-up shop in one of the centres managed by Entity F. The contract specifies the size of the space to be provided, not the actual location.

APPLICATION AND ANALYSIS EXERCISES

★ BASIC | ★ ★ MODERATE | ★ ★ ★ DIFFICULT

10.1 Determination of interest rates ★   **LO2**

On 1 July 2021, Pretty Ltd leases a machine with a fair value of $109 445 to Cool Ltd for 5 years at an annual rental (payable in advance) of $25 000, and Cool Ltd guarantees in full the estimated residual value of $15 000 on return of the asset. What would be the interest rate implicit in the lease?

(a) 9%
(b) 10%
(c) 12%
(d) 14%

10.2 Accounting by lessee ★   **LO2**

Mitch Ltd prepares the following lease payments schedule for the lease of a machine from Stark Ltd. The machine has an economic life of 6 years. The lease agreement requires four annual payments of $33 000, and the machine will be returned to Stark Ltd at the end of the lease term.

	MITCH LTD Lease payments schedule			
	Lease payments	Interest expense (10%)	Reduction in liability	Balance of liability
1 July 2021				$98 512
1 July 2022	$ 30 000	$ 9 851	$20 149	78 363
1 July 2023	30 000	7 836	22 164	56 199
1 July 2024	30 000	5 620	24 380	31 819
1 July 2025	35 000	3 181	31 819	—
	$125 000	$26 488	$98 512	

Required

The following three multiple-choice questions relate to the information provided above. Select the correct answer and show any workings required.

1. For the year ended 30 June 2022, what would Mitch Ltd record in relation to the lease?
   (a) An interest payable of $26 488
   (b) An interest payable of $nil
   (c) An interest payable of $9851
   (d) An interest payable of $7836

2. How much annual depreciation expense would Mitch Ltd record?

    (a) $24 628

    (b) $16 419

    (c) $15 585

    (d) $23 378

3. If Stark Ltd (the lessor) records a lease receivable of $102 327, the variance between this receivable and the liability of $98 512 recorded by Mitch Ltd could be due to what?

    (a) Initial direct costs paid by Stark Ltd

    (b) An unguaranteed residual value

    (c) Both of the above

    (d) Neither of the above

10.3 Accounting by lessee ★   **LO2**

On 1 July 2022, Monkey Ltd leased a plastic-moulding machine from Wise Ltd. The machine cost Wise Ltd $65 000 to manufacture and had a fair value of $77 055 on 1 July 2022. The lease agreement contained the following provisions.

Lease term	4 years
Annual rental payment, in advance on 1 July each year	$20 750
Residual value at end of the lease term	$7 500
Residual guaranteed by lessee	Nil
Interest rate implicit in lease	8%
The lease is cancellable only with the permission of the lessor.	

The expected useful life of the machine is 5 years. Monkey Ltd intends to return the machine to Wise Ltd at the end of the lease term. Included in the annual rental payment is an amount of $750 to cover the costs of maintenance and insurance paid for by the lessor.

Required

1. Prepare the lease payments schedule for Monkey Ltd (show all workings).
2. Prepare the journal entries in the books of Monkey Ltd for the year ended 30 June 2023.

10.4 Finance lease ★   **LO2, 4**

If a lease has been capitalised as a finance lease by the lessor, identify circumstances in which the lease receivable raised by the lessor will differ from the right-of-use asset raised by the lessee.

10.5 Accounting by lessee and lessor ★   **LO3, 5**

On 1 July 2023, Sherlock Ltd leased a processing plant to Holmes Ltd. The plant was purchased by Sherlock Ltd on 1 July 2023 for its fair value of $348 942. The lease agreement contained the following provisions.

Lease term	3 years
Economic life of plant	5 years
Annual rental payment, in arrears (commencing 30/6/24)	$120 000
Residual value at end of the lease term	$50 000
Residual guaranteed by lessee	$30 000
Interest rate implicit in lease	8%
The lease is cancellable only with the permission of the lessor.	

Holmes Ltd intends to return the processing plant to Sherlock Ltd at the end of the lease term. The lease has been classified as a finance lease by Sherlock Ltd.

Required

1. Prepare:

    (a) the lease payments schedule for Holmes Ltd (show all workings)

    (b) the journal entries in the records of Holmes Ltd for the year ended 30 June 2025.

2. Prepare:

    (a) the lease receipts schedule for Sherlock Ltd (show all workings)

    (b) the journal entries in the records of Sherlock Ltd for the year ended 30 June 2025.

10.6 Finance lease — lessor ★ **LO2, 4**

On 1 July 2022, Jane Plum decided she needed a new car. She went to the local car yard, North Ltd, run by Fred Peach. Jane discussed the price of a new Roadster Special with Fred, and they agreed on a price of $37 000. As North Ltd had acquired the vehicle from the manufacturer for $30 000, Fred was pleased with the deal. On learning that Jane wanted to lease the vehicle, Fred agreed to arrange for South Ltd, a local finance company, to set up the lease agreement. North Ltd then sold the car to South Ltd for $37 000.

South Ltd wrote a lease agreement, incurring initial direct costs of $1410 as a result. The lease agreement contained the following provisions.

Initial payment on 1 July 2022	$13 000
Payments on 1 July 2023 and 1 July 2024	$13 000
Guaranteed residual value at 30 June 2025	$10 000
Implicit interest rate in the lease	6%

South Ltd agreed to pay for the insurance and maintenance of the vehicle, the latter to be carried out by North Ltd at regular intervals. The cost of these services is valued at $3000 p.a.

The vehicle had an expected useful life of 4 years. The expected residual value of the vehicle at 30 June 2025 was $12 000.

Costs of maintenance and insurance incurred by South Ltd over the years ended 30 June 2023 to 30 June 2025 were $2810, $3020 and $2750 respectively. At 30 June 2025, Jane returned the vehicle to South Ltd. Assume that the lease is classified as a finance lease by South Ltd.

Required

1. Prepare the lease receipts schedule for South Ltd.
2. Prepare the journal entries in the books of South Ltd from 1 July 2022 to 30 June 2025.

10.7 Lease classification; accounting by lessor ★ **LO3, 4**

Use the information contained in exercise 10.3 to complete the following.

1. Classify the lease for Wise Ltd. Justify your answer.
2. Prepare (a) the lease receipts schedule for Wise Ltd (show all workings) and (b) the journal entries in its books for the year ended 30 June 2023.

10.8 Lease classification, accounting by lessor ★ **LO3, 5, 6**

Oceans Ltd manufactures specialised moulding machinery for both sale and lease. On 1 July 2023, Oceans Ltd leased a machine to Thirteen Ltd. The machine being leased cost Oceans Ltd $205 000 to make and its fair value at 1 July 2023 is considered to be $239 997. The terms of the lease are as follows.

The lease term is for 5 years, starting on	1 July 2023
Annual lease payment, payable on 30 June each year	$64 000
Estimated useful life of machine (scrap value $15 000)	8 years
Estimated residual value of machine at end of lease term	$8 000
Residual value guarantee by Thirteen Ltd	$5 000
Interest rate implicit in the lease	10%
The annual lease payment includes an amount of $2000 to cover annual maintenance and insurance costs.	
Thirteen Ltd may cancel the lease but only with the permission of the lessor.	
Thirteen Ltd intends to lease another machine from Oceans at the end of the lease term.	

Required

1. Classify the lease for Oceans Ltd. Justify your answer.
2. Prepare (a) the lease receipts schedule for Oceans Ltd (show all workings) and (b) the journal entries in its books for the year ended 30 June 2024.
3. Assuming that Thirteen Ltd can cancel the lease without incurring any penalties, prepare the journal entries in the books of Oceans Ltd for the year ended 30 June 2024.

10.9 Accounting by lessee and lessor ★ ★ **LO2, 5, 6**

Eliza Ltd decided to lease from Ford Ltd a car that had a fair value at 30 June 2022 of $38 960. The lease agreement contained the following provisions.

Lease term	3 years
Annual rental payments (commencing 30/6/22)	$11 200
Guaranteed residual value (expected fair value at end of lease term)	$12 000

The expected useful life of the car is 5 years. At the end of the 3-year lease term, the car was returned to Ford Ltd, which sold it for $10 000. The annual rental payments include an amount of $1200 to cover the cost of maintenance and insurance arranged and paid for by Ford Ltd.

Required

1. Prepare the journal entries for Eliza Ltd from 30 June 2022 to 30 June 2025.
2. Assuming that the lease is a finance lease from the perspective of Ford Ltd, prepare the journal entries for Ford Ltd from 30 June 2022 to 30 June 2025.
3. Assuming that the lease is an operating lease from the perspective of Ford Ltd, prepare the journal entries for Ford Ltd from 30 June 2022 to 30 June 2025.

10.10 Lease schedules and accounting by lessee and lessor ★ ★   **LO2, 6**

On 1 July 2023, Hermione Ltd leased a crane from Grainger Ltd. The crane cost Grainger Ltd $120 307, considered to be its fair value on that same day. The finance lease agreement contained the following provisions.

The lease term is for 3 years, starting on	1 July 2023
The lease is cancellable, but only with the permission from the lessor.	
Annual lease payment, payable on 30 June each year	$39 000
Estimated useful life of crane	4 years
Estimated residual value of crane at end of lease term	$22 000
Residual value guarantee by Hermione Ltd	$16 000
Interest rate implicit in the lease	7%

Required

1. Prepare the lease schedules for Hermione Ltd and Grainger Ltd.
2. Prepare the journal entries in the records of Hermione Ltd for the year ended 30 June 2024.

10.11 Accounting by lessee and lessor ★ ★   **LO2, 3, 6**

Albert Ltd entered into an agreement on 1 July 2022 to lease a processing plant with a fair value of $569 230 to Einstein Ltd. The terms of the lease agreement were as follows.

Lease term	3 years
Economic life of plant	5 years
Annual rental payment, in arrears (commencing 30/6/23)	$225 000
Residual value of plant at end of lease term	$50 000
Residual value guarantee by Einstein Ltd	$20 000
Interest rate implicit in the lease	6%
The lease is cancellable, but only with the permission of the lessor.	

At the end of the lease term, the plant is to be returned to Albert Ltd. In setting up the lease agreement Albert Ltd incurred $7350 in legal fees and stamp duty costs. The annual rental payment includes $25 000 to reimburse Albert Ltd for maintenance costs incurred on behalf of Einstein Ltd.

Required

1. Prepare a lease payments schedule and the journal entries in the records of Einstein Ltd for the year ended 30 June 2023. Show all workings.
2. Classify the lease from Albert Ltd perspective. Justify your answer.
3. Prepare a lease receipts schedule and the journal entries in the records of Albert Ltd for the year ended 30 June 2023. Show all workings.
4. Explain how and why your answers to requirements 1 and 2 would change if the lease agreement could be cancelled at any time without penalty.

10.12 Lease classification, lease accounting ★ ★ LO2, 3, 4

On 30 June 2022, Harper Ltd purchased machinery for its fair value of $42 500 and then leased it to Lee Ltd. Lee Ltd incurred $349 in costs to negotiate the lease agreement. The machine is expected to have an economic life of 5 years, after which time it will have a residual value of $2500. The lease agreement details are as follows.

Length of lease	4 years
Commencement date	30 June 2022
Annual lease payment, payable 30 June each year commencing	
30 June 2022	$12 000
Residual value at the end of the lease term	$10 000
Residual value guarantee by Lee Ltd	$8 000
Interest rate implicit in the lease	8%
The lease is cancellable, but only with the permission of Harper Ltd.	

All insurance and maintenance costs are paid by Harper Ltd and amount to $2000 per year and will be reimbursed by Lee Ltd by being included in the annual lease payment of $12 000. The machinery will be depreciated on a straight-line basis. It is expected that Lee Ltd will return the machinery at the end of the lease to Harper Ltd.

Required

1. Calculate the initial direct costs incurred by Harper Ltd to negotiate the lease agreement.
2. Describe why the lease can be considered as a finance lease by Harper Ltd, giving at least three reasons for your answer.
3. Prepare the journal entries to account for the lease in the books of Lee Ltd for the years ended 30 June 2022 and 30 June 2023.
4. Prepare the journal entries to account for the lease in the books of Harper Ltd for the year ended 30 June 2023.

10.13 Finance lease — financier lessor ★ ★ ★ LO2, 4

On 1 July 2022, Safe Ltd acquired a new car. The manager of Safe Ltd, Jack Safe, went to the local car yard, House Autos, and discussed the price of a new Racer Special with Denzel House. Jack and Denzel agreed on a price of $37 876. As House Autos had acquired the vehicle from the manufacturer for $32 000, Denzel was pleased with the deal. On discussing the financial arrangements in relation to the car, Jack decided that a lease arrangement was the most suitable. Denzel agreed to arrange for Washington Ltd, a local finance company, to set up the lease agreement. House Autos then sold the car to Washington Ltd for $37 876.

Washington Ltd wrote a lease agreement, incurring initial direct costs of $534 in the process. The lease agreement contained the following clauses.

Initial payment on 1 July 2022	$13 000
Payments on 1 July 2023 and 1 July 2024	$13 000
Interest rate implicit in the lease	6%

The lease agreement also specified for Washington Ltd to pay for the insurance and maintenance of the vehicle, the latter to be carried out by House Autos at regular intervals. A cost of $3000 per annum was included in the lease payments to cover these services.

Jack was concerned that the lease be considered an operating lease for accounting purposes. To achieve this, the lease agreement included the following terms.

- The lease was cancellable by Safe Ltd at any stage. However, if the lease was cancelled, Safe Ltd agreed to lease, on similar terms, another car from Washington Ltd.
- Safe Ltd was not required to guarantee the payment of any residual value. At the end of the lease term, 30 June 2025, or if cancelled earlier, the car would automatically revert to the lessor with no payments being required from Safe Ltd.

The vehicle had an expected economic life of 6 years. The expected fair value of the vehicle at 30 June 2025 was $12 000. Because of concern over the residual value, Washington Ltd required Jack to sign another contractual arrangement separate from the lease agreement which gave Washington Ltd the right to sell the car to Safe Ltd if the fair value of the car at the end of the lease term was less than $10 000.

Costs of maintenance and insurance paid by Washington Ltd to House Autos over the years ended 30 June 2023 to 30 June 2025 were $2810, $3020 and $2750.

At 30 June 2025, Jack returned the vehicle to Washington Ltd. The fair value of the car was determined to be $9000. Washington Ltd invoked the second agreement. With the consent of Safe Ltd, Washington Ltd sold the car to House Autos for a price of $9000 on 5 July 2025, and invoiced Safe Ltd for $1000. Safe Ltd subsequently paid this amount on 13 July 2025.

Required

Assuming the lease is classified as a finance lease for the perspective of Washington Ltd, prepare:

1. a schedule of lease payments for Safe Ltd
2. journal entries in the records of Safe Ltd for the years ended 30 June 2023, 30 June 2024 and 30 June 2025
3. a schedule of lease receipts for Washington Ltd
4. journal entries in the records of Washington Ltd for the years ended 30 June 2023, 30 June 2024 and 30 June 2025.

10.14 Lease classification, lease accounting ★ ★   **LO2, 3, 4**

As of 1 July 2022, Scarlett Ltd leases a building from Rhett Ltd. The building has a fair value at 1 July 2022 of $1 972 000. The lease agreement details are as follows.

Length of lease	10 years
Commencement date	1 July 2022
Annual lease payment, payable 30 June each year commencing 30 June 2023	$350 000
Estimated economic life of the building	10 years
Residual value at the end of the lease term	$20 000
Residual value guarantee by Scarlett Ltd	$14 000
Interest rate implicit in the lease	10%

The lease is cancellable, but a penalty equal to 50% of the remaining lease payments is applicable on cancellation. Scarlett Ltd incurred $1331 to negotiate and execute the lease agreement. All insurance and maintenance costs are paid by Rhett Ltd and are expected to amount to $30 000 per year and will be reimbursed by Scarlett Ltd by being included in the annual lease payment of $350 000. The building is to be depreciated on a straight-line basis.

Required

1. Calculate the initial direct costs incurred by Rhett Ltd to negotiate and execute the lease agreement.
2. Indicate the amounts recorded as right-of-use asset and lease liability by Scarlett Ltd and the amount recorded as lease receivable by Rhett Ltd at the beginning of the lease in their respective books.
3. Prepare the journal entries to account for the lease in the books of Scarlett Ltd for the year ended 30 June 2023.
4. Calculate the current and non-current lease liability as of 30 June 2023 relating to the lease.
5. Prepare the journal entries to account for the lease in the books of Rhett Ltd for the year ended 30 June 2023.

10.15 Lease classification, lease accounting ★ ★   **LO2, 3, 6**

On 1 July 2022, Connor Ltd purchased equipment for its fair value and then leased it to Violet Ltd, incurring $2548 in costs to prepare and execute the lease document. Violet Ltd incurred $1935 in costs to negotiate the agreement. The equipment is expected to have an economic life of 6 years, after which time it will have a residual value of $6000. The lease agreement details are as follows.

Length of lease	5 years
Commencement date	1 July 2022
Annual lease payment, payable 1 July each year commencing 1 July 2022	$15 000
Residual value at the end of the lease term, of which 50% is guaranteed by Violet Ltd	$12 000
Interest rate implicit in the lease	6%

All insurance and maintenance costs are paid by Connor Ltd and amount to $3000 per year and will be reimbursed by Violet Ltd by being included in the annual lease payment of $15 000. The equipment will be depreciated on a straight-line basis. It is expected that Violet Ltd will return the equipment to Connor Ltd at the end of the lease.

Required

1. Calculate the fair value of the leased equipment at 1 July 2022.
2. Prepare the journal entries to account for the lease in the books of Violet Ltd for the year ended 30 June 2023.
3. Prepare the journal entries to account for the lease in the books of Connor Ltd for the year ended 30 June 2023.

10.16 Lease classification, lease accounting ★ ★ **LO2, 3, 5**

Pacific Ltd has entered into an agreement to lease a crane to Masters Ltd. The lease agreement details are as follows.

Length of lease	5 years
Commencement date	1 July 2022
Annual lease payment, payable 30 June each year commencing	
30 June 2023	$12 000
Fair value of the crane at 1 July 2022	$48 776
Estimated economic life of the crane	8 years
Estimated residual value of the crane at the end of its economic life	$2 000
Residual value at the end of the lease term, of which 50% is guaranteed	
by Masters Ltd	$6 000
Interest rate implicit in the lease	9%

The lease is cancellable, but a penalty equal to 50% of the total lease payments is payable on cancellation. Masters Ltd does not intend to buy the crane at the end of the lease term. Pacific Ltd incurred $1800 to negotiate and execute the lease agreement. Pacific Ltd purchased the crane for $48 776 just before the inception of the lease.

Required

1. Prepare a schedule of lease payments for Masters Ltd.
2. Prepare journal entries to record the lease transactions for the year ended 30 June 2023 in the records of Masters Ltd.
3. State how Pacific Ltd should classify the lease. Give reasons for your answer.
4. Prepare a schedule of lease receipts for Pacific Ltd.
5. Prepare journal entries to record the lease transactions for the year ended 30 June 2023 in the records of Pacific Ltd.

10.17 Finance lease — manufacturer lessor ★ ★ ★ **LO2, 3, 6**

Stella Ltd manufactures specialised equipment for both sale and lease. On 1 July 2022, Stella Ltd leased some equipment to Freddy Ltd, incurring $1200 in costs to prepare and execute the lease document. Freddy Ltd incurred $650 in costs to negotiate the agreement. The equipment being leased cost Stella Ltd $55 072 to manufacture. The equipment is expected to have an economic life of 6 years, after which time it will have a residual value of $950. The lease agreement details are as follows.

Length of lease	5 years
Commencement date	1 July 2022
Annual lease payment, payable 30 June each year commencing	
30 June 2023	$16 000
Residual value at the end of the lease term, fully guaranteed by	
Freddy Ltd	$8 000
Interest rate implicit in the lease	8%

All insurance and maintenance costs are paid by Stella Ltd and amount to $3000 per year and will be reimbursed by Freddy Ltd by being included in the annual lease payment of $16 000. The equipment will be depreciated on a straight-line basis. It is expected that Freddy Ltd will purchase the equipment from Stella Ltd at the end of the lease.

Required
1. State how Stella Ltd should classify the lease. Give reasons for your answer.
2. Calculate the fair value of the leased equipment at 1 July 2022.
3. Prepare the journal entries to account for the lease in the books of Freddy Ltd for the year ended 30 June 2023.
4. Prepare a schedule of lease receipts for Stella Ltd.
5. Prepare the journal entries to account for the lease in the books of Stella Ltd for the year ended 30 June 2023.

10.18 Finance lease — manufacturer lessor ★ ★ ★   **LO2, 6**

Gold Ltd manufactures specialised moulding machinery for both sale and lease. On 1 July 2022, Gold Ltd leased a machine to Silver Ltd, incurring $2200 in costs to prepare and execute the lease document. The machine being leased cost Gold Ltd $220 000 to make and its fair value at 1 July 2022 is considered to be $251 990. The terms of the lease agreement are as follows.

Lease term commencing on 1 July 2022	5 years
Annual lease payment commencing on 1 July 2023	$72 000
Estimated useful life of machine (scrap value $0)	8 years
Estimated residual value of machine at end of lease term	$9 000
Residual value guarantee by Silver Ltd	$5 000
Interest rate implicit in the lease	10%
The lease is classified as a finance lease by Gold Ltd.	

The annual lease payment includes an amount of $7000 to cover annual maintenance and insurance costs. Actual executory costs for each of the 5 years were as follows.

2022–23	$7 400
2023–24	7 900
2024–25	7 700
2025–26	7 300
2026–27	7 200

Silver Ltd may cancel the lease but will incur a penalty equivalent to 2 years' payments if it does so. Silver Ltd intends to lease a new machine at the end of the lease term. The end of the reporting period for both companies is 30 June.

Required
1. Prepare a schedule of lease payments for Silver Ltd.
2. Prepare the general journal entries to record the lease transactions for the year ended 30 June 2023 in the records of Silver Ltd.
3. Prepare a schedule of lease receipts for Gold Ltd.
4. Prepare the general journal entries to record the lease transactions for the year ended 30 June 2023 in the records of Gold Ltd.

10.19 Lease classification, lease accounting ★ ★   **LO2, 6**

Ascot Ltd enters into a 5-year agreement to lease an item of machinery from Eton Ltd on 1 July 2022. Ascot Ltd incurred costs of $3928 in setting up the lease agreement. The machinery has a fair value of $492 000 at the inception of the lease and it is expected to have an economic life of 6 years, after which time it will have a residual value of $45 000. The lease agreement details are as follows.

Length of lease	5 years
Commencement date	1 July 2022
Annual lease payment, payable 30 June each year commencing 30 June 2023	$110 000
Residual value at the end of the lease term	$100 000
Residual value guarantee by Ascot Ltd	$60 000
Interest rate implicit in the lease	6%
The lease is cancellable without any penalties.	

All insurance and maintenance costs are paid by Eton Ltd and are expected to amount to $10 000 per year and will be reimbursed by Ascot Ltd by being included in the annual lease payment of $110 000. The machinery will be depreciated on a straight-line basis. It is expected that Ascot Ltd will return the machinery to Eton Ltd at the end of the lease.

Required

1. Calculate the initial direct costs incurred by Ascot Ltd to negotiate the lease agreement.
2. Prepare the journal entries to account for the lease in the books of Ascot Ltd for the year ended 30 June 2023.
3. Prepare a schedule of lease receipts for Eton Ltd.
4. Prepare the journal entries to account for the lease in the books of Eton Ltd for the year ended 30 June 2023.

ACKNOWLEDGEMENTS

Photo: © RBFried / Getty Images

Text: © 2019 Australian Accounting Standards Board (AASB). The text, graphics and layout of this publication are protected by Australian copyright law and the comparable law of other countries. No part of the publication may be reproduced, stored or transmitted in any form or by any means without the prior written permission of the AASB except as permitted by law. For reproduction or publication, permission should be sought in writing from the AASB. Requests in the first instance should be addressed to the National Director, Australian Accounting Standards Board, PO Box 204, Collins Street West, Victoria 8007.

Text: © IFRS. This publication contains copyright material of the IFRS Foundation in respect of which all rights are reserved. Reproduced by John Wiley & Sons Australia, Ltd with the permission of the IFRS Foundation. No permission granted to third parties to reproduce or distribute. For full access to IFRS Standards and the work of the IFRS Foundation please visit http://eifrs.ifrs.org. The International Accounting Standards Board, the IFRS Foundation, the authors and the publishers do not accept responsibility for any loss caused by acting or refraining from acting in reliance on the material in this publication, whether such loss is caused by negligence or otherwise.

CHAPTER 11

Financial instruments

CHAPTER AIM

This chapter explains: the principles for classifying financial instruments into financial assets, financial liabilities or equity instruments; the principles for the recognition and measurement of financial assets and financial liabilities; and the required disclosures for financial instruments.

LEARNING OBJECTIVES

After studying this chapter, you should be able to:

11.1 define a financial instrument

11.2 define a financial asset

11.3 define a financial liability

11.4 explain what is meant by a derivative and an embedded derivative

11.5 define an equity instrument

11.6 distinguish between financial liabilities and equity instruments

11.7 explain the concept of a compound financial instrument

11.8 explain the consequential effects of financial instrument classifications for dividends, interest, and gains and losses

11.9 describe the criteria for the recognition of a financial asset or financial liability

11.10 describe the conditions under which a financial asset and a financial liability must be offset

11.11 describe the requirements for the derecognition of a financial asset or a financial liability

11.12 outline the requirements for the initial measurement of a financial asset or a financial liability

11.13 outline the requirements for the subsequent measurement of a financial asset

11.14 describe the expected loss model for impairment of financial assets

11.15 outline the requirements for the subsequent measurement of a financial liability

11.16 summarise the disclosures required for financial instruments.

CONCEPTS FOR REVIEW

Before studying this chapter, you should understand and, if necessary, revise:
- the definition of an asset in the *Conceptual Framework*
- the definition of a liability in the *Conceptual Framework*.

11.1 Introduction to financial instruments

LEARNING OBJECTIVE 11.1 Define a financial instrument.

Accounting for financial instruments is governed primarily by:
- AASB 132/IAS 32 *Financial Instruments: Presentation*
- AASB 7/IFRS 7 *Financial Instruments: Disclosures*
- AASB 9/IFRS 9 *Financial Instruments*.

Paragraph 11 of AASB 132/IAS 32 defines a **financial instrument** as:

> any contract that gives rise to a financial asset of one entity and a financial liability or equity instrument of another entity.

Figure 11.1 highlights how the definition is two-sided: the contract must result in one party obtaining a financial asset and another party obtaining a financial liability or equity instrument.

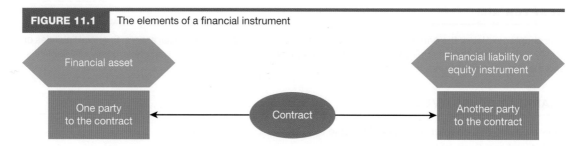

FIGURE 11.1 The elements of a financial instrument

A simple example of a financial instrument is a loan contract between a bank and its customer. The contract gives rise to a financial asset to the bank — being the right to receive cash — and a financial liability to the customer — being the obligation to pay cash.

11.1.1 Transactions that result in financial instruments

The definition of financial instruments is far-reaching. Financial instruments ultimately lead to the receipt or payment of cash or issue of an equity instrument between parties. Paragraph AG15 of AASB 132/IAS 32 separates financial instruments into:
- contracts where there are *primary instruments*, such as cash, receivables, investments and payables
- contracts where there are *derivative instruments*, such as financial options, futures and forward exchange contracts.

In contrast to primary instruments, derivative instruments (or derivatives) are instruments that *derive* their value from an underlying item, such as a share price index or interest rates.

Financial instruments may relate to singular instruments where a contract gives rise to a single financial asset, financial liability or equity instrument, such as a loan receivable, loan payable or ordinary share issued. Alternatively, financial instruments may include compound instruments where there is a combination of a financial asset, financial liability or equity instrument. An example of a compound instrument is the issue of convertible notes by a company as follows.
- The obligation to make payments of interest and principal on the convertible notes is a *financial liability*.
- The conversion option that may require the company to issue shares is an *equity instrument*.

As noted in paragraph AG7 of AASB 132/IAS 32, a contractual right or obligation to exchange financial instruments or a chain of such contractual rights and obligations is itself a financial instrument because ultimately it will lead to the receipt or payment of cash or issue of an equity instrument between the parties. It is clear from figure 11.1 that the definition of financial instrument is linked to the definitions of financial asset, financial liability and equity instrument. These definitions are explained in section 11.2.

11.1.2 Transactions that do not result in financial instruments

The following are *not* financial instruments.
- The purchase or lease of non-financial assets (e.g. inventories, property, plant and equipment or patents) (paragraph AG10 of AASB 132/IAS 32)

- Contracts that involve the prepayment of cash for goods or services (the rights and obligations relate to goods and services rather than cash; that is, financial assets and financial liabilities are not created) (AASB 132/IAS 32 paragraph AG11)
- Commodity contracts that are settled by the delivery of a non-financial asset (e.g. a forward contract to buy or sell oil, coal, iron ore, cotton, wheat or sheep that is settled only by the delivery of the physical item) (AASB 132/IAS 32 paragraph AG20)
- Rights or obligations that result from statutory requirements imposed by governments, such as tax liabilities (these rights or obligations are *not contractual*) (AASB 132/IAS 32 paragraph AG12)
- Environmental obligations imposed by governments on mining companies to restore or rehabilitate land after mining activities have ceased (AASB 132/IAS 32 paragraph AG12)
- Most warranty obligations of manufacturers (customers have rights to repairs or replacement rather than rights to a financial asset such as cash) (AASB 132/IAS 32 paragraph AG11)

Paragraph 4 of AASB 132/IAS 32 deems that certain items lie outside the scope of the accounting standards for financial instruments. The exclusions include rights or obligations relating to employee benefits, insurance contracts, share-based payment transactions, and interests in subsidiaries, associates and joint ventures.

LEARNING CHECK

- ☐ A financial instrument is any contract that gives rise to a financial asset of one entity and a financial liability or equity instrument of another entity.
- ☐ Financial instruments do not include cash transactions for the purchase or lease of physical or intangible assets, prepayments for goods or services, contracts settled by the delivery of commodities, or rights and obligations imposed by statute.
- ☐ Financial instruments ultimately lead to the receipt or payment of cash or issue of an equity instrument between parties.
- ☐ Financial instruments may involve primary financial instruments (e.g. receivables) or derivative financial instruments (e.g. option contracts) or may relate to singular instruments (e.g. shares) or compound instruments (e.g. convertible notes).

11.2 Financial assets

LEARNING OBJECTIVE 11.2 Define a financial asset.

A **financial asset** is defined in paragraph 11 of AASB 132/IAS 32 as:

> any asset that is:
> (a) cash;
> (b) an equity instrument of another entity;
> (c) a contractual right:
> (i) to receive cash or another financial asset from another entity; or
> (ii) to exchange financial assets or financial liabilities with another entity under conditions that are potentially favourable to the entity; or
> (d) a contract that will or may be settled in the entity's own equity instruments and is:
> (i) a non-derivative for which the entity is or may be obliged to receive a variable number of the entity's own equity instruments; or
> (ii) a derivative that will or may be settled other than by the exchange of a fixed amount of cash or another financial asset for a fixed number of the entity's own equity instruments.

Certain contracts settled in the entity's own equity instruments are excluded from the part (d)(ii) definition of financial asset because the contracts do not carry **financial risk**. The exclusions relate to:
- puttable financial instruments classified as equity instruments
- instruments that impose on the entity an obligation to deliver to another party a pro rata share of the net assets of the entity only on liquidation
- instruments that are contracts for the future receipt or delivery of the entity's own equity instruments.

These instruments only carry **equity risk** — that is, the risk of changes in value of the equitable or residual interest in net assets — and therefore the contracts give rise to equity instruments rather than financial assets.

A puttable financial instrument gives the holder the right to put the instrument back to the issuer for cash or another financial asset or is automatically put back on the occurrence of some future event. In contrast, a non-puttable financial instrument cannot be put back to the issuer.

Figure 11.2 provides examples for each of the categories (a) to (d) of the financial asset definition.

FIGURE 11.2	Examples of financial assets
Definition	**Examples**
Paragraph 11(a)	Cash on hand Deposit of cash with a bank or similar financial institution
Paragraph 11(b)	Shares held in another entity
Paragraph 11(c)(i)	Trade receivables Loans or advances to other entities Bills of exchange held Promissory notes held Secured, unsecured or convertible notes held Debentures held Bonds held Right to cash from a guarantor
Paragraph 11(c)(ii)	Purchased call or put options for shares in another entity Interest rate or currency rate swap agreements Forward exchange contracts Forward rate agreements Futures contracts
Paragraph 11(d)(i)	A contract to receive at a future date as many of the entity's own equity instruments as are equal in value to $100 million
Paragraph 11(d)(ii)	A contract to receive at a future date a variable number of the entity's own equity instruments as are equal in value to 100 ounces of gold at that date

11.3 Financial liabilities

LEARNING OBJECTIVE 11.3 Define a financial liability.

A **financial liability** is defined in paragraph 11 of AASB 132/IAS 32 as:

> any liability that is:
> (a) a contractual obligation:
>   (i) to deliver cash or another financial asset to another entity; or
>   (ii) to exchange financial assets or financial liabilities with another entity under conditions that are potentially unfavourable to the entity; or
> (b) a contract that will or may be settled in the entity's own equity instruments and is:
>   (i) a non-derivative for which the entity is or may be obliged to deliver a variable number of the entity's own equity instruments; or

(ii) a derivative that will or may be settled other than by the exchange of a fixed amount of cash or another financial asset for a fixed number of the entity's own equity instruments. For this purpose, rights, options or warrants to acquire a fixed number of the entity's own equity instruments for a fixed amount of any currency are equity instruments if the entity offers the rights, options or warrants pro rata to all of its existing owners of the same class of its own non-derivative equity instruments.

The entity's own equity instruments that are excluded from part (d)(ii) of the financial asset definition are also excluded from part (b)(ii) of the definition of financial liability; for example, puttable financial instruments classified as equity instruments. The excluded contracts give rise to equity instruments rather than financial liabilities because there is equity risk instead of financial risk.

Figure 11.3 sets out examples for each of the two categories (a) and (b) of the financial liability definition.

FIGURE 11.3	Examples of financial liabilities

Definition	Examples
Paragraph 11(a)(i)	Bank overdraft Trade payables Loans or advances from other entities Bills of exchange issued Promissory notes issued Secured, unsecured or convertible notes issued Debentures issued Redeemable preference shares issued Obligation to pay cash as a guarantor
Paragraph 11(a)(ii)	Sold call or put options for shares in another entity Interest rate or currency rate swap agreements Forward exchange contracts Forward rate agreements Exchange traded futures contracts
Paragraph 11(b)(i)	A contract to deliver at a future date as many of the entity's own equity instruments as are equal in value to $100 million
Paragraph 11(b)(ii)	A contract to deliver at a future date as many of the entity's own equity instruments as are equal in value to 100 ounces of gold at that date

Paragraph 19 of AASB 132/IAS 32 explains that whenever an entity may be required to deliver cash or another financial asset under the terms of the contract the definition of a financial liability is satisfied. If the contract includes an unconditional right to avoid delivering cash or another financial asset, the financial instrument is classified as equity by the issuer. An unconditional right to avoid delivering cash or another financial asset does not arise merely because the contractual obligations are subject to restrictions or are conditional on the counterparty exercising a right to redeem. Paragraph 20 of AASB 132/IAS 32 notes that a financial instrument may explicitly establish a contractual obligation to deliver cash or another financial asset or establish an obligation indirectly through its terms and conditions. An example of creating an obligation indirectly is a contract allowing for settlement by a variety of means with conditions that provide an economic reward for the delivery of cash.

LEARNING CHECK

☐ A financial liability is a contractual obligation to deliver cash or another financial asset to another entity, a contractual obligation to exchange financial assets or financial liabilities with another entity under conditions that are potentially unfavourable to the entity, and certain contracts settled in the entity's own equity instruments.

☐ Examples of financial liabilities include bank overdrafts, trade or loan payables, debentures issued, convertible notes issued, sold options and other derivatives such as forward or futures contracts.

11.4 Derivative instruments

LEARNING OBJECTIVE 11.4 Explain what is meant by a derivative and an embedded derivative.

The definitions of financial asset and financial liability include contracts that are derivatives. Appendix A of AASB 9/IFRS 9 defines a **derivative** as a contract with three characteristics:

(a) its value changes in response to the change in [the 'underlying', which may be] a specified interest rate, financial instrument price, commodity price, foreign exchange rate, index of prices or rates, credit rating or credit index, or other variable, provided in the case of a non-financial variable that the variable is not specific to a party to the contract...

(b) it requires no initial net investment or an initial net investment that is smaller than would be required for other types of contracts that would be expected to have a similar response to changes in market factors.

(c) it is settled at a future date.

The many different types of derivative instruments in the marketplace and their variety of different terms or conditions can make derivatives seem complex or difficult to understand. Fundamentally all derivatives *derive* their value from an underlying item such as a share price or an interest rate. Derivative instruments involve contractual rights and obligations that have the effect of transferring between the parties to the instrument one or more of the financial risks inherent in an underlying primary financial instrument.

On inception, derivative financial instruments are potentially favourable to one of the parties to the contract and potentially unfavourable to the other party. Accordingly, the contract for the derivative gives rise to a financial asset to one party and a financial liability to the other party. Typical examples of derivatives are futures and forward contracts, swaps and option contracts. A derivative usually has a notional amount, which is an amount of currency, a number of shares or other units specified in a contract.

Illustrative example 11.1 demonstrates how an option contract works. A call (put) option contract gives the holder right to buy (sell) a specified quantity of the underlying at a pre-determined price. The value of the option is affected by changes in value of the underlying. Option contracts usually require a premium to be paid that is less than what would be required to purchase the underlying shares or other underlying financial instruments and they are settled (unless they lapse unexercised). Thus, option contracts meet the definition of a derivative.

ILLUSTRATIVE EXAMPLE 11.1

Call option contract

In simple terms, parties to derivative financial instruments are 'taking bets' on what will happen to the price of an underlying financial instrument in the future. This example is based on a call option to purchase shares in Company Z at $3 per share. Party A acquires the call option, which is written by Party B. Party A is betting that the share price of Company Z will rise above the exercise price of $3 before the option expires, whereas Party B is betting that it will not.

Party A buys a call option from Party B that entitles it to purchase 1000 shares in Company Z at $3 per share at a specified date 6 months in the future. The shares in Company Z are the *underlying* from which the option derives its value. The option is thus a derivative financial instrument. The price at which the holder of the option may purchase the shares is known as the *exercise price* of the *option*. The amount paid for the call option by Party A is known as the option *premium*. Party A is known as the *holder* of the call option, and Party B is known as the *writer* of the call option. The date when the contract is settled is referred to as the *exercise date*.

The contract creates a contractual right for Party A to purchase the 1000 shares in Company Z at $3 per share. The contractual right is a financial asset to Party A because it may be able to acquire shares under conditions that are potentially favourable; for example, if the market price of Company Z shares increases to $4 by the exercise date, Party A will have a right to a favourable exchange because it can pay $3 per share for shares that are worth $4 per share. In contrast, the contract creates a contractual obligation for Party B to sell the shares in Company Z to Party A at $3 per share. The contractual obligation is a financial liability to Party B because it may be required to exchange the shares under potentially unfavourable conditions; for example, if the market price of Company Z shares increases to $4 by the exercise date, Party B will have an obligation to sell shares for only $3, making a loss of $1 per share.

If the share price rises above $3 after the contract is entered into, the call option is termed 'in the money'. Party A is not compelled to exercise its call option at the exercise date even if it is in the money. From Party A's perspective, it has a right to exercise the call option should it so choose. Once Party A exercises

---

its option, however, Party B is compelled to deliver the shares under the contractual obligation. If the share price is less than the exercise price of $3 the call option is termed 'out of the money'. If the option is out of the money at the exercise date, then the call option will lapse. Party A would not benefit from exercising the option if the exercise price is higher than the market price.

The nature of the holder's right and of the writer's obligation is not affected by the likelihood that the option will be exercised. The call option has a value before the exercise date even when it is out of the money because of the effects of discounting and the variability of the share price over time; for example, the share price may be $2 at the date of the contract but it is possible that the price will change to $4 at the exercise date.

Party B might decide to hedge its bet with Party A by entering into a further option contract with another party to purchase the shares at $3.50 on the same exercise date. The financial effect of the additional contract is that Party B ensures that it cannot lose more than $0.50 a share on its contract with Party A. Often a series of derivative financial instruments will be created in this way to create a desired risk position in the underlying financial asset.

11.4.1 Hybrid contracts with embedded derivatives

Derivatives may exist on a standalone basis, or they may be embedded in other financial instruments. Paragraph 4.3.1 of AASB 9/IFRS 9 defines an **embedded derivative** as:

> a component of a hybrid contract that also includes a non-derivative host — with the effect that some of the cash flows of the combined instrument vary in a way similar to a stand-alone derivative.

An embedded derivative cannot be contractually detached from the host contract, nor can it have a different counterparty from that of the host instrument.

Paragraph 4.3.3 of AASB 9/IFRS 9 specifies that if the host contract is not a financial asset, the embedded derivative must be accounted for separately if all of the following conditions are met:

(a) the economic characteristics and risks of the embedded derivative are not closely related to the economic characteristics and risks of the host;

(b) a separate instrument with the same terms as the embedded derivative would meet the definition of a derivative; and

(c) the hybrid contract is not measured at fair value with changes in fair value recognised in profit or loss (i.e. a derivative that is embedded in a financial liability at fair value through profit or loss is not separated).

Examples of embedded derivatives that may meet these three conditions include:

- a put option embedded in a debt instrument allowing the holder to require the issuer to take back the instrument for an amount of cash that varies on the basis of the change in an equity or commodity price or index; the host is a debt instrument and the variables for the embedded derivative are not related to the debt instrument
- an equity conversion feature embedded in a host convertible debt instrument; for example, a convertible note that includes an option to convert the note into a fixed number of ordinary shares of the issuer
- an option to extend the remaining term to maturity of a debt instrument without a concurrent adjustment to the market rate of interest at the time of the extension
- commodity-indexed interest or principal payments embedded in a host debt instrument or insurance contract by which the amount of interest or principal is indexed to the price of the commodity (e.g. gold).

LEARNING CHECK

☐ A derivative is a contract where the value of the contract changes in response to an underlying variable, there is little or no net investment required at the outset and settlement is a future date.

☐ The underlying variable of a derivative instrument may include a specified interest rate, financial instrument price, commodity price, foreign exchange rate, or index of prices or rates.

☐ A call option contract written over shares is one example of a derivative instrument. The holder or buyer of the call option has a contractual right to acquire shares with another party under conditions that are potentially favourable, while the writer or seller of the call option has a contractual obligation to sell shares under potentially unfavourable conditions.

▶

> ☐ An embedded derivative is a component of a hybrid contract that includes a non-derivative host with the effect that some of the cash flows of the combined instrument vary in a way similar to a standalone derivative. The embedded conversion option of a convertible note is an example of an embedded derivative.

11.5 What is an equity instrument?

LEARNING OBJECTIVE 11.5 Define an equity instrument.

Paragraph 11 of AASB 132/IAS 32 defines an **equity instrument** as:

> any contract that evidences a residual interest in the assets of an entity after deducting all of its liabilities.

Ordinary shares issued that cannot be put back to the company, referred to as non-puttable ordinary shares, are the most common type of equity instrument. The shareholders are not entitled to a fixed return on their investment but hold an equitable interest or residual interest in the net assets of the company. In a winding up, the shareholders are entitled to the balance that remains after all assets are realised and all liabilities are settled. Similarly, the periodic returns or dividends distributed to shareholders are usually out of profits after interest obligations have been met. Dividends should not be distributed to shareholders if a company does not have sufficient assets to meet its liabilities.

Paragraphs AG13 and AG14 of AASB 132/IAS 32 provide other examples of equity instruments, such as:

- warrants or call options issued that allow the holder to purchase a fixed number of non-puttable ordinary shares at a fixed amount of cash or another financial asset
- puttable financial instruments classified as equity instruments
- instruments that impose on the entity an obligation to deliver to another party a pro rata share of the net assets of the entity only on liquidation classified as equity instruments
- preference shares that do not carry an unconditional right to cash or other financial assets
- purchased call options that give the entity the right to reacquire a fixed number of its own equity instruments in exchange for a fixed amount of cash or another financial asset.

Paragraph 26 of AASB 132/IAS 32 clarifies that a derivative financial instrument allowing one party a choice over how it is settled is a financial asset or a financial liability unless all of the settlement alternatives would result in it being an equity instrument. An example is a share option that the issuer can decide to settle net in cash or by exchanging its own equity instruments. The option must be classified as a financial asset or liability because not all of the settlement options would result in equity instruments being issued. The fact that cash settlement may be required is sufficient to create a financial asset or liability.

LEARNING CHECK

> ☐ An equity instrument is a contract that evidences a residual interest in the assets of an entity after deducting all of its liabilities.
> ☐ Examples of an equity instrument include non-puttable ordinary shares, and warrants or call options that allow the holder to purchase a fixed number of non-puttable ordinary shares for a fixed amount of cash or another financial asset.

11.6 Distinguishing between financial liabilities and equity instruments

LEARNING OBJECTIVE 11.6 Distinguish between financial liabilities and equity instruments.

The distinction between financial liabilities and equity instruments is a key practical issue in accounting for financial instruments. In general, a company will prefer an equity classification because instruments included in liabilities may have adverse financial effects. If financial instruments, such as preference shares issued by the entity, are classified as liabilities:

- periodic payments on the instruments are treated as borrowing costs (i.e. interest) instead of dividends, thereby reducing reported profits

- debt covenants with financial institutions relating to gearing, solvency and other financial ratios may be breached as a result of the higher reported leverage caused by the inclusion of the financial instruments as debt
- a financial institution may breach regulatory requirements for capital adequacy that require it to maintain a certain level of capital, calculated by reference to net assets.

Paragraph 15 of AASB 132/IAS 32 requires the issuer of a financial instrument to classify the instrument, or its component parts, on initial recognition as a financial liability, a financial asset or an equity instrument in accordance with the substance of the contractual arrangement and the definitions of financial liability, financial asset and equity instrument.

An instrument can only be classified as an equity instrument if it does not include any of the conditions in the definition of financial liability; for example, the instrument cannot include any contractual obligations to deliver cash or another financial asset to another entity or to exchange financial assets or liabilities with another entity under conditions that are potentially unfavourable (AASB 132/IAS 32 paragraph 16). In effect, an instrument must only be classified as an equity instrument if the only risk that attaches to the instrument is 'equity risk'; that is, the risk of changes in value of the equitable or residual interest in the company.

11.6.1 Ordinary shares and preference shares

The substance of contractual arrangements governs the classification of a financial instrument to the issuer. Some financial instruments, such as preference shares, take the legal form of equity but are liabilities in substance (AASB 132/IAS 32 paragraph 18). Preference shares may be issued with various rights and these rights must be assessed to determine whether the shares are classified as a financial liability or an equity instrument (AASB 132/IAS 32 paragraph AG25). Redeemable preference shares give the holder the right to put the shares back to the issuing company for cash. Non-redeemable preference shares do not give this right.

Illustrative example 11.2 presents an example of the classification of share issues from the perspective of the issuing company in accordance with the contractual rights.

ILLUSTRATIVE EXAMPLE 11.2

Share issues from the perspective of the issuing company

Alberto Ltd intends to raise $1 million by issuing one million shares at an issue price of $1 each. It is considering a range of different alternatives for the type of share issue.

1. Ordinary shares

The holders of the ordinary shares are not entitled to any fixed return on, or of, their investment. In a winding up, the shareholders only receive the residual after the company's liabilities have been settled including the interest and principal on debt commitments. In accordance with paragraph 11 of AASB 132/IAS 32, the ordinary shares meet the definition of an equity instrument. The entries of Alberto Ltd to record the issue are as follows.

| Cash (financial asset) | Dr | 1 000 000 | |
| Ordinary share capital (equity) | Cr | | 1 000 000 |

2. Discretionary distributions, non-redeemable preference shares

The holders of the preference shares are entitled to a non-cumulative dividend of 5% annually at the discretion of the company. Non-cumulative means that the dividend for a particular year does not carry forward if the dividend is not paid. The preference shares are non-redeemable, which means the holders have no contractual right to return the shares to the issuer for cash. The preference shareholders rank ahead of ordinary shareholders in the event of a winding-up of the company. Paragraph AG26 of AASB 132/IAS 32 indicates that the preference shares issued will meet the definition of an equity instrument as the obligation to deliver cash to the holders is at the discretion of the company. The entries of Alberto Ltd to record the issue are as follows.

Cash (financial asset)	Dr	1 000 000	
Preference share capital (equity)	Cr		1 000 000

3. Non-discretionary distributions, redeemable (mandatory) preference shares

The holders of the preference shares are entitled to a cumulative dividend of 5% annually, which means that the entitlement to the dividend for a particular year carries forward if the dividend is not paid. The preference shares are mandatorily redeemable for cash after 5 years. There is an obligation to the holders to deliver cash for the return of capital after 5 years. In substance, the arrangement is akin to a 5-year loan at 5% p.a. Paragraph AG25 of AASB 132/IAS 32 indicates that the preference shares will meet the definition of a financial liability as there is a non-discretionary obligation to deliver cash to the holders. The entries of Alberto Ltd to record the issue are as follows.

Cash (financial asset)	Dr	1 000 000	
Preference share liability (financial liability)	Cr		1 000 000

4. Conditional distributions, redeemable (option of the holder) preference shares

The holders of the preference shares are entitled to a cumulative dividend of 5% annually subject to conditions including profitability and the shares are redeemable for cash at specific dates at the option of the holder. Accordingly, the holders are guaranteed a periodic return of 5% p.a. subject to profitability and can require the initial cash contributed be returned. Paragraph AG25 of AASB 132/IAS 32 indicates that the preference shares meet the definition of a financial liability as there are non-discretionary obligations in respect of dividends and return of capital. The entries of Alberto Ltd to record the issue are as follows.

Cash (financial asset)	Dr	1 000 000	
Preference share capital (equity)	Cr		1 000 000

5. Conditional distributions, redeemable (option of the issuer) preference shares

The holders of the preference shares are entitled to a cumulative dividend of 5% annually subject to conditions including profitability and the shares are redeemable for cash at the option of the issuing company. In this case, there is an obligation to the preference shareholders but only in respect of dividends. The intention to make distributions of dividends does not affect the classification of the shares. The company cannot be required to return the initial cash contribution. Redemption is at the discretion of the company and thus the preference shares are equity instruments (AASB 132/IAS 32 paragraph AG26). The entries of Alberto Ltd to record the issue are as follows.

Cash (financial asset)	Dr	1 000 000	
Preference share capital (equity)	Cr		1 000 000

11.6.2 Contingent settlement provisions

A financial instrument that requires an entity to deliver cash or other financial assets may have **contingent settlement provisions** — terms of settlement that are dependent on the occurrence of uncertain future events beyond the control of both the issuer and the holder. Examples of such events include changes in a share market index, the consumer price index or the issuer's future revenues. Paragraph 25 of AASB 132/IAS 32 explains that the issuer of such an instrument does not have the unconditional right to avoid delivering cash or other financial assets, which means the instrument should be classified as a financial liability. An example is preference shares that the holder can redeem for cash if, and only if, the annual revenues of the issuer fall below a specified level. In this instance, the issuer does not have an unconditional right to avoid the delivery of cash, and the preference shares must be recognised as a financial liability.

11.6.3 Contracts involving a company's own equity instruments

As stated in paragraph 21 of AASB 132/IAS 32:

> A contract is not an equity instrument solely because it may result in the receipt or delivery of the entity's own equity instruments.

Paragraph 21 of AASB 132/IAS 32 goes on to explain that a contractual obligation to deliver a variable number of the company's ordinary shares in exchange for cash or another financial asset gives rise to a financial liability rather than an equity instrument. This is because the obligation is not consistent with a residual interest in net assets. Likewise, a contractual obligation that requires a company to exchange a fixed number of its ordinary shares in exchange for a variable amount of cash or another financial asset results in a financial liability, not an equity instrument (paragraph 24). A contract that requires a company to repurchase its ordinary shares for cash or another financial asset will also usually give rise to a financial liability (paragraph 23). In contrast, a contract that will be settled by the delivery of a fixed number of a company's ordinary shares in exchange for a fixed amount of cash or another financial asset is ordinarily an equity instrument (paragraph 22).

Illustrative example 11.3 presents the classification of a company's contractual obligation to sell its own ordinary shares.

ILLUSTRATIVE EXAMPLE 11.3

Obligation for forward sale of a company's shares

Paludetto Ltd enters a forward contract to sell its own ordinary shares after seven months at a fixed forward price. The company has a contractual obligation based on the market price at the maturity date and in exchange it has a contractual right based on the forward price. The company is considering a range of alternatives for the settlement of the contract. Details of the contract include:

Contract date	1 January 2023
Maturity date	31 July 2023
Market price per share on 1 January 2023	$10
Market price per share on 30 June 2023	$13
Market price per share on 31 July 2023	$16
Fixed forward price per share on 31 July 2023	$14
Present value of forward price on 1 January 2023	$10
Number of shares under the forward contract	1 000 000
Fair value of forward contract on 1 January 2023	$nil
Fair value of forward contract on 30 June 2023	Negative $1.5 million
Fair value of forward contract on 31 July 2023	Negative $2 million

1. Net cash settlement

The contract is settled net in cash based on the difference between the forward price and market price at that time. A financial liability equal to the negative value of the contract is recognised at the end of the reporting period of 30 June. The entries of Paludetto Ltd are:

June 30	Loss on forward	Dr	1 500 000	
	Forward liability (financial liability)	Cr		1 500 000
July 31	Loss on forward	Dr	500 000	
	Forward liability (financial liability)	Dr	1 500 000	
	Cash (1 000 000 shares × ($16 − $14))	Cr		2 000 000

2. Net share settlement

The contract is settled net in shares by as many shares as is required at maturity; that is, the contract is for a variable number of shares. A financial liability equal to the negative value of the contract is recognised

▶

---

at the end of the reporting period of 30 June. There is only an equity instrument when shares are issued at maturity to settle the contract. The entries of Paludetto Ltd are as follows.

June 30	Loss on forward	Dr	1 500 000	
	Forward liability (financial liability)	Cr		1 500 000
July 31	Loss on forward	Dr	500 000	
	Forward liability (financial liability)	Dr	1 500 000	
	Share capital (125 000 shares × $16)	Cr		2 000 000

3. Shares for cash (gross physical settlement)

The contract is settled by receiving a fixed amount of cash in exchange for a fixed number of shares. In this case, the contract is settled by the physical delivery of 1 000 000 shares and there is no financial liability at the end of the reporting period of 30 June. The entries of Paludetto Ltd are as follows.

June 30	No entry			
July 31	Cash	Dr	14 000 000	
	Share capital (1 000 000 shares × $14)	Cr		14 000 000

4. Settlement options

The contract can be settled net in cash, net in shares or by the physical delivery of shares. In this case, the contract gives rise to a financial liability at 30 June because the company may have to settle otherwise than by a fixed number of its own equity instruments. The entry of Paludetto Ltd at 30 June is as follows.

| June 30 | Loss on forward | Dr | 1 500 000 | |
| | Forward liability (financial liability) | Cr | | 1 500 000 |

Source: Adapted from AASB 132, Illustrative Example 2, paragraphs IE7–IE11.

LEARNING CHECK

- ☐ The issuer of a financial instrument must classify the instrument or its component parts in accordance with the substance of the contract and the definitions of financial asset, financial liability or equity instrument.
- ☐ An instrument must only be classified as an equity instrument if it does not include any of the conditions in the definition of financial liability.
- ☐ Preference shares should be classified as financial liabilities or equity instruments by the issuer based on the terms and conditions of the issue. Preference shares that are mandatorily redeemable or redeemable at the option of the holder for cash are financial liabilities because there is an obligation to deliver cash. Preference shares that are non-redeemable or redeemable at the option of the issuer are equity instruments.
- ☐ Contracts that include a contingent settlement provision that requires cash to be delivered on the occurrence of some future event are financial liabilities.
- ☐ Contracts involving a company's own equity instruments may give rise to financial liabilities or financial assets if there is net cash settlement or net share settlement.

11.7 Compound financial instruments — convertible notes

LEARNING OBJECTIVE 11.7 Explain the concept of a compound financial instrument.

A **compound financial instrument** has characteristics that are a combination of a financial asset, financial liability or equity instrument. An issuer of a non-derivative financial instrument must determine whether it contains both a liability and an equity component and classify the component parts separately (AASB 132/IAS 32 paragraph 28). A common example of such a financial instrument is a convertible note that entitles the holder to convert the note into a fixed number of ordinary shares of the issuer (AASB 132/IAS 32 paragraph 29). From the perspective of the *issuer*, a convertible note comprises two components:

1. *financial liability*, being a contractual obligation to deliver cash in the form of interest payments and the redemption of the note principal or face value
2. *equity instrument*, being an embedded option giving the holder a right, for a specified period of time, to convert the note into a fixed number of ordinary shares of the issuer. Note that the number of shares to be issued must be fixed, otherwise the option would not meet the definition of an equity instrument.

An issuer of a convertible note must bring the issue to account by recognising a financial liability and an equity instrument. There is no revision of this two-way classification, regardless of any change in the likelihood that the conversion option will be exercised. This is because until the conversion occurs the issuer continues to have a contractual obligation to deliver cash for any interest and principal (AASB 132/IAS 32 paragraph 30).

Paragraphs 31–32 of AASB 132/IAS 32 require that the proceeds from the issue of a convertible note be allocated between the financial liability and equity components using a residual valuation method as follows.

- The financial liability component is determined as the fair value of a similar liability without the option to convert to an equity instrument. In other words, the financial liability component equals the present value of the interest and principal commitments of a non-convertible debt instrument using a discount rate appropriate to a similar term, similar credit status of the issuer and similar cash flows.
- The equity component is determined as the residual; that is, the difference, at the date of issue, between the fair value of the financial instrument (i.e. the proceeds from the note issue) and the present value of the interest and principal for the financial liability component.

Illustrative example 11.4 demonstrates the application of the residual valuation method.

ILLUSTRATIVE EXAMPLE 11.4

Accounting for convertible notes from the perspective of the issuer

On 1 July 2022, Robbo Ltd issues 2000 convertible notes. The notes have a 3-year term and are issued at a face value of $1000 per note resulting in total proceeds at the date of issue of $2 million. The notes pay interest at 6% p.a. annually in arrears. The holder of each note is entitled to convert the note into 100 ordinary shares of Robbo Ltd at specified dates.

When Robbo Ltd issues the convertible notes, the prevailing market interest rate for similar debt without conversion options is 9% p.a. The holders of the convertible notes are prepared to accept a lower interest rate given the implicit value of the conversion option.

Robbo Ltd calculates the present value of the contractual cash flows of the interest and principal for the note using the market interest rate of equivalent debt to measure the financial liability component and then deducts this amount from the note proceeds to determine the residual value of the conversion option.

Present value of principal: $2 million × 0.7722* [$T_1$, 9%, 3y]	$1 544 400
Present value of interest stream: $120 000 × 2.5313* [$T_2$, 9%, 3y]	303 756
Total liability component	1 848 156
Equity component (by deduction)	151 844
Proceeds of the note issue	$2 000 000

*From PV tables.

The entries of Robbo Ltd to record the issue are as follows.

Cash (financial asset)	Dr	2 000 000	
Convertible note liability (financial liability)	Cr		1 848 156
Option to convert notes (equity)	Cr		151 844

The option component is not subsequently remeasured and remains at $151 844. When a convertible note is converted into ordinary shares the remaining liability component for the note is transferred to share capital (AASB 132/IAS 32 paragraph AG32). The equity component remains in equity but may be transferred to a different line item within equity, such as retained earnings. If the conversion of all the notes occurred at the end of the 3-year term, the discount on the financial liability will have fully unwound; that is, the carrying amount of the liability and the face value of the notes at the date of conversion will equal $2 million. The entries of Robbo Ltd to record the conversion are as follows.

Convertible note liability (financial liability)	Dr	2 000 000	
Ordinary share capital (equity)	Cr		2 000 000

When a convertible note is redeemed for cash at maturity, the amount paid is allocated against the liability component, which is thus derecognised. The equity component for the note remains in equity, but may be transferred within equity. The entries of Robbo Ltd to record the redemption are as follows.

Convertible note liability (financial liability)	Dr	2 000 000	
Cash	Cr		2 000 000

When a convertible note is redeemed or repurchased before maturity, without change to the embedded conversion rights (i.e. the conversion rights are surrendered with the notes) the entity must allocate the consideration paid between the liability and equity components. In accordance with paragraph AG33 of AASB 132/IAS 32, the consideration is allocated to the liability component, based on its fair value, with the residual of the consideration allocated to the equity component. Gains or losses arising on the redemption or repurchase of the liability component are recognised in profit while the amount of consideration allocated to the equity component is recognised directly in equity (AASB 132/IAS 32 paragraph AG34).

A demonstration problem at the end of the chapter demonstrates the accounting approach if convertible notes are redeemed for cash before the maturity date.

Source: Adapted from AASB 132, Illustrative Example 9, paragraphs IE35–IE36.

LEARNING CHECK

☐ The issuer of a compound financial instrument must separately recognise any financial asset, financial liability and equity components.

☐ The issuer of convertible notes must, at initial recognition, separate the proceeds from the issue into the component parts of the financial instrument (i.e. a financial liability and an equity instrument) using the residual valuation method.

☐ In the residual valuation method, the financial liability component of a convertible note issue is measured as the fair value of an equivalent debt instrument without an embedded conversion option. The equity component is then measured as the residual amount; that is, the difference between the issue proceeds and the amount of the financial liability component.

11.8 Consequential effects of classifications for interest, dividends, gains and losses

LEARNING OBJECTIVE 11.8 Explain the consequential effects of financial instrument classifications for dividends, interest, and gains and losses.

The classification of financial instruments into financial assets, financial liabilities and equity instruments has consequential effects because accounting for the related distributions or gains and losses matches the presentation adopted in the statement of financial position.

Interest, dividends, losses and gains that relate to a financial liability are recognised as income or expense in profit or loss (AASB 132/IAS 32 paragraph 35). If the issuer of redeemable preference shares classifies the issue as a financial liability (e.g. scenarios 3 and 4 in illustrative example 11.2), then the issuer must recognise dividend distributions for these shares as an expense in the profit or loss. Similarly, if the issuer redeems the shares for an amount less than their carrying amount, then the issuer must recognise a gain on redemption in profit or loss.

In contrast, distributions to holders of equity instruments must be debited directly to equity (AASB 132/IAS 32 paragraph 35). If the issuer of redeemable preference shares classifies the issue as an equity instrument (e.g. scenario 5 in illustrative example 11.2), then the issuer must recognise dividend distributions for these shares directly in equity. Similarly, if the issuer redeems the shares for an amount less than their carrying amount, then the issuer must recognise the redemption directly in equity, and any difference remaining after the redemption remains in equity.

Incremental costs that are directly attributable to the issue of an equity instrument, and that would otherwise have been avoided, must be recognised as a deduction in equity (AASB 132/IAS 32 paragraph 37). Examples of such costs include registration and other regulatory fees, legal and accounting fees and stamp duties. Transaction costs for an aborted equity issue where no equity instruments are issued must be recognised in profit or loss.

LEARNING CHECK

☐ The classification of financial instruments has consequential effects because accounting for the related distributions or gains and losses matches the presentation adopted in the statement of financial position.

☐ Interest, dividends, and gains or losses that relate to items classified as financial liabilities are recognised as income or expense in the profit or loss. Accordingly, dividend distributions on mandatorily redeemable preference shares are recognised as an expense in profit or loss.

☐ Dividends or gains and losses on redemption of equity instruments are recognised directly in equity.

11.9 Recognition of financial asset or financial liability

LEARNING OBJECTIVE 11.9 Describe the criteria for the recognition of a financial asset or financial liability.

11.9.1 Subject to contractual provisions

An entity must recognise a financial asset or financial liability in the statement of financial position when it becomes a party to the contractual provisions of the instrument (AASB 9/IFRS 9 paragraph 3.1.1).

The Application Guidance of AASB 9/IFRS 9 (paragraph B3.1.2) sets out examples of the initial recognition requirement, as follows.

(a) Unconditional receivables and payables are recognised as [financial] assets or [financial] liabilities when the entity becomes a party to the contract and, as a consequence, has a legal right to receive or a legal obligation to pay cash. [Normal trade debtors and trade creditors fall into this category.]

(b) Assets to be acquired and liabilities to be incurred as a result of a firm commitment to purchase or sell goods or services are generally not recognised until at least one of the parties has performed under the agreement. [Generally, a liability for goods or services ordered does not arise until the goods or services have been shipped, delivered or rendered.]

(c) A forward contract that is within this scope of this Standard . . . is recognised as an asset or a liability on the commitment date i.e. the date of the contract. When an entity becomes a party to a forward contract, the fair values of the right and obligation are often equal, so that the net fair value of the forward contract is zero. Over the life of the forward contract, however, the rights and obligations are unlikely to be equal in value. If a forward contract has a non-zero fair value at the end of the reporting period, then it must be recognised in the statement of financial position as a financial asset or financial liability.

(d) Option contracts that are within the scope of this Standard are recognised as assets or liabilities when the holder or writer becomes a party to the contract.

(e) Planned future transactions, no matter how likely, are not assets and liabilities because the entity has not become a party to a contract.

11.9.2 Recognition of regular way purchases or sales of a financial asset

Appendix A of AASB 9/IFRS 9 defines a **regular way purchase or sale** as follows.

A purchase or sale of a financial asset under a contract whose terms require delivery of the asset within the time frame established generally by regulation or convention in the marketplace concerned.

An investment company that buys and sells shares through the ASX for its investment portfolio is an example of a regular way sale or purchase of a financial asset. The convention for the ASX marketplace, established by the ASX Operating Rules (Section 3 Trading Rules paragraph 3600), is that a trading participant must settle each trading transaction on the second business day following the date that the trade was executed on the market.

A regular way purchase or sale of financial assets is recognised in the financial statements using either trade date accounting or settlement date accounting. The trade date is the date that an entity commits to purchase or sell an asset; for example, the transaction date that a purchase of shares is reported to the ASX. The settlement date is the date that an asset is delivered to the entity; for example, the second business day after the purchase of shares is reported to the ASX when cash settlement and delivery of the shares occurs.

In trade date accounting, on the trade date, an entity buying a financial asset recognises the asset to be received from the seller and a liability to pay for it, whereas an entity selling a financial asset derecognises the asset to be delivered to the buyer and recognises a receivable and a gain or loss from the sale.

In settlement date accounting, on the settlement date, an entity buying the asset recognises the asset received while an entity selling a financial asset derecognises the asset delivered and recognises a gain or loss from sale. Illustrative example 11.5 highlights the difference between trade date accounting and settlement date accounting in the case of a purchase or sale of shares through the ASX.

ILLUSTRATIVE EXAMPLE 11.5

Trade date accounting versus settlement date accounting

Assume Sundae Ltd purchased shares through the ASX for $8000. On the other side of the trade is Scoop Ltd selling a parcel of shares that originally cost it $5000. The trade date and settlement date accounting for Sundae Ltd buying the financial asset is as follows.

Sundae Ltd buying a financial asset								
	Trade date				Settlement date			
Trade date accounting	Shares	Dr	8 000		Payable	Dr	8 000	
	Payable	Cr		8 000	Cash	Cr		8 000
Settlement date accounting	No entry				Shares	Dr	8 000	
					Cash	Cr		8 000

The trade date and settlement date accounting for Scoop Ltd selling a financial asset is as follows.

Scoop Ltd selling a financial asset								
	Trade date				Settlement date			
Trade date accounting	Receivable	Dr	8 000		Cash	Dr	8 000	
	Shares	Cr		5 000	Receivable	Cr		8 000
	Gain	Cr		3 000				
Settlement date accounting	No entry				Cash	Dr	8 000	
					Shares	Cr		5 000
					Gain	Cr		3 000

The recognition of the financial effects of a purchase or sale of shares will differ depending on whether trade date accounting or settlement date accounting applies. Consider the case where the trade date is 30 June 2023 and the settlement date is 2 July 2023. The statement of financial position of the buying entity as at 30 June 2023 will include the shares as an asset only if trade accounting applies. Similarly, the statement of profit or loss and other comprehensive income of the selling entity for the year to 30 June 2023 will include the gain or loss on the shares sold only if trade date accounting applies.

☐ An entity must recognise a financial asset or a financial liability when it becomes subject to the contractual provisions of the instrument.

☐ Unconditional receivables and payables, forward contracts and option contracts are recognised when an entity becomes a party to the contract.

☐ Firm commitments to purchase or sell goods or services are only recognised when one of the parties to the agreement has performed its contractual commitments.

☐ Planned future transactions are not recognised because there are no contractual provisions.

☐ A regular way purchase or sale of a financial asset requires the delivery of the asset within a time frame generally established by regulation or market convention and it must be recognised in the financial statements using either the trade date or settlement date.

11.10 Offsetting a financial asset and a financial liability

LEARNING OBJECTIVE 11.10 Describe the conditions under which a financial asset and a financial liability must be offset.

Paragraph 42 of AASB 132/IAS 32 requires an entity to offset a financial asset and a financial liability and present the net amount in the statement of financial position when the following two conditions are satisfied.

1. The entity has a current legally enforceable right to set off the recognised amounts.
2. The entity intends either to settle on a net basis, or to realise the asset and settle the liability simultaneously.

The rationale of offsetting (or netting off) a financial asset and a financial liability is that it reflects an entity's expected future cash flows from settling financial instruments (AASB 132/IAS 32 paragraph 43). If an entity has a right to receive or pay a single net amount and intends to do so, in substance there is only a single financial asset or single financial liability for the difference. The right of set-off must be legally enforceable and this usually stems from the terms and conditions of contracts.

Derivative instruments give rise to a financial asset and a financial liability that qualify for offsetting because the relevant contracts provide for settlement of a net position. Examples include a forward contract or a futures contract where an entity offsets its contractual right (a financial asset) against its contractual obligation (a financial liability) and presents the net amount in the statement of financial position. In illustrative example 11.3, the accounting for a forward contract with net cash settlement is based on offsetting. Only the net amount is recognised; that is, the fair value of the contract. The entity has a contractual right to cash based on the sale of shares at the forward price and this is offset against and a contractual obligation to deliver cash based on the market price of the shares at settlement.

Illustrative example 11.6 provides an example of offsetting where there is an agreement between the parties that requires amounts due or owing between them to be offset and settled on a net basis.

ILLUSTRATIVE EXAMPLE 11.6

Offsetting a financial asset and a financial liability

Company X manufactures and sells spare parts for motor vehicles. Company Y is both a customer of Company X and its agent for regional distribution. Accordingly, Company Y purchases goods from Company X on credit terms and invoices Company X for commission receivable under the agency contract. Thus, Company Y is both a trade creditor and a trade debtor of Company X. Under the terms of the agency contract, the parties have agreed to offset accounts payable and accounts receivable and to settle amounts on a net basis. At 30 June 2022 Company X has accounts receivable of $400 000 from Company Y for goods sold on credit terms but also owes accounts payable of $100 000 to Company Y for commission payable under the agency contract. The net amount receivable from Company Y is $300 000, being the excess of the gross receivable of $400 000 over the gross payable of $100 000.

In accordance with paragraph 42 of AASB 132/IAS 32, Company X offsets the accounts payable to Company Y against the accounts receivable from Company Y and presents the net amount of $300 000 in accounts receivable at 30 June 2022.

Paragraph 49 of AASB 132/IAS 32 sets out examples where the conditions for offsetting a financial asset and a financial liability are generally not satisfied, such as:

- synthetic financial instruments where a number of different financial instruments are combined to emulate the features of a single financial instrument (e.g. a series of option contracts that emulates a futures contract)
- financial assets and financial liabilities having the same primary risk exposure that involve different counterparties (e.g. assets and liabilities within a portfolio of derivative instruments)
- financial assets pledged as collateral for non-recourse financial liabilities
- financial liabilities for obligations that are expected to be recovered from a third party because of claims under insurance contracts.

LEARNING CHECK

☐ An entity must offset a financial asset and a financial liability when it has a current legally enforceable right to set off the recognised amounts and it intends either to settle on a net basis, or to realise the asset and settle the liability simultaneously.

☐ Derivative instruments frequently give rise to a financial asset and a financial liability that qualify for offsetting because the relevant contracts provide for settlement of a net position.

11.11 Derecognition of a financial asset or a financial liability

LEARNING OBJECTIVE 11.11 Describe the requirements for the derecognition of a financial asset or a financial liability.

11.11.1 Derecognition of financial asset

Derecognition of a financial asset or financial liability means the asset or liability ceases to qualify for recognition in the statement of financial position. Figure 11.4 shows the detailed conditions for derecognition of a financial asset. Paragraph 3.2.3 of AASB 9/IFRS 9 requires derecognition of a financial asset if:

- the contractual rights to cash flows from the financial asset have expired
- the entity has transferred the financial asset in such a way that it is no longer subject to the risks and rewards of ownership of the financial asset, or
- the entity has transferred the financial asset so that it no longer has control of the asset.

Paragraph B3.2.5 of the Application Guidance of AASB 9/IFRS 9 sets out examples where derecognition is not justified because an entity retains substantially all the risks and rewards of ownership of a financial asset, such as:

- securities lending agreement (i.e. an entity agrees to lend its holdings in a share or other security to a borrower for a specified period of time after which the holding must be returned to it)
- sale of shares by an entity accompanied by a deep in-the-money put option that means the shares are likely to be put back to the seller at a future date
- sale of short-term receivables by an entity accompanied by a guarantee to compensate the purchaser for any credit losses that are likely to occur.

11.11.2 Derecognition of financial liability

Derecognition of a financial liability is required when it is extinguished; that is, when the contractual obligation is discharged or cancelled or has otherwise expired (AASB 9/IFRS 9 paragraph 3.3.1). Derecognition of a financial liability typically occurs when cash consideration is transferred to settle a contractual obligation. If the amount paid on settlement is less than the carrying amount of the financial liability, then a gain is recognised in profit or loss (AASB 9/IFRS 9 paragraph 3.3.2). Derecognition of a financial liability also arises if there are substantial modifications to the terms of a loan contract such that the borrowing entity has effectively exchanged its original financial liability for a new financial liability (AASB 9/IFRS 9 paragraph 3.3.3).

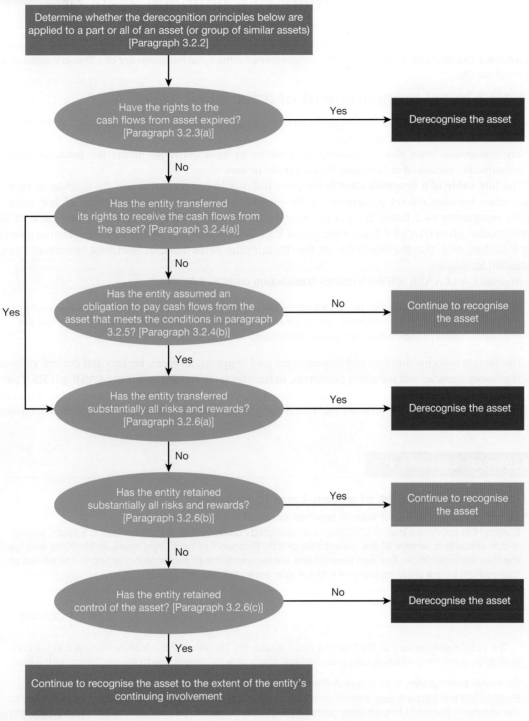

Source: AASB 9, Appendix B, paragraph B3.2.1, p. 79.

11.12 Initial measurement of a financial asset or a financial liability

LEARNING OBJECTIVE 11.12 Outline the requirements for the initial measurement of a financial asset or a financial liability.

11.12.1 Initial measurement of a financial asset

Paragraph 5.1.1 of AASB 9/IFRS 9 requires an entity to initially measure a financial asset as the sum of:
- the fair value of the financial asset, and
- any transaction costs that are directly attributable to its acquisition, unless the financial asset is subsequently measured at fair value through profit or loss.

The **fair value of a financial asset** is the price that would be received to sell the asset in an orderly transaction between market participants at the measurement date. The best evidence of fair value at initial recognition of a financial asset is normally the transaction price; that is, the fair value of the consideration given (AASB 9/IFRS 9 paragraph B5.1.2A). However, if part of the consideration given is for something other than the financial asset, then the fair value of the financial asset must be estimated using valuation techniques.

Appendix A of AASB 9/IFRS 9 defines **transaction costs** as follows.

> Incremental costs that are directly attributable to the acquisition, issue or disposal of a financial asset or financial liability... An incremental cost is one that would not have been incurred if the entity had not acquired, issued or disposed of the financial instrument.

Transaction costs include fees and commissions paid to agents, advisers, brokers and dealers, or levies by regulatory agencies and securities exchanges, or transfer taxes and stamp duties (AASB 9/IFRS 9 paragraph B5.4.8). Transaction costs do not include financing costs or internal administrative or holding costs.

Illustrative example 11.7 presents the initial measurement of a financial asset that is a long-term loan receivable.

ILLUSTRATIVE EXAMPLE 11.7

Initial measurement of a long-term loan asset

(a) Initial measurement of loan to another entity at market interest rate

Busload Ltd provides a loan of $200 000 to an unrelated company. The term of the loan is 5 years. Interest is due annually in arrears at the market rate of 5%. Busload Ltd pays legal costs of $5000 to arrange the loan documentation. The loan receivable is subsequently measured at amortised cost. The entries of Busload Ltd for the initial measurement of the loan receivable are as follows.

Loan receivable (financial asset)	Dr	205 000	
Cash	Cr		205 000

The initial measurement of the financial asset equals the fair value of the loan receivable (i.e. the consideration given for the transaction) plus the legal costs directly attributable to the origination of the loan.

(b) Initial measurement of interest-free loan to employee

Busload Ltd provides a 5-year interest-free loan of $200 000 to an employee as a reward for his loyalty to the company. Busload Ltd pays legal costs of $5000 to arrange the loan documentation. In this case, the fair value of the loan must be calculated by discounting the future cash flows using a market rate of interest for a similar loan. In accordance with paragraph B5.1.1 of the Application Guidance of AASB 9/IFRS 9, the consideration given in excess of the fair value of the loan is accounted for as an expense unless it qualifies for recognition as some other type of asset.

The present value of the future cash flows is $200 000 × 0.7835 [$T_1$, 5%, 5y] = $156 700. There is a difference of $43 300 between the consideration given for the loan (i.e. $200 000) and the fair value of the loan (i.e. $156 700). The journal entries of Busload Ltd for the initial measurement of the loan receivable are as follows.

Loan receivable (financial asset)	Dr	161 700	
Employee expenses	Dr	43 300	
Cash	Cr		205 000

An entity may determine that at initial recognition there is a difference between the transaction price and fair value of a financial asset. If the fair value is based on a quoted price in an active market or a valuation technique that uses data only from observable markets, then the entity recognises the financial asset at fair value and the difference between fair value and transaction price as a gain or loss (AASB 9/IFRS 9 Application Guidance paragraph B5.1.2A). In all other cases, initial recognition of a financial asset at fair value is adjusted for the difference; in effect, any gain or loss is deferred by being included in the recognition of the financial asset at transaction price. The deferred gain or loss may be subsequently amortised to profit or loss if it arises from a factor such as time that is priced by market participants.

Illustrative example 11.8 demonstrates initial measurement where the transaction price of a financial asset is different to fair value.

Gain on initial measurement of a financial asset

On 1 July 2021, Faith Ltd purchases 100 000 shares in Telstra Corporation Limited in an off-market transaction at a price of $4.20 each. On this day, the average market price for a Telstra share is $5.10 and during the day the shares traded in a range between $5.05 and $5.12. Faith Ltd subsequently measures share investments at fair value through the profit or loss.

Required

What are the entries of Faith Ltd for the initial measurement of its investment in the shares?

Solution

1 July 2021 — initial recognition and measurement

Investment in Telstra shares	Dr	510 000	
Gain on purchase of shares	Cr		90 000
Cash	Cr		420 000

The gain on the purchase of shares arises because of the difference between the transaction price and the market price of the Telstra shares and is calculated as 100 000 × ($5.10 − $4.20). The gain arises because the shares are purchased at a transaction price below quoted prices in an active market.

11.12.2 Initial measurement of a financial liability

Paragraph 5.1.1 of AASB 9/IFRS 9 requires an entity to initially measure a financial liability as:
• the fair value of the financial liability
• *less* any transaction costs that are directly attributable to its issue, unless the financial liability is subsequently measured at fair value through profit or loss.

The initial measurement of a financial liability is consistent with the initial measurement of a financial asset except that directly attributable transaction costs, if applicable, reduce rather than increase the carrying amount on initial recognition.

The **fair value of a financial liability** is the price that would be paid to transfer the liability to another party in an orderly transaction between market participants at the measurement date (AASB 9/IFRS 9 Appendix A). The best evidence of fair value at initial recognition of a financial liability is normally the transaction price; that is, the fair value of the consideration received (AASB 9/IFRS 9 paragraph B5.1.2A). The transaction costs for a financial liability would include any legal and accounting costs incurred by a company in relation to the issue a debt instrument.

Illustrative example 11.9 presents the initial measurement of a financial liability that is a long-term loan payable.

Initial measurement of a long-term loan payable

Initial measurement of loan from another entity at market interest rate

Togetby Ltd borrows $200 000 from an unrelated company. The term of the loan is 5 years. Interest is due annually in arrears at the market rate of 5%. Togetby Ltd reimburses the unrelated company for the legal costs of $5000 to arrange the loan documentation.

Required

What are the entries of Togetby Ltd for the initial measurement of the loan payable?

Solution

Cash	Dr	195 000	
Loan payable (financial liability)	Cr		195 000

The initial measurement of the financial liability equals the fair value of the loan payable (i.e. the consideration received for the transaction) less the legal costs directly attributable to the loan agreement.

Similar to financial assets, any difference between the transaction price and fair value of a financial liability is immediately recognised in profit or loss if the item relates to an active market.

LEARNING CHECK

- [ ] A financial asset is initially measured at its fair value plus, in the case of a financial asset that is not measured at fair value through profit or loss, any transaction costs directly attributable to the acquisition.
- [ ] A financial liability is initially measured at its fair value less, in the case of a financial liability that is not measured at fair value through profit or loss, any transaction costs directly attributable to the acquisition.
- [ ] Fair value is the price that would be received to sell an asset or paid to transfer a liability in an orderly transaction between market participants at the measurement date and the best evidence of fair value is the transaction price; that is, the consideration given or received in a transaction.
- [ ] Transaction costs include fees and commissions paid to agents, advisers, brokers and dealers or levies by regulatory agencies and securities exchanges or transfer taxes and stamp duties.

11.13 Subsequent measurement of a financial asset

LEARNING OBJECTIVE 11.13 Outline the requirements for the subsequent measurement of a financial asset.

11.13.1 Summary of requirements

Paragraph 4.1.1 of AASB 9/IFRS 9 requires an entity to classify financial assets as subsequently measured at either amortised cost or fair value.

Figure 11.5 illustrates the requirements for the subsequent measurement of financial assets at amortised cost or fair value.

There are generally three financial asset categories:

1. holdings of debt instruments — classified and measured at either amortised cost, fair value through profit or loss or fair value through other comprehensive income (OCI)
2. holdings of derivatives — classified and measured at fair value through profit loss
3. holdings of equity instruments — classified and measured at either fair value through profit or loss or fair value through OCI.

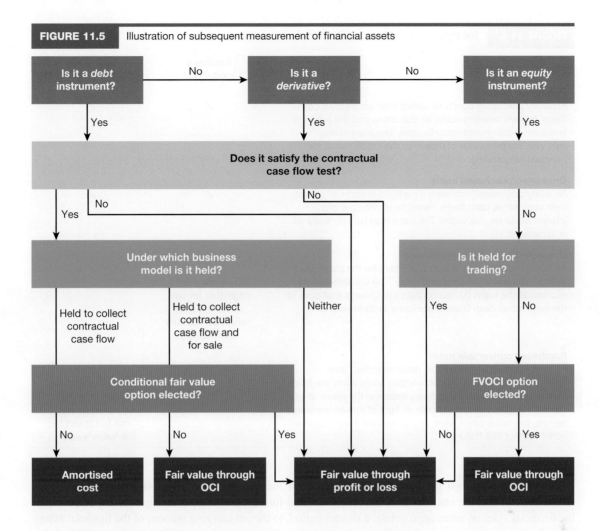

FIGURE 11.5   Illustration of subsequent measurement of financial assets

11.13.2 Measurement of financial assets at amortised cost

Paragraph 4.1.2 of AASB 9/IFRS 9 requires subsequent measurement of a financial asset at amortised cost when both of the following are satisfied.

(a) 'The financial asset is held within a business model whose objective is to hold financial assets in order to collect contractual cash flows' (**business model test**).

(b) 'The contractual terms of the financial asset give rise on specified dates to cash flows that are solely payments of principal and interest' (**cash flows characteristics test**).

The business model test is not dependent on management's intentions for an individual instrument; therefore it should ordinarily be determined at a higher level than instrument by instrument (AASB 9/IFRS 9 paragraph B4.1.2). In order to satisfy the business model test, the entity does not necessarily have to hold all the instruments to maturity; for example, it may sell some instruments to fund capital expenditures (AASB 9/IFRS 9 paragraph B4.1.3). The cash flows characteristics test requires cash flows that are 'solely principal and interest'. Accordingly, the financial assets that satisfy this test should be in the nature of debt instruments held by an entity that yield interest as consideration for the time value of money and the credit risk associated with a principal amount.

Figure 11.6 shows examples of debt instruments that do or do not satisfy both tests for classification as a financial asset at amortised cost.

Appendix A of AASB 9/IFRS 9 defines the **amortised cost of a financial asset** as:

- the amount measured at initial recognition
- *less* principal repayments
- *less/plus* the cumulative amortisation using the effective interest method of any difference between that initial amount and the maturity amount
- *less* any reduction for loss allowance.

FIGURE 11.6   The classification of financial instruments at amortised cost

	Business model test	Cash flows characteristics test
Purchased bonds An entity purchases bonds to collect their contractual cash flows. Interest receipts occur on due dates and the principal is due on a designated maturity date. The interest may vary with the time value of money or the credit risk of the principal outstanding.	✓	✓
Originated/purchased loans An entity originates/purchases a portfolio of loans to collect their contractual cash flows. Receipts of principal and interest occur on due dates. The loans may be fully secured or unsecured.	✓	✓
Originated loans for securitisation An entity originates loans with customers for the purpose of selling the loans to an unrelated entity. The unrelated entity securitises the loans by issuing debt instruments that pass on the contractual cash flows of the loans to its investors.	✗ (The loans are originated for sale rather than to collect contractual cash flows.)	✓
Purchased convertible notes An entity purchases convertible notes to collect their contractual cash flows. The convertible notes allow the holder to exchange the notes for ordinary shares in the issuer at pre-determined dates before maturity. In light of this conversion feature, the notes pay a lower rate of interest than equivalent notes without this feature.	✓	✗ (Interest is not only for the time value of money or credit risk but linked to the issuer's equity.)

The **effective interest method** allocates the interest income using the **effective interest rate** of the financial asset (i.e. the rate that discounts the estimated future cash receipts through the expected life of the financial asset or, when appropriate, a shorter period, to the net carrying amount of the financial asset). The effective interest rate must be calculated considering all contractual terms of the instrument. It includes all fees, transaction costs, premiums and discounts (Appendix A of AASB 9/IFRS 9). A calculator with a finance function is usually needed to calculate the effective interest rate. Illustrative example 11.10 shows determination of the amortised cost of a debt instrument using the effective interest rate method.

ILLUSTRATIVE EXAMPLE 11.10

Measurement of a financial asset at amortised cost

On 1 January 2022, Chang Ltd purchases a debt instrument with a remaining 3-year term for cash consideration of $1 085 868 (including transaction costs). The instrument has a principal amount of $1 250 000 (the amount payable on redemption) and interest coupon of 4.72% distributed at the end of each calendar year. The annual cash interest income is thus $59 000 ($1 250 000 × 0.0472). Using a financial calculator, the effective interest rate is calculated as 10%. The debt instrument is classified as subsequent measurement at amortised cost.

Required
Calculate the cash flows and interest income for each period and prepare the journal entries for the initial and subsequent measurement of the debt instrument.

Solution
The following table sets out the cash flows and interest income for each period, using the effective interest rate of 10%.

(A) Year	(B) Amortised cost at beginning	(C) Interest income (B) × 10%	(D) Cash flows	(E) Amortised cost at end (B + C − D)
2022	1 085 868	108 587	59 000	1 135 455
2023	1 135 455	113 545	59 000	1 190 000
2024	1 190 000	119 000	59 000	1 250 000
2024			1 250 000	—

The entries of Chang Ltd for the initial and subsequent measurement of the debt instrument held are as follows.

1 January 2022 — initial recognition and measurement

Investment in debt security	Dr	1 085 868	
Cash	Cr		1 085 868

31 December 2022 — subsequent measurement

Investment in debt security	Dr	49 587	
Cash	Dr	59 000	
Interest income	Cr		108 587

31 December 2023 — subsequent measurement

Investment in debt security	Dr	54 545	
Cash	Dr	59 000	
Interest income	Cr		113 545

31 December 2024 — subsequent measurement

Investment in debt security	Dr	60 000	
Cash	Dr	59 000	
Interest income	Cr		119 000

31 December 2024 — redemption and derecognition

Cash	Dr	1 250 000	
Investment in debt security	Cr		1 250 000

11.13.3 Measurement of financial assets at fair value

Subsequent measurement of a financial asset at fair value is the default classification under paragraph 4.1.4 of AASB 9/IFRS 9. This means that fair value must be used if a financial asset does not qualify for measurement at amortised cost. Accordingly, subsequent measurement at fair value generally applies to a broad range of financial assets other than holdings of debt instruments; that is, holdings of equity instruments and derivatives.

Fair value through other comprehensive income

AASB 9/IFRS 9 provides for a financial asset to be measured at **fair value through other comprehensive income** in two circumstances. One circumstance pertains to financial assets that meet the contractual cash flows test, such as debt securities (paragraph 4.1.2A); while the other circumstance applies to certain investments in equity instruments (paragraph 5.7.5).

In accordance with paragraph 4.1.2A of AASB 9/IFRS 9, a financial asset is recognised at fair value through other comprehensive income when both of the following conditions are satisfied:

(a) the financial asset is held within a business model whose objective [of generating returns] is achieved by both collecting contractual cash flows and selling financial assets and

(b) the contractual terms of the financial asset give rise on specified dates to cash flows that are solely payments of principal and interest [cash flows characteristics test].

Additionally, paragraph 5.7.5 of AASB 9/IFRS 9 permits the holder of an **equity instrument not held for trading** to make an irrevocable election to include changes in the fair value of that investment in other comprehensive income rather than in profit or loss. The irrevocable election must be made on initial recognition of the equity instrument. Appendix A of AASB 9/IFRS 9 indicates that to qualify as an equity instrument not held for trading an investment in shares must not be:

• acquired principally for the purpose of short-term sale

• part of a portfolio that is managed together and for which there is evidence of a recent pattern of short-term profit taking

• a derivative financial instrument (unless it is a financial guarantee contract or designated and effective hedging instrument).

Illustrative example 11.11 demonstrates fair value through other comprehensive income.

ILLUSTRATIVE EXAMPLE 11.11

Fair value through other comprehensive income

On 1 July 2022, Hold Ltd purchases 100 000 shares in Telstra Corporation Limited at a price of $5.10 each. The transaction costs for brokerage are $500. On 30 June 2023, the closing market price for a share in Telstra is $5.80. Hold Ltd has irrevocably elected to measure the share investment at fair value through other comprehensive income.

Required

What are the journal entries of Hold Ltd for the initial and subsequent measurement of its investment in the shares?

Solution

1 July 2022 — initial recognition and measurement

Investment in Telstra shares	Dr	510 500	
Cash	Cr		510 500

Transaction costs are included in the initial measurement of a financial asset that is not subsequently measured at fair value through the profit or loss.

30 June 2023 — subsequent measurement

Investment in Telstra shares	Dr	69 500	
Gain in fair value (OCI)	Cr		69 500

The gain in fair value is $69 500 calculated as $580 000 − $510 500. It is recognised in other comprehensive income (OCI) in accordance with the irrevocable election.

While the gains and losses on a share investment may be recognised in other comprehensive income, the dividends from the investment must be recognised as revenue in the profit or loss when the investor's right to receive the dividends is established (AASB 9/IFRS 9 paragraph 5.7.6).

Fair value through profit and loss

Financial assets are measured at **fair value through profit or loss** (paragraph 4.1.4 AASB 9/IFRS 9) unless they are measured at amortised cost (paragraph 4.1.2 of AASB 9/IFRS 9), at fair value through other comprehensive income (paragraph 4.1.2A of AASB 9/IFRS 9) or at fair value through other comprehensive income under an irrevocable election (paragraph 5.7.5 of AASB 9/IFRS 9).

Additionally, paragraph 4.1.5 of AASB 9/IFRS 9 allows an entity to designate irrevocably a financial asset as measured at fair value through profit or loss if it would eliminate or significantly reduce an accounting mismatch that would otherwise occur if the financial asset were measured at amortised cost, or if valuation adjustments were accounted for differently. Accounting mismatches can occur when:

- fair value gains or losses on a financial asset are recognised in other comprehensive income, while fair value gains or losses on a closely related liability are recognised in profit or loss
- fair value gains or losses on a liability are recognised in profit or loss while fair value gains or losses on the closely related financial asset are not recognised because it is measured at amortised cost.

The irrevocable designation must be made on initial recognition of the financial asset.

When accounting for financial assets at fair value through profit or loss the gains and losses that arise from fair value measurement at the end of the reporting period must be immediately recognised in the profit or loss. Illustrative example 11.12 demonstrates fair value through profit or loss.

ILLUSTRATIVE EXAMPLE 11.12

Investments at fair value through profit or loss

On 1 July 2022, Reed Ltd purchases 100 000 shares in Telstra Corporation Limited at a price of $5.10 each. The transaction costs for brokerage are $500. On 30 June 2023, the closing market price for a share in Telstra is $5.80. Reed Ltd measures its share investments at fair value through the profit or loss.

Required
What are the entries of Reed Ltd for the initial and subsequent measurement of its investment in the shares?

Solution
1 July 2022 — initial recognition and measurement

Investment in Telstra shares	Dr	510 000	
Brokerage expense	Dr	500	
Cash	Cr		510 500

Transaction costs are not included in the initial measurement of a financial asset that is subsequently measured at fair value through the profit or loss.

30 June 2023 — subsequent measurement

Investment in Telstra shares	Dr	70 000	
Gain in fair value (profit or loss)	Cr		70 000

The gain in fair value is $70 000 calculated as 100 000 × ($5.80 − $5.10).

11.13.4 Reclassification of financial assets

An entity may change its business model for managing financial assets and must reclassify any affected financial assets when this occurs (AASB 9/IFRS 9 paragraph 4.4.1). Such changes must be determined by an entity's senior management and are expected to be infrequent (paragraph B4.4.1). An example of where reclassification would be appropriate is if an entity changes its business model for a portfolio of commercial loans from hold and sell short-term to hold and collect all contractual cash flows. The appropriate reclassification in this example is from fair value through the profit or loss to amortised cost.

An entity that reclassifies a financial asset from fair value to amortised cost, initially measures the amortised cost as the fair value at the reclassification date (AASB 9/IFRS 9 paragraph 5.6.3). An entity that reclassifies a financial asset from amortised cost to fair value, initially measures the fair value as at the reclassification date. Any difference between the fair value and the previous carrying amount at amortised cost is recognised as a gain or loss in the profit or loss (paragraph 5.6.2).

- An entity must classify financial assets as either subsequently measured at amortised cost, at fair value through profit or loss, or at fair value through other comprehensive income.
- A financial asset is subsequently measured at amortised cost if an entity has a business model where the asset is held with the objective of collecting the contractual cash flows and the cash flow characteristics are solely principal and interest (e.g. purchased debt securities or purchased and originated loans).
- The amortised cost of a financial asset is the amount recognised at initial recognition less principal repayments plus/less cumulative amortisation using the effective interest method less any reduction for loss allowance.
- A financial asset is subsequently measured at fair value if subsequent measurement at amortised cost does not apply (e.g. trading portfolios of equity instruments, debt securities held short term and derivatives) or if at initial recognition an entity makes an irrevocable election to use fair value.
- Financial assets are accounted for at fair value through other comprehensive income if they meet the contractual cash flows test and are held within a business model with the objectives of generating returns both from collecting contractual cash flows and selling financial assets.
- An entity can make an irrevocable election at initial recognition to use fair value through other comprehensive income for investments in equity instruments not held for trading.
- On initial recognition an entity can irrevocably designate to account for a financial asset at fair value through profit or loss in order to avoid or substantially reduce an accounting mismatch that would otherwise occur.
- A financial asset is accounted for at fair value through profit or loss if it is not measured at amortised cost or accounted for at fair value through other comprehensive income in accordance with provisions of AASB 9/IFRS 9.
- An entity may change its business model and this may result in reclassifications of financial assets between the categories of subsequent measurement at amortised cost and subsequent measurement at fair value.

11.14 Impairment of financial assets

LEARNING OBJECTIVE 11.14 Describe the expected loss model for impairment of financial assets.

Credit loss arises when a debtor fails to pay some or all of the contractual payments, including instances of late payment. AASB 9/IFRS 9 adopts an expected loss model for the recognition of impairment losses on financial assets that are measured at amortised cost and financial assets with contractual cash flows measured at fair value through other comprehensive income. Although AASB 9/IFRS 9 deals with a range of complex situations, this discussion is confined to the general approach (paragraphs 5.5.1–5.5.11) and the simplified approach to financial assets such as trade receivables (paragraphs 5.5.15–5.5.16).

Under the general approach the entity recognises the expected credit loss for a financial asset in accordance with requirements for:

- Stage 1 — when there has not been a significant increase in credit risk since initial recognition
- Stages 2 and 3 — when there has been a significant increase in credit since initial recognition.

The entity is required to recognise an allowance for the expected credit loss. The amount of the loss allowance reflects the probability-weighted amount derived by considering the probability of a range of possible outcomes, such as payment in full, default on the last three payments and complete default. The journal entry to recognise a loss allowance is ordinarily in the following form.

| Impairment loss (profit or loss) | Dr | xxx | |
| Loss allowance | Cr | | xxx |

The loss allowance is a contra asset account that reduces the carrying amount of the financial asset. However, in the case of a financial asset classified at fair value through other comprehensive income in accordance with paragraph 4.1.2A of AASB 9/IFRS 9, the loss allowance is credited to other comprehensive income instead of recognising a loss allowance as a reduction in the carrying amount of the financial asset. Thus, although an expected credit loss is recognised, the carrying amount of the financial asset it not reduced by a loss allowance, so that the financial asset continues to be measured at fair value.

For a financial asset that is classified as Stage 1 — when there has not been a significant increase in credit risk since initial recognition — the amount of the loss allowance recognised is the expected loss for the next 12 months. Thus, for a financial asset for which the risk of default has remained the same since initial recognition, the entity recognises a loss allowance of 12 months' expected credit losses.

However, if there has been a significant change in the credit risk since initial recognition of the financial asset, the requirements for Stage 2 apply. This means that the entity must measure the loss allowance as the life-time expected credit loss.

A simplified approach is permitted for trade receivables and contracts that arise from revenue transactions within the scope of AASB 15/IFRS 15. Under the simplified approach the entity always measures the loss allowance as the life-time expected credit loss. The simplified approach can be applied to trade receivables or contract assets arising from the application of AASB 15/IFRS 15 provided:

- the receivable does not contain a significant financing component, as defined under AASB 15/IFRS 15, or
- if the receivable does contain a significant financing component, the entity chooses to measure the loss allowance as the life-time expected loss.

LEARNING CHECK

☐ AASB 9/IFRS 9 adopts an expected loss model for the recognition of impairment losses on financial assets that are measured at amortised cost and financial assets with contractual cash flows measured at fair value through other comprehensive income.

☐ The entity is required to recognise an allowance for the expected credit loss.

☐ The amount of the allowance for the expected credit loss is probability-weighted, based on a range of possible outcomes.

☐ When there has not been a significant increase in credit risk since initial recognition of the financial asset, the entity must recognise a loss allowance of 12 months' expected credit losses.

☐ When there has been a significant change in the credit risk since initial recognition of the financial asset, the entity must measure the loss allowance as the life-time expected credit loss.

11.15 Subsequent measurement of a financial liability

LEARNING OBJECTIVE 11.15 Outline the requirements for the subsequent measurement of a financial liability.

11.15.1 Summary of requirements

Paragraph 4.2.1 of AASB 9/IFRS 9 requires an entity to classify all financial liabilities as subsequently measured at amortised cost with certain exceptions including:

- financial liabilities subsequently measured at fair value through the profit or loss
- financial liabilities that arise from the transfer of financial assets that do not qualify for derecognition or when the continuing involvement in a financial asset approach applies
- financial guarantees
- commitments to provide a loan at below-market interest rates.

Figure 11.7 illustrates the requirements for the subsequent measurement of financial liabilities and it shows that there are generally four financial liability categories:

1. debt instruments issued — classified and measured at either amortised cost using the effective interest rate method or fair value through profit or loss
2. holdings of derivatives — classified and measured at fair value through profit or loss
3. financial guarantee contracts — measured at the higher of the loss allowance and the amount initially recognised pursuant to AASB 9/IFRS 9 less any cumulative income recognised in accordance with AASB 15/IFRS 15 *Revenue from Contracts with Customers*
4. commitments to provide loans below market interest rates — measured on the same basis as financial guarantee contracts.

FIGURE 11.7 Illustration of subsequent measurement of financial liabilities

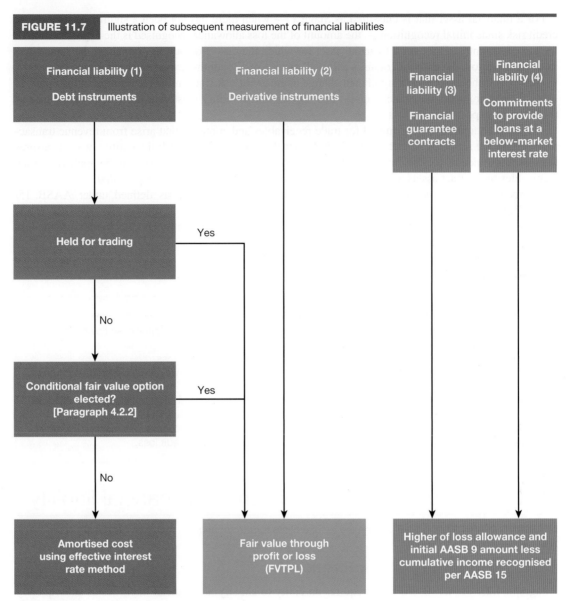

Source: Adapted from Ernst & Young (2011).

11.15.2 Measurement of financial liabilities at amortised cost

Subsequent measurement at amortised cost using the effective interest rate is the default measurement basis for financial liabilities. This contrasts to financial assets, where subsequent measurement at fair value is the default basis. Illustrative example 11.13 demonstrates the subsequent measurement of a debt instrument issued at amortised cost using the effective interest rate.

ILLUSTRATIVE EXAMPLE 11.13

Subsequent measurement of a financial liability at amortised cost

On 1 July 2022, Ali Ltd enters into an agreement to borrow $1 million from Adventure Ltd. Ali Ltd incurs transaction costs of $25 064 in respect of the agreement. Thus, the amount received less the transaction costs is $974 936. The interest to be paid is 5% for each of the first 2 years and 7% for each of the next 2 years, annually in arrears. The borrowings must be repaid after 4 years; that is, on 30 June 2026. The annual cash interest payment is $50 000 ($1 million × 0.05) for each of the first 2 years and $70 000 ($1 million × 0.07) for each of the next 2 years. Using a financial calculator, the effective interest rate is calculated as 6.67%. Ali Ltd measures the financial liability at amortised cost using the effective interest rate method.

The following table sets out the cash flows and interest expense for each period, using the effective interest rate of 6.67%.

(A) Year	(B) Amortised cost at beginning	(C) Interest income (B) × 6.67%	(D) Cash flows	(E) Amortised cost at end (B + C − D)
2023	974 936	65 028	50 000	989 964
2024	989 964	66 031	50 000	1 005 995
2025	1 005 995	67 100	70 000	1 003 095
2026	1 003 095	66 905*	70 000	1 000 000
2026			1 000 000	—

*Difference due to rounding.

Required

What are the entries of Ali Ltd for the initial and subsequent measurement of the borrowings?

Solution

1 July 2022 — initial recognition and measurement

Cash ($1 000 000 − $25 064)	Dr	974 936	
Borrowings from Adventure Ltd	Cr		974 936

30 June 2023 — subsequent measurement

Interest expense	Dr	65 028	
Borrowings from Adventure Ltd	Cr		15 028
Cash	Cr		50 000

30 June 2024 — subsequent measurement

Interest expense	Dr	66 031	
Borrowings from Adventure Ltd	Cr		16 031
Cash	Cr		50 000

30 June 2025 — subsequent measurement

Interest expense	Dr	67 100	
Borrowings from Adventure Ltd	Dr	2 900	
Cash	Cr		70 000

30 June 2026 — subsequent measurement

Interest expense	Dr	66 905	
Borrowings from Adventure Ltd	Dr	3 095	
Cash	Cr		70 000

30 June 2026 — settlement and derecognition

Borrowings from Adventure Ltd	Dr	1 000 000	
Cash	Cr		1 000 000

11.15.3 Measurement of financial liabilities at fair value

Financial liabilities may only be measured subsequently at fair value through profit or loss if they meet the required definition. Appendix A of AASB 9/IFRS 9 defines financial liabilities at fair value through the profit or loss as financial liabilities that are either:

- held for trading
- designated as fair value through profit or loss by an irrevocable election at initial recognition.

Fair value measurement of a financial liability through profit or loss means that gains or losses on remeasurement of the liability at the reporting date are recognised in the profit or loss.

Held for trading

According to Appendix A of AASB 9/IFRS 9, a financial liability is **held for trading** if the liability is:
- incurred principally for the purpose of short-term repurchase
- part of a portfolio that is managed together and for which there is evidence of a recent pattern of short-term profit taking
- a derivative financial instrument (unless it is a designated and effective hedging instrument).

Designated at fair value through profit or loss

Paragraph 4.2.2 of AASB 9/IFRS 9 allows an entity to designate a financial liability at fair value through profit or loss when doing so satisfies one of two conditions:

1. eliminates or significantly reduces an accounting mismatch between the measurement of financial liabilities and the recognition of gains and losses on them
2. management and performance of a group of financial liabilities is evaluated on a fair value basis in accordance with a documented risk management or investment strategy, and information about the group is provided internally to the entity's key management personnel as defined by AASB 124/ IAS 24 *Related Party Disclosures*.

Paragraph 5.7.7 of AASB 9/IFRS 9 requires an entity to recognise in other comprehensive income the portion of any gain or loss that is attributable to credit risk on a financial liability designated at fair value through profit or loss. The remaining portion of any gain or loss must be recognised in profit or loss. If recognition in other comprehensive income would create or enlarge an accounting mismatch, however, then paragraph 5.7.8 requires an entity to recognise the entire gain or loss in profit or loss.

Illustrative example 11.14 demonstrates the subsequent measurement of a financial liability that is a derivative contract at fair value through profit or loss.

ILLUSTRATIVE EXAMPLE 11.14

Measurement of a financial liability at fair value

On 1 March 2022, Romeo Ltd speculates on the future direction of the Australian share market by buying 50 units of ASX SPI 200 Futures with a contract maturity of September 2022. Each contract unit is valued at $25 per index point (e.g. 4000 index points equates to $100 000). Romeo Ltd's reporting date is 30 June. The values of ASX SPI 200 Futures Index at 1 March 2022 and 30 June 2022 are as follows.

Date	ASX SPI 200 Futures Index	Value of right of futures (50 × 25 × Index)	Loss on contract
1 March 2022	5 400	6 750 000	
30 June 2022	4 800	6 000 000	750 000

Required

What are the entries of Romeo Ltd for the initial and subsequent measurement of its contract for 50 units of ASX SPI 200 Futures?

Solution

1 March 2022 — initial recognition and measurement
No entry required as the right and obligation of the futures contracts are equal.

30 June 2022 — subsequent measurement

Loss in fair value (profit or loss)	Dr	750 000	
ASX SPI 200 Futures contract liability	Cr		750 000

☐ Subject to certain exceptions, an entity must classify financial liabilities as either subsequently measured at amortised cost or subsequently measured at fair value through profit or loss with the former being the default classification.

☐ A financial liability is subsequently measured at amortised cost if subsequent measurement at fair value does not apply (e.g. debt instruments not held for trading).

☐ The amortised cost of a financial liability is the amount recognised at initial recognition less principal repayments plus/less cumulative amortisation using the effective interest method.

☐ A financial liability is subsequently measured at fair value if it is held for trading or if an entity makes an irrevocable election to use fair value at initial recognition.

☐ A financial liability is held for trading if it is incurred principally for the purpose of short-term repurchase or it is part of a portfolio for short-term profit or it relates to a derivative instrument.

☐ Gains or losses arising from the fair value measurement of a financial liability at the end of the reporting period are recognised in the profit or loss, with the exception that gains or losses arising from the fair value measurement of a financial liability irrevocably designated at fair value are recognised in other comprehensive income to the extent they are attributable to changes in credit risk.

11.16 Disclosures

LEARNING OBJECTIVE 11.16 Summarise the disclosures required for financial instruments.

Paragraph 1 of AASB 7/IFRS 7 requires an entity to provide disclosures that enable users of its financial statements to evaluate:

(a) the significance of financial instruments for the entity's financial position and performance; and
(b) the nature and extent of risks arising from financial instruments to which the entity is exposed during the period and at the end of the reporting period, and how the entity manages those risks.

11.16.1 Significance of financial instruments to financial position/performance

The first part of AASB 7/IFRS 7 requires disclosures that enable users of a financial report to evaluate the significance of financial instruments to the financial position and financial performance. Figure 11.8 summarises the required disclosures by the following categories:
1. statement of financial position
2. statement of profit or loss and other comprehensive income
3. other.

FIGURE 11.8 Significance of financial instruments for financial position and financial performance

Statement of financial position	
Item	**Summary of details required test**

Categories of financial assets and financial liabilities (AASB 7/IFRS 7 paragraph 8)	• The carrying amount of the various categories of financial assets specified in AASB 9/IFRS 9:
	  – financial assets at fair value through profit or loss showing separately: (i) those mandatorily classified; and (ii) those designated as such
	  – financial assets at amortised cost
	  – financial assets at fair value through other comprehensive income, showing separately: (i) those mandatorily classified; and (ii) equity instruments for which the entity has made an irrevocable election under AASB 9/IFRS 9.
	• The carrying amount of the various categories of financial liabilities specified in AASB 9/IFRS 9:
	  – financial liabilities at fair value through profit or loss showing separately: (i) those held for trading; and (ii) those designated as such
	  – financial liabilities at amortised cost.

Statement of financial position

Item	Summary of details required test

Financial assets or financial liabilities designated at fair value through profit or loss (AASB 7/IFRS 7 paragraphs 9, 10, 10A and 11)	• Financial assets designated as measured at fair value that would otherwise be measured at amortised cost:
	  – the maximum exposure to credit risk
	  – the amount by which any credit derivatives or similar instruments mitigate the exposure to credit risk
	  – the amount of the change in fair value that is attributable to changes in the credit risk
	  – the amount of the change in the fair value of any credit derivatives or similar instruments.
	• Financial liabilities designated at fair value through profit or loss:
	  – the amount of the change in fair value that is attributable to changes in the credit risk; for example, a long-dated financial liability whose creditworthiness has deteriorated
	  – the difference between the carrying amount of the liability and the amount the entity would be contractually required to pay at maturity
	  – any transfers of the cumulative gain or loss within equity together with reasons for the transfer
	  – the amount (if any) in other comprehensive income that is realised if a financial liability is derecognised
	  – a description of the methods used to measure amounts attributed to credit risk.

Financial assets measured at fair value through other comprehensive income (AASB 7/IFRS 7 paragraphs 11A and 11B)	• Designated investments in equity instruments measured at fair value through other comprehensive income:
	  – the investments included in this category
	  – the reasons for using this alternative
	  – the fair value of each investment at the end of the reporting period
	  – dividends recognised for these investments showing separately those for: (i) investments still held; and (ii) investments derecognised.
	• Derecognised investments in equity instruments measured at fair value through other comprehensive income:
	  – the reasons for disposing of the investments
	  – the fair value of the investments at the date of disposal
	  – the cumulative gain or loss on disposal.

Reclassification of financial assets (AASB 7/IFRS 7 paragraphs 12B, 12C and 12D)	• Financial assets reclassified:
	  – the date of reclassification
	  – details of the change in business model
	  – the amount reclassified into and out of each category.
	• Financial assets reclassified to amortised cost:
	  – the effective interest rate on the date of reclassification
	  – the interest income or expense recognised
	  – the fair value of the financial assets at the end of the reporting period after the reclassification and the fair value gain or loss that would have been recognised in that period if there had not been a reclassification.

Offsetting financial assets and financial liabilities (AASB 7/IFRS 7 paragraphs 13A–13F)	• Information to enable users to evaluate the effect of netting arrangements on its financial position including:
	  – the amounts of any financial assets and financial liabilities that are set off
	  – the net amounts presented in the statement of financial position
	  – the amounts subject to an enforceable master netting arrangement or similar agreements.

Collateral (AASB 7/IFRS 7 paragraphs 14 and 15)	• Collateral given:
	  – the carrying amount of financial assets pledged as collateral (security) for liabilities or contingent liabilities
	  – the terms and conditions of any pledged collateral.
	• Collateral held:
	  – the fair value of collateral held
	  – the fair value of collateral sold or repledged and whether there is any obligation to return collateral
	  – the terms and conditions for the use of collateral held.

| Compound financial instruments with multiple embedded derivatives (AASB 7/IFRS 7 paragraph 17) | • Disclosure is required of the existence of the features of multiple embedded derivatives in compound financial instruments. |
| Defaults and breaches (AASB 7/IFRS 7 paragraphs 18 and 19) | • Loans payable at the end of the reporting period:
  – details of defaults during the period
  – the carrying amount of loans payable in default at the end of the reporting period
  – whether the default was remedied or the terms of the loans payable were renegotiated before the financial statements were authorised for issue. |

Statement of profit or loss and other comprehensive income	
Item	**Summary of details required**

Items of income, expense, gains or losses (AASB 7/IFRS 7 paragraph 20)	• Net gains or net losses on:
	  – financial assets or liabilities measured at fair value through profit of loss showing separately net gains or losses for financial assets and liabilities: (i) mandatorily classified; and (ii) designated as such
	  – for financial liabilities measured at fair value through profit or loss showing separately: (i) the amount recognised in profit or loss; and (ii) the amount recognised in other comprehensive income
	  – financial liabilities measured at amortised cost
	  – financial assets measured at amortised cost
	  – financial assets measured at fair value through other comprehensive income.
	• Total interest income and total interest expense calculated using the effective interest method for:
	  – financial assets measured at amortised cost or fair value through other comprehensive income under paragraph 4.1.2A of AASB 9/IFRS 9
	  – financial liabilities that are not at fair value through profit or loss.
	• Fee income and expense not included in determining the effective interest rate arising from:
	  – financial assets and financial liabilities that are not at fair value through profit or loss
	  – trust and other fiduciary activities.
	• An analysis of the gain or loss recognised arising from the derecognition of financial assets measured at amortised cost including the reasons for derecognising those financial assets.

Other disclosures	
Item	**Summary of details required**
Accounting policies (AASB 7/IFRS 7 paragraph 21)	• Description of accounting policies relevant to financial instruments.
Hedge accounting (AASB 7/IFRS 7 paragraph 21A)	• Disclosures about an entity's risk management strategy, hedging activities and the effect of hedging on the financial statements. • AASB 7/IFRS 7 prescribes more extensive disclosures in relation to hedging that are outside the scope of this chapter. – For further information, refer to AASB 7/IFRS 7, paragraphs 21B–24G.
Fair value (AASB 7/IFRS 7 paragraphs 25–30)	• For each class of financial assets and liabilities, the fair value of that class in a way that permits it to be compared with its carrying amount. • Disclosures of fair values are not required if the carrying amount is a reasonable approximation of fair value; for example, trade receivables. • Other details are required in respect of gains or losses that are not recognised on initial recognition of a financial asset or financial liability because fair value is determined using Level 3 inputs.

11.16.2 Risks arising from financial instruments and their management

The second part of AASB 7/IFRS 7 requires an entity to make disclosures that enable users of its financial statements to evaluate the nature and extent of the entity's exposure to risks arising from financial instruments at the end of the reporting period. Transactions in financial instruments typically result in an entity assuming or transferring **market risk**, **credit risk** or **liquidity risk** to another party. Figure 11.9 describes these risks.

FIGURE 11.9	Risks arising from financial instruments

Type of risk	Description
Market risk	• *Currency risk* — the risk that the value of a financial instrument will fluctuate because of changes in foreign exchange rates. • *Interest rate risk* — the risk that the value of a financial instrument will fluctuate because of changes in market interest rates. For example, the issuer of a financial liability that carries a fixed rate of interest is exposed to decreases in market interest rates, such that the issuer of the liability is paying a higher rate of interest than the market rate. • *Other price risk* — the risk that the value of a financial instrument will fluctuate as a result of changes in market prices (other than those arising from interest rate risk or currency risk). Market risk embodies the potential for both loss and gain.
Credit risk	The risk that one party to a financial instrument will fail to discharge an obligation and cause the other party to incur a financial loss.
Liquidity risk	The risk that an entity will encounter difficulty in meeting obligations associated with financial liabilities. This is also known as funding risk. For example, as a financial liability approaches its redemption date, the issuer may experience liquidity risk if its available financial assets are insufficient to meet its obligations.

Figure 11.10 sets out the disclosure requirements for the risks arising from financial instruments grouped into the three typical categories of market risk, credit risk and liquidity risk. Paragraph B6 of the Application Guidance to AASB 7/IFRS 7 states that the risk disclosures shall be given either in the financial statements or incorporated by cross-reference from the financial statements to some other statement, such as a management commentary or risk report.

FIGURE 11.10	Nature and extent of risks arising from financial instruments

Item	Summary of details required

Qualitative disclosures (AASB 7/IFRS 7 paragraph 33)	• For each type of risk:
	  – exposures to risk and how they arise
	  – the entity's objectives, policies and processes for managing the risk and the methods used to measure the risk
	  – any changes in exposures or managing the risk from the previous period.

Quantitative disclosures (AASB 7/IFRS 7 paragraph 34)	• For each type of risk:
	  – summary quantitative data about exposure to that risk at the end of the reporting period based on the information provided internally to key management personnel of the entity
	  – summary data for any concentration of risk; that is, financial instruments that have similar characteristics and are affected similarly by changes in economic or other conditions. For example, a risk concentration may be by geographic area, by industry or by currency.

Credit risk (paragraphs 35, 35A–35N)	• Extensive disclosure requirements for financial instruments subject to the impairment provisions of AASB 9/IFRS 9, including but by no means limited to, a reconciliation of the movement in the loss allowance, by class of financial instrument, during the period.

Credit risk — general (AASB 7/IFRS 7 paragraph 36)	• Disclosures for financial instruments to which impairment requirements do not apply, by class of financial instrument:
	  – the amount that best represents maximum exposure to credit risk at the end of the reporting period without taking into account any collateral held or other credit enhancements (e.g. guarantees) (not required for financial instruments for which the carrying amount is the best representation of the credit risk)
	  – a description of any collateral held as security and other credit enhancements and their financial effect
	  – information about the credit quality of financial assets that are neither past due or impaired.

Credit risk — collateral and other credit enhancements obtained (AASB 7/IFRS 7 paragraph 38)	• Financial or non-financial assets obtained during the period by taking possession of collateral held as security or other credit enhancements:
	  – the nature and amount of the assets
	  – policies for disposing of or use of assets which are not readily convertible to cash.

Liquidity risk (AASB 7/IFRS 7 paragraph 39)	• Maturity analysis for derivative financial liabilities showing the remaining contractual undiscounted cash flows by contractual maturities that are essential for understanding the timing of cash flows.
	• Maturity analysis for non-derivative financial liabilities showing the remaining contractual undiscounted cash flows by contractual maturities.
	• Description of how liquidity risk is managed; for example:
	  – having access to undrawn loan commitments
	  – holding readily liquid financial assets than can be sold to meet liquidity needs
	  – having diverse funding sources.

Market risk (AASB 7/IFRS 7 paragraphs 40 and 41)	• Sensitivity analysis for each type of market risk (i.e. currency risk, interest rate risk and other price risk) showing:
	  – how profit or loss and equity would have been affected by changes in the relevant risk variable that were reasonably possible at the end of the reporting period — for example, the effect on interest expense for the current year if interest rates had varied between 0.25% and 0.5%.
	• Methods and assumptions used in preparing the analysis.
	• Any changes from the previous period in the methods and assumptions used and the reasons for such changes.
	• Alternative sensitivity analysis, such as value at risk, that reflects interdependencies between market risk variables (e.g. between interest rate risk and currency risk):
	  – explanation of method used including main parameters and assumptions
	  – objective of method used and limitations.

LEARNING CHECK

☐ An entity must disclose information that enables users of its financial statements to evaluate the significance of financial instruments for its financial position including details of the carrying amounts of the various classifications of financial assets and financial liabilities.

☐ An entity must disclose information that enables users of its financial statements to evaluate the significance of financial instruments for its financial performance including details of net gains or losses, interest income and interest expense on the various classifications of financial assets and financial liabilities.

☐ An entity must also make disclosures that enable the users of its financial statements to evaluate the nature and extent of the entity's exposures to risks arising from financial instruments including market risk (i.e. currency risk, interest rate risk and other price risk), credit risk and liquidity risk.

SUMMARY

Accounting for financial instruments is covered by AASB 132/IAS 32 for presentation requirements, AASB 9/IFRS 9 for comprehensive recognition, classification and measurement rules, and AASB 7/ IFRS 7 for disclosure requirements.

AASB 132/IAS 32

- AASB 132/IAS 32 defines financial instruments, financial assets, financial liabilities and equity instruments. AASB 132/IAS 32 distinguishes equity instruments from financial liabilities on the basis that the latter include a contractual obligation to deliver cash or another financial asset to another entity or to exchange financial assets or financial liabilities with another entity under conditions that are potentially unfavourable. Accordingly, preference shares that allow for cash redemption at the option of the holder are financial liabilities.
- AASB 132/IAS 32 requires that an issuer of compound financial instruments (e.g. convertible notes) separate the financial liability component from the equity component.
- AASB 132/IAS 32 requires that interest, dividends, gains and losses be accounted for in a manner that is consistent with the statement of financial position classification of the related financial instrument.
- AASB 132/IAS 32 requires that a financial asset and a financial liability be offset if an entity has a current legally enforceable right to set off and intends to settle on a net basis or realise the asset and liability simultaneously.

AASB 9/IFRS 9

- AASB 9/IFRS 9 requires initial recognition of a financial asset or financial liability when an entity becomes a party to the contractual provisions of an instrument.
- Regular way purchases or sales of financial assets are recognised using trade date accounting or settlement date accounting.
- Initial measurement of a financial asset or financial liability is at fair value adjusted for, in the case of a financial asset or financial liability not subsequently measured at fair value through profit or loss, any directly attributable transaction costs.
- Subsequent measurement of financial assets is at fair value or amortised cost. Debt instruments that satisfy business model and cash flow characteristics tests indicating that the asset is held for its contractual cash flows of principal and interest are measured subsequently at amortised cost based on the effective interest method less any loss allowance. Debt instruments that satisfy the cash flow characteristics test but which are held within a business model to obtain returns both through the collection of contractual cash flows and the sale of financial assets are measured at fair value through other comprehensive income. An entity may also make an irrevocable election on initial recognition to account for equity instruments not held for trading as measured at fair value through other comprehensive income. An entity may under certain conditions make an irrevocable designation to measure a debt instrument at fair value through profit or loss that would otherwise be measured at amortised cost.
- Subsequent measurement of financial liabilities is at amortised cost, but there are exceptions. Debt instruments that are held for trading and derivative financial instruments are measured at fair value through profit or loss.
- Financial assets are derecognised when the contractual rights to cash flows have expired or when an entity has transferred substantially all the risks and rewards associated with ownership of the asset or no longer controls the asset.
- Financial liabilities are derecognised when the contractual obligation is discharged or cancelled or has expired.

AASB 7/IFRS 7

- AASB 7/IFRS 7 requires disclosures that enable the users of financial statements to evaluate the significance of financial instruments to the financial position and financial performance including details of the carrying amounts of the various classifications of financial assets and financial liabilities and details of net gains or losses, interest income and interest expense arising on these assets and liabilities.
- AASB 7/IFRS 7 requires disclosures that enable the users of financial statements to evaluate the nature and extent of an entity's exposures to risks arising from financial instruments including market risk (i.e. currency risk, interest rate risk and other price risk), credit risk and liquidity risk.

KEY TERMS

amortised cost of a financial asset The amount measured at initial recognition *less* principal repayments *less/plus* the cumulative amortisation using the effective interest method of any difference between that initial amount and the maturity amount *less* any reduction for loss allowance.

business model test The asset is held within a business model whose objective is to hold assets in order to collect contractual cash flows.

cash flows characteristics test The contractual terms of the financial asset give rise on specified dates to cash flows that are solely payments of principal and interest.

compound financial instrument A financial instrument that has characteristics that are a combination of a financial asset, financial liability or equity instrument.

contingent settlement provisions Terms of settlement that are dependent on the occurrence of uncertain future events beyond the control of both the issuer and the holder.

credit risk The risk that one party to a financial instrument will fail to discharge an obligation and cause the other party to incur a financial loss.

derecognition of a financial asset or financial liability The asset or liability ceases to qualify for recognition in the statement of financial position.

derivative A contract that changes value in response to an underlying variable, requires no initial net investment or an initial net investment that is smaller than would be required for other types of contracts that would be expected to have a similar response to changes in market factors, and is settled at a future date.

effective interest method Allocation of the interest income or expense using the effective interest rate of the financial asset or financial liability.

effective interest rate The rate that discounts the estimated future cash payments or receipts through the expected life of the financial liability or asset or, when appropriate, a shorter period to the net carrying amount of the financial asset.

embedded derivative A component of a hybrid contract that also includes a non-derivative host.

equity instrument Any contract that evidences a residual interest in the assets of an entity after deducting all of its liabilities.

equity instrument not held for trading An investment in shares that is not: acquired principally for short-term sale; part of a portfolio that exhibits short-term profit taking; or a derivative instrument (unless a designated and effective hedging instrument).

equity risk The risk of changes in value of the equitable or residual interest in net assets.

fair value of a financial asset The price that would be received to sell the asset in an orderly transaction between market participants at the measurement date.

fair value of a financial liability The price that would be paid to transfer the liability to another party in an orderly transaction between market participants at the measurement date.

fair value through other comprehensive income Where gains or losses arising from changes in the fair value of an investment are recognised in other comprehensive income rather than in profit or loss.

fair value through profit or loss Where gains and losses that arise from fair value measurement at the end of the reporting period are immediately recognised in the profit or loss.

financial asset Any asset that is cash; an equity instrument of another entity; a contractual right to receive cash or another financial asset from another entity, or to exchange financial assets or financial liabilities with another entity under conditions that are potentially favourable to the entity; or a contract that may be settled in the entity's own equity instruments and is a non-derivative for which the entity may be obliged to receive a variable number of the entity's own equity instruments, or a derivative that may be settled other than by the exchange of a fixed amount of cash or another financial asset for a fixed number of the entity's own equity instruments.

financial instrument Any contract that gives rise to a financial asset of one entity and a financial liability or equity instrument of another entity.

financial liability Any liability that is a contractual obligation to deliver cash or another financial asset to another entity, or to exchange financial assets or financial liabilities with another entity under conditions that are potentially unfavourable to the entity; or a contract that may be settled in the entity's own equity instruments and is a non-derivative for which the entity may be obliged to deliver a variable number of the entity's own equity instruments, or a derivative that may be settled other than by the exchange of a fixed amount of cash or another financial asset for a fixed number of the entity's own equity instruments. For this purpose, rights, options or warrants to acquire a fixed number of the entity's own equity instruments for a fixed amount of any currency are equity instruments if the entity offers the rights, options or warrants pro rata to all of its existing owners of the same class of its own non-derivative equity instruments.

financial risk The risk of a future change in a specified interest rate, financial instrument price, commodity price, foreign exchange rate, index of prices of rates, credit rating, credit index or other variable that is not specific to a party to the contract.

held for trading The status of a financial liability if it is:
- incurred principally for the purpose of short-term repurchase
- part of a portfolio that is managed together and for which there is evidence of a recent pattern of short-term profit taking
- a derivative financial instrument (unless a designated and effective hedging instrument).

liquidity risk The risk that an entity will encounter difficulty in meeting obligations associated with financial liabilities.

market risk The risk that the value of a financial instrument will fluctuate because of changes in foreign exchange rates, market interest rates or some other market prices.

regular way purchase or sale A purchase or sale of a financial asset under a contract whose terms require delivery of the asset within the time frame established generally by regulation or convention in the marketplace concerned.

transaction costs Incremental costs that are directly attributable to the acquisition, issue or disposal of a financial asset or financial liability.

DEMONSTRATION PROBLEMS

11.1 Repurchase of convertible instrument

On 1 July 2021, Tom Ltd issues 10 000, 10% convertible debentures with a 10-year maturity at a face value of $100 each. At maturity, a debenture is convertible into an ordinary share at the conversion price of $2.50 per share. Interest is payable annually in arrears on 30 June. At the date of the issue, Tom Ltd could have issued non-convertible debt with a 10-year term bearing interest at a coupon rate of 11.3% p.a. Tom Ltd uses amortised cost to subsequently measure the financial liability component of the convertible debentures.

On 1 July 2026, half way through the 10-year term, Tom Ltd repurchases all of the convertible debentures based on the fair value of $170 each. At the date of the repurchase, Tom Ltd could have issued non-convertible debt with a 5-year term bearing interest at a coupon rate of 8.16% p.a.

Required

1. Use the residual valuation method to determine the amounts of the financial liability and equity components attributable to the issue of the convertible debentures.
2. Prepare a schedule to determine the amortised cost of the financial liability up until their repurchase.
3. Use the residual valuation method to determine the amounts of the financial liability and equity components attributable to the repurchase of the convertible debentures.
4. Prepare the entries of Tom Ltd to account for the convertible debentures from the issue date to the repurchase date.

SOLUTION

1. *Issue of convertible debentures: residual valuation method*

Present value of the principal at 11.3% p.a.: $1 million (10 000 × $100) in 10 years' time	$ 342 806
Present value of the interest stream at 11.3% p.a.: $100 000 ($1 million × 10%) annually in arrears for 10 years	581 588
Total liability component	924 394
Equity component (by deduction)	75 606
Proceeds of the convertible debenture issue	$1 000 000

2. *Schedule of amortised cost of financial liability component until 30 June 2026*

(A) Year	(B) Amortised cost at beginning	(C) Interest expense (B) × 11.3%	(D) Cash flows	(E) Amortised cost at end (B + C − D)
2022	924 394	104 456	100 000	928 850
2023	928 850	104 960	100 000	933 810
2024	933 810	105 520	100 000	939 330
2025	939 330	106 144	100 000	945 474
2026	945 474	106 839	100 000	952 313

3. *Repurchase of convertible debentures: residual valuation method*

The consideration of $1 700 000 paid to redeem the debentures is allocated to the liability component and the equity component based on the same approach used in the initial allocation (AASB 132/IAS 32 paragraph AG33). This means that we first need to measure the fair value of the liability component at 30 June 2026, and then allocate that amount of the consideration to the liability component. The residual of the consideration is then allocated to the equity component.

Present value of the principal at 8.16% p.a.: $1 million (10 000 × $100) in 5 years' time	$ 675 564
Present value of the interest stream at 8.16% p.a.: $100 000 ($1 million × 10%) annually in arrears for 5 years	397 593
Total liability component	1 073 157
Equity component (by deduction)	626 843
Payment for repurchase of the convertible debenture issue	$1 700 000

The gain or loss on the liability components is determined as the difference between the allocated consideration and the carrying amount and recognised in profit or loss (AASB 132/IAS 32 paragraph AG34(a)).

Consideration allocated to the liability component	$1 073 157
Less carrying amount of the liability component	952 313
Loss on redemption of debentures	120 844

The consideration allocated to equity component is recognised directly in equity (AASB 132/IAS 32 paragraph AG34(b)).

4. *Entries of Tom Ltd from issue date to repurchase date*

TOM LTD Journal entries			
1 July 2021:			
Cash	Dr	1 000 000	
Convertible debenture liability	Cr		924 394
Option for convertible debentures (equity)	Cr		75 606
(Initial measurement of components using residual valuation method)			
30 June 2022:			
Interest expense	Dr	104 456	
Convertible debenture liability	Cr		4 456
Cash	Cr		100 000
(Subsequent measurement of liability, $924 394 + $4456 = $928 850)			
30 June 2023:			
Interest expense	Dr	104 960	
Convertible debenture liability	Cr		4 960
Cash	Cr		100 000
(Subsequent measurement of liability, $928 850 + $4960 = $933 810)			
30 June 2024:			
Interest expense	Dr	105 520	
Convertible debenture liability	Cr		5 520
Cash	Cr		100 000
(Subsequent measurement of liability, $933 810 + $5520 = $939 330)			

TOM LTD Journal entries			
30 June 2025:			
Interest expense	Dr	106 144	
Convertible debenture liability	Cr		6 144
Cash	Cr		100 000
(Subsequent measurement of liability, $939 330 + $6144 = $945 474)			
30 June 2026:			
Interest expense	Dr	106 839	
Convertible debenture liability	Cr		6 839
Cash	Cr		100 000
(Subsequent measurement of liability, $945 474 + $6839 = $952 313)			
30 June 2026:			
Convertible debenture liability	Dr	952 313	
Loss on redemption of debentures	Dr	120 844	
Option for convertible debentures (equity)	Dr	626 843	
Cash	Cr		1 700 000
(Repurchase of debentures using residual valuation method)			

The option for convertible debentures in equity after the repurchase will be a debit balance of $551 237 (i.e. $75 606 − $626 843). This amount must remain in equity. However, it could be transferred to a different account in equity; for example, an options reserve account.

11.2 Call option contract on shares (net cash settlement)

Valerian Ltd enters into a call option contract with Northern Ltd that gives Valerian Ltd the right to acquire one million shares in Petty Ltd. The options premium paid is $0.50 each. The details of the option contract are as follows.

Contract date	1 February 2022
Settlement terms	Net cash settlement
Exercise date (only at maturity)	31 July 2022
Exercise right holder	Valerian Ltd
Exercise price per share	$1.50
Share price at maturity	$1.70
Number of shares under option contract	1 000 000
Fair value of option contract on 1 February 2022	$500 000
Fair value of option contract on 30 June 2022	$300 000
Fair value of option contract at 31 July 2022	$200 000

Required

1. What financial instrument classification is appropriate for Valerian Ltd and Northern Ltd in respect of the subsequent measurement of the call option contract?
2. Prepare the entries for Valerian Ltd as the call option holder.
3. Prepare the entries for Northern Ltd as the call option writer.

SOLUTION

1. *Classification and subsequent measurement*

Valerian Ltd has purchased a financial asset. The purchased call option is a derivative that gives Valerian Ltd the right to cash if share price of Petty Ltd at maturity date exceeds the exercise price specified in the contract. A financial asset that is a derivative should be classified and subsequently measured at fair value through profit or loss.

Northern Ltd has issued a financial liability. The sold call option is a derivative that obligates Northern Ltd to deliver cash if the share price of Petty Ltd at maturity date exceeds the exercise price specified in the contract. A financial liability that is a derivative should be classified and subsequently measured at fair value through profit or loss.

2. *The entries of Valerian Ltd*

VALERIAN LTD Journal entries			

1 February 2022:
  Call option asset
    Cash
(Initial measurement at fair value)
	Dr
	Cr
		500 000	500 000

30 June 2022:
  Fair value loss (profit or loss)
    Call option asset
(Subsequent measurement at fair value through profit or loss)
	Dr
	Cr
		200 000	200 000

31 July 2022:
  Fair value loss (profit or loss)
    Call option asset
(Subsequent measurement at fair value through profit or loss
[$200 000 − $300 000])
	Dr
	Cr
		100 000	100 000

Cash Call option asset (Net cash settlement, 1 000 000 shares × [$1.70 − $1.50])	Dr Cr	200 000	200 000

3. *The entries of Northern Ltd*

NORTHERN LTD Journal entries			

1 February 2022:
  Cash
    Call option liability
(Initial measurement at fair value)
	Dr
	Cr
		500 000	500 000

30 June 2022:
  Call option liability
    Fair value gain (profit or loss)
(Subsequent measurement at fair value through profit or loss
[$300 000 − $500 000])
	Dr
	Cr
		200 000	200 000

31 July 2022:
  Call option liability
    Fair value gain (profit or loss)
(Subsequent measurement at fair value through profit or loss
[$200 000 − $300 000])
	Dr
	Cr
		100 000	100 000

Call option liability Cash (Net cash settlement, 1 000 000 shares × [$1.70 − $1.50])	Dr Cr	200 000	200 000

COMPREHENSION QUESTIONS

1 Define a financial instrument and identify transactions that give rise to financial instruments and those that do not.

2 Define a financial asset and list some common examples.

3 Define a financial liability and list some common examples.

4 Define a derivative and explain how a hybrid contract can have an embedded derivative. List some common examples of derivatives and embedded derivatives.

5 Define an equity instrument and explain how it differs from a financial liability.

6 Explain why some preference shares are recognised as financial liabilities by the issuer while others are recognised as equity instruments.

7 What is a convertible note? How does the issuer of convertible notes initially recognise the notes in its financial statements?

8 Should the dividends on preference shares be recognised directly in equity or as an expense in profit or loss?

9 The initial recognition of a financial asset or financial liability is based on a 'rights and obligations approach'. Discuss.

10 What is a regular way purchase or sale of a financial asset and what is the difference between trade date accounting and settlement date accounting?

11 When does an entity set off a financial asset and financial liability for presentation in its statement of financial position?

12 When does an entity derecognise a financial asset or financial liability?

13 How is the initial measurement of a financial asset determined? Explain how a gain or loss can arise on initial measurement of a financial asset.

14 How is the initial measurement of a financial liability determined and how does it differ to the initial measurement of a financial asset?

15 Describe the various approaches to subsequent measurement of financial assets permitted by AASB 9/IFRS 9 and the circumstances in which each approach may be applied.

16 Explain how financial assets that are debt instruments, equity instruments or derivatives may subsequently be measured.

17 Describe the subsequent measurement of financial liabilities. What is the default category for subsequent measurement of a financial liability?

18 Disclosures are required in respect of the nature and extent of risks arising from financial instruments. What are the usual risks and what details must be included in the disclosures?

CASE STUDY 11.1

FINANCIAL INSTRUMENTS IN THE GLOBAL FINANCIAL CRISIS

The global financial crisis (GFC) that began in 2007 gave rise to criticism of financial reporting, particularly in relation to the accounting treatment of financial instruments. The Financial Crisis Advisory Group (FCAG) identified four primary weaknesses:

1. difficulties in the application of fair value in illiquid markets
2. the delayed recognition of impairment losses resulting from the incurred loss approach adopted by IAS 39 *Financial Instruments: Recognition and Measurement*
3. the use of off-balance sheet financing, particularly in the US
4. the complexity of accounting standards for financial instruments.

AASB 13/IFRS 13 *Fair Value* was issued in response to concerns about the application of fair value, along with additional disclosures introduced in AASB 7/IFRS 7 when Level 3 inputs are used to measure fair value.

Critics of fair value argued that it had a pro-cyclical effect and thus worsened the effects of the GFC on the financial system. They argued that falling financial asset prices during the GFC resulted in asset write-downs by financial institutions. Consequently, financial institutions were forced to sell financial assets in order to maintain capital adequacy prices. The forced asset sales arguably fuelled further reduction in prices, which exacerbated the effects of the GFC.

Proponents of fair value countered the arguments of its critics by pointing out that, in most countries, the majority of financial assets held by financial institutions were measured using amortised cost. Further, where used, fair value provided more timely recognition of problems, thus facilitating resolution of problems and mitigating the effects of the GFC.

In relation to financial assets carried at amortised cost by financial institutions, the FCAG (2009) concluded that:

> ... the overall value of these assets has not been understated — but overstated. The incurred loss model for loan loss provisioning and difficulties in applying the model — in particular, identifying appropriate trigger points for loss recognition — in many instances has delayed the recognition of losses on loan portfolios.

Required

Discuss the concerns about the accounting treatment of financial instruments raised in response to the global financial crisis. To what extent have these concerns been addressed by AASB 9/IFRS 9 and other changes in accounting standards?

CASE STUDY 11.2

FINANCIAL INSTRUMENTS AND PERFORMANCE REPORTING

Find and read the following article: Horton, J & Macve, R 2008, '"Fair value" for financial instruments: how erasing theory is leading to unworkable global accounting standards for performance reporting', *Australian Accounting Review*, vol. 10, no. 21, May, pp. 26–39.

Required

Provide a brief summary of the authors' main criticisms.

APPLICATION AND ANALYSIS EXERCISES

★ BASIC | ★ ★ MODERATE | ★ ★ ★ DIFFICULT

11.1 Identification of financial assets, financial liabilities and equity instruments ★   **LO1, 2, 3, 5, 6**

Which of the following items qualify as a financial asset, financial liability or equity instrument within the scope of AASB 9/IFRS 9? Give reasons for your answers.

1. Cash held
2. Investment in a debt security
3. Investment in a subsidiary
4. Provision for restoration of a mine site
5. Buildings owned by the reporting entity
6. Income tax payable
7. Provision for employee benefits
8. Deferred revenue
9. Prepayments
10. Forward exchange contract
11. Investment in 3% of the ordinary shares of a private company
12. A percentage interest in an unincorporated joint venture
13. A non-controlling interest in a partnership
14. A non-controlling interest in a discretionary trust
15. An investment in an associate
16. A forward purchase contract for delivery of a commodity (e.g. wheat) that is settled only by physical delivery
17. Forward contract entered into by a gold producer to sell gold that is settled net in cash
18. Leases
19. Trade receivables
20. Loan receivables
21. Debentures issued
22. Bank borrowings
23. Ordinary shares issued
24. Call options held for shares in Telstra Corporation Limited
25. Call options written for shares in Telstra Corporation Limited
26. Convertible notes issued

11.2 Subsequent measurement of financial assets and financial liabilities ★   **LO2, 3, 13, 15**

The trainee accountant at Daffodil Ltd is unsure how to measure a number of items included in its financial records and has asked for your advice. Identify whether each of the following is a financial asset or financial liability and explain on what basis it must be subsequently measured.

1. Trade receivables
2. Primary borrowings of $2 million carrying a variable interest rate
3. 4-year government bonds held paying interest of 6% p.a.
4. Investment in a long-term portfolio of shares listed on the ASX
5. Investment in a trading portfolio of shares listed on the ASX
6. Purchased loans held for short periods before being on-sold
7. Mandatorily converting notes held, paying coupon interest of 8% p.a. — the notes must convert to a variable number of ordinary shares at the expiration of their term

8. Mandatorily redeemable preference shares with a cumulative dividend rate of 4% p.a. — the preference shares must be redeemed for cash at their expiration in 5 years, held within a business model with the objective of collecting contractual cash flows
9. Call or put options held on shares in Solar Corporation Limited
10. Call or put options written on shares in Solar Corporation Limited
11. ASX SPI 200 Futures contract with a negative fair value
12. ASX SPI 200 Futures contract with a positive fair value

11.3 Forward to buy shares ★ ★ ★ **LO5**

Wallace Ltd enters a forward contract to buy its own ordinary shares after 12 months at a fixed forward price. Wallace Ltd has a contractual obligation based on the forward price and it has a contractual right based on the market price at the maturity date. Wallace Ltd is considering a range of different alternatives for the settlement of the contract. Details of the contract are as follows.

Contract date	1 February 2023
Maturity date	31 January 2024
Market price per share on 1 February 2023	$5.00
Market price per share on 31 December 2023	$5.10
Market price per share on 31 January 2024	$5.05
Fixed forward price per share on 31 January 2024	$5.03
Present value of forward price on 1 February 2023	$5.00
Number of shares under the forward contract	2 000 000
Fair value of forward contract on 1 February 2023	$nil
Fair value of forward contract on 31 December 2023	$540 000
Fair value of forward contract on 31 January 2024	$180 000

Required

Prepare the entries of Wallace Ltd for the forward purchase contract on its own shares assuming the company has a year end of 31 December and that the contract will be settled:
1. cash for cash (net cash settlement)
2. shares for shares (net share settlement)
3. cash for shares (gross physical settlement).

11.4 Distinguishing financial liabilities from equity instruments ★ **LO6**

Determine whether Aster Ltd has a financial liability or equity instrument resulting from the issue of securities in each situation below. Give reasons for your answer.
1. Aster Ltd issues 100 000 $1 convertible notes. The notes pay interest at 7% p.a. The market rate for similar debt without the conversion option is 9%. Each note is not redeemable, but it converts at the option of the holder into however many shares that will have a value of exactly $1.
2. Aster Ltd issues 100 000 $1 redeemable convertible notes. The notes pay interest at 5% p.a. Each note converts at any time at the option of the holder into one ordinary share. The notes are redeemable at the option of the holders for cash after 5 years. Market rates for similar notes without the conversion option are 7% p.a.
3. Aster Ltd issues 100 000 $1 redeemable convertible notes. The notes pay interest at 5% p.a. Each note converts at any time at the option of the holder into one ordinary share. The notes are redeemable at the option of the issuer for cash after 5 years. If after 5 years the notes have not been redeemed or converted, they cease to carry interest. Market rates for similar notes without the conversion option are 7% p.a.
4. Aster Ltd issues 100 000 $1 redeemable convertible notes. The notes pay interest at 5% p.a. The notes are redeemable after 5 years at the option of the issuer for cash or for a variable number of shares (calculated according to a formula). If after 5 years the notes have not been redeemed or converted, they continue to carry interest at a new market rate to be determined at the expiration of the 5 years.
5. Aster Ltd issues redeemable preference shares. The shares are redeemable at the expiration of five years at the option of the holder. The shares carry a cumulative 6% dividend.
6. Aster Ltd issues redeemable preference shares. The shares carry a cumulative 6% dividend. The shares are redeemable for cash if the company makes an accounting loss in any year. Aster Ltd is highly profitable and has a history of profits and paying ordinary dividends at a yield of about 4% annually without fail for the past 25 years. The market interest rate for long-term debt at the time the preference shares were issued was 7% p.a.

11.5 Convertible notes issue including financial liability at amortised cost ★ ★   **LO7**

On 1 July 2021 Scarecrow Ltd issues convertible notes with a face value of $6 million. The convertible notes have a 20-year term and mature on 30 June 2041. Interest is payable semiannually in arrears, on 31 December and 30 June each year, and the coupon rate of interest is 7.5% p.a. At around the same point in time, companies with a similar credit rating issue debt securities without a conversion option with a coupon rate of 10% p.a., payable semiannually.

Required

1. Explain why the coupon rate to holders of the convertible notes is less than the rate of return offered to investors in the debt securities of other similar companies.
2. Determine the debt and equity components of the convertible notes issued using the residual valuation method.
3. Prepare the entries of Scarecrow Ltd to account for the convertible notes over the period 1 July 2021 to 30 June 2024.

11.6 Convertible notes issue including financial liability at amortised cost ★ ★   **LO7**

On 1 July 2024, Parade Ltd issues 2000 convertible notes. The notes have a 3-year term and are issued at par with a face value of $1000 per note, giving total proceeds at the date of issue of $2 million. The notes pay interest at 4% p.a. annually in arrears. The holder of each note is entitled to convert the note into 250 ordinary shares of Parade Ltd at contract maturity.

When the notes are issued, the prevailing market interest rate for similar debt (similar term, similar credit status of issuer and similar cash flows) without conversion options is 8% p.a. Hence, at the date of issue:

Present value of the principal: $2 million payable in 3 years' time:	$1 587 664
Present value of the interest: $80 000 ($2 million × 4%) payable annually in arrears for 3 years	206 168
Total contractual cash flows	$1 793 832

Required

Prepare the journal entries of Parade Ltd to account for the convertible notes for each year ending 30 June under the following circumstances.

1. The holders do not exercise their option and the note is repaid at the end of its term.
2. The holders exercise their conversion option at the expiration of the contract term.

11.7 Trading in shares ★ ★   **LO9**

Asha Ltd is an investment company that trades in shares on the Australian Securities Exchange. Asha Ltd measures the shares at fair value through the profit or loss. Asha Ltd makes the following trades in TelCo Limited.

Trade date	Quantity	Price	Buy/Sell	Brokerage
8 June 2022	20 000	$6.00	Buy	$1000
15 June 2022	80 000	$6.20	Buy	$1600
30 June 2022	40 000	$5.50	Sell	$800

Settlement date is T + 2 meaning that settlement of trades occurs two business days after trade date. The closing market price for shares in TelCo at 30 June 2022 is $5.60.

Required

Prepare the entries of Asha Ltd on the basis of:

1. trade date accounting
2. settlement date accounting.

11.8 Accounting for loan assets at amortised cost ★ ★   **LO12, 13, 14**

Finale Ltd is a manufacturing company that makes loans to other parties from time to time. The loan assets are classified by Finale Ltd as subsequently measured at amortised cost. Finale Ltd does not apply the simplified approach to impairment of loans receivable. In accounting for impairment losses, Finale Ltd classifies all loans as remaining at Stage 1 from inception to maturity. On 1 July 2022, Finale Ltd made the following loans.

(a) A 3-year loan of $1 million to Grate Ltd at an interest rate of 15% p.a. due annually in arrears on 30 June each year. Grate Ltd incurred transaction costs of $97 749 in respect of this loan to arrange charges for security. Finale Ltd estimates 12 months' expected credit loss as $20 000.

(b) A 3-year loan of $1 million to American Ltd at an interest rate of 10% p.a. with interest due only on settlement at 30 June 2025. Finale Ltd estimates 12 months' expected credit loss as $10 000.

(c) A 3-year loan of $1 million to an employee, Mr Whale. The loan is interest free in recognition of his loyalty to the company. Finale Ltd estimates 12 months' expected credit loss as $30 000.

Required

Prepare the entries of Finale Ltd to account for the three loans from initial recognition on 1 July 2022 to derecognition on 30 June 2025, assuming loans are paid in full on maturity.

11.9 Various financial assets and financial liabilities ★ ★   **LO12, 13**

Santiago Adventures Ltd has entered into a number of contracts that are financial instruments as follows.

(a) On 1 July 2021, the company acquired 100 000 shares in Telex Corporation Limited as a longterm investment at a cost of $500 000. The year-end market prices of Telex shares were $6.50 on 30 June 2022 and $5.50 on 30 June 2023.

(b) On 1 April 2022, the company acquired 100 000 exchange traded call options in Westside Banking Corporation Ltd at a cost of $3.00 per option. The options have an exercise price of $38.00 and mature on 22 November 2022. The options have a fair value to the holder of $4.00 each on 30 June 2022 and $5.20 each on 22 November 2022 when the options are exercised.

(c) On 1 October 2021, the company wrote 100 000 exchange traded call options in FoodCo Limited at a premium of $2.50 per option. The options have an exercise price of $40.00 and mature on 20 July 2022. FoodCo share price is $39.00 on 20 July 2022. The options have a fair value to the holder of $1.50 each on 30 June 2022 and nil each on 20 July 2022.

(d) On 1 March 2022, the company takes a sell position on 50 units of ASX SPI 200 Futures. Each contract unit is valued at $25 per index point. The ASX SPI Futures Index is 5800 on 1 March 2022, 6500 on 30 June 2022 and 5500 on 22 September 2022 when the company closes out its position.

Required

Prepare the entries of Santiago Adventures Ltd for any financial assets or financial liabilities that arise in each case.

11.10 Netting off a financial asset and financial liability ★   **LO10**

In each of the situations below, state whether the financial asset and financial liability must be offset in the books of Company X as at 30 June 2022, and explain why.

1. Company X owes Company Y $750 000, due on 30 June 2025. Company Y owes Company X $450 000, due on 30 June 2026. A legal right of set-off between the two companies is documented in writing, and the parties have indicated their intent to settle the amounts on a net basis.

2. Company X owes Company Y $750 000, due on 30 June 2023. Company Y owes Company X $450 000, due on 31 March 2023. A legal right of set-off between the two companies is documented in writing, and the parties have indicated their intent to settle amounts owing between the two parties on a net basis whenever possible.

3. Company X owes Company Y $750 000, due on 30 June 2023. Company Z owes Company X $450 000, due on 30 June 2023.

4. Company X owes Company Y $750 000, due on 30 June 2023. Company Z owes Company X $750 000, due on 30 June 2023. A legal right of set-off between the three companies is documented in writing, and the parties have indicated their intent to settle the amounts on a net basis.

5. Company X owes Company Y $750 000, due on 30 June 2024. Company X has plant and equipment with a fair value of $750 000 that it pledges to Company Y as collateral for the debt.

11.11 Purchased debt instrument with impairment ★ ★ ★   **LO9, 11, 13, 14**

On 1 January 2022, Biz Banking Ltd purchases a debt instrument with a 5-year term for its fair value of $1000 million (including transaction costs). The instrument has a principal amount of $1250 million (the amount payable on redemption) and carries fixed interest of 4.7% paid annually in arrears on 31 December. The annual cash interest income is thus $59 million ($1250 million 0.047 rounded to nearest million). Using a financial calculator, the effective interest rate is calculated as 10%. The debt instrument is classified as subsequently measured at amortised cost. At 31 December 2022 Biz Banking Ltd assesses that the credit risk of the debt instrument has not changed significantly since initial recognition and that 12 months' expected credit loss is

$1 million. There is no significant change in credit risk until 2024. During that year, the issuer of the debt instrument faces financial difficulties. By 31 December 2024 it becomes likely that the issuer of the debt instrument will be placed into receivership. The lifetime expected credit loss of the debt instrument is estimated to be $500 million on 31 December 2024, calculated by discounting the expected future cash flows at 10%. No cash flows are received during 2024. At the end of 2025, Biz Banking Ltd receives a letter stating that the issuer will be able to meet all of its remaining obligations, including interest and repayment of principal.

Required

Prepare the entries of Biz Banking Ltd for all years from initial recognition to derecognition of the financial asset.

11.12 Applying accounting theory ★ ★ ★   **LO6, 8, 13, 14**

Northern Tours Ltd needs to raise $500 000 to finance the acquisition of a new tour bus. It approached an investment bank that proposed the following alternatives:

(a) the issue of 8%, cumulative preference shares for $500 000 with a fixed redemption date 5 years from the date of issue (8% cumulative preference shares)

(b) the issue of 10%, non-cumulative, preference shares for $500 000, redeemable at the option of the issuer (10% non-cumulative preference shares).

The preference share issue is planned for 2022. The accountant prepared an abridged projected statement of financial position for Northern Tours Ltd s at 30 June 2021, based on the company's master budget. The projected statement of financial position excludes the effects of the proposed preference share issue or the investment in the new tour bus.

NORTHERN TOURS LTD Projected statement of financial position as at 30 June 2021 (abridged)			
	$		$
Assets	2 500 000	Liabilities	1 500 000
		Equity	1 000 000
	2 500 000		2 500 000

Additional information

- Northern Tours Ltd estimates profit before interest and tax (EBIT) as $420 000. This estimate is based on prior years' performance, adjusted for the effects of the additional tour bus.
- Interest expense in relation to a bank loan included in 'Liabilities' = $100 000.
- Northern Tours Ltd's bank loan includes a debt covenant which specifies a maximum leverage ratio (total liabilities/total assets) of 60%.
- The company has investigated alternative sources of funding and found that most lenders require it to have maintained interest coverage (EBIT/Interest expense) greater than 3.0.
- Management receives a bonus of 2% of profit before tax, provided the return on investment (EBIT/total assets) exceeds 12%.

Required

1. Calculate Northern Tours Ltd's leverage ratio at 30 June 2021 based on the projected statement of financial position.
2. How should the 8% cumulative preference shares be classified in accordance with AASB 132/ IAS 32? Justify your classification.
3. Prepare a journal entry to record the annual dividend payable on the 8% cumulative preference shares.
4. Using the projected figures and estimates provided, calculate Northern Tours Ltd's leverage ratio and interest coverage assuming the company issues the 8% cumulative preference shares.
5. How should the 10% non-cumulative preference shares be classified in accordance with AASB 132/IAS 32? Justify your classification.
6. Prepare a journal entry to record the annual dividend payable on the 10% non-cumulative preference shares.
7. Using the projected figures and estimates provided, calculate Northern Tours Ltd's leverage ratio and interest coverage assuming the company issues the 10% non-cumulative preference shares.

8. Compare Northern Tours Ltd's profit before tax for each financing alternative.
9. Drawing on agency theory (see chapter 2), explain which financing arrangement would be preferred by management. Where relevant, refer to your analysis of financial statement implications in parts 2 to 8.

REFERENCES

Ernst & Young 2011, *Implementing phase 1 of IFRS 9 (second edition)*, www.ey.com.
Financial Crisis Advisory Group 2009, *Report of the Financial Crisis Advisory Group*, 28 July, www.ifrs.org.

ACKNOWLEDGEMENTS

Photo: © Vintage Tone / Shutterstock.com

Photo: © TK Kurikawa / Shutterstock.com

Figure 11.4: © IFRS. This publication contains copyright material of the IFRS Foundation in respect of which all rights are reserved. Reproduced by John Wiley & Sons Australia, Ltd with the permission of the IFRS Foundation. No permission granted to third parties to reproduce or distribute. For full access to IFRS Standards and the work of the IFRS Foundation please visit http://eifrs.ifrs.org. The International Accounting Standards Board, the IFRS Foundation, the authors and the publishers do not accept responsibility for any loss caused by acting or refraining from acting in reliance on the material in this publication, whether such loss is caused by negligence or otherwise.

Text: © 2019 Australian Accounting Standards Board (AASB). The text, graphics and layout of this publication are protected by Australian copyright law and the comparable law of other countries. No part of the publication may be reproduced, stored or transmitted in any form or by any means without the prior written permission of the AASB except as permitted by law. For reproduction or publication, permission should be sought in writing from the AASB. Requests in the first instance should be addressed to the National Director, Australian Accounting Standards Board, PO Box 204, Collins Street West, Victoria 8007.

CHAPTER 12

Income taxes

CHAPTER AIM

This chapter explains how to account for company income tax in accordance with AASB 112/IAS 12 *Income Taxes*. Accounting for company income tax is based on the current and future tax consequences of transactions and events of the period, and the future recovery of assets and settlement of liabilities.

LEARNING OBJECTIVES

After studying this chapter, you should be able to:

12.1 discuss the need for an accounting standard on income taxes

12.2 discuss differences in accounting treatments and taxation treatments for a range of transactions and events

12.3 explain that some transactions and events have both current and future tax consequences

12.4 calculate and account for current income tax

12.5 calculate and account for deferred income tax

12.6 account for changes in income tax rates

12.7 explain the disclosure requirements of AASB 112/IAS 12.

CONCEPT FOR REVIEW

Before studying this chapter, you should understand and, if necessary, revise:
* how the accrual basis of accounting differs from the cash basis.

12.1 Introduction and scope

LEARNING OBJECTIVE 12.1 Discuss the need for an accounting standard on income taxes.

All companies that generate revenue, while incurring expenses, are normally subject to taxation. The tax incurred by a company in a financial year is assessed by the taxation authority (in Australia, that is the Australian Taxation Office) based on the taxation assessment rules applicable. Those rules apply in the calculation of taxable profit on which tax is payable. Those rules are not necessarily equivalent to the accounting rules used in the calculation of accounting profit. Accounting profit is calculated as the difference between revenues earned and expenses incurred, using the accrual basis of accounting. Taxable profit is the difference between taxable revenues (i.e. revenues recognised for taxation) and allowable deductions (i.e. expenses recognised for taxation). The taxation authority may not recognise all the accounting revenues as taxable when earned or all the accounting expenses as deductions when incurred or may recognise additional taxable revenues or allowable deductions not yet recognised in accounting as revenues or expenses. Therefore, there may be some differences between the taxable profit and accounting profit that will need to be taken into consideration when a company accounts for the tax effects incurred.

The tax calculated based on taxable profit (i.e. by multiplying it with the current income tax rate) reflects only the current tax effect of transactions recorded in accounting. This tax is payable to the taxation authority for the current period, so it is reflected into a current tax liability account. As a result of the differences between accounting and taxation rules, there might also be some future tax effects resulting from current transactions or accrual accounting adjustments. As long as those future tax effects are consequences of the transactions that already occurred in the current period, they should be recognised for accounting purposes as deferred tax. Together with current tax effects, those future tax effects are reflected in the **income tax** expense calculated based on the accounting profit. If those future tax effects are not recognised in accounting, the income tax expense for the current year will be misleading.

Consider the case of Wipeout Limited, as follows.

- Wipeout Limited records accounting profit before tax and before depreciation of $10 000 per annum over a 3-year period.
- Wipeout Limited has one depreciable asset that cost $600 and has a 3-year useful life.
- Wipeout Limited uses straight-line depreciation for accounting purposes, but is allowed to use a diminishing balance method for taxation purposes. As a result, it recognises $200 as an accounting depreciation expense every year, but claims $300, $200 and $100 respectively over the 3 years as tax deductions.
- The company tax rate is 30%.

Over the 3-year period, Wipeout Limited would make the calculations shown in figure 12.1.

FIGURE 12.1   Current tax liability and income tax expense

	Year 1	Year 2	Year 3
Profit before depreciation and income tax	$10 000	$10 000	$10 000
Depreciation deduction — diminishing balance method	300	200	100
Taxable profit	9 700	9 800	9 900
Current tax liability (based on a tax rate of 30%)	$ 2 910	$ 2 940	$ 2 970

	Year 1	Year 2	Year 3
Accounting profit before depreciation and income tax	$10 000	$10 000	$10 000
Depreciation expense — straight-line method	200	200	200
Accounting profit	9 800	9 800	9 800
Income tax expense (based on a tax rate of 30%)	$ 2 940	$ 2 940	$ 2 940

Figure 12.1 shows that in year 1 the current tax liability based on taxable profit after the tax deduction related to depreciation is lower than the income tax expense calculated based on accounting profit ($2910 versus $2940). While in year 2 there is no difference ($2940 versus $2940), in year 3 the difference from year 1 reverses ($2970 versus $2940). The accounting depreciation method reflects the pattern in which the economic benefits are derived from the use of the asset. If the tax depreciation is calculated using a different method, the current tax liability calculated based on the taxable profit after depreciation does not reflect the total tax effects of the way the economic benefits are derived from the asset, but only the current tax effect. However, the income tax expense for year 1 based on the accounting profit recognises the current tax liability of $2910 plus the future tax effect that seems to be deferred for year 3.

Therefore, accounting for income tax should not be based only on taxable profit or, in other words, based only on the current tax liability payable to the taxation authority. The future tax effects also need to be considered and those may reflect less or more tax to be paid in the future (that should be recognised as deferred tax assets or liabilities).

Assume there are two companies — Hanging Ltd and Ten Ltd — that have the same assets and liabilities and use the same accounting methods and policies to account for their assets and liabilities. Hanging Ltd, however, has made a tax loss in a prior period whereas Ten Ltd has not. Prior period tax losses can be used as tax deductions in following years, resulting in a reduction in the amount of tax to be paid. If income tax were accounted for purely on a current tax liability basis, then there would be no recognition in Hanging Ltd's statement of financial position that it has some future economic benefits arising from future tax deductions relating to the tax loss — those benefits should be recognised as a future (deferred) tax asset.

Future tax liabilities could also be of concern. For example, assume that while the non-current assets are still depreciable for accounting purposes for both entities, Hanging Ltd may have fully depreciated its assets for tax purposes (by using a higher depreciation rate for taxation than for accounting), whereas Ten Ltd still has some tax depreciation to claim in the future. In such circumstances, Hanging Ltd may have more future tax obligations. If income tax is accounted purely on a current tax liability basis, this liability for future tax, incurred as a result of the current treatment of tax depreciation, would not appear in Hanging Ltd's statement of financial position.

These examples demonstrate that accounting for income tax is not simply a matter of recognising the current tax liability based upon the amount of tax owing to the tax authorities in any particular year. Unless income tax is accounted for properly by incorporating the future tax consequences of the current transactions and events, the relevance of the accounting numbers is questionable.

This chapter is not concerned with the determination of numbers recognised in an entity's tax return, but rather the numbers to be used in the entity's financial statements. Accounting for income tax is governed by AASB 112/IAS 12 *Income Taxes*. The method of accounting for income tax prescribed by AASB 112/IAS 12, generally referred to as *tax-effect accounting*, recognises both current and future tax consequences of current transactions and events. In doing so, it takes into account the differences between the accounting and taxation treatments of assets and liabilities. More specifically, AASB 112/IAS 12 prescribes how to account for the current and future tax effects of current transactions and other events that are recognised in a company's financial statements and the future recovery (settlement) of the **carrying amount** of the assets (liabilities). As the objective paragraph of AASB 112/IAS 12 points out:

> The principal issue in accounting for income taxes is how to account for the current and future tax consequences of:
> (a) the future recovery (settlement) of the carrying amount of assets (liabilities) that are recognised in an entity's statement of financial position; and
> (b) transactions and other events of the current period that are recognised in an entity's financial statements.

AASB 112/IAS 12 adopts the philosophy that, as a general rule, the tax consequences of transactions that occur during a period should be 'recognised as income or an expense in the net profit or loss for the period' irrespective of when those tax effects will be realised. A transaction may have two tax 'effects'.
1. Current tax payable on profit earned for the year may be reduced or increased because the transaction is not taxable or deductible in the current year.
2. Future tax payable may be increased or reduced when that transaction becomes taxable or deductible in the future.

LEARNING CHECK

☐ There are differences in how revenues and expenses are measured for income tax purposes and how they are measured for accounting purposes. These differences must be considered in order to ensure the usefulness of the information provided in financial statements.

☐ Income tax expense should recognise both current and future tax effects of the items recorded in accounting and it is normally calculated based on the accounting profit. The current tax effects are normally reported in the current tax liability calculated based on the taxable profit, while future tax effects can give rise to a deferred tax asset or liability.

☐ Accounting for income tax is governed by AASB 112/IAS 12 *Income Taxes*.

12.2 Differences between accounting profit and taxable profit

LEARNING OBJECTIVE 12.2 Discuss differences in accounting treatments and taxation treatments for a range of transactions and events.

Accounting profit and taxable profit are determined under different sets of rules.
- **Accounting profit** is measured as the difference between accounting revenues and accounting expenses. The accounting revenues and expenses are determined in accordance with the rules established by accounting standards, normally based on accrual accounting.
- **Taxable profit** (sometimes referred to as taxable income) is calculated as the difference between taxable revenues and tax deductions allowable against those revenues. The taxable revenues and deductions are determined in accordance with the rules established by the taxation authorities, normally based on cash receipts and payments respectively.

It is unlikely that, in any given year, accounting profit will be equal to taxable profit, due to the different treatment of revenues and expenses. Table 12.1 shows some differences in treatment of some revenues and expenses between accounting — under generally accepted accounting principles (GAAP) — and taxation — under the *Income Tax Assessment Act 1997* (ITAA) in Australia.

TABLE 12.1	Examples of differences of treatment of revenues and expenses under GAAP and ITAA	
	Accounting treatment	**Taxation treatment**
Research costs	Recognised as an expense on accrual	Tax deduction on cash payment (further tax deductions possible above the actual cost)
Deferred development costs	Sometimes recognised as an asset and amortised	Tax deduction on cash payment
Goodwill impairment	Recognised as an expense on accrual	Not deductible
Entertainment outlays	Recognised as an expense when payable	Not deductible
Fines and penalties	Recognised as an expense when payable	Not deductible
Interest revenue	Recognised when receivable	Taxable income on cash receipt
Interest expense	Recognised as an expense when payable	Tax deduction on cash payment
Depreciation	Recognised as an expense on accrual	Tax deduction — but taxation depreciation rate may differ from accounting depreciation rate
Receivables (e.g. rent, interest)	Recognised as an asset and revenue on accrual	Taxable income on cash receipt
Bad and doubtful debts	Recognised as an expense when debt is doubtful	Tax deduction when debt is written off as bad
Revenue received in advance	Recognised as a liability, with revenue recognised when earned	Taxable income on receipt of cash
Accrued expenses and provisions (e.g. for long service leave, for warranties)	Recognised as an expense on accrual	Tax deduction on cash payment
Prepaid expenses (e.g. interest, rent)	Recognised as an asset, then expensed in a later period as benefits received	Tax deduction on cash payment
Exempt income (e.g. government grant)	Recognised as income on accrual	Not taxable

It should be noted, looking at table 12.1, that the different treatment of some revenues and expenses for taxation and accounting give rise to two categories of differences between taxable and accounting profit.

1. *Permanent differences* that will never reverse.
   - Some revenues may never be taxed (e.g. government grant).
   - Some expenses may never be allowed as a deduction (e.g. entertainment expenses, fines, goodwill impairment).
2. *Temporary differences* that will reverse over time.
   - Some revenues may not be recognised for taxation in the current period when earned, but in the next period when received (e.g. rent or interest receivable). That will make the taxable profit lower than the accounting profit in the current period, but in the next period accounting profit will be lower.
   - Some revenues may not be recognised for accounting in the current period as, while they are received now, they have not yet been earned, but will be earned in the next period (e.g. revenue received in advance). That will make the taxable profit higher than the accounting profit in the current period, but in the next period accounting profit will be higher.
   - Some expenses may not be recognised for taxation in the current period when incurred, but in the next period when paid (e.g. accrued expenses). That will make the taxable profit higher than the accounting profit in the current period, but in the next period accounting profit will be higher.
   - Some expenses may not be recognised for accounting in the current period when paid, but in the next period when incurred (e.g. prepayments). That will make the taxable profit lower than the accounting profit in the current period, but in the next period accounting profit will be lower.

As there is no tax effect related to permanent differences, their financial impact should be adjusted for when calculating the income tax expense based on the accounting profit. In other words, the income tax expense, incorporating both current and future tax consequences of current transactions, is calculated based on the accounting profit adjusted for permanent differences.

Temporary differences are addressed in section 12.5.3. They will give rise to future tax effects that will be recognised in accounting as future tax benefits or future tax obligations. Basically, temporary differences are responsible for the difference between income tax expense and current tax liability as they reflect the future tax consequences. Differences that result in the entity paying more tax in the future, for example when interest is received, are known as *taxable temporary differences*. Differences that result in the entity recovering tax via additional deductible expenses in the future — for example, when accrued expenses are paid — are known as *deductible temporary differences*.

LEARNING CHECK

☐ Accounting profit is measured as the difference between accounting revenues and expenses. The accounting revenues and expenses are determined in accordance with the rules established by accounting standards, normally based on accrual accounting.

☐ Taxable profit is calculated as the difference between taxable revenues and tax deductions allowable against those revenues. The taxable revenues and deductions are determined in accordance with the rules established by the taxation authorities, normally based on cash receipts and payments respectively.

☐ The differences between the accounting and taxation treatment of revenues and expenses can be classified into permanent and temporary differences. As permanent differences imply no tax effects, the accounting profit will need to be adjusted for those before calculating the income tax expense. Temporary differences are responsible for the difference between income tax expense and current tax liability, as they reflect the future tax consequences.

12.3 Current and future tax consequences of transactions and other events

LEARNING OBJECTIVE 12.3 Explain that some transactions and events have both current and future tax consequences.

Some transactions may not have any consequences for taxation. For example, an entity that pays $5000 in cash entertainment expenses for the current period is not entitled to a tax deduction on that amount in the current period or in the future.

Other transactions have only *current* period consequences for taxation. For example, if an entity pays $10 000 cash for rent of a building for the current period, a tax deduction of $10 000 is received. There is a current tax effect but no future tax effect.

Some other transactions have both *current* and *future* tax consequences. For example, assume an entity recognises interest revenue of $21 000 for the current year. Of this amount, $15 000 has been received in cash and a receivable asset has been raised for the remaining $6000. A calculation of tax payable based on cash flow requires interest revenue to be taxed only when the cash is received. Therefore, the entity will pay tax of $4500 ($15 000 × 30%) in the current year and tax of $1800 ($6000 × 30%) in the following year when the $6000 receivable is collected. In the current year, as $21 000 is recognised as accounting revenue, both the current and future tax consequences should also be recognised under income tax expense.

Therefore, accounting for income tax must take into account both current and future tax consequences of transactions. In essence, the income tax accounting must:

- prescribe the accounting treatment of the *current* tax consequences of transactions. This will give rise to current tax liabilities or current tax assets. The task is to determine an entity's liability for taxation in the current period based on an assessment of the entity's current taxable profit or tax loss determined in accordance with the tax legislation. The liability for taxation in the *current* period is recognised by a journal entry of the following form. Accounting for current tax is covered in section 12.4.

Income tax expense (current)	Dr	xxx	
Current tax liability	Cr		xxx
(Recognition of the current tax liability)			

- prescribe the accounting treatment of the *future* tax consequences of transactions. This involves an analysis of whether more tax or less tax will need to be paid in the future as a result of those transactions. From this analysis, the future tax consequences are accounted for by the recognition of deferred tax assets and deferred tax liabilities. The *deferred* or future tax assets and liabilities are recognised by a journal entry of the following form. Accounting for future tax is covered in section 12.5.

Income tax expense (deferred)	Dr	xxx	
Deferred tax asset	Dr	xxx	
Deferred tax liability	Cr		xxx
(Recognition of movement in deferred tax accounts)			

LEARNING CHECK

☐ Accounting for income tax must take into account both current and future tax consequences of transactions.

☐ The accounting treatment of the *current* tax consequences of transactions will give rise to current tax liabilities or current tax assets.

☐ The accounting treatment of the *future* tax consequences of transactions involves an analysis of whether more tax or less tax will be payable in the future. This analysis results in raising any deferred tax assets or deferred tax liabilities.

12.4 Calculation and recognition of current tax

LEARNING OBJECTIVE 12.4 Calculate and account for current income tax.

The **current tax** liability is the recognition of the tax payable to the taxation authorities in relation to the current year. The calculation of this liability involves measuring the taxable profit and multiplying it by the current tax rate (this chapter assumes that the tax rate applicable is 30% unless otherwise stated). Taxable profit can be measured based on accounting profit adjusted for the different treatment of accounting revenues and expenses for taxation purposes. The process involves the following steps.

1. Identify accounting profit for the period — as accounting profit contains the accounting revenues and accounting expenses, it is used as the starting point.
2. Determine the expenses and revenues that are treated differently for accounting and taxation.

3. Adjust for these differences by:
   - adding the accounting expenses and subtracting the tax deductions for each expense that is not deductible for tax or that differs from the deductible amount
   - subtracting the accounting revenues and adding the taxable revenues for each revenue that is not taxable or that differs from the taxable amount.

This process can be performed in a worksheet — referred to as the *current tax worksheet* — and can be expressed as follows.

> Accounting profit
>   + Accounting expenses or losses where the amounts differ from deductible amounts
>   + Taxable revenues where the amounts differ from accounting revenues or gains
>   − Deductible amounts where the amounts differ from accounting expenses or losses
>   − Accounting revenues or gains where the amounts differ from taxable revenues
>   = Taxable profit

As mentioned above, the taxation treatment of many revenues and expenses follows the cash receipts and payments related to those items; that is, cash flows. As discussed in chapter 17, the opening and ending balances from the statements of financial position for two consecutive financial years can be used to identify the net amount of changes in related assets and liabilities accounts. Supplementing that with information about accounting revenues and expenses that explain a part of the changes, we can identify the related cash flows that will explain the other part of the changes. Therefore, to determine the taxable revenues and deductible amounts, we use information from the asset and liability accounts affected, looking at the opening and ending balances and the accounting revenues or expenses that cause a movement in those balances. For example, to identify the amount that should be recognised as a tax deduction for warranty expenses, the following steps can be applied.

1. Identify the opening and ending balances of the account affected by warranty expenses (i.e. Provision for warranty). For example, assume the opening balance is $20 000 and the ending balance is $15 000.
2. Identify the likely movements that affect the balance of the Provision for warranty account (i.e. warranty expense increases it, and warranty paid decreases it). Assume that warranty expense is $30 000.
3. Identify the equation that describes the movements in the Provision for warranty account.

$$\text{Opening balance} + \text{Warranty expense} - \text{Warranty paid} = \text{Ending balance}$$

4. Calculate the warranty paid (i.e. the tax deduction related to warranty expenditure) by rewriting the previous equation based on the amounts known. The warranty paid will then be as follows.

$$\begin{aligned}\text{Warranty paid} &= \text{Opening balance (\$20\,000)} + \text{Warranty expense (\$30\,000)} - \text{Ending balance (\$15\,000)}\\ &= \$35\,000\end{aligned}$$

Another example involves determining the amount of taxable revenue related to interest revenue received in advance. To identify the amount that should be recognised as a taxable revenue, the following steps can be applied.

1. Identify the opening and ending balances of the account affected by the interest revenue received in advance (i.e. Unearned interest). Assume the opening balance is $5000 and the ending balance is $7000.
2. Identify the likely movements that affect the balance of the Unearned interest account (i.e. interest received increases it and interest revenue decreases it). Assume that interest revenue is $10 000.
3. Identify the equation that describes the movements in the Unearned interest account.

$$\text{Opening balance} + \text{Interest received} - \text{Interest revenue} = \text{Ending balance}$$

4. Calculate the interest received (i.e. the taxable revenue related to interest) by rewriting the previous equation based on the amounts known. The interest received will then be as follows.

$$\begin{aligned}\text{Interest received} &= \text{Interest revenue (\$10\,000)} + \text{Ending balance (\$7000)} - \text{Opening balance (\$5000)}\\ &= \$12\,000\end{aligned}$$

If the interest revenue is receivable in arrears, to identify the amount that should be recognised as a taxable revenue, the following steps can be applied.

1. Identify the opening and ending balances of the account affected by interest receivable (i.e. Interest receivable). Assume the opening balance is $10 000, while the ending balance is $2000.

2. Identify the likely movements that affect the balance of the Interest receivable account (i.e. interest revenue increases it and interest received decreases it). Assume that interest revenue is $6000.
3. Identify the equation that describes the movements in the Interest receivable account.

$$\text{Opening balance} + \text{Interest revenue} - \text{Interest received} = \text{Ending balance}$$

4. Calculate the interest received (i.e. the taxable revenue related to interest) by rewriting the previous equation based on the amounts known. The interest received will then be as follows.

$$\text{Interest received} = \text{Opening balance (\$10\,000)} + \text{Interest revenue (\$6000)} - \text{Ending balance (\$2000)}$$
$$= \$14\,000$$

ILLUSTRATIVE EXAMPLE 12.1

Using a current tax worksheet to determine the current tax liability

Alpha Ltd's accounting profit for the year ended 30 June 2023 was $250 450. Included in this profit were the following items of income and expenses.

Amortisation expense — development project	$30 000
Impairment of goodwill expense	7 000
Depreciation expense — equipment (15%)	40 000
Entertainment expense	12 450
Insurance expense	24 000
Doubtful debts expense	14 000
Annual leave expense	54 000
Rent revenue	25 000
Loss on equipment sold	6 667

At 30 June 2023, the company's draft statement of financial position showed the following balances.

	30 June 2023	30 June 2020
Assets		
Cash	$ 55 000	$ 65 000
Accounts receivable	295 000	277 000
Allowance for doubtful debts	(16 000)	(18 000)
Inventories	162 000	185 000
Prepaid insurance	30 000	25 000
Rent receivable	3 500	5 500
Development project	120 000	—
Accumulated amortisation — development project	(30 000)	—
Equipment	200 000	266 667
Accumulated depreciation — equipment	(90 000)	(80 000)
Goodwill	35 000	35 000
Accumulated impairment — goodwill	(14 000)	(7 000)
Deferred tax asset	?	24 900
Liabilities		
Accounts payable	310 500	294 000
Provision for annual leave	61 000	65 000
Mortgage loan	100 000	150 000
Deferred tax liability	?	57 150
Current tax liability	?	12 500

Additional information
- Taxation legislation allows Alpha Ltd to deduct 125% of the $120 000 spent on development during the year.
- Alpha Ltd has capitalised development expenditure relating to a filter project and amortises the balance over the period of expected benefit (4 years).
- The tax depreciation rate for equipment is 20% p.a. The loss on sale of equipment included in the accounting profit for the year ended 30 June 2023 refers to equipment sold on 30 June 2023 that had an original cost of $66 667 when it was purchased 3 years ago and a carrying amount at the time of sale of $36 667.

- Neither entertainment expenditure nor goodwill impairment expense is deductible for taxation purposes.
- The company income tax rate is 30%.

Required

Calculate the current income tax payable.

Solution

Before completing the worksheet, all differences between accounting and taxation figures must be identified. (*Note:* The effects of these in the current tax worksheet are seen in figure 12.2.)

(i) Amortisation expense — development project

In relation to the development costs, $120 000 has been capitalised for accounting purposes and is amortised over 4 years, being $30 000 p.a. Therefore, the accounting expense related to the development project for the year ended 30 June 2023 is $30 000. However, for taxation purposes, the taxation authority allows a tax deduction of $150 000 (being $120 000 + [25% × $120 000]). The extra 25% deduction (being $30 000 = 25% × $120 000) allowed by tax legislation is never recognised as an accounting expense, but is deductible for tax, together with the full amount of the development costs paid.

(ii) Impairment of goodwill expense

The accounting expense related to goodwill impairment is $7000. However, as no tax deduction is allowed for goodwill impairment, the tax deduction is zero.

(iii) Depreciation expense — equipment

The accounting expense related to depreciation of the equipment is $40 000. The amount of tax deduction for depreciation of equipment is $53 333 (being $266 667 × 20%).

(iv) Entertainment expense

The accounting expense related to entertainment is $12 450. No tax deduction is allowed for entertainment expenditure, so the tax deduction is zero.

(v) Insurance expense

The accounting expense related to insurance is $24 000. Insurance expenditure is deductible when paid. The existence of a Prepaid insurance asset account in the statement of financial position indicates that the insurance payment and insurance expense figures are different. It is therefore necessary to reconstruct the asset account to identify how much of the expense has already been deducted for taxation purposes. This is done as follows.

Prepaid insurance			
Balance b/d	25 000	Insurance expense	24 000
Insurance paid	29 000	Balance c/d	30 000
	54 000		54 000

For the Prepaid insurance account:

$$\text{Opening balance (\$25 000)} + \text{Insurance paid (\$29 000)} - \text{Insurance expense (\$24 000)}$$
$$= \text{Ending balance (\$30 000)}$$

The insurance paid that represents the tax deduction allowable for insurance is therefore $29 000.

(vi) Doubtful debts expense

The accounting expense related to doubtful debts is $14 000. Under taxation legislation, a tax deduction is allowed for bad debts written off. The draft statement of financial position shows that an allowance for doubtful debts was raised in the previous year, so any debts written off against that allowance are deductible in the current year. To determine the amount of that write-off, the ledger account of Allowance for doubtful debts is reconstructed as follows.

Allowance for doubtful debts			
Bad debts written off	16 000	Balance b/d	18 000
Balance c/d	16 000	Doubtful debts expense	14 000
	32 000		32 000

For the Allowance for doubtful debts account:

$$\text{Opening balance } (\$18\,000) + \text{Doubtful debts expense } (\$14\,000) - \text{Bad debts written off } (\$16\,000)$$
$$= \text{Ending balance } (\$16\,000)$$

The bad debts written off that represent the allowable tax deduction for bad debts is therefore $16 000.

(vii) Annual leave expense

The accounting expense is $54 000. Annual leave is deductible for tax purposes when paid in cash. The Provision for annual leave indicates the existence of unpaid leave. The amount of annual leave paid in the current year can be determined by reconstructing the ledger account as follows.

Provision for annual leave			
Leave paid	58 000	Balance b/d	65 000
Balance c/d	61 000	Leave expense	54 000
	119 000		119 000

For the Provision for annual leave account:

$$\text{Opening balance } (\$65\,000) + \text{Annual leave expense } (\$54\,000) - \text{Annual leave paid } (\$58\,000)$$
$$= \text{Ending balance } (\$61\,000)$$

The annual leave paid that represents the allowable tax deduction for annual leave is therefore $58 000.

(viii) Loss on equipment sold

The accounting loss on the sale of equipment is different from the gain (loss) for taxation purposes and is calculated as follows.

	Accounting	Taxation
Cost	$66 667	$66 667
Accumulated depreciation	30 000	40 000
(For tax: $66 667 × 20% × 3 years)		
Carrying amount	36 667	26 667
Proceeds	30 000	30 000
Gain (loss)	$ (6 667)	$ 3 333

Because the sales proceeds are the same amount for both accounting and taxation purposes, the difference in the gain/loss on sale is caused by the different carrying amounts under accounting and taxation for the asset sold. This difference is caused by the use of different depreciation rates. While for accounting there is an overall loss on sale of equipment of $6667 that reduces the accounting profit, for taxation there is a gain of $3333.

(ix) Rent revenue

The accounting rent revenue is $25 000. Rent revenue is taxable when received. The presence in the statement of financial position of a Rent receivable asset indicates that part of the revenue has not yet been received as cash and is not taxable in the current year. Reconstructing the ledger account shows the following.

Rent receivable			
Balance b/d	5 500	Rent received	27 000
Rent revenue	25 000	Balance c/d	3 500
	30 500		30 500

For the Rent receivable account:

$$\text{Opening balance } (\$5500) + \text{Rent revenue } (\$25\,000) - \text{Rent received } (\$27\,000) = \text{Ending balance } (\$3500)$$

The rent received that represents the taxable revenue for rent is therefore $27 000.

This chapter assumes that sales revenues are taxed when the sales of inventories are made, no matter if those sales are made for cash or on credit. If different assumptions applied, then the amounts of cash received for sales would need to be determined in order to calculate the current tax payable.

Figure 12.2 contains the current worksheet used to calculate the current tax liability for Alpha Ltd.

FIGURE 12.2 Current tax worksheet for Alpha Ltd

ALPHA LTD
Current tax worksheet
for the year ended 30 June 2023

Accounting profit			$ 250 450
Add:			
Amortisation expense — development project	(i)	$ 30 000	
Impairment of goodwill expense	(ii)	7 000	
Depreciation expense — equipment (accounting)	(iii)	40 000	
Entertainment expense	(iv)	12 450	
Insurance expense	(v)	24 000	
Doubtful debts expense	(vi)	14 000	
Annual leave expense	(vii)	54 000	
Loss on equipment sold (accounting)	(viii)	6 667	
Gain on equipment sold (tax)	(viii)	3 333	
Rent received (tax)	(ix)	27 000	218 450
			468 900
Deduct:			
Tax deduction for development project	(i)	150 000	
Tax deduction for depreciation of equipment (tax)	(iii)	53 333	
Insurance paid	(v)	29 000	
Bad debts written off	(vi)	16 000	
Annual leave paid	(vii)	58 000	
Rent revenue (accounting)	(ix)	25 000	(331 333)
Taxable profit			137 567
Current tax @ 30%			**$ 41 270**

The current tax is calculated by multiplying the taxable profit with the company tax rate. According to paragraph 12 of AASB 112/IAS 12, the current tax for the period, to the extent it is unpaid, is recognised as a liability at the end of the period. Current tax is also recognised in the income tax expense and included in the profit or loss for the period, except to the extent that it arises from transactions where the income is recognised in other comprehensive income or directly in equity (AASB 112/IAS 12 paragraph 58).

For illustrative example 12.1, the journal entry to recognise the current tax for Alpha Ltd at 30 June 2023 is as follows.

2023				
June 30	Income tax expense (current)	Dr	41 270	
	Current tax liability	Cr		41 270
	(Recognition of current income tax)			

12.4.1 Tax losses

Tax losses occur when allowable deductions exceed taxable revenues.

In Australia, tax losses can be carried forward and deducted against future taxable profits. This means that an entity that incurs a tax loss has a future tax benefit: provided it earns taxable profit in the future, it will be able to use the carried forward balances of tax losses to reduce the tax it needs to pay on that future taxable profit. This tax benefit will be recognised as an asset referred to as 'a deferred tax asset'. Deferred tax assets and their recognition are discussed further in section 12.5.

Deferred tax assets relating to tax losses are referred to in this section because of their effect in determining the measurement of the current tax liability. In dealing with tax losses it is necessary to distinguish between two events occurring at two different points of time.

1. *The creation of a carry-forward tax loss.* In the year in which a tax loss occurs, there is no liability to pay tax as there is no taxable profit. Instead a deferred tax asset is recorded to recognise the future deductibility of the tax loss. The form of the journal entry is as follows.

Deferred tax asset	Dr	xxx
Income tax revenue	Cr	xxx
(Recognition of current tax loss and the corresponding deferred tax asset)		

2. *Recoupment of a carry-forward tax loss.* In a period subsequent to that in which the tax loss was incurred, an entity may earn taxable profit. The amount of tax to be paid on that period's taxable profit may then be reduced by claiming a deduction for past tax losses. In this period, the form of the journal entry for the current period tax liability is as follows.

Income tax expense (current)	Dr	xxx
Deferred tax asset	Cr	xxx
Current tax liability	Cr	xxx
(Recognition of current tax and recoupment of the previous period's tax loss)		

One further point to note in accounting for tax losses is the effect of any *exempt income*. Exempt income is recognised as accounting income by the company but not recognised as taxable by the tax authorities; for example, certain government grants are tax exempt. The existence of exempt income has an effect both on the creation of a tax loss and the recoupment of a tax loss.

1. *Exempt income and the creation of a carry-forward tax loss.* If a tax loss occurs in a period, prior to determining any deferred tax asset arising from it, exempt income must be added back to the tax loss to calculate the tax loss after exempt income. It is this number on which the deferred tax asset is calculated. Exempt income loses its exempt status under these circumstances.
2. *Exempt income and the recoupment of a carry-forward tax loss.* If a company has earned exempt income in the current period, the deduction for past tax losses must be made firstly from the exempt income, and only after that from the taxable profit for the current period. In other words, a tax loss must first be set off against the entity's exempt income before any reduction can be made in relation to the current period's liability for tax.

ILLUSTRATIVE EXAMPLE 12.2

Creation and recoupment of carry-forward tax losses

The following information relates to Delta Designs Ltd for the year ended 30 June 2022.

Accounting loss	$ (5 600)
Exempt income included in accounting loss	2 000
Depreciation expense	14 700
Depreciation for tax	20 300
Entertainment expense (not tax-deductible)	10 000
Income tax rate	30%

The calculation of the tax loss is as follows.

DELTA DESIGNS LTD
Current tax worksheet (extract)
for the year ended 30 June 2022

Accounting loss	$ (5 600)
Add:	
Depreciation expense	14 700
Entertainment expense	10 000
	19 100
Deduct:	
Depreciation for tax	20 300
Exempt income	2 000
Tax loss before exempt income	(3 200)
Add:	
Exempt income	2 000
Tax loss after exempt income	(1 200)
Deferred tax asset @ 30%	**$ 360**

Assuming that recognition criteria for a deferred tax asset arising from tax losses (discussed further in section 12.5.1) are met, the adjusting journal entry is as follows.

2022

June 30	Deferred tax asset (tax loss)	Dr	360	
	Income tax revenue	Cr		360
	(Recognition of current tax loss)			

Delta Designs Ltd then makes a taxable profit of $23 600 for the year ending 30 June 2023. This taxable profit has been determined after considering the existence of an $800 exempt income amount arising in the current year. The prior period tax loss of $1200 (for the year ending 30 June 2022) is recouped as follows.

DELTA DESIGNS LTD
Current tax worksheet (extract)
for the year ended 30 June 2023

Taxable profit before tax loss	$23 600
Add:	
Exempt income	800
	24 400
Tax loss recouped	(1 200)
Taxable profit	23 200
Current tax liability @ 30%	**$ 6 960**

The adjusting journal entry is as follows.

2023

June 30	Income tax expense (current)	Dr	7 320	
	Deferred tax asset (tax loss)	Cr		360
	Current tax liability	Cr		6 960
	(Recognition of current tax)			

LEARNING CHECK

☐ The current tax liability is based on the company's taxable profit for the current period determined in accordance with income tax legislation.

☐ The taxable profit for the current period can be determined using a reconciliation approach based on accounting profit in the current tax worksheet.

▶

- The current tax worksheet adjusts accounting profit to come up with the taxable profit as follows:
  1. *adding* accounting expenses or losses that are not equal to tax deductions in the period
  2. *adding* taxable revenues that are not equal to accounting revenues or gains in the period
  3. *deducting* tax deductions that are not equal to accounting expenses or losses in the period
  4. *deducting* accounting revenues or gains that are not equal to taxable revenues in the period.
- The amount for current tax is determined by multiplying taxable profit by the tax rate.
- The existence of exempt income must be taken into account both in the year in which a tax loss occurs as well as in the year in which a tax loss is recouped.

12.5 Calculation and recognition of deferred tax

LEARNING OBJECTIVE 12.5 Calculate and account for deferred income tax.

Future tax consequences arise as a result of transactions and any other adjustments that affect the future amounts to be paid for tax. These transactions give rise to or adjust the assets and liabilities recognised by an entity. For example, the effects of depreciation are reflected in the carrying amounts of depreciable assets at the end of a period. Similarly, rent received in advance results in a liability being reported at the end of a period.

The calculation of **deferred tax** involves comparing the carrying amounts of assets and liabilities as recorded in the accounting statement of financial position with the amounts for these assets and liabilities that would be shown in a statement of financial position if prepared by the taxation authorities. The latter amounts are referred to as the **tax base** of an entity's assets and liabilities.

The process of accounting for deferred tax involves the following steps.

1. Determine the carrying amounts of the assets and liabilities in the statement of financial position (see section 12.5.1).
2. Determine the tax bases of these assets and liabilities (see section 12.5.2).
3. Determine the differences between the carrying amounts and the tax bases, and classify the differences into temporary taxable and deductible differences (see section 12.5.3).
4. (a) Determine the closing balances of the deferred tax asset and deferred tax liability accounts by multiplying the total deductible and taxable temporary differences respectively by the tax rate (see section 12.5.4).
   (b) Determine the adjustments to the deferred tax asset and liability accounts necessary to arrive at their closing balances, using the opening balances and the movements during the current period in these accounts (see section 12.5.5).
   (c) Prepare a journal entry recognising the adjustments to the deferred tax asset and deferred tax liability accounts, the net being the deferred income tax expense/revenue that should be recognised for the current period (see section 12.5.6).

A deferred tax worksheet is used as a part of this four-step process. An example of such a worksheet is shown in figure 12.3. The whole process is explained in detail below.

FIGURE 12.3	Deferred tax worksheet					
	Carrying amount $	Future taxable amount $	Future deductible amount $	Tax base $	Taxable temporary differences $	Deductible temporary differences $
Assets						
Plant	6 000	6 000	5 000	5 000	1 000	0
Prepaid insurance	3 000	3 000	0	0	3 000	0
Interest receivable	1 000	1 000	0	0	1 000	0
Inventories	2 000	2 000	2 000	2 000	0	0
Land — revalued	120 000	120 000	100 000	100 000	20 000	0
Loan receivable	25 000	0	0	25 000	0	0
Accounts receivable (net)	32 000	0	6 000	38 000	0	6 000
Goodwill	10 000	10 000	0	0	10 000	0

Liabilities						
Provision for annual leave	3 900	0	3 900	0	0	3 900
Accrued expenses	6 700	0	6 700	0	0	6 700
Accounts payable	34 000	0	0	34 000	0	0
Loan payable	20 000	0	0	20 000	0	0
Accrued penalties	700	0	0	700	0	0
Subscriptions received in advance	500	0	500	0	0	500
Temporary differences					35 000	17 100
Excluded differences						
Goodwill					10 000	0
Net temporary differences					**25 000**	**17 100**
Deferred tax liability					7 500	
Deferred tax asset						5 130
Beginning balances					1 000	4 000
Movements during year					60	(100)
Adjustment					**6 440**	**1 230**

12.5.1 Step 1. Determine the carrying amounts

Carrying amounts are asset and liability accounting balances *after* valuation allowances, accumulated depreciation/amortisation amounts and impairment losses have been netted off. For example, the carrying amount of accounts receivable is the balance of accounts receivable less any allowance for doubtful debts. These amounts can be read from the accounting trial balance at the end of the financial year.

12.5.2 Step 2. Determine the tax bases

Tax bases need to be determined for both assets and liabilities.

Tax base of an asset

Paragraph 5 of AASB 112/IAS 12 simply states that the tax base of an asset is the amount attributed to that asset for tax purposes. Paragraph 7 notes two ways in which the tax base of an asset can be calculated, dependent on whether the future economic benefits that are expected to be generated by the asset are taxable or not.

Economic benefits are taxable:	tax base = future deductible amount for tax purposes
Economic benefits are not taxable:	tax base = carrying amount of asset

In general, the tax base of an asset can be calculated based on the following formula.

Tax base of an asset = Future deductible amount + Carrying amount − Future taxable amount

This equation for calculating the tax base of an asset is derived from the formula in paragraph 5.1 of the now superseded AASB 1020 *Income taxes*. It is used in this text to demonstrate that the difference between the carrying amount and tax base for an asset is given by the difference between the future taxable amounts and the amount of tax deductions that can be claimed in the future as follows.

Carrying amount − Tax base of an asset = Future taxable amount − Future deductible amount

The future taxable amount for an asset is normally equal to its carrying amount unless the future economic benefits are not taxable, in which case the future taxable amount is zero. The future deductible amount is the total deductions that can be claimed in the future against the asset.

Assets that generate economic benefits that are taxable

Assets embody, by definition, expected future economic benefits; that is, an entity holding an asset expects to earn future revenue from the asset. This revenue will generally be taxed. For many assets, the carrying amount equals the future taxable economic benefits.

If an asset has a carrying amount of $1000, it is expected that the asset will generate $1000 of revenues. It may generate more, particularly where assets are recognised based on cost. However, under AASB 112/IAS 12, if the accounting records recognise only $1000 as the carrying amount of an asset, then only $1000 of expected revenue is considered as potential economic benefits that may be taxable; that is, the future taxable benefits will never exceed the carrying amount.

As noted above, where economic benefits are taxable, the tax base equals the amount deductible for tax purposes. Consider the following assets, which generate future economic benefits that are taxable.

Plant (or any other depreciable non-current asset)

Assume an item of plant has a cost of $10 000. It has been held for 2 years. The accounting rate for depreciation is 20% p.a., while the depreciation rate for taxation purposes is 25% p.a. The entity expects to generate economic benefits from this asset by using it in a manufacturing process. Note that under AASB 116/IAS 16 *Property, Plant and Equipment* 'carrying amount' is defined as the amount at which the asset is recognised net of accumulated depreciation and accumulated impairment losses. At balance date the asset for both accounting and tax purposes is recognised as follows.

	Accounting	Tax
Plant	$10 000	$10 000
Accumulated depreciation	4 000	5 000
Carrying amount	$ 6 000	$ 5 000

The amount that is deductible for tax purposes against any future taxable economic benefits is the undepreciated portion, namely $5000. Hence, for plant:

Carrying amount	= $6 000
Future taxable amount	= $6 000
Future deductible amount	= $5 000
Tax base	= $5 000

Prepaid insurance (or any other prepayments)

Assume an entity has prepaid insurance of $3000 at the end of the period. The entity expects to generate economic benefits from this asset by having insurance against unforeseen events. The asset has a carrying amount of $3000. For this asset a tax deduction was received when the insurance was paid. There is no amount deductible for tax purposes in the future. Hence, for prepaid insurance:

Carrying amount	= $3 000
Future taxable amount	= $3 000
Future deductible amount	= $ 0
Tax base	= $ 0

Interest receivable

Assume an entity has recognised an interest receivable of $1000. The entity expects to receive benefits from lending money in the form of cash interest payable to it in the future. The interest is revenue, and is assessable for tax purposes when received. There is no tax deduction available for this asset. Hence, for interest receivable:

Carrying amount	= $1 000
Future taxable amount	= $1 000
Future deductible amount	= $ 0
Tax base	= $ 0

Inventories

Assume an entity holds an inventory item that originally cost $2000. The entity expects to receive economic benefits when it sells the item. The proceeds from sale are assessable for tax purposes and the cost of the inventory item is an allowable deduction at point of sale. Hence, for inventories:

Carrying amount	= $2 000
Future taxable amount	= $2 000
Future deductible amount	= $2 000
Tax base	= $2 000

Land — revalued (or any other revalued assets when capital gains tax is applicable)
Assume the entity acquired land for resale for $100 000. The entity applies the revaluation model under AASB 116/IAS 16 *Property, Plant and Equipment* and revalues the land to $120 000. The entity expects to generate economic benefits from the asset at least equal to the revalued amount of the land. Assuming capital gains tax applies on sale of the land, the entity will receive a tax deduction for the cost of the land when the land is sold in the future. Hence, for revalued land when capital gains tax is applicable:

Carrying amount	= $120 000
Future taxable amount	= $120 000
Future deductible amount	= $100 000
Tax base	= $100 000

Assets that generate economic benefits that are not taxable

Some assets may generate future economic benefits that will not be taxable because they do not represent income (e.g. a loan receivable), were already taxed in the past (e.g. accounts receivable), or because the taxation authority decides not to tax particular potential benefits that will be realised in the future (e.g. gain on revaluation of assets where capital gains tax is not applicable).

Where the economic benefits are not taxable, the tax base equals the carrying amount. Consider the following examples.

Loan receivable
Assume an entity reports a loan receivable of $25 000. The economic benefits from this asset are not taxable as no revenue is generated. Hence, for a loan receivable:

Carrying amount	= $25 000
Future taxable amount	= $ 0
Future deductible amount	= $ 0
Tax base	= $25 000

Accounts receivable
Assume an entity has an accounts receivable balance of $32 000 and an allowance for doubtful debts of $6000. There are no economic benefits that are taxable in relation to this asset as the asset relates to the collection of cash from debtors (as mentioned in section 12.4, this chapter assumes that the sale on credit, and therefore the amount recognised in the accounts receivable, is taxed at the moment of the sale being made). A deductible amount is available in the future as, when the doubtful debts will become bad, they can be written off and claimed as a tax deduction. The best estimation of the bad debts that will be written off in the future is the allowance for doubtful debts. Therefore, the future deductible amount is equal to the allowance for doubtful debts. Hence, for accounts receivable:

Carrying amount	= $32 000
Future taxable amount	= $ 0
Future deductible amount	= $ 6 000
Tax base	= $38 000

Land — revalued (or any other revalued assets when capital gains tax is not applicable)
In the discussion of assets that generate future benefits that are taxable, the example used assumed that the entity had acquired land for resale for $100 000 and subsequently revalued it to $120 000. In that situation it was assumed that capital gains tax was applicable on sale of the asset. Assume now that there is no capital gains tax payable on the sale of the asset. On sale, the increase in value will not be taxable. Hence, for revalued land when capital gains tax is not applicable:

Carrying amount	= $120 000
Future taxable amount	= $100 000
Future deductible amount	= $100 000
Tax base	= $120 000

The above analysis of assets can be shown as in figure 12.4 (for land, assume capital gains tax was applicable).

FIGURE 12.4 Tax bases of assets

	Carrying amount	Future taxable amount	Future deductible amount	Tax base
Plant	$ 6 000	$ 6 000	$ 5 000	$ 5 000
Prepaid insurance	3 000	3 000	0	0
Interest receivable	1 000	1 000	0	0
Inventories	2 000	2 000	2 000	2 000
Land — revalued	120 000	120 000	100 000	100 000
Loan receivable	25 000	0	0	25 000
Accounts receivable (net)	32 000	0	6 000	38 000

Tax base of a liability

Unlike assets which by their nature are expected to generate income, liabilities are outflows of funds and do not generate future taxable amounts.

Paragraph 8 of AASB 112/IAS 12 describes two calculations for the tax base of a liability: all liabilities *other than* revenue received in advance; and revenue received in advance.

All liabilities other than revenue received in advance

The tax base of such a liability equals the carrying amount less any amount that will be deductible for tax purposes in respect of that liability in future periods. The formula is as follows.

$$\text{Tax base of a liability} = \text{Carrying amount} - \text{Future deductible amount}$$

Even though the future taxable amount for a liability is 0, the equation above can be written in a similar way to the equation used to determine the tax base for an asset.

$$\text{Tax base of a liability} = \text{Future taxable amount} + \text{Carrying amount} - \text{Future deductible amount}$$

As such, the difference between the tax base of a liability other than revenue received in advance and its carrying amount can be written as follows.

$$\text{Carrying amount} - \text{Tax base of a liability} = \text{Future deductible amount} - \text{Future taxable amount}$$

Therefore:
1. where the carrying amount equals the future deductible amount, the tax base is zero
2. where there is no future deductible amount, the tax base equals the carrying amount.

Where the carrying amount equals the deductible amount, the tax base is zero

Provision for annual leave

Assume an entity has a liability for annual leave of $3900. A tax deduction is available in the future when the entity pays the annual leave to its employees. Hence, for provision for annual leave:

Carrying amount	= $3 900
Future taxable amount	= $ 0
Future deductible amount	= $3 900
Tax base	= $ 0

Accrued expenses

Assume an entity has some accrued expenses not yet paid of $6700. The entity will receive a tax deduction of $6700 on payment of these expenses. Hence, for accrued expenses:

Carrying amount	= $6 700
Future taxable amount	= $ 0
Future deductible amount	= $6 700
Tax base	= $ 0

Where there is no deductible amount, the tax base equals the carrying amount

Accounts payable

Assume an entity has accounts payable of $34 000 recognised for purchases of inventories on credit. There is no amount deductible for tax purposes in future periods as the amount paid for inventory purchases is allocated as a tax deduction for inventory. Hence, for accounts payable:

Carrying amount	= $34 000
Future taxable amount	= $ 0
Future deductible amount	= $ 0
Tax base	= $34 000

Loan payable

Assume an entity has a loan of $20 000. There is no amount deductible for tax purposes in future periods as the loan payable is not directly related to any revenues or expenses (the interest payable on the loan is treated separately). Hence, for loan payable:

Carrying amount	= $20 000
Future taxable amount	= $ 0
Future deductible amount	= $ 0
Tax base	= $20 000

Accrued penalties

Assume an entity has incurred fines for safety infringements amounting to $700. The fines have not yet been paid. No tax deduction is available for fines or penalties. Hence, for accrued penalties:

Carrying amount	= $700
Future taxable amount	= $ 0
Future deductible amount	= $ 0
Tax base	= $700

Revenue received in advance

The tax base of such a liability is equal to its carrying amount less the revenue received in advance not taxable in future periods (AASB 112/IAS 12 paragraph 8). In other words, the tax base of revenue received in advance is the amount received that was not taxed in the past and will be taxed in the future. The formula is as follows.

$$\text{Tax base} = \text{Carrying amount} - \text{Revenue received in advance not taxable in future}$$

The tax is normally paid on receipt of the revenue. Therefore, the tax base is normally equal to $0.

Subscriptions received in advance

Assume an entity has received subscriptions in advance of $500. These were taxed on receipt. Hence, for subscriptions received in advance:

Carrying amount	= $500
Revenue received in advance	= $500
Tax base	= $ 0

The above analysis of liabilities can be shown as in figure 12.5. Note that the revenue received in advance not taxable in the future is put in the deductible amount column even though it is not a deductible amount. This is done for simplicity — the alternative being to create a new column in the worksheet potentially just for one item. With liabilities, both the revenue received in advance and the deductible amount are subtracted from the carrying amount to determine the tax base.

FIGURE 12.5   Tax bases of liabilities

	Carrying amount	Future taxable amount	Future deductible amount	Tax base
Provision for annual leave	$ 3 900	$0	$3 900	$ 0
Accrued expenses	6 700	0	6 700	0
Accounts payable	34 000	0	0	34 000
Loan payable	20 000	0		20 000
Accrued penalties	700	0	0	700
Subscriptions received in advance	500	0	500	0

12.5.3 Step 3. Determine and classify the temporary differences

Determine temporary differences

Paragraph 5 of AASB 112/IAS 12 defines **temporary differences** as differences between the carrying amount of an asset or liability in the statement of financial position and the asset's or liability's tax base.

Temporary differences effectively represent the expected net future taxable or deductible amounts arising from recovery of assets and settlement of liabilities at their carrying amounts. Temporary differences cannot exist where there are no future tax consequences from the realisation or settlement of an asset or liability at its carrying amount; for example, with the liability loan payable, there are no future tax consequences (i.e. no future tax deduction or assessable income) — with this liability, as shown in figure 12.5, the tax base equals the carrying amount and no temporary difference occurs.

As can be seen in figures 12.4 and 12.5, having determined both the carrying amounts and the tax bases of an entity's assets and liabilities, it is a simple task to determine the temporary differences between these amounts. Note that, according to the formulas presented above for the calculation of tax bases, differences between carrying amounts and the tax bases are equal to differences between future taxable amounts and future deductible amounts (with the exception of revenue received in advance, where the difference is equal to the revenue received in advance not taxable in the future).

Classify temporary differences

Paragraph 5 of AASB 112/IAS 12 classifies temporary differences into two types.

- **Deductible temporary differences.** These result in amounts that are deductible in determining taxable profit of future periods when the carrying amount of the asset or liability is recovered or settled. Hence, in this case, the difference between carrying amount and tax base should reflect that future deductible amounts are greater than future taxable amounts. Considering the formulas that express the difference between carrying amount and the tax base for assets and liabilities as a difference between future taxable amount and future deductible amount, the deductible temporary differences arise in the following situations:

Carrying amount of an asset < Tax base of the asset

Carrying amount of a liability > Tax base of the liability

- **Taxable temporary differences.** These result in amounts that are taxable in determining taxable profit of future periods when the carrying amount of the asset or liability is recovered or settled. Hence, in this case the difference between carrying amount and tax base should reflect that future deductible amounts are lower than future taxable amounts. Considering the formulas that express the difference between carrying amount and the tax base for assets and liabilities as a difference between future taxable amount and future deductible amount, the taxable temporary differences arise in the following situations:

Carrying amount of an asset > Tax base of the asset

Carrying amount of the liability < Tax base of the liability

Temporary differences can be calculated without the need to identify the tax base. They can simply be seen as the differences between the future taxable amounts and future deductible amounts recognised for each asset and liability.

If future taxable amount > Future deductible amount: taxable temporary difference

If future taxable amount < Future deductible amount: deductible temporary difference

A deferred tax worksheet can be prepared by combining the information in figures 12.4 and 12.5. Two extra columns are added — one for taxable temporary differences and one for deductible temporary differences. This is illustrated in figure 12.6.

FIGURE 12.6 Determining and classifying temporary differences

	Carrying amount $	Future taxable amount $	Future deductible amount $	Tax base $	Taxable temporary differences $	Deductible temporary differences $
Assets						
Plant	6 000	6 000	5 000	5 000	1 000	0
Prepaid insurance	3 000	3 000	0	0	3 000	0
Interest receivable	1 000	1 000	0	0	1 000	0
Inventories	2 000	2 000	2 000	2 000	0	0
Land — revalued	120 000	120 000	100 000	100 000	20 000	0
Loan receivable	25 000	0	0	25 000	0	0
Accounts receivable (net)	32 000	0	6 000	38 000	0	6 000
Liabilities						
Provision for annual leave	3 900	0	3 900	0	0	3 900
Accrued expenses	6 700	0	6 700	0	0	6 700
Accounts payable	34 000	0	0	34 000	0	0
Loan payable	20 000	0	0	20 000	0	0
Accrued penalties	700	0	0	700	0	0
Subscriptions received in advance	500	0	500	0	0	500
Temporary differences					**25 000**	**17 100**

Consider some of the situations raised in section 12.5.2 and their placement in figure 12.6.

Plant

The carrying amount of the asset is greater than the tax base. Hence, a taxable temporary difference arises. This is because the asset is being depreciated faster for tax purposes than accounting purposes. In a future period there will still be a recovery of the economic benefits from the asset as evidenced by a carrying amount of the asset for accounting purposes, but there will be no tax deduction for depreciation. This results in a future taxable amount greater than the future deductible amount and therefore a taxable temporary difference exists.

Prepaid insurance

The $3000 carrying amount of the prepayment is greater than the tax base of $0. Hence, a taxable temporary difference arises. In future periods the economic benefits from the prepayment will be recovered but no tax deduction will be allowed, giving rise to a future taxable amount greater than the future deductible amount.

Accounts receivable

The carrying amount for accounting purposes is net of the allowance for doubtful debts, namely $32 000, This is less than the tax base of $38 000, giving rise to a deductible temporary difference of $6000. It is expected in the future that the entity will receive a tax deduction for debts that will turn bad, while the future taxable amount is $0.

Provision for annual leave

The $3900 carrying amount of the liability is greater than the zero tax base, giving rise to a deductible temporary difference. In future periods as the entity pays its employees to take their annual leave, a tax deduction will be received, but there is no taxable amount.

Accrued expenses

The $6700 accrued expenses is greater than the zero tax base, giving rise to a deductible temporary difference. In future periods as the entity pays the accrued expenses a tax deduction will be received, but there is no taxable amount.

Subscriptions received in advance

The $500 liability is greater than the zero tax base, giving rise to a deductible temporary difference. In future periods accounting revenue will be recognised, but that was already subject to tax when received in advance. The tax on the future revenue is effectively prepaid. As such, the amount of subscription received in advance is virtually a future deductible amount and there is no future taxable amount.

Excluded differences

Paragraphs 15 and 24 of AASB 112/IAS 12 note some exceptions to the requirement that deferred tax assets and liabilities must be recognised for all taxable and deductible temporary differences. Many of these are beyond the scope of this text. The only example that is used in this text to illustrate the procedure with excluded differences is that of goodwill. Goodwill is recognised as an asset for accounting but write-offs of goodwill for impairment losses are not allowed as deductions for tax purposes. Hence, the tax base is zero. Assuming a balance of $10 000 for goodwill, if the same method is applied as before to identify any temporary differences:

Carrying amount	= $10 000
Tax base	= $ 0
Taxable temporary difference	= $10 000

However, even though a taxable temporary difference may seem to arise in relation to goodwill, recognition of any deferred tax accounts is not permitted under paragraph 15(a) of AASB 112/IAS 12 in this case. The reason for this exclusion is based on the measurement of goodwill as required by AASB 3/IFRS 3 *Business Combinations*.

Hence, the calculations shown in figure 12.6 need to be adjusted for excluded differences as shown in the deferred tax worksheet in figure 12.7.

FIGURE 12.7 Determining and classifying temporary differences including excluded differences

	Carrying amount $	Future taxable amount $	Future deductible amount $	Tax base $	Taxable temporary differences $	Deductible temporary differences $
Assets						
Plant	6 000	6 000	5 000	5 000	1 000	0
Prepaid insurance	3 000	3 000	0	0	3 000	0
Interest receivable	1 000	2 000	0	0	1 000	0
Inventories	2 000	2 000	2 000	2 000	0	0
Land	120 000	120 000	100 000	100 000	20 000	0
Loan receivable	25 000	0	0	25 000	—	0
Accounts receivable	32 000	0	6 000	38 000	0	6 000
Goodwill	10 000	10 000	0	0	10 000	0
Liabilities						
Provision for annual leave	3 900	0	3 900	0		3 900
Accrued expenses	6 700	0	6 700	0		6 700
Accounts payable	34 000	0	0	34 000	0	0
Loan payable	20 000	0	0	20 000	0	0
Accrued penalties	700	0	0	700	0	0
Subscriptions received in advance	500	0	500	0	0	500
Temporary differences						35 000	17 100
Excluded differences						
Goodwill					(10 000)	
Net temporary differences					**25 000**	**17 100**

12.5.4 Step 4(a). Determine the closing balances of deferred tax asset and deferred tax liability accounts

The existence of temporary differences gives rise to deferred tax assets or deferred tax liabilities.

Deferred tax liabilities

Deferred tax liabilities arise from the existence of taxable temporary differences; that is, where the future taxable amount is greater than the future deductible amount. The expectation of future taxable amount greater than the expected future deductions gives rise to a liability to pay tax in the future.

Deferred tax assets

Deferred tax assets arise from the existence of deductible temporary differences, where the future deductible amount is greater than the future taxable amount. The expectation of benefits from future tax deductions that are greater than the future taxable amounts gives rise to an asset. Deferred tax assets can also arise where there is a tax loss in the current period that is carrying forward to the next periods as discussed in section 12.4.

Using the last line from figure 12.7, having calculated the net temporary differences existing at the end of the period, the closing balances of deferred tax asset and deferred tax liability can be determined by multiplying the amount of the differences by the tax rate, as shown in figure 12.8.

FIGURE 12.8	Closing balances of deferred tax asset and deferred tax liability

	Taxable temporary differences $	Deductible temporary differences $
Net temporary differences	25 000	17 100
Deferred tax liability (30%)	7 500	
Deferred tax asset (30%)		5 130

Note that the balances calculated are for the *closing* balances of the deferred tax accounts at the end of the reporting period. These balances are based on the temporary differences between the carrying amounts and tax bases at the *end* of the period.

12.5.5 Step 4(b). Determine the adjustments in deferred tax asset and deferred tax liability accounts

The opening balances of the deferred tax accounts are available from the previous period's financial statements. A comparison of the opening and closing balances, taking into consideration any movements during the current period, will result in determining the adjustment necessary at the end of the current period.

Assuming the opening balance of the deferred tax liability account is $1000 and the opening balance of the deferred tax asset account is $4000, with no movements in these accounts during the period, the adjustment at the end of the period can be calculated as in figure 12.9, adding to figure 12.8.

FIGURE 12.9	Determining the adjustment in deferred tax accounts

Net temporary differences	$25 000	$17 100
Deferred tax liability (30%)	7 500	
Deferred tax asset (30%)		5 130
Beginning balances	1 000	4 000
Adjustment	**$ 6 500 Cr**	**$ 1 130 Dr**

Note that, for the deferred tax liability, the opening balance needs to be increased by $6500 to obtain a closing balance of $7500. An increase in a liability means a credit adjustment. For the deferred tax asset, an increase of $1130 is necessary to achieve a closing balance of $5130. An increase in an asset means a debit adjustment.

12.5.6 Step 4(c). Prepare the deferred tax adjustment entry

The adjusting journal entry at the end of the period is read from the last line of the deferred tax worksheet. In figure 12.9, the deferred tax liability has increased by $6500 and the deferred tax asset has increased by

$1130. The income tax expense (deferred) is a net of the adjustments in the deferred tax asset and liability accounts. The adjusting journal entry is then as follows.

Income tax expense (deferred)	Dr	5 370	
Deferred tax asset	Dr	1 130	
Deferred tax liability	Cr		6 500
(Recognition of adjustment in deferred tax accounts)			

Note that the total income tax expense for the period is a combination of the income tax expense calculated in relation to the current tax liability and the income tax expense calculated for the movement in deferred tax accounts. In other words, the income tax expense for the period is a combination of current and deferred income tax expenses.

The ledger accounts for the deferred tax accounts are then as follows.

Deferred tax asset					
01/07/22	Balance b/d	4 000	30/06/23	Balance c/d	5 130
30/06/23	Income tax expense (deferred)	1 130			
		5 130			5 130

Deferred tax liability					
30/06/23	Balance c/d	7 500	01/07/22	Balance b/d	1 000
			30/06/23	Income tax expense (deferred)	6 500
		7 500			7 500

12.5.7 Recognition criteria for deferred tax assets and liabilities

Prior to raising the journal entry in section 12.5.6, it is necessary to test whether these accounts should be recognised.

For **deferred tax liabilities**, under paragraph 16 of AASB 112/IAS 12 all deferred tax liabilities must be recognised; that is, there are no recognition criteria to be applied.

Under paragraph 28 of AASB 112/IAS 12, **deferred tax assets** can be recognised only to the extent that it is probable that taxable profit (or taxable temporary differences) will be available against which the deductible temporary differences can be utilised. A future tax deduction is a benefit only if an entity earns sufficient taxable profit in the future or has enough taxable temporary differences against which the deductions can be used. If an entity makes only tax losses in the future or has no taxable temporary differences, then tax deductions are of no benefit. Hence, the recognition criterion for deferred tax assets is based on the probability of an entity earning sufficient taxable profit in the future or having sufficient taxable temporary differences.

For *deferred tax assets arising from tax losses*, the same principle applies. The criterion is still that it must be probable that an entity earns sufficient taxable profit against which the past tax loss can be offset. However, when there is a tax loss in the current period, this is in itself strong evidence that an entity may not be able to earn taxable profit in the future. Where an entity has a history of recent tax losses, there must be convincing evidence that circumstances are going to improve for the entity in the future. Paragraph 36 of AASB 112/IAS 12 specifies a number of factors that can be used in the assessment of possible changes in the future:

- whether the entity has sufficient taxable temporary differences that will result in taxable amounts in the future against which the tax loss can be utilised
- whether the unused tax losses result from identifiable causes which are unlikely to recur
- whether tax planning opportunities are available to the entity that will create future taxable profit.

An analysis of the following areas could provide evidence that there is a change expected in the profits of the entity in the future.

- *Future budgets*. If an entity has a 5-year budget setting out future sales and expenses, this may indicate better prospects for profits for the entity in the future.
- *Causes of past/current losses*. An analysis of what caused past/current tax losses to occur may provide indications that these were one-off events (e.g. as a result of natural disasters). If these same events are not expected in the future, then this increases the probability of future profitability for the entity. The

entity may have a strong history of profits other than those giving rise to the current loss, indicating that the loss was an aberration and not a continuing condition.

- *Analysis of existing contracts and sales agreements.* If an entity has recently signed significant new contracts that will benefit the company's profits, then this may be evidence of a change in the fortunes of the company. New developments and favourable opportunities are likely to give rise to future taxable amounts.

If it were determined that the deferred tax asset raised in section 12.5.4 did not meet the recognition criteria, then the following journal entry is passed.

Income tax expense (deferred)	Dr	5 130	
Deferred tax asset	Cr		5 130
(Derecognition of deferred tax asset as recovery is no longer probable)			

12.5.8 Other movements in deferred tax accounts in the current period

One further event that could affect numbers in the deferred tax worksheet is where there are other movements in the deferred tax accounts in the current period.

An example of a movement in the *deferred tax liability* is the use by an entity of the revaluation model for property, plant and equipment (chapter 5) or intangible assets (chapter 6). Under the revaluation model assets are measured at fair value rather than cost. When an increase in the fair value of an asset is recognised, the increase is recognised in a reserve account — asset revaluation surplus — and the expected tax to be paid on the increase in earnings if capital gains tax is applicable is recognised as a deferred tax liability.

For example, if plant is measured using the revaluation model and the asset is revalued from $1000 to $1200 during the period and capital tax gains apply, then the entity passes the following entries on revaluation.

Plant	Dr	200	
Gain on revaluation of plant (other comprehensive income (OCI))	Cr		200
(Recognition of revaluation increase)			
Income tax expense (OCI)	Dr	60	
Deferred tax liability	Cr		60
(Tax effect of revaluation of plant)			
Gain on revaluation of plant (OCI)	Dr	200	
Income tax expense (OCI)	Cr		60
Asset revaluation surplus	Cr		140
(Accumulation of net revaluation gain in equity)			

In this case, the deferred tax liability increases during the period and this movement has to be taken into consideration when calculating the adjustment necessary to the deferred tax liability account at the end of the period.

An example of a movement in the *deferred tax asset* is the recovery of a tax loss. If a tax loss had been incurred in a previous period and it was recovered in the current period (see section 12.4), as a result of the current tax worksheet the following entry may have been passed.

Income tax expense (current)	Dr	2 500	
Deferred tax asset	Cr		100
Current tax liability	Cr		2 400
(Recognition of current tax)			

In this case, the deferred tax asset decreases during the period and this movement has to be taken into consideration when calculating the adjustment necessary to the deferred tax asset account at the end of the period.

These movements must be recognised in the deferred tax worksheet prior to calculation of the adjustment entry at the end of the period. Using figure 12.9 and the two movements noted above, in figure 12.10 the two movements are taken into account in the deferred tax worksheet. For the deferred tax liability, the opening balance of $1000 was increased by $60 on revaluation of the plant. Hence, an adjustment of only $6440 is necessary to get to the closing balance of $7500. For the deferred tax asset, the opening balance of $4000 was reduced by $100 on recognition of the recovery of past tax losses. An adjustment of $1230 is then necessary to get to the closing balance of $5130.

FIGURE 12.10 Determining the adjustments in the deferred tax accounts

Net temporary differences	$25 000	$17 100
Deferred tax liability (30%)	7 500	
Deferred tax asset (30%)		5 130
Beginning balances	1 000	4 000
Movements during year	60	(100)
Adjustment	**$ 6 440 Cr**	**$ 1 230 Dr**

The adjusting journal entry is then as follows.

Income tax expense (deferred)	Dr	5 210	
Deferred tax asset	Dr	1 230	
Deferred tax liability	Cr		6 440
(Recognition of adjustment in deferred tax accounts)			

The deferred tax ledger accounts would then appear as follows.

Deferred tax asset

01/07/22	Balance b/d	4 000	30/06/23	Income tax expense (current)	100
30/06/23	Income tax expense (deferred)	1 230		Balance c/d	5 130
		5 230			5 230

Deferred tax liability

30/06/23	Balance c/d	7 500	01/07/22	Balance b/d	1 000
			30/06/23	Tax on revaluation of plant	60
			30/06/23	Income tax expense (deferred)	6 440
		7 500			7 500

The completed deferred tax worksheet prepared as a result of applying the four-step process, including the treatment of movements during the period and adjustments at the end of the period in deferred tax accounts, can be seen in figure 12.3.

12.5.9 Offsetting tax assets and liabilities

In the journal entries in this section, separate accounts have been raised for deferred tax assets and deferred tax liabilities. Under paragraph 74 of AASB 112/IAS 12, these accounts can be offset against one another but only if:

(a) the entity has a legally enforceable right to set off current tax assets against current tax liabilities; and
(b) the deferred tax assets and the deferred tax liabilities relate to income taxes levied by the same taxation authority . . .

For income tax levied in Australia by the Australian Taxation Office, both of these conditions are usually met.

Current tax assets and liabilities can also be offset against each other. Under paragraph 71 of AASB 112/IAS 12, these can be offset if an entity:

(a) has a legally enforceable right to set off the recognised amounts; and
(b) intends either to settle on a net basis, or to realise the asset and settle the liability simultaneously.

These conditions are normally met for Australian entities.

☐ Carrying amounts are asset and liability accounting balances after valuation allowances, accumulated depreciation/amortisation amounts and impairment losses have been netted off.

☐ The tax base of an asset is the amount attributed to that asset for tax purposes.

☐ If an asset generates taxable economic benefits, its tax base equals the future deductible amount for tax purposes.

☐ If an asset generates economic benefits that are not taxable, its tax base equals the carrying amount of the asset.

☐ The tax base of most liabilities is found by deducting any future deductible amount from the carrying amount. Where the carrying amount equals the deductible amount, the tax base is zero. Where there is no deductible amount, the tax base equals the carrying amount.

☐ The tax base of a liability for revenue received in advance is equal to its carrying amount less the revenue received in advance not taxable in future periods.

☐ Temporary differences arise when the carrying amount of an asset or liability in the statement of financial position differs from the tax base of the asset or liability.

☐ Deductible temporary differences arise when the carrying amount of an asset is less than its tax base; and when the carrying amount of a liability is greater than its tax base.

☐ Taxable temporary differences arise when the carrying amount of an asset is greater than its tax base; and when the carrying amount of the liability is less than its tax base.

☐ AASB 112/IAS 12 requires the recognition of all deferred tax liabilities (apart from those which are excluded).

☐ Deferred tax assets can be recognised only to the extent that it is probable that the entity will have enough taxable profit (or taxable temporary differences) in the same period as the reversal of the deductible temporary differences.

☐ Recognition of deferred tax assets from tax losses is subject to the existence of strong evidence that the tax losses can be claimed in the future.

☐ The deferred tax asset and deferred tax liability are usually offset in Australia to disclose one amount for deferred tax in the statement of financial position.

12.6 Changes in tax rates

LEARNING OBJECTIVE 12.6 Account for changes in income tax rates.

When a new tax rate is enacted (or substantively enacted), the new rate should be applied in calculating the current tax liability and adjustments to deferred tax accounts during the year. It should also be applied to the deferred tax amounts recognised in prior years.

Under paragraph 51 of AASB 112/IAS 12, a journal adjustment must be passed to increase or reduce the carrying amounts of deferred tax assets and deferred tax liabilities, in order to reflect the new value of future taxable or deductible amounts. The deferred tax balances must reflect the tax consequences that would follow from the entity recovering or settling its assets and liabilities in the future; that is, at tax rates applicable then.

The adjustments to the deferred tax balances are reflected in income tax expense for the period and are shown as a movement for the period in the deferred tax worksheet as per section 12.5.6.

ILLUSTRATIVE EXAMPLE 12.3

Change of tax rate

As at 30 June 2023, the balances of deferred tax accounts for Ironman Ltd were as follows.

Deferred tax asset	$29 600
Deferred tax liability	72 800

In September 2023, the government reduced the company tax rate from 40c to 30c in the dollar, effective from 1 July 2023. The recorded deferred tax balances represent the tax effect of future taxable amounts and future deductible amounts at 40c in the dollar, so they are now overstated and must be adjusted as follows.

▶

	Deferred tax asset	Deferred tax liability
Opening balance	$29 600	$72 800
Adjustment for change in tax rate: ([40 − 30]/40)	(7 400)	(18 200)
Restated balance	$22 200	$54 600

The journal entry to recognise the effect of the change in tax rates is:

Deferred tax liability	Dr	18 200	
Deferred tax asset	Cr		7 400
Income tax expense	Cr		10 800
(Recognition of the impact of a change in tax rate on deferred tax amounts)			

LEARNING CHECK

☐ Deferred tax assets and liabilities must be restated for any announcement of a change in tax rate if that new rate will apply when those deferred tax assets and liabilities are realised.

12.7 Disclosure requirements

LEARNING OBJECTIVE 12.7 Explain the disclosure requirements of AASB 112/IAS 12.

AASB 112/IAS 12 requires extensive disclosures. The following section draws attention to some of the more important disclosures and link these with the disclosures in Wesfarmers Limited's annual report 2018.

Figure 12.11 contains the disclosure by Wesfarmers Limited of its policy in accounting for income tax. Note in particular its statements in relation to the recognition of deferred tax assets and liabilities. Also note in figure 12.11, however, that not all deferred tax assets were recognised by Wesfarmers Limited in 2018 as they did not meet the recognition criteria under AASB 112/IAS 12.

Paragraphs 79 and 80 of AASB 112/IAS 12 require the major components of income tax expense to be disclosed. These include:

- current tax expense (paragraph 80(a))
- deferred tax expense (paragraph 80(c))
- deferred tax expense relating to changes in tax rates (paragraph 80(d))
- the amount of any benefit arising from a previously unrecognised tax loss (paragraph 80(f)).

Disclosures in relation to income tax expense for Wesfarmers Limited are shown in figure 12.12.

FIGURE 12.11	Disclosure of accounting policy on income taxes, Wesfarmers

Current taxes

Current tax assets and liabilities are measured at the amount expected to be recovered from or paid to taxation authorities at the tax rates and tax laws enacted or substantively enacted by the balance sheet date.

Deferred taxes

Deferred income tax is provided using the full liability method. Deferred income tax assets are recognised for all deductible temporary differences, carried forward unused tax assets and unused tax losses, to the extent it is probable that taxable profit will be available to utilise them.

The carrying amount of deferred income tax assets is reviewed at balance sheet date and reduced to the extent that it is no longer probable that sufficient taxable profit will be available to utilise them.

Deferred income tax assets and liabilities are measured at the tax rates that are expected to apply to the year when the asset is realised or the liability is settled, based on tax rates and tax laws that have been enacted or substantively enacted at the balance sheet date.

Deferred income tax is provided on temporary differences at balance sheet date between accounting carrying amounts and the tax bases of assets and liabilities, other than for the following:

- Where they arise from the initial recognition of an asset or liability in a transaction that is not a business combination and at the time of the transaction, affects neither the accounting profit nor taxable profit or loss.
- Where taxable temporary differences relate to investments in subsidiaries, associates and interests in joint ventures:
    1. Deferred tax liabilities are not recognised if the timing of the reversal of the temporary differences can be controlled and it is probable that the temporary differences will not reverse in the foreseeable future.
    2. Deferred tax assets are not recognised if it is not probable that the temporary differences will reverse in the foreseeable future and taxable profit will not be available to utilise the temporary differences.

    Deferred tax liabilities are also not recognised on recognition of goodwill.

Income taxes relating to items recognised directly in equity are recognised in equity and not in the income statement.

Offsetting deferred tax balances

Deferred tax assets and deferred tax liabilities are offset only if a legally enforceable right exists to set off current tax assets against current tax liabilities and the deferred tax assets and liabilities relate to the same taxable entity and the same taxation authority.

Source: Wesfarmers Limited (2018, p. 110).

| **FIGURE 12.12** | Disclosures in relation to income tax expense, Wesfarmers |

3. Tax expense

	Consolidated	
	2018	**2017**
The major components of tax expense are:	**$m**	**$m**
Income statement (continuing operations)		
Current income tax expense		
Current year (paid or payable)	1 283	1 187
Adjustment for prior years	(8)	(18)
Deferred income tax expense		
Temporary differences	(29)	(7)
Adjustment for prior years	—	7
Income tax reported in the income statement	**1 246**	**1 169**
Statement of changes in equity		
Net loss on revaluing cash flow hedges	72	17
Other	—	(2)
Income tax reported in equity	**72**	**15**
Tax reconciliation (continuing operations)		
Profit before tax	3 850	3 929
Income tax at the statutory tax rate of 30%	1 155	1 179
Adjustments relating to prior years	(8)	(11)
Non-deductible items	111	9
Share of results of associates and joint venture	(12)	(18)
Other	—	10
Income tax on profit before tax	**1 246**	**1 169**

Source: Wesfarmers Limited (2018, p. 110).

Paragraph 81(ab) of AASB 112/IAS 12 requires the disclosure of income tax relating to each component of other comprehensive income. Paragraph 81(c) requires an explanation of the relationship between tax expense and accounting profit. In figure 12.12 it can be seen that the income tax expense disclosed in the statement of profit or loss and other comprehensive income is reconciled to accounting profit multiplied by the tax rate. This reconciliation allows financial statement users to understand what factors may cause this relationship to differ in the future. For example, if it is expected that an entity will earn pre-tax profits in the future of, say, $1 million, will the after-tax profit be $700 000 or some other number? Note that much of the difference in the reconciliation is caused by items that permanently differ between accounting profit and taxable profit such as entertainment expenses — an expense for accounting but not tax deductible.

Paragraph 81(g) of AASB 112 requires entities to disclose for each type of temporary difference and in respect of each type of unused tax loss the amount of deferred tax asset or deferred tax liability that has been recognised in the statement of financial position. This disclosure indicates the major reasons why the deferred tax accounts have been raised. For Wesfarmers Limited, the temporary differences giving rise to deferred tax assets and deferred tax liabilities are shown in figure 12.13. Note that the deferred tax assets are netted off against the deferred tax liabilities.

FIGURE 12.13   Disclosure of temporary differences giving rise to deferred tax assets and liabilities, Wesfarmers

	Consolidated	
	2018	2017
Deferred income tax in the balance sheet relates to the following:	$m	$m
Provisions	250	338
Employee benefits	427	417
Accrued and other payables	130	141
Borrowings	103	143
Derivatives	5	53
Trading stock	90	98
Fixed assets	273	432
Other individually insignificant balances	87	71
Deferred tax assets	1 365	1 693
Accelerated depreciation for tax purposes	212	253
Derivatives	155	148
Accrued income and other	159	155
Intangible assets	106	107
Other individually insignificant balances	41	59
Deferred tax liabilities	673	722
Net deferred tax assets	**692**	**971**
Deferred income tax in the income statement relates to the following:		
Provisions	(17)	(20)
Depreciation, amortisation and impairment	10	(23)
Other individually insignificant balances	(22)	36
Deferred tax expense	**(29)**	**(7)**

Key estimate: unrecognised deferred tax assets

Capital losses: The Group has unrecognised benefits relating to carried forward capital losses, which can only be offset against eligible capital gains. The Group has determined that at this stage future eligible capital gains to utilise the tax assets are not currently sufficiently probable. The unrecognised deferred tax assets of $119 million (2017: $127 million) relate wholly to capital losses in Australia.

Key judgement: unrecognised deferred tax liability

A deferred tax liability has not been recognised on indefinite life intangibles for which the carrying value has been assessed as recoverable through sale, consistent with the Group's practice and strategy to maximise shareholder returns.

Source: Wesfarmers Limited (2018, p. 110).

Paragraph 82(d) of AASB 101/IAS 1 *Presentation of Financial Statements* requires entities to disclose the tax expense on the face of the statement of profit or loss and other comprehensive income.

Paragraphs 54(n) and (o) of AASB 101/IAS 1 require entities to disclose liabilities and assets for current tax, deferred tax liabilities and deferred tax assets. Wesfarmers Limited discloses the income tax payable in the current liabilities section of the statement of financial position.

AASB Interpretation 23/IFRIC 23 *Uncertainty over Income Tax Treatments* specifies further disclosure requirements applicable when a firm faces uncertainties over the tax treatment with regards to recognising and measuring current and deferred tax assets and liabilities. More specifically, where there is uncertainty over the income tax treatment acceptable by the taxation authority, the firm is required to determine whether to disclose the judgements, assumptions and estimates used in determining tax profit (or loss), tax bases, unused tax losses, unused tax credit and tax rates.

☐ A company that prepares general purpose financial statements must disclose many aspects in relation to current and deferred tax, and tax losses.

☐ Key disclosures include the reconciliation between the reported income tax expense and the product of accounting profit before tax multiplied by the applicable income tax rate, and the temporary differences giving rise to deferred tax assets and liabilities.

SUMMARY

Some of the key principles contained in AASB 112/IAS 12 *Income Taxes* are as follows.
- There are differences between the accounting treatments and taxation treatments for many economic transactions.
- The current tax consequences of any transactions or events are recognised in income tax expense and current tax liabilities and assets.
- The future tax consequences of any transactions or events are recognised in income tax expense and deferred tax liabilities and assets.
- Deferred tax assets and liabilities are determined by comparing the carrying amounts of an entity's assets and liabilities at the end of a period with their tax bases.
- A comparison of tax bases and carrying amounts determines the existence of temporary differences, classified into taxable and deductible temporary differences.
- Taxable temporary differences give rise to deferred tax liabilities, and deductible temporary differences give rise to deferred tax assets.
- All deferred tax liabilities must be recognised, but deferred tax assets are only recognised if they meet specific criteria.
- Changes in tax rates are recognised with adjustments to the balances of deferred tax assets and liabilities.

KEY TERMS

accounting profit The difference between accounting revenues earned and accounting expenses incurred.

carrying amount The amount at which an asset or liability is recognised after deducting any accumulated depreciation (amortisation), accumulated impairment losses and allowances thereon.

current tax The amount of income taxes payable/recoverable in respect of the taxable profit/loss for the reporting period.

deductible temporary differences Amounts that are deductible in determining taxable profit in future periods, and arising when the carrying amount of an asset is less than its tax base and when the carrying amount of a liability is greater than its tax base.

deferred tax The amount of income tax payable/recoverable in future reporting periods in respect of temporary differences and tax losses.

deferred tax assets The amount of income tax recoverable in future reporting periods in respect of deductible temporary differences and tax losses.

deferred tax liabilities The amount of income tax payable in future reporting periods in respect of taxable temporary differences.

income tax Tax levied on company income.

tax base The amount that is attributed to an asset or liability for tax purposes.

tax losses The amount by which allowable deductions exceed taxable revenues.

taxable profit The difference between taxable revenues and tax deductions allowable against those revenues.

taxable temporary differences Amounts that are taxable in determining taxable profit in future periods, and arising when the carrying amount of an asset is greater than its tax base, and when the carrying amount of the liability is less than its tax base.

temporary differences Differences between the carrying amount of an asset or liability in the statement of financial position and the asset's or liability's tax base.

DEMONSTRATION PROBLEM

12.1 Current and deferred tax worksheets

The accounting profit before tax of Nippers Ltd for the period ended 30 June 2023 was $175 900. It included the following revenue and expense items.

Interest revenue	$11 000
Long service leave expense	7 000
Doubtful debts expense	4 200
Depreciation expense — plant (15% p.a., straight-line)	33 000
Rent expense	22 800
Entertainment expense (non-deductible)	3 900

The draft statement of financial position as at 30 June 2023 included the following assets and liabilities.

	2023	2022
Cash	$ 9 000	$ 7 500
Accounts receivable	83 000	76 800
Allowance for doubtful debts	(5 000)	(3 200)
Inventories	67 100	58 300
Interest receivable	1 000	—
Prepaid rent	2 800	2 400
Plant	220 000	220 000
Accumulated depreciation — plant	(99 000)	(66 000)
Deferred tax asset	?	30 360
Accounts payable	71 200	73 600
Provision for long service leave	64 000	61 000
Deferred tax liability	?	720

Additional information

- The tax depreciation rate for plant is 10% p.a., straight-line.
- The tax rate is 30%.
- The company has $15 000 in tax losses carried forward from the previous year. A deferred tax asset was recognised for these losses in the previous year. Taxation legislation allows such losses to be offset against future taxable profit.

Required

Prepare the worksheets and journal entries to calculate and record the current tax liability and the movements in deferred tax accounts for the year ended 30 June 2023.

SOLUTION

Current tax worksheet and journal entry

The current tax worksheet prepared from the above information is as follows (see working in the section after the worksheet).

NIPPERS LTD Current tax worksheet for the year ended 30 June 2023		
Accounting profit		$175 900
Add:		
Interest received	10 000	
Long service leave expense	7 000	
Doubtful debts expense	4 200	
Depreciation expense — plant	33 000	
Rent expense	22 800	
Entertainment expense (non-deductible)	3 900	80 900
		256 800

NIPPERS LTD		
Current tax worksheet		
for the year ended 30 June 2023		
Deduct:		
Interest revenue	11 000	
Long service leave paid	4 000	
Bad debts written off	2 400	
Depreciation for tax — plant	22 000	
Rent paid	23 200	(62 600)
Taxable profit		194 200
Less: Recoupment of tax loss		(15 000)
Net taxable profit		179 200
Current tax liability @ 30%		**$ 53 760**

Working used to prepare the current tax worksheet
There are four steps in preparing a current tax worksheet.

Step 1. Identify accounting profit for the period
The accounting profit is given: $175 900.

Step 2. Determine the expenses and revenues where there are differences in the numbers used to measure accounting profit and taxable profit
Analysing the list of revenues and expenses given in the information provided:
- *Interest revenue.* The accounting profit includes interest revenue of $11 000. Interest revenue has been accrued as there is an interest receivable account in the statement of financial position. This means that the cash received, used for taxable revenue, may differ from the accounting revenue. It is necessary to reconstruct the Interest receivable account.

Interest receivable					
01/07/22	Balance b/d	0	30/06/23	Interest received	10 000
30/06/23	Interest revenue	11 000	30/06/23	Balance c/d	1 000
		11 000			11 000

Therefore, the interest received that represents current taxable revenue is $10 000.
- *Long service leave expense.* The accounting profit includes an expense of $7000. As there is a provision for long service leave in the statement of financial position, this account must be reconstructed to determine cash payments in relation to long service leave.

Provision for long service leave					
30/06/23	Leave paid	4 000	01/07/22	Balance b/d	61 000
30/06/23	Balance c/d	64 000	30/06/23	Expense	7 000
		68 000			68 000

Therefore, the long service leave paid that represents current tax deduction is $7000.
- *Doubtful debts expense.* The accounting profit includes an expense of $4200. The statement of financial position includes an allowance for doubtful debts of $5000. This account must be reconstructed to determine the current tax deduction, being the debts written off.

Allowance for doubtful debts					
30/06/23	Debts written off	2 400	01/07/22	Balance b/d	3 200
30/06/23	Balance c/d	5 000	30/06/23	Expense	4 200
		7 400			7 400

Therefore, the debt written off that represents current tax deduction is $2400.
- *Depreciation expense.* The accounting profit includes an expense of $33 000 based on the use of a depreciation rate of 15% p.a. The depreciation rate for tax purposes is 10% p.a. giving rise to a tax deduction of $22 000, being $10\% \times \$220\,000$.

  The *accounting* accumulated depreciation is $99 000 which, at $33 000 per annum, means a 3-year depreciation period. Hence, the accumulated depreciation for tax purposes is $3 \times (10\% \times \$220\,000) = \$66\,000$.

The carrying amount of the plant for *taxation* purposes (i.e. tax base) is then:

Cost	$220 000
Accumulated tax depreciation	(66 000)
Tax base	$154 000

- *Rent expense*. The accounting profit includes an expense of $22 800. In the statement of financial position there is a prepaid rent account. This account must be reconstructed to determine the rent paid.

Prepaid rent					
01/07/22	Balance b/d	2 400	30/06/23	Rent expense	22 800
30/06/23	Rent paid	23 200	30/06/23	Balance c/d	2 800
		25 600			25 600

Therefore, the rent paid that represents current tax deduction is $23 200.

- *Entertainment expense*. Accounting profit includes an expense of $3900. However, this expense is non-deductible for tax purposes.

Step 3. Adjust accounting profit for these differences

- Add the accounting expenses not deductible for tax (entertainment expense).
- Add the accounting expenses and deduct the tax deductions where the amounts differ for accounting and tax (long service leave, doubtful debts, depreciation and rent).
- Deduct the accounting revenue and add the taxable revenue where the amounts differ for accounting and tax (interest).
- Deduct the accounting revenue where it is taxable (none arises in this problem).
    The result of this process is the determination of taxable profit.
    In this problem the taxable profit needs to be adjusted for the effects of the $15 000 in prior period tax losses. As these losses are recouped in the current period, they are deducted from the taxable profit to determine a net taxable profit.

Step 4. Multiply the net taxable profit by the current tax rate to determine the current tax liability
This process gives a figure of $53 760. The journal entry for current tax is then as follows.

Income tax expense (current)	Dr	58 260	
Current tax liability	Cr		53 760
Deferred tax asset (tax losses)	Cr		4 500

Note that, as the tax loss is recouped in the current period, the deferred tax asset raised in the year of occurrence of the tax losses (being 30% × $15 000) is now derecognised. The income tax expense is then calculated as a net of the adjustments to current tax liability and deferred tax asset.

Deferred tax worksheet and journal entry
The deferred tax worksheet is as follows.

	Carrying amount $	Future taxable amount $	Future deductible amount $	Tax base $	Taxable temporary differences $	Deductible temporary differences $
Assets						
Cash	9 000	0	0	9 000	0	0
Accounts receivable (net)	78 000	0	5 000	83 000		5 000
Inventories	67 100	67 100	67 100	67 100	0	0
Interest receivable	1 000	1 000	0	0	1 000	0
Prepaid rent	2 800	2 800	0	0	2 800	
Plant (net)	121 000	121 000	154 000	154 000		33 000
Liabilities						
Accounts payable	71 200	0	0	71 200	0	0
Provision for long service leave	64 000	0	64 000	0	0	64 000
Total temporary differences					**3 800**	**102 000**

	Carrying amount $	Future taxable amount $	Future deductible amount $	Tax base $	Taxable temporary differences $	Deductible temporary differences $
Deferred tax liability					1 140	
Deferred tax asset						30 600
Beginning balances					720	30 360
Movement during year:						
Recouped tax loss						(4 500)
Adjustment					**420 Cr**	**4 740 Dr**

Step 1. Determine the carrying amounts
These are read from the statement of financial position as at the end of the current year.

Step 2. Determine the tax bases
- *Cash.* There are no taxable economic benefits flowing from this asset. Hence, the tax base of the asset equals the carrying amount of $9000.
- *Accounts receivable.* The carrying amount for accounting purposes — in the left-hand column of the worksheet — is the balance of the accounts receivable account less the allowance for doubtful debts. The amount is $78 000, being $83 000 – $5000. This asset does not generate any future taxable economic benefits. Hence, the tax base is the gross balance of the accounts receivable account, $83 000. This can also be calculated as future deductible amount of $5000 (i.e. the allowance for doubtful debts) plus the carrying amount for accounting purposes of $78 000 minus the future taxable amount of $0.
- *Inventories.* The asset is expected to generate taxable economic benefits when the inventories are sold. The tax base is then the future deductible amount; that is, the cost of the inventories, $67 100.
- *Interest receivable.* The asset is expected to generate economic benefits that will be taxed when the interest is received. The tax base is then the future deductible amount, which is zero.
- *Prepaid rent.* The asset is expected to generate taxable economic benefits as the entity uses the rented property. The tax base is then the future deductible amount, which is zero.
- *Plant.* Depreciation for accounting purposes is calculated at 15% p.a. on a cost of $220 000, namely $33 000. The accumulated depreciation at the end of 3 years is $99 000, giving a carrying amount for plant of $121 000. For taxation the depreciation rate is 10% p.a. The carrying amount for tax purposes at the end of 3 years is then $154 000, being $220 000 less 3 × $22 000. As the plant is expected to generate taxable economic benefits as it is being used by the entity, the tax base is the future deductible amount for tax purposes. This is the part of the cost of the plant not yet claimed as a tax depreciation.
- *Provision for long service leave.* The future deductible amount for this liability is the carrying amount of $64 000. This amount is deductible as the entity pays the leave to its employees. The tax base of the liability is the carrying amount less the future deductible amount. As these are equal, the tax base is zero.
- *Accounts payable.* There is no future deductible amount for this liability. Hence the tax base is equal to the carrying amount, namely $71 200.

Step 3. Determine and classify the temporary differences
This involves comparing the carrying amounts and tax bases in the worksheet. Taxable temporary differences arise when an asset has a carrying amount greater than its tax base or when a liability has a carrying amount less than its tax base. Deductible temporary differences arise where an asset has a carrying amount less than its tax base or a liability has a carrying amount greater than its tax base. In this example, out of the assets, interest receivable and prepaid rent give rise to taxable temporary differences, while accounts receivable and plant bring deductible temporary differences. For liabilities, there is only a deductible temporary difference created by the provision for long service leave.

Step 4(a). Determine the closing balances of deferred tax asset and deferred tax liability accounts
This involves totalling the last two right-hand columns of the worksheet to obtain the total taxable temporary differences of $3800 and total deductible temporary differences of $102 000.

These totals are then multiplied by the tax rate of 30% to give a closing balance for the deferred tax liability and deferred tax asset of $1140 and $30 600 respectively.

Step 4(b). Determine the adjustments in the deferred tax asset and deferred tax liability accounts
This involves comparing the closing balances of those accounts as determined in step 4(a) with the balances as shown in the entity's statement of financial position at the end of the previous period. In this example the deferred tax liability had a beginning balance of $720 while the deferred tax asset had a beginning balance of $30 360. In relation to the deferred tax asset there was a movement in the current period in the account due to the recoupment of the tax loss as shown in the entry resulting from the current tax worksheet.

A reconstruction of these accounts showing opening balances, closing balances and movements during the period is as follows.

Deferred tax liability					
30/06/23	Balance c/d	1 140	01/07/22	Balance b/d	720
			30/06/23	Income tax expense/ revenue (deferred)	420
		1 140			1 140

Deferred tax asset					
01/07/22	Balance b/d	30 360	30/06/23	Income tax expense (current)	4 500
30/06/23	Income tax expense (deferred)	4 740	30/06/23	Balance c/d	30 600
		35 100			35 100

Step 4(c). Prepare the deferred tax adjustment entry
Based on the differences between the opening and closing balances of the deferred tax asset and liability accounts, as well as the movements in these accounts during the period identified in step 4(b), the adjustment entry for deferred tax is as follows.

Deferred tax asset		Dr	4 740
Deferred tax liability		Cr	420
Income tax expense/revenue (deferred)		Cr	4 320

COMPREHENSION QUESTIONS

1 What is the main principle of tax-effect accounting as outlined in AASB 112/IAS 12?

2 Explain how accounting profit and taxable profit differ, and how each is treated when accounting for income taxes.

3 How are the current and future tax consequences of transactions accounted for?

4 How is the taxable profit and the related current tax calculated?

5 What is a 'tax loss' and how is it accounted for?

6 What is an 'exempt income' and how does it affect the calculation or recovery of carry-forward tax losses?

7 In determining whether deferred tax assets relating to tax losses are to be recognised, what factors should be taken into consideration?

8 What are the steps in the calculation of deferred tax?

9 What is a tax base and how are the tax bases for assets and liabilities calculated?

10 Explain the meaning of a temporary difference as it relates to deferred tax calculations and give three examples.

11 Are all differences that exist at the end of the reporting period between the carrying amounts and tax bases of assets and liabilities recognised as part of deferred tax assets or deferred tax liabilities?

12 In tax-effect accounting, the temporary differences between the carrying amount and the tax base for assets and liabilities leads to the establishment of deferred tax assets and liabilities in the accounting records. List examples of temporary differences that create:
   • deferred tax assets
   • deferred tax liabilities.
13 In AASB 112/IAS 12, criteria are established for the recognition of a deferred tax asset and a deferred tax liability. Identify these criteria, and discuss any differences between the criteria for assets and those for liabilities.
14 'Despite the fact that deferred tax liabilities and assets are recognised in respect of certain assets and liabilities, the income tax expense (or benefit) of such items is always recognised in the current year.' Is this statement true? Discuss.
15 What action should be taken when a tax rate changes? Why?

CASE STUDY 12.1

TAX-EFFECT ACCOUNTING

Every year companies in Australia generally expect to have to pay some of their earnings to the Australian Government in the form of income tax. However, the amount paid to the government is rarely the amount reported as income tax expense in the statement of profit or loss and other comprehensive income.

Required

1. Explain the objectives of accounting for income tax in general purpose financial statements.
2. Explain the basic principles that are applied in accounting for income tax to meet these objectives.
3. List the steps in the calculation of deferred tax assets and liabilities.

CASE STUDY 12.2

RECOGNITION OF TAX LOSSES

Whale Ltd is engaged primarily in agricultural pursuits as well as in forestry products, including the management of its own forest reserves. Unfortunately, in the current year an eruption of a volcano in the mountain range bordering the company's operations resulted in the destruction of 40 000 hectares of standing timber, harvested logs, forestry buildings and equipment. As a result, the company recognised a $80 million tax loss in the current period. The management of Whale Ltd are debating whether it can raise a deferred tax asset in relation to this loss in the financial statements for the current period.

Required

Prepare a report to management providing advice on the recognition of a deferred tax asset and specifying the conditions, if any, under which the asset could be recognised.

CASE STUDY 12.3

DEFERRED TAX ASSET OF A LOSS MAKING COMPANY

Isa Ltd is a gold exploration company. Isa Ltd has recognised a deferred tax asset balance for tax losses in its statement of financial position for each of the past four years as follows.

	Isa Ltd ($000s)			
	2023	2024	2025	2026
Deferred tax asset	24 200	133 200	197 000	300 800

At 30 June 2026, Isa Ltd is in financial distress due to a cash shortage and bank restrictions on providing any further funds.

Required

The auditors of Isa Ltd have asked for your advice on whether a deferred tax asset should be recognised for carried forward tax losses at 30 June 2026. Discuss with reference to AASB 112/IAS 12.

CASE STUDY 12.4

DEFERRED TAX BALANCES AND DISCOUNTING

A fellow student said, 'Deferred tax liabilities and assets should be measured using a discounted cash flow model. The deferred tax is paid or refunded in the future — that could be years away — so the time value of money should be taken into account'.

Required

Refer to AASB 112/IAS 12 and comment on your fellow student's argument. Identify other assets and liabilities where discounting is required in the measurement approach.

CASE STUDY 12.5

RECOGNITION OF DEFERRED TAX ASSETS

All Sheds Ltd manufactures prefabricated sheds, ranging from industrial sheds and garden sheds down to small items such as dog kennels. In recent years, All Sheds Ltd has recorded accounting losses. The company has retrenched several of its staff after struggling to find new markets for its products.

In the prior year, the company recognised expenses and liabilities for long service leave and potential redundancy payouts. Redundancy costs and long service leave are not deductible for income tax until paid. The company recognised deferred tax assets as a result of these liabilities.

With the long service leave and redundancy entitlements being paid out to the retrenched employees in the current year, the company has now been able to claim large tax deductions for the cash payments made. The effect of these deductions is that the company has recorded a significant tax loss in the current year.

Required

1. Outline the requirements of AASB 112/IAS 12 in relation to the recognition of deferred tax assets from long service leave and retrenchment liabilities. How do these requirements differ (if at all) from the recognition requirements for deferred tax assets from tax losses?
2. Discuss whether the deferred tax asset from the employee benefits liabilities in the prior year should have been recognised. Should the tax loss in the current year be recognised as a deferred tax asset?

CASE STUDY 12.6

INCOME TAX DISCLOSURES OF TOP AUSTRALIAN COMPANIES

Select three companies listed on the ASX from different industries (e.g. Telstra, Woolworths and Fortescue Metals Group). Go to www.asx.com.au and find the most recent annual financial report of each of the three companies. Compare the information relating to income tax in the financial statements and report your findings. Your presentation should address:

- the income tax expense included in the profit or loss for the year
- any income tax included in other comprehensive income
- the current and deferred tax components of income tax expense
- whether a deferred tax asset or deferred tax liability or both is disclosed in the statement of financial position and the magnitude of their balances.

APPLICATION AND ANALYSIS EXERCISES

★ BASIC | ★ ★ MODERATE | ★ ★ ★ DIFFICULT

12.1 Tax effects of a temporary difference ★   **LO4, 5**

The following information was extracted from the records of Bowen Ltd for the year ended 30 June 2022 in relation to equipment that had cost $120 000 on 1 July 2019.

	Carrying amount $	Future taxable amount $	Future deductible amount $	Tax base $	Taxable temporary differences $	Deductible temporary differences $
Assets						
Equipment	30 000	30 000	48 000	48 000		18 000

Equipment is depreciated at 25% p.a. straight-line for accounting purposes, but the allowable rate of depreciation for taxation is 20% p.a.

Required

Assuming that no equipment is purchased or sold during the years ended 30 June 2022 to 30 June 2024, calculate the:
1. accounting expense and tax deduction for each year
2. impact of depreciation on the calculation of current tax expense for each year
3. effect on the deferred tax asset account each year.

12.2 Applying tax-effect accounting ★   LO1, 2, 3, 5

Orca Ltd applies the principles of tax-effect accounting as per AASB 112/IAS 12 in accounting for company income tax. Orca Ltd calculates depreciation expense on its plant using the straight-line method, but applies an accelerated method for tax purposes. Tax depreciation in the current year is then larger than the related accounting depreciation expense.

Orca Ltd has also recognised rent received in advance from buildings that it owns. These revenues are included in the current year's taxable profit but shown in the financial statements as a liability.

Required

1. Explain the principles underlying tax-effect accounting.
2. Determine how Orca Ltd should account for the above differences for accounting and tax.
3. Analyse under what circumstances Orca Ltd should raise deferred tax accounts and how they should be classified in the statement of financial position.

12.3 Calculation of current tax ★   LO3, 4

Mandiri Ltd made an accounting profit before tax of $80 000 for the year ended 30 June 2024. Included in the accounting profit were the following items of revenue and expense.

Donations to political parties (non-deductible)	$ 7 000
Depreciation expense — machinery (20% p.a., straight-line)	18 000
Annual leave expense	6 400
Rent revenue	12 000

For tax purposes the following applied.

Depreciation rate — machinery	25%
Annual leave paid	$ 7 800
Rent received	$10 000
Income tax rate	30%

Required

1. Calculate the current tax liability for the year ended 30 June 2024, and prepare the adjusting journal entry.
2. Explain your treatment of rent items in your answer to requirement 1.

12.4 Calculation of current tax ★   LO3, 4

Magpalitan Ltd recorded an accounting profit before tax of $100 000 for the year ended 30 June 2025. Included in the accounting profit were the following items of revenue and expense.

Entertainment expenses (non-deductible)	$ 2 000
Depreciation expense — furniture (10% p.a., straight-line)	17 000
Rent revenue	2 500

For tax purposes the following applied.

Depreciation rate — furniture	15%
Rent received	$3 000
Income tax rate	30%

Required

1. Use a current tax worksheet to calculate the current tax liability for the year ended 30 June 2025. Prepare the journal entry to record current tax.
2. Explain the future tax effect of the adjustment made in requirement 1 for rent revenue/received.

12.5 Calculation of deferred tax ★   **LO5**

The following information was extracted from the records of Sol Ltd for the year ended 30 June 2024.

SOL LTD		
Statement of financial position (extract)		
as at 30 June 2024		
Assets		
Accounts receivable	$ 50 000	
Allowance for doubtful debts	(4 000)	$ 46 000
Motor vehicles	200 000	
Accumulated depreciation — motor vehicles	(50 000)	150 000
Liabilities		
Interest payable		2 000

Additional information

- The accumulated tax depreciation for motor vehicles at 30 June 2024 was $100 000.
- The tax rate is 30%.

Required

Prepare a deferred tax worksheet to identify the temporary differences arising in respect of the assets and liabilities in the statement of financial position, and to calculate the balance of the deferred tax liability and deferred tax asset accounts at 30 June 2024. Assume the opening balances of the deferred tax accounts were $0.

12.6 Current and future tax consequences ★   **LO3**

Explain which of the following have current or future tax consequences.

1. Estimated warranty costs covering a 3-year warranty period are expensed for financial reporting purposes over a 3-year period but are treated as a tax deduction in the year in which a claim is made by a customer.
2. The company has recognised entertainment expenses in the current period for financial reporting purposes but these outlays are never deductible for tax purposes.
3. Insurance is paid 2 years in advance and a prepaid asset is recognised for accounting purposes. A tax deduction is claimed when the cash is paid.

12.7 Change in tax rates ★ ★   **LO6**

At 30 June 2023, Blue Heeler Ltd recognised a deferred tax asset of $12 000 and a deferred tax liability of $15 000. This has resulted by applying a tax rate of 30%. The Australian Government announced that it will increase the tax rate as of 1 July 2023 to 35%. In its deferred tax worksheet for the year ending 30 June 2024, Blue Heeler Ltd calculated that its taxable temporary differences were $6000 and its deductible temporary differences were $12 000.

Required

Prepare a report for the chief accountant on how the increase in the tax rate will affect the application of tax-effect accounting for the year ended 30 June 2024.

12.8 Recognition of deferred tax assets ★ ★   **LO5**

Orbost Ltd manufactures its products in Australia. In the past, Orbost Ltd has relied heavily on the export of its products to the United States. In 2022 the company's profits have declined as sales both in Australia and overseas have fallen. As a result, the company has had to retrench some of its employees as it has endeavoured to streamline its business and search for new markets.

The company has always had a generous employee scheme whereby employees were entitled to good long service leave payments as well as payments in the event of redundancy. These expenses were recognised for financial reporting purposes on an annual basis but no tax deductions were allowed until cash payments were made. The company has raised deferred tax assets in relation to these items in its financial statements.

On retrenching its employees, the company has been able to claim tax deductions for the long service leave and retrenchment payouts. This has resulted in the company recording a tax loss in 2022.

Required

Write a report to the group accountant of Orbost Ltd, covering your assessment of the company:
1. continuing to raise deferred tax assets in relation to long service leave and redundancy payouts
2. raising a deferred tax asset in relation to the current period tax loss
3. raising any deferred tax liabilities such as for depreciation of the manufacturing machinery.

12.9 Creation and reversal of temporary differences ★ ★   **LO5**

The following are all independent situations. Prepare the journal entries for deferred tax on the creation or reversal of any temporary differences. Explain in each case the nature of the temporary difference. Assume a tax rate of 30%.
1. The entity has an allowance for doubtful debts of $10 000 at the end of the reporting period relating to accounts receivable of $125 000. The prior period balances for these accounts were $8500 and $97 500 respectively. During the current period, debts worth $9250 were written off as uncollectable.
2. The entity sold a tractor at the end of the reporting period for $15 000. The tractor cost $100 000 when purchased 4 years ago, and had a carrying amount of $20 000 when sold. The tax depreciation rate for tractors of this type is 25% p.a.
3. The entity has recognised a rent receivable asset with an opening balance of $17 000 and an ending balance of $19 500 for the current year. During the year, rent of $127 000 was received in cash.
4. At the end of the reporting period, the entity has recognised a liability of $4000 in respect of outstanding fines for non-compliance with safety legislation. Such fines are not tax-deductible.

12.10 Creation and reversal of a temporary difference ★ ★   **LO5**

Injune Ltd purchased machinery on 1 July 2020 at a cost of $75 000. The machinery had an expected useful life of 5 years and was to be depreciated on a straight-line basis. The tax depreciation rate for machinery of this type is 15% p.a., straight-line. On 30 June 2022, Injune Ltd reassessed the remaining useful life of the machinery from 3 years to 2 years, and the accounting depreciation charge was adjusted accordingly. The machinery was sold on 30 June 2023 for $45 000. The company tax rate is 30%.

Required

For each of the years ended 30 June 2021, 30 June 2022 and 30 June 2023, calculate the carrying amount and the tax base of the asset and determine the appropriate deferred tax entry. Explain your answer.

12.11 Calculation of deferred tax, and adjustment entry ★ ★   **LO5**

The following information was extracted from the records of Jondaryan Ltd as at 30 June 2023.

	Carrying amount	Tax base
Asset (liability)		
Accounts receivable	$150 000	$175 000
Motor vehicles	165 000	125 000
Provision for warranty	(12 000)	0
Deposits received in advance	(15 000)	0

The depreciation rates for accounting and taxation are 15% p.a. and 25% p.a. respectively. Deposits are taxable when received, and warranty costs are deductible when paid. An allowance for doubtful debts of $25 000 has been raised against accounts receivable for accounting purposes, but such debts are deductible only when written off as uncollectable.

Required

1. Calculate the temporary differences for Jondaryan Ltd as at 30 June 2023. Justify your classification of each difference as either a deductible temporary difference or a taxable temporary difference.

2. Prepare a deferred tax worksheet and the journal entry to record deferred tax for the year ended 30 June 2023 assuming no deferred items had been raised in prior years.

12.12 Calculation of current and deferred tax, and adjustment entry ★ ★ **LO4, 5**

Shengli Ltd commences operations on 1 July 2023. One year later, on 30 June 2024, the entity prepares its first statement of comprehensive income and its first statement of financial position. The statements are prepared before considering taxation. The following information is available.

Statement of comprehensive income for the year ended 30 June 2024	
Gross profit	$ 250 000
Wages expense	(100 000)
Annual leave expense	(25 000)
Bad debts expense	(10 000)
Rent expense	(25 000)
Depreciation expense — furniture and fittings	(15 000)
Accounting profit before tax	75 000

Assets and liabilities as disclosed in the statement of financial position as at 30 June 2024	
Assets	
Cash	$ 75 000
Inventories	100 000
Accounts receivable (net)	90 000
Prepaid rent	25 000
Furniture and fittings	75 000
Accumulated depreciation — furniture and fittings	(15 000)
	350 000
Liabilities	
Accounts payable	50 000
Revenue received in advance	25 000
Loan payable	100 000
Provision for annual leave	25 000
	200 000

Additional information
- The company tax rate is assumed to be 30%.
- All salaries have been paid as at year end and are deductible for tax purposes.
- None of the annual leave has actually been paid. It is not deductible for tax purposes until it is actually paid.
- Rent was paid in advance on 1 July 2023. Actual amounts paid are allowed as a tax deduction.
- Amounts received from sales, including those on credit terms, are taxed at the time the sale is made. No bad debts were written off.
- The revenue received in advance is included in the taxable income.
- The furniture and fittings is depreciated on a straight-line basis over 5 years for accounting purposes, but over 3 years for taxation purposes. The furniture and fittings is not expected to have any residual value.

Required

1. Prepare the current tax worksheet and the journal entry to recognise current tax at 30 June 2024.
2. Prepare the deferred tax worksheet and journal entries to adjust deferred tax accounts.

12.13 Calculation of current and deferred tax, and adjustment entry ★ ★ **LO4, 5**

Bondi Ltd's accounting profit before tax for the year ended 30 June 2024 was $150 000. At 30 June 2023 and 30 June 2024, the company's draft statements of financial position showed the following balances.

	2023	2024
Assets		
Cash	$ 40 000	$ 50 000
Inventories	150 000	160 000
Accounts receivable	300 000	420 000
Allowance for doubtful debts	(15 000)	(21 500)
Prepaid insurance	20 000	15 000
Equipment	200 000	260 000
Accumulated depreciation — equipment	(100 000)	(146 000)
Buildings	400 000	400 000
Accumulated depreciation — buildings	(140 000)	(160 000)
Goodwill	40 000	40 000
Deferred tax asset	45 000	?
Liabilities		
Accounts payable	255 000	270 000
Accrued expenses	120 000	90 000
Mortgage loan	210 000	210 000
Warranty payable	70 000	50 000
Current tax liability	9 000	?
Deferred tax liability	12 000	?

Additional information
- The company tax rate is assumed to be 30%.
- During the year ended 30 June 2024, Bondi Ltd received a non-taxable royalty revenue of $20 000.
- Amounts received from sales, including those on credit terms, are taxed at the time the sale is made. Bondi Ltd recognised $20 000 in bad debts expense during the year ended 30 June 2024.
- Insurance expense incurred during the year ended 30 June 2024 was $20 000. The amounts paid in cash for insurance are allowed to be claimed as deductions for tax purposes.
- The equipment is depreciated on a straight-line basis over 5 years for accounting purposes and over 4 years for taxation purposes. The equipment is not expected to have any residual value. The only movement in the equipment account during the year ended 30 June 2024 was a result of Bondi Ltd acquiring a new equipment on 1 January 2024.
- The buildings are depreciated on a straight line basis over 20 years for accounting purposes and are not expected to have any residual value. Depreciation of buildings is not allowed to be claimed as a deduction for tax purposes. There is no movement in the buildings account during the year ended 30 June 2024.
- During the year ended 30 June 2024, Bondi Ltd paid accrued expenses of $210 000 and recognised $45 000 in warranty expense. These expenses are not deductible for tax purposes until they are actually paid.
- There are no other items that cause differences between accounting and taxable profit.
- During the year ended 30 June 2024, Bondi Ltd paid the ATO the following instalments for income tax:
  - 28 July 2023: $9000
  - 28 October 2023: $7000
  - 28 February 2024: $7500
  - 28 April 2024: $8000.

Required
1. Prepare the current tax worksheet and the journal entry to recognise current tax at 30 June 2024.
2. Prepare the deferred tax worksheet and journal entries to adjust deferred tax accounts.

12.14 Calculation of current and deferred tax, and adjustment entry ★ ★   **LO4, 5**

The profit before tax, as reported in the statement of profit and loss for Albury Ltd for the year ended 30 June 2024, amounted to $400 000, including the following revenue and expense items.

Sales revenue	$2 600 000
Interest revenue	200 000
Government grant (non-taxable)	200 000
Cost of sales	1 600 000
Bad debts expense	40 000
Depreciation expense — equipment	40 000
Depreciation expense — plant	80 000
Research and development expense	240 000
Wages expense	480 000
Long service leave expense	80 000

The statement of profit and loss for Albury Ltd for the year ended 30 June 2024 also included a gain on sale of equipment of $40 000. According to AASB 116/IAS 16, this gain is not classified as revenue, but it is nevertheless part of the accounting profit before tax for the year. The draft statements of financial position of Albury Ltd at 30 June 2023 and 30 June 2024 showed the following assets and liabilities.

	2023	2024
Assets		
Cash	$ 120 000	$ 120 000
Inventories	400 000	600 000
Accounts receivable	200 000	280 000
Allowance for doubtful debts	(20 000)	(40 000)
Interest receivable	100 000	80 000
Equipment	120 000	—
Accumulated depreciation — equipment	(60 000)	—
Plant	800 000	800 000
Accumulated depreciation — plant	(160 000)	(240 000)
Goodwill	60 000	60 000
Deferred tax asset	132 000	?
Liabilities		
Accounts payable	240 000	160 000
Wages payable	200 000	320 000
Revenue received in advance	—	80 000
Loan payable	800 000	400 000
Provision for long service leave	160 000	120 000
Deferred tax liability	96 000	?

Additional information
- In the year ended 30 June 2023, Albury Ltd had a tax loss of $260 000 that it carried over in the deferred tax asset. In June 2024, the company received an amended assessment for the year ended 30 June 2023 from the ATO, indicating that an amount of $20 000 claimed as a deduction has been disallowed. Albury Ltd has not yet adjusted its accounts to reflect the amendment.
- Amounts received from sales, including those on credit terms, are taxed at the time the sale is made. All other general taxation rules apply.
- The movement in the equipment account is caused by the sale of the equipment on 1 March 2024 for which a gain on sale of $40 000 was recognised as part of the profit before tax (see above). Albury Ltd had purchased the equipment on 1 July 2022 (with an estimated useful life of 2 years and no residual value) and for taxation purposes it claimed its full cost as a deduction at 30 June 2023.
- The plant is depreciated on a straight-line basis over 10 years for accounting purposes, but over 5 years for taxation purposes. The plant is not expected to have any residual value.
- All research and development expenses were paid in cash during the year ended 30 June 2024.
- The company tax rate is assumed to be 30% for the year ended 30 June 2023 and 28% for the year ended 30 June 2024. The balances of the deferred tax accounts at 30 June 2023 are still reflecting the 30% tax rate.

Required
1. Prepare the current tax worksheet and the journal entry to recognise current tax at 30 June 2024.
2. Prepare the deferred tax worksheet and journal entries to adjust deferred tax accounts.

Konpayi Ltd has determined its accounting profit before tax for the year ended 30 June 2023 to be $256 700. Included in this profit are the items of revenue and expense shown below.

Royalty revenue (non-taxable)	$ 8 000
Entertainment expense	1 700
Depreciation expense — buildings	7 600
Depreciation expense — plant	22 500
Doubtful debts expense	4 100
Annual leave expense	46 000
Insurance expense	4 200
Development expense	15 000

The accounting profit for Konpayi Ltd for the year ended 30 June 2023 also included a gain on sale of buildings of $5000.

The company's draft statement of financial position at 30 June 2023 showed the following assets and liabilities.

Assets		
Cash		$ 2 500
Accounts receivable	$ 21 500	
Less: Allowance for doubtful debts	(4 100)	17 400
Inventories		31 600
Prepaid insurance		4 500
Land		75 000
Buildings	170 000	
Less: Accumulated depreciation	(59 500)	110 500
Plant	150 000	
Less: Accumulated depreciation	(67 500)	82 500
Deferred tax asset (opening balance)		9 600
		333 600
Liabilities		
Accounts payable		25 000
Provision for annual leave		10 000
Deferred tax liability (opening balance)		6 000
Loan		140 000
		$181 000

Additional information
- Quarterly income tax instalments paid during the year were as follows.

28 October 2022	$18 000
28 January 2023	17 500
28 April 2023	18 000

The final balance of tax payable was due on 28 July 2023.
- The tax depreciation rate for plant (which cost $150 000, 3 years before) is 20%.
- Depreciation on buildings is not deductible for taxation purposes. The gain on sale of buildings of $5000 (see above) was recognised on buildings sold on 1 January 2023 that had cost $100 000 when acquired on 1 January 2017. The company depreciates buildings for accounting purposes at 5% p.a., straight-line. Any gain (loss) on sale of buildings is not taxable (not deductible).

- During the year, the following cash amounts were paid.

Annual leave	$52 000
Insurance	3 700

- Bad debts of $3500 were written off against the allowance for doubtful debts during the year.
- The $15 000 spent (and expensed) on development during the year is not deductible for tax purposes until 30 June 2024.
- Konpayi Ltd has tax losses amounting to $12 500 carried forward from prior years.
- The company tax rate is 30%.

Required

1. Prepare the current tax worksheet and the journal entry to recognise current tax at 30 June 2023.
2. Prepare the deferred tax worksheet and journal entries to adjust deferred tax accounts.

12.16 Calculation of movements in deferred tax accounts ★ ★   **LO5**

The statement of financial position of Labrador Ltd at 30 June 2024 showed the following assets and liabilities.

	2024	2023
Assets		
Cash	$ 40 000	$ 42 500
Inventories	85 000	77 500
Accounts receivable	250 000	240 000
Allowance for doubtful debts	(27 500)	(20 000)
Plant	250 000	250 000
Accumulated depreciation — plant	(130 000)	(105 000)
Deferred tax asset	?	20 250
Liabilities		
Accounts payable	145 000	130 000
Provision for long service leave	30 000	22 500
Rent received in advance	12 500	10 000
Deferred tax liability	?	19 050

Additional information
- Accumulated depreciation of plant for tax purposes was $157 500 at 30 June 2023, and depreciation for tax purposes for the year ended 30 June 2024 amounted to $37 500.
- The tax rate is 30%.

Required

Prepare a deferred tax worksheet to calculate the end of reporting period adjustment to deferred tax asset and liability accounts as at 30 June 2024, and show the necessary journal entry.

12.17 Calculation of current tax liability and adjusting journal entry ★ ★   **LO4**

The profit before tax, as reported in the statement of profit or loss and other comprehensive income of Miami Ltd for the year ended 30 June 2024, amounted to $60 000, including the following revenue and expense items.

Rent revenue	$3 000
Bad debts expense	6 000
Depreciation expense — plant	5 000
Annual leave expense	3 000
Long service leave expense	1 500
Entertainment costs (non-deductible)	1 800
Depreciation expense — buildings (non-deductible)	800

The statement of financial position of the company at 30 June 2024 showed the following assets and liabilities.

	2024	2023
Assets		
Cash	$ 8 000	$ 8 500
Inventories	17 000	15 500
Accounts receivable	50 000	48 000
Allowance for doubtful debts	(5 500)	(4 000)
Office supplies	2 500	2 200
Plant	50 000	50 000
Accumulated depreciation — plant	(26 000)	(21 000)
Buildings	30 000	30 000
Accumulated depreciation — buildings	(14 800)	(14 000)
Goodwill (net)	7 000	7 000
Deferred tax asset	?	4 050
Liabilities		
Accounts payable	29 000	26 000
Provision for long service leave	6 000	4 500
Provision for annual leave	4 000	3 000
Rent received in advance	2 500	2 000
Deferred tax liability	?	3 150

Additional information
- Accumulated depreciation of plant for tax purposes was $31 500 at 30 June 2023, and depreciation for tax purposes for the year ended 30 June 2024 amounted to $7500.
- The tax rate is 30%.

Required

Prepare a current tax worksheet and the journal entry to recognise the company's current tax liability as at 30 June 2024.

12.18 Calculation of current and deferred tax, and prior year amendment ★ ★ ★   LO3, 4, 5

The accounting profit before tax of Narrabri Ltd for the year ended 30 June 2023 was $66 720. It included the following revenue and expense items.

Government grant (non-taxable)	$ 5 500
Entertainment expense (non-deductible)	8 200
Doubtful debts expense	8 100
Depreciation expense — plant	24 000
Insurance expense	12 900
Annual leave expense	15 400

The accounting profit before tax for Narrabri Ltd for the year ended 30 June 2023 also included a gain on sale of plant of $3000. The draft statement of financial position as at 30 June 2023 included the following assets and liabilities.

	2023	2022
Accounts receivable	$ 156 000	$ 147 500
Allowance for doubtful debts	(6 800)	(5 200)
Prepaid insurance	3 400	5 600
Plant	240 000	290 000
Accumulated depreciation — plant	(134 400)	(130 400)
Deferred tax asset	?	9 990
Provision for annual leave	14 100	9 700
Deferred tax liability	?	9 504

Additional information
- In November 2022, the company received an amended assessment for the year ended 30 June 2022 from the tax authority. The amendment notice indicated that an amount of $4500 claimed as a deduction had been disallowed. Narrabri Ltd has not yet adjusted its accounts to reflect the amendment.

- For tax purposes, the carrying amount of plant sold was $26 000. This sale was the only movement in plant for the year.
- The tax deduction for plant depreciation was $28 800. Accumulated depreciation at 30 June 2022 for taxation purposes was $156 480.
- In the previous year, Narrabri Ltd had made a tax loss of $18 400. Narrabri Ltd recognised a deferred tax asset in respect of this loss.
- The tax rate is 30%.

Required

1. Prepare the journal entry necessary to record the amendment to the prior year's taxation return.
2. Prepare the current tax worksheet and journal entry/entries to calculate and record the current tax for the year ended 30 June 2023.
3. Justify your treatment of annual leave expense in the current tax worksheet.
4. Calculate the temporary difference as at 30 June 2023 for each of the following assets. Explain how these differences arise and why you have classified them as either deductible temporary differences or taxable temporary differences:
   (a) plant
   (b) accounts receivable.

12.19 Current and deferred tax with tax rate change ★ ★ ★   **LO4, 5, 6**

You have been asked by the accountant of Charlton Ltd to prepare the tax-effect accounting adjustments for the year ended 30 June 2023. Investigations revealed the following information.

(a) In September 2021, the Australian Government reduced the company tax rate from 40 cents to 30 cents in the dollar, effective from 1 July 2022.
(b) The profit for the year ended 30 June 2023 was $1 350 000.
(c) The assets and liabilities at 30 June 2022 and 30 June 2023 were as follows.

	2023	2022
Accounts receivable	$ 235 000	$ 200 000
Allowance for doubtful debts	(13 000)	(12 000)
Inventories	250 000	220 000
Land	100 000	100 000
Buildings	800 000	800 000
Accumulated depreciation — buildings	(99 000)	(70 000)
Equipment	600 000	600 000
Accumulated depreciation — equipment	(190 000)	(120 000)
Development expenditure — at cost	320 000	200 000
Accumulated amortisation — development expenditure	(144 000)	(80 000)
Deferred tax asset	?	29 600
Goodwill (net)	—	30 000
Accounts payable	170 000	150 000
Deferred tax liability	?	72 000
Provision for long service leave	36 000	28 000
Provision for warranty claims	32 000	34 000

(d) The company is entitled to claim a tax deduction of 125% for development expenditure in the year of expenditure. The company has adopted the accounting policy of capitalising and then amortising the expenditure over 5 years.
(e) Revenue for the year included the following.

Non-taxable income	$138 000

(f) Expenses brought to account included the following.

Depreciation — buildings	$29 000
Depreciation — equipment	70 000
Impairment — goodwill (non-deductible)	30 000
Amortisation — development expenditure	64 000

(g) Accumulated depreciation on equipment for tax purposes was $180 000 on 30 June 2022, and $285 000 on 30 June 2023.

(h) Bad debts of $14 000 were written off during the year, and warranty repairs to the value of $22 000 were carried out. There was no tax deduction for long service leave in the current year.

(i) Buildings are depreciated in the accounting records but no deduction is allowed for tax purposes.

Required

1. Prepare the journal entry to account for the change in the income tax rate announced by the Australian Government in September 2021.
2. Prepare the worksheets and journal entries to calculate and record the current tax liability, and any movements in deferred tax assets and liabilities for the year ended 30 June 2023.

12.20 Recognition of deferred tax assets ★ ★ ★   **LO5**

Paddington Ltd incurred an accounting loss of $15 120 for the year ended 30 June 2023. The current tax calculation determined that the company had incurred a tax loss of $25 000. Taxation legislation allows such losses to be carried forward and offset against future taxable profits. The company had the following temporary differences.

	30 June 2023	30 June 2022	Expected period of reversal
Deductible temporary differences:			
Accounts receivable	$24 000	$20 000	2024
Plant and equipment	10 000	15 000	2024/2025 equally
Taxable temporary differences:			
Interest receivable	3 000	5 000	2024
Prepaid insurance	20 000	40 000	2024

At 30 June 2022, Paddington Ltd had recognised a deferred tax liability of $13 500 and a deferred tax asset of $10 500 with respect to temporary differences existing at that date. No adjustment has yet been made for temporary differences existing at 30 June 2023.

Required

1. Discuss the factors that Paddington Ltd should consider in determining the amount (if any) to be recognised for deferred tax assets at 30 June 2023.
2. Calculate the amount (if any) to be recognised for deferred tax assets at 30 June 2023. Justify your answer.

12.21 Current and deferred tax ★ ★ ★   **LO4, 5**

The accounting profit before tax for the year ended 30 June 2022 for Quamby Ltd amounted to $28 500 and included the following.

Depreciation expense — motor vehicle (25% p.a., straight-line)	$ 4 500
Depreciation expense — equipment (20% p.a., straight-line)	20 000
Rent revenue	16 000
Royalty revenue (non-taxable)	5 000
Doubtful debts expense	2 300
Entertainment expense (non-deductible)	1 500
Annual leave expense	5 000
Gain on sale of equipment	1 000

The draft statement of financial position at 30 June 2022 contained the following assets and liabilities.

	2022	2021
Assets		
Cash	$ 13 200	$ 9 800
Accounts receivable	12 000	14 000
Allowance for doubtful debts	(3 000)	(2 500)
Inventories	19 000	21 500
Rent receivable	2 800	2 400
Motor vehicle	18 000	18 000
Accumulated depreciation — motor vehicle	(15 750)	(11 250)
Equipment	100 000	130 000
Accumulated depreciation — equipment	(60 000)	(52 000)
Deferred tax asset	?	6 450
Liabilities		
Accounts payable	15 655	21 500
Provision for annual leave	4 500	6 000
Current tax liability	?	8 200
Deferred tax liability	?	3 445

Additional information
- The motor vehicle is fully depreciated for tax purposes.
- The company claims tax depreciation on equipment at the rate of 15% p.a. The sale of equipment on which a gain was recognised (see above) was the only movement in the equipment account during the year and took place on 1 July 2021.
- The company tax rate is 30%.

Required

1. Prepare the current tax worksheet and the journal entry to recognise the current tax as at 30 June 2022.
2. Prepare the deferred tax worksheet and any necessary journal entries to adjust deferred tax accounts.

12.22 Current and deferred tax with prior year losses ★ ★ ★   **LO4, 5**

The accounting profit before tax of Charleville Ltd for the year ended 30 June 2023 was $175 900. It included the following revenue and expense items.

Government grant (non-taxable)	$ 5 800
Interest revenue	14 000
Long service leave expense	7 000
Doubtful debts expense	4 200
Depreciation expense — plant (15% p.a., straight-line)	33 000
Rent expense	22 800
Entertainment expense (non-deductible)	3 900

The draft statement of financial position as at 30 June 2023 included the following assets and liabilities.

	2023	2022
Cash	$ 9 000	$ 7 500
Accounts receivable	83 000	76 800
Allowance for doubtful debts	(5 000)	(3 200)
Inventories	67 100	58 300
Interest receivable	2 000	—
Prepaid rent	2 800	2 400
Plant	220 000	220 000
Accumulated depreciation — plant	(99 000)	(66 000)
Deferred tax asset	?	32 480
Accounts payable	71 200	73 600
Provision for long service leave	64 000	61 000
Deferred tax liability	?	950

Additional information
- The tax depreciation rate for plant is 10% p.a., straight-line.
- The tax rate is 30%.
- The company has $15 000 in tax losses carried forward from the previous year. A deferred tax asset was recognised for these losses. Taxation legislation allows such losses to be offset against future taxable profit.

Required

1. Prepare the worksheets and journal entries to calculate and record the current tax liability and the movements in deferred tax accounts for the year ended 30 June 2023.
2. Justify your treatment of the interest revenue in the current tax worksheet. Explain how and why this leads to the deferred tax consequence shown in the deferred tax worksheet.

REFERENCE

Wesfarmers Limited 2018, *Annual report 2018*, www.wesfarmers.com.au.

ACKNOWLEDGEMENTS

Photo: © Hero Images / Getty Images

Figures 12.11, 12.12, 12.13: © Wesfarmers Limited 2018

Text: © 2019 Australian Accounting Standards Board (AASB). The text, graphics and layout of this publication are protected by Australian copyright law and the comparable law of other countries. No part of the publication may be reproduced, stored or transmitted in any form or by any means without the prior written permission of the AASB except as permitted by law. For reproduction or publication, permission should be sought in writing from the AASB. Requests in the first instance should be addressed to the National Director, Australian Accounting Standards Board, PO Box 204, Collins Street West, Victoria 8007.

CHAPTER 13

Share capital and reserves

CHAPTER AIM

This chapter explains the two components of equity — contributed capital and reserves — and how they are reported in the statement of financial position. Besides analysing the accounting for the initial issue of shares by a company, the chapter also explains movements in share capital subsequent to the initial issue of shares, such as rights issues, placements of shares, options, share purchase plans and share buybacks.

LEARNING OBJECTIVES

After studying this chapter, you should be able to:

13.1 describe the equity of a sole proprietor, partnership and company

13.2 identify the different forms of corporate entities

13.3 outline the key features of the corporate structure

13.4 explain the nature of share capital and the different types of shares

13.5 account for the initial issue of shares

13.6 discuss the nature of, and account for, issues of shares subsequent to initial issues

13.7 discuss the rationale behind and accounting treatment of share buybacks

13.8 explain the nature of reserves and account for movements in reserves, including dividends

13.9 prepare a statement of changes in equity as well as note disclosures in relation to equity.

CONCEPT FOR REVIEW

Before studying this chapter, you should understand and, if necessary, revise:
• the differences between assets, liabilities and equity in the Conceptual Framework.

13.1 Equity

LEARNING OBJECTIVE 13.1 Describe the equity of a sole proprietor, partnership and company.

The components of the equity section of the statement of financial position are **contributed capital** and **reserves**. While the nature of capital will differ depending on the structure of the organisation — sole proprietorship, partnership or company — the key feature of contributed capital is that it consists of amounts contributed by owners. Reserves comprise equity attributable to the owners of the entity other than amounts directly contributed by the owners. An example of the equity section of the statement of financial position of a for-profit entity is shown in figure 13.1. It contains an extract from the consolidated balance sheet of Wesfarmers Limited as at 30 June 2018. Note that the key components are issued share capital, reserves and retained earnings. As discussed later in this chapter, retained earnings are also reserves.

FIGURE 13.1	Shareholders' equity, Wesfarmers			

EQUITY			2018 $m	2017 $m
Equity attributable to equity holders of the parent				
Issued capital		12	22 277	22 268
Reserved shares		12	(43)	(26)
Retained earnings		12		1 509
Reserves		12	344	190
Total equity			**22 754**	**23 941**

Source: Wesfarmers Limited (2018, p. 100).

With a *sole proprietor*, having a single owner means there is little reason for distinguishing between capital (potentially the initial investment in the business) and profits retained in the business for investment purposes. Both are simply amounts invested by the owner in the business, and withdrawals by the owner can be made from either classification of funds.

Traditionally with *partnerships*, the rights and responsibilities of the partners are specified in a partnership agreement. This document details how the profits or losses of the partnership are to be divided between the partners, including rules relating to distributions on dissolution of the partnership. In accounting for partnerships, a distinction is generally made for each partner between a capital account, to which amounts invested by a partner are credited, and a current account or retained earnings account, to which a partner's share of profits is credited and from which any drawings are debited. As with a sole proprietorship, there generally is no real distinction between capital contributed and profits retained (unless there is some other specification in the partnership agreement, which is unlikely). Both amounts represent the ongoing investment by the partners. On dissolution of the partnership, the distribution to partners is unaffected by whether an equity balance is capital or retained earnings.

With *companies*, the situation is different because their formation is generally governed by legislation, and there is normally a clear distinction made between contributed capital and profits retained in the entity. However, it should be understood that, although the laws governing companies in a particular country may require a distinction between capital and other forms of owners' equity, from an accounting point of view there is no real difference between the various classifications of owners' equity. In other words, apart from any legal restrictions such as applying to the distribution of dividends, whether an entity has $200 000 of capital and $100 000 of retained earnings, or $100 000 of capital and $200 000 of retained earnings, is of no real importance. In essence, the entity has $300 000 of equity, reflecting the shareholders' investment in the company.

This chapter concentrates on the company as the organisational form of interest, with **share capital** being the major account reflecting contributed equity or contributed capital. However, as noted above, there is no reason for the organisational form to require major differences in accounting for the equity of an entity.

LEARNING CHECK

- ☐ The equity section of the statement of financial position includes contributed capital and reserves.
- ☐ In a sole proprietorship, both capital and profits retained in the business represent amounts invested by the owner in the business.

☐ In a partnership, each partner usually has a capital account representing the partner's investment in the business and a current or retained earnings account representing the partner's share of profits. Both amounts represent the partners' investment in the business.

☐ In a company, legislation requires a clear distinction between contributed capital and reserves. Nevertheless, from an accounting theory point of view, the make-up of total equity is of no real importance.

13.2 Types of companies

LEARNING OBJECTIVE 13.2 Identify the different forms of corporate entities.

Generally, companies can be distinguished by the nature of the ownership, and the rights and responsibilities of the shareholders. Two types of companies are examined in this section: not-for-profit companies and for-profit companies.

13.2.1 Not-for-profit companies

'Not-for-profit' is not defined in International Financial Reporting Standards (IFRSs). In Australia, accounting standards issued by the Australian Accounting Standards Board (AASB) are equivalent to international standards, but sometimes contain extra paragraphs, referred to as 'Aus' paragraphs, some of which apply specifically to not-for-profit entities. For example, in paragraph Aus6.1 in Appendix A of AASB 102 *Inventories*, a **not-for-profit entity** is defined as:

> an entity whose principal objective is not the generation of profit.

Not-for-profit companies can be divided into government or public sector companies and private not-for-profit sector entities, as follows.

- Entities may be established by the government to undertake activities such as the supply of water or electricity, the provision of communications and the running of an airline. The government may own all the issued shares of the company, or a controlling interest in the entity. For the government enterprise to be classified as not-for-profit, the primary objective of the entity must be something other than the earning of profit.
- Organisations such as charities may form a company as their preferred organisational structure to limit their liability. The company may be limited by guarantee, whereby members undertake to contribute a guaranteed amount in the event the company goes into liquidation, but have no rights to dividends or distributions on liquidation. Alternatively, the company may be a non-public company, sometimes called a proprietary company or a closed corporation, where the shares are held by a limited number of shareholders and are not available for purchase by the public.

The equity section of a not-for-profit entity may be very simple, such as the example shown in figure 13.2.

FIGURE 13.2   Equity of a not-for-profit entity

Equity of the Blue Lakes Health Services	Note	$	$
Martin and Elisabeth Jones Reserve Fund	22	413 745	389 734
Other reserves	22	762 345	632 734
Accumulated funds		1 685 490	1 429 867
Total equity		**2 861 580**	**2 452 335**

13.2.2 For-profit companies

For-profit companies may take a number of forms, as follows.

- **Proprietary companies** *or closed corporations* may be established with limited membership and restrictions on obtaining funds from the public. In some countries, a distinction is made between large and small proprietary companies, with the size being measured in relation to accounting numbers such as gross revenue and gross assets as well as other variables such as the number of employees. Large proprietary companies have increased obligations in relation to the disclosure of information.

- **Public companies** *or open corporations* generally have a large number of issued shares, with the ownership being widespread. These companies rely on the public for subscription to share offers as well as the provision of debt funding via secured loans such as debentures or through unsecured loans. For-profit companies may be:
- listed — the shares are traded on a stock exchange
- unlisted — the shares are traded through brokers and financial institutions
- limited by shares — the members are liable for the debts of the company only up to any amount owing on the shares they hold
- limited by guarantee — the members undertake to contribute a guaranteed amount in the event of the company going into liquidation
- unlimited — the members are liable for all the debts of the company
- no-liability — the members are not required to pay any calls on their shares if they do not wish to continue being shareholders in the company.

The exact rights and responsibilities of shareholders in relation to the different forms of companies will differ according to the constitutions of the companies issuing the shares.

Companies also differ in size. Based on the lists published by *Fortune* magazine (2018), Wal-Mart in the United States is the largest company in the world, based on revenues of US$500.3 billion, while Apple is the most profitable with profits of US$48.3 billion. Table 13.1 shows the Australian companies that are in the *Fortune* Global 500 list.

TABLE 13.1	Australian companies in the world's top 500 (based on revenue)		
Rank in Australia	Company	Global 500 rank	Revenues (US$ billion)
1	Wesfarmers	195	51.60
2	Woolworths	228	46.18
3	BHP Group	296	38.29
4	Commonwealth Bank of Australia	349	33.89
5	Westpac Banking	414	28.57
6	Australia and New Zealand Banking Group	448	26.28
7	National Australia Bank	485	24.55

Source: Data from *Fortune* (2018).

A further distinction between companies is whether or not they are listed on a stock exchange. Large companies tend to be listed and it is these companies that seek large inflows of funds from the investing public. Table 13.2 shows the ten major stock exchanges of the world and their domestic market capitalisation as well as the Australian Securities Exchange (ASX) for comparison.

TABLE 13.2	Major stock exchanges, September 2018	
	Stock exchange	US$ billion Sept. 2018
1.	New York Stock Exchange	19 223
2.	NASDAQ	6 831
3.	London Stock Exchange	6 187
4.	Tokyo Stock Exchange	4 485
5.	Shanghai Stock Exchange	3 986
6.	Hong Kong Stock Exchange	3 325
7.	Euronext	3 321

8.	Toronto Stock Exchange	2 781
9.	Shenzhen Stock Exchange	2 285
10.	Frankfurt Stock Exchange	1 766
14.	Australian Securities Exchange	1 272

Source: Data from Forbes (2018) and Visual Capitalist (2017).

A number of Australian companies list on more than one stock exchange. For example, BHP Group lists on the NYSE (US) as well as the ASX while Kazia Therapeutics and Genetic Technologies list on the ASX and NASDAQ (US). Table 13.3 provides some statistics about the size of the ASX.

TABLE 13.3	ASX, September 2018
Domestic equity market capitalisation ($m)	$ 1 979 674
Number of listed companies	2 294
All Ords Price Index	6 326
S&P/ASX 200 Price Index	6 208
Monthly equity trading volume — Sept.	26 432 678

Source: Data from ASX (2018).

LEARNING CHECK

- ☐ Companies may be classified as for-profit or not-for-profit.
- ☐ For-profit companies may be classified as proprietary or public.
- ☐ Proprietary companies generally have limited membership and restrictions on obtaining funds from the public.
- ☐ Public companies generally rely on the public for subscriptions to share offers as well as the provision of debt funding via secured loans, such as debentures, or unsecured loans.
- ☐ For-profit companies may be listed on a stock exchange, unlisted, limited by shares, limited by guarantee, unlimited, or no-liability.

13.3 Key features of the corporate structure

LEARNING OBJECTIVE 13.3 Outline the key features of the corporate structure.

The company limited by shares is the most common type of public company and is the focus of much of our discussion. The choice of the company as the preferred form of organisational structure brings with it certain advantages, such as limited liability for shareholders. There are also some disadvantages, such as making the entity subject to greater government regulation, including the forced and detailed disclosure of information about the company. Some features of the company structure that affect the subsequent accounting for a company are described below.

13.3.1 The use of share capital

The ownership rights in a company are generally represented by shares; that is, the share capital of a company comprises a number of units or shares. Each share represents a proportional right to the net assets of the company and, within a class of shares, all shares have the same equal rights. These shares are generally transferable between parties. As a result, markets have been established to provide investors with an ability to trade in shares. Where active markets exist such as with organised stock exchanges, the fair value of a company's shares at a point in time may be reliably determined. A further advantage of transferability is that a change in ownership by one shareholder selling shares to a new investor does not have an effect on the continued existence and operation of the company.

Besides the right to share equally in the net assets, and hence the profits and losses of a company, each shareholder has other rights, including the following.

- *The right to vote for directors of the company.* This establishes the right of shareholders to have a say as owners in the strategic direction of the company. Where there is a large number of owners in a company, there is generally a separation between ownership and management. The shareholders thus employ professional managers (the directors) to manage the organisation, with these managers then providing periodic reports to the shareholders on the financial performance and position of the company. Some directors are executive directors, being employed as executives in the company, while others have non-executive roles. The directors are elected at the annual general meeting of the company, and shareholders exercise their voting rights to elect the directors. The shareholders may vote in person, or by proxy. In relation to the latter, a shareholder may authorise another party to vote on his or her behalf at the meeting; the other party could be the chairperson of the company's board.
- *The right to share in assets on the winding-up or liquidation of the company.* The rights and responsibilities of shareholders in the event of liquidation are generally covered in legislation, as are the rights of creditors to receive payment in preference to shareholders.
- *The right to share proportionately in any new issues of shares of the same class.* This right is sometimes referred to as the pre-emptive right. It ensures that a shareholder is able to retain the same proportionate ownership in a company, and that this ownership percentage cannot be diluted by the company issuing new shares to other investors, possibly at prices lower than the current fair value. However, the directors may be allowed to make limited placements of shares under certain conditions.

13.3.2 Limited liability

In a company limited by shares, when shares are issued the maximum amount payable by each shareholder is set. Even if a company incurs losses or goes into liquidation, the company cannot require a shareholder to provide additional capital. The liability of each shareholder is limited to the price of the share at the time of issue. The feature of limited liability protects shareholders by limiting the contribution required of them, which in turn places limitations on the ability of creditors to access funds for the repayment of company debts.

13.3.3 Par value and no-par value shares

In some countries, shares are issued with a specific amount stated on the share certificate, this amount being called the par value of the share. For example, a company may issue 1 million shares each with a par value of $1, the company then receiving share capital of $1 million. The only real purpose of the par value is to establish the maximum liability of the shareholder in relation to the company. The par value does not represent a fair or market value of the share. In Australia, the use of par value shares has been replaced by the issue of shares at a specified price with no par value. For example, a company may issue 1000 shares in 2021 at $3 per share, and in 2023 it may issue another 1000 shares at $5 per share. In 2023, the company then has 2000 shares and a share capital of $8000. The issue price becomes irrelevant once the shares are issued. The key variables of interest are then the number of shares issued and the amount of share capital in total.

LEARNING CHECK

- ☐ The ownership rights in a company are generally represented by shares which provide the shareholder with a number of rights.
- ☐ The liability of a shareholder in a company limited by shares is limited to the issue price of the shares.
- ☐ Shares in a public company in Australia have no par value and are issued at a price specified at time of issue.

13.4 Different forms of share capital

LEARNING OBJECTIVE 13.4 Explain the nature of share capital and the different types of shares.

Shares are issued with specific rights attached. Shares are then given different names to signify differences in rights. The two most common forms of shares are ordinary shares and preference shares.

13.4.1 Ordinary shares

The **ordinary share** is the most common form of share capital. These shares have no specific rights to any distributions of profit by the company, and ordinary shareholders are often referred to as 'residual' equity holders in that these shareholders obtain what is left after all other parties' claims have been met. Many ordinary share issues require investors to make a full payment for the shares up-front. In other cases, the shareholders pay an initial amount up-front and then, at a specified date(s), the shareholders are legally required to pay a scheduled **call**. These shares are often referred to as contributing or partly paid shares. Generally such shares entitle the holders to equal voting rights with fully paid shares, with dividends being paid on a pro rata basis. In acquiring these shares, the investors may be required to sign a client agreement with their broker before trading in these shares to acknowledge they understand the risks involved in buying partly paid shares.

Figure 13.3 shows the information provided by Wesfarmers Limited in relation to its share capital in its 2018 annual report.

FIGURE 13.3   Share capital, Wesfarmers

12. Equity and reserves (continued)

	Ordinary shares		Reserved shares	
Movement in shares on issue	'000	$m	'000	$m
At 1 July 2016	1 126 131	21 937	(2 294)	(28)
Exercise of in-substance options	—	—	206	1
Dividends applied	—	—	—	1
Issue of ordinary shares under the Wesfarmers Dividend Investment Plan	5 471	236	—	—
Issue of ordinary shares under the Wesfarmers Employee Share Acquisition Plan	2 238	92	—	—
Transfer from other reserves	—	3	—	—
At 30 June 2017 and 1 July 2017	**1 133 840**	**22 268**	**(2 088)**	**(26)**
Acquisition of shares on-market for Key Executive Equity Performance Plan (KEEPP)	—	—	(418)	(17)
Exercise of in-substance options	—	—	164	—
Transfer from other reserves	—	9	—	—
At 30 June 2018	**1 133 840**	**22 277**	**(2 342)**	**(43)**

The nature of the Group's contributed equity

Ordinary shares are fully-paid and have no par value. They carry one vote per share and the right to dividends. They bear no special terms or conditions affecting income or capital entitlements of the shareholders and are classified as equity.

Reserved shares are ordinary shares that have been repurchased by the company and are being held for future use. They include employee reserved shares, which are shares issued to employees under the share loan plan. Once the share loan has been paid in full, they are converted to ordinary shares and issued to the employee.

Incremental costs directly attributable to the issue of new shares are shown in equity as a deduction, net of tax, from the proceeds. There are no shares authorised for issue that have not been issued at reporting date.

Source: Wesfarmers Limited (2018, p. 118).

Returns to shareholders

The holders of ordinary shares have no specific rights to dividends, being residual equity holders. Whether a dividend is paid depends on the decisions made by directors. Regulations in some countries may specify from which equity accounts the dividends can be paid, or whether a company has to meet solvency tests before paying dividends. It is the directors of the company who determine the dividends to be paid in any particular year. In some cases, the directors propose a dividend at year-end, but, in accordance with the company's constitution, this proposal may have to be approved by the shareholders in the annual general meeting before payment is made. As will be seen later in this chapter (section 13.8.1), accounting for dividends is different dependent on whether a proposed dividend has to be approved by shareholders at the annual general meeting.

13.4.2 Preference shares

Another form of share capital is the **preference share**. As the name implies, holders of preference shares generally have a preferential right to dividends over the ordinary shareholders. Note firstly that the name of the instrument does not necessarily indicate the rights associated with that instrument. However, in the New South Wales Supreme Court case of *Beck v. Weinstock* [2010] NSWSC 1068, the Court held that preference shares cannot be classified as preference shares unless at the time the preference shares are issued there are on issue shares over which they have preference, generally ordinary shares.

As is discussed in chapter 11, some preference shares are in reality not equity but liabilities, or they may be compound instruments being partially debt and partially equity, sometimes referred to as hybrid securities. Classification of preference shares can have a major effect on the financial accounts, both because of the effect of the liability versus equity distinction, and the classification of the payment to preference shareholders as dividend or interest expense. As reported by Barbour (2008), in a case before the Financial Reporting Review Panel (FRRP) in the UK in 2007, the issue of whether a company's preference shares were equity or liabilities was debated. The FRRP noted in its findings in the case that presentation of the participating preference shares in accordance with IAS 32 AASB 132 *Financial Instruments: Presentation* in the 2007 accounts would have reduced net assets and shareholders' equity from £10.25 million to £7.75 million and reduced net revenue after taxation of £349 201 to a net loss after taxation of £435.

Secondly, the rights of preference shareholders may be very diverse. Some preference shares have a fixed dividend; for example, a company may issue preference shares at $10 each with a 4% dividend per annum, thus entitling each shareholder to a 40c dividend per annum. Other common features of preference shares are as follows.

- *Cumulative versus non-cumulative shares.* Where a preference share is cumulative, if a dividend is not declared in a particular year, the right to the dividend is not lost but carries over to a subsequent year. The dividends are said to be in arrears. With non-cumulative shares, if a dividend is not paid in a particular year, the right to that dividend is lost.
- *Participating versus non-participating shares.* A participating share gives the holder the right to share in extra dividends. For example, if a company has issued 8% participating preference shares and it pays a 10% dividend to the ordinary shareholders, the preference shareholders may be entitled to a further 2% dividend.
- *Convertible versus non-convertible shares.* Convertible preference shares may give the holder the right to convert the preference shares into ordinary shares. The right to convert may be at the option of the holder of the shares or at the option of the company itself. As explained in chapter 11, convertible preference shares may need to be classified into debt and equity components.
- *Converting preference shares.* With convertible preference shares, whether a conversion into ordinary shares ever occurs depends upon the exercise of an option, but with converting preference shares the terms of issue are such that the shares must convert into ordinary shares at a specified point of time. As explained in chapter 11, converting preference shares may need to be classified as debt.
- *Redeemable versus non-redeemable shares.* Subsequent to their issue, redeemable preference shares may be bought back from the shareholders by the company at a price generally established in the terms of issue of the shares. The option to redeem is normally held by the company.

The Bank of Queensland reported convertible preference shares as shown in figure 13.4.

FIGURE 13.4   Preference shares, Bank of Queensland

CPS Convertible preference shares

On 24 December 2012, the Bank issued 3 000 000 CPS. CPS were fully paid, perpetual and convertible preference shares with preferred, discretionary, non-cumulative dividends. They were not guaranteed or secured. In accordance with the ASX announcement dated 5 March 2018, BOQ confirmed the redemption of all outstanding CPS on the optional conversion/redemption date of 16 April 2018 with the redemption price of $102.44 per CPS, comprising the face value of $100 per CPS and a final dividend of $2.44 per CPS for the period from (and including) 16 October 2017 to (but excluding) the redemption date of 16 April 2018. The ASX announcement on 16 April 2018 confirmed the removal of CPS from official quotation at close of trading on 16 April 2018.

Source: Bank of Queensland (2018, p. 118).

LEARNING CHECK

- ☐ Shares are issued with specific rights attached.
- ☐ Ordinary shares give no specific rights to any distributions to shareholders of profit by the company, and ordinary shareholders' claims on the company are only paid after all other parties' claims have been met.
- ☐ Preference shares are issued with rights which may be very diverse, such as cumulative versus non-cumulative in relation to dividends.
- ☐ Preference shares generally give a preferential right to dividends over ordinary shares.

13.5 Contributed equity: issue of share capital

LEARNING OBJECTIVE 13.5 Account for the initial issue of shares.

Once a business has decided to form a public company, it will commence the procedures necessary to issue shares to the public. The initial offering of shares to the public to invest in the new company is called an **initial public offering (IPO)**. To arrange the sale of the shares, the business that wishes to float the company usually employs a promoter, such as a stockbroker or a financial institution, with expert knowledge of the legal requirements and experience in this area. Once the promoter and the managers of the business agree on the structure of the new company, a prospectus is drawn up and lodged with the regulating authority. The **prospectus** contains information about the current status of the business and its future prospects. The *Corporations Act 2001* requires companies to issue a prospectus or product disclosure statement when raising capital from retail investors.

In order to ensure that the statements in the prospectus are accurate, a process of due diligence is undertaken by an accounting firm and a report attached. To ensure that the sale of shares is successful, an underwriter may be employed. The role of the **underwriter** is to advise on such matters as the pricing of the issue, the timing of the issue and how the issue will be marketed. One of the principal reasons for using an underwriter is to ensure that all the shares are sold, as the underwriter agrees to acquire all shares that are not taken up by the public.

The costs of issuing the shares can be quite substantial and could amount to 10% of the amount raised. The costs include outlays associated with preparing and printing the relevant documentation and marketing the share issue, as well as the fees charged by the various experts consulted which could include accountants, lawyers and taxation specialists. According to paragraph 37 of AASB 132/IAS 32 *Financial Instruments: Presentation*, these costs are accounted for as a reduction in equity, effectively a reduction in share capital, provided the costs are 'incremental costs directly attributable to the equity transaction that otherwise would have been avoided'. The share capital account thus shows the net proceeds of a share issue. However, any costs of an equity transaction that is abandoned are recognised as an expense.

Any costs associated with the formation of the company that cannot be directly related to the issue of the shares, such as registration of the company name, are expensed as the cost is incurred. These outlays do not meet the definition of an asset as there are no expected future economic benefits associated with these outlays that can be controlled by the company.

13.5.1 Issue of shares

Basic issue of shares

A company may issue shares for a number of reasons such as to increase its cash for investment purposes or as part of the consideration given to acquire another business. In such cases, the overall effect of issuing shares is that the company's equity is increased as well as its assets. Any costs associated with the issue of the shares are classified as a reduction in share capital.

ILLUSTRATIVE EXAMPLE 13.1

Basic issue of shares

On 1 June 2023 Flinders Ltd issues 500 shares for cash at $10 each, incurring share issue costs of $450.

Required
Prepare the journal entries for this transaction.

Solution
Flinders Ltd records on its share register the number of shares issued, and makes the following journal entries.

June 1	Cash	Dr	5 000	
	Share capital	Cr		5 000
	(Issue of 500 $10 shares)			
	Share capital	Dr	450	
	Cash	Cr		450
	(Payment of share issue costs)			

A public issue of shares

In many cases, a company will increase its capital by offering the shares to the public, issuing a prospectus providing prospective investors with information about the future of the company. The prospective investors then apply for shares in the company, and generally pay an application fee with the **application** for shares. Note that the prospectus is *not* an invitation by the company for investors to buy shares in the company. When the prospective investors forward the application form and fee to the company, it is the investors who are offering to buy shares. It then remains for the company to accept or reject that offer.

No journal entries are raised by the company on issue of the prospectus. The first journal entries are made on receipt of cash from prospective investors. On receipt of the cash, the company records the cash received in a *cash trust account*, and raises an *application account* to record the balance prior to the issue of the shares. The cash trust account is an asset of the company, while the application account is a liability.

ILLUSTRATIVE EXAMPLE 13.2

Issue of shares to the public via prospectus

Darling Ltd needed cash for its expansion plans and decided to raise the cash by an issue of shares to the public. It published a prospectus and applications for 5000 of its shares were received during the month of January. The required application fee of $1 per share accompanied each application.

Required
What is the journal entry to record the receipt of the application fees during January?

Solution
The journal entry to record the receipt of the application fees is as follows.

Jan. 1–31	Cash trust	Dr	5 000	
	Application	Cr		5 000
	(Monies received from applicants for shares)			

The cash trust account is raised because of the nature of the legal contract between an investor and the company. In illustrative example 13.1, the journal entries illustrate the situation where a company offers to sell shares to investors, and some or all of these accept the offer. The contract between the two parties is concluded on the sale of the shares to the investors. In contrast, in illustrative example 13.2, when the company receives the application fees from investors, the contract between the two parties is not complete. At this stage the investors have made an offer to buy the shares, but this offer has not yet been accepted or rejected by the company. Hence, the monies received by the company are not equity, but a liability. At this stage the company has an obligation to return the fees to the investors as it has not yet accepted/rejected their offers to buy shares. As the cash is returnable to the applicants until the company accepts/rejects the offer, the company is unable to use the cash in its operations. It is held in trust until the decision on acceptance of offers is made.

On accepting the offers made by the applicants, the contract between the two parties is completed, the company no longer has a liability to the applicants, and the cash becomes the property of the company. The company would then issue shares to the successful applicants. The journal entries reflect the de-recognition of the application liability, the increase in equity on issue of the cash, and the change in the nature of the cash. Assuming in illustrative example 13.2 the shares were issued at the end of January with the company incurring share issue costs of $150, the journal entries are as follows.

Jan. 31	Application	Dr	5 000	
	Share capital	Cr		5 000
	(Issue of shares applied for)			
	Cash	Dr	5 000	
	Cash trust	Cr		5 000
	(Transfer from cash trust on issue of shares)			
	Share capital	Dr	150	
	Cash	Cr		150
	(Payment of share issue costs)			

There are also practical reasons for use of the cash trust and application accounts. Application monies may have to be paid back to the applicants. This could occur in the following circumstances.

- Under the terms of the prospectus, there may be a minimum number of applications that have to be received in order for the share issue to proceed — sometimes referred to as the minimum subscription. If there is not sufficient interest in the share issue from investors, the shares will not be issued and application monies will need to be returned.
- Where the share issue is highly successful and there are applications for more shares than the company wants to issue, some applicants may receive a smaller number of shares than they applied for. Excess application fees may then be returned to the applicants.

In both cases, the return of monies to unsuccessful applicants requires a journal entry of the following order — assume 200 applicants received back their $1 application fee.

	Application	Dr	200	
	Cash trust	Cr		200
	(Return of cash to unsuccessful applicants)			

Issue of partly paid shares

Shares in limited liability companies are generally issued on a fully paid basis, but in some cases shares may be issued so that part of the issue price is payable immediately and part is required to be paid later. In this case, at the appropriate date, the company has to make a call on the shareholders for the subsequent payment.

Calls on shares

On 1 August 2023 Murray Ltd issues 500 shares at $10, the terms of issue requiring the shareholders to pay $6 immediately and $4 in 1 year's time. In 1 year's time, the company makes a call on the shareholders for the remaining $4 per share, with payments to be made by 31 August 2024. Holders of 490 shares pay the required call by 31 August 2024. On 5 September, the company forfeits the shares on which the call was not paid.

Required
Prepare the journal entries required on:
1. 1 August 2023
2. 1 August 2024
3. 31 August 2024
4. 5 September 2024.

Solution
1. The initial journal entry recognises only the cash paid immediately by the shareholders.

2023				
Aug. 1	Cash	Dr	3 000	
	Share capital	Cr		3 000
	(Issue of shares)			

2. In 1 year's time, the company makes a call on the shareholders for the remaining $4 per share, with payments to be made by 31 August 2024. The call account is a receivable account, as the company expects to receive cash payments from the shareholders. At the same time, the company recognises an increase in share capital.

2024				
Aug. 1	Call	Dr	2 000	
	Share capital	Cr		2 000
	(Call of $4 on 500 shares)			

3. The holders of 490 shares pay the required call by 31 August 2024. On receipt of the call money from the shareholders the company recognises an increase in cash and a reduction in the receivable account.

2024				
Aug. 31	Cash	Dr	1 960	
	Call	Cr		1 960
	(Receipt of call money of $4 per share on 490 shares)			

4. The call account then has a remaining balance of $40. The company forfeits the shares on 5 September 2024. (Company directors may be given the power under the regulations governing the company's operations to forfeit shares where the call is not paid.)

2024				
Sept. 5	Share capital	Dr	100	
	Call	Cr		40
	Forfeited shares account	Cr		60
	(Forfeiture of 10 shares called to $10 and paid to $6 per share)			

Note:
- The share capital account is reduced by $10 per share, the sum of the amount paid and called.
- The call account is now derecognised as the amount for the unpaid calls — $4 per share — is credited to that account, giving a balance of zero.
- The amount paid by the shareholders on their shares prior to their forfeiture — $6 per share — is credited to a **forfeited shares account**. The nature of this account is dependent on the regulations of the company issuing the shares as well as the terms of issue of the shares. If the regulations require

> the balance in the forfeited shares account to be refunded to the former shareholders and the shares cancelled; the forfeited shares account is classified as a liability. If the balance in the forfeited shares account is allowed to be retained by the company and not returned to the former shareholders, the account would be called 'forfeited shares reserve' and be included in equity.

Subsequent to a forfeiture of shares, the company could decide to reissue the shares. For example, using the information in illustrative example 13.3, the company could reissue the shares on 5 November 2024 as fully paid to $10 per share on payment of $8 per share, with the forfeited shares account being used to fund the difference as well as any costs of reissue. Assuming all the shares were reissued, incurring costs of $5, and any balance of the forfeited shares account being returned to the former shareholders, the journal entries are as follows.

2024				
Nov. 5	Cash	Dr	80	
	Forfeited shares account	Dr	20	
	Share capital	Cr		100
	(Reissue of 10 shares at $10 per share on payment of $8 per share)			
	Forfeited shares account	Dr	40	
	Share issue costs payable	Cr		5
	Payable to shareholders	Cr		35
	(Share issue costs and monies refundable to shareholders)			
	Share issue costs payable	Dr	5	
	Payable to shareholders	Dr	35	
	Cash	Cr		40
	(Payment of amounts owing)			

13.5.2 Oversubscriptions

An issue of shares by a company may be so popular that it is oversubscribed; that is, there are more applications for shares than shares to be issued. Some investors may then receive an **allotment** of fewer shares than they applied for, or may not be allotted any shares at all.

Two well-known oversubscribed stocks were those associated with the initial public offerings for social networking sites Facebook and Twitter, with the latter being 30 times oversubscribed.

In most cases, excess application monies are simply refunded to the applicants. When this happens, the appropriate journal entries are as follows.

Application		Dr	xxx	
Share capital		Cr		xxx
(Issue of shares applied for)				
Application		Dr	xxx	
Cash		Dr	xxx	
Cash trust		Cr		xxx
(Transfer from cash trust and refund of excess application money)				

Depending on the company's constitution or the terms of the prospectus, an entity may retain the excess application money as an advance on future calls. In this case the journal entry is as follows.

Application		Dr	xxx	
Calls in advance		Cr		xxx
Share capital		Cr		xxx
(Issue of shares with excess application money held for future calls)				

Oversubscription of shares

Goulburn Ltd was incorporated on 1 July 2022. The directors offered to the general public 100 000 ordinary shares for subscription at an issue price of $2. The company received applications for 200 000 shares by 1 September 2022. The directors issued 150 000 shares on 15 September. The directors returned the application fees to the unsuccessful applicants who had applied for 20 000 shares. Application fees on the remaining 30 000 shares were retained as an advance on future calls as some shareholders received fewer shares than they had applied for.

Required
Prepare the journal entries.

Solution

2022				
Sept. 1	Cash trust Application (Money received on application: $2 per share on 200 000 shares)	Dr Cr	400 000	 400 000
Sept. 15	Application Share capital (Issue of shares: 150 000 shares at $2 per share)	Dr Cr	300 000	 300 000
	Application Calls in advance (Retention of application fees as calls in advance: 30 000 shares at $2 per share)	Dr Cr	60 000	 60 000
	Cash Cash trust (Transfer of cash on issue of 150 000 $2 shares and retention of excess application money for future calls — 30 000 × $2)	Dr Cr	360 000	 360 000
	Application Cash trust (Refund of application money to unsuccessful applicants: 20 000 shares at $2 per share)	Dr Cr	40 000	 40 000

LEARNING CHECK

- ☐ The initial offer of shares to the public to invest in the new company is called an initial public offering (IPO).
- ☐ The costs of issuing shares are accounted for as a reduction in share capital. The share capital account thus shows the net proceeds of a share issue.
- ☐ Any costs associated with the formation of the company that cannot be directly related to the issue of the shares are expensed as the cost is incurred.
- ☐ No journal entries are raised by the company on issue of the prospectus. The first journal entries are made on receipt of cash from prospective investors.
- ☐ Shares in limited liability companies are generally issued on a fully paid basis, but shares may be issued so that part of the issue price is payable immediately and part is required to be paid later when the company makes a call on the shareholders for the subsequent payment.
- ☐ Where shareholders do not pay calls on issued shares the company may forfeit the shares. These shares may be reissued at a later date.
- ☐ An issue of shares by a company may be so popular that it is oversubscribed. Some investors may then receive an allotment of fewer shares than they applied for, or may not be allotted any shares at all.

13.6 Contributed equity: subsequent movements in share capital

LEARNING OBJECTIVE 13.6 Discuss the nature of, and account for, issues of shares subsequent to initial issues.

Having floated the company, the directors may at a later stage decide to make changes to the share capital. This capital is sometimes referred to as **secondary capital**, and includes rights issues, placements, dividend reinvestment plans (DRPs) and share purchase plans (SPPs).

ASX Listing Rule 7.1 (ASX 2014) allows companies to issue shares of up to 15% of issued capital on a non-pro-rata basis within a 12-month period without seeking shareholder approval. Listing Rule 7.2 provides a number of exceptions that mean that issues via security purchase plans do not fall within the 15%. There are no restrictions on the number of shares that can be issued on a pro-rata basis through a renounceable rights issue or on the discount that can be offered on the share issue price under such issues. There is, however, a limit on how much can be raised through a non-renounceable offer (i.e. no greater than a 1:1 offer ratio).

The ASX Listing Rules allow small and mid-cap companies with a market capitalisation of $300 million or less and that are not included in the S&P/ASX 300 Index to:
- make additional issues within three months of shareholder approval
- issue an additional 10% of their issued capital (at a maximum 25% discount to the market price) within 12 months of shareholder approval
- issue up to 15% of their issued capital without shareholder approval.

These provisions for small and mid-cap companies were introduced in 2012 to provide a viable capital raising option for capital-intensive listed companies, minimising the need to seek shareholder approval on regular occasions through the year. Figure 13.5 is an extract from the ASX's media release explaining the new rules, the way they were devised and the rationale for them.

FIGURE 13.5	ASX placement rules for small and mid-cap companies

As part of a range of initiatives to improve the competitiveness of Australia's financial markets, ASX has finalised new listing rules to help make it easier for small to medium size companies to raise capital for investment.

The new listing rules follow extensive industry consultation and incorporate several changes from the feedback to the original proposals released in April. They have now received regulatory clearance.

ASX believes the new rules strike a balance between protecting the interests of shareholders and facilitating timely capital raisings by listed companies.

Over the last year, ASX has been developing plans to upgrade Australia's equity market and capital raising competitiveness through a series of initiatives, including these new listing rules, a faster rights issue timetable and trialling an equity research scheme. ASX will continue to promote new and better ways of raising capital for companies, which will help keep Australia a leading market to list, raise funds and invest.

The capital raising rules will come into effect from 1 August 2012. A three-month transition period has been provided for new admission requirements, which will be effective from 1 November 2012.

The key elements of the new capital raising rules are:
- Companies that are outside the S&P/ASX 300 and that also have a market capitalisation of $300 million or less can issue a further 10% of share capital in 12 months on a non-pro rata basis (i.e. by placement).
- The additional 10% requires a special resolution (at least 75% in favour) to be passed by shareholders at an annual general meeting.
- There is a maximum discount of 25% to market price at which the additional 10% can be issued.
- Additional disclosure obligations are imposed — when the special resolution is proposed, when securities are issued and when any further approval is sought — to explain matters including the purpose of the issue, impact on current shareholders, allocation policy, why the issue is via a placement and not as or in addition to a rights issue, and the fees and costs involved.

Source: ASX (2012).

In the following sections, capital raisings via share placements, rights issue, share purchase plans, dividend reinvestment plans, options and bonus issues are discussed in detail. The relative use of these forms of capital raisings in Australia is detailed in section 13.6.7.

13.6.1 Placements of shares

Rather than issue new shares through an issue to the public or current shareholders, the company may decide to place the shares with specific investors such as life insurance companies and superannuation funds. The advantages to the company of a **placement of shares** are as follows.
- *Speed*. A placement can be effected in a short period of time — 1–2 days; this lowers risks relating to movements in the market.
- *Price*. Because a placement is made to investors other than existing shareholders, and to a market that is potentially more informed and better funded, the issue price of the new shares may be closer to the market price at the date of issue. Also, the underwriting costs are lower.
- *Direction*. The shares may be placed with investors who approve of the direction of the company, or who will not interfere in the formation of company policies.
- *Prospectus*. In some cases, a placement can occur without the need for a detailed prospectus.

There are potential disadvantages to the existing shareholders from private placements in that the current shareholders will have their interest in the company diluted as a result of the placement. As a result, only limited amounts of placements of shares can occur without the approval of existing shareholders. Further disadvantages to current shareholders can occur if the company places the shares at a large discount. Again, securities laws are enacted to ensure that management cannot abuse the placement process and that current shareholders are protected.

Figure 13.6 is an extract from a typical company ASX release in relation to the placement of shares.

FIGURE 13.6	Placement of shares, Carr Industries

ASX Release
1 July 2017

Issue of placement shares
Further to the ASX announcement of 27 June 2017, Carr Industries Limited (the 'Company') is pleased to announce that the Company has completed Tranche A of the placement to raise a total $2.0 million (before costs).

Under Tranche A, 20 million new ordinary shares at $0.05 per share, raising $1 million (before costs) have been issued under the Company's capacity under Listing Rules 7.1 and 7.1A.

Subject to shareholder approval, a further 20 million new ordinary shares at $0.05 per share to raise an additional $1 million (before costs) will be issued under Tranche B.

A notice for the shareholder meeting will be issued shortly.

Following discussions with a number of creditors, the Company now intends to seek shareholder approval for the issue of up to 10 million new shares in conversion of amounts owing to creditors at the same price as the placement ($0.05). Further details will be included in the Notice of General Meeting.

A Section 708A Notice is attached.

Notice under section 708A
Carr Industries Limited ('the Company') issued 20,000,000 fully paid ordinary shares on 30 June 2017. The issued shares are part of a class of securities quoted on Australian Securities Exchange ('ASX').

The Company hereby notifies ASX under paragraph 708A(5)(e) of the Corporations Act 2001 (Cwth) (the 'Act') that:

1. the Company issued the securities without disclosure to investors under Part 6D.2 of the Act;
2. as at the date of this notice, the Company has complied with the provisions of Chapter 2M of the Corporations Act as they apply to the Company, and section 674 of the Act; and
3. as at the date of this notice, there is no information that is 'excluded information' within the meaning of sections 708A(7) and (8) of the Act.

ILLUSTRATIVE EXAMPLE 13.5

Placement of shares
Palma Ltd placed 5000 ordinary shares at $5 each with Victoria Ltd on 14 July 2022.

Required
What is the journal entry to record the placement?

Solution					
July 14	Cash		Dr	25 000	
	Share capital		Cr		25 000
	(Placement of shares)				

13.6.2 Rights issues

A **rights issue** is an offer to existing shareholders to acquire additional shares in a company in proportion to their current holding; that is, the shares are offered pro rata. For example, an offer could be made to each shareholder to buy two new shares on the basis of every ten shares currently held. If all the existing shareholders exercise their rights and take up the shares, there is no change in each shareholder's percentage ownership interest in the company. The shares are generally offered at a discount to the current market price of the shares. Shareholders have the choice to accept the offer in whole or part.

Rights issues may be renounceable or non-renounceable. If renounceable, existing shareholders may sell their rights to the new shares to another party during the offer period. Renounceable rights issues thus allow current shareholders who are unwilling to acquire the new shares themselves to receive some compensation for the dilution in shares they will experience as a result of selling their rights. As noted by the ASX (2010, p. 25):

> One of the main reasons for undertaking a non-renounceable rights issue, as opposed to a renounceable issue, is that the board believes that there is unlikely to be a market for the rights; for example, if the market for the securities of the company is illiquid. The lack of market for the rights is likely to be more of a significant issue for smaller companies and, as such, a non-renounceable rights issue may be a more viable option for smaller companies.

The ASX (2010, p. 24) made a distinction between 'traditional rights' issues and 'accelerated rights' issues. With traditional rights issues, these are conducted according to a detailed timetable prescribed in the ASX Listing Rules. However, industry has adapted these traditional issues to allow mostly larger companies to raise funds more quickly and to give boards more certainty about the funds that will be in place at a point in time (ASX 2010, p. 26). These accelerated rights issues are structured as a two-stage process with an initial or accelerated institutional component and a secondary or non-accelerated component. The advantage of accelerated rights issues is that an entity can obtain funds from institutional investors quickly, thereby reducing the risk of an overall shortfall in funding, but still allowing non-institutional investors time to consider whether they should participate in the rights offer.

Figure 13.7 provides details of a rights issue announced by Oklo Resources Limited.

FIGURE 13.7 Rights issue, Oklo Resources

ASX Announcement
2 October 2014

Non-renounceable rights issue

Oklo Resources Limited (**'Oklo' or 'Company'**) is pleased to announce the terms of a non-renounceable rights issue (**'Rights Issue'**) on the basis of one fully paid ordinary share ('Shares') for every five Shares held by shareholders at 5pm (Perth time) on 10 October 2014 (**'Record Date'**), with a registered address in Australia, New Zealand, Malaysia or Singapore (**'Eligible Shareholders'**).

The Rights Issue Shares will be offered at the price of $0.003 (0.3 cents). Based on the number of Shares on issue as at the date of this announcement, the maximum number of Shares which may be issued under the Rights Issue is 335 941 431 Shares.

The Rights Issue will raise $1 007 824 (before costs) and is fully underwritten by Taylor Collison Ltd. The underwriting fee is 6% of the gross underwritten amount ($60 469) plus 20 156 486 options with a strike price of $0.005 that will expire three years from the date of issue.

The Company's current intention is to use the net funds raised from the Rights Issue to fund further exploration at its Malian gold projects.

▸

The Record Date for determining entitlements under the Rights Issue is 10 October 2014 and the final date for receipt of applications for Shares pursuant to the Rights Issue is 23 October 2014 (subject to variation).

Details of the rights issue
Key features of the Rights Issue include:
- The Rights Issue offer is being made on the basis of one share for every 5 shares held by Eligible Shareholders on the Record Date;
- The offer price is $0.003 (0.3 cents) per Share;
- The offer will be non-renounceable and is available to all Eligible Shareholders registered on the Record Date;
- Applications and payment of funds must be received by Oklo on or before 23 October 2014 (subject to variation);
- Shares issued pursuant to the Rights Issue will rank equally with all existing fully paid shares in Oklo;
- The Shares offered under the Rights issue are expected to commence trading on 30 October 2014;
- The rights issue is fully underwritten to the amount of $1 007 824; and,
- On completion of the Rights Issue, Oklo will have 2 015 648 586 Shares on issue.
  An offer document and entitlement form will be sent to Eligible Shareholders on 14 October 2014.

Timetable

Event	Date
Offer announced and Appendix 3B and section 708AA(7) notice lodged with ASX	2 October 2014
Notice sent to Shareholders	7 October 2014
Ex Date	
(date from which securities commence trading without the Entitlement to participate in the Offer)	8 October 2014
Record Date 5pm (WST)	
(date for determining Entitlements of eligible Shareholders to participate in the Entitlement Issue)	10 October 2014
Offer Document and Entitlement and Acceptance Forms are dispatched to Shareholders	14 October 2014
Offer Opening Date	14 October 2014
Last date to extend the closing date	20 October 2014
Offer Closing Date 5pm (WST)	23 October 2014
Securities quoted on a deferred settlement basis	24 October 2014
ASX notified of under subscriptions	28 October 2014
Issue of New Shares and despatch of holding statements. Quotation on deferred settlement ends	29 October 2014
Quotation of new Shares commences	30 October 2014

The Directors may extend the Closing Date by giving at least six business days' notice to the ASX prior to the Closing Date. As such, the date the Shares are expected to commence trading on the ASX may vary.

This timetable is indicative only and is subject to change. Subject to the Corporations Act and ASX Listing Rules, Oklo reserves the right to vary the dates and times in connection with the Rights Issue, including the closing date, without prior notice.

An Appendix 3b and section 708AA(7) notice are also enclosed with this announcement.

ASX Announcement
2 October 2014

Notice under paragraph 2(f) of Section 708AA of the Corporations Act (the 'Act')
On 2 October 2014, Oklo Resources Limited (**'the Company'**) announced a pro-rata non-renounceable offer of 335 941 431 fully paid ordinary shares (**'Shares'**) each at an issue price of $0.003 (0.3 cents) per share (**'Rights Issue'**) to raise approximately $1 007 824 on the basis of one new share for every five existing fully paid ordinary shares held at 5pm (Perth time) on 10 October 2014 (**'Record Date'**) by shareholders whose registered addresses are situated in Australia, New Zealand, Malaysia and Singapore.

The Company gives notice in accordance with paragraph 2(f) of section 708AA of the Act that:
1. The Company will offer the Shares for issue without disclosure to investors under Part 6D.2 of the Act.
2. This notice is being given under paragraph (2) (f) of Section 708AA of the Act.
3. As at 2 October 2014, the Company has complied with:
   (a) The provisions of Chapter 2M of the Act as they relate to the Company; and
   (b) Section 674 of the Act.

4. As at 2 October 2014, there is no information:
   (c) That has been excluded from the continuous disclosure notice in accordance with the ASX Listing Rules; and
   (d) That investors and their professional advisors would reasonably require for the purposes of making an informed assessment of:
       (i) The assets and liabilities, financial position and performance, profits and losses and prospects of the Company; or,
       (ii) The rights and liabilities attaching to the Shares.
5. The issue of Shares under the Rights Issue will have the following potential effect on the control of Oklo:
   (a) If all Shareholders as at the Record Date take up their full entitlements under the offer, the offer will have no effect on the control of Oklo.
   (b) If the Shareholders take up only some of their entitlements under the offer, the shortfall will be taken up by the underwriter and sub-underwriters. The Company does not anticipate that the potential increase in the number of Shares held by the underwriter and sub-underwriters will have an effect on the Control of Oklo.
   (c) As at the date of this Offer Document, it is not possible to determine the precise change in control that may occur as the level of each shareholder's participation is not known.
   (d) If no Shareholders participated in the Rights Issue and the underwriter took up all of the 335 941 431 Shares offered, the underwriter's voting power in the Company would increase to 16.7%. As the Rights Issue is sub-underwritten the Company does not anticipate that the underwriter will take up all of the Shares offered.

Source: Oklo Resources Limited (2014).

A major difference between an issue of shares to the public and a rights issue is that, with the former, the offer comes from the applicant (the prospective shareholder) and it is for the company to accept or reject the offer. With a rights issue, the prospectus constitutes an offer, which may be accepted or rejected by the existing shareholder. This means that in accounting for a rights issue, there is never any need to raise a cash trust account. Further, if an application account is raised due to a time period occurring between the receipt of monies from shareholders and the date of issue of the shares, this account is not a liability but an equity account.

ILLUSTRATIVE EXAMPLE 13.6

Rights issue

Barcoo Ltd planned to raise $3.6 million from shareholders through a renounceable 1-for-6 rights issue. The terms of the issue were 6 million shares to be issued at 60c each, applications to be received by 15 April 2022. The rights issue was fully underwritten. By the due date, the company had received applications for 5 million shares from existing shareholders or parties to whom they had sold their rights. The underwriter acquired the other 1 million shares, and the shares were issued on 20 April 2022.

Required
What are the journal entries to record the rights issue?

Solution

April 15	Cash	Dr	3 000 000	
	Application	Cr		3 000 000
	(Application monies)			
	Receivable from underwriter	Dr	600 000	
	Application	Cr		600 000
	(Amount due from underwriter)			
April 20	Cash	Dr	600 000	
	Receivable from underwriter	Cr		600 000
	(Receipt from underwriter)			
	Application	Dr	3 600 000	
	Share capital	Cr		3 600 000
	(Issue of shares)			

13.6.3 Share purchase plans

A **share purchase plan** is an offer of securities up to a set dollar value to existing shareholders of a listed company. It could be made to all shareholders or a selected set of shareholders. Unlike a rights offer a share purchase plan is not a pro rata offer; that is, shareholders are not offered shares in proportion to their current holdings. For some shareholders it is an opportunity to increase their proportionate holding of shares in a company. Shareholders who do not participate will suffer a dilution of their shareholding. However, shareholders often prefer share purchase plans to placements as they allow shareholders to participate in the capital raising.

The accounting for a share purchase plan is the same as that for a share placement. The company makes the offer to the shareholders, so no cash trust is used and any application account raised is classified as equity.

Figure 13.8 is the media release issued by ANZ on 17 August 2015 in relation to its share purchase plan.

FIGURE 13.8   Share purchase plan, ANZ

Media Release
For Release: 17 August 2015

ANZ launches Share Purchase Plan Offer
ANZ today announced applications for its Share Purchase Plan Offer (SPP Offer) to raise $500 million in additional equity capital will open on Monday, 24 August 2015 with eligible shareholders able to purchase up to $15 000 worth of ANZ ordinary shares (ANZ Shares).

This capital raising is part of a program announced on 6 August 2015 to raise a total of $3 billion in equity capital to meet recently announced capital requirements for major Australian banks by the Australian Prudential Regulation Authority (APRA).

ANZ Chief Executive Officer Mike Smith said: 'We considered all the options available and determined that, on balance, a share purchase plan in conjunction with our institutional placement supports our loyal retail shareholders and completes the capital raising in a fair, timely and efficient way.

'Most of our retail shareholders will be able to apply for more shares through the SPP Offer than under a pro-rata rights issue, while many of our largest retail shareholders would have already had access to placement shares through their brokers,' Mr Smith said.

The offer price per share under the SPP Offer will be the lesser of:
- $30.95, being the offer price under the institutional placement; and
- The volume-weighted average price of ANZ Shares traded on the ASX during the 5 trading days up to, and including, the day on which the SPP Offer is scheduled to close (Tuesday, 8 September 2015) less a 2% discount, rounded down to the nearest cent.

ANZ reserves the right to scale back applications under the SPP Offer if total demand exceeds $500 million. ANZ also reserves; the right to issue new ANZ Shares or arrange for the purchase of some ANZ Shares under the SPP Offer to minimise any dilutive impact.

The SPP Offer opens on Monday, 24 August 2015 and is scheduled to close at 5.00 pm (AEST) on Tuesday, 8 September 2015.

It is open to shareholders who were registered holders of ANZ Shares at 7.00 pm (AEST) on Wednesday, 5 August 2015 (Record Date), with a registered address in Australia or New Zealand, and who are eligible to participate under the SPP Offer terms and conditions.

Source: ANZ (2015).

13.6.4 Dividend reinvestment plans

Under a **dividend reinvestment plan**, shareholders are allowed to reinvest their dividends in the company's shares rather than take the dividends as cash. The amount of funding available to the company is then dependent on the amount of dividends declared. There is no need to issue a prospectus with dividend reinvestment plans. Figure 13.9 provides an extract from a dividend investment plan operated by Wesfarmers Limited.

FIGURE 13.9 Dividend reinvestment plan, Wesfarmers

The Wesfarmers Limited Dividend Investment Plan (the 'Plan') provides a convenient way for all holders of Wesfarmers Limited shares ('Shares') to invest their dividends in new fully paid ordinary shares in the company.

The main features of the Plan include:

- At each dividend payment date, dividends on Shares nominated to be the subject of the Plan are automatically invested in Wesfarmers ordinary shares.
- Shares may be allocated under the Plan at a discount to the market price.
- Shares allocated under the Plan may, in the directors' discretion, be existing ordinary shares transferred to participants, or new Ordinary Shares issued to participants.
- Participants pay no brokerage or other costs associated with acquiring the Shares. Shares allocated under the Plan rank equally with all other ordinary shares on issue.
- Shares allocated under the Plan are registered directly in the participant's holding.
- Any cash balances in the participant's Plan account will be retained in that account until the next allocation of Shares under the Plan (without accruing interest).
- A statement is sent to participants as at each dividend payment date.
- Participants may join, vary their participation, or withdraw from the Plan at any time up to and including the business day following the record date for an allocation under the Plan.
- Participants electing partial participation can nominate a number of Shares or the percentage of their shareholding that will participate in the Plan.
- To join the Plan, shareholders need to complete the application provided with this brochure and return it to the company's Share Registry at the address shown on the form.
- A shareholder's tax position in respect of the dividend payment remains unchanged whether or not a shareholder elects to participate in the Plan.
- Participation in the Plan is entirely voluntary. Shareholders who do not apply to participate in the Plan will continue to receive their dividends in cash (paid by cheque or direct credit to their nominated bank account).

Source: Wesfarmers Limited (2018, p. 2).

Where a dividend payable exists as a liability in a company and the dividends are paid in cash the journal entry is as follows.

Dividend payable		Dr	xxx	
Cash		Cr		xxx

Where a shareholder elects to receive shares instead of cash under a dividend reinvestment plan, the journal entry is as follows.

Dividend payable		Dr	xxx	
Share capital		Cr		xxx

13.6.5 Options

A company-issued share **option** is an instrument that gives the holder the right but not the obligation to buy a certain number of shares in the company by a specified date at a stated price. For example, on 1 February 2022 a company could issue options that gave an investor the right to acquire shares in the company at $2 each, with the options having to be exercised before 31 December 2022. The option holder is taking a risk in that the share price may not reach $2 (the option is 'out of the money') or the share price may exceed $2 (the option is 'in the money').

Where the option holder exercises the option, the company increases its share capital as it issues the shares to the option holder. The company could issue these options to its employees as a part of their remuneration package; or in conjunction with another share issue, rights issue or placement as an incentive to take up the shares offered. The option may be issued free. In the case of options issued to employees, for example, the employees may receive the options as payment for past service. Alternatively, the options may only vest (i.e. be exercisable) if certain conditions are met, such as the employee remaining with the company for a specified period of time. Accounting for such options is covered in AASB 2/IFRS 2 *Share-based Payment*, the details of which are beyond the scope of this chapter. One of the key features of

AASB 2/IFRS 2 is the establishment of the measurement principles in relation to such options. In particular, paragraph 16 requires that at the date the options are granted, the fair value of the options be determined and this be used in accounting for the options. For example, assume a company at 30 June 2022 issued 100 options valued at $1 each to a key executive as a payment for past services. Each option entitled the executive to acquire a share in the company at a price of $3, the current market price of the company shares being $2.90. Assume that on 30 November the share price reached $3.10 and the executive exercised the option. The journal entries required are as follows.

June 30	Wages expense	Dr	100	
	Options	Cr		100
	(Options granted to executive)			
Nov. 30	Cash	Dr	300	
	Options	Dr	100	
	Share capital	Cr		400
	(Exercise of options issued)			

If the share price did not reach $3 within the specified life of the option, then the options would lapse. The company is then allowed to transfer the balance of the options account to other equity accounts.

Where the options are sold to investors, the company will record an increase in equity. For example, assume on 1 December 2022 Art Ltd issued 20 000 options at 50c each to acquire shares in Art Ltd at $4 per share. The initial entry recorded by Art Ltd is as follows.

Dec. 1	Cash	Dr	10 000	
	Options	Cr		10 000
	(Issue of options)			

Options generally have to be exercised by a specific date. Assume that in the case of Art Ltd the options had to be exercised by 30 June 2023, and the holders of 18 000 options exercised their rights to acquire Art Ltd shares. The journal entries required are as follows.

Dec. 1 – June 30	Cash	Dr	72 000	
	Share capital	Cr		72 000
	(Issue of shares on exercise of options:			
	18 000 shares at $4 each)			
	Options	Dr	9 000	
	Share capital	Cr		9 000
	(Transfer to share capital on exercise of options:			
	18 000 < $0.50)			

Note that the issue price of those options exercised is treated as part of share capital; in essence, these shareholders are paying $4.50 for their shares in Art Ltd. However, the journal entries shown may not always be the appropriate ones. The journal entries that need to be made when options are issued may be affected in particular jurisdictions by legal and taxation implications. For example, in Australia it is possible to 'taint' share capital by transferring amounts to that account from retained earnings or other reserves. This affects the subsequent taxation of dividends and returns of capital. The choice of equity accounts used and accounting for movements between these accounts must always be taken after gaining an understanding of legal and taxation effects.

For the options not exercised, the entity could transfer the options balance of $1000 to share capital or a reserve account including retained earnings. Again, legal and taxation implications should be considered in choosing the appropriate accounts to be used. For the example above where the holders of 2000 options did not exercise those options, the journal entry required when the options lapse is as follows.

June 30	Options	Dr	1 000	
	Options reserve	Cr		1 000
	(Transfer of lapsed options: 2000 at $0.50)			

13.6.6 Bonus issues

A **bonus issue** is an issue of shares to existing shareholders in proportion to their current shareholdings at no cost to the shareholders. The company uses its reserves balances or retained earnings to make the issue. The bonus issue is a transfer from one equity account to another, so it does not increase or decrease the equity of the company. Instead, it increases the share capital and decreases another equity account of the company.

To illustrate: assume a company has a share capital consisting of 500 000 shares. If it uses all of its $100 000 general reserve to make a 1-for-20 bonus issue, it will issue 25 000 shares pro rata to its current shareholders. The journal entry required is as follows.

General reserve	Dr	100 000	
Share capital	Cr		100 000
(Bonus issue of 25 000 shares from general reserve)			

Although the bonus issue does not have any effect on the equity of the company, empirical evidence from research into the stock market effects of bonus issues shows that share prices tend to increase as a result of bonus issues. The explanation for this effect is that the bonus issue is generally an indicator of future dividend increases. Other reasons for a company making a bonus issue include defending against a takeover bid, particularly following the revaluation of the entity's assets; providing a return to the shareholders; or lowering the current price of the company's shares in the expectation that a lower price per share may make them more tradeable.

13.6.7 Capital raising in Australia

Detailed information about the Australian capital market can be found in the submission by the Australian Securities and Investments Commission (ASIC) to the 2014 Financial Systems Inquiry established by the Australian government to determine a direction for the future of Australia's financial system (see www.fsi.gov.au for details on the inquiry).

Figure 13.10 contains an extract from ASIC's submission relating to equity market financing in Australia. Note in particular the relative proportions of capital raised from IPOs and secondary capital raisings over time. Details are also provided of the relative amounts of capital raised by the various forms of secondary capital raisings such as placements and rights issues.

FIGURE 13.10   Equity market financing in Australia

Equity market financing

634 Equity markets facilitate the issuing and trading of equity (i.e. shares), allowing companies to raise funds to conduct their business and investors to own a part of a company, with the potential to realise gains based on the future performance of the company or from trading the shares. Equity markets are an important part of the economy as they allow a company to acquire funds without incurring debt.

635 Australia enjoys a robust equity market that compares favourably with international markets in terms of comparative size and capacity to raise capital.

636 Since the Wallis Inquiry equity markets have continued to provide an important source of funding for Australian companies and economic growth. Figure 7 shows the total value of securities quoted on ASX in connection with both initial public offerings and secondary capital raisings between the 1997 and 2013 financial years by method of raising.

637 Secondary capital raisings by listed entities played a particularly important role in securing funding for domestic companies during the global financial crisis, a time of dramatically tightening conditions and uncertainty in wholesale debt and credit markets. Australia's relatively flexible framework regarding the method of raising secondary capital has been cited as a significant contributor to the ability of equity markets to address capital needs during this period.

▶

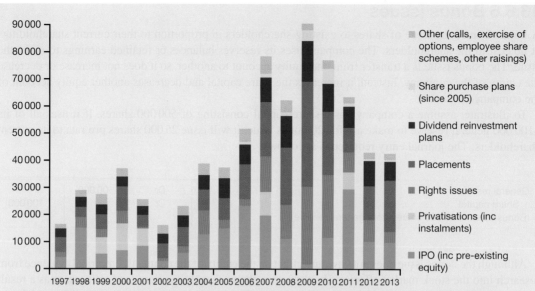

Value of initial public offering and secondary capital raised on ASX (financial years 1997–2013) ($m)

Source: AFMA Australian Financial Markets Reports 2001–2013 (based on ASX data).

638 Throughout the crisis there was significant use of share placements due to their speed and certainty as a fundraising method in volatile conditions. There was also a corresponding increase in contemporaneous share purchase plan offerings as companies sought to address the inability of existing retail holders to participate in placements. As a result, the experience of the global financial crisis generated some public debate over issues of fairness in equity fundraising.

> Note: A share purchase plan is a plan under which existing shareholders of a listed company are invited to subscribe for further shares up to a maximum monetary limit. These plans give existing members a convenient means of obtaining additional shares that are priced at a discount to the market price. ASIC has given relief to allow share purchase plans to be offered without a prospectus.

Key developments

639 As foreshadowed in the Wallis report, the growth of superannuation assets arising from Australia's compulsory superannuation scheme has had a substantial impact on domestic equity markets. A significant proportion of superannuation contributions and, as a result, Australia's $1.6 trillion pool of superannuation assets, has been allocated to equities issued to fund the growth of domestic enterprises.

640 SMSFs allocate on average one-third of total assets to Australian shares while superannuation fund default investment strategies (representing more than 43% of the superannuation assets of entities with more than four members) allocate on average 26.5% — making Australian shares the largest overall asset class for superannuation.

641 Evidence suggests that direct household investment in equities is also relatively high by international standards, with over 34% of the Australian adult population directly owning shares in 2012. Overall direct investment by households in Australian listed equities account for approximately 15% of the market, with domestic institutions owning slightly more than 40% and overseas investors slightly less than 45%.

642 Other notable developments affecting equity capital raising since the Wallis Inquiry and the global financial crisis include:

(a) innovation in capital raising methods — principally the introduction of accelerated rights issue models that combine the speed of institutional placements with the fairness of pro rata participation;

(b) increased institutional and retail shareholder activism — including the emergence of proxy advisers, new shareholder groups, and a generally heightened awareness of shareholder rights and issues such as fairness in capital raising;

(c) increased access to equity markets by companies with exposure to business operations or assets in overseas jurisdictions, or which are subject to the laws of other jurisdictions with differing systems and levels of property and governance protections, geopolitical risk and regulatory oversight;

LEARNING CHECK

☐ Directors may decide to make changes to share capital in a variety of ways, including placements of shares, rights issues, share purchase plans, dividend reinvestment plans, options and bonus share issues.

☐ Where a company makes an issue of shares or a rights issue and the offer is made by the company to the potential investor, there is no need to raise a cash trust account.

☐ A company-issued share option gives the holder the right but not the obligation to buy a certain number of shares in a company at a specified price by a specified date.

☐ If the options are exercised the issue price of the option is included in share capital.

☐ If the options are not exercised the company could transfer the options balance to share capital or other equity account, after considering any legal and taxation implications of such transfers.

13.7 Share capital: share buybacks

LEARNING OBJECTIVE 13.7 Discuss the rationale behind and accounting treatment of share buybacks.

In general, a company cannot buy shares in itself. However, under certain situations as set out in the Corporations Act, a company may decrease the number of shares issued by engaging in a **share buyback** scheme; that is, by buying back some of its own shares from current holders of those shares. A key feature of such regulations is the protection of creditors, as the company is reducing equity by using cash that would have been available to repay debt.

Some of the reasons a company may consider buying back its own shares are to:

• increase the worth per share of the remaining shares: this will depend on whether the funds used to buy back the shares were not being used effectively in the company

• manage the capital structure by reducing equity

• provide price support for issued shares; by acquiring its own shares a company demonstrates confidence in the future of the company

• most efficiently manage surplus funds held by the company; rather than pay a dividend or reinvest in other ventures the company reduces the number of shares on issue and hopefully increases earnings per share.

Accounting standards do not prescribe any accounting treatment for share buybacks. However, paragraph 33 of AASB 132/IAS 32 *Financial Instruments: Presentation* does require that on acquisition of its own shares, those shares are to be deducted from equity, and cannot be recognised as a financial asset. Further, no gain or loss can be recognised on the purchase of an entity's own financial instruments.

Consider the situation where an entity has issued the following shares over a period of years.

200 000 shares at $1.00	$200 000
100 000 shares at $1.50	150 000
200 000 shares at $2.00	400 000
500 000 shares	$750 000

Assume the total equity of the entity is as follows.

Share capital	$ 750 000
Asset revaluation surplus	20 000
Retained earnings	230 000
	$1 000 000

If the company now buys back 50 000 shares for $2.20 per share, a total of $110 000, what accounts should be affected by the buyback? Is it necessary to determine which shares from past issues have been repurchased?

In essence, the composition of the $1 million equity of the entity is relatively unimportant — it is all equity. The composition is only important if there are tax or dividend distribution issues associated with particular accounts. In the absence of such considerations, whether the equity is share capital or retained earnings is irrelevant. This is demonstrated below.

| | Equity composition | | Equity composition |
	A	or	B
Share capital (500 000 shares)	$ 750 000		$ 550 000
Asset revaluation surplus	20 000		150 000
Retained earnings	230 000		300 000
	$1 000 000		$1 000 000

The composition of equity here is *per se* irrelevant. Hence, in accounting for the share buyback, it is immaterial what accounts are affected. The $110 000 write-off could conceivably be taken totally against share capital or retained earnings, or proportionally against all three components of equity. One possible entry is as follows.

Share capital	Dr	100 000	
Retained earnings	Dr	10 000	
Cash	Cr		110 000
(Buyback of 50 000 shares for $110 000)			

Note that a company must cancel any shares it has bought back. The company is not allowed to resell or reissue those shares. This reduces the number of shares issued. Figure 13.11 provides details about the share buyback by Rio Tinto in 2017.

| FIGURE 13.11 | Share buyback, Rio Tinto |

42 Events after the balance sheet date

On 7 February 2018, the Group announced an on-market share buyback programme of US$1.0 billion Rio Tinto plc shares; this is in addition to US$1.925 billion under the US$2.5 billion programme announced on 21 September 2017, which started on 27 December 2017. Rio Tinto plc shares that have been bought back under these programmes during 2018 have been cancelled and announcements have been made to the relevant stock exchanges.

Source: Rio Tinto (2017, p. 173).

13.7.1 Treasury shares

Treasury shares is a term used for shares that an entity reacquires in itself — this term is used in paragraph 33 of AASB 132/IAS 32. However, an entity subject to the Corporations Act cannot hold treasury shares so, as shown previously in this section, shares acquired as a result of a share buyback are cancelled. However, one of the reasons a company may buy back its own shares is as part of an employee share scheme; that is, the acquired shares are to be used for the benefit of employees or salaried directors. In such cases the shares are transferred to a trust so that the entity itself does not hold the shares.

For example, if the executive share plan trust acquires 10 000 of the company's own shares at $12 per share, it would pass the following entry to record this repurchase.

Treasury shares	Dr	120 000	
Cash	Cr		120 000
(Repurchase of shares)			

On issue of the shares to employees as part of the performance plan, the entity would pass the following entry.

Employee benefits expense	Dr	120 000	
Treasury shares	Cr		120 000
(Payment of employee benefit)			

Chapter 9 contains more information on accounting for employee benefits.

Paragraph 33 of AASB 132/IAS 32 requires any treasury shares held to be deducted from equity. In its consolidated balance sheet at 30 June 2018, Qantas disclosed its treasury shares as a deduction from equity, as shown in figure 13.12.

FIGURE 13.12   Treasury shares, Qantas

EQUITY

		Qantas Group	
	Notes	2018 $m	2017 $m
Issued capital	17(A)	2 508	3 259
Treasury shares		(115)	(206)
Reserves		479	12
Retained earnings		1 084	472
Equity attributable to the members of Qantas		3 956	3 537
Non-controlling interests		3	3
Total equity		**3 959**	**3 540**

Source: Qantas Airways Ltd (2018, p. 54).

LEARNING CHECK

☐ Under certain situations as set out in the Corporations Act, a company may decrease the number of shares issued by buying back some of its own shares.

☐ Share buybacks may be conducted in order to:
 – increase the worth per share of the remaining shares
 – manage the capital structure by reducing equity
 – provide price support for issued shares
 – manage surplus funds held by the company.

☐ AASB 132/IAS 32 requires that bought back shares be deducted from equity. They cannot be recognised as a financial asset and no gain or loss can be recognised.

13.8 Reserves

LEARNING OBJECTIVE 13.8 Explain the nature of reserves and account for movements in reserves, including dividends.

'Reserves' is the generic term for all equity accounts other than contributed equity. A major component is the retained earnings account. This account accumulates the annual profit or loss earned by an entity, and is the primary account from which appropriations are made in the form of dividends. Under paragraph 88 of AASB 101/IAS 1 *Presentation of Financial Statements*, all items of income and expense recognised in a period are included in profit or loss, unless another standard requires otherwise. Hence, in general, the retained earnings account will accumulate the profit or loss earned over the life of the entity. Some standards, however, require or allow some gains and losses to be reported in other comprehensive income and accumulated in equity. Some examples are:

- revaluation of property, plant and equipment (see chapter 5)
- particular foreign exchange differences arising as a result of translation of foreign subsidiaries into a domestic currency (see chapter 24)
- re-measurements of available-for-sale financial assets (see chapter 11).

Hence, in the equity section of the statement of financial position the reserves section could include such accounts as asset revaluation surplus/reserve and foreign currency translation reserve.

13.8.1 Retained earnings

'Retained earnings' has the same meaning as 'retained profits' and 'accumulated profit or loss'. The key change in this account is the addition of the profit or loss for the current period. The main other movements in the retained earnings account are:

- dividends paid or declared
- transfers to and from reserves
- changes in accounting policy and errors (see AASB 108/IAS 8 *Accounting Policies, Changes in Accounting Estimates and Errors*, discussed in detail in chapter 18).

Dividends are a distribution from the company to its owners. Prior to changes to the Corporations Act in 2010, companies were required to pay dividends out of profits. However, as a result of the amendment to the law, this 'profits' test has been replaced with a solvency test. The purpose of the test is to ensure that a company cannot pay dividends if that has an effect on the company's ability to pay its creditors. The test, under s. 254T(1) requires that a company cannot pay dividends unless:

(a) the company's assets exceed its liabilities immediately before the dividend is declared and the excess is sufficient for the payment of the dividend; and

(b) the payment of the dividend is fair and reasonable to the company's shareholders as a whole; and

(c) the payment of the dividend does not materially prejudice the company's ability to pay its creditors.

It is now possible for a company to pay dividends out of capital. As discussed in relation to share buybacks, there seems little purpose in making any distinction between capital and reserves.

Dividends are sometimes divided into *interim* and *final* dividends. Interim dividends are paid during the financial year, while final dividends are declared by the directors at year-end for payment sometime after the end of the reporting period. In some companies, the eventual payment of the final dividends is subject to approval of the dividend by the annual general meeting. In relation to accounting for final dividends, in order for a journal entry to be raised, there must be a liability existing at the end of the year.

Hence:

- if the dividends are declared after the reporting period, no liability is recognised at the end of the reporting period (paragraph 12 of AASB 110/IAS 10 *Events after the Reporting Period*)
- if shareholder approval is required for dividends declared prior to the end of the reporting period, a liability should be recognised only when the annual general meeting approves the dividends. This is because, before that date, the entity does not have a present obligation to outlay funds.

In relation to the second point, it is expected that companies that prefer to raise a liability at year-end will change their regulations or constitution so that dividends can be declared without the need for shareholder approval.

ILLUSTRATIVE EXAMPLE 13.7

Dividends

During the period ending 30 June 2022, the following events occurred in relation to Snowy Ltd.

2021		
Sept.	25	Annual general meeting approved the final dividend of $10 000.
	30	Snowy Ltd paid the final dividend to shareholders.
2022		
Jan.	10	Snowy Ltd paid an interim dividend of $8000.
June	30	Snowy Ltd declared a final dividend of $12 000, this dividend requiring shareholder approval at the next AGM.

Required

Prepare the journal entries to record the dividend transactions of Snowy Ltd.

Solution

2021				
Sept. 25	Dividends declared Dividends payable (Dividend of $10 000 authorised by annual meeting)	Dr Cr	10 000	 10 000
30	Dividends payable Cash (Payment of dividend)	Dr Cr	10 000	 10 000
2022				
Jan. 10	Interim dividend paid Cash (Payment of interim dividend)	Dr Cr	8 000	 8 000

Notes:

1. No entry is required in relation to the final dividend of $12 000 because approval of the dividend is required at the annual general meeting before a liability is raised. A contingent liability would be recorded in the notes to the 2022 financial statements.

2. The journal entries contain temporary accounts such as 'dividends declared' and 'interim dividend paid'. These accounts are useful in preparing the statement of changes in equity (see section 13.9.2) as well as in the worksheet used in the preparation of consolidated financial statements (see chapter 26). At the end of the reporting period, these temporary accounts are transferred to retained earnings as follows.

Retained earnings
   Dividends declared
   Interim dividend paid
(Closing entry)
	Dr
	Cr
	Cr
		18 000	
			10 000
			8 000

Figure 13.13 contains an extract from the note disclosure provided by Wesfarmers Limited in its 2018 annual report.

FIGURE 13.13	Retained earnings, Wesfarmers

Consolidated	Retained earnings $m
Balance at 1 July 2016	874
Net profit for the year	2 873
Remeasurement loss on defined benefit plan, net of tax	(3)
Total other comprehensive income for the year, net of tax	(3)
Total comprehensive income for the year, net of tax	**2 870**
Equity dividends	(2 235)
Balance at 30 June 2017 and 1 July 2017	**1 509**
Net profit for the year	1 197
Remeasurement loss on defined benefit plan, net of tax	(1)
Total other comprehensive income for the year, net of tax	(1)
Total comprehensive income for the year, net of tax	**1 196**
Equity dividends	(2 529)
Balance at 30 June 2018	**176**

Source: Wesfarmers Limited (2018, p. 102).

13.8.2 Other components of equity

In accordance with paragraph 79(b) of AASB 101/IAS 1, Wesfarmers Limited reported in Note 12 of its 2018 annual report the existence of a number of reserves other than retained earnings. The nature and purpose of each of these reserves is shown in figure 13.14.

FIGURE 13.14 Reserves, Wesfarmers

Nature and purpose of reserves

Restructure tax reserve

The restructure tax reserve is used to record the recognition of tax losses arising from the equity restructuring of the Group under the 2001 ownership simplification plan.

These tax losses were generated on adoption by the Group of the tax consolidation regime.

Capital reserve

The capital reserve was used to accumulate capital profits. The reserve can be used to pay dividends or issue bonus shares.

Foreign currency translation reserve

The foreign currency translation reserve is used to record exchange differences arising from the translation of the financial statements of foreign subsidiaries.

Cash flow hedge reserve

The hedging reserve records the portion of the gain or loss on a hedging instrument in a cash flow hedge that is determined to be an effective hedge relationship.

Financial assets reserve

The financial assets reserve records fair value changes on financial assets designated at fair value through other comprehensive income.

Share-based payments reserve

The share-based payments reserve is used to recognise the value of equity-settled share-based payments provided to employees, including key management personnel, as part of their remuneration. Refer to note 28 for further details of these plans.

Source: Wesfarmers Limited (2018, p. 118).

There is no limit to the types of reserves that can be raised. However, unless an accounting standard allows or requires equity amounts to be taken directly to those reserves, the creation of reserves can occur only via transfers within equity.

Some examples of reserves other than retained earnings are discussed below.

- *Asset revaluation surplus.* According to paragraph 29 of AASB 116/IAS 16 *Property, Plant and Equipment*, subsequent to initial recognition, entities may choose between measuring the assets at cost (the cost model) or at fair value (the revaluation model). If the fair value basis is chosen, revaluation increments are recognised in other comprehensive income and accumulated in equity in an asset revaluation surplus. (Details of the accounting under a fair value basis for property, plant and equipment are covered in chapter 5.)

  Having created an asset revaluation surplus, an entity is not restricted in its subsequent disposition. It may be used for payment of dividends or be transferred to other reserve accounts including retained earnings.

- *Foreign currency translation reserve.* These differences arise when foreign operations are translated from one currency into another currency for presentation purposes, in accordance with paragraph 39 of AASB 121/IAS 21 *The Effects of Changes in Foreign Exchange Rates*. For example, an entity may be operating in Hong Kong recording its transactions in Hong Kong dollars. If the financial statements of this entity are translated into Australian dollars for presentation purposes, exchange differences are recognised in other comprehensive income and accumulated in a foreign currency translation reserve. (Details of the establishment of this reserve are found in chapter 24.)

- *Financial instruments reserve.* Some financial assets and liabilities are measured at fair value. According to paragraph 5.7.1 of AASB 9/IFRS 9 *Financial Instruments*, in general gains and losses on financial assets and liabilities that are measured at fair value are recognised in profit or loss. However, in certain circumstances, such as when the instrument is part of a hedging relationship, gains and losses are recognised in other comprehensive income and accumulated in equity.

Entities may make transfers between reserve accounts, or between reserve accounts and other equity accounts such as retained earnings. Where there is a bonus share dividend, a transfer may be made between reserve accounts and share capital. However, transfers *to* reserves such as asset revaluation surplus and foreign currency translation reserves can be made only in accordance with the accounting standard governing their creation.

When accounting for retained earnings, as when accounting for dividends, temporary accounts (namely 'transfer to/from reserve') are used, these being closed at the end of the period to retained earnings.

ILLUSTRATIVE EXAMPLE 13.8

Reserve transfers

During the period ending 30 June 2022, the following events occurred in relation to Swan Ltd.

Jan. 10	$10 000 transferred from retained earnings to general reserve
Feb. 18	$4000 transferred from asset revaluation surplus to retained earnings
June 15	Bonus share dividend of $50 000, half from general reserve and half from retained earnings

Required
Prepare the journal entries to record these transactions.

Solution

2022				
Jan. 10	Transfer to general reserve	Dr	10 000	
	General reserve	Cr		10 000
	(Transfer to general reserve)			
Feb. 18	Asset revaluation surplus	Dr	4 000	
	Transfer from asset revaluation surplus	Cr		4 000
	(Transfer from asset revaluation surplus)			
June 15	General reserve	Dr	25 000	
	Bonus dividend paid	Dr	25 000	
	Share capital	Cr		50 000
	(Bonus issue of shares)			
30	Retained earnings	Dr	31 000	
	Transfer from asset revaluation surplus	Dr	4 000	
	Transfer to general reserve	Cr		10 000
	Bonus dividend paid	Cr		25 000
	(Closing entry)			

LEARNING CHECK

☐ 'Reserves' refers to all equity accounts other than contributed equity.
☐ A major component of reserves is the retained earnings account. This account accumulates the annual profit or loss earned by an entity.
☐ The key changes in the retained earnings account are the addition of the profit or loss for the current period, dividends paid or declared, transfers to and from reserves, and changes in accounting policy and errors.
☐ If shareholder approval is required for dividends declared prior to the end of the reporting period, a liability should be recognised only once the annual general meeting approves the dividends.
☐ Unless an accounting standard allows or requires equity amounts to be taken directly to reserves, the creation of reserves can occur only via transfers within equity.

13.9 Disclosure

LEARNING OBJECTIVE 13.9 Prepare a statement of changes in equity as well as note disclosures in relation to equity.

Disclosures in relation to equity are detailed in AASB 101/IAS 1 *Presentation of Financial Statements*. The disclosures relate to specific items of equity as well as the preparation of a statement of changes in equity.

13.9.1 Specific disclosures

The specific disclosures illustrated in figure 13.15 are those required by paragraphs 79, 137 and 138 of AASB 101/IAS 1.

FIGURE 13.15	Specific disclosures on equity required by AASB 101/IAS 1

	AASB 101/ IAS 1 paragraph
Note 21: Company information Macleay Ltd is a public company registered in Sydney, Australia. The company's principal activities are the manufacture of woollen goods, ranging from clothing to furnishings for homes and offices. The company is a subsidiary of Macquarie Ltd.	138(a), (b), (c)
Note 22: Share capital and reserves The company has only one class of share capital, namely ordinary shares. Details in relation to these shares are:	79(a)
• 2 million shares have been authorised for issue by the company	(i)
• 500 000 shares have been issued fully paid to $3, and 250 000 shares have been issued at $4, but are paid only to $3 per share	(ii)
• the shares issued are no-par shares.	(iii)
Number of shares issued at 1 January 2022 500 000 Issued during 2022 250 000 Number of shares issued at 31 December 2022 750 000	(iv)
There are no restrictions on dividends payable to the shareholders.	(v)
There are no shares held by subsidiaries or associates of Macleay Ltd, and the company has not repurchased any shares issued.	(vi)
The company has issued 50 000 options to current shareholders, each option entitling the holder to buy an ordinary share in Macleay Ltd at $2.70, the options having to be exercised by 30 June 2023.	(vii)
Reserves The *plant maintenance reserve* of $140 000 was established to inform those with a financial interest in the company that it had a major claim on future funds in relation to the need to maintain the plant in accordance with Australian Government regulations. The *asset revaluation surplus* of $95 000 has arisen as the company uses the revaluation model to measure its landholdings. *Retained earnings* accumulates the annual profit or loss of the entity and the balance at reporting date represents the undistributed profits of the entity.	79(b)
Note 23: Dividends The directors of Macleay Ltd in December 2022 proposed dividends of $1 per share for fully paid shares and $0.75 for the partly paid shares, giving a total proposed dividend of $687 500. These dividends have not been recognised in the accounts because their payment is subject to approval by the shareholders at the annual general meeting.	137(a)

13.9.2 Statement of changes in equity

The statement of financial position shows the balances in the various equity accounts at the end of the period, while the comparative statement shows the balances at the beginning of the period. To explain the movement between these balances, entities are required to prepare a statement of changes in equity. In accordance with paragraph 106 of AASB 101/IAS 1, this statement reports:
- *total comprehensive income* for the period, showing separately the total amounts attributable to owners of the parent and to non-controlling interests
- the effects of *retrospective application or retrospective restatement* recognised in accordance with AASB 108/IAS 8 for each component of equity
- a *reconciliation* between the carrying amount at the *beginning* and the *end* of the period for each component of equity, separately disclosing changes resulting from:
  - profit or loss
  - each item of other comprehensive income
  - transactions with owners in their capacity as owners, showing separately contributions by and distributions to owners and changes in ownership interests in subsidiaries that do not result in a loss of control.

According to paragraph 108 of AASB 101/IAS 1, components of equity include each class of contributed equity, the accumulated balance of each class of other comprehensive income and retained earnings.

The amount of dividends recognised as distributions to owners during the period, and the related amount of dividend per share, must be disclosed, but can be disclosed in the notes or in the statement of changes in equity (AASB 101/IAS 1 paragraph 107).

Figure 13.16 is a pro-forma statement of changes in equity using a non-columnar format. Figure 13.17 uses the information disclosed by Qantas Airways Ltd in its 2018 annual report to illustrate the use of a columnar format for this statement.

FIGURE 13.16 Pro-forma note disclosures relating to the statement of changes in equity

Statement of changes in equity for the year ended 30 June 2022 ($m)							
	Note	Consolidated		Attributable to shareholders of the parent		The company	
		2022	2021	2022	2021	2022	2021
Comprehensive income							
Attributable to:							
Owners of the parent							
Non-controlling interest							
Share capital							
Balance at start of year							
Dividend reinvestment plan							
Group employee share acquisition scheme							
Group share option scheme							
New issues							
Share buyback							
Balance at end of year							
Reserves							
Asset revaluation surplus							
Balance at start of year							
Revaluation increase							
Transfers							
Balance at end of year							
Foreign currency translation reserve							
Balance at start of year							
Currency translation adjustments							
Balance at end of year							
Business combination valuation reserve							
Balance at start of year							
Increments — new business combinations							
Transfers to other reserves							
Balance at end of year							
Retained earnings							
Total income and expense for the period							
Balance of retained earnings at start of year							
Total available for appropriation							
Dividends paid or declared							
Balance of retained earnings at end of year							
Total equity at end of year							

FIGURE 13.17 Statement of changes in equity, Qantas

30 June 2018 $m	Issued capital	Treasury shares	Employee compensation reserve	Hedge reserve	Foreign currency translation reserve	Other[1] reserves	Retained earnings	Non-controlling interests	Total equity
Balance as at 1 July 2017	3 259	(206)	124	(100)	(16)	4	472	3	3 540
Total comprehensive income/(loss) for the year									
Statutory profit for the year	—	—	—	—	—	—	980	—	980
Other comprehensive income/(loss)									
Effective portion of changes in fair value of cash flow hedges, net of tax	—	—	—	559	—	—	—	—	559
Transfer of hedge reserve to the consolidated income statement, net of tax	—	—	—	(230)	—	—	—	—	(230)
Recognition of effective cash flow hedges on capitalised assets, net of tax	—	—	—	16	—	—	—	—	16
Net changes in hedge reserve for time value of options, net of tax	—	—	—	51	—	—	—	—	51
Defined benefit actuarial gains, net of tax	—	—	—	—	—	84	—	—	84
Foreign currency translation of controlled entities	—	—	—	—	3	—	—	—	3
Foreign currency translation of investments accounted for under the equity method	—	—	—	—	(3)	—	—	—	(3)
Fair value gains on investments, net of tax	—	—	—	—	—	1	—	—	1
Share of other comprehensive income of investments accounted for under the equity method	—	—	—	4	—	—	—	—	4
Total other comprehensive income	—	—	—	400	—	85	—	—	485
Total comprehensive income for the year	—	—	—	400	—	85	980	—	1 465
Transactions with owners recorded directly in equity									
Contributions by and distributions to owners									
Share buy-back	(751)	—	—	—	—	—	—	—	(751)
Dividend paid	—	—	—	—	—	—	(249)	—	(249)
Treasury shares acquired	—	(162)	—	—	—	—	—	—	(162)
Share-based payments	—	—	64	—	—	—	—	—	64
Shares vested and transferred to employees	—	253	(82)	—	—	—	(119)	—	52
Total contributions by and distributions to owners	(751)	91	(18)	—	—	—	(368)	—	(1 046)
Total transactions with owners	(751)	91	(18)	—	—	—	(368)	—	(1 046)
Balance as at 30 June 2018	2 508	(115)	106	300	(16)	89	1 084	3	3 959

1. Other reserves includes the defined benefit reserve and the fair value reserve.

The above consolidated statement of changes in equity should be read in conjunction with the accompanying notes.

Source: Qantas Airways Ltd (2018, p. 55).

☐ Disclosures in relation to equity are detailed in AASB 101/IAS 1 *Presentation of Financial Statements*.
☐ Entities are required to prepare a statement of changes in equity to explain the movements between the balances in the various equity accounts at the beginning of the period and the end of the period.

SUMMARY

This chapter has dealt with the nature of and accounting for shareholders' equity, in particular, share capital and reserves. In relation to companies:

- there are many different types of shares, with the most common being ordinary shares and preference shares
- where a company has an initial public offering, this will be preceded by the issue of a prospectus, and monies collected will be recognised in a cash trust account with a liability raised by the issuing company until the issue of the shares
- subsequent to the formation of a company, a company may raise capital via share placements, rights issues, share purchase plans and dividend reinvestment schemes
- companies may acquire their own shares as part of a buyback arrangement, but there are legal restrictions on such buybacks with companies not being allowed to hold shares in themselves
- reserves consist of retained earnings and other reserves, with some of the latter being raised as a result of application of accounting standards that require increases in equity to be recognised in other comprehensive income and accumulated in equity
- companies are required to prepare a statement of changes in equity to disclose movements within each of the equity accounts.

KEY TERMS

allotment The allocation of shares to applicants.

application The process whereby prospective shareholders apply to the company for an allotment of shares; alternatively, an account used to record the amount of money received by the company from applicants for shares.

bonus issue An issue of shares to existing shareholders in proportion to their current shareholdings at no cost to the shareholders.

call An instalment payable by shareholders on contributing or partly paid shares.

contributed capital Capital contributed by owners.

dividend reinvestment plan Shareholders are allowed to reinvest their dividends in the company's shares rather than take the dividends as cash.

forfeited shares account A liability or equity account that holds the amounts paid by the shareholders on their shares prior to their forfeiture.

initial public offering (IPO) The initial offering of shares to the public to invest in the new company.

not-for-profit entity An entity whose principal objective is not the generation of profit.

option A financial instrument that gives the holder the right to buy or sell a certain number of shares or debentures in a company by a specified date at a stipulated price.

ordinary share Shares that have no specific rights to any distributions of profit by the company. Ordinary shareholders obtain what is left after all other parties' claims have been met.

placement of shares The allocation of new shares to specific investors rather than through an issue to the public or current shareholders.

preference share Shares that confer a preferential right to dividends over the ordinary shareholders.

proprietary companies Companies with limited membership and restrictions on obtaining funds from the public.

prospectus A document required that describes the current status of a business and its future prospects.

public companies Companies that generally have a large number of issued shares and widespread ownership.

reserves Equity attributable to the owners of the entity other than amounts directly contributed by the owners.

rights issue An offer to existing shareholders to acquire additional shares in a company in proportion to their current holding.

secondary capital Changes to the original share capital, including rights issues, placements, dividend reinvestment plans and share purchase plans.

share buyback A company's purchase of its own shares from current holders of those shares.

share capital The major account reflecting contributed capital.

share purchase plan An offer of securities up to a set dollar value to existing shareholders of a listed company.

underwriter An adviser on the issue of shares that also agrees to acquire all shares that are not taken up by the public.

DEMONSTRATION PROBLEMS

13.1 Shares and options

This problem demonstrates the public issue of ordinary shares payable by instalments, the issue and exercise of options, the forfeiture of shares for non-payment of calls and the redemption of preference shares treated originally as equity out of retained earnings.

On 30 June 2022 the equity of Iota Ltd was as follows.

500 000 ordinary shares fully paid	$693 700
Options (45 000 @ 50c)	22 500
General reserve	323 100
Retained earnings	536 400

Each option entitles the holder to acquire one ordinary share at a price of $1.20 per share, exercisable by 31 March 2023. Any options not exercised by this date will lapse.

The following events occurred during the year ended 30 June 2023.

2022	
Oct. 1	A prospectus was issued offering 300 000 ordinary shares at an issue price of $1.80 per share, payable $1 on application, 40c on allotment, and 40c on a final call. The closing date for applications was 31 October 2022. The issue was underwritten at a commission of $3500.
31	Applications were received for 375 000 shares by this date.
Nov. 2	The directors allotted four shares for every five applied for, with allotment money due by 30 November 2022. In accordance with the constitution, surplus application money was transferred to allotment. The underwriting commission was paid.
30	All allotment money owing was received by this date.

2023	
Jan. 31	The first and final call was made, with money due by 28 February 2023.
Feb. 28	$112 000 call money was received by this date.
Mar. 20	The shares on which the call was unpaid were forfeited. The company is entitled to keep any balance arising from forfeiture of shares.
31	40 000 shares were allotted as a result of 40 000 options having been exercised.

Required

Prepare journal entries (in general journal form) to record the above transactions.

SOLUTION

Note that workings are shown as part of the narration where considered necessary to illustrate how figures were calculated.

2022				
Oct. 1	No entry required until shares are allotted			
31	Cash trust	Dr	375 000	
	Application	Cr		375 000
	(Money received and held in trust on application for 375 000 ordinary shares at $1 per share)			
Nov. 2	Application	Dr	300 000	
	Allotment/call	Dr	120 000	
	Share capital	Cr		420 000
	(Issue of 300 000 shares at $1.40, application being $1 per share, and 40c per share due on allotment)			

2022					
Nov. 2	Application	Dr	75 000	
	Allotment/call	Cr		75 000
	(Transfer of $75 000 surplus application money to pay for the amount due on allotment on 75 000 shares)			
	Cash	Dr	375 000	
	Cash trust	Cr		375 000
	(Transfer of money out of the trust account so that it is now available for general company use)			
	Share capital	Dr	3 500	
	Cash	Cr		3 500
	(Payment of commission to underwriter)			
30	Cash	Dr	45 000	
	Allotment/call	Cr		45 000
	(Receipt of remaining allotment money from shareholders)			
2023				
Jan. 31	Call	Dr	120 000	
	Share capital	Cr		120 000
	(Call on 300 000 shares at 40c per share payable by 28 February)			
Feb. 28	Cash	Dr	112 000	
	Call	Cr		112 000
	(Cash received on 280 000 shares at 40c for payment of the call)			
Mar. 20	Share capital	Dr	36 000	
	Call	Cr		8 000
	Forfeited shares reserve	Cr		28 000
	(Forfeiture of 20 000 shares, which had been called and paid to $1.80 per share, for non-payment of call of 40c per share, the balance being kept by the company as a reserve)			
31	Cash	Dr	48 000	
	Share capital	Cr		48 000
	(Cash received on the exercise of 40 000 options at $1.20 each)			
	Options	Dr	22 500	
	Share capital	Cr		20 000
	Options reserve	Cr		2 500
	(Write-off of options account by transferring 50c per option on 40 000 options to share capital for those that were exercised and on the 5000 lapsed options to a reserve)			

13.2 Share issues, options, rights issues, dividends, reserve transfers

The equity of Red Lobster Ltd on 1 July 2022 consisted of the following.

280 000 ordinary shares, issued at $2.40 each and called to $2.40	$672 000
Calls in arrears (24 000 shares × 80c)	(19 200)
General reserve	290 000
Retained earnings	53 780

Required

1. Prepare general journal entries to record the following transactions relating to share issues and options for the year ending 30 June 2023.

- On 15 July 2022, the directors forfeited the shares on which the call was outstanding. Forfeited shares are not to be reissued and the company's constitution requires that any forfeited amounts be refunded to the former shareholders. Refund cheques were sent on 26 July 2022. Any outstanding dividends were still payable to former shareholders.
- On 1 August 2022, a rights offer (offering 5% preference shares at an issue price of $2.80 per share) was made to existing shareholders on the basis of one preference share for every two ordinary shares held. Shares were payable in full on allotment and rights were renounceable. The issue was underwritten for a fee of $5000.
- The rights offer closed undersubscribed on 31 August 2022, and rights in respect of 40 000 shares were transferred to the underwriter. On 1 September 2022, the shares were allotted. The underwriter paid for its allotment of shares, net of its fee, on 10 September 2022. All other monies were received by 21 September 2022.
- On 1 March 2023, the directors offered for sale 100 000 options at 10c each. Each option gave the holder the right to purchase one ordinary share for $2.80 each. Options were exercisable between 1 April 2024 and 30 June 2024. The option offer closed with 80 000 applications being received. Options were duly allotted on 2 April 2023.
2. Prepare general journal entries, including any closing entries required, to record the following transactions relating to dividends and reserve transfers for the year ended 30 June 2023.
   - On 29 September 2022, the final dividend of 10c per share for the year ended 30 June 2022 was paid. The dividend had been declared on 28 June 2022. Shareholder approval is not required for a declaration of dividends.
   - On 2 January 2023, the directors declared and paid an ordinary interim share dividend of one ordinary share valued at $3, for every four ordinary shares held. The dividend was funded from the general reserve.
   - On 30 June 2023, the directors transferred $30 000 from the general reserve to retained earnings, declaring the 5% preference dividend as well as a final ordinary dividend of 8c per share. The loss for the year ended 30 June 2023 was $36 000.
3. If the company's constitution required all dividends to be approved by the shareholders at the annual general meeting before they could be paid, explain how and why your recording of the dividend payment on 29 September 2022 would change. Assume shareholder approval was granted on 20 September 2022.

SOLUTION

1. *General journal entries: share issues and options*

2022				
July 15	Share capital	Dr	57 600	
	Call	Cr		19 200
	Forfeited shares liability	Cr		38 400
	(24 000 shares are forfeited. These shares were called to $2.40 per share — so share capital is reduced by 24 000 × $2.40. The shares were forfeited for non-payment of a call of $0.80 per share — so the call account is reduced by 24 000 × $0.80. The amount already paid on the shares is $1.60 per share — so the total amount called of 24 000 × $1.60 = $38 400 is transferred to the forfeited shares liability account as this amount is required to be paid back to the former shareholders.)			
July 26	Forfeited shares liability	Dr	38 400	
	Cash	Cr		38 400
	(The balance of the forfeited shares liability is paid to the former shareholders.)			

Sept. 1	Application — preference shares	Dr	302 400	
	Receivable from underwriter	Dr	56 000	
	Share capital — preference	Cr		358 400
	(No journal entries in relation to the rights offer are made until there is a contract/transaction between the company and investors. This first occurs when the shares are allotted. After the forfeiture of the ordinary shares there were 256 000 shares still issued. On a 1-for-2 basis the company plans to issue 128 000 preference shares. Of these the underwriter will acquire 20 000 preference shares, being ½ × 40 000 ordinary shares. The company issues 128 000 preference shares at $2.80 per share. The underwriter is expected to pay for 20 000 of these shares, and the ordinary shareholders who accept the rights offer are required to pay for 108 000 of these shares; the application account is used as a receivable account here.)			
Sept. 10	Share capital — preference	Dr	5 000	
	Cash	Dr	51 000	
	Receivable from underwriter	Cr		56 000
	(The underwriter pays for 20 000 preference shares at $2.80 per share, less the fee of $5000. This fee is a cost of share issue and is accounted for as a reduction in share capital, and not as an expense.)			
Sept. 21	Cash	Dr	302 400	
	Application — preference	Cr		302 400
	(The ordinary shareholders who exercised their rights to the preference shares pay for their shares: 108 000 × $2.80.)			
2023				
Apr. 2	Cash	Dr	8 000	
	Options	Cr		8 000
	(The options are allotted on 2 April 2023, being 80 000 at $0.10 each.)			

2. *General journal entries: dividends and reserve transfers*

2022				
Sept. 29	Dividend payable	Dr	28 000	
	Cash	Cr		28 000
	(As shareholder approval was not required for these dividends, when they were declared on 28 June 2022 the company would have raised a liability to pay the dividends at that date. This liability is paid by the company on 29 September.)			
2023				
Jan. 2	General reserve	Dr	192 000	
	Share capital — ordinary	Cr		192 000
	(There are 256 000 issued ordinary shares. On the basis of 1-for-4, the company will issue 64 000 shares, at $3 each. The general reserve is used to fund the dividends.)			

June 30	General reserve	Dr	30 000	
	Transfer from general reserve	Cr		30 000
	(The transfer reduces the general reserve and increases retained earnings — note the transfer account is used rather than a direct adjustment to retained earnings itself.)			
	Dividend declared — ordinary	Dr	25 600	
	Dividend declared — preference	Dr	17 920	
	Dividends payable — ordinary	Cr		25 600
	Dividends payable — preference	Cr		17 920
	(Ordinary (256 000 + 64 000) × 8c = $25 600 Preference $358 400 × 5% = $17 920)			
	(The ordinary dividend is $0.08 per share payable on a total of 312 000 shares — (256 000 + 64 000) × $0.08 = $25 600. The preference dividend is based on 5% of $2.80 per share, and there have been 128 000 preference shares issued — 128 000 × 5% × $2.80 = $17 920.)			
	Transfer from general reserve	Dr	30 000	
	Retained earnings	Dr	49 520	
	Dividend declared — ordinary	Cr		25 600
	Dividend declared — preference	Cr		17 920
	Profit or loss summary	Cr		36 000
	(These temporary accounts are closed to retained earnings at the end of the year.)			

3. *Dividend recording*

A liability cannot be raised for a dividend declared prior to the end of reporting period if shareholder approval is required. As a consequence, no recognition of the dividend would have occurred in the prior period. When the shareholder approval is obtained, the dividends can be paid. The entry to record the payment would change to the following.

Dividend paid	Dr	28 000	
Cash	Cr		28 000

This is necessary to remove the profits being distributed from retained earnings and to record the cash payment to shareholders. No liability is recognised as the reduction in equity takes place simultaneously with the cash payment.

COMPREHENSION QUESTIONS

1 Explain the nature of a reserve. How do reserves differ from the other main components of equity?

2 The telecommunications industry in a particular country has been a part of the public sector. As a part of its privatisation agenda, the government decided to establish a limited liability company called Telecom Plus, with the issue of 10 million $3 shares. These shares were to be offered to the citizens of the country. The terms of issue were such that investors had to pay $2 on application and the other $1 per share would be called at a later time. Explain:

(a) the nature of the limited liability company, and in particular the financial obligations of acquirers of shares in the company

(b) the journal entries that would be required if applications were received for 11 million shares.

3 Explain when an options reserve would be raised.

4 Explain the difference between a renounceable and a non-renounceable rights issue.

5 A company has a share capital consisting of 100 000 shares issued at $2 per share, and 50 000 shares issued at $3 per share. Discuss the effects on the accounts if:
(a) the company buys back 20 000 shares at $4 per share
(b) the company buys back 20 000 shares at $2.50 per share.

6 When is a cash trust raised?

7 Discuss the nature of a rights issue, distinguishing between a renounceable and a non-renounceable issue.

8 What is a private placement of shares? What are the advantages and disadvantages of such a placement?

9 Discuss whether it is necessary to distinguish between the different components of equity rather than just having a single number for shareholders' equity.

10 For what reasons may a company make an appropriation of its retained earnings?

CASE STUDY 13.1

PRIVATE PLACEMENT

Mining company Aeon Metals Ltd announced plans to raise $1 150 000 through a placement of 5 227 273 ordinary fully paid shares at $0.22 per share to institutional investors to fund new surveys and drilling campaigns for its copper project. Prior to this announcement the shares of Aeon Metals Ltd were trading at around $0.26.

Required

1. Distinguish between a public share float and a private placement.
2. Assuming that the placement above proceeded, what journal entries would be required to account for it?

CASE STUDY 13.2

RIGHTS ISSUES

The following is an extract from a letter sent on 22 February 2020 by Oz Outback Ltd to its shareholders in relation to a rights issue by the company.

Dear shareholder

Renounceable rights issue — information for shareholders

On 22 February 2020 Oz Outback Ltd (the Company) announced to ASX that it was to undertake a renounceable rights issue of new ordinary shares to eligible shareholders.

Renounceable rights issue

It is proposed that the Company issue approximately 1 500 000 000 new ordinary shares at a price of $0.005 per new ordinary share to acquire three new ordinary shares for every one share held at the record date of 28 February 2020.

The rights issue is partially underwritten to a value of $1 750 000 by a number of convertible noteholders and lenders who have agreed that the face value of the convertible notes and loans they hold can be offset by them subscribing for any shortfall shares under the offer.

Any funds raised under the rights issue that are not applied to the repayment of convertible notes or loan funds will be applied towards the costs of the offer and the Company's working capital to support its focus on the development and distribution of some of the Company's products in South-East Asian markets into which the Company has recently expanded. These products include dairy and meat products from the Company's production outlets, particularly in Western Australia and the Northern Territory. Because of problems with the quality of such products currently available in South-East Asia it is believed that there is significant potential for the Company to expand its market share of the products in that region.

Applications

In the event this rights issue is not fully subscribed, the directors have determined to offer eligible shareholders the right to apply for new shares arising out of any shortfall. The shortfall facility will be made available to eligible shareholders prior to being made available to the underwriters. The number of additional new shares available will depend on the size of the shortfall.

Eligible shareholders will not be allocated additional new shares under the shortfall facility if the effect of doing so would result in that shareholder obtaining voting power in the Company in excess of 20% or if that shareholder already holds voting power in excess of 20%, increasing that voting power.

If there is still a shortfall after all applications for additional new shares from eligible shareholders have been satisfied in full (subject to the Corporations Act), the directors will call on the underwriters' commitments. To the extent that there remains any shortfall following the issue of additional new shares to the underwriters the directors reserve the right pursuant to the Corporations Act and Listing Rule 7.2 (Exception 3) to place the shortfall at an issue price per new share of not less than $0.005 within 3 months of the close of the offer on normal commercial terms.

The entitlement and acceptance form will be dispatched together with the offer document. Eligible shareholders must complete the entitlement and acceptance form in order to take up their entitlements and to apply for shortfall securities. Entitlement and acceptance forms must be properly completed and received by the Company's share registry no later than 5.00 pm (AEST) on 14 March 2020 in order for applicants to be issued new ordinary shares and shortfall securities.

Required

A client who holds shares in Oz Outback Ltd has approached you in relation to this letter. She requires you to explain the nature of a renounceable rights issue and who will receive shares in Oz Outback Ltd under the proposed rights issue. Write a report to your client providing the requested advice.

CASE STUDY 13.3

RESERVES

In its consolidated balance sheet, Qantas Airways Ltd provided the following information.

EQUITY	2018 $m	2017 $m
Issued capital	2 508	3 259
Treasury shares	(115)	(206)
Reserves	484	24
Retained earnings	955	338
Equity attributable to the members of Qantas	**3 832**	**3 415**
Non-controlling interests	—	—
Total equity	**3 832**	**3 415**

(O) Capital and reserves

iv. **Employee compensation reserve**

The fair value of equity plans granted is recognised in the employee compensation reserve over the vesting period. This reserve will be reversed against treasury shares when the underlying shares vest and transfer to the employee at the fair value. The difference between the fair value at grant date and the cost of treasury shares used is recognised in retained earnings (net of tax).

v. **Hedge reserve**

The hedge reserve comprises the effective portion of the cumulative net change in the fair value of cash flow hedging instruments and the cumulative change in fair value arising from the time value of options related to future forecast transactions.

vi. **Foreign currency translation reserve**

The foreign currency translation reserve comprises all foreign exchange differences arising from the translation of the financial statements of foreign controlled entities and investments accounted for under the equity method.

vii. **Other reserves**

Other reserves includes the defined benefit reserve comprising the remeasurements of the net defined benefit asset/(liability) which are recognised in other comprehensive income in accordance with AASB 119 *Employee Benefits* and the fair value reserve comprising of the fair value gains/(losses) on investments at fair value through other comprehensive income.

Source: Qantas Airways Ltd (2018, pp. 82, 94).

Required

Explain the nature of a reserve. Evaluate whether a company should retain reserve accounts other than retained earnings, providing examples to illustrate your analysis.

APPLICATION AND ANALYSIS EXERCISES

★ BASIC | ★ ★ MODERATE | ★ ★ ★ DIFFICULT

13.1 Cash trust accounts ★   LO5, 6

In accounting for the funds received by the company in the process of raising capital, it is sometimes necessary to raise a cash trust account. However, the cash trust account is not always an appropriate account to use.

Required

Compare the various ways in which a company may increase its share capital and analyse when a cash trust should be used in the accounting process.

13.2 Application accounts ★   LO5, 6

Lootera Ltd has announced a renounceable rights issue of 1-for-4 based on shares held at 2 July 2022. The shareholders have to exercise their rights by 31 August 2022, and pay $2 per share on application. At the end of the company's reporting period, 30 June 2022, half of the company's shareholders have applied for the new shares, and the company has received $3.5 million. The monies received have been recorded in an 'application account'. The accountant of Lootera Ltd plans to report the application account as a liability in the statement of financial position prepared at 30 June 2022, arguing that this is consistent with the accounting used for new issues of shares by the company.

Required

Write a report to the accountant of Lootera Ltd, critiquing the accountant's decision.

13.3 Repurchase of shares ★   LO7

The directors of Sand Ltd are considering spending $8 million in a repurchase of the company's shares. Some directors argue that this outlay requires the company to use a large amount of its capital that could be better put to alternative uses. They also argue that current shareholders may prefer to reward a company that grows its own business rather than artificially inflates the share price by a repurchase of shares. There is a fear among some directors that the repurchase could be a sign that the company cannot find anything better to do with its cash.

Required

Analyse these arguments and set out the main arguments in favour of a share buyback for the company in the form of a report to management of Sand Ltd.

13.4 Placement of shares ★   LO6

Fuyu Ltd is in need of an injection of capital. The directors are considering whether to raise capital via a public issue or by placing new shares with a selected group of new investors.

Required

Examine the factors that would motivate the directors to choose a placement of shares over an issue of shares to existing shareholders.

13.5 Reserves ★   LO8

Crabapple Ltd in its statement of financial position at 30 June 2022 reported the existence of two reserves:
- an asset replacement reserve created to inform shareholders of the potential amounts of funds needed to replace critical manufacturing assets in the next few years
- an assets revaluation surplus created because of the application of the revaluation model to property held by the company.

Required

Write an information release to shareholders informing them how movements in these accounts will be accounted for and the potential effects on profit or loss and other comprehensive income.

13.6 Dividends ★   LO8, 9

The directors of Beach Ltd are preparing the annual report for the company at 30 June 2022. The directors anticipate that the company will pay a dividend of $2.75 per share subsequent to the annual general meeting scheduled for 13 August 2022. This information will be included in the directors' report as well as in a release to the public concerning the annual performance of the company.

The group accountant of Beach Ltd is unsure as to whether or not the dividend should be shown as a liability in the statement of financial position at 30 June 2022.

Required

Provide a recommendation to the group accountant on what action should be undertaken in relation to accounting for the dividend.

13.7 Placement of shares, rights issues ★ LO6

The directors of Yugji Ltd are considering increasing its share capital. However they are unsure as to whether they should pursue a placement of shares or an accelerated rights issue. Some of the directors believe that this will target the same audience, namely institutional investors, and so are indifferent on which approach to take.

Required

Write a report to the directors assessing the differences between these two forms of capital raising.

13.8 Rights issue ★ LO6

West Ltd needs to raise funds for mining projects in the Northern Territory. It currently has share capital of $3 million and has issued 1.5 million shares. The directors have decided to make a non-renounceable rights issue to existing shareholders of 300 000 new shares at an issue price of $15 per share.

Rainy Day Ltd, a firm of finance brokers has agreed to fully underwrite the rights issue. West Ltd issued a prospectus on 1 April 2022 and applications closed on 3 May 2022. Costs associated with the rights issue and the eventual issue of the shares were $30 000.

Required

1. Prepare the journal entries for the rights issue and the subsequent share issue made by West Ltd, assuming that 80% of the rights were exercised by the due date.
2. Prepare the journal entries assuming that the rights issue was not underwritten and that any unexercised rights lapsed.

13.9 Issues of shares and options ★ LO6

White Ltd has been investigating the expansion of the company into new areas of development. In order to fund these new investments the company needs an increase in equity. On 1 April 2022 the company decided to make a public issue to raise $1 800 000 for new capital development. The company issued a prospectus inviting applications for 600 000 $3 shares, payable in full on application. There was an additional incentive offered by White Ltd to investors, as those shareholders who acquired more than 30 000 shares were allowed to acquire options at 50c each. These options allowed the investors to acquire shares in White Ltd at $3.20 each, the acquisition having to occur before 30 November 2022.

White Ltd had received applications for 750 000 shares and 60 000 options by 10 May. On 28 May the shares and options were allotted and money returned to unsuccessful applicants. All applicants who acquired options also received shares.

By 30 November 2022 the price of each of White's shares was $3.35. Holders of 54 000 options exercised their options in November, with the remaining options lapsing.

Required

Prepare the journal entries in the records of White Ltd in relation to the above events.

13.10 Rights issues and placement of shares ★ ★ LO6

At 1 July 2022 City Cat Ltd reported that it had a share capital of $800 000 resulting from the issue of 400 000 shares. The following transactions occurred during the year ended 30 June 2023.

1. On 10 August 2022, a renounceable 1-for-2 rights issue was made to existing shareholders. The issue price was $2 per share, payable in full on application. The issue was underwritten for a commission of $6500. The issue closed fully subscribed on 31 August, the holders of 80 000 shares having transferred their rights. The underwriting commission was paid on 4 September.
2. On 10 February 2023, 20 000 shares were privately placed with Sandy Dog Finance and Superannuation Ltd at $2 per share.

Required

Prepare the general journal entries to record the above transactions.

13.11 Dividends, calls on shares and bonus issues ★ ★ **LO6, 8, 9**

The equity of Lootera Ltd at 1 January 2023 was as follows.

Share capital		
400 000 shares fully paid	$400 000	
300 000 shares issued for $1 and paid to 50c	150 000	$550 000
General reserve		100 000
Plant maintenance reserve		40 000
Retained earnings		120 000
Total equity		**$810 000**

The following events occurred during the year.

June 25		Interim dividend of 20c per share paid, with partly paid shares receiving a proportionate dividend.
July 10		Call of 50c per share on the partly paid shares.
	31	Collection of call money.
Sept. 15		Bonus share issue of one share for each 10 shares held, at $1 per share, allocated from general reserve.
Dec. 31		Directors announce that a dividend of 15c per share will be paid in September, subject to approval at the February annual general meeting.
		Transfer of plant maintenance reserve to general reserve.
		The company earned a profit of $80 000.

Required

1. Prepare the journal entries to give effect to the above events.
2. Prepare the equity section of the statement of financial position at 31 December 2023.

13.12 Share issue, options ★ ★ **LO6, 7**

On 30 June 2021, the equity accounts of Moray Ltd consisted of the following.

400 000 'A' ordinary shares, issued at $2.50 each, fully paid	$1 000 000
75 000 6% cumulative preference shares, issued at $3 and paid to $2	155 000
Options (20 000 at 65c each)	13 000
Accumulated losses	(12 750)

As the company had incurred a loss for the year ended 30 June 2021, no dividends were declared for that year. The options were exercisable between 1 March 2022 and 30 April 2022. Each option allowed the holder to buy one 'A' ordinary share for $4.

The following transactions and events occurred during the year ended 30 June 2022.

2021		
July 25		The directors made the final call of $1 on the preference shares.
Aug. 31		All call monies were received except those owing on 5000 preference shares.
Sept. 7		The directors resolved to forfeit 5000 preference shares for non-payment of the call.
		The constitution of the company directs that forfeited amounts are not to be refunded to shareholders. The shares will not be reissued.
Nov. 1		The company issued a prospectus offering 40 000 'B' ordinary shares payable in two instalments: $3 on application and $2 on 30 November 2022. The offer closed on 30 November.
	30	Applications for 50 000 'B' ordinary shares were received.
Dec. 1		The directors resolved to allot the 'B' ordinary shares pro rata with all applicants receiving 80% of the shares applied for. Excess application monies were allowed to be held. The shares were duly allotted.
	5	Share issue costs of $8600 were paid.
2022		
April 30		The holders of 16 000 options applied to purchase shares. All monies were sent with the applications. All remaining options lapsed. The shares were duly issued.

Required

1. Prepare general journal entries to record the above transactions.
2. If Moray Ltd buys back 25 000 preference shares for $3.50 per share, what factors would its accountant have to consider in determining how best to record the transaction in the accounts?

13.13 Issue of option and shares, forfeiture of shares ★ ★   LO6, 8

Prepare ledger accounts to record the following transactions for Turtle Ltd.

2023		
July	1	A prospectus was issued inviting applications for 100 000 ordinary shares at an issue price of $3, with $2 payable on application and the balance payable on 10 June 2024. The prospectus also offered 50 000 10% preference shares at $2, fully payable on application. The issue was underwritten at a commission of $6500, allocated equally between the classes of shares.
	21	Applications closed with the ordinary share issue oversubscribed by 20 000 and the preference shares undersubscribed by 15 000.
	31	All shares were allotted, and application money refunded to unsuccessful applicants for ordinary shares.
Aug.	14	The underwriter paid amounts less commission.
Dec.	1	The directors resolved to give each ordinary shareholder, free of charge, one option for every two shares held. The options are exercisable prior to 1 June 2024 and allow each holder to acquire one ordinary share at an exercise price of $2.70. Options not exercised prior to that date lapse.
2024		
June	1	The holders of 40 000 options elected to exercise those options and 40 000 shares were issued.
	10	The balance payable on the ordinary shares was received from holders of 95 000 ordinary shares.
	15	The shares on which call money was not received were forfeited.
	25	The forfeited shares were placed with a financial institution, paid to $3 on payment of $2.80. The cash was received from the financial institution, and any balance in the forfeited shares account returned to the former shareholders. Reissue costs amounted to $550.

13.14 Share buybacks ★   LO7

The group accountant of Cruise Ltd has been given the task of accounting for a repurchase of shares by the company. The company is repurchasing 5 million shares at a cost of $2 each, paying for this in cash. However, the accountant is unsure which accounts should be reduced by the share buyback. The current equity position of the company is as follows.

	$m
Share capital	120
General reserve	50
Asset revaluation surplus	10
Retained earnings	65

Required

Write a report to the group accountant advising how to account for the buyback of shares. Provide justification for your advice.

13.15 Buyback of shares ★ ★   LO7

Budgial Ltd decided to repurchase 10% of its ordinary shares under a buyback scheme for $4.80 per share. At the date of the buyback, the equity of Budgial Ltd consisted of the following.

Share capital — 4 million shares fully paid	$4 000 000
General reserve	600 000
Retained earnings	1 100 000

The costs of the buyback scheme amounted to $9500.

Required

1. Prepare the journal entries to account for the buyback. Explain the reasons for the entries made.
2. Assume that the buyback price per share was equal to 60c per share. Prepare journal entries to record the buyback, and explain your answer.

13.16 Movements in reserves and retained earnings ★ **LO8**

Evergreen Ltd undertook the following transactions during the financial year ended 30 June 2022.
(a) Transferred $80 000 from the general reserve to retained earnings
(b) Paid an interim dividend of $45 000
(c) Transferred $36 000 from the asset revaluation surplus to the general reserve subsequent to the sale of an item of plant that was measured using the revaluation model
(d) Used the general reserve to fund the payment of 350 000 bonus shares, these being issued at $1.50 per share

Required

Prepare the journal entries in relation to these events.

13.17 Share issues, options, statement of changes in equity ★ ★ ★ **LO6, 8, 9**

On 30 June 2022, the equity accounts of Yabby Ltd consisted of the following.

180 000 ordinary shares, issued at $2.50 each, fully paid	$450 000
Options (80 000 at 75c each)*	60 000
General reserve	50 000
Forfeited shares reserve	4 000
Retained earnings	95 000

*The options were exercisable between 1 May 2023 and 31 May 2023. Each option allowed the holder to buy one ordinary share for $3 each.

Required

1. Prepare general journal entries, including any closing entries required, to record the following transactions that occurred during the year ended 30 June 2023.
   • The final 6c per share dividend for the year ended 30 June 2022 was paid on 27 September 2022. Shareholder approval to pay the dividend had been obtained at the annual general meeting on 20 September.
   • On 1 October, the directors issued a prospectus offering 60 000 ordinary shares at an issue price of $2.80, payable $2 on application and 80c as a future call. The closing date for application was 31 October 2022. The share issue was underwritten by Support Stockbrokers for a fee of $5000, payable on 15 November 2022.
   • By 31 October 2022, applications for 75 000 shares had been received.
   • On 5 November 2022, the directors allotted the shares pro rata, with applicants receiving 80% of their requested shares. The company's constitution allows excess application monies to be retained and used to offset future calls payable.
   • On 15 November 2022, the underwriting fee was paid.
   • On 31 December 2022, the directors announced an interim dividend of 3c per share payable in cash on 1 February.
   • To raise funds for expansion, the directors sold a parcel of 65 000 ordinary shares to Iron Jays Finance on 28 April 2023 at an issue price of $2.80 per share.
   • By 31 May 2023, the holders of 65 000 options had indicated that they wished to purchase shares. On 2 June 2023, 65 000 ordinary shares were issued with monies being payable by 21 June. Options not exercised duly lapsed.
   • All outstanding monies were received with respect to shares issued to option holders.
   • Profit for the year was $152 380. On 30 June 2023, the directors decided to:
     – transfer $40 000 to the general reserve
     – declare a final 10c per share dividend. Shareholder approval for this dividend will be sought at the annual general meeting in September 2023.
2. Prepare a statement of changes in equity for the year ended 30 June 2023.
3. Yabby Ltd has recognised a 'forfeited shares reserve' as part of equity. Explain how and why such a reserve would be created.

13.18 Shares, options, dividends and reserve transfers ★ ★ ★ **LO6, 8, 9**

The equity of Gugu Ltd at 30 June 2022 consisted of the following.

400 000 ordinary 'A' shares issued at $2.00, fully paid	$800 000
300 000 ordinary 'B' shares issued at $2.00, called to $1.20	360 000
50 000 6% preference shares issued at $1.50, fully paid	75 000
Share options issued at 60c, fully paid	24 000
Retained earnings	318 000

The options were exercisable before 28 February 2023. Each option entitled the holder to acquire two ordinary 'C' shares at $1.80 per share, the amount payable on notification to exercise the option.

Required

1. Prepare general journal entries to record the following transactions, which occurred during the year ended 30 June 2023.

2022	
Sept. 15	The preference dividend and the final ordinary dividend of 16c per fully paid share, both declared on 30 June 2022, were paid. The directors do not need any other party to authorise the payment of dividends.
Nov. 1	A 1-for-5 renounceable rights offer was made to ordinary 'A' shareholders at an issue price of $1.90 per share. The expiry date on the offer was 30 November 2022. The issue was underwritten at a commission of $3000.
Nov. 30	Holders of 320 000 shares accepted the rights offer, paying the required price per share, with the renounced rights being taken up by the underwriter. Ordinary 'A' shares were duly issued.
Dec. 10	Money due from the underwriter was received.
2023	
Jan. 10	The directors transferred $35 000 from retained earnings to a general reserve.
Feb. 28	As a result of options being exercised, 70 000 ordinary 'C' shares were issued. Unexercised options lapsed.
Apr. 30	The directors made a call on the ordinary 'B' shares for 80c per share. Call money was payable by 31 May.
May 31	All call money was received except for that due on 15 000 shares.
June 18	Shares on which the final call was unpaid were forfeited.
26	Forfeited shares were reissued, credited as paid to $2, for $1.80 per share, the balance of the forfeited shares account being refundable to the former shareholders.
27	Refund paid to former holders of forfeited shares.
30	The directors declared a 20c per share final dividend to be paid on 15 September 2023.

2. Prepare the equity section of the statement of financial position as at 30 June 2023.

13.19 Dividends, share issues, share buybacks, options and movements in reserves ★ ★ ★

LO6, 7, 8, 9

Chilli Crab Ltd, a company whose principal interests were in the manufacture of fine leather shoes and handbags, was formed on 1 January 2020. Prior to the 2023 period, Chilli Crab Ltd had issued 110 000 ordinary shares:

- 95 000 $30 shares were issued for cash on 1 January 2020
- 5000 shares were exchanged on 1 February 2021 for a patent that had a fair value at date of exchange of $240 000
- 10 000 shares were issued on 13 November 2022 for $50 per share.

At 1 January 2023, Chilli Crab Ltd had a balance in its retained earnings account of $750 000, while the general reserve and the asset revaluation surplus had balances of $240 000 and $180 000 respectively. The purpose of the general reserve is to reflect the need for the company to regularly replace certain of the shoe-making machinery to reflect technological changes.

Share issue costs amount to 10% of the worth of any share issue.

Required

1. Prepare the general journal entries to record the following transactions, which occurred during the 2023 financial year.

Feb. 15	Chilli Crab Ltd paid a $25 000 dividend that had been declared in December 2022. Liabilities for dividends are recognised when they are declared by the company.
May 10	10 000 shares at $55 per share were offered to the general public. These were fully subscribed and issued on 20 June 2023. On the same date, another 15 000 shares were placed with major investors at $55 per share.
June 25	The company paid a $20 000 interim dividend.
30	The company revalued land by $30 000, increasing the asset revaluation surplus by $21 000 and the deferred tax liability by $9000.
July 1	A change in the accounting standard related to insurance became effective, meaning the transitional liability was $55 000 more than the liability recognised under the previous version of the standard. This amount was recognised in other comprehensive income and accumulated in retained earnings.
22	Chilli Crab Ltd repurchased 5000 shares on the open market for $56 per share. The repurchase was accounted for by writing down share capital and retained earnings by an equal amount.
Nov. 16	Chilli Crab Ltd declared a 1-for-10 bonus issue to shareholders on record at 1 October 2023. The whole of the general reserve was used to create this bonus issue.
Dec. 1	The company issued 100 000 options at 20c each, each option entitling the holder to acquire an ordinary share in Chilli Crab Ltd at a price of $60 per share, the options to be exercised by 31 December 2024. No options had been exercised by 31 December 2023.
31	Chilli Crab Ltd calculated that its profit for the 2023 year was $150 000. It declared a $30 000 final dividend, transferred $40 000 to the general reserve, and transferred $30 000 from the asset revaluation surplus to retained earnings.

2. Prepare the statement of changes in equity for Chilli Crab Ltd for the year ended 31 December 2023.

13.20 Options, shares, dividends, reserves ★ ★ ★   **LO6, 8**

The statement of changes in equity for Aput Ltd for the year ended 30 June 2023 was as shown.

APUT LTD Statement of changes in equity for the year ended 30 June 2023	
Profit for the year	$164 370
Other comprehensive income	0
Total comprehensive income for the year	$ 164 370
Movements in equity for the year ended 30 June 2023 were:	
Share capital	
Balance at 1 July 2022	$400 000
Issue of 20 000 ordinary shares @ $2.00	40 000
Share issue costs: public issue	(6 500)
Issue of 100 000 ordinary shares @ $3.50 to public	350 000
Issue of 50 000 ordinary shares @ $3.00 on exercise of options costing 40c	170 000
Calls in advance on issue of 100 000 ordinary shares @ $3.50 to public	25 000
Balance at 30 June 2023	$978 500
Options	
Balance at 1 July 2022	$ 38 000
Transfer to share capital on exercise	(34 000)
Transfer to reserve on lapse	(4 000)
Balance at 30 June 2023	$ 0
General reserve	
Balance at 1 July 2022	$120 000
Bonus issue of shares	(80 000)
Transfer from retained earnings	45 000
Balance at 30 June 2023	$ 85 000
Options reserve	
Balance at 1 July 2022	$ 0
Transfer of lapsed options	4 000
Balance at 30 June 2023	$ 4 000

APUT LTD Statement of changes in equity for the year ended 30 June 2023	
Retained earnings	
Balance at 1 July 2022	$ 82 000
Dividends declared	(12 000)
Dividends paid	(6 000)
Transfer to general reserve	(45 000)
Profit for the period	164 370
Balance at 30 June 2023	$183 370

Required

Provide journal entries in relation to:

(a) issue of shares on exercise of options, and related transfers to/from reserves

(b) issue of shares to public

(c) dividends

(d) movements in general reserve.

Note: None of the entries should contain the account retained earnings.

REFERENCES

ANZ 2015, 'ANZ launches share purchase plan offer', media release, 17 August, www.anz.com.

Australian Securities Exchange (ASX) 2010, *Capital raising in Australia: experiences and lessons from the global financial crisis*, ASX Information Paper, 29 January, www.asx.com.au.

—— 2012, 'Helping Australian companies raise capital', media release, 25 July, www.asx.com.au.

—— 2014, *ASX listing rules*, www.asx.com.au.

—— 2018, *Market statistics*, www.asx.com.au.

Australian Securities and Investments Commission 2014, *Financial system inquiry: submission by the Australian Securities and Investments Commission*, April, www.asic.gov.au.

Bank of Queensland 2018, *Annual report 2018*, www.boq.com.au.

Barbour, C 2008, 'Debt or equity?', *CA Magazine*, October, http://icas.org.uk/TheCAArchive.

Forbes 2015, 'The world's biggest stock exchanges', www.forbes.com/pictures/eddk45iglh/the-worlds-biggest-stock-exchanges/#5a8aedb26d2b.

Fortune 2018, 'Fortune global 500', http://fortune.com/global500.

Oklo Resources Limited 2014, 'Non-renounceable rights issue', ASX announcement, 2 October, www.okloresources.com.

Qantas Airways Ltd 2018, *Annual report 2018*, www.qantas.com.au.

Rio Tinto 2017, *Annual report 2017*, www.riotinto.com/documents/RT_2017_Annual_Report.pdf.

Visual Capitalist 2017, 'The 20 largest stock exchanges in the world', April, www.visualcapitalist.com/20-largest-stock-exchanges-world.

Wesfarmers Limited 2018, *Wesfarmers Limited Dividend Investment Plan*, December, www.wesfarmers.com.au.

—— 2018, *Annual report 2018*, www.wesfarmers.com.au.

ACKNOWLEDGEMENTS

Photo: © baloon111 / Shutterstock.com

Photo: © Stock Rocket / Shutterstock.com

Figures 13.1, 13.3, 13.9, 13.13, 13.14: © Wesfarmers Limited 2018

Figure 13.4: © Bank of Queensland 2018

Figure 13.5 and text: © ASX Limited 2018. ABN 98 008 624 691. All rights reserved. This material is reproduced with the permission of ASX. This material should not be reproduced, stored in a retrieval system or transmitted in any form whether in whole or in part without the prior written permission of ASX.

Figure 13.7: © Oklo Resources Limited 2014

Figure 13.8: © ANZ 2015

Figure 13.10: © Australian Securities and Investments Commission 2014

Figure 13.11: © Rio Tinto 2017

Figures 13.12, 13.17 and case study 13.3: © Qantas Airways Ltd 2018

Text: © Sourced from the Federal Register of Legislation at 8 November 2018. For the latest information on Australian Government law, please go to https://www.legislation.gov.au.

CHAPTER 14

Share-based payment

CHAPTER AIM

Many companies provide performance-based remuneration packages to their directors. Share-based payment transactions are provided to company directors as a means of encouraging them to make decisions that will improve the overall financial performance of the business and, in turn, be in the best interests of the shareholders. This chapter explains the recognition and disclosure requirements of share-based payments in accordance with AASB 2/IFRS 2 *Share-based Payment*.

LEARNING OBJECTIVES

After studying this chapter, you should be able to:

14.1 explain the objective of AASB 2/IFRS 2

14.2 distinguish between cash-settled and equity-settled share-based payment transactions

14.3 demonstrate how equity-settled and cash-settled share-based payment transactions are recognised

14.4 explain how equity-settled share-based payment transactions are measured

14.5 explain the concept of vesting through differentiating between vesting and non-vesting conditions

14.6 explain the concept of a share option reload feature

14.7 explain how modifications to granted equity instruments are treated

14.8 demonstrate how cash-settled share-based payment transactions are measured

14.9 describe and apply the disclosure requirements of AASB 2/IFRS 2.

CONCEPTS FOR REVIEW

Before studying this chapter, you should understand and, if necessary, revise:
- the nature of share capital and different types of shares
- initial and subsequent share issues
- note disclosures in relation to shares.

14.1 Share-based payment transactions

Organisations use various mechanisms to encourage their managers and other employees to make decisions and act in ways that improve the financial performance of the organisation and, in turn, the returns to shareholders. One such mechanism is remuneration that is linked to the share price of the organisation and other accounting and performance measures.

Share plans and share option plans are an increasingly common feature of remuneration for directors, senior managers and executives, as well as many other employees as a means of aligning employees' interests with those of the shareholders, and encouraging employee retention.

Share-based payment transactions are defined in Appendix A of AASB 2/IFRS 2 *Share-based Payment* as transactions in which the entity:

(a) receives goods or services from the supplier of those goods or services (including an employee) in a share-based payment arrangement, or
(b) incurs an obligation to settle the transaction with the supplier in a share-based payment arrangement when another group entity receives those goods or services.

In other words, share-based payment transactions are those where the total amount for the goods or services reflects the value of the entity's share price. A share-based payment arrangement is an agreement between the parties to the transaction that entitles the payment to be made either in cash or other assets, or in the issue of shares. With either option, the amount paid is based on the current fair value of the equity instruments (shares or share options).

Share-based remuneration packages for directors are those in which the director is rewarded for their achievement of particular performance measures; for example, a director will be issued with 10 000 preference shares if the price of those shares stays above a nominated value for a minimum period of 3 years.

Companies offering such remuneration packages have been criticised over the years for the size of executive remuneration; for failing to align executive incentives more closely with shareholder returns (e.g. remuneration is contingent upon a minimum dividend available to shareholders); and for using short terms (1 to 3 years) for share incentives to vest rather than longer term incentives (5 to 10 years). The main concern with this last criticism is that directors/managers may only be focused on the short-term goals of the entity and not longer term planning. Companies have also been criticised for failure to disclose details of their executive performance hurdles, such as return on equity rates, which they usually justify on the basis of commercial sensitivity. Details of required disclosures and examples of actual disclosures are presented in section 14.9.

The remuneration report provided by Woolworths Group Limited in its 2018 annual report presents a rationale for engaging in share-based payment transactions with employees. It also provides examples of the types of incentives and conditions that might be incorporated into some employee share plans. The overall approach and key elements embodied in Woolworths Group Limited's executive remuneration policy from 2018 onwards are summarised in figure 14.1.

Some entities may also issue shares or share options to pay for the purchase of property or for professional advice or services. Before the issue of AASB 2/IFRS 2, there was no requirement to identify the expenses associated with this type of transaction or to measure and recognise such transactions in the financial statements of an entity. Accounting standard setters have decided that recognising the cost of share-based payments in the financial statements of entities should improve the relevance, reliability and comparability of financial information and help users of financial information to understand the economic transactions affecting entities.

AASB 2/IFRS 2 requires an entity to report the effects of share-based payment transactions on its financial performance and position, including expenses associated with transactions in which share options are granted to employees. The standard adopts the view that all share-based payment transactions ultimately lead to expense recognition, and entities must reflect the effects of such transactions in their profit or loss.

AASB 2/IFRS 2 has been amended by AASB 3/IFRS 3 *Business Combinations*. Equity instruments issued in a business combination in exchange for control of the acquiree are not within the scope of AASB 2/IFRS 2. However, AASB 2/IFRS 2 applies to equity instruments granted to employees of the acquiree in their capacity as employees. AASB 2/IFRS 2 also applies to the cancellation, replacement or modification of share-based payments arising because of a business combination or equity restructuring.

FIGURE 14.1 Remuneration principles, Woolworths

Remuneration report 2018

1. Key questions

What is our remuneration objective and guiding principles?

We have updated our remuneration principles to support the next phase of our business transformation and guide the development of the remuneration framework.

How is remuneration structured for FY18?

Woolworths Group's FY18 remuneration strategy was consistent with FY17 and continued to focus on business transformation. The diagram below provides an overview of the different remuneration components within the framework.

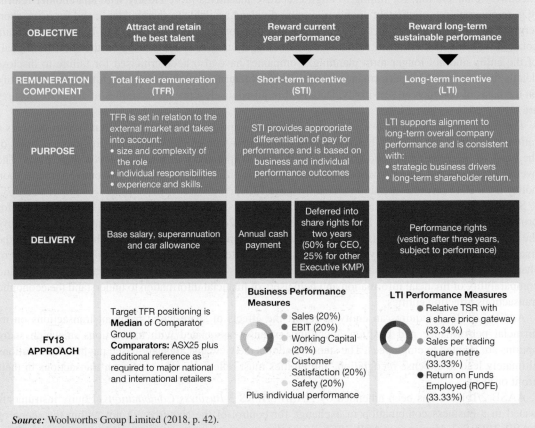

Source: Woolworths Group Limited (2018, p. 42).

14.2 Cash-settled and equity-settled share-based payment transactions

LEARNING OBJECTIVE 14.2 Distinguish between cash-settled and equity-settled share-based payment transactions.

AASB 2/IFRS 2 applies to share-based payments in which an entity acquires or receives goods or services. Goods can include inventories, consumables, property, plant or equipment, intangible assets and other non-financial forms of assets. Services, such as the provision of labour, are usually consumed immediately.

AASB 2/IFRS 2 deals with three forms of share-based payments: issue of equity (shares or share options) in exchange for the goods or services; payment of a liability by cash or other assets in exchange for the goods or services; and payments that can be either equity or cash. That is, the payment method had not been predetermined before the provision of the goods or services and one party can choose the payment method.

The accounting treatment for these transactions differs depending on the form of settlement. The three forms — **equity-settled share-based payment**, **cash-settled share-based payment** and other — and the essential features of share-based payment transactions are summarised in table 14.1.

TABLE 14.1 The form and features of share-based payment transactions

Form	Features
Equity-settled share-based payment	The entity receives goods or services as consideration for its own equity instruments; that is, the entity issues shares to another entity and receives payment for those shares in the form of goods or services provided instead of in cash.
Cash-settled share-based payment	The entity acquires goods or services by incurring liabilities for amounts based on the value of its own equities; that is, the liability amount is based on the entity's own share price and not the value of the actual goods or services they received.
Other	Entity receives or acquires goods or services and the entity, or the counterparty, has the choice of whether the transaction is settled in cash or equity.

Any transfers of an entity's equity instruments by its shareholders to parties that have supplied goods or services to the entity are considered, under paragraph 3A of AASB 2/IFRS 2, to be share-based payments (unless the transfer is clearly for a purpose other than payment for goods or services supplied to the entity). This treatment also applies to transfers of equity instruments of the entity's parent, or equity instruments of another entity in the same group as the entity, to parties that have supplied goods or services.

A transaction with an employee who holds equity instruments of the employing entity is not within the scope of AASB 2/IFRS 2 (paragraph 4). If, for example, the employee holds equity in the employer and is granted the right to acquire additional equity at a price that is less than fair value (e.g. a rights issue), the granting or exercise of that right by the employee is not governed by AASB 2/IFRS 2.

14.3 Recognition

LEARNING OBJECTIVE 14.3 Demonstrate how equity-settled and cash-settled share-based payment transactions are recognised.

Recognition of a share-based payment transaction is described in paragraph 7 of AASB 2/IFRS 2:

> An entity shall recognise the goods or services received or acquired in a share-based payment transaction when it obtains the goods or as the services are received. The entity shall recognise a corresponding increase in equity if the goods or services were received in an equity-settled share-based payment transaction, or a liability if the goods or services were acquired in a cash-settled share-based payment transaction.

Usually an expense arises from the consumption of goods or services. For example, as services are usually consumed immediately, an expense is recognised as the service is rendered. If goods are consumed over a period of time or, as in the case of inventories, sold at a later date, an expense will not be recognised until the goods are consumed or sold. Sometimes it may be necessary to recognise an expense before the goods or services are consumed or sold because they do not qualify for recognition as assets. For example, this may occur if goods are acquired as part of the research phase of a project. Even though the goods may not have been consumed, they will not qualify for recognition as assets under other accounting standards. Paragraph 8 of AASB 2/IFRS 2 explains that:

> When the goods or services received or acquired in a share-based payment transaction do not qualify for recognition as assets, they shall be recognised as expenses.

A share-based payment transaction would, depending on the principles for asset or liability recognition, be recognised in journal entries as follows.

Asset or expense	Dr	xxx	
Equity	Cr		xxx
(Recognition of an equity-settled share-based payment)			
Asset or expense	Dr	xxx	
Liability	Cr		xxx
(Recognition of a cash-settled share-based payment)			

A significant feature of AASB 2/IFRS 2 is the accounting treatment it applies to transactions settled in cash, which is different to the treatment it applies to equity-settled transactions. For *cash-settled* share-based payment transactions AASB 2/IFRS 2 paragraph 30 requires the entity to:

> measure the goods or services acquired and the liability incurred at the fair value of the liability ... Until the liability is settled, the entity shall remeasure the fair value of the liability at the end of each reporting period and at the date of settlement, with any changes in fair value recognised in profit or loss for the period.

In contrast, for share-based payment transactions that are *equity-settled*, paragraph 10 of AASB 2/IFRS 2 explains that:

> the entity shall measure the goods or services received, and the corresponding increase in equity, directly, at the fair value of the goods or services received, unless that fair value cannot be estimated reliably. If the entity cannot estimate reliably the fair value of the goods or services received, the entity shall measure their value, and the corresponding increase in equity, indirectly, by reference to the fair value of the equity instruments granted.

The recognition of share-based payment transactions requires a differential accounting treatment of changes in the fair value of equity instruments based on whether a transaction is classified as a liability or as equity. The fair value of transactions classified as equity is measured at the date the goods or services are received and subsequent value changes are ignored. In contrast, the fair value of transactions classified as liabilities (debt) are adjusted to fair value at the end of each reporting period and the resulting profit or loss is included in income.

LEARNING CHECK

☐ AASB 2/IFRS 2 requires goods or services received in a share-based payment transaction to be recognised when they are received.

☐ An increase in equity must be recognised if goods or services are received in an *equity-settled* share-based payment transaction.

☐ An increase in a liability must be recognised if the goods or services are acquired in a *cash-settled* share-based payment.

☐ When the goods or services received in a share-based payment do not qualify for recognition as an asset, they must be expensed.

☐ If a share-based payment is *settled in cash*, the liability incurred is measured at fair value and must be remeasured at the end of each reporting period (if unsettled) and at the date of settlement. Changes in fair value are recognised in profit or loss.

☐ If a share-based payment is *settled in equity*, the increase in equity is measured at the date the goods or services are received, using the fair value of those goods or services.

14.4 Equity-settled share-based payment transactions

LEARNING OBJECTIVE 14.4 Explain how equity-settled share-based payment transactions are measured.

As noted in the previous section, the goods or services received in *equity-settled* share-based payments and the corresponding increase in equity must be measured at the fair value of the goods or services unless that fair value cannot be estimated reliably (AASB 2/IFRS 2 paragraph 10). For transactions with parties other than employees, there is an assumption in AASB 2/IFRS 2 (paragraph 13) that the fair value of goods or services can be estimated reliably. In the unusual cases where the fair value cannot be reliably estimated, paragraph 10 requires that the goods or services and the corresponding increase in equity are to be measured indirectly, by reference to the fair value of the equity instruments granted at the date the goods are obtained or the service is rendered.

It is normally considered that the fair value of services received in transactions with employees cannot be reliably measured. Thus, the fair value of the services received from employees is measured by reference to the equity instruments granted.

In summary, under AASB 2/IFRS 2, equity-settled share-based payments are measured and recognised as follows.

Asset or expense Equity (Recognition of a share-based payment in which fair value of goods or services *can* be reliably estimated)	Dr Cr	Fair value of goods or services received or acquired
Asset or expense Equity (Recognition of a share-based payment where fair value of goods or services *cannot* be reliably estimated)	Dr Cr	Fair value of the equity instruments granted

14.4.1 Transactions in which services are received

Certain conditions may need to be satisfied before the counterparty in a share-based payment transaction becomes entitled to receive cash (or other assets) or equity instruments of the entity. When the conditions have been satisfied, the counterparty's entitlement has *vested*.

The term **vest** is defined in Appendix A of AASB 2/IFRS 2 as:

> To become an entitlement. Under a share-based payment arrangement, a counterparty's right to receive cash, other assets or equity instruments of the entity vests when the counterparty's entitlement is no longer conditional on the satisfaction of any vesting conditions.

Appendix A goes on to define a **vesting condition**:

> A condition that determines whether the entity receives the services that entitle the counterparty to receive cash, other assets or equity instruments of the entity, under a share-based payment arrangement. A vesting condition is either a service condition or a performance condition.

A **service condition** requires the counterparty to complete a specified period of service before becoming unconditionally entitled to a share-based payment (AASB 2/IFRS 2 Appendix A). An example of this is where a manager is required to remain employed with the entity for a minimum of 3 years. If the manager does not complete this minimum period of service during the vesting period they will lose their entitlement. During the vesting period, the entity is to presume that the required services will be received in full and paragraph 15 requires that the entity recognise the services provided each year as an increase in equity. In the event that an equity instrument *vests* immediately, no period of service is required before the counterparty is entitled to the equity instruments. At grant date, the entity recognises the full receipt of services as an increase in equity (AASB 2/IFRS 2 paragraph 14).

A **performance condition** requires the counterparty to complete a specified period of service *and* meet a specified performance target (AASB 2/IFRS 2 Appendix A). An example of a performance condition is where a manager is responsible for the entity achieving a 15% increase in profit within the service period. As with a service condition, the entity is to presume that the counterparty will complete all conditions successfully and is to recognise an increase in equity each year during the vesting period (AASB 2/IFRS 2 paragraph 15).

The granting of equity instruments in the form of share options to employees conditional on completing a 2-year period of service accounted for over the 2-year vesting period is demonstrated in illustrative example 14.1.

ILLUSTRATIVE EXAMPLE 14.1

Recognition of share options as services are rendered across the vesting period

Grattin Ltd is an insurance company. It grants 100 share options to each of its 50 employees. Each grant is conditional upon the employee working for Grattin Ltd for the next 2 years. It is assumed that each employee will satisfy the vesting conditions. At grant date, the fair value of each share option is estimated as $25.

Required

What amounts will Grattin Ltd recognise during the vesting period for the services received from the employees as consideration for the share options granted?

Solution

In accordance with paragraph 15(a) of AASB 2/IFRS 2, Grattin Ltd will recognise the following amounts.

Year	Calculation	Remuneration expense for period $	Cumulative remuneration expense $
1	$\dfrac{(100 \times 50 \text{ options}) \times \$25 \times 1 \text{ year}}{2 \text{ years}}$	62 500	62 500
2	$(100 \times 50 \text{ options}) \times \$25 - \$62\,500$	62 500	125 000

14.4.2 Transactions measured by reference to the fair value of the equity instruments granted

For share-based payments with employees and others providing similar services, it is not usually possible to measure the fair value of those services received. Paragraph 11 of AASB 2/IFRS 2 states that if this is the case:

> the entity shall measure the fair value of the services received by reference to the fair value of the equity instruments granted.

This fair value is determined by the market prices available at the *measurement date*. If market prices are not available, or if the equity instruments are subject to terms and conditions that do not apply to traded equity instruments, then a valuation technique must be used to estimate what the price of the equity instruments would have been, in an arm's length transaction, on the measurement date.

The choice of valuation technique is left to the entity. However, paragraph 17 of AASB 2/IFRS 2 specifies that the valuation technique shall be:

> consistent with generally accepted valuation methodologies for pricing financial instruments, and shall incorporate all factors and assumptions that knowledgeable, willing market participants would consider in setting the price.

Paragraph 19 of AASB 2/IFRS 2 requires that the vesting conditions, other than market conditions, be considered to ensure that any performance conditions have been satisfied. The valuation technique must also incorporate the terms and conditions of the equity instruments (e.g. whether or not an employee is entitled to receive dividends during the vesting period). For instance, many employee share options have long lives, and they are usually exercisable after the vesting period and before the end of the option's life. Option-pricing models calculate a theoretical price by using key determinants of the options.

Paragraph B6 of Appendix B of AASB 2/IFRS 2 supplies the following list of factors that option-pricing models take into account as a minimum:

(a) the exercise price of the option;
(b) the life of the option;
(c) the current price of the underlying shares;
(d) the expected volatility of the share price;
(e) the dividends expected on the shares (if appropriate); and
(f) the risk-free interest rate for the life of the option.

Expected *volatility* is a measure of the amount by which a price is expected to fluctuate during a period. Volatility is typically expressed in annualised terms, for example, daily, weekly or monthly price observations. Often there is likely to be a range of reasonable expectations about future volatility, dividends and exercise date behaviour. If so, an expected value would be calculated by weighting each amount within the range by its associated probability of occurrence.

Expectations about the future are generally based on experience and modified if the future is reasonably expected to differ from the past. For instance, if an entity with two distinctly different lines of business disposes of the one that was significantly less risky than the other, historical volatility may not be the best information on which to base reasonable expectations for the future. In other circumstances, historical information may not be available. For example, unlisted entities will have no historical share price data; likewise, newly listed entities will have little share price data available.

Whether expected dividends should be taken into account when measuring the fair value of shares or options granted depends on whether the counterparty is entitled to dividends. Generally, the assumption about expected dividends is based on publicly available information.

Paragraph B37 in Appendix B of AASB 2/IFRS 2 specifies the *risk-free* interest rate as:

> the implied yield currently available on zero-coupon government issues of the country in whose currency the exercise price is expressed, with a remaining term equal to the expected term of the option being valued It may be necessary to use an appropriate substitute, if no such government issues exist or circumstances indicate that the implied yield on zero-coupon government issues is not representative of the risk-free interest rate (for example, in high inflation economies).

Woolworths Group Limited discloses its use of an option pricing model in the determination of the fair value of options and performance rights. A relevant extract from Woolworths' 2018 annual report appears in figure 14.2. In this extract Woolworths explains that its chosen option pricing model incorporates market conditions.

FIGURE 14.2   Use of option pricing models, Woolworths

34. Employee benefits (continued)

Significant accounting policies
Share-based payments
The grant date fair value of equity-settled share-based payments is recognised as an expense proportionally over the vesting period, with a corresponding increase in equity.

The fair value of instruments with market-based performance conditions (e.g. TSR) is calculated at the date of grant using the Monte Carlo simulation model. The probability of achieving market-based performance conditions is incorporated into the determination of the fair value per instrument.

The fair value of instruments with non-market-based performance conditions (e.g. EPS, sales per trading SQM, ROFE) and service conditions and retention rights is calculated using the Black-Scholes option pricing model.

The amount recognised as an expense over the vesting period is adjusted to reflect the actual number of instruments that vest except where forfeiture is due to failure to achieve market-based performance conditions.

Source: Woolworths Group Limited (2018, p. 113).

LEARNING CHECK

☐ If the fair value of the goods and services received cannot be measured reliably, the goods or services are measured indirectly by reference to the fair value of the equity instruments granted.

☐ Vesting conditions may need to be satisfied before the counterparty in a share-based payment transaction becomes entitled to receive cash, other assets or equity instruments of the entity. The services and the corresponding increase in equity are accounted for across the vesting period as the services are rendered.

☐ It is usually considered that the fair value of services received in transactions with employees cannot be reliably measured. Therefore, the fair value of the equity instruments is used as the reliable measure. If market prices are not available, or if the equity instruments are subject to terms and conditions that do not apply to traded equity instruments, then a valuation technique must be used.

14.5 Vesting

LEARNING OBJECTIVE 14.5 Explain the concept of vesting through differentiating between vesting and non-vesting conditions.

14.5.1 Treatment of vesting conditions

If a grant of equity instruments is conditional on satisfying certain vesting conditions such as remaining in the entity's employment for a specified period of time, then the vesting conditions are not taken into account when estimating the fair value of the equity instruments. Instead, the vesting conditions are accounted for by adjusting the number of equity instruments included in the measurement of the transaction amount. Thus, the amount recognised for goods or services received as consideration for the equity instrument is based on the number of equity instruments that eventually vest. On a cumulative basis, this means that if a vesting condition is not satisfied then no amount is recognised for goods or services received.

In a situation where employees leave during the vesting period, the number of equity instruments expected to vest varies. This is demonstrated in illustrative example 14.2.

ILLUSTRATIVE EXAMPLE 14.2

Grant where the number of equity instruments expected to vest varies

Walton Company grants 100 share options to each of its 50 employees. Each grant is conditional on the employee working for the company for the next 3 years. The fair value of each share option is estimated as $25. On the basis of a weighted average probability, the company estimates that 10% of its employees will leave during the 3-year period and therefore forfeit their rights to the share options.

Required

Calculate the remuneration expense for each year and the cumulative remuneration expense given the following developments at Walton Company.

1. During the year immediately following grant date (year 1) three employees leave. At the end of year 1 the company revised its estimate of total employee departures over the full 3-year period from 10% (five employees) to 16% (eight employees).
2. During year 2 a further two employees leave, and the company revised its estimate of total employee departures across the 3-year period down to 12% (six employees).
3. During year 3 a further employee leaves, making a total of six (3 + 2 + 1) employees who have departed. A total of 4400 share options (44 employees × 100 options per employee) vested at the end of year 3.

Solution

Year	Calculation	Remuneration expense for period $	Cumulative remuneration expense $
1	$\dfrac{(5000 \text{ options} \times 84\%) \times \$25 \times 1 \text{ year}}{3 \text{ years}}$	35 000	35 000
2	$\dfrac{(5000 \text{ options} \times 88\%) \times \$25 \times 2 \text{ years}}{3 \text{ years}} - \$35\,000$	38 333	73 333
3	$(4400 \text{ options} \times \$25) - \$73\,333$	36 667	110 000

Source: Adapted from AASB 2, IG11.

In addition to continuing in service with the entity, employees may be granted equity instruments that are conditional on the achievement of a performance condition. Where the length of the vesting period varies according to when the performance condition is satisfied, paragraph 15(b) of AASB 2/IFRS 2 requires the entity to:

> estimate the length of the expected vesting period at grant date, based on the most likely outcome of the performance condition.

A grant of shares with a performance condition linked to the level of an entity's earnings and in which the length of the vesting period varies is demonstrated in illustrative example 14.3.

ILLUSTRATIVE EXAMPLE 14.3

Grant with a performance condition linked to earnings

At the beginning of year 1 Benning Ltd grants 100 shares to each of its 50 employees, conditional on the employee remaining in the company's employ during the 3-year vesting period. The shares have a fair value of $20 per share at grant date. No dividends are expected to be paid over the 3-year period. Additionally, the vesting conditions allow the shares to vest at the end of:

- year 1 if the company's earnings have increased by more than 18%
- year 2 if earnings have increased by more than 13% averaged across the 2-year period
- year 3 if earnings have increased by more than 10% averaged across the 3-year period.

By the end of year 1, Benning Ltd's earnings have increased by only 14% and three employees have left. The company expects that earnings will continue to increase at a similar rate in year 2 and the shares

▶

will vest at the end of year 2. It also expects that a further three employees will leave during year 2, and therefore that 44 employees will vest in 100 shares each at the end of year 2.

Year	Calculation	Remuneration expense for period $	Cumulative remuneration expense $
1	$\dfrac{(44^* \text{ employees} \times 100 \text{ shares}) \times \$20 \times 1 \text{ year}}{2 \text{ years}}$	44 000	44 000

*44 employees = 50 less 3 that left during year 1 less 3 expected to leave during year 2.

By the end of year 2 the company's earnings have increased by only 10%, resulting in an average of only 12% ([14% + 10%]/2) and so the shares do not vest. Two employees left during the year. The company expects that another two employees will leave during year 3 and that its earnings will increase by at least 6%, thereby achieving the average of 10% per year.

Year	Calculation	Remuneration expense for period $	Cumulative remuneration expense $
2	$\dfrac{(43^* \text{ employees} \times 100 \text{ shares}) \times \$20 \times 2 \text{ years}}{3 \text{ years}} - \$44\,000$	13 333	57 333

*43 employees = 50 less 3 that left during year 1 less 2 that left during year 2 less 2 expected to leave during year 3.

Another three employees leave during year 3 and the company's earnings have increased by 8%, resulting in an average increase of 10.67% over the 3-year period. Therefore, the performance condition has been satisfied. The 42 remaining employees (50 − [3 + 2 + 3]) are entitled to receive 100 shares each at the end of year 3.

Year	Calculation	Remuneration expense for period $	Cumulative remuneration expense $
3	([42* employees × 100 shares] × $20) − $57 333	26 667	84 000

*42 employees = 50 less 3 that left during year 1 less 2 that left during year 2 less 3 that left during year 3.

Source: Adapted from AASB 2, IG12.

An entity may also grant equity instruments to its employees with a performance condition, and the exercise price varies. This particular situation is demonstrated in illustrative example 14.4.

Because the exercise price varies depending on the outcome of a performance condition that is not a market condition, the effect of the performance condition (in this case, the possibility that the exercise price might be either $40 or $30) is not taken into account when estimating the fair value of the share options at grant date. Instead, the entity estimates the fair value of the share options at grant date and ultimately revises the transaction amount to reflect the outcome of the performance condition.

ILLUSTRATIVE EXAMPLE 14.4

Grant of equity instruments where the exercise price varies

At the beginning of year 1 Calthorpe Ltd granted 5000 share options with an exercise price of $40 to a senior executive, conditional upon the executive remaining with the company until the end of year 3. The exercise price drops to $30 if Calthorpe Ltd's earnings increase by an average of 10% per year over the 3-year period. On grant date the estimated fair value of the share options with an exercise price of $40 is $12 per option and, if the exercise price is $30, the estimated fair value of the options is $16 per option.

During year 1 the company's earnings increased by 12% and they are expected to continue to increase at this rate over the next 2 years. During year 2 the company's earnings increased by 13% and the company continued to expect that the earnings target would be achieved. During year 3 the company's earnings increased by only 3%. The earnings target was therefore not achieved and so the 5000 vested share options will have an exercise price of $40. The executive completed 3 years' service and so satisfied the service condition.

Required
Calculate the remuneration expense for each period and the cumulative remuneration expense.

Solution

Year	Calculation	Remuneration expense for period $	Cumulative remuneration expense $
1	$\dfrac{5000 \text{ options} \times \$16 \times 1 \text{ year}}{3 \text{ years}}$	26 667	26 667
2	$\dfrac{5000 \text{ options} \times \$16 \times 2 \text{ years}}{3 \text{ years}} - \$26\,667$	26 666	53 333
3	5000 options × $12 − $53 333	6 667	60 000

Source: Adapted from AASB 2, IG12.

Paragraph 21 of AASB 2/IFRS 2 requires that:

> Market conditions, such as a target share price upon which vesting (or exercisability) is conditioned, shall be taken into account when estimating the fair value of the equity instruments granted.

This means that the goods or services received from a counterparty that satisfies all other vesting conditions (such as remaining in service for a specified period of time) are recognised whether or not the market condition is satisfied.

A grant of equity instruments with a market condition is demonstrated in illustrative example 14.5.

ILLUSTRATIVE EXAMPLE 14.5

Grant with a market condition

At the beginning of year 1 Aliceville Ltd grants 5000 share options to a senior executive, conditional on that executive remaining in the company's employ until the end of year 3. The share options cannot be exercised unless the share price has increased from $15 at the beginning of year 1 to above $25 at the end of year 3. If the share price is above $25 at the end of year 3, the share options can be exercised at any time during the next 7 years (i.e. by the end of year 10). The company applies an option-pricing model that takes into account the possibility that the share price will exceed $25 at the end of year 3 and the possibility that the share price will not exceed $25 at the end of year 3. It estimates the fair value of the share options with this embedded market condition to be $9 per option. The executive completes 3 years' service with Aliceville Ltd.

Required
Calculate the remuneration expense for each period and the cumulative remuneration expense.

Solution

Year	Calculation	Remuneration expense for period $	Cumulative remuneration expense $
1	$\dfrac{5000 \text{ options} \times \$9 \times 1 \text{ year}}{3 \text{ years}}$	15 000	15 000
2	$\dfrac{5000 \text{ options} \times \$9 \times 2 \text{ years}}{3 \text{ years}} - \$15\,000$	15 000	30 000
3	(5000 options × $9) − $30 000	15 000	45 000

Source: Adapted from AASB 2, IG13.

As noted earlier, because the executive has satisfied the service condition, the company is required to recognise these amounts irrespective of the outcome of the market condition.

14.5.2 Treatment of non-vesting conditions

The process of determining whether or not a condition is a non-vesting condition or a service or performance condition, is illustrated in the flowchart in figure 14.3.

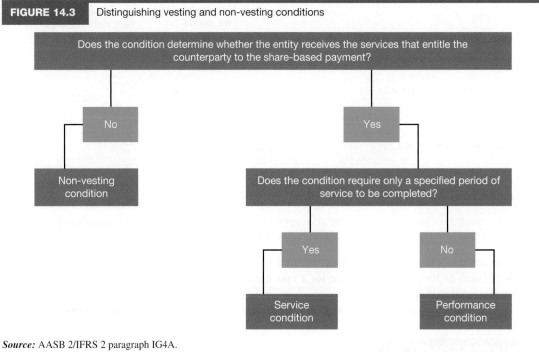

FIGURE 14.3 Distinguishing vesting and non-vesting conditions

Source: AASB 2/IFRS 2 paragraph IG4A.

14.6 Treatment of a reload feature

LEARNING OBJECTIVE 14.6 Explain the concept of a share option reload feature.

Employee share options often include features that are not found in exchange-traded options. One such feature is a *reload* which entitles the employee to be automatically granted new share options when the previously granted options are exercised using shares rather than cash to satisfy the exercise price. Although a **reload feature** can add considerably to an option's value, it is not considered feasible to value the reload feature at grant date.

Under paragraph 22 of AASB 2/IFRS 2:

> the reload feature shall not be taken into account when estimating the fair value of options granted at the measurement date. Instead, a *reload option* shall be accounted for as a new option grant, if and when a reload option is subsequently granted.

By the end of the vesting period the entity has recognised the goods or services received and the corresponding increase in equity. It is important to note that AASB 2/IFRS 2 does not allow any changes in total equity once the vesting period has expired. Paragraph 23 states that:

> the entity shall make no subsequent adjustment to total equity after vesting date. For example, the entity shall not subsequently reverse the amount recognised for services received from an employee if the vested equity instruments are later forfeited or, in the case of share options, the options are not exercised.

This restriction applies only to total equity; it does not preclude an entity from transferring amounts from one component of equity to another.

In the event that the fair value of equity instruments cannot be reliably estimated, they must instead be measured at their *intrinsic* value. Paragraph 24(a) of AASB 2/IFRS 2 states that the intrinsic value is measured:

> initially at the date the entity obtains the goods or the counterparty renders service and subsequently at the end of each reporting period and at the date of final settlement ... For a grant of share options, the share-based payment arrangement is finally settled when the options are exercised, are forfeited ... or lapse.

Any change in intrinsic value must be recognised in profit or loss. The amount to be recognised for goods or services is based on the number of equity instruments that ultimately vest or are exercised. The estimate must be revised if subsequent information indicates that the number of share options expected to vest differs from previous estimates. On vesting date, the estimate is then revised to equal the number of equity instruments that ultimately vest.

Illustrative example 14.6 provides an example of the application of the intrinsic value method of accounting for share-based payments.

ILLUSTRATIVE EXAMPLE 14.6

Grant of share options accounted for by applying the intrinsic value method

At the beginning of year 1, Brown Ltd granted 100 share options each to its 50 employees. The share options will vest at the end of year 3 if the employees remain employed by the company at that date. The share options have a life of 5 years. The exercise price is $60, which is also Brown Ltd's share price at the grant date. The company concludes that it cannot reliably estimate the fair value of the share options at the grant date.

Brown Ltd's share price during years 1–5 and the number of share options exercised during years 4–5 are set out below. Share options may be exercised only at year-end.

Year	Share price at year-end	Number of share options exercised at year-end
1	$ 63	0
2	65	0
3	75	0
4	88	2 600
5	100	1 700
		4 300

Required

Calculate the remuneration expense for each period and the cumulative remuneration expense for years 1 to 5, given the following developments at Brown Ltd.

1. At the end of year 1 three employees have left, and the company estimates that a further seven employees will leave during years 2 and 3. Hence, only 80% (40 of the original 50 employees) of the share options are expected to vest.
2. Two employees left during year 2, and the company revises its estimate of the number of share options expected to vest to 86%.
3. Two more employees leave during year 3, so there are 4300 share options vested at the end of year 3 $(100 \times [50 - (3 + 2 + 2)])$.

▶

Solution

Year	Calculation	Remuneration expense for period $	Cumulative remuneration expense $
1	$\dfrac{(50 \times 100 \text{ options} \times 80\%) \times (\$63 - \$60) \times 1 \text{ year}}{3 \text{ years}}$	4 000	4 000
2	$\dfrac{(50 \times 100 \text{ options} \times 86\%) \times (\$65 - \$60) \times 2 \text{ years}}{3 \text{ years}} - \$4000$	10 333	14 333
3	$(43 \times 100 \text{ options} \times [\$75 - \$60]) - \$14\,333$	50 167	64 500

In accordance with paragraph 24(a) of AASB 2/IFRS 2, Brown Ltd will recognise the following amounts in years 4 and 5 when the options are exercised.

Year	Calculation	Remuneration expense for period $	Cumulative remuneration expense $
4	(1700 outstanding options × [$88 − $75]) + (2600 exercised options × [$88 − $75])	55 900	120 400
5	(1700 exercised options × [$100 − $88])	20 400	140 800*

*(1700 options × [$100 − $60]) + (2600 options × [$88 − $60])
Source: Adapted from AASB 2, IG16.

If share options are forfeited after vesting date or lapse at the end of the share option's life, then paragraph 24(b) of AASB 2/IFRS 2 requires the amount previously recognised for goods or services to be reversed.

Paragraph 25 of AASB 2/IFRS 2 requires that if a grant of equity instruments is settled during the vesting period:

(a) ... the entity shall account for the settlement as an acceleration of vesting, and shall therefore recognise immediately the amount that would otherwise have been recognised for services received over the remainder of the vesting period.

(b) any payment made on settlement shall be accounted for as the repurchase of equity instruments, ie as a deduction from equity, except to the extent that the payment exceeds the intrinsic value of the equity instruments, measured at repurchase date. Any such excess shall be recognised as an expense.

LEARNING CHECK

☐ A reload feature entitles an employee to be automatically granted new options when the previously granted options are exercised using shares rather than cash to satisfy the exercise price.

☐ It is not considered feasible to value a reload feature at grant date, and thus a reload feature is accounted for as a new option if and when a reload option is subsequently granted.

☐ Having recognised the goods or services received and a corresponding increase in equity, an entity *cannot* make a subsequent adjustment to total equity after vesting date.

☐ If the fair value of equity instruments cannot be reliably estimated, they must instead be measured at their *intrinsic* value at the date goods are obtained or services are rendered, at the end of each subsequent reporting period, and at the date of final settlement (when the options are exercised, forfeited or lost). Any change in intrinsic value must be recognised in profit or loss.

14.7 Modifications to terms and conditions on which equity instruments were granted

LEARNING OBJECTIVE 14.7 Explain how modifications to granted equity instruments are treated.

An entity might choose to modify the terms and conditions on which it granted equity instruments. For example, it might change (reprice) the exercise price of share options previously granted to employees at prices that were higher than the current price of the entity's shares. It might accelerate the vesting of share options to make the options more favourable to employees; or it might remove or alter a performance condition. If the exercise price of options is modified, the fair value of the options changes. A reduction in the exercise price would increase the fair value of share options. Irrespective of any modifications to the terms and conditions on which equity instruments are granted, or a cancellation or settlement, paragraph 27 of AASB 2/IFRS 2 states the requirements for recognition as follows.

> The entity shall recognise, as a minimum, the services received measured at the grant date fair value of the equity instruments granted, unless those equity instruments do not vest because of failure to satisfy a vesting condition (other than a market condition) that was specified at grant date.

Although some companies provide for retesting to allow for the potential volatility of earnings and the cyclical nature of the market, many companies limit the retesting opportunities and others do not allow retesting at all.

The incremental effects of modifications that increase the total fair value of the share-based payment arrangement, or that are otherwise beneficial to the employee, must also be recognised. Paragraphs B43(a) and (b) in Appendix B of AASB 2/IFRS 2 explain that:

> The incremental fair value granted is the difference between the fair value of the modified equity instrument and that of the original equity instrument, both estimated as at the date of modification ... similarly, if the modification increases the number of equity instruments granted, the entity shall include the fair value of the additional equity instruments granted, measured at the date of the modification, in the measurement of the amount recognised for services received ...

If the modification occurs *during* the vesting period, the incremental fair value is included in the measurement of the amount recognised for services received from the modification date until the date when the modified equity instruments vest. This is in addition to the amount based on the grant-date fair value of the original equity instruments that is recognised over the remainder of the original vesting period. If the modification occurs *after* the vesting date, the incremental fair value is recognised immediately, or over the vesting period if the employee is required to complete an additional period of service before becoming unconditionally entitled to the modified equity instruments.

The terms or conditions of the equity instruments granted may be modified in a manner that reduces the total fair value of the share-based payment arrangement or that is not otherwise beneficial to the employee. If this occurs, then AASB 2/IFRS 2 (Appendix B paragraph B44) requires the services received as consideration to be accounted for as if that modification had not occurred (i.e. the decrease in fair value is not to be taken into account). If a cash-settled share-based payment transaction is modified to become an equity-settled share-based payment transaction, the change shall be accounted for from the date of the modification (Appendix B paragraph B44A).

14.7.1 Repurchases

If vested equity instruments are **repurchased** by the entity, AASB 2/IFRS 2 paragraph 29 specifies that:

> the payment made to the employee shall be accounted for as a deduction from equity, except to the extent that the payment exceeds the fair value of the equity instruments repurchased, measured at the repurchase date. Any such excess shall be recognised as an expense.

Illustrative example 14.7 demonstrates the accounting treatment of a repricing modification to the terms and conditions of share options.

Grant of equity instruments that are subsequently repriced

Meadow Ltd is large real estate development business. It grants 100 share options to each of its 50 employees, conditional upon the employee remaining in service over the next 3 years. The company estimates that the fair value of each option is $15. On the basis of a weighted average probability, the company also estimates that 10 employees will leave during the 3-year vesting period and therefore forfeit their rights to the share options.

Required

Calculate the remuneration expense and cumulative remuneration expense for each period, given the following developments at Meadow Ltd.

1. Four employees leave during year 1, and the company estimates that a further seven employees will leave during years 2 and 3. By the end of year 1 the company's share price has dropped, and it decides to reprice the share options. The repriced share options will vest at the end of year 3. At the date of repricing, Meadow Ltd estimates that the fair value of each of the original share options is $5 and the fair value of each repriced share option is $8. The incremental value is $3 per share option, and this amount is recognised over the remaining 2 years of the vesting period along with the remuneration expense based on the original option value of $15.
2. During year 2 a further four employees leave, and the company estimates that another four employees will leave during year 3 to bring the total expected employee departures over the 3-year vesting period to 12 employees.
3. A further three employees leave during year 3. For the remaining 39 employees (50 − [4 + 4 + 3]), the share options vested at the end of year 3.

Solution

Year	Calculation	Remuneration expense for period $	Cumulative remuneration expense $
1	$\dfrac{(50 - 11^*)\,\text{employees} \times 100\,\text{options} \times \$15 \times 1\,\text{year}}{3\,\text{years}}$	19 500	19 500

*Four employees left during year 1 and estimate of seven employees to leave during year 2.

Year	Calculation	Remuneration expense for period $	Cumulative remuneration expense $
2	$([50 - 12]\ \text{employees} \times 100\ \text{options}) \times \left(\dfrac{\$15 \times 2\,\text{years}}{3\,\text{years}} + \dfrac{\$3 \times 1\,\text{year}}{2\,\text{years}}\right) - \$19\,500$	24 200	43 700
3	$([50 - 11]\ \text{employees} \times 100\ \text{options} \times [\$15 + \$3]) - \$43\,700$	26 500	70 200

Source: Adapted from AASB 2, IG15.

☐ An entity might choose to modify the terms and conditions on which it granted equity instruments, thus changing the fair value. AASB 2/IFRS 2 requires the services received, measured at the grant-date fair value of the equity instruments, to be recognised unless those equity instruments do not vest.

☐ The incremental effects of modifications that increase the total fair value of the share-based payment arrangement, or that are otherwise beneficial to the employee, must be recognised.

☐ If vested equity instruments are repurchased, the payment made to the employee is accounted for as a deduction from equity. If the payment exceeds the fair value of the equity instruments repurchased, the excess is recognised as an expense.

14.8 Cash-settled share-based payment transactions

LEARNING OBJECTIVE 14.8 Demonstrate how cash-settled share-based payment transactions are measured.

Paragraphs 30–33D of AASB 2/IFRS 2 set out the requirements for share-based payments in which an entity incurs a liability for goods or services received, based on the price of its own equity instruments. These are known as *cash-settled* share-based payment transactions. The fair value of the liability involved is remeasured at the end of each reporting period and the date of settlement, and any changes in the fair value are recognised in profit or loss for the period. In contrast, the fair value of *equity-settled* share-based payments is determined at grant date, and remeasurement of the granted equity instruments at the end of each subsequent reporting period and settlement date does not occur.

An example of a cash-settled share-based payment is share appreciation rights that might be granted to an employee as part of a remuneration package. Share appreciation rights entitle the holder to a future cash payment (rather than an equity instrument) based on increases in the share price. Another example is where an employee is granted rights to shares that are redeemable, thus providing the employee with a right to receive a future cash payment.

Where share appreciation rights or other cash-settled share-based payments vest immediately, the goods or services and the associated liability are recognised immediately. However, if the settled share-based payments do not vest immediately, such as not vesting until the employees have served a specified period of service, the entity recognises the services received and the liability to pay for them as the services are rendered over the vesting period.

Paragraph 33 requires the liability for the cash-settled share-based payment to be measured initially and at the end of each reporting period until settled, at fair value by applying an option pricing model, taking into account the terms and conditions and the extent to which the other party, such as an employee, has rendered during that period.

Illustrative example 14.8 provides an example of the accounting treatment for cash-settled share appreciation rights.

ILLUSTRATIVE EXAMPLE 14.8

Cash-settled share appreciation rights

Bradley Ltd grants 100 share appreciation rights (SARs) to each of its 50 employees, conditional upon the employee staying with the company for the next 3 years. The company estimates the fair value of the SARs at the end of each year as shown below. The intrinsic values of the SARs at the date of exercise (which equal the cash paid out) at the end of years 3, 4 and 5 are also shown. All SARs held by employees remaining at the end of year 3 will vest.

Year	Fair value	Intrinsic value
1	$14.40	
2	$15.50	
3	$18.20	$15.00
4	$21.40	$20.00
5		$25.00

(a) During year 1 three employees leave and the company estimates that six more will leave during years 2 and 3.
(b) Four employees leave during year 2, and the company estimates that three more will leave during year 3.

▶

	Year	Calculation	Expense $	Liability $
(a)	1	$\dfrac{(50-9)\text{ employees} \times 100\,\text{SARs} \times \$14.40 \times 1\text{ year}}{3\text{ years}}$	19 680	19 680
(b)	2	$\dfrac{[50-10]\text{ employees} \times 100\,\text{SARs} \times \$15.50 \times 2\text{ years}}{3\text{ years}} - \$19\,680$	21 653	41 333

(c) Two employees leave during year 3. Therefore, a total of nine employees have left during the first 3 years.

(d) At the end of year 3, 15 employees have exercised their SARs.

(e) Another 14 employees exercise their SARs at the end of year 4.

(f) The remaining 12 employees exercise their SARs at the end of year 5.

	Year	Calculation	Expense $	Liability $
(c)	3	([50 − 9 − 15] employees × 100 SARs × $18.20) − $41 333	5 987	47 320
(d)		15 employees × 100 SARs × $15	22 500	
(e)	4	([26 − 14] employees × 100 SARs × $21.40) − $47 320	(21 640)	25 680
		14 employees × 100 SARs × $20	28 000	
(f)	5	(0 employees × 100 SARs × $25) − $25 680	(25 680)	0
		12 employees × 100 SARs × $25	30 000	
		Total	**80 500***	

*$22 500 + $28 000 + $30 000

Source: Adapted from AASB 2, IG19.

Similar to equity-settled share-based payments, cash-settled share-based payments may be conditional upon satisfying specified vesting conditions. For example, the vesting of share appreciation rights might be conditional on performance targets, such as achieving an average annual increase in profit over a three-year period, or market conditions, such as a target share price.

Paragraphs 30–33D of AASB 2/IFRS 2 prescribe principles for estimating the fair value of the liability where vesting and non-vesting conditions apply. Specifically, paragraph 33A states that vesting conditions, other than market conditions, are not taken into account in estimating the fair value of the cash-settled share-based payment. Instead, these vesting conditions are reflected in the estimate of the number of awards included in the measurement of the liability. Thus a lower number of awards are included in the measurement of the liability than would have been used if there were no vesting conditions.

Paragraph 33C specifies that market conditions, as well as non-vesting conditions, are taken into account when estimating the fair value of the cash-settled share-based payment both on initial recognition when the awards are granted and when remeasuring the liability at the end of each reporting period.

The principles of accounting for vesting and non-vesting conditions applied to cash-settled share-based payments are consistent with those applied to equity-settled share-based payments (see section 14.5.1).

14.8.1 Share-based payment transactions with cash alternatives

Some share-based payments may provide either the entity or the counterparty with the choice of having the transaction settled in cash (or other assets) or the issue of equity instruments. If the entity has incurred a liability to settle in cash or other assets, the transaction is treated as a cash-settled share-based payment. If no liability has been incurred, paragraph 34 of AASB 2/IFRS 2 requires that the transaction be treated as an equity-settled share-based payment.

Share-based payment transactions where the counterparty has settlement choice

If the counterparty to a share-based payment has the right to choose whether a transaction is settled in cash or equity instruments, a compound financial instrument has been created that includes a debt component and an equity component. The debt component represents the counterparty's right to demand a cash settlement, and the equity component represents the counterparty's right to demand settlement in equity instruments.

AASB 2/IFRS 2 (paragraphs 35 and 36) requires that transactions with employees be measured at fair value on measurement date, by taking into account the terms and conditions on which rights to cash and equity were granted:

> For transactions with parties other than employees, in which the fair value of the goods or services received is measured directly, the entity shall measure the equity component of the compound financial instrument as the difference between the fair value of the goods or services received and the fair value of the debt component, at the date when the goods or services are received.

The fair value of the debt component is measured before the fair value of the equity component (AASB 2/IFRS 2 paragraph 37), as the counterparty must forfeit the right to receive cash in order to receive equity instruments. The measurement of compound financial instruments with employees (and with other counterparties) is summarised in table 14.2.

TABLE 14.2	Measurement of compound financial instruments
Counterparty	**Measurement approach**
Employees	Measure fair value (FV) of the debt component then FV of the equity component, at measurement date, taking into account the terms and conditions on which rights to cash or equity were granted.
Parties other than employees	The equity component is the difference between FV of goods or services received and FV of the debt component, at the date the goods or services are received.

The goods or services received in respect of each component of the compound financial instrument must be accounted for separately. For the debt component, the goods or services and a liability to pay for them is recognised as the counterparty supplies the goods or services, in the same manner as other cash-settled share-based payments. For the equity component, the goods or services received and the increase in equity are recognised as the counterparty supplies the goods or services, in the same manner as other equity-settled share-based payments.

At settlement date, the liability must be remeasured to fair value. As per paragraph 39 of AASB 2/IFRS 2:

> If the entity issues equity instruments on settlement rather than paying cash, the liability shall be transferred direct to equity, as the consideration for the equity instruments issued.

If the counterparty takes a cash settlement, they are deemed to have forfeited their right to receive equity instruments. This cash payment is applied in settlement of the full liability (AASB 2/IFRS 2 paragraph 40). Any equity component previously recognised remains within equity although it can be transferred within equity.

A grant of shares with a cash alternative subsequently added that provides an employee with a settlement choice is demonstrated in illustrative example 14.9.

ILLUSTRATIVE EXAMPLE 14.9

Grant of shares with a cash alternative subsequently added

At the beginning of year 1 Scotland Ltd granted 10 000 shares with a fair value of $24 per share to a senior manager, conditional on the manager remaining in the company's employ for 3 years. By the end of year 2 the share price had dropped to $15 per share. At that date the company added a cash alternative to the grant, giving the manager the right to choose whether to receive the 10 000 shares or cash equal to the value of the shares on vesting date. On vesting date the share price had dropped to $12.

Year	Calculation	Asset/expense $	Equity $	Liability $
1	10 000 shares × $24 × 1/3 years	80 000	80 000	

The addition of the cash alternative at the end of year 2 created an obligation to settle in cash. Scotland Ltd must recognise the liability to settle in cash based on the fair value of the shares at the modification date and the extent to which the specified services have been received. The liability must be remeasured at the end of each subsequent reporting period and at the date of settlement.

Year	Calculation	Asset/expense $	Equity $	Liability $
2	(10 000 shares × $24 × 2/3 years) − $80 000	80 000	80 000	
	10 000 shares × $15 × 2/3 years		(100 000)	100 000*

Year	Calculation	Asset/expense $	Equity $	Liability $
3	(10 000 shares × $24) − $160 000	80 000	30 000	50 000*
	(10 000 shares × $12) − $150 000	(30 000)		(30 000)
	Total	**210 000**	**90 000**	**120 000****

*At the date of modification when the cash alternative is added the total liability is $150 000 ($15 × 10 000 shares). At this date a potential liability must be recognised.
**Total liability at date of settlement is $120 000 ($12 × 10 000 shares).
Source: Adapted from AASB 2, IG15.

An example of a share-based payment transaction in which an employee has a right to choose either a cash settlement or an equity settlement is demonstrated in illustrative example 14.10.

ILLUSTRATIVE EXAMPLE 14.10

Share-based payment transaction where employee has settlement choice

Norden Ltd grants to each of its 10 executives a choice of receiving a cash payment equivalent to 1000 shares or receiving 1200 shares. The grant is conditional on the completion of 3 years' service with the company. If the share alternative is chosen, the shares must be held for 2 years after vesting date. At the grant date the company's share price is $25 per share. At the end of years 1, 2 and 3 the share price is $27, $28 and $30 respectively. The company does not expect to pay dividends in the next 3 years. After taking into account the effects of post-vesting transfer restrictions, the company estimates that the grant-date fair value of the share alternative is $24 per share.

The fair value of the cash alternative is $250 000 (10 × 1000 shares × $25), and the fair value of the equity alternative is $288 000 (10 × 1200 shares × $24). Therefore, the fair value of the equity component of the compound instrument is $38 000 ($288 000 − $250 000). Norden Ltd will recognise the following amounts.

Year	Calculation	Asset/expense $	Equity $	Liability $
1	Liability component			
	(10 × 1000 × $27 × 1/3 years)	90 000		90 000
	Equity component			
	($38 000 × 1/3 years)	12 667	12 667	
2	Liability component			
	(10 × 1000 × $28 × 2/3 years) − $90 000	96 667		96 667
	Equity component			
	($38 000 × 1/3 years)	12 667	12 667	
3	Liability component			
	(10 × 1000 × $30) − $186 667	113 333		113 333
	Equity component			
	($38 000 × 1/3 years)	12 666	12 666	

At the end of year 3, the employees must choose whether to take the cash or shares. At settlement, the liability must be remeasured to its full value. If all employees choose the cash settlement, the liability is $300 000 (10 × 1000 × $30). If cash is paid on settlement it must be applied to settle the liability in full, with any previously recognised equity instrument remaining within equity.

Year	Calculation	Asset/expense $	Equity $	Liability $
End year 3	Choice 1: Cash equivalent to 10 × 1000 shares × $30			
	Cash settlement of $300 000 paid			(300 000)
	Totals	338 000	38 000	0

If the employees choose to receive shares, the liability is transferred direct to equity (AASB 2/IFRS 2 paragraph 39) as the consideration for the equity instruments that were issued. If all employees choose the equity alternative, the amount of the liability transferred to equity is $300 000.

Year	Calculation	Asset/expense $	Equity $	Liability $
End year 3	Choice 2: Equity issue of 10 × 1200 shares			
	12 000 shares issued		300 000	(300 000)
	Totals	338 000	338 000	0

Source: Adapted from AASB 2, IG22.

Share-based payment transactions where the entity has settlement choice

Where an entity has a choice of settling in cash or equity instruments, it must determine whether it has a present obligation to settle in cash. Paragraph 41 of AASB 2/IFRS 2 states that:

> The entity has a present obligation to settle in cash if the choice of settlement in equity instruments has no commercial substance (e.g. because the entity is legally prohibited from issuing shares), or the entity has a past practice or a stated policy of settling in cash, or generally settles in cash whenever the counterparty asks for cash settlement.

If a present obligation exists, the transaction must be accounted for as a cash-settled share-based payment. If a present obligation to settle in cash does not exist, the transaction is accounted for as an equity-settled arrangement (paragraphs 42 and 43).

On settlement, if the entity elects to settle in cash, paragraph 43(a) of AASB 2/IFRS 2 requires the cash payment to be accounted for as the repurchase of an equity interest, resulting in a deduction from equity. Where there is an equity settlement, no further accounting adjustments are required (paragraph 43(b)). However, paragraph 43(c) notes that:

> if the entity elects the settlement alternative with the higher fair value, as at the date of settlement, the entity shall recognise an additional expense for the excess value given.

The excess value is either the difference between the cash paid and the fair value of the equity instruments that would have been issued, or the difference between the fair value of the equity instruments issued and the amount of cash that would have been paid, whichever is applicable.

LEARNING CHECK

☐ Where share appreciation rights vest immediately, the services and the associated liability must also be recognised immediately.
☐ Where share appreciation rights do not vest until the employee has completed a specified period of service, the services received and the associated liability to pay for those services are recognised as the service is rendered. The liability is measured, initially and at the end of each reporting period until settled, at the fair value of the share appreciation rights by applying an option-pricing model that takes

▶

into account the terms and conditions on which share appreciation rights were granted, and the extent to which employees have rendered service.

☐ Some share-based payments provide either the entity or the counterparty with the choice of having the transaction settled in cash (or other assets) or the issue of equity instruments. If the entity has incurred a liability to settle in cash or other assets, the transaction is treated as a cash-settled share-based payment. If no liability has been incurred, the transaction is treated as an equity-settled share-based payment.

☐ If the entity selects the settlement alternative with the higher fair value an additional expense for the excess value given is required to be recognised.

14.9 Disclosure

LEARNING OBJECTIVE 14.9 Describe and apply the disclosure requirements of AASB 2/IFRS 2.

The global financial crisis that emerged in 2008 resulted in much criticism about the inadequacy of disclosure in regard to performance hurdles and incentives used in share-based payment transactions. Corporate executives, on the other hand, complain about the onerous reporting and disclosure requirements necessary under the accounting rules. One difficulty faced by regulators is how to reduce the volume of required information yet still retain meaningful and useful disclosure.

Paragraphs 44–52 of AASB 2/IFRS 2 prescribe various disclosures relating to share-based payments. The objective of these disclosures is to provide significant additional information to assist financial report users to understand the nature and extent of share-based payment arrangements that existed during the reporting period.

The three principles that underpin the disclosures required by AASB 2/IFRS 2 are shown in table 14.3.

TABLE 14.3   Principles underpinning the disclosures in AASB 2/IFRS 2

Disclosure principle	AASB 2/IFRS 2 paragraph
The nature and extent of the share-based payment arrangements	44 & 45
How the fair value of goods or services received, or the fair value of equity instruments granted during the period, was determined	46
The effect of share-based payment transactions on the entity's profit or loss for the period and on its financial position	50

Paragraph 45 of AASB 2/IFRS 2 specifies the disclosures necessary to give effect to the principle in paragraph 44 as including at least:

(a) a description of each type of share-based payment arrangement that existed at any time during the period, including the general terms and conditions of each arrangement, such as vesting requirements, the maximum term of options granted, and the method of settlement.

An entity with substantially similar types of share-based payments may aggregate this information unless separate disclosure of each arrangement is necessary to enable users to understand the nature and extent of the arrangements.

Other specific disclosures required in paragraph 45(b) of AASB 2/IFRS 2 are:

the number and weighted average exercise prices of share options for each of the following groups of options:
  (i) outstanding at the beginning of the period;
  (ii) granted during the period;
 (iii) forfeited during the period;
 (iv) exercised during the period;
  (v) expired during the period;
 (vi) outstanding at the end of the period; and
(vii) exercisable at the end of the period.

In relation to share options exercised during the period, the weighted average share price at the date of exercise must be disclosed. If the options were exercised on a regular basis throughout the period, the weighted average share price during the period may be disclosed instead. For share options outstanding at the end of the period, the range of exercise prices and the weighted average remaining contractual life must be disclosed. If the range of exercise prices is wide, the outstanding options must be divided into ranges that are meaningful for assessing the number and timing of additional shares that may be issued and the cash that may be received upon exercise of those options (AASB 2/IFRS 2 paragraphs 45(c) and (d)).

If the fair value of goods or services received as consideration for equity instruments of the entity has been measured indirectly by reference to the fair value of the equity instruments granted, paragraph 47 of AASB 2/IFRS 2 requires the following information to be disclosed:

(a) for share options granted during the period, the weighted average fair value of those options at the measurement date and information on how that fair value was measured, including:
  (i) the option pricing model used and the inputs to that model, including the weighted average share price, exercise price, expected volatility, option life, expected dividends, the risk-free interest rate, and any other inputs to the model, including the method used and the assumptions made to incorporate the effects of expected early exercise;
  (ii) how expected volatility was determined, including an explanation of the extent to which expected volatility was based on historical volatility; and
  (iii) whether and how any other features of the option grant were incorporated into the measurement of fair value, such as a market condition;
(b) for other equity instruments granted during the period (i.e. other than share options), the number and weighted average fair value of those equity instruments at the measurement date, and information on how that fair value was measured, including:
  (i) if fair value was not measured on the basis of an observable market price, how it was determined;
  (ii) whether and how expected dividends were incorporated into the measurement of fair value; and
  (iii) whether and how any other features of the equity instruments granted were incorporated into the measurement of fair value; and
(c) for share-based payment arrangements that were modified during the period:
  (i) an explanation of those modifications;
  (ii) the incremental fair value granted (as a result of those modifications); and
  (iii) information on how the incremental fair value granted was measured.

If the entity has measured the fair value of goods or services received during the period directly, it is required to disclose how that fair value was determined (e.g. at market price).

If the entity has rebutted the assumption that the fair value of goods or services received can be estimated reliably, it is required to disclose that fact (AASB 2/IFRS 2 paragraph 49) together with an explanation of why the presumption was rebutted.

Paragraph 51 of AASB 2/IFRS 2 gives effect to the principle that an entity must disclose information that enables financial statement users to understand the effect of share-based payments on the entity's profit or loss for the period and on its financial position. Paragraph 51 requires disclosure of at least:

(a) the total expense recognised for the period arising from share-based payment transactions in which the goods or services received did not qualify for recognition as assets . . . including separate disclosure of that portion of the total expense that arises from transactions accounted for as equity-settled share-based payment transactions;
(b) for liabilities arising from share-based payment transactions:
  (i) the total carrying amount at the end of the period; and
  (ii) the total intrinsic value at the end of the period of liabilities for which the counterparty's right to cash or other assets had vested by the end of the period.

Finally, paragraph 52 of AASB 2/IFRS 2 requires the disclosure of such other additional information as may be needed to enable the users of the financial statements to understand the nature and extent of the share-based payment arrangements; how the fair value of goods or services received, or the fair value of equity instruments granted was determined; and the effect of share-based payments on the entity's profit or loss and on its financial position.

A review of the corporate annual reports shows the large volume of space devoted to share-based payment disclosure. For example, the remuneration report in Woolworths Group Limited's 2018 annual report (discussed earlier in this chapter) comprises 20 pages.

An extract relating to share-based payment disclosures for Woolworths appears in figure 14.4.

FIGURE 14.4   Extract from the accounting policy note for share-based payment transactions, Woolworths

6.2 Employee benefits

6.2.2 Share-based payments

Performance rights by grant date

The following table summarises movements in outstanding rights for the financial period ended 24 June 2018:

Financial year	Effective date	Expiry date	No. of rights at 25 June 2017	Rights granted during year	Rights vested during year	Rights lapsed during year	No. of rights at 24 June 2018
Performance rights (LTI plan, deferred STI and RSP)							
FY13	01/07/12	01/07/17	166 103	—	—	(166 103)	—
FY14	01/07/13	01/07/18	287 763	—	—	(13 237)	274 526
FY15	01/07/14	01/07/17	212 117	—	—	(212 117)	—
FY16	01/07/15	01/07/18	595 814	—	—	(85 882)	509 932
FY17	01/07/16	01/07/19	4 646 319	39 560	—	(463 480)	4 222 399
FY18	01/07/17	01/07/21	—	5 092 828	(1 601)	(156 545)	4 934 682
Performance rights (attraction and retention)							
FY14	01/07/13 to 20/06/14	01/07/14 to 02/10/18	4 000	—	(4 000)	—	—
FY15	01/07/14 to 01/06/15	02/09/14 to 07/04/18	13 878	—	(9 000)	(4 478)	—
FY16	01/07/15 to 20/06/16	01/07/16 to 01/10/18	553 952	—	(521 258)	(20 415)	12 279
FY17	01/07/16 to 14/06/17	31/12/16 to 27/05/20	144 480	—	(40 724)	(5 768)	97 988
FY18	01/07/17 to 28/05/18	01/10/17 to 30/04/21	—	204 117	(8 708)	(970)	194 439
			6 624 126	**5 336 505**	**(5 85 691)**	**(1 128 995)**	**10 246 245**

The weighted average share price during the financial period ended 24 June 2018 was $26.78.
Source: Woolworths Group Limited (2018, p. 112).

LEARNING CHECK

☐ AASB 2/IFRS 2 prescribes various disclosures relating to share-based payments to provide information to assist financial report users to understand the share-based payment arrangements that existed during the reporting period.

☐ The key disclosure principles are: the nature and extent of the share-based payment arrangements; how the fair value of goods or services received, or the fair value of equity instruments granted during the period, was determined; and the effect of share-based payment transactions on the entity's profit or loss for the period and on its financial position.

SUMMARY

AASB 2/IFRS 2 *Share-based Payment* deals with the recognition and measurement of share-based payment transactions. Share-based payments are arrangements in which an entity receives or acquires goods or services as consideration for, or based on the price of (respectively) its own equity instruments. The main features of the standard are that it:

- requires financial statement recognition of the goods or services acquired or received under share-based payment arrangements, regardless of whether the settlement is cash or equity or whether the counterparty is an employee or another party
- employs the general principle for cash-settled transactions that the goods or services received and the liability incurred are measured at the fair value of the liability; and, until it is settled, the fair value of the liability is remeasured at the end of each reporting period and at the date of settlement and any changes in fair value are recognised in profit or loss
- employs the general principle for equity-settled transactions that the goods or services received and the corresponding increase in equity are measured at the grant date, and at the fair value of the goods or services received; and if the fair value cannot be measured reliably, the goods or services are measured indirectly by reference to the fair value of the equity instruments granted
- allows an entity to choose appropriate option-valuation models to determine fair values and to tailor those models to suit the entity's specific circumstances
- includes a lengthy set of disclosure requirements aimed at enabling financial statement users to understand the nature, extent and effect of share-based payments, and how the fair value of goods or services received or equity instruments granted was determined.

KEY TERMS

cash-settled share-based payment A transaction in which the entity acquires goods or services by incurring liabilities for amounts based on the value of its own equities.

equity-settled share-based payment A transaction in which the entity receives goods or services as consideration for its own equity instruments.

performance condition A vesting condition that requires the counterparty to complete a specified period of service and meet a specified performance target.

reload feature Entitlement of the employee to be automatically granted new share options when the previously granted options are exercised using shares rather than cash to satisfy the exercise price.

repurchase The entity buys the shares back from the employee.

service condition A vesting condition that requires the counterparty to complete a specified period of service during which services are provided to the entity.

share-based payment transactions Transactions in which the entity receives goods or services in a share-based payment arrangement or incurs an obligation to settle the transaction in a share-based payment arrangement when another group entity receives those goods or services.

vest To become an entitlement.

vesting condition Either a service condition or a performance condition. Service conditions require the counterparty to complete a specified period of service. Performance conditions require the counterparty to complete a specified period of service and specified performance targets to be met (such as a specified increase in the entity's profit over a specified period of time). A performance condition might include a market condition.

DEMONSTRATION PROBLEMS

14.1 Equity-settled share-based payment transactions

On 1 July 2022, Andrews Ltd grants 100 share options to each of its 40 senior executives. At grant date, it is estimated that the value of each share option is $25. The granting of the share options is conditional on the executive remaining in the company's employ for the next 4 years. If an executive leaves, they will forfeit their rights to the share options. The actual and estimated numbers of senior executives leaving their employ during the vesting period are as follows.

Year	Estimated Number of senior executives to leave employ	Actual Number of senior executives that left employ
1	2	5
2	2	3
3	3	2
4	2	0

As a result of the high number of senior executives that leave Andrews Ltd during years 1 and 2, the company's share price decreases by the end of year 2 and Andrews Ltd decides to reprice the share options. The company estimates the repriced share options to have a fair value of $27, an increase of $2 on their original fair value.

Required

Prepare a schedule setting out the annual and cumulative remuneration expense for each year in the vesting period.

SOLUTION

Calculate the remuneration expense to be recognised at the end of each year of the vesting period. The calculation is to include the number of executives expected to be granted share options when they vest, the number of share options to be granted, the fair value of those share options, and the result of any modifications that increase the fair value of the options or otherwise benefit the executives.

At the end of year 1, the remuneration expense to be recognised is as follows.

Year	Calculation	Remuneration expense for period	Cumulative remuneration expense
1	(40 – 7 executives) × 100 share options × $25 × 1/4	$20 625	$20 625

During the first year, five executives leave their employ at Andrews Ltd compared to an estimate of only two for that year. The entity estimates that another two executives will leave the company during the second year. Therefore, the remuneration expense to be recognised at the end of year 1 is calculated based on only 33 executives being granted the share options at the end of the vesting period.

The remuneration expense and cumulative remuneration at the end of year 2 is as follows.

Year	Calculation	Remuneration expense for period	Cumulative remuneration expense
2	[(40 – 11 executives) × 100 share options × $25 × 2/4] – $20 625	$15 625	$36 250

By the end of year 2, the number of executives that have left their employ at Andrews Ltd is eight (five in year 1 plus three in year 2), double the number estimated by the entity for that period of time. A further three executives are expected to leave during year 3. Therefore, at the end of year 2, the number of executives expected to be granted share options at the end of the vesting period is 29 (40 – 8 – 3).

At the end of year 2, Andrews Ltd's share price has dropped so management decides to reprice the share options to be granted. Paragraph B43(a) of Appendix B of AASB 2/IFRS 2 requires an entity to measure the fair value of the equity instruments immediately before and after any modifications. Andrews Ltd estimates the fair value of the repriced share options at $27, an increase of $2 in the fair value of the share options immediately before the repricing.

As per paragraph 27 of AASB 2/IFRS 2, the entity is required to recognise modification effects that result in an increase in the total fair value of the share-based payments or are otherwise beneficial to the employee. These effects are to be recognised over the remainder of the vesting period. That is, from the modification date until the date the modified equity instruments vest. This modification occurs at the end of year 2 and is therefore required to be recognised over the remaining 2 years of the 4-year vesting period.

The increase is also required to be recognised *in addition to* the amount based on the grant date fair value of the original equity instruments. Therefore, for the remainder of the vesting period (years 3 and 4) the $2 increase in the fair value of the share options will be recognised along with the original fair value of $25.

The remuneration expense and cumulative remuneration recognised at the end of year 3 is as follows.

Year	Calculation	Remuneration expense for period	Cumulative remuneration expense
3	[(40 – 12 executives) × 100 share options × ($25 × 3/4 + $2 × 1/2)] – $36 250	$19 050	$55 300

By the end of year 3 a total of 10 executives (5 + 3 + 2) have left Andrews Ltd and a further two executives are expected to leave during year 4. Therefore, the expected number of executives to be granted share options at the end of the vesting period is 28 (40 – 10 – 2).

The original price of the share options, $25, is still to be recognised for the now 3 out of 4 years of the vesting period. In addition, the $2 increase in fair value of the share options must also be recognised over years 3 and 4. Year 3 is the first year this increase is to be included. Therefore, only half of the fair value modification amount is recognised.

During the fourth and final year of the vesting period, no executives leave their employ despite Andrews Ltd estimating that another 2 executives would leave. The share options vested at the end of year 4 and the remuneration expense and cumulative remuneration at this time are calculated as follows.

Year	Calculation	Remuneration expense for period	Cumulative remuneration expense
4	[(40 – 10 executives) × 100 share options × ($25 + $2)] – $55 300	$25 700	$81 000

In summary, after a 4-year vesting period in which continuing employment was conditional, 30 executives were granted 100 share options at a fair value of $27, a total of $81 000 in remuneration. The complete remuneration schedule is shown below.

Year	Remuneration expense for period	Cumulative remuneration expense
1	$20 625	$20 625
2	$15 625	$36 250
3	$19 050	$55 300
4	$25 700	$81 000

14.2 Cash-settled share-based payment transaction

Swanson Ltd offers its senior executives share-based payment arrangements with the choice of payment in either cash or shares. On 1 July 2022, the entity grants the following options to its current senior executive, conditional on the executive remaining in that position for 3 years.

- Option 1: the right to choose a cash payment equivalent to the value of 500 shares
- Option 2: receive 750 shares (fair value at grant date is $52)

Swanson Ltd's share price for the 3-year period is as follows.

Grant date	$50
Year 1	$55
Year 2	$60
Year 3	$65

The entity does not anticipate paying any dividends on its shares over this period of time.

Required

Prepare a schedule to show the amounts to be recognised by Swanson Ltd each year under both options.

SOLUTION

Paragraphs 35–40 of AASB 2/IFRS 2 discuss the recognition criteria for share-based payments with a choice of settlement. When an entity allows employees to choose between receiving either a cash payment or equity instruments a *compound* financial instrument has been granted — one that has debt *and* equity components. The entity is required to firstly measure the fair value of the debt component and then measure the fair value of the equity component. When an entity offers a choice of settlement, it is usually structured so that the equity component is greater in value than the debt component. The entity is required to account for each component separately, then, at the settlement date, the entity remeasures the liability to its fair value. If the counterparty chooses the cash settlement option, the payment is applied as full settlement of the liability and any previously recognised equity remains in equity. Alternatively, if the counterparty chooses the equity settlement option, the previously recognised liability is transferred directly to equity as consideration for the equity instruments issued.

- *Option 1: the right to choose a cash payment equivalent to the value of 500 shares*. This option is a cash-settled share-based payment and requires Swanson Ltd to recognise a liability during the vesting period. The fair value of this option is 500 × $50 = $25 000.
- *Option 2: receive 750 shares (fair value at grant date is $52)*. This option is an equity-settled share-based payment and requires Swanson Ltd to recognise an increase in equity. The fair value of this option is 750 × $52 = $39 000.

The fair value of the equity component of the compound instrument is therefore $14 000 ($39 000 − $25 000).

The recognition of both debt and equity components at the end of year 1 are as follows.

Year	Calculation	Expense $	Equity $	Liability $	Cumulative $
1	Liability component				
	(500 shares × $55 × 1/3 years)	9 167		9 167	9 167
	Equity component				
	($14 000 × 1/3 years)	4 667	4 667		4 667

The debt (liability) component is recalculated using the current fair value at the end of each year and assumes that it remains at that current fair value for the remainder of the vesting period; that is, calculated as per the requirements of any cash-settled payment arrangement. As the equity component's fair value at grant date was $14 000 greater than the debt component at the same date, only the excess amount is required to be recognised as an equity component at the end of each year.

The recognition of both debt and equity components at the end of years 2 and 3 is therefore as follows.

Year	Calculation	Expense $	Equity $	Liability $	Cumulative $
2	Liability component				
	(500 shares × $60 × 2/3 years − $9167)	10 833		10 833	20 000
	Equity component				
	($14 000 × 1/3 years)	4 667	4 667		9 334

Year	Calculation	Expense $	Equity $	Liability $	Cumulative $
3	Liability component				
	(500 shares × $65 − $20 000)	12 500		12 500	32 500
	Equity component				
	($14 000 × 1/3 years)	4 666	4 666		14 000

The share-based payment calculations to the senior executive under each option are as follows.

Year	Calculation	Expense $	Equity $	Liability $	Cumulative $
End of year 3	*Option 1: cash-settlement* (500 shares × current FV $65)			(32 500)	—
	Option 1 totals	46 500	14 000		
	Option 2: equity-settlement (750 shares issued at $52)		32 500	(32 500)	—
	Option 2 totals	46 500	46 500	—	—

Payment and recognition under option 1

If the senior executive chooses the option for a cash-settlement at the end of the vesting period, Swanson Ltd is required to pay, to the senior executive, the liability of $32 500, which is equal to 500 shares at a fair value at settlement date of $65. The previously recognised equity of $14 000 remains in equity. This equals a total expense of $46 500 recognised for this share-based payment.

Payment and recognition under option 2

If the senior executive chooses the option for an equity-settlement at the end of the vesting period, Swanson Ltd is required to transfer the full amount of the liability over to equity. The total amount recognised as equity is $46 500, which is also the total amount recognised as an expense. This is equal to the original fair value of the equity component option of $39 000 plus the difference in fair value for the debt component between grant date and settlement date of $7500.

Debt component fair value at settlement date	$32 500
Less debt component fair value at grant date	($25 000)
Equals increase in debt component fair value	$7 500

COMPREHENSION QUESTIONS

1 Why do standard setters formulate rules on the measurement and recognition of share-based payment transactions?

2 What is the difference between equity-settled and cash-settled share-based payment transactions?

3 What is the different accounting treatment for instruments classified as debt and those classified as equity?

4 Outline the accounting treatment for the recognition of an equity-settled share-based payment transaction.

5 Explain when a counterparty's entitlement to receive equity instruments of an entity vests.

6 What are the minimum factors required under AASB 2/IFRS 2 to be taken into account in option-pricing models?

7 Distinguish between vesting and non-vesting conditions.

8 Explain what the 'repricing' of share options means.

9 Explain the measurement approach for cash-settled share-based payment transactions.

10 Are the following statements true or false?
  (a) Goods or services received in a share-based payment transaction must be recognised when they are received.
  (b) Historical volatility provides the best basis for forming reasonable expectations of the future price of share options.
  (c) Share appreciation rights entitle the holder to a future equity instrument based on the profitability of the issuer.

CASE STUDY 14.1

VESTING CONDITIONS

On 1 January 2020, Jarrod Ltd grants 2000 share options to its 10 sales staff. At this date the fair value of the share options is $50. The vesting conditions are:

* the salesperson must remain with the company for a minimum of 3 years
* the gross profit margin remains at a minimum of 40% over the next 3 years.

At the end of year 1, Jarrod Ltd adjusts the target for gross profit margin from 40% to 50%. This target proves too difficult to maintain and by the end of year 3 the gross profit margin is at 42%. At 31 December 2022, there are six sales staff employed with Jarrod Ltd. Five of these sales staff have been with the entity for the past 3 years. The other salesperson commenced employment with the entity on 1 December 2022. The fair value of the share options at the end of the vesting period is $55.

Required

With regards to the requirements of AASB 2/IFRS 2, discuss the implications of a share option grant whereby the vesting conditions are modified and subsequently not satisfied.

CASE STUDY 14.2

VESTING CONDITIONS AND SHARE OPTIONS

Sebastian Ltd grants its manager a share option plan conditional on the manager contributing 10% of his fortnightly salary of $3000 for the next 2 years. The fortnightly payments will be automatically deducted from the manager's salary and held until either: the end of the 2-year period when the manager exercises their right to the share options; or earlier, within the 2-year period, if the manager chooses to opt out of this arrangement and be refunded their contributions. Sebastian Ltd estimates the annual expense for this share-based payment plan to be $2000.

Required

Discuss the requirements of AASB 2/IFRS 2 if the manager chooses to discontinue his contributions and opts out of this share option plan after 12 months.

CASE STUDY 14.3

INCENTIVE PLANS

Visit the websites of three Australian companies and access their latest annual reports. View the remuneration report within the director's statutory report. Compare these remuneration reports and discuss your findings, especially in relation to short-term and/or long-term incentive structures.

APPLICATION AND ANALYSIS EXERCISES

★ BASIC | ★ ★ MODERATE | ★ ★ ★ DIFFICULT

14.1 Scope of AASB 2/IFRS 2 ★ **LO2**

Which of the following is a share-based payment transaction within the scope of AASB 2/IFRS 2? Give reasons for your answer.
   (a) Goods acquired from a supplier (counterparty) by incurring a liability based on the market price of the goods
   (b) An invoiced amount for professional advice provided to an entity, charged at an hourly rate, and to be settled in cash
   (c) Services provided by an employee to be settled in equity instruments of the entity
   (d) Supply of goods in return for cash or equity instruments at the discretion of the counterparty
   (e) Dividend payment to employees who are holders of an entity's shares

14.2 Categorising ★ **LO2, 3**

An entity grants 20 000 shares to a senior manager in return for services rendered.

Required

Should the entity recognise the cost of these services as a liability or a component of equity? Explain.

14.3 Recognition principles ★ LO2, 3

Mulgogi Ltd, a listed company, organises major sporting events. It acquires crowd-control equipment in return for a liability for an amount based on the price of 1000 of its own shares.

Required

Is this a share-based payment transaction? Should Mulgogi Ltd recognise the acquisition cost as an asset or an expense? Explain.

14.4 Equity-settled share-based payment transactions ★ LO3, 4

On 1 January 2022, Colette Park Ltd announces a grant of 500 share options to each of its 20 senior executives. The grant is conditional on the employee continuing to work for Colette Park Ltd for the next 3 years. The fair value of each share option is estimated to be $20. On the basis of a weighted average probability, Colette Park Ltd estimates that 10% of its senior executives will leave during the vesting period.

Required

Prepare a schedule setting out the annual and cumulative remuneration expense to be recognised by Colette Park Ltd for services rendered as consideration for the share options granted.

14.5 Share-based payment with a non-vesting condition ★ ★ ★ LO3, 4, 5

An employee is offered the opportunity to contribute 10% of their annual salary of $3000 across the next 2 years to a plan under which they receive share options. The employee's accumulated contributions to the plan may be used to exercise the options at the end of the 2-year period. The estimated annual expense for this share-based payment arrangement is $200.

Required

Prepare the necessary journal entry or entries to recognise this arrangement at the end of the first year.

14.6 Cash-settled share-based payment transactions ★ LO3, 8

An entity receives inventories from a counterparty in exchange for a liability based on the price of 4000 of the entity's own shares. At the date of receiving the inventories, the entity's shares have a market value of $12 each.

Required

Measure the value of this transaction and prepare an appropriate journal entry to recognise it.

14.7 Modifications to equity-settled share-based payment transactions ★ ★ LO4, 7

At the beginning of year 1, James Ltd grants 100 share options to each of its 120 employees, conditional on the employee remaining in the employ of James Ltd over the next 2 years. The company estimates that the fair value of the options on grant date is $12. On the basis of a weighted average probability, James Ltd estimates that 15% of its employees will leave during the vesting period. At the end of year 1, ten employees have left, and James Ltd estimates that a further five will leave during year 2. By the end of year 1, the company's share price has dropped, and it decides to reprice the share options. It estimates that the fair value of the original share options is $7 and the fair value of the repriced share options is $10. Five employees leave during year 2.

Required

Prepare a schedule setting out the remuneration expense to be recognised at the end of years 1 and 2.

14.8 Accounting for a grant where the number of equity instruments expected to vest varies ★ ★

LO7

Mitchell Ltd grants 60 share options to each of its 200 employees. Each grant is conditional on the employee working for the company for the 3 years following the grant date. On grant date, the fair value of each share option is estimated to be $18. On the basis of a weighted average probability, the company estimates that 15% of its employees will leave during the 3-year vesting period.

During year 1, 12 employees leave and the company revises its estimate of total employee departures over the full 3-year period from 15% to 18%.

Required

Prepare a schedule setting out the annual and cumulative remuneration expense for year 1.

14.9 Accounting for a grant of share options where the exercise price varies ★ ★ LO7

At the beginning of 2022, Brandon Ltd grants 4000 employee share options with an exercise price of $40 to its newly appointed chief executive officer, conditional on the executive remaining in the company's employ for the next 3 years. The exercise price drops to $30 if Brandon Ltd's earnings increase by an average of 10% per year over the 3-year period. On grant date, the estimated fair value of the employee share options with an exercise price of $30 is $22 per option. If the exercise price is $40, the options have an estimated fair value of $17 each.

During 2022, Brandon Ltd's earnings increased by 8% and are expected to continue to increase at this rate over the next 2 years.

Required

Prepare a schedule setting out the annual remuneration expense to be recognised by Brandon Ltd and the cumulative remuneration expense for 2022.

14.10 **Accounting for a grant with a market condition** ★ ★   **LO5, 7**

At the beginning of 2022, Montose Bay Ltd grants 10 000 share options to a senior marketing executive, conditional on the executive remaining in the company's employ until the end of 2024. The share options cannot be exercised unless the share price has increased from $20 at the beginning of 2022 to above $30 at the end of 2024. If the share price is above $30 at the end of 2022, the share options can be exercised at any time during the following 5 years. Montose Bay Ltd applies a binomial option-pricing model that takes into account the possibility that the share price will exceed $30 at the end of 2024 and the possibility that the share price will not exceed $30 at the end of 2024. The fair value of the share options with this market condition is estimated to be $14 per option.

Required

Calculate the annual and cumulative remuneration expense to be recognised by Montose Bay Ltd for 2022.

14.11 **Application of the intrinsic value method** ★ ★ ★   **LO6**

At the beginning of 2022, Albion Ltd grants 2000 share options to each of its 40 most senior executives. The share options have a life of 5 years and will vest at the end of year 3 if the executives remain in service until then. The exercise price is $50 and Albion Ltd's share price is also $50 at the grant date. As the company's share options have characteristics significantly different from those of other traded share options, the use of option-pricing models will not provide a reliable measure of fair value at grant date.

The company's share price during years 1–3 is shown below.

Year	Share price at year-end	Estimated number of executives departing in each year	Number of executives remaining at year-end	Number of share options exercised at year-end
1	$53	3	36	0
2	$55	2	34	0
3	$65	1	33	0

Required

Calculate the annual and cumulative remuneration expense to be recognised by Albion Ltd for each of the 3 years.

14.12 **Accounting for cash-settled share-based payment transactions** ★ ★ ★   **LO3, 8**

Ashmore Ltd grants 1000 share appreciation rights (SARs) to 10 senior managers, to be taken in cash within 2 years of vesting date on condition that the managers do not leave in the next 3 years. The SARs vest at the end of year 3. Ashmore Ltd estimates the fair value of the SARs at the end of each year in which a liability exists as shown below. The intrinsic value of the SARs at the date of exercise at the end of year 3 is also shown.

Year	Fair value	Intrinsic value	Number of managers who exercised their SARs
1	$ 8.80		
2	$11.00		
3	$20.40	$18.00	4

During year 1, one employee leaves and Ashmore Ltd estimates that a further two will leave before the end of year 3. One employee leaves during year 2 and the corporation estimates that another employee will depart during year 3. One employee leaves during year 3. At the end of year 3, four employees exercise their SARs.

Required

Prepare a schedule setting out the expense and liability that Ashmore Ltd must recognise at the end of each of the first 3 years.

14.13 Disclosure ★ ★ ★   **LO9**

Fernvale Ltd operates a share option plan for its officers, employees and consultants for up to 10% of its outstanding shares. Under this plan, the exercise price of each option equals the closing market price of the shares on the day before the grant. Each option has a term of 5 years and vests one-third on each of the 3 years following grant date. Before this financial period, Fernvale Ltd has accounted for its share option plan on settlement date and no expense has been recognised.

Required

Prepare an appropriate memorandum outlining the disclosures that will need to be made in Fernvale Ltd's financial statement following the adoption of AASB 2/IFRS 2.

REFERENCE

Woolworths Group Limited 2018, *Annual report 2018*, www.woolworthsgroup.com.au.

ACKNOWLEDGEMENTS

Photo: © Vitchanan Photography / Shutterstock.com

Photo: © Dragon Images / Shutterstock.com

Figures 14.1, 14.2, 14.4: © Woolworths Group Limited 2018

Figure 14.3 and text: © 2019 Australian Accounting Standards Board (AASB). The text, graphics and layout of this publication are protected by Australian copyright law and the comparable law of other countries. No part of the publication may be reproduced, stored or transmitted in any form or by any means without the prior written permission of the AASB except as permitted by law. For reproduction or publication, permission should be sought in writing from the AASB. Requests in the first instance should be addressed to the National Director, Australian Accounting Standards Board, PO Box 204, Collins Street West, Victoria 8007.

Text: © IFRS. This publication contains copyright material of the IFRS Foundation in respect of which all rights are reserved. Reproduced by John Wiley & Sons Australia, Ltd with the permission of the IFRS Foundation. No permission granted to third parties to reproduce or distribute. For full access to IFRS Standards and the work of the IFRS Foundation please visit http://eifrs.ifrs.org. The International Accounting Standards Board, the IFRS Foundation, the authors and the publishers do not accept responsibility for any loss caused by acting or refraining from acting in reliance on the material in this publication, whether such loss is caused by negligence or otherwise.

CHAPTER 15

Revenue

CHAPTER AIM

This chapter discusses the differences between income and revenue. The aim of this chapter is to demonstrate the accounting treatment of revenue as required for different types of events and transactions.

LEARNING OBJECTIVES

After studying this chapter, you should be able to:

15.1 describe the scope of AASB 15/IFRS 15

15.2 explain the definition of 'income' under AASB 15/IFRS 15 and distinguish it from the definition of 'revenue'

15.3 explain and apply the five steps in recognising revenue

15.4 explain and apply the recognition criteria for revenue, distinguishing between the sale of goods and the rendering of services

15.5 interpret and analyse the revenue recognition issues and disclosures arising in specific industries in practice

15.6 describe the disclosure requirements of AASB 15/IFRS 15.

CONCEPTS FOR REVIEW

Before studying this chapter, you should understand and, if necessary, revise:

• the definition of income in the *Conceptual Framework*
• the recognition criteria for income in the *Conceptual Framework*.

15.1 The scope of AASB 15/IFRS 15

LEARNING OBJECTIVE 15.1 Describe the scope of AASB 15/IFRS 15.

The main issue in accounting for revenue is in determining when the revenue is to be recognised. AASB 15/IFRS 15 establishes the principles about the nature, amount, timing and uncertainty of revenue and cash flows arising from a contract with a customer that an entity shall apply to report useful information to users of financial statements. Paragraph 31 requires revenue to be recognised when an entity satisfies a performance obligation by transferring promised goods or services (i.e. an asset) to a **customer**. An asset is transferred when the customer obtains 'control' of that asset.

AASB 15/IFRS 15 paragraph 5 states that the standard shall be applied to all contracts with customers, except:

- lease agreements — see AASB 16/IFRS 16 *Leases* (see chapter 10)
- insurance contracts — see AASB 4/IFRS 4 *Insurance Contracts*
- financial instruments and other contractual rights or obligations — see AASB 9/IFRS 9 *Financial Instruments*, AASB 10/IFRS 10 *Consolidated Financial Statements*, AASB 11/IFRS 11 *Joint Arrangements*, AASB 127/IAS 27 *Separate Financial Statements* and AASB 128/IAS 28 *Investments in Associates and Joint Ventures*
- non-monetary exchanges between entities in the same line of business to facilitate sales to customers or potential customers (e.g. an arrangement between two oil companies that agree to an exchange of oil to meet demand from their customers in different locations on a timely basis).

> **LEARNING CHECK**
>
> ☐ AASB 15/IFRS 15 applies to a contract only if the counterparty to the contract is a customer.
> ☐ AASB 15/IFRS 15 requires revenue to be recognised when the customer obtains control of a transferred asset.

15.2 The definitions of income and revenue

LEARNING OBJECTIVE 15.2 Explain the definition of 'income' under AASB 15/IFRS 15 and distinguish it from the definition of 'revenue'.

Income and expenses are directly related to an entity's financial performance (as represented by the statement of profit or loss and other comprehensive income).

15.2.1 Income

Income is defined in Appendix A of AASB 15/IFRS 15 as follows.

> Increases in economic benefits during the accounting period in the form of inflows or enhancements of assets or decreases of liabilities that result in an increase in equity, other than those relating to contributions from equity participants.

The *Conceptual Framework* (paragraph 4.68) defines income similarly:

> Income is increases in assets, or decreases in liabilities, that result in increases in equity, other than those relating to contributions from holders of equity claims.

In other words, an increase in an asset or a decrease in a liability will result in income, unless the increase or decrease results from an equity contribution (such as cash raised through share capital).

The definition of income is very broad, being based, in effect, on statement of financial position movements. The elements of the statement of financial position (assets, liabilities and equity) are defined first in the *Conceptual Framework*, before the elements of the statement of comprehensive income. Therefore, the statement of profit or loss and other comprehensive income is derived from the statement of financial position according to a strict reading of the *Conceptual Framework*. This is known as 'the asset/liability' model (see section 15.4.1).

15.2.2 Revenue

Revenue is defined in Appendix A of AASB 15/IFRS 15 as follows.

> Income arising in the course of an entity's ordinary activities.

It can be seen then that all revenue is income, but that income is a broader concept. Some income may arise other than in the course of an entity's ordinary activities. In addition to revenue, income also includes **gains**. Gains represent other items that meet the definition of income, but are not revenue. Gains include, for example, gains on disposal of non-current assets (see chapter 5) and unrealised gains on the upward revaluation of property, plant and equipment under AASB 116/IAS 16 *Property, Plant and Equipment* (see chapter 5).

The only distinguishing feature of revenue is the reference to 'an entity's ordinary activities'. Therefore, revenue is essentially a *classification* of income to distinguish between an entity's ordinary activities and other activities. AASB 15/IFRS 15 does not define ordinary activities. The distinction between sources of income that fall within ordinary activities and those that are outside ordinary activities is a matter of professional judgement.

15.2.3 Ordinary activities and gross inflows

Since ordinary activities are not defined in the *Conceptual Framework* or in AASB 15/IFRS 15, the meaning of 'ordinary' is left to entities to determine for themselves. Most companies interpret ordinary as relating to their core business operations, but this is not without some controversy.

Revenue is a gross concept, whereas gains tend to be net (although this is not always the case; e.g. unrealised gains on the upward revaluation of certain assets can be gross). AASB 101/IAS 1 *Presentation of Financial Statements* discusses this in paragraph 34:

> AASB 15 [IFRS 15] *Revenue from Contracts with Customers* requires an entity to measure revenue from contracts with customers at the amount of consideration to which the entity expects to be entitled in exchange for transferring promised goods or services. For example, the amount of revenue recognised reflects any trade discounts and volume rebates the entity allows. An entity undertakes, in the course of its ordinary activities, other transactions that do not generate revenue but are incidental to the main revenue-generating activities. An entity presents the results of such transactions, when this presentation reflects the substance of the transaction or other event, by netting any income with related expenses arising on the same transaction. For example:
>
> (a) an entity presents gains and losses on the disposal of non-current assets, including investments and operating assets, by deducting from the amount of consideration on disposal the carrying amount of the asset and related selling expenses . . .

Once an item *is* classified as revenue, the question of *gross or net* can still arise. This is addressed in paragraph B35B of AASB 15/IFRS 15, which states that an entity shall recognise revenue in the gross amount of consideration to which it expects to be entitled in exchange for those goods or services transferred. Amounts such as sales taxes and goods and services taxes are not economic benefits that flow to the entity as they are simply collected on behalf of third parties. They do not result in increases in equity and, therefore, do not meet the definition of revenue. Similarly, in an agency relationship where an entity's performance obligation is to arrange for the provision of goods or services by another party, amounts collected on behalf of the principal are not gross inflows flowing to the agent and are not to be recognised as revenue. Rather, the revenue is the amount of fee or commission received or receivable by the agent. This fee or commission might be the net amount of consideration that the entity retains after paying the other party the consideration received in exchange for the goods or services.

Figure 15.1 summarises the distinction between income and revenue.

LEARNING CHECK

☐ AASB 15/IFRS 15 defines income as increases in economic benefits during the accounting period in the form of inflows or enhancements of assets or decreases of liabilities that result in an increase in equity, other than those relating to contributions from equity participants.

☐ The definition of income is based on statement of financial position movements.

☐ Income includes revenue and gains.

- ☐ Revenue is income arising in the course of an entity's ordinary activities.
- ☐ Gains represent items that meet the definition of income, but that are not revenue.
- ☐ Revenues are usually reported in gross amounts whereas gains are reported in net.
- ☐ Gains on disposal of property, plant and equipment are prohibited from being classified as revenue.
- ☐ Amounts collected on behalf of third parties, such as sales taxes and goods and services taxes, and amounts received on behalf of the principal in an agency relationship, do not meet the definition of revenue and should be excluded from being reported as revenue.

FIGURE 15.1 Distinguishing income from revenue

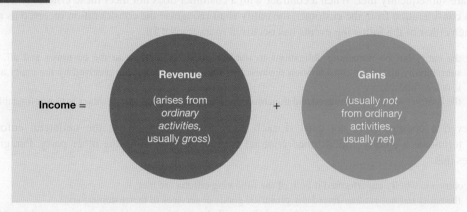

15.3 The steps in recognising revenue

LEARNING OBJECTIVE 15.3 Explain and apply the five steps in recognising revenue.

AASB 15/IFRS 15 identifies five steps in recognising revenue:
1. Identify the contract or contracts with the customer.
2. Identify the performance obligations in the contract.
3. Determine the transaction price.
4. Allocate the transaction price to the performance obligation.
5. Recognise revenue when (or as) the entity satisfies a performance obligation.

15.3.1 Step 1. Identify the contract or contracts with the customer

Appendix A of AASB 15/IFRS 15 defines a **contract** as follows.

> An agreement between two or more parties that creates enforceable rights and obligations.

For example, a typical contract for the sale of goods creates an obligation for the seller to deliver the goods, or make them available for collection, and a right to receive the agreed price when the customer has taken delivery of the goods. As described in paragraph 10 of AASB 15/IFRS 15:

> The practices and processes for establishing contracts with customers vary across legal jurisdictions, industries and entities. In addition, they may vary within an entity (for example, they may depend on the class of customer or the nature of the promised goods or services). An entity shall consider those practices and processes in determining whether and when an agreement with a customer creates enforceable rights and obligations.

AASB 15/IFRS 15 paragraph 9 requires that:

> An entity shall account for a contract with a customer that is within the scope of this Standard only when all of the following criteria are met:
> (a) the parties to the contract have approved the contract (in writing, orally or in accordance with other customary business practices) and are committed to perform their respective obligations;

(b) the entity can identify each party's rights regarding the goods or services to be transferred;

(c) the entity can identify the payment terms for the goods or services to be transferred;

(d) the contract has commercial substance (i.e. the risk, timing or amount of the entity's future cash flows is expected to change as a result of the contract); and

(e) it is probable that the entity will collect the consideration to which it will be entitled in exchange for the goods or services that will be transferred to the customer. In evaluating whether collectability of an amount of consideration is probable, an entity shall consider only the customer's ability and intention to pay that amount of consideration when it is due. The amount of consideration to which the entity will be entitled may be less than the price stated in the contract if the consideration is variable because the entity may offer the customer a price concession.

If these criteria are not met, an entity shall continue to assess the contract to determine whether these criteria are subsequently met. When a contract with a customer does not meet these criteria and an entity receives consideration from the customer, the entity shall recognise the consideration received as revenue only when either of the following events has occurred (paragraph 15):

(a) the entity has no remaining obligations to transfer goods or services to the customer and all, or substantially all, of the consideration promised by the customer has been received by the entity and is non-refundable; or

(b) the contract has been terminated and the consideration received from the customer is non-refundable.

However, a contract does not exist if each party to the contract has the unilateral enforceable right to terminate a wholly unperformed contract without compensating the other party. Paragraph 12 stipulates that:

A contract is wholly unperformed if both of the following criteria are met:

(a) the entity has not yet transferred any promised goods or services to the customer; and

(b) the entity has not yet received, and is not yet entitled to receive, any consideration in exchange for promised goods or services.

For example, if a customer placed an order for goods but cancelled the order before the goods were shipped to the customer and the customer is not required to compensate the seller on the cancellation, the sales contract is deemed to not exist and the seller shall not recognise the sales.

15.3.2 Step 2. Identify the performance obligations in the contract

When the entity enters into a contract with a customer it should identify the performance obligations (AASB 15/IFRS 15 paragraph 22). A **performance obligation** is defined in Appendix A of AASB 15/ IFRS 15 as follows.

A promise in a contract with a customer to transfer to the customer either:

(a) a good or service (or a bundle of goods or services) that is distinct; or

(b) a series of distinct goods or services that are substantially the same and that have the same pattern of transfer to the customer.

Paragraph 27 of AASB 15/IFRS 15 specifies two criteria that must both be met for a good or service to be distinct:

- the customer can benefit from the good or service on its own or in conjunction with other readily available resources
- the entity's promise to transfer the good or service to the customer is separately identifiable in the contract.

For example, a furniture store agrees to provide a bed and a desk, and separately identifies these items in the agreement with the customer. The customer can use the desk without the bed. Similarly, the customer could benefit from the bed, albeit in conjunction with readily available resources, such as sheets, without using the desk. Therefore, the bed and the desk are each distinct performance obligations of the contract with the customer. However, if a builder agreed to deliver timber to a house and to use the timber to construct an extension, could the materials be distinct goods in the contract with the customer? No, the customer would not benefit from the delivery of the timber without the builder's services to construct the extension. Further, that the builder provides a significant service of integrating the good (i.e. the timber) with other goods (any other materials used) and services promised in the contract is indicative that the delivery of the timber is not separately identifiable in the contract (AASB 15/IFRS 15 paragraph 29).

15.3.3 Step 3. Determine the transaction price

When a performance obligation is satisfied, an entity shall recognise the transaction as revenue at the transaction price. Appendix A of AASB 15/IFRS 15 defines the **transaction price** as follows.

> The amount of consideration to which the entity expects to be entitled in exchange for transferring promised goods or services to a customer, excluding amounts collected on behalf of third parties [e.g. GST].

Variable consideration

The transaction price may include fixed amounts, variable amounts or both. Sources of variation in consideration with customers include rebates for large quantities purchased over a specified period, discounts, price concessions and performance bonuses that may be dependent upon future events. For example, the transaction price could be variable if either a fixed amount is promised as a performance bonus on achievement of a specified milestone or the product was sold with a right of return.

When variable consideration arises, the entity estimates the transaction price by using either the expected value or the most likely amount.

- The *expected value* is the sum of probability-weighted amounts in a range of possible consideration amounts (AASB 15/IFRS 15 paragraph 53). An expected value may be used if an entity has a large number of contracts with similar characteristics.
- The *most likely* amount is the one most likely outcome of the contract. The most likely outcome can be used if there are only two possible outcomes (e.g. an entity either achieves a performance bonus or does not).

Once a method is selected an entity shall apply it consistently throughout the contract.

Trying to fully account for the consideration in a timely manner can increase the uncertainty of the measurement of the consideration and, hence, the revenue. AASB 15/IFRS 15 addresses this uncertainty by imposing restrictive criteria for the inclusion of variable consideration in the transaction price. Variable consideration is only included in the transaction price to the extent that it is highly probable that its inclusion will not result in a significant revenue reversal when the uncertainty is resolved. As described in paragraph 57 of AASB 15/IFRS 15:

> an entity shall consider both the likelihood and the magnitude of the revenue reversal. Factors that could increase the likelihood or the magnitude of a revenue reversal include, but are not limited to, any of the following:
> (a) the amount of consideration is highly susceptible to factors outside the entity's influence. Those factors may include volatility in a market, the judgement or actions of third parties, weather conditions and a high risk of obsolescence of the promised good or service.
> (b) the uncertainty about the amount of consideration is not expected to be resolved for a long period of time.
> (c) the entity's experience (or other evidence) with similar types of contracts is limited, or that experience (or other evidence) has limited predictive value.
> (d) the entity has a practice of either offering a broad range of price concessions or changing the payment terms and conditions of similar contracts in similar circumstances.
> (e) the contract has a large number and broad range of possible consideration amounts.

Accountants need to exercise judgement in estimating the variable component of consideration and in assessing the likelihood and significance of its potential reversal. Paragraph 59 of AASB 15/IFRS 15 requires the entity, at the end of each reporting period, to update the estimated transaction price to represent faithfully the circumstances at the end of the reporting period and the changes in circumstances during the reporting period.

Deferred consideration

In most cases, it is straightforward to calculate the fair value of the consideration received or receivable as the consideration is usually in the form of cash. The amount of cash to be paid is typically specified in an agreement. Sometimes, however, the amount to be paid is deferred for a period of time. **Deferred consideration** may take the form of interest-free credit provided to a buyer or acceptance of a note receivable bearing a below-market interest rate. In such cases, the fair value of the consideration will be less than the nominal amount of the cash receivable. Paragraph 60 of AASB 15/IFRS 15 specifies that an entity shall adjust the consideration amount for the effects of the time value of money if the timing of payments provides the customer and the entity with a significant benefit of financing the transfer of goods or services to the customer.

A significant financing component may exist regardless of whether the financing is explicitly stated in the contract or implied by the payment terms. Paragraph 61 provides that an entity shall assess whether a contract contains a financing component by considering:

(a) the difference, if any, between the amount of promised consideration and the cash selling price of the promised goods or services; and
(b) the combined effect of both of the following:
(i) the expected length of time between when the entity transfers the promised goods or services to the customer and when the customer pays for those goods or services; and
(ii) the prevailing interest rates in the relevant market.

Consideration amount shall be discounted using the discount rate that would be reflected in a separate financing transaction between the entity and its customer at contract inception. This rate can be determined by identifying the rate that discounts the nominal amount of the promised consideration to the price that customers would pay in cash for the goods and services when they transfer to the customer. Once determined, an entity shall use the same discount rate in the future.

Illustrative example 15.1 illustrates how deferred consideration should be measured under AASB 15/IFRS 15.

Measurement of deferred consideration

Chaise Ltd sells furniture and offers an interest-free period of 12 months to certain qualifying customers. Customer G qualifies for the interest-free period and purchases furniture on 30 June 2022. The current cash sales price of the furniture is $20 000. Customer G will pay $20 000 on 30 June 2023 (i.e. in 1 year's time).

The end of Chaise Ltd's reporting period is 30 June. Chaise Ltd determines that an appropriate discount rate for imputing interest to the transaction is 4% per annum. It determines that the present value of $20 000 to be received in 1 year's time is $19 230.

Required
What journal entries would Chaise Ltd record at 30 June 2022 and 30 June 2023?

Solution
At 30 June 2022, Chaise Ltd would record the following journal entry.

Receivable	Dr	20 000	
Revenue	Cr		19 230
Deferred interest	Cr		770
(To record sale of furniture with deferred consideration)			

For the year ended 30 June 2023, Chaise Ltd would record the following journal entries.

Deferred interest	Dr	770	
Interest revenue	Cr		770
(To recognise interest earned on the transaction in the statement of profit or loss and other comprehensive income)			
Cash	Dr	20 000	
Receivable	Cr		20 000
(To recognise receipt of cash)			

Exchanges or swaps

The requirements for measuring consideration where goods or services are exchanged or swapped are discussed in paragraphs 70 to 72 of AASB 15/IFRS 15 and depend on whether the swap or exchange is for goods or services of a distinct nature.

- An entity shall account for consideration payable to a customer as a reduction of the transaction price and, therefore, of revenue if it is related to an exchange for a non-distinct good or service.
- If the exchange involves a distinct good or service from the customer an entity shall account for the purchase of the good or service in the same way that it accounts for other purchases from suppliers.

When a customer promises consideration in a form other than cash, paragraph 66 of AASB 15/IFRS 15 requires the entity to measure the non-cash consideration at fair value. If the fair value of the non-cash consideration cannot be reasonably estimated, the entity measures the amount indirectly by reference to the stand-alone selling price of the goods or services promised to the customer (paragraph 67).

Illustrative example 15.2 illustrates how swaps and exchanges are accounted for under AASB 15/IFRS 15.

ILLUSTRATIVE EXAMPLE 15.2

Accounting for swaps and exchanges

Switchy Ltd swaps a container of its milk for a container of milk of Gertrudis Ltd in order to be able to deliver to a customer located closer to Gertrudis Ltd's distribution centre. The value of the container of milk is $100, which is the same for both Switchy Ltd and Gertrudis Ltd. Switchy Ltd would record the following journal entry.

Inventories — container 2	Dr	100
Inventories — container 1	Cr	100

No revenue is recorded in this transaction because the swap or exchange is for goods of a similar nature and value.

The following week, Switchy Ltd swaps a container of milk (with a value of $100) with Dairy Ltd in exchange for a container of cream. The value of Dairy Ltd's container of cream is $120. Switchy Ltd also pays $12 cash to Dairy Ltd. Switchy Ltd would record the following journal entry.

Inventories — container of cream	Dr	120
Revenue	Cr	108
Cash	Cr	12
Cost of sales	Dr	100
Inventories — container of milk	Cr	100

This transaction does generate revenue because the swap *is not* for goods of a similar nature and value. The revenue is measured at the fair value of the goods received, adjusted by the amount of any cash transferred.

15.3.4 Step 4. Allocate the transaction price to the performance obligation

When multiple performance obligations are identified in a contract with a customer, the entity must allocate the transaction price to each performance obligation. This is necessary because the revenue might be recognised at different times for the various performance obligations. Paragraph 74 of AASB 15/IFRS 15 requires the transaction price to be allocated to the performance obligations in the contract by reference to their relative **stand-alone selling prices**; that is, the price at which an entity would sell a promised good or service separately to a customer. Paragraph 79 of AASB 15/IFRS 15 stipulates that the methods for estimating the stand-alone selling price of a good or service include, but are not limited to, the:

- adjusted market assessment approach — in which an entity could evaluate the market in which it sells goods or services and estimate the price that a customer in that market would be willing to pay for those goods or services
- expected cost plus a margin approach — in which an entity forecasts its expected costs of satisfying a performance obligation and then adds an appropriate margin for that good or service.

If the transaction price allows for a discount compared with the sum of the selling prices of the separate performance obligations, the discount is allocated on the basis of relative stand-alone selling prices.

Illustrative example 15.3 illustrates how allocation of stand-alone selling prices are accounted for under AASB 15/IFRS 15.

ILLUSTRATIVE EXAMPLE 15.3

Revenue recognition for multiple-element arrangements

Sandstone Ltd provides a bundled service offering to Customer B. It charges Customer B $3000 for upfront advice and two ongoing services — 'on-call' advice and access to Sandstone Ltd's databases over a 2-year period.

Customer B pays the $3000 upfront.

Sandstone Ltd determines that, if it were to charge a separate fee for each service if sold separately, the fees would be as follows.

Upfront advice	$ 200
On-call advice	2 600
Access to databases	800

Given that the transaction price for the contract is $3000 while the stand-alone selling prices of the upfront advice, on-call advice and access to databases are $3600 in total, there is a discount of $600 ($3600 − $600). The discount is allocated to each component based on its relative stand-alone selling prices. In this example the approach results in the following allocation.

	Stand-alone selling prices $	Allocation of discount $	Allocated amount $
Upfront advice	200	200/3600 × 600 = 33	166
On-call advice	2 600	2600/3600 × 600 = 433	2 167
Access to databases	800	800/3600 × 600 = 133	667
Total	3 600		3 000

Sandstone Ltd would record the following journal entry at inception of the agreement.

Cash	Dr	3 000	
Revenue — upfront advice	Cr		166
Deferred revenue — on-call advice	Cr		2 167
Deferred revenue — access to databases	Cr		667

The deferred revenue for each of the undelivered elements (i.e. the on-call advice and the access to databases) will be recognised when those services are delivered. Because both the on-call advice and the access to databases are available to Customer B continuously over the period of the agreement, the revenue should be recognised in accordance with paragraph 35 of AASB 15/IFRS 15 (i.e. on a straight-line basis).

Since this agreement is for 2 years, in each year (assuming the financial year coincides with the agreement year) Sandstone Ltd would record the following entry.

Deferred revenue — on-call advice	Dr	1 083.50	
Deferred revenue — access to databases	Dr	333.50	
Revenue	Cr		1 417.00

By the end of the 2 years, Sandstone Ltd would have recorded total revenue of $3000, made up as follows.

Year 1	
Revenue — upfront advice	$ 166
Revenue — on-call advice and access to databases	1 417
Year 2	
Revenue — on-call advice and access to databases	1 417
Total	$3 000

This equals the total consideration agreed to at the inception of the agreement. Therefore, the allocation process does not alter the *amount* of revenue recognised; it only affects the *timing* of revenue recognition. (This should be distinguished from the case of deferred consideration where the amount of revenue *is* affected because the *payment is deferred* and this affects the fair value of the consideration.)

15.3.5 Step 5. Recognise revenue when (or as) the entity satisfies a performance obligation

Revenue is recognised when control passes to the customer. This may be at a point in time, such as when the goods are delivered to a customer, or when an airline conveys passenger to their destination. Paragraph 33 of AASB 15/IFRS 15 defines **control** as:

> the ability to direct the use of, and obtain substantially all of the remaining benefits from, the asset.

Alternatively, control over the asset (the goods or services provided to the customer) may transfer to the customer over time; that is, the performance obligation is satisfied over time. For example, consider an entity that enters into a 1-year contract to provide routine cleaning services on a weekly basis. The performance obligation is satisfied over time as the regular cleaning services are performed.

The recognition criteria will be discussed further in section 15.4.

LEARNING CHECK

☐ AASB 15/IFRS 15 identifies five steps in recognising revenue:
 1. Identify the contract or contracts with the customer.
 2. Identify the performance obligations in the contract.
 3. Determine the transaction price.
 4. Allocate the transaction price to the performance obligation.
 5. Recognise revenue when (or as) the entity satisfies a performance obligation.
☐ AASB 15/IFRS 15 requires revenue to be recognised when the entity satisfies a performance obligation and the customer obtains control of that asset.
☐ Revenue generated by exchanges or swaps for goods or services that are not of a similar nature and value shall be recorded as revenue and measured at the fair value of the goods or services received adjusted by the amount of any cash transferred.

15.4 The recognition criteria

LEARNING OBJECTIVE 15.4 Explain and apply the recognition criteria for revenue, distinguishing between the sale of goods and the rendering of services.

Before considering recognition criteria for the sale of goods, the rendering of services, interest, royalties and dividends, it is important to understand:
• the recognition criteria for income generally
• the identification of the transaction to which the recognition criteria should be applied.

15.4.1 The recognition criteria for income generally

Paragraph 5.4(a) of the *Conceptual Framework* states that:

> the recognition of income occurs at the same time as:
> (i) the initial recognition of an asset, or an increase in the carrying amount of an asset; or
> (ii) the derecognition of a liability, or a decrease in the carrying amount of a liability.

This means, in effect, that recognition of income occurs simultaneously with the recognition of increases in assets or decreases in liabilities, in accordance with the *Conceptual Framework*'s asset/liability model (see chapter 1 and section 15.2.1).

Paragraph 5.7 of the *Conceptual Framework* states that elements are only recognised if their recognition provides relevant information and a faithful representation (see chapter 1). For example, in some cases, economic benefits may not be probable until the consideration is received or until an uncertainty is removed and thus recognition may not provide relevant information. A distinction needs to be made between an uncertainty that *precludes* revenue recognition and an uncertainty that affects the *measurement* of revenue. An example of an uncertainty that *precludes* revenue recognition would be a government restriction on remitting consideration from a sale in a foreign country. In this case, no receivable and thus no revenue is recognised until the government grants permission because the test of probability of inflow of economic benefits is not met until that point.

An example of an uncertainty that affects the *measurement* of revenue would be an uncertainty regarding the collectability of an amount already included in revenue. Such an amount is recognised as an expense (commonly referred to as an 'allowance for doubtful debts') rather than as an adjustment of the amount of revenue already recognised.

Illustrative example 15.4 gives a simple example to illustrate the asset/liability model.

ILLUSTRATIVE EXAMPLE 15.4

Explaining the asset/liability model

Asha Ltd sells goods to Customer B for $100. Customer B enters into an agreement to buy the goods from Asha Ltd on 1 February for $100. Asha Ltd delivers the goods on 15 February. Customer B pays for the goods on 28 February.

On the agreement date (1 February), Asha Ltd has undertaken to deliver the goods to Customer B and Customer B has promised to pay for them. Asha Ltd has an obligation to deliver the goods and a right to receive payment once delivery has been made. However, until Asha Ltd delivers the goods it does not have an asset under the *Conceptual Framework* because it does not control the right to receive payment until delivery. Similarly, Customer B has no liability under the *Conceptual Framework* because it has no obligation to pay until delivery has been made. The agreement is thus an executory contract (also known as an agreement equally proportionately unperformed) at agreement date because neither party to the contract has performed their obligations. In the case of such agreements, no asset or liability exists under the *Conceptual Framework*.

On the delivery date (15 February), Asha Ltd has performed under the agreement and is now entitled to receive payment. Asha Ltd thus has an asset under the *Conceptual Framework*. As the right to receive payment is not an equity contribution, the increase in the asset meets the definition of income, and Asha Ltd would record the following journal entry.

Asset — receivable from Customer B	Dr	100
Income	Cr	100

On the payment date (28 February), Asha Ltd receives the cash from Customer B and records the following entry.

Cash	Dr	100
Asset — receivable from Customer B	Cr	100

The right to receive cash is replaced by the cash received.

This example illustrates how basic accrual accounting fits within the asset/liability model of the *Conceptual Framework*.

Now assume that the agreement states that from 15 February, when Asha Ltd delivers the goods, it must continue to maintain them for a year for Customer B. Customer B still pays for the goods on 28 February; however, Customer B is entitled to a refund of 20% of the amount paid if Asha Ltd does not satisfactorily maintain the goods for the year as required.

Under the asset/liability model, Asha Ltd has an obligation to maintain the goods and to refund the cash as from 15 February. Thus, it would record the following entry.

Asset — receivable from Customer B	Dr	100
Liability (obligation to maintain goods and refund cash)	Cr	20
Income	Cr	80

Under the *Conceptual Framework*, the definition of income is not met for 100% of the amount receivable because, while there has been an increase in an asset, there has also been an increase in a liability. The measurement of these amounts is not addressed in the *Conceptual Framework*.

On the payment date (28 February), Asha Ltd receives the cash from Customer B and records the following entry.

Cash	Dr	100	
Asset — receivable from Customer B	Cr		100

The right to receive cash is replaced by the cash received as in the previous case. However, Asha Ltd still has a liability as described above. When this liability is settled — for example, when the maintenance period is complete or over the period of the maintenance agreement — Asha Ltd records the following entry.

Liability (obligation to maintain goods and refund cash)	Dr	20	
Income	Cr		20

The *definition* of income is met because there has been a reduction in a liability. The *recognition criteria* for income have also been met simultaneously with the reduction of the liability because the reduction of the liability can be reliably measured at that point.

Thus, under the asset/liability model, income is recognised in two parts: the first when the receivable from Customer B is recognised; and the second when the liability to Customer B is settled.

In practice, this is no different from traditional models such as an earnings model that 'defers' revenue in order to record revenue only when it is earned. In the example above, the liability to Customer B would likely be described as 'deferred income' under an earnings model and released to income either over the maintenance agreement period or at the end of the period depending on the terms of the agreement. Therefore, in practice there is no difference between the asset/liability model and the earnings model in this case.

However, another approach that exists in practice is to record 100% of the revenue and then provide for the cost of meeting the obligation. This gives a different outcome from the asset/liability model.

15.4.2 Sale of goods

Revenue recognition in relation to contracts with customers requires an entity to satisfy performance obligations and transfer control of the asset to the customer. Paragraph 33 of AASB 15/IFRS 15 further provides that:

Goods and services are assets, even if only momentarily, when they are received and used (as in the case of many services). Control of an asset refers to the ability to direct the use of, and obtain substantially all of the remaining benefits from, the asset. Control includes the ability to prevent other entities from directing the use of, and obtaining the benefits from, an asset. The benefits of an asset are the potential cash flows (inflows or saving in outflows) that can be obtained directly or indirectly in many ways, such as by:
(a) using the asset to produce goods or provide services (including public services);
(b) using the asset to enhance the value of other assets;
(c) using the asset to settle liabilities or reduce expenses;
(d) selling or exchanging the asset;
(e) pledging the asset to secure a loan; and
(f) holding the asset.

When an entity transfers control of a product to a customer and also gives the customer the right to return the product and receive a refund of consideration paid, an entity shall recognise not only the revenue for the transferred products in the amount of consideration to which the entity expects to be entitled but also a refund liability and an asset for its rights to recover products from customers on settling the refund liability. This means the promise of an entity to accept a returned product during the return period shall not be accounted for as a performance obligation in addition to the obligation to provide a refund (AASB 15/IFRS 15 paragraphs B20–B22).

When an entity delivers a product to another party for sale to end customers, revenue cannot be recognised if the other party has no control of the product at that point in time, such as products held in a consignment arrangement. Paragraph B78 of AASB 15/IFRS 15 provides some indicators that an arrangement is a consignment arrangement:

(a) the product is controlled by the entity until a specified event occurs, such as the sale of the product to a customer of the dealer or until a specified period expires;
(b) the entity is able to require the return of the product or transfer the product to a third party (such as another dealer); and
(c) the dealer does not have an unconditional obligation to pay for the product (although it might be required to pay a deposit).

Illustrative examples 15.5–15.8 further demonstrate the application of AASB 15/IFRS 15 in respect of the sale of goods. In all cases reliable measurement is assumed.

ILLUSTRATIVE EXAMPLE 15.5

Sales of goods where the buyer delays delivery

Aaron Ltd sells goods to Customer B. Customer B requests Aaron Ltd hold delivery of the goods while it is preparing its site to be ready for delivery. Customer B formally accepts responsibility for the goods on the invoice date on the basis that it would be the usual delivery date.

Assuming the other revenue recognition criteria are met, Aaron Ltd recognises revenue on the invoice date because at that date it has transferred control of the asset to Customer B and it is probable that future economic benefits will flow (i.e. Customer B will pay for the goods because it has formally accepted responsibility for them even though they have not yet been delivered).

ILLUSTRATIVE EXAMPLE 15.6

Goods shipped subject to minor conditions

Aaron Ltd sells goods to Customer B. On the delivery date, Aaron Ltd invoices Customer B and is obliged to install the goods. The installation is minor and involves connecting the goods to an electric socket and testing that the goods perform when connected.

The key issue here is whether the installation requirement is a major or minor performance obligation of Aaron Ltd. If it is a minor performance obligation with little likelihood that it will not be met then Aaron Ltd has transferred the control of the asset to Customer B on delivery, and it is probable that future economic benefits will flow (i.e. Customer B will pay for the goods even though installation is not complete because the installation is minor and unlikely to result in non-performance of the goods).

In this case, the performance obligation is minor and therefore Aaron Ltd recognises revenue on the delivery date.

ILLUSTRATIVE EXAMPLE 15.7

Goods shipped subject to major conditions

Aaron Ltd sells goods to Customer B. On the delivery date, Aaron Ltd invoices Customer B and is obliged to install the goods. The installation is major and involves a few days' worth of work plus testing that the goods perform when installed.

In this case, the installation requirement is a major performance obligation. If Aaron Ltd does not meet the obligation, Customer B would not accept the goods and would not pay for them. Thus, Aaron Ltd has not transferred the control of the asset to Customer B on delivery, and it is not probable that future economic benefits will flow (i.e. Customer B will not accept or pay for the goods until installation is complete because the installation is major and could result in non-performance of the goods if not properly performed).

In this case, the performance obligation is significant and therefore Aaron Ltd does not recognise revenue until the installation is complete.

Consignment sales

Aaron Ltd sells goods to Customer B. The agreement between the two parties states that Customer B will hold those goods on consignment and will only pay for the goods to the extent that Customer B on-sells the goods to third parties.

In this case, Aaron Ltd has not transferred the control of the asset to Customer B on delivery, and it is not probable that future economic benefits will flow; nor, indeed, can it be argued that revenue can be reliably measured because Customer B will only pay for those goods that it on-sells to third parties. Until Company B on-sells the goods, it has no requirement to pay anything to Aaron Ltd.

Accordingly, Aaron Ltd does not recognise any revenue until Customer B has on-sold the goods.

Warranties

A warranty that accompanies a sale of goods is relevant to accounting for revenue if it is a performance obligation of the contract with a customer.

If the warranty does *not* provide the customer with a service beyond assurance that the product complies with the agreed specification, the warranty is *not* considered to be a performance obligation under the contract with the customer. This would typically be the case where the warranty is merely the warranty that the entity is legally required to provide, or a warranty that is standard for the industry. However, if the entity sells a product and charges extra for an extended warranty, the extended warranty is an additional service and therefore should be treated as a performance obligation (AASB 15 paragraphs B28–B33). The entity will then need to recognise revenue based on the extra charge when or, most commonly, over the period the performance obligation is satisfied.

15.4.3 Rendering of services

The revenue recognition criteria for the rendering of services shall be determined by reference to the performance obligations satisfied over time if the criteria stated in paragraph 35 of AASB 15/IFRS 15 are met. A performance obligation would be considered to have been satisfied over time when at least one of the following criteria is met:

(a) the customer simultaneously receives and consumes the benefits provided by the entity's performance as the entity performs [e.g. routine and recurring services such as a cleaning service];

(b) the entity's performance creates or enhances an asset (for example, work in progress) that the customer controls as the asset is created or enhanced; or

(c) the entity's performance does not create an asset with an alternative use to the entity ... and the entity has an enforceable right to payment for performance completed to date.

An entity shall consider the effects of contractual restrictions and practical limitations in assessing whether an asset has an alternative use to an entity. A contractual restriction is substantive for the asset not to have an alternative use to the entity if a customer could enforce its rights to the promised asset if the entity sought to direct the asset for another use. A practical limitation on an entity's ability to direct an asset for another use exists if significant economic losses will be incurred if an entity directs the asset for another use.

In accounting for construction contracts that carry across a number of accounting periods, individual construction contracts such as different building sites shall be accounted for separately by determining the appropriate revenue and costs to be allocated to each contract in each accounting period. Appropriate methods of measuring progress within each accounting period include output methods and input methods.

• **Output methods** recognise revenue on the basis of direct measurements of the value of the goods or services transferred to customers relative to the remaining goods or services promised under the contract. Examples include surveys of performance completed to date, appraisals of results achieved, time elapsed and units delivered. However, the information required to apply this method may not be directly observable. Hence, an input method may be necessary.

• **Input methods** recognise revenue on the basis of the entity's efforts or inputs to the satisfaction of a performance obligation, such as costs incurred, resources consumed, labour hours expended or machine hours used, relative to the total expected inputs to the satisfaction of that performance obligation.

Paragraph 44 of AASB 15/IFRS 15 requires that an entity recognise revenue for a performance obligation satisfied over time only if the entity has reliable information to reasonably measure its progress towards complete satisfaction of the performance obligation. The general requirement that the customer has control of the asset throughout the construction is also a requirement before the revenue can be recognised. If these conditions are not met, no profit is to be brought to account until they are satisfied.

Illustrative example 15.9 illustrates how the input method is applied.

ILLUSTRATIVE EXAMPLE 15.9

Measuring progress using the input method

On 1 March 2023, Paintrix Ltd enters into an agreement with Customer J to renovate Customer J's offices. The agreement states that the total consideration to be paid for the renovation will be $450 000. Paintrix Ltd expects that its total costs for the renovation will be $380 000. As at the end of its reporting period, 30 June 2023, Paintrix Ltd had incurred labour costs of $110 000 and materials costs of $150 000. Of the materials costs, $45 000 is in respect of materials that have not yet been used in the renovation. All labour costs are in respect of services performed on the renovation project. As at 30 June 2023, Customer J had made progress payments to Paintrix Ltd of $265 000.

Required
Calculate Paintrix Ltd's revenue to be recognised using the input method outlined in paragraph B19 of AASB 15/IFRS 15.

Solution

Total costs incurred to date	$260 000	
Less: Costs in respect of services not yet performed	(45 000)	
Total	$215 000	(a)
Total estimated costs	$380 000	(b)
Measurement of progress	57%	(a)/(b)
Total estimated revenue under the agreement	$450 000	(c)
Revenue to be recognised at 30 June 2023	$254 605	57% × (c)

Note that payments made by Customer J cannot be used as a basis for measuring progress towards complete satisfaction of a performance obligation under AASB 15/IFRS 15 paragraph B19(a). Also note that Paintrix Ltd will show a loss on this project as at 30 June 2023 (revenue of $254 605 less costs incurred to date of $260 000 equals a loss of $5395). This is because it has incurred materials costs of $45 000 that are not permitted to be used in measuring performance because they are in respect of services that have not yet been performed. The materials will need to be used in the provision of future services on the project. However, Paintrix Ltd could argue that it should defer the costs of $45 000 (i.e. not recognise an expense) until the related materials are used. If Paintrix Ltd deferred these costs, then it would recognise a profit of $39 605 for the period ended 30 June 2023 (revenue of $254 605 less costs incurred to date recognised as expenses of $215 000).

For each performance obligation satisfied over time, an entity shall recognise revenue over time by measuring the progress towards complete satisfaction of that performance obligation. Paragraph 40 of AASB 15/IFRS 15 requires the same method of measuring progress for each performance obligation to be applied consistently to similar performance obligations and in similar circumstances. If a performance obligation is not satisfied over time, an entity satisfies the performance obligation at a point in time. For example, an entity might charge fees for tuition over a period of time. Tuition fees would be recognised on a straight-line basis over the period of instruction.

How does this relate to the asset/liability model? Take the example of tuition fees. Assume an entity enters into an agreement to provide tuition for 1 year and charges an upfront fee of $12 000. Under the asset/liability model the entity would record the following journal entry on day 1 of the agreement.

Cash	Dr	12 000
Liability (obligation to provide tuition)	Cr	12 000

As the services are provided, the entity would record the following entry.

Liability (obligation to provide tuition)	Dr	xxx
Revenue	Cr	xxx

The asset/liability model does not prescribe how the various assets and liabilities are to be measured. Under AASB 15/IFRS 15, the first entry would be the same and the credit can also be described as 'deferred revenue'. The second and following entries are also the same as under the asset/liability model and, in addition, AASB 15/IFRS 15 prescribes that the amount recognised would be $1000 per month (i.e. on a straight-line basis over the period of the agreement).

In the asset/liability model, the credit recognised at inception of the agreement is known as a 'performance obligation'. While the terminology used is different, the concept of not recognising revenue until performance of the service has occurred is consistent between the two approaches.

If an entity does not satisfy a performance obligation 'over time', it is satisfied 'at a point in time'. For example, admission fees to an event would be recognised when the event is staged. Paragraph 38 of AASB 15/IFRS 15 provides some indicators that suggest an entity satisfies the performance obligations by transferring control of the completed services to the customer:

(a) The entity has a present right to payment for the asset . . .
(b) The customer has legal title to the asset . . .
(c) The entity has transferred physical possession of the asset . . .
(d) The customer has the significant risks and rewards of ownership of the asset . . .
(e) The customer has accepted the asset . . .

Illustrative examples 15.10–15.13 further demonstrate the application of AASB 15/IFRS 15 with regards to the rendering of services. In most of the examples one or two of the revenue recognition criteria in paragraph 38 are relatively more important to the transaction in question and these are highlighted in the examples. In all cases reliable measurement is assumed.

ILLUSTRATIVE EXAMPLE 15.10

Commissions and upfront fees

Cover Ltd is an insurance agent and provides insurance advisory services to Customer B. Cover Ltd receives a commission from insurance company Premium Ltd when Cover Ltd places Customer B's insurance policy with Premium Ltd.

The key issue with commissions is whether the revenue is recognised in full upfront or over an actual or implied service period.

In this example, Cover Ltd would record its commission revenue in full upfront if its only service was to place the related insurance policy with Customer B. However, if Cover Ltd is required to render further services to Customer B over the life of the policy then part of the commission would be deferred and recognised as revenue over the period during which the policy is in force.

Placement fees for arranging a loan

Basel Ltd is a financial adviser and provides advisory services to Customer B. Basel Ltd receives a placement fee from financial services company Farrah Ltd when Basel Ltd places Customer B's loan with Farrah Ltd.

In this case, Farrah Ltd has accepted the asset and Basel Ltd has a present right to the payment (in accordance with paragraph 38 of AASB 15/IFRS 15). As there is no further service obligation, Basel Ltd recognises its placement fee as at the date the loan is formally arranged.

Membership fees

Hockey Ltd is a sports club that charges membership fees. An upfront membership fee is payable on joining the club. In addition, an annual fee is charged at the commencement of each year. Both fees are non-refundable.

Again, the key question is whether the upfront fee contains any actual or implied ongoing service obligation. The upfront joining fee would usually not contain any ongoing service obligation and would provide membership only. If this is the case, then the joining fee would be recognised as revenue upfront. The annual fee would cover other services to be provided over the year — the key service being use of the facilities. Thus, the annual fee would be deferred and recognised as revenue over the year.

Subscription fees

Reeds Ltd is a publisher that charges non-refundable subscription fees. The subscription fee is payable each year in advance and entitles the customer to 12 magazines, one per month.

In this case, Reeds Ltd clearly has an obligation to deliver the magazines each month and thus should recognise revenue when each month's magazine is despatched to the customer.

☐ Income is recognised in the income statement when an increase in future economic benefits related to an increase in an asset or a decrease of a liability has arisen and can be measured reliably.

☐ Recognition criteria are usually applied separately to each transaction. However, in certain circumstances, it is necessary to apply the recognition criteria to the separately identifiable components of a single transaction in order to reflect the substance of the transaction.

☐ AASB 15/IFRS 15 provides guidance as to the conditions to be satisfied for an entity to recognise revenue from the sale of goods.

☐ When the outcome of a transaction involving the rendering of services can be estimated reliably, revenue associated with the transaction shall be recognised by reference to the performance obligation satisfied over time.

☐ In sales of goods where the buyer delays delivery, the seller will record the revenue accordingly if the seller has transferred the control of the asset to the buyer and it is probable that future economic benefits will flow.

☐ Revenue is normally recognised when the buyer accepts delivery, and installation and inspection are complete. However, where there is a major performance obligation, such as major installation, revenue can be recognised only when the performance obligation is met.

☐ If the recipient undertakes to sell the goods on behalf of the shipper in a consignment sale, revenue is recognised by the shipper when the goods are sold by the recipient to a third party.

☐ Insurance agency commissions received which do not require the agent to render further service are recognised as revenue by the agent on the effective commencement or renewal dates of the related policies. However, if the agent will be required to render further services during the life of the policy, that part of the commission is deferred and recognised as revenue over the period during which the policy is in force.

15.5 Revenue recognition issues in various industries in practice

LEARNING OBJECTIVE 15.5 Interpret and analyse the revenue recognition issues and disclosures arising in specific industries in practice.

Before addressing various industry issues, it is important to understand the principles for distinguishing between a principal and an agent in a transaction and for determining revenue in multiple-element transactions.

15.5.1 The principal/agent distinction

AASB 15/IFRS 15 includes revenue recognition with regards to transactions involving the principal–agent relationship. Paragraphs B35B and B36 state:

B35B. When (or as) an entity that is a principal satisfies a performance obligation, the entity recognises revenue in the gross amount of consideration to which it expects to be entitled in exchange for the specified good or service transferred.

B36. ... When (or as) an entity that is an agent satisfies a performance obligation, the entity recognises revenue in the amount of any fee or commission to which it expects to be entitled in exchange for arranging for the specified goods or services to be provided by the other party. An entity's fee or commission might be the net amount of consideration that the entity retains after paying the other party the consideration received in exchange for the goods or services to be provided by that party.

The key distinction is whether the principal or agent is exposed to the transfer of assets associated with the sale of goods or the rendering of services. Table 15.1 explains the indicators that help make this distinction.

TABLE 15.1   Indicators of whether an entity is acting as an agent or principal in a transaction

Feature of transaction	Principal	Agent
Responsibility for providing the goods and services	Primarily responsible for acceptable delivery of goods or services to the customer	Not responsible for acceptability to the customer; if the customer is not satisfied the agent will have recourse to the principal
Inventories risk — loss or damage, holding costs	Has inventories risk before or after the customer order and during shipping or on return	Has no inventories risk
Ability to set prices or provide additional goods or services	Has latitude in setting prices, can offer additional goods or services	Cannot amend prices or provide additional goods or services
Customer's credit risk (risk that the customer will not be able to pay for the goods or services once delivered)	Bears the credit risk for the amount receivable from the customer	Does not bear the credit risk
Pre-determined fee or commission for services	Usually does not earn a pre-determined fee or commission	Usually earns a pre-determined fee or commission

15.5.2 Telecommunications

Numerous revenue recognition issues arise in the telecommunications industry, including multiple-element arrangements such as those described above, upfront connection fees, the sale of handsets via distributors and fees from third-party content providers.

Multiple-element arrangements

Questions have been raised as to whether, in an arrangement where a handset is provided 'free' to a customer together with a contract for services, the cost of the handset to the provider could be recorded as a customer acquisition cost and capitalised as an asset. The principle was articulated in AASB 15/IFRS 15, which specified how the revenue side of the transaction should be accounted for, but did not address whether the costs can be deferred or how to determine whether components are separate or part of the multiple-element arrangement.

The key question is whether the provision of the handset forms part of a multiple-element arrangement or whether it is a separate transaction. This is often dependent on the facts and circumstances of the particular arrangement. If the provision of the handset is considered to be a separate transaction (e.g. because it is provided to the customer by a distributor who has no right of return to the telecommunications company and bears all the risks and rewards associated with the provision of the handset to the customer) then the cost of the handset to the telecommunications company should be treated as an expense when it is provided because there is no relationship to ongoing service revenue.

However, if the provision of the handset is considered to be an integral part of the service arrangement with the customer (e.g. because it is provided to the customer as part of its services agreement with the telecommunications company) then the cost of the handset to the telecommunications company could be deferred on the basis that the revenue from the entire arrangement is recognised over the period of the agreement.

Telstra Corporation Limited applies the former view in accounting policy note 3.2.2 to its 2018 financial statements, as illustrated in figure 15.2.

FIGURE 15.2   Deferred expenditure, Telstra

3.2 Goodwill and other intangible assets

3.2.2 Recognition and measurement

Deferred expenditure

Deferred expenditure mainly includes direct incremental costs of establishing a customer contract, costs incurred for basic access installation and connection fees for existing and new services, as well as deferred costs related to the revised nbn Definitive Agreements.

Significant items of expenditure are deferred to the extent that they are recoverable from future revenue and will contribute to our future earning capacity. Any costs in excess of future revenue are recognised immediately in the income statement.

We amortise deferred expenditure over the average period in which the related benefits are expected to be realised. The amortisation expense is recognised in our operating expenses.

Source: Telstra Corporation Limited (2018, p. 85).

Upfront connection fees

The key issue with fees received for connecting a customer to the telecommunications network is whether the revenue is recognised in full upfront or over an actual or implied service period. Most telecommunications companies consider the fee to form part of a multiple-element service arrangement with the customer, as illustrated in figure 15.3.

Sale of handsets via distributors

The key issue here is whether the distribution channels used by telecommunications companies are agents for the telecommunications company or whether they act in their own right as principals in a transaction with customers. Paragraph B36 of AASB 15/IFRS 15 makes it clear that where an entity acts as an agent it recognises only its commission received and the key distinction between agent and principal is based on the nature of its promise in fulfilling the performance obligation. An entity is a principal if it will provide the specified goods or services itself, but if it will arrange for the other party to provide those goods or services it is an agent. Say, for example, a distributor sells handsets to customers and at the same time signs them up to a service agreement with the telecommunications company. The telecommunications company provides the handsets to the distributor and pays a commission to the distributor when it signs up a customer to a services agreement with the telecommunications company. The customer can return the handset to the distributor if it is faulty and the distributor must replace the handset at its own cost. This indicates that the distributor acts as a principal in respect of the handset but as an agent in respect of the services. From the telecommunications company's perspective, the revenue, if any, it receives from the sale of the handsets to the distributor is recognised at the date of sale (and related costs are expensed) rather than being recognised over the service period as discussed in the section on multiple-element arrangements.

Fees from third-party content providers

The agent versus principal question is also fundamental in cases where third parties provide content (such as ringtones, transport updates and games) to mobile phone customers. The content can either be purchased separately by the customer or included in a price plan.

The telecommunications company usually receives a fee from the third party content provider for every subscriber to that content. The question is whether the telecommunications company should record gross revenue from the sale of services including the content, with an expense for the cost of the content, or the net amount (i.e. the amount attributable to the content provided to the customer less the cost of the content to the telecommunications company).

The answer, again, lies in analysing the facts and circumstances of each arrangement. In general terms, where the telecommunications company is simply acting as a vehicle for the third party's content and the third party is directly responsible to the customer for issues such as accuracy of the data provided, then the telecommunications should only record the net amount as revenue.

Alternatively, if the telecommunications company brands the content as its own and takes full responsibility to the customer for its accuracy then it should record the revenue gross.

Summary of revenue recognition issues

The extract in figure 15.3, from the accounting policy notes to the financial statements of Telstra Corporation Limited, serves as a summary of revenue recognition issues in the telecommunications industry.

FIGURE 15.3   Revenue recognition, Telstra

2.2 Income (continued)

2.2.1 Recognition and measurement

Revenue represents the fair value of the consideration received or receivable. Revenue is recorded net of sales returns, trade allowances, discounts, sales incentives, duties and taxes. We generate revenue and other income primarily from the following business activities:

Category	Recognition and measurement
Sale of services	*Telecommunication services* Revenue from: • calls is earned on completion of the call • internet and data is earned on a straight-line basis over the period of service provided, unless another method better represents the stage of completion. Installation and connection fees that are not considered to be separate services are deferred and recognised over the average estimated customer life.

Category	Recognition and measurement
	Rent of network facilities
	We earn rent mainly from access to retail and wholesale fixed and mobile networks and from the rent of dedicated lines, customer equipment, property, plant and equipment and other facilities. The revenue from providing access to the network is recorded on an accrual basis over the rental period.
	Advertising and subscription service
	Revenue from online advertising services is recognised when displayed or over the stated display period for advertisements published on the websites or when the services have been rendered for promotional activities. Subscription revenue is recognised on a straight-line basis over the subscription period.
Sale of goods	Revenue from the sale of goods includes revenue from the sale of customer equipment and other goods. This revenue is recorded on delivery of the goods sold.
Construction contracts	We record construction revenue and profit on a percentage of contract completion basis. The percentage or completion is calculated based on estimated costs to complete the contract. This does not apply to short duration contracts (less than one month) where revenue is only recorded upon contract completion.
	Profits are recognised when:
	• the stage of contract completion can be reliably determined
	• costs to date can be clearly identified
	• total contract revenues to be received and costs to complete can be reliably estimated.
Lease income	We earn income from operating subleases of mobile handsets offered to our retail customers (Telstra as a lessor), which we lease from a third party in a back-to-back arrangement (Telstra as a lessee). We also earn income from property leases. Lease income is recognised as other revenue on a straight-line basis over the lease term. Expenses arising from the head lease are recognised as other expenses (refer to note 2.3).
Government grants	Government grants are recognised where there is reasonable assurance that the grant will be received and Telstra will comply with all attached conditions.
	Government grants relating to costs are deferred and recognised in the income statement over the period necessary to match them with the costs that they are intended to compensate.
Interest income	We record interest income on an accrual basis. For financial assets, interest income is determined by the effective yield on the instrument.

The following paragraphs further explain how we measure and recognise revenue generated from our business activities.

(a) Revenue arrangements with multiple deliverables

Where two or more revenue-generating activities or deliverables are sold under a single arrangement, each deliverable that is considered to have a value to the customer on a standalone basis is accounted for as a separate unit of account.

We allocate the consideration from the revenue arrangement to its separate units based on the relative standalone selling prices of each unit. In the absence of a standalone selling price, the item is measured based on the best estimate of the selling price of that unit. The amount allocated to a delivered item is limited to the amount that is not contingent upon the delivery of additional items or meeting other specified performance conditions (non-contingent amount).

(b) Principal versus agency relationship (gross versus net revenue recognition)

Generally, we record the full gross amount of sales proceeds as revenue. However, if we are acting as an agent, revenue is recorded on a net basis.

(c) Sales incentives

We provide cash and non-cash sales incentives. The incentives are accrued when it is probable that the customer will earn the incentives. Cash sales incentives are generally recorded as a reduction in revenue and allocated to each product/service contributing towards the earning of the incentive. The allocation is based on the relative amounts of revenue earned for each product and service, unless a more appropriate methodology is available.

A non-cash sales incentive is considered to be a separate deliverable in a multiple deliverables arrangement regardless of whether it is provided to customers at the commencement of a contract or is an amount that can be used to buy future products and services. A portion of the total revenue under the arrangement is allocated to the non-cash incentive in accordance with the policy for multiple deliverables arrangements. The sales revenue allocated to the incentive is recognised when the customer redeems the reward and we provide the product or service or when the right to purchase additional goods or services is forfeited.

Source: Telstra Corporation Limited (2018, pp. 70–1).

15.5.3 Retail

The extract in figure 15.4, from the 2018 annual report of Woolworths Group Limited, serves as a summary of revenue recognition in the retail industry.

FIGURE 15.4   Revenue recognition, Woolworths

1.2 Significant accounting policies

1.2.2 Revenue

Revenue is measured at the fair value of consideration received or receivable on the basis that it meets the recognition criteria set out as follows:

Sale of goods and services

Revenue is recognised when the significant risks and rewards of ownership have been transferred to the customer, when it is probable the revenue will be received and the amount of revenue can be reliably measured. Service revenue is recognised based on the stage of completion of the contract with the customer.

Source: Woolworths Group Limited (2018, p. 67).
Note: The note to Woolworths' financial statements refers to the transfer of the significant risks and rewards of ownership, because Woolworths did not early adopt AASB 15/IFRS 15, and was reporting in accordance with the now superseded AASB 118/IAS 18.

15.5.4 Airline

The airline industry has long offered customers frequent flyer programs. Some airlines previously accounted for their frequent flyer programs by providing for the incremental cost of flying the passenger when the award credits are redeemed, rather than by allocating the consideration between the components. This means the airlines recognised all the revenue at the time of the sales transaction and at the same time provided for the expected incremental cost.

The extract in figure 15.5 provides Qantas Airways Ltd's accounting policy notes for the recognition of revenue in the company's 2018 annual report.

FIGURE 15.5   Revenue recognition, Qantas

(F) Revenue recognition

I. **Passenger and freight revenue**

Passenger and freight revenue is measured at the fair value of the consideration received, net of sales discounts, passenger and freight interline/IATA commission and Goods and Services Tax. Passenger revenue and freight revenue is recognised when passengers or freight are uplifted. Unused tickets are recognised as revenue using estimates based on the terms and conditions of the ticket, historic trends and experience.

Passenger recoveries (including fuel surcharge on passenger tickets) are included in net passenger revenue. Freight fuel surcharge is included in net freight revenue.

Revenue from ancillary passenger revenue, passenger services fees, lease capacity revenue and air charter revenue is recognised as revenue when the services are provided.

Receipts for advanced passenger ticket sales or freight sales which have not yet been availed or recognised as revenue are deferred on the balance sheet as revenue received in advance.

II. **Frequent Flyer marketing revenue**

Marketing revenue associated with the issuance of Frequent Flyer points is recognised when the service is performed (typically on the issuance of the point). Marketing revenue is measured as the difference between the cash received on issuance of a point and the amount deferred as unrecognised redemption revenue.

III. **Frequent Flyer redemption revenue**

Revenue received for the issuance of points is deferred as a liability (revenue received in advance) until the points are redeemed or, in the case of Qantas Group flight redemption, the passenger is uplifted. Redemption revenue is measured based on the weighted average fair value of the points redeemed. The fair value of the awards is reduced to take into account the proportion of points that are expected

▶

to expire (breakage). Redemption revenue arising from Qantas Group flight redemptions is recognised in passenger revenue. Redemptions on other airlines are recognised in other revenue.

Source: Qantas Airways Ltd (2018, pp. 88–9).

15.6 Disclosure requirements of AASB 15/IFRS 15

LEARNING OBJECTIVE 15.6 Describe the disclosure requirements of AASB 15/IFRS 15.

Disclosure requirements for the recognition of revenue are listed in paragraph 110 of AASB 15/IFRS 15 and require an entity to disclose both qualitative and quantitative information about:

* the contracts with customers
* the significant judgements and changes in the judgements made
* any assets recognised from the costs to fulfil a contract with a customer.

An entity shall consider the level of detail necessary to satisfy the disclosure objective and how much emphasis to place on each of the various requirements. An entity can use discretion to determine whether to disaggregate items that have substantially different characteristics or to aggregate a large amount of insignificant detail.

SUMMARY

The definition of *income* in AASB 15/IFRS 15 and the *Conceptual Framework* is very broad, being based, in effect, on statement of financial position movements. This is known as 'the asset/liability' model. The definition of income includes both revenue and gains, with different criteria for each. AASB 15/IFRS 15 deals only with revenue from contracts with customers while other relevant standards deal with gains.

AASB 15/IFRS 15 adopts five steps in recognising revenue.
1. Identify the contracts with the customer.
2. Identify the performance obligations in the contract.
3. Determine the transaction price.
4. Allocate the transaction price to the performance obligation.
5. Recognise revenue when the entity satisfies a performance obligation.

The key criterion for recognising revenue in relation to contracts with customers is whether 'control' of the related good or service has been transferred to the customer. The recognition criteria for rendering of services shall be determined by reference to the performance obligations satisfied 'over time' if the criteria stated in paragraph 35 of AASB 15/IFRS 15 are met. If not, an entity satisfies the performance obligation 'at a point in time'.

KEY TERMS

contract An agreement between two or more parties that creates enforceable rights and obligations.

control The ability to direct the use of, and obtain substantially all of the remaining benefits from, the asset.

customer A party that has contracted with an entity to obtain goods or services that are an output of the entity's ordinary activities in exchange for consideration.

deferred consideration Interest-free credit provided to a buyer or acceptance of a note receivable bearing a below-market interest rate.

gains Other items that meet the definition of income and may, or may not, arise in the course of the ordinary activities of an entity. Gains represent increases in economic benefits and as such are no different in nature from revenue.

income Increases in assets, or decreases in liabilities, that result in increases in equity, other than those relating to contributions from holders of equity claims.

input methods To recognise revenue on the basis of the entity's efforts or inputs to the satisfaction of a performance obligation (for example, resources consumed, labour hours expended, costs incurred, time elapsed or machine hours used) relative to the total expected inputs to the satisfaction of that performance obligation.

output methods To recognise revenue on the basis of direct measurements of the value to the customer of the goods or services transferred to date relative to the remaining goods or services promised under the contract.

performance obligation A promise in a contract with a customer to transfer to the customer either:
(a) a good or service (or a bundle of goods or services) that is distinct; or (b) a series of distinct goods or services that are substantially the same and that have the same pattern of transfer to the customer.

revenue Income arising in the course of an entity's ordinary activities.

stand-alone selling price The price at which an entity would sell a promised good or service separately to a customer.

transaction price The amount of consideration to which an entity expects to be entitled in exchange for transferring promised goods or services to a customer, excluding amounts collected on behalf of third parties.

DEMONSTRATION PROBLEM

15.1 Servicing fees included in the price of a product

Cascade Ltd sells goods to Gardener Ltd. Gardener Ltd enters into an agreement to buy the goods from Cascade Ltd for $60 000 on 1 September 2023. Cascade Ltd delivers the goods on 10 September 2023. Gardener Ltd pays for the goods on 30 September 2023.

The agreement states that, from the date of delivery, Cascade Ltd must provide maintenance for these goods for the first 12 months. Gardener Ltd is entitled to a refund of 15% of the amount paid if Cascade Ltd does not satisfactorily maintain the goods for the year as required.

Required

Prepare the journal entries to be recorded by Cascade Ltd as per the recognition criteria in AASB 15/IFRS 15.

SOLUTION

Under the *Conceptual Framework*'s asset/liability model, the definition of income is not met for 100% of the amount receivable because, while there has been an increase in an asset, there has also been an increase in a liability — Cascade Ltd's obligation to maintain the goods for 12 months and to refund the cash as from 10 September 2023. Cascade Ltd shall recognise the revenue on sales of goods when the goods are delivered (control transferred) as the performance obligation is satisfied at a point in time; and recognise the maintenance service in the next 12 months as the performance obligation is only satisfied over a period of time. Therefore, on this date, Cascade Ltd would record the following entry.

Sept. 10	Asset — accounts receivable — Gardener Ltd	Dr	60 000	
	Liability (obligation to maintain goods and refund cash)	Cr		9 000
	Sales revenue	Cr		51 000

The agreement for the transaction entitles Gardener Ltd to a refund of 15% if the maintenance is not performed satisfactorily or for the full 12-month period. Therefore, Cascade Ltd recognises $9000 as the liability/obligation.

Sept. 30	Cash	Dr	60 000	
	Asset — accounts receivable — Gardener Ltd	Cr		60 000
	(To record the receipt of cash from Gardener Ltd)			

Over the period of the maintenance agreement Cascade Ltd records the following entry.

	Liability (obligation to maintain goods and refund cash)	Dr	9 000	
	Services revenue	Cr		9 000
	(To record services revenue as the services are provided to Gardener Ltd)			

COMPREHENSION QUESTIONS

1 What are the key distinctions between 'income' and 'revenue'? Why do you think the AASB/IASB made these distinctions?
2 What is the 'asset/liability' model for the definition and recognition of income under the *Conceptual Framework*? Does it give a different outcome from other models permitted under AASB 15/IFRS 15?
3 What are the recognition criteria for income under the *Conceptual Framework*? How do these differ from the key stated purpose of AASB 15/IFRS 15?
4 What is a multiple-element transaction? Give two examples and discuss how AASB 15/IFRS 15 applies to such transactions.
5 Compare and contrast the revenue recognition criteria for the sale of goods with those for the rendering of services.

CASE STUDY 15.1

PAYMENT BY INSTALMENTS

Robinson Ltd is entering into a contract to sell boat products to Harris Ltd for $50 000. The agreement allows Harris Ltd to pay for these goods by equal instalments, the first instalment being required on delivery and the remainder to be paid every 6 months for the next 2 years. The boat products are delivered to Harris Ltd on 1 January 2023. Robinson Ltd determine that an appropriate discount rate for interest on this transaction is 5% per annum.

Required

Advise Robinson Ltd on how the company is to account for the revenue from this transaction.

CASE STUDY 15.2

PAYMENT IN ADVANCE

Sahara Ltd sells goods to Jackson Ltd. The agreement between the two parties states that Jackson Ltd pays for the goods in advance of delivery which will occur in 12 months' time. Control of the goods passes to Jackson Ltd at the date of delivery. Jackson Ltd pays $40 000 to Sahara Ltd on 1 July 2022. Sahara Ltd delivers the goods to Jackson Ltd on 1 July 2023.

Required

Advise Sahara Ltd on how to appropriately recognise the revenue from this transaction.

CASE STUDY 15.3

REVENUE RECOGNITION AND MEASUREMENT

Access the ASX website (www.asx.com.au) and search for companies within the Commercial and Professional Services industry. Choose three companies from this industry, access their most recent annual reports, and provide a comparison of their notes to the financial statements that discuss their recognition and measurement of revenue.

APPLICATION AND ANALYSIS EXERCISES

★ BASIC | ★ ★ MODERATE | ★ ★ ★ DIFFICULT

15.1 Definitions ★   **LO1, 2, 4**

State which of the following meets the definition of 'revenue' under AASB 15/IFRS 15 for Toys2U Ltd, a retailer of toys. Give reasons for your answer.

1. Sales tax collected on behalf of the taxing authority
2. Gain on the sale of an investment property
3. Amounts receivable from customers who have purchased toys
4. Gain on the sale of equity securities held as investments
5. Revaluation increase on the revaluation of operating properties under AASB 116/IAS 16

15.2 Definitions, scope ★   **LO1, 2, 3**

State whether each of the following is true or false.

1. 'Income' means the same as 'revenue'.
2. 'Gains' are always recognised net under IFRSs.
3. 'Revenue' must always be in respect of an entity's ordinary operations.
4. 'Gains' must always be outside of an entity's ordinary operations.
5. Services provided under a construction contract are accounted for under AASB 15/IFRS 15.

15.3 Measurement ★   **LO3**

State whether each of the following is true or false.

1. Revenue is measured at the fair value of the consideration given by the seller.
2. Revenue is measured at the transaction price that is allocated to that performance obligation.
3. If payment for the goods or services is deferred, the fair value of the consideration will be less than the nominal amount of the cash receivable.
4. A swap or exchange for goods or services of a similar nature and value generates revenue.
5. Collectability of amounts due from customers is a measurement issue, not a recognition issue.

15.4 Recognition ★   **LO4**

What is an 'executory contract'? How does this affect the dates on which revenue is recognised under the conceptual framework?

15.5 Measurement — dates for recognition ★ ★   **LO4**

SodaPop Ltd sells plastic bottles. Wholesale customers that purchase more than 10 000 bottles per month are entitled to a discount of 8% on their purchases. On 1 March 2022, Customer P ordered 20 crates of bottles from SodaPop Ltd. Each crate contains 1000 bottles. The normal selling price per crate is $450. SodaPop Ltd delivered the 20 crates on 15 March 2022. Customer P paid for the goods on 15 April 2022. The end of SodaPop Ltd's reporting period is 30 June.

Required

Prepare the journal entries to record this transaction by SodaPop Ltd for the year ended 30 June 2022.

15.6 Revenue recognition — rendering of services ★ ★   **LO4**

On 1 February 2023, FastNet Ltd entered into an agreement with Smith Ltd to develop a new database system (both hardware and software) for Smith Ltd. The agreement states that the total consideration to be paid for the system will be $430 000. FastNet Ltd expects that its total costs for the system will be $335 000. As the end of its reporting period, 30 June 2023, FastNet Ltd had incurred labour costs of $65 000 and materials costs of $180 000. Of the materials costs, $30 000 is in respect of materials that have not yet been used on the system. Of the labour costs, $12 500 is an advance payment to a subcontractor who had not performed their work on the project as at 30 June 2023. As at 30 June 2023, Smith Ltd had made progress payments to FastNet Ltd of $250 000.

FastNet Ltd calculates the measurement of progress using input methods in accordance with paragraph B18 of AASB 15/IFRS 15.

Required

Calculate the revenue to be recognised by FastNet Ltd for the year ended 30 June 2023 and prepare the journal entries to record the transactions described. Assume all of FastNet Ltd's costs are paid for in cash.

15.7 Revenue recognition — sale of goods ★ ★   **LO4**

In each of the following situations, state at which date, if any, revenue will be recognised.

1. A contract for the sale of goods is entered into on 1 May 2022. The goods are delivered on 15 May 2022. The buyer pays for the goods on 30 May 2022. The contract contains a clause that entitles the buyer to rescind the purchase at any time. This is in addition to normal warranty conditions.

2. A contract for the sale of goods is entered into on 1 May 2022. The goods are delivered on 15 May 2022. The buyer pays for the goods on 30 May 2022. The contract contains a clause that entitles the buyer to return the goods up until 30 June 2022 if the goods do not perform according to their specification.

3. A contract for the sale of goods is entered into on 1 May 2022. The goods are delivered on 15 May 2022. The contract contains a clause that states that the buyer shall pay only for those goods that it sells to a third party for the period ended 31 August 2022. Any goods not sold to a third party by that date will be returned to the seller.

4. Retail goods are sold with normal provisions allowing the customer to return the goods if the goods do not perform satisfactorily. The goods are invoiced on 1 May 2022 and the customer pays cash for them on that date.

15.8 Multiple-element arrangement ★ ★   **LO3, 4**

All Star Ltd provides a bundled service offering to Bruce Ltd. It charges Bruce Ltd $28 000 for initial connection to its network and two ongoing services — access to the network for 1 year and 'on-call troubleshooting' advice for that year.

Bruce Ltd pays the $28 000 upfront, on 1 July 2023. All Star Ltd determines that, if it were to charge a separate fee for each service if sold separately, the fee would be as follows.

Connection fee	$ 5 000
Access fee	9 000
Troubleshooting	18 000

The end of All Star Ltd's reporting period is 30 June.

Required

Prepare the journal entries to record this transaction in accordance with AASB 15/IFRS 15 for the year ended 30 June 2024, assuming All Star Ltd applies the relative fair value approach. Show all workings.

15.9 Revenue recognition — rendering of services ★ ★ ★   **LO3, 4**

In each of the following situations, state at which date(s), if any, revenue will be recognised.

1. A contract for the rendering of services is entered into on 1 May 2023. The services are delivered on 15 May 2023. The buyer pays for the services on 30 May 2023.

2. A contract for the rendering of services is entered into on 1 May 2023. The services are delivered continuously over a 1-year period commencing on 15 May 2023. The buyer pays for all the services on 30 May 2023.

3. A contract for the rendering of services is entered into on 1 May 2023. The services are delivered continuously over a 1-year period commencing on 15 May 2023. The buyer pays for the services on a monthly basis, commencing on 15 May 2023.

4. Lemon Ltd is an insurance agent and provides insurance advisory services to Customer B. Lemon Ltd receives a commission from insurance company Ibis Ltd when Lemon Ltd places Customer B's insurance policy with Ibis Ltd, on 1 April 2023. Lemon Ltd has no further obligation to provide services to Customer B.

5. Lemon Ltd is an insurance agent and provides insurance advisory services to Customer B. Lemon Ltd receives a commission from insurance company Ibis Ltd when Lemon Ltd places Customer B's insurance policy with Ibis Ltd, on 1 April 2023. Lemon Ltd is required to provide ongoing services to Customer B until 1 April 2024. Additional amounts are charged for these services. All amounts are at market rates.

6. Citrus Ltd receives a non-refundable upfront fee from Customer B for investment advice, on 1 March 2023. Under the agreement with Customer B, Citrus Ltd must provide ongoing management services until 1 March 2024. An additional amount is charged for these services. The upfront fee is higher than the market rate for equivalent initial investment advice services.

15.10 Agent vs. principal ★ ★   **LO5**

Discuss how an entity would determine whether it acts as an agent or principal in sales transactions. In your answer, discuss the distinguishing features between an agency versus principal relationship and the consequences for revenue recognition.

15.11 Telecommunications multiple-element arrangement ★ ★ ★   **LO5**

Network Ltd is a telecommunications company that offers a variety of services to its customers including fixed-line telephone services, mobile phone services and internet services. It uses numerous distributors to sell its mobile phone services. Customers purchase a phone handset from the distributor and at the same time can sign up to a contract with Network Ltd for a period of 12 months or 24 months for the provision of network access for a fixed fee. Calls are charged separately if they exceed a certain limit per month. If the customer enters into a 12-month contract, the handset is sold to them for 40% less than the quoted market price. If the customer enters into a 24-month contract, the handset is sold to them for 50% less than the quoted market price. The distributor earns a commission from Network Ltd based on a percentage of the consideration for each contract entered into — 12% for a 12-month contract and 15% for a 24-month contract.

Network Ltd sells its handsets to its distributors at 50% less than market price on the basis that the distributor will use the handset to entice customers to enter into the contracts with Network Ltd.

If the customer has any problems with the handset during or after the period of the contract (up to a maximum of 2 years), the customer has recourse to the distributor who must replace the handset at its own cost. In the case of a handset manufactured by Network Ltd, the distributor will source the handset from Network Ltd, which will sell it to the distributor at 50% less than market value.

The distributor sells handsets to customers even if they do not sign up to any services agreement with Network Ltd. In such cases, the customers are charged the market price for the handsets. The distributor also sells other handsets (i.e. not only those of Network Ltd).

Network Ltd has determined that the distributor is acting as its agent in respect of the service contracts but not in respect of its handsets.

Additional information

Handset cost to Network Ltd	$200
Handset market price	$320
12-month contract, price charged to customers	$80 per month, all paid upfront
24-month contract, price charged to customers	$60 per month, all paid upfront

Required

Discuss the revenue recognition issues that arise out of the transactions described (a) for Network Ltd and (b) for the distributor. Ignore discounting.

Logistics Ltd provides professional advisory services to develop internal and external reporting systems to facilitate the integration of various forms of capital (financial, mechanical, human, intellectual, natural and social) in the business models of their clients. The contracts take up to 18 months, culminating in the delivery of a report to clients outlining the design of integrated information systems, as well as specifications and procedures for implementation.

Until recently, Logistics Ltd progressively recognised revenue from providing services in accordance with AASB 118/IAS 18 *Revenue*. It recognised revenue and expenses, and hence profit, based on the stage of completion of its contracts with customers.

With the move to AASB 15/IFRS 15 *Revenue from Contracts with Customers*, the company needs to change the way it accounts for revenue. It is not permitted to recognise revenue under AASB 15/IFRS 15 until the report is delivered to the customer on completion of the contract.

The financial accountant estimated that the change in accounting policy would result in a 30% reduction in revenue and a 50% reduction in profit in the year of adoption of the new standard. The managing director thought this would be misleading to investors because the amount of work and cash inflows were expected to remain stable. She complained that 'Investors will think Logistics Ltd is performing poorly and the share price will decline'.

Required

Drawing on your understanding of the efficient markets hypothesis (refer to chapter 2), prepare a response to the managing director's concern. Include in your response any recommended action that Logistics Ltd could take to reduce the likelihood of a negative impact on its share price.

REFERENCES

Qantas Airways Ltd 2018, *Annual report 2018*, www.qantas.com.au.
Telstra Corporation Limited 2018, *Annual report 2018*, www.telstra.com.au.
Woolworths Group Limited 2018, *Annual report 2018*, www.woolworthsgroup.com.au.

ACKNOWLEDGEMENTS

Photo: © Diego Cervo / Shutterstock.com
Photo: © Rawpixel.com / Shutterstock.com
Figures 15.2, 15.3: © Telstra Corporation Limited 2018
Figure 15.4: © Woolworths Group Limited 2018
Figure 15.5: © Qantas Airways Ltd 2018

CHAPTER 16

Presentation of financial statements

CHAPTER AIM

This chapter discusses the reporting requirements of AASB 101/IAS 1 *Presentation of Financial Statements*, which prescribes the basis for the presentation of a statement of financial position, a statement of profit or loss and other comprehensive income, a statement of changes in equity, and related notes.

LEARNING OBJECTIVES

After studying this chapter, you should be able to:

16.1 describe the main components of financial statements

16.2 explain the general principles underlying the preparation and presentation of financial statements

16.3 explain the requirements of the statement of financial position

16.4 explain the requirements of the statement of profit or loss and other comprehensive income

16.5 explain the requirements of the statement of changes in equity

16.6 discuss other disclosures required by AASB 101/IAS 1 in the notes to the financial statements.

CONCEPTS FOR REVIEW

Before studying this chapter, you should understand and, if necessary, revise:

• the different types of companies that can be formed under the *Corporations Act 2001*
• the concepts of general purpose financial reporting and reporting entity
• the objectives of financial statements
• the definition, recognition and measurement of the elements of financial statements such as income, expenses, assets, liabilities and equity.

16.1 Components of financial statements

LEARNING OBJECTIVE 16.1 Describe the main components of financial statements.

The overall principles and other considerations relating to the presentation of financial statements are contained in AASB 101/IAS 1 *Presentation of Financial Statements*. A **complete set of financial statements** is defined in paragraph 10 as comprising:

   (a) a statement of financial position as at the end of the period;
   (b) a statement of profit or loss and other comprehensive income for the period;
   (c) a statement of changes in equity for the period;
   (d) a statement of cash flows for the period;
   (e) notes, comprising a summary of significant accounting policies and other explanatory information;
  (ea) comparative information in respect of the preceding period as specified in paragraphs 38 and 38A; and
   (f) a statement of financial position as at the beginning of the preceding period when an entity applies an accounting policy retrospectively or makes a retrospective restatement of items in its financial statements, or when it reclassifies items in its financial statements in accordance with paragraphs 40A–40D.

While AASB 101/IAS 1 refers to the statements as a 'statement of financial position', a 'statement of profit or loss and other comprehensive income', a 'statement of changes in equity' and a 'statement of cash flows', reporting entities may use other labels when presenting these financial statements in accordance with AASB 101/IAS 1. For example, an entity may choose to label its statement of financial position a 'balance sheet' and its statement of profit or loss and other comprehensive income a 'statement of comprehensive income'.

Paragraph 38 of AASB 101/IAS 1 requires an entity to present:

> comparative information in respect of the preceding period for all amounts reported in the current period's financial statements. An entity shall include comparative information for narrative and descriptive information if it is relevant to understanding the current period's financial statements.

Paragraph 38A of AASB 101/IAS 1 states:

> An entity shall present, as a minimum, two statements of financial position, two statements of profit or loss and other comprehensive income, two separate statements of profit or loss (if presented), two statements of cash flows and two statements of changes in equity, and related notes.

Each component of the financial statements must be clearly identified in the financial statements and distinguished from other information reported in the same document (AASB 101/IAS 1 paragraphs 49–51). Entities often present other information, such as certain financial ratios or a narrative review of operations by management or the directors. These reports are sometimes referred to as 'management discussion and analysis'. In Australia entities are obliged under the *Corporations Act 2001* to prepare a 'directors' report' that covers, among other matters, commentary on the results of operations and financial position of the entity. In addition, some entities voluntarily prepare sustainability reports or corporate social responsibility reports. This other information is reported outside the financial statements and is not within the scope of pronouncements issued by the Australian Accounting Standards Board (AASB).

This chapter deals with the requirements of AASB 101/IAS 1 for the presentation of the statement of financial position, the statement of profit or loss and other comprehensive income, the statement of changes in equity and notes. AASB 101/IAS 1 applies to all general purpose financial statements, except that its requirements relating to the structure and content of financial statements are not applicable to half-year financial reports. The structure and content requirements of half-year financial reports are contained in AASB 134/IAS 34 *Interim Financial Reporting*. This chapter also deals with various requirements of AASB 1054 *Australian Additional Disclosures*, AASB 108/IAS 8 *Accounting Policies, Changes in Accounting Estimates and Errors* and AASB 110/IAS 10 *Events after the Reporting Period*. These standards predominantly prescribe disclosure requirements, although AASB 108/IAS 8 and AASB 110/IAS 10 also contain certain measurement requirements. AASB 1054 specifies additional disclosure requirements that are broadly applicable to entities that prepare general purpose financial statements in accordance with Australian accounting standards.

Other Australian equivalents of International Financial Reporting Standards (IFRSs) mandate disclosures relating to specific financial statement elements and transactions and events, as well as their recognition and measurement. Specific required disclosures relevant to the topics of the various chapters of this text are outlined in those chapters. The statement of cash flows is considered in chapter 17.

16.2 General features of financial statements

LEARNING OBJECTIVE 16.2 Explain the general principles underlying the preparation and presentation of financial statements.

AASB 101/IAS 1 describes eight general principles that need to be applied in the presentation of financial statements. These requirements are intended to ensure that the financial statements of an entity are a faithful presentation of its financial position, financial performance and cash flows in accordance with the *Conceptual Framework*. The principles are:
1. fair presentation and compliance with standards
2. going concern
3. accrual basis of accounting
4. materiality and aggregation
5. offsetting
6. frequency of reporting
7. comparative information
8. consistency of presentation.

16.2.1 Fair presentation and compliance with standards

Paragraph 15 of AASB 101/IAS 1 states that financial statements shall present fairly the financial position, financial performance and cash flows of an entity. It elaborates on 'fair presentation' as follows.

Fair presentation requires the faithful representation of the effects of transactions, other events and conditions in accordance with the definitions and recognition criteria for assets, liabilities, income and expenses set out in the *Conceptual Framework for Financial Reporting* (*Conceptual Framework*). The application of [accounting standards], with additional disclosure when necessary, is presumed to result in financial statements that achieve a fair presentation.

Paragraph 17 of AASB 101/IAS 1 elaborates on the meaning of 'fair presentation' as including:
• selecting and applying accounting policies in accordance with AASB 108/IAS 8
• presenting information that is in a manner that provides relevant, reliable, comparable and understandable information
• providing additional disclosures to assist the understanding of users, where necessary, to those specified by accounting standards.

The last sentence of paragraph 15 of AASB 101/IAS 1 is very significant. There is an assumption that compliance with accounting standards, accompanied by additional disclosure, if necessary, will result in fair presentation.

16.2.2 Going concern

Paragraph 25 of AASB 101/IAS 1 states that financial statements shall be prepared on a **going concern** basis unless management intends to either liquidate the entity or cease trading, or has no realistic alternative but to do so. The conceptual framework makes a similar underlying assumption. When management is aware of any material uncertainties that cast doubt upon the entity's ability to continue as a going concern, those uncertainties must be disclosed (AASB 101/IAS 1 paragraph 25). When financial statements are not prepared on a going concern basis, that fact must be disclosed, together with the basis on which the financial statements are prepared and the reason why the entity is not regarded as a going concern.

If, for example, an entity has been placed in receivership and it is anticipated that liquidation will follow, the going concern assumption would be inappropriate. In such circumstances, the financial statements would typically be prepared on a 'liquidation' basis, which means that assets and liabilities are measured at the amounts expected to be received or settled on liquidation. In the case of assets, this will often be a 'fire-sale' value rather than a fair market value (for discussion of fair value measurement, see chapter 3).

16.2.3 Accrual basis of accounting

Financial statements, except for the statement of cash flows, must be prepared using the **accrual basis of accounting** (AASB 101/IAS 1 paragraph 27). Under this accrual basis, the effects of all transactions and other events are recognised in the accounting records when they occur, rather than when cash or its equivalent is received or paid. Financial statements prepared on the accrual basis inform users not only of past transactions involving the receipt and payment of cash but also of obligations to pay cash in the future and of amounts owing to the entity in the form of receivables. Accrual accounting is expected to provide a better basis for assessing the entity's past and future performance than information solely about cash receipts and payments during that period. When using the accrual basis, an entity recognises items as assets, liabilities, equity, income and expenses when they satisfy the definitions and recognition criteria for those elements in the *Conceptual Framework* (AASB 101/IAS 1 paragraph 28). See paragraphs 1.17–1.19 and chapter 5 of the *Conceptual Framework* and chapter 1 of this text for further details.

16.2.4 Materiality and aggregation

Paragraph 7 of AASB 101/IAS 1 defines 'material' as follows.

> Omissions or misstatements of items are material if they could, individually or collectively, influence the economic decisions that users make on the basis of the financial statements. Materiality depends on the size and nature of the omission or misstatement judged in the surrounding circumstances. The size or nature of the item, or a combination of both, could be the determining factor.

Each material class of similar items must be presented separately in the financial statements in accordance with paragraph 29 of AASB 101/IAS 1. Items of a dissimilar nature or function must be presented separately unless they are immaterial. When applying this requirement, an entity shall not reduce the understandability of its financial statements by obscuring material information with immaterial information or by aggregating material items that have different natures and functions (AASB 101/IAS 1 paragraph 30A). Paragraph 31 states that an entity need not provide a specific disclosure required by an accounting standard if the information is not material. This applies even if the accounting standards contain a list of specific requirements or describes them as minimum requirements. Conversely, paragraph 31 requires an entity to consider providing additional disclosures when mere compliance with the specific requirements in accounting standards is insufficient to enable users to understand the impact of particular transactions and conditions on the entity's financial position and financial performance.

Financial statements result from processing large volumes of transactions that are then aggregated into classes according to their nature or function. These classes form the line items on the statement of financial position, statement of comprehensive income, statement of changes in equity, and statement of cash flows. The minimum line items specified by AASB 101/IAS 1 are discussed in sections 16.3, 16.4 and 16.5 and in chapter 17 (in relation to the statement of cash flows).

16.2.5 Offsetting

Paragraph 32 of AASB 101/IAS 1 states that assets and liabilities, and income and expenses, shall not be offset unless required or permitted by an accounting standard. For example, AASB 132/IAS 32 *Financial Instruments: Presentation* defines a right of set-off in respect of *financial* assets and liabilities (discussed further in chapter 11). For items to be offset under AASB 132/IAS 32, there must be a *legal right* of set-off. This means that there must be a legal agreement documenting the right of the parties to settle amounts owed to/from each other on a net basis. For users of financial statements, however, the disadvantage of offsetting is that aggregation leads to loss of information. Paragraphs 34 and 35 identify situations where offsetting would be appropriate. These include:

- gains and losses on the disposal of non-current assets, which should be reported net instead of separately reporting the gross proceeds as income and the cost of the asset disposed of as an expense
- expenditure related to a provision recognised in accordance with AASB 137/IAS 37 (see chapter 8) that may be offset against an amount reimbursed under a contractual arrangement with a third party
- gains and losses arising from a group of similar transactions, such as gains and losses arising from foreign exchange or from financial instruments held for trading. A net gain or loss may be reported, rather than separately reporting the gains and the losses. However, a gain or loss must be reported separately if it is material.

16.2.6 Frequency of reporting

Paragraph 36 of AASB 101/IAS 1 requires that financial statements be presented at least annually. If an entity's reporting period changes, the length of the reporting period will be greater or less than a year in the period of the change. For example, if an entity with a reporting period ending on 30 September changed its reporting period to end on 30 June, the first financial statements it prepares for the period ending 30 June would cover a 9-month period. When this occurs, paragraph 36 of AASB 101/IAS 1 requires the entity to disclose the reason for the longer or shorter reporting period and the fact that the amounts presented in the financial statements are not entirely comparable.

16.2.7 Comparative information

AASB 101/IAS 1 requires the disclosure of comparative information in respect of the preceding period for all amounts reported in the financial statements, unless otherwise permitted by an accounting standard (paragraph 38). This extends to narrative information where the comparative narrative information is relevant to understanding the current period financial statements; for example details of a contingent liability, where the development of the issue over time is relevant to users. Paragraph 38A of AASB 101/ IAS 1 requires that an entity shall present at least two statements of financial position, two statements of profit or loss and other comprehensive income, two separate statements of profit or loss (if presented), two statements of cash flows and two statements of changes in equity, and related notes. Paragraph 38C of AASB 101/IAS 1 provides that an entity may present additional comparative information beyond the minimum required, provided that the additional information is prepared in accordance with accounting standards. For example, an entity may choose to provide a third statement of cash flows as an additional comparative statement.

Due to changed circumstances, or in order to provide a fair representation, an entity may change the classification of items reported in financial statements. For example, an entity may reclassify a non-current asset as held-for-sale if the entity plans to recover its carrying amount principally through a sale transaction rather than through continuing use, in accordance with AASB 5/IFRS 5 *Non-current Assets Held for Sale and Discontinued Operations*. When the presentation or classification of an item in the financial statements is changed, the entity must reclassify comparative amounts, to the extent practicable (AASB 101/IAS 1 paragraph 41). Further, the entity must present a statement of financial position for the end of the current period, the end of the preceding period, and the beginning of the previous period (AASB 101/IAS 1 paragraphs 40A and 40B). Thus, in the event of a change in the presentation or classification of items presented in financial statements, at least three statements of financial position must be presented.

16.2.8 Consistency of presentation

Paragraph 45 of AASB 101/IAS 1 requires that the presentation and classification of items in the financial statements be retained from one period to the next unless:

(a) it is apparent, following a significant change in the nature of the entity's operations or a review of its financial statements, that another presentation or classification would be more appropriate having regard to the criteria for the selection and application of accounting policies in AASB 108 [IAS 8]; or

(b) an [accounting standard] requires a change in presentation.

When such a change is made, the comparative information must also be reclassified. For example, as discussed in section 16.3.1, an entity may present its assets and liabilities in current and non-current classifications or in order of liquidity where this presentation is more reliable and relevant. If, after a change in operations, an entity elects to reclassify its assets and liabilities from the current/non-current presentation to the liquidity-based presentation, the comparative financial information must also be reclassified.

☐ The eight general features of financial statements are:
  – fair presentation and compliance with standards
  – going concern
  – accrual basis of accounting
  – materiality and aggregation
  – offsetting
  – frequency of reporting
  – comparative information
  – consistency of presentation.
☐ Offsetting of assets and liabilities, and income and expenses, is appropriate in certain situations.

16.3 Statement of financial position

LEARNING OBJECTIVE 16.3 Explain the requirements of the statement of financial position.

As discussed in chapter 1, a major purpose of financial statements is to provide information about an entity's financial position. The **statement of financial position** serves this purpose because it summarises the elements directly related to the measurement of financial position: an entity's assets, liabilities and equity. It thus provides the basic information for evaluating an entity's capital structure and analysing its liquidity, solvency and financial flexibility. It also provides a basis for calculating rates of return (e.g. return on total assets and equity, and measures of solvency and liquidity).

16.3.1 Statement of financial position classifications

The statement of financial position presents a structured summary of the assets, liabilities and equity of an entity. Assets and liabilities are classified in a manner that facilitates the evaluation of an entity's financial structure and its liquidity, solvency and financial flexibility. Consequently, assets and liabilities are classified according to their function in the operations of the entity concerned and their liquidity and financial flexibility characteristics.

Paragraph 60 of AASB 101/IAS 1 requires an entity to classify assets and liabilities as current or non-current in its statement of financial position, except when a presentation based on liquidity is considered to provide more relevant and reliable information. When that exception arises, all assets and liabilities are required to be presented broadly in order of liquidity.

According to paragraph 66 of AASB 101/IAS 1:

An entity shall classify an asset as current when:
(a) it expects to realise the asset, or intends to sell or consume it, in its normal operating cycle;
(b) it holds the asset primarily for the purpose of trading;
(c) it expects to realise the asset within twelve months after the reporting period; or
(d) the asset is cash or a cash equivalent (as defined in AASB 107 [IAS 7]) unless the asset is restricted
    from being exchanged or used to settle a liability for at least twelve months after the reporting period.
An entity shall classify all other assets as non-current.

Paragraph 69 of AASB 101/IAS 1 stipulates that:

An entity shall classify a liability as current when:
(a) it expects to settle the liability in its normal operating cycle;
(b) it holds the liability primarily for the purpose of trading;
(c) the liability is due to be settled within twelve months after the reporting period; or
(d) it does not have an unconditional right to defer settlement of the liability for at least twelve months after
    the reporting period (see paragraph 73). Terms of a liability that could, at the option of the counterparty,
    result in its settlement by the issue of equity instruments do not affect its classification.
An entity shall classify all other liabilities as non-current.

For example, inventories are classified as current because they are held primarily for trading purposes. When an entity applies the current/non-current classification, assets and liabilities that do not meet the criteria for classification as current are classified as non-current.

Paragraph 73 of AASB 101/IAS 1 explains that if an entity has the discretion to refinance or roll over an obligation for at least 12 months after the reporting period under the terms of an existing loan facility, and expects to do so, the obligation is classified as non-current, even if it would otherwise be due within 12 months of the end of the reporting period. This would amount to the unconditional right referred to in paragraph 69(d). The criteria for classifying liabilities as current or non-current are based solely on the conditions existing at the end of the reporting period. For example, if an entity had a long-term loan that fell due in August 2020 and entered into an agreement after 30 June 2020 to refinance or to reschedule payments on the loan, the liability would be classified as current in the statement of financial position at 30 June 2020, in accordance with paragraph 72. Similarly, paragraph 74 explains that if an entity breaches an undertaking under a long-term loan agreement during the reporting period with the effect that the loan is repayable on demand, the loan is classified as current. However, the loan should be classified as non-current if the lender agrees by the end of the reporting period to waive the right to demand immediate repayment for at least 12 months after the reporting period (paragraph 75).

Figure 16.1 shows the classification of assets in the statement of financial position of Telstra Corporation Limited, while figure 16.2 shows the classification of liabilities. Note that some of Telstra's provisions, borrowings, derivative financial liabilities and revenue received in advance are classified as current liabilities and some as non-current liabilities.

FIGURE 16.1	Current and non-current assets, Telstra			

| | | | As at 30 June | |
| | | | 2018 | 2017 |
Telstra Group		Note	$m	$m
Current assets				
Cash and cash equivalents		2.6	629	938
Trade and other receivables		3.3	5 018	5 468
Inventories		3.4	801	893
Derivative financial assets		4.3	75	21
Current tax receivables			6	11
Prepayments			548	531
Total current assets			7 077	7 862
Non-current assets				
Trade and other receivables		3.3	1 012	1 039
Inventories		3.4	19	29
Investments — accounted for using the equity method		6.3	1 237	194
Investments — other		4.4	36	292
Property, plant and equipment		3.1	22 108	21 350
Intangible assets		3.2	9 180	9 558
Derivative financial assets		4.3	1 897	1 623
Deferred tax assets		2.4	54	44
Defined benefit asset		5.3	250	142
Total non-current assets			35 793	34 271
Total assets			**42 870**	**42 133**

Source: Telstra Corporation Limited (2018, p. 61).

FIGURE 16.2	Current and non-current liabilities, Telstra			

| | | | As at 30 June | |
| | | | 2018 | 2017 |
Telstra Group		Note	$m	$m
Current liabilities				
Trade and other payables		3.5	4 835	4 189
Employee benefits		5.1	868	865
Other provisions			118	190
Borrowings		4.3	1 635	2 476
Derivative financial liabilities		4.3	1	42
Current tax payables			132	161
Revenue received in advance			1 227	1 236
Total current liabilities			8 816	9 159

Telstra Group	Note	As at 30 June 2018 $m	As at 30 June 2017 $m
Non-current liabilities			
Other payables	3.5	65	70
Employee benefits	5.1	157	160
Other provisions		171	134
Borrowings	4.3	15 316	14 808
Derivative financial liabilities	4.3	388	536
Deferred tax liabilities	2.4	1 624	1 539
Defined benefit liability	5.3	7	6
Revenue received in advance		1 312	1 161
Total non-current liabilities		19 040	18 414
Total liabilities		**27 856**	**27 573**

Source: Telstra Corporation Limited (2018, p. 61).

The current/non-current classification is ordinarily considered to be more relevant when an entity has a clearly identifiable **operating cycle**. This is because it distinguishes between those assets and liabilities that are expected to circulate within the entity's operating cycle and those used in the entity's long-term operations.

The typical cycle operates from cash, purchase of inventories (in the case of a manufacturer, production) and then receivables through sales of inventories and finally back to cash through collection of the receivables. The average time of the operating cycle varies with the nature of the operations and may extend beyond 12 months. Long operating cycles are common in real estate development, construction and forestry.

Current assets may include inventories and receivables that are expected to be sold, consumed or realised as part of the normal operating cycle beyond 12 months after the reporting period. Similarly, current liabilities may include payables that are expected to be settled more than 12 months after the reporting period if the operating cycle exceeds 12 months. Because of these possibilities paragraph 61 of AASB 101/IAS 1 requires that irrespective of whether assets and liabilities are classified on the current/non-current basis or in order of liquidity:

> ... an entity shall disclose the amount expected to be recovered or settled after more than twelve months for each asset and liability line item that combines amounts expected to be recovered or settled:
> (a) no more than twelve months after the reporting period, and
> (b) more than twelve months after the reporting period.

A presentation based broadly on order of liquidity is usually considered to be more relevant than a current/non-current presentation for the assets and liabilities of financial institutions. This is because financial institutions do not supply goods or services within a clearly identifiable operating cycle.

Figure 16.3 shows Westpac Banking Corporation's consolidated statement of financial position (balance sheet), in which the assets and liabilities of the group are presented in order of liquidity.

The classification of assets and liabilities as current or non-current is a particularly important issue for calculating summary indicators to assess an entity's liquidity and solvency.

FIGURE 16.3 Consolidated statement of financial position, Westpac

	Note	Consolidated 2018 $m	Consolidated 2017 $m
Assets			
Cash and balances with central banks		26 431	18 397
Receivables due from other financial institutions	10	5 790	7 128
Trading securities and financial assets designated at fair value	11	22 134	25 324
Derivative financial instruments	21	24 101	24 033
Available-for-sale securities	12	61 119	60 710
Loans	13	709 690	684 919
Life insurance assets	15	9 450	10 643
Regulatory deposits with central banks overseas		1 355	1 048
Due from subsidiaries		—	—
Investments in subsidiaries		—	—

Investments in associates	35	115	60
Property and equipment		1 329	1 487
Deferred tax assets	7	1 180	1 112
Intangible assets	26	11 763	11 652
Other assets	27	5 135	5 362
Total assets		879 592	851 875
Liabilities			
Payables due to other financial institutions	16	18 137	21 907
Deposits and other borrowings	17	559 285	533 591
Other financial liabilities at fair value through income statement	18	4 297	4 056
Derivative financial instruments	21	24 407	25 375
Debt issues	19	172 596	168 356
Current tax liabilities		296	308
Life insurance liabilities	15	7 597	9 019
Due to subsidiaries		—	—
Provisions	28	1 928	1 639
Deferred tax liabilities	7	18	10
Other liabilities	29	9 193	8 606
Total liabilities excluding loan capital		797 754	772 867
Loan capital	20	17 265	17 666
Total liabilities		815 019	790 533
Net assets		**64 573**	**61 342**
Shareholders' equity			
Share capital:			
— Ordinary share capital	32	36 054	34 889
— Treasury shares and RSP treasury shares	32	(493)	(495)
Reserves	32	1 077	794
Retained profits		27 883	26 100
Total equity attributable to owners of Westpac Banking Corporation		64 521	61 288
Non-controlling interests	32	52	54
Total shareholders' equity and non-controlling interests		**64 573**	**61 342**

Source: Westpac Banking Corporation (2018, p. 144).

An entity's current ratio (current assets to current liabilities) is often used as an indicator of liquidity and solvency. Lenders may also include terms in debt contracts requiring the borrower to maintain a minimum ratio of current assets to current liabilities. This is known as a 'negative pledge'. If the entity falls below that ratio then the financier has the right to demand repayment of the borrowing, which may, in turn, affect the assessment of whether the entity is a going concern.

16.3.2 Information required to be presented in the statement of financial position

AASB 101/IAS 1 does not prescribe a standard format that must be adopted for the statement of financial position. Rather, it prescribes a list of items that are considered to be sufficiently different in nature or function to warrant presentation in the statement of financial position as separate line items. These items are listed in paragraph 54:

  (a) property, plant and equipment;
  (b) investment property;
  (c) intangible assets;
  (d) financial assets (excluding amounts under (e), (h) and (i));
  (e) investments accounted for using the equity method;
  (f) biological assets within the scope of AASB 141 [IAS 41] *Agriculture;*
  (g) inventories;
  (h) trade and other receivables;
  (i) cash and cash equivalents;
  (j) the total of assets classified as held for sale and assets included in disposal groups classified as held for sale in accordance with AASB 5 [IFRS 5] *Non-current Assets Held for Sale and Discontinued Operations;*
  (k) trade and other payables;

(l) provisions;

(m) financial liabilities (excluding amounts shown under (k) and (l));

(n) liabilities and assets for current tax, as defined in AASB 112 [IAS 12] *Income Taxes*;

(o) deferred tax liabilities and deferred tax assets, as defined in AASB 112 [IAS 12];

(p) liabilities included in disposal groups classified as held for sale in accordance with AASB 5 [IFRS 5];

(q) non-controlling interests, presented within equity; and

(r) issued capital and reserves attributable to owners of the parent.

Paragraph 55 of AASB 101/IAS 1 requires additional line items, headings and subtotals to be presented in the statement of financial position when their inclusion is relevant to an understanding of the entity's financial position. Paragraph 55A further requires that:

When an entity presents subtotals in accordance with paragraph 55, those subtotals shall:

(a) be comprised of line items made up of amounts recognised and measured in accordance with [the accounting standards];

(b) be presented and labelled in a manner that makes the line items that constitute the subtotal clear and understandable;

(c) be consistent from period to period, in accordance with paragraph 45; and

(d) not be displayed with more prominence than the subtotals and totals required in [the accounting standards] for the statement of financial position.

Paragraph 58 explains that the judgement on whether additional items should be separately presented is based on an assessment of:

(a) the nature and liquidity of assets;

(b) the function of assets within the entity; and

(c) the amounts, nature and timing of liabilities.

For example, Telstra Corporation Limited includes 'trade and other payables' of $4 835 000 000 as a separate line item, in addition to 'revenue received in advance' of $1 227 000 000 in the current liabilities section of its statement of financial position as shown in figure 16.2. The trade and other payables pertains to trade and other payables to creditors on receipt of goods or services. The revenue received in advance is the amount received from customers before goods or services are provided to them. The same separate items are provided in the non-current liabilities section of the statement of financial position.

Figure 16.4 shows the disclosures made in Telstra's statement of financial position concerning the issued capital and reserves attributable to owners of the parent and non-controlling interests.

| **FIGURE 16.4** | Equity, Telstra |

		As at 30 June	
		2018	2017
Telstra Group	**Note**	**$m**	**$m**
Equity			
Share capital	4.2	4 428	4 421
Reserves	4.2	(117)	(105)
Retained profits		10 716	10 225
Equity available to Telstra Entity shareholders		15 027	14 541
Non-controlling interests		(13)	19
Total equity		**15 014**	**14 560**

Source: Telstra Corporation Limited (2018, p. 61).

16.3.3 Information required to be presented in the statement of financial position or in the notes

To provide greater transparency and enhance the understandability of the statement of financial position, paragraph 77 of AASB 101/IAS 1 requires the subclassification of line items to be reported either in the statement or in the notes. For example, an entity might provide subclassification of intangible assets as brand names, licences and patents. Paragraph 78 of AASB 101/IAS 1 explains that subclassifications of line items in the statement of financial position are also dependent on the size, nature and function of the amounts involved. Judgement about the need for subclassifications should be made with regard to the same factors previously outlined when judging whether additional line items should be presented in the statement of financial position (see section 16.2.4). In some cases, the subclassifications are governed by a specific accounting standard. For example, AASB 116/IAS 16 *Property, Plant and Equipment* requires items of property, plant and equipment to be disaggregated into classes (see chapter 5). Entities typically report land and buildings as a separate class from machinery and equipment. Another example is receivables that can be disaggregated into amounts receivable from trade customers, receivable from related parties, prepayments and other amounts.

Figure 16.5 shows the subclassifications of trade and other payables in note 3.5 to the 2018 statement of financial position of Telstra Corporation Limited. Telstra subclassifies its payables as trade creditors, accrued expenses, accrued capital expenditure, accrued interest, contingent consideration and other creditors. Note 3.5 also includes information about payables classified as current and non-current liabilities (see section 16.3.1 for details).

FIGURE 16.5	Trade and other payables, Telstra		

		As at 30 June	
Telstra Group		**2018** **$m**	**2017** **$m**
Current			
Trade creditors		1 588	1 185
Accrued expenses		1 891	1 733
Accrued capital expenditure		341	438
Accrued interest		264	256
Contingent consideration		4	4
Other creditors		747	573
		4 835	4 189
Non-current			
Contingent consideration		—	4
Other creditors		65	66
		65	70

Trade creditors and other creditors are non-interest bearing liabilities. Our payment terms vary but we generally make payments within 30 to 45 days from the invoice date.

Source: Telstra Corporation Limited (2018, p. 89).

In addition, paragraph 79 of AASB 101/IAS 1 requires an entity to disclose the following, either in the statement of financial position or in the notes:

(a) for each class of share capital:
   (i) the number of shares authorised;
   (ii) the number of shares issued and fully paid, and issued but not fully paid;
   (iii) par value per share, or that the shares have no par value;
   (iv) a reconciliation of the number of shares outstanding at the beginning and at the end of the period;
   (v) the rights, preferences and restrictions attaching to that class including restrictions on the distribution of dividends and the repayment of capital;
   (vi) shares in the entity held by the entity or by its subsidiaries or associates; and
   (vii) shares reserved for issue under options and contracts for the sale of shares, including terms and amounts; and
(b) a description of the nature and purpose of each reserve within equity.

Paragraph 80 of AASB 101/IAS 1 requires that entities that are not companies, and therefore do not have share capital, must disclose equivalent information to that required by paragraph 79(a) for each category of equity interests. For example, a unit trust would report on the number of units authorised by the trust deed, details about units issued, par value, a reconciliation of the number of units at the beginning and end of the period, rights to and restrictions on distributions, equity held in subsidiaries and units reserved under options and contracts.

16.3.4 Limitations of the statement of financial position

The view of an entity's financial position presented by the statement of financial position is by no means perfect and is often criticised by some commentators as being of limited value. These limitations primarily arise from:

- the optional measurement of certain assets at historical cost or depreciated historical cost rather than at a current value, such as fair value (see chapter 3)
- the mandatory omission of intangible self-generated assets from the statement of financial position as a result of the recognition and measurement requirements of AASB 138/IAS 38 *Intangible Assets*; examples include successful research expenditure, brand names and mastheads (see chapter 6)
- financial engineering that frequently leads to off-balance-sheet rights and obligations
- the aggregation of amounts that are measured inconsistently. For example, it is questionable to add the cost of a non-current asset and the fair value of a different asset.

The notes to the financial statements are an important source of information that can assist to mitigate the effects of these limitations.

LEARNING CHECK

☐ The information to be presented in the statement of financial position includes, as a minimum, prescribed asset, liability and equity items.

☐ A required order or format for the statement of financial position is not prescribed, but guidance is provided in AASB 101/IAS 1.

☐ All assets and liabilities are usually classified as either current or non-current. Note that an entity's operating cycle, which is the key to classification as current or non-current, may be longer than 12 months.

16.4 Statement of profit or loss and other comprehensive income

LEARNING OBJECTIVE 16.4 Explain the requirements of the statement of profit or loss and other comprehensive income.

The **statement of profit or loss and other comprehensive income** is the prime source of information about an entity's financial performance. The statement of profit or loss and other comprehensive income can also be used to assist users to predict an entity's future performance and future cash flows. The ability to identify likely non-recurring items of income or expense is of particular significance in forming expectations about future profits and cash flows.

16.4.1 Items of comprehensive income

The statement of profit or loss and other comprehensive income reports on all transactions and valuation adjustments affecting net assets other than transactions with 'owners as owners'. It includes items that are recognised through profit or loss which finds its way into equity in retained profits compared to recognition directly against reserves. Profit or loss is the most common measure of an entity's performance. It is used in the determination of other summary indicators, such as earnings per share and the return on equity. Profitability ratios may be used in contracts, such as management bonus plans.

While the statement of profit or loss and other comprehensive income incorporates all income and expenses, a distinction is made between profit or loss for the period and other comprehensive income. However, the distinction between items recognised in profit or loss and those recognised in other comprehensive income is dependent upon prescriptions of accounting standards and accounting policy choices, rather than being driven by conceptual differences. For example, AASB 116/IAS 16 requires asset revaluation losses to be recognised in profit or loss, unless reversing a previous revaluation gain. However, AASB 116/IAS 16 also requires asset revaluation gains to be recognised in other comprehensive income, unless reversing a previous revaluation loss (see chapter 5). Accordingly, a revaluation loss would be reported in profit or loss while a revaluation gain would be reported below the profit line in other comprehensive income.

16.4.2 Information required to be presented in the statement of profit or loss and other comprehensive income

AASB 101/IAS 1 does not prescribe a standard format for the statement of profit or loss and other comprehensive income. It does, however, require that the statement of profit or loss and other comprehensive income be presented either as:

- a single statement with profit or loss and other comprehensive income presented in two sections; the two sections are to be presented together with the profit or loss section presented first followed directly by the other comprehensive income section
- a separate statement of profit or loss immediately followed by a statement of comprehensive income.

In a business combination where a parent owns less than 100% of the shares in a subsidiary, the equity in the subsidiary not attributable to the parent is referred to as the non-controlling interest (see chapters 25–30 for further information). Paragraph 81B of AASB 101/IAS 1 requires disclosure of the following items, in addition to the profit or loss and other comprehensive income sections, as allocations of profit or loss and other comprehensive income for the period:

   (a) profit or loss for the period attributable to:
      (i) non-controlling interests; and
      (ii) owners of the parent.
   (b) comprehensive income for the period attributable to:
      (i) non-controlling interests; and
      (ii) owners of the parent.

The paragraph further states that if the entity presents profit or loss in a separate statement it shall present (a) in that statement (see chapter 29).

The following sections will examine the items that are considered to be of sufficient importance to the reporting of the performance of an entity to warrant their presentation in the statement of profit or loss and other comprehensive income. The profit or loss section and the other comprehensive income section are considered separately.

Profit or loss section

Profit or loss is the total of income less expenses, excluding the items of other comprehensive income (AASB 101/IAS 1 paragraph 7). Paragraph 82 lists the items that must be presented in the profit or loss section:

   (a) revenue, presenting separately interest revenue calculated using the effective interest method;
  (aa) gains and losses arising from the derecognition of financial assets measured at amortised cost;
   (b) finance costs;
  (ba) impairment losses (including reversals of impairment losses or impairment gains) determined in accordance with Section 5.5 of AASB 9 [IFRS 9];
   (c) share of the profit or loss of associates and joint ventures accounted for using the equity method;
  (ca) if a financial asset is reclassified out of the amortised cost measurement category so that it is measured at fair value through profit or loss, any gain or loss arising from a difference between the previous amortised cost of the financial asset and its fair value at the reclassification date (as defined in AASB 9 [IFRS 9]);
  (cb) if a financial asset is reclassified out of the fair value through other comprehensive income measurement category so that it is measured at fair value through profit or loss, any cumulative gain or loss previously recognised in other comprehensive income that is reclassified to profit or loss;
   (d) tax expense;
  (ea) a single amount for the total of discontinued operations (see AASB 5 [IFRS 5]).

Other comprehensive income section

Paragraph 82A of AASB 101/IAS 1 states:

The other comprehensive income section shall present line items for the amounts for the period of:
   (a) items of other comprehensive income (excluding amounts in paragraph (b)), classified by nature and grouped into those that, in accordance with other [accounting standards]:
      (i) will not be reclassified subsequently to profit or loss; and
      (ii) will be reclassified subsequently to profit or loss when specific conditions are met.

(b) the share of the other comprehensive income of associates and joint ventures accounted for using the equity method, separated into the share of items that, in accordance with other [accounting standards]:
  (i) will not be reclassified subsequently to profit or loss; and
  (ii) will be reclassified subsequently to profit or loss when specific conditions are met.

Paragraph 7 of AASB 101/IAS 1 lists examples of the items of other comprehensive income, including:
- the effective portion of gains and losses on hedging instruments in cash flow hedges in accordance with AASB 9/IFRS 9 (see chapter 11)
- changes in revaluation surplus recognised in accordance with AASB 116/IAS 16 (see chapter 5)
- foreign currency gains and losses on translation of foreign operations in accordance with AASB 121/IAS 21 (see chapter 24)
- remeasurement of defined benefit plans recognised in accordance with AASB 119/IAS 19 (see chapter 9).

The share of other comprehensive income of associates and joint ventures accounted for using the equity method refers to the investor's proportionate share of other comprehensive income, such as an asset revaluation, recognised by an associate or joint venture entity (see chapters 31 and 32). Items classified as other comprehensive income may be reported net of tax in the statement of profit or loss and other comprehensive income. Alternatively, each item of other comprehensive income may be shown on a before-tax basis, along with an aggregate amount of income tax relating to other comprehensive income.

Additional line items and labelling

Paragraph 85 of AASB 101/IAS 1 requires additional line items, headings and subtotals to be presented in the statement of profit or loss and other comprehensive income when such presentation is relevant to an understanding of the entity's financial performance. Disclosure of additional line items may help users to understand the entity's performance and to make predictions about future earnings and cash flow because items may vary in frequency and the extent to which they recur. Paragraph 85B further requires that the line items presented in profit or loss and other comprehensive income statements shall reconcile any subtotals presented in accordance with paragraph 85 with the subtotals or totals required in accounting standards for such statements. The subtotals shall be presented and labelled in a manner that makes the line items that constitute the subtotal clear and understandable, and shall be consistent from period to period (paragraph 85A). Paragraph 86 further explains that materiality and the nature and function of the items of income and expense should be considered in making judgements concerning the inclusion of additional line items.

An entity may also amend the descriptions used and the ordering of items when this is necessary to explain the elements of financial performance. However, paragraph 87 of AASB 101/IAS 1 specifically prohibits the presentation of any items of income and expense as 'extraordinary items' either in the statement of profit or loss and other comprehensive income or in the notes. 'Extraordinary items' had previously been defined as 'income or expenses that arise from events or transactions that are clearly distinct from the ordinary activities of the enterprise and therefore are not expected to recur frequently or regularly' (e.g. a loss on the disposal of part of the business). Presentation of extraordinary items as a separate item distracts users from or undermines the statutory profit. The AASB/IASB concluded that items previously reported as extraordinary items did not warrant presentation as a separate item of comprehensive income.

Limitations of the statement of profit or loss and other comprehensive income

Like the view of an entity's financial position presented by the statement of financial position, the view of an entity's performance presented by the statement of profit or loss and other comprehensive income is by no means perfect. Limitations can arise from:
- the mandatory expensing of expenditure relating to intangible self-generated assets as required by AASB 138/IAS 38 (see chapter 6)
- deliberate earnings management through the making of biased judgements relating to the measurement of items of income or expense, such as an impairment loss, or recognising costs as assets instead of expenses with the objective of smoothing earnings or projecting an image of earnings growth.

16.4.3 Information required to be presented in the statement of profit or loss and other comprehensive income or in the notes

To enhance the understandability of the statement of profit or loss and other comprehensive income, paragraph 97 of AASB 101/IAS 1 requires the separate disclosure of the nature and amount of material items of income and expense. Paragraph 98 identifies circumstances that would give rise to the separate disclosure of items of income and expense:

    (a) write-downs of inventories to net realisable value or of property, plant and equipment to recoverable amount, as well as reversals of such write-downs;
    (b) restructurings of the activities of an entity and reversals of any provisions for the costs of restructuring;
    (c) disposals of items of property, plant and equipment;
    (d) disposals of investments;
    (e) discontinued operations;
    (f) litigation settlements; and
    (g) other reversals of provisions.

Disclosure of material items is important to users of financial statements wishing to predict the likely future sustainability of the reported profit. This is particularly so for items that vary in frequency and in the likelihood of occurrence.

Paragraph 99 of AASB 101/IAS 1 requires an entity to present an analysis of expenses classified either by their 'nature' or 'function' within the entity whichever provides the more relevant and reliable information. Expenses are subclassified to represent the components of financial performance that may differ in terms of frequency, potential for gain or loss and predictability. Under the 'nature of expense' method, an entity aggregates expenses within profit or loss according to their nature (e.g. purchases of material, transport expenses, employee benefits expense, depreciation expense and advertising expenses). This method may be simple to apply because no allocations of expenses to functional classifications are necessary. The 'function of expense' method (also known as 'cost of sales' method) classifies expenses according to their function as part of cost of sales (e.g. costs of sales, distribution expenses and administrative expenses). This method provides more information to users than the classification of expenses by nature. Disclosure of the subclassification of expenses helps users of financial statements to identify relationships between expenses and various measures of the volume of activity, such as sales revenue. If the classification of expenses is by function, the entity must disclose additional information about the nature of expenses, including depreciation and amortisation expense and employee benefits expense, because it is useful for predicting future cash flows (AASB 101/IAS 1 paragraph 105).

Some income and expense items are required to be initially recognised in other comprehensive income and subsequently reclassified to profit or loss. For example, as discussed in chapter 23, gains and losses on cash flow hedges may be initially recognised in other comprehensive income and accumulated in equity, and transferred to profit or loss when the hedged item affects profit or loss. The subsequent recognition in profit or loss of an item previously recognised in other comprehensive income is referred to as a reclassification adjustment in AASB 101/IAS 1. In practice, it is also commonly referred to as recycling of gains and losses through profit or loss but the standard setters use the term 'reclassification' to enhance convergence between IFRSs and US GAAP.

Not all items recognised in other comprehensive income are subject to potential reclassification. For example, revaluation gains recognised in accordance with AASB 116/IAS 16 are not reclassified to profit or loss.

Paragraph 92 of AASB 101/IAS 1 requires the disclosure of **reclassification adjustments** relating to items of other comprehensive income. A reclassification adjustment is included with the related item of other comprehensive income in the period that the adjustment is reclassified to profit or loss. These amounts may have been recognised in other comprehensive income in a previous period. They could also have been recognised in other comprehensive income in the same period. For example, some of the deferred gain or loss accumulated in equity pertaining to a cash flow hedge that is reclassified to profit or loss may have been recognised in other comprehensive income in the current reporting period.

In accounting for a reclassification adjustment, gains previously recognised in other comprehensive income are deducted from other comprehensive income in the period in which they are recognised in profit or loss. This is to avoid double counting of the gain. Conversely, losses previously recognised in other comprehensive income are added back to other comprehensive income in the period in which they are recognised in profit or loss. Illustrative example 16.1 demonstrates how to present a reclassification adjustment in the statement of profit or loss and other comprehensive income.

Reclassification adjustment

Tasman Ltd is a small manufacturing company. It held a net investment in a foreign operation, called Abel Ltd. The foreign currency gains and losses on translation of the financial statements of Abel Ltd are recognised in other comprehensive income and accumulated in the 'foreign currency translation reserve' in equity, in accordance with AASB 121/IAS 21 *The Effects of Changes in Foreign Exchange Rates*.

On 1 July 2022, Tasman Ltd disposed of its net investment in Abel Ltd at a loss of $28 000. At that time the accumulated credit in the 'foreign currency translation reserve' in relation to the net investment in Abel Ltd was $15 000, of which $5000 had been recognised in the year ended 30 June 2022. There was no income tax associated with the accumulated foreign currency gain. Tasman Ltd revalued land in accordance with the fair value measurement basis permitted by AASB 116/IAS 16, resulting in a gain of $18 000 net of tax for the year ended 30 June 2023 (2022: $12 000). These were the only items of other comprehensive income for the year ended 30 June 2023 and the year ended 30 June 2022.

TASMAN LTD			
Statements of profit or loss and other comprehensive income			
for the year ended 30 June			
	Notes	2023 $'000	2022 $'000
Revenue	2	980	740
Cost of sales	3	(400)	(300)
Selling and administrative expenses	4	(210)	(200)
Finance costs	4	(100)	(100)
Reclassification of foreign currency gain on translation of financial statements of net investment in foreign operation	5	15	—
Loss on disposal of net investment		(28)	—
Profit before taxation		**257**	**140**
Income tax expense	6	(100)	(40)
Profit for the year		**157**	**100**
Other comprehensive income			
Items that will not be reclassified to profit or loss:			
Gain on revaluation, net of tax	7	18	12
		18	12
Items that may be reclassified subsequently to profit or loss:			
Foreign currency gain on translation of foreign operations	8	—	5
Reclassification adjustment for gains on translation of foreign operations	8	(15)	—
		(15)	5
Other comprehensive income for the year, net of tax		3	17
Total comprehensive income for the year		**160**	**117**
Profit attributable to:			
Owners of Tasman Ltd		150	95
Non-controlling interests		7	5
		157	100
Total comprehensive income attributable to:			
Owners of Tasman Ltd		153	112
Non-controlling interests		7	5
		160	117

Prior to the disposal of the net investment in Abel Ltd, Tasman Ltd had accumulated foreign currency gains of $15 000 on the translation of the financial statements of Abel Ltd. The foreign currency gain had been recognised in other comprehensive income over several periods, including an amount of $5000, which was recognised in 2022. Now that Tasman Ltd has disposed of its net investment in Abel Ltd the accumulated gain of $15 000 must be reclassified to profit. To avoid double counting of the foreign currency gain, it is deducted from other comprehensive income and added to profit. Thus, the reclassification adjustment of $15 000 has no net effect on total comprehensive income in 2023 because it increases profit by $15 000 and decreases other comprehensive income by the same amount.

16.4.4 Illustrative statements of profit or loss and other comprehensive income

The guidance on implementing AASB 101/IAS 1 that accompanies, but is not part of, the standard includes illustrative statements of profit or loss and other comprehensive income. Figures 16.6 and 16.7 provide illustrative examples of statements of profit or loss and other comprehensive income (adapted from the guidance on implementing AASB 101/IAS 1). Figure 16.6 illustrates the statement of profit of loss and other comprehensive income as a single statement, with expenses classified according to function and figure 16.7 illustrates the statement of profit or loss and other comprehensive income in two statements, with expenses classified according to nature.

FIGURE 16.6 Statement of profit or loss and other comprehensive income in one statement with expenses classified according to function

XYZ GROUP
Statement of profit or loss and other comprehensive income
for the year ended 31 December 2023

	2023 $'000	2022 $'000
Revenue	390 000	355 000
Cost of sales	(245 000)	(230 000)
Gross profit	145 000	125 000
Other income	20 667	11 300
Distribution costs	(9 000)	(8 700)
Administrative expenses	(20 000)	(21 000)
Other expenses	(2 100)	(1 200)
Finance costs	(8 000)	(7 500)
Share of profit of associates	35 100	30 100
Profit before tax	**161 667**	**128 000**
Income tax expense	(40 417)	(32 000)
Profit for the year from continuing operations	**121 250**	**96 000**
Loss for the year from discontinued operations	—	(30 500)
Profit for the year	**121 250**	**65 500**
Other comprehensive income		
Items that will not be reclassified to profit or loss:		
Gains on property revaluation	933	3 367
Investments in equity instruments	(24 000)	26 667
Remeasurements of defined benefit pension plans	(667)	1 333
Share of gain (loss) on property revaluation of associates	400	(700)
Income tax relating to items that will not be reclassified	5 834	(7 667)
	(17 500)	23 000
Items that may be reclassified subsequently to profit or loss:		
Exchange differences on translating foreign operations	5 334	10 667
Cash flow hedges	(667)	(4 000)
Income tax relating to items that may be reclassified	(1 167)	1 167
	3 500	5 000
Other comprehensive income for the year, net of tax	(14 000)	28 000
Total comprehensive income for the year	**107 250**	**93 500**
Profit attributable to:		
Owners of the parent	97 000	52 400
Non-controlling interests	24 250	13 100
	121 250	65 500
Total comprehensive income attributable to:		
Owners of the parent	85 800	74 800
Non-controlling interests	21 450	18 700
	107 250	93 500
Earnings per share (in currency units):		
Basic and diluted	0.46	0.30

Source: Adapted from IASB (2016, pp. B1901–2).

FIGURE 16.7 Statement of profit or loss and other comprehensive income in two statements with expenses classified according to nature

XYZ GROUP
Statement of profit or loss and other comprehensive income
for the year ended 31 December 2023

	2023 $'000	2022 $'000
Revenue	390 000	355 000
Other income	20 667	11 300
Changes in inventories of finished goods and work in progress	(115 100)	(107 900)
Work performed by the entity and capitalised	16 000	15 000
Raw materials and consumables used	(96 000)	(92 000)
Employee benefits expense	(45 000)	(43 000)
Depreciation and amortisation expense	(19 000)	(17 000)
Impairment of property, plant and equipment	(4 000)	—
Other expenses	(6 000)	(5 500)
Finance costs	(15 000)	(18 000)
Share of profit of associates	35 100	30 100
Profit before tax	**161 667**	**128 000**
Income tax expense	(40 417)	(32 000)
Profit for the year from continuing operations	**121 250**	**96 000**
Loss for the year from discontinued operations	—	(30 500)
Profit for the year	**121 250**	**65 500**
Profit attributable to:		
Owners of the parent	97 000	52 400
Non-controlling interests	24 250	13 100
	121 250	65 500
Earnings per share (in currency units):		
Basic and diluted	0.46	0.30
Profit for the year	**121 250**	**65 500**
Other comprehensive income		
Items that will not be reclassified to profit or loss:		
Gains on property revaluation	933	3 367
Investments in equity instruments	(24 000)	26 667
Remeasurements of defined benefit pension plans	(667)	1 333
Share of gain (loss) on property revaluation of associates	400	(700)
Income tax relating to items that will not be reclassified	5 834	(7 667)
	(17 500)	23 000
Items that may be reclassified subsequently to profit or loss:		
Exchange differences on translating foreign operations	5 334	10 667
Cash flow hedges	(667)	(4 000)
Income tax relating to items that may be reclassified	(1 167)	1 667
	3 500	5 000
Other comprehensive income for the year, net of tax	(14 000)	28 000
Total comprehensive income for the year	**107 250**	**93 500**
Total comprehensive income attributable to:		
Owners of the parent	85 800	74 800
Non-controlling interests	21 450	18 700
	107 250	93 500

Source: Adapted from IASB (2016, pp. B1904–5).

Note that the earnings per share is disclosed pursuant to the requirements of AASB 133/IAS 33 *Earnings per Share*.

LEARNING CHECK

☐ The statement of profit or loss and other comprehensive income is the prime source of information about an entity's financial performance. It can be used to assist users to predict an entity's future performance and future cash flows.

☐ The statement of profit or loss and other comprehensive income must be presented either as:
  – a single statement with profit or loss and other comprehensive income presented in two sections
  – a separate statement of profit or loss immediately followed by a statement of comprehensive income.

□ An entity shall present an analysis of expenses classified either by their 'nature' or 'function' within the entity, whichever provides the more relevant and reliable information.

□ Some items, such as foreign currency gain on translation of foreign operations, initially recognised in other comprehensive income as unrealised gain will need to be reclassified to profit or loss when it becomes realised subsequently in order to avoid double counting.

□ However, not all items recognised in other comprehensive income are subject to potential reclassification. For example, revaluation gain and remeasurements of defined benefit plans are not reclassified to profit or loss.

□ Entities are encouraged to present the analysis of expenses in the statement of profit or loss and other comprehensive income.

16.5 Statement of changes in equity

LEARNING OBJECTIVE 16.5 Explain the requirements of the statement of changes in equity.

The **statement of changes in equity** provides a reconciliation of the opening and closing amounts of each component of equity for the period. The purpose of the statement of changes in equity is to report transactions with owners, such as the issue of new shares and the payment of dividends, and the effects of any retrospective adjustments to beginning-of-period components of equity.

16.5.1 Presentation of the statement of changes in equity

The statement of changes in equity is usually presented in a tabular format. The various components of equity, such as share capital, retained earnings and revaluation surplus, are listed in separate columns. The opening balance, current period movements and closing balance are shown in different rows. As for the other financial statements, comparative amounts are required to be reported in the statement of changes in equity. The comparative figures are usually presented in a separate table from the current period figures. See figure 16.8 for presentation of the statement of changes in equity. Figure 16.8 shows the consolidated statement of changes in equity of the Qantas Group. Qantas provides the analysis of other comprehensive income in the statement but discloses information about dividends in the notes. Note 6 (see figure 16.9) also provides information about dividend imputation credits, which are discussed in section 16.6.4.

16.5.2 Information required to be reported in the statement of changes in equity

Paragraph 106 of AASB 101/IAS 1 requires the following information to be presented in the statement of changes in equity:

(a) total comprehensive income for the period, showing separately the total amounts attributable to owners of the parent and to non-controlling interests;

(b) for each component of equity, the effects of retrospective application or retrospective restatement recognised in accordance with AASB 108 [IAS 8]; and

(c) [deleted]

(d) for each component of equity, a reconciliation between the carrying amount at the beginning and the end of the period, separately (as a minimum) disclosing changes resulting from:
  (i) profit or loss;
  (ii) other comprehensive income; and
  (iii) transactions with owners in their capacity as owners, showing separately contributions by and distributions to owners and changes in ownership interests in subsidiaries that do not result in a loss of control.

The components of equity referred to in these disclosure requirements include each class of contributed equity, retained earnings and the amounts accumulated in equity for each class of items recognised in other comprehensive income, such as the asset revaluation surplus and the foreign currency translation reserve.

FIGURE 16.8 Consolidated statement of changes in equity, Qantas

Consolidated statement of changes in equity
For the year ended 30 June 2018

30 June 2018 $m	Issued capital	Treasury shares	Employee compensation reserve	Hedge reserve	Foreign currency translation reserve	Other reserves	Retained earnings	Non-controlling interests	Total equity
Balance as at 1 July 2017	3 259	(206)	124	(100)	(16)	4	472	3	3 540
Total comprehensive income/(loss) for the year									
Statutory profit for the year	—	—	—	—	—	—	980	—	980
Other comprehensive income/(loss)									
Effective portion of changes in fair value of cash flow hedges, net of tax	—	—	—	559	—	—	—	—	559
Transfer of hedge reserve to the consolidated income statement, net of tax	—	—	—	(230)	—	—	—	—	(230)
Recognition of effective cash flow hedges on capitalised assets, net of tax	—	—	—	16	—	—	—	—	16
Net changes in hedge reserve for time value of options, net of tax	—	—	—	51	—	—	—	—	51
Defined benefit actuarial losses, net of tax	—	—	—	—	—	84	—	—	84
Foreign currency translation of controlled entities	—	—	—	—	3	—	—	—	3
Foreign currency translation of investments accounted for under the equity method	—	—	—	—	(3)	—	—	—	(3)
Fair value gains on investments, net of tax	—	—	—	—	—	1	—	—	1
Share of other comprehensive income of investments accounted for under the equity method	—	—	—	4	—	—	—	—	4
Total other comprehensive income/(loss)	—	—	—	400	—	85	—	—	485
Total comprehensive income/(loss) for the year	—	—	—	400	—	85	980	—	1 465
Transactions with owners recorded directly in equity									
Contributions by and distributions to owners									
Share buy-back	(751)	—	—	—	—	—	—	—	(751)
Dividend paid	—	—	—	—	—	—	(249)	—	(249)
Treasury shares acquired	—	(162)	—	—	—	—	—	—	(162)
Share-based payments	—	—	64	—	—	—	—	—	64
Shares vested and transferred to employees	—	253	(82)	—	—	—	(119)	—	52
Total contributions by and distributions to owners	(751)	91	(18)	—	—	—	(368)	—	(1 046)
Total transactions with owners	(751)	91	(18)	—	—	—	(368)	—	(1 046)
Balance as at 30 June 2018	2 508	(115)	106	300	(16)	89	1 084	3	3 959

Source: Qantas Airways Ltd (2018, p. 55).

FIGURE 16.9   Dividends distributed, Qantas

Dividends and other shareholder distributions

(A) Dividends declared and paid

In August 2018, the Directors declared a fully franked final dividend of ten cents per ordinary share totalling $168 million. The record date for determining entitlements to the final dividend is 6 September 2018. The dividend will be paid on 10 October 2018.

During the year ended 30 June 2018, the Group paid two unfranked dividends of seven cents per ordinary share totalling $249 million ($127 million on 13 October 2017 and $122 million on 12 April 2018). Dividends of $0.3 million were paid to non–controlling interest shareholders by non–wholly owned controlled entities.

(C) Franking account

	2018 $m	2017 $m
Total franking account balance at 30 per cent	5	—

The above amount represents the balance of the franking account as at 30 June, after taking into account adjustments for:
- franking credits that will arise from the payment of income tax payable for the current year
- franking credits that will arise from the receipt of dividends recognised as receivables at the year end
- franking credits that may be prevented from being distributed in subsequent years.

The ability to utilise the franking credits is dependent upon there being sufficient available profits to declare dividends.

Source: Qantas Airways Ltd (2018, pp. 63–4).

According to paragraph 107 of AASB 101/IAS 1, an entity must disclose both the amount of dividends recognised as distributions to owners (shareholders) during the period and the related amount per share either in the statement of changes in equity or in the notes. Note the requirement to provide details of an owner-related equity transaction, such as dividends, in the statement of changes in equity or notes, and not as part of the statement of profit or loss and other comprehensive income.

Profit (loss) for the period increases (decreases) retained earnings. Other items of comprehensive income affect other components of equity. For example, a gain on revaluing assets, net of its tax effect, increases the asset revaluation surplus.

LEARNING CHECK

☐ The purpose of the statement of changes in equity is to report transactions with owners such as the issue of shares and the payment of dividends.

☐ It provides a reconciliation of the opening and closing amounts of each component of equity for the period.

16.6 Notes

LEARNING OBJECTIVE 16.6 Discuss other disclosures required by AASB 101/IAS 1 in the notes to the financial statements.

Notes are an integral part of the financial statements. Their purpose is to enhance the understandability of the statement of financial position, statement of profit or loss and other comprehensive income, statement of cash flows and statement of changes in equity. As far as practicable, each item in these statements is cross-referenced to any related information in the notes (AASB 101/IAS 1 paragraph 113).

Information must be disclosed in the notes in accordance with paragraph 112 of AASB 101/IAS 1 is:
- information about the basis of preparation of the financial statements and the specific accounting policies used, in accordance with paragraphs 117–24

- information required by other accounting standards unless presented elsewhere in the financial statements
- other information that is not presented elsewhere in the financial statements but is relevant to understanding them.

As discussed in this chapter, AASB 101/IAS 1 allows some information to be presented either in the notes or in the financial statements, such as the statement of financial position or the statement of profit or loss and other comprehensive income. Paragraphs 113 and 114 require an entity to present notes in a systematic manner by considering the effect on the understandability and comparability of its financial statements. Examples of systematic ordering or grouping of the notes (paragraph 114) include:

(a) giving prominence to the areas of its activities that the entity considers to be most relevant to an understanding of its financial performance and financial position, such as grouping together information about particular operating activities;

(b) grouping together information about items measured similarly such as assets measured at fair value; or

(c) following the order of the line items in the statement(s) of profit or loss and other comprehensive income and the statement of financial position.

We will first consider the statements about compliance with IFRSs and with Australian accounting standards, followed by the summary of significant accounting policies used and sources of estimation uncertainty, information relating to items in the financial statements, and other disclosures.

16.6.1 Compliance with IFRSs and Australian accounting standards

In Australia, an entity is required by AASB 1054 (paragraph 9) to disclose whether the financial statements are general purpose financial statements or special purpose financial statements.

An explicit and unreserved statement of compliance with IFRSs should be made if, and only if, the financial statements comply with all the requirements of IFRSs (AASB 101/IAS 1 paragraph 16). Similarly, an explicit and unreserved statement of compliance with Australian accounting standards should be made if, and only if, the financial statements comply with all the requirements of Australian accounting standards (AASB 1054 paragraph 7).

For many entities, compliance with Australian accounting standards results in compliance with IFRSs. However, some Australian accounting standards allow some entities, such as not-for-profit entities, to use alternative policies, such as measurement at depreciated replacement cost, that are not consistent with IFRSs.

In extremely rare circumstances, management may conclude that compliance with a requirement in an Australian accounting standard would be so misleading that it would conflict with the objective of financial statements. However, most entities in Australia that prepare general purpose financial statements are not permitted to depart from the requirements of Australian accounting standards (AASB 101 paragraph Aus19.1). Rather, if management of these entities conclude that compliance with a requirement in an Australian accounting standard would be so misleading as to conflict with the decision usefulness objective, paragraph 23 of AASB 101/IAS 1 requires disclosure of the title of the relevant accounting standard, the nature of the requirement, the reason for management's conclusion that compliance is misleading, and the adjustments necessary to each item for each period presented to achieve a fair presentation.

Entities that are not prohibited by the relevant regulatory framework from departing from Australian accounting standards may do so in the extremely rare circumstances in which management concludes that compliance with a requirement in an Australian accounting standard would be so misleading that it would conflict with the objective of financial statements, in accordance with paragraph 19. When assessing whether compliance would be misleading, management must consider why the objectives of financial statements would not be achieved in the current circumstances and how the entity's circumstances differ from other entities that do comply with the requirement. When an entity that is not prohibited from doing so by the relevant regulatory framework departs from an Australian accounting standard in accordance with paragraph 19, the disclosures required by paragraph 20 are:

- that management has concluded that the financial statements present fairly the entity's financial position, financial performance and cash flows
- that the financial statements are in compliance with Australian accounting standards except for the specific departure to achieve a fair presentation
- the title of the standard from which the entity has departed

- the nature of the departure
- the treatment required by the standard
- why the treatment would be so misleading in the circumstances that it would be in conflict with the objectives of financial statements specified in the *Conceptual Framework*
- the financial effect of the departure on each item in the financial statements for each period presented.

Paragraph 16 of AASB 101/IAS 1 requires entities to include a statement of compliance with IFRSs, if applicable, in the statement about the basis of preparation of the financial statements, except not-for-profit entities. Only entities that comply with all the requirements of IFRSs are allowed to make an explicit and unreserved statement of such compliance. As noted in paragraph Aus16.2:

> Compliance with Australian accounting standards by for-profit entities will not necessarily lead to compliance with IFRSs. This circumstance arises when the entity is a for-profit government department to which particular Standards apply, such as AASB 1004 *Contributions*, and to which Aus paragraphs in various other Australian Accounting Standards apply, and the entity applies a requirement that is inconsistent with an IFRS requirement.

Entities that apply reduced disclosure requirements would not be able to state compliance with IFRSs (paragraph RDR16.1). See section 1.1.2 and AASB 1053 *Application of Tiers of Australian Accounting Standards* for details pertaining to reduced disclosure requirements.

16.6.2 Statement of significant accounting policies

Accounting policies are the specific principles, bases, conventions, rules and practices applied by an entity in preparing and presenting financial statements (AASB 108/IAS 8 paragraph 5). Accounting policies are discussed in detail in chapter 18.

In deciding whether to disclose particulars of an accounting policy, managers must consider its relevance in assisting users to understand how transactions and events have been reported in the financial statements. In some cases, disclosure is prescribed by other accounting standards. For example, AASB 116/IAS 16 requires disclosure of the depreciation methods used for each class of property, plant and equipment (paragraph 73(b)) (see chapter 5).

Paragraph 13 of AASB 101/IAS 1 requires that an appropriate accounting policy shall be selected and applied consistently for similar transactions, other events and conditions, unless an accounting standard specifically requires or permits categorisation of items for which different policies may be appropriate. This means, an entity can only change its accounting policy if it is required by an accounting standard or it results in more reliable and relevant information about the effects of the transactions (paragraph 14).

Paragraph 117 of AASB 101/IAS 1 explains that the summary of significant accounting policies should include the measurement bases used. For example, an entity should disclose whether cost or fair value has been used in measuring property, plant and equipment subsequent to initial recognition. (Paragraph 73(a) of AASB 116/IAS 16 requires disclosure of the measurement basis used to determine the gross carrying amount for each class of property, plant and equipment) (see chapter 5).

Paragraph 8 of AASB 1054 requires disclosure of the statutory basis or other regulatory framework, if any, under which financial statements are prepared and whether the entity is a for-profit or not-for-profit entity. For example, Note 1 of the financial statements of Telstra Corporation Limited (2018, p. 64) for the year ended 30 June 2018 states:

> This financial report is a general purpose financial report, prepared by a 'for-profit' entity, in accordance with the requirements of the Australian Corporations Act 2001, Accounting Standards applicable in Australia and other authoritative pronouncements of the Australian Accounting Standards Board (AASB). It also complies with International Financial Reporting Standards (IFRS) and Interpretations published by the International Accounting Standards Board (IASB).

Sources of estimation uncertainty

An entity must disclose information about the assumptions concerning the future, and other major sources of estimation uncertainty at the end of the reporting period, that have a significant risk of causing material adjustments to the carrying amounts of assets and liabilities within the next financial year (e.g. assumptions about growth rates used in measuring the recoverable amount of major assets) (AASB 101/IAS 1 paragraph 125). While this information does not need to form part of the summary of significant accounting policies, it is not uncommon for entities to include the disclosures about measurement uncertainty in that section of the notes.

Paragraph 122 of AASB 101/IAS 1 also requires disclosure of the judgements that management has made in applying accounting standards. This requirement applies to those judgements that have the most significant effect on the amounts recognised in financial statements. For example, judgement about whether substantially all the risks and rewards of ownership have been transferred by a lease required in applying AASB 117/IAS 17 *Leases* would often have a significant effect on amounts reported in financial statements (see chapter 10). The disclosures made in accordance with paragraph 122 form part of the summary of accounting policies.

Figure 16.10 illustrates an extract from the notes of Telstra's financial statements. The extract is of the statement of the basis of preparation of the financial statements. Note that Telstra includes the statement of compliance with the Australian *Corporations Act 2001*, AASBs and IFRSs in the statement of basis of preparation of the financial report and discloses the uncertainty of accounting estimates.

FIGURE 16.10   Basis of preparation of the financial statements, Telstra

1.1 Basis of preparation of the financial report

This financial report is a general purpose financial report, prepared by a 'for profit' entity, in accordance with the requirements of the Australian Corporations Act 2001, Accounting Standards applicable in Australia and other authoritative pronouncements of the Australian Accounting Standards Board (AASB). It also complies with International Financial Reporting Standards (IFRS) and Interpretations published by the International Accounting Standards Board (IASB).

The financial report is presented in Australian dollars and, unless otherwise stated, all values have been rounded to the nearest million dollars ($m) under the option available under the Australian Securities and Investments Commission (ASIC) Corporations (Rounding in Financial/Directors' Report) Instrument 2016/191. The functional currency of the Telstra Entity and its Australian controlled entities is Australian dollars. The functional currency of certain non-Australian controlled entities is not Australian dollars. The results of these entities are translated into Australian dollars in accordance with our accounting policy in note 7.1.

The financial report is prepared in accordance with historical cost, except for some categories of financial instruments, which are recorded at fair value.

1.2 Key accounting estimates and judgements

Preparing the financial report requires management to make estimates and judgements. The accounting policies and significant management judgments and estimates used in the preparation of the financial report and any changes thereto are set out in the relevant notes. They can be located within the following notes:

Key accounting estimates and judgements	Note	Page
Impact of nbn Infrastructure Services Agreement (ISA) on sales revenue and other income	2.2	72
Estimating provision for income tax	2.4	75
Unrecognised deferred tax assets	2.4	76
Cash generating units (CGUs) for impairment assessment	3.1	80
Useful lives and residual values of tangible assets	3.1	80
Impact of nbn Infrastructure Services Agreement (ISA) on our fixed asset base	3.1	81
Determining CGUs and their recoverable amount for impairment assessment	3.2	83
Capitalisation of development costs	3.2	86
Determining fair value of identifiable intangible assets	3.2	86
Useful lives of intangible assets	3.2	86
Estimating allowance for doubtful debts	3.3	87
Estimating net realisable value	3.4	88
Long service leave provision	5.1	109
Defined benefit plan	5.3	117
Accounting for business combinations	6.1	119
Significant influence over our investments	6.3	127
Joint control of our investments	6.3	127

Note 7.1 includes our accounting policy on foreign currency translation, changes in accounting policies and a summary of new accounting standards to be applied in future reporting periods.

Source: Telstra Corporation Limited (2018, p. 64).

16.6.3 Information about capital

Paragraph 134 of AASB 101/IAS 1 requires disclosure of information that enables users of financial statements to evaluate the entity's management of capital. This requirement encompasses qualitative information about objectives, policies and processes, including a description of what is managed as capital, the nature of any externally imposed capital requirements, whether the entity has complied with externally imposed requirements, and, if the entity has not complied with external requirements, the implications of non-compliance.

Quantitative disclosures are also required, including summary data of what is managed as capital. This may differ from reported equity because an entity may exclude some components of equity, such as deferred amounts pertaining to cash flow hedges, from what is managed as capital, while including some items that are classified as liabilities, such as subordinated debt.

The standard adopts a management perspective by focusing on how capital is viewed by management, rather than prescribing specific definitions of capital for the purposes of the disclosures. The entity is required to base its capital disclosures on the information provided internally to key management personnel (AASB 101/IAS 1 paragraph 135).

16.6.4 Other disclosures

AASB 101/IAS 1 prescribes other disclosures, including certain information about dividends and corporate details, such as the legal structure.

Paragraph 51 of AASB 101/IAS 1 requires the following disclosures:
- the name of the reporting entity and any change in that name from the preceding reporting date
- whether the financial statements cover the individual entity or a group of entities
- the date of the end of the reporting period or the reporting period covered by the financial statements, whichever is appropriate to that component of the financial statements (the date of the end of the reporting period is appropriate for the statement of financial position, and the reporting period is appropriate for statements that report on flows, such as the statement of profit or loss and other comprehensive income)
- the presentation currency, as defined in AASB 121/IAS 21 *The Effects of Changes in Foreign Exchange Rates*
- the level of rounding used in presenting amounts in the financial statements, usually thousands or millions.

It is not uncommon for dividends to be proposed or declared (i.e. approved by the appropriate authorising body, such as the directors) after the reporting date but before the financial statements are issued. Unless the dividends are declared before the end of the reporting period they cannot be recognised in the financial statements. AASB 110/IAS 10 *Events after the Reporting Period* requires disclosure in the notes of any dividends that have been proposed or declared before the release of the financial statements but not recognised in the financial statements. Paragraph 137(a) of AASB 101/IAS 1 requires the disclosure to include the amount of the dividends that have been proposed or declared but not recognised, and the related amount per share. The amount of any cumulative preference dividends that have not been recognised as liabilities also must be disclosed (paragraph 137(b)).

AASB 101/IAS 1 also requires disclosure of certain non-financial information. The prescribed disclosures include (paragraph 138):
- the legal form of the entity, such as whether it is a company or a trust
- the country of incorporation
- the address of the registered office or the principal place of business (if different from the registered office)
- a description of the nature of the entity's operations and its principal activities
- the name of the parent and the ultimate parent of the group
- if a limited-life company, the length of the limited life.

Additional disclosures pertaining to **audit fees** and dividend imputation credits are required by AASB 1054. Paragraph 10 of AASB 1054 requires disclosure of fees paid to auditors or reviewers, distinguishing between payments for:
- audit or review of the financial statements of the entity
- non-audit services, detailing the nature and amount for each type of non-audit service, such as tax advice.

Dividend imputation was adopted in Australia in 1987. Prior to the introduction of dividend imputation, company profit was effectively taxed twice: once when the company was assessed on its taxable income, and again when the after-tax profit was distributed to shareholders as a dividend. Dividend imputation effectively allows the shareholder a credit for the tax that the company has already paid in relation to the profits from which the dividend is distributed.

Dividends can be fully franked, partially franked or unfranked. A fully franked dividend is one on which the shareholder, as a taxpayer, may be eligible to claim full tax credit for income tax previously paid by the company on the profit. A partially franked dividend arises where the company has not paid enough income tax on the profit to be able to pass on a full dividend imputation (franking) credit to the shareholder. Thus, the tax credit only attaches to part of the dividend. For example, a $2.00 dividend may have a franked component of $1.50 and an unfranked component of $0.50. If a company has not paid tax or has already passed on to shareholders all available dividend imputation credits, its dividends will be unfranked. From the shareholder's perspective, the dividend is assessable income, but there is no dividend imputation credit to offset the assessable income.

Fully franked dividends are more valuable than unfranked dividends to individual shareholders who are eligible to claim the franking credit. Thus, information about dividend imputation credits available is relevant to shareholders and potential shareholders of the company. An entity must disclose the amount of the dividend imputation credits available at the reporting date for use in subsequent reporting periods in accordance with paragraph 13 of AASB 1054. The Qantas Group's disclosures about dividend imputation credits were illustrated in figure 16.9.

16.6.5 Illustrative examples of financial statements

The IASB issues implementation guidance to accompany IFRSs. While not forming part of the standard, the guidance issued by the IASB is available on the AASB website. Part 1 of the IAS 1 Implementation Guidance (IAS 1 IG) includes illustrative examples of the presentation of financial statements. Two of the examples of the statement of profit or loss and other comprehensive income were reproduced as figures 16.6 and 16.7. You may wish to refer to Part 1 of IAS 1 IG for examples of other statements as well as additional examples of the statement of profit or loss and other comprehensive income. Part 2 of IAS 1 IG illustrates the determination of reclassification adjustments, while part 3 illustrates capital disclosures.

LEARNING CHECK

- ☐ Notes are provided to help users understand information in the financial statements.
- ☐ In addition to the requirements of AASB 101/IAS 1, notes are required by a number of standards relevant to particular transactions.
- ☐ Notes may provide information not presented in the financial statements.
- ☐ Notes are normally presented in this order:
    - statement of compliance with accounting standards
    - summary of significant accounting policies
    - information relating to items in the financial statements
    - other disclosures.
- ☐ An entity must disclose in the summary of significant accounting policies:
    - the measurement basis used in preparing the financial statements
    - any other relevant policies.
- ☐ An entity must disclose in the notes information about assumptions concerning the future and other key sources of estimation uncertainty at the end of the reporting period.
- ☐ An entity is required to disclose information to enable users of its financial statements to evaluate the entity's objectives, policies and processes for managing capital.
- ☐ AASB 101/IAS 1 and AASB 1054 require information regarding dividends, company details and audit fees to be disclosed.

SUMMARY

AASB 101/IAS 1 *Presentation of Financial Statements* and AASB 1054 *Australian Additional Disclosures* deal with fundamental disclosures and considerations that underpin financial statement presentation.

AASB 101/IAS 1 prescribes overall considerations to be applied in the preparation of financial statements, and the structure and content of financial statements. A complete set of financial statements comprises:
- a statement of financial position
- a statement of profit or loss and other comprehensive income
- a statement of cash flows
- a statement of changes in equity
- notes, comprising a summary of significant accounting policies and other explanatory information
- a statement of financial position as at the beginning of the earliest comparative period when certain changes are made retrospectively or items in the financial statements are reclassified.

The prescribed disclosures are designed to enhance the understandability of the financial statements to the users of general purpose financial statements in their economic decision making and to improve comparability of an entity's financial statements both with other entities and from previous periods. AASB 1054 prescribes additional disclosures required by the AASB beyond those required by IFRSs.

KEY TERMS

accrual basis of accounting Accounting in which the effects of all transactions and other events are recognised in the accounting records when they occur, rather than when cash or its equivalent is received or paid.

audit fees Payments for audit or review of the financial statements of the entity.

complete set of financial statements A statement of financial position as at the end of the period; a statement of profit or loss and other comprehensive income for the period; a statement of changes in equity for the period; a statement of cash flows for the period; notes, comprising a summary of significant accounting policies and other explanatory information; comparative information in respect of the preceding period; and a statement of financial position as at the beginning of the preceding period when an entity applies an accounting policy retrospectively or makes a retrospective restatement of items in its financial statements, or when it reclassifies items in its financial statements.

going concern The ability of the entity to continue in business for the foreseeable future.

notes Part of the financial statements provided to enhance the understandability of the statement of financial position, statement of profit or loss and other comprehensive income, statement of cash flows and statement of changes in equity.

operating cycle The time period between the acquisition of assets for processing and their realisation in cash or cash equivalents.

reclassification adjustments Amounts that were recognised in other comprehensive income in a previous period (or the current period) but are reclassified to the current period's profit or loss when the relevant item is derecognised.

statement of changes in equity A financial statement that provides a reconciliation of the opening and closing amounts of each component of equity for the period.

statement of financial position A financial statement that summarises an entity's assets, liabilities and equity.

statement of profit or loss and other comprehensive income A financial statement that summarises an entity's financial performance.

DEMONSTRATION PROBLEMS

16.1 Preparation of financial statements in accordance with AASB 101/IAS 1

The internal statement of profit or loss and other comprehensive income and statement of financial position of Pink Ltd are reproduced here as figures 16.11 and 16.12.

FIGURE 16.11 Statement of profit or loss and other comprehensive income of Pink Ltd for internal purposes

PINK LTD
Statement of profit or loss and other comprehensive income
for the year ended 30 June 2023

INCOME			
Revenues			
Sales		$1 545 000	
Less: Sales returns		5 000	$1 540 000
Services revenue			260 000
Other income			
Proceeds on sale of office furniture			20 000
Total income			1 820 000
EXPENSES			
Selling expenses			
Cost of sales	$942 800		
Freight inwards	6 000		
Total cost of sales		948 800	
Freight outwards		7 000	
Advertising expense		10 000	
Sales staff salaries expense		205 000	
Sales staff vehicle expense		15 000	
Telephone expense		12 500	
Depreciation — motor vehicles		30 000	
Depreciation — store equipment		12 000	
Depreciation — retail store		25 000	
Total selling expenses		1 265 300	
Administrative expenses			
Rates expense		15 000	
Insurance expense		16 000	
Administrative staff salaries expense		197 000	
Carrying amount of office furniture sold		17 000	
Depreciation — office furniture		18 000	
Total administrative expenses		263 000	
Financial expenses			
Rent expense		16 500	
Sales discount allowed		10 000	
Interest expense		1 500	
Bad debts expense		7 900	
Total financial expenses		35 900	
Total expenses			1 564 200
Profit before income tax			**255 800**
Income tax expense (30%)			(76 740)
Profit for the year			**179 060**
Other comprehensive income			
Gain on revaluation of retail store			60 000
Total comprehensive income			**$ 239 060**

FIGURE 16.12 Statement of financial position of Pink Ltd for internal purposes

PINK LTD
Statement of financial position
as at 30 June 2023

Current assets		
Cash		$ 64 000
Accounts receivable	$ 218 000	
Allowance for doubtful debts	(10 900)	207 100
Inventories		250 000
Prepaid insurance		4 000
Prepaid rent		2 000
Total current assets		527 100

Non-current assets		
Land (at cost)		100 000
Retail store (at fair value)		435 000
Motor vehicles (at cost)	300 000	
Accumulated depreciation	(180 000)	120 000
Store equipment (at cost)	60 000	
Accumulated depreciation	(27 000)	33 000
Office furniture (at cost)	90 000	
Accumulated depreciation	(38 000)	52 000
Goodwill (at cost)		140 000
Development costs		100 000
Total non-current assets		980 000
Total assets		1 507 100
Current liabilities		
Accounts payable		60 000
Salaries payable		9 000
Interest payable		300
Current tax liability		76 740
GST payable		8 000
Ordinary dividend payable		80 000
Preference dividend payable		40 000
Total current liabilities		274 040
Non-current liabilities		
Loan payable		12 000
Total non-current liabilities		12 000
Total liabilities		286 040
Net assets		**$1 221 060**
Equity		
Share capital		
400 000 ordinary shares issued and paid to $1		$ 400 000
500 000 preference shares issued and paid to $1		500 000
		900 000
Less: Share issue costs		(13 000)
Net share capital		887 000
Reserves		
Revaluation surplus	$ 160 000	
General reserve	75 000	
Retained earnings	99 060	
Total reserves		334 060
Total equity		**$1 221 060**

The internal financial statements are prepared based on the following additional information.

- An external valuer estimated the fair value of the retail store at $435 000. The carrying amount as at 30 June 2023 was $375 000. Assume a tax rate of 30%. The deferred tax effect has not been recorded.
- $10 000 has been transferred from retained earnings to the general reserve.
- A final dividend was declared (on 30 June 2023) out of retained earnings on ordinary shares at 20c per share and a dividend of 8% on preference shares.

Required

Prepare the following financial statements for external disclosure by Pink Ltd in accordance with the requirements of AASB 101/IAS 1 *Presentation of Financial Statements* (ignoring notes and comparative amounts):

1. a statement of profit or loss and other comprehensive income (classify expenses according to function)
2. a statement of financial position
3. a statement of changes in equity.

SOLUTION

The information in the internal financial statements, aggregated where necessary, provides the information for various line items in the financial statements prepared in accordance with the requirements of AASB 101/IAS 1 as outlined in this chapter.

1. *Statement of profit or loss and other comprehensive income*

Figure 16.13 illustrates the statement of profit or loss and other comprehensive income. The necessary calculations are explained after the figure.

FIGURE 16.13   Statement of profit or loss and other comprehensive income, Pink Ltd

PINK LTD Statement of profit or loss and other comprehensive income for the year ended 30 June 2023	
Revenue[a]	$1 540 000
Cost of sales	(948 800)
Gross profit	591 200
Services revenue	260 000
Other income[b]	3 000
Selling expenses[c]	(316 500)
Administrative expenses[d]	(246 000)
Other expenses[e]	(34 400)
Finance costs[f]	(1 500)
Profit before income tax	**255 800**
Income tax expense	(76 740)
Profit for the year	**179 060**
Other comprehensive income	
Items that will not be reclassified to profit or loss:	
Gain on revaluation of retail store	60 000
Income tax relating to items not reclassified	(18 000)
Other comprehensive income for the year, net of tax	42 000
Total comprehensive income for the year	**$ 221 060**

Calculations for figure 16.13

(a) *Revenue* of $1 540 000 was calculated as $1 545 000 (sales, net) less $5000 (sales returns).

(b) *Other income* of $3000 represents a gain from disposal of office furniture calculated as $20 000 (sale proceeds) less $17 000 (carrying amount).

(c) *Selling expenses* of $316 500 were calculated as $1 265 300 (total selling expenses according to the internal statement of profit or loss and other comprehensive income) less $948 800 (cost of sales).

(d) *Administrative expenses* of $246 000 were calculated as $263 000 (total administrative expenses according to the internal statement of profit or loss and other comprehensive income) less $17 000 (carrying amount of office furniture sold).

(e) *Other expenses* of $34 400 were calculated as $35 900 (total financial expenses according to the internal statement of profit or loss and other comprehensive income) less $1500 (interest expense).

(f) *Finance costs* expense of $1500 represents interest expense.

2. *Statement of financial position*

Figure 16.14 illustrates the statement of financial position. The necessary calculations are explained after the figure.

FIGURE 16.14   Statement of financial position, Pink Ltd

PINK LTD Statement of financial position as at 30 June 2023	
ASSETS	
Current assets	
Cash and cash equivalents	$ 64 000
Trade and other receivables[a]	213 100
Inventories	250 000
Total current assets	527 100
Non-current assets	
Property, plant and equipment[b]	740 000
Intangible assets[c]	240 000
Total non-current assets	980 000
Total assets	1 507 100

LIABILITIES	
Current liabilities	
Trade and other payables[(d)]	197 300
Current tax payable	76 740
Total current liabilities	274 040
Non-current liabilities	
Long-term borrowings	12 000
Deferred tax liabilities[(e)]	18 000
Total non-current liabilities	30 000
Total liabilities	304 040
Net assets	**$1 203 060**
EQUITY	
Share capital	$ 887 000
Reserves[(e, f)]	217 000
Retained earnings	99 060
Total equity	**$1 203 060**

Calculations for figure 16.14

(a) *Trade and other receivables* of $213 100 was calculated as $207 100 (accounts receivable, net) plus $4000 (prepaid insurance) plus $2000 (prepaid rent).

(b) *Property, plant and equipment* of $740 000 was calculated as $980 000 (total non-current assets according to the internal statement of financial position) less $140 000 (goodwill) less $100 000 (development costs).

(c) *Intangible assets* of $240 000 was calculated as $140 000 (goodwill) plus $100 000 (development costs).

(d) *Trade and other payables* of $197 300 was calculated as $60 000 (accounts payable) plus $9000 (salaries payable) plus $300 (interest payable) plus $8000 (GST payable) plus $120 000 (ordinary and preference dividends payable). GST payable is treated as part of trade and other payables, not current tax liabilities, in the statement of financial position, as required by AASB Interpretation 1031 *Accounting for the Goods and Services Tax (GST) paragraph 9*.

(e) As noted in the additional information provided, Pink Ltd has revalued its retail store upwards by $60 000. Applying AASB 112/IAS 12 *Income Taxes* and using the tax rate of 30%, this results in:
  • a *deferred tax liability* of $18 000 (30% × $60 000)
  • an increase in the revaluation surplus during the current period of $42 000 [$60 000 × (1 − 30%)].
    See chapters 5 and 12 for the treatment of revaluation increases and the associated tax effect.

(f) *Reserves* of $217 000 were calculated as $75 000 (general reserve) plus $142 000 (revaluation surplus, comprising $100 000
  [beginning] plus $42 000 [increase during the current period]).

3. *Statement of changes in equity*

Figure 16.15 illustrates the statement of changes in equity for Pink Ltd. The necessary calculations are provided after the figure.

FIGURE 16.15	Statement of changes in equity, Pink Ltd

PINK LTD					
Statement of changes in equity					
for the year ended 30 June 2023					
	Share capital	General reserve	Revaluation surplus[(a)]	Retained earnings	Total equity
Balance at 1 July 2022	**$887 000**	**$65 000**	**$100 000**	**$ 50 000**	**$1 102 000**
Total comprehensive income for the year	—	—	42 000	179 060	221 060
Dividend declared — ordinary	—	—	—	(80 000)	(80 000)
Dividend declared — preference	—	—	—	(40 000)	(40 000)
Transfer to general reserve	—	10 000	—	(10 000)	—
Balance at 30 June 2023	**$887 000**	**$75 000**	**$142 000**	**$ 99 060**	**$1 203 060**
Ordinary dividends: 20c per share					
Preference dividends: 8c pershare					

Calculations for figure 16.15

(a) As noted in the additional information provided, Pink Ltd revalued its retail store upwards by $60 000. Applying AASB 112/IAS 12 *Income Taxes* and using the tax rate of 30%, this results in:
  • a deferred tax liability of $18 000 (30% × $60 000)
  • an increase in the revaluation surplus during the current period of $42 000 [$60 000 × (1 − 30%)].
    See chapters 5 and 12 for the treatment of revaluation increases and the associated tax effect.

16.2 Revision of the financial statements and preparation of appropriate notes

A new company, Mars Ltd, has prepared its first financial statements, as shown, for internal purposes.

MARS LTD		
Statement of profit or loss and other comprehensive income		
for the period from incorporation (18 September 2023) to 30 June 2024		
Profit before income tax but after charging:		$255 000
Employee benefits expense	$30 000	
Interest on debentures	20 000	
Depreciation of plant	30 000	
Amortisation of patents and trademarks	20 000	
Impairment of goodwill	15 000	
Doubtful debts	5 000	
Accounting and audit expense	10 000	
Less: Income tax expense		80 500
		174 500
Extraordinary item (net of tax)		
Profit on sale of shares in Saturn Ltd		10 500
Total available for appropriation		185 000
Less: Proposed dividend		100 000
Retained earnings at 30 June 2024		**$ 85 000**

MARS LTD					
Statement of financial position					
as at 30 June 2024					
EQUITY			NON-CURRENT ASSETS		
1 000 000 ordinary			Land (revalued)		$1 016 000
shares called and					
paid to 80c each	$800 000		Plant (at cost $250 000		
Retained earnings	85 000		*less* depreciation		
			$30 000)		220 000
Revaluation surplus			Goodwill (at cost		
(Land)	11 200	$ 896 200	$115 000 *less*		
			impairment $15 000)		100 000
NON-CURRENT			Patents and trademarks		
LIABILITIES			(at cost $150 000 *less*		
			amortisation $20 000)		130 000
8% debentures	500 000				1 466 000
Deferred tax liability	4 800	504 800			
CURRENT LIABILITIES			CURRENT ASSETS		
Accounts and bills			Inventories (finished		
payable	260 000		goods)	$150 000	
Provision for taxation	85 000		Debtors (*less* allowance		
			for doubtful		
			debts $5000)	130 000	
Dividend payable	100 000				
Employee benefits	20 000	465 000	Cash at bank	120 000	400 000
		$1 866 000			$1 866 000

Additional information
- 8% debentures were issued to the public on 1 January 2024 for a term of 7 years.
- On 1 November 2023, shares were purchased in Saturn Ltd at a cost of $20 000. These shares were subsequently sold on 31 March 2024 for $35 000.
- Sales revenue amounted to $1 000 000 and raw materials used totalled $830 000.
- Revenue from services amounted to $65 000.
- The dividend payable does not require shareholder approval.
- Accounting and audit expense of $10 000 comprised $7000 for audit work and $3000 for taxation advice.
- On 30 June 2024, land was revalued from $1 000 000 to $1 016 000.
- Tax rate is 30%.

Required

1. Revise the financial statements to comply with the requirements of AASB 101/IAS 1 *Presentation of Financial Statements*, classifying expenses according to nature. Assume an income tax rate of 30%.
2. Prepare any appropriate notes to these financial statements in accordance with the requirements of AASB 101/IAS 1.

SOLUTION

1. *Present financial statements as per AASB 101/IAS 1*

   Figure 16.16 illustrates the statement of profit or loss and other comprehensive income, figure 16.17 illustrates the statement of financial position, figure 16.18 illustrates the statement of changes in equity and figure 16.19 illustrates the notes required by AASB 101/IAS 1. Details regarding the calculation of figures are provided, where appropriate, following each of the financial statements.

FIGURE 16.16	Statement of profit or loss and other comprehensive income, Mars Ltd

MARS LTD Statement of profit or loss and other comprehensive income for the period from 18 September 2023 to 30 June 2024	
Revenue[a]	$1 065 000
Other income[b]	15 000
Changes in inventories of finished goods[c]	150 000
Raw materials used	(830 000)
Employee benefits expense	(30 000)
Depreciation of plant	(30 000)
Amortisation of patents and trademarks	(20 000)
Impairment of goodwill	(15 000)
Doubtful debts	(5 000)
Accounting and audit expense	(10 000)
Finance costs	(20 000)
Profit before income tax	**270 000**
Income tax expense[d]	(85 000)
Profit for the period	**185 000**
Other comprehensive income	
Items that will not be reclassified to profit or loss:	
Gain on revaluation of land	16 000
Income tax relating to items not reclassified[e]	(4 800)
Other comprehensive income for the period, net of tax	11 200
Total comprehensive income for the period	**$ 196 200**

Calculations for figure 16.16
(a) *Revenue* of $1 065 000 is calculated as $1 000 000 (sales revenue) plus $65 000 (services revenue).
(b) *Other income* of $15 000 represents a gain on sale of shares in Saturn Ltd calculated as $35 000 (sale price) less $20 000 (cost).
(c) *Changes in inventories of finished goods* represents the increase in the value of inventories from nil (18 September 2023) to $150 000 (30 June 2024).
(d) *Income tax expense* of $85 000 is calculated as $80 500 (as per question) plus $4500 (income tax on sale of shares in Saturn Ltd [30% × $15 000]).
(e) *Income tax relating to items not reclassified* is calculated as 30% × $16 000 = $4800.

FIGURE 16.17	Statement of financial position, Mars Ltd

MARS LTD Statement of financial position as at 30 June 2024	
ASSETS	
Current assets	
Cash and cash equivalents	$120 000
Trade and other receivables	130 000
Inventories	150 000
Total current assets	400 000

MARS LTD	
Statement of financial position	
as at 30 June 2024	
Non-current assets	
Land	$1 016 000
Property, plant and equipment	220 000
Goodwill	100 000
Other intangible assets	130 000
Total non-current assets	1 466 000
Total assets	1 866 000
LIABILITIES	
Current liabilities	
Trade and other payables[(a)]	360 000
Current tax payable	85 000
Short-term provisions	20 000
Total current liabilities	465 000
Non-current liabilities	
Long-term borrowings	500 000
Deferred tax liability	4 800
Total non-current liabilities	504 800
Total liabilities	969 800
Net assets	**$ 896 200**
EQUITY	
Share capital	$ 800 000
Retained earnings	85 000
Revaluation surplus[(b)]	11 200
Total equity	**$ 896 200**

(a) *Trade and other payables* of $360 000 equals $260 000 (accounts and bills payable) plus $100 000 (dividend payable).
(b) *Revaluation surplus* of $11 200 equals $16 000 (gain on revaluation of land) less $4800 (deferred tax liability [30% × $16 000]).

FIGURE 16.18	Statement of changes in equity, Mars Ltd

MARS LTD			
Statement of changes in equity			
for the period ended 30 June 2024			
	Share capital	Retained earnings	Revaluation surplus	Total
---	---	---	---	---
Balance at 18 September 2023	—	—	—	—
Total comprehensive income for the period	—	$ 185 000	$ 11 200	$ 196 200
Issue of ordinary shares	$ 800 000	—	—	800 000
Dividend declared — ordinary shares	—	(100 000)	—	(100 000)
Balance at 30 June 2024	**$ 800 000**	**85 000**	**$ 11 200**	**$ 896 200**

2. *Prepare appropriate notes*

    The notes below are only those required in accordance with AASB 101/IAS 1. Additional notes would also need to be provided in accordance with the disclosure requirements of other standards, for example:

- details of accounting policies in accordance with AASB 108/IAS 8 (see chapter 18)
- various details for classes of property, plant and equipment in accordance with AASB 116/IAS 16 (see chapter 5)
- details of intangible assets in accordance with AASB 138/IAS 38 (see chapter 6)
- classifications of inventories in accordance with AASB 102/IAS 2 *Inventories* (see chapter 4)
- various details for classes of provisions in accordance with AASB 137/IAS 37 *Provisions, Contingent Liabilities and Contingent Assets* (see chapter 8).

    Information regarding sources of estimation uncertainty is required to be disclosed in accordance with paragraphs 125–133 of AASB 101/IAS 1 (see also section 16.6.2). As this information is usually unique to each entity, and given that no information relating to estimation uncertainty was provided in the question, these details do not appear in the notes.

FIGURE 16.19 Notes required by AASB 101/IAS 1, Mars Ltd

Notes to the financial statements for the period ending 30 June 2024

Note 1. Summary of significant accounting policies

Statement of compliance

The financial statements are general purpose financial statements which have been prepared in accordance with the requirements of the *Corporations Act 2001*, Australian accounting standards which include Australian equivalents to international financial reporting standards (AIFRSs) and AASB Interpretations. Compliance with AIFRSs ensures the financial statements and notes comply with international financial reporting standards.

Basis of preparation

The financial statements have been prepared on the historical cost basis, except where stated otherwise.

Dividends

Dividends per ordinary share 10c per share.

Note 2. Share capital

Share capital:	
1 000 000 ordinary shares paid to 80c per share	$800 000

Shares issued during the year

1 000 000 ordinary shares were issued as paid to 80c per share to finance the operations of the company. There were no shares issued at the beginning of the reporting period.

Ordinary shares

Ordinary shares entitle the holder to receive dividends and, in the event of winding up, to participate in the proceeds from the sale of assets in proportion to the number of and amounts paid up on shares held. Ordinary shareholders are entitled to one vote in person or by proxy, per share, at a meeting of the company [assumed].

Note 3. Audit fees

Amounts paid or payable to the auditor for:	
Audit or review of the financial statements of the entity	$ 7 000
Non-audit services — taxation advice	3 000
	$10 000

COMPREHENSION QUESTIONS

1 Discuss the eight overall considerations to be applied in the presentation of financial statements. Of these, which are more subjective? Explain your answer.

2 Why is it important for entities to disclose the measurement bases used in preparing the financial statements?

3 What is the purpose of a statement of financial position? What comprises a complete set of financial statements in accordance with AASB 101/IAS 1?

4 What are the major limitations of a statement of financial position as a source of information for users of general purpose financial statements?

5 Under what circumstances are assets and liabilities ordinarily classified broadly in order of liquidity rather than on a current/non-current classification?

6 Can an asset that is not realisable within 12 months be classified as a current asset? If so, under what circumstances?

7 Explain the difference between classification of expenses by nature and by function.

8 Does the separate identification of profit and items of other comprehensive income provide a meaningful distinction between the effects of different types of non-owner transactions and events?

9 What is the objective of a statement of changes in equity?

10 Why is a summary of accounting policies important to ensuring the understandability of financial statements to users of general purpose financial statements?

11 Provide an example of a judgement made in preparing the financial statements that can lead to estimation uncertainty at the end of the reporting period. Describe the disclosures that would be required in the notes.

12 What disclosures are required in the notes in regard to accounting policy judgements?

CASE STUDY 16.1

ANALYSIS OF EXPENSES

Review the published financial reports of the following companies and report on the information applicable to the statement of profit or loss and other comprehensive income. Determine whether the expenses are classified by nature or function. Give some possible reasons for the different methods of classification of expenses used.

- Bayer Group
- Qantas Airways Ltd
- Sigma Pharmaceuticals Ltd
- Telstra Corporation Limited

CASE STUDY 16.2

MEASUREMENT BASIS USED

A first-time shareholder has approached you requesting some advice. The shareholder has received the company's annual report and noticed the following statement in the summary of significant accounting policies.

> The financial report has been prepared on the basis of historical cost, except for the revaluation of certain non-current assets which is explained in the notes.

Required

Explain to the shareholder why this statement is included in the accounting policy note.

CASE STUDY 16.3

MANAGEMENT JUDGEMENTS

Any judgements made by management when applying the entity's accounting policies that have a significant effect on amounts recognised in the financial statements must also be disclosed. What judgements do you think are made by management?

CASE STUDY 16.4

FORMATS FOR STATEMENT OF PROFIT OR LOSS AND OTHER COMPREHENSIVE INCOME

The accountant for Moonshine Ltd has heard that following recent changes to accounting standards, the income statement now has a new title and companies now have a choice regarding the presentation of income and expense items recognised in a period. However, the accountant is unsure of the exact requirements following changes to accounting standards.

Required

As you are a recent university accounting graduate, the accountant seeks your assistance and requests that you provide information to Moonshine Ltd about this apparent presentation choice and whether the income statement now has a new title.

APPLICATION AND ANALYSIS EXERCISES

★ BASIC | ★ ★ MODERATE | ★ ★ ★ DIFFICULT

16.1 Fair presentation ★   LO2

The directors of an Australian company that is required to prepare financial reports under the Corporations Act conclude that applying the requirements of AASB 136 *Impairment of Assets* would not provide a fair presentation because the resulting $120 000 impairment loss is temporary.

Required

Advise the directors how this problem should be addressed in the financial statements in accordance with AASB 101.

16.2 Materiality and aggregation ★   LO2

Indicate whether each of the following statements is true or false.
1. A material item is determined solely on the basis of its size.
2. A class of assets or liabilities is determined by reference to items of a similar nature or function.
3. Inventories and trade accounts receivable may be aggregated in the statement of financial position.
4. Cash and cash equivalents may be aggregated in the statement of financial position.

16.3 Classification of items in the statement of financial position ★   LO3

The general ledger trial balance of Thomas Ltd includes the following accounts that are reported in the statement of financial position.

(a)	Trade receivables	(g)	Debentures payable
(b)	Work in progress	(h)	Preference share capital
(c)	Trade creditors	(i)	Unearned revenue
(d)	Prepayments	(j)	Accrued salaries
(e)	Property	(k)	Trading securities held
(f)	Goodwill	(l)	Share capital

Thomas Ltd classifies assets and liabilities into current and non-current categories and uses the minimum line items permitted under AASB 101/IAS 1.

Required

Assume you are the accountant responsible for preparing the statement of financial position of Thomas Ltd. In which caption and classification on the statement of financial position would you include each of the above accounts? If you need additional information to finalise your decision as to the appropriate classification or caption, indicate what information you require.

16.4 Current asset and liability classifications ★   LO3

The general ledger trial balance of David Ltd at 30 June 2022 includes the following asset and liability accounts.

(a)	Interest payable	$	4 000
(b)	Trade receivables		200 000
(c)	Accounts payable		170 000
(d)	Prepayments		24 000
(e)	Inventories of finished goods		240 000
(f)	Allowance for doubtful debts		16 000
(g)	Cash		20 000
(h)	Accrued wages and salaries		40 000
(i)	Inventories of raw materials		120 000
(j)	Loan (due 31 October 2022)		200 000
(k)	Lease liability		150 000
(l)	Current tax payable		60 000

Additional information
- The lease liability (k) includes an amount of $26 000 for lease payments due before 30 June 2023.
- The company classifies assets and liabilities using a current/non-current basis.

Required

Prepare the current assets and current liabilities sections of the statement of financial position of David Ltd as at 30 June 2022, using the minimum line items permitted under AASB 101/IAS 1.

16.5 Current asset classifications ★   **LO3**

The general ledger trial balance of Madeleine Ltd includes the following asset accounts at 30 June 2022.

(a)	Inventories	$250 000
(b)	Trade receivables	300 000
(c)	Prepaid insurance	20 000
(d)	Listed investments held for trading purposes at fair value	50 000
(e)	Investments in financial assets	200 000
(f)	Cash	75 000
(g)	Deferred tax asset	37 500

Additional information

• Madeleine Ltd's investments in financial assets are part of a long-term investment strategy.
• The company classifies assets and liabilities using a current/non-current basis.

Required

Prepare the current asset section of the statement of financial position of Madeleine Ltd as at 30 June 2022, using the minimum line items permitted under AASB 101/IAS 1.

16.6 Statement of profit or loss and other comprehensive income ★   **LO4**

The general ledger trial balance of DEF Ltd includes the following accounts at 30 June 2022.

(a)	Sales revenue	$1 800 000
(b)	Interest income	36 000
(c)	Gain on sale of plant	7 500
(d)	Valuation gain on trading securities	30 000
(e)	Dividend revenue	7 500
(f)	Cost of sales	1 260 000
(g)	Finance expenses	27 000
(h)	Selling and distribution expenses	114 000
(i)	Administrative expenses	52 500
(j)	Income tax expense	127 500

Additional information

• DEF Ltd recognised a loss on valuation of $1500 net of tax for financial assets recognised at fair value through other comprehensive income. No financial assets were sold during the year.
• A gain of $6000 net of tax was recognised on the revaluation of land.
• DEF Ltd uses the single statement format for the statement of profit or loss and other comprehensive income.
• DEF Ltd classifies expenses by function.

Required

Prepare the statement of profit or loss and other comprehensive income of DEF Ltd for the year ended 30 June 2022, showing the analysis of expenses in the statement.

16.7 Statement of profit or loss and other comprehensive income ★   **LO4**

The general ledger trial balance of Dion Ltd includes the following accounts at 30 June 2022.

(a)	Sales revenue	$750 000
(b)	Interest revenue	25 000
(c)	Gain on sale of plant and equipment	10 000
(d)	Cost of sales	400 000
(e)	Finance expenses	15 000
(f)	Selling and distribution costs	50 000
(g)	Administrative expenses	30 000
(h)	Income tax expense	50 000

Additional information

- A revaluation gain of $14 000 net of tax was recognised for financial assets recognised at fair value through other comprehensive income held during 2022. This gain may subsequently be reclassified.
- No financial assets recognised at fair value through other comprehensive income were sold during the year.
- Dion Ltd uses the single statement format for the statement of profit or loss and other comprehensive income and classifies expenses by function.

Required

Prepare the statement of profit or loss and other comprehensive income of Dion Ltd for the year ended 30 June 2022, showing the analysis of expenses in the statement.

16.8 Statement of changes in equity ★   **LO5**

The shareholders' equity section of the statement of financial position of Ark Ltd at 30 June 2022 is as follows.

	2022	2021
Share capital	$100 000	$ 80 000
General reserve	25 000	20 000
Foreign currency translation reserve	37 000	30 000
Retained earnings	85 000	80 000
	$247 000	$210 000

Additional information

- Ark Ltd issued 8000 shares at $2.50 each on 31 May 2022 for cash.
- A transfer of $5000 was made from retained earnings to the general reserve.
- Comprehensive income for the year was $72 000, including a foreign currency translation gain of $7000 recognised in other comprehensive income.
- Dividends paid during 2022: final dividend for 2021, $25 000; interim dividend, $30 000.

Required

Prepare the statement of changes in equity of Ark Ltd for the year ended 30 June 2022 in accordance with AASB 101/IAS 1.

16.9 Materiality, offsetting ★   **LO2**

Fine Company Ltd is a retailer that imports about 30% of its goods. The following foreign exchange gains and losses were recognised in profit during the year.

	Loss $m	Gain $m
Foreign currency borrowings with Bank L	50	
Forward exchange contracts used as hedging instruments		1
Forward exchange contracts not used as hedges	3	
Foreign currency borrowings with Bank S		10

Materiality has been determined as $5 million for items recognised in profit or loss.

Required

Identify which of the above gains and losses are permitted to be offset in Fine Company Ltd's financial statements.

16.10 Preparation of a statement of financial position ★   **LO3**

The summarised general ledger trial balance of Jayden Ltd, a manufacturing company, includes the following accounts at 30 June 2022.

	Dr	Cr
Cash	$ 175 000	
Deposits (at call)	36 000	
Trade debtors	1 744 000	
Allowance for doubtful debts		$ 80 000
Sundry debtors	320 000	
Prepayments	141 000	
Raw materials inventories	490 000	
Work in progress	151 000	
Finished goods inventories	1 042 000	
Investments in listed companies	52 000	
Land (at valuation)	250 000	
Buildings (at cost)	1 030 000	
Accumulated depreciation — buildings		120 000
Plant and equipment	8 275 000	
Accumulated depreciation — plant and equipment		3 726 000
Leased assets	775 000	
Accumulated amortisation — leased assets		310 000
Goodwill	3 200 000	
Accumulated impairment — goodwill		670 000
Patents	110 000	
Trade creditors		1 617 000
Sundry creditors and accruals		840 000
Bank loans		2 215 000
Debentures		675 000
Other loans		800 000
Lease liabilities		350 000
Current tax payable		152 000
Deferred tax liability		420 000
Provision for employment benefits		275 000
Provision for restructuring		412 000
Provision for warranty		42 000
Share capital		3 500 000
Investments revaluation surplus		25 000
Land revaluation surplus		81 000
Retained earnings		1 481 000
	$17 791 000	$17 791 000

Additional information
- Bank loans and 'other loans' are all repayable beyond 1 year.
- $300 000 of the debentures is repayable within 1 year.
- Lease liabilities include $125 000 repayable within 1 year.
- Investments in companies are long-term investments. Revaluation gains and losses will not be reclassified.
- Provision for employment benefits includes $192 000 payable within 1 year.
- The planned restructuring is intended to be completed within 1 year.
- Provision for warranty includes $20 000 estimated to be incurred beyond 1 year.

Required

Prepare the statement of financial position of Jayden Ltd at 30 June 2022 in accordance with AASB 101/IAS 1, using the captions that a listed entity is likely to use.

16.11 Preparation of a statement of financial position ★ **LO3**

The summarised general ledger trial balance of Dominic Ltd, a manufacturing company, includes the following accounts at 30 June 2022.

	Dr	Cr
Cash deposits	$ 234 000	
Trade debtors	1 163 000	
Allowance for doubtful debts		$ 50 000
Sundry debtors	270 000	
Prepayments	94 000	
Sundry loans (current)	20 000	
Raw materials on hand	493 000	

Finished goods	695 000
Investments in unlisted companies	30 000
Land (at cost)	234 000
Buildings (at cost)	687 000
Accumulated depreciation — buildings	80 000
Plant and equipment (at cost)	6 329 000
Accumulated depreciation — plant and equipment	3 036 000
Goodwill	1 850 000
Brand names	40 000
Patents	25 000
Deferred tax asset	189 000
Trade creditors	1 078 000
Sundry creditors and accruals	685 000
Bank overdraft	115 000
Bank loans	1 273 000
Other loans	646 000
Current tax payable	74 000
Provision for employee benefits	222 000
Dividends payable	100 000
Provision for warranty	20 000
Share capital	3 459 000
Retained earnings	1 515 000
	$12 353 000 $12 353 000

Additional information
- The bank overdraft is payable on demand and forms part of cash equivalents.
- Bank loans include amounts repayable within 1 year $480 000.
- Other loans outstanding are repayable within 1 year.
- Provision for employee benefits includes $124 000 payable within 1 year.
- Provision for warranty is in respect of a 6-month warranty given over certain goods sold.
- The investments in unlisted companies are long-term investments.

Required

Prepare the statement of financial position of Dominic Ltd at 30 June 2022 in accordance with AASB 101/IAS 1, using the captions that a listed company is likely to use.

16.12 Preparation of a statement of financial position ★ **LO3**

The summarised general ledger trial balance of Daniel Ltd, an investment company, includes the following accounts at 30 June 2022.

	Dr	Cr
Cash at bank	$ 14 000	
Deposits (at call)	224 869	
Dividends receivable	22 693	
Interest receivable	478	
Settlements receivable	9 900	
Trading securities	74 455	
Investments in listed securities	1 880 000	
Deferred tax asset	655	
Settlements payable		$ 14 805
Interest payable		280
Other payables		83
Current tax payable		242
Provision for employee benefits		752
Deferred tax liability		56 414
Share capital		1 500 000
Revaluation surplus — investments		376 090
Retained earnings		278 384
	$2 227 050	$2 227 050

Additional information
- Provision for employee benefits includes $280 payable within 1 year.
- Investments in listed securities are held as long-term investments. Revaluation gains and losses will not be reclassified.

- The deferred tax asset and deferred tax liability do not satisfy the criteria for offsetting in accordance with AASB 112/IAS 12.

Required

Prepare the statement of financial position of Daniel Ltd at 30 June 2022 in accordance with AASB 101/IAS 1, using the captions that a listed company is likely to use.

16.13 **Preparation of a statement of profit or loss and other comprehensive income** ★ **LO4**

The general ledger trial balance of Caitlin Ltd, an investment company, includes the following revenue and expense items for the year ended 30 June 2022.

	Dr	Cr
Dividends from investments		$920 000
Distributions from trusts		60 000
Interest on deposits		80 000
Interest income from bank bills		10 000
Income from dealing in securities and derivatives (held for trading purposes)		40 000
Loss on credit derivatives (held for trading)	$ 60 000	
Other income		10 000
Interest expense	15 000	
Administrative salaries and wages	30 000	
Sundry administrative expenses	45 000	
Income tax expense	280 000	

Additional information

- The revaluation gain for financial assets recognised at fair value through other comprehensive income held during the year ended 30 June 2022 was $70 000. The related tax was $21 000. Revaluation gains and losses will not be reclassified.
- No financial assets were sold during the year ended 30 June 2022.
- Caitlin Ltd uses the single statement format for the statement of profit or loss and other comprehensive income.
- Caitlin Ltd presents an analysis of expenses by function in the statement of profit or loss and other comprehensive income.

Required

Prepare the statement of profit or loss and other comprehensive income of Medico Ltd for the year ended 30 June 2022 in accordance with AASB 101/IAS 1, showing the analysis of expenses by function in the statement.

16.14 **Preparation of a statement of profit or loss and other comprehensive income** ★ **LO4**

The general ledger trial balance of Medico Ltd, a medical manufacturing and research company, includes the following accounts at 30 June 2022.

	Dr	Cr
Sales revenue		$2 600 000
Interest income		4 000
Gain on sale of plant		52 000
Rental income		4 000
Royalty income		20 000
Other revenue		2 000
Cost of sales	$1 640 000	
Interest on borrowings	66 000	
Sundry borrowing costs	2 000	
Research expense	102 000	
Advertising expense	50 000	
Sales staff salaries	194 000	
Amortisation of patents	14 000	
Freight out	64 000	
Shipping supplies	32 000	
Depreciation on sales equipment	10 000	
Administrative salaries	144 000	
Legal and professional fees	26 000	
Office rent expense	60 000	

Insurance expense	28 000
Depreciation of office equipment	32 000
Stationery and supplies	10 000
Miscellaneous expenses	4 000
Income tax expense	62 000

Additional information
- Land was revalued upward by $200 000 during the year ended 30 June 2022. The related tax was $60 000.
- Medico Ltd uses the single statement format for the statement of profit or loss and other comprehensive income.

Required

Prepare the statement of profit or loss and other comprehensive income of Medico Ltd for the year ended 30 June 2022 in accordance with AASB 101/IAS 1, showing the analysis of expenses by function in the statement.

16.15 Statement of profit or loss and other comprehensive income ★ ★   **LO4**

The general ledger trial balance of Anastasia Ltd includes the following accounts at 30 June 2022.

(a)	Sales revenue	$975 000
(b)	Interest income	20 000
(c)	Share of profit of associates	15 000
(d)	Gain on sale of financial assets	10 000
(e)	Decrease in inventories of finished goods	25 000
(f)	Raw materials and consumables used	350 000
(g)	Employee benefit expenses	150 000
(h)	Loss on translation of foreign operations (nil tax effect)	30 000
(i)	Depreciation of property, plant and equipment	45 000
(j)	Impairment loss on property	80 000
(k)	Finance costs	35 000
(l)	Other expenses	45 000
(m)	Income tax expense	75 000

Additional information
- The financial assets are bonds that are measured at fair value, with changes in fair value recognised through the statement of profit or loss. When held-for-sale financial assets from this category are sold, the accumulated amount recognised in equity for the asset is reclassified to profit or loss. Movements in the financial assets revaluation reserve during the year ended 30 June 2022 comprised:
  - gross revaluation increases recognised $44 000 (related deferred income tax $14 000)
  - gross reclassifications on sale of the financial assets $10 000 gain (related income tax $3000).
- Anastasia Ltd uses the single statement format for the statement of profit or loss and other comprehensive income.
- Anastasia Ltd presents an analysis of expenses by nature in the statement of profit or loss and other comprehensive income.

Required

Prepare the statement of profit or loss and other comprehensive income of Anastasia Ltd for the year ended 30 June 2022.

16.16 Presentation of items in the financial statements ★ ★   **LO2, 3, 4, 5, 6**

Consider the following items for Xavier Ltd at 30 June 2022.
- (a) Loss on revaluation of financial assets recognised at fair value through other comprehensive income
- (b) Finance expenses
- (c) Aggregate amount of dividends declared and paid during the year
- (d) Revaluation loss on building (not reversing any previous revaluation)
- (e) Allowance for doubtful debts
- (f) Transfer from retained earnings to general reserve
- (g) Contractual commitments under an operating lease
- (h) Deferred tax liability

Required

State whether each item is reported in:

1. the statement of financial position
2. profit or loss in the statement of profit or loss and other comprehensive income
3. other comprehensive income in the statement of profit or loss and other comprehensive income
4. the statement of changes in equity
5. the notes to the financial statements.

16.17 Presentation of items in the financial statements ★ ★   **LO2, 3, 4, 5, 6**

Consider the following items for Kateri Ltd at 30 June 2022.

(a) Contingent liabilities
(b) Dividends paid
(c) Cash and cash equivalents
(d) Capital contributed during the year
(e) Revaluation gain on land (not reversing any previous revaluation)
(f) Judgements that management has made in classifying financial assets
(g) Income tax expense
(h) Provisions

Required

State whether each item is reported in:

1. the statement of financial position
2. profit or loss in the statement of profit or loss and other comprehensive income
3. other comprehensive income in the statement of profit or loss and other comprehensive income
4. the statement of changes in equity
5. the notes to the financial statements.

16.18 Preparation of a statement of financial position and statement of profit or loss and other comprehensive income ★ ★   **LO3, 4**

The summarised general ledger trial balance of Roisin Ltd, a spare parts manufacturer, for the year ended 30 June 2022 is detailed below.

	Dr	Cr
Sales of goods		$7 760 000
Share of profits of associates		36 000
Rent received		9 000
Other income		6 000
Cost of sales	$5 378 000	
Distribution expenses	243 000	
Sales and marketing expenses	1 467 000	
Administration expenses	520 000	
Interest expense	74 000	
Other borrowing expenses	6 000	
Income tax expense	141 000	
Cash at bank	20 000	
Deposits (at call)	150 000	
Trade debtors	740 000	
Allowance for doubtful debts		24 000
Other debtors	154 000	
Employee share plan loans	260 000	
Raw materials inventories	53 000	
Finished goods inventories	1 190 000	
Investment in associates	375 000	
Land and buildings	426 000	
Accumulated depreciation — buildings		61 000
Plant and equipment	2 100 000	
Accumulated depreciation — plant and equipment		940 000
Financial assets recognised at fair value through other comprehensive income	60 000	
Goodwill	1 450 000	
Bank loans		111 000
Other loans		810 000
Trade creditors		820 000
Provision for employee benefits		153 000

Provision for restructuring		62 000
Provision for warranty		40 000
Income tax payable		30 000
Deferred tax liability		100 000
Issued capital		3 220 000
Retained earnings, 1 July 2021		760 000
Dividends paid	150 000	
Financial assets revaluation reserve		15 000
	$14 957 000	$14 957 000

Additional information
- Employee share plan loans receivable include $40 000 due within 1 year.
- $30 000 of bank loans is repayable within 1 year.
- $375 000 of other loans is repayable within 1 year.
- Provision for employee benefits includes $108 000 payable within 1 year.
- The planned restructuring is intended to be fully implemented within 1 year.
- Provision for warranty is in respect of a 6-month warranty on certain goods sold.
- The financial assets were acquired during the current year and were revalued upward by $23 000 at the end of the reporting period. The related income tax was $8000.
- The financial assets are equity securities which the entity elected to recognise at fair value through other comprehensive income. The accumulated gain or loss will not be reclassified.
- Roisin Ltd uses the single statement format for the statement of profit or loss and other comprehensive income and presents an analysis of expenses by function in the statement.

Required

Prepare the statement of financial position and statement of profit or loss and other comprehensive income of Roisin Ltd for the year ended 30 June 2022 in accordance with AASB 101/IAS 1, using statement captions that a listed company is likely to use.

16.19 Preparation of a statement of financial position, statement of profit or loss and other comprehensive income and statement of changes in equity ★ ★ ★   **LO3, 4, 5**

The summarised general ledger trial balance of Flip Ltd, a manufacturing company, for the year ended 30 June 2022 is detailed below.

	Dr	Cr
Sales revenue		$5 000 000
Interest income		22 000
Sundry income		25 000
Change in inventories of work in progress	$ 125 000	
Change in inventories of finished goods		60 000
Raw materials used	2 200 000	
Employee benefit expense	950 000	
Depreciation expense	226 000	
Amortisation — patent	25 000	
Rental expense	70 000	
Advertising expense	142 000	
Insurance expense	45 000	
Freight out expense	133 000	
Doubtful debts expense	10 000	
Interest expense	30 000	
Other expenses	8 000	
Income tax expense	320 000	
Cash	4 000	
Cash on deposit (at call)	80 000	
Trade debtors	495 000	
Allowance for doubtful debts		18 000
Other debtors	27 000	
Raw materials inventories, 30 June 2022	320 000	
Finished goods inventories, 30 June 2022	385 000	
Land	94 000	
Buildings	220 000	
Accumulated depreciation — land and buildings		52 000
Plant and equipment	1 380 000	

	Dr	Cr
Accumulated depreciation — plant and equipment		320 000
Patents	140 000	
Accumulated amortisation — patent		50 000
Goodwill	620 000	
Bank loans		92 000
Other loans		450 000
Trade creditors		452 000
Provision for employee benefits		120 000
Income tax payable		35 000
Deferred tax liability		140 000
Retained earnings, 30 June 2021		310 000
Dividends paid	210 000	
Share capital		1 137 000
Dividends reinvested		41 000
Deferred cash flow hedge (equity)	65 000	
	$8 324 000	$8 324 000

Additional information
- $20 000 of bank loans is repayable within 1 year.
- $90 000 of other loans is repayable within 1 year.
- Flip Ltd uses the single statement format for the statement of profit or loss and other comprehensive income and presents an analysis of expenses by nature in the statement.

Required

Prepare the statement of financial position, statement of profit or loss and other comprehensive income and statement of changes in equity of Flip Ltd for the year ended 30 June 2022 in accordance with the requirements of AASB 101/IAS 1, using statement captions that a listed company is likely to use.

16.20 **Preparation of a statement of financial position, statement of profit or loss and other comprehensive income and statement of changes in equity** ★ ★ ★   **LO3, 4, 5**

The summarised general ledger trial balance of Cob Ltd, a manufacturing company, for the year ended 30 June 2022 is detailed below.

	Dr	Cr
Sales of goods		$4 769 000
Interest income		6 000
Cost of sales	$3 287 000	
Distribution expenses	86 000	
Sales and marketing expenses	820 000	
Administration expenses	252 000	
Interest expense	44 000	
Other borrowing expenses	4 000	
Income tax expense	85 000	
Cash on hand	4 000	
Cash on deposit, at call	100 000	
Trade debtors	450 000	
Allowance for doubtful debts		14 000
Other debtors	93 000	
Raw materials inventories	188 000	
Finished goods inventories	714 000	
Financial assets recognised at fair value through other comprehensive income	225 000	
Land and buildings	257 000	
Accumulated depreciation — buildings		36 000
Plant and equipment	1 260 000	
Accumulated depreciation — plant and equipment		564 000
Patents	48 000	
Amortisation of patent		3 000
Goodwill	870 000	
Bank loans		66 000
Other loans		570 000
Trade creditors		510 000
Provision for employee benefits		93 000
Warranty provision		37 000

Current tax payable		25 000
Deferred tax liability		135 000
Retained earnings, 30 June 2021		326 000
Dividends paid	150 000	
Land revaluation surplus		50 000
Financial assets revaluation surplus		42 000
Share capital		1 691 000
	$8 937 000	$8 937 000

Additional information
- Shares were issued during 2022 for $120 000.
- Share capital was $1 541 000 at 30 June 2021.
- Of the $150 000 dividend, $30 000 was reinvested as part of a dividend reinvestment plan.
- The balances of the land revaluation surplus and the financial assets revaluation surplus at 30 June 2021 were $15 000 credit and $35 000 credit respectively. Both the land revaluation surplus and financial assets surplus may be reclassified subsequently to profit or loss.
- The following revaluations were recognised during the year ended 30 June 2022: land revalued upward by $50 000 (related income tax $15 000) and financial assets revalued upward by $10 000 (related income tax $3000).
- The financial assets are held as part of a long-term investment strategy.
- $45 000 of bank loans is repayable within 1 year.
- $80 000 of other loans is repayable within 1 year.
- The provision for employee benefits includes $57 000 payable within 1 year.
- The warranty provision is in respect of a 12-month warranty given on certain goods sold.
- Cob Ltd uses the single statement format for the statement of profit or loss and other comprehensive income and classifies expenses by function within the statement.

Required

Prepare the statement of financial position, statement of profit or loss and other comprehensive income and statement of changes in equity of Cob Ltd for the year ended 30 June 2022 in accordance with the requirements of AASB 101/IAS 1, using statement captions that a listed company is likely to use.

REFERENCES

Qantas Airways Ltd 2018, *Annual report 2018*, www.qantas.com.au.
Telstra Corporation Limited 2018, *Annual report 2018*, www.telstra.com.au.
Westpac Banking Corporation 2018, *Annual report 2018*, www.westpac.com.au.

ACKNOWLEDGEMENTS

Photo: © humphery / Shutterstock.com
Figures 16.1, 16.2, 16.4, 16.5, 16.10 and text: © Telstra Corporation Limited 2018
Figure 16.3: © Westpac Banking Corporation, *Annual report 2018*
Figures 16.8, 16.9: © Qantas Airways Ltd 2018
Text: © 2019 Australian Accounting Standards Board (AASB). The text, graphics and layout of this publication are protected by Australian copyright law and the comparable law of other countries. No part of the publication may be reproduced, stored or transmitted in any form or by any means without the prior written permission of the AASB except as permitted by law. For reproduction or publication, permission should be sought in writing from the AASB. Requests in the first instance should be addressed to the National Director, Australian Accounting Standards Board, PO Box 204, Collins Street West, Victoria 8007.

CHAPTER 17

Statement of cash flows

CHAPTER AIM

Ultimately, all existing and potential investors, lenders and other creditors would like to obtain cash from their investment. Consequently, information about an entity's receipts and payments is of fundamental importance to users of financial statements. The statement of cash flows provides this information by reporting cash inflows and outflows classified into operating, investing and financing activities, and the net movement in cash and cash equivalents during the period. This chapter explains how to present a statement of cash flows in accordance with AASB 107/IAS 7 *Statement of Cash Flows* and demonstrates the techniques, including worksheets, that can be used to prepare a statement of cash flows for entities with complex transactions.

LEARNING OBJECTIVES

After studying this chapter, you should be able to:

17.1 explain the purpose of a statement of cash flows

17.2 define cash and cash equivalents

17.3 classify cash inflows and outflows into operating, investing and financing activities

17.4 contrast the direct and indirect methods of presenting cash flows from operating activities

17.5 prepare a statement of cash flows

17.6 prepare other disclosures required or encouraged by AASB 107/IAS 7.

CONCEPTS FOR REVIEW

Before studying this chapter, you should understand and, if necessary, revise:

- accrual accounting
- asset revaluations
- tax-effect accounting
- the statement of profit or loss and other comprehensive income
- the statement of financial position.

17.1 Purpose of a statement of cash flows

LEARNING OBJECTIVE 17.1 Explain the purpose of a statement of cash flows.

The overall purpose of a statement of cash flows is to present information about the changes in cash and cash equivalents of an entity during the period, classified by operating, investing and financing activities. The statement of cash flows can assist investors, creditors and other users of financial statements to evaluate:

- the entity's ability to generate cash and cash equivalents
- the entity's ability to affect the amount, timing and certainty of generating future cash flows
- the entity's need to utilise cash and cash equivalents.

The classification of cash flows as arising from operating activities, investment activities and finance activities is useful in analysing the movement in cash and cash equivalents during the period. In the long term, the entity's ability to generate cash flows from operating activities in order to finance investment and pay dividends is critical to its survival. When an entity borrows money to finance investments in its operating capacity, it needs to generate sufficient cash flows from its operations to service its debt (i.e. interest and repayments) and pay dividends to its shareholders. Users of financial statements can compare cash generated from operating activities with expected cash outflows for loan repayments, dividends and planned investments.

When used in conjunction with other financial statements, information about cash flows assists users of financial statements to:

- predict future cash flows
- evaluate an entity's financial structure (including liquidity) and its ability to meet its obligations and to pay dividends
- understand the reasons for the difference between profit or loss for a period and the net cash flow from operating activities (the reasons for the differences are often helpful in evaluating the quality of earnings of an entity)
- compare the operating performance of different entities (because net operating cash flows reported in the statement of cash flows are unaffected by different accounting choices and judgements under accrual accounting used in determining the profit or loss of an entity)
- develop models to assess and compare the present value of the expected future cash flows of different entities.

LEARNING CHECK

- ☐ The statement of cash flows reports on changes in cash and cash equivalents, classified as arising from:
  - operating activities
  - investing activities
  - financing activities.
- ☐ The statement can be used to assess:
  - the ability of an entity to generate cash and cash equivalents
  - the entity's need to utilise cash and cash equivalents
  - the entity's ability to affect the timing, amount and certainty of future cash flows.

17.2 Defining cash and cash equivalents

LEARNING OBJECTIVE 17.2 Define cash and cash equivalents.

Cash and **cash equivalents** are defined in paragraph 6 of AASB 107/IAS 7 as follows.

Cash comprises cash on hand and demand deposits.

Cash equivalents are short-term, highly liquid investments that are readily convertible to known amounts of cash and which are subject to an insignificant risk of changes in value.

Paragraph 7 of AASB 107/IAS 7 explains that cash equivalents are held for the purpose of meeting short-term cash commitments, and not for investment or other purposes. Cash equivalents must be convertible into a known amount of cash. This means the amount of cash that will be received must be known at the time of the initial investment. Since a cash-equivalent investment must by definition be readily convertible to cash and have an insignificant risk of changing in value, an investment will qualify as a cash equivalent only if it has a short maturity (usually three months or less). Examples of cash and cash equivalents include:

- cash on hand
- cash at bank
- short-term money market securities
- 90-day term deposits.

Equity investments typically do not qualify as cash equivalents, but it is necessary to consider their substance; equity instruments such as preference shares acquired shortly before their specified maturity date may fall within the definition of cash equivalents.

Bank borrowings are ordinarily classified as a financing activity, except for bank overdrafts that are repayable on demand and which form an integral part of an entity's cash management. Such overdrafts may fluctuate from being overdrawn to being positive. In Australia, bank overdrafts are often included as a component of cash and cash equivalents. Thus, the amount of cash and cash equivalents reported in the statement of cash flows may differ from 'cash and short-term deposits' reported in the statement of financial position because cash and cash equivalents may include a bank overdraft, which would be reported as a liability in the statement of financial position. This is illustrated in figure 17.1 in the reconciliation between cash and cash equivalents reported in the statement of cash flows and related items reported in the statement of financial position.

FIGURE 17.1	Composition of cash and cash equivalents		
		2021 $'000	2020 $'000
Cash and short-term deposits		4 500	4 900
Bank overdraft		(1 200)	(1 100)
Cash assets		**3 300**	**3 800**

The definitions of cash and cash equivalents used in AASB 107/IAS 7 are summarised in figure 17.2.

FIGURE 17.2	Concepts of cash and cash equivalents used in AASB 107/IAS 7		
	Form	**Conditions**	**Examples**
Cash	Cash on hand		Notes and coins
	Demand deposits		Call deposits held at financial institutions
Cash equivalents	Short-term, highly liquid investments	Readily convertible into known amounts of cash and subject to an insignificant risk of change in value	Bank bills Non-bank bills Deposits on short-term money market, such as 7-day deposits
	Bank overdraft	Repayable on demand and form an integral part of an entity's cash management	Cheque account that is in overdraft

The statement of cash flows reports on changes in aggregate cash and cash equivalents. Therefore, movements between items classified as cash and cash equivalents, such as a transfer from cash at bank to a 90-day term deposit, are not reported in the statement of cash flows.

LEARNING CHECK

- ☐ The statement of cash flows reports on movements in cash and cash equivalents.
- ☐ Cash equivalents are short-term highly liquid investments that are readily convertible into known amounts of cash, and which are subject to an insignificant risk of changes in value.
- ☐ Bank overdrafts are considered part of cash and cash equivalents if the overdrafts are repayable on demand and form an integral part of the entity's cash management function.

17.3 Classifying cash flow activities

LEARNING OBJECTIVE 17.3 Classify cash inflows and outflows into operating, investing and financing activities.

Cash flow activities reported in the statement of cash flows are classified into **operating activities**, **investing activities** and **financing activities**. Paragraph 6 of AASB 107/IAS 7 defines these activities as follows.

> *Operating activities* are the principal revenue-producing activities of the entity and other activities that are not investing or financing activities.
>
> *Investing activities* are the acquisition and disposal of long-term assets and other investments not included in cash equivalents.
>
> *Financing activities* are activities that result in changes in the size and composition of the contributed equity and borrowings of the entity.

Only expenditures that result in a recognised asset in the statement of financial position are eligible for classification as investing activities. For example, Green Ltd incurs expenditure of $50 000 on research for a carbon-neutral air conditioner. Expenditure incurred in the research phase must be recognised as an expense in accordance with AASB 138/IAS 38 *Intangible Assets*. Accordingly, the cash paid in relation to the research project is not classified as an investing cash flow because it has not resulted in the recognition of an asset in the statement of financial position of Green Ltd.

Note that the operating activities category is a default category because it includes all activities that are not classified as either investing activities or financing activities. Figure 17.3 provides a summary of the typical cash receipts and payments of an entity, classified by activity.

FIGURE 17.3 Typical cash receipts and payments classified by activity

	Cash inflows	Cash outflows
Operating activities (generally associated with revenues and expenses)	From sale of goods or services From cash advances and loans made by *financial institutions* relating to the entity's main revenue-producing activities	To suppliers for goods To employees for services To other persons/entities for expenses To lenders for interest and other borrowing costs (or financing activity) To governments for income and other taxes
Investing activities (generally movements in non-current assets)	From sale of property, plant and equipment From sale of shares and debentures of other entities From repayment of advances and loans to other entities From interest received (or operating activity) From dividends received (or operating activity)	To purchase property, plant and equipment To purchase shares and debentures of other entities To lend money to other entities
Financing activities (generally movements in non-current liabilities and equity)	From issue of shares From issuing debentures and notes From borrowings (loans and mortgages)	To shareholders for share buybacks and redemption of preference shares To shareholders for dividends paid (or an operating activity) To debenture holders for redemption of debt To lenders to repay borrowings

17.3.1 Classifying interest and dividends received and paid

AASB 107/IAS 7 does not prescribe how interest and dividends received and paid should be classified. Rather, paragraph 31 requires cash flows from interest and dividends received and paid to be disclosed separately and classified in a consistent manner from period to period as operating, investing or financing activities. Paragraph 33 explains that interest paid and interest and dividends received are usually classified as operating cash flows for a financial institution, but there is no consensus on the classification of these cash flows for other entities. This is because interest paid and interest and dividends received may be classified as operating cash flows — they may be viewed as entering into the determination of profit or loss — or as financing cash flows (for interest paid) and investing cash flows (for interest and dividends received), being viewed as the costs of financing or the returns on investments respectively. Paragraph 34 notes that dividends paid may be classified as financing cash flows because they are a cost of obtaining equity finance or as cash from operating activities, to assist users to determine the ability of the entity to pay dividends from operating cash flows.

As shown in figure 17.4, Bega Cheese Limited classifies interest paid (finance costs) as operating cash flows. Interest received is classified as investing cash flows. Dividends paid are classified as financing cash flows.

FIGURE 17.4	Statement of cash flows, Bega Cheese			

| | | | CONSOLIDATED | |
| | | | 2018 | 2017 |
		Notes	$'000	$'000
Cash flows from operating activities				
Receipts from customers inclusive of goods and services tax			1 499 943	1 274 872
Payments to suppliers and employees inclusive of goods and services tax			(1 404 944)	(1 190 698)
Interest and other costs of financing paid			(10 676)	(3 228)
Income taxes paid		7f	(25 759)	(10 727)
Net cash inflow from operating activities		19	58 564	70 221
Cash flows from investing activities				
Proceeds from sale of shares in listed companies			2 700	—
Payments for shares in listed companies			(623)	—
Interest received			854	437
Dividend received			25	15
Payments for property, plant and equipment		11	(26 998)	(26 568)
Net proceeds from sale of property, plant and equipment			10 014	188 921
Tax paid on sale of infant nutritional assets			(53 438)	—
Payments for intangible assets		12	(19 570)	(12 611)
Payments for acquisition of Bega Foods		26	(452 726)	—
Payments for acquisition of PCA, net of cash required		26	(11 658)	—
Payments related to corporate activity			(13 916)	(13 147)
Joint venture distributions received		24	500	1 063
Net cash (outflow)/inflow from investing activities			(564 836)	138 110
Cash flows from financing activities				
Proceeds from borrowings			69 693	198 280
Repayment of borrowings			(45 944)	(45 671)
Payment of finance lease liabilities			(1 881)	—
Net proceeds from issue of shares			49 971	120 195
Dividends paid to members			(19 431)	(15 260)
Net cash inflow from financing activities			52 408	257 544
Net (decrease)/increase in cash and cash equivalents			(453 864)	465 875
Cash and cash equivalents at the beginning of the year			475 533	9 658
Cash and cash equivalents at the end of the year		19	**21 669**	**475 533**

Source: Bega Cheese Limited (2018, p. 39).

17.3.2 Classifying taxes on income

Paragraph 35 of AASB 107/IAS 7 requires that income tax paid be separately disclosed in the statement of cash flows and classified as cash flows from operating activities, unless it can be specifically identified with financing or investing activities.

As noted in paragraph 36, although the tax expense can often be readily identified with investing and financing activities, the associated cash payments may arise in different periods, making it very difficult and often impracticable to classify tax payments as cash flows from investing and financing activities. For this reason, taxes paid are usually classified as cash flows from operating activities.

Refer to figure 17.4 to identify the income tax paid reported by Bega Cheese Limited in the operating activities section of the statement of cash flows.

17.4 Format of the statement of cash flows

LEARNING OBJECTIVE 17.4 Contrast the direct and indirect methods of presenting cash flows from operating activities.

The general format of a statement of cash flows follows the three cash flow activities. Cash flows from operating activities are presented first, followed by cash flows from investing activities and then those from financing activities. The resultant net increase or decrease in cash and cash equivalents during the period is then used to report the movement in cash and cash equivalents from the balance at the beginning of the period to the balance at the end of the period.

A typical format of a statement of cash flows is presented in figure 17.5.

FIGURE 17.5	Typical format of a statement of cash flows using the direct method of reporting cash flows from operating activities

Statement of cash flows		
for the year ended 31 December ...		
Cash flows from operating activities		
Cash receipts from customers	$ xxx	
Cash paid to suppliers and employees	(xxx)	
Cash generated from operations	xxx	
Interest received	xxx	
Interest paid	(xxx)	
Income taxes paid	(xxx)	
Net cash from operating activities		$ xxx
Cash flows from investing activities		
Acquisition of subsidiary, net of cash acquired	(xxx)	
Purchase of property and plant	(xxx)	
Proceeds from sale of plant	xxx	
Net cash used in investing activities		(xxx)
Cash flows from financing activities		
Proceeds from share issue	xxx	
Proceeds from borrowings	xxx	
Payment of borrowings	(xxx)	
Dividends paid	(xxx)	
Net cash from financing activities		xxx
Net increase in cash and cash equivalents		xxx
Cash and cash equivalents at beginning of year		xxx
Cash and cash equivalents at end of year		**$ xxx**

17.4.1 Reporting cash flows from operating activities

Paragraph 18 of AASB 107/IAS 7 provides that cash flows from operating activities may be reported using one of two methods:

- the *direct method* — whereby major classes of cash receipts and gross cash payments are disclosed
- the *indirect method* — whereby profit or loss is adjusted for the effects of transactions of a non-cash nature, any deferrals or accruals of past or future operating cash receipts or payments, and items of income or expense associated with investing or financing cash flows. Alternatively, the cash flows from operations may be presented under the indirect method by adjusting revenues for changes in receivables and adjusting expenses for changes in inventories, payables and other accruals (AASB 107/IAS 7 paragraph 20).

Although both methods are permitted, AASB 107/IAS 7 explicitly encourages the use of the direct method.

Figure 17.5 illustrates the typical format of a statement of cash flows that uses the direct method. You may have noticed that Bega Cheese Limited (figure 17.4) also uses the direct method to present cash flows from operating activities.

Figure 17.6 illustrates the typical format of the indirect method of reporting cash flows from operating activities. As can be seen in figure 17.6, depreciation expense is added back to profit in calculating cash flows from operating activities. This is because depreciation expense reduces profit but has no effect on cash flows. The loss on the sale of investment is added back to profit because it reduces profit but does not affect cash flows from operating activities. Conversely, a gain on the disposal of equipment would be deducted from profit in calculating cash flows from operations. The related cash flow (i.e. the cash proceeds on the sale of the equipment) is included in cash flows from investing activities.

| FIGURE 17.6 | Typical format for the indirect method of reporting cash flows from operating activities |

Statement of cash flows for the year ended 31 December ...	
Profit before tax	$ xxx
Adjustments for:	
Depreciation	xxx
Foreign exchange loss	xxx
Loss on sale of equipment	xxx
Interest income	(xxx)
Interest expense	xxx
Increase in trade and other receivables	(xxx)
Decrease in inventories	xxx
Increase in accounts payable	xxx
Decrease in accrued liabilities	(xxx)
Cash generated from operations	xxx
Interest received	xxx
Interest paid	(xxx)
Income taxes paid	(xxx)
Net cash from operating activities	**$ xxx**

Profit is adjusted for the difference between an amount recognised in profit and the corresponding operating cash flows, such as the change in receivables. This process is explained in more detail in section 17.7. Note that in applying the indirect method, an adjustment is made for the total amount of interest income, rather than for the difference between interest income measured on an accrual basis and the amount of interest received. This is because paragraph 31 of AASB 107/IAS 7 requires disclosure of interest received in the statement of cash flows, irrespective of whether cash flows from operating activities are presented using the direct method or the indirect method. Similarly, dividends received and interest paid must be disclosed separately in the statement of cash flows.

In Australia, if the direct method of reporting cash flows from operating activities is used, a reconciliation between the net cash flows from operating activities and profit or loss must be disclosed in the notes in accordance with paragraph 16 of AASB 1054 *Additional Australian Disclosures*. As the gross amount of cash paid for income taxes is reported in the statement of cash flows, the reconciliation note commences with profit rather than profit before tax. Similarly, it is not necessary to deduct total interest and dividend income, or add back total interest paid, because gross amounts of interest received, dividend received and interest paid are reported in the statement of cash flows. Accordingly, profit is adjusted for the difference between each of these items reported on an accrual basis and the related cash flows.

17.4.2 Reporting cash flows from investing and financing activities

Paragraph 21 of AASB 107/IAS 7 requires separate reporting of the major classes of gross cash receipts and gross cash payments arising from investing and financing activities, except for certain cash flows (outlined in the following section) that may be reported on a net basis. For example, if an entity borrows money to repay another long-term loan, it must report a gross financing cash inflow for the amount borrowed and gross financing cash outflow for the repayment of the original loan.

17.4.3 Reporting cash flows on a net basis

Paragraph 22 of AASB 107/IAS 7 allows the following cash flows to be reported on a net basis:

(a) cash receipts and payments on behalf of customers when the cash flows reflect the activities of the customer rather than those of the entity; and

(b) cash receipts and payments for items in which the turnover is quick, the amounts are large, and the maturities are short.

Paragraph 23 of AASB 107/IAS 7 identifies examples of cash receipts and payments covered by paragraph 22(a), including the acceptance and repayment of a bank's demand deposits. For example, assume an entity finances some of its operations with a 90-day bill acceptance facility with its bank. This means that the entity writes commercial bills, giving rise to a contractual obligation to pay the face value of the bill. The bank accepts the bill and pays the entity a discounted amount, with the difference being interest effectively paid by the entity. Thus, the entity is borrowing the discounted amount of the bill and repaying the face value, which is the sum of the amount borrowed and interest. The entity will have cash inflows from financing activities each time a commercial bill is accepted by the bank and cash outflows from financing activities each time one of its commercial bills matures. Paragraph 22(b) permits the entity to offset the cash received for the 90-day bills against the repayment on maturity, such that only the net movement in the level of borrowing is reported. However, if the entity finances its operations through 180-day bills, it would have to report the related cash receipts and payments on a gross basis because this would not be a short-term borrowing as referred to in paragraphs 22 and 23.

Other examples of cash flows referred to in paragraph 22(a) of AASB 107/IAS 7 include the receipt of funds and payment of funds held for customers by an investment entity and rents collected from tenants by an agent and paid to the owners of the properties (paragraph 23). Examples of cash receipts and payments referred to in paragraph 22(b) are principal amounts relating to credit card customers, and the purchase and sale of investments and other short-term borrowings (usually those that have a maturity period of three months or less) (paragraph 23A).

Paragraph 24 of AASB 107/IAS 7 permits the following cash flows to be reported on a net basis by financial institutions:

(a) cash receipts and payments for the acceptance and repayment of deposits with a fixed maturity date;

(b) the placement of deposits with and withdrawal of deposits from other financial institutions; and

(c) cash advances and loans made to customers and the repayment of those advances and loans.

LEARNING CHECK

☐ The statement of cash flows shows the major classes of cash flows classified as being from operating, investing and financing activities.

☐ Cash flows from operating activities may be presented using the direct method, in which gross cash inflows and outflows are presented, or the indirect method, which commences with profit and presents adjustments to derive net cash generated by operating activities.

☐ If the direct method of reporting cash from operations is used, the entity must also disclose a reconciliation between net cash from operating activities and profit or loss.

☐ Gross cash receipts and gross cash payments must be reported for cash flows from investing and financing activities.

☐ Certain individual cash flows must be disclosed; for example, interest and dividends received or paid.

17.5 Preparing a statement of cash flows

LEARNING OBJECTIVE 17.5 Prepare a statement of cash flows.

Unlike the statement of financial position and statement of profit or loss and other comprehensive income, the statement of cash flows is *not* prepared from an entity's general ledger trial balance. Preparation requires information to be compiled concerning the cash inflows and cash outflows of the relevant entity over the period covered by the statement. It is possible to compile the required information through a detailed analysis and summary of the entity's records of cash receipts and cash payments, such as cash receipts and cash payments journals. Ordinarily, though, a statement of cash flows is prepared by using comparative statements of financial position to determine the net amount of changes in assets, liabilities and equities over the period. The comparative statements of financial position are supplemented by various items of information from the statement of profit or loss and other comprehensive income and additional information extracted from the accounting records of the entity to enable certain cash receipts and payments to be fully identified. This method of preparation is demonstrated in simplified form using the information presented for Rose Ltd in figure 17.7. The same method can be used to prepare a consolidated statement of cash flows for a group of entities.

FIGURE 17.7	Financial statements and additional accounting information, Rose Ltd

ROSE LTD
Statement of profit or loss and other comprehensive income
for the year ended 31 December 2022

Revenue	
Sales revenue	$800 000
Interest income	5 000
Gain on sale of plant	4 000
	809 000
Expenses	
Cost of sales	$480 000
Wages and salaries expense	120 000
Depreciation — plant and equipment	25 000
Interest expense	4 000
Other expenses	76 000
	705 000
Profit before tax	104 000
Income tax expense	30 000
Profit for the year	74 000
Other comprehensive income	
Gain on equity investments	2 000
Income tax	(600)
Other comprehensive income net of tax	1 400
Total comprehensive income for the year	**$ 75 400**

ROSE LTD			
Comparative statements of financial position			
as at:			
	31 December 2021	31 December 2022	Increase (decrease)
Cash at bank	$ 60 000	$ 56 550	$ (3 450)
Accounts receivable	70 000	79 000	9 000
Inventories	65 000	70 000	5 000
Prepayments	8 000	9 500	1 500
Interest receivable	150	100	(50)
Plant and equipment[a]	150 000	165 000	15 000
Investments (at FV through OCI)	12 000	14 000	2 000
Intangible assets[b]	—	15 000	15 000
	$365 150	$409 150	
Accounts payable	$ 42 000	$ 45 000	3 000
Wages and salaries payable	4 000	5 000	1 000
Accrued interest	—	200	200
Other expenses payable	3 000	1 800	(1 200)
Current tax payable	14 000	16 000	2 000
Deferred tax liability	5 000	8 600	3 600
Long-term borrowings[c]	60 000	70 000	10 000
Share capital	200 000	200 000	—
Retained earnings[d]	37 150	61 150	24 000
Financial asset revaluation reserve	—	1 400	1 400
	$365 150	$409 150	

Additional information extracted from the company's records
(a) Plant that had a carrying amount of $10 000 was sold for $14 000 cash. New equipment purchased for cash amounted to $50 000.
(b) Intangible assets ($15 000) were acquired for cash.
(c) A borrowing of $10 000 was made during the year and received in cash.
(d) Dividends paid in cash were $50 000.

17.5.1 Cash flows from operating activities

Ascertaining the net cash flows from operating activities is the first step in preparing a statement of cash flows. The process used varies according to whether the direct or the indirect method of disclosure is used.

First, we will work through the approach used for the direct method, which utilises a series of equations to calculate gross cash inflows and gross cash outflows for items required to be shown in the statement of cash flows.

Determining cash receipts from customers

The starting point for determining how much cash was received from customers is the sales revenue reported in the statement of profit or loss and other comprehensive income. However, this figure reflects sales made by the entity during the period irrespective of whether the customers have paid for their purchases. Credit sales are recorded by a debit to accounts receivable and a credit to sales revenue. Thus, sales revenue reflects sales that occur in the current period, but cash received from customers includes sales made in the previous period if cash is not collected until the current period, and excludes sales made in the current period if customers have not paid by the end of the current period. Hence, cash received from customers (assuming there have been no bad debts written off or settlement discounts given) equals:

$$\text{Sales revenue} + \text{Beginning accounts receivable} - \text{Ending accounts receivable}$$

Using the Rose Ltd information from figure 17.7, receipts from customers is determined as follows.

Sales revenue	$800 000
+ Beginning accounts receivable	70 000
Cash collectable from customers	870 000
− Ending accounts receivable	(79 000)
Receipts from customers	$791 000

The entity may offer settlement discounts to customers for prompt or early payment of their accounts. For example, if a customer who owes $100 takes advantage of an offer of a 5% discount for prompt payment, the customer would pay $95 only to settle the receivable, and the entity would record the discount allowed expense of $5 for the non-cash reduction in receivables. Settlement discounts are accounted for as a non-cash expense (discount allowed) in profit or loss and a reduction in accounts receivable. Thus, settlement discounts allowed reduce the amount of cash that can be collected from customers. Accordingly, discount allowed must be adjusted for in calculating cash receipts from customers. Similarly, adjustment would be necessary for bad debts written off if the entity used the direct write-off method of accounting for uncollectable debts. Calculation of cash receipts from customers under the allowance method of accounting for uncollectable debts is considered later in this chapter.

The logic of this calculation is apparent from the following summarised accounts receivable account in the general ledger for the year.

Accounts receivable			
Opening balance	70 000	Bad debts expense	—
Sales revenue	800 000	Discount allowed	—
		Cash receipts	791 000
		Closing balance	79 000
	870 000		870 000

The summarised general ledger account above can be reconstructed from the statement of financial position including comparative amounts (the opening and closing balances) and statement of profit or loss and other comprehensive income (bad debts expense, discount allowed and sales revenue). The cash receipts amount is then determined as the 'plug' figure (balancing item) in the accounts receivable account.

The above approach may be simplified by working with the change in receivables over the period. Under this approach, cash received from customers (assuming there are no bad debts written off or discounts allowed) equals:

$$\text{Sales revenue} - \text{Increase in accounts receivable}$$
or

$$+ \text{Decrease in accounts receivable}$$

Thus, cash received from customers for Rose Ltd can alternatively be determined as follows.

$$\$800\,000 - \$9000 = \$791\,000$$

Determining interest received

A similar approach is used to determine interest received, which equals:

Interest revenue − Increase in interest receivable

or

+ Decrease in interest receivable

Thus, Rose Ltd's interest received is as follows.

$$\$5000 + \$50 = \$5050$$

Determining cash paid to suppliers and employees

Payments to suppliers may comprise purchases of inventories and payments for services. However, not all inventories purchased during the year are reflected in profit or loss as cost of sales, because cost of sales includes beginning inventories and excludes ending inventories. The cost of purchases of inventories made during the period equals:

Cost of sales − Beginning inventories + Ending inventories

Alternatively, this could be expressed as follows.

Cost of sales + Increase in inventories

or

− Decrease in inventories

Using a similar approach to that outlined for cash receipts from customers, it is then necessary to adjust for accounts payable at the beginning and end of the period to arrive at cash paid to suppliers for purchases of inventories. Thus, cash paid to suppliers of inventories is calculated as follows.

Purchases of inventories + Beginning accounts payable − Ending accounts payable

Alternatively, this could be expressed as follows.

Purchases of inventories + Decrease in accounts payable

or

− Increase in accounts payable

As shown in figure 17.7, Rose Ltd's comparative statements of financial position report an increase in inventories of $5000 and in accounts payable of $3000. Hence, cash paid to suppliers for purchases is calculated as follows.

Cost of sales	$480 000
+ Increase in inventories	5 000
Purchases for year	485 000
− Increase in accounts payable	(3 000)
Payments to suppliers for purchases of inventories	$482 000

If the entity receives a discount from its suppliers for prompt or early payment of accounts payable the settlement discount received is accounted for as interest revenue and a reduction in accounts payable. Thus, settlement discounts reduce the amount of cash paid to suppliers and must be deducted in calculating cash paid to suppliers. This treatment assumes the supplier's invoice was initially recorded at the gross amount.

The logic of the previous calculations incorporating the adjustment for discount received is apparent from the following summarised inventories and accounts payable (for inventories) accounts in the general ledger for the year.

Inventories			
Opening balance	65 000	Cost of sales	480 000
Purchases	485 000	Closing balance	70 000
	550 000		550 000

Accounts payable			
Discount received	–	Opening balance	42 000
Cash payments	482 000	Purchases	485 000
Closing balance	45 000		
	527 000		527 000

The summarised general ledger accounts above can be reconstructed from the information contained in the comparative statements of financial position (the opening and closing balances) and the statement of profit or loss and other comprehensive income (cost of sales). The purchases amount is then determined by the difference in the inventories account and inserted on the credit side of the accounts payable account. The amount of cash payments can then be determined as the 'plug' figure in reconciling the accounts payable account.

A similar approach is taken to determine the amount of payments made to suppliers for services and to employees. Adjustments must be made to the relevant expenses recognised in profit or loss for changes in the beginning and ending amounts of prepayments and relevant accounts payable and accrued liabilities. Thus, the amount of cash paid to suppliers for services is calculated as follows.

> Expenses charged in profit or loss – Beginning prepayments
> + Ending prepayments
> + Beginning accounts payable/accruals
> – Ending accounts payable/accruals

Alternatively, this could be expressed as follows.

> Expenses charged in profit or loss + Increase in prepayments
> or
> – Decrease in prepayments
> + Decrease in accounts payable/accruals
> or
> – Increase in accounts payable/accruals

Rose Ltd's comparative statements of financial position show the following.

Increase in prepayments	$ 1 500
Increase in wages and salaries payable	1 000
Decrease in other expenses payable	(1 200)

Thus, cash paid to suppliers of services is calculated as follows.

Other expenses	$76 000
+ Increase in prepayments	1 500
+ Decrease in other expenses payable	1 200
Payments to suppliers of services	$78 700

Similarly, cash paid to employees is calculated as follows.

Wages and salaries expense	$120 000
– Increase in wages and salaries payable	1 000
Payments to employees	$119 000

Using the previous calculations, total payments to suppliers and employees to be reported in the statement of cash flows comprises the following.

Payments to suppliers for purchases	$482 000
Payments to suppliers for services	78 700
Payments to employees	119 000
Total payments to suppliers and employees	$679 700

Determining interest paid

Using the same approach as for other expenses, Rose Ltd's interest paid is determined as follows.

Interest expense	$4 000
– Increase in accrued interest	200
Interest paid	$3 800

Determining income tax paid

The determination of income tax paid can be complicated because in addition to current tax payable, the application of tax-effect accounting can give rise to deferred tax assets and deferred tax liabilities. Further, some of the movements in the current and deferred tax accounts might not be reflected in the income tax expense recognised in profit or loss. Certain gains and losses and associated tax effects are recognised in other comprehensive income (OCI) and accumulated in equity accounts. For example, as explained in chapter 12, deferred tax may arise from a revaluation of property, plant and equipment that causes a difference between the carrying amount and tax base of those assets, thereby resulting in a charge for income tax being made to the revaluation surplus account. As a result, it is often simpler to reconstruct the deferred tax liability account to determine the allocation of income tax expense. We can use this reconstruction to determine the deferred component of income tax expense recognised in profit or loss, if this is not already identified in the statement of profit or loss and other comprehensive income.

Deferred tax liability			
		Opening balance	5 000
		Tax effect recognised in OCI	600
Closing balance	8 600	Income tax expense (deferred)	3 000
	8 600		8 600

The above summarised general ledger account can be reconstructed from the comparative statements of financial position (opening and closing balances) and the statement of profit or loss and other comprehensive income. The income tax expense shown in the reconstruction of the deferred tax liability account is the deferred component of income tax expense; that is, the amount of income tax expense pertaining to the movement in deferred tax balances.

The movement in the deferred tax liability account for Rose Ltd can be summarised as follows.

Beginning balance	$5 000
+ Tax recognised directly in OCI	600
+ Income tax expense (deferred)	3 000
Ending balance	$8 600

The current component of income tax expense can then be calculated by deducting the deferred component of income tax expense from the total income tax expense recognised in profit or loss. The current component of income tax expense for Rose Ltd can be calculated as follows.

Income tax expense	$30 000
– Income tax expense (deferred)	(3 000)
Income tax expense (current)	$27 000

The beginning balance of current tax payable of $14 000 is increased by the current component of income tax expense, $27 000. If no payments were made, the ending balance would be $41 000. However, as the ending balance is only $16 000, we can conclude that the amount of income tax paid must have been $25 000. To illustrate, the movement in Rose Ltd's current tax payable account may be summarised as follows.

Beginning balance	$ 14 000
+ Income tax expense (current)	27 000
– Income tax paid	(25 000)
Ending balance	$ 16 000

For Rose Ltd, the amount of income tax paid consists of the final balance in respect of the previous year's current tax payable, and instalments (e.g. quarterly) in respect of the current year. The income tax expense may include an adjustment for any under or over accrual for current tax payable at the beginning of the period.

Summarising cash flows from operating activities

Using the direct method, the cash flows from the operating activities section of Rose Ltd's statement of cash flows for the year are presented in figure 17.8.

FIGURE 17.8	Cash flows from operating activities (direct method), Rose Ltd

ROSE LTD
Statement of cash flows (extract)
for the year ended 31 December 2022

Cash flows from operating activities	
Cash receipts from customers	$ 791 000
Cash paid to suppliers and employees	(679 700)
Cash generated from operations	111 300
Interest received*	5 050
Interest paid**	(3 800)
Income taxes paid	(25 000)
Net cash from operating activities	**$ 87 550**
Reconciliation note	
Profit for the period	$ 74 000
Adjustments for:	
Depreciation	25 000
Gain on sale of plant	(4 000)
Increase in accounts receivable	(9 000)
Decrease in interest receivable	50
Increase in inventories	(5 000)
Increase in prepayments	(1 500)
Increase in accounts payable	3 000
Increase in accrued interest	200
Decrease in other payables including salaries and wages payable	(200)
Increase in current tax payable	2 000
Increase in deferred tax liability	3 000
Net cash from operating activities	**$ 87 550**

*May be classified as investing
**May be classified as financing

Figure 17.8 includes a note reconciling profit for the period to net cash from operating activities. The purpose of this note is to explain the difference between net cash provided by operating activities and profit reported in the statement of profit or loss and other comprehensive income. The increase in wages and salaries payable of $1000 and the decrease in other expenses payable of $1200 are combined as one line item and shown as a net reduction of $200 in the reconciliation note. The increase in deferred tax liability that forms part of the reconciliation between profit and net cash from operating activities is $3000 but the movement in the deferred tax liability is $3600 according to the comparative statements of financial position. The difference arises because $600 of the increase in the deferred tax liability pertains to amounts reported in OCI. The $600 deferred tax item reported in OCI does not form part of the reconciliation between profit and net cash from operations because it is not included in profit.

The presentation of Rose Ltd's cash flows from operating activities under the indirect method is shown in figure 17.9. In this illustration, wages and salaries payable and other expenses payable are combined as one line item. Under the indirect method Rose Ltd adjusts for the full amount of the interest income, interest expense and income tax expense so that the amount of cash received or paid for each item is disclosed separately in the statement of cash flows.

ROSE LTD
Statement of cash flows (extract)
for the year ended 31 December 2022

Cash flows from operating activities	
Profit before tax	$104 000
Adjustment for:	
Depreciation	25 000
Interest income	(5 000)
Gain on sale of plant	(4 000)
Interest expense	4 000
Increase in accounts receivable	(9 000)
Increase in inventories	(5 000)
Increase in prepayments	(1 500)
Increase in accounts payable	3 000
Decrease in other payables	(200)
Cash generated from operations	111 300
Interest received*	5 050
Interest paid**	(3 800)
Income taxes paid	(25 000)
Net cash from operating activities	**$ 87 550**

*May be classified as investing
**May be classified as financing

17.5.2 Cash flows from investing activities

Determining cash flows from investing activities requires identifying cash inflows and outflows relating to the acquisition and disposal of long-term assets and other investments not included in cash equivalents.

The comparative statements of financial position of Rose Ltd in figure 17.7 show that plant has increased by $15 000, investments by $2000 and intangible assets by $15 000. To determine the cash flows relating to these increases, it is necessary to analyse the underlying transactions.

The plant reported in the statement of financial position is net of accumulated depreciation. The net increase in plant reflects the recording of acquisitions, disposals and depreciation. Using the data provided, the analysis of the plant movement (which is net of accumulated depreciation) is as follows.

Beginning balance	$150 000
Acquisitions	50 000
Disposals	(10 000)
Depreciation for year	(25 000)
Ending balance	$165 000

Plant with a carrying amount of $10 000 was sold, as stated in the additional information (a). This amount is shown as a deducted from the beginning net carrying amount for plant and equipment.

The additional information provided in figure 17.7 states that the acquisitions were made for cash during the period, so no adjustment is necessary for year-end payables. Assuming that there were no outstanding payables for plant purchases at the beginning of the year, the cash flow for plant acquisitions for the year is $50 000 (note (a) in figure 17.7). (If payables for plant purchases were outstanding at the beginning of the period, the amount would need to be included in cash paid for purchases of plant during the current period.)

The gain or loss on disposal of plant is the difference between the carrying amount and the proceeds on the sale of plant. Thus, the proceeds on sale of plant can be calculated as follows.

Carrying amount of plant sold + Gain on disposal of plant

or

− Loss on disposal of plant

For Rose Ltd, the calculation is as follows.

$$\$10\,000 + 4\,000 = \$14\,000$$

However, the proceeds from the sale of plant equals the cash inflow for the year only if there are no outstanding receivables arising from the sale of plant at either the beginning or the end of the year. If receivables for the sale of plant exist, the cash inflow is determined using the approach that was previously outlined for sales revenue and accounts receivable. For simplicity, it is assumed that Rose Ltd had no receivables outstanding, at the beginning or end of the year, arising from the sale of plant.

Issues similar to those outlined for the acquisition of plant arise in respect of investments and intangible assets. The comparative statements of financial position for Rose Ltd show that the movement in intangible assets equals the additional cash acquisitions made during the period, as detailed in the additional information presented in figure 17.7. Note, however, that the movement in intangible assets equals the cash outflows for the year only if it is assumed that there were no related accounts payable at the beginning or end of the year that were settled during the year. If payables exist, the cash outflow is determined using the approach that was previously outlined for cash paid to suppliers and employees.

Investments increased by $2000 during the year, as shown in the comparative statements of financial position. This increase relates to the gain on revaluation of equity investments reported in the statement of profit or loss and other comprehensive income. Thus, the movement in investments does not affect cash flows from investing activities. Using the above information, the cash flows from investing activities reported in Rose Ltd's statement of cash flows for 2022 are presented in figure 17.10.

FIGURE 17.10 Cash flows from investing activities, Rose Ltd

ROSE LTD	
Statement of cash flows (extract)	
for the year ended 31 December 2022	
Cash flows from investing activities	
Purchase of intangible assets	$(15 000)
Purchase of plant	(50 000)
Proceeds from sale of plant	14 000
Net cash used in investing activities	**$(51 000)**

17.5.3 Cash flows from financing activities

Determining cash flows from financing activities requires identification of cash flows that resulted in changes in the size and composition of contributed equity and borrowings.

The additional information (c) in figure 17.7 confirms that the increase in borrowings of $10 000 derived from the comparative statements of financial position of Rose Ltd arose from an additional borrowing received in cash. It would normally be necessary to analyse the net movement in borrowings in order to identify whether the movement reflects repayments and additional borrowings, and whether any new borrowings arose from non-cash transactions, such as entering into a long term lease of equipment (see chapter 10).

If the entity had issued shares during the period this would be reflected in a change in share capital. An alternative source of information about capital contributions is the statement of changes in equity. Any share issues for non-cash consideration, such as shares issued as part of a dividend reinvestment scheme, should be deducted from the movement in share capital to determine cash proceeds from share issues. Rose Ltd's share capital is unchanged at $200 000, as shown in figure 17.7.

Dividends distributed by the entity can be identified by analysing the change in retained earnings. Profit increases retained earnings and losses decrease retained earnings. Dividends decrease retained earnings. Any non-cash dividends should be deducted from total dividends to determine cash dividends paid. Information about dividends is also reported in the statement of changes in equity. The movement in Rose Ltd's retained earnings of $24 000 reflects:

Profit for the period	$ 74 000	
Dividends (paid in cash)	(50 000)	((d) in figure 17.7)
Net movement	$ 24 000	

Using the previous information, the financing cash flow section of Rose Ltd's statement of cash flows for 2022 is presented in figure 17.11.

FIGURE 17.11	Cash flows from financing activities, Rose Ltd

ROSE LTD Statement of cash flows (extract) for the year ended 31 December 2022	
Cash flows from financing activities	
Proceeds from borrowings	$ 10 000
Dividends paid*	(50 000)
Net cash used in financing activities	**$(40 000)**

*May be classified as an operating cash flow

All that remains to complete the statement of cash flows for Rose Ltd is the determination of the net increase or decrease for the period in cash held, and to use this net change to reconcile cash at the beginning and end of the year.

The complete statement of cash flows for Rose Ltd (using the direct method for reporting cash flows from operating activities) is shown in figure 17.12. The balance of cash at year-end of $56 550 shown in figure 17.12 agrees with the cash at bank balance shown in the statement of financial position at 31 December 2022 in figure 17.7. There are no cash equivalents such as short-term deposits or a bank overdraft.

FIGURE 17.12	Complete statement of cash flows, Rose Ltd

ROSE LTD Statement of cash flows for the year ended 31 December 2022		
Cash flows from operating activities		
Cash receipts from customers	$ 791 000	
Cash paid to suppliers and employees	(679 700)	
Cash generated from operations	111 300	
Interest received	5 050	
Interest paid	(3 800)	
Income taxes paid	(25 000)	
Net cash from operating activities		$ 87 550
Cash flows from investing activities		
Purchase of intangible assets	(15 000)	
Purchase of plant	(50 000)	
Proceeds from sale of plant	14 000	
Net cash used in investing activities		(51 000)
Cash flows from financing activities		
Proceeds from borrowings	10 000	
Dividends paid	(50 000)	
Net cash used in financing activities		(40 000)
Net decrease in cash and cash equivalents		(3 450)
Cash and cash equivalents at beginning of year		60 000
Cash and cash equivalents at end of year		**$ 56 550**

LEARNING CHECK

☐ The statement of cash flows can be prepared using an equation approach, which is useful for calculating gross cash flows for specific items required to be presented when the direct method of presenting operating cash flows is applied.

☐ Alternatively, amounts reported in the statement of cash flows can be determined by reconstructing general ledger accounts.

☐ The sum of cash provided by or used in operating, investing and financing activities is the net increase or decrease in cash and cash equivalents.

☐ The net increase (decrease) in cash and cash equivalents is added to (subtracted from) cash and cash equivalents at the beginning of the year in presenting the amount of cash and cash equivalents at the end of the year in the statement of cash flows.

17.6 Other disclosures

LEARNING OBJECTIVE 17.6 Prepare other disclosures required or encouraged by AASB 107/IAS 7.

AASB 107/IAS 7 prescribes additional disclosures in the notes to the financial statements, including:

- information about the components of cash and cash equivalents
- changes in ownership interests of subsidiaries and other businesses
- non-cash investing and financing transactions.

Additional information is often necessary to obtain a complete picture of the change in an entity's financial position because not all transactions are simple cash transactions. Significant changes can result from the acquisition or disposal of subsidiaries or other business units, or from financing and investing transactions that do not involve cash flows in the current period.

17.6.1 Components of cash and cash equivalents

The components of cash and cash equivalents must be disclosed and reconciled to amounts reported in the statement of financial position. The reconciliation provides better transparency of how items are reported in the financial statements. For example, cash and cash equivalents may comprise cash, short-term deposits and an overdraft. The end-of-period amount of cash and cash equivalents reported in the statement of cash flows may differ from that reported in the statement of financial position because the cash and short-term deposits are reported as current assets while the overdraft is a liability. Figure 17.1 illustrates the reconciliation between cash and cash equivalents in the statement of cash flows with the corresponding item reported in the statement of financial position.

Paragraph 48 of AASB 107/IAS 7 requires disclosure of the amount of significant cash and cash-equivalent balances held that are not available for general use. For example, foreign exchange controls in some countries may affect the general availability of the cash held by a foreign subsidiary.

17.6.2 Changes in ownership interests of subsidiaries and other businesses

Chapters 25 to 32 deal with the financial reporting of consolidated groups of entities. When a parent entity obtains control of another entity, or loses control of an existing subsidiary, the comparative consolidated statement of financial position of the group before and after the acquisition or disposal will frequently reflect significant changes in the assets and liabilities arising from the acquisition or disposal. Financial statement users need to be aware of the effects of changes in ownership and control in order to understand the change in financial position of the consolidated group. AASB 107/IAS 7 specifies additional reporting requirements relating to changes in control of subsidiaries and other businesses as follows.

39. The aggregate cash flows arising from obtaining or losing control of subsidiaries or other businesses shall be presented separately and classified as investing activities.
40. An entity shall disclose, in aggregate, in respect of both obtaining or losing control of subsidiaries or other businesses during the period each of the following:
    (a) the total consideration paid or received;
    (b) the portion of the consideration consisting of cash and cash equivalents;
    (c) the amount of cash and cash equivalents in the subsidiaries or other businesses over which control is obtained or lost; and
    (d) the amount of the assets and liabilities other than cash or cash equivalents in the subsidiaries or other businesses over which control is obtained or lost, summarised by each major category.

Paragraph 39 of AASB 107/IAS 7 requires the aggregate cash flow effects of obtaining control of subsidiaries or other businesses to be reported as one item in the investing activities section of the statement of cash flows. When an entity obtains control of a subsidiary or other business, any cash and cash equivalents acquired are deducted from the cash consideration paid in determining the cash flow effects of obtaining control. An example is presented in illustrative example 17.1.

Cash flow effects of obtaining control of another business

Brut Ltd is a catering business. In 2021 it obtained control over party supplies company Champagne Ltd by acquiring all of the ordinary shares of Champagne Ltd. Brut Ltd paid consideration of $1 500 000 in cash. Champagne Ltd held cash and cash equivalents of $100 000 at the time of the acquisition. Thus, the cash flow effect for Brut Ltd of obtaining control of Champagne Ltd is $1 400 000 (i.e. $1 500 000 − $100 000). This would be reported as a cash outflow from investing activities in Brut

Ltd's consolidated statement of cash flows. This is illustrated in figure 17.13, which shows the investing activities section of Brut Ltd's consolidated statement of cash flows.

Similarly, paragraph 39 of AASB 107/IAS 7 requires the aggregate cash flow effects of losing control of subsidiaries or other businesses to be reported as one item in the investing activities section of the statement of cash flows. If an entity loses control of a subsidiary or other business, any cash and cash equivalents held by that subsidiary or other business at the time of the disposal are deducted from the cash consideration received in reporting the cash flow effects of losing control. For example, Brut Ltd sold its retail business in 2021 to Empire Ltd for consideration of $9 000 000, comprising cash of $8 000 000 and shares in Empire Ltd with a fair value of $1 000 000. The retail business held cash of $100 000, which was transferred to Empire Ltd with the sale of the business. The net cash proceeds of the sale of the retail business is $7 900 000, being the cash component of the consideration less the $100 000 cash held by the retail business. Figure 17.13 illustrates the net reporting of the cash proceeds of the sale.

FIGURE 17.13 Investing activities section of statement of cash flows of Brut Ltd for the year ended 30 June 2021

	2021 $'000	2020 $'000
Cash flows from investing activities		
Payments for property, plant and equipment	(5 500)	(4 800)
Proceeds from sale of business (net of cash held)	7 900	
Payment for purchase of business (net of cash acquired)	(1 400)	—
Proceeds from the sale of property, plant and equipment	1 100	1 300
Net cash from (used in) investing activities	**2 100**	**(3 500)**

Separate presentation of the cash flow effects of transactions to obtain or to surrender control of subsidiaries or other businesses is required. The cash flow effects of transactions resulting in the loss of control, such as the sale of a subsidiary, are not deducted from the cash flows of transactions that obtain control, such as the acquisitions of a subsidiary. Both the aggregate cash flow effects of obtaining control of subsidiaries and other businesses and the aggregate cash flow effects of losing control of subsidiaries and other businesses are reported separately in the investing activities section of the statement of cash flows as shown in figure 17.13.

Disclosures provided by Brut Ltd in accordance with paragraph 40 (a)–(c) of AASB 107/IAS 7 are shown in figure 17.14.

FIGURE 17.14 Selected disclosures about transactions resulting in the acquisition or loss of control over other entities by Brut Ltd for the year ended 30 June 2021

During the year Brut Ltd obtained control of Champagne Ltd by acquiring all of the ordinary shares of Champagne Ltd. All of the consideration was paid in cash. Details of the consideration and analysis of the cash flows are summarised below.

Total consideration (included in cash flows from investing activities)	$1 500 000
Cash acquired in subsidiary (included in cash flows from investing activities)	(100 000)
Net cash flows on acquisition	$1 400 000

During the year Brut Ltd sold its retail business for total consideration of $9 000 000. Details of the consideration and analysis of the cash flows are summarised below.

Total consideration, comprising cash and equity investments	$9 000 000
Cash consideration (included in cash flows from investing activities)	8 000 000
Cash acquired in subsidiary (included in cash flows from investing activities)	(100 000)
Net cash flows on disposal of the business	$7 900 000

17.6.3 Non-cash transactions

Not all investing or financing transactions involve current cash flows, although such transactions may significantly affect the financial structure of the entity. Non-cash investing and financing transactions need to be understood in order to comprehend the change in financial position of an entity. Examples include:

- acquisition of assets by means of a lease or by assuming other liabilities
- acquisition of assets or an entity by means of an equity issue
- conversion of debt to equity
- conversion of preference shares to ordinary shares
- refinancing of long-term debt
- payment of dividends through a dividend reinvestment scheme.

In regard to non-cash transactions, paragraph 43 of AASB 107/IAS 7 states:

Investing and financing transactions that do not require the use of cash or cash equivalents shall be excluded from a statement of cash flows. Such transactions shall be disclosed elsewhere in the financial statements in a way that provides all the relevant information about these investing and financing activities.

Figure 17.15 illustrates Brut Ltd's disclosure of non-cash investing and financing activities in the notes to its financial statements. Brut Ltd acquired plant and equipment under a lease which was initially accounted for as an increase in property, plant and equipment and an increase in liabilities. The other major non-cash transaction is the purchase of plant, equipment and leasehold improvements for which the company has not yet paid. Comparative figures for 2020 are shown in parentheses.

FIGURE 17.15   Non-cash investing and financing activities of Brut Ltd for the year ended 30 June 2021

During the financial year Brut Ltd:
 (i) Acquired plant and equipment under finance leases with an aggregate value of $6 000 000 (2020: $5 600 000).
(ii) Acquired shares in another entity in partial consideration for the sale of its retail business (2020: nil). The fair value of the shares was $1 000 000 at the time of acquisition (refer note 14).

17.6.4 Disclosures that are encouraged but not required

Paragraph 50 of AASB 107/IAS 7 encourages, but does not require, additional information that may be relevant to users in understanding the financial position and liquidity of an entity. They are:

(a) the amount of undrawn borrowing facilities that may be available for future operating activities and to settle capital commitments, indicating any restrictions on the use of these facilities;
(b) [deleted]

(c) the aggregate amount of cash flows that represent increases in operating capacity separately from those cash flows that are required to maintain operating capacity; and

(d) the amount of the cash flows arising from the operating, investing and financing activities of each reportable segment (see AASB 8 [IFRS 8] *Operating Segments*).

SUMMARY

AASB 107/IAS 7 *Statement of Cash Flows* is a disclosure standard requiring the presentation of a statement of cash flows as an integral part of an entity's financial statements.

- The statement of cash flows is particularly useful to investors, lenders and others when evaluating an entity's ability to generate cash and cash equivalents, and to meet its obligations and pay dividends.
- The statement of cash flows is required to report cash flows classified into operating, investing and financing activities, as well as the net movement in cash and cash equivalents during the period.
- Net cash flows from operating activities may be presented using either the direct or the indirect method.
- AASB 107/IAS 7 requires additional information to be presented elsewhere in the financial statements concerning investing and financing activities that do not involve cash flows and are therefore excluded from a statement of cash flows.
- AASB 107/IAS 7 requires additional disclosures relating to the cash flow effects of obtaining or losing control of subsidiaries and other businesses.

KEY TERMS

cash Cash on hand and demand deposits.

cash equivalents Short-term, highly liquid investments that are readily convertible to known amounts of cash and which are subject to an insignificant risk of changes in value.

financing activities Activities that result in changes in the size and composition of the contributed equity and borrowings of the entity.

investing activities The acquisition and disposal of long-term assets and other investments not included in cash equivalents.

operating activities The principal revenue-producing activities of the entity and other activities that are not investing or financing activities.

DEMONSTRATION PROBLEM

17.1 Preparing a statement of cash flows using a worksheet

Figure 17.16 presents the financial statements of Lyrebird Ltd followed by other information used in the preparation of the statement of cash flows. The worksheet is shown in figure 17.17. An explanation of the reconciling adjustments follows the worksheet. The indirect method is used to present cash flows from operating activities in figure 17.18. Finally, the presentation of the operating cash flows using the direct method is illustrated, with supporting workings and explanations.

FIGURE 17.16   Financial statements of Lyrebird Ltd

LYREBIRD LTD Comparative statements of financial position as at:			
	31 December 2021	31 December 2022	Increase (decrease)
Cash	$ 60 000	$ 69 800	$ 9 800
Short-term deposits	120 000	140 000	20 000
Accounts receivable, net	140 000	190 000	50 000
Inventories	130 000	155 000	25 000
Prepayments	16 000	19 000	3 000
Interest receivable	300	200	(100)
Investment in associate	40 000	45 000	5 000
Land	80 000	120 000	40 000
Plant	300 000	420 000	120 000
Accumulated depreciation	(50 000)	(65 000)	(15 000)
Intangible assets	90 000	60 000	(30 000)
	$926 300	$1 154 000	$227 700
Accounts payable	$ 84 000	$ 90 000	$ 6 000
Accrued liabilities	14 000	12 000	(2 000)
Current tax payable	28 000	32 000	4 000

	31 December 2021	31 December 2022	Increase (decrease)
Deferred tax liability	20 000	25 000	5 000
Borrowings	120 000	180 000	60 000
Share capital	600 000	680 000	80 000
Retained earnings	60 300	135 000	74 700
	$926 300	$1 154 000	$227 700

LYREBIRD LTD
Statement of profit or loss and other comprehensive income
for the year ended 31 December 2022

Revenue		
Sales revenue		$1 600 000
Interest		10 000
Share of profits of associate		10 000
Gain on sale of plant		8 000
		1 628 000
Expenses		
Cost of sales	$960 000	
Wages and salaries	240 000	
Depreciation — plant	40 000	
Impairment — intangible assets	30 000	
Interest	12 000	
Doubtful debts	8 000	
Other expenses	132 000	1 422 000
Profit before tax		206 000
Income tax expense		(65 000)
Profit for the year		141 000
Other comprehensive income		—
Total comprehensive income		**$ 141 000**

Other information used in worksheet			
(a)	Changes in equity:	Share capital	Retained earnings
	Balance at 31 December 2021	$600 000	$ 60 300
	Profit for the year	—	141 000
	Dividends		
	— cash	—	(36 300)
	— reinvested under dividend scheme	30 000	(30 000)
	Cash share issue	50 000	—
	Balance at 31 December 2022	$680 000	$135 000
(b)	Investment in associate (equity method)		
	Balance at 31 December 2021		$ 40 000
	Share of profit of associate		10 000
	Dividend received		(5 000)
	Balance at 31 December 2022		$ 45 000
(c)	Land		
	Additional land acquired		$ 40 000
	Finance provided by vendor		(35 000)
	Cash paid		$ 5 000
(d)	Plant		
	Acquisitions		$180 000
	Cash paid		171 000
	Accounts payable outstanding at year-end		9 000
			$180 000
	Disposals — cost		$ 60 000
	Accumulated depreciation		(25 000)
	Proceeds received in cash		43 000
(e)	Intangible assets		
	There were no acquisitions or disposals.		
	Impairment write-down		30 000

(f)	Accounts payable comprises:	2021	2022
	Purchase of inventories	$ 49 000	$ 56 000
	Purchase of plant	15 000	9 000
	Other purchases	20 000	25 000
	Balance at 31 December	$ 84 000	$ 90 000
(g)	Accrued liabilities comprises accruals for:		
	Interest	$ 1 200	$ 2 100
	Wages, salaries and other expenses	12 800	9 900
	Balance at 31 December	$ 14 000	$ 12 000
(h)	Increase in borrowings of $ 60 000 reflects:		
	Land vendor finance		$ 35 000
	Additional cash borrowing		25 000
			$ 60 000
(i)	Income tax expense comprises:		
	Income tax expense (current)		$ 60 000
	Income tax expense (deferred)		5 000
			$ 65 000
(j)	Movement in current tax payable:		
	Balance at 31 December 2021		$ 28 000
	Income tax expense		60 000
	Payments made		(56 000)
	Balance at 31 December 2022		$ 32 000

SOLUTION

FIGURE 17.17	Statement of cash flows worksheet

LYREBIRD LTD
Statement of cash flows worksheet
for year ended 31 December 2022

	Balance 31/12/21	Debits		Credits		Balance 31/12/22
Cash	$ 60 000	(26)	$ 9 800			$ 69 800
Short-term deposits	120 000	(27)	20 000			140 000
Accounts receivable, net	140 000	(2)	50 000			190 000
Interest receivable	300			(13)	$ 100	200
Inventories	130 000	(3)	25 000			155 000
Prepayments	16 000	(4)	3 000			19 000
Investment in associate	40 000	(7)	5 000			45 000
Land	80 000	(18)	5 000			120 000
		(19)	35 000			
Plant	300 000	(9)	8 000	(21)	43 000	420 000
		(19)	180 000	(22)	25 000	
Accumulated depreciation	(50 000)	(22)	25 000	(10)	40 000	(65 000)
Intangible assets	90 000			(11)	30 000	60 000
	$926 300					$1 154 000
Accounts payable	$ 84 000	(20)	6 000	(5)	12 000	$ 90 000
Accrued liabilities	14 000	(6)	2 900	(14)	900	12 000
Current tax payable	28 000			(16)	4 000	32 000
Deferred tax liability	20 000			(17)	5 000	25 000
Borrowings	120 000			(19)	35 000	
				(28)	25 000	180 000
Share capital	600 000			(23)	50 000	
				(24)	30 000	680 000
Retained earnings	60 300	(15)	65 000	(1)	206 000	
		(24)	30 000			
		(25)	36 300			135 000
	$926 300					$1 154 000

LYREBIRD LTD
Statement of cash flows worksheet
for year ended 31 December 2022

Statement of cash flows data	Balance 31/12/21	Debits		Credits		Balance 31/12/22
Operating activities						
Profit before tax		(1)	$206 000			$ 206 000
Increase in accounts receivable				(2)	$ 50 000	(50 000)
Increase in inventories				(3)	25 000	(25 000)
Increase in prepayments				(4)	3 000	(3 000)
Increase in accounts payable		(5)	12 000			12 000
Decrease in accrued liabilities				(6)	2 900	(2 900)
Share of profits of associate				(7)	10 000	(10 000)
Interest income				(8)	10 000	(10 000)
Gain on sale of plant				(9)	8 000	(8 000)
Depreciation — plant		(10)	40 000			40 000
Impairment — intangible assets		(11)	30 000			30 000
Interest expense		(12)	12 000			12 000
Cash generated from operations			300 000		108 900	191 100
Interest received		(8)	10 000			
		(13)	100			10 100
Dividend received from associate		(7)	5 000			5 000
Interest paid		(14)	900	(12)	12 000	(11 100)
Income tax paid		(16)	4 000			
		(17)	5 000	(15)	65 000	(56 000)
Net cash from operating activities			325 000		185 900	139 100
Investing activities						
Purchase of land				(18)	5 000	(5 000)
Purchase of plant				(19)	180 000	
				(20)	6 000	(186 000)
Proceeds from sale of plant		(21)	43 000			43 000
Net cash used in investing activities			43 000		191 000	(148 000)
Financing activities						
Proceeds from borrowings		(28)	25 000			25 000
Proceeds from share issue		(23)	50 000			50 000
Payment of cash dividends				(25)	36 300	(36 300)
Net cash flows from financing activities			75 000		36 300	38 700
Net increase in cash and cash equivalents			443 000		413 200	$ 29 800
Increase in cash				(26)	9 800	
Increase in short-term deposits				(27)	20 000	
			$443 000		$443 000	

Explanation of reconciling adjustments in worksheet

Explanations of the reconciling adjustments for each line item of the worksheet are provided below in the same order as they appear in the worksheet, commencing with profit before tax.

Profit before tax

When using the indirect method of presenting cash flows from operating activities, the profit before tax of $206 000 is the starting point. Accordingly, an adjustment (1) is made to retained earnings to reflect the profit before tax for the year, and a separate adjustment (15) is made for income tax expense.

Increase in net accounts receivable

The net increase in accounts receivable of $50 000 reflects the excess of sales revenue over the cash collected from receivables. It must therefore be deducted from profit before tax (adjustment 2). Because the indirect method is being used, there is no need to include separate adjustments for bad debts written off, changes in any allowance for doubtful debts or discounts allowed. Such adjustments are necessary to determine cash flows from customers under the direct method only.

Increase in inventories
The increase in inventories of $25 000 represents the amount by which purchases of inventories exceed the amount included in profit or loss for the cost of goods sold (adjustment 3).

Prepayments
The increase in prepayments of $3000 is an operating cash outflow during the period that is not reflected in profit before tax (adjustment 4).

Accounts payable
Based on 'other information, item (f)' in figure 17.17, accounts payable comprise the following.

	2021	2022	Increase (decrease)	
Amount arising from the:				
Purchase of inventories and services	$69 000	$81 000	$12 000	(Adjustment 5)
Purchase of plant	15 000	9 000	(6 000)	(Adjustment 20)
	$84 000	$90 000	$ 6 000	

The increase in accounts payable arising from the purchase of inventories and services reflects the amount by which the purchases exceed the payments. It does not involve an operating cash outflow for the period. In this example, the increase in accounts payable partly offsets the increase in inventories reflected in adjustment 3.

The reduction in accounts payable arising from the purchase of plant of $6000 increases the cash outflow for the purchase of plant (adjustment 20).

Accrued liabilities
Based on 'other information, item (g)' in figure 17.17, accrued liabilities comprise the following.

	2021	2022	Increase (decrease)
Amount arising from:			
Accrued interest	$ 1 200	$ 2 100	$ 900
Other	12 800	9 900	(2 900)
	$14 000	$12 000	$(2 000)

The reduction in other accrued liabilities increases the operating cash outflows for the year and is reflected in adjustment 6. The increase in accrued interest payable does not involve a cash flow and is reflected in adjustment 14, as part of the calculation of interest paid.

Share of profits of associate
The investment in associate (accounted for under the equity method) increased by $5000, comprising the share of profits of the associate of $10 000, net of a dividend received of $5000. The $10 000 share of profits is excluded from cash generated from operations and the $5000 dividend received is included in net cash from operating activities. The $5000 net increase in the investment does not represent a cash flow and this is reflected in the $10 000 adjustment, net of the $5000 dividend (adjustment 7).

Interest income
When completing the worksheet, interest income is initially transferred out of profit before tax in order to arrive at cash generated from operations (adjustment 8), and is then increased by the reduction in interest receivable of $100 (adjustment 13) to arrive at the interest cash inflow. Alternatively, the interest cash inflow could be classified as an investing activity.

Gain on sale of plant
Note that the accumulated depreciation for the plant sold is transferred to the plant account and that the gross proceeds from the sale of the plant are shown as a credit adjustment. These transfers are consistent with the following journal entries.

Accumulated depreciation	Dr	25 000	
Plant	Cr		25 000
(Closing accumulated depreciation against the plant account on disposal of the plant)			

The carrying amount of the plant sold is $35 000.

Cash	Dr	43 000	
Plant	Cr		35 000
Gain on sale of plant	Cr		8 000
(Disposal of plant)			

Plant is reduced by $35 000, being the net effect of the credit to plant for the cash proceeds from the sale $43 000 (Cr), and debit against plant for the gain on disposal of $8000 (Dr). Gain on disposal of plant of $8000 is not a cash inflow, so it is deducted from profit before tax in arriving at net cash from operating activities (adjustment 9). A separate adjustment is made for the proceeds from sale of plant of $43 000 as an investing cash flow. The reduction in plant for plant sold of $60 000 comprises the following adjustments.

Proceeds	$43 000	(Adjustment 21)
– Gain on sale	(8 000)	(Adjustment 9)
+ Accumulated depreciation	25 000	(Adjustment 22)
Cost of plant sold	$60 000	

Depreciation of plant and impairment of intangible assets
Both of these expenses in the statement of profit or loss and other comprehensive income do not constitute cash flows in the current period, so they are added back in arriving at net cash from operating activities (depreciation adjustment 10 of $40 000 and impairment adjustment 11 of $30 000).

Interest expense
Interest expense is initially transferred out of profit before tax in order to arrive at cash generated from operations (adjustment 12). It is then reduced by the increase in accrued interest $900 (adjustment 14), to arrive at the interest cash outflow. The calculation is shown earlier in the explanation of accrued liabilities, above. Alternatively, the interest cash outflow could be classified as a financing activity.

Income tax paid
Income tax expense of $65 000 (adjustment 15) is reduced by the increase in current tax payable of $4000 (adjustment 16) and the increase in deferred tax liability of $5000 (adjustment 17) to determine the income tax cash outflow of $56 000. In this example, there are no tax charges — such as on revaluation surplus or translation reserve increases — made directly to equity accounts. This is evident because there are no items of other comprehensive income reported in the statement of profit or loss and other comprehensive income.

Purchase of land and plant
Additional land was acquired at a cost of $40 000, with $35 000 being financed by the vendor. Adjustment 18 records the cash outflow of $5000 and adjustment 19 records the non-cash component of $35 000. The other side of the adjustment is made to borrowings.
Plant acquisitions for the year are $180 000 (adjustment 19). This amount is increased by the reduction in plant accounts payable of $6000 (adjustment 20); this is discussed in the explanation of accounts payable, above.

Proceeds from borrowings
The cash proceeds from borrowings of $25 000 (adjustment 28) comprise the gross increase in borrowings of $60 000 ($180 000 − $120 000) reduced by the $35 000 of land vendor finance (adjustment 19); this is discussed in the explanation of the purchase of land and plant, above.

Proceeds from share issue and payment of cash dividends

To determine the proceeds from share issue (adjustment 23), the increase in share capital of $80 000 ($680 000 − $600 000) is reduced by the $30 000 of reinvested dividends (adjustment 24) because these dividends did not involve a cash inflow. Similarly, cash flows from financing activities include only the $36 300 of dividends paid in cash (adjustment 25).

Increase in cash and short-term deposits

Short-term deposits are considered to be cash equivalents. Therefore, the increase is included in the net increase in cash and cash equivalents for the period of $29 800 (adjustments 26 and 27).

Figure 17.18 contains Lyrebird Ltd's statement of cash flows for the year ended 31 December 2022 (without prior year comparatives).

FIGURE 17.18	Statement of cash flows of Lyrebird Ltd

LYREBIRD LTD
Statement of cash flows
for year ended 31 December 2022

Cash flows from operating activities		
Profit before tax	$206 000	
Adjustments for:		
Depreciation	40 000	
Impairment of intangible assets	30 000	
Gain on sale of plant	(8 000)	
Share of profits of associate	(10 000)	
Interest income	(10 000)	
Interest expense	12 000	
Increase in receivables	(50 000)	
Increase in inventories	(25 000)	
Increase in prepayments	(3 000)	
Increase in accounts payable	12 000	
Decrease in accrued liabilities	(2 900)	
Cash generated from operations	191 100	
Interest received	10 100	
Dividend received from associate	5 000	
Interest paid	(11 100)	
Income taxes paid	(56 000)	
Net cash from operating activities		$139 100
Cash flows from investing activities		
Purchase of land (Note A)	(5 000)	
Purchase of plant	(186 000)	
Proceeds from sale of plant	43 000	
Net cash used in investing activities		(148 000)
Cash flows from financing activities		
Proceeds from borrowings	25 000	
Proceeds from share issue (Note B)	50 000	
Dividends paid (Note B)	(36 300)	
Net cash from financing activities		38 700
Net increase in cash and cash equivalents		29 800
Cash and cash equivalents at beginning of year (Note C)		180 000
Cash and cash equivalents at end of year (Note C)		$209 800

Notes

(A) Land

During the year, land at a cost of $40 000 was acquired by means of vendor finance of $35 000 and a cash payment of $5000.

(B) Dividends

During the year, shareholders elected to reinvest dividends amounting to $30 000 under the company's dividend share reinvestment scheme. (This information will be reported in the company's statement of changes in equity, so a cross-reference to that statement may be used instead of this note.)

(C) Cash and cash equivalents

Cash and cash equivalents included in the statement of cash flows comprise the following amounts reported in the statement of financial position.

	2022	2021
Cash	$ 69 800	$ 60 000
Short-term deposits	140 000	120 000
Cash and cash equivalents at end of year	$209 800	$180 000

The current period, 2022, is shown on the left in the note because it is customary to present the current year first, followed by the comparative figures, reading from left to right. However, comparative data were presented in the worksheets to facilitate working from left to right in calculating movements in line items used to determine cash flows.

If the direct method of presenting operating cash flows is used, the cash receipts from customers and cash paid to suppliers and employees can be determined by reconstructing the relevant general ledger accounts or by using the equations previously given. For the purposes of this example, it is assumed that net accounts receivable comprises the following.

	2019	2020
Accounts receivable	$160 000	$215 000
Allowance for doubtful debts	(20 000)	(25 000)
	$140 000	$190 000

It is further assumed that bad debts of $3000 were deducted from the allowance for doubtful debts and the remaining allowance for doubtful debts was increased by a charge to profit or loss of $8000 (refer to the statement of profit or loss and other comprehensive income).

As demonstrated previously, the summarised general ledger accounts can be reconstructed from the statement of financial position and supplementary information (opening and closing balances), and statement of profit or loss and other comprehensive income and supplementary information (bad debts and sales). The cash receipts amount is then determined as the balancing figure.

The reconstructed accounts receivable and allowance for doubtful debts general ledger accounts would appear as follows.

Accounts receivable			
Opening balance	160 000	Bad debts write-off	3 000
Sales revenue	1 600 000	Cash received	1 542 000
		Closing balance	215 000
	1 760 000		1 760 000

Allowance for doubtful debts			
Bad debts write-off	3 000	Opening balance	20 000
Closing balance	25 000	Doubtful debts expense	8 000
	28 000		28 000

Cash paid to suppliers of inventories can be determined by reconstructing the relevant general ledger accounts. The purchases amount is determined as the difference between the opening and closing balances (obtained from the statement of financial position) and cost of sales (obtained from the statement of profit or loss and other comprehensive income). The determined amount of purchases is then recorded in the accounts payable (for inventories) account to calculate the cash payments to suppliers of inventories. This is shown as follows.

Inventories			
Opening balance	130 000	Cost of sales	960 000
Purchases	985 000	Closing balance	155 000
	1 115 000		1 115 000

Accounts payable — inventories purchases			
Cash payments	978 000	Opening balance	49 000
Closing balance	56 000	Purchases	985 000
	1 034 000		1 034 000

Cash paid to other suppliers and employees can be similarly determined or calculated by using the equations previously given. Cash payments to other suppliers and employees comprise the following.

Wages and salaries	$240 000
Other expenses	132 000
	372 000
Prepayments increase	3 000
Increase (decrease) in accounts payable for other purchases (other information note f)	(5 000)
Accruals liabilities (other information note g)	2 900
Total payments to employees and other suppliers of services	$372 900

Using the above calculations, total payments to suppliers and employees comprise the following.

Payments for:	
Inventories	$ 978 000
Service providers	372 900
	$1 350 900

Using the above calculations, cash flows from operating activities presented under the direct method are shown in figure 17.19.

FIGURE 17.19	Cash flows from operating activities using the direct method

Cash flow from operating activities	
Cash received from customers	$ 1 542 000
Cash payments to suppliers and employees	(1 350 900)
Cash generated from operations	191 100
Interest received	10 100
Dividend received from associate	5 000
Interest paid	(11 100)
Income taxes paid	(56 000)
Net cash from operating activities	$ 139 100

COMPREHENSION QUESTIONS

1 What is the purpose of a statement of cash flows?
2 How might a statement of cash flows be used?
3 What is the meaning of 'cash equivalent'?
4 Explain the required classifications of cash flows under AASB 107/IAS 7.
5 What sources of information are usually required to prepare a statement of cash flows?
6 Explain the differences between the presentation of cash flows from operating activities under the direct method and their presentation under the indirect method. Do you consider one method to be more useful than the other? Why?
7 The statement of cash flows is said to be of assistance in evaluating the financial strength of an entity, yet the statement can exclude significant non-cash transactions that can materially affect the financial strength of an entity. How does AASB 107/IAS 7 seek to overcome this issue?
8 An entity may report significant profits over a number of successive years and still experience negative net cash flows from its operating activities. How can this happen?
9 An entity may report significant accounting losses over a number of successive years and still report positive net cash flows from operating activities over the same period. How can this happen?
10 What supplementary disclosures are required when a consolidated statement of cash flows is being prepared for a group that has obtained or lost control of a subsidiary?

CASE STUDY 17.1

INCREASING CASH FLOW, DECREASING PROFIT

Lana Ferdinand, the owner-manager of a small proprietary company, had carefully monitored the cash position over the past financial year, and was pleased to note at the end of the year that the cash position was strong, and had shown a healthy 50% increase over the year. When presented with the statement of profit or loss for the year, she was dismayed to note that profit had deteriorated significantly. In her anger, she accuses you of having made errors in the accounting since 'such a silly situation could not possibly exist'.

Required

Explain how you would respond to Lana Ferdinand.

CASE STUDY 17.2

CLASSIFICATION OF CASH FLOWS

The accountant for Delta Ltd prepared the following statement of cash flows.

DELTA LTD Statement of cash flows for the year ended 30 June 2022	$'000
Cash flows from operating activities	
Cash received from customers	870
Cash paid to suppliers of goods and services	(650)
Interest received	40
Interest paid	(200)
Income tax paid	(100)
Net cash outflow from operating activities	(40)
Cash flows from investing activities	
Cash received from sale of investments	300
Cash paid for purchase of property, plant and equipment	(400)
Net cash outflow from investing activities	(100)
Cash flows from financing activities	
Proceeds from borrowings	160
Dividends paid	(30)
Net cash inflow from financing activities	130
Net decrease in cash and cash equivalents	(10)
Cash and cash equivalents at the beginning of the year	15
Cash and cash equivalents at the end of the year	**5**

The managers were worried that investors would be displeased by the negative operating cash flow and that the company's share price might fall as a result. One manager suggested that the interest paid and interest received might be classified as financing cash flows and investing cash flows respectively, so that the company's cash flow would look better.

Required

1. Calculate the net cash flows for each activity if Delta Ltd reclassified interest paid and interest received as suggested by the manager.
2. Drawing on your understanding of the efficient market hypothesis (see chapter 2), is the change in the classification of interest paid or received in the statement of cash flows likely to make a difference to the share price? Give reasons for your answer.

CASE STUDY 17.3

CASH FLOWS OF TOP AUSTRALIAN COMPANIES

Select three ASX-listed companies from different industries (e.g. metals and mining, telecommunication services, consumer staples). Go to www.asx.com.au and find the most recent annual financial statements of the three companies.

Required

Compare the companies' statements of cash flows and report your findings, especially with respect to the major categories of operating activities, investing activities and financing activities.

APPLICATION AND ANALYSIS EXERCISES

★ BASIC | ★ ★ MODERATE | ★ ★ ★ DIFFICULT

17.1 Cash received from customers ★   LO5

At 30 June 2021, Ruby Ltd had net accounts receivable of $360 000. At 30 June 2022, accounts receivable were $440 000 and sales for the year amounted to $1 500 000. Doubtful debts expense was $75 000 for the year. Discount allowed was $45 000 for the year.

Required

Calculate cash received from customers by Ruby Ltd for the year ended 30 June 2022.

17.2 Cash payments to suppliers ★   LO5

Purple Ltd had the following balances.

	30 June 2021	30 June 2022
Inventories	$510 000	$630 000
Accounts payable for inventories purchases	103 000	95 000

Cost of sales was $2 400 000 for the year ended 30 June 2022.

Required

Calculate cash payments to suppliers for the year ended 30 June 2022.

17.3 Cash received from customers ★   LO5

At 30 June 2021, Orange Ltd had accounts receivable of $200 000. At 30 June 2022, accounts receivable were $240 000 and sales for the year amounted to $2 100 000. Bad debts amounting to $50 000 had been written off during the year, and discounts of $17 000 had been allowed in respect of payments from customers made within prescribed credit terms. Orange Ltd did not have an allowance for doubtful debts in either year.

Required

Calculate cash received from customers for the year ended 30 June 2022.

17.4 Financing cash flows ★   LO5

The following information has been compiled from the accounting records of Marshall Ltd for the year ended 30 June 2022.

Dividends — paid	$50 000
— dividend reinvestment scheme	30 000
Additional cash borrowing	75 000
Issue of shares — cash	75 000
— dividend reinvestment	30 000

Required

Determine the amount of net cash from financing activities Marshall Ltd would report in its statement of cash flows for the year ended 30 June 2022.

17.5 Net investing cash flows ★ ★   LO5

The statement of financial position of Lily Ltd at 30 June 2022 recorded the following items.

	30 June 2021	30 June 2022
Land, at independent valuation	$ 500 000	$ 600 000
Plant, at cost	350 000	425 000
Accumulated depreciation	(100 000)	(140 000)
Investments at fair value through OCI	150 000	200 000
Goodwill	125 000	100 000
Land revaluation surplus	100 000	170 000
Investments revaluation reserve	25 000	55 000

Additional information
- Impairment of goodwill was $25 000 in the year ended 30 June 2022.
- There were no acquisitions or disposals of land.
- There were no disposals of plant or investments.
- The land revaluation surplus increase is net of deferred tax of $30 000.
- The investments revaluation reserve increase for the year is net of deferred tax of $10 000.

Required

Prepare the investing section of the statement of cash flows for Lily Ltd for the year ended 30 June 2022.

17.6 Investing cash flows ★   **LO5**

The following information has been compiled from the accounting records of Robin Ltd for the year ended 30 June 2022.

Purchase of land, with the vendor financing $100 000 for 2 years	$350 000
Purchase of plant	250 000
Sale of plant:	
Carrying amount	50 000
Cash proceeds	42 000

Required

Determine the amount of investing net cash outflows Robin Ltd would report in its statement of cash flows for the year ended 30 June 2022.

17.7 Net financing cash flows ★ ★   **LO5**

The following information has been extracted from the accounting records of Barney Ltd.

	30 June 2021	30 June 2022
Borrowings	$100 000	$200 000
Share capital	200 000	250 000
Property revaluation surplus	50 000	60 000
Retained earnings	75 000	95 000

Additional information
- Borrowings of $20 000 were repaid during the year to 30 June 2022. New borrowings include $50 000 vendor finance arising on the acquisition of a property.
- The increase in share capital includes $30 000 arising from the company's dividend reinvestment scheme.
- The movement in retained earnings comprises profit for the year $90 000, net of dividends $70 000.
- There were no dividends payable reported in the statement of financial position at either 30 June 2021 or 30 June 2022.

Required

Prepare the financing section of the statement of cash flows for Barney Ltd for the year ended 30 June 2022.

17.8 Cash receipts from customers and cash paid to suppliers and employees ★ ★   **LO5**

The accounting records of Stella Ltd recorded the following information.

	30 June 2021	30 June 2022
Accounts receivable	$80 000	$ 100 000
Inventories	64 000	68 000
Prepaid expenses	2 000	6 000
Accounts payable for inventories purchased	30 000	32 000
Employee liabilities	10 000	11 000
Other accruals (including accrued interest:		
2021: $1400; 2022: $1700)	8 000	7 600
Sales revenue		1 200 000
Cost of sales		960 000
Expenses (including $10 000 depreciation and		
$4000 interest)		150 000

Required

1. Calculate the amount of cash received from customers during the year ended 30 June 2022.
2. Calculate the amount of cash paid to suppliers and employees during the year ended 30 June 2022.

17.9 Preparation of a statement of cash flows ★ ★   **LO3, 5**

A summarised comparative statement of financial position of Graham Ltd is presented below.

	30 June 2021	30 June 2022
Cash	$ 54 000	$ 82 000
Trade receivables	94 000	146 000
Investments	35 000	30 000
Plant	260 000	360 000
Accumulated depreciation	(90 000)	(120 000)
	$353 000	$ 498 000
Trade accounts payable	$ 95 000	$ 122 000
Deferred tax liability		10 000
Share capital	200 000	250 000
Retained earnings	58 000	109 000
Investment revaluation surplus	—	7 000
	$353 000	$ 498 000

Additional information
- An investment was sold for $18 000. There was no gain or loss accumulated in the investment revaluation reserve in respect of this investment.
- There were no disposals of plant.
- The profit for the year was $97 000, after income tax expense of $38 000.
- A dividend of $42 000 was paid during the year.
- The only item of other comprehensive income was a gain on revaluation of financial investments and its associated tax effect.

Required

Using the indirect method of presenting cash flows from operating activities, prepare a statement of cash flows in accordance with AASB 107/IAS 7 for the year ended 30 June 2022.

17.10 Preparation of a statement of cash flows ★ ★   **LO4, 5**

A summarised comparative statement of financial position of Charlton Ltd is presented below.

	30 June 2021	30 June 2022
Cash	$ 96 000	$ 49 000
Accounts receivable (net)	147 000	163 000
Prepayments	20 000	15 000
Inventories	60 000	104 000
Land	40 000	40 000
Plant	368 000	420 000
Accumulated depreciation	(45 000)	(70 000)
Deferred tax asset	20 000	24 000
	$706 000	$745 000
Accounts payable	$140 000	$152 000
Accrued liabilities	36 000	42 000
Current tax payable	24 000	31 000
Dividend payable	56 000	50 000
Borrowings	73 000	75 000
Share capital	335 000	345 000
Retained earnings	42 000	50 000
	$706 000	$745 000

Additional information
- Plant additions amounted to $72 000. Plant with a carrying value of $15 000 (cost $20 000, accumulated depreciation $5000) was sold for $22 000. The proceeds for the sale of plant had not been received by 30 June 2022.
- Accounts payable at 30 June 2021 include $34 000 arising from the acquisition of plant.
- Accrued liabilities include accrued interest of $3000 at 30 June 2021 and $4000 at 30 June 2022.

- The increase in share capital of $10 000 arose from the reinvestment of dividends.
- The profit for the year ended 30 June 2022 was $92 000, after interest expense of $6000 and income tax expense of $46 000. There were no other items of comprehensive income.
- Dividends declared out of profits for the year were: interim dividend $34 000, final dividend $50 000.

Required

Using the indirect method of presenting cash flows from operating activities, prepare a statement of cash flows in accordance with AASB 107/IAS 7 for the year ended 30 June 2022.

17.11 Preparation of a statement of cash flows ★ ★   **LO3, 4, 5**

A summarised comparative statement of financial position of Findlay Ltd is presented below.

	30 June 2021	30 June 2022
Cash	$ 40 000	$ 182 000
Trade receivables	130 000	180 000
Inventories	116 000	124 000
Prepayments	20 000	24 000
Land	160 000	180 000
Plant	540 000	640 000
Accumulated depreciation	(120 000)	(184 000)
	$ 906 000	$1 146 000
Accounts payable	$ 90 000	$ 96 000
Borrowings	320 000	400 000
Share capital	400 000	460 000
Retained earnings	96 000	190 000
	$ 906 000	$1 146 000

Additional information
- There were no disposals of land or plant during the year.
- A $60 000 borrowing was settled through the issue of ordinary shares. There were no other repayments of borrowings.
- Profit for the year was $240 000, interest expense was $28 000, and income tax expense was $82 000. There were no items of other comprehensive income.
- A $146 000 dividend was paid during the year.
- Sales revenue for the year was $600 000. There was no other revenue.

Required

1. Using the indirect method of presenting cash flows from operating activities, prepare a statement of cash flows in accordance with AASB 107/IAS 7 for the year ended 30 June 2022.
2. Prepare the operating section of the statement of cash flows using the direct method.

17.12 Presentation of a statement of cash flows ★ ★   **LO3, 5**

A summarised comparative statement of financial position of Danica Ltd is presented below, together with the statement of profit or loss and other comprehensive income for the year ended 30 June 2022.

	30 June 2021	30 June 2022
Cash	$ 30 000	$ 68 000
Trade receivables	46 000	70 000
Inventories	30 000	32 000
Investments at fair value through OCI	35 000	40 000
Plant	125 000	150 000
Accumulated depreciation	(23 000)	(35 000)
	$243 000	$325 000
Accounts payable	$ 39 000	$ 43 000
Accrued interest	3 000	5 000
Current tax payable	10 000	12 000
Deferred tax liability	–	1 500
Borrowings	60 000	100 000
Share capital	100 000	100 000
Retained earnings	31 000	60 000
Investment revaluation reserve	–	3 500
	$243 000	$325 000

DANICA LTD
Statement of profit or loss and other comprehensive income
for the year ended 30 June 2022

Sales	$ 700 000
Cost of sales	(483 000)
Gross profit	217 000
Distribution costs	(62 000)
Administration costs	(74 000)
Interest	(6 000)
Profit before tax	75 000
Income tax expense	(23 000)
Profit for the year	52 000
Other comprehensive income	
Gain on revaluation of investments (net of tax)	3 500
Total comprehensive income	**$ 55 500**

Additional information
- There were no disposals of investments or plant during the year.
- A dividend of $23 000 was paid during the year.
- The deferred tax liability is in relation to investments.

Required

Using the direct method of presenting cash flows from operating activities, prepare a statement of cash flows in accordance with AASB 107/IAS 7 for the year ended 30 June 2022.

17.13 Preparation of a statement of cash flows ★ ★ **LO3, 4, 5**

A summarised comparative statement of financial position of Bronze Ltd is presented below, together with a statement of profit or loss and other comprehensive income for the year ended 30 June 2022.

	30 June 2021	30 June 2022
Cash	$ 45 000	$ 35 000
Trade receivables	69 000	105 000
Allowance for doubtful debts	(3 000)	(6 000)
Inventories	45 000	67 000
Equity investments	53 000	60 000
Plant	187 000	225 000
Accumulated depreciation	(35 000)	(53 000)
	$361 000	$433 000
Accounts payable	$ 65 000	$ 75 000
Accrued interest	5 000	7 000
Current tax payable	15 000	18 000
Deferred tax	30 000	37 000
Borrowings	80 000	100 000
Share capital	100 000	100 000
Investment revaluation reserve	2 000	7 000
Retained earnings	64 000	89 000
	$361 000	$433 000

BRONZE LTD
Statement of profit or loss and other comprehensive income
for the year ended 30 June 2022

Sales	$1 035 000
Cost of sales	(774 000)
Gross profit	261 000
Distribution costs	(76 000)
Administration costs	(96 000)
Interest expense	(7 000)
Profit before tax	82 000
Income tax expense	(24 000)
Profit for the year	58 000

BRONZE LTD	
Statement of profit or loss and other comprehensive income	
for the year ended 30 June 2022	
Other comprehensive income	
Gain on revaluation of investments (net of tax)	5 000
Total comprehensive income	**$ 63 000**

Additional information

- The movement in the allowance for doubtful debts for the year comprises the following.

Balance at 30 June 2021	$ 3 000
Charge for year	5 000
Bad debts written off	(2 000)
Balance at 30 June 2022	$ 6 000

- Equity investments are shares in other companies that are measured at fair value, with increases/decreases being recognised in other comprehensive income, and accumulated in the investment revaluation reserve until investments are sold.
- There were no disposals of plant during the year.
- A dividend of $33 000 was paid during the year.
- There were no acquisitions or disposals of investments during the year.

Required

1. Using the direct method of presenting cash flows from operating activities, prepare a statement of cash flows in accordance with AASB 107/IAS 7 for the year ended 30 June 2022.
2. Prepare the operating activities section of the statement of cash flows using the indirect method of presentation.

17.14 Preparation of a statement of cash flows ★ ★   **LO3, 5**

A comparative statement of financial position of Adele Ltd is presented below.

	30 June 2021	30 June 2022
Cash	$ 60 000	$109 000
Trade receivables	92 000	102 000
Inventories	50 000	80 000
Land (at valuation)	25 000	31 000
Plant	230 000	260 000
Accumulated depreciation	(45 000)	(60 000)
	$412 000	$522 000
Accounts payable	$ 75 000	$ 77 500
Accrued interest	6 000	8 000
Other accrued liabilities	22 500	21 500
Current tax payable	15 000	17 000
Provision for employee benefits	19 000	21 000
Dividend payable	—	30 000
Borrowings	47 500	52 500
Deferred tax liability	29 000	19 500
Share capital	175 000	190 000
Revaluation surplus	6 000	10 000
Retained earnings	17 000	75 000
	$412 000	$522 000

ADELE LTD	
Statement of profit or loss and other comprehensive income	
for the year ended 30 June 2022	
Sales	$ 1 790 000
Cost of sales	(1 432 000)
Gross profit	358 000
Gain on sale of plant	8 000
Dividend income	2 000
Distribution costs	(92 500)

Administrative costs	(80 000)
Interest expense	(4 000)
Other costs	(20 000)
Profit before tax	171 500
Income tax expense	(51 500)
Profit for the year	120 000
Other comprehensive income	
Gain on asset revaluation (net of tax)	4 000
Total comprehensive income	**$ 124 000**

Additional information
- The increase to the revaluation surplus is net of deferred tax of $2000.
- Plant with a carrying amount of $30 000 (cost $42 500, accumulated depreciation $12 500) was sold for $38 000.
- Accounts payable at 30 June 2022 include $11 000 in respect of plant acquisitions.
- There were borrowing repayments of $15 000 during the year.
- The increase in share capital of $15 000 arose from the company's dividend reinvestment scheme.
- Dividends declared out of profits for the year were: interim dividend $32 000, final dividend $30 000.

Required

Using the direct method of presenting cash flows from operating activities, prepare a statement of cash flows in accordance with AASB 107/IAS 7 for the year ended 30 June 2022, including a reconciliation of cash flows arising from operating activities and profit in accordance with AASB 1054.

17.15 Preparation of statement of cash flows information ★ ★   **LO2, 3, 4, 5**

The statement of profit or loss and other comprehensive income and comparative statements of financial position of Amber Ltd are as follows.

AMBER LTD		
Statement of financial position		
as at 31 December		
	2021	**2022**
Current assets		
Deposits at call	$ 19 000	$ 30 000
Accounts receivable	340 000	320 000
Allowance for doubtful debts	(19 000)	(15 000)
Inventories	654 000	670 000
Prepayments	52 000	55 000
	1 046 000	1 060 000
Non-current assets		
Land	400 000	400 000
Buildings	1 175 000	1 850 000
Accumulated depreciation — buildings	(200 000)	(235 000)
Plant	850 000	940 000
Accumulated depreciation — plant	(375 000)	(452 000)
	1 850 000	2 503 000
Total assets	**$2 896 000**	**$3 563 000**
Current liabilities		
Bank overdraft	$ 140 000	$ 49 000
Accounts payable	553 000	570 000
Interest payable	25 000	30 000
Final dividend payable	205 000	230 000
Current tax payable	70 000	77 000
	993 000	956 000
Non-current liabilities		
Borrowings	900 000	1 300 000
Deferred tax liability	12 000	16 000
	912 000	1 316 000
Total liabilities	1 905 000	2 272 000

▶

	2021	2022
Equity		
Share capital	800 000	1 000 000
Retained earnings	191 000	291 000
	991 000	1 291 000
Total liabilities and equity	**$2 896 000**	**$3 563 000**

AMBER LTD
Statement of profit or loss and other comprehensive income
for the year ended 31 December 2022

Sales	$8 550 000
Less: Cost of sales	4 517 000
Gross profit	4 033 000
Gain on sale of plant	18 000
	4 051 000
Distribution costs	(1 635 000)
Administration costs	(1 566 000)
Interest	(70 000)
Profit before tax	780 000
Income tax expense	(250 000)
Profit for the period	530 000
Other comprehensive income	—
Total comprehensive income	**$ 530 000**

The following additional information has been extracted from the accounting records of Amber Ltd.

(a)	Movement in allowance for doubtful debts:	
	Balance 31 December 2021	$ 19 000
	Charge for year	7 000
	Bad debts written off	(11 000)
	Balance 31 December 2022	$ 15 000

(b) Building additions were completed. There were no disposals.

(c) The movement in plant and accumulated depreciation on plant comprised the following.

	Cost	Accumulated depreciation
Balance 31 December 2021	$ 850 000	$375 000
Additions — cash	160 000	—
Disposals	(70 000)	(50 000)
Depreciation	—	127 000
Balance 31 December 2022	$ 940 000	$452 000

(d) There was no outstanding interest payable at year-end.

(e) Income tax expense comprised:

Income tax currently payable	$ 246 000
Deferred income tax	4 000
	$ 250 000

(f) Additional cash borrowings $ 400 000

(g) Movement in equity

	Share capital	Retained earnings
Balance 31 December 2021	$ 800 000	$191 000
Additional shares issued for cash	200 000	—
Profit for the period		530 000
Interim dividend — cash	—	(200 000)
Final dividend payable		(230 000)
Balance 31 December 2022	$1 000 000	$291 000

Required

1. Prepare a summary of cash flows from operating activities using the indirect method of presentation.
2. Prepare a summary of cash flows from investing activities.
3. Prepare a summary of cash flows from financing activities.
4. Prepare a summary of cash flows from operating activities using the direct method of presentation.

17.16 Preparing a statement of cash flows with notes ★ ★ ★   **LO2, 3, 5, 6**

The statement of profit or loss and other comprehensive income and comparative statements of financial position of Dolphin Ltd were as follows.

DOLPHIN LTD Statement of financial position as at 31 December		
	2021	2022
Current assets		
Cash at bank	$ 92 000	$ 104 000
Cash deposits (30-day)	80 000	140 000
Accounts receivable	220 000	234 000
Allowance for doubtful debts	(24 000)	(32 000)
Interest receivable	4 000	6 000
Inventories	588 000	640 000
Prepayments	26 000	18 000
	986 000	1 110 000
Non-current assets		
Land	200 000	280 000
Plant	1 200 000	1 400 000
Accumulated depreciation	(280 000)	(360 000)
Investments in associate	160 000	184 000
Brand names	240 000	180 000
	1 520 000	1 684 000
Total assets	**$ 2 506 000**	**$ 2 794 000**
Current liabilities		
Accounts payable	$ 360 000	$ 392 000
Accrued liabilities	170 000	184 000
Current tax payable	80 000	86 000
Current portion of long-term borrowings	40 000	40 000
	650 000	702 000
Non-current liabilities		
Borrowings	196 000	276 000
Deferred tax liability	70 000	80 000
Provision for employee benefits	80 000	86 000
	346 000	442 000
Total liabilities	996 000	1 144 000
Equity		
Share capital	1 000 000	1 060 000
Retained earnings	510 000	590 000
	1 510 000	1 650 000
Total liabilities and equity	**$ 2 506 000**	**$ 2 794 000**

DOLPHIN LTD Statement of profit or loss and other comprehensive income for the year ended 31 December 2022	
Sales	$ 3 560 000
Cost of sales	(2 060 000)
Gross profit	1 500 000
Interest	4 000
Share of profits of associate	40 000
Gain on sale of plant	16 000
Total income	1 560 000

DOLPHIN LTD	
Statement of profit or loss and other comprehensive income	
for the year ended 31 December 2022	
Expenses	
Salaries and wages	704 000
Depreciation	100 000
Discount allowed	16 000
Doubtful debts	12 000
Interest	42 000
Other (including impairment of brand names $30 000)	372 000
	1 246 000
Profit before tax	314 000
Income tax expense	(94 000)
Profit for the period	220 000
Other comprehensive income	—
Total comprehensive income	**$ 220 000**

The following additional information has been extracted from the accounting records of Dolphin Ltd.

(a)	30-day cash deposits are used in the course of the daily cash management of the company.	
(b)	Movement in allowance for doubtful debts:	
	Balance 31 December 2021	$ 24 000
	Charge for year	12 000
	Bad debts written off	(4 000)
	Balance 31 December 2022	$ 32 000
(c)	Land	
	Additional cash purchase	$ 80 000
(d)	Plant	
	Purchases for year (including $50 000 acquired by a lease)	$300 000
(e)	Disposals of plant	
	Cost of disposals	$100 000
	Accumulated depreciation	(20 000)
(f)	Investments in associate	
	Share of profit	$ 40 000
	Dividends received	16 000
(g)	Accounts payable	
	Includes amounts owing in respect of plant purchases:	
	31 December 2021	$ 24 000
	31 December 2022	36 000
(h)	Accrued liabilities	
	Includes accrued interest payable:	
	31 December 2021	$ 8 000
	31 December 2022	10 000
(i)	Income tax expense comprises:	
	Current tax payable	$ 84 000
	Deferred tax	10 000
	Income tax expense	$ 94 000
(j)	Dividends paid	
	Under a dividend reinvestment scheme, shareholders have the right to receive additional shares in lieu of cash dividends.	
	Dividends paid comprised:	
	Dividends paid in cash during the year	$ 80 000
	Dividends reinvested	60 000
	Total dividends	$140 000

Required

1. Using the direct method of presenting cash flows from operating activities, prepare a statement of cash flows in accordance with AASB 107/IAS 7 for the year ended 31 December 2022.
2. Prepare a note reconciling profit to cash flows from operating activities in accordance with AASB 1054.
3. Prepare any other notes to the statement of cash flows that you consider are required by AASB 107/IAS 7.

17.17 **Analysis of differences between profit and cash flows from operations** ★ ★ ★ **LO1, 5**

Obtain the financial statements of Bega Cheese Limited for 2018, which includes 2017 comparative figures. The company's profit for 2017 was $138 748 000. However, cash used in operations was $70 221 000 during the same period.

Required

Prepare a report for non-accountants to:

1. explain how a company can make a profit without generating positive net operating cash flows during the same period
2. identify the major factors contributing to the difference between Bega Cheese Limited's profit and cash from operating activities during 2017.

REFERENCE

Bega Cheese Limited 2018, *Annual report 2018*, www.begacheese.com.au.

ACKNOWLEDGEMENTS

Photo: © Hero Images / Getty Images

Figure 17.4: © Bega Cheese Limited 2018

Text: © 2019 Australian Accounting Standards Board (AASB). The text, graphics and layout of this publication are protected by Australian copyright law and the comparable law of other countries. No part of the publication may be reproduced, stored or transmitted in any form or by any means without the prior written permission of the AASB except as permitted by law. For reproduction or publication, permission should be sought in writing from the AASB. Requests in the first instance should be addressed to the National Director, Australian Accounting Standards Board, PO Box 204, Collins Street West, Victoria 8007.

CHAPTER 18

Accounting policies and other disclosures

CHAPTER AIM

This chapter examines the issues for preparers of general purpose financial statements with regard to the selection and changing of accounting policies, changes in accounting estimates and the correction of errors. It also considers the nature of events affecting an entity that occur after the reporting period and their implications for disclosure.

LEARNING OBJECTIVES

After studying this chapter, you should be able to:

18.1 describe how accounting policies and changes to accounting policies are disclosed in general purpose financial statements

18.2 describe how changes in accounting estimates are accounted for and disclosed in general purpose financial statements

18.3 explain how prior period errors arise, and how they are accounted for and disclosed in general purpose financial statements

18.4 explain the requirements when it is impracticable to make retrospective adjustments for changes in accounting policies or correction of errors

18.5 describe the concept of materiality and how material items are identified

18.6 explain the difference between types of events occurring after the end of the reporting period and how they are to be treated in the financial statements.

CONCEPTS FOR REVIEW

Before studying this chapter, you should understand and, if necessary, revise:

- the regulatory framework governing financial reporting in Australia including the requirements of the *Corporations Act 2001*
- the *Conceptual Framework* and the objective of general purpose financial reporting
- the reporting requirements of AASB 101/IAS 1 *Presentation of Financial Statements*.

18.1 Accounting policies

LEARNING OBJECTIVE 18.1 Describe how accounting policies and changes to accounting policies are disclosed in general purpose financial statements.

Chapter 1 introduced the notion that the objective of financial statements is to provide information about the financial position, financial performance and cash flows of an entity that is useful to a wide range of users in making economic decisions. In evaluating such information users need to know the bases upon which the financial statements have been prepared. Paragraph 5 of AASB 108/IAS 8 *Accounting Policies, Changes in Accounting Estimates and Errors* defines **accounting policies** as:

> the specific principles, bases, conventions, rules and practices applied by an entity in preparing and presenting financial statements.

This section considers the requirements relating to the disclosure of accounting policies and disclosure of changes to accounting policies in general purpose financial statements.

18.1.1 Disclosure of accounting policies

Paragraph 117 of AASB 101/IAS 1 requires an entity to disclose its significant accounting policies. Accounting policy disclosures are often quite extensive. The details may be prescribed by other accounting standards or be a matter for management judgement. The notes to the financial statements begin with general information about the basis upon which the financial statements have been prepared.

First, the note usually states that the financial statements are general purpose financial statements. The note also discloses the statutory basis or other reporting framework, if any, under which the financial statements are prepared and whether the entity is a for-profit or not-for-profit entity (AASB 1054 *Australian Additional Disclosures* paragraph 8). This information enables users of the statements to understand the basis on which they have been prepared. Specifically, the note must state whether the statements are prepared in accordance with accounting standards and interpretations.

Second, the note should disclose the measurement basis or bases used in preparing the financial statements. Such information could relate to an overall measurement base or a measurement base applied to specific items within the financial statements.

As the going concern basis and accrual accounting are prescribed by AASB 101/IAS 1 paragraphs 25 and 27, no mention of them is necessary unless there is material uncertainty about the company's ability to continue as a going concern. If such uncertainty exists, paragraph 25 requires disclosure of the nature of the uncertainty. For example, significant doubt may exist about a company's ability to obtain renewal of financing loans and, hence, its ability to continue to operate.

Where the financial statements have not been prepared on a going concern basis, paragraph 25 requires the company to disclose that fact, the reasons for not applying the going concern basis and the basis used. A company in liquidation or expecting to wind up its operations would normally apply the liquidation basis whereby assets and liabilities would be recorded at the amounts expected to be realised on sale or required on settlement.

For entities that are a going concern, the majority of companies will use the historical cost measurement basis for individual items, but other bases such as fair value, current cost, net market value or present value may also be used. Where more than one basis is used, the class of assets or liabilities to which each measurement basis is applied must be disclosed. An example of this disclosure is:

> These financial statements have been prepared on the basis of historical cost, except for certain assets, which, as noted, are at fair value.

Third, the notes should provide a description of accounting policies. This may be provided in summary form in a single note disclosure or provided throughout the notes as they relate to each line item. Paragraph 119 of AASB 101/IAS 1 states that the information provided should allow users to understand how transactions and other events are reflected in the reported financial performance and position, but leaves the detail to management judgement. When deciding how much detail to provide about individual accounting policies, management should consider:

- the likely users of the financial report and their information needs
- the nature of the company's operations

- whether accounting policies are presented by accounting standards or 'voluntarily' adopted by management
- whether policies are selected from alternatives allowed in accounting standards.

In many cases, standard setters have already made this judgement as some accounting standards prescribe the information to be disclosed about accounting policies. Paragraph 36(a) of AASB 102/IAS 2 *Inventories* requires disclosure of the accounting policies adopted in measuring inventories including the cost formula used. Paragraph 73 of AASB 116/IAS 16 *Property, Plant and Equipment* requires entities to disclose for each class of property, plant and equipment the measurement bases used (cost or revaluation) for determining the gross carrying amount.

Fourth, the notes should disclose those judgements, apart from those involving estimations, that management has made in the process of applying the entity's accounting policies that have the most significant effect on the amounts recognised in the financial statements (AASB 101/IAS 1 paragraph 122). Some of these judgements are already required to be disclosed by other accounting standards. For example, paragraph 9(a) of AASB 12/IFRS 12 *Disclosure of Interests in Other Entities* requires an entity to disclose the significant judgements and assumptions made in determining that it does not control another entity even though it holds more than half of the voting rights of the other entity.

Finally, the notes should disclose information about the assumptions made concerning the future, and other major sources of estimation uncertainty at the end of the reporting period that have a significant risk of causing a material adjustment to the carrying amounts of assets and liabilities within the next financial year. In respect of those assets and liabilities, the note should include details of their nature and carrying amount at the end of the reporting period (AASB 101/IAS 1 paragraph 125). The assumptions to be disclosed relate to management's most difficult subjective or complex judgements, such as:
- provisions subject to the future outcome of litigation in progress
- long-term employee benefits such as superannuation obligations
- the recoverable amount of specialised classes of property, plant and equipment.

These disclosures do not apply to assets and liabilities carried at fair value (paragraph 128). Paragraph 129 illustrates the disclosures to be made about these assumptions.

In figure 18.1, Note 1 shows the accompanying accounting policy note to the financial statements of CSR Limited, which provides an example of the disclosure noted above, and Note 12 provides specific disclosures relating to property, plant and equipment.

| FIGURE 18.1 | Example of disclosure of accounting policies, CSR |

Notes to the financial report

1 Basis of preparation
This section sets out the basis upon which the CSR group's financial statements are prepared as a whole. Significant and other accounting policies that summarise the measurement basis used and are relevant to an understanding of the financial statements are provided throughout the notes to the financial statements. All other accounting policies are outlined in note 33.

Statement of compliance: CSR Limited is a limited company incorporated in Australia whose shares are publicly traded on the Australian Securities Exchange.

This general purpose financial report is prepared in accordance with the *Corporations Act 2001* and applicable Accounting Standards and Interpretations, and complies with other requirements of the law. CSR Limited is a 'for profit' entity. The financial report includes the consolidated financial statements of CSR Limited and its controlled entities (CSR group).

Accounting Standards include Australian Accounting Standards. Compliance with Australian Accounting Standards ensures that the financial statements and notes of the company and the CSR group comply with International Financial Reporting Standards.

Basis of preparation: The financial report is based on historical cost, except for certain financial assets and liabilities which are at fair value.

In preparing this financial report, the CSR group is required to make estimates and assumptions about carrying values of assets and liabilities. These estimates and assumptions are based on historical experience and various other factors that are believed to be reasonable under the circumstances. Actual results may differ from these estimates. The estimates and underlying assumptions are reviewed on an ongoing basis.

The accounting policies adopted are consistent with those of the previous year, unless otherwise stated.

Basis of consolidation: The consolidated financial statements have been prepared by aggregating the financial statements of all the entities that comprise the CSR group, being CSR Limited and its controlled entities. In these consolidated financial statements:

- results of each controlled entity are included from the date CSR Limited obtained control and until such time as it ceased to control an entity; and
- all inter-entity balances and transactions are eliminated.

Control is achieved where CSR Limited is exposed to, or has rights to, variable returns from its involvement with an entity and has the ability to affect those returns through its power to direct the activities of the entity. Entities controlled by CSR Limited are under no obligation to accept responsibility for liabilities of other common controlled entities except where such an obligation has been specifically undertaken.

Business combinations: Non-controlling interests in the results and equity of subsidiaries are shown separately in the statement of financial performance, statement of comprehensive income, statement of financial position and statement of changes in equity respectively. The effects of all transactions with non-controlling interests are recorded in equity if there is no change in control. Where there is a loss of control, any remaining interest in the entity is remeasured to fair value and a gain or loss is recognised in the income statement. Any losses are allocated to the non-controlling interest in subsidiaries even if the accumulated losses should exceed the non-controlling interest in the individual subsidiary's equity.

Comparative information: Where applicable, comparative information has been reclassified in order to comply with current period disclosure requirements, the impact of which is not material to the financial report.

Rounding: Unless otherwise shown in the financial statements, amounts have been rounded to the nearest tenth of a million dollars and are shown by $million. CSR Limited is a company of the kind referred to in the Australian Securities and Investments Commission (ASIC) Corporations (Rounding in Financial/Directors' Reports) Instrument 2016/191, dated 24 March 2016.

Currency: Unless otherwise shown in the financial statements, amounts are in Australian dollars, which is the CSR group's functional currency.

New or revised accounting standards: As outlined below, the CSR group has adopted all amendments to Australian Accounting Standards which became applicable for the CSR group from 1 April 2018.

AASB 15 *Revenue from Contracts with Customers* ('AASB 15'): The CSR group has adopted AASB 15 from 1 April 2018 which resulted in changes in accounting policies. The new standard is based on the principle that revenue is recognised when control of a good or service transfers to a customer, that is, the 'notion of control' replaces the existing 'notion of risks and rewards'. Refer to note 5.

AASB 9 *Financial Instruments* ('AASB 9'): The CSR group adopted phase 1 (classification and measurement of financial assets and liabilities) and phase 3 (hedge accounting) of AASB 9 as issued in December 2013, which resulted in changes to accounting policies and retrospective adjustments in the CSR Annual Report for the year ended 31 March 2015. The CSR group has adopted phase 2 (impairment, including expected credit loss) of AASB 9 from 1 April 2018. Phase 2 has not materially impacted the financial report of the CSR group. Refer to note 11.

New standards not yet applicable: Other than AASB 16 *Leases*, standards not yet applicable are not expected to have a material impact on the CSR group. Refer to note 30 for further disclosure on the impact of AASB 16 *Leases*.

Critical accounting judgments and key sources of estimation uncertainty: Critical judgments and key assumptions that management has made in the process of applying the CSR group's accounting policies and that have the most significant effect on the amounts recognised in the financial statements are detailed in the notes below:

Note	Judgment/estimation
12	Asset impairment
14	Measurement of provisions for restoration and environmental rehabilitation and legal claims
14	Provision for uninsured losses and future claims
14, 15	Product liability
24	Classification of joint arrangements

NOTES TO THE FINANCIAL REPORT: The notes are organised into the following sections.

Financial performance overview: provides a breakdown of individual line items in the statement of financial performance, and other information that is considered most relevant to users of the annual report.

▶

Balance sheet items: provides a breakdown of individual line items in the statement of financial position that are considered most relevant to users of the annual report.

Capital structure and risk management: provides information about the capital management practices of the CSR group and shareholder returns for the year. This section also discusses the CSR group's exposure to various financial risks, explains how these affect the CSR group's financial position and performance and what the CSR group does to manage these risks.

Group structure: explains aspects of the CSR group structure and the impact of this structure on the financial position and performance of the CSR group.

Other:
- provides information on items which require disclosure to comply with Australian Accounting Standards and other regulatory pronouncements; and
- provides information about items that are not recognised in the financial statements but could potentially have a significant impact on the CSR group's financial position and performance.

12 Property, plant and equipment and intangible assets
i) Property, plant and equipment

$ million	Note	Land and buildings 2019	2018	Plant and equipment 2019	2018	Total 2019	2018
Cost or written down value		341.0	378.9	1 306.4	1 540.9	1 647.4	1 919.8
Accumulated depreciation and impairment		(88.3)	(108.3)	(849.5)	(978.1)	(937.8)	(1 086.4)
Net carrying amount		**252.7**	**270.6**	**456.9**	**562.8**	**709.6**	**833.4**
Net carrying amount at 1 April		270.6	291.6	562.8	556.6	833.4	848.2
Capital expenditure		23.9	0.8	90.9	78.8	114.8	79.6
Disposed		—	(0.3)	(1.9)	(3.4)	(1.9)	(3.7)
Disposal of discontinued operations	9	(37.4)	—	(91.0)	—	(128.4)	—
Depreciation — continuing operations	6	(8.0)	(9.4)	(49.7)	(52.9)	(57.7)	(62.3)
Depreciation — discontinued operations	6	(1.1)	(1.1)	(9.7)	(13.0)	(10.8)	(14.1)
Impairments — continuing operations		—	(0.1)	(6.2)	(1.6)	(6.2)	(1.7)
Impairments — discontinued operations		(0.3)	—	(26.4)	—	(26.7)	—
Exchange differences		—	—	(0.3)	(0.1)	(0.3)	(0.1)
Acquisitions — business combinations	10	—	—	0.5	0.1	0.5	0.1
Transferred from (to) intangible assets	12ii)	—	0.5	(7.8)	(4.6)	(7.8)	(4.1)
Transferred from (to) inventories & other assets		5.0	(11.4)	(4.3)	2.9	0.7	(8.5)
Balance at 31 March		**252.7**	**270.6**	**456.9**	**562.8**	**709.6**	**833.4**

ii) Goodwill and other intangible assets

$ million	Note	Goodwill 2019	2018	Software 2019	2018	Other 2019	2018	Total other intangible assets 2019	2018
Cost		57.2	98.1	87.8	89.6	46.1	48.3	133.9	137.9
Accumulated amortisation and impairment		—	—	(74.2)	(72.5)	(36.0)	(20.9)	(110.2)	(93.4)
Net carrying amount		**57.2**	**98.1**	**13.6**	**17.1**	**10.1**	**27.4**	**23.7**	**44.5**

$ million	Note	Goodwill 2019	Goodwill 2018	Software 2019	Software 2018	Other 2019	Other 2018	Total other intangible assets 2019	Total other intangible assets 2018
Net carrying amount at 1 April		98.1	97.1	17.1	17.9	27.4	28.8	44.5	46.7
Capital expenditure		–	–	0.3	3.1	–	–	0.3	3.1
Disposed		–	–	(0.1)	(0.1)	–	–	(0.1)	(0.1)
Amortisation — continuing operations	6	–	–	(5.7)	(5.7)	(1.6)	(1.8)	(7.3)	(7.5)
Amortisation — discontinued operations	6	–	–	(0.3)	(0.5)	–	–	(0.3)	(0.5)
Impairments — continuing operations		(9.8)	–	(0.7)	(1.3)	(15.3)	–	(16.0)	(1.3)
Impairments — discontinued operations		(30.7)	–	(4.9)	–	(0.4)	–	(5.3)	–
Exchange differences		(0.4)	0.8	0.1	–	–	–	0.1	–
Acquisitions — business combinations	10	–	0.2	–	–	–	–	–	–
Transferred from plant & equipment	12i)	–	–	7.8	4.1	–	–	7.8	4.1
Transferred from software to other intangible assets		–	–	–	(0.4)	–	0.4	–	–
Balance at 31 March		**57.2**	**98.1**	**13.6**	**17.1**	**10.1**	**27.4**	**23.7**	**44.5**

Recognition and measurement

- **Property, plant and equipment:** assets acquired are recorded at historical cost of acquisition less depreciation. Historical cost includes expenditure that is directly attributable to the acquisition of items. Subsequent costs are included in the asset's carrying amount or recognised as a separate asset, as appropriate, only when it is probable that future economic benefits associated with the item will flow to the group and the cost of the item can be measured reliably. All other repairs and maintenance are charged to profit or loss during the reporting period in which they are incurred. The assets' residual values and useful lives are reviewed, and adjusted if appropriate, at the end of each reporting period. An asset's carrying amount is written down immediately to its recoverable amount if the asset's carrying amount is greater than its estimated recoverable amount.

- **Depreciation/amortisation:** assets are depreciated or amortised at rates based upon their expected economic life using the straight-line method. Land, goodwill and trade names with indefinite lives are not depreciated or amortised. Useful lives are as follows: buildings 10 to 40 years; plant and equipment two to 40 years; and systems software and other intangible assets two to eight years.

- **Software:** developed internally or acquired externally, is initially measured at cost and includes development expenditure. Subsequently, these assets are carried at cost less accumulated amortisation and impairment losses.

- **Other intangible assets:** including trade names and customer lists obtained through acquiring businesses, are measured at fair value at the date of acquisition. Trade names of $1.6 million (2018: $16.9 million) that have an indefinite life are assessed for recoverability annually. Customer lists and all other trade names that have a defined useful life are amortised and subsequently carried net of accumulated amortisation. Intangible assets not obtained through acquiring businesses are measured at cost. These assets are subsequently carried at cost less accumulated amortisation and impairment losses.

- **Goodwill:** represents the excess of the cost of acquisition over the fair value of the identifiable assets and liabilities acquired. Goodwill is not amortised, but tested annually and whenever there is an indicator of impairment.

Critical accounting estimate — carrying value assessment

The CSR group tests property, plant and equipment and intangible assets for impairment to ensure they are not carried at above their recoverable amounts:

- at least annually for goodwill and trade names with indefinite lives; and
- where there is an indication that the assets may be impaired (which is assessed at least each reporting date).

These tests for impairment are performed by assessing the recoverable amount of each individual asset or, if this is not possible, then the recoverable amount of the cash generating unit (CGU) to which the asset belongs. CGUs are the lowest levels at which assets are grouped and generate separately identifiable cash flows. The recoverable amount is the higher of an asset or a CGU's fair value less costs of disposal and value in use. The value in use calculations are based on discounted cash flows expected to arise from the asset. Management judgment is required in these valuations to forecast future cash flows and a suitable discount rate in order to calculate the present value of these future cash flows. Future cash flows take into consideration forecast changes in the building cycle, aluminium prices and exchange rates where appropriate.

If the recoverable amount of a CGU is estimated to be less than its carrying amount, the carrying amount of the CGU is reduced to its recoverable amount with any impairment recognised immediately in the statement of financial performance.

The carrying amount of goodwill and trade names with indefinite lives forms part of the Building Products segment: $57.2 million and $1.6 million retrospectively (31 March 2018: $66.9 million and $16.9 million retrospectively)) and Glass segment: $nil (31 March 2018: $31.2 million of goodwill).

In accordance with AASB 136 *Impairment of Assets*, an impairment assessment has been performed for the Roofing CGU at 31 March 2019.

Roofing cash generating unit

The Roofing CGU has experienced a shortfall in earnings when compared to internal forecasts, with the business experiencing weaker demand. Future cash flows from the Roofing CGU have been reforecast to reflect current trading and market conditions.

Following a detailed value in use impairment review of future cash flow projections, an impairment charge of $32.8 million has been recorded in the statement of financial performance for 31 March 2019. This impairment charge has been allocated to goodwill ($9.8 million), other intangible assets ($16.0 million), plant and equipment ($6.2 million) and equity accounted investments ($0.8 million). Refer to note 25. This impairment charge fully impairs all goodwill and indefinite life intangibles previously recognised for the Roofing CGU.

Given that the impairment assessment is a critical accounting estimate and the estimated recoverable amount of the Roofing CGU is now equal to its carrying amount, key assumptions and sensitivities in relation to the impairment assessment performed for the Roofing CGU at 31 March 2019 is set out below:

Key assumptions for the Roofing CGU:
- Post-tax discount rate: 10.0%
- Terminal growth rate: 2.5%
- Cash flows: cash flows are modelled over a five year period with a terminal value used from year six onwards. The first five years represent financial plans forecast by management based on the CSR group's view of business activity, with average assumptions applied in the terminal year to ensure the cash flows are sufficiently stable to calculate the terminal value.

Impact of reasonable possible changes in key assumptions have been considered:
- Post-tax discount rate increases from 10.0% to 10.5%: result in an additional impairment charge to plant and equipment of $3.5 million.
- Long term growth rate decreases from 2.5% to 2.0%: result in an additional impairment charge to plant and equipment of $3.5 million.
- Business cash contribution reduces by 10% for each year modelled: result in an additional impairment charge to plant and equipment of $6.3 million.

No other reasonable possible changes in key assumptions have been identified.

Glass cash generating unit

In accordance with AASB 136 *Impairment of Assets*, an impairment assessment was performed for the Glass CGU at 30 September 2018. Following a detailed value in use impairment review of future cash flow projections, an impairment charge of $63.3 million was recorded in the statement of financial performance for 30 September 2018. This impairment charge was allocated to goodwill ($30.7 million), other intangible assets ($5.3 million), plant and equipment ($26.7 million) and other assets ($0.6 million). This impairment charge fully impaired all goodwill previously recognised for the Glass CGU. In addition, onerous lease provisions of $10.6 million and other provisions of $0.5 million were recorded at 30 September 2018.

The sale of the Glass CGU was announced on 28 November 2018 and completed on 31 January 2019. The Glass CGU is reported in the current period as a discontinued operation. Refer to note 9.

Source: CSR Limited (2019, pp. 59, 68–69).

When a new accounting standard has been issued but has not yet come into effect, paragraphs 30 and 31 of AASB 108/IAS 8 require the company to disclose:
- the title of the new standard
- the nature of the future change in accounting policy

- the date the company proposes to adopt the standard or the effective date required
- a discussion of the impact the initial application of the standard is expected to have on the entity's financial statements or, if that impact is not known or reasonably estimable, a statement to that effect.

An example of such a disclosure is provided in figure 18.2, which is an extract from Note 30 to the financial statements of CSR Limited.

FIGURE 18.2   Example of disclosure for new accounting standard that has not yet come into effect, CSR

Notes to the financial report

30 Commitments and contingencies

i) Commitments

Impact of new standards not yet applicable: AASB 16 Leases ('AASB 16'):
Released on 23 February 2016 and will primarily affect the accounting treatment of leases by lessees and will result in the recognition of almost all leases on the statement of financial position. The standard removes the current distinction between operating and financing leases and requires recognition of an asset (the right to use the leased item) and a financial liability to pay rentals for almost all lease contracts.

The group has selected and implemented a system solution to capture all leases in scope and perform the accounting entries in compliance with all aspects of AASB 16. The standard will be first applicable for the year commencing 1 April 2019 and the group is currently in the final stages of determining the final impact on the consolidated financial statements.

The estimated impact on the CSR group on the consolidated statement of financial position as at 1 April 2019 and on the consolidated statement of financial performance for the year ending 31 March 2020 is set out below:

$ million	
New lease liabilities	205 to 225
New right-of-use (ROU) assets	155 to 175
Decrease in retained earnings	20 to 30
Increase in earnings before interest and tax (EBIT)	3 to 8
Decrease in net profit after tax	1 to 3

The group plans to adopt AASB 16 *Leases* using the modified retrospective approach. Therefore, the net effect of the new lease liabilities and right-to-use assets, adjusted for deferred tax, will be recognised in retained earnings, with no restatement of comparative information.

To date the most significant impact identified is in respect of the ROU asset and lease liability for property leases. The nature of the expense related to those leases will change because AASB 16 replaces the straight-line lease expense with a depreciation charge for ROU assets and interest expense on lease liabilities.

The group plans to apply practical expedients including: low-value and short-term lease exemptions (i.e. continue to recognise operating lease expense for low-value and short-term leases), portfolio application for forklifts and motor vehicles (i.e. use of a single discount rate to these portfolios), exclusion of initial direct costs and outgoings on all lease portfolios.

Source: CSR Limited (2019, p. 91).

18.1.2 Disclosure of changes in accounting policies

Paragraph 13 of AASB 108/IAS 8 requires that an entity must apply accounting policies consistently for similar transactions, events or conditions unless otherwise required by an accounting standard. Accordingly, paragraph 14 specifies only two circumstances in which an entity is permitted to change an accounting policy. These are:
- if the change is *required* by an accounting standard
- if the change, *made voluntarily*, results in the financial statements providing reliable and more relevant information about the effects of transactions, other events or conditions on the entity's financial position, financial performance or cash flows.

Disclosure requirements for both of these changes in accounting policies are now considered.

Adoption of a new or revised accounting standard

If a change in an accounting policy is made as a result of the adoption of a new or revised accounting standard, paragraph 28 of AASB 108/IAS 8 requires an entity to disclose:

- the title of the standard
- when applicable, that the change is made in accordance with the transitional provisions of the standard, a description of those provisions and provisions that might have an effect on future periods
- the nature of the change in accounting policy
- to the extent practicable, the amount of the adjustment for the current and previous periods to each financial statement line item affected and, if applicable, the basic and diluted earnings per share
- the amount of any adjustment to periods prior to those presented to the extent practicable
- if comparative information has not been restated because it is impracticable to do so, the circumstances that prevented retrospective application and a description of how and from when the change in accounting policy has been applied.

An example of the disclosure required for the adoption of new and revised accounting standards is shown in figure 18.3.

FIGURE 18.3   Example of disclosure for adoption of new and revised accounting standard, CSR

Notes to the financial report

5 Revenue
Recognition and measurement
From 1 April 2018, the CSR group adopted AASB 15 *Revenue from Contracts with Customers* ('AASB 15') and applied the modified retrospective approach. The new standard is based on the principle that revenue is recognised when control of a good or service transfers to a customer, that is, the 'notion of control' replaces the existing 'notion of risks and rewards'. The impact of this change in accounting standard is not material to the CSR group as the 'notion of control' is closely aligned to the 'notion of risks and rewards' for CSR revenue streams.

11 Working capital
Recognition and measurement
Trade receivables: are recognised initially at fair value and are subsequently measured at amortised cost. The CSR group has adopted phase 2 of AASB 9 *Financial Instruments*, which requires an expected credit loss ('ECL') model as opposed to an incurred credit loss model under AASB 139 *Financial Instruments: Recognition and Measurement*. The ECL model requires the CSR group to account for expected credit losses and changes in those expected credit losses at each reporting date to reflect changes in credit risk since initial recognition of the financial assets. AASB 9 also requires a simplified approach for measuring the loss allowance at an amount equal to lifetime ECL for trade receivables, contract assets and lease receivables in certain circumstances. Accordingly, the CSR group's allowance for doubtful debts calculation applies the expected loss model and takes into consideration the likely level of bad debts (based on historical experience) as well as any known 'at risk' receivables. Bad debts are written off against the allowance account and any other change in the allowance account is recognised in the statement of financial performance.

Source: CSR Limited (2019, pp. 63, 67).

In some cases, an accounting standard may allow companies the option to adopt the standard before they are required to do so (or 'early adopt'). For example, when AASB 15/IFRS 15 *Revenue from Contracts with Customers* was issued in December 2014, it was to be applied to annual reporting periods beginning on or after 1 January 2017 (subsequently amended to 1 January 2018); however, early adoption of this standard was permitted by paragraph Aus4.3.

Voluntary changes in accounting policies

For a voluntary accounting policy change, the disclosures required by paragraph 29 of AASB 108/IAS 8 are:

- the nature of the change
- the reasons that applying the new accounting policy provides reliable and more relevant information
- to the extent practicable, the amount of the adjustment for the current and previous periods to each financial statement line item affected and, if applicable, the basic and diluted earnings per share

- the amount of the adjustment relating to periods prior to those presented to the extent practicable
- if retrospective application is impracticable, the circumstances that led to the existence of that condition and a description of how and from when the change in accounting policy was applied. Paragraph 5 of AASB 108/IAS 8 defines **retrospective application** as applying a new accounting policy to transactions, other events and conditions as if that policy had always been applied.

As noted above, entities can claim relief from retrospective application of a voluntary change on the basis that such application was impractical. In its 'Exposure Draft ED/2018/1 *Accounting Policy Changes* (Proposed amendments to IAS 8)', the IASB proposed to extend this relief, or lower the impractical threshold, to entities on the basis that the cost to the entity to provide such information exceeds the expected benefits to users. Importantly, this relief extension would only apply to instances where the entity 'voluntarily changes an accounting policy to reflect explanatory material included in agenda decisions published by the IFRS Interpretations Committee' (IASB 2018, p. 4). The rationale for this proposal is that it is common for entities to voluntarily change an accounting policy due to such agenda decisions. As the background paragraph in the introduction to the Exposure Draft goes on to state, 'An agenda decision is non-authoritative and, therefore, any resulting change is not required by IFRS Standards' (IASB 2018, p. 4).

Figure 18.4 gives an example regarding disclosures needed for a change in an accounting policy.

FIGURE 18.4	Example of disclosure resulting from a change in accounting policy

	26 Changes in accounting policies
AASB108(28)(a)–(d) AASB16(C5)(b),(C7)	As explained in note 25(a) above, the group has adopted the amendments made to AASB 16 *Leases* retrospectively from 1 January 2018, but has not restated comparatives for the 2017 reporting period as permitted under the specific transition provisions in the standard.
AASB16(C8),(C12)(a)	On adoption of AASB 16, the group recognised lease liabilities in relation to leases which had previously been classified as 'operating leases' under the principles of AASB 117 *Leases*. These liabilities were measured at the present value of the remaining lease payments, discounted using the lessee's incremental borrowing rate as of 1 January 2018. The weighted average lessee's incremental borrowing rate applied to the lease liabilities on 1 January 2018 was xx.x%.

AASB16(C12)(b)		2018 $'000
	Operating lease commitments disclosed as at 31 December 2017	x xxx
	Discounted using the group's incremental borrowing rate of xx.x%	x xxx
	Add: finance lease liabilities recognised as at 31 December 2017	x xxx
	(Less): short-term leases recognised on a straight-line basis as expense	(xxx)
	(Less): low-value leases recognised on a straight-line basis as expense	(xxx)
	(Less): contracts reassessed as service agreements	(xxx)
	Add/(less): adjustments as a result of different treatment of extension and termination options	xx
	Add/(less): adjustments relating to changes in the index or rate affecting variable payments	xx
	Lease liability recognised as at 1 January 2018	**x xxx**

AASB16(C8)(b)(ii)	The associated right-of-use assets for property leases were measured on a retrospective basis as if the new rules had always been applied. Other right-of use assets were measured at the amount equal to the lease liability, adjusted by the amount of any prepaid or accrued lease payments relating to that lease recognised in the balance sheet as at 31 December 2017. Property, plant and equipment increased by $x xxx 000 on 1 January 2018, prepayments reduced by $xxx 000 and trade and other payables by $xxx 000. The net impact on retained earnings on 1 January 2018 was $xxx 000.
AASB16(C13),(C10)	In applying AASB 16 for the first time, the group has used the following practical expedients permitted by the standard: • the use of a single discount rate to a portfolio of leases with reasonably similar characteristics • the accounting for operating leases with a remaining lease term of less than 12 months as at 1 January 2018 as short-term leases

- the exclusion of initial direct costs for the measurement of the right-of-use asset at the date of initial application, and
- the use of hindsight in determining the lease term where the contract contains options to extend or terminate the lease.

AASB16(C4)	The group has also elected not to apply AASB 16 to contracts that were not identified as containing a lease under AASB 117 and Interpretation 4 *Determining whether an Arrangement contains a Lease*.

Source: PricewaterhouseCoopers (2018, pp. 321–2).

LEARNING CHECK

☐ Accounting policies are necessary to provide guidance in accounting for specific transactions and events.

☐ Accounting policies are normally prescribed by accounting standards.

☐ Accounting policies used in the preparation of financial statements need to be disclosed in the notes.

☐ Accounting policies may be changed only when required by an accounting standard or if such a change will improve the reliability or relevance of reported information.

☐ Accounting policy changes must be applied retrospectively unless it is impracticable to do so.

18.2 Changes in accounting estimates

LEARNING OBJECTIVE 18.2 Describe how changes in accounting estimates are accounted for and disclosed in general purpose financial statements.

As stated in paragraph 33 of AASB 108/IAS 8:

> The use of reasonable estimates is an essential part of the preparation of financial statements and does not undermine their reliability.

In business, many estimates are made of accounting information because of the uncertainty of future events. For example, a company may estimate its doubtful debts expense for the year based on a percentage of the year's sales; depreciation expense is always based on an estimate of useful life, residual value and pattern of use of future economic benefits; and employee benefits liabilities such as long service leave and superannuation are based on actuarial calculations using estimated discount rates.

Therefore, it is not surprising that companies will revise their accounting estimates as new information becomes available or subsequent developments occur, such as an asset becoming obsolete or a change in the circumstances on which an estimate was based. AASB 108/IAS 8 provides for the recognition and disclosure of changes in accounting estimates and their effects on the financial statements. Paragraph 36 requires the effect of a **change in an accounting estimate** to be recognised *prospectively* by including it in profit or loss in the reporting period of the change and, if applicable, the profit or loss in any future reporting periods affected by the change. Accounting estimates recognised in previous periods must not be revised with retrospective effect to financial statements of previous periods. If a change in an accounting estimate gives rise to changes in assets, liabilities or equity, the change must be recognised by adjusting the carrying amount of the related asset, liability or equity item in the period of the change (paragraph 37). Paragraph 39 requires disclosure of the nature and amount of any change in an accounting estimate that affects the financial performance or financial position of the current reporting period or any future reporting periods (if possible).

The standard does not indicate where the information regarding a change in an accounting estimate is to be disclosed. However, it is likely that the relevant information will be disclosed in the notes. According to paragraph 40 of AASB 108/IAS 8, the information concerning the effect on future periods of a change in an accounting estimate need not be disclosed if estimating it is impracticable, but the entity must disclose that fact. No explanation as to why it is impracticable to estimate the effect of the change is required.

Note that a change in an accounting estimate must be distinguished from a change in accounting policy. In any given situation, if there are difficulties in distinguishing between a change in an accounting estimate and a change in an accounting policy, paragraph 35 of AASB 108/IAS 8 requires the change to be treated as a change in an accounting estimate. Illustrative example 18.1 illustrates the AASB 108/IAS 8 requirements for changes in accounting estimates.

Disclosure of a change in accounting estimates

Brontebuck Ltd acquired a printing press on 1 July 2020 for $240 000. At that date, the useful life of the press was estimated to be 5 years, at the end of which the press would have an estimated residual value of $60 000. Accordingly, the press was depreciated using the straight-line method at $36 000 p.a. ([$240 000 – $60 000] ÷ 5) for the years ended 30 June 2021 and 30 June 2022. On 1 July 2022, because of technological developments in the printing industry, the accountant revised the useful life of the press to 4 years in total and the residual value to $6000. As per the requirements of AASB 108/IAS 8, the new estimates were applied in calculating the depreciation charge for both the 2023 and the 2024 financial years as follows.

$$Carrying\ amount\ at\ 30\ June\ 2022 = \$240\,000 - \$72\,000\ (2\ years \times \$36\,000)$$
$$= \$168\,000$$
$$Depreciation\ charge = \$168\,000 - New\ residual\ value\ (\$6000) \div Revised\ useful\ life\ (2\ more\ years)$$
$$= (\$168\,000 - \$6000) \div 2$$
$$= \$81\,000\ p.a.$$

Required

How would Brontebuck Ltd disclose the change in accounting estimates?

Solution

The following note would be included in the financial statements as at 30 June 2023.

> At the beginning of the financial year, the total useful life to the company of the printing press was revised downwards from 5 to 4 years, and the residual value at the end of that useful life was revised downwards from $60 000 to $6000. For each of the remaining 2 years of the asset's life, including the current financial year, depreciation expense will be increased by $45 000, from the original estimate of $36 000, to $81 000.

LEARNING CHECK

☐ Material changes in accounting estimates must be recognised prospectively by applying the change to the current and future (if applicable) accounting periods.

☐ The nature and amount of a change in accounting estimates must be disclosed for both the current period and for all future periods unless it is impracticable to determine future effects.

☐ If there are difficulties in distinguishing between a change in an accounting policy or a change in an accounting estimate, the change should be treated as a change in an accounting estimate.

18.3 Errors

LEARNING OBJECTIVE 18.3 Explain how prior period errors arise, and how they are accounted for and disclosed in general purpose financial statements.

Paragraphs 41–49 of AASB 108/IAS 8 consider the treatment of errors made by an entity in the preparation of its financial statements. **Prior period errors** are omissions from, and other misstatements in, the entity's financial statements for one or more previous reporting periods that are discovered in the current period. Such errors can occur for a number of reasons, including calculation errors, mistakes in applying accounting policies, oversights or misinterpretation of facts, and fraud (paragraph 5).

According to paragraph 42 of AASB 108/IAS 8, the correction of a material error that occurred in a previous period is to be accounted for by a **retrospective restatement** in the first financial statements issued after the discovery of the error; in other words, previously reported information has to be corrected. This is achieved either by restating the comparative amounts if the error occurred in the previous financial period, or by restating the opening balances of assets, liabilities and equity in the comparative period if the error occurred in a period before the beginning of the period covered by the comparative figures; that is, more than one period before the start of the current financial year. The aim is to present financial statements (restated) as if the error had never occurred by correcting the error in the comparative information for the previous period(s) in which it occurred. However, comparative information need not be restated if this is impracticable (paragraph 43) (see section 7.4).

The standard seems to imply that errors relate only to previous periods. For example, paragraph 46 of AASB 108/IAS 8 notes:

> The correction of a prior period error is excluded from profit or loss for the period in which the error is discovered.

However, an error may be detected in the current period that has an effect both on the current period and on a previous period. For example, a depreciable asset may not have been depreciated, and when this error is discovered adjustments will be necessary to both the current period's depreciation expense and previous period's depreciation expense.

When an error is discovered, according to AASB 108/IAS 8 paragraph 49 the company must disclose:
- the nature of the error
- for each previous period presented, to the extent practicable, the amount of the correction for (a) each financial statement line affected, and (b) if applicable, basic and diluted earnings per share
- the amount of the correction relating to periods before those presented in comparative information
- if retrospective restatement is impracticable for a particular prior period, the circumstances that caused that condition and a description of how and from when the error has been corrected.

Illustrative example 18.2 is based on data provided in the Implementation Guidance on AASB 108/IAS 8 and illustrates the disclosure requirements for the treatment of errors.

ILLUSTRATIVE EXAMPLE 18.2

Disclosure requirements for the treatment of errors

During 2021, Roedeer Ltd discovered that inventories to the value of $6500 that had been recognised as sold during 2020 were incorrectly included in inventories as at 31 December 2020. The income tax rate was 30% for 2021 and 2020.

The following financial information was provided *before* the error was adjusted in accordance with the requirements of AASB 108/IAS 8.

ROEDEER LTD		
Statement of profit or loss and other comprehensive income		
for the year ended 31 December 2021		
	2021	2020
Revenue	$104 000	$ 73 500
Cost of sales	(80 000)	(53 500)
Correction of error	(6 500)	—
Profit before income tax	17 500	20 000
Income tax expense	(5 250)	(6 000)
Profit after income tax	12 250	14 000
Retained earnings (beginning)	34 000	20 000
Retained earnings (end)	46 250	34 000

Required

How should the correction of the inventories error be disclosed in the statement of profit or loss and other comprehensive income?

Solution

The correction of the $6500 inventories error should be disclosed in the statement of profit or loss and other comprehensive income as follows.

	2021	Restated 2020
Revenue	$104 000	$ 73 500
Cost of sales	(80 000)	(60 000)
Profit before income tax	24 000	13 500
Income tax expense	(7 200)	(4 050)
Profit after income tax	16 800	9 450

Note X. Error in inventories

Inventories worth $6500 had been recognised as sold in 2020, but was incorrectly included in inventories at 31 December 2020. This error was corrected during 2021. Restated financial information for 2020 is presented above as if the error had not been made. The effect of the restatement on the financial statements for 2020 is as follows.

	Effect on 2020
Increase in cost of sales	$6 500
Decrease in income tax expense	1 950
Decrease in profit for the year	4 550
Decrease in inventories	6 500
Decrease in income tax payable	1 950
Decrease in equity	4 550

Restatement of 2020 financial information in the statement of financial position and the statement of changes in equity would also be required but is not illustrated here.

Figure 18.5 gives an example of the disclosure required following the discovery of accounting errors.

FIGURE 18.5 Example of disclosure of accounting errors

(b) Correction of error in accounting for leasing contract

AASB108 (49)(a)	In September 2018, a subsidiary undertook a detailed review of its leasing contracts and discovered that the terms and conditions of a contract for the lease of equipment had been misinterpreted. As a consequence, the equipment had been incorrectly accounted for as a finance lease rather than as an operating lease.
AASB108 (49)(b)(i), (c) AASB112 (81)(a)	The error has been corrected by restating each of the affected financial statement line items for the prior periods as follows.

Balance sheet (extract)	31 December 2017 $'000	Increase/ (decrease) $'000	31 December 2017 (Restated) $'000	31 December 2016 $'000	Increase/ (decrease) $'000	1 January 2016 (Restated) $'000
Property, plant and equipment	106 380	(1 300)	105 080	94 695	(1 550)	93 145
Deferred tax asset	5 040	(108)	4 932	3 735	(93)	3 642
Non-current borrowings	(80 619)	1 289	(79 330)	(77 741)	1 491	(76 250)
Current borrowings	(8 988)	238	(8 750)	(8 104)	235	(7 869)
Net assets	116 935	119	117 054	95 643	83	95 726
Retained earnings	(36 254)	(119)	(36 373)	(21 024)	(83)	(21 107)
Total equity	(116 935)	(119)	(117 054)	(95 643)	(83)	(95 726)

Statement of profit or loss (extract)	2017 $'000	Profit increase/ (decrease) $'000	2017 (Restated) $'000
Cost of sales of goods	(65 216)	(25)	(65 241)
Finance costs	(6 348)	76	(6 272)
Profit before income tax	**40 388**	**51**	**40 439**
Income tax expense	(11 806)	(15)	(11 821)
Profit from discontinued operation	399	—	399
Profit for the period	**28 981**	**36**	**29 017**
Profit is attributable to:			
Owners of VALUE ACCOUNTS Holdings Limited	26 662	36	26 698
Non-controlling interests	2 319	—	2 319
	28 981	**36**	**29 017**
Statement of comprehensive income (extract)			
Profit for the period	28 981	36	29 017
Other comprehensive income for the period	3 554	—	3 554
Total comprehensive income for the period	**32 535**	**36**	**32 571**
Total comprehensive income is attributable to:			
Owners of VALUE ACCOUNTS Holdings Limited	29 959	36	29 995
Non-controlling interests	2 576	—	2 576
	32 535	**36**	**32 571**

AASB108
(49)(b)(ii)

Basic and diluted per share for the prior year have also been restated. The amount of the correction for both basic and diluted earnings per share was an increase of $0.1 cents per share.
    The correction further affected some of the amounts disclosed in note 5(b) and note 18. Depreciation expense for the prior year was reduced by $250 000 and rental expense relating to operating leases increased by $275 000.

New illustration

The amounts disclosed above for the 2017 reporting period, and for the balance sheets as at 1 January and 31 December 2017 are before restatements for the change in accounting policy disclosed in note 26.

Source: PricewaterhouseCoopers (2018, pp. 155–6).

LEARNING CHECK

☐ Errors may occur in financial statements because of mathematical mistakes, mistakes in applying accounting policies, oversights or misinterpretations of facts, and fraud.

☐ Material prior period errors must be corrected retrospectively in the first financial statements issued after their discovery.

☐ Comprehensive disclosures of the error(s) and its effect on the results and balances of previous year must be made in the notes to the financial statements.

18.4 Impracticability in respect of retrospective adjustments for accounting policy changes or correction of errors

LEARNING OBJECTIVE 18.4 Explain the requirements when it is impracticable to make retrospective adjustments for changes in accounting policies or correction of errors.

As noted previously, AASB 108/IAS 8 requires retrospective application of a change in accounting policy and retrospective restatement for material prior period errors except where such application is impracticable (paragraphs 23–25 and 43–45).

The terms 'retrospective application' and 'retrospective restatement' are defined in paragraph 5 of AASB 108/IAS 8:

Retrospective application is applying a new accounting policy to transactions, other events and conditions as if that policy had always been applied.

Retrospective restatement is correcting the recognition, measurement and disclosure of amounts of elements of financial statements as if a prior period error had never occurred.

Impracticable refers to the inability of a company to apply a requirement of AASB 108/IAS 8 after making every reasonable effort to do so (paragraph 5). For example, in some circumstances the data may not have been collected in prior periods to adjust comparative information in a way that allows retrospective application of a new accounting policy (paragraph 50).

To avoid misapplication of the impracticability clause, paragraph 5 of AASB 108/IAS 8 states that it is impracticable to make a retrospective adjustment or restatement if:

    (a) the effects of the retrospective application or retrospective restatement are not determinable;

    (b) the retrospective application or retrospective restatement requires assumptions about what management's intent would have been in that period; or

    (c) the retrospective application or retrospective restatement requires significant estimates of amounts and it is impossible to distinguish objectively information about those estimates that:

        (i) provides evidence of circumstances that existed on the date(s) as at which those amounts are to be recognised, measured or disclosed; and

        (ii) would have been available when the financial statements for that prior period were authorised for issue from other information.

Thus, by this definition, the standard setters have effectively limited the application of the clause to a set number of circumstances. Managers cannot simply claim impracticability to avoid the cost and effort of making retrospective adjustments. If retrospective adjustments are not practicable, the changes are made prospectively; that is, to current and future periods only.

The IASB's ED/2018/1 proposes to provide application guidance in an Appendix to IAS 8. If implemented, paragraphs A2 to A5 of Appendix A will incorporate paragraphs 50 to 53 of the current standard. Paragraphs A6 to A10 will provide guidance in relation to the cost–benefit determination relating to instances where voluntary changes arise from an agenda decision. It should be apparent that this will require significant judgement by preparers of financial statements. The key points to note from these potential guidance paragraphs are as follows.

- The entity must make this assessment by considering all relevant facts and circumstances.
- Assessing the expected benefits to users is an entity-specific consideration. The entity should consider how the absence of the information that would be provided by retrospective application could affect the decisions of users. The entity should consider:
  - the nature and magnitude of the change, noting that the more significant the nature and magnitude of the change is, the more likely the user's decisions could be affected, and the more likely users would benefit from the information
  - the pervasiveness of the change across the financial statements, noting that the more pervasive the change, the greater the likelihood it could affect the user's decisions
  - the degree of significance the change would have on trend information
  - the extent of the departure from retrospective application.
- The entity should consider the additional costs and effort the entity could reasonably expect to incur from the retrospective application. This assessment will require the entity to consider, amongst other things, whether the information required is reasonably available without undue cost and effort.

LEARNING CHECK

☐ If it is impracticable to retrospectively restate the figures for the previous years due to changes in an accounting policy or correction of an error, then they must be restated prospectively.

18.5 Materiality

LEARNING OBJECTIVE 18.5 Describe the concept of materiality and how material items are identified.

As discussed in chapter 1, the *Conceptual Framework* identifies relevance as a fundamental qualitative characteristic of useful financial information. **Materiality** is a key aspect of relevance. Paragraph 2.11 states:

> Information is material if omitting, misstating or obscuring it could reasonably be expected to influence decisions that the primary users of general purpose financial reports make on the basis of those reports, which provide financial information about a specific reporting entity. In other words, materiality is an entity-specific aspect of relevance based on the nature or magnitude, or both, of the items to which the information relates in the context of the individual entity's financial report. Consequently, the Board cannot specify a uniform quantitative threshold for materiality or predetermine what could be material in a particular situation.

Materiality is, therefore, based on qualitative as well as quantitative factors. Materiality is also entity-specific — what is material to one entity may not be material to another. In keeping with the broad notion that IFRS standards are principles-based rather than rules-based, the IASB did not see it appropriate to specify quantitative thresholds. These two points place the onus on preparers of financial statements to exercise professional judgement in determining how the concept of materiality should be applied.

Paragraph 5 of AASB 108 (which is identical to paragraph 7 of AASB 101) provides the following:

> Omissions or misstatements of items are material if they could, individually or collectively, influence the economic decisions that users make on the basis of the financial statements. Materiality depends on the size and nature of the omission or misstatement judged in the surrounding circumstances. The size or nature of the item, or a combination of both, could be the determining factor.

Consideration of the materiality of an item or a group of items is required in relation to erroneous or omitted items, particularly when preparing financial statements. An error involves misstatement of either an amount or a fact, or misapplication of an accounting standard. A sales invoice posted as $500 000 instead of $50 000, an expense classified as an asset, or inventories carried at a cost that is greater than net realisable value are all examples of errors. Only material errors need to be adjusted. Items of amount or information that have not been included in the financial statements are omissions. An invoice which has not been posted or impairment losses recognised which have not been disclosed are examples of omissions.

The assessment of materiality is a matter of judgement in light of the particular circumstances of the reporting entity. An understatement of $50 000 may be material to one entity but immaterial to another. To assess whether items are material, their size and nature are normally considered together, although it is possible for items to be deemed material purely on the basis of either their size or their nature.

LEARNING CHECK

- ☐ The notion of materiality assists accountants in making judgements about the level of acceptable error, the degree of precision required and the extent of disclosure required in financial statements.
- ☐ In determining whether an item is material, consideration must be given to both its size and nature.
- ☐ The assessment of materiality is a matter of judgement.

18.6 Events occurring after the end of the reporting period

LEARNING OBJECTIVE 18.6 Explain the difference between types of events occurring after the end of the reporting period and how they are to be treated in the financial statements.

Financial statements are prepared to present the financial position of a company or an entity at a certain date and to record the results of its operations for the financial year ended on that date. The financial statements are to be prepared on the basis of conditions which exist at the end of the reporting period, but there can be events after that date which identify or clarify such conditions. In order to provide full disclosure and a guide to the handling of economic events arising after the end of the reporting period, AASB 110/IAS 10 *Events after the Reporting Period* was issued.

Paragraph 3 of AASB 110/IAS 10 defines **events after the reporting period** as follows.

Events after the reporting period are those events, favourable and unfavourable, that occur between the end of the reporting period and the date when the financial statements are authorised for issue.

The financial statements are authorised for issue on the day the directors' declaration is signed. Paragraph 17 of AASB 110/IAS 10 requires the company to disclose the date of authorisation and who gave that authorisation. Because this information is included on the directors' declaration attached to the financial statements, no specific disclosure note is required.

Events that occur between the end of the reporting period and the date the accounts are authorised may provide information relating to circumstances that arose on or prior to the reporting date while others may provide information relating to circumstances that have arisen since the reporting date. Accordingly, AASB 110/IAS 10 differentiates events that occur within this time into two types.

The first type of event is described by paragraph 3 of AASB 110/IAS 10 as events occurring between the end of the reporting period and the date the financial statements are authorised for issue and that provide evidence of conditions that existed at the end of the reporting period. The standard refers to these as **adjusting events after the end of the reporting period**. For convenience, they are hereafter referred to as adjusting events. Examples of adjusting events include the settlement after the end of the reporting period of a court case and for which no liability or an estimated liability had been brought to account, or the bankruptcy of a customer after the end of the reporting period (as this usually confirms that a loss already existed at the end of the reporting period). Paragraph 8 of AASB 110/IAS 10 requires the financial effect of adjusting events to be reflected in the financial statements prepared at the end of the reporting period. Thus, an adjustment must be made to the financial statements before publication. Adjustments may be required to recognise an amount, adjust an existing balance, reclassify an item or change a disclosure note.

The second type of event — **non-adjusting events after the end of the reporting period** — is described by paragraph 3 of AASB 110/IAS 10 as events that are indicative of conditions that arose after the end of the reporting period. Examples of non-adjusting events include a flood or fire after the end of the reporting period that destroys a company's buildings and plant, or a major business combination occurring after the end of the reporting period. Characteristically, these events are material in relation to the future operations or results of a company.

Further examples of both types of events can be found in paragraph 9 (adjusting events) and paragraph 22 (non-adjusting events) of AASB 110/IAS 10.

Non-adjusting events must be disclosed by way of note to the financial statements. Paragraph 21 of AASB 110/IAS 10 requires the note to include a description of the nature of each event and an estimate, if possible, of the financial effect of each event. If the financial effect of the event cannot be reliably estimated, the note should disclose this fact.

Paragraph 21 of AASB 110/IAS 10 requires the disclosure of non-adjusting events only if the effect of such events is material. For adjusting events, no specific reference is made to materiality but, generally, adjustments would not be made for immaterial events.

If an event after the reporting date leads management to determine that the entity will liquidate or cease trading, intentionally or otherwise, paragraph 14 of AASB 110/IAS 10 prohibits the entity from preparing its accounts on a going concern basis. Accordingly, the financial statements would need to be redrafted using liquidation values for the entity's net assets as these values would be deemed more relevant to the circumstances of the entity and the needs of the user.

ILLUSTRATIVE EXAMPLE 18.3

Events occurring after the end of the reporting period

The end of the reporting period of Llama Ltd is 30 June 2023. The following events have taken place since the end of the reporting period.

1. On 15 July 2023, the company settled and paid a personal injury claim from a former employee arising out of an accident that occurred in November 2022. Damages amounted to $65 000.
2. On 31 August 2023, a building owned by the company was severely damaged by storm resulting in uninsured damages of $150 000.
3. On 17 September 2023, the company issued 200 000 fully paid shares to acquire the net assets of JMC Pty Ltd. All events are deemed to be material by reason of both nature and/or amount.

Required

Assuming the accounts are authorised after 17 September, how must the events be classified, reported and disclosed?

Solution

The settlement of the personal injury claim provides new evidence in relation to a condition — the injury claim (reporting a present obligation) — which existed at the end of the reporting period and is therefore an adjusting event and requires a journal entry as follows.

2023				
June 30	Compensation expenses	Dr	65 000	
	Claims payable	Cr		65 000
	(Damages payable under injury claim to former employee)			

The flood damage and the share issue relate to conditions that arose after the end of the reporting period and therefore are non-adjusting events requiring note disclosure only as follows.

Note X. Non-adjusting events occurring after the end of the reporting period

On 31 August 2023, a storm severely damaged a building owned by the company. Uninsured damages amounted to $150 000.

On 17 September 2023, the company issued 200 000 fully paid shares at an issue price of $1.50 each to acquire the net assets of JMC Pty Ltd.

Note: If the accounts were authorised on 15 September, no disclosure regarding the share issue would be required.

LEARNING CHECK

☐ Material events occurring after the end of the reporting period, providing additional information about conditions existing at the end of the reporting period, require adjusting journal entries to be prepared.

☐ Material events providing information about conditions occurring after the end of the reporting period may require disclosure if they are likely to affect users' economic decisions.

SUMMARY

Three key aspects of preparing general purpose financial statements are the:
- setting of appropriate accounting policies
- determination of material information
- appropriate treatment of events after the end of the reporting period.

All important accounting policies must be disclosed by companies in a note to the financial statements (usually note 1 or 2). Changes to accounting policies can be made in limited circumstances only and extensive disclosures must be made of the reasons for such changes and the impact of the changes on past, present and future financial statements.

Material changes in accounting estimates, such as depreciation and doubtful debts, must be recognised prospectively by applying the change to current year profit or loss and carrying amounts. The nature and amount of the change and any effects on a future period's results must be disclosed in the notes to the statements.

Errors in financial statements may arise from mistakes, oversight or fraud. Material errors in a prior period's figures must be retrospectively adjusted as soon as they are found by restating the comparative figures and disclosing the full impact of the error(s) on prior year results and carrying amount in the notes to the current year's financial statements.

While retrospective adjustments are required for changes in accounting policies and correction of errors, this is not required where it is impracticable, in which case the changes are made prospectively.

Information is material if its omission, misstatement or non-disclosure has the potential, individually or collectively, to influence the economic decisions of users made on the basis of the financial statements. Materiality is a concept essential to the preparation and presentation of general purpose financial statements, because the notion of materiality guides the margin of error acceptable, the degree of precision required and the extent of disclosure required.

Events after the end of the reporting period are those events, favourable and unfavourable, that occur between the end of the reporting period and the date when the financial statements are authorised for issue. There are two types of events:
- adjusting, which change the financial statements
- non-adjusting, which require disclosure in the notes.

KEY TERMS

accounting policies The specific principles, bases, conventions, rules and practices applied by an entity in preparing and presenting financial statements.

adjusting events after the end of the reporting period Events that occur between the end of the reporting period and the date that the financial statements are authorised for issue and that provide evidence of conditions that existed at the end of the reporting period.

change in an accounting estimate An adjustment of the carrying amount of an asset or a liability, or the amount of the periodic consumption of an asset, that results from the assessment of the present status of, and expected future benefits and obligations associated with, assets and liabilities. Changes in accounting estimates result from new information or a new development and, accordingly, are not corrections of errors.

events after the reporting period Events, which could be favourable or unfavourable, that occur between the end of the reporting period and the date that the financial statements are authorised for issue.

impracticable Applying a requirement to retrospectively restate comparative figures or retrospectively apply an accounting policy is impracticable when the entity cannot apply it after making every reasonable effort to do so.

materiality The notion of materiality guides the margin of error acceptable, the degree of precision required and the extent of the disclosure required when preparing general purpose financial statements.

non-adjusting events after the end of the reporting period Events that occur between the end of the reporting period and the date when the financial statements are authorised for issue and that are indicative of conditions that arose after the reporting period.

prior period errors Omissions from, and other misstatements in, the entity's financial statements for one or more previous reporting periods that are discovered in the current period.

retrospective application Applying a new accounting policy to transactions, other events and conditions as if that policy had always been applied.

retrospective restatement A correction of the recognition, measurement and disclosure of amounts of elements of financial statements as if a prior period error had never occurred.

DEMONSTRATION PROBLEMS

18.1 Accounting policies

At 30 June 2021, the statement of financial position of Yak Ltd contained an intangible asset worth $800 000 relating to the brand name 'Shangri La Shirts', which has been successfully developed by the business over the past decade. The asset was recognised on 30 June 2020 at a 'directors' valuation'.

In order to demonstrate the result of a change in accounting policy, imagine that Australia first adopted international accounting standards on 1 January 2022. AASB 138/IAS 38 *Intangible Assets* specifically prohibits the recognition of internally generated brands on the grounds that expenditure on such items cannot be distinguished from the cost of developing the business as a whole. Accordingly, Yak Ltd must change its accounting policy in relation to brands as from 1 January 2022.

Required

Prepare any journal entries and financial statement note disclosures that Yak Ltd must make for the year ended 30 June 2022 as a result of the change in policy (ignore any tax effects).

SOLUTION

Paragraph 19(a) of AASB 108 states that if the change in accounting policy arises on initial application of an Australian accounting standard, the change is to be accounted for in accordance with the specific transitional provisions. The transitional provisions in IAS 38 were deleted by the AASB for AASB 138; hence, there are no such provisions in AASB 138. AASB 108 paragraph 19(b) states that if no transitional provisions apply then the change in policy is to be applied retrospectively.

AASB 108 paragraph 22 states that retrospective application requires the company to adjust the opening balance of each affected component of equity for the earliest prior period presented and the other comparative amounts disclosed for each prior period presented as if the new accounting policy had always been applied.

Under the new accounting policy, no asset can be recognised for the brand name, hence the existing asset must be derecognised. The original journal entry to recognise the asset would have been as follows.

2020				
June 30	Brand name	Dr	800 000	
	Revenue on recognition	Cr		800 000
	(Recognition of brand name at directors' valuation)			

This revenue account would have been closed off to retained earnings via the profit or loss summary on 30 June 2020. Thus, a retrospective adjustment must be made to the opening balance of retained earnings in the current year to remove this prior period revenue. The derecognition journal entry is as follows.

2022				
June 30	Retained earnings (opening)	Dr	800 000	
	Brand name	Cr		800 000
	(Derecognition of brand name on change of accounting policy)			

Disclosures relating to this change of accounting policy are determined by paragraph 28 of AASB 108. An appropriate note would be as follows.

Summary of significant accounting policies

Change in accounting policy

An adjustment of $800 000 has been made to the opening balance of retained earnings for the year ended 30 June 2022, representing the effect of a change in accounting policy for the recognition of brand name costs upon the initial adoption of AASB 138 *Intangible Assets*. AASB 138 prohibits the recognition of brands as the costs of developing such assets cannot be distinguished from the costs of developing the business as a whole. Accordingly, the brand name asset has been derecognised. Comparative information for intangible assets and retained earnings has been restated to reflect the change in accounting policy.

18.2 Events occurring after the end of the reporting period

The following events of Roedeer Ltd occurred after the end of the reporting period of 30 June 2022.

(a) On 1 July 2022, tenders were called for the provision of courier services to the company. A 2-year contract worth $150 000 was awarded to Gazelle Pty Ltd on 23 July 2022.

(b) On 7 July 2022, the directors resolved to sell a block of land in Bunbury owned by the company. The land was purchased for $25 000 a number of years ago with the intention of constructing a branch office in that city. This plan has now been abandoned so the land is to be sold for an expected net return of $2.6 million.

(c) On 16 July 2022, 150 000 ordinary shares worth $2.50 each were issued by the company following a successful public share offer.

(d) On 17 July 2022, creditors invoices worth $57 000 for the provision of administrative services up to 30 June 2022 were received.

All the events are material and all occurred prior to the date the financial statements were authorised for issue.

Required

Classify the events occurring after the end of the reporting period as adjusting or non-adjusting. Account for the events in accordance with AASB 110/IAS 10.

SOLUTION

(a) The tender relates to the provision of courier services in the future, so this is a material non-adjusting event. A note disclosure required by paragraph 21 of AASB 110/IAS 10 would be as follows.

Note X. Events occurring after the end of the reporting period
On 23 July 2022, a contract was awarded to Gazelle Pty Ltd for the provision of courier services worth $150 000 to the company over the next 2 years.

(b) The sale of the block of land provides new information with respect to the company's asset (land) and is a material adjusting event. Since the directors intend to sell the land immediately after the end of the reporting period, it should be reclassified from the asset category 'Property, plant and equipment' to the category 'Non-current assets held for sale' as per paragraph 6 of AASB 5/IFRS 5 *Non-current Assets Held for Sale and Discontinued Operations*. No change in value is necessary as the land's cost is the lower of carrying amount and fair value less costs of disposal, as required by paragraph 15.

(c) The issue of shares relates to conditions existing after the end of the reporting period, so this is a material non-adjusting event. A note disclosure required by paragraph 21 of AASB 110/IAS 10 would be as follows.

Note X. Events occurring after the end of the reporting period
On 16 July 2022, 150 000 ordinary shares of $2.50 each were issued by the company after a public share offer.

(d) The receipt of creditors' invoices provides additional information about liabilities outstanding at the end of the reporting period and expense incurred for the financial year being reported, so this is a material adjusting event. The adjusting journal entry would be as follows.

2022			
June 30	Administrative services expense	Dr	57 000	
	Accounts payable	Cr		57 000
	(Recognition of outstanding invoices)			

COMPREHENSION QUESTIONS

1 What disclosures are required by AASB 101/IAS 1 regarding accounting policies?
2 Why would an accounting estimate change and how is the change accounted for?
3 What is a prior period error? How and when is it corrected?
4 What is the difference between 'retrospective application' and 'retrospective restatement'?
5 When is it impracticable to make a retrospective change in an accounting policy or a retrospective restatement to correct an error?
6 Outline the concept of materiality as it applies to financial reporting.
7 Explain the difference between adjusting and non-adjusting events occurring after the end of the reporting period. Describe the difference in the way such events impact on the preparation of financial statements.

CASE STUDY 18.1

ACCOUNTING ESTIMATES

The board of directors of Good Company Ltd has resolved to change the company's accounting policy for capitalising gains or losses on its cash flow hedges recognised in other comprehensive income. To date, such gains or losses were capitalised to hedged items, but the directors now believe that taking such gains or losses to profit or loss is a more appropriate treatment. Due to a recent computer virus, all data from the non-current asset register, including specific depreciation details from prior periods, has been destroyed.

Required

The board of directors has approached you for advice regarding the disclosures, if any, that are required for this change in accounting policy.

CASE STUDY 18.2

ACCOUNTING POLICIES

Refer to case study 18.1. Assume the change in the accounting policy for capitalising hedge gains or losses was due to the issue of a revised accounting standard, AASB 9/IAS 9 *Financial Instruments,* which requires all hedge gains or losses to be taken to profit or loss, thereby removing the choice to capitalise.

Required

Advise the company of the disclosures, if any, that are required by this change in accounting policy.

CASE STUDY 18.3

MATERIALITY

Antelope Ltd is a catering company specialising in providing catering services to remote area mine sites. The company has operations in Australia but during the current year it acquired significant long-term contracts in Pakistan and Nigeria. AASB 8/IFRS 8 *Operating Segments* requires entities to disclose material segment information but Antelope Ltd has failed to comply with this requirement.

Required

Discuss whether the non-disclosure by Antelope Ltd of information about operations in Pakistan and Nigeria would be material.

CASE STUDY 18.4

EVENT OCCURRING AFTER THE END OF THE REPORTING PERIOD

The statement of financial position of Waterbuck Ltd as at 30 June 2023 includes an asset 'Debenture money receivable $500 000' and a liability 'Debentures $500 000'. Note 12 to the accounts reveals that the issue of the debentures to a private investor was approved by the board of directors on 28 June 2023 but the debenture issue did not take place until 17 July 2023.

Required

Comment on the accounting treatment of Waterbuck Ltd's debenture issue in accordance with the requirements of AASB 110/IAS 10.

CASE STUDY 18.5

COMPLIANCE WITH ACCOUNTING POLICY DISCLOSURE REQUIREMENTS

Accounting policy disclosures contained in Notes 1 and 12 from CSR Limited's 2019 annual report were provided in figure 18.1.

Required

Provide a brief description of CSR's accounting policies with respect to:
1. compliance
2. currency
3. depreciation
4. rounding.

APPLICATION AND ANALYSIS EXERCISES

★ BASIC | ★ ★ MODERATE | ★ ★ ★ DIFFICULT

18.1 Annual reporting requirements, true and fair view ★   LO1, 5

The directors of an Australian company, Mulga Ltd, have formed the view that compliance with a particular AASB standard will mean the company's financial statements will not provide a true and fair view, which is contrary to the Corporations Act.

Required

Advise the directors how this problem can be resolved when preparing the company's financial statements in accordance with AASB 101/IAS 1.

18.2 Accounting policies ★   LO1

Lin Ltd has provided the following information to help with the preparation of the accounting policy note to the financial statements for the year ended 30 June 2024.

- Lin Ltd values its inventories at the lower of cost and net realisable value. Costs are assigned to inventories as follows.
  (a) Raw materials — purchase cost on a first-in-first-out basis
  (b) Work in progress — cost of direct material and labour and a proportion of manufacturing overheads based on normal operating capacity
  (c) Finished goods — same as work in progress
- Items of plant and equipment are measured using the cost basis.
- Land and buildings are measured using the fair value basis. Independent valuations of land and buildings are obtained every year unless circumstances indicate that an earlier valuation is required. The valuations are based on the amount that could be exchanged between a knowledgeable willing buyer and a knowledgeable willing seller in an arm's-length transaction on the valuation date. Where the carrying amount of land and buildings is materially different from its fair value, valuation adjustments are made. Valuation increases are credited to an asset revaluation surplus unless they are reversed against a previous valuation decrease. Valuation decreases are expensed unless they are reversed against a previous valuation increase.
- Buildings, plant and equipment are depreciated on a straight-line basis so as to write off the cost or other value of each asset less estimated residual value at the end of the life of the asset over its expected useful life. Depreciation of assets starts when they are installed and ready for use. Depreciation rates used by the company are as follows.

Buildings		5%
Plant and equipment		15–25%

- Receivables are carried at nominal amounts less any allowance for doubtful debts. An estimate of doubtful debts is recognised when collection of the full nominal amount is no longer probable. Bad debts are written off as incurred. Credit sales are on 30-day terms.
- In determining cash flows for the year, the company includes in the cash balance all cash on hand and in banks net of any outstanding bank overdrafts. Long term cash deposits are not part of the daily cash management function and are regarded as investments.
- The company recognises liabilities for the following employee entitlements accrued as at the end of the reporting period: wages and salaries, annual leave and long service leave. Such liabilities are measured as required by AASB 119/IAS 19 *Employee Benefits*.

Required

Prepare the accounting policy note for inclusion in the financial statements of Lin Ltd as at 30 June 2024. This task may require you to research the accounting policy disclosure requirements of applicable accounting standards.

18.3 Accounting estimates and errors ★   **LO2, 3**

Yung Ltd estimates its future liability for repairs to products sold with a 12-month warranty as a percentage of its net credit sales. Warranty expense and actual repair costs for the last 2 years ending 30 June were as follows.

	Warranty provisions	Actual costs
2021–22	$10 000	$16 000
2022–23	11 000	18 250

Required

Comment on Yung Ltd's accounting method for warranty liabilities. What action should be taken with respect to the accounting estimates? If an investigation during 2023–24 finds that the figure for warranty expense was incorrectly calculated for 2022–23 and should have been $17 500, what action is required under AASB 108/IAS 8?

18.4 Events after the reporting period ★   **LO6**

Magpie Ltd operates a fleet of fishing trawlers. The following events took place after the end of the reporting period, 30 June 2022, but before the date the accounts were authorised, 15 September 2022.

(a) On 17 July 2022, Magpie Ltd's main fishing fleet was sunk during a freak storm. Insurance will cover the replacement of the vessels but lost sales representing $275 000 in profits are not covered.

(b) On 19 July 2022 Magpie Ltd took delivery of a fishing net for its prawn trawler. The net was purchased from a UK manufacturer on delivered duty paid shipping terms and was in transit at the end of the reporting period. An inspection of the net revealed significant structural flaws and the net was returned to the supplier on 28 July 2022. Magpie Ltd is to receive a full refund of the $325 000 purchase price which had been paid in advance on 29 June 2022.

(c) On 29 August 2022 a lawsuit was lodged against the company by the families of crew members drowned in the 17 July storm, alleging negligence, and claiming $2 million in damages. No date has as yet been set for the court hearing.

(d) On 1 September 2022 the directors resolved to issue to the public 8 000, 5% debentures of $10 each, payable $5 on application and $5 on allotment.

Required

Classify each event as an adjusting or non-adjusting event after the end of the reporting period. Explain your decisions.

18.5 Accounting policies and accounting estimates ★   **LO1**

The following relate to Dog Ltd.

(a) The useful life of depreciable plant is determined as being 5 years.

(b) Dog Ltd depreciates non-current assets.

(c) Dog Ltd uses straight-line depreciation.

(d) Dog Ltd determines that it will calculate its warranty provision using past experience of products returned for repair under warranty.

(e) The current year's warranty provision is calculated by providing for 1% of current year sales, based on last year's warranty claimed amounting to 1% of sales.

Required

Indicate whether each item is an accounting policy or an accounting estimate.

18.6 Materiality and events after the reporting period ★ ★   **LO5, 6**

The following information has been made available to you to assist in the preparation of the financial statements of Alys Ltd for the year ended 30 June 2024.

(a) The company has been involved in a dispute with a government environment agency relating to the release of noxious gases from its manufacturing plant in early June 2024. An expert investigation was conducted to determine if the company was at fault. The draft financial report already discloses a contingent liability in the notes detailing the investigation and estimating the potential damages at $1.25 million. The investigator's report, released on 1 August 2024, found Alys Ltd to be responsible for the release and damages amounting to $1 500 000 were payable by the company.

(b) On 9 July 2024, the sales manager raised credit notes worth $30 000 relating to sales of faulty goods in the last 2 weeks of June 2024.

(c) On 25 September 2024, the company received notification that a customer owing $130 000 had gone into liquidation. The liquidator advised that unsecured creditors are likely to receive a distribution of only 20c in the dollar. The liquidation was caused by a flood in July 2024 which destroyed the customer's operating plant and warehouse. The damage was not covered by insurance.

Alys Ltd's draft profit for the year ended 30 June 2024 is $720 000.

Required

In relation to the above events or transactions, prepare the necessary notes or general journal entries to comply with applicable accounting standards.

18.7 Events after the reporting period ★ ★   **LO6**

Monty Ltd has provided the following information concerning events occurring between the end of the reporting period and the date the accounts were authorised. This information is to be considered in the preparation of the financial statements for the year ended 30 June 2022.

(a) On 17 July 2022, a firebomb destroyed four of the company's transport vehicles, resulting in damages of $600 000. Insurance will cover $450 000 of the damages, but payment of the insurance claim has been delayed by a police investigation. As a result of the loss of these vehicles, the company's delivery schedules have been severely disrupted.

(b) On 18 July 2022, the release of a superior and cheaper product by a competitor caused a major decline in demand for Monty Ltd's Product X. In an effort to sell remaining stock of the product, Monty Ltd has reduced its selling price to 50% of cost. Inventories on hand at 30 June 2022 were recorded at their cost of $306 000.

(c) On 15 August 2022, the Department of Occupational Health and Safety charged the company over unsafe storage practices that resulted in the leakage of toxic materials into a local creek. The leakage occurred on 3 July 2022. If found to be negligent by the court, the company will have to pay a fine of $250 000 plus legal and clean-up costs in excess of $175 000.

(d) On 21 August 2022, the purchasing manager discovered that a batch of invoices relating to June inventories purchases had not been processed. The invoices totalled $58 480.

(e) On 30 August 2022, the company issued a prospectus offering 6000 10% debentures of $150 each for public subscription. The debentures are redeemable on 1 October 2025. Interest is payable annually in arrears. The debentures are secured by a floating charge over the company's assets.

Required

Assume all events and transactions are material.

1. Classify the events as either adjusting or non-adjusting events after the end of the reporting period. Justify your classification.

2. Based on your answer to requirement 1, prepare the necessary journal entries or note disclosures to comply with the requirements of AASB 110/IAS 10.

18.8 Errors ★ ★   **LO3**

The annual audit of the accounting records and draft financial statements of Mala Ltd as at 30 June 2022 revealed the following errors and omissions.

(a) Credit notes totalling $52 000 relating to June sales were posted against sales made in July.

(b) The purchase price of $71 200 for a new vehicle on 1 January 2021 was posted to the vehicle maintenance expense account. Motor vehicles are depreciated at 25% p.a. straight-line.

(c) A manufacturing assembly line has been taken out of operation pending its sale. The asset had a carrying amount of $40 000 as at 30 June 2022 and is likely to be sold for a profit.

(d) No disclosure has been made about a fire in the warehouse during May that caused damage worth $280 000. The warehouse and its contents are fully insured.

(e) No adjustment to the allowance for doubtful debts has been made to reflect the fact that a major debtor owing $31 500 went into liquidation after the end of the reporting period. Correspondence with the liquidator indicates that the expected payout will be no more than 10c in the dollar.

Required

Assume all errors and omissions are material. Prepare the necessary adjustments (if any) for each item.

18.9 Materiality, errors and events after the reporting period   ★ ★   **LO5, 6**

You are currently auditing the financial statements and records of Badger Ltd for the year ended 30 June 2024. In the course of your investigations you uncover the following transactions that occurred after the end of the reporting period but which appear to relate to the financial year ended 30 June 2024.

(a) Warranty costs raised for goods returned in the final two weeks of June 2024 were posted as July 2024 sales returns. The goods returned were worth $16 500.

(b) On 16 September 2024, there was a fire in the company's main warehouse. Loss of inventories was covered by insurance but there was significant disruption to the flow of production output. The financial effects of the disruption are estimated to be $150 000, and are not covered by insurance.

(c) Badger Ltd manufactures textiles and purchases raw cotton from overseas. A shipment of cotton was in transit at the end of the reporting period and, given that the price per bale is determined by quality, an estimated cost of $125 000 was recognised. The cotton duly arrived on 18 July 2024 and after examination it was determined that the cost will be $163 000.

(d) On 23 July 2024, a favourable judgement was handed down in a lawsuit lodged by Badger Ltd against a major supplier for damages arising from poor-quality materials delivered in April 2023. The damages and costs awarded to Badger Ltd totalled $1 500 000. The draft accounts currently report this as a contingent asset.

Required

1. Discuss how you would determine whether or not each of the above events is material, stating any additional information you would require in making your determination.

2. Assuming each of these events is considered material and occurred prior to the date the accounts were authorised, explain which, if any, are adjusting or non-adjusting events after the reporting period.

18.10 Accounting policies, accounting estimates and errors   ★ ★   **LO1, 2, 4**

In order to comply with AASB 108/IAS 8, determine whether the following changes should be accounted for prospectively or retrospectively.

1. A change in accounting estimate
2. A voluntary change in an accounting policy
3. A change in accounting policy required by a new or revised accounting standard
4. An immaterial error discovered in the current year, relating to a transaction recorded 3 years ago
5. A material error discovered in the current year, relating to a transaction recorded 3 years ago (management determines that retrospective application would cause undue cost and effort)

18.11 Changes in accounting estimates   ★ ★   **LO2**

On 1 July 2016, Swan Ltd acquired a building for $12 500 000 with an estimated life of 25 years and a residual value of nil. Swan Ltd uses the straight-line method of depreciation. Based on expert advice provided to Swan Ltd in 2022, it was decided the building should be depreciated over a total period of 20 years.

At 1 July 2021, details for the building were as follows.

Cost	$12 500 000
Accumulated depreciation	(2 500 000)
Carrying amount	$10 000 000

Required

Prepare the accounting policy note required by AASB 108/IAS 8 for this change in an accounting estimate by Swan Ltd for the year ended 30 June 2022. Show all workings.

18.12 Accounting policies and changes in accounting estimates ★ ★ ★   **LO1, 2**

Camel Ltd traditionally estimated its allowance for doubtful debts as a percentage of net credit sales for the year. An analysis of the variance between the allowance amount and the actual bad debts written off for the past 5 years has shown significant unfavourable discrepancies. In the previous year (ended 30 June 2023) the allowance was estimated at $24 000, but bad debts written off during the current year were $11 200 more than allowed for. Consequently, the accountant has decided to change the method of estimation from a percentage of net credit sales to an analysis of the accounts receivable balances. This analysis estimated that the allowance for doubtful debts should be $35 600 as at 30 June 2024 (the current year).

Required

1. Show the following for the year ended 30 June 2024:
   (a) the ledger account for the allowance for doubtful debts
   (b) the end of the reporting period adjusting journal entry.
2. Justify your accounting treatment in requirement 1 with reference to the requirements of AASB 108/IAS 8.
3. Explain how and why the change in method of estimation should be disclosed by Camel Ltd.

18.13 Accounting policies ★ ★ ★   **LO1**

At a meeting on 16 June 2022, the directors of Alpaca Ltd decided to change the company's accounting policy in regard to research and development expenditure.

- In previous years, research and development expenditure had been capitalised and amortised over 3 years. In line with this policy, $150 000 was capitalised on 1 January 2021.
- The new policy is to write off all research and development to expense when incurred.
- During the year ended 30 June 2022, the company spent a further $86 000 on research and development which was capitalised on 1 January 2022.
- Research and development expenditure is allowable as a deduction for tax purposes when incurred.

Required

Prepare any note disclosures required by AASB 108/IAS 8 in respect of the change in accounting policy. Show all workings.

REFERENCES

CSR Limited 2019, *Annual report 2019*, www.csr.com.au.
IASB 2018, 'Exposure Draft ED/2018/1 *Accounting Policy Changes* (Proposed amendments to IAS 8)', IFRS Foundation, www.ifrs.org.
PricewaterhouseCoopers 2018, *Value Accounts Holdings Limited*, www.pwc.com.au.

ACKNOWLEDGEMENTS

Photo: © alterfalter / Shutterstock.com
Photo: © Paolo Cipriani / Getty Images
Figures 18.1, 18.2, 18.3: © CSR Limited 2019
Figures 18.4, 18.5: © PricewaterhouseCoopers 2018
Text: © 2019 Australian Accounting Standards Board (AASB). The text, graphics and layout of this publication are protected by Australian copyright law and the comparable law of other countries. No part of the publication may be reproduced, stored or transmitted in any form or by any means without the prior written permission of the AASB except as permitted by law. For reproduction or publication, permission

should be sought in writing from the AASB. Requests in the first instance should be addressed to the National Director, Australian Accounting Standards Board, PO Box 204, Collins Street West, Victoria 8007.

CHAPTER 19

Earnings per share

CHAPTER AIM

The purpose of this chapter is to examine and understand the earnings per share information that is presented in a reporting entity's financial statements in accordance with AASB 133/IAS 33 *Earnings per Share*. The principles for the calculation of basic and diluted earnings per share are demonstrated along with the presentation requirements of the standards.

LEARNING OBJECTIVES

After studying this chapter, you should be able to:

19.1 explain the objective of AASB 133/IAS 33

19.2 discuss the application and scope of AASB 133/IAS 33

19.3 discuss the components of basic earnings per share and examine how it is measured

19.4 explain the concept of diluted earnings per share and how it is measured

19.5 explain the need for retrospective adjustment of earnings per share

19.6 describe and apply the disclosure requirements of AASB 133/IAS 33.

CONCEPTS FOR REVIEW

Before studying this chapter, you should understand and, if necessary, revise:

- the preparation of the statement of profit or loss and other comprehensive income
- share-based payments
- the nature of share capital and the difference between preference and ordinary shares
- initial share issues and subsequent issues.

19.1 Objective of AASB 133/IAS 33

LEARNING OBJECTIVE 19.1 Explain the objective of AASB 133/IAS 33.

Earnings per share, commonly known as EPS, is a ratio that is calculated by dividing the profit or loss (earnings) attributable to ordinary shareholders of a parent entity by the weighted average number of ordinary shares the entity has on issue during the reporting period.

The main focus of AASB 133/IAS 33 is to provide for consistency in the determination and measurement of an entity's earnings per ordinary share so that comparisons can be made 'between different entities in the same reporting period and between different reporting periods for the same entity' (paragraph 1).

EPS is used by investors as a measure of an entity's profitability. In general, the higher the EPS the more profitable the entity. An increase in EPS over a number of years indicates the entity is in a strong financial position and may, therefore, be a relatively reliable investment. Conversely, a decreasing trend indicates a decline in the entity's financial position and, perhaps, a more risky investment. Any change in an entity's EPS may lead to a change in the entity's share price. The Remuneration Report in Woolworths Group Limited's 2018 annual report includes a comparative summary of EPS over 5 years, showing a decrease in EPS from 196.5 (2014) to 110.2 (2016), then a slight increase to 119.4 (2017) and 132.6 (2018). This summary is shown in figure 19.1.

FIGURE 19.1	Remuneration report, Woolworths

2.5 Five year performance perspective

The following table represents the business performance outcomes over a five-year period which is aligned to the STI and LTI outcomes for Executive KMP.

FINANCIAL YEAR		FY14	FY15	FY16	FY17	FY18
Basic EPS[1] — Total Group	(cents per share)	196.5	195.2	110.2	119.4	132.6
Total dividend	(cents per share)	137	139	77	84	103[2]
Share price	(year end closing $)	35.66	27.39	20.56	25.36	29.96
TSR[3]	(%)	12.9	(18.5)	(22.6)	26.8	22.4
STI outcome	(average)	91.3	0	0	114.2[4]	98.0[4]
LTI	(average)	46.25	N/A[5]	N/A[5]	0	0

1. Before significant items.
2. The FY18 total dividend includes a special dividend of 10 cents per share.
3. TSR represents the total shareholder return over the year, which includes changes in the share price as well as dividends and other capital returns that are assumed to be reinvested into Woolworths Group shares.
4. Based on the average STI outcome for Executive KMP, including individual performance modifiers. Outcomes are a percentage of target, including individual performance modifiers.
5. There were no LTI plans due to vest in FY15 and FY16.

Source: Woolworths Group Limited (2018, p. 50).

EPS is used as a key performance indicator when determining the remuneration entitlements of directors and executives. For example, Woolworths Group Limited uses EPS targets as performance hurdles in its short-term and long-term incentive plans for the company's executives, as shown in the last two rows of figure 19.1.

The utility of EPS has been criticised on the basis of the flexibility that entities have in choosing accounting methods when determining their profit. While accounting policy *choice* enables entities to select the accounting methods that are the most appropriate to reflect their actual business operations, it results in inconsistencies between entities in the determination of their profit. For example, entities may select the depreciation method that best reflects the pattern of usage of their physical assets (see AASB 116/IAS 16 *Property, Plant and Equipment* paragraph 60). If one entity chooses the straight-line method then a constant charge is made against its profit across the useful life of its assets. However, if another entity selects the diminishing balance method, then the expense charged against its profit will decrease over its assets' useful lives. When considering the results of an entity's earnings per share, users of this information need to be aware that different accounting methods used by entities have a direct effect on the EPS calculation.

Another limitation to the utility of the EPS ratio for comparison purposes is that it can be altered simply by changes in the number of shares on issue. For example, the number of shares used in the calculation of EPS will be altered if the entity issues bonus ordinary shares. AASB 133/IAS 33 aims to ensure that a consistently determined number of ordinary shares is maintained in order to enhance the comparability of financial reports.

Despite the limitations of EPS as an indicator of the performance of an entity, it is widely used in share analysis.

LEARNING CHECK

- ☐ AASB 133/IAS 33 *Earnings per Share* prescribes the principles for the calculation and presentation of earnings per share.
- ☐ Under AASB 133/IAS 33, the earnings per share, or EPS, ratio is calculated by dividing the profit or loss (earnings) attributable to ordinary shareholders of a parent entity by the weighted average number of ordinary shares the entity has on issue during the reporting period.
- ☐ EPS is a key performance indicator for entities over time and for comparison between entities.
- ☐ The utility of EPS has been criticised because of the flexibility that entities have in choosing accounting methods when determining their profit. This is a limitation that has a direct effect on the EPS calculation.
- ☐ AASB 133/IAS 33 aims to ensure that a consistently determined number of ordinary shares is maintained to ensure consistency in the EPS calculation which, in turn, enhances the comparability of the financial reports.

19.2 Application and scope

LEARNING OBJECTIVE 19.2 Discuss the application and scope of AASB 133/IAS 33.

Only certain types of entities are required to provide information about their earnings per share. AASB 133/IAS 33 applies to an entity, or the parent of a consolidated group, whose **ordinary shares** or **potential ordinary shares** are publicly traded (paragraph 2).

Some examples of potential ordinary shares are included in paragraph 7 of AASB 133/IAS 33:

(a) financial liabilities or equity instruments, including preference shares, that are convertible into ordinary shares;
(b) options and warrants;
(c) shares that would be issued upon the satisfaction of conditions resulting from contractual arrangements, such as the purchase of a business or other assets.

If an entity presents both consolidated and separate financial statements (see chapter 26), the required disclosures need only be determined on the basis of consolidated information. However, the parent entity earnings per share information may be helpful to some users of the financial statements. Entities have the option of also disclosing earnings per share figures for the parent entity, but, as noted in paragraph 4 of AASB 133/IAS 33, such separate disclosures shall not be shown in the consolidated financial statements.

The earnings per share information presented by Woolworths Group Limited in its 2018 annual report is shown in figure 19.2.

FIGURE 19.2	Shareholder value and financial strength, Woolworths

Shareholder value and financial strength

		2018 52 weeks	2017 52 weeks	2016 52 weeks	2015 52 weeks	2014 52 weeks
Shareholder value						
Ordinary share price closing	($)	29.96	25.36	20.56	27.39	35.66
Market capitalisation	($bn)	39.2	32.8	26.3	34.7	44.9
Weighted average shares on issue	(m)	1 300.5	1 283.9	1 263.5	1 256.6	1 248.0

		2018 52 weeks	2017 52 weeks	2016 52 weeks	2015 52 weeks	2014 52 weeks
Basic EPS continuing operations before significant items	(cents per share)	123.4	110.8	116.8	203.9	196.5
Total dividend	(cents per share)	93.0	84.0	77.0	139.0	137.0
Payout ratio before significant items	(%)	70.7	70.7	70.4	71.7	70.3
Financial strength						
Fixed charges cover	(items)	2.6	2.5	2.3	2.9	3.0

The five year summary has been condensed to include financial information and metrics considered key to the Annual Report. The full version of the five year summary can be found on the Woolworths Group website. Visit www.woolworthsgroup.com.au.

Source: Woolworths Group Limited (2018, p. 124).

LEARNING CHECK

☐ AASB 133/IAS 33 applies to the calculation and presentation of earnings per share by reporting entities whose ordinary shares or potential ordinary shares are publicly traded, or are in the process of being issued in public markets, or an entity that discloses earnings per share.

☐ If an entity presents both consolidated and separate financial statements, the AASB 133/IAS 33 disclosures need only be determined on the basis of consolidated information. Entities have the option of also disclosing earnings per share figures for the parent entity, but this information can only be presented in the parent's separate financial statements (not in the consolidated financial statements).

19.3 Basic earnings per share

LEARNING OBJECTIVE 19.3 Discuss the components of basic earnings per share and examine how it is measured.

There are two earnings per share ratios:
- basic earnings per share
- diluted earnings per share.

The formula for calculating **basic earnings per share** is described in paragraph 10 of AASB 133/IAS 33 and shown in figure 19.3.

FIGURE 19.3	Basic earnings per share ratio

$$\frac{\text{Profit attributable to ordinary shareholders of the parent entity}}{\text{Weighted average number of ordinary shares outstanding during the reporting period}}$$

19.3.1 Earnings

The 'earnings' amount to be included in the calculation must only include income and expenses attributable to ordinary shareholders. All amounts directly attributable to preference shares must be excluded. Therefore, the profit of the entity is to be adjusted for any tax expense relating directly to preference shares and any dividends on preference shares that have been classified as liabilities. The remaining company tax expense is a normal component of the profit of an entity, and therefore it is a normal part of the calculation of profit. The calculation of 'earnings' is demonstrated in figure 19.4.

FIGURE 19.4	Earnings calculation to exclude tax expense and preference dividends

Profit before tax expense	100 000	
Less: Tax expense	(30 000)	
Profit after tax	70 000	
Less: Preference dividends	(10 000)	
Profit attributable to ordinary equity holders (earnings)	60 000	(numerator of the EPS ratio)

The preference dividends to be deducted from profit or loss are the after-tax amounts, and for *non-cumulative* preference dividends they are to include any amounts declared during the period (AASB 133/IAS 33 paragraph 14(a)). In respect of *cumulative* preference dividends, paragraph 14(b) requires the after-tax preference dividend amount to be deducted from profit or loss whether or not the dividends have been declared. Note, the amount used for preference dividends can only be the amount relating to the *current* reporting period and 'does not include the amount of any preference dividends for cumulative preference shares paid or declared during the current period in respect of previous periods' (AASB 133/IAS 33 paragraph 14(b)).

Increasing rate preference shares

Increasing rate preference shares are securities that provide for either a low initial dividend to compensate an entity for selling its shares at a discount; or, they provide for an above-market dividend in later periods to compensate investors for buying the entity's securities at a premium. If an entity issues increasing rate preference shares then paragraph 15 of AASB 133/IAS 33 requires any discount or premium on the original issue to be amortised to retained earnings and treated as a preference dividend for the calculation of earnings per share.

Repurchases and conversion of preference shares

If an entity chooses to repurchase preference shares it has on issue, any gain or loss resulting from the change in fair value of those shares is charged to retained earnings as a return to preference shareholders. Paragraph 16 of AASB 133/IAS 33 requires these gains/losses to be excluded from the calculation of profit or loss attributable to ordinary equity holders. Similarly, if preference shares are converted to ordinary shares, any gain or loss on fair value of these converted shares must also be excluded from the calculation (AASB 133/IAS 33 paragraphs 17 and 18).

The treatment of cumulative and non-cumulative dividends is demonstrated in illustrative example 19.1.

ILLUSTRATIVE EXAMPLE 19.1

Non-cumulative and cumulative preference dividends

Jasmine Ltd is a cosmetics manufacturer. The company has 200 000 Class A preference shares on issue, each carrying a non-cumulative dividend right of 5% of the $1 issue value of the share. A non-cumulative dividend was declared during the reporting period. The company also has 400 000 Class B preference shares outstanding, which carry a cumulative dividend right of 4% per share based on the issue value of $1 per share. The company has a profit for the period from continuing operations amounting to $2 million, and tax is payable at the rate of 30%.

Calculate the earnings (profit attributable to ordinary shareholders) that will be used in the calculation of basic EPS for Jasmine Ltd.

Solution

The determination of earnings to exclude tax expense and preference dividends is as follows.

Calculation	$
Profit before tax	2 000 000
Tax expense	(600 000)
Profit after tax	1 400 000
Preference dividends	(26 000)*
Profit attributable to ordinary equity holders	1 374 000

*([200 000 × 5%] + [400 000 × 4%])

The amount to be used in the numerator of the EPS ratio is therefore $1 374 000.

19.3.2 Shares

As the earnings per share calculation is focused on the ordinary equity of an entity, the denominator in the calculation contains only ordinary share capital. Table 19.1 lists the actions that may be taken by an entity regarding their share capital and the impact each action will have on the number of ordinary shares used in the EPS calculation.

TABLE 19.1   Share capital actions

Action regarding share capital	Increase or decrease to the number of ordinary shares
New issue of ordinary shares during a reporting period	Increase
Repurchase of ordinary shares	Decrease
Forfeiture of ordinary shares (shares are not reissued)	Decrease
Splitting of ordinary shares	Increase
Consolidating/combining ordinary shares	Decrease
Conversion of convertible preference shares into ordinary shares	Increase

Paragraph 19 of AASB 133/IAS 33 requires the number of ordinary shares used in the calculation of basic EPS to be 'the weighted average number of ordinary shares outstanding during the period'.

This weighted average takes into consideration variations in the number of outstanding shares during the year. The number of ordinary shares outstanding at the beginning of the reporting period is adjusted for the number of ordinary shares bought back and/or issued during the period. The adjusted number of ordinary shares is then multiplied by a time-weighting factor which is described in paragraph 20 of AASB 133/IAS 33 as:

> the number of days that the shares are outstanding as a proportion of the total number of days in the period.

If the entity has a number of adjustments to their ordinary shares during the year then a 'reasonable approximation' is deemed adequate in the calculation of the weighted average number of shares. Shares are included in the calculation from the date that the consideration for shares is receivable, which is usually the issue date. Paragraph 21 of AASB 133/IAS 33 provides examples of included ordinary share issues, summarised in table 19.2.

TABLE 19.2   Inclusions for weighted average number of ordinary shares

Ordinary share issue	Date of inclusion
Shares issued in exchange for cash	Date the cash is receivable
Shares issued on a voluntary reinvestment of dividends	Date the dividends are reinvested
Shares issued as a result of a conversion of a debt instrument to ordinary shares	Date the interest ceases to accrue
Shares issued in place of interest or principal on other financial instruments	Date the interest ceases to accrue
Shares issued in exchange for the settlement of a liability	Date of settlement
Shares issued as consideration for the acquisition of an asset other than cash	Date of acquisition
Shares issued for the rendering of services	Date the services are rendered

In respect of ordinary shares issued as part of the consideration in a business combination, they are to be included from the acquisition date as this reflects the date from which the acquiree's profits are included in the acquirer's income (AASB 133/IAS 33 paragraph 22).

Share consolidation and share repurchase

While a consolidation of shares will decrease the number of shares on issue, there is no corresponding reduction in the entity's resources. In contrast, when a repurchase occurs, the entity's resources (e.g. cash) will also be reduced. Shares that are repurchased and held by the issuing entity are called **treasury shares**. If a purchase of treasury shares occurs, then the weighted average number of shares outstanding for the period in which the transaction takes place must be adjusted for the reduction in the number of shares from the date of the repurchase (AASB 133/IAS 33 paragraph 29).

The calculation of the weighted average number of ordinary shares where a new share issue and a share repurchase have occurred during the period is demonstrated in illustrative example 19.2.

ILLUSTRATIVE EXAMPLE 19.2

Determining the weighted average number of shares

Brodie Ltd has 22 000 ordinary shares on issue at 1 January 2023 which is the beginning of its reporting period. On 30 June 2023, it issued a further 5000 ordinary shares for cash. On 1 November 2023, Brodie Ltd repurchased 500 shares at fair value in a market transaction.

		Issued shares	Treasury shares	Shares outstanding
1 January 2023	Balance at the beginning of the year	22 000	1 500	20 500
30 June 2023	Issue of new ordinary shares for cash	5 000		25 500
1 November 2023	Repurchase of issued shares		500	25 000
31 December 2023	Balance at the end of the year	27 000	2 000	25 000

The weighted average number of shares for use in the earnings per share calculation is determined as follows.

$$= (20\,500 \times 6/12) + (25\,500 \times 4/12) + (25\,000 \times 2/12)$$
$$= 10\,250 + 8500 + 4167$$
$$= 22\,917 \text{ shares}$$

Source: Adapted from AASB 133/IAS 33, Example 2.

Contingently issuable shares

An entity may enter into a **contingent share agreement** whereby the issue of shares is dependent upon specific conditions being met. If the specified conditions are not due to expire until a future reporting period then, at the end of the current reporting period, the entity will have **contingently issuable ordinary shares** outstanding. These are defined in paragraph 5 of AASB 133/IAS 33 as:

> ordinary shares issuable for little or no cash or other consideration upon the satisfaction of specified conditions in a contingent share agreement.

If an entity has contingently issuable shares they must be treated as outstanding and only included in the calculation of basic earnings per share from the date when all necessary conditions have been satisfied (AASB 133/IAS 33 paragraph 24).

Bonus issues and share splits

If an entity announces a bonus issue of shares or if it splits issued shares, thereby increasing the number of shares outstanding, there is usually no consideration involved and therefore no corresponding increase in the entity's resources. In this situation, paragraph 28 of AASB 133/IAS 33 requires the number of ordinary shares outstanding before the split to be adjusted proportionately as per the split arrangements. For example, under a 2-for-1 bonus issue, multiplying the number of ordinary shares outstanding before the bonus issue by 2 determines the number of additional ordinary shares. This adjustment is to be treated as if it had occurred before the beginning of the current period. Therefore, if the EPS for prior years is reported on the current financial statements, the calculation for each of those prior years must be adjusted for this bonus issue. The effect of a bonus issue of shares on the basic earnings per share calculation is demonstrated in illustrative example 19.3.

Bonus issue of shares

Harry Ltd determined its profit attributable to ordinary shareholders for the reporting period ended 30 June 2023 as $560 000 (2022: $520 000). The number of ordinary shares on issue up to 31 October 2022 was 75 000. Harry Ltd announced a 2-for-1 bonus issue of shares, effective for each ordinary share outstanding at 31 October 2022.

Basic earnings per share is calculated as follows.

Bonus issue on 1 November 2022	$75\,000 \times 2 = 150\,000$
Basic earnings per share 30 June 2023	$\dfrac{\$560\,000}{75\,000 + 150\,000} = \$2.49$
Basic earnings per share 30 June 2022	$\dfrac{\$520\,000}{75\,000 + 150\,000} = \$2.31$

Because the bonus shares were issued for no consideration, the event is treated as if it had occurred before the beginning of the 2022 reporting period, the earliest period presented in the financial statements (AASB 133/IAS 33 paragraph 28).

Source: Adapted from AASB 133/IAS 33, Example 3.

Rights issues

With a bonus issue, as the shares are usually issued for no consideration, there is an increase in the number of shares outstanding, which is not accompanied by a corresponding increase in the resources of the issuing entity. In a rights issue the exercise price is usually lower than the fair value of the shares issued. This means that the rights issue includes a bonus element. In this case, the application guidance in AASB 133/IAS 33 (paragraph A2) requires that the number of ordinary shares used in the calculation of earnings per share, for all periods before the rights issue, is to be the number of ordinary shares outstanding before the rights issue multiplied by an adjustment factor. The components of the adjustment factor are shown in figure 19.5.

FIGURE 19.5   Adjustment factor for rights issues containing a bonus element

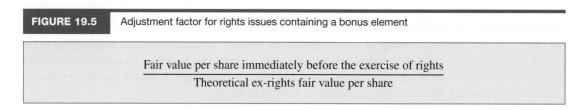

$$\frac{\text{Fair value per share immediately before the exercise of rights}}{\text{Theoretical ex-rights fair value per share}}$$

The calculation for the denominator in the adjustment factor is shown in figure 19.6.

FIGURE 19.6   Theoretical ex-rights value per share

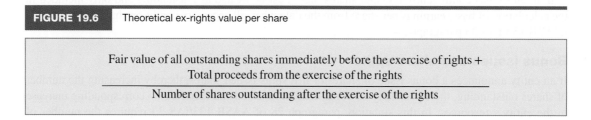

$$\frac{\begin{array}{c}\text{Fair value of all outstanding shares immediately before the exercise of rights} + \\ \text{Total proceeds from the exercise of the rights}\end{array}}{\text{Number of shares outstanding after the exercise of the rights}}$$

Fair value is the share price at the close of the last day on which the shares were traded together with the rights (cum-rights). The calculation of basic earnings per share where there is a rights issue during the period is demonstrated in illustrative example 19.4.

Rights issue

Georgou Ltd determined its profit attributable to ordinary shareholders for the reporting period ended 30 June 2023 as $5000. At the beginning of the reporting period the company had 1000 ordinary shares on issue. It announced a rights issue with the following details.

- Date of rights issue, 1 July 2022
- Last date to exercise rights, 1 September 2022
- One new share for each four outstanding (250 total)
- Exercise price, $10
- Market price of one share immediately before exercise on 1 September 2022, $12

Determine the theoretical ex-rights value per share

$$\frac{\text{Fair value of all outstanding shares immediately before the exercise of rights} +}{\text{Number of shares outstanding after the exercise of the rights}}$$

$$\frac{(\$12 \times 1000 \text{ shares}) + (\$10 \times 250 \text{ shares})}{1000 \text{ shares} + 250 \text{ shares}} = \$11.60$$

Determine the adjustment factor

$$\frac{\text{Fair value per share immediately before the exercise of rights}}{\text{Theoretical ex-rights fair value per share}} = \frac{\$12}{\$11.60}$$

$$= 1.03$$

Basic earnings per share is calculated as follows.

$$\text{Profit attributable to ordinary shareholders 30 June 2023} = \frac{500}{\left(100 \times 1.03 \times \frac{2}{12}\right) + \left(1250 \times \frac{10}{12}\right)}$$

$$= \$4.12$$

Source: Adapted from AASB 133/IAS 33, Example 4.

☐ Earnings per share is measured by dividing profit (or loss) attributable to ordinary shareholders by the weighted average number of ordinary shares outstanding during the period. This measurement approach results in a ratio known as 'basic' earnings per share.

☐ The profit or loss used in the calculation of basic earnings per share must be from continuing operations and must exclude any income or expense attributable to ordinary shareholders that has been recognised in the reporting period (i.e. any tax expense and any dividends on preference shares that have been classified as liabilities will be deducted as part of the determination of profit).

☐ If the number of shares on issue changes during the reporting period, the number of ordinary shares used in the calculation of basic earnings per share is adjusted by a time-weighting factor.

19.4 Diluted earnings per share

LEARNING OBJECTIVE 19.4 Explain the concept of diluted earnings per share and how it is measured.

In addition to calculating the basic earnings per share ratio, if an entity has options, warrants, contingently issuable shares or convertible securities, then AASB 133/IAS 33 requires an entity to also recognise the effect of potential dilution to its earnings per share ratio. **Dilution** is defined in paragraph 5 of AASB 133/IAS 33 as:

> a reduction in earnings per share or an increase in loss per share resulting from the assumption that convertible instruments are converted, that options or warrants are exercised, or that ordinary shares are issued upon the satisfaction of specified conditions.

Adjustments are to be made to both the profit or loss attributable to ordinary shareholders and the weighted average number of ordinary shares. The profit or loss attributable to ordinary shareholders is increased by the after-tax amount of dividends, interest on dilutive potential ordinary shares, and any other changes to income or expense that would result from the conversion of the potential dilutive shares. The weighted average number of ordinary shares is increased by the weighted average number of additional ordinary shares that would be outstanding if the potential dilutive shares are converted (AASB 133/IAS 33 paragraph 32).

According to AASB 133/IAS 33 (paragraph 41), potential ordinary shares are dilutive 'when, and only when, their conversion to ordinary shares would decrease earnings per share or increase loss per share from continuing operations'.

Potential ordinary shares can be antidilutive; that is, they have the opposite effect of dilutive shares. **Antidilution** occurs when the conversion of the potential ordinary shares 'would increase earnings per share or decrease loss per share from continuing operations' (AASB 133/IAS 33 paragraph 43).

19.4.1 Earnings

For the purposes of calculating diluted earnings per share, the profit or loss attributable to ordinary shareholders is to be adjusted by the after-tax effect of (AASB 133/IAS 33 paragraph 33):

(a) any dividends or other items related to dilutive potential ordinary shares deducted . . . ;
(b) any interest recognised in the period related to dilutive potential ordinary shares; and
(c) any other changes in income or expense that would result from the conversion of the dilutive potential ordinary shares.

If potential ordinary shares were to be converted, any dividends or interest payable in relation to those dilutive securities would no longer arise. Instead the new ordinary shares would be entitled to participate in profit. Therefore, the profit or loss is adjusted for the items in paragraph 33(a)–(c), along with any related tax effect. Consequential changes may also include a reduction in interest expense related to potential ordinary shares resulting in an increase in profit. Therefore, '[f]or the purpose of calculating diluted earnings per share, profit or loss attributable to ordinary equity holders of the parent entity is adjusted for any such consequential changes in income or expense' (AASB 133/IAS 33 paragraph 35).

19.4.2 Shares

The diluted earnings per share ratio must also include an adjustment to increase the weighted average number of ordinary shares by the amount of the ordinary shares that would be issued on the conversion of the dilutive securities. Paragraph 36 of AASB 133/IAS 33 deems that the potential ordinary shares are to be regarded as having been 'converted into ordinary shares at the beginning of the period or, if later, the date of the issue of the potential ordinary shares'.

The potential ordinary shares shall be weighted for the period that they are outstanding. If any of the dilutive securities lapse or are cancelled, they are included in the calculation only for the portion of time during which they are outstanding. Any dilutive securities that are converted into ordinary shares during the period are included in the calculation of diluted earnings per share from the beginning of the period to the date of conversion (AASB 133/IAS 33 paragraph 38). If the terms of dilutive securities include more than one basis for conversion into ordinary shares then, under paragraph 39, 'the calculation assumes the most advantageous conversion rate or exercise price from the standpoint of the holder of the potential ordinary shares'.

Dilutive potential ordinary shares

Potential ordinary shares are treated as dilutive 'when, and only when, their conversion to ordinary shares would decrease earnings per share or increase loss per share from continuing operations' (AASB 133/IAS 33 paragraph 41). The conversion, exercise or other issue of potential ordinary shares that would have an antidilutive effect on earnings per share is not assumed in the calculation of diluted earnings per share (paragraph 43).

To obtain the maximum *dilution* of basic earnings per share each issue or series of potential ordinary shares is to be considered separately and in sequence from most dilutive to least dilutive. This means that 'dilutive potential ordinary shares with the lowest "earnings per incremental share" are included in the diluted earnings per share calculation before those with a higher earnings per incremental share' (AASB 133/IAS 33 paragraph 44). The first series of potential ordinary shares to be included are generally options and warrants as they have no effect on the numerator (profit or loss) of the calculation.

Options and warrants

The assumed proceeds from **options** and **warrants** are regarded as received from the issue of ordinary shares at the average market price during the period. The options and warrants are deemed to be dilutive when their issue price is less than this average market price. The calculation for diluted earnings per share treats the issue of potential ordinary shares, such as options, as consisting of both the following (AASB 133/IAS 33 paragraph 46):

(a) a contract to issue a certain number of the ordinary shares at their average market price during the period. Such ordinary shares are assumed to be fairly priced and to be neither dilutive nor antidilutive. They are ignored in the calculation of diluted earnings per share.

(b) a contract to issue the remaining ordinary shares for no consideration. Such ordinary shares generate no proceeds and have no effect on profit or loss attributable to ordinary shares outstanding. Therefore, such shares are dilutive and are added to the number of ordinary shares outstanding in the calculation of diluted earnings per share.

The amount of the dilution is determined as the average market price of ordinary shares during the period minus the exercise price of the options. The difference between the number of ordinary shares issued and the number that would have been issued at the average market price is treated as an issue of ordinary shares for no consideration. The application guidance to AASB 133/IAS 33 indicates that a simple average of the weekly or monthly closing prices of ordinary shares is usually adequate for determining the average market price. However, this approach will need to be adjusted when share prices fluctuate widely (paragraphs A4–A5).

Employee share options and non-vested ordinary shares are regarded as options in the calculation of diluted earnings per share even though they may be contingent on vesting (AASB 133/IAS 33 paragraph 48).

The effect of share options on basic and diluted earnings per share is demonstrated in illustrative example 19.5.

ILLUSTRATIVE EXAMPLE 19.5

Effect of share options on earnings per share

Starview Ltd determined its profit attributable to ordinary shareholders for the reporting period ended 30 June 2023 as $250 000. The average market price of the entity's shares during the period is $2.00 per share. The weighted average number of ordinary shares on issue during the period is 750 000. The weighted average number of shares under share options arrangements during the year is 125 000 and the exercise price of shares under option is $1.20.

	Earnings $	Shares	Per share $
Basic earnings per share is calculated as follows:			
Profit attributable to ordinary shareholders for the reporting period ended 30 June 2023	250 000		
Weighted average shares on issue during the period		750 000	
Basic earnings per share			0.33
Diluted earnings per share is calculated as follows:			
Weighted average number of shares under option		125 000	

	Earnings $	Shares	Per share $
Weighted average number of shares that would have been issued at average market price is (125 000 × $1.20)/$2.00		(75 000)	
Diluted earnings per share	250 000	800 000	0.31

Source: Adapted from AASB 133/IAS 33, Example 5.

Convertible securities

If convertible preference shares are dilutive they are included in the diluted earnings per share. They are regarded as antidilutive when the amount of the dividend declared or accumulated for the current period on the convertible preference shares is greater than the basic earnings per share. Similarly, convertible debt is antidilutive whenever its interest (net of tax and other changes in income or expenses) per ordinary share obtainable on conversion exceeds basic earnings per share (AASB 133/IAS 33 paragraph 50).

Contingently issuable shares

Contingently issuable shares, such as performance-based employee share options, are included in the diluted earnings per share calculation from the later of:
- the beginning of the period
- the date of the contingent share agreement.

Where the conditions are not satisfied, the number of contingently issuable shares included in the calculation of diluted earnings per share is based on the number of shares that would be issuable if the end of the period were the end of the contingency period (AASB 133/IAS 33 paragraph 52).

When calculating the diluted earnings per share for contingently issuable shares that are conditional on a specified profit figure being attained or maintained over a number of periods, and the vesting period ends in a future financial period, the additional ordinary shares are treated as outstanding if the effect is dilutive. The number of contingently issuable shares to be included in the calculation is based on the number of ordinary shares that would be issued if the amount of earnings at the end of the reporting period were the amount of earnings at the end of the contingency period (AASB 133/IAS 33 paragraph 53).

The calculation is the same if the contingently issuable shares are conditional on the achievement of a future market price. That is, the calculation is based on the number of ordinary shares that would be issued if the market price at the end of the reporting period were the market price at the end of the contingency period. However, if the vesting condition requires an average market price to be maintained over a vesting period which ends at a future date, then the calculation is to use the average (market price) for the period of time that has lapsed. Furthermore, it is explained that the calculation of 'basic' earnings per share 'does not include such contingently issuable ordinary shares until the end of the contingency period because not all necessary conditions have been satisfied' (AASB 133/IAS 33 paragraph 54).

If the number of contingently issuable ordinary shares is dependent on *both* future earnings and future prices of ordinary shares, then these contingently issuable shares are not included in the diluted earnings per share calculation unless both specified conditions are met.

Contracts that may be settled in ordinary shares or cash

If an entity has issued a contract that may be settled in cash or ordinary shares at the entity's option, then, for the purposes of calculating earnings per share, the contract is assumed to be settled in ordinary shares (AASB 133/IAS 33 paragraph 58). If the result of these potential ordinary shares is dilutive they are to be included in the diluted earnings per share. Alternatively, for contracts that can be settled in cash or ordinary shares at the holder's option, paragraph 60 requires the more dilutive option of the cash settlement or share settlement to be included in the calculation of diluted earnings per share. Such contracts could include an option that provides the holder with settlement choice of cash or ordinary shares.

As mentioned, when determining the dilutive effect of 'potential' ordinary shares, each issue or series of dilutive securities is considered in sequence from most dilutive to least dilutive (AASB 133/IAS 33 paragraph 44). Securities with the lowest earnings impact per additional share are included in the calculation first. Determining the order in which to include dilutive securities is demonstrated in illustrative example 19.6.

Calculation of weighted average number when more than one issue of potentially dilutive securities exist

Rosy Ltd extracted the following information from its financial records in order to determine its basic earnings per share and diluted earnings per share for its reporting period ended 30 June 2023.

Profit from continuing operations	$36 400
Less: Dividends on preference shares	(6 400)
Profit from continuing operations attributable to ordinary shareholders	30 000
Loss from discontinued operations	(8 000)
Profit attributable to ordinary shareholders	$22 000
Ordinary shares on issue	5 000
Average market price of one ordinary share during the period	$7.50

Potential ordinary shares (potentially dilutive securities):

1. Options	15 000 with an exercise price of $6.00
2. Convertible preference shares	1600 shares with an issue value of $100 entitled to a cumulative dividend of $12 per share. Each preference share is convertible to two ordinary shares.

Required

Determine Rosy Ltd's basic earnings per share and diluted earnings per share for the period ended 30 June 2023.

Solution

Step 1. Determine the increase in earnings attributable to ordinary shareholders on conversion of potential ordinary shares

Options	
Increase in earnings	$0
Additional shares issued for no consideration	
15 000 × ($7.50 − $6.00)/$7.50	3 000
Earnings per additional share	$0
Convertible preference shares	
Increase in earnings [(1600 × $100) × ($12/$100)]	$19 200
Additional shares (2 × 1600)	3 200
Earnings per additional share	$6.00

The dilutive securities are included in the earnings per share calculation in the following order.
1. Options (lowest earnings impact per incremental share)
2. Convertible preference shares (highest earnings impact per incremental share)

Step 2. Determine dilutive effect of convertible securities

	$	Shares	$ per share	
Profit from continuing operations attributable to ordinary shareholders	30 000	5 000	6.00	
Increase in earnings from options	0	3 000		
	30 000	8 000	3.75	Dilutive
Increase in earnings from convertible preference shares*	19 200	3 200		
	49 200	11 200	4.39	Antidilutive

*As the convertible preference shares increased diluted earnings per share they would be considered antidilutive and ignored in the calculation of diluted earnings per share.

Step 3. Calculate basic EPS and diluted EPS

	Basic EPS $	Diluted EPS $
Profit from continuing operations attributable to ordinary shareholders	6.00	3.75
Loss from discontinued operations attributable to ordinary shareholders		
($8000)/5000	(1.60)	
($8000)/8000		(1.00)
Profit attributable to ordinary shareholders		
$22 000/5000	4.40	
$22 000/8000		2.75

Source: Adapted from AASB 133/IAS 33, Example 9.

19.5 Retrospective adjustments

LEARNING OBJECTIVE 19.5 Explain the need for retrospective adjustment of earnings per share.

Retrospective adjustments are made to restate the values of relevant items so enable valid comparisons across time. If, for example, the number of issued shares increases during a reporting period as a result of a bonus issue for no consideration, then the operating profit for the whole period in which the bonus issue occurred will be attributable to the increased number of shares and not to the lesser number of shares outstanding at the beginning of the reporting period. AASB 133/IAS 33 requires basic and diluted earnings per share to be adjusted retrospectively if:

• the number of ordinary shares or potential ordinary shares outstanding *increases* as a result of capitalisation, a bonus issue, or a share split; or
• the number *decreases* as a result of a consolidation (reverse share split).

The retrospective adjustment also applies for the period from the end of the reporting period up to the date the financial statements are authorised. In addition, retrospective adjustments are required for all periods presented for the effects of errors and adjustments resulting from changes in accounting policies (AASB 133/IAS 33 paragraph 64).

19.6 Disclosure

LEARNING OBJECTIVE 19.6 Describe and apply the disclosure requirements of AASB 133/IAS 33.

The basic earnings per share and diluted earnings per share ratios must be presented in an entity's statement of profit or loss and other comprehensive income for each class of ordinary shares that has a different right to share in profit for the period (AASB 133/IAS 33 paragraph 66). They must be presented even if a loss has resulted per share and the amounts are negative (paragraph 69). If the items of profit or loss are presented in a separate statement then the basic and diluted earnings per share ratios are required to be presented in that separate statement (paragraph 67A). If the diluted earnings per share ratio is presented for one period, then it must be shown for all periods that are presented in the financial statements, even if it is the same as the basic earnings per share (paragraph 67). Paragraph 68 requires:

> An entity that reports a discontinued operation shall disclose the basic and diluted amounts per share for the discontinued operation either in the statement of comprehensive income or in the notes.

Paragraphs 70–73A of AASB 133/IAS 33 prescribe various disclosures relating to earnings per share. The objective of these disclosures is to provide sufficient additional information to assist financial statement users to understand the composition of the earnings per share ratios. Paragraph 70 requires an entity to disclose:

(a) the amounts used as the numerators in calculating basic and diluted earnings per share, and a reconciliation of those amounts to profit or loss attributable to the parent entity for the period. The reconciliation shall include the individual effect of each class of instruments that affects earnings per share.
(b) the weighted average number of ordinary shares used as the denominator in calculating basic and diluted earnings per share, and a reconciliation of these denominators to each other. The reconciliation shall include the individual effect of each class of instruments that affects earnings per share.
(c) instruments (including contingently issuable shares) that could potentially dilute basic earnings per share in the future, but were not included in the calculation of diluted earnings per share because they are antidilutive for the period(s) presented.
(d) a description of ordinary share transactions or potential ordinary share transactions, other than those accounted for in accordance with paragraph 64, that occur after the reporting period and that would have changed significantly the number of ordinary shares or potential ordinary shares outstanding at the end of the period if those transactions had occurred before the end of the reporting period.

Examples of transactions in paragraph 70(d) are presented in paragraph 71:

(a) an issue of shares for cash;
(b) an issue of shares when the proceeds are used to repay debt or preference shares outstanding at the end of the reporting period;
(c) the redemption of ordinary shares outstanding;
(d) the conversion or exercise of potential ordinary shares outstanding at the end of the reporting period into ordinary shares;
(e) an issue of options, warrants, or convertible instruments; and
(f) the achievement of conditions that would result in the issue of contingently issuable shares.

Woolworths Group Limited includes reconciliations of the earnings amounts and the weighted average number of shares used in its basic and diluted earnings per share calculation in note 4 of its 2018 annual report. These reconciliations are presented in figure 19.7. These reconciliations produce the EPS figures shown earlier in figure 19.2.

If, in addition to calculating basic and diluted earnings per share, an entity uses a numerator other than the one required by AASB 133/IAS 33, then it must still use the denominator (weighted average number of ordinary shares) as prescribed under AASB 133/IAS 33. These additional ratios must be displayed as the prescribed basic EPS and diluted EPS ratios and presented in the notes to the financial statements. The basis on which the numerator is determined, including whether the amounts per share are before or after tax, must also be disclosed (paragraph 73).

AASB 133/IAS 33 (paragraph 72) also encourages the voluntary disclosure of the terms and conditions of financial instruments and contracts that incorporate terms and conditions affecting the measurement of basic and diluted earnings per share.

FIGURE 19.7   Earnings per share disclosure, Woolworths

4. Capital structure, finance and risk management

4.1 Earnings per share	2018	2017
Profit for the period attributable to equity holders of the parent entity used in earnings per share ($m)		
Continuing operations	1 605	1 422
Discontinued operations	119	112
	1 724	1 534
Weighted average number of shares used in earnings per share (shares, millions)[1]		
Basic earnings per share	1 300.5	1 283.9
Diluted earnings per share[2]	1 303.9	1 287.3
Basic earnings per share (cents per share)[1]		
Continuing operations	123.4	110.8
Discontinued operations	9.2	8.6
	132.6	119.4
Diluted earnings per share[1,2]		
Continuing operations	123.1	110.5
Discontinued operations	9.2	8.6
	132.3	119.1

1. Weighted average number of shares has been adjusted to remove treasury shares held by Woolworths Custodian Pty Ltd (as trustee of various employee share trusts).
2. Includes 3.4 million (2017: 3.4 million) shares deemed to be issued for no consideration in respect of employee options and performance rights.

Source: Woolworths Group Limited (2018, p. 88).

LEARNING CHECK

☐ The basic earnings per share and diluted earnings per share ratios must be presented in an entity's statement of profit or loss and other comprehensive income even if the amounts are negative.

☐ If the items of profit or loss are presented in a separate statement then the basic and diluted earnings per share ratios are required to be presented in that separate statement.

☐ Basic earnings per share and diluted earnings per share must be displayed with equal prominence and must be calculated for each class of ordinary shares that have different rights to share in the profit of the period.

☐ If diluted earnings per share is presented for one period, then it must be shown for all periods that are presented in the financial statements.

☐ If the entity has a discontinued operation, then it must calculate and disclose the basic and diluted earnings per share ratios for the discontinued operation in the statement of profit or loss and other comprehensive income.

SUMMARY

AASB 133/IAS 33 provides principles for the calculation and presentation of basic and diluted earnings per share. Earnings per share (EPS) is a ratio used to compare the after-tax profit available to ordinary shareholders of an entity on a per share basis with that of previous reporting periods and other entities. It is calculated by dividing profit or loss (earnings) attributable to ordinary shareholders, by the weighted average number of ordinary shares outstanding during a reporting period.

The objective of AASB 133/IAS 33 is to improve the information provided by reporting entities, and the consistency of comparisons between entities and across different time periods.

The main features of AASB 133/IAS 33 are that it requires:
- the profit (or loss) used in the calculation of basic earnings per share to be from continuing operations. This means that any tax expense and dividends on preference shares that have been classified as liabilities will be deducted as part of the determination of profit
- the denominator in the calculation to contain only ordinary shares
- the number of ordinary shares used in the calculation of basic earnings per share to be adjusted by a time-weighting factor, which is the number of days in the reporting period that the shares are outstanding as a proportion of the total number of days in the period.

In addition to calculating the basic earnings per share ratio, if an entity has options, warrants, contingently issuable shares or securities that are convertible to ordinary shares, AASB 133/IAS 33 requires the effect of dilution to be recognised in the entity's earnings per share. Adjustments to calculate diluted earnings per share must be made to:
- the profit (or loss) attributable to the ordinary shareholders for the after-tax amount of dividends, interest or other income or expenses that would no longer arise if the dilutive securities were converted into ordinary shares
- increase the weighted average number of ordinary shares outstanding to reflect what the weighted average would have been assuming that all potential ordinary shares (dilutive securities) had been converted.

KEY TERMS

antidilution An increase in earnings per share or a reduction in loss per share resulting from the assumption that convertible instruments are converted, that options or warrants are exercised, or that ordinary shares are issued upon the satisfaction of specified conditions.

basic earnings per share Basic earnings per share is calculated by dividing profit or loss attributable to ordinary equity holders of the parent entity by the weighted average number of ordinary shares outstanding during the period.

contingent share agreement An agreement to issue shares that is dependent on the satisfaction of specified conditions.

contingently issuable ordinary shares Ordinary shares issuable for little or no cash or other consideration upon the satisfaction of specified conditions in a contingent share agreement.

dilution A reduction in earnings per share or an increase in loss per share resulting from the assumption that convertible instruments are converted, that options or warrants are exercised, or that ordinary shares are issued upon the satisfaction of specified conditions.

earnings per share A ratio calculated by comparing an entity's profit with the number of ordinary shares it has on issue.

increasing rate preference shares Securities that provide for either a low initial dividend to compensate an entity for selling its shares at a discount or provide for an above-market dividend in later periods to compensate investors for buying the entity's securities at a premium.

options A financial instrument that gives the holder the right to buy or sell a certain number of shares or debentures in a company by a specified date at a stipulated price.

ordinary shares Shares that have no specific rights to any distributions of profit by the company. Ordinary shareholders obtain what is left after all other parties' claims have been met.

potential ordinary share A financial instrument or other contract that may entitle its holder to ordinary shares.

retrospective adjustments A restatement of the values of relevant items to enable valid comparisons across time.

treasury shares Shares reacquired by the issuing entity.
warrants Financial instruments that give the holder the right to purchase ordinary shares.

DEMONSTRATION PROBLEM

19.1 Basic EPS and diluted EPS

For the financial year ending 30 June 2024, Tower Ltd extracted the following information from its financial statements to determine the year's basic earnings per share and diluted earnings per share.

Before tax profit from continuing operations	$2 750 000
Ordinary shares, 150 000 issued at $2	300 000
(this figure includes an additional 50 000 ordinary shares issued on 1/10/23 for cash)	
5% non-cumulative preference shares, 500 000 issued at $1	500 000
Average market price for one ordinary share during the year	$15

Additional information

- Tower Ltd entered into a market transaction on 1 December 2023 to repurchase 12 000 ordinary shares at fair value.
- Convertible preference shares: 40 000 shares with an issue value of $100 per share, a cumulative dividend of $15 per share. Each preference share is convertible to 1 ordinary share. Holders of 38 000 convertible preference shares converted their shares into ordinary shares on 1 May 2024.
- The tax rate is 30%.

Required

For Tower Ltd for the year ending 30 June 2024, calculate the:

1. basic earnings per share
2. diluted earnings per share.

SOLUTION

1. *Basic earnings per share*

The formula to calculate the basic earnings per share is as follows.

$$\frac{\text{Profit attributable to ordinary shareholders of the parent entity}}{\text{Weighted average number of ordinary shares outstanding during the period}}$$

First, we need to determine *profit attributable to ordinary shareholders* as follows.

Before tax profit from continuing operations	$2 750 000
Less: Income tax expense*	(825 000)
After tax profit from continuing operations	1 925 000
Preference dividends**	(25 000)
Profit attributable to ordinary shareholders	$1 900 000

*Income tax expense is calculated at 30% of the before tax profit from continuing operations.
**The preference dividends for the year are deducted as they are payable to preference shareholders and not attributable to ordinary shareholders. The amount of $25 000 for preference dividends is calculated as: 500 000 preference shares × 5%.

Second, we need to determine the *weighted average number of ordinary shares outstanding during the period* as follows.

		Issued shares	Treasury shares	Shares outstanding	No. of months	Weighted average
2023						
July 1	Balance of ordinary shares at beginning of period	100 000		100 000		
Oct. 1	Issue of new ordinary shares for cash			150 000	3	25 000
Dec. 1	Repurchase of issued shares	50 000	12 000	138 000	2	25 000
2024						
May 1	Conversion of preference shares	38 000		176 000	5	57 500
June 30	Balance of ordinary shares at end of period	188 000	12 000	176 000	2	29 333
					12	**136 833**

A weighted average is used because the number of ordinary shares on issue can vary during the financial year. The number of ordinary shares at the beginning of the financial period is adjusted for the number of ordinary shares issued or repurchased during the year. A time-factor is then considered to reflect the number of days or months those shares were outstanding before another issue or repurchase took place. For example, Tower Ltd had 100 000 shares outstanding at 1 July 2023. On 1 October 2023, Tower Ltd issued an additional 50 000 ordinary shares, thus increasing the number of ordinary shares outstanding to 150 000. Therefore, the amount of 100 000 ordinary shares outstanding only applies for a period of 3 months out of the 12 months in the year. The time-weighting factor for that period is therefore 3/12. The weighted average number of ordinary shares for that period of time is calculated as: 100 000 shares × 3/12 = 25 000 shares. A summary of each weighted-average calculation is provided below.

	Shares outstanding	No. of months	Weighted average	Weighted average calculation
2023				
July 1	100 000			
Oct. 1	150 000	3	25 000	(100 000 × 3/12)
Dec. 1	138 000	2	25 000	(150 000 × 2/12)
2024				
May 1	176 000	5	57 500	(138 000 × 5/12)
June 30	176 000	2	29 333	(176 000 × 2/12)
		12	136 833	

Finally, the basic earnings per share for Tower Ltd for the year ending 30 June 2024 can now be calculated.

$$\frac{\text{Profit attributable to ordinary shareholders}}{\text{Weighted average number of ordinary shares}} = \frac{\$1\,900\,000}{136\,833}$$
$$= \$13.89$$

2. *Diluted earnings per share*

The calculation for diluted earnings per share uses the weighted average number of ordinary shares that would be issued *assuming* the conversion or issue of any dilutive potential ordinary shares occurs during the financial year. For each group of dilutive potential ordinary shares the increase in earnings attributable to ordinary shareholders needs to be considered along with their dilutive effect. In this example, only the convertible preference shares need to be considered by Tower Ltd for the financial year ending 30 June 2024.

The number of convertible preference shares issued was 40 000. However, only 38 000 preference shares were converted to ordinary shares on a 1-for-1 basis. The profit or loss attributed to ordinary shareholders is to be adjusted for the effect of the dividends that would have been paid on those preference shares if they had not been converted to ordinary shares. The cumulative dividend per share was $15 and they were issued at $100 per share. Therefore, the dividend on these 38 000 preference shares would have been: (38 000 × $100) × ($15/$100) = $3 800 000 × 0.15 = $570 000. This amount is equal to the increase in earnings that would occur upon the conversion of these preference shares.

The weighted average number of ordinary shares outstanding will be increased by the number of ordinary shares issued: 38 000. The additional earnings per share is $15, calculated as $570 000/38 000.

Calculating the dilutive effect helps to determine whether the potential ordinary shares are dilutive or antidilutive.
- If *dilutive*, they will reduce earnings per share or increase the loss per share.
- If *antidilutive*, they will increase the earnings per share or reduce the loss per share.

A control number is required in establishing whether the potential ordinary shares are dilutive or antidilutive. This control number is the *profit or loss from continuing operations attributable to the parent*.

The effect of each potential ordinary shares situation on the calculation of diluted earnings per share is as follows.

	$	Shares	$ per share	
Profit from continuing operations attributable to ordinary shareholders	1 900 000	136 833	13.89	
Increase in earnings from convertible preference shares	570 000	38 000		
	2 470 000	174 833	14.13	Antidilutive

The convertible preference shares are determined to be antidilutive as they have the effect of *increasing* the dilutive earnings per share from 13.89 to 14.1. Therefore, they are not included and the diluted EPS is calculated to be the same as the basic EPS. For the year ending 30 June 2024, the earnings per share for Tower Ltd would be disclosed in the notes to the financial statements as follows.

	Basic EPS	Diluted EPS
Profit from continuing operations attributable to ordinary shareholders	13.89	13.89

COMPREHENSION QUESTIONS

1 What is the earnings per share ratio used for?

2 What are the components in the numerator and the denominator in the earnings per share calculation?

3 Where are the earnings per share figures for a parent entity presented?

4 Why is a time-weighting factor used to determine the number of shares that is used in the calculation of basic earnings per share?

5 What is the treatment applied to treasury shares when calculating the weighted average number of shares used in the earnings per share calculation?

6 Distinguish between basic earnings per share and diluted earnings per share.

7 Explain the effect of potential ordinary shares on the calculation of diluted earnings per share.

8 Explain how the amount of dilution from options is determined.

9 When determining the amount of the proceeds from options and warrants, how is the average share price established?

10 Why are retrospective adjustments made to earnings per share ratios?

11 Where are the basic and diluted earnings per share ratios presented in a set of financial statements?

CASE STUDY 19.1

CONTINGENTLY ISSUABLE ORDINARY SHARES

The directors of Carter Limited are not sure how to, or if they should, include ordinary shares issuable under employee share-based payment schemes in the calculation of the company's earnings per share.

Required

Advise the directors on the considerations required regarding contingently issuable ordinary shares as per AASB 133/IAS 33.

CASE STUDY 19.2

EARNINGS PER SHARE REPORTED IN NOTES

Visit the websites of three Australian companies in the energy industry and access their latest annual reports. Compare the income statements and the notes to the financial statements with regards to information provided on the companies' earnings per share. Report your findings, particularly in relation to items affecting the diluted earnings per share.

CASE STUDY 19.3

COMPARING EARNINGS PER SHARE

Access the 2018 annual report of Wesfarmers Limited and compare the basic and diluted EPS results to those of Woolworths Group Limited for 2018 as provided in this chapter. Discuss which company appeared to have the better earnings per share results.

APPLICATION AND ANALYSIS EXERCISES

★ BASIC | ★ ★ MODERATE | ★ ★ ★ DIFFICULT

19.1 Scope of AASB 133/IAS 33 ★   **LO2**

If an entity presents both consolidated and separate financial statements, which statements are used for the calculation of basic earnings per share? Give reasons for your answer.

19.2 Components of basic earnings per share ★   **LO3**

Which of the following is a component of earnings used in the calculation of basic earnings per share? Give reasons for your answer.

(a) Profit before tax expense

(b) Preference dividends declared during the period

(c) Income tax expense

(d) Profit from discontinued operations

(e) Prior year dividend paid to holders of cumulative preference shares

19.3 Measuring basic earnings per share ★   **LO3**

On 30 June 2023, Samira Ltd determines profit attributable to ordinary shareholders as $600 000. At the beginning of the reporting period the company had 2 400 000 ordinary shares outstanding. The company had no share issues during the period.

Required

Calculate Samira Ltd's 2023 basic earnings per share ratio.

19.4 Theoretical ex-rights value ★ ★   **LO3**

Tully Ltd has 60 000 ordinary shares on issue. The company announced a 1-for-3 rights issue with an exercise price of $5 for each right. The market price of one ordinary share immediately before the exercise of the rights was $7.

Required

Determine the theoretical ex-rights value per share.

19.5 Rights adjustment factor and adjusted basic earnings per share ★ ★   **LO3**

Assume that in exercise 19.4 Tully Ltd announced the rights issue at the beginning of its reporting period (1 July 2023) and the last date for exercising the rights was 1 October 2023. Tully Ltd announced profit attributable to ordinary shareholders of $329 175 for the full reporting period.

Required

Use the theoretical ex-rights value per share determined in exercise 19.4 to calculate the adjustment factor, and calculate adjusted basic earnings per share.

19.6 Categorising ★   **LO3**

An entity announces a share split to occur in the current reporting period. There is no consideration payable by existing shareholders and therefore no corresponding increase in the entity's resources.

Required

Should the entity recognise the additional shares in the weighted average number of shares used in calculating basic earnings per share? Explain.

19.7 Bonus issue of shares ★ ★   **LO3**

On 1 January 2022, Rangeville Ltd has 50 000 ordinary shares outstanding. On 1 March 2022, the company announces a bonus issue of 2 shares for every share held on that date. At year end, Rangeville Ltd's profit attributable to ordinary shareholders amounts to $225 000 (2021: $150 000).

Required

Calculate the 2022 and 2021 basic earnings per share amounts that Rangeville Ltd must disclose in its financial statements for the year ended 31 December 2022.

19.8 Measurement principles ★   **LO3**

The directors of Singh Group have decided to repurchase 200 000 ordinary shares in an 'on-market' arm's length transaction.

Required

Are the treasury shares acquired in this transaction included in the weighted average number of shares outstanding when determining basic earnings per share? Explain your answer.

19.9 Effect of share options on diluted earnings per share ★ ★   **LO4**

Ryan Ltd determines its profit attributable to ordinary shareholders for the reporting period ended 30 June 2023 as $48 000.

The company has calculated its weighted average number of ordinary shares on issue during the period as 240 000. The weighted average number of shares under share options arrangements during the period is 12 000.

The average market price of the entity's shares during the period is $1.20 per share, and the exercise price of shares under option is $0.75.

Required

Prepare a schedule setting out the calculation of basic and diluted earnings per share.

19.10 Determining the additional shares from potentially dilutive options ★ ★   **LO4**

Tenham Ltd has 30 000 ordinary shares outstanding during the reporting period ended 30 June 2024. The average market price of its ordinary shares during the period was $6.75 per share. The company also has 7500 options on issue with an exercise price of $6.00 each.

Required

Calculate the additional shares attributable to ordinary shareholders from the potentially dilutive options.

19.11 Theoretical ex-rights value, rights adjustment factor and basic earnings per share ★ ★ ★   **LO5**

At the beginning of the current reporting period (1 January 2023 – 31 December 2023) Daintree Ltd has 60 000 ordinary shares on issue. The company announced a 1-for-5 rights issue on 1 January 2023. The exercise price is $2 and the last date to exercise the rights is 1 April 2023. The market price of one share immediately before exercise on 1 April 2023 was $3. At the end of the current reporting period, Daintree Ltd determined profit attributable to ordinary shareholders at $244 650.

Required

Determine the theoretical ex-rights value per share, the rights adjustment factor, and the basic earnings per share.

19.12 Disclosure ★ ★ ★   **LO6**

Lismore Ltd operates an executive performance share plan. Under this plan, the company grants rights to employees which are convertible into ordinary shares of the company. It also grants options under the plan. The options have a term of 5 years and are converted into ordinary shares when the executives satisfy their individual performance conditions. The options granted during the current reporting period are considered antidilutive; however, in past years the options granted have been dilutive.

Required

Prepare an appropriate note to be included in the financial statements of Lismore Ltd disclosing the information concerning the classification of potential ordinary shares.

REFERENCE

Woolworths Group Limited 2018, *Annual report 2018*, www.woolworthsgroup.com.au.

ACKNOWLEDGEMENTS

Photo: © S_L / Shutterstock.com

Photo: © John Warburton-Lee Photography / Alamy Stock Photo

Figures 19.1, 19.2, 19.7: © Woolworths Group Limited 2018

Text: © 2019 Australian Accounting Standards Board (AASB). The text, graphics and layout of this publication are protected by Australian copyright law and the comparable law of other countries. No part of the publication may be reproduced, stored or transmitted in any form or by any means without the prior written permission of the AASB except as permitted by law. For reproduction or publication, permission should be sought in writing from the AASB. Requests in the first instance should be addressed to the National Director, Australian Accounting Standards Board, PO Box 204, Collins Street West, Victoria 8007.

CHAPTER 20

Operating segments

CHAPTER AIM

General purpose financial statements present aggregated information about an entity. Users, however, should be able to evaluate the individual business activities and economic environments in which the entity engages and operates. This chapter focuses on the application of AASB 8/IFRS 8 *Operating Segments* and how preparers identify and disclose such segments.

LEARNING OBJECTIVES

After studying this chapter, you should be able to:

20.1 discuss the objectives of financial reporting by segments

20.2 identify the types of entities that are within the scope of AASB 8/IFRS 8

20.3 explain the controversy surrounding the issuance of AASB 8/IFRS 8

20.4 identify operating segments in accordance with AASB 8/IFRS 8

20.5 apply the definition of reportable segments

20.6 explain the disclosure requirements of AASB 8/IFRS 8

20.7 analyse disclosures made by companies applying AASB 8/IFRS 8.

CONCEPTS FOR REVIEW

Before studying this chapter, you should understand and, if necessary, revise:

- the *Conceptual Framework*
- the objectives of financial reporting.

20.1 Objectives of financial reporting by segments

LEARNING OBJECTIVE 20.1 Discuss the objectives of financial reporting by segments.

AASB 8/IFRS 8 *Operating Segments* is primarily a disclosure standard and is particularly relevant for large organisations that operate in different geographical locations and/or offer a diverse range of products or services.

Paragraph 1 of AASB 8/IFRS 8 sets out the standard's core principle as follows.

> An entity shall disclose information to enable users of its financial statements to evaluate the nature and financial effects of the business activities in which it engages and the economic environments in which it operates.

An **operating segment** is defined in paragraph 5 of AASB 8/IFRS 8 as a component of an entity:

(a) that engages in business activities from which it may earn revenues and incur expenses (including revenues and expenses relating to transactions with other components of the same entity),

(b) whose operating results are regularly reviewed by the entity's chief operating decision maker to make decisions about resources to be allocated to the segment and assess its performance, and

(c) for which discrete financial information is available.

Many entities operate in multiple geographical areas or provide products or services that are subject to differing rates of profitability, opportunities for growth, future prospects and risks. Information about an entity's operating segments is relevant to assessing the risks and returns of a diversified or multinational entity where often that information cannot be determined from aggregated data. Therefore, segment information is regarded as necessary to help users of financial statements:

- better understand the entity's past performance
- better assess the entity's risks and returns
- make more informed judgements about the entity as a whole.

Many securities analysts rely on the segment disclosures to help them assess not only an entity's past performance but also to help them predict future performance. Segment disclosures are widely regarded as some of the most useful disclosures in financial statements because of the extent to which they disaggregate financial information into meaningful and often revealing groupings. For example, an entity may appear profitable on a consolidated basis, but segment disclosures may reveal that one part of the business is performing poorly while another part is performing well. The part that is performing poorly may be significant to the entity as a whole and over time continued poor performance by that part (or segment) may cause the entire entity's performance to suffer. This is the kind of information that affects an entity's share price because analysts frequently look at predicted future cash flows in making their share price determinations.

On the other hand, preparers of financial statements may not wish to reveal too much information on a disaggregated basis to their competitors. Some may consider the disclosure requirements of AASB 8/IFRS 8 to be too revealing. For example, a user may be able to determine an entity's profit margin by segment when reading the segment disclosures. This is a key reason why it is unlikely that entities would volunteer to disclose segment information (see section 20.2). Another reason is that it is often a time-consuming exercise to prepare the segment disclosures.

LEARNING CHECK

☐ AASB 8/IFRS 8 *Operating Segments* requires an entity to disclose information to enable the users of its financial statements to evaluate the nature and financial effects of its business activities and operating environments.

☐ An operating segment is a component of an entity that engages in business activities from which it earns revenue and incurs expenses (including revenues and expenses from transactions with other components of the same entity), whose operating results are regularly reviewed by the entity's chief operating decision maker and for which discrete financial information is available.

☐ Segment disclosures are some of the most useful disclosures in financial statements because of the extent to which they disaggregate financial information into meaningful, and often revealing, groupings.

☐ Preparers of financial statements may be reluctant to report segment information because it can be time-consuming and costly, and can reveal more information than the entity would prefer.

20.2 Scope

LEARNING OBJECTIVE 20.2 Identify the types of entities that are within the scope of AASB 8/IFRS 8.

AASB 8/IFRS 8 applies to the financial statements of an entity 'whose debt or equity instruments are traded in a public market' or 'that files, or is in the process of filing, its financial statements with a securities commission or other regulatory organisation for the purpose of issuing any class of instruments in a public market' (paragraph 2(a)). Most commonly 'traded in a public market' would mean a public securities exchange such as the Australian Securities Exchange (ASX).

Where financial statements contain both consolidated financial statements and the parent's separate financial statements (see chapter 26), segment information is required only for the consolidated financial statements (AASB 8/IFRS 8 paragraph 4). However, if consolidated financial statements are not prepared, and the entity is within the scope of the standard, it must apply the standard in its separate or individual financial statements.

If an entity voluntarily chooses to disclose segment information, then it must fully comply with AASB 8/IFRS 8; otherwise it must not describe the disclosed information as segment information (paragraph 3). Voluntary disclosure may occur, for example, where a large public company that is not listed, but has a large number of dependent users (e.g. minority shareholders, employees and creditors), elects to provide segment information. However, voluntary segment disclosures are not expected to be common, for reasons discussed in section 20.1.

LEARNING CHECK

☐ AASB 8/IFRS 8 applies to entities whose debt or equity instruments are traded in a public market or that are in the process of issuing instruments in a public market.

☐ If consolidated financial statements and the parent's separate financial statements are prepared, segment information is required only for the consolidated financial statements.

☐ If consolidated financial statements are not prepared and the entity is within the scope of AASB 8/IFRS 8, then the entity must comply with the standard in its separate or individual financial statements.

☐ Voluntary disclosures claiming to be information about segments must comply with AASB 8/IFRS 8.

20.3 A controversial standard

LEARNING OBJECTIVE 20.3 Explain the controversy surrounding the issuance of AASB 8/IFRS 8.

In November 2006, the IASB issued IFRS 8 *Operating Segments* to replace IAS 14 *Segment Reporting*. The Australian Accounting Standards Board (AASB) issued the Australian equivalent to IFRS 8 as AASB 8 *Operating Segments* in February 2007. AASB 8 was applicable for annual reporting periods beginning on or after 1 January 2009, with early adoption permitted.

The project to develop a new standard on segment reporting was part of the IASB's program for achieving convergence with standards issued by the US Financial Accounting Standards Board (FASB). The starting point was to identify the key differences between the existing standards of the IASB (IAS 14 *Segment Reporting*) and FASB (SFAS 131 *Disclosures about Segments of an Enterprise and Related Information*). In summary, the three main differences were as follows.

1. IAS 14 required segments to be identified either by the goods and services provided to customers or by geographic region whereas SFAS 131 required segments to be identified according to those used by management for internal review.
2. IAS 14 required each reported line item to be measured on a basis consistent with that used in preparing the financial statements in accordance with IFRS whereas SFAS 131 required line item disclosures to be measured according to the basis used by management for internal review.
3. IAS 14 required disclosure of specific and defined line items for each segment whereas SFAS 131 required only the disclosure of non-defined line items regularly reported to management for internal review.

In essence, the IASB had previously taken a more prescriptive view as to how segments should be identified and disclosed whereas the same disclosures under FASB standards were driven by the nature of the segment information provided to management for internal decision making.

The result of the project was to propose a new standard, IFRS 8 *Operating Segments* that adopted the management-perspective approach favoured by the United States. At the time, the IASB justified this decision on the following grounds.

- It would allow users of financial statements to see the operations of the entity through the eyes of management.
- Given such information was already generated from the company's internal reporting systems, the requirements of IFRS 8 could be implemented without any significant additional or recurring cost.

In 2006, the IASB issued exposure draft ED 8 *Operating Segments* proposing the new standard. During the public consultation process that followed, responses were mixed and within the European community a degree of controversy ensued. While some agreed with the views expressed by the IASB, others voiced — and in some cases formally lodged — strong objections. They preferred the prescriptive style of IAS 14, arguing that by giving preparers discretion under the proposed management approach the objectivity of financial statements would be compromised as preparers sought to control the content of segment disclosures. This would lead to the release of inconsistent data, not just from company to company, but also, with organisational change, year to year, resulting in a loss of trend data.

Before it can be formally adopted, an IASB standard requires the endorsement of the European Parliament. The endorsement resolution of IFRS 8 in November 2007 included a statement that the IASB should carry out a review of the new standard 2 years after its implementation. Interestingly, it was not until July 2013, 6 years later, that the IASB released its report and feedback statement titled 'Post-implementation Review: IFRS 8 Operating Segments'. This report was the first of its kind and was the result of an extensive consultative process seeking views from a range of stakeholders. While views from investors were mixed, preparers generally thought the standard worked well. Auditors, accounting firms, standard setters and regulators generally supported the standard, but made some suggestions to improve its application. Overall, the IASB concluded that despite some concerns, the feedback did not suggest any 'significant failings' in the standard. They did concede, however, that there was scope to improve some aspects of the standard and identified some areas that 'warrant further investigation'. The likely outcome is that IFRS 8 — and therefore AASB 8 — will be subject to some amendments in the coming years.

LEARNING CHECK

- ☐ AASB 8/IFRS 8 requires entities to report segment information in the same way that information is reported internally for management purposes.
- ☐ The adoption of IFRS 8 in Europe was contentious, with some arguing that the management approach was insufficiently prescriptive compared to the previous standard, IAS 14. Similar reservations were expressed when Australia adopted AASB 8 in 2007 in place of AASB 114.
- ☐ Results of a review of IFRS 8 conducted by the IASB and released in July 2013 revealed there was general support for the principles of the standard but the IASB undertook to continue investigating concerns that were raised.
- ☐ It is likely that amendments will be made to AASB 8/IFRS 8 in the future.

20.4 Operating segments

LEARNING OBJECTIVE 20.4 Identify operating segments in accordance with AASB 8/IFRS 8.

The term **chief operating decision maker** (CODM) identifies a function, not necessarily a manager with a specific title (AASB 8/IFRS 8 paragraph 7). That function may be a group of people (e.g. an executive committee). Generally, an operating segment has a segment manager who is directly accountable to the CODM. As with the CODM, the term 'segment manager' identifies a function, not necessarily a manager with a specific title. A single manager may be the segment manager for more than one operating segment and the CODM may also be the segment manager for one or more operating segments (paragraph 9). When an entity has a matrix structure, for example, with some managers responsible for different product and service lines and other managers responsible for specific geographical areas, and the CODM regularly reviews the operating results for both sets of components, the entity uses the core principle (see section 20.1) to determine its operating segments (paragraph 10).

As was discussed in section 20.3, this 'management' approach to identifying operating segments is a departure from the more prescriptive style of other standards. The view by some is that this approach has the potential to meet the needs of preparers of financial statements who seek to control the information contained therein when the objective of general purpose financial reports and the accounting standards that underlie these should be to serve the needs of investors and other users of these statements. Figure 20.1 summarises the key decision points in identifying operating segments.

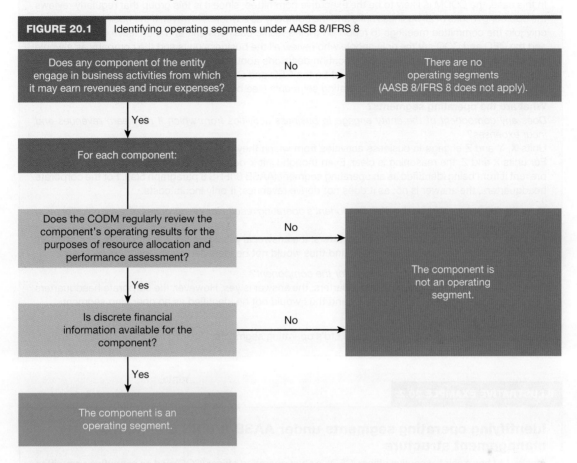

Illustrative examples 20.1 and 20.2 examine the process to identify operating segments.

ILLUSTRATIVE EXAMPLE 20.1

Identifying operating segments under AASB 8/IFRS 8 — divisional management structure

Anstead Ltd has a chief executive officer (CEO), a chief operating officer (COO) and an executive committee comprising the CEO, COO and the heads (general managers) of three business units — units X, Y and Z. Every month, financial information is presented to the executive committee for each of business units X, Y and Z and for Anstead Ltd in order to assess the performance of each business unit and of the company as a whole. Units X, Y and Z each generate revenue and incur expenses from their business activities. Unit Y derives the majority of its revenue from Unit Z. Corporate headquarter costs that are not allocated to units X, Y or Z are also reported separately each month to the executive committee in order to determine the overall results for Anstead Ltd.

Required
Identify the CODM and the operating segments of Anstead Ltd.

Solution

Who is the CODM?

In this case, the CODM is likely to be the executive committee, since it is this group that regularly reviews the operating results of all business units and the company as a whole. However, if the business unit heads only join the committee meetings to report on their specific business unit and then leave the meeting — and the CEO and COO are the only people who review all the business units and the company as a whole and are the ones who make resource allocation decisions about, for example, changing the structure of the business units — then the CODM would be the CEO and COO. In practice, this would not make any difference to the identification of the operating segments (see below).

What are the operating segments?

Does any component of the entity engage in business activities from which it may earn revenues and incur expenses?

Units X, Y and Z engage in business activities from which they may earn revenues and incur expenses. For units X and Z, the reasoning is clear. Even though Unit Y derives its revenue internally, this does not prevent it from being identified as an operating segment (AASB 8/IFRS 8 paragraph 5(a)). For the corporate headquarters, the answer is no, as it does not derive revenues; it only incurs costs.

Does the CODM regularly review the component's operating results for the purposes of resource allocation and performance assessment?

For units X, Y, Z and the corporate headquarters, the answer is yes. However, the corporate headquarters has already failed the first decision point and thus would not be identified as an operating segment.

Is discrete financial information available for the component?

For units X, Y, Z and the corporate headquarters, the answer is yes. However, the corporate headquarters has already failed the first decision point and thus would not be identified as an operating segment.

Conclusion

Units X, Y and Z are identified as Anstead Ltd's operating segments.

ILLUSTRATIVE EXAMPLE 20.2

Identifying operating segments under AASB 8/IFRS 8 — matrix management structure

Ainsley Ltd has a chief executive officer (CEO), a chief operating officer (COO) and an executive committee comprising the CEO, COO and the heads (general managers) of three business units organised according to the company's main products — units X, Y and Z. The company also operates in two distinct geographic regions — Oceania and North America. The heads of these geographic regions attend executive committee meetings, have input into decisions about the distribution of the company's products into their geographic regions and give their views on the performance of the company's products in their regions. Every month, financial information is presented to the executive committee for each of business units X, Y and Z, geographic regions Oceania and North America and for Ainsley Ltd as a whole in order to assess the performance of each business unit, each geographic region and of the company overall. Corporate headquarter costs that are not allocated to units X, Y or Z or to the geographic regions are also reported separately each month to the executive committee in order to determine the results for Ainsley Ltd as a whole. There is necessarily an overlap between the financial information presented for each of units X, Y and Z and the Oceania and North American geographic regions because the product performance reported for each unit is reported again, with that of the other two product units, by geographic region.

Required

Identify the CODM and the operating segments of Ainsley Ltd.

Solution

Who is the CODM?

In this case, the CODM is likely to be the executive committee, since it is the group that regularly reviews the operating results of all business units, geographic regions and the company as a whole. However, the heads of the geographic regions do not appear to be able to make decisions about all business units and the company as a whole; rather, they only have input into the impact of product decisions on their geographic regions. This fact may influence the determination of operating segments (see the conclusion).

What are the operating segments?

Does any component of the entity engage in business activities from which it may earn revenues and incur expenses?

For units X, Y and Z, the answer is clearly yes. For the geographic regions, the answer is also yes, even though the revenues are generated from deployment of the products from units X, Y and Z in the regions. For the corporate headquarters, the answer is no as it does not derive revenues; it only incurs costs.

Does the CODM regularly review the component's operating results for the purposes of resource allocation and performance assessment?
For units X, Y, Z, the geographic regions and the corporate headquarters, the answer is yes. However, the corporate headquarters has already failed the first decision point and thus would not be identified as an operating segment.

Is discrete financial information available for the component?
For units X, Y, Z, the geographic regions and the corporate headquarters, the answer is yes. However, the corporate headquarters has already failed the first decision point and thus would not be identified as an operating segment.

Conclusion
This leaves the entity potentially having two sets of operating segments — units X, Y and Z; and geographic regions Oceania and North America. It is in this situation that paragraph 10 of AASB 8/IFRS 8 directs the entity to the core principle of the standard to decide which set will best 'enable users of its financial statements to evaluate the nature and financial effects of the business activities in which it engages and the economic environments in which it operates'. In this situation, management must exercise judgement. Arguably, in this case, identifying units X, Y and Z as the operating segments best reflects the core principle because the organisation of the company along product lines seems to be dominant over the organisation by geographic lines (as reflected in the slightly lower impact on decision making by the geographic region heads).

LEARNING CHECK

- ☐ The chief operating decision maker (CODM) is a function rather than a specific title and may comprise a group of people rather than an individual.
- ☐ AASB 8/IFRS 8 is seen to be somewhat controversial on the grounds that the 'management' approach in identifying operating segments contradicts the generally prescriptive nature of other accounting standards.

20.5 Reportable segments

LEARNING OBJECTIVE 20.5 Apply the definition of reportable segments.

20.5.1 Identifying reportable segments

Having identified any operating segments the next step is to identify which of these are **reportable segments**. Paragraph 11 of AASB 8/IFRS 8 states that an entity shall report separately information about each operating segment that:

(a) has been identified [as an operating segment] or results from aggregating two or more of those segments in accordance with paragraph 12, and
(b) exceeds the quantitative thresholds in paragraph 13.

The quantitative thresholds

Paragraph 13 of AASB 8/IFRS 8 outlines the quantitative thresholds to apply in the determination of a reportable segment.

An entity shall report separately information about an operating segment that meets any of the following quantitative thresholds:
(a) Its reported revenue, including both sales to external customers and intersegment sales or transfers, is 10 per cent or more of the combined revenue, internal and external, of all operating segments.
(b) The absolute amount of its reported profit or loss is 10 per cent or more of the greater, in absolute amount, of (i) the combined reported profit of all operating segments that did not report a loss and (ii) the combined reported loss of all operating segments that reported a loss.
(c) Its assets are 10 per cent or more of the combined assets of all operating segments.

Upon first reading, paragraph 13(b) may seem confusing. In essence, the preparer must add up the profits of all the operating segments (ignoring any losses) then add up the losses of all the operating segments (ignoring any profits). Whichever of these totals is greater in absolute terms then becomes the base figure against which any individual operating segment's profit or loss is measured in determining whether or not the 10% threshold has been exceeded. Consider illustrative example 20.3.

ILLUSTRATIVE EXAMPLE 20.3

Applying the quantitative thresholds

A reporting entity identifies five operating segments with the following profits/(losses).

Unit	A	B	C	D	E	Total all segments
Profit/(loss)	50	80	(5)	10	(20)	115

Required
Identify the reportable segments of the entity.

Solution
The absolute sum of the profits reported by units A, B and D = 140. The absolute sum of the losses reported by units C and E = 25.

The absolute sum of the profits is the greater so the profits and losses of all five units are measured in absolute terms against 140 to determine the quantitative threshold.

On this basis, units A, B and E would be reportable segments on the basis of the 10% profit or loss threshold.

Paragraph 13 of AASB 8/IFRS 8 goes on to say that if management believes that information about an operating segment would be useful to users of financial statements, it may treat that segment as a reportable segment even if the quantitative thresholds are not met.

The aggregation criteria

The aggregation criteria in paragraph 12 of AASB 8/IFRS 8 provide that two or more operating segments may be aggregated into a single operating segment if aggregation is consistent with the core principle of the standard, the segments have similar economic characteristics and the segments are similar in *each* of:

(a) the nature of the products and services;
(b) the nature of the production processes;
(c) the type or class of customer for their products and services;
(d) the methods used to distribute their products or provide their services; and
(e) if applicable, the nature of the regulatory environment, for example, banking, insurance or public utilities.

An entity may combine operating segments that do not meet the quantitative thresholds to produce a reportable segment only if the segments have similar economic characteristics and meet the aggregation criteria of paragraph 12 (AASB 8/IFRS 8 paragraph 14).

The 75% threshold

Paragraph 15 of AASB 8/IFRS 8 requires that an entity must keep identifying operating segments as reportable (even if they do not meet the criteria in paragraph 13) until at least 75% of the entity's revenue is included in reportable segments. Importantly, segment revenue here is *external* revenue only and the total revenue is that of the consolidated group.

What happens to segments that are not reportable?

Paragraph 16 of AASB 8/IFRS 8 states that business activities and operating segments that are not reportable must be combined and disclosed as 'all other segments' separately from the reconciling items required by paragraph 28 (see section 20.6.5).

Vertically integrated businesses

As noted above, AASB 8/IFRS 8 does not distinguish between revenues and expenses from transactions with third parties and those from transactions *within the group* for the purposes of identifying operating segments (paragraph 5). Therefore, in an entity with internal vertically integrated businesses, it is possible that such internal businesses might be identified as operating segments under AASB 8/IFRS 8.

How many segments are enough?

Paragraph 19 of AASB 8/IFRS 8 provides additional guidance to entities regarding the maximum number of reportable segments — indicating that once ten segments have been identified as reportable it is reasonable to consider whether a practical limit has been reached.

Figure 20.2 summarises the key decision points in identifying reportable segments, and continues from figure 20.1.

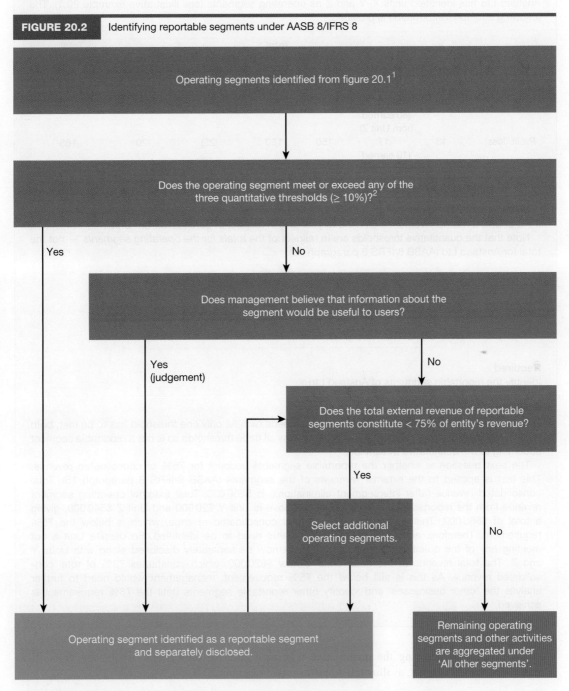

| FIGURE 20.2 | Identifying reportable segments under AASB 8/IFRS 8 |

1. Operating segments may be aggregated if they have similar economic characteristics and are similar in each of the aggregation criteria.
2. Operating segments may be combined if they have similar economic characteristics and are similar in the majority of the aggregation criteria.

20.5.2 Applying the definition of reportable segments

Building on illustrative example 20.1, example 20.4 illustrates how Anstead Ltd identifies its reportable segments under AASB 8/IFRS 8.

ILLUSTRATIVE EXAMPLE 20.4

Identifying reportable segments under AASB 8/IFRS 8

Anstead Ltd has identified units X, Y and Z as operating segments (see illustrative example 20.1). The following additional information is provided.

	Unit X $'000	Unit Y $'000	Unit Z $'000	Total operating segments $'000	Corporate headquarters $'000	Other businesses $'000	Total Anstead Ltd (consolidated) $'000
Revenue	60	100 (80 earned from Unit Z)	540	700	—	230	850
Profit/(loss)	13	17 (10 earned from Unit Z)	150	180	(25)	20	165
Assets	200	600	1 250	2 050	250	200	2 500

Management has determined that units X, Y and Z do not meet the aggregation criteria of AASB 8/IFRS 8. Unit Z has no inventories on hand at year-end in respect of purchases from Unit Y.

Note that the quantitative thresholds are in respect of the *totals for the operating segments* — not the total for Anstead Ltd (AASB 8/IFRS 8 paragraph 13).

	Revenue % of total	Profit % of total	Assets % of total
Unit X	8.6	7.2	9.7
Unit Y	14.3	9.5	29.3
Unit Z	77.1	83.3	61.0

Required
Identify the reportable segments of Anstead Ltd.

Solution
Unit Z exceeds all three thresholds while Unit Y exceeds two. As only one threshold has to be met, both these units are reportable segments. Unit X falls below all three thresholds so is not a reportable segment according to the quantitative thresholds.

The next question is whether the reportable segments account for 75% of consolidated revenue. This test is applied to the *external* revenues of the segments (AASB 8/IFRS 8 paragraph 15). Total consolidated revenue (after intersegment eliminations) is $850 000. Total external operating segment revenue from the reportable segments identified above is Unit Y $20 000 and Unit Z $540 000, giving a total of $560 000. This constitutes 66% of total consolidated revenue, which is below the 75% requirement. Therefore, additional operating segments need to be identified. So despite Unit X not meeting any of the quantitative thresholds, it must now be separately disclosed along with Units Y and Z. The total revenue of the three units is now $620 000, which constitutes 73% of total consolidated revenue. As this is still below the 75% requirement, management would need to further analyse the 'other businesses' and identify other reportable segments until the 75% requirement is achieved.

Another aspect of applying the quantitative criteria is that the allocations of relevant amounts to segments needs to occur first, as illustrated in illustrative example 20.5.

Applying the requirements — determining segment revenue, expense, assets and liabilities

The following financial information is reported to the CODM for diversified manufacturing company Beenleigh Ltd for the year ended 30 June 2020.

	Wine $m	Water heaters $m	Olive oil $m	All segments $m
Segment revenue	150	90	10	250
Segment result (profit)	14	5	1	20
Segment assets	500	200	100	800

Additional information
- Total consolidated revenue of Beenleigh Ltd is $253 million.
- Total consolidated profit — after income tax expense of $5 million, interest income of $1 million and a gain on disposal of investments of $2 million — is $8 million.
- Total consolidated liabilities of Beenleigh Ltd are $200 million.
- Liabilities include borrowings of $150 million and their related interest expense of $10 million.
- Liabilities of $40 million are trade creditors and other payables directly attributable to the wine segment.
- Liabilities of $10 million are trade creditors and other payables directly attributable to the water heaters segment.
- All assets and related depreciation have been allocated to the business segments.

Required
Determine the allocation of segment revenue, expense, assets and liabilities.

Solution
The allocation of segment revenue, expense, assets and liabilities is determined as follows.

	Wine $m	Water heaters $m	Olive oil $m	Unallocated $m	Consolidated $m
Revenue	150	90	10	3[a]	253
Expenses	(136)	(85)	(9)	(15)	(245)
Segment result (profit)	14	5	1	(12)[b]	8
Assets	500	200	100	—	800
Liabilities	40	10	—	150[c]	200

(a) Interest income and gain on disposal of investments.
(b) $3 million revenue and $15 million expenses (interest expense and income tax expense).
(c) Borrowings are not allocated because the segments' operations are not primarily of a financial nature.

This example also shows that before an entity can apply the quantitative criteria to determine its reportable segments it needs first to calculate correctly the segment allocations and unallocated amounts.

☐ An entity must report information separately for each identified operating segment that exceeds any of the quantitative thresholds relating to revenue, profit or loss and assets.
☐ Segments that meet certain aggregation criteria may be combined for reporting purposes.
☐ At least 75% of the entity's total revenue must be included in reportable segments.
☐ Segments that are not reportable must be combined and reported as 'all other segments'.

20.6 Disclosure

LEARNING OBJECTIVE 20.6 Explain the disclosure requirements of AASB 8/IFRS 8.

As explained in section 20.3, the approach to disclosure is a key point of difference between AASB 8/IFRS 8 and its predecessor AASB 114/IAS 14. While AASB 114/IAS 14 was prescriptive, AASB 8/IFRS 8 sets out an approach in which operating segment disclosure is determined according to how management internally evaluates and measures the performance of its operations.

The general principle of disclosure is set out in paragraph 20 of AASB 8/IFRS 8, which is, in effect, a restatement of the core principle of the standard:

> An entity shall disclose information to enable users of its financial statements to evaluate the nature and financial effects of the business activities in which it engages and the economic environments in which it operates.

To give effect to this principle, paragraph 21 requires an entity to disclose:

(a) general information as described in paragraph 22;

(b) information about reported segment profit or loss, including specified revenues and expenses included in reported segment profit or loss, segment assets, segment liabilities and the basis of measurement, as described in paragraphs 23–27; and

(c) reconciliations of the totals of segment revenues, reported segment profit or loss, segment assets, segment liabilities and other material segment items to corresponding entity amounts as described in paragraph 28.

20.6.1 General information

Under paragraph 22 of AASB 8/IFRS 8, an entity shall disclose:
- factors used to identify the entity's reportable segments, including the basis of organisation
- types of products or services from which each reportable segment derives its revenues.

In complying with the first point, for example, management would disclose whether it identified operating segments based on products or services, or geographic regions, and whether segments have been aggregated.

20.6.2 Information about profit or loss, assets and liabilities

Paragraph 23 of AASB 8/IFRS 8 states that an entity shall report 'a measure' of profit or loss and, if such amounts are regularly provided to the CODM, 'a measure' of total assets and total liabilities for each reportable segment.

The amount of each segment item reported shall be the measure reported to the CODM for the purposes of making decisions about allocating resources to the segment and assessing its performance (AASB 8/IFRS 8 paragraph 25). In other words, whatever the CODM uses to measure and assess the operating segment is what is disclosed under AASB 8/IFRS 8. This extends to the allocation of amounts of profit or loss and assets and liabilities to segments. If the CODM uses information based on amounts that are allocated to segments, then those amounts should be allocated for the purposes of disclosing 'a measure'.

In respect of segment profit or loss, paragraph 23 of AASB 8/IFRS 8 requires certain line items to be disclosed *only* if these items are included in the measure of segment profit or loss reported to the CODM, or are otherwise regularly provided to the CODM:

(a) revenues from external customers;

(b) revenues from transactions with other operating segments of the same entity;

(c) interest revenue;

(d) interest expense;

(e) depreciation and amortisation;

(f) material items of income and expense disclosed in accordance with paragraph 97 of AASB 101 *Presentation of Financial Statements*;

(g) the entity's interest in the profit or loss of associates and joint ventures accounted for by the equity method;

(h) income tax expense or income; and

(i) material non-cash items other than depreciation and amortisation.

Interest revenue and interest expense may be reported on a net basis only if a majority of the segment's revenues are from interest and the CODM relies primarily on net interest revenue to assess the performance of the segment. This may be the case, for example, in the banking industry.

In respect of segment assets, certain line items are also required (AASB 8/IFRS 8 paragraph 24) to be disclosed only if these items are included in the measure of segment assets reported to the CODM, or are otherwise regularly provided to the CODM:
- the amount of investment in associates and joint ventures accounted for by the equity method
- the amounts of additions to non-current assets (with certain exceptions).

The notable feature of these disclosure requirements is the lack of prescription: if the items listed (with the exception of a measure of segment profit or loss, which must always be disclosed) are reported to the CODM then they must be disclosed. What is not reported internally need not be disclosed externally. Furthermore, *how* the amount of an item is measured internally is how the amount is measured externally for that item in the segment disclosure, even if the measurement basis is not in accordance with accounting standards.

20.6.3 Measurement

Because management has discretion in how segment information is measured for internal decision making, paragraph 27 of AASB 8/IFRS 8 requires the entity to provide an explanation of such measurements of profit or loss, and, if applicable, assets and liabilities, for each reportable segment. This includes the following.

- The basis of accounting for transactions between reportable segments.
- The nature of any differences between the measurements of the reportable segments' profits or losses and the entity's profit or loss before income taxes and discontinued operations (i.e. the profit or loss reported in the statement of profit or loss and other comprehensive income in accordance with accounting standards). For example, the CODM may apply the cash basis for measuring the segment profit or loss, which clearly differs from the accrual basis mandated by accounting standards. The CODM may determine 'cash profit' to be profit or loss before fair value movements, depreciation and amortisation, and impairment charges.
- The nature of any differences between the measurements of the reportable segments' assets and the entity's assets. For example, this could include accounting policies and policies for allocation of jointly used assets.
- The nature of any differences between the measurements of the reportable segments' liabilities and the entity's liabilities. For example, this could include accounting policies and policies for allocation of jointly utilised liabilities.
- The nature of any changes from prior periods in the measurement methods used to determine reported segment profit or loss and the effect, if any, of those changes on the measure of segment profit or loss. For example, if the CODM decides to change the measure of segment profit or loss used from one that excludes fair value movements to one that includes fair value movements, this fact would need to be disclosed together with the impact on reported segment profit or loss.
- The nature and effect of any asymmetrical allocations to reportable segments. For example, an entity might allocate depreciation expense to a segment without allocating the related depreciable assets to that segment.

20.6.4 Reconciliations

Paragraph 28 of AASB 8/IFRS 8 requires an entity to provide reconciliations of all of the following.

- The total of the reportable segments' revenues to the entity's revenue. In illustrative example 20.4, ignoring the identification of additional segments to meet the 75% threshold, this would be a reconciliation of total operating segments' revenues of $700 000 to Anstead Ltd's revenue of $850 000.
- The total of the reportable segments' measures of profit or loss to the entity's profit or loss before income tax and discontinued operations (or, if items such as income tax are allocated to segments, to profit or loss after income tax). In illustrative example 20.4, ignoring the identification of additional segments to meet the 75% threshold, this would be a reconciliation of total operating segments' profit of $180 000 to Anstead Ltd's profit of $165 000.
- The total of the reportable segments' assets (if reported) to the entity's assets. In illustrative example 20.4, ignoring the identification of additional segments to meet the 75% threshold, this would be a reconciliation of total operating segments' assets of $2.05 million to Anstead Ltd's assets of $2.5 million.
- The total of the reportable segments' liabilities (if reported) to the entity's liabilities.
- The total of the reportable segments' amounts for every other material item of information disclosed to the corresponding amount for the entity. This would include, for example, the line items disclosed under paragraphs 23 and 24 of AASB 8/IFRS 8, if the amount disclosed differs from that disclosed in the entity's statement of profit or loss and other comprehensive income or statement of financial position.

All material reconciling items must be separately identified and described. Using illustrative example 20.4, assuming the amounts are material, Anstead Ltd would need to disclose its reconciliation of total reportable segments' profit to the entity profit as follows.

	$'000
Total reportable segments' profit	180
Less: Inter-segment profit	(10)
Less: Corporate headquarters costs not allocated to reportable segments	(25)
Add: Profit from other businesses not identified as reportable segments	20
Total Anstead Ltd profit	165

20.6.5 Entity-wide disclosures

The following disclosures apply to all entities subject to AASB 8/IFRS 8, including those that have only one reportable segment (unless the information is already provided as part of the reportable segment information).

- *Information about products and services:* revenues from external customers for *each product or service* or each group of similar products or services. In this case, the amount of revenues must be based on the financial information used to produce the entity's financial statements, *not* based on amounts reported to the CODM. If the information is not available and the cost to develop it would be excessive, the entity need not disclose the information but it must state this fact (AASB 8/IFRS 8 paragraph 32). This requirement is potentially onerous in that it is possible that one reportable segment includes numerous products and/or services.
- *Information about geographical areas:* revenues from external customers and non-current assets (i) attributed to/located in the entity's country of domicile and (ii) attributed to/located in foreign countries. If revenues or non-current assets attributed to/located in an individual foreign country are material, those revenues/assets shall be disclosed separately. The entity must also disclose the basis for attributing revenues from external customers to individual countries. In this case, as in paragraph 32, the amount of revenues and assets must be based on the financial information used to produce the entity's financial statements. If the information is not available and the cost to develop it would be excessive then the entity need not disclose the information but it must state this fact (AASB 8/IFRS 8 paragraph 33).
- *Information about major customers:* if revenues from transactions with a single external customer amount to 10% or more of an entity's revenues, disclose that fact, the total amount of revenues from each such customer, and the segment or segments reporting the revenues. The identity of the customer or customers does not have to be disclosed.

20.6.6 Comparative information

There are a few circumstances in which comparative information must be restated or otherwise taken into account.

- If an operating segment was a reportable segment for the immediately preceding prior period but is not for the current period, and management decides that the segment is of continuing significance, information about that segment must continue to be reported in the current period (AASB 8/IFRS 8 paragraph 17).
- If an operating segment becomes a reportable segment for the current period, comparative information must be restated to reflect the newly reportable segment, even if that segment did not meet the criteria for reportability in the prior period. This is required unless the information is not available and the cost to develop it would be excessive (AASB 8/IFRS 8 paragraph 18).
- If management changes its measure of segment profit or loss, paragraph 27(e) requires disclosure of the nature and effect of that change, as discussed above. The standard does not specify whether comparative information must be restated in this circumstance. However, applying the principles of AASB 108/IAS 8 *Accounting Policies, Changes in Accounting Estimates and Errors* and the general principle apparent in AASB 8/IFRS 8 in respect of consistency of comparative information, one would expect the comparative information to be restated in this circumstance.
- If an entity changes the structure of its internal organisation in a manner that causes the composition of its reportable segments to change, the corresponding information for prior periods, including interim periods, must be restated. This applies unless the information is not available and the cost to develop

it would be excessive (AASB 8/IFRS 8 paragraph 29). Note that in this case the exemption from restatement applies to each individual item of disclosure. This could result in restatement of some items and not of others.

- If an entity changes the structure of its internal organisation in a manner that causes the composition of its reportable segments to change and the corresponding information for prior periods is *not* restated, the entity must disclose the segment information for the current period on both the old and the new basis. This applies unless the information is not available and the cost to develop it would be excessive (AASB 8/IFRS 8 paragraph 30).

LEARNING CHECK

☐ AASB 8/IFRS 8 sets out an approach in which segment disclosure is determined according to how management internally evaluates and measures the performance of its operations.

☐ Entities must disclose general information about the basis of its organisation and the types of products or services from which operating segment revenue is derived.

☐ For each operating segment, entities are required to disclose information about profit or loss and, where such information is regularly provided to the CODM, assets and liabilities; how these items were measured for internal evaluation; and reconciliations of these measurements with totals reported by the entity.

☐ All entities subject to AASB 8/IFRS 8 must report certain information about products and services, geographical areas and major customers.

☐ In certain circumstances, entities may need to restate or take into account comparative information.

20.7 Applying the disclosures in practice

LEARNING OBJECTIVE 20.7 Analyse disclosures made by companies applying AASB 8/IFRS 8.

The following examples illustrate how two Australian companies have applied the requirements of AASB 8/IFRS 8.

Figure 20.3 is an extract from the 2018 annual report of Woolworths Group Limited, a major retailing company listed on the ASX.

FIGURE 20.3 Segment disclosures note, Woolworths

Notes to the consolidated financial statements

2 GROUP PERFORMANCE

2.1 Segment disclosures from continuing operations

2.1.1 Operating segment reporting
Reportable segments are identified on the basis of internal reports on the business units of the Group that are regularly reviewed by the Chief Executive Officer in order to allocate resources to the segment and assess its performance. These business units offer different products and services and are managed separately.

The Group's reportable segments are as follows:
- **Australian Food** — procurement of food products for resale to customers in Australia;
- **New Zealand Food** — procurement of food and drinks for resale to customers in New Zealand;
- **Endeavour Drinks** — procurement of drinks for resale to customers in Australia;
- **BIG W** — procurement of discount general merchandise products for resale to customers in Australia;
- **Hotels** — provision of leisure and hospitality services including food and drinks, accommodation, entertainment and gaming in Australia; and
- **Other** — consists of the Group's other operating segments that are not separately reportable as well as various support functions including property and central overhead costs.

There are varying levels of integration between the Australian Food, Endeavour Drinks and Hotels reportable segments. This includes the common usage of property and services and administration functions. Inter-segment pricing is determined on an arm's length basis.

Performance is measured based on segment earnings before interest and tax (EBIT) which is consistent with the way management monitor and report the performance of these segments.

▶

2018	Australian Food $m	New Zealand Food $m	Endeavour Drinks $m	Big W $m	Hotels $m	Other $m	Consolidated continuing operations $m
Revenue from the sale of goods and services	37 379	5 898	8 271	3 566	1 612	–	56 726
Other operating revenue	235	4				–	239
Inter-segment revenue	–	–				17	17
Segment revenue	37 614	5 902	8 271	3 566	1 612	17	56 982
Eliminations						(17)	(17)
Unallocated revenue[1]						222	222
Total revenue	**37 614**	**5 902**	**8 271**	**3 566**	**1 612**	**222**	**57 187**
Earnings/(loss) before interest and tax	1 757	262	516	(110)	259	(136)	2 548
Financing costs							(154)
Profit before income tax							2 394
Income tax expense							(718)
Profit for the period from continuing operations							**1 676**
Depreciation and amortisation	673	117	87	80	102	44	1 103
Capital expenditure[2]	1 179	197	169	95	157	139	1 936
2017							
Revenue from the sale of goods and services	35 836	5 843	7 913	3 542	1 553	154[5]	54 841
Other operating revenue	188	5				–	193
Inter-segment revenue	–	–				87	87
Segment revenue	36 024	5 848	7 913	3 542	1 553	241	55 121
Eliminations[3]						(87)	(87)
Unallocated revenue[1]						244	244
Total revenue	**36 024**	**5 848**	**7 913**	**3 542**	**1 553**	**398**	**55 278**
Earnings/(loss) before interest and tax	1 603	292	503	(151)	233	(154)	2 326
Financing costs							(194)
Profit before income tax							2 132
Income tax expense							(651)
Profit for the period from continuing operations							**1 481**
Depreciation and amortisation	618	111	85	79	105	40	1 038
Impairment of non-financial assets[4]	–	–	17	21	–	–	38
Capital expenditure[2]	918	182	116	31	112	481	1 840

Table notes

1. Unallocated revenue is comprised of rent and other revenue from non-operating activities across the Group.
2. Capital expenditure is comprised of property, plant and equipment additions and intangible asset acquisitions.
3. Due to a realignment in the operating model for the Group's international procurement function in the current year, the prior period comparatives have been reclassified to conform.
4. Refer to Note 3.5 for further detail on the impairment of non-financial assets.
5. Revenue from the sale of goods in Other relates to EziBuy. The sale of EziBuy completed on 25 June 2017.

2.1.2 Geographical information

The table below provides information on the geographical location of revenue from continuing operations and non-current assets (excluding financial instruments, deferred tax assets and inter-company receivables). Revenue from external customers is allocated to a geography based on the location in which the sales originated. Non-current assets are allocated based on the location of the operation to which they relate.

	Australia		New Zealand		Consolidated continuing operations	
	2018 A$m	2017 A$m	2018 A$m	2017 A$m	2018 A$m	2017 A$m
Revenue from the sale of goods and services	50 797	48 808	5 929	6 033	56 726	54 841
Other operating revenue	235	188	4	5	239	193
Other revenue	175	201	47	43	222	244
Revenue from external customers	51 207	49 197	5 980	6 081	57 187	55 278
Non-current assets	12 487	11 873	3 253	3 287	15 740	15 160

Source: Woolworths Group Limited (2018, pp. 72–3).

Points to note about figure 20.3

1. The group has identified six reportable segments, based on different products and services that require different technology and marketing strategies.
2. There is no disclosure of segment assets or liabilities. This indicates that these are not reported internally to the CODM.
3. Of the six segments, Australian Food contributes 65.8% of the group's revenues ($37 614/$57 187) and 69.0% of the group's EBIT. It is also interesting to note the loss reported by the Big W segment. This highlights how segment disclosures enable a more detailed and insightful analysis of the group's results.
4. The geographical information disclosures (as required by paragraph 33) show that the majority of the group's external revenues are generated from Australian customers and that most of the group's non-current assets are also based in Australia.
5. The disclosures about products and services required by paragraph 32 are not made separately because each segment is defined based on its different products and services.
6. In the absence of a statement to the contrary, Woolworths Group Limited has no single customer from whom greater than 10% of the group's revenue is generated.

The second example, presented in figure 20.4, comes from the 2018 annual report of Wesfarmers Limited, another ASX-listed company, which operates in the retail and industrial sectors.

FIGURE 20.4   Segment information note, Wesfarmers

Segment information for the year ended 30 June 2018

The Group's operating segments are organised and managed separately according to the nature of the products and services provided.

Each segment represents a strategic business unit that offers different products and operates in different industries and markets. The Board and executive management team (the chief operating decision-makers) monitor the operating results of the business units separately for the purpose of making decisions about resource allocation and performance assessment.

The types of products and services from which each reportable segment derives its revenues are disclosed below. Segment performance is evaluated based on operating profit or loss (segment result), which in certain respects, is presented differently from operating profit or loss in the consolidated financial statements.

Interest income and expenditure are not allocated to operating segments, as this type of activity is managed on a Group basis.

Transfer prices between business segments are set on an arm's length basis in a manner similar to transactions with third parties. Segment revenue, expenses and results include transfers between business segments. Those transfers are eliminated on consolidation and are not considered material.

The operating segments and their respective types of products and services are as follows:

Retail
Bunnings
- Retailer of building material and home and garden improvement products; and
- Servicing project builders and the housing Industry.

Coles
- Super market and liquor retailer, including a hotel portfolio;
- Retailer of fuel and operator of convenience stores; and
- Coles property business operator.

Officeworks
- Retailer and supplier of office products and solutions for home, small-to-medium sized businesses and education.

Department Stores
Kmart
- Retailer of apparel and general merchandise, including toys, leisure, entertainment, home and consumables; and
- Provision of automotive service, repairs and tyre service.

Target
- Retailer of apparel, homewares and general merchandise, including accessories, electricals and toys.

Industrials
Industrial and Safety (WIS)
- Supplier and distributor of maintenance, repair and operating products;
- Manufacturer and marketing of industrial gases and equipment;
- Supplier, manufacturer and distributor of workwear clothing in Australia and internationally;
- Specialised supplier and distributor of industrial safety products and services; and
- Provider of risk management and compliance services.

Chemicals, Energy and Fertilisers (WesCEF)
- Manufacturer and marketing of chemicals for industry, mining and mineral processing;
- Manufacturer and marketing of broadacre and horticultural fertilisers;
- National marketing and distributor of LPG and LNG; and
- LPG and LNG extraction for domestic and export markets.

Resources
- Interest in the Bengalla joint operation.

Other
Includes:
- *Forest products:* non-controlling interest in Wespine Industries Pty Ltd;
- *Property:* non-controlling interest in BWP Trust;
- *Investment banking:* non-controlling interest in Gresham Partners Group Limited;
- *Private equity investment:* non-controlling interests in Gresham Private Equity Fund No. 2; and
- *Corporate:* includes treasury, head office, central support functions and other corporate entity expenses. Corporate is not considered an operating segment and includes activities that are not allocated to other operating segments.

Revenues by segment for FY2018
From continuing operations

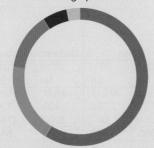

	$m
● Coles	39 388
● Bunnings	12 544
● Department Stores	8 837
● Industrials	3 980
● Officeworks	2 142

Seasonality

Revenue and earnings of various businesses are affected by seasonality and cyclicality as follows:

- For retail divisions, earnings are typically greater in the December half of the financial year due to the impact of the Christmas holiday shopping period;
- For Resources, the majority of the entity's coal contracted tonnages are renewed on an annual basis; and
- For Chemicals, Energy and Fertilisers, earnings are typically greater in the second half of the financial year due to the impact of the Western Australian winter season break on fertiliser sales.

Geographical information

The table below provides information on the geographical location of revenue and non-current assets (other than financial instruments, deferred tax assets and pension assets). Revenue from external customers is allocated to a geography based on the location of the operation in which it was derived. Non-current assets are allocated based on the location of the operation to which they relate. Revenue and non-current assets relating to discontinued operations have been excluded.

	Revenue		Non-current assets	
	2018 $m	2017 $m	2018 $m	2017 $m
Australia	64 909	63 073	26 856	27 170
New Zealand	1 912	1 774	203	303
United Kingdom	42	47	4	5
Other foreign countries	20	19	6	4
	66 883	64 913	27 069	27 482

Continuing operations

	Bunnings		Coles		Department stores		Office works	
	2018 $m	2017 $m	2018 $m	2017 $m	2018 $m	2017 $m	2018 $m	2017 $m
Segment revenue	12 544	11 514	39 388	39 217	8 837	8 528	2 142	1 964
Adjusted EBITDA	1 683	1 505	2 151	2 256	862	739	181	168
Depreciation and amortisation	(179)	(171)	(651)	(647)	(202)	(196)	(25)	(24)
Segment result	**1 504**	**1 334**	**1 500**	**1 609**	**660**	**543**	**156**	**144**
Items not included in segment result	—	—	—	—	(306)	—	—	—
EBIT								
Finance costs								
Profit before income tax expense								
Income tax expense								
Profit attributable to members of the parent								
Others segment information								
Segment assets	5 025	4 846	21 180	21 140	3 617	3 928	1 452	1 401
Investments in associates and joint venture	17	17	—	—	—	—	—	—
Tax assets								
Total assets								
Segment liabilities	(1 875)	(1 785)	(4 561)	(4 245)	(1 482)	(1 423)	(532)	(488)
Tax liabilities								
Interest-bearing liabilities								
Total liabilities								
Other net assets	(3 098)	(2 825)	(10)	(209)	(47)	(142)	8	(25)
Net assets	69	253	16 609	16 686	2 088	2 363	928	888
Capital expenditure	497	367	762	811	293	222	45	36
Share net profit or loss of associates and joint venture included in EBIT	—	—	—	—	—	—	—	—

											Discontinued operations	
	Industrials											
	WIS		WesCEF		Resources		Other		Consolidated			
	2018 $m	2017 $m	2018 $m	2017 $m	2018 $m	2017 $m	2018 $m	2017 $m	2018 $m	2017 $m	2018 $m	2017 $m
	1 750	1 776	1 830	1 639	400	287	(8)	(12)	66 883	64 913	2 995	3 531
	159	158	469	472	190	107	(130)	(53)	5 565	5 352	6	316
	(41)	(43)	(79)	(77)	(18)	(16)	(3)	(1)	(1 198)	(1 175)	(85)	(91)
	118	115	390	395	172	91	(133)	(54)	4 367	4 177	(79)	225
	—	—	—	—	—	—	—	—	(306)	—	(1 186)	—
									4 061	4 177	(1 265)	225
									(211)	(248)	(10)	(16)
									3 850	3 929	(1 275)	209
									(1 246)	(1 169)	(132)	(96)
									2 604	2 760	(1 407)	113
	1 698	1 661	1 539	1 484	263	260	719	1 121	35 493	35 841	—	2 600
	—	—	202	183			529	503	748	703	—	—
							692	971	692	971	—	—
									36 933	37 515	—	2 600
	(335)	(385)	(355)	(270)	(68)	(63)	(548)	(684)	(9 756)	(9 343)	—	(1 126)
							(299)	(292)	(299)	(292)	—	—
							(4 124)	(5 143)	(4 124)	(5 413)	—	—
									(14 179)	(15 048)	—	(1 126)
	(631)	(585)	(745)	(793)	(191)	(91)	4 714	6 681	—	2 011	—	(2 011)
	732	691	641	604	4	106	1 683	2 887	22 754	24 478	—	(537)
	50	34	60	44	14	13	2	—	1 723	1 527	139	156
	—	—	41	61	—	—	56	86	97	147	—	—

Source: Wesfarmers Limited (2018, pp. 105–7).

Note: During the course of 2018, Wesfarmers demerged Coles, which is now listed separately on the ASX.

While the segment disclosures look quite similar, it is interesting to note the following comparisons and contrasts between Wesfarmers Limited and Woolworths Group Limited.

- Wesfarmers Limited's disclosure note specifically refers to the board and executive management team as its chief operating decision makers.
- Wesfarmers Limited's segment information includes allocations for assets and liabilities, a clear indication that the CODM considers this when reviewing segment performance.
- While no specific statement is made, the absence of a disclosure about major customers confirms there is no single customer from which greater than 10% of the entity's revenue is derived.
- The geographical information indicates Wesfarmers Limited's concentration in Australia is greater than Woolworths Group Limited's with 97% of revenue and over 99% of non-current assets allocated to this location.

LEARNING CHECK

☐ Segment disclosures in published accounts can be quite extensive and provide a useful insight to the operations of an entity.

☐ Segment disclosures from one company to another may vary according to the information provided to the CODM for internal review.

SUMMARY

AASB 8/IFRS 8 *Operating Segments* is primarily a disclosure standard and is particularly relevant for large organisations that operate in different geographical locations and/or in diverse businesses. Information about an entity's segments is relevant to assessing the risks and returns of a diversified or multinational entity where often that information cannot be determined from aggregated data.

AASB 8/IFRS 8 adopted a management approach to identifying segments rather than prescribing segment disclosures. This means segment disclosure is determined according to how management internally evaluates and measures the performance of its operations. Segment disclosures from one company to another may vary according to the information provided to the CODM for internal review. This management approach may enable investors to evaluate the company on the same basis used by management in its decision making; however, many argue that management can take advantage of the discretion provided in IFRS 8 in order to control the information provided to users. AASB 8/IFRS 8 has, thus, been a controversial standard.

Under AASB 8/IFRS 8, an entity must report information separately for each identified operating segment that exceeds any of the quantitative thresholds relating to revenue, profit or loss and assets. Segments that meet certain aggregation criteria may be combined for reporting purposes. At least 75% of the entity's total revenue must be included in reportable segments. Segments that are not reportable must be combined and reported as 'all other segments'.

Entities are required to disclose general information about the basis of their organisation and the types of products or services from which operating segment revenue is derived. For each operating segment, entities are required to disclose information about profit or loss and, where such information is regularly provided to the CODM, assets and liabilities; how these items were measured for internal evaluation; and reconciliations of these measurements with totals reported by the entity. All entities subject to AASB 8/IFRS 8 must report certain information about products and services, geographical areas and major customers. In certain circumstances, entities may need to restate or take into account comparative information. Segment disclosures in published accounts can be quite extensive and provide a useful insight to the operations of an entity.

KEY TERMS

chief operating decision maker The person or group responsible for making operating decisions across the entity.

operating segment A component of an entity that engages in business activities from which it may earn revenues and incur expenses (including revenues and expenses relating to transactions with other components of the same entity); whose operating results are regularly reviewed by the entity's chief operating decision maker to make decisions about resources to be allocated to the segment and assess its performance; and for which discrete financial information is available.

reportable segments Operating segments for which an entity reports separate information.

COMPREHENSION QUESTIONS

1 Segment disclosures are widely regarded as some of the most useful disclosures in financial statements because of the extent to which they disaggregate financial information into meaningful and often revealing groupings. Discuss this assertion by reference to the objectives of financial reporting by segments.

2 AASB 8/IFRS 8 anticipates that some entities not within its scope might voluntarily disclose segment information. Do you think many reporting entities would voluntarily provide these disclosures? Explain your answer.

3 Explain what the 'management approach' used in AASB 8/IFRS 8 means.

4 Discuss the concerns raised about IFRS 8 (AASB 8) when it was first introduced. Compare the views of users and preparers when analysing these concerns. Do you think the concerns expressed by users will eventuate?

5 Distinguish between an operating segment and a reportable segment.

6 Describe how an entity determines its chief operating decision maker.

7 The 75% threshold relating to revenue refers to 'external revenue'. Explain what is meant by external revenue and how a segment could generate revenue that is not external.

8 Explain why the disclosure requirements of AASB 8/IFRS 8 are said to be less prescriptive compared with those of other standards.

9 Evaluate whether the reconciliations required by paragraph 28 of AASB 8/IFRS 8 address a concern about lack of comparability between entities caused by management's ability to select any measurement basis it chooses in reporting segment information.

10 AASB 8/IFRS 8 requires entities to disclose information about products and services, geographical areas and major customers. Discuss why such information may benefit users of financial statements.

CASE STUDY 20.1

CONTROVERSY OVER IFRS 8

Download the document 'EU Adoption of the IFRS 8 Standard on Operating Segments'. Refer to the section headed 'Segment Reporting' and prepare a summary of the four sets of questions raised by the author in relation to the adoption of IFRS 8.

CASE STUDY 20.2

EXPERIENCE OF IFRS 8

Download the document 'Post-implementation Review: Operating Segments'. Referring to page 7 of this document, prepare a brief report that summarises the key issues identified in the feedback received by the IASB with respect to areas for improvement and amendment to IFRS 8.

APPLICATION AND ANALYSIS EXERCISES

★ BASIC | ★ ★ MODERATE | ★ ★ ★ DIFFICULT

20.1 Defining operating segments ★   LO4

AASB 8/IFRS 8 sets out three criteria that need to be met in order to identify an operating segment.

Required

List and briefly explain the three criteria.

20.2 Aggregating operating segments ★   LO5

Yosemite Ltd is a listed manufacturing company. It produces most of its products in Australia but exports 90% of these products to the United States, Canada and Germany. It has only one main product line: scientific equipment. Yosemite Ltd is organised internally into two main business units: local and export. The export business unit is in turn divided into two sub-units: North America and Germany (North America includes Canada). Each business unit reports separate financial and operational information to the chief executive officer (CEO) and chief financial officer (CFO) who are identified as the CODM. The results of the two business units are then aggregated to form the consolidated financial information. Details of the identified operating segments are as follows.

	United States	Canada	Germany	Australia
Economic and political conditions	Stable	Stable. Closely related to US environment	Stable	Stable
Relationships between operations	Closely linked to Canadian operations	Closely linked to US operations	Self-sustaining	Self-sustaining
Proximity of operations	Closely linked to Canadian operations	Closely linked to US operations	Not close to other operations	Not close to other operations
Special risks	None	None	Stricter regulations	Small market
Exchange control regulations	None	None	None	None
Currency risks	Low	Low to medium	Low	Low to medium

Required

Identify which operating segments, if any, meet the aggregation criteria of paragraph 12 of AASB 8/IFRS 8. Give reasons for your answer.

20.3 Identifying reportable segments ⋆ **LO5**

Using the information from exercise 20.2, identify Yosemite Ltd's reportable segments.

20.4 Identifying reportable segments ⋆ ⋆ **LO5**

Carnarvon Ltd is a listed diversified retail company. Its stores are located mainly in Australia. It has three main types of stores: general department stores, liquor stores and specialist toy stores. Each of these stores has different products, customer types and distribution processes. In accordance with AASB 8/IFRS 8, Carnarvon Ltd has identified three operating segments: general department stores, liquor stores and specialist toy stores.

All three business units earn most of their revenue from external customers. Total consolidated revenue of Carnarvon Ltd is $800 million.

	General department stores $m	Liquor stores $m	Toy stores $m	All segments $m
Revenue	500	220	80	800
Segment result (profit)	28	9	6	43
Assets	800	350	150	1 300

Required

Identify Carnarvon Ltd's reportable segments in accordance with AASB 8/IFRS 8. Explain your answer.

20.5 Analysing the information provided ⋆ ⋆ **LO5**

Using the information provided about Carnarvon Ltd in exercise 20.4, analyse the relative profitability of the reportable segments.

20.6 Disclosures ⋆ ⋆ **LO5, 6**

Mobility Ltd, a listed manufacturing company, has two reportable segments, A and B. Both A and B are manufacturing segments.

Required

For each item listed, state whether or not it would be disclosed for each of the reportable segments, identify the segments for which it would be disclosed and explain what other disclosures, if any, are required in accordance with AASB 8/IFRS 8.

1. Interest income — not reported to the CODM on a segment basis but regularly provided to the CODM for the group as a whole
2. Dividend income — not reported to the CODM on a segment basis but regularly provided to the CODM for the group as a whole
3. Share of profits from investments in equity-method associates attributable to Segment A — reported to the CODM for Segment A
4. Interest expense — not reported to the CODM on a segment basis but regularly provided to the CODM for the group as a whole
5. Revenues from external customers for each of Segment A and Segment B
6. The amount of investments in associates accounted for using the equity method attributable to Segment A
7. Payables and trade creditors attributable to Segment B but not reported to the CODM
8. Borrowing costs that have been capitalised for Segment B and are regularly reported to the CODM

20.7 Disclosures ⋆ ⋆ **LO5, 6**

Jenkins Ltd has three reportable segments, A, B and C, which represent distinct geographical areas. The CODM receives financial information about the geographical areas. Segment A produces Product P and Product Y. Segment B produces Product P only. Segment C produces Product Y and sells Service Z. The following financial information about each segment is reported to the CODM.

• Revenues from external customers
• Earnings before interest, depreciation and amortisation and tax (EBITDA)
• Depreciation and amortisation

Required

State whether each of the following statements is true or false, by reference to the relevant requirements of AASB 8/IFRS 8.

1. Jenkins Ltd must disclose EBITDA for each reportable segment.
2. Jenkins Ltd must disclose total assets for each reportable segment.
3. Jenkins Ltd must reconcile the total EBITDA of segments A, B and C to its reported profit determined in accordance with accounting standards before income tax and discontinued operations.
4. Jenkins Ltd must disclose total liabilities for each reportable segment.
5. Jenkins Ltd must disclose depreciation and amortisation for each reportable segment.
6. Jenkins Ltd must disclose revenue from external customers for each of Product P, Product Y and Service Z.

20.8 Reportable segments, allocating amounts to segments ★ ★   **LO5, 6, 7**

Simeon Ltd is a listed diversified retail company. Its stores are located mainly in Australia. It has three main types of stores: general department stores, liquor stores and specialist toy stores. Each of these stores has different products, customer types and distribution processes. Simeon Ltd has three business units: general department stores, liquor stores and specialist toy stores.

For the year ended 30 June 2022 each business unit reported the following financial information to Simeon Ltd's CODM.

	General department stores $m	Liquor stores $m	Toy stores $m	All segments $m
Revenue	800	200	100	1 100
Segment result (profit)	30	14	8	52
Assets	1 800	400	200	2 400

Total consolidated revenue of Simeon Ltd for the year ended 30 June 2022 is $1600 million. Included in general department stores' revenue is $100 million of revenue from toy stores. As at the end of the reporting period toy stores owed general department stores $90 million. This amount is included in general department stores' assets. Within the general department stores business unit there are five different legal entities including legal entities Y and Z. As at 30 June 2022 legal entity Z owed $46 million to legal entity Y. These amounts have not been eliminated in determining the assets of the general department stores segment. Intersegment asset balances are reported to the CODM but are not used by the CODM as the basis for determining reportable segments. Intrasegment assets are reported to the CODM and are eliminated in determining reportable segments.

Required

State whether the following statements are true or false. Give reasons for your answers.

1. Simeon Ltd has three reportable segments.
2. The revenue figure that should be used by the general department stores segment for the purposes of determining whether or not it is a reportable segment is $700 million.
3. Simeon Ltd must disclose the toy store's segment liabilities after deducting the $90 million owed to general department stores.
4. The assets figure that should be used by the general department stores segment for the purposes of determining whether or not it is a reportable segment is $1800 million.
5. The assets figure that should be used by the general department stores segment for the purposes of determining whether or not it is a reportable segment is $1710 million.
6. The assets figure that should be used by the general department stores segment for the purposes of determining whether or not it is a reportable segment is $1754 million.
7. Simeon Ltd must disclose a reconciliation of total segment assets to its consolidated assets of $2264 million.

20.9 Disclosing segment information ★ ★ ★   **LO5, 6**

Nambour Ltd is a diversified manufacturing company. The CODM has been presented with the following information concerning eight operating segments that have been identified.

	A	B	C	D	E	F	G	H
Revenue	150	50	25	25	20	15	10	5
Profits	38	5	7		6		2	3
Losses				(4)		(7)		
Assets	750	500	100	150	300	50	100	50

Nambour Ltd has no unallocated revenue.

Required

Show how this information would be presented in the operating segment disclosure note in the accounts.

20.10 Identifying reportable segments ★ ★ ★   **LO5, 6**

The following information concerning eight operating segments has been presented to the CODM of a large retail company.

Segment	Total revenue	Internal revenue	External revenue
A	120	10	110
B	90	—	90
C	60	—	60
D	30	—	30
E	24	—	24
F	20	—	20
G	36	20	16
H	10	—	10
All segments	390	30	360
		Unallocated revenue	40
		Total entity revenue	400

Required

1. Determine which of the segments A to H are reportable segments under AASB 8/IFRS 8.
2. Prepare a reconciliation of the total reportable segment revenue with the total revenue of the entity.

20.11 Analysing the segment information ★ ★ ★   **LO7**

Jarek Ltd is a listed diversified manufacturing company. It is listed on the London Stock Exchange and produces most of its products in China and India. Its markets are in the European Union and the Asia–Pacific region. It produces three types of products and services: home furniture, office furniture and soft furnishings.

The CODM has determined that Jarek Ltd's operating segments should be based on geographical markets and has identified the reportable segments as listed below. The following information is reported to the CODM for each of the markets.

1. Earnings before interest, depreciation and amortisation and taxation (EBITDA)
2. Revenues from external customers

The following table sets out the financial information provided to the CODM for the year ended 31 December 2023. Each operating segment has been identified as a reportable segment.

	France $	Germany $	United Kingdom $	India $	China $	Australia and New Zealand $
Revenue from external customers	22 300 000	35 654 000	21 587 600	5 356 800	7 324 800	8 763 400
Intersegment revenue	—	—	—	10 000 000	10 000 000	—
EBITDA	6 400 000	7 325 000	5 325 000	5 324 000	7 625 000	2 325 000

Other information disclosed in the company's 31 December 2023 financial statements includes:
(a) total consolidated revenue: $125 000 000
(b) intersegment revenues represent wholesale sales from China and India to the other operating segments
(c) net profit before taxation: $25 625 000
(d) total consolidated assets: $1 041 670 000
(e) revenue from external customers for each type of product:
    (i) home furniture: $78 525 000
    (ii) office furniture: $17 700 000
    (iii) soft furnishings: $28 775 000.

Required
Analyse Jarek Ltd's business with reference to its reported segment information. Show all workings to support your analysis.

REFERENCES

Wesfarmers Limited 2018, *Annual report 2018*, www.wesfarmers.com.au.
Woolworths Group Limited 2018, *Annual report 2018*, www.woolworthsgroup.com.au.

ACKNOWLEDGEMENTS

Photo: © Caiaimage / Getty Images
Photo: © Scott Kenneth Brodie / Shutterstock.com
Photo: © Victor Wong / Shutterstock.com
Photo: © Nils Versemann / Shutterstock.com
Photo: © Nils Versemann / Shutterstock.com
Figure 20.3: © Woolworths Group Limited 2018
Figure 20.4: © Wesfarmers Limited 2018
Text: © 2019 Australian Accounting Standards Board (AASB). The text, graphics and layout of this publication are protected by Australian copyright law and the comparable law of other countries. No part of the publication may be reproduced, stored or transmitted in any form or by any means without the prior written permission of the AASB except as permitted by law. For reproduction or publication, permission should be sought in writing from the AASB. Requests in the first instance should be addressed to the National Director, Australian Accounting Standards Board, PO Box 204, Collins Street West, Victoria 8007.
Text: © IFRS. This publication contains copyright material of the IFRS Foundation in respect of which all rights are reserved. Reproduced by John Wiley & Sons Australia, Ltd with the permission of the IFRS Foundation. No permission granted to third parties to reproduce or distribute. For full access to IFRS Standards and the work of the IFRS Foundation please visit http://eifrs.ifrs.org. The International Accounting Standards Board, the IFRS Foundation, the authors and the publishers do not accept responsibility for any loss caused by acting or refraining from acting in reliance on the material in this publication, whether such loss is caused by negligence or otherwise.

CHAPTER 21

Related party disclosures

CHAPTER AIM

Related entities regularly enter into business transactions with each other. The simple existence of a related party relationship has the potential to affect the financial performance and position of an entity. This chapter describes AASB 124/IAS 24 *Related Party Disclosures*, which requires entities to provide users of financial statements with knowledge of business relationships, related party transactions, outstanding balances and commitments with related parties that may affect assessments of the business risks faced by entities.

LEARNING OBJECTIVES

After studying this chapter, you should be able to:

21.1 explain the objective, application and scope of AASB 124/IAS 24 *Related Party Disclosures*

21.2 identify an entity's related parties

21.3 identify relationships that do not give rise to a related party relationship as envisaged under AASB 124/ IAS 24

21.4 describe and apply the disclosures required by AASB 124/IAS 24

21.5 explain why a government-related entity may have a partial exemption from related party disclosures.

CONCEPTS FOR REVIEW

Before studying this chapter, you should understand and, if necessary, revise:
- the meaning of a parent–subsidiary relationship
- the difference between an associated entity and a joint venture operation.

21.1 Objective, application and scope of AASB 124/IAS 24

LEARNING OBJECTIVE 21.1 Explain the objective, application and scope of AASB 124/IAS 24 *Related Party Disclosures*.

Entities often establish relationships with other entities and individuals, and enter into business transactions together. For example, groups of entities may conduct their business activities through subsidiary organisations, associated entities or joint venture operations. If an entity engages in transactions with other closely connected entities there is a danger that the economics of the transaction may not be the same had the transaction been negotiated by independent parties in an arm's length arrangement. For example, an entity might have an incentive to shift risks and returns in the form of profits or losses, income or expense flows, or assets or liabilities to a party that it is able to influence or control.

AASB 124/IAS 24 *Related Party Disclosures* is primarily a disclosure standard. It is particularly relevant for entities that have established relationships with related parties, and that have transacted with those parties. The standard has been revised a number of times to simplify and clarify the definition and meaning of a related party and to provide a partial exemption from the disclosure requirements for government-related entities. The objective of AASB 124/IAS 24, described in paragraph 1, is to:

> ensure that an entity's financial statements contain the disclosures necessary to draw attention to the possibility that its financial position and profit or loss may have been affected by the existence of related parties and by transactions and outstanding balances, including commitments, with such parties.

Due to the relationship between an entity and a related party they may enter into transactions with each other under different terms and conditions than they would if they were unrelated parties. For example, as described in paragraph 6 of AASB 124/IAS 24, 'an entity that sells goods to its parent at cost might not sell on those terms to another customer'. Any profit that could have been obtained from a transaction with an external party is forgone due to the influence of the parent–subsidiary relationship.

Furthermore, the financial position of an entity may be affected even without the existence of a related party transaction. An example given in paragraph 7 of AASB 124/IAS 24 is 'a subsidiary may terminate relations with a trading partner on acquisition by the parent of a fellow subsidiary engaged in the same activity as the former trading partner'; that is, the subsidiary may cease trade with an entity that provides the same goods/services as the newly acquired subsidiary in the group.

Paragraph 2 of AASB 124/IAS 24 requires the standard to be applied in:

(a) identifying related party relationships and transactions;
(b) identifying outstanding balances, including commitments, between an entity and its related parties;
(c) identifying the circumstances in which disclosure of the items in (a) and (b) is required; and
(d) determining the disclosures to be made about those items.

The standard includes a reminder that intragroup transactions (between a parent and its subsidiaries) are already disclosed in the entity's financial statements, and that related party transactions and outstanding balances are eliminated from the consolidated financial statements of the group as per AASB 10/IFRS 10 *Consolidated Financial Statements* or AASB 127/IAS 27 *Separate Financial Statements*.

An alternative to the disclosure of related party transactions, balances and commitments could be to restate the events as though they had occurred between independent parties in arm's length transactions. However, in many instances the value of the events and their impacts would be very difficult — if not impossible — to determine, as comparable transactions simply may not exist.

When determining the disclosures necessary to provide sufficient knowledge to financial statement users, the major issues that must be considered include identifying related parties and related party arrangements, and deciding on the type and extent of the disclosure to be made.

The notes to the consolidated financial statements for Woolworths Group Limited includes related party disclosures as shown in figure 21.1.

5.5 Related parties

Transactions within the Group

During the financial period and previous financial periods, Woolworths Group Limited advanced loans to, received and repaid loans from, and provided treasury, accounting, legal, taxation and administrative services to other entities within the Group.

Entities within the Group also exchanged goods and services in sale and purchase transactions. All transactions occurred on the basis of normal commercial terms and conditions. Balances and transactions between the Company and its subsidiaries, which are related parties of the Company, have been eliminated on consolidation and are not disclosed in this Note.

Directors and Key Management Personnel

All transactions with directors and Key Management Personnel (including their related parties) were conducted on an arm's length basis in the ordinary course of business and under normal terms and conditions for customers and employees. These transactions are considered trivial or domestic in nature. Related parties of Key Management Personnel who are employees received normal employee benefits on standard terms and conditions.

Disclosures relating to directors and Key Management Personnel are set out in Note 6.3 and in the Remuneration Report.

Source: Woolworths Group Limited (2018, p. 109).

LEARNING CHECK

- [ ] The objective of disclosing related party information is to ensure that the users of financial statements are provided with sufficient knowledge to undertake an independent assessment of the risks and opportunities facing entities that engage in related party transactions.
- [ ] A related party is a person or entity that is related to the entity that is preparing its financial statements.
- [ ] Related parties may enter into transactions on terms and conditions that would not apply to unrelated parties. Knowledge of business relationships, related party transactions, outstanding balances and commitments with related parties may affect assessments of the business risks faced by entities.
- [ ] Related party relationships, transactions, outstanding balances and commitments are disclosed in the consolidated and separate financial statements of a parent, venturer or investor presented in accordance with AASB 10/IFRS 10 *Consolidated Financial Statements* or AASB 127/IAS 27 *Separate Financial Statements*. Intragroup transactions and balances are eliminated from consolidated financial statements.
- [ ] The major issues that must be considered include identifying related parties and related party arrangements, and deciding on the type and extent of the disclosure to be made.

21.2 Identifying related parties

LEARNING OBJECTIVE 21.2 Identify an entity's related parties.

AASB 124/IAS 24 applies to the identification of **related party** relationships and transactions, and outstanding balances and commitments with related parties.

The conditions indicating whether one party is considered to be related to another are summarised in table 21.1.

TABLE 21.1   Definition of a related party — AASB 124/IAS 24 paragraph 9(a), (b)

Part a — A person or a close member of that person's family is related to a reporting entity if that person:

(i) has control or joint control of the reporting entity;
(ii) has significant influence over the reporting entity; or
(iii) is a member of the key management personnel of the reporting entity or of a parent of the reporting entity.

(i) The entity and the reporting entity are members of the same group (which means that each parent, subsidiary and fellow subsidiary is related to the others).

(ii) One entity is an associate or joint venture of the other entity (or an associate or joint venture of a member of a group of which the other entity is a member).

(iii) Both entities are joint ventures of the same third party.

(iv) One entity is a joint venture of a third entity and the other entity is an associate of the third entity.

(v) The entity is a post-employment benefit plan for the benefit of employees of either the reporting entity or an entity related to the reporting entity. If the reporting entity is itself such a plan, the sponsoring employers are also related to the reporting entity.

(vi) The entity is controlled or jointly controlled by a person identified in part (a).

(vii) A person identified in (a)(i) has significant influence over the entity or is a member of the key management personnel of the entity (or of a parent of the entity).

(viii) The entity, or any member of a group of which it is a part, provides key management personnel services to the reporting entity or to the parent of the reporting entity.

Source: AASB 124, paragraph 9.

21.2.1 A close member of the family of a person

Under paragraph 9 of AASB 124/IAS 24, close members of the family of a person are:

> those family members who may be expected to influence, or be influenced by, that person in their dealings with the entity and include:
> (a) that person's children and spouse or domestic partner;
> (b) children of that person's spouse or domestic partner; and
> (c) dependants of that person or that person's spouse or domestic partner.

21.2.2 Control, joint control, significant influence

AASB 124/IAS 24 requires the meanings of the terms control, joint control and significant influence to be defined as per their meanings specified in other standards.

Control is defined in paragraph 6 of AASB 10/IFRS 10:

> An investor controls an investee when it is exposed, or has rights, to variable returns from its involvement with the investee and has the ability to affect those returns through its power over the investee.

Joint control is defined in paragraph 3 of AASB 128/IAS 28 *Investments in Associates and Joint Ventures* as:

> the contractually agreed sharing of control of an arrangement, which exists only when decisions about the relevant activities require the unanimous consent of the parties sharing control.

Significant influence is defined in paragraph 3 of AASB 128/IAS 28 as:

> the power to participate in the financial and operating policy decisions of the investee but is not control or joint control of those policies.

Determination of whether a close family relationship has related party disclosure consequences is demonstrated in illustrative example 21.1.

ILLUSTRATIVE EXAMPLE 21.1

Close family members with control or significant influence

Charlie has a controlling investment in Delta Ltd. He is married to Mary, who holds an investment in Gamma Ltd that gives her significant influence over that company.

Required
Analyse the related party relationships.

21.2.3 Key management personnel

Under paragraph 9 of AASB 124/IAS 24, **key management personnel** are:

> those persons having authority and responsibility for planning, directing and controlling the activities of the entity, directly or indirectly, including any director (whether executive or otherwise) of that entity.

An example of key management personnel identified by Woolworths Group Limited, and disclosed in that company's 2018 annual report, is shown in figure 21.2.

FIGURE 21.2   Key management personnel, Woolworths

EXECUTIVE KMP
Brad Banducci
Chief Executive Officer
Steve Donohue
Managing Director, Endeavour Drinks
David Marr
Chief Financial Officer
Claire Peters
Managing Director, Woolworths Supermarkets
Martin Smith
Managing Director, Endeavour Drinks
Colin Storrie
Group Portfolio Director

Source: Woolworths Group Limited (2018, p. 43).

Determining whether a party is related to a member of key management personnel is demonstrated in illustrative example 21.2.

ILLUSTRATIVE EXAMPLE 21.2

Key management personnel

Lee has a 100% interest in Homestyle Ltd and he is also a member of the key management personnel of Country Ltd. Tenham Ltd has a controlling interest in Country Ltd.

In this set of circumstances:

- for Country Ltd's financial statements, Homestyle Ltd is a related entity because Lee controls Homestyle Ltd and he is also a member of the key management personnel of Country Ltd
- for Homestyle Ltd's financial statements, Country Ltd is a related entity because Lee controls Homestyle Ltd and he is also a member of Country Ltd's key management personnel.

Source: Adapted from AASB 124, Illustrative Example 3.

21.2.4 An associate of the entity

Under paragraph 9 of AASB 124/IAS 24, any party that is determined to be an associate of the reporting entity is also considered to be a related party. An **associated entity** is one 'over which the investor has significant influence' (AASB 128/IAS 28 *Investments in Associates and Joint Ventures* paragraph 3). Under paragraph 27 of AASB 128/IAS 28, an associate includes subsidiaries of the associate. For example, an investor that has significant influence over an associate is related to the associate's subsidiary.

21.2.5 A joint venture

Any relationship that is determined to be a joint venture as defined in AASB 128/IAS 28 is regarded as a related party. Paragraph 3 of AASB 128/IAS 28 defines a **joint venture** as:

> a joint arrangement whereby the parties that have joint control of the arrangement have rights to the net assets of the arrangement.

As per paragraph 27 of AASB 128/IAS 28, a joint venture includes subsidiaries of the joint venture.

21.2.6 Post-employment benefit plan

Post-employment benefits include 'pensions, other retirement benefits, post-employment life insurance and post-employment medical care' (AASB 124/IAS 24 paragraph 9). AASB 124/IAS 24 does not provide an indication of why post-employment benefits are defined as related parties. However, an entity sponsoring a post-employment benefit plan is likely to have either control or significant influence over the plan. There may also be obligations or commitments outstanding at the end of a reporting period.

LEARNING CHECK

- Related party entities include:
  - entities in the same parent–subsidiary group
  - associates
  - joint ventures
  - post-employment benefit plans
  - entities that are controlled or jointly controlled by a related party person
  - related party persons with significant influence over an entity, including close family members and where a person or entity is a member of the key management personnel of a reporting entity.
- Paragraphs 9a and 9b of AASB 124/IAS 24 define when a person or an entity is a related party to a reporting entity.

21.3 Relationships that are not related parties

LEARNING OBJECTIVE 21.3 Identify relationships that do not give rise to a related party relationship as envisaged under AASB 124/IAS 24.

When considering the existence of related party relationships that require specific disclosures under AASB 124/IAS 24, it is helpful to know which relationships have been specifically excluded from the context of the standard. Paragraph 10 clearly states that it is the *substance* — not merely the legal form — of a relationship or transaction that is important. An example of a non-related party transaction would be the offer of trade discounts between an entity and one of its major customers. The trade discounts are offered based on the bulk purchases made by the customer (a normal business transaction) and not due to the entity's reliance on their continued trade. The relationships that are *not* regarded as related parties by AASB 124/IAS 24 are listed in paragraph 11. These are summarised in figure 21.3.

FIGURE 21.3 Relationships that are not regarded as related parties

---

Two entities simply because they have a director in common
Two entities simply because they have a member of key management personnel in common
Two entities simply because a member of the key management personnel of one entity has significant influence over the other entity
Two venturers simply because they share joint control over a joint venture

The following entities simply by virtue of normal dealings with an entity

 (i) Providers of finance
 (ii) Trade unions
 (iii) Public utilities
 (iv) Departments and agencies of a government that does not control, jointly control or significantly influence the reporting entity

The following entities simply by virtue of the economic dependence that arises from transacting a significant volume of business with a party

 (i) a customer
 (ii) a supplier
 (iii) a franchisor
 (iv) a distributor or general agent

Source: Adapted from AASB 124, paragraph 11.

LEARNING CHECK

☐ It is the *substance* of the relationship — not merely the legal form — that determines whether a related party relationship exists. There are specific relationships that are considered not to be related parties as per the context of AASB 124/IAS 24.

21.4 Disclosure

LEARNING OBJECTIVE 21.4 Describe and apply the disclosures required by AASB 124/IAS 24.

In order for users of financial statements to form a view about the effects of the related party relationships of an entity, paragraph 13 of AASB 124/IAS 24 requires the disclosure of the relationship where control exists, irrespective of whether there have been transactions between the parties. If there have been transactions, then the nature of the relationship, together with sufficient information to enable an understanding of the potential effect of the transactions on the financial statements, must be disclosed.

21.4.1 Related party transactions and related party relationships

If the relationship is between parent and subsidiary entities, the identification of the parties is in addition to the disclosure requirements of AASB 12/IFRS 12 *Disclosures of Interests in Other Entities*, AASB 127/IAS 27 *Separate Financial Statements* and AASB 128/IAS 28 *Investments in Associates and Joint Ventures*. If the parent entity or the ultimate controlling entity does not make financial statements publicly available, then under paragraph 13 of AASB 124/IAS 24 the name of the closest parent that does so must be disclosed.

All entities

To assist users of financial statements to form their view about the effects of related party relationships on an entity, paragraph 19 of AASB 24/IAS 24 requires a range of information to be disclosed separately for each:
- parent
- entity with joint control or significant influence
- subsidiary
- associate
- joint venture in which the entity is a venturer
- key management personnel
- other related party.

The minimum disclosures are detailed under paragraph 18 of AASB 124/IAS 24 and include:

 (a) the amount of the transactions;
 (b) the amount of outstanding balances, including commitments, and:
  (i) their terms and conditions, including whether they are secured, and the nature of the consideration to be provided in settlement; and
  (ii) details of any guarantees given or received;

(c) provisions for doubtful debts related to the amount of outstanding balances; and

(d) the expense recognised during the period in respect of bad or doubtful debts due from related parties.

A major focus of the disclosure requirements of AASB 124/IAS 24 is directed towards revealing the remuneration arrangements made for key management personnel. These requirements are intended to improve the transparency of related party relationships with directors and influential senior executives. These disclosures, contained in paragraph 17, are required in total for each of a range of categories:

(a) short-term employee benefits;
(b) post-employment benefits;
(c) other long-term benefits;
(d) termination benefits; and
(e) share-based payment.

Although the term 'compensation' is used in AASB 124/IAS 24 to describe benefits paid to employees, the term 'remuneration' refers to the same concept. According to the Productivity Commission (2010, p. iv):

> The remuneration of company directors and executives is an issue which has attracted considerable interest from shareholders, business groups and the wider community. Concerns have been raised over excessive remuneration practices, particularly as we face almost unprecedented turmoil in global financial and equity markets . . . The crisis has also highlighted the need to maintain a robust regulatory framework that promotes transparency and accountability on remuneration practices, and better aligns the interests of shareholders and the community with the performance and reward structures of Australia's corporate directors and executives.

The key management personnel remuneration disclosures provided by Woolworths Group Limited in its 2018 financial statements are shown in figure 21.4.

| FIGURE 21.4 | Key management personnel remuneration, Woolworths |

6.3 Key management personnel

The total remuneration for key management personnel of the Group is as follows:

	2018 $	2017 $
Short-term employee benefits	14 217 931	14 176 416
Post-employment benefits	297 319	334 138
Other long-term benefits	139 776	116 035
Share-based payments	10 500 022	6 206 191
	25 155 048	20 832 780

Equity instrument disclosures relating to key management personnel

Details of equity instruments provided as compensation to key management personnel and shares issued on exercise of these instruments, together with the terms and conditions of the instruments, are disclosed in Section 5.1 of the Remuneration Report.

Source: Woolworths Group Limited (2018, p. 116).

Examples of related party transactions that must be disclosed are provided in paragraph 21 of AASB 124/IAS 24 and include:
• the purchases or sales of goods or services whether incomplete or finished
• the acquisition or disposal of property and other assets
• the provision or receipt of services
• lease arrangements
• transfers of research and development
• transfers under licence agreements
• transfers under finance arrangements (including loans and equity contributions)
• provisions of guarantees

- commitments including executory contracts
- the settlement of liabilities on behalf of the entity or by the entity on behalf of a related party.

An example of transactions with related parties and key management personnel is shown in the notes accompanying Woolworths Group Limited's 2018 annual report and is shown in figure 21.5.

| FIGURE 21.5 | Transactions with directors and other key management personnel, Woolworths |

Remuneration report

5.2 KMP share right movements

The table below summarises the share rights granted as part of the Non-executive Director Equity Plan introduced in January 2018 (see Section 3.3). No share rights were vested or lapsed as at 24 June 2018.

Non-executive directors	Share rights granted under the Non-executive Directors Equity Plan	
	No.	$[1]
G M Cairns	1 781	49 983
J R Broadbent	1 246	34 968
H S Kramer	547	15 352
S L McKenna	—	—
S R Perkins	2 898	81 332
K A Tesija	—	—
M J Ullmer	2 137	59 975
Total	8 609	241 610

1. Amount represents Non-executive Director fees sacrificed.

The table below summarises the movements during the year in holdings of share right interests in Woolworths Group Limited for current Executive KMP. A share right entitles the holder to one ordinary fully paid Woolworths Group Limited share, subject to applicable performance and vesting conditions.

Executive KMP		Opening balance No.	Share rights granted No.	$[1]	Share rights lapsed[2] No.	$	Share rights lapsed[3] No.	Closing balance No.
B L Banducci	FY18	342 570	254 242	5 472 037	—	—	(23 731)	573 081
	FY17	122 680	241 220	4 769 723	(21 330)	461 181	—	342 570
S J Donohue[4]	FY18	108 352	66 257	1 340 379	(14 011)	359 727	(3 444)	157 154
D P Marr	FY18	265 953	108 738	2,275,506	(16 912)	433 023	(36 638)	321 141
	FY17	170 020	116 702	2 375 664	(16 219)	336 187	(4 550)	265 953
C E Peters	FY18	143 590	101 544	2 054 235	(19 133)	517 060	—	226 001
	FY17	—	145 587	3 140 868	(1 997)	51 792	—	143 590
M R Smith	FY18	98 334	79 078	1 426 903	—	—	(8 773)	168 639
	FY17	28 741	71 593	1 457 395	—	—	(2 000)	98 334
C G Storrie	FY18	91 700	66 257	1 340 379	(9 855)	269 876	—	148 102
	FY17	19 180	81 845	1 666 091	(9 325)	243 878	—	91 700
Total	FY18	1 050 499	676 116	13 909 439	(59 911)	1 579 687	(72 586)	1 594 118
	FY17	340 621	656 947	13 409 741	(48 871)	1 093 038	(6 550)	942 147

No share rights held by Executive KMP were forfeited during the year.

1. Share rights granted is the total fair value of share rights granted during the year determined by an independent actuary. This will be recognised in employee benefits expense over the vesting period of the share right, in accordance with Australian Accounting Standards.
2. The value of share rights vested during the year is calculated based on the VWAP of Woolworths Group Limited shares traded in the five days prior to and including the date of vesting.
3. The number of share rights which lapsed as a result of failure to meet performance hurdles relates to the FY13 LTI plan and FY15 LTI plan.
4. Mr Donohue held share rights prior to his appointment effective 1 April 2018.

Source: Woolworths Group Limited (2018, p. 56).

- ☐ A relationship where control exists must be disclosed, irrespective of whether there have been transactions between the parties.
- ☐ If there have been transactions in a relationship where control exists, the nature of the relationship, together with sufficient information to enable an understanding of the potential effect of the transactions on the financial statements, must be disclosed.
- ☐ A range of information is required to be disclosed separately for each parent, entity with joint control or significant influence, subsidiary, associate, joint venture in which the entity is a venturer, key management personnel and other related parties.
- ☐ The minimum disclosures are the amount of the transactions, the amount of the outstanding balances and commitments, provisions for doubtful debts related to outstanding balances and the expense recognised during the period in respect of bad or doubtful debts due from related parties.
- ☐ AASB 124/IAS 24 requires disclosure of the remuneration arrangements for key management personnel, including short-term employee benefits, post-employment benefits, other long-term benefits, termination benefits and share-based payment.

21.5 Government-related entities

LEARNING OBJECTIVE 21.5 Explain why a government-related entity may have a partial exemption from related party disclosures.

A number of countries have a sizeable number of entities that are controlled by the government. Often the practical difficulties and costs for government-controlled entities of complying with the extensive disclosure requirements of AASB 124/IAS 24 are likely to outweigh the benefits to financial statement users. Accordingly, paragraph 25 provides an exemption from some of the disclosure requirements for transactions between entities that are controlled, jointly controlled or significantly influenced by a government, and with other entities that are related because they are controlled by the same government. The exemption from disclosure for **government-related entities** is demonstrated in illustrative example 21.3.

ILLUSTRATIVE EXAMPLE 21.3

Exemption from disclosure for government-related entities

A local government organisation directly controls two entities — Armidale Ltd and Bowen Ltd — and indirectly controls Emerald Ltd, Fitzroy Ltd, Jondaryan Ltd and Somerset Ltd. Mr Mitchell is a key person in the management of Armidale Ltd.

Required
Determine the extent to which Emerald Ltd can apply the partial exemption in paragraph 25 of AASB 124/IAS 24.

Solution
The exemption in paragraph 25 can be applied by Emerald Ltd for transactions with the local government entity and for transactions with Armidale Ltd, Bowen Ltd, Fitzroy Ltd, Jondaryan Ltd and Somerset Ltd.
  The exemption cannot be applied for transactions with key management personnel (Mr Mitchell).

Source: Adapted from AASB 124, Illustrative Example 1.

If an entity chooses to apply the exemption, it is still required to identify the government to which it is related and to provide a range of other relevant disclosures under paragraph 26 of AASB 124/IAS 24. These include:

- the nature of the relationship
- the nature and amount of each individually significant transaction
- either a qualitative or a quantitative indication of the extent of other transactions that are, in aggregate, significant.

In addition, when determining the level of detail to be disclosed, the entity should not only consider the closeness of the relationship with the related parties, but should also consider the level of significance of the actual transaction. Paragraph 27 of AASB 124/IAS 24 requires the entity to consider whether the transaction is:

(a) significant in terms of size;
(b) carried out on non-market terms;
(c) outside normal day-to-day business operations, such as the purchase and sale of businesses;
(d) disclosed to regulatory or supervisory authorities;
(e) reported to senior management;
(f) subject to shareholder approval.

LEARNING CHECK

☐ AASB 124/IAS 24 provides an exemption from some of the disclosure requirements for transactions between entities that are controlled, jointly controlled or significantly influenced by a government, and with other entities that are related because they are controlled by the same government.
☐ If an entity chooses to apply the exemption, it is still required to identify the government to which it is related and to disclose the nature of the relationship; the nature and amount of each individually significant transaction; and either a qualitative or a quantitative indication of the extent of other transactions that are, in aggregate, significant.

SUMMARY

AASB 124/IAS 24 *Related Party Disclosures* is a disclosure standard that defines related party relationships and prescribes the events, transactions, balances and commitments that must be revealed in the financial statements and reports of disclosing entities. As related party relationships can be expected to affect the profit or loss or the financial position of an entity, disclosures about them are particularly helpful to investors, lenders and other users when they evaluate and assess the risks and opportunities facing entities. The main features of AASB 124/IAS 24 are that it:
- considers key management personnel and their close family members to be related parties
- considers compensation benefits for key management personnel to be related party transactions
- requires additional disclosure regarding key management personnel compensation arrangements for a number of employment benefits including share-based payments.

Determining when related party relationships exist and identifying the circumstances in which disclosures about such relationships must be made involves a certain amount of judgement. In making that judgement, entities must take into account the definitions of related parties provided in AASB 124/IAS 24. The definition of related parties includes:
- relationships affected by control or significant influence or joint venture arrangements
- key management personnel.

KEY TERMS

associated entity An entity over which the investor has significant influence.

control The ability to direct the use of, and obtain substantially all of the remaining benefits from, the asset.

government-related entities Entities that are controlled, jointly controlled or significantly influenced by a government.

joint control The contractually agreed sharing of control of an arrangement, which exists only when decisions about the relevant activities require the unanimous consent of the parties sharing control.

joint venture A joint arrangement whereby the parties that have joint control of the arrangement have rights to the net assets of the arrangement.

key management personnel Those persons having authority and responsibility for planning, directing and controlling the activities of the entity, directly or indirectly.

post-employment benefits Benefits, other than termination benefits, that are payable after completion of employment, typically after the employee retires; includes pensions, other retirement benefits, post-employment life insurance and post-employment medical care.

related party A person or entity that is related to the entity that is preparing its financial statements.

significant influence The power to participate in the financial and operating policy decisions of the investee, but not control or joint control of those policies.

COMPREHENSION QUESTIONS

1 Why do standard setters formulate rules for the disclosure of related party relationships?

2 Explain how the mere existence of a related party relationship might have the potential to affect transactions with other parties.

3 Explain why key management personnel are regarded as related parties.

4 An alternative to disclosing information about related parties is to restate related party events as though they had occurred between independent parties in arm's length transactions. Explain why this approach has not been adopted by the standard setters.

5 Explain why a parent company and its subsidiary entities are regarded as related parties.

6 Outline the rationale for including an employer-sponsored post-employment benefit plan as a related party of the employer entity.

7 Distinguish between control, joint control and significant influence.

8 Provide four examples of related party transactions that must be disclosed by a related party disclosing entity.

9 AASB 124/IAS 24 requires the identity of key management personnel to be disclosed. Explain how an entity determines whether an employee is a member of key management personnel.

CASE STUDY 21.1

EXECUTIVE REMUNERATION

The following text outlines the purpose of the Australian Government Productivity Commission's public inquiry into executive remuneration.

> The Productivity Commission was asked to undertake a public inquiry into the regulatory framework around remuneration of directors and executives of companies regulated under the Corporations Act.
>
> This inquiry has concluded. The Commission's final report was provided to the Australian Government on 19 December 2009. The Government publicly released the report on 4 January 2010.
>
> Specifically, the Commission was requested to consider:
> - trends in director and executive remuneration in Australia and internationally
> - the effectiveness of the existing framework for the oversight, accountability and transparency of director and executive remuneration practices
> - the role of institutional and retail shareholders in the development, setting, reporting and consideration of remuneration practices
> - any mechanisms that would better align the interests of boards and executives with those of shareholders and the wider community
> - the effectiveness of the international responses to remuneration issues arising from the global financial crisis.
>
> In undertaking the inquiry, the Commission liaised with the Australia's Future Tax System Review and the Australian Prudential Regulation Authority.
>
> The Commission has made recommendations on how the existing framework governing remuneration practices in Australia could be improved.
>
> *Source:* Productivity Commission (2014).

Required

Go to the website of the Australian Government's Productivity Commission (www.pc.gov.au) and locate the above project summary. Follow the link to the government's response and discuss whether or not you agree with the responses provided for each recommendation. Consider the explanation provided by the government regarding any variances to the Commission's recommendations.

CASE STUDY 21.2

RELATED PARTY DISCLOSURES

Choose the most recent annual report of two Australian publicly listed companies (other than Woolworths Group Limited). Locate the remuneration report and the financial statement notes dealing with related party disclosures. Compare the details provided by each company. Do you consider there is too much/not enough disclosure about related party relationships (including key management personnel remuneration), transactions, balances and commitments? Explain.

CASE STUDY 21.3

RELATED PARTY LOANS

At the end of the 2018 financial reporting period, Bank of Queensland had a number of outstanding loans/advances to related parties, including a balance of $1.9 million to key management personnel.

Required

Locate Note 6.4 in Bank of Queensland's 2018 annual report (www.boq.com.au/Shareholder-centre/financial-information/Annual-Report) and write a report on the appropriateness of the disclosures of the related party transactions to (1) key management personnel and (2) other related parties. Your report should explain why the AASB/IASB requires information about loans with key management personnel to be disclosed. It should also include a summary of the other related party disclosures included in Note 6.4.

APPLICATION AND ANALYSIS EXERCISES

★ BASIC | ★ ★ MODERATE | ★ ★ ★ DIFFICULT

21.1 Scope of AASB 124/IAS 24 ★   LO2, 3

Which of the following are related parties of an entity within the scope of AASB 124/IAS 24? Give reasons for your answer.

(a) A person who has the authority to plan, direct and control the activities of the entity

(b) The domestic partner and children of a director of the entity

(c) The non-dependant sister of a director of the entity

(d) A subsidiary company that is directly controlled by the entity

(e) Dividend payment to employees who are holders of an entity's shares

21.2 Recognition principles ★   LO2, 3

Felix Anderson is a newly appointed director of Elite Sports Ltd, a listed company that organises major sporting events. Felix has provided consultancy services to Elite Sports Ltd for the past 10 years. In the most recent financial year these services amounted to $400 000.

Required

Determine whether the consultancy service provided by Felix is a related party transaction that should be disclosed in the financial statements of Elite Sports Ltd. Explain your answer.

21.3 Recognition principles ★   LO2, 3

The Golden Years Company operates a pension scheme that offers defined benefit pensions for the benefit of the company's employees. At the end of the reporting period, the present value of the defined benefit obligation is $85 million and the fair value of the defined benefit scheme assets is $90 million.

Required

Is the pension scheme a related party of the The Golden Years Company? Explain.

21.4 Determining whether parties are related ★ ★   LO2, 3

Hasan holds 100% of the shares in Matheson Ltd and he is also a director of Sinaga Ltd. All of the shares in Sinaga Ltd are held by Roberts Ltd.

Required

Determine the related party relationships for Matheson Ltd.

21.5 Identifying related party transactions ★ ★ ★   LO3

Many entities have transactions with related parties which occur under normal terms and conditions. For example, banks provide a wide range of banking and other financial services and products, some of which are used by bank directors and their close family members.

Required

Choose one entity from each of the following three business sectors and identify the types of transactions (e.g. goods and services) that the entities might engage in with related parties under normal commercial terms and conditions.

(a) Transport sector

(b) Retailing sector

(c) Construction sector

21.6 Determining whether transactions are related party transactions ★ ★   LO2, 3, 4

Which of the following is a related party transaction and, under AASB 124/IAS 24, requires disclosure in the annual financial statements?

(a) A performance-related amount paid to the directors of the entity

(b) A loan for $100 000 that was made to a retired director of an entity, and which was written off as an uncollectible debt during the current financial year

(c) A loan of $30 000 advanced to the chief financial officer of an entity and which is outstanding at the end of the reporting period

(d) An annual cash bonus amount paid to factory workers employed by the entity

21.7 Disclosure ★ ★   LO4

During the period ended 30 June 2023, Ru Li, an employee of Westside Company, purchased goods from the company on normal commercial terms and conditions. Li receives remuneration consisting of cash and other short-term benefits amounting to $240 000. During the 30 June 2023 financial year, Li also received a grant of 75 000 options from the company that is conditional on her continuing to work for the company for the next 3 years. Li is considered to be a member of the key management personnel of the Westside Company.

Required

Prepare appropriate disclosures reflecting the related party relationship and transactions between Westside Company and its employee Ru Li for the period ended 30 June 2023.

21.8 Exemption from disclosure for government-related entities ★ ★   **LO5**

Buffer Zone is a government organisation which directly controls another entity, Evergreen Ltd, and through its interest in Evergreen Ltd it indirectly controls Olive Ltd and Rose Ltd.

Required

Determine the extent to which Olive Ltd can apply the partial disclosure exemption for government-related entities.

REFERENCES

Productivity Commission 2010, *Executive remuneration in Australia, Productivity Commission inquiry report*, Australian Government, p. iv.

—— 2014, *Executive remuneration*, www.pc.gov.au.

Woolworths Group Limited 2018, *Annual report 2018*, www.woolworthsgroup.com.au.

ACKNOWLEDGEMENTS

Photo: © Jacob Wackerhausen / iStockphoto

Photo: © g-stockstudio / Shutterstock.com

Figures 21.1, 21.2, 21.4, 21.5: © Woolworths Group Limited 2018

Text: © 2019 Australian Accounting Standards Board (AASB). The text, graphics and layout of this publication are protected by Australian copyright law and the comparable law of other countries. No part of the publication may be reproduced, stored or transmitted in any form or by any means without the prior written permission of the AASB except as permitted by law. For reproduction or publication, permission should be sought in writing from the AASB. Requests in the first instance should be addressed to the National Director, Australian Accounting Standards Board, PO Box 204, Collins Street West, Victoria 8007.

Text: © IFRS. This publication contains copyright material of the IFRS Foundation in respect of which all rights are reserved. Reproduced by John Wiley & Sons Australia, Ltd with the permission of the IFRS Foundation. No permission granted to third parties to reproduce or distribute. For full access to IFRS Standards and the work of the IFRS Foundation please visit http://eifrs.ifrs.org. The International Accounting Standards Board, the IFRS Foundation, the authors and the publishers do not accept responsibility for any loss caused by acting or refraining from acting in reliance on the material in this publication, whether such loss is caused by negligence or otherwise.

Text: © Productivity Commission 2010, 2014

CHAPTER 22

Sustainability and corporate social responsibility reporting

CHAPTER AIM

This chapter examines social, environmental and governance reporting issues, which organisations are increasingly required to consider as part of their internal and external reporting processes. Specifically, the chapter considers organisational performance beyond financial performance.

LEARNING OBJECTIVES

After studying this chapter, you should be able to:

22.1 explain why an entity might adopt sustainable development and corporate social responsibility practices

22.2 discuss stakeholder influence on sustainable business practice

22.3 describe a range of methods used to report on social and environmental performance

22.4 describe the commonly used guidelines for sustainability reporting

22.5 evaluate the implications of climate change for accounting.

CONCEPT FOR REVIEW

Before studying this chapter, you should understand and, if necessary, revise:
• the regulation of financial reporting.

22.1 Sustainability and corporate social responsibility

LEARNING OBJECTIVE 22.1 Explain why an entity might adopt sustainable development and corporate social responsibility practices.

Although shareholders are traditionally seen as the most important stakeholders with regard to financial performance, a broader range of stakeholders is increasingly evaluating organisations on their social and environmental performance. The term **sustainability reporting** refers to reporting on social and environmental aspects of an organisation's operations.

The concept of corporate social responsibility (CSR) traditionally focuses on organisations' impacts on society. It highlights that while companies may primarily be focused on making profits, they also have an effect on, and responsibility to, society. Specifically, the notion of an organisation's 'social contract' refers to an expectation (rather than a formal agreement) that organisations act in ways acceptable to society. This notion includes acting within the law, but also extends to areas which may not be specifically covered by legislation in all countries (e.g. ensuring fair working conditions, providing a safe workplace for employees, and minimising environmental pollution). While the term CSR is sometimes used to consider environmental issues, the broader term 'sustainability' was introduced to encompass both social and environmental issues.

22.1.1 Origins of sustainability and corporate social responsibility

Sustainable development was identified as a significant issue by the United Nations in 1987, when it commissioned a report, *Our Common Future*. The report defined sustainable development as 'development that meets the needs of the present without compromising the ability of future generations to meet their own needs' (United Nations World Commission on Environment and Development 1987). This definition recognises that organisations' operations affect:

- the economy
- the environment
- society.

Hence, organisations have a responsibility not only to the financial interests of shareholders, but also to the broader interests of all stakeholders — both current and future generations. This definition highlights the importance of both intergenerational and intragenerational equity. **Intergenerational equity** has a long-term focus and recognises that consumption of resources should not affect the quality of life of future generations. **Intragenerational equity** relates to the ability to meet the needs of current generations. Together, intragenerational and intergenerational equity have been termed **eco-justice**. The concept of sustainability also considers what is known as **eco-efficiency** — a focus on the efficient use of resources to minimise the impact on the environment. While the definition of sustainability has received widespread debate, there is general agreement that it involves preservation and maintenance of the environment and involves some duty of social justice (Gray 2010).

The term 'corporate social responsibility' was popularised in the 1960s, with an explicit focus on organisations' responsibility to society. Given organisations use and control the majority of the Earth's resources, they have a responsibility to consider how their operations affect society, and to act in an appropriate (socially acceptable) manner. Hence, it became increasingly acknowledged that while it is essential for private sector organisations to make profits in order to continue operations, they must also consider their effects on the environment and society for current and future generations.

22.1.2 Reasons for adopting sustainable and corporate social responsibility practices

Embracing sustainability could make good business sense for an organisation. Various reasons for companies adopting sustainable practices include:

- compliance with mandatory obligations
- voluntary activity, guided by an organisation's ethical or moral position
- strategic activity, which benefits the environment, society and the organisation.

Compliance with environmental and social regulations (e.g. controlling pollution in accordance with the Environment Protection Act and meeting product safety standards for consumers) is essential for organisations, so that they do not incur penalties or suffer decreased profits through loss of market share due to poor reputation. This has been referred to as a *risk management approach* to sustainability or CSR.

Sustainability or CSR activity may also be undertaken voluntarily by organisations that choose to engage in activities beyond those required by law (e.g. philanthropy and recycling initiatives). Such activities may be guided by the organisation's ethical or moral stance (i.e. because they feel it is the 'right' thing to do). This is often referred to as an *altruistic approach* to CSR. There is also an argument that organisations that proactively adopt sustainability practices (i.e. those beyond what is required by law) may benefit from enhanced reputation and increased market share, resulting in increased profits.

Another reason for undertaking a specific sustainability or CSR activity is that it can generate dual benefits — helping the environment and/or society and the organisation in terms of its own core business operations. This is referred to as a *strategic approach* to sustainability or CSR. A strategic approach involves activities such as a mining company in a remote area training local unemployed people, who may later work for the organisation. Such training creates 'shared value' for both the organisation and society more broadly.

Figure 22.1 highlights how BHP Group Limited sees the sustainability of its operations affecting both internal and external stakeholders. Figure 22.2 shows ANZ Bank's approach to sustainability through its sustainability framework.

| FIGURE 22.1 | Material sustainability issues, BHP Group |

Our people
We look to create a culture of care and trusted relationships with our people through strong leadership and open communication.

Environment
We aim to minimise the environmental impacts from our activities and work in partnership with others to support environmental resilience.

Putting health and safety first, being environmentally responsible and supporting our communities.

Society
We support the development of diversified and resilient local economies that contribute to improved quality of life beyond the life of our operations.

Source: BHP Group Limited (2018, p. 9).

| FIGURE 22.2 | Corporate sustainability framework, ANZ |

Our Corporate Sustainability Framework

Our Corporate Sustainability Framework supports our business strategy and is aligned with the bank's purpose. The Framework has three key areas of focus:

- **Fair and responsible banking**
  Earn trust by keeping pace with the changing expectations of our stakeholders, maintaining high standards of conduct and understanding the social and environmental impacts of our business decisions.

▶

- **Social and economic participation**
  Build strong customer relationships and connect with our communities, supporting a diverse and inclusive society in which everyone can participate.
- **Sustainable growth**
  Create opportunities for all our customers and enable sustainable growth for individuals, businesses and industry.

SUSTAINABLE GROWTH

FAIR AND RESPONSIBLE BANKING

SHAPE A WORLD WHERE PEOPLE AND COMMUNITIES THRIVE

SOCIAL AND ECONOMIC PARTICIPATION

Source: ANZ (2017, p. 6).

While the costs of sustainability or CSR practices have been noted by companies, it has also been acknowledged that there are potential costs (e.g. loss of market share or decreased profits) associated with not adopting these practices. As such, sustainability-related expenses have also been viewed as long-term investments for an organisation. Essentially, however, sustainability and CSR practices remain largely discretionary. Hence, beyond compliance with legislation (e.g. the Workplace Health and Safety Act), organisations can choose whether they adopt sustainability or CSR practices (and if so, what type) .

In some countries (e.g. Indonesia), large private sector and public sector organisations are required by law to allocate a percentage of their profits to CSR activities. In most countries, however (including Australia, USA and UK), such activities (beyond basic CSR compliance) are encouraged rather than formally required. Encouragement may take the form of mechanisms such as tax deductions (e.g. for donations to charities) or emissions trading schemes (discussed in section 22.5).

LEARNING CHECK

☐ Sustainability reporting refers to reporting on social and environmental aspects of an organisation's operations.

☐ Corporate social responsibility (CSR) traditionally focuses on organisations' impacts on society. While CSR is sometimes used to consider environmental issues, the broader term 'sustainability' was introduced to encompass both social and environmental issues.

☐ Organisations' operations not only affect the economy, but also the environment and society. Hence, they have a responsibility not only to the financial interests of shareholders, but also to the broader interests of all stakeholders — both current (intragenerational equity) and future generations (intergenerational equity).

☐ Intergenerational equity has a long-term focus and recognises that consumption of resources should not affect the quality of life of future generations. Intragenerational equity relates to the ability to meet the needs of the current generation(s).

□ Organisations that proactively adopt sustainability practices (i.e. those beyond what is required by law) may benefit from enhanced reputation and increased market share, resulting in increased profits.

□ Beyond compliance with legislation, organisations can choose whether to adopt sustainability or CSR practices, as these practices are largely discretionary.

22.2 Stakeholder influences

LEARNING OBJECTIVE 22.2 Discuss stakeholder influence on sustainable business practice.

An understanding of why organisations adopt sustainable reporting practices can be gained by examining the range of organisational stakeholders and how their influence has changed over time. Traditionally, shareholders were seen as the primary stakeholder and organisations' primary objective was to maximise profits and shareholder value (whilst operating within the requirements of the law). Contemporary organisations must now consider a range of **stakeholders** — individuals and organisations affected by a company's operations — in their decision making. These might include employees, customers, suppliers, the media, government, superannuation funds and other institutional investors, lenders and community groups. Some sustainability frameworks (e.g. the Global Reporting Initiative, discussed in section 22.3) require organisations to undertake stakeholder assessment as part of their reporting process. Similarly, businesses, as part of their operations, identify and engage with stakeholders as a means of reducing risk and managing reputation.

Figure 22.3 provides examples of stakeholders and why they might be interested in corporate sustainability.

FIGURE 22.3	Stakeholder interests in corporate sustainability
Shareholders	Sustainability can improve entity value. Others consider sustainability issues in their investment decisions.
Customers	Some customers are interested in the source of products and actively seek 'green' or 'fair trade' products.
Fund investors	Some investors seek investments which provide financial and social returns (i.e. profits and social benefits).
Community groups	These groups are concerned with services and facilities offered in the local community, and the associated social and environmental implications (e.g. job creation, health and greenhouse gas emissions).
Media	The media can voice concerns of other stakeholders as well as set the public agenda relating to corporate sustainability issues.
Government and regulators	In some jurisdictions government and regulators monitor mandatory reporting of sustainability or environmental issues (e.g. Environmental Protection Authority).
Creditors or banks	Financial institutions need to consider the environmental impacts of projects they fund.

Stakeholders are increasingly concerned with issues of sustainability. Growing recognition of social and environmental issues has contributed to this increase. Such issues include:

- human rights (e.g. child labour, exploitative labour conditions in developing countries where people may work under poor conditions)
- employee rights (e.g. remuneration, safe workplace standards)
- philanthropy and charitable giving
- ethical and transparent business practices
- corporate governance (appropriate and transparent policies)
- pollution and environmental harm (e.g. logging, inappropriate use of non-renewable resources)
- environmental protection, and environmentally sustainable business operations
- product and process quality (e.g. safety of products, use of animal testing)
- unethical products (e.g. socially irresponsible products, weapons)
- climate change (e.g. the impact corporations have on global warming).

Figure 22.4 details Telstra's approach to **stakeholder engagement** as reflected in its Bigger Picture 2018 Sustainability Report.

FIGURE 22.4	Stakeholder engagement, Telstra	
Stakeholder group	**How we engage**	**Key sustainability topics**
Customers Our customers are residential consumers, small to medium enterprises, large companies and organisations, as well as government	Customer service channels including face-to-face, online and calls, external market research, social media, newsletters and white papers, Telecommunications Industry Ombudsman (TIO), regular messages issued through the mobile safety information SMS campaign and face-to-face consumer forums	• Customer experience • Privacy and data security • Business resilience • Ethics, values and governance
Communities We engage with our communities wherever we operate, including non-profit organisations and program partners, as well as community groups and individuals local to our operations	Team of Community Engage-ment Specialists, ongoing engagement through Corporate Affairs, Telstra stores and Telstra Country Wide, online channels, feedback surveys, sustainability programs and partnerships, community consultation, individual meetings and proactive community engagement in response to EME concerns and mobile base station consultation projects	• Customer experience • Business resilience • Ethics, values and governance • Health, safety and wellbeing • Human rights
Employees/potential employees Our workforce is large and diverse, with more than 32 000 employees in over 20 countries	Annual employee engagement survey, employee networking and engagement through internal social media channels, intranet corporate news, grievance mechanisms, performance reviews, and regu-lar team/departmental/company-wide meetings	• Customer experience • Privacy and data security • Business resilience • Health, safety and wellbeing • Cyber safety
Government We engage with government ministers and staff at local, state and federal levels in Australia, and internationally. Engagement can be with ministers, party leaders and department staff	Ongoing personal engagement, newsletters, online channels, public policy participation, government inquiries, feedback surveys, complaints/inquiries, information requests and partnerships	• Privacy and data security • Business resilience • Cyber safety • Network investment • Societal impacts of technology
Industry We engage with our sector peers and competitors, as well as ICT and telecommunications specific associations	Participation in industry associations, memberships such as Groupe Speciale Mobile Association (GSMA), Joint Audit Committee (JAC) and Global e-Sustainability Initiative (GeSI)	• Customer experience • Supply chain sustainability • Energy and emissions • Social and environmental sustainability • Ethics, values and governance
Shareholders and investment community Our investment community comprises institutional investors, buy and sell-side analysts, as well as around 1.4 million shareholders, some of whom invest with social and environmental preferences	Half year and full year briefings, investor days, investor road-shows, investor meetings, ASX announcements, direct phone and email correspondence, Telstra annual general meeting, Telstra website, online Telstra Exchange	• Customer experience • Privacy and data security • Business resilience • Regulatory change • Industry disruption and competition

Media We regularly engage with representatives from print, radio, TV, social and online media at a local, national and international level	Ongoing direct engagement with our communications, investor relations and media teams, media releases interviews	• Industry disruption and competition • Business resilience	• Customer experience • Privacy and data security • Network investments
Unions We work closely with the relevant employee trade unions including Community and Public Sector Union, Communications Electrical Plumbing Union and Professionals Australia	Formal consultation meetings and correspondence, ongoing engagement through Work Health Safety representatives	• Workplace relations • Health, safety and wellbeing	• Growing inequality • People capability • Industry disruption and competition
Suppliers We engage with more than 6000 suppliers, located across 45 countries around the world	Ongoing engagement by our procurement team, supplier surveys, ongoing assessments and onsite audits, participation in JAC-appointed audits and GeSI initiatives, commenced roll out of the Supplier Governance Framework, quarterly contractor HSE Forum with major suppliers of our construction workforce, ongoing collaboration with the Indigenous Workforce Program and activities under our Indigenous Labour Program, direct engagement of suppliers with higher potential human rights risks	• Privacy and data security • Ethics, values and governance • Supply chain sustainability	• Energy and emissions • New growth and business expansion
Regulators We work closely with industry regulators in all our markets	Participation in reviews conducted by regulators, information provision under various reporting requirements, ongoing regulatory inspections, ongoing regular engagement, newsletters, participation in industry bodies	• Customer experience • Ethics, values and governance	• Regulatory change • Industry disruption and competition

Source: Telstra Corporation Limited (2018, pp. 4–5).

The relationship between organisations and their stakeholders is complex. The extent to which an organisation will consider its stakeholders is often related to the power or influence of those stakeholders. Managers need to determine which stakeholders they should consider in their actions and manage these (at times) competing interests.

A stakeholder's power is related to the degree of control they have over resources required by the organisation (Ullmann 1985). The more necessary the resources controlled by a stakeholder are to the success of the organisation, the more likely it is that managers will address that stakeholder's concerns. One of the major roles of managers is to consider the relative importance of each of their stakeholders in meeting the organisation's strategic objectives, and to manage these relationships accordingly. For example, when a mining company wants to develop a mine site, there would be several stakeholders involved. These include government organisations responsible for approving the project, local businesses which may be affected by it (either positively due to increased business activity or negatively due to disruption/competition), local residents who may be affected (either positively due to employment opportunities or negatively due to disruption, inconvenience or a decrease in land values), land owners who may be directly affected (if the mining company needs to access their land) and environmental lobby groups who may be opposed to the mine. From the mining company's perspective, different stakeholder groups will be considered to have different levels of power, with government typically considered one of the most powerful groups, as government decides whether to authorise the project.

22.2.1 Ethical investment

Ethical investment and ethical investment funds represent a growing influence on corporate sustainability performance and reporting. Entities are challenged by social, environmental and regulatory pressures as institutional investors increasingly voice their concerns about the economic, financial and regulatory risks of business (see social and environmental issues detailed in the previous section). In the context of global warming, for example, many institutional investors have increased their demand for sustainability reporting by becoming signatories to the **CDP** (formerly the Carbon Disclosure Project). The CDP represents several large institutional investors, holding assets of more than US$100 trillion, such as Goldman Sachs, Catholic Super and Bank of America Merrill Lynch. These investors are concerned about the risks associated with climate change, and are thus calling for more information about how companies are addressing the challenges of climate change. The CDP questions companies about their policies, particularly in regard to lowering emissions and climate change resilience (CDP 2016).

The CDP is a voluntary effort to encourage standardised reporting procedures for companies to provide investors with relevant information about the business risks and opportunities from climate change (Kolk, Levy & Pinkse 2008). However, the lack of rigorous greenhouse gas emission disclosure guidelines and associated global regulation, means reports are often not standardised, making comparability difficult.

In the context of other social and environmental issues, sustainability reporting has become increasingly important for organisations to communicate how their operations address these issues. (Section 22.4 details guidelines available to organisations in preparing this information. However, similar to greenhouse gas emission disclosure requirements, reports are often not standardised, limiting comparability across organisations.)

In addition to direct investment in an ethical investment fund, investors have the opportunity to identify investments from benchmark indices. These indices categorise investments on the basis of sustainability in addition to financial performance. Launched in 1999, the Dow Jones Sustainability Indices (DJSIs) track the financial performance of the leading sustainability-driven companies worldwide. Based on the cooperation of S&P Dow Jones Indices and Sustainable Asset Management — an international investment group — the DJSIs provide asset managers with objective benchmarks to manage sustainability portfolios. In addition to providing information to investors, the DJSIs provide feedback to participating companies on their sustainability performance, and how they rank compared to industry averages. Similarly, the Australian Sustainable Asset Management Sustainability Index provides benchmarks for investors and feedback to companies with respect to their sustainability performance.

LEARNING CHECK

☐ Contemporary entities must consider a range of stakeholders in their decision making (e.g. employees, customers and suppliers), and stakeholders are increasingly concerned with issues of sustainability.

☐ The relationship between organisations and their stakeholders is complex. The extent to which an organisation will consider its stakeholders and address their concerns is often related to their power or influence.

☐ Ethical investment and ethical investment funds represent a growing influence on corporate sustainability performance and reporting. Ethical investment fund investors have the opportunity to identify investments from benchmark indices that categorise investments on the basis of sustainability in addition to financial performance.

22.3 Sustainability reporting

LEARNING OBJECTIVE 22.3 Describe a range of methods used to report on social and environmental performance.

Sustainability issues, and particularly those resulting from climate change, have an increasing influence on the business environment and, in turn, on the role of accountants. The need to measure and report on social and environmental performance (e.g. greenhouse gas emissions) has impacts on an organisation's information systems and reporting practices. Although the term 'sustainability reporting' is now commonly adopted, a number of other terms are also often used (e.g. corporate social reporting; corporate social responsibility reporting; triple bottom line reporting; environmental reporting; social audit; environmental, social and governance reports; and stakeholder reports). Many of these terms are used interchangeably.

While the term triple bottom line (TBL) reporting was commonly used until about 2006, the term 'sustainability reporting' is now commonly adopted.

The term 'triple bottom line reporting' was introduced in the late 1990s and refers to reporting on three aspects of performance — financial, environmental and social (Elkington 1997). A triple bottom line report or **sustainability report** refers to a report that not only presents information about the financial performance of an entity, but also provides information upon which stakeholders can judge the environmental and social performance. A well implemented sustainability reporting system can be used as part of a broader framework to integrate sustainability into business management decisions (Suggett & Goodsir 2002).

Sustainability reports are prepared by a range of organisations from various sectors, including for-profit organisations, not-for-profit organisations and the public sector.

The Australian Government, in producing guidelines to assist Australian entities determine appropriate environmental indicators, identified the following benefits of sustainability reporting (Department of the Environment and Heritage 2003, p. 6).

> *Embedding sound corporate governance and ethics systems throughout all levels of an organisation.* Currently many corporate governance initiatives are focused at the Board level. TBL helps ensure a values-driven culture is integrated at all levels.
>
> *Improved management of risk through enhanced management systems and performance monitoring.* This may also lead to more robust resource allocation decisions and business planning, as risks are better understood.
>
> *Formalising and enhancing communication with key stakeholders such as the finance sector, suppliers, community and customers.* This allows an organisation to have a more proactive approach to addressing future needs and concerns.
>
> *Attracting and retaining competent staff by demonstrating an organisation is focused on values and its long-term existence.*
>
> *Ability to benchmark performance both within industries and across industries.* This may lead to a competitive advantage with customers and suppliers, as well as enhanced access to capital as the finance sector continues to consider non-financial performance within credit and investment decisions.

While the extent of organisations presenting sustainability reports has increased, there is no required format, resulting in significant variation. Reporting in many countries is currently voluntary and organisations have developed their own measurement and reporting formats. Hence, reporting and disclosure (in terms of what and how organisations report) is largely discretionary and often not directly comparable. Further, such information may be presented as a separate report (e.g. CSR or environmental report), or combined and included in a company's annual report (i.e. 'integrated reporting').

22.3.1 Integrated reporting

Integrated reporting is an initiative designed to improve sustainability reporting and integrate it more closely with financial reporting and governance reporting (i.e. reporting on the rules, processes and laws within which an organisation operates or is governed). The development of integrated reporting followed the global financial crisis and resulted from a perceived need for a new economic model to protect a range of stakeholders (e.g. businesses, investors, employees and society) from subsequent crises. Governments and business leaders recognise the need for a change in emphasis of corporate reporting given it currently does not adequately reflect material environmental, social and governance factors such as resource usage, social impacts, human rights and how businesses may contribute to climate change (Stevenson 2011).

In 2010, the Prince of Wales' Accounting for Sustainability Project (A4S) and Global Reporting Initiative (GRI) formed the International Integrated Reporting Committee, now known as the International Integrated Reporting Council (IIRC). The IIRC members represent a cross-section of society, including members from the corporate, accounting, securities, regulatory, non-governmental organisation (NGO), intergovernmental organisation (IGO) and standard-setting sectors. The mission of the IIRC is 'to establish integrated reporting and thinking within mainstream business practice as the norm in the public and private sectors'. The IIRC believes integrated thinking and reporting will result in efficient and productive capital (resource) allocation, being forces for financial stability and sustainability.

In 2013, the IIRC developed its International Integrated Reporting Framework. The framework requires information about organisations' strategy, governance, impacts, performance and prospects, and aims to 'secure the adoption of Integrated Reporting by report preparers and gain the support of regulators and investors'. Figure 22.5 lists the framework's guiding principles and content elements.

Guiding Principles

The following Guiding Principles underpin the preparation of an integrated report, informing the content of the report and how information is presented:

- *Strategic focus and future orientation:* An integrated report should provide insight into the organization's strategy, and how it relates to the organization's ability to create value in the short, medium and long term, and to its use of and effects on the capitals
- *Connectivity of information:* An integrated report should show a holistic picture of the combination, interrelatedness and dependencies between the factors that affect the organization's ability to create value over time
- *Stakeholder relationships:* An integrated report should provide insight into the nature and quality of the organization's relationships with its key stakeholders, including how and to what extent the organization understands, takes into account and responds to their legitimate needs and interests
- *Materiality:* An integrated report should disclose information about matters that substantively affect the organization's ability to create value over the short, medium and long term
- *Conciseness:* An integrated report should be concise
- *Reliability and completeness:* An integrated report should include all material matters, both positive and negative, in a balanced way and without material error
- *Consistency and comparability:* The information in an integrated report should be presented: (a) on a basis that is consistent over time; and (b) in a way that enables comparison with other organizations to the extent it is material to the organization's own ability to create value over time.

Content Elements

An integrated report includes eight Content Elements that are fundamentally linked to each other and are not mutually exclusive:

- *Organizational overview and external environment:* What does the organization do and what are the circumstances under which it operates?
- *Governance:* How does the organization's governance structure support its ability to create value in the short, medium and long term?
- *Business model:* What is the organization's business model?
- *Risks and opportunities:* What are the specific risks and opportunities that affect the organization's ability to create value over the short, medium and long term, and how is the organization dealing with them?
- *Strategy and resource allocation:* Where does the organization want to go and how does it intend to get there?
- *Performance:* To what extent has the organization achieved its strategic objectives for the period and what are its outcomes in terms of effects on the capitals?
- *Outlook:* What challenges and uncertainties is the organization likely to encounter in pursuing its strategy, and what are the potential implications for its business model and future performance?
- *Basis of presentation:* How does the organization determine what matters to include in the integrated report and how are such matters quantified or evaluated?

Source: International Integrated Reporting Committee (2013, p. 5).

However, beyond these principles and elements, there is limited guidance regarding the specific format and detail expected in these reports. Hence, until more detailed guidance or regulation is introduced, comparability seems unlikely. Further information about the IIRC can be found on its website, www.integratedreporting.org.

22.3.2 Environmental reporting

Environmental reporting is a subset of sustainability reporting. When preparing sustainability reports, organisations generally include information about their environmental performance and impacts. This may be presented as a separate section of the annual report, in a separate environmental report or as part of a comprehensive sustainability or CSR report.

Research on environmental disclosure has largely examined this issue in terms of an organisation's **social contract**, arguing that organisations can only continue to exist in society if they operate within a value system consistent with that society (Gray, Owen & Adams 1996). This means that an organisation must appear to consider the rights of the public at large, not just its shareholders.

Organisations that have been subject to scrutiny due to concerns of poor environmental performance (e.g. high emissions, large oil spills) have subsequently been found to provide greater levels of environmental information (Deegan & Rankin 1996). In addition, other companies operating in industries where there has been a large environmental problem may also respond with increased disclosure to promote transparency. By way of example, following the BP oil spill in the Gulf of Mexico in 2010, increased disclosure on environmental issues was noted not only in BP's annual report, but also in a number of other oil companies' annual reports.

Another factor that could affect environmental reporting is firm reputation and strategic risk management. Managers have a desire to manage stakeholder views of environmental performance in an effort to portray the firm as environmentally and socially responsible, with the expectation that effective environmental or social risk management will lead to increased earnings and investment in the company.

LEARNING CHECK

☐ A number of terms are commonly used for sustainability reporting (e.g. corporate social reporting, corporate social responsibility reporting, triple bottom line reporting, environmental reporting, social audit, environmental, social and governance reporting and stakeholder reporting). Many of these terms are used interchangeably.

☐ Sustainability reports are prepared by a range of organisations from various sectors, including not-for-profit entities and the public sector; however, there has been limited guidance on appropriate methods of developing sustainability reports.

☐ Reporting in many countries is voluntary and organisations have developed their own measurement and reporting formats, resulting in poor comparability of these reports.

☐ Integrated reporting is an initiative designed to improve sustainability reporting and integrate it more closely with financial and governance reporting. The IIRC has introduced a framework which includes guiding principles and content elements, but to date there is limited guidance regarding the specific format and detail expected in these reports.

☐ Environmental reporting is a subset of sustainability reporting. When preparing sustainability reports, organisations generally include information about their environmental performance and impacts.

22.4 Guidelines for sustainability and CSR reporting

LEARNING OBJECTIVE 22.4 Describe the commonly used guidelines for sustainability reporting.

There is a range of guidelines on sustainability reporting. The United Nations (UN) has been responsible for a number of these, including the UN Global Compact with principles on human rights, labour, environment and anti-corruption. Corporate entities joining the Global Compact are required to communicate annually on their progress by submitting an annual 'Communication on Progress' report. Non-business participants are required to submit a 'Communication on Engagement' report every two years. The key information to be included in these reports includes a statement of ongoing commitment to the Global Compact, a description of practical actions the company has taken to implement the Global Compact's key principles, and a measurement of outcomes. The UN Global Compact coordinates with other sustainability and CSR reporting frameworks, including the Global Reporting Initiative (GRI) (see section 22.4.1) Sustainability Reporting Standards.

The UN has also produced the Principles for Responsible Investment, a set of investment principles aimed at integrating social and environmental factors into financial practices. Signatory companies (usually institutional investors) are required to communicate their application of the principles annually to the UN.

In 2008, the United Nations Conference on Trade and Development (UNCTAD) produced guidance on the use of corporate sustainability indicators in annual reports. The objective of the document, which was developed with reference to the GRI's guidelines and the International Financial Reporting Standards, is to provide detailed guidance on the preparation of reports using selected indicators. The guidance discusses key stakeholders and their information needs, including an overview of users, their uses for corporate responsibility reporting, and selected indicators, along with detailed guidance for reporting on each of these indicators. The selected indicators are presented in figure 22.6.

The Organisation for Economic Co-operation and Development's (OECD) *Guidelines for Multinational Enterprises* includes a section on disclosure, which encourages multinational enterprises to provide disclosures on their non-financial performance in addition to financial performance. AccountAbility's AA1000 series provides principles-based standards for sustainability reporting.

FIGURE 22.6   Overview of selected corporate sustainability indicators

Group	Indicator
Trade, investment and linkages	• Total revenues • Value of imports versus exports • Total new investments • Local purchasing
Employment creation and labour practices	• Total workforce with breakdown by employment type, employment contract and gender • Employee wages and benefits with breakdown by employment type and gender • Total number and rate of employee turnover broken down by gender • Percentage of employees covered by collective agreements
Technology and human resources development	• Expenditure on research and development • Average hours of training per year per employee broken down by employee category • Expenditure on employee training per year per employee broken down by employee category
Health and safety	• Cost of employee health and safety • Work days lost to occupational accidents, injuries and illness
Government and community contributions	• Payments to government • Voluntary contributions to civil society
Corruption	• Number of convictions for violations of corruption related laws or regulations and amount of fines paid/payable

Source: United Nations (2008, pp. 17–18).

The International Organization for Standardization (ISO) has developed standards dealing with a range of issues. Of relevance to sustainability reporting is the ISO 14000 series on environmental management and the ISO 26000 guidance standard on social responsibility. ISO 14001 requires management to develop a policy of communication of environmental performance. ISO 26000, issued in 2010, requires organisations to demonstrate their accountability by reporting significant impacts related to social responsibility to concerned stakeholders.

22.4.1 Global Reporting Initiative

The GRI was launched in 1997 as an initiative to develop a globally accepted reporting framework to enhance the quality of sustainability reporting. It is a joint initiative of the Coalition of Environmentally Responsible Economies (CERES) and the United Nations Environment Program (UNEP). The aim is to enhance transparency, comparability and clarity, amongst other principles.

The GRI developed a framework of principles and performance indicators that organisations could use to measure and report their economic, social and environmental performance. GRI's initial *Sustainability Reporting Guidelines* were produced in 2000 and revised over time, with the fourth-generation (G4) Guidelines being released in 2013. In 1 July 2018 the guidelines were replaced by the GRI Sustainability Reporting Standards.

The standards were developed through years of consultation with experts and stakeholders and are intended to represent global best practice for reporting on economic, environmental and social impacts. Organisations that adopt the GRI Standards use three universal standards: GRI 101: *Foundation*, GRI 102: *General Disclosures* and GRI 103: *Management Approach* and then apply topic-specific economic, environmental and social standards that suit the characteristics of the organisation and its activities. Organisations using the standards product a report that is either:

• *a report in accordance with the GRI standards* — the report complies with all of the requirements in the GRI standards, or
• *a GRI-referenced report* — the report has merely drawn on GRI standards for guidance to assist the reporting of specific information.

The GRI Sustainability Reporting Standards are intended to:

• enable any organisation to understand and communicate about their impacts on the economy, the environment and society
• provide flexibility to meet all sustainability reporting needs
• serve as a reference for policy makers and regulators.

Figure 22.7 lists the GRI Sustainability Reporting Standards.

| FIGURE 22.7 | Global Reporting Initiative Sustainability Reporting Standards |

Universal Standards

The 100 series of the GRI Standards includes three universal Standards applicable for every organization preparing a sustainability report. They guide reporters in using the Standards, reporting an organization's relevant contextual information, and reporting how its material topics are managed.

GRI 101: Foundation 2016 (containing Standard Interpretation 1)
GRI 102: General Disclosures 2016
GRI 103: Management Approach 2016

Economic Standards

The 200 series of the GRI Standards include topic-specific Standards used to report information on an organization's material impacts related to economic topics.

GRI 201: Economic Performance 2016
GRI 202: Market Presence 2016
GRI 203: Indirect Economic Impacts 2016
GRI 204: Procurement Practices 2016
GRI 205: Anti-corruption 2016
GRI 206: Anti-competitive Behavior 2016

Environment Standards

The 300 series of the GRI Standards include topic-specific Standards used to report information on an organization's material impacts related to environmental topics.

GRI 301: Materials 2016
GRI 302: Energy 2016
GRI 303: Water and Effluents 2018
GRI 304: Biodiversity 2016
GRI 305: Emissions 2016
GRI 306: Effluents and Waste 2016
GRI 307: Environmental Compliance 2016
GRI 308: Supplier Environmental Assessment 2016

Social Standards

The 400 series of the GRI Standards include topic-specific Standards used to report information on an organization's material impacts related to social topics.

GRI 401: Employment 2016 (containing Standard Interpretation 1)
GRI 402: Labor/Management Relations 2016
GRI 403: Occupational Health and Safety 2018
GRI 404: Training and Education 2016
GRI 405: Diversity and Equal Opportunity 2016
GRI 406: Non-discrimination 2016
GRI 407: Freedom of Association and Collective Bargaining 2016
GRI 408: Child Labor 2016
GRI 409: Forced or Compulsory Labor 2016
GRI 410: Security Practices 2016
GRI 411: Rights of Indigenous Peoples 2016
GRI 412: Human Rights Assessment 2016
GRI 413: Local Communities 2016
GRI 414: Supplier Social Assessment 2016
GRI 415: Public Policy 2016
GRI 416: Customer Health and Safety 2016
GRI 417: Marketing and Labeling 2016
GRI 418: Customer Privacy 2016
GRI 419: Socioeconomic Compliance 2016

Source: Global Reporting Initiative (2018).

22.4.2 Mandatory sustainability and CSR reporting requirements

There are increasing instances of mandatory environmental, social and governance reporting requirements around the world, some of which are considered in this section. Figure 22.8 summarises some of the key reporting requirements for various countries.

FIGURE 22.8 Global corporate social responsibility disclosure requirements

Australia

Under the Financial Services Reform Act, issuers of financial products are obliged to disclose the extent to which labour standards or environmental, social or ethical considerations are taken into account in the selection, retention or realisation of an investment. The Corporations Act requires some disclosure of violations of environmental legislation in listed companies' annual reports. The ASX requires companies to disclose if they have material exposure to 'environmental and social sustainability risks' and, if so, identify how they plan to manage and mitigate this risk. Companies listed on ASX must disclose if they have developed a code of conduct on environmental risks and controls. ASX mandates that all products with an investment component disclose the extent to which environmental and social considerations are taken into account in investment selection, retention and realisation.

China

An influential directive strongly encourages state-owned enterprises to follow sound CSR practices. The government's 'Green Securities' policy requires listed companies to disclose more information about their environmental record.

Denmark

Companies are required to disclose their CSR activities and use of environmental resources. Companies with 'significant environmental impacts' are obligated to publish green accounts.

France

Companies are required to include ESG information in their annual reports. Listed companies must disclose data on 40 labour and social criteria. Public pension funds are required to disclose how their investment policy guidelines have addressed social and environmental considerations. CSR reporting and social and environmental information obligation for listed companies and other large companies is subject to independent third-party verification.

Hong Kong

The Hong Kong Stock Exchange requires board diversity for listed companies (based on age, gender, culture and professional experience). Companies have to comply or explain their reasoning for not adhering to the requirements.

India

Mandatory for companies with net worth of more than Rs 500 crore (1 crore is 10 000 000 rupees), or turnover of Rs 1000 crore to adopt a CSR policy and establish a CSR committee. Companies with a minimum net worth of Rs 500 crore, turnover of Rs 500 crore or profit of Rs 5 crore are required to spend at least 2% of their 3-year average annual net profit on social welfare initiatives.

Specified corporations must submit an annual environmental audit. The Securities and Exchange Board of India mandates listed companies report on Environmental, Social and Governance initiatives undertaken by them.

Indonesia

Law requires listed companies to report on the effects of their activities on society and the environment. Failure to do so necessitates an explanation for not disclosing this information. Companies involved in operations that affect natural resources are obligated to create and implement CSR programs.

Japan

Specified companies and government agencies are required to produce annual reports on their activities related to the environment including amount of greenhouse gas emissions and total amount of waste generated.

Malaysia

Listed companies are required to publish CSR information in their annual report.

Norway

Large companies are required to disclose information on how they integrate social responsibility into their business strategies. Listed companies must publish a statement on the companies' principles for corporate governance. Environmental issues are to be included in companies' directors' reports.

Saudi Arabia

Launched the Saudi Arabian Responsible Competitiveness Index (SARCI), evaluating a company's strategy, management, engagement processes and performance systems.

Singapore

The Code on Corporate Governance provides principles and guidelines for corporate governance, for which companies are required to disclose compliance. Sustainability reporting is mandatory for listed companies, disclosing a company's economic, environmental and social impacts.

South Africa

The Mineral Resources and Petroleum Bill requires certain companies to disclose to the government how they will address the social impacts of their operations. The Broad-Based Black Empowerment Act requires disclosure on corporate initiatives regarding black empowerment. King III requires integrated sustainability reporting and third party assurance.

Taiwan

The financial markets regulator requires all public and listed companies to disclose their CSR performance, including measurements the company has adopted with regards to environmental protection, community participation, contribution to society, social and public interests, consumer rights and interest, and the state of implementation. Taiwan Stock Exchange (TWSE) has an index that focuses on corporate governance and corporate social responsibility.

United Kingdom

Companies listed on the London Stock Exchange are required to disclose information on environmental, workplace, social, and community matters that are material to their business, including greenhouse gas emissions. Pension managers must provide a written statement dictating the extent to which social, environmental or ethical considerations are taken into account in investment decisions. The Modern Slavery Act of 2015 requires company to disclose what they do to combat modern slavery, human trafficking and child labour throughout their supply chain (Islam 2018).

United States of America

The Mandatory Reporting of Greenhouse Gases rule requires large emitters of greenhouse gases to collect and report data with respect to their greenhouse gas emissions. The New York Stock Exchange requires listed companies to 'adopt and disclose a code of business conduct and ethics'. The California Transparency in Supply Chains Act of 2010 requires large retail and manufacturing firms in that state to disclose their efforts to eliminate slavery and human trafficking from their supply chains (Islam 2018). The US Global Conflict Mineral Rule requires firms to disclose efforts to combat human trafficking in global minerals supply chains (Islam 2018).

Source: Extracts from Hauser Institute for Civil Society (2015). From the Initiative For Responsible Investment Working Paper 'Corporate Social Responsibility Disclosure Efforts by National Governments and Stock Exchanges'.

22.4.3 Social and environmental management systems

With increased interest in sustainable reporting, interest in **social and environmental management systems** has also intensified. These systems (typically software) help organisations to measure, record and manage their social and environmental performance. Implementation of these systems indicates an organisation's commitment to better monitor, manage, measure and report social and environmental matters. These systems not only provide organisations with social and environmental management tools, but also facilitate communication to stakeholders, along with organisational learning.

The international standard ISO 14001 *Environmental Management* governs environmental management systems and relates to their development and audit. It requires certifying companies to establish and maintain communication (both internally and externally); develop policies, objectives and targets; and assess environmental performance against these requirements. ISO 26000 *Social Responsibility* provides guidance on social responsibility for organisations to act in an ethical and transparent way.

☐ There is a range of guidelines on sustainability reporting, including from the United Nations, the Organisation for Economic Co-operation and Development and the International Organization for Standardization.

☐ The most widely recognised guidelines are those provided by the Global Reporting Initiative (GRI). The GRI Sustainability Reporting Standards provide a comprehensive framework for organisations to measure and report their economic, social and environmental performance.

☐ Mandatory environmental, social and governance reporting requirements are increasing around the world, but they vary between countries.

☐ Social and environmental management systems help organisations to measure, record and manage their social and environmental performance.

22.5 Climate change and accounting

LEARNING OBJECTIVE 22.5 Evaluate the implications of climate change for accounting.

One of the most pressing sustainability issues is climate change. The United Nations Framework Convention on Climate Change (UNFCCC) developed the **Kyoto Protocol** to achieve international action to mitigate human-induced climate change. The Kyoto Protocol commits signatories to achieving greenhouse gas or carbon emission reductions.

Under the Kyoto Protocol, countries were allocated allowed emissions based on agreed targets. If countries' actual emissions are less than their agreed targets, unused emission allowances can be traded. Carbon credits can also be received for investing in carbon efficient initiatives. The Kyoto Protocol came into force in 2005 and relates to two commitment periods: 2008–2012 and 2013–2020. However, a number of countries withdrew from the Protocol or did not commit to second-round targets (e.g. Canada, the United States and New Zealand).

A new agreement was adopted in 2015 (the **Paris Agreement**), to be implemented from 2020 with the aim of constraining global average temperature increase to no more than 1.5 °C over the long-term. The Paris Agreement outlines a broad approach towards a global emissions trading market as a mechanism to reduce carbon emissions.

The following section examines emissions schemes and the accounting issues that stem from climate change and emissions trading.

22.5.1 Emissions reduction schemes

One response being used around the globe to mitigate climate change is the development of emissions reduction schemes. These can be in the form of either an emissions trading scheme or a carbon tax. An **emissions trading scheme (ETS)** is often referred to as a cap and trade scheme, as it allows participants to trade excess emissions permits. Emissions trading schemes work differently in different jurisdictions, but essentially governments create tradeable emissions permits based on the Kyoto target. Permits are given to business, sold or auctioned. A cap or limit is set on the level of emissions permitted by organisations. Organisations are required to obtain permits that equal the amount of their emissions. If their emissions levels exceed the amount allowed based on the permits held, they are required to buy additional permits to avoid substantial fines. This has led to the creation of secondary markets where greenhouse gas permits can be bought or sold, with the price being determined by market demand and supply. Over time governments can lower the cap, thus moving towards achieving a country's national emissions reduction target.

The alternative is a carbon tax based on the amount of emissions. There is no cap set on the level of emissions and it has been argued that a carbon tax is less likely to lead to a reduction in emissions because of this. However, the alternative view is that a carbon tax sends an immediate price signal to the market that the organisation's operations result in greenhouse gas emissions, affecting society.

Governments in a number of countries have introduced an ETS, including Japan, the United States, New Zealand, China and India. The most established ETS is the European Union Emissions Trading Scheme (EU ETS), which commenced in 2005 and remains the world's largest, encompassing all EU member states as well as Iceland, Norway and Liechtenstein. The EU ETS is collectively responsible for almost half of the EU's emissions of carbon dioxide.

The New Zealand government pledged to cut greenhouse gas emissions by between 10 and 20% on 1990 levels by 2020 (New Zealand Ministry for the Environment 2011). The New Zealand ETS puts obligations on certain industries to account for the greenhouse gas emissions that result from their activities. The New Zealand ETS is based around a trade in units, with the New Zealand Unit (NZU), allocated by the government. Emitting firms have to surrender these to the government annually and purchase additional units where actual emissions exceed allocated units, while those who remove rather than emit greenhouse gases (e.g. the forestry sector) can receive units.

In Australia in 2008, the then Labor Australian Government proposed the Carbon Pollution Reduction Scheme (CPRS), being a market-based solution designed to encourage business to invest in greenhouse gas emission reductions (Garnaut 2008). The CPRS had many detractors, however, particularly from the powerful mining and energy lobby groups which argued that their industries would lose competitive advantage if greenhouse gases were priced. In 2011, the Australian House of Representatives passed a Clean Energy legislative package, putting a price on carbon as an incentive to invest in clean energies, thus reducing pollution. A fixed carbon price of $23 a tonne applied from 1 July 2012, with the intention of moving to a flexible price from 1 July 2015. In 2013, however, the Liberal–National Coalition Government came into power and repealed the carbon tax in the following year, with the intention of replacing it with an alternative scheme, which had not been implemented at the time of writing.

While emissions trading schemes generally target high emitters, it is anticipated that every business is affected in some way (e.g. through increased power or transport costs). There is an increase in demand by some businesses for products to be carbon neutral, or for suppliers to disclose their carbon footprint. However, a criticism of various ETS is that they were initially too generous in allocating permits, thus reduction in emissions was not sufficiently encouraged.

An ETS results in both benefits and costs. While benefits extend to the population in general, and companies through strategic and/or financial advantage, costs to organisations include the costs of future investments to mitigate and manage emissions, the costs to meet reporting requirements and costs for compliance and monitoring (Bui, Fowler & Hunt 2009). Measurement, reporting, and verification (third-party assurance) are also challenges for companies, some of which rely on theoretical calculation rather than actual measurements.

If the ETS operates as a market scheme there are likely to be additional costs or at the very least price fluctuations and uncertainty involved in the event that carbon credits need to be purchased, as well as indirect costs for people and organisations more broadly, resulting from higher electricity prices.

Multinational corporations are particularly affected by the development of ETSs, due to different schemes being implemented in different countries. This results in differing institutional constraints and reporting requirements across the locations in which they operate.

22.5.2 Accounting for carbon emissions

As previously mentioned, ETSs are either currently operating or proposed across a number of jurisdictions. Despite this, there is currently no guidance on how to account for carbon pollution permits or emissions trading activities. In 2004, prior to the commencement of the EU ETS, the IASB issued IFRIC 3 *Emission Rights*. There was, however, considerable criticism of the proposal, with many arguing it involved inconsistent accounting of assets and liabilities and potential volatility. Following these criticisms it was subsequently withdrawn. In the United States, the Emerging Issues Task Force also attempted to address the issue of accounting for carbon emissions, but this was subsequently removed from their agenda and remains unresolved.

The operation of a carbon trading scheme creates a number of short-term and long-term financial implications for organisations. In the short term, organisations are required to account for both purchased and allocated emissions allowances. One issue facing organisations is how to account for allowances allocated by government on an annual basis. Are they to be recorded at fair value or at cost — effectively zero? Should there be a difference in treatment for allocated versus purchased emissions allowances? The treatment of allowances is likely to be related to their classification as either an intangible asset or a financial instrument.

Organisations also need to consider how to account for their obligation to the government at the end of the reporting period to 'pay' for their emissions. It has also been suggested that organisations should be permitted to use hedge accounting to reduce the risk associated with their allowance asset and emissions liability (Cook 2009).

Climate change also has an impact on traditional financial accounting as it affects the value of assets and asset impairment decisions. Climate change can affect the value of physical assets such as land, and assets used to produce products no longer in demand due to changes in consumer preference to 'green' products and technologies. Climate change also affects the disclosure of risk and risk management strategies required in financial reports.

LEARNING CHECK

☐ One of the most pressing sustainability issues is climate change.

☐ The Kyoto Protocol is an agreement which commits signatories to achieve greenhouse gas or carbon emission reductions. It relates to two commitment periods: 2008–2012 and 2013–2020, with the Paris Agreement to be implemented from 2020.

☐ ETSs and carbon taxes are two approaches to reduce environmental pollution.

☐ The European Union ETS is the world's largest, and a number of other countries have introduced similar schemes.

☐ Accounting for carbon emissions is challenging, and has a significant effect on the value of assets and liabilities.

SUMMARY

Sustainability relates to development that meets the needs of the present without compromising the ability of future generations to meet their own needs. Increasing awareness of the importance of sustainable development to business has resulted in increased sustainability reporting. A number of terms are commonly used for sustainability reporting:

- Sustainability reporting (also known as triple bottom line or TBL reporting) refers to performance in three main areas: financial, environmental and social.
- Sustainability, TBL or corporate social responsibility reports have been presented by a range of Australian companies, not-for-profit organisations and government departments.
- Integrated reporting is a recent initiative designed to improve sustainability reporting and integrate it more closely with financial and governance reporting.
- Social and environmental reporting are subsets of sustainability reporting. Currently, no required format for social or environmental reporting exists.

The most widely recognised reporting guideline is the Global Reporting Initiative (GRI) Sustainability Reporting Standards, a globally accepted reporting framework to enhance the quality of sustainability reporting.

Ethical investment and ethical funds pose a growing influence on corporate sustainability behaviour. Institutional investors have increased their demand for sustainability reporting through signing up to the Carbon Disclosure Project. In addition, investment in ethical funds has increased substantially in recent years.

One response to mitigate climate change is the introduction of emissions trading schemes (ETS). An ETS is a system designed to control emissions by allowing participants to trade excess emissions permits. While emissions trading schemes generally target high emitters, every organisation is expected to be affected in some way. There is currently no guidance on how to account for carbon pollution permits or emissions trading activities.

KEY TERMS

CDP A group of large institutional investors aiming to encourage standardised reporting procedures for companies to provide investors with relevant information about the business risks and opportunities from climate change. Formerly known as the Carbon Disclosure Project.

eco-efficiency A focus on the efficient use of resources to minimise the impact on the environment.

eco-justice A combination of intragenerational and intergenerational equity.

emissions trading scheme (ETS) A scheme designed to reduce greenhouse gas emissions by placing a cost on emissions.

ethical investment An investment approach based on an assessment of the ethical standards of entities.

integrated reporting An initiative designed to improve sustainability reporting and integrate it more closely with financial reporting and governance reporting.

intergenerational equity The concept that consumption of resources should not affect the quality of life of future generations.

intragenerational equity The ability to meet the needs of current generations.

Kyoto Protocol An international agreement that commits signatories to reducing greenhouse gas emissions.

Paris Agreement The successor to the Kyoto Protocol — an international agreement that commits signatories to keeping global temperature increase to 1.5 °C.

social and environmental management systems Systems (typically software) that help organisations to measure, record and manage their social and environmental performance.

social contract The expectation that an organisation will operate within the values of its society.

stakeholder engagement The ways in which an entity interacts with its stakeholders.

stakeholders Individuals and organisations affected by a company's operations.

sustainability report A report that not only presents information about the financial performance of an entity, but provides information upon which stakeholders can also judge the environmental and social performance. Also known as a triple bottom line report.

sustainability reporting Reporting on social, environmental and financial aspects of an organisation's operations.

sustainable development Development that meets the needs of the present without compromising the ability of future generations to meet their own needs.

COMPREHENSION QUESTIONS

1 Explain the meaning of sustainability.

2 Explain the difference between eco-justice and eco-efficiency, and outline how both might relate to business activities.

3 What reasons might an entity provide for adopting sustainable development?

4 Identify what information entities are likely to provide if they use sustainability reporting.

5 Explain the difference between sustainability reporting and traditional financial reporting.

6 What benefits should entities expect from preparing sustainability reports?

7 What is international integrated reporting and how does it differ from the current financial reporting system?

8 What is the Global Reporting Initiative, and what is its purpose?

9 Identify four corporate stakeholders and explain how they affect a business's operations.

10 Identify why you would expect the finance sector — and investment funds in particular — to have an interest in climate change. Identify how ethical investment can affect corporate decision making regarding sustainable business operations.

11 Explain what an environmental management system is and how it can be used to improve environmental performance.

12 Explain how emissions trading schemes are likely to affect financial reporting.

CASE STUDY 22.1

SUSTAINABILITY REPORTING

The manager of Gladstone Ltd is not convinced of the scientific evidence behind climate change, and does not consider it necessary to adopt changes in the company's operations that would decrease its greenhouse gas emissions. Gladstone Ltd's accountant, however, has argued that if the company does not decrease its greenhouse gas emissions, the company's carbon footprint will begin to appear on its statement of financial position with the introduction of a carbon emissions trading scheme.

Required

Explain what the accountant means when they say a carbon footprint will appear on the statement of financial position, and whether this 'footprint' would be visible to investors.

CASE STUDY 22.2

COSTS AND BENEFITS OF ENVIRONMENTALLY FRIENDLY BUSINESS PRACTICES

The directors of Perth Ltd are concerned about the increased costs proposed by the company in adopting new, more environmentally friendly technology. Management has argued that the company was 'always going to pay a price for carbon reduction', but contends the short-term costs will be outweighed by the long-term benefits.

Required

Explain what benefits management might be referring to.

CASE STUDY 22.3

STAKEHOLDERS

Darwin Ltd wants to focus on 'people, profits, planet'. The board of directors has proposed linking top managers' pay to broad measures of environmental sustainability, and worker and customer satisfaction. The board proposes that bonuses for management will be linked to targets such as the reduction of greenhouse gas emissions and energy use, the introduction of new environmentally friendly products and improvements in workforce morale.

Required

Advise the board of the potential implications, both positive and negative, of the proposed remuneration policy.

CASE STUDY 22.4

ETHICAL INVESTMENT

The report *Carbon counts 2011: The carbon footprints of Australian superannuation investment managers* examines 14 of the largest superannuation funds in Australia, accounting for $36 billion in equity holdings, and looks at the greenhouse gas emissions associated with 88 equity portfolios that employ different investment styles. The report is considered to have a significant impact on the investment strategies of superannuation funds.

Required

Outline the type of influence the report may have.

CASE STUDY 22.5

ETHICAL INVESTMENT

Refer again to the report mentioned in case study 22.4. While some investment categories have a smaller carbon footprint than others (due to a focus on different industries), it has been argued that it is not just the size of the carbon footprint that it important, but also the relative performance of companies within an industry group. The board of Onslow Ltd has proposed a review of the company's superannuation fund portfolio to shift from overweight carbon-efficient companies to underweight carbon-intensive companies.

Required

Explain what the board means in relation to these terms.

APPLICATION AND ANALYSIS EXERCISES

★ BASIC | ★ ★ MODERATE | ★ ★ ★ DIFFICULT

22.1 Sustainability reporting ★ ★   LO1, 2, 3, 4

Obtain the most recent sustainability report by Shell (Royal Dutch Shell plc).

Required

Prepare a report that addresses the following issues.
1. Shell's vision and mission statement, and how these might relate to sustainability (if at all)
2. Shell's stakeholders and how the company has engaged with each of stakeholder group
3. Governance mechanisms in place on the board of directors to address sustainability
4. How Shell links sustainability to its risk management systems
5. Any guidance Shell used in implementing environmental and social performance and reporting systems

22.2 Stakeholder engagement ★ ★   LO2

This chapter has identified a range of stakeholders that managers should consider when determining sustainability performance and reporting. Determine how managers should engage with each of these stakeholders and document what sustainability issues they would be likely to discuss during this engagement process.

22.3 Sustainability index ★   LO2

Explain the purpose of the Dow Jones Sustainability Indices.

22.4 Reporting ★ ★ ★   LO3

Explain the difference between an integrated report and a CSR report. What are some of the benefits and limitations of each?

22.5 Impact on financial reporting ★ ★   LO3, 4

There are no IFRS accounting standards for the reporting of social and environmental activities. Evaluate what issues this presents for the preparation of financial reports.

22.6 Sustainability — developing countries ★ ★   LO1, 2, 5

You are the accountant of a company that is considering expanding its operations to a developing country. The CEO has asked for a report outlining what issues the company should consider from a sustainability perspective when making this decision. Outline some of the key issues to be included in the report.

22.7 ETS ★ ★ ★   **LO5**

Explain the difference between an emissions trading scheme and a carbon tax. What are some of the benefits and limitations of each?

22.8 ETS ★ ★   **LO5**

Research and prepare a report on the different approaches for accounting for carbon emissions under the EU ETS.

REFERENCES

ANZ 2017, *Corporate sustainability review 2017*, www.anz.com.

Australian Government Department of the Environment and Heritage 2003, *Triple bottom line reporting in Australia: a guide to reporting against environmental indicators*, Commonwealth of Australia, Canberra.

BHP Group Limited 2018, *Sustainability report 2018*, www.bhp.com.

Bui, B, Fowler, C & Hunt, C 2009, 'Costs of an ETS', *Chartered Accountants Journal*, vol. 88, no. 9, pp. 36–8.

CDP 2016, 'About us', www.cdp.net.

Cook, A 2009, 'Emissions rights: from costless activity to market operations', *Accounting, Organizations and Society*, vol. 34, nos. 3/4, pp. 456–68.

Deegan, C & Rankin, M 1996, 'Do Australian companies report environmental news objectively? An analysis of environmental disclosures by firms prosecuted successfully by the Environmental Protection Authority', *Accounting, Auditing & Accountability Journal*, vol. 9, no. 2, pp. 52–67.

Elkington, J 1997, *Cannibals with forks — the triple bottom line of 21st century business*, Capstone Publishing, Oxford.

Garnaut, R 2008, *The Garnaut climate change review final report*, Cambridge University Press, Melbourne.

Global Reporting Initiative 2018, *Sustainability Reporting Standards*, www.globalreporting.org.

Gray, R 2010, 'Is accounting for sustainability actually accounting for sustainability . . . and how would we know? An exploration of narratives of organisations and the planet', *Accounting, Organizations and Society*, vol. 35, iss. 1, pp. 47–62.

Gray, R, Owen, D & Adams, C 1996, *Accounting and accountability*, Prentice Hall, Hertfordshire, UK.

Hauser Institute for Civil Society 2015, *Corporate social responsibility disclosure efforts by national governments and stock exchanges*, Initiative for Responsible Investment, Harvard University, hausercenter.org.

International Integrated Reporting Committee 2013, *The international framework*, www.integratedreporting.org.

Islam, MA 2018, 'What is corporate social responsibility — and does it work?', *The Conversation*, https://theconversation.com/what-is-corporate-social-responsibility-and-does-it-work-89710.

Kolk, A, Levy, D & Pinkse, J 2008, 'Corporate responses in an emerging climate regime: the institutionalization and commensuration of carbon disclosure', *European Accounting Review*, vol. 17, no. 4, pp. 719–45.

New Zealand Ministry for the Environment 2011, *The New Zealand emissions trading scheme*, Wellington, www.mfe.govt.nz/ets.

Stevenson, N 2011, 'New dawn for reporting', *Accountancy futures: critical issues for tomorrow's profession*, 3rd edn, ACCA, pp. 10–13.

Suggett, D & Goodsir, B 2002, *Triple bottom line measurement and reporting in Australia. Making it tangible*, The Allen Consulting Group, Melbourne.

Telstra Corporation Limited 2018, *Bigger Picture 2018 Sustainability Report: Global Reporting Initiative and United Nations Global Compact Index,* https://exchange.telstra.com.au/sustainability/data-downloads.

Ullmann, AA 1985, 'Data in search of a theory: a critical examination of the relationship among social disclosure and economic performance of US firms', *Academy of Management Review*, vol. 10, no. 3, pp. 540–57.

United Nations Conference on Trade and Development (UNCTAD) 2008, *Guidance on corporate responsibility indicators in annual reports*, United Nations, New York and Geneva.

United Nations World Commission on Environment and Development 1987, *Our common future — the Brundlandt report*, University of Oxford Press, Oxford.

ACKNOWLEDGEMENTS

Figure 22.1: © BHP Group Limited 2018

Figure 22.2: © ANZ 2017

Figure 22.4: © Telstra Corporation Limited 2018

Figure 22.5: © International Integrated Reporting Council 2013

Figure 22.6: United Nations 2008. © Public Domain

Figure 22.7: © Global Reporting Initiative 2018

Figure 22.8: © Hauser Institute for Civil Society 2015

Text: Department of the Environment and Heritage 2003. © Commonwealth of Australia

CHAPTER 23

Foreign currency transactions and forward exchange contracts

CHAPTER AIM

This chapter explains how to account for foreign currency transactions in accordance with AASB 121/IAS 21 *The Effects of Changes in Foreign Exchange Rates*. The chapter also explains how to account for hedging relationships using forward exchange contracts in accordance with AASB 9/IFRS 9 *Financial Instruments*.

LEARNING OBJECTIVES

After studying this chapter, you should be able to:

23.1 explain the need to translate foreign currency transactions

23.2 explain how exchange rates function

23.3 prepare entries for the initial measurement of foreign currency items at transaction date

23.4 define and describe monetary and non-monetary items

23.5 describe how foreign exchange differences affect monetary assets or liabilities

23.6 prepare entries for the subsequent measurement of monetary items that are denominated in foreign currency

23.7 prepare entries for the subsequent measurement of non-monetary items that are denominated in foreign currency

23.8 explain what is meant by 'foreign exchange risk' and the circumstances in which it can arise

23.9 describe a 'forward exchange contract'

23.10 explain hedge accounting

23.11 describe the disclosures required in the financial report relating to foreign currency transactions.

CONCEPT FOR REVIEW

Before studying this chapter, you should understand and, if necessary, revise:
- accounting for financial instruments.

23.1 The need for translation of foreign currency transactions

LEARNING OBJECTIVE 23.1 Explain the need to translate foreign currency transactions.

An Australian company may engage in operating, investing or financing activities that involve entering into transactions denominated in a currency other than Australian dollars (A$). Reporting the effects of such transactions in the original foreign currencies would not be useful to financial report users who are normally interested in the company's overall financial position, financial performance and cash flows. Therefore, it is necessary to translate these effects into a single currency. If the financial statements of the company are presented in A$, then the financial effects of all transactions have to be recorded and reported in A$, including transactions denominated in foreign currencies such as United States dollars (US$), New Zealand dollars (NZ$), pounds (£), euros (€), Chinese yuan (元) or Japanese yen (¥).

Accounting for foreign currency transactions is regulated by AASB 121/IAS 21 *The Effects of Changes in Foreign Exchange Rates*. AASB 121/IAS 21 covers the:

- initial measurement of the financial statement elements that arise from foreign currency transactions
- subsequent measurement of assets and liabilities that arise from foreign currency transactions, including subsequent measurement at the end of a reporting period
- treatment of any exchange differences that arise from the subsequent measurement of assets and liabilities denominated in foreign currency
- translation of the financial statements of foreign operations (e.g. subsidiaries and associates).

This chapter deals with the translation of the effects of foreign currency transactions, including the initial and subsequent measurement of financial statement elements that arise from foreign currency transactions and the treatment of any exchange differences. This chapter also explains how the requirements of AASB 9/IFRS 9 *Financial Instruments* apply to accounting for hedging transactions that involve forward exchange contracts that are designed to protect a firm against losses from fluctuations in foreign exchange rates. Chapter 24 covers how to translate the financial statements of a foreign operation.

AASB 121/IAS 21 distinguishes between the denomination currency or settlement currency for a transaction and the measurement currency that applies for accounting purposes. The standard requires a company to account for a transaction denominated in foreign currency by measuring the transaction in the company's functional currency (paragraph 21).

23.1.1 Functional currency

Paragraph 8 of AASB 121/IAS 21 defines the **functional currency** of a company as:

> the currency of the primary economic environment in which the company operates.

The primary economic environment of a company is the one in which the company primarily generates and expends cash (paragraph 9). Normally, the functional currency of an Australian company is A$ because the company primarily generates and expends cash in Australia.

In determining the functional currency of an Australian company, AASB 121/IAS 21 (paragraph 9) gives priority to the following three indicators.

1. The currency that mainly affects the sales prices for its goods and services, which is usually the currency in which the sales prices are denominated and settled
2. The currency of the country whose competitive forces and regulations mainly determine the sales prices of its goods and services
3. The currency that mainly influences labour, material and other costs of providing its goods or services, which is usually the currency in which such costs are denominated and settled

An Australian company that competes for customers in the Australian marketplace by selling locally manufactured goods or providing services from local employees would generally have A$ as the functional currency, as that will satisfy all three indicators. An example of an Australian company where A$ is the functional currency is Ramsay Health Care Limited, a local company providing health care services to Australian communities.

The functional currency for an Australian company may not be obvious when the three indicators provide mixed results. An Australian company may produce commodities from mines in the Pilbara region of Western Australia (e.g. gold, copper, aluminium, lead, nickel, tin, zinc, silver and iron ore), but the commodity prices may be denominated in US$. In this case, the US$ is the currency that mainly affects sales prices, while the A$ is the currency that mainly affects costs.

If the three main indicators yield mixed results, AASB 121/IAS 21 requires management to use its judgement to determine the functional currency that most faithfully represents the economic effects of the underlying transactions, events and conditions (paragraph 12). In exercising this judgement, paragraph 10 suggests that management may consider the following two additional indicators.

- The currency in which funds from issuing debt and equity instruments are generated
- The currency in which receipts from operating activities are banked and retained

An example of an Australian company that yields mixed results based on the three main indicators is Fortescue Metals Group Limited (Fortescue), which mines iron ore in Western Australia, predominantly for Chinese customers. Fortescue noted in its 2018 annual report that management have determined that the functional currency is US$.

The functional currency of an Australian company determined to be A$ or some other currency would remain the same from one reporting period to the next unless the company's underlying transactions, events and conditions changed in such a way as to justify a change in the functional currency (AASB 121/IAS 21 paragraph 13).

23.1.2 Types of foreign currency transactions

AASB 121/IAS 21 describes a **foreign currency transaction** as a transaction that is denominated or requires settlement in a foreign currency (paragraph 20). In this regard, any currency other than the company's functional currency is a foreign currency (paragraph 8). An Australian company with a functional currency of A$ may enter into various foreign currency transactions with other entities as follows.

- Buy or sell goods or services at prices denominated in a foreign currency.
- Acquire or dispose of plant and equipment at prices denominated in a foreign currency.
- Borrow or lend funds where the amounts payable or receivable are denominated in a foreign currency.

For example, an Australian company may import materials for use in a manufacturing process (e.g. a dress maker and fashion house that imports silk from a French supplier for the price of €200 000). Alternatively, an Australian food producer may export cheese to Japan for the price of ¥400 000. Qantas Airways Limited may acquire a new aeroplane from the Boeing Company in the United States at the price of US$72 000 000. An Australian company may borrow £500 000 to purchase land in the West Midlands of England and subsequently pay interest of £25 000 p.a.

In each case, the Australian company must recognise the financial effects of the foreign currency transaction by translating the foreign currency amounts (i.e. €200 000, ¥400 000, US$72 000 000, £500 000 and £25 000) into the functional currency of A$. The translation is based on the exchange rate between the foreign currency and the functional currency.

LEARNING CHECK

☐ A company must account for a transaction denominated in foreign currency by measuring the transaction in the company's functional currency, which for an Australian company is commonly A$.

☐ The functional currency is the currency of the primary economic environment in which the company operates. The primary economic environment is the one in which the company primarily generates and expends cash.

☐ A foreign currency transaction involves a currency other than the functional currency.

☐ An Australian company with a functional currency of A$ enters into a foreign currency transaction if it imports or exports goods in a currency other than A$ or borrows or lends funds in a currency other than A$.

23.2 Exchange rates

LEARNING OBJECTIVE 23.2 Explain how exchange rates function.

A person who has travelled outside their country of residence would be aware that foreign currency can be bought or sold through banks or other financial institutions (that act as foreign exchange dealers) at specified exchange rates. A person departing Australia will exchange Australian dollars (A$) to buy foreign currency such as euros (€), pounds (£) or US dollars (US$). A person returning to Australia may exchange foreign currency for A$. AASB 121/IAS 21 describes an **exchange rate** as the ratio of exchange for two currencies (paragraph 8). A **spot exchange rate** is the exchange rate for immediate delivery at a particular point in time whereas the **closing rate** is the spot exchange rate at the end of the reporting period (paragraph 8).

Foreign exchange dealers may quote the exchange rates using the *indirect form* of quotation, which sets out the equivalent amount of foreign currency for one unit of local currency. In Australia, this form is also preferred by the media in the presentation of financial news. For Australia, an example of the indirect form of quotation is as follows.

Indirect form: A$1.00 equals US$0.6961/0.7754

The exchange rate shown in the indirect form above sets out the prices for buying and selling A$1.00 as follows.
- US$0.6961 is the *buying* rate for A$1.00, being the price the *foreign exchange dealer will pay* to buy A$1.00 from a customer.
- US$0.7754 is the *selling* rate for A$1.00, being the price the *foreign exchange dealer will ask* to sell A$1.00 to a customer.

Accordingly, a person travelling to the United States will sell A$ (and buy US$) based on the exchange rate of A$1.00 equals US$0.6961. A person returning from the United States will sell US$ (and buy A$) based on the exchange rate of A$1.00 equals US$0.7754. The difference between the buying (bid) and selling (ask) rates is known as the bid–ask spread and it provides a profit margin to the foreign exchange dealer for acting as the medium through which market participants buy and sell currencies.

An alternative approach is to present exchange rates using the *direct form* of quotation that sets out the equivalent amount of local currency for one unit of foreign currency. For Australia, an example of the direct form of quotation is as follows.

Direct form: US$1.00 equals A$1.2897/1.4366

The exchange rate shown in direct form sets out the prices for buying and selling US$1.00 as follows.
- A$1.2897 is the *buying* rate for US$1.00, being the price the *foreign exchange dealer will pay* to buy US$1.00 from a customer.
- A$1.4366 is the *selling* rate for US$1.00, being the price the *foreign exchange dealer will ask* to sell US$1.00 to a customer.

As a foreign exchange dealer buying US$ with A$ is essentially selling A$ in the process, the rates shown in the direct form of quotation are the reciprocals of the relevant exchange rates shown in the indirect form of quotation; that is, 1 US$0.6961 equals A$1.4366 and 1 US$0.7754 equals A$1.2897. The foreign exchange dealer that buys A$ at the rate of A$1.00 equals US$0.6961 is essentially selling US$ at the rate of US$1.00 equals A$1.4366. The foreign exchange dealer that sells A$ at the rate of A$1.00 equals US$0.7754 is essentially buying US$ at the rate of US$1.00 equals A$1.2897. In general, the:
- buying rate under the indirect form of quotation is the inverse of the selling rate under the direct form of quotation
- selling rate under the indirect form of quotation is the inverse of the buying rate under the direct form of quotation.

The application of exchange rates to translate foreign currency balances into A$ is demonstrated next by a simple example. Assume an Australian company has a foreign currency payable of US$5000 that must be translated into A$ using the exchange rates shown in this section. In the first instance, it is necessary to determine whether the buying or selling rate should be used for the purpose of the translation. The liability balance denominated in US$ means that the Australian company has an obligation to pay US$, which means it needs to sell A$ to get the US$ necessary to settle its obligation; therefore, it will need to find a foreign exchange dealer willing to buy A$ and sell US$. In this case, the relevant exchange rate for translation is either the foreign exchange dealer's buying rate for A$ (in the indirect form of quotation) or their selling rate for US$ (in the direct form of quotation). Accordingly, the translation of the foreign currency payable of US$5000 proceeds as follows.

Translation of foreign currency payable			
Indirect:	US$5000 ÷ 0.6961	equals	A$7183
Direct:	US$5000 × 1.4366	equals	A$7183

This example highlights a rule of thumb that can be relied on when translating foreign currency balances; that is, translation is a process of division if rates are expressed in indirect form (A$1.00 = US$ equivalent) and multiplication if rates are expressed in direct form (US$1.00 = A$ equivalent).

In contrast, an Australian company with a foreign currency receivable of US$5000 has an asset balance denominated in US$ and a right to receive US$. In this case, the Australian company wanting A$ will need to consider selling US$ received to buy A$ and therefore will need to find a foreign exchange dealer willing to sell A$ and buy US$. The relevant exchange rate for translation is then either the foreign exchange dealer's selling rate for A$ (in the indirect form of quotation) or the buying rate for US$ (in the direct form of quotation). Accordingly, the translation of the foreign currency receivable of US$5000 proceeds as follows.

Translation of foreign currency receivable

Indirect:	US$5000 ÷ 0.7754	equals	A$6448
Direct:	US$5000 × 1.2897	equals	A$6448

In the remainder of this chapter and in the end-of-chapter questions, exchange rates may be expressed using either the indirect or direct form of quotation. In order to keep the focus on the key translation issues, however, a single rate rather than separate selling and buying rates is normally shown.

LEARNING CHECK

- ☐ An exchange rate is the ratio of exchange for two currencies. A spot exchange rate is the rate for immediate delivery at a point in time. The closing exchange rate is the rate at the end of the reporting period.
- ☐ Exchange rates can be quoted in indirect form for one unit of local currency (e.g. A$1.00) or in direct form for one unit of foreign currency (e.g. US$1.00).
- ☐ Exchange rates are usually quoted by the foreign currency dealer showing a buying/bid rate and selling/ask rate.
- ☐ A foreign currency amount can be translated into A$ by dividing the foreign currency amount by the rate of exchange expressed in indirect form.
- ☐ A foreign currency amount can be translated into A$ by multiplying the foreign currency amount by the rate of exchange expressed in direct form.

23.3 Initial measurement at the transaction date

LEARNING OBJECTIVE 23.3 Prepare entries for the initial measurement of foreign currency items at transaction date.

The logical question that arises in accounting for foreign currency transactions is: which exchange rates should be used to translate the foreign currency balances?

Consistent with historical cost accounting, the financial statement items that arise from a foreign currency transaction should be measured on initial recognition using the historical exchange rate at the date of the transaction; that is, the spot exchange rate at the date of the transaction. Paragraph 21 of AASB 121/IAS 21 requires that a foreign currency transaction be recorded on initial recognition in A$ by applying the spot exchange rate at the date of the transaction to the foreign currency amount. The requirement to translate at the **transaction date** applies to all foreign currency transactions. The requirement means that each asset, liability or item of equity that arises from entering into a foreign currency transaction must be initially recognised and measured using the spot exchange rate at the date of the transaction. The spot exchange rate also applies to any items of revenue or expense that are attributable to the transaction.

The general principle applicable to the acquisition or disposal of an asset is that the date of the transaction depends on when control of the future economic benefits embodied in the asset are obtained from or transferred to another entity. AASB 102/IAS 2 *Inventories* (paragraph 6) indicates that inventories are recognised only if the definition of an asset in the *Conceptual Framework* is satisfied. AASB 116/IAS 16 *Property, Plant and Equipment* (paragraph 7) states that the initial recognition of an item arises only when it is probable that the future economic benefits will flow to the entity and the cost can be measured reliably. In relation to revenue recognition in the case of sale of goods to customers, AASB 15/IFRS 15 *Revenue from Contracts with Customers* requires an entity to satisfy performance obligations and transfer control of the asset to the customer.

In most instances, the terms of agreements between a company and its foreign customers or suppliers will determine the date of the transaction for the sale or purchase of goods. A free on board (FOB) clause is usually included in contracts stipulating who has title to the goods during shipment. A contract that is FOB destination means that the seller retains ownership while the goods are in transit and ownership changes only at the point when the buyer has received the goods into its stores. A contract that is FOB shipping point means that the seller retains ownership of the goods only to the point when the goods are placed on the ship. In this case, ownership changes at the point when the seller transfers the goods to the specific carrier agreed with the buyer. Another contract variant is FOB origin, which means the seller bears responsibility for the goods while the goods remain in the country of origin.

A simple example demonstrates the initial recognition and measurement of financial statement items at the transaction date. At 1 May 2022, a company acquires a machine on credit terms from a foreign supplier for a price of US\$300 000 when the prevailing exchange rate is US\$1.00 = A\$1.20. In accordance with paragraph 21 of AASB 121/IAS 21, the journal entry of the company to record the purchase of the machine is as follows.

2022				
May 1	Machine (cost)	Dr	360 000	
	Payable to foreign supplier	Cr		360 000
	(Initial recognition of machine and payable at transaction date using spot rate, US$300 000 × 1.20)			

A practical issue concerns how to deal with a multitude of purchase transactions in the same foreign currency during the reporting period. In these circumstances, the spot rate on the transaction date may be replaced by an average exchange rate for the period when those multiple transactions took place, identified as the transaction period. Paragraph 22 of AASB 121/IAS 21 allows an average exchange rate to be applied against the total transactions in a foreign currency for the period provided that exchange rates have not fluctuated significantly. An example would be the translation of all inventories purchases made in US\$ during the month of February 2022 using the average exchange rate with the A\$ for that month. In effect, the translation of the total inventories purchases for the month using the average exchange rate should not be materially different from the total derived from translating each separate purchase transaction in the month using the relevant daily exchange rates.

If revenues or expenses denominated in foreign currency are earned or incurred evenly during a period (e.g. interest revenue or expense), they are translated using the average rate for that period. It should be noted that revenues and expenses denominated in foreign currency are not to be remeasured after the initial recognition. This is in accordance with accrual accounting that recognises the revenues when they are earned and expenses when they are incurred.

LEARNING CHECK

☐ The financial statement items that arise from a foreign currency transaction should be measured on initial recognition using the historical exchange rate at the date of the transaction; that is, the spot exchange rate at the date of the transaction.

☐ The date of the transaction depends on when control of the future economic benefits embodied in the asset are obtained from or transferred to another entity.

☐ The terms of agreements between a company and its foreign customers or suppliers will determine the date of the transaction for the sale or purchase of goods.

☐ When dealing with a multitude of purchase transactions in the same foreign currency during the reporting period, the spot rate on the transaction date may be replaced by an average exchange rate for the transaction period.

☐ If revenues or expenses denominated in foreign currency are earned or incurred evenly during a period, they are translated using the average rate for that period.

23.4 Monetary and non-monetary items

LEARNING OBJECTIVE 23.4 Define and describe monetary and non-monetary items.

Subsequent measurement of financial statement items resulting from a foreign currency transaction depends on whether the items are monetary or non-monetary items.

AASB 121/IAS 21 defines **monetary items** as units of currency held and assets and liabilities to be received or paid in a fixed or determinable amount of currency (paragraph 8). A monetary item therefore refers to cash or another item that constitutes a claim to cash or an obligation to pay cash. An Australian company with a functional currency of A$ could have monetary items denominated in foreign currency, such as:

- cash at bank of US$60 000
- accounts payable of €200 000
- accounts receivable of ¥400 000
- payable for plant purchase of US$72 000 000
- borrowings of £500 000
- interest payable of £20 000.

Monetary items should not be confused with financial assets. Shares held in companies listed on the Australian Securities Exchange (ASX) are financial assets and can easily be converted into cash through sale. The shares held, however, do not represent a claim to a fixed number of dollars or currency and therefore do not constitute a monetary item. In contrast, foreign currency borrowings is a monetary item because it represents an obligation to pay a fixed number of foreign currency units, even if exchange rate movements cause the obligation measured in A$ to vary.

A **non-monetary item** is an asset or liability that is not a monetary item. Examples of non-monetary items include inventories and property, plant and equipment.

LEARNING CHECK

☐ Monetary items are units of currency held and assets and liabilities to be received or paid in fixed or determinable amounts of currency.
☐ Not all financial assets are monetary items.
☐ Non-monetary items are assets and liabilities that are not monetary items.

23.5 Foreign exchange differences for monetary items

LEARNING OBJECTIVE 23.5 Describe how foreign exchange differences affect monetary assets or liabilities.

AASB 121/IAS 21 defines a **foreign exchange difference** as the difference resulting from translating a given number of units of one currency into another currency at different exchange rates (paragraph 8). Exchange differences arise whenever a foreign currency balance is remeasured using an exchange rate that is different to the one applied previously.

23.5.1 Realised and unrealised gains or losses from exchange differences

Foreign currency transactions that involve the recognition of a monetary asset or liability usually give rise to a foreign exchange difference because the monetary item is settled after its initial recognition when exchange rates have changed. An example is a credit sale of inventories to a customer for US$100 where the sale and cash receipt occur during the same financial period. Assume that at the date of the transaction the spot rate is US$1.00 = A$1.20, but at the date of settlement (cash receipt) the spot rate has changed to US$1.00 = A$1.50. Figure 23.1 illustrates that a realised exchange gain of $30 results within a single reporting period.

A realised exchange gain that is attributable to a single reporting period is recognised in profit or loss for that period and does not present any special accounting problem given that it occurs in the same period as the sales transaction. A realised exchange gain, however, may relate to more than one reporting period. An example is where a credit sale transaction occurs in a reporting period, but the date of cash receipt belongs to the next reporting period. Assume that at the date of the transaction the spot rate is US$1.00 = A$1.20, at the end of the reporting period the spot rate is US$1.00 = A$1.40 and at the date of cash settlement the spot rate is US$1.00 = A$1.50. Figure 23.2 illustrates a realised gain that relates to two reporting periods.

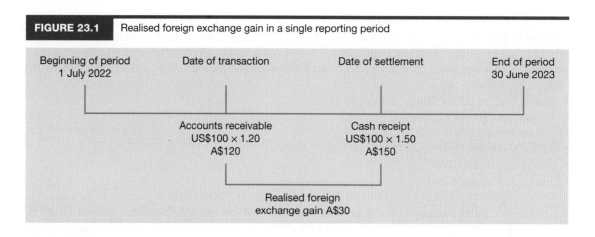

FIGURE 23.1 Realised foreign exchange gain in a single reporting period

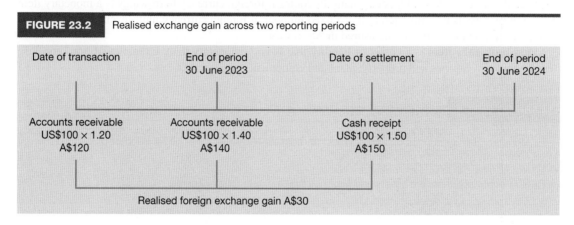

FIGURE 23.2 Realised exchange gain across two reporting periods

The issue that arises if a realised exchange difference does not occur in a single reporting period is whether unrealised exchange gains and losses should be recognised. The question turns on how monetary items are translated at the end of the reporting period. If a receivable of US$100 at 30 June 2023 is translated using the spot rate of 1.40, then an unrealised exchange gain of A$20 (A$140 less A$120) must be recognised for the year. AASB 121/IAS 21 mandates this approach and requires that exchange gains and losses be immediately recognised in the profit or loss as they arise. This is known as the 'immediate recognition method' of accounting for exchange gains and losses. The immediate recognition method is consistent with accrual accounting because the accounting for exchange gains and losses is not dependent on a cash transaction. It should be noted though that the immediate recognition method treats the financing arrangement for a foreign currency transaction as a separate matter from the underlying transaction; that is, the measurement of a foreign currency receivable is separate from the recognition and measurement of the sale that gave rise to the receivable.

23.5.2 The relationship between exchange rates and exchange differences

The illustrations in figures 23.1 and 23.2 highlight that the nature of foreign exchange differences depends on the foreign currency monetary item and how exchange rates change. In the example shown, the translated A$ amount of the US$ receivable increases as the direct exchange rate for US$1.00 increases from A$1.20 to A$1.50 and results in a foreign exchange gain of A$30. Consider the position of a receivable for US$100 if the direct exchange rate for US$1.00 decreased from A$1.40 to A$1.30 (US$ decreases in value relative to A$). In this case, the translated amount of the receivable would decrease from A$140 to A$130 and result in a foreign exchange loss of A$10. Alternatively, a payable for US$100 would decrease from A$140 to A$130 and result in a foreign exchange gain of A$10.

It is possible to generalise the relationships between foreign currency monetary items, exchange rate changes and exchange differences. Figure 23.3 sets out these relationships.

Change in exchange rate		Foreign currency monetary item	
		Payable US$	Receivable US$
Increase in direct rate US$1 = A$# Decrease in indirect rate A$1 = US$#	US$ appreciates (increases) in value compared to A$	Increase in A$ amount ⇒ Exchange loss	Increase in A$ amount ⇒ Exchange gain
Decrease in direct rate US$1 = A$# Increase in indirect rate A$1 = US$#	A$ appreciates (increases) in value compared to US$	Decrease in A$ amount ⇒ Exchange gain	Decrease in A$ amount ⇒ Exchange loss

If the change in the exchange rate shows that *the foreign currency increases in value relative to the functional currency* (either by an increase in the direct rate of quotation or, equivalently, a decrease in the indirect rate):

- a monetary asset denominated in foreign currency will increase when translated into the less valuable functional currency, giving rise to a foreign exchange gain as the company is effectively entitled to receive more units of functional currency
- a monetary liability denominated in foreign currency will increase when translated into the less valuable functional currency, giving rise to a foreign exchange loss as the company is effectively asked to pay more units of functional currency.

If the change in the exchange rate shows that *the foreign currency decreases in value relative to the functional currency* (either by a decrease in the direct rate of quotation or, equivalently, an increase in the indirect rate):

- a monetary asset denominated in foreign currency will decrease when translated into the more valuable functional currency, giving rise to a foreign exchange loss as the company is effectively entitled to receive less units of functional currency
- a monetary liability denominated in foreign currency will decrease when translated into the more valuable functional currency, giving rise to a foreign exchange gain as the company is effectively asked to pay less units of functional currency.

LEARNING CHECK

- ☐ Foreign exchange differences arise whenever a foreign currency balance is measured using an exchange rate that is different to the one applied at initial measurement or at the end of a reporting period.
- ☐ A realised exchange difference arises on the cash settlement of a monetary asset or liability based on the change in the exchange rate from initial recognition to cash settlement of the monetary asset or liability.
- ☐ An unrealised exchange difference arises on the remeasurement of a monetary asset or liability at the end of the reporting period.
- ☐ Exchanges gains (losses) on a monetary asset arise if there is an increase (decrease) in the direct rate of exchange or decrease (increase) in the indirect rate of exchange.
- ☐ Exchanges gains (losses) on a monetary liability arise if there is a decrease (increase) in the direct rate of exchange or an increase (decrease) in the indirect rate of exchange.

23.6 Subsequent measurement of foreign currency monetary items

LEARNING OBJECTIVE 23.6 Prepare entries for the subsequent measurement of monetary items that are denominated in foreign currency.

Accounting for transactions that involve foreign currency monetary items can potentially involve three stages based on the date of the transaction, the end of the reporting period and the date of cash settlement. Figure 23.4 illustrates the three stages.

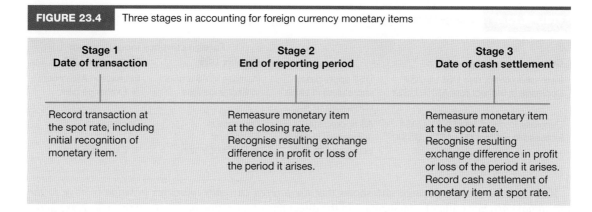

FIGURE 23.4	Three stages in accounting for foreign currency monetary items

Stage 1 Date of transaction	Stage 2 End of reporting period	Stage 3 Date of cash settlement
Record transaction at the spot rate, including initial recognition of monetary item.	Remeasure monetary item at the closing rate. Recognise resulting exchange difference in profit or loss of the period it arises.	Remeasure monetary item at the spot rate. Recognise resulting exchange difference in profit or loss of the period it arises. Record cash settlement of monetary item at spot rate.

In the first stage, the financial statement elements that arise on the transaction date, including any monetary items, are initially recognised and measured using the spot exchange rate. In the second stage, the monetary item that is outstanding at the end of the reporting period is subsequently measured using the closing exchange rate. In the third stage, the monetary item is subsequently measured at its settlement date using the spot exchange rate. The exchange differences that results from these remeasurements are recognised as exchange gains or losses in the profit or loss of the period in which they arise. The cash settlement of the monetary item is also recorded using the spot exchange rate at the settlement date.

The three stages shown in figure 23.4 provide a general guide to accounting for monetary items denominated in foreign currency. The three stages do not apply if the cash settlement of the monetary item occurs before the end of the reporting period. In this case, there is a remeasurement of the monetary item at the settlement date but not at the end of the reporting period; that is, only the first and third stages would apply. The first stage was addressed in section 23.3. The other stages are addressed next.

23.6.1 Measurement of foreign currency monetary items at the end of the reporting period

Paragraph 23(a) of AASB 121/IAS 21 requires that foreign currency monetary items outstanding at the end of the reporting period be translated using the closing exchange rate. This requirement means that a foreign currency monetary item is remeasured from its translated amount at the date of initial recognition to the translated amount based on the spot exchange rate at the end of the reporting period. In effect, the foreign currency monetary item is restated to its realisable amount in A$ at the end of the reporting period.

The subsequent measurement of a foreign currency monetary item at the end of the reporting period results in an exchange difference if the relevant exchange rate has changed after initial measurement at the date of the transaction. The exchange difference equals the change in the number of A$ that are equivalent to the foreign currency amount. AASB 121/IAS 21 generally requires that an exchange difference resulting from the subsequent measurement of a monetary item be recognised in the profit or loss in the period that it arises (paragraph 28). A simple example demonstrates the subsequent measurement of a foreign currency monetary item and recognition of the exchange difference at the end of the reporting period.

At 1 May 2023, a company acquires a machine on credit terms from a foreign supplier for a price of US$300 000 when the prevailing exchange rate is US$1.00 = A$1.20. At the end of the reporting period, on 30 June 2023, the exchange rate is US$1.00 = A$1.60. In accordance with AASB 121/ IAS 21 (paragraphs 23 and 28), the journal entry to remeasure the outstanding foreign currency monetary item at 30 June 2023 is as follows.

2023				
June 30	Foreign exchange loss	Dr	120 000	
	Payable to foreign supplier	Cr		120 000
	(Increase in foreign currency payable at the end of the reporting period using closing rate, US$300 000 × 1.60 less US$300 000 × 1.20)			

The journal entry for the subsequent measurement of the foreign currency payable increases the A$ amount by A$120 000 from A$360 000 at the date of the transaction to A$480 000 at the end of the reporting period. The increase in the monetary liability gives rise to a foreign exchange loss of A$120 000 that is recognised in the profit or loss of the period. The foreign exchange loss is an unrealised loss because it relates to an outstanding monetary item at the end of the reporting period. A realised foreign exchange difference will occur in a future period when the monetary item is settled in cash.

23.6.2 Measurement of foreign currency monetary items at settlement date

Paragraph 29 of AASB 121/IAS 21 indicates that a foreign currency monetary item must also be remeasured at **settlement date**. The need for subsequent measurement arises because settlement involves the receipt or payment of foreign currency at a particular date; that is, cash is received or paid. In A$ terms, the amount of cash received or paid is determined by the foreign currency amount translated at the spot exchange rate at the date of settlement. The A$ amount of the monetary item in the accounting records has to correspond with the cash received or paid at the time of settlement. Accordingly, it is necessary to remeasure the foreign currency monetary item using the spot exchange rate at the date of settlement.

If the settlement date occurs in the same reporting period as the transaction date, then the monetary item will have been previously measured at the transaction date. If the settlement date occurs after the end of a reporting period (as shown in figure 23.4), then the monetary item will have been previously measured at the end of that reporting period. The subsequent measurement of a foreign currency monetary item at settlement date results in an exchange difference relative to the previous measurement if the exchange rate changes. The exchange difference from subsequent measurement of a foreign currency monetary item at settlement date is generally recognised in the profit or loss in the period that it arises (AASB 121/IAS 21 paragraph 28). A simple example demonstrates the subsequent measurement of a foreign currency monetary item at settlement date, the recognition of the resulting exchange difference and the cash settlement of the monetary item.

On 1 May 2023, a company acquires a machine on credit terms from a foreign supplier for a price of US$300 000 when the prevailing exchange rate is US$1.00 = A$1.20. On that day, the company recognises an accounts payable in A$ of A$360 000 (US$300 000 × 1.20). At the end of the reporting period, on 30 June 2023, the exchange rate is US$1.00 = A$1.60. As a result, the company recognises an increase in the accounts payable to A$480 000 (US$300 000 × 1.60). On 15 July 2023, the foreign supplier account is paid in full when the exchange rate is US$1.00 = A$1.50. Before settlement is recognised, the amount in the accounts payable must be remeasured based on the exchange rate existing at settlement date. In accordance with paragraphs 28 and 29 of AASB 121/IAS 21, the journal entry to remeasure the foreign currency monetary item at settlement date is as follows.

2023				
July 15	Payable to foreign supplier	Dr	30 000	
	Foreign exchange gain	Cr		30 000
	(Decrease in foreign currency payable at settlement date using spot rate, US$300 000 × 1.50 less US$300 000 × 1.60)			

The journal entry for the measurement of the foreign currency payable at settlement date decreases the A$ amount by A$30 000 from A$480 000 recognised at the end of the previous reporting period to A$450 000 at the date of settlement. The decrease in the monetary liability gives rise to a foreign exchange gain of A$30 000 that is recognised in the profit or loss of the period.

The cash settlement of the foreign payable is a foreign currency cash flow. Paragraph 25 of AASB 107/IAS 7 *Statement of Cash Flows* requires that a foreign currency cash flow is translated at the spot exchange rate at the date of the cash flow. Accordingly, the journal entry to record the cash settlement of the foreign currency payable at the settlement date is as follows.

2023				
July 15	Payable to foreign supplier	Dr	450 000	
	Cash at bank	Cr		450 000
	(Cash payment for settlement of foreign currency payable at settlement date using spot rate, US$300 000 × 1.50)			

On the transaction date of 1 May 2023, a monetary liability of A\$360 000 is booked. At the settlement date of 15 July 2023, the monetary liability is settled by a cash payment of A\$450 000. The realised exchange difference, therefore, is a loss of \$90 000. In accounting for the foreign currency monetary item, however, exchange differences are recognised before realisation. An exchange loss of \$120 000 is recognised at the end of the reporting period at 30 June 2023 and an exchange gain of \$30 000 is recognised at the settlement date of 15 July 2023. The net amount of the two recognised exchange differences reconciles to the realised exchange loss of \$90 000 (i.e. \$120 000 loss and \$30 000 gain equate to a net loss of \$90 000).

The timing of the recognition of exchange differences is a key feature of AASB 121/IAS 21. An unrealised exchange loss of \$120 000 is recognised in the annual reporting period ended 30 June 2023 and then an exchange gain of \$30 000 is recognised in the annual reporting period ended 30 June 2024. In accordance with the accrual basis of accounting, the standard recognises exchange differences in the reporting periods in which the exchange differences arise. Recognition of foreign exchange gains or losses does not depend on cash transactions.

It is worth noting that the two journal entries for the subsequent measurement of the foreign currency monetary item and the cash payment at the settlement date can be combined into a single journal entry, if desired, as follows.

2023				
July 15	Payable to foreign supplier	Dr	480 000	
	Foreign exchange gain	Cr		30 000
	Cash at bank	Cr		450 000
	(Subsequent measurement and settlement of foreign currency payable at settlement date)			

23.6.3 Illustrative examples

This section further demonstrates the stages of accounting shown in figure 23.4 using a variety of examples in respect of the recognition and measurement of foreign currency monetary items. All of examples relate to Oz Ltd, an Australian company listed on the ASX, which prepares general purpose financial statements at 30 June each year. Assume Oz Ltd uses a periodic inventories system.

ILLUSTRATIVE EXAMPLE 23.1

Exporting goods on credit terms

On 13 May 2023, Oz Ltd sells inventories to a US customer, Reagan Inc., for an agreed price of US\$40 000. On 12 August 2023, Oz Ltd receives cash in full payment of the sales invoice. Relevant exchange rates are as follows.

13 May 2023 — transaction date	A\$1 = US\$0.74
30 June 2023 — end of the reporting period	A\$1 = US\$0.77
12 August 2023 — settlement date	A\$1 = US\$0.80

The accounts receivable balance (i.e. the monetary item) is translated at the spot exchange at the three dates as follows.

Date	Accounts receivable in A\$	Increase/(decrease)
13 May 2023	US\$40 000 ÷ 0.74 = \$54 054	
30 June 2023	US\$40 000 ÷ 0.77 = \$51 948	(\$2 106)
12 August 2023	US\$40 000 ÷ 0.80 = \$50 000	(\$1 948)

The journal entries of Oz Ltd to record the initial recognition and measurement of the accounts receivable together with its subsequent measurement and settlement are as follows.

Journals for the year ending 30 June 2023

2023				
May 13	Accounts receivable Sales revenue (Initial recognition and measurement of accounts receivable at transaction date using spot rate, US$40 000 ÷ 0.74)	Dr Cr	54 054	54 054
June 30	Foreign exchange loss Accounts receivable (Decrease in accounts receivable at end of reporting period using closing rate, US$40 000 ÷ 0.77 less US$40 000 ÷ 0.74)	Dr Cr	2 106	2 106

Journals for the year ending 30 June 2024

2023				
Aug. 12	Foreign exchange loss Accounts receivable (Decrease in accounts receivable at settlement date using spot rate, US$40 000 ÷ 0.80 less US$40 000 ÷ 0.77)	Dr Cr	1 948	1 948
Aug. 12	Cash at bank Accounts receivable (Cash receipt on settlement of customer account using spot rate, US$40 000 ÷ 0.80)	Dr Cr	50 000	50 000

Brief observations concerning this example are as follows.
(a) Oz Ltd's statement of financial position at 30 June 2023 includes accounts receivable of $51 948 (i.e. $54 054 − $2106). Oz Ltd's statement of profit or loss and other comprehensive income for the year to 30 June 2023 includes a foreign exchange loss of $2106.
(b) Oz Ltd's statement of profit or loss and other comprehensive income for the year to 30 June 2024 includes a foreign exchange loss of $1948.
(c) Oz Ltd incurs a realised foreign exchange difference on the accounts receivable equal to a loss of $4054 (i.e. $54 054 − $50 000) and this includes the exchange losses recognised for the years ended 30 June 2023 and 30 June 2024 amounting to $2106 and $1948 respectively.
(d) Oz Ltd's recognition of the foreign exchange differences is consistent with the movement in exchange rates during the reporting periods. The A$ appreciates in value relative to the US$ and therefore the accounts receivable of US$40 000 decreases in A$ value, giving rise to foreign exchange losses.

ILLUSTRATIVE EXAMPLE 23.2

Importing goods on credit terms

Oz Ltd purchases raw materials from a New Zealand company, Clark Ltd, for the agreed price of NZ$500 000. The purchase contract is FOB destination. On 15 May 2023, Oz Ltd orders the materials. On 20 May 2023, Clark Ltd ships the materials. On 15 July 2023, Oz Ltd receives the materials into its factory. On 10 September 2023, Oz Ltd pays for the materials. Relevant exchange rates are as follows.

15 July 2023 — transaction date	NZ$1 = A$0.88
10 September 2023 — settlement date	NZ$1 = A$0.80

The accounts payable balance (i.e. the monetary item) is translated at the spot exchange rates at the two dates as follows.

Date	Accounts payable in A$	Increase/(decrease)
15 July 2023	NZ$500 000 × 0.88 = $440 000	
10 September 2023	NZ$500 000 × 0.80 = $400 000	($40 000)

The journal entries of Oz Ltd to record the initial recognition and measurement of the accounts payable and its subsequent measurement and settlement are as follows.

Journals for the year ending 30 June 2024

2023				
July 15	Raw materials Accounts payable (Initial recognition and measurement of accounts payable at transaction date using spot rate, NZ$500 000 × 0.88)	Dr Cr	440 000	440 000
Sept. 10	Accounts payable Foreign exchange gain (Decrease in accounts payable at the settlement date using spot rate, NZ$500 000 × 0.88 less NZ$500 000 × 0.80)	Dr Cr	40 000	40 000
Sept. 10	Accounts payable Cash at bank (Cash payment for settlement of supplier account using spot rate, NZ$500 000 × 0.80)	Dr Cr	400 000	400 000

Brief observations concerning this example are as follows.

(a) Oz Ltd recognises the purchase of raw materials when the goods are in its factory based on the FOB destination contract.

(b) Oz Ltd does not have an outstanding monetary item in respect of the foreign currency transaction at the end of a reporting period. In this case only translations at the transaction date and settlement date are relevant.

(c) The exchange rate movements after the date of acquisition of the raw materials have no bearing on the measurement of raw materials cost. The cost of the raw materials in A$ terms is the historical cost in NZ$ translated at the historical exchange rate when the raw materials were purchased.

(d) Oz Ltd's profit or loss for the year to 30 June 2024 includes the foreign exchange gain of $40 000.

ILLUSTRATIVE EXAMPLE 23.3

Consulting revenue and foreign currency bank account

Oz Ltd provides consulting services to the Italian company, Berlusconi SpA, over the period 1 April 2023 to 30 April 2023 in return for €20 000 per day. On 30 April 2023, Oz Ltd receives a cheque of €600 000 in full payment for the services provided and deposits it into a new bank account denominated in €. There are no other transactions in € and the balance of the bank account at 30 June 2023 remains at €600 000. Relevant exchange rates are as follows.

30 April 2023 — date of cash receipt	A$1 = €0.78
Average for April 2023 — transaction period	A$1 = €0.77
30 June 2023 — end of the reporting period	A$1 = €0.80

The cash at bank balance (i.e. the monetary item) is translated at the spot exchange rates at the two dates as follows.

Date	Cash at bank in A$	Increase/(decrease)
30 April 2023	€600 000 ÷ €0.78 = $769 231	
30 June 2023	€600 000 ÷ €0.80 = $750 000	($19 231)

The journal entries of Oz Ltd to record the initial recognition and measurement of the cash receipt for consulting services and the subsequent measurement of the bank balance denominated in euros are as follows.

Journals for the year ending 30 June 2023

2023				
April 30	Cash at bank	Dr	769 231	
	Foreign exchange loss	Dr	9 990	
	Consulting revenue	Cr		779 221
	(Recognition of consulting revenue for April 2023 using average rate, €600 000 ÷ 0.77, and initial recognition and measurement of cash at bank using spot rate, €600 000 ÷ 0.78)			
June 30	Foreign exchange loss	Dr	19 231	
	Cash at bank	Cr		19 231
	(Decrease in cash at bank at the end of the reporting period using closing rate, €600 000 ÷ 0.80 less €600 000 ÷ 0.78)			

Brief observations concerning this example are as follows.

(a) Oz Ltd's statement of financial position at 30 June 2023 includes a foreign currency cash balance equal to $750 000 (i.e. $769 231 − $19 231). Oz Ltd's statement of profit or loss and other comprehensive income for the year to 30 June 2023 includes net foreign exchange losses of $29 221 (i.e. $9990 + $19 231).

(b) Oz Ltd's euros bank account at the end of the reporting period is a monetary item and is measured at the closing exchange rate (i.e. €600 000 ÷ 0.80).

(c) Oz Ltd recognises the consulting revenue on an accruals basis over the period the revenue was generated by translating at the relevant average exchange rate. In contrast, the revenue from the sale of inventories or plant is generated on the date of the sale transaction.

ILLUSTRATIVE EXAMPLE 23.4

Foreign currency borrowings

On 1 July 2022, Oz Ltd enters a loan agreement with the Bank of England plc to borrow £300 000 for a period of 5 years. The interest on the borrowings is payable half-yearly in arrears at the fixed interest rate of 6% p.a. with interest payments of £9000 (£300 000 × 6% × ½ year) due on 31 December and 30 June each year. Oz Ltd prepares half-yearly reports and its reporting periods end 30 June and 31 December each year. The following exchange rates are applicable for the annual financial period to 30 June 2023.

1 July 2022 — date of transaction	A$1 = £0.60
Average July–Dec 2022 — interest period	A$1 = £0.62
31 December 2022 — end of the reporting period	A$1 = £0.64
Average Jan–June 2023 — interest period	A$1 = £0.59
30 June 2023 — end of the reporting period	A$1 = £0.56

The bank borrowings balance (i.e. the monetary item) is translated at the spot exchange rates at the three dates as follows.

Date	Bank borrowings in A$	Increase/(decrease)
1 July 2022	£300 000 ÷ £0.60 = $500 000	
31 December 2022	£300 000 ÷ £0.64 = $468 750	($31 250)
30 June 2023	£300 000 ÷ £0.56 = $535 714	$66 964

The journal entries of Oz Ltd to record the initial recognition and measurement of the borrowings, the interest on the borrowings and the subsequent measurement of the borrowings at the end of the reporting periods are as follows.

▶

Journals for 1 July to 31 December 2022

2022				
July 1	Cash at bank Borrowings (non-current) (Initial recognition and measurement of borrowings at transaction date using spot rate, £300 000 ÷ 0.60)	Dr Cr	500 000	500 000

Dec. 31	Interest expense
	   Foreign exchange gain
	   Cash at bank
	(Recognition of interest expense for the December half-year using average rate, £9000 ÷ 0.62, and cash payment for interest using the spot rate, £9000 ÷ 0.64)
		Dr
		Cr
		Cr
			14 516	453
				14 063

Dec. 31	Borrowings (non-current) Foreign exchange gain (Decrease in borrowing at end of reporting period using closing rate, £300 000 ÷ 0.64 less £300 000 ÷ 0.60)	Dr Cr	31 250	31 250

Journals for 1 January to 30 June 2023

2023				
June 30	Interest expense Foreign exchange loss Cash at bank (Recognition of interest expense for the June half-year using average rate, £9000 ÷ 0.59, and cash payment for interest using the spot rate, and £9000 ÷ 0.56)	Dr Dr Cr	15 254 817	16 071
June 30	Foreign exchange loss Borrowings (non-current) (Increase in borrowing at end of reporting period using closing rate, £300 000 ÷ 0.56 less £300 000 ÷ 0.64)	Dr Cr	66 964	66 964

Brief observations concerning this example are as follows.

(a) Oz Ltd's statement of financial position at 30 June 2023 includes foreign currency borrowings equal to $535 714 (i.e. £300 000 ÷ 0.56). Oz Ltd's statement of profit or loss and other comprehensive income for the year to 30 June 2023 includes financing charges of $30 134 (i.e. $14 516 − $453 + $15 254 + $817) and a net foreign exchange loss of $35 714 (i.e. $31 250 − $66 964).

(b) Oz Ltd recognises interest expense for a reporting period on an accruals basis by translating at the relevant average exchange rate.

(c) In this example, the payment of interest corresponds with the end of the reporting periods. In other cases, an amount for interest payable may be recognised at the end of each reporting period and, as a monetary item, it would be translated using the applicable closing rate.

(d) In this example, there are no repayments of loan principal until the end of the 5-year term. If the borrowings were partly repaid before the end of the 5-year term, then the requirement to remeasure the monetary item at settlement date applies. Each time principal is repaid it is necessary to restate the outstanding amount of the borrowings before the repayment using the spot rate.

LEARNING CHECK

☐ Accounting for transactions that involve foreign currency monetary items can potentially involve two subsequent measurements after the date of the transaction: at the end of the reporting period and at the date of cash settlement.

☐ At the end of the reporting period, a foreign currency monetary item is remeasured using the closing exchange rate and any resulting foreign exchange difference is recognised in profit or loss.

☐ At the date of settlement, a foreign currency monetary item is remeasured using the spot exchange rate and any resulting foreign exchange difference is recognised in profit or loss.

23.7 Subsequent measurement of foreign currency non-monetary items

LEARNING OBJECTIVE 23.7 Prepare entries for the subsequent measurement of non-monetary items that are denominated in foreign currency.

AASB 121/IAS 21 (paragraph 23(b)) requires that a non-monetary item measured in terms of historical cost in a foreign currency be translated using the exchange rate at the date of the historical transaction. The subsequent measurement of a non-monetary item will not give rise to any exchange differences if the original translated cost continues to apply. This section explains three scenarios where exchange differences do affect the measurement of a non-monetary asset. The first scenario is exchange differences in the nature of interest costs that relate to a 'qualifying asset'. The second scenario is exchange differences on a non-monetary asset that is subsequently measured at fair value rather than historical cost. The third scenario is the recognition of inventories write-downs and impairment losses on other assets.

23.7.1 Qualifying assets

A **qualifying asset** is an asset that necessarily takes a substantial period of time to get ready for its intended use (AASB 123/IAS 23 paragraph 5). Examples of qualifying assets are:
- inventories that require a substantial period of time to bring them to a saleable position
- assets resulting from development and construction activities in the extractive industries
- manufacturing plants
- power generation facilities
- investment properties.

In accordance with paragraph 8 of AASB 123/IAS 23 *Borrowing Costs*, the cost of a qualifying asset includes borrowing costs that are directly attributable to the acquisition, construction or production of that asset. Borrowing costs are interest and other costs that are incurred in borrowing funds. Borrowing costs attributable to a qualifying asset are capitalised until the construction of the asset is complete and it is ready for use. Borrowing costs may include foreign exchange differences on foreign currency borrowings to the extent that they are regarded as an adjustment to interest costs (paragraph 6). Figure 23.5 illustrates the required accounting approach.

FIGURE 23.5 Borrowing costs and qualifying assets

In the example included in figure 23.5, foreign exchange differences in the nature of interest costs are included in the cost of the qualifying asset up until 31 December 2022. After this date, there is no longer a qualifying asset and the foreign exchange differences are recognised immediately in the profit or loss of the period. The required approach is demonstrated by illustrative example 23.5.

ILLUSTRATIVE EXAMPLE 23.5

Foreign exchange borrowings on a qualifying asset

On 1 July 2022, Oz Ltd enters a loan agreement with the Bank of England plc to borrow £300 000 and uses the funds to acquire components for construction of a manufacturing plant. By 31 December 2022, when the plant is ready to use, further costs of A$100 000 have been paid to finish its construction. The interest on the borrowings is payable half-yearly in arrears at the fixed interest rate of 6% p.a. with interest payments of £9000 (£300 000 × 6% × ½ year) due on 31 December and 30 June each year. ▶

Oz Ltd prepares half-yearly reports and its reporting periods end 30 June and 31 December each year. The following exchange rates are applicable for the annual financial period to 30 June 2023.

1 July 2022	A$1 = £0.60
Average July–Dec 2022	A$1 = £0.62
31 December 2022	A$1 = £0.64
Average Jan–June 2023	A$1 = £0.59
30 June 2023	A$1 = £0.56

The journal entries of Oz Ltd to record the cost of the qualifying asset and the interest costs on the borrowings are as follows.

Journals for 1 July to 31 December 2022

2022				
July 1	Plant under construction	Dr	500 000	
	Borrowings (non-current)	Cr		500 000
	(Initial recognition and measurement of borrowings at transaction date using spot rate, £300 000 ÷ 0.60 = $500 000)			
Dec. 31	Plant under construction	Dr	14 063	
	Cash at bank	Cr		14 063
	(Capitalisation of interest costs for the December half-year comprised of interest expense, £9000 ÷ 0.62 = $14 516, and foreign exchange gain, £9000 ÷ 0.62 less £9000 ÷ 0.64 = $453)			
Dec. 31	Plant under construction	Dr	100 000	
	Cash at bank	Cr		100 000
	(Additional costs paid to finalise construction of the manufacturing plant)			
Dec. 31	Plant (cost)	Dr	614 063	
	Plant under construction	Cr		614 063
	(Reclassification of asset on the date it ceases to be a qualifying asset, $500 000 + $14 063 + $100 000 = $614 063)			

Journal for 1 January to 30 June 2023

2023				
June 30	Interest expense	Dr	15 254	
	Foreign exchange loss	Dr	817	
	Cash at bank	Cr		16 071
	(Recognition of interest expense for the June half-year, £9000 ÷ 0.59 = $15 254 and foreign exchange loss, £9000 ÷ 0.59 less £9000 ÷ 0.56 = $817)			

As illustrated in illustrative example 23.4, journal entries are also required for the subsequent measurement of the foreign currency borrowings at 31 December 2022 and 30 June 2023. These journals are omitted from the analysis here in order to focus on how the cost of the qualifying asset is determined.

23.7.2 Revalued assets

In accordance with paragraph 23 of AASB 121/IAS 21, non-monetary items that are measured at fair value in a foreign currency are translated using the exchange rate at the date that the fair value is determined. In this case, exchange differences on the asset can arise because exchange rates have changed from the date of acquiring the asset (or from the date of a previous revaluation) to the date of the current revaluation. AASB 121/IAS 21 requires that any exchange difference attributable to the revaluation is recognised consistently with the gain or loss on revaluation. If a gain or loss on revaluation of land is recognised in other comprehensive income, then any foreign exchange component of that gain or loss is also recognised in other comprehensive income (paragraph 30). The required approach is demonstrated by illustrative example 23.6.

Foreign exchange differences on a revalued asset

On 15 July 2022, Oz Ltd acquires land in California for a cash consideration of US$800 000. Subsequently at 15 May 2023, Oz Ltd revalues the land to its fair value of US$1 200 000. A revaluation gain before income tax of US$400 000 is to be brought to account in other comprehensive income for the year to 30 June 2023. Relevant exchange rates and translated amounts are as follows.

15 July 2022	A$1 = US$0.80	Land US$800 000 ÷ 0.80 = $1 000 000
15 May 2023	A$1 = US$0.75	Land US$1 200 000 ÷ 0.75 = 1 600 000
		Revaluation gain on land $ 600 000

The journal entries of Oz Ltd to record the initial recognition and measurement of the land at cost and subsequent measurement at fair value are as follows.

Journals for the year ending 30 June 2023

2022				
July 15	Land	Dr	1 000 000	
	Cash at bank	Cr		1 000 000
	(Initial recognition and measurement of land at transaction date using spot rate)			
2023				
May 15	Land	Dr	600 000	
	Gain on revaluation (OCI)	Cr		600 000
	(Revaluation of land to fair value using the spot rate at the date of revaluation)			

There are two components included in the gain on revaluation of the land of $600 000:
- the translated revaluation gain on the land; that is, US$400 000 ÷ 0.75 = $533 333
- a foreign exchange gain on the land; that is, US$800 000 ÷ 0.75 less US$800 000 ÷ 0.80 = $66 667.

In accordance with AASB 121/IAS 21 both components are recognised in other comprehensive income. A similar approach would apply if the revaluation of land to fair value involved a loss on revaluation instead of a gain. In this case, however, the loss on revaluation and any exchange differences are recognised in the profit or loss rather than in other comprehensive income. The accounting standard requirements for the revaluation of property, plant and equipment are covered in further detail in chapter 5.

23.7.3 Inventories write-downs and impairment

Paragraph 25 of AASB 121/IAS 21 notes that the carrying amount for certain non-monetary assets must be determined after making a comparison between the asset's carrying amount (i.e. book value) and some other value. In the case of inventories, the required measurement rule in AASB 102/IAS 2 *Inventories* (paragraph 9) is the lower of cost and net realisable value. If inventories on hand is to be sold in a foreign currency, then the net realisable value of the inventories in the functional currency (e.g. A$) is determined as the net realisable value in foreign currency translated by the spot exchange rate at the date this value is determined (AASB 121/IAS 21 paragraph 25). The effect of the translation could result in an inventories write-down in the functional currency (e.g. A$) whereas there would be no write-down of inventories if measurement was presented in the foreign currency. This point is demonstrated by illustrative example 23.7.

Foreign exchange differences on inventories write-downs

On 1 January 2023, Oz Ltd acquires inventories for a cash consideration of US$80 000. The inventories are still on hand at 30 June 2023 and have a net realisable value of US$80 000; that is, equal to the original cost in US$. Relevant exchange rates and translated amounts are as follows.

▶

1 January 2023	A$1 = US$0.72	Inventories US$80 000 ÷ 0.72 = $111 111
30 June 2023	A$1 = US$0.77	Inventories US$80 000 ÷ 0.77 = 103 896
		Inventories write-down $ 7 215

The journal entries of Oz Ltd to record the initial recognition and measurement of the inventories at cost and subsequent measurement at realisable value are as follows.

Journals for the year ending 30 June 2023

2023				
Jan. 1	Inventories	Dr	111 111	
	Cash at bank	Cr		111 111
	(Initial recognition and measurement of inventories at transaction date using spot rate)			
June 30	Inventories write-down expense	Dr	7 215	
	Inventories	Cr		7 215
	(Remeasurement of inventories to net realisable value at the end of the reporting period)			

Similarly, AASB 136/IAS 36 *Impairment of Assets* may require impairment testing where the carrying amount of an asset is compared to its recoverable amount in foreign currency translated into functional currency (e.g. A$). The recoverable amount of an asset is the higher of its fair value less costs to sell and its value in use (AASB 136/IAS 36 paragraph 6). These values would be translated using the spot exchange rate at the date the recoverable amount calculation is made (paragraph 54). The accounting standard requirements for the recognition of impairment of assets are covered in further detail in chapter 7.

LEARNING CHECK

☐ Borrowing costs including foreign exchange differences are included in the initial measurement of a qualifying asset; that is, an asset that necessarily takes a substantial period of time to get ready for its intended use.

☐ A non-monetary asset revalued to fair value is translated using the spot exchange rate at the date of the revaluation.

☐ Inventories written down to net realisable value are translated using the spot exchange rate at the date of the write-down.

☐ Recoverable amount is calculated for assets subject to impairment testing. The recoverable amount is translated using the spot exchange rate at the date of the recoverable amount calculation.

23.8 Foreign exchange risk

LEARNING OBJECTIVE 23.8 Explain what is meant by 'foreign exchange risk' and the circumstances in which it can arise.

Foreign exchange risk (also known as foreign currency risk or simply currency risk) is the risk that an entity's financial position, financial performance or cash flows will be affected by fluctuations in exchange rates.

In an accounting context, foreign exchange risk may relate to:

• recognised assets and liabilities
• unrecognised firm commitments to buy or sell an asset
• a forecast or planned transaction to buy or sell an asset.

Examples of a recognised asset include an accounts receivable from the sale of goods denominated in a foreign currency or a loan receivable from lending funds denominated in foreign currency. Examples of a recognised liability include an accounts payable from purchasing goods denominated in foreign currency or borrowings denominated in foreign currency. The nature of foreign exchange risk for recognised assets and liabilities is highlighted in the illustrative examples in section 23.6. In illustrative example 23.1, as an exporter of goods, Oz Ltd recognises an account receivable of $54 054 at the date of sale, but due to the fluctuation in the A$/US$ exchange rate it only collects $50 000 from the customer at the date of settlement, resulting in a foreign exchange loss of $4054.

A firm commitment means the entity has entered a binding agreement for the exchange of a specified quantity of resources at a specified price on a specified future date (AASB 9/IFRS 9 Appendix A). An **unrecognised firm commitment** is a firm commitment that the entity is yet to recognise for accounting purposes. In general, a binding agreement is not recognised for accounting purposes if the parties to the agreement have not performed their commitments under the agreement; that is, the agreement is equally proportionately unperformed. An unrecognised firm commitment becomes a recognised asset or liability at the point in time where the execution of the agreement has transferred control of resources or resulted in a present obligation. An Australian company may have a firm commitment to purchase an asset in 2 months' time for a specified amount in foreign currency; for example, an agreement to purchase new plant from a foreign supplier for US$500 000. The company does not recognise the firm commitment for accounting purposes because the agreement is unperformed; that is, the risks and rewards of plant ownership are yet to be transferred. Nonetheless, there is a foreign exchange risk associated with the firm commitment because the A$/US$ exchange rate may fluctuate before the date of recognition of the asset. Assume that before the US$500 000 asset purchase is recognised the exchange rate fluctuates from US$1.00 = A$1.40 to US$1.00 = $1.50. The financial effect from the date of the firm commitment to the date of recognition is that the A$ cost of the plant increases by $50 000 from $700 000 to $750 000.

A **forecast transaction** is an uncommitted but anticipated future transaction (AASB 9/IFRS 9 Appendix A). A highly probable forecast transaction is a forecast transaction where the odds are significantly in favour of the transaction taking place. Examples of highly probable forecast transactions include planned sales or purchases of goods denominated in foreign currency in the forthcoming period where the plans are consistent with the entity's experience from prior periods. An Australian company may have planned to make export sales to customers in the United States of US$900 000 in the coming year. The sales cannot be recognised for accounting purposes until the transactions occur. Consequently, there is a foreign exchange risk that the annual export sales in A$ will be significantly higher or lower than envisaged at the start of the year because of fluctuations in the A$/US$ exchange rate.

An Australian company may take action or enter into arrangements with the objective of mitigating foreign exchange risk — in particular, the possible adverse financial effects of fluctuations in exchange rates. These actions or arrangements are known as **hedging transactions** for foreign exchange risk. The most common form of hedging transaction is entering into forward exchange contracts.

LEARNING CHECK

☐ Foreign exchange risk is the risk that an entity's financial position, financial performance or cash flows will be affected by fluctuations in exchange rates.
☐ Foreign exchange risk may relate to recognised assets and liabilities, unrecognised firm commitments or planned foreign currency transactions.

23.9 Forward exchange contracts

LEARNING OBJECTIVE 23.9 Describe a 'forward exchange contract'.

23.9.1 The nature of a forward contract

A **forward exchange contract** is an agreement between two parties to exchange a specified quantity of one currency for another at a specified exchange rate on a specified future date. The specified exchange rate in the contract is known as the **forward rate**. In accordance with AASB 9/IFRS 9 *Financial Instruments* (Appendix A), a forward exchange contract is a derivative because it is a contract with three characteristics:
1. its value changes in response to changes in an underlying item, being changes in exchange rates
2. it requires no initial investment
3. it is settled at a future date.

The advantage of using a forward exchange contract is the ease of acquisition and its flexibility. Contracts are readily available from financial institutions and can be arranged for settlement at specific dates and for specific amounts of foreign currency. An Australian company may enter a forward exchange contract to buy or sell foreign currency in exchange of A$ for speculative reasons or to protect itself from foreign exchange risk. When a company enters into a foreign exchange contract to protect itself from foreign exchange risk, the contract will act as a hedge.

If an Australian company enters a forward exchange contract to *buy* foreign currency, then the following apply.
- The company has a contractual obligation to provide A$ at the settlement date and that obligation is a liability fixed at the forward rate.
- The company has a contractual right to receive foreign currency at the settlement date and that right is an asset that is realised at the spot rate at the end of the contract.
- The company's contractual obligation (at the forward rate) and contractual right (at the spot rate at the end of the contract) are settled on a net basis at the end of the contract.

If the Australian company enters a forward exchange contract to *sell* foreign currency, then the following apply.
- The company has a contractual right to receive A$ at the settlement date and that right is an asset fixed at the forward rate.
- The company has a contractual obligation to provide foreign currency at the settlement date and that obligation is a liability that is realised at the spot rate at the end of the contract.
- The company's contractual right (at the forward rate) and contractual obligation (at the spot rate at the end of the contract) are settled on a net basis at the end of the contract.

23.9.2 The fair value of a forward contract

The fair value of a forward contract at a point in time equals the discounted amount of the gain or loss that would result if another forward contract with the same settlement date as the original contract was entered into at that point in time. Therefore, the fair value is determined by the difference between the forward rate of the original contract and the forward rate of a new contract available in the market at a particular point in time with the same settlement date as the original contract. It should be noted that the fair value of a forward contract at the date of contract inception is $nil.

The fair value of a forward contract is demonstrated using an example of an Australian company that enters an agreement with a financial institution to buy US$100 000 at the forward rate of US$1.00 = A$1.30. The contract is entered into on 1 October 2022 for the settlement date of 31 March 2023. Figure 23.6 shows the spot and forward exchange rates relevant to this 6-month forward contract to buy US$100 000.

FIGURE 23.6	Spot rates versus forward rates	

	Spot rate	**Forward rate (for 31/3/2023)**
1 October 2022 — date of contract inception	US$1 = A$1.30	US$1 = A$1.35
31 December 2022 — end of reporting period	US$1 = A$1.32	US$1 = A$1.36
31 March 2023 — date of contract settlement	US$1 = A$1.33	US$1 = A$1.33

Figure 23.6 highlights that the forward rate will usually differ from the spot rate at the date of entering the contract. The difference between the forward and spot rates at 1 October 2022 is explained by the theory of interest rate parity as follows.

$$\text{Forward rate A\$1.35} = \frac{(1 + \text{Australian 6-month interest rate})}{(1 + \text{United States 6-month interest rate})} \times \text{Spot rate A\$1.30}$$

In this example, the forward rate is priced higher than the prevailing spot rate at the date of entering the contract so that the company is willing to pay a premium to fix the rate of exchange at a future date. At 1 October 2022, the company can buy US$100 000 at the spot rate for A$130 000; however, if it wishes to buy US$100 000 at the 6-month forward rate the cost is set to A$135 000. It is also possible that the forward rate at the date of entering the contract is set at a discount over the spot rate. This would be the case if the company could buy US$100 000 at a 6-month forward rate less than A$1.30. At the date of entering the contract, there may be a premium or discount; however, the fair value of the contract at inception is $nil.

Figure 23.6 also highlights that spot and forward rates fluctuate across time. At 31 December 2022, the forward rate for exchange for 31 March 2023 is A$1.36, meaning that in order to buy US$100 000, an entity would have to pay A$136 000 at 31 March 2023. This indicates that the original forward contract is more valuable for the company than the current available contract as it allows the company to buy US$100 000 by paying only A$135 000 at 31 March 2023. As such, the fair value at 31 December 2022 of the forward contract entered into on 1 October 2022 is the present value of A$1000 (A$136 000 − A$135 000, or US$100 000 × (1.36 − 1.35)). Accordingly, the fair value of a forward contract after inception is determined as the present value of the difference between the foreign currency position at the original forward rate (A$135 000) and the foreign currency position at the forward rate applicable at the date of measurement (A$136 000).

Figure 23.6 also shows that on 31 March 2023, the settlement of forward contract to buy US$100 000 at A$1.35 results in realised exchange loss calculated by reference to the spot rate at that date. At the date of settlement, the company has an obligation to buy US$100 000 for the payment of A$135 000 (at the original forward rate of A$1.35); however, the foreign currency to be received only has a value of A$133 000 (at the spot rate of A$1.33). The fair value of the contract is a net loss of A$2000, which equates to the realised exchange loss on the contract.

In the example, it is apparent that the value of the forward contract changes through time with fluctuations in forward rates, spot rates and interest rates. Assume a 0% discount rate for fair value calculations to simplify the analysis. The fair values of the forward contract to buy US$100 000 through time are as follows: at 1 October 2022 $nil, at 31 December 2022 positive A$1000, and at 31 March 2023 negative A$2000.

The change in the fair value of a forward contract between two dates is based on the difference between the forward rates for contracts with the same settlement dates entered into at those two dates. In the example, the change in the fair value of the forward contract between 31 December 2022 and 31 March 2023 is negative A$3000, which is US$100 000 × (1.33 − 1.36). Nevertheless, the change in the fair value of a forward contract can be expressed as comprising:

- the change in the spot element of the forward contract (referred to as the intrinsic value of the forward contract) equal to the change in spot rates multiplied by the foreign currency
- the change in the forward element of the forward contract (referred to as the time value of the forward contract) equal to the change in premium or discount multiplied by the foreign currency.

In the example, the change in the fair value between 31 December 2022 and 31 March 2023 of negative A$3000 can be expressed as US$100 000 × (1.33 − 1.32) + US$100 000 × (0 − 0.04). In general, the change in fair value of a forward contract between two dates can be expressed per unit of foreign currency as follows.

$$FV_2 - FV_1 = FR_2 - FR_1 = (SR_2 - SR_1) + (FR_2 - SR_2) - (FR_1 - SR_1) = (SR_2 - SR_1) + (P_2 - P_1)$$

where:

FV_1 and FV_2, FR_1 and FR_2, SR_1 and SR_2, and P_1 and P_2 are denoting the fair values, forward rates, spot rates and premiums over the two dates.

Figure 23.7 shows the change in the fair value of forward contract to buy US$100 000 by reference to the change in the spot and forward elements.

FIGURE 23.7 Spot and forward elements of the change in fair value of a forward contract

Date	Spot rate	Forward rate (for 31/3/23)	Premium (discount)	Change in contract fair value	Change in spot element	Change in forward element
1 Oct. 2022	A$1.30	A$1.35	A$0.05	$nil	—	—
31 Dec. 2022	A$1.32	A$1.36	A$0.04	A$0.01	A$0.02	(A$0.01)
31 Mar. 2023	A$1.33	A$1.33	$nil	(A$0.03)	A$0.01	(A$0.04)
Change in rates				(A$0.02)	A$0.03	(A$0.05)
Foreign currency US$				100 000	100 000	100 000
Change in fair value				(A$2 000)	A$3 000	(A$5 000)

The calculation of the fair value of forward contracts to sell foreign currency should take into consideration that any increase in the forward rates expressed using the direct from of quotation is reflecting an increase in the value of the foreign currency; as the contract obligates the company to sell foreign currency based on the fixed rate set at the inception of the contract, that indicates a potential loss for the company and therefore a decrease in the fair value of the contract. Therefore, all the differences that indicate gains and increases in value for forward contracts to buy foreign currency will indicate losses and decreases in value for forward contracts to sell foreign currency.

23.9.3 Accounting where there is no hedging relationship

Paragraph AG18 of AASB 132/IAS 32 *Financial Instruments: Presentation* states that the contractual right and obligation of a forward contract constitutes a financial asset or financial liability respectively.

AASB 9/IFRS 9 requires that a financial asset or financial liability that is a derivative (e.g. a forward exchange contract) be subsequently measured at fair value (paragraphs 4.1.4 and 4.2.1) at the end of each reporting period and right before settlement. The gain or loss on a forward exchange contract measured at fair value is recognised in profit or loss unless it is part of a hedging relationship (paragraph 5.71). Accounting for a forward exchange contract where there is no hedging relationship is demonstrated in illustrative examples 23.8 and 23.9.

ILLUSTRATIVE EXAMPLE 23.8

Forward contract to buy foreign currency

On 1 October 2022, Oz Ltd enters a forward exchange contract to buy US$100 000 in 6 months' time at 31 March 2023. The contract is entered into for speculative purposes as the management of Oz Ltd believe that future economic conditions will lead to an appreciation in the US$ relative to the A$. Relevant exchange rates are as follows.

	Spot rate	Forward rate (for 31/3/2023)
1 October 2022 — date of contract inception	US$1 = A$1.30	US$1 = A$1.35
31 December 2022 — end of reporting period	US$1 = A$1.32	US$1 = A$1.36
31 March 2023 — date of contract settlement	US$1 = A$1.33	US$1 = A$1.33

Assume a discount rate of 0% to simplify the fair value calculations. The fair value at a point in time can be determined as the number of units of foreign currency subject to the contract multiplied by the difference between the forward rate at that point in time and the forward rate of the original contract. Equivalently, it can be calculated as the difference between the contract right and the contract obligation at that point in time. The forward rates at different points in time are considered to estimate the spot rate at the end of the contract and therefore the contract right is calculated based on them. The contract obligation is fixed at the forward rate set at the contract inception. Therefore, the fair values of the forward contract across the three dates are as follows.

Date	Contract right (varies)	Contract obligation (fixed)	Fair value	Change
1 Oct. 2022	US$100 000 × 1.35 = $135 000	US$100 000 × 1.35 = $135 000	$nil	—
31 Dec. 2022	US$100 000 × 1.36 = $136 000	US$100 000 × 1.35 = $135 000	$1 000	$1 000
31 Mar. 2023	US$100 000 × 1.33 = $133 000	US$100 000 × 1.35 = $135 000	($2 000)	($3 000)

The journal entries of Oz Ltd are as follows. Please note that there is no entry recorded at the date of contract inception as the fair value of contract is $nil.

Journals for the year ending 30 June 2023

2022				
Oct. 1	No entry			
Dec. 31	Forward contract	Dr	1 000	
	Gain on forward contract	Cr		1 000
	(Subsequent measurement of forward contract to buy US$100 000 at the end of the reporting period)			
2023				
Mar. 31	Loss on forward contract	Dr	3 000	
	Forward contract	Cr		3 000
	(Subsequent measurement of forward contract to buy US$100 000 at settlement date)			
Mar. 31	Forward contract	Dr	2 000	
	Cash	Cr		2 000
	(Settlement of forward contract to buy US$100 000 resulting in realised exchange loss of $2000)			

Forward contract to sell foreign currency

On 1 July 2022, Oz Ltd enters a forward exchange contract to sell US$100 000 in 9 months' time at 31 March 2023. The contract is entered into for speculative purposes as the management of Oz Ltd believe that future economic conditions will result in the US$ declining in value relative to the A$. Relevant exchange rates are as follows.

	Spot rate	Forward rate (for 31/3/2023)
1 July 2022 — date of contract inception	US$1 = A$1.40	US$1 = A$1.45
31 December 2022 — end of reporting period	US$1 = A$1.38	US$1 = A$1.42
31 March 2023 — date of contract settlement	US$1 = A$1.33	US$1 = A$1.33

Assume a discount rate of 0% for fair value calculations to simplify the analysis. The fair value at a point in time can be determined as the number of units of foreign currency subject to the contract multiplied by the difference between the forward rate of the original contract and the forward rate at that point in time. Equivalently, it can be calculated as the difference between the contract right and the contract obligation at that point in time. The forward rates at different points in time are considered to estimate the spot rate at the end of the contract and therefore in this case the contract obligation to provide US$ is calculated based on them. The contract right to receive A$ is fixed at the forward rate set at the contract inception. Therefore, the fair values of the forward contract across the three dates are as follows.

Date	Contract right (fixed)	Contract obligation(varies)	Fair value	Change
1 Oct. 2022	US$100 000 × 1.45 = $145 000	US$100 000 × 1.45 = $145 000	$nil	—
31 Dec. 2022	US$100 000 × 1.45 = $145 000	US$100 000 × 1.42 = $142 000	$3 000	$3 000
31 Mar. 2023	US$100 000 × 1.45 = $145 000	US$100 000 × 1.33 = $133 000	$12 000	$9 000

The journal entries of Oz Ltd are as follows.

Journals for the year ending 30 June 2023

2022				
July 1	No entry			
Dec. 31	Forward contract	Dr	3 000	
	Gain on forward contract	Cr		3 000
	(Subsequent measurement of forward contract to sell US$100 000 at the end of the reporting period)			
2023				
Mar. 31	Forward contract	Dr	9 000	
	Gain on forward contract	Cr		9 000
	(Subsequent measurement of forward contract to sell US$100 000 at settlement date)			
Mar. 31	Cash	Dr	12 000	
	Forward contract	Cr		12 000
	(Settlement of forward contract to sell US$100 000 resulting in realised exchange loss of $12 000)			

- ☐ A forward exchange contract is an agreement between two parties to exchange a specified quantity of one currency for another at a specified exchange rate known as the forward rate.
- ☐ A forward contract has the following three characteristics: (1) its fair value changes with changes in exchange rates; (2) it requires no initial outlay; and (3) it is settled at a future date on a net basis.
- ☐ A forward exchange contract to buy foreign currency involves a right to receive foreign currency and an obligation to pay A$ that is fixed at the forward rate.
- ☐ A forward exchange contract to sell foreign currency involves a right to receive A$ fixed at the forward rate and an obligation to provide foreign currency.
- ☐ The fair value of a forward contract at a point in time equals the discounted amount of the gain or loss that would result if another forward contract with the same settlement date as the original contract was entered into.

▶

□ The fair value of a forward exchange contract to buy foreign currency at a point in time is calculated as the number of foreign currency units multiplied by the difference between the forward rate at that point in time and the forward rate of the original contract. Any increases after the contract inception in the forward rate expressed using the direct form of quotation increases the fair value of the forward exchange contract to buy foreign currency.

□ The fair value of a forward exchange contract to sell foreign currency at a point in time is calculated as the number of foreign currency units multiplied by the difference between the forward rate of the original contract and the forward rate at that point in time. Any increases after the contract inception in the forward rate expressed using the direct form of quotation decreases the fair value of the forward exchange contract to sell foreign currency.

□ A forward exchange contract that is not associated with hedging activity is measured at fair value at the end of the reporting period and at settlement date, with any resulting gain or loss recognised in the profit or loss.

23.10 Forward exchange contracts with hedging

LEARNING OBJECTIVE 23.10 Explain hedge accounting.

A forward contract is a financial instrument that may be used to manage or hedge against foreign exchange risk. A forward contract is a hedging instrument used to mitigate the possible adverse effects of changes in exchange rates on a hedged item arising from a foreign currency transaction. When there is a hedge, the foreign exchange gains or losses on one transaction (e.g. hedge contract — the hedging instrument) will offset losses or gains on another (e.g. accounts payable for inventory purchase — the hedged item).

23.10.1 Hedging relationships that qualify for hedge accounting

According to paragraph 6.4.1 of AASB 9/IFRS 9, hedge accounting applies to **hedging relationships** that meet the following three conditions.
1. The hedging relationship consists of eligible hedging instruments and hedged items.
2. The hedging relationship meets hedge effectiveness requirements.
3. The hedging relationship is formally designated and documented.

Eligible hedging instruments and hedged items

Paragraph 6.2.1 of AASB 9/IFRS 9 allows the **hedging instrument** in a hedging relationship to be a derivative measured at fair value through profit or loss; for example, a forward contract to buy or sell foreign currency. In order to qualify as an eligible hedging instrument, a forward contract must have been entered into with a party external to the reporting entity (paragraph 6.2.3). The forward contract may be designated as a hedging instrument in its entirety or in some proportion based on its intrinsic value (paragraph 6.2.4).

The **hedged item** in a hedging relationship includes any of the following (paragraph 6.3.1):
• a recognised asset or liability in the statement of financial position
• an unrecognised firm commitment
• a highly probable forecast transaction.

A brief discussion of each of those items was included in section 23.8, which addressed foreign exchange risk. Only assets, liabilities, firm commitments or highly probable forecast transactions that are with external parties to the reporting entity can be designated as hedged items (paragraph 6.3.5). The hedged item can be a single item or a group of items; for example, a planned purchase transaction or a series of planned purchase transactions denominated in foreign currency (AASB 9/IFRS 9 paragraph 6.3.1). In the case of a group of items there are additional conditions for eligibility, including that the items in the group are managed on a group basis for risk management purposes (paragraph 6.6.1). A hedged item must also be reliably measurable (paragraph 6.3.2).

Hedge effectiveness

In accordance with paragraph B6.4.1 of AASB 9/IFRS 9, the hedge effectiveness of a forward contract means the extent to which changes in the fair value of the forward contract offset changes in the fair value or cash flows of the hedged item.

Hedge effectiveness is ascertained from the following.
- There is an economic relationship between the hedging instrument and the hedged item.
- The effect of credit risk does not dominate the economic relationship between the hedging instrument and the hedged item.
- The hedge ratio of the hedging relationship reflects actual quantities and is consistent with the purpose of hedge accounting.

An economic relationship between a forward exchange contract and the hedged item would normally be indicated by the values of each moving in an opposite direction when exchange rates change (AASB 9/ IFRS 9 paragraph B6.4.3). The hedge ratio refers to the relationship between the quantity of the hedging instrument and the quantity of the hedged item in terms of their relative weighting, for example, a forward contract to buy US$80 000 for a planned purchase transaction of US$100 000 has a hedging ratio of 80% (AASB 9/IFRS 9 Appendix A).

An entity must assess whether a hedging relationship meets the hedging effectiveness requirements at the inception of the hedging relationship, at the end of each reporting period and whenever there is a significant change in hedging circumstances (AASB 9/IFRS 9 paragraph B6.4.12). The details on how to assess hedging effectiveness are beyond the scope of this chapter.

Formal designation and documentation

A hedging relationship has to be formally designated and documented at its inception to qualify for hedge accounting. Under paragraph 6.4.1(b) of AASB 9/IFRS 9, the documentation must identify:
- the hedging instrument
- the hedged item
- the entity's risk management objective and strategy for undertaking the hedge
- the nature of the risk being hedged
- how the entity will assess whether the hedging relationship meets the hedge effectiveness requirements, including the analysis of sources of hedge ineffectiveness and how the hedge ratio is determined.

23.10.2 Accounting for hedging relationships

Hedge accounting applies to the following three types of hedging relationships (AASB 9/IFRS 9 paragraph 6.5.2):
1. a fair value hedge
2. a cash flow hedge
3. a hedge of a net investment in a foreign operation.

This section explains accounting for a fair value hedge and a cash flow hedge where the hedging instrument is a forward contract. Accounting for a hedge of the net investment in a foreign operation is beyond the scope of the chapter.

A **fair value hedge** is a hedge of the exposure to *changes in the fair value* of a recognised asset or liability or an unrecognised firm commitment or some component thereof that is attributable to a particular risk and could affect profit or loss (AASB 9/IFRS 9 paragraph 6.5.2(a)). Examples of a fair value hedge of foreign exchange risk using a forward contract are:
- a forward contract to buy US$ hedging recognised accounts payable in US$
- a forward contract to buy US$ hedging recognised borrowings in US$
- a forward contract to buy US$ hedging an unrecognised firm commitment to purchase goods in US$
- a forward contract to sell US$ hedging recognised accounts receivable in US$
- a forward contract to sell US$ hedging a recognised loan receivable in US$
- a forward contract to sell US$ hedging an unrecognised firm commitment to sell goods in US$.

A **cash flow hedge** is a hedge of the exposure to the variability in future cash flows that is attributable to a particular risk that is associated with all, or some component of, a recognised asset or liability or a highly probable forecast transaction and could affect profit or loss (AASB 9/IFRS 9 paragraph 6.5.2(b)). A hedge of the foreign exchange risk of an unrecognised firm commitment may also be treated as a cash flow hedge (paragraph 6.5.4). In contrast to a fair value hedge, a cash flow hedge relates to the *future cash flows* associated with a recognised asset or liability or a future transaction rather than changes in the fair value of a hedged item. Examples of a cash flow hedge of foreign exchange risk using a forward contract are:
- a forward contract to buy US$ hedging a highly probable purchase of inventories in US$
- a forward contract to buy US$ hedging future interest payments on variable rate debt in US$

- a forward contract to buy US$ hedging an unrecognised firm commitment to purchase goods in US$
- a forward contract to sell US$ hedging a highly probable sale of inventories in US$
- a forward contract to sell US$ hedging future interest receipts on a variable rate loan receivable in US$
- a forward contract to sell US$ hedging an unrecognised firm commitment to sell goods in US$.

Accounting for a fair value hedge of a recognised monetary item

Paragraph 6.5.8(a) of AASB 9/IFRS 9 requires that when accounting for a fair value hedge, the gain or loss on the subsequent measurement of the hedging instrument — the forward contract — is recognised in profit or loss if the hedged item is a recognised monetary asset or liability; for example, an accounts receivable or accounts payable. The profit or loss for the period therefore includes the exchange loss (gain) on a foreign currency monetary item together with the gain (loss) on a forward contract. The required hedge accounting approach is demonstrated in illustrative example 23.10.

ILLUSTRATIVE EXAMPLE 23.10

Fair value hedge of a recognised monetary item

On 1 June 2023, Oz Ltd purchases inventories for US$500 000 with the invoice to be paid on 1 September 2023. On the same date as the inventories purchase, Oz Ltd enters into a forward exchange contract to buy US$500 000 on 1 September 2023. Assume a discount rate of 0% for fair value calculations to simplify the analysis. Relevant exchange rates are as follows.

	Spot rate	Forward rate (for 1/9/2023)
1 June 2023	US$1 = A$1.43	US$1 = A$1.47
30 June 2023	US$1 = A$1.39	US$1 = A$1.42
1 Sept. 2023	US$1 = A$1.50	US$1 = A$1.50

The accounts payable of US$500 000 is translated at spot rates and the right under the forward contract to buy US$500 000 is measured at forward rates as follows.

Date	Accounts payable spot rate	Gain/(loss) spot rate	Contract fair value forward rate	Gain/(loss) forward rate
1 June 2023	$715 000	—	—	—
30 June 2023	$695 000	$20 000	($25 000)	($25 000)
1 Sept. 2023	$750 000	($55 000)	$15 000	$40 000
Realised gain/(loss)		($35 000)		$15 000

It should be noted that the changes in the spot exchange rates increase the A$ amount of the accounts payable by $35 000 from the transaction date to the settlement date (i.e. $750 000 − $715 000). Similarly, the fair value of the forward contract increases by $15 000 from the transaction date to the settlement date. In this hedging relationship, the exchange loss incurred on the accounts payable is offset by the gain on the forward contract. The net effect of the hedging relationship is a loss of $20 000 (i.e. $35 000 loss net of $15 000 gain). This net effect is guaranteed at the date the forward contract is entered into (i.e. contract obligation fixed at $735 000 net of accounts payable $715 000) and is given by the premium at the contract inception multiplied by number of units of foreign currency. In the absence of the forward contract, the loss arising on the recognised liability (the accounts payable) would have been $35 000.

The journal entries of Oz Ltd for the year to 30 June 2023 are as follows.

Journals for the year ending 30 June 2023

2023				
June 1	Inventories 　　Accounts payable (Initial recognition and measurement of accounts payable at transaction date using spot rate)	Dr Cr	715 000	715 000
June 30	Accounts payable 　　Foreign exchange gain (Foreign exchange gain on remeasurement of accounts payable to spot rate recognised in profit or loss)	Dr Cr	20 000	20 000
June 30	Loss on forward contract 　　Forward contract (Loss on forward contract on remeasurement to fair value recognised in profit or loss)	Dr Cr	25 000	25 000

At 30 June 2023, the end of the reporting period, the statement of financial position will include liabilities in respect of accounts payable of $695 000 and a forward contract of $25 000. The journal entries of Oz Ltd for the year to 30 June 2024 are as follows.

2023				
Sept. 1	Foreign exchange loss	Dr	55 000	
	Accounts payable	Cr		55 000
	(Foreign exchange loss on remeasurement of accounts payable to spot rate recognised in profit or loss)			
Sept. 1	Accounts payable	Dr	750 000	
	Cash at bank	Cr		750 000
	(Cash settlement of the account)			
Sept. 1	Forward contract	Dr	40 000	
	Gain on forward contract	Cr		40 000
	(Gain on forward contract on remeasurement to fair value recognised in profit or loss)			
Sept. 1	Cash at bank	Dr	15 000	
	Forward contract	Cr		15 000
	(Cash settlement of the contract)			

In this example, it is apparent that the gains and losses on the remeasurement of the accounts payable and forward contract are immediately recognised in the profit or loss. The total gains and losses recognised for accounting purposes reconcile to the realised exchange loss on the accounts payable and the realised gain on the fair value of the forward contract (i.e. $20 000 − $25 000 − $55 000 + $40 000 = −$35 000 + $15 000).

Accounting for a fair value hedge of an unrecognised firm commitment

Recall that a firm commitment is a binding agreement for the exchange of a specified quantity of resources at a specified price on a specified future date or dates, while an unrecognised firm commitment is a firm commitment that has not been recognised in the financial statements.

Paragraph 6.5.8(a) of AASB 9/IFRS 9 requires that in accounting for a fair value hedge, the gain or loss on the subsequent measurement of the hedging instrument — the forward contract — is also recognised in profit or loss if the hedged item is an unrecognised firm commitment. In addition, the change in the fair value of the unrecognised firm commitment is recognised as an asset or liability with a corresponding gain or loss recognised in the profit or loss (paragraph 6.5.8(b)). An example is a forward contract hedging an unrecognised firm commitment to purchase plant from a foreign supplier. The fair values of the forward contract and unrecognised firm commitment change through time after the entity has entered into these arrangements. Subsequently, the acquisition of the plant is recognised after the contractual obligations in respect of the purchase have been met. The initial measurement of the plant at cost includes the cumulative change in the fair value of the firm commitment previously recognised as an asset or liability (paragraph 6.5.9). The required hedge accounting approach is demonstrated in illustrative example 23.11.

ILLUSTRATIVE EXAMPLE 23.11

Fair value hedge of an unrecognised firm commitment

On 1 April 2023, Oz Ltd enters into a firm commitment with a foreign supplier to buy a machine for US$500 000. The ownership of the machine and the consideration for the purchase are transferred on 31 July 2023. On the same day as entering the firm commitment, Oz Ltd enters into a forward exchange contract to buy US$500 000 on 31 July 2023. Assume a discount rate of 0% for fair value calculations to simplify the analysis. Relevant exchange rates are as follows.

	Spot rate	Forward rate (for 31/7/2023)
1 April 2023	US$1 = A$1.41	US$1 = A$1.46
30 June 2023	US$1 = A$1.39	US$1 = A$1.42
31 July 2023	US$1 = A$1.48	US$1 = A$1.48

In order to measure fair values of the firm commitment to expend US$500 000 and the forward contract to buy US$500 000 forward rates are applied as follows.

Date	Commitment (outlay) forward rate	Gain/(loss) forward rate	Contract fair value forward rate	Gain/(loss) forward rate
1 Apr. 2023	$730 000	—	—	—
30 June 2023	$710 000	$20 000	($20 000)	($20 000)
31 July 2023	$740 000	($30 000)	$10 000	$30 000
Realised gain/(loss)		($10 000)		$10 000

The required accounting approach is to separately recognise the financial effects of the changes in the fair value of the forward contract and the firm commitment. The journal entries of Oz Ltd for the year ending 30 June 2023 are as follows.

Journals for the year ending 30 June 2023

2023				
June 30	Loss on forward contract Forward contract (Loss on forward contract on remeasurement to fair value recognised in profit or loss)	Dr Cr	20 000	20 000
June 30	Unrecognised firm commitment Gain on unrecognised firm commitment (Gain on unrecognised firm commitment arising from change in fair value)	Dr Cr	20 000	20 000

At 30 June 2023, the end of the reporting period, the statement of financial position will include a liability in respect of the forward contract of $20 000 and an asset for an unrecognised firm commitment of $20 000. The journal entries of Oz Ltd for the year to 30 June 2024 are as follows.

Journals for the year ending 30 June 2024

2023				
July 31	Forward contract Gain on forward contract (Gain on forward contract on remeasurement to fair value recognised in profit or loss)	Dr Cr	30 000	30 000
July 31	Cash at bank Forward contract (Cash settlement of the contract)	Dr Cr	10 000	10 000
July 31	Loss on unrecognised firm commitment Unrecognised firm commitment (Loss on unrecognised firm commitment arising from change in fair value)	Dr Cr	30 000	30 000
July 31	Machine (cost) Unrecognised firm commitment Cash at bank (Recognition of cumulative changes in the fair value of the unrecognised firm commitment into the cost of acquisition of machine)	Dr Dr Cr	730 000 10 000	740 000

The nature of this hedging relationship is that the forward contract to buy US$500 000 locks in the A$ cost of the machine purchase at $730 000. If the forward contract had not been entered into, the machine cost recognised on the transaction date of 31 July 2023 would be $740 000.

A similar approach applies to the recognition of revenue arising from meeting a firm commitment to sell goods. The measurement of the revenue is adjusted to include the cumulative change in the fair value of the firm commitment that was previously recognised as an asset or liability. Assume Oz Ltd has:
- a firm commitment to sell goods to a customer on 31 July 2023 for US$500 000
- a forward exchange contract to sell US$500 000 based on the forward rate of US$1.00 = A$1.46 due for settlement on 31 July 2023.

Oz Ltd would recognise sales revenue of $730 000 (i.e. US$500 000 × 1.46) after including the cumulative change in the fair value of the firm commitment to the date of the sale transaction. In this case, the hedging relationship locks in the A$ amount recognised for the revenue and gross profit on the transaction. In the absence of the hedge, revenue recognised would be $740 000 (i.e. US$500 000 × 1.48). It should be noted, however, that if the spot rate on 31 July 2023 was US$1.00 = A$1.40, then the revenue recognised would be only $700 000 (i.e. US$500 000 × 1.40).

Accounting for a cash flow hedge of a highly probable forecast transaction

Recall that a highly probable forecast transaction is a forecast transaction where the odds are significantly in favour of the transaction taking place.

Paragraph 6.5.11(b) of AASB 9/IFRS 9 requires that in accounting for a cash flow hedge, the gain or loss on the subsequent measurement of the hedging instrument — the forward contract — is included in other comprehensive income and recognised to a cash flow hedge reserve in equity. If a hedged forecast transaction results in the recognition of a non-financial asset or non-financial liability, then the amount in the cash flow hedge reserve is removed and included in the initial measurement of that asset or liability (paragraph 6.5.11(d)(i)). In other cases, the amount in the cash flow reserve is reclassified subsequently to profit or loss in the same period or periods that the hedged future cash flows affect the profit or loss; for example, in the period that a forecast sale transaction occurs (paragraph 6.5.11(d)(ii)). The required hedge accounting approach is demonstrated in illustrative example 23.12.

ILLUSTRATIVE EXAMPLE 23.12

Cash flow hedge of a highly probable forecast transaction

On 1 April 2023, Oz Ltd enters into a forward exchange contract to sell US$500 000 on 31 July 2023. The forward contract is designated as a hedge for a sales transaction of US$500 000 that Oz Ltd expects to have with a US customer on 31 July 2023. The sales transaction is highly probable based on past experience. Assume a discount rate of 0% for fair value calculations to simplify the analysis. Relevant exchange rates are as follows.

	Spot rate	Forward rate (for 31/7/2023)
1 April 2023	US$1 = A$1.41	US$1 = A$1.46
30 June 2023	US$1 = A$1.39	US$1 = A$1.42
31 July 2023	US$1 = A$1.48	US$1 = A$1.48

In order to measure fair values of the hedged item (i.e. the future sale transaction) and the forward contract to sell US$500 000, forward rates are applied as follows.

Date	Hedged future sale forward rate	Gain/(loss) forward rate	Forward contract (obligation) forward rate	Gain/(loss) forward rate
1 Apr. 2023	$730 000	—	$730 000	
30 June 2023	$710 000	($20 000)	$710 000	$20 000
31 July 2023	$740 000	$30 000	$740 000	($30 000)
Realised gain/(loss)		$10 000		($10 000)

The required accounting approach is to include the changes in the fair value of the forward contract in a cash flow hedge reserve and then reclassify the amount into the profit or loss when the sales transaction occurs. The journal entries of Oz Ltd are as follows.

Journals for the year ending 30 June 2023

2023				
June 30	Forward contract	Dr	20 000	
	Gain on forward contract to reserve (OCI)	Cr		20 000
	(Gain on forward contract on remeasurement to fair value recognised to cash flow hedge reserve)			

At 30 June 2023, the end of the reporting period, the statement of financial position will include an asset of $20 000 in respect of the forward contract and a cash flow hedge reserve of $20 000 in equity. The journal entries of Oz Ltd for the year to 30 June 2024 are as follows.

▶

Journals for the year ending 30 June 2024

2023					
July 31	Loss on forward contract to reserve (OCI)	Dr	30 000		
	Forward contract	Cr		20 000	
	Cash at bank	Cr		10 000	
	(Loss on forward contract on remeasurement to fair value recognised to cash flow hedge reserve and cash settlement of the contract)				
July 31	Accounts receivable	Dr	740 000		
	Reclassification adjustment from reserve (OCI)	Cr		10 000	
	Sales revenue	Cr		730 000	
	(Reclassification adjustment of the cumulative changes in the cash flow hedge on recognition of the sale)				

The nature of this hedging relationship is that the forward contract to sell US$500 000 locks in the A$ amount to be recognised in the profit or loss when the sale occurs at $730 000 (i.e. US$500 000 × 1.46). The balance in the cash flow reserve after the reclassification adjustment is $nil. The profit or loss for the period includes the sale and the reclassification adjustment. AASB 9/IFRS 9 is silent about how the reclassification adjustment should be reported in the profit or loss. In this example, the reclassification adjustment is included as part of the sales revenue for the period rather than reported as a separate item; that is, the reclassification adjustment of $10 000 reduces the sales revenue recognised.

A similar approach applies to the recognition of inventories arising from a highly probable purchase transaction. The measurement of the inventories is adjusted to include the cumulative change in the fair value of the forward contract that is included in the cash flow reserve. Assume Oz Ltd has:

- a planned purchase of inventories on 31 July 2023 for US$500 000
- a forward exchange contract to buy US$500 000 based on the forward rate of US$1.00 = A$1.46 due for settlement on 31 July 2023.

Oz Ltd would recognise inventories of $730 000 (i.e. US$500 000 × 1.46) after the inclusion of a reclassification adjustment for an exchange gain of $10 000. In this case, the hedging relationship locks in the A$ amount recognised for inventories. In the absence of the hedge, the inventories would be recognised at $740 000 (i.e. US$500 000 × 1.48). It should be noted, however, that if the spot rate on 31 July 2023 was US$1.00 = A$1.90, then the inventories recognised would be $950 000 (i.e. US$500 000 × 1.9).

23.11 Disclosures

LEARNING OBJECTIVE 23.11 Describe the disclosures required in the financial report relating to foreign currency transactions.

Paragraph 52 of AASB 121/IAS 21 requires that the financial report disclose:

- the amount of exchange differences recognised in the profit or loss for the period other than those that relate to financial instruments measured at fair value through profit or loss
- the net exchange differences recognised in other comprehensive income and accumulated in a separate component of equity and reconciliation of such exchange differences at the beginning and end of the period.

If there is a change in the functional currency, that fact and the reason for the change must also be disclosed (AASB 121/IAS 21 paragraph 54).

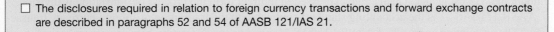

LEARNING CHECK

☐ The disclosures required in relation to foreign currency transactions and forward exchange contracts are described in paragraphs 52 and 54 of AASB 121/IAS 21.

SUMMARY

An Australian company that operates primarily in the local economic environment has a functional currency of A$. If the company transacts in foreign currencies, the resulting accounting balances must be translated into A$ for inclusion into the company's financial statements. This includes the translation of foreign currency amounts for assets, liabilities, equities, revenues, expenses and cash flows. Examples of foreign currency transactions include the sale or purchase of inventories, the acquisition of non-current assets such as plant or land, and borrowings or loans made.

Exchange rates are the means of translating foreign currency amounts. An exchange rate is the ratio of exchange for two currencies. A spot exchange rate is the rate at a point in time. An average exchange rate can be calculated by averaging spot exchange rates over a period of time. The closing exchange rate is the rate at the end of the reporting period. A forward exchange rate is a rate specified for a future date. Exchanges rates for the A$ are expressed in direct form for one unit of foreign currency or in indirect form for one unit of A$. In order to translate a foreign currency amount into A$ using an exchange rate expressed in direct form, the process of translation is multiplication. In order to translate a foreign currency amount into A$ using an exchange rate expressed in indirect form the process of translation is division.

AASB 121/IAS 21 is the accounting standard applicable to the translation of foreign currency transactions. The accounting approach of AASB 121/IAS 21 relies on the distinction between monetary items and non-monetary items. A monetary item is effectively defined as cash or a claim to cash; for example, cash, receivables, payables, borrowings and loans. Foreign currency transactions that involve monetary items are translated in three steps:

1. *the date of the transaction:* initial recognition and measurement of financial statement items using the spot exchange rate
2. *end of the reporting period:* subsequent measurement of outstanding monetary item using the closing exchange rate and resulting exchange difference recognised to profit or loss
3. *cash settlement date:* subsequent measurement of outstanding monetary item using the spot exchange rate and resulting exchange differences recognised to profit or loss together with cash settlement recorded using the spot exchange rate.

Non-monetary items such as inventories or plant that are measured at cost must be translated at the historical exchange rate at the date of the transaction. Non-monetary items that are remeasured to fair value, recoverable amount or net realisable value are remeasured using the spot exchange rate at the date of remeasurement. The resulting exchange difference is included as part of the gain or loss arising from the asset's remeasurement.

Foreign exchange risk arises from foreign currency transactions because fluctuations in exchange rates can affect the financial position, financial performance or cash flows of an entity. Foreign exchange risk may relate to recognised assets and liabilities (e.g. accounts payable) or unrecognised firm commitments (e.g. a contract to purchase plant) or a forecast transaction in the future (e.g. a planned purchase of inventories). Forward exchange contracts may be used to hedge against foreign exchange risk. These contracts involve an agreement to exchange a specified quantity of one currency for another on a future date based on a specified forward exchange rate. A forward contract to buy foreign currency hedges an underlying position where a cash outflow or monetary liability arises; for example, settlement of an account payable. A forward contract that sells foreign currency hedges an underlying position where a cash inflow or monetary asset arises; for example, settlement of an account receivable.

A forward contract is a derivative pursuant to AASB 9/IFRS 9 *Financial Instruments*. A forward contract is initially measured at $nil and subsequently at fair value. The fair value of a forward contract is calculated by reference to the gain or loss that would arise if the contract was closed out by taking the reverse position. The gain or loss should be discounted for the time value of money. The gain or loss from the subsequent measurement of a forward contract that is not designated as a hedging instrument is immediately recognised in the profit or loss.

A forward contract designated as a hedging instrument for a hedged item that is a recognised asset or liability is referred to as a fair value hedge. The gain or loss on a forward contract in a fair value hedge is immediately recognised to the profit or loss. A forward contract designated as a hedging instrument for a hedged item that is a highly probable forecast transaction is referred to as a cash flow hedge. The gain or loss on a forward contract that is a cash flow hedge is recognised in other comprehensive income and a cash flow hedge reserve. When the forecast transaction occurs, the gain or loss in the cash flow reserve is removed and included in the amount of a recognised asset or liability or reclassified in other comprehensive income and recognised to the profit or loss. A forward contract designated as a hedging instrument for a firm commitment may be recognised as fair value hedge or a cash flow hedge. The gain or loss on the unrecognised firm commitment is recognised consistently with the gain or loss on the forward contract; that is, in the profit or loss or in other comprehensive income.

KEY TERMS

cash flow hedge A hedge of the exposure to the variability in cash flows that is attributable to a particular risk that is associated with all, or some component of, a recognised asset or liability or a highly probably forecast transaction and could affect profit or loss.

closing rate The spot exchange rate at the end of the reporting period.

exchange rate The ratio of exchange between two currencies.

fair value hedge A hedge of the exposure to changes in the fair value of a recognised asset or liability or an unrecognised firm commitment or some component thereof that is attributable to a particular risk and could affect profit or loss.

forecast transaction An uncommitted but anticipated future transaction.

foreign currency transaction A transaction that is denominated or requires settlement in a foreign currency.

foreign exchange difference The difference resulting from translating a given number of units of one currency into another currency at different exchange rates.

foreign exchange risk The risk that an entity's financial position, financial performance or cash flows will be affected by fluctuations in exchange rates.

forward exchange contract An agreement between two parties to exchange a specified quantity of one currency for another at a specified exchange rate on a specified future date.

forward rate The exchange rate specified in a forward exchange contract.

functional currency The currency of the primary economic environment in which the company operates.

hedged item A recognised asset or liability, unrecognised firm commitment or highly probable forecast transaction in a hedging relationship.

hedging instrument A financial instrument used in a hedging relationship.

hedging relationships Combinations of one or more hedged items.

hedging transactions Arrangements designed to mitigate foreign exchange risk.

monetary items Units of currency held and assets and liabilities to be received or paid in a fixed or determinable amount of currency.

non-monetary item An asset or liability that is not receivable or payable in foreign currency.

qualifying asset An asset that necessarily takes a substantial period of time to get ready for its intended use.

settlement date The day on which cash is received or paid.

spot exchange rate The exchange rate at a point of time for immediate delivery of the currency in an exchange.

transaction date When control of the future economic benefits embodied in an asset are obtained from or transferred to another entity.

unrecognised firm commitment A firm commitment that the entity is yet to recognise for accounting purposes.

DEMONSTRATION PROBLEMS

23.1 Accounts payable repaid in instalments

Paradise Ltd is an Australian company that makes and sells curtains. On 1 March 2023, Paradise Ltd ordered fabric from a French company at an invoice cost of €500 000 on terms FOB destination. On 30 April 2023, the goods were delivered into stores. The agreed payment arrangements are that 10% of the total amount owing would be paid on delivery, 50% 2 months after delivery, and the remaining 40% 4 months after delivery. The end of the reporting period for Paradise Ltd is 30 June. Paradise Ltd prepares its financial statements in accordance with applicable accounting standards including AASB 121/IAS 21. The following exchange rates are applicable.

1 March 2023	A$1 = €0.50
30 April 2023	A$1 = €0.60
30 June 2023	A$1 = €0.70
31 August 2023	A$1 = €0.80

Required

Prepare the journal entries of Paradise Ltd necessary to record the above transactions in its accounting records.

SOLUTION

2023				
April 30	Inventories Accounts payable (To record credit purchase of inventories at the transaction date using the spot rate, €500 000/€0.60 = $833 333)	Dr Cr	833 333	833 333
April 30	Accounts payable Cash at bank (To record first payment of 10% of invoice, €50 000/€0.60 = $83 333. The remaining balance is €450 000/€0.60 = $750 000)	Dr Cr	83 333	83 333
June 30	Accounts payable Foreign exchange gain (Remeasurement of the balance remaining in accounts payable using the closing rate, €450 000/€0.70 less €450 000/€0.60 = $107 143)	Dr Cr	107 143	107 143
June 30	Accounts payable Cash at bank (To record second payment of 50% of invoice, €250 000/€0.70 = $357 143. The remaining balance is €200 000/€0.70 = $285 714)	Dr Cr	357 143	357 143
Aug. 31	Accounts payable Foreign exchange gain (Remeasurement of the balance remaining in accounts payable using the spot rate, €200 000/€0.80 less €200 000/€0.70 = 35 714)	Dr Cr	35 714	35 714
Aug. 31	Accounts payable Cash at bank (To record third and final payment of 40% of invoice, €200 000/€0.80 = $250 000)	Dr Cr	250 000	250 000

23.2 Cash flow hedge of forecast transaction then fair value hedge of recognised item

On 1 November 2022 Crying Sun Ltd ordered inventories to the value of US$500 000 on FOB destination terms. On 31 January 2023, the inventories were delivered. On 1 November 2022, Crying Sun Ltd also entered into a forward exchange contract to buy US$500 000 with a settlement date of 28 February 2023 (the date when the invoice for the inventories is due to be paid) to hedge against the foreign exchange risk attached to the purchase of and payment for the inventories. There is a cash flow hedge to the date of the purchase transaction and then a fair value hedge to the date the invoice is paid. Crying Sun Ltd has a financial year ending 31 December.

Relevant exchange rates are as follows.

	Spot rate	Forward rate (for 28/2/2023)
1 November 2022	A$1 = US$1.00	A$1 = US$0.95
31 December 2022	A$1 = US$0.90	A$1 = US$0.89
31 January 2023	A$1 = US$0.85	A$1 = US$0.84
28 February 2023	A$1 = US$0.75	A$1 = US$0.75

Required

Prepare the journal entries of Crying Sun Ltd necessary to record the above transactions in its accounting records. Assume a discount rate of 0% when calculating the fair value of the forward contract.

SOLUTION

2022					
Dec. 31	Forward contract		Dr	35 482	
	Gain on forward contract to reserve (OCI)		Cr		35 482
	(To record gain on forward contract for a cash flow hedge, US$500 000/0.89 less US$500 000/0.95 = $35 482)				
2023					
Jan. 31	Forward contract		Dr	33 440	
	Gain on forward contract to reserve (OCI)		Cr		33 440
	(To record gain on forward contract for a cash flow hedge, US$500 000/0.84 less US$500 000/0.89 = $33 440)				
Jan. 31	Inventories		Dr	519 313	
	Transfer from cash flow hedge reserve		Dr	68 922	
	Accounts payable		Cr		588 235
	(To record the accounts payable, US$500 000/0.85 = $588 235, and the cost of inventories after removing the amount in the cash flow hedge reserve)				
Feb. 28	Foreign exchange loss		Dr	78 432	
	Accounts payable		Cr		78 432
	(To record foreign exchange loss on accounts payable to date of settlement, US$500 000/0.75 less US$500 000/0.85 = $78 432)				
Feb. 28	Accounts payable		Dr	666 667	
	Cash at bank		Cr		666 667
	(To record settlement of accounts payable, US$500 000/0.75)				
Feb. 28	Forward contract		Dr	71 429	
	Gain on forward contract		Cr		71 429
	(To record gain on forward contract for a fair value hedge to date of settlement, US$500 000/0.75 less US$500 000/0.84 = $71 429)				
Feb. 28	Cash at bank		Dr	140 351	
	Forward contract		Cr		140 351
	(To record settlement of forward contract and the realised cash gain, US$500 000/0.75 less US$500 000/0.95)				

It is worth noting that the settlement of the accounts payable and forward contract results in a net outlay of $526 316 (i.e. $666 667 less $140 351). This is the net outlay guaranteed by the hedging relationship, being US$500 000 at the forward rate of A$1.00 = US$0.95.

COMPREHENSION QUESTIONS

1 Explain the financial reporting issue that arises when a company enters into foreign currency transactions. Provide examples of various foreign currency transactions and indicate whether each transaction involves the initial recognition of a monetary item or non-monetary item or both.

2 Explain what is meant by the term 'functional currency'.

3 Describe the indicators used in determining the functional currency of an entity.

4 Explain what is meant by a spot exchange rate, closing exchange rate and forward exchange rate.

5 Illustrate the direct and indirect methods of quoting exchange rates.

6 Explain how the items that arise from foreign currency transactions are translated into the functional currency when initially recognised in the accounting records.

7 Describe how the transaction date is determined for the purpose of initially recognising items arising from foreign currency transactions.

8 Explain the distinction between monetary and non-monetary items.

9 Explain what is meant by the term 'exchange difference'. Distinguish between an unrealised exchange loss and a realised exchange loss. Provide an overview of the accounting requirements of AASB 121/IAS 21 in relation to foreign currency transactions and exchange differences.

10 Describe how monetary items designated in a foreign currency are subsequently remeasured under AASB 121/IAS 21. At what dates does the remeasurement occur?

11 Describe the conditions under which non-monetary items designated in a foreign currency are subsequently remeasured under AASB 121/IAS 21.

12 Explain what is meant by the term 'qualifying asset'. Describe the accounting treatment for exchange differences that relate to qualifying assets.

13 If land or inventories are designated in foreign currency, how should the recoverable amount of the land or realisable value of the inventories be measured?

14 What is meant by foreign exchange risk? How can forward exchange contracts be used to manage foreign exchange risk?

15 Explain how the fair value of a forward contract is measured at inception date, at the end of the reporting period and at settlement date.

16 Distinguish between a fair value hedge and a cash flow hedge that uses a forward exchange contract as the hedging instrument. Describe the accounting treatment of any gains or losses on a forward contract that qualifies for hedge accounting.

CASE STUDY 23.1

RECOGNITION OF LIABILITIES

You are the technical accounting consultant of a Big 4 accounting firm. One of your clients is an Australian travel company that arranges package tours to overseas destinations. The client states: 'When we arrange accommodation in foreign hotels we recognise a liability at the spot rate. Then when we pay for the accommodation any exchange gain or loss is included in the profit or loss. We believe that we are complying with AASB 121/IAS 21'.

Required

Do you agree with the client's position? Explain why.

CASE STUDY 23.2

RECOGNITION METHODS

AASB 121/IAS 21 mandates the immediate recognition method where exchange differences on monetary items are recognised in the profit or loss in the period of exchange rate movement. Other methods such as 'defer and amortise' or 'recognition on realisation' are not permitted.

Required

Do you agree that the correct decision has been made from the point of view of the *Conceptual Framework*? Are there other reasons to prefer the immediate recognition method?

APPLICATION AND ANALYSIS EXERCISES

★ BASIC | ★ ★ MODERATE | ★ ★ ★ DIFFICULT

23.1 Translation of various foreign currency transactions and balances ★   **LO3, 6**

On 1 June 2023, Laurie Ltd, an Australian company with a functional currency of A$, entered into a number of transactions in NZ$ when the exchange rate was A$1.00 = NZ$1.30. Any assets arising from the NZ$ transactions are still on hand and any liabilities remain unsettled. On 30 June 2023, the exchange rate is A$1.00 = NZ$1.20.

Required

Translate each of the following items for initial and subsequent measurement as appropriate.
1. Sales revenue and accounts receivable of NZ$20 000
2. Inventories and accounts payable of NZ$32 000
3. Plant NZ$72 000
4. Interest-free borrowings of NZ$125 000

23.2 Translation of various foreign currency transactions and balances ★   **LO6, 7**

Know Your Product Ltd is an Australian company with a functional currency of A$. The company entered into a number of transactions denominated in US$ during the year ended 30 June 2023. The closing exchange rate is A$1.00 = US$0.77.

Required

Determine the translated amount that will be included in the financial statements for each of the following transactions or events.

1. Land at cost of US$600 0000 acquired on 1 February 2023 when the exchange rate is A$1.00 = US$0.67.
2. Land revalued to US$900 000 on 30 June 2023 that had cost US$600 000 on 1 February 2023 when the exchange rate was A$1.00 = US$0.67.
3. Credit sale of US$240 000 on 12 March 2023 when the exchange rate is A$1.00 = US$0.68. Received cash from debtor of US$120 000 on 30 June 2023.
4. Credit purchase of inventories of US$320 000 on 15 June 2023 when the exchange rate is A$1.00 = US$0.62. The creditor remains unpaid at 30 June 2023.
5. A loan payable of US$500 000 arranged on 1 January 2023 when the exchange rate is A$1.00 = US$0.60. On 30 June 2023, the outstanding interest on the loan is US$50 000.
6. A 6-month forward contract to buy US$2 000 000 entered into on 1 April 2023 at the forward rate of A$1.00 = US$0.75. On 30 June 2023, the forward rate for a 3-month forward to buy US$2 000 000 is A$1.00 = US$0.70. Assume a 3-month discount rate of 2% applies at 30 June 2023.

23.3 Translation of consulting service expense ★   **LO3, 6, 7**

Koala Ltd is an Australian company that receives management consulting services from Spin Incorporated. On 15 June 2023, Koala Ltd received an invoice from Spin Incorporated amounting to US$5 million for services provided over the period 1 January 2023 to 31 May 2023. On 15 July 2023, Koala Ltd paid the invoice. The functional currency of Koala Ltd is A$ and its financial year ends on 30 June. Applicable exchange rates are as follows.

1 Jan. 2023	A$1 = US$0.70
31 May 2023	A$1 = US$0.64
Average 1 Jan. 2023 to 31 May 2023	A$1 = US$0.65
15 June 2023	A$1 = US$0.62
30 June 2023	A$1 = US$0.60
15 July 2023	A$1 = US$0.58

Required

Prepare the entries of Koala Ltd to record the effects of the management fee transaction in accordance with AASB 121/IAS 21.

23.4 Translation of purchase of inventories on credit terms ★   **LO3, 6, 7**

Stranded Ltd is an Australian company that purchases inventories from Hammers plc, which is an English company. The following information is relevant to a recent acquisition of inventories for £200 000 pursuant to a contract with terms including FOB shipping point.

Date	Event	Exchange rate
11 May 2023	Inventories shipped	A$1 = £0.41
22 June 2023	Inventories delivered	A$1 = £0.42
30 June 2023	End of reporting period	A$1 = £0.43
31 July 2023	Cash payment of £300 000 to Hammers plc	A$1 = £0.39

Required

Prepare the journal entries of Stranded Ltd that relate to the foreign currency purchase of inventories in accordance with AASB 121/IAS 21. How would your answer change if the inventories acquired had a net realisable value of £170 000 at 30 June 2023?

23.5 Translation of sale of inventories on credit terms ★   **LO3, 6, 7**

Tropic Ltd is an Australian company that makes and sells small electronic goods. On 1 February 2023, a customer from the United States ordered some goods from Tropic Ltd at an invoice cost of US$400 000 on terms FOB destination. On 30 April 2023, the goods were delivered to the customer. The agreed payment arrangements are that 30% of the total amount owing would be paid on delivery, 20% 3 months after delivery, and the remaining 50% 4 months after delivery. The end of the reporting period for Tropic Ltd is 30 June. The following exchange rates are applicable.

1 February 2023	A$1 = US$0.75
30 April 2023	A$1 = US$0.73
30 June 2023	A$1 = US$0.68
31 July 2023	A$1 = US$0.72
31 August 2023	A$1 = US$0.76

Required

Prepare the journal entries of Tropic Ltd necessary to record the above transactions in its accounting records.

23.6 Translation of foreign currency borrowings and interest costs ★   **LO3, 6**

On 1 October 2022, the Australian company Run Down Ltd enters a loan agreement with the Bank of Scotland to borrow £2 000 000 for a period of 5 years. The interest on the borrowings is payable half-yearly in arrears at the fixed interest rate of 10% p.a. with interest payments of £100 000 (i.e. £2 000 000 × 10% × ½ year) due on 31 March and 30 September each year. The functional currency of Run Down Ltd is A$. It has reporting periods ending on 31 December and 30 June. Applicable exchange rates during the financial period ending 30 June 2023 are as follows.

1 Oct. 2022	A$1 = £0.42
31 Dec. 2022	A$1 = £0.40
31 Mar. 2023	A$1 = £0.38
30 June 2023	A$1 = £0.36

Required

In accordance with AASB 121/IAS 21, prepare the entries of Run Down Ltd to record the borrowing transaction, the borrowing costs expense, the borrowings costs paid and the remeasurement of the borrowings at the end of the reporting period.

23.7 Translation of purchase of plant, sale of inventories and interest free loan ★ ★   **LO3, 6, 7**

Apples Ltd is an Australian company. The functional currency of Apples Ltd is A$. It has reporting periods ending on 31 December and 30 June. During the year ended 30 June 2023, Apples Ltd entered into various foreign currency transactions in euros (€) as follows.

(a) On 15 November 2022, Apples Ltd ordered plant costing €400 000 from an Italian company under an FOB destination contract. On 30 November 2022, the plant was delivered. On 25 January 2023, the invoice for the plant purchase was paid.

(b) On 30 November 2022, Apples Ltd sold inventories to a German customer for the agreed price of €250 000. The inventories had a cost of $175 000. On 31 January 2023, the sales invoice was paid by the customer.

(c) On 1 July 2022, Apples Ltd made an interest-free loan to a related French company, Attitude Cavaliere, for €500 000. The term of the loan is set at 5 years, at which time Attitude Cavaliere will be required to arrange its debt finances independently.

Applicable exchange rates are as follows.

1 July 2022	€1 = A$1.27
15 Nov. 2022	€1 = A$1.20
30 Nov. 2022	€1 = A$1.30
31 Dec. 2022	€1 = A$1.25
25 Jan. 2023	€1 = A$1.23
31 Jan. 2023	€1 = A$1.21
30 June 2023	€1 = A$1.35

Required

In accordance with AASB 121/IAS 21, prepare the entries of Apples Ltd for the half year to 31 December 2022 and the full year to 30 June 2022.

23.8 Translation of purchases of inventories on credit terms ★ ★   **LO3, 7**

You are the financial controller of Delight Ltd, an Australian company listed on the ASX that distributes imported food products in the local market. The functional currency of Delight Ltd is A$. Delight Ltd's purchases of inventories in foreign currency during the year ended 30 June 2023 are set out below. Exchange rates at delivery date, shipment date, the end of the reporting period and payment date are expressed to A$1.

Supplier	Madras Curry Monster	Thai Satay Saucy	Russian Caviary	Turkish Delightful	German Sausagez
Foreign currency	Indian rupee (IR)	Thai baht (THB)	Russian rouble (RR)	Turkish lire (TL)	Euros (€)
Invoice amount	3 000 000	900 000	40 000 000	80 000 000	500 000
Contract basis	FOB shipping	FOB destination	FOB shipping	FOB shipping	FOB destination
Shipment date	20 Jul. 2022	31 Jul. 2022	1 Nov. 2022	31 Mar. 2023	30 Apr. 2023
Delivery date	31 Jul. 2022	30 Aug. 2022	31 Dec. 2022	30 Apr. 2023	30 Jun. 2023
Payment date	30 Sept. 2022	31 Oct. 2022	31 Jan. 2023	31 Jul. 2023	31 Aug. 2023
Rate on delivery	IR 10	THB 2	RR 1 000	TL 10 000	€0.80
Rate on shipping	IR 12	THB 3	RR 2 000	TL 10 500	€0.78
Rate at the end of the reporting period	IR 18	THB 10	RR 1 800	TL 10 750	€0.70
Rate on payment	IR 15	THB 4	RR 500	TL 11 000	€0.75

Required

In accordance with AASB 121/IAS 21, prepare the necessary entries in relation to the inventories purchase transactions up until and including 31 August 2023.

23.9 Translation of sales of inventories on credit terms ★ ★ **LO3, 6, 7**

You are the financial controller of Valley Vines Ltd, an Australian company listed on the ASX that sells premium Australian wines into overseas markets. Valley Vines' sales of inventories in foreign currency during the year ended 30 June 2023 are set out below. Exchange rates at delivery date, shipment date, the end of the reporting period and payment date are expressed to A$1.

Customer	Israel #3	Dubai #6	Turkey #4	Egypt #8	United States #9
Foreign currency	Israeli shekel (NIS)	Dubai dirham (AED)	Turkish lire (TL)	Egyptian dinar (ED)	US dollar (US$)
Invoice amount	4 500 000	30 000 000	20 000 000 000	750 000 000	4 000 000
Contract basis	FOB shipping	FOB shipping	FOB destination	FOB destination	FOB shipping
Delivery date	30 Aug. 2022	31 Oct. 2022	31 Jan. 2023	31 Mar. 2023	30 Apr. 2023
Shipment date	31 Jul. 2022	30 Sept. 2022	30 Nov. 2022	28 Feb. 2023	15 Apr. 2023
Cash receipt date	31 Oct. 2022	5 Feb. 2023	31 Mar. 2023	31 Jul. 2023	31 Aug. 2023
Rate on delivery	NIS 1.6	AED 3.5	TL 9 500	ED 5 000	US$0.75
Rate on shipment	NIS 1.4	AED 4.0	TL 9 000	ED 5 500	US$0.80
Rate at the end of the reporting period	NIS 1.2	AED 3.8	TL 10 750	ED 5 750	US$0.88
Rate on cash receipt	NIS 1.3	AED 4.2	TL 10 500	ED 6 000	US$0.86

Required

In accordance with AASB 121/IAS 21, prepare the necessary entries in relation to the sale transactions up until and including 31 August 2023.

23.10 Qualifying assets ★ ★ **LO3, 6, 7**

On 1 July 2022, Remote Ltd, an Australian company that has A$ as its functional currency, enters a loan agreement with a lender in Hong Kong to borrow HK$800 000 and uses the funds to acquire components for construction of a warehouse. By 31 December 2022, when the warehouse is ready to use, further costs of A$100 000 have been paid to finish its construction. The interest on the borrowings is payable half-yearly in arrears at the fixed interest rate of 10% p.a. with interest payments of HK$40 000 (HK$800 000 × 10% × ½ year) due on 31 December and 30 June each year. Remote Ltd prepares half-yearly reports and its reporting periods end 30 June and 31 December each year. The following exchange rates are applicable for the annual financial period to 30 June 2023.

1 July 2022	A$1 = HK$5.60
Average July–Dec. 2022	A$1 = HK$5.65
31 Dec. 2022	A$1 = HK$5.70
Average Jan.–June 2023	A$1 = HK$5.72
30 June 2023	A$1 = HK$5.75

Required

In accordance with AASB 121/IAS 21, prepare the necessary entries in relation to the transactions up until and including 30 June 2023.

23.11 Revalued assets and inventory write-downs ★ ★   **LO3, 6, 7**

On 15 July 2022, Adelaide Ltd, an Australian company that has A$ as its functional currency, acquires land in Paris, France, for a cash consideration of €500 000. On 1 January 2023, Adelaide Ltd acquires inventories on credit for €75 000. Subsequently at 30 June 2023, Adelaide Ltd revalues the land to its fair value of €700 000. The inventories are still on hand at 30 June 2023 and have a net realisable value of €70 000. On 1 August 2023, Adelaide Ltd pays in full the inventories purchased. Relevant exchange rates are as follows.

15 July 2022	A$1 = €0.85
1 Jan. 2023	A$1 = €0.80
30 June 2023	A$1 = €0.82
1 Aug. 2023	A$1 = €0.83

Required

In accordance with AASB 121/IAS 21, prepare the necessary entries for Adelaide Ltd up until and including 1 August 2023.

23.12 Forward contract with no hedging ★ ★   **LO3, 6, 10**

On 1 February 2023, Rosewood Ltd, an Australian company that has A$ as its functional currency, enters a forward exchange contract to buy £200 000 in 6 months' time at 31 July 2023. The contract is entered into for speculative purposes as the management of Rosewood Ltd believe that future economic conditions will lead to an appreciation in the £ relative to the A$. Relevant exchange rates are as follows.

	Spot rate	Forward rate (for 31/7/2023)
1 Feb. 2023 — date of contract inception	£1 = A$1.68	£1 = A$1.80
30 June 2023 — end of reporting period	£1 = A$1.72	£1 = A$1.82
31 July 2023 — date of contract settlement	£1 = A$1.65	£1 = A$1.65

Assume a discount rate of 0% for fair value calculations.

Required

1. Prepare the necessary entries for Rosewood Ltd up until and including 31 July 2023 in accordance with AASB 121/IAS 21.
2. Assuming that the forward contract entered is to sell £200 000, prepare the necessary entries for Rosewood Ltd up until and including 31 July 2023. The other features of the contract stay the same.

23.13 Forward contract with fair value hedging ★ ★   **LO10**

On 1 May 2024, Edmund Ltd, an Australian company that has A$ as its functional currency, purchases inventories for US$200 000 with the invoice to be paid on 30 October 2024. On the same date as the inventories purchase, Edmund Ltd enters into a forward exchange contract to buy US$200 000 on 30 October 2024. Assume a discount rate of 0% for fair value calculations. Relevant exchange rates are as follows.

	Spot rate	Forward rate (for 30/10/2024)
1 May 2024	US$1 = A$1.53	US$1 = A$1.57
30 June 2024	US$1 = A$1.56	US$1 = A$1.60
30 October 2024	US$1 = A$1.48	US$1 = A$1.48

Required

Prepare the necessary entries for Edmund Ltd up until and including 30 October 2024 in accordance with AASB 121/IAS 21.

23.14 Forward contract with fair value hedging ★ ★ **LO10**

On 1 March 2024, Frank Ltd, an Australian company that has A$ as its functional currency, enters into a firm commitment with a foreign supplier to buy an equipment for US$500 000. The ownership of the equipment and the consideration for the purchase are transferred on 31 August 2024. On the same day as entering the firm commitment, Frank Ltd enters into a forward exchange contract to buy US$500 000 on 31 August 2024. Assume a discount rate of 0% for fair value calculations. Relevant exchange rates are as follows.

	Spot rate	Forward rate (for 31/8/2024)
1 March 2024	US$1 = A$1.36	US$1 = A$1.39
30 June 2024	US$1 = A$1.37	US$1 = A$1.41
31 August 2024	US$1 = A$1.38	US$1 = A$1.38

Required

Prepare the necessary entries for Frank Ltd up until and including 31 August 2024 in accordance with AASB 121/IAS 21.

23.15 Forward contract with cash flow hedging ★ ★ **LO10**

On 1 January 2023, Toby Ltd, an Australian company that has A$ as its functional currency, enters into a forward exchange contract to sell €300 000 on 31 August 2023. The forward contract is designated as a hedge for a sales transaction of €300 000 that Toby Ltd expects to have with a German customer on 31 August 2023. The sales transaction is highly probable based on past experience. Assume a discount rate of 0% for fair value calculations. Relevant exchange rates are as follows.

	Spot rate	Forward rate (for 31/8/2023)
1 January 2023	€1 = A$1.27	€1 = A$1.32
30 June 2023	€1 = A$1.30	€1 = A$1.35
31 August 2023	€1 = A$1.36	€1 = A$1.36

Required

Prepare the necessary entries for Toby Ltd up until and including 31 August 2023 in accordance with AASB 121/IAS 21.

23.16 Purchase of inventories paid in instalments; borrowing hedged by forward contract ★ ★ **LO3, 6, 10**

You are the finance director of the Australian listed company Fire Ltd, which has a functional currency in A$. Fire Ltd purchases goods from Hong Kong and has borrowings from a US bank. The company's financial year ends on 30 June 2023. Fire Ltd entered the following transactions during the year.

(a) Fire Ltd purchased inventories from a Hong Kong supplier for HK$2 700 000 on 15 April 2023. The purchase contract is settled in three equal instalments of HK$900 000. The following exchange rates apply.

15 Apr. 2023	Date of purchase HK$2 700 000	A$1 = HK$5.99
31 May 2023	1st payment of HK$900 000	A$1 = HK$6.01
30 June 2023	End of the reporting period	A$1 = HK$6.21
31 Aug. 2023	2nd payment of HK$900 000	A$1 = HK$6.18
30 Sept. 2023	3rd payment of HK$900 000	A$1 = HK$6.24

(b) On 1 January 2023, Fire Ltd borrowed US$3 000 000 from an investment bank in the United States for a 12-month period. The borrowing has a fixed rate of interest at 10% p.a. payable at 6-month intervals. On 1 April 2023, Fire Ltd entered a 9-month forward contract to buy US$2 500 000 in order to hedge against the foreign exchange risk on the US$ loan principal. The following exchange rates apply.

Date	Spot rate	Forward rate (for 31/12/2023)
1 Jan. 2023	A$1 = US$0.89	A$1 = US$0.84
1 Apr. 2023	A$1 = US$0.86	A$1 = US$0.82
30 June 2023	A$1 = US$0.85	A$1 = US$0.79
31 Dec. 2023	A$1 = US$0.80	A$1 = US$0.80

Assume a 0% discount rate for fair value calculations.

Required

Prepare the entries of Fire Ltd to account for its foreign currency transactions in accordance with AASB 121/IAS 21.

23.17 Purchase of inventories paid in instalments; borrowing with hedged interest commitment; purchase of inventories with hedged liability to supplier ★ ★ ★   LO3, 7, 10

You are the finance director of Gripweed Ltd, an Australian company listed on the ASX. The company is an importer of goods from overseas markets. The company's financial year ends on 30 June 2023. The company entered the following transactions during the year.

(a) Gripweed Ltd purchased inventories from a Hong Kong supplier for HK$300 000. The title to the goods passes to the company on delivery. The payment for the inventories is due in equal instalments. The following exchange rates are applicable.

22 Apr. 2023	Date of order for inventories	A$1 = HK$8.40
30 Apr. 2023	Date of delivery for inventories	A$1 = HK$8.90
31 May 2023	1st payment of HK$100 000	A$1 = HK$8.96
30 June 2023	2nd payment of HK$100 000	A$1 = HK$8.99
31 July 2023	3rd payment of HK$100 000	A$1 = HK$9.44

(b) Gripweed Ltd purchased land in Japan on 1 July 2022 for ¥60 000 000. The land is subsequently revalued on 30 June 2023 to its fair value of ¥90 000 000. The following exchange rates are applicable.

1 July 2022	Date of acquisition of land	A$1 = ¥180
30 June 2023	Date of revaluation of land	A$1 = ¥265

(c) Gripweed Ltd arranged interest-only borrowings on 1 January 2023 for US$20 000 000. The borrowings have a 10-year term and interest is paid half-yearly at the rate of 7.6% p.a. Gripweed Ltd took out a 6-month forward exchange contract on 1 January 2023 as a hedge against the initial interest payment due. The following exchange rates are applicable.

	Spot rate	Forward rate (for 30/6/2023)
1 Jan. 2023	A$1 = US$0.80	A$1 = US$0.75
30 June 2023	A$1 = US$0.65	A$1 = US$0.65

(d) Gripweed Ltd purchases inventories on 1 May 2023 from an English supplier for £450 000. On the same date, Gripweed enters a 3-month forward exchange contract to buy £450 000 to hedge its liability to the supplier. On 31 July 2023, the supplier is paid and the forward contract is settled. The following exchange rates are applicable.

	Spot rate	Forward rate (for 31/7/2023)
1 May 2023	A$1 = £0.64	A$1 = £0.62
30 June 2023	A$1 = £0.52	A$1 = £0.47
31 July 2023	A$1 = £0.37	A$1 = £0.37

(e) Assume the same facts as part (d) except that the date of the purchase of inventories is 31 July 2023 and at 1 May 2023 it is a highly probable forecast transaction.

Required

Prepare the entries of Gripweed Ltd to account for its foreign currency transactions in accordance with AASB 121/IAS 21. Assume a 0% discount rate for fair value calculations. Explain the techniques applied in respect of each transaction.

23.18 Sale of inventories with no hedge, fair value hedge and cash flow hedge ★ ★ ★   **LO3, 7, 10**

Cool Ltd is an Australian mining company listed on the ASX. The company is an exporter of iron ore to overseas steel mills. The company's functional currency is A$ and its financial year ends on 30 June 2023. The company entered various sale transactions during the year. Relevant exchange rates are as follows.

	Spot rate	Forward rate (for 31/7/2023)
1 Apr. 2023	A$1 = US$0.78	A$1 = US$0.75
1 June 2023	A$1 = US$0.76	A$1 = US$0.72
30 June 2023	A$1 = US$0.78	A$1 = US$0.74
31 July 2023	A$1 = US$0.80	A$1 = US$0.80

(a) On 1 April 2023, Cool Ltd sold iron ore to a Japanese customer for US$2 500 000. On 31 July 2023, the customer paid for the iron ore.

(b) On 1 June 2023, Cool Ltd sold iron ore to a Chinese customer for US$4 250 000. On 31 July 2023, the customer paid for the iron ore. On 1 June 2023, the company entered into a forward exchange contract to sell US$4 250 000, which it designated as a hedge of the customer account.

(c) On 1 April 2023, in anticipation of a highly probable transaction with its Korean customer, Cool Ltd entered into a forward exchange contract to sell US$1 500 000 as a hedging instrument. The forward contract has a settlement date of 31 July 2023. On 1 June 2023, Cool Ltd sold iron ore to a Korean customer for US$1 500 000. On 31 July 2023, the customer paid for the iron ore.

Required

Prepare the entries of Cool Ltd to account for its foreign currency transactions in accordance with AASB 121/IAS 21. Assume a 0% discount rate for fair value calculations.

23.19 Hedged firm commitment; hedged highly probable forecast transaction; hedged recognised liability; and borrowings and interest attributable to a qualifying asset ★ ★ ★   **LO3, 7, 10**

Aloha Ltd is an Australian company that purchases inventories and specialised equipment from US suppliers. The company's functional currency is A$ and its financial year ends on 30 June 2023. The company entered various transactions denominated in US$ during the year. Assume a discount rate of 0% for fair value calculations. Relevant exchange rates are as follows.

	Spot rate	Forward rate (for 31/8/2023)
1 Jan. 2023	A$1 = US$0.85	A$1 = US$0.83
1 Mar. 2023	A$1 = US$0.79	A$1 = US$0.76
1 May 2023	A$1 = US$0.75	A$1 = US$0.73
30 June 2023	A$1 = US$0.70	A$1 = US$0.67
31 Aug. 2023	A$1 = US$0.77	A$1 = US$0.77

(a) On 1 March 2023, Aloha Ltd entered into a firm commitment with a US company to build a new equipment item for US$1 800 000. On 31 August 2023, the item of equipment is delivered and installed and recognised as an asset in Aloha Ltd's accounting records. On 1 March 2023, Aloha Ltd entered a 6-month forward contract to buy US$1 800 000 for settlement on 31 August 2023. The forward contract is designated as a hedging instrument for an unrecognised firm commitment.

(b) On 31 August 2023, Aloha Ltd acquired inventories, as normal around this time of year, from a US supplier for US$5 000 000. On 1 January 2023, Aloha Ltd entered an 8-month forward contract to buy US$5 000 000 for settlement on 31 August 2023. The forward contract is designated as a hedging instrument for a highly probable forecast inventories purchase transaction.

(c) On 1 May 2023, Aloha Ltd acquired inventories from a US supplier for US$500 000. The invoice is paid in full on 31 August 2023. On 1 May 2023, Aloha Ltd entered a 4-month forward exchange contract to buy US$500 000 for settlement on 31 August 2023. The forward contract is designated as a hedging instrument for a recognised liability.

(d) On 1 January 2023, Aloha Ltd commenced the construction of an item of specialised plant. The estimated construction period for the plant is 18 months. On 1 January 2023, Aloha Ltd borrowed US$18 000 000 to finance the construction of the plant. The interest on the borrowings is 10% p.a. paid at the end of each year. The average exchange rate for the period 1 January 2023 to 30 June 2023 is A$1.00 = US$0.825.

Required

Prepare the entries of Aloha Ltd to account for its foreign currency transactions in accordance with AASB 121/IAS 21. Assume a 0% discount rate for fair value calculations.

ACKNOWLEDGEMENTS

Photo: © Dmitry Kalinovsky / Shutterstock.com
Photo: © Syda Productions / Shutterstock.com

CHAPTER 24

Translation of foreign currency financial statements

CHAPTER AIM

Companies may prepare their financial statements in one currency but translate them into another currency for presentation purposes. This chapter discusses the application of AASB 121/IAS 21 *The Effects of Changes in Foreign Exchange Rates* to the translation of an entity's financial statements into another currency.

LEARNING OBJECTIVES

After studying this chapter, you should be able to:

24.1 discuss the need for translation of foreign entities' financial statements

24.2 explain the difference between functional and presentation currencies

24.3 understand the main methods used in the translation process

24.4 translate a set of financial statements from local currency into the functional currency and account for exchange differences

24.5 translate a set of financial statements from functional currency into the presentation currency and account for exchange differences

24.6 prepare the disclosures required by AASB 121/IAS 21.

CONCEPT FOR REVIEW

Before studying this chapter, you should understand and, if necessary, revise:
* the format of financial statements prepared under AASB 101/IAS 1 *Presentation of Financial Statements*.

24.1 Introduction and scope

LEARNING OBJECTIVE 24.1 Discuss the need for translation of foreign entities' financial statements.

Many Australian companies have operations in overseas locations as well as in Australia. Two accounting issues that such companies face are as follows.

1. What currency will be used for accounting in the overseas location itself?
2. What currency will be used for the preparation of the consolidated financial statements of the entity as a whole?

If we look at some Australian companies we find a diversity of currencies being used.

The Fortescue Metals Group Ltd (Fortescue) was formed in 2003. Initially an exploration company, Fortescue has since transitioned into one of the world's largest producers and seaborne traders of iron ore. Operating in the Pilbara region of Western Australia, the company shipped more than 170 million tonnes of iron in the year ended 30 June 2018. Fortescue's major markets are in Asia, particularly China.

In 2009, Fortescue adopted the US dollar (US$) as its *functional currency*. A company's functional currency is the currency of the primary economic environment in which the entity operates. It is determined with reference to the underlying economic substance of the company's transactions and operating context.

Iron ore prices are denominated in US dollars and thus Fortescue's iron ore sales generate significant US dollar cash inflows. In addition, the company's secured notes and subordinated loan note are denominated in US dollars and so will generate substantial US dollar cash inflows and outflows in the future. Thus, Fortescue uses the US dollar for accounting within the company and its subsidiaries. Fortescue also uses the US dollar as its presentation currency for reporting to shareholders (Fortescue 2018).

The US dollar is also the currency in which the financial statements of Rio Tinto Limited are presented as it 'most reliably reflects the Group's global business performance' (Rio Tinto Limited 2017, p. 118). However, for many of its offshore locations, the currency used for its accounts is the local currency rather than either the US or the Australian dollar. Hence, the financial statements of the overseas operations must be translated into US dollars for presentation in the group's financial statements.

For many Australian companies, the currency used for presentation of the group's financial statements is the Australian dollar, while their overseas operations use multiple currencies depending on which country the overseas operation is located in. In Note 19 of its 2018 annual report Wesfarmers Limited noted that 'all subsidiaries are incorporated in Australia' unless otherwise identified, and, with some exceptions, 'all entities utilise the functional currency of the country of incorporation' (Wesfarmers Limited 2018, p. 135). In relation to its overseas subsidiaries the functional currency is not always the Australian dollar. Figure 24.1 lists the countries of incorporation of Wesfarmers' overseas subsidiaries. The overseas subsidiaries keep their accounts in the local currency (with a small number of exceptions, noted in figure 24.1).

FIGURE 24.1   Countries of incorporation and functional currencies of overseas subsidiaries, Wesfarmers

Bangladesh	Republic of Ireland
Bermuda	New Zealand
Cayman Islands	Portugal
China	Singapore
Hong Kong	United Arab Emirates
India	United Kingdom
Indonesia	United States of America

All entities utilise the functional currency of the country of incorporation with the exception of Wesfarmers Risk Management Limited and Target Australia Sourcing (Shanghai) Co Ltd, which utilise the Australian dollar and KAS International Trading (Shanghai) Company Limited, PT Blackwoods Indonesia and Wesfarmers Oil & Gas Pty Ltd, which utilise the US dollar.

Source: Wesfarmers Limited (2018, p. 135).

The financial statements of these overseas subsidiaries are then translated into Australian dollars for inclusion in the consolidated financial statements of Wesfarmers Limited, presented in Australian dollars, as described in figure 24.2.

| FIGURE 24.2 | Foreign currency translation, Wesfarmers |

Foreign currency

As at the reporting date, the assets and liabilities of overseas subsidiaries are translated into Australian dollars at the rate of exchange ruling at the balance sheet date and the income statements are translated at the average exchange rates for the year. The exchange differences arising on the retranslation are taken directly to a separate component of equity.

Transactions in foreign currencies are initially recorded in the functional currency at the exchange rates ruling at the date of the transaction. Monetary assets and liabilities denominated in foreign currencies are translated at the rate of exchange ruling at the balance sheet date. Exchange differences arising from the application of these procedures are taken to the income statement, with the exception of differences on foreign currency borrowings that provide a hedge against a net investment in a foreign entity, which are taken directly to equity until the disposal of the net investment and are then recognised in the income statement. Tax charges and credits attributable to exchange differences on those borrowings are also recognised in equity.

Source: Wesfarmers Limited (2018, p. 103).

The purpose of this chapter is to discuss the process for translating the financial statements of a foreign entity into the financial statement presentation currency for presentation purposes. This may also involve the translation of a foreign entity's financial statements into its functional currency first. The relevant accounting standard applied in the translation process is AASB 121/IAS 21 *The Effects of Changes in Foreign Exchange Rates.*

LEARNING CHECK

☐ The financial statements of an overseas subsidiary may be recorded in a foreign currency and translated into Australian dollars for the purpose of combining those statements with the financial statements of the parent Australian company.

☐ The financial statements of an Australian company may be prepared in Australian dollars and translated into a foreign currency for presentation purposes.

24.2 Functional and presentation currencies

LEARNING OBJECTIVE 24.2 Explain the difference between functional and presentation currencies.

Paragraph 3 of AASB 121/IAS 21 outlines two translation processes, which are discussed in this chapter:
1. translating the results and financial position of foreign operations that are included in the financial statements of the entity into the functional currency (section 24.4)
2. translating an entity's results and financial position into a presentation currency (section 24.5).

In order to understand these processes, it is necessary to distinguish between three different types of currencies: local currency, functional currency and presentation currency. Not all foreign subsidiaries experience all these three currencies. Local currency is not defined in AASB 121/IAS 21. The other two terms are defined in paragraph 8.
• **Local currency**. This is the currency of the country in which the foreign operation is based.
• **Functional currency**. This is the currency of the primary economic environment in which the foreign entity operates. This may be the Australian currency, that of the foreign operation, or the currency of another foreign entity.
• **Presentation currency**. This is the currency in which the financial statements are presented by the reporting entity.

To illustrate, consider Kangaroo Ltd, which is an Australian company, and its subsidiary Paris Ltd, which is based in France. The operations in France are to sell goods manufactured in China. In this case, Paris Ltd would most likely maintain its accounts in euros, the local currency, while the functional currency could be the Chinese renminbi (RMB), reflecting the major economic operations in China. However, for presentation in the consolidated financial statements of Kangaroo Ltd, the presentation currency could be the Australian dollar. As the accounts of Paris Ltd are maintained in euros, they may firstly have to be translated into the functional currency, the RMB, and then translated again into the Australian dollar for presentation purposes. It is these two translation processes that are referred to at the beginning of this section.

There is no requirement under Australian accounting standards for an entity to present its financial statements in Australian dollars. The financial statements may be presented in any currency (AASB 121/IAS 21 paragraph 38). The choice is based on what the management of an entity believes will provide the most relevant information to the users of the financial statements. As noted in section 24.1, while Fortescue and Rio Tinto Limited have chosen to use the US dollar as their presentation currency, companies such as Wesfarmers Limited have chosen the Australian dollar. Choosing the functional currency is a much more involved process and requires management judgement.

24.2.1 Functional currency

As discussed in chapter 23, according to AASB 121/IAS 21 the functional currency is the currency of the primary economic environment in which the entity operates. To understand how two entities could have different functional currencies, consider the following two situations.

1. An Australian company, Koala Ltd, establishes a subsidiary in Beijing, Great Wall Ltd. Great Wall Ltd acquires buildings and equipment and manufactures products in Beijing. Chinese labour is used in the manufacturing process and profits are used to reinvest in Great Wall Ltd. After the determination of Great Wall Ltd's profits, where financially prudent, dividends are remitted to Koala Ltd. On examining the economics of the relationship between the two companies, the subsidiary is not just acting as an extension of the parent. Apart from the initial investment, the cash flows, both inflows and outflows, are dependent on the economic environment of China rather than Australia. The effect of a change in the **exchange rate** between Australia and China has no immediate effect on the operations of the Chinese subsidiary. It certainly affects the worth of the parent's investment in the subsidiary, but it has no immediate cash flow effect on the parent. In this circumstance, the primary economic environment in which Great Wall Ltd operates is China. The functional currency of Great Wall Ltd is then the Chinese RMB rather than the Australian dollar.

2. An Australian parent company, Emu Ltd, establishes a subsidiary in Beijing, Summer Palace Ltd. Emu Ltd sends the components to make washing machines to Summer Palace Ltd. The machines are assembled in Beijing and, on completion, are sent back to Australia for sale to Australian customers. Summer Palace Ltd is financed by Emu Ltd. In this scenario, an analysis of the economics of the relationship between Emu Ltd and Summer Palace Ltd is that the primary economic environment affecting Summer Palace Ltd is Australia. The foreign subsidiary is a direct extension or an integral component of the Australian company. All costs apart from the labour costs are affected by price changes in Australia; selling prices of the inventories are dependent on Australia's supply and demand; and all finances are made in Australian dollars. In this case, the functional currency of Summer Place Ltd is the Australian dollar and not the Chinese RMB. However, Summer Palace Ltd may keep its accounting records in RMB.

In determining the functional currency of a foreign operation of a reporting entity it is then necessary to analyse the underlying economics of the situation.

24.2.2 Identifying the functional currency of a foreign operation

The determination of the functional currency of an entity requires judgement. According to paragraph 9 of AASB 121/IAS 21, the key economic factor to consider is: *in which economic environment does an entity primarily generate and expend cash?* Generation of cash is primarily from sale of goods and services while expenditure is for inventories and services such as labour.

The following factors, given in paragraph 9(a) and (b) of AASB 121/IAS 21, should be considered in answering this question.
• Which currency mainly influences sales prices for goods and services?
• What is the currency of the country whose competitive forces and regulations mainly determine the sales price of its goods and services?
• What is the currency that mainly influences labour, material and other costs of providing goods and services?

These are the primary indicators of which currency is the functional currency. Table 24.1 provides a tabular representation of these indicators that can be used in determining whether the functional currency of the foreign operation of a reporting entity is the same as the functional currency of the entity.

TABLE 24.1

TABLE 24.1 **Primary economic indicators of functional currency**

Economic indicators	Indicators pointing to foreign operation's currency as functional currency	Indicators pointing to reporting entity's currency as functional currency
Sales prices	Prices are not primarily responsive in the short term to exchange rate changes. They are determined primarily by local conditions.	Prices are primarily responsive to exchange rate changes in the short term and are determined primarily by worldwide competition.
Sales markets	There are active local markets, although there may be significant amounts of exports.	Sales are mostly in the country of the reporting entity, or denominated in the reporting entity's currency.
Expenses	Production costs and operating expenses are determined primarily by local conditions.	Production costs and operating expenses are obtained primarily from reporting entity sources.

If answers to the above questions do not supply a clear answer on what the functional currency is, then paragraph 10 of AASB 121/IAS 21 provides further factors that may also provide evidence of an entity's functional currency. These factors can be expressed in terms of further questions that should be asked.
- In which currency are the funds from financing activities, such as issue of debt and equity instruments, generated?
- In which currency are the funds from operations normally retained?

These are the financing indicators of functional currency. Table 24.2 illustrates these indicators.

TABLE 24.2 **Financing economic indicators of functional currency**

Economic indicators	Indicators pointing to foreign operation's currency as functional currency	Indicators pointing to reporting entity's currency as functional currency
Financing	Funds are primarily denominated in the local currency, and come from the foreign operation's activities including local fund raising.	Funds are primarily from the reporting entity as a result of that entity's fundraising activities, or the reporting entity is expected to service the debt of the foreign operation.
Retention of funds	Profits generated by the foreign operation are retained in the foreign entity and used for its expansion.	Profits are remitted to the reporting entity.

The activities of a foreign operation may also provide clues on what is the functional currency. In this regard, paragraph 11 of AASB 121/IAS 21 provides additional factors to be considered in determining the functional currency of a foreign operation. These can be expressed in the form of the following questions that may be asked.
- Are the activities of the foreign operation carried out as an extension of the reporting entity, rather than being carried out with a significant degree of autonomy?
- Are the transactions with the reporting entity a high or a low proportion of the foreign operation's activities?
- Do the cash flows from the activities of the foreign operation directly affect the cash flows of the reporting entity, and are they readily available for remittance to it?
- Are the cash flows from the activities of the foreign operation sufficient to service existing and normally expected debt obligations without funds having to be made available from the reporting entity?

Table 24.3 provides a discussion of these activity indicators.

Paragraph 12 of AASB 121/IAS 21 notes that management may have to use its judgement to determine the functional currency, the objective being to choose the currency that most faithfully represents the economic effects of the underlying transactions, events and conditions. Priority is given to the primary factors in paragraph 9 before the indicators in paragraphs 10 and 11 are considered. The latter indicators provide supporting evidence to the information provided by considering the primary factors.

Hence, in situations where the functional currency is that of the foreign operation, it should be expected that the foreign operation is a self-contained operation and primarily operating independently within a particular country or economic environment. The daily operations of the foreign operation both in terms of inputs and outputs are independent from the economic environment of the reporting entity. The funding of the foreign operation primarily comes from its own operations or from successful fundraising activities that it undertakes. The cash flows of the reporting entity are then not affected to any great extent by the activities of the foreign operation.

TABLE 24.3	Activity economic indicators of functional currency	
Economic indicators	Indicators pointing to foreign operation's currency as functional currency	Indicators pointing to reporting entity's currency as functional currency
Autonomy	The foreign operation operates as an independent entity, having little interaction either in terms of inputs or outputs with the reporting entity.	The foreign operation obtains raw materials from the reporting entity and sells the output in the reporting entity's country.
Intercompany transactions	There is a low volume of intragroup transactions and there is not an extensive interrelationship between the operations of the foreign operation and those of the reporting entity. However, the foreign entity may rely on the reporting entity's competitive advantages, such as patents and trademarks.	There is a high volume of intragroup transactions; there is an extensive interrelationship between the operations of the reporting entity and those of the foreign operation or the foreign operation is an investment or financing device for the reporting entity.
Cash flows	The cash outlaid on goods and services is paid to entities other than the reporting entity, and cash inflows from sales are from entities other than the reporting entity.	The foreign operation pays the reporting entity for goods and services and receives revenues from sales of output to the reporting entity.
Servicing of debt obligations	The foreign operation generates sufficient cash to be able to service its own debt obligations.	The foreign operation relies on the reporting entity to supply funds to pay the debts incurred by the foreign operation.

In situations where the functional currency of the foreign operation is that of the reporting entity, it should be seen that the foreign operation is acting as an extension of the reporting entity itself. The cash flows of the foreign operation are integrated with the reporting entity in that products are acquired from the reporting entity or from that entity's country, and sales are made to the reporting entity, or in that entity's country. The cash flows of the reporting entity are affected by the activities of the foreign operation. Funding for the foreign operation comes primarily from the reporting entity.

As in all situations, the economic environment must be examined to determine where the cash is primarily generated and expended.

LEARNING CHECK

☐ The functional currency is the currency of the primary economic environment in which the foreign entity operates.

☐ The rationale behind the choice of an entity's functional currency is based on reflecting the underlying economics of the situation.

☐ The determination of an entity's functional currency requires judgement and is based upon an analysis of a number of factors or economic indicators which assist in the analysis of the economic environment in which the entity operates.

24.3 The translation process

LEARNING OBJECTIVE 24.3 Understand the main methods used in the translation process.

Once the functional currency has been identified it may be necessary to translate a foreign operation's financial statements from one currency to another.

Assume that the financial records of a Chinese foreign operation, Hangzhou Ltd, are kept in the local currency (RMB) and that the Australian reporting entity, Tasmania Ltd, presents the consolidated financial statements in its functional currency, namely the Australian dollar (A$). There are three possible translation scenarios.

1. *The local currency is the functional currency.* As the accounts of Hangzhou Ltd are kept in the local currency RMB, which is also the functional currency, no translation process to convert to functional currency is necessary. However, the functional currency of Tasmania Ltd is different from that of Hangzhou Ltd. In this case, as the consolidated financial statements of Tasmania Ltd are presented in A$, it is necessary to translate the financial statements of Hangzhou Ltd from the functional currency of RMB into the presentation currency of A$.

2. *The functional currency of the foreign operation is the Australian dollar.* The accounts of Hangzhou Ltd are kept in RMB. The first translation process is to translate the financial statements of Hangzhou Ltd from the local currency of RMB into the functional currency of A$. As A$ is the presentation currency of Tasmania Ltd, there is no need for any further translation process to be undertaken.

3. *The functional currency of the foreign operation is the currency of a third country.* Because Hangzhou Ltd sells its products in Europe and obtains its finance from European banks, it has been assessed that the functional currency of Hangzhou Ltd is the euro (€). The first translation process is to translate the financial statements from the local currency of RMB into the functional currency of €. The second translation process is to translate from the functional currency of € into the presentation currency of A$.

There are, therefore, two translation processes: translation from local currency into functional currency and translation from functional currency into presentation currency. There are also two methods used for these processes. The accounting standards do not give names to these methods; however, in this text, for ease of referral, they are called the 'temporal method' and the 'current rate method'. These methods are explained in sections 24.4 and 24.5.

Figure 24.3 demonstrates the translation process under these three scenarios and where the two translation methods are used. The currencies are based on the example of Tasmania Ltd and Hangzhou Ltd.

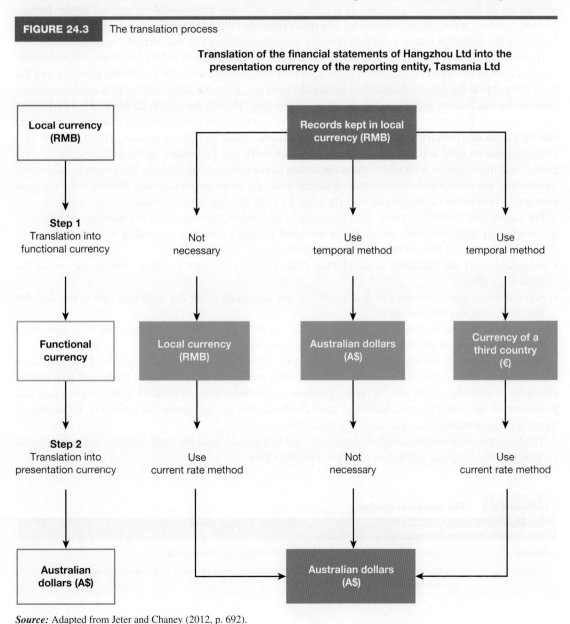

| **FIGURE 24.3** | The translation process |

Translation of the financial statements of Hangzhou Ltd into the presentation currency of the reporting entity, Tasmania Ltd

Source: Adapted from Jeter and Chaney (2012, p. 692).

24.4 Translation into the functional currency — the temporal method

LEARNING OBJECTIVE 24.4 Translate a set of financial statements from local currency into the functional currency and account for exchange differences.

The basic principle established in paragraph 21 of AASB 121/IAS 21 of recording a foreign currency transaction in the functional currency is that the spot exchange rate should be applied to the foreign currency amount at the date of transaction. The **spot exchange rate** is defined in paragraph 8 of AASB 121/IAS 21 as the exchange rate at a point of time for immediate delivery of the currency in an exchange.

Hence, in translating the *revenues and expenses* in the statement of profit or loss and other comprehensive income, each item should be translated at the spot exchange rate between the functional currency and the local currency on the date the transaction occurred. However, given the large number of transactions being reported by the foreign operation, this is often not possible. Hence, paragraph 22 of AASB 121/IAS 21 allows the use of a rate that approximates the actual rate at the transaction date; for example, an average rate for a week or a month might be used for all transactions occurring in those periods. The extent to which averaging can be used depends on the extent to which there is a fluctuation in the exchange rate over a period, and the evenness with which the transactions occur within those periods. For example, where the transactions are made evenly throughout a financial year (e.g. there are no seasonal effects) and there is an even movement of the exchange rate over the year, a yearly average could be used.

For *assets and liabilities*, these are effectively translated at the rates that the carrying amounts of the assets and liabilities were measured in the local currency records. According to paragraph 23 of AASB 121/IAS 21, at the end of each reporting period:

• *monetary items* are translated at the **closing rate**, which is the spot exchange rate at the end of the reporting period
• *non-monetary items measured at historical cost* are translated using the exchange rate at the date the historical cost was determined
• *non-monetary items measured at fair value, realisable value or recoverable amount* are translated using the exchange rates at the dates those values were measured.

Monetary items are defined in paragraph 8 of AASB 121/IAS 21 as units of currency held and assets and liabilities to be received or paid in a fixed or determinable number of units of money. Paragraph 16 provides examples of monetary liabilities, including pensions and other employee benefits to be paid in cash, and provisions to be settled in cash, including cash dividends that are recognised as a liability. Examples of monetary assets include cash and accounts receivable.

The basic principles of the translation method used to translate from the local currency to the functional currency — the temporal method — are shown in table 24.4.

TABLE 24.4	The temporal method
Statement of financial position	
Assets	Assets should first be classified as monetary or non-monetary.
Monetary	Monetary assets are translated at the rate existing at the end of the reporting period; that is, the closing rate.

Non-monetary	For a non-monetary asset, the exchange rate used is the rate current at the date at which the recorded amount for the asset has been entered into the accounts. Hence, for non-monetary assets recorded at historical cost, the rates used are those existing when the historical cost was recorded. For non-monetary assets that have been revalued, whether upwards or downwards, the exchange rates used will relate to the dates of revaluation.
Liabilities	Liabilities should first be classified as monetary or non-monetary.
Monetary	As with monetary assets, the closing rate is used.
Non-monetary	As with non-monetary assets, the exchange rate at the date the liability was measured is used.

Equity	In selecting the appropriate exchange rate, two factors are important.
	    First, equity is divided into pre-acquisition and post-acquisition equity. Where a reporting entity acquires an investment in a foreign operation, then the equity recorded by the foreign operation at acquisition date is pre-acquisition equity. If a reporting entity establishes a foreign operation, the equity used to form the foreign operation is pre-acquisition equity. Equity earned by the foreign operation subsequent to acquisition date is post-acquisition equity.
	    Second, movements in other reserves and retained earnings constituting transfers within equity are treated differently from other reserves such as asset revaluation surpluses which are created by the application of the revaluation model.

Share capital	The capital is translated at the rate existing at acquisition or investment.
Other reserves	If pre-acquisition, the reserves are translated at the rate existing at acquisition date. If the reserves are post-acquisition and result from internal transfers, the rate used is that current at the date the amounts transferred were originally recognised in equity. If the reserves are post-acquisition and not created from internal transfers, the rate used is that current at the date the reserves are first recognised in the accounts.
Statement of profit or loss and other comprehensive income	
Retained earnings	If pre-acquisition, the retained earnings are translated at the rate of exchange current at the acquisition date. Post-acquisition profits are carried forward balances from translation of previous periods' statements of profit or loss and other comprehensive income.
Revenues	These are translated at the rates current at the dates the transactions occurred, but an approximation such as an average rate for a period may be used.
Expenses	These are translated at the rates current at the dates the transactions occurred, but an approximation such as an average rate for a period may be used. For expenses that relate to non-monetary assets, such as depreciation and amortisation, the rates applicable are those used to translate the related non-monetary assets.
Dividends paid	These are translated at the rate current at the date of payment.
Dividends declared	These are translated at the rate current at the date of declaration.

According to paragraph 34 of AASB 121/IAS 21, the object of this translation process, based upon using historical rates, is to produce the same amounts in functional currency that would have occurred had the items been recorded initially in the functional currency. In other words, the translation process seeks to achieve the numbers that would have been recorded if the transactions had occurred in the functional currency rather than in the local currency. For example, assume Tasmania Ltd owned the Chinese company Hangzhou Ltd. Hangzhou Ltd bought a vehicle for RMB140 000 when the exchange rate was A$1 = RMB7. On the date the vehicle was acquired the A$ equivalent of RMB140 000 is A$20 000. By translating the non-monetary asset at historical rates, the vehicle is always translated back to the amount that the Australian reporting entity would have paid if it had bought the vehicle itself in Australian dollars.

The application of the rates as described in table 24.4 will result in an exchange difference being calculated. An **exchange difference** arises mainly because the foreign operation's monetary items are translated at closing rates while the non-monetary items are translated at historical rates. Also, revenues and expenses which give rise to monetary items such as cash, receivables and payables are translated at the rates current during the period when the transactions occurred. In other words, not all items in the financial statements are being translated at the same rate. Hence, there has to be a balancing item which is the exchange difference. This exchange difference can be explained by examining the movements in the monetary items over the period. An example of this appears in illustrative example 24.1.

In accordance with paragraph 28 of AASB 121/IAS 21, exchange differences that arise on translating local currencies to functional currencies are recognised in *profit or loss for the period in which they arise.*

ILLUSTRATIVE EXAMPLE 24.1

Translation into the functional currency

Changi Ltd, a company operating in Singapore, is a wholly owned subsidiary of Perth Ltd, a company listed in Australia. Perth Ltd formed Changi Ltd on 1 July 2022 with an investment of A$310 000. Changi Ltd's records and financial statements are prepared in Singaporean dollars (S$). Changi Ltd has prepared the following financial information at 30 June 2023.

CHANGI LTD Statement of financial position as at 30 June 2023	S$
Current assets	
Inventories	210 000
Monetary assets	190 000
Total current assets	400 000
Non-current assets	
Land — acquired 1/7/22	100 000
Buildings — acquired 1/10/22	120 000
Plant and equipment — acquired 1/11/22	110 000
Accumulated depreciation — plant and equipment	(10 000)
Deferred tax asset	10 000
Total non-current assets	330 000
Total assets	730 000
Current liabilities	
Current tax liability	70 000
Borrowings	50 000
Payables	100 000
Total current liabilities	220 000
Non-current liabilities	
Borrowings	150 000
Total liabilities	370 000
Net assets	**360 000**
Equity	
Share capital	310 000
Retained earnings	50 000
Total equity	**360 000**

CHANGI LTD Statement of profit or loss and other comprehensive income for the year ended 30 June 2023	S$	S$
Sales revenue		1 200 000
Cost of sales:		
Purchases	1 020 000	
Ending inventories	210 000	810 000
Gross profit		390 000

Expenses:		
Selling	120 000	
Depreciation	10 000	
Interest	20 000	
Other	90 000	240 000
Profit before income tax		**150 000**
Income tax expense		60 000
Profit for the period		**90 000**

The only movement in equity, other than in profit, was a dividend paid during the period of S$40 000.

Additional information
- Exchange rates over the period 1 July 2022 to 30 June 2023 were as follows.

	S$1.00 = A$
1 July 2022	1.00
1 October 2022	0.95
1 November 2022	0.90
1 January 2023	0.85
1 April 2023	0.73
30 June 2023	0.75
Average rate for year	0.85
Average rate for November 2022 – June 2023	0.80
Average rate for April 2023 – June 2023	0.77

- Proceeds of long-term borrowings were received on 1 July 2022 and are payable in four annual instalments commencing 1 July 2023. Interest expense relates to this loan.
- The inventories on hand at balance date represents approximately the final 3 months' purchases (April–June 2023).
- Revenues and expenses are spread evenly throughout the year.
- Deferred tax asset relates to a temporary deductible difference for the plant and equipment caused by depreciation.
- The dividends were paid on 1 April 2023.

Required
The functional currency is determined to be the Australian dollar. Translate the financial statements of Changi Ltd into the functional currency.

Solution
The translation process is as shown in figure 24.4.

FIGURE 24.4	Translation into functional currency

	S$	Rate	A$
Sales	1 200 000	0.85	1 020 000
Cost of sales:			
Purchases	1 020 000	0.85	867 000
Ending inventories	210 000	0.77	161 700
	810 000		705 300
Gross profit	90 000		314 700
Expenses:			
Selling	120 000	0.85	102 000
Depreciation	10 000	0.90	9 000
Interest	20 000	0.85	17 000
Other	90 000	0.85	76 500
	240 000		204 500

	S$	Rate	A$
			110 200
Foreign exchange translation loss			**2 200**
Profit before tax	150 000		108 000
Income tax expense	60 000	0.85	51 000
Profit for the period	90 000		57 000
Retained earnings at 1/7/22	0		0
	90 000		57 000
Dividends paid	40 000	0.72	28 800
Retained earnings at 30/6/23	50 000		28 200
Share capital	310 000	1.00	310 000
Total equity	**360 000**		**338 200**
Non-current borrowings	150 000	0.75	112 500
Current tax liability	70 000	0.75	52 500
Current borrowings	50 000	0.75	37 500
Payables	100 000	0.75	75 000
Total liabilities	**370 000**		**277 500**
Inventories	210 000	0.77	161 700
Monetary assets	190 000	0.75	142 500
Land	100 000	1.00	100 000
Buildings	120 000	0.95	114 000
Plant and equipment	110 000	0.90	99 000
Accumulated depreciation	(10 000)	0.90	(9 000)
Deferred tax asset	10 000	0.75	7 500
Total assets	**730 000**		**615 700**

In relation to the exchange rates used, note the following.
- For revenues and expenses, in general the average rate of 0.85 is used. Depreciation, however, is translated using the same rate as applied to the related asset in the statement of financial position: 0.90.
- Monetary assets and liabilities are translated at the current rate of 0.75.
- Non-monetary assets are translated at the historical rates — the rates existing when the assets were first acquired.

As explained previously, the exchange gain/loss for the period can be determined by examining the movements in the monetary items over the period.

From figure 24.4, the net monetary assets of Changi Ltd at 30 June 2023 consist of the following.

	S$
Monetary assets	190 000
Deferred tax asset	10 000
Borrowings: non-current	(150 000)
Borrowings: current	(50 000)
Current tax liability	(70 000)
Payables	(100 000)
Net monetary assets at 30/6/23	(170 000)

The net monetary assets at 1 July 2022 were S$310 000 (equivalent to the A$310 000 initial investment as the exchange rate was S$1 = A$1). During the period, the increases in net monetary assets are generated by the sales, while the decreases are generated by all the expenses and purchases. The exchange differences are calculated by comparing the difference between the exchange rate used in the translation process and the current rate at the end of the reporting period on all those items that cause changes in net monetary assets as follows.

	S$	Current rate less rate applied	A$ gain (loss)
Net monetary assets at 1 July 2022	310 000	(0.75 − 1.00)	(77 500)
Increases in net monetary assets:			
Sales	1 200 000	(0.75 − 0.85)	(120 000)
	1 510 000		(197 500)

Decreases in net monetary assets:				
Land		(100 000)	(0.75 − 1.00)	25 000
Buildings		(120 000)	(0.75 − 0.95)	24 000
Plant and equipment		(110 000)	(0.75 − 0.90)	16 500
Purchases		(1 020 000)	(0.75 − 0.85)	102 000
Selling expenses		(120 000)	(0.75 − 0.85)	12 000
Interest		(20 000)	(0.75 − 0.85)	2 000
Other expenses		(90 000)	(0.75 − 0.85)	9 000
Dividend paid		(40 000)	(0.75 − 0.72)	(1 200)
Income tax expense*		(60 000)	(0.75 − 0.85)	6 000
		(1 680 000)		195 300
Net monetary assets at 30 June 2023		(170 000)		(2 200)
*The entry for the period is:			S$	S$
Income tax expense	Dr		60 000	
Deferred tax asset	Dr		10 000	
Current tax liability	Cr			70 000

In preparing the translated financial statements for the following period, it should be noted that the balance of retained earnings as at 30 June 2023, as translated in figure 24.4, is carried forward into the next period. In other words, there is no direct translation of the retained earnings (opening balance) within the translation process in years subsequent to the initial translation.

The exchange gain/loss for the period can also be determined as a balancing item after all the financial statement items were translated based on the applicable rates. Having translated all the assets and liabilities, the translated amount of total equity can be calculated as the difference between the translated assets and liabilities. The gain/loss will be equal to the difference between this translated amount of total equity and all the other amounts translated that belong to equity. Basically, the calculation is done by going backwards from the translated amount of total equity to the profit before tax and before the exchange gain/loss. In the example, based on the translated amounts of total assets of $615 700 and total liabilities of $277 500, the translated amount of total equity is determined as $338 200 ($615 700 – $277 500). As the translated amount of the other equity is $310 000, the translated amount of Retained earnings at 30 June 2020 should be $28 200. As that recognises the profit after tax, including any exchange gain/loss for the period, after dividend paid of $28 800, the translated amount of the profit after tax is $57 000 and therefore the translated amount of profit before tax is $108 000. As the profit before tax excluding any exchange gain/loss for the period is translated to $110 200, the amount of foreign exchange loss is $2200.

☐ The basic principle is that the spot exchange rate should be applied to the foreign currency at the date of the transaction.

☐ Revenues and expenses are translated at the spot exchange rate between the functional currency and the local currency at the date each transaction occurred. However, a rate that approximates the actual rate, such as an average rate for a period, can be used.

☐ Assets and liabilities are normally translated at historical rates for non-monetary items and closing rates for monetary items.

☐ An exchange difference may arise because the foreign operation's monetary items are translated at closing rates while the non-monetary items are translated at historical rates.

☐ Exchange differences that arise on translating local currencies to functional currencies are recognised in profit or loss for the period in which they arise.

24.5 Translation from the functional currency into the presentation currency — the current rate method

LEARNING OBJECTIVE 24.5 Translate a set of financial statements from functional currency into the presentation currency and account for exchange differences.

Having prepared the financial statements of all entities within a group using their functional currencies, it is then necessary to translate the financial statements into a presentation currency prior to aggregating the financial statements together to present consolidated financial statements. For example, assume an Australian reporting entity has two subsidiaries, one in Malaysia whose functional currency is the Malaysian ringgit and the other a Hong Kong company whose functional currency is the HK dollar. If the presentation currency selected is the Australian dollar, then both sets of financial statements would have to be translated from their functional currencies into Australian dollars prior to being consolidated with the financial statements of the Australian parent.

The process for translating from the functional currency to the presentation currency is described in paragraph 39 of AASB 121/IAS 21 and involves using the following procedures.

- Translate the assets and liabilities at the closing rate at the date of the statement of financial position.
- Translate the revenues and expenses at the spot rates at the dates of the transactions.
- Translate other equity items based on the distinction between pre- and post-acquisition equity.
- Recognise resulting exchange differences in other comprehensive income and accumulate it into a foreign exchange reserve.

In relation to these procedures, note:

(a) For most revenues and expenses apart from depreciation the translation is the same as the process used when translating from local currency to the functional currency. For practical reasons, a rate that approximates the exchange rate at the date of the transaction can be used, such as an average rate for the period, unless the exchange rates fluctuate significantly during the period (see AASB 121/IAS 21 paragraph 40).

(b) According to paragraph 41 of AASB 121/IAS 21, the exchange difference is recognised in other comprehensive income and not as profit or loss. Having been recognised in other comprehensive income, it is accumulated in equity using a 'foreign currency translation reserve'. The exchange difference is not recognised in profit or loss because the changes in exchange rate have little or no direct effect on the present and future cash flows from operations. In other words, the operations of the entity are affected by the functional currency rather than the presentation currency.

As with the temporal method, application of the current rate method gives rise to an exchange difference. The exchange difference arises because of two reasons. *First*, the revenue and expense items are translated at rates different from the closing rate which is used for all assets and liabilities. *Second*, the opening net assets are translated at a closing rate different from the previous closing rate; that is, a vehicle held at 30 June 2023 is translated at the closing rate at that date, whereas at 30 June 2024, the closing rate at that date is used for the same vehicle. The exchange difference can then be measured by assessing the differences in the rates used for both revenue/expense items and the differences in opening and closing rates on the net assets at the beginning of the period.

The basic principles of the translation method used to translate from the functional currency to the presentation currency — the current rate method — are shown in table 24.5.

TABLE 24.5	The current rate method
Statement of financial position	
Assets	All assets, whether current or non-current, monetary or non-monetary, are translated at the closing rate, which is the exchange rate current at the end of the reporting period. This includes all contra-asset accounts such as accumulated depreciation and allowance for doubtful debts.
Liabilities	All liabilities are translated at the same rate as for assets, namely the closing rate current at the end of the reporting period.

Equity	In selecting the appropriate exchange rate, two factors are important.
	    First, equity is divided into pre-acquisition and post-acquisition equity. Where a reporting entity acquires an investment in a foreign operation, then the equity recorded by the foreign operation at acquisition date is pre-acquisition equity. If a reporting entity establishes a foreign operation, the equity used to form the foreign operation is pre-acquisition equity. Equity earned by the foreign operation subsequent to acquisition date is post-acquisition equity.
	    Second, movements in other reserves and retained earnings constituting transfers within equity are treated differently from other reserves such as asset revaluation surpluses which are created by the application of the revaluation model.

Share capital	If on hand at acquisition date or created by investment, this is translated at the rate current at acquisition date or investment. If created by transfer from a reserve, such as general reserve via a bonus issue, this is translated at the rate current at the date the amounts transferred were originally recognised in equity.

Other reserves	If on hand at acquisition date, these are translated at the exchange rate existing at acquisition date. If reserves are post-acquisition and created by an internal transfer within equity, they are translated at the rate existing at the date the reserve from which the transfer was made was originally recognised in the accounts. If post-acquisition and not the result of an internal transfer (e.g. an asset revaluation surplus), the rate used is that current at the date the reserve is recognised in the accounts.		
Retained earnings	If on hand at acquisition date, they are translated at the exchange rate existing at acquisition. Post-acquisition profits are carried forward balances from translation of previous periods' statements of profit or loss and other comprehensive income.		

Statement of profit or loss and other comprehensive income

Revenues and expenses	These are translated at the rates current at the applicable transaction dates. For items that occur regularly throughout the period, such as purchases of inventories and sales, for practical reasons average or standard rates that approximate the relevant rates may be employed. In relation to items such as depreciation, which are allocations for a period, even though they may be recognised in the accounts only at year-end (because they reflect events occurring throughout the period) an average-for-the-period exchange rate may be used.
Dividends paid/declared	These are translated at the rates current when the dividends were paid or declared.
Transfer to/from reserves	If these are transfers internal to equity, the rate used for the transfer and the reserve created is the rate existing when the amounts transferred were originally recognised in equity.

ILLUSTRATIVE EXAMPLE 24.2

Translation into the presentation currency

The same example used in illustrative example 24.1 is used here. The functional currency of Changi Ltd is Singapore dollars and the presentation currency is Australian dollars. The translation is then as follows.

	S$	Rate	A$
Sales	1 200 000	0.85	1 020 000
Cost of sales:			
Purchases	1 020 000	0.85	867 000
Ending inventories	210 000	0.77	161 700
	810 000		705 300
Gross profit	390 000		314 700
Expenses:			
Selling	120 000	0.85	102 000
Depreciation	10 000	0.80	8 000
Interest	20 000	0.85	17 000
Other	90 000	0.85	76 500
	240 000		203 500
Profit before tax	150 000		111 200
Income tax expense	60 000	0.85	51 000
Profit for the period	90 000		60 200
Retained earnings at 1/7/22	0		0
	90 000		60 200
Dividends paid	40 000	0.72	28 800

	S$	Rate	A$
Retained earnings at 30/6/23	50 000		31 400
Share capital	310 000	1.00	310 000
Foreign currency translation reserve			**(71 400)**
Total equity	**360 000**		**270 000**
Non-current borrowings	150 000	0.75	112 500
Current tax liability	70 000	0.75	52 500
Current borrowings	50 000	0.75	37 500
Payables	100 000	0.75	75 000
Total liabilities	**370 000**		**277 500**
Inventories	210 000	0.75	(157 500)
Monetary assets	190 000	0.75	142 500
Land	100 000	0.75	75 000
Buildings	120 000	0.75	90 000
Plant and equipment	110 000	0.75	82 500
Accumulated depreciation	(10 000)	0.75	(7 500)
Deferred tax asset	10 000	0.75	7 500
Total assets	**730 000**		**547 500**

In relation to the exchange rates used, note the following.
- Revenues and expenses — including depreciation expense — are generally translated at the average exchange rate, namely 0.85.
- Assets and liabilities are translated at the closing rate, namely 0.75.
- The exchange difference arising as a result of the translation is A$(71 400) — there has been an exchange loss over the period, which is recognised in other comprehensive income and accumulated in equity. This loss arises for two reasons as follows.
  1. The revenue and expense items and the dividend are translated at the rates at the date of the transactions or average rates and not the closing rate.

Recorded profit after dividend	=	S$50 000
Profit after dividend as translated	=	A$31 400
Profit after dividend × closing rate	=	S$50 000 × 0.75
	=	A$37 500
Translation gain/(loss)		A$37 500 −
		A$31 400
	=	A$6 100

  2. The opening net assets are translated at a rate different from the closing rate.

Net assets at 1 July 2022	=	S$310 000
Net assets at 1 July 2022 × opening rate	=	S$310 000 × 1.00
	=	A$310 000
Net assets at 1 July 2022 × closing rate	=	S$310 000 × 0.75
	=	A$232 500
Translation gain/(loss)	=	A$(77 500)
The total translation loss is then	=	A$6 100 + A$(77 500)
Total translation loss	=	A$(71 400)

The amount in foreign currency translation reserve for the period can also be determined as a balancing item after all the financial statement items were translated based on the applicable rates. Having translated all the assets and liabilities, the translated amount of total equity can be calculated as the difference between the translated assets and liabilities. The gain/loss will be equal to the difference between this translated amount of total equity and all the other amounts translated that belong to equity. Basically, the calculation is done by going backwards from the translated amount of total equity to the foreign currency translation reserve. In the example, based on the translated amounts of total assets of $547 500 and total liabilities of $277 500, the translated amount of total equity is determined as $270 000 ($547 500 − $277 500). As the translated amount of the other equity is $341 400 (share capital of $310 000 and retained earnings of $31 400), the amount of foreign currency translation reserve is $(71 400).

The translation of the financial statements from the functional currency into the presentation currency should not change the way in which the underlying items are measured or have any effect on the financial information being presented. Rather the translation process should just express the underlying amounts in a different currency. However, note that in illustrative example 24.2 this effect is not achieved. For example, consider the profit to equity ratio at the end of the reporting period.

		S$	A$
Profit to equity ratio	=	$90 000/$360 000	$59 700/$270 000
	=	0.25	0.28

The ratios will only be the same if *all* items in the statement of profit or loss and other comprehensive income are translated at the closing rate, the same as the assets and the liabilities. Using the exchange rate at date of transaction for revenues and expenses means that retaining the same ratios before and after translation is not possible. According to paragraph 17 of the Basis of Conclusions to AASB 121/IAS 21, the International Accounting Standards Board (IASB) considered the use of a translation method that translates all items at the closing rate. The advantages of such a method is that it is simple to apply, does not generate exchange differences from applying different rates to revenue/expense items, and it does not change ratios such as return on assets. The IASB, however, rejected this method.

24.5.1 Choice of a presentation currency

As stated in paragraph 10 of the Basis of Conclusions to AASB 121/IAS 21, the IASB considered whether an entity should be permitted to present its financial statements in a currency other than its functional currency. The functional currency, being the currency of the primary economic environment in which the entity operates, most usefully reflects the economic effect of transactions and events on the entity. Where an entity has subsidiaries that have different functional currencies, management could choose a functional currency based upon which currency management uses when controlling and monitoring the financial performance of the group. Some argue that with globalisation entities should be permitted to present their financial statements in any currency.

As noted in section 24.1, Fortescue uses US dollars as its presentation currency based upon the argument that the US$ is its functional currency and so presenting its financial statements in US dollars best portrays the economic environment in which the entity operates.

When the AASB in Australia issued an exposure draft requesting responses to whether or not Australian accounting standards should require the use of the Australian dollar as the presentation currency, the following response was given by the Rinker Group Limited (sourced from AASB 2003, p. 7), which wanted to use US dollars as its presentation currency.

> It is our view that mandated presentation currency is not now appropriate to the circumstances of Rinker and that adoption of an Australian converged standard which is identical to the proposals outlined in the improvement to AASB 121 would serve the users of our financial reports far better.
>
> While Rinker is domiciled in Australia, is listed on the Australian [Securities] Exchange and currently has a shareholder base which is approximately 80% Australian, it is overwhelmingly a US economic entity. Over 80% of its revenue, profit, and assets are in the US. Ninety-nine percent of its debt is in the US. The clearly stated strategy of the company is to grow in the US. One of the characteristics of the industry in which Rinker participates (heavy building materials) is that revenues and costs are totally denominated in the local currency (US revenue and costs are completely in US dollars; Australian revenue and costs are completely in Australian dollars). As a result, variances in US dollar/Australian dollar exchange rates represent purely translation variances with no economic impact on the intrinsic value of the entity . . .
>
> . . . mandated reporting in Australian dollars may provide misleading information to the users of financial reports, particularly in periods when there are significant movements in the US dollar/Australian dollar exchange rates . . .

In the AASB papers summarising these responses, the example shown in figure 24.5 was provided to illustrate the point being made by Rinker.

The financial statements in the functional currency show the financial performance and position of the entity in the currency that primarily affects the operations of that entity. The translation process should not result in a different performance/position being shown. Note the effect on the comparative analysis of the change in exchange rates. The only way that the problem is overcome is if, in comparing the 2003 results with the 2002 results, the 2002 results are translated at the 2003 exchange rate rather than the 2002 rate. In other words, comparative figures must be continuously updated for exchange rate changes.

FIGURE 24.5 Illustration of the argument against mandated presentation currency

	2001	2002	2003
Debtors — US$	10	13	16
Actual growth	—	30%	23%
Exchange rate: A$1 = US$	0.5	0.56	0.67
Translate to presentation currency — A$			
Debtors — A$	20	23	24
Growth reported	—	15%	4%
Difference between growth rates	—	15%	19%

Source: AASB (2003, p. 4).

LEARNING CHECK

☐ Revenues and expenses are translated at the spot exchange rate between the functional currency and the presentation currency at the date each transaction occurred. However, a rate that approximates the actual rate, such as an average rate for a period, can be used.

☐ Assets and liabilities are translated at the closing rate at the date of the statement of financial position.

☐ Exchange differences arise because: (a) revenues and expenses are translated at rates other than the closing rate; and (b) the opening net assets are translated at a closing rate different from that at the end of the financial period.

☐ Any exchange difference is recognised in other comprehensive income and accumulated in equity using an account such as a foreign currency translation reserve.

24.6 Disclosure

LEARNING OBJECTIVE 24.6 Prepare the disclosures required by AASB 121/IAS 21.

Paragraphs 51 to 57 of AASB 121/IAS 21 require an entity to disclose:

- the amount of exchange differences included in profit or loss for the period (paragraph 51(a))
- net exchange differences classified in a separate component of equity, and a reconciliation of the amount of such exchange differences at the beginning and end of the period (paragraph 52(b))
- when the presentation currency of the parent entity is different from the functional currency:
  - the fact that they are different
  - the functional currency
  - the reason for using a different presentation currency (paragraph 53)
- when there is a change in the functional currency, the fact that such a change has occurred and the reason for the change (paragraph 54).

Wesfarmers Limited's accounting policy in relation to foreign currency translation was shown in figure 24.2. Figure 24.6 shows the exchange difference disclosures in the group's statement of comprehensive income and statement of changes in equity and its disclosure of movements in its foreign currency translation reserve from its 2018 annual report.

FIGURE 24.6 Statement of comprehensive income and statement of changes in equity, Wesfarmers

Statement of comprehensive income for the year ended 30 June 2018		Consolidated	
	Note	2018 $m	Restated 2017 $m
Profit attributable to members of the parent		1 197	2 873
Other comprehensive income			
Items that may be reclassified to profit or loss:			
Foreign currency translation reserve	12		

	Note		
Exchange differences on translation of foreign operations		(7)	(2)
Exchange differences recognised in the income statement on disposal of foreign operations		(2)	—
Cash flow hedge reserve	12		
Unrealised gains/(losses) on cash flow hedges		96	(136)
Realised losses transferred to net profit		29	92
Realised losses transferred to non-financial assets		114	84
Share of associates and joint venture reserves	18	(7)	—
Tax effect	3	(72)	(17)
Items that will not be reclassified to profit or loss:			
Retained earnings	12		
Remeasurement loss on defined benefit plan		(1)	(5)
Tax effect	3	—	2
Other comprehensive income for the year, net of tax		**150**	**18**
Total comprehensive income for the year, net of tax, attributable to members of the parent arising from:			
Continuing operations			
Continuing operations		2 754	2 784
Discontinued operations		(1 407)	107
		1 347	**2 891**

Statement of changes in equity
for the year ended 30 June 2018

		Attributable to equity holders of the parent					
Consolidated	Note	Issued capital $m	Reserved shares $m	Retained earnings $m	Hedging reserve $m	Other reserves $m	Total equity $m
Balance at 1 July 2016		21 937	(28)	874	(105)	271	22 949
Net profit for the year		—	—	2 873	—	—	2 873
Other comprehensive income							
Exchange differences on translation of foreign operations	12	—	—	—	—	(2)	(2)
Changes in the fair value of cash flow hedges, net of tax	12	—	—	—	23	—	23
Remeasurement loss on defined benefit plan, net of tax	12	—	—	(3)	—	—	(3)
Total other comprehensive income for the year, net of tax		—	—	(3)	23	(2)	18
Total comprehensive income for the year, net of tax		—	—	2 870	23	(2)	2 891
Share-based payment transactions	12	3	—	—	—	3	6
Issue of shares	12	328	—	—	—	—	328
Proceeds from exercise of in-substance options	12	—	1	—	—	—	1
Equity dividends	11	—	1	(2 235)	—	—	(2 234)
		331	2	(2 235)	—	3	(1 899)
Balance at 30 June 2017 and 1 July 2017		**22 268**	**(26)**	**1 509**	**(82)**	**272**	**23 941**
Net profit for the year		—	—	1 197	—	—	1 197
Other comprehensive income							
Exchange differences on translation of foreign operations	12	—	—	—	—	(7)	(7)
Exchange differences recognised in the income statement on disposal of foreign operations	12	—	—	—	—	(2)	(2)

Statement of changes in equity for the year ended 30 June 2018							
		Attributable to equity holders of the parent					
Consolidated	**Note**	**Issued capital $m**	**Reserved shares $m**	**Retained earnings $m**	**Hedging reserve $m**	**Other reserves $m**	**Total equity $m**
Changes in the fair value of cash flow hedges, net of tax	12	–	–	–	160	–	160
Remeasurement loss on defined benefit plan, net of tax	12	–	–	(1)	–	–	(1)
Total other comprehensive income for the year, net of tax		–	–	(1)	160	(9)	150
Total comprehensive income for the year, net of tax		–	–	1 196	160	(9)	1 347
Share-based payment transactions	12	9	–	–	–	3	12
Acquisition of shares on-market for Key Executive Equity Performance Plan (KEEPP)	12	–	(17)	–	–	–	(17)
Equity dividends	11	–	–	(2 529)	–	–	(2 529)
		9	(17)	(2 529)	–	3	(2 534)
Balance at 30 June 2018		**22 277**	**(43)**	**176**	**78**	**266**	**22 754**

12. Equity and reserves (continued)

Foreign currency translation reserve

The foreign currency translation reserve is used to record exchange differences arising from the translation of the financial statements of foreign subsidiaries.

Consolidated	**Retained earnings $m**	**Restructure tax reserve $m**	**Capital reserve $m**	**Foreign currency translation reserve $m**	**Cash flow hedge reserve $m**	**Financial assets reserve $m**	**Share-based payments reserve $m**
Balance at 1 July 2016	874	150	24	54	(105)	5	38
Net profit	2 873	–	–	–	–	–	–
Dividends	(2 235)	–	–	–	–	–	–
Remeasurement loss on defined benefit plan, net of tax	(3)	–	–	–	–	–	–
Net loss on financial instruments recognised in equity	–	–	–	–	(136)	–	–
Realised gains transferred to balance sheet/ net profit	–	–	–	–	176	–	–
Tax effect of transfers and revaluations	–	–	–	–	(17)	–	–
Currency translation differences	–	–	–	(2)	–	–	–
Share-based payment transactions	–	–	–	–	–	–	3
Balance at 30 June 2017 and 1 July 2017	**1 509**	**150**	**24**	**52**	**(82)**	**5**	**41**

Net profit	1 197	—	—	—	—	—	—
Dividends	(2 529)	—	—	—	—	—	—
Remeasurement loss on defined benefit plan, net of tax	(1)	—	—	—	—	—	—
Net loss on financial instruments recognised in equity	—	—	—	—	96	—	—
Realised losses transferred to balance sheet/net profit	—	—	—	—	143	—	—
Share of associates and joint venture reserve	—	—	—	(7)	—	—	—
Tax effect of transfers and revaluations	—	—	—	—	(72)	—	—
Currency translation differences	—	—	—	(7)	—	—	—
Exchange differences recognised in the income statement on disposal of foreign operations	—	—	—	(2)	—	—	—
Share-based payment transactions	—	—	—	—	—	—	3
Balance at 30 June 2018	**176**	**150**	**24**	**43**	**78**	**5**	**44**

Source: Wesfarmers Limited (2018, pp. 99, 102, 118–19).

LEARNING CHECK

☐ AASB 121/IAS 21 requires an entity to make disclosures about the translation of financial statements into other currencies.

☐ Exchange differences included in profit or loss must be disclosed.

☐ If the presentation currency is different from the functional currency this fact must be disclosed as well as the functional currency and the reason for using a different presentation currency.

☐ Movements in the foreign currency translation reserve must be disclosed.

SUMMARY

This chapter has covered the principles of accounting for the effects of changes in foreign exchange rates as contained in AASB 121/IAS 21 *The Effects of Changes in Foreign Exchange Rates*. Some of the key principles are as follows.

- The financial statements of a foreign operation must be translated into its functional currency.
- The functional currency is the currency of the primary economic environment in which the entity operates.
- Determination of the functional currency is a matter of judgement, primarily dependent on the environment in which the foreign operation generates and expends cash.
- Translation from local currency to functional currency requires the application of the temporal method under which non-monetary assets and liabilities are translated at historical exchange rates.
- Foreign exchange differences arising from translation under the temporal method are recognised in profit or loss.
- The financial statements of a foreign operation, translated or prepared in its functional currency, may be translated into a presentation currency.
- Australian reporting entities may choose any currency as their presentation currency.
- Translation from functional currency into presentation currency requires the application of the current rate method under which assets and liabilities at the end of the reporting period are translated at closing rates.
- Foreign exchange differences arising from translation under the current rate method are recognised in other comprehensive income and accumulated in equity.

KEY TERMS

closing rate The spot exchange rate at the end of the reporting period.

exchange difference The difference resulting from translating a certain amount of one currency into another at different exchange rates.

exchange rate The ratio of exchange between two currencies.

functional currency The currency of the primary economic environment in which the company operates.

local currency The currency of the country in which the foreign operation is based.

monetary items Units of currency held and assets and liabilities to be received or paid in a fixed or determinable amount of currency.

presentation currency The currency in which the financial statements are presented by the reporting entity.

spot exchange rate The exchange rate at a point of time for immediate delivery of the currency in an exchange.

DEMONSTRATION PROBLEM

24.1 Translation of financial statements using both the temporal and current rate methods

On 1 July 2024, an Australian company, Uluru Ltd, acquired all the issued capital of a Swedish company, Stockholm Ltd, for $997 400. At the date of acquisition, the equity of Stockholm Ltd consisted of the following.

	Krona (K)
Share capital	800 000
General reserve	200 000
Retained earnings	635 000

The internal financial statements of Stockholm Ltd at 30 June 2025 are shown below.

Statement of profit or loss and other comprehensive income		
	K	K
Revenues		2 585 000
Cost of sales:		
Opening stock	600 000	
Purchases	1 800 000	
	2 400 000	
Closing stock	580 000	1 820 000
Gross profit		765 000
Expenses:		
Depreciation	125 000	
Other	270 000	395 000
Profit before income tax		370 000
Income tax expense		200 000
Profit for the period		170 000
Retained earnings as at 1 July 2024		635 000
		805 000
Dividend paid		100 000
Retained earnings as at 30 June 2025		705 000

Statement of financial position		
	1/7/24 K	30/6/25 K
Current assets		
Cash and receivables	500 000	500 000
Inventories	600 000	580 000
Total current assets	1 100 000	1 080 000
Non-current assets		
Land	300 000	300 000
Buildings	700 000	700 000
Accumulated depreciation	(100 000)	(130 000)
Plant	800 000	900 000
Accumulated depreciation	(235 000)	(330 000)
Total non-current assets	1 465 000	1 440 000
Total assets	2 565 000	2 520 000
Current liabilities	350 000	235 000
Non-current liabilities		
Notes — issued September 2024	580 000	580 000
Total liabilities	930 000	815 000
Net assets	**1 635 000**	**1 705 000**
Equity		
Share capital	800 000	800 000
General reserve	200 000	200 000
Retained earnings	635 000	705 000
Total equity	**1 635 000**	**1 705 000**

Additional information

• Exchange rates for the Swedish krona were as follows.

	1K = A$
1 July 2024	0.54
Average 2024–25	0.52
1 January 2025	0.53
30 June 2025	0.50
Average January–June 2025	0.55
Average for the last 4 months of the 2024–25 period	0.51

• Stockholm Ltd acquired additional plant for K100 000 on 1 January 2025 by issuing a note for K80 000 and paying the balance in cash.

- Sales, purchases and other expenses were incurred evenly throughout the year.
- Depreciation for the period in krona was as follows.

Buildings	30 000
Plant	
— acquired before 1 July 2024	85 000
— acquired on 1 January 2025	10 000

- The inventories is valued on a FIFO basis. The opening stock was acquired when the exchange rate was 0.55, and the closing stock was acquired during the last 4 months of the 2024–25 period.
- Dividends of K50 000 were paid on 1 July 2024 and 1 January 2025.
- The tax rate for Stockholm Ltd is 25%.

Required

Translate the accounts of the foreign subsidiary, Stockholm Ltd, into Australian dollars at 30 June 2025, assuming the following.

1. The functional currency is the Swedish krona, and the presentation currency is the Australian dollar. Verify the translation difference.
2. The functional currency is the Australian dollar, as is the presentation currency. Verify the translation difference.

SOLUTION

1. *Translation of accounts from functional currency to presentation currency*

	K	K	Rate	$'000
Revenue		2 585 000	0.52	1 344 200
Cost of sales:				
Opening stock	600 000		0.54	324 000
Purchases	1 800 000		0.52	936 000
	2 400 000			1 260 000
Closing stock	580 000		0.51	295 800
Cost of sales		1 820 000		964 200
Gross profit		765 000		380 000
Depreciation	115 000		0.52	59 800
	10 000		0.55	5 500
Other expenses	270 000		0.52	140 400
		395 000		205 700
		370 000		174 300
Income tax expense		200 000	0.52	104 000
Profit for the period		170 000		70 300
Retained earnings as at 1/7/24		635 000	0.54	342 900
		805 000		413 200
Dividend paid		50 000	0.54	27 000
		50 000	0.53	26 500
Retained earnings as at 30/6/25		705 000		359 700
Share capital		800 000	0.54	432 000
General reserve		200 000	0.54	108 000
Foreign currency translation reserve				**(47 200)**
		1 705 000		852 500
Cash and receivables		500 000	0.50	250 000
Inventories		580 000	0.50	290 000
Land		300 000	0.50	150 000
Buildings		700 000	0.50	350 000
Accumulated depreciation		(130 000)	0.50	(65 000)
Plant		900 000	0.50	450 000
Accumulated depreciation		(330 000)	0.50	(165 000)
		2 520 000		1 260 000
Current liabilities		235 000	0.50	117 500
Notes		580 000	0.50	290 000
		815 000		407 500
Net assets		1 705 000		852 500

Verification of foreign currency translation reserve (FCTR)

Change in net investment			
Opening net assets	=	K1 635 000	
Opening net assets × closing exchange rate	=	1 635 000 × 0.50	
	=	$817 500	
Opening net assets × beginning exchange rate	=	1 635 000 × 0.54	
	=	$882 900	
Translation gain/(loss)	=	$(65 400)	
Profit or loss and other comprehensive income			
Change in retained earnings	=	K705 000 − K635 000	
	=	K70 000	
Change × ending exchange rate	=	K70 000 × 0.50	
	=	$35 000	
Change as translated	=	$359 700 − $340 900	
	=	$16 800	
Translation gain/(loss)	=	$35 000−$16 800	
	=	$18 200	
Balance of FCTR	=	$(65 400) + $18 200	
	=	$(47 200)	

2. *Translation from local currency to functional currency*

	K	Rate	$
Revenue	2 585 000	0.52	1 344 200
Cost of sales:			
Opening stock	600 000	0.54	324 000
Purchases	1 800 000	0.52	936 000
	2 400 000		1 260 000
Closing stock	580 000	0.51	295 800
Cost of sales	1 820 000		964 200
Gross profit	765 000		380 000
Depreciation	115 000	0.54	62 100
	10 000	0.53	5 300
Other expenses	270 000	0.52	140 400
	395 000		207 200
	370 000		172 200
Foreign exchange gain			**17 400**
			189 600
Income tax expense	200 000	0.52	104 000
Profit for the period	170 000		85 600
Retained earnings as at 1/7/24	635 000	0.54	342 900
	805 000		428 500
Dividend paid	50 000	0.54	27 000
	50 000	0.53	26 500
	100 000		53 500
Retained earnings as at 30/6/25	705 000		375 000
Share capital	800 000	0.54	432 000
General reserve	200 000	0.54	108 000
Total equity	**1 705 000**		**915 000**
Cash and receivables	500 000	0.50	250 000
Inventories	580 000	0.51	295 800
Land	300 000	0.54	162 000
Buildings	700 000	0.54	378 000
Accumulated depreciation	(130 000)	0.54	(70 200)
Plant	800 000	0.54	432 000
	100 000	0.53	53 000
Accumulated depreciation	(320 000)	0.54	(172 800)
	(10 000)	0.53	(5 300)
Total assets	2 520 000		1 322 500
Current liabilities	235 000	0.50	117 500
Notes	580 000	0.50	290 000
Total liabilities	815 000		407 500
Net assets	**1 705 000**		**915 000**

Verification of exchange gain

	K	Current rate less rate applied	A$ Gain/(loss)
Net monetary assets at 1/7/24	(430 000)	(0.54 − 0.50)	17 200
Increases: Sales	2 585 000	(0.52 − 0.50)	(51 700)
	2 155 000		(34 500)
Decreases:	1 800 000	(0.52 − 0.50)	36 000
Purchases	270 000	(0.52 − 0.50)	5 400
Other expenses	200 000	(0.52 − 0.50)	4 000
Income tax expense	50 000	(0.54 − 0.50)	2 000
Dividends	50 000	(0.53 − 0.50)	1 500
Acquisition of plant	100 000	(0.53 − 0.50)	3 000
	2 470 000		51 900
Net monetary assets at 30/6/25	(315 000)		
Foreign exchange gain/(loss)			17 400

COMPREHENSION QUESTIONS

1 Why are financial statements translated from one currency to another?

2 What is meant by 'functional currency'?

3 What is the rationale behind the choice of an exchange rate as an entity's functional currency?

4 What guidelines are used to determine the functional currency of an entity?

5 How are statement of profit or loss and other comprehensive income items translated from the local currency into the functional currency?

6 How are statement of financial position items translated from the local currency into the functional currency?

7 How are foreign exchange gains and losses calculated when translating from local currency to functional currency?

8 What is meant by 'presentation currency'?

9 How are statement of profit or loss and other comprehensive income items translated from functional currency to presentation currency?

10 How are statement of financial position items translated from functional currency to presentation currency?

11 What causes a foreign currency translation reserve to arise?

12 Why are gains/losses on translation into the presentation currency taken to a foreign currency translation reserve rather than to profit or loss for the period?

13 Discuss the differences in the translation process when translating from a local currency to a functional currency compared with translating from a functional currency to a presentation currency.

CASE STUDY 24.1

FINANCIAL REPORTING

In Note 29 (p. 87) of the 2018 annual report of the Qantas Group, the following information was provided.

(D) FOREIGN CURRENCY

(i) Foreign Currency Transactions

Transactions in foreign currencies are translated into the respective functional currencies of the Group's companies at the exchange rates at the date of the transactions.

Monetary assets and liabilities denominated in foreign currencies are translated into the functional currency at the exchange rate at the reporting date. Non-monetary assets and liabilities that are measured at fair value in a foreign currency are translated into the functional currency at the exchange rate when the fair value was determined. Non-monetary items that are measured based on historical cost in a foreign currency are translated at the exchange rate at the date of the transactions. Foreign currency differences are generally recognised in the Consolidated Income Statement.

(ii) Foreign Operations

The assets and liabilities of foreign operations, including goodwill and fair value adjustments arising on acquisition, are translated into AUD at the exchange rates at the reporting date. The income and expenses of foreign operations are translated into AUD at the exchange rates at the date of the transactions.

Foreign currency differences are recognised in the Consolidated Statement of Comprehensive Income and accumulated in the Foreign Currency Translation Reserve, except to the extent that the translation difference is allocated to non-controlling interests.

When a foreign operation is disposed of in its entirety or partially such that control, significant influence or joint control is lost, the cumulative amount in the Foreign Currency Translation Reserve related to that foreign operation is reclassified to the Consolidated Income Statement as part of the gain or loss on disposal. If the Group disposes of part of its interests in a subsidiary but retains control, then the relevant proportion of the cumulative amount is reattributed to non-controlling interests. When the Group disposes of only part of an associate or joint venture while retaining significant influence or joint control, the relevant proportion of the cumulative amount is reclassified to the Consolidated Income Statement.

Required

Explain this note to a reader of the Qantas report.

CASE STUDY 24.2

FINANCIAL REPORTING

In its 2018 annual report (p. 135), Wesfarmers Limited notes all subsidiaries (with some exceptions) are incorporated in Australia and therefore produce their financial statements in Australian dollars. However, there are a number of subsidiaries that were not incorporated in Australia and therefore adopt the functional currency of the country of incorporation. For example, Bunnings (NZ) Ltd for which the functional currency is the New Zealand dollar (NZD), and Wesfarmers Risk Management (Singapore) Pte Ltd for which the functional currency is the Singapore dollar (SGD).

Required

Discuss the translation process that will occur so that these subsidiaries can be included in the consolidated financial statements of Wesfarmers Limited.

Note: Case studies 24.3 and 24.4 are adapted from Radford (1996).

CASE STUDY 24.3

DETERMINATION OF FUNCTIONAL CURRENCY

Case A

A Malaysian operation manufactures a product using Malaysian materials and labour. Specialised equipment and senior operations staff are supplied by its Australian parent. Reimbursement invoices for these services are denominated in the Malaysian ringgit. The product is sold in the Malaysian market at a price, denominated in Malaysian ringgit, which is determined by competition with similar locally produced products. The foreign operation retains sufficient cash to meet wages and day-to-day operating costs and further investment needs, with only a very small amount being paid as dividends to the Australian parent. The receipt of dividends from the foreign operation is not important to the parent's cash management function. Long-term financing is arranged and serviced by the Malaysian operation.

Case B

A Korean operation is a wholly owned subsidiary of an Australian company which regards the operation as a long-term investment, and thus takes no part in the day-to-day decision making of the operation. The operation purchases parts from various non-related Australian manufacturers for assembly by Korean labour. The finished product is exported to a number of countries but South Korea is still the major market. Consequently, sales prices are mainly determined by competition within South Korea.

Required

In relation to these cases, discuss the choice of a functional currency.

CASE STUDY 24.4

DETERMINATION OF FUNCTIONAL CURRENCY

Case A

An Indonesian operation manufactures a product using Indonesian materials and labour. Patented processes and senior operations staff are supplied by its Australian parent. Reimbursement invoices for these services are denominated in Australian dollars. The product is sold in the Australian market at a price, denominated in Australian dollars, that is determined by competition with similar locally produced products. The Indonesian operation remits all revenue to the Australian parent, retaining only sufficient cash to meet wages and day-to-day operating costs. The receipt of cash from the Indonesian operation is important to the parent's cash management function. Long-term financing is arranged and serviced by the parent.

Case B

A New Zealand operation is a wholly owned subsidiary of an Australian company. The parent regards the operation as a strategic investment and all financial and operational decisions are made by Australian management. The New Zealand operation purchases parts from various non-related Australian manufacturers for assembly in New Zealand. The finished product is exported to a number of countries with Australia as the major market. Consequently, sales prices are determined by competition within Australia.

Required

In relation to these cases, discuss which currency is the functional currency of the foreign entity.

CASE STUDY 24.5

DETERMINATION OF FUNCTIONAL CURRENCY

Foreign Ltd is a Queensland software developer that specialises in software that controls the operations of open cut mining. To exploit opportunities in the US market, the firm has established a wholly owned subsidiary operating in Atlanta, Georgia. The operations of the subsidiary (Opencut Inc.) essentially involve the marketing of software initially developed in Australia but which is further developed by the US subsidiary to suit the special requirements of particular US customers. Foreign Ltd does not charge Opencut Inc. for the software successfully amended and marketed in the United States. At this stage no dividends have been paid by Opencut Inc., however, it is expected that dividends will commence within 12 months. With respect to working capital, Opencut Inc. has a 'revolving credit' agreement (overdraft facility) with the Bank of Georgia, which has been guaranteed by the Australian parent.

Required

Discuss the process of translating the financial statements of Opencut Inc. for consolidation with Foreign Ltd.

CASE STUDY 24.6

DETERMINATION OF FUNCTIONAL CURRENCY

Victory Ltd is an Australian company with two overseas subsidiaries, one in Indonesia and the other in South Korea. The Indonesian subsidiary has as its major activity the distribution in Indonesia of Victory Ltd's products. It has been agreed that the subsidiary will, for a period of time, retain all profits in order to expand its distribution network in Indonesia. In the past it has remitted most of its profits to the Australian parent company.

The South Korean subsidiary has been established to manufacture a range of products for the South-East Asian market. There is also an expectation that it could in the future become the major manufacturing plant for Victory Ltd and provide a supply of products for the Australian market.

Required

Based on the above, determine the functional currency of the foreign subsidiaries. Explain your choice.

APPLICATION AND ANALYSIS EXERCISES

★ BASIC | ★ ★ MODERATE | ★ ★ ★ DIFFICULT

24.1 Multiple choice ★   LO2, 3, 4

Select the best answer for each of the following items.

1. The account balances of a foreign subsidiary are to be translated from the local currency into the functional currency. The functional currency is:
   (a) the currency in which the transactions are recorded by the foreign entity
   (b) the Australian dollar
   (c) the local currency of the foreign subsidiary in which the records are maintained
   (d) the currency of the primary economic environment in which the entity operates.

2. When the functional currency of a foreign subsidiary in Singapore is the Australian dollar (A$), translation gains and losses resulting from translating the financial statements of the Singapore subsidiary into A$ for presentation purposes should be included:
   (a) in the statement of profit or loss and other comprehensive income in the period in which they arise
   (b) in other comprehensive income and accumulated in equity
   (c) as a deferred item in the statement of financial position.

3. In order to translate the financial statements of a foreign subsidiary into Australian dollars for consolidation of those statements with those of the parent, it is necessary to identify the functional currency. Which of the following factors indicates that the functional currency is the local currency of the foreign subsidiary?
   (a) Financing of the subsidiary is primarily from local sources.
   (b) Sales contracts are determined in Australian dollars.
   (c) There is a high volume of transactions between the two entities.
   (d) Profits generated by the foreign subsidiary are remitted to the Australian parent entity.

4. The temporal method is being applied to translate the financial statements of a foreign entity into its functional currency. The historical exchange rate should be used to translate:
   (a) plant measured at cost, but not the related depreciation expense and accumulated depreciation
   (b) plant measured at cost and the related accumulated depreciation, but not the related depreciation expense
   (c) plant measured at cost, the related accumulated depreciation and the related depreciation expense.

24.2 Identifying the exchange rate ★   LO3

The accounts listed below are those for Sentosa Ltd, a foreign subsidiary in Singapore, that maintains its accounting records in Singapore dollars (S$). The parent is an Australian company, Dreamscapes Ltd. In the spaces provided indicate the exchange rates that would be applied in translating the accounts shown in the financial statements of the Singapore subsidiary into Australian dollars (A$) assuming:

(a) the functional currency is the A$
(b) the functional currency is the S$.

Use the following letters to identify the appropriate exchange rate:
H — historical exchange rate
C — current exchange rate
A — average exchange rate for the current period.

Account	Exchange rate if the functional currency is:	
	A$	S$
Cash	_____	_____
Prepaid expenses	_____	_____
Inventories at cost	_____	_____
Inventories at net realisable value	_____	_____

| Account | Exchange rate if the functional currency is: | |
	A$	S$
Plant at cost		
Accumulated depreciation — plant		
Goodwill		
Accounts payable		
Debentures		
Capital		
Sales		
Wages expense		
Depreciation expense		

24.3 Translation into functional currency ★   LO4, 5

Jurong Ltd, a company incorporated in Singapore, acquired all the issued shares of Victoria Ltd, a Hong Kong company, on 1 July 2022. The trial balance of Victoria Ltd at 30 June 2023 was as follows.

	HK$ Dr	HK$ Cr
Share capital		400 000
Retained earnings (1/7/22)		120 000
General reserve		50 000
Payables		80 000
Deferred tax liability		60 000
Current tax liability		10 000
Provisions		40 000
Sales		305 000
Proceeds on sale of land		125 000
Accumulated depreciation — plant		170 000
Plant	460 000	
Land	200 000	
Cash	120 000	
Accounts receivable	150 000	
Inventories at 1 July 2022	30 000	
Purchases	130 000	
Depreciation — plant	78 000	
Carrying amount of land sold	100 000	
Income tax expense	25 000	
Other expenses	67 000	
	1 360 000	1 360 000

Additional information

- Exchange rates based on equivalence to HK$1 were as follows.

	S$
1 July 2022	0.20
8 October 2022	0.25
1 December 2022	0.28
1 January 2023	0.30
2 April 2023	0.27
30 June 2023	0.22
Average for last quarter 2022–23	0.24
Average for 2022–23	0.26

- Inventories were acquired evenly throughout the year. The closing inventories of HK$30 000 were acquired during the last quarter of the year.
- Sales and other expenses occurred evenly throughout the year.
- The Hong Kong tax rate is 20%.
- The land on hand at the beginning of the year was sold on 8 October 2022. The land on hand at the end of the year was acquired on 1 December 2022.
- Movements in plant over the year ended 30 June 2023 were as follows.

	HK$
Plant at 1 July 2022	300 000
Acquisitions — 8 October 2022	100 000
— 2 April 2023	60 000
Plant at 30 June 2023	460 000

Depreciation on plant is measured at 20% p.a. on cost. Where assets are acquired during a month, a full month's depreciation is charged.
- The functional currency of the Victoria Ltd is the Singaporean dollar.

Required
1. Prepare the financial statements of Victoria Ltd in Singaporean dollars at 30 June 2023.
2. Verify the foreign currency translation adjustment.

24.4 Translation into functional and presentation currency ★ **LO4, 5**

Perth Ltd is a manufacturer of sheepskin products in Australia. It is a wholly owned subsidiary of a Hong Kong company, Kowloon Ltd. The following assets are held by Perth Ltd at 30 June 2022.

Plant:	Cost A$	Useful life (years)	Acquisition date	Exchange rate on acquisition date (A$1 = HK$)
Tanner	40 000	5	10/8/18	5.4
Benches	20 000	8	8/3/20	5.8
Presses	70 000	7	6/10/21	6.2

Plant is depreciated on a straight-line basis, with zero residual values. All assets acquired in the first half of a month are allocated a full month's depreciation.

Inventories:
- At 1 July 2021, the inventories on hand of A$25 000 was acquired during the last month of the period ended 30 June 2021.
- Inventories acquired during the period ended 30 June 2022 was acquired evenly throughout the period. Total purchases of A$420 000 were acquired during that period.
- The inventories of A$30 000 on hand at 30 June 2022 was acquired during June 2022.
- Relevant exchange rates (quoted as A$1 = HK$) are as follows.

Average for June 2021	7.2
1 July 2021	7.0
Average for 2021–22	7.5
Average for June 2022	7.7
Average for October 2021 – June 2022	7.6
30 June 2022	7.8

Required
1. Assuming the functional currency for Perth Ltd is the A$, calculate the:
   (a) balances for the plant items and inventories in HK$ at 30 June 2022
   (b) depreciation and cost of sales amounts in HK$ in the statement of profit or loss and other comprehensive income for the period ended 30 June 2022.
2. Assuming the functional currency is the HK$ and the presentation currency is A$, calculate the:
   (a) balances for the plant items and inventories in HK$ at 30 June 2022
   (b) depreciation and cost of sales amounts in HK$ in the statement of profit or loss and other comprehensive income for the period ended 30 June 2022.

On 1 July 2023, Orbost Ltd, an Australian company, acquired the issued shares of Chicago Ltd, a company incorporated in the United States. The draft statement of profit or loss and other comprehensive income and statement of financial position of Chicago Ltd at 30 June 2024 were as follows.

	US$	US$
Sales revenues		4 800 000
Cost of sales:		
Opening inventories	420 000	
Purchases	2 520 000	
	2 940 000	
Closing inventories	840 000	2 100 000
Gross profit		2 700 000
Expenses:		
Depreciation	270 000	
Other	810 000	1 080 000
Profit before income tax		1 620 000
Income tax expense		600 000
Profit		1 020 000
Retained earnings as at 1 July 2023		600 000
		1 620 000
Dividend paid	360 000	
Dividend declared	600 000	960 000
Retained earnings as at 30 June 2024		660 000

	2024 US$	2023 US$
Current assets		
Inventories	840 000	420 000
Accounts receivable	60 000	390 000
Cash	60 000	1 710 000
Total current assets	960 000	2 520 000
Non-current assets		
Patent	240 000	240 000
Plant	2 160 000	1 800 000
Accumulated depreciation	(390 000)	(240 000)
Land	1 500 000	900 000
Buildings	2 760 000	2 460 000
Accumulated depreciation	(360 000)	(240 000)
Total non-current assets	5 910 000	4 920 000
Total assets	6 870 000	7 440 000
Current liabilities		
Provisions	900 000	1 860 000
Dividends payable	600 000	—
Accounts payable	960 000	2 820 000
Total current liabilities	2 460 000	4 680 000
Non-current liabilities		
Loan from Orbost Ltd	1 590 000	—
Total liabilities	4 050 000	4 680 000
Net assets	**2 820 000**	**2 760 000**
Equity		
Share capital	2 160 000	2 160 000
Retained earnings	660 000	600 000
Total equity	**2 820 000**	**2 760 000**

Additional information

- On 1 January 2024, Chicago Ltd acquired new plant for US$120 000. This plant is depreciated over a 5-year period.
- On 1 April 2024, Chicago Ltd acquired US$200 000 worth of land.
- On 1 October 2023, Chicago Ltd acquired US$100 000 worth of new buildings. These buildings are depreciated evenly over a 10-year period.

- The interim dividend was paid on 1 January 2024, half of which was from profits earned prior to 1 July 2023, while the dividend payable was declared on 30 June 2024.
- Sales, purchases and expenses occurred evenly throughout the period. The inventories on hand at 30 June 2024 were acquired during June 2024.
- The loan of US$530 000 from Orbost Ltd was granted on 1 July 2023. The interest rate is 8% p.a. Interest is paid on 30 June and 1 January each year.
- The exchange rates for the financial year were as follows.

	US$1 = A$
1 July 2023	2.00
1 October 2023	1.80
1 January 2024	1.70
1 April 2024	1.60
30 June 2024	1.50
Average for October 2023 – June 2024	1.65
Average for June 2024	1.52
Average for 2023–24	1.75

Required

1. If the functional currency for Chicago Ltd is the Australian dollar, prepare the financial statements of Chicago Ltd at 30 June 2024 in the functional currency.
2. Verify the foreign currency translation adjustment.

24.6 Translation into presentation currency ★ ★   **LO5**

Use the information in exercise 24.5 and assume an average exchange rate of 1.70 for January–June 2024.

Required

1. If the functional currency for Chicago Ltd is the US dollar, prepare the financial statements of Chicago Ltd at 30 June 2024 in the presentation currency of the Australian dollar.
2. Verify the foreign currency translation adjustment.

24.7 Translation into functional currency ★ ★   **LO5**

On 1 January 2022, Southern Ltd formed a company, Cross Ltd, in the United States to sell Australian products such as boomerangs and cuddly toy koalas and kangaroos. The initial capital was US$500 000. On 1 February 2022, a lease was signed on a shop for US$20 000, payable on the first day of each month. On 15 February 2022, store furnishings were acquired for US$448 000; these were expected to have a useful life of 4 years. On 10 June 2022, more fittings were acquired at a cost of US$124 000, again with an expected life of 4 years.

Additional information

- Where non-current assets are acquired during a month, a full month's depreciation is applied.
- The tax rate in the United States is 20%, while the tax rate in Australia is 30%.
- The functional currency for Cross Ltd is the Australian dollar.
- Exchange rates for the financial year were (A$1 = US$) as follows.

1 January 2022	0.72
1 February	0.75
15 February	0.76
10 June	0.78
30 June	0.77
Average for first half year	0.75
30 September	0.78
1 December	0.81
Average for second half year	0.77
31 December 2022	0.82

- Sales in the first half of the year amounted to US$210 000.
- Expenses, other than depreciation, leases costs, and purchases in the first half of the year amounted to US$60 000.
- Financial information relating to Cross Ltd for the year ended 31 December 2022 is as follows.

	US$
Sales revenue	680 000
Closing inventories	20 000
Accumulated depreciation — furniture and fittings	120 750
Accounts payable	40 000
Share capital	500 000
	1 360 750
Lease expenses	220 000
Purchases	230 000
Inventories	20 000
Other expenses	150 000
Depreciation — furniture and fittings	120 750
Furniture and fittings	572 000
Cash	14 600
Accounts receivable	33 400
	1 360 750

Required

Translate the financial statements of Cross Ltd into Australian dollars for inclusion in the consolidated financial statements of Southern Ltd at 31 December 2022.

24.8 Translation into presentation currency ★ ★ **LO5**

On 1 July 2021 Pictures Ltd, an Australian company, acquired shares in North Point Ltd, a company based in Hong Kong. At this date, the equity of North Point Ltd was as follows.

	HK$
Share capital	200 000
General reserve	100 000
Retained earnings	300 000

At 30 June 2021 and 2023, the retained earnings balances of North Point Ltd were HK$400 000 and HK$450 000 respectively. All transactions occurred evenly throughout these years. The internal financial statements of the two companies at 30 June 2024 were as follows.

Statements of profit or loss and other comprehensive income		
	Pictures Ltd A$	North Point Ltd HK$
Sales	700 000	595 000
Cost of sales	300 000	400 000
	400 000	195 000
Expenses	210 200	100 000
	189 800	95 000
Dividend revenue	12 000	—
Profit before income tax	201 800	95 000
Tax expense	51 800	20 000
Profit	150 000	75 000
Retained earnings as at 1/7/23	750 000	450 000
	900 000	525 000
Dividend paid	100 000	25 000
Retained earnings as at 30/6/24	800 000	500 000

Statements of financial position		
	Pictures Ltd A$	North Point Ltd HK$
Current assets	311 520	250 000
Shares in North Point Ltd	288 480	—
Property, plant and equipment (net)	700 000	500 000
Patents and trademarks	100 000	150 000
Total assets	1 400 000	900 000
Liabilities	100 000	100 000
Net assets	**1 300 000**	**800 000**

Equity		
Share capital	500 000	200 000
General reserve	–	100 000
Retained earnings	800 000	500 000
Total equity	**1 300 000**	**800 000**

Additional information

- The dividend paid by North Point Ltd was paid (and recognised as dividend revenue of A$12 000 by Pictures Ltd) on 1 May 2024.
- Some relevant exchange rates are as follows.

1 July 2021	HK$1 = A$0.60
Average for 2021–22	0.62
1 July 2022	0.65
Average for 2022–23	0.68
1 July 2023	0.70
Average for 2023–24	0.65
1 May 2024	0.60
30 June 2024	0.58

Required

Translate the financial statements of North Point Ltd as at 30 June 2024 into the presentation currency of Australian dollars, assuming that the functional currency is the Hong Kong dollar.

24.9 Translation into presentation currency ★ ★ **LO5**

Lion Ltd is an international company resident in Singapore. It acquired the issued shares of an Australian company, Drake Ltd, on 1 July 2022 for A$700 000.

At 30 June 2023, the following information was available about the two companies.

	Lion Ltd S$	Drake Ltd A$
Share capital	560 000	350 000
Retained earnings as at 1/7/22	330 000	170 000
Provisions	34 000	30 000
Payables	14 000	40 000
Sales	620 000	310 000
Dividend revenue	6 400	0
Accumulated depreciation — plant	210 000	160 000
	1 785 400	1 060 000
Cash	92 100	30 000
Accounts receivable	145 300	115 000
Inventories	110 000	80 000
Shares in Drake Ltd	336 000	0
Buildings (net)	84 000	220 000
Plant	420 000	400 000
Cost of sales	390 000	120 000
Depreciation — plant	85 000	40 000
Tax expense	23 000	15 000
Other expenses	50 000	10 000
Dividend paid	20 000	10 000
Dividend declared	30 000	20 000
	1 785 400	1 060 000

Additional information

- Sales, purchases and other expenses were incurred evenly throughout the period ended 30 June 2023. The dividend paid by Drake Ltd was received by Lion Ltd on 1 January 2023, while the dividend declared by Drake Ltd was announced on 30 June 2023.
- Drake Ltd acquired A$100 000 additional new plant on 1 January 2023. Of the depreciation charged in the period ended 30 June 2023, A$8000 related to the new plant.
- The rates of exchange between the Australian dollar and the Singapore dollar were (expressed as A$1 = S$) as follows.

1 July 2022	0.60
1 December 2022	0.64
1 January 2023	0.68
30 June 2023	0.70
Average for January–June 2023	0.72
Average for 2022–23	0.65

- The functional currency of Drake Ltd is the Australian dollar.

Required

1. Translate the financial statements of Drake Ltd into Singapore dollars for inclusion in the consolidated financial statements of Lion Ltd.
2. Verify the foreign currency translation adjustment.

24.10 Translation into functional and presentation currency ★ ★ ★   **LO4, 5**

Canberra Ltd, an Australian company, acquired all the issued shares of Washington Ltd, a US company, on 1 January 2023. At this date, the net assets of Washington Ltd are shown below.

	US$
Property, plant and equipment	310 000
Accumulated depreciation	(60 000)
	250 000
Cash	20 000
Inventories	40 000
Accounts receivable	20 000
Total assets	330 000
Accounts payable	30 000
Net assets	300 000

The trial balance prepared by the US company Washington Ltd at 31 December 2023 contained the following information.

	US$ Dr	US$ Cr
Share capital		200 000
Retained earnings		100 000
Accounts payable		84 000
Sales		180 000
Accumulated depreciation — plant and equipment		90 000
Property, plant and equipment	310 000	
Accounts receivable	80 000	
Inventories	90 000	
Cash	24 000	
Cost of sales	60 000	
Depreciation	30 000	
Administrative expenses	4 000	
Rent expenses	6 000	
Insurance expenses	5 000	
Wages expenses	41 000	
Other expenses	4 000	
	654 000	654 000

Additional information

- No property, plant and equipment were acquired in the period ended 31 December 2023.
- All sales and expenses incurred evenly throughout the period. The inventories on hand at the end of the year were acquired during December 2023.
- Exchange rates were (A$1 = US$) as follows.

1 January 2023	0.52
31 December 2023	0.60
Average for December 2023	0.58
Average for 2023	0.56

- The functional currency for Washington Ltd is the US dollar.

Required

1. Prepare the financial statements of Washington Ltd at 31 December 2023 in the presentation currency of Australian dollars.
2. Verify the foreign currency translation adjustment.
3. Discuss the differences that would occur if the functional currency of Washington Ltd was the Australian dollar.
4. If the functional currency was the Australian dollar, calculate the foreign currency translation adjustment.

24.11 Translation into functional and presentation currency ★★★   **LO4, 5**

On 1 July 2023, Toowoomba Ltd, an Australian company, acquired all the issued shares of Sussex Ltd, a UK company. At this date, the equity of Sussex Ltd consisted of the following.

	£
Share capital	800 000
Retained earnings	200 000

The financial statements of Sussex Ltd at 30 June 2024 were as follows.

Statement of comprehensive income for Sussex Ltd for the year ended 30 June 2024	
	£
Sales	2 000 000
Cost of sales	
Opening inventories	(400 000)
Purchases	(900 000)
Ending inventories	200 000
	(1 100 000)
Depreciation	(100 000)
Other expenses	(500 000)
Profit before tax	300 000
Income tax expense	(100 000)
Profit after tax	200 000

Statement of financial position for Sussex Ltd as at 30 June 2024	
	£
Plant and equipment	1 500 000
Accumulated depreciation	(300 000)
	1 200 000
Cash	100 000
Inventories	200 000
Accounts receivable	100 000
Total assets	1 600 000
Accounts payable	100 000
Bank loan	300 000
Total liabilities	400 000
Net assets	1 200 000
Share capital	800 000
Retained earnings	400 000

Additional information

- Exchange rates for the year ended 30 June 2024 were as follows (£1 = A$).

1 July 2023	1.80
1 March 2024	1.82
1 April 2024	1.78
1 May 2024	1.84
Average for May–June 2024	1.85
Average for 2023–24	1.79
30 June 2024	1.76

- Sales, purchases and other expenses were incurred evenly throughout the year.
- The ending inventory was acquired on 1 March 2024 by paying cash of £20 000 and the balance on credit.
- The plant at 30 June 2024 includes a new plant acquired for £120 000 on 1 May 2024 by paying cash.
- Depreciation on plant and equipment is calculated at 10% p.a. on cost.
- The bank loan was taken out on 1 April 2024, with interest rate at 8% p.a. paid quarterly on 30 June, 30 September, 31 December and 31 March each year. The interest expense on the loan for the year was included under 'Other expenses' in the statement of comprehensive income.

Required

1. Assuming the functional currency for Sussex Ltd is the Australian dollar, translate the financial statements of Sussex Ltd into the functional currency.
2. Assuming the functional currency for Sussex Ltd is the UK pound and the presentation currency of Toowoomba Ltd's group is Australian dollars, translate the financial statements of Sussex Ltd into the presentation currency.

REFERENCES

AASB 2003, *Presentation currency of Australian financial reports* (Agenda paper 12.2), collation of submissions on the invitation to comment, meeting of the AASB, 15–16 October, Glenelg, South Australia.

Fortescue Metals Group Ltd 2018, *2018 annual report*, www.fmgl.com.au.

Jeter, DC & Chaney, PK 2012, *Advanced accounting*, 5th edn, John Wiley Sons, Inc.

Qantas Airways Ltd 2018, *Annual report 2018*, www.qantas.com.au.

Radford, J 1996, *Foreign currency translation: clarity or confusion?*, Curtin University of Technology, Perth, Western Australia.

Rio Tinto Limited 2017, *Annual report 2017*, www.riotinto.com.

Wesfarmers Limited 2018, *2018 annual report*, www.wesfarmers.com.au.

ACKNOWLEDGEMENTS

Photo: © mystockicons / iStockphoto

Photo: © Bankoo / Shutterstock.com

Figures 24.1, 24.2, 24.6: © Wesfarmers Limited 2018

Figure 24.5: © IFRS. This publication contains copyright material of the IFRS Foundation in respect of which all rights are reserved. Reproduced by John Wiley & Sons Australia, Ltd with the permission of the IFRS Foundation. No permission granted to third parties to reproduce or distribute. For full access to IFRS Standards and the work of the IFRS Foundation please visit http://eifrs.ifrs.org. The International Accounting Standards Board, the IFRS Foundation, the authors and the publishers do not accept responsibility for any loss caused by acting or refraining from acting in reliance on the material in this publication, whether such loss is caused by negligence or otherwise.

Case study 24.1: © Qantas Airways Ltd 2018

Text: © 2019 Australian Accounting Standards Board (AASB). The text, graphics and layout of this publication are protected by Australian copyright law and the comparable law of other countries. No part of the publication may be reproduced, stored or transmitted in any form or by any means without the prior written permission of the AASB except as permitted by law. For reproduction or publication, permission should be sought in writing from the AASB. Requests in the first instance should be addressed to the National Director, Australian Accounting Standards Board, PO Box 204, Collins Street West, Victoria 8007.

CHAPTER 25

Business combinations

CHAPTER AIM

An entity seeking investment opportunities may engage in transactions in which it acquires assets and possibly assumes liabilities. This chapter considers the application of AASB 3/IFRS 3 *Business Combinations* and how it is applied in reporting such transactions in financial statements.

LEARNING OBJECTIVES

After studying this chapter, you should be able to:

25.1 explain the objective of AASB 3/IFRS 3

25.2 determine whether a transaction is a business combination

25.3 explain the key steps in the acquisition method

25.4 explain the nature of an acquirer and key factors in the identification of an acquirer

25.5 identify the acquisition date

25.6 explain when to recognise and how to measure the identifiable assets acquired and liabilities assumed by an acquirer

25.7 discuss the nature of goodwill and how it is measured as well as how to measure a gain on bargain purchase

25.8 identify the disclosures required by AASB 3/IFRS 3.

CONCEPTS FOR REVIEW

Before studying this chapter, you should understand and, if necessary, revise:
* accounting for intangible assets
* the principles for measurement of fair value.

25.1 Objective of AASB 3/IFRS 3

LEARNING OBJECTIVE 25.1 Explain the objective of AASB 3/IFRS 3.

Australian internet company Arq Group Limited (formerly Melbourne IT Ltd) — probably best known for its domain name registration business — acquired digital marketing company WME Group in 2017 for $38 687 000 funded through $29 415 000 in equity and $9 272 000 in debt. The acquisition improved Arq Group's ability to service demand for digital marketing solutions in the small- and medium-sized enterprise (SME) sector (Arq Group 2018).

The purpose of this chapter is to analyse the accounting for **business combinations**, a term used in accounting standards to describe the sort of transaction undertaken between Arq Group (the **acquirer**) and WME Group (the **acquiree**). Specifically, a business combination occurs when an acquirer obtains control of another **business** or businesses. This chapter focuses on the accounting undertaken by the acquirer. The issues that will be investigated are as follows.

- Which assets and liabilities of the acquired entity — the acquiree — will be recognised by the acquirer, and how will these be measured?
- What happens if the acquirer pays an amount that exceeds the fair value of the net assets of the acquiree?
- What happens if the acquirer pays an amount less than the fair value of the acquiree's net assets?
- What information about such transactions is the acquirer required to disclose in its financial statements that will enable users to evaluate the nature and financial effects of the business combination?

In addressing these questions, the relevant accounting standard is AASB 3/IFRS 3 *Business Combinations*.

Business combinations may take various forms. We will consider two forms.

1. An acquisition in which the acquirer purchases assets, and possibly assumes liabilities, of the acquiree, subsequently recognising these assets and liabilities in its own accounts. The entity from whom the business was acquired will then either continue to operate with a reduced level of assets and liabilities (if only a portion of its net assets are acquired) or may liquidate (if all its net assets are acquired). Importantly, in this instance the acquiree is identified as the net assets acquired, not the entity from whom the net assets were acquired.

2. An acquisition in which the acquirer purchases sufficient shares in another entity to obtain control of that entity and hence control that entity's net assets. In this case, the entity from whom the net assets were acquired is the acquiree and does not liquidate, but continues its operations with no change in its assets and liabilities. In this instance the transaction is between the acquirer and the shareholders of the other entity and the acquiree is identified as the entity (represented by net assets) over whom control is obtained.

The same accounting principles apply in both situations. In this chapter the accounting is directed primarily at the first situation, namely the direct acquisition of assets and liabilities from another entity. The indirect acquisition is addressed in chapters 28–30. However, the principles discussed in this chapter apply to both types of acquisitions, as the economic substance of the transactions is the same; it is only the form of the business combination that differs.

Figure 25.1 shows details of the WME Group acquisition undertaken by Arq Group.

FIGURE 25.1	Business combinations, Arq Group

Section D: Group structure — D1. Business combinations

There have been no acquisitions during the year ended 31 December 2018.

Acquisitions in 2017

(a) Web Marketing Experts Pty Ltd, Nothing But Web Pty Ltd, Results First Ltd

On 31 May 2017, Arq Group Limited (formerly 'Melbourne IT Ltd') acquired 100% of WME Group. WME Group is a leading provider of end-to-end digital marketing solutions including search engine optimisation, search engine advertising and web design, for purchase consideration of $38 687 000 (including working capital and net debt adjustment). The acquisition was funded through a combination of equity and debt (approximately $29 415 000 and $9 272 000 respectively). The acquisition of WME Group further strengthened the Group's capabilities to provide complete digital marketing solutions to small and medium businesses across Australia and New Zealand.

Assets acquired and liabilities assumed

The fair values of the identifiable assets and liabilities of WME Group as at the date of acquisition were:

Fair value recognised on acquisition

	$'000s
Assets	
Cash and cash equivalents	1 104
Trade and other receivables	4 746
Property, plant and equipment	390
Intangible assets	3 801
Other assets	419
	10 460
Liabilities	
Trade and other payables	1 578
Provisions	428
Income in advance	1 256
Current tax liability	2 509
Deferred tax liability	962
	6 733
Total identifiable net assets at fair value	3 727
Goodwill and other intangibles arising on acquisition	34 960
Purchase consideration	38 687

As at 31 December 2018, the Group has completed the fair value assessment on the net assets acquired including current and deferred tax liabilities. There have been no significant changes to the fair value assessment presented in the financial statements for the year ended 31 December 2017.

From the date of acquisition to 31 December 2017, WME Group has contributed $13 473 000 to the revenue and $3 330 000 to the profit after tax attributable to members of the parent. If the combination had taken place at the beginning of the prior year, Group revenue would have been $207 511 000 and profit after tax attributable to members of the parent would have been $16 008 000.

Purchase consideration

	$'000s
Cash paid	25 000
Working capital adjustment	(3 734)
Net debt adjustment	5 256
Contingent consideration liability	12 165
	38 687

On 21 August 2017, the net of the working capital adjustment of ($3 734 000) and the net debt adjustment of $5 256 000 has been refunded.

On 13 September 2017, contingent consideration of $12 165 000 was paid which has been included in the cash flows from investing activities.

On 5 June 2018, contingent consideration of $157 000 was paid as the final settlement of contingent consideration for amounts held in escrow.

Transaction costs associated with the acquisition of WME Group of $794 000 were expensed through the Statement of Comprehensive Income and equity raising costs totalling $1 807 000 were taken directly to equity for the year ended 31 December 2017. This was included in the cash flows from financing activities.

Analysis of cash flows on acquisition

	$'000s
Purchase consideration paid	25 000
Net cash acquired	(1 104)
Net cash flow on acquisition (included in cash flows from investing activities)	23 896

Source: Arq Group Limited (2018, pp. 126–7).

25.2 Determining whether a transaction is a business combination

LEARNING OBJECTIVE 25.2 Determine whether a transaction is a business combination.

Companies are continually changing the composition of their assets and liabilities. Assets such as inventories are acquired on a regular basis while plant and equipment is acquired less often. In other circumstances a group of assets or net assets is acquired. The nature of the assets acquired dictates the accounting standard to be applied in recognising the transaction. Where the assets acquired and liabilities assumed constitute a business, the transaction is described as a business combination and AASB 3/ IFRS 3 is applied. For other acquisitions of assets not constituting a business (non-business acquisitions), AASB 116/IAS 16 *Property, Plant and Equipment* or — if the assets are financial instruments — AASB 9/IFRS 9 *Financial Instruments* is applied.

There are two key differences between the accounting for a business combination and accounting for a non-business acquisition.

1. In a business combination, the assets acquired and liabilities assumed are measured at fair value, whereas for a non-business acquisition, the assets acquired are measured at cost.
2. A business combination may give rise to the recognition of 'goodwill' or, less commonly, a 'bargain purchase', neither of which are recognised in a non-business acquisition.

The focus of this chapter is where the acquisition of net assets is deemed to be a business combination. There are two key conditions to be satisfied in order for a business combination to occur.

1. *The assets or net assets acquired must be a business.* The key feature of a business is that it must be capable of providing a return to the acquirer. The application guidance provided by paragraph B7 of AASB 3/IFRS 3 indicates that a business consists of inputs (i.e. economic resources) to which processes (e.g. strategic management or operational processes) are applied, which then have the ability to create outputs. To be a business, an entity does not have to produce outputs — it only has to be capable of providing a return. Hence, an entity still in the development stage, such as a mining operation that is currently exploring but not yet producing ore, can still be classed as a business. The acquisition of assets may or may not include the acquisition of processes. The definition of a business under AASB 3/ IFRS 3 is still satisfied if the acquirer integrates the acquired business into its own inputs and processes in order to generate a return. Such a return may, for example, take the form of a cost saving.

   Consider the situation in figure 25.2 in which X Ltd acquires the supermarket division from Y Ltd in exchange for shares. In this situation X Ltd obtains control of a group of integrated net assets, namely the supermarket division from Y Ltd. As the supermarket division is capable of providing a return to X Ltd it is identified as a business. X Ltd is identified as the acquirer undertaking a business combination and will account for its acquisition by applying AASB 3/IFRS 3. Note that the acquiree is the supermarket division, not Y Ltd.

   In contrast, Y Ltd is acquiring an investment in the equity instruments of X Ltd. This investment is a single asset and does not constitute a business. Y Ltd will apply AASB 9/IFRS 9 *Financial Instruments* in accounting for its acquisition of financial assets. It is important then to analyse the nature of the economic transaction in order to select the relevant accounting standard to apply to that transaction.

2. *The acquirer must obtain control of that business.* Control exists when an entity has the power to direct the future benefits of the assets acquired and has the ability to get varying, rather than fixed,

returns from using those assets. The term 'control' is the same as that applied in AASB 10/IFRS 10 *Consolidated Financial Statements* and is explained in more detail in chapter 26.

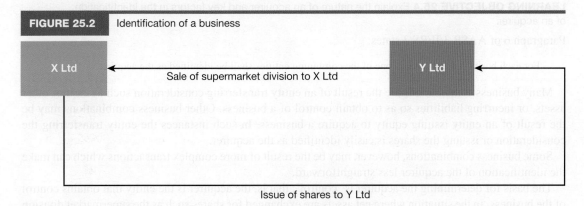

FIGURE 25.2 Identification of a business

X Ltd ← Sale of supermarket division to X Ltd — Y Ltd ←

Issue of shares to Y Ltd

25.3 The acquisition method

LEARNING OBJECTIVE 25.3 Explain the key steps in the acquisition method.

Under AASB 3/IFRS 3 the acquirer must account for each business combination by applying what is known as the 'acquisition method'.

Paragraph 5 of AASB 3/IFRS 3 lists the four key steps required by the acquisition method.

Step 1. Identify the acquirer.

Step 2. Determine the acquisition date.

Step 3. Recognise and measure the identifiable assets acquired, the liabilities assumed and any non-controlling interest in the acquiree.

Step 4. Recognise and measure goodwill or a gain from a bargain purchase.

The acquisition method is applied on the acquisition date, which is the date the acquirer obtains control of the acquiree.

Each of the four steps in the acquisition method is analysed in the following sections.

25.4 Step 1. Identify the acquirer

LEARNING OBJECTIVE 25.4 Explain the nature of an acquirer and key factors in the identification of an acquirer.

Paragraph 6 of AASB 3/IFRS 3 states:

> For each business combination, one of the combining entities shall be identified as the acquirer.

Many business combinations are the result of an entity transferring consideration such as cash or other assets, or incurring liabilities so as to obtain control of a business. Other business combinations may be the result of an entity issuing equity to acquire a business. In such instances the entity transferring the consideration or issuing the shares is easily identified as the acquirer.

Some business combinations, however, may be the result of more complex transactions which can make the identification of the acquirer less straightforward.

The basis for determining the acquirer is 'control'; that is, the acquirer is the entity that obtains control of the business. In the situation where net assets are exchanged for shares such as the supermarket division in figure 25.2, the identification of the acquirer is relatively easy in that, as a result of the exchange, the supermarket division is under the control of X Ltd.

In other situations, where one entity obtains control of another by means of an exchange of shares, the identification of the acquirer may be more difficult. Consider the situation where Entity A initiates discussions with Entity B to enter into a business combination. To effect the combination, Entity A instigates the formation of a new company, Entity C, and installs its own managers to run it. Entity C in turn issues shares to acquire all the equity of both entities A and B. The subsequent organisational structure is shown in figure 25.3.

| FIGURE 25.3 | Identification of an acquirer |

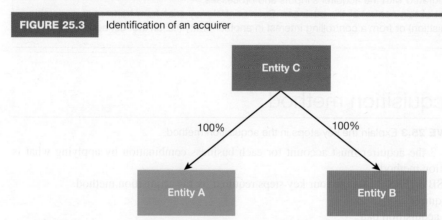

Figure 25.3 appears to suggest that Entity C may be the acquiring entity. However, Entity C was created by Entity A to formalise the organisational structure and to manage the merged entities. It played no part in the negotiations between Entity A and Entity B prior to the merger and hence cannot be the acquirer.

The determination of an acquirer may require judgement based on an analysis of the acquisition transaction. Paragraphs B15 to B18 of AASB 3/IFRS 3 provide guidance in determining which entity is the acquirer, identifying the following factors and circumstances to consider when shares are exchanged between entities to effect a business combination.

- *What are the relative voting rights in the combined entity after the business combination?* The acquirer is usually the entity whose owners have the largest portion of the voting rights in the combined entity.
- *Is there a large non-controlling voting interest in the combined entity?* As discussed in chapter 29, the acquirer is usually the entity that has the largest non-controlling voting interest in an entity that has a widely dispersed ownership.
- *What is the composition of the governing body of the combined entity?* The acquirer is usually the combining entity whose owners have the ability to elect, appoint or remove a majority of the members of the governing body of the combined entity. In relation to the entities in figure 25.3, prior to the business combination, both Entity A and Entity B had boards of directors. After the combination, the key board of directors will be that of Entity C. In determining which entity was the acquirer it would be useful to analyse the composition of the board of Entity C to see whether the majority of the directors come from the former board of Entity A or of Entity B.

- *What is the composition of the senior management of the combined entity?* The acquirer is usually the combining entity whose (former) management dominates the management of the combined entity.
- *What are the terms of the exchange of equity interests?* The acquirer is usually the entity that pays a premium over the pre-combination fair value of the other entity's shares.
- *Which of the combining entities is larger?* Relative size could be measured by reference to the fair value of the entity, revenue or profit. We would expect the acquirer to be the larger of the combining entities, making the smaller entities the acquiree(s).
- *Which entity initiated the transaction?* Typically the entity that is the acquirer is the one that undertakes action to take over the acquiree.

The determination of the acquirer is an important step under the acquisition method, as it affects the accounting for the business combination. As we will see in *step 3*, the assets and liabilities of the acquiree are measured at their acquisition date fair values. Applying the above paragraphs to the example from figure 25.3, Entity A would be deemed the acquiring entity and considered to have acquired the assets and liabilities of Entity B.

LEARNING CHECK

☐ In a business combination one of the combining entities must be identified as the acquirer.
☐ In many circumstances this identification is relatively straightforward.
☐ In more complex business combinations the identification of an acquirer requires judgement and AASB 3/IFRS 3 provides indicators to assist in making this judgement.

25.5 Step 2. Determine the acquisition date

LEARNING OBJECTIVE 25.5 Identify the acquisition date.

Paragraph 8 of AASB 3/IFRS 3 requires the acquirer to identify the **acquisition date**, which is the date on which it obtains control of the acquiree. In any transaction, including a business combination, identifying when control passes to the acquirer and thus identifying the acquisition date should be quite obvious. Consider, however, the following sequence of events in a business combination:

- the date the contract is signed
- the date the purchase consideration is transferred between the entities
- the date on which assets are physically transferred from one location to another
- the date on which an offer becomes unconditional.

These dates may be important, but aspects of a transaction such as physical transfer of assets or signing of a document do not determine the acquisition date. The key element of a business combination is the transfer of control and it is the defining factor in determining the acquisition date.

The significance of the acquisition date relates to the fact that it determines what fair values are applied to the measurement of the following components of the business combination.

1. *The identifiable assets and liabilities acquired.* The identifiable assets and liabilities of the acquiree are measured at their fair values, but these may change on a day-to-day basis. The acquisition date will determine the point at which such fair values should be measured.
2. *Measurement of the fair value of the consideration transferred.* The consideration transferred by the acquirer is measured as the sum of the fair values of assets given, liabilities undertaken or equity issued in exchange for the net assets or shares of the acquiree. For example, if the consideration consists of shares in the acquirer, and the acquirer is listed on a securities exchange, the market price of the acquirer's shares may fluctuate on a daily basis. The choice of date will determine the fair value measurement applied.
3. *Measurement of the non-controlling interest in an acquiree.* This occurs only when the acquirer acquires shares — as opposed to actual assets or net assets — in the acquiree. The acquirer need acquire only enough shares (say 60%) to obtain a controlling interest in the acquiree. The non-controlling interest — the other 40% of shares — is measured at fair value at acquisition date. Accounting for the non-controlling interest is discussed in chapter 29.
4. *Measurement of any previously held equity interest in an acquiree.* The acquirer may have held an equity interest in the acquiree prior to the business combination. For example, an acquirer may own 20% of the shares of an entity and then acquire a further 40% to give it a controlling interest in the acquiree. This situation is discussed in chapter 26. Alternatively, an acquirer may own 20% of the shares

of an entity and then acquire all the net assets of that entity, with the latter going into liquidation. In this case, the acquirer effectively gives up its investment in the acquiree as part of the business combination. In both circumstances, the 20% holding in the acquiree is recorded as an asset in the records of the acquirer prior to the business combination. It is necessary to measure the fair value of this asset at acquisition date as a part of the accounting for the business combination. Again, fair values vary over time and it is necessary to determine the acquisition date in order to measure the fair value in accounting for the business combination.

Determining the acquisition date will also impact on the measurement of subsequent earnings of the combined entities.

LEARNING CHECK

☐ The acquisition date is the date on which the acquirer gains control of the acquiree.
☐ Determination of the acquisition date affects the measurement of fair value for all components of a business combination.

25.6 Step 3. Recognise and measure identifiable assets acquired and liabilities assumed

LEARNING OBJECTIVE 25.6 Explain when to recognise and how to measure the identifiable assets acquired and liabilities assumed by an acquirer.

As noted in section 25.5, measurement of the non-controlling interest in the acquiree is applicable only in the case of the indirect acquisition where the acquirer acquires shares rather than net assets in the acquiree, and is discussed in chapter 29. This section deals with direct acquisitions, the situation where the acquirer acquires assets and assumes liabilities in the acquiree, these being transferred from the acquiree to the acquirer as a part of the business combination.

It should be noted that *Step 3* is concerned with the recognition and measurement of *identifiable* assets and liabilities. The concept of identifiability is discussed in chapter 6 as the term arises in AASB 138/ IAS 38 *Intangible Assets*. For an asset to be identifiable, it must be separable or arise from contractual or other legal rights. Goodwill, not being separable, is not an identifiable asset.

25.6.1 Recognition

Paragraph 10 of AASB 3/IFRS 3 states:

> As of the acquisition date, the acquirer shall recognise, separately from goodwill, the identifiable assets acquired, the liabilities assumed and any non-controlling interest in the acquiree. Recognition of identifiable assets acquired and liabilities assumed is subject to the conditions specified in paragraphs 11 and 12.

Paragraph 11 of AASB 3/IFRS 3 requires that assets and liabilities recognised in a business combination must meet the definitions prescribed in the *Conceptual Framework for Financial Reporting* (*Conceptual Framework*) as follows.

- 'An asset is a present economic resource controlled by the entity as a result of past events' (paragraph 4.3).
- 'A liability is a present obligation of the entity to transfer an economic resource as a result of past events' (paragraph 4.26).

AASB 3/IFRS 3 requires fair value to be applied to the net assets acquired in a business combination. If a fair value reflects a market price then future benefits by way of cash flows in or out can be assumed to be probable and value can be assumed to be capable of reliable measurement. The use of a fair value may require judgement, but judgement does not necessarily make such measurement unreliable.

Paragraph 12 of AASB 3/IFRS 3 imposes the condition that the item acquired or assumed must be part of the business acquired rather than the result of a separate transaction. An example of this criteria being applied is where a potential acquiree has a receivable for an unresolved claim against the potential acquirer. As part of the agreement to combine, the acquirer agrees to settle the claim against the acquiree, and transfers funds to the acquiree as a result. It is necessary to separate out this transaction from the business combination, and separate out the consideration paid for the assets and liabilities of the acquiree from the monies paid to settle the claim by the acquiree.

In recognising all the assets and liabilities of a business that has been acquired, there may be assets and liabilities that have not been recognised by the acquiree but are recognisable by the acquirer. The assets and liabilities recognised by an acquiree are subject to the recognition criteria in the specific standards that were applied by the acquiree. An example is that of intangible assets. An acquiree in applying AASB 138/IAS 38 *Intangible Assets* may not have recognised some internally generated intangible assets such as brands. However, for the acquirer, these brands are acquired intangible assets and are recognisable under both AASB 3/IFRS 3 and AASB 138/IAS 38.

Similarly, the recognition of liabilities by an acquiree is subject to the recognition criteria in AASB 137/IAS 37 *Provisions, contingent liabilities and contingent assets*. Some liabilities classified as contingent liabilities under AASB 137/IAS 37 may be able to be recognised as liabilities in accordance with AASB 3/IFRS 3 (paragraphs 22 and 23). For example, a guarantee for a loan might not be recognised as a liability by the acquiree applying AASB 137/IAS 37, yet be recognised at fair value under AASB 3/IFRS 3. Recall that paragraph 11 of AASB 3/IFRS 3 requires that an identifiable asset or liability recognised in a business combination satisfy the definition of an asset or liability in the *Conceptual Framework*. At the time of writing, the IASB and AASB have issued an exposure draft ((AASB ED290/IASB ED/2019/3) proposing an exception for liabilities that come within the scope of AASB 137/IAS 37. The effect of the proposed exception is that such liabilities recognised in a business combination should satisfy the definition of a liability in AASB 137/IAS 37, rather than the broader definition adopted by the *Conceptual Framework*.

25.6.2 Measurement

Paragraph 18 of AASB 3/IFRS 3 requires that identifiable assets acquired and liabilities assumed are measured at their acquisition-date fair values.

Information about fair value measurement is found in AASB 13/IFRS 13 *Fair Value Measurement* (see chapter 3). Fair value is an exit price, being the price that would be received to sell an asset or paid to transfer a liability in an orderly transaction between market participants at the measurement date. This price is measured using one of three possible valuation techniques:

- the market approach
- the income approach
- the cost approach.

Inputs into the valuation techniques are classified into a fair value hierarchy with the inputs being prioritised into three levels: Level 1, Level 2 and Level 3.

- Level 1 inputs are quoted prices in an active market for identical assets and liabilities.
- Level 2 inputs are quoted market prices that are observable for the asset or liability, either directly (i.e. as prices) or indirectly (i.e. derived from prices).
- Level 3 inputs are not based on observable market data.

It may be that the measurement of the acquired assets and liabilities is not completed by the end of the accounting period. This may happen, for example, where an acquisition occurs close to the end of an accounting period. In this situation, paragraph 45 of AASB 3/IFRS 3 requires the acquirer to prepare provisional best estimates of fair value, and report these provisional amounts in its financial statements. These will be adjusted to the fair values when the amounts are subsequently determined. The measurement period in which the adjustments can be made cannot exceed 1 year after the acquisition date.

ILLUSTRATIVE EXAMPLE 25.1

Identifiable assets acquired and liabilities assumed

The following details relate to a business combination. Assume a *Step 1* analysis has identified Burleigh Ltd as the acquirer as it controls the assets and liabilities of Heads Ltd subsequent to the combination, and a *Step 2* analysis has determined an acquisition date of 1 July 2023.

The financial position of Heads Ltd at 1 July 2023, with the identifiable assets and liabilities measured at both their carrying amounts in the records of Heads Ltd as well as fair value, was as follows.

	Carrying amount	Fair value
Share capital:		
Preference shares: 6000 fully paid shares	$ 12 000	
Ordinary shares: 30 000 fully paid shares	60 000	
Retained earnings	36 000	
Debentures	8 000	$ 8 160
Accounts payable	16 000	16 000
	$132 000	
Plant and equipment	84 000	72 000
Accumulated depreciation — plant and equipment	(20 000)	
Inventories	36 000	40 000
Accounts receivable	32 000	28 000
Brands	—	10 000
	$132 000	

At 1 July 2023, Burleigh Ltd acquires all the assets and some of the liabilities of Heads Ltd, with Heads Ltd going into liquidation. The terms of the acquisition are as follows.

1. Burleigh Ltd is to take over all the assets of Heads Ltd as well as the accounts payable of Heads Ltd.
2. Costs of liquidation of Heads Ltd will be $700 and are to be paid with funds supplied by Burleigh Ltd.
3. Preference shareholders of Heads Ltd are to receive two fully paid preference shares in Burleigh Ltd for every three shares held or alternatively, $2 per share in cash payable at acquisition date.
4. Ordinary shareholders of Heads Ltd are to receive two fully paid ordinary shares in Burleigh Ltd for every share held or, alternatively, $5.00 in cash, payable half at acquisition date and half on 30 June 2024. The incremental borrowing rate for Burleigh Ltd is 10% p.a.
5. Ordinary shares issued by Burleigh Ltd have a fair value of $2.20 per share, while preference shares issued by Burleigh Ltd have a fair value of $2.00 per share. Holders of 3000 preference shares and 5000 ordinary shares elect to receive the cash.
6. Costs of issuing and registering the shares issued by Burleigh Ltd amount to $80 for the preference shares and $200 for the ordinary shares.
7. Debenture holders of Heads Ltd are to be paid in cash out of funds provided by Burleigh Ltd. These debentures have a fair value of $102 per $100 debenture.
8. Costs associated with the business combination and incurred by Burleigh Ltd amount to $2000.
9. Apart from the deferred payment of cash to the ordinary shareholders, other cash payments were to be made on 1 August 2023. Shares were also to be issued by that date.

Required
What will the acquirer, Burleigh Ltd, recognise in relation to the acquisition of Heads Ltd?

Solution
Using the information above, the application of *Step 3* will result in Burleigh Ltd recognising the following identifiable assets acquired and liabilities assumed in relation to Heads Ltd, measured at fair value.

Plant and equipment	$ 72 000
Inventories	40 000
Accounts receivable	28 000
Brands	10 000
	150 000
Accounts payable	(16 000)
	$134 000

Note that Burleigh Ltd recognises brands as an intangible asset that it is acquiring, but, under accounting standards, Heads Ltd was not able to recognise this internally generated asset.

LEARNING CHECK

☐ The acquiree must recognise identifiable assets acquired and liabilities assumed at their acquisition-date fair values.

☐ The recognition of assets and liabilities is not subject to normal recognition criteria, although AASB 3/IFRS 3 makes recognition subject to two main conditions: the definitions of assets and liabilities must be met and the item acquired or assumed must be part of the business acquired.

25.7 Step 4. Recognise and measure goodwill and a gain on bargain purchase

LEARNING OBJECTIVE 25.7 Discuss the nature of goodwill and how it is measured as well as how to measure a gain on bargain purchase.

The final step under the acquisition method is to determine whether goodwill or a gain on bargain purchase arises from the business combination. This determination is made by comparing the consideration transferred by the acquirer with the fair value of the identifiable assets acquired and liabilities assumed in the business (determined in *Step 3*).

25.7.1 Consideration transferred

Consideration transferred refers to what the acquirer gives up in order to acquire the net assets of the acquiree. According to paragraph 37 of AASB 3/IFRS 3, the measurement is made at acquisition date, and consists of the sum of the fair values of everything transferred by the acquirer to the former owners of the acquiree. Hence:

Consideration transferred = Fair value of *assets* transferred by the acquirer to the acquiree
+ Fair value of *liabilities* incurred by the acquirer to former owners of the acquiree
+ Fair value of *equity* interest issued by the acquirer to the acquiree

Note that, whereas the focus of *Step 3* was on the assets and liabilities of the *acquiree*, the calculation of the consideration transferred is on what is transferred by the *acquirer*.

In a specific exchange, the consideration transferred to the acquiree could include just one form of consideration, such as cash, but could equally well consist of a number of forms such as cash, non-current assets, shares and contingent consideration.

Cash

The fair value of cash or a cash equivalent is normally readily determinable. In the event there is a significant time difference between acquisition date and settlement, the acquirer assigns a fair value to the deferred payment based on the amount the entity would have to borrow to settle the debt immediately. The entity's incremental borrowing rate would be the discount rate normally applied to any deferred payment.

Use of cash, including a deferred payment, to acquire net assets in the acquiree, results in the following form of journal entry at acquisition date.

Net assets (of the business being acquired)	Dr	xxx	
Cash (the immediate payment)	Cr		xxx
Payable to acquiree (the deferred payment)	Cr		xxx
(Acquisition of net assets with partially deferred payment)			

On the settlement date when the deferred payment is made to the acquiree, the interest component is recognised as follows.

Payable to acquiree	Dr	xxx	
Interest expense	Dr	xxx	
Cash	Cr		xxx
(Payment of deferred amount)			

Non-monetary assets

Non-monetary assets are assets such as property, plant and equipment, investments, licences and patents.

Where the acquirer agrees to transfer any non-monetary assets to the acquiree as part of the consideration, the acquirer is effectively selling that asset to the acquiree. Where the carrying amount of the transferred asset differs from its fair value, a gain or loss is recognised at acquisition date. To account for this, under paragraph 38 of AASB 3/IFRS 3, the acquirer remeasures the transferred non-monetary asset to fair value. The difference between the fair value and the carrying amount of the asset is recognised in profit or loss.

To illustrate, assume an item of plant is transferred to the acquiree as part of the consideration transferred. If the acquirer had recorded the plant at cost of $180 with an accumulated depreciation of $30, and the fair value of the plant was $155, the acquirer would record the following journal entries at acquisition date.

Accumulated depreciation	Dr	30
Plant	Cr	25
Gain	Cr	5
(Remeasurement as part of consideration transferred in a business combination)		
Net assets acquired	Dr	xxx
Plant	Cr	155
Other consideration payable	Cr	xxx
(Acquisition of net assets from acquiree)		

Equity instruments

If an acquirer issues its own shares as consideration, it needs to determine the fair value of those shares at acquisition date. For listed entities, reference is made to the quoted price of the shares on the securities exchange.

In issuing shares as part of the consideration paid, transaction costs such as stamp duties, professional advisers' fees, underwriting costs and brokerage fees may be incurred. Paragraph 53 of AASB 3/IFRS 3 requires that these costs be accounted for in accordance with AASB 132/IAS 32 *Financial Instruments: Presentation* and AASB 9/IFRS 9 *Financial Instruments*. Transaction costs of an equity transaction shall be accounted for as a deduction from equity, rather than an expense. The rationale for this accounting treatment is that such costs (net of any related tax benefit) reduce the proceeds from the equity issue.

To illustrate, assume an acquirer issues 40 000 shares as consideration for a business consisting of identifiable assets having a fair value of $250 000 and liabilities having a fair value of $50 000. If these shares have a fair value of $5 per share and costs of $300 were incurred to issue the shares, then the acquirer would record the following entries at acquisition date.

Identifiable assets	Dr	250 000
Liabilities	Cr	50 000
Share capital	Cr	200 000
(Acquisition of business via share issue)		
Share capital	Dr	300
Cash	Cr	300
(Costs of issuing shares)		

Liabilities

The fair values of liabilities are calculated in accordance with AASB 13/IFRS 13 *Fair Value Measurement*. In many cases the measurement will be undertaken by determining the present value of expected future cash outflows. Future losses or expected outlays arising as a result of the business combination, such as reorganisation of a factory, are not liabilities of the acquirer and should not be included in the calculation of the consideration transferred.

Costs of arranging and issuing debt instruments are an integral part of the liability issue and are included in the initial measurement of the liability, consistent with the accounting for the costs of issuing equity instruments.

Contingent consideration

Appendix A of AASB 3/IFRS 3 provides the following definition of **contingent consideration**.

> Usually, an obligation of the acquirer to transfer additional assets or equity interests to the former owners of an acquiree as part of the exchange for control of the acquiree if specified future events occur or conditions are met. However, contingent consideration also may give the acquirer the right to the return of previously transferred consideration if specified conditions are met.

In some business combinations the former owner of the acquiree may be concerned about the value of the consideration received because of the uncertainty of future events. The acquiree may then specify that contingent consideration be built into the acquisition agreement. The contingent consideration will require the acquirer to pay further consideration to the acquiree in the future if certain specified future events occur or conditions are met.

Two examples of contingent consideration are as follows.

1. The acquiree received shares issued by the acquirer as part of the consideration transferred instead of cash. The acquiree is uncertain about the future market price of the acquirer's shares. The acquisition agreement then contained a clause whereby if the market value of the acquirer's shares declined within the 12 months following the acquisition date, the acquiree would be entitled to a further cash consideration.

2. The acquiree received shares in the acquiree as part of the consideration transferred. The acquiree requires cash flow in the years following the acquisition date. A clause in the combination agreement could require the acquirer to make further cash payments to the acquiree if the acquirer's business did not achieve certain specified sales and/or profit targets over a specified period subsequent to the acquisition date.

As the agreement at acquisition date includes the clauses about the contingent consideration, paragraph 39 of AASB 3/IFRS 3 requires the fair value of the contingent consideration to be included in the measurement of the consideration transferred. The acquirer will need to classify an obligation to pay contingent consideration as a liability or equity based upon definitions given in AASB 132/IAS 32. For example, where the future consideration payable consists of financial instruments, is this consideration equity or a liability?

According to paragraph 58 of AASB 3/IFRS 3, accounting for contingent consideration occurs not only at acquisition date, but the equity or liability account raised at acquisition date must be accounted for in periods subsequent to acquisition date. Accounting for contingent consideration subsequent to acquisition date is as follows.

- Where the consideration was classified as *equity*, it is not remeasured and any subsequent settlement is accounted for within equity. To illustrate, assume that at acquisition date it was calculated that the fair value of the consideration would consist of the issue of 20 000 shares in the acquirer having a fair value of $5 per share. If it was subsequently estimated that 40 000 shares would be required to be issued, then no overall change in equity occurs as equity is effectively adjusted by the issue of 40 000 shares at $2.50 per share.

- Where the contingent consideration is classified as a liability that is a financial instrument, any movement in the fair value is recognised as a gain or loss recognised in profit or loss or in other comprehensive income in accordance with AASB 9/IFRS 9.

25.7.2 Acquisition-related costs

As noted in paragraph 53 of AASB 3/IFRS 3, acquisition-related costs are costs incurred by the acquirer in undertaking the business combination. Examples of these costs are: finder's fees, advisory, accounting, valuation and other professional or consulting fees.

In AASB 116/IAS 16 *Property, Plant and Equipment*, directly attributable costs are capitalised into the cost of acquisition of these assets. However, acquisition-related costs incurred in a business combination are accounted for as expenses in the period in which they occur. The key reasons for this are:

- acquisition-related costs are not part of the fair value exchange between acquirer and acquiree
- they are separate transactions for which the buyer pays the fair value for the services received
- these amounts do not generally represent assets of the acquirer at acquisition date because the benefits obtained are consumed as the services are received.

The AASB 3/IFRS 3 accounting for these outlays is a result of the decision by the standard setters to record identifiable assets acquired and liabilities assumed at fair value. In contrast, under AASB 116/IAS 16 and AASB 138/IAS 38, assets acquired are recorded initially at cost.

Consideration transferred

This example builds on illustrative example 25.1.

The consideration transferred is determined by observing all the assets given up by the acquirer, liabilities assumed by the acquirer, and shares issued by the acquirer. In this example, Burleigh Ltd gives up cash and issues shares to Heads Ltd. The consideration transferred is measured at fair value.

Consideration transferred

			Fair value	
Cash:	Costs of liquidation of Heads Ltd		$ 700	
	Preference shareholders (3000 × $2)		6 000	
	Ordinary shareholders:			
	Payable immediately $\left(5000 \times \frac{1}{2} \times \$5\right)$		12 500	
	Payable later $\left(5000 \times \frac{1}{2} \times \$5 \times 0.909\,091\right)^{*}$		11 364	
	Debenture holders, including premium ($8000 × 1.02)		8 160	$ 38 724
Shares:	Preference shareholders $\left(\frac{2}{3} \times 3000 \times \$2.00\right)$		4 000	
	Ordinary shareholders $\left(\frac{2}{1} \times 25\,000 \times \$2.20\right)$		110 000	114 000
Consideration transferred				$152 724

*$11 364 is the cash payable in 1 year's time discounted at 10% p.a.

Without providing the detail on the net assets acquired, but concentrating on the consideration transferred, the journal entries in Burleigh Ltd at acquisition date are as follows.

2023				
July 1	Net assets acquired	Dr	152 724	
	Deferred consideration payable	Cr		11 364
	Consideration payable	Cr		27 360
	Share capital — preference	Cr		4 000
	Share capital — ordinary	Cr		110 000
	(Acquisition of Heads Ltd)			
	Acquisition-related expenses	Dr	2 000	
	Cash	Cr		2 000
	(Acquisition-related expenses)			
Aug. 1	Consideration payable	Dr	27 360	
	Cash	Cr		27 360
	(Payment of consideration to Heads Ltd)			
	Share capital — ordinary	Dr	200	
	Share capital — preference	Dr	80	
	Cash	Cr		280
	(Share issue costs)			
2024				
June 30	Deferred consideration payable	Dr	11 364	
	Interest expense	Dr	1 136	
	Cash	Cr		12 500
	(Balance of consideration paid)			

25.7.3 Goodwill

According to paragraph 32 of AASB 3/IFRS 3, goodwill is measured at acquisition date and occurs when consideration transferred *plus* the non-controlling interest in the acquiree *plus* the acquirer's previously held equity interest in the acquiree *is greater than* the net fair value of the identifiable assets acquired and liabilities assumed.

As the existence of a non-controlling interest and a previously held equity interest arise in business combinations only where the acquirer buys the shares of an acquiree (see chapters 28–30), these calculations are not applicable to circumstances where an acquirer buys assets or net assets of an acquiree. Hence, in the business combinations discussed in this chapter, **goodwill** arises *when the consideration transferred is greater than the net fair value of identifiable assets acquired and liabilities assumed.*

The rationale here is that if the amount paid for the business is greater than the fair value of the identifiable net assets acquired, then the acquirer has been prepared to pay a premium to acquire some form of unidentifiable benefit, which is referred to as goodwill.

Measurement of goodwill

As noted above:

Goodwill	=	Consideration transferred
		less
		Net fair value of identifiable assets acquired and liabilities assumed

To determine goodwill in a business combination, an acquisition analysis is undertaken at acquisition date and the consideration transferred is compared with the net fair value of the identifiable assets acquired and liabilities assumed.

ILLUSTRATIVE EXAMPLE 25.3

Acquisition analysis and goodwill

The net fair value of the identifiable assets and liabilities of Heads Ltd was calculated in illustrative example 25.1 while the consideration transferred was calculated in illustrative example 25.2.

Required
1. Using the information from illustrative examples 25.1 and 25.2, prepare an acquisition analysis.
2. Prepare the journal entries of the acquirer, Burleigh Ltd.

Solution
1. *Acquisition analysis*
   Net fair value of identifiable assets acquired and liabilities assumed of Heads Ltd are as follows.

Plant and equipment	$ 72 000
Inventories	40 000
Accounts receivable	28 000
Brands	10 000
	150 000
Accounts payable	16 000
Fair value of net assets acquired	$134 000

Consideration transferred

				Fair value
Cash:	Costs of liquidation of Heads Ltd		$ 700	
	Preference shareholders (3000 × $2)		6 000	
	Ordinary shareholders:			
	Payable immediately $\left(5000 \times \frac{1}{2} \times \$5\right)$		12 500	
	Payable later $\left(5000 \times \frac{1}{2} \times \$5 \times 0.909091\right)$		11 364	
	Debenture holders, including premium ($8000 × 1.02)		8 160	$ 38 724
Shares:	Preference shareholders $\left(\frac{2}{3} \times 3000 \times \$2.00\right)$		4 000	
	Ordinary shareholders $\left(\frac{2}{1} \times 25 000 \times \$2.20\right)$		110 000	114 000
Consideration transferred				$152 724

▶

Goodwill

Consideration transferred	=	$152 724
Less: Fair value of net assets acquired	=	$134 000
Goodwill	=	$ 18 724

2. *Journal entries*

The journal entries in the records of the acquirer, Burleigh Ltd, in relation to the business combination with Heads Ltd are then as follows.

2023					
July 1	Equipment		Dr	72 000	
	Inventories		Dr	40 000	
	Accounts receivable		Dr	28 000	
	Brands		Dr	10 000	
	Goodwill		Dr	18 724	
	Accounts payable		Cr		16 000
	Deferred consideration payable		Cr		11 364
	Consideration payable		Cr		27 360
	Share capital — preference		Cr		4 000
	Share capital — ordinary		Cr		110 000
	(Acquisition of Heads Ltd)				
	Acquisition-related expenses		Dr	2 000	
	Cash		Cr		2 000
	(Acquisition-related expenses)				
Aug. 1	Consideration payable		Dr	27 360	
	Cash		Cr		27 360
	(Payment of consideration to Heads Ltd)				
	Share capital — ordinary		Dr	200	
	Share capital — preference		Dr	80	
	Cash		Cr		280
	(Share issue costs)				
2024					
June 30	Deferred consideration payable		Dr	11 364	
	Interest expense		Dr	1 136	
	Cash		Cr		12 500
	(Balance of consideration paid)				

In relation to the measurement of goodwill, the following should be noted.

- Goodwill is not measured directly, for example, by reference to a market. Instead it is recognised as a residual based upon two other calculations.
- Being a residual measure, there is no attempt in a business combination to measure the total goodwill of the business acquired. Goodwill would, for example, be understated if the acquirer was able to acquire a business for less than its fair value; that is, a lower consideration transferred leads to a smaller measure of goodwill.
- Only acquired goodwill is recognised. As noted in chapter 6, entities do not recognise internally generated goodwill.
- Goodwill is not amortised, but is subject to an annual impairment test — see chapter 7.
- To ensure that goodwill includes only unidentifiable assets, it is essential that:
  - the consideration be measured accurately
  - the measurement of the identifiable assets acquired and liabilities assumed be at fair value rather than at their original carrying amounts in the acquiree, and
  - all intangible assets are recognised.

Referring back to figure 25.1, Note D1 of Arq Group's 2018 annual report provides summary details of the consideration and fair value of net assets acquired in determining $34.96 million of intangibles and goodwill arising from its acquisition of WME Group.

Nature of goodwill

Goodwill is recognised as an asset in a business combination at acquisition date. It represents the economic benefits arising from other assets of the acquiree that are not individually identified and separately recognised.

In a business combination, an acquirer is required to recognise all assets that are capable of being individually identified and recognised. The criterion of 'being individually identified' relates to the characteristic of 'identifiability' as used in AASB 138/IAS 38 *Intangible Assets*, and is used to distinguish intangible assets from goodwill.

The future economic benefits associated with goodwill may arise from synergy between the identifiable assets acquired. Alternatively, the benefits may arise from assets that individually do not qualify for recognition in the financial statements but for which the acquirer is prepared to make a payment in a business combination.

Johnson and Petrone (1998, p. 296) used the descriptor of 'core goodwill', arguing that there were two main components of goodwill. These two components are referred to as 'going-concern goodwill' and 'combination' goodwill'. This is represented diagrammatically in figure 25.4.

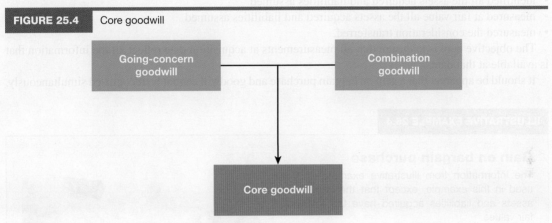

| FIGURE 25.4 | Core goodwill |

Source: Adapted from Johnson and Petrone (1998).

Combination goodwill arises from the combination of the acquirer's and acquiree's businesses. It stems from the synergies that result from the combination. For example, an acquirer may have access to supplies of high-quality sand suitable for glass making, while the acquiree may be involved in the manufacture of glass products. By combining the two entities, the joint entities are capable of producing more economic benefits — cheaper manufacture of glass products — than if the entities were separate.

Going-concern goodwill relates to the 'going concern' of the acquiree's existing business. This element of core goodwill relates solely to the acquiree, not the acquirer. The acquiree may be able to earn a higher return on an assembled collection of net assets than would be expected from those net assets operating separately. This reflects synergies of the assets as well as factors relating to market imperfections such as an ability to earn a monopoly profit, or where there are barriers to competitors entering a particular market. It may also relate to factors such as good working relations with employees, or the innovative ideas produced within the acquiree's business.

It is important to analyse the composition of goodwill. The acquirer paid a part of the consideration transferred for the goodwill, and the reasons for the expenditure of that money should be able to be explained. To enable users to evaluate the value recorded for goodwill, acquirers are required under paragraph B64(e) of AASB 3/IFRS 3 to disclose a qualitative description of the factors that make up the goodwill recognised, such as expected synergies from combining operations of the acquiree and the acquirer, intangible assets that do not qualify for separate recognition or other factors.

Arq Group allocated goodwill to each of its cash-generating units, which were expected to benefit from the synergies created by the combination.

25.7.4 Gain on bargain purchase

Where an entity pays a consideration *less* than the net fair value of the identifiable assets acquired, the acquirer is seen to have made a bargain purchase. The acquirer recognises this **gain on bargain purchase** in profit or loss in the period of the acquisition.

As noted above:

Gain on bargain purchase	=	Net fair value of the identifiable assets acquired and liabilities assumed *less* Consideration transferred

The existence of a bargain purchase is considered by the standard setters to be an anomalous transaction because, typically, parties to the business combination do not knowingly sell assets at amounts lower than their fair values. It may occur because of the acquirer's negotiation skills, or, more likely, because of a forced sale in which the seller is required to liquidate.

Before a gain on bargain purchase can be recognised, paragraph 36 of AASB 3/IFRS 3 requires the acquirer to *reassess* whether it has correctly:

- identified all the assets acquired and liabilities assumed
- measured at fair value all the assets acquired and liabilities assumed
- measured the consideration transferred.

The objective here is to ensure that all measurements at acquisition date reflect all the information that is available at that date.

It should be apparent that a gain on bargain purchase and goodwill cannot be recognised simultaneously.

ILLUSTRATIVE EXAMPLE 25.4

Gain on bargain purchase

The information from illustrative example 25.1 is used in this example, except that the identifiable assets and liabilities acquired have the following fair values.

Equipment	$ 90 000
Inventories	50 000
Accounts receivable	28 000
Brands	12 000
	180 000
Accounts payable	16 000
	$164 000

Required

1. Prepare an acquisition analysis.
2. Prepare the first journal entry in Burleigh Ltd to record the acquisition of the net assets of Heads Ltd, assuming the reassessment process did not result in any changes in the fair values calculated.

Solution

1. *Acquisition analysis*

   The acquisition analysis now shows the following.

Fair value of net assets acquired	=	$164 000
Less: Consideration transferred	=	$152 724
Gain on bargain purchase	=	$ 11 276

2. *Journal entries*

   Assuming the reassessment process did not result in any changes to the fair values calculated, the first journal entry in Burleigh Ltd to record the acquisition of the net assets of Heads Ltd is as follows.

2023					
July 1	Equipment		Dr	90 000	
	Inventories		Dr	50 000	
	Accounts receivable		Dr	28 000	
	Brands		Dr	12 000	
	Accounts payable		Cr		16 000
	Deferred consideration payable		Cr		11 364
	Consideration payable		Cr		27 360
	Share capital — preference		Cr		4 000
	Share capital — ordinary		Cr		110 000
	Gain (profit or loss)		Cr		11 276
	(Acquisition of Heads Ltd)				

LEARNING CHECK

☐ The consideration transferred is the sum of the fair values of the components given up by the acquirer, excluding any directly attributable costs, which are expensed.

☐ Goodwill is a residual measured by consideration transferred less net fair value of identifiable assets acquired less liabilities assumed.

☐ Goodwill is subject to an annual impairment test.

☐ Core goodwill consists of going-concern goodwill and combination goodwill.

☐ A gain on bargain purchase arises in the unlikely event that the acquirer transfers consideration that is less than the net fair value of identifiable assets acquired less liabilities assumed.

☐ A gain on bargain purchase is recognised only after reassessments are made.

☐ A gain on bargain purchase is recognised in profit or loss in the year it arises.

25.8 Disclosures

LEARNING OBJECTIVE 25.8 Identify the disclosures required by AASB 3/IFRS 3.

Paragraph 59 of AASB 3/IFRS 3 outlines the general principle relating to disclosures stating that acquirers shall disclose information that enables users of its financial statements to evaluate the nature and financial effect of a business combination.

Appendix B of AASB 3/IFRS 3, which is an integral part of the standard, provides guidance to assist preparers in applying the standard in the preparation of financial statements. Paragraph B64 specifies a number of items required to be disclosed to ensure the objective in paragraph 59 is met. These include:

- name and description of the acquiree
- the acquisition date
- the primary reasons for the business combination
- a qualitative description of the factors that make up goodwill
- the acquisition-date fair values of the total consideration transferred as well as the acquisition-date fair values of each major class of consideration
- information concerning contingent consideration
- the amounts recognised as of acquisition date for each class of assets acquired and liabilities assumed
- any gain on bargain purchase, and reasons why the transaction resulted in a gain.

Paragraph 61 of AASB 3/IFRS 3 requires the disclosure of information to assist in the evaluation of the financial effects of all adjustments recognised in the current period that relate to business combinations occurring in *previous* periods. Paragraph B67 details disclosures required in meeting the information objective in paragraph 61.

LEARNING CHECK

☐ AASB 3/IFRS 3 requires extensive disclosures relating to business combinations so that users of financial statements can understand the financial effects of the transactions.

SUMMARY

AASB 3/IFRS 3 *Business Combinations* deals with the accounting for business combinations by an acquirer. The standard:

- specifies the application of the acquisition method in accounting for a business combination
- requires that an acquirer be identified for each business combination
- requires that the consideration transferred by the acquirer to the acquiree be measured at acquisition date at the sum of the fair values of the assets given up, liabilities undertaken and equity instruments issued by the acquirer
- requires that the acquirer measure the identifiable assets acquired and liabilities assumed at fair value at acquisition date
- specifies that goodwill be measured as the excess of the consideration transferred over the net fair value of the identifiable assets acquired and liabilities assumed
- specifies that a gain on bargain purchase be recognised when the consideration transferred is less than the net fair value of the identifiable assets acquired and liabilities assumed.

KEY TERMS

acquiree The business or businesses of which the acquirer obtains control in a business combination.

acquirer The entity that obtains control of the acquiree.

acquisition date The date on which the acquirer obtains control of the acquiree.

business An integrated set of activities and assets that is capable of being conducted and managed for the purpose of providing a return in the form of dividends, lower costs or other economic benefits directly to investors or other owners, members or participants.

business combination A transaction or other event in which an acquirer obtains control of one or more businesses.

contingent consideration Usually, an obligation of the acquirer to transfer additional assets or equity interests to the former owners of an acquiree as part of the exchange for control of the acquiree if specified future events occur or conditions are met. However, contingent consideration also may give the acquirer the right to the return of previously transferred consideration if specified conditions are met.

contingent liability (a) A possible obligation that arises from past events and whose existence will be confirmed only by the occurrence or non-occurrence of one or more uncertain future events not wholly within the control of the entity; or (b) a present obligation that arises from past events but is not recognised because: (i) it is not probable that an outflow of resources embodying economic benefits will be required to settle the obligation; or (ii) the amount of the obligation cannot be measured with sufficient reliability.

gain on bargain purchase When the consideration transferred is less than the net fair value of identifiable assets acquired and liabilities assumed.

goodwill An asset representing the future economic benefits arising from other assets acquired in a business combination that are not individually identified and separately recognised.

DEMONSTRATION PROBLEM

25.1 Business combinations

On 1 January 2022, Jack Ltd concluded agreements to acquire all the assets and liabilities of Jill Ltd. Jill Ltd would then liquidate. The statements of financial position of both companies at that date were as follows.

	Jack Ltd	Jill Ltd
Cash	$ 20 000	$ 1 000
Accounts receivable	35 000	19 000
Inventories	52 000	26 500
Property, plant and equipment (net)	270 500	144 500

Goodwill	10 000	5 000
Financial assets	54 000	18 000
	$441 500	$214 000
Accounts payable	$ 68 000	$ 76 000
Loan payable	—	40 000
Share capital — $1 shares	300 000	80 000
Retained earnings	73 500	18 000
	$441 500	$214 000

The notes to Jill Ltd's accounts reported a contingent liability relating to a loan guarantee. A liability was not recognised by Jill Ltd for the loan guarantee because of the low likelihood of it generating an outflow of economic benefits and the difficulty of measuring the amount to be paid.

In exchange for all the assets and liabilities of Jill Ltd, Jack Ltd agreed to give the following.

- Shareholders in Jill Ltd are to receive, for every four shares held in Jill Ltd, three shares in Jack Ltd and $1.00 in cash. Each Jack Ltd share has a fair value at 1 January 2022 of $1.80.
- Cash to cover the liquidation costs of Jill Ltd, which is expected to be $6000.

Jack Ltd assessed the fair values of the recorded identifiable assets of Jill Ltd as follows.

Cash	$ 1 000
Receivables	17 500
Inventories	32 000
Property, plant and equipment	165 500
Financial assets	19 000

Jill Ltd had also been undertaking research into new manufacturing equipment and had expensed a total of $10 000 research costs. Jack Ltd assessed that the fair value of the in-process research was $2000. All liabilities were recorded at fair value and the contingent liability was assessed to have a fair value of $1500.

External accounting advice and valuers' fees incurred by Jack Ltd amounted to $3000. The cash payable to Jill Ltd and the acquisition-related expenses were paid subsequent to the acquisition date.

Required

Prepare the acquisition analysis at 1 January 2022 and the journal entries in Jack Ltd relating to its acquisition of Jill Ltd.

SOLUTION

***Step 1.* Identify the acquirer**

As Jack Ltd is obtaining control of the assets and liabilities of Jill Ltd, Jack Ltd is the acquirer.

***Step 2.* Determine the acquisition date**

The acquisition date is 1 January 2022 as this is the date the agreements are concluded and it is assumed that Jack Ltd obtains control of the net assets of Jill Ltd on this date.

***Step 3.* Recognise and measure the identifiable asset acquired and liabilities assumed**

Acquisition analysis

(a) *What are the identifiable assets and liabilities recognised by Jack Ltd, and how will they be measured in the records of Jack Ltd?*

Providing the assets and liabilities meet the definitions in the *Conceptual Framework*, there are no other recognition criteria. The identifiable assets acquired and liabilities assumed are measured at fair value.

The in-process research in Jill Ltd meets the definition of an asset. It is internally generated by Jill Ltd but is an acquired intangible for Jack Ltd. It will be recognised as an asset by Jack Ltd at its fair value of $2000. The contingent liability in Jill Ltd also meets the definition of a liability. Its measurement in a business combination is at fair value according to AASB 3/ IFRS 3. Therefore, Jack Ltd will recognise it as a provision for guarantee for $1500.

Note that any goodwill recorded by Jill Ltd is not an identifiable asset recognised by Jack Ltd. Goodwill recognised by Jack Ltd is measured as a residual and not by independent valuation. The identifiable assets and liabilities acquired are then as follows.

Cash	$ 1 000
Accounts receivable	17 500
Inventories	32 000
Property, plant and equipment	165 500
Financial assets	19 000
In-process research	2 000
	237 000
Provision for guarantee	1 500
Loan payable	40 000
Accounts payable	76 000
	$117 500

Net fair value of identifiable assets acquired and liabilities assumed = $119 500

(b) *What is the consideration transferred?*

The consideration transferred consists of the sum of the fair values of the assets given up, the liabilities assumed and equity instruments issued by the acquirer. In this example, the acquirer gives up an asset — cash — and issues equity instruments, namely shares in Jack Ltd.

The consideration transferred consists of the following.

Shares:	Number of shares issued by Jill Ltd	80 000	
	Shares issued by Jack Ltd: $\frac{3}{4} \times 80\,000$	60 000	
	Fair value of shares issued by Jack Ltd: 60 000 × $1.80		$108 000
Cash:	For shareholders: 80 000/4 × $1.00	$20 000	
	For liquidation costs of Jill Ltd	6 000	26 000
Consideration transferred			$134 000

Step 4. What is the goodwill acquired or gain on bargain purchase?

In this example, the consideration transferred is greater than the net fair value of the identifiable assets acquired and liabilities assumed, so goodwill is recognised.

$$\text{Goodwill} = \$134\,000 - \$119\,500 = \$14\,500$$

Journal entries in Jack Ltd at 1 January 2022.

Cash	Dr	1 000	
Accounts receivable	Dr	17 500	
Inventories	Dr	32 000	
Property, plant and equipment	Dr	165 500	
Financial assets	Dr	19 000	
In-process research	Dr	2 000	
Goodwill	Dr	14 500	
Accounts payable	Cr		76 000
Loan payable	Cr		40 000
Provision for guarantee	Cr		1 500
Share capital	Cr		108 000
Payable to Jill Ltd	Cr		26 000
(Acquisition of assets and liabilities of Jill Ltd)			
Payable to Jill Ltd	Dr	26 000	
Cash	Cr		26 000
(Payment of consideration transferred)			
Acquisition-related expenses	Dr	3 000	
Cash	Cr		3 000
(Expenses incurred in relation to acquisition of Jill Ltd)			

COMPREHENSION QUESTIONS

1 What is meant by a 'business combination'?

2 Discuss the importance of identifying the acquisition date.

3 What is meant by 'contingent consideration' and how is it accounted for?

4 Explain the key components of 'core' goodwill.

5 What recognition criteria are applied to assets and liabilities acquired in a business combination?

6 How is an acquirer identified?

7 Explain the key steps in the acquisition method.

8 How is the consideration transferred calculated?

9 How is a gain on bargain purchase accounted for?

10 Why is it important to identify an acquirer in a business combination?

CASE STUDY 25.1

APPLYING AASB 3/IFRS 3

Water Ltd has recently undertaken a business combination with Lily Ltd. At the start of negotiations, Water Ltd owned 30% of the shares of Lily Ltd. The current discussions between the two entities concerned Water Ltd's acquisition of the remaining 70% of shares of Lily Ltd. The negotiations began on 1 January 2022 and enough shareholders in Lily Ltd agreed to the deal by 30 September 2022. The purchase agreement was for shareholders in Lily Ltd to receive in exchange shares in Water Ltd. Over the negotiation period, the share price of Water Ltd shares reached a low of $5.40 and a high of $6.20.

The accountant for Water Ltd, Mr Spencer, knows that AASB 3/IFRS 3 has to be applied in accounting for business combinations. However, he is confused as to how to account for the original 30% investment in Lily Ltd, what share price to use to account for the issue of Water Ltd's shares, and how the varying dates such as the date of exchange and acquisition date will affect the accounting for the business combination.

Required

Provide Mr Spencer with advice on the issues that are confusing him.

CASE STUDY 25.2

ACCOUNTING FOR GOODWILL

Silver Ltd has acquired a major manufacturing division from Lining Ltd. The accountant, Mr Wilson, has shown the board of directors of Silver Ltd the financial information regarding the acquisition. Mr Wilson calculated a residual amount of $45 000 to be reported as goodwill in the accounts. The directors are not sure whether they want to record goodwill on Silver Ltd's statement of financial position. Some directors are not sure what goodwill is or why the company has bought it. Other directors even query whether goodwill is an asset, with some being concerned with future effects on the statement of profit or loss and other comprehensive income.

Required

Prepare a report for Mr Wilson to present to the directors to help them understand the nature of goodwill and how to account for it.

CASE STUDY 25.3

IDENTIFYING THE ACQUIRER

White Ltd has been negotiating with Cloud Ltd for several months, and agreements have finally been reached for the two companies to combine. In considering the accounting for the combined entities, management realises that, in applying AASB 3/IFRS 3, an acquirer must be identified. However, there is debate among the accounting staff as to which entity is the acquirer.

Required

1. What factors/indicators should management consider in determining which entity is the acquirer?

2. Why is it necessary to identify an acquirer? In particular, what differences in accounting would arise if White Ltd or Cloud Ltd were identified as the acquirer?

CASE STUDY 25.4

ACCOUNTING FOR RESEARCH

Terry Ltd has acquired all the net assets of Graham Ltd with the latter going into liquidation. Both companies operate in the area of testing and manufacturing pharmaceutical products. One of the main reasons that Terry Ltd sought to acquire Graham Ltd was that the latter company had an impressive record in the development of drugs for the cure of some mosquito-related diseases. Graham Ltd employed a number of scientists who were considered to be international experts in their area and at the leading edge of research in their field. Much of the recent work undertaken by these scientists was classified for accounting purposes as research, and as per AASB 138/IAS 38 *Intangible Assets* was expensed by Graham Ltd. However, in deciding what it would pay to take over Graham Ltd, Terry Ltd had paid a sizeable amount of money for the ongoing research being undertaken by Graham Ltd as it was expected that it would be successful eventually.

The accountant for Terry Ltd, Ms Tully, has suggested that the amount paid by Terry Ltd for this research should be shown as goodwill in the company's statement of financial position. However, the directors of the company do not believe that this faithfully represents the true nature of the assets acquired in the business combination, and want to recognise this as an asset separately from goodwill. Ms Tully believes that this will not be in accordance with AASB 138/IAS 38.

Required

Provide the directors with advice on the accounting for the aforementioned transaction.

CASE STUDY 25.5

ACCOUNTING FOR ACQUISITION-RELATED COSTS

One of the responsibilities of the group accountant for Southland Ltd, Mr Henry, is to explain to the company's board of directors the accounting principles applied by the company in preparing the annual report. Having analysed AASB 3/IFRS 3, Mr Henry is puzzled by the requirement in paragraph 53 that any acquisition-related costs such as fees for lawyers and valuers should be expensed. Mr Henry has analysed other accounting standards such as AASB 116/IAS 16 *Property, Plant and Equipment* and notes that under this standard such costs are capitalised into the cost of any property, plant and equipment acquired. She therefore believes that to expense such costs in accounting for a business combination would not be consistent with accounting for acquisitions of other assets.

Further, Mr Henry believes that to expense such costs would result in a loss being reported in the statement of profit or loss and other comprehensive income in the period the business combination occurs. She is not sure how she will explain to the board of directors that the company makes a loss every time it enters a business combination. She believes the directors will wonder why the company enters into business combinations if immediate losses occur — surely losses indicate that bad decisions have been made by the company.

Required

Prepare a report for Mr Henry on how she should explain the accounting for acquisition-related costs to the board of directors.

APPLICATION AND ANALYSIS EXERCISES

★ BASIC | ★ ★ MODERATE | ★ ★ ★ DIFFICULT

25.1 Accounting by an acquirer ★

LO6

On 1 July 2023, Sonic Ltd acquired the following assets and liabilities from Screwdriver Ltd.

	Carrying amount	Fair value
Land	$ 600 000	$ 700 000
Plant (cost $800 000)	560 000	580 000
Inventories	160 000	170 000
Cash	30 000	30 000
Accounts payable	(40 000)	(40 000)
Loans	(160 000)	(160 000)

In exchange for these assets and liabilities, Sonic Ltd issued 200 000 shares that had been issued for $2.20 per share but at 1 July 2023 had a fair value of $4.50 per share.

Required

1. Prepare the journal entries in the records of Sonic Ltd to account for the acquisition of the assets and liabilities of Screwdriver Ltd.
2. Prepare the journal entries assuming that the fair value of Sonic Ltd shares was $4 per share.

25.2 Accounting by an acquirer ★ **LO6**

Tony Ltd acquired all the assets and liabilities of Jennings Ltd on 1 July 2024. At this date, the assets and liabilities of Jennings Ltd consisted of the following.

	Carrying amount	Fair value
Current assets	$1 000 000	$ 980 000
Non-current assets	4 000 000	4 220 000
	5 000 000	5 200 000
Liabilities	500 000	500 000
	$4 500 000	$4 700 000
Share capital — 100 000 shares	$3 000 000	
Reserves	1 500 000	
	$4 500 000	

In exchange for these net assets, Tony Ltd agreed to:
- issue 10 Tony Ltd shares for every Jennings Ltd share — Tony Ltd shares were considered to have a fair value of $10 per share; costs of share issue were $500
- transfer a patent to the former shareholders of Jennings Ltd — the patent was carried in the records of Tony Ltd at $350 000 but was considered to have a fair value of $1 million
- pay $5.20 per share in cash to each of the former shareholders of Jennings Ltd.
  Tony Ltd incurred $10 000 in costs associated with the acquisition of these net assets.

Required

1. Prepare an acquisition analysis in relation to this acquisition.
2. Prepare the journal entries in Tony Ltd to record the acquisition at 1 July 2024.

25.3 Accounting by an acquirer ★ ★ **LO6**

David Ltd, a supplier of snooker equipment, agreed to acquire the business of a rival company, Tennant Ltd, taking over all assets and liabilities as at 1 June 2023.

The price agreed on was $60 000, payable $20 000 in cash and the balance by the issue to the selling company of 16 000 fully paid shares in David Ltd, these shares having a fair value of $2.50 per share.

The trial balances of the two companies as at 1 June 2023 were as follows.

	David Ltd		Tennant Ltd	
	Dr	Cr	Dr	Cr
Share capital		$100 000		$ 90 000
Retained earnings		12 000	$ 24 000	
Accounts payable		2 000		20 000
Cash	$ 30 000		—	
Plant (net)	50 000		30 000	
Inventories	14 000		26 000	
Accounts receivable	8 000		20 000	
Government bonds	12 000		—	
Goodwill	—		10 000	—
	$114 000	$114 000	$110 000	$110 000

All the identifiable net assets of Tennant Ltd were recorded by Tennant Ltd at fair value except for the inventories, which were considered to be worth $28 000 (assume no tax effect). The plant had an expected remaining life of 5 years.

The business combination was completed and Tennant Ltd went into liquidation. David Ltd incurred incidental costs of $500 in relation to the acquisition. Costs of issuing shares in David Ltd were $400.

Required

1. Prepare the journal entries in the records of David Ltd to record the business combination.
2. Show the statement of financial position of David Ltd after completion of the business combination.

25.4 Consideration transferred ★ ★

On 1 September 2022, the directors of Toby Ltd approached the directors of Bailey Ltd with the following proposal for the acquisition of the issued shares of Bailey Ltd, conditional on acceptance by 90% of the shareholders of Bailey Ltd by 30 November 2022.

- Two fully paid ordinary shares in Toby Ltd plus $6.20 cash for every preference share in Bailey Ltd, payable at acquisition date.
- Three fully paid ordinary shares in Toby Ltd plus $2.40 cash for every ordinary share in Bailey Ltd. Half the cash is payable at acquisition, and the other half in 1 year's time.

By 30 November, 90% of the ordinary shareholders and all of the preference shareholders of Bailey Ltd had accepted the offer. The directors of Toby Ltd decided *not* to acquire the remaining ordinary shares. Share transfer forms covering the transfer were dated 30 November 2022, and showed a price per Toby Ltd ordinary share of $8.40. Toby Ltd's incremental borrowing rate is 8% p.a.

Toby Ltd then appointed a new board of directors of Bailey Ltd. This board took office on 1 December 2022 and immediately:

- revalued the asset Shares in Other Companies to its market value (assume no tax effect)
- used the surplus so created to make a bonus issue of $64 000 to ordinary shareholders, each shareholder being allocated two ordinary shares for every ten ordinary shares held.

The statement of financial position of Bailey Ltd at 30 November 2022 was as follows.

BAILEY LTD Statement of financial position as at 30 November 2022		
Current assets		$ 240 000
Non-current assets		
Land and buildings	$406 000	
Plant and equipment	336 000	
Less: Accumulated depreciation	(90 000)	
Shares in other companies listed on stock exchange at cost (market $380 000)	60 000	
Government bonds, at cost	100 000	
Total non-current assets		812 000
Total assets		1 052 000
Current liabilities		60 000
Net assets		**$ 992 000**
Equity		
Share capital		
160 000 ordinary shares fully paid	$320 000	
100 000 6% preference shares fully paid	200 000	$ 520 000
Retained earnings		472 000
Total equity		**$ 992 000**

Required

Prepare all journal entries (in general form) to record the above transactions in the records of (a) Toby Ltd and (b) Bailey Ltd.

25.5 Accounting by an acquirer ★ ★

Penny Ltd is seeking to expand its share of the widgets market and has negotiated to take over the operations of Robinson Ltd on 1 January 2024. The statements of financial position of the two companies as at 31 December 2023 were as follows.

	Penny Ltd	Robinson Ltd
Cash	$ 23 000	$ 12 000
Accounts receivable	25 000	34 700
Inventories	35 500	27 600
Freehold land	150 000	100 000
Buildings (net)	60 000	30 000
Plant and equipment (net)	65 000	46 000
Goodwill	25 000	2 000
	$383 500	$252 300

Accounts payable	$ 56 000	$ 45 100
Mortgage loan	50 000	44 000
Debentures	100 000	52 500
Share capital — 100 000 shares	100 000	—
— 60 000 shares	—	60 000
Other reserves	28 500	26 800
Retained earnings	49 000	23 900
	$383 500	$252 300

Penny Ltd is to acquire all the identifiable assets, except cash, of Robinson Ltd. The assets of Robinson Ltd are all recorded at fair value except the following.

	Fair value
Inventories	$ 39 000
Freehold land	130 000
Buildings	40 000

In exchange, Penny Ltd is to provide sufficient extra cash to allow Robinson Ltd to repay all of its outstanding debts and its liquidation costs of $2400, plus two fully paid shares in Penny Ltd for every three shares held in Robinson Ltd. The fair value of a share in Penny Ltd is $3.20.

Costs of issuing the shares were $1200.

Required

Prepare the acquisition analysis and journal entries to record the business combination in the records of Penny Ltd.

25.6 Accounting for business combination by acquirer ★ ★   **LO6**

Police Ltd and Box Ltd are small family-owned companies engaged in vegetable growing and distribution. The Jones family owns the shares in Box Ltd and the Tyler family owns the shares in Police Ltd. The head of the Jones family wishes to retire but his two sons are not interested in carrying on the family business. Accordingly, on 1 July 2024, Police Ltd is to take over the operations of Box Ltd, which will then liquidate. Police Ltd is asset-rich but has limited overdraft facilities so the following arrangement has been made.

Police Ltd is to acquire all of the assets, except cash, delivery trucks and motor vehicles, of Box Ltd and will assume all of the liabilities except accounts payable. In return, Police Ltd is to give the shareholders of Box Ltd a block of vacant land, two delivery vehicles and sufficient additional cash to enable the company to pay off the accounts payable and the liquidation costs of $1500. On the liquidation of Box Ltd, Mr Jones is to receive the land and the motor vehicles and his two sons are to receive the delivery trucks. The land and vehicles had the following market values at 30 June 2024.

	Carrying amount	Fair value
Freehold land	$50 000	$120 000
Delivery trucks	30 000	28 000

The statements of financial position of the two companies as at 30 June 2021 were as follows.

	Police Ltd	Box Ltd
Cash	$ 3 500	$ 2 000
Accounts receivable	25 000	15 000
Freehold land	250 000	100 000
Buildings (net)	25 000	30 000
Cultivation equipment (net)	65 000	46 000
Irrigation equipment	16 000	22 000
Delivery trucks	45 000	36 000
Motor vehicles	25 000	32 000
	$454 500	$283 000

	Police Ltd	Box Ltd
Accounts payable	$ 26 000	$ 23 500
Loan — Bank of Gallifrey	150 000	80 000
Loan — Williams Bros	35 000	35 000
Loan — Smith Corp.	70 000	52 500
Share capital — 100 000 shares	100 000	0
— 60 000 shares	0	60 000
Reserves	28 500	0
Retained earnings	45 000	32 000
	$454 500	$283 000

All the assets of Box Ltd are recorded at fair value, with the exception of the following.

	Fair value
Freehold land	$120 000
Buildings	40 000
Cultivation equipment	40 000
Motor vehicle	34 000

Required

1. Prepare the acquisition analysis and the journal entries to record the acquisition of Box Ltd's operations in the records of Police Ltd.
2. Prepare the statement of financial position of Police Ltd after the business combination.

25.7 Accounting for business combination by acquirer ★ ★ ★ LO6

Yarra Ltd and River Ltd are two family-owned flax-producing companies in Victoria. Yarra Ltd is owned by the Jones family and the Smith family owns River Ltd. The Jones family has only one son and he is engaged to be married to the daughter of the Smith family. Because the son is currently managing Yarra Ltd, it is proposed that, after the wedding, he should manage both companies. As a result, it is agreed by the two families that Yarra Ltd should take over the net assets of River Ltd.

The statement of financial position of River Ltd immediately before the takeover is as follows.

	Carrying amount	Fair value
Cash	$ 10 000	$ 10 000
Accounts receivable	70 000	62 500
Land	310 000	420 000
Buildings (net)	265 000	275 000
Farm equipment (net)	180 000	182 000
Irrigation equipment (net)	110 000	112 500
Vehicles (net)	80 000	86 000
	$1 025 000	
Accounts payable	$ 40 000	40 000
Loan — Trevally Bank	240 000	240 000
Share capital	335 000	
Retained earnings	410 000	
	$1 025 000	

The takeover agreement specified the following details.

- Yarra Ltd is to acquire all the assets of River Ltd except for cash, and one of the vehicles (having a carrying amount of $22 500 and a fair value of $24 000), and assume all the liabilities except for the loan from the Trevally Bank. River Ltd is then to go into liquidation. The vehicle is to be transferred to Mr and Mrs Smith.
- Yarra Ltd is to supply sufficient cash to enable the debt to the Trevally Bank to be paid off and to cover the liquidation costs of $2750. It will also give $75 000 to be distributed to Mr and Mrs Smith to help pay the costs of the wedding.
- Yarra Ltd is also to give a piece of its own prime land to River Ltd to be distributed to Mr and Mrs Smith, this eventually being available to be given to any offspring of the forthcoming marriage. The piece of land in question has a carrying amount of $40 000 and a fair value of $110 000.
- Yarra Ltd is to issue 50 000 shares, these having a fair value of $14 per share, to be distributed via River Ltd to the soon to-be-married-daughter of Mr and Mrs Smith, who is currently a shareholder in River Ltd.

The takeover proceeded as per the agreement, with Yarra Ltd incurring incidental costs of $12 500 and share issue costs of $9000.

Required

Prepare the acquisition analysis and the journal entries to record the acquisition of River Ltd in the records of Yarra Ltd.

25.8 Acquisition analysis ★ ★ ★ LO6

On 1 July 2024, Donna Ltd and Noble Ltd sign an agreement whereby the operations of Noble Ltd are to be taken over by Donna Ltd. Noble Ltd will liquidate after the transfer is complete. The statements of financial position of the two companies on that day were as follows.

	Donna Ltd	Noble Ltd
Cash	$ 50 000	$ 20 000
Accounts receivable	75 000	56 000
Inventories	46 000	29 000
Land	65 000	0
Plant and equipment	180 000	167 000
Accumulated depreciation — plant and equipment	(60 000)	(40 000)
Patents	10 000	0
Shares in London Ltd	0	26 000
Debentures in Jack Ltd (nominal value)	10 000	0
	$376 000	$258 000
Accounts payable	$ 62 000	$ 31 000
Mortgage loan	75 000	21 500
10% debentures (face value)	100 000	30 000
Contributed equity:		
Ordinary shares of $1, fully paid	100 000	0
A class shares of $2, fully paid	0	40 000
B class shares of $1, fully paid		60 000
Retained earnings	39 000	75 500
	$376 000	$258 000

Donna Ltd is to acquire all the assets of Noble Ltd (except for cash). The assets of Noble Ltd are recorded at their fair values except for the following.

	Carrying amount	Fair value
Inventories	$ 29 000	$ 39 200
Plant and equipment	127 000	140 000
Shares in London Ltd	26 000	22 500

In exchange, the A class shareholders of Noble Ltd are to receive one 7% debenture in Donna Ltd, redeemable on 1 July 2025, for every share held in Noble Ltd. The fair value of each debenture is $3.50. Donna Ltd will also provide one of its patents to be held jointly by the A class shareholders of Noble Ltd and for which they will receive future royalties. The patent is carried at $4000 in the records of Donna Ltd, but is considered to have a fair value of $5000.

The B class shareholders of Noble Ltd are to receive two shares in Donna Ltd for every three shares held in Noble Ltd. The fair value of each Donna Ltd share is $2.70. Costs to issue these shares amount to $900. Additionally, Donna Ltd is to provide Noble Ltd with sufficient cash, additional to that already held, to enable Noble Ltd to pay its liabilities. The outstanding debentures are to be redeemed at a 10% premium. Annual leave entitlements of $16 200 outstanding at 1 July 2024 and expected liquidation costs of $5000 have not been recognised by Noble Ltd. Costs incurred in arranging the business combination amounted to $1600.

Required

Prepare the journal entries in the records of Donna Ltd to record the acquisition of Noble Ltd.

25.9 Accounting for a business combination by the acquirer ★ ★ ★ LO6

Cyborg Ltd was having difficulty in raising finance for expansion while Dalek Ltd was interested in achieving economies by marketing a wider range of products. They entered discussions on how they could mutually achieve added benefits to both companies. They prepared the following financial positions of the companies at 30 June 2023.

	Cyborg Ltd	Dalek Ltd
Share capital		
160 000 shares	$ 160 000	
360 000 shares		$360 000
Retained earnings	48 000	120 000
	208 000	480 000
Liabilities		
Debentures (secured by floating charge)	80 000	—
Accounts payable	168 000	48 000
	248 000	48 000
Total equity and liabilities	$ 456 000	$528 000
Assets		
Cash	$ 48 000	$ 96 000
Accounts receivable	72 000	80 000
Inventories (at cost)	172 000	188 000
Land and buildings (at cost)	92 000	76 000
Plant and machinery (at cost)	208 000	164 000
Accumulated depreciation on plant and machinery	(136 000)	(76 000)
Total assets	$ 456 000	$528 000

It was agreed that it would be mutually advantageous for Cyborg Ltd to specialise in manufacturing, and for marketing, purchasing and promotion to be handled by Dalek Ltd. Accordingly, Dalek Ltd sold *part* of its assets to Cyborg Ltd on 1 July 2023, the identifiable assets acquired having the following fair values.

Inventories	$88 000 (cost $60 000)
Land and buildings	$136 000 (carrying amount $40 000)
Plant and machinery	$108 000 (cost $152 000, accumulated depreciation $72 000)

The acquisition was satisfied by the issue of 160 000 'A' ordinary shares (fully paid) in Cyborg Ltd.

Required

1. Assuming the assets acquired constitute a business, show the journal entries to record the above transactions in the records of Cyborg Ltd:
   (a) if the fair value of the 'A' ordinary shares of Cyborg Ltd was $2 per share
   (b) if the fair value of the 'A' ordinary shares of Cyborg Ltd was $2.20 per share.
2. Show the statement of financial position of Cyborg Ltd after the transactions, assuming the fair value of Cyborg's Ltd's 'A' ordinary shares was $2.20 per share.

25.10 Accounting for acquisitions of a business and shares in another entity ★ ★ ★   **LO6**
Blink Ltd is seeking to expand its share of the men's products market and has negotiated to acquire the operations of Weeping Ltd and the shares of Angel Ltd.

At 1 July 2023, the trial balances of the three companies were as follows.

	Blink Ltd	Weeping Ltd	Angel Ltd
Cash	$145 000	$ 5 200	$ 84 000
Accounts receivable	34 000	21 300	12 000
Inventories	56 000	30 000	25 400
Shares in listed companies	16 000	22 000	7 000
Land and buildings (net)	70 000	40 000	36 000
Plant and equipment (net)	130 000	105 000	25 000
Goodwill (net)	6 000	5 000	5 600
	$457 000	$228 500	$195 000
Accounts payable	$ 65 000	$ 40 000	$ 29 000
Bank overdraft	0	0	1 500
Debentures	50 000	0	100 000
Mortgage loan	100 000	30 000	0
Contributed equity			
Ordinary shares of $1, fully paid	200 000	150 000	60 000
Other reserves	15 000	6 500	2 500
Retained earnings (30/6/23)	27 000	2 000	2 000
	$457 000	$228 500	$195 000

Weeping Ltd

Blink Ltd is to acquire all assets (except cash and shares in listed companies) of Weeping Ltd. Acquisition related costs are expected to be $7600. The net assets of Weeping Ltd are recorded at fair value except for the following.

	Carrying amount	Fair value
Inventories	$ 30 000	$ 26 000
Land and buildings	40 000	80 000
Shares in listed companies	22 000	18 000
Accounts payable	(40 000)	(49 100)
Accrued leave	0	(29 700)

In exchange, the shareholders of Weeping Ltd are to receive, for every three Weeping Ltd shares held, one Blink Ltd share worth $2.50 each. Costs to issue these shares are $950. Additionally, Blink Ltd will transfer to Weeping Ltd its 'shares in listed companies' asset, which has a fair value of $15 000. These shares, together with those already owned by Weeping Ltd will be sold and the proceeds distributed to the Weeping Ltd shareholders. Assume that the shares were sold for their fair values.

Blink Ltd will also give Weeping Ltd sufficient additional cash to enable Weeping Ltd to pay all its creditors. Weeping Ltd will then liquidate. Liquidation costs are estimated to be $8700.

Angel Ltd

Blink Ltd is to acquire all the issued shares of Angel Ltd. In exchange, the shareholders of Angel Ltd are to receive:

- one Blink Ltd share, worth $2.50
- $1.50 cash for every two Angel Ltd shares held.

Required

1. Prepare the acquisition analysis and journal entries to record the acquisitions in the records of Blink Ltd.
2. Explain in detail why, if Weeping Ltd has recorded a goodwill asset of $5000, Blink Ltd calculates the goodwill acquired via an acquisition analysis. Why does Blink Ltd not determine a fair value for the goodwill asset and record that figure as it has done for other assets acquired from Weeping Ltd?
3. Shortly after the business combination, the liquidator of Weeping Ltd receives a valid claim of $25 000 from a creditor. As Blink Ltd has agreed to provide sufficient cash to pay all the liabilities of Weeping Ltd at acquisition date, the liquidator requests and receives a cheque for $25 000 from Blink Ltd. How should Blink Ltd record this payment? Why?

25.11 Acquisition of two businesses ★ ★ ★ **LO6**

Amy Ltd is a manufacturer of specialised industrial equipment seeking to diversify its operations. After protracted negotiations, the directors decided to purchase the assets and liabilities of Pond Ltd and the spare parts retail division of Rory Ltd.

At 30 June 2024 the statements of financial position of the three entities were as follows.

	Amy Ltd	Pond Ltd	Rory Ltd
Land and buildings (net)	$ 60 000	$ 25 000	$ 40 000
Plant and equipment (net)	100 000	36 000	76 000
Office equipment (net)	16 000	4 000	6 000
Shares in listed companies	24 000	15 000	20 800
Debentures in listed companies	20 000	0	0
Accounts receivable	35 000	26 000	42 000
Inventories	150 000	54 000	30 200
Cash	59 000	11 000	9 000
Goodwill	0	7 000	0
	$464 000	$178 000	$224 000
Accounts payable	$ 26 000	$ 14 000	$ 27 000
Current tax liability	21 000	6 000	7 000
Provision for leave	36 000	10 000	17 500
Bank loan	83 000	16 000	43 500

	Amy Ltd	Pond Ltd	Rory Ltd
Debentures	60 000	50 000	0
Share capital (issued at $1, fully paid)	200 000	60 000	90 000
Retained earnings	38 000	22 000	39 000
	$464 000	$178 000	$224 000

The acquisition agreement details are as follows.

Pond Ltd

Amy Ltd is to acquire all the identifiable assets (other than cash) and liabilities (other than debentures, provisions and tax liabilities) of Pond Ltd for the following purchase consideration.

- Shareholders in Pond Ltd are to receive three shares in Amy Ltd, credited as fully paid, in exchange for every four shares held. The shares in Amy Ltd are to be issued at their fair value of $3 per share. Costs of share issue amounted to $2000.
- Amy Ltd is to provide sufficient cash which, when added to the cash already held, will enable Pond Ltd to pay out the current tax liability and provision for leave, to redeem the debentures at a premium of 5%, and to pay its liquidation expenses of $2500.

The fair values of the assets and liabilities of Pond Ltd are equal to their carrying amounts with the exception of the following.

	Fair value
Land and buildings	$60 000
Plant and equipment	50 000

Incidental costs associated with the acquisition amount to $2500.

Rory Ltd

Amy Ltd is to acquire the spare parts retail business of Rory Ltd. The following information isavailable concerning that business, relative to the whole of Rory Ltd.

	Total amount	Spare parts division	
	Carrying amount	Carrying amount	Fair value
Land and buildings (net)	$40 000	$20 000	$30 000
Plant and equipment (net)	76 000	32 000	34 500
Office equipment (net)	6 000	2 000	2 500
Accounts receivable	42 000	21 000	20 000
Inventories	30 200	12 000	12 000
Accounts payable	27 000	14 000	14 000
Provision for leave	17 500	7 000	7 000

The divisional net assets are to be acquired for $10 000 cash, plus 11 000 ordinary shares in Amy Ltd issued at their fair value of $3, plus the land and buildings that have been purchased from Pond Ltd.

Incidental costs associated with the acquisition are $1000.

Required

1. Prepare the acquisition analysis for the acquisition transactions of Amy Ltd.
2. Prepare the journal entries for the acquisition transactions in the records of Amy Ltd.

25.12 Accounting by acquirer, liquidation journal entries by acquiree ★ ★ ★   **LO6, 7**

The financial statements of Sicily Ltd at 1 August 2022 contained the following information.

Assets		Equity	
Vehicles	$ 90 000	Share capital: 150 000 shares	$144 000
Accumulated depreciation	(13 200)	Retained earnings	76 800
Delivery trucks	105 000	Total equity	220 800
Accumulated depreciation	(18 600)	Liabilities	
Machinery	59 400	Loans	192 000
Accumulated depreciation	(9 000)	Provisions	84 000
Buildings	144 000	Payables	126 000
Accumulated depreciation	(12 000)	Accounts payable	56 400
Land	240 000	Total liabilities	458 400

Cash	6 000	
Accounts receivable	36 000	
Inventories	51 600	
Total assets	**$679 200**	**Total equity and liabilities** $679 200

Sicily Ltd is involved in the manufacture of fine Italian leather handbags. The company was established by the de Niro brothers over 100 years ago. The family became very wealthy as their handbags were prized by the fashion conscious in the community. However, the current manager, Roberto de Niro, wishes to retire and offers to sell the business to his main rival, Al Ltd, which is headed up by the manager and owner, Vito Corleone.

Vito and Roberto come to an agreement by which Al Ltd will take over Sicily Ltd. Al Ltd will acquire all the assets of Sicily Ltd except for the cash and the motor vehicles. In exchange, Al Ltd will give the shareholders of Sicily Ltd a block of land valued at $288 000 and a motor vehicle valued at $61 200. These assets are currently held by Al Ltd. The land is carried at cost of $120 000 while the motor vehicle is carried at $60 000, being cost of $63 000 and accumulated depreciation of $3000. Al Ltd will also provide sufficient additional cash to enable Sicily Ltd to pay off the accounts payable and the liquidation expenses of $3600. On liquidation of Sicily Ltd, the land and the motor vehicles will be distributed to members of the de Niro family.

Al Ltd incurred legal and valuation costs of $6000 in undertaking the business combination.

The assets and liabilities of Sicily Ltd are recorded at amounts equal to fair value except for the following.

	Fair value
Land	$300 000
Buildings	168 000
Machinery	60 000
Delivery trucks	90 000
Inventories	60 000

Al Ltd also recognised the brand 'Sicily' that was not recognised in the records of Sicily Ltd as it was an internally developed brand. It was calculated that this brand had a fair value of $78 000.

Required

Prepare the journal entries in Al Ltd to record the acquisition of the assets and liabilities of Sicily Ltd.

25.13 Accounting by the acquirer, liquidation of the acquiree ★ ★ ★   **LO6, 7**

Rove Ltd is a manufacturer of frozen foods in Fitzroy. The company's products include many forms of vegetables and meats but one item lacking in its product range is frozen fish. The board of Rove Ltd decided to investigate a takeover of a Tasmanian company, McManus Ltd, whose prime product was the packaging of frozen Huon salmon. The reason this company was of particular interest was that Rove Ltd already owned a number of factories in Hobart some of which were underutilised. If McManus were acquired, then Rove Ltd would liquidate the company and transfer all the processing work to its other Hobart factories.

The financial statements of McManus Ltd at 1 December 2022 showed the following information.

Plant	$133 600
Accumulated depreciation — plant	(32 000)
Land	20 800
Cash	16 000
Accounts receivable	44 800
Inventories	23 200
Total assets	**206 400**
Accounts payable	24 800
Provisions	24 000
Loans	17 200
Total liabilities	**66 000**
Share capital — 60 000 A ordinary shares	48 000
— 40 000 B ordinary shares	32 000
Retained earnings	60 400
Total equity	**$140 400**

All the assets and liabilities of McManus Ltd were recorded at amounts equal to fair value except as follows.

	Fair value
Plant	$112 000
Land	35 800
Inventories	28 000

McManus Ltd also had a brand 'Comec' that was not recorded by the company because it had been internally generated. It was valued at $10 000. McManus Ltd had not recorded the interest accrued on the loans amounting to $22 800 or annual leave entitlements of $13 000.

Rove Ltd decided to acquire all the assets of McManus Ltd except for the cash. In exchange for these assets, Rove Ltd agreed to provide:

- two shares in Rove Ltd for every three A ordinary shares held in McManus Ltd. The fair value of each Rove Ltd share was agreed to be $2.16.
- artworks to the owners of the B ordinary shares held in McManus Ltd. (These artworks were held in the records of Rove Ltd at $40 000 and valued at $58 000.)
- sufficient additional cash to enable McManus Ltd to pay off its liabilities including the expected liquidation costs of $4000.

The business combination occurred on 1 December 2022. Legal and accounting costs incurred by Rove Ltd in undertaking this business combination amounted to $1300. Costs to issue the shares to the A ordinary shareholders of McManus Ltd were $700.

Required

Prepare the journal entries in the records of Rove Ltd at 1 December 2022 to record the business combination.

REFERENCES

Arq Group Limited 2018, *Annual report 2018*, https://arq.group
Johnson, LT & Petrone, KR 1998, 'Is goodwill an asset?', *Accounting Horizons*, vol. 12, no. 3, pp. 293–303.

ACKNOWLEDGEMENTS

Photo: © fizkes / Shutterstock.com
Photo: © Sirinarth Mekvorawuth / Getty Images
Figure 25.1: © Arq Group Limited 2018

CHAPTER 26

Consolidation: controlled entities

CHAPTER AIM

When a group of entities combine their activities to become a single consolidated economic entity, they do not have to relinquish their legal status as individual entities. However, they do need to work together towards a common set of objectives that are normally imposed by the dominant entity in the group. This dominant entity is said to have control over the other entities and is recognised as being the parent entity; the other entities are called subsidiaries or controlled entities. This group of entities needs to disclose its financial position, financial performance and cash flows in a set of financial statements separate from the statements of the individual entities within the group. These statements are known as consolidated financial statements. This chapter focuses on discussing the general principles used in the preparation of consolidated financial statements, based on AASB 10/IFRS 10 *Consolidated Financial Statements* with additional reference to AASB 3/ IFRS 3 *Business Combinations*.

LEARNING OBJECTIVES

After studying this chapter, you should be able to:

26.1 explain the purpose of consolidated financial statements

26.2 discuss the meaning and application of the criterion of control

26.3 describe the consolidation process

26.4 explain the circumstances under which a parent entity may be exempt from preparing consolidated financial statements

26.5 discuss the disclosure requirements related to consolidated entities.

CONCEPTS FOR REVIEW

Before studying this chapter, you should understand and, if necessary, revise:

• the concept of 'control' in the definition of an asset in the *Conceptual Framework*
• the concept of a business combination.

26.1 Consolidated financial statements

LEARNING OBJECTIVE 26.1 Explain the purpose of consolidated financial statements.

The majority of entities listed on public stock exchanges such as the Australian Securities Exchange (ASX) are groups of entities that have combined their activities in pursuit of common objectives. For example, the ASX-listed Woolworths Group Limited consists of separate legal entities, each being separately incorporated in countries including the United States, New Zealand, India, Hong Kong, China, Singapore, Macau and Australia. Each of those entities that together form a group prepares its own financial statements, showing its financial position, financial performance and cash flows. However, preparation of an additional set of financial statements for the group — consolidated financial statements — is required to show the group's financial position, financial performance and cash flows as those of a single economic entity.

Consolidated financial statements are defined in Appendix A of AASB 10/IFRS 10 *Consolidated Financial Statements* as follows.

> The financial statements of a group in which the assets, liabilities, equity, income, expenses and cash flows of the parent and its subsidiaries are presented as those of a single economic entity.

As stated in paragraph B86 of AASB 10/IFRS 10, consolidated financial statements 'combine like items of assets, liabilities, equity, income, expenses and cash flows' of the entities in the group. The purpose of preparing consolidated financial statements is to show the combined financial position, financial performance and cash flows of the group of entities as if they were a single economic entity. As such, they consist of a consolidated statement of financial position, a consolidated statement of profit or loss and other comprehensive income, a consolidated statement of changes in equity and a consolidated statement of cash flows. These consolidated statements reflect only the effects of transactions with external parties to the group.

AASB 10/IFRS 10 governs the preparation of consolidated financial statements and contains the definitions of the main theoretical concepts used to identify a group of entities for which consolidated financial statements may need to be prepared. As such, Appendix A of AASB 10/IFRS 10 provides the following definitions.

Group A parent and its subsidiaries.
Parent An entity that controls one or more entities.
Subsidiary An entity that is controlled by another entity.

The parent–subsidiary relationship is a special case of an investor–investee relationship, where the investor (the parent) has control over the investee (the subsidiary). Note that in a group there can be only one parent. The control cannot be shared.

Consider figure 26.1. Assuming that Laura Ltd controls Toby Ltd, both entities form a group in which Laura Ltd is the parent entity and Toby Ltd is the subsidiary.

FIGURE 26.1	A simple group of entities

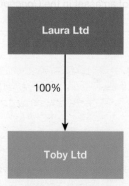

Note, however, that for a number of entities that are interconnected there may be a main group and, within it, a number of subgroups, each with its own unique parent. Consider figure 26.2. Assuming that George Ltd controls all the other entities in the figure, all the entities form a main group, where George Ltd is the parent entity and all the other entities are subsidiaries. If Fred Ltd controls Rick Ltd, together they form a subgroup, where Fred Ltd is the parent and Rick Ltd is the subsidiary. The existence of subgroups inside the main group does not mean that a group may have more than one parent. Fred Ltd is the parent entity only in the Fred Ltd–Rick Ltd subgroup and it is a subsidiary in George Ltd's main group.

FIGURE 26.2   A group of entities that contains a subgroup

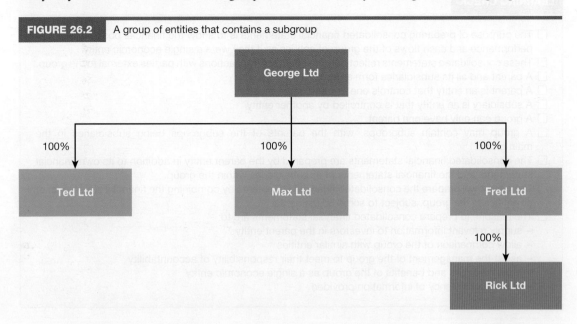

No matter how complex the structure of an actual group is, it is very important to identify the entity that is the parent of the group, as this entity is required to prepare consolidated financial statements in addition to its own financial statements and the financial statements of all subsidiaries within the group. The parent will prepare the consolidated financial statements by combining the financial statements of all entities in the group, subject to some adjustments.

Together with understanding what the consolidated financial statements are and who prepares them, it is important to understand the *reasons* that the regulators require the parent entity to prepare those statements. Some of those reasons are as follows.

1. *To supply relevant information to investors in the parent entity.* The information obtained from the consolidated financial statements is relevant to investors in the parent entity. A shareholder's wealth in the parent is dependent not only on how that entity performs, but also on the performance of the other entities controlled by the parent. To require these investors, in analysing their investment, to source their information from the financial statements of each of the entities comprising the group would place a large cost burden on those investors.

2. *To allow comparison of the group with similar entities.* Some entities are organised into a group structure such that different activities are undertaken by separate entities within the group. Other entities are organised differently, with some having all activities conducted within the one entity. Access to consolidated financial statements makes comparisons across these entities an easier task for the users of financial statements.

3. *To assist in the discharge of accountability by management of the group.* A key purpose of financial reporting is the discharge of accountability by management. The consolidated financial statements report the assets under the control of the group, together with the claims on those assets, as well as the performance obtained in the management of those assets. Based on the information contained within these statements, the management of the group can be held accountable for their actions.

4. *To report the risks and benefits of the group as a single economic entity.* There are risks associated with managing an entity, and an entity rarely obtains control of another without also obtaining significant opportunities to benefit from that control. The consolidated financial statements allow an assessment of these risks and benefits. Note, however, that the benefits from intragroup transactions are eliminated when preparing consolidated financial statements, as those statements should only reflect the effects of transactions with external parties.

5. *To ensure consistency of information provided to users.* The consolidated financial statements are prepared after adjusting the separate financial statements of the entities within the group for the

different accounting policies applied, making sure that all the items reported are combined after being recognised and measured consistently.

26.2 Control

LEARNING OBJECTIVE 26.2 Discuss the meaning and application of the criterion of control.

As seen in the definitions of *parent* and *subsidiary*, under AASB 10/IFRS 10, *control* is the criterion for the existence of a parent–subsidiary relationship between an investor and an investee. Determination of whether control exists is *a matter of judgement*. In many situations it will not be clear cut that one entity controls another, and a determination will have to be made by considering all available facts and circumstances (AASB 10/IFRS 10 paragraph 8). Hence, it is important to understand the meaning of the term 'control' and what evidence may be accumulated to determine whether control exists. As noted later in this section, AASB 10/IFRS 10 provides factors to be considered in determining whether control exists.

Control of an investee is defined in Appendix A of AASB 10/IFRS 10 as follows.

> An investor controls an investee when the investor is exposed, or has rights, to variable returns from its involvement with the investee and has the ability to affect those returns through its power over the investee.

Based on this definition, paragraph 7 of AASB 10/IFRS 10 identifies three elements that must be held by an investor in order for it to have control:

 (a) power over the investee . . .
 (b) exposure, or rights, to variable returns from its involvement with the investee . . .
 (c) the ability to use its power over the investee to affect the amount of the investor's returns.

The third element provides the link between the first two elements, as presented in figure 26.3. These three elements are discussed in detail in the following sections.

FIGURE 26.3	The concept of control according to AASB 10/IFRS 10

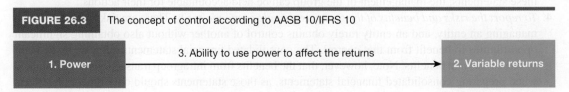

26.2.1 Power

Power is defined in Appendix A of AASB 10/IFRS 10 as follows:

> Existing rights that give the current ability to direct the relevant activities.

Based on this definition, four characteristics of power can be identified.

1. Power is related to relevant activities.
2. Power arises from existing rights.
3. Power is the ability to direct.
4. The ability to direct must be current to have power.

These characteristics are described in detail next.

Power is related to relevant activities

Relevant activities are defined in Appendix A of AASB 10/IFRS 10 as:

> ...activities of the investee that significantly affect the investee's returns.

Paragraph B11 of AASB 10/IFRS 10 provides examples of some possible relevant activities, including:
- selling and purchasing goods and services
- managing financial assets
- selecting, acquiring and disposing of assets
- researching and developing new products
- determining a funding structure or obtaining funding.

The determination of relevant activities may change over time and differ between entities based on the purpose and design of the investees; hence, it may be necessary to analyse the purpose and design of the investees in order to identify the relevant activities. That analysis will also allow the investors to properly identify how decisions about the relevant activities are made, so that they can determine whether they have the necessary rights to direct those activities. If some relevant activities are directed by an investor and some by others, each investor needs to determine whether it is able to direct the activities that most significantly affect the investee's returns.

Power arises from existing rights

Paragraph B15 of AASB 10/IFRS 10 provides examples of the rights that determine the existence of power, such as:
- voting rights
- rights to appoint, reassign or remove members of an investee's key management personnel
- rights to appoint or remove another entity that participates in management decisions
- rights to direct the investee to enter into, or veto any changes to, transactions that affect the investee's returns.

However, as those examples are not exhaustive, to assist in determining whether certain rights give rise to power, paragraph B18 of AASB 10/IFRS 10 suggests the consideration of evidence of whether:

(a) The investor can, without having the contractual right to do so, appoint or approve the investee's key management personnel who have the ability to direct the relevant activities.

(b) The investor can, without having the contractual right to do so, direct the investee to enter into, or can veto any changes to, significant transactions for the benefit of the investor.

(c) The investor can dominate either the nominations process for electing members of the investee's governing body or the obtaining of proxies from other holders of voting rights.

(d) The investee's key management personnel are related parties of the investor (for example, the chief executive officer of the investee and the chief executive officer of the investor are the same person).

(e) The majority of the members of the investee's governing body are related parties of the investor.

Voting rights

As paragraph B35 of AASB 10/IFRS 10 states, where an investor holds more than half of the voting rights of the investee, the investor has power provided that:

(a) the relevant activities are directed by a vote of the holder of the majority of voting shares, or

(b) a majority of the members of the governing body that directs the relevant activities are appointed by a vote of the holder of the majority of the voting rights.

In the absence of other evidence, if an investor holds a majority of voting rights, those two conditions are usually satisfied. Therefore, in those circumstances, it is assumed that the investor has the power over the investee. An exception exists in the case of the so-called structured entities defined in Appendix A of AASB 12/IFRS 12 *Disclosure of Interests in Other Entities*. A structured entity is an entity that has been designed so that voting or similar rights are not the dominant factor in deciding who controls the entity, such as when any voting rights relate to administrative tasks only and the relevant activities are directed by means of contractual arrangements.

Where an investor holds less than 50% of the voting shares of an investee, the determination of whether the investor has power over the investee is more difficult. In determining the existence of power, together with the size of the investor's voting interest, it is necessary to examine the potential actions of the holders of the other shares in the investee. Some factors to assist in this process are as follows.

- *Attendance at annual general meetings.* The probability of shareholders attending the general meeting and exercising their voting rights may be lessened by their level of their voting interest and geographical location.
- *Level of dilution and disorganisation or apathy of the remaining shareholders.* Holders of small parcels of shares are often not organised into voting blocks.
- *The existence of contracts.* As noted in paragraph B39 of AASB 10/IFRS 10, a contractual arrangement between an investor and other holders of shares may give the investor sufficient voting rights to have power.

A number of problems arise in assessing the existence of power based on the actions and characteristics of the remaining shareholders where the investor holds less than a majority of voting shares. First, there is the question of temporary control. If the identification of the parent is based on factors that may change over time, there is a danger of a change in the identity of the parent over time. For example, the percentage of votes cast at general meetings may historically be 70%, but in a particular year it may be 50%. A shareholder with 30% of the voting shares has control in the latter circumstance but not in the former. Similarly, consider the situation where there are two substantial block holdings of voting shares, meaning that neither has power over the investee. One of the holders of a substantial block of shares may then sell its shares to a large number of buyers. The other holder of a substantial block may suddenly find that it has the power to control, regardless of whether this investor wants to exercise control or not.

Second, the ability of an entity to control another entity may rely on the relationships with other entities. For example, a holder of 40% of the voting shares may be 'friendly' with the holder of another 11% of shares. The 11% shareholder might be a financial institution that has invested in the holder of the 40% interest and plans to vote with that entity to increase its potential for repayment of loans. However, business relationships and loyalties are not always permanent.

Different classes of shares may have different voting rights. However, unless otherwise specified in the company's constitution, each shareholder has one vote for each share held. Therefore, it is normally assumed that the percentage of ownership interest of an investor in an investee is equivalent to the percentage of voting rights that this investor holds in the investee.

Paragraphs B47–B50 of AASB 10/IFRS 10 discuss the issue of whether potential voting rights should be considered in assessing the existence of power. These rights may be transferable to voting rights, such as those within a share option or convertible instrument (paragraph B47). If the potential voting rights can be easily converted by the investor into voting rights at any point in time with no restriction or significant loss, they must be taken into consideration when assessing the existence of power.

Power is the ability to direct

There is a distinction between ability to direct and actually directing. An entity that has the ability to direct may decide not to exercise that ability and allow another entity to actually direct. For example, Entity C may have two owners — Entity A that owns 55% of the shares in Entity C and Entity B that holds the remaining 45% of issued shares. Entity A may have the ability to direct the activities of Entity C but, as it is an investment company and holds shares purely for cash flow via dividends, may not desire to be involved in the management of other entities. Entity B may then actually undertake the management of Entity C. Even so, Entity A is the parent as it has the ability to direct the activities of Entity C, regardless of whether it decides to use this ability or not. Entity B will always be considered as the holder of a **non-controlling interest**.

Note also that, in order to be considered to have the ability to direct, the investor should have practical ability to exercise its rights. According to paragraph B22 of AASB 10/IFRS 10, that means that the investor's rights should be **substantive rights**. Judgement is required in assessing whether rights are substantive. Paragraph B23 of AASB 10/IFRS 10 provides some factors to consider in making that determination.

- *Whether there are any barriers — economic or otherwise — that prevent a holder from exercising the rights.* Examples of such barriers are financial penalties, terms and conditions that make it unlikely that rights will be exercised, and the absence of specialised services necessary for exercising the rights. Paragraph B23(a) provides a detailed list of possible barriers.
- *Where more than one party is involved, whether there is a mechanism in place to enable those parties to practically exercise the rights.*
- *Whether the party or parties that hold the rights would benefit from the exercise of those rights*; for example, potential voting rights.

Paragraph B24 of AASB 10/IFRS 10 adds that for rights to be substantive, they must be exercisable when decisions about the direction of the relevant activities need to be made.

If the rights are purely protective rights, the holder does not have power (AASB 10/IFRS 10 paragraph 14). **Protective rights** are defined in Appendix A of AASB 10/IFRS 10 as follows.

> Rights designed to protect the interest of the party holding those rights without giving that party power over the entity to which those rights relate.

Paragraph B28 provides examples of protective rights, which include:

(a) a lender's right to restrict a borrower from undertaking activities that could significantly change the credit risk of the borrower to the detriment of the lender.

(b) the right of a party holding a non-controlling interest in an investee to approve capital expenditure greater than that required in the ordinary course of business, or to approve the issue of equity or debt instruments.

(c) the right of a lender to seize the assets of a borrower if the borrower fails to meet specified loan repayment conditions.

The ability to direct must be current

The investor must be currently able to exercise its rights to direct in order to be considered to have power over the investee. However, there are circumstances where power is still held by an investor even though there may be a time period that needs to pass, or an activity that needs to be undertaken, before the right to direct can be currently exercisable. Paragraph B24 of AASB 10/IFRS 10 provides examples of these circumstances.

26.2.2 Exposure or rights to variable returns

Besides having power to direct the relevant activities of an investee, an investor must also have the rights to variable returns from that investee if they are to have control over the investee.

Where an investor holds ordinary shares in an investee, it is entitled to receive returns in the form of dividends, changes in the value of the investment, or residual interests on liquidation. These returns can be positive or negative — hence the use of the term 'returns' rather than 'benefits'. If debt securities are held, the return is in the form of interest. Other returns may include:

- returns from structuring activities with the investee (e.g. obtaining a secure supply of raw materials, access to a port facility, or a distribution network)
- returns from denying or regulating access to an investee's assets (e.g. obtaining control of a patent for a competing product and stopping production)
- returns from economies of scale
- remuneration from provision of services, such as servicing of assets, and management.

The returns that an investor that has control over an investee receives must have the potential to vary based on the performance of the investee. Paragraph B57 of AASB 10/IFRS 10 provides examples of such variable returns as:

- dividends from ordinary shares that will change based on the profit performance of the investee
- fixed interest payments from a bond, as they expose the investor to the credit risk of the issuer of the bond, namely the investee
- fixed performance fees for management of the investee's assets, as they expose the investor to the performance risk of the investee.

If the returns that the investor is entitled to receive are not variable based on the performance of the investee, the investor cannot recognise that they have control over the investee. As such, if the investor only invests in the debt instruments issued by the investee and receives returns in the form of interest that is not linked to the performance of the investee, then the investor does not have control over the investee.

26.2.3 Ability to use power to affect returns

Besides having power to direct the relevant activities of the investee and rights to variable returns from the involvement with the investee, a parent must have the ability to use its power over the investee to affect the variable returns received from the investee. This requires that the parent be able to use its power to increase its benefits and limit its losses from the subsidiary's relevant activities. There is then a link between the holding of the power and the returns receivable. However, there is no specification of the level of returns to be received. AASB 10/IFRS 10 only requires that some variable returns be receivable and that the parent by its actions can affect the amount of those returns.

26.2.4 Agents

In determining whether control exists over an investee, an investor with decision-making rights needs to assess whether it is a principal or an **agent**. According to paragraph B58 of AASB 10/IFRS 10:

> An agent is a party primarily engaged to act on behalf and for the benefit of another party or parties (the principal(s)) and therefore does not control the investee when it exercises its decision-making authority.

Paragraph B60 of AASB 10/IFRS 10 provides a number of factors to consider in determining whether a decision maker is a principal or an agent, such as:

- the scope of its decision-making authority over the investee — this relates to the range of activities that the decision maker is permitted to direct
- the rights held by other parties (e.g. whether another entity has substantive removal rights over the decision maker)
- the remuneration to which it is entitled in accordance with the remuneration agreement — the remuneration of an agent would be expected to be commensurate with the level of skills needed to provide the management service while the remuneration agreement would contain terms and conditions normally included in arrangements for similar services
- the decision maker's exposure to variability of returns from other interest that it holds in the investee — the greater the decision maker's exposure to variable returns from its involvement in the investee, the more likely it is that the decision maker is not an agent.

Where a decision maker is determined to be an agent, it is the principal that may be considered the controlling entity over the investee.

LEARNING CHECK

- ☐ The criterion for the existence of a parent–subsidiary relationship that determines the need for consolidation is that of control.
- ☐ There are three characteristics of control: (1) power over an investee, (2) exposure or rights to variable returns from the investee and (3) the ability to use power over the investee to affect the amount of the investor's returns.
- ☐ Power is the current ability to direct the relevant activities of an investee and arises from existing rights.
- ☐ Relevant activities of the investee are those activities that significantly affect the investee's returns.
- ☐ An investor's rights that gives power over the investee need to be able to be exercised (i.e. be substantive) and cannot be only protective.
- ☐ The returns to an investor must have the potential to vary as a result of the performance of the investee.
- ☐ There is a link between power and returns in that an investor must have the ability to use its power to affect its returns from its investment.
- ☐ An agent does not have control over an entity when it exercises its decision-making rights on behalf of the principal.

26.3 Consolidation process

AASB 10/IFRS 10 establishes the principles for the preparation of consolidated financial statements. In applying AASB 10/IFRS 10 in the preparation of the consolidated financial statements, AASB 3/IFRS 3 *Business Combinations* is also considered. The consolidated financial statements are prepared by combining the financial statements of the individual entities within the group (i.e. adding items in individual statements line by line), subject to some very important adjustments. These adjustments include the elimination of intragroup shareholdings, as well as the removal of the effects of intragroup transactions — because the group as an entity cannot have investments in itself, assets receivable from within itself, liabilities payable to itself or profits or losses generated from transactions with itself. These eliminations will be addressed in chapters 27 and 28 respectively. Further issues associated with the preparation of consolidated financial statements are discussed in chapters 29 and 30.

The process of adding the financial statements together in order to prepare consolidated financial statements can be seen in its simplest form in figure 26.4. In this example there are two entities in the group, P Ltd and S Ltd. The consolidated financial statements are prepared by first adding together the assets and liabilities of both entities, followed by the adjustments necessary to eliminate intragroup shareholdings and the effects on intragroup transactions. In chapter 27 a consolidation worksheet is used to describe this process.

FIGURE 26.4   The consolidation process

	P Ltd		S Ltd		Adjustments		Consolidation of P Ltd and S Ltd
Current assets	$xxx	+	$xxx	+/−	$xxx	=	$xxx
Non-current assets	xxx	+	xxx	+/−	xxx	=	xxx
Total assets	xxx		xxx		xxx		xxx
Current liabilities	xxx	+	xxx	+/−	xxx	=	xxx
Non-current liabilities	xxx	+	xxx	+/−	xxx	=	xxx
Total liabilities	xxx		xxx		xxx		xxx
Net assets	$xxx		$xxx		xxx		$xxx

Note that the consolidation process does *not* involve making adjustments to the individual financial statements or in the accounts of the entities in the group. The consolidated financial statements are an additional set of financial statements and are prepared using a worksheet to facilitate the addition and adjustment process. Note also that, when preparing the consolidated financial statements, paragraph 19 of AASB 10/IFRS 10 requires the use of uniform accounting policies for like transactions and other events in similar circumstances. If the reporting periods of the parent and subsidiaries differ, the subsidiaries must prepare, for consolidation purposes, additional financial information as of the same date and for the same period as the financial statements of the parent. If it is impracticable to prepare this additional information, the most recent financial statements of subsidiaries with a different reporting period to the parent will be used for consolidation purposes provided that:

- those financial statements are adjusted for the effects of significant transactions or events that occur between the date of those financial statements and the date of the consolidated financial statements
- the difference between the date of those subsidiaries' financial statements and that of the consolidated financial statements shall be no more than 3 months
- the length of the reporting periods and any difference between the dates of the financial statements shall be the same from period to period.

LEARNING CHECK

☐ AASB 10/IFRS 10 establishes the principles for the preparation of consolidated financial statements. In applying AASB 10/IFRS 10 in the preparation of the consolidated financial statements, AASB 3/IFRS 3 is also considered. ▶

□ The process of consolidation requires the aggregation of the financial statements of the parent and all of its subsidiaries, subject to some adjustments.
□ The aggregation process does not affect the financial statements or the accounts of entities within the group.

26.4 Circumstances where a parent may not prepare consolidated financial statements

LEARNING OBJECTIVE 26.4 Explain the circumstances under which a parent entity may be exempt from preparing consolidated financial statements.

Paragraph 4(a) of AASB 10/IFRS 10 requires *each* parent to prepare consolidated financial statements, except in those circumstances where it meets *all* of the following conditions:

  (i) it is a wholly-owned subsidiary or is a partially-owned subsidiary of another entity and all its other owners, including those not otherwise entitled to vote, have been informed about, and do not object to, the parent not presenting consolidated financial statements;
 (ii) its debt or equity instruments are not traded in a public market (a domestic or foreign stock exchange or an over-the-counter market, including local and regional markets);
(iii) it did not file, nor is it in the process of filing, its financial statements with a securities commission or other regulatory organisation for the purpose of issuing any class of instruments in a public market; and
(iv) its ultimate or any intermediate parent produces consolidated financial statements that are available for public use and comply with IFRSs, in which subsidiaries are consolidated or are measured at fair value through profit or loss in accordance with this Standard.

Consider the group structure in figure 26.5. A Ltd is a parent entity with two subsidiaries. B Ltd is also a parent with C Ltd being its subsidiary. Is B Ltd required to prepare consolidated financial statements?

FIGURE 26.5	A parent and its subsidiaries

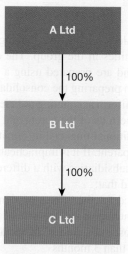

In line with the conditions in paragraph 4(a) of AASB 10/IFRS 10, in order to determine if B Ltd needs to prepare consolidated financial statements, the following questions are asked.
- *Is B Ltd itself a wholly owned subsidiary?* In figure 26.5, B Ltd is a wholly owned subsidiary of A Ltd and hence meets the first condition in paragraph 4(a)(i). Note also in paragraph 4(a)(i) that even if A Ltd owned only, say, 80% of B Ltd making B Ltd a partially owned subsidiary, B Ltd will meet the first condition in paragraph 4(a)(i) if the holders of the 20% non-controlling interest in B Ltd have been informed about and do not object to B Ltd not presenting consolidated financial statements.
- *Are the debt or equity instruments of B Ltd traded in a public market?* If these instruments are traded in a public market then there are potential users interested in a set of consolidated financial statements

from B Ltd. If B Ltd is a wholly owned subsidiary, it is unlikely that its equity instruments would be traded in a public market, but its debts instruments may still be traded.

- *Has B Ltd filed its financial reports with a regulatory agency for the purpose of issuing any class of instruments in a public market?*
- *Has A Ltd produced consolidated financial statements complying with IFRS?*

In September 2010, the AASB issued Exposure Draft ED 205 *Extending Relief from Consolidation, the Equity Method and Proportionate Consolidation*. The AASB was concerned about the effects of condition (iv) in paragraph 4(a) of AASB 10/IFRS 10 in circumstances where, because of the effects of the reduced disclosure requirements (as part of AASB's Differential Reporting Project), the ultimate or the intermediary parents may not have prepared IFRS-compliant consolidated financial statements. Using the group structure in figure 26.5, if A Ltd had not prepared consolidated financial statements that were IFRS-compliant, B Ltd would have to prepare consolidated financial statements as condition (iv) in paragraph 4(a) of AASB 10/IFRS 10 would not be satisfied. ED 205 intended to provide relief to B Ltd from preparing consolidated financial statements. Hence, the AASB added paragraph Aus4.1 to AASB 10 to extend the relief from preparing consolidated financial statements currently provided under paragraph 4 of AASB 10/IFRS 10. To apply paragraph Aus4.1, a parent must still meet conditions (i)–(iii). If that parent has an ultimate or intermediate parent that prepares consolidated financial statements available for public use, then according to paragraph Aus4.1 it does not have to prepare consolidated financial statements under certain conditions. Paragraph Aus4.1 of AASB 10 states:

> Notwithstanding paragraph 4(a)(iv), a parent that meets the criteria in paragraphs 4(a)(i), 4(a)(ii) and 4(a)(iii) need not present consolidated financial statements if its ultimate or any intermediate parent produces financial statements available for public use in which subsidiaries are consolidated or are measured at fair value through profit or loss in accordance with this Standard and:
> (a) the parent and its ultimate or intermediate parent are:
>   (i) both not-for-profit entities complying with Australian Accounting Standards; or
>   (ii) both entities complying with Australian Accounting Standards — Reduced Disclosure Requirements; or
> (b) the parent is an entity complying with Australian Accounting Standards — Reduced Disclosure Requirements and its ultimate or intermediate parent is a not-for-profit entity complying with Australian Accounting Standards.

The AASB has also added paragraph Aus4.2 to AASB 10:

> Notwithstanding paragraphs 4(a) and Aus4.1, the ultimate Australian parent shall present consolidated financial statements that consolidate its investments in subsidiaries in accordance with this Standard when the ultimate Australian parent is required by legislation to comply with Australian Accounting Standards except if the ultimate Australian parent is required, in accordance with paragraph 31 of this Standard, to measure all of its subsidiaries at fair value through profit or loss.

Consider again figure 26.5. Assume that A Ltd is a Hong Kong company and B Ltd and C Ltd are its Australian subsidiaries. B Ltd is then the ultimate Australian parent. If B Ltd is required by legislation to comply with Australian accounting standards, then it is required to prepare consolidated financial statements containing the financial statements of B Ltd and C Ltd.

Paragraph 31 of AASB 10/IFRS 10 provides another exception to the principle that parents shall consolidate their subsidiaries. Paragraph 31 requires a parent that is an investment entity to measure its investments in subsidiaries, other than those that provide services that relate to the investment entity's investment activities, at fair value through profit or loss in accordance with AASB 9/IFRS 9 *Financial Instruments* instead of consolidating them. An investment entity is defined in Appendix A of AASB 10 as follows.

> An entity that:
> (a) obtains funds from one or more investors for the purpose of providing those investor(s) with investment management services;
> (b) commits to its investor(s) that its business purpose is to invest funds solely for returns from capital appreciation, investment income, or both; and
> (c) measures and evaluates the performance of substantially all of its investments on a fair value basis.

An example of such an investment entity would be where a number of investors establish a limited partnership that has control of a number of entities in which it has invested solely for the purpose of capital appreciation, investment income — such as dividends, interest or rental income — or both.

Paragraphs B85A–B85W of AASB 10 provide guidance on determining whether an entity is an investment entity.

To help assess whether an entity is an investment entity, paragraph 28 of AASB 10 provides the following as typical characteristics of an investment entity:

(a) it has more than one investment (see paragraphs B85O–B85P);
(b) it has more than one investor (see paragraphs B85Q–B85S);
(c) it has investors that are not related parties of the entity (see paragraphs B85T–B85U); and
(d) it has ownership interests in the form of equity or similar interests (see paragraphs B85V–B85W).

The absence of any of these typical characteristics does not necessarily disqualify an entity from being classified as an investment entity. An investment entity that does not have all of these typical characteristics provides additional disclosure required by paragraph 9A of AASB 12 [IFRS 12].

LEARNING CHECK

☐ Parent entities are required to prepare consolidated financial statements.
☐ Parent entities that meet all the conditions in paragraph 4(a) of AASB 10/IFRS 10 are exempted from preparing consolidated financial statements.
☐ The AASB has provided some relief from the preparation of consolidated financial statements where the parent in a group does not meet all the conditions to be exempted from preparing consolidated financial statements due to the ultimate or intermediary parent of that parent being subject to reduced disclosure requirements or not being an Australian entity.
☐ Another exception to the requirement for parents to consolidate their subsidiaries exists where the parent is an investment entity.

26.5 Disclosure

LEARNING OBJECTIVE 26.5 Discuss the disclosure requirements related to consolidated entities.

There are no disclosures specified in AASB 10/IFRS 10. AASB 12/IFRS 12 *Disclosure of Interests in Other Entities* outlines the disclosures required in the consolidated financial statements. If a parent is required to prepare consolidated financial statements, it will still need to prepare its own separate financial statements. AASB 127/IAS 27 *Separate Financial Statements* sets out, among other things, disclosures required in the separate financial statements of the parent.

26.5.1 Disclosures required by AASB 12/IFRS 12

The key objective of AASB 12/IFRS 12 is stated in paragraph 1:

The objective of this Standard is to require an entity to disclose information that enables users of its financial statements to evaluate:
(a) the nature of, and risks associated with, its *interests in other entities*; and
(b) the effects of those interests on its financial position, financial performance and cash flows.

Notice the emphasis on the ability of users of financial statements to be able to evaluate risks. In the introduction to IFRS 12 *Disclosure of Interests in Other Entities*, in paragraph IN5, the IASB noted that 'the global financial crisis that started in 2007 highlighted a lack of transparency about the risks to which a reporting entity was exposed from its involvement with structured entities'. As a result, IFRS 12 and, by extension, AASB 12, requires an entity to disclose the significant judgements and assumptions it has made in determining the nature of its interest in another entity (paragraph 2(a)), and, in particular, judgements, assumptions and changes in these in relation to subsidiaries (paragraph 7). Paragraph 9 of AASB 12/IFRS 12 provides the following examples of situations where it is necessary to disclose significant judgements and assumptions:

• where an entity does not control another entity but it holds more than half of the voting rights in the other entity
• where an entity controls another entity but it holds less than half of the voting rights of the other entity
• where an entity is an agent or a principal.

To assist users in understanding the nature of the group, paragraph 10 of AASB 12/IFRS 12 states the following.

An entity shall disclose information that enables users of its consolidated financial statements
- (a) to understand:
    - (i) the composition of the group; and
    - (ii) the interest that non-controlling interests have in the group's activities and cash flows (paragraph 12); and
- (b) to evaluate:
    - (i) the nature and extent of significant restrictions on its ability to access or use assets, and settle liabilities, of the group (paragraph 13);
    - (ii) the nature of, and changes in, the risks associated with its interests in consolidated structured entities (paragraphs 14–17);
    - (iii) the consequences of changes in its ownership interest in a subsidiary that do not result in a loss of control (paragraph 18); and
    - (iv) the consequences of losing control of a subsidiary during the reporting period (paragraph 19).

Where the financial statements of a subsidiary are as of a date that differs from that of the parent, the entity must disclose both the date used by the subsidiary as well as the reason for using a different date (paragraph 11). As the parent controls the subsidiary, the choice of a different date must be one made by the parent and not the subsidiary.

Where a non-controlling interest exists in a subsidiary, paragraph 12 of AASB 12/IFRS 12 requires that an entity disclose for each such subsidiary:
- (a) the name of the subsidiary
- (b) the principal place of business (and country of incorporation if different from the principal place of business) of the subsidiary
- (c) the proportion of ownership interests held by non-controlling interests
- (d) the proportion of voting rights held by non-controlling interests, if different from the proportion of ownership interests held
- (e) the profit or loss allocated to non-controlling interests of the subsidiary during the reporting period
- (f) accumulated non-controlling interests of the subsidiary at the end of the reporting period
- (g) summarised financial information about the subsidiary (see paragraph B10).

Paragraph B10 of AASB 12/IFRS 12 states the following.

> For each subsidiary that has non-controlling interests that are material to the reporting entity, an entity shall disclose:
> - (a) dividends paid to non-controlling interests.
> - (b) summarised financial information about the assets, liabilities, profit or loss and cash flows of the subsidiary that enables users to understand the interest that non-controlling interests have in the group's activities and cash flows. That information might include but is not limited to, for example, current assets, non-current assets, current liabilities, non-current liabilities, revenue, profit or loss and total comprehensive income.

Paragraph B11 notes that the summarised financial information is required *before* adjusting for intragroup transactions. Paragraph 13 of AASB 12/IFRS 12 provides disclosures required where an entity has significant restrictions on its ability to access or use the assets or settle the liabilities of the group.

Paragraph 14 of AASB 12/IFRS 12 deals with consolidated structured entities. In Appendix A, a **structured entity** is defined as follows.

> An entity that has been designed so that voting or similar rights are not the dominant factor in deciding who controls the entity, such as when any voting rights relate to administrative tasks only and the relevant activities are directed by means of contractual arrangements.

Paragraphs B22–B24 of AASB 12/IFRS 12 provide further information about structured entities. According to paragraph B22, a structured entity may have the following features.
- (a) restricted activities.
- (b) a narrow and well-defined objective, such as to effect a tax-efficient lease, carry out research and development activities, provide a source of capital or funding to an entity or provide investment opportunities for investors by passing on risks and rewards associated with the assets of the structured entity to investors.
- (c) insufficient equity to permit the structured entity to finance its activities without subordinated financial support.
- (d) financing in the form of multiple contractually linked instruments to investors that create concentrations of credit or other risks (tranches).

The following examples of entities that are regarded as structured entities are noted in paragraph B23:

(a) securitisation vehicles.
(b) asset-backed financings.
(c) some investment funds.

Disclosures in relation to consolidated structured entities required by AASB 12/IFRS 12 include:

- the terms of any contractual arrangement that could require a parent or its subsidiaries to supply financial support to a consolidated structured entity
- information about the provision of financial support supplied without the parent or its subsidiaries having a contractual obligation to do so
- current intentions to provide financial or other support to a consolidated structured entity.

Where the structured entity is *not* consolidated, paragraphs 24–31 of AASB 12/IFRS 12 provide information on the disclosures required. As these structured entities are not consolidated, it is important that users are aware of any risks associated with involvement with these entities. In particular, paragraph 26 requires disclosure about an entity's:

> interests in unconsolidated structured entities, including, but not limited to, the nature, purpose, size and activities of the structured entity and how the structured entity is financed.

To assist in the evaluation of risks associated with unconsolidated structured entities, paragraph 29 of AASB 12/IFRS 12 requires an entity to disclose in tabular format, unless another format is more appropriate, a summary of:

(a) the carrying amounts of the assets and liabilities recognised in its financial statements relating to its interests in unconsolidated structured entities.
(b) the line items in the statement of financial position in which those assets and liabilities are recognised.
(c) the amount that best represents the entity's maximum exposure to loss from its interests in unconsolidated structured entities, including how the maximum exposure to loss is determined. If an entity cannot quantify its maximum exposure to loss from its interests in unconsolidated structured entities it shall disclose that fact and the reasons.
(d) a comparison of the carrying amounts of the assets and liabilities of the entity that relate to its interests in unconsolidated structured entities and the entity's maximum exposure to loss from those entities.

Paragraphs 18 and 19 set out disclosures required where there are changes in the parent's ownership interest in a subsidiary as well as when a parent loses control of a subsidiary. These situations are discussed in chapter 30.

26.5.2 Disclosures required by AASB 127/IAS 27

Paragraph 4 of AASB 127/IAS 27 contains the following definition of **separate financial statements**.

> Separate financial statements are those presented by an entity in which the entity could elect, subject to the requirements in this Standard, to account for its investments in subsidiaries, joint ventures and associates either at cost, in accordance with AASB 9 [IFRS 9] *Financial Instruments,* or using the equity method as described in AASB 128 [IAS 28] *Investments in Associates and Joint Ventures.*

There are two situations in which separate financial statements are prepared.

1. *Where a parent is exempted from preparing consolidated financial statements in accordance with paragraph 4(a) of AASB 10/IFRS 10.*

   In this case, paragraph 16 of AASB 127/IAS 27 requires the parent to supply the following information in the separate financial statements prepared by the parent:

   (a) the fact that the financial statements are separate financial statements; that the exemption from consolidation has been used; the name and principal place of business (and country of incorporation, if different) of the entity whose consolidated financial statements that comply with International Financial Reporting Standards have been produced for public use; and the address where those consolidated financial statements are obtainable.

(b) a list of significant investments in subsidiaries, joint ventures and associates, including:
    (i) the name of those investees.
    (ii) the principal place of business (and country of incorporation, if different) of those investees.
    (iii) its proportion of the ownership interest (and its proportion of voting rights, if different) held in those investees.
(c) a description of the method used to account for the investments listed under (b).

2. *Where a parent prepares separate financial statements in addition to consolidated financial statements.*
Historically, the *Corporations Act 2001* required parents to present parent entity financial statements together with consolidated financial statements within the annual report. A discussion paper prepared by Cotter (2003) researched the relevance of parent entity financial reports for consolidated entities and proposed the removal of the requirement for parent entity financial reports to be published in the annual report. The *Corporations Amendment (Corporate Reporting Reform) Act 2010* amended the *Corporations Act 2001* so that those reporting entities that present consolidated financial statements are no longer required to present parent entity financial statements. This change applied for financial reports for the year ended 30 June 2010 onwards. However, reporting entities that choose to still present parent entity financial statements are allowed to do so.

Paragraph 17 of AASB 127/IAS 27 requires the following information to be disclosed in the separate financial statements:

(a) the fact that the statements are separate financial statements and the reasons why those statements are prepared if not required by law.
(b) a list of significant investments in subsidiaries, joint ventures and associates, including:
    (i) the name of those investees.
    (ii) the principal place of business (and country of incorporation, if different) of those investees.
    (iii) its proportion of the ownership interest (and its proportion of the voting rights, if different) held in those investees.
(c) a description of the method used to account for the investments listed under (b).

LEARNING CHECK

☐ AASB 10/IFRS 10 does not contain disclosure requirements for consolidated financial statements.

☐ AASB 12/IFRS 12 contains disclosure requirements for consolidated financial statements.

☐ AASB 12/IFRS 12 requires specific disclosures for structured entities. A structured entity is an entity that has been designed so that voting or similar rights are not the dominant factor in deciding who controls the entity.

☐ AASB 127/IAS 27 contains requirements relating to the information to be disclosed in the separate financial statements prepared by a parent.

SUMMARY

Where entities form relationships with other entities, accounting standards often require additional disclosure so that users of financial statements can understand the economic substance of the entities involved. Where an entity is classified as a subsidiary of another, the parent, AASB 10/IFRS 10 establishes principles for the preparation of consolidated financial statements. AASB 3/IFRS 3 will also need to be applied as the formation of a parent–subsidiary relationship is normally a result of a business combination.

The existence of a parent–subsidiary relationship is determined by whether one entity has control over another. The existence of control requires the assessment of the power an entity has over another entity, whether the investor is exposed or has rights to variable returns from its involvement in the investee, and the ability of the investor to use its power over the investee to affect the amount of those returns. This analysis requires the accountant to exercise judgement in analysing the specific relationships between entities, since the existence of control is not simply a matter of determining whether an entity owns a majority of shares in another.

The consolidated financial statements are in addition to those prepared for either the parent or a subsidiary as separate legal entities. The consolidated financial statements are prepared by adding the financial statements of a parent and each of its subsidiaries, with adjustments being made during this process.

In general, parent entities are responsible for the preparation of the consolidated financial statements. However, AASB 10/IFRS 10 exempts some parent entities that meet specified criteria from the preparation of these statements.

AASB 10/IFRS 10 does not contain disclosure requirements for consolidated financial statements. The disclosure requirements are found in AASB 12/IFRS 12. AASB 127/IAS 27 contains disclosure requirements for the separate financial statements prepared by the parent.

KEY TERMS

agent A party primarily engaged to act on behalf and for the benefit of another party or parties (the principal(s)) which therefore does not control the investee when it exercises its decision-making authority.

consolidated financial statements The financial statements of a group in which the assets, liabilities, equity, income, expenses and cash flows of the parent and its subsidiaries are presented as those of a single economic entity.

control of an investee An investor controls an investee when the investor is exposed, or has rights, to variable returns from its involvement with the investee and has the ability to affect those returns through its power over the investee.

group A parent and its subsidiaries.

non-controlling interest (NCI) Equity in a subsidiary not attributable, directly or indirectly, to a parent.

parent An entity that controls one or more entities.

power Existing rights that give the current ability to direct the relevant activities.

protective rights Rights designed to protect the interest of the party holding those rights without giving that party power over the entity to which those rights relate.

relevant activities Activities of the investee that significantly affect the investee's returns.

separate financial statements Statements presented by a parent or an investor with joint control of, or significant influence over, an investee, in which the investments are accounted for at cost in accordance with AASB 9/IFRS 9.

structured entity An entity that has been designed so that voting or similar rights are not the dominant factor in deciding who controls the entity.

subsidiary An entity that is controlled by another entity.

substantive rights Rights that the rights holder has the practical ability to exercise.

COMPREHENSION QUESTIONS

1 What are the consolidated financial statements?
2 What is the purpose of preparing consolidated financial statements?
3 What is a group, a parent and a subsidiary?
4 What is a parent–subsidiary relationship?

5 How many parents can a group have?

6 Why do the regulators require the parent entity to prepare consolidated financial statements?

7 What is meant by the term 'control'?

8 What are the key elements of control?

9 When does an investor have power over an investee?

10 What are 'relevant' activities?

11 What are substantive rights and protective rights?

12 What are variable returns?

13 What benefits could be sought by an entity that obtains control over another entity?

14 What is the link between ownership interest and control?

15 When are potential voting rights considered in determining if one entity controls another?

16 Explain the link between power and returns.

17 What is an agent or a principal?

18 Describe the consolidation process.

19 Which entities are required to prepare consolidated financial statements and which entities are exempted?

20 What is the key objective of AASB 12/IFRS 12?

21 What needs to be disclosed according to AASB 12/IFRS 12 for each subsidiary where a non-controlling interest exists?

22 What is a structured entity?

23 When does a parent need to prepare separate financial statements according to AASB 127/IAS 27?

24 What needs to be disclosed in the separate financial statements prepared by a parent according to AASB 127/IAS 27?

CASE STUDY 26.1

NATURE OF CONTROL

The following comment was received by the IASB on 6 April 2009 from the Swedish Financial Reporting Board in response to the issue of Exposure Draft (ED) 10 *Consolidated Financial Statements* (the predecessor of IFRS 10).

> We agree that consolidated financial statements would be improved, if they include entities under 'de facto' control. However, the problem is to establish which entities are really under 'de facto' control. There are situations where it is very clear that the dominant shareholder de facto controls another entity, but there are also lots of situations, where it is not clear that the dominant shareholder de facto controls the other entity. We suggest that the requirement for consolidation based on 'de facto' control is restricted to situations, where it is beyond reasonable doubt that control really exists.

Required

Discuss whether AASB 10/IFRS 10 in its current form has the problem raised by the Swedish Financial Reporting Board.

CASE STUDY 26.2

POWER AND RELEVANT ACTIVITIES

According to paragraph BC43 of the Basis for Conclusions on AASB 10/IFRS 10 *Consolidated Financial Statements*:

> Respondents to ED 10 did not object to changing the definition of control to power to direct the activities of an investee. Many were confused, however, about what the Board meant by 'power to direct' and which 'activities' the Board had in mind. They asked for a clear articulation of the principle behind the term 'power to direct'. They also expressed the view that power should relate to significant activities of an investee, and not those activities that have little effect on the investee's returns.

Required

Discuss whether AASB 10/IFRS 10 addressed the comments made by the respondents to ED 10.

CASE STUDY 26.3

RIGHTS TO VARIABLE RETURNS

Some have argued that the criteria for consolidation should refer to significant variable returns. These parties argue that the consolidated financial statements are not meaningful if they include subsidiaries in which the parent's level of rights to variable returns is less than 50% or is not significant.

Required

Discuss:

1. the place of a returns criterion in the definition of control
2. possible returns that could occur as a result of obtaining control of another entity
3. the need to place a specified level of returns in the definition of control.

APPLICATION AND ANALYSIS EXERCISES

★ BASIC | ★ ★ MODERATE | ★ ★ ★ DIFFICULT

26.1 Parent–subsidiary relationship ★   LO1, 2, 3

Visit the website of Woolworths Group Limited (www.woolworthsgroup.com.au) and retrieve the most recent annual report.

Required

1. Identify and discuss the principles of consolidation used as disclosed in note 1 to the consolidated financial statements.
2. Identify the subsidiaries, as disclosed in the notes to the consolidated financial statements, describing the differences between the wholly owned and partially owned subsidiaries.
3. Discuss potential reasons the regulators require Woolworths Group Limited to prepare consolidated financial statements.

26.2 Parent–subsidiary relationship ★ ★ ★   LO2

In the following independent situations, determine whether a parent–subsidiary relationship exists, and which entity, if any, is a parent.

1. Tom Ltd is a company that was hurt by a major downturn in the economy. It previously obtained a significant loan from Jenson Bank, and when Tom Ltd was unable to make its loan repayments, the bank made an agreement with Tom Ltd to become involved in the management of the company. Under the agreement between the two entities, Tom Ltd's managers had to obtain authority from the bank for acquisitions over $10 000 and were required to have bank approval for the company's budgets.
2. Sawyer Ltd is a major financing company whose interest in investing is return on the investment. Sawyer Ltd does not get involved in the management of its investments. If an investee is not managed properly, Sawyer Ltd sells its shares in that investee and selects a more profitable investee to invest in. It previously held a 35% interest in Anderson Ltd as well as providing substantial convertible debt finance to that entity. Recently, Anderson Ltd was having cash flow difficulties and persuaded Sawyer Ltd to convert some of the convertible debt into equity so as to ease the effects of interest payments on cash flow. As a result, Sawyer Ltd's equity interest in Anderson Ltd increased to 52%. Sawyer Ltd still wanted to remain a passive investor, with no changes in the directors on the board of Anderson Ltd. These directors were appointed by the holders of the 48% of shares not held by Sawyer Ltd.

26.3 Voting rights ★   LO2

Falco Ltd owns 40% of the shares of Skye Ltd; no other party owns more than 3% of the shares. The annual general meeting of Skye Ltd is to be held in one month's time. Historically, only the holders of around 75% of the shares were present and voted in each of the previous years' annual meetings.

Required

Discuss the potential for Skye Ltd to be classified as a subsidiary of Falco Ltd.

26.4 Voting rights ★   LO2

Alvin Ltd has 37% of the voting interest in Theodore Ltd. An investment bank with which Alvin Ltd has business relationships holds a 15% voting interest in Theodore Ltd. Because of the closeness of the business relationship with the bank, Alvin Ltd believes it can rely on the bank's support to ensure it cannot be outvoted at general meetings of Theodore Ltd. However, there is no guarantee that the bank will always support Alvin Ltd.

Required

Discuss whether Alvin Ltd is a parent of Theodore Ltd.

26.5 Options ★ LO2

Rose Ltd, Lily Ltd and Carnation Ltd each own one-third of the ordinary shares that carry voting rights at a general meeting of shareholders of Bloom Ltd. Rose Ltd, Lily Ltd and Carnation Ltd each have the right to appoint two directors to the board of Bloom Ltd. Rose Ltd also owns call options that are exercisable at a fixed price at any time and, if exercised, would increase Rose Ltd's voting rights in Bloom Ltd to 60%, while Lily Ltd's and Carnation Ltd's would become 20% each. The management of Rose Ltd does not intend to exercise the call options.

Required

Discuss whether Bloom Ltd is a subsidiary of any of the other entities.

26.6 Options ★ ★ LO2

Thomas Ltd and Jackson Ltd own 80% and 20% respectively of the ordinary shares that carry voting rights at a general meeting of shareholders of Stanmar Ltd. Thomas Ltd sells half of its interest to Benson Ltd and buys call options from Benson Ltd that are exercisable at any time at a premium to the market price when issued and, if exercised, would give Thomas Ltd its original 80% voting rights. At the end of the current financial period, the options are out of the money.

Required

Discuss whether Thomas Ltd is the parent of Stanmar Ltd.

26.7 Parent–subsidiary relationship ★ ★ ★ LO2

In the following independent situations, determine whether a parent–subsidiary relationship exists and which entity, if any, is a parent.

1. Bernadette Ltd and Howard Ltd each hold 50% of the shares in Raj Ltd, all companies being involved in the computer software industry. Bernadette Ltd agrees that Howard Ltd should provide the management of Raj Ltd because of the expertise provided by its managing director, Barry Kripke. Howard Ltd receives a management fee for providing its expertise.

2. Penny Ltd has recently acquired a 35% interest in Leonard Ltd, a company that has discovered large deposits of iron ore. Penny Ltd has extensive experience in the mining industry and, as a result, has been able to have four of its directors elected to the board of Leonard Ltd, which has six directors in total.

3. Amy Ltd holds 30% of the shares issued by Sheldon Ltd. The other shareholders come from mixed backgrounds, but each holds on average 10% of shares in Sheldon Ltd. Only three of the other shareholders have an interest in the management of the company. There are seven directors of Sheldon Ltd. Four of these are appointed by Amy Ltd. The other three directors are appointed by the three other shareholders who have an interest in the management of the company. Most of the remaining shareholders live outside Australia and rarely attend annual general meetings of Sheldon Ltd unless they have other business to attend to in the country around the same time as the annual general meetings are held.

26.8 Relevant activities ★ LO2

Oliver Ltd and Felicity Ltd decide to establish a new entity, Arrow Ltd. The purpose of Arrow Ltd is to develop and market a new car seat designed for use by babies when travelling in a car. Oliver Ltd and Felicity Ltd have specific roles in the new company and have unilateral ability to make all decisions in relation to their specified roles. Oliver Ltd has agreed that it will be responsible for developing the new car seat and obtaining all the approvals from the relevant safety bodies in Australia. Once the seat has been designed and all safety approvals have been received, Felicity Ltd will manufacture and market the product.

Required

Discuss the activities undertaken by Oliver Ltd and Felicity Ltd in relation to the determination of which entity controls Arrow Ltd.

26.9 Determining subsidiary status ★ ★ LO2

During the current financial period, Laurel Ltd acquired 40% of the ordinary shares of Lance Ltd. Under the company's constitution, each share is entitled to one vote. On the basis of past experience, only 65% of the eligible votes are typically cast at the annual general meetings of Lance Ltd. No other shareholder holds a major block of shares in Lance Ltd.

The directors of Laurel Ltd argue that they are not required under AASB 10/IFRS 10 to include Lance Ltd as a subsidiary in Laurel Ltd's consolidated financial statements as there is no conclusive evidence that Laurel Ltd can control the relevant activities of Lance Ltd. The auditors of Laurel Ltd disagree, referring specifically to the votes cast in the past years.

Required

Provide a report to Laurel Ltd on whether it should regard Lance Ltd as a subsidiary in its preparation of consolidated financial statements.

26.10 Convertible debt ★ ★ LO2

Barry Ltd and Allen Ltd own 55% and 45% respectively of the ordinary shares that carry voting rights at a general meeting of shareholders of Flash Ltd. Allen Ltd also holds debt instruments that are convertible into ordinary shares of Flash Ltd. The debt can be converted at a substantial price, in comparison with Allen Ltd's net assets, at any time, and if converted would require Allen Ltd to borrow additional funds to make the payment. If the debt were to be converted, Allen Ltd would hold 70% of the voting rights and Barry Ltd's interest would reduce to 30%. Given the effect of increasing its debt on its debt–equity ratio, Allen Ltd does not believe that it has the financial ability to enter into conversion of the debt.

Required

Discuss whether Allen Ltd is a parent of Flash Ltd.

26.11 Control ★ ★ ★ LO2

Barney Ltd has acquired, during the current year, the following investments in shares issued by other companies.

Ted Ltd	$120 000 (40% of issued capital)
Mosby Ltd	$117 000 (35% of issued capital)

Barney Ltd is unsure how to account for these investments and has asked you, as the auditor, for some professional advice.

Specifically, Barney Ltd is concerned that it may need to consider those entities as subsidiaries under AASB 10/IFRS 10. To help you, the company has provided the following information about the two investee companies.

Ted Ltd

- The remaining shares in Ted Ltd are owned by a diverse group of investors, each of which holds a small parcel of shares.
- Historically, only a small number of the shareholders attend the general meetings or question the actions of the directors.
- The current board of directors has five members, of which three are retiring at the next annual general meeting. Barney Ltd has nominated three new directors to replace the ones that are retiring and expects that they will be appointed at the next annual general meeting.

Mosby Ltd

- The remaining shares in Mosby Ltd are owned by a small group of investors, each of which owns approximately 15% of the issued shares. One of these shareholders is Ted Ltd, which owns 17%.
- The shareholders take a keen interest in the running of the company and attend all meetings.
- Two of the other shareholders, including Ted Ltd, already have representatives on the board of directors who have indicated their intention of nominating for re-election.

Required

1. Advise Barney Ltd as to whether, under AASB 10/IFRS 10, it controls Ted Ltd and/or Mosby Ltd. Support your conclusion.
2. Would your conclusion be different if the remaining shares in Ted Ltd were owned by three institutional investors each holding 20%? If so, why?

26.12 Entities required to prepare consolidated financial statements ★ ★ ★ LO2, 4

In the following independent situations, discuss which entity, if any, may be a parent required to prepare consolidated financial statements under AASB 10/IFRS 10.

1. Lily Ltd owns 100% of the shares of Aldrin Ltd, which owns 100% of the shares of Mira Ltd. All companies prepare their own financial reports under AASB/IFRS accounting standards. Although the shares of Aldrin Ltd are not traded on any public stock exchange, it is in the process of issuing debt instruments in a public market.

2. Marshall Ltd owns 80% of the shares of Eriksen Ltd, which owns 100% of the shares of New York Ltd. All companies prepare their own financial reports under AASB/IFRS accounting standards. Although the shares of Eriksen Ltd are not traded on any public stock exchange, its debt instruments are publicly traded.

3. Barney Ltd owns 100% of the shares of Stinson Ltd, which owns 80% of the shares of Harris Ltd. All companies prepare their own financial reports under AASB/IFRS accounting standards. Stinson Ltd does not have debt or equity instruments traded in a public market, nor does it intend to issue any.

REFERENCE

Cotter, J 2003, 'Relevance of parent entity financial reports', discussion paper, Australian Accounting Standards Board, www.aasb.gov.au.

ACKNOWLEDGEMENTS

Text: © 2019 Australian Accounting Standards Board (AASB). The text, graphics and layout of this publication are protected by Australian copyright law and the comparable law of other countries. No part of the publication may be reproduced, stored or transmitted in any form or by any means without the prior written permission of the AASB except as permitted by law. For reproduction or publication, permission should be sought in writing from the AASB. Requests in the first instance should be addressed to the National Director, Australian Accounting Standards Board, PO Box 204, Collins Street West, Victoria 8007.

Text: © IFRS. This publication contains copyright material of the IFRS Foundation in respect of which all rights are reserved. Reproduced by John Wiley & Sons Australia, Ltd with the permission of the IFRS Foundation. No permission granted to third parties to reproduce or distribute. For full access to IFRS Standards and the work of the IFRS Foundation please visit http://eifrs.ifrs.org. The International Accounting Standards Board, the IFRS Foundation, the authors and the publishers do not accept responsibility for any loss caused by acting or refraining from acting in reliance on the material in this publication, whether such loss is caused by negligence or otherwise.

CHAPTER 27

Consolidation: wholly owned entities

CHAPTER AIM

This chapter discusses the application of AASB 10/IFRS 10 *Consolidated Financial Statements* to wholly owned entities. When a parent owns 100% of the share capital in another entity (a special case of a parent–subsidiary relationship), it will need to prepare consolidated financial statements unless the circumstances discussed in chapter 26 (section 26.4) are all present. The process to prepare those statements, which involves adding together the individual statements line by line, subject to some important consolidation adjustments, is briefly discussed in section 26.3. In this chapter the aim is to discuss the consolidation process in the case of wholly owned entities. The discussion focuses on how to prepare specific consolidation adjustment entries — in particular the business combination valuation entries and the pre-acquisition entries — and post them in the consolidation worksheet in order to prepare consolidated financial statements.

LEARNING OBJECTIVES

After studying this chapter, you should be able to:

27.1 discuss the consolidation process in the case of wholly owned entities and the initial adjustments required in the consolidation worksheet

27.2 explain how a consolidation worksheet is used

27.3 prepare an acquisition analysis for the parent's acquisition of a subsidiary

27.4 prepare the consolidation worksheet entries at the acquisition date, being the business combination valuation entries and the pre-acquisition entries

27.5 prepare the consolidation worksheet entries in periods subsequent to the acquisition date

27.6 prepare the consolidation worksheet entries where the subsidiary revalues its assets at acquisition date

27.7 prepare the disclosures required by AASB 3/IFRS 3 and AASB 12/IFRS 12.

CONCEPTS FOR REVIEW

Before studying this chapter, you should understand and, if necessary, revise:
• accounting for a business combination
• the consolidation method and the concept of control.

27.1 Consolidation process in the case of wholly owned entities

LEARNING OBJECTIVE 27.1 Discuss the consolidation process in the case of wholly owned entities and the initial adjustments required in the consolidation worksheet.

This chapter discusses the preparation of consolidated financial statements for a group that was created by a parent acquiring 100% of the shares in other entities. The main accounting standard referred to in this chapter is AASB 10/IFRS 10 *Consolidated Financial Statements*. The chapter also references AASB 3/IFRS 3 *Business Combinations*, as the parent's acquisition of shares in a subsidiary is simply one form of a business combination. Specifically, this chapter will refer to the acquisition method used to account for business combinations described in AASB 3/IFRS 3 as this method is applicable to the preparation of consolidated financial statements. Chapter 25 discusses this method in detail and therefore an in-depth understanding of that chapter is essential for the preparation of consolidated financial statements.

As discussed in chapter 26, under AASB 10/IFRS 10 **consolidated financial statements** are the result of combining the financial statements of a parent and all its subsidiaries. (The determination of whether an entity is a **parent** or a **subsidiary** is also discussed in chapter 26.) The consolidated financial statements of a parent and its subsidiaries include information about a subsidiary from the date the parent obtains control of the subsidiary; that is, from the acquisition date. A subsidiary continues to be included in the parent's consolidated financial statements until the parent no longer controls that entity.

In this chapter, the only business combinations considered are those where the parent acquires its controlling interest in a subsidiary and, as a result, owns all the issued shares of the subsidiary — the subsidiary is then a wholly owned subsidiary. This may occur by the parent buying all the shares in a subsidiary in one transaction, or by the parent acquiring the remaining shares after having previously acquired a non-controlling interest in the subsidiary. Therefore, in this chapter, the **group** under discussion is one where:

- there are only two entities within the group — one parent and one subsidiary (see figure 27.1)
- both entities have share capital
- the parent owns all the issued shares of the subsidiary; that is, the subsidiary is wholly owned (partially owned subsidiaries, where it is necessary to account for the non-controlling interest, are covered in chapter 29)
- there are no intragroup transactions between the parent and its subsidiary after the acquisition date (chapter 28 discusses the case of intragroup transactions subsequent to acquisition date).

FIGURE 27.1	The group structure considered in this chapter

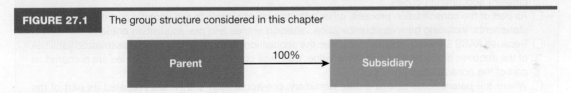

The consolidated financial statements are prepared by adding together, line by line, the financial statements of the parent and its subsidiary in the consolidation process subject to some very important consolidation adjustments. First, the financial statements that are added together must be comparable. Therefore, *before undertaking the consolidation process* it may be necessary to make adjustments in relation to the content of the financial statements of the subsidiary.

- If the end of a subsidiary's reporting period does not coincide with the end of the parent's reporting period, adjustments must be made for the effects of significant transactions and events that occur between those dates, with additional financial statements being prepared where it is practicable to do so (AASB 10/IFRS 10 paragraphs B92–B93). In most such cases, the subsidiary will prepare adjusted financial statements as at the end of the parent's reporting period, so that adjustments are not necessary on consolidation. Where the preparation of adjusted financial statements is unduly costly, the financial statements of the subsidiary prepared at a different date from the parent may be used, subject to adjustments for significant transactions. However, as paragraph B93 states, for this to be a viable option, the difference between the ends of the reporting periods can be no longer than 3 months. Further, the length of the reporting periods, as well as any difference between the ends of the reporting periods, must be the same from period to period.

- The consolidated financial statements are to be prepared using uniform accounting policies for like transactions and other events in similar circumstances (AASB 10/IFRS 10 paragraph 19). Where the parent and the subsidiary used different policies, adjustments are made so that like transactions are accounted for under a uniform policy in the consolidated financial statements (normally the policy used by the parent).

Second, *as part of the consolidation process*, a number of other adjustments are made to the parent's and the subsidiary's statements, these being expressed in the form of journal entries.

- As required by AASB 3/IFRS 3, at the acquisition date the acquirer must recognise the identifiable assets acquired and liabilities assumed of the subsidiary at fair value. Adjusting the carrying amounts of the subsidiary's assets and liabilities to fair value and recognising any identifiable assets acquired and liabilities assumed as part of the business combination, but not recorded by the subsidiary, is a part of the consolidation process. The entries used to make these adjustments are referred to in this chapter as the *business combination valuation entries*. As noted in section 27.2, these adjusting entries are generally not made in the records of the subsidiary itself, but in a consolidation worksheet.

- Where the parent has an ownership interest (i.e. owns shares) in a subsidiary, another set of adjusting entries are made, referred to in this chapter as the *pre-acquisition entries*. As noted in paragraph B86(b) of AASB 10/IFRS 10, this involves eliminating the carrying amount of the parent's investment in the subsidiary and the parent's portion of pre-acquisition equity in the subsidiary. This avoids double counting of the group's assets and equity. The name of these entries is derived from the fact that the equity of the subsidiary at the acquisition date is referred to as pre-acquisition equity, and it is this equity that is being eliminated. These entries are also made in the consolidation worksheet, not in the records of the subsidiary.

- The third set of adjustments is for transactions between the entities within the group subsequent to the acquisition date, including sales of inventories or non-current assets. These intragroup transactions are referred to in paragraph B86(c) of AASB 10/IFRS 10. Adjustments for these transactions are discussed in detail in chapter 28.

LEARNING CHECK

☐ The consolidated financial statements are prepared by adding together, line by line, the financial statements of the parent and its subsidiary in the consolidation process.

☐ Before undertaking the consolidation process, adjustments must be made to the subsidiary's statements where the parent entity and the subsidiary have different ends of reporting periods or use different accounting policies.

☐ As part of the consolidation process, other adjustments are made to the parent's and the subsidiary's statements, including business combination valuation entries and pre-acquisition entries.

☐ Because AASB 3/IFRS 3 requires that under the acquisition method the identifiable assets and liabilities of the acquiree are to be reported at fair value, business combination valuation entries are prepared as part of the consolidation process.

☐ Where the parent holds shares in the subsidiary, pre-acquisition entries are prepared as part of the consolidation process in order to prevent double counting of the group's assets and equity.

27.2 Consolidation worksheets

LEARNING OBJECTIVE 27.2 Explain how a consolidation worksheet is used.

The consolidated financial statements are prepared by adding together the financial statements of the parent and the subsidiary, subject to the consolidation adjustments. The financial statements that are added together are the statements of financial position, statements of profit or loss and other comprehensive income, statements of changes in equity and statements of cash flows.

A worksheet or computer spreadsheet is often used to facilitate the addition process and to make the business combination valuation and pre-acquisition entry adjustments. From the worksheet, the following statements are prepared: the consolidated statement of financial position, consolidated statement of profit or loss and other comprehensive income and consolidated statement of changes in equity. Consolidated statements of cash flows must also be prepared, but these are not covered in this text.

The format for the worksheet is presented in figure 27.2, which contains the information used for the consolidation of the financial statements of the parent, Parent Ltd, and the subsidiary, Subsidiary Ltd.

FIGURE 27.2   Consolidation worksheet — basic format

Financial statements	Parent Ltd	Subsidiary Ltd		Adjustments			Group
				Dr	Cr		
Retained earnings	25 000	12 000	1	12 000			25 000
Share capital	37 000	15 000	1	15 000			37 000
Total equity	**62 000**	**27 000**					**62 000**
Shares in Subsidiary Ltd	27 000	—			27 000	1	—
Other assets	35 000	27 000					62 000
Total assets	**62 000**	**27 000**					**62 000**

Note the following points about the worksheet.

- Column 1 contains the names of the accounts, as the financial statements are combined on a line-by-line basis.
- Columns 2 and 3 contain the financial information for the parent, Parent Ltd, and its subsidiary, Subsidiary Ltd. This information is obtained from the financial statements of the separate legal entities. The number of columns is expanded if there are more subsidiaries within the group.
- The next four columns, headed 'Adjustments', are used to post and reference the adjustments required in the consolidation process. These include the business combination valuation entries, pre-acquisition entries and the adjustments for intragroup transactions. These adjustments, written in the form of journal entries in the consolidation journal, are recorded in the worksheet, separately from the individual records of the parent and subsidiary, so they do not affect the individual financial statements. Where there are many adjustments, each journal entry should be numbered so that it is clear which items are being affected by a particular adjustment entry. In figure 27.2 there is only one worksheet entry, hence the number '1' is entered against each item affected by that entry. The worksheet adjustment entry is as follows.

(1)	Retained earnings (opening balance)	Dr	12 000	
	Share capital	Dr	15 000	
	Shares in Subsidiary Ltd	Cr		27 000

- The last column, headed 'Group', includes the calculated consolidated amounts for each line item, together with totals and subtotals. The figures in the 'Group' column provide the information for preparing the consolidated statement of profit or loss and other comprehensive income, consolidated statement of changes in equity and consolidated statement of financial position. These statements will not include all the line items in the consolidation worksheet. However, information for the notes to these statements is also obtained from line items in the worksheet.
- The figures for each individual line item in the 'Group' column (excluding totals and subtotals) arise through addition and subtraction based on the general rules of debits and credits as you proceed horizontally across the worksheet. For example, for share capital:

$37 000$ (Parent Ltd) + $15 000$ (Subsidiary Ltd) − $15 000$ (the debit side adjustment) = $37 000$

- In the 'Group' column, the totals and subtotals are the result of adding the preceding items in that column rather than totalling items across the rows. For example, the total consolidated equity of $62 000 is determined by adding the consolidated retained earnings balance of $25 000 and the consolidated share capital balance of $37 000, both these balances appearing in the 'Group' column.

prepared to convert the added-together financial statements of the parent and subsidiary to the financial statements of the group.

☐ The consolidation worksheet entries do not have an impact on the individual statements of the parent and the subsidiary because the consolidation worksheet is separate from the individual records.

27.3 The acquisition analysis

LEARNING OBJECTIVE 27.3 Prepare an acquisition analysis for the parent's acquisition of a subsidiary.

According to AASB 3/IFRS 3 and as described in chapter 25, entities need to account for business combinations using the acquisition method. As part of the acquisition method, an acquisition analysis is conducted at acquisition date because it is necessary to recognise all the identifiable assets and liabilities of the subsidiary at fair value (including those previously not recorded by the subsidiary), and to determine whether there has been any goodwill acquired or whether a gain on bargain purchase has occurred. The acquisition analysis is considered the first step in the consolidation process as it identifies the information necessary for making both the business combination valuation and pre-acquisition entry adjustments for the consolidation worksheet.

The end result of the acquisition analysis will be the determination of whether there is any goodwill acquired or gain on bargain purchase. Paragraph 32 of AASB 3/IFRS 3 sets out the measurement of goodwill as follows.

> The acquirer shall recognise goodwill as of the acquisition date measured as the excess of (a) over (b) below:
> (a) the aggregate of:
>   (i) the consideration transferred measured in accordance with this Standard, which generally requires acquisition-date fair value (see paragraph 37);
>   (ii) the amount of any non-controlling interest in the acquiree measured in accordance with this Standard; and
>   (iii) in a business combination achieved in stages (see paragraphs 41 and 42), the acquisition-date fair value of the acquirer's previously held *equity interest* in the acquiree.
> (b) the net of the acquisition-date amounts of the identifiable assets acquired and the liabilities assumed measured in accordance with this Standard.

If (a) is less than (b), no goodwill is acquired and the difference will be recognised as gain on bargain purchase. In this chapter, because the parent acquires all the shares in the subsidiary, there is no effect due to (a)(ii). However, because of (a)(iii), the acquisition analysis is affected by whether at acquisition date the parent has previously acquired any equity interests in the subsidiary.

27.3.1 Parent has no previously held equity interest in the subsidiary

In this case, the parent acquires all the shares of the subsidiary at acquisition date in one transaction. In terms of paragraph 32 of AASB 3/IFRS 3, goodwill arises when the consideration transferred (paragraph 32(a)(i)) is greater than the net fair value of the identifiable assets and liabilities acquired (paragraph 32(b)). Where the reverse occurs, a gain on bargain purchase is recognised.

Consider the example in figure 27.3.

FIGURE 27.3	Information at acquisition date

On 1 July 2022, Parent Ltd acquired all the issued share capital of Subsidiary Ltd, giving in exchange 100 000 shares in Parent Ltd, these having a fair value of $5 per share. At acquisition date, the statements of financial position of Parent Ltd and Subsidiary Ltd, and the fair values of Subsidiary Ltd's assets and liabilities, were as follows.

	Parent Ltd	Subsidiary Ltd	
	Carrying amount	Carrying amount	Fair value
EQUITY AND LIABILITIES			
Equity			
Share capital	$550 000	$300 000	
Retained earnings	350 000	140 000	
Total equity	900 000	440 000	
Liabilities			
Provisions	30 000	60 000	$60 000
Payables	27 000	34 000	34 000
Deferred tax liabilities	10 000	6 000	6 000
Total liabilities	67 000	100 000	
Total equity and liabilities	**$967 000**	**$540 000**	
ASSETS			
Land	$120 000	$150 000	170 000
Equipment	620 000	480 000	330 000
Accumulated depreciation — equipment	(380 000)	(170 000)	
Shares in Subsidiary Ltd	500 000		
Inventories	92 000	75 000	80 000
Cash	15 000	5 000	5 000
Total assets	**$967 000**	**$540 000**	

At acquisition date, Subsidiary Ltd has an unrecorded patent with a fair value of $20 000 and a contingent liability with a fair value of $15 000. This contingent liability relates to a loan guarantee made by Subsidiary Ltd which did not recognise a liability in its records because it did not consider it could reliably measure the liability. The tax rate is 30%.

The acquisition analysis consists of calculating and comparing the fair value of the consideration transferred and the net fair value of the identifiable assets and liabilities of the subsidiary at acquisition date. The net fair value of the identifiable assets and liabilities of the subsidiary could be calculated by revaluing the assets and liabilities of the subsidiary from the carrying amounts to fair values, remembering that, under AASB 112/IAS 12 *Income Taxes*, where there is a difference between the carrying amount and the tax base caused by a revaluation, the tax effect of such a difference has to be recognised as a deferred tax liability or asset. However, the calculation of the net fair value of the identifiable assets and liabilities of the subsidiary is done in a simpler way, starting with the recorded equity of the subsidiary, which represents the recorded net assets of the subsidiary at their carrying amounts. If the subsidiary recorded goodwill from a previous business combination, the calculation has to eliminate it from the amount recognised as the recorded net assets of the subsidiary — because only the value of net identifiable assets is required (this case is discussed in section 27.4.4). Next, the differences between the fair values of the assets and their carrying amounts, adjusted for tax, are added and the differences between the fair values of the liabilities and their carrying amounts, adjusted for tax, are subtracted. The last step is to add and subtract the fair values of the assets and liabilities respectively that were not previously recognised by the subsidiary, also adjusted for tax.

In the example in figure 27.3, the recorded equity of the subsidiary consists of:

$$\$300\,000 \text{ capital} + \$140\,000 \text{ retained earnings}$$

An equity account is raised relating to the differences between fair value and carrying amounts for assets and liabilities recorded by Subsidiary Ltd — as well as for assets and liabilities not recognised by the subsidiary but recognised as being acquired as part of the business combination — referred to in this chapter as the *business combination valuation reserve* (BCVR). However, only the after-tax differences will be recognised in this reserve as the equity and the net assets are only affected by the after-tax differences. This reserve is not an account recognised in the subsidiary's records, but it is recognised in the consolidation process as part of the business combination valuation entries. For example, for land there is a difference of $20 000 between the fair value and its carrying amount and, on revaluation of the land to fair value, a business combination valuation reserve of $14 000 (i.e. $20 000(1 − 30%), where 30% is the tax rate) is raised. For provision for guarantee, recognised on consolidation in relation to the contingent liability for the loan guarantee, a negative amount of $10 500 (i.e. $15 000(1 − 30%)) will be recognised in business combination valuation reserve, as liabilities decrease the value of equity or net assets. This reserve is recognising the adjustments to the recorded equity necessary to reflect the net fair value of equity, which, in the absence of previously recorded goodwill, would be equal to the net fair value of the identifiable assets and liabilities of the subsidiary.

The consideration transferred has to be measured at fair value at acquisition date and adjusted for the dividends declared prior to acquisition and payable after acquisition to the parent. As those dividends can be considered to be a refund on the consideration transferred, they will be deducted from the value of the consideration transferred (this case is discussed in section 27.4.5).

The acquisition analysis, including the determination of the acquired goodwill, is as shown in figure 27.4.

FIGURE 27.4	Acquisition analysis — no previously held equity interests

At 1 July 2022:

Net fair value of identifiable assets and liabilities
of Subsidiary Ltd = $300 000 + $140 000 (equity)
+ ($170 000 − $150 000)(1 − 30%) (BCVR — land)
+ ($330 000 − $310 000)(1 − 30%) (BCVR — equipment)
+ ($80 000 − $75 000)(1 − 30%) (BCVR — inventories)
+ $20 000(1 − 30%) (BCVR — patent)
− $15 000(1 − 30%) (BCVR — provision for guarantee)
= $475 000

Consideration transferred = 100 000 shares × $5
= $500 000

Goodwill = $500 000 − $475 000
= $25 000

27.3.2 Parent has previously held equity interest in the subsidiary

The situation described in figure 27.3 will be used here, the only difference being that on 1 July 2022 Parent Ltd acquires 80% (i.e. 240 000) of the shares in Subsidiary Ltd, giving in exchange 80 000 shares in Parent Ltd (these having a fair value of $5 per share). Parent Ltd had previously acquired the other 20% (i.e. 60 000) of the shares of Subsidiary Ltd for $75 000. At 1 July 2022, this previous investment in Subsidiary Ltd was recorded by Parent Ltd at $92 000. This investment was classified as a financial instrument and measured at fair value, with $17 000 having previously been recognised in other comprehensive income. At 1 July 2022, these shares had a fair value of $100 000.

In accordance with paragraph 42 of AASB 3/IFRS 3, Parent Ltd normally revalues the previously held investment to fair value, recognising the increase in profit or loss. However, if Parent Ltd had elected under paragraph 5.7.5 of AASB 9/IFRS 9 *Financial Instruments* to present changes in fair value in other comprehensive income, such changes would be recognised in other comprehensive income. The journal entries in Parent Ltd at acquisition date, both for the previously held investment as well as the acquisition of the remaining shares in Subsidiary Ltd, are as follows.

Shares in Subsidiary Ltd	Dr	8 000	
Gain on investment	Cr		8 000
(Revaluation to fair value)			
Shares in Subsidiary Ltd	Dr	400 000	
Share capital	Cr		400 000
(Acquisition of shares in Subsidiary Ltd by issuing and transferring 80 000 shares at $5 per share)			

The acquisition analysis is shown in figure 27.5.

FIGURE 27.5   Acquisition analysis — previously held equity interests

At 1 July 2022:

Net fair value of identifiable assets and liabilities
of Subsidiary Ltd

$$= \$300\,000 + \$140\,000 \text{ (equity)}$$
$$+ (\$170\,000 - \$150\,000)(1 - 30\%) \text{ (BCVR — land)}$$
$$+ (\$330\,000 - \$310\,000)(1 - 30\%) \text{ (BCVR — equipment)}$$
$$+ (\$80\,000 - \$75\,000)(1 - 30\%) \text{ (BCVR — inventories)}$$
$$+ \$20\,000(1 - 30\%) \text{ (BCVR — patent)}$$
$$- \$15\,000(1 - 30\%) \text{ (BCVR — provision for guarantee)}$$
$$= \$475\,000$$

Consideration transferred

$$= 80\,000 \text{ shares} \times \$5$$
$$= \$400\,000$$

Fair value of previously held equity interests $= \$100\,000$

Aggregate investment

$$= \$400\,000 + \$100\,000$$
$$= \$500\,000$$

Goodwill

$$= \$500\,000 - \$475\,000$$
$$= \$25\,000$$

LEARNING CHECK

☐ The acquisition analysis for a wholly owned subsidiary consists of calculating and comparing the net fair value of the identifiable assets and liabilities of the subsidiary at acquisition date with the investment by the parent in the subsidiary's shares at fair value and determining whether any goodwill or gain on bargain purchase has arisen as a part of the business combination.

☐ The acquisition analysis starts with the value of shareholders' equity (net assets) recorded by the subsidiary at acquisition date, from which the value of previously recorded goodwill (an unidentifiable asset) is deducted to come up with the book value of the net identifiable assets and liabilities of the subsidiary.

☐ The acquisition analysis then includes after-tax adjustments for differences between carrying amounts and fair values at acquisition date of the identifiable assets and liabilities recorded by the subsidiary and for the recognition of identifiable assets and liabilities not previously recognised in the records of the subsidiary. These adjustments to the book value of the net identifiable assets and liabilities of the subsidiary result in the net fair value of the identifiable assets and liabilities of the subsidiary at acquisition date.

☐ The investment by the parent in the subsidiary's shares at fair value includes the fair value of the consideration transferred and the fair value of the previously held ownership interest in the subsidiary.

☐ The consideration transferred is reduced for any dividends payable to the parent that were declared prior to the acquisition, as they are considered as a refund of a part of the consideration transferred.

☐ Where at acquisition date the parent holds shares in the subsidiary that it has previously acquired, this investment must be revalued to fair value at acquisition date and recognise the resulting gain or loss, if any, in profit or loss or other comprehensive income, as appropriate.

☐ The acquisition analysis ends with the determination of whether there is any goodwill acquired or gain on bargain purchase by comparing the consideration transferred (adjusted for dividends payable declared prior to acquisition) plus the fair value at acquisition date of the previously held investment to the net fair value of the identifiable assets and liabilities of the subsidiary at acquisition date.

27.4 Consolidation worksheet entries at the acquisition date

LEARNING OBJECTIVE 27.4 Prepare the consolidation worksheet entries at the acquisition date, being the business combination valuation entries and the pre-acquisition entries.

As noted earlier, the consolidation process does not result in any entries being made in the actual records of either the parent or the subsidiary. The adjustment entries are made on the consolidation journal and posted in the consolidation worksheet. Given that the consolidation process for each period starts by adding together the individual financial statements of the subsidiary and the parent prepared for that period, the adjustments posted in a previous period do not carry over. Hence, adjustment entries need to be passed in each worksheet prepared, and these entries may change over time. This section of the chapter analyses the adjustment entries that would be passed in a consolidation worksheet prepared *at the acquisition date*.

27.4.1 Business combination valuation entries

In figure 27.3, there are three identifiable assets recognised by the subsidiary with fair values that differ from their carrying amounts at acquisition date. There is also an intangible asset and a contingent liability not previously recognised by the subsidiary that should be recognised as part of the business combination. The identifiable assets and liabilities that require adjustment to fair value can be easily identified by reference to the acquisition analyses in figures 27.4 and 27.5, namely land, equipment, inventories, patent and the unrecorded provision for guarantee. Goodwill also has to be recognised on consolidation. These differences are all recognised using business combination valuation entries (see section 27.6 for a discussion on making some of these adjustments in the records of the subsidiary itself). Consolidation worksheet adjustment entries for each of these assets and the unrecorded liability are given in figure 27.6.

FIGURE 27.6	Business combination valuation entries at acquisition date

Business combination valuation entries				
(1)	Land	Dr	20 000	
	Deferred tax liability	Cr		6 000
	Business combination valuation reserve	Cr		14 000
(2)	Accumulated depreciation — equipment	Dr	170 000	
	Equipment	Cr		150 000
	Deferred tax liability	Cr		6 000
	Business combination valuation reserve	Cr		14 000
(3)	Inventories	Dr	5 000	
	Deferred tax liability	Cr		1 500
	Business combination valuation reserve	Cr		3 500
(4)	Patent	Dr	20 000	
	Deferred tax liability	Cr		6 000
	Business combination valuation reserve	Cr		14 000
(5)	Business combination valuation reserve	Dr	10 500	
	Deferred tax asset	Dr	4 500	
	Provision for loan guarantee	Cr		15 000
(6)	Goodwill	Dr	25 000	
	Business combination valuation reserve	Cr		25 000

Note that the increase in value of identifiable assets and the recognition of identifiable assets not previously recognised by the subsidiary give rise to business combination valuation reserves, as discussed previously, but also to deferred tax liabilities. The tax effects for those adjustments for assets are recognised as deferred tax liabilities because the carrying amounts of those assets increase, while the tax bases are assumed to not change and that will increase the taxable temporary differences. On the other hand, the recognition of liabilities not previously recognised by the subsidiary give rise to negative amounts in business combination valuation reserves, as discussed previously, but also to deferred tax assets. The tax effects for those adjustments for liabilities are recognised as deferred tax assets because the carrying amounts of those liabilities increase, while the tax bases are 0 and that will increase the deductible temporary differences. The goodwill adjustment does not give rise to a deferred tax asset or liability as the temporary difference created is an excluded difference under AASB 112/IAS 12. The total balance of the business combination valuation reserve is $60 000. Because it recognises the value adjustments for the subsidiary's net assets at acquisition date, the business combination valuation reserve is considered to be part of the pre-acquisition equity of the subsidiary. The valuation entries are posted in the adjustment columns of the worksheet, which is illustrated in section 27.4.3.

27.4.2 Pre-acquisition entries

As noted in paragraph B86(b) of AASB 10/IFRS 10, the pre-acquisition entries are required to eliminate the carrying amount of the parent's investment in the subsidiary and the parent's portion of pre-acquisition equity. The pre-acquisition entries at acquisition date, then, involve two areas:
- the investment account 'Shares in Subsidiary Ltd', as shown in the financial statements of the parent
- the equity of the subsidiary at the acquisition date (i.e. the pre-acquisition equity). The pre-acquisition equity is not just the equity recorded by the subsidiary but includes the business combination valuation reserve recognised on consolidation via the business combination valuation entries.

Using the example in figure 27.3, and reading the information from the acquisition analysis in figure 27.4 (including the business combination valuation reserve for the revalued assets, patent, goodwill and the contingent liability), the pre-acquisition entry at acquisition date is as shown in figure 27.7. The pre-acquisition entry in this figure is numbered (7) because there were six previous business combination valuation entries as shown in figure 27.6.

FIGURE 27.7	Pre-acquisition entry at acquisition date			
Pre-acquisition entry				
(7)	Retained earnings (1/7/22)	Dr	140 000	
	Share capital	Dr	300 000	
	Business combination valuation reserve	Dr	60 000	
	Shares in Subsidiary Ltd	Cr		500 000

The pre-acquisition entry is necessary to avoid overstating the assets, liabilities and equity of the group. To illustrate, consider the information in figure 27.3 relating to Parent Ltd's acquisition of the shares in Subsidiary Ltd. Having acquired the shares in Subsidiary Ltd, Parent Ltd records as an asset the investment account 'Shares in Subsidiary Ltd' at $500 000. This asset represents the actual net assets of Subsidiary Ltd; that is, the ownership of the shares gives Parent Ltd the right to the assets and liabilities of Subsidiary Ltd. To include both the asset investment account 'Shares in Subsidiary Ltd' and the assets and liabilities of Subsidiary Ltd in the consolidated statement of financial position would double count the assets and liabilities of the subsidiary. On consolidation, the investment account is therefore eliminated.

Similarly, Parent Ltd has equity of $900 000, which represents its net assets including the investment account, 'Shares in Subsidiary Ltd'. Because the investment in the subsidiary represents the actual net assets of Subsidiary Ltd, or, in other words, the equity of the subsidiary, the equity of the parent effectively includes the equity of the subsidiary. To include both the equity of the subsidiary at acquisition date and the equity of the parent in the consolidated statement of financial position would double count the pre-acquisition equity of the subsidiary. On consolidation, the equity of the subsidiary at acquisition date is therefore eliminated.

A further explanation for the elimination in the pre-acquisition entry of the investment account and the pre-acquisition equity of the subsidiary is that the investment account cannot be recognised in the consolidated financial statements as it represents, from the group's perspective, an investment in itself. Therefore, the investment account recognised by the parent is eliminated first. This elimination makes sure that the group's assets are now properly recorded, recognising the parent's assets minus the investment in the subsidiary, plus, as a result of the business combination valuation entries above, the subsidiary's identifiable assets recorded at fair value plus goodwill, as the following equation shows.

$$
\begin{aligned}
\text{Group's assets} &= \text{Parent's assets} - \text{Investment in subsidiary} + \text{Subsidiary's identifiable} \\
&\quad \text{assets at fair value} + \text{Goodwill} \\
&= \text{Parent's assets} + \text{Subsidiary's identifiable assets at fair value} \\
&\quad - (\text{Investment in subsidiary} - \text{Goodwill})
\end{aligned}
$$

However, at acquisition date, goodwill is the excess of the investment over the subsidiary's identifiable assets minus liabilities recorded at fair value; as such, the difference between the investment in the subsidiary and goodwill is equal to the subsidiary's identifiable assets minus liabilities recorded at fair value, and therefore:

$$
\begin{aligned}
\text{Group's assets} &= \text{Parent's assets} + \text{Subsidiary's identifiable assets at fair value} - \text{Subsidiary's} \\
&\quad \text{identifiable net assets at fair value} \\
&= \text{Parent's assets} + \text{Subsidiary's liabilities at fair value}
\end{aligned}
$$

According to the fundamental accounting equation (i.e. assets = liabilities + equity), and knowing that the group's liabilities include the parent's liabilities plus the subsidiary's liabilities at fair value, the group's equity can be written as follows.

Group's equity = Group's assets − Group's liabilities

= Parent's assets + Subsidiary's liabilities at fair value

− (Parent's liabilities + Subsidiary's liabilities at fair value)

= Parent's assets − Parent's liabilities

= Parent's equity

As such, at acquisition date, the equity of the group should be equal to the parent's equity only and therefore the subsidiary's equity (including the business combination valuation reserve) should be eliminated from the aggregated amount of the parent's and the subsidiary's equity before the amount can be recognised in the consolidated financial statements.

27.4.3 Consolidation worksheet

Figure 27.8 contains the consolidation worksheet prepared at acquisition date, with adjustments being made as business combination valuation entries and pre-acquisition entries. The right-hand column reflects the consolidated amounts that will be posted in the consolidated statement of financial position. In relation to this column, note the following.

- The assets of the subsidiary are carried forward into the consolidated statement of financial position at fair value, due to the adjustments in the business combination valuation entries.
- With the business combination valuation reserve, the business combination valuation entry establishes the reserve, and the pre-acquisition entry eliminates it because it is by nature part of pre-acquisition equity.
- In relation to the two equity accounts recorded in the separate statements of the parent and the subsidiary prior to consolidation — share capital and retained earnings — only the parent's balances are carried into the consolidated statement of financial position. At acquisition date, all the equity of the subsidiary is pre-acquisition equity and is eliminated in the pre-acquisition entries.

FIGURE 27.8 Consolidation worksheet at acquisition date

Financial statements	Parent Ltd	Subsidiary Ltd		Dr	Cr		Group
				Adjustments			
Retained earnings (1/7/22)	350 000	140 000	7	140 000			350 000
Share capital	550 000	300 000	7	300 000			550 000
Business combination			5	10 500	14 000	1	—
valuation reserve			7	60 000	14 000	2	
					3 500	3	
					14 000	4	
					25 000	6	
	900 000	440 000					900 000
Provisions	30 000	60 000			15 000	5	105 000
Payables	27 000	34 000					61 000
Deferred tax liabilities (net							
of deferred tax assets)	10 000	6 000	5	4 500	6 000	1	31 000
					6 000	2	
					1 500	3	
					6 000	4	
	67 000	100 000					197 000
Total equity and liabilities	967 000	540 000					1 097 000
Cash	15 000	5 000					20 000
Land	120 000	150 000	1	20 000			290 000
Equipment	620 000	480 000			150 000	2	950 000
Accumulated depreciation	(380 000)	(170 000)	2	170 000			(380 000)
Shares in Subsidiary Ltd	500 000	—			500 000	7	—
Inventories	92 000	75 000	3	5 000			172 000
Patent	—	—	4	20 000			20 000
Goodwill	—	—	6	25 000			25 000
Total assets	967 000	540 000					1 097 000

27.4.4 Subsidiary has recorded goodwill at acquisition date

In the example used in section 27.4.3, at acquisition date the subsidiary did not have any recorded goodwill. Consider the situation where the assets recorded by the subsidiary at acquisition date are the same as in figure 27.3 except that now there is recorded goodwill, as follows.

	Subsidiary Ltd	
	Carrying amount	Fair value
Cash	$ 5 000	$ 5 000
Land	150 000	170 000
Equipment	480 000	330 000
Accumulated depreciation — equipment	(170 000)	
Goodwill	**10 000**	
Inventories	75 000	80 000
	$550 000	

The acquisition analysis, assuming no previously held equity interests by the parent, is then as follows.

Net fair value of identifiable assets and liabilities of Subsidiary Ltd	= $300 000 + $140 000 (equity)
	+ ($170 000 − $150 000)(1 − 30%) (BCVR — land)
	+ ($330 000 − $310 000)(1 − 30%) (BCVR — equipment)
	+ ($80 000 − $75 000)(1 − 30%) (BCVR — inventories)
	+ $20 000(1 − 30%) (BCVR — patent)
	− $15 000(1 − 30%) (BCVR — provision for guarantee)
	− **$10 000 (goodwill)**
	= $465 000
Consideration transferred	= 100 000 × $5
	= $500 000
Goodwill	= $500 000 − $465 000
	= $35 000
Recorded goodwill	= **$10 000**
Unrecorded goodwill	= **$25 000**

Note that, since the first calculation in the acquisition analysis relates to the fair value of the *identifiable* assets, the goodwill of the subsidiary (i.e. an unidentifiable asset) must be subtracted. Further, it is necessary to calculate the additional goodwill not recorded by the subsidiary, this being the amount that should be recognised on consolidation. The amount of goodwill that would be recognised in the business combination valuation entry is $25 000.

(6)	Goodwill	Dr	25 000	
	Business combination valuation reserve	Cr		25 000

The pre-acquisition entry is as follows.

(7)	Retained earnings (1/7/22)	Dr	140 000	
	Share capital	Dr	300 000	
	Business combination valuation reserve	Dr	60 000	
	Shares in Subsidiary Ltd	Cr		500 000

Note that the journal entry is the same as in the case when the subsidiary has not recorded any goodwill prior to the acquisition. However, the line item for goodwill in the consolidation worksheet is different due to previously recorded goodwill and would show the following.

			Adjustments		
Financial statements	Parent Ltd	Subsidiary Ltd	Dr	Cr	Group
Goodwill	—	10 000	6	25 000		35 000

The consolidated statement of financial position thus shows the total goodwill of the consolidated entity. Any accumulated impairment losses related to goodwill recorded by the subsidiary at acquisition date must be eliminated in the consolidation worksheet. If the total goodwill of the consolidated entity is impaired after acquisition, the impaired goodwill could be either that recognised by the subsidiary prior to consolidation or that recognised on consolidation, based on whether the subsidiary or the group, treated as cash generating units, are impaired respectively. If the goodwill recorded by the subsidiary is impaired, no adjustment is required on consolidation for the impairment of that goodwill as the impairment is recorded in the subsidiary's accounts. If the goodwill recognised on consolidation is impaired, this is done via the consolidation entries.

27.4.5 Subsidiary has recorded dividends at acquisition date

Using the information in figure 27.3, assume that one of the payables at acquisition date is a dividend payable of $10 000. The parent can acquire the shares in the subsidiary on a *cum div.* or an *ex div.* basis.

If the shares are acquired on a *cum div.* basis, then the parent acquires the right to the dividend declared by the subsidiary prior to the acquisition date. In this case, if Parent Ltd transfers shares worth $500 000 for the shares in Subsidiary Ltd, then the entry it passes to record the business combination in its own records is as follows.

Shares in Subsidiary Ltd	Dr	490 000	
Dividend receivable	Dr	10 000	
Share capital	Cr		500 000

Therefore, the parent acquires two assets — the investment in the subsidiary and the dividend receivable. In calculating the goodwill in the subsidiary, using the information in figure 27.3, the acquisition analysis is as follows.

Net fair value of identifiable assets and liabilities of Subsidiary Ltd	= $300 000 + $140 000 (equity)
	+ ($170 000 − $150 000)(1 − 30%) (BCVR — land)
	+ ($330 000 − $310 000)(1 − 30%) (BCVR — equipment)
	+ ($80 000 − $75 000)(1 − 30%) (BCVR — inventories)
	+ $20 000(1 − 30%) (BCVR — patent)
	− $15 000(1 − 30%) (BCVR — provision for guarantee)
	= $475 000
Consideration transferred	= **(100 000 × $5) − $10 000 (dividend receivable)**
	= **$490 000**
Goodwill	= $490 000 − $475 000
	= $15 000

The fair value of the consideration paid for the net assets of the subsidiary is that recognised in the investment in the subsidiary account, excluding the dividend receivable. This dividend can be considered a refund of the consideration transferred that decreases the cost of the investment. The pre-acquisition entry is, therefore as follows.

(7)	Retained earnings (1/7/22)	Dr	140 000	
	Share capital	Dr	300 000	
	Business combination valuation reserve	Dr	50 000	
	Shares in Subsidiary Ltd	Cr		490 000

However, a further consolidation worksheet entry is also required.

Dividend payable	Dr	10 000	
Dividend receivable	Cr		10 000

This last entry is necessary so that the consolidated statement of financial position shows only the assets and liabilities of the group; that is, only those benefits receivable from, and obligations payable to, entities external to the group. In relation to the dividend receivable recorded by Parent Ltd, this is not an asset of the group, because the group does not expect to receive dividends from a party external to it. Similarly, the dividend payable recorded by the subsidiary is not a liability of the group. That dividend will be paid within the group, not to entities outside the group. Therefore, the entry eliminates the intragroup dividend.

If the shares are acquired on an *ex div.* basis, then the parent only acquires the shares and it is not entitled to receive the dividend declared by the subsidiary prior to the acquisition. The dividend has no effect on the acquisition analysis. If Parent Ltd had transferred a consideration worth $500 000 for the shares in Subsidiary Ltd on an *ex div.* basis, then the acquisition analysis is exactly the same as in figure 27.4 and the pre-acquisition entry is the same as in figure 27.7.

27.4.6 Gain on bargain purchase

In figure 27.3, Parent Ltd transferred a consideration worth $500 000 for the shares in Subsidiary Ltd. Consider the situation where Parent Ltd paid $470 000 for these shares. The acquisition analysis is as shown in figure 27.9.

FIGURE 27.9	Acquisition analysis — gain on bargain purchase

Net fair value of identifiable assets and liabilities
of Subsidiary Ltd
= $300 000 + $140 000 (equity)
+ ($170 000 − $150 000)(1 − 30%) (BCVR — land)
+ ($330 000 − $310 000)(1 − 30%) (BCVR — equipment)
+ ($80 000 − $75 000)(1 − 30%) (BCVR — inventories)
+ $20 000(1 − 30%) (BCVR — patent)
− $15 000(1 − 30%) (BCVR — provision for guarantee)
= $475 000

Consideration transferred = $470 000

Gain on bargain purchase = $475 000 − $470 000
= $5000

As the net fair value of the identifiable assets and liabilities of the subsidiary is greater than the consideration transferred, in accordance with paragraph 36 of AASB 3/IFRS 3 the acquirer must firstly reassess the identification and measurement of the subsidiary's identifiable assets and liabilities as well as the measurement of the consideration transferred. The expectation under AASB 3/IFRS 3 is that the excess of the net fair value over the consideration transferred is usually the result of measurement errors rather than being a real gain to the acquirer. However, having confirmed the identification and measurement of both amounts paid and net assets acquired, if an excess still exists, under paragraph 34 it is recognised immediately in profit as a gain on bargain purchase.

The existence of a gain on bargain purchase has no effect on the business combination valuation entries unless, as discussed in section 27.4.4, the subsidiary has previously recorded goodwill. In that case, a business combination revaluation entry crediting goodwill and debiting business combination valuation reserve for the amount of goodwill recorded by the subsidiary would be required. (If impairment losses have been recognised on that goodwill, the journal entry would include a credit to goodwill for the amount of goodwill recorded by the subsidiary at cost, a debit for business combination valuation reserve for the carrying amount of goodwill and another debit for the accumulated impairment losses on this goodwill.) That is because the previously recorded goodwill has to be eliminated. Nevertheless, the gain on bargain purchase has to be recognised at acquisition date in the pre-acquisition entry and it is not eliminated as it is part of post-acquisition equity. The pre-acquisition entry for the situation in figure 27.9 is as shown in figure 27.10. Note that this entry eliminates the pre-acquisition equity and the investment account and recognises the gain on bargain purchase.

FIGURE 27.10	Pre-acquisition entry at acquisition date — gain on bargain purchase

	Pre-acquisition entry			
(7)	Retained earnings (1/7/22)	Dr	140 000	
	Share capital	Dr	300 000	
	Business combination valuation reserve	Dr	35 000	
	Gain on bargain purchase	Cr		5 000
	Shares in Subsidiary Ltd	Cr		470 000

LEARNING CHECK

☐ Business combination valuation entries at acquisition date are used to recognise the identifiable assets and liabilities of the subsidiary at fair value and the previously unrecorded goodwill. As a result of these entries, a business combination valuation reserve is recognised on consolidation as part of pre-acquisition equity.

☐ Pre-acquisition entries at acquisition date eliminate the pre-acquisition equity of the subsidiary and the investment account recorded by the parent.

☐ When the subsidiary has recorded goodwill at acquisition date, adjustments must be made in the acquisition analysis to determine the amount of goodwill to be recognised in the consolidation worksheet.

▶

☐ When the subsidiary has recorded a dividend payable at acquisition date and the parent recognised it as dividend receivable on acquisition, adjustments must be made in the acquisition analysis when calculating the consideration transferred for the net assets of the subsidiary.

☐ If the acquisition analysis determined the existence of a gain on bargain purchase and not goodwill, the gain on bargain purchase will be recognised in the pre-acquisition entry at acquisition date. If the subsidiary had a previously recorded goodwill, that goodwill will have to be eliminated as part of the business combination valuation entries at acquisition date.

27.5 Consolidation worksheet entries subsequent to the acquisition date

LEARNING OBJECTIVE 27.5 Prepare the consolidation worksheet entries in periods subsequent to the acquisition date.

At acquisition date, the business combination valuation entries result in the economic entity (i.e. the group) recognising assets and liabilities of the subsidiary at fair value, including those that were not previously recognised by the subsidiary. Subsequently, changes in these assets and liabilities occur as assets are depreciated or sold, liabilities settled and goodwill impaired. Movements in pre-acquisition equity also occur as dividends are declared or paid from pre-acquisition equity and transfers are made within pre-acquisition equity.

27.5.1 Business combination valuation entries

In the example used in figure 27.3, business combination valuation entries were made for five items: land, equipment, inventories, patent and the provision for guarantee. In this section, a 3-year time period subsequent to the acquisition date, 1 July 2022, is analysed (giving an end of reporting period of 30 June 2025) with the following events occurring.
- The land is sold in the period ended 30 June 2025.
- The equipment is depreciated on a straight-line basis over a 5-year period after acquisition.
- The inventories on hand at 1 July 2022 are all sold by 30 June 2023, the end of the first year after acquisition date.
- The patent has an indefinite life, and is tested for impairment annually, with an impairment loss of $5000 recognised in the period ended 30 June 2024.
- The provision for the guarantee results in a payment of $10 000 in June 2023, with no further liability existing.
- Goodwill is written down by $5000 in the period ended 30 June 2024 as a result of an impairment test.

Each of the assets and liabilities will now be analysed separately with the consolidation worksheet subsequently shown for the period ended 30 June 2025.

Land

At acquisition date, 1 July 2022, the business combination valuation entry is as follows.

Land	Dr	20 000	
Deferred tax liability	Cr		6 000
Business combination valuation reserve	Cr		14 000

This entry will be repeated in all future periods until the period when the land is derecognised even though the entry was posted in the previous periods. That is because the entry was posted in the consolidation journal and did not have any effect on the individual statements of the subsidiary; as a result, it did not carry forward to the next period. At 30 June 2023, because the land is still on hand, the same business combination valuation entry is made in the consolidation worksheet used to prepare the consolidated financial statements at that date. It is assumed that the asset is not held for sale in this period and is recorded at cost.

Assume that in the period ended 30 June 2024 the land is classified as held for sale and is accounted for under AASB 5/IFRS 5 *Non-current Assets Held for Sale and Discontinued Operations*. The land is then recorded at the lower of its carrying amount and fair value less costs of disposal. Assuming the carrying amount is the lower value, then the business combination valuation entry in the consolidation worksheet prepared at 30 June 2024 is the same as that for 30 June 2023.

Assume that in the period ended 30 June 2025 the land is sold for $200 000, incurring $1000 in costs to sell. Subsidiary Ltd will record a gain on sale of $49 000 (i.e. $200 000 − $150 000 − $1000). From the group's perspective, the gain on sale is only $29 000 (i.e. $200 000 − $170 000 − $1000). Hence, on consolidation, an adjustment to reduce the recorded gain by $20 000 is required. The factor causing the difference in gain on sale is the cost of the land sold. The cost of the land is greater to the group than to the subsidiary. As the asset has been sold, there will not be any temporary differences to recognise as a deferred tax liability anymore. Note, however, that due to the reduction in the recorded gain, an adjustment needs to be made to income tax expense to reduce it as well.

The business combination valuation entry at 30 June 2025 is as follows.

Gain on sale of land	Dr	20 000
Income tax expense	Cr	6 000
Business combination valuation reserve	Cr	14 000

Alternatively, if Subsidiary Ltd sold the land for $120 000, incurring $1000 in costs to sell, it would record in its accounts a loss on sale of $31 000. From the group's perspective, the loss on sale is $51 000. Hence, on consolidation, an adjustment to increase the recorded loss by $20 000 is required. Therefore, if the subsidiary's financial statements show a loss on sale of land, the business combination valuation entry will be as follows.

Loss on sale of land	Dr	20 000
Income tax expense	Cr	6 000
Business combination valuation reserve	Cr	14 000

Where revalued assets are derecognised, as noted in paragraph 41 of AASB 116/IAS 16 *Property, Plant and Equipment*, it is usual business practice to transfer the revaluation surplus to retained earnings. If this principle is applied on consolidation, then in the year of sale of the land another business combination valuation entry is posted as follows.

Business combination valuation reserve	Dr	14 000
Transfer from business combination valuation reserve	Cr	14 000

The entry that adjusts the gain or loss on sale of land can be combined with the entry that recognises the transfer from business combination valuation reserve to retained earnings into one entry as follows.

Gain on sale of land/Loss on sale of land	Dr	20 000
Income tax expense	Cr	6 000
Transfer from business combination valuation reserve	Cr	14 000

Because this entry has no net effect on retained earnings in subsequent periods (when all the accounts involved will transfer to retained earnings), no consolidation worksheet entries are required after the period when the land was sold. Another explanation is that as the asset is derecognised by the subsidiary, the fair value increment that should have been recognised at acquisition date is now 'realised' and recognised under subsidiary's profits, which in subsequent periods are in the subsidiary's retained earnings — in essence, that is equivalent to having recognised that value increment in the subsidiary's accounts and therefore no further adjustments are necessary.

Equipment

The business combination valuation entry at 1 July 2022 is as follows.

Accumulated depreciation — equipment	Dr	170 000
Equipment	Cr	150 000
Deferred tax liability	Cr	6 000
Business combination valuation reserve	Cr	14 000

This entry will be repeated until the period when the equipment is derecognised. However, the asset is depreciated on a straight-line basis evenly over a 5-year period, equivalent to a rate of depreciation of 20% p.a. Because the asset is recognised by the group at an amount that is $20 000 greater than that recognised in the records of the subsidiary, the depreciation expense to the group must also be greater in every period by 20% × $20 000. Also, as the depreciation increases, the difference between the carrying amount and tax base decreases and the taxable temporary difference at acquisition date is partly reversed every period. Therefore, the deferred tax liability recognised at acquisition date is progressively reversed, with the movement being in proportion to depreciation charges — in this case 20% p.a. The adjustments for depreciation and the related tax effects are recognised in the consolidation worksheet valuation entries in the periods subsequent to acquisition date up to the period when the asset is fully depreciated or sold.

The business combination valuation entries for equipment at 30 June 2023 are as follows.

Accumulated depreciation — equipment	Dr	170 000	
Equipment	Cr		150 000
Deferred tax liability	Cr		6 000
Business combination valuation reserve	Cr		14 000
Depreciation expense	Dr	4 000	
Accumulated depreciation — equipment	Cr		4 000
(20% × $20 000 p.a.)			
Deferred tax liability	Dr	1 200	
Income tax expense	Cr		1 200
(20% × $6000, or 30% × $4000 p.a.)			

Note that the first entry is the same as that made at acquisition date, with the other two entries reflecting subsequent depreciation and tax-effect changes.

The valuation entries at 30 June 2025 reflect the need to adjust for 3 years' depreciation (i.e. for two previous periods and one current period) as follows.

Accumulated depreciation — equipment	Dr	170 000	
Equipment	Cr		150 000
Deferred tax liability	Cr		6 000
Business combination valuation reserve	Cr		14 000
Depreciation expense	Dr	4 000	
Retained earnings (1/7/24)	Dr	8 000	
Accumulated depreciation — equipment	Cr		12 000
(20% × $20 000 p.a.)			
Deferred tax liability	Dr	3 600	
Income tax expense	Cr		1 200
Retained earnings (1/7/24)	Cr		2 400
(20% × $6000, or 30% × $4000 p.a.)			

Note that the previous periods' adjustments to depreciation and the related tax effects are recognised against retained earnings (opening balance), while the current period's adjustments are recorded against the actual expense accounts. That is because the previous depreciation and income tax expenses are closed to retained earnings at the end of the previous period that they relate to.

The equipment is fully depreciated by 30 June 2027. In the subsidiary's financial statements, neither the equipment nor the related accumulated depreciation is shown as the asset is derecognised by the subsidiary. The consolidation worksheet adjustment must then relate to:

- current period's depreciation: $4000
- the tax effect of the adjustment to the current period's depreciation: 30% × $4000 = $1200
- prior periods' depreciation: 4 years at $4000 per annum = $16 000. As the prior periods' depreciation and its tax effect should be in the retained earnings (opening balance), but on opposite sides (i.e. depreciation on debit, income tax on credit), only the net after-tax adjustment for prior periods' depreciation needs to be posted under retained earnings (opening balance) now: (1 − 30%) × $16 000 = $11 200
- the business combination valuation reserve is then transferred to retained earnings as the asset is fully consumed.

The relevant entry is as follows.

Depreciation expense	Dr	4 000	
Income tax expense	Cr		1 200
Retained earnings (1/7/26)	Dr	11 200	
Transfer from business combination valuation reserve	Cr		14 000

The entries may also be expressed as follows.

Accumulated depreciation — equipment	Dr	170 000	
Equipment	Cr		150 000
Deferred tax liability	Cr		6 000
Business combination valuation reserve	Cr		14 000
Depreciation expense	Dr	4 000	
Retained earnings (1/7/26)	Dr	16 000	
Accumulated depreciation — equipment			20 000
(20% × $20 000 p.a.)			
Deferred tax liability	Dr	6 000	
Income tax expense	Cr		1 200
Retained earnings (1/7/26)	Cr		4 800
(20% × $6000, or 30% × $4000 p.a.)			

Since the equipment is fully consumed and then derecognised, two further entries are required.

Equipment	Dr	150 000	
Accumulated depreciation — equipment	Cr		150 000
Business combination valuation reserve	Dr	14 000	
Transfer from business combination valuation reserve	Cr		14 000

It is recommended that the more complicated set of entries be avoided, as the single-entry adjustment concentrates on adjusting those accounts on the left-hand side of the worksheets that need to be adjusted in order to show the group picture on the right-hand side of the worksheet.

In future periods after the asset is derecognised, no further business combination valuation entries will be required. The value increment for equipment as of acquisition date would have been recognised in the retained earnings by the subsidiary and, in essence, that is equivalent to having been already recorded by the group.

If the equipment had been sold on 1 January 2027, then the worksheet adjustment entry at 30 June 2027 would be similar to that where the asset is fully depreciated. The only difference is that there needs to be an adjustment to the gain on sale of equipment (or to the loss on sale if that is recorded by the subsidiary) to reflect the adjustment to the undepreciated portion of the asset. The consolidation worksheet adjustment must then relate to:

- the current period's depreciation (half a year's depreciation): $\frac{1}{2} \times \$4000 = \$2000$
- the undepreciated portion of the asset at point of sale affecting the gain or loss on the asset sold: $\frac{1}{2} \times \$4000 = \$2000$
- the tax effect of both the adjustment to the current period's depreciation and the gain or loss on the asset: $30\% \times \$4000 = \$1200$
- prior periods' depreciation: 4 years at $4000 per annum = $16 000. As in the previous example, this must be tax-effected so that the adjustment for prior periods' depreciation is $11 200 (i.e. $16 000 × (1 − 30%)).
- the business combination valuation reserve is then transferred to retained earnings as the asset is derecognised.

The relevant entry is as follows.

Depreciation expense	Dr	2 000	
Gain on sale of equipment/Loss on sale of equipment	Dr	2 000	
Income tax expense	Cr		1 200
Retained earnings (1/7/26)	Dr	11 200	
Transfer from business combination valuation reserve	Cr		14 000

Again, as the asset is derecognised in the current period and the fair value increment as of acquisition date is realised by the subsidiary, no further business combination valuation entries will be required in the next periods.

Inventories

The valuation entry for inventories at acquisition date, 1 July 2022, is as follows.

Inventories	Dr	5 000	
Deferred tax liability	Cr		1 500
Business combination valuation reserve	Cr		3 500

The key event affecting the subsequent accounting for inventories is the sale of the inventories by the subsidiary. If the inventories are sold in the period ended 30 June 2023, the subsidiary records cost of sales at the carrying amount of $75 000, whereas the cost to the group is $80 000. Therefore, in the consolidation worksheet, a $5000 adjustment to cost of sales is required. As the inventories are sold, the deferred tax liability does not exist anymore; however, as a result of the adjustment to cost of sales that decreases the profit, a decrease in income tax expense should be recognised. As with land and equipment, the business combination valuation reserve is transferred to retained earnings because the asset is derecognised.

The valuation entry at 30 June 2023 is then as follows.

Cost of sales	Dr	5 000	
Income tax expense	Cr		1 500
Transfer from business combination valuation reserve	Cr		3 500

No consolidation worksheet entry is required in subsequent years as inventories were all sold in the current period and the relevant fair value increment at acquisition date would have been already recognised by the subsidiary in the retained earnings for those subsequent years.

If at 30 June 2023 only 80% of the inventories had been sold, then the valuation entry must reflect adjustments both to cost of sales and ending inventories. The consolidation worksheet valuation entries, reflecting the adjustments for the 80% inventories sold and the 20% still on hand, are respectively as follows.

Cost of sales	Dr	4 000	
Income tax expense	Cr		1 200
Transfer from business combination valuation reserve	Cr		2 800
Inventories	Dr	1 000	
Deferred tax liability	Cr		300
Business combination valuation reserve	Cr		700

Assuming the remaining 20% inventories is sold by 30 June 2024, the valuation entry in the consolidation worksheet prepared at that date is as follows.

Cost of sales	Dr	1 000	
Income tax expense	Cr		300
Transfer from business combination valuation reserve	Cr		700

There won't be any further entries for the next periods as the inventories were all sold by the beginning of the next periods.

Patent

The business combination valuation entry at acquisition date, 1 July 2022, is as follows.

Patent	Dr	20 000	
Deferred tax liability	Cr		6 000
Business combination valuation reserve	Cr		14 000

This entry is used in each year that the patent continues to have an indefinite life. A change occurs only if there is an impairment loss. In this example, an impairment loss of $5000 occurs in the period ended 30 June 2024. The business combination valuation entries at 30 June 2024 are as follows.

Patent	Dr	20 000	
Deferred tax liability	Cr		6 000
Business combination valuation reserve	Cr		14 000
Impairment loss	Dr	5 000	
Accumulated impairment losses	Cr		5 000
Deferred tax liability	Dr	1 500	
Income tax expense	Cr		1 500

The entries at 30 June 2025 are as follows.

Patent	Dr	20 000	
Deferred tax liability	Cr		6 000
Business combination valuation reserve	Cr		14 000
Retained earnings (1/7/24)	Dr	3 500	
Deferred tax liability	Dr	1 500	
Accumulated impairment losses	Cr		5 000

These entries will be repeated in the next periods without changes to the extent that the patent is not derecognised or further impaired.

Liability — provision for loan guarantee

The business combination valuation entry at 1 July 2022 is as follows.

Business combination valuation reserve	Dr	10 500	
Deferred tax asset	Dr	4 500	
Provision for loan guarantee	Cr		15 000

If the liability is paid or otherwise derecognised, the above entry changes. In this example, a payment of $10 000 is made during the year ended 30 June 2023 in relation to this liability. The subsidiary records an expense of $10 000. Since the liability was recognised by the group at acquisition date, now the group should not recognise the expense; therefore, the expense recognised by the subsidiary must be eliminated on consolidation. Further, a gain of $5000 must be recognised by the group as the liability recognised by the group for $15 000 is settled for $10 000. The business combination valuation entry at 30 June 2023 is as follows.

Transfer from business combination valuation reserve	Dr	10 500	
Income tax expense	Dr	4 500	
Expense	Cr		10 000
Gain on derecognition of loan guarantee	Cr		5 000

No entry is required on 30 June 2024 or 30 June 2025 or in any subsequent periods. That is because, as in the case of identifiable assets undervalued or not recorded at acquisition date that were sold or fully depreciated in prior periods, the effect of the liability incurred by the group is now recorded by the subsidiary in the retained earnings, where it should be from the group's perspective as well.

Goodwill

The entry at 1 July 2022 is as follows.

| Goodwill | Dr | 25 000 | |
| Business combination valuation reserve | Cr | | 25 000 |

In the consolidation worksheet prepared at 30 June 2024, the business combination valuation entry will recognise the $25 000 goodwill acquired as above. However, impairment tests for goodwill are undertaken annually. Goodwill is written down by $5000 in the period ended 30 June 2024 as a result of an impairment test. Therefore, a further entry is required to recognise the impairment of the goodwill.

| Impairment loss | Dr | 5 000 | |
| Accumulated impairment losses | Cr | | 5 000 |

The entries at 30 June 2025 are as follows.

Goodwill		Dr	25 000	
Business combination valuation reserve		Cr		25 000
Retained earnings (1/7/24)		Dr	5 000	
Accumulated impairment losses		Cr		5 000

The business combination valuation entries at 30 June 2025 are as shown in figure 27.11.

FIGURE 27.11   Business combination valuation entries at 30 June 2025

(1)	Gain on sale of land	Dr	20 000	
	Income tax expense	Cr		6 000
	Transfer from business combination valuation reserve	Cr		14 000
(2)	Accumulated depreciation — equipment	Dr	170 000	
	Equipment	Cr		150 000
	Deferred tax liability	Cr		6 000
	Business combination valuation reserve	Cr		14 000
	Depreciation expense	Dr	4 000	
	Retained earnings (1/7/24)	Dr	8 000	
	Accumulated depreciation — equipment	Cr		12 000
	(20% × $20 000 p.a.)			
	Deferred tax liability	Dr	3 600	
	Income tax expense	Cr		1 200
	Retained earnings (1/7/24)	Cr		2 400
	(20% × $6000, or 30% × $4000 p.a.)			
(3)	Patent	Dr	20 000	
	Deferred tax liability	Cr		6 000
	Business combination valuation reserve	Cr		14 000
	Retained earnings (1/7/24)	Dr	3 500	
	Deferred tax liability	Dr	1 500	
	Accumulated impairment losses	Cr		5 000
(4)	Goodwill	Dr	25 000	
	Business combination valuation reserve	Cr		25 000
	Retained earnings (1/7/24)	Dr	5 000	
	Accumulated impairment losses	Cr		5 000

Figure 27.12 summarises the events that have an impact on those assets for each of the periods after the acquisition date until 30 June 2025.

FIGURE 27.12   Events that have an impact on assets or liabilities recognised in business combination valuation entries

Item	Period ended 30 June 2023	Period ended 30 June 2024	Period ended 30 June 2025
Land	—	—	Sold
Equipment	Partly depreciated	Partly depreciated	Partly depreciated
Inventories	Sold	—	—
Patent	—	Partly impaired	—
Provision for guarantee	Settled	—	—
Goodwill	—	Partly impaired	—

Note that in any period after acquisition, business combination valuation entries are prepared for the assets and liabilities that were not recorded at fair value at acquisition date to the extent that they are still on hand with the subsidiary at the beginning of that period.

- If they are sold, fully depreciated or settled by the beginning of that period, no business combination valuation entries need to be prepared for those items (in the example above, according to figure 27.12, inventories and provision for guarantee have been derecognised prior to 1 July 2024, so no business combination valuation entries are prepared at 30 June 2025).
- If they are still on hand with the subsidiary at the beginning of that period, but they are sold, fully depreciated or settled by the end of the current period, business combination valuation entries only

need to be prepared to adjust the gains or losses generated by the sale and the expenses generated by depreciation, amortisation or impairment of assets or settlement of liabilities, recognising also the tax effects (in the example above, according to figure 27.12, land is still on hand at 1 July 2024, but is derecognised prior to 30 June 2025, so business combination valuation entries are prepared at 30 June 2025 to adjust the gain on sale of the land and the tax effects).

- If they are still on hand with the subsidiary at the end of that period, business combination valuation entries need to be prepared to adjust the expenses generated by the depreciation, amortisation or impairment of assets or the gains from the partial settlement of liabilities, recognising also the tax effects, but also to adjust the actual assets and liabilities to the fair value at the beginning of the current period (in the example above, according to figure 27.12, equipment, patent and goodwill are still on hand at 30 June 2025, so business combination valuation entries are prepared at 30 June 2025 to adjust the depreciation expenses for equipment, impairment losses for patent and goodwill, recognising also the tax effects, but also to adjust those assets to the fair value at the beginning of the current period).

If adjustments are needed to expenses for the previous periods, those adjustments are posted against retained earnings (opening balance).

27.5.2 Pre-acquisition entries

The pre-acquisition entry at acquisition date, relating to the example in figure 27.3, is as follows.

Retained earnings (1/7/22)	Dr	140 000
Share capital	Dr	300 000
Business combination valuation reserve	Dr	60 000
Shares in Subsidiary Ltd	Cr	500 000

There are two events that can cause a change in this entry after acquisition date:

- changes in the pre-acquisition equity, due to transfers between pre-acquisition equity accounts, including transfers from business combination valuation reserve, other transfers between pre-acquisition reserves and bonus share dividends
- changes in the investment account recognised by the parent, due to impairment as a result of pre-acquisition dividends or due to the parent paying calls on the partly paid shares of the subsidiary. Note that this text assumes across all chapters on consolidation issues that the parent recognises its investment in the subsidiary at cost in accordance with paragraph 10(a) of AASB 127.

In any particular year, some of these events would have occurred in previous periods, and some will occur in the current period. The pre-acquisition entries for the current period consist of (a) a combined pre-acquisition entry as at the beginning of the current period (i.e. the pre-acquisition entry at the acquisition date adjusted for the effects of all pre-acquisition equity changes and changes in the investment account recognised by the parent up to the beginning of the current period) and (b) entries relating to those changes in the current period.

Note that, as discussed in section 27.4.6, in the presence of a gain on bargain purchase, the pre-acquisition entry at acquisition date should recognise this gain as a part of the consolidated profit for the period starting at acquisition date, and not eliminate it. This is because it is considered to belong to post-acquisition equity. In subsequent periods after the acquisition date, the gain on bargain purchase is included in retained earnings (opening balance) and therefore essentially can be considered as a reduction in the debit adjustment to the opening balance of retained earnings posted in pre-acquisition entries.

Changes in the pre-acquisition equity

Changes in the pre-acquisition equity are due to transfers between pre-acquisition equity accounts, including transfers from business combination valuation reserve, other transfers between pre-acquisition reserves and bonus share dividends. Each of those changes and how they affect the pre-acquisition entries will be addressed next.

Transfers from business combination valuation reserve

A special case of transfers between pre-acquisition equity accounts that cause changes in the pre-acquisition equity is a transfer from business combination valuation reserve to retained earnings. This transfer is an example of a transfer between pre-acquisition reserves.

For the items adjusted by business combination valuation entries, according to figure 27.12, three events since acquisition date have caused a change in business combination valuation reserve.

Two of these occurred in the year ending 30 June 2023:
- the sale of inventories on hand at acquisition date
- the payment and write-off of the loan guarantee liability.

In both cases, the adjustment was made to transfer from business combination valuation reserve in the business combination valuation entries at 30 June 2023.

This transfer affects the pre-acquisition entry because the business combination valuation reserves for those items are recognised first at acquisition date and therefore are part of pre-acquisition equity. If the business combination valuation entry recognises now a *transfer from* the business combination valuation reserve, instead of a business combination valuation reserve, an adjustment in the pre-acquisition entries must also be made to the transfer account. This is done by adding another entry to the pre-acquisition entries in the year of transfer (see below) after recording the first pre-acquisition entry that was adjusted only for the pre-acquisition equity changes up to the beginning of the current period. The need to make this extra adjustment in the pre-acquisition entries should be obvious from the business combination valuation entries for this period. It is only if there is a transfer in the business combination valuation entries that this flows through to the extra pre-acquisition entry. This extra pre-acquisition entry eliminates the effects of the current period transfer by reversing the transfer. This entry is needed because the first pre-acquisition entry eliminated the pre-acquisition equity adjusted only for the transfers prior to the beginning of the current period. If during the current period there are some extra transfers, the eliminated amounts from each individual equity account are not exactly the same as the amounts that existed in those accounts before elimination. To make sure the right amounts are eliminated, the current period's transfers need to be reversed. A question that may be asked regarding this treatment is why the first pre-acquisition entry is not adjusted for the current period's transfers in the first place. The answer is that the transfers to or from retained earnings during the current period are recorded in separate accounts (e.g. transfer from business combination valuation reserve, transfer to general reserve, bonus share dividend) that will be closed to retained earnings only at the end of the current period.

The pre-acquisition entries at 30 June 2023 affected by the sale of inventories and the payment of the liability for loan guarantee are then as follows.

Retained earnings (1/7/22)	Dr	140 000	
Share capital	Dr	300 000	
Business combination valuation reserve	Dr	60 000	
Shares in Subsidiary Ltd	Cr		500 000
Business combination valuation reserve	Dr	7 000	
Transfer from business combination valuation reserve	Cr		7 000
($3500 inventories and $(10 500) loan guarantee liability)			

In the consolidation worksheet at 30 June 2024, assuming no other current transfers or events, the pre-acquisition entry is the combination of the two entries from the previous period's worksheet.

Retained earnings (1/7/23)*	Dr	133 000	
Share capital	Dr	300 000	
Business combination valuation reserve**	Dr	67 000	
Shares in Subsidiary Ltd	Cr		500 000

*$140 000 + $3500 (inventories) − $10 500 (loan guarantee)
**$60 000 − $3500 (inventories) + $10 500 (loan guarantee)

Note that as the inventories and the guarantee are derecognised, the effects of their fair value adjustments that should have been recognised as of acquisition date are in essence recognised in the subsidiary's accounts under retained earnings and should be eliminated from there, as they represent pre-acquisition equity.

In the period ended 30 June 2025 (the current period) pre-acquisition balances are affected by the sale of the land. As can be seen from the business combination valuation entry for land in section 27.5.1, in the current period there is a transfer from the business combination valuation reserve to retained earnings of $14 000. This requires the following entry to be included in the pre-acquisition entries for the current period, together with the pre-acquisition entry from the previous period's worksheet.

Transfer from business combination valuation reserve	Dr	14 000	
Business combination valuation reserve	Cr		14 000

In summary, the pre-acquisition entries to be passed in the consolidation worksheet at 30 June 2025 are as shown in figure 27.13. These are affected by the sale of inventories and payment of the loan guarantee in the period ended 30 June 2023 and the sale of land in the period ended 30 June 2025.

FIGURE 27.13	Pre-acquisition entries at 30 June 2025

(5)	Retained earnings (1/7/24)*	Dr	133 000	
	Share capital	Dr	300 000	
	Business combination valuation reserve**	Dr	67 000	
	Shares in Subsidiary Ltd	Cr		500 000
	Transfer from business combination valuation reserve	Dr	14 000	
	Business combination valuation reserve	Cr		14 000

*$140 000 + $3500 (inventories) − $10 500 (loan guarantee)
**$60 000 − $3500 (inventories) + $10 500 (loan guarantee)

Figure 27.14 shows the consolidation worksheet at 30 June 2025 containing the adjustment entries from figures 27.11 and 27.13.

FIGURE 27.14	Consolidation worksheet at 30 June 2025

Financial statements	Parent Ltd	Subsidiary Ltd	Adjustments Dr		Adjustments Cr		Group
Revenues	120 000	95 000					215 000
Expenses	(85 000)	(72 000)	2	4 000			(161 000)
	35 000	23 000					54 000
Gain on sale of non-current assets	15 000	31 000	1	20 000			26 000
Profit before tax	50 000	54 000					80 000
Income tax expense	(15 000)	(21 000)			6 000	1	(28 800)
					1 200	2	
Profit for the period	35 000	33 000					51 200
Retained earnings (1/7/24)	420 000	220 000	2	8 000	2 400	2	491 400
			3	5 000			
			4	5 000			
			5	133 000			
Transfer from business combination valuation reserve	—	—	5	14 000	14 000	1	—
Retained earnings (30/6/25)	455 000	253 000					542 600
Share capital	550 000	300 000	5	300 000			550 000
Business combination valuation reserve	—		5	67 000	14 000	2	
					14 000	3	
					25 000	4	
					14 000	5	—
	1 005 000	553 000					1 092 600
Provisions	40 000	40 000					80 000
Payables	32 000	24 000					56 000
Deferred tax liabilities	12 000	16 000	2	3 600	6 000	2	36 400
					6 000	3	
	84 000	80 000					172 400
Total equity and liabilities	1 089 000	633 000					1 265 000
Cash	65 000	95 000					160 000
Land	170 000	50 000					220 000
Equipment	750 000	683 000			150 000	2	1 283 000
Accumulated depreciation	(448 000)	(270 000)	2	170 000	12 000	2	(560 000)
Shares in Subsidiary Ltd	500 000	—			500 000	5	—
Inventories	52 000	75 000					127 000
Patent	—	—	3	20 000			20 000
Accumulated impairment losses	—	—			5 000	3	(5 000)
Goodwill	—	—	4	25 000			25 000
Accumulated impairment losses	—	—			5 000	4	(5 000)
Total assets	1 089 000	633 000					1 265 000

Other transfers between pre-acquisition reserve accounts

Other than the transfers from business combination valuation reserve to retained earnings, a subsidiary may record some other transfers between pre-acquisition reserves. From time to time the subsidiary may transfer pre-acquisition retained earnings to other reserves, or make transfers from other pre-acquisition reserves to retained earnings. In all of those cases, the transfers need to be reversed if they happen during the current period, or recognised as an adjustment to the first pre-acquisition entry if they happen during the previous periods. Note that the transfers from or to retained earnings are recognised in separate accounts called 'Transfer from X' or 'Transfer to X', where X designates the other equity account involved in the transfer; for example, if a transfer is made from general reserve to retained earnings, it is recognised in the account named 'Transfer from general reserve'; if a transfer is made to general reserve from retained earnings, it is recognised in the account named 'Transfer to general reserve'. Additionally, all the transfers from or to retained earnings will be recognised as an increase or a decrease at the date of transfer respectively in the other reserve account involved in the transfer.

All these transfers from pre-acquisition equity do not cause any change in the total pre-acquisition equity, but simply change its composition. Therefore, there is no change in the investment account recorded by the parent entity. In fact, the parent is unaffected by these transfers.

For the cases illustrated below, assume that the first pre-acquisition entry for the year ending 30 June 2023, that does not take into consideration the effect of reserve transfers that occur during the current period, is as follows.

Retained earnings (1/7/22)	Dr	140 000
Share capital	Dr	300 000
Business combination valuation reserve	Dr	60 000
Shares in Subsidiary Ltd	Cr	500 000

Case 1: Transfers from retained earnings to other reserves

Assume that in the period ended 30 June 2023 the subsidiary transfers $4000 to general reserve from pre-acquisition retained earnings. The entry passed in the subsidiary as a result of the transfer is as follows.

Transfer to general reserve	Dr	4 000
General reserve	Cr	4 000

The pre-acquisition entries for the period ended 30 June 2023 are shown in figure 27.15.

FIGURE 27.15	Pre-acquisition entries — transfer to general reserve in the current period

Retained earnings (1/7/22)	Dr	140 000
Share capital	Dr	300 000
Business combination valuation reserve	Dr	60 000
Shares in Subsidiary Ltd	Cr	500 000
General reserve	Dr	4 000
Transfer to general reserve	Cr	4 000

As both the transfer to general reserve and the general reserve accounts are pre-acquisition equity in nature, they are eliminated as part of the pre-acquisition entries by reversing the journal entry recognised by the subsidiary. Without this reversal, the consolidated accounts would still include the general reserve created by the transfer, because the first pre-acquisition entry that was not adjusted for the current transfer would not eliminate it. Nevertheless, in the next period, the pre-acquisition entry that eliminates the investment against the pre-acquisition equity of the subsidiary is adjusted for this transfer and therefore the only pre-acquisition entry in subsequent periods is as follows.

Retained earnings (opening balance)*	Dr	136 000	
Share capital	Dr	300 000	
Business combination valuation reserve	Dr	60 000	
General reserve	Dr	4 000	
Shares in Subsidiary Ltd	Cr		500 000

*$140 000 − $4000

Case 2: Transfers to retained earnings from other reserves

This case uses the information in case 1, in which a $4000 general reserve was created. Assume that in the period ended 30 June 2024 the subsidiary transfers $1000 to retained earnings from this general reserve. The entry passed in the subsidiary as a result of the transfer is as follows.

| General reserve | Dr | 1 000 | |
| Transfer from general reserve | Cr | | 1 000 |

The pre-acquisition entries for the period ended 30 June 2024 are shown in figure 27.16.

FIGURE 27.16   Pre-acquisition entries — transfer from general reserve in the current period

Retained earnings (1/7/23)	Dr	136 000	
Share capital	Dr	300 000	
Business combination valuation reserve	Dr	60 000	
General reserve	Dr	4 000	
Shares in Subsidiary Ltd	Cr		500 000
Transfer from general reserve	Dr	1 000	
General reserve	Cr		1 000

Since both the transfer from general reserve and general reserve accounts are pre-acquisition equity in nature, they are eliminated as part of the pre-acquisition entry. The pre-acquisition entry in subsequent periods is as follows.

Retained earnings (opening balance)*	Dr	137 000	
Share capital	Dr	300 000	
Business combination valuation reserve	Dr	60 000	
General reserve	Dr	3 000	
Shares in Subsidiary Ltd	Cr		500 000

*$140 000 − $4000 + $1000

Bonus share dividends

Another example of transfers between pre-acquisition equity accounts is the distribution of the bonus dividends. Bonus share dividends involve a subsidiary issuing shares as dividends instead of paying cash. The effect of this is a transfer of pre-acquisition equity from one account to another, which needs to be eliminated in the pre-acquisition entry. As before, the transfer will be eliminated in the period of transfer by reversing the entry recognised by the subsidiary; in the next periods, it will be considered as an adjustment to the first pre-acquisition entry that eliminates the investment against the pre-acquisition equity.

Assume that in the period ended 30 June 2023 the subsidiary distributes a dividend of $3000 from pre-acquisition retained earnings by issuing bonus shares. The entries passed as a result of the dividend are as follows.

Parent Ltd	Subsidiary Ltd			
No entry required	Bonus dividend paid	Dr	3 000	
	Share capital	Cr		3 000

The effect of this bonus dividend is to increase the share capital of the subsidiary by $3000 and to reduce the retained earnings of the subsidiary by the same amount. There is no overall change in the pre-acquisition equity of the subsidiary, just a transfer from one equity account to another. Accordingly, there is no change in the balance of the investment account in the records of the parent. No entry is required by the parent because its share of wealth in the subsidiary is unchanged by the bonus share issue. However, on consolidation, the entry recorded by the subsidiary needs to be reversed.

The pre-acquisition entries for the period ended 30 June 2023 are shown in figure 27.17.

Retained earnings (1/7/22)	Dr	140 000	
Share capital	Dr	300 000	
Business combination valuation reserve	Dr	60 000	
Shares in Subsidiary Ltd	Cr		500 000
Share capital	Dr	3 000	
Bonus dividend paid	Cr		3 000

The pre-acquisition entry in subsequent periods is as follows.

Retained earnings (opening balance)*	Dr	137 000	
Share capital	Dr	303 000	
Business combination valuation reserve	Dr	60 000	
Shares in Subsidiary Ltd	Cr		500 000

*$140 000 − $3000

Note that bonus share dividends can be distributed from other pre-acquisition equity accounts as well, not just retained earnings. In those cases, the consolidation journal entries will be the same, except that in the period of transfer instead of recording a credit to bonus dividend paid, a credit to the other pre-acquisition equity account involved will be recorded, while in the next periods an adjustment will not be made against the opening balance of retained earnings, but against the balance of the other pre-acquisition equity account involved.

Changes in the investment account recognised by the parent

Changes in the investment account recognised by the parent are in the form of impairment due to pre-acquisition dividends distributions or increases due to calls paid on partly paid shares of the subsidiary. These changes and how they impact the pre-acquisition entries will be discussed next.

Pre-acquisition dividends

Prior to July 2008, AASB 127/IAS 27 *Consolidated and Separate Financial Statements* described a cost method in relation to accounting for a parent's investment in a subsidiary. The equity of the subsidiary was then classified into pre-acquisition and post-acquisition components based upon whether the equity existed before or after the acquisition date. Dividends from pre-acquisition equity were accounted for as a recovery of a parent's investment in a subsidiary and recognised as a reduction in the cost of the investment. Dividends from post-acquisition equity were accounted for by the parent as revenue.

In July 2008, the AASB incorporated amendments made by the IASB to IAS 27 into AASB 127. In response to the 2008 changes proposed by the IASB that an investor was to recognise as income all dividends received from a subsidiary, the AASB issued the following statement.

> While the AASB considers that the proposed changes are a departure from a conceptually pure application of the cost method, the AASB acknowledges that it is suitable on pragmatic grounds. The AASB also notes that it can be argued that the identification of particular dividends as being sourced from either pre- or post-acquisition retained earnings is arbitrary in many circumstances.

The AASB thus recognised that the amendments departed from the application of the cost method and that its agreement with the IASB changes was on pragmatic grounds.

These amendments required that all dividends paid or payable by a subsidiary were to be accounted for as revenue by the parent. AASB 9/IFRS 9 *Financial Instruments* in paragraph 5.7.6 reinforced this accounting treatment for dividends. Note, however, as discussed in section 27.4.5, that the dividends declared by the subsidiary prior to the acquisition of the subsidiary on a *cum div.* basis by the parent are still treated as a refund on the consideration transferred; that is, as a recovery of a parent's investment in a subsidiary and recognised as a reduction in the cost of the investment.

In 2011, the AASB issued a new AASB 127 *Separate Financial Statements*, amended further in 2014. Paragraph 12 of the current standard states the following.

> Dividends from a subsidiary, a joint venture or an associate are recognised in the separate financial statements of an entity when the entity's right to receive the dividend is established. The dividend is recognised in profit or loss unless the entity elects to use the equity method, in which case the dividend is recognised as a reduction from the carrying amount of the investment.

Remember that the assumption used in this text is that the parent recognises its investment in subsidiaries at cost, subject to impairment, not using the equity method. As such, dividends declared after acquisition and paid or payable by the subsidiary to a parent are recognised as revenue in the profit or loss of the parent. In relation to dividends, there is no need to classify the equity of the subsidiary into pre-acquisition and post-acquisition equity. However, the dividends from pre-acquisition equity are, by definition, a distribution of pre-acquisition equity, which decreases the pre-acquisition equity and may reduce the value of the investment recognised by the parent. By treating those dividends as revenue, the parent may overstate its income. To reduce any risk of any possible overstatement of income by a parent, the IASB looked at the impairment testing of the investment account recorded by the parent. If the investment account decreases in value as a result of the dividends from pre-acquisition equity, an impairment loss needs to be recognised. To determine whether there is an impairment of the investment account that should be recognised as a result of dividends distribution, paragraph 12(h) of AASB 136/IAS 36 *Impairment of Assets* contains a scenario that may provide evidence that the impairment of the investment account occurred:

> for an investment in a subsidiary, joint venture or associate, the investor recognises a dividend from the investment and evidence is available that:
> (i) the carrying amount of the investment in the separate financial statements exceeds the carrying amounts in the consolidated financial statements of the investee's net assets, including associated goodwill; or
> (ii) the dividend exceeds the total comprehensive income of the subsidiary, joint venture or associate in the period the dividend is declared.

Note, however, that pre-acquisition dividends that cause the impairment of the investment account determine another adjustment to be posted in the pre-acquisition entry for the period when the dividend was declared. Assume that in the period ended 30 June 2023 the subsidiary declares a dividend of $1000 from pre-acquisition retained earnings. As a result of this, it is observed that the investment account was impaired by $1000. The entries passed as a result of the dividend are as follows.

Parent Ltd				Subsidiary Ltd			
Dividend receivable	Dr	1 000		Dividend declared	Dr	1 000	
Dividend revenue	Cr		1 000	Dividend payable	Cr		1 000
Impairment loss	Dr	1 000					
	Cr						
Accumulated impairment losses — shares in Subsidiary Ltd			1 000				

The pre-acquisition entries for the period ended 30 June 2023 will need to eliminate these accounts recorded by the individual entities by reversing the entries, together with the elimination of the pre-acquisition equity and the investment account, as shown in figure 27.18.

FIGURE 27.18	Pre-acquisition entries — dividend provided for in the current period

Retained earnings (1/7/22)	Dr	140 000	
Share capital	Dr	300 000	
Business combination valuation reserve	Dr	60 000	
Shares in Subsidiary Ltd	Cr		500 000
Dividend revenue	Dr	1 000	
Dividend receivable	Cr		1 000
Dividend payable	Dr	1 000	
Dividend declared	Cr		1 000
Accumulated impairment losses — shares in Subsidiary Ltd	Dr	1 000	
Impairment loss	Cr		1 000

If the dividend has been paid prior to the end of the period when the dividend was declared, the pre-acquisition entries would be as follows.

Retained earnings (1/7/22)	Dr	140 000	
Share capital	Dr	300 000	
Business combination valuation reserve	Dr	60 000	
Shares in Subsidiary Ltd	Cr		500 000
Dividend revenue	Dr	1 000	
Dividend paid	Cr		1 000
Accumulated impairment losses — shares in Subsidiary Ltd	Dr	1 000	
Impairment loss	Cr		1 000

Note that the elimination of dividend receivable and dividend payable is not recognised anymore as those accounts are not in the subsidiary's accounts as the dividend is paid.

In the next periods after the period when dividend was declared, only the reversal of the impairment loss will be recognised in the pre-acquisition entry (but with a credit to retained earnings (opening balance) instead of impairment loss) because:
- the assumption is that the dividend is paid and therefore dividend receivable and dividend payable are not recognised anymore in the parent's and subsidiary's accounts respectively
- dividend revenue and dividend declared have been closed to retained earnings (opening balance), with zero net effect on consolidated retained earnings
- impairment loss from the previous period is now in retained earnings (opening balance).

Retained earnings (opening balance)	Dr	140 000	
Share capital	Dr	300 000	
Business combination valuation reserve	Dr	60 000	
Shares in Subsidiary Ltd	Cr		500 000
Accumulated impairment losses — shares in Subsidiary Ltd	Dr	1 000	
Retained earnings (opening balance)	Cr		1 000

Calls on partly paid shares of the subsidiary

If the subsidiary had partly paid shares on acquisition, after the acquisition date it can issue a call asking for a part or all of the remaining amount to be paid. If the parent owns 100% of the subsidiary, it will have to pay 100% of the instalment money called. If the call is not paid yet, there will not be any effects on the investment account. However, the payment of call money will increase the investment account and that will be recognised as a change in the investment account that will need to be eliminated in the pre-acquisition entry.

Assume that in the period ended 30 June 2023, a call for $10 000 was issued by the subsidiary and paid by the parent. The entries passed as a result of the call paid are as follows.

Parent Ltd				Subsidiary Ltd			
Shares in Subsidiary Ltd	Dr	10 000		Cash	Dr	10 000	
Cash	Cr		10 000	Share capital	Cr		10 000

In the pre-acquisition entries for the current period, an additional adjustment will be posted to eliminate the effects of the call.

Retained earnings (1/7/22)	Dr	140 000	
Share capital	Dr	300 000	
Business combination valuation reserve	Dr	60 000	
Shares in Subsidiary Ltd	Cr		500 000
Share capital	Dr	10 000	
Shares in Subsidiary Ltd	Cr		10 000

The pre-acquisition entry in subsequent periods is as follows.

Retained earnings (opening balance)	Dr	140 000	
Share capital	Dr	310 000	
Business combination valuation reserve	Dr	60 000	
Shares in Subsidiary Ltd	Cr		510 000

- [ ] In any period after acquisition, business combination valuation entries are prepared for the assets and liabilities that were not recorded at fair value at acquisition date to the extent that they are still on hand with the subsidiary at the beginning of that period.
- [ ] If adjustments are needed to expenses for the previous periods, those adjustments are posted against retained earnings (opening balance).
- [ ] In any period after acquisition, pre-acquisition entries are adjusted for changes in the pre-acquisition equity due to transfers between pre-acquisition equity accounts and changes in the investment account recognised by the parent due to impairment as a result of pre-acquisition dividends or due to the parent paying calls on the partly paid shares of the subsidiary.
- [ ] The pre-acquisition entries for any period after acquisition consist of the pre-acquisition entry at the acquisition date adjusted for the effects of all those changes up to the beginning of the current period — and entries relating to those changes in pre-acquisition equity in the current period.
- [ ] In the presence of a gain on bargain purchase, in subsequent periods after the acquisition date, the gain on bargain purchase is included in retained earnings (opening balance) and therefore reduces the adjustment to the opening balance of retained earnings posted in pre-acquisition entries.

27.6 Consolidation worksheet entries when the subsidiary revalues its assets at acquisition date

LEARNING OBJECTIVE 27.6 Prepare the consolidation worksheet entries where the subsidiary revalues its assets at acquisition date.

AASB 3/IFRS 3 does not discuss whether the revaluation of the assets of the subsidiary at acquisition date should be done in the consolidation worksheet or in the records of the subsidiary. Most entities will make their adjustments in the consolidation worksheet, mainly for two reasons.

- Adjustments to fair value for assets such as goodwill and inventories are not allowed in the actual records of the subsidiary. Goodwill is not allowed to be revalued and inventories should always be recognised at the lowest of the cost and net realisable value, not at fair value.
- The revaluation of non-current assets in the records of the subsidiary require the subsidiary to adopt the revaluation model of accounting for the whole class of assets that those assets belong to, and to use that model in all post-acquisition periods. Applying the revaluation model for whole classes of assets each year may be too costly for the subsidiary and, therefore, not preferable.

Nevertheless, some subsidiaries may decide to revalue some of the assets for which the fair value was different from the carrying amount at acquisition date in their own accounts. In that case, there will not be any business combination valuation entries for the revalued assets. Moreover, the pre-acquisition entries will change. Note that the business combination valuation entries applied in the consolidation worksheet for property, plant and equipment assets in this chapter are of the same form as those applied for property, plant and equipment in chapter 5. The difference is that the after-tax revaluation increment was recognised as business combination valuation reserve and not asset revaluation surplus. If the subsidiary revalues some assets in its own accounts, an asset revaluation surplus will be recognised and, being part of pre-acquisition equity, it will need to be considered when preparing the pre-acquisition entries. As asset revaluation surplus behaves in the same manner as business combination valuation reserve, the pre-acquisition entries will be affected if the revalued asset is derecognised, as the asset revaluation surplus will be transferred to retained earnings. Nevertheless, as the asset revaluation surplus or its transfer to retained earnings will be eliminated in pre-acquisition entries just like the business combination valuation reserve and its transfer, the consolidated financial statements at acquisition date are the same regardless of whether revaluation occurs on consolidation or in the records of the subsidiary.

- □ There are costs associated with applying the revaluation model in the subsidiary's accounts, which may result in an entity preferring to make value adjustments in the consolidation worksheet.
- □ If the subsidiary decides to revalue some assets at acquisition date in its own accounts, an asset revaluation surplus is raised; being a part of pre-acquisition equity in nature, in the pre-acquisition entry this asset revaluation surplus is eliminated and the transfer from it is reversed in the period of transfer.

27.7 Disclosure

LEARNING OBJECTIVE 27.7 Prepare the disclosures required by AASB 3/IFRS 3 and AASB 12/IFRS 12.

Paragraphs B64–B67 of Appendix B to AASB 3/IFRS 3 cover the disclosure of information about business combinations. These paragraphs require an acquirer to disclose information that enables users of its financial statements to evaluate the nature and financial effect of business combinations that occurred during the reporting period, as well as those that occur between the end of the reporting period and when the financial statements are authorised for issue. Examples of disclosures required by these paragraphs are given in figure 27.19.

FIGURE 27.19	Disclosure for business combinations

Note 4. Business combinations	AASB 3/IFRS 3 paragraph
On 20 October 2022, Libra Ltd acquired 100% of the voting shares of Pisces Ltd, a listed company specialising in the manufacture of electronic parts for sound equipment. The primary reason for the acquisition was to gain access to specialist knowledge relating to electronic systems. Control was obtained by acquisition of all the shares of Pisces Ltd.	B64(a), (b), (c)
	64(d)
To acquire this ownership interest, Libra Ltd issued 600 000 ordinary shares, valued at $2.50 per share, which rank equally for dividends after the acquisition date. The fair value is based on the published market price at acquisition date.	B64(f)(iv)
The total consideration transferred was $1 800 000 and consisted of the following.	B64(f)

	$'000
Shares issued, at fair value	1 500
Cash paid	240
Cash payable in 2 years' time	60
Total consideration transferred	1 800

The fair values and the carrying amounts of the assets acquired and liabilities assumed in Pisces Ltd as at 20 October 2022 were as follows.   **B64(f)**

	Fair value $'000	Carrying amount $'000
Property, plant and equipment	1 240	1 020
Receivables	340	340
Inventories	160	130
Intangible assets	302	22
Goodwill	54	0
	2 096	1 512
Payables	152	152
Provisions	103	103
Deferred tax liabilities	41	41
	296	296
Fair value of net assets of Pisces Ltd	1 800	

	AASB 3/IFRS 3 paragraph
Goodwill in Pisces Ltd can be attributed to the synergies existing within the company, and relate to the high level of training given to the staff as well as the professional expertise of the employees. Further, there exist in-process research activities in Pisces Ltd for which it was impossible to determine reliable fair values for the separate recognition of intangible assets.	B64(e)

	B64(q)(i)

Pisces Ltd earned a profit for the period from 20 October 2022 to 30 June 2023 of $520 000. This has been included in the consolidated statement of profit or loss and other comprehensive income for the year ended 30 June 2023.

None of the above information has been prepared on a provisional basis.

B67

The consolidated profit is shown in the consolidated statement of profit or loss and other comprehensive income at $5 652 000, which includes the $520 000 contributed by Pisces Ltd from 20 October 2022 to the end of the period. If Pisces Ltd had been acquired at 1 July 2022, it is estimated that the consolidated entity would have reported the following.

B64(q)(ii)

	$'000
Consolidated revenue	36 654
Consolidated profit	6 341

In relation to the business combination in the period ended 30 June 2022 when Libra Ltd acquired all the shares in Orion Ltd, an adjustment was made in the current period relating to the provisional measurement of specialised equipment held by Orion Ltd. A loss of $250 000 was recognised in the current reporting period because of the write-down of this equipment.

B67(a)(iii)

Included in the current period profit are gains on the sale of land acquired as a part of the business combination with Pisces Ltd. The gain amounted to $100 000 and arose due to an upsurge in demand for inner-city properties.

B67(e)

B67(d)

Goodwill	$'000
Gross amount at 1 July 2022	120
Accumulated impairment losses	(15)
Carrying amount at 1 July 2022	105
Goodwill recognised in current period	54
Carrying amount at 30 June 2023	159
Gross amount at 30 June 2023	174
Accumulated impairment losses	(15)
Carrying amount at 30 June 2023	159

AASB 12/IFRS 12 *Disclosure of Interests in Other Entities* also requires disclosures in relation to a parent's interest in its subsidiaries. Figure 27.20 illustrates some of these disclosures.

FIGURE 27.20   Disclosures concerning subsidiaries

Note 5. Subsidiaries	AASB 12/IFRS 12 paragraph
Aries Ltd has a 40% interest in Virgo Ltd. Although it has less than half the voting power, Aries Ltd believes it has control of Virgo Ltd. Aries Ltd is able to exercise this control because the remaining ownership in Virgo Ltd is diverse and widely spread, with the next single largest ownership block being 11%.	9(b)
Aries Ltd has invested in a special purpose entity established by Pictor Ltd. Pictor Ltd established Cetus Ltd as a vehicle for distributing the sailing boats it makes. Aries Ltd currently owns 60% of the shares issued by Cetus Ltd. However, because of the limited decisions that the board of Cetus Ltd can make owing to the constitution of that entity, Aries Ltd believes that it does not have any real control over the operations of Cetus Ltd, so it sees its role in Cetus Ltd as that of an investor.	9(a)
Aries Ltd has a wholly owned subsidiary, Gemini Ltd, which operates within the electricity generating industry. The end of its reporting period is 31 May. Gemini Ltd continues to use this date because the government regulating authority requires all entities within the industry to provide financial information to it based on financial position at that date.	11
Aries Ltd has a wholly owned subsidiary, Hercules Ltd, in the country of Mambo. Because of constraints on assets leaving the country recently imposed by the new military government, there are major restrictions on the subsidiary being able to transfer funds to Aries Ltd.	10(b)(i)

Disclosures in relation to subsidiaries are set out in AASB 12/IFRS 12 *Disclosure of Interests in Other Entities*. These are discussed in chapter 26. Note, however, the following extract from paragraph 10.

An entity shall disclose information that enables users of its consolidated financial statements

(a) to understand:
    (i) the composition of the group; and
    (ii) the interest that non-controlling interests have in the group's activities and cash flows (paragraph 12); and

(b) to evaluate:
    (i) the nature and extent of significant restrictions on its ability to access or use assets, and settle liabilities, of the group (paragraph 13);
    (ii) the nature of, and changes in, the risks associated with its interests in consolidated structured entities (paragraphs 14–17) . . .

LEARNING CHECK

☐ An acquirer is required by AASB 3/IFRS 3 to disclose information in its financial statements to enable users to evaluate the nature and financial effect of each business combination during the reporting period.

☐ AASB 12/IFRS 12 establishes the disclosures relating to a parent's interests in subsidiaries.

SUMMARY

This chapter covers the consolidation process used in the preparation of the consolidated financial statements for a group consisting of a parent and a wholly owned subsidiary. Because of the requirements of AASB 3/IFRS 3 to recognise the identifiable assets acquired and liabilities assumed of an acquired entity at fair value, an initial adjustment to be made on consolidation concerns any assets or liabilities for which there are differences between fair value and carrying amount at the acquisition date. Further, although some intangible assets and liabilities of the subsidiary may not have been recognised in the subsidiary's records, they are recognised as part of the business combination.

The preparation of the consolidated financial statements is done using a consolidation worksheet, the left-hand columns of which contain the individual financial statements of the members of the group. The adjustment columns contain the consolidation worksheet entries that adjust the right-hand columns that form the consolidated financial statements. The adjustment entries have no effect on the actual financial records of the parent and its subsidiaries and they do not carry over from period to period.

At acquisition date, an acquisition analysis is undertaken. The key purposes of this analysis are to determine the fair values of the identifiable assets and liabilities of the subsidiary, and to calculate any goodwill or gain on bargain purchase arising from the business combination. From this analysis, the main consolidation worksheet adjustment entries at acquisition date are the business combination valuation entries (to adjust carrying amounts of the subsidiaries' identifiable assets and liabilities to fair value) and the pre-acquisition entries (to eliminate the pre-acquisition equity against the investment asset recognised by the parent).

In preparing consolidated financial statements in periods after acquisition date, the consolidation worksheet will contain business combination valuation entries and pre-acquisition entries. However, these entries are not necessarily the same as those posted at acquisition date. If there are changes to the assets and liabilities of the subsidiaries since acquisition date, or there have been movements in pre-acquisition equity or the investment account recognised by the parent, changes must be made to these entries.

KEY TERMS

consolidated financial statements The financial statements of a group in which the assets, liabilities, equity, income, expenses and cash flows of the parent and its subsidiaries are presented as those of a single economic entity.

group A parent and its subsidiaries.

parent An entity that controls one or more entities.

subsidiary An entity that is controlled by another entity.

DEMONSTRATION PROBLEMS

27.1 Consolidated financial statements after acquisition date

On 1 July 2021, Pegasus Ltd acquired 100% of the issued shares of Taurus Ltd on a *cum div.* basis. The fair value of the consideration paid was measured at $335 000. At this date, the records of Taurus Ltd included the following information.

Share capital	$200 000
General reserve	5 000
Retained earnings	100 000
Dividend payable	20 000
Goodwill	5 000

The dividend recognised as a liability at 1 July 2021 was paid in August 2021. At 1 July 2021, all the identifiable assets and liabilities of Taurus Ltd were recorded in the subsidiary's books at fair value except for the following assets.

	Carrying amount	Fair value
Inventories	$ 40 000	$ 43 000
Plant (cost $240 000)	180 000	185 000

The inventories were all sold by 30 June 2022. The plant has a further 5-year life and is depreciated on a straight-line basis. Goodwill was not impaired in any period. When assets are sold or fully consumed, any related business combination valuation reserve is transferred to retained earnings. The tax rate is 30%.

The summarised financial statements of the entities within the group at 30 June 2023 are as shown in figure 27.21. The transfer to general reserve in the period ended 30 June 2023 was from profits earned before acquisition date.

FIGURE 27.21 Summarised financial statements for Pegasus Ltd and Taurus Ltd at 30 June 2023

Financial statements	Pegasus Ltd	Taurus Ltd
Revenues	$ 125 000	$ 90 000
Expenses	(85 000)	(65 000)
Profit before tax	40 000	25 000
Income tax expense	(15 500)	(10 200)
Profit for the period	24 500	14 800
Retained earnings (1/7/22)	150 000	85 000
Transfer to general reserve	(20 000)	(15 000)
Retained earnings (30/6/23)	154 500	84 800
Share capital	500 000	200 000
General reserve	50 000	20 000
Financial assets reserve (1/7/22)	2 000	3 000
Gain on financial assets	12 000	10 000
Financial assets reserve (30/6/23)	14 000	13 000
Plant revaluation surplus (1/7/22)	8 000	5 000
Gain on plant revaluation	28 000	22 000
Plant revaluation surplus (30/6/23)	36 000	27 000
Total equity	754 500	344 800
Deferred tax liabilities	11 000	16 000
Other liabilities	50 000	20 000
Total liabilities	61 000	36 000
Total equity and liabilities	$ 815 500	$380 800
Cash	$ 25 000	$ 5 000
Inventories	60 000	85 000
Financial assets	50 000	40 000
Plant	500 000	300 000
Accumulated depreciation − plant	(160 000)	(80 000)
Shares in Taurus Ltd	315 000	−
Fixtures and fittings	40 000	38 000
Accumulated depreciation − fixtures and fittings	(14 500)	(12 200)
Goodwill	−	5 000
Total assets	$ 815 500	$380 800

Required

Prepare the consolidated financial statements for Pegasus Ltd at 30 June 2023.

SOLUTION

The first step in the consolidation process is the acquisition analysis, shown below. This involves comparing the net fair value of the identifiable assets and liabilities of the subsidiary with the fair value of consideration transferred at acquisition date and determining the existence of goodwill or gain on bargain purchase. For this analysis, it is necessary to identify the following.

• *The equity of the subsidiary at acquisition date.* This consists of $200 000 share capital, $5000 general reserve and $100 000 retained earnings; this represents the recorded (book) value of the net assets of the subsidiary at acquisition date.

• *Any goodwill previously recorded by the subsidiary.* Goodwill is an *unidentifiable* asset, but it is included in the net assets of the subsidiary at acquisition date if it was previously recorded by the subsidiary; because it is the fair value of *identifiable* net assets that needs to be calculated based on the value of net assets recorded in the equity of the subsidiary at acquisition date, goodwill *previously recorded by the subsidiary* must be deducted from the value of equity of the subsidiary at acquisition date; in this problem, the subsidiary has previously recorded goodwill of $5000.

- *Differences between the carrying amounts of recorded identifiable assets and liabilities of the subsidiary and their fair values at acquisition date, as well as the fair values of any unrecorded identifiable assets and liabilities of the subsidiary recognised as part of the business combination.* Those differences are identified for inventories for which there is a $3000 difference (i.e. $43 000 − $40 000) and plant for which there is a $5000 difference (i.e. $185 000 − $180 000). These differences are recognised in the acquisition analysis in the business combination valuation reserve on an after-tax basis, that is, the differences are multiplied by (1 − tax rate), and are added to the equity of the subsidiary at acquisition date to get to the net fair value of identifiable assets and liabilities of the subsidiary at acquisition date.

- *Dividends payable recorded by the subsidiary at acquisition date.* If the parent acquired the shares in the subsidiary on an *ex div.* basis, these dividends have no effect on the acquisition analysis. The acquisition in this problem was made on a *cum div.* basis. This means that the cost of the combination of $335 000 paid by the parent was for both the shares in the subsidiary (or, in other words, for the net assets of the subsidiary) and the dividends receivable. Hence, the consideration transferred must be adjusted for the amount paid for the dividends receivable, that is, $20 000 to get to the net consideration transferred that recognises only the payment for the net assets of the subsidiary; it is this net consideration transferred that is compared against the fair value of the net identifiable assets to determine if goodwill has been acquired.

- *Any previously held interest in the subsidiary by the parent.* If the parent had some shares in the subsidiary prior to acquiring the rest of the shares that gave it 100% interest, the fair value of that previously held interest has to be added to the fair value of the net consideration transferred for the remaining shares before it is compared against the fair value of the net identifiable assets; in this problem, there is no previously held interest.

Acquisition analysis
At 1 July 2021:

Net fair value of identifiable assets and liabilities of Taurus Ltd	= $200 000 + $5000 + $100 000 (equity)
	− $5000 (goodwill recorded)
	+ ($5000)(1 − 30%) (BCVR — plant)
	+ ($3000)(1 − 30%) (BCVR — inventories)
	= $305 600
Consideration transferred	= $335 000 − $20 000 (dividend receivable)
	= $315 000
Goodwill	= $315 000 − $305 600
	= $9400
Unrecorded goodwill	= $9400 − $5000
	= $4400

When the net fair value of the identifiable assets and liabilities acquired is compared with the net consideration transferred, it is found that the latter is the greater amount — the difference between the two numbers is goodwill. In this problem, the goodwill of the subsidiary is $9400. This is the amount that will be reported in the consolidated statement of financial position if prepared at acquisition date. As the subsidiary has already recorded goodwill of $5000, the adjustment necessary in the consolidation worksheet is $4400 — only the unrecorded goodwill needs to be recorded on consolidation.

Consolidation worksheet adjustment entries at 30 June 2023
The consolidation worksheet entries should be prepared based on the acquisition analysis, but taking into consideration any changes in the assets or liabilities for which calculation adjustments were considered there and any transfers from pre-acquisition equity and changes in the investment account that occurred post-acquisition.

1. *Business combination valuation entries at 30 June 2023*

The business combination entries at 30 June 2023 are affected by changes in the assets and liabilities for which calculation adjustments were considered in the acquisition analysis.

The inventories have been sold by 30 June 2022 (i.e. prior to the beginning of the current period), so there is no need to prepare a business combination valuation entry. The value increment for inventories as of acquisition date is now recognised in the retained earnings of the subsidiary as the subsidiary realised this increment through the sale.

The plant is still on hand within the group. The first adjustment entry is the same as that prepared at the acquisition date to adjust the plant account. The accumulated depreciation of $60 000 (i.e. $240 000 − $180 000) is eliminated and the plant reduced from the historical cost of $240 000 to fair value of $185 000 by an amount of $55 000. The $5000 difference between carrying amount and fair value is split between deferred tax liability (30%) and business combination valuation reserve (70%). This entry is used in every period while the asset continues to be held by the subsidiary.

The second business combination valuation entry for plant reflects the fact that the plant is being depreciated by the subsidiary on a straight-line basis over a 5-year period, but based on an undervalued depreciable amount; that is, the carrying amount at acquisition date of $180 000. From the point of view of the group, the depreciation should be based on the fair value at acquisition date of $185 000. The fair value adjustment to the plant at acquisition date was $5000. Using a 20% depreciation rate, depreciation needs to be adjusted each year by $1000. Because the acquisition date was 1 July 2021 and the end of the reporting period is 30 June 2023, there is a 2-year time period between these two dates, with one year belonging to the previous period. The business combination valuation entry for plant has to include adjustments for current period depreciation and 1-year prior period depreciation. The current period depreciation is adjusted via depreciation expense, whereas prior period depreciation affects retained earnings (opening balance). Total depreciation adjustment of $2000 is recorded against accumulated depreciation.

The third business combination valuation entry for plant recognises the tax effect of the second entry above. As the asset is used and benefits flow to the entity, the deferred tax liability recognised in the first adjustment entry is partly reversed based on how many years have passed out of the useful life. This can be explained based on the change in the carrying amount of the asset as a result of the adjustment to accumulated depreciation from the second adjustment entry. In the worksheet entry discussed in the previous paragraph, accumulated depreciation was increased by $2000. This affected the carrying amount of the asset, and caused a decrease in the taxable temporary difference between it and the tax base of the asset. This results in the decrease of the deferred tax liability raised in the first business combination valuation entry for plant. The amount of the decrease is equal to the adjustment to accumulated depreciation times the tax rate: $2000 × 30% = $600. The adjustment to current depreciation expense decreases the profit and, therefore, the income tax expense is also decreased by $300 (the adjustment to depreciation expense of $1000 × the 30% tax rate). The adjustment to the previous period's depreciation expense decreases the previous period's profit and, therefore, the previous period's income tax expense is also decreased by $300 (the adjustment for previous period depreciation to retained earnings of $1000 × the 30% tax rate), which is recognised as an increase in retained earnings as the previous period's income tax expense is now in the retained earnings.

The final business combination valuation entry relates to the recognition of goodwill acquired in the business combination not previously recognised by the subsidiary in its accounts. At acquisition date, according to the acquisition analysis the parent acquired $9400 goodwill in the subsidiary. However, as the subsidiary had already recognised $5000 goodwill, only the additional $4400 goodwill is recognised on consolidation as having been acquired by the group.

The business combination valuation entries at 30 June 2023 are then as follows.

Accumulated depreciation — plant	Dr	60 000	
Plant	Cr		55 000
Deferred tax liability	Cr		1 500
Business combination valuation reserve	Cr		3 500
Depreciation expense	Dr	1 000	
Retained earnings (1/7/22)	Dr	1 000	
Accumulated depreciation — plant	Cr		2 000
(20% × $5000 p.a. for 2 years)			
Deferred tax liability	Dr	600	
Income tax expense	Cr		300
Retained earnings (1/7/22)	Cr		300
Goodwill	Dr	4 400	
Business combination valuation reserve	Cr		4 400

2. *Pre-acquisition entries at 30 June 2023*

The pre-acquisition entries at acquisition date can be read from the acquisition analysis. The differences between carrying amounts and fair values of the subsidiary's identifiable assets and liabilities are reflected in the business combination valuation reserve which is eliminated together with the other equity accounts recognised by the subsidiary at acquisition date, as it is a part of pre-acquisition equities. The entries at 1 July 2021 (acquisition date) is as follows.

Retained earnings (1/7/21)	Dr	100 000	
Share capital	Dr	200 000	
General reserve	Dr	5 000	
Business combination valuation reserve	Dr	10 000	
Shares in Taurus Ltd	Cr		315 000
Dividend payable	Dr	20 000	
Dividend receivable	Cr		20 000

Note the entry relating to the $20 000 dividend; because the dividend is paid in August 2021, the dividend payable and receivable of $20 000 will not exist in the individual accounts of the subsidiary and the parent and therefore the entry will not need to be repeated in further periods.

The first entry changes for periods after the acquisition date because of events affecting pre-acquisition equity that occur in the previous periods and are related to pre-acquisition equity transfers and changes in the investment account. In this problem, the only event between the acquisition date and the *beginning* of the current period affecting the pre-acquisition entry is the transfer for the inventories sold from business combination valuation reserve to retained earnings, meaning that the business combination valuation reserve that needs to be eliminated has been reduced by $2100, while the retained earnings (opening balance) that also needs to be eliminated is increased by the same amount.

The pre-acquisition entry at the beginning of the period ended 30 June 2023 is then as follows.

Retained earnings (1/7/22)*	Dr	102 100	
Share capital	Dr	200 000	
General reserve	Dr	5 000	
Business combination valuation reserve**	Dr	7 900	
Shares in Taurus Ltd	Cr		315 000

*$100 000 + $2100 (BCVR − inventories)
**$10 000 − $2100 (BCVR − inventories)

A further event in the *current* period that affects the balances of pre-acquisition equity is the transfer made by the subsidiary to general reserve of $15 000 — the subsidiary increased its general reserve and reduced its retained earnings using a transfer account; this affects the balances of pre-acquisition equity in specific accounts. An extra entry needs to be posted under the pre-acquisition entries to reverse this current period's transfer.

The extra entry required is as follows.

General reserve	Dr	15 000	
Transfer to general reserve	Cr		15 000

Both the business combination valuation entries and the pre-acquisition entries are then posted on the consolidation worksheet as shown in figure 27.22.

The consolidated figures that will be included in the consolidated financial statements are extracted from the last column of the consolidation worksheet shown in figure 27.22. Therefore, the consolidated financial statements of profit and loss and other comprehensive income, of changes in equity and of financial position for Pegasus Ltd's group at 30 June 2023 are as shown in figure 27.23.

FIGURE 27.22 Consolidation worksheet at 30 June 2023

Financial statements	Pegasus Ltd	Taurus Ltd	Adjustments Dr		Cr		Group
Revenues	125 000	90 000					215 000
Expenses	(85 000)	(65 000)	1 000	1			(151 000)
Profit before tax	40 000	25 000					64 000
Income tax expense	(15 500)	(10 200)			300	1	(25 400)
Profit for the period	24 500	14 800					38 600
Retained earnings (1/7/22)	150 000	85 000	1 000	1	300	1	132 200
			102 100	2			
	174 500	99 800					170 800
Transfer to general reserve	(20 000)	(15 000)			15 000	2	(20 000)
Retained earnings (30/6/23)	154 500	84 800					150 800
Share capital	500 000	200 000	200 000	2			500 000
Business combination valuation reserve	—	—	7 900	2	3 500	1	—
					4 400	1	
General reserve	50 000	20 000	5 000	2			50 000
			15 000	2			
Financial assets reserve (1/7/22)	2 000	3 000					5 000
Gain on financial assets	12 000	10 000					22 000
Financial assets reserve (30/6/23)	14 000	13 000					27 000
Plant revaluation surplus (1/7/22)	8 000	5 000					13 000
Gain on plant revaluation	28 000	22 000					50 000
Plant revaluation surplus (30/6/23)	36 000	27 000					63 000
Total equity	754 500	344 800					790 800
Deferred tax liabilities	11 000	16 000	600	1	1 500	1	27 900
Other liabilities	50 000	20 000					70 000
Total liabilities	61 000	36 000					97 900
Total equity and liabilities	815 500	380 800					888 700
Cash	25 000	5 000					30 000
Inventories	60 000	85 000					145 000
Financial assets	50 000	40 000					90 000
Plant	500 000	300 000			55 000	1	745 000
Accumulated depreciation — plant	(160 000)	(80 000)	60 000	1	2 000	1	(182 000)
Shares in Taurus Ltd	315 000	—			315 000	2	—
Fixtures and fittings	40 000	38 000					78 000
Accumulated depreciation — fixtures and fittings	(14 500)	(12 200)					(26 700)
Goodwill	—	5 000	4 400	1			9 400
Total assets	815 500	380 800	397 000		397 000		888 700

FIGURE 27.23 (a) Consolidated statement of profit or loss and other comprehensive income

PEGASUS LTD
Consolidated statement of profit or loss and other comprehensive income
for the year ended 30 June 2023

Revenues	$215 000
Expenses	(151 000)
Profit before tax	**64 000**
Income tax expense	(25 400)
Profit for the period	**38 600**
Other comprehensive income	
Revaluation of financial assets	22 000
Gain on plant revaluation	50 000
Other comprehensive income for the year net of tax	72 000
Total comprehensive income for the year	**$ 110 600**

PEGASUS LTD
Consolidated statement of changes in equity
for the year ended 30 June 2023

Total comprehensive income for the year	$110 600
Retained earnings balance at 1 July 2022	$132 200
Profit for the period	38 600
Transfer to general reserve	(20 000)
Retained earnings balance at 30 June 2023	$150 800
General reserve balance at 1 July 2022	$ 30 000
Transfer from retained earnings	20 000
General reserve balance at 30 June 2023	$ 50 000
Financial assets reserve at 1 July 2022	$ 5 000
Gain for the year	22 000
Financial assets reserve at 30 June 2023	$ 27 000
Plant revaluation surplus at 1 July 2022	$ 13 000
Gain for the year	50 000
Plant revaluation surplus at 30 June 2023	$ 63 000
Share capital balance at 1 July 2022	$500 000
Share capital balance at 30 June 2023	$500 000

PEGASUS LTD
Consolidated statement of financial position
as at 30 June 2023

EQUITY AND LIABILITIES		
Equity		
Share capital		$500 000
Other components of equity		140 000
Retained earnings		150 800
Total equity		790 800
Non-current liabilities		
Deferred tax liabilities		27 900
Other		70 000
Total non-current liabilities		97 900
Total equity and liabilities		**$888 700**
ASSETS		
Non-current assets		
Plant	$ 745 000	
Accumulated depreciation	(182 000)	$563 000
Fixtures and fittings	78 000	
Accumulated depreciation	(26 700)	51 300
Goodwill		9 400
Total non-current assets		623 700
Current assets		
Cash		30 000
Inventories		145 000
Financial assets		90 000
Total current assets		265 000
Total assets		**$888 700**

27.2 Consolidation worksheet entries on and after acquisition date

On 30 September 2021, Sagittarius Ltd acquired 80% of the shares of Aquila Ltd for $2.50 per share in cash. The recorded equity of Aquila Ltd at that date consisted of the following.

Share capital (10 000 shares)	$10 000
General reserve	3 000
Retained earnings	12 000

Sagittarius Ltd had previously acquired 20% of the shares of Aquila Ltd for $3500. The fair value of this investment at 30 September 2021 was $4000.

At acquisition date, all the identifiable assets and liabilities of Aquila Ltd were recorded at fair value except for some machinery and inventories whose carrying amounts were each $2000 less than their fair values. The machinery had a further 5-year life. All inventories were sold by Aquila Ltd before December 2021. The tax rate is 30%.

In a previous period, Aquila Ltd had purchased some goodwill that had been written down to a carrying amount of $2000 as at 30 September 2021. Aquila Ltd had developed a business magazine containing economic indicators for the coal industry. The magazine was widely sought after. Sagittarius Ltd placed a value of $1500 on the masthead of this magazine. The intangible asset, not recognised by Aquila Ltd at 30 September 2021 as it was internally generated, was considered to have an indefinite life.

At 30 September 2021, Crater Ltd had sued Aquila Ltd for alleged damaging statements made in the magazine, and a court case was in progress. Although it considered that a present obligation for damages existed, Aquila Ltd had not recognised any liability because it did not believe that the liability recognition criteria could be met. Sagittarius Ltd assessed potential damages at a fair value at 30 September 2021 of $2000. In January 2023, the court handed down its decision, and Aquila Ltd was required to pay damages of $2500.

The end of the reporting period for both companies is 30 June. Between 30 September 2021 and 30 June 2022, the following movements occurred in the records of Aquila Ltd.

- Aquila Ltd transferred $3000 from pre-acquisition retained earnings to the general reserve.
- Aquila Ltd had declared and paid a bonus share dividend of one share for every two shares held at 1 October 2021 partly out of the general reserve ($3000) and the remainder out of the retained earnings.

Required

1. Prepare the consolidation worksheet adjustment entries for consolidation of the financial statements of Sagittarius Ltd and Aquila Ltd on:
   (a) 30 September 2021
   (b) 30 June 2022.
2. Assuming no further movements in pre-acquisition equity of Aquila Ltd, prepare the consolidation worksheet entries at 30 June 2023.

SOLUTION

The first step in the preparation of consolidation worksheet adjustment entries is to prepare the acquisition analysis at acquisition date. This requires the identification of:

- *the recorded equity of the subsidiary at acquisition date*. This consists of $10 000 share capital, $3000 general reserve and $12 000 retained earnings.
- *any goodwill previously recorded by the subsidiary*. The subsidiary has recorded goodwill of $2000.
- *differences between carrying amounts and fair values for identifiable assets recorded by the subsidiary*. The differences arise for machinery ($2000) and inventories ($2000).
- *the fair value of identifiable assets and liabilities not recognised by the subsidiary but recognised as part of the business combination*. The group recognises a masthead with a fair value of $1500 and a provision for damages with a fair value of $2000.
- *any dividends payable by the subsidiary at acquisition date*. There are none in this problem.
- *any previously held interest in the subsidiary by the parent*. The fair value of the previously held investment in the subsidiary by the parent is $4000.

Acquisition analysis at 30 September 2021

Net fair value of identifiable assets and liabilitiesof Aquila Ltd	= ($10 000 + $12 000 + $3000) (equity) − $2000 (goodwill recorded) + $2000(1 − 30%) (BCVR — machinery) + $2000(1 − 30%) (BCVR — inventories) + $1500(1 − 30%) (BCVR — masthead) − $2000(1 − 30%) (BCVR — provision for damages) = $25 450
Consideration transferred	= 80% × 10 000 × $2.50 = $20 000
Fair value of previously held investment	= $4000
Aggregate amount of investment	= $20 000 + $4000 = $24 000
Gain on bargain purchase	= $25 450 − $24 000 = $1450
Adjustment to goodwill	= ($2000)

The aggregate of the investment in Aquila Ltd is $1450 lower than the net fair value of the identifiable assets and liabilities of the subsidiary. Therefore, a gain on bargain purchase needs to be recognised and there is no goodwill. As the subsidiary has recorded $2000 goodwill, the adjustment on consolidation for goodwill needs to write off this goodwill.

1 a. *Consolidation worksheet entries at 30 September 2021*

(i) *Business combination valuation entries*

The business combination valuation entries are used to adjust the carrying amount of the subsidiary's recorded assets to fair value, to recognise assets and liabilities not recorded by the subsidiary and to write off goodwill recorded by the subsidiary. These adjustments have all been identified in the acquisition analysis. In recognising the assets and liabilities at fair value, the adjustments affect the business combination valuation reserve (70% of the adjustment; i.e. 1 − tax rate) and deferred tax accounts (30% of the adjustment). The entries at acquisition date are as follows.

Machinery	Dr	2 000	
Deferred tax liability	Cr		600
Business combination valuation reserve	Cr		1 400
Inventories	Dr	2 000	
Deferred tax liability	Cr		600
Business combination valuation reserve	Cr		1 400
Masthead	Dr	1 500	
Deferred tax liability	Cr		450
Business combination valuation reserve	Cr		1 050
Business combination valuation reserve	Dr	1 400	
Deferred tax asset	Dr	600	
Provision for damages	Cr		2 000
Business combination valuation reserve	Dr	2 000	
Goodwill	Cr		2 000

Note that with the liability, there is an overall decrease in the business combination valuation reserve as a negative amount is recognised in it, and the tax adjustment is to a deferred tax asset. For goodwill, the business combination valuation reserve is further decreased as goodwill is written off, but there is no tax effect.

(ii) *Pre-acquisition entry*

The pre-acquisition entry at acquisition date can be read from the acquisition analysis. The entry eliminates the pre-acquisition equity of the subsidiary, including the business combination valuation reserve as recognised in the previous set of entries, and the investment account as recorded by the parent and recognises the gain on bargain purchase as part of post-acquisition equity. The entry at acquisition date is as follows.

Retained earnings (30/9/18)	Dr	12 000	
Share capital	Dr	10 000	
General reserve	Dr	3 000	
Business combination valuation reserve	Dr	450	
Gain on bargain purchase	Cr		1 450
Shares in Aquila Ltd	Cr		24 000

1 b. *Consolidation worksheet entries at 30 June 2022*

These entries are at the end of the first period since acquisition date, and cover 9 months.

(i) *Business combination valuation entries*

As the machinery is still on hand at the end on the current period, the business combination valuation entry that was recorded at acquisition date is repeated now. However, there needs to be an additional entry to adjust the depreciation for 9 months based on the difference between carrying amount in the subsidiary and fair value. The adjustment is to current period depreciation and amounts to $300 $\left(\text{i.e. } \frac{9}{12} \times \frac{\$2000}{5}\right)$ as the machinery has a further 5-year life at acquisition date. The adjustment to depreciation changes the carrying amount of the asset. This changes the taxable temporary difference between the carrying amount and the tax base of the machinery. As a result, the deferred tax liability raised on adjusting the machinery to fair value is reversed. The reversal is $90 — that is, 30% × the depreciation adjustment of $300. A decrease in income tax expense is also recognised as the depreciation expense adjustment decreases the current profit.

Machinery	Dr	2 000	
Deferred tax liability	Cr		600
Business combination valuation reserve	Cr		1 400
Depreciation expense	Dr	300	
Accumulated depreciation	Cr		300
$\left(\frac{9}{12} \times \frac{1}{5} \times \$2000\right)$			
Deferred tax liability	Dr	90	
Income tax expense	Cr		90

The inventories on hand at acquisition date are sold by December 2021. The adjustment is made to cost of sales instead of inventories, because the cost of sales to the group should be recognised as $2000 higher than that recorded by the subsidiary on the sale of the inventories. As the cost of sales are increased, the current period profit decreases and so does the income tax expense. As the asset is sold, there is no deferred tax effect anymore and the group transfers the business combination valuation reserve to retained earnings. The entry for inventories is as follows.

Cost of sales	Dr	2 000	
Income tax expense	Cr		600
Transfer from business combination valuation reserve	Cr		1 400

As the masthead is still on hand at the end of the current period and is not subject to amortisation or impairment, there is no change to the entry for the masthead.

Masthead	Dr	1 500	
Deferred tax liability	Cr		450
Business combination valuation reserve	Cr		1 050

As the provision for damages should still be recognised as the damages were not yet paid prior to the end of the current period, there is no change to the entry for the provision for damages. This entry would change if the subsidiary itself recognised a liability or the liability was settled or changed in value.

Business combination valuation reserve	Dr	1 400	
Deferred tax asset	Dr	600	
Provision for damages	Cr		2 000

There is no change to the entry for goodwill. This entry would change if the subsidiary itself derecognised the goodwill or recognised an impairment; in the latter case, the impairment of goodwill will also be eliminated in the pre-acquisition entries.

| Business combination valuation reserve | Dr | 2 000 | |
| Goodwill | Cr | | 2 000 |

(ii) *Pre-acquisition entries*

The first pre-acquisition entry at 30 June 2022, which should normally be adjusted for the transfers between pre-acquisition equity accounts or changes in the investment account prior to the beginning of the period, is the same as that at acquisition date as 30 June 2022 is the end of the period during which the acquisition took place.

Retained earnings (30/9/21)	Dr	12 000	
Share capital	Dr	10 000	
General reserve	Dr	3 000	
Business combination valuation reserve	Dr	450	
Gain on bargain purchase	Cr		1 450
Shares in Aquila Ltd	Cr		24 000

For events occurring in the current period that affect pre-acquisition equity or the investment balances, additional entries are posted as pre-acquisition entries to reverse their effects. There are no events that affect the investment balance. However, in the current period, the following events affect the pre-acquisition equity.

- *$1400 transfer from business combination valuation reserve to retained earnings as the inventories on hand at acquisition date were sold in the current period.* As can be seen from the related business combination valuation entry, on sale of the inventories the related business combination valuation reserve is transferred to retained earnings. Hence, the business combination valuation reserve is reduced and retained earnings increased by recognising an account called transfer from business combination valuation reserve — this account needs to be eliminated and the business combination valuation reserve needs to be increased to the amount prior to the transfer by reversing the entry that recognised the transfer.
- *$3000 transfer to general reserve from pre-acquisition retained earnings.* This decreases retained earnings by recognising a temporary account called transfer to general reserve and increases the general reserve.
- *$5000 bonus share dividend.* This increases share capital by $5000 and reduces the equity accounts from which the bonus share dividend was distributed: general reserve decreases by $3000 and retained earnings by $2000, the latter recognised in a separate account called bonus dividend paid.

The journal entries posted as pre-acquisition entries to reverse those effects at 30 June 2022 are then as follows.

Transfer from business combination valuation reserve	Dr	1 400	
Business combination valuation reserve	Cr		1 400
General reserve	Dr	3 000	
Transfer to general reserve	Cr		3 000
Share capital	Dr	5 000	
General reserve	Cr		3 000
Bonus dividend paid	Cr		2 000

2. *Consolidation worksheet entries at 30 June 2023*

This is 1 year after the last set of entries and $1\frac{3}{4}$ years since acquisition date. One year belongs to the current period, while 9 months are from the last period.

(i) Business combination valuation entries

The first adjustment entry raised at acquisition date and at 30 June 2022 for the machinery to recognise the fair value increment is still used now as the machinery is still on hand at the beginning of the current period. In terms of depreciation adjustments, the entry prepared at 30 June 2022 will require some changes. The depreciation adjustments now should be for $1\frac{3}{4}$ years since acquisition date. Current period depreciation expense is adjusted for a full year's depreciation adjustment and the adjustment for prior period depreciation expense for $\frac{3}{4}$ of a year affects retained earnings (opening balance). Using the asset results in changes in the carrying amount of the asset, and further results in reversing the deferred tax liability raised in the first adjustment entry. The current period income tax expense is affected by the adjustment to the current period depreciation, while the adjustment for the previous depreciation, which affects retained earnings, also affects last year's income tax expense, requiring a further adjustment to retained earnings.

Machinery	Dr	2 000	
Deferred tax liability	Cr		600
Business combination valuation reserve	Cr		1 400
Depreciation expense*	Dr	400	
Retained earnings (1/7/22)**	Dr	300	
Accumulated depreciation	Cr		700
Deferred tax liability	Dr	210	
Income tax expense	Cr		120
Retained earnings (1/7/22)	Cr		90

$*\frac{1}{5} \times \$2000$ p.a.

$**\frac{1}{5} \times \$2000 \times \frac{3}{4}$

There is still no change to the adjustment for the masthead as nothing happens to the masthead by 30 June 2023.

Masthead	Dr	1 500	
Deferred tax liability	Cr		450
Business combination valuation reserve	Cr		1 050

In January 2023, the court determined that the subsidiary was to pay damages of $2500. As the liability is settled, the business combination valuation reserve is transferred to retained earnings. In settling the liability, the subsidiary raised a damages expense of $2500. Since the group recognised the liability for damages at acquisition date for $2000, the expense to the group on payment of $2500 is only the additional amount of $500 (i.e. $2500 − $2000). Since $2500 damages expense was recorded by the subsidiary, and the group wants to report only $500 damages expense, the consolidation adjustment is a $2000 reduction in damages expense. Further, no deferred tax asset is recognised after settlement of the liability, but a current tax effect needs to be recorded as an adjustment to income tax expense due to the adjustment to damages expense.

Transfer from business combination valuation reserve	Dr	1 400	
Income tax expense	Dr	600	
Damages expense	Cr		2 000

There is still no change to the entry for goodwill as nothing happens to the goodwill by 30 June 2023.

Business combination valuation reserve	Dr	2 000	
Goodwill	Cr		2 000

(ii) *Pre-acquisition entries*

The first pre-acquisition entry that is adjusted for the impact of transfers between pre-acquisition equity accounts and changes in the investment account that occur prior to the beginning of the year, 1 July 2022, is the sum of the entries made in the consolidation worksheet at 30 June 2022. The gain on bargain purchase, the transfers accounts and the bonus share dividend account are affecting the retained earnings (opening balance) and should be adjusted there. As such, each line in the first pre-acquisition entry now can be calculated by adjusting the balance at acquisition date for all events affecting that balance between acquisition date and the beginning of the current period, as follows.

Retained earnings (1/7/22):

$6950 = $12 000 (balance at acquisition date) − $1450 (gain on bargain purchase) + $1400 (transfer from BCVR — inventories) − $3000 (transfer to general reserve from retained earnings) − $2000 (bonus share dividend from retained earnings)

Share capital:

$15 000 = $10 000 (balance at acquisition date) + $2000 (bonus share dividend from retained earnings) + $3000 (bonus share dividend from general reserve)

General reserve:

$3000 = $3000 (balance at acquisition date) + $3000 (transfer to general reserve from retained earnings) − $3000 (bonus share dividend from general reserve)

Business combination valuation reserve:

($950) = $450 (balance at acquisition date) − $1400 (transfer from BCVR — inventories)

Shares in Aquila Ltd:

There is no change to this account.

Note that the gain on bargain purchase should be recognised now as part of retained earnings (1/7/22) by crediting that account as it belongs to the period of acquisition that ended at 30 June 2022; however, that will reverse a part of the debit to retained earnings (1/7/22) necessary to eliminate the pre-acquisition retained earnings and, therefore, the gain on bargain purchase is considered above as a deduction in the calculation of the adjustment to retained earnings (1/7/22). The entry is then as follows.

Retained earnings (1/7/22)	Dr	6 950	
Share capital	Dr	15 000	
General reserve	Dr	3 000	
Business combination valuation reserve	Cr		950
Shares in Aquila Ltd	Cr		24 000

Note that for business combination valuation reserve, a negative amount of ($950) needs to be eliminated and this is done by crediting the account.

Other entries are required for events occurring in the current period that affect accounts in the pre-acquisition entry. In this problem, there is only one such event. In the current period the contingent liability was settled, resulting in a transfer from business combination valuation reserve to retained earnings. As the business combination valuation reserve for the liability is a negative amount, the effect on the pre-acquisition equity is that the business combination valuation reserve has been increased by $1400; also retained earnings decreases by $1400, but this is recognised in the current period transfer account. In the pre-acquisition entry, this effect needs to be reversed as follows.

Business combination valuation reserve	Dr	1 400	
Transfer from business combination valuation reserve			
	Cr		1 400

COMPREHENSION QUESTIONS

1 Briefly describe the consolidation process in the case of wholly owned entities.
2 Explain the initial adjustments that may be required before undertaking the consolidation process.
3 Explain the adjustments that may be required as part of the consolidation process.
4 Explain the purpose and format of the consolidated worksheet.
5 Explain the purpose of the acquisition analysis in the preparation of consolidated financial statements.
6 How does AASB 3/IFRS 3 *Business Combinations* affect the acquisition analysis?
7 At the date the parent acquires a controlling interest in a subsidiary, if the carrying amounts of the subsidiary's identifiable assets are not equal to their fair values, explain why adjustments to these assets are required in the preparation of the consolidated financial statements.
8 If the parent assesses that some of the subsidiary's identifiable assets and liabilities are not recorded by the subsidiary at acquisition date, explain why adjustments to these assets and liabilities are required in the preparation of the consolidated financial statements.
9 Explain the purpose of the business combination valuation entries in the preparation of consolidated financial statements.
10 Explain the purpose of the pre-acquisition entries in the preparation of consolidated financial statements.
11 When there is a dividend payable by the subsidiary at acquisition date, under what conditions should it be taken into consideration in preparing the pre-acquisition entries?
12 Is it necessary to distinguish pre-acquisition dividends from post-acquisition dividends? Why?
13 If the subsidiary has recorded goodwill in its records at acquisition date, how does this affect the acquisition analysis, the business combination valuation entries and the pre-acquisition entries?
14 Explain how the existence of a gain on bargain purchase affects the pre-acquisition entries, both in the year of acquisition and in subsequent years.
15 Why are some adjustment entries in the previous period's consolidation worksheet also made in the current period's worksheet?
16 Explain how and why the business combination valuation entries will be adjusted in subsequent years after the acquisition date.
17 Explain how and why the pre-acquisition entries will be adjusted in subsequent years after the acquisition date.
18 Using an example, explain how the business combination entries affect the pre-acquisition entries, both at acquisition date and in the subsequent years.
19 Explain the choices that may be available to revalue the identifiable assets recorded by the subsidiary at carrying amounts different from fair value at the acquisition date.
20 At acquisition date, the subsidiary may have the choice to revalue (or not) in its own accounts the identifiable assets previously recorded at carrying amounts different from fair value. Discuss how the business combination entries and the pre-acquisition entries will be affected by this choice.

CASE STUDY 27.1

UNRECORDED ASSETS

Lynx Ltd has just acquired all the issued shares of Indus Ltd. The accounting staff at Lynx Ltd has been analysing the assets and liabilities acquired as a result of this business combination. This analysis found that Indus Ltd had been expensing its research outlays in accordance with AASB 138/IAS 38 *Intangible Assets*. Over the past 3 years before the acquisition, the company has expensed a total of $20 000, including $8000 immediately before the acquisition date. One of the reasons that Lynx Ltd acquired Indus Ltd was its promising research findings in an area that could benefit the products being produced by Lynx Ltd.

There is disagreement among the accounting staff as to how to account for the research outlays of Indus Ltd. Some of the staff argue that, since it is research expenditure, the correct accounting treatment is to expense it, and so no adjustments need to be done on consolidation. Other members of the accounting staff believe that it should be recognised on consolidation as an asset, but are unsure of the accounting entries to use, and are concerned about the future effects of recognition of an asset.

Required

Advise the accountants that prepare the consolidated financial statements of Lynx Ltd on what accounting choice is the most appropriate in these circumstances.

CASE STUDY 27.2

UNRECORDED LIABILITY

Scorpio Ltd has finally concluded its negotiations to acquire Norma Ltd, and has secured ownership of all the shares of Norma Ltd. One of the areas of discussion during the negotiation process was the current court case that Norma Ltd was involved in. The company was being sued by some former employees who were retrenched, but are now claiming damages for unfair dismissal. The company did not believe that it owed these employees anything. However, realising that industrial relations was an uncertain area, particularly given the country's current confusing industrial relations laws, it had raised a note to the accounts issued before the takeover by Scorpio Ltd reporting the existence of the court case as a contingent liability. No monetary amount was disclosed, but the company's lawyers had placed a $56 700 amount on the probable payout to settle the case.

The accounting staff of Scorpio Ltd are unsure of the effect of this contingent liability on the accounting for the consolidated group after the acquisition. Some argue that it is not a liability of the group and so should not be recognised on consolidation, but are willing to accept some form of note disclosure. A further concern being raised is the effects on the accounts, depending on whether Norma Ltd wins or loses the case. If Norma Ltd wins the court case, it will not have to pay out any damages and could get reimbursement of its court costs, estimated to be around $40 000.

Required

Give your opinion on the treatment of the contingent liability at acquisition date for consolidation purposes, as well as any subsequent effects when Norma Ltd either wins or loses the case.

CASE STUDY 27.3

MISVALUED AND UNRECORDED ASSETS AND LIABILITIES

Mensa Ltd has acquired all the shares of Careers Ltd. The accountant for Mensa Ltd, having studied the requirements of AASB 3/IFRS 3 *Business Combinations*, realises that all the identifiable assets and liabilities of Careers Ltd must be recognised in the consolidated financial statements at fair value. Although she understands the need to revalue items recorded by the subsidiary at carrying amounts different from fair value and to recognise previously unrecorded assets or liabilities at fair value, she is unsure of a number of matters associated with accounting for these assets and liabilities. She has approached you and asked for your advice.

Required

Write a report for the accountant at Mensa Ltd advising on the following issues.

1. Should the adjustments to fair value be made in the consolidation worksheet or in the accounts of Careers Ltd?
2. What equity accounts should be used when revaluing or recognising assets and liabilities?
3. Do these equity accounts remain in existence indefinitely, since they do not seem to be related to the equity accounts recognised by Careers Ltd itself?

CASE STUDY 27.4

GOODWILL

When Hydra Ltd acquired the shares of Draco Ltd, one of the assets in the statement of financial position of Draco Ltd was $15 000 goodwill, which had been recognised by Draco Ltd upon its acquisition of a business from Valhalla Ltd. Having prepared the acquisition analysis as part of the process of preparing the consolidated financial statements for Hydra Ltd, the group accountant has asked for your opinion.

Required

Provide advice on the following issues.

1. How does the goodwill previously recorded by the subsidiary affect the accounting for the group's goodwill?
2. If, in subsequent years, goodwill is impaired, for example by $10 000, should the impairment loss be recognised in the records of Hydra Ltd or as a consolidation adjustment?

CASE STUDY 27.5

GAIN ON BARGAIN PURCHASE

The accountant for Carina Ltd, Ms Finn, has sought your advice on an accounting issue that has been puzzling her. When preparing the acquisition analysis relating to Carina Ltd's acquisition of Lyra Ltd, she calculated that there was a gain on bargain purchase of $10 000. Being unsure of how to account for this, she was informed by professional acquaintances that this should be recognised as income. However, she reasoned that this would increase the consolidated profit in the first year after acquisition date. As she is aware that the pre-acquisition equity of the subsidiary needs to be eliminated on consolidation, she is unsure of whether this profit is all post- or pre-acquisition profit or a mixture of the two.

Required

Compile a detailed report on the nature of the gain on bargain purchase, its recognition on acquisition and the effects of its recognition on subsequent consolidated financial statements.

APPLICATION AND ANALYSIS EXERCISES

★ BASIC | ★ ★ MODERATE | ★ ★ ★ DIFFICULT

27.1 Acquisition analysis, acquisition date entries ★   **LO3, 4**

On 1 July 2022, Keith Ltd acquired the remaining 80% of the issued shares that it did not previously own in Urban Ltd, transferring 400 000 Keith Ltd shares to Urban Ltd's former shareholders. At that date, the financial statements of Urban Ltd showed the following information.

Share capital	$700 000
Asset revaluation surplus	140 000
Retained earnings	460 000

All the assets and liabilities of Urban Ltd were recorded at amounts equal to their fair values at the acquisition date. The fair value of Keith Ltd's shares at acquisition date was $3.50 per share. The previously held interest by Keith Ltd in Urban Ltd (i.e. 20% of the issued shares) was recognised in Keith Ltd's accounts at the fair value at 1 July 2022 of $260 000. Keith Ltd incurred $25 000 in acquisition-related costs, including $12 000 in share issue costs.

Required

1. Prepare the acquisition analysis at 1 July 2022.
2. Prepare the journal entries for Keith Ltd to recognise the additional investment in Urban Ltd at 1 July 2022.
3. Prepare the consolidation worksheet entries for Keith Ltd's group at 1 July 2022.

27.2 Acquisition analysis, acquisition date entries ★   **LO3, 4**

On 1 July 2022, Michael Ltd acquired all the issued shares of Andrew Ltd, paying $60 000 cash and transferring 50 000 of its own shares to Andrew Ltd's former shareholders. At that date, the financial statements of Andrew Ltd showed the following information.

Share capital	$50 000
General reserve	25 000
Retained earnings	75 000

All the assets and liabilities of Andrew Ltd were recorded at amounts equal to their fair values at the acquisition date. The fair value of Michael Ltd's shares at acquisition date was $2 per share. Michael Ltd incurred $15 000 in acquisition-related costs that included $2500 as share issue costs.

Required

1. Prepare the acquisition analysis at 1 July 2022.
2. Prepare the journal entries for Michael Ltd to recognise the investment in Andrew Ltd at 1 July 2022.
3. Prepare the consolidation worksheet entries for Michael Ltd's group at 1 July 2022.

27.3 Undervalued and unrecorded assets ★　　　　　　　　　　　　　　　　　**LO3, 6**

On 1 July 2022, Nicole Ltd acquired all the issued shares of Kidman Ltd, paying $250 000 cash. At that date, the financial statements of Kidman Ltd showed the following information.

Share capital	$100 000
Retained earnings	100 000

All the assets and liabilities of Kidman Ltd were recorded at amounts equal to their fair values at the acquisition date, except some inventories recorded at $10 000 below their fair value. Also, Nicole Ltd identified at acquisition date a patent with a fair value of $40 000 that Kidman Ltd has not recorded in its own accounts.

Required

1. Prepare the acquisition analysis at 1 July 2022.
2. Prepare the consolidation worksheet entries for Nicole Ltd's group at 1 July 2022.
3. Discuss how the answers for 1 and 2 above would change if the Nicole Ltd paid only $200 000 cash for the shares in Kidman Ltd.

27.4 Undervalued and unrecorded assets, unrecorded liabilities ★　　　　　　　**LO3, 4**

On 1 July 2022, Dean Ltd acquired all the issued shares of Lewis Ltd for a cash consideration of $1 000 000. At that date, the financial statements of Lewis Ltd showed the following information.

Share capital	$650 000
General reserve	20 000
Retained earnings	250 000

All the assets and liabilities of Lewis Ltd were recorded at amounts equal to their fair values at the acquisition date, except some equipment recorded at $50 000 below its fair value with a related accumulated depreciation of $80 000. Also, Dean Ltd identified at acquisition date a contingent liability related to a lawsuit where Lewis Ltd was sued by a former supplier and attached a fair value of $40 000 to that liability.

Required

1. Prepare the acquisition analysis at 1 July 2022.
2. Prepare the consolidation worksheet entries for Dean Ltd's group at 1 July 2022, assuming that Lewis Ltd has not revalued the equipment in its own accounts.
3. Prepare the consolidation worksheet entries for Dean Ltd's group at 1 July 2022, assuming that Lewis Ltd has revalued the equipment in its own accounts.

27.5 Pre- and post-acquisition dividends ★　　　　　　　　　　　　　　　　**LO3, 4, 5**

On 1 July 2022, George Ltd acquired all the issued shares (*cum div.*) of Ezra Ltd for $480 000. At that date, the financial statements of Ezra Ltd showed the following information.

Share capital	$200 000
General reserve	100 000
Retained earnings	140 000
Dividend payable	40 000

All the assets and liabilities of George Ltd were recorded at amounts equal to their fair values at the acquisition date. The dividend payable reported at 1 July 2022 by Ezra Ltd was paid on 15 August 2022. Ezra Ltd paid a further dividend of $50 000 on 2 February 2023 from post-acquisition profits.

Required

1. Prepare the acquisition analysis at 1 July 2022.
2. Prepare the consolidation worksheet entries for George Ltd's group at 1 July 2022.
3. Prepare the consolidation worksheet entries for George Ltd's group at 30 June 2023.
4. Discuss how the entries for 2 and 3 above would change if the shares were bought on an *ex div.* basis.

27.6 Previously recorded goodwill ★ **LO4, 5**

On 1 July 2022, Shawn Ltd acquired all the issued shares of Mendes Ltd for $153 000. At this date the equity of Mendes Ltd was recorded as follows.

Share capital	$80 000
General reserve	30 000
Retained earnings	40 000

All the identifiable assets and liabilities were recorded at amounts equal to their fair values.

Required

1. Prepare the consolidation worksheet entries for Shawn Ltd's group at 1 July 2022 and 30 June 2023.
2. Prepare the consolidation worksheet entries for Shawn Ltd's group at 1 July 2022 and 30 June 2023, assuming Shawn Ltd paid $148 000 for the shares in Mendes Ltd.
3. Prepare the consolidation worksheet entries for Shawn Ltd's group at 1 July 2022 and 30 June 2023, assuming Shawn Ltd paid $145 000 for the shares in Mendes Ltd and Mendes Ltd had goodwill of $4000 recorded prior to the acquisition.

27.7 Pre-acquisition dividends, previously recorded goodwill ★ **LO3, 4, 5**

On 1 January 2023, Daniel Ltd acquired all the issued shares (*cum div.*) of Powter Ltd for $526 000. At that date the equity of Powter Ltd was recorded as follows.

Share capital	$300 000
General reserve	80 000
Retained earnings	120 000

On 1 January 2023, the records of Powter Ltd showed that the company had previously recorded a goodwill at cost of $10 000. Further, Powter Ltd had a dividend payable of $20 000, the dividend to be paid in March 2023. All other assets and liabilities were carried at amounts equal to their fair values.

Required

1. Prepare the acquisition analysis at 1 January 2023.
2. Prepare the consolidation worksheet entries for Daniel Ltd's group at 1 January 2023.
3. Prepare the consolidation worksheet entries for Daniel Ltd's group at 30 June 2023.
4. Discuss how the entries for 2 and 3 above would change if the consideration transferred was $249 000.

27.8 Pre-acquisition reserves transfers ★ **LO3, 4, 5**

On 1 July 2022, Kate Ltd acquired all the issued shares of Miller Ltd for $200 000. The financial statements of Miller Ltd showed its equity at that date to be as follows.

Share capital (20 000 shares)	$100 000
General reserve	40 000
Retained earnings	60 000

All the assets and liabilities of Miller Ltd were recorded at amounts equal to their fair values at that date.

During the year ending 30 June 2023, Miller Ltd undertook the following actions.

- On 10 September 2022, Miller Ltd paid a dividend of $20 000 from the profits earned prior to 1 July 2022.
- On 1 January 2023, Miller Ltd transferred $15 000 from the general reserve existing at 1 July 2022 to retained earnings.
- On 28 June 2023, Miller Ltd declared a dividend of $20 000 from the profits earned after 1 July 2022 to be paid on 15 August 2023.

Required

1. Prepare the acquisition analysis at 1 July 2022.
2. Prepare the consolidation worksheet entries for Kate Ltd's group at 1 July 2022.
3. Prepare the consolidation worksheet entries for Kate Ltd's group at 30 June 2023.

27.9 Undervalued and unrecorded assets, unrecorded liabilities ★   LO3, 4

In the year ended 30 June 2018, Sam Ltd acquired 40% of the issued shares of Hunt Ltd for $72 000. This acquisition did not give Sam Ltd control of Hunt Ltd, because the ownership of Hunt Ltd was held by a small number of shareholders (Hunt Ltd was developed as a family business in 2004). On 1 July 2022, Sam Ltd approached these family members following a death in the family and persuaded them to sell the remainder of the shares in Hunt Ltd to Sam Ltd for $137 700 on a *cum div.* basis.

Information about the two companies at 1 July 2022 included the following.

- Sam Ltd recorded its original investment in Hunt Ltd at fair value, with changes in fair value being recognised in profit or loss. At 1 July 2022, the investment was recorded at $91 800.
- The equity of Hunt Ltd at 1 July 2022 consisted of $144 000 share capital and $36 000 retained earnings.
- Included in the assets and liabilities recorded by Hunt Ltd at 1 July 2022 were goodwill of $5400 (net of accumulated impairment losses of $3600) and dividend payable of $4500.
- On the acquisition date all the identifiable assets and liabilities of Hunt Ltd were recorded at carrying amounts equal to their fair values except for inventories for which the fair value of $39 600 was $3600 greater than its carrying amount, and equipment for which the fair value of $94 500 was greater than the carrying amount, this being cost of $108 000 less accumulated depreciation of $18 000.
- Sam Ltd discovered that Hunt Ltd had two assets that had not been recorded by Hunt Ltd. These were internally generated patents that had a fair value of $45 000 and in-process research and development for which Hunt Ltd had expensed $90 000, but Sam Ltd considered that an asset was created with a fair value of $18 000.
- In the notes to the financial statements at 30 June 2022, Hunt Ltd had reported the existence of a contingent liability relating to guarantees for loans. Sam Ltd determined that this liability had a fair value of $9000 at 1 July 2022.

The tax rate is 30%.

Required

1. Prepare the acquisition analysis at 1 July 2022.
2. Prepare the consolidation worksheet entries for Sam Ltd's group at 1 July 2022.

27.10 Previously recorded goodwill, pre-acquisition reserves transfers ★

On 1 July 2021, Calum Ltd acquired all the issued shares (*ex div.*) of Scott Ltd. At this date the financial statements of Scott Ltd showed the following balances in its accounts.

Share capital	$300 000
General reserve	80 000
Retained earnings	160 000
Dividend payable	40 000
Goodwill	20 000

At 1 July 2021, all the identifiable assets and liabilities of Scott Ltd were recorded at amounts equal to their fair values.

The financial statements of Calum Ltd and Scott Ltd at 30 June 2022 contained the following information.

	Calum Ltd	Scott Ltd
Profit for the period	$ 70 000	$ 50 000
Retained earnings (1/7/21)	180 000	160 000
Transfer from general reserve	0	20 000
Retained earnings (30/6/22)	250 000	230 000
Share capital	1 400 000	300 000
General reserve	184 000	60 000
Total equity	1 834 000	590 000
Provisions	60 000	40 000
Payables	30 000	50 000
Long-term loans	100 000	220 000
Total liabilities	190 000	310 000
Total equity and liabilities	**$2 024 000**	**$ 900 000**

	Calum Ltd	Scott Ltd
Plant	$1 200 000	$ 1 640 000
Accumulated depreciation — plant	(590 000)	(1 300 000)
Fixtures	600 000	240 000
Accumulated depreciation — fixtures	(360 000)	(160 000)
Land	400 000	280 000
Brands	100 000	60 000
Shares in Scott Ltd	544 000	0
Goodwill	0	20 000
Inventories	90 000	80 000
Cash	10 000	14 000
Receivables	30 000	26 000
Total assets	**$2 024 000**	**$ 900 000**

Required

1. Prepare the acquisition analysis at 1 July 2021.
2. Prepare the consolidation worksheet entries for Calum Ltd's group at 30 June 2022.
3. Prepare the consolidated financial statements for Calum Ltd's group at 30 June 2022.

27.11 **Undervalued assets, pre-acquisition reserves transfers** ★   **LO3, 4, 5**

On 1 July 2022, Birds Ltd acquired all the issued shares of Tokyo Ltd for $174 800. At this date the equity of Tokyo Ltd consisted of share capital of $80 000 and retained earnings of $68 800. All the identifiable assets and liabilities of Tokyo Ltd were recorded at amounts equal to fair value except for the following.

	Carrying amount	Fair value
Patent	$60 000	$72 000
Plant (cost $80 000)	40 000	48 000
Inventories	21 600	28 000

The patent was considered to have an indefinite life. It was estimated that the plant had a further life of 10 years, and was depreciated on a straight-line basis. All the inventories were sold by 30 June 2023.

In May 2023, Tokyo Ltd transferred $20 000 from the retained earnings on hand at 1 July 2022 to a general reserve. In June 2023, Tokyo Ltd conducted an impairment test on the patent and on the goodwill acquired. As a result, the goodwill was considered to be impaired by $1200. The tax rate is 30%.

Required

1. Prepare the acquisition analysis at 1 July 2022.
2. Prepare the consolidation worksheet entries for Birds Ltd's group at 1 July 2022.
3. Prepare the consolidation worksheet entries for Birds Ltd's group at 30 June 2023.

27.12 **Undervalued assets, pre-acquisition reserves transfers** ★   **LO3, 4, 5**

Billy Ltd acquired all the issued shares of Joel Ltd on 1 January 2022 for $36 000. At this date the equity of Joel Ltd consisted of the following.

Share capital	$25 000
General reserve	6 250
Retained earnings	2 500

All the identifiable assets and liabilities of Joel Ltd were recorded at amounts equal to their fair values except for the following.

	Carrying amount	Fair value
Inventories	$ 6 000	$ 8 000
Plant (cost $35 000)	25 000	26 000

Of the inventories on hand at 1 January 2022, 90% was sold by 30 June 2022. The remainder was sold by 30 June 2023. The plant was considered to have a further 2-year useful life with benefits to be received equally in each of those years. The tax rate is 30%.

Required

1. Prepare the acquisition analysis at 1 January 2022.
2. Prepare the consolidation worksheet entries for Billy Ltd's group at 30 June 2022.
3. Prepare the consolidation worksheet entries for Billy Ltd's group at 30 June 2023.
4. Prepare the consolidation worksheet entries for Billy Ltd's group at 30 June 2024.

27.13 Undervalued assets, pre-acquisition reserves transfers ★ ★   **LO3, 4, 6, 7**

Bruno Ltd acquired all the issued shares (*ex div.*) of Mars Ltd on 1 July 2021 for $110 000. At this date Mars Ltd recorded a dividend payable of $10 000 and equity of the following.

Share capital	$54 000
Retained earnings	36 000
Asset revaluation surplus	18 000

All the identifiable assets and liabilities of Mars Ltd were recorded at amounts equal to their fair values at acquisition date except for the following.

	Carrying amount	Fair value
Inventories	$14 000	$16 000
Machinery (cost $100 000)	92 500	94 000

Of the inventories, 90% was sold by 30 June 2022. The remainder was sold by 30 June 2023. The machinery was considered to have a further 5-year life and it is depreciated on a straight-line basis.

Both Mars Ltd and Bruno Ltd use the revaluation model for land. At 1 July 2021, the balance of Bruno Ltd's asset revaluation surplus was $13 500.

In May 2022, Mars Ltd transferred $3000 from the retained earnings at 1 July 2021 to a general reserve.

The tax rate is 30%.

The following information was provided by the two companies at 30 June 2022.

	Bruno Ltd	Mars Ltd
Profit before tax	$ 120 000	$ 12 500
Income tax expense	(56 000)	(4 200)
Profit for the year	64 000	8 300
Retained earnings (1/7/21)	80 000	36 000
	144 000	44 300
Transfer to general reserve	(0)	(3 000)
Retained earnings (30/6/22)	$ 144 000	$ 41 300
Share capital	$ 360 000	$ 54 000
Retained earnings	144 000	41 300
General reserve	10 000	3 000
Asset revaluation surplus	18 500	20 000
Liabilities	42 500	13 000
	$ 575 000	$131 300
Land	$ 160 000	$ 20 000
Plant and machinery	360 000	125 600
Accumulated depreciation — plant and machinery	(110 000)	(33 000)
Inventories	55 000	18 700
Shares in Mars Ltd	110 000	0
	$ 575 000	$131 300

Required

1. Prepare the acquisition analysis at 1 July 2021.
2. Prepare the consolidation worksheet entries for Bruno Ltd's group at 30 June 2022.
3. Prepare the consolidated financial statements for Bruno Ltd's group at 30 June 2022.

27.14 Undervalued and unrecorded assets, pre-acquisition reserves transfers ★ ★ **LO3, 4, 5, 7**

On 1 July 2021, Cold Ltd held an investment in the shares in Chisel Ltd previously measured at $9300. Cold Ltd uses the fair value method to measure this investment with movements in fair value being recognised in profit or loss. Cold Ltd had acquired these shares 2 years earlier for $6150. The shares had a fair value at 1 July 2021 of $10 000.

On 1 July 2021, Cold Ltd acquired the remaining 80% of the shares (*cum div.*) in Chisel Ltd. The consideration for these shares consisted of 15 000 shares in Cold Ltd valued at $2.00 per share plus a brand that was carried in the records of Cold Ltd at $10 000 (net of accumulated amortisation of $1500), but the fair value at acquisition date is $12 400.

On 1 July 2021, the equity of Chisel Ltd consisted of the following.

Share capital	$25 000
Retained earnings	16 000

At this date, Chisel Ltd had in its accounts a dividend payable of $3000, which was paid on 15 August 2028. Chisel Ltd had also recorded goodwill of $2500, net of accumulated impairment losses of $3500. Chisel Ltd had an unrecorded asset relating to internally generated trademarks that had a fair value of $4000. These had a future expected useful life of 8 years. All other identifiable assets and liabilities of Chisel Ltd were recorded at amounts equal to fair value except for the following.

	Carrying amount	Fair value
Plant (cost $45 000)	$37 000	$40 000
Inventories	9 000	11 500

The plant was expected to have a further 6-year useful life. In relation to the inventories held at 1 July 2021, 90% was sold by 30 June 2022 and the rest by 30 June 2023. The tax rate is 30%.

In June 2022, Chisel Ltd transferred $1000 from retained earnings on hand at 1 July 2021 to the general reserve, and a further $1500 in June 2023.

The following information was provided by the two companies at 30 June 2023.

	Cold Ltd	Chisel Ltd
Profit before tax	$ 30 000	$ 27 500
Income tax expense	(11 000)	(9 000)
Profit for the year	19 000	18 500
Retained earnings (1/7/22)	22 000	19 000
	41 000	37 500
Transfer to general reserve	(12 000)	(2 500)
Retained earnings (30/6/23)	$ 29 000	$ 35 000
Share capital	$ 75 000	$ 25 000
General reserve	21 000	3 500
Retained earnings	29 000	35 000
Total equity	125 000	63 500
Provisions	27 500	6 000
Payables	17 500	4 000
Total liabilities	45 000	10 000
Total equity and liabilities	**$170 000**	**$ 73 500**
Cash	$ 12 500	$ 7 000
Accounts receivable	25 000	12 500
Inventories	20 000	18 500
Goodwill	0	6 000
Accumulated impairment losses	0	(3 500)
Shares in Chisel Ltd	50 000	0
Plant	105 000	45 000
Accumulated depreciation — plant	(42 500)	(12 000)
Total assets	**$170 000**	**$ 73 500**

Required

1. Prepare the journal entries for Cold Ltd at 1 July 2021 in relation to the investment in Chisel Ltd and for the receipt of the dividend in August 2021.
2. Prepare the consolidation worksheet for Cold Ltd's group at 30 June 2023.
3. Prepare the consolidated financial statements for Cold Ltd's group at 30 June 2023.

27.15 Undervalued and unrecorded assets, unrecorded liabilities, pre-acquisition reserves transfers ★ ★   **LO4, 5**

On 1 August 2019, Ed Ltd acquired 10% of the shares in Sherran Ltd for $8000. Ed Ltd used the fair value method to measure this investment with movements in fair value being recognised in profit or loss. At 1 July 2021, the fair value of this investment was $15 400. The original investment in Sherran Ltd was due to the fact that Sherran Ltd was undertaking research into particular microbiological elements that could influence the profitability of Ed Ltd. With the continuing success of this research, Ed Ltd decided to acquire the remaining shares (*cum div.*) in Sherran Ltd.

On 1 July 2021, Ed Ltd made an offer to buy the remaining shares in Sherran Ltd for $151 000 cash. This offer was accepted by the shareholders of Sherran Ltd. On 1 July 2021, immediately after the business combination, the statements of financial position of Ed Ltd and Sherran Ltd were as follows.

	Ed Ltd	Sherran Ltd
Share capital	$130 000	$ 90 000
General reserve	56 500	12 000
Retained earnings	93 500	36 000
Total equity	280 000	138 000
Dividend payable	25 000	12 600
Other liabilities	75 000	25 000
Total liabilities	100 000	37 600
Total equity and liabilities	**$380 000**	**$175 600**
Cash	$11 000	$20 600
Receivables	25 200	20 000
Other assets	10 000	8 000
Shares in Sherran Ltd	153 800	0
Inventories	55 000	42 000
Plant and equipment	210 000	107 000
Accumulated depreciation — plant and equipment	(85 000)	(22 000)
Total assets	**$380 000**	**$175 600**

On analysing the financial statements of Sherran Ltd, Ed Ltd determined that all the assets and liabilities recorded by Sherran Ltd were shown at amounts equal to their fair values except for the following.

	Carrying amount	Fair value
Plant and equipment (cost $46 000)	$35 000	$43 000
Inventories	42 000	46 000

The plant and equipment is expected to have a further 4-year useful life and is depreciated on a straight-line basis. The inventories were all sold by 30 June 2022.

Sherran Ltd had expensed all the outlays on research and development. Ed Ltd considered that an asset was created and placed a fair value of $12 000 on this asset at 1 July 2021. The research and development is amortised evenly over a 10-year period. Sherran Ltd also had reported a contingent liability at 30 June 2021 in relation to claims by customers for damaged goods. Ed Ltd placed a fair value of $3000 on these claims at 1 July 2021. The claims by customers were settled in May 2022 for $2800.

The tax rate is 30%.

Required

1. Prepare the consolidated financial statements for Ed Ltd's group at 1 July 2021.
2. Prepare the consolidation worksheet entries for Ed Ltd's group at 30 June 2022.

27.16 Undervalued and unrecorded assets, unrecorded liabilities, pre-acquisition reserves transfers ★ ★
LO3, 5, 7

Garth Ltd is a major Australian manufacturer of women's clothing. One of its major competitors was Brooks Ltd whose business was established by a French family over 30 years ago. It had won numerous awards for its designs and has established a number of brands that have been successful, especially with teenagers.

In order to expand its business as well as to increase its market power, Garth Ltd acquired on 1 July 2019 all the issued shares (*cum div.*) of Brooks Ltd for $330 000. At this date, the equity of Brooks Ltd was as follows.

Share capital	$200 000
General reserve	20 000
Retained earnings	50 000

All the identifiable assets and liabilities of Brooks Ltd were recorded at amounts equal to their fair values except for the following.

	Carrying amount	Fair value
Plant (cost $220 000)	$180 000	$186 000
Land	190 000	210 000
Inventories	20 000	28 000

The plant's expected remaining useful life was 5 years with benefits being expected evenly over that period. The plant was sold on 1 January 2022 for $187 000. The land was sold in February 2021 for $250 000. Of the inventories, 90% was sold by 30 June 2020 and the rest by 30 June 2021.

At 1 July 2019, Brooks Ltd had recorded a dividend payable of $10 000 that was paid in September 2019. Brooks Ltd also had some unrecorded assets, in particular the brands relating to the clothing sold in the teenage market. Garth Ltd valued these brands at $12 000 and assessed them to have an indefinite life. In the notes to its financial statements at 30 June 2019, Brooks Ltd disclosed a contingent liability relating to a guarantee it had made to one of its related companies. Garth Ltd assessed the fair value of the guarantee payable as being $10 000. In August 2021, Brooks Ltd was required to pay $2500 in relation to the guarantee.

All transfers to the general reserve made by Brooks Ltd have been from retained earnings earned prior to 1 July 2019. The tax rate is 30%.

The financial information provided by the two companies at 30 June 2022 is as follows.

	Garth Ltd	Brooks Ltd
Revenues	$190 000	$110 000
Expenses	(80 000)	(76 000)
	110 000	34 000
Gains on sale of non-current assets	5 000	4 000
Profit before tax	115 000	38 000
Income tax expense	(40 000)	(6 000)
Profit for the year	75 000	32 000
Other comprehensive income		
Gains on revaluation of plant	12 000	0
Comprehensive income for the year	$ 87 000	$ 32 000
Profit for the year	$ 75 000	$ 32 000
Retained earnings (1/7/21)	80 000	88 000
	155 000	120 000
Dividend paid	(34 000)	0
Transfer to general reserve	0	(15 000)
	(34 000)	(15 000)
Retained earnings (30/6/22)	$121 000	$105 000

Share capital	$ 280 000	$200 000
General reserve	20 000	48 000
Asset revaluation surplus	24 000	0
Retained earnings	121 000	105 000
Total equity	445 000	353 000
Provisions	15 000	12 000
Payables	40 000	8 000
Total liabilities	55 000	20 000
Total equity and liabilities	**$ 500 000**	**$373 000**
Cash	$ 12 000	$ 30 000
Accounts receivable	28 000	12 000
Inventories	30 000	51 000
Plant	230 000	320 000
Accumulated depreciation — plant	(120 000)	(40 000)
Shares in Brooks Ltd	320 000	0
Total assets	**$ 500 000**	**$373 000**

Required

1. Prepare the acquisition analysis at 1 July 2019.
2. Prepare the consolidation worksheet entries for Garth Ltd's group at 30 June 2022.
3. Prepare the consolidated financial statements for Garth Ltd's group at 30 June 2022.

27.17 Undervalued and unrecorded assets, pre-acquisition reserves transfers ★ ★ ★   **LO5**

Imagine Ltd acquired all the issued shares (*cum div.*) of Dragons Ltd on 1 July 2021. At this date the statement of financial position of Dragons Ltd included the following information.

	Carrying amount	Fair value
Plant	$1 000 000	$882 000
Accumulated depreciation — plant	(128 000)	
Goodwill	24 000	
Receivables	76 000	76 000
Cash	25 000	25 000
Inventories	75 000	95 000
	1 072 000	
Share capital (120 000 shares)	600 000	
General reserve	116 000	
Retained earnings	220 000	
Provisions	96 000	96 000
Dividend payable	40 000	40 000
	1 072 000	

The plant was considered to have a further 10-year life and is depreciated on a straight-line basis. The goodwill on hand at 1 July 2021 was written off as the result of an impairment test conducted in June 2023. All the inventories were sold by 30 June 2022. The dividend payable at 1 July 2018 was paid in August 2021. The assets recognised by Dragons Ltd did not include an internally generated patent of Dragons Ltd that was valued by Imagine Ltd at $50 000. Its useful life was considered to be 5 years, with benefits being received equally over that period.

In exchange for the shares in Dragons Ltd, Imagine Ltd gave the following as consideration.

- 250 000 shares in Imagine Ltd, each share having a fair value of $2.00
- Cash of $200 000
- Artworks having a fair value of $300 000

    Imagine Ltd incurred legal and accounting costs of $25 000 and share issue costs of $20 000.

    In January 2025, Dragons Ltd paid a bonus dividend of $200 000, being one share for every three shares held, the dividend being paid from retained earnings on hand at 1 July 2021.

    The tax rate is 30%.

Required

Prepare the consolidation worksheet entries for Imagine Ltd's group at 30 June 2026.

27.18 Undervalued and unrecorded assets, unrecorded liabilities, pre-acquisition reserves transfers ★ ★ ★ LO5

James Ltd operates a number of supermarkets with an emphasis on supplying high-quality produce. The operations of Blunt Ltd are primarily in the fine fruit market. Believing that the acquisition of Blunt Ltd would enable James Ltd to expand its supply to its customers, James Ltd commenced actions to acquire the shares of Blunt Ltd. On 1 July 2019, James Ltd acquired all the issued shares (*cum div.*) of Blunt Ltd for $123 500. At this date the equity of Blunt Ltd consisted of the following.

Share capital	$100 000
Reserves	5 000
Retained earnings	10 000

On 1 July 2019, Blunt Ltd had recorded a dividend payable of $6000 and goodwill of $5000 (net of accumulated impairment losses of $7000). The dividend was paid in August 2019. In the previous year's annual report Blunt Ltd had reported the existence of a contingent liability for damages based upon a lawsuit by a customer who had slipped on some fallen fruit in one of the stores operated by Blunt Ltd. James Ltd calculated that this liability had a fair value of $10 000. Blunt Ltd also had some customer databases that were not recorded as assets but James Ltd placed a fair value of $6000 on these items. Blunt Ltd believed that the databases had a future life of 4 years.

All of the identifiable assets and liabilities of Blunt Ltd were recorded at amounts equal to their fair values except for the following.

	Carrying amount	Fair value
Plant (cost $120 000)	$94 000	$96 000
Land	80 000	85 000
Inventories	20 000	24 000

The plant had an expected remaining useful life of 10 years. The land was sold by Blunt Ltd in February 2021. The inventories were all sold by 30 June 2020.

In February 2022, Blunt Ltd transferred $3000 of the reserves on hand at 1 July 2019 to retained earnings. The remaining $2000 was transferred to retained earnings in February 2023.

The court case involving the damages sought by the customer was settled in May 2023. Blunt Ltd was required to pay $7500 to the customer.

Required

Prepare the consolidation worksheet entries for James Ltd's group at 30 June 2023.

27.19 Undervalued assets, unrecorded liabilities, pre-acquisition reserves transfers ★ ★ ★ LO5

On 1 July 2021, Jessica Ltd acquired all the issued shares (*ex div.*) of Mauboy Ltd for $227 500. At this date the equity of Mauboy Ltd consisted of the following.

Share capital (100 000 partly paid shares)	$150 000
General reserve	34 000
Retained earnings	20 000

At acquisition date, Mauboy Ltd reported a dividend payable of $8000. All the identifiable assets and liabilities of Mauboy Ltd were recorded at amounts equal to their fair values except for the following.

	Carrying amount	Fair value
Plant (cost $200 000)	$175 000	$190 000
Land	150 000	155 000
Inventories	32 000	40 000

The plant was considered to have a further 3-year useful life. The land was sold in January 2022 for $170 000. Of the above inventories, 90% was sold by 30 June 2022 and the remainder was sold by 30 June 2023. Mauboy Ltd had recorded goodwill of $2000 (net of accumulated impairment losses of $12 000). Mauboy Ltd was involved in a court case that could potentially result in the company paying damages to customers. Jessica Ltd calculated the fair value of this liability to be $8000, but Mauboy Ltd had not recorded any liability.

The following events occurred in the year ending 30 June 2022.

- On 12 August 2021, Mauboy Ltd paid the dividend that existed at 1 July 2021.
- On 1 December 2021, Mauboy Ltd transferred $17 000 from the general reserve existing at 1 July 2021 to retained earnings.
- On 1 January 2022, Mauboy Ltd made a call of 10c per share on its issued shares. All call money was received by 31 January 2022.
- On 29 June 2022, Jessica Ltd reassessed the liability of Mauboy Ltd in relation to the court case as the chances of winning the case had improved. The fair value was now considered to be $2000.

Required

Prepare the consolidation worksheet entries for Jessica Ltd's group at 30 June 2022.

27.20 Undervalued and unrecorded assets, unrecorded liabilities, pre-acquisition reserves transfers ★ ★ ★   **LO3, 5, 7**

Jersey Ltd acquired all the issued shares (*ex div.*) of Boys Ltd on 1 July 2020 for $492 000. At this date the equity of Boys Ltd consisted of the following.

Share capital	$260 000
General reserve	100 000
Retained earnings	81 000

At the acquisition date all the identifiable assets and liabilities of Boys Ltd were recorded at amounts equal to the fair value except for the following.

	Carrying amount	Fair value
Plant (cost $460 000)	$400 000	$420 000
Land	200 000	240 000
Inventories	60 000	76 000

The plant was considered to have a further 5-year life. The plant was sold for $310 000 on 1 January 2022. The land was sold on 1 February 2021 for $300 000. The inventories were all sold by 30 June 2021. Also at acquisition date Boys Ltd had recorded a dividend payable of $14 000 and goodwill (net of accumulated impairment losses of $26 000) of $10 000. Boys Ltd had not recorded an internally generated brand that Jersey Ltd considered to have a fair value of $24 000. The brand was considered to have an indefinite life. Also not recorded by Boys Ltd was a contingent liability relating to a current court case in which Boys Ltd was involved with a supplier that was seeking compensation. Jersey Ltd placed a fair value of $30 000 on this liability. This court case was settled in May 2022 at which time Boys Ltd was required to pay damages of $32 000.

In February 2021, Boys Ltd transferred $20 000 from the general reserve on hand at 1 July 2020 to retained earnings. A further $30 000 was transferred in February 2022.

Both companies have an equity account entitled 'Other components of equity' that recognise certain gains and losses from financial assets. At 1 July 2021, the balances of these accounts were $60 000 for Jersey Ltd and $30 000 for Boys Ltd.

The financial statements of the two companies at 30 June 2022 contained the following information.

	Jersey Ltd	Boys Ltd
Revenues	$ 260 000	$ 128 000
Expenses	(140 000)	(84 000)
Trading profit	120 000	44 000
Gains (losses) on sale of non-current assets	60 000	16 000
Profit before tax	180 000	60 000
Income tax expense	(40 000)	(10 000)
Profit for the period	140 000	50 000
Retained earnings (1/7/21)	666 000	110 000
Transfer from general reserve	60 000	30 000
	866 000	190 000
Dividend paid	(40 000)	0
Retained earnings (30/6/22)	826 000	190 000
Share capital	300 000	260 000
General reserve	20 000	40 000
Other components of equity	50 000	36 000
Total equity	1 196 000	526 000
Accounts payable	80 000	20 000
Deferred tax liability	36 000	20 000
Other non-current liabilities	496 000	460 000
Total liabilities	612 000	500 000
Total equity and liabilities	**$1 808 000**	**$1 026 000**
Plant	$ 860 000	$ 776 000
Accumulated depreciation — plant	(364 000)	(440 000)
Land	300 000	400 000
Brands	160 000	0
Shares in Boys Ltd	492 000	0
Financial assets	220 000	210 000
Cash	20 000	10 000
Inventories	80 000	60 000
Goodwill	40 000	36 000
Accumulated impairment losses	0	(26 000)
Total assets	**$1 808 000**	**$1 026 000**

Required

1. Prepare the acquisition analysis at 1 July 2020.
2. Prepare the consolidation worksheet entries for Jersey Ltd's group at 30 June 2022.
3. Prepare the consolidated financial statements for Jersey Ltd's group at 30 June 2022.

ACKNOWLEDGEMENTS

Text: © 2019 Australian Accounting Standards Board (AASB). The text, graphics and layout of this publication are protected by Australian copyright law and the comparable law of other countries. No part of the publication may be reproduced, stored or transmitted in any form or by any means without the prior written permission of the AASB except as permitted by law. For reproduction or publication, permission should be sought in writing from the AASB. Requests in the first instance should be addressed to the National Director, Australian Accounting Standards Board, PO Box 204, Collins Street West, Victoria 8007.

Text: © IFRS. This publication contains copyright material of the IFRS Foundation in respect of which all rights are reserved. Reproduced by John Wiley & Sons Australia, Ltd with the permission of the IFRS Foundation. No permission granted to third parties to reproduce or distribute. For full access to IFRS Standards and the work of the IFRS Foundation please visit http://eifrs.ifrs.org. The International Accounting Standards Board, the IFRS Foundation, the authors and the publishers do not accept responsibility for any loss caused by acting or refraining from acting in reliance on the material in this publication, whether such loss is caused by negligence or otherwise.

CHAPTER 28

Consolidation: intragroup transactions

CHAPTER AIM

This chapter discusses the application of AASB 10/IFRS 10 *Consolidated Financial Statements* with regards to transactions between the entities within a group that has wholly owned subsidiaries. The chapter builds on chapter 27, which discussed the preparation of the consolidated financial statements of a parent and its wholly owned subsidiary. Specifically, chapter 27 addressed business combination valuation entries and pre-acquisition entries. The main topic of this chapter is how to prepare further adjustments in the consolidation worksheet to adjust for transactions occurring between a parent and its subsidiary, such as the sale of inventories from the parent to its subsidiary at a profit.

LEARNING OBJECTIVES

After studying this chapter, you should be able to:

28.1 explain the need for making adjustments for intragroup transactions

28.2 outline the adjustment process and the key questions to consider

28.3 prepare worksheet entries for intragroup transactions involving profits or losses in beginning and ending inventories

28.4 prepare worksheet entries for intragroup transactions involving profits or losses on the transfer of property, plant and equipment in both the current and previous periods

28.5 prepare worksheet entries for intragroup services

28.6 prepare worksheet entries for intragroup dividends

28.7 prepare worksheet entries for intragroup borrowings.

CONCEPTS FOR REVIEW

Before studying this chapter, you should understand and, if necessary, revise:

• the nature of the consolidated group and the purpose of preparing consolidated financial statements

• the preparation of business combination valuation entries and pre-acquisition entries

• the use and format of the consolidation worksheet.

28.1 The need for intragroup adjustments

LEARNING OBJECTIVE 28.1 Explain the need for making adjustments for intragroup transactions.

The consolidation process involves adding together the financial statements of the parent and its subsidiaries, subject to some adjustments. A consolidation worksheet is used for this process. In chapter 27, two sets of adjustments were made in the adjustment columns of the worksheet, namely the business combination valuation entries and the pre-acquisition entries.

In this chapter, further adjustments are made in the worksheet adjustment columns. These adjustments are to eliminate the effects of intragroup transactions, whether or not profits or losses are made by members of the group through trading with each other. These adjustments are made to ensure that the financial position and financial performance of the group are not understated or overstated.

A key point to remember is that the **consolidated financial statements** are the statements of a **group** and are presented as those of a *single economic entity*. The consolidated financial statements should then show only the effects of transactions with entities *external* to the economic entity. This means that:

- consolidated *revenues* are earned only from transactions with entities external to the group
- consolidated *expenses* are incurred only from transactions with entities external to the group
- consolidated *profit* arises only in relation to transactions with entities external to the group
- consolidated *assets* are recorded at the cost to the group, not necessarily the cost to the legal entity that owns them
- consolidated *liabilities* are obligations to entities external to the group.

This chapter focuses on the adjustments for transactions made within a group, and analyses transactions involving inventories, non-current assets (property, plant and equipment), services, dividends and borrowings. The accounting standard that is applied is AASB 10/IFRS 10 *Consolidated Financial Statements*.

LEARNING CHECK

- ☐ The consolidated financial statements should report only the effects of transactions between the group and external entities.
- ☐ Adjustments are necessary to remove the effects of transactions between the entities within the group.

28.2 The adjustment process

LEARNING OBJECTIVE 28.2 Outline the adjustment process and the key questions to consider.

The requirement for the full adjustment for the effects of intragroup transactions is stated in paragraph B86(c) of AASB 10/IFRS 10:

> eliminate in full intragroup assets and liabilities, equity, income, expenses and cash flows relating to transactions between entities of the group (profits or losses resulting from intragroup transactions that are recognised in assets, such as inventory and fixed assets, are eliminated in full). Intragroup losses may indicate an impairment that requires recognition in the consolidated financial statements.

These adjustments are made in the worksheet adjustment columns and, as such, do not carry over to the next period. The adjustments posted in one period may need to be repeated (under the same or a slightly different format) in the next period to the extent that the effects of prior period intragroup transactions are still present in the individual accounts of the legal entities involved.

Remember that, in general, the effects of transactions are recognised by individual entities in accounts disclosed in the individual statements of financial position (i.e. assets, liabilities and equity) and/or accounts disclosed in the individual statements of comprehensive income (i.e. expenses and income). The accounts from the individual statements of comprehensive income are closed at the end of each period to the retained earnings account. In the consolidation worksheet, the consolidation adjustments to the accounts disclosed in the individual statements of financial position will be repeated every period against those accounts as long as the effects of the intragroup transactions are still present. However, the consolidation adjustments to the accounts disclosed in the individual statements of comprehensive income will be posted in the consolidation worksheet against those accounts only in the period of the intragroup transactions; in the next periods, those adjustments will be posted to the opening balance of the retained earnings account as long as the effects of the intragroup transactions are still present in that account. Therefore, it is critically important when determining an adjustment entry to firstly classify the underlying economic transaction as a 'prior period' transaction or a 'current period' transaction, especially when adjusting income and expenses accounts.

- The effects of *current* period transactions on the current period income and expenses are present in accounts such as sales, cost of sales, depreciation expense and income tax expense.
- The effects of *prior* period transactions on the prior period income and expenses are present in the retained earnings account (opening balance), while their effects on the current period income and expenses are present in the respective accounts.

If a transaction is not correctly classified, an incorrect adjustment entry can result. Hence, when determining the appropriate adjustment entry, the first question that should be asked is as follows.

1. *Is this a prior period or a current period transaction?* If it is a current period transaction, its effects will be eliminated against the respective accounts. If it is a prior period transaction, the effects on prior period income and expenses accounts will be eliminated against the retained earnings account (opening balance), while its effects on current period accounts will be eliminated against the respective accounts.

   Further, when determining the appropriate adjustment entry for a particular transaction, it is useful to consider the way in which the consolidation worksheet is used.

   - The left-hand side of the worksheet contains the legal entities' amounts recorded in the individual accounts, incorporating the effects of all transactions, both intragroup and with entities external to the group.
   - The right-hand side of the worksheet contains the group amounts that should be recorded in the consolidated accounts, incorporating only the effects of transactions with external entities to the group.
   - The adjustment columns are the adjustments necessary to get from the legal entities' amounts to the group amounts.

   Therefore, the next questions to be asked when analysing an intragroup transaction are as follows.

2. *What has been recorded by the legal entities?* That is, what accounts on the left-hand side of the worksheet contain amounts arising from, or affected by, the intragroup transaction and what are the amounts recorded in those accounts?

3. *What should be reported by the group?* That is, what amounts should the group report on the right-hand side of the worksheet for the individual accounts affected by the intragroup transaction?

4. *What adjustments are necessary to get from the legal entities' amounts to the group amounts?* That is, the adjustments are determined by comparing what has been recorded by the legal entities to what the group needs to report.

   In analysing intragroup transactions involving inventories, non-current assets and other items, it is these questions that will be asked. Note that the flow of the transaction is unimportant; that is, the adjustment entry is the same whether the parent sells an asset to a subsidiary, or whether a subsidiary sells it to the parent. The transaction is within the economic entity in both cases and, therefore, its effects need to be eliminated in full.

   Note further that the adjustment process is *not* aimed at showing the group position as if the transaction had not occurred. The transaction has occurred. Potentially, a transfer of an asset within a group may change the use of the asset; for example, an item of plant in one entity may be transferred to another entity which sells second-hand plant. The latter entity would classify the item as inventories. The purpose of the consolidation adjustment entries is to adjust for the *effects* of the transaction on the amounts recorded.

The fifth question that should be asked when analysing an intragroup transaction is:

5. *What is the tax effect of the adjustments made?* Having determined the consolidation adjustment for the intragroup transaction, the tax-effect consequences need to be considered. Obviously, not all adjustments have tax consequences. The only adjustment entries that have tax consequences are those where profits or losses are eliminated (current tax effect) and carrying amounts of assets or liabilities are adjusted (deferred tax effect).

According to paragraph B86(c) of AASB 10/IFRS 10:

> AASB 112 [IAS 12] *Income Taxes* applies to temporary differences that arise from the elimination of profits and losses resulting from intragroup transactions.

Further, according to paragraph 11 of AASB 112/IAS 12:

> In consolidated financial statements, temporary differences are determined by comparing the carrying amounts of assets and liabilities in the consolidated financial statements with the appropriate tax base. The tax base is determined by reference to a consolidated tax return in those jurisdictions in which such a return is filed. In other jurisdictions, the tax base is determined by reference to the tax returns of each entity in the group.

In this text, it is assumed that the group does not prepare a consolidated tax return. Therefore, the tax base of an asset or a liability is the tax base as recognised by the individual legal entity that holds the asset or liability and it is not affected by the consolidation adjustment. Any difference between the carrying amount of an asset or liability and its tax base in a legal entity within the group is accounted for by the legal entity. However, on consolidation, adjustments may be made to the carrying amounts of assets or liabilities when eliminating intragroup profit or losses and these will create extra temporary differences. In such cases, any associated tax effect must be considered. Under AASB 112/IAS 12, deferred tax accounts must be raised where there are temporary differences between the carrying amount of an asset or a liability and its tax base.

Therefore, immediately following the adjustment entries that eliminate intragroup profits or losses and adjust the carrying amount of assets or liabilities, a further tax-effect adjustment would be made. This adjustment will recognise the deferred tax account affected by the change in the temporary difference.

As mentioned above, in this text it is assumed that the parent and each subsidiary are separate tax-paying entities. However, in Australia, groups comprising a parent and its wholly owned subsidiaries can elect to be treated as a single entity for tax purposes under the tax consolidation system. Such entities prepare a consolidated tax return. Under such a scheme, the tax-effect adjustments demonstrated in this chapter would not apply.

In summary, the five questions are as follows.
1. Is this a prior period or a current period transaction?
2. What has been recorded by the legal entities?
3. What should be reported by the group?
4. What adjustments are necessary to get from the legal entities' amounts to the group amounts?
5. What is the tax effect of the adjustments made?

Realisation of intragroup profits or losses

The adjustment for intragroup transactions may involve elimination of profits or losses. According to paragraph B86(c) of AASB 10/IFRS 10:

> profits or losses resulting from intragroup transactions that are recognised in assets, such as inventory and fixed assets, are eliminated in full.

Therefore, intragroup profits or losses that require consolidation adjustments are those 'recognised in assets' (i.e. those that affect the carrying amount of assets recognised by the legal entities). As a result of these profits or losses, those assets are overstated or understated respectively. These profits or losses can be described as 'unrealised profits' and 'unrealised losses'. The test for realisation is the involvement of an external entity in relation to the item affected by the intragroup transaction. If an inventories item is transferred from a subsidiary to the parent entity (or vice versa), no external entity is involved in that transaction. The profit or loss made by the subsidiary is unrealised to the group. If the parent then sells that inventories item to a party external to the group, the intragroup profit or loss becomes realised to the group. This may result in the group recognising the profit or loss in a different period from that in which it is recognised by the legal entity and, therefore, adjustments may still need to be made.

Handy hints

It is important to understand the reasons the adjustments are made in the consolidation worksheet and how they are determined. In this text, each line in the adjustment entries is explained separately to ensure a proper understanding. No line item in an adjustment entry is made just as a balancing item. However, in preparing the worksheet entries, it is not necessary to go through some of the detailed calculations necessary for explanatory purposes. In the sections that follow, handy hints are given to assist in an easier preparation of an adjustment entry.

☐ Adjustments are required for both previous periods and current period intragroup transactions to the extent that the effects of those transactions are still present in the individual accounts of the entities involved.

☐ Adjustments are determined by comparing the amounts recognised in the individual accounts affected with the amounts that the group should recognise.

☐ Where adjustments for intragroup transactions affect the carrying amounts of assets and liabilities, further adjustments are made for the tax effect of those adjustments.

☐ The profits or losses generated from intragroup transfers of assets are considered unrealised from the group's perspective and eliminated on consolidation until such moment when those assets are transferred to external entities.

28.3 Inventories

LEARNING OBJECTIVE 28.3 Prepare worksheet entries for intragroup transactions involving profits or losses in beginning and ending inventories.

In the following examples, assume that Laura Ltd owns all the share capital of George Ltd, and that the consolidation process is being carried out on 30 June 2022, for the period ending on that date. Assume also a tax rate of 30%. For all entries shown for the individual entities, assume the use of a perpetual inventories system.

28.3.1 Sales of inventories in the current period

Example

On 1 June 2022, Laura Ltd sold inventories to George Ltd for $10 000 cash. The inventories had previously cost Laura Ltd $8000. What are the consolidation adjustment entries for the period ending 30 June 2022 to eliminate the effects of this intragroup sale?

1. Is this a prior period or a current period transaction?
The intragroup transaction is a current period transaction; only current period accounts will be affected in the worksheet adjustment entries.

Case 1. The inventories remain unsold at 30 June 2022
2. What has been recorded by the legal entities?
Laura Ltd would have made the following entries on the intragroup sale of the inventories.

LAURA LTD			
Cash	Dr	10 000	
Sales	Cr		10 000
Cost of sales	Dr	8 000	
Inventories	Cr		8 000

George Ltd would have made the following entry.

GEORGE LTD			
Inventories	Dr	10 000	
Cash	Cr		10 000

The journal entries recognise the effects on cash, sales, cost of sales and inventories. However, as the value of cash does not change by being transferred intragroup, in the analysis of the intragroup transaction there is no need to consider the cash account. The amounts recorded by the individual legal entities in the relevant accounts affected by the intragroup transaction, together with the sum of the amounts in each of those accounts across both entities are as follows.

	Laura Ltd	George Ltd	Sum
Sales	$10 000	$ 0	$10 000
Cost of sales	8 000	0	8 000
Inventories	0	10 000	10 000

3. What should be reported by the group?

From the group's perspective, no sale has been made to an external entity. Hence, there have been no sales or related cost of sales, and inventories should be valued at the original cost to the group: $8000.

4. What adjustments are necessary to get from the legal entities' amounts to the group amounts?

A comparison between the sum of the amounts recorded by the legal entities in the relevant accounts and the amounts that should be reported by the group shows the following.

	Sum	Group	Difference
Sales	$10 000	$ 0	$(10 000)
Cost of sales	8 000	0	(8 000)
Inventories	10 000	8 000	(2 000)

Therefore, the aggregate figures recorded by the legal entities need to be adjusted. Sales revenue, cost of sales and inventories need to be decreased by $10 000, $8000 and $2000 respectively. The adjustment entry posted in the consolidation worksheet (and not in the journals of the subsidiary or the parent) at 30 June 2022 is as follows.

Consolidation			
Sales	Dr	10 000	
Cost of sales	Cr		8 000
Inventories	Cr		2 000

5. What is the tax effect of the adjustments made?

In this example, the adjustment entry above reduces the profit by $2000 (i.e. the intragroup profit), as sales revenue decreases by a greater amount than cost of sales ($10 000 versus $8000). The decrease in profit decreases income tax expense by 30% of the decrease in profit. At the same time, the carrying amount of inventories is reduced by $2000, with no effect on the tax base. The decrease in the carrying amount of inventories creates an extra deductible temporary difference of $2000, giving rise to a deferred tax asset of 30% of $2000. The deferred tax asset can also be seen as recognising a tax benefit for the group generated by the fact that, as Laura Ltd recognises the profit on the intragroup sale, they have to pay tax on it, but, from the group's perspective, this represents a prepayment of tax as the profit is not recognised by the group. Therefore, to recognise the tax effect of the adjustment, the second consolidation worksheet adjustment entry is as follows.

Consolidation			
Deferred tax asset	Dr	600	
Income tax expense	Cr		600

Figure 28.1 shows the consolidation worksheet for this simple case after posting the adjustment entries. The worksheet displays the individual figures reported by the parent (Laura Ltd) and the subsidiary (George Ltd) in their individual financial statements in the first two columns. The worksheet also includes the consolidated figures in the last column where inventories are recorded at the cost to the group of $8000, while the sales revenue, cost of sales and the profit are reported as $0, as from the point of view of the group no sale has taken place and no profit should be recognised. However, inventories are still recorded at $10 000 in the individual accounts of George Ltd, while sales revenue, cost of sales and the profit is still recorded as $10 000, $8000 and $2000 respectively in the individual accounts of Laura Ltd. Also, a deferred tax asset is recognised in the consolidated accounts for the income tax expense recognised by Laura Ltd.

FIGURE 28.1 Consolidation worksheet

	Laura Ltd	George Ltd	Adjustments Dr	Cr	Group
Statement of financial position (extract)					
Cash	$10 000	$(10 000)			$ 0
Inventories		10 000		$2 000	8 000
Deferred tax asset			$ 600		600
Current tax liability	600				600
Statement of comprehensive income (extract)					
Sales	$10 000		$10 000		$ 0
Cost of sales	8 000			$8 000	0
Gross profit	2 000				0
Income tax expense	600			600	0
Profit after tax	1 400				0

Case 2. The inventories are all on-sold by 30 June 2022 to external entities

Assume that George Ltd had sold all the inventories for $11 000 to external entities.

2. What has been recorded by the legal entities?

The journal entries recorded by the legal entities would have been the same as in case 1, with two extra entries by George Ltd to recognise the external sale. Given a total cost of the inventories to George Ltd of $10 000, this gives a cost of inventories sold recognised by George Ltd of $10 000.

GEORGE LTD			
Cash		Dr	11 000	
Sales		Cr		11 000
Cost of sales		Dr	10 000	
Inventories		Cr		10 000

The amounts recorded by the individual legal entities in the relevant accounts affected by the intragroup transaction, together with the sum of the amounts in each of those accounts across both entities are as follows.

	Laura Ltd	George Ltd	Sum
Sales	$10 000	$11 000	$21 000
Cost of sales	8 000	10 000	18 000
Inventories	0	0	0

3. What should be reported by the group?

The sale by George Ltd to external entities is recognised by the group, as it involves external entities. The cost of sales from the group perspective is the original cost to Laura Ltd, not the price paid intragroup by George Ltd. Therefore, the amounts for the group should be as follows.

	Group
Sales	$11 000
Cost of sales	8 000
Inventories	0

4. What adjustments are necessary to get from the legal entities' amounts to the group amounts?

A comparison between the sum of the amounts recorded by the legal entities in the relevant accounts and the amounts that should be reported by the group shows the following.

	Sum	Group	Difference
Sales	$21 000	$11 000	$(10 000)
Cost of sales	18 000	8 000	(10 000)
Inventories	0	0	0

The consolidation worksheet adjustment entry at 30 June 2022 is then as follows.

Consolidation			
Sales	Dr	10 000	
Cost of sales	Cr		10 000

5. What is the tax effect of the adjustments made?

No tax-effect entry is necessary, as the first adjustment entry does not increase or decrease the overall profit (the decrease in sales revenue, an income account, is compensated by the decrease of the same amount in cost of sales, an expense account), or the carrying amount of any asset or liability.

Case 3. The inventories are partially on-sold by 30 June 2022 to external entities

Assume that George Ltd had sold 80% of the inventories for $8500 to external entities.

2. What has been recorded by the legal entities?

The entries recorded by the legal entities would have been the same as in case 1, with two extra entries recognised by George Ltd when they made the external sale. Given a total cost of the inventories to George Ltd of $10 000, this gives a cost of inventories sold recorded by George Ltd of $8000 (i.e. 80% × $10 000).

GEORGE LTD			
Cash	Dr	8 500	
Sales	Cr		8 500
Cost of sales	Dr	8 000	
Inventories	Cr		8 000

Further, the cost of the inventories still held by George Ltd is $2000 (i.e. 20% × $10 000). Therefore, the amounts recorded by the individual legal entities in the relevant accounts affected by the intragroup transaction, together with the sum of the amounts in each of those accounts across both entities are as follows.

	Laura Ltd	George Ltd	Sum
Sales	$10 000	$8 500	$18 500
Cost of sales	8 000	8 000	16 000
Inventories	0	2 000	2 000

3. What should be reported by the group?

The sale by George Ltd to external entities is recognised by the group, as it involves external entities. The cost of sales from the group perspective is $6400, being 80% of the original cost to Laura Ltd. The cost to the group of inventories remaining in George Ltd is $1600 (i.e. 20% × $8000). The amounts for the group are as follows.

	Group
Sales	$8 500
Cost of sales	6 400
Inventories	1 600

4. What adjustments are necessary to get from the legal entities' amounts to the group amounts?

A comparison between the sum of the amounts recorded by the legal entities in the relevant accounts and the amounts that should be reported by the group shows the following.

	Sum	Group	Difference
Sales	$18 500	$8 500	$(10 000)
Cost of sales	16 000	6 400	(9 600)
Inventories	2 000	1 600	(400)

The consolidation worksheet adjustment entry at 30 June 2022 is as follows.

Consolidation			
Sales	Dr	10 000	
Cost of sales	Cr		9 600
Inventories	Cr		400

5. What is the tax effect of the adjustments made?

In this example, the adjustment entry above reduces the profit by $400, as sales revenue decreases by a greater amount than cost of sales ($10 000 versus $9600). The decrease in profit decreases income tax expense by 30% of $400. At the same time, the adjustment entry decreases the carrying amount of inventories by $400, while the tax base is not affected. The decrease in the carrying amount of inventories creates an extra deductible temporary difference between the carrying amount and the tax base, giving rise to a deferred tax asset of 30% of $400. Therefore, to recognise the tax effect of the adjustment, the second consolidation worksheet adjustment entry is as follows.

Consolidation			
Deferred tax asset	Dr	120	
Income tax expense	Cr		120

Realisation of intragroup profits or losses

In the case 1 example, the before-tax profit of the group is *lower* than that recognised by the legal entities by $2000 (being *$0* versus *sales $10 000 – cost of sales $8000*). This difference is unrealised profit as it has not yet been recognised by the group. It relates to inventories that are still on hand and not yet on-sold to external entities. *As all inventories transferred intragroup are still on hand with the group, the entire profit on the intragroup sale is unrealised.* The profit will be recognised by the group when the inventories are sold to external entities.

In the case 2 example, the before-tax profit of the group is *equal* to that recognised by the legal entities (being *sales $11 000 – cost of sales $8000* versus *sales $21 000 – cost of sales $18 000*). The profit on the intragroup sale (being *sales $10 000 – cost of sales $8000*) is realised profit as it has been included in the profit recognised by the group. It relates to inventories that have been on-sold to external entities. As all inventories transferred intragroup are on-sold, the entire profit on the intragroup sale is realised. In other words, *as none of the inventories transferred intragroup is still on hand, there is no unrealised profit.*

In the case 3 example, the before-tax profit of the group is *lower* than that recognised by the legal entities by $400 (being *sales $8500 – cost of sales $6400* versus *sales $18 500 – cost of sales $16 000*). This difference is unrealised profit as it has not yet been recognised by the group. It relates to inventories still on hand and not yet on-sold to external entities. As 20% of the inventories transferred intragroup are still on hand with the group, 20% of the profit on the intragroup sale is unrealised. As 80% of the inventories transferred intragroup are on-sold to external entities, 80% of the profit on the intragroup sale is realised.

Handy hints

In preparing the adjustment entries for inventories sold intragroup for a profit within the current period, note the following.

- In all cases, regardless of the amount of inventories on-sold, the adjustment to *sales* is always the amount of the sales within the group (i.e. $10 000).
- The adjustment to *inventories* is always equal to the percentage (%) of inventories still on hand within the group multiplied by the profit on the sale within the group (i.e. the unrealised profit = % of inventories still on hand × (transfer price − original cost)).

Case 1: none sold	100% × $2000 = $2 000
Case 2: all sold	0% × $2000 = $ 0
Case 3: 80% sold	20% × $2000 = $ 400

- The adjustment to *cost of sales* can be determined as a balancing item once the adjustments to *sales* and *inventories* have been determined (as the difference between the adjustment to *sales* and the adjustment to *inventories*).

Case 1: none sold	$10 000 – $2 000 =	$ 8 000
Case 2: all sold	$10 000 – $ 0 =	$10 000
Case 3: 80% sold	$10 000 – $ 400 =	$ 9 600

- The *tax effect* adjustment is always equal to the tax rate multiplied by the unrealised profit and is posted as a debit to deferred tax asset and a credit to income tax expense.

Case 1: none sold	30% × $2 000 = $600
Case 2: all sold	30% × $ 0 = $ 0
Case 3: 80% sold	30% × $ 400 = $120

- Note that the amount for which the inventories are on-sold to external entities after the intragroup transfer does not matter in the adjustments. As such, it does not make a difference whether the external sales are made at a profit or loss.

28.3.2 Sales of inventories in the prior period

Any inventories sold within the group in a prior period and remaining on hand at the end of that period are still on hand at the beginning of the next period. As such, the unrealised profit related to inventories still on hand at the end of the prior period is still unrealised at the beginning of the next period. In all the examples in this section where inventories are still on hand at the beginning of a period, the assumption used is that inventories will be on-sold to external entities before the end of that period. This assumption ensures that unrealised profits in beginning inventories become realised by the end of the period.

Example

On 1 June 2021, Laura Ltd sold $10 000 worth of inventories to George Ltd for cash. The inventories had previously cost Laura Ltd $8000. Of these inventories, 20% were not sold outside the group before 30 June 2021. These remaining inventories were all sold by George Ltd to external entities before 30 June 2022 for $2200. What are the adjustment entries in the consolidation worksheet prepared at 30 June 2022 to eliminate the effects of the intragroup sale?

1. Is this a prior period or a current period transaction?
The intragroup transaction is a prior period transaction. The legal entities recorded a profit on sale of inventories in the period ended 30 June 2021. Being a prior period event, we should expect to adjust prior period accounts such as retained earnings (opening balance), together with current period accounts.

2. What has been recorded by the legal entities?
Because the inventories were transferred within the group in the prior period, the retained earnings (opening balance) contains profit in relation to the inventories still on hand at the beginning of the period that is unrealised from the group perspective. This equals $400 (i.e. 20% × ($10 000 – $8000)). Note that the tax effects are ignored at this stage. They will be considered when addressing question 5.

To recognise the effect of the external sale, two journal entries are posted by George Ltd. Given a total cost of the inventories to George Ltd of $10 000, this gives a cost of inventories sold during the current period of $2000 (i.e. 20% × $10 000).

GEORGE LTD			
Cash	Dr	2 200	
Sales	Cr		2 200
Cost of sales	Dr	2 000	
Inventories	Cr		2 000

The entities would have recorded the following amounts in relation to the inventories on hand at the beginning of the current period (on-sold by the end of the period to external entities).

	Laura Ltd	George Ltd	Sum
Retained earnings (1/7/21)	$400	$ 0	$ 400
Sales	0	2 200	2 200
Cost of sales	0	2 000	2 000
Inventories	0	0	0

3. What should be reported by the group?

The sale by George Ltd to external entities is recognised by the group, as it involves external entities. The cost of sales is $1600, being 20% of the original cost to Laura Ltd. No inventories are on hand at the end of the reporting period. The amounts for the group are as follows.

	Group
Retained earnings (1/7/21)	$ 0
Sales	2 200
Cost of sales	1 600
Inventories	0

4. What adjustments are necessary to get from the legal entities' amounts to the group amounts?

A comparison shows the following.

	Sum	Group	Difference
Retained earnings (1/7/21)	$ 400	$ 0	$(400)
Sales	2 200	2 200	0
Cost of sales	2 000	1 600	(400)
Inventories	0	0	0

The first consolidation worksheet adjustment entry at 30 June 2022 is as follows.

Consolidation			
Retained earnings (1/7/21)		Dr	400
Cost of sales		Cr		400

5. What is the tax effect of the adjustments made?

The adjustment entry has no effect on the carrying amount of any asset or liability; hence, there is no deferred tax-effect entry required. However, it does have an effect on the prior period and current period profits, decreasing the former and increasing the latter. As a result, the income tax expense for the prior period has to decrease, leading to an increase in the opening balance of the retained earnings account, while the income tax expense for the current period has to increase.

The second consolidation worksheet adjustment entry at 30 June 2022 is as follows.

Consolidation			
Income tax expense		Dr	120
Retained earnings (1/7/21)		Cr		120

The two consolidation adjustment entries can be combined into one as follows.

Consolidation			
Retained earnings (1/7/21)		Dr	280
Income tax expense		Dr	120
Cost of sales		Cr		400

Realisation of intragroup profits

Note that the consolidation adjustment entries in this example ensure that:
- the group's retained earnings (opening balance) is $280 less than the retained earnings (opening balance) recognised by the legal entities (as the unrealised profit in beginning inventories should be eliminated from the prior period profits)
- the group's current period after-tax profit is $280 greater than the current period after-tax profit recorded by the legal entities (as the unrealised profit in beginning inventories is realised in the current period).

While the legal entities recognised the after-tax profit of $280 in the period ended 30 June 2021, the group recognised it in the period ended 30 June 2022, as it was then that the external entities were involved in the sale. The adjustment entry transfers the unrealised profit from the prior period to the current period when it was realised. As there is no unrealised profit anymore, there is no need for any worksheet adjustments in future periods.

Handy hints

In preparing the consolidation adjustment entry for profit remaining in inventories on hand at the beginning of the current period, to the extent that the inventories are on-sold to external entities by the end of the current period, note the following.

- The adjustment to *retained earnings (opening balance)* is the after-tax profit on transferred inventories remaining on hand at the beginning of the period (also known as after-tax unrealised profit in beginning inventories).
- The adjustment to *cost of sales* is the before-tax profit on inventories on hand at the beginning of the period (also known as before-tax unrealised profit in beginning inventories).
- The adjustment to *income tax expense* is the tax rate times the adjustment to cost of sales.
- Note that the amount for which the inventories are on-sold to external entities after the intragroup transfer does not matter in the adjustments. As such, it does not make a difference whether the external sales are made at a profit or loss.
- Note that only the amount of unrealised profit in beginning inventories is needed in the adjustments; the amount for which the inventories are transferred intragroup in the prior period does not matter *per se*.

ILLUSTRATIVE EXAMPLE 28.1

Intragroup transactions involving transfers of inventories

Sandy Ltd acquired all the issued shares of Beach Ltd on 1 January 2024. The following transactions occurred between the two entities since then.

(a) On 1 June 2024, Sandy Ltd sold inventories to Beach Ltd for $12 000, these inventories previously costing Sandy Ltd $10 000. By 30 June 2024, Beach Ltd had on-sold 20% of these inventories to external entities for $3000. The other 80% was all sold to external entities by 30 June 2025 for $13 000.
(b) During the period ended 30 June 2025, Beach Ltd sold inventories to Sandy Ltd for $6000, this being at cost plus 20% mark-up. Of these inventories, $1200 remained on hand in Sandy Ltd at 30 June 2025.
The tax rate is 30%.

Required

Prepare the consolidation worksheet entries for Sandy Ltd at 30 June 2025 in relation to the intragroup transfers of inventories.

Solution

The required consolidation worksheet entries are as follows.

(a) *Sale of inventories in previous period*

Retained earnings (1/7/24)	Dr	1 120	
Income tax expense	Dr	480	
Cost of sales	Cr		1 600

Workings
- The intragroup transaction is a prior period transaction involving inventories still on hand with the group at the beginning of the current period.
- Profit after tax on the inventories still on hand at 1 July 2024 is $1120 (i.e. 80% × ($12 000 − $10 000) × (1 − 30%)). Retained earnings (opening balance) should be adjusted for this after-tax unrealised profit.
- The adjustment to cost of sales is $1600 (i.e. 80% × ($12 000 − $10 000)), equal to the before-tax unrealised profit.
- The adjustment to income tax expense is the tax rate times the adjustment to cost of sales (i.e. 30% × $1600 = $480).

(b) *Sale of inventories in current period*

Sales	Dr	6 000	
Cost of sales	Cr		5 800
Inventories	Cr		200
Deferred tax asset	Dr	60	
Income tax expense	Cr		60

Workings
- This is a current period transaction involving inventories still on hand at the end of the current period.
- Sales within the group are $6000 and they need to be eliminated in full.
- The inventories remaining on hand at 30 June 2025 are recorded by Sandy Ltd at $1200. As this represents 20% of the total inventories transferred intragroup of $6000, the cost to the group of these inventories is $1000 (i.e. 20% × $6000/(1 + 20% mark-up)). The adjustment to inventories is then $200 (i.e. the unrealised profit of $1200 – $1000).
- Cost of sales recorded by the members of the group is $5000 (i.e. $6000/(1 + 20% mark-up)) for Beach Ltd and $4800 (i.e. $6000 – $1200 or essentially 80% × $6000) for Sandy Ltd; a total of $9800. Cost of sales for the group is $4000 (i.e. 80% × $6000/(1 + 20% mark-up)). The adjustment to cost of sales is then $5800. This could also be calculated as a balancing item having determined the adjustments for sales and inventories (i.e. the difference between the adjustment to sales of $6000 and the adjustment to inventories of $200).
- As the carrying amount of inventories is reduced by $200, a deferred tax asset of $60 (i.e. 30% × $200) is raised. This deferred tax asset recognises that the tax paid on the unrealised profit is a prepayment of tax from the group's perspective; that is, a tax benefit.

LEARNING CHECK

- ☐ Adjustments for current period inventories transfers affect current period profit accounts such as sales and cost of sales.
- ☐ Adjustments for prior period inventories transfers are only made for prior period unrealised profits or losses remaining in beginning inventories and affect the retained earnings account.
- ☐ To the extent that the inventories transferred intragroup are still with the group at the end of the current period, adjustments are also made to the inventories account.
- ☐ Where unrealised profit remains in ending inventories, the carrying amount of inventories is affected and a deferred tax-effect adjustment is required. Where the entire profit in beginning inventories is realised, only a current tax-effect adjustment is required.

28.4 Property, plant and equipment

LEARNING OBJECTIVE 28.4 Prepare worksheet entries for intragroup transactions involving profits or losses on the transfer of property, plant and equipment in both the current and previous periods.

Besides transferring inventories, it is possible for property, plant and equipment to be transferred within the group. The worksheet adjustment entries are shown in two parts:
1. entries to adjust for any profit or loss on transfer of the assets
2. entries relating to any depreciation of the assets after transfer.

As realisation of the profit or loss on transfer can be obtained through the depreciation of the transferred asset (and not necessarily through the sale of the asset to an external entity), the depreciation entries are covered in section 28.4.2 in conjunction with the discussion on profit realisation.

If a non-depreciable asset such as land is transferred, only the first of the above two sets of entries is required, and realisation of the profit or loss occurs, as with inventories, on sale of the asset to an external entity.

28.4.1 Sale of property, plant and equipment

Example

On 1 July 2022, George Ltd sold some plant to Laura Ltd for $18 500 cash. It had a carrying amount in George Ltd at time of sale of $18 000. Depreciation charged on plant by George Ltd is 10% p.a. on cost, while Laura Ltd applies a rate of 6% p.a. on cost. The income tax rate is 30%. What are the consolidation adjustment worksheet entries at 30 June 2023 to eliminate the effects of this intragroup sale?

1. Is this a prior period or a current period transaction?
The intragroup transaction is a current period transaction.

2. What has been recorded by the legal entities?
The journal entries in the records of George Ltd and Laura Ltd at the date of sale, 1 July 2022, are as follows.

GEORGE LTD			
Cash		Dr	18 500	
Gain on sale of plant		Cr		500
Plant		Cr		18 000

LAURA LTD			
Plant		Dr	18 500	
Cash		Cr		18 500

3. What should be reported by the group?
From the group's viewpoint there has been no sale of plant to an external entity. Hence there has been no sale and no gain on sale, and the cost of the plant to the group is the carrying amount of the asset at the time of transfer from George Ltd to Laura Ltd, namely $18 000.

4. What adjustments are necessary to get from the legal entities' amounts to the group amounts?
A comparison shows the following.

	Legal entities	Group	Difference
Gain on sale of plant	$ 500	$ 0	$(500)
Plant	18 500	18 000	(500)

Note: The column 'Legal entities' reflects the sum of the amounts recorded separately by the legal entities.

The consolidation worksheet adjustment entry is as follows.

Consolidation			
Gain on sale of plant		Dr	500	
Plant		Cr		500

5. What is the tax effect of the adjustments made?
In the consolidation worksheet entry above, the carrying amount of the plant is reduced by $500, while its tax base is not affected. This creates an additional deductible temporary difference between carrying amount and tax base of $500. Hence, a deferred tax asset is raised. Also, as the elimination of the gain on sale decreased the profit, the income tax expense should be reduced as well. Therefore, the second consolidation worksheet adjustment entry that recognises the tax effect is as follows.

Consolidation			
Deferred tax asset		Dr	150	
Income tax expense		Cr		150

Note that the adjustment entries for a current period's intragroup sale of assets at a loss are very similar to the adjustment entries discussed above for an intragroup sale of assets at a profit. If on 1 July 2022, George Ltd sold the plant with the original carrying amount of $18 000 to Laura Ltd for $17 500 cash, the first consolidation adjustment worksheet entry at 30 June 2023 will need to eliminate the loss of sale of plant of $500 recognised by George Ltd.

Consolidation			
Plant		Dr	500	
Loss on sale of plant		Cr		500

In the consolidation worksheet entry above, the carrying amount of the plant and the profit for the period are increased by $500, resulting in an additional taxable temporary difference and in an increase in income tax expense respectively. Therefore, the second consolidation worksheet adjustment entry that recognises the tax effect would be as follows.

Consolidation		
Income tax expense	Dr	150
Deferred tax liability	Cr	150

Handy hints

In preparing the consolidation adjustment entry for intragroup sale, for a profit, of non-current assets remaining on hand at the end of the current period, note the following.

- The adjustment to both *gain on sale* and the *non-current asset* is the difference between the intragroup sale price and the carrying amount at the point of sale (i.e. intragroup profit).
- The *tax effect* adjustment is always equal to the tax rate multiplied by the intragroup profit and is posted as a debit to deferred tax asset and a credit to income tax expense.

What are the consolidation worksheet entries at 30 June 2024 to eliminate the effects of this intragroup sale?

1. Is this a prior period or a current period transaction?
The entries at 30 June 2024 will account for the transfer of plant as a *prior period* transaction as the sale occurred on 1 July 2022.

2. What has been recorded by the legal entities?
The transaction occurred in a prior period, so the retained earnings (opening balance) includes a gain on sale of $500. The plant is recorded at a cost of $18 500.

3. What should be reported by the group?
From the group's perspective, no transaction occurred with an external entity so there was no prior period gain, and the cost of the plant to the group is $18 000.

4. What adjustments are necessary to get from the legal entities' amounts to the group amounts?
A comparison shows the following.

	Legal entities	Group	Difference
Retained earnings (1/7/23)	$ 500	$ 0	$(500)
Plant	18 500	18 000	(500)

Note: The column 'Legal entities' reflects the sum of the amounts recorded separately by the legal entities.

The consolidation worksheet adjustment entry at 30 June 2024 is as follows.

Consolidation		
Retained earnings (1/7/23)	Dr	500
Plant	Cr	500

5. What is the tax effect of the adjustments made?
The adjustment entry decreases the carrying amount of the plant, with no effect on the tax base; hence, a deductible temporary difference arises, which creates a deferred tax asset. Also, the entry has an effect on the prior period profit, decreasing it. As a result, the income tax expense for the prior period has to decrease, leading to an increase in the opening balance of the retained earnings account.

The second consolidation worksheet adjustment entry at 30 June 2024 is as follows.

Consolidation		
Deferred tax asset	Dr	150
Retained earnings (1/7/23)	Cr	150

These two entries can be combined into the following.

Consolidation			
Retained earnings (1/7/23)	Dr	350	
Deferred tax asset	Dr	150	
Plant	Cr		500

Handy hints

In preparing the consolidation adjustment entry for prior period intragroup sale of non-current assets remaining on hand at the end of the current period, note the following.
- The adjustment to the *non-current asset* is the difference between the intragroup sale price of the asset and its carrying amount at the point of sale (i.e. intragroup profit).
- The adjustment to the *retained earnings (opening balance)* is the after-tax intragroup profit.
- The *tax effect* adjustment is always equal to the tax rate multiplied by the intragroup profit and is posted as a debit to deferred tax asset.

Note also that the above entry would be used in each period that the plant stays on hand, until it gets sold or reaches the end of the useful life.

28.4.2 Depreciation and realisation of profits

Depreciation is generally measured as a function of the cost of the asset. As the cost of the asset to the group is different from that recorded by the legal entity holding the asset, it is necessary to make adjustments in relation to depreciation.

In the example in section 28.4.1 it was noted that the depreciation rate used by George Ltd was 10% p.a., different from that used by Laura Ltd of 6% p.a. This would occur if the asset changed its pattern of use on transfer from one entity to another. The depreciation charged must reflect the pattern of use in the entity holding the asset. Hence, the appropriate depreciation rate for the group is that used by the entity holding the asset; in the example, that entity is Laura Ltd as George Ltd sold the asset to Laura Ltd. The rate to be applied by the group is then 6% p.a.

What are the consolidation adjustment entries for depreciation that need to be posted in the consolidation worksheet at 30 June 2023?

1. Is this a prior period or a current period transaction?
The transaction is a current period transaction.

2. What has been recorded by the legal entities?
The journal entry in the records of Laura Ltd to record the depreciation in the first year of holding the asset is as follows.

LAURA LTD			
Depreciation expense	Dr	1 110	
Accumulated depreciation	Cr		1 110
(6% × $18 500)			

3. What should be reported by the group?
If the cost of the plant to the group is $18 000, while the depreciation rate is 6%, the annual depreciation is $1080 (i.e. 6% × $18 000).

4. What adjustments are necessary to get from the legal entities' amounts to the group amounts?
A comparison shows the following.

	Legal entities	Group	Difference
Depreciation expense	$1 110	$1 080	$(30)
Accumulated depreciation	1 100	1 080	(30)

Note: The column 'Legal entities' reflects the sum of the amounts recorded separately by the legal entities.

The consolidation worksheet adjustment entry at 30 June 2023 is as follows.

Consolidation			
Accumulated depreciation		Dr	30
Depreciation expense		Cr	30

5. What is the tax effect of the adjustments made?

The previous entry reduced accumulated depreciation and an expense and hence increased the carrying amount of the asset and the profit, respectively. The increase in the carrying amount with no effect on the tax base gives rise to a difference between carrying amount and tax base. This difference is a reversal of the initial deductible temporary difference recognised when the gain on sale was eliminated and the carrying amount of the plant was decreased. For the initial temporary difference, a deferred tax asset was recognised; now, that deferred tax asset needs to be reduced by an amount equal to the tax rate times the adjustment to accumulated depreciation (i.e. 30% × $30). Note that the reversal to the deferred tax asset could also be calculated as the depreciation rate times the deferred tax asset balance initially raised on adjusting for the gain on sale of the plant (i.e. 6% × $150).

The second consolidation worksheet adjustment entry recognising the tax effect is as follows.

Consolidation			
Income tax expense		Dr	9
Deferred tax asset		Cr	9

Handy hints

In preparing the consolidation adjustment entry for depreciation affected by current period intragroup sale of non-current assets remaining on hand at the end of the current period, note the following.

- The adjustment per annum to the *accumulated depreciation* and *depreciation expense* is the difference between the intragroup selling price of the asset and its carrying amount at the time of the intragroup sale (i.e. intragroup profit) times the depreciation rate. If the asset was within the group only for a proportion of the full year during the current period after the intragroup sale, the adjustment per annum needs to be multiplied by that proportion before it is included in the consolidation adjustment entry.
- The *tax effect* adjustment is equal to the tax rate multiplied by the adjustment to *accumulated depreciation* or *depreciation expense* and is posted as a debit to *income tax expense* and a credit to *deferred tax asset*.

What are the consolidation adjustment entries for depreciation that need to be posted in the consolidation worksheet at 30 June 2024?

1. Is this a prior period or a current period transaction?

As the intragroup sale occurred in the prior period, this intragroup transaction is a prior period transaction.

2. What has been recorded by the legal entities?

Laura Ltd has recorded prior period depreciation expense of $1110 (which has decreased the opening balance of retained earnings) and current period expense of $1110.

3. What should be reported by the group?

The group recognises depreciation expense of $1080 p.a. in both the current and prior periods.

4. What adjustments are necessary to get from the legal entities' amounts to the group amounts?

A comparison shows the following.

	Legal entities	Group	Difference
Retained earnings (1/7/23)	$(1 110)	$(1 080)	$ 30
Depreciation expense	1 110	1 080	(30)
Accumulated depreciation	2 220	2 160	(60)

The consolidation worksheet adjustment entry at 30 June 2024 in relation to depreciation is as follows.

Consolidation			
Accumulated depreciation		Dr	60
Depreciation expense		Cr	30
Retained earnings (1/7/23)		Cr	30

It should be understood that the worksheet entries in *subsequent* periods will adjust the same accounts as in the period ended 30 June 2024 to the extent that the asset is still within the group at the beginning of the period. There will be a current period depreciation expense adjustment, the retained earnings (opening balance) will be adjusted for the number of prior periods times the annual depreciation expense adjustment, and the accumulated depreciation will be adjusted by the sum of the depreciation adjustments for the current and prior periods.

5. What is the tax effect of the adjustments made?

The previous entry reduced accumulated depreciation and a current expense and increased the opening balance of retained earnings; hence, it increased the carrying amount of the asset and the current and prior profits, respectively. The increase in the carrying amount gives rise to a difference between carrying amount and tax base. This difference is a reversal of the initial deductible temporary difference recognised when the gain on sale was eliminated and the carrying amount of the plant was decreased. For the initial temporary difference, a deferred tax asset was recognised; now that deferred tax asset needs to be reduced by an amount equal to the tax rate times the adjustment to accumulated depreciation (i.e. $30\% \times \$60$). Note that the reversal to the deferred tax asset could also be calculated as the depreciation rate times the deferred tax asset balance initially raised on adjusting for the gain on sale of the plant and times the number of years (or part-years) since the intragroup sale until the end of the current period (i.e. $6\% \times \$150 \times 2$ years).

The increases in the current and prior profits give rise to increases in income tax expense for the current and prior periods. These will be recognised by increasing income tax expense and decreasing the opening balance of retained earnings respectively.

The consolidation worksheet adjustment entry is as follows.

Consolidation			
Retained earnings (1/7/23)	Dr	9	
Income tax expense	Dr	9	
Deferred tax asset	Cr		18

Handy hints

In preparing the consolidation adjustment entry for depreciation affected by prior period intragroup sale of non-current assets remaining on hand at the end of the current period, note the following.

- The adjustment per annum to the *depreciation expense* is the difference between the intragroup sale price of the asset and its carrying amount before the intragroup sale (i.e. intragroup profit) times the depreciation rate.
- The adjustment to the *retained earnings (opening balance)* is the adjustment per annum to the depreciation expense times the period in years from the intragroup sale to the beginning of the current period.
- The adjustment to the *accumulated depreciation* is the adjustment to the depreciation expense plus the adjustment to the *retained earnings (opening balance)*.
- The *tax effect* adjustment is:
  - reversing *deferred tax asset* by the tax rate multiplied by the adjustment to accumulated depreciation
  - increasing *income tax expense* by the tax rate multiplied by the adjustment to current *depreciation expense*
  - decreasing *retained earnings (opening balance)* by the tax rate multiplied by the adjustment to prior *depreciation expenses*.

Realisation of intragroup profits or losses

Realisation of profits or losses normally occurs when an external entity is involved in the transaction. With inventories, the point of realisation is easy to determine as realisation occurs when the transferred inventories are on-sold to the external entity. With depreciable assets, determining when the gain or loss on sale becomes realised to the group is not as simple. The depreciable asset normally remains within the group and is used in production rather than being sold to external entities. No external entity may ever become *directly* involved with the depreciable asset. Hence, to determine the realisation of profit or loss, an assumption must be made about the realisation process, as it may not be observed just by noting an external transaction.

The realisation of the profit or loss on a depreciable asset transferred within the group is *assumed* to occur when the future benefits embodied in the asset are consumed by the group. In other words, the depreciable asset transferred within the group may not be sold to an external entity, but will be used up within the group to generate benefits for the group. As the asset is used up within the group, the benefits are received by the group. A useful measure of the pattern of benefits received by the group can be obtained by reference to the depreciation charged on the asset, since the depreciation allocation is related to the pattern of benefits obtained from the use of the assets. Hence, for depreciable assets, the involvement of external entities in the transaction occurs on an indirect basis with the assumption being made that realisation of intragroup profits occurs in a pattern consistent with the allocation of the depreciation of the non-current asset.

Consider the consolidation worksheet entries at 30 June 2024 in the above example. The consolidation worksheet adjustment for the gain on sale was as follows.

Retained earnings (1/7/23)	Dr	350
Deferred tax asset	Dr	150
Plant	Cr		500

This entry reduces prior period after-tax profit by $350; that is, there is $350 of unrealised profit. The group has not recognised this profit of $350 which has been recognised by the legal entities.

The consolidation worksheet entries for depreciation are as follows.

Accumulated depreciation	Dr	60
Depreciation expense	Cr		30
Retained earnings (1/7/23)	Cr		30
Retained earnings (1/7/23)	Dr	9
Income tax expense	Dr	9
Deferred tax asset	Cr		18

A credit to depreciation expense is a reduction in expenses, and hence an increase in profit. In these two entries, the after-tax profit is increased by $21 (i.e. $30 increase in profit through depreciation adjustment – $9 increase in tax expense), both for the current period and for the prior period. That is, as the asset is depreciated, in each period the profit for the group is $21 greater than that recorded by the legal entities. That amount is equivalent to the profit on the intragroup sale (i.e. $350) times the depreciation rate (i.e. 6%). As such, it can be said that the $350 intragroup profit is being realised by the group at 6% p.a. Over the life of the asset, the whole $350 will become realised to the group.

Hence, while normally intragroup profit or loss is realised with the on-sale of the transferred asset to external entities, with depreciable assets, realisation occurs also as the asset is depreciated. Nevertheless, the depreciable assets can also be on-sold to external entities and that will also realise the remaining unrealised profits or losses on the initial intragroup transfer.

28.4.3 Change in classification of transferred assets

It is possible for an item that is transferred within the group to be regarded by the seller as a non-current asset and by the buyer as inventories or vice versa. Consider the following examples.

Example 1

On 1 June 2023, Laura Ltd sells a machine to George Ltd for $20 000 cash, with Laura Ltd classifying the machine as a depreciable asset and George Ltd classifying it as inventories (i.e. George Ltd is a seller of second-hand machinery). The carrying amount of the asset in the books of Laura Ltd was $16 000 on that date. The asset is still on hand with the group at 30 June 2023. What are the consolidation adjustment entries that are posted in the consolidation worksheet to eliminate the effects of this transaction at 30 June 2023?

To answer this requirement, the five questions discussed at the beginning of the chapter can be applied.

1. Is this a prior period or a current period transaction?
As the intragroup sale occurs in the current period, this intragroup transaction is a current period transaction.

2. What has been recorded by the legal entities?

Laura Ltd records a gain on sale of $4000, while George Ltd records inventories of $20 000. The legal entities also record an increase in cash and a decrease in cash respectively for the same amount (i.e. $20 000). However, as the value of cash does not change by being transferred intragroup (as opposed to the value of machinery reclassified as inventories), there is no need to take cash into consideration when preparing consolidation adjustments.

3. What should be reported by the group?

From the group's perspective, the intragroup gain on sale should not be recognised. The asset should be recorded as inventories (as from now on, it is going to be used as inventories by the entity that has the asset in the group, and not as machinery), but with an amount equal to the carrying amount at the date of the intragroup sale (i.e. $16 000).

4. What adjustments are necessary to get from the legal entities' amounts to the group amounts?

Given the differences between the items and the amounts recorded by the legal entities and those that should be reported by the group, the gain on sale should be eliminated, while inventories should decrease from $20 000 to $16 000. Therefore, the consolidation worksheet entry should be as follows.

Gain on sale	Dr	4 000	
Inventories	Cr		4 000

Note that, as the asset is now classified as inventories, there is no depreciation recorded by the owner of the asset. As the group should not recognise any depreciation either, there is no need for any depreciation adjustments to be posted in the consolidation worksheet.

5. What is the tax effect of the adjustments made?

As the first adjustment entry decreases the profit by $4000 by eliminating the gain on sale, the group should recognise a decrease in income tax expense of 30% times $4000. Also, the carrying amount of the inventories is decreased with no impact on the tax base, creating an extra deductible temporary difference of $4000 that gives rise to a deferred tax asset of 30% times $4000. Therefore, the second consolidation worksheet entry should be as follows.

Deferred tax asset	Dr	1 200	
Income tax expense	Cr		1 200

Note that if the inventories item was sold by the end of the current period to external entities, the first consolidation adjustment entry will include a credit to cost of sales, instead of inventories and the effect on the profit and the carrying amount of inventories will be zero. As such, there will not be any tax effect entry.

Handy hints

In preparing the consolidation adjustment entry for current period intragroup transfer of non-current assets to inventories still on hand at the end of the period, note the following.
- The adjustment to both *gain on sale* and *inventories* is the difference between the intragroup sale price and the carrying amount at the point of sale (i.e. intragroup profit).
- The *tax effect* adjustment is equal to the tax rate multiplied by the intragroup profit and is posted as a debit to deferred tax asset and a credit to income tax expense.

In preparing the consolidation adjustment entry for current period intragroup transfer of non-current assets to inventories sold by the end of the period, note the following.
- The adjustment to both *gain on sale* and *cost of sales* is the difference between the intragroup sale price and the carrying amount at the point of intragroup sale (i.e. intragroup profit).
- There is no *tax effect* adjustment as the intragroup profit is realised and no net adjustment to profit or carrying amount of assets was necessary.

Example 2

On 1 July 2022, Laura Ltd sells a machine to George Ltd for $20 000 cash, with Laura Ltd classifying the machine as inventories and George Ltd classifying it as machinery (i.e. Laura Ltd is a manufacturer of machinery). The cost of the asset in the books of Laura Ltd was $16 000 on that date. The asset is depreciated by George Ltd at a rate of 10% p.a. on cost and is still on hand with the group at 30 June 2023. What are the consolidation adjustment entries that are posted in the consolidation worksheet to eliminate the effects of this transaction at 30 June 2023?

1. Is this a prior period or a current period transaction?
As the sale occurs at the beginning of the current period, this intragroup transaction is a current period transaction.

2. What has been recorded by the legal entities?
Laura Ltd records sales revenue of $20 000 and cost of sales of $16 000 as from its perspective, this is a sale of inventories. George Ltd records machinery of $20 000. Moreover, as the asset is depreciable, a depreciation expense is recognised by George Ltd in accumulated depreciation (i.e. 10% × $20 000 = $2000).

The legal entities record also an increase in cash and a decrease in cash respectively for the same amount (i.e. $20 000). However, the value of cash does not change by being transferred intragroup (as opposed to the value of inventories reclassified as machinery), so there is no need to take cash into consideration when preparing consolidation adjustments.

3. What should be reported by the group?
From the group's perspective, the intragroup sale should not be recognised. The asset should be recorded as machinery (as from now on, it is going to be used as machinery by the entity that has the asset in the group, and not as inventories), but with an original amount equal to the cost at the date of the intragroup sale (i.e. $16 000). Moreover, as the asset is depreciable, a depreciation expense needs to be recognised by the group in accumulated depreciation based on the original cost to the group (i.e. 10% × $16 000 = $1600).

4. What adjustments are necessary to get from the legal entities' amounts to the group amounts?
Given the differences between the items and the amounts recorded by the legal entities and those that should be reported by the group, the sales and the cost of sales should be eliminated and the machinery should decrease from $20 000 to $16 000. Also, the depreciation expense and the accumulated depreciation should be reduced by $400 (i.e. $2000 – $1600). Therefore, the consolidation worksheet entries should be as follows.

Sales	Dr	20 000	
Cost of sales	Cr		16 000
Machinery	Cr		4 000
Accumulated depreciation	Dr	400	
Depreciation expense	Cr		400

5. What is the tax effect of the adjustments made?
As the first adjustment entry decreases the profit by $4000 by eliminating the sales of $20 000 and cost of sales of $16 000, the group should recognise a decrease in income tax expense of 30% × $4000. Also, the carrying amount of the machinery is decreased with no impact on the tax base, creating an extra deductible temporary difference of $4000 that gives rise to a deferred tax asset of 30% × $4000. Therefore, the first tax consolidation worksheet entry should be as follows.

Deferred tax asset	Dr	1 200	
Income tax expense	Cr		1 200

However, the second consolidation adjustment entry that decreases the depreciation expense increases the profit by $400 (effectively realising a part of the gain from the intragroup transfer) and increases the carrying amount of the asset. The former effect increases the income tax expense by 30% × $400. The latter effect reverses the deductible temporary difference that created a deferred tax asset by 10% of the original amount recognised (i.e. 10% × 30% × $4000). Therefore, the second tax consolidation worksheet entry should be as follows.

Income tax expense	Dr	120	
Deferred tax asset	Cr		120

Handy hints

In preparing the consolidation adjustment entries for current period intragroup transfer of inventories to non-current assets still on hand at the end of the period, note the following.

- The adjustment to *sales revenue* is the intragroup sale price.
- The adjustment to *cost of sales* is the original cost of inventories sold intragroup.
- The adjustment to the *non-current asset* is the difference between the sale price and the original cost (i.e. intragroup profit).
- The adjustment to the *depreciation expense* per annum is the depreciation rate times the intragroup profit.
- The *tax effect* adjustment for the elimination of the gain on the intragroup transfer is equal to the tax rate multiplied by the intragroup profit and is posted as a debit to deferred tax asset and a credit to income tax expense.
- The *tax effect* adjustment for depreciation is equal to the tax rate multiplied by the adjustment to depreciation expense and is posted as a credit to deferred tax asset and a debit to income tax expense.

In preparing the consolidation adjustment entries for prior period intragroup transfer of inventories to non-current assets still on hand at the end of the current period, note the following.

- The adjustment to the *retained earnings (opening balance)* and *non-current asset* is the difference between the sale price and the original cost (i.e. intragroup profit).
- The adjustment to the *depreciation expense* per annum is the depreciation rate times the intragroup profit. The adjustment to current depreciation expense will be posted against the depreciation expense account, while the adjustment to depreciation expenses of prior periods will be posted against the retained earnings (opening balance).
- The *tax effect* adjustment for the elimination of the gain on the intragroup transfer is equal to the tax rate multiplied by the intragroup profit and is posted as a credit to retained earnings (opening balance) and a debit to deferred tax asset.
- The *tax effect* adjustment for depreciation is equal to the tax rate multiplied by the adjustment to depreciation expense. The tax adjustment for current depreciation expense will be posted against the income tax expense account, while the tax adjustment for depreciation expenses of prior periods will be posted against the retained earnings (opening balance). A credit to deferred tax asset will also be posted equal to the tax rate multiplied by the total adjustment to current and prior depreciation expenses.

ILLUSTRATIVE EXAMPLE 28.2

Intragroup transactions involving non-current assets

Toowoomba Ltd owns all the issued shares of Mandurah Ltd. The following transactions occurred.

(a) On 1 January 2021, Mandurah Ltd sold an item of plant to Toowoomba Ltd for $120 000. At time of sale, this asset had a carrying amount in the records of Mandurah Ltd of $115 000. The asset is to be depreciated on a straight-line basis at 10% p.a. on cost and it is still on hand with Toowoomba Ltd at 30 June 2023.

(b) On 16 May 2023, Toowoomba Ltd sold equipment to Mandurah Ltd for $50 000, this asset having a carrying amount at time of sale of $40 000. The equipment was regarded by Toowoomba Ltd as a depreciable non-current asset, being depreciated at 10% p.a. on cost, whereas Mandurah Ltd records the equipment as inventories. The asset was sold by Mandurah Ltd to an external entity before 30 June 2023.

Required

Prepare the consolidation worksheet adjustment entries for the preparation of consolidated financial statements at 30 June 2023. The tax rate is 30%.

Solution

The required entries for the consolidation worksheet at 30 June 2023 are as follows.

(a) *Sale of plant in prior period*

Retained earnings (1/7/22)	Dr	3 500	
Deferred tax asset	Dr	1 500	
Plant	Cr		5 000
Accumulated depreciation	Dr	1 250	
Depreciation expense	Cr		500
Retained earnings (1/7/22)	Cr		750
Income tax expense	Dr	150	
Retained earnings (1/7/22)	Dr	225	
Deferred tax asset	Cr		375

Workings
- This intragroup transaction is a prior period transaction involving the sale of a non-current asset.
- Profit after tax on the intragroup sale is $3500 (i.e. ($120 000 – $115 000) × (1 – 30%)); retained earnings (opening balance) needs to be adjusted for this after-tax intragroup profit.
- The adjustment to the carrying amount of plant is $5000 (i.e. $120 000 – $115 000), equal to the before-tax profit on the intragroup sale; this adjustment gives rise to a deferred tax asset of $1500 (i.e. 30% × $5000).
- The adjustment per annum to the current *depreciation expense* is the intragroup profit times the depreciation rate (i.e. 10% × $5000 = $500).
- The adjustment to the *retained earnings (opening balance) for prior periods depreciation* is the adjustment per annum to the depreciation expense multiplied by the time period from the intragroup sale to the beginning of the current period (i.e. $500 × 1.5 years = $750).
- The adjustment to the *accumulated depreciation* is the adjustment to the current depreciation expense plus the adjustment to the *retained earnings (opening balance)*.
- The *tax effect* related to the depreciation adjustment is:
  - reversing *deferred tax asset* by the tax rate multiplied by the adjustment to *accumulated depreciation*
  - increasing *income tax expense* by the tax rate multiplied by the adjustment to current *depreciation expense*
  - decreasing *retained earnings (opening balance)* by the tax rate multiplied by the adjustment to prior *depreciation expenses*.

(b) *Sale of equipment in current period, and classified as inventories by buyer*

Gain on sale of equipment	Dr	10 000	
Cost of sales	Cr		10 000

Workings
- The intragroup transaction is a current period transaction involving a non-current asset transferred intragroup as inventories and then sold to external entities by the end of the current period.
- The adjustment to *gain on sale* and *cost of sales* is $10 000 (i.e. $50 000 – $40 000), equal to the before-tax profit on the intragroup transfer.
- No tax effect adjustment is necessary as the inventories were sold to external entities by the end of the current period.

LEARNING CHECK

☐ Adjustments for the gain/loss on sale of property, plant and equipment are made in all periods in which the assets are still within the group.

☐ Where the transferred assets are depreciable, adjustments are made to the depreciation expense account (for the current period depreciation) or to the retained earnings account (for the previous periods' depreciation), the adjustments being a proportion of the gain/loss on sale based on the depreciation rate per year and the time period for which the asset is depreciated after the intragroup sale.

☐ As depreciation reflects the use of the asset by the group, the depreciation adjustments are considered to be realising a part of the gain/loss on the intragroup sale of property, plant and equipment.

☐ As the adjustments for intragroup sale of property, plant and equipment that are still on hand with the group affect the profit and the carrying amount of assets, adjustments for the tax effects are also required.

28.5 Intragroup services

LEARNING OBJECTIVE 28.5 Prepare worksheet entries for intragroup services.

Many different examples of services between a parent and its subsidiary exist, as follows.

- Laura Ltd may lend some specialist personnel to George Ltd for a limited period of time to perform a particular task for George Ltd. For this service, Laura Ltd may charge George Ltd a certain fee, or expect George Ltd to perform other services in return.
- George Ltd may lease or rent an item of plant or a warehouse from Laura Ltd or vice versa.
- George Ltd may exist solely for the purpose of carrying out some specific task, such as research activities for the parent, and a fee for such activities is charged. In this situation, all service revenue earned by the subsidiary is paid for by the parent, and must be adjusted in the consolidation process.

Example

During the period ended 30 June 2022, Laura Ltd offered George Ltd the services of an employee who had specialist marketing skills. The employee served with George Ltd for 2 months, and in return for the services George Ltd paid $80 000 to Laura Ltd. What are the consolidation worksheet entries at 30 June 2022 to eliminate the effects of this intragroup transaction?

1. Is this a prior period or a current period transaction?
This intragroup transaction is a current period transaction.

2. What has been recorded by the legal entities?
The entries recorded by the legal entities are as follows.

LAURA LTD			
Cash	Dr	80 000	
Service revenue	Cr		80 000

GEORGE LTD			
Service expense	Dr	80 000	
Cash	Cr		80 000

3. What should be reported by the group?
There has been no external entity involved in this transaction. To the group there is no expense or revenue.

4. What adjustments are necessary to get from the legal entities' amounts to the group amounts?
A comparison shows the following.

	Legal entities	Group	Difference
Service revenue	$80 000	0	$(80 000)
Service expense	80 000	0	(80 000)

The consolidation worksheet adjustment entry is as follows.

Consolidation			
Service revenue	Dr	80 000	
Service expense	Cr		80 000

5. What is the tax effect of the adjustments made?
The consolidation worksheet adjustment entry does not affect the carrying amount of any asset or liability or the overall profit. Therefore, there is no tax-effect adjustment.

Realisation of intragroup profits or losses

With the transfer of services within the group, the consolidation adjustments do not affect the profit of the group. In a transaction involving a payment by a parent to a subsidiary, or vice versa, for services rendered, the client shows an expense and the service provider shows a revenue. The net effect on the group's profit is zero. Hence, from the group's perspective, there are no unrealised profits or losses from intragroup services.

Handy hints

In preparing the consolidation adjustment entries for current period intragroup services, note the following.
- The adjustment to *service revenue* and *service expense* is the intragroup fee charged for those services.
- If the intragroup services have not been paid by the end of the current period, an adjustment to *fees receivable* and *fees payable* is also required for the amount unpaid.
- There is no tax adjustment.
- Note that no adjustment needs to be posted in the subsequent periods, unless the fee remains unpaid by the end of a future period (in those cases, an adjustment to *fees receivable* and *fees payable* will still be required for the amount unpaid).

LEARNING CHECK

- ☐ Adjustments for previous periods' intragroup services affect only statement of financial position accounts, but only if the fees have not been paid.
- ☐ Adjustments for current period intragroup services affect statement of profit or loss and other comprehensive income accounts and statement of financial position accounts if the fees have not been paid and only statement of profit or loss and other comprehensive income accounts if the fees have been paid.
- ☐ It is not necessary to have a tax-effect adjustment when adjusting for intragroup services.
- ☐ Profits/losses on intragroup services are considered immediately realised to the group.

28.6 Dividends

LEARNING OBJECTIVE 28.6 Prepare worksheet entries for intragroup dividends.

Where a parent owns all the shares in a subsidiary, all dividends paid/payable by the subsidiary are received/receivable by the parent. The subsidiary may pay the dividends from pre-acquisition or post-acquisition equity. According to paragraph 12 of AASB 127/IAS 27 *Separate Financial Statements*:

> Dividends from a subsidiary, a joint venture or an associate are recognised in the separate financial statements of an entity when the entity's right to receive the dividend is established. The dividend is recognised in profit or loss unless the entity elects to use the equity method, in which case the dividend is recognised as a reduction from the carrying amount of the investment.

Remember that the assumption used in this text is that the parent recognises its investment in subsidiaries at cost, subject to impairment, not using the equity method. If dividends from pre-acquisition equity cause a decrease in the value of the investment, an impairment loss may be recognised by the parent on the investment in subsidiary account. The impairment loss will have to be eliminated on consolidation, together with all the other effects of the intragroup dividends.

28.6.1 Dividends declared in the current period but not paid

Example

On 25 June 2022, George Ltd declares a dividend of $10 000. At the end of the period, the dividend remains unpaid. What are the consolidation worksheet entries at 30 June 2022 to eliminate the effects of this intragroup transaction?

1. Is this a prior period or a current period transaction?
This intragroup transaction is a current period transaction.

2. What has been recorded by the legal entities?
The entries in the legal entities' records are as follows.

GEORGE LTD			
Dividend declared	Dr	10 000	
Dividend payable	Cr		10 000

LAURA LTD		
Dividend receivable	Dr	10 000
Dividend revenue	Cr	10 000

3. What should be reported by the group?

From the group's point of view there is no revenue or reduction in retained earnings as no external entity is involved with the transaction. In relation to the liability dividend payable, the obligation is not to pay monies to any entity external to the group. In relation to the asset dividend receivable, the group does not expect to receive monies from entities external to the group.

4. What adjustments are necessary to get from the legal entities' amounts to the group amounts?

A comparison shows the following.

	Legal entities	Group	Difference
Dividend declared	$10 000	0	$(10 000)
Dividend payable	10 000	0	(10 000)
Dividend receivable	10 000	0	(10 000)
Dividend revenue	10 000	0	(10 000)

The consolidation worksheet adjustment entries are as follows.

Consolidation		
Dividend payable	Dr	10 000
Dividend declared	Cr	10 000
Dividend revenue	Dr	10 000
Dividend receivable	Cr	10 000

5. What is the tax effect of the adjustments made?

The carrying amount of both an asset and a liability are affected by these adjustment entries. However, no tax-effect entry is necessary as there is no effect on the net assets.

What are the consolidation worksheet entries at 30 June 2023 to eliminate the effects of this intragroup transaction?

Assume the dividend declared in June 2022 is paid in August 2022. At 30 June 2023, the declaration of intragroup dividends on 25 June 2022 would be considered as a prior period transaction. However, there is no adjustment required in relation to retained earnings (opening balance) as the dividend declared and dividend revenue recognised in the prior period had a zero net effect on the consolidated retained earnings. As the dividend was paid in August 2022, in the consolidation worksheet at 30 June 2023 there are no accounts on the left-hand side of the worksheet relating to the dividend; that is, the dividend receivable and dividend payable were closed on payment of the dividend. Hence, there are no adjustment entries required in the 2023 worksheet or in any other future worksheet with regards to the dividends declared in 2022 and paid in 2023.

Handy hints

In preparing the consolidation adjustment entries for current period dividends declared and not yet paid, note the following.

- The adjustment to *dividend revenue, dividend declared, dividend receivable* and *dividend payable* is the amount of dividend declared intragroup.
- There is no tax adjustment.
- Note that no adjustment needs to be posted in the subsequent periods.

28.6.2 Dividends declared and paid in the current period

Example

In January 2022, George Ltd pays an interim dividend of $6000. What are the consolidation worksheet entries at 30 June 2022 to eliminate the effects of this intragroup transaction?

1. Is this a prior period or a current period transaction?

This intragroup transaction is a current period transaction.

2. What has been recorded by the legal entities?

The entries passed by Laura Ltd and George Ltd in January 2022 are as follows.

LAURA LTD			
Cash		Dr	6 000	
Dividend revenue		Cr		6 000

GEORGE LTD			
Interim dividend paid		Dr	6 000	
Cash		Cr		6 000

3. What should be reported by the group?

The group has not entered into any transaction with external entities. The group has earned no revenue nor incurred any expense.

4. What adjustments are necessary to get from the legal entities' amounts to the group amounts?

A comparison shows the following.

	Legal entities	Group	Difference
Dividend revenue	$6 000	0	$(6 000)
Interim dividend paid	6 000	0	(6 000)

The consolidation worksheet adjustment entry at 30 June 2022 is as follows.

Consolidation			
Dividend revenue		Dr	6 000	
Interim dividend paid		Cr		6 000

5. What is the tax effect of the adjustments made?

As no carrying amount of asset or liability is affected by the entry, there is no tax-effect entry required.

There is no consolidation worksheet adjustment required in periods subsequent to 30 June 2022 as the individual accounts are closed to the retained earnings and do not have any net impact on the consolidated figures.

Handy hints

In preparing the consolidation adjustment entries for current period dividends declared and paid, note the following.
- The adjustment to *dividend revenue* and *dividend declared* is the amount of dividend declared intragroup.
- There is no tax adjustment.
- No adjustment needs to be posted in the subsequent periods.

28.6.3 Bonus share dividends

Example

Assume a bonus share dividend of $5000 is paid by George Ltd out of post-acquisition profits on 1 June 2022. What are the consolidation worksheet entries at 30 June 2022 to eliminate the effects of this intragroup transaction?

The journal entry made by George Ltd is as follows.

GEORGE LTD			
Bonus share dividend		Dr	5 000	
Share capital		Cr		5 000

Since the bonus share dividend is paid by George Ltd out of post-acquisition profits, these profits, which for consolidation purposes are normally available for dividends, have been capitalised as share capital.

In the records of Laura Ltd, no entry is required as the bonus share dividend does not give Laura Ltd an increased share of George Ltd; that is, Laura Ltd receives nothing that it did not previously own.

For consolidation purposes, two alternative adjustments are possible.

1. Eliminate the bonus dividend paid against the share capital of George Ltd; that is, reverse the entry made by the subsidiary to record the dividend as follows.

Consolidation			
Share capital		Dr	5 000	
Bonus share dividend		Cr		5 000

If this entry is used, the fact that George Ltd has provided for a bonus dividend does not appear in the consolidated financial statements unless disclosed by way of a note. The consolidated retained earnings balance will include profits that have been distributed as bonus shares and are not available for the payment of dividends.

2. Do not eliminate the bonus dividend paid but set up a new capitalised profits reserve in the consolidation worksheet. The entry is as follows.

Consolidation			
Share capital		Dr	5 000	
Capitalised profits reserve		Cr		5 000

The purpose of creating this reserve is to disclose the fact that part of the retained earnings of the group has been distributed by the subsidiary and is therefore no longer available for payment of dividends to the parent.

Alternative (2) is recommended as the preferred treatment of bonus share dividends on consolidation as it raises the capitalised profits reserve in the consolidated financial statements as a non-distributable reserve.

ILLUSTRATIVE EXAMPLE 28.3

Intragroup dividends

Grey Ltd owns all the issued shares of Dolphin Ltd, having acquired them for $250 000 on 1 January 2022. In preparing the consolidated financial statements at 30 June 2024, the accountant documented the following transactions.

2023	
Jan. 15	Dolphin Ltd paid an interim dividend of $10 000.
June 25	Dolphin Ltd declared a dividend of $15 000, this being recognised in the records of both entities.
Aug. 1	The $15 000 dividend declared on 25 June was paid by Dolphin Ltd.
2024	
Jan. 18	Dolphin Ltd paid an interim dividend of $12 000.
June 23	Dolphin Ltd declared a dividend of $18 000, this being recognised in the records of both entities.

The tax rate is 30%.

Required

Prepare the consolidation worksheet adjustment entries for the preparation of consolidated financial statements at 30 June 2024.

Solution

The required consolidation worksheet entries are as follows.

1. *Interim dividend paid*

Dividend revenue		Dr	12 000	
Dividend paid		Cr		12 000

2. *Final dividend declared*

Dividend payable	Dr	18 000	
Dividend declared	Cr		18 000
Dividend revenue	Dr	18 000	
Dividend receivable	Cr		18 000

LEARNING CHECK

☐ Dividends from subsidiary are recognised as revenue by the parent and do not affect the investment in the subsidiary.

☐ Consolidation adjustments affect both the dividend accounts raised by the subsidiary and those raised by the parent.

☐ Consolidated financial statements show only the effects of dividends paid or payable to entities outside the group.

☐ There are no tax-effect entries relating to adjustments for dividends.

28.7 Intragroup borrowings

LEARNING OBJECTIVE 28.7 Prepare worksheet entries for intragroup borrowings.

Members of a group often borrow and lend money among themselves, and may charge and pay interest on the money borrowed. In some cases, an entity may be set up within the group solely for the purpose of handling group finances and for borrowing money on international money markets and then offering the funds via intragroup borrowings to the other entities within the group. Consolidation adjustments are necessary in relation to these intragroup borrowings and interest thereon because these transactions create assets and liabilities, and revenues and expenses, that do not exist in terms of the group's relationship with external entities.

Example

On 1 July 2022, Laura Ltd lends $100 000 to George Ltd, charging interest of $9000 p.a. What are the consolidation worksheet entries at 30 June 2023 to eliminate the effects of this intragroup transaction?

1. Is this a prior period or a current period transaction?
This intragroup transaction is a current period transaction.

2. What has been recorded by the legal entities?
The entries are as follows.

LAURA LTD			
Advance to George Ltd	Dr	100 000	
Cash	Cr		100 000
Cash	Dr	9 000	
Interest revenue	Cr		9 000

GEORGE LTD			
Cash	Dr	100 000	
Advance from Laura Ltd	Cr		100 000
Interest expense	Dr	9 000	
Cash	Cr		9 000

3. What should be reported by the group?
From the group's perspective, there is no loan made to an external entity. Hence, no asset or liability exists in relation to an external entity, and no revenues or expenses have been incurred.

4. What adjustments are necessary to get from the legal entities' amounts to the group amounts?
A comparison shows the following.

	Legal entities	Group	Difference
Advance to George Ltd	$100 000	0	$(100 000)
Advance from Laura Ltd	100 000	0	(100 000)
Interest revenue	9 000	0	(9 000)
Interest expense	9 000	0	(9 000)

The consolidation worksheet adjustment entries are as follows.

Consolidation			
Advance from Laura Ltd	Dr	100 000	
Advance to George Ltd	Cr		100 000
Interest revenue	Dr	9 000	
Interest expense	Cr		9 000

While the loan remains in existence, the same worksheet entries are required in each period's worksheet.

5. What is the tax effect of the adjustments made?
The effect on net assets is zero. Hence, no tax-effect entry is necessary.

Handy hints

In preparing the consolidation adjustment entries for intragroup borrowings, note the following.

- The adjustment to *intragroup liability* (e.g. *Advance from X Ltd*) and *intragroup receivable* (e.g. *Advance to Y Ltd*) is the amount of intragroup borrowings.
- The adjustment to *interest revenue* and *interest expense* is the amount of interest incurred on the intragroup borrowing during the current period. If some interest remains unpaid at the end of the period, an adjustment to *interest receivable* and *interest payable* for the amount unpaid is also required. If some interest is paid in advance, an adjustment to *interest received in advance* and *prepaid interest* is also required.
- There is no tax adjustment.
- No adjustment needs to be posted in the subsequent periods.

ILLUSTRATIVE EXAMPLE 28.4

Intragroup debentures

On 1 January 2022, Janelle Ltd issues 1000 $100 debentures with an interest rate of 15% p.a. payable on 1 January of each year. Adam Ltd, a wholly owned subsidiary of Janelle Ltd, acquires half the debentures issued. The journal entries made by Janelle Ltd and Adam Ltd for the year ended 30 June 2019 are as follows.

JANELLE LTD				
2022				
Jan. 1	Cash		Dr	100 000	
	Debentures		Cr		100 000
	(Issue of debentures)				
June 30	Interest expense		Dr	7 500	
	Interest payable		Cr		7 500
	(Accrued interest payable of 15% for 6 months)				

ADAM LTD

2022			
Jan. 1	Debentures in Janelle Ltd	Dr	50 000
	Cash	Cr	50 000
	(Debentures acquired)		
June 30	Interest receivable	Dr	3 750
	Interest revenue	Cr	3 750
	(Accrued interest revenue)		

The consolidation entries to adjust for the entries recorded in the legal entities are as follows.

Consolidation

Debentures	Dr	50 000
Debentures in Janelle Ltd	Cr	50 000
Interest payable	Dr	3 750
Interest receivable	Cr	3 750
Interest revenue	Dr	3 750
Interest expense	Cr	3 750

LEARNING CHECK

☐ Intragroup borrowings result in assets in one entity of the group and liabilities in another. Interest payments result in revenues in one entity of the group and expenses in another. Adjustments are necessary to eliminate those effects recorded by the entities within the group.

☐ There are no tax-effect entries relating to adjustments for intragroup borrowings.

SUMMARY

This chapter has dealt with the accounting for intragroup transactions when preparing the consolidation worksheet in accordance with AASB 10/IFRS 10 *Consolidated Financial Statements*. The key points are as follows.

- The group recognises only profits or losses on transactions between the group and entities external to the group.
- The adjustment entries do not affect the records or financial statements of the parent and subsidiaries, even though there may be a record in general journal form of the adjustment entries passed in a worksheet.
- When determining the relevant adjustment entries, the transactions need to be classified into current and prior period transactions.
- The key questions to be answered when preparing the consolidation adjustments for the intragroup transactions are as follows.
    1. Is this a prior period or a current period transaction?
    2. What has been recorded by the legal entities?
    3. What should be reported by the group?
    4. What adjustments are necessary to get from the legal entities' amounts to the group amounts?
    5. What is the tax effect of the adjustments made?

KEY TERMS

consolidated financial statements The financial statements of a group in which the assets, liabilities, equity, income, expenses and cash flows of the parent and its subsidiaries are presented as those of a single economic entity.

group A parent and its subsidiaries.

DEMONSTRATION PROBLEM

28.1 Comprehensive problem

On 1 July 2019, Bull Ltd acquired all the share capital of Shark Ltd for $472 000. At that date, Shark Ltd's equity consisted of the following.

Share capital	$300 000
General reserve	96 000
Retained earnings	56 000

At 1 July 2019, all the identifiable assets and liabilities of Shark Ltd were recorded at fair value. Financial information for Bull Ltd and Shark Ltd for the period ended 30 June 2023 is presented in the left-hand columns of the worksheet in figure 28.2.

Additional information

- On 1 January 2023, Shark Ltd sold inventories costing $30 000 to Bull Ltd for $50 000. Half of the inventories were sold to external entities for $28 000 by 30 June 2023.
- On 1 January 2022, Shark Ltd sold an inventories item costing $2000 to Bull Ltd for $4000. Bull Ltd treated this item as equipment and depreciated it at 5% p.a. on a straight-line basis.
- In the period ended 30 June 2021, Bull Ltd sold land to Shark Ltd for $40 000, which was $20 000 above cost. The land is still held by Shark Ltd at 30 June 2023.
- At 1 July 2022, there was a $6000 profit in the inventories of Bull Ltd from goods acquired from Shark Ltd for $30 000 in the previous period.
- The tax rate is 30%.

Required

Prepare the consolidated financial statements for the period ended 30 June 2023.

SOLUTION

The first step is to determine the business combination valuation and pre-acquisition entries at 30 June 2023. These entries are prepared after undertaking an acquisition analysis for Bull Ltd's acquisition of all the shares in Shark Ltd.

At 1 July 2019:

Net fair value of the identifiable assets and liabilities of Shark Ltd	= $300 000 + $96 000 + $56 000
	= $452 000
Consideration transferred	= $472 000
Goodwill	= $20 000

Consolidation worksheet entries

1. *Business combination valuation entry*

As all the identifiable assets and liabilities of Shark Ltd are recorded at amounts equal to their fair values, the only business combination valuation entry required is that for goodwill.

Goodwill	Dr	20 000	
Business combination valuation reserve	Cr		20 000

2. *Pre-acquisition entry*

The entry at 30 June 2023 is the same as that at acquisition date as there have not been any events affecting that entry since acquisition date (i.e. no transfers from pre-acquisition equity).

Retained earnings (1/7/22)	Dr	56 000	
Share capital	Dr	300 000	
General reserve	Dr	96 000	
Business combination valuation reserve	Dr	20 000	
Shares in Shark Ltd	Cr		472 000

The next step is to prepare the adjustment entries for intragroup transactions.

3. *Profit in ending inventories*

Sales	Dr	50 000	
Cost of sales	Cr		40 000
Inventories	Cr		10 000
Deferred tax asset	Dr	3 000	
Income tax expense	Cr		3 000

Workings

- The transaction on 1 January 2023 involving Shark Ltd selling inventories to Bull Ltd is a current period transaction involving inventories still on hand at the end of the current period.
- Sales within the group are $50 000 and should be eliminated.
- The entire profit on the intragroup sale is $20 000 (i.e. $50 000 − $30 000). The inventories remaining on hand with Bull Ltd at 30 June 2023 are half of the inventories sold intragroup. Therefore, the unrealised profit is $10 000 and that gives the adjustment to inventories (i.e. they should be adjusted from half of $50 000 to half of $30 000).
- Cost of sales recorded by the members of the group is $30 000 for Shark Ltd and $25 000 for Bull Ltd (i.e. half of $50 000, as only half was sold by Bull Ltd); a total of $55 000. Cost of sales for the group is $15 000 (i.e. half of $30 000, the original cost to the group). The adjustment to cost of sales is then $40 000. This could also be calculated as a balancing item having determined the adjustments for sales and inventories (i.e. the difference between the adjustment to sales of $50 000 and the adjustment to inventories of $10 000).
- As the carrying amount of inventories is reduced by $10 000, a deferred tax asset of $3000 (i.e. 30% × $10 000) is raised. Given there is no deferred tax asset in the worksheet in figure 28.2, the adjustment can be included in the worksheet as a debit against the deferred tax liability line item.

4. *Sale in prior period of inventories, classified as equipment*

Retained earnings (1/7/22)	Dr	1 400	
Deferred tax asset	Dr	600	
Equipment	Cr		2 000

Workings
- The intragroup transaction on 1 January 2022 is a prior period transaction involving an intragroup transfer of an inventories item reclassified as a non-current asset.
- Profit after tax on this intragroup transfer is $1400 (i.e. ($4000 − $2000) × (1 − 30%)); retained earnings (opening balance) needs to be adjusted for this after-tax intragroup profit.
- The adjustment to the *non-current asset* is the difference between the transfer price and the original cost (i.e. the intragroup profit).
- As the carrying amount of equipment is reduced by $2000 with no effect on the tax base, a deferred tax asset of $600 (i.e. 30% × $2000) is raised.

5. *Depreciation*

Accumulated depreciation	Dr	150	
Depreciation expense	Cr		100
Retained earnings (1/7/22)	Cr		50
Income tax expense	Dr	30	
Retained earnings (1/7/22)	Dr	15	
Deferred tax asset	Cr		45

Workings
- The adjustment to the *depreciation expense* per annum is the depreciation rate applied by the current owner, Bull Ltd, times the intragroup profit (i.e. 5% × $2000 = $100). The adjustment to current depreciation expense (i.e. 1 full year worth of depreciation expense adjustment, $100) will be posted against the depreciation expense account, while the adjustment to depreciation expenses of prior periods (i.e. only half a year worth of depreciation expense adjustment as the asset was with Bull Ltd only for half a year in the prior period) will be posted against the retained earnings (opening balance).
- The *tax effect* adjustment for depreciation is equal to the tax rate multiplied by the adjustment for depreciation presented above. The tax adjustment for current depreciation expense will be posted against the income tax expense account by debiting it with $30 (i.e. 30% × $100), while the tax adjustment for depreciation expenses of prior periods will be posted against the retained earnings (opening balance) by debiting it with $15 (i.e. 30% × $50). A credit to deferred tax asset will also be posted equal to the tax rate multiplied by the total adjustment to current and prior depreciation expenses (i.e. 30% × ($100 + $50)) to reverse a part of the deferred tax asset recognised as a result of the profit on sale.

6. *Profit on sale of land in previous period*

Retained earnings (1/7/22)	Dr	14 000	
Deferred tax asset	Dr	6 000	
Land	Cr		20 000

Workings
- The intragroup transaction during the period ended 30 June 2021 is a prior period transaction involving the sale of a non-current asset.
- Profit after tax on this intragroup sale recorded in the prior period is $14 000 (i.e. $20 000 × (1 − 30%)); retained earnings (opening balance) needs to be adjusted for this after-tax intragroup profit.
- The adjustment to land is $20 000, equal to the before-tax profit on the intragroup sale, which gives rise to a deferred tax asset of $6000 (30% × $20 000).

7. *Profit in beginning inventories*

Retained earnings (1/7/22)	Dr	4 200	
Income tax expense	Dr	1 800	
Cost of sales	Cr		6 000

Workings

- The intragroup transaction addressed here is a prior period transaction involving inventories still on hand at the beginning of the current period.
- Profit after tax remaining in inventories at 1 July 2022 is $4200 (i.e. $6000 × (1 − 30%)); retained earnings (opening balance) needs to be adjusted for this after-tax unrealised profit.
- The adjustment to cost of sales is $6000, equal to the before-tax profit remaining in inventories held at the beginning of the period.
- The adjustment to income tax expense is the tax rate times the adjustment to cost of sales (i.e. $1800).

8. *Dividend paid*

The financial statements in figure 28.2 show that Bull Ltd has recorded dividend revenue of $5000, while Shark Ltd has recorded dividend paid of $5000. The consolidation worksheet entry is as follows.

| Dividend revenue | Dr | 5 000 | |
| Dividend paid | Cr | | 5 000 |

Workings

- This is a current period transaction involving intragroup dividends paid.
- This consolidation adjustment entry eliminates the revenue raised by Bull Ltd and the dividend paid recognised by Shark Ltd. From the group's point of view, there are no revenues and no reduction in retained earnings caused by these dividends.

9. *Loan: Bull Ltd to Shark Ltd*

The financial statements in figure 28.2 show that Bull Ltd has recorded loan receivable of $5000, while Shark Ltd has recorded loan payable of $5000. The consolidation worksheet entry is as follows.

| Loan payable to Bull Ltd | Dr | 5 000 | |
| Loan receivable from Shark Ltd | Cr | | 5 000 |

Workings

- The loan may have been made in a previous period or the current period. The consolidation worksheet entry will be the same: this entry eliminates the receivable raised by the parent and the payable raised by the subsidiary. From the group's point of view, there are no loans payable or receivable to entities external to the group.

10. *Interest on loan*

The financial statements in figure 28.2 show that Bull Ltd has recorded interest revenue of $500, while Shark Ltd has recorded interest expense of $500. The consolidation worksheet entry is as follows.

| Interest revenue from Shark Ltd | Dr | 500 | |
| Interest expense to Bull Ltd | Cr | | 500 |

Workings

- This intragroup transaction is a current period transaction involving interest payments.
- Bull Ltd records interest revenue of $500 and Shark Ltd records interest expense of $500. No interest was incurred or earned by the group from entities external to the group, so these accounts must be eliminated on consolidation.

11. *Service: Bull Ltd to Shark Ltd*

The financial statements in figure 28.2 show that Bull Ltd has recorded service revenue of $5000, while Shark Ltd has recorded service expense of $5000. The consolidation worksheet entry is as follows.

| Service revenue from Shark Ltd | Dr | 5 000 | |
| Service expense to Bull Ltd | Cr | | 5 000 |

Workings
- This is a current period transaction involving intragroup services.
- This consolidation adjustment entry eliminates the revenue raised by Bull Ltd and the expense raised by Shark Ltd. From the group's point of view, there are no revenues earned or expenses incurred.

Figure 28.2 shows the completed worksheet for preparation of the consolidated financial statements of Bull Ltd and its subsidiary Shark Ltd at 30 June 2023.

Once the effects of all adjustments are added or subtracted horizontally in the worksheet to calculate figures in the right-hand 'group' column, the consolidated financial statements can be prepared, as shown in figure 28.3(a), (b) and (c).

FIGURE 28.2 Consolidation worksheet

Financial statements	Bull Ltd	Shark Ltd		Dr	Cr		Group
				Adjustments			
Sales revenue	$1 190 500	$ 933 500	3	$50 000			$ 2 074 000
Cost of sales	(888 000)	(670 000)			$40 000	3	(1 512 000)
					6 000	7	
Wages and salaries	(62 500)	(32 000)					(94 500)
Depreciation	(5 200)	(4 800)			100	5	(9 900)
Service expense to Bull Ltd	0	(5 000)			5 000	11	0
Interest expense to Bull Ltd	0	(500)			500	10	0
Other expenses	(4 000)	0					(4 000)
Total expenses	(959 700)	(712 300)					(1 620 400)
Service revenue from Shark Ltd	5 000	0	11	5 000			0
Interest revenue from Shark Ltd	500	0	10	500			0
Dividend revenue	5 000	0	8	5 000			0
Profit before income tax	241 300	221 200					453 600
Income tax expense	(97 120)	(118 480)	5	30	3 000	3	(214 430)
			7	1 800			
Profit for the period	144 180	102 720					239 170
Retained earnings (1/7/22)	100 820	70 280	2	56 000	50	5	95 535
			4	1 400			
			5	15			
			6	14 000			
			7	4 200			
	245 000	173 000					334 705
Dividend paid	(80 000)	(5 000)			5 000	8	(80 000)
Retained earnings (30/6/23)	165 000	168 000					254 705
Share capital	500 000	300 000	2	300 000			500 000
Business combination valuation reserve			2	20 000	20 000	1	—
General reserve	135 000	96 000	2	96 000			135 000
	800 000	564 000					889 705
Other components of equity (1/7/22)	4 000	12 000					16 000
Gains on financial assets	1 000	6 000					7 000
Other components of equity (30/6/23)	5 000	18 000					23 000
Total equity	805 000	582 000					912 705
Loan payable to Bull Ltd	0	5 000	9	5 000			0

			Ref	Dr	Cr	Ref	
Deferred tax liability	52 000	30 000	3	3 000	45	5	72 445
			4	600			
			6	6 000			
Total equity and liabilities	$ 857 000	$ 617 000					$ 985 150
Shares in Shark Ltd	$ 472 000	$ 0			$472 000	2	$ 0
Cash	75 000	78 000					153 000
Inventories	168 000	36 000			10 000	3	194 000
Other current assets	10 000	300 000					310 000
Loan receivable from Shark Ltd	5 000	0			5 000	9	0
Financial assets	15 000	68 000				4	83 000
Plant and equipment	52 000	28 000			2 000		78 000
Accumulated depreciation — plant and equipment	(10 000)	(13 000)	5	$ 150			(22 850)
Land	70 000	120 000			20 000	6	170 000
Goodwill	0	0	1	20 000			20 000
	$ 857 000	$ 617 000		$578 195	$578 195		$ 985 150

FIGURE 28.3 (a) Consolidated statement of profit or loss and other comprehensive income

BULL LTD
Consolidated statement of profit or loss and other comprehensive income
for the period ended 30 June 2023

Sales revenue	$ 2 074 000
Cost of sales	(1 512 000)
Gross profit	562 000
Wages and salaries	(94 500)
Depreciation expense	(9 900)
Other expenses	(4 000)
Total expenses	(108 400)
Profit before income tax	453 600
Income tax expense	(214 430)
Profit for the period	**239 170**
Other comprehensive income	
Gain on financial assets	7 000
TOTAL COMPREHENSIVE INCOME FOR THE PERIOD	**$ 246 170**

FIGURE 28.3 (b) Consolidated statement of changes in equity

BULL LTD
Consolidated statement of changes in equity
for the period ended 30 June 2023

Total comprehensive income for the period	$246 170
Retained earnings at 1 July 2022	$ 95 535
Profit for the period	239 170
Dividend paid	(80 000)
Retained earnings at 30 June 2023	$254 705
General reserve at 1 July 2022	$135 000
General reserve at 30 June 2023	$135 000

BULL LTD	
Consolidated statement of changes in equity	
for the period ended 30 June 2023	
Other components of equity at 1 July 2022	$ 16 000
Increases in financial assets	7 000
Other components of equity at 30 June 2023	$ 23 000
Share capital at 1 July 2022	$500 000
Share capital at 30 June 2023	$500 000

FIGURE 28.3	(c) Consolidated statement of financial position

BULL LTD		
Consolidated statement of financial position		
as at 30 June 2023		
Current assets		
Cash		$153 000
Inventories		194 000
Other current assets		310 000
Total current assets		657 000
Non-current assets		
Financial assets		83 000
Plant and equipment	$ 78 000	
Accumulated depreciation — plant and equipment	(22 850)	55 150
Land		170 000
Goodwill		20 000
Total non-current assets		328 150
Total assets		985 150
Non-current liabilities		
Deferred tax liability		72 445
Net assets		**$912 705**
Equity		
Share capital		$500 000
General reserve		135 000
Retained earnings		254 705
Other components of equity		23 000
Total equity		**$912 705**

COMPREHENSION QUESTIONS

1 Why is it necessary to make adjustments for intragroup transactions?

2 Why is it important to identify intragroup transactions as current or previous period transactions?

3 In making consolidation worksheet adjustments for intragroup transactions, sometimes tax-effect entries are made. Why?

4 What are the key questions to consider when preparing consolidation worksheet adjustments for intragroup transactions?

5 What is meant by 'realisation of intragroup profits or losses'?

6 With regards to intragroup transfers of inventories, are adjustments for current period transfers different from adjustments for such transfers happening in a previous period? Explain.

7 When are profits realised in relation to inventories transfers within the group?

8 Where a current period intragroup transaction involves a depreciable asset, why is depreciation expense adjusted?

9 Where a previous period intragroup transaction involves a depreciable asset, why is retained earnings adjusted?

10 When are profits realised on transfers of depreciable assets within the group?

11 Are tax effect-entries required when adjusting for intragroup services or intragroup borrowings? Explain.

12 Are adjustments for post-acquisition intragroup dividends different from those for pre-acquisition intragroup dividends? Explain.

CASE STUDY 28.1

CONSOLIDATION ADJUSTMENTS

Janelle Ltd sold inventories during the current period to its wholly owned subsidiary, Adam Ltd, for $15 000. These items previously cost Janelle Ltd $12 000. Adam Ltd subsequently sold half the items to Nambour Ltd, an external entity, for $8000. The income tax rate is 30%.

The group accountant for Janelle Ltd, Bob Jones, maintains that the appropriate consolidation adjustment entries are as follows.

Sales	Dr	15 000	
Cost of sales	Cr		13 000
Inventories	Cr		2 000
Deferred tax asset	Dr	300	
Income tax expense	Cr		300

Required

1. Discuss whether the entries suggested by Bob Jones are correct, explaining on a line-by-line basis the correct adjustment entries.
2. Determine the consolidation worksheet entries in the following period, assuming the remaining inventories are on-sold to external parties, and explain the adjustments on a line-by-line basis.

CASE STUDY 28.2

DEPRECIATION EXPENSE

At the beginning of the current period, Janelle Ltd sold a depreciable asset to its wholly owned subsidiary, Adam Ltd, for $80 000. Janelle Ltd had originally paid $200 000 for this asset, and by the time of sale to Adam Ltd had charged accumulated depreciation of $150 000. This asset is used differently in Adam Ltd from how it was used in Janelle Ltd; thus, whereas Janelle Ltd used a 10% p.a. straight-line depreciation method, Adam Ltd uses a 20% p.a. straight-line depreciation method.

In calculating the depreciation expense for the consolidated group (as opposed to that recorded by Adam Ltd), the group accountant, Roger Moore, is unsure of which amount the depreciation rate should be applied to ($200 000, $50 000 or $80 000) and which depreciation rate to use (10% or 20%).

Required

Provide a detailed response, explaining which depreciation rate should be used and to what amount it should be applied.

APPLICATION AND ANALYSIS EXERCISES

★ BASIC | ★ ★ MODERATE | ★ ★ ★ DIFFICULT

28.1 Current and prior periods intragroup transfers of inventories ★   LO2, 3

Joey Ltd owns all of the share capital of Chandler Ltd. The income tax rate is 30%. The following transactions took place during the periods ended 30 June 2022 or 30 June 2023.

(a) In January 2023, Joey Ltd sells inventories to Chandler Ltd for $45 000 in cash. The inventories had previously cost Joey Ltd $30 000, and remain unsold by Chandler Ltd at the end of the period.

(b) In February 2023, Joey Ltd sells inventories to Chandler Ltd for $51 000 in cash. These inventories had previously cost Joey Ltd $36 000 and are on-sold externally on 2 April 2023.

(c) In February 2023, Chandler Ltd sells inventories to Joey Ltd for $66 000 in cash (original cost to Chandler Ltd was $48 000) and half are on-sold externally by 30 June 2023.

(d) In March 2023, Joey Ltd sold inventories for $30 000 to Zara Ltd, an external entity. These inventories were transferred from Chandler Ltd on 1 June 2022. The inventories had originally cost Chandler Ltd $18 000, and were sold to Joey Ltd for $36 000.

Required

In relation to the above intragroup transactions:

1. prepare adjusting journal entries for the consolidation worksheet at 30 June 2023
2. explain in detail why you made each adjusting journal entry.

28.2 Current and prior periods intragroup transfers of inventories ★ 　　　　　　　**LO2, 3**

Monica Ltd owns all the share capital of Phoebe Ltd. The income tax rate is 30%. The following transactions took place during the periods ended 30 June 2022 or 30 June 2023.

(a) On 1 May 2022, Monica Ltd sold inventories to Phoebe Ltd for $5000 on credit, recording a profit of $1000. Half of the inventories were unsold by Phoebe Ltd at 30 June 2022 and none at 30 June 2023. Phoebe Ltd paid half the amount owed on 15 June 2022 and the rest on 1 July 2022.

(b) On 10 June 2022, Phoebe Ltd sold inventories to Monica Ltd for $18 000 in cash. The inventories had previously cost Phoebe Ltd $14 000. Half of these inventories were unsold by Monica Ltd at 30 June 2022 and 30% at 30 June 2023.

(c) On 1 January 2023, Phoebe Ltd sold inventories costing $5000 to Monica Ltd at a transfer price of $8000, paid in cash. The entire inventories were sold by Monica Ltd to external entities by 30 June 2023.

Required

In relation to the above intragroup transactions:

1. prepare adjusting journal entries for the consolidation worksheet at 30 June 2022 and 30 June 2023

2. explain in detail why you made each adjusting journal entry.

28.3 Current and prior periods intragroup transfers of non-current assets ★ 　　　　**LO2, 4**

Sophie Ltd owns all the share capital of Ruby Ltd. The income tax rate is 30%. The following transactions took place during the periods ended 30 June 2022 or 30 June 2023.

(a) On 1 July 2021, Sophie Ltd sold a motor vehicle to Ruby Ltd for $15 000. This had a carrying amount to Sophie Ltd of $12 000. Both entities depreciate motor vehicles at a rate of 10% p.a. on cost.

(b) Ruby Ltd manufactures items of machinery which are used as property, plant and equipment by other companies, including Sophie Ltd. On 1 January 2022, Ruby Ltd sold such an item to Sophie Ltd for $62 000, its cost to Ruby Ltd being only $55 000 to manufacture. Sophie Ltd charges depreciation on these machines at 20% p.a. on the diminishing value.

(c) Sophie Ltd manufactures certain items which it then markets through Ruby Ltd. During the period ended 30 June 2023, Sophie Ltd sold for $12 000 items to Ruby Ltd at cost plus 20%. By 30 June 2023, Ruby Ltd has sold to external entities 75% of these transferred items.

(d) Ruby Ltd also sells second-hand machinery. Sophie Ltd sold one of its depreciable assets (original cost $40 000, accumulated depreciation $32 000) to Ruby Ltd for $5000 on 1 January 2023. Ruby Ltd had not on-sold the item by 30 June 2023.

(e) Ruby Ltd sold a depreciable asset (carrying amount of $22 000) to Sophie Ltd on 1 January 2022 for $25 000. Both entities charge depreciation in relation to these items at a rate of 10% p.a. On 31 December 2022, Sophie Ltd sold this asset to Dubbo Ltd, an external entity, for $20 000.

Required

In relation to the above intragroup transactions:

1. prepare adjusting journal entries for the consolidation worksheet at 30 June 2022 and 30 June 2023

2. explain in detail why you made each adjusting journal entry.

28.4 Current and prior periods intragroup transfers of non-current assets ★ ★ 　　　**LO2, 4**

Fred Ltd owns all the share capital of Wilma Ltd. The income tax rate is 30%. The following transactions took place during the periods ended 30 June 2022 or 30 June 2023.

(a) Wilma Ltd sold some land to Fred Ltd in December 2021. The land had originally cost Wilma Ltd $25 000, but was sold to Fred Ltd for only $20 000. To help Fred Ltd pay for the land, Wilma Ltd gave Fred Ltd an interest-free loan of $12 000, and the balance was paid in cash. The land was sold to external entities in June 2022 for $30 000 and immediately after that, Fred Ltd paid the amount owed to Wilma Ltd.

(b) On 1 July 2021, Fred Ltd sold equipment costing $10 000 to Wilma Ltd for $12 000. Fred Ltd had not charged any depreciation on the asset before the sale as it just purchased it from an external entity. Both entities depreciate items of equipment at 10% p.a. on cost. The equipment is still held by Wilma Ltd at 30 June 2023.

(c) On 1 July 2021, Wilma Ltd sold a building to Fred Ltd for $200 000 in cash. This item had an original cost of $500 000 and accumulated depreciation for Wilma Ltd at time of sale of $250 000. The remaining useful life of that building is estimated to be 10 years and the future economic benefits are assumed to be derived consistently throughout the life. The building was sold to external entities on 1 April 2023 for $210 000.

(d) On 1 July 2022, Fred Ltd sold an item regarded as equipment, to Wilma Ltd which regarded it as inventories. At the time of the sale, the carrying amount of the item to Fred Ltd was $5000 and it was sold to Wilma Ltd for $4000. The item is sold to an external entity by Wilma Ltd by 30 June 2023.

(e) On 1 October 2022, Fred Ltd sold an item of machinery to Wilma Ltd for $6000. This item had cost Fred Ltd $4000. Fred Ltd regarded this item as inventories whereas Wilma Ltd intended to use it as a non-current asset. Wilma Ltd charges depreciation at the rate of 10% p.a. on cost. The machine was sold to external entities on 1 April 2023 for $5000.

Required

In relation to the above intragroup transactions:

1. prepare adjusting journal entries for the consolidation worksheet at 30 June 2022 and 30 June 2023
2. explain in detail why you made each adjusting journal entry.

28.5 Current period intragroup transfers of inventories and non-current assets ★   LO2, 3, 4

Rachel Ltd owns all the share capital of Green Ltd. The income tax rate is 30%. During the period ended 30 June 2023, the following transactions took place.

(a) Green Ltd sold inventories costing $75 000 to Rachel Ltd. Green Ltd recorded a $15 000 profit before tax on these transactions. At 30 June 2023, Rachel Ltd has none of these goods still on hand.

(b) Rachel Ltd sold inventories costing $12 000 to Green Ltd for $27 000. By 30 June 2023, one-third of these were sold to Willow Ltd for $14 250 and one-third to Layla Ltd for $13 500; the rest are still on hand with Green Ltd. Willow Ltd and Layla Ltd are external entities.

(c) On 1 January 2023, Rachel Ltd sold land for cash to Green Ltd at $30 000 above cost. The land is still on hand with Green Ltd.

(d) Green Ltd sold a warehouse to Rachel Ltd for $150 000 on 1 July 2022. The carrying amount of this warehouse recognised by Green Ltd at the time of sale was $123 000. Rachel Ltd charges depreciation at a rate of 5% p.a. on cost.

Required

In relation to the above intragroup transactions:

1. prepare adjusting journal entries for the consolidation worksheet at 30 June 2023
2. explain in detail why you made each adjusting journal entry.

28.6 Current and prior period intragroup services ★   LO2, 5

Darcy Ltd owns all the share capital of Isabella Ltd. The following intragroup transactions took place during the periods ended 30 June 2022 or 30 June 2023.

(a) Isabella Ltd paid $20 000 during the period ended 30 July 2022 and $40 000 during the period ended 30 June 2023 as management fees for services provided by Darcy Ltd.

(b) Isabella Ltd rented a spare warehouse to Darcy Ltd starting from 1 July 2021 for 1 year. The total charge for the rental was $30 000, and Darcy Ltd paid this amount to Isabella Ltd on 1 January 2022.

(c) Isabella Ltd rented a spare warehouse from Darcy Ltd for $50 000 p.a. The rental contract started at 1 January 2022, and the payments are made annually in advance on 1 January.

Required

In relation to the above intragroup transactions:

1. prepare adjusting journal entries for the consolidation worksheet at 30 June 2022 and 30 June 2023
2. explain in detail why you made each adjusting journal entry.

28.7 Current and prior period intragroup dividends ★   LO2, 6

Maggie Ltd owns all the share capital of Taylor Ltd. The following intragroup transactions took place during the periods ended 30 June 2022 or 30 June 2023.

(a) During the period ended 30 June 2022, Taylor Ltd paid an interim dividend of $40 000 out of pre-acquisition profits. As a result, the investment in Taylor Ltd is considered to be impaired by $40 000.

(b) On 30 June 2022, Taylor Ltd declared a final dividend of $25 000 out of post-acquisition profits.

(c) During the period ended 30 June 2023, Taylor Ltd paid an interim dividend of $30 000 out of post-acquisition profits.

(d) On 30 June 2023, Taylor Ltd declared a final dividend of $50 000 out of post-acquisition profits.

Required

In relation to the above intragroup transactions:

1. prepare adjusting journal entries for the consolidation worksheet at 30 June 2022 and 30 June 2023

2. explain in detail why you made each adjusting journal entry.

28.8 Current and prior period intragroup debentures ★ ★   **LO2, 7**

Ross Ltd owns all the share capital of Geller Ltd. The following transactions are independent.

(a) On 1 January 2022, Geller Ltd issues 20 000 debentures at the nominal value of $20 with an interest rate of 8% p.a., payable half-yearly on 30 June and 31 December each year. Debentures are to be redeemed after 3 years. Ross Ltd takes 100% of the debentures issued.

(b) On 1 January 2022, Geller Ltd issues 20 000 debentures at the nominal value of $20 with an interest rate of 8% p.a., payable half-yearly on 30 June and 31 December each year. Debentures are to be redeemed after 3 years. Ross Ltd takes 50% of the debentures issued.

(c) On 1 January 2022, Geller Ltd issues 20 000 debentures at the nominal value of $20 with an interest rate of 8% p.a., payable half-yearly on 30 June and 31 December each year. Debentures are to be redeemed after 3 years. Ross Ltd takes 25% of the debentures issued. On 31 March 2022, Ross Ltd acquired another 25% of these debentures *cum div.* on the open market for $9 each.

Required

In relation to the above intragroup transactions:

1. prepare adjusting journal entries for the consolidation worksheet at 30 June 2022 and 30 June 2023

2. explain in detail why you made each adjusting journal entry.

28.9 Current and prior period intragroup borrowings ★   **LO2, 7**

Tony Ltd owns all the share capital of Sean Ltd. The following transactions are independent.

(a) Sean Ltd gives $50 000 as an interest-free loan to Tony Ltd on 1 July 2021. Tony Ltd made a $20 000 repayment by 30 June 2022.

(b) Sean Ltd borrows $50 000 from Tony Ltd on 1 July 2021 with an interest rate of 6% p.a. The interest is to be paid annually in arrears, starting on 30 June 2022.

(c) Sean Ltd borrows $50 000 from Tony Ltd on 31 December 2021 with an interest rate of 6% p.a. The interest is to be paid annually in advance, starting on 31 December 2021.

(d) Sean Ltd borrows $50 000 from Tony Ltd on 31 December 2021 with an interest rate of 6% p.a. The interest is to be paid biannually in arrears, starting on 30 June 2022.

(e) Sean Ltd borrows $50 000 from Tony Ltd on 1 July 2021 with an interest rate of 6% p.a. The interest is to be paid biannually in advance, starting on 1 July 2021.

Required

In relation to the above intragroup transactions:

1. prepare adjusting journal entries for the consolidation worksheet at 30 June 2022 and 30 June 2023

2. explain in detail why you made each adjusting journal entry.

28.10 Intragroup transfers of inventories, non-current assets, services and dividends ★ **LO2, 3, 4, 5, 6**

Karen Ltd owns all the share capital of Anne Ltd. The income tax rate is 30%. The following transactions took place during the periods ended 30 June 2021 to 30 June 2023.

(a) In February 2021, Karen Ltd sold inventories to Anne Ltd for $6000, at a mark-up of 20% on cost. One-quarter of these inventories were unsold by Anne Ltd at 30 June 2021 to external entities, and none at 30 June 2022.

(b) On 1 January 2021, Anne Ltd sold a new tractor to Karen Ltd for $20 000. This had cost Anne Ltd $16 000 on that day. Both entities charged depreciation at the rate of 10% p.a. on the diminishing balance. The tractor was still on hand with Karen Ltd at 30 June 2023.

(c) A non-current asset with a carrying amount of $1000 was sold by Karen Ltd to Anne Ltd for $800 on 1 January 2023. Anne Ltd intended to use this item as inventories, being a seller of second-hand goods. The item was still on hand at 30 June 2023.

(d) Anne Ltd rented a spare warehouse to Karen Ltd starting from 1 July 2022 for 1 year. The total charge for the rental was $300, and Karen Ltd paid half of this amount to Anne Ltd on 1 January 2023 and the rest is to be paid on 1 July 2023.

(e) In December 2022, Anne Ltd paid a $1500 interim dividend.

(f) During March 2023, Anne Ltd declared a $3000 dividend. The dividend was paid in August 2023.

Required

In relation to the above intragroup transactions:

1. prepare adjusting journal entries for the consolidation worksheet at 30 June 2022 and 30 June 2023

2. explain in detail why you made each adjusting journal entry.

28.11 Intragroup transfers of inventories, non-current assets, services and borrowings ★ ★   **LO2, 3, 4, 5, 7**

Kaitlyn Ltd owns all the share capital of Eve Ltd. The income tax rate is 30%. The following transactions took place during the periods ended 30 June 2022 or 30 June 2023.

(a) On 1 May 2022, Eve Ltd sold inventories costing $600 to Kaitlyn Ltd for $1200 on credit. On 30 June 2022, only half of these goods had been sold by Kaitlyn Ltd to external entities, and Kaitlyn Ltd had paid $600 to Eve Ltd. All remaining inventories were sold to external entities by 30 June 2023 and Kaitlyn Ltd paid the outstanding amount to Eve Ltd on 5 May 2023.

(b) On 1 January 2022, Kaitlyn Ltd sold an item of plant to Eve Ltd for $10 000. Immediately before the sale, Kaitlyn Ltd had the item of plant on its accounts for $12 000. Kaitlyn Ltd depreciated items at 5% p.a. on the diminishing balance and Eve Ltd used the straight-line method over 10 years.

(c) An inventories item with a cost of $4000 was sold by Kaitlyn Ltd to Eve Ltd for $3600 on 1 January 2023. Eve Ltd intended to use this item as equipment. Both entities charge depreciation at the rate of 10% p.a. on the diminishing balance on non-current assets. The item was still on hand at 30 June 2023.

(d) Kaitlyn Ltd provided management services to Eve Ltd during the period ended 30 June 2023. The total charge for those services was $5000, and that was unpaid at 30 June 2023.

(e) Kaitlyn Ltd borrows $60 000 from Eve Ltd on 1 July 2021 with an interest rate of 6% p.a. The loan is for 5 years. The interest is to be paid biannually in arrears, starting on 31 December 2021.

Required

In relation to the above intragroup transactions:

1. prepare adjusting journal entries for the consolidation worksheet at 30 June 2022 and 30 June 2023

2. explain in detail why you made each adjusting journal entry.

28.12 Consolidation worksheet with pre-acquisition equity transfers and intragroup transactions ★   **LO3, 4, 5, 6, 7**

On 1 January 2020, Olivia Ltd acquired all the share capital of Chloe Ltd for $300 000. The equity of Chloe Ltd at 1 January 2020 was as follows.

Share capital	$200 000
Retained earnings	50 000
General reserve	20 000

At this date, all identifiable assets and liabilities of Chloe Ltd were recorded at fair value.

On 1 May 2023, Chloe Ltd transferred $15 000 from the general reserve (pre-acquisition) to retained earnings. The income tax rate is 30%.

The following information has been provided about transactions between the two entities.

(a) The beginning and ending inventories of Olivia Ltd and Chloe Ltd in relation to the current period ended on 31 December 2023 included the following inventories transferred intragroup.

	Olivia Ltd	Chloe Ltd
Beginning inventories:		
Transfer price	$2 000	$1 200
Original cost	1 400	800
Ending inventories:		
Transfer price	500	900
Original cost	300	700

Olivia Ltd sold inventories to Chloe Ltd during the current period for $3000. This was $500 above the cost of the inventories to Olivia Ltd. Chloe Ltd sold inventories to Olivia Ltd in the current period for $2500, recording a pre-tax profit of $800.

(b) Olivia Ltd sold an inventories item to Chloe Ltd on 1 July 2023 for use as machinery. The item cost Olivia Ltd $4000 and was sold to Chloe Ltd for $6000. Chloe Ltd depreciated the item at a rate of 10% p.a. on cost.

(c) On 31 December 2023, Chloe Ltd owes Olivia Ltd $1000 for items sold on credit.

(d) Chloe Ltd undertook an advertising campaign for Olivia Ltd during the period ended 31 December 2023. Olivia Ltd was charged and paid $8000 to Chloe Ltd for this service.

(e) Olivia Ltd received dividends totalling $63 000 during the current period ended 31 December 2023 from Chloe Ltd. These dividends were declared in the current period out of post-acquisition profits.

Required

1. Prepare the acquisition analysis at 1 January 2020.
2. Prepare the business combination valuation entries and pre-acquisition entries at 1 January 2020.
3. Prepare the business combination valuation entries and pre-acquisition entries at 31 December 2023.
4. Prepare the consolidation worksheet journal entries to eliminate the effects of intragroup transactions at 31 December 2023.

28.13 Consolidation with differences between carrying amount and fair value at acquisition date, impairment of goodwill and intragroup transactions ★   LO1, 2, 3, 4, 5, 6, 7

Financial information for Skye Ltd and its 100% owned subsidiary, Blue Ltd, for the period ended 31 December 2023 is provided below.

	Skye Ltd	Blue Ltd
Sales revenue	$50 000	$47 200
Dividend revenue	2 000	0
Gain on sale of property, plant and equipment	2 000	4 000
Other income	2 000	4 000
Total income	56 000	55 200
Cost of sales	42 000	36 000
Other expenses	6 000	2 000
Total expenses	48 000	38 000
Profit before income tax	8 000	17 200
Income tax expense	2 700	3 900
Profit for the period	5 300	13 300
Retained earnings (1/1/23)	12 000	6 000
	17 300	19 300
Interim dividend paid	5 000	2 000
Retained earnings (31/12/23)	$12 300	$17 300

Skye Ltd acquired its shares in Blue Ltd at 1 January 2023 for $40 000 on a *cum div.* basis. At that date, Blue Ltd recorded share capital of $20 000. Blue Ltd had declared prior to the acquisition a dividend of $6000 that was paid in March 2023.

At 1 January 2023, all identifiable assets and liabilities of Blue Ltd were recorded at fair value except for inventories, for which the carrying amount was $800 less than fair value. Some of the inventories have been a little slow to sell, and 10% of it is still on hand at 31 December 2023. Inventories on hand in Blue Ltd at 31 December 2023 also includes some items acquired from Skye Ltd during the period ended 31 December 2023. These were sold by Skye Ltd for $10 000, at a profit before tax of $2000.

Half of the goodwill on acquisition of Blue Ltd by Skye Ltd was written off as the result of an impairment test on 31 December 2023.

During March 2023, Skye Ltd provided some management services to Blue Ltd at a fee of $1000 paid by 31 December 2023.

On 1 July 2023, Blue Ltd sold machinery to Skye Ltd at a gain of $4000. This machinery had a carrying amount to Blue Ltd of $40 000, and was considered by Skye Ltd to have a further 5-year useful life.

By 31 December 2023, the financial assets acquired by Skye Ltd and Blue Ltd from external entities increased in value by $2000 and $1300 respectively with gains and losses being recognised in other comprehensive income.

The income tax rate is 30%.

Required

1. Prepare the acquisition analysis at 1 January 2023.
2. Prepare the business combination valuation entries and pre-acquisition entries at 1 January 2023.
3. Prepare the business combination valuation entries and pre-acquisition entries at 31 December 2023.
4. Prepare the consolidation worksheet journal entries to eliminate the effects of intragroup transactions at 31 December 2023.
5. Discuss the concept of 'realisation' using the intragroup transactions in this question to illustrate the concept.
6. Prepare the consolidation worksheet for the preparation of the consolidated financial statements for the period ended 31 December 2023.
7. Prepare the consolidated statement of profit or loss and other comprehensive income for Skye Ltd and its subsidiary, Blue Ltd, at 31 December 2023.

28.14 Consolidation with differences between carrying amount and fair value at acquisition date and intragroup transactions ★   **LO3, 4, 5, 6, 7**

Waltzing Ltd purchased 100% of the shares of Matilda Ltd on 1 July 2020 for $50 000. At that date the equity of the two entities was as follows.

	Waltzing Ltd	Matilda Ltd
Asset revaluation surplus	$25 000	$ 4 000
Retained earnings	14 500	2 800
Share capital	50 000	40 000

At 1 July 2020, all the identifiable assets and liabilities of Matilda Ltd were recorded at fair value except for the following.

	Carrying amount	Fair value
Inventories	$ 3 000	$ 3 500
Plant and equipment (cost $80 000)	60 000	61 000

All of the inventories were sold by December 2020. The plant and equipment had a further 5-year useful life. Any valuation adjustments are made on consolidation.

Financial information for Waltzing Ltd and Matilda Ltd for the period ended 30 June 2022 is as follows.

	Waltzing Ltd	Matilda Ltd
Sales revenue	$39 000	$20 000
Dividend revenue	2 200	800
Total income	41 200	20 800
Cost of sales	30 000	15 000
Other expenses	5 400	2 500
Total expenses	35 400	17 500
Gross profit	5 800	3 300
Gain on sale of furniture	0	250
Profit before income tax	5 800	3 550
Income tax expense	1 500	1 100

	Waltzing Ltd	Matilda Ltd
Profit for the period	4 300	2 450
Retained earnings (1/7/21)	7 250	1 400
	11 550	3 850
Interim dividend paid	2 000	1 000
Final dividend declared	4 000	1 200
	6 000	2 200
Retained earnings (30/6/22)	$ 5 500	$ 1 650

Additional information

- Waltzing Ltd records dividend receivable as revenue when dividends are declared.
- The beginning inventories of Matilda Ltd at 1 July 2021 included goods which cost Matilda Ltd $1000. Matilda Ltd purchased these inventories from Waltzing Ltd at cost plus 33% mark-up.
- Intragroup sales totalled $5000 for the period ended 30 June 2022. Sales from Waltzing Ltd to Matilda Ltd, at cost plus 10% mark-up, amounted to $2800. The ending inventories of Waltzing Ltd included goods which cost Waltzing Ltd $2200. Waltzing Ltd purchased these inventories from Matilda Ltd at cost plus 10% mark-up.
- On 31 December 2021, Matilda Ltd sold Waltzing Ltd office furniture for $1500. This furniture originally cost Matilda Ltd $1500 and was written down to $1250 just before the intragroup sale. Waltzing Ltd depreciates furniture at the rate of 10% p.a. on cost.
- The asset revaluation surplus relates to land. The following movements occurred in this account.

	Waltzing Ltd	Matilda Ltd
1 July 2020 to 30 June 2021	$1 500	$(250)
1 July 2021 to 30 June 2022	1 000	250

- The income tax rate is 30%.

Required

1. Prepare the acquisition analysis at 1 July 2020.
2. Prepare the business combination valuation entries and pre-acquisition entries at 1 July 2020.
3. Prepare the business combination valuation entries and pre-acquisition entries at 30 June 2022.
4. Prepare the consolidation worksheet journal entries to eliminate the effects of intragroup transactions at 30 June 2022.
5. Prepare the consolidation worksheet for the preparation of the consolidated financial statements for the period ended 30 June 2022.
6. Prepare the consolidated statement of profit or loss and other comprehensive income for the period ended 30 June 2022.

ACKNOWLEDGEMENTS

Photo: © wavebreakmedia / Shutterstock.com

Photo: © Brand X / Getty Images

Text: © 2019 Australian Accounting Standards Board (AASB). The text, graphics and layout of this publication are protected by Australian copyright law and the comparable law of other countries. No part of the publication may be reproduced, stored or transmitted in any form or by any means without the prior written permission of the AASB except as permitted by law. For reproduction or publication, permission should be sought in writing from the AASB. Requests in the first instance should be addressed to the National Director, Australian Accounting Standards Board, PO Box 204, Collins Street West, Victoria 8007.

Text: © IFRS. This publication contains copyright material of the IFRS Foundation in respect of which all rights are reserved. Reproduced by John Wiley & Sons Australia, Ltd with the permission of the IFRS Foundation. No permission granted to third parties to reproduce or distribute. For full access to IFRS Standards and the work of the IFRS Foundation please visit http://eifrs.ifrs.org. The International Accounting Standards Board, the IFRS Foundation, the authors and the publishers do not accept responsibility for any loss caused by acting or refraining from acting in reliance on the material in this publication, whether such loss is caused by negligence or otherwise.

CHAPTER 29

Consolidation: non-controlling interest

CHAPTER AIM

This chapter discusses the application of AASB 10/IFRS 10 *Consolidated Financial Statements* to a group structure where the parent owns less than 100% of the shares of a subsidiary. This case requires the distinction between the parent interest in the subsidiary and the remaining (i.e. non-controlling) interest. The objective of this chapter is to explain the nature of the non-controlling interest and to describe the measurement of the non-controlling interest in the subsidiary's equity, the preparation of consolidation worksheet adjustment entries necessary in the presence of non-controlling interest and the subsequent disclosure of that interest in the consolidated financial statements.

LEARNING OBJECTIVES

After studying this chapter, you should be able to:

29.1 discuss the nature of the non-controlling interest (NCI)

29.2 explain the principles of measurement and disclosure of the NCI

29.3 explain how the consolidation worksheet is changed by the presence of the NCI

29.4 identify how the existence of the NCI affects the consolidation process, particularly the measurement of goodwill

29.5 explain how the NCI is calculated in a three-step process

29.6 identify how the existence of intragroup transactions affects the measurement of the NCI

29.7 explain how a gain on bargain purchase affects the measurement of the NCI

29.8 identify the disclosures required in relation to the NCI.

CONCEPTS FOR REVIEW

Before studying this chapter, you should understand and, if necessary, revise:
- the nature of the group
- the acquisition analysis and the structure of the consolidation worksheet for wholly owned subsidiaries
- the rationale for valuation adjustments and pre-acquisition equity elimination for wholly owned subsidiaries
- the business combination valuation entries and pre-acquisition entries posted in the consolidation worksheet for wholly owned subsidiaries
- the rationale for adjustments for the impact of intragroup transactions
- the concept of profit realisation in relation to intragroup transactions
- the adjustment entries for intragroup transactions posted in the consolidation worksheet.

29.1 The nature of a non-controlling interest

LEARNING OBJECTIVE 29.1 Discuss the nature of the non-controlling interest (NCI).

In Australia, many entities have mainly wholly owned subsidiaries. However, some entities still prefer to have less than 100% ownership interest in some subsidiaries. Ernst & Young (2010, p. 2) provide four potential reasons for this preference:

1. to decrease the cash needed as consideration to acquire the control over the subsidiary
2. to incentivise the executives of the subsidiary to manage the entity to increase shareholder value by allowing executives to hold a part of the ownership interest as non-controlling interest
3. to comply with regulatory requirements, such as competition laws, which may prevent an entity from acquiring 100% of a competitor, customer or supplier
4. to partner with local investors to limit risk and exposure when expanding into emerging markets.

Therefore, after discussing the case of wholly owned subsidiaries in chapters 27 and 28, we now need to consider the case of partially owned subsidiaries. According to the concept of consolidation adopted by AASB/IASB, a group consists of all the assets and liabilities of the parent and its subsidiaries, regardless of the ownership that the parent entity has in its subsidiaries. However, where a parent owns less than 100% of the shares in a subsidiary, other entities own the remaining non-controlling interest. Appendix A of AASB 10/IFRS 10 *Consolidated Financial Statements* defines **non-controlling interest (NCI)** as:

> equity in a subsidiary not attributable, directly or indirectly, to a parent.

The non-controlling interest is still regarded as equity of the group. Hence, there are effectively two equity parties in the group: the owners of the parent and the NCI. Classification of the NCI as equity affects both the calculation of the NCI as well as how it is disclosed in the consolidated financial statements. Measurement and disclosure of the NCI are mainly determined by AASB 10/IFRS 10 and AASB 101/IAS 1 *Presentation of Financial Statements*.

LEARNING CHECK

- ☐ Many entities have mainly wholly owned subsidiaries, but some entities still prefer partially owned subsidiaries.
- ☐ Reasons for preferring partially owned subsidiaries include limited financial resources, executive and shareholders' interest alignment, regulatory requirements or risk protection.
- ☐ In a subsidiary that is not wholly owned by the parent there are two ownership interests: the parent and the non-controlling interest (NCI).
- ☐ The non-controlling interest is defined as equity in a subsidiary not attributable, directly or indirectly, to a parent.
- ☐ Classification of the NCI as equity affects the calculation of the NCI and how it is disclosed in the consolidated financial statements.
- ☐ Measurement and disclosure of the NCI are mainly determined by AASB 10/IFRS 10 *Consolidated Financial Statements* and AASB 101/IAS 1 *Presentation of Financial Statements*.

29.2 Measurement and disclosure of the NCI share of equity

LEARNING OBJECTIVE 29.2 Explain the principles of measurement and disclosure of the NCI.

Before looking at the detailed mechanics of calculating the NCI share of equity, it is useful to understand the measurement principles relating to the NCI and how the NCI is disclosed in the consolidated financial statements.

29.2.1 Measurement of the NCI share of equity

The NCI, being a part of the equity in the subsidiary, contributes to the equity of the consolidated group and so is entitled to a share of consolidated equity. Nevertheless, the measurement of the NCI share of equity involves firstly allocating to the NCI a part of the subsidiary's equity proportionate to the ownership interest that it holds in the subsidiary. However, because the subsidiary's equity is affected by profits or losses made in relation to transactions within the group, the calculation of the NCI is affected by the existence of intragroup transactions. The NCI is only entitled to the share of the subsidiary's equity that is reflected in the consolidated equity. In other words, the NCI is entitled to a share of the equity of the subsidiary adjusted for the effects of profits or losses made on intragroup transactions. This is discussed in more detail in section 29.6.

29.2.2 Disclosure of NCI

The consolidated financial statements show the financial position and financial performance of the group as a single economic entity. However, the presentation of the total equity of the group in the consolidated financial statements is such that the equity attributable to the owners of the parent is shown separately from the equity attributable to the NCI. The reason the accounting standards ask for separate disclosure of the parent and NCI share of equity is that the owners of the parent want to determine the profitability and the equity of the group that will accrue to them, separate from that belonging to the NCI. As such, disclosure of the NCI is required in the consolidated statement of profit or loss and other comprehensive income, the consolidated statement of changes in equity and the consolidated statement of financial position.

Statement of profit or loss and other comprehensive income

According to paragraph 81B of AASB 101/IAS 1:

> An entity shall present the following items, in addition to the profit or loss and other comprehensive income sections, as allocation of profit or loss and other comprehensive income for the period:
> (a) profit or loss for the period attributable to:
>   (i) non-controlling interests, and
>   (ii) owners of the parent.
> (b) comprehensive income for the period attributable to:
>   (i) non-controlling interests, and
>   (ii) owners of the parent.
> If an entity presents profit or loss in a separate statement it shall present (a) in that statement.

Note that in terms of the various line items in the statement, such as revenues and expenses, there is no requirement to separate the amounts attributable to owners of the parent and those attributable to the NCI.

Figure 29.1 shows how the consolidated statement of profit or loss and other comprehensive income may be shown.

FIGURE 29.1	Disclosure of the NCI in the statement of profit or loss and other comprehensive income

WALLABY LTD **Consolidated statement of profit or loss and other comprehensive income** for the year ended 30 June 2023	2023 $m	2022 $m
Revenue	500	450
Expenses	280	260
Gross profit	220	190
Finance costs	40	35
	180	155
Share of after-tax profit of associates	30	25
Profit before tax	**210**	**180**
Income tax expense	(28)	(22)
Profit for the year	**182**	**158**
Other comprehensive income	31	24
Total comprehensive income for the year	**213**	**182**
Profit attributable to:		
Owners of the parent	151	140
Non-controlling interests	31	18
	182	158
Total comprehensive income attributable to:		
Owners of the parent	179	160
Non-controlling interests	34	22
	213	182

Statement of changes in equity

According to paragraph 106 of AASB 101/IAS 1:

> The statement of changes in equity includes the following information:
> (a) total comprehensive income for the period, showing separately the total amounts attributable to owners of the parent and to non-controlling interests ...

There is no requirement to show the NCI share of each equity account. Figure 29.2 provides an example of disclosures in the consolidated statement of changes of equity.

FIGURE 29.2 Disclosure of NCI in the statement of changes in equity

	Share capital $m	Revaluation surplus $m	Translation reserve $m	Retained earnings $m	Total $m	Non-controlling interest $m	Owners of the parent $m
		WALLABY LTD Consolidated statement of changes in equity (extract) for the year ended 30 June 2023					
			Equity				
Balance at 1 July 2022	400	120	100	250	870	130	740
Changes in accounting policy	–	–	–	–			
Total comprehensive income for the period	–	21	10	182	213	34	179
Dividends	–	–	–	(150)	(150)	(10)	(140)
Issue of share capital	–	–	–	–	–	–	–
Balance at 30 June 2023	400	141	110	282	933	154	779

Statement of financial position

According to paragraph 22 of AASB 10/IFRS 10:

> A parent shall present non-controlling interests in the consolidated statement of financial position within equity, separately from the equity of the owners of the parent.

Paragraph 54(q) of AASB 101/IAS 1 confirms this requirement.

The NCI share of the different categories of equity does not need to be separately disclosed. Note that the consolidated assets and liabilities are those for the whole of the group; it is only the equity that is divided into parent and NCI shares. Figure 29.3 shows how the equity may be disclosed in a consolidated statement of financial position in the presence of NCI.

FIGURE 29.3 Disclosure of NCI in the statement of financial position

WALLABY LTD Consolidated statement of financial position (extract) as at 30 June 2023	2023 $m	2022 $m
Equity		
Share capital	400	400
Other reserves	251	220
Retained earnings	282	250
Total equity	933	870
Non-controlling interests	154	130
Equity attributable to owners of the parent	779	740

29.3 The consolidation worksheet in the presence of NCI

LEARNING OBJECTIVE 29.3 Explain how the consolidation worksheet is changed by the presence of the NCI.

The consolidation worksheet used for a wholly owned subsidiary is changed to enable the disclosures required where NCI exists in a subsidiary. Figure 29.4 contains a pro-forma example of such a worksheet. (The assets and liabilities section is not included, as it is not affected by the presence of NCI.) In relation to this worksheet, note the following.

- As in the case of wholly owned subsidiaries, the column on the right of the 'Adjustments' column is named 'Group'. The 'Adjustments' column contains the business combination valuation reserve (BCVR) and pre-acquisition entries and the adjustments for intragroup transactions. Combining these adjustments with the financial statement numbers of both the parent and subsidiary provides the group (consolidated) amounts. Note that the consolidated amounts related to equity include the equity attributable to the owners of the parent and to NCI. For example, the consolidated share capital is $200, being the sum of the share capital attributable to the owners of the parent and to the NCI.

- Two columns (one for debit and one for credit entries) collectively named 'NCI' are added to the normal worksheet that was used for wholly owned subsidiaries. These columns record the NCI journal entries prepared in order to transfer the NCI share of each *individual consolidated equity* account from the consolidated amounts to an account that recognises the NCI share of *total consolidated equity* (see later in this chapter). For example, the NCI share of consolidated share capital of $40 is transferred from the consolidated share capital amount (by being included on the 'NCI' debit column in the 'Share capital' line) to the NCI share of total equity (by being on the 'NCI' credit column in the new 'Total equity: NCI' line described below).

- One more column, named 'Parent', is added which contains the parent share of consolidated equity. This share is calculated by adjusting the consolidated amounts related to equity from the 'Group' column for the NCI journal entries posted in the 'NCI' columns. The adjustments are made according to the general rules of debits and credits. For example, the parent share of consolidated share capital ($160) is calculated as the consolidated amount ($200 from the 'Group' column) minus the NCI share ($40 from the 'NCI' debit column). This is because share capital is a credit account, and the NCI share is going to be subtracted from the consolidated share capital to get to the parent share. In contrast, dividend paid has a debit balance, so the NCI share of $2 is extracted from the consolidated amount of $10 via the 'NCI' credit column to get the parent share of $8.

- Two new lines are added in the worksheet, namely 'Total equity: parent' and 'Total equity: NCI'. These lines contain amounts that show the parent share and the NCI share of total consolidated equity respectively.
  – 'Total equity: parent' is determined by adding together the amounts in the 'Parent' column for all individual equity accounts.
  – 'Total equity: NCI' is determined by subtracting the sum of the amounts for this line in the 'NCI' debit column (i.e. $2 + $2) from the sum of the amounts in the 'NCI' credit column (i.e. $10 + $36 + $40 + $4 + $4). The resulting amount is written in the 'Parent' column.

The sum of the amounts included in these two lines in the 'Parent' column equal the total consolidated equity shown in the 'Group' column.

The disclosures detailed in section 29.2.2 should be able to be read from this worksheet.

FIGURE 29.4 Consolidation worksheet for a group containing NCI (extract)

Financial statements	Parent Ltd	Sub Ltd	Adjustments Dr	Adjustments Cr	Group	NCI Dr	NCI Cr	Parent
Revenues					100			
Expenses	—	—			20			
					80			
Income tax expense	—	—			25			
Profit after tax					55	*1* 10		45
Retained earnings (op. bal.)	—	—			145	*2* 36		109
					200			154
Interim dividend paid					10		2 *3*	8
Final dividend declared	—	—			10		2 *4*	8
	—	—			20			16
Retained earnings (cl. bal.)					180			138
Share capital					200	*5* 40		160
Other reserves					20	*6* 4		16
BCVR	—	—			20	*7* 4		16
Total equity: parent								330
Total equity: NCI						*3* 2	10 *1*	90
						4 2	36 *2*	
							40 *5*	
							4 *6*	
							4 *7*	
Total equity	—	—			420	98	98	420

LEARNING CHECK

☐ There is no NCI share extracted from the assets or liabilities section of the worksheet as NCI receives a share of equity only.

☐ Because it is necessary to distinguish between the parent share and the NCI share of equity in the consolidated financial statements, extra columns and lines are added in the consolidation worksheet to divide the consolidated equity into the NCI and parent share.

☐ Two columns are added that record the NCI journal entries necessary to transfer the NCI share of individual equity accounts out of the respective accounts and into an account that recognises the NCI share of total consolidated equity.

☐ One extra column is added that includes the parent share of the individual equity accounts calculated by extracting from the consolidated amounts of each individual equity account the NCI share according to the NCI journal entries.

☐ Two lines are added to separately record the NCI and parent share of total consolidated equity.

29.4 The effects of the NCI on the goodwill recognised in the consolidation process

LEARNING OBJECTIVE 29.4 Identify how the existence of the NCI affects the consolidation process, particularly the measurement of goodwill.

The first step in the consolidation process is the acquisition analysis. From this analysis the amount of goodwill to be recognised is determined.

Paragraph 32 of AASB 3/IFRS 3 *Business Combinations* states:

> The acquirer shall recognise goodwill as of the acquisition date measured as the excess of (a) over (b) below:
>
> (a) the aggregate of:
>> (i) the consideration transferred measured in accordance with this Standard, which generally requires acquisition-date fair value (see paragraph 37);
>> (ii) the amount of any non-controlling interest in the acquiree measured in accordance with this Standard; and
>> (iii) in a business combination achieved in stages (see paragraphs 41 and 42), the acquisition-date fair value of the acquirer's previously held equity interests in the acquiree.
>
> (b) the net of the acquisition-date amounts of the identifiable assets acquired and the liabilities assumed measured in accordance with this Standard.

Therefore, in order to determine the amount of goodwill as part of the acquisition analysis, we need to be aware of the methods prescribed by the standard to measure non-controlling interest.

Paragraph 19 of AASB 3/IFRS 3 states:

> For each business combination, the acquirer shall measure at the acquisition date components of non-controlling interests in the acquiree that are present ownership interests and entitle their holders to a proportionate share of the entity's net assets in the event of liquidation at either:
>
> (a) fair value; or
>
> (b) the present ownership instruments' proportionate share in the recognised amounts of the acquiree's identifiable net assets.

The choice of each alternative measurement prescribed in paragraph 19 of AASB 3/IFRS 3 affects the determination of goodwill and the subsequent consolidation adjustments. Where the first alternative is used, goodwill attributable to both the NCI and the parent is measured. Under the second alternative, only the goodwill attributable to the parent is measured, with no goodwill recognised for NCI. The methods are sometimes referred to as the 'full goodwill' and the 'partial goodwill' methods (see paragraph BC205 in the Basis for Conclusions on AASB 3/IFRS 3). These terms are used in this chapter.

These methods are demonstrated in sections 29.4.1 and 29.4.2 and the reasons for the standard setters allowing these two optional measurements, as well as factors to consider when choosing between the methods, are discussed in section 29.4.3.

29.4.1 Full goodwill method

Under this method, at acquisition date, the NCI in the subsidiary is measured at fair value. The fair value is determined on the basis of the market prices for shares not acquired by the parent, or, if these are not available, a valuation technique is used.

It is not sufficient to use the consideration paid by the parent to measure the fair value of the NCI. For example, if a parent paid $80 000 for 80% of the shares of a subsidiary, then the fair value of the NCI cannot be assumed to be $20 000 (i.e. 20% × $80 000/80%). It may be that the parent paid a premium in order to obtain the controlling interest in the subsidiary. Moreover, the consideration paid by the parent normally relates to the expected synergies arising from the combination of the parent and the subsidiary. The parent would increase the consideration transferred due to these synergies. However, some of these synergies may result in increased earnings in the parent and not in the subsidiary. In this case, the NCI does not receive any share of those synergies. Hence, the consideration paid by the parent could not be used to measure the fair value of the NCI in the subsidiary.

ILLUSTRATIVE EXAMPLE 29.1

Full goodwill method

P Ltd paid $169 600 for 80% of the shares of S Ltd on 1 July 2023. All identifiable assets and liabilities of the subsidiary were recorded at fair value at acquisition date, except for land for which the fair value was $10 000 greater than its carrying amount. Valuation adjustments are made in the consolidation worksheet. The tax rate is 30%. The NCI in S Ltd was considered to have a fair value of $42 000 and P Ltd uses the full goodwill method. At acquisition date, the equity of S Ltd consisted of the following.

▶

Share capital	$100 000
General reserve	60 000
Retained earnings	40 000

The acquisition analysis is as follows.

Net fair value of identifiable assets and liabilities of S Ltd	= $100 000 + $60 000 + $40 000
	+ $10 000(1 − 30%) (BCVR — land)
	= $207 000
(a) Consideration transferred	= $169 600
(b) NCI in S Ltd	= $42 000
Aggregate of (a) and (b)	= $211 600
Goodwill	= $211 600 − $207 000
	= $4600
Fair value of S Ltd	= $42 000/20%
	= $210 000
Net fair value of identifiable assets and liabilities of S Ltd	= $207 000
Goodwill of S Ltd	= $210 000 − $207 000
	= $3000
Goodwill	= $4600
Goodwill of S Ltd	= $3000
Control premium	= $4600 − $3000
	= $1600

Note the following.
- The total goodwill of $4600 calculated in the acquisition analysis consists of both the goodwill of the subsidiary and a control premium paid by the parent over the fair value of the shares acquired to obtain control over the subsidiary. The goodwill of the subsidiary will be allocated proportionally to the parent and NCI, but the control premium is only attributable to the parent.
- As the fair value of the shares that the NCI has (20%) is determined to be $42 000, if P Ltd acquired 80% of S Ltd, it would expect to pay $168 000 (i.e. 80% × $42 000/20). As P Ltd paid $169 600, it then paid a control premium of $1600.
- The goodwill attributable to P Ltd — including both its share of S Ltd's goodwill and the control premium — could be calculated as follows.

Net fair value of identifiable assets and liabilities attributable to P Ltd	= 80% × $207 000
	= $165 600
Consideration transferred	= $169 600
Goodwill attributable to P Ltd	= $169 600 − $165 600
	= $4000

- The goodwill attributable to NCI could be calculated as follows.

Net fair value of identifiable assets and liabilities attributable to NCI	= 20% × $207 000
	= $41 400
NCI	= $42 000
Goodwill attributable to NCI	= $42 000 − $41 400
	= $600

- Effectively the total goodwill of $4600 is broken down as follows.

Control premium paid by P Ltd	= $1600
Parent's share of S Ltd's goodwill	= $2400 [$4000 − $1600
	or 80% × $3000]
NCI share of S Ltd's goodwill	= $600 [20% × $3000]

To account for the goodwill, a business combination valuation reserve (BCVR) is raised for the goodwill of the subsidiary ($3000). This reserve is then attributed on a proportional basis to the parent and the NCI ($2400 to the parent and $600 to the NCI).

The control premium part of goodwill is recognised in the pre-acquisition entry as the earnings from this part of the goodwill will flow only into the parent's earnings — if this part of the goodwill would be recognised in BCVR, a part will be incorrectly attributed to NCI when the NCI share of individual equity accounts (including BCVR) is measured.

The consolidation worksheet entries are as follows.

1. *Business combination valuation entries*

Two BCVR entries are required: one for the revaluation of the land to fair value, and the second to recognise the goodwill of the subsidiary that does not include the control premium.

Land	Dr	10 000	
Deferred tax liability	Cr		3 000
BCVR	Cr		7 000
(Revaluation of land)			
Goodwill	Dr	3 000	
BCVR	Cr		3 000
(Recognition of goodwill of S Ltd)			

2. *Pre-acquisition entry*

In relation to the equity on hand at acquisition date, only 80% is attributable to the parent and 20% is attributable to the NCI. The pre-acquisition entry relates to the investment by the parent in the subsidiary, and thus relates to 80% of the amounts shown in the acquisition analysis as subsidiary's equity. The adjustments in the pre-acquisition entry then consist of:

- eliminating the investment account recognised by the parent in the subsidiary
- eliminating 80% of the recorded equity of the subsidiary at acquisition date
- eliminating 80% of the BCVR recognised as a result of differences between fair value and carrying amounts of the subsidiary's identifiable assets and liabilities at acquisition date
- eliminating 80% of the BCVR recognised for the goodwill of the subsidiary
- recognising the goodwill attributed only to the parent entity (the control premium).

Retained earnings [80% × $40 000]	Dr	32 000	
Share capital [80% × $100 000]	Dr	80 000	
General reserve [80% × $60 000]	Dr	48 000	
BCVR [80% × ($7000 + $3000)]	Dr	8 000	
Goodwill	Dr	1 600	
Shares in S Ltd	Cr		169 600

29.4.2 Partial goodwill method

Under the second option, at acquisition date the NCI is measured at the NCI's proportionate share of the acquiree's identifiable assets and liabilities. The NCI therefore does not get a share of any goodwill as goodwill is not an identifiable asset. The only goodwill recognised is that attributable to the parent; hence, the term 'partial' goodwill. This goodwill (that belongs to the parent) will be calculated as follows.

> Goodwill   = Consideration transferred at fair value
>   + Previously acquired investment by parent at fair value
>   − Parent share of the net fair value of identifiable assets and liabilities of subsidiary

ILLUSTRATIVE EXAMPLE 29.2

Partial goodwill method

From illustrative example 29.1, P Ltd paid $169 600 for 80% of the shares of S Ltd on 1 July 2023. On this date, all identifiable assets and liabilities of S Ltd were recorded at fair value, except for land for which the fair value was $10 000 greater than its carrying amount. Valuation adjustments are made in the consolidation worksheet. The tax rate is 30%. At acquisition date, the equity of S Ltd consisted of the following.

Share capital	$100 000
General reserve	60 000
Retained earnings	40 000

▶

The NCI is measured at the proportionate share of the net fair value of the identifiable assets and liabilities in the subsidiary at acquisition date.

The acquisition analysis is as follows.

Net fair value of identifiable assets and liabilities of S Ltd	= $100 000 + $60 000 + $40 000
	+ $10 000(1 – 30%) (BCVR — land)
	= $207 000
(a) Consideration transferred	= $169 600
(b) NCI in S Ltd	= 20% × $207 000
	= $41 400
Aggregate of (a) and (b)	= $211 000
Goodwill	= $211 000 – $207 000
	= $4000

Note that the $4000 goodwill under this partial method is the same as the parent's share of goodwill including the control premium calculated in section 29.4.1 under the full goodwill method.

The consolidation worksheet entries are as follows.

1. *Business combination valuation entry*

   Note that there is no BCVR entry for goodwill because there is no goodwill that can be allocated both to the parent and NCI. The goodwill under the partial goodwill method only belongs to the parent and is recognised in the pre-acquisition entry.

Land	Dr	10 000
Deferred tax liability	Cr	3 000
BCVR	Cr	7 000

2. *Pre-acquisition entry*

   In relation to the equity on hand at acquisition date, only 80% is attributable to the parent, and 20% is attributable to the NCI. The pre-acquisition entry relates to the investment by the parent in the subsidiary, and thus relates to 80% of the equity amounts shown in the acquisition analysis. The adjustments in the pre-acquisition entry then consist of:
   - eliminating the investment account recognised by the parent in the subsidiary
   - eliminating 80% of the recorded equity of the subsidiary at acquisition date
   - eliminating 80% of the BCVR recognised as a result of differences between fair value and carrying amounts of the subsidiary's identifiable assets and liabilities at acquisition date
   - recognising the goodwill attributed only to the parent entity.

Retained earnings [80% × $40 000]	Dr	32 000
Share capital [80% × $100 000]	Dr	80 000
General reserve [80% × $60 000]	Dr	48 000
BCVR [80% × $7000]	Dr	5 600
Goodwill	Dr	4 000
Shares in S Ltd	Cr	169 600

29.4.3 Analysing the two methods

For each business combination resulting in a parent owning less than 100% of shares in the subsidiary, the parent must choose which method of measuring NCI it adopts. A parent can use the full goodwill method for some partially owned subsidiaries and the partial goodwill method for others.

Why did the standard setters allow a choice of methods?

It is unusual for the standard setters to allow a choice of methods as this leads to non-comparability of financial statements between entities. However, when preparing IFRS 3, on which AASB 3 is based, the IASB members could not agree on the use of the fair value measurement for NCI (i.e. the full goodwill method) and so both methods were allowed (see AASB 3/IFRS 3 BC210 and BC213).

Some reasons for the disagreement related to the use of the full goodwill method are (see AASB 3/IFRS 3 BC213–214):
- it is more costly to measure the NCI at fair value
- there is not sufficient evidence to assess the marginal benefits of reporting the acquisition-date fair value of the NCI.

What is the effect of choosing one method over the other?

Choosing one method over the other results in different outcomes as follows.
1. The reported amounts at acquisition date will be different. The amounts recognised for goodwill and the NCI share of equity would be higher under the full goodwill method.
2. If the goodwill is tested for impairment subsequent to acquisition date, the test is less complex under the full goodwill method. Further, any impairment of goodwill will be recognised for the entire subsidiary under the full goodwill method, but only for the parent's share of the goodwill under the partial goodwill method.
3. Where a parent acquires some or all of the NCI subsequent to obtaining control, there is a lower negative impact on equity attributable to the parent shareholders under the full goodwill method due to the NCI being recognised at a higher carrying amount.

Ernst & Young (2010) provides a detailed discussion of these outcomes.

LEARNING CHECK

- ☐ In order to determine the amount of goodwill as part of the consolidation process, we need to be aware of the methods prescribed by AASB 3/IFRS 3 to measure non-controlling interest.
- ☐ AASB 3/IFRS 3 provides two alternative methods for measuring the NCI at acquisition date that directly affect the goodwill recognised.
- ☐ Under the full goodwill method, the NCI is measured at fair value at acquisition date, and goodwill is separated between goodwill of subsidiary (recognised in the business combination valuation entries) and control premium (recognised in the pre-acquisition entries).
- ☐ Under the partial goodwill method, the NCI is measured as a proportion of the net fair value of the identifiable assets and liabilities of the subsidiary at acquisition date. As such, NCI does not get a share of goodwill. Only the parent's share of goodwill is recognised and this is done in the pre-acquisition entries.
- ☐ IASB and AASB decided to allow the use of these two alternative methods even though this decision has some disadvantages for both users (affects comparability of financial information) and preparers of financial statements (increases preparation costs).

29.5 Calculating the NCI share of recorded equity

LEARNING OBJECTIVE 29.5 Explain how the NCI is calculated in a three-step process.

The NCI share of consolidated equity is calculated in two stages:
1. the NCI share of 'recorded equity', which is the equity contained in the records of the subsidiary itself plus any BCVR recognised at acquisition date
2. the adjustments to the NCI share of recorded equity due to the effects of intragroup transactions.

This section of the chapter covers the detailed mechanics of calculating the NCI share of recorded equity. The adjustments to the NCI due to intragroup transactions are covered in section 29.6.

29.5.1 Basic principles

The NCI is entitled to a share of the recorded equity of the subsidiary as measured at the end of the period for which the consolidated financial statements are being prepared. This share is calculated in three steps:
1. the measurement of the NCI share of equity of the subsidiary at acquisition date
2. the measurement of the NCI share of the changes in subsidiary equity between the acquisition date and the beginning of the current period for which the consolidated financial statements are being prepared
3. the measurement of the NCI share of the changes in subsidiary equity in the current period.

The calculation could be represented diagrammatically, as shown in figure 29.5.

FIGURE 29.5   Calculating the NCI share of equity

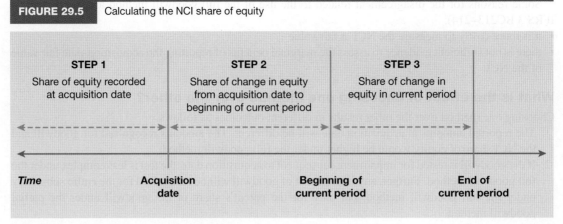

Source: Peter Gerhardy, Ernst & Young, Adelaide.

Illustrative example 29.3 demonstrates this procedure.

ILLUSTRATIVE EXAMPLE 29.3

Measurement of NCI as a three-step process

Consider the calculation of the NCI share of retained earnings over a 5-year period. Assume the following information in relation to House Ltd.

Retained earnings as at 1 July 2016	$10 000
Retained earnings as at 30 June 2020	50 000
Profit for the current period ended 30 June 2021	15 000
Retained earnings as at 30 June 2021	65 000

Assume that Opera Ltd had acquired 80% of the share capital of House Ltd at 1 July 2016, and the consolidated financial statements were being prepared at 30 June 2021. The 20% NCI in House Ltd is entitled to a share of the retained earnings balance at 30 June 2021 of $65 000, a share equal to $13 000. This share is calculated in three steps.

Step 1. A share of the balance at 1 July 2016 (20% × $10 000)	=	$ 2 000
Step 2. A share of the change in retained earnings from the acquisition date to the		
beginning of the current period (20% × ($50 000 − $10 000))	=	8 000
Step 3. A share of the current period increase in retained earnings (20% × $15 000)	=	3 000
		$13 000

Note that, in calculating the NCI share of retained earnings of House Ltd at 30 June 2022 (one year after the above calculation), the total of steps 1 and 2 would be $13 000, as calculated above. Step 3 would be the calculation of the share of changes in retained earnings in the period ended 30 June 2022.

The separate calculations in these three steps are not based on a division of equity into pre-acquisition and post-acquisition equity. The division of equity is based on *time periods* and this three-step process is needed because changes in equity are recorded for accounting purposes on a period-by-period basis.

The journal entries posted in the NCI columns of the consolidation worksheet to reflect the NCI share of equity are based on this three-step approach. The three steps are further illustrated in the next sections.

29.5.2 Step 1. Measurement of the NCI at acquisition date

This section describes step 1 in the calculation of the NCI share of equity at acquisition date and illustrates the effects that the existence of the NCI has on the acquisition analysis, BCVR entries and pre-acquisition entries at acquisition date. The acquisition analysis and the consolidation worksheet entries at acquisition date are affected by whether the full goodwill or partial goodwill method is used in the measurement of the NCI at acquisition date.

Full goodwill method

Consolidation worksheet entries at acquisition date

On 1 July 2019, Tweed Ltd acquired 60% of the shares of Heads Ltd for $45 000 when the equity of Heads Ltd consisted of the following.

Share capital	$40 000
General reserve	2 000
Retained earnings	2 000

At acquisition date, all the identifiable assets and liabilities of Heads Ltd were recorded at fair value except for equipment and inventories.

	Carrying amount	Fair value
Equipment (cost $250 000)	$180 000	$200 000
Inventories	40 000	50 000

The tax rate is 30%. The fair value of the NCI in Heads Ltd at 1 July 2019 was $28 000.

Acquisition analysis

Net fair value of identifiable assets and liabilities of Heads Ltd	= $40 000 (share capital)
	+ $2000 (general reserve)
	+ $2000 (retained earnings)
	+ $20 000(1 − 30%) (BCVR — equipment)
	+ $10 000(1 − 30%) (BCVR — inventories)
	= $65 000
(a) Consideration transferred	= $45 000
(b) NCI in Heads Ltd	= $28 000
Aggregate of (a) and (b)	= $73 000
Goodwill	= $73 000 − $65 000
	= $8000
Fair value of Heads Ltd	= $28 000/40%
	= $70 000
Net fair value of identifiable assets and liabilities of Heads Ltd	= $65 000
Goodwill of Heads Ltd	= $70 000 − $65 000
	= $5000
	= $8000
Goodwill	= $5000
Goodwill of Heads Ltd control premium	= $8000 − $5000
	= $3000

Where NCI exists, as the parent acquires only a part of the ownership interest in the subsidiary, the parent is entitled to a proportionate share of the equity in the subsidiary. As NCI is measured at fair value in this example (and therefore the full goodwill method is applied), the parent is entitled to the proportionate share of the goodwill recognised for the subsidiary, together with the control premium.

1. *Business combination valuation entries*

The BCVR entries, other than that required to recognise goodwill, are unaffected by the existence of NCI. In the case of full goodwill method, the BCVR entry for goodwill will recognise only the goodwill of the subsidiary, excluding the control premium. Therefore, the BCVR entries in the consolidation worksheet (see figure 29.6) prepared at acquisition date are as follows.

Accumulated depreciation — equipment	Dr	70 000	
Equipment	Cr		50 000
Deferred tax liability	Cr		6 000
BCVR	Cr		14 000
Inventories	Dr	10 000	
Deferred tax liability	Cr		3 000
BCVR	Cr		7 000
Goodwill	Dr	5 000	
BCVR	Cr		5 000

The total BCVR at acquisition date is $26 000. The BCVR is part of pre-acquisition equity because it is recognised on consolidation at acquisition date. The NCI is entitled to a proportionate share of this reserve.

2. *Pre-acquisition entry*

The pre-acquisition entry at acquisition date is prepared using the information from the acquisition analysis. The parent's proportional share of the various equity accounts of the subsidiary, as well as the parent's share of the BCVR, are eliminated against the investment account, while the control premium is recognised in the goodwill account. In this illustrative example, the pre-acquisition entry is as follows.

Retained earnings (1/7/19) [60% × $2000]	Dr	1 200	
Share capital [60% × $40 000]	Dr	24 000	
BCVR [60% × $26 000]	Dr	15 600	
General reserve [60% × $2000]	Dr	1 200	
Goodwill	Dr	3 000	
Shares in Heads Ltd	Cr		45 000

3. *NCI share of equity at acquisition date*

The NCI at acquisition date (step 1 in the calculation of NCI) is determined as the proportional share of the equity recorded by the subsidiary at that date and the valuation reserves recorded on consolidation.

Share capital	40% × $40 000	= $16 000
General reserve	40% × $2000	= 800
BCVR	40% × $26 000	= 10 400
Retained earnings	40% × $2000	= 800
		$28 000

The following entry is then passed in the NCI columns of the consolidation worksheet.

Retained earnings (1/7/19)	Dr	800	
Share capital	Dr	16 000	
BCVR	Dr	10 400	
General reserve	Dr	800	
NCI	Cr		28 000

This entry makes sure that the remaining amounts in the individual pre-acquisition equity accounts (the part belonging to the NCI, after the part belonging to the parent was eliminated in the pre-acquisition entry) are transferred to the NCI account that recognises the NCI's part of the consolidated equity. This entry is passed as the step 1 NCI entry in *all* subsequent consolidation worksheets. *It is never* changed as it should always reflect the NCI's share of consolidated equity *as of acquisition date*. Any subsequent changes in pre-acquisition equity are addressed in the step 2 and step 3 NCI calculation.

Figure 29.6 shows an extract from the consolidation worksheet for Tweed Ltd and its subsidiary, Heads Ltd, at acquisition date. Only the equity section of the worksheet is shown as only this section is used in the calculation of NCI.

FIGURE 29.6 Consolidation worksheet (extract) at acquisition date: full goodwill method

Financial statements	Tweed Ltd	Heads Ltd	Adjustments		Dr	Cr		Group	NCI		Dr	Cr		Parent
Retained earnings (1/7/19)	50 000	2 000	2	1 200				50 800		3	800			50 000
Share capital	100 000	40 000	2	24 000				116 000		3	16 000			100 000
General reserve	20 000	2 000	2	1 200				20 800		3	800			20 000
BCVR			2	15 600	14 000	1		10 400		3	10 400			0
					7 000	1								
Total equity: parent					5 000	1								170 000
Total equity: NCI												28 000	3	28 000
Total equity	170 000	44 000						198 000			28 000	28 000		198 000

Partial goodwill method

ILLUSTRATIVE EXAMPLE 29.5

Consolidation worksheet entries at acquisition date

On 1 July 2019, Tweed Ltd acquired 60% of the shares of Heads Ltd for $45 000 when the equity of Heads Ltd consisted of the following.

Share capital	$40 000
General reserve	2 000
Retained earnings	2 000

At acquisition date, all the identifiable assets and liabilities of Heads Ltd were recorded at fair value except for equipment and inventories.

	Carrying amount	Fair value
Equipment (cost $250 000)	$180 000	$200 000
Inventories	40 000	50 000

The tax rate is 30%. The NCI at acquisition date is measured based on the proportionate share of the net fair value of identifiable assets and liabilities of Heads Ltd.

Acquisition analysis

Net fair value of identifiable assets and liabilities of Heads Ltd	= $40 000 (share capital)
	+ $2000 (general reserve)
	+ $2000 (retained earnings)
	+ $20 000(1 − 30%) (BCVR — equipment)
	+ $10 000(1 − 30%) (BCVR — inventories)
	= $65 000
(a) Consideration transferred	= $45 000
(b) NCI in Heads Ltd	= 40% × $65 000
	= $26 000
Aggregate of (a) and (b)	= $71 000
Goodwill	= $71 000 − $65 000
	= $6000

1. *Business combination valuation entries*

The BCVR entries for equipment and inventories at acquisition date are unaffected by the existence of the NCI. These entries are the same as for the full goodwill method in illustrative example 29.4.

Accumulated depreciation — equipment	Dr	70 000	
Equipment	Cr		50 000
Deferred tax liability	Cr		6 000
BCVR	Cr		14 000
Inventories	Dr	10 000	
Deferred tax liability	Cr		3 000
BCVR	Cr		7 000

The total BCVR balance is $21 000. Note that there is no BCVR entry for goodwill under the partial goodwill method. Under this method, only the parent's share of goodwill is recognised, and this is done in the pre-acquisition entry.

2. *Pre-acquisition entries*

The pre-acquisition entry at acquisition date is as follows.

Retained earnings (1/7/19) [60% × $2000]	Dr	1 200	
Share capital [60% × $40 000]	Dr	24 000	
BCVR [60% × $21 000]	Dr	12 600	
General reserve [60% × $2000]	Dr	1 200	
Goodwill	Dr	6 000	
Shares in Heads Ltd	Cr		45 000

As previously mentioned, under the partial goodwill method only the parent's share of the goodwill will be recognised in this entry. The parent's share of the equity accounts in the subsidiary at acquisition date (including the share of the BCVR account) will be eliminated against the investment account recognised by the parent in the subsidiary.

3. *NCI share of equity at acquisition date*

The NCI at acquisition date (the step 1 NCI) is determined as the proportional share of the equity recorded by the subsidiary at that date and the valuation reserves recorded on consolidation.

Share capital	40% × $40 000	= $16 000
General reserve	40% × $2000	= 800
BCVR	40% × $21 000	= 8 400
Retained earnings	40% × $2000	= 800
		$26 000

The following entry is then passed in the NCI columns of the consolidation worksheet at acquisition date.

Retained earnings (1/7/19)	Dr	800	
Share capital	Dr	16 000	
BCVR	Dr	8 400	
General reserve	Dr	800	
NCI	Cr		26 000

This entry is passed as the step 1 NCI entry in *all* subsequent consolidation worksheets. *It is never changed*. Any subsequent changes in pre-acquisition equity are addressed in the step 2 and step 3 NCI calculation.

Figure 29.7 shows an extract from the consolidation worksheet for Tweed Ltd and its subsidiary, Heads Ltd, at acquisition date. Only the equity section of the worksheet is shown.

Financial statements	Tweed Ltd	Heads Ltd	Adjustments Dr		Cr		NCI Group	Dr		Cr	Parent
Retained earnings (1/7/19)	50 000	2 000	2	1 200			50 800	3	800		50 000
Share capital	100 000	40 000	2	24 000			116 000	3	16 000		100 000
General reserve	20 000	2 000	2	1 200			20 800	3	800		20 000
BCVR			2	12 600	14 000	1	8 400	3	8 400		0
					7 000	1					
Total equity: parent											170 000
Total equity: NCI										26 000 3	26 000
Total equity	170 000	44 000					196 000		26 000	26 000	196 000

29.5.3 Step 2. Measurement of the NCI share of changes in equity between acquisition date and beginning of the current period

In illustrative examples 29.4 and 29.5, Tweed Ltd acquired shares in Heads Ltd on 1 July 2019. To illustrate steps 2 and 3 in the measurement of the NCI, we will consider the preparation of the consolidated financial statements 3 years after acquisition date — at 30 June 2022.

The entries prepared in this section are based on illustrative example 29.5 where the partial goodwill method is used. Remember, however, that the effects of the events occurring subsequent to acquisition date on all entries are the same for the full goodwill method.

The following information is available for the assets that were undervalued at acquisition date.

- All inventories on hand at 1 July 2019 are sold by 30 June 2020.
- The equipment has an expected useful life of 5 years.

In the 3 years after acquisition date, Heads Ltd recorded some changes in equity detailed in figure 29.8.

FIGURE 29.8   Changes in equity since acquisition date

	2019–20	2020–21	2021–22
Retained earnings (opening balance)	$ 2 000	$ 7 800	$16 000
Profit for the period	8 000	12 000	15 000
	10 000	19 800	31 000
Transfer from general reserve	0	0	500
Transfer to general reserve	0	1 000	0
Dividend paid	1 000	1 200	1 500
Dividend declared	1 200	1 600	2 000
Retained earnings (closing balance)	$ 7 800	$16 000	$28 000
Share capital	$40 000	$40 000	$40 000
General reserve	$ 2 000	$ 3 000	$ 2 500

To prepare the step 2 NCI journal entries, it is necessary to note any changes in the equity of the subsidiary between the acquisition date and the beginning of the current period. These will generally be movements in retained earnings and reserves.

In this example, using information from figure 29.8 together with the information about the assets that were undervalued at acquisition date, three changes in the equity of the subsidiary during the period from the acquisition date until the beginning of the current period are identified.

1. Retained earnings increased from $2000 to $16 000 as reported in the financial statements.
2. As a result of the sale during the period ended 30 June 2020 of inventories undervalued at acquisition date, $7000 is considered transferred from business combination valuation reserve to retained earnings.
3. General reserve increased from $2000 to $3000 as a result of a transfer from retained earnings.

These changes are addressed below to calculate and to account for their impact on the NCI.

1. Retained earnings

According to the information from figure 29.8, the balance of the retained earnings account has increased by $14 000 from $2000 at acquisition date to $16 000 at 30 June 2021. The NCI share of retained earnings will therefore increase by 40% × $14 000 = $5600.

However, the NCI share of changes in retained earnings must also take into account the impact on post-acquisition retained earnings of the adjustment consolidation worksheet entries (i.e. the BCVR entries). That is because the NCI is entitled to a share in the retained earnings that are calculated based on those adjustments. The business combination valuation entries at 30 June 2022, the end of the current reporting period, are as follows.

Accumulated depreciation — equipment	Dr	70 000	
Equipment	Cr		50 000
Deferred tax liability	Cr		6 000
BCVR	Cr		14 000
Depreciation expense	Dr	4 000	
Retained earnings (1/7/21)	Dr	8 000	
Accumulated depreciation — equipment	Cr		12 000
(20% × $20 000 p.a.)			
Deferred tax liability	Dr	3 600	
Income tax expense	Cr		1 200
Retained earnings (1/7/21)	Cr		2 400
(30% × $4000 p.a.)			

Note that there is no BCVR entry for inventories as this undervalued asset at acquisition date was sold prior to the beginning of the current period.

In the business combination valuation entries above, there is a net debit adjustment to retained earnings (1/7/21) of $5600 in relation to the after-tax effects of depreciating the equipment (i.e. the $8000 adjustment for previous periods' depreciation before tax less the $2400 adjustment for the tax effect). Hence, the NCI share of changes in retained earnings is determined by calculating the change in retained earnings reported in the financial statements over the period from acquisition date until the beginning of the current period (1/7/21), less the adjustment recorded in the BCVR entries during the current period against the opening balance of retained earnings relating to depreciation of the equipment. The NCI entry will include a debit to the opening balance of the retained earnings account and a credit to the NCI account to recognise the NCI share of changes in retained earnings separately from the parent's share of those changes as follows.

Retained earnings (1/7/21)	Dr	3 360	
NCI	Cr		3 360
(40% × [$16 000 − $2000 − ($8000 − $2400)])			

Note that this applies only when there is a net increase in the retained earnings after adjustments for the BCVR entries that have an impact on the opening balance of retained earnings. In the case of a net decrease, the journal entry includes a debit to NCI and a credit to retained earnings for the NCI's share of the decrease.

In this example, the only adjustment to the opening balance of the retained earnings in the BCVR entries is that relating to the depreciation of equipment. In other examples, there may be a number of adjustments. In general, those adjustments will be related to:

- previous periods' depreciation adjustments for the non-current assets revalued in the consolidation worksheet
- previous periods' impairment of the goodwill recognised in BCVR.

All such adjustments must be taken into account in calculating the NCI share of changes in retained earnings under step 2 NCI. The BCVR entries may also include transfers from BCVR to retained earnings for assets revalued at acquisition date that were disposed of or reached the end of their useful life in the current period, or for contingent liabilities recognised at acquisition date and settled or revalued during the current period; as those entries affect the closing balance of retained earnings and not the opening balance, they would not be taken into account in calculating the NCI share of changes in retained earnings under step 2 NCI — instead, they will be considered under step 3 NCI (as discussed later).

2. BCVR

The sale of inventories in the period ended 30 June 2020 resulted in a transfer from the BCVR to retained earnings that was recorded in the BCVR entries for that period. The after tax profit/loss on this sale of inventories would have been recorded in the subsidiary's retained earnings, and the NCI would have received a share when the changes in retained earnings were considered above (i.e. it is part of the $16 000 balance in retained earnings at 1/7/21). However, this profit/loss includes the value adjustment that was recognised as part of BCVR at acquisition date and considered as part of NCI in the step 1 NCI calculation. Therefore, the NCI now double counts the value adjustment for inventories. Hence, the NCI should be decreased by 40% × $7000 = $2800. Moreover, in the step 1 NCI, BCVR is debited with the NCI share of BCVR recognised at acquisition date; as the BCVR is now lower because of the sale of inventories, the NCI share of BCVR must be decreased. Therefore, the adjustment journal entry will need to reverse the entry recorded in the step 1 NCI calculation that recognised the NCI share of BCVR at acquisition date for the BCVR attributable to the inventories sold. Hence, the NCI entry now is as follows.

NCI		Dr	2 800
BCVR		Cr		2 800

3. General reserve

In the period ended 30 June 2021, $1000 was transferred from retained earnings to the general reserve. The NCI share of general reserve will increase by 40% × $1000 = $400. The NCI entry now will recognise this by crediting NCI and eliminating from the general reserve the part of the changes that belong to NCI as follows.

General reserve		Dr	400
NCI		Cr		400

Summary

The three entries above recognise the NCI share of the changes in equity up to the beginning of the current period by transferring it from the individual consolidated equity accounts to the NCI account and making sure that only the parent share remains in those accounts. These entries may be combined into a single journal entry. The combined entry for step 2 NCI calculation at 30 June 2022 passed in the NCI columns of the consolidation worksheet is as follows.

Retained earnings (1/7/21)		Dr	3 360
General reserve		Dr	400
BCVR		Cr		2 800
NCI		Cr		960

In general, the changes in equity in the previous periods up to the beginning of the current period necessary to be identified for the step 2 NCI entry include changes in retained earnings, adjusted for the impact of BCVR entries for the current period on the opening balance of retained earnings, transfers to/from reserves, and changes in share capital.

29.5.4 Step 3. Measurement of the NCI share of changes in equity in the current period

Using the information from figure 29.8 together with the information about the assets that were undervalued at acquisition date, three changes in the equity of the subsidiary during the current period are identified.
1. Profit for the period (after tax) was recorded as $15 000.
2. There was a transfer from general reserve to retained earnings of $500.
3. Dividends paid amounted to $1500, while dividends declared were $2000.
   These changes are addressed below to calculate and to account for their impact on NCI.

1. Profit

During the current period, Heads Ltd recorded a profit after tax of $15 000. The NCI is entitled to a 40% share of this profit. However, similar to the treatment of changes in retained earnings in the step 2 NCI calculation detailed in section 29.5.3, the profit of the subsidiary needs to be adjusted for the impact of the BCVR entries recorded in the current period. The adjustments to current period profit need to be determined by taking into account all items in the BCVR entries that affect current period profit.

The information for this adjustment is taken from the BCVR entries at 30 June 2022 as shown in section 29.5.3. In these entries there is a debit adjustment to depreciation expense of $4000 and a credit adjustment to income tax expense of $1200, which result in a net decrease of the current profit by $2800.

The NCI share of current profit of the subsidiary is then:

$$40\% \times (\$15\,000 - (\$4000 - \$1200)) = \$4880$$

The NCI worksheet entry in the NCI columns of the worksheet is then as follows.

NCI share of profit or loss	Dr	4 880	
NCI	Cr		4 880
(40% × [$15 000 − ($4000 − $1200)])			

The adjustment recorded as 'NCI share of profit or loss' is posted in the consolidation worksheet against the profit of the subsidiary to remove the NCI share of that profit and transfer it to the NCI.

2. Transfer from general reserve

During the current period, Heads Ltd transferred $500 from general reserve to retained earnings. This transaction does not change the amount of total equity because it is a transfer between equity accounts, so there is also no change to the NCI. However, the NCI share of general reserve has decreased and the NCI share of retained earnings has increased. Nevertheless, the transfer was recognised by the subsidiary in its own accounts, including both the NCI share and the parent share of that transfer. In order to separate between the NCI and the parent share of the transfer, in the NCI columns of the consolidation worksheet we reverse the initial journal entry that recorded the transfer, but only for the NCI share, so that in the last column of the worksheet we only have the effects of the transfer on the parent. We use the 'transfer from general reserve' account and not retained earnings as it is a current period transfer.

The consolidation worksheet entry in the NCI columns is as follows.

Transfer from general reserve	Dr	200	
General reserve	Cr		200
(40% × $500)			

Note that in relation to transfers to or from equity accounts, for measurement of the NCI, it is irrelevant whether the movement involves pre- or post-acquisition equity. The NCI receives a share of total equity. However, for the parent share, the movement involving pre-acquisition equity needs to be considered in the adjustments in the pre-acquisition entries.

3. Dividends

During the current period, Heads Ltd paid a dividend of $1500 and declared a dividend of $2000. Dividends are a reduction in retained earnings. The NCI share of equity is reduced as a result of the payment or declaration of dividends. The 'dividend paid' and 'dividend declared' accounts recorded by the subsidiary recognise both the NCI and the parent share of those dividends; to separate between them, in the NCI columns of the consolidation worksheet we credit those accounts and debit NCI by the NCI share of dividends as follows.

NCI	Dr	600	
Dividend paid	Cr		600
(40% × $1500)			
NCI	Dr	800	
Dividend declared	Cr		800
(40% × $2000)			

In general, the changes in equity in the current period necessary to be identified for the step 3 NCI entry include profit/(loss) earned, adjusted for the impact of BCVR entries on the current profit, current transfers to/from reserves, dividends paid/declared and changes in share capital in the current period. These current changes are similar to the previous period changes considered in step 2, with the exception of the retained earnings being replaced by profit/(loss) and the inclusion of dividends for the current period. The dividends paid/declared from previous periods do not need to be considered in step 2 as they decrease the opening balance of retained earnings and therefore the change in retained earnings that is considered there already accounts for them.

29.5.5 Posting the NCI entries into the consolidation worksheet

An extract from the consolidation worksheet prepared at 30 June 2022 is shown in figure 29.9. This contains the impact on equity of BCVR entries shown in section 29.5.3 (entry 1), the pre-acquisition entry at 30 June 2022 (entry 2), step 1 NCI entry (entry 3), step 2 NCI entry (entry 4), and the step 3 NCI entry (entry 5). It also contains as entry (6) the adjustment for the current period's intragroup dividend paid/payable. Note that entries 1, 2 and 6 are recorded in the 'Adjustments' column to adjust the individual accounts in order to calculate the consolidated amounts, while entries 3, 4 and 5 are posted in the 'NCI' columns to transfer the NCI share of the particular equity accounts from the consolidated equity to the NCI.

FIGURE 29.9 Consolidation worksheet with NCI columns

Financial statements	Tweed Ltd	Heads Ltd		Adjustments Dr		Cr		Group		NCI Dr		Cr		Parent
Profit/(loss) for the period	20 000	15 000	1	4 000		1 200	1	30 100	5	4 880				25 220
			6	900										
			6	1 200										
Retained earnings (1/7/21)	25 000	16 000	1	8 000		2 400	1	30 000	3	800				25 840
			2	5 400					4	3 360				
Transfer from general reserve	0	500						500	5	200				300
	45 000	31 500						60 600						51 360
Dividend paid	10 000	1 500				900	6	10 600				600	5	10 000
Dividend declared	5 000	2 000				1 200	6	5 800				800	5	5 000
	15 000	3 500						16 400						15 000
Retained earnings (30/6/22)	30 000	28 000						44 200						36 360
Share capital	100 000	40 000	2	24 000				116 000	3	16 000				100 000
General reserve	20 000	2 500	2	1 200				21 300	3	800		200	5	20 300
									4	400				
BCVR	0	0	2	8 400		14 000	1	5 600	3	8 400		2 800	4	0
Total equity: parent														156 660
Total equity: NCI									5	600		26 000	3	30 440
									5	800		960	4	
												4 880	5	
Total equity	150 000	70 500						187 100		37 280		37 280		187 100

29.6 Adjusting NCI for the effects of intragroup transactions

LEARNING OBJECTIVE 29.6 Identify how the existence of intragroup transactions affects the measurement of the NCI.

As noted in chapter 28, the full effects of the transactions between the parent and its subsidiaries are adjusted for on consolidation. This occurs regardless of the level of ownership of the parent in the subsidiary. As a result, the adjustments for intragroup transactions provided in chapter 28 are the same regardless of whether the subsidiary is wholly owned or partially owned by the parent. Note, however, that in the case of dividends declared/paid by the subsidiary, only the dividends to the parent are intragroup dividends and will be eliminated on consolidation. With dividend transactions in a partially owned subsidiary situation, the same accounts are adjusted as in chapter 28, but the amounts are calculated on a proportional basis, using the parent's percentage ownership in the subsidiary.

ILLUSTRATIVE EXAMPLE 29.6

Dividends

P Ltd owns 80% of the share capital of S Ltd. In the current period, the subsidiary pays a $1000 dividend and declares a further $1500 dividend. The adjustment entries in the consolidation worksheet in the current period are as follows.

Dividend revenue	Dr	800	
Dividend paid	Cr		800
(80% × $1000)			
Dividend payable	Dr	1 200	
Dividend declared	Cr		1 200
(80% × $1500)			
Dividend revenue	Dr	1 200	
Dividend receivable	Cr		1 200
(80% × $1500)			

Note that the dividend payable of $1500 as shown in the subsidiary's financial statements is only partially eliminated, while the dividend revenue and dividend receivable of $1200 recognised in the parent's financial statements are entirely eliminated. The consolidated financial statements will still show a liability of $300, being the amount payable by the group to the NCI. However, the NCI share of dividends paid/declared will be transferred from the 'dividend paid' and 'dividend declared' accounts and be recognised as a decrease in the NCI account balance. That is because the amount of dividend paid/declared reduces the equity and, with it, the part that belongs to NCI. Therefore, the NCI adjustment entries (as discussed in step 3 NCI under section 29.5.4) will include the following entries for dividends paid/declared during the current period.

NCI	Dr	200	
Dividend paid	Cr		200
(20% × $1000)			
NCI	Dr	300	
Dividend declared	Cr		300
(20% × $1500)			

We address other examples of intragroup transactions in the presence of NCI below. Consider the situation where Surf Ltd owns 80% of the shares of Sand Ltd. During the current period, Sand Ltd sells inventories to Surf Ltd for $18 000, recording a profit of $2000. The inventories are unsold by the end of the period.

The consolidation worksheet adjustment entries for the intragroup transaction are as follows.

Sales	Dr	18 000	
Cost of sales	Cr		16 000
Inventories	Cr		2 000
Deferred tax asset	Dr	600	
Income tax expense	Cr		600

The adjustment is made because the group cannot recognise the $1400 after-tax profit on sale of the inventories within the group. As a result of the adjustment, the consolidated profit is less than the sum of the recorded profits of the entities within the group by $1400.

The NCI is entitled to a share of the subsidiary's profit as reflected in the consolidated profit. However, in the step 3 NCI calculation described in section 29.5.4, the NCI is given a share of recorded profit of the subsidiary. This means that the equity attributed to the NCI in section 29.5.4 is overstated because, as a result of the intragroup transaction, the recorded profit is larger than the subsidiary's profit as reflected in the consolidated profit.

To ensure the NCI only gets a share of the consolidated profit, further NCI entries are made in relation to the effects of intragroup transactions. However, not all intragroup transactions have an effect on the NCI share of equity. Note two features of the intragroup transactions that will affect the NCI calculation.

- *The transactions must affect profit/loss and not only individual accounts of income and expenses.* The NCI receives a share of equity and within that, a share of consolidated profit. Hence, transactions that do not affect profit will give rise to an adjustment to the NCI. For example, where there is a loan between the parent and the subsidiary, adjustments are made to eliminate the loan payable and the loan receivable and maybe interest revenue and interest expense. However, given that the amount of interest revenue and interest expense is the same, their eliminations have no net effect on profit/loss and hence no NCI effect. In other words, in order to affect the NCI calculation, the intragroup transaction should have some unrealised profits in the current or previous periods.
- *The transactions must affect the profit/loss of the subsidiary.* The NCI receives a share of the equity of the group contributed by the subsidiary, not by the parent. Therefore, in order to be considered in the calculation of NCI, the intragroup transactions must affect the profit/loss of the subsidiary. Hence, if the parent sells inventories to the subsidiary for a profit, there is no effect on the NCI as the profit is made by the parent. If the subsidiary sells inventories to the parent at a profit, there is an NCI effect.

The example above involving Surf Ltd and Sand Ltd has the two required features.
1. The sale of inventories had a net effect on profit.
2. The sale was from Sand Ltd to Surf Ltd; that is, the subsidiary recorded the profit.

Therefore, this transaction affects the calculation of the NCI.

The adjustments to the NCI for an intragroup transaction are determined when the adjustments are made for the full effects of the intragroup transaction in the 'Adjustment' column of the consolidation worksheet. That is, having noted the journal entry for the intragroup transaction, the next journal entry is for the NCI effect. In the Surf Ltd–Sand Ltd example, that entry to recognise the NCI effect is as follows.

NCI	Dr	280	
NCI share of profit or loss	Cr		280
(20% × $1400)			

This entry reduces the NCI in total due to the reduction of the NCI share of profit. As explained above, the reduction in the NCI share of profit is due to the fact that the step 3 NCI calculation based on recorded profit has overstated the NCI share of group equity. The credit adjustment to 'NCI share of profit or loss' does not recognise an increase in the NCI share of profit; instead, this adjustment is posted because the adjustment for the intragroup transaction eliminated the unrealised profit in full from the consolidated profit; as the last column of the worksheet needs to reflect the parent's share of the consolidated profit that only needs to be reduced by the parent's share of the unrealised profit, the NCI's share of the unrealised profit is added back.

Illustrative example 29.7 provides more examples of intragroup transactions and explanation of their effects on the NCI consolidation worksheet entries.

ILLUSTRATIVE EXAMPLE 29.7

NCI and intragroup transactions

Rip Ltd owns 80% of the issued shares of Curl Ltd. At 30 June 2023, the following information is available.

(a) In July 2022, Rip Ltd sold to external entities $2000 worth of inventories that had been sold to it by Curl Ltd in May 2022 at a profit before tax to Curl Ltd of $500.

(b) In February 2023, Rip Ltd sold $10 000 worth of inventories to Curl Ltd, recording a profit before tax of $2000. At 30 June 2023, 20% of these inventories remained unsold by Curl Ltd, the rest having been sold to external entities.

(c) In March 2020, Curl Ltd sold $12 000 worth of inventories to Rip Ltd at a mark-up of 20%. At 30 June 2023, $1200 of these inventories remained unsold by Rip Ltd.

(d) At 1 July 2021, Rip Ltd purchased plant from Curl Ltd for $100 000. At that date, this plant had a carrying amount of $90 000 in the accounts of Curl Ltd.

(e) At 30 June 2023, Rip Ltd recorded depreciation of $10 000 in relation to plant sold to it by Curl Ltd on 1 July 2021. Rip Ltd uses a 10% p.a. straight-line depreciation method for plant.

Required

Given a tax rate of 30%, prepare the consolidation worksheet entries to eliminate the effects of the intragroup transactions as at 30 June 2023, considering the effect on NCI where applicable.

Solution

(a) *Sale of inventories in prior period: Curl Ltd to Rip Ltd*

Note that the heading for this entry identifies the timing of the transaction (i.e. it occurred in a prior period) and also the flow of the transaction within the group (i.e. the subsidiary sold to the parent). Both of these pieces of information are used in determining the consolidation worksheet entries. This intragroup transaction generated a profit before tax for the subsidiary of $500 in the previous period that is now realised.

The entry in the 'Adjustment' column of the worksheet for this intragroup transaction is as follows.

Retained earnings (1/7/22)	Dr	350	
Income tax expense	Dr	150	
Cost of sales	Cr		500

This entry has two effects on equity. There is a prior period effect and a current period effect. The entry requires a reduction in prior period after-tax profit of $350 and an increase in current period after-tax profit of $350. That means that the consolidated profit in the prior period is $350 less than the recorded profit and the consolidated profit in the current period is $350 higher than the recorded profit. However, the net effect on the consolidated equity is zero.

As the flow of the transaction is from subsidiary to parent, the entry has NCI effects. Therefore, an NCI entry needs to be prepared. As the adjustment entry to eliminate the effects of the intragroup transaction has a zero net effect on the consolidated equity, the NCI entry should not include any debit or credit to the NCI account. However, as the adjustment entry to eliminate the effects of the intragroup transaction for the consolidated entity decreased the retained earnings (opening balance) and increased the current profit by the unrealised profit in beginning inventories, the NCI's share of it needs to be added back to retained earnings (opening balance) and subtracted from the current profit; that will ensure that in the last column of the worksheet the parent's share of the consolidated profit and the retained earnings (opening balance) is only adjusted for the parent's share of the profit on the intragroup transaction.

In conclusion, the entry in the NCI columns of the worksheet is as follows.

NCI share of profit or loss	Dr	70	
Retained earnings (1/7/22)	Cr		70
(20% × $350)			

(b) *Sale of inventories in current period: Rip Ltd to Curl Ltd*

The consolidation worksheet entry in the 'Adjustment' column for the intragroup transaction is as follows.

Sales	Dr	10 000	
Cost of sales	Cr		9 600
Inventories	Cr		400
Deferred tax asset	Dr	120	
Income tax expense	Cr		120

Because the sale is from parent to subsidiary, there is no NCI adjustment required, even though the transaction has a net effect on the profit.

(c) *Sale of inventories in current period: Curl Ltd to Rip Ltd*

The entries in the 'Adjustment' column of the worksheet for the intragroup transaction are as follows.

Sales	Dr	12 000	
Cost of sales	Cr		11 800
Inventories	Cr		200
Deferred tax asset	Dr	60	
Income tax expense	Cr		60

The intragroup transaction generated a profit before tax for the subsidiary of $200 in the current period that is unrealised from the point of view of the group. The adjustment entry requires a reduction of $140 in current period after-tax profit. Therefore, the consolidated profit is $140 less than that recorded by the subsidiary in the current period.

Because the sale is from subsidiary to parent, there are NCI effects. As the adjustment entry to eliminate the effects of the intragroup transaction for the consolidated entity decreased the current profit by the unrealised profit in inventories, the NCI's share of it needs to be added back to the current profit; that will ensure that in the last column of the worksheet the parent's share of the consolidated profit is only adjusted for the parent's share of the profit on the intragroup transaction. The reduction in the NCI share of total equity is recognised as a debit to the NCI account.

Therefore, the following entry is prepared in the NCI columns of the worksheet.

NCI	Dr	28	
NCI share of profit or loss	Cr		28
(20% × $140)			

(d) *Sale of plant in prior period: Curl Ltd to Rip Ltd*

The entry in the 'Adjustment' columns of the worksheet for the intragroup transaction is as follows.

Retained earnings (1/7/22)	Dr	7 000	
Deferred tax asset	Dr	3 000	
Plant	Cr		10 000

This adjustment entry reduces the prior period profit by $7000, the profit on the intragroup sale which was unrealised at the moment of sale. As the profit on sale of the plant was made by the subsidiary selling the asset to the parent, there are NCI effects. The NCI entry must then reduce the NCI total share of equity by NCI share of the unrealised profit from the prior period intragroup sale − $1400 (i.e. 20% × $7000). Also, as the adjustment entry to eliminate the effects of the intragroup transaction for the consolidated entity decreased the prior period profit by the unrealised profit, the NCI's share of it needs to be added back to the retained earnings (opening balance); that will ensure that in the last column of the worksheet the parent's share of the consolidated retained earnings is only adjusted for the parent's share of the profit on the intragroup transaction. Therefore, the entry in the NCI columns of the worksheet is as follows.

NCI	Dr	1 400	
Retained earnings (1/7/22)	Cr		1 400
(20% × $7000)			

(e) *Depreciation on plant sold in prior period: Curl Ltd to Rip Ltd*
The entries in the 'Adjustment' columns of the worksheet for the intragroup transaction are as follows.

Accumulated depreciation — plant	Dr	2 000	
Depreciation expense	Cr		1 000
Retained earnings (1/7/22)	Cr		1 000
Retained earnings (1/7/22)	Dr	300	
Income tax expense	Dr	300	
Deferred tax asset	Cr		600

These entries follow from that in (d). As the plant is used within the group, profit on sale of the asset is partly realised by the group — this is evidenced by the fact that the credit adjustment to depreciation expense increases group profit. The above adjustment entries increase the consolidated after-tax profit in both the prior and the current period by $700 each. That is, in both the current and prior periods, the consolidated profit is higher than recorded profit.

The NCI entry must then recognise an increase in the NCI share of current period profit as well as of the prior period profit, leading to an increase in the NCI share of equity in total. As in the previous NCI entries, this is done in a way that is somewhat counterintuitive as the NCI share of profit or loss and of retained earnings (opening balance) are debited; however, this is done in order to remove the NCI share of that increase from the consolidated amounts for current and prior period profits so that only the parent's share of that increase is shown in the last column of the consolidation worksheet.

The entry in the NCI column of the worksheet is as follows.

NCI share of profit or loss	Dr	140	
Retained earnings (1/7/22)	Dr	140	
NCI	Cr		280
(20% × $700 p.a.)			

Note the NCI entries in both (d) and (e). In the NCI entry in (d), the NCI is reduced by $1400. The plant has a 10-year life and the benefits from using the plant are assumed to be received evenly by the group over that period. In the NCI entry in (e), the NCI share of total equity is being increased by $140 p.a., i.e. $1400/10 years. Hence, over the life of the asset, the NCI share of the equity is being increased by $140 p.a. so that at the end of the life of the asset the whole of the $1400 reduction in NCI recognised on the intragroup sale of the plant will be reversed.

LEARNING CHECK

☐ Since the NCI is entitled to a share of consolidated equity, it is necessary to adjust the NCI share of equity for the effects of intragroup transactions.

☐ In the case of dividends, only the dividends paid/declared to the parent are intragroup dividends and will need to be adjusted on consolidation. Dividends paid/declared to NCI reduce the NCI share of total consolidated equity.

☐ Since the NCI is calculated in relation to the equity of the subsidiary, not all intragroup transactions affect the calculation of the NCI, but only those where the equity and more specifically the profit of the subsidiary is affected.

29.7 Gain on bargain purchase

LEARNING OBJECTIVE 29.7 Explain how a gain on bargain purchase affects the measurement of the NCI.

In the rare case that a gain on bargain purchase arises as a result of a business combination, such a gain has no effect on the calculation of the NCI share of equity. The gain is made by the *parent* paying less than the net fair value of the identifiable assets acquired and liabilities assumed of the subsidiary. The NCI receives a share of the net assets of the subsidiary, and has no involvement with the gain on bargain purchase.

To illustrate, assume a subsidiary has $80 000 in total equity at acquisition date, consisting of share capital of $50 000 and retained earnings of $30 000.

All identifiable assets and liabilities of the subsidiary are recorded at amounts equal to fair value at acquisition date, which means that the net fair value of the identifiable assets and liabilities of the subsidiary is equal to the total equity. If the parent acquired 80% of the shares of the subsidiary for $63 000, then the acquisition analysis, assuming that NCI is measured at its proportionate share of the net fair value of the identifiable assets and liabilities of the subsidiary at acquisition date, is as follows.

Net fair value of the identifiable assets and liabilities of the subsidiary	= $80 000
(a) Consideration transferred	= $63 000
(b) NCI in subsidiary	= 20% × $80 000
	= $16 000
Aggregate of (a) and (b)	= $79 000
Gain on bargain purchase	= $80 000 − $79 000
	= $1000

It should be noted that although not stated in the accounting standards, when the parent recognises a gain on bargain purchase, the measurement of non-controlling interest at acquisition date is always going to be based on the fair value of its proportionate share of the identifiable assets and liabilities of the subsidiary at acquisition date; in other words, in cases involving gain on bargain purchase, the NCI should not be measured at fair value of the shares it owns. The consolidation worksheet entries at acquisition date are as follows.

1. Business combination valuation entry
No entry required as there are no valuation adjustments required and no goodwill to be recognised.

2. Pre-acquisition entry

Share capital	Dr	40 000	
Retained earnings	Dr	24 000	
Gain on bargain purchase	Cr		1 000
Shares in subsidiary	Cr		63 000

3. NCI (step 1)

Share capital	Dr	10 000	
Retained earnings	Dr	6 000	
NCI	Cr		16 000

Note that, as mentioned above, the NCI does not receive any share of the gain on bargain purchase.

29.8 Disclosure

LEARNING OBJECTIVE 29.8 Identify the disclosures required in relation to the NCI.

The specific disclosure requirements with regards to NCI within the consolidated statement of profit or loss and other comprehensive income, consolidated statement of changes in equity and consolidated statement of financial position are discussed in section 29.2.2 as stipulated in AASB 10/IFRS 10 and AASB 101/IAS 1. AASB 12/IFRS 12 *Disclosure of Interests in Other Entities* also contains some disclosures requirements for subsidiaries in which there are NCI. Paragraph 12 of AASB 12/IFRS 12 states:

> An entity shall disclose for each of its subsidiaries that have non-controlling interests that are material to the reporting entity:
> (a) the name of the subsidiary.
> (b) the principal place of business (and country of incorporation if different from the principal place of business) of the subsidiary.
> (c) the proportion of ownership interests held by non-controlling interests.
> (d) the proportion of voting rights held by non-controlling interests, if different from the proportion of ownership interests held.
> (e) the profit or loss allocated to non-controlling interests of the subsidiary during the reporting period.
> (f) accumulated non-controlling interests of the subsidiary at the end of the reporting period.
> (g) summarised financial information about the subsidiary (see paragraph B10).

SUMMARY

This chapter describes the accounting procedures necessary where a parent has less than 100% ownership interest in a subsidiary (i.e. NCI exists in the subsidiary). Accounting for the NCI is established in AASB 10/IFRS 10 *Consolidated Financial Statements*. Some key points are as follows.

- NCI is classified as equity, and is entitled to a proportionate share of consolidated equity contributed by the subsidiary calculated in three steps.
- The accounting standards allow alternative methods of calculating goodwill when NCI is present, namely the full goodwill method and the partial goodwill method.
- The BCVR entries apart from those related to goodwill are the same regardless of the existence of NCI.
- The pre-acquisition entries are prepared using the parent's proportionate share of subsidiary equity.
- The existence of intragroup transactions affects the calculation of the NCI only to the extent that there is profit or loss on the intragroup transaction recognised by the subsidiary that is unrealised from the point of view of the group at the beginning or at the end of the period.

KEY TERM

non-controlling interest (NCI) Equity in a subsidiary not attributable, directly or indirectly, to a parent.

DEMONSTRATION PROBLEM

29.1 Consolidated financial statements

Beach Ltd acquired 80% of the shares of Boys Ltd on 1 July 2019 for $540 000, when the equity of Boys Ltd consisted of the following.

Share capital	$500 000
General reserve	80 000
Retained earnings	50 000
Asset revaluation surplus	20 000

All identifiable assets and liabilities of Boys Ltd are recorded at fair value at this date except for inventories for which the fair value was $10 000 greater than carrying amount, and plant which had a carrying amount of $150 000 (net of $40 000 accumulated depreciation) and a fair value of $170 000. The inventories were all sold by 30 June 2020, and the plant had a further 5-year life with depreciation based on the straight-line method. Valuation adjustments on consolidation are made in the consolidation worksheet.

Financial information for both companies at 30 June 2023 is as follows.

	Beach Ltd	Boys Ltd
Sales revenue	$ 720 000	$ 530 000
Other revenue	240 000	120 000
	960 000	650 000
Cost of sales	(610 000)	(410 000)
Other expenses	(230 000)	(160 000)
	(840 000)	(570 000)
Profit before tax	120 000	80 000
Tax expense	(40 000)	(25 000)
Profit for the period	80 000	55 000
Retained earnings at 1/7/22	200 000	112 000
	280 000	167 000
Dividend paid	(20 000)	(10 000)
Dividend declared	(25 000)	(15 000)
	(45 000)	(25 000)
Retained earnings at 30/6/23	235 000	142 000
Share capital	600 000	500 000
Asset revaluation surplus*	20 000	60 000
General reserve	80 000	100 000
Total equity	935 000	802 000

	Beach Ltd	Boys Ltd
Dividend payable	25 000	15 000
Other liabilities	25 000	25 000
Total liabilities	50 000	40 000
Total equity and liabilities	$ 985 000	$ 842 000
Receivables	$ 80 000	$ 30 000
Inventories	100 000	170 000
Plant and equipment	200 000	500 000
Accumulated depreciation — plant and equipment	(115 000)	(88 000)
Land	100 000	80 000
Shares in Boys Ltd	540 000	—
Deferred tax assets	50 000	40 000
Other assets	30 000	110 000
Total assets	$ 985 000	$ 842 000

*The balances of the surplus at 1 July 2022 were $35 000 (Beach Ltd) and $50 000 (Boys Ltd).

The following information provides details on transactions that took place between Beach Ltd and Boys Ltd after acquisition date.

(a) During the period ended 30 June 2023, Boys Ltd sold inventories to Beach Ltd for $23 000, recording a profit before tax of $3000. Beach Ltd has since sold half of these items to external entities.

(b) During the period ended 30 June 2023, Beach Ltd sold inventories to Boys Ltd for $18 000, recording a profit before tax of $2000. Boys Ltd has not on-sold any of these items.

(c) On 1 June 2023, Boys Ltd paid $1000 to Beach Ltd for services rendered.

(d) During the period ended 30 June 2023, Boys Ltd sold inventories to Beach Ltd. At 30 June 2022, Beach Ltd still had inventories on hand on which Boys Ltd had recorded a before-tax profit of $4000; the rest was sold to external entities.

(e) On 1 July 2021, Boys Ltd sold plant to Beach Ltd for $150 000, recording a profit of $20 000 before tax. Beach Ltd applies a 10% p.a. straight-line method of depreciation in relation to these assets.

Required

1. Given an income tax rate of 30%, prepare the consolidated financial statements for Beach Ltd for the year ended 30 June 2023 using the *partial goodwill method* to measure the NCI at acquisition date.

2. What differences would occur in the consolidation worksheet entries at 30 June 2023 if the *full goodwill method* was used to calculate the non-controlling interest at acquisition date? Assume the fair value of the NCI in the subsidiary at acquisition date is $134 500.

SOLUTION

1. *Consolidated financial statements using the partial goodwill method*

The first step in solving this problem is to prepare the acquisition analysis. Determining the net fair value of identifiable assets and liabilities is the same as for wholly owned subsidiaries. Where the NCI exists, it is necessary to determine the net fair value attributable to the NCI.

In this problem, the parent acquired 80% of the shares of the subsidiary. The net fair value of the identifiable assets and liabilities of the subsidiary is compared with the consideration transferred plus the NCI measured as a proportion of the net fair value acquired under the partial goodwill method, and a goodwill or gain is determined. Note that the goodwill or gain is only attributable to the parent, since the residual so calculated relates to what was paid by the parent and the proportion of net fair value of the identifiable assets and liabilities of the subsidiary acquired by the parent.

Acquisition analysis

Net fair value of the identifiable assets and liabilities of Boys Ltd	= $500 000 + $80 000 + $50 000 + $20 000 + $10 000(1 − 30%) (BCVR — inventories) + $20 000(1 − 30%) (BCVR — plant) = $671 000
(a) Consideration transferred	= $540 000
(b) NCI in Boys Ltd	= 20% × $671 000 = $134 200
Aggregate of (a) and (b)	= $674 200
Goodwill	= $674 200 − $671 000 = $3200

Consolidation worksheet entries at 30 June 2023

(1) *Business combination valuation entries*

The business combination valuation entries except for goodwill are unaffected by the existence of the NCI. Under AASB 3/IFRS 3, all identifiable assets and liabilities acquired in the subsidiary must be measured at fair value. This principle is unaffected by the existence of the NCI. As the inventories undervalued at acquisition date were sold by 30 June 2020, there are no BCVR entries for inventories at 30 June 2023.

Accumulated depreciation — plant and equipment	Dr	40 000	
Plant	Cr		20 000
Deferred tax liability	Cr		6 000
BCVR	Cr		14 000
Depreciation expense	Dr	4 000	
Retained earnings (1/7/22)	Dr	12 000	16 000
Accumulated depreciation — plant and equipment	Cr		
Deferred tax liability	Dr	4 800	
Income tax expense	Cr		1 200
Retained earnings (1/7/22)	Cr		3 600

(2) *Pre-acquisition entry*

Retained earnings (1/7/22)	Dr	45 600	
Share capital	Dr	400 000	
General reserve	Dr	64 000	
Asset revaluation surplus (1/7/22)	Dr	16 000	
BCVR	Dr	11 200	
Goodwill	Dr	3 200	
Shares in Boys Ltd	Cr		540 000

This pre-acquisition entry differs from the entries prepared for a wholly owned subsidiary in that the adjustment to equity accounts is for the parent's share of the equity accounts. This is because the consideration transferred was only for the parent's share of equity (80%). Hence, the adjustment to equity accounts is for 80% of the normal adjustment.

For retained earnings (1/7/22), the amount to be posted in the entry must take into account the fact that the inventories on hand at acquisition date have been sold during the previous periods and the BCVR transferred to retained earnings: (80% × \$50 000) (opening balance) + (80% × \$7000) (BCVR — inventories). For share capital, general reserve and asset revaluation surplus, the amounts of adjustments are \$400 000 (80% × \$500 000), \$64 000 (80% × \$80 000) and \$16 000 (80% × \$20 000) respectively, as it is assumed that no transfers in or out those accounts happened prior to the beginning of the current period. The adjustment to the BCVR relates solely to the plant as the inventories have been sold during the previous periods: 80% × \$14 000 (BCVR — plant), while the goodwill is recognised according to the amount determined in the acquisition analysis.

The next three adjustment entries relate to the calculation of the NCI in the three-step process. These entries are passed in the 'NCI' columns of the worksheet, not in the 'Adjustment' column to distinguish between the NCI and the parent share of the consolidated equity.

(3) *NCI share of equity at acquisition date, 1 July 2019 (step 1)*

Step 1 calculates the NCI share of the equity of the subsidiary at acquisition date, including the recorded equity plus any BCVR raised on consolidation at acquisition date.

Pre-acquisition equity of Boys Ltd		20%
Retained earnings (1/7/19)	\$ 50 000	\$ 10 000
Share capital	500 000	100 000
General reserve	80 000	16 000
Asset revaluation surplus	20 000	4 000
BCVR	21 000	4 200
		\$134 200

The worksheet entry in the 'NCI' column at 30 June 2023 to recognise the NCI at acquisition date is as follows.

Retained earnings (1/7/22)	Dr	10 000
Share capital	Dr	100 000
General reserve	Dr	16 000
Asset revaluation surplus (1/7/22)	Dr	4 000
BCVR	Dr	4 200
NCI	Cr	134 200

Note that the adjustments to the equity accounts are on the debit side of the respective accounts, because these amounts will be subtracted from the balances in the 'Group' column in order to determine the parent's share of equity. On the other hand, the NCI account has a credit adjustment because the NCI is classified as equity and this journal entry recognises it.

(4) *NCI share of changes in equity from 1 July 2019 to 30 June 2022 (step 2)*

Step 2 calculates the NCI share of equity between the acquisition date and the beginning of the current period, that is, between 1 July 2019 and 30 June 2022. This requires the calculation of movements in the subsidiary's equity accounts between these two dates. These movements are visible in the financial statements of the subsidiary and in the BCVR entries prepared at the end of the current period.

General reserve

The balance at 30 June 2022, read from the financial information at 30 June 2023 and observing no transfers in the current period, is $100 000. The difference between this and the balance at 1 July 2019 of $80 000 is $20 000. The NCI is entitled to 20% of this increase in equity. The combination of step 1 and step 2 effectively gives the NCI a 20% share of the total $100 000 balance.

Retained earnings

The balance at 30 June 2022 is the same as the opening balance in the current period, which is read from the financial information provided, namely $112 000. The difference between this amount and the balance recorded by the subsidiary at acquisition date reflects movements recorded by the subsidiary, such as post-acquisition profits, reserve transfers and dividends. What is not reflected in the difference calculated are the amounts affecting the opening balance of retained earnings in the current period not recorded by the subsidiary but recognised on consolidation in the BCVR entries prepared in the current period. In this problem, the entry that needs to be taken into account here is the one adjusting the prior periods' depreciation of the plant on hand at acquisition date (3 years' worth) and the related tax effects. The NCI in relation to changes in retained earnings (1/7/22) is therefore as follows.

20% × ($112 000 balance at 1/7/19 − $50 000 balance at acquisition date − ($12 000 − $3600) prior periods' after tax depreciation adjustment on plant)

Asset revaluation surplus

The balance at acquisition date is $20 000 and the balance at 30 June 2022 is $50 000. The NCI is entitled to 20% of the difference between these two amounts, namely $6000.

BCVR

The balance at acquisition date was $21 000. As a result of the sale of the inventories, the business combination valuation reserve at 30 June 2022 is only $14 000, a reduction of $7000, a result of the transfer from this reserve to retained earnings. Since the reserve has decreased in amount, this results in a decrease in the NCI share of this account.

A summary of these movements in the equity accounts from 1 July 2019 to 30 June 2022 is then as follows.

	Change in equity	20%
General reserve ($100 000 − $80 000)	$20 000	$ 4 000
Retained earnings ($112 000 − $50 000 − ($12 000 − $3600))	53 600	10 720
Asset revaluation surplus ($50 000 − $20 000)	30 000	6 000
BCVR ($14 000 − $21 000)	(7 000)	(1 400)

Therefore, the worksheet entry in the 'NCI' column is as follows.

Retained earnings (1/7/22)	Dr	10 720	
General reserve	Dr	4 000	
Asset revaluation surplus (1/7/22)	Dr	6 000	
BCVR	Cr		1 400
NCI	Cr		19 320

(5) *NCI share of changes in equity from 1 July 2022 to 30 June 2023 (step 3)*

Steps 1 and 2 determine the NCI share of equity recorded up to the beginning of the current year. Step 3 calculates the NCI share of changes in equity in the current year — 1 July 2022 to 30 June 2023. The combination of all three steps determines the NCI share of equity at the end of the reporting period.

There are a number of changes in equity in the current period, with each change attracting its own adjustment entry in the NCI columns of the worksheet.

Profit for the period

The NCI receives a share of recorded profit of the subsidiary. Similar to step 2, this is adjusted for the after-tax depreciation adjustment recorded in the BCVR entries in the current period for the plant on hand at acquisition date. The NCI share of the current profit is then 20% × ($55 000 − ($4000 − $1200)).

The worksheet entry in the 'NCI' column, to recognise the NCI share of the current profit of the subsidiary, is as follows.

NCI share of profit or loss	Dr	10 440	
NCI	Cr		10 440

The first line in the above entry is a debit because in the consolidation worksheet this is deducted from the consolidated profit in order to calculate the parent share of profit. Note that, somewhat counterintuitively, increases in the NCI share of profit require a debit adjustment to this account and decreases in the NCI share of profit require a credit adjustment.

Dividend paid

The dividend paid by the subsidiary reduces the equity of the subsidiary. The adjustment needs to reduce the NCI share of equity, while eliminating the NCI share of dividends paid from the consolidated amount.

The entry in the 'NCI' column of the worksheet is as follows.

NCI	Dr	2 000	
Dividend paid	Cr		2 000
(20% × $10 000)			

Dividend declared

As with the dividend paid, the NCI has been given its share of equity before the declaration of dividends. Because the dividend declared reduces the equity of the subsidiary, the NCI share of equity is also reduced, while eliminating the NCI share of dividends declared from the consolidated amount.

The entry in the 'NCI' column of the worksheet is as follows.

NCI	Dr	3 000	
Dividend declared	Cr		3 000
(20% × $15 000)			

Asset revaluation surplus

The balance of the subsidiary's asset revaluation surplus at 1 July 2022 was $50 000. The balance at 30 June 2023 is $60 000. The NCI share of equity is increased by 20% of this change during the period. The debit adjustment is recognised in the worksheet against the gains/losses on asset revaluation account disclosed in other comprehensive income as this account reflects the increase in the surplus balance for the current period. The adjustment is a debit because it needs to reduce the consolidated gain so that the left-hand column of the worksheet headed 'Parent' shows only the parent share of the gain.

The entry in the 'NCI' column of the worksheet is as follows.

Gains/losses on asset revaluation	Dr	2 000
NCI	Cr	2 000
(20% × ($60 000 − $50 000))		

Intragroup transactions

(6) *Dividend paid*

The entry in the 'Adjustment' column of the consolidation worksheet to adjust for the intragroup dividend out of the $10 000 dividend paid is as follows.

Dividend revenue	Dr	8 000
Dividend paid	Cr	8 000
(80% × $10 000)		

(7) *Dividend declared*

The subsidiary declared a dividend of $15 000 of which $12 000 is payable within the group. The entries in the 'Adjustment' column of the worksheet are as follows.

Dividend payable	Dr	12 000
Dividend declared	Cr	12 000
Dividend revenue	Dr	12 000
Dividend receivable	Cr	12 000

The NCI adjustment for this dividend was already posted above under (5).

(8) *Sale* of *inventories in the current period: Boys Ltd to Beach Ltd*

The worksheet entries in the 'Adjustment' column are as follows.

Sales	Dr	23 000
Cost of sales	Cr	21 500
Inventories	Cr	1 500
(Unrealised profit on sale of inventories, 50% × $3000)		
Deferred tax asset	Dr	450
Income tax expense	Cr	450
(Tax effect, 30% × $1500)		

(9) *Adjustment to NCI: unrealised profit in ending inventories*

The profit on sale was made by the subsidiary. The NCI is therefore affected. The total after-tax profit on the intragroup sale of inventories was $2100 (i.e. $3000 − $900 tax). However, since half the inventories are sold to an external entity, this portion is realised. The adjustment to the NCI relates only to the unrealised profits remaining in inventories still on hand (half of $2100, or $1050). The related adjustment entry (8) reduces after-tax profit by $1050 and makes the consolidated profit lower than recorded profit.

The transaction occurs in the current period. Therefore, the NCI share of current profit is reduced as is the total NCI share of equity. The worksheet entry in the 'NCI' column of the worksheet is as follows.

NCI	Dr	210
NCI share of profit or loss	Cr	210
(20% × $1050)		

The debit adjustment shows a reduction in total equity attributable to the NCI. The credit adjustment is necessary so the last column of the worksheet will show the parent's share of the consolidated profit adjusted only for the parent's share of the unrealised profit. This entry can also be seen as an adjustment to the entry in NCI step 3 that recognised the NCI share of the current profit. As that entry considered the profit before the elimination of unrealised profit on the intragroup transaction, it overstated the NCI share of current profit; this overstatement is corrected by reversing that entry for the NCI share of unrealised profit.

(10) *Sale of inventories in the current period: Beach Ltd to Boys Ltd*

The entries in the 'Adjustment' column of the worksheet to eliminate in full the effects of this intragroup transaction are as follows.

Sales	Dr	18 000	
Cost of sales	Cr		16 000
Inventories	Cr		2 000
Deferred tax asset	Dr	600	
Income tax expense	Cr		600

Because the profit on this intragroup transaction is made by the parent and does not directly affect the equity of the subsidiary, there is no need to make any further adjustment to the NCI share of equity.

(11) *Payment for services: Boys Ltd to Beach Ltd*

The entry in the 'Adjustment' column of the worksheet to eliminate in full the effects of this intragroup transaction is as follows.

Other revenues	Dr	1 000	
Other expenses	Cr		1 000

The profit of the subsidiary is affected by this transaction. However, the consolidated profit, and with that, the total consolidated equity, is unaffected by this adjustment as the revenues are adjusted for the same amount as expenses. Hence, there is no need to make any adjustment to the NCI share of equity.

(12) *Sale of inventories in previous period: Boys Ltd to Beach Ltd*

The entries in the 'Adjustment' column of the worksheet to eliminate in full the effects of this intragroup transaction are as follows.

Retained earnings (1/7/22)	Dr	2 800	
Income tax expense	Dr	1 200	
Cost of sales	Cr		4 000

(13) *Adjustment to NCI: unrealised profit in beginning inventories*

The profit on this transaction was made by the subsidiary, so an adjustment to the NCI share of equity is required. There are two effects on the NCI because the transaction affects both the prior period's and the current period's figures. The adjustment entry (12) reduces prior period profit by $2800 and increases current period profit by $2800. The NCI's share of those adjustments needs to be added back to retained earnings (opening balance) and subtracted from the current profit; that will ensure that in the last column of the worksheet the parent's share of the consolidated profit and the retained earnings (opening balance) is only adjusted for the parent's share of the profit on the intragroup transaction. Total equity is not affected. The NCI adjustment then should not include any adjustment to the NCI share of total equity.

The NCI entry in the 'NCI' column of the worksheet is as follows.

NCI share of profit or loss	Dr	560	
Retained earnings (1/7/22)	Cr		560

(14) *Sale of depreciable asset in the previous period: Boys Ltd to Beach Ltd*

The sale occurred at the beginning of the previous period. Because the transaction occurred in the previous period, the subsidiary's recorded retained earnings (opening balance) contains an after-tax unrealised profit of $14 000.

The entries in the 'Adjustment' column of the worksheet to eliminate in full the effects of this intragroup transaction are as follows.

Retained earnings (1/7/22)	Dr	14 000
Deferred tax asset	Dr	6 000
Plant and equipment	Cr	20 000

(15) *Adjustment to NCI: unrealised profit in depreciable asset sold in the previous period*
The subsidiary recorded the profit on this intragroup transaction, so the NCI is affected. The adjustment entry (14) reduces prior period after-tax profit by $14 000. The NCI adjustment then needs to reduce the NCI share of total equity by the NCI share (20%) of $14 000. The NCI's share of this profit needs to be added back to retained earnings (opening balance); that will ensure that in the last column of the consolidation worksheet the parent's share of the retained earnings (opening balance) is only adjusted for the parent's share of the $14 000 profit on the intragroup transaction.

The worksheet entry in the 'NCI' column is as follows.

NCI	Dr	2 800
Retained earnings (1/7/22)	Cr	2 800

Worksheet entries relating to the sale of the asset and the associated NCI adjustment are made in each year of the asset's life. Realisation of this profit is dealt with in relation to the depreciation adjustment entry.

(16) *Depreciation on non-current asset sold in the previous period: Boys Ltd to Beach Ltd*
The entries in the 'Adjustment' column of the worksheet reflect the depreciation of the transferred asset over a 2-year period on a straight-line basis, given an overall asset life of 10 years.

Accumulated depreciation — plant and equipment	Dr	4 000
Depreciation expense	Cr	2 000
Retained earnings (1/7/22)	Cr	2 000
(Depreciation of 10% × $20 000 p.a. for 2 years)		
Retained earnings (1/7/22)	Dr	600
Income tax expense	Dr	600
Deferred tax asset	Cr	1 200

The assumption made in relation to the $14 000 unrealised profit is that realisation will occur over the life of the asset as the benefits of the depreciable asset are consumed by the group. The profit is then realised in proportion to the depreciation charged on the asset. As can be seen from the adjustment entry (16), the after-tax adjustment to depreciation expense is $1400 (being $2000 – $600). In other words, the $14 000 profit recognised at the date of the intragroup sale by the subsidiary will be recognised as realised to the extent of $1400 p.a. over the next 10 years. Hence, $1400 is realised in the period ended 30 June 2022, and a further $1400 is realised in the period ended 30 June 2023.

(17) *Adjustment to NCI: realisation of profit via depreciation for non-current asset sold in the previous period — Boys Ltd to Beach Ltd*
The related 'Adjustment' entry (16) increases both prior period profit and current period profit by $1400 p.a. The NCI entry then recognises the increases in the NCI share of both prior period profit and current period profit by eliminating it from the consolidated amounts, as well as increasing the NCI share of total equity.

The worksheet entry in the 'NCI' column is as follows.

NCI share of profit or loss	Dr	280
Retained earnings (1/7/22)	Dr	280
NCI	Cr	560
(20% × $1400 p.a.)		

In each of the 10 years following the intragroup transfer of the asset, the group realises an extra $1400 profit. This increases the NCI share of profit by $280 per year, and effectively reverses the reduction in the NCI share of profit relating to the gain on sale shown in entry (15). As the profit becomes realised over time, the NCI share of equity increases. Combining the effects of entries (15) and (17), the effect on NCI share of retained earnings (opening balance) over time is as follows.

NCI share of retained earnings (1/7/22)	$2800 less $280
NCI share of retained earnings (1/7/23)	$2800 less (2 × $280)
NCI share of retained earnings (1/7/24)	$2800 less (3 × $280)
NCI share of retained earnings (1/7/25)	$2800 less (4 × $280)

In the period ended 30 June 2031, the profit becomes fully realised as the asset becomes fully depreciated. In the period ended 30 June 2032, no adjustments are necessary in relation to the intragroup transfer of the depreciable asset.

The consolidation worksheet for Beach Ltd at 30 June 2023 is shown in figure 29.10.

FIGURE 29.10   *Consolidation* worksheet showing NCI and the effects of intragroup transaction

Financial statements	Beach Ltd	Boys Ltd		Adjustments Dr		Cr	Group		NCI Dr		Cr		Parent
Sales revenue	720 000	530 000	8	23 000			1 209 000						
			10	18 000									
Other revenues	240 000	120 000	6	8 000			339 000						
			7	12 000									
			11	1 000									
	960 000	650 000					1 548 000						
Cost of sales	(610 000)	(410 000)			21 500	8	(978 500)						
					16 000	10							
					4 000	12							
Other expenses	(230 000)	(160 000)	1	4 000	1 000	11	(391 000)						
					2 000	16							
	(840 000)	(570 000)					(1 369 500)						
Profit before tax	120 000	80 000					178 500						
Tax expense	(40 000)	(25 000)	12	1 200	1 200	1	(64 550)						
			16	600	600	10							
					450	8							
Profit	80 000	55 000					113 950	5	10 440	210	9		102 880
								13	560				
								17	280				
Retained earnings (1/7/22)	200 000	112 000	1	12 000	3 600	1	242 600	3	10 000	560	13		224 960
			2	45 600	2 000	16		4	10 720	2 800	15		
			12	2 800				17	280				
			14	14 000									
	280 000	167 000	16	600			356 550						327 840
Dividend paid	(20 000)	(10 000)			8 000	6	(22 000)			2 000	5		(20 000)
Dividend declared	(25 000)	(15 000)			12 000	7	(28 000)			3 000	5		(25 000)
	(45 000)	(25 000)					(50 000)						(45 000)

Financial statements	Beach Ltd	Boys Ltd	Adjustments				Group	NCI				Parent
				Dr	Cr				Dr	Cr		
Retained earnings (30/6/23)	235 000	142 000					306 550					282 840
Share capital	600 000	500 000	2	400 000			700 000	3	100 000			600 000
General reserve	80 000	100 000	2	64 000			116 000	3	16 000			96 000
								4	4 000			
BCVR	0	0	2	11 200	14 000	1	2 800	3	4 200	1 400	4	0
	915 000	742 000					1 125 350					978 840
Asset revaluation surplus (1/7/22)	35 000	50 000	1	16 000			69 000	3	4 000			59 000
								4	6 000			
Gains/losses on asset revaluation	(15 000)	10 000					(5 000)	5	2 000			(7 000)
Asset revaluation surplus (30/6/23)	20 000	60 000					64 000					52 000
Total equity: parent												1 030 840
Total equity: NCI								5	2 000	134 200	3	158 510
								5	3 000	19 320	4	
								9	210	10 440	5	
								1	2 800	2 000	5	
										560	17	
Total equity	935 000	802 000					1 189 350		182 370	182 370		1 189 350
Dividend payable	25 000	15 000	7	12 000			28 000					
Other liabilities	25 000	25 000	1	4 800	6 000	1	51 200					
Total liabilities	50 000	40 000					79 200					
Total equity and liabilities	985 000	842 000					1 268 550					
Receivables	80 000	30 000			12 000	6	98 000					
Inventories	100 000	170 000			1 500	8	266 500					
					2 000	10						
Plant and equipment	200 000	500 000			20 000	1	660 000					
					20 000	14						
Accumulated depreciation — plant and equipment	(115 000)	(88 000)	1	40 000	16 000	1	(175 000)					
			16	4 000								
Land	100 000	80 000					180 000					
Shares in Boys Ltd	540 000	0			540 000	2	0					
Deferred tax asset	50 000	40 000	8	450	1 200	16	95 850					
			10	600								
			14	6 000								
Goodwill	0	0	2	3 200			3 200					
Other assets	30 000	110 000					140 000					
Total assets	985 000	842 000		705 050	705 050		1 268 550					

The consolidated financial statements for Beach Ltd and its subsidiary, Boys Ltd, for the year ended 30 June 2023 are as shown in figure 29.11(a), (b) and (c).

FIGURE 29.11	(a) Consolidated statement of profit or loss and other comprehensive income

BEACH LTD
Consolidated statement of profit or loss and comprehensive income
for the year ended 30 June 2023

Revenue	
Sales	$ 1 209 000
Other	339 000
Total revenue	1 548 000
Expenses	
Cost of sales	(978 500)
Other	(391 000)
Total expenses	(1 369 500)
Profit before tax	**178 500**
Income tax expense	(64 550)
Profit for the period	**113 950**
Other comprehensive income	
Revaluation decreases	(5 000)
Total comprehensive income	**$ 108 950**
Profit attributable to:	
Owners of the parent	$ 102 880
Non-controlling interest	11 070
	$ 113 950
Comprehensive income attributable to:	
Owners of the parent	$ 95 880
Non-controlling interest	13 070
	$ 108 950

FIGURE 29.11	(b) Consolidated statement of changes in equity

BEACH LTD
Consolidated statement of changes in equity
for the year ended 30 June 2023

	Equity						
	Share capital	Retained earnings	General reserve	Asset revaluation surplus	Total: owners of the parent	Total: NCI	Total equity
Balance at 1 July 2022	$600 000	$224 960	$96 000	$59 000	$ 979 960	$150 440	$1 130 400
Total comprehensive income		102 880		(7 000)	95 880	13 070	108 950
Dividends paid		(20 000)			(20 000)	(2 000)	(22 000)
Dividends declared	(25 000)				(25 000)	(3 000)	(28 000)
Balance at 30 June 2023	$600 000	$282 840	$96 000	$52 000	$1 030 840	$158 510	$1 189 350

FIGURE 29.11 (c) Consolidated statement of financial position

BEACH LTD
Consolidated statement of financial position
as at 30 June 2023

ASSETS	
Current assets	
Receivables	$ 98 000
Inventories	266 500
Total current assets	364 500
Non-current assets	
Plant and equipment	660 000
Accumulated depreciation — plant and equipment	(175 000)
Land	180 000
Deferred tax asset	95 850
Goodwill	3 200
Other	140 000
Total non-current assets	904 050
Total assets	1 268 550
LIABILITIES	
Current liabilities: dividend payable	28 000
Non-current liabilities	51 200
Total liabilities	79 200
Net assets	**$1 189 350**
EQUITY	
Share capital	$ 600 000
General reserve	96 000
Asset revaluation surplus	52 000
Retained earnings	282 840
Parent interest	1 030 840
Non-controlling interest	158 510
Total equity	**$1 189 350**

2. *Consolidation worksheet changes under full goodwill method*

Under the full goodwill method, the acquisition analysis would change as goodwill is calculated by taking into consideration the fair value of the NCI in the subsidiary.

Acquisition analysis

Net fair value of the identifiable assets and liabilities of Boys Ltd	= $500 000 + $80 000 + $50 000 + $20 000 + $10 000(1 − 30%) (BCVR — inventories) + $20 000(1 − 30%) (BCVR — plant)
	= $671 000
(a) Consideration transferred	= $540 000
(b) NCI in Boys Ltd	= $134 500
Aggregate of (a) and (b)	= $674 500
Goodwill	= $674 500 − $671 000
	= $3500
Fair value of Boys Ltd	= $134 500/20%
	= $672 500
Net fair value of the identifiable assets and liabilities of Boys Ltd	= $671 000
Goodwill of Boys Ltd	= $672 500 − $671 000
	= $1500
Goodwill	= $3500
Goodwill of Boys Ltd	= $1500
Control premium	**= $2000**

Consolidation worksheet entries at 30 June 2023

(1) *Business combination valuation entries*

Because the full goodwill method is used, an extra BCVR entry is needed in relation to goodwill of subsidiary, excluding the control premium. The latter will be recorded in the pre-acquisition entries.

Goodwill	Dr	1 500	
BCVR	Cr		1 500

(2) *Pre-acquisition entries*

Retained earnings (1/7/22)	Dr	45 600	
Share capital	Dr	400 000	
General reserve	Dr	64 000	
Asset revaluation surplus (1/7/22)	Dr	16 000	
BCVR [80% × ($14 000 + $1500)]	Dr	12 400	
Goodwill	Dr	2 000	
Shares in Boys Ltd	Cr		540 000

(3) *NCI share of equity at acquisition date, 1 July 2019 (step 1)*

Under the full goodwill method, NCI at acquisition date will change as goodwill of the subsidiary has been recognised in the BCVR. The NCI share of equity is calculated to be as follows.

Pre-acquisition equity of Boys Ltd	
Retained earnings (1/7/22): 20% × $50 000	= $ 10 000
Share capital: 20% × $500 000	= 100 000
General reserve: 20% × $80 000	= 16 000
Asset revaluation surplus (1/7/22): 20% × $20 000	= 4 000
Business combination valuation reserve: 20% × ($14 000 + $7000 + $1500)	= 4 500
	$134 500

The worksheet entry in the 'NCI' column is as follows.

Retained earnings (1/7/22)	Dr	10 000	
Share capital	Dr	100 000	
General reserve	Dr	16 000	
Asset revaluation surplus (1/7/22)	Dr	4 000	
BCVR	Dr	4 500	
NCI	Cr		134 500

No other changes are required.

COMPREHENSION QUESTIONS

1 What is meant by the term 'non-controlling interest' (NCI)?

2 Explain whether the NCI is better classified as debt or equity.

3 Explain whether the NCI is entitled to a share of subsidiary equity or some other amount.

4 For what lines in the financial statements is it necessary to provide a break-down into parent entity share and NCI share?

5 Describe the format of the consolidation worksheet prepared in the presence of the NCI.

6 Why is it necessary to change the format of the worksheet where the NCI exists in the group?

7 What is the impact on goodwill of the two methods prescribed by AASB 3/IFRS 3 to measure NCI?

8 Describe the disadvantages of the two methods prescribed by AASB 3/IFRS 3 to measure NCI for users and preparers of financial information.

9 If a step approach is used in the calculation of the NCI share of equity, what are the steps involved?

10 How does the existence of the NCI affect the business combination valuation entries?

11 How does the existence of the NCI affect the pre-acquisition entries?

12 Explain how business combination valuation entries may affect the calculation of NCI in step 2 and step 3.

13 What are two events that could occur between the acquisition date and the beginning of the current period that could affect the calculation of the NCI share of retained earnings?

14 Explain whether an NCI adjustment needs to be made for all intragroup transactions.

15 Explain how the adjustment for intragroup transactions affects the calculation of the NCI share of equity.

16 Explain how the gain on bargain purchase affects the measurement of the NCI.

17 Identify the disclosures required in relation to the NCI.

CASE STUDY 29.1

CLASSIFICATION OF THE NCI

Bruce Williams is the accountant for Vintage Cars Ltd. This entity has an 80% holding in the entity Antique Parts Ltd. Bruce is concerned that the consolidated financial statements prepared under AASB 10/IFRS 10 may be misleading. He believes that the NCI in Antique Parts Ltd does not belong to the group and it should be treated as a liability, rather than as a part of consolidated equity.

He therefore wants to prepare the consolidated financial statements showing the NCI in Antique Parts Ltd under liabilities in the statement of financial position, and for the statement of profit and loss and other comprehensive income and the statement of changes in equity to show the profit numbers relating to the parent shareholders only.

Required

Discuss the differences that would arise in the consolidated financial statements if the NCI were classified as debt rather than equity, and the reasons the standard setters have chosen the equity classification of NCI in AASB 10/IFRS 10.

CASE STUDY 29.2

CHOICE OF FULL OR PARTIAL GOODWILL METHODS

The following statement appears in Note 1 of the annual report of Margaret Ltd.

> On an acquisition-by-acquisition basis, the Group recognises any non-controlling interest in the acquiree either at fair value or at the non-controlling interest's proportionate share of the acquiree's net identifiable assets.

Required

Discuss under what circumstances Margaret Ltd would choose one method over the other in recognising any non-controlling interest in an acquiree.

CASE STUDY 29.3

REALISATION OF PROFITS

The consolidated financial statements of Submarine Ltd are being prepared by the group accountant, Raz Putin. He is currently in dispute with the auditors over the need to adjust the NCI share of equity for intragroup transactions. He believes that would be unnecessary. He argues that, as the NCI group of shareholders has an equity interest in the subsidiary, it is entitled to a share of what the subsidiary records as equity, including the profit obtained from all transactions.

He also disputes with the auditors the notion of 'realisation' of profit in relation to the NCI. If realisation requires the involvement of an external entity in a transaction, then in relation to transactions such as intragroup transfers of vehicles and services or interest payments, the profit will never be realised as those transactions never involve external entities. As a result, the most appropriate accounting is to give the NCI a share of subsidiary equity and not be concerned with the fictitious involvement of external entities.

Required

Write a report to Raz convincing him that his arguments are fallacious.

CASE STUDY 29.4

CALCULATION OF NCI

In December 2022, William Ltd acquired 60% of the issued shares of Thomas Ltd. The accountant for William Ltd, Nikki Romanov, is concerned about the approach she should take in preparing the consolidated financial statements for the newly established group. In particular, she is concerned about the calculation of the NCI share of equity, particularly in the years after acquisition date. She has heard accountants in other companies talking about a 'step' approach, and in particular how this makes accounting in periods after the acquisition date very easy.

Required

Prepare a report for Nikki, explaining the step approach for the calculation of NCI and the effects of this approach in the years after acquisition date.

CASE STUDY 29.5

INTRAGROUP TRANSACTIONS

Because Joshua Cement Works Ltd has a number of subsidiaries, the accountant, Evelyn Chen, is required to prepare a set of consolidated financial statements for the group. She is concerned about the calculation of the NCI share of equity particularly where there are intragroup transactions. The auditors require that when adjustments are made for intragroup transactions, the effects of these transactions on the NCI should also be adjusted for. Evelyn has two concerns.

1. Why is it necessary to adjust the NCI share of equity for the effects of intragroup transactions?
2. Is it necessary to make NCI adjustments in relation to *all* intragroup transactions?

Required

Prepare a report for Evelyn, explaining these two areas of concern.

APPLICATION AND ANALYSIS EXERCISES

★ BASIC | ★ ★ MODERATE | ★ ★ ★ DIFFICULT

29.1 Full and partial goodwill method ★   LO4

On 1 July 2022, Rainbow Ltd acquired 80% of the issued shares of Lorikeet Ltd for $165 000. At this date, the equity of Lorikeet Ltd was as follows.

Share capital	$200 000
General reserve	80 000
Retained earnings	100 000

At acquisition date, all the identifiable assets and liabilities of Lorikeet Ltd were recorded at amounts equal to fair value. At 30 June 2024, the equity of Lorikeet Ltd consisted of the following.

Share capital	$200 000
General reserve	100 000
Retained earnings	160 000

A transfer from pre-acquisition retained earnings to general reserve of $20 000 was made during the year ended 30 June 2023. During the year ended 30 June 2024, Lorikeet Ltd recorded a profit of $30 000.

Required

Prepare the consolidated worksheet entries at 30 June 2024 for Rainbow Ltd assuming the following.

1. At 1 July 2022, the fair value of the non-controlling interest was $80 000 and Rainbow Ltd adopts the full goodwill method.
2. Rainbow Ltd adopts the partial goodwill method.

29.2 Full and partial goodwill method ★
LO4

Hare Ltd acquired 90% of the issued shares (*cum div.*) of Tortoise Ltd on 1 July 2021 for $711 000. At this date, the equity of Tortoise Ltd consisted of the following.

Share capital	$375 000
Asset revaluation surplus	90 000
Retained earnings	240 000

At acquisition date, all the identifiable assets and liabilities of Tortoise Ltd were recorded at amounts equal to their fair value. Tortoise Ltd had recorded a dividend payable of $10 000, which was paid in August 2021, and goodwill of $5000.

At 30 June 2023, the equity of Tortoise Ltd consisted of the following.

Share capital	$375 000
Asset revaluation surplus	120 000
Retained earnings	330 000

During the year ended 30 June 2023, Tortoise Ltd recorded a profit of $60 000.

Required

Prepare the consolidated worksheet entries at 30 June 2023 for Hare Ltd assuming the following.

1. At 1 July 2021, the fair value of the non-controlling interest was $75 000 and Hare Ltd adopts the full goodwill method.
2. Hare Ltd adopts the partial goodwill method.

29.3 Partial goodwill method, gain on bargain purchase ★
LO4, 7

Black Ltd acquired 90% of the issued shares of Swan Ltd for $107 600 on 1 July 2022. At this date, the equity of Swan Ltd consisted of the following.

Share capital	$80 000
Retained earnings	40 000

At acquisition date, all the identifiable assets and liabilities of Swan Ltd were recorded at amounts equal to their fair value. At 30 June 2023, the equity of Swan Ltd consisted of the following.

Share capital	$80 000
General reserve	10 000
Retained earnings	45 000

During the year ended 30 June 2023, Swan Ltd recorded a profit of $15 000. The general reserve was created from a transfer from the retained earnings existing at 1 July 2022.

Required

Prepare the consolidated worksheet entries at 30 June 2023 for Black Ltd assuming Black Ltd adopts the partial goodwill method.

29.4 Undervalued assets, full and partial goodwill method ★
LO4, 7

On 1 July 2022, Jane Ltd acquired 75% of the issued shares of Austen Ltd for $360 000. At this date, the equity of Austen Ltd consisted of share capital of $200 000 and retained earnings of $130 000. All the identifiable assets and liabilities of Austen Ltd were recorded at amounts equal to fair value except for the following.

	Carrying amount	Fair value
Machine (cost $25 000)	$ 10 000	$ 12 000
Plant (cost $200 000)	100 000	140 000
Inventories	25 000	33 000

Austen Ltd also had an internally generated patent not recognised at 1 July 2022. Jane Ltd assessed the fair value of that patent at $50 000. The tax rate is 30%.

1. Prepare the acquisition analysis at 1 July 2022 assuming that Jane Ltd used the partial goodwill method.
2. Prepare the acquisition analysis at 1 July 2022 assuming that Jane Ltd used the full goodwill method and the fair value of the non-controlling interest at 1 July 2022 was $110 000.

29.5 Undervalued assets, full and partial goodwill method ★   **LO3, 4, 7**

On 1 July 2022, Sugar Ltd acquired 90% of the shares of Glider Ltd for $435 240. At this date, the equity of Glider Ltd consisted of share capital of $300 000 and retained earnings of $120 000. All the identifiable assets and liabilities of Glider Ltd were recorded at amounts equal to fair value except for the following.

	Carrying amount	Fair value
Land	$ 80 000	$ 95 000
Plant (cost $380 000)	300 000	330 000
Inventories	15 000	18 000

The land is still on hand with Glider Ltd at 30 June 2023. The plant was considered to have a further 10-year life. All the inventories were sold by 30 June 2023. The tax rate is 30%. Sugar Ltd uses the partial goodwill method.

During the year ended 30 June 2023, Glider Ltd recorded a profit of $30 000.

Required

1. Prepare the consolidation worksheet entries for the preparation of the consolidated financial statements of Sugar Ltd at 30 June 2023.
2. Prepare the consolidation worksheet entries if Sugar Ltd used the full goodwill method, assuming the fair value of the non-controlling interest at 1 July 2022 was $47 700.

29.6 Undervalued assets, full and partial goodwill method ★   **LO3, 4, 5**

On 1 July 2022, James Ltd acquired 90% of the issued shares of Cameron Ltd for $145 080. The equity of Cameron Ltd at this date consisted of:

Share capital	$100 000
Retained earnings	40 000

The carrying amounts and fair values of the assets and liabilities recorded by Cameron Ltd at 1 July 2022 were as follows.

	Carrying amount	Fair value
Inventories	$ 5 000	$ 6 000
Fittings (net)	10 000	10 000
Land	45 000	50 000
Machinery (net)	100 000	110 000
Liabilities	20 000	20 000

All inventories on hand at 1 July 2022 are sold by 30 June 2023. The fittings and machinery have a further 10-year life beyond 1 July 2022, with benefits to be received evenly over this period. Differences between carrying amounts and fair values are recognised in the consolidation worksheet. James Ltd uses the partial goodwill method. The tax rate is 30%.

Required

1. Prepare the acquisition analysis at acquisition date.
2. Prepare the business combination valuation entries and the pre-acquisition entry at acquisition date.
3. Prepare the journal entry to recognise NCI at acquisition date.
4. Prepare the consolidation worksheet entries at 30 June 2023. Assume a profit for Cameron Ltd for the year ended 30 June 2023 of $20 000 and no other changes in Cameron Ltd's equity since the acquisition date.
5. Identify and prepare the journal entries in requirements 2 to 4 that will change if the full goodwill method is used. Assume a fair value for NCI on 1 July 2022 of $15 900.

29.7 Undervalued assets, partial goodwill method, dividends ★ **LO3, 4, 5, 6**

On 1 July 2019, Leo Ltd acquired 80% of the issued shares of Sayer Ltd for $240 000 when the equity of Sayer Ltd consisted of the following.

Share capital	$160 000
General reserve	10 000
Retained earnings	59 000

At this date, all identifiable assets and liabilities of Sayer Ltd were recorded at fair value except for the following.

	Carrying amount	Fair value
Inventories	$10 000	$14 000
Plant (cost $220 000)	90 000	99 000
Land	70 000	87 000

Half of the inventories were sold by 30 June 2020 and the remainder by 30 June 2021. The plant has a further 3-year life beyond 1 July 2019, with benefits to be received evenly over this period. The land was sold on 1 March 2023 to an external party. Adjustments for the differences between carrying amounts and fair values are to be made in the consolidation worksheet. Leo Ltd uses the partial goodwill method. The tax rate is 30%.

During the 4 years since acquisition, Sayer Ltd has recorded the following annual results and declared the following dividends.

Year ended	Profit (loss)	Dividends
30 June 2020	$15 000	$ 5 000
30 June 2021	20 000	10 000
30 June 2022	(5 000)	1 000
30 June 2023	20 000	14 000

Dividends were paid within 6 weeks of the end of each period. There have been no transfers to or from the general reserve since the acquisition date.

Required
1. Prepare the consolidation worksheet entries as at 1 July 2019.
2. Prepare the consolidation worksheet entries for the year ended 30 June 2020.
3. Prepare the consolidation worksheet entries for the year ended 30 June 2021.
4. Prepare the consolidation worksheet entries for the year ended 30 June 2022.
5. Prepare the consolidation worksheet entries for the year ended 30 June 2023.

29.8 Undervalued assets, partial goodwill method ★ **LO3, 4, 5, 6**

On 1 July 2019, Errol Ltd acquired 75% of the issued shares of Flynn Ltd for $503 000 when the equity of Flynn Ltd consisted of the following.

Share capital	$320 000
General reserve	80 000
Retained earnings	160 000

At this date, all identifiable assets and liabilities of Flynn Ltd were recorded at fair value except for the following.

	Carrying amount	Fair value
Inventories	$ 80 000	$ 96 000
Machinery (cost $200 000)	140 000	164 000
Land	200 000	280 000

All the inventories were sold by 30 June 2020. The Machinery has a further 3-year life beyond 1 July 2019, with benefits to be received evenly over this period. The land was sold on 1 March 2022 for $300 000. Adjustments for the differences between carrying amounts and fair values are to be made in the consolidation worksheet except for land which is to be measured in Flynn Ltd's accounts at fair value. Errol Ltd uses the partial goodwill method. The tax rate is 30%.

During the 4 years since acquisition, Flynn Ltd has recorded the following annual results.

Year ended	Profit (loss)	Total comprehensive income
30 June 2020	$ 40 000	$ 48 000
30 June 2021	92 000	112 000
30 June 2022	(24 000)	4 000
30 June 2023	88 000	88 000

The other comprehensive income item relates to gains/losses on revaluation of land. There have been no transfers to or from the general reserve or any dividends paid or declared by Flynn Ltd since the acquisition date.

Required
1. Prepare the consolidation worksheet entries as at 1 July 2019.
2. Prepare the consolidation worksheet entries for the year ended 30 June 2020.
3. Prepare the consolidation worksheet entries for the year ended 30 June 2021.
4. Prepare the consolidation worksheet entries for the year ended 30 June 2022.
5. Prepare the consolidation worksheet entries for the year ended 30 June 2023.

29.9 Undervalued assets, full goodwill method ★ ★   **LO3, 4, 5, 6**

On 1 July 2019, Charlie Ltd acquired 60% of the issued shares of Chapman Ltd for $111 700 when the equity of Chapman Ltd consisted of the following.

Share capital	$120 000
General reserve	10 000
Retained earnings	30 000

At this date, the identifiable assets and liabilities of Chapman Ltd were recorded at fair value except for the following assets.

	Carrying amount	Fair value
Inventories	$45 000	$50 000
Equipment (cost $80 000)	65 000	75 000
Land	80 000	90 000

Half of the inventories on hand at acquisition date were sold by 30 June 2020, with the remainder being sold during the year ended 30 June 2021. The equipment had a further 5-year life beyond 1 July 2019, with benefits to be received evenly over this period. The equipment was sold on 1 January 2021 for $70 000. Adjustments for the differences between carrying amounts and fair values are to be made in the consolidation worksheet. At 30 June 2022, the goodwill recorded on acquisition was written down by $3000 as the result of an impairment test. The tax rate is 30%.

Charlie Ltd uses the full goodwill method. The fair value of the non-controlling interest at 1 July 2019 was $74 100.

During the 3 years since acquisition, Chapman Ltd has recorded the following annual results.

Year ended	Profit
30 June 2020	$15 000
30 June 2021	27 000
30 June 2022	12 000

There have been no transfers to or from the general reserve or any dividend paid or declared by Chapman Ltd since the acquisition date.

Required
1. Prepare the consolidation worksheet entries as at 1 July 2019.
2. Prepare the consolidation worksheet entries for the year ended 30 June 2020.
3. Prepare the consolidation worksheet entries for the year ended 30 June 2021.
4. Prepare the consolidation worksheet entries for the year ended 30 June 2022.

29.10 Undervalued assets, full goodwill method ★   **LO3, 4, 5, 6**

On 1 July 2022, Huntsman Ltd acquired 90% the issued shares of Spider Ltd for $140 300. At this date the equity of Spider Ltd consisted of share capital of $100 000 and retained earnings of $50 000. All the identifiable assets and liabilities of Spider Ltd were recorded at amounts equal to fair value at 1 July 2022, except for plant for which the carrying amount of $80 000 (net of accumulated depreciation of $40 000) was $3000 less than the fair value. The plant was estimated to have a further 3-year life beyond 1 July 2022, with the benefits expected to flow evenly over the period. Huntsman Ltd uses the full goodwill method. The fair value of the non-controlling interest at 1 July 2022 was $15 500.

The following annual results were recorded by Spider Ltd following the business combination.

Year ended	Profit/(loss)	Other items of comprehensive income
30 June 2023	$ 8 000	$2 000
30 June 2024	9 000	3 000
30 June 2025	10 000	4 000
30 June 2026	11 000	5 000

The other items of comprehensive income relate to the gains on revaluation of land of Spider Ltd. The tax rate is 30%.

Required

1. Prepare the consolidation worksheet entries as at 1 July 2022.
2. Prepare the consolidation worksheet entries for the year ended 30 June 2023.
3. Prepare the consolidation worksheet entries for the year ended 30 June 2024.
4. Prepare the consolidation worksheet entries for the year ended 30 June 2025.
5. Prepare the consolidation worksheet entries for the year ended 30 June 2026.

29.11 Undervalued assets, full goodwill method ★   **LO3, 4, 5, 6**

On 1 July 2022, Fur Ltd acquired 75% of the issued shares of Seal Ltd for $191 000 when the equity of Seal Ltd consisted of share capital of $120 000 and retained earnings of $90 000. At this date, all the identifiable assets and liabilities of Seal Ltd were recorded at amounts equal to their fair values except for the following.

	Carrying amount	Fair value
Inventories	$20 000	$ 26 000
Land	80 000	110 000
Machinery (cost $68 000)	48 000	57 000

In relation to these assets, the following information is available.

- All the inventories were sold by 30 June 2023.
- The land was revalued in the records of Seal Ltd immediately after the business combination. It was subsequently sold by Seal Ltd on 1 June 2024 for $113 000. At this date, the recorded gains on revaluation of this land taken to other comprehensive income were $3000, the land being revalued to fair value by Seal Ltd immediately prior to sale.
- The machinery was considered to have a further useful life of 3 years.
  The fair value of the non-controlling interest in Seal Ltd at 1 July 2022 was $63 000. Fur Ltd uses the full goodwill method.
  The following annual results were recorded by Seal Ltd following the business combination.

Year ended	Profit/(loss)	Other items of comprehensive income
30 June 2023	$15 000	$ 3 000
30 June 2024	34 500	7 500
30 June 2025	(9 000)	10 500
30 June 2026	33 000	4 000

The other items of comprehensive income relate to gains/(losses) on the revaluation of land which is measured at fair value in the records of Seal Ltd.

The tax rate is 30%.

Required

1. Prepare the consolidation worksheet entries as at 1 July 2022.
2. Prepare the consolidation worksheet entries for the year ended 30 June 2023.
3. Prepare the consolidation worksheet entries for the year ended 30 June 2024.
4. Prepare the consolidation worksheet entries for the year ended 30 June 2025.
5. Prepare the consolidation worksheet entries for the year ended 30 June 2026.

29.12 Undervalued assets, partial goodwill method ★   **LO3, 4, 5**

Bradley Ltd purchased 75% of the issued shares of Cooper Ltd for $500 000 on 1 July 2016 when the equity of Cooper Ltd was as follows.

Share capital	$200 000
General reserve	120 000
Retained earnings	80 000

At this date, Cooper Ltd had not recorded any goodwill, and all identifiable assets and liabilities were recorded at fair value except for the following assets.

	Carrying amount	Fair value
Inventories	$140 000	$200 000
Equipment (cost $340 000)	300 000	380 000
Land	100 000	200 000

All the inventories on hand at 1 July 2016 were sold by 30 June 2017. The equipment has a remaining useful life of 10 years, with benefits to be received evenly over this period. Differences between carrying amounts and fair values are recognised in the consolidation worksheet. The NCI at acquisition date is measured based on the proportionate share of the identifiable assets and liabilities in Cooper Ltd. The tax rate is 30%.

At 30 June 2022, the trial balances of Bradley Ltd and Cooper Ltd are as follows.

	Bradley Ltd	Cooper Ltd
Current assets	$ 324 000	$ 168 000
Shares in Cooper Ltd	500 000	—
Equipment	851 000	380 000
Land	220 000	100 000
Cost of sales	450 000	70 000
Other expenses	130 000	14 000
Income tax expense	100 000	10 000
	$ 2 575 000	$ 742 000
Share capital	$ 800 000	$ 200 000
General reserve	120 000	160 000
Retained earnings (1/7/21)	240 000	150 000
Sales revenue	1 021 200	160 000
Payables	145 800	24 000
Accumulated depreciation — equipment	248 000	48 000
	$ 2 575 000	$ 742 000

Required

1. Prepare the acquisition analysis at acquisition date.
2. Prepare the business combination valuation entries and the pre-acquisition entry at acquisition date.
3. Prepare the journal entry to recognise NCI at acquisition date.

4. Prepare the consolidation worksheet entries at 30 June 2017. Assume a profit for Cooper Ltd for the year ended 30 June 2017 of $80 000 and no other changes in Cooper Ltd's equity since the acquisition date.
5. Prepare the consolidation worksheet entries at 30 June 2022.
6. Prepare the consolidated financial statements at 30 June 2022.

29.13 Undervalued and unrecorded assets, partial and full goodwill method ★ ★   **LO3, 4, 5**

On 1 July 2020, Adam Ltd acquired 80% of the issued shares (*cum div.*) of Mosely Ltd for $202 000 when the equity of Mosely Ltd consisted of the following.

Share capital — 100 000 shares	$100 000
General reserve	40 000
Retained earnings	50 000

At this date, the carrying amounts and fair values of the assets of Mosely Ltd were as follows.

	Carrying amount	Fair value
Land	$70 000	$90 000
Plant (cost $100 000)	80 000	85 000
Fittings (cost $40 000)	20 000	20 000
Goodwill	5 000	10 000

At 1 July 2020, Mosely Ltd had not recorded an internally generated trademark that Adam Ltd considered to have a fair value of $50 000. This intangible asset was considered to have an indefinite useful life. Both plant and fittings were expected to have a further 5-year useful life beyond 1 July 2020, with benefits being received evenly over those periods. The plant was sold on 1 January 2023. Any adjustment for the differences between carrying amounts and fair values is recognised in the consolidation worksheet. Adam Ltd uses the partial goodwill method.

Additional information

• In August 2020, the dividend payable of $5000 on hand at 1 July 2020 was paid by Mosely Ltd.
• The following profits were recorded by Mosely Ltd.

For the year ended 30 June 2021	$20 000
For the year ended 30 June 2022	25 000
For the year ended 30 June 2023	30 000

• In June 2022, Mosely Ltd transferred out of post-acquisition profits $5000 to general reserve, and in June 2023, a further $6000 was transferred.
• Dividends declared or paid since 1 July 2020 are:
  – $8000 dividend declared in June 2021, paid in August 2021
  – $6000 dividend declared in June 2022, paid in August 2022
  – $5000 dividend paid in December 2022
  – $8000 dividend declared in June 2023, expected to be paid in August 2023.

Required

1. Prepare the worksheet entries for the preparation of the consolidated financial statements of Adam Ltd and its subsidiary, Mosely Ltd, at 30 June 2023.
2. Prepare the worksheet entries that would differ from those in requirement 1 if Adam Ltd uses the full goodwill method. Assume the value of the non-controlling interest at 1 July 2020 was $49 250.

29.14 Undervalued and unrecorded assets, full goodwill method ★ ★   **LO3, 4, 5, 6, 7**

On 1 July 2019, Riley Ltd acquired 70% of the issued shares (*cum div.*) of Tyler Ltd for $141 950. At this date, the equity of Tyler Ltd consisted of the following.

Share capital	$100 000
General reserve	31 000
Retained earnings	25 000
Other components of equity	9 000

Tyler Ltd's records showed a dividend payable at 1 July 2019 of $10 000. The dividend was paid on 1 November 2019.

A comparison of the carrying amounts and fair values of the assets of Tyler Ltd at 1 July 2019 revealed the following.

	Carrying amount	Fair value
Plant (cost $75 000)	$45 000	$60 000
Vehicles (cost $40 000)	23 000	23 000
Goodwill	10 000	10 000

Both plant and vehicles were expected to have a further 5-year life beyond the acquisition date, with benefits being received evenly over those periods. The plant was sold on 30 June 2022. Tyler Ltd had not recorded an internally generated brand name that was considered by Riley Ltd to have a fair value of $20 000. The brand name is regarded as having an indefinite useful life. Adjustments for the differences in carrying amounts and fair values are recognised in the consolidation worksheet. At 30 June 2020, goodwill was considered to be impaired by $1000, and a further impairment loss of $2000 was recognised by 30 June 2021. Riley Ltd uses the full goodwill method. The fair value of the NCI at 1 July 2019 was $57 000. The tax rate is 30%.

Additional information
- The dividends paid and declared since 1 July 2019 are:
  - $10 000 dividend declared in June 2020, paid in October 2020
  - $5000 dividend declared in June 2021, paid in September 2021
  - $8000 dividend paid in April 2022.
- In June 2021, Tyler Ltd transferred an amount of $20 000 from the pre-acquisition general reserve to retained earnings.
- The other components of equity account reflects movements in the fair values of financial assets. The balances of this account at 1 July 2021 were $4000 for Riley Ltd and $11 000 for Tyler Ltd.
- On 30 June 2022, the financial data of both companies were as follows.

	Riley Ltd	Tyler Ltd
Revenues	$280 000	$190 000
Expenses	220 000	140 000
Profit before tax	60 000	50 000
Income tax expense	26 000	14 000
Profit for the period	34 000	36 000
Retained earnings (1/7/21)	76 000	65 000
Total available for appropriation	110 000	101 000
Dividend paid	20 000	8 000
Retained earnings (30/6/22)	90 000	93 000
Share capital	100 000	100 000
General reserve	44 000	11 000
Other components of equity	6 000	9 000
Payables	20 000	12 000
	$260 000	$225 000
Cash	$ 22 050	$ 43 000
Financial assets	20 000	30 000
Vehicles	35 000	50 000
Accumulated depreciation — vehicles	(12 000)	(30 000)
Plant and equipment	80 000	120 000
Accumulated depreciation — plant and equipment	(50 000)	(75 000)
Land	30 000	—
Goodwill	—	10 000
Accumulated impairment — goodwill	—	(3 000)
Trademarks	—	80 000
Shares in Tyler Ltd	134 950	—
	$260 000	$225 000

Required

Prepare the consolidated financial statements of Riley Ltd as at 30 June 2022.

29.15 Undervalued assets, partial goodwill method, intragroup transactions ★ ★   **LO3, 4, 5, 6**

On 1 July 2022, Isabel Ltd acquired 80% of the issued shares of Darcy Ltd for $794 400. On that date, the statement of financial position of Darcy Ltd consisted of the following.

Share capital	$ 750 000
General reserve	30 000
Asset revaluation surplus	45 000
Retained earnings	30 000
Liabilities	540 000
	$1 395 000
Cash	$ 105 000
Inventories	210 000
Land	195 000
Plant and equipment	900 000
Accumulated depreciation — plant and equipment	(390 000)
Trademark	300 000
Goodwill	75 000
	$1 395 000

At 1 July 2022, all identifiable assets and liabilities of Darcy Ltd were recorded at fair value except for the following.

	Carrying amount	Fair value
Inventories	$210 000	$240 000
Land	195 000	255 000
Plant and equipment (cost $300 000)	510 000	570 000
Trademark	300 000	330 000

During the year ended 30 June 2023, all inventories on hand at the beginning of the year were sold, and the land was sold on 28 February 2023 to Outback Ltd, an external party, for $210 000. The plant and equipment had a further 5-year life beyond 1 July 2022 and was expected to be used evenly over that time. The trademark was considered to have an indefinite life. Any adjustments for differences at acquisition date between carrying amounts and fair values are made in the consolidation worksheet. Isabel Ltd uses the partial goodwill method. The tax rate is assumed to be 30%.

Financial information for Isabel Ltd and Darcy Ltd for the year ended 30 June 2023 is as follows.

	Isabel Ltd	Darcy Ltd
Sales revenue	$600 000	$516 000
Other income	225 000	90 000
	825 000	606 000
Cost of sales	486 000	384 000
Other expenses	159 000	93 000
	645 000	477 000
Profit from trading	180 000	129 000
Gains/(losses) on sale of non-current assets	30 000	15 000
Profit before tax	210 000	144 000
Income tax expense	60 000	54 000
Profit for the period	150 000	90 000
Retained earnings (1/7/22)	90 000	30 000
Transfer from general reserve	—	24 000
	240 000	144 000

Interim dividend paid	36 000	30 000
Final dividend declared	18 000	12 000
	54 000	42 000
Retained earnings (30/6/23)	$186 000	$102 000
Asset revaluation surplus (1/7/22)		$ 45 000
Gain on revaluation of specialised plant		15 000
Asset revaluation surplus (30/6/23)		$ 60 000

The transfer from general reserve for Darcy Ltd is from pre-acquisition equity. During the year ended 30 June 2023, Darcy Ltd sold inventories to Isabel Ltd for $24 000. The original cost of these items to Darcy Ltd was $15 000. One-third of these inventories were still on hand at the end of the year.

On 31 March 2023, Darcy Ltd transferred an item of plant with a carrying amount of $30 000 to Isabel Ltd for $45 000. Isabel Ltd treated this item as inventories. The item was still on hand at the end of the year. Darcy Ltd applied a 20% p.a. depreciation rate to this type of plant.

Required

1. Prepare the consolidation worksheet entries necessary for preparation of the consolidated financial statements for Isabel Ltd and its subsidiary for the year ended 30 June 2023.
2. Prepare the consolidated statement of profit or loss and other comprehensive income and statement of changes in equity for Isabel Ltd and its subsidiary at 30 June 2023.

29.16 Full goodwill method, intragroup transactions ★ ★   **LO4, 6**

On 1 July 2017, Nathan Ltd acquired 75% of the issued shares of Jones Ltd at a cost of $27 600. At this date, the equity of Jones Ltd consisted of the following.

Ordinary shares — ($1 each fully paid)	$30 000
Retained earnings	6 000

At 1 July 2017, Jones Ltd had not recorded any goodwill, and all the identifiable assets and liabilities of Jones Ltd were recorded at fair value. Nathan Ltd uses the full goodwill method. The fair value of the non-controlling interest in Jones Ltd at 1 July 2017 was $9000.

The trial balances of the two companies as at 30 June 2022 are as follows.

Trial balances				
as at 30 June 2022				
	Nathan Ltd		Jones Ltd	
	Dr	Cr	Dr	Cr
Share capital		$ 40 000		$ 30 000
Retained earnings (1/7/21)		19 000		14 500
Other components of equity		—		5 000
Current tax liability		8 500		2 900
Plant	$ 30 000		$ 60 000	
Accumulated depreciation — plant		17 000		30 500
Shares in Jones Ltd	27 600		—	
10% debentures in Jones Ltd	2 500		—	
Inventories	12 000		15 500	
Cash	14 050		500	
Financial assets	—		11 000	
Deferred tax asset	2 000		5 000	
Sales revenue		50 000		80 000
Cost of sales	34 000		58 500	
Selling expenses	4 000		6 000	
Other expenses	1 500		1 500	
Financial expenses	1 500		2 000	

Trial balances as at 30 June 2022				
	Nathan Ltd		Jones Ltd	
	Dr	Cr	Dr	Cr
Income tax expense	5 000		5 500	
Interest received from debentures		250	—	
Dividend revenue		1 800	—	
Dividend paid	—		2 400	
10% debentures	2 400			5 000
	$136 550	$136 550	$167 900	$167 900

Additional information

- Intragroup sales of inventories for the year ended 30 June 2022 from Jones Ltd to Nathan Ltd: $19 000.
- Unrealised profits on inventories held at 1 July 2021: inventories held by Nathan Ltd purchased from Jones Ltd at a profit before tax of $800.
- Unrealised profits on inventories held at 30 June 2022: inventories held by Nathan Ltd purchased from Jones Ltd at a profit before tax of $1200.
- The other components of equity account relates to financial assets held by Jones Ltd. The balance of this account at 1 July 2021 was $4000.
- The tax rate is 30%.

Required

Prepare the consolidated financial statements for Nathan Ltd for the year ended 30 June 2022.

29.17 Undervalued assets, partial goodwill method, intragroup transactions ★ ★   LO4, 6

On 1 July 2021, Matthew Ltd paid $236 400 for 75% of the issued shares of Crawley Ltd. At this date, the equity of Crawley Ltd consisted of the following.

Share capital (200 000 shares)	$ 200 000
General reserve	80 000
Retained earnings	40 000

A comparison of the carrying amounts and fair values of Crawley Ltd's assets at the acquisition date showed the following.

	Carrying amount	Fair value
Land	$184 000	$200 000
Plant (cost $150 000)	100 000	120 000
Inventories	65 000	90 000
Accounts receivable	40 000	35 000
Goodwill	4 000	—

In relation to these assets, the following information is available.
- The plant had a further 5-year life but was sold on 1 January 2023.
- All the inventories were sold by 30 June 2022.
- All the accounts receivable were collected by 30 June 2022.

Any valuation reserves arising on consolidation are transferred on realisation of the asset to retained earnings. Matthew Ltd uses the partial goodwill method.

The following transactions occurred between 1 July 2021 and 30 June 2023.

2022

Jan.	1	Crawley Ltd transferred $20 000 from general reserve to retained earnings.
Feb.	11	Crawley Ltd paid an $8000 dividend, half being from profits earned prior to 1 July 2021.
	21	Crawley Ltd sold inventories to Matthew Ltd for $50 000 recording a before-tax profit of
March		$10 000. The tax rate is 30%.
June	25	Crawley Ltd declared a $15 000 dividend.
	30	Crawley Ltd recorded a profit of $130 000. One-quarter of the inventories sold by Crawley Ltd to Matthew Ltd on 21 March 2022 are still on hand with Matthew Ltd.
Aug	14	The $15 000 dividend declared by Crawley Ltd was paid.
Sept.	21	The remaining inventories in Matthew Ltd sold to it by Crawley Ltd were sold outside the group.

2023

Jan.	1	Crawley Ltd paid a $16 000 dividend.
June	30	Crawley Ltd recorded a profit of $150 000.

Required

Prepare the consolidation worksheet entries for the preparation of consolidated financial statements by Matthew Ltd at 30 June 2023.

29.18 Undervalued assets, full and partial goodwill method, intragroup transactions ★ ★ **LO3, 4, 6**

On 1 July 2018, Robert Ltd acquired 75% of the issued shares of Grantham Ltd for $160 000. The following balances appeared in the records of Grantham Ltd at this date.

Share capital	$80 000
General reserve	8 000
Retained earnings	40 000

At 1 July 2018, all the identifiable assets and liabilities of Grantham Ltd were recorded at fair value except for the following.

	Carrying amount	Fair value
Machinery (cost $144 000)	$120 000	$160 000
Inventories	64 000	80 000
Receivables	80 000	72 000

The machinery had a remaining useful life of 5 years beyond 1 July 2018, with benefits to be received on a straight-line basis over the period. The machinery was sold by Grantham Ltd on 1 January 2023 for $16 000. By 30 June 2019, receivables had all been collected and inventories sold. Any adjustments for differences at acquisition date between carrying amounts and fair values are made in the consolidation worksheet.

For the year ended 30 June 2023, the following information is available.

- Intragroup sales were: Grantham Ltd to Robert Ltd — $80 000. The mark-up on cost of all sales was 25%.
- At 30 June 2023, inventories of Robert Ltd included $8000 of items acquired from Grantham Ltd.
- At 1 July 2022, inventories of Robert Ltd included goods of $4000 resulting from a sale on 1 March 2022 of non-current assets by Grantham Ltd at a before-tax profit of $800. These items were on-sold to external entities by Robert Ltd on 1 September 2022. This class of non-current assets is depreciated using a 10% p.a. depreciation rate on a straight-line basis.
- On 1 January 2023, Grantham Ltd sold an item of plant to Robert Ltd for $8000 at a before-tax profit of $2400. For plant assets, Grantham Ltd applies a 10% p.a. straight-line depreciation rate, while Robert Ltd uses a 2.5% p.a. straight-line rate.
- The tax rate is 30%.
- Financial information for the year ended 30 June 2023 includes the following.

	Robert Ltd	Grantham Ltd
Sales revenue	$ 336 000	$ 204 000
Dividend revenue	12 000	–
Other revenue	48 000	32 000
Total revenue	396 000	236 000
Cost of sales	232 000	104 000
Other expenses		
Selling and administrative (including depreciation)	16 000	8 000
Financial	32 000	24 000
Total expenses	280 000	136 000
Profit from trading	116 000	100 000
Gains/(losses) on sale of non-current assets	16 000	4 000
Profit before tax	132 000	104 000
Income tax expense	52 800	41 600
Profit for the period	79 200	62 400
Retained earnings (1/7/22)	160 000	80 000
	239 200	142 400
Transfer to general reserve	15 200	4 000
Interim dividend paid	16 000	32 000
Final dividend declared	16 000	16 000
	47 200	52 000
Retained earnings (30/6/23)	$ 192 000	$ 90 400
Asset revaluation surplus (1/7/22)	$ 12 000	$ 8 000
Gains on property revaluation	4 000	2 000
Asset revaluation surplus (30/6/23)	$ 16 000	$ 10 000

Required

1. Prepare the consolidation worksheet entries for the preparation of the consolidated financial statements for Robert Ltd at 30 June 2023 using the partial goodwill method.
2. Prepare the entries that would change in requirement 1 above if the full goodwill method were used. The fair value of the NCI at 1 July 2018 was $51 600.

29.19 **Undervalued assets, partial goodwill method, intragroup transactions** ★ ★ **LO3, 4, 5, 6**

On 1 July 2021, Richard Ltd acquired 80% of the issued shares (*cum div.*) of Carson Ltd for $166 400. At this date, the equity of Carson Ltd consisted of the following.

Share capital	$120 000
General reserve	24 000
Retained earnings	16 000

At 1 July 2021, one of the liabilities of Carson Ltd was a dividend payable of $10 000. This dividend was paid on 1 September 2021. One of the assets recorded by Carson Ltd was goodwill of $5000. Richard Ltd uses the partial goodwill method.

At 1 July 2021, all the identifiable assets and liabilities of Carson Ltd were recorded at amounts equal to their fair values except for the following.

	Carrying amount	Fair value
Plant (cost $100 000)	$80 000	$88 000
Land	60 000	80 000
Inventories	40 000	52 000

In relation to these assets, the following information is available.

- The plant had an expected useful life of 4 years.
- Land is revalued in the records of Carson Ltd at acquisition date. The land on hand at 1 July 2021 was sold by Carson Ltd on 8 February 2023. On sale any related asset revaluation surplus is transferred to retained earnings.
- The inventories were all sold by 30 June 2022.

Additional information

- During the period ended 30 June 2022, Carson Ltd transferred $8000 from the general reserve existing at 1 July 2021 to retained earnings.
- At 30 June 2022, Carson Ltd recognised gains on revaluation of land of $6000 in other comprehensive income for the period.
- In June 2022, Carson Ltd sold inventories to Richard Ltd for $7000. The inventories had originally cost Carson Ltd $5000. 20% of these inventories remained unsold by Richard Ltd at 30 June 2022.
- During the 2022–23 period ended 30 June 2023, Carson Ltd sold inventories to Richard Ltd for $120 000. At 30 June 2023, Richard Ltd holds inventories sold to it by Carson Ltd for $20 000 which had cost Carson Ltd $15 000.
- On 1 January 2023, Carson Ltd sold an inventories item to Richard Ltd at a before-tax profit of $5000. The original cost of this item to Carson Ltd is $10 000. This asset was classified as plant by Richard Ltd and depreciated over a 5-year period.
- The tax rate is 30%.
- Financial information provided by the companies at 30 June 2023 was as follows.

	Richard Ltd	Carson Ltd
Sales revenue	$ 910 000	$ 624 000
Other revenue	60 000	65 600
Total revenue	970 000	689 600
Cost of sales	(625 000)	(464 000)
Other expenses	(225 000)	(129 600)
Total expenses	(850 000)	(593 600)
Profit before tax	120 000	96 000
Tax expense	(30 000)	(32 000)
Profit for the period	90 000	64 000
Retained earnings at 1 July 2022	100 000	48 000
Transfer from asset revaluation surplus	—	14 000
Transfer to general reserve	—	(12 000)
Dividend paid	(20 000)	(12 000)
Dividend declared	(30 000)	(6 000)
Retained earnings at 30 June 2023	140 000	96 000
Share capital	400 000	120 000
General reserve	—	28 000
Asset revaluation surplus	—	10 000
Total equity	540 000	254 000
Provisions	40 000	30 000
Payables	30 000	40 000
Deferred tax liabilities	12 000	15 000
Non-current liabilities	83 000	65 000
Total liabilities	165 000	150 000
Total equity and liabilities	$ 705 000	$ 404 000
Shares in Carson Ltd	$ 158 400	—
Plant	800 000	$ 320 000
Accumulated depreciation — plant	(544 000)	(120 000)
Land	60 000	90 000
Intangible assets	75 000	60 000
Deferred tax assets	15 000	8 000
Cash	20 000	5 000
Receivables	40 600	6 000
Inventories	80 000	30 000
Goodwill	—	5 000
Total assets	$ 705 000	$ 404 000

Required

Prepare the consolidation worksheet for the preparation of consolidated financial statements for Richard Ltd at 30 June 2023.

29.20 Undervalued assets, full goodwill method, intragroup transactions   ★ ★   **LO3, 4, 5, 6**

Mary Ltd acquired 75% of the issued shares of Edith Ltd on 1 July 2018. In exchange for these shares, Mary Ltd gave a consideration of $26 000 cash and 10 000 shares in Mary Ltd, these having a fair value of $2 each. At this date, the shareholders' equity of Edith Ltd consisted of the following.

Share capital (15 000 shares)	$45 000	
Retained earnings	9 000	

At this date all the identifiable assets and liabilities of Edith Ltd were recorded at amounts equal to their fair values except for plant for which the fair value was $2000 greater than the carrying amount of $25 000 (original cost was $35 000). The plant was expected to have a further 5-year life. The fair value of the non-controlling interest at 1 July 2018 was $15 000. Mary Ltd uses the full goodwill method. The tax rate is 30%.

Assets held by Edith Ltd at 30 June 2023 include financial assets. Gains and losses on these assets are recognised in other comprehensive income. During the year ended 30 June 2023, Edith Ltd recorded gains of $1500 on these assets. Financial information supplied by the two companies at 30 June 2023 was as follows.

	Mary Ltd	Edith Ltd
Sales revenue	$ 75 000	$ 118 000
Interest revenue	375	1 000
Dividend revenue	2 700	1 000
	78 075	120 000
Cost of sales	(51 000)	(87 750)
Financial expenses	(2 250)	(3 000)
Selling expenses	(6 000)	(9 000)
Other expenses	(2 250)	(2 250)
	(61 500)	(102 000)
Profit before tax	16 575	18 000
Income tax expense	(7 500)	(8 200)
Profit for the year	9 075	9 800
Retained earnings (1/7/22)	28 900	21 700
	37 975	31 500
Dividend paid	(4 000)	(3 600)
Retained earnings (30/6/23)	33 975	27 900
Share capital	60 000	45 000
Other components of equity	—	7 500
Total equity	93 975	80 400
Current liabilities	12 750	4 350
Non-current liabilities: Loans	—	7 500
Total liabilities	12 750	11 850
Total equity and liabilities	$ 106 725	$ 92 250
Plant	$ 45 000	$90 000
Accumulated depreciation — plant	(25 500)	(45 750)
Shares in Edith Ltd	46 000	—
Loans to Edith Ltd	3 750	—
Inventories	13 400	23 250
Cash	21 075	750
Financial assets	—	16 500
Deferred tax assets	3 000	7 500
Total assets	$ 106 725	$ 92 250

Additional information
- At 1 July 2022, Mary Ltd held inventories that had been sold to it by Edith Ltd in the previous year at a profit of $1200.
- During the year ended 30 June 2023, Edith Ltd sold inventories to Mary Ltd for $28 500. At 30 June 2023, Mary Ltd still had on hand inventories that had been sold to it by Edith Ltd for a profit of $1800 before tax.
- Interest of $375 was paid to Mary Ltd by Edith Ltd on both 30 June 2022 and 30 June 2023.

Required

Prepare the consolidated financial statements of Mary Ltd for the year ended 30 June 2023.

29.21 Undervalued assets, full and partial goodwill method, intragroup transactions ★ ★ **LO3, 4, 5, 6**

On 1 July 2018, Downton Ltd acquired 75% of the issued shares (*cum div.*) of Abbey Ltd for $135 000. At this date the equity of Abbey Ltd consisted of the following.

Share capital	$60 000
General reserve	6 000
Retained earnings	30 000

At the date of the business combination, all the identifiable assets and liabilities of Abbey Ltd had carrying amounts equal to their fair values except for the following.

	Carrying amount	Fair value
Plant (cost $120 000)	$80 000	$110 000
Inventories	50 000	62 000
Receivables	66 000	60 000

The plant had a further useful life of 5 years. It was sold by Abbey Ltd to external entities on 1 April 2023 for $6000. By 30 June 2019, all the inventories were sold to entities outside the group. Also, by 30 June 2019, receivables of $66 000 had been collected. One of the liabilities of Abbey Ltd at 1 July 2018 was dividend payable of $20 000. The tax rate is 30%. Downton Ltd uses the partial goodwill method.

Additional information

- At 30 June 2022, inventories of Downton Ltd included assets sold to it by Abbey Ltd for a before-tax profit of $600. These items were sold to external entities during the year ended 30 June 2023.
- During the year ended 30 June 2023, Abbey Ltd had sold inventories to Downton Ltd for $120 000. The mark-up on sales was 25% on cost. At 30 June 2023, Downton Ltd still had some of these inventories on hand that were acquired from Abbey Ltd for $6000.
- On 1 January 2023, Abbey Ltd sold a plant to Downton Ltd for a before-tax profit of $2400. This plant was carried at $3000 (original cost $40 000) in the records of Abbey Ltd at the time of sale. Depreciation on this type of plant is calculated using a 20% p.a. straight-line method.
- Financial information provided by Abbey Ltd concerning events affecting it during the year ended 30 June 2023 was as follows.

Profit for the year	$ 46 800
Retained earnings at 1 July 2022	60 000
	106 800
Dividend paid	(24 000)
Dividend declared	(12 000)
Transfer to general reserve	(3 000)
	(39 000)
Retained earnings at 30 June 2023	$ 67 800

The transfer to general reserve is from post-acquisition retained earnings. Abbey Ltd also reported a comprehensive income for the year ended 30 June 2023 of $48 300, which included gains on revaluation of land of $750, as the asset revaluation surplus in relation to the land had increased from $6000 to $7500 over the year.

Required

1. Prepare the consolidation worksheet entries for the preparation of the consolidated financial statements of Downton Ltd at 30 June 2023.
2. Prepare the consolidation worksheet entries at 30 June 2023 if Downton Ltd had used the full goodwill method and the fair value of the non-controlling interest at 1 July 2018 was $39 000.

REFERENCE

Ernst & Young 2010, *Controlling the effects of a non-controlling interest*, EYGM no. AU0467, March, www.ey.com.

ACKNOWLEDGEMENTS

Photo: © ESB Professional / Shutterstock.com

Figure 29.5: © Peter Gerhardy

Text: © 2019 Australian Accounting Standards Board (AASB). The text, graphics and layout of this publication are protected by Australian copyright law and the comparable law of other countries. No part of the publication may be reproduced, stored or transmitted in any form or by any means without the prior written permission of the AASB except as permitted by law. For reproduction or publication, permission should be sought in writing from the AASB. Requests in the first instance should be addressed to the National Director, Australian Accounting Standards Board, PO Box 204, Collins Street West, Victoria 8007.

Text: © IFRS. This publication contains copyright material of the IFRS Foundation in respect of which all rights are reserved. Reproduced by John Wiley & Sons Australia, Ltd with the permission of the IFRS Foundation. No permission granted to third parties to reproduce or distribute. For full access to IFRS Standards and the work of the IFRS Foundation please visit http://eifrs.ifrs.org. The International Accounting Standards Board, the IFRS Foundation, the authors and the publishers do not accept responsibility for any loss caused by acting or refraining from acting in reliance on the material in this publication, whether such loss is caused by negligence or otherwise.

CHAPTER 30

Consolidation: other issues

CHAPTER AIM

This chapter discusses the application of AASB 10/IFRS 10 *Consolidated Financial Statements* to consolidation issues involving multiple subsidiary group structures. The chapter also addresses changes in the equity held by a parent in a subsidiary, dealing with situations where the parent increases its shareholding in a subsidiary as well as situations where a parent reduces its shareholding in a subsidiary. In the latter case the parent may retain control or lose control of the subsidiary.

LEARNING OBJECTIVES

After studying this chapter, you should be able to:

30.1 understand different ways in which a group can be formed and how ownership interests in that group can be changed

30.2 explain the difference between direct non-controlling interest (DNCI) and indirect non-controlling interest (INCI)

30.3 prepare the consolidated financial statements for a multiple subsidiary structure

30.4 explain the effects on the consolidation process where the acquisition is non-sequential

30.5 explain how to account for changes in ownership interests by a parent in a group.

CONCEPTS FOR REVIEW

Before studying this chapter, you should understand and, if necessary, revise:
- the concept of a group for consolidation purposes
- the nature and measurement of the non-controlling interest (NCI).

30.1 Introduction and scope

LEARNING OBJECTIVE 30.1 Understand different ways in which a group can be formed and how ownership interests in that group can be changed.

The purpose of this chapter is to discuss some advanced issues raised in the preparation of consolidated financial statements. In chapters 26–29 the basic principles used in the preparation of consolidated financial statements were presented. These principles will continue to be applied in this chapter, but the application will be to more complex group structures or will involve dealing with changes in ownership within the group. Therefore, two main issues are discussed in this chapter.

The first issue is the preparation of consolidated financial statements for a group structure where the parent has control over two subsidiaries but the parent has an ownership interest in only one of those subsidiaries. In chapter 29 the group under discussion consisted of two companies in which the parent had a partial interest in a subsidiary. In that subsidiary there were two sets of parties that hold ownership interests, the **parent** and the **non-controlling interest (NCI)**. Remember that an entity controls another entity if, for example, it holds, directly or indirectly, the majority of voting rights in the other entity. The voting rights are given by the ownership interests and this text assumes that one voting right is attached to each share. As such, in the group structure in figure 30.1, P Ltd directly controls A Ltd through its ownership interest in A Ltd. However, P Ltd has indirect control of B Ltd through A Ltd. Therefore, P Ltd is the parent of two subsidiaries, A Ltd and B Ltd, although it only has an ownership interest in A Ltd. P Ltd is the **ultimate parent**, while A Ltd, as well as being P Ltd's subsidiary, is the **immediate parent** of B Ltd; for ease of interpretation, B Ltd will be referred to as the **ultimate subsidiary**. Moreover, the NCI in A Ltd has an indirect interest in B Ltd through the ownership interest of A Ltd in B Ltd. As such, in this group structure, the NCI is classified into direct NCI (DNCI) and indirect NCI (INCI). This classification and the calculation of the NCI and its components are discussed in section 30.2.

In preparing the consolidated financial statements for complex group structures such as those in figure 30.1, the timing of the acquisition of the ownership interests is important. Two situations are discussed in this chapter.

- First, there is the situation where P Ltd acquired its ownership interest in A Ltd before A Ltd acquired its ownership interest in B Ltd. In this chapter this is referred to as a sequential acquisition — P Ltd controls A Ltd before A Ltd controls B Ltd (in other words, the ultimate parent controls the immediate parent *before* the immediate parent controls the ultimate subsidiary).
- Second, there is the situation where A Ltd acquired its ownership interest in B Ltd before P Ltd acquired its ownership interest in A Ltd. This is referred to as a non-sequential acquisition — A Ltd controls B Ltd before P Ltd controls A Ltd (in other words, the ultimate parent controls the immediate parent *after* the immediate parent controls the ultimate subsidiary).

The preparation of consolidated financial statements for a multiple subsidiary structure is discussed in section 30.3. The additional issues encountered in the preparation of consolidated financial statements where the multiple subsidiary structure is created through a non-sequential acquisition are discussed in section 30.4.

The second issue discussed in this chapter involves a parent and its subsidiary and changes in the ownership of the parent in the subsidiary subsequent to the group being formed. A number of situations are possible.

- The parent acquires additional shares in a subsidiary — discussed in section 30.5.2.
- The parent sells part of its shares in a subsidiary but retains control of the subsidiary — discussed in section 30.5.3.
- The parent sells part of its shares in a subsidiary and loses control of the subsidiary — discussed in section 30.5.4.

30.2 Direct and indirect non-controlling interest

LEARNING OBJECTIVE 30.2 Explain the difference between direct non-controlling interest (DNCI) and indirect non-controlling interest (INCI).

One feature of multiple subsidiary structures where a parent has an interest in a subsidiary that is itself a parent of another subsidiary is the need to classify the NCI ownership in the subsidiaries into **direct non-controlling interest (DNCI)** and **indirect non-controlling interest (INCI)**.

A DNCI exists where the NCI owns shares in a subsidiary. An INCI exists in a subsidiary where that subsidiary is owned by a partially owned subsidiary in the group. The NCI in the partially owned subsidiary is the INCI in the other subsidiary.

Consider the group in figure 30.1.

| FIGURE 30.1 | Group with both INCI and DNCI |

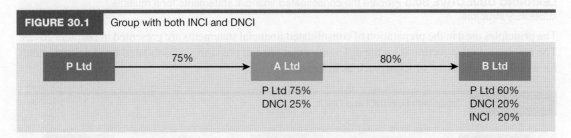

In relation to A Ltd there is only one NCI. The NCI has a direct ownership in this entity. Hence, the NCI of 25% is classified as a DNCI.

In relation to B Ltd there is both a DNCI and an INCI. Because A Ltd owns 80% of the shares of B Ltd, there is an NCI that holds shares directly in B Ltd and that is referred to as DNCI in B Ltd of 20%. However, A Ltd owns 80% of B Ltd and A Ltd has two owners: P Ltd (75%) and its DNCI (25%). Hence, P Ltd indirectly owns 60% of B Ltd (i.e. 75% × 80%), and the DNCI in A Ltd indirectly owns 20% of B Ltd (i.e. 25% × 80%). The indirect ownership in B Ltd held by DNCI in A Ltd is referred to as an INCI in B Ltd. Essentially, the direct ownership by A Ltd in B Ltd (80%) can be expressed as the sum of the indirect ownership in B Ltd by P Ltd (60%) and INCI (20%).

Figure 30.2 provides another example of the existence of an INCI. The INCI in B Ltd exists because there is a DNCI in A Ltd. The 30% DNCI in A Ltd owns 30% × 60% (18%) of B Ltd, giving rise to an 18% INCI in B Ltd. Similar to the case in figure 30.1, the direct ownership by A Ltd in B Ltd (60%) can be expressed as the sum of the indirect ownership in B Ltd by P Ltd (42%) and INCI (18%).

Note that, in both figures 30.1 and 30.2, if P Ltd's ownership in A Ltd was changed to 100%, there would be no INCI in B Ltd. For an INCI to exist in an entity there has to be a DNCI in the immediate parent of that entity.

| FIGURE 30.2 | Indirect and direct NCI |

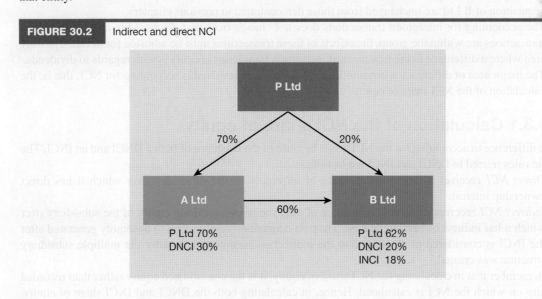

30.3 Preparing consolidated financial statements for a multiple subsidiary structure

LEARNING OBJECTIVE 30.3 Prepare the consolidated financial statements for a multiple subsidiary structure.

The principles used in the preparation of consolidated financial statements are presented in chapters 26–29. The emphasis in this section is on the *differences* that arise in preparing consolidated financial statements for a multiple subsidiary structure such as in figure 30.3.

FIGURE 30.3	Group with both INCI and DNCI

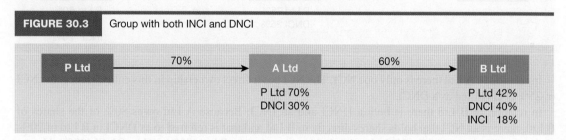

In general, when preparing consolidated financial statements for group structures such as that in figure 30.3, note the following.
- The steps involved in preparing the consolidation worksheet are essentially the same as outlined in previous chapters.
- There are two business combinations rather than one. The combination of P Ltd and A Ltd and the combination of A Ltd and B Ltd are analysed separately in exactly the same fashion as for any two-entity combination because these combinations each involve two companies. It does not matter which of the two combinations is analysed first.
- The acquisition analysis, business combination valuation entries and pre-acquisition entries for P Ltd's acquisition of A Ltd are unchanged from those demonstrated in previous chapters.
- The acquisition analysis, business combination valuation entries and pre-acquisition entries for A Ltd's acquisition of B Ltd are unchanged from those demonstrated in previous chapters.
- The accounting for intragroup transactions does not change from that discussed in chapter 28. If the transactions are within the group, the effects of these transactions must be adjusted for in full. The only area where a difference in the treatment of intragroup transactions occurs is with regards to dividends.
- The major area of difference when multiple subsidiaries are involved is accounting for NCI; that is, the calculation of the NCI share of equity.

30.3.1 Calculation of the NCI share of equity

The difference in accounting for the NCI arises because of the existence of both a DNCI and an INCI. The basic rules related to DNCI and INCI are as follows.
- *Direct NCI* receives a proportionate share of *all* equity of the subsidiary over which it has direct ownership interest.
- *Indirect NCI* receives a proportionate share of only the *post-acquisition* equity of the subsidiary over which it has indirect ownership interest. The post-acquisition equity refers to the equity generated after the INCI is considered to be entitled to the indirect ownership; that is, after the multiple subsidiary structure was created.

Remember that in calculating the NCI share of equity, it is the consolidated equity rather than recorded equity on which the NCI is calculated. Hence, in calculating both the DNCI and INCI share of equity, adjustments must be made to eliminate any unrealised profits/losses arising from transactions within the group.

The calculation of the DNCI share of equity is therefore the same as the calculation of NCI illustrated in chapter 29. The extra adjustments have to be made for the INCI as it receives a share of post-acquisition equity only. First, however, why is the INCI limited to a share of post-acquisition equity only? Consider the group of P Ltd in figure 30.3.

In analysing why the INCI receives a share of post-acquisition equity only, it is important to remember that an INCI arises only when a partly owned subsidiary holds shares in another subsidiary. In figure 30.3, the INCI arises in B Ltd only because there exists a DNCI in A Ltd. The DNCI in A Ltd is the same group of shareholders as the INCI in B Ltd.

The DNCI in A Ltd is entitled to a share of the net assets of A Ltd. This share is calculated as a 30% share of the equity of A Ltd. However, one of the assets of A Ltd is the investment 'Shares in B Ltd' which reflects the right of A Ltd to 60% of the net assets of B Ltd. Because the INCI in B Ltd is the same party as the DNCI in A Ltd, it would be double counting to give the INCI a share of the equity of B Ltd relating to the pre-acquisition net assets of B Ltd. The double-counting issue arises because the investment, Shares in B Ltd, reflects the pre-acquisition equity (i.e. net assets) of B Ltd. When B Ltd earns post-acquisition equity, represented by post-acquisition net assets, this equity is not reflected in A Ltd because the investment account, Shares in B Ltd, is assumed to be recorded at cost. Hence, the double-counting issue does not arise in relation to B Ltd's post-acquisition equity, and the INCI is given a share of the post-acquisition equity of B Ltd.

As explained in previous chapters, the identifiable assets or liabilities of a subsidiary recorded at acquisition date at amounts that differ from fair value or not recorded at all will affect the *pre-acquisition* equity. As those assets and liabilities are used, disposed or settled, post-acquisition expenses may be understated or overstated and gains or losses that are part of pre-acquisition equity may be recognised by the subsidiary post-acquisition — the business combination valuation entries and the pre-acquisition entries will adjust for those. As the INCI receives a share of post-acquisition equity only, the adjustment to equity reflected through these pre-acquisition entries must be considered when calculating the INCI share of equity to make sure only the proportionate share of pre-acquisition equity is allocated to INCI.

As explained in chapter 29, AASB 3/IFRS 3 *Business Combinations* allows a choice between the full goodwill and the partial goodwill methods. This choice has no effect on post-acquisition equity. Hence, the calculation of the INCI share of equity is unaffected by which goodwill method is used. *In this chapter, the partial goodwill method is used in all examples dealing with DNCI and INCI.*

As further explained in chapter 29, the calculation of the NCI share of equity takes place in three steps:
1. share of equity at acquisition date
2. share of changes in equity from acquisition date to the beginning of the current period
3. share of changes in equity in the current period.

There are only *two steps* in calculating the INCI share of equity. Since, by definition, all the equity on hand at acquisition date is *pre-acquisition*, the INCI does not receive a share of equity at that date.

ILLUSTRATIVE EXAMPLE 30.1

Calculation of the NCI share of equity

Using the example in figure 30.3, assume A Ltd pays, at 1 July 2021, $55 200 for its 60% interest in B Ltd when the equity of B Ltd is as follows.

Share capital	$40 000
General reserve	30 000
Retained earnings	15 000

At acquisition date, all the identifiable assets and liabilities of B Ltd are recorded at fair value except for the following.

	Carrying amount	Fair value
Plant	$50 000	$55 000
Inventories	20 000	25 000

The plant is expected to last a further 5 years. Of the inventories, 90% are sold by 30 June 2022 and the remainder by 30 June 2023. The tax rate is 30%.

For the accounting period ending 30 June 2023, the after-tax profit of B Ltd is $10 000, and the opening balance of retained earnings (at 1/7/19) is $24 000.

Assume that P Ltd already had 70% ownership interest in A Ltd prior to 1 July 2021.

Required

Prepare the consolidation worksheet entries relating to A Ltd's acquisition of B Ltd, including the NCI entries relating to B Ltd, required for the preparation of the consolidated financial statements at 30 June 2023.

Solution

Net fair value of identifiable assets and liabilities of B Ltd	= $40 000 (share capital) + $30 000 (general reserve)
	+ $15 000 (retained earnings)
	+ $5000(1 − 30%) (BCVR — plant)
	+ $5000(1 − 30%) (BCVR — inventories)
	= $92 000
(a) Consideration transferred	= $55 200
(b) NCI in B Ltd	= 40% × $92 000
	= $36 800
Aggregate of (a) and (b)	= $92 000
Goodwill	= Nil

The consolidation worksheet entries at *30 June 2023* are as follows.

(1) Business combination valuation entries

Plant	Dr	5 000	
Deferred tax liability	Cr		1 500
BCVR	Cr		3 500
Depreciation expense	Dr	1 000	
Retained earnings (1/7/22)	Dr	1 000	
Accumulated depreciation	Cr		2 000
(20% × $5000 p.a.)			
Deferred tax liability	Dr	600	
Income tax expense	Cr		300
Retained earnings (1/7/22)	Cr		300
Cost of sales	Dr	500	
Income tax expense	Cr		150
Transfer from BCVR	Cr		350

(2) Pre-acquisition entries
At 1 July 2021:

Retained earnings (1/7/21)	Dr	9 000	
Share capital	Dr	24 000	
General reserve	Dr	18 000	
BCVR	Dr	4 200	
Shares in B Ltd	Cr		55 200
(60% of equity balances)			

As of 30 June 2023, all inventories have been sold, resulting in a transfer of business combination valuation reserve to retained earnings.

Retained earnings (1/7/22)*	Dr	10 890	
Share capital	Dr	24 000	
General reserve	Dr	18 000	
BCVR**	Dr	2 310	
Shares in B Ltd	Cr		55 200
Transfer from BCVR	Dr	210	
BCVR	Cr		210
(60% × $350)			

*$10 890 = 60% × [$15 000 + 90% × ($5000 − $1500) (inventories sold in previous period)]
**$2310 = $4200 − 60% × [90% × ($5000 − $1500)]

(3) NCI share of equity at acquisition date, 1 July 2021 (step 1)

The DNCI receives a share of the equity on hand at acquisition date. Since this equity is pre-acquisition, the INCI does not receive a share. The entry in the NCI columns is as follows.

Retained earnings (1/7/22)	Dr	6 000	
Share capital	Dr	16 000	
General reserve	Dr	12 000	
BCVR*	Dr	2 800	
NCI	Cr		36 800
(40% of balances)			

*$2800 = 40% of BCVR of $7000 at acquisition date

(4) NCI share of changes in equity from 1 July 2021 to 30 June 2022 (step 2)

DNCI share

The DNCI of 40% in B Ltd is entitled to a share of the change in equity from 1 July 2021 to 30 June 2022.

The retained earnings balance has changed from $15 000 at acquisition date to $24 000 at 30 June 2022. To recognise the correct share of consolidated post-acquisition equity attributable to DNCI, an adjustment must be made for the depreciation of plant for the period ended 30 June 2022 as evidenced in the business combination valuation entry (that entry included a debit to retained earnings of $1000 and a credit of $300). The entry in the NCI columns of the worksheet is as follows.

Retained earnings (1/7/22)	Dr	3 320	
NCI	Cr		3 320
(40% × [$24 000 − $15 000 − ($1000 − $300)])			

The DNCI is also affected by the transfer of $3150 (90% × [$5000 − $1500]) from the business combination valuation reserve on sale of 90% of the inventories in the period ended 30 June 2022. As the amount was already allocated to DNCI at acquisition date when it was recorded under BCVR and again now when it is part of retained earnings, the following entry is posted to avoid double counting.

NCI	Dr	1 260	
BCVR	Cr		1 260
(40% × 90% × [$5000 − $1500])			

INCI share

The INCI of 18% in B Ltd is entitled to a share of post-acquisition changes in equity over this period.

The retained earnings balance of $24 000 at 30 June 2022 contains two items relating to pre-acquisition equity:
- the $15 000 balance on hand at acquisition date
- a $3150 transfer from business combination valuation reserve relating to the 90% of inventories sold.

Also, according to the business combination valuation entries, the retained earnings recorded by the subsidiary needs to be decreased due to the after-tax depreciation expense adjustment for the plant for the period ended 30 June 2022.

Therefore, the post-acquisition equity in the retained earnings (1/7/22) balance is as follows.

$$\$24\,000 - \$18\,150 - (\$1000 - \$300) = \$5150$$

The INCI share of this is $927, being 18% × $5150. The worksheet entry at 30 June 2023 in the NCI columns is as follows.

Retained earnings (1/7/22)	Dr	927	
NCI	Cr		927

There is no need for any entry relating to the business combination valuation reserve. First, this is pre-acquisition equity and, second, the effects of the transfer have been taken into consideration in the grossing-up process with retained earnings.

(5) NCI share of equity from 1 July 2022 to 30 June 2023 (step 3)
During this period, B Ltd records an after-tax profit of $10 000.

DNCI share
The DNCI share of profit is adjusted for the effects of the depreciation on plant and the sale of the rest of the inventories, as evidenced in the business combination valuation entry. The entry in the NCI columns of the worksheet is as follows.

NCI share of profit	Dr	3 580	
NCI	Cr		3 580
(40% × [$10 000 − ($1000 − $300) − ($500 − $150)])			

Besides the increase in equity caused by the earning of profit, the equity of B Ltd in the current period is affected by the transfer from business combination valuation reserve to retained earnings of $350 as a result of the sale of inventories that were on hand at acquisition date. This equity change is a movement within pre-acquisition equity and therefore affects only the DNCI, not the INCI. The entry in the NCI columns of the worksheet is as follows.

Transfer from BCVR	Dr	140	
BCVR	Cr		140
(40% × $350)			

INCI share
As with the DNCI calculation, an adjustment must be made for the depreciation on the plant and the sale of the remaining inventories during the current period. The entry in the NCI columns is as follows.

NCI share of profit	Dr	1 611	
NCI	Cr		1 611
(18% × [$10 000 − ($1000 − $300) − ($500 − $150)])			

30.3.2 The effects of intragroup transactions on the calculation of the NCI

As noted earlier, the adjustments for the effects of transactions within the group in structures such as in figure 30.3 are the same as those for the two-company structure illustrated in chapter 29. The effects of the transactions must be adjusted in full regardless of the amount of NCI existing in any entity.

What must be considered is the effect on the NCI of such adjustments. The key to this is determining which entity recorded the profit on the transaction. Using the structure in figure 30.3:

- if A Ltd earned the profit/loss — whether by selling to P Ltd or B Ltd — the NCI adjustment is based on the 30% DNCI in A Ltd
- if B Ltd made the profit/loss — whether by selling to P Ltd or A Ltd — the NCI adjustment is based on the total NCI in B Ltd of 58% — that is, the sum of the 40% DNCI and 18% INCI.

To illustrate, assume that during the current period B Ltd sold $25 000 worth of inventories to P Ltd at a profit before tax of $5000. The inventories are still on hand at the end of the current year. The consolidation worksheet entries are as follows.

Sale of inventories: B Ltd to P Ltd

Sales	Dr	25 000	
Cost of sales	Cr		20 000
Inventories	Cr		5 000
Deferred tax asset	Dr	1 500	
Income tax expense	Cr		1 500

Adjustment to NCI in B Ltd

NCI	Dr	2 030	
NCI share of profit	Cr		2 030
([40% + 18%] × [$5000 – $1500])			

Where items of property, plant and equipment are transferred within the group, the effects of the depreciation adjustments must be taken into account. For example, assume B Ltd at the beginning of the previous year sold plant to A Ltd for $800 000 at a profit before tax of $20 000, with the asset having an expected life of 5 years. The consolidation worksheet entries are as follows.

Transfer of plant: B Ltd to A Ltd

Retained earnings (opening balance)	Dr	14 000	
Deferred tax asset	Dr	6 000	
Plant	Cr		20 000

Adjustment to NCI

NCI	Dr	8 120	
Retained earnings (opening balance)	Cr		8 120
([40% + 18%] × $14 000)			

Depreciation of plant

Accumulated depreciation	Dr	8 000	
Depreciation expense	Cr		4 000
Retained earnings (opening balance)	Cr		4 000
(Depreciation of 20% × $20 000 p.a.)			
Income tax expense	Dr	1 200	
Retained earnings (opening balance)	Dr	1 200	
Deferred tax asset	Cr		2 400

Adjustment to NCI in B Ltd

Retained earnings (opening balance)	Dr	1 624	
NCI share of profit	Dr	1 624	
NCI	Cr		3 248
([40% + 18%] × $2800 = $1624)			

30.3.3 Dividends

Following the explanation from the calculation of NCI in chapter 29, in calculating the DNCI share of retained earnings, the DNCI is given a share of opening balance of retained earnings and current period's profits adjusted by a share of current dividends paid and declared, and transfers to and from reserves. The INCI is allocated a share of the current period's post-acquisition profits, opening balance of post-acquisition retained earnings, and transfers to and from post-acquisition reserves. The INCI share of these balances is not reduced via allocation of dividend paid or declared. In this regard, consider the following consolidation worksheet in relation to dividends paid by B Ltd (using the structure in figure 30.3). An extract from the worksheet shows that the adjustment for the intragroup transaction and the allocation to the 40% DNCI in B Ltd eliminates the total balance of the dividend paid.

Financial statements	P Ltd	A Ltd	B Ltd	Adjustments Dr	Cr	Non-controlling interest Dr	Cr	Consolidation
Dividend paid	—	—	2 000		1 200		800	—

No dividend is paid directly to the INCI. The INCI in B Ltd, being the same shareholders as the DNCI in A Ltd, receives a share of the profit of A Ltd, which includes dividend revenue from B Ltd. When the DNCI in A Ltd receives a share of the profit of A Ltd, it receives a share of the profit of B Ltd because the dividend paid by B Ltd is a distribution of B Ltd's profit. This raises a problem of double counting, because the INCI of B Ltd, which receives a share of the profit of B Ltd, is the same party as the DNCI in A Ltd, which receives a share of the profit of B Ltd via the dividend revenue from B Ltd included in the profit of A Ltd.

Assume that the changes in retained earnings for the period ended 30 June 2023 are as follows.

	P Ltd	A Ltd	B Ltd
Profit for the period	$ 40 000	$28 000	$10 000
Retained earnings (opening balance)	90 000	25 000	24 000
	130 000	53 000	34 000
Dividend paid	10 000	3 000	2 000
Dividend declared	10 000	5 000	3 000
Transfer to reserves	10 000	5 000	6 000
	30 000	13 000	11 000
Retained earnings (closing balance)	$100 000	$40 000	$23 000

The DNCI of 30% in A Ltd and the DNCI of 40% in B Ltd receive their share of all equity accounts within the respective entities as follows.

	DNCI — A Ltd	DNCI — B Ltd
	30%	40%
Profit for the period	$ 8 400	$ 4 000
Retained earnings (opening balance)	7 500	9 600
	15 900	13 600
Dividend paid	900	800
Dividend declared	1 500	1 200
Transfer to reserves	1 500	2 400
	3 900	4 400
Retained earnings (closing balance)	$12 000	$ 9 200

Dividend paid in the current period

In the group illustrated in figure 30.3, the profit of A Ltd includes $1200 dividend revenue (60% × $2000); that is, A Ltd's share of the dividend paid by B Ltd from its current profit. The issue here is that, if the INCI in B Ltd is allocated a share of the profit of B Ltd and the DNCI in A Ltd is allocated a share of the profit of A Ltd (which includes the dividend revenue from B Ltd), then, because the DNCI and the INCI are the same party, the calculation of the NCI share of equity involves double counting.

In calculating the NCI share of equity, it is necessary to make an adjustment to eliminate the double counting. This could be done by adjusting the INCI of B Ltd's equity or the DNCI share of A Ltd's equity, since the problem is caused by the fact that A Ltd has recognised some of B Ltd's profit via dividend revenue. In this text, the adjustment is made to the DNCI share of A Ltd's equity in step 3 of the calculation of the NCI share of equity; that is, in calculating the NCI share of changes in equity in the current period. Hence, when making the adjustment for the $2000 dividend paid from B Ltd to A Ltd, there are two consolidation worksheet entries, the first adjusting for intragroup transactions and the second in step 3 of the calculation of NCI as follows.

Dividend paid by B Ltd			
Dividend revenue	Dr	1 200	
Dividend paid	Cr		1 200
(60% × $2000)			
Step 3. NCI calculation			
NCI	Dr	800	
Dividend paid	Cr		800
(40% × $2000)			
NCI	Dr	360	
NCI share of profit	Cr		360
(Reduction of the DNCI share of profit in A Ltd since the latter includes the dividend from B Ltd: 30% × $1200 or 18% × $2000)			

Dividend declared in the current period

B Ltd has declared a $3000 dividend but not paid it by the end of the period. A Ltd will still recognise 60% of this, $1800, as dividend revenue. Hence, the same double-counting problem that arose with dividend paid also arises with dividend declared. An extra entry to overcome the double counting problem is again required. The consolidation worksheet entries are as follows.

Dividend declared by B Ltd			
Dividend payable	Dr	1 800	
Dividend declared	Cr		1 800
(60% × $3000)			
Dividend revenue	Dr	1 800	
Dividend receivable	Cr		1 800
Step 3. NCI calculation for A Ltd			
NCI	Dr	1 200	
Dividend paid	Cr		1 200
(40% × $3000)			
NCI	Dr	540	
NCI share of profit	Cr		540
(30% × $1800 or 18% × $3000)			

LEARNING CHECK

☐ The calculation of the DNCI share of equity differs from that for the INCI share of equity.

☐ The DNCI receives a share of all equity of the subsidiary whereas the INCI receives a share of post-acquisition equity only.

☐ Where adjustments are made for intragroup transactions, the existence of both DNCI and INCI may need to be taken into account.

☐ In calculating the NCI share of equity where dividends are paid/payable within the group, adjustments may be necessary to ensure double counting for INCI's share of dividends does not occur.

30.4 Non-sequential acquisitions

LEARNING OBJECTIVE 30.4 Explain the effects on the consolidation process where the acquisition is non-sequential.

In accounting for multiple subsidiary structures, the accounting treatment depends on the sequence in which the acquisitions occurred. In this chapter, a **sequential acquisition** is one where P Ltd acquires its shares in A Ltd before A Ltd acquires its shares in B Ltd, or both acquisitions occur on the same date. A **non-sequential acquisition** is one where A Ltd acquires its shares in B Ltd before P Ltd acquires its shares in A Ltd. Previous examples used in this chapter assumed that the multiple subsidiary structure was created via sequential acquisitions. While the principles discussed in terms of preparing consolidated financial statements in the presence of INCI still apply for non-sequential acquisitions, a further issue needs to be addressed here.

Consider the group in figure 30.4 in which Y Ltd is a subsidiary of X Ltd and Z Ltd is a subsidiary of Y Ltd.

FIGURE 30.4 Group with both INCI and DNCI

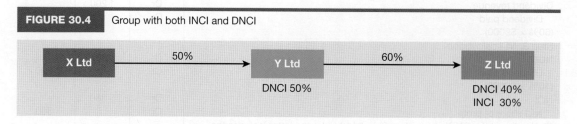

Consider the situation where the sequence in which the two acquisitions occurred was as follows.

1 July 2022: Y Ltd acquired its interest in Z Ltd
1 July 2023: X Ltd acquired its interest in Y Ltd

The problem that the non-sequential acquisition causes is that, in relation to X Ltd's acquisition of Y Ltd, one of the assets of Y Ltd is 'Shares in Z Ltd'. At the date of X Ltd's acquisition in Y Ltd, the fair value of the investment 'Shares in Z Ltd' may have increased owing to the increased worth of Z Ltd. In other words, when X Ltd considers the fair value of the consideration to pay for shares in Y Ltd, it considers not only the value of Y Ltd but also the value of Z Ltd. The fair value of Y Ltd's investment in Z Ltd relates to the increased worth of Z Ltd between 1 July 2022 and 1 July 2023.

Assume Y Ltd acquired its 60% interest in Z Ltd on 1 July 2022 for $420 when the financial position of Z Ltd was as follows.

	Carrying amount	Fair value
Share capital	$300	
Retained earnings	230	
	$530	
Land	$200	$300
Other assets	330	330
	$530	

The acquisition analysis of Y Ltd's acquisition of Z Ltd is then as follows.

Net fair value of identifiable assets and liabilities of Z Ltd	= $300 + $230 + $100(1 − 30%) (BCVR − land)	
	= $600	
(a) Consideration transferred	= $420	
(b) Non-controlling interest in Z Ltd	= 40% × $600	
	= $240	
Aggregate of (a) and (b)	= $660	
Goodwill acquired	= $660 − $600	
	= $60	

The consolidation worksheet entries at acquisition date, 1 July 2022, for this acquisition are as follows.

Business combination valuation entry — Z Ltd		
Land	Dr	100
Deferred tax liability	Cr	30
BCVR	Cr	70
Pre-acquisition entry — Z Ltd		
Share capital [60% × $300]	Dr	180
Retained earnings (1/7/22) [60% × $230]	Dr	138
BCVR [60% × $70]	Dr	42
Goodwill	Dr	60
Shares in Z Ltd	Cr	420
DNCI at 1 July 2019 — Z Ltd		
Share capital [40% × $300]	Dr	120
Retained earnings (1/7/22) [40% × $230]	Dr	92
BCVR [40% × $70]	Dr	28
NCI	Cr	240

On 1 July 2023, X Ltd acquires 50% of the shares in Y Ltd for $650 when the financial positions of Y Ltd and Z Ltd are as follows.

Y Ltd	Carrying amount	Fair value	Z Ltd	Carrying amount	Fair value
Share capital	$500		Share capital	$300	
Retained earnings	600		Retained earnings	300	
Shares in Z Ltd	420	$540	Land	200	$400
Other assets	680	680	Other assets	400	400

Hence, in relation to Z Ltd at 1 July 2023 compared to 1 July 2022:

• retained earnings has increased by $70 (i.e. from $230 to $300)
• land has increased its fair value by a further $100 (i.e. from $300 to $400).

Consolidation worksheet entries at 1 July 2023:
Because X Ltd acquires the group consisting of Y Ltd and Z Ltd, the consolidation worksheet entries for both Y Ltd and Z Ltd are prepared at 1 July 2023.

(1) Business combination valuation entries — Z Ltd

Land	Dr	100	
Deferred tax liability	Cr		30
BCVR	Cr		70
Land	Dr	100	
Deferred tax liability	Cr		30
BCVR	Cr		70

It is useful to recognise the increases in valuation separately as only the first increase is part of pre-acquisition equity from the point of view of the parent and DNCI.

(2) Pre-acquisition entries — Z Ltd
The first pre-acquisition entry for Z Ltd is the same as the one prepared at 1 July 2022.

Share capital [60% × $300]	Dr	180	
Retained earnings (1/7/23) [60% × $230]	Dr	138	
BCVR [60% × $70]	Dr	42	
Goodwill	Dr	60	
Shares in Z Ltd	Cr		420

The second entry refers to the changes in pre-acquisition equity of Z Ltd up to 1 July 2023.

Retained earnings (1/7/23) [60% × $70]	Dr	42	
BCVR [60% × $70]	Dr	42	
Goodwill*	Dr	36	
Shares in Z Ltd	Cr		120

*This reflects Y Ltd's share of the extra goodwill in Z Ltd between 1 July 2022 and 1 July 2023. This extra goodwill is calculated as the difference between the increase in the fair value of the investment account Shares in Z Ltd and the increase in the net fair value of identifiable assets of Z Ltd (i.e. the increase in the value of equity in this case). The goodwill of Z Ltd is not revalued at 1 July 2023; hence, there is no share of equity recognised as for assets such as land.

The last entry above eliminates the extra worth in Z Ltd which is reflected in the Shares in Z Ltd account of Y Ltd. Considering that the original $420 in that account was eliminated in the pre-acquisition entries recognised for the acquisition of Z Ltd by Y Ltd, the whole fair value of this account is now eliminated.

(3) 40% DNCI at 1 July 2022 — Z Ltd

Share capital [40% × $300]	Dr	120	
Retained earnings (1/7/23) [40% × $230]	Dr	92	
BCVR [40% × $70]	Dr	28	
NCI	Cr		240

(4) 40% DNCI share of equity from 1 July 2022 to 1 July 2023 — Z Ltd

Retained earnings (1/7/23)	Dr	28	
NCI	Cr		28
(40% × $70)			
BCVR	Dr	28	
NCI	Cr		28
(40% × $70 land)			

The INCI receives no amount of equity of Z Ltd at this stage because the INCI can only be recognised once the entire multiple subsidiary structure is created; that is, on 1 July 2023.

(5) Business combination valuation entry — Y Ltd

Shares in Z Ltd	Dr	120	
BCVR	Cr		120
($540 – $420)			

(6) Pre-acquisition entries — Y Ltd
This is based on the following acquisition analysis for X Ltd and Y Ltd.

Net fair value of identifiable assets and liabilities of Y Ltd	= $500 + $600 + $120 (BCVR — shares in Z Ltd)
	= $1220
(a) Consideration transferred	= $650
(b) Non-controlling interest in Y Ltd	= 50% × $1220
	= $610
Aggregate of (a) and (b)	= $1260
Goodwill acquired	= $1260 – $1220
	= $40

Share capital [50% × $500]	Dr	250	
Retained earnings (1/7/23) [50% × $600]	Dr	300	
BCVR [50% × $120]	Dr	60	
Goodwill	Dr	40	
Shares in Y Ltd	Cr		650

(7) 50% DNCI — Y Ltd

Share capital [50% × $500]	Dr	250	
Retained earnings (1/7/23) [50% × $600]	Dr	300	
BCVR [50% × $120]	Dr	60	
NCI	Cr		610

The consolidation worksheet at 1 July 2023 is shown in figure 30.5. For retained earnings, share capital and the business combination valuation reserve, the consolidation amounts are those for X Ltd (i.e. there are no post-acquisition subsidiary amounts in these accounts attributable to the parent).

FIGURE 30.5	Consolidation worksheet: non-sequential acquisitions

Financial statements	X Ltd	Y Ltd	Z Ltd	Adjustments				NCI			Consolidation
					Dr	Cr			Dr	Cr	
Retained earnings	800	600	300	2	138		3		92		800
				6	300		4		28		
				2	42		7		300		
Share capital	900	500	300	2	180		3		120		900
				6	250		7		250		
BCVR	—	—	—	2	42	70	1	3	28		—
				6	60	70	1	4	28		
				2	42	120	5	7	60		

Liabilities	—	—	—			30	*1*			60
						30	*1*			
NCI								240	*3*	906
								28	*4*	
								28	*4*	
								610	*7*	
	__1 700__	__1 100__	__600__							__2 666__
Shares in Y Ltd	650	—	—	*5*		650	*6*			—
Shares in Z Ltd	—	420		*5*	120	420	*2*			
						120	*2*			
Land			200	*1*	100					400
				1	100					
Other assets	1 050	680	400							2 130
Goodwill	—	—	—	*2*	60					136
				6	40					
				2	36					
	__1 700__	__1 100__	__600__		__1 510__	__1 510__		__906__	__906__	__2 666__

30.5 Changes in ownership interests by a parent in a group

LEARNING OBJECTIVE 30.5 Explain how to account for changes in ownership interests by a parent in a group.

In previous chapters on consolidation the situations discussed are where the parent obtains control of a subsidiary and there is no subsequent change in the ownership interest of the parent in the subsidiary. In this section three situations are discussed in which the parent's interest in a subsidiary is changed subsequent to the initial obtaining of control, as follows.

- A parent acquires additional shares in a subsidiary. For example, P Ltd owns 60% of the shares of a subsidiary and then acquired a further 20% interest. The NCI was 40% but is reduced to 20% as a result of the parent's acquiring additional shares. This situation is discussed in section 30.5.2.
- A parent sells shares in a subsidiary but retains control of the subsidiary. For example, P Ltd owns 80% of the shares in a subsidiary but sells some of those shares and its interest is now 60%. This level of ownership interest is sufficient for P Ltd to still control the subsidiary. The NCI was 20% but increases to 40%. This situation is discussed in section 30.5.3.
- A parent sells shares in a subsidiary and loses control of the subsidiary. For example, P Ltd owns 60% of the shares in a subsidiary, but sells some of its shares and its interest is now 40%. This level of ownership is not sufficient to retain control. The former subsidiary must no longer be included in the consolidated financial statements of P Ltd. This situation is discussed in section 30.5.4.

30.5.1 Changes in ownership interests without loss of control

As discussed in chapter 29, AASB 10/IFRS 10 requires both the parent interest and the NCI to be classified as equity. Where the parent acquires additional shares in a subsidiary or where the parent sells shares in a subsidiary but still retains control, there is no change in the economic entity. Both the parent and the subsidiary are still within the economic entity. These changes in ownership interests cannot then give rise to gains or losses to the economic entity. They are accounted for as equity transactions, as they are transactions between the owners and not with entities outside the group.

Where the parent acquires additional shares in the subsidiary this transaction is not a business combination as the parent already had control of the subsidiary. Hence, there is no need to adjust the identifiable assets and liabilities of the subsidiary to fair values or to measure goodwill in relation to the transaction involving acquisition of additional shares.

Note paragraphs 23 and B96 of AASB 10/IFRS 10:

23. Changes in a parent's ownership interest in a subsidiary that do not result in the parent losing control of the subsidiary are equity transactions (ie transactions with owners in their capacity as owners).

B96. When the proportion of the equity held by non-controlling interests changes, an entity shall adjust the carrying amounts of the controlling and non-controlling interests to reflect the changes in their relative interests in the subsidiary. The entity shall recognise directly in equity any difference between the amount by which the non-controlling interests are adjusted and the fair value of the consideration paid or received, and attribute it to the owners of the parent.

Hence, when such transactions occur:
- the carrying amounts of the parent's interest and the NCI are adjusted to reflect the change in the respective ownership interests
- where the consideration paid or received by the parent on acquisition or sale of shares in the subsidiary exceeds the carrying value of the relevant interest in the subsidiary sold to the parent or sold by the parent, the difference is recognised directly in equity and is attributable to the parent's interest.

The parent and the NCI will negotiate the consideration paid on these transactions based on an assessment of the fair value of the subsidiary. In contrast, the relative interests of the parent and the NCI in the subsidiary, as reflected in the consolidated financial statements, are based on the carrying amounts of the net assets of the subsidiary. It is this difference that gives rise to the amount being recognised directly in equity.

This method of accounting for the relative interests applies in all circumstances, regardless of whether the measurement of the NCI is based on the full or partial goodwill method.

30.5.2 Acquisition of additional shares by the parent subsequent to date of acquisition

ILLUSTRATIVE EXAMPLE 30.2

Accounting for the acquisition of additional shares by the parent

P Ltd acquired a 60% interest in S Ltd for $12 000 on 1 July 2021 when the equity of S Ltd was as follows.

Share capital	$10 000
Retained earnings	8 000

The identifiable assets and liabilities of S Ltd were all measured at amounts equal to their fair value except for plant for which the fair value was $1000 greater than its carrying amount. The plant had a further economic life of 5 years. The fair value of the NCI in S Ltd was considered to be $8000 and the full goodwill method is used.

Assume that at 1 July 2023, P Ltd acquired a further 20% of the shares in S Ltd for $5000 when the recorded equity of S Ltd consisted of the following.

Share capital	$10 000
Retained earnings	10 000

Required

Prepare the consolidation worksheet entries relating to P Ltd's investment in S Ltd at 1 July 2023.

Solution

Acquisition analysis at 1 July 2021

Net fair value of identifiable assets and liabilities of S Ltd	=	$10 000 + $8000 (recorded equity)
		+ $1000(1 − 30%) (BCVR — plant)
	=	$18 700
(a) Consideration transferred	=	$12 000
(b) NCI in S Ltd	=	$8000
Aggregate of (a) and (b)	=	$20 000
Goodwill	=	$20 000 − $18 700
	=	$1300
Fair value of S Ltd	=	$8000/40%
	=	$20 000
Goodwill of S Ltd	=	$20 000 − $18 700
	=	$1300
Control premium	=	$1300 − $1300
	=	Nil

As P Ltd paid $12 000 for 60% of S Ltd, which had a fair value of $20 000 (i.e. $8000/40%), there is no control premium — all the goodwill will be recognised in BCVR.

At 1 July 2023, P Ltd would pass the following entry in its records to recognise the acquisition of additional shares.

Shares in S Ltd	Dr	5 000	
Cash	Cr		5 000

The consolidation worksheet entries at 1 July 2023 — immediately prior to the acquisition of additional shares — are as follows.

(1) Business combination valuation entries

Plant	Dr	1 000	
Deferred tax liability	Cr		300
BCVR	Cr		700
Retained earnings (1/7/23)	Dr	400	
Accumulated depreciation	Cr		400
Deferred tax liability	Dr	120	
Retained earnings (1/7/23)	Cr		120
Goodwill	Dr	1 300	
BCVR	Cr		1 300

(2) Pre-acquisition entry

Retained earnings (1/7/23)	Dr	4 800	
Share capital	Dr	6 000	
BCVR	Dr	1 200	
Shares in S Ltd	Cr		12 000

(3) NCI entries

Retained earnings (1/7/23)	Dr	3 200	
Share capital	Dr	4 000	
BCVR	Dr	800	
NCI	Cr		8 000
Retained earnings (1/7/23)	Dr	688	
NCI	Cr		688
(40% × [$10 000 − $8000 − ($400 − $120)])			

On the acquisition of the further 20% of the shares in S Ltd for $5000, the following issues are considered.

- As the acquisition of additional shares is not a business combination there is no additional business combination valuation entry and no changes in the original business combination valuation entries (as in (1) above).

- There is no change to the original pre-acquisition entry as it still reflects what occurred at the initial business combination (as in (2) above).
- The NCI has changed from 40% to 20%. Journal entry (3) recognises the NCI share of equity up to the date of the parent acquiring additional shares in the subsidiary; in this example the date is 1 July 2023. At this date a further consolidation entry is required to recognise the reduction in the share of equity attributable to the NCI. Before this further acquisition, as per entry (3), the total share of the NCI is $8688 (i.e. $8000 + $688). As the share of the NCI has halved, the NCI share of equity is reduced by $4344 (i.e. ½ × $8688). This is then reflected in the NCI share of each of the equity accounts being halved; for example, in relation to share capital, the NCI share was $4000, and it is reduced by half, namely $2000. A further consolidation worksheet entry is then required to reflect the reduction in the NCI share of equity.

(4) Reduction in the NCI share of equity

NCI	Dr	4 344
Share capital	Cr	2 000
Retained earnings (1/7/23)	Cr	1 944
BCVR	Cr	400
(50% of NCI share at 1/7/23)		

- Just as the NCI share of the individual equity accounts at 1 July 2023 has reduced, the parent's share has increased. The parent has acquired a further 20% interest in the subsidiary. The equity lost by the NCI as shown in (4) above is now attributable to the parent. It is this equity that was acquired for the additional $5000 investment by the parent. Hence, an entry (entry (5) below) is necessary to eliminate the equity acquired by the parent and the investment account of the parent. As noted in section 30.5.1, the consideration paid by the parent for the additional shares is based on an assessment of the fair value of the subsidiary, not the recorded equity of the subsidiary. This difference is not a gain/loss but is recognised as equity. In entry (5) below the difference is recognised as a movement in the retained earnings account in the current period — note the adjustment is not to the opening balance of retained earnings. The amount is determined as the amount necessary to balance the entry.

The further entry required in the consolidation worksheet immediately after the acquisition of additional shares by the parent is as follows.

(5) Elimination of additional investment in S Ltd

Share capital	Dr	2 000
Retained earnings (1/7/23)	Dr	1 944
BCVR	Dr	400
Retained earnings*	Dr	656
Shares in S Ltd	Cr	5 000

*This difference could alternatively be recognised in a separate reserve account. However, just as the business combination valuation reserve is eventually transferred to retained earnings, any separate reserve would probably eventually be transferred to retained earnings. Also, the balance is most likely to be a debit balance as the consideration paid will probably be higher than the book value of the extra equity that the parent is now entitled to.

Below are the extracts from the consolidation worksheet relating to retained earnings, before and after the acquisition of additional shares, assuming P Ltd has a balance of zero (for simplicity).

Before the acquisition of additional shares by the parent

Financial statements	P Ltd	S Ltd	Adjustments Dr		Cr		Group	NCI Dr		Cr	Parent
Retained earnings (1/7/23)	—	10 000	*1* *2*	400 4 800	120	*1*	4 920	*3* *3*	3 200 688		1 032

Financial statements	P Ltd	S Ltd	Adjustments				Group	NCI				Parent
				Dr	Cr				Dr	Cr		
Retained earnings (1/7/23)	—	10 000	1 2 5	400 4 800 1 944	120	1	2 976	3 3	3 200 688	1 944	4	1 032
Adjustment on share acquisition			5	656								(656)

At 30 June 2024, the NCI entries would include 20% of the profit for the current period.

30.5.3 Sale of shares by parent with retention of control

The example used here is the same as that in section 30.5.2 (illustrative example 30.2) except that at 1 July 2023 it is assumed that P Ltd, instead of buying an additional 20% of shares in S Ltd, sells 5% of the shares issued by S Ltd. The selling price of the shares by P Ltd is $1250.

At 1 July 2023, on sale of its shares in S Ltd, P Ltd records the following entry.

Cash	Dr	1 250
Shares in S Ltd [$12 000/60% × 5%]	Cr	1 000
Gain on sale of shares	Cr	250

The NCI share of S Ltd's equity increases from 40% to 45%.

The consolidation worksheet entries for the period ended 30 June 2024 are as follows.

(1) Business combination valuation entry

These entries are the same as in illustrative example 30.2 as the group is unchanged.

(2) Pre-acquisition entry

In illustrative example 30.2, the pre-acquisition entry related to P Ltd's holding of 60% of the shares of S Ltd. As P Ltd has sold 5% of the shares of S Ltd, this entry now relates only to the remaining 55% of the shares of S Ltd. The pre-acquisition entry subsequent to the sale of shares is based on 55% of the pre-acquisition equity balances of S Ltd at 1 July 2021 as follows.

Retained earnings (1/7/23) [55% × $8000]	Dr	4 400
Share capital [55% × $10 000]	Dr	5 500
BCVR [55% × $2000]	Dr	1 100
Shares in S Ltd [$12 000 – $1000]	Cr	11 000

(3) NCI entries

These entries before the sale by P Ltd of 5% of its shareholding in S Ltd reflect the NCI's 40% share of S Ltd's equity as at 1 July 2023.

Retained earnings (1/7/23)	Dr	3 200
Share capital	Dr	4 000
BCVR	Dr	800
NCI	Cr	8 000
Retained earnings (1/7/23)	Dr	688
NCI	Cr	688
(40% × [$10 000 – $8000 – ($400 – $120)])		

However, as a result of P Ltd selling some of its shares in S Ltd, the NCI's share of S Ltd has increased to 45%. This increased share is recognised in a further consolidation worksheet entry — entry (4).

(4) Increase in the NCI share of equity

The NCI has increased from 40% to 45%. The NCI therefore is entitled to a further 5% of the equity of S Ltd at 1 July 2023 as follows.

Retained earnings (1/7/23) [5% × ($10 000 – ($400 – $120))]	Dr	486
Share capital [5% × $10 000]	Dr	500
BCVR [5% × ($700 + $1300)]	Dr	100
NCI	Cr	1 086

(5) Elimination of the gain recorded by P Ltd

P Ltd recorded a gain on sale of its shares in S Ltd of $250. As noted in section 30.5.1 the economic entity should not recognise the gain or loss on sale of shares as part of the profit, but as an adjustment to equity. On consolidation the gain recorded by P Ltd as part of the current profit is then eliminated. The entry is as follows.

Gain on sale of shares	Dr	250	
Retained earnings (1/7/23)	Cr		86
Other reserves	Cr		164

In relation to this entry note the following.

(i) The first line of the entry results in the elimination of the gain recorded by P Ltd so that the group shows no gain on sale of shares in the subsidiary as part of the profit in the consolidated financial statements.

(ii) The gain on sale recorded by P Ltd must be adjusted by any post-acquisition equity already recognised by the group in relation to the shares sold. The adjustment to retained earnings (1/7/23) of $86 reflects the fact that there have been post-acquisition profits recorded by the subsidiary. This is calculated as follows.

Profits recorded by S Ltd subsequent to acquisition date	= $10 000 – $8000
	= $2000
Post-acquisition portion	= $2000 – ($400 – $120) (after-tax depreciation adjustments for plant)
	= $1720
Amount relating to 5% of shares sold	= 5% × $1720
	= $86

As the group has already recognised $86 increased equity, on sale of the shares an increase in equity of only $164 instead of $250 is recognised by the group. This amount relates to the increased worth of the subsidiary not yet recognised by the group. This can also be calculated assuming that, if P Ltd sold 5% of the subsidiary for $1250, then the whole subsidiary at the time of sale was worth $25 000 (i.e. $1250/5%) and therefore:

Fair value of net assets of subsidiary	= $25 000
Recorded net assets of subsidiary	= $20 000
Net assets recognised by the group	= $20 000 + ($1000 – $400) (plant)
	– ($300 – $120) (deferred tax liability)
	+ $1300 (goodwill)
	= $21 720
Unrecognised net assets	= $25 000 – $21 720
	= $3280
Amount relating to 5% of shares sold	= 5% × $3280
	= $164

(iii) The third line of the above journal entry recognises the $164 not previously recognised by the group. As noted in section 30.5.1, in accordance with AASB 10/IFRS 10 this amount is recognised directly in equity. This could be as a movement in retained earnings as used in illustrative example 30.2 or in a reserve account because AASB 10/IFRS 10 does not specify any particular equity account to be used. In this journal entry, the account 'other reserves' is used.

The following entry will be required in consolidation worksheets subsequent to the period ended 30 June 2024.

Retained earnings (opening balance)	Dr	164	
Other reserves	Cr		164

If the balance in other reserves were transferred to retained earnings, future consolidation entries would not be necessary.

Note the change in the consolidation worksheet for the gain on sale, retained earnings (opening balance) and other reserves accounts as a result of the sale of shares. Below are the related extracts from the consolidation worksheet before and after the sale of shares, assuming P Ltd has a balance of zero in retained earnings (for simplicity).

Before the sale of shares

Financial statements	P Ltd	S Ltd	Adjustments Dr		Cr		Group	NCI Dr		Cr	Parent
Retained earnings (1/7/23)	—	10 000	1 2	400 4 800	120	1	4 920	3 3	3 200 688		1 032

After the sale of shares

Financial statements	P Ltd	S Ltd	Adjustments Dr		Cr		Group	NCI Dr		Cr	Parent
Gain	250		5	250							—
Retained earnings (1/7/23)	—	10 000	1 2	400 4 400	120 86	1 5	5 406	3 3 4	3 200 688 486		1 032
Other reserves	—	—			164						164

Note that the equity of the parent as shown in the consolidated financial statements has increased by $164, shown in 'other reserves'. The parent itself recorded a gain of $250. At 30 June 2024, the NCI would be allocated 45% of the post-acquisition profits of S Ltd earned subsequent to the sale of shares by the parent.

30.5.4 Changes in ownership interests with loss of control

A parent may lose control of a subsidiary for a number of reasons, such as:
- it may sell shares in the subsidiary such that another entity has the controlling interest
- there may be a change in the dispersion in the holding of shares by entities comprising the NCI such that a parent with less than a 50% holding loses control
- a subsidiary may become subject to the control of a government, court, administrator or regulator
- there may be a change in a contractual arrangement.

In this section the example will relate to a situation where the parent sells some of its shares in a subsidiary and as a result loses control of the subsidiary.

Having lost control, but retained an investment in the former subsidiary, in accordance with paragraph 25 of AASB 10/IFRS 10, the investor will record that remaining investment in accordance with AASB 9/IFRS 9 *Financial Instruments*, namely at fair value. The measurement of the remaining asset at fair value is factored into the calculation of any gain/loss on disposal of the shares in the subsidiary.

The example used here is based on illustrative example 30.2 where P Ltd originally acquired 60% of the issued shares of S Ltd; however, it is considered that on 1 July 2023 P Ltd sold 20% of the shares in S Ltd for $5000. It is assumed that this sale causes P Ltd to lose control of S Ltd.

If P Ltd sold 20% of the shares in S Ltd for $5000, then it is assumed that the fair value of its remaining investment in S Ltd (40%) is $10 000 (i.e. $5000/20% × 40%). After the sale of shares in the subsidiary the remaining investment held by P Ltd is recorded at $8000 (being $12 000/60% × 40%). It is also assumed that any changes in fair value are recognised in profit or loss.

On sale of the shares in S Ltd, P Ltd would pass the following entry to reflect both the sale of the shares and the remeasurement of the remaining investment in S Ltd to fair value.

Cash	Dr	5 000	
Shares in S Ltd*	Cr		2 000
Gain on shares in S Ltd**	Cr		3 000

*$12 000 cost of initial investment – $10 000 fair value of remaining investment
**($5000 – $12 000/60% × 20%) gain on sale + ($10 000 – $12 000/60% × 40%) gain on revaluation of remaining investment

In accordance with paragraphs 25 and B98 of AASB 10/IFRS 10, the parent will:
1. derecognise the assets and liabilities of the former subsidiary based on the carrying amounts at the date when control was lost
2. derecognise the carrying amount of any NCI in the former subsidiary at the date when control was lost
3. recognise the fair value of the consideration received
4. recognise any investment retained in the former subsidiary at its fair value at the date when control was lost
5. recognise any gain/loss in profit or loss attributable to the parent.

The gain/loss from the group's perspective is calculated as follows.

Gain/loss = Fair value of the proceeds (if any) from the transaction that resulted in loss of control
+ Fair value of any retained investment in the former subsidiary at the date when control is lost
– Parent's share of the carrying amount in the group of the net assets at the date when control is lost

If the group uses the full goodwill method in relation to the NCI then on consolidation the goodwill relating to the control premium is also recognised (via the pre-acquisition entry adjustment in the consolidation worksheet). This goodwill is also included in the parent's share of the carrying amount in the group of the net assets at the date the control is lost.

In relation to the example where P Ltd sells some of its shares in S Ltd, the gain on sale is calculated as follows.

Gain	= $5000 (proceeds on sale)
	+ $10 000 (fair value of remaining investment)
	– $13 032 (P Ltd's share of S Ltd's net assets)*
	= $1968
*S Ltd's net assets	= $20 000 (recorded by subsidiary)
	+ $1300 (goodwill)
	+ ($1000 – $400) (plant revaluation adjusted for depreciation)
	– ($300 – $120) (deferred tax liability related to plant revaluation)
	= $21 720
P Ltd's share of S Ltd's net assets	= 60% × $21 720
	= $13 032

Hence, the recorded gain of $3000 must be adjusted on consolidation to the real gain to the parent of $1968 — an adjustment of $1032.

The consolidated worksheet entry in the year of sale is as follows.

Gain on shares in S Ltd	Dr	1 032	
Retained earnings (1/7/23)	Cr		1 032

This entry achieves two things.
• It adjusts the gain on sale from that recorded to the real gain to the parent.
• It reinstates the opening balance of the retained earnings account prior to sale.

Note the consolidation worksheet in relation to retained earnings prior to sale as follows.

Before the sale of shares

Financial statements	P Ltd	S Ltd		Adjustments				Group		NCI			Parent
				Dr	Cr					Dr	Cr		
Retained earnings (1/7/23)	—	10 000	1	400	120	1		4 920	3	3 200			1 032
			2	4 800					3	688			

Subsequent to sale, the financial statements of the subsidiary will not be included in the consolidation worksheet — although derecognition of the assets and liabilities of the subsidiary as well as the NCI will need to be disclosed. The worksheet after the sale would show the following.

After the sale of shares

Financial statements	P Ltd	S Ltd		Adjustments				Group		NCI			Parent
				Dr	Cr					Dr	Cr		
Gain	3 000			1 032									1 968
Retained earnings (1/7/23)	—	—			1 032								1 032

Note that the opening balance of retained earnings is reinstated and the real gain on sale of shares will be reported.

30.5.5 Disclosures relating to changes in ownership interests

AASB 12/IFRS 12 *Disclosure of Interests in Other Entities* requires disclosures to be made where there are changes in ownership interests.

Paragraph 18 of AASB 12/IFRS 12 sets out the disclosure required where there are changes in a parent's ownership interest in a subsidiary that do not result in a loss of control:

> An entity shall present a schedule that shows the effects on the equity attributable to owners of the parent of any changes in its ownership interest in a subsidiary that do not result in a loss of control.

Paragraph 19 of AASB 12/IFRS 12 sets out the disclosure required where a parent loses control of a subsidiary during the reporting period:

> An entity shall disclose the gain or loss, if any, calculated in accordance with paragraph 25 of AASB 10, and:
> (a) the portion of that gain or loss attributable to measuring any investment retained in the former subsidiary at its fair value at the date when control is lost; and
> (b) the line item(s) in profit or loss in which the gain or loss is recognised (if not presented separately).

LEARNING CHECK

☐ Where changes in ownership interests occur subsequent to the parent obtaining control of a subsidiary, these changes do not give rise to gains or losses to the economic entity.

☐ The acquisition of additional shares by a parent, subsequent to the acquisition date is not a business combination, and there is no measurement of fair values of subsidiary assets and liabilities or calculation of goodwill associated with this transaction.

☐ Where a parent sells shares in a subsidiary but loses control, the calculation of the gain/loss on the transaction includes the measurement of the fair value of any retained non-controlling interest in the former subsidiary at the date when control is lost.

☐ AASB 12/IFRS 12 requires disclosures to be made where there are changes in ownership interests.

SUMMARY

Accounting standards require the separation of consolidated equity into parent interest and non-controlling interest (NCI). One complication in the calculation of NCI is that, where a group has multiple subsidiaries, it may be necessary to classify the NCI into direct non-controlling interest (DNCI) and indirect non-controlling interest (INCI), because the calculation of the DNCI share of equity differs from that of the INCI. In particular, the INCI does not receive a share of all the equity of a subsidiary, but is entitled to a share of post-acquisition equity only. The existence of an INCI must be taken into account where dividends are paid within a group because, without adjustment for the INCI, double counting of the NCI share of equity may occur.

Where a parent has a number of subsidiaries, the timing of the acquisition of those subsidiaries is important in preparing the consolidation adjustments. Sequential acquisitions arise where the parent acquires its interest in a subsidiary before or on the same date as that subsidiary acquires an interest in its own subsidiary. Non-sequential acquisitions arise where a parent acquires an interest in a subsidiary that already is a parent; that is, it has its own subsidiary. In non-sequential acquisitions, the complicating factor is that one of the assets that may have a carrying amount different from fair value is the investment in a subsidiary previously acquired. The fair value of the investment reflects increases in the worth of the underlying net assets in that subsidiary.

Where the parent acquires additional shares in a subsidiary or where the parent sells shares in a subsidiary but still retains control, there is no change in the economic entity. Both the parent and the subsidiary are still within the economic entity. These changes in ownership interests cannot then give rise to gains or losses recognised as profit to the economic entity. They are accounted for as equity transactions, as they are transactions between the owners and not with entities outside the group.

Where the parent sells some of its shares in a subsidiary and as a result loses control of the subsidiary, but retains an investment in the former subsidiary, in accordance with paragraph 25 of AASB 10/IFRS 10, the investor will record that remaining investment in accordance with AASB 9/IFRS 9 *Financial Instruments*, namely at fair value. The measurement of the remaining asset at fair value is factored into the calculation of any gain/loss on disposal of the shares in the subsidiary. The gain/loss on disposal is recognised in the profit or loss.

KEY TERMS

direct non-controlling interest (DNCI) The NCI that directly owns shares in a subsidiary.

immediate parent The subsidiary in a multiple subsidiary structure that directly controls the ultimate subsidiary and is controlled by the ultimate parent.

indirect non-controlling interest (INCI) The NCI that indirectly owns shares in a subsidiary. Where a subsidiary is owned by a partially owned subsidiary in a group, the DNCI in the partially owned subsidiary is the INCI in the other subsidiary.

non-controlling interest (NCI) Equity in a subsidiary not attributable, directly or indirectly, to a parent.

non-sequential acquisition An acquisition in which the immediate parent in a multiple subsidiary structure acquires its shares in the ultimate subsidiary before the ultimate parent acquires its shares in the immediate parent.

parent An entity that controls one or more entities.

sequential acquisition An acquisition in which the ultimate parent acquires its shares in the immediate parent before the immediate parent acquires its shares in the ultimate subsidiary, or both acquisitions occur on the same date.

ultimate parent The parent in a multiple subsidiary structure that controls directly or indirectly all the subsidiaries in the group, including the immediate parent.

ultimate subsidiary The subsidiary in a multiple subsidiary structure that is controlled directly by the immediate parent and indirectly by the ultimate parent.

DEMONSTRATION PROBLEMS

30.1 Effects of intragroup transactions on the calculation of the NCI

On 1 July 2021, Australia Ltd acquired 60% of the issued shares (*cum div.*) of Bangladesh Ltd for $163 980. On the same day, Bangladesh Ltd acquired 75% of the issued shares of Bhutan Ltd for

$129 050. At this date, an extract from the statement of financial position of Bangladesh Ltd and Bhutan Ltd disclosed the following.

	Bangladesh Ltd	Bhutan Ltd
Share capital	$240 000	$164 000
General reserve	8 000	—
Retained earnings	1 600	2 400
Dividend payable	14 400	—

The dividend payable by Bangladesh Ltd was subsequently paid. No other dividends have been paid from pre-acquisition equity.

On 1 July 2021, all the identifiable assets and liabilities of Bhutan Ltd were recorded at fair value except for some non-monetary assets. A comparison of the non-monetary assets' carrying amounts and fair values revealed the following information.

	Bhutan Ltd	
	Carrying amount	Fair value
Inventories	$ 5 000	$ 6 000
Plant (cost $160 000)	128 000	133 000
Land	56 000	60 000

All inventories were sold by 30 June 2022. The plant was expected to provide further benefits evenly over the next 5 years. The land is still held by Bhutan Ltd at 30 June 2023.

On 1 July 2021 all the identifiable assets and liabilities of Bangladesh Ltd were recorded at fair value except for the following.

	Bangladesh Ltd	
	Carrying amount	Fair value
Inventories	$ 6 000	$ 8 000
Plant (cost $147 000)	126 000	130 000

All inventories were sold by 30 June 2022. The plant was expected to provide further benefits evenly over the next 4 years. At 1 July 2021, Bangladesh Ltd had in its accounts a goodwill with a balance of $6000. The financial data as at 30 June 2023 of the three companies are shown below.

Additional information
- Sales and purchases during the period ended 30 June 2023 included the following transactions.
  - Sales by Bangladesh Ltd to Australia Ltd invoiced at cost plus 33% were $12 000.
  - Sales by Bhutan Ltd to Australia Ltd invoiced at cost plus 25% were $36 000.
- Inventories on hand of Australia Ltd at 30 June 2023 included $1600 acquired from Bangladesh Ltd and $1200 acquired from Bhutan Ltd.
- Inventories of Bangladesh Ltd at 1 July 2022 included goods received from Bhutan Ltd on which Bhutan Ltd recognised $160 profit.
- Receivables and payables included $3600 owing by Australia Ltd to Bangladesh Ltd.
- The tax rate is 30%.

	Australia Ltd	Bangladesh Ltd	Bhutan Ltd
Sales revenue	$675 360	$444 800	$290 000
Dividend revenue	18 720	13 200	—
Debenture interest	—	3 200	3 840
Total revenue	694 080	461 200	293 840
Cost of sales	490 400	333 600	232 000
Other expenses	44 080	42 800	20 000
Total expenses	534 480	376 400	252 000
Profit before tax	159 600	84 800	41 840
Income tax expense	64 000	32 000	16 000
Profit for the period	95 600	52 800	25 840
Retained earnings (1/7/22)	4 000	10 400	8 800
	99 600	63 200	34 640

	Australia Ltd	Bangladesh Ltd	Bhutan Ltd
Dividend paid	20 000	14 400	8 000
Dividend declared	30 000	16 800	9 600
	50 000	31 200	17 600
Retained earnings (30/6/23)	49 600	32 000	17 040
Share capital	420 000	240 000	164 000
General reserve	12 000	16 000	8 000
Total equity	481 600	288 000	189 040
8% Debentures	160 000		
Provisions	20 000	29 600	16 000
Dividend payable	30 000	16 800	9 600
Current tax liability	64 400	32 000	16 000
Total liabilities	274 400	78 400	41 600
Total equity and liabilities	$ 756 000	$ 366 400	$ 230 640
Inventories	$ 5 600	$ 4 400	$ 5 120
Receivables	21 860	15 550	1 520
Cash	28 000	10 600	21 600
8% debentures in Australia Ltd	—	40 000	48 000
Shares in Bangladesh Ltd	155 340	—	—
Shares in Bhutan Ltd	—	129 050	—
Plant	500 000	147 000	160 000
Accumulated depreciation	(204 000)	(63 000)	(64 000)
Land	200 000	70 000	56 000
Deferred tax asset	32 000	6 800	2 400
Goodwill	17 200	6 000	—
Total assets	$ 756 000	$ 366 400	$ 230 640

Required

Prepare the consolidated financial statements for Australia Ltd and its subsidiaries as at 30 June 2023.

SOLUTION

The *first step* in the consolidation process is to establish the structure of the group and percentage ownership of the NCI — see figure 30.6.

FIGURE 30.6	The structure of the group

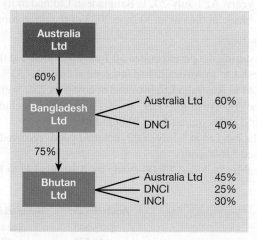

The *next step* is to prepare the acquisition analysis, the business combination valuation and pre-acquisition entries, and the NCI entries for both acquisitions.

Acquisition analysis: Bangladesh Ltd and Bhutan Ltd

Net fair value of identifiable assets and liabilities of Bhutan Ltd

= $164 000 (share capital) + $2400 (retained earnings)
+ $1000(1 − 30%) (BCVR — inventories)
+ $5000(1 − 30%) (BCVR — plant)
+ $4000(1 − 30%) (BCVR — land)
= $173 400

(a) Consideration transferred		= $129 050	
(b) NCI in Bhutan Ltd		= 25% × $173 400	
		= $43 350	
Aggregate of (a) and (b)		= $172 400	
Gain on bargain purchase		= $173 400 − $172 400	
		= $1000	

(1) Business combination valuation entries: Bangladesh Ltd and Bhutan Ltd

The business combination valuation entries at 1 July 2021 are as follows.

Inventories	Dr	1 000	
Deferred tax liability	Cr		300
BCVR	Cr		700
Accumulated depreciation — plant	Dr	32 000	
Plant	Cr		27 000
Deferred tax liability	Cr		1 500
BCVR	Cr		3 500
Land	Dr	4 000	
Deferred tax liability	Cr		1 200
BCVR	Cr		2 800

The inventories were all sold in the period ended 30 June 2022, so no further business combination valuation entries are required for inventories at 30 June 2023. At 30 June 2023, the valuation entries for plant require adjustment to reflect additional depreciation of $1000 p.a., being one-fifth of $5000. The land is still held by Bhutan Ltd at 30 June 2023. Therefore, the business combination valuation entries at 30 June 2023 are as follows.

Accumulated depreciation — plant	Dr	32 000	
Plant	Cr		27 000
Deferred tax liability	Cr		1 500
BCVR	Cr		3 500
Depreciation expense	Dr	1 000	
Retained earnings (1/7/22)	Dr	1 000	
Accumulated depreciation — plant	Cr		2 000
Deferred tax liability	Dr	600	
Income tax expense	Cr		300
Retained earnings (1/7/22)	Cr		300
Land	Dr	4 000	
Deferred tax liability	Cr		1 200
BCVR	Cr		2 800

(2) Pre-acquisition entry: Bangladesh Ltd and Bhutan Ltd

The pre-acquisition entry at 1 July 2021 is as follows.

Retained earnings (1/7/21)	Dr	1 800	
Share capital	Dr	123 000	
BCVR	Dr	5 250	
Gain on bargain purchase	Cr		1 000
Shares in Bhutan Ltd	Cr		129 050

The inventories are all sold in the period ended 30 June 2022, and therefore the related business combination valuation reserve (75% × $700) is transferred to retained earnings in that period. Both plant and land are still held by Bhutan Ltd.

At 30 June 2023, the pre-acquisition entry becomes the following.

Retained earnings (1/7/22)*	Dr	1 325	
Share capital	Dr	123 000	
BCVR	Dr	4 725	
Shares in Bhutan Ltd	Cr		129 050

*$1800 − $1000 gain on bargain purchase + (75% × $700) BCVR for inventories

(3) NCI share of equity in Bhutan Ltd at 1 July 2021 (step 1)

Retained earnings (1/7/22)	Dr	600
Share capital	Dr	41 000
BCVR	Dr	1 750
NCI	Cr	43 350

(4) NCI share of changes in equity in Bhutan Ltd from 1 July 2021 to 30 June 2022 (step 2)
Changes in retained earnings

DNCI (25%)

Retained earnings of Bhutan Ltd at 30 June 2022 have increased by $6400; that is, from $2400 to $8800, but adjustments must be made for the after-tax depreciation of plant up to 30 June 2022, as shown in the business combination valuation entries. As such, the DNCI share of changes in equity from 1 July 2021 to 30 June 2022 is recognised in the following worksheet entry.

Retained earnings (1/7/22)	Dr	1 425
NCI	Cr	1 425
(25% × [$6400 − ($1000 − $300)])		

INCI (30%)

The INCI receives a share of post-acquisition equity only. As shown above in the calculation of the DNCI share of changes in retained earnings from 1 July 2021 to 30 June 2022, retained earnings have increased by $6400, but a part of this increase is due to the BCVR (pre-acquisition equity) of $700 for inventory undervalued at acquisition date sold during this period. Considering the further adjustments needed for the after-tax depreciation of plant $700 (i.e. $1000 − $300), the INCI share of post-acquisition retained earnings is as follows.

$$30\% \times [\$6400 - \$700 - (\$1000 - \$300)] = \$1500$$

The worksheet entry to recognise this share is as follows.

Retained earnings (1/7/22)	Dr	1 500
NCI	Cr	1 500

Changes in BCVR

The business combination valuation reserve has decreased because the reserve in relation to inventories has been transferred to retained earnings. This affects the DNCI only because it relates to pre-acquisition profits.

DNCI (25%)

NCI	Dr	175
BCVR	Cr	175
(25% × $700)		

Changes in general reserve

The general reserve has increased from a zero balance at acquisition date to $8000, an increase of $8000. Assuming that this has resulted from a transfer from post-acquisition retained earnings, both the DNCI and INCI are affected.

DNCI (25%) and INCI (30%)

General reserve	Dr	4 400
NCI	Cr	4 400
([25% + 30%] × $8000)		

(5) NCI share of equity in Bhutan Ltd from 1 July 2022 to 30 June 2023 (step 3)

Because there is no adjustment to the current period profit in the pre-acquisition entry, both the DNCI and INCI receive a share of the recorded profit of $25 840 adjusted for the after-tax adjustment for the current period's depreciation of plant as follows.

NCI share of profit	Dr	13 827	
NCI	Cr		13 827
([25% + 30%] × [$25 840 − ($1000 − $300)])			

Bhutan Ltd has paid a dividend of $8000. This affects the DNCI only now (see below for further details).

NCI	Dr	2 000	
Dividend paid	Cr		2 000
(25% × $8000)			

Bhutan Ltd has declared a dividend of $9600. Only the DNCI is affected now (see below for further effects).

NCI	Dr	2 400	
Dividend declared	Cr		2 400
(25% × $9600)			

The next step is to deal with the other acquisition, Australia Ltd's acquisition of Bangladesh Ltd.

Acquisition analysis: Australia Ltd and Bangladesh Ltd

Net fair value of identifiable assets and liabilities of Bangladesh Ltd	=	$240 000 (capital) + $8000 (general reserve) + $1600 (retained earnings) + $2000(1 − 30%) (BCVR — inventories) + $4000(1 − 30%) (BCVR — plant) − $6000 (goodwill)
	=	$247 800
(a) Consideration transferred	=	$163 980 − (60% × $14 400) (dividend)
	=	$155 340
(b) NCI in Bangladesh Ltd	=	40% × $247 800
	=	$99 120
Aggregate of (a) and (b)	=	$254 460
Goodwill acquired by Australia Ltd	=	$6660

Note that, as the partial goodwill method is applied in this chapter for all examples with a multiple subsidiary group structure, including this demonstration problem, the previously recorded goodwill from Bangladesh Ltd's individual accounts has to be written off in the business combination valuation entries; otherwise, a share of it will be allocated to NCI. The goodwill acquired by Australia Ltd of $6660 calculated in the acquisition analysis above is then recorded in the pre-acquisition entry to ensure it is not allocated to NCI.

(6) Business combination valuation entries: Australia Ltd and Bangladesh Ltd
The entries at 30 June 2023 take into account that the inventories are sold in the period ended 30 June 2022 (and therefore no further entries are required for it now), and over the two years since acquisition, the depreciation of the plant is adjusted at $1000 p.a., being one quarter of $4000. The entries at 30 June 2023 are as follows.

Accumulated depreciation — plant	Dr	21 000	
Plant	Cr		17 000
Deferred tax liability	Cr		1 200
BCVR	Cr		2 800
Depreciation expense	Dr	1 000	
Retained earnings (1/7/22)	Dr	1 000	
Accumulated depreciation — plant	Cr		2 000
Deferred tax liability	Dr	600	
Income tax expense	Cr		300
Retained earnings (1/7/22)	Cr		300
BCVR	Dr	6 000	
Goodwill	Cr		6 000

(7) Pre-acquisition entries: Australia Ltd and Bangladesh Ltd

The pre-acquisition entries at 1 July 2021 are as follows.

Retained earnings (1/7/21)	Dr	960	
Share capital	Dr	144 000	
General reserve	Dr	4 800	
BCVR*	Cr		1 080
Goodwill	Dr	6 660	
Shares in Bangladesh Ltd	Cr		155 340
Dividend payable	Dr	8 640	
Dividend receivable	Cr		8 640

*60% × ($6000 recorded goodwill – $1400 BCVR for inventories – $2800 BCVR for plant)

By 30 June 2023, the dividend has been paid and the inventories sold with the relevant business combination valuation reserve transferred to retained earnings. Therefore, the pre-acquisition entry at 30 June 2023 is as follows.

Retained earnings (1/7/22)	Dr	1 800	
Share capital	Dr	144 000	
General reserve	Dr	4 800	
BCVR*	Cr		1 920
Goodwill	Dr	6 660	
Shares in Bangladesh Ltd	Cr		155 340

*60% × ($6000 recorded goodwill – $2800 BCVR for plant)

(8) NCI share of equity in Bangladesh Ltd at 1 July 2021 (step 1)

Retained earnings (1/7/22)	Dr	640	
Share capital	Dr	96 000	
General reserve	Dr	3 200	
BCVR	Cr		720
NCI	Cr		99 120
(40% of balances at acquisition)			

(9) NCI share of changes in equity in Bangladesh Ltd from 1 July 2021 to 30 June 2022 (step 2)

Changes in retained earnings

The retained earnings for Bangladesh Ltd have increased from $1600 to $10 400, an increase of $8800. This has to be adjusted for the after-tax depreciation adjustment on plant, $1000 – $300. As such, the entry to recognise the NCI's share of those changes is as follows.

Retained earnings (1/7/22)	Dr	3 240	
NCI	Cr		3 240
(40% × [$8800 – ($1000 – $300)])			

Changes in BCVR

The business combination valuation reserve relating to inventories has been transferred to retained earnings. As such, the entry to recognise the NCI's share of those changes is as follows.

NCI	Dr	560	
BCVR	Cr		560
(40% × $1400)			

Changes in general reserve

The general reserve has increased from $8000 to $16 000. As such, the entry to recognise the NCI's share of those changes is as follows.

General reserve	Dr	3 200	
NCI	Cr		3 200
(40% × $8000)			

(10) NCI share of equity in Bangladesh Ltd from 1 July 2022 to 30 June 2022 (step 3)

Current profit

The current period profit is $52 800, and is adjusted for the after-tax depreciation adjustment on plant for the current period. As such, the entry to recognise the NCI's share of current profit is as follows.

NCI share of profit		Dr	20 840	
NCI		Cr		20 840
(40% × ($52 800 − [$1000 − $300]))				

Dividend paid by Bangladesh Ltd of $14 400

NCI		Dr	5 760	
Dividend paid		Cr		5 760
(40% × $14 400)				

Dividend declared by Bangladesh Ltd of $16 800

NCI		Dr	6 720	
Dividend declared		Cr		6 720

Dividend revenue from Bhutan Ltd of $13 200

Bhutan Ltd paid a dividend of $8000 and declared a dividend of $9600. Bangladesh Ltd therefore recorded dividend revenue of $13 200 (i.e. 75% × ($8000 + $9600)). As the INCI has received a share of the profit of Bhutan Ltd, to avoid double counting the DNCI in Bangladesh Ltd must be adjusted in relation to this dividend revenue.

NCI		Dr	5 280	
NCI share of profit		Cr		5 280
(40% × $13 200)				

Intragroup transactions

(11) Dividend paid by Bhutan Ltd

Dividend revenue		Dr	6 000	
Interim dividend paid		Cr		6 000
(75% × $8000)				

(12) Dividend declared by Bhutan Ltd

Dividend payable		Dr	7 200	
Dividend declared		Cr		7 200
(75% × $9600)				
Dividend revenue		Dr	7 200	
Dividend receivable		Cr		7 200

(13) Dividend paid by Bangladesh Ltd

Dividend revenue		Dr	8 640	
Interim dividend paid		Cr		8 640
(60% × $14 400)				

(14) Dividend declared by Bangladesh Ltd

Dividend payable		Dr	10 080	
Dividend declared		Cr		10 080
(60% × $16 800)				
Dividend revenue		Dr	10 080	
Dividend receivable		Cr		10 080

(15) Profit in ending inventories: Sales by Bangladesh Ltd to Australia Ltd

Sales revenue	Dr	12 000	
Cost of sales	Cr		11 600
Inventories	Cr		400
Deferred tax asset	Dr	120	
Income tax expense	Cr		120

(16) Adjustment to NCI in Bangladesh Ltd

NCI	Dr	112	
NCI share of profit	Cr		112
(40% × [$400 − $120])			

(17) Profit in ending inventories: Sales by Bhutan Ltd to Australia Ltd

Sales revenue	Dr	36 000	
Cost of sales	Cr		35 760
Inventories	Cr		240
Deferred tax asset	Dr	72	
Income tax expense	Cr		72

(18) Adjustment to NCI in Bhutan Ltd

NCI	Dr	92	
NCI share of profit	Cr		92
([25% + 30%] × [$240 − $72])			

(19) Profit in opening inventories: Sales by Bhutan Ltd to Bangladesh Ltd

Retained earnings (1/7/22)	Dr	112	
Income tax expense	Dr	48	
Cost of sales	Cr		160

(20) Adjustment to NCI in Bhutan Ltd

NCI share of profit	Dr	62	
Retained earnings (1/7/22)	Cr		62
([25% + 30%] × [$160 − $48])			

(21) Intragroup receivables and payables

Payables	Dr	3 600	
Receivables	Cr		3 600

(22) Intragroup debentures in Australia Ltd
Intragroup debentures held amount to $88 000 ($40 000 by Bangladesh Ltd and $48 000 by Bhutan Ltd).

8% debentures	Dr	88 000	
8% debentures in Australia Ltd	Cr		88 000

(23) Intragroup debenture interest paid by Australia Ltd
Assuming that the intragroup debentures were held for the entire year ended 30 June 2023, the interest paid was 8% of $88 000.

Debenture interest revenue	Dr	7 040	
Debenture interest expense	Cr		7 040

The consolidation worksheet is shown in figure 30.7.

FIGURE 30.7 Consolidation worksheet

Financial statements	Australia Ltd $	Bangladesh Ltd $	Bhutan Ltd $	Adjustments Dr $ (ref)	Adjustments Cr $ (ref)	Group $	Non-controlling interest Dr $ (ref)	Non-controlling interest Cr $ (ref)	Parent $
Sales revenue	675 360	444 800	290 000	12 000 (15)	11 600 (15)	1 362 160			
Dividend revenue	18 720	13 200	—	36 000 (17)	35 760 (17)	—			
				6 000 (11)	160 (19)				
				7 200 (12)	7 040 (23)				
				8 640 (13)					
				10 080 (14)					
Debenture interest	—	3 200	3 840	7 040 (23)					
Total revenue	694 080	461 200	293 840			1 362 160			
Cost of sales	490 400	333 600	232 000			1 008 480			
Other expenses	44 080	42 800	20 000	1 000 (1)	7 040 (23)	101 840			
				1 000 (6)					
Total expenses	534 480	376 400	252 000			1 110 320			
Profit before tax	159 600	84 800	41 840			251 840			
Tax expense	64 000	32 000	16 000	48 (19)	300 (1)	111 256			
					300 (6)				
					120 (15)				
					72 (17)				
Profit for the period	95 600	52 800	25 840			140 584	13 827 (5)	5 280 (10)	111 339
							20 840 (10)	112 (16)	
							62 (20)	92 (18)	
								62 (20)	
Retained earnings (1/7/22)	4 000	10 400	8 800	1 000 (1)	300 (1)	18 563	600 (3)		11 220
				1 325 (2)	300 (6)		1 425 (4)		
				1 000 (6)			1 500 (4)		
				1 800 (7)			640 (8)		
				112 (19)			3 240 (9)		
Dividend paid	99 600 / 20 000	63 200 / 14 400	34 640 / 8 000		6 000 (11)	159 147 / 27 760		2 000 (5)	122 559 / 20 000
					7 200 (12)			5 760 (10)	
Dividend declared	30 000	16 800	9 600		8 640 (13)	39 120		2 400 (5)	30 000
					10 080 (14)			6 720 (10)	
Retained earnings (30/6/23)	50 000	31 200	17 600			66 880			50 000
Retained earnings (30/6/23)	49 600	32 000	17 040	123 000 (2)		92 267	41 000 (3)		72 559
				144 000 (7)			96 000 (8)		
Share capital	420 000	240 000	164 000			557 000			420 000
General reserve	12 000	16 000	8 000	4 800 (7)		31 200	4 400 (4)		20 400
							3 200 (8)		
							3 200 (9)		

Financial statements	Australia Ltd $	Bangladesh Ltd $	Bhutan Ltd $	Adjustments Dr (ref)	Adjustments Dr $	Adjustments Cr $	Adjustments Cr (ref)	Group $	NCI Dr (ref)	NCI Dr $	NCI Cr $	NCI Cr (ref)	Parent $
BCVR	—	—	—	2 6	4 725 6 000	3 500 2 800 2 800 1 920	1 1 6 7	295	3	1 750	175 720 560	4 8 9	—
Total equity: parent													512 959
Total equity: NCI													167 803
Total equity	481 600	288 000	189 040					680 762	4 5 5 9 10 10 10 16 18	175 2 000 2 400 560 5 760 6 720 5 280 112 92 __214 783__	43 350 1 425 1 500 4 400 13 827 99 120 3 240 3 200 20 840 __214 783__	3 4 5 4 4 5 8 9 9 10	680 762
Debentures	160 000	—	—	22	88 000			72 000					
Provisions	20 000	29 600	16 000	21	3 600			62 000					
Dividend payable	30 000	16 800	9 600	12 14	7 200 10 080			39 120					
Current tax liability	64 400	32 000	16 000					112 400					
Deferred tax liability	—	—	—	1 6	600 600	1 500 1 200 1 200	1 1 6	2 700					
Total liabilities	274 400	78 400	41 600					288 220					
Total equity and liabilities	756 000	366 400	230 640					968 982					
Inventories	5 600	4 400	5 120			400 240	15 17	14 480					
Receivables	21 860	15 550	1 520			3 600 7 200 10 080	21 12 14	18 050					
Cash	28 000	10 600	21 600					60 200					
Debentures in Australia Ltd	—	40 000	48 000			88 000	22	—					
Shares in Bangladesh Ltd	155 340	—	—			155 340	7	—					
Shares in Bhutan Ltd	—	129 050	—			129 050	2	—					
Plant	500 000	147 000	160 000			27 000 17 000	1 6	763 000					
Accumulated depreciation	(204 000)	(63 000)	(64 000)	1 6	32 000 21 000	2 000 2 000	1 6	(282 000)					
Land	200 000	70 000	56 000	1	4 000			330 000					
Deferred tax asset	32 000	6 800	2 400	15 17	120 72			41 392					
Goodwill	17 200	6 000	—	7	6 660	6 000	6	23 860					
Total assets	756 000	366 400	230 640		__550 702__	__550 702__		968 982					

The consolidated financial statements for Australia Ltd at 30 June 2023 are shown in figure 30.8(a), (b) and (c).

FIGURE 30.8   **(a)** Consolidated statement of profit or loss and other comprehensive income

AUSTRALIA LTD	
Consolidated statement of profit or loss and other comprehensive income	
for financial year ended 30 June 2023	
Revenue: Sales	$1 362 160
Expenses	
Cost of sales	1 008 480
Other	101 840
Total expenses	1 110 320
Profit before income tax	251 840
Income tax expense	(111 256)
Profit for the period	**140 584**
Other comprehensive income	0
Total comprehensive income	**$ 140 584**
Attributable to:	
Owners of the parent	$ 111 339
Non-controlling interest	29 245
	$ 140 584

FIGURE 30.8   **(b)** Consolidated statement of changes in equity

AUSTRALIA LTD		
Consolidated statement of changes in equity		
for the year ended 30 June 2023		
Total comprehensive income for the period		$140 584
Attributable to:		
Owners of the parent		111 339
Non-controlling interest		29 245
	Consolidated	Parent
Share capital		
Balance, beginning of year	$557 000	$420 000
Balance, end of year	$557 000	$420 000
General reserve		
Balance, beginning of year	$ 31 200	$ 20 400
Balance, end of year	$ 31 200	$ 20 400
Retained earnings		
Balance, beginning of year	$ 18 563	$ 11 220
Profit for the period	140 584	111 339
Dividends paid and declared	(66 880)	(50 000)
Balance, end of year	$ 92 267	$ 72 559

FIGURE 30.8   **(c)** Consolidated statement of financial position

AUSTRALIA LTD	
Consolidated statement of financial position	
as at 30 June 2023	
ASSETS	
Current assets	
Inventories	$ 14 480
Receivables	18 050
Cash	60 200
Total current assets	92 730

AUSTRALIA LTD
Consolidated statement of financial position
as at 30 June 2023

Non-current assets	
Plant and equipment	763 000
Accumulated depreciation — plant and equipment	(282 000)
Land	330 000
Deferred tax assets	41 392
Goodwill	23 860
Total non-current assets	876 252
Total assets	968 982
LIABILITIES	
Current liabilities	
Provisions	62 000
Dividends payable	39 120
Current tax liabilities	112 400
Total current liabilities	213 520
Non-current liabilities	
Debentures	72 000
Deferred tax liabilities	2 700
Total non-current liabilities	74 700
Total liabilities	288 220
Net assets	**$ 680 762**
EQUITY	
Share capital	$ 420 000
Other reserves: general	20 400
Retained earnings	72 559
Owners of the parent	512 959
Non-controlling interest	167 803
Total equity	**$ 680 762**

30.2 Effects of changes in ownership interests

Trial balances for Rose Ltd and Wood Ltd at 30 June 2023 were as follows.

	Rose Ltd	Wood Ltd
Current assets	$ 176 000	$ 89 000
Shares in Wood Ltd	180 000	—
Plant (net)	747 500	298 000
Dividends declared	80 000	40 000
Cost of sales	610 000	260 000
Other expenses	190 000	55 000
	$1 983 500	$742 000
Share capital		
— 400 000 shares	$ 400 000	
— 200 000 shares		$200 000
Retained earnings (1/7/22)	238 700	80 000
General reserve	150 000	30 000
Sales	970 000	400 000
Gain on loss of control of subsidiary	145 000	—
Liabilities	79 800	32 000
	$1 983 500	$742 000

Rose Ltd acquired its 80% interest in Wood Ltd for $215 000 on 1 January 2021 when the shareholders' equity of Wood Ltd consisted of the following.

Share capital	$200 000
General reserve	20 000
Retained earnings	40 000

At the date of acquisition, all the identifiable net assets of Wood Ltd were recorded at fair value except for some plant for which the fair value was $5000 greater than the carrying amount. The plant had an expected useful life of 5 years.

On 1 January 2023, Rose Ltd sold 80 000 shares (i.e. 40% of the issued shares) in Wood Ltd for $180 000. At 1 January 2023 Wood Ltd had recorded an interim profit after tax of $40 000 based on sales of $190 000, cost of sales of $120 000 and other expenses of $30 000. The fair value of the shares in Wood Ltd does not change between 1 January 2023 and 30 June 2023.

Required

Prepare the consolidation worksheets at 30 June 2023 for the following independent situations.

1. Wood Ltd does not remain a subsidiary of Rose Ltd after 1 January 2023.
2. Wood Ltd's status as a subsidiary of Rose Ltd is unaffected by the sale of shares in January 2023. In relation to the trial balance at 30 June 2023, assume that the balance of Shares in Wood Ltd is $107 500 and the balance of Plant is $820 000. Also, assume that the gain on sale of shares where control is not lost is $72 500 and liabilities are $152 300 — see the worksheet in Part 2 for these changes.

SOLUTION

Acquisition analysis at 1 January 2021

Net fair value of identifiable assets and liabilities of Wood Ltd	= $200 000 + $20 000 + $40 000
	+ $5000(1 − 30%) (BCVR − plant)
	= $263 500
(a) Consideration transferred	= $215 000
(b) NCI in Wood Ltd	= 20% × $263 500
	= $52 700
Aggregate of (a) and (b)	= $267 700
Goodwill	= $4200

Worksheet entries at 1 January 2023 — prior to sale

Business combination valuation entries

Plant	Dr	5 000	
Deferred tax liability	Cr		1 500
BCVR	Cr		3 500
Depreciation expense	Dr	500	
Retained earnings (1/7/22)	Dr	1 500	
Accumulated depreciation — plant	Cr		2 000
Deferred tax liability	Dr	600	
Income tax expense	Cr		150
Retained earnings (1/7/22)	Cr		450

Pre-acquisition entry

Retained earnings (1/7/22)	Dr	32 000	
Share capital	Dr	160 000	
General reserve	Dr	16 000	
BCVR	Dr	2 800	
Goodwill	Dr	4 200	
Shares in Wood Ltd	Cr		215 000

1. *Sale of shares with loss of control of subsidiary*

Rose Ltd would pass a journal entry in its own records to recognise the gain on sale of the shares in Wood Ltd of $72 500 (being proceeds of $180 000 less cost of shares sold of $215 000/80% × 40%) as well as the gain on re-measurement of the remaining shares to fair value of $72 500 (being fair value of $180 000 less cost of shares remaining of $215 000/80% × 40%). Rose Ltd would also recognise the receipt of cash and would adjust the balance of the investment account to reflect the value of the remaining interest in Wood Ltd. The entry recorded by Rose Ltd at 1 January 2023 is then as follows.

Cash	Dr	180 000	
Shares in Wood Ltd ($215 000 − $180 000)	Cr		35 000
Gain on shares in Wood Ltd ($72 500 + $72 500)	Cr		145 000

However, the economic entity will need to calculate the real gain/loss to the parent. The calculation is as follows.

Real gain = $180 000 [proceeds on sale] + $180 000 [fair value of remaining investment]
            + $285 880 [Rose Ltd's share of Wood Ltd's net assets]*
          = $74 120

*80% × ($200 000 [share capital] + $80 000 [retained earnings (1/7/22)] + $40 000 [profit up to 1/7/23] + $30 000 [general reserve] + ($5000 − $2000) [plant revaluation — net of depreciation] − ($1500 − $600) [deferred tax liability related to plant revaluation — net of depreciation]) + $4200 [goodwill] = $281 680 + $4200 = $285 880

Hence, in the consolidation worksheet the recorded gain of $145 000 must be reduced by $70 880 to show the real gain of $74 120.

Worksheet entries at 30 June 2023

(1) As Wood Ltd is no longer a subsidiary of Rose Ltd, its financial statements are not added to those of the rest of the group. The first consolidation worksheet entry (i) adjusts for the gain on sale recorded by Rose Ltd and (ii) reinstates the equity earned by the group for the first 6 months of the year (from 1 July 2022 to 1 January 2023) while Wood Ltd was still a subsidiary of Rose Ltd. As the sale of the subsidiary occurred halfway through the year, the consolidated financial statements of Rose Ltd must include the post-acquisition equity of Wood Ltd up to the point of sale. As Wood Ltd is no longer a subsidiary, the balances in the reserves must be transferred out to record the movement. The consolidation worksheet entry is as follows.

Gain on shares in Wood Ltd	Dr	70 880	
Cost of sales	Dr	120 000	
Other expenses [$30 000 + $500 − $150]	Dr	30 350	
Sales	Cr		190 000
Transfer from general reserve [$30 000 − 80% × $20 000]	Cr		14 000
Transfer from BCVR [$3500 − 80% × $3500]	Cr		700
Retained earnings (1/7/19) [$80 000 − $32 000 − ($1500 − $450)]	Cr		46 950
Reduction in equity on sale of subsidiary	Dr	30 420	

(2) The second consolidation worksheet entry deals with the fact that there was a NCI of 20% in relation to Wood Ltd within the group for the first half of the year. In worksheet entry (1) above, the group's equity for the first half of the year was reinstated into the consolidated financial statements. In entry (2) the NCI share of this equity is separated out. As Wood Ltd is no longer a subsidiary after the sale of shares, the NCI share of equity must also be derecognised. Hence the second worksheet entry both brings into the group the NCI (20%) share of equity of Wood Ltd for the first half of the year, and derecognises the NCI on sale of the subsidiary. The entry in the NCI columns of the consolidation worksheet is as follows.

Share of profit [20% × ($40 000 − ($500 − $150))]	Dr	7 930	
Transfer from general reserve [20% × $30 000]	Dr	6 000	
Transfer from BCVR [20% × $3500]	Dr	700	
Retained earnings (1/7/22) [20% × ($80 000 − ($1500 − $450))]	Dr	15 790	
Reduction in equity on sale of subsidiary	Cr		30 420

The consolidation worksheet at 30 June 2023 is as follows.

Financial statements	Rose Ltd	Adjustments Dr		Adjustments Cr		NCI Dr	NCI Cr	Consolidation
Sales revenue	970 000			190 000	1			1 160 000
Cost of sales	610 000	1	120 000					730 000
	360 000							430 000
Expenses	190 000	1	30 350					220 350
	170 000							209 650
Gain on sale of shares	145 000	1	70 880					74 120

	Rose Ltd		Dr			Cr		Group
Profit	315 000							283 770
NCI share					2	7 930		7 930
Rose Ltd share								275 840
Retained earnings (1/7/22)	238 700		46 950	1	2	15 790		269 860
	553 700							545 700
Transfer from general reserve	—		14 000	1	2	6 000		8 000
Transfer from BCVR	—		700	1	2	700		—
								553 700
Reduction in equity on sale of subsidiary	—	1	30 420			30 420	2	—
								553 700
Dividends declared	80 000							80 000
Retained earnings (30/6/23)	473 700							473 700
Share capital	400 000							400 000
General reserve	150 000							150 000
Liabilities	79 800							79 800
	1 103 500							1 103 500
Current assets	176 000							176 000
Shares in Wood Ltd	180 000							180 000
Plant (net)	747 500							747 500
	1 103 500							1 103 500

2. *Sale of shares without loss of control of subsidiary*

On sale of the shares in Wood Ltd, Rose Ltd would record the following entry in its own records.

Cash	Dr	180 000	
Shares in Wood Ltd	Cr		107 500
Gain on sale of shares in Wood Ltd	Cr		72 500

The consolidation worksheet entries at 30 June 2023 are as follows.

(1) Business combination valuation entries

These are the same entries as at 1 January 2023 adjusted for a further half-year's depreciation on the plant of $500 and related tax effects.

Plant	Dr	5 000	
Deferred tax liability	Cr		1 500
BCVR	Cr		3 500
Depreciation expense	Dr	1 000	
Retained earnings (1/7/22)	Dr	1 500	
Accumulated depreciation — plant	Cr		2 500
Deferred tax liability	Dr	750	
Income tax expense	Cr		300
Retained earnings (1/7/22)	Cr		450

(2) Pre-acquisition entry

As half of the original investment was sold by Rose Ltd, the pre-acquisition entry is now half of what it was prior to the sale of shares as follows.

Retained earnings (1/7/22)	Dr	16 000	
Share capital	Dr	80 000	
General reserve	Dr	8 000	
BCVR	Dr	1 400	
Goodwill	Dr	2 100	
Shares in Wood Ltd	Cr		107 500

(3) NCI share of equity at 1 January 2021

Retained earnings (1/7/22)	Dr	8 000	
Share capital	Dr	40 000	
General reserve	Dr	4 000	
BCVR	Dr	700	
NCI	Cr		52 700
(20% of balances at 1/1/21)			

(4) NCI share of changes in equity from 1 January 2021 to 30 June 2022

Retained earnings (1/7/22)*	Dr	7 790	
General reserve**	Dr	2 000	
NCI	Cr		9 790

*20% × [$80 000 − $40 000 − ($1500 − $450)]
**20% × ($30 000 − $20 000)

(5) NCI share of equity from 30 June 2022 to 1 January 2023 (date of sale of shares)

NCI share of profit	Dr	7 930	
NCI	Cr		7 930
(20% × [$40 000 − ($500 − $150)])			

(6) Increase in NCI share of equity as a result of sale of shares — NCI increases from 20% to 60%

NCI share of profit*	Dr	15 860	
Retained earnings (1/7/22)**	Dr	31 580	
Share capital***	Dr	80 000	
General reserve****	Dr	12 000	
BCVR*****	Dr	1 400	
NCI	Cr		140 840

*40% × [$40 000 − ($500 − $150)]
**40% × [$80 000 − ($1500 − $450)]
***40% × $200 000
****40% × $30 000
*****40% × $3500

(7) Adjustment to gain on sale of shares by Rose Ltd

Gain on sale of shares	Dr	72 500	
Retained earnings (1/7/22)	Cr		15 580
Transfer from general reserve	Cr		4 000
Other reserves	Cr		52 920

This entry adjusts the gain on sale for the post-acquisition equity previously recognised by the group in relation to the shares sold.

    Retained earnings (1/7/22): 40% × [$80 000 − ($40 000 − ($1500 − $450) pre–acquisition]
    Transfer from general reserve: 40% × ($30 000 − $20 000)

The entry transfers the balance of the gain on sale to equity, in this example the account 'other reserves' is used, but any equity account could be used.

The effect of this entry ensures the opening balances of the equity accounts are then the same as the closing balances in the previous year's consolidated statement of financial position. To illustrate, note the retained earnings line in the consolidation worksheet both before and after the sale.

Before the sale of shares

Financial statements	Rose Ltd	Wood Ltd		Adjustments Dr	Cr		Group		NCI Dr	Cr	Parent
Retained earnings (30/6/22)	238 700	80 000	1	1 500	450	1	285 650	3	8 000		269 860
			2	32 000				4	7 790		

After the sale of shares

Financial statements	Rose Ltd	Wood Ltd	Adjustments Dr		Cr		Group		NCI Dr		Cr	Parent
Retained earnings (30/6/22)	238 700	80 000	*1*	1 500	450	*1*	317 230	*3*	8 000			269 860
			2	16 000	15 580	*7*		*4*	7 790			
								6	31 580			

(8) NCI share of equity from 1 January 2023 to 30 June 2023 — the NCI is now 60%

								Dr	26 790	
NCI share of profit										
NCI								Cr		26 790
(60% × [$85 000 − $40 000 − ($500 − $150)])										

(9) Dividends declared

								Dr	16 000	
Liabilities										
Dividends declared								Cr		16 000
(40% × $40 000)										

(10) NCI adjustment

								Dr	24 000	
NCI										
Dividends declared								Cr		24 000
(60% × $40 000)										

The consolidation worksheet at 30 June 2023 is as follows.

Financial statements	Rose Ltd	Wood Ltd	Adjustments Dr		Cr			NCI Dr		Cr	Parent
Sales revenue	970 000	400 000									1 370 000
Cost of sales	610 000	260 000									870 000
	360 000	140 000									500 000
Expenses	190 000	55 000	*1*	1 000	300	*1*					245 700
	170 000	85 000									254 300
Gain on sale	72 500		*7*	72 500							—
Profit	242 500										254 300
NCI share								*5*	7 930		50 580
								6	15 860		
								8	26 790		
Rose Ltd share											203 720
Retained earnings (1/7/22)	238 700	80 000	*1*	1 500	450	*1*		*3*	8 000		269 860
			2	16 000	15 580	*7*		*4*	7 790		
								6	31 580		
	481 200	165 000									473 580

Financial statements	Rose Ltd	Wood Ltd	Adjustments Dr		Cr			NCI Dr	Cr		Parent
Transfer from general reserve					4 000	7					4 000
											477 580
Dividends declared	80 000	40 000			16 000	8			24 000	9	80 000
Retained earnings (30/6/23)	401 200	125 000									397 580
Capital	400 000	200 000	80 000	2			3	40 000			400 000
							6	80 000			
BCVR	–	–	1 400	2	3 500	1	3	700			–
							6	1 400			
General reserve	150 000	30 000	8 000	2			3	4 000			154 000
							4	2 000			
							6	12 000			
Other reserves					52 920	7					52 920
Liabilities	152 300	32 000	750	1	1 500	1					169 050
			16 000	8							
NCI							9	24 000	52 700	3	214 050
									9 790	4	
									7 930	5	
									140 840	6	
									26 790	8	
	1 103 500	387 000									1 387 600
Current assets	176 000	89 000									265 000
Shares in Wood Ltd	107 500				107 500	2					–
Goodwill			2 100	2							2 100
Plant (net)	820 000	298 000	5 000	1	2 500	1					1 120 500
	1 103 500	387 000									1 387 600

COMPREHENSION QUESTIONS

1 Discuss the two types of NCI that may exist in a multiple subsidiary group structure.
2 Explain the difference in the calculation of the direct and indirect NCI.
3 Why does the indirect NCI receive a share of only *post-acquisition* equity?
4 What effect does the existence of a direct and an indirect NCI have on the adjustments for intragroup transactions?
5 What effect does the existence of a direct and an indirect NCI have on the adjustments for dividends paid within a group?
6 Explain sequential and non-sequential acquisitions.
7 Explain the effects on the consolidation process when the acquisition is non-sequential.
8 Explain how to account for further acquisition of shares by a parent in a subsidiary.
9 Explain how to account for sales of shares by a parent in a subsidiary that do not result in loss of control.
10 Explain how to account for changes in ownership interests by a parent in a group that result in loss of control.
11 What are the disclosure requirements relating to changes in ownership interest by a parent in a group?

CASE STUDY 30.1

NON-CONTROLLING INTEREST

P Ltd owns 20% of the issued shares of B Ltd. In recent months it has been in takeover discussions with A Ltd, and agreement has finally been reached between the different parties on the acquisition by P Ltd of 60% of the issued shares of A Ltd. One of the assets of A Ltd is a 70% holding in B Ltd. The group accountant of P Ltd has been examining the new group under the control of P Ltd and considering the implications for the preparation of consolidated financial statements. One of the members of the accounting team, Mei Fen, has raised the issue of accounting for indirect non-controlling interests. According to Mei Fen, in the new group structure there are both direct and indirect non-controlling interests, and she argues that different measurements are required for these two types. The group accountant has asked you to determine the non-controlling interests in the new group, differentiating between different non-controlling interest groups, and to explain the difference, if any, in the calculation of their interests in group equity.

Required

Prepare a report for the group accountant.

CASE STUDY 30.2

DIVIDENDS AND NON-CONTROLLING INTERESTS

Andrew Brown is the group accountant for P Ltd. P Ltd owns 60% of A Ltd which owns 70% of B Ltd. He has just completed the preparation of the consolidated financial statements of the group, and is discussing issues raised by the auditors. The auditors have raised concerns about the accounting for a dividend paid by B Ltd to A Ltd in the current period. They argue that consolidation adjustments are necessary to avoid double counting the non-controlling interest's share of equity. Andrew has asked for your advice concerning the effect of the payment of such a dividend on the determination of the non-controlling interest share of equity.

Required

Write a report to Andrew explaining the non-controlling interests that exist within the group, and how the calculation of their interests is affected by payment of dividends within the group.

CASE STUDY 30.3

CHANGES IN OWNERSHIP INTERESTS

At 1 July 2021, Christina Ltd acquires 60% of the issued shares of Adeline Ltd, enough to give Christina Ltd control. At 30 June 2022, Christina Ltd acquires a further 10%. One year later, on 30 June 2023, Christina Ltd sells 20% of the issued shares of Adeline Ltd, but because of the dispersion of the other shareholders, it still controls Adeline Ltd. On 30 June 2024, Christina Ltd further sells 30% of the issued shares in Adeline Ltd and loses control.

Required

Write a report explaining the accounting treatment of the changes in the ownership interest by Christina Ltd in Adeline Ltd at different points in time.

APPLICATION AND ANALYSIS EXERCISES

★ BASIC | ★ ★ MODERATE | ★ ★ ★ DIFFICULT

30.1 Calculation of the non-controlling interest, multiple subsidiaries, acquisitions on the same date ★ **LO3**

On 1 July 2020, Fiji Ltd acquired 75% of the issued shares of India Ltd at a cost of $560 000 and India Ltd acquired 80% of the issued shares of Japan Ltd at a cost of $270 000. At acquisition date, the equity of India Ltd and Japan Ltd was as follows.

	India Ltd	Japan Ltd
Share capital	$300 000	$280 000
General reserve	40 000	—
Retained earnings	100 000	40 000

At 1 July 2020, all identifiable assets and liabilities of India Ltd and Japan Ltd were recorded at fair value. On 30 June 2022, India Ltd transferred the general reserve to retained earnings and declared a dividend of $20 000 which was paid on 1 November 2022.

On 30 June 2024, India Ltd and Japan Ltd provided the following information.

	India Ltd	Japan Ltd
Profit before income tax	$ 96 000	$ 64 000
Income tax expense	40 000	30 000
Profit	56 000	34 000
Retained earnings (1/7/23)	150 000	84 000
	206 000	118 000
Transfer to general reserve	—	40 000
Dividend paid	20 000	—
Dividend declared	30 000	20 000
	50 000	60 000
Retained earnings (30/6/24)	$156 000	$ 58 000

Required

Calculate the non-controlling interest's share in retained earnings at 30 June 2024 for India Ltd and Japan Ltd.

30.2 **Consolidation worksheet entries, multiple subsidiaries, acquisitions on the same date** ★ **LO3**

On 1 July 2020, Laos Ltd acquired 70% of the issued shares of Maldives Ltd for $100 000 and Maldives Ltd acquired 60% of the issued shares of Malaysia Ltd for $70 000. The equity of the companies at 1 July 2020 was as follows.

	Maldives Ltd	Malaysia Ltd
Share capital	$100 000	$80 000
Retained earnings	40 000	30 000

At 1 July 2020, all the identifiable assets and liabilities of both Maldives Ltd and Malaysia Ltd were recorded at fair value.

At 30 June 2023, the financial data of the three companies were as follows.

	Laos Ltd	Maldives Ltd	Malaysia Ltd
Sales revenue	$120 000	$102 000	$ 84 000
Other revenue	60 000	44 000	36 000
Total revenues	180 000	146 000	120 000
Cost of sales	90 000	80 000	72 000
Other expenses	60 000	41 000	26 000
Total expenses	150 000	121 000	98 000
Profit before income tax	30 000	25 000	22 000
Income tax expense	8 000	8 000	5 000
Profit for the period	22 000	17 000	17 000
Retained earnings (1/7/22)	55 000	46 000	25 000
Total available for appropriation	77 000	63 000	42 000
Dividend paid	15 000	10 000	5 000
Retained earnings (30/6/23)	62 000	53 000	37 000
Share capital	148 000	100 000	80 000
Net assets	$210 000	$153 000	$117 000

Since 1 July 2020, the following transactions have occurred between the three companies.

- On 1 July 2022, Malaysia Ltd sold a motor vehicle to Maldives Ltd for $25 000. The carrying amount of the vehicle at the date of sale was $23 000. Vehicles are depreciated at 30% p.a. on a straight-line basis.
- During the year ended 30 June 2023, Maldives Ltd sold inventories valued at $20 000 to Laos Ltd, this having cost Maldives Ltd $15 000. Half of the inventories are still on hand at 30 June 2023.

The tax rate is 30%.

Required

Prepare the consolidation worksheet journal entries for the year ended 30 June 2023.

30.3 Consolidation worksheet entries, multiple subsidiaries, acquisitions on the same date ★ **LO3**

On 1 July 2021, Canada Ltd acquired 80% of the issued shares of China Ltd and China Ltd acquired 75% of the issued shares of Chile Ltd. All shares were acquired on a *cum div.* basis.

The equity of China Ltd and Chile Ltd at 1 July 2021 consisted of the following items.

	China Ltd	Chile Ltd
Share capital	$80 000	$60 000
Asset revaluation surplus	5 000	—
Retained earnings	1 000	4 000
Dividend payable	8 000	5 000

At 1 July 2021, all identifiable assets and liabilities of China Ltd and Chile Ltd were recorded at fair value. No goodwill or gain on bargain purchase arose in any of the acquisitions.

The financial statements of the three companies at 30 June 2023 contained the following information.

	Canada Ltd	China Ltd	Chile Ltd
Share capital	$130 000	$80 000	$60 000
Asset revaluation surplus	—	5 000	—
Retained earnings (1/7/22)	10 000	10 500	13 000
Dividend payable	13 000	8 000	6 000
Profit	4 000	2 000	1 500

The dividends payable refer to dividends declared out of profits for the year ended 30 June 2023. Since 1 July 2021, the following intragroup transactions have occurred.

(a) China Ltd sold to Chile Ltd an item of machinery for $12 000 on 31 December 2021. The machinery had originally cost China Ltd $14 000 and at the time of sale had been depreciated to $11 200. Chile Ltd charges depreciation at 10% p.a. straight-line on this machinery.

(b) During the year ended 30 June 2023, inventories were sold by Chile Ltd to China Ltd at 25% mark-up on cost. Inventories for which China Ltd paid $4000 to Chile Ltd are included in the inventories of China Ltd as at 30 June 2023. The tax rate is 30%.

Required

Prepare the consolidation worksheet entries for the year ended 30 June 2023.

30.4 Consolidated financial statements, multiple subsidiaries, acquisitions on the same date ★ ★ **LO3**

Pakistan Ltd acquired 75% of the issued shares of Peru Ltd on 1 July 2019 for $1 900 000. The identifiable assets and liabilities of Peru Ltd were recorded at fair value at acquisition date. The equity of Peru Ltd consisted of the following items.

Share capital	$ 500 000
General reserve	800 000
Retained earnings	1 200 000
	$2 500 000

On the same date, Peru Ltd acquired 60% of the issued shares of Philippines Ltd for $1 100 000. The identifiable assets and liabilities of Philippines Ltd were also recorded at fair value. The equity of Philippines Ltd consisted of the following items.

Share capital	$ 660 000
General reserve	500 000
Retained earnings	500 000
	$1 660 000

The financial information provided by the three companies for the year ended 30 June 2024 is as follows.

	Pakistan Ltd	Peru Ltd	Philippines Ltd
Sales revenue	$2 850 000	$1 100 000	$ 880 000
Other revenue	420 000	200 000	60 000
Total revenues	3 270 000	1 300 000	940 000
Cost of sales	1 410 000	520 000	380 000
Other expenses	200 000	80 000	110 000
Total expenses	1 610 000	600 000	490 000
Profit before income tax	1 660 000	700 000	450 000
Income tax expense	580 000	160 000	140 000
Profit	1 080 000	540 000	310 000
Retained earnings (1/7/23)	4 070 000	2 300 000	1 120 000
Total available for appropriation	5 150 000	2 840 000	1 430 000
Dividend paid	400 000	160 000	80 000
Dividend declared	400 000	200 000	90 000
Transfer to general reserve	100 000	50 000	40 000
	900 000	410 000	210 000
Retained earnings (30/6/24)	$4 250 000	$2 430 000	$1 220 000

The following additional information was obtained.

- All transfers to general reserve were from post-acquisition profits.
- Included in the plant and machinery of Philippines Ltd was a machine sold by Peru Ltd on 30 June 2021 for $75 000. The asset had originally cost $130 000 and it had been written down to $60 000 prior to the intragroup sale. Philippines Ltd depreciates the machine on a straight-line basis over 5 years, with no residual value.
- Philippines Ltd had transferred one of its motor vehicles (carrying amount of $15 000) to Pakistan Ltd on 31 March 2023 for $12 000. Pakistan Ltd regarded this vehicle as part of its inventories. The vehicle was sold by Pakistan Ltd to external entities on 31 July 2023.
- The tax rate is 30%.

Required

Prepare the consolidated statement of profit or loss and other comprehensive income and statement of changes in equity (not including movements in the general reserve and share capital) for the group for the year ended 30 June 2024.

30.5 Calculation of the non-controlling interest, multiple subsidiaries, acquisitions on the same date ★   **LO3**

On 1 July 2022, Nauru Ltd acquired 60% of the issued shares of Nepal Ltd for $450 000, and Nepal Ltd acquired 80% of the issued shares of New Zealand Ltd for $285 000.

It was considered that Nauru Ltd exercised control over Nepal Ltd and New Zealand Ltd. At acquisition date, the equity for Nepal Ltd and New Zealand Ltd was as follows.

	Nepal Ltd	New Zealand Ltd
Share capital	$300 000	$210 000
General reserve	195 000	105 000
Retained earnings	120 000	30 000

At 1 July 2022, all the identifiable assets and liabilities of both Nepal Ltd and New Zealand Ltd were recorded at fair value.

Three years later, the companies provided the following information.

	Nepal Ltd	New Zealand Ltd
Profit before income tax	$ 36 000	$27 000
Income tax expense	15 000	11 250
Profit	21 000	15 750
Retained earnings (1/7/24)	132 000	41 250
	153 000	57 000
Dividend declared	15 000	12 000
Retained earnings (30/6/25)	$138 000	$45 000

There was a transfer to reserves of $6000 from pre-acquisition profits in the period ended 30 June 2024 by New Zealand Ltd.

Required

Calculate the non-controlling interest's share of retained earnings at 30 June 2025 of Nepal Ltd and New Zealand Ltd.

30.6 Consolidated financial statements, multiple subsidiaries, acquisitions on the same date ★ ★   **LO3**

On 1 July 2019, the following balances appeared in the ledgers of the following three companies.

	Russia Ltd	Samoa Ltd	Singapore Ltd
Retained earnings	$20 000	$10 000	$ 5 000
General reserve	8 000	2 000	1 000
Dividend payable	4 000	2 000	—
Share capital	80 000	60 000	20 000

The dividends payable on 1 July 2019 were paid in October 2019.

For the year ended 30 June 2024, the following information is available.

- Inter-company sales were:
  - Samoa Ltd to Russia Ltd — $20 000
  - Singapore Ltd to Russia Ltd — $15 000.
- The mark-up on cost on all sales was 25%.
- At 30 June 2024, inventories of Russia Ltd included:
  - $1000 of goods purchased from Samoa Ltd
  - $1800 of goods purchased from Singapore Ltd.
- The income tax rate is 30%.
- Russia Ltd paid $67 200 for 80% of the issued shares of Samoa Ltd at 1 July 2019 when all identifiable assets and liabilities of Samoa Ltd were recorded at fair value.
- Samoa Ltd paid $18 750 for 75% of the issued shares of Singapore Ltd at 1 July 2019 when all identifiable assets and liabilities of Singapore Ltd were recorded at fair value as follows.

Receivables	$ 9 000
Inventories	10 000
Plant	20 000
Total assets	39 000
Liabilities	13 000
Net assets	$26 000

- The plant has an expected remaining useful life of 5 years. By 30 June 2020, all receivables had been collected and inventories sold.

The financial information for the year ended 30 June 2024 for all three companies was as follows.

	Russia Ltd	Samoa Ltd	Singapore Ltd
Sales revenue	$ 98 400	$ 48 500	$30 000
Cost of sales	61 000	29 000	13 000
Gross profit	37 400	19 500	17 000
Expenses			
Selling and administrative			
(including depreciation)	10 000	5 000	3 000
Financial	3 000	1 000	1 000
	13 000	6 000	4 000

	Russia Ltd	Samoa Ltd	Singapore Ltd
	24 400	13 500	13 000
Dividend revenue	3 200	4 500	—
Profit before income tax	27 600	18 000	13 000
Income tax expense	12 000	8 100	5 200
Profit	15 600	9 900	7 800
Retained earnings (1/7/23)	40 000	20 000	10 000
Total available for appropriation	55 600	29 900	17 800
Transfer to general reserve	4 000	1 900	—
Dividend paid	5 000	2 000	4 000
Dividend declared	5 000	2 000	2 000
	14 000	5 900	6 000
Retained earnings (30/6/24)	41 600	24 000	11 800
General reserve	12 000	3 900	1 000
Share capital	80 000	60 000	20 000
Total equity	$133 600	$ 87 900	$32 800
Receivables	$ 18 000	$ 25 000	$11 000
Inventories	25 000	26 400	13 800
Shares in Samoa Ltd	65 600	—	
Shares in Singapore Ltd	—	18 750	
Plant	50 000	39 750	20 000
Total assets	158 600	109 900	44 800
Provisions	20 000	20 000	10 000
Dividend payable	5 000	2 000	2 000
Total liabilities	25 000	22 000	12 000
Net assets	$133 600	$ 87 900	$32 800

Required

Prepare the consolidated financial statements for Russia Ltd's group and all its subsidiaries at 30 June 2024.

30.7 Consolidation worksheet, consolidated financial statements, multiple subsidiaries, acquisitions on the same date ★ ★ **LO3**

On 1 July 2023, Vanuatu Ltd acquired 80% of the issued shares in Vietnam Ltd (*cum div.*) for $44 760. At this date, Vietnam Ltd had not recorded any goodwill and all its identifiable net assets were recorded at fair value except for land and inventories for which the differences between the carrying amount and fair value at acquisition date were as follows.

	Carrying amount	Fair value
Land	$ 8 000	$10 000
Inventories	12 000	15 000

Half of the inventories remained on hand at 30 June 2024. Immediately after the acquisition date, Vietnam Ltd revalued the land to fair value. The land was still on hand at 30 June 2024.

At 1 July 2023, Vietnam Ltd acquired 75% of the issued shares of Brunei Ltd for $15 300. Brunei Ltd had not recorded any goodwill and all its identifiable assets and liabilities were recorded at fair value except for inventories for which the difference between the carrying amount and fair value at acquisition date was as follows.

	Carrying amount	Fair value
Inventories	$10 000	$14 000

All the inventories were sold by 30 June 2024.

At the acquisition date, the financial statements of the three companies showed the following.

	Vanuatu Ltd	Vietnam Ltd	Brunei Ltd
Share capital	$80 000	$32 000	$20 000
General reserve	20 000	3 200	—
Asset revaluation surplus	16 000	6 400	—
Retained earnings	6 400	4 800	(3 200)
Dividend payable	12 000	3 200	—

The following information was provided for the year ended 30 June 2024.

	Vanuatu Ltd	Vietnam Ltd	Brunei Ltd
Sales revenue	$108 000	$72 000	$54 000
Cost of sales	72 000	61 200	40 500
Gross profit	36 000	10 800	13 500
Less: Distribution and administrative expenses	9 000	2 700	2 880
	27 000	8 100	10 620
Plus: Interim dividend revenue	1 280	1 500	—
Profit before income tax	28 280	9 600	10 620
Income tax expense	8 480	1 920	2 400
Profit	19 800	7 680	8 220
Retained earnings (1/7/23)	6 400	4 800	(3 200)
	26 200	12 480	5 020
Less: Dividend paid	4 000	—	1 000
Dividend declared	4 000	1 600	1 000
	8 000	1 600	2 000
Retained earnings (30/6/24)	$ 18 200	$10 880	$ 3 020

Additional information
- Dividends declared for the year ended 30 June 2023 were duly paid.
- Intragroup purchases (at cost plus $33^{1/3}\%$) were as follows.
  - Vanuatu Ltd from Vietnam Ltd — $43 200
  - Vietnam Ltd from Brunei Ltd — $37 800
- Intragroup purchases valued at cost to the purchasing company were included in inventories at 30 June 2024, as follows.
  - Vanuatu Ltd — $5400
  - Vietnam Ltd — $4500
- The tax rate is 30%.

Required
1. Prepare the consolidation worksheet entries for the preparation of the consolidated financial statements of Vanuatu Ltd at 30 June 2024.
2. Prepare the consolidated statement of profit or loss and other comprehensive income and statement of changes in equity (not including movements in share capital and other reserves) at 30 June 2024.

30.8 Consolidation worksheet entries, sequential acquisitions ★ ★   **LO3**

On 1 July 2022, Brunei Ltd acquired (*ex div.*) 80% of the issued shares of Bhutan Ltd for $146 400. At this date, the equity of Bhutan Ltd consisted of the following.

Share capital	$100 000
General reserve	50 000
Retained earnings	20 000

In the accounts at this date, Bhutan Ltd had recorded a dividend payable of $5000 and goodwill of $13 000. All the identifiable assets and liabilities of Bhutan Ltd were recorded at fair value except for the following.

	Carrying amount	Fair value
Plant (cost $120 000)	$90 000	$100 000
Inventories	40 000	45 000

The plant has a further 5-year useful life, and is depreciated using the straight-line method. Of the inventories, 90% were sold by 30 June 2023, the remaining 10% being sold by 30 June 2024.

During the period ended 30 June 2023, Bhutan Ltd recorded a profit of $40 000 and there were no changes in reserves. During the period ended 30 June 2024, Bhutan Ltd recorded a profit of $36 000, and recorded a transfer to general reserve of $6000.

On 1 January 2023, Bhutan Ltd acquired 50% of the issued shares of Burma Ltd for $57 000, giving it the capacity to control that entity. At this date, the equity of Burma Ltd consisted of the following.

Share capital	$80 000
General reserve	40 000
Retained earnings	(10 000)

The identifiable assets and liabilities of Burma Ltd consisted of the following.

	Carrying amount	Fair value
Land	$50 000	$56 000
Plant (cost $110 000)	80 000	82 000
Inventories	10 000	12 000

All the inventories on hand at 1 January 2023 was sold by 30 June 2023. The plant had a further 10-year useful life, and was depreciated using the straight-line method. The land was sold by Burma Ltd in the period ended 30 June 2024.

The profit of Burma Ltd for the period from 1 January 2023 to 30 June 2023 was $8000. There were no movements in the general reserve during this period. During the period ended 30 June 2024, Burma Ltd earned a $20 000 profit. Burma Ltd also transferred $20 000 from general reserve to retained earnings during the period ended 30 June 2024.

Assume a tax rate of 30%.

Required

Prepare the consolidation worksheet entries for the preparation of the consolidated financial statements of Brunei Ltd at 30 June 2024.

30.9 Consolidation worksheet entries, multiple subsidiaries, acquisitions on the same date ★ ★   **LO3**

The statements of financial position of Tonga Ltd, Thailand Ltd and Tuvalu Ltd for the year ended 30 June 2023 are as follows.

	Tonga Ltd	Thailand Ltd	Tuvalu Ltd
Share capital	$300 000	$100 000	$42 000
Retained earnings	120 000	36 000	8 000
Dividend payable	60 000	20 000	12 000
	$480 000	$156 000	$62 000
Non-current assets	$240 000	$ 40 000	$20 000
Shares in Thailand Ltd	111 600	—	—
Shares in Tuvalu Ltd	—	42 000	—
Inventories	20 000	50 000	40 000
Receivables	108 400	24 000	2 000
	$480 000	$156 000	$62 000

For the year ended 30 June 2023, Thailand Ltd and Tuvalu Ltd recorded a profit of $4000 and $2000 respectively.

Thailand Ltd holds 90% of the issued shares of Tuvalu Ltd since their acquisition on 1 July 2020 for a total consideration of $41 460. At the acquisition date, Tuvalu Ltd's equity comprised of the following items.

Share capital (42 000 shares)	$42 000
Retained earning	2 000

At this date, all identifiable assets and liabilities of Tuvalu Ltd were recorded at fair value except for some plant for which the fair value of $16 000 was $2000 greater than the carrying amount (i.e. original cost of $17 000 less accumulated depreciation of $3000). The plant was expected to last a further 5 years.

On 1 July 2020, the directors of Tonga Ltd made a successful offer for 90 000 of Thailand Ltd's fully paid shares. The consideration was $109 980 and, at the acquisition date, Thailand Ltd's equity comprised of the following items.

Share capital (100 000 shares)	$100 000
Retained earnings	8 000

At this date, all identifiable assets and liabilities of Tonga Ltd were recorded at fair value except for some machinery whose fair value was $6000 greater than its recorded amount of $12 000, the latter being $20 000 cost less accumulated depreciation of $8000. The machinery was expected to have a further useful life of 3 years.

Required

Prepare the consolidation worksheet entries for the preparation of the consolidated financial statements of Tonga Ltd's group and all its subsidiaries at 30 June 2023.

30.10 Consolidation worksheet entries, non-sequential acquisitions ★ ★ ★   **LO3, 4**

On 1 July 2022, Indonesia Ltd acquired 75% of the issued shares of India Ltd for $320 000. At this date the statement of financial position of India Ltd was as follows.

Current assets	$ 20 000
Non-current assets	500 000
	520 000
Liabilities	(120 000)
Net assets	$400 000
Share capital	$100 000
General reserve	100 000
Retained earnings	200 000
Total equity	$400 000

All the identifiable assets and liabilities of India Ltd were recorded at fair value except for some land for which the fair value was $10 000 greater than the carrying amount and some depreciable assets with a further 5-year useful life for which the fair value was $12 000 greater than the carrying amount. The tax rate is 30%.

On 1 July 2024, Palau Ltd acquired 60% of the issued shares of Indonesia Ltd for $350 000. At this date, the statement of financial position of Indonesia Ltd was as follows.

Current assets		$ 120 000
Non-current assets		
Investment in India Ltd	$320 000	
Other	280 000	600 000
		720 000
Liabilities		(220 000)
Net assets		$ 500 000
Share capital		$ 200 000
Retained earnings		300 000
		$ 500 000

All the identifiable assets and liabilities of Indonesia Ltd were recorded at fair value except for the investment in India Ltd which had a fair value of $400 000. The statement of financial position of India Ltd at 1 July 2024 was as follows.

Current assets	$ 30 000
Non-current assets	600 000
	630 000
Liabilities	(130 000)
	$ 500 000
Share capital	$ 100 000
General reserve	120 000
Retained earnings	280 000
	$ 500 000

All the identifiable assets and liabilities of India Ltd at this date were recorded at fair value except for the land held at 1 July 2022 which, at 1 July 2024, had a fair value of $20 000 greater than carrying amount, and the depreciable assets which have a further 3-year useful life have a fair value of $8000 greater than carrying amount.

Financial information about Palau Ltd, Indonesia Ltd and India Ltd at 30 June 2025 is as follows.

	Palau Ltd	Indonesia Ltd	India Ltd
Current assets	$ 200 000	$150 000	$ 35 000
Non-current assets			
Investment in Indonesia Ltd	350 000		—
Investment in India Ltd	—	320 000	—
Land	100 000	50 000	40 000
Depreciable assets	500 000	400 000	620 000
Accumulated depreciation	(80 000)	(80 000)	(40 000)
Total assets	1 070 000	840 000	655 000
Total liabilities	250 000	260 000	120 000
Net assets	$ 820 000	$580 000	$535 000
Share capital	$ 300 000	$200 000	$100 000
General reserve	200 000	—	120 000
Retained earnings (1/7/24)	150 000	300 000	280 000
Profit for the period	170 000	80 000	35 000
Total equity	$ 820 000	$580 000	$535 000

Required

Prepare the worksheet entries for the consolidated financial statements of Palau Ltd's group at 30 June 2025.

30.11 Consolidated financial statements, multiple subsidiaries, acquisitions on the same date ★ ★ ★   **LO3**

On 1 July 2023, United States Ltd acquired 60% of the issued shares of Peru Ltd for $54 000. On the same day, Peru Ltd acquired 80% of the issued shares (*cum div.*) of Canada Ltd for $35 800. At the acquisition date, Peru Ltd's and Canada Ltd's financial statements showed the following balances.

	Peru Ltd	Canada Ltd
Share capital	$50 000	$30 000
General reserve	15 000	10 000
Retained earnings	7 500	4 000
Dividend payable	—	2 500

The dividend of Canada Ltd was paid later in the year ended 30 June 2024.

On 1 July 2023, all identifiable assets and liabilities of Peru Ltd and Canada Ltd were recorded at fair values except for the following.

	Peru Ltd		Canada Ltd	
	Carrying amount	Fair value	Carrying amount	Fair value
Plant and machinery (cost $40 000)	$30 000	$40 000	—	—
Inventories	20 000	25 000	$15 000	$20 000
Vehicles (cost $40 000)	—	—	25 000	27 500

The vehicles have an expected useful life of 4 years and the plant is expected to last a further 10 years. Benefits are expected to be received evenly over these periods. All inventories on hand at 1 July 2023 were sold by 30 June 2024.

The financial statements of the three companies at 30 June 2024 are as follows.

	United States Ltd	Peru Ltd	Canada Ltd
Sales revenue	$ 260 000	$ 182 500	$57 500
Other revenue	80 000	52 500	29 000
	340 000	235 000	86 500
Cost of sales	205 000	95 000	43 000
Other expenses	73 000	9 000	21 000
	278 000	185 000	64 000
Profit before income tax	62 000	5 000	22 500
Income tax expense	25 500	20 000	10 000
Profit	36 500	30 000	12 500
Retained earnings (1/7/23)	12 000	7 500	4 000
	48 500	37 500	16 500
Interim dividend paid	5 000	7 500	1 500
Final dividend declared	8 000	4 000	2 000
Transfer to general reserve	12 500	3 000	2 000
	25 500	14 500	5 500
Retained earnings (30/6/24)	23 000	23 000	11 000
Share capital	125 000	50 000	30 000
General reserve	72 500	18 000	12 000
Bank overdraft	10 500	3 000	10 000
Provisions	20 500	15 000	10 000
Current tax liability	27 500	21 000	13 000
Deferred tax liability	12 500	6 000	4 000
Dividend payable	8 000	4 000	2 000
	$ 299 500	$ 140 000	$ 92 000
Bank	$ 24 500	$ 12 500	$16 000
Receivables	30 600	8 500	8 000
Inventories	51 500	20 900	34 000
Dividend receivable	2 400	1 600	—
Shares in Peru Ltd	54 000	—	—
Shares in Canada Ltd	—	33 800	—
Deferred tax asset	10 500	7 700	4 000
Plant	100 000	90 000	—
Accumulated depreciation — plant	(24 000)	(35 000)	—
Vehicles	65 000	—	50 000
Accumulated depreciation — vehicles	(15 000)	—	(20 000)
	$2 995 000	$ 140 000	$ 92 000

Additional information
(a) Included in the ending inventories of Peru Ltd at 30 June 2024 was inventories purchased from Canada Ltd for $5000. This had originally cost Canada Ltd $4000.
(b) United States Ltd had sold inventories to Canada Ltd during the period ended 30 June 2024 for $12 500. This had cost United States Ltd $10 000. Half of this has been sold to external parties by Canada Ltd during the period for $7500.
(c) The tax rate is 30%.

Required

Prepare the consolidated financial statements for United States Ltd and its subsidiaries, Peru Ltd and Canada Ltd, for the period ending 30 June 2024.

30.12 Sale of shares with loss of control ★★ **LO5**

X Ltd acquired 80% of the issued shares of Y Ltd for $350 000 on 1 July 2023 when the equity of Y Ltd consisted of $200 000 capital and $150 000 retained earnings. At this date the carrying amounts of Y Ltd's identifiable assets and liabilities were not different from fair value except for plant for which the fair value was $5000 greater than the carrying amount. The plant had a further 5-year useful life.

On 30 June 2025, X Ltd sold all its interest in Y Ltd for $600 000 when the financial statements of Y Ltd showed the following.

Sales revenue	$450 000
Expenses	387 500
Profit	62 500
Retained earnings (1/7/24)	250 000
Retained earnings (30/6/25)	312 500
Share capital	200 000
Total equity	$512 500
Net assets	$512 500

Required

Prepare the consolidation worksheet entries for X Ltd at 30 June 2025.

30.13 Sale of shares with no loss of control ★ ★   **LO5**

On 1 July 2023, A Ltd acquired 80% of the shares issued by B Ltd for $85 000. At this date, the shareholders' equity of B Ltd consisted of share capital of $80 000 and retained earnings of $20 000. All identifiable assets were recorded at amounts equal to fair value except for plant for which the fair value was $4000 greater than the carrying amount. The plant had a further 4-year useful life. The partial goodwill method is used on consolidation.

On 1 July 2025, A Ltd sold a quarter of its shareholding in B Ltd for $48 000 cash. The financial statements of A Ltd and B Ltd at this date prior to the sale were as follows.

	A Ltd	B Ltd
Share capital	$100 000	$ 80 000
General reserve	20 000	10 000
Retained earnings	100 000	70 000
Liabilities	20 000	12 000
	$240 000	$172 000
Shares in B Ltd	$ 85 000	
Other assets	155 000	$172 000
	$240 000	$172 000

Required

Prepare the consolidation worksheet at 1 July 2025 after the sale of shares by A Ltd, assuming that the sale did not result in A Ltd losing control of B Ltd.

30.14 Acquisition of additional shares in subsidiary by parent ★ ★   **LO5**

On 1 July 2023, K Ltd acquired 60% of the issued shares of L Ltd for $66 000 cash when the equity of L Ltd consisted of share capital of $80 000 and retained earnings of $20 000. All the identifiable assets and liabilities of L Ltd were recorded at amounts equal to fair value except for plant for which the fair value was $4000 greater than carrying amount. The plant had a further 4-year useful life. The partial goodwill method is used on consolidation.

On 1 July 2025, K Ltd acquired a further 20% of the issued shares of Ltd for $26 000. At this date, the shareholders' equity of L Ltd consisted of $80 000 share capital and $40 000 retained earnings.

Required

Prepare the consolidation worksheet entries for the year ended 30 June 2026.

30.15 Acquisition of additional shares in a subsidiary by parent ★ ★   **LO5**

Peter Ltd acquired 80% of the issued shares of Sam Ltd on 1 July 2021 for $32 000 when equity of Sam Ltd consisted of the following.

Share capital	$20 000
Retained earnings	16 000

All the identifiable assets and liabilities of Sam Ltd were recorded at amounts equal to their fair values at this date except for plant for which the fair value was $2000 greater than the carrying amount. The remaining economic life of the plant was 5 years. The fair value of the non-controlling interest was $8000. The full goodwill method was used on consolidation.

On 1 July 2023, Peter Ltd acquired a further 20% of the issued shares of Sam Ltd for $10 000 when the shareholders' equity of Sam Ltd was as follows.

Share capital	$20 000
Retained earnings	20 000

Required

Prepare the consolidation worksheet entries at 1 July 2023 immediately after Peter Ltd's acquisition of further shares in Sam Ltd.

30.16 **Sale of shares in subsidiary by parent resulting in loss of control** ★ ★ **LO5**

Insomnia Ltd acquired 80% of the issued shares of Sleepy Ltd on 1 July 2021 for $101 875 when the shareholders' equity of Sleepy Ltd consisted of the following.

Share capital	$62 500
Retained earnings	50 000

All the identifiable assets and liabilities of Sleepy Ltd were recorded at amounts equal to their fair values, except for plant for which the fair value was $6250 greater than the carrying amount. The remaining economic life of the plant was 5 years. The fair value of the non-controlling interest was $25 000. The full goodwill method was used on consolidation.

On 1 July 2023, Insomnia Ltd sold 40% of the issued shares of Sleepy Ltd (i.e. 1/2 of its holdings) for $62 500. Shareholders' equity of Sleepy Ltd at this date consisted of share capital of $62 500 and retained earnings of $62 500. As a result of this sale, Insomnia Ltd lost control of Sleepy Ltd.

Required

1. Prepare the journal entries in Insomnia Ltd to record the sale of shares in Sleepy Ltd and any gain/loss on sale.
2. Prepare the consolidation worksheet entries at 1 July 2023 immediately after Insomnia Ltd sold its shares in Sleepy Ltd.

30.17 **Sale of shares in subsidiary by parent without loss of control** ★ ★ **LO5**

Pretty Ltd acquired 80% of the issued shares of Smart Ltd on 1 July 2021 for $61 125 when the shareholders' equity of Smart Ltd consisted of the following.

Share capital	$37 500
Retained earnings	30 000

All the identifiable assets and liabilities of Smart Ltd were recorded at amounts equal to their fair values except for plant for which the fair value was $3750 greater than carrying amount. The remaining economic life of the plant was 5 years. The fair value of the non-controlling interest was $15 000. The full goodwill method was used on consolidation.

On 1 July 2023, Pretty Ltd sold 16% of the issued shares of Smart Ltd (i.e. 1/5 of its holdings) for $15 000. Shareholders' equity of Smart Ltd at this date consisted of share capital of $37 500 and retained earnings of $37 500.

Required

Prepare the consolidation worksheet entries at 1 July 2023 immediately after Pretty Ltd sold its shares in Smart Ltd.

30.18 **Consolidation worksheet entries, analysis of non-controlling interest, sequential acquisitions** ★ ★ ★ **LO2, 3, 4, 5**

A client of yours is the chief accountant of Comoros Ltd which, at 30 June 2023, has two subsidiaries, Cook Islands Ltd and Chile Ltd. He is unsure how to prepare the consolidated financial statements and has asked for your help. He has provided you with the information below concerning the group, and has determined a series of questions for which he wants clear, well-written answers. Provide the answers to these questions. Assume a tax rate of 30%.

Part A

Comoros Ltd acquired 40% of the issued shares of Cook Islands Ltd on 1 July 2020 for a total consideration of $79 400, consisting of $9400 cash and 14 000 Comoros Ltd shares having an estimated fair value of $5 per share. The equity of Cook Islands Ltd at this date is as follows.

Share capital	$100 000
General reserve	50 000
Retained earnings	40 000

All the identifiable assets and liabilities of Cook Islands Ltd were recorded at fair value except for plant (carrying amount $60 000, net of $10 000 depreciation) for which the fair value was $65 000. The plant has a further 5-year useful life.

During January 2021, Cook Islands Ltd paid a dividend of $5000. Further, in January 2021, a transfer to retained earnings of $4000 was made from the general reserve established before 1 July 2020.

Required

1. Prepare the business combination valuation entries and pre-acquisition entries in relation to Comoros Ltd's acquisition of Cook Islands Ltd at 30 June 2021, assuming Cook Islands Ltd is a subsidiary of Comoros Ltd at this date.
2. Explain how the calculations used in requirement 1 meet the requirements of AASB 3/IFRS 3 *Business Combinations*.
3. If Comoros Ltd acquired its shares in Cook Islands Ltd at 1 July 2020, but did not achieve control until 1 July 2021 when the retained earnings of Cook Islands Ltd were $60 000 and the fair value of plant was $30 000 greater than the carrying amount, should the fair values be measured at 1 July 2020, or at 1 July 2021 when Comoros Ltd obtained control of Cook Islands Ltd? Explain your answer, referring to requirements of appropriate accounting standards.
4. If Cook Islands Ltd earned a $10 000 profit between 1 July 2020 and 30 June 2021, determine the non-controlling interest's share of Cook Islands Ltd's equity at 30 June 2021.
5. Explain your calculation of the non-controlling interest's share of profit in requirement 4.

Part B

Cook Islands Ltd acquired 75% of the issued shares of Chile Ltd at 1 January 2021 for $137 000 when the equity of Chile Ltd consisted of $100 000 capital and $62 000 retained earnings which included profit of $12 000 earned after 1 July 2020. At acquisition date, all the identifiable assets and liabilities of Chile Ltd were recorded at fair value except for the following assets.

	Carrying amount	Fair value
Land	$80 000	$90 000
Plant (net of accumulated depreciation of $15 000)	60 000	65 000
Inventories	20 000	25 000

Of the inventories, 90% were sold by 30 June 2021 and the remainder by 30 June 2022. The land was sold in January 2023 for $120 000. The plant has a further 5-year useful life.

Required

Prepare the business combination valuation entries and pre-acquisition entries in relation to Cook Islands Ltd's acquisition of Chile Ltd at 30 June 2021 and 30 June 2023.

Part C

The following transactions affect the preparation of consolidated financial statements of Comoros Ltd's group at 30 June 2023.

(a) Sale of inventories in June 2022 from Chile Ltd to Comoros Ltd — the inventories cost Chile Ltd $2000, and were sold to Comoros Ltd for $3000. At 30 June 2023, Comoros Ltd did not hold any of these inventories.
(b) Sale of plant on 1 January 2022 from Chile Ltd to Comoros Ltd — the plant had a carrying amount in Chile Ltd of $12 000 at time of sale, and was sold for $15 000. The plant had a further 5-year useful life.
(c) Dividend of $10 000 declared in June 2023 by Chile Ltd to be paid in August 2023.
(d) Payment of a $4500 management fee from Chile Ltd to Comoros Ltd in February 2023.

Required

In relation to the preparation of the consolidated financial statements for Comoros Ltd's group at 30 June 2023, complete the following.

1. Provide consolidation worksheet journal entries for the above transactions, including related non-controlling interest adjustments.
2. Explain the adjustment entry for transaction (a).
3. Explain the non-controlling interest adjustment entry in relation to transaction (c).
4. If the retained earnings (1/7/22) of Chile Ltd was $80 000 and the profit for the period ended 30 June 2023 was $10 000, calculate the non-controlling interests share of Chile Ltd's equity at 30 June 2023, assuming no changes in reserves.
5. The calculation of non-controlling interest is based on the concept of sharing only those profits that are realised to the group. Explain this concept, showing how it is implemented using transactions (a), (b) and (d).

ACKNOWLEDGEMENTS

Photo: © Odua Images / Shutterstock.com

Photo: © wutzkohphoto / Shutterstock.com

Text: © 2019 Australian Accounting Standards Board (AASB). The text, graphics and layout of this publication are protected by Australian copyright law and the comparable law of other countries. No part of the publication may be reproduced, stored or transmitted in any form or by any means without the prior written permission of the AASB except as permitted by law. For reproduction or publication, permission should be sought in writing from the AASB. Requests in the first instance should be addressed to the National Director, Australian Accounting Standards Board, PO Box 204, Collins Street West, Victoria 8007.

Text: © IFRS. This publication contains copyright material of the IFRS Foundation in respect of which all rights are reserved. Reproduced by John Wiley & Sons Australia, Ltd with the permission of the IFRS Foundation. No permission granted to third parties to reproduce or distribute. For full access to IFRS Standards and the work of the IFRS Foundation please visit http://eifrs.ifrs.org. The International Accounting Standards Board, the IFRS Foundation, the authors and the publishers do not accept responsibility for any loss caused by acting or refraining from acting in reliance on the material in this publication, whether such loss is caused by negligence or otherwise.

CHAPTER 31

Associates and joint ventures

CHAPTER AIM

This chapter discusses the application of AASB 128/IAS 28 *Investments in Associates and Joint Ventures*. The objectives of this standard are to prescribe the accounting for investments in associates and to set out the requirements for the application of the equity method when accounting for investments in associates and joint ventures.

LEARNING OBJECTIVES

After studying this chapter, you should be able to:

31.1 explain the nature of associates and joint ventures

31.2 discuss the concepts of significant influence and joint control

31.3 explain the rationale for the equity method and the different sets of financial statements in which it may be applied

31.4 apply the equity method to an investment in an associate

31.5 adjust the application of the equity method for fair value/carrying amount differences of identifiable assets and liabilities at acquisition date and account for goodwill or gain on bargain purchase at acquisition

31.6 account for the effects of inter-entity transactions

31.7 account for associates and joint ventures where these entities incur losses

31.8 discuss the disclosures required in relation to associates and joint ventures.

CONCEPTS FOR REVIEW

Before studying this chapter, you should understand and, if necessary, revise:

- the nature of goodwill or gain on bargain purchase in a business combination including fair value increments at acquisition
- incremental and decremental revaluations of non-current assets
- accounting for unrealised gains arising from intragroup transactions between entities within a group
- the criteria for identifying parent entities and subsidiaries and the requirement to prepare consolidated financial statements.

31.1 Introduction and scope

LEARNING OBJECTIVE 31.1 Explain the nature of associates and joint ventures.

An equity investment is where one entity holds shares in another entity. Where such an investment exceeds 50% we generally identify that the investor has control over the investee, giving rise to a parent–subsidiary relationship. As we saw in chapters 26–30 of this text, the parent entity is required to prepare consolidated financial statements under AASB 10/IFRS 10 *Consolidated Financial Statements* (i.e. a set of financial statements of the parent and its subsidiaries presented as those of a single economic entity).

Other equity investments may be relatively insignificant and simply carried at either cost or fair value under AASB 9/IFRS 9 *Financial Instruments*. Other investments may involve less than 50% ownership and yet still be significant. For example, in the disclosure note reproduced in figure 31.1, one of Australia's largest listed companies, Wesfarmers Limited, lists its interests in a diverse range of associates. These investments are in the range of 20% to 50%, below the level indicative of control yet *they are not insignificant*. All are accounted for using the *equity method of accounting*.

FIGURE 31.1	Investments in associates and joint ventures, Wesfarmers

18. Associates and joint arrangements

	CONSOLIDATED	
	2018 $m	2017 $m
Investments in associates	731	686
Interests in joint ventures	17	17
	748	703
Net profits from operations of associates	92	117
Other comprehensive income of associates	(8)	(7)
Profit/(loss) from operations of joint venture	5	30
Other comprehensive income of joint venture	1	7
Total comprehensive income	90	147

Investments in associates
Recognition and measurement

The Group's investments in its associates, being entities in which the Group has significant influence and are neither subsidiaries nor jointly controlled assets, are accounted for using the equity method. Under this method, the investment in associates is carried in the consolidated balance sheet at cost plus post-acquisition changes in the Group's share of the associates' net assets.

Goodwill relating to associates is included in the carrying amount of the investment and is not amortised. After application of the equity method, the Group determines whether it is necessary to recognise any additional impairment loss with respect to the Group's investment. The Group's income statement reflects the Group's share of the associate's result.

Where there has been a change recognised directly in the associate's equity, the Group recognises its share of any changes and discloses this in the consolidated statement of comprehensive income.

Where the reporting dates of the associates and the Group vary, management accounts of the associate for the period to the Group's balance date are used for equity accounting. The associates' accounting policies are consistent with those used by the Group for like transactions and events in similar circumstances.

Investment properties owned by associates are initially measured at cost, including transaction costs. Subsequent to initial recognition, investment properties are stated at fair value, which reflects market conditions at the balance sheet date. Gains or losses arising from changes in the fair values of investment properties are recognised in profit or loss of the associate, in the year in which they arise. This is consistent with the Group's policy.

Interests in joint arrangements
Recognition and measurement

The Group recognises its share of the assets, liabilities, expenses and income from the use and output of its joint operations. The Group's investment in its joint venture is accounted for using the equity method of accounting.

Key judgement: control and significant influence

The Group has a number of management agreements with associates and joint arrangements it considers when determining whether it has control, joint control or significant influence. The Group assesses whether it has the power to direct the relevant activities of the investee by considering the rights it holds to appoint or remove key management and the decision-making rights and scope of powers specified in the contract.

Where the Group has the unilateral power to direct the relevant activities of an investee, the Group then assesses whether the power it holds is for its own benefit (acting as principal) or for the benefit of others (acting as agent). This determination is based on a number of factors including an assessment of the magnitude and variability of the Group's exposure to variable returns associated with its involvement with the investee. In an agency capacity, the Group is considered to be acting on behalf of other parties and therefore does not control the investee when it exercises its decision-making powers.

Interests in associates and joint arrangements

Associates	Principal activity	Reporting date	Country of incorporation	2018 %	2017 %
Australian Energy Consortium Pty Ltd[1]	Oil and gas	31 December	Australia	27.4	27.4
Bengalla Coal Sales Company Pty Limited	Sales agent	31 December	Australia	40.0	40.0
Bengalla Mining Company Pty Limited	Management company	31 December	Australia	40.0	40.0
BWP Trust	Property investment	30 June	Australia	24.8	24.8
Gresham Partners Group Limited	Investment banking	30 September	Australia	50.0	50.0
Gresham Private Equity Funds	Private equity fund	30 June	Australia	(a)	(a)
Queensland Nitrates Management Pty Ltd	Chemical manufacture	30 June	Australia	50.0	50.0
Queensland Nitrates Pty Ltd	Chemical manufacture	30 June	Australia	50.0	50.0
Wespine Industries Pty Ltd	Pine sawmillers	30 June	Australia	50.0	50.0

Joint operations	Principal activity	Reporting date	Country of incorporation	%	%
Sodium Cyanide	Sodium cyanide manufacture	30 June	Australia	75.0	75.0
Bengalla	Coal mining	31 December	Australia	40.0	40.0
ISPT	Property ownership	30 June	Australia	25.0	25.0

Joint ventures	Principal activity	Reporting date	Country of incorporation	%	%
BPI NO 1 Pty Ltd	Property management	30 June	Australia	(b)	(b)

[1] Australian Energy Consortium Pty Ltd has a 50.0 per cent interest in Quadrant Energy Holdings Pty Ltd.

(a) Gresham Private Equity Funds: Whilst the Group's interest in the unit holders' funds of Gresham Private Equity Fund No. 2 amounts to greater than 50.0 per cent, it is not a controlled entity as the Group does not have the practical ability to direct their relevant activities. Such control requires a unit holders' resolution of 75.0 per cent of votes pursuant to the Funds' trust deeds.

(b) BPI NO 1 Pty Ltd: Whilst the Group owns the only equity share in BPI NO 1 Pty Ltd, the Group's effective interest approximates 50.0 per cent and joint control is effected through contractual arrangements with the joint venture partner.

Source: Wesfarmers Limited (2018, p. 131).

The purpose of this chapter is to detail the nature of associates and joint ventures and to set out how they are accounted for. The appropriate accounting standard is AASB 128/IAS 28 *Investments in Associates and Joint Ventures.* Under AASB 128/IAS 28, the equity method is applied to both associates and joint ventures. Accounting for joint arrangements is covered by AASB 11/IFRS 11 *Joint Arrangements* (see chapter 32).

LEARNING CHECK

☐ An equity investment refers to an entity's investment in shares of another entity.

☐ An equity investment may result in the investee being deemed an associate or a joint venture.

☐ AASB 128/IAS 28 *Investments in Associates and Joint Ventures* requires the equity method to be applied to both associates and joint ventures.

31.2 Identifying associates and joint ventures

LEARNING OBJECTIVE 31.2 Discuss the concepts of significant influence and joint control.

31.2.1 Associates

An **associate** is defined in paragraph 3 of AASB 128/IAS 28 as:

> an entity over which the investor has significant influence.

The same paragraph defines **significant influence** as:

> the power to participate in the financial and operating policy decisions of the investee but is not control or joint control of those policies.

The key features of this definition are as follows.

- The investor has the power or the capacity to affect the decisions made in relation to the investee. As with the concept of control used in determining the parent–subsidiary relationship, an investor is not required to actually exercise this power to influence. It is only necessary that an investor has the ability to do so.
- The specific power is that of being able *to participate in the financial and operating policy decisions* of the investee but significant influence falls short of control over such decisions.

The preparer is required to exercise judgement in determining the existence of significant influence over another entity. Paragraphs 5 to 9 of AASB 128/IAS 28 provide guidance to assist in this determination. Specifically, paragraph 5 states:

> If an entity holds, directly or indirectly (e.g. through subsidiaries), 20 per cent or more of the voting power of the investee, it is presumed that the entity has significant influence, unless it can be clearly demonstrated that this is not the case. Conversely, if the entity holds, directly or indirectly (e.g. through subsidiaries), less than 20 per cent of the voting power of the investee, it is presumed that the entity does not have significant influence, unless such influence can be clearly demonstrated.

The distinction between a direct and an indirect holding in an associate is depicted in figure 31.2.

| FIGURE 31.2 | Direct and indirect associate relationships |

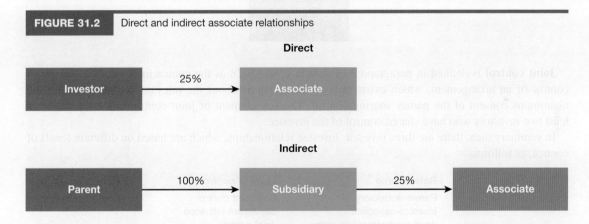

So, while 20% of the voting power over an investee is the quantitative indicator, there is scope for other factors to override this determination either side of this threshold. For example, an entity may have 25% of the voting power in an investee while another entity holds 60%. Despite their voting power exceeding 20%, the fact that another entity has control may lead the preparer to the conclusion that they do not have significant influence over the investee.

There is no requirement that the investor holds any shares, or has any beneficial interest in the associate. However, as discussed later, the application of the equity method is possible only where the investor holds shares in the associate. In other cases, the investor is required to make specific disclosures in its financial statements.

According to paragraph 6 of AASB 128/IAS 28, the existence of significant influence by an entity is usually evidenced in one or more of the following ways:

(a) representation on the board of directors or equivalent governing body of the investee;
(b) participation in policy-making processes, including participation in decisions about dividends or other distributions;
(c) material transactions between the entity and its investee;
(d) interchange of managerial personnel; or
(e) provision of essential technical information.

Due to the voting power the investor typically has in the investee, the most common form of participation is that of representation on the board of directors.

31.2.2 Joint ventures

A **joint arrangement** is defined in paragraph 3 of AASB 128/IAS 28 as an arrangement of which two or more parties have joint control.

The key feature of a joint arrangement is that of joint control. The most obvious example of joint control is where two entities each hold 50% of the shares of a third entity as shown in figure 31.3.

| FIGURE 31.3 | Example of joint control of a joint venture |

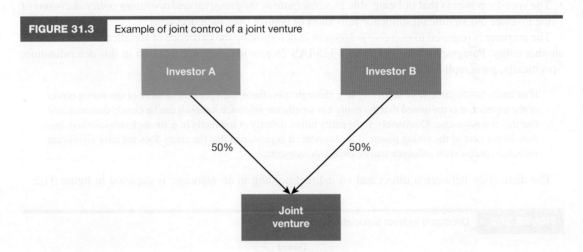

Joint control is defined in paragraph 3 of AASB 128/IAS 28 as the contractually agreed sharing of control of an arrangement, which exists only when decisions about the relevant activities require the unanimous consent of the parties sharing control. The key element of joint control is there must be at least two investors who have shared control of the investee.

In summary then, there are three investor–investee relationships, which are based on different levels of control, as follows.

Relationship	Level of control
Parent–subsidiary	Dominant control
Investor–associate	Significant influence
Joint arrangement–investee	Joint control

According to paragraph 14 of AASB 11/IFRS 11, an investor in a joint arrangement must determine whether the arrangement is a joint operation or a joint venture. This classification depends on the rights and obligations of the parties to the arrangement. Joint ventures are accounted for under AASB 128/IAS 28 while joint operations are accounted for under AASB 11/IFRS 11. This distinction is covered in detail in chapter 32. In this chapter, it is sufficient to note that a **joint venture** is an arrangement where the investor has a right to an investment in the investee. The investee will have the following features.

- The legal form of the investee and the contractual arrangements are such that the investor does not have rights to the assets and obligations for the liabilities of the investee.
- The investee has been designed to have a trade of its own and as such must directly face the risks arising from the activities it undertakes, such as demand, credit or inventories risks.

In the examples used in this chapter, an investor will hold between 20% and 50% of the shares in an investee. The classification of that investment as an investor–associate relationship or a joint venture will depend on whether the investor has significant influence over or joint control of the investee. The subsequent accounting for either structure is the same.

31.3 The equity method of accounting: rationale and application

LEARNING OBJECTIVE 31.3 Explain the rationale for the equity method and the different sets of financial statements in which it may be applied.

The method of accounting used to account for an investor's interest in an associate or joint venture is known as the equity method of accounting.

Paragraph 3 of AASB 128/IAS 28 describes the **equity method** as:

> a method of accounting whereby the investment is initially recognised at cost and adjusted thereafter for the post-acquisition change in the investor's share of the investee's net assets. The investor's profit or loss includes its share of the investee's profit or loss and the investor's other comprehensive income includes its share of the investee's other comprehensive income.

31.3.1 Rationale for the equity method

Paragraph 11 of AASB 128/IAS 28 provides an insight into the standard setters' rationale for the equity method by making the following points.

• The recognition of income on the basis of dividends earned by an investor from investments in an associate or joint venture may not adequately reflect the performance of the investee.

• Because the investor has joint control of, or significant influence over, the investee, the investor has an interest in the associate's or joint venture's performance and return on investment.

• The equity method requires the investor to include its share of the profit or loss of such an investee in its own financial statements thereby providing more informative reporting of the investor's net assets and profit or loss.

Under the cost method, the only information provided about the associate's performance would be in relation to dividends received or receivable from the associate.

The equity method is designed to provide more information than that provided by the cost method, but less than that given under the consolidation method. However, as stated in paragraph 26 of AASB 128/IAS 28:

> Many of the procedures that are appropriate for the application of the equity method are similar to the consolidation procedures described in AASB 10 [IFRS 10]. Furthermore, the concepts underlying the procedures used in accounting for the acquisition of a subsidiary are also adopted in accounting for the acquisition of an investment in an associate or a joint venture.

Because of the similarity with the principles and procedures of consolidation, the equity method has sometimes been described as 'one-line consolidation'. Importantly, however, the equity method as applied under AASB 128/IAS 28 is not entirely consistent with consolidation principles.

The standard setters do not explain why the equity method is preferred to the fair value method. Further, where there is a departure from consolidation principles, AASB 128/IAS 28 does not supply a justification for the departure. This makes it difficult to evaluate the equity method on the basis of it being a one-line consolidation method or simply another measurement method competing with fair value.

31.3.2 Application of the equity method: consolidation worksheet or investor's accounts

According to paragraph 16 of AASB 128/IAS 28, an entity that has joint control of, or significant influence over an investee must apply the equity method to account for such investments. At what stage during the preparation of financial statements the equity method is applied depends upon whether the investor is also a parent.

(a) *Where the investor is a parent and prepares consolidated financial statements*. If the parent or any subsidiaries have investments in associates or joint ventures, the equity method is applied to such investments in the consolidated financial statements. Under the *Corporations Act 2001*, consolidated financial statements must disclose financial information regarding the parent entity such as total assets, total liabilities and profit or loss. Under an ASIC Class Order CO 10/654 such information may be presented either by including the primary financial statements of the parent entity alongside the consolidated financial statements of the group or by way of a note disclosure to the accounts containing summarised financial information about the parent entity. Regardless of this choice, the standard that applies to presenting this information is AASB 127/IAS 27 *Separate Financial Statements*. Paragraph 10 of this standard requires investments in subsidiaries, joint ventures and associates to be accounted for either at cost or in accordance with AASB 9/IFRS 9.

Accordingly, the parent entity typically carries any investments in associates or joint ventures at cost in its individual accounts and any dividends from associates or joint ventures are recognised in profit or loss as revenue. The consolidation process then applies the equity method of accounting to these investments through eliminations and adjustments. Remember that as consolidation entries are not permanent, this conversion must be done at each reporting date.

(b) *Where the investor is not a parent and so does not prepare consolidated financial statements*. In this case, the investor applies the equity method to its investments in associates and joint ventures in its individual accounting records. Subsequently, the effects of the equity method flow directly into the financial statements of the investor.

It is possible that a non-parent entity with investments in associates or joint ventures could prepare separate financial statements under AASB 127/IAS 27. In such circumstances, the same principles that applied to the parent entity would apply to the non-parent but in this text we assume that no separate financial statements are prepared and, where no consolidated financial statements are prepared, the equity method is applied in the records of the investor.

LEARNING CHECK

☐ The equity method is sometimes described as a one-line consolidation method.

☐ Standard setters consider the equity method a better measure of the investor's success in influencing the returns and performance of an associate or joint venture.

☐ Where an entity prepares consolidated financial statements, the equity method is applied to associates of the parent and its subsidiaries in the consolidated financial statements, and not in the separate accounts of the parent.

☐ Where an entity does not prepare consolidated financial statements, the equity method is applied to investments in associates in the accounts of the investor.

31.4 Applying the equity method: basic principles

LEARNING OBJECTIVE 31.4 Apply the equity method to an investment in an associate.

The investor applies the equity method in accounting for its investment in the investee, being either an associate or a joint venture investee, from the date it acquires significant influence. Paragraph 10 of AASB 128/IAS 28 describes the basics of the equity method. There are four key steps in its application.

1. Recognise the *initial investment* in the investee at cost. If the investment has already been recorded at fair value, an adjustment must be made to restate the investment back to its original cost.
2. Increase or decrease the carrying amount of the investment by the investor's share of the *profit or loss* of the investee after the acquisition date — that is, post-acquisition profit or loss.
3. Reduce the carrying amount of the investment by *distributions*, such as dividends, received from the investee.
4. Increase or decrease the carrying amount of the investment for the investor's share of changes arising in the investee's *other comprehensive income*. Such changes include those arising from the revaluation of assets where the movements are recognised in the reserves of the investee's equity rather than in profit or loss.

Although potential voting rights may be considered in the assessment of significant influence, it is the equity interest that is used in any of the above calculations of proportionate share.

ILLUSTRATIVE EXAMPLE 31.1

Basic application of the equity method

In this example, the investor owns 25% of the shares of the investee. Assuming this investment is sufficient to give the investor significant influence over the investee, the investee is then an associate of the investor. The equity method is applied to account for the investment. The same journal entries are used if there were four investors in the investee, each having a 25% interest in the investee and the investors had joint control over the investee; that is, the investee is a joint venture.

Part A. Investor does not prepare consolidated financial statements
On 1 July 2023, Kangaroo Ltd acquired 25% of the shares of Joey Ltd for $42 500. At this date, all the identifiable assets and liabilities of Joey Ltd were recorded at amounts equal to fair value, and the equity of Joey Ltd consisted of the following.

Share capital	$100 000
General reserve	30 000
Asset revaluation surplus	20 000
Retained earnings	20 000

During the 2023–24 year, Joey Ltd reported an after-tax profit of $25 000. As reported in other comprehensive income, the asset revaluation surplus increased by $5000. Joey Ltd paid a $4000 dividend and transferred $3000 to general reserve.

Step 1. Recognition of the initial investment
At 1 July 2023, Kangaroo Ltd would record the investment in Joey Ltd at a cost of $42 500.

July 1	Investments in associates and joint ventures	Dr	42 500	
	Cash	Cr		42 500
	(25% investment in associate/joint venture)			

Step 2. Recognition of the share of profit or loss of associate/joint venture
At 30 June 2024, the investee has reported a profit for the year of $25 000. Under the equity method the investor recognises a 25% share of this profit as income and increases the investment in the associate/ joint venture with the following journal entry.

June 30	Investments in associates and joint ventures	Dr	6 250	
	Share of profit or loss of associates and joint ventures	Cr		6 250
	(Share of profit or loss of associate/joint venture:			
	25% × $25 000)			

The share of profit or loss of associates and joint ventures is disclosed as a separate line item in the statement of profit or loss and other comprehensive income in accordance with paragraph 82(c) of AASB 101/IAS 1.

Step 3. Recognition of share of other comprehensive income: increase in asset revaluation surplus

The asset revaluation surplus has increased by $5000, with this also being reported by the investee in other comprehensive income. This is post-acquisition equity and the investor is entitled to a 25% share. The investment in the associate/joint venture is increased, and the share of other comprehensive income is recognised, this being then accumulated in equity. The journal entries in the records of the investor at 30 June 2024 are as follows.

June 30	Investments in associates and joint ventures	Dr	1 250	
	Share of other comprehensive income of associates and joint ventures	Cr		1 250
	(Share of revaluation increase: 25% × $5000)			
June 30	Share of other comprehensive Income of associates and joint ventures	Dr	1 250	
	Asset revaluation surplus	Cr		1 250
	(Accumulation of revaluation increase in equity)			

Paragraph 82A of AASB 101/IAS 1 requires that the share of other comprehensive income of associates and joint ventures be disclosed separately in the other comprehensive income section of the statement of profit or loss and other comprehensive income.

The general reserve has also been increased by $3000. However, there is no need to pass any journal entries relating to this transfer from current profits to reserves because there is no net change in the equity of the investee. The investor, under step 2 above, recognised its share of the investee's profit. This includes a share of the amount transferred to general reserve. To recognise a share of the general reserve as well as a share of the profit would double count the investor's share of equity.

Step 4. Adjustment for dividend paid by associate/joint venture

In the current period, the investee paid a dividend of $4000. Under the equity method, the investor recognises its share of the investee's profit as income. If dividends are a distribution of such profits, then to recognise dividends as income would be double counting. Accordingly, under the equity method the dividend is not recognised as revenue by the investor; rather it reduces the investor's share of the equity of the investee. Hence, the investor passes a journal entry to recognise the receipt of cash on payment of the dividend and reduces its investment in the investee.

The entry at 30 June 2024 is as follows.

June 30	Cash	Dr	1 000	
	Investments in associates and joint ventures	Cr		1 000
	(Adjustment for dividend paid by associate/joint venture: 25% × $4000)			

Note that if the dividend had been declared by the investee but not paid, the investor would recognise a dividend receivable instead of cash and still reduce its investment in the investee. Also, this entry would be recorded on the date the dividend was declared and/or received. In this example this date was assumed to be 30 June.

At 30 June 2024, the carrying amount of the investment in the associate is measured at $49 000.

Cost at acquisition	$42 500
Share of profit	6 250
Share of OCI	1 250
Dividend	(1 000)
Carrying amount at 30/6/24	$49 000

Part B. Investor prepares consolidated financial statements

In this circumstance, the entry shown in step 1 would be recorded by the investor, as the investment in the associate is carried at cost. The entries relating to the equity method, however, are *not* made in the investor's accounting records but in the consolidation worksheet instead. The journal entries shown in steps 2 and 3 in Part A above are common to those that would appear in the consolidation journal and the consolidation worksheet at 30 June 2024.

The entry that differs where the investor prepares a consolidation worksheet is that shown in step 5 for the dividend paid.

Because the investor carries the investment at cost, and does not recognise any share of profit in its individual records, the cash dividend from the investee is recognised as revenue. To avoid the double counting mentioned previously the worksheet entry must eliminate the dividend revenue recorded by the investor and reduce the carrying amount of investment in the associate.

The consolidation worksheet entry at 30 June 2024 is as follows.

June 30	Dividend revenue	Dr	1 000	
	Investments in associates and joint ventures	Cr		1 000
	(Adjustment for dividend paid by associate/joint venture: 25% × $4000)			

If the dividend had been declared but not paid, the adjustment entry would be the same as above.

LEARNING CHECK

☐ The equity method is applied from the date the investor obtains significant influence over the investee.

☐ The investment in an associate/joint venture is initially recorded at cost.

☐ The equity method requires the carrying amount of the investment in an associate/joint venture to be increased or decreased for the investor's share of the post-acquisition movements in the equity of the associate/joint venture.

☐ The investor's share of current period profit or loss of associates and joint ventures is disclosed as a separate line item in the investor's statement of profit or loss and other comprehensive income.

☐ The investor's share of other comprehensive income of associates and joint ventures is disclosed as a separate line item in the investor's statement of profit or loss and other comprehensive income.

☐ Dividends from the investee are recognised as reductions in the carrying amount of the investment.

☐ Where dividends are paid/declared by an associate/joint venture and the investor does not prepare consolidated financial statements, no dividend revenue is recognised by the investor.

☐ Where dividends are paid/declared by an associate/joint venture and the investor prepares consolidated financial statements, the dividend revenue recognised in the parent's accounts is eliminated on consolidation.

31.5 Applying the equity method: goodwill and fair value adjustments

LEARNING OBJECTIVE 31.5 Adjust the application of the equity method for fair value/carrying amount differences of identifiable assets and liabilities at acquisition date and account for goodwill or gain on bargain purchase at acquisition.

Paragraph 32 of AASB 128/IAS 28 requires an investment to be accounted for using the equity method from the date it becomes an associate or joint venture. The equity method subsequently requires that an investor recognise its share of the post-acquisition equity of the investee.

As with any equity investments, when the investor acquires its interest in the associate or joint venture, it pays (or gives up) consideration based on its assessment of the fair value of the investee at that date. The consideration paid by the investor includes:

• the recorded equity of the investee, equal to the recorded carrying amounts of the assets and liabilities of the investee
• the differences between the carrying amounts of the assets and liabilities of the investee and the fair values of these assets and liabilities
• the fair values of any assets and liabilities not recognised by the investee
• any goodwill existing in the investee.

As the investment is initially recognised at cost, the initial carrying amount of the investor's interest in the investee reflects all of these amounts — the pre-acquisition equity of the investee effectively equals the sum of the fair values of the assets and liabilities of the investee (recorded and unrecorded) and the cost of any goodwill acquired.

The investee does not record all the pre-acquisition equity at acquisition date. It may, however, recognise some of it subsequent to acquisition date. For example, assume the investee's sole asset at acquisition date was land that was recorded at acquisition date at \$100 000 but had a fair value at that date of \$120 000. Although the investee's recorded equity at acquisition date is \$100 000 the real pre-acquisition equity is \$114 000 after taking into account the deferred tax effect. If in the year following the acquisition date the investee sold the land for \$120 000, the before-tax gain on sale of \$20 000 from the investor's perspective is the realisation of pre-acquisition equity, not a post-acquisition change in equity. Under the application of the equity method, the carrying amount of the investor's investment in the investee should not be increased by a share of this gain.

In order for post-acquisition changes in the equity of the investee to be identified, an analysis is undertaken at acquisition date to identify the pre-acquisition equity. This is done in the same way as demonstrated in chapters 26–30 when accounting for a parent's acquisition in a subsidiary.

The acquisition analysis involves comparing the cost of the investment in the associate/joint venture with the net fair value of the identifiable assets and liabilities of the investee, determining whether any goodwill or excess arose at acquisition date.

In applying the equity method, the share of the investee's post-acquisition profit or loss is adjusted for differences between carrying amounts and fair values of identifiable assets and liabilities at acquisition date and for any impairment of the investment. These adjustments are only notional adjustments; that is, they are not made in the records of the investee but are simply used in the calculation of the investor's share of post-acquisition equity of the investee. Because the investor's share of post-acquisition profit or loss of the investee is after tax, these adjustments are also calculated on an after-tax basis.

Illustrative example 31.2 shows the accounting for fair value/carrying amount differences at acquisition date and goodwill acquired by the investor. Illustrative example 31.3 shows the accounting where an excess occurs.

ILLUSTRATIVE EXAMPLE 31.2

Goodwill and fair value adjustments

On 1 July 2021, Emu Ltd acquired 25% of the shares of Bilby Ltd for \$49 375. At this date, the equity of Bilby Ltd consisted of the following.

Share capital	\$100 000
General reserve	50 000
Retained earnings	20 000

At the acquisition date, all the identifiable assets and liabilities of Bilby Ltd were recorded at fair value, except for plant for which the fair value was \$10 000 greater than its carrying amount, and inventories whose fair value was \$5000 greater than its cost. The tax rate is 30%. The plant has a further 5-year life. The inventories were all sold by 30 June 2022. In the reporting period ending 30 June 2022, Bilby Ltd reported a profit of \$15 000.

The acquisition analysis at 1 July 2021 is as follows.

Net fair value of the identifiable assets and liabilities of Bilby Ltd	= (\$100 000 + \$50 000 + \$20 000) (equity)
	+ \$10 000(1 − 30%) (plant)
	+ \$5000(1 − 30%) (inventories)
	= \$180 500
Net fair value acquired by Emu Ltd	= 25% × \$180 500
	= \$45 125
Cost of investment	= \$49 375
Goodwill	= \$4250

The analysis has determined that Emu Ltd has acquired goodwill of \$4250 in Bilby Ltd. This goodwill is already included in the carrying amount of the investment and is not separately recognised as it is in a business combination. Paragraph 42 of AASB 128/IAS 28 points out that, as goodwill in an associate or joint venture is not separately recognised, it is not separately tested for impairment. Instead, the investment is tested for impairment as a single asset. Unlike a cash-generating unit where impairment is first allocated to goodwill and can never be reversed, any impairment of an investment in an associate or joint venture is recognised against the investment and can be reversed in subsequent periods.

As the investee reports its profit or loss post-acquisition, it does so depreciating its assets according to the investee's carrying amounts. Paragraph 32 of AASB 128/IAS 28 requires appropriate adjustments be made to the investee's profit or loss to account for depreciation of assets based on their acquisition-date fair values. The \$7000 after-tax fair value increment in the plant is allocated as a short-depreciation adjustment against the investee's profit over the next 5 years as follows.

$$\text{Depreciation adjustment} = [\$10\,000\,(1 - 30\%)]/5 \text{ years}$$
$$= \$1400$$

Similarly, the investee will allocate the acquisition-date carrying amount for inventories to cost of sales when determining its profit. AASB 128/IAS 28 requires the investee's profit to be adjusted to account for the fair value of these inventories as follows.

$$\text{Inventories adjustment} = \$5000\,(1 - 30\%)$$
$$= \$3500$$

Hence, the investor's share of post-acquisition equity at 30 June 2022 is as follows.

Recorded profit of Bilby Ltd		$ 15 000
Pre-acquisition adjustments		
Depreciation of plant	$(1 400)	
Sale of inventories	(3 500)	(4 900)
		10 100
Investor's share of post-acquisition profit (25%)		$ 2 525

The journal entry to reflect the application of the equity method to the investment in the investee is as follows.

Investment in Bilby Ltd	Dr	2 525	
Share of profit or loss of associates and joint ventures	Cr		2 525
(Recognition of share of post-acquisition profit of investee)			

This entry is the same regardless of whether the investor prepares consolidated financial statements or the entries are made in the records of the investor.

ILLUSTRATIVE EXAMPLE 31.3

Excess

In the event that the analysis of the acquisition identifies the consideration to be less than the fair value of the investee's identifiable net assets, paragraph 32 of AASB 128/IAS 28 requires this excess to be included as income in the determination of the investor's share of the investee's profit or loss in the period in which the investment is acquired.

Assume in illustrative example 31.2 that the cost of the investment was $45 000. The acquisition analysis would then show the following.

Net fair value acquired by Emu Ltd	= 25% × $180 500
	= $45 125
Cost of investment	= $45 000
Excess	= $125

The amount of the adjustment needed in applying equity-method accounting to the investment in the associate at 30 June 2022 is then as follows.

Recorded profit of Bilby Ltd		$15 000
Pre-acquisition adjustments		
Depreciation of plant	$(1 400)	
Sale of inventories	(3 500)	(4 900)
		10 100
Investor's share of post-acquisition profit (25%)		2 525
Adjustment for excess		125
		$ 2 650

Note that the excess relates to the investor's 25% investment in the investee and so is added after the pre-acquisition adjustments are made to the recorded profit.

The journal entry to reflect the application of the equity method to the investment in the investee is as follows.

Investment in Bilby Ltd	Dr	2 650	
Share of profit or loss of associates and joint ventures	Cr		2 650
(Recognition of share of post-acquisition profit of investee)			

31.5.1 Applying the equity method across multiple years

In illustrative examples 31.2 and 31.3, the journal entries are determined for the year following the investor's acquisition of shares in the associate/joint venture. In subsequent years the entries required will differ, dependent on whether the investor prepares consolidated financial statements.

- *If the investor does not prepare consolidated financial statements.* There are no extra issues to consider in this situation. As the journal entries passed by the investor are recognised in its accounts, the carrying amount of the investment at any time reflects the cumulative net effect of equity method accounting since acquisition.
- *If the investor prepares consolidated financial statements.* The complication that arises here is that all the journal entries are passed in the consolidation worksheet and not in the records of the investor. At any time, the carrying amount of the investment will remain at cost. Hence, in years subsequent to the acquisition, the worksheet journal entries will need to recognise not only the equity method entries of the current period, but also the cumulative effects of all prior periods' equity method entries. This will require recognition of all prior periods' shares of profit or loss and other comprehensive income as well as eliminating all prior periods' dividend income from retained profits against the carrying amount of the investment. The consolidated worksheet entries are shown in illustrative example 31.4.

ILLUSTRATIVE EXAMPLE 31.4

Multiple periods

On 1 July 2022, Platypus Ltd acquired 40% of the shares of Koala Ltd for $122 400. The equity of Koala Ltd at acquisition date consisted of the following.

Ordinary share capital	$200 000
Retained earnings	80 000

At 1 July 2022, all the identifiable assets and liabilities of Koala Ltd were recorded at fair value except for the following.

	Carrying amount	Fair value
Machinery	$140 000	$160 000
Inventories	35 000	45 000

By 30 June 2023, the inventories on hand at 1 July 2022 had been sold by Koala Ltd. The machinery was expected to provide future benefits evenly over the next 2 years and then be scrapped. The tax rate is 30%.

Dividends declared at 30 June are paid within the following 3 months, with liabilities being raised at the date of declaration.

In January 2025, Koala Ltd revalued furniture upwards by $6000, affecting the asset revaluation surplus by $4200.

The financial statements of Koala Ltd over three periods contained the following information.

	30 June 2023	30 June 2024	30 June 2025
Profit or loss	$ 40 000	$ 60 000	$ 70 000
Retained earnings (opening balance)	80 000	98 000	123 000
	120 000	158 000	193 000
Dividend paid	(5 000)	(10 000)	(15 000)
Dividend declared	(7 000)	(15 000)	(20 000)
Transfer to general reserve	(10 000)	(10 000)	0
	(22 000)	(35 000)	(35 000)
Retained earnings (closing balance)	$ 98 000	$123 000	$158 000

Required

Prepare the entries in the consolidation worksheet of Platypus Ltd to apply the equity method to its investment in Koala Ltd for each of the 3 years ending 30 June 2023, 2024 and 2025.

Solution

Acquisition analysis

Net fair value of identifiable assets and liabilities of Koala Ltd	= $200 000 + $80 000 (equity)
	+ $20 000(1 − 30%) (machinery)
	+ $10 000(1 − 30%) (inventories)
	= $301 000
Net fair value acquired by Platypus Ltd	= 40% × $301 000
	= $120 400
Cost of investment	= $122 400
Goodwill	= $2000
Pre-acquisition effects:	
Depreciation of machinery p.a. after tax	= 50% × $20 000(1 − 30%)
	= $7000
After tax profit on sale of inventories	= $10 000(1 − 30%)
	= $7000

Consolidation worksheet 30 June 2023

Workings

Recorded profit of investee		$ 40 000
Pre-acquisition adjustments:		
Inventories	$(7 000)	
Depreciation of machinery	(7 000)	(14 000)
		26 000
Investor's share — 40%		$ 10 400

The entries in the consolidation worksheet of Platypus Ltd at 30 June 2023 are as follows.

June 30	Investments in associates and joint ventures	Dr	10 400	
	Share of profit or loss of associates and joint ventures	Cr		10 400
	(Recognition of equity-accounted profit of Koala Ltd)			
	Dividend revenue	Dr	4 800	
	Investments in associates and joint ventures	Cr		4 800
	(Adjustments for dividends from Koala Ltd: 40% × [$5000 + $7000])			

Note that the net increase in in the carrying amount of the investment for the year equals $5600 (i.e. $10 400 − $4800).

Consolidation worksheet 30 June 2024

Share of prior period's equity

The first journal entry in the consolidation worksheet recognises the investor's share of the movement in equity of the investee in the prior period. The only account affected by prior period movements is retained earnings. Note that the movement in the general reserve has to be added back to retained earnings as this was effectively a transfer from profit. The calculation of the investor's share of prior period movements in equity is as follows.

Movement in retained earnings since acquisition date

($98 000 − $80 000)		$ 18 000
Movement in general reserve		10 000
Pre-acquisition adjustments		
Depreciation	$(7 000)	
Inventories	(7 000)	(14 000)
		14 000
Investor's share — 40%		$ 5 600

The consolidation worksheet entry at 30 June 2024 is as follows.

Investment in associates and joint ventures	Dr	5 600	
Retained earnings (1/7/23)	Cr		5 600
(Recognition of equity-accounted prior period profit of Koala Ltd)			

Note that the above entry is necessary because the equity accounting entries are made in the consolidation worksheet and not in the actual records of the investor.

Share of current period equity

The next set of entries relates to the investor's share of equity for the 2023–24 year.

Workings

Recorded profit of investee		$60 000
Pre-acquisition adjustments		
Depreciation of machinery	(7 000)	(7 000)
		53 000
Investor's share — 40%		$21 200

The entries in the consolidation worksheet at 30 June 2024 reflecting the effects of the profit generated and the dividends declared/paid are as follows.

Investment in associates and joint ventures	Dr	21 200	
Share of profit or loss of associates and joint ventures	Cr		21 200
(Recognition of equity-accounted profit of Koala Ltd)			
Dividend revenue	Dr	10 000	
Investment in associates and joint ventures	Cr		10 000
(Adjustments for dividends from Koala Ltd: 40% × [$10 000 + $15 000])			

Note that the net increase in equity and in the investment account as a result of applying the equity method is $16 800 (i.e. $5600 + $21 200 − $10 000).

Consolidation worksheet 30 June 2025

Share of prior period equity

The first journal entry in the consolidation worksheet recognises the investor's share of the movement in equity of the investee in the prior period. The calculation of the investor's share of prior period movements in equity is as follows.

Movement in retained earnings since acquisition date

($123 000 − $80 000)		$ 43 000
Movement in general reserve		20 000
Pre-acquisition adjustments		
Depreciation: 2 × $7000	(14 000)	
Inventories	(7 000)	(21 000)
		42 000
Investor's share — 40%		$ 16 800

The consolidation worksheet entry at 30 June 2025 is as follows.

June 30	Investments in associates and joint ventures	Dr	16 800	
	Retained earnings (1/7/24)	Cr		16 800
	(Recognition of equity-accounted prior period profit of Koala Ltd)			

Share of current period equity

The next set of entries relates to the investor's share of equity for the 2024–25 year.

Recorded profit of investee	$70 000
Pre-acquisition adjustments	
Nil	Nil
	70 000
Investor's share — 40%	$28 000
Other comprehensive income of investee	
$6000(1 − 30%)	$ 4 200
Investor's share — 40%	$ 1 680

The entries in the consolidation worksheet at 30 June 2025 reflecting the effects of the profit and other comprehensive income generated and the dividends declared/paid are as follows.

June 30	Investment in associates and joint ventures	Dr	28 000	
	Share of profit or loss of associates and joint ventures	Cr		28 000
	(Recognition of equity-accounted profit of Koala Ltd)			
	Investment in associates and joint ventures	Dr	1 680	
	Share of other comprehensive income of associates and	Cr		1 680
	joint ventures			
	(Share of revaluation increase)			
	Share of other comprehensive income of associates and	Dr	1 680	
	joint ventures			
	Asset revaluation surplus	Cr		1 680
	(Accumulation of revaluation increase in equity)			
	Dividend revenue	Dr	14 000	
	Investment in associates and joint ventures	Cr		14 000
	(Adjustment for dividends from Koala Ltd: 40% × [$15 000 + $20 000])			

LEARNING CHECK

- ☐ Goodwill arising from the acquisition of an associate or joint venture is not separately recognised. Accordingly, goodwill is not tested separately for impairment.
- ☐ Excess on acquisition is recognised along with share of profit of the investee at the first reporting date after acquisition.
- ☐ Calculation of adjustments for differences between carrying amounts and fair values is always on an after-tax basis.
- ☐ Where differences between fair values and carrying amounts exist at acquisition date for the investee's identifiable assets and liabilities, subsequent equity recognised by the associate may include pre-acquisition adjustments relating to these differences.
- ☐ Prior to calculating the investor's share, reported profit of an associate or joint venture must first be adjusted to account for fair value differences at acquisition.
- ☐ Where the investor prepares consolidated financial statements, the equity method is applied in the consolidation worksheet. As consolidation entries are never posted, the effects of all prior periods' equity method adjustments must be accounted for along with the current period's adjustments.

31.6 Applying the equity method — inter-entity transactions

LEARNING OBJECTIVE 31.6 Account for the effects of inter-entity transactions.

As detailed in chapter 28, in the preparation of consolidated financial statements, adjustments are made to eliminate the effects of transactions between a parent and its subsidiaries, and between the subsidiaries themselves. The rationale for these adjustments is that the consolidated financial statements show only the results of transactions between the group and entities external to the group. The group is regarded as a single economic entity. The adjustment procedure requires the full effect of the transaction to be eliminated and the adjustments are made against the particular accounts affected by the transactions.

As stated in paragraph 26 of AASB 128/IAS 28, many of the procedures that are appropriate for the application of the equity method are similar to consolidation procedures described in AASB 10/IFRS 10. Where a parent or its consolidated subsidiaries undertake transactions with an associate or a joint venture, adjustments must be made for unrealised gains and losses on those transactions.

The principles for adjusting the effects of inter-entity transactions under equity accounting are as follows.

- *Adjustments are made for transactions between an associate/joint venture and the investor that give rise to unrealised profits and losses.* Such transactions include the sale of inventories from the investor to the investee. Realisation of the profits or losses on these transactions occurs when the asset on which the profit or loss accrued is sold to an external entity, or as the future benefits embodied in the asset are consumed.

  Unlike consolidation, there is no need to adjust for transactions between the investor and the investee — only any unrealised gains or losses arising from those transactions. Therefore, transactions such as a loan between the entities, or the payment of interest on the loan, do not require an adjustment under equity accounting.

- *Adjustments for transactions between an investor and an investee are done on a proportional basis, determined in accordance with the investor's ownership interest in the investee.* This differs from consolidation adjustments where the adjustments are made on a 100% basis, and are unaffected by the parent's ownership interest in the subsidiary.

- *Adjustments are made on an after-tax basis to the share of profit or loss of associates and joint ventures and investment in associates and joint ventures accounts.* AASB 128/IAS 28 does not detail which accounts should be adjusted under the equity method. For example, if an investee sells inventories to an investor at a profit, should the inventories account of the investor be adjusted? In this chapter, the only accounts adjusted are the Share of profits or losses in associates and joint ventures account and the Investments in associates and joint ventures account — no adjustments are made to specific accounts of the investor or investee.

  Note that the adjustments are made on an after-tax basis as the equity method recognises a share of after-tax profits only.

The adjustments are the same for all transactions regardless of whether they are upstream (where an associate/joint venture sells to an investor) or downstream (where an investor sells to an associate/joint venture). The direction of the transaction is irrelevant in determining the accounts affected by the application of the equity method.

It is difficult to find a rationale for the adjustments for inter-entity transactions under the equity method of accounting as applied under AASB 128/IAS 28. Unlike subsidiaries, associates and joint ventures are not part of the single economic entity and so the consolidation rationale is not applicable. The main argument for the method used is simplicity. However, the method does lead to some strange results. For example, where an investor sells inventories to an investee, the adjustment is to the share of profit or loss of associates and joint ventures account even though the profit was made by the investor and not the investee. The incremental change to the investment account does not therefore reflect only changes in the equity of the investee, but includes unrealised profits made by the investor.

31.6.1 Examples of inter-entity transactions

In the following examples, assume:
- the reporting period is for the year ending 30 June 2024
- the investor, Tasmanian Ltd, owns 25% of Devil Ltd. Tasmanian Ltd acquired its ownership interest in Devil Ltd 2 years prior on 1 July 2022, when the retained earnings balance of Devil Ltd was $100 000. At this date, all the identifiable assets and liabilities of Devil Ltd were recorded at fair value
- at 30 June 2023, the retained earnings balance in Devil Ltd is $140 000, and the profit recorded for the 2023–24 period is $30 000. The tax rate is 30%.

The adjustment entries may differ according to whether they are made in the consolidation worksheet or in the accounting records of the investor. Differences in particular arise where the effects of a transaction occur across 2 or more years.

Example 1. Sale of inventories from associate to investor in the current period

During the 2023–24 period, Devil Ltd sold $5000 worth of inventories to Tasmanian Ltd. These items had previously cost Devil Ltd $3000. All the items remain unsold by the investor at 30 June 2024.

The calculations for applying the equity method are as follows.

2022–23 period	
Change in retained earnings since acquisition date: $140 000 – $100 000	$40 000
Investor's share — 25%	$10 000
2023–24 period	
Current period profit	$30 000
Adjustments for inter-entity transactions	
Unrealised after-tax profit in ending inventories: $2000(1 – 30%)	(1 400)
	28 600
Investor's share — 25%	$ 7 150

If the investor prepares consolidated financial statements, the entries in the consolidation worksheet at 30 June 2024 to apply the equity method to its associate/joint venture are as follows.

June 30	Investment in associates and joint ventures	Dr	10 000	
	Retained earnings (1/7/23)	Cr		10 000
	Investment in associates and joint ventures	Dr	7 150	
	Share of profit or loss of associates and joint ventures	Cr		7 150

If the investor does not prepare consolidated financial statements, the entries are made in the records of the investor. The first entry would be made at 30 June 2023 and only the second entry from above would be made at 30 June 2024.

Example 2. Sale of inventories from investor to associate in the current period

Details are the same as in example 1, except that Tasmanian Ltd sells the inventories to Devil Ltd.

The calculations and journal entries are exactly the same as in example 1. The flow of the transaction, whether upstream or downstream, does not affect the accounting for the unrealised gain.

Example 3. Sale of inventories in the current period, part remaining unsold

During the 2023–24 period, Devil Ltd sold $5000 worth of inventories to Tasmanian Ltd. These items had previously cost Devil Ltd $3000. Half of the items remain unsold by Tasmanian Ltd at 30 June 2024.

The increment to the investment account is calculated in a similar way to example 1, but the adjustment is based only on the unrealised gain remaining in inventories on hand at the end of the period. The calculations are as follows.

2022–23 period	
As for example 1: Investor's share — 25%	$10 000
2023–24 period	
Current period profit	$30 000
Adjustment for inter-entity transactions	
Unrealised after-tax profit in ending inventories: $1000(1 – 30%)	(700)
	29 300
Investor's share — 25%	$ 7 325

If the investor prepares consolidated financial statements, at 30 June 2024, the entries in the consolidation worksheet to apply the equity method to its associate are as follows.

June 30	Investment in associates and joint ventures	Dr	10 000	
	Retained earnings (1/7/23)	Cr		10 000
	Investment in associates and joint ventures	Dr	7 325	
	Share of profit or loss of associates and joint ventures	Cr		7 325

If the investor does not prepare consolidated financial statements, in the 2023–24 period only the second of the above two entries is required.

Example 4. Sale of inventories in the previous period

During the 2022–23 period, Tasmanian Ltd sold $5000 worth of inventories to Devil Ltd. These items had previously cost Tasmanian Ltd $3000. All the items remain unsold by Devil Ltd at 30 June 2023. These were all sold to other entities by 30 June 2024.

The calculations for applying the equity method are as follows.

2022–23 period	
Change in retained earnings since acquisition date: $140 000 – $100 000	$40 000
Adjustment for inter-entity transactions	
Unrealised after-tax profit in ending inventories: $2000(1 – 30%)	(1 400)
	38 600
Investor's share — 25%	$ 9 650
2023–24 period	
Current period's profit	$30 000
Adjustment for inter-entity transactions	
Realised after-tax profit in opening inventories: $2000(1 – 30%)	1 400
	31 400
Investor's share — 25%	$ 7 850

In the 2023–24 period, the profit that was unrealised in the previous period becomes realised. Hence, the amount is *added back* in the calculation of the 2023–24 share of equity. Across the two periods, the net effect is zero as the unrealised gain in 2022–23 is offset when it is realised in 2023–24.

If the investor prepares consolidated financial statements at 30 June 2024, the entries in the consolidation worksheet to apply the equity method to its associate are as follows.

June 30	Investment in associates and joint ventures	Dr	9 650	
	Retained earnings (1/7/23)	Cr		9 650
	Investment in associates and joint ventures	Dr	7 850	
	Share of profit or loss of associates and joint ventures	Cr		7 850

If the investor does not prepare consolidated statements, the only entry passed at 30 June 2024 is the second entry above.

Example 5. Sale of depreciable non-current asset

On 1 July 2022, Devil Ltd sold an item of plant to Tasmanian Ltd for $8000. The carrying amount of the asset on this date in Devil Ltd's records was $3000. The plant had a remaining useful life of 5 years.

The calculations for applying the equity method are as follows.

2022–23 period	
Change in retained earnings since acquisition date	$40 000
Adjustments for inter-entity transactions	
Unrealised after-tax gain on sale of plant: $5000(1 – 30%)	(3 500)
Realised after-tax gain on sale of plant: $\frac{1}{5} \times \$3500$	700
	37 200
Investor's share — 25%	$ 9 300

Note that at the time of sale of the plant the gain on the sale is unrealised. The profit is realised as the asset is consumed or used by the entity holding the asset. The consumption of benefits is measured by the depreciation of the asset. Hence, as the plant is depreciated on a straight-line basis over a 5-year period, one-fifth of the profit is realised in each year after the inter-entity transfer.

2023–24 period	
Current period profit	$30 000
Adjustment for inter-entity transactions	
Realised after-tax gain on sale of plant: $\frac{1}{5} \times \$3500$	700
	30 700
Investor's share — 25%	$ 7 675

A further one-fifth of the unrealised profit is realised in the 2023–24 period as the benefits from the asset are further consumed. By the end of the 5-year period, the whole of the profit is realised.

If the investor prepares consolidated financial statements at 30 June 2024, the entries in the consolidation worksheet to apply the equity method to its associate/joint venture are as follows.

June 30	Investment in associates and joint ventures	Dr	9 300	
	Retained earnings (1/7/23)	Cr		9 300
	Investment in associates and joint ventures	Dr	7 675	
	Share of profit or loss of associates and joint ventures	Cr		7 675

If the investor does not prepare consolidated statements, only the second of the above entries is passed at 30 June 2024.

Example 6. Payment of interest

On 1 July 2022, Tasmanian Ltd loaned $10 000 to Devil Ltd. Interest of $1000 p.a. was paid by Devil Ltd.

Although the profit of Devil Ltd includes the interest expense from this transaction, no adjustment is required because the revenue/expense on the transaction is assumed to be realised. Profits are considered to be unrealised only when they are recognised in the carrying amount of an asset transferred upstream or downstream between the investor and the associate or joint venture.

ILLUSTRATIVE EXAMPLE 31.5

Equity method of accounting

On 1 July 2021, Dingo Ltd paid $2 696 000 for 40% of the shares of Numbat Ltd, a company involved in the manufacture of garden equipment. At that date, the equity of Numbat Ltd consisted of the following.

Share capital — 3 000 000 shares	$3 000 000
Retained earnings	3 000 000

At 1 July 2021, all the identifiable net assets of Numbat Ltd were recorded at fair value except for the following.

	Carrying amount	Fair value
Inventories	$1 000 000	$1 200 000
Plant (cost $3 200 000)	2 500 000	3 000 000

The inventories were all sold by 30 June 2022. The plant had a further expected useful life of 10 years.

Additional information
(a) On 1 July 2022, Dingo Ltd held inventories sold to it by Numbat Ltd at a profit before income tax of $150 000. This was all sold by 30 June 2023.
(b) In February 2023, Numbat Ltd sold inventories to Dingo Ltd at a profit before income tax of $600 000. Half of this was still held by Dingo Ltd at 30 June 2023.
(c) On 30 June 2023, Numbat Ltd held inventories sold to it by Dingo Ltd at a profit before income tax of $250 000. This had been sold to Numbat Ltd for $2 000 000.
(d) On 2 July 2021, Numbat Ltd sold some equipment to Dingo Ltd for $1 500 000, with Numbat Ltd recording a profit before income tax of $ 400 000. The equipment had a further 4-year life, with benefits expected to occur evenly in these years.
(e) In June 2022, Numbat Ltd provided for a dividend of $1 000 000. This dividend was paid in August 2022. Dividend revenue is recognised when the dividend is provided for.
(f) The balances in the general reserve have resulted from transfers from retained earnings.
(g) The tax rate is 30%.
(h) Each share in Numbat Ltd has a fair value at 30 June 2023 of $4.

The consolidated financial statements of Dingo Ltd and the financial statements of Numbat Ltd at 30 June 2023, not including the equity-accounted figures, are as follows.

Statements of profit or loss and other comprehensive income
for the year ended 30 June 2023

	Dingo Ltd $'000	Numbat Ltd $'000
Revenue	25 000	18 600
Expenses	19 200	13 600
Profit before tax	5 800	5 000
Income tax expense	2 200	1 100
Profit for the period	**3 600**	**3 900**
Other comprehensive income: revaluation gains	0	400
Total comprehensive income	**3 600**	**4 300**

Statements of changes in equity
for the year ended 30 June 2023

	Dingo Ltd $'000	Numbat Ltd $'000
Total comprehensive income	3 600	4 300
Retained earnings as at 1/7/22	4 000	4 000
Profit	3 600	3 900
	7 600	7 900
Transfer to general reserve	—	1 000
Dividend paid	3 000	1 500
Dividend provided	1 500	1 000
	4 500	3 500
Retained earnings as at 30/6/23	3 100	4 400
Asset revaluation surplus as at 1/7/22	—	200
Increase in 2022–23		400
Asset revaluation surplus as at 30/6/23		600
General reserve as at 1/7/22	1 000	1 500
Increase in 2022–23	—	1 000
General reserve at 30/6/23	1 000	2 500

Statements of financial position
as at 30 June 2023

	Dingo Ltd $'000	Numbat Ltd $'000
EQUITY AND LIABILITIES		
Equity		
Share capital	8 000	3 000
Asset revaluation surplus	—	600
General reserve	1 000	2 500
Retained earnings	3 100	4 400
Total equity	12 100	10 500
Total liabilities	1 500	1 400
Total equity and liabilities	**13 600**	**11 900**
ASSETS		
Current assets		
Inventories	4 000	2 000
Receivables	1 000	900
	5 000	2 900
Non-current assets		
Property, plant and equipment	5 904	
Investment in Numbat Ltd	2 696	9 000
	8 600	9 000
Total assets	**13 600**	**11 900**

Required

Prepare the consolidated financial statements of Dingo Ltd at 30 June 2023, applying the equity method of accounting to the investment in Numbat Ltd.

Solution

The first step is to prepare an acquisition analysis which compares at acquisition date, 1 July 2021, the cost of the investment in Numbat Ltd and the share of the net fair value of the identifiable assets and liabilities of Numbat Ltd. This analysis is the same as the acquisition analysis used in preparing consolidated financial statements, and results in the determination of any goodwill or excess.

Acquisition analysis

At 1 July 2021:	
Net fair value of identifiable assets and liabilities of Numbat Ltd	= ($3 000 000 + $3 000 000) (equity)
	+ $200 000(1 − 30%) (inventories)
	+ $500 000(1 − 30%) (plant)
	= $6 490 000
Net fair value acquired by Dingo Ltd	= 40% × $6 490 000
	= $2 596 000
Cost of investment	= $2 696 000
Goodwill	= $100 000

As a result of the analysis, the effects of the adjustments to assets on hand at acquisition date can be calculated. In relation to the plant, there is a $500 000 difference between the fair value and the carrying amount at acquisition date. As a result, the reported profits of the associate after acquisition date will include amounts that were paid for by the investor at acquisition date. The equity method recognises a share of post-acquisition equity only. The plant is being depreciated by the associate at 20% p.a. straight-line. The after-tax effect of the depreciation each year is calculated as follows.

$$\text{Depreciation of plant p.a.} = \left[\$500\,000\,(1 - 30\%)\right] / 10\,\text{years}$$
$$= \$35\,000$$

In each of the 10 years subsequent to the acquisition date, the reported profit of the associate is reduced by $35 000 p.a. prior to calculating the investor's share of post-acquisition equity.

In relation to inventories, there is a $200 000 difference between fair value and carrying amount at acquisition date. When the associate sells the inventories, it will report a profit that includes pre-acquisition equity to the investor. The after-tax effect on profit on sale of the inventories is as follows.

$$\text{Pre-acquisition inventories effect} = \$200\,000\,(1 - 30\%)$$
$$= \$140\,000$$

In the year of sale of the inventories, the investor's share of the reported profit of the associate is reduced by $140 000 prior to calculating the investor's share of post-acquisition equity.

Consolidation worksheet entries — 30 June 2023

The investor's share of the post-acquisition equity of the associate to be recognised on consolidation is calculated in two steps: a share of post-acquisition equity between the acquisition date and the beginning of the current period, and a share of the current period's post-acquisition equity. A third step is necessary to adjust for dividends paid/payable by the investee.

(1) Share of changes in post-acquisition equity in previous periods

The calculation is based on post-acquisition movements in the retained earnings account and other reserve accounts created by transfers from retained earnings, and adjusted for the effects of inter-entity transactions. The consolidation worksheet entry for the investor's share of the associate's post-acquisition equity recognised between the date of acquisition and the beginning of the current period is calculated as follows.

	$'000	$'000
Retained earnings:		
Post-acquisition retained earnings from acquisition date to		
beginning of the current period: $4 000 000 − $3 000 000		1 000
Change in general reserve in previous periods		1 500
		2 500

	$'000	$'000
Pre-acquisition adjustments		
Depreciation of plant	(35)	
Sale of inventories	(140)	(175)
Post-acquisition retained earnings		2 325
Adjustments for inter-entity transactions		
Inventories on hand at 30/6/23: $150 000(1 − 30%)	(105)	
Unrealised profit on sale of equipment		
Original gain $400 000(1 − 30%) less depreciation p.a. of $\frac{1}{4} \times \$280\,000$	(210)	(315)
		2 010
Investor's share (40%) of retained earnings at 1/7/22		804
Asset revaluation surplus:		
Share of asset revaluation surplus in previous periods: 40% × $200 000		80
Total increase in equity-accounted carrying amount in previous periods		884

The consolidation worksheet entry in relation to previous period's equity is as follows.

Investments in associates and joint ventures	Dr	884 000	
Retained earnings (1/7/22)	Cr		804 000
Asset revaluation surplus	Cr		80 000
(Recognition of equity-accounted share of prior period's equity)			

In relation to the above entry and calculations, note the following.

Retained earnings (1/7/22)

- *Retained earnings.* The change is calculated as the difference between the recorded balance at acquisition date and the balance at the beginning of the current period.
- *General reserve.* The change in this equity amount is calculated in the same way as for retained earnings. There was no balance at acquisition date. The balance at the beginning of the period, as can be seen in the statement of changes in equity, was $1.5 million. Hence, this entire amount is an increase in post-acquisition equity.
- *Determination of post-acquisition equity.* The movement in recorded retained earnings is not all post-acquisition equity. The investor recognised the fair value of the assets and liabilities of the associate at acquisition date, and not the carrying amount in the associate. Where there are movements in these assets and liabilities, some of the profits recognised by the associate are pre-acquisition and not post-acquisition. There were two assets at acquisition date for which the fair value differed from carrying amount as follows.
  - *Plant.* The fair value was $500 000 greater than the carrying amount. As calculated in the acquisition analysis, since the asset has a 10-year life, in relation to the investor's share the pre-acquisition after-tax amount included in reported equity of the associate is $14 000 p.a.
  - *Inventories.* The fair value was $200 000 greater than carrying amount. As calculated in the acquisition analysis, since the inventories was sold after the acquisition date, in relation to the investor's share the pre-acquisition effect is $56 000.

Hence, the change in post-acquisition retained earnings between acquisition date and the beginning of the current period is $2 325 000.

- *Inter-entity transactions.* Where either the investor or investee has recognised unrealised profits or losses on transactions with the other party, adjustments are made to eliminate these. In this example, the additional information details four inter-entity transactions, two of which relate to previous periods, namely (a) and (b) as follows.
  - (a) On 1 July 2022, the investee sold inventories to the investor at a profit before tax of $150 000. This was unrealised at 30 June 2019. The investor's share of the recorded change in equity is then reduced by $42 000 after-tax profit.
  - (b) On 2 July 2021, the investee recognised an after-tax profit of $280 000 on the sale of equipment to the investor. This profit is realised as the benefits from the asset are consumed. The rate of consumption is measured via depreciation. As the asset has a 4-year life, one-quarter of this after-tax profit is realised each year. Hence, the investor's share of the unrealised portion at 30 June 2022, one year after the transaction, is $84 000 being 40% of the original after-tax profit of $280 000 less ¼ of $280 000.

The investor's share of post-acquisition retained earnings, adjusted for unrealised profits on inter-entity transactions is then $804 000.

Asset revaluation surplus

There was no asset revaluation surplus recognised in the investee at acquisition date. As per the statement of comprehensive income, the balance at 1 July 2022 was $200 000. Hence, this entire amount is a post-acquisition change in equity and the investor's 40% share of this is $80 000.

Investment in associate/joint venture — Numbat Ltd

The investor's total share of post-acquisition equity of the investee up to the beginning of the current period is, therefore, $884 000. This amount is then added to the investment in associates and joint ventures account, with increases recognised in the relevant equity accounts of the investor.

(2) *Share of post-acquisition profit in the current period*

In part (1), the investor's share of the previous period's post-acquisition equity was calculated. In this part, the calculation is of the investor's share of the post-acquisition equity of the investee relating to the current period. In this example, increases in equity arise due to the investee's earning of a profit and recording of other comprehensive income relating to increases in the asset revaluation surplus.

The calculations and required consolidation adjustment entries are shown below.

	$'000	$'000
Recorded profit:		3 900
Pre-acquisition adjustments		
Depreciation of plant		(35)
Post-acquisition profit		3 865
Adjustments for inter-entity transactions		
Realised profit in opening inventories	105	
Unrealised profit in Dingo Ltd's ending inventories: $\frac{1}{2} \times \$600\,000\,(1 - 30\%)$	(210)	
Unrealised profit in Numbat Ltd's ending inventories: $\$250\,000(1 - 30\%)$	(175)	
Realised profit on plant: $\frac{1}{4} \times \$280\,000$	70	(210)
		3 655
Investor's share (40%) of associate/joint venture		1 462
Other comprehensive income:		
Share of increase in asset revaluation surplus: $40\% \times \$400\,000$		160
Total increase in equity-accounted carrying amount in current period		1 622

The consolidation worksheet entries are as follows.

Investments in associates and joint ventures	Dr	1 462 000	
Share of profit or loss of associates and joint ventures	Cr		1 462 000
(Share of profit or loss of associate/joint venture)			
Investments in associates and joint ventures	Dr	160 000	
Share of other comprehensive income of associates and joint ventures	Cr		160 000
(Share of revaluation increase)			
Share of other comprehensive income of associates and joint ventures	Dr	160 000	
Asset revaluation surplus	Cr		160 000
(Accumulation of revaluation increase in equity)			

In relation to these calculations and entry, note the following.

Profit or loss for the period

- *Share of profit or loss of associate.* The associate reports an after-tax profit for the year of $3 900 000. This profit needs to be adjusted for any unrealised profits or losses at the end of the period arising from transactions between the investor and the associate.

    However, this profit is not all post-acquisition profit. Movements in assets and liabilities on hand at acquisition date when fair values differed from carrying amounts give rise to pre-acquisition elements in recorded profits. In the current period, because the plant on hand at acquisition date was recognised by the investor at fair value, the extra depreciation on the plant reflects pre-acquisition equity. As calculated in the acquisition analysis the pre-acquisition effect is $35 000 p.a. This is subtracted from the profit of the period profit to give the post-acquisition profit for the period.

- *Inter-entity transactions.* In this problem there are four transactions noted in the additional information that affect the current period, namely (a)–(d).

(a) The inventories on hand at 1 July 2022 is all sold by 30 June 2023. The profit on the inter-entity sale was unrealised at the beginning of the current period but is realised in the current period. The after-tax profit on sale of the inventories was $105 000. Since the profit is realised in the current period, it is added to the reported profit of the associate. Note that $105 000 is subtracted in the calculation of the investor's share of previous period equity and is added to the calculation of the investor's share of current period profit. Since the profit is now realised, there is no need to make an adjustment in future periods.

(b) In February 2023, the associate sold inventories to the investor at an after-tax profit of $420 000. Since half of the inventories is still on hand at 30 June 2023, there is unrealised profit at the end of the reporting period of $210 000. This amount is subtracted from reported profit because the investor's share relates to realised profit only.

(c) In the current period, the investor sold inventories to the associate for an after-tax profit of $175 000. Since these inventories remain on hand at the end of the reporting period, the unrealised profit is subtracted from reported profit.

(d) The gain on sale of equipment was adjusted for in the calculation of the investor's share of previous period equity. As noted in that calculation, the unrealised profit on sale is realised as the asset is used up and depreciated. The amount realised each year is in proportion to depreciation, namely one-quarter p.a. The amount of the gain realised in the current period is then $\frac{1}{4} \times \$280\,000$, that is, $70 000. Being realised profit, it is added back to recorded profit.

The total post-acquisition profit of the investee adjusted for the effects of inter-entity transactions is then $3 655 000, and the investor's 40% share is $1 462 000.

Other comprehensive income

From the statement of changes in equity it can be seen that the asset revaluation surplus has increased by $400 000 in the current period. The investor is entitled to 40% of this, that is, $160 000. This is recognised in other comprehensive income and accumulated in the asset revaluation surplus.

Investment in associate/joint venture — Numbat Ltd

The investor's share of current period post-acquisition equity is then $1 622 000, which increases the investor's investment in the associate. This amount is disaggregated by separate line items in the consolidated statement of comprehensive income for the share of profit of the associate, $1 462 000, and share of other comprehensive income of associate, $160 000.

(3) *Dividends paid and provided for by associate/joint venture*

A further entry is necessary to take into account reductions in the investee's equity in the current period because of dividends. In the current period, Numbat Ltd paid a $1.5 million dividend and declared a $1 million dividend. Because the investor recognises dividend revenue when the dividends are declared, it would recognise dividend revenue of $1 million (i.e. 40% × [$1.5 million + $1 million]).

The following entry eliminates, on consolidation, the dividend revenue recorded by the investor. This is because in parts (1) and (2) above, the investor's equity has been increased by its share of the equity of the associate/joint venture from which the dividends were paid/declared. Similarly, it is also necessary to reduce the investment in the associate as the share of equity in the associate as calculated in parts (1) and (2) has been reduced by the payment/declaration of the dividend. The consolidation worksheet entry is as follows.

Dividend revenue	Dr	1 000 000	
Investments in associates and joint ventures	Cr		1 000 000
(Adjustment for dividends paid/payable by investee: 40% × [$1 500 000 + $1 000 000])			

(4) *Total investment*

On the basis of the above worksheet entries, the carrying amount of the investment in the associate/ joint venture, Numbat Ltd, is as follows.

$$\$2\,696\,000 + \$884\,000 + \$1\,622\,000 - \$1\,000\,000 = \$4\,202\,000$$

The consolidated financial statements of Dingo Ltd at 30 June 2023, including the investment in the associate/joint venture accounted for under the equity method, are as follows.

DINGO LTD Consolidated statement of profit or loss and other comprehensive income for year ended 30 June 2023	
	$'000
Revenue ($25 000 000 − $1 000 000 dividend eliminated)	24 000
Expenses	(19 200)
Share of profit or loss of associates and joint ventures accounted for using the equity method	1 462
Profit before tax	**6 262**
Income tax expense	(2 200)
Profit for the year	**4 062**
Other comprehensive income	
Share of other comprehensive income of associates and joint ventures accounted for using the equity method	160
Total comprehensive income for the year	**4 222**

DINGO LTD Consolidated statement of changes in equity for year ended 30 June 2023	
	$'000
Total comprehensive income for the year	4 222
Retained earnings at 1/7/22 ($4 000 000 + $804 000)	4 804
Profit or loss for the year	4 062
	8 866
Dividend paid	(3 000)
Dividend provided	(1 500)
Retained earnings at 30/6/23	4 366
Asset revaluation surplus at 1/7/22 ($nil + $80 000)	80
Revaluation increases ($nil + $160 000)	160
Asset revaluation surplus at 30/6/23	240
General reserve at 1/7/22	1 000
General reserve at 30/6/23	1 000

DINGO LTD Consolidated statement of financial position as at 30 June 2023	
	$'000
EQUITY AND LIABILITIES	
Equity	
Share capital	8 000
Asset revaluation surplus	240
General reserve	1 000
Retained earnings	4 366
Total equity	13 606
Total liabilities	1 500
Total equity and liabilities	**15 106**
ASSETS	
Current assets	
Inventories	4 000
Receivables	1 000
	5 000
Non-current assets	
Property, plant and equipment	5 904
Investment in associates and joint ventures	4 202
	10 106
Total assets	**15 106**

31.7 Share of losses of an associate or joint venture

LEARNING OBJECTIVE 31.7 Account for associates and joint ventures where these entities incur losses.

Under the equity method of accounting, profits of the associate increase the carrying amount of the investment while losses and dividends reduce the carrying amount. It is possible then, that if an associate incurred substantial and/or sustained losses the carrying amount of the investment could be eliminated. Paragraph 38 of AASB 128/IAS 28 states:

> If an entity's share of losses of an associate or a joint venture equals or exceeds its interest in the associate or joint venture, the entity discontinues recognising its share of further losses.

In other words, once the carrying amount is reduced to zero the equity method ceases. Logically, an investor cannot have a negative investment.

There may be circumstances where the investment in the associate or joint venture consists of more than just the carrying amount of the investment in the associate or joint venture. The investor's interest in the associate/joint venture may also include other long-term interests in the associate/joint venture, such as preference shares or long-term receivables or loans. So, the carrying amount of the investment in associates and joint ventures account is first reduced to zero, and any further losses in excess of this are then applied against any other components of the investor's interest in the associate/joint venture in the reverse order of their priority in liquidation. The rationale is that, if the associate/joint venture is making losses, then the probability of the other investments in the associate/joint venture being realised is lessened.

Paragraph 39 of AASB 128/IAS 28 states:

> If the associate or joint venture subsequently reports profits, the entity resumes recognising its share of those profits only after its share of the profits equals the share of losses not recognised.

In other words, after the carrying amount of the associate or joint venture is reduced to zero, the investor must still keep track of any share of additional losses. If the investee subsequently recovers to start generating profits, the investor's share of these profits must first offset the unrecognised losses before resuming the equity method of accounting.

In situations where the associate initially records losses, there may be indications that the investment is impaired, in which case the investor should apply AASB 136/IAS 36 *Impairment of Assets*. Paragraph 42 of AASB 128/IAS 28 states that, in determining the value in use of the investment, an investor estimates:

(a) its share of the present value of the estimated future cash flows expected to be generated by the associate or joint venture, including the cash flows from the operations of the associate or joint venture and the proceeds from the ultimate disposal of the investment; or

(b) the present value of the estimated future cash flows expected to arise from dividends to be received from the investment and from its ultimate disposal.

Under appropriate assumptions, both methods give the same result.

Share of losses of the associate

On 1 July 2019, Koala Ltd acquired 25% of the shares of Bear Ltd for $100 000. At that date, the equity of Bear Ltd was $400 000, with all identifiable assets and liabilities being measured at amounts equal to fair value. Table 31.1 shows the profits and losses made by the associate over the first 5 years of operations after 1 July 2019, with their effects on the carrying amount of the investment.

TABLE 31.1	Profits and losses made by associate over first 5 years of operations				
Year	Profit/(loss)	Share of profit or loss	Cumulative share	Equity-accounted carrying amount of investment	Unrecognised losses
2019–20	$ 20 000	$ 5 000	$ 5 000	$105 000	$ 0
2020–21	(200 000)	(50 000)	(45 000)	55 000	0
2021–22	(300 000)	(75 000)	(120 000)	0	20 000
2022–23	60 000	15 000	(105 000)	0	5 000
2023–24	100 000	25 000	(80 000)	20 000	0

Table 31.1 shows that the investment account is initially recorded by Koala Ltd at $100 000, and is progressively adjusted for Koala Ltd's share of the profits and losses of Bear Ltd. In the 2021–22 year, the share of the loss of the associate exceeds the carrying amount of the investment, the investor discontinues recognising its share of future losses. Even though profits are recorded by the associate in the 2022–23 year, the balance of the investment stays at zero because the profits are not sufficient to offset losses not recognised.

The journal entries in the consolidation worksheets of Koala Ltd over these periods are as follows.

30 June 2020			
Investment in associates and joint ventures	Dr	5 000	
Share of profit or loss of associates and joint ventures	Cr		5 000
30 June 2021			
Share of profit or loss of associates and joint ventures	Dr	50 000	
Retained earnings (1/7/20)	Cr		5 000
Investment in associates and joint ventures	Cr		45 000
30 June 2022			
Share of profit or loss of associates and joint ventures	Dr	55 000	
Retained earnings (1/7/21)	Dr	45 000	
Investment in associates and joint ventures	Cr		100 000
30 June 2023			
Retained earnings (1/7/22)	Dr	100 000	
Investment in associates and joint ventures	Cr		100 000
30 June 2024			
Retained earnings (1/7/23)	Dr	100 000	
Share of profit or loss of associates and joint ventures	Cr		20 000
Investment in associates and joint ventures	Cr		80 000

LEARNING CHECK

☐ The investor's share of losses of an associate is recognised but only to the point where the carrying amount of the investment in the associate is zero.

☐ The share of losses may be offset against other investments the investor has in the associate, such as long-term receivables.

☐ If, after reporting losses, an associate earns a profit, the investor recognises a share of profits only after the share of profits exceeds the share of past losses not recognised.

31.8 Disclosure

LEARNING OBJECTIVE 31.8 Discuss the disclosures required in relation to associates and joint ventures.

AASB 128/IAS 28 does not address the disclosure requirements in relation to investments in associates and joint ventures. Instead, a separate standard, AASB 12/IFRS 12 *Disclosure of Interests in Other Entities*, provides the guidance relating to disclosure of such investments.

Paragraph 1 of AASB 12/IFRS 12 states the standard's key objective:

> The objective of this Standard is to require an entity to disclose information that enables users of its financial statements to evaluate:
> (a) the nature of, and risks associated with, its interests in other entities; and
> (b) the effects of those interests on its financial position, financial performance and cash flows.

It is interesting to note the emphasis on the ability of users of financial statements to be able to evaluate risks. In its introduction to IFRS 12 the IASB noted in paragraph IN5 that the global financial crisis that started in 2007 highlighted a lack of transparency about the risks to which a reporting entity was exposed from its involvement with structured entities. With respect to associates and joint ventures, paragraph 7 of AASB 12/IFRS 12 requires an entity to disclose information about significant judgements and assumptions it has made in determining that it had joint control or significant influence over another entity.

Paragraph 9 of AASB 12/IFRS 12 provides examples of situations where it is necessary for an investor to disclose significant judgements and assumptions in relation to associates:

- where it does not have significant influence even though it holds 20% or more of the voting rights of another entity
- where it has significant influence even though it holds less than 20% of the voting rights of another entity.

Paragraph 20 of AASB 12/IFRS 12 requires an entity to disclose information that enables users to evaluate the nature, extent and financial effects of its interest in associates and joint ventures, including the nature and effects of its contractual relationship with the other investors with joint control of, or significant influence over, the same investments. To achieve this, paragraph 21 of AASB 12/IFRS 12 requires disclosures:

> (a) for each joint arrangement and associate that is material to the reporting entity:
>   (i) the name of the joint arrangement or associate.
>   (ii) the nature of the entity's relationship with the joint arrangement or associate (by, for example, describing the nature of the activities of the joint arrangement or associate and whether they are strategic to the entity's activities).
>   (iii) the principal place of business (and country of incorporation, if applicable and different from the principal place of business) of the joint arrangement or associate.
>   (iv) the proportion of ownership interest or participating share held by the entity and, if different, the proportion of voting rights held (if applicable).
> (b) for each joint venture and associate that is material to the reporting entity:
>   (i) whether the investment in the joint venture or associate is measured using the equity method or at fair value.
>   (ii) summarised financial information about the joint venture or associate as specified in paragraphs B12 and B13.
>   (iii) if the joint venture or associate is accounted for using the equity method, the fair value of its investment in the joint venture or associate, if there is a quoted market price for the investment.
> (c) financial information as specified in paragraph B16 about the entity's investments in joint ventures and associates that are not individually material:
>   (i) in aggregate for all individually immaterial joint ventures and, separately,
>   (ii) in aggregate for all individually immaterial associates.

The summarised information in paragraph (b)(ii) above consists of:

> B12. For each joint venture and associate that is material to the reporting entity, an entity shall disclose:
>   (a) dividends received from the joint venture or associate.
>   (b) summarised financial information for the joint venture or associate (see paragraphs B14 and B15) including, but not necessarily limited to:
>   (i) current assets.
>   (ii) non-current assets.
>   (iii) current liabilities.
>   (iv) non-current liabilities.

(v) revenue.

(vi) profit or loss from continuing operations.

(vii) post-tax profit or loss from discontinued operations.

(viii) other comprehensive income.

(ix) total comprehensive income.

B13. In addition to the summarised financial information required by paragraph B12, an entity shall disclose for each joint venture that is material to the reporting entity the amount of:

(a) cash and cash equivalents included in paragraph B12(b)(i).

(b) current financial liabilities (excluding trade and other payables and provisions) included in paragraph B12(b)(iii).

(c) non-current financial liabilities (excluding trade and other payables and provisions) included in paragraph B12(b)(iv).

(d) depreciation and amortisation.

(e) interest income.

(f) interest expense.

(g) income tax expense or income.

Paragraph 22 of AASB 12/IFRS 12 also requires disclosures relating to the following.

• *Significant restrictions on the ability of associates or joint ventures to transfer funds to the investor.* These transfers could relate to dividend payments or repayment of loans.

• *Different reporting dates used by the investor and an associate or joint venture.* The disclosure consists of stating the date at the end of the reporting period for the associate as well the reason for using a different period or date.

• *The unrecognised share of losses of an associate or joint venture.* An investor must disclose the unrecognised share of losses made by an associate both for the reporting period and cumulatively where the equity method has been discontinued.

Where the carrying amount of an associate or joint venture is immaterial, an entity must disclose an aggregated carrying amount of all the individually immaterial investments. Further, paragraph B16 of AASB 12/IFRS 12 requires an entity to disclose the aggregated amount of its share of those joint ventures' or associates':

(a) profit or loss from continuing operations.

(b) post-tax profit or loss from discontinued operations.

(c) other comprehensive income.

(d) total comprehensive income.

Figure 31.4 shows the disclosures provided in relation to investments in joint ventures and associates by CSR Limited.

FIGURE 31.4	Disclosures related to joint ventures and associates, CSR

23 Equity accounting information

Carrying amount ($million) Entity[1]	2018			2017		
	Long-term loan	Equity accounted investment	Net investment	Long-term loan	Equity accounted investment	Net investment
Building products						
Rondo Building Services Pty Limited[2]	—	18.8	18.8	—	14.5	14.5
Gypsum Resources Trust Australia[2]	12.0	—	12.0	12.0	—	12.0

New Zealand						
Brick						
Distributors[3]	–	7.9	7.9	–	7.8	7.8
Other[2]	2.4	3.0	5.4	3.1	3.3	6.4
Total investment	**14.4**	**29.2**	**43.6**	**14.4**	**25.5**	**39.9**

1. The CSR group's interest in these entities is 50% (2017: 50%).
2. Entities incorporated in Australia.
3. Entity is a limited partnership in New Zealand.

Recognition and measurement

Investments in joint venture and associate entities have been accounted for under the equity method in the CSR group financial statements. CSR's share of net profit/loss of joint venture entities is recorded in the statement of financial performance.

Purchases and sales of goods and services to joint venture entities are on normal terms and conditions.

i) Net investment in joint ventures.

$million	2018	2017
Opening net investment	**39.9**	**61.0**
Share of net profit before income tax	18.1	21.0
Share of income tax	(5.4)	(6.3)
Dividends and distributions received	(9.5)	(14.2)
Write-down of equity accounted investment	(0.4)	–
Disposal of investment in joint venture	–	(21.4)
Foreign currency translation and other	0.9	(0.2)
Closing net investment	**43.6**	**39.9**

ii) Summarised financial information of joint venture entities.

$million	2018	2017
Statement of financial position		
Current assets	96.6	92.5
Non-current assets	22.1	22.3
Current liabilities	58.7	50.0
Non-current liabilities	3.3	2.3
Statement of financial performance		
Revenue	273.5	293.3
Share of net profit (loss) after tax		
Viridian Glass New Zealand[1]	–	(0.3)
Rondo Pty Limited	12.4	14.4
Other	0.3	0.6

1. The CSR group held a 58% interest in Viridian Glass Limited Partnership until 30 June 2016 when the remaining 42% interest was acquired. Refer to note 8 for further detail. In the year ended 31 March 2017, contribution to net profit is for the three month period ended 30 June 2016.

iii) Balances and transactions with joint venture entities.

$million	2018	2017
Current loans payable to CSR	0.1	0.1
Non-current loans payable to CSR	11.3	11.3
Purchases of goods and services	24.4	46.3
Sales of goods and services	2.8	3.3

Source: CSR Limited (2018, p. 85).

LEARNING CHECK

☐ Disclosure requirements relating to investments in associates are contained in AASB 12/IFRS 12 *Disclosure of Interests in Other Entities.*

☐ An entity must disclose information about significant judgements and assumptions made in determining that it has joint control or significant influence over another entity.

☐ For each material investment in associates or joint ventures, detailed summarised financial information must be disclosed and all individually immaterial investments aggregated.

SUMMARY

This chapter has covered the principles of accounting for investments in associates and joint ventures as contained in AASB 128/IAS 28 *Investments in Associates and Joint Ventures*. Some of the key principles are as follows.

- Besides subsidiaries, an entity may have investments in other entities, known as associates and joint ventures, with which the entity has a special relationship.
- An entity over which an investor has significant influence in the determination of financial and operating policy decisions is referred to as an associate.
- When an investor is involved in an investment where there is a contractually agreed sharing of control such that decisions require the unanimous consent of the parties sharing control, the investor has joint control over the investee, which is referred to as a joint venture.
- The equity method is designed to provide more information about an investment than generally supplied under the cost method, but provides less information than supplied under the consolidation method.
- Under the equity method, an investor recognises increases and decreases in the carrying amount of its investment in an investee and increases and decreases in its equity based upon the investor's proportionate interest in the equity of the investee.
- In applying the equity method, adjustments to equity balances recorded by the investee are made to eliminate any pre-acquisition equity.
- Adjustments are made to eliminate the effects of unrealised gains and losses arising from inter-entity transactions. These are made for both upstream and downstream transactions with amounts being calculated based on the investor's proportional interest in the investee.
- The carrying amount of an investment in an associate or joint venture cannot be reduced below zero. Where an investee incurs further losses, the application of the equity method is discontinued. The equity method resumes once the investor's share of the investee's profits exceeds the investor's share of unrecognised losses.
- AASB 12/IFRS 12 *Disclosure of Interests in Other Entities* provides guidance for significant disclosures required by investors with investments in other entities, including associates and joint ventures.

KEY TERMS

associate An entity over which the investor has significant influence.

equity method A method of accounting whereby the investment is initially recognised at cost and adjusted thereafter for the post-acquisition change in the investor's share of the investee's net assets. The investor's profit or loss includes its share of the investee's profit or loss and the investor's other comprehensive income includes its share of the investee's other comprehensive income.

joint arrangement A contractual arrangement in which the parties involved have joint control over the decision making in relation to the joint arrangement.

joint control The contractually agreed sharing of control of an arrangement, which exists only when decisions about the relevant activities require the unanimous consent of the parties sharing control.

joint venture A joint arrangement whereby the parties that have joint control of the arrangement have rights to the net assets of the arrangement.

significant influence The power to participate in the financial and operating policy decisions of the investee, but not control or joint control of those policies.

COMPREHENSION QUESTIONS

1 What is an associate entity?
2 Why are associates distinguished from other investments held by the investor?
3 Discuss the similarities and differences between the criteria used to identify subsidiaries and those used to identify associates.
4 What is meant by 'significant influence'?
5 What factors could be used to indicate the existence of significant influence?
6 What is a joint venture?
7 What is meant by 'joint control'?

8 How does joint control differ from control as applied on consolidation?

9 Discuss the relative merits of accounting for investments by the cost method, the fair value method and the equity method.

10 Outline the accounting adjustments required in relation to transactions between the investor and an associate/joint venture. Critically evaluate the rationale for these adjustments.

11 Compare the accounting for the effects of inter-entity transactions for transactions between parent entities and subsidiaries and between investors and associates/joint ventures.

12 Discuss whether the equity method should be viewed as a form of consolidation or a valuation technique.

13 Explain why equity accounting is sometimes referred to as 'one-line consolidation'.

14 Explain the differences in application of the equity method of accounting where the method is applied in the records of the investor compared with the application in the consolidation worksheet of the investor.

15 Explain the treatment of dividends from the associate under the equity method of accounting.

CASE STUDY 31.1

SIGNIFICANT INFLUENCE

The accountant of Cornett Chocolates Ltd, Ms Fraulein, has been advised by her auditors that the entity's investment in Concertina's Milk Ltd should be accounted for using the equity method of accounting. Cornett Chocolates Ltd holds only 20.2% of the voting shares currently issued by Concertina's Milk Ltd. Since the investment was undertaken purely for cash flow reasons based on the potential dividend stream from the investment, Ms Fraulein does not believe that Cornett Chocolates Ltd exerts significant influence over the investee.

Required

Discuss the factors that Ms Fraulein should investigate in determining whether an investor–associate relationship exists, and what avenues are available so that the equity method of accounting does not have to be applied.

CASE STUDY 31.2

NATURE OF A JOINT VENTURE

A shareholder of CSR Limited has come to you confused about something they have seen in Note 23 of the company's 2018 annual report. Under the heading *Equity Accounting Information* CSR lists Viridian Glass, a New Zealand-based glass products firm, as an investment in which it holds a 58% ownership interest. The shareholder believes that only ownership interests between 20% and 50% qualify for equity accounting and that investments over 50% should be treated as subsidiaries and consolidated in the financial statements.

Required

Prepare a response to the shareholder outlining why CSR could deem it appropriate to carry their 58% investment in Viridian Glass under the equity method of accounting.

CASE STUDY 31.3

Talvez Ltd, a publicly listed company, has a 19.5% shareholding in another entity. The accountant is considering whether or not this investment satisfies the definition of an associate under AASB 128/IAS 28 and the impacts the decision will have on the company's financial statements.

Required

Compare and contrast the impacts on the financial statements of applying the equity method to an investment with those of applying the cost method to the same investment.

CASE STUDY 31.4

EQUITY ACCOUNTING

Event Hospitality & Entertainment Limited provided the following information in its 2018 annual report.

Notes to the financial statements for the year ended 30 June 2018
Section 5 — group composition
5.3 — interests in other entities
Accounting policy
Interests in equity accounted investees
The Group's interests in equity accounted investees comprise interests in associates and interests in joint ventures. Associates are those entities in which the Group has significant influence, but not control or joint control, over the financial and operating policies. Significant influence is presumed to exist when the Group holds between 20% and 50% of the voting power of another entity.

Interests in associates and joint ventures (see below) are accounted for using the equity method. They are recognised initially at cost, which includes transaction costs. Subsequent to initial recognition, the consolidated financial statements include the Group's share of the profit or loss and other comprehensive income of equity accounted investees, until the date on which significant influence or joint control ceases.

Unrealised gains arising from transactions with equity accounted investees are eliminated to the extent of the Group's interest in the entity. Unrealised losses are eliminated in the same way as unrealised gains, but only to the extent that there is no evidence of impairment.

Joint arrangements
A joint arrangement is an arrangement of which two or more parties have joint control, in which the parties are bound by a contractual arrangement, and the contractual arrangement gives two or more of those parties joint control of the arrangement.

The Group classifies its interests in joint arrangements as either joint operations or joint ventures depending on the Group's rights to the assets and obligations for the liabilities of the arrangements. When making this assessment, the Group considers the structure of the arrangements, the legal form of any separate vehicles, the contractual terms of the arrangements and other facts and circumstances.

The Group's interests in joint operations, which are arrangements in which the parties have rights to the assets and obligations for the liabilities, are accounted for on the basis of the Group's interest in those assets and liabilities. The Group's interests in joint ventures, which are arrangements in which the parties have rights to the net assets, are equity accounted.

Source: Event Hospitality & Entertainment Limited (2018, p. 73).

Required

Some investors in Event Hospitality & Entertainment Ltd who have limited accounting knowledge, particularly about equity accounting, have asked you to provide a report to them commenting on:
1. the difference between significant influence and control
2. the differences between associates, joint ventures and joint arrangements
3. how the date of significant influence is determined
4. what is meant by the term unrealised gains and losses and why they are eliminated.

APPLICATION AND ANALYSIS EXERCISES

★ BASIC | ★ ★ MODERATE | ★ ★ ★ DIFFICULT

31.1 Adjustments where investor prepares and does not prepare consolidated financial
statements ★   **LO3, 4, 5**

Duckbill Ltd acquired a 30% interest in Platypus Ltd for $75 000 cash on 1 July 2021. The directors of Duckbill Ltd believe this investment represents significant influence over the investee. The equity of Platypus Ltd at the acquisition date was as follows.

Share capital	$ 45 000
Retained earnings	180 000

All the identifiable assets and liabilities of Platypus Ltd were recorded at fair value. Profits and dividends for the years ended 30 June 2022 to 2024 were as follows.

	Profit before tax	Income tax expense	Dividends paid
2022	$120 000	$45 000	$120 000
2023	105 000	37 500	30 000
2024	90 000	30 000	15 000

Required

1. Prepare journal entries in the records of Duckbill Ltd for each of the years ended 30 June 2022 to 2024 in relation to its investment in the associate, Platypus Ltd. (Assume Duckbill Ltd does not prepare consolidated financial statements.)
2. Prepare the consolidation worksheet entries to account for Duckbill Ltd's interest in the associate/joint venture, Platypus Ltd. (Assume Duckbill Ltd does prepare consolidated financial statements.)
3. Calculate the carrying amount of the investment in Platypus Ltd at 30 June 2024.

31.2 Accounting for an associate/joint venture by an investor ★   **LO4**

On 1 July 2022, Pygmy Ltd issued ordinary shares to acquire a 40% interest in Possum Ltd. On this date, these issued shares had a fair value of $170 000. The directors of Pygmy Ltd believe that they have significant influence over the financial and operating policy decisions of Possum Ltd. The share capital, reserves and retained earnings of Possum Ltd at the acquisition date and at 30 June 2023 were as follows.

	1 July 2022	30 June 2023
Share capital	$300 000	$300 000
Asset revaluation surplus	—	100 000
General reserve	—	15 000
Retained earnings	100 000	109 000
	$400 000	$524 000

At 1 July 2022, all the identifiable assets and liabilities of Possum Ltd were recorded at fair value. The following is applicable to Possum Ltd for the year to 30 June 2023.

- Profit (after income tax expense of $11 000): $39 000.
- Increase in reserves:
  – general (transferred from retained earnings): $15 000
  – asset revaluation (revaluation of freehold land and buildings at 30 June 2023): $100 000
- Dividends paid to shareholders: $15 000.
- The tax rate is 30%.
- Pygmy Ltd does not prepare consolidated financial statements.

Required

Prepare the journal entries in the records of Pygmy Ltd for the year ended 30 June 2023 in relation to its investment in the associate, Possum Ltd.

31.3 Investor prepares consolidated financial statements, multiple periods ★ ★   **LO4, 5**

On 1 July 2021, Ground Ltd purchased 30% of the shares of Hog Ltd for $180 000. At this date, the ledger balances of Hog Ltd were as follows.

Capital	450 000	Assets	675 000
Other reserves	90 000	Less: Liabilities	90 000
Retained earnings	45 000		
	585 000		585 000

At 1 July 2021, all the identifiable assets and liabilities of Hog Ltd were recorded at fair value except for plant whose fair value was $15 000 greater than carrying amount. This plant has an expected future life of 5 years, the benefits being received evenly over this period. Dividend revenue is recognised when dividends are declared. The tax rate is 30%.

The results of Hog Ltd for the next 3 years were as follows.

	30 June 2022	30 June 2023	30 June 2024
Profit/(loss) before income tax	$150 000	$120 000	$(15 000)
Income tax expense	60 000	60 000	—
Profit/(loss)	90 000	60 000	(15 000)
Dividend declared and paid	45 000	15 000	6 000
Dividend declared	30 000	15 000	3 000

Required

Prepare, in journal entry format, for the years ending 30 June 2022, 2023 and 2024, the consolidation worksheet adjustments to include the equity-accounted results for the associate, Hog Ltd, in the consolidated financial statements of Ground Ltd.

31.4 Adjustments where investor does and does not prepare consolidated financial statements ★ ★   **LO4, 5, 6**

On 1 July 2021, Saltwater Ltd acquired a 30% interest in one of its suppliers, Crocodile Ltd, at a cost of $13 650. The directors of Saltwater Ltd believe they exert 'significant influence' over Crocodile Ltd.

The equity of Crocodile Ltd at acquisition date was as follows.

Share capital (20 000 shares)	$20 000
Retained earnings	10 000

All the identifiable assets and liabilities of Crocodile Ltd at 1 July 2021 were recorded at fair values except for some depreciable non-current assets with a fair value of $15 000 greater than carrying amount. These depreciable assets are expected to have a further 5-year life.

Additional information

- At 30 June 2023, Saltwater Ltd had inventories costing $100 000 (2022: $60 000) on hand which had been purchased from Crocodile Ltd. A profit before tax of $30 000 (2022: $10 000) had been made on the sale.
- All companies adopt the recommendations of AASB 112 regarding tax-effect accounting. Assume a tax rate of 30% applies.
- Information about income and changes in equity of Crocodile Ltd as at 30 June 2023 is as follows.

Profit before tax		$360 000
Income tax expense		180 000
Profit		180 000
Retained earnings at 1/7/22		50 000
		230 000
Dividend paid	$50 000	
Dividend declared	50 000	100 000
Retained earnings at 30/6/23		$130 000

- All dividends may be assumed to be out of the profit for the current year. Dividend revenue is recognised when declared by investees.
- The equity of Crocodile Ltd at 30 June 2023 was as follows.

Share capital	$ 20 000
Asset revaluation surplus	30 000
General reserve	5 000
Retained earnings	130 000

The asset revaluation surplus arose from a revaluation of freehold land made at 30 June 2023. The general reserve arose from a transfer from retained earnings in June 2022.

Required

1. Assume Saltwater Ltd does not prepare consolidated financial statements. Prepare the journal entries in the records of Saltwater Ltd for the year ended 30 June 2023 in relation to the investment in Crocodile Ltd.

2. Assume Saltwater Ltd does prepare consolidated financial statements. Prepare the consolidated worksheet entries for the year ended 30 June 2023 for inclusion of the equity-accounted results of Crocodile Ltd.

31.5 Accounting for an associate within — and where there are no — consolidated financial statements ★ ★   **LO3, 4, 5**

On 1 July 2021, Flying Ltd purchased 40% of the shares of Fox Ltd for $63 200. At that date, equity of Fox Ltd consisted of the following.

Share capital	$125 000
Retained earnings	11 000

At 1 July 2021, the identifiable assets and liabilities of Fox Ltd were recorded at fair value. Information about income and changes in equity for both companies for the year ended 30 June 2024 was as follows.

	Flying Ltd	Fox Ltd
Profit before tax	$26 000	$23 500
Income tax expense	10 600	5 400
Profit	15 400	18 100
Retained earnings (1/7/23)	18 000	16 000
	33 400	34 100
Dividend paid	5 000	4 000
Dividend declared	10 000	5 000
	15 000	9 000
Retained earnings (30/6/24)	$18 400	$25 100

Additional information
- Flying Ltd recognises dividends as revenue when they are declared by the investee.
- On 31 December 2022, Fox Ltd sold Flying Ltd a motor vehicle for $12 000. The vehicle had originally cost Fox Ltd $18 000 and was written down to $9000 for both tax and accounting purposes at time of sale to Flying Ltd. Both companies depreciated motor vehicles at the rate of 20% p.a. on cost.
- The beginning inventories of Fox Ltd included goods at $4000 bought from Flying Ltd; their cost to Flying Ltd was $3200.
- The ending inventories of Flying Ltd included goods purchased from Fox Ltd at a profit before tax of $1600.
- The tax rate is 30%.

Required
1. Prepare the journal entries in the records of Flying Ltd to account for the investment in Fox Ltd under the equity method for the year ended 30 June 2024 assuming Flying Ltd does not prepare consolidated financial statements.
2. Prepare the consolidation worksheet entries in relation to the investment in Fox Ltd, assuming Flying Ltd does prepare consolidated financial statements at 30 June 2024.

31.6 Consolidation worksheet entries including investments in joint ventures ★ ★ ★   **LO3, 4**

You are given the following details for the year ended 30 June 2023.

	Echidna Ltd	Kangaroo Ltd	Kookaburra Ltd
Profit before tax	$400 000	$120 000	$100 000
Income tax expense	124 000	40 000	24 000
Profit	276 000	80 000	76 000
Retained earnings at 1 July 2022	80 000	48 000	44 000
	356 000	128 000	120 000
Dividend paid	56 000	24 000	8 000
Dividend declared	60 000	16 000	32 000
Transfer to general reserve			
(from current period's profit)	40 000	20 000	24 000
	156 000	60 000	64 000
Retained earnings at 30 June 2023	$200 000	$ 68 000	$ 56 000

Additional information

- Echidna Ltd owns 80% of the participating shares in Kangaroo Ltd and 20% of the shares in Kookaburra Ltd. Echidna Ltd has entered into a contractual arrangement with four other venturers in relation to Kookaburra Ltd, and the five investors have a joint control arrangement in relation to Kookaburra Ltd.
- On 1 July 2021, all identifiable assets and liabilities of Kangaroo Ltd were recorded at fair value. Echidna Ltd purchased 80% of Kangaroo Ltd's shares on 1 July 2021, and paid $20 000 for goodwill, none of which had been recorded on Kangaroo Ltd's records. Echidna Ltd uses the partial goodwill method.
- At the date Echidna Ltd acquired its shares in Kookaburra Ltd, Kookaburra Ltd's recorded equity was as follows.

Share capital	$400 000
General reserve	60 000
Retained earnings	20 000

All the identifiable assets and liabilities of Kookaburra Ltd were recorded at fair value.

Echidna Ltd paid $100 000 for its shares in Kookaburra Ltd on 1 July 2021. There was $12 000 transferred to general reserve by Kookaburra Ltd in the year ended 30 June 2022, out of equity earned since 1 July 2021.

- Included in the beginning inventories of Echidna Ltd were profits before tax made by Kangaroo Ltd: $20 000; Kookaburra Ltd: $12 000.
- Included in the ending inventories of Echidna Ltd were profits before tax made by Kookaburra Ltd: $16 000.
- Kookaburra Ltd had recorded a profit (net of $2000 tax) of $8000 in selling certain non-current assets to Echidna Ltd on 1 January 2023. Echidna Ltd treats the items as non-current assets and charges depreciation at the rate of 25% p.a. straight-line from that date.
- Echidna Ltd purchased for $40 000 an item of plant from Kangaroo Ltd on 1 September 2021. The carrying amount of the asset at that date was $28 000. The asset was depreciated at the rate of 20% p.a. straight-line from 1 September 2021.
- During the year ended 30 June 2023, Kookaburra Ltd has revalued upwards one of its non-current assets by $32 000. There had been no previous downward revaluations.
- Dividend revenue is recognised when dividends are declared.
- The tax rate is 30%.

Required

Prepare the consolidation worksheet entries (in journal form) needed for the consolidated statements for the year ended 30 June 2023 for Echidna Ltd and its subsidiary Kangaroo Ltd. Include the equity-accounted results of Kookaburra Ltd.

31.7 Inter-entity transactions where investor does not prepare consolidated financial statements ★ **LO6**

Dolphin Ltd owns 25% of the shares of its associate, Shark Ltd. At the acquisition date, there were no differences between the fair values and the carrying amounts of the identifiable assets and liabilities of Shark Ltd.

For 2022–23, Shark Ltd recorded a profit of $200 000. During this period, Shark Ltd paid a $20 000 dividend, declared in June 2022, and an interim dividend of $16 000. The tax rate is 30%.

The following transactions have occurred between Dolphin Ltd and Shark Ltd.

- On 1 July 2021, Shark Ltd sold a non-current asset costing $20 000 to Dolphin Ltd for $24 000. Dolphin Ltd applies a 10% p.a. on cost straight-line method of depreciation.
- On 1 January 2023, Shark Ltd sold an item of plant to Dolphin Ltd for $30 000. The carrying amount of the asset to Shark Ltd at time of sale was $22 000. Dolphin Ltd applies a 15% p.a. straight-line method of depreciation.
- A non-current asset with a carrying amount of $40 000 was sold by Shark Ltd to Dolphin Ltd for $56 000 on 1 June 2023. Dolphin Ltd regarded the item as inventories and still had the item on hand at 30 June 2023.
- On 1 July 2021, Dolphin Ltd sold an item of machinery to Shark Ltd for $14 000. This item had cost Dolphin Ltd $8000. Dolphin Ltd regarded this item as inventories whereas Shark Ltd intended to use the item as a non-current asset. Shark Ltd applied a 10% p.a. on cost straight-line depreciation method.

Dolphin Ltd applies the equity method in accounting for its investment in Shark Ltd.

Dolphin Ltd does not prepare consolidated financial statements.

Required

Prepare the journal entries of Dolphin Ltd for the year ended 30 June 2023 in relation to its investment in Shark Ltd.

31.8 Inter-entity transactions where investor has no subsidiaries ★   **LO6**

Dibbler Ltd acquired 20% of the ordinary shares of Potoroo Ltd on 1 July 2022. At this date, all the identifiable assets and liabilities of Potoroo Ltd were recorded at fair value. An analysis of the acquisition showed that $2000 of goodwill was acquired.

Dibbler Ltd has no subsidiaries, and records its investment in the associate, Potoroo Ltd, in accordance with AASB 128. In the 20234 period, Potoroo Ltd recorded a profit of $100 000, paid an interim dividend of $10 000 and, in June 2024, declared a further dividend of $15 000. In June 2023, Potoroo Ltd had declared a $20 000 dividend, which was paid in August 2023. Dibbler Ltd recognises dividends as revenue when they are received.

The following transactions have occurred between the two entities (all transactions are independent unless specified).

- In January 2024, Potoroo Ltd sold inventories to Dibbler Ltd for $15 000. These inventories had previously cost Potoroo Ltd $10 000, and remains unsold by Dibbler Ltd at the end of the period.
- In February 2024, Dibbler Ltd sold inventories to Potoroo Ltd at a before-tax profit of $5000. Half of this was sold by Potoroo Ltd before 30 June 2024.
- In June 2023, Potoroo Ltd sold inventories to Dibbler Ltd for $18 000. These inventories had cost Potoroo Ltd $12 000. At 30 June 2023, these inventories remained unsold by Dibbler Ltd. However, it was all sold by Dibbler Ltd before 30 June 2024.
- The tax rate is 30%.

Required

Prepare the journal entries in the records of Dibbler Ltd in relation to its investment in Potoroo Ltd for the year ended 30 June 2024.

31.9 Consolidated financial statements including investments in associates ★ ★ ★   **LO3, 4, 5, 7**

Box Ltd acquired 90% of the ordinary shares of Jelly Ltd on 1 July 2018 at a cost of $150 750. At that date the equity of Jelly Ltd was as follows.

Share capital (100 000 shares)	$100 000
General reserve	8 000
Retained earnings	12 000

At 1 July 2018, all the identifiable assets and liabilities of Jelly Ltd were at fair value except for the following assets.

	Carrying amount	Fair value
Inventories	$10 000	$15 000
Depreciable assets	25 000	35 000

The inventories was all sold by 30 June 2019. Depreciable assets have an expected further 5-year life, with depreciation being calculated on a straight-line basis. Valuation adjustments are made on consolidation.

Box Ltd uses the partial goodwill method.

On 1 July 2021, Box Ltd acquired 25% of the capital of Fish Ltd for $3500 entering into a joint venture with three other venturers. All the identifiable assets and liabilities of Fish Ltd were recorded at fair value except for the following.

	Carrying amount	Fair value
Inventories	$1 000	$1 500
Depreciable assets	6 000	7 000

All these inventories were sold in the 12 months after 1 July 2021. The depreciable assets were considered to have a further 5-year life.

Information on Fish Ltd's equity position is as follows.

	1 July 2021	30 June 2022
Share capital	$10 000	$10 000
General reserve	–	2 000
Retained earnings	2 150	4 000

For the year ended 30 June 2023, Fish Ltd recorded a profit before tax of $2600 and an income tax expense of $600. Fish Ltd paid a dividend of $200 in January 2023. Box Ltd regards Fish Ltd as a joint venture investee.

During the year ended 30 June 2023, Fish Ltd sold inventories to Jelly Ltd for $6000. The cost of these inventories to Fish Ltd was $4000. Jelly Ltd has resold only 20% of these items. However, Jelly Ltd made a profit before tax of $500 on the resale of these items.

On 1 January 2022, Box Ltd sold Fish Ltd a motor vehicle for $4000, at a profit before tax of $800 to Box Ltd. Both companies treat motor vehicles as non-current assets. Both companies charge depreciation at 20% p.a. on the diminishing balance.

Assume a tax rate of 30%.

Information about income and changes in equity for Box Ltd and its subsidiary, Jelly Ltd, for the year ended 30 June 2023 is as follows.

	Box Ltd	Jelly Ltd
Sales revenue	$200 000	$60 000
Less: Cost of sales	110 000	30 000
Gross profit	90 000	30 000
Less: Depreciation	16 000	4 000
Other expenses	22 000	3 000
	38 000	7 000
	52 000	23 000
Plus: Other revenue	30 000	5 000
Profit before income tax	82 000	28 000
Less: Income tax expense	20 000	10 000
Profit	62 000	18 000
Plus: Retained earnings (1/7/22)	120 000	80 000
	182 000	98 000
Less: Dividend paid	20 000	4 000
Retained earnings (30/6/23)	$162 000	$94 000

Required

1. Prepare the consolidated statement of profit or loss and other comprehensive income of Box Ltd and its subsidiary Jelly Ltd as at 30 June 2023.
2. In the consolidated statement of financial position, what would be the balance of the investment shares in Fish Ltd?

REFERENCES

CSR Limited 2018, *Annual report 2018*, www.csr.com.au.
Event Hospitality & Entertainment Limited 2018, *Annual report 2018*, www.evt.com.
Wesfarmers Limited 2018, *2018 annual report*, www.wesfarmers.com.au.

ACKNOWLEDGEMENTS

Figure 31.1: © Wesfarmers Limited 2018
Figure 31.4: © CSR Limited 2018
Case study 31.4: © Event Hospitality & Entertainment Limited 2018

CHAPTER 32

Joint arrangements

CHAPTER AIM

This chapter discusses the application of AASB 11/IFRS 11 *Joint Arrangements*. The objective of this standard is to establish principles for financial reporting by entities that have an interest in arrangements that are controlled jointly. To meet this objective, the standard provides a definition of joint control, criteria to classify joint arrangements into joint ventures and joint operations, and principles for accounting for joint arrangements.

LEARNING OBJECTIVES

After studying this chapter, you should be able to:

32.1 discuss the use of joint arrangements by companies to structure their business

32.2 explain the nature of a joint arrangement and how to classify joint arrangements into joint ventures and joint operations

32.3 explain the accounting undertaken by a joint operation

32.4 prepare the journal entries required by a joint operator to recognise its share of the assets, liabilities, revenues and expenses of the joint operation

32.5 discuss the disclosures required in relation to joint operations.

CONCEPTS FOR REVIEW

Before studying this chapter, you should understand and, if necessary, revise:

• the nature of associates and joint ventures
• the concepts of significant influence and joint control.

32.1 Introduction and scope

LEARNING OBJECTIVE 32.1 Discuss the use of joint arrangements by companies to structure their business.

This chapter is concerned with situations where entities join together to seek a common goal. These entities sign contracts requiring them to act together and to agree on the major decisions involving the entities' activities in relation to specified projects. The purpose of joining together may be for varied reasons. Sometimes, it is to share costs or to manage the risk involved in a project. Alternatively, it may be to provide the parties with access to new technology or new markets. These contractual arrangements, if they meet certain conditions, are described as **joint arrangements**, the key feature of which is that the parties involved have joint control over the decision making in relation to the joint arrangement.

Joint arrangements can be established for many reasons such as the joint development of new technologies where there are risks in terms of eventual success, the need for application of specialised skills such as in the manufacture of aircraft, or where a joint product may be more acceptable to the market such as a tourist resort partnering with an airline to provide 'fly and stay' packages to travellers. CSR Limited and Boral Limited issued a press release to announce their proposal 'to form a joint venture to combine their brick operations on the east coast of Australia'. Part of the press release is reproduced in figure 32.1.

FIGURE 32.1	Proposal to form a joint venture, Boral and CSR

> ## Proposal to form a joint venture, Boral and CSR
>
> The proposed joint venture will be owned 60% by CSR and 40% by Boral reflecting the relative valuation of the two businesses. There is no cash consideration as part of the proposed joint venture.
>
> Brick demand in Australia has experienced a sustained structural decline, with bricks becoming an increasingly smaller component of the broader cladding market. Lower brick demand has resulted in declining capacity utilisation, reduced profitability, plant curtailments and closures.
>
> The proposed transaction will enable both Boral and CSR to access additional operational and overhead efficiencies that would otherwise be unavailable to the parties acting independently.
>
> With combined revenue in the order of $230 million, initial overhead savings of $7–$10 million per annum are expected following the formation of the joint venture and integration of the businesses. Longer term, consolidation of selected manufacturing sites will lower per unit costs of production and enable both companies to develop selected high value land assets without impacting product range and operational capability. It also positions the business to deliver returns that recover the cost of capital through building cycles ...
>
> ### Benefits of the proposed transaction
> The proposed transaction will enable Boral and CSR to deliver a number of efficiencies that would be unavailable to the parties acting independently including:
> - Consolidate overhead costs including sales, administrative and marketing through a single management structure.
> - Develop more efficient freight and distribution networks, leveraging the location of the combined manufacturing footprint to improve service and reduce costs.
> - Potentially rationalise the number of sites in some states, particularly where sites have been mothballed while investing in other sites to improve operational and technical efficiency.
> - Allow redevelopment of certain land assets over time, without foregoing the ability to provide a similar product range and operational capability.
>
> Cost synergies as a result of the formation of the joint venture are expected to position the combined business to recover the cost of capital over the longer term. This in turn will ensure the sustainability of the Boral and CSR bricks businesses.
>
> *Source:* CSR Limited (2014).

Joint arrangements do not need to have investors that have equal interests in the project. As explained later in this chapter, decision making of the arrangement on a joint control basis is a key element of a joint arrangement and requires the unanimous agreement of all parties involved.

This chapter examines accounting standard AASB 11/IFRS 11 *Joint Arrangements*. The standard deals with both joint ventures and joint operations. While accounting for joint ventures is discussed in chapter 31 of this text, this chapter focuses on accounting for joint operations.

32.2 Joint arrangements: characteristics and classification

LEARNING OBJECTIVE 32.2 Explain the nature of a joint arrangement and how to classify joint arrangements into joint ventures and joint operations.

32.2.1 The characteristics of a joint arrangement

The term 'arrangement' describes an activity, operation or specific grouping of assets and liabilities, which may or may not form a legal entity such as a company. As described in paragraph 4 of AASB 11/IFRS 11, a joint arrangement arises where two or more entities have an arrangement between each other such that these entities have joint control of the arrangement. For example, Entity A and Entity B may agree to form Entity C and the management of Entity C is under the joint control of both Entity A and Entity B.

Paragraph 5 of AASB 11/IFRS 11 lists the two main characteristics of a joint arrangement:

1. the parties are bound by a contractual arrangement
2. the contractual arrangement gives two or more of those parties joint control of the arrangement.

Contractual arrangement

The agreement between the parties is in the form of a contract, which would generally be in writing. The contractual arrangement may be written into the articles of association or constitution of the entities themselves.

As described in paragraph B4 of Appendix B of AASB 11/IFRS 11, the agreement sets out the terms under which the parties agree to participate in relation to the joint activity. It would contain such matters as:

(a) the purpose, activity and duration of the joint arrangement.
(b) how the members of the board of directors, or equivalent governing body, of the joint arrangement, are appointed.
(c) the decision-making process: the matters requiring decisions from the parties, the voting rights of the parties and the required level of support for those matters. The decision-making process reflected in the contractual arrangement establishes joint control of the arrangement.
(d) the capital or other contributions required of the parties.
(e) how the parties share assets, liabilities, revenues, expenses or profit or loss relating to the joint arrangement.

An example of where a contractual arrangement is necessary in order for a joint arrangement to exist is shown in figure 32.2.

FIGURE 32.2 Contractual arrangements

Assume an arrangement in which A and B each have 35% of the voting rights in the arrangement with the remaining 30% being widely dispersed. Decisions about the relevant activities require approval by a majority of the voting rights.

If there is a contractual arrangement between A and B which specifies that decisions about the relevant activities of the arrangement require both A and B agreeing, then A and B have joint control over the arrangement. No decision about the relevant activities can be made without the agreement of both A and B.

In the absence of such an agreement, no entity has any form of control over the arrangement as a decision can be made about the relevant activities if any combination of either A, B or C agree to it. In

Joint control

The criterion that identifies a contractual arrangement as a joint arrangement is that of joint control. Joint control is defined in Appendix A of AASB 11/IFRS 11 as:

[t]he contractually agreed sharing of control of an arrangement which exists only when decisions about the relevant activities require the unanimous consent of the parties sharing control.

Note the two key characteristics of joint control:
1. there exists a contractually agreed sharing of control
2. the agreement is that decisions about the relevant activities require the *unanimous* consent of the parties sharing control (i.e. no party can make a unilateral decision about relevant activities).

Each party that has joint control is referred to as a joint venture or a joint operator. Other entities in the joint arrangement are a *party to a joint arrangement*. If in the example in figure 32.2 there is a contractual agreement between A and B, then A and B are joint venturers or joint operators while the holders of the widely dispersed 30% of voting interests are parties to the joint arrangement.

Where a joint arrangement exists there is no single entity that has control. The joint venturers/operators must act together to manage the affairs of the arrangement.

In assessing whether joint control exists, judgement will need to be exercised, and all facts and circumstances will need to be examined (AASB 11/IFRS 11 paragraph 12). If the facts and circumstances change, paragraph 13 requires a reassessment of the existence of joint control.

Note that the agreement may not use the term 'joint control' but the existence of joint control may be implicit in the arrangement. For example, consider a situation where A and B each have 50% of the voting interest in an arrangement and under the terms of the contract any decision about relevant activities requires at least 51% of the votes. In such a case, decisions can be made only where A and B agree. The terms of the contract required A and B to act jointly even if the contractual agreement does not refer to joint control.

There are two steps in the assessment of the existence of joint control.
1. Assess whether the parties to the arrangement have *control*. Control is defined in Appendix A of AASB 10/IFRS 10 *Consolidated Financial Statements* and exists in a joint arrangement when two or more investors in the arrangement are exposed, or have rights, to variable returns from their involvement with the arrangement, and have the ability to affect those returns through their power over the arrangement. Control must be over the 'relevant' activities. These are also defined in AASB 10/IFRS 10 and refer to those activities of the arrangement that significantly affect the returns of the arrangement.
2. Assess whether two or more parties have *joint control*. The control over the arrangement must be in the hands of more than one party to the arrangement. This assessment requires the determination of the existence of a contractual arrangement requiring the unanimous consent of the parties sharing control in relation to the relevant activities.

32.2.2 The classification of a joint arrangement

Having determined that a joint arrangement exists, it is then necessary to classify it. There are two types of joint arrangements, namely joint ventures and joint operations. Appendix A of AASB 11/IFRS 11 defines a **joint venture** as:

[a] joint arrangement whereby the parties that have joint control of the arrangement have rights to the net assets of the arrangement.

It defines a **joint operation** as:

[a] joint arrangement whereby the parties that have **joint control** of the arrangement have rights to the assets, and obligations for the liabilities, relating to the arrangement.

The parties to a joint venture are called **joint venturers**. The parties to a joint operation are called **joint operators**.

Note in particular that paragraph 14 of AASB 11/IFRS 11 states that the key element in the classification of a joint arrangement is the rights and obligations of the parties to the arrangement. For a joint operation the rights pertain to the rights and obligations associated with *individual* assets and liabilities, whereas with a joint venture, the rights and obligations pertain to the *net assets* (i.e. the investment in net assets).

The assessment of the classification of a joint arrangement is not straightforward; it requires judgement.

According to paragraph 17 of AASB 11/IFRS 11, the assessment of the rights and obligations in an arrangement involves analysing four factors:

1. the structure of the arrangement
2. the legal form of the arrangement
3. the terms agreed to by the parties in the contractual arrangement
4. any other relevant facts and circumstances.

Each of these factors will be considered separately.

1. Structure of the arrangement

The main issue here is whether or not the arrangement is structured through a 'separate vehicle'. A **separate vehicle** is defined in Appendix A of AASB 11/IFRS 11 as:

> [a] separately identifiable financial structure, including separate legal entities or entities recognised by statute, regardless of whether those entities have a legal personality.

A separate vehicle would include a company. For example, if Qantas Airways Ltd and Cathay Pacific Airways Limited formed a company, Viking Airlines, to manage flights between countries such as Sweden, Finland, Norway and Denmark, then Viking Airlines would be a separate vehicle.

If the joint arrangement *is not* structured through a separate vehicle, then, as stated in paragraph B16 of AASB 11/IFRS 11, the arrangement is classified as a joint operation. The contractual arrangement would establish the parties' rights to the assets and obligations for the liabilities of the arrangement as well as the rights to revenues and obligations for expenses of the arrangement. For example, the government may put out tenders to build a fighter aircraft for the Australian Air Force. Three companies put in a joint tender which is successful. The three companies establish a joint arrangement under which Company A builds the engines for the aircraft, Company B builds the aircraft itself, while Company C is responsible for the computer software for the aircraft. Each company is then responsible for a specific task and uses its own assets and incurs its own liabilities in relation to the agreed task.

If the joint arrangement *is* structured through a separate vehicle, then the arrangement can be either a joint operation or a joint venture. This determination is based on an analysis of the remaining three factors noted above. This classification process may be expressed in the form of a decision tree as shown in figure 32.3.

2. The legal form of the separate vehicle

In considering the legal form of the separate vehicle the main area of interest is how the legal form affects the rights to the assets and obligations for the liabilities. If the legal form establishes rights to *individual assets and obligations*, the arrangement is a joint operation. If the legal form establishes rights to the *net assets* of the arrangement, then the arrangement is a joint venture.

To establish the arrangement as a joint operation, the legal form of the separate vehicle must not establish a separation between the parties and the separate vehicle. The assets and liabilities of the separate vehicle must be the parties' assets and liabilities, and not those of the separate vehicle itself.

Note, however, that an assessment of the legal form may not be sufficient. The terms of the contractual arrangement may override the legal form. In other words, just because the legal form of the separate vehicle is a company does not mean that the arrangement is a joint venture.

3. The terms of the contractual arrangement

Generally the choice of the legal form of the arrangement would be such as to reflect the rights and obligations of the parties to the arrangement. However, in other cases, the terms of the contractual arrangement may override the rights and obligations conferred by the legal form chosen. For example, the form of the structured vehicle may be an incorporated entity. Being an incorporated entity, the entity is separate from the owners of the entity. Incorporation establishes that the assets and liabilities of the entity are separate from those of the owners of the entity. The legal form is such that the owners have rights to the net assets of the entity. However, the contractual arrangement could be written such that the owners are given an interest in the individual assets of the incorporated entity and are responsible for the liabilities of the incorporated entity. The legal form would have suggested that a joint venture exists; however, the terms of the contractual arrangement have modified the legal form such that the arrangement is a joint operation.

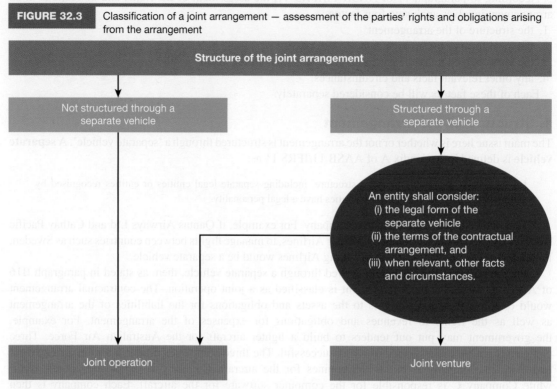

FIGURE 32.3 Classification of a joint arrangement — assessment of the parties' rights and obligations arising from the arrangement

Source: AASB 11, Appendix B.

4. Other facts and circumstances

The terms of the contractual arrangement may not specify the rights and obligations of the parties to the assets and liabilities of the joint arrangements. An assessment of other facts and circumstances of the arrangement may assist in classifying the arrangement.

One fact to consider is whether the arrangement is designed to provide *output* to the parties to the arrangement. In the example used above where Qantas Airways Ltd and Cathay Pacific Airways Limited established Viking Airlines, it would be usual for Viking Airlines to be managed with the objective of producing a profit for the company with dividends being paid to the owners of that company. However, in other situations, a joint arrangement may be established with the objective of producing a product that is distributed to the owners of the company who then decide on how to use or sell that product. The profit is then generated by the owners of the company subsequent to receipt of the output from the joint arrangement. These forms of joint arrangements are generally classified as joint operations. For example, two companies may agree to work together to produce bottled water from a mountain spring. The agreement is that the output from the arrangement, namely bottled water, is then distributed to each of the joint operators. Each operator is then responsible for distributing the bottled water under its own label for sale and marketing purposes. The joint operation manufactures the product and determines a cost of the output to the joint operators. The parties to the joint arrangement have a right to substantially all the economic benefits of the assets held by the arrangement.

Another feature of such an arrangement is, as a result of the decision to supply the output of the joint arrangement to the parties themselves, there is no cash inflow to the joint arrangement from the sale of the product. The joint arrangement relies solely on the parties to the arrangement for the supply of cash to continue the operations of the arrangement as well as to pay for the liabilities incurred by the arrangement. The parties themselves are then responsible for the liabilities of the arrangement as the latter has no facility to be able to generate cash for the settlement of liabilities.

Figure 32.4 contains an example of where the structured vehicle is an incorporated entity. The assets and liabilities of the incorporated entity are those of the entity. However, the facts and circumstances are such that the incorporated entity produces output that is distributed to the owners of the incorporated entity. Note the form of the arrangement given in figure 32.4 leads to the conclusion that the incorporated entity is a joint operation, not a joint venture.

FIGURE 32.4   Facts and circumstances affecting classification of joint arrangements

Assume that two parties structure a joint arrangement in an incorporated entity (Entity C) in which each party has a 50% ownership interest. The purpose of the arrangement is to manufacture materials required by the parties for their own individual manufacturing processes. The arrangement ensures that the parties operate the facility that produces the materials to the quantity and quality specifications of the parties.

The legal form of Entity C (an incorporated entity) through which the activities are conducted initially indicates that the assets and liabilities held in Entity C are the assets and liabilities of Entity C. The contractual arrangement between the parties does not specify that the parties have rights to the assets or obligations for the liabilities of Entity C. Accordingly, the legal form of Entity C and the terms of the contractual arrangement indicate that the arrangement is a joint venture.

However, the parties also consider the following aspects of the arrangement:
- The parties agreed to purchase all the output produced by Entity C in a ratio of 50:50. Entity C cannot sell any of the output to third parties, unless this is approved by the two parties to the arrangement. Because the purpose of the arrangement is to provide the parties with output they require, such sales to third parties are expected to be uncommon and not material.
- The price of the output sold to the parties is set by both parties at a level that is designed to cover the costs of production and administrative expenses incurred by Entity C. On the basis of this operating model, the arrangement is intended to operate at a break-even level.

From the fact pattern above, the following facts and circumstances are relevant:
- The obligation of the parties to purchase all the output produced by Entity C reflects the exclusive dependence of Entity C upon the parties for the generation of cash flows and, thus, the parties have an obligation to fund the settlement of the liabilities of Entity C.
- The fact that the parties have rights to all the output produced by Entity C means that the parties are consuming, and therefore have rights to, all the economic benefits of the assets of Entity C.

These facts and circumstances indicate that the arrangement is a joint operation. The conclusion about the classification of the joint arrangement in these circumstances would not change if, instead of the parties using their share of the output themselves in a subsequent manufacturing process, the parties sold their share of the output to third parties.

If the parties changed the terms of the contractual arrangement so that the arrangement was able to sell output to third parties, this would result in Entity C assuming demand, inventories and credit risks. In that scenario, such a change in the facts and circumstances would require reassessment of the classification of the joint arrangement. Such facts and circumstances would indicate that the arrangement is a joint venture.

Source: AASB 11, Appendix B, Example 5.

The classification of a joint arrangement structured through a separate vehicle may be seen as a decision tree as shown in figure 32.5.

LEARNING CHECK

- ☐ A joint arrangement has two main characteristics:
  - the parties are bound by a contractual arrangement
  - the contractual arrangement gives two or more parties joint control of the arrangement.
- ☐ Joint arrangements can be classified into joint operations and joint ventures. The key element in the classification is the determination of the rights and obligations of the parties to the arrangement.
- ☐ For a joint operation the rights pertain to the rights and obligations associated with individual assets and liabilities, whereas with a joint venture the rights and obligations pertain to the net assets; that is, the investment in net assets.
- ☐ The process of classification requires an analysis of four factors:
  - the structure of the arrangement
  - the legal form of the arrangement
  - the terms agreed to by the parties in the contractual arrangement
  - any other relevant facts and circumstances.

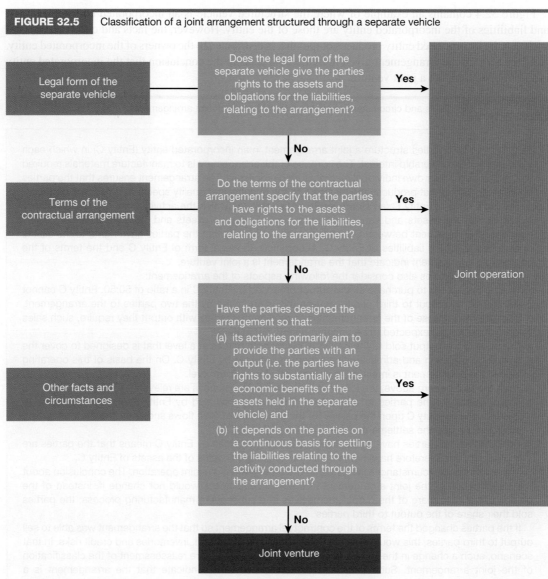

FIGURE 32.5 Classification of a joint arrangement structured through a separate vehicle

Legal form of the separate vehicle

Does the legal form of the separate vehicle give the parties rights to the assets and obligations for the liabilities, relating to the arrangement? — **Yes** →

No ↓

Terms of the contractual arrangement

Do the terms of the contractual arrangement specify that the parties have rights to the assets and obligations for the liabilities, relating to the arrangement? — **Yes** →

No ↓

Other facts and circumstances

Have the parties designed the arrangement so that:
(a) its activities primarily aim to provide the parties with an output (i.e. the parties have rights to substantially all the economic benefits of the assets held in the separate vehicle) and
(b) it depends on the parties on a continuous basis for settling the liabilities relating to the activity conducted through the arrangement? — **Yes** →

No ↓

Joint operation

Joint venture

Source: AASB 11, Appendix B.

32.3 Accounting for joint arrangements

LEARNING OBJECTIVE 32.3 Explain the accounting undertaken by a joint operation.

The accounting for a joint venture is different from that of a joint operation. Regarding a joint venture, the joint venturers have an interest in the investment in the joint arrangement. The accounting for this interest is done by application of the equity method in accordance with AASB 128/IAS 28 *Investments in Associates and Joint Ventures*. The details of accounting for joint ventures are given in chapter 31.

32.3.1 Accounting by the joint operation itself

Where the joint operation is undertaken outside a formal structure, such as a corporation or partnership, separate accounting records do not need to be kept for the joint operation. However, for accountability reasons it is expected that the joint operation agreement would require these records.

AASB 11/IFRS 11 does not provide standards on accounting for the joint operation itself. If the joint operation does not sell the output produced, but rather distributes it to the operators, there is no profit or loss account raised by the operation. In preparing accounts for the joint operation, the main purpose is to accumulate costs as incurred. These are capitalised into a work in progress account, which is transferred to the operators as inventories. Further, the joint operation's accounts provide information about the assets and liabilities relating to the joint operation as well as the contributions from the operators. Hence, a statement of financial position is the joint operation's main financial statement.

Illustrative example 32.1 demonstrates the accounting system within the joint operation. The journal entries represent the establishment of the joint operation and its activities throughout the year. Transactions that occur regularly throughout the year, such as payment of wages, are accumulated into one entry.

From this example it can be seen that the costs of producing the output are accumulated in the joint operation's accounts, and the inventories, at cost, are distributed to the joint operators. In this example, all costs are capitalised into inventories. In some cases, the costs may be transferred to the operators' accounts as expenses and matched in the records of the operators with the revenue from sale of the output. For example, if the joint operation involved exploring for minerals, it may be desirable to expense the costs of exploration and evaluation rather than capitalise them for allocation to future inventories. Similarly, where depreciation is charged on non-current assets, the depreciation expense may not, as in this example, be charged in the accounts of the joint operation itself. Instead, a charge for depreciation may be made in the records of each operator.

ILLUSTRATIVE EXAMPLE 32.1

Accounting by an unincorporated joint operation

On 1 July 2025, X Ltd and Y Ltd signed an agreement to form a joint operation to manufacture a product called Plasboard. This product is used in the packaging industry and has the advantages of the strength and protection qualities of cardboard as well as the flexibility and durability of plastic.

To commence the operation, both operators contributed $1 500 000 in cash. In the example it is assumed that not all the raw materials are used during the period, and not all finished goods have been transferred to the operators.

The journal entries in the joint operation's accounts for the year ended 30 June 2026 are as follows.

Contributions of cash by the operators

Cash	Dr	3 000 000	
X Ltd — contribution	Cr		1 500 000
Y Ltd — contribution	Cr		1 500 000
(Contributions by operators)			

Use of cash and loan to buy equipment and raw materials

Equipment	Dr	800 000	
Cash	Cr		500 000
Loan — equipment	Cr		300 000
(Acquisition of equipment)			
Raw materials	Dr	650 000	
Trade creditors	Cr		650 000
(Acquisition of materials)			

Payment of wages

Wages — management	Dr	200 000	
Wages — other	Dr	520 000	
Cash	Cr		700 000
Accrued wages	Cr		20 000
(Annual wages)			

▶

Borrowing from the bank

Cash		Dr	500 000
Bank loan		Cr	500 000
(Amount borrowed)			

Repayment of loan and other expenses

Loan — equipment		Dr	100 000
Cash		Cr	100 000
(Part payment for loan on equipment)			
Trade creditors		Dr	420 000
Cash		Cr	420 000
(Payment of trade creditors)			
Overhead expenses		Dr	1 300 000
Cash		Cr	1 300 000
(Payment of manufacturing expenses such as electricity)			

Depreciation of equipment

Depreciation expense		Dr	80 000
Accumulated depreciation		Cr	80 000
(Depreciation of equipment)			

Transfer of expenses to work in progress

Work in progress		Dr	2 580 000
Wages		Cr	720 000
Raw materials		Cr	480 000
Overhead expenses		Cr	1 300 000
Depreciation expense		Cr	80 000
(Allocating of costs to work in progress)			

Transfer from work in progress to inventories

Inventories		Dr	1 800 000
Work in progress		Cr	1 800 000
(Allocation to finished goods inventories)			

Transfer of inventories to operators throughout the year

X Ltd		Dr	800 000
Y Ltd		Dr	800 000
Inventories		Cr	1 600 000
(Delivery of output to operators)			

The major ledger accounts of interest in relation to the joint operation are as follows.

Cash			
Contribution — X Ltd	1 500 000	Equipment	500 000
Contribution — Y Ltd	1 500 000	Wages	700 000
Bank loan	500 000	Loan — equipment	100 000
		Trade creditors	420 000
		Overhead expenses	
		Balance c/d	1 300 000
			480 000
	3 500 000		3 500 000
Balance b/d	480 000		

Work in progress			
Wages	720 000	Inventories	1 800 000
Raw materials	480 000		
Overhead	1 300 000		
Depreciation	80 000	Balance c/d	780 000
	2 580 000		2 580 000
Balance c/d	780 000		

The statement of financial position of the joint operation at 30 June 2026 would be as follows.

Statement of financial position as at 30 June 2026		
Current assets		
Raw materials	$ 170 000	
Inventories	200 000	
Work in progress	780 000	
Cash	480 000	
Total current assets		$1 630 000
Non-current assets		
Equipment	800 000	
Accumulated depreciation	(80 000)	720 000
Total assets		2 350 000
Current liabilities		
Trade creditors	230 000	
Accrued wages	20 000	
Total current liabilities		250 000
Non-current liabilities		
Bank loan	500 000	
Loan — equipment	200 000	
Total non-current liabilities		700 000
Total liabilities		950 000
Net assets		**$1 400 000**
Joint operators' equity		
X Ltd: Contributions — at 1/7/25	$1 500 000	
Cost of inventories distributed	(800 000)	$ 700 000
Y Ltd: Contributions — at 1/7/25	1 500 000	
Cost of inventories distributed	(800 000)	700 000
Total joint operators' equity		**$1 400 000**

32.4 Accounting by a joint operator

LEARNING OBJECTIVE 32.4 Prepare the journal entries required by a joint operator to recognise its share of the assets, liabilities, revenues and expenses of the joint operation.

The key feature of a joint operation is that the joint operator has an interest in the individual assets and liabilities of the joint operation. In the situation where the joint operation produces an output which is distributed to the joint operators, the joint operator will receive a share of the output of the joint operation as well as be responsible for a share of the expenses of the operation that are not capitalised into the cost of the output.

Hence, each joint operator needs to recognise in its own accounts:
(a) its share of any jointly held assets
(b) its share of any jointly held liabilities
(c) its revenue from the sale of any output received from the joint operation
(d) its share of any revenue from the sale of any product that is jointly constructed by the joint operators
(e) its share of any expenses incurred by the joint operation
(f) its expenses incurred in construction of a joint product.

Hence, in accounting for a joint operation where output is distributed to the joint operators, each joint operator will view the accounts of the joint operation as shown in section 32.3.1 and calculate its share of each of the relevant accounts. At the end of each period, each venturer will analyse and account for movements in those accounts.

32.4.1 Contributions of cash to a joint operation

Illustrative example 32.2 demonstrates the entries required when joint operators' contribute cash to a joint operation.

ILLUSTRATIVE EXAMPLE 32.2

Contribution of cash by a joint operator

On 1 July 2022, Sydney Ltd and Melbourne Ltd establish a joint operation to manufacture a product. Each company has a 50% interest in the operation and shares output equally. To commence the operation, both companies contribute cash of $1 500 000 on 1 July 2022. Each operator depreciates equipment at 10% p.a. on cost.

The following information was extracted from the accounts and financial statements of the joint operation as at 30 June 2023.

Statement of financial position (extract) as at 30 June 2023	
Assets	
Cash	$ 420 000
Raw materials	100 000
Work in progress	650 000
Inventories	200 000
Equipment	1 500 000
Total assets	2 870 000
Liabilities	
Accounts payable (raw materials)	120 000
Accrued expenses (wages)	150 000
Bank loan	1 000 000
Total liabilities	1 270 000
Net assets	**$1 600 000**

Cash receipts and payments for the year ended 30 June 2023	Payments	Receipts
Contributions		$3 000 000
Bank loan		1 000 000
Equipment (purchased 3/7/22)	$1 500 000	
Wages	500 000	
Accounts payable (raw materials)	380 000	
Overhead expenses	1 200 000	
	$3 580 000	$4 000 000

Costs incurred for the year ended 30 June 2023	
Wages	$ 650 000
Raw materials	400 000
Overhead expenses	1 200 000
	2 250 000
Less: Cost of inventories	1 600 000
Work in progress at 30/6/23	$ 650 000

Required

Prepare the journal entries in the records of Sydney Ltd and Melbourne Ltd for the year ended 30 June 2023.

Solution

Records of Sydney Ltd

At 1 July 2022, Sydney Ltd records its interest in the joint operation, the asset cash being distinguished as an asset in a joint operation by the use of (JO).

Cash in joint operation (JO)	Dr	1 500 000	
Cash	Cr		1 500 000
(Contribution of cash to joint operation)			

At 30 June 2023, the joint operation has used the cash to acquire various assets, undertake loans, incur expenses and manufacture inventories. As a contributor of 50% of the cash into the joint operation, Sydney Ltd is entitled to 50% of all the assets, liabilities, expenses and output of the joint operation.

From the statement of financial position of the joint operation, it should be noted that the net assets of the joint operation amount to $1 600 000 (i.e. $2 870 000 – $1 270 000). The inventories in the statement of financial position amount to $200 000. From the costs incurred information, it can be seen that the joint operation has produced $1 600 000 worth of inventories. If only $200 000 is still on hand in the joint operation, then $1 400 000 worth of inventories must have been transferred to the joint operators (i.e. $700 000 each).

On transfer of inventories to the joint operators, the joint operation reduces the inventories balance and reduces the equity contribution of the joint operators. The contributions section of the statement of financial position of the joint operation at the end of the period, after the transfer of inventories, is as follows.

Sydney Ltd:	Initial contribution	$1 500 000	
	Less: Inventories transferred	(700 000)	$ 800 000
Melbourne Ltd:	Initial contribution	1 500 000	
	Less: Inventories transferred	(700 000)	800 000
			$1 600 000

At 30 June 2023, Sydney Ltd makes the following entry in its records to replace 'cash in JO' with a 50% share of each of the accounts — assets and liabilities — in the statement of financial position of the joint operation at 30 June 2023. The entry also recognises the inventories of $700 000 transferred to Sydney Ltd from the joint operation.

Raw material in JO [$100 000/2]	Dr	50 000	
Work in progress in JO [$650 000/2]	Dr	325 000	
Inventories in JO [$200 000/2]	Dr	100 000	
Equipment in JO [$1 500 000/2]	Dr	750 000	
Inventories [$1 400 000/2]	Dr	700 000	
Accounts payable in JO [$120 000/2]	Cr		60 000
Accrued expenses in JO [$150 000/2]	Cr		75 000
Bank loan in JO [$1 ;000 000/2]	Cr		500 000
Cash in JO [$1 500 000 – ($420 000/2)]	Cr		1 290 000

Note that Sydney Ltd's share of cash in the joint operation is calculated by finding the difference between the share at the beginning of the period, the initial contribution in this example, and the share at the end of the period.

Sydney Ltd depreciates the equipment in its own records. Therefore, having recognised an asset at $750 000, Sydney Ltd would also pass the following entry at 30 June 2023.

Depreciation expense [10% × $750 000]	Dr	75 000	
Accumulated depreciation	Cr		75 000
(Depreciation on equipment in the joint operation)			

Records of Melbourne Ltd

As Melbourne Ltd contributed the same asset (cash of $1 500 000) to the joint operation as Sydney Ltd, the journal entries in the records of Melbourne Ltd would be the same as that in Sydney Ltd.

32.4.2 Contributions of assets to a joint operation

In illustrative example 32.2, the joint operators contributed cash to the joint operation. However, in some cases a joint operator may contribute assets other than cash to the joint operation. For example, one of the joint operators in a mining arrangement may also manufacture mining equipment. This joint operator may contribute equipment to the joint operation while the other operators may contribute cash.

Where an operator contributes a non-current asset to the joint operation, the value of the contribution is effectively the fair value of that non-current asset. Hence, if one operator contributed $100 000 cash and the other operator a non-current asset, then for both parties to agree to join there would have to be agreement that the non-current asset being contributed had a fair value of $100 000. If all operators contributed non-current assets, then some form of valuation of the contributions would need to be made by the parties involved.

However, as the transaction is not an arm's length transaction, a joint operator contributing assets other than cash cannot transfer the asset at fair value to the joint operation and recognise a full profit on the transaction (AASB 11/IFRS 11 paragraph B34). The joint operator can only recognise gains and losses on such transactions to the extent of the other parties' interests in the joint operation.

Assume operator Alice Ltd carries a non-current asset *at fair value* in its accounts; for example, an item of plant for $100 000. If this asset is contributed to a joint operation whereas the other operator, Springs Ltd, contributes cash of $100 000, the journal entry to record the contribution in the records of Alice Ltd is as follows.

Cash in JO [$100 000/2]	Dr	50 000
Plant in JO [$100 000/2]	Dr	50 000
Plant	Cr		100 000

In the records of Springs Ltd, the entry is as follows.

Cash in JO [$100 000/2]	Dr	50 000
Plant in JO [$100 000/2]	Dr	50 000
Cash	Cr		100 000

Note that in the records of both operators the plant in the joint operation is recorded at the same amount, namely $50 000.

However, the accounting records of an operator that contributes a non-current asset is more complicated when the operator carries the contributed asset in its records at an amount *less than fair value*.

In contributing an asset to the joint operation, the operator is effectively selling a proportion of that asset to the other joint operators, and retaining a proportion for itself. Where the carrying amount of the asset is lower than the fair value, the operator makes a profit on selling the proportion of the asset to the other operators. The profit is the difference between the fair value and carrying amount of the proportion of the asset sold.

Assume Alice Ltd contributed a non-current asset with a fair value of $100 000, and a carrying amount of $80 000, while Springs Ltd contributed cash of $100 000. Alice Ltd can then recognise a profit on sale of half the non-current asset, namely $10 000 (being $\frac{1}{2}$ ($100 000 − $80 000)). The entry in the records of Alice Ltd is as follows.

Cash in JO [$100 000/2]	Dr	50 000
Plant in JO [$80 000/2]	Dr	40 000
Gain on sale of plant [$20 000/2]	Cr		10 000
Plant	Cr		80 000

The whole of the plant is given up by the operator, with half being sold to the other operator at a profit and the other half being the asset held in the joint operation. Note that Alice Ltd has recognised the plant in the joint operation at half of the carrying amount and not at half of the fair value.

For Springs Ltd, the entry in its records is different from Alice Ltd, being as follows.

Cash in JO [$100 000/2]	Dr	50 000
Plant in JO [$100 000/2]	Dr	50 000
Cash	Cr		100 000

Note that Springs Ltd has recognised the non-current asset in its records at half of fair value. Hence, Alice Ltd and Springs Ltd have their equal share of the plant in the joint operation recognised in their records at different amounts.

The fact that the operators have the non-current asset recorded at different amounts in their records affects the calculation of the cost of the inventories distributed to the operators from the joint operation. If the asset is depreciated, and the depreciation included in the cost of inventories, then, as the operators have the asset recorded at different amounts, the depreciation expense for each of the operators differs and so does the cost of inventories transferred.

Where the asset is depreciated in the joint operation's records, this depreciation is based on the fair value of the asset. For Springs Ltd, the depreciation charge is then the appropriate one and no adjustment is necessary. However, for Alice Ltd, an adjustment is necessary, as the depreciation charged by the joint operation is too great. As the depreciation is capitalised into inventories and work in progress in the records of the joint operation, when Alice Ltd recognises its share of the assets of the joint operation in its accounts, a further entry is necessary to reduce the balances of the inventories-related accounts. This extra entry in Alice Ltd's records is demonstrated in illustrative example 32.3.

ILLUSTRATIVE EXAMPLE 32.3

Contribution of a non-current asset by an operator

On 1 July 2022, Tweed Ltd and Heads Ltd established a joint operation to manufacture a product. Each company has a 50% interest in the operation and shares output equally. To commence the operation, on 1 July 2022, Tweed Ltd contributed cash of $1 500 000 and Heads Ltd contributed equipment which had a carrying amount of $1 000 000, and a fair value of $1 500 000. The equipment is depreciated in the joint operation's accounts at 10% p.a. on cost.

The following information was extracted from the joint operation's financial statements as at 30 June 2023.

Statement of financial position (extract) as at 30 June 2023	
Assets	
Cash	$ 420 000
Raw materials	100 000
Work in progress	800 000
Inventories	200 000
Equipment	1 500 000
Accumulated depreciation — equipment	(150 000)
Total assets	2 870 000
Liabilities	
Accounts payable	120 000
Accrued expenses (wages)	150 000
Bank loan	1 000 000
Total liabilities	1 270 000
Net assets	**$1 600 000**

Cash receipts and payments for the year ended 30 June 2023		
	Payments	Receipts
Contributions		$1 500 000
Bank loan		1 000 000
Wages	$ 500 000	
Accounts payable (raw materials)	380 000	
Overhead expenses	1 200 000	
	$2 080 000	$2 500 000

▶

Costs incurred		
for the year ended 30 June 2023		
Wages		$ 650 000
Raw materials		400 000
Depreciation		150 000
Overhead expenses		1 200 000
		2 400 000
Less: Cost of inventories		1 600 000
Work in progress at 30 June 2023		$ 800 000

Required

Prepare the journal entries in the records of each of the operators for the year ended 30 June 2023.

Solution

Records of Tweed Ltd

In this example, Tweed Ltd contributes cash to the joint operation, and Heads Ltd contributes equipment. At 1 July 2022, Tweed Ltd gives up the cash contribution and recognises a share of the cash and the equipment in the joint operation. Tweed Ltd will recognise a share of the fair value of the asset. The entry is as follows.

Cash in JO [$1 500 000/2]	Dr	750 000	
Equipment in JO [$1 500 000/2]	Dr	750 000	
Cash	Cr		1 500 000

At 30 June 2023, Tweed Ltd recognises a share of the assets and liabilities in the statement of financial position of the joint operation. Note that the joint operation has produced inventories of $1 600 000, of which $1 400 000 has been transferred to the operators. Further, the joint operation has depreciated the equipment, the depreciation being based on the fair value of the equipment.

The entry at 30 June 2023 in Tweed Ltd's accounts is as follows.

Raw material in JO [$100 000/2]	Dr	50 000	
Work in progress in JO [$800 000/2]	Dr	400 000	
Inventories in JO [$200 000/2]	Dr	100 000	
Inventories [$1 400 000/2]	Dr	700 000	
Accumulated depreciation — equipment in JO [$150 000/2]	Cr		75 000
Accounts payable in JO [$120 000/2]	Cr		60 000
Accrued expenses in JO [$150 000/2]	Cr		75 000
Bank loan in JO [$1 000 000/2]	Cr		500 000
Cash in JO [$750 000 − ($420 000/2)]	Cr		540 000

As depreciation has been based on fair value in the joint operation, and Tweed Ltd has its share of the equipment in the joint operation recorded at fair value, the correct amount of depreciation has been capitalised into the cost of inventories. No adjusting entry is necessary.

Records of Heads Ltd

At 1 July 2022, Heads Ltd contributes equipment to the joint operation, this having a carrying amount in Heads Ltd different from the fair value of the asset. In recording its contribution to the joint operation, Heads Ltd therefore recognises a gain on selling half of the equipment to Tweed Ltd. Heads Ltd's share of the equipment in the joint operation is then based on the original carrying amount of the asset.

The entry is as follows.

Cash in JO [$1 500 000/2]	Dr	750 000	
Equipment in JO [$1 000 000/2]	Dr	500 000	
Gain on sale of equipment [$500 000/2]	Cr		250 000
Equipment	Cr		1 000 000

At 30 June 2023, Heads Ltd recognises its share of the accounts in the statement of financial position of the joint operation as well as its share of the inventories transferred from the joint operation.

The entry is as follows.

Raw material in JO [$100 000/2]	Dr	50 000	
Work in progress in JO [$800 000/2]	Dr	400 000	
Inventories in JO [$200 000/2]	Dr	100 000	
Inventories [$1 400 000/2]	Dr	700 000	
Accumulated depreciation — equipment in JO [$150 000/2]	Cr		75 000
Accounts payable in JO [$120 000/2]	Cr		60 000
Accrued expenses in JO [$150 000/2]	Cr		75 000
Bank loan in JO [$1 000 000/2]	Cr		500 000
Cash in JO [$750 000 − ($420 000/2)]	Cr		540 000

Note that this entry is the same as that for Tweed Ltd.

The depreciation recognised by Tweed Ltd is $75 000, which is based on the fair value of the asset. However, the equipment in the joint operation has been recognised by Heads Ltd at only $500 000, which is half of the original carrying amount. Heads Ltd needs to recognise only $50 000 depreciation, which is 10% of $500 000. Hence, whereas the work in progress and inventories recognised by Heads Ltd includes depreciation of $75 000, the real cost of these assets to Heads Ltd is less, to the amount of $25 000. A further entry is necessary to reduce the accumulated depreciation recognised by Heads Ltd and to reduce the cost of the work in progress and inventories relating to the joint operation. This means that the cost of these assets to Heads Ltd is different from that recognised by Tweed Ltd. This is because the cost of the equipment in the joint operation is less for Heads Ltd than for Tweed Ltd.

As the depreciation is capitalised into work in progress and inventories (both that amount still on hand in the joint operation as well as that transferred to Heads Ltd), the adjustment to depreciation is proportionately allocated across these accounts as follows.

		Share of $25 000	
Work in progress	$ 400 000	1/3	$ 8 333
Inventories in JO	100 000	1/12	2 083
Inventories	700 000	7/12	14 584
	$1 200 000		$25 000

The entry in the records of Heads Ltd to adjust the accumulated depreciation and the cost of the inventories-related accounts is as follows.

Accumulated depreciation — equipment in JO [10% × ($750 000 − $500 000)]	Dr	25 000	
Work in progress in JO	Cr		8 333
Inventories in JO	Cr		2 083
Inventories	Cr		14 584

32.4.3 Management fees paid to a joint operator

It is common for one of the joint operators to act in a management position for the joint operation. In such circumstances, the joint operation will pay a management fee to the joint operator for its management services.

In accounting for these payments, the joint operation pays cash to a joint operator, with the cost of the service being capitalised into work in progress and inventories produced by the joint operation. For a joint operator that does not supply the service there are no accounting adjustments necessary because of the transaction. For the joint operator that does supply the service, normally it would incur a cost to supply the service and earn a profit on the supply of that service. In accounting for its interest in the joint operation, the operator supplying the service has to consider the following.

- As with supplying assets other than cash as part of the initial contribution, a joint operator cannot earn a profit on supplying services to itself.
- As the joint operation capitalises the amount paid to the operator into the cost of work in progress and inventories, an adjustment is necessary to the inventories-related accounts of that operator because the cost of these items to the operator supplying the services is less than that to the other operator(s).

Management fees paid to a joint operator

Margaret Ltd and River Ltd have formed a joint operation and share equally in the output of that operation. During the current period ending 30 June 2023, the joint operation pays a management fee of $400 000 to Margaret Ltd. The cost to Margaret Ltd of supplying management services to the joint operation is $320 000. At the end of the current period, Margaret Ltd's share of the inventories-related assets from the joint operation as recorded for Margaret Ltd is as follows.

Work in progress in JO	$300 000
Inventories in JO	200 000
Inventories	500 000

The joint operation has capitalised the management services fee of $400 000 into the cost of these assets. In the records of Margaret Ltd at 30 June 2023, the following entries are required.

Cash	Dr	400 000	
Fee revenue	Cr		400 000
(Revenue on payment of the service fee by the joint operation)			
Cost of supplying services	Dr	320 000	
Cash	Cr		320 000
(Cost of supplying the services)			

The total profit to Margaret Ltd on supplying the management service is $80 000. Half this profit is made on supplying services to River Ltd and the other $40 000 on supplying services to itself. An adjustment is necessary to eliminate the revenue and the expense on supplying services to itself. The following entry eliminates from the fee revenue only the amount of the expense — the profit element in the revenue is eliminated in the next entry.

Fee revenue [$320 000/2]	Dr	160 000	
Cost of supplying services	Cr		160 000
(Adjustment for the profit on Margaret Ltd supplying services to itself)			

The profit element on supplying services to itself, $40 000, is proportionately adjusted across the inventories-related assets as follows.

			Share of $40 000
Inventories in JO	$ 200 000	20%	$ 8 000
Inventories	500 000	50%	20 000
Work in progress in JO	300 000	30%	12 000
	$1 000 000		$40 000

The journal entry is as follows.

Fee revenue	Dr	40 000	
Inventories in JO	Cr		8 000
Inventories	Cr		20 000
Work in progress in JO	Cr		12 000
(Adjustment for the cost of the inventories-related assets from the joint operation)			

Note that the combination of this entry and the immediately preceding one results in adjusting fee revenue for a total of $200 000, which is half the revenue paid by the joint operation to Margaret Ltd.

If Margaret Ltd had provided the services but the joint operation had not yet paid the fee by the end of the period, the liabilities of the joint operation need to be adjusted. Further, the fee receivable account of $400 000 raised by Margaret Ltd needs to be adjusted. The entry is as follows.

Accruals in JO	Dr	200 000	
Fee receivable	Cr		200 000
(Management fee due from joint operation)			

LEARNING CHECK

- ☐ Each joint operator needs to recognise in its own accounts its share of any jointly held assets, any jointly held liabilities, any revenue from the sale of jointly produced output, any expenses incurred by the joint operation, and its own expenses incurred in construction of a joint product.
- ☐ Where an operator contributes a non-current asset to the joint operation, the value of the contribution is effectively the fair value of that non-current asset.
- ☐ A joint operator contributing assets other than cash cannot transfer the asset at fair value to the joint operation and recognise a full profit on the transaction. The joint operator can only recognise gains and losses on such transactions to the extent of the other parties' interests in the joint operation.
- ☐ If a joint operator supplies management services to the joint operation, it cannot earn a profit on supplying services to itself. Adjustments may be necessary to inventories-related accounts where the cost of the supplied services is less to the operator that supplies the services than the cost to other joint operator(s).

32.5 Disclosure

LEARNING OBJECTIVE 32.5 Discuss the disclosures required in relation to joint operations.

AASB 12/IFRS 12 *Disclosure of Interests in Other Entities* contains the disclosures required for interests in joint arrangements. Paragraph 20 requires an entity to disclose sufficient information about joint operations to enable users of its financial statements to evaluate the nature, extent and financial effects of its interests in joint arrangements, including the nature of its contractual relationship with other investors with joint control over joint arrangements.

For each joint arrangement, paragraph 21 of AASB 12/IFRS 12 requires that the following be disclosed:
- the name of the joint arrangement
- the nature of the entity's relationship with the joint arrangement (by, for example, describing the nature of the activities of the joint arrangement and whether it is strategic to the entity's activities)
- the principal place of business (and country incorporation, if applicable and different from the principal place of business) of the joint arrangement
- the proportion of ownership interest or participating share held by the entity and, if different, the proportion of voting rights held (if applicable).

In regard to joint operations, each joint operator includes the relevant amounts for assets, liabilities, revenues and expenses in its own records. The assets are actual assets of the joint operator, and the operator is responsible for the liabilities recognised. There is no specific requirement to show the items associated with a joint operation separately from other assets and liabilities of the operator. However, some entities may consider these to be a separate class of assets and provide information in the notes to the financial statements regarding assets and liabilities associated with joint operations.

In note 18 of its 2018 annual report, Wesfarmers Limited provided the information about the recognition and measurement policies for its interests in joint arrangements as follows.

> The Group recognises its share of the assets, liabilities, expenses and income from the use and output of its joint operations. The Group's investment in joint ventures is accounted for using the equity method of accounting.

Also in note 18 of Wesfarmers Limited's 2018 annual report, as shown in figure 32.6, is the specific information required by paragraph 21 of AASB 12/IFRS 12 about the group's joint operations.

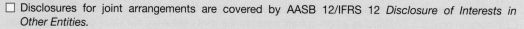

FIGURE 32.6 Disclosures about joint operations, Wesfarmers

Joint operations	Principal activity	Reporting date	Country of incorporation	Ownership 2016 %	2015 %
Sodium Cyanide	Sodium cyanide manufacture	30 June	Australia	75.0	75%
Bengalla	Coal mining	31 December	Australia	40.0	40.0
ISPT	Property ownership	30 June	Australia	25.0	25.0

Source: Wesfarmers Limited (2018, p. 131).

SUMMARY

This chapter has covered the principles of accounting for joint arrangements, particularly joint operations, as contained in AASB 11/IFRS 11 *Joint Arrangements*. Some of the key principles are as follows.

- A joint arrangement is an arrangement between a number of parties in which two or more parties have joint control.
- A joint arrangement has two key characteristics, namely the parties are bound by a contractual agreement, and this agreement gives two or more parties joint control over the arrangement.
- Joint control exists when decisions about relevant activities require the unanimous consent of the parties sharing control.
- There are two types of joint arrangement, namely joint ventures and joint operations.
- The classification of a joint arrangement is dependent on the rights and obligations of the parties to the arrangement.
- With a joint arrangement the parties that have joint control have rights to the assets and obligations for the liabilities relating to the arrangement.
- With a joint venture, the parties that have joint control have rights to the net assets of the arrangement.
- Where a joint arrangement is not structured through a separate vehicle it is a joint operation.
- Where a joint arrangement is structured through a separate vehicle, its classification depends on an analysis of the legal form of the separate vehicle, the terms of the contractual arrangement and other relevant facts and circumstances.
- For a joint operation, a joint operator must recognise its share of the assets and liabilities of the arrangement, as well as its revenues and expenses associated with the arrangement.

KEY TERMS

joint arrangement A contractual arrangement in which the parties involved have joint control over the decision making in relation to the joint arrangement.

joint control The contractually agreed sharing of control of an arrangement, which exists only when decisions about the relevant activities require the unanimous consent of the parties sharing control.

joint operation A joint arrangement whereby the parties that have joint control of the arrangement have rights to the assets, and obligations for the liabilities, relating to the arrangement.

joint operators The parties to a joint operation.

joint venture A joint arrangement whereby the parties that have joint control of the arrangement have rights to the net assets of the arrangement.

joint venturers The parties to a joint venture.

separate vehicle A separately identifiable financial structure, including separate legal entities or entities recognised by statute, regardless of whether those entities have a legal personality.

DEMONSTRATION PROBLEM

32.1 Movements in assets, depreciation

Frank Fizz Ltd has discovered a new way of providing that extra fizz to soft drinks necessary to capturing the next generation of young people. To exploit this new invention, it enters into a joint agreement with two other soft drink manufacturers, Koke Ltd and Popsi Ltd. The agreement in relation to the joint operation was signed on 1 July 2022. The agreement contains the following specifications.

- Frank Fizz Ltd is to have a 50% interest in the joint operation, with Frank Fizz Ltd supplying the patent for the secret extra fizz to the joint operation. At 1 July 2022, the fair value of the patent is considered to be at $10 million. Frank Fizz Ltd has capitalised outlays during the development of the new formula for fizz and has capitalised costs of $7 million at 1 July 2022. The patent is amortised in the records of each of the joint operators, and not included in the cost of inventories. The patent is expected to have a 10-year life.
- Koke Ltd is to have a 25% interest in the joint operation, supplying $5 million cash to the joint operation.

- Popsi Ltd is to have a 25% interest in the joint operation. Popsi Ltd is to supply plant and equipment to the joint operation at a fair value of $5 million. The plant and equipment is currently recorded in the records of Popsi Ltd at a carrying amount of $4 million (related accumulated depreciation is $1 million). The plant and equipment has an expected remaining useful life of 5 years. Popsi Ltd is to play a major role in the management of the joint operation, and will be paid a management fee of $200 000 p.a. The expected cost to Popsi Ltd of supplying these services is $170 000. The fee was paid on 25 June 2023.

Information in relation to the operations of the joint operation at the end of the first year, 30 June 2023, is as follows.

Statement of financial position	
Cash	$ 1 200 000
Work in progress	200 000
Plant and equipment	6 000 000
Accumulated depreciation	(1 200 000)
Patent	10 000 000
	$16 200 000
Joint operators' equity	$14 800 000
Trade creditors	600 000
Accrued expenses	800 000
	$16 200 000

Statement of cash flows		
Cash balance at 1/7/22		$5 000 000
Less:		
Wages and salaries	$ 860 000	
Supplies and materials	1 520 000	
Plant and equipment	1 000 000	
Administration expenses	420 000	3 800 000
Cash balance at 30/6/23		$1 200 000

Costs of production	
Wages and salaries	$1 560 000
Supplies and materials	2 120 000
Administration expenses	520 000
Depreciation — plant and equipment	1 200 000
	5 400 000
Work in progress at 30 June 2023	(200 000)
Cost of inventories produced	$5 200 000

Required

Prepare the journal entries in the records of each of the joint operators for the year ending 30 June 2023.

SOLUTION

Records of Frank Fizz Ltd

Frank Fizz Ltd has a 50% interest in the joint operation. This entitles it to a 50% interest in the $5 million cash supplied by Koke Ltd and the $5 million plant and equipment supplied by Popsi Ltd. Frank Fizz Ltd supplies the patent. It then has a 50% interest in the patent now held by the joint operation. As it is contributing the patent its share is 50% of the carrying amount in its own records at time of contribution, namely $7 million. The value of the patent is $10 million, so Frank Fizz Ltd makes a profit on the patent contributed to the joint operation, but only to the extent of the other parties' interests in the joint operation, namely 50% of the difference between the fair value of the patent and its carrying amount. The initial entry in the records of Frank Fizz Ltd to record the contributions to the joint operation is as follows.

1 July 2022	Cash in JO	Dr	2 500 000		(1/2 × $5 000 000)
	Plant and equipment in JO	Dr	2 500 000		(1/2 × $5 000 000)
	Patent in JO	Dr	3 500 000		(1/2 × $7 000 000)
	Gain on sale of patent	Cr		1 500 000	(1/2 × [$10 000 000 − $7 000 000])
	Patent	Cr		7 000 000	
	(Investment in joint operation)				

The patent is amortised in the records of each joint operator. The amortisation expense is based on a 10-year life and an initial cost of $3 500 000. The entry at end of the first year is as follows.

30 June 2023	Amortisation expense — patent in JO	Dr	350 000		(10% × $3 500 000)
	Accumulated amortisation — patent in JO	Cr		350 000	
	(Amortisation on asset held in joint operation)				

At the end of the first year Frank Fizz Ltd recognises the changes in the assets and liabilities held by the joint operation over the financial year. Hence, it recognises 50% of the assets and liabilities held by the joint operation at the end of the year, as shown in the statement of financial position prepared by the joint operation, adjusting for asset and liability balances held at the beginning of the year. Plant and equipment has increased from $5 million to $6 million over the year — only the share of the increase is recognised at the end of the first year. With cash, there has been a decrease from the $5 million at the beginning of the year to $1 200 000 at the end of the year — a decrease of $3 800 000. The joint operation has produced inventories of $5 200 000, which have been distributed to the joint operators. Frank Fizz Ltd recognises its 50% share of the inventories — note it is now held by Frank Fizz Ltd and not the joint operation. The entry is as follows.

	Work in progress in JO	Dr	100 000		(1/2 × 200 000)
	Plant and equipment in JO	Dr	500 000		(1/2 × $1 000 000)
	Inventories	Dr	2 600 000		(1/2 × $5 200 000)
	Accumulated depreciation on plant and equipment in JO	Cr		600 000	(1/2 × $1 200 000)
	Trade creditors in JO	Cr		300 000	(1/2 × $600 000)
	Accrued expenses in JO	Cr		400 000	(1/2 × $800 000)
	Cash in JO	Cr		1 900 000	(1/2 × $3 800 000)
	(Adjustment to investment in joint operation)				

Records of Koke Ltd (25%)

Koke Ltd has a 25% share in the joint operation. To record the establishment of the joint operation, Koke Ltd recognises its 25% share of the fair value of the assets supplied by the joint operators and its giving up of the $5 million cash contribution. The entry is as follows.

1 July 2022	Patent in JO	Dr	2 500 000		(1/4 × $10 000 000)
	Cash in JO	Dr	1 250 000		(1/4 × $5 000 000)
	Plant and equipment in JO	Dr	1 250 000		(1/4 × $5 000 000)
	Cash	Cr		5 000 000	
	(Investment in joint operation)				

At the end of the first year of operation Koke Ltd recognises the amortisation of the patent writing off the cost of the patent over a 10-year period. The entry is as follows.

30 June 2023	Amortisation expense — patent in JO	Dr	250 000		(10% × $2 500 000)
	Accumulated amortisation — patent in JO	Cr		250 000	
	(Amortisation on asset held in joint operation)				

At the end of the first year Koke Ltd recognises its share of the changes in the assets and liabilities held by the joint operation. The procedure is the same as shown previously for Frank Fizz Ltd, except that Koke Ltd has only a 25% share in the joint operation. The entry is as follows.

Work in progress in JO	Dr	50 000		(1/4 × $200 000)
Plant and equipment in JO	Dr	250 000		(1/4 × $1 000 000)
Inventories	Dr	1 300 000		(1/4 × $5 200 000)
Accumulated depreciation — plant and equipment in JO	Cr		300 000	(1/4 × $1 200 000)
Trade creditors in JO	Cr		150 000	(1/4 × $600 000)
Accrued expenses in JO	Cr		200 000	(1/4 × $800 000)
Cash in JO	Cr		950 000	(1/4 × $3 800 000)
(Adjustment to investment in joint operation)				

Records of Popsi Ltd (25%)

Popsi Ltd has a 25% share in the joint operation. Popsi Ltd supplies plant and equipment to the joint operation. This plant and equipment is recorded by Popsi Ltd at $4 million but has a fair value of $5 million. The effect here is the same as that used by Frank Fizz Ltd in relation to its contribution of the patent. Popsi Ltd records its 25% share of the assets contributed to the joint operation. However, in relation to the plant and equipment it supplies, it recognises a 25% share of the carrying amount of $4 million. It also derecognises the plant and equipment recorded at $5 million and related accumulated depreciation of $1 million, as the asset now belongs to the joint operation. As the fair value of the asset is greater than its carrying amount at time of contribution, Popsi Ltd recognises a profit but only to the extent of the interests of the other joint operators, namely 75% of $5 million fair value less $4 million carrying amount. The entry is as follows.

1 July 2022	Cash in JO	Dr	1 250 000		(1/4 × $5 000 000)
	Plant and equipment in JO	Dr	1 000 000		(1/4 × $4 000 000)
	Patent in JO	Dr	2 500 000		(1/4 × $10 000 000)
	Accumulated depreciation — plant and equipment in JO	Dr	1 000 000		
	Gain on sale of plant and equipment			750 000	(3/4 × [$5 000 000 − $4 000 000])
	Plant and equipment	Cr		5 000 000	
	(Investment in joint operation)				

At the end of the first year Popsi Ltd recognises the amortisation of the patent. The entry is as follows.

30 June 2023	Amortisation expense —patent in JO	Dr	250 000		(10% × $2 500 000)
	Accumulated amortisation — patent in JO	Cr		250 000	
	(Amortisation of patent held in joint operation)				
	Work in progress in JO	Dr	50 000		(1/4 × $200 000)
	Plant and equipment in JO	Dr	250 000		(1/4 × $1 000 000)
	Inventories	Dr	1 300 000		(1/4 × $5 200 000)
	Accumulated depreciation — plant and equipment in JO	Cr		300 000	(1/4 × $1 200 000)
	Trade creditors in JO	Cr		150 000	(1/4 × $600 000)
	Accrued expenses in JO	Cr		200 000	(1/4 × $800 000)
	Cash in JO	Cr		950 000	(1/4 × $3 800 000)
	(Adjustment to investment in joint operation)				

The joint operation has calculated depreciation on plant and equipment based on 20% p.a. on cost. However, as Popsi Ltd contributed the original plant and equipment the cost of this asset is less to Popsi Ltd than to the other joint operators — Popsi Ltd recognises a cost of $4 million dollars whereas the other joint operators and the joint operation itself use a cost of $5 million. Hence, an adjustment to the depreciation charge needs to be determined based on Popsi Ltd's 25% share of the depreciation relating to the $1 million difference in recognised cost. The depreciation expense recognised by the joint venture was capitalised into the cost of inventories, affecting both the work-in-progress and the cost of finished inventories. The adjustment is then Popsi Ltd's 25% share of the 20% depreciation on the $1 million lower cost (i.e. $50 000). Hence, Popsi Ltd passes an entry that reduces the amount recognised for accumulated depreciation on the plant and equipment by $50 000, as well as a reduction in the cost of the inventories received and the carrying amount of the work in progress in the joint operation. In relation to the latter two assets the amount of the reduction is determined on a proportional basis as shown in the working below.

Working: Share of $50 000 difference relating to depreciation

Inventories	$1 300 000	$1 300 000/$1 350 000	$48 000
Work in progress	50 000	$50 000/$1 350 000	2 000
	$1 350 000		$50 000

The entry is as follows.

Accumulated depreciation — plant and equipment in JO	Dr	50 000		(1/4 × 1/5 × $1 000 000)
Inventories	Cr		48 000	
Work in progress in JO	Cr		2 000	
(Adjustment to depreciation on plant and equipment held in joint operation)				

Popsi Ltd receives a management fee of $200 000 per annum. This is recognised in its records as revenue. The cost of supplying these services is $170 000. This is recognised as an expense. The entries to recognise the revenue and related expense are as follows.

Cash	Dr	200 000	
Fee revenue	Cr		200 000
(Revenue on payment of services fee by joint operation)			
Cost of supplying services	Dr	170 000	
Cash	Cr		170 000
(Cost of supplying services to joint operation)			

Via the above two entries, Popsi Ltd has recognised a profit of $30 000 on supplying a service to the joint operation. However, it cannot recognise a profit on supplying services to itself. Hence, both the revenue and the related expense need to be reduced. The revenue is to be reduced by Popsi Ltd's 25% interest in the $200 000 revenue, namely $50 000 and the expense is reduced by Popsi Ltd's 25% interest in the $170 000 expenses, namely $42 500. As the joint operation has capitalised the cost of the administrative service into the cost of inventories, the cost of the inventories transferred from the joint operation to Popsi Ltd and the cost of the work in progress in the joint operation must be reduced by the profit element of $7500 (i.e. $50 000 − $42 500). The adjustment to the inventories and work in progress is done on a proportional basis.

Fee revenue	Dr	50 000		(1/4 × $ 200 000)
Cost of supplying services	Cr		42 500	(1/4 × $170 000)
Inventories	Cr		7 222	(1 300 000/$1 350 000 × $7 500)
Work in progress in JO	Cr		278	(50 000/$1 350 000 × $7 500)
(Adjustment to accounts relating to supply of management services to the joint operation)				

COMPREHENSION QUESTIONS

1 What is a joint arrangement?
2 What is meant by 'joint control'?
3 How does joint control differ from control as used in classifying subsidiaries?
4 How does a joint venture differ from a joint operation?
5 What are the key steps in classifying a joint arrangement into joint ventures and joint operations?
6 How are joint ventures accounted for?
7 How are joint operations accounted for?

CASE STUDY 32.1

CLASSIFICATION OF A JOINT ARRANGEMENT

Falls Ltd and Creek Ltd decided to jointly undertake the manufacture of an electric car. They formed Silver Ltd, which will manufacture the car. Falls Ltd and Creek Ltd provide the various parts for the manufacture of the car, which is assembled by Silver Ltd.

Falls Ltd and Creek Ltd each hold 50% of the voting rights in Silver Ltd and receive 50% of the cars produced by Silver Ltd. Falls Ltd and Creek Ltd then sell the cars in their own geographic region. The constitution of Silver Ltd requires that the operations of the company must be in accordance with a business plan prepared annually, and to which both Falls Ltd and Creek Ltd both agree. Silver Ltd has six directors, with three being appointed by Falls Ltd and three by Creek Ltd.

Required

Evaluate whether a joint arrangement exists and how it should be classified.

CASE STUDY 32.2

EXISTENCE AND CLASSIFICATION OF A JOINT ARRANGEMENT

The Chinese mining company Changchun Mining Ltd and the Australian mining company Seal Rush Ltd have agreed to set up a separate company, Dragon Rush Ltd, to mine for Seal in Australia. The Australian government has issued permits to the Australian company to mine for Seal in specified areas of Australia.

The companies have set up a joint operating agreement which contains the following provisions.

- The assets and liabilities of Dragon Rush Ltd are those of that company and not of the parties owning shares in Dragon Rush Ltd.
- Dragon Rush Ltd has a board of directors that will consist of six persons, three provided by each of Changchun Mining Ltd and Seal Rush Ltd. Each of these companies has a 50% ownership in Dragon Rush Ltd. For any resolution to be passed by the board, there has to be unanimous consent of all directors.
- Seal Rush Ltd will provide the management team for Dragon Rush Ltd for which a management fee will be paid by Dragon Rush Ltd. However, all budget matters and work programs have to be approved by the board of Dragon Rush Ltd.
- The rights and obligations arising from the exploration development and production activities of Dragon Rush Ltd are to be shared by all parties to the joint arrangement. In particular, the parties will share in the production obtained from the mining activities and all costs associated with the work undertaken.
- If cash is required for ongoing mining activities, the board of Dragon Rush Ltd may make calls on the parties owning shares in that company.

Required

Discuss whether a joint arrangement exists and whether it should be classified as a joint venture or a joint operation.

CASE STUDY 32.3

CLASSIFICATION OF A JOINT ARRANGEMENT

Two smaller banks that operate in Australia are the Ballarat Bank and the St Martins Bank. These have in the past primarily offered domestic banking services to their customers. However, in recent times, these customers have made increasing demands for international currency transactions and access to offshore banking arrangements. As both banks individually are not prepared to undertake the risks associated with international operations on their own, they have decided to join together to provide these services to their customers.

To this end, they have formed the Overseas Bank. This bank is regarded as a separate vehicle in its own right, with the assets and liabilities of the Overseas Bank being those of the bank itself. The Ballarat Bank and St Martins bank will each hold a 50% interest in the Overseas Bank. These two banks have signed an agreement such that all major decisions in relation to the Overseas Bank require the unanimous agreement of the two banks. The board of the Overseas Bank will consist of an equal number of representatives of these two banks.

The Ballarat Bank and the St Martins bank have agreed to provide initial funding to establish the Overseas Bank and have also agreed on a mechanism for further cash inflows if required.

Required

Discuss whether a joint arrangement exists and how it should be classified.

CASE STUDY 32.4

ACCOUNTING FOR AN ASSET USED BY A NUMBER OF COMPANIES

Raby Ltd and Bay Ltd are companies that have newly discovered oil wells in a Middle-Eastern country. There is some distance to the nearest port and, rather than build separate pipelines, they have agreed to jointly build a pipeline to the port and share the use of the pipeline for transporting oil. The management of the pipeline is conducted in accordance with an agreement between Raby Ltd and Bay Ltd, which requires unanimous agreement in relation to such issues as maintenance and future expansion or contraction of the pipeline. Kalgoorlie Ltd also has oil wells in the area and has agreed to use any excess capacity of the pipeline.

Required

Discuss how you would account for the pipeline.

APPLICATION AND ANALYSIS EXERCISES

★ BASIC | ★ ★ MODERATE | ★ ★ ★ DIFFICULT

32.1 Contributions of cash ★   LO3, 4

Seal Ltd's main area of interest is the production of glass products. Manatee Ltd manufactures products that require the employment of artists with skills in fine etchings. After negotiations, on 1 July 2022 the executives of both companies reached an agreement to establish a joint operation that would be involved in the production of fine glass tableware. Under the contractual agreement, both operators agreed to invest $210 000 each in the joint operation. Each party to the joint operation would have a 50% interest in the joint operation and the output of the joint operation would be distributed equally to each operator.

After the first year of operation the following information about the joint operation was provided at 30 June 2023.

Cash	$ 49 000
Inventories:	
Finished goods	14 000
Work in progress	28 000
Raw materials	28 000
Plant	175 000
Accumulated depreciation	(35 000)
Total assets	$259 000
Creditors	$ 35 000
Accrued expenses	14 000
Total liabilities	$ 49 000

The joint operation reported the following costs incurred during the financial year.

Salaries and wages	$ 98 000
Raw materials	63 000
Other expenses including depreciation	91 000
Total costs incurred	252 000
Cost of inventories	224 000
Work in progress at 30 June 2023	$ 28 000

The joint operation also reported the following cash receipts and payments for the year ending 30 June 2023.

Receipts		
Contributions by operators		$420 000
Payments		
Acquisition of plant at 1 July 2022	$175 000	
Acquisition of raw material	56 000	
Salaries and wages	84 000	
Other expenses	56 000	371 000
Cash balance at 30 June 2023		$ 49 000

Required

In relation to the joint operation for the year ending 30 June 2023 prepare the journal entries in the records of Manatee Ltd.

32.2 Contribution of plant ★ LO3, 4

On 1 July 2022, Sea Ltd and Lion Ltd signed a contractual agreement to form a joint operation for the manufacture of kitchen products. The agreement provided that Lion Ltd would contribute $240 000 in cash while Sea Ltd would provide $40 000 in cash as well as manufacturing equipment currently held by Sea Ltd that had a fair value of $200 000. The equipment was currently recorded by Sea Ltd at a carrying amount of $180 000, net of accumulated depreciation of $30 000.

The agreement provided that each operator would receive half of the output of the joint operation. Depreciation on equipment is charged at 20% p.a. on cost, based on the expected pattern of use in the joint operation.

Financial information provided by the joint operation at 30 June 2023 was as follows.

Statement of financial position (partial)			
Cash	$ 56 000	Accounts payable	$ 40 000
Raw materials	32 000	Accrued wages	16 000
Inventories (undistributed)	16 000	Loan	200 000
Work in progress	32 000		
Equipment	400 000		
Accumulated depreciation	(80 000)		
	$456 000		$256 000

Cash receipts and payments

	Payments	Receipts
Contributions		$280 000
Loan		200 000
Purchase of raw materials	$ 64 000	
Wages	96 000	
Purchase of equipment (2 July 2022)	200 000	
Other expenses	64 000	
	$424 000	$480 000

Costs incurred

Wages	$112 000
Raw materials	72 000
Overheads including depreciation on equipment	144 000
	328 000
Cost of inventories	(296 000)
Work in progress at 30 June 2023	$ 32 000

Required

Prepare the journal entries in the records of Sea Ltd in relation to the joint operation for the year ending 30 June 2023.

32.3 Sharing output ★

LO3, 4

On 1 July 2022, Darwin Ltd entered into a joint agreement with Broome Ltd to form an unincorporated entity to produce a new type of widget.

It was agreed that each party to the agreement would share the output equally.

Darwin Ltd's initial contribution consisted of $2 000 000 cash and Broome Ltd contributed machinery that was recorded in the records of Broome Ltd at $1 900 000. During the first year of operation both parties contributed a further $3 000 000 each.

On 30 June 2023, the venture manager provided the following statements (in $'000).

Costs incurred

Wages	$1 840
Supplies	2 800
Overheads	2 200
	6 840
Cost of inventories	4 840
Work in progress at 30 June 2023	$2 000

Receipts and payments

Receipts:		
Original contributions		$2 000
Additional contributions		6 000
		8 000
Payments:		
Machinery (2/7/22)	$ 800	
Wages	1 800	
Supplies	3 000	
Overheads	2 100	
Operating expenses	200	7 900
Closing cash balance		$ 100

Assets and liabilities	
Assets	
Cash	$ 100
Machinery	2 800
Supplies	400
Work in progress	2 000
Total assets	5 300
Liabilities	
Accrued wages	40
Creditors	300
Total liabilities	340
Net assets	$4 960

Each joint operator depreciates machinery at 20% p.a. on cost in its own records.

Required

1. Prepare the journal entries in the records of Darwin Ltd and Broome Ltd in relation to the joint operation.
2. Prepare the journal entries in the records of Broome Ltd assuming that the joint operation, not the operators, had depreciated the machinery and included that expense in the cost of inventories transferred.

32.4 Unincorporated joint operation ★ **LO3, 4**

On 1 July 2021, Platypus Ltd entered into a joint agreement with Otter Ltd to establish an unincorporated joint operation to manufacture timber-felling equipment. It was agreed that the output of the operation would be shared in the proportions Platypus Ltd 60% and Otter Ltd 40%.

To commence the operations, contributions were as follows.

- Platypus Ltd: cash of $550 000 and equipment having a carrying amount of $150 000 and a fair value of $200 000
- Otter Ltd: cash of $300 000 and plant having a carrying amount of $225 000 and a fair value of $200 000

Otter Ltd revalued the plant it contributed to fair value prior to its transfer to the joint operation. Plant and equipment was depreciated (to the nearest month) in the joint operation's books at 20% p.a. on cost. During December 2021, an additional $500 000 cash was contributed by the operators in the same proportion as their initial contributions.

The following information, in relation to the joint operations for the year ended 30 June 2022, was provided by the operation manager.

(a) *Costs incurred for the year ended 30 June 2022*

Wages	$ 200 000
Raw materials	600 000
Overheads	325 000
Depreciation	102 500
	1 227 500
Less: Cost of inventories	1 002 500
Work in progress at 30 June 2022	$ 225 000

(b) *Receipts and payments for year ended 30 June 2022*

	Payments	Receipts
Contributions		$1 350 000
Plant (3 January 2022)	$ 225 000	
Wages	175 000	
Accounts payable	490 000	
Overhead costs	305 000	
Operating expenses	20 000	
	$1 215 000	$1 350 000

(c) *Assets and liabilities at 30 June 2022*

	Dr	Cr
Cash	135 000	
Raw materials	50 000	
Work in progress	225 000	
Inventories	127 500	
Plant and equipment	625 000	
Accumulated depreciation — plant and equipment		102 500
Accounts payable		160 000
Accrued expenses — wages and overheads		45 000

Required

Prepare the journal entries in the records of Platypus Ltd in relation to the joint operation for the year ended 30 June 2022. (Round all amounts to the nearest dollar and show all relevant workings.)

32.5 Share of output ★ ★ ★   LO3, 4

Alice Ltd is a mining company operating in Victoria. Its main areas of mining are open-pit gold mines and iron ore mines. In 2022 while exploring for ore the company discovered a major source of spring water suitable for bottling for human consumption. Alice Ltd believed the find was commercially significant. Given its lack of past expertise in the bottled water industry Alice Ltd decided to establish a joint operation with Springs Ltd to operate a factory to produce bottled water. The joint operation agreement was signed on 1 January 2023, with Alice Ltd and Springs Ltd having a 50% share in the unincorporated joint operation.

The initial contributions by the two operators were as follows.

Alice Ltd:	
Capitalised expenses	$ 800 000
Equipment	800 000
Cash	2 400 000
Springs Ltd:	
Cash	4 000 000

The capitalised expenses were recorded in the books of Alice Ltd at $320 000, while the equipment was recorded at a carrying amount of $640 000. In order to supply the cash, Alice Ltd borrowed $800 000 of its required contribution. It is expected that the reserves of water will be depleted within 10 years, and the equipment is expected to have a similar useful life.

On 1 June 2023, the joint operation was ready to start producing bottles of water. The joint operation's accounts at 30 June 2024 contained the following information.

Statement of financial position (extract)		
	2024	2023
Work in progress		$ 200 000
Capitalised costs	$ 800 000	800 000
Plant and equipment	8 160 000	7 760 000
Cash	80 000	240 000
Accounts payable — plant	(240 000)	(800 000)
Accrued expenses — wages etc.	(160 000)	(200 000)

Cash receipts and payments (extract)		
	2024	
	Payments	Receipts
Materials and supplies	$480 000	
Administration	160 000	
Wages	560 000	
Accounts payable — plant	960 000	
Contributions from joint operators		$2 000 000

The output of the first year's operations was distributed equally to the joint operators. Production in the first year was estimated to be 15% of the reserves. At 30 June 2024, Alice Ltd held 10% of its share of output in inventories, having sold the rest to its customers for $2 000 000. Expenses of the joint operation incurred up to 30 June 2024 were allocated to the operators.

Because of some damage to the environment caused by the establishment of the pumping station to extract the water, there is a potential restoration cost to be incurred at closure of the joint operation. Whether this will be required will depend on the result of current legal inquiries.

Required

Prepare the journal entries in the records of Alice Ltd for the periods ending 30 June 2023 and 2024.

32.6 Operators share output ★ ★ ★ **LO3, 4**

On 1 July 2023, Dalby Ltd entered into a joint operation agreement with Chinchilla Ltd to manufacture stevedoring equipment. It was agreed that each party to the agreement would share the output equally.

To commence the operation, contributions were as follows.
- Dalby Ltd: cash of $2 000 000 and equipment having a $400 000 carrying amount and a fair value of $600 000
- Chinchilla Ltd: cash of $1 800 000 and plant having a carrying amount of $900 000 and a fair value of $800 000

Chinchilla Ltd revalued the plant it contributed to the joint operation prior to its transfer to the joint operation.

Plant and equipment is depreciated (to the nearest month) in the joint operation's books at 20% p.a. on cost.

During December 2023, both parties contributed an additional $1 500 000 cash.

The following information, in relation to the joint operation's operations for the year ended 30 June 2024, was provided by the operations manager.

(a) *Costs incurred for the year ended 30 June 2024*

Wages	$1 200 000
Raw materials	2 150 000
Overheads	1 860 000
Depreciation	470 000
	5 680 000
Less: Cost of inventories	2 580 000
Work in progress at 30 June 2024	$3 100 000

(b) *Receipts and payments for the year ended 30 June 2024*

	Payments	Receipts
Contributions		$6 800 000
Plant (10 July 2023)	$ 950 000	
Wages	1 150 000	
Accounts payable	1 980 000	
Overhead costs	1 810 000	
Operating expenses	440 000	
	$ 6 330 000	$6 800 000

(c) *Assets and liabilities as at 30 June 2024*

	Dr	Cr
Cash	470 000	
Raw materials	360 000	
Work in progress	3 100 000	
Inventories	580 000	
Plant and equipment	2 350 000	
Accumulated depreciation — plant and equipment		470 000
Accounts payable		530 000
Accrued expenses		100 000

Required

Prepare the journal entries in the records of Dalby Ltd and Chinchilla Ltd in relation to the joint operation for the year ended 30 June 2024.

After prospecting unsuccessfully for a number of years for gold, in November 2023 Greens Pool Ltd finally found an economically viable deposit. Realising that it did not have sufficient expertise to operate a gold mine successfully, Greens Pool Ltd formed an unincorporated joint operation with Apollo Bay Ltd, agreeing to share the output of the mine equally. It was agreed that the two operators would initially contribute the following assets.

Greens Pool Ltd:	
Capitalised exploration costs, including permits licences, and mining rights, currently recorded by Greens Pool Ltd at $100 000	$400 000
Cash	350 000
Apollo Bay Ltd:	
Cash	750 000

The joint operation commenced on 1 January 2024. By 31 December 2024, the mine had been operating successfully. It was reliably estimated at the commencement of the project that the mine had expected reserves of 50 000 tonnes.

In the first year following commencement, 2500 tonnes of gold was extracted, while in 2025, 5000 tonnes was extracted. This output was distributed to the operators equally.

All costs except general administration costs were capitalised into the cost of the output, with depreciation of equipment and capitalised exploration costs being written off in proportion to the depletion of the reserves. General administration expenses were allocated to the operators equally.

The financial statements of the joint operation over the first 2 years of operation showed the following information.

Cash receipts and payments		
	2024	**2025**
Balance at 1 January	—	$ 150 000
Contributions from operators	$1 100 000	600 000
	1 100 000	750 000
Plant and equipment	400 000	95 000
Wages	300 000	330 000
Materials	100 000	120 000
General administration	150 000	150 000
	950 000	695 000
Balance at 31 December	$ 150 000	$ 55 000

Statement of financial position		
	2024	**2025**
Capitalised exploration costs	$ 380 000	$ 340 000
Plant and equipment	400 000	495 000
Accumulated depreciation	(20 000)	(70 000)
Cash	150 000	55 000)
Materials	25 000	20 000
	935 000	840 000
Accrued wages	5 000	10 000
Accounts payable (materials)	10 000	15 000
	15 000	25 000
Net assets	$ 920 000	$ 815 000
Operators' equity		
Contributions as at 1 January		920 000
Additional contributions	1 500 000	600 000
	1 500 000	1 520 000
Less: Output distributed	430 000	555 000
Allocation: general administration	150 000	150 000
	580 000	705 000
Balance at 31 December	$ 920 000	$ 815 000

Required

Prepare the journal entries in the records of Greens Pool Ltd to record its interest in the joint operation for the years ending 31 December 2024 and 2025.

32.8 **Management fees supplied by one of the joint operators** ★ **LO4**

On 1 July 2022, Broome Ltd and Kalbarri Ltd agreed to a joint operation that would be involved in the production of furniture. The contractual arrangement required both parties to invest $270 000 cash in the joint operation with each party having a 50% interest. Under the contractual arrangement the joint operation would distribute the output equally to each venturer.

The joint operation agreed to pay Broome Ltd $30 000 p.a. to supply management services to the joint operation. The cost to Broome Ltd to supply these services is $24 000.

At 30 June 2023 the joint operation reported the following information.

Statement of financial position (partial)			
Cash	$ 33 000	Accounts payable	$45 000
Raw materials	36 000	Accrued wages	18 000
Inventories (undistributed)	20 000		
Work in progress	54 000		
Machinery	225 000		
Accumulated depreciation	(45 000)		
	$323 000		$63 000

Cash receipts and payments		
	Payments	Receipts
Contributions		$540 000
Purchase of raw materials	$ 72 000	
Wages	108 000	
Purchase of equipment (2 July 2022)	225 000	
Management services (supplied by Broome Ltd)	30 000	
Other expenses	72 000	
	$507 000	$540 000

Costs incurred	
Wages	$ 126 000
Raw materials	81 000
Management services	30 000
Overheads including depreciation	117 000
	354 000
Cost of inventories	(300 000)
Work in progress at 30 June 2023	$ 54 000

Required

Prepare the journal entries in the records of Broome Ltd in relation to the joint operation for the year ending 30 June 2023.

32.9 **Operators share output** ★ ★ **LO4**

Walrus Ltd enters into an arrangement with another operator, Whale Ltd, to establish an unincorporated joint operation to produce a drug that assists both hayfever sufferers and those with sinus problems. To produce the drug requires a combination of the technical and pharmaceutical knowledge of both companies. Each company will receive an equal share of the output of the drug, which they will retail through their own preferred outlets, potentially under different names. Walrus Ltd agrees to manage the project for a fee of $100 000 p.a. Walrus Ltd estimates that it will cost $80 000 to provide the service. The management fee is capitalised into the cost of inventories produced.

The operation commences on 1 January 2023, with each operator providing $1 000 000 cash. At the end of the first year, the statement of financial position of the joint operation showed the following.

Assets	
Vehicles	$ 200 000
Accumulated depreciation	(50 000)
Equipment	820 000
Accumulated depreciation	(60 000)
Inventories	80 000
Work in progress	320 000
Materials	210 000
Total assets	1 520 000
Liabilities	
Provisions	80 000
Payables	40 000
	120 000
Net assets	**$1 400 000**
Operators' equity	
Initial contributions	2 000 000
Inventories delivered	(400 000)
General administration costs	(200 000)
Total equity	**$1 400 000**

Required
1. Prepare the journal entries in the records of Walrus Ltd during 2023.
2. What differences would occur if the management fee paid to Walrus Ltd were treated as general administration costs?

32.10 Unincorporated joint operation managed by one of the operators ★ ★ ★   LO4

During 2021, discussions took place between Cairns Ltd, a company concerned with the design of specialised tools and machines, and two companies, Townsville Ltd and Mackay Ltd, which could potentially assist in the manufacture of a new tool. The new tool is called SmartTool and is to be used in the making of high grade mining instruments. On 1 June 2022, the three companies agreed to form an unincorporated joint operation to achieve this purpose. It was agreed that the relative interests in the joint operation would be as follows.

Cairns Ltd	50%
Townsville Ltd	25%
Mackay Ltd	25%

It was further agreed that Mackay Ltd would undertake a management role in relation to the new operation, being responsible for operating decisions and for record keeping. Mackay Ltd would be paid a management fee by the joint operation of $30 000.

In establishing the joint operation, the various parties agreed to provide the following assets as their initial contribution.

- Cairns Ltd was to provide the patent to SmartTool, which was being recorded by Cairns Ltd at a capitalised development cost of $2 100 000. The operators agreed that this asset had a fair value of $3 500 000, with an expected useful life of 10 years.
- Townsville Ltd was to provide cash of $1 500 000.
- Mackay Ltd was to provide the basic plant and equipment to manufacture the new tool. The plant and equipment was recorded in the books of Mackay Ltd at $900 000, but the operators agreed that it had a fair value of $1 5000 000. The plant and equipment was estimated to have a further useful life of 5 years.

During the first period of its operation, the output of the joint operation was distributed to each of the operators in proportion to their agreed interests. By 30 June 2023, Mackay Ltd had sold 80% of the output received from the joint operation for $450 000. The joint operation had not paid the management fee to Mackay Ltd by 30 June 2023.

Information from the financial statements of the joint operation as at 30 June 2023 is as follows.

Assets	
Cash	$ 60 000
Plant and equipment	1 620 000
Accumulated depreciation	(312 000)
Patent	3 000 000
Accumulated depreciation	(300 000)
Office equipment	132 000
Accumulated depreciation	(13 200)
Work in progress	60 000
Liabilities	
Creditors — for materials	204 000
Accruals — salaries etc., including the management fee	168 000
Cash payments	
Salaries	330 000
Materials	732 000
Operating expenses	126 000

Required
1. Prepare the journal entries in the records of Cairns Ltd and Townsville Ltd at the commencement of the joint operation.
2. Prepare the journal entries in the records of Mackay Ltd for the financial year ending 30 June 2023.

REFERENCES

CSR Limited 2014, *CSR and Boral propose to form East Coast Bricks JV*, www.csr.com.au.
Wesfarmers Limited 2018, *2018 annual report*, www.wesfarmers.com.au.

ACKNOWLEDGEMENTS

Photo: © AzmanL / Getty Images
Photo: © blue jean images RF / Getty Images
Figure 32.1: © CSR Limited 2014
Figure 32.3, 32.4, 32.5 and text: © 2019 Australian Accounting Standards Board (AASB). The text, graphics and layout of this publication are protected by Australian copyright law and the comparable law of other countries. No part of the publication may be reproduced, stored or transmitted in any form or by any means without the prior written permission of the AASB except as permitted by law. For reproduction or publication, permission should be sought in writing from the AASB. Requests in the first instance should be addressed to the National Director, Australian Accounting Standards Board, PO Box 204, Collins Street West, Victoria 8007.
Figure 32.6 and text: © Wesfarmers Limited 2018
Text: © IFRS. This publication contains copyright material of the IFRS Foundation in respect of which all rights are reserved. Reproduced by John Wiley & Sons Australia, Ltd with the permission of the IFRS Foundation. No permission granted to third parties to reproduce or distribute. For full access to IFRS Standards and the work of the IFRS Foundation please visit http://eifrs.ifrs.org. The International Accounting Standards Board, the IFRS Foundation, the authors and the publishers do not accept responsibility for any loss caused by acting or refraining from acting in reliance on the material in this publication, whether such loss is caused by negligence or otherwise.

CHAPTER 33

Insolvency and liquidation

CHAPTER AIM

The aim of this chapter is to consider the legal requirements when a company is unable to pay its debts, and the accounting procedures for liquidating a company. The chapter also describes the duties and powers of the person handling the liquidation (the liquidator), the order of priority of payment of the company's debts during the course of the liquidation and the payments, if any, to shareholders.

LEARNING OBJECTIVES

After studying this chapter, you should be able to:

33.1 describe the meaning of insolvency

33.2 describe the role of a receiver appointed by a secured creditor

33.3 describe the meaning of administration and identify the requirements imposed on an administrator and on directors of an insolvent company

33.4 describe the meaning of liquidation and the liquidator's duties, and compare the two modes of liquidation

33.5 describe the powers of a liquidator

33.6 determine how a company's debts are proven for liquidation

33.7 determine the order of priority of payment of the company's debts on liquidation

33.8 determine the rights and obligations of contributories on liquidation

33.9 prepare the accounting records necessary for the liquidation of a company.

CONCEPTS FOR REVIEW

Before studying this chapter, you should understand and, if necessary, revise:
- the different types of shares that may be issued by a company
- the accounting procedures for the issue, calls and forfeiture of partly paid shares.

33.1 Insolvency

LEARNING OBJECTIVE 33.1 Describe the meaning of insolvency.

One of the main advantages of the corporate form of organisation is that the life of the corporation does not cease on the retirement or death of any of its members. Nevertheless, a corporation's life is not unlimited and may end for various reasons, one of the most common being the lack of financial resources necessary to continue to operate (i.e. insolvency).

Section 95A of the *Corporations Act 2001* provides a definition of **solvent** and **insolvent** with reference to a person, but the definition can be extended to a company, which is considered a legal person.

(1) A person is solvent if, and only if, the person is able to pay all the person's debts, as and when they become due and payable.

(2) A person who is not solvent is insolvent.

The Corporations Act provides extensive guidance on the rights of members and creditors whenever the life of the company is in danger of drawing to a close due to financial difficulties. The Corporations Act attempts to avoid the liquidation or winding up (these terms can be used interchangeably) of companies in certain circumstances by allowing the appointment of receivers and/or administrators to protect the rights of creditors and members, and to help the company through any financial difficulties it may face. Liquidation proceedings are then undertaken only if the company cannot be saved.

The Australian Securities and Investments Commission (ASIC) website, www.asic.gov.au, provides guidance for directors, shareholders and creditors when a company becomes insolvent. For example, ASIC instructs directors that, if their company is insolvent, they must act not only on behalf of shareholders, but also on behalf of creditors and not allow the company to go further into debt. Unless it is possible to promptly restructure, refinance or obtain equity funding to recapitalise the company, generally the options are to appoint a voluntary administrator or a liquidator. However, the first signs of potential or existing insolvency may be detected by creditors, who may then initiate the receivership for the satisfaction of their claims before it is too late.

> **LEARNING CHECK**
>
> ☐ Insolvency occurs when a company is unable to pay its debts as and when they fall due and payable.

33.2 Receivership

LEARNING OBJECTIVE 33.2 Describe the role of a receiver appointed by a secured creditor.

Receivership is the first form of external administration prescribed by the Corporations Act and involves a receiver, receiver–manager or other **controller** being appointed to take possession or control of the property of the company for the purpose of enforcing a security interest. Unless the receiver is given the status of manager, he or she cannot enter into transactions such as buying or selling the company's property. In most cases, a **receiver–manager** is appointed. Section 416 of the Corporations Act specifies that, unless the contrary intention appears, a reference to a receiver of property of a corporation refers to a receiver–manager. In general, receivers are privately appointed at the instigation of a secured creditor who is given such power in his or her trust deed.

A **secured creditor** is someone who has a 'charge' over some or all of the company's assets to secure a debt owed by the company. Two types of secured creditor are recognised under the Corporations Act:

- a creditor secured by a **non-circulating security interest** (formerly known as a specific charge), such as a mortgage, lien or bill of sale
- a creditor secured by a **circulating security interest** (formerly known as a floating charge), which commonly occurs with debentures.

A receiver can also be appointed by a court. The power of a court to appoint a receiver is given by statute, and the court will make such an appointment when it perceives that it is just and convenient that such an order be made. The court would generally be required to make the order when a situation arises that is not covered by a trust deed or the strict letter of the security arrangement, or where parties other than secured creditors are seeking the appointment of a receiver. A court-appointed receiver needs the permission of the court to sell property of the company.

The **receiver** is responsible to the secured creditor or to the court, not to the company, but also has the same general duties as a company director. The receiver's role is to:

- collect and sell enough of the charged assets to repay the debt owed to the secured creditor
- pay out the money collected in the order required by the Corporations Act
- report to ASIC any offences or other irregular matters they discover in performing their duties.

In performing those duties a receiver has great powers, as stipulated in s. 420 of the Corporations Act.

> (1) Subject to this section, a receiver of property of a corporation has power to do, in Australia and elsewhere, all things necessary or convenient to be done for or in connection with, or as incidental to, the attainment of the objectives for which the receiver was appointed.

A receiver must always be a registered liquidator and according to s. 418(1) of the Corporations Act cannot be a person that:

> (a) is a secured party in relation to any property (including PPSA retention of title property) of the corporation; or
>
> (b) is an auditor or a director, secretary, senior manager or employee of the corporation; or
>
> (c) is a director, secretary, senior manager or employee of a body corporate that is a secured party in relation to any property (including PPSA retention of title property) of the corporation; or
>
> (d) is not a registered liquidator; or
>
> (e) is a director, secretary, senior manager or employee of a body corporate related to the corporation; or
>
> (f) unless ASIC directs in writing that this paragraph does not apply in relation to the person in relation to the corporation — has at any time within the last 12 months been a director, secretary, senior manager, employee or promoter of the corporation or of a related body corporate.

'PPSA' noted above refers to the *Personal Property Securities Act 2009*.

In accordance with s. 429(2)(b) of the Corporations Act, when a receiver is appointed, the company is required to submit to them within 14 days a **report as to affairs** of the company in accordance with ASIC's Form 507 'Report as to affairs' available on the ASIC website. The purpose of the report as to affairs is to provide information concerning the company's estimated realisable value of assets and any expected surplus or deficiency of assets after deducting creditors' claims. Furthermore, a receiver may require certain persons such as current and former officers and employees of the company to verify by a statement in writing and submit a report containing certain specified information as to the company's affairs (s. 430(1)). Any costs or expenses incurred by the officer or employee must be paid by the receiver out of their receipts from selling the company's property (s. 430(3)).

A receiver is required to open a special bank account (Corporations Act s. 421(1)) and, in accordance with s. 432, to lodge a **statement of receipts and payments** every 6 months, using ASIC's Form 524 'Presentation of accounts and statement' available on the ASIC website.

One problem a receiver may face is if they have been appointed under a circulating security interest. Section 433 of the Corporations Act indicates that certain other types of debts must be paid in priority to any claims for principal and interest under the circulating security interest. The debts having priority are listed in s. 433(3). Note that this list applies when the company is not in the process of being wound up.

> (3) In the case of a company, the receiver or other person taking possession or assuming control of property of the company must pay, out of the property coming into his, her or its hands, the following debts or amounts in priority to any claim for principal or interest in respect of the debentures:
>
> (a) first, any amount that in a winding up is payable in priority to unsecured debts pursuant to section 562;
>
> (b) next, if an auditor of the company had applied to ASIC under subsection 329(6) for consent to his, her or its resignation as auditor and ASIC had refused that consent before the relevant date — the reasonable fees and expenses of the auditor incurred during the period beginning on the day of the refusal and ending on the relevant date;
>
> (c) subject to subsections (6) and (7), next, any debt or amount that in a winding up is payable in priority to other unsecured debts pursuant to paragraph 556(1)(e), (g) or (h) or section 560.

Under s. 433(3)(c), wages, superannuation contributions, the superannuation guarantee charge, long service leave, sick leave and retrenchment payments are to be given priority over circulating security interests.

Neither state nor Commonwealth governments are entitled to any particular priority under these provisions. Therefore, unremitted pay-as-you-go (PAYG) tax deductions under the *Income Tax Assessment Act 1997* need only be paid by the receiver if they acquire control of all of the company's property. Otherwise, the PAYG deductions shall be paid by any liquidator appointed subsequent to the receivership.

Once the security is paid off, the receiver may simply resign. Alternatively, a winding up order may be made even though a receiver is in possession of the property of the company. The receivership still continues, and the receiver may be appointed as the liquidator. If a separate liquidator is appointed, the receiver is entitled to remain in control of the property on which the security is based. He or she still has the power to hold and dispose of relevant property, including the power to use the company's name for that purpose.

LEARNING CHECK

☐ Receivers are usually appointed by secured creditors such as mortgage holders. The main effect of appointing a receiver–manager is that the secured property can be sold to repay the debt of the secured creditor. The receiver is responsible to the secured creditor, not to the company.

☐ If the receiver is appointed by secured creditors under a circulating security interest, the receiver will need to repay certain preferential unsecured debts, such as wages, superannuation contributions, the superannuation guarantee charge, leave entitlements and retrenchment payments ahead of any payment to the secured creditor.

33.3 Administration

LEARNING OBJECTIVE 33.3 Describe the meaning of administration and identify the requirements imposed on an administrator and on directors of an insolvent company.

Administration is the second form prescribed in the Corporations Act of placing the control of a company in the hands of external parties when it faces financial difficulties. This form is addressed in Part 5.3A of the Act. The purpose of Part 5.3A is set out in s. 435A as follows.

> The object of this Part ... is to provide for the business, property and affairs of an insolvent company to be administered in a way that:
> (a) maximises the chances of the company, or as much as possible of its business, continuing in existence; or
> (b) if it is not possible for the company or its business to continue in existence — results in a better return for the company's creditors and members than would result from an immediate winding up of the company.

The onus of responsibility for insolvency falls squarely on the directors of a company, and the directors may be liable for prosecution under the Corporations Act if they allow the company to continue to trade while it is insolvent. According to s. 436A, directors are expected to appoint a voluntary administrator to the company even before it becomes insolvent.

> (1) A company may, by writing, appoint an administrator of the company if the board has resolved to the effect that:
> (a) in the opinion of the directors voting for the resolution, the company is insolvent, or is likely to become insolvent at some future time; and
> (b) an administrator of the company should be appointed.

An administrator may be appointed also by a liquidator or provisional liquidator if he or she believes that the company is or will become insolvent (Corporations Act s. 436B), or by a secured creditor who is entitled to enforce a charge on the whole, or substantially the whole, of a company's property (s. 436C).

According to ASIC, administration is designed to resolve the company's future direction quickly. An independent and suitably qualified person — the administrator — takes full control of the company in an attempt to save either the company or the company's business.

Section 437A(1) sets out the role of an **administrator** as follows.

> While a company is under administration, the administrator:
> (a) has control of the company's business, property and affairs; and
> (b) may carry on that business and manage that property and those affairs; and

(c) may terminate or dispose of all or part of that business, and may dispose of any of that property; and

(d) may perform any function, and exercise any power, that the company or any of its officers could perform or exercise if the company were not under administration.

The administrator takes over all the powers of the company and its directors (s. 437C). According to s. 437D, only the administrator can deal with company's property and any such transaction or dealing is void under s. 437D(2) unless:

(a) the administrator entered into it on the company's behalf; or

(b) the administrator consented to it in writing before it was entered into; or

(c) it was entered into under an order of the court.

The administrator must report to ASIC on possible offences by officers who continue to trade on the company's behalf. Section 437E of the Corporations Act provides that an order for compensation of losses can be served on any officer who undertakes a transaction which is void under s. 437D. Furthermore, a transfer of shares in a company or alteration of status of shareholders during an administration is not effective unless the administrator gives his or her written consent, or the court permits (s. 437F). The administrator or the court will need to be satisfied that the transfer of shares, or the alteration in the status of shareholders, is in the best interest of the company as a whole and does not breach other sections of the Corporations Act that deal with the rights of shareholders.

According to ASIC's website and s. 438A of the Corporations Act, the administrator, after taking control of the company, must investigate and report to creditors information as to the company's business, property, affairs and financial circumstances, and on the three options available to creditors. The options available to creditors are to:

1. end the administration and return the company to the directors' control
2. approve a deed of company arrangement through which the company will pay all or part of its debts and then be free of those debts
3. wind-up the company and appoint a liquidator.

The company's directors are required under the Corporations Act to help the administrator in performing their necessary tasks. According to s. 438B(1)–(3):

(1) As soon as practicable after the administration of a company begins, each director must:

(a) deliver to the administrator all books in the director's possession that relate to the company, other than books that the director is entitled, as against the company and the administrator, to retain; and

(b) if the director knows where other books relating to the company are — tell the administrator where those books are.

(2) Within 5 business days after the administration of a company begins or such longer period as the administrator allows, the directors must give to the administrator a report in the prescribed form about the company's business, property, affairs and financial circumstances.

(2A) The administrator must, within 5 business days after receiving a report under subsection (2), lodge a copy of the report.

(3) A director of a company under administration must:

(a) attend on the administrator at such times; and

(b) give the administrator such information about the company's business, property, affairs and financial circumstances; as the administrator reasonably requires.

The administrator must give an opinion on each option and recommend which option is in the best interests of creditors (Corporations Act s. 439A). The creditors then make the decision as to which option should be taken (s. 439C). If option 2 is taken, the administrator will continue his or her duties in order to see the deed of company arrangement through to its end, if suitable to the creditors. Chapter 5, Division 10 of the Corporations Act imposes many additional requirements on an administrator in exercising a deed of company arrangement, but these requirements are not covered in detail here. If option 3 is taken, the administrator can become the company's liquidator and, according to s. 446A, the liquidation process will proceed under the requirements of a creditors' voluntary winding up. According to s. 440A, 'a company under administration cannot be wound up voluntarily, except as provided by section 446A'. If an application for an order to wind up a company has been made to the court, and if the company is under administration, the court is required to adjourn the hearing of that application if it is satisfied that it is in the interests of the company's creditors for the company to continue under administration rather than be wound up. The court also cannot appoint a provisional liquidator of a company if the company is under administration and the court is satisfied that it is in the interests of the company's creditors for the company to continue under the administrator.

An administrator is not required to report to shareholders on the progress or outcome of the administration. Shareholders do not get to vote on the future of the company in these circumstances.

Additional powers are given to the administrator under s. 442A of the Corporations Act, which states:

> Without limiting section 437A, the administrator of a company under administration has power to do any of the following:
> (a) remove from office a director of the company;
> (b) appoint a person as such a director, whether to fill a vacancy or not;
> (c) execute a document, bring or defend proceedings, or do anything else, in the company's name and on its behalf;
> (d) whatever else is necessary for the purposes of this Part.

The administrator has the power to sell or close down the company's business or sell individual assets in the lead up to the creditors' decision on the company's future. If any of the company's property is secured under a charge, lien, pledge or lease, ss. 442B and 442C of the Corporations Act allow the administrator to deal with that property and to sell it, but only with the written consent of the security holders or the court. The court may only give leave to dispose of the property if it is satisfied that arrangements have been made to protect adequately the interests of the secured creditors. Under s. 442CC, if the administrator disposes of the property by way of sale, and, if the proceeds of sale equal or exceed the total of the secured debts, the administrator must set aside so much of the net proceeds as equals the total of those debts and apply the amount so set aside in paying those debts. However, if the proceeds of sale fall short of the total of the secured debts, then the administrator must set aside the net proceeds and apply the amount towards paying those debts in order of priority. If the amount is insufficient to fully pay debts of the same priority, they must be paid proportionately, and if any of those debts is not fully paid the debt that remains unpaid may be recovered from the company as an unsecured debt.

Even though the administrator is given wide powers under the Corporations Act, they are also given wide responsibilities. For example, under s. 443A, the administrator of a company is liable for debts incurred in the performance or exercise of any of their functions and powers as administrator, for:

(a) services rendered; or
(b) goods bought; or
(c) property hired, leased, used or occupied, including property consisting of goods that is subject to a lease that gives rise to a PPSA security interest in the goods; or
(d) the repayment of money borrowed; or
(e) interest in respect of money borrowed; or
(f) borrowing costs.

Under s. 443BA of the Corporations Act, the administrator of a company is also liable to pay to the Commissioner of Taxation amounts payable under the Income *Tax Assessment Act 1997*. Apart from these responsibilities, the administrator of a company under administration is not liable for other debts of the company.

According to s. 438E of the Corporations Act, an administrator is required to keep proper accounting records and to submit a statement of receipts and payments to creditors every 6 months using ASIC's Form 524, similarly to the receiver. If the administrator is in the process of executing a deed of company arrangement with creditors, a statement of receipts and payments must also be presented under the requirements of s. 445J.

LEARNING CHECK

☐ When insolvency occurs, the Corporations Act provides for an insolvent company to be administered in a way that maximises the chances of the company continuing in existence; or if that is not possible, results in a better return for the company's creditors and members than would result from an immediate winding up of the company.

□ The administrator, after taking control of the company, must investigate and report to creditors information as to the company's business, property, affairs and financial circumstances, and offer an opinion as to the best of three options available to creditors.
1. End the voluntary administration and return the company to the directors' control.
2. Approve a deed of company arrangement through which the company will pay all or part of its debts and then be free of those debts.
3. Wind up the company and appoint a liquidator.
□ The administrator must regularly submit to creditors a statement of receipts and payments in accordance with ASIC's Form 524.

33.4 Liquidation

LEARNING OBJECTIVE 33.4 Describe the meaning of liquidation and the liquidator's duties, and compare the two modes of liquidation.

Liquidation or winding up is the third form of external administration prescribed by the Corporations Act. **Liquidation** is a process whereby a company is dissolved, at which point the company ceases to be a legal entity. There are two modes of winding up a company:
- winding up by the court, addressed in Parts 5.4 to 5.4B and 5.6 of the Corporations Act
- voluntary winding up, addressed in Parts 5.5 and 5.6.

33.4.1 Winding up by the court

General grounds on which a company may be wound up by the court are listed in s. 461 of the Corporations Act as follows.

The court may order the winding up of a company if:
(a) the company has by special resolution resolved that it be wound up by the court; or
(c) the company does not commence business within one year from its incorporation or suspends its business for a whole year; or
(d) the company has no members; or
(e) directors have acted in affairs of the company in their own interests rather than in the interests of the members as a whole, or in any other manner whatsoever that appears to be unfair or unjust to other members; or
(f) affairs of the company are being conducted in a manner that is oppressive or unfairly prejudicial to, or unfairly discriminatory against, a member or members or in a manner that is contrary to the interests of the members as a whole; or
(g) an act or omission, or a proposed act or omission, by or on behalf of the company, or a resolution, or a proposed resolution, of a class of members of the company, was or would be oppressive or unfairly prejudicial to, or unfairly discriminatory against, a member or members or was or would be contrary to the interests of the members as a whole; or
(h) ASIC has stated in a report prepared under Division 1 of Part 3 of the ASIC Act, that, in its opinion:
  (i) the company cannot pay its debts and should be wound up; or
  (ii) it is in the interests of the public, of the members, or of the creditors, that the company should be wound up; or
(k) the court is of opinion that it is just and equitable that the company be wound up.

However, the most common reason for winding up by the court is insolvency. Under ss. 459P, 462 and 464 of the Corporations Act, various people and institutions may apply for the winding up of an insolvent company. These include the company itself, a creditor, a director, ASIC and a contributory. A contributory is defined in s. 9 and refers to the holders or immediate past holders of shares in the company. They will need to fill in the appropriate prescribed form, advertise the application, and serve the application on the company within 14 days (s. 465A). On hearing the application, the court may then issue an order to wind up the company, and the liquidation of the company is said to have commenced on the day of the winding up order, unless the company has been previously operating under an administrator. In this circumstance, the date of commencement is the day on which the administration began (see ss. 513A and 513C).

A provisional liquidator may be appointed at any time after the filing of the application (s. 472(2)) in order to see that the status quo of the company is maintained; that is, that the assets are not quickly drained from the company. On the day that the court issues the winding up order, it appoints a **liquidator** (s. 472(1)). It is common practice for the provisional liquidator (if any) to be appointed liquidator.

Once a company commences winding up, be it by a court order or voluntarily, the company is required in every public document and in every negotiable instrument of the company to include the words 'in liquidation' after its name (s. 541).

The liquidator's task is to:
- take possession of the company's assets under s. 474(1)
- realise the assets, or to carry on business as necessary for the beneficial disposal of the assets (s. 477(1))
- determine the creditors and order of priority of payment
- pay the creditors
- distribute the balance of funds (if any) to shareholders, or if necessary (or possible) to make calls on shareholders for extra funds to meet creditors' claims
- bring about the dissolution of the company.

Officers of the company are required to provide every reasonable assistance so the liquidator can carry out his or her duties (s. 530A). Furthermore, the directors and secretary of the company are required under s. 475 to submit a report as to the company's affairs to the liquidator no later than 14 days after the making of the winding up order, unless there are special reasons for not doing so, in which case an extension of time may be granted.

The report as to affairs under s. 475(1) of the Corporations Act must be presented as per ASIC's Form 507 'Report as to affairs' available on the ASIC website. The report as to affairs must be made out as at the date of the winding up order or at an earlier date if so specified by the liquidator (s. 475(1)). The aim of the report as to affairs is to provide information concerning the company's estimated realisable values of assets and any expected surplus or deficiency of assets after deducting creditors' claims. It is really a statement of financial position prepared on a realisation basis excluding the usual reporting assumptions of going concern and historical cost.

Once the liquidator has received the report as to affairs, they are required under s. 476 of the Corporations Act to lodge a preliminary report with ASIC, normally within 2 months, containing the following details.
- In the case of a company having a share capital — the amount of capital issued, subscribed and paid up
- The estimated amounts of assets and liabilities of the company
- If the company has failed — the causes of the failure
- Whether, in the liquidator's opinion, further enquiry is desirable regarding the promotion, formation or insolvency of the company or the conduct of the business of the company

After the liquidator has realised all the property, discharged the liability to creditors, and made a final return (if any) to contributories, he or she may apply to the court for the company to be deregistered (Corporations Act s. 480). When the order is made that the company be deregistered under s. 481(5), ASIC must deregister the company and the company ceases to exist (ss. 601AC and 601AD).

33.4.2 Voluntary winding up

If an application has been filed with the court on the grounds that the company is insolvent, or the court has ordered that the company be wound up in insolvency or the company is a trustee company that is in the course of administering or managing real estates, the company is not entitled to be wound up voluntarily unless leave is granted by the court (Corporations Act s. 490).

The basis for a voluntary winding up under Part 5.5 of the Corporations Act is the passing of a special resolution to wind up (s. 491) and the appointment of a liquidator in a general members' meeting (s. 495(1)). The special resolution may propose the winding up to be under the control of members (known as members' voluntary wind up) or creditors (known as creditors' voluntary wind up).

The members' voluntary wind up is only possible when the company is solvent to make sure creditors' interests are not overlooked. Therefore, where the members propose to wind up the company voluntarily under their control, the majority of directors are required, in accordance with s. 494(1) of the Corporations Act, to make a written declaration that they have made an inquiry into the affairs of the company and they have formed an opinion that the company will be able to pay its debts in full within a period not exceeding 12 months after the commencement of the winding up. The prescribed form for such a **declaration of solvency** is ASIC's Form 520 'Declaration of solvency' available on the ASIC website. This form details a **statement of affairs** (i.e. a statement of the estimated realisable values of assets and amounts payable for liabilities) to be included with the declaration, as required by s. 494(2) of the Corporations Act.

There must be attached to the declaration a statement of affairs of the company showing, in the prescribed form:

(a) the property of the company, and the total amount expected to be realised from that property; and

(b) the liabilities of the company; and

(c) the estimated expenses of winding up;

made up to the latest practicable date before the making of the declaration.

If the directors refuse to sign a declaration of solvency, the winding up thereafter proceeds under the control of creditors, as a creditors' voluntary winding up.

If the directors sign a declaration of solvency, but the liquidator forms the opinion that the company will not be able to pay its debts in full within the period stated in the declaration of solvency, the liquidator must do *one* of the following, under s. 496(1) of the Corporations Act.

• Apply under s. 459P for the company to be wound up in insolvency.

• Appoint an administrator of the company under s. 436B.

• Convene a meeting of the company's creditors.

If the liquidator selects the third option, the winding up thereafter proceeds as if it was a creditors' voluntary winding up.

In a *creditors' voluntary winding up*, as s. 497(1) of the Corporations Act states the following.

The liquidator of the company must, within 10 business days after the day of the meeting of the company at which the resolution for voluntary winding up is passed:

(a) send to each creditor:

(i) a summary of the affairs of the company in the prescribed form; and

(ii) a list setting out the names of all creditors, the addresses of those creditors and the estimated amounts of their claims, as shown in the records of the company; and

(b) lodge a copy of the documents sent in accordance with paragraph (a).

A **summary of affairs** provides less detail than a report as to affairs under s. 475 and must be completed in accordance with ASIC's Form 509 'Presentation of summary of affairs of a company' available on the ASIC website.

Within 5 days of the meeting at which the resolution for voluntary winding up is passed, the directors of the company must give the liquidator a report as to the company's business, property, affairs and financial circumstances (Corporations Act s. 497(4)). The creditors' meeting may also nominate a person to be liquidator, and if that person nominated is different from the person nominated previously at the members' meeting, the person nominated by the creditors will be the liquidator (s. 499).

The liquidator then proceeds to wind up the company. Once the affairs are fully wound up, the liquidator must prepare an account showing how the winding up has been conducted and the property disposed of (Corporations Act s. 509). The liquidator must lodge a return with ASIC on the basis that the affairs of the company are fully wound up. On the expiration of 3 months after the lodging of this return, s. 509(1) states that ASIC must deregister the company.

LEARNING CHECK

☐ Once a company commences winding up, one of the first tasks to be undertaken is the preparation of a report as to affairs, the format of which is found in ASIC's Form 507.

☐ The main purpose of a report as to affairs is to estimate the realisable value of the company's assets and to assess whether there is a surplus or deficiency for the members.

☐ Insolvency is one of the main reasons for a company to be wound up by a court order.

☐ A voluntary winding up is initiated by the members of a company and may be under the control of either the members or the creditors of the company.

☐ If an application for winding up the company already exists or the company is subject to winding up by the court, the company is not entitled to be wound up voluntarily unless leave is granted by the court.

☐ In a members' voluntary winding up, the members control the winding up process and, because of that, only a solvent company can be subject to a members' voluntary winding up; to ensure this is the case, a declaration of solvency needs to be prepared in accordance with ASIC's Form 520.

☐ In a creditors' voluntary winding up, creditors control the winding up process. No declaration of solvency exists and creditors must be sent a summary of affairs (in accordance with ASIC's Form 509) attached to the notice of the forthcoming creditors' meeting.

▶

☐ The liquidator must present an account showing how the winding up has been conducted and the property disposed of either at a meeting of members or, in the case of a creditors' voluntary winding up, at a meeting of members and creditors, and then lodge it with ASIC, which then deregisters the company.

33.5 Powers of a liquidator

LEARNING OBJECTIVE 33.5 Describe the powers of a liquidator.

In the case of a company being *wound up by the court*, the powers of the liquidator are specified in s. 477 of the Corporations Act. Section 477(1) states that the liquidator may:

- carry on the business of the company so far as is necessary for its beneficial disposal or winding up
- pay any class of creditors in full (subject to the provisions of s. 556)
- make compromises or arrangements with creditors or people claiming to be creditors
- come to agreements regarding calls, liabilities and claims existing between the company and a contributory or other debtor, and take any security for the payment of such calls, liabilities and claims. According to s. 477(2) of the Corporations Act, a liquidator may also:
- enter into legal proceedings on behalf of the company
- appoint a solicitor to help with the duties
- sell/dispose of property of the company
- exercise the court's powers under s. 483(3) in relation to making calls on contributories
- deal with all deeds, receipts and other documents of the company, using the company's seal when necessary
- subject to the *Bankruptcy Act 1966*, prove the bankruptcy of contributories or debtors of the company or under any deed executed under that Act
- deal with bills of exchange or promissory notes on behalf of the company
- obtain credit where necessary
- use any legal methods to obtain payment of money due from a contributory or a debtor, or from the estate of a deceased contributory or debtor
- appoint an agent to do what the liquidator cannot do in person
- do everything else that is necessary to wind up the affairs of the company and distribute its property.

Normally, a liquidator must not make concessions on a debt to the company if the amount claimed by the company is $20 000 or more. The liquidator is also entitled to inspect the records of the company and it is illegal to try to stop this (Corporations Act s. 477(2A) and (3)).

The liquidator's powers given by s. 477 of the Corporations Act are controlled by the court; any creditor or contributory or ASIC may apply to the court regarding the liquidator's proposed exercise of these powers (s. 477(6)).

In the case of a *voluntary winding up*, the liquidator's powers are specified in s. 506 of the Corporations Act. The liquidator can:

- exercise any powers the Corporations Act confers on a liquidator in a winding up in insolvency or by the court
- exercise the power under s. 478 of a liquidator appointed by the court to settle a list of contributors
- exercise the court's powers under s. 483(3) in relation to making calls on contributories
- exercise the power of the court of fixing a time when debts and claims must be proved
- convene a general meeting of the company to obtain agreement for matters as the liquidator thinks fit.

As with a court winding up, the liquidator must not make concessions on any debts except as under s. 477(2A) of the Corporations Act. The liquidator must then pay the debts of the company and sort out the rights of the contributories (s. 506(3)).

The liquidator is required to keep proper records in which entries with details of proceedings of meetings must be made. Also, similarly to the administrator, the liquidator must regularly submit to creditors a statement of receipts and payments in accordance with ASIC's Form 524 as per s. 539(1) of the Corporations Act. Creditors and contributories, or their agents, are entitled to inspect these records, unless the court orders otherwise (s. 531).

□ In a winding up by the court, the liquidator has powers specified under s. 477 of the Corporations Act, including carrying on the business, selling properties of the company, collecting calls from contributories on partly paid shares, and paying creditors before winding up the company.

□ In a voluntary winding up, the liquidator's powers are specified by s. 506 and include all the powers given by s. 477.

□ A liquidator is required to keep proper records, containing entries and proceedings of meetings, and should prepare statements of receipts and payments in accordance with ASIC's Form 524.

33.6 Identifying the company's debts on liquidation

LEARNING OBJECTIVE 33.6 Determine how a company's debts are proven for liquidation.

Section 553 of the Corporations Act entitles all creditors' claims to be admissible to proof against the company in liquidation.

(1) Subject to this Division [Division 6] and Division 8, in every winding up, all debts payable by, and all claims against, the company (present or future, certain or contingent, ascertained or sounding only in damages), being debts or claims the circumstances giving rise to which occurred before the relevant date, are admissible to proof against the company...

(2) Where, after the relevant date, an order is made under section 91 of the ASIC Act against a company that is being wound up, the amount that, pursuant to the order, the company is liable to pay is admissible to proof against the company.

The actual procedures to be followed if proof of debts is required by the liquidator are provided in Corporations Regulations 5.6.39 to 5.6.57. Debts may be admitted by the liquidator without formal proof; however, if a formal proof is requested, the creditor must complete Form 535 'Formal proof of debt or claim' found in Schedule 2 of the Regulations (Corporations Act s. 553D).

The size of any debt (including a debt that is for or includes interest) is calculated for the purposes of the winding up as at the relevant date (Corporations Act s. 554), which is defined in s. 9 as the day on which the winding up is taken to have begun, in accordance with ss. 513A–513C.

□ All debts payable by or claims against the company up to the relevant date are admissible for proof against the company.

□ The liquidator must determine which debts are admissible and which are not.

33.7 Ranking the company's debts on liquidation

LEARNING OBJECTIVE 33.7 Determine the order of priority of payment of the company's debts on liquidation.

The general principle regarding priority of payment of debts in liquidation is stated in s. 555 of the Corporations Act as follows.

Except as otherwise provided by this Act, all debts and claims proved in a winding up rank equally and, if the property of the company is insufficient to meet them in full, they must be paid proportionately.

The Act, however, allows many exceptions to the general rule. According to the Act, four different categories of creditors can be identified, listed in order of priority of payment:
- secured creditors
- preferential unsecured creditors
- ordinary unsecured creditors
- deferred creditors.

33.7.1 Secured creditors

A secured creditor is a creditor secured over a non-circulating or circulating security interest. In receiving payment for a debt on the winding up of an insolvent company, each type of secured creditor has three choices of action available to them under the Corporations Act.

1. Surrender the security and prove for the whole amount of the debt as an unsecured creditor (s. 554E(3)).
2. Realise the asset(s) subject to the security, and prove for the balance (if any) not recovered from the asset(s) unless the liquidator is not satisfied that the realisation has been effected in good faith and in a proper manner (s. 554E(4)).
3. Estimate the value of the security and prove for the balance. The liquidator may redeem the security by paying to the creditor the amount of the estimated value of the security (s. 554F). In this situation, the liquidator usually has a statutory lien or commercial law lien over the funds realised for his or her expenses and fees (remuneration) to the extent that they pertain to the realisation of the secured assets.

Creditors secured by a non-circulating security interest

Creditors secured by a non-circulating interest have a charge against specific property, and hold a registered mortgage, bill of sale or lien over that property. Control of the property rests with the secured creditor. The liquidator has no control; however, the property may be dealt with in either of two ways.

1. Provided the creditor agrees, the liquidator may pay the secured creditor the amount claimed and claim the property.
2. The creditor may proceed with due legal action to sell the property, returning any money in excess of his or her claim to the liquidator.

The advantage to a secured creditor of choosing the second option is that the property covered by the non-circulating security interest does not pass through the liquidator.

In the situation where the property does not realise the total claim of the secured creditor, the balance of the claim is no longer secured and the creditor must prove in the liquidation for the balance of the claim as an unsecured creditor. (Such a creditor is referred to as a **partly secured creditor** in the summary of affairs).

Note that under s. 124 of the Corporations Act, the company also has the power to mortgage the company's uncalled capital. However, the principle of limited liability, as spelled out in s. 516, applies in that no additional amounts can be called to satisfy secured creditors (or any other creditor):

> if the company is a company limited by shares, a member need not contribute more than the amount (if any) unpaid on the shares in respect of which the member is liable as a present or past member.

Creditors secured by a circulating security interest

Creditors secured by a circulating security interest hold a charge relating to all assets of the company; that is, it 'floats' over whatever assets the company has at a particular time. When a liquidator is appointed, the circulating security interest takes form ('crystallises') over specific assets and the circulating security interest holder ranks as a secured creditor. This type of security is advantageous to a company since it does not restrict the management of specific assets. These creditors are secured and have preference of payment over unsecured creditors. However, s. 561 of the Corporations Act sets out three debts which, if there are limited funds, must be paid in the following order in preference to a claim secured by a circulating security interest.

1. Wages and superannuation contributions payable by the company for services rendered by employees before the relevant date, but not exceeding $2000 in respect of an excluded employee of the company (ss. 556(1)(e) and 556(1A)).
2. All amounts due on or before the relevant date to employees through industrial awards and for leave of absence, but not exceeding $1500 in the case of an excluded employee of the company. These amounts include long service leave, recreation leave, sick leave, superannuation contributions, and amounts due to any person who has advanced money to the company for the purpose of paying such employee entitlements (ss. 556(1)(g), 556(1B), 558 and 560).
3. Retrenchment payments payable to employees of the company (other than excluded employees, i.e. a director of the company, or a spouse or relative of the director) (ss. 556(1)(h) and 556(1C)).

33.7.2 Preferential unsecured creditors

Preferential unsecured creditors are those creditors who are given preferential treatment over other unsecured creditors. Section 556 of the Corporations Act lists, in order of priority of payment, 13 classes of debt that belong to preferential unsecured creditors:

1. expenses incurred by the administrator or liquidator in preserving, realising or getting in property of the company or in carrying on the company's business
2. first applicant's costs incurred to obtain a winding up order by the court
3. debts incurred by an administrator or liquidator that are to be indemnified
4. costs incurred by directors for preparing the report as to affairs in the case of winding up by court
5. costs incurred by directors for preparing the summary of affairs in the case of voluntary winding up
6. costs of auditing the liquidator's accounts where the audit was required by ASIC
7. costs incurred by the administrator or liquidator
8. administrator's or liquidator's fee (called deferred expenses in s. 556)
9. costs incurred by the members of the committee of inspection
10. wages and superannuation contributions payable by the company for services rendered by employees before the relevant date, but not exceeding $2000 in respect of an excluded employee of the company
11. workers' injury compensation claims
12. all amounts due on or before the relevant date to employees through industrial awards and for leave of absence, but not exceeding $1500 in the case of an excluded employee of the company
13. retrenchment payments payable to employees of the company (other than excluded employees).

33.7.3 Ordinary unsecured creditors

Ordinary unsecured creditors are creditors whose debts have no preferential treatment and are the last to be paid before funds are returned to contributories. As specified in s. 555 of the Corporations Act, the debts rank equally, and if the property of the company is insufficient to meet them in full, they are to be paid proportionately. Unsecured creditors include trade creditors, rent payable, audit fees payable (for normal year-end audit), directors' fees payable (excluding any salary up to $2000 paid to directors as employees of the firm, which have preferential ranking under s. 556), telephone and internet bills, goods and services tax, rates, fringe benefits tax and PAYG income tax instalments payable to the Australian Taxation Office.

In relation to ordinary unsecured creditors, note the following.

- Although creditors such as electricity authorities and telecommunications companies are unsecured, they often obtain preferential payment by threatening to withdraw their services.
- Local Government Acts and State Land Tax Acts may empower the authority to charge the land for unpaid rates and taxes. For example, all municipal rates levied by a local government authority in Western Australia act as a charge against the relevant land according to s. 576 of the Local Government Act. In the event of land being transferred, the Act provides for the remittance of the rates outstanding from the proceeds of the sale of the land. A council has the power of sale over land where the municipal rates are outstanding for a period of more than 3 years. The effect of these provisions within the Local Government Act is to render rates preferential in terms of priority of payment, as the rates must be paid before a secured creditor is able to exercise the right to sell real property.

33.7.4 Deferred creditors

Deferred creditors hold, in effect, certain debts that are payable to the contributories of the company ahead of repayments of capital to those contributories. Depending on the constitution of the company, arrears of preference dividends whether declared or otherwise, any ordinary dividends payable, and any calls paid in advance by contributories may be paid ahead of any returns of capital. However, as per s. 563A of the Corporations Act, such debts are deferred until all unsecured creditors are paid in full. Claims by shareholders under a buyback arrangement are also deferred creditors (s. 563AA). Contributories' rights to receive dividends and calls in advance are further discussed in section 33.8.

☐ Creditors are paid in order of priority, which is usually the following order: creditors secured by a non-circulating security interest (specific charge), creditors secured by a circulating security interest (floating charge), preferential unsecured creditors, ordinary unsecured creditors and then deferred creditors.

☐ In cases of insolvency, some preferential unsecured creditors rank for payment ahead of creditors secured by a circulating security interest, namely wages payable, leave payable and retrenchment payments payable.

33.8 Rights of contributories on liquidation

LEARNING OBJECTIVE 33.8 Determine the rights and obligations of contributories on liquidation.

In respect of a limited company, a **contributory** is defined in s. 9 of the Corporations Act as follows.

> (a) in relation to a company (other than a no liability company):
>> (i) a person liable as a member or past member to contribute to the property of the company if it is wound up; and
>> (ii) for a company with a share capital — a holder of fully paid shares in the company; and
>> (iii) before the final determination of the persons who are contributories because of sub-paragraphs (i) and (ii) — a person alleged to be such a contributory. . .

Note that the liability extends to past members as well as to present members. The liability of contributories is specified in Part 5.6, Division 2, of the Corporations Act. Note the following points.

- Present or past members must contribute to the company's property enough money to pay the company's debts and liabilities and costs of the winding up, and to adjust the rights of contributories among themselves (s. 515).
- In the case of a limited liability company, present and past members do not have to contribute more than the amount unpaid on the shares (for a company limited by shares) or the amount undertaken to contribute (for a company limited by guarantee) for which each is liable as a past or present member (ss. 516–518).
- Past members do not have to contribute money for a debt or liability of the company which occurred after they ceased to be members (s. 520).
- Past members do not need to contribute if they were not members for more than a year before the commencement of the winding up (s. 521), unless prior to winding up, the company changed from an unlimited company to a limited company under s. 164 and the past member was a member at the time of the change (s. 523(a)).
- Past members only need to contribute if it appears to the court that the existing members cannot satisfy the contributions they are liable to make under the Act (s. 522) or if prior to winding up, the company changed from an unlimited company to a limited company and no person who was a member at that time is a member at the commencement of the winding up (s. 523(b)).

In accordance with ss. 478 and 506(1)(c), the liquidator is required to make a list of the contributories. The list is divided into two parts (s. 478(3)):

1. contributories in their own right
2. people who are contributories by virtue of representing, or being liable for the debts of, other people.

The list of contributories is prima facie evidence of the liabilities of people named in the list of contributories (ss. 478(4) and 506(2)). People whose names are on the list must be notified by the liquidator and are given time (21 days after service of the notice or any further period if allowed by the court) to appeal against their inclusion (Corporations Regulations 5.6.62).

The contributories have claims over the share capital contributed, but those claims can only be satisfied once the creditors' claims are fully satisfied. Therefore, the following three possible situations can arise in relation to contributories' claims:

1. insufficient funds exist to pay creditors, requiring calls to be made on contributories
2. sufficient funds exist to meet creditors' claims, but not to repay all share capital to contributories
3. surplus funds exist over and above creditors' and contributories' claims.

33.8.1 Insufficient funds to pay creditors

If there are insufficient funds to pay the creditors and partly paid shares exist, the court is empowered, in a winding up by the court, to issue an order to make calls on all or any of the contributories to the extent of their liability, to be paid into a bank account kept by the liquidator (Corporations Act s. 483(3) and (4)). In a voluntary winding up, power to make calls on contributories is conferred on the liquidator by s. 506(1)(d). To enforce payment of the call, the liquidator may bring a court action against the contributory. Section 527 of the Corporations Act states that the liability of a contributory is of the nature of a specialty debt, and is payable when calls are made for enforcing the liability.

Once all shares have been paid in full, any deficiency of funds must be borne by creditors in the reverse order of priority of payment. Thus, deferred creditors suffer losses first, followed by unsecured creditors, then preferential unsecured creditors, and so on.

33.8.2 Sufficient funds to pay creditors, but not to repay all share capital to contributories

Most liquidations in Australia do not have sufficient funds to pay creditors; hence, it is rare for a company to return any capital to its contributories. In a situation where there is sufficient money to pay all creditors in full *but not all* contributories in full, the company is faced with a 'deficiency' of funds for contributories. The overriding principle is that any distribution of this deficiency, and of money, to contributories must be made in accordance with the company's constitution. A constitution may give preference shareholders priority claim over ordinary shareholders as to return of capital. If so, then preference shareholders' claims must be satisfied in full before any funds are paid to ordinary shareholders. However, preference shareholders do not have this priority claim to return of capital unless it is specifically stated in the company's constitution.

The requirements of companies' constitutions as to return of capital vary. For example, many constitutions may contain statements based on the repealed Table A of Schedule 1 to the Corporations Act as follows.

> 97. (1) If the company is wound up, the liquidator may, with the sanction of a special resolution, divide among the members in kind the whole or any part of the property of the company and may for that purpose set such value as he [/she] considers fair upon any property to be so divided and may determine how the division is to be carried out as between the members or different classes of members.

This paragraph effectively gives the liquidator, in consultation with the members, the power to determine the final distribution to be made to shareholders. Any distribution calculation then is approved by a special resolution of members. In the case of disputes, the liquidator may need to seek advice from the court. Generally, in the absence of clear statements in the company's constitution and in the absence of legal precedent, the Corporations Act is unclear as to the appropriate final distribution to shareholders. In the absence of agreement among shareholders, some liquidators in practice may refer the ultimate distribution decision to ASIC.

Some of the more modern company constitutions are worded along the following lines and these words probably express the current intention of the Act.

> Any deficiency of funds on the winding up of a company is to be borne by each shareholder in accordance with the number of shares held, irrespective of the issue price of those shares. If any shares are partly paid, the amount unpaid on those shares is to be treated as property of the company.

In this circumstance, it does not matter how much is paid to the company by each shareholder under the terms of the share issue. All fully paid shareholders receive the same payout per share from the remaining funds, even though some may have paid $2 per share and others $7 per share. However, if the shares are partly paid, the unpaid amount on those shares represents part of the property of the company to be distributed to shareholders. Thus, shareholders who have fully paid shares are not at a disadvantage compared with those who hold partly paid shares, as the shareholders with partly paid shares will be liable for the remaining instalments before any cash is distributed to them.

Distribution of cash to contributories

Assume the following data.

Share capital:
200 000 'A' ordinary shares issued for $1 and paid to 25c	$ 50 000
550 000 'B' ordinary shares issued and fully paid at $1	550 000
	$600 000

- Cash available for payment to contributories is $240 000.
- The constitution states that contributories rank equally per share as to return of capital. Figure 33.1 illustrates the distribution of cash per share.

FIGURE 33.1	Distribution of cash to contributories

	No. of shares	Paid to	Notional call	Notional refund 52c	Actual refund (call)	Deficiency share
'A' ordinary	200 000	$ 50 000	$150 000	$104 000	$ (46 000)	$ 96 000
'B' ordinary	550 000	550 000	—	286 000	286 000	264 000
	750 000	600 000	150 000	$390 000	$240 000	$ 36 000
Cash available		(240 000)	240 000			
Deficiency		$ 360 000				
Total notional cash			$390 000			

Total notional cash per share = $390 000 ÷ 750 000 = 52c per share

From figure 33.1, note that the company calculates the notional cash available for payment to all shareholders as the cash available of $240 000 plus a notional call on the partly paid 'A' ordinary shares of $150 000 up to their full issue price. Thus, $390 000 is potentially available for distribution across 750 000 shares. As all shares participate equally in the final distribution, this is equivalent to 52c per share. The 'B' ordinary shares, being fully paid, are therefore entitled to receive $286 000 (i.e. 52c × 550 000 shares). As the notional call on the 'A' ordinary shares to make them fully paid ($150 000) is greater than the notional refund on these shares ($104 000, i.e. 52c × 200 000 shares), the holders of those shares will be called to pay a total of $46 000 (23c per share). Figure 33.1 also shows that, as a result of the final distribution to shareholders, the total deficiency of funds to contributories of $360 000 (i.e. $600 000 − $240 000) is shared between 'A' ordinary shareholders — who lose $96 000 ($50 000 paid-up capital + $46 000 call) and 'B' ordinary shareholders — who lose $264 000 ($550 000 paid-up capital − $286 000 refund).

When making a call on contributories, two general principles are followed by the liquidator, as illustrated in figure 33.1.
- No share is fully called up unless all the uncalled capital is required to meet claims.
- The call should be equal to the amount needed to meet the creditors' claims and to adjust the rights of contributories, after giving due consideration to the probability that some contributories may fail to pay the call.

Thus, in the above example, although a call of 23c per share is required on the 'A' ordinary shareholders to adjust the rights of all classes, it is likely that not all shareholders will pay the call. If the liquidator is unable to receive calls from some shareholders, those shares will be forfeited and excluded from any calculation of distribution on liquidation. Further calls may then be required on those shareholders who did not default on the earlier call, to the extent of the issue price of those shares. Alternatively, the liquidator may initiate legal proceedings against the defaulting shareholder in order to recover the amount due, if such proceedings are not too costly.

33.8.3 Surplus funds over and above creditors' and contributories' claims

As with the sharing of any deficiency and repayment of funds to contributories, the rights of contributories to participate in a surplus of funds should be specified in the constitution. Preference shareholders may or may not be entitled to share in a surplus with ordinary shareholders, depending on the constitution. Any provision in the constitution that gives preference shareholders a prior claim as to return of capital does not automatically give them a right to participate in a surplus on liquidation. As in figure 33.1, the contributories may rank equally per share and therefore the apportionment may be based on the number of shares and not on the amount paid up. Furthermore, if there are surplus funds and one or more classes of shares have unpaid calls, the liquidator may simply refund the amount due to the shareholders who are in arrears less calls and related interest due.

Procedures for distributing a surplus to contributories are set down in Corporations Regulations 5.6.71 and 5.6.72.

33.8.4 Calls in advance and arrears of dividends

Two further matters affecting payment to contributories are calls in advance and arrears of dividends.

Calls in advance

The constitution may deal with this situation; however, in the absence of such guidance, calls in advance with related interest will be repaid before any payments are made to shareholders, and after all payments have been made to creditors. Note s. 563A of the Corporations Act reaffirms that money due to members is to be paid only after all other creditors have been paid in full; that is, shareholders with calls in advance are effectively deferred creditors. However, calls in advance on shares with a priority as to return of capital must be repaid in full before any payment of calls in advance on other shares.

Arrears of dividends

Once again the constitution must be consulted — there may be provision for prior payment of arrears of dividend on liquidation. If there is no guidance in the constitution, and if the dividend is a legal debt but not paid, those shareholders have a prior claim over other returns of capital to shareholders but rank after unsecured creditors; that is, shareholders with dividends in arrears are deferred creditors. If no dividend declaration has been made and the constitution is silent, there can be no claim for arrears of dividend unless the terms of the share issue so provide.

LEARNING CHECK

- ☐ In a company limited by shares, contributories are required to pay up to a maximum of the issue price of the shares in respect to which they are liable as a present or past member in order to pay creditors in full.
- ☐ The rights of contributories, in both a deficiency and surplus situation, are determined by the requirements laid down in the company's constitution.
- ☐ If the constitution is silent, then a deficiency is borne by each shareholder, preference and ordinary, in accordance with the number of shares held.
- ☐ Calls in advance, to the extent that they do not need to be called up by the liquidator, are repaid to shareholders after all creditors have been paid and before any distribution of capital to shareholders.
- ☐ Dividends that are a legal debt must be paid after all creditors have been paid, and dividends undeclared are not paid unless the constitution specifically says so.

33.9 Accounting for liquidation

LEARNING OBJECTIVE 33.9 Prepare the accounting records necessary for the liquidation of a company.

In terms of accounting requirements on liquidation, five main tasks are to be performed:
1. preparation of various reports by the company for the liquidator: a report as to affairs (Form 507), a summary of affairs (Form 509) in a creditors' voluntary winding up, and a declaration of solvency (Form 520) in a members' voluntary winding up
2. realisation of the assets

3. possession of assets by secured creditors
4. payment to the creditors in order of priority
5. return of capital and surplus (if any) to contributories (shareholders).

33.9.1 Reports prepared by the company for the liquidator

Illustrative example 33.2 demonstrates a summary of affairs prepared in the case of a creditors' voluntary winding up. This report is shown on the grounds of simplicity for learning purposes, as it avoids preparation of detailed schedules required by the report as to affairs. Preparation of a summary of affairs is illustrated using the format specified in ASIC's Form 509, entitled 'Presentation of summary of affairs of a company' (see the ASIC website for a copy of this form).

ILLUSTRATIVE EXAMPLE 33.2

Summary of affairs

Fern Ltd resolved to wind up its affairs on 31 December 2023. Its statement of financial position prepared for internal purposes is shown in figure 33.2.

FIGURE 33.2   Statement of financial position of the company winding up

FERN LTD **Statement of financial position** as at 31 December 2023		
Current assets		
Inventories	$130 000	
Trade receivables (net)	100 000	
Interest receivable on bonds	50	
Total current assets		$230 050
Non-current assets		
Freehold property	85 000	
Plant and machinery (net)	33 875	
Goodwill	25 000	
8% investments (due 31/03/26)	5 000	
Total non-current assets		148 875
Total assets		378 925
Current liabilities		
Trade creditors	115 000	
Bank overdraft (secured on freehold property)	25 000	
Other liabilities	8 925	
Total current liabilities		148 925
Non-current liabilities		
10% debentures (secured by a circulating security interest)	50 000	
12% unsecured notes	100 000	
Total non-current liabilities		150 000
Total liabilities		298 925
Net assets		**$ 80 000**
Share capital		
25 000 10% preference shares issued at $1 and fully paid		$ 25 000
60 000 ordinary shares issued at $1 and partly paid	$ 60 000	
Less: Calls in arrears 5000 × 25c	(1 250)	58 750
		83 750
Reserves		
Retained earnings		(3 750)
Total equity		**$ 80 000**

Additional information

(a) Other liabilities included the following.

Wages payable (for one person)	$2 500
Directors' fees payable	2 000
Goods and services tax payable	1 500
Rates payable for year ended 31/12/23	1 000
Long service leave payable	750
Sick leave payable	375
Workers compensation payable	300
PAYG tax instalment payable	500
	$8 925

(b) Assets were expected to realise the following estimated values.

Freehold property	$135 000
Plant and machinery	20 000
Trade receivables	90 000
Goodwill	nil
8% investments to be sold 'cum div.'	5 000
Inventories	95 000
Calls in arrears	nil

Required

Prepare a summary of affairs as at 31 December 2023 for Fern Ltd.

Solution

ASIC's Form 509 is used in the preparation of a summary of affairs (see figure 33.3). Details are included in the body of the statement where necessary.

FIGURE 33.3	Summary of affairs, Fern Ltd

FERN LTD
Summary of affairs
Assets and liabilities as at 31 December 2023

	Valuation (show whether cost or net book amount)	Estimated realisable values
1. Assets not specifically charged:		
(a) Interest in land	—	—
(b) Sundry debtors: Trade receivables (net book amount)	$ 100 000	$ 90 000
Calls in arrears	1 250	—
(c) Cash on hand	—	—
(d) Cash at bank	—	—
(e) Stock as detailed in inventories	130 000	9 000
(f) Work in progress as detailed in inventories	—	—
(g) Plant and machinery as detailed in inventories (net book amount)	33 875	20 000
(h) Other assets: 8% investments	5 000	5 000
Interest on bonds	50	—
Goodwill (net carrying amount)	25 000	—
	295 175	210 000
2. Assets subject to specific charges: Freehold property $ 85 000		
Less: Amounts owing (25 000)	60 000	110 000
Total assets	**355 175**	**320 000**
Total estimated realisable values		**320 000**

3. *Less:* Preferential creditors entitled to priority over the
   holders of debentures under any floating charge

Wages	(2 500)	
Long service leave	(750)	
Sick leave	(375)	(3 625)
		316 375

4. *Less:* Amounts owing and secured by floating charge
   over company's assets

10% debentures		(50 000)
		266 375

5. *Less:* Preferential creditors

Workers compensation		(300)
Estimated amount available for unsecured creditors		266 075

6. Creditors (unsecured)

Rates	1 000	
GST	1 500	
Directors' fees	2 000	
Unsecured notes	100 000	
Trade creditors	115 000	
PAYG tax instalments	500	220 000
		46 075

7. Balances owing to partly secured creditors —
8. Contingent assets, estimated to produce —
9. Contingent liabilities estimated to rank for estimated
   deficiency/surplus —

Estimated surplus (subject to costs of liquidation)		$ 46 075
Share capital		
Issued: 25 000 10% preference shares issued at $1	25 000	
60 000 ordinary shares issued at $1	60 000	$ 85 000
Paid up: 25 000 10% preference shares	25 000	
55 000 ordinary shares fully paid	55 000	
5 000 ordinary shares paid to 75c	3 750	$ 83 750

Note the following points.

(a) Estimated realisable value for assets subject to specific charges: $135 000 (estimated realisable value of freehold property) − $25 000 (bank overdraft secured on freehold property) = $110 000.

(b) Three creditors (wages, long service leave and sick leave) are given preference over circulating security interests (floating charge), assuming that wages were not payable to an excluded employee.

(c) All unsecured creditors rank equally.

33.9.2 Realisation of the assets

The realisation of assets is accounted for in the company's records using a liquidation account and a liquidator's receipts and payments account. Note that this latter account is actually a cash account that recognises the cash of the company now controlled by the liquidator; however, given that the information included there is exactly the same as that required to be included in the statement of receipts and payments according to ASIC Form 524, in this text is it identified as the liquidator's receipts and payments account. The cash available at the liquidation date is recognised as the beginning balance of the liquidator's receipts and payments account. As the liquidation process begins, first the carrying amounts of all assets that will be sold by the liquidator (i.e. except cash and assets subject to a security interest) are transferred to the liquidation account. If the carrying amount of an asset is the result of a balance in the asset account adjusted for a related contra-account (e.g. the carrying amount of a non-current asset is the balance in the asset account minus the related accumulated depreciation), the balance in the asset account is written off as a credit to the asset against a debit to the liquidation account, while the balance of the related contra-account is written off by debiting the contra-account against a credit to the liquidation account.

Liquidation	Dr	xxx	
Carrying amounts of assets transferred	Cr		xxx

Second, on realisation (sale) of the assets by the liquidator, the liquidator's receipts and payments account is debited and the liquidation account is credited by the proceeds on sale.

Liquidator's receipts and payments	Dr	xxx	
Liquidation	Cr		xxx

After these initial entries, the liquidation account and the liquidator's receipts and payments account appear in the company's records as shown below.

Liquidation		
Carrying amounts of assets transferred (excluding cash and assets subject to a security interest)	xxx	Proceeds of sale by liquidator	xxx

Liquidator's receipts and payments	
Beginning balance	xxx
Proceeds of sale by liquidator	xxx

33.9.3 Possession of assets by secured creditors

Assets over which a non-circulating security interest (i.e. a fixed charge) is held are commonly taken into possession by the secured creditor and sold. Any net proceeds after payment of the security are then handed over to the liquidator. To account for this, the following entry is passed in the records of the liquidating company (assuming the asset is sold for a gain).

Liquidator's receipts and payments	Dr	xxx	
Secured creditor	Dr	xxx	
Secured asset	Cr		xxx
Liquidation	Cr		xxx

Note that the gain on sale represents the excess of the sale proceeds of the secured asset over the carrying amount of the asset and is recognised as a credit to the liquidation account. If the secured asset was sold for a loss, the credit to the liquidation account would be replaced by a debit for the amount of loss. The liquidator's receipts and payments account will record the net proceeds after payment of the security. For example, if the secured asset had a carrying amount of $15 000 and was sold by the secured creditor for $18 000, while the security interest was $13 000, the liquidator will recognise a gain on disposal of secured asset of $3000 (i.e. $18 000 − $15 000) as a credit to the liquidation account, while the secured creditor will hand over to the liquidator $5000 in cash (i.e. $18 000 − $13 000), which will be recognised as a debit to the liquidator's receipts and payments account.

As the unsecured and secured assets not taken into possession by the secured creditor were already debited to the liquidation account in the first step and the net proceeds of disposal of these assets are credited to the liquidation account, the balance of the liquidation account represents, after the adjustments for the secured assets, the gain/loss on liquidation of all the assets.

Liquidation			
Carrying amounts of assets transferred (excluding cash and assets subject to a security interest)	xxx	Proceeds of sale by liquidator	xxx
		Gain on disposal of secured asset after satisfaction of the secured creditor	xxx

Liquidator's receipts and payments	
Beginning balance	xxx
Proceeds of sale by liquidator	xxx
Net amounts received from secured creditors	xxx

33.9.4 Payment to other creditors in order of priority

The liquidator needs to pay off the remaining creditors in strict order of priority from the balance of the liquidator's receipts and payments account, which includes the proceeds of sale of the assets. However, if that balance is not enough to cover those claims and the shares are only partly paid, the company will issue calls on contributories to pay further amounts due on the shares. The money received on calls will increase the balance of the liquidator's receipts and payments account, being recognised as a debit to it.

In the course of determining a list of creditors, the liquidator is likely to find certain liabilities that were not recorded in the company's records; for example, liquidation expenses and remuneration, and unrecorded interest payable. Such unrecorded liabilities, in effect, increase the loss or reduce the gain on liquidation, and are best accounted for by debiting the liquidation account and crediting the appropriate liability accounts.

In some cases, certain creditors may be willing to settle for an amount lower than the carrying amount of the debt. This represents a discount given to the company by those creditors and should be accounted for by debiting the appropriate liability accounts and crediting the liquidation account, thus increasing the gain on liquidation of the net assets. Next, the payment of creditors' claims will be recognised as a credit to the liquidator's receipts and payments account.

Considering the discussion above and after the payment to other creditors in order of priority, the liquidation account and the liquidator's receipts and payments account will appear in the company's records as shown below.

Liquidation			
Carrying amounts of assets transferred (excluding cash and assets subject to a security interest)	xxx	Proceeds of sale by liquidator	xxx
		Gain on disposal of secured asset after satisfaction of the secured creditor	xxx
Unrecorded liabilities, for example:		Discounts given by creditors	xxx
Liquidation expenses	xxx		
Interest payable	xxx		

Liquidator's receipts and payments			
Beginning balance	xxx	Payment to other creditors in order of priority	xxx
Proceeds of sale by liquidator	xxx		
Net amounts received from secured creditors	xxx		
Calls on contributories	xxx		

33.9.5 Return of capital to contributories

After the payment to creditors, the remaining cash should be distributed to contributories as a return of capital. The accounting procedures to return capital to contributories are as follows.

1. Calculate the appropriate distribution of funds for each class of shareholder in accordance with the rights of contributories as discussed in section 33.8.
2. Make any necessary further calls on the various classes of partly paid shares and recognise the money received on those calls as a debit to the liquidator's receipts and payments account.
3. Transfer share capital to a shareholders' distribution account. If there is more than one class of shares, separate shareholders' distribution accounts may be used for each class, or one account may be used with multiple columns. In this text one account is used for simplicity. If there are shares with calls in arrears, and the liquidator is unable to recover these calls, it is important that the shares be forfeited *before* share capital is transferred to shareholders' distribution. Any forfeited shares reserve is treated as part of the gain on liquidation and is not refunded to the previous shareholders.
4. Transfer all reserve accounts (including any forfeited shares reserve from the previous step and retained earnings) to the liquidation account. Note that if the retained earnings account has a debit balance (i.e. accumulated losses), its balance is transferred to the debit side of the liquidation account; otherwise, to the credit side, together with the other reserves. The balance of the liquidation account after these transfers represents the ultimate deficiency (if it is on the credit side) or surplus (if it is on the debit side) to be borne by/distributed to contributories.
5. Pay any appropriate capital distribution to the various classes of shareholders by crediting the liquidator's receipts and payments account and debiting the shareholders' distribution account.
6. Transfer the balance of the liquidation account (representing the deficiency or surplus) to the shareholders' distribution account. At this point, all accounts in the ledger should be closed.

The basic format for the liquidation, liquidator's receipts and payments, and shareholders' distribution accounts is as follows (assuming the company has a credit balance in retained earnings and a deficiency on liquidation).

Liquidation			
Carrying amounts of assets transferred (excluding cash and assets subject to a security interest)	xxx	Proceeds of sale by liquidator	xxx
		Gain on disposal of secured asset after satisfaction of the secured creditor	xxx
Unrecorded liabilities, for example:		Discounts given by creditors	xxx
Liquidation expenses	xxx	Other reserves and retained earnings (accumulated profits)	xxx
Interest payable	xxx		
		Balance (deficiency) transferred to Shareholders' Distribution account	xxx

Liquidator's receipts and payments			
Beginning balance	xxx	Payment to other creditors in order of priority	xxx
Proceeds of sale by liquidator	xxx	Distribution of cash to contributories	xxx
Net amounts received from secured creditors	xxx		
Calls on contributories	xxx		

Shareholders' distribution			
Distribution of cash to contributories	xxx	Share capital	xxx
Balance (deficiency) of the liquidation account transferred	xxx		

SUMMARY

When a company is experiencing financial difficulties, a receiver may be appointed by secured creditors to take possession of the company's property over which a security is held. The receiver can then sell the property, pay the secured creditor, and hand any surplus cash back to the company's management, to an administrator or to a liquidator if the company is to be wound up.

When a company is in danger of becoming insolvent, the intention of the Corporations Act is to keep it in business if possible. Hence, the Corporations Act provides for the appointment of an administrator to take over the affairs of a company which is potentially insolvent. The administrator's role is to meet with creditors in order to determine whether the company should continue to operate, enter into a deed of company arrangement or wind up the company.

There are two ways for a company to be wound up: a voluntary winding up and a winding up under a court order. One of the main reasons for a company to be wound up by a court order is that the company is insolvent. When a company commences winding up by the court, one of the first tasks to be undertaken is the preparation of a report as to affairs, the main purpose of which is to estimate the realisable value of the company's assets and to assess whether there is a surplus or deficiency for the members.

A voluntary winding up may be put in place by either the members or the creditors of a company. If the company is insolvent, it is not entitled to be wound up voluntarily unless leave is granted by the court. In a members' voluntary winding up, there is usually a declaration of solvency prepared. In a creditors' voluntary winding up, both creditors and members control the winding up process. No declaration of solvency exists and creditors must be sent a summary of affairs.

The liquidator has many powers, including carrying on the business, selling properties of the company, collecting calls from contributories, and paying creditors before winding up the company. The liquidator is required to keep proper records, containing entries and proceedings of meetings, and to prepare a statement of receipts and payments.

All debts payable by or claims against the company up to the relevant date are admissible for proof against the company and the liquidator must determine which debts to admit and which to reject. Creditors are paid in order of priority, usually as follows: (1) creditors secured by a non-circulating security interest (specific charge), (2) creditors secured by a circulating security interest (floating charge), (3) preferential unsecured creditors, (4) ordinary unsecured creditors and (5) deferred creditors. However, in cases of insolvency, some preferential unsecured creditors — wages payable, leave payable and retrenchment payments payable — rank for payment ahead of creditors secured by a circulating security interest.

The rights of contributories, in both a deficiency and surplus situation, are determined by the requirements laid down in the company's constitution. But if the constitution is silent, then a deficiency is borne by each shareholder, preference and ordinary, in accordance with the number of shares held. Calls in advance with related interest will be repaid before any payments are made to shareholders, and after all payments have been made to creditors, unless the constitution says otherwise. Dividends that are a legal debt must be paid after all creditors; dividends undeclared or in arrears are not paid unless the constitution specifically says so.

In accounting for the liquidation process, after the report as to affairs is prepared, the major accounts used for liquidation are the liquidation account, the shareholders' distribution account and the liquidator's receipts and payments account. The main purpose of the liquidation account is to calculate the deficiency or surplus on liquidation and to show how it is distributed between contributories, whereas the shareholders' distribution account shows the capital amount due to contributories, the share of surplus or deficiency on liquidation, and the final cash payments to each class of contributories. The liquidator's receipts and payments account is basically a summary of all the receipts and payments, including the cash balance at the beginning of the liquidation process, and it forms the basis on which the statement of receipts and payments is prepared.

KEY TERMS

administration The second form of external administration prescribed by the Corporations Act. Administration provides for the business, property and affairs of an insolvent company to be administered in a way that maximises the chances of the company, or as much as possible of its business, continuing in existence; or if it is not possible for the company or its business to continue in existence — results in a better return for the company's creditors and members than would otherwise result from an immediate winding up of the company.

administrator An independent and suitably qualified person appointed to take *full* control of a company in an attempt to save either the company or the company's business.

circulating security interest A floating charge over all of a company.

contributory A person liable as a member or past member to contribute to the property of the company if it is wound up.

controller A receiver, or receiver–manager or anyone else who is in possession, or has control, of the property of a company for the purpose of enforcing a security interest.

declaration of solvency A statement by the majority of directors that they have made an inquiry into the affairs of the company and they have formed an opinion that the company will be able to pay its debts in full within a period not exceeding 12 months after the commencement of a members' voluntary winding up.

deferred creditors Creditors that hold certain debts that are payable to the contributories of the company ahead of repayments of capital to those contributories.

insolvent Not solvent, that is, unable to pay all debts as and when they become due and payable.

liquidation The third form of external administration prescribed by the Corporations Act. The process whereby a company is dissolved, at which point the company ceases to be a legal entity.

liquidator An external administrator appointed to dissolve the company.

non-circulating security interest A fixed charge over a company's property, such as a mortgage, lien or bill of sale.

ordinary unsecured creditors Creditors whose debts have no preferential treatment under the Corporations Act and are the last to be paid before funds are returned to contributories.

partly secured creditor A creditor whose charge over property does not realise the creditor's total claim. The balance of the claim is no longer secured and the creditor must prove in the liquidation for the balance of the claim as an unsecured creditor.

preferential unsecured creditors Those creditors who, under the Corporations Act, are given preferential treatment over other unsecured creditors.

receiver An external administrator appointed by a court or secured creditor to collect and sell enough of the charged assets to repay the debt owed to the secured creditor, pay out the money collected in the order required by the Corporations Act, and report to ASIC any offences or other irregular matters they discover in performing their duties.

receiver–manager A receiver with the additional power to buy or sell the company's property.

receivership The first form of external administration prescribed by the Corporations Act. Receivership involves a receiver, receiver–manager or controller being appointed by a court or by secured creditors in order to protect the security of those creditors.

report as to affairs A report as to the financial status of a company at commencement of external administration.

secured creditor Someone who has a 'charge' over some or all of the company's assets, to secure a debt owed by the company.

solvent Able to pay all debts as and when they become due and payable.

statement of affairs A statement of the estimated realisable values of assets and amounts payable for liabilities and the estimated expenses of winding up.

statement of receipts and payments A 6-monthly set of accounts showing the progress of the administration of a company.

summary of affairs A report as to the financial status of a company at commencement of a creditors' voluntary winding up.

DEMONSTRATION PROBLEMS

33.1 Journals and ledgers on liquidation

Cycad Ltd is in liquidation under a court order. The statement of financial position as at 30 June 2023 is contained in figure 33.4.

FIGURE 33.4   Statement of financial position of Cycad Ltd

CYCAD LTD
Statement of financial position
as at 30 June 2023

Share capital			Non-current assets	$59 310
Preference:				
10 000 shares fully paid at $4	$ 40 000		Current assets	
			Cash	$1 500	
			Trade receivables (net)	4 300	5 800
Ordinary:				
(First issue)			Total assets	65 110
25 000 shares fully paid at $1	25 000		Current liabilities	
(Second issue)			Trade creditors	16 000
25 000 shares issued for $1 and				
paid to 50c	12 500			
(Third issue)				
5000 shares issued for $1 and paid				
to 75c	3 750			
Reserves	81 250			
Retained earnings	(32 140)			
Total equity	**$ 49 110**		**Net assets**	**$49 110**

The order of priority provided in the constitution for repayment of capital is: (1) preference shares and (2) ordinary shares.

The non-current assets were realised at $55 000 and trade receivables were collected, except $800; the latter amount proved to be irrecoverable.

Liquidator's remuneration was fixed at 1% of gross proceeds of assets (excluding bank balance) and the liquidator's expenses amounted to $115. Any calls on shares made by the liquidator are duly collected.

Required

1. Prepare journal entries to liquidate Cycad Ltd.
2. Prepare the liquidation account, the shareholders' distribution account, and the liquidator's receipts and payments account.

SOLUTION

The solution is contained in figure 33.5.

FIGURE 33.5   Journal and ledgers of Cycad Ltd on liquidation

Journal of Cycad Ltd			
Liquidation	Dr	63 610	
Non-current assets	Cr		59 310
Trade receivables	Cr		4 300
(Transfer of all assets except cash)			
Liquidator's receipts and payments	Dr	58 500	
Liquidation	Cr		58 500
(Proceeds on sale of non-current assets and trade receivables)			
Liquidation	Dr	700	
Liquidation expenses payable	Cr		115
Liquidator's remuneration payable	Cr		585
(Unrecorded liability for liquidator's remuneration $585 and expenses $115)			
Liquidation	Dr	32 140	
Retained earnings	Cr		32 140
(Transfer of accumulated losses)			
Liquidation expenses payable	Dr	115	
Liquidator's remuneration payable	Dr	585	
Trade creditors	Dr	16 000	
Liquidator's receipts and payments	Cr		16 700
(Liabilities paid in order of priority)			

		Dr	Cr
Call — 2nd issue ordinary		4 750	
Share capital — 2nd issue ordinary			4 750
(Call on 2nd issue ordinary shares)			
Liquidator's receipts and payments		4 750	
Call — 2nd issue ordinary			4 750
(Receipt of cash)			
Share capital — preference		40 000	
Share capital — 1st issue ordinary		25 000	
Share capital — 2nd issue ordinary		17 250	
Share capital — 3rd issue ordinary		3 750	
Shareholders' distribution			86 000
(Transfer of share capital)			
Shareholders' distribution		40 000	
Liquidator's receipts and payments			40 000
(Payment to preference shareholders)			
Shareholders' distribution		8 050	
Liquidator's receipts and payments			8 050
(Cash paid to 1st issue and 3rd issue ordinary shares)			
Shareholders' distribution		37 950	
Liquidation			37 950
(Transfer of deficiency on liquidation)			

Liquidation

Carrying amounts of assets transferred:		Proceeds of sale by liquidator	58 500
Non-current assets	59 310	Deficiency transferred to Shareholders'	
Trade receivables	4 300	distribution account:	
Liquidation expenses	115	1st issue ordinary	17 250
Liquidator's remuneration	585	2nd issue ordinary	17 250
Retained earnings	32 140	3rd issue ordinary	3 450
	94 450		94 450

Liquidator's receipts and payments

Beginning balance	1 500	Liquidation expenses	115
Proceeds of sale by liquidator:		Liquidator's remuneration	585
Non-current assets	55 000	Trade creditors	16 000
Trade receivables	3 500	Payment to preference shares	40 000
		Payment to 1st issue ordinary	7 750
Calls on 2nd issue ordinary	4 750	Payment to 3rd issue ordinary	300
	64 750		64 750

Shareholders' distribution

Payment to preference shares	40 000	Share capital:	
Payment to 1st issue ordinary	7 750	Preference	40 000
Payment to 3rd issue ordinary	300	1st issue ordinary	25 000
Deficiency of the liquidation account		2nd issue ordinary	17 250
transferred	37 950	3rd issue ordinary	3 750
	86 000		86 000

Note:

(a) After paying all liabilities, there is $43 300 available for shareholders; that is, from the liquidator's receipts and payments account: $1500 (cash available at the beginning) + $55 000 (proceeds from the sale of non-current assets) + $3500 (proceeds from trade receivables) − $115 (payment of liquidation expenses) − $585 (payment of liquidator's remuneration) − $16 000 (payment of trade creditors). Since preference share capital of $40 000 is to be refunded first, this leaves $3300 available for ordinary shareholders.

(b) The ordinary share capital before any further calls equals $41 250; that is, from the statement of financial position at 30 June 2023: $25 000 (first issue) + $12 500 (second issue) + $3750 (third issue) — hence, there is a deficiency to be borne by ordinary shareholders of $37 950 (i.e. $41 250 − $3300).

(c) The notional cash available is $17 050 (which includes further calls up to the issue price of all shares); that is, $3300 (cash available before calls) + $12 500 (calls on second issue) + $1250 (calls on third issue) — this is shared by ordinary shareholders in accordance with the ratio of the number of shares. Figure 33.6 illustrates how the distribution of cash is calculated.

(d) A call of $4750 is made on the second issue of ordinary shares. Note that the notional calls are larger and extend to all partly paid shares, but they were offset by the notional refunds that second and third issue ordinary shares are entitled to receive, according to figure 33.6. When the call is received, total cash available is $3300 + $4750 = $8050, which is then paid by the liquidator to first issue ordinary shares, $7750, and third issue ordinary shares, $300.

FIGURE 33.6 Distribution of cash

	No. of shares	Paid to	Notional call	Notional refund 31c	Actual refund (call)	Deficiency share
First issue ordinary	25 000	$25 000	—	$ 7 750	$ 7 750	$17 250
Second issue ordinary	25 000	12 500	$12 500	7 750	(4 750)	17 250
Third issue ordinary	5 000	3 750	1 250	1 550	300	3 450
	55 000	41 250	13 750	$17 050	$ 3 300	$37 950
Cash available		(3 300)	3 300			
Deficiency		$37 950				
Total notional cash			$17 050			

Total notional cash per share = $17 050 ÷ 55 000 = 31c per share

33.2 Arrears of preference dividends, creditor discounts, secured creditors

This example includes, in addition to the issues addressed in the previous example, the treatment on liquidation of:

- contra-asset accounts (e.g. accumulated depreciation)
- secured creditors
- arrears of preference dividends
- forfeiture of share due to calls in arrears
- discount given by creditors.

Palm Ltd went into liquidation under a court order on 30 June 2023. Figure 33.7 shows the company's statement of financial position at that date.

FIGURE 33.7 Statement of financial position of Palm Ltd

PALM LTD
Statement of financial position
as at 30 June 2023

Assets		
Receivables		$20 400
Inventories		20 500
Freehold property		18 000
Plant and machinery	$ 30 000	
Less: Accumulated depreciation — plant and machinery	(15 000)	15 000
Goodwill		4 000
Total assets		77 900
Liabilities		
12% debentures (secured by circulating security interest)		9 000
Bank overdraft (secured by non-circulating interest on freehold property)		6 000
Unsecured creditors:		
Accounts payable	12 950	
Accrued liabilities	1 950	14 900
Total liabilities		29 900
Net assets		**$48 000**

Share capital			
14 000 10% preference shares fully paid at $1			$14 000
20 000 'A' ordinary shares paid to $1.55 and issued for $2			31 000
10 000 'B' ordinary shares issued for $1 and called to 75c		$ 7 500	
Less: Calls in arrears 2000 shares at 25c		(500)	7 000
Total share capital			52 000
Reserves			
Retained earnings			(4 000)
Total equity			**$48 000**

Note:
(a) Arrears of preference dividend were $1400 (1 year to 30 June 2023).
(b) Accounts payable were prepared to settle their claims at a discounted amount of $11 950.
(c) The liquidator was able to receive the following amounts for assets.

Plant and machinery	$ 6 000
Goodwill	—
Receivables	20 000
Inventories	16 000

(d) The freehold property was sold by the bank from which Palm Ltd secured the bank overdraft for $23 000 and, after settlement of local government rates and the overdraft, the remainder was transferred to the liquidator.
(e) The item 'Accrued liabilities' in the statement of financial position of Palm Ltd from figure 33.7 included the following.

Local government rates payable on freehold property for year ended 30/6/2023	$ 500
Directors' fees payable	400
GST payable	250
Rent payable	150
Accrued advertising costs payable	250
Wages payable	250
Telephone account payable	150
	$1 950

The liquidator forfeited all 'B' ordinary shares on which calls were in arrears because of the non-collectability of such arrears.

After meeting all liabilities, and receiving the payment for their expenses, $650, and their remuneration, $950, the liquidator distributed the remaining balance of cash to shareholders on 30 September 2023.

The constitution of the company states that arrears of dividends are to be paid in the event of liquidation.

All shares are to rank equally, based on the number of shares held, in distributing any surplus or deficiency.

Required
1. Prepare journal entries to record the liquidation of Palm Ltd.
2. Prepare the liquidator's receipts and payments account.
3. Prepare the liquidation account.
4. Prepare the shareholders' distribution account.
5. Prepare a statement showing how the surplus or deficiency on liquidation is apportioned among Palm Ltd's shareholders.

SOLUTION
Figure 33.8 illustrates each part of the required liquidation records.

FIGURE 33.8   Liquidation records of Palm Ltd

1.	**Journal of Palm Ltd**			
Liquidation		Dr	74 900	
Receivables		Cr		20 400
Inventories		Cr		20 500
Plant and machinery		Cr		30 000
Goodwill		Cr		4 000
(Asset accounts transferred to liquidation)				
Accumulated depreciation — plant and machinery		Dr	15 000	
Liquidation		Cr		15 000
(Contra-asset transferred to liquidation)				
Liquidator's receipts and payments		Dr	42 000	
Liquidation		Cr		42 000
(Proceeds on sale of assets)				
Liquidator's receipts and payments		Dr	16 500	
Bank overdraft		Dr	6 000	
Accrued liabilities — local government rates		Dr	500	
Freehold property		Cr		18 000
Liquidation		Cr		5 000
(Receipt of net amount after sale of secured asset by bank.				
Gain of $5000 = $23 000 [sale proceeds of freehold property]				
− $18 000 [carrying amount of freehold property])				
Liquidation		Dr	3 000	
Liquidation expenses payable		Cr		650
Liquidator's remuneration payable		Cr		950
Preference dividend payable		Cr		1 400
(Unrecorded liability for liquidation expenses and remuneration,				
and arrears of preference dividends)				
Accounts payable		Dr	1 000	
Liquidation		Cr		1 000
(Discount provided by accounts payable)				
Share capital — 'B' ordinary		Dr	1 500	
Call — 'B' ordinary		Cr		500
Forfeited shares reserve		Cr		1 000
(Forfeiture of 2000 'B' ordinary shares due to unpaid calls;				
the holders of those shares paid only 50c per share before				
the forfeiture)				
Liquidation		Dr	4 000	
Retained earnings		Cr		4 000
(Reserves transferred to liquidation)				
Forfeited shares reserve		Dr	1 000	
Liquidation		Cr		1 000
(Reserves transferred to liquidation)				
Liquidation expenses payable		Dr	650	
Liquidator's remuneration payable		Dr	950	
Debentures		Dr	9 000	
Wages payable		Dr	250	
Accounts payable		Dr	11 950	
Rent payable		Dr	150	
Directors' fees payable		Dr	400	
Accrued advertising costs payable		Dr	250	
GST payable		Dr	250	
Telephone account payable		Dr	150	
Preference dividend payable		Dr	1 400	
Liquidator's receipts and payments		Cr		25 400
(Creditors paid in order of priority)				
Share capital — preference		Dr	14 000	
— 'A' ordinary		Dr	31 000	
— 'B' ordinary		Dr	6 000	
Shareholders' distribution		Cr		51 000
(Transfer of share capital to shareholders' distribution)				

		Dr	33 100	
Shareholders' distribution		Dr	33 100	
Liquidator's receipts and payments		Cr		33 100
(Cash distribution to shareholders:				
Preference $14 700; 'A' ordinary $12 000; 'B' ordinary $6400)				
Shareholders' distribution		Dr	17 900	
Liquidation		Cr		17 900
(Deficiency/(surplus) shared as follows:				
Preference $(700); 'A' ordinary $19 000; 'B' ordinary $(400))				

2.   Liquidator's receipts and payments

Proceeds of sale by liquidator:		Liquidation expenses	650
Plant and machinery	6 000	Liquidator's remuneration	950
Receivables	20 000	Debentures	9 000
Inventories	16 000	Wages payable	250
	42 000	Accounts payable	11 950
		Rent payable	150
Net amounts received from secured		Directors' fees payable	400
creditors	16 500	Accrued advertising costs payable	250
		GST payable	250
		Telephone account payable	150
		Preference dividend payable	1 400
			25 400
		Distribution of cash to contributories:	
		Preference	14 200
		'A' ordinary	12 000
		'B' ordinary	6 400
	$58 500		58 500

Note: Cash available for shareholders is $58 500 − $25 400 = $33 100.

3.   Liquidation

Carrying amount of assets transferred	74 900	Accumulated depreciation — plant	15 000
Liquidation expenses	650	Proceeds on sale by liquidator	42 000
Liquidator's remuneration	950	Gain on disposal of secured asset	5 000
Preference dividend payable	1 400	Accounts payable (discount)	1 000
Retained earnings	4 000	Forfeited shares reserve	1 000
	81 900		64 000
Surplus transferred to shareholders'			
distribution account:			
Preference	700	Deficiency transferred to shareholders'	
'B' ordinary	400	distribution account:	
	1 100	'A' ordinary	19 000
	83 000		83 000

Note: Deficiency on liquidation = $81 900 − $64 000 = $17 900.

4.   Shareholders' distribution

Distribution of cash to contributories:		Share capital:	
Preference	14 700	Preference	14 000
'A' ordinary	12 000	'A' ordinary	31 000
'B' ordinary	6 400	'B' ordinary	6 000
Deficiency of the liquidation account		Surplus of the liquidation account	
transferred:		transferred:	
'A' ordinary	19 000	Preference	700
		'B' ordinary	400
	51 000		51 000

	No. of shares	Paid to	Notional call	Notional refund $1.05	Actual refund (call)	Deficiency/ (surplus) share
Preference	14 000	$ 14 000	—	$14 700	$14 700	$ (700)
'A' ordinary	20 000	31 000	$ 9 000	21 000	12 000	19 000
'B' ordinary	8 000	6 000	2 000	8 400	6 400	(400)
	42 000	51 000	11 000	$44 100	$33 100	$17 900
Cash available		(33 100)	33 100			
Deficiency		$ 17 900				
Total notional cash			$44 100			

Total notional cash per share = $44 100 ÷ 42 000 = $1.05 per share

Note: Arrears of dividend are paid as a deferred claim after all unsecured creditors are paid in full. Where the dividends are not to be paid, the company would ignore the arrears of dividends.

33.3 Receivership followed by liquidation

This problem introduces a receiver, who firstly realises the assets to pay a secured creditor. The receiver uses a realisation account for this purpose. The realisation account is similar in nature to the liquidation account, and simply records the assets taken over by the receiver and sold. Any gain or loss on sale is recorded in profit and transferred to retained earnings.

The receiver completes their task by paying the secured creditors the money owed, as recorded in the receiver's receipts and payments account, but only after their wages are paid.

In this question, it is assumed that the company is then placed into liquidation. Hence, the receiver transfers any money left over to the liquidator.

The trial balance of Boab Ltd as at 30 June 2022 is as shown in figure 33.9.

FIGURE 33.9	Trial balance of Boab Ltd

BOAB LTD
Trial balance
as at 30 June 2022

	Dr	Cr
Capital (shares of $1 each fully paid)		$ 400 000
Retained earnings		154 000
12% debentures		520 000
Goodwill and patents	$ 185 000	
Freehold property	350 000	
Plant and machinery (net)	352 000	
Delivery vans (net) (subject to hire purchase)	224 000	
Cars (net) (subject to bill of sale — registered)	145 000	
Accounts receivable	116 200	
Bank overdraft		11 000
Accounts payable		287 200
	$1 372 200	$1 372 200

Accounts payable of $287 200 as shown in figure 33.9 included the following.

Trade creditors	$113 800
Land tax payable	13 000
Municipal rates due	4 200
Rent (1 March to 30 June)	12 800
Owing on hire purchase	34 000
Owing on bill of sale	26 000
Wages	51 600
Interest on debentures	31 200
Interest on bank overdraft	600

At 30 June 2022, a receiver is appointed on behalf of the debenture holders who are secured by a circulating security interest over the company's assets. The receiver is to be paid a remuneration of $3000 per week.

By 28 July 2022, the receiver has realised the freehold property for $375 000 and a portion (carrying amount $200 000) of the plant and machinery for $290 000. As well as the receiver's remuneration, there are sundry expenses of $5400.

On 28 July 2022, the receiver, after meeting those expenses and liabilities that are entitled to preferential treatment, pays the debenture holders in full (including interest to date, which includes an additional amount of $5200 for July) and hands the balance to the liquidator.

On completion of the receivership, the company goes into liquidation and a liquidator is appointed at a fixed remuneration of $180 000.

The remainder of the plant and machinery is sold by the liquidator for $200 000. The cars are taken over by the holder of the bill of sale and sold for $101 000, with $75 000 (net) being sent to the liquidator. The delivery vans are sold for $210 000. Accounts receivable are realised for $111 200. Goodwill and patents are considered worthless. Expenses of liquidation amount to $33 000. Debts accrued between 30 June 2022 and 28 July 2022 consist of wages of $48 000 and sick leave of $3600.

Required

1. Prepare the receiver's receipts and payments account.
2. Prepare the receiver's realisation account.
3. Prepare the liquidator's receipts and payments account.
4. Prepare the liquidation account.

SOLUTION

The solution is contained in figure 33.10.

FIGURE 33.10	Records of receivership followed by liquidation

1. **Receiver's receipts and payments**

Proceeds of sale by receiver:			Receiver's expenses		5 400
Freehold property		375 000	Receiver's remuneration		
Plant and machinery		290 000	(4 weeks × $3000)		12 000
			Wages		51 600
			Debenture holders:		
			Principal	520 000	
			Interest ($31 200 + $5200)	36 400	556 400
			Balance (to liquidator)		39 600
		665 000			665 000

2. **Receiver's realisation**

Carrying amounts of assets transferred:			Proceeds of sale by receiver:	
Freehold property		350 000	Freehold property	375 000
Plant and machinery		200 000	Plant and machinery	290 000
Receiver's expenses		5 400		
Receiver's remuneration		12 000		
Interest on debentures		5 200		
Profit or loss (gain)		92 400		
		665 000		665 000

3. **Liquidator's receipts and payments**

Balance (from receiver)		39 600	Bank overdraft and interest	
Proceeds of sale by liquidator:			($11 000 + $600)	$ 11 600
Plant and machinery		200 000	Liquidator's expenses	33 000
Delivery vans	210 000		Liquidator's remuneration	180 000
			Wages	48 000
Less: Owing on hire			Sick leave	3 600
purchase	(34 000)	176 000		

3.		Liquidator's receipts and payments		
Accounts receivable	111 200	Trade creditors		113 800
		Municipal rates due		4 200
Amounts received from secured creditors:		Land tax payable		13 000
Cars	75 000	Rent		12 800
		Distribution of cash to contributories		181 800
	601 800			601 800

4.		Liquidation		
Carrying amounts of assets transferred:		Proceeds from sale:		
Plant and machinery ($352 000 – $200 000)	152 000	Plant and machinery		200 000
Delivery vans	224 000	Delivery vans		210 000
Accounts receivable	116 200	Accounts receivable		111 200
Goodwill and patents	185 000	Retained earnings ($154 000 + $92 400)		246 400
Loss on disposal of cars ($145 000 – $101 000)	44 000			
Wages	48 000			
Sick leave	3 600			
Liquidator's expenses	33 000	Deficiency transferred to shareholders' distribution account		218 200
Liquidator's remuneration	180 000			
	985 800			985 800

COMPREHENSION QUESTIONS

1 Describe the meaning of 'insolvency' with regards to companies.
2 Briefly describe the procedures through which the Corporations Act attempts to avoid liquidation of companies if possible.
3 Who can appoint a receiver for a company facing financial difficulties?
4 Outline the role and powers of a receiver appointed by a secured creditor.
5 Who can appoint a voluntary administrator?
6 Outline the role of an administrator appointed to a company which is insolvent.
7 Outline the role of directors before and during voluntary administration.
8 Briefly discuss the ways in which a company may be wound up, indicating the likely circumstances in which each is applicable.
9 What is the purpose of the report as to affairs (Form 507), the summary of affairs (Form 509) and the statement of receipts and payments (Form 524)?
10 Outline the powers of a liquidator in winding up a company (a) under a court order and (b) in a voluntary winding up.
11 Describe how a company's debts are identified and admitted on liquidation.
12 Discuss the order of priority of payment in the event of winding up a company.
13 Who are the contributories of a company? Explain.
14 Outline the principles to be followed in apportioning a deficiency among creditors and contributories.
15 If there is a surplus on liquidation, discuss how the surplus is to be apportioned among contributories.
16 What must a liquidator do if he or she is unable to collect unpaid call money from shareholders?
17 Arrears of dividends are paid in the winding up process in certain circumstances. Outline those circumstances.
18 Describe the accounts used in accounting for a liquidation.

CASE STUDY 33.1

LIQUIDATION OF A FAMILY COMPANY

Assume that you are the managing director of a small, family-owned proprietary company operating in Australia. The members of the company have decided to wind up its operations for family reasons. The company has been trading profitably and has had no problem in paying its accounts when they fall due.

Required

Visit the ASIC website and investigate what you must do in order to wind up the company properly in accordance with the law. Report your findings and show details of the forms that must be completed.

CASE STUDY 33.2

CURRENT LIQUIDATIONS OF PREVIOUSLY LISTED COMPANIES

Visit www.delisted.com.au or a similar website and present brief details of three companies that have been listed on the securities exchange, and that are currently going through the process of liquidation. Provide reasons (if possible) for such liquidations occurring.

APPLICATION AND ANALYSIS EXERCISES

★ BASIC | ★ ★ MODERATE | ★ ★ ★ DIFFICULT

33.1 Order of priority for paying creditors ★   **LO7**

Flea Ltd, whose capital consisted of $25 000 in fully paid shares, was wound up as a result of a court order. Its liquidator realised $335 825 from the sale of the company's assets. This amount included $85 000 from the proceeds on sale of the company's land and buildings.

Debts proved and admitted were as follows.

Unsecured notes	$ 50 000
Debentures (secured by circulating security interest)	150 000
First mortgage on land and buildings	50 000
Trade accounts payable	40 000
PAYG tax instalment	390
Fringe benefits tax	1 000
Directors' fees	1 500
GST	995
Employees' holiday pay	2 500
Employees' wages — 5 employees for 2 weeks at $400 per week	2 000
Secretary's salary — 3 weeks at $240 per week	360
Managing director's salary — 4 weeks at $600 per week	1 200
Sales commission	250
Liquidation expenses	1 500
Second mortgage on land and buildings	40 000
Liquidator's remuneration	4 000

Required

Show the order of priority of payment of debts for Flea Ltd and calculate the amount payable to the company's trade accounts payable.

33.2 Distribution to different classes of shareholders ★   **LO8**

On 1 September 2023, Mouse Ltd went into liquidation. At that date, the equity of Mouse Ltd comprised the following.

200 000 ordinary shares issued for $2 and paid to $1.50	$300 000
300 000 ordinary shares issued for $1 and fully paid	300 000
	$600 000

Required

Prepare a statement detailing the distribution of cash to shareholders assuming that after realising the assets and paying all creditors, the liquidator had the following cash available to distribute to shareholders.

(a) $0

(b) $50 000

(c) $150 000

(d) $250 000

33.3 Distribution to different classes of shareholders ★   LO8

On 31 May 2023, White Ant Ltd went into liquidation. At that date, the equity of White Ant Ltd comprised the following.

200 000 preference shares issued for $1 paid to 50c	$100 000
500 000 ordinary shares issued for $1 paid to 80c	400 000
	$500 000

After realising the assets and paying all creditors, the liquidator had $150 000 cash available to distribute to shareholders.

Required

1. Prepare a statement detailing the distribution of cash to shareholders assuming the company's constitution was silent regarding the rights of shareholders upon winding up.
2. Prepare a statement detailing the distribution of cash to shareholders assuming the company's constitution provides that upon winding up, preference shareholders are preferential as to return of capital.

33.4 Distribution to different classes of shareholders ★   LO8

On 1 December 2023, Elephant Ltd went into liquidation. At that date, the equity of Elephant Ltd comprised the following.

200 000 'A' ordinary shares issued for $2 and paid to $1.55	$310 000
300 000 'B' ordinary shares issued for $1 and fully paid	300 000
	$610 000

After realising the assets and paying all creditors, the liquidator had $60 000 cash available to distribute to shareholders.

Required

1. Prepare a statement of the distribution to shareholders supported by a detailed explanation of the apportionment of any cash among the various classes of shareholders.
2. How will the statement of the cash distribution to shareholders change if the ordinary shares 'A' were paid to:
   (a) $1.25
   (b) $1.75?

33.5 Distribution to different classes of shareholders ★   LO8

On 1 December 2023, Leo Ltd went into liquidation. At that date, the equity of Leo Ltd comprised the following.

200 000 'A' ordinary shares issued for $2 and paid to $1	$200 000
300 000 'B' ordinary shares issued for $1 and fully paid	300 000
	$500 000

After realising the assets and paying all creditors, the liquidator had $100 000 cash available to distribute to shareholders.

Required

1. Prepare a statement of the distribution to shareholders supported by a detailed explanation of the apportionment of any cash among the various classes of shareholders.
2. How would the statement of the cash distribution to shareholders change if both ordinary shares 'A' and 'B' were fully paid at 1 December 2023?
3. How would the statement of the cash distribution to shareholders change if the ordinary shares 'A' were fully paid, while ordinary shares 'B' were only paid to 75c at 1 December 2023?
4. How would the statement of the cash distribution to shareholders change if the ordinary shares 'A' were partly paid to $1, while ordinary shares 'B' were only paid to 75c at 1 December 2023?

33.6 Distribution to different classes of shareholders ★ **LO8**

On 1 December 2023, Hippo Ltd went into liquidation. At that date, the equity of Hippo Ltd comprised the following.

900 000 preference shares fully paid to $1, to be redeemed for $1.10	$ 900 000
600 000 'A' ordinary shares issued for $1 and fully paid	600 000
1 200 000 'B' ordinary shares issued for $2 and fully paid	2 400 000
	$3 900 000

After realising the assets and paying all creditors, the liquidator had $1 350 000 cash available to distribute to shareholders. The order of priority provided in the constitution for repayment of capital is: (1) preference and (2) ordinary.

Required

1. Prepare a statement of the distribution to shareholders supported by a detailed explanation of the apportionment of any cash among the various classes of shareholders.
2. How will the statement of the cash distribution to shareholders change if the ordinary shares 'B' were partly paid to:
   (a) 50c
   (b) $1.40
   (c) $1.70?
3. If all the shares were ranked equally according to the constitution in distributing any surplus or deficiency, how would the statement of the cash distribution to shareholders change?

33.7 Distribution to different classes of shareholders ★ **LO8**

On 1 December 2023, Rui Ltd went into liquidation. At that date, the equity of Rui Ltd comprised the following.

300 000 preference shares fully paid to $1, to be redeemed for $1.10	$ 300 000
200 000 'A' ordinary shares issued for $1 and paid to 50c	100 000
400 000 'B' ordinary shares issued for $2 and paid to $1.75	700 000
	$1 000 000

After realising the assets and paying all creditors, the liquidator had $250 000 cash available to distribute to shareholders. The order of priority provided in the constitution for repayment of capital is: (1) preference and (2) ordinary.

Required

1. Prepare a statement of the distribution to shareholders supported by a detailed explanation of the apportionment of any cash among the various classes of shareholders.
2. How would the statement of the cash distribution to shareholders change if the available cash for distribution after realising the assets and paying all creditors was:
   (a) $400 000
   (b) $640 000?
3. If all the shares were ranked equally according to the constitution in distributing any surplus or deficiency, how would the statement of the cash distribution to shareholders in requirements 1 and 2 change?

33.8 Distribution to different classes of shareholders ★ ★ **LO8**

On 30 April 2023, Puppy Ltd went into voluntary liquidation. At that date, equity comprised the following.

Share capital:	
200 000 preference shares issued for $1 and fully paid	$ 200 000
440 000 ordinary shares issued for $1 and fully paid	440 000
320 000 'A' ordinary shares issued for $1 and paid to 60c	192 000
40 000 'B' ordinary shares issued for $1 and paid to 50c	20 000
	852 000
Retained earnings (accumulated losses)	(512 000)
Total equity	$ 340 000

The liquidator proceeded to realise all of the company's assets. The loss on liquidation amounted to $64 000 and, after paying sundry creditors, there was a cash balance of $212 000 available for distribution to the shareholders. (The constitution gives preference shareholders a prior claim to return of capital, and other shareholders are to rank equally, based on the number of shares held.)

Required

Prepare a statement of the distribution to shareholders supported by a detailed explanation of the apportionment of any cash among the various classes of shareholders.

33.9 Distribution to different classes of shareholders ★ **LO8**

On 1 December 2023, Submarine Ltd went into liquidation. At that date, the equity of Submarine Ltd comprised the following.

300 000 preference shares fully paid to $1, to be redeemed for $1.10	$ 300 000
200 000 'A' ordinary shares issued for $1 and paid to 50c	100 000
400 000 'B' ordinary shares issued for $2 and paid to $1.50	600 000
	$1 000 000

After realising the assets and paying all creditors, the liquidator had $420 000 cash available to distribute to shareholders. The order of priority provided in the constitution for repayment of capital is: (1) preference and (2) ordinary.

Required

1. Prepare a statement of the distribution to shareholders supported by a detailed explanation of the apportionment of any cash among the various classes of shareholders.
2. How would the statement of the cash distribution to shareholders change if the available cash for distribution was only $300 000 after realising the assets and paying all creditors?
3. If all the shares were ranked equally according to the constitution in distributing any surplus or deficiency, how would the statement of the cash distribution to shareholders in requirements 1 and 2 change?

33.10 Three main ledger accounts for liquidation ★ ★ **LO9**

Mammal Ltd went into voluntary liquidation on 30 June 2023. Its summarised statement of financial position at that date was as follows.

MAMMAL LTD					
Statement of financial position					
as at 30 June 2023					
Equity			Current assets		
Share capital:			Receivables	$10 000	
160 000 shares issued at a price of			Inventories	12 000	
$1, called to 50c	$ 80 000				
Less: Calls in arrears (40 000 at 25c)	(10 000)		Cash	8 000	$ 30 000
			Non-current assets		
			Land	40 000	
			Plant	18 000	58 000
			Total assets		88 000
			Current liabilities		
			Payables		(18 000)
Total equity	**$ 70 000**		**Net assets**		**$ 70 000**

All assets realised amounted to $60 000. Calls in arrears were fully collected. Payables allowed a $1000 discount. Costs of liquidation were $5000.

Required

Record the above in the liquidation account, the liquidator's receipts and payments account and the shareholders' distribution account.

33.11 Receipts and payments with final distribution to shareholders ★ ★ **LO8, 9**

Jellyfish Ltd went into liquidation on 30 June 2024, its equity being as follows.

10 000 10% preference shares each fully paid at $1
5 000 first issue ordinary shares each fully paid at $1
25 000 second issue ordinary shares issued for $1 and paid to 50c
Retained earnings (credit balance) of $750

The constitution states that preference shares carry the right to payment of arrears of dividends whether declared or undeclared up to the commencement of the winding up.

The last preference dividend was paid to 30 June 2023. To adjust the rights of contributories, the liquidator made a call of 50c per share on the second issue ordinary shares.

All call money was received except that in respect of 250, second issue ordinary shares. This money proved to be irrecoverable and the shares were subsequently forfeited.

Claims admitted for payment amounted to $8435, assets realised amounted to $15 000, and liquidation expenses to $75.

Liquidator's remuneration was fixed at 1% of gross proceeds from sale of assets.

Required

1. Prepare the liquidator's receipts and payments account.
2. Provide a statement showing the final distribution to shareholders, based on the statement in the constitution that all shares, by number, rank equally on distribution of final cash.

33.12 Order of payment of debt and shareholders' distributions ★ ★   **LO8, 9**

Oatmeal Ltd went into liquidation on 31 March 2023, its equity being as follows.

75 000 ordinary shares issued and fully paid	$175 000
Retained earnings (accumulated losses)	(35 600)
	$139 400

Debts proved and admitted for payment by the liquidator were as follows.

Debentures (secured by circulating security interest)	$100 000
Mortgage loan (secured over land and buildings)	240 000
Unpaid annual leave	45 800
Employee retrenchment payments	56 400
Director's salary	8 400
Directors' fees	2 400
PAYG tax instalments	6 200
Accounts payable	125 000
Liquidation expenses	1 300
Liquidator's remuneration	5 000

The land and buildings were seized by the secured creditor and sold to repay the mortgage loan. Surplus funds amounting to $5000 were forwarded to the liquidator. All other assets were sold and realised $230 000. Any calls which the liquidator may need to make are expected to be recoverable.

Required

Prepare the liquidator's receipts and payments account and the shareholders' distribution account for Oatmeal Ltd. (Show all calculations.)

33.13 Journal entries and ledger accounts for liquidation ★ ★   **LO9**

The trial balance of Mantis Ltd on 1 June 2023, the date on which the court ordered that the company be wound up, is presented below.

MANTIS LTD		
Trial balance		
as at 1 June 2023		
	Debit	Credit
Cash	$ 9 000	
Inventories	188 800	
Plant and machinery	211 400	

MANTIS LTD		
Trial balance		
as at 1 June 2023		
Land and buildings	60 000	
Retained earnings (accumulated losses)	80 800	
Accounts payable		$160 000
Mortgage (secured over land and buildings)		40 000
Share capital: 350 000 ordinary shares issued for $1 each, fully paid		350 000
	$550 000	$550 000

Additional information

(a) The sale of assets realised the following amounts in cash.
  • Inventories $120 000
  • Plant and machinery $140 000

(b) The mortgage holder took possession of the land and buildings and sold them for $90 000 and after settlement of the debt paid any excess funds to the liquidator.

(c) Liquidation costs amounted to $19 000.

(d) The liquidator paid all liabilities.

Required

1. Prepare journal entries to wind up the affairs of Mantis Ltd.
2. Prepare the liquidation account, the liquidator's receipts and payments account and the shareholders' distribution account.

33.14 Summary of affairs ★ ★   **LO9**

The trial balance below is of Flower Ltd's accounts as at 30 June 2023.

FLOWER LTD		
Trial balance		
as at 30 June 2023		
	Debit	Credit
Share capital		$ 630 000
Calls in arrears (on 16 000 shares)	$ 4 000	
Calls in advance		3 000
Revaluation surplus		5 000
Retained earnings	145 000	
Land	182 000	
Buildings	300 000	
Accumulated depreciation — buildings		72 000
Plant	340 000	
Accumulated depreciation — plant		40 000
Cash at bank	30 000	
Inventories	100 000	
Accounts receivable	95 000	
Bills receivable	80 000	
Goodwill	50 000	
12% debentures		200 000
Mortgage payable		220 000
Secured creditor (for plant)		50 000
Unsecured creditors		106 000
	$1 326 000	$1 326 000

Share capital consisted of 700 000 ordinary shares, issued at a price of $1 and called to 90c. It was decided on 30 June 2023 to wind up Flower Ltd.

Additional information

• Debentures are secured by circulating security interest; mortgage is secured over buildings.
• Assets are estimated to realise the following amounts.

Land	$180 000
Buildings	200 000
Inventories	70 000
Plant	200 000

Bills receivable		58 000
Accounts receivable		87 000
Calls in arrears		3 000
Goodwill		—

- There is an impending lawsuit against the company. Expected damages payout is $30 000.
- Unsecured creditors comprise the following.

Accounts payable		$ 85 000
GST		4 000
Director's salary		7 000
Directors' fees		6 000
Local government rates		4 000
		$106 000

Required

Present a summary of affairs to send to creditors.

33.15 Ledger accounts for liquidation ★ ★ ★   **LO9**

A court order for the winding up of Salamander Ltd was made on 31 March 2023. A statement of financial position prepared on that date was as follows.

SALAMANDER LTD Statement of financial position as at 31 March 2023		
Current assets		
Cash at bank	$ 4 000	
Cash in hand	300	
Accounts receivable	46 500	
Inventories	49 500	
Total current assets		$100 300
Non-current assets		
Plant and equipment (net)	96 200	
Land and buildings (net)	30 000	
Goodwill	39 500	
Total non-current assets		165 700
Total assets		266 000
Current liabilities		
Accounts payable	29 300	
PAYG tax instalments	5 700	
Accrued expenses	5 000	
Total current liabilities		40 000
Non-current liabilities		
2000 $20 10% debentures	40 000	
11% mortgage on land and buildings	20 000	
Total non-current liabilities		60 000
Total liabilities		100 000
Net assets		**$166 000**
Share capital		
20 000 7% cumulative preference shares issued for $2, called to $1.50 each	$ 30 000	
100 000 ordinary shares issued for $2, called to $1.50 each	150 000	$180 000
Less: Calls in arrears: 2000 ordinary shares at 50c		(1000)
		179 000
Reserves		
Retained earnings		(13 000)
Total equity		**$166 000**

Note: Arrears of preference dividends amounted to $4200.

Additional information

- Accrued expenses included the following.

Interest on mortgage	$1 000
Interest on debentures	800
Wages (four employees, $800 each)	3 200

- Assets are expected to realise the following amounts.

Accounts receivable	$16 400	
Inventories	10 500	
Plant and equipment	30 000	
Unpaid calls	500	(1000 at 50c)

- The mortgage holder took possession of the land and buildings and sold them for $60 000, paying any surplus to the liquidator.
- The debentures are secured by a circulating security interest over the assets of Salamander Ltd.
- On 1 May 2023, the liquidator realised the assets in (b) for the above amounts. The balance of the unpaid calls was treated as irrecoverable and the shares were forfeited.
- On 1 June 2023, the liquidator paid all liabilities and adjusted the rights of shareholders. The constitution gives preference shareholders the right to receive arrears of dividend.
- Uncalled capital (where required to be called up) proved to be recoverable.
- The winding up of the company was completed on 1 July 2023, costs of liquidation being $3000.

Required

1. Prepare the liquidation account and the shareholders' distribution account (show clearly any working in relation to the final distribution to shareholders).
2. Prepare the liquidator's receipts and payments account.

33.16 Order of payment of debts, journal entries for liquidation surplus ★ ★ **LO7, 9**

Glowworm Ltd went into voluntary liquidation on 30 June 2024. The statement of financial position prepared on that date is as follows.

GLOWWORM LTD Statement of financial position as at 30 June 2024		
Current assets		
Cash		$ 32 000
Inventories		126 000
Accounts receivable	$ 72 200	
Less: Allowance for doubtful debts	(8 200)	64 000
Non-current assets		
Plant and equipment	336 000	
Less: Accumulated depreciation — plant and equipment	(70 400)	265 600
Land		181 200
Shares in listed companies		104 000
Total assets		772 800
Current liabilities		
Accounts payable		86 400
Other payables		32 200
Non-current liabilities		
Mortgage on land		170 000
Debentures		300 000
Total liabilities		588 600
Net assets		**$184 200**
Equity		
Share capital:		
Preference: 40 000 shares, issued at $1, fully paid	$ 40 000	
Ordinary 'A' 50 000 shares, issued at $1, fully paid	50 000	
Ordinary 'B' 40 000 shares, issued at $1, called to 60c	24 000	$114 000
General reserve		14 000
Retained earnings		56 200
Total equity		**$184 200**

Additional information

- Liquidator's remuneration and expenses amounted to $3600.
- Other payables of $32 200 comprised the following.

Wages payable — employees	$12 000
Wages payable — managing director	5 600
Annual leave payable — employees	8 800
Income tax payable	4 000
Telephone bill payable	1 800

- The debentures are secured by a circulating security interest over the company's assets.
- The mortgage holder took possession of the land and sold it for $163 400.
- Other assets realised the following amounts.

Inventories	$108 000
Accounts receivable	52 000
Plant and equipment	268 000
Shares in listed companies	122 000

- Uncalled capital (if required to be called up) is recoverable.
- Preference shareholders are preferential as to dividends and return of capital. The constitution does not provide any further rights for preference shareholders.
- In relation to return of capital, ordinary 'A' shareholders and ordinary 'B' shareholders rank equally after preference shareholders.

Required

1. List the debts paid by the liquidator in their order of priority of payment.
2. Prepare journal entries to wind up Glowworm Ltd.

33.17 Sale of assets, final distribution to shareholders ★ ★ ★   **LO7, 8, 9**

As a result of a court order, Spider Ltd went into liquidation on 30 June 2023. A statement of financial position prepared on that date was as follows.

SPIDER LTD Statement of financial position as at 30 June 2023		
Equity		
Share capital:		
80 000 preference shares, issued at $2 and paid to $1		$ 80 000
136 000 'A' ordinary shares, issued for $2, called to $1.50		204 000
100 000 'B' ordinary shares, issued for $1, called to 75c		75 000
		359 000
Less: Calls in arrears:		
24 000 'A' ordinary shares	$ (6 000)	
2400 'B' ordinary shares	(600)	(6 600)
		352 400
Calls in advance: 4000 'A' ordinary shares at 50c		2 000
General reserve		51 600
Retained earnings (accumulated losses)		(26 000)
Total equity		**$ 380 000**
Current assets		
Cash		$ 1 800
Accounts receivable	$ 111 000	
Allowance for doubtful debts	(2 000)	109 000
Inventories		39 200
Total current assets		150 000
Non-current assets		
Land		140 000
Buildings	432 000	
Less: Accumulated depreciation — buildings	(326 000)	106 000
Plant and equipment	210 000	
Less: Accumulated depreciation — plant and equipment	(160 000)	50 000

SPIDER LTD
Statement of financial position
as at 30 June 2023

Goodwill	44 000	
Less: Accumulated impairment losses — goodwill	(8 000)	36 000
Total non-current assets		332 000
Total assets		482 000
Current liabilities		
Loan (unsecured)		12 000
Creditors and accruals		50 000
Total current liabilities		62 000
Non-current liabilities		
Mortgage (secured on land and buildings)		40 000
Total non-current liabilities		40 000
Total liabilities		102 000
Net assets		**$380 000**

Additional information

(a) The company's constitution was silent as to return of capital in the event of a winding up.

(b) The mortgage holder took possession of the land and buildings, sold them for $286 000, paid off the mortgage plus interest owing of $1600 and refunded the difference to the liquidator.

(c) The liquidator was able to realise the following amounts for the assets.

Plant and equipment	$ 49 000
Inventories	34 000
Accounts receivable	107 000
	$190 000

(d) The ledger account 'Creditors and accruals' comprised the following.

Workers compensation owing to employee	$10 000
Company income tax owing	20 000
Annual leave owing to a director's son	4 000
Trade creditors	16 000
	$50 000

(e) Additional liabilities accepted by the liquidator and not yet recorded were as follows.

Interest accrued on mortgage	$ 1 600
Salaries owing to two directors ($30 000 + $32 000)	62 000
Retrenchment payments owing to four employees	40 000
Wages owing to 14 employees	270 000
	$373 600

(f) All calls in arrears were received by the liquidator, except from 4000 'A' ordinary shares. These shares were forfeited.

(g) Calls in advance were not paid back before the final distribution by the liquidator. Uncalled capital (where required to be called up) on final distribution proved to be recoverable.

(h) Liquidation expenses amounted to $7600.

Required

1. Prepare the journal entry in Spider Ltd's records to record the sale by the mortgage holder of the land and buildings, and the receipt of any net cash from the mortgage holder.
2. Prepare the liquidation account.
3. Show all workings for calculation of the final distribution of deficiency or surplus to shareholders.
4. Prepare the liquidator's receipts and payments account, showing clearly the order of priority of payment of liabilities.

Hornet Ltd went into voluntary liquidation on 1 January 2024, at which date the statement of financial position was as shown below.

HORNET LTD Statement of financial position as at 1 January 2024				
LIABILITIES AND EQUITY			**ASSETS**	
Share capital:			Land and buildings (net)	$125 000
200 000 ordinary shares fully paid	$230 000		Plant (net)	200 000
Retained earnings	5 000		Fixed deposit	5 000
Mortgage loan	75 000		Accounts receivable	49 000
Debentures	50 000		Investments	25 000
Bank overdraft	40 000		Inventories	60 000
Accounts payable	40 000			
Other payables	24 000			
	$464 000			$464 000

Additional information

(a) Creditors were called on to prove their debts. The liquidator discovered the following.
  - Debenture interest of $3750 was due on 1 January 2024.
  - The Hive Bank holds a mortgage over the plant as security against the overdraft; as the bank has waived its right to seize the plant, the liquidator has undertaken to sell the asset and repay the overdraft.
  - The mortgage loan is secured over land and buildings; the mortgagee has decided to sell the assets to recover the amount owing.
  - The debentures are secured by a circulating security interest over inventories.
  - Other payables comprise loans from directors, made on 1 December 2023.

(b) Assets realised the following amounts.

Land and buildings	$200 000	
Less: Rates and selling expenses	(8 000)	
Less: Mortgage loan	(75 000)	$117 000
Plant and equipment		195 000
Fixed deposit		6 000
Accounts receivable		45 000
Investments		15 000
Inventories		50 000
		$428 000

(c) The liquidator made the following payments.

Debentures	$ 50 000
Debenture interest	3 750
Bank overdraft	40 000
Accounts payable (in full settlement)	38 000
Other payables	24 000
Additional amounts not recorded in the records:	
Liquidator's remuneration	12 500
Liquidation expenses	5 500
Holiday pay — employee	2 000
Retrenchment payment — employee	5 000
Income tax penalty	1 500
	$182 250

Required

1. Prepare the liquidation account.
2. Prepare the liquidator's receipts and payments.
3. Prepare the shareholders' distribution account.

Mandarinia Ltd went into liquidation on 31 March 2023. The report as to affairs prepared at that date is as follows.

MANDARINIA LTD
Report as to affairs
as at 31 March 2023

	Valuation	Estimated realisable value
(1) Assets not specifically charged:		
Calls in arrears (1000 ordinary shares at 25c)	$ 250	$ 200
Cash on hand	50	50
Sundry debtors	24 400	18 100
Inventories	51 900	17 940
	76 600	36 290

(2) Assets subject to specific charge	Carrying amount	Estimated realisable value		
Land	$40 000	$40 900		
Less: Mortgage and accrued interest	24 500	24 500	15 500	16 400
			$92 100	52 690
Total estimated realisable value				52 690
(3) *Less:* Preferential creditors entitled to priority over the holders of a floating charge				(600)
				52 090
(4) *Less:* Amount owing under floating charge — bank overdraft				(19 440)
				32 650
(5) *Less:* Other preferential claims				(1 400)
				31 250
(6) *Less:* Unsecured creditors — ordinary				(13 450)
Estimated surplus subject to liquidation expenses				$ 17 800
Share capital				
Paid-up capital:				
Issued preference shares: 42 000 shares fully paid at $1				$ 42 000
Issued ordinary shares: 60 000 shares called to 60c, issued for $1				36 000
Called capital				78 000
Calls on ordinary shares paid in advance: 4000 shares at 40c each				1 600
				$ 79 600
Balance of retained earnings account, 31/3/23				$ 22 390 Dr

Except for the return of capital to shareholders, liquidation of the company was completed at 30 September 2023. The liquidator's receipts and payments account for the 6 months ended 30 September 2023 is as follows.

Liquidator's receipts and payments			
Receipts		*Payments*	
Cash in hand	50	Bank overdraft	19 440
Receivables	17 260	Liquidation expenses	1 130
Inventories	34 020	Liquidator's remuneration	2 400
Land (net)	24 000	Preferential creditors	2 000
Calls in arrears	250	Unsecured creditors *less* discount	13 410
		Surplus available to shareholders	37 200
	75 580		75 580

The mortgage holder had taken possession of the land, sold it for $49 000, and paid the surplus to the liquidator after fully satisfying the mortgage claim.

Preference shares are preferred to return of capital. All uncalled capital proved recoverable.

Required

Prepare the liquidation account and the shareholders' distribution account as they will appear after repayment of capital.

The trial balance of Mouse Ltd on 1 September 2024, the date on which the court ordered that the company be wound up, is presented below.

MOUSE LTD Trial balance as at 1 September 2024		
	Debit	Credit
Bank overdraft (secured over land and buildings)		$114 000
Accounts payable		91 000
Accrued expenses		2 000
Unsecured notes		150 000
Debentures (secured by a circulating security interest over the company's assets)		200 000
Share capital: 7% preference issued at $1		50 000
'A' ordinary issued at $1		200 000
'B' ordinary issued at $1		40 000
'C' ordinary issued at $1		20 000
Allowance for doubtful debts		1 000
Accumulated depreciation — vehicles		17 000
Accumulated depreciation — plant and equipment		40 000
Cash	$ 100	
Accounts receivable	97 000	
Inventories	146 400	
Shares in Bee Pty Ltd	17 500	
Vehicles	29 000	
Plant and equipment	181 000	
Land and buildings (net)	250 000	
Goodwill	24 000	
Retained earnings	180 000	
	$925 000	$925 000

Additional information

(a) Share capital consisted of the following.
- 50 000 7% preference shares fully paid
- 200 000 'A' ordinary shares fully paid
- 100 000 'B' ordinary shares paid to 40c
- 100 000 'C' ordinary shares paid to 20c

The constitution provided that preference shareholders were preferential as to return of capital in a winding up, and 'C' ordinary shareholders were deferred as to return of capital until all other classes of shares had been paid in full.

(b) Proceeds from sale of assets (the bank agreed to allow the liquidator to sell the land and buildings) were as follows.

Accounts receivable	$ 71 000
Inventories	100 000
Shares in Bee Pty Ltd	10 000
Vehicles	10 000
Plant and equipment	116 000
Land and buildings	240 000

(c) The liquidator called up the uncalled balance on 'B' ordinary shares and 'C' ordinary shares. Holders of 10 000 'C' ordinary shares and 10 000 'B' ordinary shares failed to pay the call and these shares were subsequently forfeited.

(d) Payments made by liquidator after negotiation with creditors were as follows.

Liquidation expenses	$ 2 100
Liquidator's remuneration	4 000
Bank overdraft and interest	116 000
Accounts payable	89 000
Accrued expenses	2 200
Unsecured notes and interest	154 500
Debentures and interest	206 000

Required

1. Prepare journal entries to wind up the affairs of Mouse Ltd.
2. Prepare the liquidation account, the liquidator's receipts and payments account and the shareholders' distribution account, clearly showing the share of cash for each class of shares.

33.21 Journal entries, given a report as to affairs ★ ★   **LO9**

At 31 July 2023, the liquidator of PPY Ltd, who had been appointed by the court, prepared the report as to affairs shown below.

PPY LTD Report as to affairs as at 31 July 2023		
	Valuation	Estimated realisable value
(1) Assets not specifically charged:		
Interest in land	—	—
Sundry debtors	$ 58 000	$ 36 000
Cash on hand	—	—
Cash at bank	1 000	1 000
Inventories	122 000	94 000
Work-in-progress	—	—
Plant and equipment at cost/value	82 000	44 000
Other assets — bills receivable	48 000	28 000
	311 000	203 000
(2) Assets subject to specific charge:		
Land and buildings	91 000	80 000
Less: Amounts owing (mortgage)	(70 000)	(70 000)
	21 000	10 000
	$332 000	213 000
Total estimated realisable value		213 000
(3) *Less:* Preferential creditors entitled to priority over floating charge:		
claims by employees — salaries and wages		(1 400)
		211 600
(4) *Less:* Amounts owing and secured by floating charge —		
debentures		(30 000)
(5) *Less:* Preferential creditors		—
		181 600
(6) Balances owing to unsecured creditors:		
Trade creditors	$ (93 000)	
Income tax payable	(4 000)	(97 000)
Estimated surplus subject to liquidation expenses		$ 84 600
Share capital		
Issued: 90 000 ordinary shares fully paid		$125 000
50 000 6% preference shares, fully paid		
		50 000
Total share capital		$175 000
Retained earnings		$ 19 000 Cr

Additional information

(a) Accumulated depreciation on plant and equipment was recorded at $14 000.

(b) Arrears of cumulative preference dividend totalled $12 000. The constitution gives the preference shareholders priority of payment of arrears of preference dividends. All shares rank equally per share as to return of capital.

(c) Of the $93 000 trade creditors recognised by the liquidator, PPY Ltd had not recorded $3000. Further, PPY Ltd had not recorded unpaid salaries and wages amounting to $1400.

(d) At the completion of the winding up, the following additional information was available.
- Interest accrued on mortgage was $2000, and on debentures $1200.
- Liquidation expenses were $800, and liquidator's remuneration was $4000.
- No bill receivable was dishonoured.
- All other creditors were paid the amounts reported in the report as to affairs.
- Land and buildings realised $75 000.
- All other assets realised the amounts estimated.

(e) In relation to the land and buildings, the mortgagee sold the assets and remitted to the liquidator any amount in excess of the debt due.

Required

Prepare the journal entries in PPY Ltd to wind up the company. (Show calculations for the distribution of cash to shareholders.)

33.22 **Report as to affairs and ledger accounts** ★ ★   **LO9**

The statement of financial position of Horse Ltd below was prepared at 30 June 2023, before liquidation proceedings commenced.

HORSE LTD Statement of financial position as at 30 June 2023		
Equity		
Share capital:		
60 000 10% preference shares issued at $1, fully paid		$ 60 000
40 000 ordinary shares called to 75c, issued at $1	$30 000	
Less: Calls in arrears 25c on 10 000 ordinary shares	(2 500)	27 500
		87 500
Retained earnings		(12 620)
Total equity		74 880
Liabilities		
Accounts payable	39 800	
GST payable	200	
Rent payable	180	
Telephone account payable	500	
Electricity account payable	600	
PAYG tax instalment	840	
Wages payable	1 400	
Managing director's salary payable	4 700	
Fringe benefits tax payable	900	
Bank overdraft (secured by circulating security interest)	18 000	
Mortgage payable (secured on freehold)	90 000	
Partly secured creditor (holding $5000 security on plant)	16 000	173 120
Total equity and liabilities		**$248 000**
Assets		
Freehold land and buildings (net)		$114 000
Plant (net)		25 000
Inventories		68 000
Bills receivable		3 400
Accounts receivable		31 000
Cash on hand		6 600
Total assets		**$248 000**

Additional information

(a) It is estimated that $2000 of the calls in arrears would be received.

(b) The estimated sales values of the assets are as follows.

Freehold land and buildings	$120 000
Inventories	58 000
Accounts receivable	22 000
Bills receivable	3 400
Plant (including $10 000 on plant over which a security is held)	20 000

Required

1. Prepare a summary of affairs as at 30 June 2023.
2. Assuming that the liquidator realises all assets (including land and buildings, and plant) and calls in arrears at the amounts estimated, forfeits those shares that do not pay the call, pays the creditors at the amounts as listed in the statement of financial position (except for accounts payable who settle out at $38 000) and distributes the balance after deducting liquidator's expenses of $1900 and liquidator's remuneration of $5700, prepare the liquidation account, the shareholders' distribution account, and the liquidator's receipts and payments account. The constitution provides that all shares rank equally, per share, as to return of capital.

33.23 Receivership and liquidation ★ ★ ★   **LO9**

On 31 March 2023, you were appointed receiver, at a remuneration of 5% of the gross proceeds on sale of assets, in respect of Cicada Ltd. Your appointment was made by the ACE Bank, which held an equitable mortgage over the assets of Cicada Ltd, in respect of an advance of $42 000 which was still owing.

On 30 April 2023, Cicada Ltd went into voluntary liquidation and you were appointed liquidator for the purposes of the winding up.

The trial balance of Cicada Ltd at 31 March 2023 is as follows.

CICADA LTD Trial balance as at 31 March 2023	
Debits	
Inventories	$ 30 000
Plant — subject to hire purchase agreement with Equipment Hire Co. Ltd	3 000
Other plant	24 000
Work in progress	12 240
Accounts receivable	39 840
Retained earnings	23 400
	$132 480
Credits	
Share capital (80 000 shares issued for $1 and paid to 60c)	$ 48 000
ACE Bank	42 000
Accounts payable	35 940
Long service leave payable to retrenched employee	2 100
Local council rates payable	1 800
PAYG tax deductions from employees (to be remitted to the Australian Taxation Office)	600
Wages owing to Y. Young (2 weeks to 31 March 2023, at $720 per week)	1 440
Amount still owing as retrenchment payment	600
	$132 480

All assets were sold by you in your capacity as receiver, the proceeds of which amounted to $72 000. To achieve this, you had to spend $1200 to complete the work in progress. Expenses of advertising and stocktaking amounted to $1200.

You made the appropriate payments from the receivership funds. After this was completed, you retired from the receivership. You were then appointed liquidator and proceeded with the distribution of funds in hand under the liquidation. Liquidator's expenses amounted to $600.

Required

1. Prepare the receiver's receipts and payments account.
2. Prepare the final receipts and payments account of the liquidator, showing in detail the order in which the funds in hand are distributed.

ACKNOWLEDGEMENTS

Photo: © Kittie and Minnie / Shutterstock.com

Text: Sourced from the Federal Register of Legislation at 8 November 2018. For the latest information on Australian Government law please go to https://www.legislation.gov.au.

CHAPTER 34

Accounting for mineral resources

CHAPTER AIM

This chapter describes the unique accounting issues faced by entities involved in the mineral resources industry, and accounting for mineral resources in accordance with AASB 6/IFRS 6 *Exploration for and Evaluation of Mineral Resources*.

LEARNING OBJECTIVES

After studying this chapter, you should be able to:

34.1 explain the context of mineral resources and that entities involved in extractive activities are often faced with unique and challenging accounting issues

34.2 describe the objective of AASB 6/IFRS 6

34.3 apply the necessary judgement in determining the nature of the activities and related costs considered to be within the limited scope of AASB 6/IFRS 6

34.4 evaluate the accounting policy options available for exploration and evaluation assets under AASB 6/IFRS 6

34.5 analyse costs incurred during the exploration and evaluation phase of extractive activities in order to apply the area of interest method as set out in AASB 6/IFRS 6

34.6 demonstrate understanding of the presentation requirements of AASB 6/IFRS 6 and industry practices

34.7 evaluate the appropriateness of continued capitalisation of costs incurred during the exploration and evaluation phase of extractive activities

34.8 apply the disclosure requirements of AASB 6/IFRS 6

34.9 discuss the possible future developments related to accounting for the extractive industries.

CONCEPTS FOR REVIEW

Before studying this chapter, you should understand and, if necessary, revise:

- the concept of an asset in the *Conceptual Framework*
- the concept of an expense in the *Conceptual Framework*
- depreciation, amortisation and impairment of tangible and intangible assets.

34.1 Mineral resources in context

LEARNING OBJECTIVE 34.1 Explain the context of mineral resources and that entities involved in extractive activities are often faced with unique and challenging accounting issues.

The mineral resources industry is a key pillar of the Australian economy, employing more than 200 000 people (Minerals Council of Australia 2017). In 2017, the industry's export income represented over half (54%) of Australia's total exported goods and services (Minerals Council of Australia 2018). A number of large multinational mining companies operate in Australia, including BHP Group, Newcrest, Rio Tinto, Alcoa, Chalco, Shenhua, Alcan and Glencore. There are also many small mining and mineral exploration companies listed on the Australian Securities Exchange (ASX). The industry spends significant amounts on new capital investment, exploration, and research and development. It is an important source of employment in regional Australia.

This chapter focuses on how to account for costs related to exploration and evaluation of mineral resources, which is governed by AASB 6/IFRS 6 *Exploration for and Evaluation of Mineral Resources*. AASB 6/IFRS 6 is the only industry-specific standard applicable to what are commonly referred to as the extractive industries.

The **extractive industries** are 'those industries involved in finding and removing wasting natural resources located in or near the Earth's crust' (International Accounting Standards Committee 2000). The term 'wasting natural resources' means non-renewable or non-replaceable resources, and includes minerals (e.g. iron ore, alumina, lead, coal, gold, nickel, zinc and uranium) and oil and gas (e.g. petroleum, crude oil and coal seam gas).

The Minerals Council of Australia views the industry's main activities in terms of exploration, extraction and processing, but the International Accounting Standards Board (2010) describes five main activities: prospecting, exploration, evaluation, development and production. These are summarised in figure 34.1.

FIGURE 34.1	Description of extractive activities
Prospecting	Searching for geological features that, based on geological, topographical, geophysical and historical data, suggest the potential presence of mineral deposits or oil or gas-bearing formations.
Exploration	Studying areas identified via prospecting to determine the likely quantity and quality of ore that is present. Exploration often involves drilling or digging for samples.
Evaluation	Determining whether extraction of mineral deposits, oil or gas is technically feasible and commercially viable.
Development	Establishing access to the site (e.g. roads and rail facilities, platforms or rigs at sea), access to the mineral reserve itself (e.g. excavations, tunnels and wells) and developing site infrastructure to support the workforce.
Production	Taking the mineral resources from the Earth and processing them into a marketable product.

AASB 6/IFRS 6 provides limited guidance for all extractive industries and offers different accounting policy alternatives. Many of the financial reporting issues that affect entities in the extractive industries are a result of the environment in which they operate. The financial statements of such entities need to reflect the risks and rewards to which they are exposed. Aside from government and environmental influences, the main features of activities undertaken in the extractive industries are as follows.

- High risk with the potential for (but no guarantee of) high rewards — costs are often incurred in the hope of finding mineral resources in producible (sufficiently profitable or 'commercial') quantities. Sometimes those costs can be very high, yet lead to no significant resource finds. On the other hand, some highly valuable mineral resource discoveries occur at very little cost. This makes the accounting for costs incurred in finding mineral resources particularly challenging.
- Time and cost to produce — once mineral reserves are discovered, there can be considerable additional expenditure involved in developing and producing those reserves, coupled with a significant time lag between commencement of the exploration activities and production of the reserves. This raises issues associated with the likelihood and extent of economic benefits from such expenditures, which can make impairment assessments more difficult.

☐ Extractive industries are those involved in finding and removing wasting natural resources located in or near the Earth's crust.

☐ Extractive activities include: prospecting, exploration, evaluation, development and production.

☐ AASB 6/IFRS 6 *Exploration for and Evaluation of Mineral Resources* provides limited guidance for all extractive industries and offers different accounting policy alternatives.

☐ Extractive industries are subject to high risks with the potential for (but no guarantee of) high rewards. This makes the accounting for costs incurred in finding mineral resources challenging.

☐ There can be considerable additional time and expenditure between exploration activities and production. This raises issues associated with the likelihood and magnitude of economic benefits from such expenditures, which can make impairment assessments more difficult.

34.2 Objective of AASB 6/IFRS 6

LEARNING OBJECTIVE 34.2 Describe the objective of AASB 6/IFRS 6.

According to paragraph 1 of AASB 6/IFRS 6, the objective of the standard is limited to specifying the financial reporting for the 'exploration for and evaluation of mineral resources', which is defined in appendix A of the standard as follows.

> The search for mineral resources, including minerals, oil, natural gas and similar non-regenerative [non-renewable] resources after the entity has obtained legal rights to explore in a specific area, as well as the determination of the technical feasibility and commercial viability of extracting the mineral resource.

More specifically, paragraph 2 of AASB 6/IFRS 6 restricts the objectives of the standard to making limited improvements to existing accounting practices for exploration and evaluation (E&E) expenditures, specifying when entities need to assess E&E assets for impairment in accordance with AASB 136/IAS 36 *Impairment of Assets*, and requiring certain disclosures.

☐ The objective of AASB 6/IFRS 6 is limited to financial reporting for the exploration for and evaluation of mineral resources.

☐ AASB 6/IFRS 6 specifies when entities need to assess E&E assets for impairment in accordance with AASB 136/IAS 36 *Impairment of Assets* and requires certain disclosures.

34.3 Scope of AASB 6/IFRS 6

LEARNING OBJECTIVE 34.3 Apply the necessary judgement in determining the nature of the activities and related costs considered to be within the limited scope of AASB 6/IFRS 6.

The scope of AASB 6/IFRS 6 is specifically limited to accounting for E&E expenditures and, as noted in paragraph 4, it 'does not address other aspects of accounting by entities engaged in the exploration for and evaluation of mineral resources'. In other words, AASB 6/IFRS 6 does not deal with the prospecting, development and production activities described in figure 34.1. Therefore, it does not provide guidance on other industry-specific issues that may arise during the E&E phase. Figure 34.2 illustrates the scope of AASB 6/IFRS 6.

☐ AASB 6/IFRS 6 is limited to accounting for exploration and evaluation expenditure.

☐ AASB 6/IFRS 6 does not address accounting for other related activities such as prospecting, development or production.

FIGURE 34.2 | Scope of AASB 6/IFRS 6

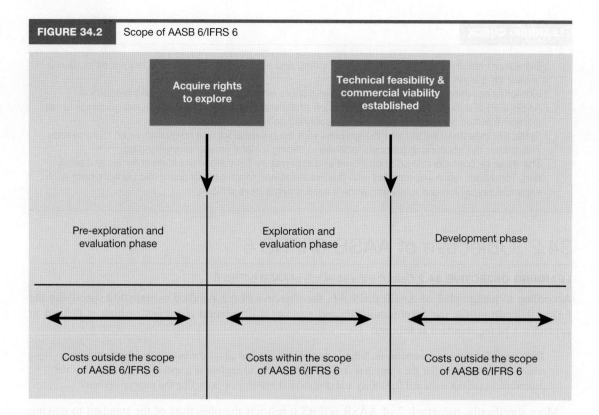

34.4 Recognition of exploration and evaluation assets

LEARNING OBJECTIVE 34.4 Evaluate the accounting policy options available for exploration and evaluation assets under AASB 6/IFRS 6.

34.4.1 Temporary exemption from AASB 108/IAS 8 paragraphs 11 and 12

Entities involved in extractive activities follow a large variety of accounting practices which, as described in paragraph BC17 of the Basis for Conclusions of IFRS 6, range 'from deferring capitalising on the balance sheet nearly all exploration and evaluation expenditure to recognising all such expenditure in profit or loss as incurred'. Paragraph 6 of AASB 6/IFRS 6 requires that an entity recognising E&E assets (i.e. capitalising expenditure as an asset) should apply paragraph 10 of AASB 108/IAS 8 *Accounting Policies, Changes in Accounting Estimates and Errors* as well as paragraphs Aus7.1 and Aus7.2 of AASB 6. Hence, management should use its judgement in developing and applying an accounting policy to ensure it results in information that is relevant and reliable. Accounting policies regarding E&E typically relate to 'areas of interest'. Appendix B of AASB 6 defines an **area of interest** as follows.

An individual geological area which is considered to constitute a favourable environment for the presence of a mineral deposit or an oil or natural gas field, or has been proved to contain such a deposit or field.

Paragraph Aus7.3 of AASB 6 notes the following.

In most cases, an area of interest will comprise a single mine or deposit or a separate oil or gas field.

Under paragraphs 11 and 12 of AASB 108/IAS 8, management is required to consider various sources of authoritative guidance (i.e. rules and regulations) when developing accounting policies for items not addressed by a specific accounting standard. Under AASB 6/IFRS 6, however, an exemption is available from this requirement. This exemption effectively allows the continued application or use of much of the existing industry accounting practices for recognition and measurement of E&E assets and expenditures.

Historically, other than expensing all E&E costs as incurred, the most common methods used by entities in the extractive industries to account for costs incurred prior to production ('pre-production costs') are the:

- successful efforts method
- area of interest method
- full cost method.

Under the successful efforts method, only those costs directly related to the discovery, acquisition or development of specific, distinct mineral reserves are capitalised and accumulated as part of a cost centre. This is usually at the individual licence level, with a separate licence held for each development site.

The area of interest method as described in AASB 6/IFRS 6 is similar to the successful efforts method, except that it uses an area of interest (rather than an individual licence) as the cost centre. (In some cases, there may be several licences for one area of interest.)

The full cost method generally involves the capitalisation of all costs incurred in prospecting, acquiring mineral interests, exploration, appraisal, development and construction — accumulated in large cost centres. This is normally done at the country level, such that entities operating in more than one country will disclose separate amounts for their operations in each country. The full cost method is not consistent with the *Conceptual Framework* and as a result cannot be used outside of the E&E phase. The area of interest method is used in Australia, and is discussed further below.

34.4.2 Treatment of exploration and evaluation expenditures in Australia

The Australian experience differs to some extent from international experience because, prior to the adoption of IFRSs in Australia, there was an existing standard, AASB 1022 *Accounting for the Extractive Industries*, which permitted the capitalisation of E&E expenditure using the area of interest method, provided certain tests were satisfied. As a result, when the Australian Accounting Standards Board (AASB) issued AASB 6 in Australia, it inserted Australia-specific guidance. Paragraphs Aus7.1 and Aus7.2 of AASB 6 require that for each area of interest, E&E costs:

- be expensed as incurred, or
- be partially or fully capitalised, provided the rights to tenure (exploration rights) of the area of interest are current, assuming one or both of the following is also satisfied:
  - the E&E costs are expected to be recouped through sale or successful development and exploitation
  - at the end of the reporting period, the E&E activities in the area of interest are not at a stage that would permit assessment of the existence or otherwise of economically recoverable reserves, and active and significant operations in (or in relation to) the area of interest are continuing.

Figure 34.3 details the E&E accounting policy from BHP Group Limited's 2018 annual report, which reflects the AASB 6 area of interest method for capitalisation of petroleum E&E activities, compared to a policy of expensing most E&E costs associated with minerals activities.

FIGURE 34.3   E&E expenditure accounting policy, BHP Group

Exploration and evaluation

Exploration costs are incurred to discover mineral and petroleum resources. Evaluation costs are incurred to assess the technical feasibility and commercial viability of resources found.

Exploration and evaluation expenditure is charged to the income statement as incurred, except in the following circumstances in which case the expenditure may be capitalised:

In respect of minerals activities:

- the exploration and evaluation activity is within an area of interest that was previously acquired as an asset acquisition or in a business combination and measured at fair value on acquisition; or
- the existence of a commercially viable mineral deposit has been established.

In respect of petroleum activities:

- the exploration and evaluation activity is within an area of interest for which it is expected that the expenditure will be recouped by future exploitation or sale; or
- exploration and evaluation activity has not reached a stage that permits a reasonable assessment of the existence of commercially recoverable reserves.

A regular review of each area of interest is undertaken to determine the appropriateness of continuing to carry forward costs in relation to that area. Capitalised costs are only carried forward to the extent that they are expected to be recovered though the successful exploitation of the area of interest or alternatively by its sale. To the extent that capitalised expenditure is no longer expected to be recovered, it is charged to the income statement.

Key judgements and estimates

Exploration and evaluation expenditure results in certain items of expenditure being capitalised for an area of interest where it is considered likely to be recoverable by future exploitation or sale, or where the activities have not reached a stage that permits a reasonable assessment of the existence of reserves. This policy requires management to make certain estimates and assumptions as to future events and circumstances, in particular whether an economically viable extraction operation can be established. These estimates and assumptions may change as new information becomes available. If, after having capitalised the expenditure under the policy, a judgement is made that recovery of the expenditure is unlikely, the relevant capitalised amount will be written off to the income statement.

Source: BHP Group Limited (2018, p. 177).

LEARNING CHECK

☐ AASB 6 provides temporary exemption from paragraphs 11 and 12 of AASB 108/IAS 8, hence providing for the continued application or use of the existing industry accounting practices for recognition and measurement of E&E assets and expenditure.

☐ In accordance with AASB 6, in Australia the area of interest method is permitted and E&E expenditure is either expensed or partially or fully capitalised where certain tests are satisfied.

34.5 Measurement of exploration and evaluation assets

LEARNING OBJECTIVE 34.5 Analyse costs incurred during the exploration and evaluation phase of extractive activities in order to apply the area of interest method as set out in AASB 6/IFRS 6.

34.5.1 Measurement at recognition

Regardless of the method used, paragraph 8 of AASB 6/IFRS 6 states that E&E assets must initially be measured at cost. This raises the question of what types of E&E expenditures qualify for capitalisation as E&E assets. Paragraph 9 of AASB 6/IFRS 6 provides the following guidance.

> An entity shall determine an accounting policy specifying which expenditures are recognised as exploration and evaluation assets and apply the policy consistently. In making this determination, an entity considers the degree to which the expenditure can be associated with finding specific mineral resources. The following are examples of expenditures that might be included in the initial measurement of exploration and evaluation assets (the list is not exhaustive):
> (a) acquisition of rights to explore;
> (b) topographical, geological, geochemical and geophysical studies;
> (c) exploratory drilling;
> (d) trenching;
> (e) sampling; and
> (f) activities in relation to evaluating the technical feasibility and commercial viability of extracting a mineral resource.

Additional Australian specific guidance is also included in AASB 6 that clarifies the following.

- In allocating direct and indirect costs to an area of interest, internal costs should not be treated any differently to external costs such as fees for contractors or consultants (paragraph Aus9.1).
- The costs of acquiring leases or other rights of tenure in the area of interest would normally form part of the E&E asset for the relevant area of interest (paragraph Aus9.2).
- Depreciation applicable to assets used in E&E activities is an indirect cost that qualifies for allocation to an area of interest (paragraph Aus9.3).
- Only general and administrative costs that directly relate to operational activities in the relevant area of interest can be capitalised (e.g. payroll costs for staff involved in E&E operations) while all other

general and administrative type costs (e.g. salary costs of general management) must be expensed as incurred (paragraph Aus9.4).

Figure 34.4 and illustrative example 34.1 classify the typical general and administrative costs of an entity involved in E&E activities between those related directly to E&E activities, which would likely qualify for capitalisation, versus those that are only indirectly related to E&E activities, and therefore would be expensed as incurred.

FIGURE 34.4   Classification of typical general and administrative expenses as direct versus indirect

Direct	Indirect
• Office supplies used specifically in the administration of E&E operations • Bank fees for banking activities associated with E&E operations • Payroll processing for E&E activity operations personnel • Audit fees for audit reporting on E&E activity operations • Liability insurance for E&E activity operations • Rent and utilities for premises used for E&E activity operations	• Directors' fees • Secretarial and share registry expenses • Salaries and other expenses of general management

---

ILLUSTRATIVE EXAMPLE 34.1

Classification of general and administrative expenses as direct versus indirect

Burbank Mining Limited undertakes exploration and evaluation activities and has incurred the following expenses.

	$
Office supplies used specifically in the administration of E&E operations	100 000
Secretarial and share registry expenses	50 000
Bank fees for banking activities associated with E&E operations	50 000
Payroll processing for E&E activity operations personnel	200 000
Directors' fees	250 000
Audit fees for audit reporting on E&E activity operations	300 000
Salaries and other expenses of general management	400 000
Liability insurance for E&E activity operations	300 000
Rent and utilities for premises used for E&E activity operations	100 000

Required
Advise Burbank Mining Limited which amounts should be capitalised and which amounts should be expensed.

Solution
The following costs are considered directly relevant to Burbank Mining Limited's E&E activities and should therefore be capitalised.

	$
Office supplies used specifically in the administration of E&E operations	100 000
Bank fees for banking activities associated with E&E operations	50 000
Payroll processing for E&E activity operations personnel	200 000
Audit fees for audit reporting on E&E activity operations	300 000
Liability insurance for E&E activity operations	300 000
Rent and utilities for premises used for E&E activity operations	100 000
Total	**1 050 000**

The following costs are not considered directly relevant to Burbank Mining Limited's E&E activities, and should therefore be expensed.

	$
Secretarial and share registry expenses	50 000
Directors' fees	250 000
Salaries and other expenses of general management	400 000
Total	**700 000**

Paragraphs 5 and 10 of AASB 6/IFRS 6 also indicate that costs related to activities undertaken prior to the commencement of E&E activities (which is presumed to be before the entity has obtained the legal rights to explore a specific area) and costs incurred for the development of mineral resources after the E&E phase are not covered by the standard, and therefore should be accounted for in accordance with other applicable IFRSs and the *Conceptual Framework*. In practice, this usually results in the immediate expensing of costs incurred prior to obtaining exploration licences and the treatment of development costs as intangible assets accounted for under AASB 138/IAS 38 *Intangible Assets* (AASB 6/IFRS 6 paragraph 10) or property, plant and equipment accounted for under AASB 116/IAS 16 *Property, Plant and Equipment* (AASB 6/IFRS 6 paragraph 12).

34.5.2 Obligations for removal and restoration

According to paragraph 11 of AASB 6/IFRS 6, obligations for **removal and restoration** incurred as a result of E&E activities are recognised in accordance with AASB 137/IAS 37 *Provisions, Contingent Liabilities and Contingent Assets* (see chapter 8). This means that if an entity has an obligation to restore an area of interest damaged by its E&E activities, it must recognise a liability for that restoration as the related damage is identified. This is a complex and highly judgement-driven process because of the significant degree of estimation involved and the impact of laws and regulations applicable to each area of interest. Also, if mineral resources are found as a result of the E&E activities undertaken and the area is developed into a producing asset, the remediation (or restoration) of the site will not occur until those resources are exhausted and production ceases, which could be a long period of time.

In practice, any damage caused to a site during the E&E phase is usually immaterial compared with the damage caused during construction of production facilities after confirming the existence and ability to extract commercial quantities of mineral resources in the area. Therefore, most of the liability for removal and restoration tends to be recognised during the construction period, which is after the E&E phase covered by AASB 6/IFRS 6.

34.5.3 Measurement after recognition

Under paragraph 12 of AASB 6/IFRS 6, subsequent to initial recognition E&E assets shall be measured using the cost model or the revaluation model. The implications of using the revaluation model will differ depending on the extent to which the components of E&E assets are classified as property, plant and equipment under AASB 116/IAS 16 or intangible assets under AASB 138/IAS 38. The classification issue is discussed further in section 34.6.1.

The revaluation model in AASB 138/IAS 38 requires the existence of an active market (discussed in chapter 6). However, the revaluation model in AASB 116/IAS 16 only requires that fair value be measured reliably (discussed in chapter 5).

According to paragraph 15 of AASB 6/IFRS 6, regardless of which model is selected (cost or revaluation), it must be applied consistently to all E&E assets. However, it is extremely rare for the revaluation model to be used in the extractive industries.

34.5.4 Changes in accounting policies

Paragraph 13 of AASB 6/IFRS 6 allows an entity to change its accounting policies related to E&E expenditures on the condition that the change 'makes the financial statements more relevant to the economic decision-making needs of users and no less reliable, or more reliable and no less relevant to those needs'. In assessing the relevance and reliability of the change, entities are directed to the criteria in AASB 108/IAS 8, although they are not expected to fully comply with those criteria. In addition, the AASB inserted an Australia-specific paragraph (Aus13.1) specifying that any such change must still result in a policy that is consistent with the Australia-specific guidance (discussed in section 34.4.2). An example of an acceptable change in accounting policy following this guidance would be a change from capitalising E&E expenditures using the area of interest method to expensing of all E&E expenditures until the technical feasibility and commercial viability of extracting mineral reserves is established.

34.5.5 Depreciation and amortisation

For E&E assets that are subsequently developed and moved into production, the entity must devise an accounting policy to depreciate or amortise those assets over their estimated useful lives. Commonly, the useful lives of mineral resources are directly linked to the life of the underlying economically recoverable reserves (i.e. those reserves that are commercially viable (profitable) to extract). As a result, these assets are usually depreciated, using the unit-of-production method, to the residual value expected at the conclusion of production. 'The underlying principle of the unit-of-production method is that capitalised costs associated with a cost centre are incurred to find and develop the commercially producible mineral reserves in that cost centre, so that each unit produced from the centre is assigned an equal amount of cost' (International Accounting Standards Committee 2000, paragraph 7.19).

There are some assets, such as drilling rigs and similar equipment, that are used in more than one area of interest or have a useful life that is shorter or longer than that of the underlying reserves. Such assets are normally depreciated using the straight-line method, which means they are depreciated evenly over the time period during which they are expected to provide economic benefits to the entity. Accordingly, the straight-line method allocates an equal amount of cost to each year, while the unit-of-production method allocates an equal amount of cost to each unit produced. Hence, the unit-of-production method would result in no depreciation being recognised during the E&E phase because production would not have commenced.

There are numerous ways in which an entity could calculate a depreciation charge under the unit-of-production method; however, the most common formula is as follows.

$$\text{Depreciation charge for the period} = \text{Current period's production} \times \frac{\text{Net book value of the asset at the beginning of the period}}{\text{Opening reserves estimated at the beginning of the period}}$$

Illustrative example 34.2 provides an illustration of the application of the above formula.

ILLUSTRATIVE EXAMPLE 34.2

Application of the unit-of-production method

Monterey Mining Limited's production for the 2023 year was 40 000 barrels of oil. At the beginning of the period, the net book value of the equipment used to produce the oil was $1 250 000. The opening reserves estimated at the beginning of the period were 250 000 barrels of oil.

Required
Calculate the depreciation charge on the equipment for the 2023 year.

Solution
Using the unit-of-production formula, the following depreciation charge would apply.

$$\frac{40\,000}{250\,000} \times \$1\,250\,000 = \$200\,000$$

34.6 Presentation

LEARNING OBJECTIVE 34.6 Demonstrate understanding of the presentation requirements of AASB 6/IFRS 6 and industry practices.

34.6.1 Classification of E&E assets

AASB 6/IFRS 6 requires E&E assets to be classified as either tangible or intangible. For example, paragraph 16 of the standard notes that drilling rights are treated as intangible assets, while vehicles and drilling rigs are treated as tangible assets. Figure 34.5 demonstrates the typical components of E&E assets, classified between tangible and intangible, highlighting that the majority of E&E assets are classified as intangible assets. As a result, they are measured using the cost model because of the restrictive requirements associated with use of the AASB 138/IAS 38 revaluation model (as discussed in chapter 6). Note that even though equipment used in E&E activities is classified as a tangible asset, the consumption of that equipment, which is reflected through depreciation charges, may qualify for capitalisation as part of an intangible E&E asset if that equipment is being consumed in the E&E activities associated with the intangible E&E asset.

FIGURE 34.5	Typical components of E&E assets classified as tangible versus intangible assets

Tangible	Intangible
• Vehicles and drilling rigs • Costs of replacing major parts of equipment used in E&E activities • Costs of major inspections of equipment used in E&E activities	• Acquisition of rights to explore (e.g. drilling rights and exploration licences) • Topographical, geological, geochemical and geophysical study costs • Deferred costs associated with consumables (e.g. materials and fuel used, contractor payments, employee remuneration)

34.6.2 Reclassification of E&E assets

Once the technical feasibility (i.e. that extraction is possible) and commercial viability (i.e. that the project is expected to be profitable) of extracting a mineral resource have been established for a particular area of interest, paragraph 17 of AASB 6/IFRS 6 requires that the related E&E asset be tested for impairment and then reclassified and accounted for under AASB 116/IAS 16 or AASB 138/IAS 38 as appropriate. If no resources are found as a result of the E&E activities in a specific area, the E&E assets related to that area would normally be impaired and therefore written off as an expense.

The technical feasibility and commercial viability of extracting a mineral resource are normally considered to be established once an entity has confirmed the existence of 'economically recoverable reserves', which Appendix B of AASB 6 defines as follows.

> The estimated quantity of product in an area of interest that can be expected to be profitably extracted, processed and sold under current and foreseeable economic conditions.

Any costs incurred after this stage are specifically outside the scope of AASB 6/IFRS 6 and should not be recognised as E&E assets. Instead the *Conceptual Framework* and AASB 138/IAS 38 should be applied in developing accounting policies for these assets. In practical terms, this means that until a feasibility study is complete and development is approved, accumulated capitalised costs are classified as E&E assets within the scope of AASB 6/IFRS 6.

34.7 Impairment

LEARNING OBJECTIVE 34.7 Evaluate the appropriateness of continued capitalisation of costs incurred during the exploration and evaluation phase of extractive activities.

34.7.1 Recognition and measurement

E&E assets are normally not amortised until (and if) they reach the production phase. However, they must still be assessed for impairment. Given E&E assets do not normally generate cash inflows and due to the nature of E&E activities, there is often not enough information available to reliably estimate their recoverable amount. Paragraph 18 of AASB 6/IFRS 6 requires E&E assets to be assessed for impairment when 'facts and circumstances suggest that the carrying amount of an exploration and evaluation asset exceeds the recoverable amount'. Once an entity has concluded that an E&E asset may be impaired, AASB 136/IAS 36 must be used to measure, present and disclose that impairment in the financial statements, subject to two important modifications set out in paragraphs 20 and 21 of AASB 6/IFRS 6:

- separate impairment testing 'triggers' for E&E assets
- groups of cash-generating units can be used in impairment testing.
  The concept of a cash-generating unit is discussed in chapter 7.

Under paragraph 20 of AASB 6/IFRS 6, one or more of the following facts and circumstances are considered indicators of impairment of E&E assets (although this list is not exhaustive).

- The exploration rights for the specific area have expired or are expected to expire in the near future and there is no expectation of renewal.
- There is no budget or plan for further substantive E&E expenditure in the specific area.
- The entity has decided to discontinue E&E activities in the specific area due to such activities not leading to the discovery of commercially viable quantities of mineral resources.
- The entity has established that the book value of the E&E asset is unlikely to be recovered in full from successful development or sale.

With respect to expiry of exploration rights, the term 'near future' is generally accepted to mean 12 months from the end of the reporting period. In addition, the above list does not include finding that an exploratory or development well does not contain oil or gas in commercial quantities (commonly referred to as finding a 'dry hole'). The reason for this is that often dry holes are merely a function of identifying or defining the exploration area. Alternatively, depending on the nature of the mineral resources (e.g. shale gas), a number of dry holes are needed before the entity can conclude that there are not commercial quantities of resources present. However, if a dry hole marks the end of budgeted or planned exploration activity, it would be considered an indicator of impairment.

Other impairment indicators not listed in AASB 6/IFRS 6 might include decreases in market prices of the relevant mineral resources, adverse regulatory or taxation changes, liquidity restrictions affecting access to funding for E&E activities, civil unrest affecting access to the specific area, and natural disasters causing damage or restricting access to the specific area.

34.7.2 Specifying the level at which E&E assets are assessed for impairment

In determining the level at which to assess E&E assets for impairment (e.g. individual licence, area of interest, country), entities are required to determine an accounting policy for allocating those E&E assets to cash-generating units or groups of cash-generating units. Further, paragraph 21 of AASB 6/IFRS 6 requires that each cash-generating unit or group of cash-generating units to which an E&E asset is allocated must not be larger than an operating segment determined in accordance with AASB 8/IFRS 8 *Operating Segments* (discussed in chapter 20).

Despite this ability to aggregate cash-generating units for E&E asset impairment testing purposes, the AASB inserted Australia-specific guidance (paragraph Aus22.1) into AASB 6, limiting the level at which an E&E asset may be tested for impairment. This limit applies to a level no larger than the area of interest to which the E&E asset relates, consistent with the AASB's area of interest approach for measurement and recognition.

It is important to note that although an impairment loss on an E&E asset is reversible under AASB 136/IAS 36, in practice sometimes an E&E asset is completely written off when an impairment is recognised because no further future economic benefits are expected.

LEARNING CHECK

☐ AASB 6/IFRS 6 requires E&E assets to be assessed for impairment when 'facts and circumstances suggest that the carrying amount [of an exploration and evaluation asset] exceeds the recoverable amount'.

☐ Where E&E assets may be impaired, AASB 136/IAS 36 is applied, subject to two modifications required by AASB 6/IFRS 6, namely specific impairment testing triggers are used and groups of cash-generating units can be used.

☐ AASB 6/IFRS 6 requires that each cash-generating unit or group of cash-generating units to which an E&E asset is allocated must not be larger than an operating segment determined in accordance with AASB 8/IFRS 8.

34.8 Disclosure

LEARNING OBJECTIVE 34.8 Apply the disclosure requirements of AASB 6/IFRS 6.

Paragraphs 23 to 25 of AASB 6/IFRS 6 detail the disclosures required relating to E&E expenditures. Such disclosures include:

- accounting policies applicable to E&E expenditures and E&E assets
- the amounts of assets, liabilities, income, expenses, operating cash flows and investing cash flows related to E&E activities.

Further, the disclosure requirements of AASB 116/IAS 16 or AASB 138/IAS 38 must also be applied depending on whether E&E assets have been classified as tangible or intangible assets respectively.

Examples of some of the disclosures have been provided throughout this chapter; however, figure 34.6 provides a comprehensive illustration of all disclosures required by AASB 6/IFRS 6.

FIGURE 34.6   Example disclosures required by AASB 6/IFRS 6 in the notes to the financial statements

---

Note 1. Summary of accounting policies (extract)

Exploration and evaluation expenditures

Once the legal right to explore has been acquired, exploration and evaluation expenditure is charged to profit or loss as incurred, unless the directors conclude that a future economic benefit is more likely than not to be realised. These costs include materials and fuel used, surveying costs, drilling costs and payments made to contractors.

In evaluating if expenditures meet the criteria to be capitalised, several different sources of information are utilised. The information that is used to determine the probability of future benefits depends on the extent of exploration and evaluation that has been performed.

Exploration and evaluation expenditure incurred on areas of interest where a resource has not yet been established is expensed as incurred until sufficient evaluation has occurred in order to establish a resource. Costs expensed during this phase are included in 'exploration expenditure' in profit or loss.

Upon the establishment of a resource (at which point the Company considers it probable that economic benefits will be realised), the Company capitalises any further evaluation costs incurred for the particular area of interest to exploration and evaluation assets up to the point when a reserve is established.

Once reserves are established and development is approved, exploration and evaluation assets are tested for impairment and transferred to 'Mines under construction'. No amortisation is charged during the exploration and evaluation phase.

Note 2. Operating (loss)/profit (extract)

	2022 $'000	2021 $'000
Operating (loss)/profit is stated after (charging)/crediting:		
Impairment of exploration and evaluation assets (a)	(146)	(6)
Reversal of previously impaired exploration and evaluation assets (b)	25	—
Exploration and evaluation costs written off	(10)	(5)
Gain on sale of exploration and evaluation assets	118	94

(a) The Company's rights to explore one of its areas of interest expired during the current reporting period and the local authority responsible for granting such rights has declined renewal of those rights on the basis that the area contains habitat considered vital to support an endangered species, and no significant mineral reserves have been identified to date. As a result, the Company has fully provided for the write-off of exploration and evaluation assets associated with this area of interest. The impairment charge is included in exploration and evaluation expenses.

(b) The Company has reversed some of the previously recorded impairment charge related to the Gold Mine. These reversals resulted from a positive change in the estimates used to determine the asset's recoverable amount, subsequent to the impairment losses being recognised. The reversal of the previously booked impairment charge is included as an adjustment to the provision for impairment of exploration and evaluation expenditure.

Note 3. Exploration and evaluation assets

	2022 $'000	2021 $'000
E&E expenditure as at 1 July	524	361
Additions	358	293
Unsuccessful exploration expenditure derecognised	(10)	(5)
Disposals	(52)	(25)
Transfer to mines under construction	(101)	(100)
E&E expenditure as at 30 June	719	524
Provision for impairment as at 1 July	(23)	(17)
Impairment charge for the year	(146)	(6)
Reversal of previously booked impairments	25	—
Provision for impairment as at 30 June	(144)	(23)
Net book value as at 30 June	575	501

34.9 Developments and contemporary issues

LEARNING OBJECTIVE 34.9 Discuss the possible future developments related to accounting for the extractive industries.

34.9.1 Accounting for waste removal costs

In surface mining operations, it is necessary to remove rocks, soil and other waste materials, which are commonly referred to as **overburden**, to access the relevant mineral deposits for extraction purposes. The costs incurred in such activities are referred to as 'stripping costs'.

In some mining operations, the stripping costs will vary significantly from period to period because of variations in the thickness of the layer of overburden, the physical properties of the ore body and operational requirements that determine when overburden can be removed. Interpretation 20/IFRIC 20 *Stripping costs in the production phase of a surface mine* clarifies when production stripping costs should be recognised as an asset, and how they should initially and subsequently be measured. If stripping costs are incurred during the development phase of a mine then these costs are generally capitalised and then systematically amortised once production begins, typically using the unit of production method.

Production stripping costs however are thought to have two possible benefits: create inventories whereby AASB 102/IAS 2 *Inventories* would apply, or improve access to the ore which is to be mined in the future. It is possible that inventories are created as stripping during the production phase accesses deeper layers of materials, where the ratio of ore to waste increases. Where the stripping improves access to the ore that is to be mined in the future, then the costs may be capitalised as 'stripping activity asset', provided certain requirements are satisfied. These requirements include:

- the costs will lead to probable future economic benefits
- the costs can be measured reliably
- the body of ore to which the costs relate can be identified.

34.9.2 The IASB's extractive activities project

In 2004, the IASB set up an international project team comprising staff from the national standard setters in Australia, Canada, Norway and South Africa to undertake a detailed assessment of accounting for extractive activities. The project team's findings and recommendations are presented in their discussion paper (DP) entitled, *Discussion Paper on Extractive Activities* (2010). The DP was substantially narrower in scope than many commentators had predicted and Interpretation 20/IFRIC 20 (discussed above) was subsequently issued. In December 2012, the IASB discontinued this project and activated a broader research project on intangible assets as part of its response to its Agenda Consultation 2011 (a public agenda consultation process to determine its future work plans). This broader project 'Intangible assets, including extractive activities and research & development activities' is designed to assess the feasibility of developing one set of reporting requirements for investigative, exploratory and developmental activities across a wide range of activities. It has been formally activated as an IASB-only research project with a DP to follow.

> **LEARNING CHECK**
>
> ☐ Interpretation 20/IFRIC 20 clarifies when production stripping costs should be recognised as an asset, and how they should initially and subsequently be measured.
>
> ☐ 'Intangible assets, including extractive activities and research & development activities' is the focus of an IASB research project, to assess the feasibility of developing one set of reporting requirements for investigative, exploratory and developmental activities across a wide range of activities.

SUMMARY

The principal issues in the financial reporting for E&E expenditures are the recognition and measurement of E&E assets, assessing impairment of E&E assets, and determining appropriate disclosures to identify and explain the amounts in the entity's financial statements arising from the exploration for and evaluation of mineral resources.

AASB 6/IFRS 6:

- provides guidance on when capitalisation of costs related to E&E activities should commence and the identification of which elements of that cost should be capitalised
- requires that after the initial recognition of the asset, a decision has to be made about whether to apply the cost model or the revaluation model
- specifies that the asset must be assessed for impairment when impairment indicators are present, including determining the level within the entity at which the test should be applied (which is limited to a level no larger than the area of interest to which the E&E asset relates)
- requires specific disclosures to be made in relation to the accounting policies for E&E assets and the amounts recognised in the financial statements related to E&E activities.

KEY TERMS

area of interest An individual geological area which is considered to constitute a favourable environment for the presence of a mineral deposit or an oil or natural gas field, or has been proved to contain such a deposit or field.

extractive industries Those industries involved in finding and removing non-renewable natural resources located in or near the Earth's crust.

overburden Rocks, soil and other waste materials that must be removed to access mineral deposits for extraction purposes.

removal and restoration An obligation to restore an area of interest damaged by E&E activities.

COMPREHENSION QUESTIONS

1. Discuss the complexities and considerations an entity involved in the extractive industries may face in determining the accounting policies to apply to expenditures it incurs.
2. Discuss the scope of expenditures to which AASB 6 is limited.
3. Explain the measurement options of E&E assets available to companies, subsequent to initial recognition.
4. If an entity wants to change its accounting policies applicable to E&E expenditures, discuss the issues it should consider.
5. Explain how E&E assets should be classified in the financial statements.
6. Discuss the two specific modifications a company could make to the impairment testing of E&E assets compared to other assets under AASB 136/IAS 36.
7. Explain how E&E assets that are subsequently developed into producing assets are most commonly depreciated.
8. Discuss the contemporary issues related to accounting for extractive activities.

CASE STUDY 34.1

AREA OF INTEREST

Redwoods Mining Limited has exploration licences for two areas. The first is in north-western Australia and is at the prospecting stage. The second is several hundred kilometres east and is in the exploration stage. The company's management wants to treat the projects as one area of interest and does not believe that AASB 6 will apply.

Required

Discuss whether you agree with management's view.

CASE STUDY 34.2

CAPITALISING COSTS

The accountant of Local Oil Limited has recommended to management that the company capitalise its E&E costs, as this will increase the company's assets and have no effect on profit or loss.

Required

Discuss whether you agree with the accountant's advice.

CASE STUDY 34.3

USEFUL LIFE OF AN ASSET

Pearl Mining Limited has a number of depreciable assets which it uses in a particular area of interest.

Required

Discuss the factors you would need to consider in determining the depreciable period (useful life) of the asset.

APPLICATION AND ANALYSIS EXERCISES

★ BASIC | ★ ★ MODERATE | ★ ★ ★ DIFFICULT

34.1 Obligations for removal and restoration ★   LO5

The management of Oil Ltd is concerned that the E&E activities it has commenced in a specific area will cause significant damage to the surrounding environment, and the government of the country where the area of interest is located has attached strict conditions to the exploration licence for that area. Those conditions require that Oil Ltd return the environment to its original condition.

Required

What are the implications of the above scenario for Oil Ltd's financial statements?

34.2 Specifying the level at which E&E assets are assessed for impairment ★ ★ ★   LO6

E&E activity in one of LNG Ltd's areas of interest has not reached a stage that permits a reasonable assessment of the existence of economically recoverable reserves. The exploration licence for that area is still current and LNG Ltd intends to continue E&E activities in that area. One of the wells drilled by LNG Ltd in that area during the period did not result in the finding of any mineral reserves. However, other wells drilled in the area have resulted in mineral reserve findings.

Required

What alternatives does LNG Ltd have for determining the level at which to assess its E&E assets for impairment in that area of interest?

34.3 Application of the revaluation model ★ ★   LO6

Gold Ltd classifies its E&E assets as intangible assets. A new accountant has just been employed and has suggested that Gold Ltd should change its accounting policy for E&E assets from its existing cost model to the fair value model under AASB 138/IAS 38 because it would provide more relevant information.

Required

What might prevent Gold Ltd from being able to make this change in accounting policy?

34.4 Change in accounting policy ★ ★   LO7

Oil Sands Ltd is a company involved in the search for, production of and sale of oil and gas resources. The company has been following an accounting policy of expensing all of its E&E costs as incurred since adoption of AASB 6/IFRS 6. However, it has noted that its most significant competitor follows a policy of capitalising such costs on an area of interest basis. This makes the competitor's profit look better in some years than Oil Sands Ltd's profit.

Required

Discuss whether Oil Sands Ltd can change its accounting policy to capitalise all of its E&E costs to match its competitor's accounting policy.

34.5 Elements of cost of E&E assets ★ ★ **LO7**

Mining Ltd has acquired a licence to explore a new area of interest and its accounting policy is to fully capitalise all of its E&E expenditures on an area of interest basis. During the period, costs have been incurred in relation to:

(a) the acquisition of speculative seismic data in relation to the area of interest to be used to determine whether to apply for an exploration licence for that area

(b) labour costs of engineers to analyse the seismic data obtained

(c) the exploration licence fee

(d) legal costs associated with obtaining the exploration licence

(e) labour costs for engineers to carry out topographical, geological, geochemical and geophysical studies on the area after obtaining the exploration licence

(f) payroll-related costs for that labour

(g) contractors' fees for exploratory drilling

(h) hire of drilling equipment.

Required

Which of the above items would qualify for capitalisation as part of the E&E asset under AASB 6/IFRS 6?

34.6 Impairment of E&E assets ★ **LO7**

During the year ended 30 June 2023, the management of LPG Ltd has been analysing its engineering reports for a specific area of interest, which indicate that sample drilling has not resulted in any findings that confirm the existence of oil and gas in that area. As a result, LPG Ltd is reluctant to invest any further funds in exploring the area. An E&E asset with a carrying value of $1.8 million exists in relation to that asset as at 30 June 2023.

Required

What is the possible impact of this decision on LPG Ltd's financial statements as at 30 June 2023?

34.7 Recognition of E&E assets ★ ★ **LO7**

Ore Ltd has incurred the following costs during the period in relation to a specific area of interest. Its accounting policy is to capitalise all E&E costs on an area of interest basis.

Cash paid to acquire seismic study from government that is selling exploration rights for the area (GST exempt)	$ 9 000
Cash paid to acquire exploration rights for the area from government (GST exempt)	30 000
Cash paid to acquire fencing materials to mark out the area of interest, including GST of $240	26 400
Contractor fees for labour to set up the fencing, including GST of $150	1 650
Contractor fees for exploratory drilling, including GST of $7500	82 500
Hire of drilling equipment for contractor use, including GST of $1500	16 500
Salary of project manager hired specifically to manage E&E activities in the area	180 000
Stationery and other office supplies used by the project manager, including GST of $90	990
Ore Ltd non-executive directors' fees paid during the period	480 000

Required

Determine the amount of the E&E asset to be capitalised by Ore Ltd in relation to the area of interest.

34.8 Measurement of E&E assets ★ ★ ★ **LO4, 5, 6**

During the year ended 30 June 2023, Resources Ltd explored four different areas of interest and spent $200 000 in each. The results of E&E activities suggested that Areas A, B and C may contain mineral reserves so the company acquired leases over these three areas. The leases cost $300 000, $440 000 and $360 000 respectively.

During the year ended 30 June 2024, Resources Ltd commenced a drilling program to evaluate Areas A, B and C. Eight exploratory wells were drilled, five in Area A, two in Area B and one in Area C at a cost of $240 000 each. The five wells drilled in Area A did not result in any mineral resource findings (i.e. they were dry holes). The two wells drilled in Area B indicated that the company had discovered economically recoverable reserves. Management was uncertain about the likelihood of finding economically recoverable reserves for the well in Area C as some mineral reserves were found but not enough to be considered economically recoverable at this stage. Therefore, Resources Ltd decided to continue E&E activities in Area C as of 30 June 2024. Area A was abandoned, and, after incurring costs of $100 000 to confirm the technical feasibility and commercial viability of extracting the mineral resources, development of Area B commenced.

During the year ended 30 June 2025, to evaluate the area of interest further, three more wells were drilled in Area B. Of these, two were dry. Each well cost $280 000. The successful wells in Area B were developed for a total cost of $600 000. Expenditure on additional plant and equipment related to development was $650 000. After further dry wells costing $350 000 were drilled in Area C, management concluded that Area C did not contain any commercially viable quantities of mineral resources, so it was abandoned.

These costs are summarised as follows.

Costs incurred for each area of interest						
		A	B	C	D	Total
30/06/2023	Exploration	200 000	200 000	200 000	200 000	800 000
	Leases	300 000	440 000	360 000	—	1 100 000
30/06/2024	Dry wells	1 200 000	—	—	—	1 200 000
	Other wells	—	480 000	240 000	—	720 000
	Technical feasibility/ commercial viability costs	—	100 000	—	—	100 000
30/06/2025	Dry wells	—	560 000	350 000	—	910 000
	Other wells	—	280 000	—	—	280 000
	Development	—	600 000	—	—	600 000
	PPE	—	650 000	—	—	650 000
Total		1 700 000	3 310 000	1 150 000	200 000	6 360 000

Required

Determine what amounts would be recognised as an expense in the profit or loss versus capitalised as an asset, in relation to each area of interest for each financial year assuming Resources Ltd:

1. expenses all of its E&E costs as incurred
2. capitalises all E&E costs on an area of interest basis
3. capitalises successful E&E costs on an area of interest basis (i.e. expenses dry holes).

REFERENCES

BHP Group Limited 2018, *2018 annual report*, www.bhp.com.
International Accounting Standards Board 2010, *Discussion Paper DP/2010/1 Extractive activities*, April, www.ifrs.org.
International Accounting Standards Committee 2000, *Extractive industries*, issue paper, IASC, November, www.ifrs.org.
Minerals Council of Australia 2017, 'Employment and skills', www.minerals.org.au.
—— 2018, *Annual report 2017*, www.minerals.org.au.

ACKNOWLEDGEMENTS

Photo: © chain45154 / Getty Images
Figure 34.3: © BHP Group Limited 2018
Text: © 2019 Australian Accounting Standards Board (AASB). The text, graphics and layout of this publication are protected by Australian copyright law and the comparable law of other countries. No part of the publication may be reproduced, stored or transmitted in any form or by any means without the prior written permission of the AASB except as permitted by law. For reproduction or publication, permission should be sought in writing from the AASB. Requests in the first instance should be addressed to the National Director, Australian Accounting Standards Board, PO Box 204, Collins Street West, Victoria 8007.
Text: © IFRS. This publication contains copyright material of the IFRS Foundation in respect of which all rights are reserved. Reproduced by John Wiley & Sons Australia, Ltd with the permission of the IFRS Foundation. No permission granted to third parties to reproduce or distribute. For full access to IFRS Standards and the work of the IFRS Foundation please visit http://eifrs.ifrs.org. The International Accounting Standards Board, the IFRS Foundation, the authors and the publishers do not accept responsibility for any loss caused by acting or refraining from acting in reliance on the material in this publication, whether such loss is caused by negligence or otherwise.

Agriculture

CHAPTER AIM

This chapter describes accounting for agriculture in accordance with AASB 141/IAS 41 *Agriculture*.

LEARNING OBJECTIVES

After studying this chapter, you should be able to:

35.1 explain the background to the development of AASB 141/IAS 41

35.2 distinguish between agricultural activities, agricultural produce and biological assets

35.3 explain the different accounting treatment required before and after harvest

35.4 explain the recognition criteria for biological assets and agricultural produce

35.5 analyse the meaning of 'fair value' when applied to biological assets and agricultural produce

35.6 explain the practical implications of measuring these assets at fair value, including interpreting the disclosures made by companies applying the standard

35.7 examine the interaction between AASB 141/IAS 41 and AASB 120/IAS 20 *Accounting for Government Grants and Disclosure of Government Assistance*

35.8 examine the interaction between AASB 141/IAS 41 and AASB 116/IAS 16 *Property, Plant and Equipment* and AASB 140/IAS 40 *Investment Property*

35.9 describe the disclosure requirements of AASB 141/IAS 41

35.10 apply the recognition and measurement requirements of AASB 141/IAS 41 to a simple statement of profit or loss and other comprehensive income and statement of financial position.

CONCEPTS FOR REVIEW

Before studying this chapter, you should understand and, if necessary, revise:
- the concept of an asset in the *Conceptual Framework*
- depreciation and impairment of tangible assets
- AASB 13/IFRS 13 *Fair Value Measurement*.

35.1 Introduction to AASB 141/IAS 41

LEARNING OBJECTIVE 35.1 Explain the background to the development of AASB 141/IAS 41.

IAS 41 was issued by the International Accounting Standards Committee (IASC) in February 2001 and confirmed as part of the core set of standards to be issued by the International Accounting Standards Board (IASB) in April 2001. The IASC generally develops standards relevant to all businesses, but decided agriculture required a separate standard. This was primarily because of the diversity in accounting for agricultural activity in practice, due to:

- the specific exclusion of assets related to agricultural activity from other standards at the time
- the piecemeal approach to accounting guidelines for agricultural activity developed by national standard setters (with the exception of Australia, which had developed and applied a standard on self-generating and regenerating assets, or SGARAs)
- the nature of agricultural activity creating uncertainty or conflicts when applying traditional accounting models.

The IASC also acknowledged the increasing scale of agricultural operations and associated need to attract capital from investors, which increased the need to develop standards for the general purpose financial statements of the entities involved.

IAS 41 was a controversial standard when it was first issued, mainly because of the requirement to measure assets related to agricultural activity at fair value, with movements in fair value recognised in profit or loss.

In Australia, the standard on SGARAs was issued as AASB 1037 and applied to financial years ending on or after 30 June 2000. This standard was controversial in Australia for the same reasons that IAS 41 was controversial. As part of Australia's adoption of IFRSs in 2005, AASB 141 replaced AASB 1037.

In May 2011, the IASB issued IFRS 13 *Fair Value Measurement* (which amended IAS 41). This standard was adopted in Australia as AASB 13, effective for annual periods beginning on or after 1 January 2013. AASB 13/IFRS 13 combines into one standard all of the requirements regarding *how to* measure fair value, rather than being dispersed throughout multiple standards. It does *not* detail requirements regarding *when to* use fair value as the measurement basis, which are addressed in other standards such as AASB 141/IAS 41 *Agriculture*.

LEARNING CHECK

☐ The IASC regarded agriculture as an industry with a particular need for its own standard due to the diversity in accounting for agricultural activity in practice.

☐ IAS 41 was issued by the IASC in 2001 and AASB 141 *Agriculture* was adopted as its equivalent in Australia in 2005.

☐ AASB 141/IAS 41 is a controversial standard because it requires that assets related to agricultural activity be measured at fair value, with movements in fair value recognised in profit or loss.

35.2 Scope and key definitions

LEARNING OBJECTIVE 35.2 Distinguish between agricultural activities, agricultural produce and biological assets.

35.2.1 Scope

AASB 141/IAS 41 applies to accounting for the following when they relate to agricultural activity:
1. biological assets
2. agricultural produce
3. government grants.

The standard does not apply to land, bearer plants or intangible assets related to agricultural activity (AASB 141/IAS 41 paragraphs 2 and 21). Land related to agricultural activity is recognised and measured by applying either AASB 116/IAS 16 *Property, Plant and Equipment* or AASB 140/IAS 40 *Investment Property*, whichever is appropriate in the circumstances. So, for example, if the land meets the definition of an investment property it is measured using either the fair value model or the cost model — an accounting policy choice permitted by AASB 140/IAS 40. Note that 'investment property' is defined in paragraph 5 of AASB 140/IAS 40 as:

> property (land or a building — or part of a building — or both) held (by the owner or by the lessee under a finance lease) to earn rentals or for capital appreciation or both, rather than for:
> (a) use in the production or supply of goods or services or for administrative purposes; or
> (b) sale in the ordinary course of business.

If the land does *not* meet the definition of an investment property then it must be recognised and measured by applying AASB 116/IAS 16 (see chapter 5). AASB 116/IAS 16 allows an accounting policy choice between the cost model and the revaluation model. The cost model under AASB 140/IAS 40 is the same as that under AASB 116/IAS 16. However, the fair value model under AASB 140/IAS 40 differs from the revaluation model under AASB 116/IAS 16. Under AASB 140/IAS 40, fair value movements are recognised in profit or loss. Under AASB 116/IAS 16, the treatment of revaluation adjustments is recognised in profit and loss or other comprehensive income (OCI), depending on whether it is a revaluation increment or decrement (see chapter 5).

The impact of the accounting policy choice in respect of land is discussed further in section 35.8.

Bearer plants, such as fruit trees and grape vines, are recognised and measured by applying AASB 116/IAS 16.

Intangible assets related to agricultural activity are accounted for under AASB 138/IAS 38 *Intangible Assets* (see chapter 6).

35.2.2 Key definitions

Paragraph 5 of AASB 141/IAS 41 contains the following important definitions.

Agricultural activity:
the management by an entity of the biological transformation and harvest of biological assets for sale or for conversion into agricultural produce or into additional biological assets.

Agricultural produce:
the harvested product of the entity's biological assets.

Bearer plant:
a living plant that:
(a) is used in the production or supply of agricultural produce;
(b) is expected to bear produce for more than one period; and
(c) has a remote likelihood of being sold as agricultural produce, except for incidental scrap sales.

Biological asset:
a living animal or plant.

Biological transformation:
the processes of growth, degeneration, production, and procreation that cause qualitative or quantitative changes in a biological asset.

Harvest:
the detachment of produce from a biological asset or the cessation of a biological asset's life processes.

Agricultural activity covers a diverse range of activities. However, paragraph 6 of AASB 141/IAS 41 states that there are three common features that exist within this diversity.
- *Capability to change.* Living plants and animals are capable of biological transformation (e.g. growth).
- *Management of change.* Management facilitates biological transformation. For example, management of a vineyard or orchard by providing nutrients, water and protection from pests, facilitates the growth of the vines and trees. This can be distinguished from unmanaged biological change such as the growth of fish in the ocean. Thus, ocean fishing is not an agricultural activity.
- *Measurement of change.* The change in quality (e.g. ripeness, protein content or fibre strength) or quantity (e.g. weight, cubic metres or diameter) resulting from biological transformation is measured and monitored as a routine management function.

35.3 The harvest distinction

LEARNING OBJECTIVE 35.3 Explain the different accounting treatment required before and after harvest.

There is a very important distinction between agricultural produce, which is the harvested product of the entity's biological assets, and products that result from processing after harvest. AASB 141/IAS 41 applies only to the harvested product *at the point of harvest*. Thereafter, AASB 102/IAS 2 *Inventories*, or another applicable standard is applied.

AASB 141/IAS 41 includes examples to illustrate the difference between biological assets, agricultural produce and products that are the result of processing after harvest, a summary of which is detailed in table 35.1 (paragraph 4 of AASB 141/IAS 41).

| TABLE 35.1 | Distinction between biological assets, agricultural produce and products that are a result of processing after harvest |

Biological assets	Agricultural produce	Products that are the result of processing after harvest
Sheep	Wool	Yarn, carpet
Trees in a timber plantation	Felled trees	Logs, lumber
Dairy cattle	Milk	Cheese
Pigs	Carcass	Sausages, cured hams
Cotton plants	Harvested cotton	Thread, clothing
Sugarcane	Harvested cane	Sugar
Tobacco plants	Picked leaves	Cured tobacco
Tea bushes	Picked leaves	Tea
Grape vines	Picked grapes	Wine
Fruit trees	Picked fruit	Processed fruit
Oil palms	Picked fruit	Palm oil
Rubber trees	Harvested latex	Rubber products

Some plants, for example, tea bushes, grape vines, oil palms and rubber trees, usually meet the definition of a bearer plant and are within the scope of AASB 116 [IAS 16]. However, the produce growing on bearer plants, for example, tea leaves, grapes, oil palm fruit and latex, is within the scope of AASB 141 [IAS 41].
Source: AASB 141/IAS 41, paragraph 4.

One of the initial criticisms of AASB 141/IAS 41 was that it requires assets for which there is often not an active or ready market to be measured at fair value, while assets with an active and ready market are measured at cost under AASB 102/IAS 2. For example, it can be difficult to determine a fair value for immature trees in a plantation because there may not be an active or ready market for trees not yet fully grown. In contrast, there would be a much more easily identifiable market value for lumber or wooden furniture. The IASB rejected criticisms of the fair value model for biological assets and agricultural produce but provided a concession by permitting an exemption from following the fair value requirement when fair value cannot be reliably measured. This is discussed further in section 35.5.2.

Arguments were made that in some cases processing after harvest was akin to biological transformation (e.g. wine production from grapes and cheese production from milk) and therefore should not be subject to the 'at the harvest point' distinction. While the IASB acknowledged this issue, there was no change to IAS 41, as the IASB considered that it would be difficult to differentiate these circumstances from other manufacturing processes (e.g. transforming wood into furniture).

LEARNING CHECK

☐ AASB 141/IAS 41 applies only to agricultural produce at the point of harvest.

☐ AASB 102/IAS 2, or another applicable standard, is applied to products that are the result of processing after harvest.

☐ AASB 141/IAS 41 has been criticised for requiring assets (for which there is often not an active or ready market) to be measured at fair value, while assets with an active and ready market are measured at cost under AASB 102/IAS 2.

35.4 The recognition criteria for biological assets and agricultural produce

LEARNING OBJECTIVE 35.4 Explain the recognition criteria for biological assets and agricultural produce.

35.4.1 The recognition criteria

Paragraph 10 of AASB 141/IAS 41 states that an entity shall recognise a biological asset or agricultural produce when, and only when:

(a) the entity controls the asset as a result of past events;
(b) it is probable that future economic benefits associated with the asset will flow to the entity; and
(c) the fair value or cost of the asset can be measured reliably.

Note that (a) reflects one of the characteristics of the *definition* of an asset in the *Conceptual Framework* (control) while (b) and (c) relate to the recognition criteria in the *Conceptual Framework*.

35.4.2 The problem with 'control'

The issue of control can be problematic in the agricultural industry where leases or management agreements are involved. For example, a vineyard may be owned by one entity but managed by another. Because the definition of 'agricultural activity' talks about 'the management' by an entity of the biological transformation of biological assets it is possible to confuse management with control. Therefore, it is important to distinguish between these two concepts.

Illustrative example 35.1 demonstrates the distinction between management and control.

ILLUSTRATIVE EXAMPLE 35.1

Distinguishing management from control of biological assets and agricultural produce

Avoca Ltd owns Vineyard Tamar. Avoca Ltd invests in many vineyards and so appoints Manager M to manage Vineyard Tamar. Manager M is responsible for all the operations of the vineyard including daily care, regular maintenance, harvesting of the grapes and storage of the grapes after harvest. The grapes are then sent to be processed into wine by the winemaker.

Manager M and the winemaker are not related parties of Avoca Ltd. Avoca Ltd pays Manager M a management fee for its services. The fee includes reimbursement of all costs incurred by Manager M

▶

---

plus an agreed fixed margin. Avoca Ltd pays the winemaker a production fee for its services. The fee includes reimbursement of all costs incurred by the winemaker plus an agreed fixed margin.

All sales and marketing of the bottled wine is managed by a distributor. The distributor is not a related party of Avoca Ltd. Avoca Ltd pays the distributor a fee for its services. The fee includes reimbursement of all costs incurred by the distributor plus an agreed fixed margin.

Required

1. Who controls the biological asset (the vines)? Avoca Ltd or Manager M?
2. Who controls the agricultural produce (the grapes)? Avoca Ltd, Manager M, the winemaker or the distributor?

Solution

In order to answer these questions, a number of issues must be considered.

Control. According to the *Conceptual Framework* (paragraph 4.20):

> an entity controls an economic resource if it has the present ability to direct the use of the economic resource and obtain the economic benefits that may flow from it. Control includes the present ability to prevent other parties from directing the use of the economic resource and from obtaining the economic benefits that may flow from it.

What are the economic benefits that may flow from the vines and grapes? These would be the growth of the vines so as to produce grapes and the revenues to be earned by either selling the grapes or by processing them into wine to sell.

Who obtains the economic benefits? Manager M, the winemaker and distributor are each paid a fee for their services. Thus, Avoca Ltd benefits from any increases in value beyond the recovery of costs plus the fixed margin. Manager M, the winemaker and the distributor do not share in these excess profits because their return is fixed.

Who has the present ability to direct the use of the vines and the grapes? While Manager M manages the daily operations of the vineyard it does so on behalf of Avoca Ltd. Similarly, the winemaker makes the wine on behalf of Avoca Ltd, and the distributor sells the wine on behalf of Avoca Ltd. Thus, Avoca Ltd has the ability to sell or pledge the vines and the grapes even though, in practice, the sale of the grapes is conducted by Manager M on behalf of Avoca Ltd. These entities all act as agents of Avoca Ltd.

So we can conclude that Avoca Ltd controls the biological assets and agricultural produce under paragraph 10 of AASB 141/IAS 41. Therefore, Avoca Ltd should recognise these assets (assuming the other requirements of paragraph 10 are met).

However, the agricultural activity as defined in paragraph 5 of AASB 141/IAS 41 is carried out by Manager M. It is the entity that manages the transformation of the vines into grapes. Does this mean that Manager M applies AASB 141/IAS 41 while Avoca Ltd does not? Since we have concluded that Avoca Ltd controls the biological assets and agricultural produce, these assets must be recognised by Avoca Ltd. If Manager M were to apply AASB 141/IAS 41 it would apply the standard to nothing since it does not control the assets in question. Therefore, it is reasonable to conclude that Manager M conducts the agricultural activity on behalf of Avoca Ltd, and thus Avoca Ltd should apply AASB 141/IAS 41. However, this argument could be challenged on the basis of applying the recognition criteria of the standard before the scope section.

LEARNING CHECK

☐ Under AASB 141/IAS 41 an entity shall recognise a biological asset or agricultural produce when, and only when, the entity controls the asset as a result of past events, it is probable that future economic benefits associated with the asset will flow to the entity, and the fair value or cost of the asset can be measured reliably.

☐ The issue of control can be problematic in the agricultural industry where leases or management agreements are involved and it is important to distinguish between 'control' and 'management'.

35.5 Measurement at fair value

LEARNING OBJECTIVE 35.5 Analyse the meaning of 'fair value' when applied to biological assets and agricultural produce.

35.5.1 Measurement requirement

Paragraph 12 of AASB 141/IAS 41 states the following.

> A biological asset shall be measured on initial recognition and at the end of each reporting period at its fair value less costs to sell, except for the case described in paragraph 30 where the fair value cannot be measured reliably.

Paragraph 13 of AASB 141/IAS 41 states the following.

> Agricultural produce harvested from an entity's biological assets shall be measured at its fair value less costs to sell at the point of harvest. Such measurement is the cost at that date when applying AASB 102 [IAS 2] *Inventories* or another applicable Standard.

'Fair value' is defined in paragraph 8 as:

> the price that would be received to sell an asset or paid to transfer a liability in an orderly transaction between market participants at the measurement date.

'Costs to sell' are defined in paragraph 5 as:

> the incremental costs directly attributable to the disposal of an asset, excluding finance costs and income taxes.

Costs to sell include commissions to brokers and dealers, levies by regulatory agencies and commodity exchanges, and transfer taxes and duties. Costs to sell exclude transport and other costs necessary to get assets to a market. However, such transport costs are deducted in determining fair value (AASB 13/IFRS 13 paragraph 26).

Note, as bearer plants are outside the scope of AASB 141/IAS 41, they should be accounted for as property, plant and equipment in accordance with AASB 116/IAS 16. Hence, companies are required to measure bearer plants initially at cost, and thereafter have an option to apply either the cost or the revaluation model (see chapter 5). However, the produce growing on the bearer plants is a biological asset measured at fair value less costs to sell, as detailed above.

35.5.2 Arguments for and against the use of fair value

When IAS 41 was first proposed as Exposure Draft E65, the requirement to use fair value as the measurement basis was controversial. The arguments for and against the use of fair value are summarised in table 35.2 (AASB 141 Basis for Conclusions paragraphs B14–B21).

TABLE 35.2	Arguments for and against the use of fair value for measuring biological assets	
	Case for fair value	**Case against fair value**
Biological transformation has a direct relationship to changes in expectations of future economic benefits to the entity.	✓	
The relationship between cost incurrence and future economic benefits is weak particularly for biological assets that take a long time to mature.	✓	

(continued)

TABLE 35.2 *(continued)*

	Case for fair value	Case against fair value
Relevance	✓ (Many biological assets are traded in active markets; long production cycles mean that the change in asset value is more relevant than a period-end measure of costs incurred.)	✓ (Market prices at the end of the reporting period may not bear a close relationship to the prices at which the assets will be sold.)
Reliability	✓ (Active markets provide reliable information; allocation of costs is arbitrary when there are joint products and joint costs.)	✓ (Cost of historical transactions is more reliable and objective; market prices are often volatile and cyclical; uncertainty regarding active market prices for assets that have a long growth period.)
Comparability and understandability	✓ (Different sources of animals and plants — home grown or purchased — should not be measured differently, which would be the outcome under a historical cost model.)	✓ (Reporting of unrealised gains and losses is not useful to users.)

The board decided to proceed with the requirement to use fair value, but acknowledged the argument that fair value can not always be measured reliably (e.g. where market prices are not available and alternative estimates of fair value are clearly unreliable). This resulted in the exception in paragraph 30, which states:

> There is a presumption that fair value can be measured reliably for a biological asset. However, that presumption can be rebutted only on initial recognition for a biological asset for which quoted market prices are not available and for which alternative fair value measurements are determined to be clearly unreliable. In such a case, that biological asset shall be measured at its cost less any accumulated depreciation and any accumulated impairment losses. Once the fair value of such a biological asset becomes reliably measurable, an entity shall measure it at its fair value less costs to sell.

It is important to note that this exception can be applied only on initial recognition of the asset. For example, in Australia where AASB 1037 was being applied prior to the adoption of IFRSs, companies had already recognised their biological assets and were measuring them at fair value. Hence, they could not take advantage of the exception in paragraph 30, because the assets had already been recognised.

In addition, the exception applies only to biological assets, not to agricultural produce. AASB 141/IAS 41 takes the view that the fair value of agricultural produce at the point of harvest can always be measured reliably (paragraph 32).

35.5.3 How to apply the fair value measurement requirement

Under AASB 13/IFRS 13, fair value is the price that would be received to sell an asset or paid to transfer a liability in an orderly transaction in the principal (or most advantageous) market at the measurement date under current market conditions (i.e. an exit price) regardless of whether that price is directly observable or estimated using another valuation technique (paragraph 24). Consideration should be given to the three-level fair value hierarchy to determine the appropriate valuation approach:

- *Level 1:* based on quoted prices (unadjusted) in active markets for identical assets or liabilities that the entity can access at the measurement date
- *Level 2:* based on inputs other than quoted prices included within Level 1 that are observable for the asset or liability, either directly or indirectly (e.g. prices for similar assets)
- *Level 3:* based on unobservable inputs for the asset or liability. Unobservable inputs shall reflect the assumptions that market participants would use when pricing the asset or liability, including assumptions about risk (e.g. a NPV calculation).

AASB 141/IAS 41 (paragraphs 15–25) includes guidance on how to apply the fair value measurement requirement.

- Biological assets or agricultural assets may be grouped according to significant attributes such as age or quality (e.g. all 'A' grade cattle may be grouped and a fair value determined for that group).

- AASB 141/IAS 41 requires the spot price (the current market price) be used for determining fair value. This applies even when a company has entered into a contract to sell its biological assets or agricultural produce (e.g. cotton) at a future point in time at a set price (known as a forward price).
- Cost may sometimes approximate fair value, particularly when:
  1. little biological transformation has taken place since initial cost incurrence (e.g. seedlings planted immediately prior to the end of a reporting period), or
  2. the impact of the biological transformation on price is not expected to be material (e.g. the initial period of growth in a 30-year pine tree plantation production cycle).
- Where biological assets are attached to land and there is no separate market for the assets without the land, the entity may use information regarding the combined assets to determine the fair value of the biological assets. For example, the fair value of the raw land may be deducted from the fair value of the combined assets to arrive at the fair value of the biological assets.

In determining fair value, AASB 13/IFRS 13 requires that an entity use valuation techniques appropriate to the circumstances and for which sufficient data are available to measure fair value, maximising the use of relevant observable inputs and minimising the use of unobservable inputs (paragraph 61). Illustrative example 35.2 details the calculation of fair value using Level 2 inputs. (See chapter 3 for a more detailed discussion of the fair value measurement hierarchy, observable inputs, and unobservable outputs under AASB 13/IFRS 13.)

A widely used valuation technique is the income approach (AASB 13/IFRS 13 paragraph 62), under which net present value is an acceptable measure (see B5–B11). This involves calculating the present value of expected net cash flows from the asset, discounted at a current market-determined rate. Note that the objective of this calculation is to determine the fair value of the asset in its *present* condition.

In practice, entities may need to work out the cash flows from a biological asset in its mature state (e.g. mature forest) and work backwards to then calculate the cash flows from the asset in its immature state (e.g. immature forest). Future biological transformation may be taken into account in determining fair value because the buyer would assess the potential for the asset to reach maturity in determining how much to pay for the asset in its immature state (see paragraph B13 of AASB 13/IFRS 13). In addition, AASB 141/IAS 41 refers to 'biological transformation or harvest' where appropriate, to clarify that a harvested asset is not the same as a growing asset. Therefore, a market value for a growing asset may be calculated based on its potential to continue to grow and be harvested, taking into account risk factors regarding the potential growth of the asset.

ILLUSTRATIVE EXAMPLE 35.2

Calculating fair value

Lilydale Ltd owns dairy cattle. The market value of cattle is calculated by reference to the litres of milk able to be produced and the lactation rate of the cows. Cattle are regularly sold at auction. Costs incurred to transport the cattle to auction are $500 per truck. The normal capacity of a truck is approximately 200 cattle.

Lilydale Ltd has determined that, based on latest auction prices close to the end of the reporting period, a mature cow's market value is 5000 litres × lactation rate (0.5) × price of milk ($0.35) = $875 and a heifer's market value is 2000 litres × 0.5 × $0.35 = $350.

At the end of the reporting period, Lilydale Ltd had 1000 mature cows and 400 heifers.

Transport costs are deducted in determining fair value in accordance with AASB 13/IFRS 13. The approximate cost per cow is $500/200 = $2.50. Thus the market value for each cow is $875 − $2.50 = $872.50. The market value for each heifer is $350 − $2.50 = $347.50. The fair value as at the end of the reporting period is thus as follows.

$$
\begin{array}{rl}
1000 \times \$872.50 = & \$\ \ 872\,500 \\
400 \times \$347.50 = & \$\ \ 139\,000 \\
& \$1\,011\,500
\end{array}
$$

35.5.4 Gains and losses

Paragraph 26 of AASB 141/IAS 41 states that:

> A gain or loss arising on initial recognition of a biological asset at fair value less costs to sell and from a change in fair value less costs to sell of a biological asset shall be included in profit or loss for the period in which it arises.

Paragraph 28 of AASB 141/IAS 41 contains a similar requirement for agricultural produce except that it does not refer to a change in fair value of agricultural produce. This is because agricultural produce is recognised and measured only at the point of harvest (see AASB 141/IAS 41 paragraphs 1(b) and 13) and this amount becomes its cost for ongoing measurement under AASB 102/IAS 2 or another applicable standard. Thus, there is no remeasurement to fair value of agricultural produce whereas biological assets are remeasured to fair value at the end of each reporting period.

Illustrative example 35.3 explains how gains or losses on initial recognition (sometimes referred to as 'day one profits/losses') may occur.

ILLUSTRATIVE EXAMPLE 35.3

Gains or losses on initial recognition of biological assets and agricultural produce

In the case of biological assets, a gain may arise on initial recognition when, for example, an animal is born. If the fair value of a newborn calf is $50. On initial recognition of the newborn animal, the journal entry would be as follows.

Biological asset	Dr	50	
Profit or loss	Cr		50
(To record the acquisition of the newborn calf)			

In the case of agricultural produce a gain or loss on initial recognition may arise as a result of harvesting. For example, say the fair value of a tonne of grapes is $20, then on initial recognition of the grapes, the following journal entry is required.

Agricultural produce	Dr	20	
Profit or loss	Cr		20
(To recognise the grapes at fair value)			

A change in fair value of a biological asset is recorded as a gain or loss at the end of each reporting period. Illustrative example 35.4 details the relevant journal entries.

ILLUSTRATIVE EXAMPLE 35.4

Recording a change in fair value of a biological asset

Assume that at 30 June 2020 (the end of the reporting period) the fair value of Franklin Ltd's vines was $2 500 000. As at 30 June 2021, Franklin Ltd determines the following.

Fair value of the grapes harvested at 31 March 2021	500 000
Costs to sell the grapes	10 000
Fair value of the vines as at 31 March 2021	3 100 000

Franklin Ltd determines that there is no change in fair value of the vines between 31 March 2021 and 30 June 2021 and so uses the valuation as at 31 March for the purposes of the end of reporting period valuation.

The carrying amount of the vines is determined under AASB 116/IAS 16, using either the cost or revaluation model. Franklin Ltd adopts the revaluation model in applying AASB 116/IAS 16 to account for the grape vines.

The change in fair value of the vines is therefore $3 100 000 less $2 500 000 = $600 000.

The fair value of the grapes as at 30 June 2021 is calculated as follows.

$500 000 less $10 000 (costs to sell) = $490 000

The journal entries as at 30 June 2018 are as follows.

PPE asset — vines	Dr	600 000	
OCI	Cr		600 000
(To record the change in fair value of the vines)			
Agricultural produce — grapes	Dr	490 000	
Profit or loss	Cr		490 000
(To record the grapes at fair value)			

LEARNING CHECK

☐ AASB 141/IAS 41 requires that a biological asset be measured on initial recognition and at the end of each reporting period at its fair value less costs to sell, except where the fair value cannot be measured reliably.

☐ AASB 141/IAS 41 states that agricultural produce harvested from an entity's biological assets shall be measured at its fair value less costs to sell at the point of harvest. Costs to sell include commissions to brokers and dealers, levies by regulatory agencies and commodity exchanges and transfer taxes and duties.

☐ Fair value is determined based on a three-level hierarchy under AASB 13/IFRS 13. Valuation techniques such as net present value may be used under Level 3, where Level 1 and 2 data are not available.

☐ A gain or loss arising on initial recognition of a biological asset at fair value less costs to sell and from a change in fair value less costs to sell of a biological asset shall be included in profit or loss for the period in which it arises.

☐ A gain arising on initial recognition of agricultural produce (at fair value less costs to sell) shall be included in profit or loss for the period in which it arises. Agricultural produce is recognised and measured only at the point of harvest, and this amount becomes its cost for ongoing measurement under AASB 102/IAS 2 (or another applicable standard).

☐ Bearer plants are outside the scope of AASB 141/IAS 41, and instead accounted for as property, plant, and equipment under AASB 116/IAS 16 using the cost or revaluation model.

35.6 Practical implementation issues with the use of fair value

LEARNING OBJECTIVE 35.6 Explain the practical implications of measuring these assets at fair value, including interpreting the disclosures made by companies applying the standard.

Determining fair value in the agricultural industry creates some practical difficulties, particularly in the case of immature biological assets such as young trees in a forest or young salmon in a salmon farm.

35.6.1 Immature biological assets

During 2005 and 2006, as IAS 41 was first being implemented in Europe, there was controversy in the salmon farming industry over the measurement of immature salmon. A practice was emerging of measuring live immature salmon at cost on the basis that fair value could not be reliably measured. The regulator intervened and required that the *live* immature salmon be measured at fair value based on *slaughtered* immature salmon values (being similar assets), for which there was an active market. The rationale given was that slaughtered salmon sold whole and gutted should, in an accounting sense, be considered similar to live salmon and this also applies to immature farmed salmon. According to AASB 13/IFRS 13, the fair value of assets should be based on their present location and condition (e.g. including weight and quality at the end of the reporting period). Hence, live salmon should be valued based on observable prices in an active market of slaughtered salmon in the weight class (adjusted for conversion from live weight to slaughter weight) in which the salmon would be sold if it were slaughtered at the end of the reporting period (The Committee of European Securities Regulators 2007).

It is interesting to observe the nature of disclosures made by companies applying the fair value requirements of IAS 41 in these circumstances. Figure 35.1 presents the disclosures of the Scottish Salmon Company in its 2018 annual report.

FIGURE 35.1 Disclosures illustrating AASB 141/IAS 41 practical implementation, Scottish Salmon Company

Note 16 — biological assets

	2018 (£'000s)	2017 (£'000s)
Book value of live fish	84 207	64 775
Book value of smolt	7 066	4 231
Total book value of biological assets	91 273	69 006
Fair value adjustments on biological assets in the consolidated statement of financial position		
The Scottish Salmon Company Limited	38 327	26 094
Total fair value adjustment in the consolidated statement of financial position	38 327	26 094
Total value of biological assets in the consolidated statement of financial position	**129 600**	**95 100**
Reconciliation of changes in value of live fish		
Opening fair value of live fish at 1 January	95 100	80 167
Fair value adjustment at 1 January	(26 094)	(25 800)
Fair value adjustment at 31 December	38 327	26 094
Net fair value adjustment taken to consolidated statement of comprehensive income	**12 233**	**294**
Increase due to purchases and capitalisation of costs	113 402	102 341
Decreases due to harvests	(95 995)	(74 914)
Decreases due to mortalities and culls	(2 206)	(17 019)
Fair value of live fish at 31 December	**122 534**	**90 869**
Book value of smolt	7 066	4 231
Fair value of live fish	122 534	90 869
Total value of biological assets in the consolidated statement of financial position	**129 600**	**95 100**
Volumes of biological assets (in tonnes)		
Volume of biological assets harvested during the year (GWT)	29 913	25 272
Volume of biological assets in the sea at year end (LWT)	21 176	16 472
Split as follows:		
Juvenile fish < 1 kg	1 442	1 791
Harvestable fish > 1 kg	19 734	14 681

Valuation of biological assets

IAS 41 requires that biological assets are accounted for at estimated fair value net of harvesting costs, processing and selling. Fair value is measured using the income approach, in accordance with IFRS 13, and is categorised into level 3 in the fair value hierarchy as the inputs include unobservable inputs.

Valuation model

The valuation under the income approach is completed based on a valuation model. This begins with forecasting revenues by estimating the fair value of ready to harvest fish, based on market prices. Whilst there is no clear defined published market price for Scottish farmed salmon, the Group considers the development in its contract and spot prices and utilises future published prices for Norwegian salmon as a base price and applies an uplift to cover the average historic Scottish premium.

The valuation model is then completed for each site individually taking into account the following unobservable inputs on forecasted costs:

- volume of fish in the sea
- growth rates
- survival rates
- on-growing costs including feed costs and feed conversion ratios
- harvesting costs
- gutting costs
- freight costs.

These inputs also take into account any specific factors (such as disease) on a regional basis.

The above extract highlights a few key points.

1. The company has disclosed separately the 'live fish' and the 'smolt'. (Smolt is immature live salmon.)
2. The company makes the point that the valuation model is based on uncertain assumptions and that relatively small changes in these assumptions could have a significant impact on the valuation of the biological assets.
3. The disclosures include a description of the valuation technique and inputs used in measuring fair value, in accordance with the disclosure requirements in paragraph 93 of AASB 13/IFRS 13 for fair value measures using Level 2 or Level 3 inputs.
4. The company also discloses the reconciliation required by paragraph 50 of AASB 141/IAS 41. It has elected to separate the book value from the fair value in the reconciliation and to indicate the cumulative effect of fair value adjustments over time on the statement of financial position. This is not required by the standard and may imply some concern about the requirement to use fair value. This is also evident in the 'Key figures' section that precedes the financial statements (Scottish Salmon Company 2018, p. 4) where some of the key performance ratios are cited 'before biomass fair value adjustment'.

35.6.2 Disclosure practices

It is common for companies applying AASB 141/IAS 41 to separately disclose the fair value movements attributable to agricultural assets, either in the statement of profit or loss and other comprehensive income or in the notes, and in information reported outside the financial statements to investors such as in 'investor packs' or 'financial commentaries'. This is because companies want to highlight the fair value movements as being separate from other forms of income.

The extract in figure 35.2 from Treasury Wine Estates Ltd's 2018 annual report illustrates this point.

FIGURE 35.2 Separate disclosure of fair value movements attributable to agricultural assets, Treasury Wine Estates

	Profit report Financial performance				
	Reported currency			Constant currency	
A$m (unless otherwise stated)	F18	F17	Change	F17	Change
Volume (m 9Le cases)	34.6	36.4	(5.1)%*	36.4	(5.1)%*
Net sales revenue (NSR)	2 429.0	2 401.7	1.1%*	2 387.9	1.7%*
NSR per case ($)	70.25	65.96	6.5%	65.58	7.1%
Other revenue	67.4	132.5	(49.1)%	131.3	(43.7)%

A$m (unless otherwise stated)	Reported currency			Constant currency	
	F18	F17	Change	F17	Change
Cost of goods sold	(1 435.6)	(1 568.3)	8.5%	(1 560.7)	8.0%
Cost of goods sold per case ($)	41.52	43.07	3.6%	42.86	3.1%
Gross profit	1 060.8	965.9	9.8%	958.5	10.7%*
Gross profit margin (% of NSR)	43.7%	40.2%	8.7%	40.1%	9.0%
Cost of doing business	(530.6)	(510.8)	(3.9)%	(509.3)	(4.2)%
Cost of doing business margin (% of NSR)	21.8%	21.3%	(0.5)ppts	21.3%	(0.5)ppts
EBITS	**530.2**	**455.1**	**16.5%**	**449.2**	**18.0%**
EBITS margin (%)	21.8%	19.0%	2.8ppts	18.8%	3.0ppts
SGARA	(15.1)	(5.7)	NM#	(5.2)	NM#
EBIT	**515.1**	**449.4**	**14.6%**	**444.0**	**16.0%**
Net finance costs	(33.4)	(27.1)	(23.2)%	(26.7)	(25.1)%
Tax expense	(116.7)	(130.4)	10.5%	(131.4)	11.2%
Net profit after tax (before material items)	**365.0**	**291.9**	**25.0%**	**285.9**	**27.7%**
Material items (after tax)	(4.6)	(22.0)	79.1%	(21.0)	78.1%
Non-controlling interests	(0.1)	(0.8)	87.5%	(0.8)	87.5%
Net profit after tax	**360.3**	**269.1**	**33.9%**	**264.1**	**36.4%**
Reported EPS (A¢)	49.7	36.5	36.2%		
Net profit after tax (before material items and SGARA)	**376.0**	**293.4**	**28.2%**	**286.9**	**31.1%**
EPS (before material items and SGARA) (A¢)	51.8	39.8	30.2%*		
Average no. of shares (m)	725.7	736.8			
Dividend (A¢)	33.0	26.0	23%		

*As part of TWE's route-to-market transition in the US, TWE proactively restocked a former distributor partner primarily in states where TWE is now directly distributing. These actions resulted in a negative impact to volume, NSR and gross profit in TWE's F18 results.

#Not meaningful

Source: Treasury Wine Estates Ltd (2018, p. 20).

LEARNING CHECK

☐ Determining fair value in the agricultural industry creates some practical difficulties, particularly in the case of immature biological assets where uncertain assumptions are required and small changes in these assumptions could have a significant impact on the valuation of the biological assets.

☐ AASB 13/IFRS 13 requires disclosures including a description of the valuation techniques and inputs used in determining fair value using Level 2 or Level 3 inputs, and the effect of changes in the assumptions where fair value would change significantly.

☐ AASB 141/IAS 41 requires disclosure of a reconciliation of the changes in value of the biological assets for each year.

☐ It is common for companies applying AASB 141/IAS 41 to separately disclose the fair value movements attributable to agricultural assets.

35.7 Government grants

LEARNING OBJECTIVE 35.7 Examine the interaction between AASB 141/IAS 41 and AASB 120/IAS 20 *Accounting for Government Grants and Disclosure of Government Assistance.*

Sometimes entities may receive government grants in respect of agricultural activity. AASB 141/IAS 41 prescribes how these should be accounted for where biological assets are measured at fair value, distinguishing between conditional and unconditional government grants.

1. Unconditional government grants are recognised as income when the grant becomes receivable (paragraph 34).
2. Conditional government grants are recognised as income when the conditions attaching to the grant are met (paragraph 35).

Note that if biological assets are not measured at fair value (i.e. where the exemption in paragraph 30 applies) then AASB 120/IAS 20 *Accounting for Government Grants and Disclosure of Government Assistance* applies. AASB 120/IAS 20 allows various choices in accounting for government grants, including deferral of the revenue and permitting the grant to be offset against the cost of the asset. These approaches are not permitted for biological assets measured at fair value under AASB 141/IAS 41. Note that bearer plants are excluded from the scope of biological assets under AASB 141/IAS 41. As such, government grants relating to bearer plants are subject to AASB 120/IAS 20.

Illustrative example 35.5 demonstrates how conditional and unconditional government grants are accounted for when biological assets are measured at fair value.

ILLUSTRATIVE EXAMPLE 35.5

Conditional and unconditional government grants

Bicheno Ltd engages in agricultural activities and measures its biological assets at fair value in accordance with AASB 141/IAS 41. In 2022, Bicheno Ltd received two grants from the government. Grant A, of $10 000, was notified to the company on 7 January 2022 and had no conditions attaching to it. The grant was received on 14 March 2022. Grant B, of $50 000, was notified to the company on 31 January 2022. Grant B had the following condition attached to it: 'Bicheno Ltd must continue to operate its agricultural activities in the East Cost area until at least 31 January 2030. If Bicheno discontinues all or part of its operations in the East Coast area before that date then Bicheno shall immediately repay Grant B in full'. Grant B was received on 14 April 2022.

The end of Bicheno Ltd's reporting period is 30 June. The journal entries for Bicheno Ltd for the year ended 30 June 2022 would be as follows.

Receivables	Dr	10 000	
Income	Cr		10 000
(To recognise the unconditional Grant A when it became receivable on 7 January)			
Cash	Dr	10 000	
Receivables	Cr		10 000
(To recognise receipt of the cash on 14 March)			
Cash	Dr	50 000	
Performance obligation	Cr		50 000
(To recognise the cash received on 14 April and the corresponding obligation to comply with the conditions of Grant B)			

Grant B is thus recorded as a liability until such time as the conditions are met. Note that if the conditions attaching to Grant B permitted Bicheno Ltd to retain some of the grant based on the passing of time (e.g. by means of a formula), then Bicheno Ltd would be able to gradually recognise the grant as income over the period of time.

LEARNING CHECK

☐ AASB 141/IAS 41 prescribes how government grants related to agricultural activity should be accounted for where biological assets are measured at fair value.

☐ Unconditional government grants are recognised as income when the grant becomes receivable.

☐ Conditional government grants are recognised as income when the conditions attaching to the grant are satisfied.

35.8 The interaction between AASB 141/IAS 41 and AASB 116/IAS 16 and AASB 140/IAS 40

LEARNING OBJECTIVE 35.8 Examine the interaction between AASB 141/IAS 41 and AASB 116/IAS 16 *Property, Plant and Equipment* and AASB 140/IAS 40 *Investment Property*.

As noted in section 35.2.1, AASB 141/IAS 41 does not apply to land related to agricultural activity. Rather, an entity follows AASB 116/IAS 16 or AASB 140/IAS 40, depending on the circumstances. If the land meets the definition of an investment property (see section 35.2.1) it is measured using either the cost model or the fair value model under AASB 140/IAS 40. Thus, land related to agricultural activity that is an investment property may be measured either (a) at cost or (b) at fair value with changes in fair value being taken to the profit or loss. However, the agricultural assets attaching to that land (e.g. forests) must be measured at fair value under AASB 141/IAS 41.

If the land does not meet the definition of an investment property it must be accounted for under AASB 116/IAS 16. AASB 116/IAS 16 also allows a choice between the cost method and the revaluation method. Under the revaluation method, changes in fair value are taken to OCI rather than through profit or loss for upward revaluations (see chapter 5). Table 35.3 summarises the accounting choices available.

TABLE 35.3	**Accounting policy choices available in respect of land related to agricultural activity**			
	Land that is an investment property (AASB 140/IAS 40)		**Land that is not an investment property (AASB 116/IAS 16)**	
Accounting policy choice	Cost model	Fair value model	Cost model	Revaluation model
Increase in fair value over cost	Not recognised	Recognised in profit or loss	Not recognised	Recognised in OCI
Decrease in fair value	Recognised in profit or loss	Recognised in profit or loss	Recorded in profit or loss	Record in profit or loss, except to the extent that it reverses a previous upward revaluation for which there is accumulated credit in the revaluation surplus in equity

The related agricultural assets must be measured at fair value in accordance with AASB 141/IAS 41. The accounting policy choices for land mean that an entity could have a mixed measurement basis for its agricultural activities, with inconsistencies between the treatment of the land and the biological assets growing on the land.

The IASB considered this issue and commented as follows in the Basis for Conclusions (paragraphs 56–7).

> Some argue that land attached to biological assets related to agricultural activity should also be measured at its fair value for consistency of measurement. They also argue that it is sometimes difficult to measure the fair value of such biological assets separately from the land since an active market often exists for the combined assets (that is, land and biological assets; for example, trees in a plantation forest).

However, the IASB rejected this approach.

☐ Land related to agricultural activity that is an investment property may be measured either at cost and tested for impairment under AASB 116/IAS 16, or at fair value with changes in fair value being taken to the profit or loss.
☐ Agricultural assets attaching to land must be measured at fair value under AASB 141/IAS 41.
☐ If land related to agricultural activity does not meet the definition of an investment property it must be accounted for under AASB 116/IAS 16, which allows a choice between the cost method and the revaluation method.
☐ The accounting policy choices for land mean that an entity could have a mixed measurement basis for its agricultural activities, with inconsistencies between the treatment of the land and the biological assets growing on the land.

35.9 Disclosure requirements

LEARNING OBJECTIVE 35.9 Describe the disclosure requirements of AASB 141/IAS 41.

Paragraphs 40 through 57 set out the disclosure requirements of AASB 141/IAS 41. These are divided into three sections:

1. general
2. additional disclosures for biological assets where fair value cannot be measured reliably
3. government grants.

The requirements are summarised below.

35.9.1 General disclosures

General disclosure requirements are contained in paragraphs 40 to 53 of AASB 141/IAS 41 and include:

- aggregate gain or loss for the period on initial recognition (biological assets and agricultural produce) and as a result of fair value movements (biological assets)
- description of each group of biological assets (groups may be determined based on consumable (e.g. crops) versus bearer (e.g. wool sheep) biological assets, or based on mature versus immature biological assets (or both)
- description of the nature of activities involving each group of biological assets
- non-financial measures or estimates of the physical quantities of biological assets at the end of the period and output of agricultural produce during the period
- details of biological assets whose title is restricted or which has been pledged as security, commitments for the development or acquisition of biological assets and financial risk management strategies related to agricultural activity
- reconciliation of the changes in the carrying amount of biological assets between the beginning and end of the current period.

Entities are also encouraged, but not required, to disclose separately the fair value changes attributable to physical changes and price changes.

35.9.2 Additional disclosures for biological assets where fair value cannot be measured reliably

Where fair value cannot be measured reliably, paragraphs 54–56 of AASB 141/IAS 41 require additional disclosures, including:

- a description of the biological assets, an explanation of why fair value cannot be measured reliably, the range of estimates within which fair value is likely to lie, the depreciation method and rates/useful lives used, the gross carrying amount and accumulated depreciation at the beginning and end of the period
- gain or loss on disposal, impairment losses and depreciation — shown separately in the reconciliation required under 'General' disclosures
- specified details if the fair value becomes reliably measurable during the period.

AASB 13/IFRS 13 contains additional disclosure requirements (see chapter 3).

35.9.3 Government grants

Paragraph 57 requires disclosure of the nature and extent of government grants recognised, unfulfilled conditions and other contingencies attaching to government grants and significant decreases expected in the level of government grants.

LEARNING CHECK

☐ AASB 141/IAS 41 requires general disclosures, additional disclosures for biological assets where fair value cannot be measured reliably and government grants.

35.10 Preparing financial statements when applying AASB 141/IAS 41

LEARNING OBJECTIVE 35.10 Apply the recognition and measurement requirements of AASB 141/IAS 41 to a simple statement of profit or loss and other comprehensive income and statement of financial position.

Illustrative example 35.6 shows how a company would present its statement of profit or loss and other comprehensive income and statement of financial position when applying AASB 141/IAS 41.

ILLUSTRATIVE EXAMPLE 35.6

Preparing a statement of profit or loss and other comprehensive income and statement of financial position under AASB 141/IAS 41

Burnie Ltd owns dairy cattle and has an end of reporting period of 30 June.

At 1 July 2022, Burnie Ltd had 900 cows and 200 heifers, with a fair value (less costs to sell) of $800 per cow and $320 per heifer.

During the year ended 30 June 2023 the following occurred.
1. 200 new cows were purchased at $810 each.
2. 50 heifers matured into cows.
3. 5 heifers died.
4. 100 cows were sold for $830 each.
5. Salaries and other operating costs were $60 000.

Burnie Ltd owns the farmland, which was purchased for $1.5 million. The land is measured at cost under AASB 116/IAS 16. As at 30 June 2023 the market value of the land was assessed at $5.6 million.

Burnie Ltd also has plant and equipment which was purchased for $1 000 000 and is depreciated over its expected useful life of 10 years. As at 1 July 2022, the plant and equipment was 2 years old.

As at 30 June 2023, the fair value (less costs to sell) is determined as $850 per cow and $350 per heifer. Burnie Ltd has determined that these are the appropriate fair values to use for the purposes of transfers and deaths of heifers.

The price change between a heifer and a cow at the time of maturity during the year was estimated to be $500.

During the year, Burnie Ltd produced milk with a fair value less costs to sell of $500 000.

Workings

1. Reconciliation of movements in livestock

	Cows	Fair value	Heifers	Fair value
Balance as at 1 July 2022	900	$720 000	200	$ 64 000
Purchases	200	162 000	—	
Sales	(100)	(83 000)	—	
Transfer to cows	50	17 500	(5)	(17 500)
Deaths			(5)	(1 750)
Balance as at 30 June 2023	1 050	892 500	145	50 750
Increase in fair value:				
– attributable to physical change		25 000		
– attributable to price change		51 000		6 000

2. Reconciliation of movements in fair value — cows

Physical balance (assuming FIFO)	Change in fair value	Total
Opening balance 900 @ $800		
Sold 100 @ $830	100 @ $30	$ 3 000
Balance 800 @ $800		
Year end 800 @ $850	800 @ $50	$40 000
Purchased 200 @ $810		
Year end 200 @ $850	200 @ $40	$ 8 000
Total attributable to fair value changes		$51 000
Heifers 50 @ $350		
Year end 50 @ $850	50 @ $500	$25 000
	(all attributable to physical change)	

---

3. Reconciliation of movements in fair value — heifers

Physical balance (assuming FIFO)	Change in fair value	Total
Opening balance 200 @ $320		
Transfer 50 @ $350	50 @ $30	$ 1 500
Balance 150 @ $320		
Year end 150 @ $350	150 @ $30	4 500
Total attributable to fair value changes		6 000
Died 5 @ $350	5 @ $350 (all value lost)	(1 750)
Total		**$ 4 250**

4. Property, plant and equipment

Land measured at cost, no impairment as market value exceeds carrying amount as at 30 June 2023.

Plant and equipment	
Cost	$1 000 000
Accumulated depreciation as at 1 July 2022	(200 000)
Balance as at 1 July 2022	800 000
Annual depreciation	(100 000)
Balance as at 30 June 2022:	
Land	1 500 000
Plant and equipment	800 000
Total	$2 300 000
Balance as at 30 June 2023:	
Land	$1 500 000
Plant and equipment	700 000
Total	$2 200 000

BURNIE LTD
Statement of profit or loss and other comprehensive income (extract)
for the year ended 30 June 2023

Fair value of milk produced	$ 500 000
Net gains arising from changes in fair value less costs to sell of dairy livestock (note y)	80 250
Depreciation expense	(100 000)
Other operating expenses	(60 000)
Profit from operations	420 250
Income tax expense	xxx
Profit for the year	xxx

BURNIE LTD
Statement of financial position (extract)
as at 30 June 2023

	2023	2022
Assets		
Non-current assets		
Dairy livestock — immature	$ 50 750	$ 64 000
Dairy livestock — mature	892 500	720 000
Subtotal — biological assets	943 250	784 000
Property, plant and equipment	2 200 000	2 300 000

Note y

Biological assets

Reconciliation of carrying amounts of dairy livestock

Carrying amount at 1 July 2022	$784 000
Increases due to purchases	162 000

Note y	
Increase in fair value less costs to sell:	
– attributable to price changes	57 000
– attributable to physical changes	25 000
Total increase in fair value less costs to sell	82 000
Decreases due to deaths	(1 750)
Net increase in fair value	80 250
Decreases due to sales	(83 000)
Carrying amount as at 30 June 2023	943 250

LEARNING CHECK

☐ AASB 141/IAS 41 requires disclosure of the biological assets in the financial statements including a reconciliation of the movement in their values.

SUMMARY

IAS 41 was a controversial standard when it was first issued, mainly because of its requirement to measure assets related to agricultural activity at fair value, with gains and losses arising from movements in fair value recognised in profit or loss. The IASB rejected criticisms of the fair value model for biological assets and agricultural produce but permitted an exemption when fair value cannot be reliably measured. The IASB also included guidance in the standard on how to apply the fair value measurement requirement. Additionally, the standards were subsequently revised to exclude bearer plants from the scope of AASB 141/IAS 41 and, instead, to bring them within the scope of AASB 116/IAS 16.

AASB 141/IAS 41 distinguishes between biological assets, agricultural produce and products that are the result of processing after harvest, and prescribes different accounting treatments for each category. The interaction between AASB 141/IAS 41, AASB 116/IAS 16 and AASB 140/IAS 40 is very important to understand and apply, particularly since, in the agricultural industry, it is common to find different parties involved in owning and managing agricultural assets.

KEY TERMS

agricultural activity The management by an entity of the biological transformation and harvest of biological assets for sale or for conversion into agricultural produce or into additional biological assets.

agricultural produce The harvested product of the entity's biological assets.

bearer plant A living plant that is used in the production or supply of agricultural produce and which is expected to bear produce for more than one period.

biological asset A living animal or plant.

biological transformation The processes of growth, degeneration, production, and procreation that cause qualitative or quantitative changes in a biological asset.

harvest The detachment of produce from a biological asset or the cessation of a biological asset's life processes.

COMPREHENSION QUESTIONS

1 Explain why IAS 41 was a controversial standard when it was issued.

2 Explain why the concept of 'control' is problematic when applying the recognition criteria of AASB 141/IAS 41.

3 What are the arguments for and against the use of fair value as the measurement basis for biological assets and agricultural produce? Explain why the IASB decided to require fair value.

4 How is the risk that future cash flows pertaining to biological assets may not eventuate as predicted taken into account when determining the fair value of a biological asset using the present value of net cash flows method?

5 How does a gain arise on initial recognition of a biological asset or agricultural produce?

6 Why is agricultural produce not remeasured to fair value during a reporting period?

7 Discuss the three-level hierarchy for determining fair value under AASB 13/IFRS 13 in the context of the ruling in respect of immature salmon.

CASE STUDY 35.1

ACCOUNTING FOR IMMATURE CROPS

The manager of Smithton Ltd does not believe that the company's immature crops belong in the calculation of biological assets, as there is no active market for immature crops, and they are not yet at the point of harvest.

Required

Advise the manager whether this position meets the requirements of AASB 141/IAS 41.

CASE STUDY 35.2

INTERACTION BETWEEN STANDARDS

The accountant of Fingal Ltd has presented land and a pine tree plantation as a single asset on the basis that the two are interrelated, with one component being worth almost nothing without the other.

Required

Advise the accountant whether this position is acceptable.

CASE STUDY 35.3

CONTROL

The lessee of West Coast Wines Ltd manages the vineyards under a lease. It has included vineyards as an asset in its accounting records as it is responsible for the management and harvest.

Required

Discuss whether this approach is acceptable under AASB 141/IAS 41.

APPLICATION AND ANALYSIS EXERCISES

★ BASIC | ★★ MODERATE | ★★★ DIFFICULT

35.1 Agricultural activity — definitions ★   LO2

State which of the following meets the definition of 'agricultural activity' in AASB 141/IAS 41. Give reasons for your answer.

1. Pig farming
2. Ocean fishing
3. Clearing forests to create farmland
4. Salmon farming
5. Managing vineyards

35.2 Agricultural activity — definitions ★   LO2

State whether the following are (a) biological assets, (b) agricultural produce (c) products that result from processing after harvest or (d) bearer plants.

1. Living pigs
2. Living sheep
3. Pigs' carcasses
4. Pork sausages
5. Trees growing in a plantation forest
6. Furniture
7. Olive trees
8. Olives
9. Olive oil
10. Vines growing in a vineyard

35.3 Application of theory to accounting ★★★   LO3

Acres Ltd is a listed company with a large dairy farm. The fair value of the company's herd of cows declined as a result of a drop in the price of milk. The managing director is very worried about the impact that recognising the loss might have on the company's share price, claiming 'Investors will think the company is performing poorly, even though we have long-term contracts for delivery of milk'. The managing director suggests disclosing the decline in fair value in the notes instead of recognising it in the financial statements.

Required

Prepare a response to the managing director addressing:

1. whether her suggestion complies with the requirements of AASB 141/IAS 41
2. the potential implications of the efficient market hypothesis for the impact of the recognition of the loss on the company's share price, noting any assumptions in your argument
3. the implications of the efficient market hypothesis for the managing director's strategy of disclosing the change in fair value in the notes instead of recognising it in the financial statements.

35.4 Agricultural activity — measurement ★ **LO3, 4, 5**

For each of the items listed, state whether they would be measured (a) at fair value under AASB 141, (b) at the lower of cost and net realisable value under AASB 102/IAS 2 or (c) at cost or fair value under AASB 116/IAS 16.

1. Living pigs
2. Living sheep
3. Pigs' carcasses
4. Pork sausages
5. Trees growing in a plantation forest
6. Furniture
7. Olive trees
8. Olives
9. Olive oil
10. Vines growing in a vineyard

35.5 Fair value determination ★ ★ **LO5, 6**

Which of the following is included in determining the fair value of a biological asset that does not have an active market and which has a 5-year production cycle?

1. Revenue from sale in 5 years' time
2. Costs of growing for 5 years
3. Financing costs on borrowings taken out to fund the growing costs
4. Taxation on taxable income generated from sale in 5 years' time
5. Discount rate that reflects expected variability in cash flows

35.6 Fair value determination ★ **LO5, 6**

Wynyard Ltd owns a plantation forest. As at the end of the reporting period the fair value of the plantation forest including the land was $10.5 million. Wynyard Ltd needs to determine the fair value of the trees excluding the land to comply with AASB 141/IAS 41 at the end of its reporting period. How does Wynyard Ltd determine the fair value of the trees?

35.7 Accounting for a government grant ★ ★ ★ **LO7**

Severn Oaks Ltd engages in agricultural activities and measures its biological assets at fair value in accordance with AASB 141/IAS 41. In 2022, Severn Oaks Ltd received a grant of $475 000 from the government. The grant was notified to the company on 31 March 2022. The terms and conditions of the grant were as follows.

> This grant is effective from 1 July 2022. Severn Oaks Ltd must continue to employ staff from Area A in its agricultural activities until at least 30 June 2027. If Severn Oaks Ltd ceases to employ staff from Area A before that date then Severn Oaks Ltd shall immediately repay the grant. The amount to be repaid shall be calculated according to the following formula.
>
> $$A = B - (C \times D)$$
>
> where:
> A = amount to be repaid
> B = amount of initial grant
> C = number of years the company has employed staff in Area A
> D = $85 000.

The end of Severn Oaks Ltd's reporting period is 30 June. The grant was received on 15 April 2022.

Required

Prepare the journal entries to account for the grant by Severn Oaks Ltd for the years ended 30 June 2022 and 30 June 2023, assuming Severn Oaks Ltd complies with the conditions of the grant.

35.8 Disclosure of biological assets ★ ★ **LO9**

State whether each of the following is true or false.

1. Companies applying AASB 141/IAS 41 must disclose separately the fair value (less costs to sell) of mature and immature biological assets.
2. A vineyard planted on land classified as an investment property by the owner must be recognised and measured as part of that investment property.
3. An entity using the exemption in paragraph 30 of AASB 141/IAS 41 for a particular biological asset must apply AASB 120/IAS 20 if it receives a government grant in respect of that asset.
4. If agricultural produce cannot be reliably measured then it may be accounted for at cost under paragraph 30 of AASB 141/IAS 41.

35.9 Preparation of financial statements applying AASB 141/IAS 41 ★ ★ ★ **LO10**

Heavenleigh Ltd owns sheep and the end of its reporting period is 30 June. The sheep are held to produce wool.

At 1 July 2022, Heavenleigh Ltd had 8000 sheep and 400 lambs, with a fair value (less costs to sell) of $180 per sheep and $60 per lamb.

During the year ended 30 June 2023 the following occurred.

- 500 new sheep were purchased at $190 each.
- 120 lambs matured into sheep.
- 8 lambs died.
- 50 lambs were born.
- 300 sheep were sold for $260 each.
- Salaries and other operating costs were $82 000.

Heavenleigh Ltd owns the farmland, which was purchased for $2.5 million. The land is measured at fair value using the revaluation model under AASB 116/IAS 16. As at 30 June 2023, the fair value of the land was assessed at $3.6 million ($3.2 million as at 30 June 2022).

Heavenleigh Ltd also has plant and equipment, which was purchased for $1 million and is depreciated over its expected useful life of 10 years. As at 1 July 2022, the plant and equipment was 2 years old.

As at 30 June 2023, the fair value (less costs to sell) is determined as $260 per sheep and $65 per lamb. Heavenleigh Ltd has determined that these are the appropriate fair values to use for the purposes of transfers, births and deaths of lambs.

The price change between a lamb and a sheep at the time of maturity during the year was estimated to be $205.

During the year Heavenleigh Ltd produced wool with a fair value less costs to sell of $564 000.

Required

Prepare the relevant extracts from the statement of profit or loss and other comprehensive income and statement of financial performance and the reconciliation required by paragraph 50 of AASB 141/IAS 41 for Heavenleigh Ltd in accordance with AASB 141/IAS 41 for the year ended 30 June 2023. Show all workings.

REFERENCES

Committee of European Securities Regulators 2007, *Extract from EECS's database of enforcement decisions*, Ref: 07–120.

The Scottish Salmon Company 2018, *Annual report 2017*, www.scottishsalmon.com.

Treasury Wine Estates Ltd 2018, *Annual report 2018,* Treasury Wine Estates Ltd, www.tweglobal.com.

ACKNOWLEDGEMENTS

Photo: © Lukasz Szwaj / Shutterstock.com

Photo: © Goodluz / Shutterstock.com

Figure 35.1: © The Scottish Salmon Company 2018

Figure 35.2: © Treasury Wine Estates Ltd 2018

APPENDIX

Present value tables

TABLE 1	Present value of $1: PVIF $= 1/(1 + k)^t$																		
Period	**1%**	**2%**	**3%**	**4%**	**5%**	**6%**	**7%**	**8%**	**9%**	**10%**	**12%**	**14%**	**15%**	**16%**	**18%**	**20%**	**24%**	**28%**	**32%**	**36%**
1	0.9901	0.9804	0.9709	0.9615	0.9524	0.9434	0.9346	0.9259	0.9174	0.9091	0.8929	0.8772	0.8696	0.8621	0.8475	0.8333	0.8065	0.7813	0.7576	0.7353
2	0.9803	0.9612	0.9426	0.9246	0.9070	0.8900	0.8734	0.8573	0.8417	0.8264	0.7972	0.7695	0.7561	0.7432	0.7182	0.6944	0.6504	0.6104	0.5739	0.5407
3	0.9706	0.9423	0.9151	0.8890	0.8638	0.8396	0.8163	0.7938	0.7722	0.7513	0.7118	0.6750	0.6575	0.6407	0.6086	0.5787	0.5245	0.4768	0.4348	0.3975
4	0.9610	0.9238	0.8885	0.8548	0.8227	0.7921	0.7629	0.7350	0.7084	0.6830	0.6355	0.5921	0.5718	0.5523	0.5158	0.4823	0.4230	0.3725	0.3294	0.2923
5	0.9515	0.9057	0.8626	0.8219	0.7835	0.7473	0.7130	0.6806	0.6499	0.6209	0.5674	0.5194	0.4972	0.4761	0.4371	0.4019	0.3411	0.2910	0.2495	0.2149
6	0.9420	0.8880	0.8375	0.7903	0.7462	0.7050	0.6663	0.6302	0.5963	0.5645	0.5066	0.4556	0.4323	0.4104	0.3704	0.3349	0.2751	0.2274	0.1890	0.1580
7	0.9327	0.8706	0.8131	0.7599	0.7107	0.6651	0.6227	0.5835	0.5470	0.5132	0.4523	0.3996	0.3759	0.3538	0.3139	0.2791	0.2218	0.1776	0.1432	0.1162
8	0.9235	0.8535	0.7894	0.7307	0.6768	0.6274	0.5820	0.5403	0.5019	0.4665	0.4039	0.3506	0.3269	0.3050	0.2660	0.2326	0.1789	0.1388	0.1085	0.0854
9	0.9143	0.8368	0.7664	0.7026	0.6446	0.5919	0.5439	0.5002	0.4604	0.4241	0.3606	0.3075	0.2843	0.2630	0.2255	0.1938	0.1443	0.1084	0.0822	0.0628
10	0.9053	0.8203	0.7441	0.6756	0.6139	0.5584	0.5083	0.4632	0.4224	0.3855	0.3220	0.2697	0.2472	0.2267	0.1911	0.1615	0.1164	0.0847	0.0623	0.0462
11	0.8963	0.8043	0.7224	0.6496	0.5847	0.5268	0.4751	0.4289	0.3875	0.3505	0.2875	0.2366	0.2149	0.1954	0.1619	0.1346	0.0938	0.0662	0.0472	0.0340
12	0.8874	0.7885	0.7014	0.6246	0.5568	0.4970	0.4440	0.3971	0.3555	0.3186	0.2567	0.2076	0.1869	0.1685	0.1372	0.1122	0.0757	0.0517	0.0357	0.0250
13	0.8787	0.7730	0.6810	0.6006	0.5303	0.4688	0.4150	0.3677	0.3262	0.2897	0.2292	0.1821	0.1625	0.1452	0.1163	0.0935	0.0610	0.0404	0.0271	0.0184
14	0.8700	0.7579	0.6611	0.5775	0.5051	0.4423	0.3878	0.3405	0.2992	0.2633	0.2046	0.1597	0.1413	0.1252	0.0985	0.0779	0.0492	0.0316	0.0205	0.0135
15	0.8613	0.7430	0.6419	0.5553	0.4810	0.4173	0.3624	0.3152	0.2745	0.2394	0.1827	0.1401	0.1229	0.1079	0.0835	0.0649	0.0397	0.0247	0.0155	0.0099
16	0.8528	0.7284	0.6232	0.5339	0.4581	0.3936	0.3387	0.2919	0.2519	0.2176	0.1631	0.1229	0.1069	0.0930	0.0708	0.0541	0.0320	0.0193	0.0118	0.0073
17	0.8444	0.7142	0.6050	0.5134	0.4363	0.3714	0.3166	0.2703	0.2311	0.1978	0.1456	0.1078	0.0929	0.0802	0.0600	0.0451	0.0258	0.0150	0.0089	0.0054
18	0.8360	0.7002	0.5874	0.4936	0.4155	0.3503	0.2959	0.2502	0.2120	0.1799	0.1300	0.0946	0.0808	0.0691	0.0508	0.0376	0.0208	0.0118	0.0068	0.0039
19	0.8277	0.6864	0.5703	0.4746	0.3957	0.3305	0.2765	0.2317	0.1945	0.1635	0.1161	0.0829	0.0703	0.0596	0.0431	0.0313	0.0168	0.0092	0.0051	0.0029
20	0.8195	0.6730	0.5537	0.4564	0.3769	0.3118	0.2584	0.2145	0.1784	0.1486	0.1037	0.0728	0.0611	0.0514	0.0365	0.0261	0.0135	0.0072	0.0039	0.0021
25	0.7798	0.6095	0.4776	0.3751	0.2953	0.2330	0.1842	0.1460	0.1160	0.0923	0.0588	0.0378	0.0304	0.0245	0.0160	0.0105	0.0046	0.0021	0.0010	0.0005
30	0.7419	0.5521	0.4120	0.3083	0.2314	0.1741	0.1314	0.0994	0.0754	0.0573	0.0334	0.0196	0.0151	0.0116	0.0070	0.0042	0.0016	0.0006	0.0002	0.0001
40	0.6717	0.4529	0.3066	0.2083	0.1420	0.0972	0.0668	0.0460	0.0318	0.0221	0.0107	0.0053	0.0037	0.0026	0.0013	0.0007	0.0002	0.0001	—	—
50	0.6080	0.3715	0.2281	0.1407	0.0872	0.0543	0.0339	0.0213	0.0134	0.0085	0.0035	0.0014	0.0009	0.0006	0.0003	0.0001	—	—	—	—
60	0.5504	0.3048	0.1697	0.0951	0.0535	0.0303	0.0173	0.0099	0.0057	0.0033	0.0011	0.0004	0.0002	0.0001	—	—	—	—	—	—

TABLE 2 Present value of an annuity of \$1 per period for *n* periods:

$$PVIFA = \sum_{t-1}^{n} \frac{1}{(1+k)^t}$$

$$= \frac{1 - \frac{1}{(1+k)^n}}{k}$$

Number of payments	1%	2%	3%	4%	5%	6%	7%	8%	9%	10%	12%	14%	15%	16%	18%	20%	24%	28%	32%
1	0.9901	0.9804	0.9709	0.9615	0.9524	0.9434	0.9346	0.9259	0.9174	0.9091	0.8929	0.8772	0.8696	0.8621	0.8475	0.8333	0.8065	0.7813	0.7576
2	1.9704	1.9416	1.9135	1.8861	1.8594	1.8334	1.8080	1.7833	1.7591	1.7355	1.6901	1.6467	1.6257	1.6052	1.5656	1.5278	1.4568	1.3916	1.3315
3	2.9410	2.8839	2.8286	2.7751	2.7232	2.6730	2.6243	2.5771	2.5313	2.4869	2.4018	2.3216	2.2832	2.2459	2.1743	2.1065	1.9813	1.8684	1.7663
4	3.9020	3.8077	3.7171	3.6299	3.5460	3.4651	3.3872	3.3121	3.2397	3.1699	3.0373	2.9137	2.8550	2.7982	2.6901	2.5887	2.4043	2.2410	2.0957
5	4.8534	4.7135	4.5797	4.4518	4.3295	4.2124	4.1002	3.9927	3.8897	3.7908	3.6048	3.4331	3.3522	3.2743	3.1272	2.9906	2.7454	2.5320	2.3452
6	5.7955	5.6014	5.4172	5.2421	5.0757	4.9173	4.7665	4.6229	4.4859	4.3553	4.1114	3.8887	3.7845	3.6847	3.4976	3.3255	3.0205	2.7594	2.5342
7	6.7282	6.4720	6.2303	6.0021	5.7864	5.5824	5.3893	5.2064	5.0330	4.8684	4.5638	4.2883	4.1604	4.0386	3.8115	3.6046	3.2423	2.9370	2.6775
8	7.6517	7.3255	7.0197	6.7327	6.4632	6.2098	5.9713	5.7466	5.5348	5.3349	4.9676	4.6389	4.4873	4.3436	4.0776	3.8372	3.4212	3.0758	2.7860
9	8.5660	8.1622	7.7861	7.4353	7.1078	6.8017	6.5152	6.2469	5.9952	5.7590	5.3282	4.9464	4.7716	4.6065	4.3030	4.0310	3.5655	3.1842	2.8681
10	9.4713	8.9826	8.5302	8.1109	7.7217	7.3601	7.0236	6.7101	6.4177	6.1446	5.6502	5.2161	5.0188	4.8332	4.4941	4.1925	3.6819	3.2689	2.9304
11	10.3876	9.7868	9.2526	8.7605	8.3064	7.8869	7.4987	7.1390	6.8052	6.4951	5.9377	5.4527	5.2337	5.0286	4.6560	4.3271	3.7757	3.3351	2.9776
12	11.2551	10.5753	9.9540	9.3851	8.8633	8.3838	7.9427	7.5361	7.1607	6.8137	6.1944	5.6603	5.4206	5.1971	4.7932	4.4392	3.8514	3.3868	3.0133
13	12.1337	11.3484	10.6350	9.9856	9.3936	8.8527	8.3577	7.9038	7.4869	7.1034	6.4235	5.8424	5.5831	5.3423	4.9095	4.5327	3.9124	3.4272	3.0404
14	13.0037	12.1062	11.2961	10.5631	9.8986	9.2950	8.7455	8.2442	7.7862	7.3667	6.6282	6.0021	5.7245	5.4675	5.0081	4.6106	3.9616	3.4587	3.0609
15	13.8651	12.8493	11.9379	11.1184	10.3797	9.7122	9.1079	8.5595	8.0607	7.6061	6.8109	6.1422	5.8474	5.5755	5.0916	4.6755	4.0013	3.4834	3.0764
16	14.7179	13.5777	12.5611	11.6523	10.8378	10.1059	9.4466	8.8514	8.3126	7.8237	6.9740	6.2651	5.9542	5.6685	5.1624	4.7296	4.0333	3.5026	3.0882
17	15.5623	14.2919	13.1661	12.1657	11.2741	10.4773	9.7632	9.1216	8.5436	8.0216	7.1196	6.3729	6.0472	5.7487	5.2223	4.7746	4.0591	3.5177	3.0971
18	16.3983	14.9920	13.7535	12.6593	11.6896	10.8276	10.0591	9.3719	8.7556	8.2014	7.2497	6.4674	6.1280	5.8178	5.2732	4.8122	4.0799	3.5294	3.1039
19	17.2260	15.6785	14.3238	13.1339	12.0853	11.1581	10.3356	9.6036	8.9501	8.3649	7.3658	6.5504	6.1982	5.8775	5.3162	4.8435	4.0967	3.5386	3.1090
20	18.0456	16.3514	14.8775	13.5903	12.4622	11.4699	10.5940	9.8181	9.1285	8.5136	7.4694	6.6231	6.2593	5.9288	5.3527	4.8696	4.1103	3.5458	3.1129
25	22.0232	19.5235	17.4131	15.6221	14.0939	12.7834	11.6536	10.6748	9.8226	9.0770	7.8431	6.8729	6.4641	6.0971	5.4669	4.9476	4.1474	3.5640	3.1220
30	25.8077	22.3965	19.6004	17.2920	15.3725	13.7648	12.4090	11.2578	10.2737	9.4269	8.0552	7.0027	6.5660	6.1772	5.5168	4.9789	4.1601	3.5693	3.1242
40	32.8347	27.3555	23.1148	19.7928	17.1591	15.0463	13.3317	11.9246	10.7574	9.7791	8.2438	7.1050	6.6418	6.2335	5.5482	4.9966	4.1659	3.5712	3.1250
50	39.1961	31.4236	25.7298	21.4822	18.2559	15.7619	13.8007	12.2335	10.9617	9.9148	8.3045	7.1327	6.6605	6.2463	5.5541	4.9995	4.1666	3.5714	3.1250
60	44.9550	34.7609	27.6756	22.6235	18.9293	16.1614	14.0392	12.3766	11.0480	9.9672	8.3240	7.1401	6.6651	6.2402	5.5553	4.9999	4.1667	3.5714	3.1250

INDEX

Note: Figures and tables are indicated by *f* and *t*, respectively, following the page reference.